MICHIGAN
RULES OF COURT

VOLUME I – STATE

2020

THOMSON REUTERS

Mat. #42622788

ISBN 978–1–539–21254–6

PREFACE

Designed for use in the office or courtroom, this pamphlet contains the Michigan state rules.

WHAT'S NEW

Michigan Court Rules, Volume I – State, 2020, includes rules and associated material governing practice before the Michigan state courts. It is current with amendments received through January 1, 2020.

CONTACT US

For additional information or research assistance, call the reference attorneys at 1-800-REF-ATTY (1-800-733-2889). Contact our U.S. legal editorial department directly with your questions and suggestions by e-mail at editors.us-legal@tr.com.

Thank you for subscribing to this product. Should you have any questions regarding this product please contact Customer Service at 1-800-328-4880 or by fax at 1-800-340-9378. If you would like to inquire about related publications, or to place an order, please contact us at 1-888-728-7677 or visit us at legalsolutions.thomsonreuters.com.

THE PUBLISHER

February 2020

THOMSON REUTERS PROVIEW™

TABLE OF CONTENTS

———

MICHIGAN COURT RULES OF 1985

Effective March 1, 1985

1

CASE FILE MANAGEMENT STANDARDS

Case–Type Codes

(A) Circuit Court Case–Type Code List. The following case-type code list must be used in circuit court as provided in Standard 3.3.1.1 of the Michigan Trial Court Records Management Standards. The bracketed letters are the case-type codes.

(1) *Appeals.*

(a) Agencies [AA]. All matters from administrative agencies other than the Michigan Employment Security Commission and the Michigan Secretary of State. Includes appeal of any county clerk action taken under MCL 28.421 *et seq.*

(b) Employment Security Commission [AE]. All matters regarding Michigan Employment Security Commission actions.

(c) Parole Board Decisions [AP]. Appeals in parole board decisions.

(d) Criminal Appeals [AR]. All criminal appeals from a lower court when filed in a higher court.

(e) Civil Appeals [AV]. All civil appeals from a lower court when filed in a higher court.

(2) *Administrative Review, Superintending Control, Extraordinary Writs.*

(a) Habeas Corpus [AH]. All writs of habeas corpus governed by MCR 3.303 and MCR 3.304 except habeas corpus to obtain custody of a child.

(b) Licensing and Vehicles [AL]. All matters regarding Secretary of State actions.

(c) Superintending Control [AS]. All matters involving superintending control or supervisory control powers of the court.

(d) Writs [AW]. All actions for mandamus not filed in the Court of Claims and all quo warranto and other writs.

(3) *Criminal.*

(a) Extradition/Detainer [AX]. All extradition and detainer matters initiated by Michigan to other states.

(b) Capital Felonies [FC]. Capital felony cases in which life sentence is possible and a larger number of peremptory jury challenges is provided.

(c) Noncapital Felonies [FH].

(d) Juvenile Felonies [FJ]. Juvenile offenses committed by juveniles and waived to the criminal division of the circuit court under MCR 3.950. Includes life offenses committed by juveniles in which the prosecuting attorney has authorized the filing of a criminal complaint and warrant under MCR 6.907 instead of proceeding in the family division of the circuit court.

(4) *Civil Damage Suits.*

(a) Property Damage, Auto Negligence [ND]. All complaints of property damage, but not personal injury, involving the use of a motor vehicle.

(b) No–Fault Automobile Insurance [NF]. All claims for first-party personal protection benefits and first-party property protection benefits under the no-fault automobile insurance act.

(c) Medical Malpractice [NH]. All claims involving health-care provider malpractice.

(d) Personal Injury, Auto Negligence [NI]. All complaints of personal injury, or personal injury and property damage, involving the use of a motor vehicle.

(e) Other Professional Malpractice [NM]. All claims involving professional malpractice other than health-care provider malpractice.

(f) Other Personal Injury [NO]. All other claims involving liability for personal injury not otherwise coded.

(g) Products Liability [NP]. All claims involving products liability.

(h) Liquor Control [NS]. All claims involving liability under the liquor control code.

(i) Other Damage Suits [NZ]. All other claims for damages.

(5) *Other Civil Matters.*

(a) Business Claims [CB]. All claims in which all or part of the action includes a business or commercial dispute under MCL 600.8035.

(b) Condemnation [CC]. All condemnation proceedings.

(c) Employment Discrimination [CD]. All complaints of employment discrimination.

(d) Environment [CE]. All environmental matters such as zoning, pollution, etc.

(e) Forfeiture Claims [CF]. All claims of interest in property seized under the Controlled Substance that may be subject to forfeiture.

(f) Housing and Real Estate [CH]. All housing, real estate, foreclosure, land contracts, and other property proceedings (except landlord-tenant and land contract summary proceedings).

(g) Contracts [CK]. All proceedings involving contractual obligations not otherwise coded.

(h) Labor Relations [CL]. All labor-management matters except employment discrimination.

(i) Antitrust, Franchising, and Trade Regulation [CP]. All complaints regarding unlawful trade practices including but not limited to pricing and advertising of consumer items, regulation of watercraft, restraint of trade and monopolies, Consumer Protection Act, Farm and Utility Equipment Franchise Act, franchise investment law, motor vehicle dealer agreements, and the Motor Fuel Distribution Act.

(j) Corporate Receivership [CR]. All corporate receivership proceedings.

(k) General Civil [CZ]. All other civil actions not otherwise coded.

(*l*) Proceedings to Restore, Establish, or Correct Records [PC]. All proceedings to restore, establish, or correct records that are assigned a new case number (not brought under an existing case).

(m) Claim and Delivery [PD]. All complaints to recover personal property that are assigned a new case number (not brought under an existing case).

(n) Receivers in Supplemental Proceedings [PR]. All proceedings appointing a receiver that are assigned a new case number (not brought under an existing case).

(*o*) Supplemental Proceedings [PS]. All supplemental proceedings that are assigned a new case number (not brought under an existing case).

(p) Miscellaneous Proceedings [PZ]. All other matters assigned a new case number (not brought under an existing case), including the following matters: grand jury and multicounty grand jury, and applications for restoration of firearms rights under MCL 28.424.

(6) *Family Division—Domestic Relations.*

(a) Custody [DC]. All habeas corpus to obtain custody of a child; order to show cause for custody of a child; other custody, or custody and support proceedings when no divorce action has been filed; or actions under the Uniform Child Custody Jurisdiction Enforcement Act. Also used for intrastate transfers of postjudgment custody or custody and support proceedings where no divorce action has been filed.

(b) Divorce, Minor Children [DM]. All complaints for divorce, separate maintenance, or annulment when minor children are involved. Also used for intrastate transfers of postjudgment divorce; divorce and custody; or divorce, custody, and support complaints when minor children are involved.

(c) Divorce, No Children [DO]. All complaints for divorce, separate maintenance, or annulment when no minor children are involved. Also used for intrastate transfers of postjudgment divorce complaints when no minor children are involved.

(d) Paternity [DP]. All questions of paternity; paternity and custody; or paternity, custody, and support. Also used for intrastate transfers of postjudgment paternity; paternity and custody; or paternity, custody, and support complaints.

(e) Other Support [DS]. All support matters under the Family Support Act. Also used for intrastate transfers of postjudgment support matters under the Family Support Act.

(f) Other Domestic Relations Matters [DZ]. All other prejudgment matters involving domestic relations proceedings not otherwise coded. Also used for intrastate transfers of other postjudgment matters involving domestic relations proceedings not otherwise coded.

(g) Assist with Discovery [UD]. All proceedings to assist with discovery or to compel a response to a discovery order issued by another state's tribunal.

(h) UIFSA Establishment [UE]. All support and paternity establishment proceedings incoming from another state.

(i) UIFSA Filing [UF]. All outgoing requests to another state or country initiating enforcement, modification, income withholding, or redirection of support orders not issued in this state.

(j) UIFSA Initiation [UI]. All support and paternity establishment proceedings outgoing to another state.

(k) UIFSA Registration of Orders for Modification [UM]. All incoming registrations of another state's orders for the specific purpose of modification.

(*l*) UIFSA Registration of Orders for Enforcement [UN]. All incoming registrations of another state's orders for the specific purpose of enforcement.

(7) *Family Division—Proceedings under Juvenile Code.*

(a) Designated Juvenile Offenses [DJ]. All juvenile offenses designated by the prosecutor or court to be heard in the family division of circuit court in the same manner as an adult criminal case is heard in the criminal division of the circuit court.

(b) Delinquency Proceedings [DL]. All delinquency proceedings initiated by petition under the juvenile code or initiated by Uniform Law Citation for various minor offenses not in the Motor Vehicle Code.

(c) Juvenile Guardianship [JG]. All juvenile guardianships created by order under the juvenile code, MCL 712A.19a and MCL 712A.19c

(d) Child Protective Proceedings [NA]. All child protective proceedings initiated by petition under the juvenile code.

(e) Personal Protection Actions Brought Under the Juvenile Code [PJ]. All petitions seeking a personal protection order against a respondent under the age of 18. Includes proceedings conducted for violation of personal protection orders issued under the juvenile code when heard by a county other than the county that issued the personal protection order.

(f) Traffic and Local Ordinance [TL]. All traffic and local ordinance issued on a Uniform Law Citation under the Motor Vehicle Code or local corresponding ordinance.

(8) *Family Division—Proceedings under Adoption Code.*

(a) Adult Adoptions [AB]. All adult adoptions.

(b) Agency International Adoptions [AC]. All foreign children adoptions.

(c) Direct Placement Adoptions [AD]. All direct placement adoptions including temporary placements prior to filing of petition for direct placement.

(d) Relative Adoptions [AF]. All adoptions by relatives including relative guardians, but not including stepparent adoptions.

(e) Safe Delivery of Newborn Adoptions [AG]. All adoptions resulting from safe delivery of newborn proceedings.

(f) Permanent Ward Adoptions (state ward or court ward) [AM]. All state or court ward adoptions resulting from child protective proceedings.

(g) Nonrelative Adoptions [AN]. All adoptions by guardians who are not relatives.

(h) Agency Other Adoptions [AO]. All other private or public agency adoptions not otherwise designated.

(i) Adoption Miscellaneous [AU]. Releases for adoption (including those executed out–of–court), ex parte petitions to issue notice of intent to release for adoption, and notices of intent to claim paternity.

(j) Stepparent Adoptions [AY]. All adoptions by stepparents.

(9) *Family Division—Miscellaneous Proceedings.*

(a) Emancipation of Minor [EM]. All emancipation proceedings initiated under the Status of Minors and Emancipation Act.

(b) Infectious Disease [ID]. All proceedings under the public health code for treatment of infectious disease or testing for infectious disease.

(c) Safe Delivery of Newborn Child [NB]. All proceedings involving a newborn child surrendered under MCL 712.1 *et seq.*

(d) Name Change [NC]. All name change proceedings.

(e) Personal Protection Against Stalking [PH]. All personal protection proceedings under MCL 600.2950a when there is no domestic relationship between the parties and the respondent is not under the age of 18.

(f) Personal Protection in Domestic Relationships [PP]. All personal protection proceedings under MCL 600.2950 and/or MCL 600.2950a when there is a domestic relationship between the parties and the respondent is not under the age of 18.

(g) Waiver of Parental Consent to Obtain Abortion [PW]. All waiver of parental consent proceedings under the Parental Rights Restoration Act.

(h) Young Adult Voluntary Foster Care Act [VF]. All petitions filed under MCL 400.655.

(i) Violation Proceedings on Out-of-County Personal Protection Order—Revised Judicature Act [VP]. All proceedings conducted for violation of personal protection orders issued under MCL 600.2950 or MCL 600.2950a when heard by a county other than the county that issued the personal protection order. This case is filed as "In the Matter of."

(10) *Family Division—Ancillary Proceedings.* Use case-type codes listed in (C) for matters filed in the probate court that may alternatively be filed in the family division of circuit court as an ancillary proceeding.

(11) *Court of Claims.*

(a) Habeas Corpus [MA]. All writs of habeas corpus not governed by MCR 3.303 and MCR 3.304.

(b) Mandamus [MB]. All actions for mandamus against state officials and departments.

(c) Highway Defect [MD]. All claims involving highway defects.

(d) Medical Malpractice [MH]. All claims involving health-care provider malpractice.

(e) Contracts [MK]. All other proceedings involving contractual obligations not otherwise coded.

(f) Constitutional Claims [MM]. All claims for money damages brought under the Michigan Constitution.

(g) Prisoner Litigation [MP]. All claims for money damages against the State of Michigan filed by state prisoners.

(h) Tax–Related Suits [MT]. All claims involving liability for state taxes.

(i) Other Damage Suits [MZ]. All other claims not otherwise coded.

(B) District Court Case–Type Code List. The following case-type code list must be used in district court as provided in Standard 3.3.1.1 of the Michigan Trial Court Records Management Standards. The bracketed letters are the case-type codes.

(1) *Criminal.*

(a) Extradition/Detainer [EX]. All extradition and detainer matters initiated by Michigan to other states.

(b) Felony Criminal [FY]. All felony nontraffic cases. Includes life offenses committed by juveniles in which the prosecuting attorney has authorized the filing of a criminal complaint and warrant under MCR 6.907 instead of proceeding in the family division of the circuit court, and specified offenses committed by juveniles and waived to the criminal division of the circuit court under MCR 3.950.

(c) Ordinance Misdemeanor Criminal [OM]. All nontraffic misdemeanor offenses issued under ordinance.

(d) Statute Misdemeanor Criminal [SM]. All nontraffic misdemeanor offenses issued under statute.

(2) *Traffic.*

(a) Felony Drunk Driving [FD]. All felony drunk-driving cases.

(b) Felony Traffic [FT]. All felony traffic cases except drunk driving.

(c) Ordinance Misdemeanor Drunk Driving [OD]. All drunk-driving misdemeanor offenses issued under ordinance.

(d) Ordinance Civil Infraction Traffic [OI]. All traffic civil infraction offenses issued under ordinance.

(e) Ordinance Misdemeanor Traffic [OT]. All traffic misdemeanor offenses issued under ordinance except drunk driving.

(f) Statute Misdemeanor Drunk Driving [SD]. All drunk-driving misdemeanor offenses issued under statute.

(g) Statute Civil Infraction Traffic [SI]. All traffic civil infraction offenses issued under statute.

(h) Statute Misdemeanor Traffic [ST]. All traffic misdemeanor offenses issued under statute except drunk driving.

(3) *Nontraffic Civil Infraction and Parking.*

(a) Ordinance Parking [OK]. All parking offenses issued under ordinance.

(b) Ordinance Civil Infraction Nontraffic [ON]. All nontraffic civil infraction offenses issued under ordinance.

(c) Statute Parking [SK]. All parking offenses issued under statute.

(d) Statute Civil Infraction Nontraffic [SN]. All nontraffic civil infraction offenses issued under statute.

(4) *Civil Damage Suits.*

(a) General Civil [GC]. All civil cases for money damages except small claims, landlord-tenant, and land contract.

(b) Miscellaneous Civil [GZ]. All nonmonetary claims including coroner's inquests, claim and delivery without money judgment, drug forfeitures, other summary proceedings not relating to landlord-tenant and land contract, and proceedings under the public health code for testing for infectious disease.

(c) Small Claims [SC]. All civil claims for the recovery of money that does not exceed the jurisdictional limit in MCL 600.8401.

(5) *Housing and Real Estate Suits.*

(a) Landlord–Tenant Summary Proceedings [LT].

(b) Land Contract Summary Proceedings [SP].

(C) Probate Court Case–Type Code List. The following case-type code list must be used in probate court as provided in Standard 3.3.1.1 of the Michigan Trial Court Records Management Standards. The bracketed letters are the case-type codes.

(1) *Estates, Trusts, Wills.*

(a) Decedent Estates, Supervised Administration [DA]. All matters involving decedent estates in which administration is supervised.

(b) Decedent Estates, Unsupervised Administration and Nonadministered Estates [DE]. All matters involving decedent estates in which either administration is unsupervised or the estate is not administered.

(c) Determination of Heirs (separate proceeding) [DH]. All matters to determine heirs as a separate proceeding.

(d) Small Estates [PE]. All assignments of estates where gross estate assets do not exceed $15,000 (as adjusted for inflation).

(e) Trust Registration [TR]. All requests to register trusts.

(f) Trust, Testamentary [TT]. All trusts that take effect on the death of the settlor.

(g) Trust Inter Vivos [TV]. All trusts which are operative during the lifetime of the settlor.

(2) *Guardianships and Conservatorships.* These case types may also be filed in the family division of circuit court as an ancillary proceeding.

(a) Adult Conservatorship [CA]. All matters involving conservatorship of adults.

(b) Minor Conservatorship [CY]. All matters involving conservatorship of minors.

(c) Developmental Disability Guardianship [DD]. All matters involving guardianship of individuals with developmental disability, both adults and minors.

(d) Adult Guardianship [GA]. All matters involving full guardianship of incapacitated individuals.

(e) Limited Guardianship of Adult [GL]. All matters involving limited guardianship of incapacitated individuals.

(f) Minor Guardianship [GM]. All matters involving full guardianship of minors.

(g) Limited Guardianship of Minor [LG]. All matters involving limited guardianship of minors.

(h) Protective Orders [PO]. All protective orders requested under the estates and protected individuals code except when filed in conjunction with a petition for conservatorship. All petitions filed under MCL 333.5682 regarding POST forms except when filed in conjunction with a petition for guardianship.

(3) *Mental Illness Proceedings and Judicial Admission.* These case types may also be filed in the family division of circuit court as an ancillary proceeding.

(a) Judicial Admission [JA]. All matters involving judicial admission of individuals with developmental disability.

(b) Mental Illness Proceedings [MI]. All mental illness and substance use disorder proceedings brought under the mental health code.

(4) *Civil and Miscellaneous Proceedings.*

(a) Delayed Registration of Birth [BR]. All petitions and orders on denial of application for delayed registration of birth pursuant to MCL 333.2828 and petitions and orders for delayed registration of foreign birth pursuant to MCL 333.2830.

(b) Civil [CZ]. All civil matters commenced under MCR 5.101(C).

(c) Miscellaneous Matters [ML]. All other matters filed with the probate court for judicial or administrative action including but not limited to: appeal of land owner on an assessment made by the county road commissioner or state highway commissioner under Chapter 247; appeal of a determination made by the department of treasury under the Michigan Estate Tax Act; appeal by an adoptee, the adoptee's guardian, or the adoptive parent or parents of a determination made by the department of health and human services under the Social Welfare Act; appeal of a determination made by the drain commission under the Drain Code of 1956; appeal of a redetermination of ability to pay for mental health services made under the mental health code; condemnation proceedings; death by accident or disaster; filing of letters by foreign personal representative; kidney transplants; lost instruments; opening of safe deposit box; support of poor persons; and uniform transfers/gifts to minors acts.

[Amended effective January 18, 2018, 501 Mich; January 1, 2019, 502 Mich; July 1, 2019, 503 Mich.]

CHAPTER 1. GENERAL PROVISIONS

Effective March 1, 1985

SUBCHAPTER 1.100 APPLICABILITY; CONSTRUCTION

Rule 1.101 Title; Citation

These rules are the "Michigan Court Rules of 1985". An individual rule may be referred to as "Michigan Court Rule _____", and cited by the symbol "MCR _____". For example, this rule may be cited as MCR 1.101.

[Adopted effective March 1, 1985.]

Comments

Staff Comment to 1985 Adoption

MCR 1.101 corresponds to the second paragraph of GCR 1963, 11.1.

The Michigan Court Rules of 1985 are based on the proposal of the Committee To Revise and Consolidate the Court Rules, which was originally published in 1978. See 402A Mich. Revisions were made in response to comments received, and additional proposals were developed that had not been included in the earlier publication. On July 29, 1983, the Supreme Court ordered that the revised draft be published for comment. See 417A Mich. A committee of judges and lawyers was appointed to review the comments and to advise the Court as to whether further modifications should be made. After the submission of the committee report, the Supreme Court again considered the rules and adopted them in the present form.

These rules replace the General Court Rules of 1963, the Rules of the Court of Claims, the District Court Rules, the Probate Court Rules of 1972, and the Juvenile Court Rules of 1969. They take into account all amendments of the former rules through July 31, 1984. The Michigan Court Rules do not replace the Michigan Rules of Evidence, the Code of Professional Responsibility and Canons, the Code of Judicial Conduct, the Rules Concerning the State Bar, and the Rules for the Board of Law Examiners.

Rule 1.102 Effective Date

These rules take effect on March 1, 1985. They govern all proceedings in actions brought on or after that date, and all further proceedings in actions then pending. A court may permit a pending action to proceed under the former rules if it finds that the application of these rules to that action would not be feasible or would work injustice.

[Adopted effective March 1, 1985.]

Comments

Staff Comment to 1985 Adoption

MCR 1.102 is comparable to GCR 1963, 14.

Rule 1.103 Applicability

The Michigan Court Rules govern practice and procedure in all courts established by the constitution and laws of the State of Michigan. Rules stated to be applicable only in a specific court or only to a specific type of proceeding apply only to that court or to that type of proceeding and control over general rules.

[Adopted effective March 1, 1985.]

Comments

Staff Comment to 1985 Adoption

MCR 1.103 revises GCR 1963, 11, covering the applicability of the rules to the various courts. The Michigan Court Rules differ from the General Court Rules of 1963 in that a single set of rules is made applicable to all courts. However, various rules are by their terms applicable only in certain courts or to certain types of proceedings. Several chapters include provisions as to the applicability of the rules within each. See MCR 3.001, 4.001, 5.001, 6.001.

Rule 1.104 Statutory Practice Provisions

Rules of practice set forth in any statute, if not in conflict with any of these rules, are effective until superseded by rules adopted by the Supreme Court.

[Adopted effective March 1, 1985.]

Comments

Staff Comment to 1985 Adoption

MCR 1.104 is substantially the same as GCR 1963, 16.

Rule 1.105. Construction

These rules are to be construed, administered, and employed by the parties and the court to secure the just, speedy, and economical determination of every action and to avoid the consequences of error that does not affect the substantial rights of the parties.

[Adopted effective March 1, 1985. Amended June 19, 2019, effective January 1, 2020, 503 Mich.]

Comments

Staff Comment to 1985 Adoption

MCR 1.105 is substantially the same as GCR 1963, 13.

Staff Comment to 2020 Amendment

These amendments are based on a proposal created by a special committee of the State Bar of Michigan and approved for submission to the Court by the Bar's Representative Assembly. The rules require mandatory discovery disclosure in many cases, adopt a presumptive limit on interrogatories (20 in most cases, but 35 in domestic relations proceedings) and limit a deposition to 7 hours. The amendments also update the rules to more specifically address issues related to electronically stored information, and encourage early action on discovery issues during the discovery period.

The amendment of MCR 2.309(A)(2) sets a presumptive limit of twenty interrogatories for each separately represented party. Several commenters suggested that the term "discrete subpart" be more explicitly defined. But the rule's reference to "a discrete subpart" is intended to draw guidance from federal courts construing FR Civ P 30(a)(1). Generally, subparts are not separately counted if they are logically or factually subsumed within and necessarily related to the primary question. In upholding the limit, parties and courts should also pragmatically balance the overall goals of discovery and the admonition of MCR 1.105. Further, the intent of the provision at MCR 2.301(B)(4) is to ensure that parties responding to discovery requests have the full time period to do so as provided for under these rules prior to the expiration of the discovery period.

Rule 1.106 Catch Lines

The catch lines of a rule are not part of the rule and may not be used to construe the rule more broadly or more narrowly than the text indicates.

[Adopted effective March 1, 1985.]

Comments

Staff Comment to 1985 Adoption

MCR 1.106 is substantially the same as GCR 1963, 15.

Rule 1.107 Number

Words used in the singular also apply to the plural, where appropriate.

[Adopted effective March 1, 1985.]

Comments

Staff Comment to 1985 Adoption

MCR 1.107 is new.

Rule 1.108.   Computation of Time

In computing a period of time prescribed or allowed by these rules, by court order, or by statute, the following rules apply:

(1) The day of the act, event, or default after which the designated period of time begins to run is not included. The last day of the period is included, unless it is a Saturday, Sunday, legal holiday, or day on which the court is closed pursuant to court order; in that event the period runs until the end of the next day that is not a Saturday, Sunday, legal holiday, or day on which the court is closed pursuant to court order.

(2) If a period is measured by a number of weeks, the last day of the period is the same day of the week as the day on which the period began.

(3) If a period is measured by months or years, the last day of the period is the same day of the month as the day on which the period began. If what would otherwise be the final month does not include that day, the last day of the period is the last day of that month. For example, "2 months" after January 31 is March 31, and "3 months" after January 31 is April 30.

[Adopted effective March 1, 1985. Amended effective September 21, 2010, 487 Mich.]

Comments

Staff Comment to 1985 Adoption

MCR 1.108 includes the provisions of GCR 108.6 regarding computation of time.

In addition, new language is added covering computation of time periods measured in weeks, months, and years, based in part on PCR 108.4.

Staff Comment to 2010 Amendment

The amendment of MCR 1.108(1) extends the rule to any day that the court has ordered a court closure. A time period would be extended to the next day the court is open.

Rule 1.109.   Court Records Defined; Document Defined; Filing Standards; Signatures; Electronic Filing and Service; Access

Rule 1.109 effective until December 31, 2020. See following Rule 8.119, effective January 1, 2021.

(A) Court Records Defined.

(1) Court records are defined by MCR 8.119 and this subrule. Court records are recorded information of any kind that has been created by the court or filed with the court in accordance with Michigan Court Rules. Court records may be created using any means and may be maintained in any medium authorized by these court rules provided those records comply with other provisions of law and these court rules.

(a) Court records include, but are not limited to:

(i) documents, attachments to documents, discovery materials, and other materials filed with the clerk of the court,

(ii) documents, recordings, data, and other recorded information created or handled by the court, including all data produced in conjunction with the use of any system for the purpose of transmitting, accessing, reproducing, or maintaining court records.

(b) For purposes of this subrule:

(i) Documents include, but are not limited to, pleadings, orders, and judgments.

(ii) Recordings refer to audio and video recordings (whether analog or digital), stenotapes, log notes, and other related records.

(iii) Data refers to any information entered in the case management system that is not ordinarily reduced to a document, but that is still recorded information, and any data entered into or created by the statewide electronic-filing system.

(iv) Other recorded information includes, but is not limited to, notices, bench warrants, arrest warrants, and other process issued by the court that do not have to be maintained on paper or digital image.

(2) Discovery materials that are not filed with the clerk of the court are not court records. Exhibits that are maintained by the court reporter or other authorized staff pursuant to MCR 2.518 or MCR 3.930 during the pendency of a proceeding are not court records.

(B) Document Defined.   A document means a record produced on paper or a digital image of a record originally produced on paper or originally created by an approved electronic means, the output of which is readable by sight and can be printed to 8 ½ × 11 inch paper without manipulation.

(C) Filing With Court Defined.   Pleadings and other documents and materials filed with the court as required by these court rules must be filed with the clerk of the court in accordance with MCR 1.109(D), except that the judge to whom the case is assigned may accept materials for filing when circumstances warrant. A judge who does so shall note the filing date on the materials and immediately transmit them to the clerk. It is the responsibility of the party who presented the materials to the judge to confirm that they have been filed with the clerk. If the clerk records the receipt of materials on a date other than the filing date, the clerk shall record the filing date in the case history.

(D) Filing Standards.

(1) *Form and Captions of Documents.*

(a) All documents prepared for filing in the courts of this state and all documents prepared by the court for placement in a case file must be legible and in the English language, comply with standards established by the State Court Administrative Office, and be on good quality 8½ by 11 inch paper or transmitted through an approved electronic means and maintained as a digital image. The font size must be 12 or 13 point for body text and no less than 10 point for footnotes, except with regard to forms approved by the State Court Administrative Office. Transcripts filed with the court must contain only a single transcript page per document page, not multiple pages combined on a single document page.

(b) The first part of every document must contain a caption stating:

(i) the name of the court;

(ii) the names of the parties or the title of the action or proceeding, subject to (c);

(iii) the case number, including a prefix of the year filed and a two-letter suffix for the case-type code from a list provided by the State Court Administrator pursuant to MCR 8.117, according to the principal subject matter of the proceeding;

(iv) the identification of the document;

(v) the name, business address, telephone number, and state bar number of each attorney appearing in the case; and

(vi) the name, an address, and telephone number of each party appearing without an attorney.

(c) In a civil action initiating document, the title of the action must include the names of all the parties, with the plaintiff's name placed first. In subsequent documents, it is sufficient to state the name of the first party on each side with an appropriate indication of other parties, such as "et al."

(d) In a case filed under the juvenile code, the caption must also contain a petition number, where appropriate.

(e) If an action has been assigned to a particular judge in a multi-judge court, the name of that judge must be included in the caption of a document later filed with the court.

(f) An affidavit must be verified by oath or affirmation.

(g) Pursuant to Administrative Order No. 2006–2, a filer is prohibited from filing a document that contains another person's social security number except when the number is required or allowed by statute, court rule, court order, or for purposes of collection activity when it is required for identification.

(2) *Case Initiation Information.* A party filing a case initiating document and a party filing any response or answer to a case initiating document shall provide specified case information in the form and manner established by the State Court Administrative Office and as specified in other applicable rules. At a minimum, specified case information shall include the name, an address for service, an e-mail address, and a telephone number of every party, and:

(a) in a civil action, either of the following statements:

(i) There is no other pending or resolved civil action arising out of the transaction or occurrence alleged in the complaint, or

(ii) A civil action between these parties or other parties arising out of the transaction or occurrence alleged in the complaint has been previously filed in [this court]/ [_____ Court], where it was given case number _____ and was assigned to Judge _____. The action [remains]/[is no longer] pending.

(b) in proceedings governed by chapters 3.200 and 3.900, except for outgoing requests to other states and incoming registration actions filed under the Revised Uniform Reciprocal Enforcement of Support Act, MCL 780.151 *et seq.* and the Uniform Interstate Family Support Act, MCL 552.2101 *et seq.*, either of the following statements, if known:

(i) There are no pending or resolved cases within the jurisdiction of the family division of the circuit court involving the family or family members of the person[s] who [is/are] the subject of the complaint or petition, or

(ii) There is one or more pending or resolved cases within the jurisdiction of the family division of the circuit court involving the family or family members of the person[s] who [is/are] the subject of the complaint or petition. I have filed a completed case inventory listing those cases.

(3) *Verification.* Except when otherwise specifically provided by rule or statute, a document need not be verified or accompanied by an affidavit. If a document is required or permitted to be verified, it may be verified by

(a) oath or affirmation of the party or of someone having knowledge of the facts stated; or

(b) except as to an affidavit, including the following signed and dated declaration:

"I declare under the penalties of perjury that this _____ has been examined by me and that its contents are true to the best of my information, knowledge, and belief." Any requirement of law that a document filed with the probate court must be sworn may be also met by this declaration.

In addition to the sanctions provided by subrule (E), a person who knowingly makes a false declaration under this subrule may be found in contempt of court.

(4) All other materials submitted for filing shall be prepared in accordance with this subrule and standards established by the State Court Administrative Office. An attachment or discovery material that is submitted for filing shall be made part of the public case file unless otherwise confidential.

(5) Except where electronic filing is implemented, all original documents filed on paper may be reproduced and maintained by the court as a digital image in place of the paper original in accordance with standards established by the State Court Administrative Office. Any document reproduced under this subrule replaces the paper as the official record.

(6) A clerk of the court may reject nonconforming documents as prescribed by MCR 8.119.

(7) Electronic filing and electronic service of documents is governed by subrule (G) and the policies and standards of the State Court Administrative Office.

(8) *Filing Documents Under Seal.* Public documents may not be filed under seal except when the court has previously entered an order in the case under MCR 2.302(C). However, a document may be made nonpublic temporarily before an order is entered as follows:

(a) A filer may request that a public document be made nonpublic temporarily when filing a motion to seal a document under MCR 8.119(I). As part of the filing, the filer shall provide a proposed order granting the motion to seal and shall identify each document that is to be sealed under the order. The filer shall bear the burden of establishing good cause for sealing the document.

(b) Pending the court's order, the filer shall serve on all the parties:

(i) copies of the motion to seal and the request to make each document nonpublic temporarily,

(ii) each document to be sealed, and

(iii) the proposed order.

(c) The clerk of the court shall ensure that the documents identified in the motion are made nonpublic pending entry of the order.

(d) Before entering an order sealing a document under this rule, the court shall comply with MCR 8.119(I). On entry of the order on the motion, the clerk shall seal only those documents stated in the court's order and shall remove the nonpublic status of any of the documents that were not stated in the order.

(E) Signatures.

(1) A signature, as required by these court rules and law, means a written signature as defined by MCL 8.3q or an electronic signature as defined by this subrule.

(2) *Requirement.* Every document filed shall be signed by the person filing it or by at least one attorney of record. A party who is not represented by an attorney must sign the document. In probate proceedings the following also applies:

(a) When a person is represented by an attorney, the signature of the attorney is required on any paper filed in a form approved by the State Court Administrator only if the form includes a place for a signature.

(b) An application, petition, or other paper may be signed by the attorney for the petitioner, except that an inventory, account, acceptance of appointment, and sworn closing statement must be signed by the fiduciary or trustee. A receipt for assets must be signed by the person entitled to the assets.

(3) *Failure to Sign.* If a document is not signed, it shall be stricken unless it is signed promptly after the omission is called to the attention of the party.

(4) An electronic signature is acceptable in accordance with this subrule.

(a) An electronic signature means an electronic sound, symbol, or process, attached to or logically associated with a record and executed or adopted by a person with the intent to sign the record. The following form is acceptable: /s/ *John L. Smith*.

(b) Retention of a signature electronically affixed to a document that will be retained by the court in electronic format must not be dependent upon the mechanism that was used to affix that signature.

(5) *Effect of Signature.* The signature of a person filing a document, whether or not represented by an attorney, constitutes a certification by the signer that:

(a) he or she has read the document;

(b) to the best of his or her knowledge, information, and belief formed after reasonable inquiry, the document is well grounded in fact and is warranted by existing law or a good-faith argument for the extension, modification, or reversal of existing law; and

(c) the document is not interposed for any improper purpose, such as to harass or to cause unnecessary delay or needless increase in the cost of litigation.

(6) *Sanctions for Violation.* If a document is signed in violation of this rule, the court, on the motion of a party or on its own initiative, shall impose upon the person who signed it, a represented party, or both, an appropriate sanction, which may include an order to pay to the other party or parties the amount of the reasonable expenses incurred because of the filing of the document, including reasonable attorney fees. The court may not assess punitive damages.

(7) *Sanctions for Frivolous Claims and Defenses.* In addition to sanctions under this rule, a party pleading a frivolous claim or defense is subject to costs as provided in MCR 2.625(A)(2). The court may not assess punitive damages.

(F) Requests for access to public court records shall be granted in accordance with MCR 8.119(H).

(G) Electronic Filing and Service.

(1) *Definitions.* For purposes of this subrule:

(a) "Authorized user" means a user of the e-filing system who is registered to file, serve, and receive documents and related data through approved electronic means. A court may revoke user authorization for good cause as determined by the court, including but not limited to a security breach.

(b) "Electronic filing" or "e-filing" means the electronic transmission of data and documents to the court through the electronic-filing system.

(c) "Electronic-filing system" means a system provided by the State Court Administrative Office that permits electronic transmission of data and documents.

(d) "Electronic notification" means the electronic transmission of information from the court to authorized users through the electronic-filing system. This does not apply to service of documents. See subrule (f).

(e) "Electronic service" or "e-service" means the electronic service of information by means of the electronic-filing system under this rule. It does not include service by alternative electronic service under MCR 2.107(C)(4).

(f) "Notice of electronic filing or service" means a notice automatically generated by the e-filing system at the time a document is filed or served.

(2) *Electronic–Filing and Electronic–Service Standards.* Courts shall implement electronic filing and electronic service capabilities in accordance with this rule and shall comply with the standards established by the State Court Administrative Office. Confidential and nonpublic information must be electronically filed or electronically served in compliance with these standards to ensure secure transmission of the information.

(3) *Scope and Applicability.*

(a) A court shall:

(i) accept electronic filing and permit electronic service of documents;

(ii) comply with the electronic-filing guidelines and plans approved by the State Court Administrative Office; and

(iii) maintain electronic documents in accordance with the standards established by the State Court Administrative Office.

(b) A court may allow documents, including but not limited to materials related to case evaluations or inventory information for decedent estates, to be transmitted to the court for purposes other than filing in a case file.

(c) Non–Electronic Materials. Courts must accommodate the filing and serving of materials that cannot be filed or served electronically.

(d) Converting Paper Documents. The clerk of the court shall convert to electronic format any document filed on paper.

(e) A court may electronically serve notices, orders, opinions, and other documents by means of the electronic-filing system.

(f) For the required case types, attorneys must electronically file documents in courts where electronic filing has been implemented. All other filers are required to electronically file documents only in courts that have been granted approval to mandate electronic filing by the State Court Administrative Office under AO 2019-XX.

(g) Where electronic filing is mandated, a party may file paper documents with that court and be served with paper documents according to subrule (G)(6)(a)(ii) if the party can demonstrate good cause for an exemption. For purposes of this rule, a court shall consider the following factors in determining whether the party has demonstrated good cause:

(i) Whether the person has a lack of reliable access to an electronic device that includes access to the Internet;

(ii) Whether the person must travel an unreasonable distance to access a public computer or has limited access to transportation and is unable to access the e-Filing system from home;

(iii) Whether the person has the technical ability to use and understand email and electronic filing software;

(iv) Whether access from a home computer system or the ability to gain access at a public computer terminal present a safety issue for the person;

(v) Any other relevant factor raised by a person.

(h) Upon request, the following persons are exempt from electronic filing without the need to demonstrate good cause:

(i) a person who has a disability that prevents or limits the person's ability to use the electronic filing system;

(ii) a person who has limited English proficiency that prevents or limits the person's ability to use the electronic filing system; and

(iii) a party who is confined by governmental authority, including but not limited to an individual who is incarcerated in a jail or prison facility, detained in a juvenile facility, or committed to a medical or mental health facility.

(i) A request for an exemption must be filed with the court in paper where the individual's case will be or has been filed. If the individual filed paper documents at the same time as the request for exemption, the clerk shall process the documents for filing. If the documents meet the filing requirements of subrule (D), they will be considered filed on the day they were submitted.

(i) The request for an exemption must be on a form approved by the State Court Administrative Office and verified under MCR 1.109(D)(3). There is no fee for the request.

(ii) The request must specify the reasons that prevent the individual from filing electronically. The individual may file supporting documents along with the request for the court's consideration.

(iii) A judge must review the request and any supporting documentation and issue an order granting or denying the request within two business days of the date the request was filed.

(iv) The clerk of the court must promptly mail the order to the individual. The clerk must place the request, any supporting documentation, and the order in the case file. If there is no case file, the documents must be maintained in a group file.

(v) An exemption granted under this rule is valid only for the court in which it was filed and for the life of the case unless the individual exempted from filing electronically registers with the electronic-filing system. In that event, the individual waives the exemption and becomes subject to the rules of electronic filing and the requirements of the electronic-filing system. An individual who waives an exemption under this rule may file another request for exemption.

(4) *Official Court Record.* The electronic version of any document filed with or generated by the court under this rule and any case initiation data transmitted in accordance with subrule (D)(2) is an official court record.

(5) *Electronic–Filing Process.*

(a) General Provisions.

(i) Specified case information, including e-mail addresses for achieving electronic service, shall be provided electronically by the authorized user in the form and manner established by the State Court Administrative Office pursuant to subrule (D)(2).

(ii) The authorized user has the responsibility of ensuring that a filing has been received by the electronic-filing system. If the authorized user discovers that the version of the document available for viewing through the e-filing system does not depict the document as submitted, the authorized user shall notify the clerk of the court immediately and resubmit the filing if necessary. In the event of a controversy between the clerk of the court and the authorized user, the authorized user may file a motion with the court under subrule (G)(7).

(iii) If the clerk of the court rejects a submitted document pursuant to MCR 8.119(C), the clerk shall notify the authorized user of the rejection and the reason for the rejection. A rejected document shall not become part of the official court record and the rejection shall be recorded in an electronic-filing transaction from the court to the authorized user in accordance with subrule (c).

(b) Time and Effect of Electronic Filing. A document submitted electronically is deemed filed with the court when the transmission to the electronic-filing system is completed and the required filing fees have been paid or waived. If a document is submitted with a request to waive the filing fees, no fees will be charged at the time of filing and the document is deemed filed on the date the document was submitted to the court. A transmission is completed when the transaction is recorded as prescribed in subrule (c). Regardless of the date a filing is accepted by the clerk of the court, the date of filing is the date submitted. Electronic filing is not restricted by the operating hours of a court and any document submitted at or before 11:59 p.m. of a business day is deemed filed on that business day. Any document submitted on a Saturday, Sunday, legal holiday, or other day on which the court is closed pursuant to court order is deemed filed on the next business day.

(c) Electronic–Filing Transaction. On receipt of a submission or on rejection of a submission for nonpayment, the electronic-filing system shall record the filing transaction and send a notice of receipt of the submission and payment or rejection to the authorized user. When the filing transaction is date and time stamped, the electronic-filing system shall record the filing transaction and send a notice of electronic-filing to the authorized user. If the filing is rejected, the electronic-filing system shall record the rejection and send a notice of the rejection to the authorized user. The system shall maintain for every court a record of each submission, payment, filing, and rejection transaction in accordance with the records retention and disposal schedules and standards established by the State Court Administrative Office. A notice of electronic filing shall include the date and time of the transaction, the name of the authorized user filing the document(s), the type of document, the name of the authorized user receiving the notice, and a hyperlink to the filed or rejected document(s).

(d) Documents Under Seal. Except for documents filed pursuant to a protective order issued under MCR 2.302(C), a party seeking to file a document under seal must comply with subrule (D)(8).

(6) *Electronic–Service Process.*

(a) General Provisions.

(i) Service of process of case initiating documents shall be made in accordance with the rules and laws required for the particular case type.

(ii) Service of process of all other documents electronically filed shall be accomplished electronically among authorized users through the electronic-filing system unless one or more parties have been exempted from electronic filing, or a party has not filed a response or answer or has not registered with the electronic-filing system and that party's e-mail address is unknown. In those circumstances, service shall be made on that party by any other method required by Michigan Court Rules.

(iii) Delivery of documents through the electronic-filing system in conformity with these rules is valid and effective personal service and is proof of service under Michigan Court Rules.

(iv) Except for service of process of initiating documents and as otherwise directed by the court or court rule, service may be performed simultaneously with filing.

(v) When a court rule permits service by mail, service may be accomplished electronically under this subrule.

(b) Time and Effect. A document served electronically through the electronic-filing system in conformity with all applicable requirements of this rule is considered served when the transmission to the recipient's e-mail address is completed. A transmission is completed when the transaction is recorded as prescribed in subrule (c).

(c) Electronic–Service Transaction. On transmission of a document, the electronic-filing system shall record the service transaction. The system shall maintain for every court a record of each service transaction in accordance with the state-approved records retention and disposal schedules and standards established by the State Court Administrative Office.

(7) *Transmission Failures.*

(a) In the event the electronic-filing system fails to transmit a document submitted for filing, the authorized user may file a motion requesting that the court enter an order permitting the document to be deemed filed on the date it was first attempted to be sent electronically. The authorized user must prove to the court's satisfaction that:

(i) the filing was attempted at the time asserted by the authorized user;

(ii) the electronic-filing system failed to transmit the electronic document; and

(iii) the transmission failure was not caused, in whole or in part, by any action or inaction of the authorized user. A transmission failure caused by a problem with a filer's telephone line, ISP, hardware, or software shall be attributed to the filer.

(b) Scheduled system outages, such as for system maintenance, shall be posted on the MiFILE website.

(c) Notice shall be provided on the MiFILE website and/or the One Court of Justice website if the electronic-filing system becomes unavailable for an extended or indefinite period. The notice shall indicate that filers are responsible for filing documents on paper and serving paper in another manner required by Michigan Court Rules in order to meet any deadlines imposed by statute or court rule.

[Adopted February 22, 1990, effective January 1, 1991, 434 Mich. Amended September 30, 2003, effective January 1, 2004, 469 Mich. Amended effective May 24, 2012, 491 Mich. Amended October 31, 2012, effective January 1, 2013, 493 Mich; May 30, 2018, effective September 1, 2018, 501 Mich. Amended March 20, 2019, effective May 1, 2019, 503 Mich. Amended effective August 14, 2019, 503 Mich. Amended June 5, 2019, effective September 1, 2019, 503 Mich. Amended effective September 11, 2019, 503 Mich. Amended September 18, 2019 effective January 1, 2020, 503 Mich.]

Rule 1.109. Court Records Defined; Document Defined; Filing Standards; Signatures; Electronic Filing and Service; Access

Rule 1.109 effective January 1, 2021. See previous Rule 1.109, effective until December 31, 2020.

(A) Court Records Defined.

(1) Court records are defined by MCR 8.119 and this subrule. Court records are recorded information of any kind that has been created by the court or filed with the court in accordance with Michigan Court Rules. Court records may be created using any means and may be maintained in any medium authorized by these court rules provided those records comply with other provisions of law and these court rules.

(a) Court records include, but are not limited to:

(i) documents, attachments to documents, discovery materials, and other materials filed with the clerk of the court,

(ii) documents, recordings, data, and other recorded information created or handled by the court, including all data produced in conjunction with the use of any system for the purpose of transmitting, accessing, reproducing, or maintaining court records.

(b) For purposes of this subrule:

(i) Documents include, but are not limited to, pleadings, orders, and judgments.

(ii) Recordings refer to audio and video recordings (whether analog or digital), stenotapes, log notes, and other related records.

(iii) Data refers to any information entered in the case management system that is not ordinarily reduced to a document, but that is still recorded information, and any data entered into or created by the statewide electronic-filing system.

(iv) Other recorded information includes, but is not limited to, notices, bench warrants, arrest warrants, and other process issued by the court that do not have to be maintained on paper or digital image.

(2) Discovery materials that are not filed with the clerk of the court are not court records. Exhibits that are maintained by the court reporter or other authorized staff pursuant to MCR 2.518 or MCR 3.930 during the pendency of a proceeding are not court records.

(B) Document Defined. A document means a record produced on paper or a digital image of a record originally produced on paper or originally created by an approved electronic means, the output of which is readable by sight and can be printed to $8 \frac{1}{2} \times 11$ inch paper without manipulation.

(C) Filing With Court Defined. Pleadings and other documents and materials filed with the court as required by these court rules must be filed with the clerk of the court in accordance with MCR 1.109(D), except that the judge to whom the case is assigned may accept materials for filing when circumstances warrant. A judge who does so shall note the filing date on the materials and immediately transmit them to the clerk. It is the responsibility of the party who presented the materials to the judge to confirm that they have been filed with the clerk. If the clerk records the receipt of materials on a date other than the filing date, the clerk shall record the filing date in the case history.

(D) Filing Standards.

(1) *Form and Captions of Documents.*

(a) All documents prepared for filing in the courts of this state and all documents prepared by the court for placement in a case file must be legible and in the English language, comply with standards established by the State Court Administrative Office, and be on good quality 8½ by 11 inch paper or transmitted through an approved electronic means and maintained as a digital image. The font size must be 12 or 13 point for body text and no less than 10 point for footnotes, except with regard to forms approved by the State Court Administrative Office. Transcripts filed with the court must contain only a single transcript page per document page, not multiple pages combined on a single document page.

(b) The first part of every document must contain a caption stating:

(i) the name of the court;

(ii) the names of the parties or the title of the action or proceeding, subject to (c);

(iii) the case number, including a prefix of the year filed and a two-letter suffix for the case-type code from a list provided by the State Court Administrator pursuant to MCR 8.117, according to the principal subject matter of the proceeding;

(iv) the identification of the document;

(v) the name, business address, telephone number, and state bar number of each attorney appearing in the case; and

(vi) the name, an address, and telephone number of each party appearing without an attorney.

(c) In a civil action initiating document, the title of the action must include the names of all the parties, with the plaintiff's name placed first. In subsequent documents, it is sufficient to state the name of the first party on each side with an appropriate indication of other parties, such as "et al."

(d) In a case filed under the juvenile code, the caption must also contain a petition number, where appropriate.

(e) If an action has been assigned to a particular judge in a multi-judge court, the name of that judge must be included in the caption of a document later filed with the court.

(f) An affidavit must be verified by oath or affirmation.

(2) *Case Initiation Information.* A party filing a case initiating document and a party filing any response or answer to a case initiating document shall provide specified case information in the form and manner established by the State Court Administrative Office and as specified in other applicable rules. At a minimum, specified case information shall include the name, an address for service, an e-mail address, and a telephone number of every party, and:

(a) in a civil action, either of the following statements:

(i) There is no other pending or resolved civil action arising out of the transaction or occurrence alleged in the complaint, or

(ii) A civil action between these parties or other parties arising out of the transaction or occurrence alleged in the complaint has been previously filed in [this court]/ [_____ Court], where it was given case number _____ and was assigned to Judge _____. The action [remains]/[is no longer] pending.

(b) in proceedings governed by chapters 3.200 and 3.900, except for outgoing requests to other states and incoming registration actions filed under the Revised Uniform Reciprocal Enforcement of Support Act, MCL 780.151 *et seq.* and the Uniform Interstate Family Support Act, MCL 552.2101 *et seq.*, either of the following statements, if known:

(i) There are no pending or resolved cases within the jurisdiction of the family division of the circuit court involving the family or family members of the person[s] who [is/are] the subject of the complaint or petition, or

(ii) There is one or more pending or resolved cases within the jurisdiction of the family division of the circuit court involving the family or family members of the person[s] who [is/are] the subject of the complaint or petition. I have filed a completed case inventory listing those cases.

(3) *Verification.* Except when otherwise specifically provided by rule or statute, a document need not be verified or accompanied by an affidavit. If a document is required or permitted to be verified, it may be verified by

(a) oath or affirmation of the party or of someone having knowledge of the facts stated; or

(b) except as to an affidavit, including the following signed and dated declaration:

"I declare under the penalties of perjury that this _____ has been examined by me and that its contents are true to the best of my information, knowledge, and belief." Any requirement of law that a document filed with the probate court must be sworn may be also met by this declaration.

In addition to the sanctions provided by subrule (E), a person who knowingly makes a false declaration under this subrule may be found in contempt of court.

(4) All other materials submitted for filing shall be prepared in accordance with this subrule and standards established by the State Court Administrative Office. An attachment or discovery material that is submitted for filing shall be made part of the public case file unless otherwise confidential.

(5) Except where electronic filing is implemented, all original documents filed on paper may be reproduced and maintained by the court as a digital image in place of the paper original in accordance with standards established by the State Court Administrative Office. Any document reproduced under this subrule replaces the paper as the official record.

(6) A clerk of the court may reject nonconforming documents as prescribed by MCR 8.119.

(7) Electronic filing and electronic service of documents is governed by subrule (G) and the policies and standards of the State Court Administrative Office.

(8) *Filing Documents Under Seal.* Public documents may not be filed under seal except when the court has previously entered an order in the case under MCR 2.302(C). However, a document may be made nonpublic temporarily before an order is entered as follows:

(a) A filer may request that a public document be made nonpublic temporarily when filing a motion to seal a document under MCR 8.119(I). As part of the filing, the filer shall provide a proposed order granting the motion to seal and shall identify each document that is to be sealed under the order. The filer shall bear the burden of establishing good cause for sealing the document.

(b) Pending the court's order, the filer shall serve on all the parties:

(i) copies of the motion to seal and the request to make each document nonpublic temporarily,

(ii) each document to be sealed, and

(iii) the proposed order.

(c) The clerk of the court shall ensure that the documents identified in the motion are made nonpublic pending entry of the order.

(d) Before entering an order sealing a document under this rule, the court shall comply with MCR 8.119(I). On entry of the order on the motion, the clerk shall seal only those documents stated in the court's order and shall remove the nonpublic status of any of the documents that were not stated in the order.

(9) *Personal Identifying Information.*

(a) The following personal identifying information is protected and shall not be included in any public document or attachment filed with the court except as provided by these rules:

(i) date of birth,

(ii) social security number or national identification number,

(iii) driver's license number or state-issued personal identification card number,

(iv) passport number, and

(v) financial account numbers.

(b) Filing, Accessing, and Serving Personal Identifying Information

(i) All protected personal identifying information listed in this rule that is required by law or court rule to be filed with the court or that is necessary to the court for purposes of identifying a particular person in a case must be provided to the court in the form and manner established by the State Court Administrative Office.

(ii) Where a social security number is required to be filed with the court, it shall be the last four digits only. This requirement does not apply to documents required to be filed with the friend of the court that are not placed in the court's legal file under MCR 8.119(D).

(iii) If a party is required to include protected personal identifying information in a public document filed with the court, the party shall file the document with the protected personal identifying information redacted, along with a personal identifying information form approved by the State Court Administrative Office under subrule (i). The personal identifying information form must identify each item of redacted information and specify an appropriate reference that uniquely corresponds to each item of redacted information listed. All references in the case to the redacted identifiers listed in the personal identifying information form will be understood to refer to the corresponding complete identifier. A party may amend the personal identifying information form as of right. Fields for protected personal identifying information will not be included in SCAO-approved court forms.

(iv) Protected personal identifying information provided under this subrule is nonpublic and available, as required for case activity or as otherwise authorized by law or these court rules, only to the parties to the case; interested persons as defined in these court rules; and other persons, entities, or agencies entitled by law or these court rules to access nonpublic records filed with the court.

(v) A party may stipulate in writing to allow access to his or her protected personal identifying information to any person, entity, or agency.

(vi) A party or a court is not exempt from the requirement to serve a nonpublic document containing protected personal identifying information that has been filed with the court under subrule (i), except by court order in accordance with subrule (vii).

(vii) Upon a finding of just cause, on the court's own motion or on motion of the party, the court may order any personal identifying information be made confidential. The order shall identify the party, person, or entity to whom access is restricted. If a party's home address or telephone number is made confidential, the order shall designate an alternative address for serving documents on that party or provide an alternative telephone number for making contact with that party for purposes of case activity.

(c) Local court forms shall not contain fields for protected personal identifying information. A court shall not reject a document for filing, dismiss a case, or take other negative action against a party for failure to file protected personal identifying information on a local court form.

(d) Failure to Comply.

(i) A party waives the protection of personal identifying information as to the party's own protected information by filing it in a public document and not providing it in the form and manner established under this rule.

(ii) If a party fails to comply with the requirements of this rule, the court may, upon motion or its own initiative, seal the improperly filed documents and order new redacted documents to be prepared and filed.

(e) Protected personal identifying information provided to the court as required by subrule (c) shall be entered into the court's case management system in accordance with standards established by the State Court Administrative Office. The information shall be maintained for the purposes for which it was collected and for which its use is authorized by federal or state law or court rule; however, it shall not be included or displayed as case history under MCR 8.119(D)(1).

(10) Request for Copy of Public Document with Protected Personal Identifying Information; Redacting Personal Identifying Information; Responsibility; Certifying Original Record; Other.

(a) The responsibility for excluding or redacting personal identifying information listed in subrule (9) from all documents filed with or offered to the court rests solely with the parties and their attorneys. The clerk of the court is not required to review, redact, or screen documents at time of filing for personal identifying information, protected or otherwise, whether filed electronically or on paper.

(b) Dissemination of social security numbers by the courts is restricted to the purposes for which its use is authorized by federal or state law. When a court receives a request for copies of any public document filed on or after March 1, 2006, the court must review the document and redact all social security numbers on the copy. This requirement does not apply to certified copies or true copies when they are required by law, or copies made for those uses for which the social security number was provided.

(c) Redacting Personal Identifying Information.

(i) Protected personal identifying information contained in a document and filed with the court shall be redacted by the clerk of the court on written request by the person to whom it applies. The clerk of the court shall process the request promptly. The request does not require a motion fee, must specify the protected personal identifying information to be redacted, and shall be maintained in the case file as a nonpublic document.

(ii) Personal identifying information that is not protected as identified in this rule may also be redacted or made confidential or nonpublic. The party or person whose personal identifying information is in a public document filed with the court may file an ex parte motion asking the court to direct the clerk to redact the information from that document or to make the information either confidential or nonpublic. The court may schedule a hearing on the motion at its discretion. The court shall enter such an order if the party or person's privacy interest outweighs the public's interest in the information. The motion shall be on a form approved by the state court administrative office, must specify the personal identifying information to be redacted, and shall be maintained in the case file as a nonpublic document.

(iii) A party or person whose protected personal identifying information is in an exhibit offered for hearing or trial may file a written request that the information be redacted. The request does not require a motion fee, must specify the protected personal identifying information to be redacted, and shall be maintained in the case file as a nonpublic document. The court shall enter such an order if the party or person's privacy interest outweighs the public's interest in the information.

(d) Certifying a Record. The clerk of the court may certify a redacted record as a true copy of an original record on file with the court by stating that information has been redacted in accordance with law or court rule, or sealed as ordered by the court.

(e) Maintenance of Redacted or Restricted Access Personal Identifying Information. A document from which personal identifying information has been redacted shall be maintained in accordance with standards established by the State Court Administrative Office.

(E) Signatures.

(1) A signature, as required by these court rules and law, means a written signature as defined by MCL 8.3q or an electronic signature as defined by this subrule.

(2) *Requirement.* Every document filed shall be signed by the person filing it or by at least one attorney of record. A party who is not represented by an attorney must sign the document. In probate proceedings the following also applies:

(a) When a person is represented by an attorney, the signature of the attorney is required on any paper filed in a form approved by the State Court Administrator only if the form includes a place for a signature.

(b) An application, petition, or other paper may be signed by the attorney for the petitioner, except that an inventory, account, acceptance of appointment, and sworn closing statement must be signed by the fiduciary or trustee. A receipt for assets must be signed by the person entitled to the assets.

(3) *Failure to Sign.* If a document is not signed, it shall be stricken unless it is signed promptly after the omission is called to the attention of the party.

(4) An electronic signature is acceptable in accordance with this subrule.

(a) An electronic signature means an electronic sound, symbol, or process, attached to or logically associated with a record and executed or adopted by a person with the intent to sign the record. The following form is acceptable: /s/ *John L. Smith.*

(b) Retention of a signature electronically affixed to a document that will be retained by the court in electronic format must not be dependent upon the mechanism that was used to affix that signature.

(5) *Effect of Signature.* The signature of a person filing a document, whether or not represented by an attorney, constitutes a certification by the signer that:

(a) he or she has read the document;

(b) to the best of his or her knowledge, information, and belief formed after reasonable inquiry, the document is well grounded in fact and is warranted by existing law or a good-faith argument for the extension, modification, or reversal of existing law; and

(c) the document is not interposed for any improper purpose, such as to harass or to cause unnecessary delay or needless increase in the cost of litigation.

(6) *Sanctions for Violation.* If a document is signed in violation of this rule, the court, on the motion of a party or on its own initiative, shall impose upon the person who signed it, a represented party, or both, an appropriate sanction, which may include an order to pay to the other party or parties the amount of the reasonable expenses incurred because of the filing of the document, including reasonable attorney fees. The court may not assess punitive damages.

(7) *Sanctions for Frivolous Claims and Defenses.* In addition to sanctions under this rule, a party pleading a frivolous claim or defense is subject to costs as provided in MCR 2.625(A)(2). The court may not assess punitive damages.

(F) Requests for access to public court records shall be granted in accordance with MCR 8.119(H).

(G) **Electronic Filing and Service.**

(1) *Definitions.* For purposes of this subrule:

(a) "Authorized user" means a user of the e-filing system who is registered to file, serve, and receive documents and related data through approved electronic means. A court may revoke user authorization for good cause as determined by the court, including but not limited to a security breach.

(b) "Electronic filing" or "e-filing" means the electronic transmission of data and documents to the court through the electronic-filing system.

(c) "Electronic-filing system" means a system provided by the State Court Administrative Office that permits electronic transmission of data and documents.

(d) "Electronic notification" means the electronic transmission of information from the court to authorized users through the electronic-filing system. This does not apply to service of documents. See subrule (f).

(e) "Electronic service" or "e-service" means the electronic service of information by means of the electronic-filing system under this rule. It does not include service by alternative electronic service under MCR 2.107(C)(4).

(f) "Notice of electronic filing or service" means a notice automatically generated by the e-filing system at the time a document is filed or served.

(2) *Electronic–Filing and Electronic–Service Standards.* Courts shall implement electronic filing and electronic service capabilities in accordance with this rule and shall comply with the standards established by the State Court Administrative Office. Confidential and nonpublic information must be elec-tronically filed or electronically served in compliance with these standards to ensure secure transmission of the information.

(3) *Scope and Applicability.*

(a) A court shall:

(i) accept electronic filing and permit electronic service of documents;

(ii) comply with the electronic-filing guidelines and plans approved by the State Court Administrative Office; and

(iii) maintain electronic documents in accordance with the standards established by the State Court Administrative Office.

(b) A court may allow documents, including but not limited to materials related to case evaluations or inventory information for decedent estates, to be transmitted to the court for purposes other than filing in a case file.

(c) Non–Electronic Materials. Courts must accommodate the filing and serving of materials that cannot be filed or served electronically.

(d) Converting Paper Documents. The clerk of the court shall convert to electronic format any document filed on paper.

(e) A court may electronically serve notices, orders, opinions, and other documents by means of the electronic-filing system.

(f) For the required case types, attorneys must electronically file documents in courts where electronic filing has been implemented. All other filers are required to electronically file documents only in courts that have been granted approval to mandate electronic filing by the State Court Administrative Office under AO 2019-XX.

(g) Where electronic filing is mandated, a party may file paper documents with that court and be served with paper documents according to subrule (G)(6)(a)(ii) if the party can demonstrate good cause for an exemption. For purposes of this rule, a court shall consider the following factors in determining whether the party has demonstrated good cause:

(i) Whether the person has a lack of reliable access to an electronic device that includes access to the Internet;

(ii) Whether the person must travel an unreasonable distance to access a public computer or has limited access to transportation and is unable to access the e-Filing system from home;

(iii) Whether the person has the technical ability to use and understand email and electronic filing software;

(iv) Whether access from a home computer system or the ability to gain access at a public computer terminal present a safety issue for the person;

(v) Any other relevant factor raised by a person.

(h) Upon request, the following persons are exempt from electronic filing without the need to demonstrate good cause:

(i) a person who has a disability that prevents or limits the person's ability to use the electronic filing system;

(ii) a person who has limited English proficiency that prevents or limits the person's ability to use the electronic filing system; and

(iii) a party who is confined by governmental authority, including but not limited to an individual who is incarcerated in a jail or prison facility, detained in a juvenile facility, or committed to a medical or mental health facility.

(i) A request for an exemption must be filed with the court in paper where the individual's case will be or has been filed. If the individual filed paper documents at the same time as the request for exemption, the clerk shall process the documents for filing. If the documents meet the filing requirements of subrule (D), they will be considered filed on the day they were submitted.

(i) The request for an exemption must be on a form approved by the State Court Administrative Office and verified under MCR 1.109(D)(3). There is no fee for the request.

(ii) The request must specify the reasons that prevent the individual from filing electronically. The individual may file supporting documents along with the request for the court's consideration.

(iii) A judge must review the request and any supporting documentation and issue an order granting or denying the request within two business days of the date the request was filed.

(iv) The clerk of the court must promptly mail the order to the individual. The clerk must place the request, any supporting documentation, and the order in the case file. If there is no case file, the documents must be maintained in a group file.

(v) An exemption granted under this rule is valid only for the court in which it was filed and for the life of the case unless the individual exempted from filing electronically registers with the electronic-filing system. In that event, the individual waives the exemption and becomes subject to the rules of electronic filing and the requirements of the electronic-filing system. An individual who waives an exemption under this rule may file another request for exemption.

(4) *Official Court Record.* The electronic version of any document filed with or generated by the court under this rule and any case initiation data transmitted in accordance with subrule (D)(2) is an official court record.

(5) *Electronic–Filing Process.*

(a) General Provisions.

(i) Specified case information, including e-mail addresses for achieving electronic service, shall be provided electronically by the authorized user in the form and manner established by the State Court Administrative Office pursuant to subrule (D)(2).

(ii) The authorized user has the responsibility of ensuring that a filing has been received by the electronic-filing system. If the authorized user discovers that the version of the document available for viewing through the e-filing system does not depict the document as submitted, the authorized user shall notify the clerk of the court immediately and resubmit the filing if necessary. In the event of a controversy between the clerk of the court and the authorized user, the authorized user may file a motion with the court under subrule (G)(7).

(iii) If the clerk of the court rejects a submitted document pursuant to MCR 8.119(C), the clerk shall notify the authorized user of the rejection and the reason for the

rejection. A rejected document shall not become part of the official court record and the rejection shall be recorded in an electronic-filing transaction from the court to the authorized user in accordance with subrule (c).

(b) Time and Effect of Electronic Filing. A document submitted electronically is deemed filed with the court when the transmission to the electronic-filing system is completed and the required filing fees have been paid or waived. If a document is submitted with a request to waive the filing fees, no fees will be charged at the time of filing and the document is deemed filed on the date the document was submitted to the court. A transmission is completed when the transaction is recorded as prescribed in subrule (c). Regardless of the date a filing is accepted by the clerk of the court, the date of filing is the date submitted. Electronic filing is not restricted by the operating hours of a court and any document submitted at or before 11:59 p.m. of a business day is deemed filed on that business day. Any document submitted on a Saturday, Sunday, legal holiday, or other day on which the court is closed pursuant to court order is deemed filed on the next business day.

(c) Electronic–Filing Transaction. On receipt of a submission or on rejection of a submission for nonpayment, the electronic-filing system shall record the filing transaction and send a notice of receipt of the submission and payment or rejection to the authorized user. When the filing transaction is date and time stamped, the electronic-filing system shall record the filing transaction and send a notice of electronic-filing to the authorized user. If the filing is rejected, the electronic-filing system shall record the rejection and send a notice of the rejection to the authorized user. The system shall maintain for every court a record of each submission, payment, filing, and rejection transaction in accordance with the records retention and disposal schedules and standards established by the State Court Administrative Office. A notice of electronic filing shall include the date and time of the transaction, the name of the authorized user filing the document(s), the type of document, the name of the authorized user receiving the notice, and a hyperlink to the filed or rejected document(s).

(d) Documents Under Seal. Except for documents filed pursuant to a protective order issued under MCR 2.302(C), a party seeking to file a document under seal must comply with subrule (D)(8).

(6) *Electronic–Service Process.*

(a) General Provisions.

(i) Service of process of case initiating documents shall be made in accordance with the rules and laws required for the particular case type.

(ii) Service of process of all other documents electronically filed shall be accomplished electronically among authorized users through the electronic-filing system unless one or more parties have been exempted from electronic filing, or a party has not filed a response or answer or has not registered with the electronic-filing system and that party's e-mail address is unknown. In those circumstances, service shall be made on that party by any other method required by Michigan Court Rules.

(iii) Delivery of documents through the electronic-filing system in conformity with these rules is valid and effective personal service and is proof of service under Michigan Court Rules.

(iv) Except for service of process of initiating documents and as otherwise directed by the court or court rule, service may be performed simultaneously with filing.

(v) When a court rule permits service by mail, service may be accomplished electronically under this subrule.

(b) Time and Effect. A document served electronically through the electronic-filing system in conformity with all applicable requirements of this rule is considered served when the transmission to the recipient's e-mail address is completed. A transmission is completed when the transaction is recorded as prescribed in subrule (c).

(c) Electronic–Service Transaction. On transmission of a document, the electronic-filing system shall record the service transaction. The system shall maintain for every court a record of each service transaction in accordance with the state-approved records retention and disposal schedules and standards established by the State Court Administrative Office.

(7) *Transmission Failures.*

(a) In the event the electronic-filing system fails to transmit a document submitted for filing, the authorized user may file a motion requesting that the court enter an order permitting the document to be deemed filed on the date it was first attempted to be sent electronically. The authorized user must prove to the court's satisfaction that:

(i) the filing was attempted at the time asserted by the authorized user;

(ii) the electronic-filing system failed to transmit the electronic document; and

(iii) the transmission failure was not caused, in whole or in part, by any action or inaction of the authorized user. A transmission failure caused by a problem with a filer's telephone line, ISP, hardware, or software shall be attributed to the filer.

(b) Scheduled system outages, such as for system maintenance, shall be posted on the MiFILE website.

(c) Notice shall be provided on the MiFILE website and/or the One Court of Justice website if the electronic-filing system becomes unavailable for an extended or indefinite period. The notice shall indicate that filers are responsible for filing documents on paper and serving paper in another manner required by Michigan Court Rules in order to meet any deadlines imposed by statute or court rule.

(H) Definitions. The following definitions apply to case records as defined in MCR 8.119(D) and (E).

(1) "Confidential" means that a case record is nonpublic and accessible only to those individuals or entities specified in statute or court rule. A confidential record is accessible to parties only as specified in statute or court rule.

(2) "Nonpublic" means that a case record is not accessible to the public. A nonpublic case record is accessible to parties and only those other individuals or entities specified in statute or court rule. A record may be made nonpublic only pursuant to statute or court rule. A court may not make a record nonpublic by court order.

(3) "Redact" means to obscure individual items of information within an otherwise publicly accessible document.

(4) "Redacted document" means a copy of an original document in which items of information have been redacted.

(5) "Sealed" means that a document or portion of a document is sealed by court order pursuant to MCR 8.119(I). Except as required by statute, an entire case may not be sealed.

[Adopted February 22, 1990, effective January 1, 1991, 434 Mich. Amended September 30, 2003, effective January 1, 2004, 469 Mich. Amended effective May 24, 2012, 491 Mich. Amended October 31, 2012, effective January 1, 2013, 493 Mich; May 30, 2018, effective September 1, 2018, 501 Mich. Amended March 20, 2019, effective May 1, 2019, 503 Mich. Amended effective August 14, 2019, 503 Mich. Amended June 5, 2019, effective September 1, 2019, 503 Mich. Amended effective September 11, 2019, 503 Mich. Amended September 18, 2019, effective January 1, 2020, 503 Mich; May 22, 2019, effective January 1, 2021, 503 Mich.]

Comments

Staff Comment to 1991 Adoption

A proposal to require the use of letter-size paper for pleadings and other papers filed in Michigan courts has been under consideration for several years. See Administrative Order 1987–8.

New MCR 1.109, effective January 1, 1991, adopts such a requirement, consistent with the trend in many other jurisdictions, including the federal courts.

The requirement does not apply to attachments, though parties are encouraged to reproduce them on 8½–by–11-inch paper as well.

Staff Comment to 2004 Amendment

The September 30, 2003 amendment of Rules 1.109 and 2.113 of the Michigan Court Rules, effective January 1, 2004, established a uniform type-size standard for all papers filed in Michigan courts. This conforms to the 12-point minimum that is required for briefs filed at the Court of Appeals, MCR 7.212(B), and applications and briefs filed at the Supreme Court, MCR 7.302, 7.304, 7.306, and 7.309. There is an exception for court forms approved by the State Court Administrative Office. The change does not preclude the filing of typewritten or legible handwritten pleadings, provided they meet the size requirements.

Staff Comment to 2012 Amendment

This amendment explicitly allows for the use of an electronic signature, and allows notarization by electronic process.

Staff Comment to 2013 Amendment

The amendments of these rules update the rules making them less "paper" focused and reflecting the use of electronic technology in the way courts process court records. The amendments also clarify and delineate the types of records and other materials maintained by a court, and clarify how access is provided.

Staff Comment to 2018 Amendment

The amendments in this order are intended to begin moving trial courts toward a statewide uniform e-Filing process. In addition, the order moves existing language into MCR 1.109 as a way to, for the first time, include most filing requirements in one single rule, instead of scattered in various rules. The order largely mirrors the administrative orders that most e-Filing pilot projects have operated under, but contains some significant new provisions. For example, courts are required to maintain documents in an electronic document management system, and the electronic record is the official court record.

Staff Comment to May, 2019 Amendment

The amendments of Rules 1.109, 2.102, 2.104, 2.106, 2.107, 2.117, 2.119, 2.403, 2.503, 2.506, 2.508, 2.518, 2.602, 2.603, 2.621, 3.101, 3.104, 3.203, 3.205, 3.210, 3.302, 3.607, 3.613, 3.614, 3.705, 3.801, 3.802, 3.805, 3.806, 4.201, 4.202, 4.303, 4.306, 5.001, 5.104, 5.105, 5.107, 5.108, 5.113, 5.117, 5.118, 5.119, 5.120, 5.125, 5.126, 5.132, 5.162, 5.202, 5.203, 5.205, 5.302, 5.304, 5.307, 5.308, 5.309, 5.310, 5.311, 5.313, 5.402, 5.404, 5.405, 5.409, 5.501, and 5.784 and addition of Rule 3.618 of the Michigan Court Rules are an expected progression necessary for design and implementation of the statewide electronic-filing system. These particular amendments will assist in implementing the goals of the project.

Staff Comment to August, 2019 Amendment

These amendments update cross-references and make other nonsubstantive revisions to clarify the rules.

Staff Comment to September 1, 2019 Amendment

The amendment of MCR 1.109 provides a single statewide process for requesting an exemption from the requirement to e-File, including both an automatic exemption for certain persons, and a list of factors for the court to consider when determining whether to exempt a person from the requirement to e-File.

Staff Comment to September 11, 2019 Amendment

The amendments of MCR 1.109, 3.206, 3.931, and 3.961 enable family division courts to use the required case inventory form to administer cases while keeping the information confidential. This change is intended to prevent providing information that could affect the safety of domestic violence victims and their children.

Staff Comment to 2020 Amendment

The amendments of MCR 1.109, 2.107, 2.113, 2.116, 2.119, 2.222, 2.223, 2.225, 2.227, 3.206, 3.211, 3.212, 3.214, 3.303, 3.903, 3.921, 3.925, 3.926, 3.931, 3.933, 3.942, 3.950, 3.961, 3.971, 3.972, 4.002, 4.101, 4.201, 4.202, 4.302, 5.128, 5.302, 5.731, 6.101, 6.615, 8.105, and 8.119 and rescission of MCR 2.226 and 8.125 continue the process for design and implementation of the statewide electronic-filing system.

Staff Comment to 2021 Amendment

The amendments make certain personal identifying information nonpublic and clarify the process regarding redaction.

Rule 1.110   Collection of Fines and Costs

Fines, costs, and other financial obligations imposed by the court must be paid at the time of assessment, except when the court allows otherwise, for good cause shown.

[Adopted October 23, 2001, effective January 1, 2002, 465 Mich.]

Comments

Staff Comment to 2001 Adoption

The October 23, 2001 addition of MCR 1.110, effective January 1, 2002, stated the expectation that fines, fees, costs, and other financial obligations imposed by courts are due at the time of assessment, absent good cause shown. This is consistent with pilot programs that have been conducted in some courts, and with the assessment standards set forth in *Michigan Trial Court Collections: A Design and Implementation Guide for Collections Programs*.

Rule 1.111.   Foreign Language Interpreters

(A) Definitions. When used in this rule, the following words and phrases have the following definitions:

(1) "Case or Court Proceeding" means any hearing, trial, or other appearance before any court in this state in an action, appeal, or other proceeding, including any matter conducted by a judge, magistrate, referee, or other hearing officer.

(2) "Party" means a person named as a party or a person with legal decision-making authority in the case or court proceeding.

(3) A person is "financially able to pay for interpretation costs" if the court determines that requiring reimbursement of interpretation costs will not pose an unreasonable burden on the person's ability to have meaningful access to the court. For purposes of this rule, a person is financially able to pay for interpretation costs when:

(a) The person's family or household income is greater than 125% of the federal poverty level; and

(b) An assessment of interpretation costs at the conclusion of the litigation would not unreasonably impede the person's ability to defend or pursue the claims involved in the matter.

(4) "Certified foreign language interpreter" means a person who has:

(a) passed a foreign language interpreter test administered by the State Court Administrative Office or a similar state or federal test approved by the state court administrator,

(b) met all the requirements established by the state court administrator for this interpreter classification, and

(c) registered with the State Court Administrative Office.

(5) "Interpret" and "interpretation" mean the oral rendering of spoken communication from one language to another without change in meaning.

(6) "Qualified foreign language interpreter" means:

(a) A person who provides interpretation services, provided that the person has:

(i) registered with the State Court Administrative Office; and

(ii) passed the consecutive portion of a foreign language interpreter test administered by the State Court Administrative Office or a similar state or federal test approved by the state court administrator (if testing exists for the language), and is actively engaged in becoming certified; and

(iii) met the requirements established by the state court administrator for this interpreter classification; and

(iv) been determined by the court after voir dire to be competent to provide interpretation services for the proceeding in which the interpreter is providing services, or

(b) A person who works for an entity that provides in-person interpretation services provided that:

(i) both the entity and the person have registered with the State Court Administrative Office; and

(ii) the person has met the requirements established by the state court administrator for this interpreter classification; and

(iii) the person has been determined by the court after voir dire to be competent to provide interpretation services for the proceeding in which the interpreter is providing services, or

(c) A person who works for an entity that provides interpretation services by telecommunication equipment, provided that:

(i) the entity has registered with the State Court Administrative Office; and

(ii) the entity has met the requirements established by the state court administrator for this interpreter classification; and

(iii) the person has been determined by the court after voir dire to be competent to provide interpretation services for the proceeding in which the interpreter is providing services.

(B) Appointment of a Foreign Language Interpreter.

(1) If a person requests a foreign language interpreter and the court determines such services are necessary for the person to meaningfully participate in the case or court proceeding, or on the court's own determination that foreign language interpreter services are necessary for a person to meaningfully participate in the case or court proceeding, the court shall appoint a foreign language interpreter for that person if the person is a witness testifying in a civil or criminal case or court proceeding or is a party.

(2) The court may appoint a foreign language interpreter for a person other than a party or witness who has a substantial interest in the case or court proceeding.

(3) In order to determine whether the services of a foreign language interpreter are necessary for a person to meaningfully participate under subrule (B)(1), the court shall rely upon a request by an LEP individual (or a request made on behalf of an LEP individual) or prior notice in the record. If no such requests have been made, the court may conduct an examination of the person on the record to determine whether such services are necessary. During the examination, the court may use a foreign language interpreter. For purposes of this examination, the court is not required to comply with the requirements of subrule (F) and the foreign language interpreter may participate remotely.

(C) Waiver of Appointment of Foreign Language Interpreter. A person may waive the right to a foreign language interpreter established under subrule (B)(1) unless the court determines that the interpreter is required for the protection of the person's rights and the integrity of the case or court proceeding. The court must find on the record that a person's waiver of an interpreter is knowing and voluntary. When accepting the person's waiver, the court may use a foreign language interpreter. For purposes of this waiver, the court is not required to comply with the requirements of subrule (F) and the foreign language interpreter may participate remotely.

(D) Recordings. The court may make a recording of anything said by a foreign language interpreter or a limited English proficient person while testifying or responding to a colloquy during those portions of the proceedings.

(E) Avoidance of Potential Conflicts of Interest.

(1) The court should use all reasonable efforts to avoid potential conflicts of interest when appointing a person as a foreign language interpreter and shall state its reasons on the record for appointing the person if any of the following applies:

(a) The interpreter is compensated by a business owned or controlled by a party or a witness;

(b) The interpreter is a friend, a family member, or a household member of a party or witness;

(c) The interpreter is a potential witness;

(d) The interpreter is a law enforcement officer;

(e) The interpreter has a pecuniary or other interest in the outcome of the case;

(f) The appointment of the interpreter would not serve to protect a party's rights or ensure the integrity of the proceedings;

(g) The interpreter does have, or may have, a perceived conflict of interest;

(h) The appointment of the interpreter creates an appearance of impropriety.

(2) A court employee may interpret legal proceedings as follows:

(a) The court may employ a person as an interpreter. The employee must meet the minimum requirements for interpreters established by subrule (A)(4). The state court administrator may authorize the court to hire a person who does not meet the minimum requirements established by subrule (A)(4) for good cause including the unavailability of a certification test for the foreign language and the absence of certified interpreters for the foreign language in the geographic area in which the court sits. The court seeking authorization from the state court administrator shall provide proof of the employee's competency to act as an interpreter and shall submit a plan for the employee to meet the minimum requirements established by subrule (A)(4) within a reasonable time.

(b) The court may use an employee as an interpreter if the employee meets the minimum requirements for interpreters established by this rule and is not otherwise disqualified.

(F) Appointment of Foreign Language Interpreters.

(1) When the court appoints a foreign language interpreter under subrule (B)(1), the court shall appoint a certified foreign language interpreter whenever practicable. If a certified foreign language interpreter is not reasonably available, and after considering the gravity of the proceedings and whether the matter should be rescheduled, the court may appoint a qualified foreign language interpreter who meets the qualifications in (A)(6). The court shall make a record of its reasons for using a qualified foreign language interpreter.

(2) If neither a certified foreign language interpreter nor a qualified foreign language interpreter is reasonably available, and after considering the gravity of the proceeding and whether the matter should be rescheduled, the court may appoint a person whom the court determines through voir dire to be capable of conveying the intent and content of the speaker's words sufficiently to allow the court to conduct the proceeding without prejudice to the limited English proficient person.

(3) The court shall appoint a single interpreter for a case or court proceeding. The court may appoint more than one interpreter after consideration of the nature and duration of the proceeding; the number of parties in interest and witnesses requiring an interpreter; the primary languages of those persons; and the quality of the remote technology that may be utilized when deemed necessary by the court to ensure effective communication in any case or court proceeding.

(4) The court may set reasonable compensation for interpreters who are appointed by the court. Court–appointed interpreter costs are to be paid out of funds provided by law or by the court.

(5) If a party is financially able to pay for interpretation costs, the court may order the party to reimburse the court for all or a portion of interpretation costs.

(6) Any doubts as to eligibility for interpreter services should be resolved in favor of appointment of an interpreter.

(7) At the time of determining eligibility, the court shall inform the party or witness of the penalties for making a false statement. The party has the continuing obligation to inform the court of any change in financial status and, upon request of the court, the party must submit financial information.

(G) Administration of Oath or Affirmation to Interpreters. The court shall administer an oath or affirmation to a foreign language interpreter substantially conforming to the following: "Do you solemnly swear or affirm that you will truly, accurately, and impartially interpret in the matter now before the court and not divulge confidential communications, so help you God?"

(H) Request for Review.

(1) Any time a court denies a request for the appointment of a foreign language interpreter or orders reimbursement of interpretation costs, it shall do so by written order.

(2) An LEP individual may immediately request review of the denial of appointment of a foreign language interpreter or an assessment for the reimbursement of interpretation costs. A request for review must be submitted to the court within 56 days after entry of the order.

    (a) In a court having two or more judges, the chief judge shall decide the request for review de novo.

    (b) In a single-judge court, or if the denial was issued by a chief judge, the judge shall refer the request for review to the state court administrator for assignment to another judge, who shall decide the request de novo.

    (c) A pending request for review under this subrule stays the underlying litigation.

    (d) A pending request for review under this subrule must be decided on an expedited basis.

    (e) No motion fee is required for a request for review made under this subrule.

[Adopted effective September 11, 2013, 495 Mich. Amended effective January 29, 2014, pending public comment, 495 Mich. Amended effective May 7, 2014, 495 Mich. Amended May 22, 2019, effective September 1, 2019, 502 Mich.]

Comments

Comments of Supreme Court to 2013 Adoption

The Michigan Supreme Court embraces the goal of providing access to all the courts of this State. This includes interpreter services for persons with Limited English Proficiency (LEP), to ensure that they have meaningful access to our courts.

The rules we adopt today provide court-appointed foreign language interpreters for truly needy LEP persons to support their access to justice, while not compelling taxpayers to bear the burden for LEP persons who can afford to pay for this service.

Our rules provide for court interpreters without cost to indigent LEP persons. If a party is financially able to pay for interpretation costs, the court may order the party to reimburse the court at the conclusion of the case or court proceeding. Moreover, our rules provide additional protection by allowing the trial judge to provide a court interpreter without cost to any LEP party, based on the judge's finding that assessing costs for the interpreter would limit that person's access to court.

Some history is in order. In August 2010, under the leadership of then–Chief Justice Marilyn Kelly, the Supreme Court convened a steering committee of judges and court administrators to develop proposals addressing access to court services for LEP individuals. The steering committee produced a court rule proposal specifying the procedures for appointment of an interpreter in Michigan's trial courts, as well as creating a structure for certifying various levels of interpreters, and creating a board to produce recommended requirements for interpreters and handle any misconduct claims.

Since February 2011, the Court has also worked cooperatively with the United States Department of Justice to improve the ability of LEP persons to access Michigan's courts. The Court's staff has communicated regularly with the Department, sharing numerous versions of the proposed court rules, exchanging ideas for the hiring and training of interpreters, and devising new and innovative ways to provide interpreter services at low or reduced costs. The Justice Department, through its administrative investigation function, has identified areas for improvement in individual trial courts across the state.

As a result of the dedicated work of the LEP committee, as well as the helpful and productive discussions with the Justice Department, the Court has fashioned a rule that reasonably accommodates access to the courts for LEP individuals with limited resources, and provides additional protection by allowing the trial judge to make a fact-based individualized determination whether assessment of costs would limit an LEP person's access to the court. This is a truly "flexible and fact-dependent standard." 67 *Fed. Reg.* 41459 (June 18, 2002). In fact, the rule is an individualized assessment that balances the four factors of (1) the number or proportion of LEP persons eligible to be served or likely to be encountered in court; (2) the frequency with which LEP individuals come into contact with the courts; (3) the nature and importance of the court system in people's lives; and (4) the resources available and costs. *Id.* The rules the Court has adopted strike the balance between ensuring meaningful access while not imposing undue burdens on Michigan's local courts. *Id.*

The Court has adopted a rule that focuses on the critical legal requirement: *meaningful access.* Under Rule 1.111(B)(1), a court is required to provide an interpreter for a party or witness if the court determines one is needed for either the party or the witness to meaningfully participate. LEP services are provided to all who have a need for them, and, under the rule, only parties who are able to pay for them are subject to reimbursement at the conclusion of the matter. In determining whether a party has the ability to reimburse for interpreter services, the court will impose costs only if the party has income above 125% of the federal poverty level *and* the court finds assessment of the interpreter costs would not unreasonably impede the person's ability to pursue or defend a claim. In other words, Rules 1.111(A)(4) and (B)(1) ensure that there will be no chilling effect on the LEP person's opportunity to pursue or defend a legal action.

Further, the rule we adopt is a frank acknowledgement that our trial courts— and indeed, our State's economy—are under severe financial stress and cannot, without explicit legal authority, be required to provide, at taxpayer expense, interpreter services for all LEP persons regardless of their means.

We will conduct appropriate educational programs with state court judges, administrators, and stakeholders as we work to implement this significant change in Michigan's procedure for appointment of foreign language interpreters.

Staff Comment to January 2014 Amendment

The amendments of MCR 1.111 make technical revisions and insert an interim review process for cases in which a court denies a request for an interpreter or orders reimbursement of interpretation costs. These revisions are adopted with immediate effect, but pending public comment and a future public hearing.

Staff Comment to May 2014 Amendment

These amendments reflect changes that correct minor technical errors that have occurred in drafting or the changes respond to recent adopted rule revisions, which occasionally inadvertently create incorrect cross-references in other rules.

Staff Comment to 2019 Amendment

The amendments of MCR 1.111 and 8.127 require additional testing for qualified interpreters and include a minor revision in the timing for recertification applications. The amendments, proposed by the Foreign Language Board of Review, promote greater confidence that a qualified foreign language interpreter is proficient in the language and reduce the possibility that renewals are delayed.

SUBCHAPTER 1.200   AMENDMENT OF MICHIGAN COURT RULES

Rule 1.201   Amendment Procedure

(A) Notice of Proposed Amendment. Before amending the Michigan Court Rules or other sets of rules within its jurisdiction, the Supreme Court will notify the secretary of the State Bar of Michigan and the state court administrator of the proposed amendment, and the manner and date for submitting comments. The notice also will be posted on the Court's website, http://courts.mi.gov/courts/michigansupremecourt/rules/court-rules-admin-matters/pages/default.aspx.[1]

(B) Notice to Bar. The state bar secretary shall notify the appropriate state bar committees or sections of the proposed amendment, and the manner and date for submitting comments. Unless otherwise directed by the Court, the proposed amendment shall be published in the Michigan Bar Journal.

(C) Notice to Judges. The state court administrator shall notify the presidents of the Michigan Judges Association, the Michigan District Judges Association, and the Michigan Probate and Juvenile Court Judges Association of the proposed amendment, and the manner and date for submitting comments.

(D) Exceptions. The Court may modify or dispense with the notice requirements of this rule if it determines that there is a need for immediate action or if the proposed amendment would not significantly affect the delivery of justice.

(E) Administrative Public Hearings. The Court will conduct a public hearing pursuant to Supreme Court Administrative Order 1997–11 before acting on a proposed amendment that requires notice, unless there is a need for immediate action, in which event the amendment will be considered at a public hearing following adoption. Public hearing agendas will be posted on the Court's website.

[Adopted effective March 1, 1985. Amended July 30, 2001, effective September 1, 2001, 465 Mich. Amended effective May 7, 2014, 495 Mich.]

1 Web address likely should be: https://courts.michigan.gov/courts/michigan supremecourt/rules/court-rules-admin-matters/pages/default.aspx.

Comments

Staff Comment to 1985 Adoption

MCR 1.201 retains the basic procedure for amendment of the rules found in GCR 1963, 933.

Subrule (B) adds a reference to publication in the Michigan Bar Journal because of the practice of publishing proposed amendments.

In subrule (C) the reference to the committees of the "judicial conference" is replaced by references to notification of the presidents of the various judges associations.

Staff Comment to 2001 Amendment

The July 30, 2001, amendment of subrule (A), effective September 1, 2001, added notice that rule proposals are posted on the Supreme Court's website. The amendment also recognized that the notice process applies to other sets of rules within the Court's jurisdiction, *e.g.*, the Michigan Rules of Evidence, the Michigan Rules of Professional Conduct, the Rules Governing the State Bar of Michigan, the Rules for the Board of Law Examiners, and the Michigan Code of Judicial Conduct. The amendment of subrule (D) provided that the Court may dispense with the notice requirements for changes that do not significantly affect the delivery of justice. The addition of subrule (E) incorporated the public hearing provisions of Supreme Court Administrative Order 1997–11.

Staff Comment to 2014 Amendment

These amendments reflect changes that correct minor technical errors that have occurred in drafting or the changes respond to recent adopted rule revisions, which occasionally inadvertently create incorrect cross-references in other rules.

CHAPTER 2. CIVIL PROCEDURE

Effective March 1, 1985

SUBCHAPTER 2.000   GENERAL PROVISIONS

Rule 2.001   Applicability

The rules in this chapter govern procedure in all civil proceedings in all courts established by the constitution and laws of the State of Michigan, except where the limited jurisdiction of a court makes a rule inherently inapplicable or where a rule applicable to a specific court or a specific type of proceeding provides a different procedure.

[Adopted effective March 1, 1985.]

Comments

Staff Comment to 1985 Adoption

MCR 2.001 is new, and states the applicability of the rules of civil procedure in chapter 2. They apply to all cases in all courts unless there is a specific rule applicable to the matter or the civil procedure rules are inherently inapplicable because of the limited jurisdiction of a court.

Rule 2.002.   Waiver of Fees for Indigent Persons

(A) Applicability and Scope.

(1) Only an individual is eligible for the waiver of fees under this rule. A private or public organization is not eligible for a waiver of fees unless an applicable statute provides that no fee(s) shall be required.

(2) Except as provided in subrule (I), for the purpose of this rule "fees" applies only to fees required by MCL 600.857, MCL 600.880, MCL 600.880a, MCL 600.880b, MCL 600.880c, MCL 600.1027, MCL 600.1986, MCL 600.2529, MCL 600.5756, MCL 600.8371, MCL 600.8420, MCL 700.2517, MCL 700.5104, and MCL 722.717.

(3) A request to waive fees must be filed in each case for which a waiver is requested. A request cannot be applied to multiple cases involving the same individual.

(4) If fees are waived under this rule before judgment, the waiver continues through the date of judgment unless ordered otherwise under subrule (J). If fees are waived under this rule postjudgment, the waiver continues through the date of adjudication of the postjudgment proceedings. If jurisdiction of the case is transferred to another court, the waiver continues in the receiving court according to this rule unless ordered otherwise by the receiving court under subrule (J). If an interlocutory appeal is filed in another court, the waiver continues in the appellate court.

(5) If the case is appealed, the waiver is void in the appellate court. A request to waive appellate filing fees may be filed in the appellate court in accordance with this rule.

(B) Request for Waiver of Fees. A request to waive fees must accompany the documents the individual is filing with the court. The request must be on a form approved by the State Court Administrative Office entitled "Fee Waiver Request." Except as provided in (K), no additional documentation may be required. The information contained on the form shall be nonpublic. The request must be verified in accordance with MCR 1.109(D)(3)(b) and may be signed either

(1) by the individual in whose behalf the request is made; or

(2) by a person having personal knowledge of the facts required to be shown, if the individual in whose behalf the request is made is unable to sign it because of minority or other disability.

(C) Persons Receiving Public Assistance. If a party shows that he or she is receiving any form of means-tested public assistance, the clerk of the court must waive payment of fees as to that party on a form approved by the State Court Administrative Office. For purposes of this rule, means-tested public assistance includes but is not limited to:

(1) Food Assistance Program through the State of Michigan;

(2) Medicaid;

(3) Family Independence Program through the State of Michigan;

(4) Women, Infants, and Children benefits;

(5) Supplemental Security Income through the federal government; or

(6) Any other federal, state, or locally administered means-tested income or benefit.

The clerk of the court must provide a copy of the signed waiver of fees to the individual. The waiver shall be nonpublic.

(D) Representation by a Legal Services Program. If a party is represented by a legal services program that is a grantee of the federal Legal Services Corporation or the Michigan State Bar Foundation, or by a law school clinic that provides services on the basis of indigence, the clerk of the court must waive payment of fees as to that party on a form approved by the State Court Administrative Office.

The clerk of the court must provide a copy of the signed waiver of fees to the individual. The waiver shall be nonpublic.

(E) If the clerk of the court is unable to waive fees under (C) or (D), the clerk shall immediately submit the request for judicial review.

(F) Other Indigent Individuals. If an individual shows that he or she is unable because of indigence to pay fees, the court shall order those fees waived. The court must waive fees when the individual lives in a household with gross income under 125% of the federal poverty guidelines. The court must also waive fees when gross household income is above 125% of the federal poverty guidelines if the payment of fees would constitute a financial hardship on the individual.

(G) Order Regarding a Request to Waive Fees. A judge shall enter an order either granting or denying a request made under (E) or (F) within three business days and such order shall be nonpublic. If required financial information is not provided in the waiver request, the judge may deny the waiver. An order denying shall indicate the reason for denial. The order granting a request must include a statement that the person for whom fees are waived is required to notify the court when the reason for waiver no longer exists.

(1) The clerk of the court shall send a copy of the order to the individual. If the court denied the request, the clerk shall also send a notice that to preserve the filing date the individual must pay the fees within 14 days from the date the clerk sends notice of the order or the filing will be rejected.

(2) De Novo Review of Fee Waiver Denials.

(a) Request for De Novo Review. If the court denies a request for fee waiver, the individual may file a request for de novo review within 14 days of the notice denying the waiver. There is no motion fee for the request. A request for de novo review automatically stays the case or preserves the filing date until the review is decided. A de novo review must be held within 14 days of receiving the request.

(b) Review.

(i) If the court holds a hearing on the request for de novo review, it shall be closed and held on the record. The clerk of the court shall serve notice of the review at least 9 days before the time set for the hearing if served by mail, or at least 7 days before the time set for the hearing if served by delivery under MCR 2.107(C)(1) or (2). The Michigan Rules of Evidence do not apply at this hearing.

(ii) If a hearing is held, the individual shall bring documents to verify the statements made in the fee waiver request and request for de novo review. The court may question the individual regarding the statements made in the requests.

(c) Chief Judge Ruling, Judicial Assignment.

(i) In a court having two or more judges, the chief judge shall decide the request for de novo review. In a single-judge court, or if the order denying waiver was issued by the chief judge, the judge shall refer the request to the state court administrator for assignment to another judge, who shall decide the request for de novo review.

(ii) The court shall enter an order reflecting its decision on the de novo review. If the court denies the request, it shall explain its reasoning in the order.

(H) Domestic Relations Cases; Payment of Fees by Spouse. If a party entitled to relief in an action for divorce, separate maintenance, annulment, or affirmation of marriage is qualified for waiver of filing fees under subrule (C), (D), or (F) and is also entitled to an order requiring the other party to pay attorney fees, the court shall order waiver of payment of those fees and shall require the other party to pay them, unless the other party is also qualified to have filing fees waived under subrule (C) or (D) or (F).

(I) Payment of Service Fees and Costs of Publication for Indigent Individuals. If payment of fees has been waived for an individual and service of process must be made by an official process server or by publication, the court shall order the service fees or costs of publication paid by the county or funding unit in which the action is pending, if the individual files an ex parte affidavit stating facts showing the necessity for that type of service of process. If known at the time, the affidavit may be included in or with the request to waive fees.

(J) Reinstatement of Requirement to Pay Fees. If the payment of fees has been waived under this rule, the court may on its own initiative order the individual for whom the fees were

waived to pay those fees when, upon a finding of fact, the court determines the reason for the waiver no longer exists. If an order to reinstate fees is entered, the individual must pay the fees as ordered. If fees are reinstated, the court shall not delay entry of orders or judgments or in any other way delay the progress of the case pending payment of the fees.

(K) Review of Fee Waiver Petitions. Only if a court finds that a request for a fee waiver is incomplete or if a court has a reasonable belief that a request is inaccurate, the court may conduct further inquiries reasonably necessary to prove indigence or financial hardship. Any hearing regarding these further inquiries shall be on the record. The notice of hearing shall indicate the specific issues that are subject to further inquiry.

[Adopted effective March 1, 1985. Amended May 2, 1995, effective July 1, 1995, 448 Mich; December 5, 2018, effective January 1, 2019, 502 Mich. Amended effective January 23, 2019, 502 Mich.]

Comments

Staff Comment to 1985 Adoption

MCR 2.002 is substantially the same as GCR 1963, 120.

Staff Comment to 1995 Amendment

The amendments of MCR 2.002, effective July 1, 1995, add a new subrule (A)(2) defining "fees and costs," as meaning only filing fees required by law, excluding such costs and expenses as transcript preparation. There are corresponding adjustments in subrules (C) and (D).

Staff Comment to 2018 Amendment

This order clarifies and updates MCR 2.002 (regarding determination of indigence for purposes of filing fees) by establishing a more streamlined procedure to be used in an e-Filing (and paper) environment, creating a threshold level of indigence (125% of the federal poverty level) and implementing a de novo review procedure.

Staff Comment to 2019 Amendment

This order makes corrections and technical changes to the rule and clarifies the existing language. The changes were recommended by the State Bar of Michigan workgroup on consistent fee waivers.

Rule 2.003   Disqualification of Judge

(A) Applicability. This rule applies to all judges, including justices of the Michigan Supreme Court, unless a specific provision is stated to apply only to judges of a certain court. The word "judge" includes a justice of the Michigan Supreme Court.

(B) Who May Raise. A party may raise the issue of a judge's disqualification by motion or the judge may raise it.

(C) Grounds.

(1) Disqualification of a judge is warranted for reasons that include, but are not limited to, the following:

(a) The judge is biased or prejudiced for or against a party or attorney.

(b) The judge, based on objective and reasonable perceptions, has either (i) a serious risk of actual bias impacting the due process rights of a party as enunciated in *Caperton v Massey*, [556 US 868]; 129 S Ct 2252; 173 L Ed 2d 1208 (2009), or (ii) has failed to adhere to the appearance of impropriety standard set forth in Canon 2 of the Michigan Code of Judicial Conduct.

(c) The judge has personal knowledge of disputed evidentiary facts concerning the proceeding.

(d) The judge has been consulted or employed as an attorney in the matter in controversy.

(e) The judge was a partner of a party, attorney for a party, or a member of a law firm representing a party within the preceding two years.

(f) The judge knows that he or she, individually or as a fiduciary, or the judge's spouse, parent or child wherever residing, or any other member of the judge's family residing in the judge's household, has more than a de minimis economic interest in the subject matter in controversy that could be substantially impacted by the proceeding.

(g) The judge or the judge's spouse, or a person within the third degree of relationship to either of them, or the spouse of such a person:

(i) is a party to the proceeding, or an officer, director, or trustee of a party;

(ii) is acting as a lawyer in the proceeding;

(iii) is known by the judge to have a more than de minimis interest that could be substantially affected by the proceeding;

(iv) is to the judge's knowledge likely to be a material witness in the proceeding.

(2) *Disqualification not Warranted.*

(a) A judge is not disqualified merely because the judge's former law clerk is an attorney of record for a party in an action that is before the judge or is associated with a law firm representing a party in an action that is before the judge.

(b) A judge is not disqualified based solely upon campaign speech protected by *Republican Party of Minn v White*, 536 US 765 (2002), so long as such speech does not demonstrate bias or prejudice or an appearance of bias or prejudice for or against a party or an attorney involved in the action.

(D) Procedure.

(1)(a) *Time for Filing in the Trial Courts.* To avoid delaying trial and inconveniencing the witnesses, all motions for disqualification must be filed within 14 days of the discovery of the grounds for disqualification. If the discovery is made within 14 days of the trial date, the motion must be made forthwith.

(b) *Time for Filing in the Court of Appeals.* All motions for disqualification must be filed within 14 days of disclosure of the judges' assignment to the case or within 14 days of the discovery of the grounds for disqualification. If a party discovers the grounds for disqualification within 14 days of a scheduled oral argument or argument on the application for leave to appeal, the motion must be made forthwith.

(c) *Time for Filing in the Supreme Court.* If an appellant is aware of grounds for disqualification of a justice, the appellant must file a motion to disqualify with the application for leave to appeal. All other motions must be filed within 28 days after the filing of the application for leave to appeal or within 28 days of the discovery of the grounds for disqualification. If a party discovers the grounds for disqualification within 28 days of a scheduled oral argument or argument on the application for leave to appeal, the motion must be made forthwith.

All requests for review by the entire Court pursuant to subsection (3)(b) must be made within 14 days of the entry of the decision by the individual justice.

(d) *Untimely Motions.* Untimely motions in the trial court, the Court of Appeals, and the Supreme Court may be granted for good cause shown. If a motion is not timely filed in the trial court, the Court of Appeals, or the Supreme Court, untimeliness is a factor in deciding whether the motion should be granted.

(2) *All Grounds to Be Included; Affidavit.* In any motion under this rule, the moving party must include all grounds for disqualification that are known at the time the motion is filed. An affidavit must accompany the motion.

(3) *Ruling.*

(a) For courts other than the Supreme Court, the challenged judge shall decide the motion. If the challenged judge denies the motion,

(i) in a court having two or more judges, on the request of a party, the challenged judge shall refer the motion to the chief judge, who shall decide the motion de novo;

(ii) in a single-judge court, or if the challenged judge is the chief judge, on the request of a party, the challenged judge shall refer the motion to the state court administrator for assignment to another judge, who shall decide the motion de novo.

(b) In the Supreme Court, if a justice's participation in a case is challenged by a written motion or if the issue of participation is raised by the justice himself or herself, the challenged justice shall decide the issue and publish his or her reasons about whether to participate.

If the challenged justice denies the motion for disqualification, a party may move for the motion to be decided by the entire Court. The entire Court shall then decide the motion for disqualification de novo. The Court's decision shall include the reasons for its grant or denial of the motion for disqualification. The Court shall issue a written order containing a statement of reasons for its grant or denial of the motion for disqualification. Any concurring or dissenting statements shall be in writing.

(4) *If Disqualification Motion is Granted.*

(a) For courts other than the Supreme Court, when a judge is disqualified, the action must be assigned to another judge of the same court, or, if one is not available, the state court administrator shall assign another judge.

(b) In the Supreme Court, when a justice is disqualified, the underlying action will be decided by the remaining justices of the Court.

(E) Waiver of Disqualification. Parties to the proceeding may waive disqualification even where it appears that there may be grounds for disqualification of the judge. Such waiver may occur whether the grounds for disqualification were raised by a party or by the judge, so long as the judge is willing to participate. Any agreement to waive the disqualification must be made by all parties to the litigation and shall be in writing or placed on the record.

[Adopted effective March 1, 1985. Amended July 10, 1995, effective September 1, 1995, 449 Mich. Amended effective November 25, 2009, 485 Mich; March 16, 2010, 485 Mich.]

Comments

Staff Comment to 1985 Adoption

MCR 2.003 is based on GCR 1963, 912.

Under subrule (B)(3) a judge is disqualified not only as to a proceeding in which the judge was consulted or employed as counsel (see GCR 1963, 912.2[a][3]), but also when the judge was consulted or employed as counsel in the matter in controversy, even before it reached the litigation stage.

Subrule (C)(1) changes the time when the motion must be filed. A party must file a motion within 14 days after learning of the ground for disqualification, rather than 10 days after the case is assigned to a judge or 10 days before trial. However, if the discovery is made within 14 days of trial, the motion must be made forthwith. This would cover situations in which the assignment of the judge is not made until shortly before the trial date.

Subrule (C)(2) removes the language limiting a party to one motion to disqualify per judge. Additional grounds for disqualification might be discovered later. However, the party must include all grounds that are known at the time the motion is filed.

Staff Comment to 1995 Amendment

The July 10, 1995 amendments of MCR 2.003, and Rules 3A, 3D, 6C, and 7B of the Michigan Code of Judicial Conduct, and new MCR 9.227 and Rule 7D of the Michigan Code of Judicial Conduct, are based on the proposed revision of the Michigan Code of Judicial Conduct submitted by the State Bar Representative Assembly. See 442 Mich 1216 (1993). They are effective September 1, 1995.

Staff Comment to 2009 Amendment

The amendments adopted by the Court in this order explicitly apply the judicial disqualification rule to all state judges, including Supreme Court Justices. In addition, the amendments revise disqualification standards and establish procedures for the disqualification process.

Staff Comment to 2010 Amendment

The amendment of MCR 2.003(D) establishes time requirements for filing motions for disqualification in the trial courts, Court of Appeals, and the Supreme Court.

Rule 2.004   Incarcerated Parties

(A) This subrule applies to

(1) domestic relations actions involving minor children, and

(2) other actions involving the custody, guardianship, neglect, or foster-care placement of minor children, or the termination of parental rights,

in which a party is incarcerated under the jurisdiction of the Department of Corrections.

(B) The party seeking an order regarding a minor child shall

(1) contact the department to confirm the incarceration and the incarcerated party's prison number and location;

(2) serve the incarcerated person with the petition or motion seeking an order regarding the minor child, and file proof with the court that the papers were served; and

(3) file with the court the petition or motion seeking an order regarding the minor child, stating that a party is incarcerated and providing the party's prison number and location; the caption of the petition or motion shall state that a telephonic or video hearing is required by this rule.

(C) When all the requirements of subrule (B) have been accomplished to the court's satisfaction, the court shall issue an order requesting the department, or the facility where the party is located if it is not a department facility, to allow that party to participate with the court or its designee by way of a noncollect and unmonitored telephone call or by videoconferencing technology in a hearing or conference, including a friend of the court adjudicative hearing or meeting. The order shall include the date and time for the hearing or conference, and the prisoner's name and prison identification number, and shall be served at least 7 days before the hearing or conference by the court upon the parties and the warden or supervisor of the facility where the incarcerated party resides. The initial telephone call or videoconference shall be conducted in accordance with subrule (E). If the prisoner indicates an interest in participating in subsequent proceedings following an initial telephone call or videoconference pursuant to subrule (E), the court shall issue an order in accordance with this subrule for each subsequent hearing or conference.

(D) All court documents or correspondence mailed to the incarcerated party concerning any matter covered by this rule shall include the name and the prison number of the incarcerated party on the envelope.

(E) The purpose of the initial telephone call or videoconference with the incarcerated party, as described in subrule (C), is to determine

(1) whether the incarcerated party has received adequate notice of the proceedings and has had an opportunity to respond and to participate,

(2) whether counsel is necessary in matters allowing for the appointment of counsel to assure that the incarcerated party's access to the court is protected,

(3) whether the incarcerated party is capable of self-representation, if that is the party's choice,

(4) how the incarcerated party can communicate with the court or the friend of the court during the pendency of the action, and whether the party needs special assistance for such communication, including participation by way of additional telephone calls or videoconferencing technology as permitted by the Michigan Court Rules, and

(5) the scheduling and nature of future proceedings, to the extent practicable, and the manner in which the incarcerated party may participate.

(F) A court may not grant the relief requested by the moving party concerning the minor child if the incarcerated party has not been offered the opportunity to participate in the proceedings, as described in this rule. This provision shall not apply if the incarcerated party actually does participate in a telephone call or video conference, or if the court determines that immediate action is necessary on a temporary basis to protect the minor child.

(G) The court may impose sanctions if it finds that an attempt was made to keep information about the case from an incarcerated party in order to deny that party access to the courts.

[Formerly Rule 3.220, adopted November 1, 2002, effective January 1, 2003, 467 Mich. Renumbered Rule 2.004 and amended, November 1, 2002, effective January 1, 2003, 469 Mich. Amended October 1, 2014, effective January 1, 2015, 497 Mich; September 21, 2016, effective January 1, 2017, 500 Mich.]

Comments

Staff Comment to 2003 Adoption

The November 1, 2002, enactment of MCR 3.220, effective January 1, 2003, is based on a proposal made in conjunction with the settlement agreement in the Court of Claims of that portion of *Cain v Dep't of Corrections*, 88–61119–AZ, 93–15000–CM, and 96–16341–CM, that pertains to women prisoners.

Staff Comment to 2003 Amendment and Renumbering

MCR 2.004, effective January 1, 2003, is based on a proposal made in conjunction with the settlement agreement in the Court of Claims of that portion of *Cain v Dep't of Corrections*, 88–61119–AZ, 93–15000–CM, and 96–16341–CM, that pertains to women prisoners. The rule initially was adopted in November 2002 as MCR 3.220, but was amended and renumbered as Rule 2.004 in December 2002 to clarify the scope of the rule and to eliminate other potential confusion.

Staff Comment to 2015 Amendment

The amendments of MCR 2.004 allow an inmate's participation by video or videoconferencing.

Staff Comment to 2017 Amendment

These amendments permit courts to expand the use of videoconferencing technology in many court proceedings, and clarify the proceedings at which videoconferencing technology may be used.

SUBCHAPTER 2.100 COMMENCEMENT OF ACTION; SERVICE OF PROCESS; PLEADINGS; MOTIONS

Rule 2.101 Form and Commencement of Action

(A) Form of Action. There is one form of action known as a "civil action."

(B) Commencement of Action. A civil action is commenced by filing a complaint with a court.

[Adopted effective March 1, 1985.]

Comments

Staff Comment to 1985 Adoption

MCR 2.101 includes the provisions of GCR 1963, 12 (subrule [A]) and 101 (subrule [B]).

Rule 2.102 Summons; Expiration of Summons; Dismissal of Action for Failure to Serve

(A) Issuance. On the filing of a complaint, the court clerk shall issue a summons to be served as provided in MCR 2.103 and 2.105. A separate summons may issue against a particular defendant or group of defendants. A duplicate summons may be issued from time to time and is as valid as the original summons.

(B) Form. A summons must be issued "In the name of the people of the State of Michigan," under the seal of the court that issued it. It must be directed to the defendant, and include

(1) the name and address of the court,

(2) the names of the parties,

(3) the case number,

(4) the name and address of the plaintiff's attorney or the address of a plaintiff appearing without an attorney,

(5) the defendant's address, if known,

(6) the name of the court clerk,

(7) the date on which the summons was issued,

(8) the last date on which the summons is valid,

(9) a statement that the summons is invalid unless served on or before the last date on which it is valid,

(10) the time within which the defendant is required to answer or take other action, and

(11) a notice that if the defendant fails to answer or take other action within the time allowed, judgment may be entered against the defendant for the relief demanded in the complaint.

(C) Amendment. At any time on terms that are just, a court may allow process or proof of service of process to be amended, unless it clearly appears that to do so would materially prejudice the substantive rights of the party against whom the process issued. An amendment relates back to the date of the original issuance or service of process unless the court determines that relation back would unfairly prejudice the party against whom the process issued.

(D) Expiration. A summons expires 91 days after the date the summons is issued. However, within those 91 days, on a showing of due diligence by the plaintiff in attempting to serve the original summons, the judge to whom the action is assigned may order a second summons to issue for a definite period not exceeding 1 year from the date the summons is issued. If such an extension is granted, the new summons expires at the end of the extended period. The judge may impose just conditions on the issuance of the second summons. Duplicate summons issued under subrule (A) do not extend the life of the original summons. The running of the 91–day period is tolled while a motion challenging the sufficiency of the summons or of the service of the summons is pending.

(E) Dismissal as to Defendant Not Served.

(1) On the expiration of the summons as provided in subrule (D), the action is deemed dismissed without prejudice as to a defendant who has not been served with process as provided in these rules, unless the defendant has submitted to the court's jurisdiction. As to a defendant added as a party after the filing of the first complaint in the action, the time provided in this rule runs from the filing of the first pleading that names that defendant as a party.

(2) After the time stated in subrule (E)(1), the clerk shall examine the court records and enter an order dismissing the action as to a defendant who has not been served with process or submitted to the court's jurisdiction. The clerk's failure to enter a dismissal order does not continue an action deemed dismissed.

(3) The clerk shall give notice of the entry of a dismissal order under MCR 2.107 and record the date of the notice in the case file. The failure to give notice does not affect the dismissal.

(F) Setting Aside Dismissal. A court may set aside the dismissal of the action as to a defendant under subrule (E) only on stipulation of the parties or when all of the following conditions are met:

(1) within the time provided in subrule (D), service of process was in fact made on the dismissed defendant, or the defendant submitted to the court's jurisdiction;

(2) proof of service of process was filed or the failure to file is excused for good cause shown;

(3) the motion to set aside the dismissal was filed within 28 days after notice of the order of dismissal was given, or, if notice of dismissal was not given, the motion was promptly filed after the plaintiff learned of the dismissal.

(G) Exception; Summary Proceedings to Recover Possession of Realty. Subrules (D), (E), and (F) do not apply to summary proceedings governed by MCL 600.5701–600.5759 and by subchapter 4.200 of these rules.

[Adopted effective March 1, 1985. Amended June 11, 1991, effective October 1, 1991, 437 Mich; September 9, 2003, effective January 1, 2004, 469 Mich; March 20, 2019, effective May 1, 2019, 502 Mich.]

Comments

Staff Comment to 1985 Adoption

MCR 2.102 is comparable to GCR 1963, 102 and DCR 102.7.

Subrule (A) corresponds to GCR 1963, 102.1. The rule is revised to make clear that, while the clerk issues the summons, the clerk is not responsible for having it served.

Subrule (B) is similar to GCR 1963, 102.2, covering the requirements for the information to be included in the summons. The new provision adds several items, including the date of issuance, the file number, the defendant's address, the last date on which the summons is valid, and a statement that the summons is invalid unless served before that date. There is also a change in the language of subrule (B)(11). GCR 1963, 102.2 states that a judgment "will be" rendered against a defendant who fails to answer. Subrule (B)(11) says that judgment "may be" entered.

Subrule (C) includes additional language regarding the effective date of an amendment: The amendment relates back to the date of the original issuance or service of process unless the court determines that relation back would unfairly prejudice the opposing party.

Subrule (D) is comparable to GCR 1963, 102.4. A provision is added that the 182-day life of a summons is tolled while a motion challenging the summons or its service is pending.

Subrule (E) is comparable to GCR 102.5. Language is added in subrule (E)(1) to clarify the application of the rule to a defendant who is added after the first complaint is filed. The 182-day period runs from the filing of the first pleading that names that defendant as a party.

Subrule (F) is based on GCR 1963, 102.6. Language is added allowing a dismissal to be set aside on stipulation.

In subrule (F)(1) the condition of a motion to set aside a dismissal is changed from a requirement that service was made within 180 days to a requirement that service was made within the time permitted by subrule (D). This takes account of the possibility that the court may have extended the time for service or that the time may have been tolled while a motion challenging service was pending.

In subrule (F)(3) language is added to cover the time for filing a motion to set aside a dismissal in circumstances in which the clerk failed to give notice of the dismissal. In such a case the motion must be filed promptly after the plaintiff learns of the dismissal.

MCR 2.102(G) excepts summary proceedings to recover possession of real estate from the dismissal rule, as had DCR 102.7. The rules governing those procedures include their own provisions regarding service. See subchapter 4.200.

Staff Comment to 1991 Amendment

The [October 1, 1991] amendment of MCR 2.102(D) shortens the time for expiration of a summons from 182 days to 91 days.

Staff Comment to 2004 Amendment

The September 9, 2003 amendment of subrule (D), effective January 1, 2004, substituted the phrase "due diligence by the plaintiff in attempting to serve the original summons" for the "good cause" requirement in the former subrule. This is consistent with *Bush v Beemer*, 224 Mich App 457 (1997). Cf. *Richards v McNamee*, 240 Mich App 444 (2000). In any event, the relevant statute of limitations would not be tolled unless the complaint were timely filed *and* the requirements of MCL 600.5856 were met before the expiration of the period of limitation. See *Gladych v New Family Homes, Inc*, 468 Mich 594 (2003).

Staff Comment to 2019 Amendment

The amendments of Rules 1.109, 2.102, 2.104, 2.106, 2.107, 2.117, 2.119, 2.403, 2.503, 2.506, 2.508, 2.518, 2.602, 2.603, 2.621, 3.101, 3.104, 3.203, 3.205, 3.210, 3.302, 3.607, 3.613, 3.614, 3.705, 3.801, 3.802, 3.805, 3.806, 4.201, 4.202, 4.303, 4.306, 5.001, 5.104, 5.105, 5.107, 5.108, 5.113, 5.117, 5.118, 5.119, 5.120, 5.125, 5.126, 5.132, 5.162, 5.202, 5.203, 5.205, 5.302, 5.304, 5.307, 5.308, 5.309, 5.310, 5.311, 5.313, 5.402, 5.404, 5.405, 5.409, 5.501, and 5.784 and addition of Rule 3.618 of the Michigan Court Rules are an expected progression necessary for design and implementation of the statewide electronic-filing system. These particular amendments will assist in implementing the goals of the project.

Rule 2.103   Process; Who May Serve

(A) Service Generally. Process in civil actions may be served by any legally competent adult who is not a party or an officer of a corporate party.

(B) Service Requiring Seizure of Property. A writ of restitution or process requiring the seizure or attachment of property may only be served by

(1) a sheriff or deputy sheriff, or a bailiff or court officer appointed by the court for that purpose,

(2) an officer of the Department of State Police in an action in which the state is a party, or

(3) a police officer of an incorporated city or village in an action in which the city or village is a party.

A writ of garnishment may be served by any person authorized by subrule (A).

(C) Service in a Governmental Institution. If personal service of process is to be made on a person in a governmental institution, hospital, or home, service must be made by the person in charge of the institution or by someone designated by that person.

(D) Process Requiring Arrest. Process in civil proceedings requiring the arrest of a person may be served only by a sheriff, deputy sheriff, or police officer, or by a court officer appointed by the court for that purpose.

[Adopted effective March 1, 1985.]

Comments

Staff Comment to 1985 Adoption

MCR 2.103 includes provisions from both GCR 1963, 103 and DCR 103.

Subrule (A) is similar to GCR 1963, 103(1), and allows any competent adult other than a party or an officer of a corporate party to serve a summons and complaint. The effect is to expand the class of persons who can serve process in the district court. Compare DCR 103.1, under which persons other than the officers listed in MCL 600.8321 could serve process only with leave of court. As under GCR 1963, 103(1), the attorney for a party may serve process.

In addition, the term "any person of suitable age and discretion" in GCR 1963, 103(1) is changed to "any legally competent adult".

Subrule (B) contains the substance of DCR 103.3, regarding service requiring seizure of property.

Subrule (C) is similar to GCR 1963, 103(2) and DCR 103.2. However, the rule is modified to allow the person in charge of the institution to designate anyone to serve process, not only a member of the institution staff. See PCR 103.2.

Subrule (D) is based on GCR 1963, 103(3) and DCR 103.3. Process requiring the arrest of a person may only be served by a law enforcement officer or a court officer appointed for that purpose.

Rule 2.104   Process; Proof of Service

(A) Requirements. Proof of service may be made by

(1) written acknowledgment of the receipt of a summons and a copy of the complaint, dated and signed by the person to whom the service is directed or by a person authorized under these rules to receive the service of process;

(2) a certificate stating the facts of service, including the manner, time, date, and place of service, if service is made within the State of Michigan by

(a) a sheriff,

(b) a deputy sheriff or bailiff, if that officer holds office in the county in which the court issuing the process is held,

(c) an appointed court officer,

(d) an attorney for a party; or

(3) a written statement of the facts of service, verified under MCR 1.109(D)(3). The statement shall include the manner, time, date, and place of service, and indicate the process server's official capacity, if any.

The place of service must be described by giving the address where the service was made or, if the service was not made at a particular address, by another description of the location.

(B) Failure to File. Failure to file proof of service does not affect the validity of the service.

(C) Publication, Posting, and Mailing. If the manner of service used requires sending a copy of the summons and complaint by mail, the party requesting issuance of the summons is responsible for arranging the mailing and filing proof of service. Proof of publication, posting, and mailing under MCR 2.106 is governed by MCR 2.106(G).

[Adopted effective March 1, 1985. Amended March 20, 2019, effective May 1, 2019, 502 Mich.]

Comments

Staff Comment to 1985 Adoption

MCR 2.104 is comparable to GCR 1963, 104.

In subrule (A)(2)(b) references to "coroners" and "constables" are deleted.

Subrule (A)(2)(d) adds the attorney for a party to the list of persons who may prove service by filing a certificate of service.

Language is added at the end of subrule (A) to require greater specificity regarding the place of service than is found in GCR 1963, 104(1).

New subrule (C) makes clear that MCR 2.106(G) governs proof of publication, posting, and mailing under that rule.

The [March 1, 1985] amendment of MCR 2.104(C) adds an explicit statement that when a copy of the summons and complaint are required to be sent by mail, the party who secured the issuance of the summons is responsible for the mailing and proof of service.

Staff Comment to 2019 Amendment

The amendments of Rules 1.109, 2.102, 2.104, 2.106, 2.107, 2.117, 2.119, 2.403, 2.503, 2.506, 2.508, 2.518, 2.602, 2.603, 2.621, 3.101, 3.104, 3.203, 3.205, 3.210, 3.302, 3.607, 3.613, 3.614, 3.705, 3.801, 3.802, 3.805, 3.806, 4.201, 4.202, 4.303, 4.306, 5.001, 5.104, 5.105, 5.107, 5.108, 5.113, 5.117, 5.118, 5.119, 5.120, 5.125, 5.126, 5.132, 5.162, 5.202, 5.203, 5.205, 5.302, 5.304, 5.307, 5.308, 5.309, 5.310, 5.311, 5.313, 5.402, 5.404, 5.405, 5.409, 5.501, and 5.784 and addition of Rule 3.618 of the Michigan Court Rules are an expected progression necessary for design and implementation of the statewide electronic-filing system. These particular amendments will assist in implementing the goals of the project.

Rule 2.105. Process; Manner of Service

(A) Individuals. Process may be served on a resident or nonresident individual by

(1) delivering a summons and a copy of the complaint to the defendant personally; or

(2) sending a summons and a copy of the complaint by registered or certified mail, return receipt requested, and delivery restricted to the addressee. Service is made when the defendant acknowledges receipt of the mail. A copy of the return receipt signed by the defendant must be attached to proof showing service under subrule (A)(2).

(B) Individuals; Substituted Service. Service of process may be made

(1) on a nonresident individual, by

(a) serving a summons and a copy of the complaint in Michigan on an agent, employee, representative, sales representative, or servant of the defendant, and

(b) sending a summons and a copy of the complaint by registered mail addressed to the defendant at his or her last known address;

(2) on a minor, by serving a summons and a copy of the complaint on a person having care and control of the minor and with whom he or she resides;

(3) on a defendant for whom a guardian or conservator has been appointed and is acting, by serving a summons and a copy of the complaint on the guardian or conservator;

(4) on an individual doing business under an assumed name, by

(a) serving a summons and copy of the complaint on the person in charge of an office or business establishment of the individual, and

(b) sending a summons and a copy of the complaint by registered mail addressed to the individual at his or her usual residence or last known address.

(C) Partnerships; Limited Partnerships. Service of process on a partnership or limited partnership may be made by

(1) serving a summons and a copy of the complaint on any general partner or agent for service of process; or

(2) serving a summons and a copy of the complaint on the person in charge of a partnership office or business establishment and sending a summons and a copy of the complaint by registered mail, addressed to a general partner or agent for service of process at his or her usual residence or last known address.

(D) Private Corporations, Domestic and Foreign. Service of process on a domestic or foreign corporation may be made by

(1) serving a summons and a copy of the complaint on an officer or the resident agent;

(2) serving a summons and a copy of the complaint on a director, trustee, or person in charge of an office or business establishment of the corporation and sending a summons and a copy of the complaint by registered mail, addressed to the principal office of the corporation;

(3) serving a summons and a copy of the complaint on the last presiding officer, president, cashier, secretary, or treasurer of a corporation that has ceased to do business by failing to keep up its organization by the appointment of officers or otherwise, or whose term of existence has expired;

(4) sending a summons and a copy of the complaint by registered mail to the corporation or an appropriate corporation officer and to the Michigan Bureau of Commercial Services, Corporation Division if

(a) the corporation has failed to appoint and maintain a resident agent or to file a certificate of that appointment as required by law;

(b) the corporation has failed to keep up its organization by the appointment of officers or otherwise; or

(c) the corporation's term of existence has expired.

(E) Partnership Associations; Unincorporated Voluntary Associations. Service of process on a partnership association or an unincorporated voluntary association may be made by

(1) serving a summons and a copy of the complaint on an officer, director, trustee, agent, or person in charge of an office or business establishment of the association, and

(2) sending a summons and a copy of the complaint by registered mail, addressed to an office of the association. If an office cannot be located, a summons and a copy of the complaint may be sent by registered mail to a member of the association other than the person on whom the summons and complaint was served.

(F) Service on Insurer. To the extent that it is permitted by statute, service on an insurer may be satisfied by providing two summonses and a copy of the complaint to the Commissioner of the Office of Financial and Insurance Regulation via delivery or registered mail.

(G) Public Corporations. Service of process on a public, municipal, quasi-municipal, or governmental corporation, unincorporated board, or public body may be made by serving a summons and a copy of the complaint on:

(1) the chairperson of the board of commissioners or the county clerk of a county;

(2) the mayor, the city clerk, or the city attorney of a city;

(3) the president, the clerk, or a trustee of a village;

(4) the supervisor or the township clerk of a township;

(5) the president, the secretary, or the treasurer of a school district;

(6) the president or the secretary of the Michigan State Board of Education;

(7) the president, the secretary, or other member of the governing body of a corporate body or an unincorporated board having control of a state institution;

(8) the president, the chairperson, the secretary, the manager, or the clerk of any other public body organized or existing under the constitution or laws of Michigan, when no other method of service is specially provided by statute.

The service of process may be made on an officer having substantially the same duties as those named or described above, irrespective of title. In any case, service may be made by serving a summons and a copy of the complaint on a person in charge of the office of an officer on whom service may be made and sending a summons and a copy of the complaint by registered mail addressed to the officer at his or her office.

(H) Agent Authorized by Appointment or by Law.

(1) Service of process on a defendant may be made by serving a summons and a copy of the complaint on an agent authorized by written appointment or by law to receive service of process.

(2) Whenever, pursuant to statute or court rule, service of process is to be made on a nongovernmental defendant by service on a public officer, service on the public officer may be made by registered mail addressed to his or her office.

(I) Discretion of the Court.

(1) On a showing that service of process cannot reasonably be made as provided by this rule, the court may by order permit service of process to be made in any other manner reasonably calculated to give the defendant actual notice of the proceedings and an opportunity to be heard.

(2) A request for an order under the rule must be made in a verified motion dated not more than 14 days before it is filed. The motion must set forth sufficient facts to show that process cannot be served under this rule and must state the defendant's address or last known address, or that no address of the defendant is known. If the name or present address of the defendant is unknown, the moving party must set forth facts showing diligent inquiry to ascertain it. A hearing on the motion is not required unless the court so directs.

(3) Service of process may not be made under this subrule before entry of the court's order permitting it.

(J) Jurisdiction; Range of Service; Effect of Improper Service.

(1) Provisions for service of process contained in these rules are intended to satisfy the due process requirement that a defendant be informed of an action by the best means available under the circumstances. These rules are not intended to limit or expand the jurisdiction given the Michigan courts over a defendant. The jurisdiction of a court over a defendant is governed by the United States Constitution and the constitution and laws of the State of Michigan. See MCL 600.701 *et seq.*

(2) There is no territorial limitation on the range of process issued by a Michigan court.

(3) An action shall not be dismissed for improper service of process unless the service failed to inform the defendant of the action within the time provided in these rules for service.

(K) Registered and Certified Mail.

(1) If a rule uses the term "registered mail," that term includes the term "certified mail," and the term "registered mail, return receipt requested." includes the term "certified mail, return receipt requested". However, if certified mail is used, the receipt of mailing must be postmarked by the post office.

(2) If a rule uses the term "certified mail," a postmarked receipt of mailing is not required. Registered mail may be used when a rule requires certified mail.

[Adopted effective March 1, 1985. Amended effective September 28, 2011, 490 Mich. Amended March 28, 2018, effective May 1, 2018, 501 Mich.]

Comments

Staff Comment to 1985 Adoption

MCR 2.105 is based on GCR 1963, 105, and includes some provisions from GCR 1963, 106.1.

Subrule (A)(2) provides that service on an individual may be made by registered or certified mail with delivery restricted to the addressee. A copy of the return receipt signed by the defendant must be attached to the proof of service.

There are corresponding changes in subrules (C)–(E) that would permit service by mail on persons who are served as representatives of organizations. The prior rule spoke of "leaving" the summons and a copy of the complaint with these persons. GCR 1963, 105.3–105.6.

In subrule (B), regarding substituted service on individuals, a person's conservator is added as a representative on whom service may be made.

The provisions of GCR 1963, 105.4 regarding service on insurers are moved from the section dealing with private corporations to a new subrule (F) in recognition that insurance companies need not be corporations. MCL 500.106. The reference to service on a "resident agent" is deleted. The statute from which that term was drawn (CL 1970, 500.1404) has been repealed.

Additional detail has been added in subrule (I) regarding court orders for service where service under the rule cannot reasonably be made. Some of the procedural provisions are taken from GCR 1963, 106.1. The authority to order such other methods of service on the ground that the defendant resides outside of Michigan is deleted.

In subrule (J)(1), regarding the limits on jurisdiction of the courts, a reference to the United States Constitution is added.

Subrule (J)(3) is a new provision regarding the remedy when service is found to have been improper. Dismissal is required only if the attempt to serve did not give the defendant notice of the action within the time provided for service by the rules.

Subrule (K) clarifies the use of the terms "registered mail" and "certified mail".

The forms contained in GCR 1963, 105.10–105.15 are deleted. The function of approving forms had been delegated to the state court administrator.

Staff Comment to 2011 Amendment

The above noted changes are minor revisions of the rules that have been recommended to the Court to correct cross references and to reflect other technical changes.

Staff Comment to 2018 Amendment

The amendment of MCR 2.105 adds reference to service on the "agent for service of process" so that it is consistent with MCL 449.1105(a)(2).

Rule 2.106   Notice by Posting or Publication

(A) Availability. This rule governs service of process by publication or posting pursuant to an order under MCR 2.105(I).

(B) Procedure. A request for an order permitting service under this rule shall be made by motion in the manner provided in MCR 2.105(I). In ruling on the motion, the court shall determine whether mailing is required under subrules (D)(2) or (E)(2).

(C) Notice of Action; Contents.

(1) The order directing that notice be given to a defendant under this rule must include

(a) the name of the court,

(b) the names of the parties,

(c) a statement describing the nature of the proceedings,

(d) directions as to where and when to answer or take other action permitted by law or court rule, and

(e) a statement as to the effect of failure to answer or take other action.

(2) If the names of some or all defendants are unknown, the order must describe the relationship of the unknown defendants to the matter to be litigated in the best way possible, as, for example, unknown claimants, unknown owners, or unknown heirs, devisees, or assignees of a named person.

(D) Publication of Order; Mailing. If the court orders notice by publication, the defendant shall be notified of the action by

(1) publishing a copy of the order once each week for 3 consecutive weeks, or for such further time as the court may require, in a newspaper in the county where the defendant resides, if known, and if not, in the county where the action is pending; and

(2) sending a copy of the order to the defendant at his or her last known address by registered mail, return receipt requested, before the date of the last publication. If the plaintiff does not know the present or last known address of the defendant, and cannot ascertain it after diligent inquiry, mailing a copy of the order is not required. The moving party is responsible for arranging for the mailing and proof of mailing.

(E) Posting; Mailing. If the court orders notice by posting, the defendant shall be notified of the action by

(1) posting a copy of the order in the courthouse and 2 or more other public places as the court may direct for 3 continuous weeks or for such further time as the court may require; and

(2) sending a copy of the order to the defendant at his or her last known address by registered mail, return receipt requested, before the last week of posting. If the plaintiff does not know the present or last known address of the defendant, and cannot ascertain it after diligent inquiry, mailing a copy of the

order is not required. The moving party is responsible for arranging for the mailing and proof of mailing.

The order must designate who is to post the notice and file proof of posting. Only a person listed in MCR 2.103(B)(1), (2), or (3) may be designated.

(F) Newspaper Defined.

(1) The term "newspaper" as used in this rule is limited to a newspaper published in the English language for the dissemination of general news and information or for the dissemination of legal news. The newspaper must have a bona fide list of paying subscribers or have been published at least once a week in the same community without interruption for at least 2 years, and have been established, published, and circulated at least once a week without interruption for at least 1 year in the county where publication is to occur.

(2) If no newspaper qualifies in the county where publication is to be made under subrule (D)(1) the term "newspaper" includes a newspaper that by this rule is qualified to publish notice of actions commenced in an adjoining county.

(G) Proof of Service. Service of process made pursuant to this rule may be proven as follows:

(1) Publication must be proven by an affidavit of the publisher or the publisher's agent

(a) stating facts establishing the qualification of the newspaper in which the order was published,

(b) setting out a copy of the published order, and

(c) stating the dates on which it was published.

(2) Posting must be proven by a verified statement of the person designated in the order under subrule (E) attesting that a copy of the order was posted for the required time in the courthouse in a conspicuous place open to the public and in the other places as ordered by the court.

(3) Mailing must be proven by a verified statement. The person signing the verified statement must attach a copy of the order as mailed, and a return receipt.

[Adopted effective March 1, 1985. Amended March 20, 2019, effective May 1, 2019, 502 Mich.]

Comments

Staff Comment to 1985 Adoption

MCR 2.106 is similar to GCR 1963, 106. The principal change is the deletion of the limitation of GCR 106 to actions in which personal jurisdiction is not required. Rather, MCR 2.106 is written to prescribe the procedure for giving of notice by publication or posting where such notice is authorized by order under MCR 2.105(I). The procedures for requesting an order are placed in MCR 2.105(I).

The [March 1, 1985] amendment of MCR 2.106(C)(1) modifies the language to make clear that when an order is entered permitting notice by publication or posting, the order itself must include the specific information required by the rule.

Subrule (D)(1) requires that a publication be made in the county in which the defendant resides, if known. Under GCR 1963, 106.4, the publication must be made in the county in which the action is pending. Subrule (D)(1) also reduces the required number of weeks of publication from 4 (see GCR 1963, 106.3[1]) to 3.

Subrule (E) adds provisions specifying the manner of notice by posting applicable when posting is ordered by the court.

Subrules (D)(2) and (E)(2) provide that it is the plaintiff who is responsible for the mailing that accompanies notice under this rule. In addition, those provisions specify that the mailing in conjunction with a publication or posting of notice must be by registered mail.

The forms found in GCR 1963, 106.8–106.12 are deleted.

Staff Comment to 2019 Amendment

The amendments of Rules 1.109, 2.102, 2.104, 2.106, 2.107, 2.117, 2.119, 2.403, 2.503, 2.506, 2.508, 2.518, 2.602, 2.603, 2.621, 3.101, 3.104, 3.203, 3.205, 3.210, 3.302,

3.607, 3.613, 3.614, 3.705, 3.801, 3.802, 3.805, 3.806, 4.201, 4.202, 4.303, 4.306, 5.001, 5.104, 5.105, 5.107, 5.108, 5.113, 5.117, 5.118, 5.119, 5.120, 5.125, 5.126, 5.132, 5.162, 5.202, 5.203, 5.205, 5.302, 5.304, 5.307, 5.308, 5.309, 5.310, 5.311, 5.313, 5.402, 5.404, 5.405, 5.409, 5.501, and 5.784 and addition of Rule 3.618 of the Michigan Court Rules are an expected progression necessary for design and implementation of the statewide electronic-filing system. These particular amendments will assist in implementing the goals of the project.

Rule 2.107. Service and Filing of Pleadings and Other Documents

(A) Service; When Required.

(1) Unless otherwise stated in this rule, every party who has filed a pleading, an appearance, or a motion must be served with a copy of every document later filed in the action. A nonparty who has filed a motion or appeared in response to a motion need only be served with documents that relate to that motion.

(2) Except as provided in MCR 2.603, after a default is entered against a party, further service of documents need not be made on that party unless he or she has filed an appearance or a written demand for service of documents. However, a pleading that states a new claim for relief against a party in default must be served in the manner provided by MCR 2.105.

(3) If an attorney appears on behalf of a person who has not received a copy of the complaint, a copy of the complaint must be delivered to the attorney on request.

(4) All documents filed on behalf of a defendant must be served on all other defendants not in default.

(B) Service on Attorney or Party.

(1) Service required or permitted to be made on a party for whom an attorney has appeared in the action must be made on the attorney except as follows:

(a) The original service of the summons and complaint must be made on the party as provided by MCR 2.105;

(b) When a contempt proceeding for disobeying a court order is initiated, the notice or order must be personally delivered to the party, unless the court orders otherwise;

(c) After a final judgment or final order has been entered and the time for an appeal of right has passed, documents must be served on the party unless the rule governing the particular postjudgment procedure specifically allows service on the attorney;

(d) The court may order service on the party;

(e) If an attorney files a notice of limited appearance under MCR 2.117 on behalf of a self-represented party, service of every document later filed in the action must continue to be made on the party, and must also be made on the limited scope attorney for the duration of the limited appearance. At the request of the limited scope attorney, and if circumstances warrant, the court may order service to be made only on the party.

(2) If two or more attorneys represent the same party, service of documents on one of the attorneys is sufficient. An attorney who represents more than one party is entitled to service of only one copy of a document.

(3) If a party prosecutes or defends the action on his or her own behalf, service of documents must be made on the party in the manner provided by subrule (C).

(C) Manner of Service. Except under MCR 1.109(G)(6)(a), service of a copy of a document on an attorney must be made by delivery or by mailing to the attorney at his or her last known business address or, if the attorney does not have a business address, then to his or her last known residence address. Except under MCR 1.109(G)(6)(a), service on a party must be made by delivery or by mailing to the party at the address stated in the party's pleadings.

(1) *Delivery to Attorney.* Delivery of a copy to an attorney within this rule means

(a) handing it to the attorney personally, serving it electronically under MCR 1.109(G)(6)(a), or, if agreed to by the parties, e-mailing it to the attorney as allowed under MCR 2.107(C)(4);

(b) leaving it at the attorney's office with the person in charge or, if no one is in charge or present, by leaving it in a conspicuous place; or

(c) if the office is closed or the attorney has no office, by leaving it at the attorney's usual residence with some person of suitable age and discretion residing there.

(2) *Delivery to Party.* Delivery of a copy to a party within this rule means

(a) handing it to the party personally, serving it electronically under MCR 1.109(G)(6)(a), or, if agreed to by the parties, e-mailing it to the party as allowed under MCR 2.107(C)(4); or

(b) leaving it at the party's usual residence with some person of suitable age and discretion residing there.

(3) *Mailing.* Mailing a copy under this rule means enclosing it in a sealed envelope with first class postage fully prepaid, addressed to the person to be served, and depositing the envelope and its contents in the United States mail. Service by mail is complete at the time of mailing.

(4) *Alternative Electronic Service.*

(a) Except as provided by MCR 1.109(G)(6)(a)(ii), the parties may agree to alternative electronic service among themselves by filing a stipulation in that case. Some or all of the parties may also agree to alternative electronic service of notices and court documents in a particular case by a court or a friend of the court by filing an agreement with the court or friend of the court respectively. Alternative electronic service may be by any of the following methods:

(i) e-mail,

(ii) text message, or

(iii) alert consisting of an e-mail or text message to log into a secure website to view notices and court papers.

(b) Obligation to Provide and Update Information.

(i) The agreement for alternative electronic service shall set forth the e-mail addresses or phone numbers for service. Attorneys who agree to e-mail service shall include the same e-mail address currently on file with the State Bar of Michigan. If an attorney is not a member of the State Bar of Michigan, the email address shall be the e-mail address currently on file with the appropriate registering agency in the state of the attorney's admission. Parties or attorneys who have agreed to alternative electronic service under this subrule shall immediately notify, as required, the court or the friend of the court if the e-mail address or phone number for service changes.

(ii) The agreement for service by text message or text message alert shall set forth the phone number for service. Parties or attorneys who have agreed to service by text message or text message alert under this subrule shall immediately notify, as required, the court or the friend of the court if the phone number for service changes.

(c) The party or attorney shall set forth in the agreement all limitations and conditions concerning e-mail or text message service, including but not limited to:

(i) the maximum size of the document that may be attached to an e-mail or text message,

(ii) designation of exhibits as separate documents,

(iii) the obligation (if any) to furnish paper copies of e-mailed or text message documents, and

(iv) the names and e-mail addresses of other individuals in the office of an attorney of record designated to receive e-mail service on behalf of a party.

(d) Documents served by e-mail or text message must be in PDF format or other format that prevents the alteration of the document contents. Documents served by alert must be in PDF format or other format for which a free downloadable reader is available.

(e) A document served by alternative electronic service that the court or friend of the court or his or her authorized designee is required to sign may be signed in accordance with MCR 1.109(E).

(f) Each e-mail or text message that transmits a document or provides an alert to log in to view a document shall identify in the e-mail subject line or at the beginning of the text message the name of the court, case name, case number, and the title of each document being sent.

(g) An alternative electronic service transmission sent at or before 11:59 p.m. shall be deemed to be served on that day. If the transmission is sent on a Saturday, Sunday, legal holiday, or other day on which the court is closed pursuant to court order, it is deemed to be served on the next business day.

(h) A party or attorney may withdraw from an agreement for alternative electronic service by notifying the party or parties, court, and the friend of the court, as appropriate, in writing and shall take effect immediately.

(i) Alternative electronic service is complete upon transmission, unless the party, court, or friend of the court making service learns that the attempted service did not reach the intended recipient. If an alternative electronic service transmission is undeliverable, the entity responsible for serving the document must serve the document by regular mail under MCR 2.107(C)(3) or by delivery under MCR 2.107(C)(1) or (2), and include a copy of the return notice indicating that the electronic transmission was undeliverable. The court or friend of the court must also retain a notice that the electronic transmission was undeliverable.

(j) The party, court, or friend of the court shall maintain an archived record of sent items that shall not be purged until a judgment or final order is entered and all appeals have been completed.

(k) This rule does not require the court or the friend of the court to create functionality it does not have nor accommodate more than one standard for alternative electronic service.

(l) The party or attorney requesting electronic service under this subrule is required to submit a request to initiate, update, modify, or withdraw from electronic service to the court independently from the friend of the court office.

(D) Proof of Service. Except as otherwise provided by MCR 2.104, 2.105, or 2.106, proof of service of documents required or permitted to be served must be by written acknowledgment of service, or a written statement by the individual who served the documents verified under MCR 1.109(D)(3). The proof of service may be included at the end of the document as filed. Proof of service must be filed promptly and at least at or before a hearing to which the document relates.

(E) Service Prescribed by Court. When service of documents after the original complaint cannot reasonably be made because there is no attorney of record, because the party cannot be found, or for any other reason, the court, for good cause on ex parte application, may direct in what manner and on whom service may be made.

(F) Numerous Parties. In an action in which there is an unusually large number of parties on the same side, the court on motion or on its own initiative may order that

(1) they need not serve their documents on each other;

(2) responses to their pleadings need only be served on the party to whose pleading the response is made;

(3) a cross-claim, counterclaim, or allegation in an answer demanding a reply is deemed denied by the parties not served; and

(4) the filing of a pleading and service on an adverse party constitutes notice of it to all parties.

A copy of the order must be served on all parties in the manner the court directs.

[Adopted effective March 1, 1985. Amended September 9, 2003, effective January 1, 2004, 469 Mich; March 14, 2007, effective May 1, 2007, 477 Mich; October 16, 2007, effective January 1, 2008, 479 Mich; September 30, 2008, effective January 1, 2009, 482 Mich; October 31, 2012, effective January 1, 2013, 493 Mich; January 29, 2014, effective May 1, 2014, 495 Mich; September 20, 2017, effective January 1, 2018, 501 Mich; May 30, 2018, effective September 1, 2018, 501 Mich; August 30, 2018, effective September 1, 2018, 502 Mich; March 20, 2019, effective May 1, 2019, 502 Mich; September 18, 2019, effective January 1, 2020, 503 Mich.]

Comments

Staff Comment to 1985 Adoption

MCR 2.107 is based on GCR 1963, 107.

In subrule (A)(1) a provision is added requiring that a nonparty who has filed a motion or appeared in response to a motion be served with papers that relate to the motion. This would be expected to arise most commonly with motions to intervene or motions with regard to discovery requests directed to a nonparty.

Subrule (A)(2), covering service of papers on a party in default, includes a cross-reference to MCR 2.603, which adds several requirements of notice to a defaulted party.

Subrule (B)(1)(c) specifies for how long parties may continue to serve an attorney who has appeared in the action. This addition is related to MCR 2.117(C), covering the duration of an attorney's appearance.

Subrule (D) permits a proof of service of papers to be included in the body of the document itself. Subrule (D) also adds language regarding the time for filing a proof of service to cover the circumstance in which there is no hearing involved. In such cases proof of service must be filed "promptly".

Staff Comment to 2004 Amendment

The September 9, 2003 amendment of MCR 2.107(G), effective January 1, 2004, continues to give judges the discretion to accept papers for filing when circumstances warrant, but requires the party who presented the papers to confirm that they have been properly filed with the clerk of the court.

Staff Comment to March, 2007 Amendment

This amendment corrects an incorrect reference.

Staff Comment to October, 2007 Amendment

The amendments allow parties to stipulate to agree to e-discovery, or service of papers among the parties, by e-mail. Further, the amendments require that court clerks note the date pleadings are filed if that date is different than the date the filing is docketed.

The e-discovery rules allow parties or those represented by attorneys to stipulate to service by e-mail. The stipulation establishes the maximum document size, the designation of exhibits as separate documents, the persons who are entitled to receive an e-mailed document other than the party or attorney, and the obligation, if any, to furnish paper copies of e-mailed documents. The rule also requires that the subject line of an e-mail that contains a document or has a document attached indicate the court, case number, party name, and title of the document being sent. Documents are required to be in a format, such as PDF, that precludes alteration, and a designation of "s/" or "/s/" is sufficient for a signature. Documents e-mailed after 4:30 p.m. Eastern Time are considered filed the next day, and service by e-mail is equivalent to service by delivery. Service is complete upon transmission, unless the sender receives notice that the e-mail did not reach the intended address. An e-mail sender is required to maintain an archived record of sent items until the case concludes, including the disposition of all appeals.

Staff Comment to 2008 Amendment

The amendments allow parties or attorneys to voluntarily agree to receive notices and other documents from the court by e-mail, similar to the current ability of parties to stipulate to serve one another by e-mail.

Staff Comment to 2013 Amendment

The amendments of these rules update the rules making them less "paper" focused and reflecting the use of electronic technology in the way courts process court records. The amendments also clarify and delineate the types of records and other materials maintained by a court, and clarify how access is provided.

Staff Comment to 2014 Amendment

The amendment of MCR 2.107 provides clarification by adding the phrase "final order" so that after either a final judgment or final order has entered, papers should be served on the party after the time for appeal has passed. The amendment of MCR 2.117 states that the duration of an attorney's appearance extends until a final judgment or final order is entered. This amendment is intended to clarify that representation by an attorney who appears in a postjudgment motion ends with the final order related to that matter (after the period for appeal of right has passed).

Staff Comment to January, 2018 Amendment

The amendments of Rules 1.0, 1.2, 4.2, and 4.3 of the Michigan Rules of Professional Conduct and Rules 2.107, 2.117, and 6.001 of the Michigan Court Rules were submitted to the Court by the State Bar of Michigan Representative Assembly. The rules are intended to provide guidance for attorneys and clients who would prefer to engage in a limited scope representation. The rules allow for such an agreement "preferably in writing," and enable an attorney to file a notice of LSR with the court when the representation is undertaken as well as a termination notice when the representation has ended. The rules also explicitly allow attorneys to provide document preparation services for a self-represented litigant without having to file an appearance with the court.

Staff Comment to First September, 2018 Amendment

The amendments in this order are intended to begin moving trial courts toward a statewide uniform e-Filing process. In addition, the order moves existing language into MCR 1.109 as a way to, for the first time, include most filing requirements in one single rule, instead of scattered in various rules. The order largely mirrors the administrative orders that most e-Filing pilot projects have operated under, but contains some significant new provisions. For example, courts are required to maintain documents in an electronic document management system, and the electronic record is the official court record.

Staff Comment to Second September, 2018 Amendment

These amendments update cross-references in the rules, and are intended to reflect changes that are necessary as a result of the Court's recent e-Filing rules amendments.

Staff Comment to 2019 Amendment

The amendments of Rules 1.109, 2.102, 2.104, 2.106, 2.107, 2.117, 2.119, 2.403, 2.503, 2.506, 2.508, 2.518, 2.602, 2.603, 2.621, 3.101, 3.104, 3.203, 3.205, 3.210, 3.302, 3.607, 3.613, 3.614, 3.705, 3.801, 3.802, 3.805, 3.806, 4.201, 4.202, 4.303, 4.306, 5.001, 5.104, 5.105, 5.107, 5.108, 5.113, 5.117, 5.118, 5.119, 5.120, 5.125, 5.126, 5.132, 5.162, 5.202, 5.203, 5.205, 5.302, 5.304, 5.307, 5.308, 5.309, 5.310, 5.311, 5.313, 5.402, 5.404, 5.405, 5.409, 5.501, and 5.784 and addition of Rule 3.618 of the Michigan Court Rules are an expected progression necessary for design and implementation of the statewide electronic-filing system. These particular amendments will assist in implementing the goals of the project.

Staff Comment to 2020 Amendment

The amendments of MCR 1.109, 2.107, 2.113, 2.116, 2.119, 2.222, 2.223, 2.225, 2.227, 3.206, 3.211, 3.212, 3.214, 3.303, 3.903, 3.921, 3.925, 3.926, 3.931, 3.933, 3.942, 3.950, 3.961, 3.971, 3.972, 4.002, 4.101, 4.201, 4.202, 4.302, 5.128, 5.302, 5.731, 6.101, 6.615, 8.105, and 8.119 and rescission of MCR 2.226 and 8.125 continue the process for design and implementation of the statewide electronic-filing system.

Rule 2.108. Time

(A) Time for Service and Filing of Pleadings.

(1) A defendant must serve and file an answer or take other action permitted by law or these rules within 21 days after being served with the summons and a copy of the complaint in Michigan in the manner provided in MCR 2.105(A)(1).

(2) If service of the summons and a copy of the complaint is made outside Michigan, or if the manner of service used requires the summons and a copy of the complaint to be sent by registered mail addressed to the defendant, the defendant must serve and file an answer or take other action permitted by law or these rules within 28 days after service.

(3) When service is made in accordance with MCR 2.106, the court shall allow a reasonable time for the defendant to answer or take other action permitted by law or these rules, but may not prescribe a time less than 28 days after publication or posting is completed.

(4) A party served with a pleading stating a cross-claim or counterclaim against that party must serve and file an answer or take other action permitted by law or these rules within 21 days after service.

(5) A party served with a pleading to which a reply is required or permitted may serve and file a reply within 21 days after service of the pleading to which it is directed.

(6) In an action alleging medical malpractice filed on or after October 1, 1986, unless the defendant has responded as provided in subrule (A)(1) or (2), the defendant must serve and file an answer within 21 days after being served with the notice of filing the security for costs or the affidavit in lieu of such security required by MCL 600.2912d.

(B) Time for Filing Motion in Response to Pleading. A motion raising a defense or an objection to a pleading must be served and filed within the time for filing the responsive pleading or, if no responsive pleading is required, within 21 days after service of the pleading to which the motion is directed.

(C) Effect of Particular Motions and Amendments. When a motion or an amended pleading is filed, the time for pleading set in subrule (A) is altered as follows, unless a different time is set by the court:

(1) If a motion under MCR 2.116 made before filing a responsive pleading is denied, the moving party must serve and file a responsive pleading within 21 days after notice of the denial. However, if the moving party, within 21 days, files an application for leave to appeal from the order, the time is

extended until 21 days after the denial of the application unless the appellate court orders otherwise.

(2) An order granting a motion under MCR 2.116 must set the time for service and filing of the amended pleading, if one is allowed.

(3) The response to a supplemental pleading or to a pleading amended either as of right or by leave of court must be served and filed within the time remaining for response to the original pleading or within 21 days after service of the supplemental or amended pleading, whichever period is longer.

(4) If the court has granted a motion for more definite statement, the responsive pleading must be served and filed within 21 days after the more definite statement is served.

(D) Time for Service of Order to Show Cause. An order to show cause must set the time for service of the order and for the hearing, and may set the time for answer to the complaint or response to the motion on which the order is based.

(E) Extension of Time. A court may, with notice to the other parties who have appeared, extend the time for serving and filing a pleading or motion or the doing of another act, if the request is made before the expiration of the period originally prescribed. After the expiration of the original period, the court may, on motion, permit a party to act if the failure to act was the result of excusable neglect. However, if a rule governing a particular act limits the authority to extend the time, those limitations must be observed. MCR 2.603(D) applies if a default has been entered.

(F) Unaffected by Expiration of Term. The time provided for the doing of an act or the holding of a proceeding is not affected or limited by the continuation or expiration of a term of court. The continuation or expiration of a term of court does not affect the power of a court to do an act or conduct a proceeding in a civil action pending before it.

[Adopted effective March 1, 1985. Amended December 11, 1986, effective December 12, 1986, 426 Mich.]

Comments

Staff Comment to 1985 Adoption

MCR 2.108 is based on GCR 1963, 108. Throughout the Michigan Court Rules, time limits for periods of up to 6 months are expressed in multiples of 7 days, except for very short periods, certain statutorily prescribed times, and certain administrative provisions that do not affect the conduct of litigation.

The provisions of GCR 1963, 108.6, regarding computation of time, are moved to MCR 1.108.

The [March 1, 1985] amendment of MCR 2.108(A)(1) and (2) changes the time within which a defendant served by registered or certified mail under MCR 2.105(A)(2) must respond from 21 days to 28 days.

The [March 1, 1985] amendment of MCR 2.108(A)(4) corrects a typographical error, substituting "permitted" for "permitting".

Subrule (C)(4) is slightly different from GCR 1963, 108.3(4). The provision regarding the time for filing a more definite statement is omitted; that subject is covered by MCR 2.115. Subrule (C)(4) only states when the responsive pleading is required.

GCR 1963, 108 was not consistent in its use of the terms "file" and "serve". In several provisions, only one of those terms was used, while the intention seemed to be that both filing and service were required. See, e.g., GCR 1963, 108.2, 108.4. Both terms are used in MCR 2.108.

The time for service of motions and affidavits, covered by GCR 1963, 108.4, is moved to the motion practice rule, MCR 2.119.

GCR 1963, 108.7(1), which provided an extra 2 days to act when a paper was mailed out of the county, is omitted.

Language is added in MCR 2.108(E) regarding the trial judge's authority to extend the time for various acts. If a specific rule places limitations on the judge's authority to do so, the specific provision controls, rather than this general one.

Rule 2.109   Security for Costs

(A) Motion. On motion of a party against whom a claim has been asserted in a civil action, if it appears reasonable and proper, the court may order the opposing party to file with the court clerk a bond with surety as required by the court in an amount sufficient to cover all costs and other recoverable expenses that may be awarded by the trial court, or, if the claiming party appeals, by the trial and appellate courts. The court shall determine the amount in its discretion. MCR 3.604(E) and (F) govern objections to the surety.

(B) Exceptions. Subrule (A) does not apply in the following circumstances:

(1) The court may allow a party to proceed without furnishing security for costs if the party's pleading states a legitimate claim and the party shows by affidavit that he or she is financially unable to furnish a security bond.

(2) Security shall not be required of

(a) the United States or an agency or instrumentality of the United States;

(b) the State of Michigan or a governmental unit of the state, including but not limited to a public, municipal, quasi-municipal or governmental corporation, unincorporated board, public body, or political subdivision; or

(c) an officer of a governmental unit or agency exempt from security who brings an action in his or her official capacity.

(C) Modification of Order. The court may order new or additional security at any time on just terms,

(1) if the party or the surety moves out of Michigan, or

(2) if the original amount of the bond proves insufficient.

A person who becomes a new or additional surety is liable for all costs from the commencement of the action, as if he or she had been the original surety.

[Adopted effective March 1, 1985. Amended December 11, 1986, effective December 12, 1986, 426 Mich; March 24, 1998, effective April 1, 1998, 456 Mich.]

Comments

Staff Comment to 1985 Adoption

MCR 2.109 corresponds to GCR 1963, 109. The principal change is that the court will have the authority to require the posting of security not only by a plaintiff, but also by any other party asserting a claim in the action. Some counterclaims or cross-claims might greatly expand the scope of the litigation, making it appropriate to require a defendant to post security.

In subrule (A) a cross-reference is added to the provisions of the general bond rule regarding objections to sureties.

In subrule (B)(1) the language of GCR 1963, 109(1), regarding the showing required to avoid the need to post security, is modified slightly in light of *Gaffier v St Johns Hospital*, 68 Mich App 474 (1976).

Staff Comment to 1998 Amendment

The amendment of MCR 2.109 makes technical changes necessary in light of statutory amendments and corrects cross-references.

The amendment of MCR 2.109 relates to amendments of MCL 600.2912d, 600.2912e, by 1993 PA 78.

Rule 2.110   Pleadings

(A) Definition of "Pleading." The term "pleading" includes only:

(1) a complaint,

(2) a cross-claim,

(3) a counterclaim,

(4) a third-party complaint,

(5) an answer to a complaint, cross-claim, counterclaim, or third-party complaint, and

(6) a reply to an answer.

No other form of pleading is allowed.

(B) When Responsive Pleading Required. A party must file and serve a responsive pleading to

(1) a complaint,

(2) a counterclaim,

(3) a cross-claim,

(4) a third-party complaint, or

(5) an answer demanding a reply.

(C) Designation of Cross-Claim or Counterclaim. A cross-claim or a counterclaim may be combined with an answer. The counterclaim or cross-claim must be clearly designated as such.

(1) A responsive pleading is not required to a cross-claim or counterclaim that is not clearly designated as such in the answer.

(2) If a party has raised a cross-claim or counterclaim in the answer, but has not designated it as such, the court may treat the pleading as if it had been properly designated and require the party to amend the pleading, direct the opposing party to file a responsive pleading, or enter another appropriate order.

(3) The court may treat a cross-claim or counterclaim designated as a defense, or a defense designated as a cross-claim or counterclaim, as if the designation had been proper and issue an appropriate order.

[Adopted effective March 1, 1985.]

Comments

Staff Comment to 1985 Adoption

MCR 2.110 is based on GCR 1963, 110.1 and 111.7.

Subrule (A) defines the term "pleading," and subrule (B) specifies when a responsive pleading is required. In addition to the required responsive pleadings, the party always has the option of filing a reply to an answer.

Subrule (C) provides more detail regarding the treatment of misdesignated cross-claims and counterclaims than was found in GCR 1963, 111.7.

Several provisions of GCR 1963, 110 are not included in MCR 2.110. The provisions on motions (GCR 1963, 110.2) are moved to the motion practice rule, MCR 2.119. The rule of construction found in GCR 1963, 110.3 is deleted as unnecessary in light of MCR 1.105.

Rule 2.111   General Rules of Pleading

(A) Pleading to Be Concise and Direct; Inconsistent Claims.

(1) Each allegation of a pleading must be clear, concise, and direct.

(2) Inconsistent claims or defenses are not objectionable. A party may

   (a) allege two or more statements of fact in the alternative when in doubt about which of the statements is true;

   (b) state as many separate claims or defenses as the party has, regardless of consistency and whether they are based on legal or equitable grounds or on both.

All statements made in a pleading are subject to the requirements of MCR 1.109(D)(3) and (E).

(B) Statement of Claim. A complaint, counterclaim, cross-claim, or third-party complaint must contain the following:

(1) A statement of the facts, without repetition, on which the pleader relies in stating the cause of action, with the specific allegations necessary reasonably to inform the adverse party of the nature of the claims the adverse party is called on to defend; and

(2) A demand for judgment for the relief that the pleader seeks. If the pleader seeks an award of money, a specific amount must be stated if the claim is for a sum certain or a sum that can by computation be made certain, or if the amount sought is $25,000 or less. Otherwise, a specific amount may not be stated, and the pleading must include allegations that show that the claim is within the jurisdiction of the court. Declaratory relief may be claimed in cases of actual controversy. See MCR 2.605. Relief in the alternative or relief of several different types may be demanded.

(C) Form of Responsive Pleading. As to each allegation on which the adverse party relies, a responsive pleading must

(1) state an explicit admission or denial;

(2) plead no contest; or

(3) state that the pleader lacks knowledge or information sufficient to form a belief as to the truth of an allegation, which has the effect of a denial.

(D) Form of Denials. Each denial must state the substance of the matters on which the pleader will rely to support the denial.

(E) Effect of Failure to Deny.

(1) Allegations in a pleading that requires a responsive pleading, other than allegations of the amount of damage or the nature of the relief demanded, are admitted if not denied in the responsive pleading.

(2) Allegations in a pleading that does not require a responsive pleading are taken as denied.

(3) A pleading of no contest, provided for in subrule (C)(2), permits the action to proceed without proof of the claim or part of the claim to which the pleading is directed. Pleading no contest has the effect of an admission only for purposes of the pending action.

(F) Defenses; Requirement That Defense Be Pleaded.

(1) *Pleading Multiple Defenses.* A pleader may assert as many defenses, legal or equitable or both, as the pleader has against an opposing party. A defense is not waived by being joined with other defenses.

(2) *Defenses Must Be Pleaded; Exceptions.* A party against whom a cause of action has been asserted by complaint, cross-claim, counterclaim, or third-party claim must assert in a responsive pleading the defenses the party has against the claim. A defense not asserted in the responsive pleading or by motion as provided by these rules is waived, except for the defenses of lack of jurisdiction over the subject matter of the action, and failure to state a claim on which relief can be granted. However,

   (a) a party who has asserted a defense by motion filed pursuant to MCR 2.116 before filing a responsive pleading need not again assert that defense in a responsive pleading later filed;

(b) if a pleading states a claim for relief to which a responsive pleading is not required, a defense to that claim may be asserted at the trial unless a pretrial conference summary pursuant to MCR 2.401(C) has limited the issues to be tried.

(3) *Affirmative Defenses.* Affirmative defenses must be stated in a party's responsive pleading, either as originally filed or as amended in accordance with MCR 2.118. Under a separate and distinct heading, a party must state the facts constituting

(a) an affirmative defense, such as contributory negligence; the existence of an agreement to arbitrate; assumption of risk; payment; release; satisfaction; discharge; license; fraud; duress; estoppel; statute of frauds; statute of limitations; immunity granted by law; want or failure of consideration; or that an instrument or transaction is void, voidable, or cannot be recovered on by reason of statute or nondelivery;

(b) a defense that by reason of other affirmative matter seeks to avoid the legal effect of or defeat the claim of the opposing party, in whole or in part;

(c) a ground of defense that, if not raised in the pleading, would be likely to take the adverse party by surprise.

[Adopted effective March 1, 1985. Amended September 22, 1989, effective December 1, 1989, 433 Mich; January 17, 1992, effective April 1, 1992, 439 Mich; March 24, 1998, effective April 1, 1998, 456 Mich; August 30, 2018, effective September 1, 2018, 502 Mich.]

Comments

Staff Comment to 1985 Adoption

MCR 2.111 is based on GCR 1963, 111. The provisions are reorganized, and several are moved to other rules. GCR 1963, 111.8, concerning counterclaims, is relocated to MCR 2.203, which contains the general counterclaim provisions. GCR 1963, 111.10, which provided for submission of a case to the court on stipulated facts, is relocated to the summary disposition rule, MCR 2.116.

In addition, there are several other changes. Subrule (B)(2) includes a requirement that a pleader include a statement of a specific ad damnum if the claim is for a sum certain or an amount that can be computed. In addition, a specific amount must always be stated in actions in which no more than $10,000 is sought.

Subrule (F)(2) includes a slight modification of GCR 1963, 111.3. In general, a defense that a party is not required to plead can be raised at trial. However, a pretrial order under MCR 2.401(C) may limit the issues to be tried.

The [March 1, 1985] amendment of MCR 2.111(F)(3)(a) adds "immunity granted by law" to the list of affirmative defenses that must be pleaded.

GCR 1963, 111.6, regarding unwarranted claims and denials, is omitted. A much more detailed rule covering that subject is included as MCR 2.114.

Staff Comment to 1992 Amendment

The 1992 amendments of MCR 2.111 were designed to confirm the right of a party to amend a pleading to add or modify affirmative defenses. This right of amendment is governed by MCR 2.118. To the extent that *Campbell v St John Hospital*, 434 Mich 608, 615-617; 455 NW2d 695 (1990), had been understood to preclude amendment of affirmative defenses, including defenses related to the Malpractice Arbitration Act (MCL 600.5040 et seq.), the rule of Campbell was modified by these amendments.

Staff Comment to 1998 Amendment

The amendment of MCR 2.111 makes technical changes necessary in light of statutory amendments and corrects cross-references.

The amendment of MCR 2.111 is based on statutes amended by 1996 PA 388. The change in MCR 2.111(B)(2) applies to actions filed on or after January 1, 1998, the effective date of the statute increasing the jurisdictional limit of the district court.

Staff Comment to 2018 Amendment

These amendments update cross-references in the rules, and are intended to reflect changes that are necessary as a result of the Court's recent e-Filing rules amendments.

Rule 2.112   Pleading Special Matters

(A) Capacity; Legal Existence.

(1) Except to the extent required to show jurisdiction of a court, it is not necessary to allege

(a) the capacity of a party to sue,

(b) the authority of a party to sue or be sued in a representative capacity, or

(c) the legal existence of an organized association of persons that is made a party.

(2) A party wishing to raise an issue about

(a) the legal existence of a party,

(b) the capacity of a party to sue or be sued, or

(c) the authority of a party to sue or be sued in a representative capacity,

must do so by specific allegation, including supporting facts peculiarly within the pleader's knowledge.

(B) Fraud, Mistake, or Condition of Mind.

(1) In allegations of fraud or mistake, the circumstances constituting fraud or mistake must be stated with particularity.

(2) Malice, intent, knowledge, and other conditions of mind may be alleged generally.

(C) Conditions Precedent.

(1) In pleading performance or occurrence of conditions precedent, it is sufficient to allege generally that all conditions precedent have been performed or have occurred.

(2) A denial of performance or occurrence must be made specifically and with particularity.

(D) Action on Policy of Insurance.

(1) In an action on a policy of insurance, it is sufficient to allege

(a) the execution, date, and amount of the policy,

(b) the premium paid or to be paid,

(c) the property or risk insured,

(d) the interest of the insured, and

(e) the loss.

(2) A defense of

(a) breach of condition, agreement, representation, or warranty of a policy of insurance or of an application for a policy; or

(b) failure to furnish proof of loss as required by the policy

must be stated specifically and with particularity.

(E) Action on Written Instrument.

(1) In an action on a written instrument, the execution of the instrument and the handwriting of the defendant are admitted unless the defendant specifically denies the execution or the handwriting and supports the denial with an affidavit filed with the answer. The court may, for good cause, extend the time for filing the affidavits.

(2) This subrule also applies to an action against an indorser and to a party against whom a counterclaim or a cross-claim on a written instrument is filed.

(F) Official Document or Act. In pleading an official document or official act, it is sufficient to allege that the document was issued or the act done in compliance with law.

(G) Judgment. A judgment or decision of a domestic or foreign court, a tribal court of a federally recognized Indian tribe, a judicial or quasi-judicial tribunal, or a board or officer, must be alleged with sufficient particularity to identify it; it is not necessary to state facts showing jurisdiction to render it.

(H) Statutes, Ordinances, or Charters. In pleading a statute, ordinance, or municipal charter, it is sufficient to identify it, without stating its substance, except as provided in subrule (M).

(I) Special Damages. When items of special damage are claimed, they must be specifically stated.

(J) Law of Other Jurisdictions; Notice in Pleadings. A party who intends to rely on or raise an issue concerning the law of

(1) a state other than Michigan,

(2) a United States territory,

(3) a foreign nation or unit thereof, or

(4) a federally recognized Indian tribe

must give notice of that intention either in his or her pleadings or in a written notice served by the close of discovery.

(K) Fault of Nonparties; Notice.

(1) *Applicability.* This subrule applies to actions based on tort or another legal theory seeking damages for personal injury, property damage, or wrongful death to which MCL 600.2957 and MCL 600.6304, as amended by 1995 PA 249, apply.

(2) *Notice Requirement.* Notwithstanding MCL 600.6304, the trier of fact shall not assess the fault of a nonparty unless notice has been given as provided in this subrule.

(3) *Notice.*

(a) A party against whom a claim is asserted may give notice of a claim that a nonparty is wholly or partially at fault. A notice filed by one party identifying a particular nonparty serves as notice by all parties as to that nonparty.

(b) The notice shall designate the nonparty and set forth the nonparty's name and last known address, or the best identification of the nonparty that is possible, together with a brief statement of the basis for believing the nonparty is at fault.

(c) The notice must be filed within 91 days after the party files its first responsive pleading. On motion, the court shall allow a later filing of the notice on a showing that the facts on which the notice is based were not and could not with reasonable diligence have been known to the moving party earlier, provided that the late filing of the notice does not result in unfair prejudice to the opposing party.

(4) *Amendment Adding Party.* A party served with a notice under this subrule may file an amended pleading stating a claim or claims against the nonparty within 91 days of service of the

first notice identifying that nonparty. The court may permit later amendment as provided in MCR 2.118.

(L) Medical Malpractice Actions.

(1) In an action alleging medical malpractice filed on or after October 1, 1993, each party must file an affidavit as provided in MCL 600.2912d and 600.2912e. Notice of filing the affidavit must be promptly served on the opposing party. If the opposing party has appeared in the action, the notice may be served in the manner provided by MCR 2.107. If the opposing party has not appeared, the notice must be served in the manner provided by MCR 2.105. Proof of service of the notice must be promptly filed with the court.

(2) In a medical malpractice action, unless the court allows a later challenge for good cause:

(a) all challenges to a notice of intent to sue must be made by motion, filed pursuant to MCR 2.119, at the time the defendant files its first response to the complaint, whether by answer or motion, and

(b) all challenges to an affidavit of merit or affidavit of meritorious defense, including challenges to the qualifications of the signer, must be made by motion, filed pursuant to MCR 2.119, within 63 days of service of the affidavit on the opposing party. An affidavit of merit or meritorious defense may be amended in accordance with the terms and conditions set forth in MCR 2.118 and MCL 600.2301.

(M) Headlee Amendment Actions. In an action brought pursuant to Const 1963, art 9, § 32, alleging a violation of Const 1963, art 9, §§ 25–34, the pleadings shall set forth with particularity the factual basis for the alleged violation or a defense and indicate whether there are any factual questions that are anticipated to require resolution by the court. In an action involving Const 1963, art 9, § 29, the plaintiff shall state with particularity the type and extent of the harm and whether there has been a violation of either the first or second sentence of that section. In an action involving the second sentence of Const 1963, art 9, § 29, the plaintiff shall state with particularity the activity or service involved. The pleadings shall identify all statutes involved in the case, and the parties shall append to their pleadings copies of all ordinances and municipal charter provisions involved, and any available documentary evidence supportive of a claim or defense. The parties may supplement their pleadings with additional documentary evidence as it becomes available to them.

(N) A party whose cause of action is to collect a consumer debt as defined in the Michigan collection practices act (MCL 445.251[a] and [d]) must also include the following information in its complaint:

(1) the name of the creditor (as defined in MCL 445.251[e] and [f]), and

(2) the corresponding account number or identification number, or if none is available, information sufficient to identify the alleged debt, and

(3) the balance due to date.

(O) Business and Commercial Disputes.

(1) If a case involves a business or commercial dispute as defined in MCL 600.8031, and the court maintains a business court docket, a party shall verify on the face of the party's initial pleading that the case meets the statutory requirements

to be assigned to the business court. If a cross-claim, counterclaim, third-party complaint, amendment, or any other modification of the action includes a business or commercial dispute, a party shall verify on the face of the party's pleading that the case meets the statutory requirements to be assigned to the business court.

(2) If a party files a pleading alleging a business or commercial dispute as defined in MCL 600.8031 but fails to verify that the case meets the statutory requirements to be assigned to the business court as required in subsection (1) of this subrule, any party to the action may thereafter file a motion for determination that the case is eligible for assignment to the business court.

(3) On the motion of a party or the court's own initiative, if the court determines that the action meets the statutory requirements of MCL 600. 8031, the court shall assign the case to the business court.

(4) A party may file a motion requesting the chief judge review a decision made under subsection 3. The chief judge's ruling is not an order that may be appealed.

[Statements by Kelly, Corrigan, Young, and Markman, JJ., appear in 485 Mich.]

[Adopted effective March 1, 1985. Amended May 14, 1996, effective July 1, 1996, 451 Mich; November 6, 1996, effective February 1, 1997, 453 Mich; March 24, 1998, effective April 1, 1998, 456 Mich; November 27, 2007, effective January 1, 2008, 480 Mich; January 20, 2009, effective May 1, 2009, 483 Mich; September 9, 2009, effective January 1, 2010, 485 Mich; February 16, 2010, effective May 1, 2010, 485 Mich; November 10, 2011, effective January 1, 2012, 490 Mich; June 5, 2013, effective September 1, 2013, 494 Mich.]

Comments

Staff Comment to 1985 Adoption

MCR 2.112 is comparable to GCR 1963, 112. The only change is the addition of a requirement that a party intending to rely on foreign law must give notice of that intention by the close of discovery. See subrule (J).

The provisions of GCR 1963, 602, regarding actions on written instruments, are moved to this rule as subrule (E).

Staff Comment to 1996 Amendment

The 1996 amendment of MCR 2.112(G) and (J) was prompted by proposals from the Indian Tribal Court/State Trial Court Forum and from the State Bar of Michigan. The adopted rule reflects a synthesis of those sources, of a corresponding rule of the North Dakota Supreme Court, and of the model rules generated by the Michigan Indian Judicial Association.

Staff Comment to 1997 Amendment

The November 6 amendment of MCR 2.112, relates to statutory changes made by 1995 PA 161 and 1995 PA 249.

New MCR 2.112(K) governs the procedure for identifying nonparties whose conduct is claimed to be a cause of the injury, and for adding them as parties. See MCL 600.2957 and MCL 600.6304.

Staff Comment to 1998 Amendment

The March 24, 1998 [effective April 1, 1998], amendment of MCR 2.112 makes technical changes necessary in light of statutory amendments and corrects cross-references.

The amendment of MCR 2.112 relates to amendments of MCL 600.2912d, 600.2912e, by 1993 PA 78.

Staff Comment to January, 2009 Amendment

The amendment of MCR 2.112 clarifies that the subrule provisions apply to actions based on tort or another legal theory seeking damages for personal injury,

property damage, or wrongful death to which MCL 600.2957 and MCL 600.6304 apply, and more closely parallels the statutory provisions on which it is based. A similar change has been made in MCR 2.403(O)(10), which was also based on MCL 600.6304.

Staff Comment to September, 2008 Amendment

The amendments of MCR 2.112 impose specific pleading requirements for a case that is a consumer debt action under the Michigan collection practices act, which will provide defendants with relevant information regarding the alleged debt. The amendments of MCR 3.101 require those who seek a garnishment to provide specific information regarding the interest and costs related to the judgment.

Staff Comment to 2019 Amendment

The amendments of MCR 2.112 set a limit on the period for raising challenges to affidavits of merit and meritorious defense and notices of intent in medical malpractice actions. The amendments also allow revision under MCR 2.118 and MCL 600.2301. The amendment of MCR 2.118 explicitly states that the amended affidavit of merit or meritorious defense relates back to the date of the affidavit's original filing.

Staff Comment to 2011 Amendment

The existing fact-specific pleading requirements in MCR 2.112(M) are retained and expanded to promote earlier consideration whether facts must be established in the case. The amendments of MCR 2.625 clarify that costs, including reasonable attorney fees, are recoverable in a Headlee action. The amendment of MCR 7.206(D)(3) allows parties to utilize electronic filing in Headlee cases, as well as other extraordinary writs or original actions filed in the Court of Appeals. The amendments of MCR 7.206 create a new specific subsection (7.206[E]) regarding the procedure for filing a Headlee action as an original proceeding in the Court of Appeals. The amendment of MCR 7.213 is intended to clarify that Headlee actions are considered priority matters in the Court of Appeals.

Staff Comment to 2013 Amendment

The amendments of MCR 2.112 provide a means to identify business court cases and the placement of those matters on the business court docket. The amendment of MCR 8.119 allows business court opinions to be published.

Rule 2.113. Form, Captioning, Signing, and Verifying of Documents

(A) Applicability. The form, captioning, signing, and verifying of all documents are prescribed in MCR 1.109(D) and (E).

(B) Paragraphs; Separate Statements.

(1) All allegations must be made in numbered paragraphs, and the paragraphs of a responsive pleading must be numbered to correspond to the numbers of the paragraphs being answered.

(2) The content of each paragraph must be limited as far as practicable to a single set of circumstances.

(3) Each statement of a claim for relief founded on a single transaction or occurrence or on separate transactions or occurrences, and each defense other than a denial, must be stated in a separately numbered count or defense.

(C) Written Instruments.

(1) If a claim or defense is based on a written instrument, a copy of the instrument or its pertinent parts must be attached to the pleading and labeled according to standards established by the State Court Administrative Office unless the instrument is

(a) a matter of public record in the county in which the action is commenced and its location in the record is stated in the pleading;

(b) in the possession of the adverse party and the pleading so states;

(c) inaccessible to the pleader and the pleading so states, giving the reason; or

(d) of a nature that attaching the instrument would be unnecessary or impractical and the pleading so states, giving the reason.

(2) An attachment or reference to an attachment under subrule (C)(1)(a) or (b) is a part of the pleading for all purposes.

(D) Adoption by Reference. Statements in a pleading may be adopted by reference only in another part of the same pleading.

[Adopted effective March 1, 1985. Amended April 13, 1989, effective July 1, 1989, 432 Mich; September 11, 1991, effective November 1, 1991, 438 Mich. Amended effective November 30, 1999, 461 Mich; May 23, 2000, 462 Mich. Amended September 30, 2003, effective January 1, 2004, 469 Mich; October 31, 2012, effective January 1, 2013, 493 Mich; May 30, 2018, effective September 1, 2018, 501 Mich. Amended effective August 14, 2019, 503 Mich. Amended September 18, 2019, effective January 1, 2020, 503 Mich.]

Comments

Staff Comment to 1985 Adoption

MCR 2.113 includes provisions from GCR 1963, 110.2(2) and 113. The rules regarding the form of pleadings and papers are included in this rule. Signing of papers is covered in rule 2.114.

Under subrule (A), the rules on the form, captioning, and signing of pleadings apply to all papers. However, affidavits must be verified by oath or affirmation.

Subrule (C)(1), which covers the contents of the caption, adds several new requirements. The case-type code (see MCR 8.117) must be included. In addition, the telephone number of the attorney, or of a pleading party appearing without an attorney, must be included. And subrule (C)(1)(h) requires the name and state bar number of each attorney who has appeared. The requirement was adopted in Supreme Court Administrative Order No. 1983–5.

Subrule (C)(2) specifies the language in which the plaintiff must make the required certification (see MCR 8.112 and GCR 1963, 926.4) regarding prior or pending actions involving the same parties and subject matter. In addition, the rule covers the possibility that an earlier action may have been transferred, rather than dismissed.

In subrule (E)(1) language is added requiring that the paragraphs of the responsive pleading be numbered to correspond to the numbering of the pleading being answered.

Subrule (F) eliminates the exception for insurance policies from the general rule that written instruments on which a claim or defense is based must be attached. Compare GCR 1963, 113.4.

Under subrule (G) adoption by reference is permitted only with regard to other parts of the same document. Compare GCR 1963, 113.5.

Staff Comment to 1989 Amendment

The [April 13, 1989] amendment to MCR 2.113(C)(2) requires the filing attorney's statement to include a reference to other known cases arising out of the same transaction or occurrence as the action being filed, even where such other cases do not involve the same parties.

Staff Comment to 1991 Amendment

The [November 1,] 1991 amendment of MCR 2.113(C)(2) was designed to clarify a plaintiff's initial obligation to disclose the existence of related civil litigation.

Staff Comment to 1999 Amendment

The amendment of MCR 2.113 is to accommodate statewide records standards applicable to all courts and all clerks of the courts as developed and recommended by the Michigan Trial Court Case File Management Standards Committee.

Staff Comment to 2000 Amendment

These amendments [effective May 23, 2000] are made to allow for flexibility in making changes to case classification codes. Case classification codes are used principally for administrative purposes by trial courts and the State Court Administrator for collecting management information regarding case and for identifying the administrative processing of cases.

The notice requirements of MCR 1.201 were dispensed with in order that several changes in case classification codes required with the implementation of the Estates and Protected Individuals Code, MCL 700.1101 *et seq.*, could be implemented immediately by the State Court Administrator. The Estates and Protected Individuals Code became effective April 1, 2000. This matter will be included on the Court's future public hearing agenda for the purpose of receiving comments.

The State Court Administrator will incorporate case classification codes in the Case File Management Standards maintained by that office. The State Court

Administrator will publish a revised case classification code schedule immediately, and will periodically publish case classification codes for the benefit of the public and the bar.

Staff Comment to 2004 Amendment

The September 30, 2003 amendment of Rules 1.109 and 2.113 of the Michigan Court Rules, effective January 1, 2004, established a uniform type-size standard for all papers filed in Michigan courts. This conforms to the 12-point minimum that is required for briefs filed at the Court of Appeals, MCR 7.212(B), and applications and briefs filed at the Supreme Court, MCR 7.302, 7.304, 7.306, and 7.309. There is an exception for court forms approved by the State Court Administrative Office. The change does not preclude the filing of typewritten or legible handwritten pleadings, provided they meet the size requirements.

Staff Comment to 2013 Amendment

The amendments of these rules update the rules making them less "paper" focused and reflecting the use of electronic technology in the way courts process court records. The amendments also clarify and delineate the types of records and other materials maintained by a court, and clarify how access is provided.

Staff Comment to 2018 Amendment

The amendments in this order are intended to begin moving trial courts toward a statewide uniform e-Filing process. In addition, the order moves existing language into MCR 1.109 as a way to, for the first time, include most filing requirements in one single rule, instead of scattered in various rules. The order largely mirrors the administrative orders that most e-Filing pilot projects have operated under, but contains some significant new provisions. For example, courts are required to maintain documents in an electronic document management system, and the electronic record is the official court record.

Staff Comment to 2019 Amendment

These amendments update cross-references and make other nonsubstantive revisions to clarify the rules.

Staff Comment to 2020 Amendment

The amendments of MCR 1.109, 2.107, 2.113, 2.116, 2.119, 2.222, 2.223, 2.225, 2.227, 3.206, 3.211, 3.212, 3.214, 3.303, 3.903, 3.921, 3.925, 3.926, 3.931, 3.933, 3.942, 3.950, 3.961, 3.971, 3.972, 4.002, 4.101, 4.201, 4.202, 4.302, 5.128, 5.302, 5.731, 6.101, 6.615, 8.105, and 8.119 and rescission of MCR 2.226 and 8.125 continue the process for design and implementation of the statewide electronic-filing system.

Rule 2.114. Signatures of Attorneys and Parties; Verification; Effect; Sanctions [Repealed effective September 1, 2018.]

Rule 2.115 Motion to Correct or to Strike Pleadings

(A) Motion for More Definite Statement. If a pleading is so vague or ambiguous that it fails to comply with the requirements of these rules, an opposing party may move for a more definite statement before filing a responsive pleading. The motion must point out the defects complained of and the details desired. If the motion is granted and is not obeyed within 14 days after notice of the order, or within such other time as the court may set, the court may strike the pleading to which the motion was directed or enter an order it deems just.

(B) Motion to Strike. On motion by a party or on the court's own initiative, the court may strike from a pleading redundant, immaterial, impertinent, scandalous, or indecent matter, or may strike all or part of a pleading not drawn in conformity with these rules.

[Adopted effective March 1, 1985.]

Comments

Staff Comment to 1985 Adoption

MCR 2.115 is substantially the same as GCR 1963, 115.

Rule 2.116 Summary Disposition

(A) Judgment on Stipulated Facts.

(1) The parties to a civil action may submit an agreed-upon stipulation of facts to the court.

(2) If the parties have stipulated to facts sufficient to enable the court to render judgment in the action, the court shall do so.

(B) Motion.

(1) A party may move for dismissal of or judgment on all or part of a claim in accordance with this rule. A party against whom a defense is asserted may move under this rule for summary disposition of the defense. A request for dismissal without prejudice under MCL 600.2912c must be made by motion under MCR 2.116 and MCR 2.119.

(2) A motion under this rule may be filed at any time consistent with subrule (D) and subrule (G)(1), but the hearing on a motion brought by a party asserting a claim shall not take place until at least 28 days after the opposing party was served with the pleading stating the claim.

(C) Grounds. The motion may be based on one or more of these grounds, and must specify the grounds on which it is based:

(1) The court lacks jurisdiction over the person or property.

(2) The process issued in the action was insufficient.

(3) The service of process was insufficient.

(4) The court lacks jurisdiction of the subject matter.

(5) The party asserting the claim lacks the legal capacity to sue.

(6) Another action has been initiated between the same parties involving the same claim.

(7) Entry of judgment, dismissal of the action, or other relief is appropriate because of release, payment, prior judgment, immunity granted by law, statute of limitations, statute of frauds, an agreement to arbitrate or to litigate in a different forum, infancy or other disability of the moving party, or assignment or other disposition of the claim before commencement of the action.

(8) The opposing party has failed to state a claim on which relief can be granted.

(9) The opposing party has failed to state a valid defense to the claim asserted against him or her.

(10) Except as to the amount of damages, there is no genuine issue as to any material fact, and the moving party is entitled to judgment or partial judgment as a matter of law.

(D) Time to Raise Defenses and Objections. The grounds listed in subrule (C) must be raised as follows:

(1) The grounds listed in subrule (C)(1), (2), and (3) must be raised in a party's first motion under this rule or in the party's responsive pleading, whichever is filed first, or they are waived.

(2) The grounds listed in subrule (C)(5), (6), and (7) must be raised in a party's responsive pleading, unless the grounds are stated in a motion filed under this rule prior to the party's first responsive pleading. Amendment of a responsive pleading is governed by MCR 2.118.

(3) The grounds listed in subrule (C)(4) and the ground of governmental immunity may be raised at any time, regardless of whether the motion is filed after the expiration of the period in which to file dispositive motions under a scheduling order entered pursuant to MCR 2.401.

(4) The grounds listed in subrule (C)(8), (9), and (10) may be raised at any time, unless a period in which to file dispositive motions is established under a scheduling order entered pursuant to MCR 2.401. It is within the trial court's discretion to allow a motion filed under this subsection to be considered if the motion is filed after such period.

(E) Consolidation; Successive Motions.

(1) A party may combine in a single motion as many defenses or objections as the party has based on any of the grounds enumerated in this rule.

(2) No defense or objection is waived by being joined with one or more other defenses or objections.

(3) A party may file more than one motion under this rule, subject to the provisions of subrule (F).

(F) Motion or Affidavit Filed in Bad Faith. A party or an attorney found by the court to have filed a motion or an affidavit in violation of the provisions of MCR 1.109(D)(3) and (E) may, in addition to the imposition of other penalties prescribed by that rule, be found guilty of contempt.

(G) Affidavits; Hearing.

(1) Except as otherwise provided in this subrule, MCR 2.119 applies to motions brought under this rule.

(a) Unless a different period is set by the court,

(i) a written motion under this rule with supporting brief and any affidavits must be filed and served at least 21 days before the time set for the hearing, and

(ii) any response to the motion (including brief and any affidavits) must be filed and served at least 7 days before the hearing.

(iii) the moving party or parties may file a reply brief in support of the motion. Reply briefs must be confined to rebuttal of the arguments in the nonmoving party or parties' response brief and must be limited to 5 pages. The reply brief must be filed and served at least 4 days before the hearing.

(iv) no additional or supplemental briefs may be filed without leave of the court.

(b) If the court sets a different time for filing and serving a motion, or a reply brief, its authorization must be endorsed in writing on the face of the notice of hearing or made by separate order.

(c) Except where electronic filing has been implemented, a copy of a motion, response (including brief and any affidavits), or reply brief filed under this rule must be provided by counsel to the office of the judge hearing the motion. The judge's copy must be clearly marked JUDGE'S COPY on the cover sheet; that notation may be handwritten. Where electronic filing has been implemented, a judge's copy shall not be required.

(2) Except as to a motion based on subrule (C)(8) or (9), affidavits, depositions, admissions, or other documentary evidence may be submitted by a party to support or oppose the grounds asserted in the motion.

(3) Affidavits, depositions, admissions, or other documentary evidence in support of the grounds asserted in the motion are required

(a) when the grounds asserted do not appear on the face of the pleadings, or

(b) when judgment is sought based on subrule (C)(10).

(4) A motion under subrule (C)(10) must specifically identify the issues as to which the moving party believes there is no genuine issue as to any material fact. When a motion under subrule (C)(10) is made and supported as provided in this rule, an adverse party may not rest upon the mere allegations or denials of his or her pleading, but must, by affidavits or as otherwise provided in this rule, set forth specific facts showing that there is a genuine issue for trial. If the adverse party does not so respond, judgment, if appropriate, shall be entered against him or her.

(5) The affidavits, together with the pleadings, depositions, admissions, and documentary evidence then filed in the action or submitted by the parties, must be considered by the court when the motion is based on subrule (C)(1)–(7) or (10). Only the pleadings may be considered when the motion is based on subrule (C)(8) or (9).

(6) Affidavits, depositions, admissions, and documentary evidence offered in support of or in opposition to a motion based on subrule (C)(1)—(7) or (10) shall only be considered to the extent that the content or substance would be admissible as evidence to establish or deny the grounds stated in the motion.

(H) Affidavits Unavailable.

(1) A party may show by affidavit that the facts necessary to support the party's position cannot be presented because the facts are known only to persons whose affidavits the party cannot procure. The affidavit must

(a) name these persons and state why their testimony cannot be procured, and

(b) state the nature of the probable testimony of these persons and the reason for the party's belief that these persons would testify to those facts.

(2) When this kind of affidavit is filed, the court may enter an appropriate order, including an order

(a) denying the motion, or

(b) allowing additional time to permit the affidavit to be supported by further affidavits, or by depositions, answers to interrogatories, or other discovery.

(I) Disposition by Court; Immediate Trial.

(1) If the pleadings show that a party is entitled to judgment as a matter of law, or if the affidavits or other proofs show that there is no genuine issue of material fact, the court shall render judgment without delay.

(2) If it appears to the court that the opposing party, rather than the moving party, is entitled to judgment, the court may render judgment in favor of the opposing party.

(3) A court may, under proper circumstances, order immediate trial to resolve any disputed issue of fact, and judgment may be entered forthwith if the proofs show that a party is entitled to judgment on the facts as determined by the court. An immediate trial may be ordered if the grounds asserted are based on subrules (C)(1) through (C)(6), or if the motion is based on subrule (C)(7) and a jury trial as of right has not been demanded on or before the date set for hearing. If the motion is based on subrule (C)(7) and a jury trial has been demanded, the court may order immediate trial, but must afford the parties a jury trial as to issues raised by the motion as to which there is a right to trial by jury.

(4) The court may postpone until trial the hearing and decision on a matter involving disputed issues of fact brought before it under this rule.

(5) If the grounds asserted are based on subrule (C)(8), (9), or (10), the court shall give the parties an opportunity to amend their pleadings as provided by MCR 2.118, unless the evidence then before the court shows that amendment would not be justified.

(J) Motion Denied; Case Not Fully Adjudicated on Motion.

(1) If a motion under this rule is denied, or if the decision does not dispose of the entire action or grant all the relief demanded, the action must proceed to final judgment. The court may:

(a) set the time for further pleadings or amendments required;

(b) examine the evidence before it and, by questioning the attorneys, ascertain what material facts are without substantial controversy, including the extent to which damages are not disputed; and

(c) set the date on which all discovery must be completed.

(2) A party aggrieved by a decision of the court entered under this rule may:

(a) seek interlocutory leave to appeal as provided for by these rules;

(b) claim an immediate appeal as of right if the judgment entered by the court constitutes a final judgment under MCR 2.604(B); or

(c) proceed to final judgment and raise errors of the court committed under this rule in an appeal taken from final judgment.

[Adopted effective March 1, 1985. Amended December 11, 1986, effective December 12, 1986, 426 Mich; October 18, 1990, effective January 1, 1991, 436 Mich; January 17, 1992, effective April 1, 1992, 439 Mich. Amended effective September 19, 1995, 450 Mich. Amended October 3, 2000, effective January 1, 2001, 463 Mich; May 22, 2007, effective September 1, 2007, 478 Mich; October 3, 2012, effective January 1, 2013, Mich; May 24, 2017, effective September 1, 2017, 500 Mich; August 30, 2018, effective September 1, 2018, 502 Mich; September 18, 2019, effective January 1, 2020, 503 Mich.]

Comments

Staff Comment to 1985 Adoption

MCR 2.116 consolidates and reorganizes the provisions regarding summary disposition of claims or defenses found in GCR 1963, 111.10, 116, and 117. Much of the substance of the rules remains the same, although procedural provisions formerly applicable only to rule 116 or rule 117 are made applicable to all portions of the new rule.

Subrule (A) is the procedure for judgment on stipulated facts found in GCR 1963, 111.10.

Subrule (B) is derived from GCR 1963, 117.1. The language is modified to indicate that not all such motions seek "judgment" on a claim. Sometimes the relief sought is dismissal (for example, when the motion challenges service of process or jurisdiction).

Under GCR 1963, 117.1 a party seeking to recover on a claim could not file a motion until the adverse party had responded. Under subrule (B)(2), the motion may be *filed* at any time, but the claimant may not notice it for hearing until the time for answer has passed.

The [March 1, 1985] amendment of MCR 2.116(B)(2) corrects the cross-reference to subrule (D), which covers the time for raising defenses.

Subrule (C) collects the various grounds for accelerated and summary judgment found in GCR 1963, 116.1 and 117.2.

Subrule (D) collects the various provisions regarding the time when these grounds must be raised. See GCR 1963, 116.1, 116.2. The provision should be read in conjunction with MCR 2.111(F), which covers the subject of when defenses must be raised, and MCR 2.118(D), under which an amended pleading relates back to the date the original pleading was filed.

Subrule (E) is based on GCR 1963, 116.2.

Subrule (F) replaces the provisions of GCR 1963, 116.5, regarding affidavits made in bad faith, with a reference to MCR 2.114, which covers the subject of bad faith signing of papers.

Subrule (G), regarding affidavits, is based on GCR 116.3 and 117.3. The rule makes clear that affidavits as well as other evidentiary materials submitted in connection with a motion must be considered by the court when the motion is based on subrules (C)(1)–(7) or (10). However, when the motion is based on subrule (C)(8) (failure to state a claim) or subrule (C)(9) (failure to state a defense), only the pleadings may be considered.

Subrule (G)(4) is new. It requires a party moving for summary judgment under subrule (C)(10) (lack of genuine issue of material fact) to specify the issues as to which it is claimed that there is no factual dispute. Further, language taken from FR Civ P 56(e) is added, requiring the party opposing the motion to respond with affidavits or other evidentiary materials to show the existence of a factual dispute, rather than relying on the allegations or denials in pleadings.

Subrule (H) covers procedure when a party shows that affidavits are unavailable. It is derived from GCR 1963, 116.6.

Subrule (I) includes the provisions regarding disposition of the motion found in GCR 1963, 116.3 and 117.3. In addition, under subrule (I)(2), an immediate trial of disputed factual issues raised by a motion under subrule (C)(7) may be held despite the fact that a jury has been demanded. The immediate trial would, however, be by jury.

The [March 1, 1985] amendment of MCR 2.116(I)(1) adds the word "material" in the reference to genuine issues of fact, making the language consistent with MCR 2.116(C)(10).

Subrule (J) includes the provisions regarding further proceedings when the motion is denied or the case is not fully decided on motion. See GCR 1963, 117.4. In addition, subrule (J)(2) contains new provisions clarifying the appellate options of a party aggrieved by the court's decision.

In addition, the provisions of GCR 1963, 116.4 regarding the form of affidavits are moved to the motion practice rule. MCR 2.119. The motion practice rule is expressly made applicable to MCR 2.116. See MCR 2.116(G)(1).

Staff Comment to 1990 Amendment

The 1990 amendments to MCR 2.116(G)(1) [effective January 1, 1991] were designed to give the parties and the court additional time to prepare for a hearing on a motion for summary disposition. The 1990 amendments to MCR 2.116(B)(2) [effective January 1, 1991] added a cross-reference to MCR 2.116(G)(1) and clarified a previously ambiguous provision concerning the scheduling of a hearing on a motion brought by a party asserting a claim.

Staff Comment to 1992 Amendment

The 1992 amendments of MCR 2.116 were designed to confirm the right of a party to amend a pleading to add or modify affirmative defenses. This right of amendment is governed by MCR 2.118. To the extent that Campbell v St John Hospital, 434 Mich 608, 615-617; 455 NW2d 695 (1990), had been understood to preclude amendment of affirmative defenses, including defenses related to the Malpractice Arbitration Act (MCL 600.5040 et seq.), the rule of Campbell was modified by these amendments.

Staff Comment to 1995 Amendment

The amendment of MCR 2.116(J)(2) corrects cross-references to MCR 2.604 that were no longer correct after MCR 2.604 was amended on May 16, 1995, and further amended on September 19, 1995.

Staff Comment to 2000 Amendment

The October 3, 2000, amendment of MCR 2.116(G), effective January 1, 2001, specifies that materials submitted in support of or opposition to a motion under MCR 2.116 (C)(1)—(7) or (10) may only be considered to the extent that their content or substance would be admissible. See *Maiden v Rozwood*, 461 Mich 109 (1999).

Staff Comment to 2007 Amendment

The amendments of MCR 2.116 clarify that motions for summary disposition based on governmental immunity or lack of subject-matter jurisdiction may be filed even if the time set for filing dispositive motions in a scheduling order has expired. Defects in subject-matter jurisdiction cannot be waived and may be raised at any time. *People v Erwin*, 212 Mich App 55, 64 (1995); *People v*

Richards, 205 Mich App 438, 444 (1994). Likewise, governmental immunity may be raised at any time. See *Mack v Detroit*, 467 Mich 186, 197 n 13 (2002).

The amendments also clarify that it is within the court's discretion to consider a motion based on the grounds set forth in MCR 2.116(C)(8), (9), or (10), if the motion is filed after the period for dispositive motions established in a scheduling order has expired. This clarification reflects the holding in *People v Grove*, 455 Mich 439 (1997), that it was within the trial court's discretion to decline to accept a plea agreement offered after the date set forth in the scheduling order for accepting such an agreement had passed.

Staff Comment to 2013 Amendment

Inclusion of the revised language in MCR 2.116(C)(7) clarifies the procedure for bringing a motion for summary disposition on the grounds of a forum selection clause.

Staff Comment to 2017 Amendment

The amendments, originally submitted in a slightly different form by the State Bar of Michigan Representative Assembly, amend the rules regarding motions for summary disposition to allow for the filing of reply briefs only in summary disposition proceedings.

Staff Comment to 2018 Amendment

These amendments update cross-references in the rules, and are intended to reflect changes that are necessary as a result of the Court's recent e-Filing rules amendments.

Staff Comment to 2020 Amendment

The amendments of MCR 1.109, 2.107, 2.113, 2.116, 2.119, 2.222, 2.223, 2.225, 2.227, 3.206, 3.211, 3.212, 3.214, 3.303, 3.903, 3.921, 3.925, 3.926, 3.931, 3.933, 3.942, 3.950, 3.961, 3.971, 3.972, 4.002, 4.101, 4.201, 4.202, 4.302, 5.128, 5.302, 5.731, 6.101, 6.615, 8.105, and 8.119 and rescission of MCR 2.226 and 8.125 continue the process for design and implementation of the statewide electronic-filing system.

Rule 2.117.   Appearances

(A) Appearance by Party.

(1) A party may appear in an action by filing a notice to that effect or by physically appearing before the court for that purpose. In the latter event, the party must promptly file a written appearance and serve it on all persons entitled to service. A written appearance must comply with the caption requirements in MCR 1.109(D)(1)(b).

(2) Filing an appearance without taking any other action toward prosecution or defense of the action neither confers nor enlarges the jurisdiction of the court over the party. An appearance entitles a party to be served with all documents as provided by MCR 2.107(A). In all other respects, the party is treated as if the appearance had not been filed.

(B) Appearance by Attorney.

(1) *In General.* An attorney may appear by an act indicating that the attorney represents a party in the action. An appearance by an attorney for a party is deemed an appearance by the party. Unless a particular rule indicates otherwise, any act required to be performed by a party may be performed by the attorney representing the party.

(2) *Notice of Appearance.*

(a) If an appearance is made in a manner not involving the filing of a document with the court, the attorney must promptly file a written appearance and serve it on the parties entitled to service. The written appearance must comply with the caption requirements in MCR 1.109(D)(1)(b).

(b) If an attorney files an appearance, but takes no other action toward prosecution or defense of the action, the appearance entitles the attorney to be served with all documents as provided by MCR 2.107(A).

(c) Pursuant to MRPC 1.2(b), a party to a civil action may appear through an attorney for limited purposes during the course of an action, including, but not limited to, depositions, hearings, discovery, and motion practice, if the following conditions are satisfied:

(i) The attorney files and serves a notice of limited appearance with the court before or during the relevant action or proceeding, and all parties of record are served with the limited entry of appearance; and

(ii) The notice of limited appearance identifies the limitation of the scope by date, time period, and/or subject matter.

(d) An attorney who has filed a notice of limited appearance must restrict activities in accordance with the notice or any amended limited appearance. Should an attorney's representation exceed the scope of the limited appearance, opposing counsel (by motion), or the court (by order to show cause), may set a hearing to establish the actual scope of the representation.

(3) *Appearance by Law Firm.*

(a) A pleading, appearance, motion, or other document filed by a law firm on behalf of a client is deemed the appearance of the individual attorney first filing a document in the action. All notices required by these rules may be served on that individual. That attorney's appearance continues until an order of substitution or withdrawal is entered, or a confirming notice of withdrawal of a notice of limited appearance is filed as provided by subrule (C)(3). This subrule is not intended to prohibit other attorneys in the law firm from appearing in the action on behalf of the party.

(b) The appearance of an attorney is deemed to be the appearance of every member of the law firm. Any attorney in the firm may be required by the court to conduct a court ordered conference or trial.

(C) Duration of Appearance by Attorney.

(1) Unless otherwise stated or ordered by the court, an attorney's appearance applies only in the court in which it is made, or to which the action is transferred, until a final judgment or final order is entered disposing of all claims by or against the party whom the attorney represents and the time for appeal of right has passed. The appearance applies in an appeal taken before entry of final judgment or final order by the trial court.

(2) Unless otherwise stated in this rule, an attorney who has entered an appearance may withdraw from the action or be substituted for only on order of the court.

(3) An attorney who has filed a notice of limited appearance pursuant to MCR 2.117(B)(2)(c) and MRPC 1.2(b) may withdraw by filing a notice of withdrawal from limited appearance with the court, served on all parties of record, stating that the attorney's limited representation has concluded and the attorney has taken all actions necessitated by the limited representation, and providing to the court a current service address and telephone number for the self-represented litigant. If the notice of withdrawal from limited appearance is signed by the client, it shall be effective immediately upon filing and service. If it is not signed by the client, it shall become effective 14 days after filing and service, unless the self-represented client files and serves a written objection to the withdrawal on the grounds that the attorney did not complete the agreed upon services.

(D) Nonappearance of Attorney Assisting in Document Preparation. An attorney who assists in the preparation of pleadings or other documents without signing them, as authorized in MRPC 1.2(b), has not filed an appearance and shall not be deemed to have done so. This provision shall not be construed to prevent the court from investigating issues concerning the preparation of such a document.

(E) Service of Documents After Removal of Appearance. If an attorney has filed a limited appearance or the attorney is removed from the case for any other reason, the attorney shall not continue to be served with documents in the case after the limited appearance ends or after an order is entered removing the attorney from the case.

[Adopted effective March 1, 1985. Amended January 29, 2014, effective May 1, 2014, 495 Mich; September 20, 2017, effective January 1, 2018, 501 Mich; March 20, 2019, effective May 1, 2019, 502 Mich.]

Comments

Staff Comment to 1985 Adoption

MCR 2.117 is largely new and governs appearances by parties and attorneys.

Under subrule (A) a party may appear by filing a written notice of appearance, which may follow a physical appearance before the court. The only effect of such an appearance is to entitle the party to receive copies of papers as provided by MCR 2.107(A).

Subrule (B) governs appearances by attorneys. In general, an attorney who has appeared for a party may act for the party in the action. See subrule (B)(1). As in the case of a party, an attorney's appearance may be in the form of filing a notice of appearance, with no further action being taken. The effect is the same: the attorney is entitled to receive copies of papers filed. See subrule (B)(2)(b).

Subrule (B)(3) governs appearances by a law firm. Notices may be served on the individual attorney who first signs a paper filed in the case. However, the rule is not meant to prevent other attorneys in the firm from appearing. The appearance is also deemed to be the appearance of every other member of the law firm, and the court may order another attorney in the firm to appear at a conference or for trial.

Subrule (C) governs the duration of an attorney's appearance. An appearance applies only until the time for an appeal of right from the final judgment has passed. Thereafter, the attorney is deemed not to represent the party, and service of further notices must be on the party. The attorney's appearance does apply in an appeal taken before entry of final judgment. See subrule (C)(1). Otherwise, an appearance in the trial court does not apply on appeal. The rules governing appeals to circuit court (MCR 7.101[D][1]) and the Court of Appeals (MCR 7.204[G]) require the filing of a new appearance for an appellee.

Under subrule (C)(2) a court order is required for withdrawal or substitution of an attorney.

Staff Comment to 2014 Amendment

The amendment of MCR 2.107 provides clarification by adding the phrase "final order" so that after either a final judgment or final order has entered, papers should be served on the party after the time for appeal has passed. The amendment of MCR 2.117 states that the duration of an attorney's appearance extends until a final judgment or final order is entered. This amendment is intended to clarify that representation by an attorney who appears in a postjudgment motion ends with the final order related to that matter (after the period for appeal of right has passed).

Staff Comment to 2017 Amendment

The amendments of Rules 1.0, 1.2, 4.2, and 4.3 of the Michigan Rules of Professional Conduct and Rules 2.107, 2.117, and 6.001 of the Michigan Court Rules were submitted to the Court by the State Bar of Michigan Representative Assembly. The rules are intended to provide guidance for attorneys and clients who would prefer to engage in a limited scope representation. The rules allow for such an agreement "preferably in writing," and enable an attorney to file a notice of LSR with the court when the representation is undertaken as well as a termination notice when the representation has ended. The rules also explicitly allow attorneys to provide document preparation services for a self-represented litigant without having to file an appearance with the court.

Staff Comment to 2019 Amendment

The amendments of Rules 1.109, 2.102, 2.104, 2.106, 2.107, 2.117, 2.119, 2.403, 2.503, 2.506, 2.508, 2.518, 2.602, 2.603, 2.621, 3.101, 3.104, 3.203, 3.205, 3.210, 3.302, 3.607, 3.613, 3.614, 3.705, 3.801, 3.802, 3.805, 3.806, 4.201, 4.202, 4.303, 4.306, 5.001,

5.104, 5.105, 5.107, 5.108, 5.113, 5.117, 5.118, 5.119, 5.120, 5.125, 5.126, 5.132, 5.162, 5.202, 5.203, 5.205, 5.302, 5.304, 5.307, 5.308, 5.309, 5.310, 5.311, 5.313, 5.402, 5.404, 5.405, 5.409, 5.501, and 5.784 and addition of Rule 3.618 of the Michigan Court Rules are an expected progression necessary for design and implementation of the statewide electronic-filing system. These particular amendments will assist in implementing the goals of the project.

Rule 2.118   Amended and Supplemental Pleadings

(A) Amendments.

(1) A party may amend a pleading once as a matter of course within 14 days after being served with a responsive pleading by an adverse party, or within 14 days after serving the pleading if it does not require a responsive pleading.

(2) Except as provided in subrule (A)(1), a party may amend a pleading only by leave of the court or by written consent of the adverse party. Leave shall be freely given when justice so requires.

(3) On a finding that inexcusable delay in requesting an amendment has caused or will cause the adverse party additional expense that would have been unnecessary had the request for amendment been filed earlier, the court may condition the order allowing amendment on the offending party's reimbursing the adverse party for the additional expense, including reasonable attorney fees.

(4) Amendments must be filed in writing, dated, and numbered consecutively, and must comply with MCR 2.113. Unless otherwise indicated, an amended pleading supersedes the former pleading.

(B) Response to Amendments. Within the time prescribed by MCR 2.108, a party served with an amendment to a pleading requiring a response under MCR 2.110(B) must

(1) serve and file a pleading in response to the amended pleading, or

(2) serve and file a notice that the party's pleading filed in response to the opposing party's earlier pleading will stand as the response to the amended pleading.

(C) Amendments to Conform to the Evidence.

(1) When issues not raised by the pleadings are tried by express or implied consent of the parties, they are treated as if they had been raised by the pleadings. In that case, amendment of the pleadings to conform to the evidence and to raise those issues may be made on motion of a party at any time, even after judgment.

(2) If evidence is objected to at trial on the ground that it is not within the issues raised by the pleadings, amendment to conform to that proof shall not be allowed unless the party seeking to amend satisfies the court that the amendment and the admission of the evidence would not prejudice the objecting party in maintaining his or her action or defense on the merits. The court may grant an adjournment to enable the objecting party to meet the evidence.

(D) Relation Back of Amendments. An amendment that adds a claim or a defense relates back to the date of the original pleading if the claim or defense asserted in the amended pleading arose out of the conduct, transaction, or occurrence set forth, or attempted to be set forth, in the original pleading. In a medical malpractice action, an amendment of an affidavit of merit or affidavit of meritorious defense relates back to the date of the original filing of the affidavit.

(E) Supplemental Pleadings. On motion of a party the court may, on reasonable notice and on just terms, permit the party to serve a supplemental pleading to state transactions or events that have happened since the date of the pleading sought to be supplemented, whether or not the original pleading is defective in its statement of a claim for relief or a defense. The court may order the adverse party to plead, specifying the time allowed for pleading.

[Adopted effective March 1, 1985. Amended October 24, 2000, effective January 1, 2001, 463 Mich; February 16, 2010, effective May 1, 2010, 485 Mich.]

Comments

Staff Comment to 1985 Adoption

MCR 2.118 is based on GCR 1963, 118.

Under subrule (A)(3), the court may order the amending party to compensate the opposing party for the additional expense caused by a late amendment.

Subrule (B) modifies the language of GCR 1963, 118.2 regarding responses to amended pleadings. Within the time allowed, the party must either serve and file a responsive pleading or serve and file a notice that the pleading on file in response to the earlier pleading will stand as the response to the amended one.

Staff Comment to 2000 Amendment

The October 24, 2000, amendment of MCR 2.118, effective January 1, 2001, clarifies that the relation-back doctrine pertains to the addition of claims and defenses.

Staff Comment to 2010 Amendment

The amendments of MCR 2.112 set a limit on the period for raising challenges to affidavits of merit and meritorious defense and notices of intent in medical malpractice actions. The amendments also allow revision under MCR 2.118 and MCL 600.2301. The amendment of MCR 2.118 explicitly states that the amended affidavit of merit or meritorious defense relates back to the date of the affidavit's original filing.

Rule 2.119   Motion Practice

(A) Form of Motions.

(1) An application to the court for an order in a pending action must be by motion. Unless made during a hearing or trial, a motion must

(a) be in writing,

(b) state with particularity the grounds and authority on which it is based,

(c) state the relief or order sought, and

(d) be signed by the party or attorney as provided in MCR 1.109(D)(3) and (E).

(2) A motion or response to a motion that presents an issue of law must be accompanied by a brief citing the authority on which it is based, and must comply with the provisions of MCR 7.215(C) regarding citation of unpublished Court of Appeals opinions.

(a) Except as permitted by the court, the combined length of any motion and brief, or of a response and brief, may not exceed 20 pages double spaced, exclusive of attachments and exhibits.

(b) Except as permitted by the court or as otherwise provided in these rules, no reply briefs, additional briefs, or supplemental briefs may be filed.

(c) Quotations and footnotes may be single-spaced. At least one-inch margins must be used, and printing shall not be smaller than 12-point type.

(d) Except where electronic filing has been implemented, a copy of a motion or response (including brief) filed under this rule must be provided by counsel to the office of the judge hearing the motion. The judge's copy must be clearly marked JUDGE'S COPY on the cover sheet; that notation may be handwritten. Where electronic filing has been implemented, a judge's copy shall not be required.

(3) A motion and notice of the hearing on it may be combined in the same document.

(4) If a contested motion is filed after rejection of a proposed order under subrule (D), a copy of the rejected order and an affidavit establishing the rejection must be filed with the motion.

(B) Form of Affidavits.

(1) If an affidavit is filed in support of or in opposition to a motion, it must:

(a) be made on personal knowledge;

(b) state with particularity facts admissible as evidence establishing or denying the grounds stated in the motion; and

(c) show affirmatively that the affiant, if sworn as a witness, can testify competently to the facts stated in the affidavit.

(2) Sworn or certified copies of all documents or parts of documents referred to in an affidavit must be attached to the affidavit unless the documents:

(a) have already been filed in the action;

(b) are matters of public record in the county in which the action is pending;

(c) are in the possession of the adverse party, and this fact is stated in the affidavit or the motion; or

(d) are of such nature that attaching them would be unreasonable or impracticable, and this fact and the reasons are stated in the affidavit or the motion.

(C) Time for Service and Filing of Motions and Responses.

(1) Unless a different period is set by these rules or by the court for good cause, a written motion (other than one that may be heard ex parte), notice of the hearing on the motion, and any supporting brief or affidavits must be served as follows:

(a) at least 9 days before the time set for the hearing, if served by first-class mail, or

(b) at least 7 days before the time set for the hearing, if served by delivery under MCR 2.107(C)(1) or (2) or MCR 1.109(G)(6)(a).

(2) Unless a different period is set by these rules or by the court for good cause, any response to a motion (including a brief or affidavits) required or permitted by these rules must be served as follows:

(a) at least 5 days before the hearing, if served by first-class mail, or

(b) at least 3 days before the hearing, if served by delivery under MCR 2.107(C)(1) or (2) or MCR 1.109(G)(6)(a).

(3) If the court sets a different time for serving a motion or response its authorization must be endorsed in writing on the face of the notice of hearing or made by separate order.

(4) Unless the court sets a different time, a motion must be filed at least 7 days before the hearing, and any response to a motion required or permitted by these rules must be filed at least 3 days before the hearing.

(D) Uncontested Orders.

(1) Before filing a motion, a party may serve on the opposite party a copy of a proposed order and a request to stipulate to the court's entry of the proposed order.

(2) On receipt of a request to stipulate, a party may

(a) stipulate to the entry of the order by signing the following statement at the end of the proposed order: "I stipulate to the entry of the above order"; or

(b) waive notice and hearing on the entry of an order by signing the following statement at the end of the proposed order: "Notice and hearing on entry of the above order is waived."

A proposed order is deemed rejected unless it is stipulated to or notice and hearing are waived within 7 days after it is served.

(3) If the parties have stipulated to the entry of a proposed order or waived notice and hearing, the court may enter the order. If the court declines to enter the order, it shall notify the moving party that a hearing on the motion is required. The matter then proceeds as a contested motion under subrule (E).

(4) The moving party must serve a copy of an order entered by the court pursuant to subrule (D)(3) on the parties entitled to notice under MCR 2.107, or notify them that the court requires the matter to be heard as a contested motion.

(5) Notwithstanding the provisions of subrule (D)(3), stipulations and orders for adjournment are governed by MCR 2.503.

(E) Contested Motions.

(1) Contested motions should be noticed for hearing at the time designated by the court for the hearing of motions. A motion will be heard on the day for which it is noticed, unless the court otherwise directs. If a motion cannot be heard on the day it is noticed, the court may schedule a new hearing date or the moving party may renotice the hearing.

(2) When a motion is based on facts not appearing of record, the court may hear the motion on affidavits presented by the parties, or may direct that the motion be heard wholly or partly on oral testimony or deposition.

(3) A court may, in its discretion, dispense with or limit oral arguments on motions, and may require the parties to file briefs in support of and in opposition to a motion.

(4) Appearance at the hearing is governed by the following:

(a) A party who, pursuant to subrule (D)(2), has previously rejected the proposed order before the court must either

(i) appear at the hearing held on the motion, or

(ii) before the hearing, file a response containing a concise statement of reasons in opposition to the motion and supporting authorities.

A party who fails to comply with this subrule is subject to assessment of costs under subrule (E)(4)(c).

(b) Unless excused by the court, the moving party must appear at a hearing on the motion. A moving party who fails to appear is subject to assessment of costs under subrule (E)(4)(c); in addition, the court may assess a penalty not to exceed $100, payable to the clerk of the court.

(c) If a party violates the provisions of subrule (E)(4)(a) or (b), the court shall assess costs against the offending party, that party's attorney, or both, equal to the expenses reasonably incurred by the opposing party in appearing at the hearing, including reasonable attorney fees, unless the circumstances make an award of expenses unjust.

(F) Motions for Rehearing or Reconsideration.

(1) Unless another rule provides a different procedure for reconsideration of a decision (see, e.g., MCR 2.604[A], 2.612), a motion for rehearing or reconsideration of the decision on a motion must be served and filed not later than 21 days after entry of an order deciding the motion.

(2) No response to the motion may be filed, and there is no oral argument, unless the court otherwise directs.

(3) Generally, and without restricting the discretion of the court, a motion for rehearing or reconsideration which merely presents the same issues ruled on by the court, either expressly or by reasonable implication, will not be granted. The moving party must demonstrate a palpable error by which the court and the parties have been misled and show that a different disposition of the motion must result from correction of the error.

(G) Motion Fees.
The following provisions apply to actions in which a motion fee is required:

(1) A motion fee must be paid on the filing of any request for an order in a pending action, whether the request is entitled "motion," "petition," "application," or otherwise.

(2) The clerk shall charge a single motion fee for all motions filed at the same time in an action regardless of the number of separately captioned documents filed or the number of distinct or alternative requests for relief included in the motions.

(3) A motion fee may not be charged:

(a) in criminal cases;

(b) for a notice of settlement of a proposed judgment or order under MCR 2.602(B);

(c) for a request for an order waiving fees under MCR 2.002 or MCL 600.2529(4) or MCL 600.8371(6);

(d) if the motion is filed at the same time as another document in the same action as to which a fee is required; or

(e) for entry of an uncontested order under subrule (D).

[Adopted effective March 1, 1985. Amended August 23, 1989, effective October 1, 1989, 437 Mich; June 25, 1991, effective October 1, 1991, 437 Mich; June 8, 1995, effective September 1, 1995, 449 Mich. Amended effective September 19, 1995, 450 Mich; February 4, 1997, 454 Mich. Amended March 24, 1998, effective April 1, 1998, 456 Mich; September 30, 2003, effective October 1, 2003, 469 Mich; May 28, 2008, effective September 1, 2008, 481 Mich; March 23, 2016, effective May 1, 2016, 499 Mich; May 24, 2017, effective September 1, 2017, 500 Mich; August 30, 2018, effective September 1, 2018, 502 Mich; March 20, 2019, effective May 1, 2019, 502 Mich; September 18, 2019, effective January 1, 2020, 503 Mich.]

Comments

Staff Comment to 1985 Adoption

MCR 2.119 provides considerably more detail than did the prior motion practice rule, GCR 1963, 119. It brings together a number of provisions from various sections of the General Court Rules and adds several new provisions.

Subrule (A)(1), governing the basic form of motions, is taken from GCR 1963, 110.2. The signing requirements of MCR 2.114 apply. The remainder of subrule (A) consists of new provisions allowing a notice of hearing to be combined with the motion in a single document, and requiring that a rejected order be attached to a contested motion filed thereafter.

Subrule (B), governing the form of affidavits, is taken from GCR 1963, 116.4.

Subrule (C) replaces GCR 1963, 108.4, which provided for 4 days' notice of motions. The notice time is lengthened to 9 days if the motion is served by mail and 7 days if it is delivered to the opposing party. Similarly, subrule (C)(2) changes the time for response by the opposing party to 5 days (service by mail) or 3 days (delivery). Finally, the rule expressly provides the times by which the motions and responses must be filed. See subrule (C)(4). The court is authorized to set different time limits, but must do so in writing on the notice of hearing or in a separate order. See subrule (C)(3).

The [March 1, 1985] amendment of MCR 2.119(C)(4) explicitly authorizes the court to modify the time for filing motions and responses to motions.

Subrule (D) is a new provision creating an optional procedure for seeking uncontested orders. A party may serve a proposed order on the other parties, requesting stipulation to the entry of the order. The other parties may stipulate to the entry of the order or waive notice of hearing on its entry with language specified in subrule (D)(2). If they do, the court shall either enter the order or notify the moving party that a hearing is required. The moving party is responsible for notice of the court's actions. Subrule (D)(5) provides that MCR 2.503 governs stipulations for adjournment. A party may choose to file the motion without having used the uncontested order procedure, or may use a less formal method of seeking agreement; however, the opposing party would not be subject to the cost sanctions of subrule (E)(4).

Subrule (E) governs the procedure regarding contested motions, which may be used: (1) without resort to the uncontested order procedure, (2) following rejection of a proposed order under the uncontested order procedure, or (3) because the court has declined to enter an order to which the parties have stipulated. Subrules (E)(1) and (3) are based on the current motion practice provisions of GCR 1963, 119. Subrule (E)(4) creates the requirement that the moving party, and any other party who has previously rejected the proposed order, appear at the hearing or face the possible imposition of costs.

Subrule (E)(2) is a new provision based on FR Civ P 43(e). It gives the judge the option of making certain factual decisions relevant to motions on the affidavits filed, or of directing that depositions or in-court testimony be taken. The rule would not apply to at least some motions under MCR 2.116, which has its own provisions regarding the manner in which the judge is to consider a motion.

Subrule (F) adds a new provision covering motions for rehearing or reconsideration. It is similar to local rule 17(k) of the United States District Court for the Eastern District of Michigan. Such a motion must be filed and served within 7 days after the entry of the order disposing of the motion, and there is to be no response or oral argument unless directed by the court.

Subrule (G) contains the motion fee provisions found in Administrative Order 1978–6. Under the present statute, MCL 600.2529, motion fees are required only in circuit court in counties with populations of more than 100,000. Another exception is added: no fee is required for entry of an uncontested order under subrule (D).

Staff Comment to 1989 Amendment

There are two changes [in the October 1, 1989 amendment] in MCR 2.119(F)(1). First, the rule is expressly made inapplicable where other rules provide different procedures for seeking reconsideration of decisions. Second, the time limit on motions for reconsideration is increased from 7 to 14 days.

Staff Comment to 1991 Amendment

The [October 1,] 1991 amendment of Rule 2.119(A) was the product of a proposal by the Michigan Judges Association and of earlier proposals that had been developed in conjunction with the work of the Caseflow Management Coordinating Committee and the Caseflow Management Rules Committee. The 20-page limit on briefs accords with rules that have been promulgated by the United States District Court for the Eastern District of Michigan and for the Western District of Michigan.

Staff Comment to September 1, 1995 Amendment

The 1995 amendment of MCR 2.119(A)(2) changed some of the technical requirements for motions, responses, and accompanying briefs.

Staff Comment to September 19, 1995 Amendment

The amendment of MCR 2.119(F)(1) corrects cross-references to MCR 2.604 that were no longer correct after MCR 2.604 was amended on May 16, 1995, and further amended on September 19, 1995.

Staff Comment to 1997 Amendment

The February 4, 1997, amendment to MCR 2.119(G) adjusts the reference to the statute that establishes the fees for filing motions.

Staff Comment to 1998 Amendment

The amendment of MCR 2.119 makes technical changes necessary in light of statutory amendments and corrects cross-references.

The amendment of MCR 2.119 is based on statutes amended by 1996 PA 388.

Staff Comment to 2003 Amendment

The amendment of Rule 2.119 of the Michigan Court Rules was adopted September 30, 2003, effective October 1, 2003, without publication for comment. The Court suspended the notice provisions of MCR 1.201 in light of the October 1, 2003, effective date of 2003 PA 138, which amended various provisions of the Revised Judicature Act relating to court filing fees.

Staff Comment to 2008 Amendment

The amendments of MCR 7.204 and MCR 7.205 clarify that a party who seeks to appeal to the Court of Appeals has 21 days after the entry of an order deciding a motion for new trial, a motion for rehearing or reconsideration, or a motion for other relief from the order or judgment appealed to file a claim of appeal or an application for leave to appeal, if the motion is filed within the initial 21–day appeal period. The amendments also limit the ability of the trial court to extend the 21–day period under MCR 7.204(A)(1)(b), MCR 7.205(A)(2), and MCR 7.205(F)(3)(b) to situations in which good cause is shown.

For consistency with the amendments of MCR 7.204 and MCR 7.205, and to eliminate a conflict between MCR 2.119(F)(1) and MCR 7.204(A)(1)(b), the time limit for filing a motion for rehearing or reconsideration in the trial court under MCR 2.119(F)(1) is increased from 14 to 21 days.

Staff Comment to 2016 Amendment

An unpublished opinion may be cited, for example, if there is no published authority on a given legal proposition or if it is necessary to demonstrate a conflict in interpretation of the law. The changes in MCR 2.119 and MCR 7.212 provide cross-references to MCR 7.215(C).

Staff Comment to 2017 Amendment

The amendments, originally submitted in a slightly different form by the State Bar of Michigan Representative Assembly, amend the rules regarding motions for summary disposition to allow for the filing of reply briefs only in summary disposition proceedings.

Staff Comment to 2018 Amendment

These amendments update cross-references in the rules, and are intended to reflect changes that are necessary as a result of the Court's recent e-Filing rules amendments.

Staff Comment to 2019 Amendment

The amendments of Rules 1.109, 2.102, 2.104, 2.106, 2.107, 2.117, 2.119, 2.403, 2.503, 2.506, 2.508, 2.518, 2.602, 2.603, 2.621, 3.101, 3.104, 3.203, 3.205, 3.210, 3.302, 3.607, 3.613, 3.614, 3.705, 3.801, 3.802, 3.805, 3.806, 4.201, 4.202, 4.303, 4.306, 5.001, 5.104, 5.105, 5.107, 5.108, 5.113, 5.117, 5.118, 5.119, 5.120, 5.125, 5.126, 5.132, 5.162, 5.202, 5.203, 5.205, 5.302, 5.304, 5.307, 5.308, 5.309, 5.310, 5.311, 5.313, 5.402, 5.404, 5.405, 5.409, 5.501, and 5.784 and addition of Rule 3.618 of the Michigan Court Rules are an expected progression necessary for design and implementation of the statewide electronic-filing system. These particular amendments will assist in implementing the goals of the project.

Staff Comment to 2020 Amendment

The amendments of MCR 1.109, 2.107, 2.113, 2.116, 2.119, 2.222, 2.223, 2.225, 2.227, 3.206, 3.211, 3.212, 3.214, 3.303, 3.903, 3.921, 3.925, 3.926, 3.931, 3.933, 3.942, 3.950, 3.961, 3.971, 3.972, 4.002, 4.101, 4.201, 4.202, 4.302, 5.128, 5.302, 5.731, 6.101, 6.615, 8.105, and 8.119 and rescission of MCR 2.226 and 8.125 continue the process for design and implementation of the statewide electronic-filing system.

SUBCHAPTER 2.200 PARTIES; JOINDER OF CLAIMS AND PARTIES; VENUE; TRANSFER OF ACTIONS

Rule 2.201 Parties Plaintiff and Defendant; Capacity

(A) Designation of Parties. The party who commences a civil action is designated as plaintiff and the adverse party as defendant. In an appeal the relative position of the parties and their designations as plaintiff and defendant are the same, but they are also designated as appellant and appellee.

(B) Real Party in Interest. An action must be prosecuted in the name of the real party in interest, subject to the following provisions:

(1) A personal representative, guardian, conservator, trustee of an express trust, a party with whom or in whose name a contract has been made for the benefit of another, or a person authorized by statute may sue in his or her own name without joining the party for whose benefit the action is brought.

(2) An action on the bond of a public officer required to give bond to the people of the state may be brought in the name of the person to whom the right on the bond accrues.

(3) An action on a bond, contract, or undertaking made with an officer of the state or of a governmental unit, including but not limited to a public, municipal, quasi-municipal, or governmental corporation, an unincorporated board, a public body, or a political subdivision, may be brought in the name of the state or the governmental unit for whose benefit the contract was made.

(4) An action to prevent illegal expenditure of state funds or to test the constitutionality of a statute relating to such an expenditure may be brought:

(a) in the name of a domestic nonprofit corporation organized for civic, protective, or improvement purposes; or

(b) in the names of at least 5 residents of Michigan who own property assessed for direct taxation by the county where they reside.

(C) Capacity to Sue or Be Sued.

(1) A natural person may sue or be sued in his or her own name.

(2) A person conducting a business under a name subject to certification under the assumed name statute may be sued in that name in an action arising out of the conduct of that business.

(3) A partnership, partnership association, or unincorporated voluntary association having a distinguishing name may sue or be sued in its partnership or association name, in the names of any of its members designated as such, or both.

(4) A domestic or a foreign corporation may sue or be sued in its corporate name, unless a statute provides otherwise.

(5) Actions to which the state or a governmental unit (including but not limited to a public, municipal, quasi-munici-pal, or governmental corporation, an unincorporated board, a public body, or a political subdivision) is a party may be brought by or against the state or governmental unit in its own name, or in the name of an officer authorized to sue or be sued on its behalf. An officer of the state or governmental unit must be sued in the officer's official capacity to enforce the performance of an official duty. An officer who sues or is sued in his or her official capacity may be described as a party by official title and not by name, but the court may require the name to be added.

(D) Unknown Parties; Procedure.

(1) Persons who are or may be interested in the subject matter of an action, but whose names cannot be ascertained on diligent inquiry, may be made parties by being described as:

(a) unknown claimants;

(b) unknown owners; or

(c) unknown heirs, devisees, or assignees of a deceased person who may have been interested in the subject matter of the action.

If it cannot be ascertained on diligent inquiry whether a person who is or may be interested in the subject matter of the action is alive or dead, what disposition the person may have made of his or her interest, or where the person resides if alive, the person and everyone claiming under him or her may be made parties by naming the person and adding "or [his or her] unknown heirs, devisees, or assignees."

(2) The names and descriptions of the persons sought to be made parties, with a statement of the efforts made to identify and locate them, must be stated in the complaint and verified by oath or affirmation by the plaintiff or someone having knowledge of the facts in the plaintiff's behalf. The court may require a more specific description to be made by amendment.

(3) A publication giving notice to persons who cannot be personally served must include the description of unknown persons as set forth in the complaint or amended complaint.

(4) The publication and all later proceedings in the action are conducted as if the unknown parties were designated by their proper names. The judgment rendered determines the nature, validity, and extent of the rights of all parties.

(5) A person desiring to appear and show his or her interest in the subject matter of the action must proceed under MCR 2.209. Subject to that rule, the person may be made a party in his or her proper name.

(E) Minors and Incompetent Persons. This subrule does not apply to proceedings under chapter 5.

(1) *Representation.*

(a) If a minor or incompetent person has a conservator, actions may be brought and must be defended by the conservator on behalf of the minor or incompetent person.

(b) If a minor or incompetent person does not have a conservator to represent the person as plaintiff, the court shall appoint a competent and responsible person to appear as next friend on his or her behalf, and the next friend is responsible for the costs of the action.

(c) If the minor or incompetent person does not have a conservator to represent the person as defendant, the action may not proceed until the court appoints a guardian ad litem, who is not responsible for the costs of the action unless, by reason of personal misconduct, he or she is specifically charged costs by the court. It is unnecessary to appoint a representative for a minor accused of a civil infraction.

(2) *Appointment of Representative.*

(a) Appointment of a next friend or guardian ad litem shall be made by the court as follows:

(i) if the party is a minor 14 years of age or older, on the minor's nomination, accompanied by a written consent of the person to be appointed;

(ii) if the party is a minor under 14 years of age or an incompetent person, on the nomination of the party's next of kin or of another relative or friend the court deems suitable, accompanied by a written consent of the person to be appointed; or

(iii) if a nomination is not made or approved within 21 days after service of process, on motion of the court or of a party.

(b) The court may refuse to appoint a representative it deems unsuitable.

(c) The order appointing a person next friend or guardian ad litem must be promptly filed with the clerk of the court.

(3) *Security.*

(a) Except for costs and expenses awarded to the next friend or guardian ad litem or the represented party, a person appointed under this subrule may not receive money or property belonging to the minor or incompetent party or awarded to that party in the action, unless he or she gives security as the court directs.

(b) The court may require that the conservator representing a minor or incompetent party give security as the court directs before receiving the party's money or property.

(4) *Incompetency While Action Pending.* A party who becomes incompetent while an action is pending may be represented by his or her conservator, or the court may appoint a next friend or guardian ad litem as if the action had been commenced after the appointment.

[Adopted effective March 1, 1985. Amended January 16, 1992, effective April 1, 1992, 439 Mich.]

Comments

Staff Comment to 1985 Adoption

MCR 2.201 is substantially the same as GCR 1963, 201.

The term "conservator" is added in subrule (B)(1) to conform to the Revised Probate Code.

Language is added to subrule (E)(1)(c) to make clear that it is not necessary to appoint a representative for a minor accused of a civil infraction. See MCL 257.741(5).

Staff Comment to 1992 Amendment

Subrule (E) is amended [effective April 1, 1992] to make clear that its terms do not apply to proceedings under chapter 5.

Rule 2.202   Substitution of Parties

(A) Death.

(1) If a party dies and the claim is not thereby extinguished, the court may order substitution of the proper parties.

(a) A motion for substitution may be made by a party, or by the successor or representative of the deceased party.

(b) Unless a motion for substitution is made within 91 days after filing and service of a statement of the fact of the death, the action must be dismissed as to the deceased party, unless the party seeking substitution shows that there would be no prejudice to any other party from allowing later substitution.

(c) Service of the statement or motion must be made on the parties as provided in MCR 2.107, and on persons not parties as provided in MCR 2.105.

(2) If one or more of the plaintiffs or one or more of the defendants in an action dies, and the right sought to be enforced survives only to the surviving plaintiffs or only against the surviving defendants, the action does not abate. A party or attorney who learns that a party has died must promptly file a notice of the death.

(B) Transfer or Change of Interest. If there is a change or transfer of interest, the action may be continued by or against the original party in his or her original capacity, unless the court, on motion supported by affidavit, directs that the person to whom the interest is transferred be substituted for or joined with the original party, or directs that the original party be made a party in another capacity. Notice must be given as provided in subrule (A)(1)(c).

(C) Public Officers; Death or Separation From Office. When an officer of the class described in MCR 2.201(C)(5) is a party to an action and during its pendency dies, resigns, or otherwise ceases to hold office, the action may be continued and maintained by or against the officer's successor without a formal order of substitution.

(D) Substitution at Any Stage. Substitution of parties under this rule may be ordered by the court either before or after judgment or by the Court of Appeals or Supreme Court pending appeal. If substitution is ordered, the court may require additional security to be given.

[Adopted effective March 1, 1985.]

Rule 2.203 Joinder of Claims, Counterclaims, and Cross–Claims

(A) Compulsory Joinder. In a pleading that states a claim against an opposing party, the pleader must join every claim that the pleader has against that opposing party at the time of serving the pleading, if it arises out of the transaction or occurrence that is the subject matter of the action and does not require for its adjudication the presence of third parties over whom the court cannot acquire jurisdiction.

(B) Permissive Joinder. A pleader may join as either independent or alternate claims as many claims, legal or equitable, as the pleader has against an opposing party. If a claim is one previously cognizable only after another claim has been prosecuted to a conclusion, the two claims may be joined in a single action; but the court may grant relief only in accordance with the substantive rights of the parties.

(C) Counterclaim Exceeding Opposing Claim. A counterclaim may, but need not, diminish or defeat the recovery sought by the opposing party. It may claim relief exceeding in amount or different in kind from that sought in the pleading of the opposing party.

(D) Cross-Claim Against Co-party. A pleading may state as a cross-claim a claim by one party against a co-party arising out of the transaction or occurrence that is the subject matter of the original action or of a counterclaim, or that relates to property that is the subject matter of the original action. The cross-claim may include a claim that the party against whom it is asserted is or may be liable to the cross-claimant for all or part of a claim asserted in the action against the cross-claimant.

(E) Time for Filing Counterclaim or Cross-Claim. A counterclaim or cross-claim must be filed with the answer or filed as an amendment in the manner provided by MCR 2.118. If a motion to amend to state a counterclaim or cross-claim is denied, the litigation of that claim in another action is not precluded unless the court specifies otherwise.

(F) Separate Trials; Separate Judgment. If the court orders separate trials as provided in MCR 2.505(B), judgment on a claim, counterclaim, or cross-claim may be rendered in accordance with the terms of MCR 2.604 when the court has jurisdiction to do so. The judgment may be rendered even if the claims of the opposing party have been dismissed or otherwise disposed of.

(G) Joining Additional Parties.

(1) *Persons Who May be Joined.* Persons other than those made parties to the original action may be made parties to a counterclaim or cross-claim, subject to MCR 2.205 and 2.206.

(2) *Summons.* On the filing of a counterclaim or cross-claim adding new parties, the court clerk shall issue a summons for each new party in the same manner as on the filing of a complaint, as provided in MCR 2.102(A)–(C). Unless the court orders otherwise, the summons is valid for 21 days after the court issues it.

[Adopted effective March 1, 1985. Amended February 2, 1999, effective June 1, 1999, 459 Mich; October 1, 2014, effective January 1, 2015, 497 Mich.]

Rule 2.204 Third–Party Practice

(A) When Defendant May Bring in Third Party.

(1) Subject to the provisions of MCL 500.3030, any time after commencement of an action, a defending party, as a third-party plaintiff, may serve a summons and complaint on a person not a party to the action who is or may be liable to the third-party plaintiff for all or part of the plaintiff's claim. The third-party plaintiff need not obtain leave to make the service if the third-party complaint is filed within 21 days after the third-party plaintiff's original answer was filed. Otherwise, leave on motion with notice to all parties is required. Unless the court orders otherwise, the summons issued on the filing of a third-party complaint is valid for 21 days after it is issued, and must include the expiration date. See MCR 2.102(B)(8).

(2) Within the time provided by MCR 2.108(A)(1)–(3), the person served with the summons and third-party complaint (the "third-party defendant") must respond to the third-party plaintiff's claim as provided in MCR 2.111, and may file counterclaims against the third-party plaintiff and cross-claims against other parties as provided in MCR 2.203. The third-party defendant may assert against the plaintiff any defenses which the third-party plaintiff has to the plaintiff's claim. The third-party defendant may also assert a claim against the plaintiff arising out of the transaction or occurrence that is the subject matter of the plaintiff's claim against the third-party plaintiff.

(3) The plaintiff may assert a claim against the third-party defendant arising out of the transaction or occurrence that is the subject matter of the plaintiff's claim against the third-party plaintiff, and the third-party defendant must respond as provided in MCR 2.111 and may file counterclaims and cross-claims as provided in MCR 2.203.

(4) A party may move for severance, separate trial, or dismissal of the third-party claim. The court may direct entry of a final judgment on either the original claim or the third-party claim, in accordance with MCR 2.604(B).

(5) A third-party defendant may proceed under this rule against a person not a party to the action who is or may be liable to the third-party defendant for all or part of a claim made in the action against the third-party defendant.

(B) When Plaintiff May Bring in Third Party. A plaintiff against whom a claim or counterclaim is asserted may bring in a third party under this rule to the same extent as a defendant.

(C) Exception; Small Claims. The provisions of this rule do not apply to actions in the small claims division of the district court.

[Adopted effective March 1, 1985. Amended effective September 19, 1995, 450 Mich.]

Comments

Staff Comment to 1985 Adoption

The [March 1, 1985] amendment of MCR 2.204(A)(1) modifies the provisions regarding the filing and serving of a third-party complaint. Leave of court is not required if the third-party complaint is filed within 21 days after the defendant's original answer, and served within 21 days thereafter. Language is also added requiring that the summons specify its expiration date.

The [March 1, 1985] amendment of MCR 2.204(A)(2) makes explicit the requirement that a party served with a third-party complaint must answer or otherwise respond within the same time limits as applicable to other complaints. See MCR 2.108(A)(1)–(3).

Staff Comment to 1995 Amendment

The amendment of MCR 2.204(A)(4) corrects cross-references to MCR 2.604 that were no longer correct after MCR 2.604 was amended on May 16, 1995, and further amended on September 19, 1995.

Rule 2.205   Necessary Joinder of Parties

(A) Necessary Joinder. Subject to the provisions of subrule (B) and MCR 3.501, persons having such interests in the subject matter of an action that their presence in the action is essential to permit the court to render complete relief must be made parties and aligned as plaintiffs or defendants in accordance with their respective interests.

(B) Effect of Failure to Join. When persons described in subrule (A) have not been made parties and are subject to the jurisdiction of the court, the court shall order them summoned to appear in the action, and may prescribe the time and order of pleading. If jurisdiction over those persons can be acquired only by their consent or voluntary appearance, the court may proceed with the action and grant appropriate relief to persons who are parties to prevent a failure of justice. In determining whether to proceed, the court shall consider

(1) whether a valid judgment may be rendered in favor of the plaintiff in the absence of the person not joined;

(2) whether the plaintiff would have another effective remedy if the action is dismissed because of the nonjoinder;

(3) the prejudice to the defendant or to the person not joined that may result from the nonjoinder; and

(4) whether the prejudice, if any, may be avoided or lessened by a protective order or a provision included in the final judgment.

Notwithstanding the failure to join a person who should have been joined, the court may render a judgment against the plaintiff whenever it is determined that the plaintiff is not entitled to relief as a matter of substantive law.

(C) Names of Omitted Persons and Reasons for Nonjoinder to Be Pleaded. In a pleading in which relief is asked, the pleader must state the names, if known, of persons who are not joined, but who ought to be parties if complete relief is to be accorded to those already parties, and must state why they are not joined.

[Adopted effective March 1, 1985.]

Comments

Staff Comment to 1985 Adoption

MCR 2.205 is substantially the same as GCR 1963, 205.

Rule 2.206   Permissive Joinder of Parties

(A) Permissive Joinder.

(1) All persons may join in one action as plaintiffs

(a) if they assert a right to relief jointly, severally, or in the alternative, in respect of or arising out of the same transaction, occurrence, or series of transactions or occurrences and if a question of law or fact common to all of the plaintiffs will arise in the action; or

(b) if their presence in the action will promote the convenient administration of justice.

(2) All persons may be joined in one action as defendants

(a) if there is asserted against them jointly, severally, or in the alternative, a right to relief in respect of or arising out of the same transaction, occurrence, or series of transactions or occurrences and if a question of law or fact common to all of the defendants will arise in the action; or

(b) if their presence in the action will promote the convenient administration of justice.

(3) A plaintiff or defendant need not be interested in obtaining or defending against all the relief demanded. Judgment may be rendered for one or more of the parties against one or more of the parties as the rights and liabilities of the parties are determined.

(B) Separate Trials. The court may enter orders to prevent a party from being embarrassed, delayed, or put to expense by the joinder of a person against whom the party asserts no claim and who asserts no claim against the party,

and may order separate trials or enter other orders to prevent delay or prejudice.
[Adopted effective March 1, 1985.]

Comments

Staff Comment to 1985 Adoption

MCR 2.206 is substantially the same as GCR 1963, 206.

Rule 2.207 Misjoinder and Nonjoinder of Parties

Misjoinder of parties is not a ground for dismissal of an action. Parties may be added or dropped by order of the court on motion of a party or on the court's own initiative at any stage of the action and on terms that are just. When the presence of persons other than the original parties to the action is required to grant complete relief in the determination of a counterclaim or cross-claim, the court shall order those persons to be brought in as defendants if jurisdiction over them can be obtained. A claim against a party may be severed and proceeded with separately.
[Adopted effective March 1, 1985.]

Comments

Staff Comment to 1985 Adoption

MCR 2.207 is substantially the same as GCR 1963, 207.

Rule 2.209 Intervention

(A) Intervention of Right. On timely application a person has a right to intervene in an action:

(1) when a Michigan statute or court rule confers an unconditional right to intervene;

(2) by stipulation of all the parties; or

(3) when the applicant claims an interest relating to the property or transaction which is the subject of the action and is so situated that the disposition of the action may as a practical matter impair or impede the applicant's ability to protect that interest, unless the applicant's interest is adequately represented by existing parties.

(B) Permissive Intervention. On timely application a person may intervene in an action

(1) when a Michigan statute or court rule confers a conditional right to intervene; or

(2) when an applicant's claim or defense and the main action have a question of law or fact in common.

In exercising its discretion, the court shall consider whether the intervention will unduly delay or prejudice the adjudication of the rights of the original parties.

(C) Procedure. A person seeking to intervene must apply to the court by motion and give notice in writing to all parties under MCR 2.107. The motion must

(1) state the grounds for intervention, and

(2) be accompanied by a pleading stating the claim or defense for which intervention is sought.

(D) Notice to Attorney General. When the validity of a Michigan statute or a rule or regulation included in the Michigan Administrative Code is in question in an action to which the state or an officer or agency of the state is not a party, the court may require that notice be given to the Attorney General, specifying the pertinent statute, rule, or regulation.
[Adopted effective March 1, 1985.]

Comments

Staff Comment to 1985 Adoption

MCR 2.209 is based on GCR 1963, 209. A requirement of a timely application to exercise intervention of right is added in subrule (A). See FR Civ P 24(a).

There is a corresponding change in subrule (C), to recognize that a motion to intervene is always required.

Rule 2.221 Motion for Change of Venue

(A) Time to File. A motion for change of venue must be filed before or at the time the defendant files an answer.

(B) Late Motion. Untimeliness is not a ground for denial of a motion filed after the answer if the court is satisfied that the facts on which the motion is based were not and could not with reasonable diligence have been known to the moving party more than 14 days before the motion was filed.

(C) Waiver. An objection to venue is waived if it is not raised within the time limits imposed by this rule.
[Adopted effective March 1, 1985.]

Comments

Staff Comment to 1985 Adoption

MCR 2.221 includes the provisions found in GCR 1963, 401, 402, and 409.

The only substantive changes are in subrule (B). Unlike the practice under GCR 1963, 402, a plaintiff is permitted to file a late motion for a change of venue.

In addition, the language of GCR 1963, 402 is modified to remove the possible implication that the judge must grant the motion if the moving party demonstrates that the grounds are newly discovered. The fact that the grounds are newly discovered only removes untimeliness as a basis for denying the motion.

Rule 2.222 Change of Venue; Venue Proper

(A) Grounds. The court may order a change of venue of a civil action, or of an appeal from an order or decision of a state board, commission, or agency authorized to promulgate rules or regulations, for the convenience of parties and witnesses or when an impartial trial cannot be had where the action is pending. In the case of appellate review of administrative proceedings, venue may also be changed for the convenience of the attorneys.

(B) Motion Required. If the venue of the action is proper, the court may not change the venue on its own initiative, but may do so only on motion of a party.

(C) Multiple Claims. If multiple claims are joined in an action, and the venue of one or more of them would have been improper if the claims had been brought in separate actions, the defendant may move to separate the claims and to transfer those as to which venue would have been improper. The court has discretion to

(1) order the transfer of all claims,

(2) order the separation and transfer moved for, or

(3) retain the entire action for trial.

(D) Order for Change of Venue; Case Records.

(1) The transferring court must enter all necessary orders pertaining to the certification and transfer of the action to the receiving court. The court must order the party that moved for change of venue to pay the applicable statutory filing fee to the receiving court, unless fees have been waived in accordance with MCR 2.002.

(2) The transferring court must serve the order on the parties and send a copy to the receiving court. The clerk of the transferring court must prepare the case records for transfer in accordance with the orders entered under subrule (1) and the Michigan Trial Court Records Management Standards and send them to the receiving court by a secure method.

(3) The receiving court must temporarily suspend payment of the filing fee and open a case pending payment of the filing fee as ordered by the transferring court. The receiving court must notify the party that moved for change of venue of the new case number in the receiving court, the amount due, and the due date.

(E) Payment of Filing and Jury Fees.

(1) The party that moved for change of venue must pay to the receiving court within 28 days of the date of the transfer order the applicable filing fee as ordered by the transferring court. No further action may be had in the case until payment is made. If the fee is not paid to the receiving court within 28 days of the date of the order, the receiving court must order the case transferred back to the transferring court.

(2) If a jury fee has been paid, the clerk of the transferring court must forward it to the clerk of the receiving court as soon as possible after the case records have been transferred.

[Adopted effective March 1, 1985. Amended November 6, 1996, effective February 1, 1997, 453 Mich; May 22, 2007, effective September 1, 2007, 478 Mich; September 18, 2019, effective January 1, 2020, 503 Mich.]

Comments

Staff Comment to 1985 Adoption

MCR 2.222 includes provisions from GCR 1963, 403 and 406.

A new subrule (B) is added to emphasize that if the venue of a civil action is proper, the court may not change venue on its own initiative.

Subrule (C) includes the provisions formerly found in GCR 1963, 406(2), covering the possible remedies when multiple claims are joined and there would not be an independent basis for venue as to some of them. The provisions of GCR 1963, 406(1) regarding improperly joined claims are deleted.

New subrule (D) provides that if a change of venue is granted, the moving party is required to pay the filing fee applicable in the court to which the case is transferred.

The amendment of MCR 2.222(D) [entered January 25, 1985, effective March 1, 1985] adds provisions regarding the transfer of jury fees when venue is changed. If the fee had been paid in the court in which the action was filed, the clerk is to forward it to the clerk of the court to which the action is to be transferred.

The references in the former rules to the "county" in which the action is pending are changed because of the application of the rules to the district court.

Staff Comment to 1997 Amendment

The November 6 amendment of MCR 2.222, relates to statutory changes made by 1995 PA 161 and 1995 PA 249.

Staff Comment to 2007 Amendment

This amendment was adopted to address the situation in which a party moves for change of venue and an order is entered changing venue but the movant fails to pay the filing fee in the transferee court. In such a situation, the original court loses jurisdiction upon entry of the order transferring venue, but the transferee court does not gain jurisdiction until the appropriate filing fee has been paid. The amendment requires that the moving party submit a negotiable instrument in the amount of the filing fee for the transferee court before or at the time the order changing venue is entered, thereby ensuring that there will not be a jurisdictional gap.

Staff Comment to 2020 Amendment

The amendments of MCR 1.109, 2.107, 2.113, 2.116, 2.119, 2.222, 2.223, 2.225, 2.227, 3.206, 3.211, 3.212, 3.214, 3.303, 3.903, 3.921, 3.925, 3.926, 3.931, 3.933, 3.942, 3.950, 3.961, 3.971, 3.972, 4.002, 4.101, 4.201, 4.202, 4.302, 5.128, 5.302, 5.731, 6.101, 6.615, 8.105, and 8.119 and rescission of MCR 2.226 and 8.125 continue the process for design and implementation of the statewide electronic-filing system.

Rule 2.223 Change of Venue; Venue Improper

(A) Motion; Court's Own Initiative. If the venue of a civil action is improper, the court

(1) shall order a change of venue on timely motion of a defendant, or

(2) may order a change of venue on its own initiative with notice to the parties and opportunity for them to be heard on the venue question.

If venue is changed because the action was brought where venue was not proper, the action may be transferred only to a county in which venue would have been proper.

(B) Order for Change of Venue; Case Records.

(1) The transferring court must enter all necessary orders pertaining to the certification and transfer of the action to the receiving court. The court must order the plaintiff to pay the applicable statutory filing fee directly to the receiving court, unless fees have been waived in accordance with MCR 2.002. The court may also order the plaintiff to pay reasonable compensation and attorney fees to the defendant if the case was filed in the wrong court.

(2) The transferring court must serve the order on the parties and send a copy to the receiving court. The clerk of the transferring court must prepare the case records for transfer in accordance with the orders entered under subrule (1) and the Michigan Trial Court Records Management Standards and send them to the receiving court by a secure method.

(3) The receiving court shall temporarily suspend payment of the filing fee and open a case pending payment of the filing fee and costs as ordered by the transferring court. The receiving court must notify the plaintiff of the new case number in the receiving court, the amount due, and the due date.

(C) Payment of Filing and Jury Fees After Change of Venue.

(1) The plaintiff must pay to the receiving court within 28 days of the date of the transfer order the applicable filing fee, costs, and expenses as ordered by the transferring court or the receiving court will dismiss the action. No further proceedings may be had in the action until payment has been made.

(2) If a jury fee has been paid, the clerk of the transferring court must forward it to the clerk of the receiving court as soon as possible after the case records have been transferred.

(3) MCL 600.1653 applies to tort actions filed on or after October 1, 1986.

[Adopted effective March 1, 1985. Amended November 6, 1996, effective February 1, 1997, 453 Mich; September 18, 2019, effective January 1, 2020, 503 Mich.]

Comments

Staff Comment to 1985 Adoption

MCR 2.223 is comparable to GCR 1963, 404.

Subrule (A)(2) adds a requirement that before the court may change venue on its own initiative it must give the parties notice and opportunity to be heard on the venue question.

Subrule (B)(1) provides that one of the costs that the plaintiff must pay is a new filing fee in the court to which the action is transferred. Unlike the comparable provision in MCR 2.222(D), this cost will always be imposed on the plaintiff, rather than on whichever party moved for a change of venue, because it is the plaintiff who selected the wrong forum.

The amendment of MCR 2.223(B) [entered January 25, 1985, effective March 1, 1985] adds provisions regarding the transfer of jury fees when venue is changed.

If the fee had been paid in the court in which the action was filed, the clerk is to forward it to the clerk of the court to which the action is to be transferred.

Staff Comment to 1997 Amendment

The November 6 amendment of MCR 2.223, relates to statutory changes made by 1995 PA 161 and 1995 PA 249.

Staff Comment to 2020 Amendment

The amendments of MCR 1.109, 2.107, 2.113, 2.116, 2.119, 2.222, 2.223, 2.225, 2.227, 3.206, 3.211, 3.212, 3.214, 3.303, 3.903, 3.921, 3.925, 3.926, 3.931, 3.933, 3.942, 3.950, 3.961, 3.971, 3.972, 4.002, 4.101, 4.201, 4.202, 4.302, 5.128, 5.302, 5.731, 6.101, 6.615, 8.105, and 8.119 and rescission of MCR 2.226 and 8.125 continue the process for design and implementation of the statewide electronic-filing system.

Rule 2.224.   Change of Venue in Tort Actions [Repealed effective February 1, 1997]

Rule 2.225.   Joinder of Party to Control Venue

(A) Joinder Not in Good Faith. On a defendant's motion, venue must be changed on a showing that the venue of the action is proper only because of the joinder of a codefendant who was not joined in good faith but only to control venue.

(B) Order for Change of Venue; Case Records.

(1) The transferring court must enter all necessary orders pertaining to the certification and transfer of the action to the receiving court. The court must order the plaintiff to pay the applicable statutory filing fee directly to the receiving court, unless fees have been waived in accordance with MCR 2.002. The court may also order the plaintiff to pay reasonable compensation and attorney fees to the defendant when necessary to accomplish the transfer.

(2) The transferring court must serve the order on the parties and send a copy to the receiving court. The clerk of the court must prepare the case records for transfer in accordance with the orders entered under subrule (1) and the Michigan Trial Court Records Management Standards and send them to the receiving court by a secure method.

(3) The receiving court shall temporarily suspend payment of the filing fee and open a case pending payment of the filing fee and costs as ordered by the transferring court. The receiving court must notify the plaintiff of the new case number in the receiving court, the amount due, and the due date.

(C) Payment of Filing and Jury Fees After Transfer.

(1) The plaintiff must pay to the receiving court within 28 days of the date of the transfer order the applicable filing fee and any expenses or attorney fees as ordered by the transferring court or the receiving court will dismiss the action.

(2) If a jury fee has been paid, the clerk of the transferring court must forward it to the clerk of the receiving court as soon as possible after the case records have been transferred. [Adopted effective March 1, 1985. Amended September 18, 2019, effective January 1, 2020, 503 Mich.]

Comments

Staff Comment to 1985 Adoption

MCR 2.225 is comparable to GCR 1963, 407.

In subrule (A) the word "may" is changed to "must" to require a change of venue on the showing of bad faith joinder of parties.

As in MCR 2.222 and 2.223, the rule requires the payment of an additional filing fee in the court to which the action is transferred. This cost will always be imposed on the plaintiff because the transfer results from the bad faith of the plaintiff in joining parties.

References to the "county" in which the action is pending are changed because of the application of the rule to the district court. In addition, the reference to a

defendant being "established" in the county is changed in view of the amendment of the venue statute to delete that concept. See 1976 PA 375, amending MCL 600.1621.

The amendment of MCR 2.225 [entered on January 25, 1985, effective March 1, 1985] adds provisions regarding the transfer of jury fees when venue is changed. If the fee had been paid in the court in which the action was filed, the clerk is to forward it to the clerk of the court to which the action is to be transferred.

Staff Comment to 2020 Amendment

The amendments of MCR 1.109, 2.107, 2.113, 2.116, 2.119, 2.222, 2.223, 2.225, 2.227, 3.206, 3.211, 3.212, 3.214, 3.303, 3.903, 3.921, 3.925, 3.926, 3.931, 3.933, 3.942, 3.950, 3.961, 3.971, 3.972, 4.002, 4.101, 4.201, 4.202, 4.302, 5.128, 5.302, 5.731, 6.101, 6.615, 8.105, and 8.119 and rescission of MCR 2.226 and 8.125 continue the process for design and implementation of the statewide electronic-filing system.

Rule 2.226.   Change of Venue; Orders [Repealed effective January 1, 2020.]

Rule 2.227   Transfer of Actions on Finding of Lack of Jurisdiction

(A) Transfer to Court Which Has Jurisdiction. When the court in which a civil action is pending determines that it lacks jurisdiction of the subject matter of the action, but that some other Michigan court would have jurisdiction of the action, the court may order the action transferred to the other court in a place where venue would be proper. If the question of jurisdiction is raised by the court on its own initiative, the action may not be transferred until the parties are given notice and an opportunity to be heard on the jurisdictional issue.

(B) Order Transferring Jurisdiction; Case Records.

(1) The transferring court must enter all necessary orders pertaining to the certification and transfer of the action to the receiving court. The court must order the plaintiff to pay the applicable statutory filing fee directly to the receiving court, unless fees have been waived in accordance with MCR 2.002. The court may also order the plaintiff to pay reasonable compensation and attorney fees to the defendant for filing the case in the wrong court.

(2) The transferring court must serve the order on the parties and send a copy to the receiving court. The clerk of the court must prepare the case records for transfer in accordance with the orders entered under subrule (1) and the Michigan Trial Court Records Management Standards and send them to the receiving court by a secure method.

(3) The receiving court shall temporarily suspend payment of the filing fee and open a case pending payment of the filing fee and costs as ordered by the transferring court. The receiving court must notify the plaintiff of the new case number in the receiving court, the amount due, and the due date.

(C) Payment of Filing and Jury Fees After Transfer.

(1) The plaintiff must pay to the receiving court within 28 days of the date of the transfer order the applicable filing fee and must submit proof of the payment of any expenses as ordered by the transferring court or the receiving court will dismiss the action.

(2) If a jury fee has been paid, the clerk of the transferring court must forward it to the clerk of the receiving court as soon as possible after the case records have been transferred.

(D) Procedure After Transfer.

(1) The action proceeds in the receiving court as if it had been originally filed there. If further pleadings are required or allowed, the time for filing them runs from the date the filing

fee is paid under subrule (C)(1). The receiving court may order the filing of new or amended pleadings. If part of the action remains pending in the transferring court, certified copies of the papers filed may be forwarded, with the cost to be paid by the plaintiff.

(2) If a defendant had not been served with process at the time the action was transferred, the plaintiff must obtain the issuance of a new summons from the receiving court.

(3) A waiver of jury trial in the court in which the action was originally filed is ineffective after transfer. A party who had waived trial by jury may demand a jury trial after transfer by filing a demand and paying the applicable jury fee within 28 days after the filing fee is paid under subrule (C)(1). A demand for a jury trial in the court in which the action was originally filed is preserved after transfer.

(E) Relation to Other Transfer Provisions. This rule does not affect transfers (pursuant to other rules or statutes) of actions over which the transferring court had jurisdiction.

[Adopted effective March 1, 1985. Amended September 18, 2019, effective January 1, 2020, 503 Mich.]

Comments

Staff Comment to 1985 Adoption

MCR 2.227 creates a new procedure permitting a court which determines that it lacks jurisdiction of an action to transfer it to an appropriate court, rather than dismiss it. Under subrule (A)(1) the procedure is discretionary, and the court may not make such an order on its own initiative without giving the parties an opportunity to be heard.

Under subrule (A)(2), as a condition of transfer the court is to require the plaintiff to pay appropriate costs. In effect, this gives the plaintiff control over whether the case will be transferred. If the plaintiff does not pay the costs within the appropriate period, the court is to dismiss the action. In many cases, the plaintiff might prefer to simply start a new action in the appropriate court.

Subrule (B) includes provisions covering procedure after transfer, including such matters as the time for further pleadings after the records are sent by the transferring court, issuance of a new summons if the defendant had not been served at the time of transfer, and the continuing effect of a demand for or waiver of jury trial after transfer.

Subrule (C) makes clear that these provisions do not affect the transfer of cases pursuant to other rules or statutes when the transferring court had jurisdiction. See, e.g., MCR 4.002, 4.003; MCL 700.022(3).

Staff Comment to 2020 Amendment

The amendments of MCR 1.109, 2.107, 2.113, 2.116, 2.119, 2.222, 2.223, 2.225, 2.227, 3.206, 3.211, 3.212, 3.214, 3.303, 3.903, 3.921, 3.925, 3.926, 3.931, 3.933, 3.942, 3.950, 3.961, 3.971, 3.972, 4.002, 4.101, 4.201, 4.202, 4.302, 5.128, 5.302, 5.731, 6.101, 6.615, 8.105, and 8.119 and rescission of MCR 2.226 and 8.125 continue the process for design and implementation of the statewide electronic-filing system.

Rule 2.228   Transfer to the Court of Claims

(A) A notice of transfer to the Court of Claims must be provided before or at the time the defendant files an answer.

(B) After the time provided in subrule (A)—

(1) If the court in which a civil action is pending has concurrent jurisdiction with the Court of Claims, the defendant must seek leave to file a notice of transfer and the court may grant leave if it is satisfied that the facts on which the motion is based were not and could not with reasonable diligence have been known to the moving party more than 14 days before the motion was filed.

(2) If the court in which a civil action is pending does not have subject matter jurisdiction because the case is within the exclusive jurisdiction of the Court of Claims, MCR 2.227 governs.

[Adopted September 20, 2018, effective January 1, 2019, 502 Mich.]

Comments

Staff Comment to 2019 Adoption

MCL 600.6404(3) allows defendant to transfer a case to the Court of Claims. This rule requires such a transfer to be made at or before the time the defendant files an answer, which is the same period mandated for change of venue under MCR 2.221. The proposal arose from the Court's consideration of *Baynesan v Wayne State University* (docket 154435), in which defendant waited until just a month before trial before transferring a case he could have transferred nearly a year sooner. In subrule (B), the rule distinguishes between courts with concurrent jurisdiction and courts without concurrent jurisdiction when an untimely notice of transfer is filed.

SUBCHAPTER 2.300   DISCOVERY

Rule 2.301.   Availability and Timing of Discovery

(A) Availability of Discovery.

(1) In a case where initial disclosures are required, a party may seek discovery only after the party serves its initial disclosures under MCR 2.302(A). Otherwise, a party may seek discovery after commencement of the action when authorized by these rules, by stipulation, or by court order.

(2) In actions in the district court, no discovery is permitted before entry of judgment except by leave of the court or on the stipulation of all parties. A motion for discovery may not be filed unless the discovery sought has previously been requested and refused.

(3) Notwithstanding the provisions of this or any other rule, discovery is not permitted in actions in the small claims division of the district court or in civil infraction actions.

(4) After a post judgment motion is filed in a domestic relations action as defined by subchapter 3.200 of these rules, parties may obtain discovery by any means provided in subchapter 2.300 of these rules.

(B) Completion of Discovery.

(1) In circuit and probate court, the time for completion of discovery shall be set by an order entered under MCR 2.401(B).

(2) In an action in which discovery is available only on leave of the court or by stipulation, the order or stipulation shall set a time for completion of discovery. A time set by stipulation may not delay the scheduling of the action for trial.

(3) After the time for completion of discovery, a deposition of a witness taken solely for the purpose of preservation of testimony may be taken at any time before commencement of trial without leave of court.

(4) Unless ordered otherwise, a date for the completion of discovery means the serving party shall initiate the discovery by a time that provides for a response or appearance, per these rules, before the completion date. As may be reasonable under the circumstances, or by leave of court, motions with regard to discovery may be brought after the date for completion of discovery.

(C) Course of Discovery. The court may control the scope, order, and amount of discovery, consistent with these rules.

[Adopted effective March 1, 1985. Amended effective October 1, 1991, 437 Mich. Amended June 19, 2019, effective January 1, 2020, 503 Mich.]

Comments

Staff Comment to 1985 Adoption

MCR 2.301 covers the time for completion of discovery. The corresponding provision of the General Court Rules is GCR 1963, 301.7, which sets the discovery cutoff at the pretrial conference or the waiver of a pretrial conference. Under MCR 2.301 discovery must be completed 1 year after an answer is filed unless the court sets another date.

Subrule (B) is related to MCR 2.302(A)(2), which provides that in district court discovery is available only by stipulation or a court order. In such a case, the order or stipulation providing for discovery is to set the time for completion of discovery, but is not to delay trial of the action.

Subrule (C) creates an exception for the taking of a deposition to preserve testimony. Such a deposition may be taken without court order at any time before commencement of trial.

The amendment of MCR 2.301, effective October 1, 1991, is based on the recommendations of the Caseflow Management Rules Committee, appointed by the Supreme Court on July 28, 1989. The committee was appointed to consider the comments received on several of the proposed court rule amendments submitted by the Caseflow Management Coordinating Committee, which were published for comment on January 17, 1989. A detailed explanation of the proposals can be found in the report of the Caseflow Management Rules Committee, 435 Mich 1210.

In addition, on June 11, 1991, the Court entered Administrative Order No. 1991-4, which directs the State Court Administrative Office and the trial courts to cooperate in developing and implementing caseflow management plans.

Staff Comment to 1991 Amendment

MCR 2.301(A) is amended [effective October 1, 1991] by deleting the provision setting one year as the time for completion of discovery in the absence of an order providing otherwise. Setting the time for completion of discovery, and other events in the case, is to be done by scheduling orders under MCR 2.401(B)(2).

Staff Comment to 2020 Amendment

These amendments are based on a proposal created by a special committee of the State Bar of Michigan and approved for submission to the Court by the Bar's Representative Assembly. The rules require mandatory discovery disclosure in many cases, adopt a presumptive limit on interrogatories (20 in most cases, but 35 in domestic relations proceedings) and limit a deposition to 7 hours. The amendments also update the rules to more specifically address issues related to electronically stored information, and encourage early action on discovery issues during the discovery period.

The amendment of MCR 2.309(A)(2) sets a presumptive limit of twenty interrogatories for each separately represented party. Several commenters suggested that the term "discrete subpart" be more explicitly defined. But the rule's reference to "a discrete subpart" is intended to draw guidance from federal courts construing FR Civ P 30(a)(1). Generally, subparts are not separately counted if they are logically or factually subsumed within and necessarily related to the primary question. In upholding the limit, parties and courts should also pragmatically balance the overall goals of discovery and the admonition of MCR 1.105. Further, the intent of the provision at MCR 2.301(B)(4) is to ensure that parties responding to discovery requests have the full time period to do so as provided for under these rules prior to the expiration of the discovery period.

Rule 2.302. Duty to Disclose; General Rules Governing Discovery

(A) Required Initial Disclosures.

(1) *In General.* Except as exempted by these rules, stipulation, or court order, a party must, without awaiting a discovery request, provide to the other parties:

(a) the factual basis of the party's claims and defenses;

(b) the legal theories on which the party's claims and defenses are based, including, if necessary for a reasonable understanding of the claim or defense, citations to relevant legal authorities;

(c) the name and, if known, the address and telephone number of each individual likely to have discoverable information—along with the subjects of that information—that the disclosing party may use to support its claims or defenses, unless the use would be solely for impeachment;

(d) a copy—or a description by category and location—of all documents, ESI, and tangible things that the disclosing party has in its possession, custody, or control and may use to support its claims or defenses, unless the use would be solely for impeachment;

(e) a description by category and location of all documents, ESI, and tangible things that are not in the disclosing party's possession, custody, or control that the disclosing party may use to support its claims or defenses, unless the use would be solely for impeachment. The description must include the name and, if known, the address and telephone number of the person who has possession, custody, or control of the material;

(f) a computation of each category of damages claimed by the disclosing party, who must also make available for inspection and copying as under MCR 2.310 the documents or other evidentiary material, unless privileged or protected from disclosure, on which each computation is based, including materials bearing on the nature and extent of injuries suffered;

(g) a copy (or an opportunity to inspect a copy) of pertinent portions of any insurance, indemnity, security equivalent, or suretyship agreement under which another person may be liable to satisfy all or part of a possible judgment in the action or to indemnify or reimburse for payments made to satisfy the judgment, including self-insured retention and limitations on coverage, indemnity, or reimbursement for amounts available to satisfy a judgment; and

(h) the anticipated subject areas of expert testimony.

(2) *Additional Disclosures for No–Fault Cases.* In addition to the disclosures under subrule (A)(1), in a case asserting a first-party claim for benefits under the Michigan no-fault act, MCL 500.3101, *et seq.*, the following disclosures must be made without awaiting a discovery request:

(a) A defendant from whom no-fault benefits are claimed must disclose:

(i) a copy of the first-party claim file and a privilege log for any redactions and

(ii) the payments the insurance company has made on the claim.

(b) The plaintiff must disclose all applicable claims, including all of the following information within the plaintiff's possession, custody, or control:

(i) the identity of those who provided medical, household, and attendant care services to plaintiff,

(ii) all provider bills or outstanding balances for which the plaintiff seeks reimbursement,

(iii) the name, address, and phone number of plaintiff's employers, and

(iv) the additional disclosures under subrule (A)(3).

(3) *Additional Disclosures by Claimants for Damages for Personal Injury.* A party claiming damages for injury arising from a mental or physical condition must provide the other parties with executed medical record authorizations in the form approved by the State Court Administrative Office or in a form agreed by the parties for all persons, institutions, hospitals, and other custodians in actual possession of medical information

relating to the condition, unless the party asserts privilege pursuant to MCR 2.314(B).

(4) *Cases Exempt from Initial Disclosure.* Unless otherwise stipulated or ordered, the following are exempt from initial disclosure under subrule (A)(1)–(3):

(a) an appeal to the circuit court under subchapter 7.100;

(b) an action in district court (see MCR 2.301[A][2]);

(c) an action under subchapter 3.200;

(d) an action brought without an attorney by a person in the custody of the United States, a state, or a state subdivision;

(e) an action to enforce or quash an administrative summons or a subpoena;

(f) a proceeding ancillary to a proceeding in another court, including an action for a subpoena under MCR 2.305(E) or (F);

(g) an action to compel or stay arbitration or to confirm, vacate, enforce, modify, or correct an arbitration award;

(h) an action for collection of penalties, fines, forfeitures, or forfeited recognizances under MCR 3.605;

(i) personal protection proceedings under subchapter 3.700; and

(j) an action for habeas corpus under MCR 3.303 and 3.304.

(5) *Time for Initial Disclosures.*

(a) Application of Time Limits. These deadlines apply unless a stipulation or order sets a different time.

(b) In General.

(i) A party that files a complaint, counterclaim, cross-claim, or third-party complaint must serve its initial disclosures within 14 days after any opposing party files an answer to that pleading.

(ii) A party answering a complaint, counterclaim, cross-claim, or third-party complaint must serve its initial disclosures within the later of 14 days after the opposing party's disclosures are due or 28 days after the party files its answer.

(iii) A party serving disclosures need only serve parties that have appeared. The party must serve later-appearing parties within 14 days of the appearance.

(c) Parties Served or Joined Later. A party first served or otherwise joined after the time for initial disclosures under subrule (A)(5)(a) or (b) must serve its initial disclosures within 14 days after filing the party's first pleading, unless a stipulation or order sets a different time.

(6) *Basis for Initial Disclosure; Unacceptable Excuses.* A party must serve initial disclosures based on the information then reasonably available to the party. However, a party is not excused from making disclosures because the party has not fully investigated the case or because the party challenges the sufficiency of another party's disclosures or because another party has not made its disclosures.

(7) *Form of Disclosures.* Disclosures under subrule (A) are subject to MCR 2.302(G), must be in writing, signed, and served, and a proof of service must be promptly filed.

(B) Scope of Discovery.

(1) *In General.* Parties may obtain discovery regarding any non-privileged matter that is relevant to any party's claims or defenses and proportional to the needs of the case, taking into account all pertinent factors, including whether the burden or expense of the proposed discovery outweighs its likely benefit, the complexity of the case, the importance of the issues at stake in the action, the amount in controversy, and the parties' resources and access to relevant information. Information within the scope of discovery need not be admissible in evidence to be discoverable.

(2) *Insurance Agreements.* A party may obtain discovery of the existence and contents of an insurance agreement under which a person carrying on an insurance business may be liable to satisfy part or all of a judgment which may be entered in the action or to indemnify or reimburse for payments made to satisfy the judgment. Information concerning the insurance agreement is not by reason of disclosure admissible at trial. For purposes of this subrule, an application for insurance is not part of an insurance agreement.

(3) *Trial Preparation; Materials.*

(a) Subject to the provisions of subrule (B)(4), a party may obtain discovery of documents and tangible things otherwise discoverable under subrule (B)(1) and prepared in anticipation of litigation or for trial by or for another party or another party's representative (including an attorney, consultant, surety, indemnitor, insurer, or agent) only on a showing that the party seeking discovery has substantial need of the materials in the preparation of the case and is unable without undue hardship to obtain the substantial equivalent of the materials by other means. In ordering discovery of such materials when the required showing has been made, the court shall protect against disclosure of the mental impressions, conclusions, opinions, or legal theories of an attorney or other representative of a party concerning the litigation.

(b) Without the showing required by subrule (B)(3)(a), a party or a nonparty may obtain a statement concerning the action or its subject matter previously made by the person making the request. A nonparty whose request is refused may move for a court order. The provisions of MCR 2.313(A)(5) apply to the award of expenses incurred in relation to the motion.

(c) For purposes of subrule (B)(3)(b), a statement previously made is

(i) a written statement signed or otherwise adopted or approved by the person making it; or

(ii) a stenographic, mechanical, electrical, or other recording, or a transcription of it, which is a substantially verbatim recital of an oral statement by the person making it and contemporaneously recorded.

(4) *Trial Preparation; Experts.* Discovery of facts known and opinions held by experts, otherwise discoverable under the provisions of subrule (B)(1) and acquired or developed in anticipation of litigation or for trial, may be obtained only as follows:

(a)(i) A party may through interrogatories require another party to identify each person whom the other party expects to call as an expert witness at trial, to state the subject matter about which the expert is expected to testify, and to state the substance of the facts and opinions to which the expert is expected to testify and a summary of the grounds for each opinion.

(ii) A party may take the deposition of a person whom the other party expects to call as an expert witness at trial. The party taking the deposition may notice that the deposition is to be taken for the purpose of discovery only and that it shall not be admissible at trial except for the purpose of impeachment, without the necessity of obtaining a protective order as set forth in MCR 2.302(C)(7).

(iii) On motion, the court may order further discovery by other means, subject to such restrictions as to scope and such provisions (pursuant to subrule [B][4][c]) concerning fees and expenses as the court deems appropriate.

(b) A party may not discover the identity of and facts known or opinions held by an expert who has been retained or specially employed by another party in anticipation of litigation or preparation for trial and who is not expected to be called as a witness at trial, except

(i) as provided in MCR 2.311, or

(ii) where an order has been entered on a showing of exceptional circumstances under which it is impracticable for the party seeking discovery to obtain facts or opinions on the same subject by other means.

(c) Unless manifest injustice would result

(i) the court shall require that the party seeking discovery under subrules (B)(4)(a)(ii) or (iii) or (B)(4)(b) pay the expert a reasonable fee for time spent in a deposition, but not including preparation time; and

(ii) with respect to discovery obtained under subrule (B)(4)(a)(ii) or (iii), the court may require, and with respect to discovery obtained under subrule (B)(4)(b) the court shall require, the party seeking discovery to pay the other party a fair portion of the fees and expenses reasonably incurred by the latter party in obtaining facts and opinions from the expert.

(d) A party may depose a witness that he or she expects to call as an expert at trial. The deposition may be taken at any time before trial on reasonable notice to the opposite party, and may be offered as evidence at trial as provided in MCR 2.308(A). The court need not adjourn the trial because of the unavailability of expert witnesses or their depositions.

(e) Subrule (B)(3)(a) protects drafts of any interrogatory answer required under subrule (B)(4)(a)(i), regardless of the form in which the draft is recorded.

(f) Subrule (B)(3)(a) protects communications between the party's attorney and any expert witness under subrule (B)(4), regardless of the form of the communications, except to the extent that the communications:

(i) relate to compensation for the expert's study or testimony;

(ii) identify facts or data that the party's attorney provided and that the expert considered in forming the opinions to be expressed; or

(iii) identify assumptions that the party's attorney provided and that the expert relied on in forming the opinions to be expressed.

(5) *Duty to Preserve ESI.* A party has the same obligation to preserve ESI as it does for all other types of information.

(6) *Limitation of Discovery of ESI.* A party need not provide discovery of ESI from sources that the party identifies as not reasonably accessible because of undue burden or cost. On motion to compel discovery or for a protective order, the party from whom discovery is sought must show that the information is not reasonably accessible because of undue burden or cost. If that showing is made, the court may nonetheless order discovery if the requesting party shows good cause, considering proportionality under subrule (B)(1) and the limitations of subrule (C). The court may specify conditions for the discovery, including allocation of the expense, and may limit the frequency or extent of discovery of ESI (whether or not the ESI is from a source that is reasonably accessible).

(7) *Information Inadvertently Produced.* If information that is subject to a claim of privilege or of protection as trial-preparation material is produced in discovery, the party making the claim may notify any party that received the information of the claim and the basis for it. After being notified, a party must promptly return, sequester, or destroy the specified information and any copies it has and may not use or disclose the information until the claim is resolved. A receiving party may promptly present the information to the court under seal for a determination of the claim. If the receiving party disclosed the information before being notified, it must take reasonable steps to retrieve it. The producing party must preserve the information until the claim is resolved.

(C) Protective Orders. On motion by a party or by the person from whom discovery is sought, and on reasonable notice and for good cause shown, the court in which the action is pending may issue any order that justice requires to protect a party or person from annoyance, embarrassment, oppression, or undue burden or expense, including one or more of the following orders:

(1) that the discovery not be had;

(2) that the discovery may be had only on specified terms and conditions, including a designation of the time or place;

(3) that the discovery may be had only by a method of discovery other than that selected by the party seeking discovery;

(4) that certain matters not be inquired into, or that the scope of the discovery be limited to certain matters;

(5) that discovery be conducted with no one present except persons designated by the court;

(6) that a deposition, after being sealed, be opened only by order of the court;

(7) that a deposition shall be taken only for the purpose of discovery and shall not be admissible in evidence except for the purpose of impeachment;

(8) that a trade secret or other confidential research, development, or commercial information not be disclosed or be disclosed only in a designated way;

(9) that the parties simultaneously file specified documents or information enclosed in sealed envelopes to be opened as directed by the court.

If the motion for a protective order is denied in whole or in part, the court may, on terms and conditions as are just, order that a party or person provide or permit discovery. The provisions of MCR 2.313(A)(5) apply to the award of expenses incurred in relation to the motion.

(D) Sequence of Discovery. Unless the court orders otherwise, methods of discovery may be used in any sequence, and the fact that a party is conducting discovery, whether by deposition or otherwise, does not operate to delay another party's discovery.

(E) Supplementing Disclosures and Responses.

(1) *Duty to Supplement.*

(a) In General. A party that has made a disclosure under MCR 2.302(A)—or that has responded to an interrogatory, request for production, or request for admission—must supplement or correct its disclosure or response:

(i) in a timely manner if the party learns that in some material respect the disclosure or response is incomplete or incorrect, and if the additional or corrective information has not otherwise been made known to the other parties during the discovery process or in writing or

(ii) as ordered by the court.

(b) Order, Agreement, or Request. A duty to supplement disclosures or responses may be imposed by order of the court, agreement of the parties, or at any time before trial through requests for supplementation.

(2) *Failure to Supplement.* If the court finds, by way of motion or otherwise, that a party has not supplemented disclosures or responses as required by this subrule, the court may enter an order as is just, including an order providing the sanctions stated in MCR 2.313(B), and, in particular, MCR 2.313(B)(2)(b).

(F) Changes to Discovery Procedure. A court order or written and filed stipulation of the affected parties may:

(1) provide that depositions may be taken before any person, at any time or place, on any notice, and in any manner, and when so taken may be used like other depositions; and

(2) change the disclosure requirements in MCR 2.302(A) and the limits on interrogatories in MCR 2.309(A)(2); and

(3) modify or waive the other procedures of these rules regarding discovery so long as not inconsistent with a court order, but a stipulation may not change scheduling order deadlines without court approval.

(G) Signing of Disclosures, Discovery Requests, Responses, and Objections; Sanctions.

(1) In addition to any other signature required by these rules, every disclosure under MCR 2.302(A), every request for discovery, and every response or objection to such a request made by a party represented by an attorney shall be signed by at least one attorney of record. A party who is not represented by an attorney must sign the disclosure, request, response, or objection.

(2) If a disclosure, request, response, or objection is not signed, it shall be stricken unless it is signed promptly after the omission is called to the attention of the party making the disclosure, request, response, or objection, and another party need not take any action with respect to it until it is signed.

(3) The signature of the attorney or party constitutes a certification that he or she has read the disclosure, request, response, or objection, and that to the best of the signer's

knowledge, information, and belief formed after a reasonable inquiry:

(a) the disclosure is

(i) complete and correct as of the time it is made; and

(ii) consistent with these rules and warranted by existing law or a good faith argument for the extension, modification, or reversal of existing law.

(b) the discovery request, response, or objection is:

(i) consistent with these rules and warranted by existing law or a good faith argument for the extension, modification, or reversal of existing law;

(ii) not interposed for any improper purpose, such as to harass or to cause unnecessary delay or needless increase in the cost of litigation; and

(iii) not unreasonable or unduly burdensome or expensive, given the needs of the case, the disclosure and discovery already had in the case, the amount in controversy, and the importance of the issues at stake in the litigation.

(4) If a certification is made in violation of this rule, the court, on the motion of a party or on its own initiative, may impose upon the person who made the certification, the party on whose behalf the disclosure, request, response, or objection is made, or both, an appropriate sanction, which may include an order to pay the amount of the reasonable expenses incurred because of the violation, including reasonable attorney fees.

(H) Filing and Service of Disclosure and Discovery Materials.

(1) Unless required by a particular rule, disclosures, requests, responses, depositions, and other discovery materials may not be filed with the court except as follows:

(a) If the materials are to be used in connection with a motion, they must either be filed separately or be attached to the motion, response, or an accompanying affidavit.

(b) If the materials are to be used at trial, they must be made an exhibit under MCR 2.518 or MCR 3.930.

(c) The court may order disclosure or discovery materials to be filed.

(2) Copies of disclosure and discovery materials served under these rules must be served on all parties, unless the court has entered an order under MCR 2.107(F).

(3) On appeal, only disclosure and discovery materials that were filed or made exhibits are part of the record on appeal.

(4) MCR 2.316 governs removal and destruction of disclosure and discovery materials.

[Adopted effective March 1, 1985. Amended March 16, 1989, effective June 1, 1989, 432 Mich; December 17, 1990, effective March 1, 1991, 437 Mich; March 5, 1993, effective June 1, 1993, 442 Mich; June 7, 1994, effective September 1, 1994, 445 Mich; December 16, 2008, effective January 1, 2009, 482 Mich; October 31, 2012, effective January 1, 2013, 493 Mich; June 4, 2014, effective September 1, 2014, 496 Mich; October 1, 2014, effective January 1, 2015, 497 Mich; June 19, 2019, effective January 1, 2020, 503 Mich.]

Comments

Staff Comment to 1985 Adoption

MCR 2.302 collects the general provisions governing discovery. There was no counterpart to the rule in the General Court Rules, although certain aspects of it were covered by rules spread throughout the discovery subchapter. The rule is organized in the manner of FR Civ P 26. Although the discovery rules continue to include some provisions not found in the federal rules, in general, the Michigan

Court Rules make Michigan discovery practice far more like federal procedure than was the case under the General Court Rules.

Subrule (A) includes the general statement as to the availability of discovery. Subrule (A)(1) is based on FR Civ P 26(a). The General Court Rules had comparable provisions at the beginning of the rule covering each method of discovery. See, e.g., GCR 1963, 302.1 (depositions), 309.1 (interrogatories), 310.1 (motion to produce or permit inspection).

In addition, the rule retains two major limitations on discovery applicable to the district court. As under DCR 302.2, no discovery is allowed except on court order or stipulation. See subrule (A)(2). Additional language is included to make clear that discovery is allowed after judgment, for example, under MCR 2.621 or 3.101(J). Second, subrule (A)(3) carries forward the provision of DCR 302.6 that discovery is not allowed in the small claims division of the district court, and adds a prohibition on discovery in civil infraction actions.

Subrule (B) governs the general subject of the scope of discovery. It is modeled on FR Civ P 26(b). Most of the material was not included in the General Court Rules.

Subrule (B)(1) changes the scope of discovery to the federal formulation by eliminating the admissibility requirement found in GCR 1963, 302.2(1) (and incorporated in GCR 1963, 309.4 and 310.1). The second paragraph of FR Civ P 26(b)(1), covering court orders limiting discovery, is omitted; however, such orders would be allowed under subrules (A)(1) and (C).

Subrule (B)(1)(b) retains the substance of GCR 1963, 302.2(1), forbidding a party who has invoked a privilege at a deposition from introducing at trial the testimony of the witness pertaining to the evidence objected to at the deposition. Note that there is a related provision regarding privileges with respect to medical information in MCR 2.314(B).

Subrules (B)(2), covering discovery of insurance agreements, and (B)(3), limiting the discoverability of documents and things prepared by the other party in anticipation of litigation or trial, are basically the same as FR Civ P 26(b)(2) and (3). There were no corresponding provisions in the former Michigan rules.

In subrule (B)(4), in addition to the methods of discovery regarding expert witnesses that are provided by FR Civ P 26(b)(4), a party is permitted to take the deposition of an expert witness that the opposing party intends to call at trial. This is consistent with prior Michigan practice. The cost provisions in subrule (B)(4)(c) are modified from the corresponding provisions of the federal rule because of the availability of depositions of experts.

Subrule (B)(4)(d) is a provision not found in FR Civ P 26. It permits a party to take the deposition of a witness whom that party expects to call as an expert at trial. Use of such a deposition at trial is governed by MCR 2.308(A)(1)(c)(i). The General Court Rules included such a provision only with regard to the Wayne and Genesee circuit courts. GCR 1963, 302.7, 302.8.

Subrule (C) is based on FR Civ P 26(c). The prior Michigan rules had several provisions regarding protective orders. For example, GCR 1963, 306.2, 307.4, and 309.5 included many of the same principles as subrule (C). However, several new protective order provisions are added. Subrule (C)(5), like FR Civ P 26(c)(5), permits the court to order that a deposition is to be taken with no one present except those permitted by the order. By contrast, GCR 1963, 306.2 did not allow exclusion of a party. Second, subrule (C)(7) adds to the list of possible protective orders found in FR Civ P 26(c) and GCR 1963, 306.2, that a deposition may be taken only for the purpose of discovery and will not be admissible at trial.

The [March 1, 1985] amendment of MCR 2.302(C)(7) specifies that a protective order that a deposition is to be taken only for the purpose of discovery and will not be admissible in evidence does not preclude the use of the deposition for purpose of impeachment.

Subrule (D), covering the sequence and timing of discovery, is taken from FR Civ P 26(d). There was no comparable provision in the General Court Rules.

Subrule (E), supplementation of responses, is based on FR Civ P 26(e). There was no comparable Michigan provision, although GCR 1963, 309.2 (applicable only in Wayne circuit court) treated interrogatories asking for the identification of witnesses as "continuing" questions. In addition to the provisions of the federal rule, subrule (E)(2) provides sanctions for failure to supplement.

Subrule (F), governing stipulations regarding discovery, is taken from FR Civ P 29. The only similar provision in the General Court Rules was GCR 1963, 302.2(2), which applied only to depositions.

Subrule (G) is based on the August 1, 1983, amendment of FR Civ P 26, which added the provisions regarding the signing of discovery requests and responses, and sanctions for violation of the rule. The rule is similar to MCR 2.114, governing signing of other papers. In addition to any other signature required (see, e.g., MCR 2.309[B][3]), discovery requests and responses must be signed by an attorney if the party is represented by an attorney. The effect of a signature on a discovery request or response is a certification similar to that required by MCR 2.114 as to other papers. See subrule (G)(3). Similar sanctions are imposed for a certification made in violation of the rule. See subrule (G)(4).

Subrule (H) is a new provision governing the filing of discovery materials, which differs from both prior Michigan practice and the federal rules. Unless a particular rule requires a filing (see, e.g., MCR 2.312[F]), filing is required only when the materials are to be used in connection with a motion or at trial. Only those discovery materials that were filed or made an exhibit are considered part of the record on appeal. In a number of places throughout the other discovery rules, references to filing of various papers are deleted to be consistent with subrule (H).

The [March 1, 1985] amendment of MCR 2.302(H) adds a requirement that discovery materials be served on all parties. The general rule requiring service, MCR 2.107(A)(1), applies to papers "filed". Under MCR 2.302(H), most discovery materials will not be filed.

Staff Comment to 1989 Amendment

MCR 2.302(H)(4) was amended [June 1, 1989] to add reference to a new rule, MCR 2.316, authorizing removal and destruction of certain discovery material.

Staff Comment to 1991 Amendment

The [March 1,] 1991 amendment changed a cross-reference in subrule (B)(4)(d) in order to acknowledge a previous amendment to MCR 2.308(A).

Staff Comment to 1993 Amendment

The March 5, 1993, amendment of MCR 2.302(B)(4)(b), effective June 1, 1993, deals with the subject of discovery of the identity of experts who have been retained or specially employed in anticipation of or during litigation but who are not expected to be called as witnesses. Case law has produced varying answers regarding whether the limitations on discovery of facts known or opinions held by such experts also extends to their identities. Decisions such as *Sucoe v Oakwood Hosp Corp*, 185 MichApp 484 (1990), *vacated in part* 439 Mich 914 (1992), have held that a party seeking the identity of such experts need not show exceptional circumstances. Others, such as *Ager v Jane C Stormont Hosp*, 622 F2d 496 (CA 10, 1980), have held that the extraordinary circumstances requirement does apply to identity. The amendment adopts the latter view.

The remaining changes in the language and structure of the rule are meant to clarify, rather than change, the current provision.

Staff Comment to 1994 Amendment

[Under the amendment effective September 1, 1994,] the language of former MCR 2.302(B)(1)(b) is moved to the deposition rule as new MCR 2.306(D)(4), and a cross reference to MCR 2.314 is added.

Staff Comment to 2008 Amendment

These amendments update Michigan's discovery rules as they relate to electronically stored information. The provisions of the proposal at MCR 2.302(B)(6) and MCR 2.506(A)(3) allow the court to shift the cost of discovery to the requesting party if discovery is requested from sources that are not reasonably accessible, and prohibit sanctions if information is lost or destroyed as a result of a good-faith, routine record destruction policy or "litigation hold" procedures. The "safe harbor" provision provided in MCR 2.302(B)(5) and in MCR 2.313 applies when information is lost or destroyed under a routine electronic information system, if the operation of the system was performed in good faith. Good faith may be shown by a party's actions to attempt to preserve information as part of a "litigation hold" that would otherwise have been lost or destroyed under an electronic information system.

The new language of MCR 2.302 and MCR 2.506 also allows parties to determine the format in which the information should be produced, and how to handle a situation in which protected information is inadvertently produced.

Staff Comment to 2013 Amendment

The amendments of these rules update the rules making them less "paper" focused and reflecting the use of electronic technology in the way courts process court records. The amendments also clarify and delineate the types of records and other materials maintained by a court, and clarify how access is provided.

Staff Comment to 2014 Amendment

The amendment of MCR 2.302 clarifies that discovery is available in post-judgment proceedings in domestic relations matters.

Staff Comment to 2015 Amendment

The amendment of MCR 2.302 allows any party to schedule a discovery-only deposition without the need to obtain stipulation of the other party or parties or approval of the court.

Staff Comment to 2020 Amendment

These amendments are based on a proposal created by a special committee of the State Bar of Michigan and approved for submission to the Court by the Bar's Representative Assembly. The rules require mandatory discovery disclosure in many cases, adopt a presumptive limit on interrogatories (20 in most cases, but 35 in domestic relations proceedings) and limit a deposition to 7 hours. The amendments also update the rules to more specifically address issues related to electronically stored information, and encourage early action on discovery issues during the discovery period.

The amendment of MCR 2.309(A)(2) sets a presumptive limit of twenty interrogatories for each separately represented party. Several commenters suggested that the term "discrete subpart" be more explicitly defined. But the rule's reference to "a discrete subpart" is intended to draw guidance from federal courts construing FR Civ P 30(a)(1). Generally, subparts are not separately counted if they are logically or factually subsumed within and necessarily related to the primary question. In upholding the limit, parties and courts should also pragmatically balance the overall goals of discovery and the admonition of MCR 1.105. Further, the intent of the provision at MCR 2.301(B)(4) is to ensure that parties responding to discovery requests have the full time period to do so as provided for under these rules prior to the expiration of the discovery period.

Rule 2.303 Depositions Before Action or Pending Appeal

(A) Before Action.

(1) *Petition.* A person who desires to perpetuate his or her own testimony or that of another person, for use as evidence and not for the purpose of discovery, regarding a matter that may be cognizable in a Michigan court may file a verified petition in the circuit court of the county of the residence of an expected adverse party. The petition must be entitled in the name of the petitioner and must show:

(a) that the petitioner expects to be a party to an action cognizable in a Michigan court but is presently unable to bring it or cause it to be brought and the reasons why;

(b) the subject matter of the expected action and the petitioner's interest in it;

(c) the facts sought to be established by the proposed testimony and the reasons for desiring to perpetuate it;

(d) the names or a description of the persons that the petitioner expects will be adverse parties and their addresses so far as known; and

(e) the names and addresses of the persons to be examined and the substance of the testimony that the petitioner expects to elicit from each.

The petition must ask for an order authorizing the petitioner to take the depositions of the persons to be examined named in the petition for the purpose of perpetuating their testimony.

(2) *Notice and Service.* The petitioner shall serve a notice on each person named in the petition as an expected adverse party, together with a copy of the petition, stating that the petitioner will apply to the court, at a specified time and place, for the order described in the petition. At least 21 days before the date of hearing, the notice must be served in the manner provided in MCR 2.105 for service of summons. If service cannot be made on an expected adverse party with due diligence, the court may issue an order as is just for service by publication or otherwise, and shall appoint, for persons not served in the manner provided in MCR 2.105, an attorney to represent them, and to cross-examine the deponent. If an expected adverse party is a minor or an incompetent person, the law relating to minors and incompetents, including MCR 2.201(E), applies.

(3) *Order and Examination.* If the court is satisfied that the perpetuation of the testimony may prevent a failure or delay of justice, it shall issue an order designating or describing the persons whose depositions may be taken and specifying the subject matter of the examination and whether the depositions

are to be taken on oral examination or written interrogatories. The depositions may then be taken in accordance with these rules. In addition the court may issue orders of the character provided for by MCR 2.310 and 2.311.

(4) *Use of Deposition.*

(a) If a deposition to perpetuate testimony is taken under these rules, it may be used in an action involving the same subject matter subsequently brought in a Michigan court, in accordance with MCR 2.308.

(b) If a deposition to perpetuate testimony has been taken under the Federal Rules of Civil Procedure, or the rules of another state, the court may, if it finds that the deposition was taken in substantial compliance with these rules, allow the deposition to be used as if it had been taken under these rules.

(B) Pending Appeal. If an appeal has been taken from a judgment of a trial court, or before the taking of an appeal if the time for appeal has not expired, the court in which the judgment was rendered may allow the taking of the depositions of witnesses to perpetuate their testimony for use if there are further proceedings in that court. The party who wishes to perpetuate the testimony may move for leave to take the depositions, with the same notice and service of the motion as if the action were then pending in the trial court. The motion must show

(1) the names and addresses of the persons to be examined and the substance of the testimony that the party expects to elicit from each; and

(2) the reasons for perpetuating their testimony.

If the court finds that the perpetuation of testimony is proper to avoid a failure or delay of justice, it may issue an order allowing the depositions to be taken and may issue orders of the character provided for by MCR 2.310 and 2.311. The depositions may then be taken and used in the same manner and under the same conditions prescribed in these rules for depositions taken in actions pending before the court.

[Adopted effective March 1, 1985.]

Comments

Staff Comment to 1985 Adoption

MCR 2.303 is similar to GCR 1963, 303, which was virtually identical to FR Civ P 27.

Under subrule (A)(4)(b), the fact that a deposition was taken in conformity with the rules of another jurisdiction does not necessarily make the deposition admissible. The rule merely puts such a deposition on the same footing as one taken under these rules.

Rule 2.304 Persons Before Whom Depositions May Be Taken

(A) Within the United States. Within the United States or within a territory or insular possession subject to the dominion of the United States, depositions may be taken

(1) before a person authorized to administer oaths by the laws of Michigan, the United States, or the place where the examination is held;

(2) before a person appointed by the court in which the action is pending; or

(3) before a person on whom the parties agree by stipulation under MCR 2.302(F)(1).

A person acting under subrule (A)(2) or (3) has the power to administer oaths, take testimony, and do all other acts necessary to take a deposition.

(B) In Foreign Countries. In a foreign country, depositions may be taken

(1) on notice before a person authorized to administer oaths in the place in which the examination is held, by either the law of that place or of the United States; or

(2) before a person commissioned by the court, and a person so commissioned has the power by virtue of the commission to administer a necessary oath and take testimony; or

(3) pursuant to a letter rogatory.

A commission or a letter rogatory may be issued on motion and notice and on terms that are just and appropriate. It is not requisite to the issuance of a commission or a letter rogatory that the taking of the deposition in another manner is impracticable or inconvenient; both a commission and a letter rogatory may be issued in a proper case. A notice or commission may designate the person before whom the deposition is to be taken either by name or descriptive title. A letter rogatory may be addressed "To the Appropriate Authority in [*name of country*]." Evidence obtained in response to a letter rogatory need not be excluded merely because it is not a verbatim transcript or the testimony was not taken under oath, or because of a similar departure from the requirements for depositions taken within the United States under these rules.

(C) Disqualification for Interest. Unless the parties agree otherwise by stipulation in writing or on the record, a deposition may not be taken before a person who is

(1) a relative or employee of or an attorney for a party,

(2) a relative or employee of an attorney for a party, or

(3) financially interested in the action.

[Adopted effective March 1, 1985.]

Comments

Staff Comment to 1985 Adoption

MCR 2.304 is comparable to GCR 1963, 304. However, subrule (B), regarding the taking of depositions in foreign countries, is changed to more closely parallel FR Civ P 28(b). Compare GCR 1963, 304.2.

Rule 2.305. Discovery Subpoena to a Non–Party

(A) General Provisions.

(1) A represented party may issue a subpoena to a non-party for a deposition, production or inspection of documents, inspection of tangible things, or entry to land upon court order or after all parties have had a reasonable opportunity to obtain an attorney, as determined under MCR 2.306(A). An unrepresented party may move the court for issuance of non-party discovery subpoenas. MCR 2.306(B)(1)–(2) and (C)–(G) apply to a subpoena under this rule. This rule governs discovery from a non-party under MCR 2.303(A)(4), 2.307, 2.310(D) or 2.315. MCR 2.506(A)(2) and (3) apply to any request for production of ESI. A subpoena for hospital records is governed by MCR 2.506(I).

(2) A subpoena may provide that it is solely for producing documents or other tangible things for inspection and copying, and that the party does not intend to examine the deponent. The subpoena shall specify whether an inspection is requested or whether the subpoena may be satisfied by delivering a copy

of the requested documents. Any request for documents shall indicate that the subpoenaing party will pay reasonable copying costs.

(3) A subpoena shall provide a minimum of 14 days after service of the subpoena (or a shorter time if the court directs) for the requested act. The subpoenaing party may file a motion to compel compliance with the subpoena under MCR 2.313(A). The motion must include a copy of the request and proof of service of the subpoena. The movant must serve the motion on the non-party as provided in MCR 2.105.

(4) A subpoena issued under this rule is subject to the provisions of MCR 2.302(C), and the court in which the action is pending or in which the subpoena is served, on timely motion made by a party or the subpoenaed non-party before the time specified in the subpoena for compliance, may:

(a) quash or modify the subpoena if it is unreasonable or oppressive;

(b) enter an order permitted by MCR 2.302(C); or

(c) conditionally deny the motion on prepayment by the party on whose behalf the subpoena is issued of the reasonable cost of producing documents or other tangible things.

The non-party's obligation to respond to the subpoena is stayed until the motion is resolved.

(5) Service of a subpoena on the deponent must be made as provided in MCR 2.506(G). A copy of the subpoena must be served on all other parties on the date of issuance.

(6) In a subpoena for a non-party deposition, a party may name as the deponent a public or private corporation, partnership, association, or governmental agency and describe with reasonable particularity the matters on which examination is requested. The subpoena shall be served at least 14 days prior to the scheduled deposition. No later than 10 days after being served with the subpoena, the subpoenaed entity may serve objections, or file a motion for protective order, upon which the party seeking discovery may either proceed on topics as to which there was no objection or move to enforce the subpoena. The organization named must designate one or more officers, directors, managing agents, or other persons, who consent to testify on its behalf, and may set forth, for each person designated, the matters on which the person will testify. The deposition of each produced witness may not exceed one day of seven hours. The persons designated shall testify to matters known or reasonably available to the organization.

(7) Upon written request from another party and payment of reasonable copying costs, the subpoenaing party shall provide copies of documents received pursuant to a subpoena.

(B) Place of Compliance. Except for a subpoena for delivery of copies of documents only under subrule (A)(2), a non-party served with a subpoena in Michigan may be required to comply with the subpoena only in the county where the deponent resides, is employed, has its principal place of business or transacts relevant business; or at the location of the things to be inspected or land to be entered; or at another convenient place specified by order of the court.

(C) Petition to Courts Outside Michigan. When the place of compliance is in another state, territory, or country, the subpoenaing party may petition a court of that state, territory, or country for a subpoena or equivalent process.

(D) Action Pending in Another Country. An officer or a person authorized by the laws of another country to issue a subpoena in Michigan, with or without a commission, in an action pending in a court of that country may submit an application to a court of record in the county in which the subpoenaed person resides, is employed, has its principal place of business, transacts relevant business, or is found, for a subpoena. The court may hear and act on the application with or without notice, as the court directs.

(E) Action Pending in Another State or Territory. A person may request issuance of a subpoena in this state for an action pending in another state or territory under the Uniform Interstate Depositions and Discovery Act, MCL 600.2201 *et seq.*, to require a person to attend a deposition, to produce and permit inspection and copying of materials, or to permit inspection of premises under the control of the person.

[Adopted effective March 1, 1985. Amended September 22, 1998, effective December 1, 1998, 459 Mich; October 2, 2013, effective January 1, 2014, 495 Mich; May 25, 2016, effective September 1, 2016, 499 Mich; June 19, 2019, effective January 1, 2020, 503 Mich.]

Comments

Staff Comment to 1985 Adoption

MCR 2.305 is based on GCR 1963, 305.

The main substantive change is the addition of subrule (B) covering the subject of subpoenas directing the production of documents or other tangible things. When such a subpoena is directed to a party deponent, the procedures of MCR 2.310, regarding requests to produce, apply.

In addition, in subrule (A)(1), the reference to the subpoena being issued by the clerk is deleted in view of the change in MCR 2.506, which permits subpoenas to be signed by the attorney for a party.

Staff Comment to 1998 Amendment

The amendment of Rule 2.305 was suggested by the Representative Assembly of the State Bar of Michigan. The changes made clear that nonparty records-only discovery subpoenas are authorized. The normal procedure for noticing a deposition applies to records-only subpoenas, and the procedure in MCR 2.310 still pertains to requests to a nonparty for entry on land or production of items for testing or sampling. The time for responding to a document subpoena or a document request under Rule 2.305(B)(1) was changed from seven to fourteen days. The amendment also made nonsubstantive changes to clarify and simplify language.

Staff Comment to 2014 Amendment

The changes of MCR 2.305 make subrule (E) applicable only to actions pending in another country, while new subrule (F) cross references the Uniform Interstate Depositions and Discovery Act, which establishes the procedures to be used in seeking a deposition or discovery subpoena in Michigan for use in an action that is pending in another state or territory.

Staff Comment to 2016 Amendment

The amendment of MCR 2.305 clarifies that subpoenas requesting the production of documents shall be issued only after defendant has had reasonable time after the complaint is filed and served to obtain an attorney, as described in MCR 2.306(A)(1).

Staff Comment to 2020 Amendment

These amendments are based on a proposal created by a special committee of the State Bar of Michigan and approved for submission to the Court by the Bar's Representative Assembly. The rules require mandatory discovery disclosure in many cases, adopt a presumptive limit on interrogatories (20 in most cases, but 35 in domestic relations proceedings) and limit a deposition to 7 hours. The amendments also update the rules to more specifically address issues related to electronically stored information, and encourage early action on discovery issues during the discovery period.

The amendment of MCR 2.309(A)(2) sets a presumptive limit of twenty interrogatories for each separately represented party. Several commenters suggested that the term "discrete subpart" be more explicitly defined. But the rule's reference to "a discrete subpart" is intended to draw guidance from federal courts construing FR Civ P 30(a)(1). Generally, subparts are not separately counted if they are logically or factually subsumed within and necessarily related to the primary question. In upholding the limit, parties and courts should also

pragmatically balance the overall goals of discovery and the admonition of MCR 1.105. Further, the intent of the provision at MCR 2.301(B)(4) is to ensure that parties responding to discovery requests have the full time period to do so as provided for under these rules prior to the expiration of the discovery period.

Rule 2.306. Depositions on Oral Examination of a Party

(A) When Depositions May Be Taken; Limits.

(1) Subject to MCR 2.301(A) and these rules, after commencement of the action, a party may take the testimony of a party by deposition on oral examination. Leave of court, granted with or without notice, must be obtained if the plaintiff seeks to take a deposition before the defendant has had a reasonable time to obtain an attorney. A reasonable time is deemed to have elapsed if:

(a) the defendant has filed an answer;

(b) the defendant's attorney has filed an appearance;

(c) the defendant has served notice of the taking of a deposition or has taken other action seeking discovery;

(d) the defendant has filed a motion under MCR 2.116; or

(e) 28 days have expired after service of the summons and complaint on a defendant or after service made under MCR 2.106.

(2) The deposition of a person confined in prison or of a patient in a state home, institution, or hospital for the mentally ill or mentally handicapped, or any other state hospital, home, or institution, may be taken only by leave of court on terms as the court provides.

(3) A deposition may not exceed one day of seven hours.

(B) Notice of Examination; Production of Documents and Things.

(1) A party desiring to take the deposition of a party on oral examination must give reasonable notice in writing to every other party to the action. The notice must state:

(a) the time and place for taking the deposition, and

(b) the name and address of each person to be examined, if known, or, if the name is not known, a general description sufficient to identify the person or the particular class or group to which the person belongs.

(2) The notice may be accompanied by a request for the production of documents and tangible things at the taking of the deposition. MCR 2.310 applies to the request.

(3) In a notice, a party may name as the deponent a public or private corporation, partnership, association, or governmental agency and describe with reasonable particularity the matters on which examination is requested. The notice shall be served at least 14 days prior to the scheduled deposition. No later than 10 days after being served with the notice, the noticed entity may serve objections or file a motion for protective order, upon which the party seeking discovery may either proceed on topics as to which there was no objection or motion, or move to enforce the notice. The organization named must designate one or more officers, directors, or managing agents, or other persons, who consent to testify on its behalf, and may set forth, for each person designated, the matters on which the person will testify. The deposition of each produced witness may not exceed one day of seven hours. The persons designated shall testify to matters known or reasonably available to the organi-

zation. This subrule does not preclude taking a deposition by another procedure authorized in these rules.

(C) Conduct of Deposition; Examination and Cross-Examination; Manner of Recording; Objections; Communicating with Deponent.

(1) *Examination of Deponent.*

(a) The person before whom the deposition is to be taken must put the witness on oath.

(b) Examination and cross-examination of the witness shall proceed as permitted at a trial under the Michigan Rules of Evidence.

(c) In lieu of participating in the oral examination, a party may send written questions to the person conducting the examination, who shall propound them to the witness and record the witness's answers.

(2) *Recording of Deposition.* The person before whom the deposition is taken shall personally, or by someone acting under his or her direction and in his or her presence, record the testimony of the witness.

(a) The testimony must be taken stenographically or recorded by other means in accordance with this subrule. The testimony need not be transcribed unless requested by one of the parties.

(b) While the testimony is being taken, a party, as a matter of right, may also make a record of it by nonsecret mechanical or electronic means, except that video recording is governed by MCR 2.315. Any use of the recording in court is within the discretion of the court. A person making such a record must furnish a duplicate of the record to another party at the request and expense of the other party.

(3) *Recording by Nonstenographic Means.* The court may order, or the parties may stipulate, that the testimony at a deposition be recorded by other than stenographic means.

(a) The order or stipulation must designate the manner of recording and preserving the deposition, and may include other provisions to assure that the recorded testimony will be accurate and trustworthy. A deposition in the form of a recording may be filed with the court as are other depositions.

(b) If a deposition is taken by other than stenographic means on order of the court, a party may nevertheless arrange to have a stenographic transcription made at that party's own expense.

(c) Before a deposition taken by other than stenographic means may be used in court it must be transcribed unless the court enters an order waiving transcription. The costs of transcription are borne by the parties as determined by the court.

(d) Subrule (C)(3) does not apply to video depositions, which are governed by MCR 2.315.

(4) *Objections During Deposition.*

(a) All objections made at the deposition, including objections to

(i) the qualifications of the person taking the deposition,

(ii) the manner of taking it,

(iii) the evidence presented, or

(iv) the conduct of a party, must be noted on the record by the person before whom the deposition is taken. Subject to limitation imposed by an order under MCR 2.302(C) or subrule (D) of this rule, evidence objected to on grounds other than privilege shall be taken subject to the objections.

(b) An objection during a deposition must be stated concisely in a civil and nonsuggestive manner.

(c) Objections are limited to

(i) objections that would be waived under MCR 2.308(C)(2) or (3), and

(ii) those necessary to preserve a privilege or other legal protection or to enforce a limitation ordered by the court.

(5) *Communicating with Deponent.*

(a) A person may instruct a deponent not to answer only when necessary to preserve a privilege or other legal protection, to enforce a limitation ordered by the court, or to present a motion under MCR 2.306(D)(1).

(b) A deponent may not communicate with another person while a question is pending, except to decide whether to assert a privilege or other legal protection.

(c) For purposes of this rule, "communicate" includes electronic communication conducted by text message, email or other transmission using an electronic device.

(D) Motion to Terminate or Limit Examination; Sanctions; Asserting Privilege.

(1) *Motion.* At any time during the taking of the deposition, on motion of a party or of the deponent and on a showing that the examination is being conducted in bad faith or in a manner unreasonably to annoy, embarrass, or oppress the deponent or party, or that the matter inquired about is privileged, a court in which the action is pending or the court in the county or district where the deposition is being taken may order the person conducting the examination to cease taking the deposition, or may limit the scope and manner of the taking of the deposition as provided in MCR 2.302(C). If the order entered terminates the examination, it may resume only on order of the court in which the action is pending.

(2) *Sanctions.* On motion, the court may impose an appropriate sanction—including the reasonable expenses and attorney fees incurred by any party—on a person who impedes, delays, or frustrates the fair examination of the deponent or otherwise violates this rule.

(3) *Suspending Deposition.* On demand of the objecting party or deponent, the taking of the deposition must be suspended for the time necessary to move for an order. MCR 2.313(A)(5) applies to the award of expenses incurred in relation to the motion.

(4) *Raising Privilege Before Deposition.* If a party knows before the time scheduled for the taking of a deposition that he or she will assert that the matter to be inquired about is privileged, the party must move to prevent the taking of the deposition before its occurrence or be subject to costs under subrule (G).

(5) *Failure to Assert Privilege.* A party who has a privilege regarding part or all of the testimony of a deponent must either assert the privilege at the deposition or lose the privilege as to that testimony for purposes of the action. A party who claims a

privilege at a deposition may not at the trial offer the testimony of the deponent pertaining to the evidence objected to at the deposition. A party who asserts a privilege regarding medical information is subject to the provisions of MCR 2.314(B).

(E) Exhibits. Documents and things produced for inspection during the examination of the witness must, on the request of a party, be marked for identification and annexed to the deposition, if practicable, and may be inspected and copied by a party, except as follows:

(1) The person producing the materials may substitute copies to be marked for identification, if he or she affords to all parties fair opportunity to verify the copies by comparison with the originals.

(2) If the person producing the materials requests their return, the person conducting the examination or the stenographer must mark them, give each party an opportunity to inspect and copy them, and return them to the person producing them, and the materials may then be used in the same manner as if annexed to the deposition. A party may move for an order that the original be annexed to and filed with the deposition, pending final disposition of the action.

(F) Certification and Transcription; Filing; Copies.

(1) If transcription is requested by a party, the person conducting the examination or the stenographer must certify on the deposition that the witness was duly sworn and that the deposition is a true record of the testimony given by the witness. A deposition transcribed and certified in accordance with subrule (F) need not be submitted to the witness for examination and signature.

(2) On payment of reasonable charges, the person conducting the examination shall furnish a copy of the deposition to a party or to the deponent. Where transcription is requested by a party other than the party requesting the deposition, the court may order, or the parties may stipulate, that the expense of transcription or a portion of it be paid by the party making the request.

(3) Except as provided in subrule (C)(3) or in MCR 2.315(E), a deposition may not be filed with the court unless it has first been transcribed. If a party requests that the transcript be filed, the person conducting the examination or the stenographer shall, after transcription and certification:

(a) securely seal the transcript in an envelope endorsed with the title and file number of the action and marked "Deposition of [*name of witness,*]" and promptly file it with the court in which the action is pending or send it by registered or certified mail to the clerk of that court for filing;

(b) give prompt notice of its filing to all other parties, unless the parties agree otherwise by stipulation in writing or on the record.

(G) Failure to Attend or to Serve Subpoena; Expenses.

(1) If the party giving the notice of the taking of a deposition fails to attend and proceed with the deposition and another party attends in person or by attorney pursuant to the notice, the court may order the party giving the notice to pay to the other party the reasonable expenses incurred in attending, including reasonable attorney fees.

(2) If the party giving the notice of the taking of a deposition of a witness fails to serve a subpoena on the witness, and the witness because of the failure does not attend, and if another party attends in person or by attorney because he or she expects the deposition of that witness to be taken, the court may order the party giving the notice to pay to the other party the reasonable expenses incurred in attending, including reasonable attorney fees.

[Adopted effective March 1, 1985. Amended June 7, 1994, effective September 1, 1994, 445 Mich; May 30, 2008, effective September 1, 2008, 480 Mich; June 30, 2008, effective September 30, 2008, 481 Mich; May 25, 2016, effective September 1, 2016, 499 Mich; June 19, 2019, effective January 1, 2020, 503 Mich.]

Comments

Staff Comment to 1985 Adoption

MCR 2.306 contains the basic deposition procedures drawn from GCR 1963, 302 and 306 and FR Civ P 30.

Subrule (A) covers when depositions may be taken. The only limitation is on depositions taken by the plaintiff. GCR 1963, 302.1 simply provided that they could be taken after commencement of the action, and FR Civ P 30(a) permits a plaintiff to take a deposition 30 days after service of the summons and complaint. Subrule (A)(1) lists the events that trigger the plaintiff's right to take a deposition.

Subrule (A)(2) carries forward the requirement of GCR 1963, 302.2(2) that the deposition of a person confined in a prison or state institution may be taken only by leave of the court.

Subrule (B) contains the various notice provisions, some of which were covered by GCR 1963, 306.1. Subrules (B)(4) and (5) are comparable to FR Civ P 30(b)(5) and (6), and were not found in the former Michigan rules.

Subrule (C) brings together various provisions regarding the conduct and recording of depositions, found in GCR 1963, 302.3 and 306.4, and FR Civ P 30(b)(4) and (c).

Subrule (D) is comparable to GCR 1963, 306.4. Subrule (D)(3) is new. A deponent who knows that he or she will assert a privilege at the deposition is required to raise the matter by motion in advance or be subject to costs.

Subrule (E) adds the substance of FR Civ P 30(f), regarding the annexing of documents and things produced for inspection at a deposition.

Subrule (F) includes the provisions on certification, transcription, and filing of depositions, the subject formerly covered by GCR 1963, 306.6. The filing provisions are modified in light of MCR 2.302(H). Subrule (F)(1) eliminates the requirement, previously found in GCR 1963, 306.5 (and FR Civ P 30[b][4]), that the deposition transcript be submitted to the witness for review and signing. Parties would not be prohibited from doing so, however.

Subrule (G) is substantially the same as GCR 1963, 306.7 (and FR Civ P 30[g]).

Staff Comment to 1994 Amendment

[Under the September 1, 1994 amendment,] the language of former MCR 2.302(B)(1)(b) is moved to the deposition rule as new MCR 2.306(D)(4), and a cross reference to MCR 2.314 is added.

Staff Comment to 2008 Amendment

These amendments require that objections to questions asked at a deposition be concise, and be stated in a civil and nonsuggestive manner. The purpose of these amendments is to prohibit the practice of counsel interposing "speaking objections" that are designed to instruct the witness. Further, the amendments require that objections and instructions not to answer a question be limited to a claim of privilege or other legal basis, and prohibit a deponent from conferring with anyone while a question is pending, except to confer with counsel regarding assertion of a privilege or other legal protection. Finally, the amendments add specific language allowing a court to impose sanctions, including reasonable attorney fees and costs, on a person who impedes, delays, or frustrates the fair examination of the deponent or otherwise violates the rule.

Staff Comment to 2016 Amendment

The amendments of MCR 2.306(C)(5) and (C)(5)(b) replace references to the word "conferring" or "confer" with "communicating" or "communicate." The amendment of MCR 2.306(C)(5)(c) clarifies that the term "communicate" includes electronic transmission by text message, email or other electronic manner.

Staff Comment to 2020 Amendment

These amendments are based on a proposal created by a special committee of the State Bar of Michigan and approved for submission to the Court by the Bar's Representative Assembly. The rules require mandatory discovery disclosure in many cases, adopt a presumptive limit on interrogatories (20 in most cases, but 35 in domestic relations proceedings) and limit a deposition to 7 hours. The amendments also update the rules to more specifically address issues related to electronically stored information, and encourage early action on discovery issues during the discovery period.

The amendment of MCR 2.309(A)(2) sets a presumptive limit of twenty interrogatories for each separately represented party. Several commenters suggested that the term "discrete subpart" be more explicitly defined. But the rule's reference to "a discrete subpart" is intended to draw guidance from federal courts construing FR Civ P 30(a)(1). Generally, subparts are not separately counted if they are logically or factually subsumed within and necessarily related to the primary question. In upholding the limit, parties and courts should also pragmatically balance the overall goals of discovery and the admonition of MCR 1.105. Further, the intent of the provision at MCR 2.301(B)(4) is to ensure that parties responding to discovery requests have the full time period to do so as provided for under these rules prior to the expiration of the discovery period.

Rule 2.307. Depositions on Written Questions

(A) Serving Questions; Notice.

(1) Under the same circumstances and under the same limitations as set out in MCR 2.305(A) and MCR 2.306(A), a party may take the testimony of a person, including a party, by deposition on written questions. The attendance of non-party witnesses may be compelled by the use of a subpoena as provided in MCR 2.305. A deposition on written questions may be taken of a public or private corporation or partnership or association or governmental agency in accordance with the provisions of MCR 2.305(A)(6) or 2.306(B)(3).

(2) A party desiring to take a deposition on written questions shall serve them on every other party with a notice stating

(a) the name and address of the person who is to answer them, if known, and, if the name is not known, a general description sufficient to identify the person or the particular class or group to which the person belongs; and

(b) the name or descriptive title and address of the person before whom the deposition is to be taken.

(3) Within 14 days after the notice and written questions are served, a party may serve cross-questions on all other parties. Within 7 days after being served with cross-questions, a party may serve redirect questions on all other parties. Within 7 days after being served with redirect questions, a party may serve recross-questions on all other parties. The parties, by stipulation in writing, or the court, for cause shown, may extend or shorten the time requirements.

(B) Taking of Responses and Preparation of Record.
A copy of the notice, any stipulation, and copies of all questions served must be delivered by the party who proposed the deposition to the person before whom the deposition will be taken as stated in the notice. The person before whom the deposition is to be taken must proceed promptly to take the testimony of the witness in response to the questions, and, if requested, to transcribe, certify, and file the deposition in the manner provided by MCR 2.306(C), (E), and (F), attaching the copy of the notice, the questions, and any stipulations of the parties.

[Adopted effective March 1, 1985. Amended June 19, 2019, effective January 1, 2020, 503 Mich.]

Comments

Staff Comment to 1985 Adoption

MCR 2.307 is comparable to GCR 1963, 307.

The rule is modified (including the deletion of former GCR 1963, 307.3) because of the change in the rules regarding filing of discovery materials. See MCR 2.302(H).

The language of former GCR 1963, 307.4 is deleted; the subject of protective orders is covered by the general discovery provisions in MCR 2.302(C).

Staff Comment to 2020 Amendment

These amendments are based on a proposal created by a special committee of the State Bar of Michigan and approved for submission to the Court by the Bar's Representative Assembly. The rules require mandatory discovery disclosure in many cases, adopt a presumptive limit on interrogatories (20 in most cases, but 35 in domestic relations proceedings) and limit a deposition to 7 hours. The amendments also update the rules to more specifically address issues related to electronically stored information, and encourage early action on discovery issues during the discovery period.

The amendment of MCR 2.309(A)(2) sets a presumptive limit of twenty interrogatories for each separately represented party. Several commenters suggested that the term "discrete subpart" be more explicitly defined. But the rule's reference to "a discrete subpart" is intended to draw guidance from federal courts construing FR Civ P 30(a)(1). Generally, subparts are not separately counted if they are logically or factually subsumed within and necessarily related to the primary question. In upholding the limit, parties and courts should also pragmatically balance the overall goals of discovery and the admonition of MCR 1.105. Further, the intent of the provision at MCR 2.301(B)(4) is to ensure that parties responding to discovery requests have the full time period to do so as provided for under these rules prior to the expiration of the discovery period.

Rule 2.308 Use of Depositions in Court Proceedings

(A) In General. Depositions or parts thereof shall be admissible at trial or on the hearing of a motion or in an interlocutory proceeding only as provided in the Michigan Rules of Evidence.

(B) Objections to Admissibility. Subject to the provisions of subrule (C) and MCR 2.306(C)(4), objection may be made at the trial or hearing to receiving in evidence a deposition or part of a deposition for any reason that would require the exclusion of the evidence.

(C) Effect of Errors or Irregularities in Depositions.

(1) *Notice.* Errors or irregularities in the notice for taking a deposition are waived unless written objection is promptly served on the party giving notice.

(2) *Disqualification of Person Before Whom Taken.* Objection to taking a deposition because of disqualification of the person before whom it is to be taken is waived unless made before the taking of the deposition begins or as soon thereafter as the disqualification becomes known or could be discovered with reasonable diligence.

(3) *Taking of Deposition.*

(a) Objections to the competency of a witness or to the competency, relevancy, or materiality of testimony are not waived by failure to make them before or during the taking of a deposition, unless the ground of the objection is one which might have been obviated or removed if presented at that time.

(b) Errors and irregularities occurring at the deposition in the manner of taking the deposition, in the form of the questions or answers, in the oath or affirmation, or in the conduct of parties and errors of any other kind which might be cured if promptly presented, are waived unless seasonable objection is made at the taking of the deposition.

(c) Objections to the form of written questions submitted under MCR 2.307 are waived unless served in writing on the party propounding them within the time allowed for serving the succeeding cross-questions or other questions and within 7 days after service of the last questions authorized.

(d) On motion and notice a party may request a ruling by the court on an objection in advance of the trial.

(4) Certification, Transcription, and Filing of Deposition. Errors and irregularities in the manner in which the testimony is transcribed or the deposition is prepared, signed, certified, sealed, endorsed, transmitted, filed, or otherwise dealt with by the person before whom it was taken are waived unless a motion objecting to the deposition is filed within a reasonable time.

(5) Harmless Error. None of the foregoing errors or irregularities, even when not waived, or any others, preclude or restrict the use of the deposition, except insofar as the court finds that the errors substantially destroy the value of the deposition as evidence or render its use unfair or prejudicial.

[Adopted effective March 1, 1985. Amended July 24, 1989, effective December 1, 1989, 432 Mich.]

Comments

Staff Comment to 1985 Adoption

MCR 2.308 brings together the various provisions on use of depositions in court proceedings previously found in GCR 1963, 302.4, 302.5, and 308. It is very similar to FR Civ P 32. The federal rule, however, does not include the harmless error provision found in subrule (C)(5) (and GCR 1963, 308.5).

The rule does not include the language previously found in GCR 1963, 302.4(4), providing that when a party introduces only part of a deposition, another party may introduce other parts. That subject is now covered by MRE 106.

Staff Comment to 1989 Amendment

Former subrule (A) mostly duplicated provisions in the Michigan Rules of Evidence. See, e.g., MRE 106, 803(18), and 804. The [December 1, 1989] amendment eliminates the overlap, and the possibility of conflict, by explicitly deferring to the MRE provisions. MRE 804(b) [was] amended concurrently.

Rule 2.309.   Interrogatories to Parties

(A) Availability; Procedure for Service; Limits.

(1) A party may serve on another party written interrogatories to be answered by the party served or, if the party served is a public or private corporation, partnership, association, or governmental agency, by an officer or agent. Subject to MCR 2.302(B), interrogatories may, without leave of court, be served:

(a) on the plaintiff after commencement of the action or

(b) on a defendant with or after the service of the summons and complaint on that defendant.

(2) Each separately represented party may serve no more than twenty interrogatories upon each party. A discrete subpart of an interrogatory counts as a separate interrogatory.

(B) Answers and Objections.

(1) Each interrogatory must be answered separately and fully in writing under oath. The answers must include such information as is available to the party served or that the party could obtain from his or her employees, agents, representatives, sureties, or indemnitors. If the answering party objects to an interrogatory, the reasons for the objection must be stated in lieu of an answer.

(2) The answering party shall repeat each interrogatory or subquestion immediately before the answer to it.

(3) The answers must be signed by the person making them and the objections signed by the attorney or an unrepresented party making them.

(4) The party on whom the interrogatories are served must serve the answers and objections, if any, on all other parties within 28 days after the interrogatories are served, except that a defendant may serve answers within 42 days after being served with the summons and complaint. The court may allow a longer or shorter time and, for good cause shown, may excuse service on parties other than the party who served the interrogatories.

(C) Motion to Compel Answers. The party submitting the interrogatories may move for an order under MCR 2.313(A) with respect to an objection to or other failure to answer an interrogatory. If the motion is based on the failure to serve answers, proof of service of the interrogatories must be filed with the motion. The motion must state that the movant has in good faith conferred or attempted to confer with the party not making the disclosure in an effort to secure the disclosure without court action.

(D) Scope; Use at Trial.

(1) An interrogatory may relate to matters that can be inquired into under MCR 2.302(B).

(2) An interrogatory otherwise proper is not necessarily objectionable merely because an answer to the interrogatory involves an opinion or contention that relates to fact or the application of law to fact, but the court may order that an interrogatory need not be answered until after designated discovery has been completed or until a pretrial conference or other later time.

(3) The answer to an interrogatory may be used to the extent permitted by the rules of evidence.

(E) Option to Produce Business Records. Where the answer to an interrogatory may be derived from

(1) the business records of the party on whom the interrogatory has been served,

(2) an examination, audit, or inspection of business records, or

(3) a compilation, abstract, or summary based on such records,

and the burden of deriving the answer is substantially the same for the party serving the interrogatory as for the party served, it is a sufficient answer to the interrogatory to specify the records from which the answer may be derived and to afford to the party serving the interrogatory reasonable opportunity to examine, audit, or inspect the records and to make copies, compilations, abstracts, or summaries. A specification shall be in sufficient detail to permit the interrogating party to identify, as readily as can the party served, the records from which the answer may be derived.

[Adopted effective March 1, 1985. Amended July 16, 2002, effective January 1, 2003, 466 Mich; June 19, 2019, effective January 1, 2020, 503 Mich.]

Comments

Staff Comment to 1985 Adoption

MCR 2.309 is drawn from GCR 1963, 309 and FR CIV P 33.

The time provisions are changed to roughly coincide with those of FR Civ P 33(a): the party served has 28 days to answer (versus 15 days in GCR 1963, 309.2). The defendant may answer within 42 days after being served with the summons and complaint, if the interrogatories are served with or soon after the summons and complaint. There was a related provision in GCR 1963, 309.1—the plaintiff must wait 10 days after commencing the action before serving interrogatories.

Subrule (B)(3) adds a requirement that the answering party repeat the interrogatory immediately before the answer.

The burden of bringing disputes regarding interrogatories to the attention of the court by motion is placed on the party submitting the interrogatories, rather than the answering party. Compare subrule (C) with GCR 1963, 309.3.

Consistent with the other provisions on the scope of discovery, subrule (D)(2) adopts language from FR Civ P 33(b) providing that interrogatories may seek answers that involve opinions or application of law to fact.

Under subrule (D)(3) use of interrogatories is governed by the rules of evidence. GCR 1963, 309.4 incorporated the rule regarding use of depositions.

Subrule (E) adopts the substance of FR Civ P 33(c), giving the answering party the option to produce business records in certain circumstances.

Staff Comment to 2002 Amendment

The July 16, 2002 amendments of subrules 2.309(C), 2.310(C)(3), and 2.312(3), effective January 1, 2003, require that discovery motions include a statement that the movant has in good faith conferred or attempted to confer with the party not making the disclosure in an effort to secure the disclosure without court action. Subrule 2.310(C)(6) was added to clarify the respective responsibilities for the costs of discovery.

Staff Comment to 2020 Amendment

These amendments are based on a proposal created by a special committee of the State Bar of Michigan and approved for submission to the Court by the Bar's Representative Assembly. The rules require mandatory discovery disclosure in many cases, adopt a presumptive limit on interrogatories (20 in most cases, but 35 in domestic relations proceedings) and limit a deposition to 7 hours. The amendments also update the rules to more specifically address issues related to electronically stored information, and encourage early action on discovery issues during the discovery period.

The amendment of MCR 2.309(A)(2) sets a presumptive limit of twenty interrogatories for each separately represented party. Several commenters suggested that the term "discrete subpart" be more explicitly defined. But the rule's reference to "a discrete subpart" is intended to draw guidance from federal courts construing FR Civ P 30(a)(1). Generally, subparts are not separately counted if they are logically or factually subsumed within and necessarily related to the primary question. In upholding the limit, parties and courts should also pragmatically balance the overall goals of discovery and the admonition of MCR 1.105. Further, the intent of the provision at MCR 2.301(B)(4) is to ensure that parties responding to discovery requests have the full time period to do so as provided for under these rules prior to the expiration of the discovery period.

Rule 2.310. Requests for Production of Documents and Other Things; Entry on Land for Inspection and Other Purposes

(A) Definitions. For the purpose of this subchapter,

(1) "Documents" includes writings, drawings, graphs, charts, photographs, sound recordings, images, and other data or data compilations stored in any medium, including ESI.

(2) "ESI" means electronically stored information, regardless of format, system, or properties.

(3) "Entry on land" means entry upon designated land or other property in the possession or control of the person on whom the request is served for the purpose of inspecting, measuring, surveying, photographing, testing, or sampling the property or a designated object or operation on the property, within the scope of MCR 2.302(B).

(B) Scope.

(1) A party may serve on another party a request

(a) to produce and permit the requesting party, or someone acting for that party,

(i) to inspect and copy designated documents or

(ii) to inspect and copy, test, or sample other tangible things that constitute or contain matters within the scope of MCR 2.302(B) and that are in the possession, custody, or control of the party on whom the request is served; or

(b) to permit entry on land.

(2) A party may serve on a nonparty a request

(a) to produce and permit the requesting party or someone acting for that party to inspect and test or sample tangible things that constitute or contain matters within the scope of

MCR 2.302(B) and that are in the possession, custody, or control of the person on whom the request is served; or

(b) to permit entry on land.

(C) Request to Party.

(1) The request may, without leave of court, be served on the plaintiff after commencement of the action and on the defendant with or after the service of the summons and complaint on that defendant. The request must list the items to be inspected, either by individual item or by category, and describe each item and category with reasonable particularity. The request must specify a reasonable time, place, and manner of making the inspection and performing the related acts, as well as the form or forms in which electronically stored information is to be produced, subject to objection.

(2) The party on whom the request is served must serve a written response within 28 days after service of the request, except that a defendant may serve a response within 42 days after being served with the summons and complaint. The court may allow a longer or shorter time. With respect to each item or category, the response must state that inspection and related activities will be permitted as requested or that the request is objected to, in which event the reasons for objection must be stated. If objection is made to part of an item or category, the part must be specified. If the request does not specify the form or forms in which electronically stored information is to be produced, the party responding to the request must produce the information in a form or forms in which the party ordinarily maintains it, or in a form or forms that is or are reasonably usable. A party producing electronically stored information need only produce the same information in one form.

(3) The party submitting the request may move for an order under MCR 2.313(A) with respect to an objection to or a failure to respond to the request or a part of it, or failure to permit inspection as requested. If the motion is based on a failure to respond to a request, proof of service of the request must be filed with the motion. The motion must state that the movant has in good faith conferred or attempted to confer with the party not making the disclosure in an effort to secure the disclosure without court action.

(4) The party to whom the request is submitted may seek a protective order under MCR 2.302(C).

(5) A party who produces documents for inspection shall produce them as they are kept in the usual course of business or shall organize and label them to correspond with the categories in the request.

(6) Unless otherwise ordered by the court for good cause, the party producing items for inspection shall bear the cost of assembling them and the party requesting the items shall bear any copying costs.

[Adopted effective March 1, 1985. Amended September 22, 1998, effective December 1, 1998, 459 Mich; June 21, 2000, effective September 1, 2000, 462 Mich; July 16, 2002, effective January 1, 2003, 466 Mich; December 16, 2008, effective January 1, 2009, 482 Mich; June 19, 2019, effective January 1, 2020, 503 Mich.]

Comments

Staff Comment to 1985 Adoption

MCR 2.310 is based on FR Civ P 34.

The rule adopts the federal formulation of requiring a party to serve a request for production of documents or things or permission to enter land before seeking a court order as was required by GCR 1963, 310.1. The time provisions are similar to those of FR Civ P 34(b)—the party served with the request has 28 days to respond (except that a defendant has at least 42 days after being served with the summons and complaint).

In subrule (C) a new procedure is created for serving a request to produce or permit entry on land on a nonparty. Both the former Michigan rule (GCR 1963, 310) and FR Civ P 34 limit the procedure to requests to parties, although they leave open the possibility of independent actions against nonparties. The procedure parallels that for requests to parties, although service of both the request and of any subsequent motion must be made in the manner provided by MCR 2.105. Subrule (C)(5) permits the court to order the party seeking discovery to pay reasonable expenses incurred by the person complying with the request.

The [March 1, 1985] amendment of MCR 2.310(C)(1) makes more specific the cross-reference to MCR 2.306.

Staff Comment to 1998 Amendment

The amendment of Rule 2.310 was suggested by the Representative Assembly of the State Bar of Michigan. The changes made clear that nonparty records-only discovery subpoenas are authorized. The normal procedure for noticing a deposition applies to records-only subpoenas, and the procedure in MCR 2.310 still pertains to requests to a nonparty for entry on land or production of items for testing or sampling. The time for responding under Rule 2.310(C)(2) was changed from 28 to 14 days. The amendment also made nonsubstantive changes to clarify and simplify language.

Staff Comment to 2000 Amendment

The June 21, 2000 amendment of MCR 2.310(C)(2), effective September 1, 2000, increased the period from 14 to 28 days the time for a party to respond to a request under the court rule. The change was recommended by the Representative Assembly of the State Bar of Michigan.

Staff Comment to 2002 Amendment

The July 16, 2002 amendments of subrules 2.309(C), 2.310(C)(3), and 2.312(3), effective January 1, 2003, require that discovery motions include a statement that the movant has in good faith conferred or attempted to confer with the party not making the disclosure in an effort to secure the disclosure without court action. Subrule 2.310(C)(6) was added to clarify the respective responsibilities for the costs of discovery.

Staff Comment to 2008 Amendment

These amendments update Michigan's discovery rules as they relate to electronically stored information. The provisions of the proposal at MCR 2.302(B)(6) and MCR 2.506(A)(3) allow the court to shift the cost of discovery to the requesting party if discovery is requested from sources that are not reasonably accessible, and prohibit sanctions if information is lost or destroyed as a result of a good-faith, routine record destruction policy or "litigation hold" procedures. The "safe harbor" provision provided in MCR 2.302(B)(5) and in MCR 2.313 applies when information is lost or destroyed under a routine electronic information system, if the operation of the system was performed in good faith. Good faith may be shown by a party's actions to attempt to preserve information as part of a "litigation hold" that would otherwise have been lost or destroyed under an electronic information system.

The new language of MCR 2.302 and MCR 2.506 also allows parties to determine the format in which the information should be produced, and how to handle a situation in which protected information is inadvertently produced.

Staff Comment to 2020 Amendment

These amendments are based on a proposal created by a special committee of the State Bar of Michigan and approved for submission to the Court by the Bar's Representative Assembly. The rules require mandatory discovery disclosure in many cases, adopt a presumptive limit on interrogatories (20 in most cases, but 35 in domestic relations proceedings) and limit a deposition to 7 hours. The amendments also update the rules to more specifically address issues related to electronically stored information, and encourage early action on discovery issues during the discovery period.

The amendment of MCR 2.309(A)(2) sets a presumptive limit of twenty interrogatories for each separately represented party. Several commenters suggested that the term "discrete subpart" be more explicitly defined. But the rule's reference to "a discrete subpart" is intended to draw guidance from federal courts construing FR Civ P 30(a)(1). Generally, subparts are not separately counted if they are logically or factually subsumed within and necessarily related to the primary question. In upholding the limit, parties and courts should also pragmatically balance the overall goals of discovery and the admonition of MCR 1.105. Further, the intent of the provision at MCR 2.301(B)(4) is to ensure that parties responding to discovery requests have the full time period to do so as provided for under these rules prior to the expiration of the discovery period.

Rule 2.311   Physical and Mental Examination of Persons

(A) Order for Examination. When the mental or physical condition (including the blood group) of a party, or of a person in the custody or under the legal control of a party, is in controversy, the court in which the action is pending may order the party to submit to a physical or mental or blood examination by a physician (or other appropriate professional) or to produce for examination the person in the party's custody or legal control. The order may be entered only on motion for good cause with notice to the person to be examined and to all parties. The order must specify the time, place, manner, conditions, and scope of the examination and the person or persons by whom it is to be made, and may provide that the attorney for the person to be examined may be present at the examination.

(B) Report of Examining Physician.

(1) If requested by the party against whom an order is entered under subrule (A) or by the person examined, the party causing the examination to be made must deliver to the requesting person a copy of a detailed written report of the examining physician setting out the findings, including results of all tests made, diagnosis, and conclusions, together with like reports on all earlier examinations of the same condition, and must make available for inspection and examination x-rays, cardiograms, and other diagnostic aids.

(2) After delivery of the report, the party causing the examination to be made is entitled on request to receive from the party against whom the order is made a similar report of any examination previously or thereafter made of the same condition, and to a similar inspection of all diagnostic aids unless, in the case of a report on the examination of a nonparty, the party shows that he or she is unable to obtain it.

(3) If either party or a person examined refuses to deliver a report, the court on motion and notice may enter an order requiring delivery on terms as are just, and if a physician refuses or fails to comply with this rule, the court may order the physician to appear for a discovery deposition.

(4) By requesting and obtaining a report on the examination ordered under this rule, or by taking the deposition of the examiner, the person examined waives any privilege he or she may have in that action, or another action involving the same controversy, regarding the testimony of every other person who has examined or may thereafter examine the person as to the same mental or physical condition.

(5) Subrule (B) applies to examinations made by agreement of the parties, unless the agreement expressly provides otherwise.

(6) Subrule (B) does not preclude discovery of a report of an examining physician or the taking of a deposition of the physician under any other rule.

[Adopted effective March 1, 1985.]

Comments

Staff Comment to 1985 Adoption

MCR 2.311 is based on GCR 1963, 311 and FR Civ P 35.

In the last sentence of subrule (A), the word "must" is changed to "may", allowing the trial court to direct that the examination take place without the attorney for the party being examined present.

New subrule (B)(5) is added to make clear that the provisions also apply to examinations conducted by agreement of the parties, unless the agreement provides otherwise.

Rule 2.312. Request For Admission

(A) Availability; Scope. Within the time for completion of discovery, a party may serve on another party a written request for the admission of the truth of a matter within the scope of MCR 2.302(B) stated in the request that relates to statements or opinions of fact or the application of law to fact, including the genuineness of documents described in the request. Copies of the documents must be served with the request unless they have been or are otherwise furnished or made available for inspection and copying. The request must clearly identify in the caption and before each request that it is a Request for Admission. Each matter of which an admission is requested must be stated separately.

(B) Answer; Objection.

(1) Each matter as to which a request is made is deemed admitted unless, within 28 days after service of the request, or within a shorter or longer time as the court may allow, the party to whom the request is directed serves on the party requesting the admission a written answer or objection addressed to the matter. Unless the court orders a shorter time a defendant may serve an answer or objection within 42 days after being served with the summons and complaint.

(2) The answer must specifically deny the matter or state in detail the reasons why the answering party cannot truthfully admit or deny it. A denial must fairly meet the substance of the request, and when good faith requires that a party qualify an answer or deny only part of the matter of which an admission is requested, the party must specify the parts that are admitted and denied.

(3) An answering party may not give lack of information or knowledge as a reason for failure to admit or deny unless the party states that he or she has made reasonable inquiry and that the information known or readily obtainable is insufficient to enable the party to admit or deny.

(4) If an objection is made, the reasons must be stated. A party who considers that a matter of which an admission has been requested presents a genuine issue for trial may not, on that ground alone, object to the request. The party may, subject to the provisions of MCR 2.313(C), deny the matter or state reasons why he or she cannot admit or deny it.

(C) Motion Regarding Answer or Objection. The party who has requested the admission may move to determine the sufficiency of the answer or objection. The motion must state that the movant has in good faith conferred or attempted to confer with the party not making the disclosure in an effort to secure the disclosure without court action. Unless the court determines that an objection is justified, it shall order that an answer be served. If the court determines that an answer does not comply with the requirements of the rule, it may order either that the matter is admitted, or that an amended answer be served. The court may, in lieu of one of these orders, determine that final disposition of the request be made at a pretrial conference or at a designated time before trial. The provisions of MCR 2.313(A)(5) apply to the award of expenses incurred in relation to the motion.

(D) Effect of Admission.

(1) A matter admitted under this rule is conclusively established unless the court on motion permits withdrawal or amendment of an admission. For good cause the court may allow a party to amend or withdraw an admission. The court may condition amendment or withdrawal of the admission on terms that are just.

(2) An admission made by a party under this rule is for the purpose of the pending action only and is not an admission for another purpose, nor may it be used against the party in another proceeding.

(E) Public Records.

(1) A party intending to use as evidence

(a) a record that a public official is required by federal, state, or municipal authority to receive for filing or recording or is given custody of by law, or

(b) a memorial of a public official,

may prepare a copy, synopsis, or abstract of the record, insofar as it is to be used, and serve it on the adverse party sufficiently in advance of trial to allow the adverse party a reasonable opportunity to determine its accuracy.

(2) The copy, synopsis, or abstract is then admissible in evidence as admitted facts in the action, if otherwise admissible, except insofar as its inaccuracy is pointed out by the adverse party in an affidavit filed and served within a reasonable time before trial.

(F) Filing With Court. Requests and responses under this rule must be filed with the court either before service or within a reasonable time thereafter.

[Adopted effective March 1, 1985. Amended July 16, 2002, effective January 1, 2003, 466 Mich; June 19, 2019, effective January 1, 2020, 503 Mich.]

Comments

Staff Comment to 1985 Adoption

MCR 2.312 is drawn from GCR 1963, 312 and FR Civ P 36.

Subrule (A) adopts the federal formulation of the scope of requests for admission, allowing a request to ask for admissions regarding the application of law to fact. Compare GCR 1963, 312.1 with FR Civ P 36(a).

The time for response is the same as for interrogatories and requests to produce, and is comparable to that in FR Civ P 36(a) (28 days; as to a defendant, at least 42 days after service of the summons and complaint). GCR 1963, 312.1 required a response within 10 days.

As in the interrogatory rule, MCR 2.309(C), subrule (C) adopts the federal practice of placing the burden of filing a motion on the requesting party if there is a dispute. Compare FR Civ P 36(a) with GCR 1963, 312.1.

Subrule (F) excepts requests for admission from the general rule regarding filing of discovery materials. See MCR 2.302(H).

Staff Comment to 2002 Amendment

The July 16, 2002 amendments of subrules 2.309(C), 2.310(C)(3), and 2.312(3), effective January 1, 2003, require that discovery motions include a statement that the movant has in good faith conferred or attempted to confer with the party not making the disclosure in an effort to secure the disclosure without court action. Subrule 2.310(C)(6) was added to clarify the respective responsibilities for the costs of discovery.

Staff Comment to 2020 Amendment

These amendments are based on a proposal created by a special committee of the State Bar of Michigan and approved for submission to the Court by the Bar's Representative Assembly. The rules require mandatory discovery disclosure in many cases, adopt a presumptive limit on interrogatories (20 in most cases, but 35 in domestic relations proceedings) and limit a deposition to 7 hours. The amendments also update the rules to more specifically address issues related to electronically stored information, and encourage early action on discovery issues during the discovery period.

The amendment of MCR 2.309(A)(2) sets a presumptive limit of twenty interrogatories for each separately represented party. Several commenters suggested that the term "discrete subpart" be more explicitly defined. But the rule's reference to "a discrete subpart" is intended to draw guidance from federal courts construing FR Civ P 30(a)(1). Generally, subparts are not separately counted if they are logically or factually subsumed within and necessarily related to the primary question. In upholding the limit, parties and courts should also pragmatically balance the overall goals of discovery and the admonition of MCR 1.105. Further, the intent of the provision at MCR 2.301(B)(4) is to ensure that parties responding to discovery requests have the full time period to do so as provided for under these rules prior to the expiration of the discovery period.

Rule 2.313. Failure to Serve Disclosure or to Provide or to Permit Discovery; Sanctions

(A) Motion for Order Compelling Disclosure or Discovery. A party, on reasonable notice to other parties and all persons affected, may apply for an order compelling disclosure or discovery as follows:

(1) *Appropriate Court.* A motion for an order under this rule may be made to the court in which the action is pending, or, as to a matter relating to a deposition in, or non-party subpoena served outside of, the county where the action is pending, to a court in that county.

(2) *Motion.*

(a) To Compel Disclosure. If a party fails to serve a disclosure required by MCR 2.302(A), another party may move to compel disclosure and for appropriate sanctions.

(b) To Compel Discovery. If

(i) a deponent fails to answer a question propounded or submitted under MCR 2.306 or 2.307,

(ii) a corporation or other entity fails to make a designation under MCR 2.306(B)(3) or 2.307(A)(1),

(iii) a party fails to answer an interrogatory submitted under MCR 2.309(A) and (B),

(iv) in response to a request for inspection submitted under MCR 2.310, a person fails to respond that inspection will be permitted as requested, or

(v) If a party; an officer, director, or managing agent of a party; or a person designated under MCR 2.306(B)(3) or 2.307(A)(1) to testify on behalf of a party fails to appear before the person who is to take his or her deposition, after being served with a proper notice, the party seeking discovery may move for an order compelling compliance. When taking a deposition on oral examination, the proponent of the question may complete or adjourn the examination before applying for an order.

(c) To compel compliance with a non-party discovery subpoena. If a recipient of a non-party discovery subpoena under MCR 2.305 fails to comply, the issuing party may move to compel compliance. When taking a deposition on oral examination, the proponent of the question may complete or adjourn the examination before applying for an order. The motion must include a copy of the subpoena and proof of service of the subpoena. The movant must serve the motion on the person from whom discovery is sought as provided in MCR 2.105.

(3) *Ruling; Protective Order.* If the court denies the motion in whole or in part, it may enter a protective order that it could have entered on motion made under MCR 2.302(C).

(4) *Evasive or Incomplete Disclosure, Answer, or Response.* For purposes of this subrule an evasive or incomplete disclosure, answer, or response must be treated as a failure to disclose, answer, or respond.

(5) *Award of Expenses of Motion.*

(a) If the motion is granted—or if the disclosure or requested discovery is provided after the motion was filed—, the court may, after opportunity for hearing, require the party or deponent whose conduct necessitated the motion or the party or attorney advising such conduct, or both, to pay to the moving party the reasonable expenses incurred as a result of the conduct and in making the motion, including attorney fees, unless the court finds that the moving party filed the motion before attempting in good faith to obtain the disclosure or discovery without court action, the opposition to the motion was substantially justified, or other circumstances make an award unjust.

(b) If the motion is denied, the court may, after opportunity for hearing, require the moving party or the attorney advising the motion, or both, to pay to the person who opposed the motion the reasonable expenses incurred in opposing the motion, including attorney fees, unless the court finds that the making of the motion was substantially justified or that other circumstances make an award of expenses unjust.

(c) If the motion is granted in part and denied in part, the court may, after opportunity for hearing, apportion the reasonable expenses incurred in relation to the motion among the parties and other persons in a just manner.

(6) *Additional Sanctions.* The court in which the action is pending may order such sanctions as are just. Among others, it may take an action authorized under subrule (B)(2)(a), (b), and (c).

(B) Failure to Comply With Order.

(1) *Sanctions by Court Where Deposition Is Taken.* If a deponent fails to be sworn or to answer a question after being directed to do so by a court in the county or district in which the deposition is being taken, the failure may be considered a contempt of that court.

(2) *Sanctions by Court in Which Action Is Pending.* If a party or an officer, director, or managing agent of a party, or a person designated under MCR 2.306(B)(5) or 2.307(A)(1) to testify on behalf of a party, fails to obey an order to provide or permit discovery, including an order entered under subrule (A) of this rule or under MCR 2.311, the court in which the action is pending may order such sanctions as are just, including, but not limited to the following:

(a) an order that the matters regarding which the order was entered or other designated facts may be taken to be established for the purposes of the action in accordance with the claim of the party obtaining the order;

(b) an order refusing to allow the disobedient party to support or oppose designated claims or defenses, or prohibiting the party from introducing designated matters into evidence;

(c) an order striking pleadings or parts of pleadings, staying further proceedings until the order is obeyed, dismissing the action or proceeding or a part of it, or rendering a judgment by default against the disobedient party;

(d) in lieu of or in addition to the foregoing orders, an order treating as a contempt of court the failure to obey an order, except an order to submit to a physical or mental examination;

(e) where a party has failed to comply with an order under MCR 2.311(A) requiring the party to produce another for examination, such orders as are listed in subrules (B)(2)(a), (b), and (c), unless the party failing to comply shows that he or she is unable to produce such person for examination.

In lieu of or in addition to the foregoing orders, the court may require the party failing to obey the order or the attorney advising the party, or both, to pay the reasonable expenses, including attorney fees, caused by the failure, unless the court finds that the failure was substantially justified or that other circumstances make an award of expenses unjust.

(C) Failure to Disclose, Supplement, or Admit.

(1) *Failure to Disclose or Supplement.* If a party fails to provide information or identify a witness as required by MCR 2.302(A) or (E), the party is not allowed to use that information or witness to supply evidence on a motion, at a hearing, or at a trial, unless the failure was substantially justified or is harmless. In addition to or instead of this sanction, the court, on motion and after giving an opportunity to be heard:

(a) may order payment of the reasonable expenses, including attorney fees, caused by the failure;

(b) may inform the jury of the party's failure; and

(c) may impose other appropriate sanctions, including any of the orders listed in MCR 2.313(B)(2)(a)–(c).

(2) *Failure to Admit.* If a party denies the genuineness of a document, or the truth of a matter as requested under MCR 2.312, and if the party requesting the admission later proves the genuineness of the document or the truth of the matter, the requesting party may move for an order requiring the other party to pay the expenses incurred in making that proof, including attorney fees. The court shall enter the order unless it finds that

(a) the request was held objectionable pursuant to MCR 2.312,

(b) the admission sought was of no substantial importance,

(c) the party failing to admit had reasonable ground to believe that he or she might prevail on the matter, or

(d) there was other good reason for the failure to admit.

(D) Failure to Preserve ESI. If ESI that should have been preserved in the anticipation or conduct of litigation is lost because a party failed to take reasonable steps to preserve it, and it cannot be restored or replaced through additional discovery, the court:

(1) upon finding prejudice to another party from loss of the information, may order measures no greater than necessary to cure the prejudice or

(2) only upon finding that the party acted with the intent to deprive another party of the information's use in the litigation, may order appropriate remedies, including:

(a) a presumption that the lost information was unfavorable to the party;

(b) a jury instruction directing that the jury may or must presume the information was unfavorable to the party; or

(c) dismissal of the action or entry of a default judgment.

[Adopted effective March 1, 1985. Amended December 16, 2008, effective January 1, 2009, 482 Mich; June 19, 2019, effective January 1, 2020, 503 Mich.]

Comments

Staff Comment to 1985 Adoption

MCR 2.313 is based on GCR 1963, 313 and FR Civ P 37. The rule follows the structure of the federal rule but does not require that a motion regarding a deposition be brought in the county where the deposition is held. This is consistent with the practice under GCR 1963, 313.1(1).

The rule provides greater detail regarding award of costs than did GCR 1963, 313. Compare subrules (A)(5), (B)(2), and (D)(2) with GCR 1963, 313.1(3) and (4). As under the corresponding federal provisions, the cost sanctions may be imposed on an attorney for a party as well as on the party. See FR Civ P 37(a)(4), 37(b)(2), 37(d).

Staff Comment to 2008 Amendment

These amendments update Michigan's discovery rules as they relate to electronically stored information. The provisions of the proposal at MCR 2.302(B)(6) and MCR 2.506(A)(3) allow the court to shift the cost of discovery to the requesting party if discovery is requested from sources that are not reasonably accessible, and prohibit sanctions if information is lost or destroyed as a result of a good-faith, routine record destruction policy or "litigation hold" procedures. The "safe harbor" provision provided in MCR 2.302(B)(5) and in MCR 2.313 applies when information is lost or destroyed under a routine electronic information system, if the operation of the system was performed in good faith. Good faith may be shown by a party's actions to attempt to preserve information as part of a "litigation hold" that would otherwise have been lost or destroyed under an electronic information system.

The new language of MCR 2.302 and MCR 2.506 also allows parties to determine the format in which the information should be produced, and how to handle a situation in which protected information is inadvertently produced.

Staff Comment to 2020 Amendment

These amendments are based on a proposal created by a special committee of the State Bar of Michigan and approved for submission to the Court by the Bar's Representative Assembly. The rules require mandatory discovery disclosure in many cases, adopt a presumptive limit on interrogatories (20 in most cases, but 35 in domestic relations proceedings) and limit a deposition to 7 hours. The amendments also update the rules to more specifically address issues related to electronically stored information, and encourage early action on discovery issues during the discovery period.

The amendment of MCR 2.309(A)(2) sets a presumptive limit of twenty interrogatories for each separately represented party. Several commenters suggested that the term "discrete subpart" be more explicitly defined. But the rule's reference to "a discrete subpart" is intended to draw guidance from federal courts construing FR Civ P 30(a)(1). Generally, subparts are not separately counted if they are logically or factually subsumed within and necessarily related to the primary question. In upholding the limit, parties and courts should also pragmatically balance the overall goals of discovery and the admonition of MCR 1.105. Further, the intent of the provision at MCR 2.301(B)(4) is to ensure that parties responding to discovery requests have the full time period to do so as provided for under these rules prior to the expiration of the discovery period.

Rule 2.314. Discovery of Medical Information Concerning Party

(A) Scope of Rule.

(1) When a mental or physical condition of a party is in controversy, medical information about the condition is subject to discovery under these rules to the extent that

(a) the information is otherwise discoverable under MCR 2.302(B), and

(b) the party does not assert that the information is subject to a valid privilege.

(2) Medical information subject to discovery includes, but is not limited to, medical records in the possession or control of a physician, hospital, or other custodian, and medical knowledge discoverable by deposition or interrogatories.

(3) For purposes of this rule, medical information about a mental or physical condition of a party is within the control of the party, even if the information is not in the party's immediate physical possession.

(B) Privilege; Assertion; Waiver; Effects.

(1) A party who has a valid privilege may assert the privilege and prevent discovery of medical information relating to his or her mental or physical condition. The privilege must be asserted in the party's disclosure under 2.302(A), in written response to a request for production of documents under MCR 2.310, in answers to interrogatories under MCR 2.309(B), before or during the taking of a deposition, or by moving for a protective order under MCR 2.302(C). A privilege not timely asserted is waived in that action, but is not waived for the purposes of any other action.

(2) Unless the court orders otherwise, if a party asserts that the medical information is subject to a privilege and the assertion has the effect of preventing discovery of medical information that must be disclosed or is otherwise discoverable under MCR 2.302(B), the party may not thereafter present or introduce any physical, documentary, or testimonial evidence relating to the party's medical history or mental or physical condition.

(C) Response by Party to Request for Medical Information.

(1) A party who is served with a request for production of medical information under MCR 2.310 must either:

(a) make the information available for inspection and copying as requested;

(b) assert that the information is privileged;

(c) object to the request as permitted by MCR 2.310(C)(2); or

(d) furnish the requesting party with signed authorizations in the form approved by the state court administrator sufficient in number to enable the requesting party to obtain the information requested from persons, institutions, hospitals, and other custodians in actual possession of the information requested.

(2) A party responding to a request for medical information as permitted by subrule (C)(1)(d) must also inform the adverse party of the physical location of the information requested.

(D) Release of Medical Information by Custodian.

(1) A physician, hospital, or other custodian of medical information (referred to in this rule as the "custodian") shall comply with a properly authorized request for the medical information within 28 days after the receipt of the request, or, if at the time the request is made the patient is hospitalized for the mental or physical condition for which the medical information is sought, within 28 days after the patient's discharge or release. The court may extend or shorten these time limits for good cause.

(2) In responding to a request for medical information under this rule, the custodian will be deemed to have complied with the request if the custodian

(a) makes the information reasonably available for inspection and copying; or

(b) delivers to the requesting party the original information or a true and exact copy of the original information accompanied by a sworn certificate in the form approved by the state court administrator, signed by the custodian verifying that the copy is a true and complete reproduction of the original information.

(3) If it is essential that an original document be examined when the authenticity of the document, questions of interpretation of handwriting, or similar questions arise, the custodian must permit reasonable inspection of the original document by the requesting party and by experts retained to examine the information.

(4) If x-rays or other records incapable of reproduction are requested, the custodian may inform the requesting party that these records exist, but have not been delivered pursuant to subrule (D)(2). Delivery of the records may be conditioned on the requesting party or the party's agent signing a receipt that includes a promise that the records will be returned to the custodian after a reasonable time for inspection purposes has elapsed.

(5) In complying with subrule (D)(2), the custodian is entitled to receive reasonable reimbursement in advance for expenses of compliance.

(6) If a custodian does not respond within the time permitted by subrule (D)(1) to a party's authorized request for medical information, a subpoena may be issued under MCR 2.305(A)(2), directing that the custodian present the information for examination and copying at the time and place stated in the subpoena.

(E) Persons Not Parties. Medical information concerning persons not parties to the action is not discoverable under this rule.

[Adopted effective March 1, 1985. Amended June 7, 1994, effective September 1, 1994, 445 Mich; March 14, 2007, effective May 1, 2007, 477 Mich; June 19, 2019, effective January 1, 2020, 503 Mich.]

Comments

Staff Comment to 1985 Adoption

MCR 2.314 is largely new and covers discovery of medical records of a party via a request for production under MCR 2.310. There were related provisions in GCR 1963, 506.7 regarding subpoenas for production of hospital records.

Subrule (B) covers privileges regarding medical information and in general requires a party to decide whether or not to assert the privilege at the discovery stage. Under subrule (B)(1), if the party does not assert the privilege in response to a request to produce, it is waived. Under subrule (B)(2) if the party asserts the privilege and thereby prevents discovery of the information, the party is precluded from introducing testimony at trial relating to the party's medical history or condition. However, the court may modify this procedure.

Under subrule (C), when a party is served with a request for production of his or her medical records, the party must make the records available, assert they are privileged, object to the request, or furnish authorization forms that will enable the adverse party to obtain the records from medical records custodians.

The provisions regarding compliance by custodians of medical records are in subrule (D). The state court administrator is to approve forms for use in connection with this procedure.

Subrule (E) makes clear that the rule does not preclude discovery of medical records in other ways permitted by these rules.

Staff Comment to 1994 Amendment

Several changes are made in MCR 2.314, the rule regarding discovery of medical information. As amended [effective September 1, 1994], the rule applies the preclusive effect of subrule (B)(1) to a party who asserts a privilege as to medical information in connection with depositions and interrogatories as well as to requests for production of documents. See *Gibson v Bronson Methodist Hosp*, 445 Mich 331, 517 N.W.2d 736 (Mich 1994).

Staff Comment to 2007 Amendment

This amendment corrects an incorrect reference.

Staff Comment to 2020 Amendment

These amendments are based on a proposal created by a special committee of the State Bar of Michigan and approved for submission to the Court by the Bar's Representative Assembly. The rules require mandatory discovery disclosure in many cases, adopt a presumptive limit on interrogatories (20 in most cases, but 35 in domestic relations proceedings) and limit a deposition to 7 hours. The amendments also update the rules to more specifically address issues related to electronically stored information, and encourage early action on discovery issues during the discovery period.

The amendment of MCR 2.309(A)(2) sets a presumptive limit of twenty interrogatories for each separately represented party. Several commenters suggested that the term "discrete subpart" be more explicitly defined. But the rule's reference to "a discrete subpart" is intended to draw guidance from federal courts construing FR Civ P 30(a)(1). Generally, subparts are not separately counted if they are logically or factually subsumed within and necessarily related to the primary question. In upholding the limit, parties and courts should also pragmatically balance the overall goals of discovery and the admonition of MCR 1.105. Further, the intent of the provision at MCR 2.301(B)(4) is to ensure that parties responding to discovery requests have the full time period to do so as provided for under these rules prior to the expiration of the discovery period.

Rule 2.315   Video Depositions

(A) When Permitted. Depositions authorized under MCR 2.303 and 2.306 may be taken by means of simultaneous audio and visual electronic recording without leave of the court or stipulation of the parties, provided the deposition is taken in accordance with this rule.

(B) Rules Governing. Except as provided in this rule, the taking of video depositions is governed by the rules governing the taking of other depositions unless the nature of the video deposition makes compliance impossible or unnecessary.

(C) Procedure.

(1) A notice of the taking of a video deposition and a subpoena for attendance at the deposition must state that the deposition is to be visually recorded.

(2) A video deposition must be timed by means of a digital clock or clocks capable of displaying the hours, minutes, and seconds. The clock or clocks must be in the picture at all times during the taking of the deposition.

(3) A video deposition must begin with a statement on camera of the date, time, and place at which the recording is being made, the title of the action, and the identification of the attorneys.

(4) The person being deposed must be sworn as a witness on camera by an authorized person.

(5) More than one camera may be used, in sequence or simultaneously.

(6) The parties may make audio recordings while the video deposition is being taken.

(7) At the conclusion of the deposition a statement must be made on camera that the deposition is completed.

(D) Custody of Tape and Copies.

(1) The person making the video recording must retain possession of it. The video recording must be securely sealed and marked for identification purposes.

(2) The parties may purchase audio or audio-visual copies of the recording from the operator.

(E) Filing; Notice of Filing. If a party requests that the deposition be filed, the person who made the recording shall

(1) file the recording with the court under MCR 2.306(F)(3), together with an affidavit identifying the recording, stating the total elapsed time, and attesting that no alterations, additions, or deletions other than those ordered by the court have been made;

(2) give the notice required by MCR 2.306(F)(3), and

(3) serve copies of the recording on all parties who have requested them under MCR 2.315(D)(2).

(F) Use as Evidence; Objections.

(1) A video deposition may not be used in a court proceeding unless it has been filed with the court.

(2) Except as modified by this rule, the use of video depositions in court proceedings is governed by MCR 2.308.

(3) A party who seeks to use a video deposition at trial must provide the court with either

(a) a transcript of the deposition, which shall be used for ruling on any objections, or

(b) a stipulation by all parties that there are no objections to the deposition and that the recording (or an agreed portion of it) may be played.

(4) When a video deposition is used in a court proceeding, the court must indicate on the record what portions of the recording have been played. The court reporter or recorder need not make a record of the statements in the recording.

(G) Custody of Video Deposition After Filing. After filing, a video deposition shall remain in the custody of the court unless the court orders the recording stored elsewhere for technical reasons or because of special storage problems. The order directing the storage must direct the custodian to keep the recordings sealed until the further order of the court. Video depositions filed with the court shall have the same status as other depositions and documents filed with the court, and may be reproduced, preserved, destroyed, or salvaged as directed by order of the court.

(H) Appeal. On appeal the recording remains part of the record and shall be transmitted with it. A party may request that the appellate court view portions of the video deposition. If a transcript was not provided to the court under subrule (F)(3), the appellant must arrange and pay for the preparation of a transcript to be included in the record on appeal.

(I) Costs. The costs of taking a video deposition and the cost for its use in evidence may be taxed as costs as provided by MCR 2.625 in the same manner as depositions recorded in other ways.

[Adopted effective March 1, 1985.]

Comments

Staff Comment to 1985 Adoption

MCR 2.315 is based on GCR 1963, 315.

Subrule (E) modifies the filing and notice of filing provisions to be consistent with the general deposition provisions of MCR 2.306(F). The video recording need only be filed if requested by a party, and the person who made the recording, rather than the clerk, is responsible for giving notice of the filing. Compare GCR 1963, 315.5.

Subrule (F) revises the provisions regarding the use of a video deposition as evidence and the procedure for objections to material in the deposition. GCR 1963, 315.6(2) directed the judge to rule on objections after viewing the video tape. Under subrule (F)(3), the party seeking to introduce the recording must either provide a transcript for use in ruling on objections, or obtain the stipulation of all parties that there is no objection to the deposition and that all or part of it may be played. The court reporter or recorder need not make a record of the playing of the deposition. However, the court must indicate on the record what portions have been played.

There are related provisions regarding video depositions on appeal in subrule (H). The recording itself is part of the record, and may be viewed by the appellate court. In addition, if a transcript was not provided for use by the trial court in ruling on objections, the appellant must have the deposition transcribed for the appeal.

Rule 2.316. Removal of Disclosure and Discovery Materials from File

(A) Definition. For the purpose of this rule, "disclosure material" means disclosures under MCR 2.302(A) and "discovery material" means deposition transcripts, audio or video recordings of depositions, interrogatories, documents produced during discovery and made a part of the court file, and answers to interrogatories and requests to admit.

(B) Removal from File. In civil actions, disclosure and discovery materials may be removed from files and destroyed in the manner provided in this rule.

(1) *By Stipulation.* If the parties stipulate to the removal of disclosure and discovery materials from the file, the clerk may remove the materials and dispose of them in the manner provided in the stipulation.

(2) *By the Clerk.*

(a) The clerk may initiate the removal of disclosure and discovery materials from the file in the following circumstances.

(i) If an appeal has not been taken, 18 months after entry of judgment on the merits or dismissal of the action.

(ii) If an appeal has been taken, 91 days after the appellate proceedings are concluded, unless the action is remanded for further proceedings in the trial court.

(b) The clerk shall notify the parties and counsel of record, when possible, that disclosure and discovery materials will be removed from the file of the action and destroyed on a specified date at least 28 days after the notice is served unless within that time

(i) the party who filed the disclosure or discovery materials retrieves them from the clerk's office or

(ii) a party files a written objection to removal of disclosure or discovery materials from the file.

If an objection to removal of disclosure or discovery materials is filed, the materials may not be removed unless the court so orders after notice and opportunity for the objecting party to be heard. The clerk shall schedule a hearing and give notice to the parties. The rules governing motion practice apply.

(3) *By Order.* On motion of a party, or on its own initiative after notice and hearing, the court may order disclosure and discovery materials removed at any other time on a finding that the materials are no longer necessary. However, no disclosure or discovery materials may be destroyed by court personnel or the clerk until the periods set forth in subrule (2)(a)(i) or (2)(a)(ii) have passed.

[Adopted March 16, 1989, effective June 1, 1989, 432 Mich. Amended June 19, 2019, effective January 1, 2020, 503 Mich.]

Comments

Staff Comment to 1989 Adoption

The Michigan Judges Association recommended adoption of this rule to reduce costs and lessen the physical burden of maintaining voluminous discovery materials that cannot or will not be utilized in the trial of civil cases.

Staff Comment to 2020 Amendment

These amendments are based on a proposal created by a special committee of the State Bar of Michigan and approved for submission to the Court by the Bar's Representative Assembly. The rules require mandatory discovery disclosure in many cases, adopt a presumptive limit on interrogatories (20 in most cases, but 35 in domestic relations proceedings) and limit a deposition to 7 hours. The amendments also update the rules to more specifically address issues related to electronically stored information, and encourage early action on discovery issues during the discovery period.

The amendment of MCR 2.309(A)(2) sets a presumptive limit of twenty interrogatories for each separately represented party. Several commenters suggested that the term "discrete subpart" be more explicitly defined. But the rule's reference to "a discrete subpart" is intended to draw guidance from federal courts construing FR Civ P 30(a)(1). Generally, subparts are not separately counted if they are logically or factually subsumed within and necessarily related to the primary question. In upholding the limit, parties and courts should also pragmatically balance the overall goals of discovery and the admonition of MCR 1.105. Further, the intent of the provision at MCR 2.301(B)(4) is to ensure that parties responding to discovery requests have the full time period to do so as provided for under these rules prior to the expiration of the discovery period.

SUBCHAPTER 2.400 PRETRIAL PROCEDURE; ALTERNATIVE DISPUTE RESOLUTION; OFFERS OF JUDGMENT; SETTLEMENTS

Rule 2.401. Pretrial Procedures; Conferences; Scheduling Orders

(A) Time; Discretion of Court. At any time after the commencement of the action, on its own initiative or the request of a party, the court may direct that the attorneys for the parties, alone or with the parties, appear for a conference. The court shall give reasonable notice of the scheduling of a conference. More than one conference may be held in an action.

(B) Early Scheduling Conference and Order.

(1) *Early Scheduling Conference.* The court may direct that an early scheduling conference be held. During this conference the court should consider any matters that will facilitate the fair and expeditious disposition of the action, including:

(a) whether jurisdiction and venue are proper or whether the case is frivolous;

(b) whether to refer the case to an alternative dispute resolution procedure under MCR 2.410;

(c) the complexity of a particular case and enter a scheduling order setting time limitations for the processing of the case and establishing dates when future actions should begin or be completed in the case;

(d) disclosure, discovery, preservation, and claims of privilege of ESI;

(e) the simplification of the issues;

(f) the amount of time necessary for discovery, staging of discovery, and any modification to the extent of discovery;

(g) the necessity or desirability of amendments to the pleadings;

(h) the possibility of obtaining admissions of fact and of documents to avoid unnecessary proof;

(i) the form and content of the pretrial order;

(j) the timing of disclosures under MCR 2.302(A);

(k) the limitation of the number of expert witnesses, whether to have a separate discovery period for experts, whether to require preparation and disclosure of testifying expert reports, and whether to specify expert disclosure deadlines;

(l) the consolidation of actions for trial, the separation of issues, and the order of trial when some issues are to be tried by a jury and some by the court;

(m) the possibility of settlement;

(n) whether mediation, case evaluation, or some other form of alternative dispute resolution would be appropriate for the case, and what mechanisms are available to provide such services;

(o) the identity of the witnesses to testify at trial;

(p) the estimated length of trial;

(q) whether all claims arising out of the transaction or occurrence that is the subject matter of the action have been joined as required by MCR 2.203(A); and

(r) other matters that may aid in the disposition of the action.

(2) *Scheduling Order.*

(a) At an early scheduling conference under subrule (B)(1), or at such other time as the court concludes that such an order would facilitate the progress of the case, the court shall establish times for events and adopt other provisions the court deems appropriate, including

(i) the initiation or completion of an ADR process,

(ii) the amendment of pleadings, adding of parties, or filing of motions,

(iii) what, if any, changes should be made in the timing, form, or requirement for disclosures under MCR 2.302(A),

(iv) what, if any, changes should be made to the limitations on discovery imposed under these rules and whether other presumptive limitations should be established,

(v) the completion of discovery,

(vi) the exchange of witness lists under subrule (H)(2)(h), and

(vii) the scheduling of a pretrial conference, a settlement conference, or trial.

More than one such order may be entered in a case.

(b) The scheduling of events under this subrule shall take into consideration the nature and complexity of the case, including the issues involved, the number and location of parties and potential witnesses, including experts, the extent of expected and necessary discovery, and the availability of reasonably certain trial dates.

(c) The scheduling order also may include provisions concerning initial disclosure, discovery of ESI, any agreements the parties reach for asserting claims of privilege or for protection as trial-preparation material after production, preserving discoverable information, and the form in which ESI shall be produced.

(d) Whenever reasonably practical, the scheduling of events under this subrule shall be made after meaningful consultation with all counsel of record.

(i) If a scheduling order is entered under this subrule in a manner that does not permit meaningful advance consultation with counsel, within 14 days after entry of the order, a party may file and serve a written request for amendment of the order detailing the reasons why the order should be amended.

(ii) Upon receiving such a written request, the court shall reconsider the order in light of the objections raised by the parties. Whether the reconsideration occurs at a conference or in some other manner, the court must either enter a new scheduling order or notify the parties in writing that the court declines to amend the order. The court must schedule a conference, enter the new order, or send the written notice, within 14 days after receiving the request.

(iii) The submission of a request pursuant to this subrule, or the failure to submit such a request, does not preclude a party from filing a motion to modify a scheduling order.

(C) Discovery Planning.

(1) Upon court order or written request by another party, the parties must confer among themselves and prepare a proposed discovery plan. The attorneys of record and all unrepresented parties that have appeared are jointly responsible for arranging the conference and for attempting in good faith to agree on a proposed discovery plan.

(2) A proposed discovery plan must address all disclosure and discovery matters, including the matters set forth in subrule (B), and propose deadlines for completion of disclosure and discovery. The parties must show good cause to request a change in deadlines set by a scheduling order.

(3) A discovery plan, noting any disagreements between the parties, may be submitted to the court as part of a stipulation or motion. The court may enter an order governing disclosure, discovery, and any other case management matter the court deems appropriate.

(4) If a party or attorney fails to participate in good faith in developing and submitting a proposed discovery plan, the court may enter an appropriate sanction, including payment of attorney fees and costs caused by the failure.

(D) Order for Trial Briefs. The court may direct the attorneys to furnish trial briefs as to any or all of the issues involved in the action.

(E) Appearance of Counsel. The attorneys attending the conference shall be thoroughly familiar with the case and have the authority necessary to fully participate in the conference. The court may direct that the attorneys who intend to try the case attend the conference.

(F) Presence of Parties at Conference. If the court anticipates meaningful discussion of settlement, the court may direct that the parties to the action, agents of parties, representatives of lienholders, or representatives of insurance carriers, or other persons:

(1) be present at the conference or be immediately available at the time of the conference; and

(2) have information and authority adequate for responsible and effective participation in the conference for all purposes, including settlement.

The court's order may require the availability of a specified individual; provided, however, that the availability of a substitute who has the information and authority required by subrule (F)(2) shall constitute compliance with the order.

The court's order may specify whether the availability is to be in person or by telephone.

This subrule does not apply to an early scheduling conference held pursuant to subrule (B).

(G) Failure to Attend or to Participate.

(1) Failure of a party or the party's attorney or other representative to attend a scheduled conference or to have information and authority adequate for responsible and effective participation in the conference for all purposes, including settlement, as directed by the court, may constitute a default to which MCR 2.603 is applicable or a ground for dismissal under MCR 2.504(B).

(2) The court shall excuse a failure to attend a conference or to participate as directed by the court, and shall enter a just order other than one of default or dismissal, if the court finds that

(a) entry of an order of default or dismissal would cause manifest injustice; or

(b) the failure was not due to the culpable negligence of the party or the party's attorney.

The court may condition the order on the payment by the offending party or attorney of reasonable expenses as provided in MCR 2.313(B)(2).

(H) Final Pretrial Conference and Order.

(1) If the court finds at a final pretrial conference that due to a lack of reasonable diligence by a party the action is not ready for trial, the court may enter an appropriate order to facilitate preparation of the action for trial and may require the offending party to pay the reasonable expenses, including attorney fees, caused by the lack of diligence.

(2) The court may hold a final pretrial conference to facilitate preparation of the action for trial and to formulate a trial plan. The conference may be combined with a settlement conference. At least one lead attorney who will conduct the trial for each party and any unrepresented party shall attend the conference. At the conference the parties may discuss the following, and the court may order the parties to prepare, either before or after the conference, a joint final pretrial order that may provide for:

(a) scheduling motions in limine;

(b) a concise statement of plaintiff's claims, including legal theories;

(c) a concise statement of defendant's defenses and claims, including crossclaims and claims of third-party plaintiffs, and defenses of cross defendants or third-party defendants, including legal theories;

(d) a statement of any stipulated facts or other matters;

(e) issues of fact to be litigated;

(f) issues of law to be litigated;

(g) evidence problems likely to arise at trial;

(h) a list of witnesses to be called unless reasonable notice is given that they will not be called, and a list of witnesses that may be called, listed by category as follows:

(i) live lay witnesses;

(ii) lay deposition transcripts or videos including resolving objections and identifying portions to be read or played;

(iii) live expert witnesses; and

(iv) expert deposition transcripts or videos including resolving objections and identifying portions to be read or played.

(i) a list of exhibits with stipulations or objections to admissibility;

(j) an itemized statement of damages and stipulations to those items not in dispute;

(k) estimated length of trial:

(i) time for plaintiff's proofs;

(ii) time for defendant's proofs; and

(iii) whether it is a jury or nonjury trial.

(*l*) trial date and schedule;

(m) whether the parties will agree to arbitration;

(n) a statement that counsel have met, conferred and considered the possibility of settlement and alternative dispute resolution, giving place, time and date and the current status of these negotiations as well as plans for further negotiations;

(*o*) rules governing conduct of trial;

(p) jury instructions;

(q) trial briefs;

(r) voir dire; and

(s) any other appropriate matter.

(I) Witness Lists.

(1) No later than the time directed by the court under subrule (B)(2)(a), the parties shall file and serve witness lists. The witness list must include:

(a) the name of each witness, and the witness' address, if known; however, records custodians whose testimony would be limited to providing the foundation for the admission of records may be identified generally;

(b) whether the witness is an expert, and the field of expertise.

(2) The court may order that any witness not listed in accordance with this rule will be prohibited from testifying at trial except upon good cause shown.

(3) This subrule does not prevent a party from obtaining an earlier disclosure of witness information by other discovery means as provided in these rules.

(J) ESI Conference, Plan and Order.

(1) *ESI Conference.* Where a case is reasonably likely to include the discovery of ESI, parties may agree to an ESI Conference, the judge may order the parties to hold an ESI Conference, or a party may file a motion requesting an ESI Conference. At the ESI Conference, the parties shall consider:

(a) any issues relating to preservation of discoverable information, including adoption of a preservation plan for potentially relevant ESI;

(b) identification of potentially relevant types, categories, and time frames of ESI;

(c) identification of potentially relevant sources of ESI and whether the ESI is reasonably accessible;

(d) disclosure of the manner in which ESI is maintained;

(e) implementation of a preservation plan for potentially relevant ESI;

(f) the form in which each type of ESI will be produced;

(g) what metadata, if any, will be produced;

(h) the time to produce ESI;

(i) the method for asserting or preserving claims of privilege or protection of trial preparation materials, including whether such claims may be asserted after production;

(j) privilege log format and related issues;

(k) the method for asserting or preserving confidential and proprietary status of information either of a party or a person not a party to the proceeding;

(*l*) whether allocation among the parties of the expense of production is appropriate; and

(m) any other issue related to the discovery of ESI.

(2) *ESI Discovery Plan.* Within 14 days after an ESI Conference, the parties shall file with the court an ESI discovery plan and a statement concerning any issues upon which the parties cannot agree. Unless the parties agree otherwise, the attorney for the plaintiff shall be responsible for submitting the ESI discovery plan to the court. The ESI discovery plan may include:

(a) a statement of the issues in the case and a brief factual outline;

(b) a schedule of discovery including discovery of ESI;

(c) a defined scope of preservation of information and appropriate conditions for terminating the duty to preserve prior to the final resolution of the case;

(d) the forms in which ESI will be produced; and

(e) the sources of any ESI that are not reasonably accessible because of undue burden or cost.

(3) *ESI Competence.* Attorneys who participate in an ESI Conference or who appear at a conference addressing ESI issues must be sufficiently versed in matters relating to their clients' technological systems to competently address ESI issues; counsel may bring a client representative or outside expert to assist in such discussions.

(4) *ESI Order.* The court may enter an order governing the discovery of ESI pursuant to the parties' ESI discovery plan, upon motion of a party, by stipulation of the parties, or on its own.

[Adopted effective March 1, 1985. Amended June 11, 1991, effective October 1, 1991, 437 Mich; May 8, 2000, effective August 1, 2000, 462 Mich; January 31, 2003, effective May 1, 2003, 467 Mich; December 16, 2008, effective January 1, 2009, 482 Mich; June 19, 2019, effective January 1, 2020, 503 Mich.]

Comments

Staff Comment to 1985 Adoption

MCR 2.401 is comparable to GCR 1963, 301.

Subrule (A) makes the holding of a pretrial conference optional. Under GCR 1963, 301.1 such conferences were required, although Wayne circuit local rule 301.1 made them optional in that court and GCR 1963, 301.8 permitted the parties to waive the pretrial conference in other counties. Despite the general rule that the holding of a conference is optional, under subrule (A)(2) one must be held if requested by a party within 182 days after the filing of an answer, if that would not delay the trial.

Subrule (B) covers the matters that may be considered at the pretrial conference. Added to the list found in GCR 1963, 301.1 are the necessity for additional time for discovery (see MCR 2.301), and the appropriateness of mediation under MCR 2.403.

Under subrule (C) the court may direct the attorneys to prepare the summary of the results of the conference.

Subrule (C)(3) differs slightly from GCR 1963, 301.3. The latter said that a party is not to be deprived of the right to present evidence on issues raised by the pleadings unless they were waived at the pretrial conference. Subrule (C)(3) takes account of the fact that some issues need not be pleaded in order to be preserved for trial, but rather may be preserved by motion. See MCR 2.111(F)(2)(a).

Subrule (E) retains the provision of GCR 1963, 301.5 allowing the court to require the parties to be present or available at the conference. There is a new, related provision in MCR 2.506(A)(2), which also applies to insurance representatives.

New language is added in subrule (F) regarding sanctions for failure to appear at a conference. Dismissal is added as a possible sanction. In addition, the court may excuse the failure to appear under certain circumstances.

The protracted litigation provision of GCR 1963, 301.6 is omitted.

Staff Comment to 1991 Amendment

There are extensive revisions of MCR 2.401 [effective October 1, 1991], governing pretrial procedure and conferences. In addition to adjustments in a number of the other subrules, new provisions are added regarding scheduling orders [subrule (B)(2)], attendance of attorneys at conferences [subrule (E)], and service of witness lists [subrule (I)].

Staff Comment to 2000 Amendment

The amendment is based on the recommendations of the Michigan Supreme Court Dispute Resolution Task Force, which was published for comment on May 10, 1999, see 459 Mich 1251, and was the subject of a series of public hearings across the state.

The Task Force report, issued in January 1999, and its addendum report, issued in January 2000 after receipt of comments, should be consulted for the background and details of the amendment. Basically, the change is as follows.

MCR 2.401 is amended to direct consideration of alternative dispute resolution processes at scheduling and pretrial conferences.

Staff Comment to 2003 Amendment

MCR 2.401(F) and (G), MCR 2.410(D)(2) and (3), MCR 2.506(A), and MCR 7.213(A) were amended January 31, 2003, effective May 1, 2003. Before the amendments, each of these subrules included a requirement that someone with "authority to settle" (or similar language) attend the type of proceeding described in each subrule. The amendments substituted the more flexible requirement that the person attending the proceeding have "information and authority adequate for responsible and effective participation" in settlement discussions.

The 2003 amendments of MCR 2.401(G) and MCR 2.410(D)(3) de-emphasized the use of defaults as sanctions for a party's failure to comply fully with an order. The amended rules allow entry of a default, but tilt in favor of less drastic sanctions.

Staff Comment to 2009 Amendment

These amendments update Michigan's discovery rules as they relate to electronically stored information. The provisions of the proposal at MCR 2.302(B)(6) and MCR 2.506(A)(3) allow the court to shift the cost of discovery to the requesting party if discovery is requested from sources that are not reasonably accessible, and prohibit sanctions if information is lost or destroyed as a result of a good-faith, routine record destruction policy or "litigation hold" procedures. The "safe harbor" provision provided in MCR 2.302(B)(5) and in MCR 2.313 applies when information is lost or destroyed under a routine electronic information system, if the operation of the system was performed in good faith. Good faith may be shown by a party's actions to attempt to preserve information as part of a "litigation hold" that would otherwise have been lost or destroyed under an electronic information system.

The new language of MCR 2.302 and MCR 2.506 also allows parties to determine the format in which the information should be produced, and how to handle a situation in which protected information is inadvertently produced.

Staff Comment to 2020 Amendment

These amendments are based on a proposal created by a special committee of the State Bar of Michigan and approved for submission to the Court by the Bar's Representative Assembly. The rules require mandatory discovery disclosure in many cases, adopt a presumptive limit on interrogatories (20 in most cases, but 35 in domestic relations proceedings) and limit a deposition to 7 hours. The amendments also update the rules to more specifically address issues related to electronically stored information, and encourage early action on discovery issues during the discovery period.

The amendment of MCR 2.309(A)(2) sets a presumptive limit of twenty interrogatories for each separately represented party. Several commenters suggested that the term "discrete subpart" be more explicitly defined. But the rule's reference to "a discrete subpart" is intended to draw guidance from federal courts construing FR Civ P 30(a)(1). Generally, subparts are not separately counted if they are logically or factually subsumed within and necessarily related to the primary question. In upholding the limit, parties and courts should also pragmatically balance the overall goals of discovery and the admonition of MCR 1.105. Further, the intent of the provision at MCR 2.301(B)(4) is to ensure that parties responding to discovery requests have the full time period to do so as provided for under these rules prior to the expiration of the discovery period.

Rule 2.402   Use of Communication Equipment

(A) Definition. "Communication equipment" means a conference telephone or other electronic device that permits all those appearing or participating to hear and speak to each other.

(B) Use. A court may, on its own initiative or on the written request of a party, direct that communication equipment be used for a motion hearing, pretrial conference, scheduling conference, or status conference. The court must give notice to the parties before directing on its own initiative that communication equipment be used. A party wanting to use communication equipment must submit a written request to the court at least 7 days before the day on which such equipment is sought to be used, and serve a copy on the other parties, unless good cause is shown to waive this requirement. The requesting party also must provide a copy of the request to the office of the judge to whom the request is directed. The court may, with the consent of all parties or for good cause, direct that the testimony of a witness be taken through communication equipment. A verbatim record of the proceeding must still be made.

(C) Burden of Expense. The party who initiates the use of communication equipment shall pay the cost for its use, unless the court otherwise directs. If the use of communication equipment is initiated by the court, the cost for its use is to be shared equally, unless the court otherwise directs.

[Adopted effective March 1, 1985. Amended June 2, 1998, effective September 1, 1998, 457 Mich; June 1, 2000, effective September 1, 2000, 462 Mich.]

Comments

Staff Comment to 1985 Adoption

MCR 2.402 is substantially the same as GCR 1963, 918.

Staff Comment to 1998 Amendment

The June 1998 amendment of MCR 2.402(B), effective September 1, 1998, was suggested by the Michigan Judges Association. The amendment permits a court to arrange for a witness to testify through communication equipment "for good cause," as well as if all parties consent.

Staff Comment to 2000 Amendment

The June 21, 2000 amendments of MCR 2.402 (B) and (C), effective September 1, 2000, added a scheduling conference to the list of proceedings for which communication equipment may be used, allowed discretion for late requests, required that a copy of the request be provided to the office of the judge to whom it is directed, and assigned the cost for using communication equipment to the requesting party.

Rule 2.403   Case Evaluation

(A) Scope and Applicability of Rule.

(1) A court may submit to case evaluation any civil action in which the relief sought is primarily money damages or division of property.

(2) Case evaluation of tort cases filed in circuit court is mandatory beginning with actions filed after the effective dates of Chapters 49 and 49A of the Revised Judicature Act, as added by 1986 PA 178.

(3) A court may exempt claims seeking equitable relief from case evaluation for good cause shown on motion or by stipulation of the parties if the court finds that case evaluation of such claims would be inappropriate.

(4) Cases filed in district court may be submitted to case evaluation under this rule. The time periods set forth in subrules (B)(1), (G)(1), (L)(1) and (L)(2) may be shortened at the discretion of the district judge to whom the case is assigned.

(B) Selection of Cases.

(1) The judge to whom an action is assigned or the chief judge may select it for case evaluation by written order after the filing of the answer

   (a) on written stipulation by the parties,

   (b) on written motion by a party, or

   (c) on the judge's own initiative.

(2) Selection of an action for case evaluation has no effect on the normal progress of the action toward trial.

(C) Objections to Case Evaluation.

(1) To object to case evaluation, a party must file a written motion to remove from case evaluation and a notice of hearing of the motion and serve a copy on the attorneys of record and the ADR clerk within 14 days after notice of the order assigning the action to case evaluation. The motion must be set for hearing within 14 days after it is filed, unless the court orders otherwise.

(2) A timely motion must be heard before the case is submitted to case evaluation.

(D) Case Evaluation Panel.

(1) Case evaluation panels shall be composed of 3 persons.

(2) The procedure for selecting case evaluation panels is as provided in MCR 2.404.

(3) A judge may be selected as a member of a case evaluation panel, but may not preside at the trial of any action in which he or she served as a case evaluator.

(4) A case evaluator may not be called as a witness at trial.

(E) Disqualification of Case Evaluators. The rule for disqualification of a case evaluator is the same as that provided in MCR 2.003 for the disqualification of a judge.

(F) ADR Clerk. The court shall designate the ADR clerk specified under MCR 2.410, or some other person, to administer the case evaluation program. In this rule and MCR 2.404, "ADR clerk" refers to the person so designated.

(G) Scheduling Case Evaluation Hearing.

(1) The ADR clerk shall set a time and place for the hearing and send notice to the case evaluators and the attorneys at least 42 days before the date set.

(2) Adjournments may be granted only for good cause, in accordance with MCR 2.503.

(H) Fees.

(1) Each party must send a check for $75 made payable in the manner and within the time specified in the notice of the case evaluation hearing. However, if a judge is a member of the panel, the fee is $50. If the order for case evaluation directs that payment be made to the ADR clerk, the ADR clerk shall arrange payment to the case evaluators. Except by stipulation and court order, the parties may not make any other payment of fees or expenses to the case evaluators than that provided in this subrule.

(2) Only a single fee is required of each party, even where there are counterclaims, cross-claims, or third-party claims. A person entitled to a fee waiver under MCR 2.002 is entitled to a waiver of fees under this rule.

(3) If one claim is derivative of another (e.g., husband-wife, parent-child) they must be treated as a single claim, with one fee to be paid and a single award made by the case evaluators.

(4) Fees paid pursuant to subrule (H) shall be refunded to the parties if

(a) the court sets aside the order submitting the case to case evaluation or on its own initiative adjourns the case evaluation hearing, or

(b) the parties notify the ADR clerk in writing at least 14 days before the case evaluation hearing of the settlement, dismissal, or entry of judgment disposing of the action, or of an order of adjournment on stipulation or the motion of a party.

If case evaluation is rescheduled at a later time, the fee provisions of subrule (H) apply regardless of whether previously paid fees have been refunded.

(5) Fees paid pursuant to subrule (H) shall not be refunded to the parties if

(a) in the case of an adjournment, the adjournment order sets a new date for case evaluation and the fees are applied to the new date, or

(b) the request for and granting of adjournment is made within 14 days of the scheduled case evaluation, unless waived for good cause.

Penalties for late filing of papers under subrule (I)(2) are not to be refunded.

(I) Submission of Summary and Supporting Documents.

(1) Unless otherwise provided in the notice of hearing, at least 14 days before the hearing, each party shall

(a) serve a copy of the case evaluation summary and supporting documents in accordance with MCR 2.107, and

(b) file a proof of service and three copies of a case evaluation summary and supporting documents with the ADR clerk.

(2) Each failure to timely file and serve the materials identified in subrule (1) and each subsequent filing of supplemental materials within 14 days of the hearing, subjects the offending attorney or party to a $150 penalty to be paid in the manner specified in the notice of the case evaluation hearing. An offending attorney shall not charge the penalty to the client, unless the client agreed in writing to be responsible for the penalty.

(3) The case evaluation summary shall consist of a concise summary setting forth that party's factual and legal position on issues presented by the action. Except as permitted by the court, the summary shall not exceed 20 pages double spaced, exclusive of attachments. Quotations and footnotes may be single spaced. At least one inch margins must be used, and printing shall not be smaller than 12–point font.

(J) Conduct of Hearing.

(1) A party has the right, but is not required, to attend a case evaluation hearing. If scars, disfigurement, or other unusual conditions exist, they may be demonstrated to the panel by a personal appearance; however, no testimony will be taken or permitted of any party.

(2) The rules of evidence do not apply before the case evaluation panel. Factual information having a bearing on damages or liability must be supported by documentary evidence, if possible.

(3) Oral Presentation shall be limited to 15 minutes per side unless multiple parties or unusual circumstances warrant additional time. Information on settlement negotiations not protected under MCR 2.412 and applicable insurance policy limits shall be disclosed at the request of the case evaluation panel.

(4) Statements by the attorneys and the briefs or summaries are not admissible in any court or evidentiary proceeding.

(5) Counsel or the parties may not engage in ex parte communications with the case evaluators concerning the action prior to the hearing. After the evaluation, the case evaluators need not respond to inquiries by the parties or counsel regarding the proceeding or the evaluation.

(K) Decision.

(1) Within 14 days after the hearing, the panel will make an evaluation and submit the evaluation to the ADR clerk. If an evaluation is made immediately following the hearing, the panel will provide a copy to the attorney for each party of its evaluation in writing. If an evaluation is not made immediately following the hearing, the evaluation must be served by the ADR clerk on each party within 14 days after the hearing. If an award is not unanimous, the evaluation must so indicate.

(2) Except as provided in subrule (H)(3), the evaluation must include a separate award as to each plaintiff's claim against each defendant and as to each cross-claim, counterclaim, or third-party claim that has been filed in the action. For the purpose of this subrule, all such claims filed by any one party against any other party shall be treated as a single claim.

(3) The evaluation may not include a separate award on any claim for equitable relief, but the panel may consider such claims in determining the amount of an award.

(4) In a tort case to which MCL 600.4915(2) or MCL 600.4963(2) applies, if the panel unanimously finds that a party's action or defense as to any other party is frivolous, the panel shall so indicate on the evaluation. For the purpose of this rule, an action or defense is "frivolous" if, as to all of a plaintiff's claims or all of a defendant's defenses to liability, at least 1 of the following conditions is met:

(a) The party's primary purpose in initiating the action or asserting the defense was to harass, embarrass, or injure the opposing party.

(b) The party had no reasonable basis to believe that the facts underlying that party's legal position were in fact true.

(c) The party's legal position was devoid of arguable legal merit.

(5) In an action alleging medical malpractice to which MCL 600.4915 applies, the evaluation must include a specific finding that

(a) there has been a breach of the applicable standard of care,

(b) there has not been a breach of the applicable standard of care, or

(c) reasonable minds could differ as to whether there has been a breach of the applicable standard of care.

(L) Acceptance or Rejection of Evaluation.

(1) Each party shall file a written acceptance or rejection of the panel's evaluation with the ADR clerk within 28 days after service of the panel's evaluation. Even if there are separate awards on multiple claims, the party must either accept or reject the evaluation in its entirety as to a particular opposing party. The failure to file a written acceptance or rejection within 28 days constitutes rejection.

(2) There may be no disclosure of a party's acceptance or rejection of the panel's evaluation until the expiration of the 28–day period, at which time the ADR clerk shall send a notice indicating each party's acceptance or rejection of the panel's evaluation.

(3) In case evaluations involving multiple parties the following rules apply:

(a) Each party has the option of accepting all of the awards covering the claims by or against that party or of accepting some and rejecting others. However, as to any particular opposing party, the party must either accept or reject the evaluation in its entirety.

(b) A party who accepts all of the awards may specifically indicate that he or she intends the acceptance to be effective only if

(i) all opposing parties accept, and/or

(ii) the opposing parties accept as to specified coparties.

If such a limitation is not included in the acceptance, an accepting party is deemed to have agreed to entry of judgment, or dismissal as provided in subrule (M)(1), as to that party and those of the opposing parties who accept, with the action to continue between the accepting party and those opposing parties who reject.

(c) If a party makes a limited acceptance under subrule (L)(3)(b) and some of the opposing parties accept and others reject, for the purposes of the cost provisions of subrule (O) the party who made the limited acceptance is deemed to have rejected as to those opposing parties who accept.

(M) Effect of Acceptance of Evaluation.

(1) If all the parties accept the panel's evaluation, judgment will be entered in accordance with the evaluation, unless the amount of the award is paid within 28 days after notification of the acceptances, in which case the court shall dismiss the action with prejudice. The judgment or dismissal shall be deemed to dispose of all claims in the action and includes all fees, costs, and interest to the date it is entered, except for cases involving

rights to personal protection insurance benefits under MCL 500.3101 *et seq.*, for which judgment or dismissal shall not be deemed to dispose of claims that have not accrued as of the date of the case evaluation hearing.

(2) If only a part of an action has been submitted to case evaluation pursuant to subrule (A)(3) and all of the parties accept the panel's evaluation, the court shall enter an order disposing of only those claims.

(3) In a case involving multiple parties, judgment, or dismissal as provided in subrule (1), shall be entered as to those opposing parties who have accepted the portions of the evaluation that apply to them.

(N) Proceedings After Rejection.

(1) If all or part of the evaluation of the case evaluation panel is rejected, the action proceeds to trial in the normal fashion.

(2) If a party's claim or defense was found to be frivolous under subrule (K)(4), that party may request that the court review the panel's finding by filing a motion within 14 days after the ADR clerk sends notice of the rejection of the case evaluation award.

(a) The motion shall be submitted to the court on the case evaluation summaries and documents that were considered by the case evaluation panel. No other exhibits or testimony may be submitted. However, oral argument on the motion shall be permitted.

(b) After reviewing the materials submitted, the court shall determine whether the action or defense is frivolous.

(c) If the court agrees with the panel's determination, the provisions of subrule (N)(3) apply, except that the bond must be filed within 28 days after the entry of the court's order determining the action or defense to be frivolous.

(d) The judge who hears a motion under this subrule may not preside at a nonjury trial of the action.

(3) Except as provided in subrule (2), if a party's claim or defense was found to be frivolous under subrule (K)(4), that party shall post a cash or surety bond, pursuant to MCR 3.604, in the amount of $5,000 for each party against whom the action or defense was determined to be frivolous.

(a) The bond must be posted within 56 days after the case evaluation hearing or at least 14 days before trial, whichever is earlier.

(b) If a surety bond is filed, an insurance company that insures the defendant against a claim made in the action may not act as the surety.

(c) If the bond is not posted as required by this rule, the court shall dismiss a claim found to have been frivolous, and enter the default of a defendant whose defense was found to be frivolous. The action shall proceed to trial as to the remaining claims and parties, and as to the amount of damages against a defendant in default.

(d) If judgment is entered against the party who posted the bond, the bond shall be used to pay any costs awarded against that party by the court under any applicable law or court rule. MCR 3.604 applies to proceedings to enforce the bond.

(4) The ADR clerk shall place a copy of the case evaluation and the parties' acceptances and rejections in a sealed envelope for filing with the clerk of the court. In a nonjury action, the

envelope may not be opened and the parties may not reveal the amount of the evaluation until the judge has rendered judgment.

(O) Rejecting Party's Liability for Costs.

(1) If a party has rejected an evaluation and the action proceeds to verdict, that party must pay the opposing party's actual costs unless the verdict is more favorable to the rejecting party than the case evaluation. However, if the opposing party has also rejected the evaluation, a party is entitled to costs only if the verdict is more favorable to that party than the case evaluation.

(2) For the purpose of this rule "verdict" includes,

(a) a jury verdict,

(b) a judgment by the court after a nonjury trial,

(c) a judgment entered as a result of a ruling on a motion after rejection of the case evaluation.

(3) For the purpose of subrule (O)(1), a verdict must be adjusted by adding to it assessable costs and interest on the amount of the verdict from the filing of the complaint to the date of the case evaluation, and, if applicable, by making the adjustment of future damages as provided by MCL 600.6306. After this adjustment, the verdict is considered more favorable to a defendant if it is more than 10 percent below the evaluation, and is considered more favorable to the plaintiff if it is more than 10 percent above the evaluation. If the evaluation was zero, a verdict finding that a defendant is not liable to the plaintiff shall be deemed more favorable to the defendant.

(4) In cases involving multiple parties, the following rules apply:

(a) Except as provided in subrule (O)(4)(b), in determining whether the verdict is more favorable to a party than the case evaluation, the court shall consider only the amount of the evaluation and verdict as to the particular pair of parties, rather than the aggregate evaluation or verdict as to all parties. However, costs may not be imposed on a plaintiff who obtains an aggregate verdict more favorable to the plaintiff than the aggregate evaluation.

(b) If the verdict against more than one defendant is based on their joint and several liability, the plaintiff may not recover costs unless the verdict is more favorable to the plaintiff than the total case evaluation as to those defendants, and a defendant may not recover costs unless the verdict is more favorable to that defendant than the case evaluation as to that defendant.

(c) Except as provided by subrule (O)(10), in a personal injury action, for the purpose of subrule (O)(1), the verdict against a particular defendant shall not be adjusted by applying that defendant's proportion of fault as determined under MCL 600.6304(1)-(2).

(5) If the verdict awards equitable relief, costs may be awarded if the court determines that

(a) taking into account both monetary relief (adjusted as provided in subrule [O][3]) and equitable relief, the verdict is not more favorable to the rejecting party than the evaluation, or, in situations where both parties have rejected the evaluation, the verdict in favor of the party seeking costs is more favorable than the case evaluation, and

(b) it is fair to award costs under all of the circumstances.

(6) For the purpose of this rule, actual costs are

(a) those costs taxable in any civil action, and

(b) a reasonable attorney fee based on a reasonable hourly or daily rate as determined by the trial judge for services necessitated by the rejection of the case evaluation, which may include legal services provided by attorneys representing themselves or the entity for whom they work, including the time and labor of any legal assistant as defined by MCR 2.626.

For the purpose of determining taxable costs under this subrule and under MCR 2.625, the party entitled to recover actual costs under this rule shall be considered the prevailing party.

(7) Costs shall not be awarded if the case evaluation award was not unanimous. If case evaluation results in a nonunanimous award, a case may be ordered to a subsequent case evaluation hearing conducted without reference to the prior case evaluation award, or other alternative dispute resolution processes, at the expense of the parties, pursuant to MCR 2.410(C)(1).

(8) A request for costs under this subrule must be filed and served within 28 days after the entry of the judgment or entry of an order denying a timely motion

(i) for a new trial,

(ii) to set aside the judgment, or

(iii) for rehearing or reconsideration.

(9) In an action under MCL 436.1801, if the plaintiff rejects the award against the minor or alleged intoxicated person, or is deemed to have rejected such an award under subrule (L)(3)(c), the court shall not award costs against the plaintiff in favor of the minor or alleged intoxicated person unless it finds that the rejection was not motivated by the need to comply with MCL 436.1801(5).

(10) For the purpose of subrule (O)(1), in an action filed on or after March 28, 1996, and based on tort or another legal theory seeking damages for personal injury, property damage, or wrongful death, a verdict awarding damages shall be adjusted for relative fault as provided by MCL 600.6304.

(11) If the "verdict" is the result of a motion as provided by subrule (O)(2)(c), the court may, in the interest of justice, refuse to award actual costs.

[Adopted effective March 1, 1985. Amended January 22, 1987 effective April 1, 1987, 428 Mich; August 12, 1987, effective October 1, 1987, 429 Mich; September 25, 1987, effective December 1, 1987, 429 Mich; October 3, 1987, effective January 1, 1988, 429 Mich; December 21, 1989, effective March 31, 1990, 434 Mich. Amended effective July 2, 1991, 437 Mich. Amended December 1, 1994, effective February 1, 1995, 447 Mich; November 6, 1996, effective February 1, 1997, 453 Mich; May 8, 1997, effective October 1, 1997, 454 Mich; May 9, 2000, effective August 1, 2000, 462 Mich; January 20, 2009, effective May 1, 2009, 483 Mich; April 5, 2011, effective September 1, 2011, 489 Mich; December 21, 2011, effective May 1, 2012, 490 Mich; October 2, 2013, effective January 1, 2014, 495 Mich; September 23, 2015, effective January 1, 2016, 498 Mich. Amended effective March 9, 2016, 499 Mich; March 20, 2019, effective May 1, 2019, 502 Mich.]

Comments

Staff Comment to 1985 Adoption

MCR 2.403 corresponds to GCR 1963, 316. There are a number of revisions.

Subrule (A) deletes the authorization for a separate procedure for the Third Judicial Circuit. However, one of the key features of the third circuit rule is adopted for statewide use. Under subrule (L)(1), failure to file an acceptance or rejection of a mediation award within the time provided constitutes acceptance of the award, unlike the practice under GCR 1963, 316.6(H)(1), which made failure to file an acceptance the equivalent of rejection. The time for accepting or rejecting the award is set at 28 days.

Subrule (C)(2) is changed from the corresponding language of GCR 1963, 316.3(B). Under the latter provision, a motion to remove a case from mediation stayed mediation proceedings. Subrule (C)(2) does not include the stay provision, but says instead that such a motion must be heard before the case is submitted to mediation.

Subrules (F)–(O) are reorganized and rewritten, although only a few substantive changes are included.

First, subrule (H)(1) does not direct that the checks by which the parties pay the mediation fee are to be payable to the attorney mediators, as had GCR 1963, 316.6(C)(1). Rather, the checks are to be made payable in the manner specified in the mediation notice. In some courts the mediation program might be arranged so that it is more convenient to have the checks payable to the mediation clerk or the court clerk.

Subrule (I) not only requires that the parties submit documents relating to the issues to be mediated, but also that they supply briefs or summaries setting forth their legal or factual positions on the issues. Failure to submit either document to the mediation clerk at least 7 days before the hearing date subjects the party to the cost penalty imposed by subrule (I)(2). Under the corresponding provision, GCR 1963, 316.6(E), the penalty provisions applied only to the documents. Submission of the brief or summary was optional.

Under GCR 1963, 316.6(F)(3), the mediators were not permitted to inquire into settlement negotiations. Subrule (J)(3) modifies the prohibition. The mediators may inquire unless a party objects. This is similar to the provision of the former third circuit local rule 403.12.

Several provisions of the rule are modified to deal with the situation in which there is more than one party on a side. Subrule (H)(1) makes clear that only a single fee is required of each party even where there are counterclaims, cross-claims, or third-party claims. Second, subrule (K)(2) specifies that the evaluation must include a separate award as to each cross-claim, counterclaim, or third-party claim, although all claims between any two parties are treated as a single claim. Finally, under subrule (L)(3), parties are permitted to accept some, but less than all, of the individual awards. Judgment will be entered as to those pairs of parties who have accepted. See subrule (M)(2). However, a party has the option of making a "conditional" acceptance of the entire award, specifying that if fewer than all of the opposing parties accept, the party making the conditional acceptance should be taken as rejecting as to all of them. A party may be willing to accept the award in its entirety if that has the effect of eliminating the need for a trial. However, if the case is going to be tried anyway, the party may prefer to have a trial as to all opposing parties. For the purpose of applying the cost provisions, a party making a conditional acceptance is treated as having rejected the award as to those opposing parties who accepted it. See subrule (L)(3)(c).

The [March 1, 1985] amendment of MCR 2.403(N)(2) deletes the requirement that the mediation clerk return copies of mediation documents to the attorney who submitted them.

The [March 1, 1985] amendment of MCR 2.403(O)(1) revises the language regarding the liability for costs of a party who rejects a mediation evaluation, correcting an unintended change from GCR 316.7(b). The rejecting party is liable for costs unless that party improves its position by at least 10 percent (unless the other party has rejected, in which case a party is liable for costs only if the opponent improves its position by at least 10 percent).

Finally, subrule (O)(4) adopts the principle, found in the third circuit local rule 403.15, that where the mediation panel's award is not unanimous, costs are not to be awarded against a rejecting party. Subrule (K)(1) requires that if the award is not unanimous, it must so indicate.

Staff Comment to January, 1987 Amendment

The amendments of MCR 2.403(K) and (N) [adopted January 22, 1987] deal with the relationship between mediation and removal of cases from circuit to district court under MCL 600.641. The language adopted is that recommended by a committee appointed to evaluate the mediation process. See volume 426B of Michigan Reports.

New MCR 2.403(K) [adopted January 22, 1987] provides that if a mediation award does not exceed the jurisdictional limitation on the district court, the mediators must include a statement as to whether the damages sustained, without regard to liability questions, exceed the district court jurisdictional limit.

A corresponding amendment of MCR 2.403(N) [adopted January 22, 1987] requires that this statement be provided to the circuit judge when the judge is informed that the award does not exceed the district court jurisdictional limit.

Subrule (N)(2) provides that in a nonjury case not only must the evaluation itself be sealed until the judge has entered judgment, but the parties are forbidden to tell the judge about the mediation award. Compare GCR 1963, 316.6(H)(2).

Staff Comment to October, 1987 Amendment

The August 12, 1987, amendment of subrule (A) relates to the adoption of the new domestic relations mediation rule, MCR 3.211, effective October 1, 1987.

Staff Comment to December, 1987 Amendment

The September 25, 1987, amendments of MCR 2.403 [effective December 1, 1987] grew out of the work of the Mediation Evaluation Committee appointed on April 4, 1986. A detailed explanation of its proposals can be found in the Committee's report, which was published as Volume 426B of Michigan Reports. Several other parts of the Committee's recommendations had been acted upon in previous orders amending MCR 2.403, 428 Mich cxlvii, MCR 4.003, 428 Mich clix, and adopting new MCR 3.211, 428 Mich cxlix.

The amendment of subrule (A)(1) emphasizes that mediation is intended for use in cases involving money damages and division of property, but leaves open the possibility of submitting cases in which other kinds of relief are sought. There are related changes in subrules (K)(3) and (O)(5) dealing with the form of mediation evaluations and the awarding of costs.

New subrule (A)(2) deals with probate proceedings, permitting submission to mediation of portions of such proceedings.

Subrule (I)(1) is amended to require that a proof of service on the opposing party be submitted with the other mediation documents.

The amendment to subrule (K)(2) clarifies that a separate award must be made as to plaintiff's claim against each defendant.

There are a series of changes in subrule (O), which concerns the award of costs following rejection of a mediation evaluation.

New subrule (O)(2) defines "verdict."

Language is added to subrule (O)(3) [formerly (O)(2)] to provide that a verdict is considered "more favorable" to a defendant than a mediation award when both the award and the verdict are zero.

New subrule (O)(4) adds several provisions for determining liability for costs in cases involving multiple parties.

Subrule (O)(6) [formerly (O)(3)] is amended to provide that the attorney fee component of costs awarded under the rule is to be computed on a reasonable hourly or daily rate.

Several other recommendations of the Mediation Evaluation Committee remain under study. In addition, other provisions of the proposal published for comment [see 65 Michigan Bar Journal 1157 (November, 1986)] relate to the mediation provisions of 1986 PA 178, which are being considered by a separate committee appointed to study the mediation of medical malpractice actions.

Staff Comment to 1988 Amendment

The October 23, 1987, amendments to MCR 2.403 [effective January 1, 1988] relate to the mediation provisions of 1986 PA 178, MCL 600.4901–600.4969. The amendments are effective January 1, 1988. Although a number of subrules are unaffected by the amendments, the text of the entire rule is set forth to avoid confusion in light of the September 25, 1987, amendments to the rule, which take effect on December 1, 1987.

New subrule (A)(2) implements the requirements of MCL 600.4903 and MCL 600.4951, which direct that all tort cases be mediated. The trial court may except a case on motion for good cause.

New subrule (D)(4) implements MCL 600.4905, which directs that in medical malpractice cases the mediation panel include two health care professionals. The new provision spells out the procedure for making designations of health care professionals, including provisions dealing with cases in which there is more than one party on a side or in which the defendants have different specialties or fields of practice. Subrule (D)(4)(c) provides that the mediation hearing is to proceed with fewer than five mediators if a party fails to make a designation or a designated person does not appear at the hearing.

New subrule (D)(5) prohibits the calling of a mediator as a witness at trial.

Subrule (G)(1) is amended to provide that the notice of the mediation hearing must be given 56 days in advance, in order to give the parties time to locate and designate health care professionals to serve on the mediation panel.

In subrule (H), the fee is increased to $125 in medical malpractice cases, since there are two additional mediators. The rule also expressly provides that the parties may not make any payments to mediators other than as provided in the rule.

Subrule (I)(1) is amended to require five copies of mediation documents in medical malpractice cases.

There is a minor change in subrule (I)(2) regarding payment of penalties to mediators to take account of the possibility of non-lawyers serving as mediators.

Subrule (K)(5) is added and subrule (N)(1) is amended to implement the provisions of MCL 600.4915(2) and MCL 600.4963(2), which require the posting of a bond by a party whose claim or defense the mediation panel unanimously finds to be frivolous.

New subrule (K)(6) implements MCL 600.4915(1), which requires that the evaluation in medical malpractice cases include a specific finding on the applicable standard of care.

Staff Comment to 1989 Amendment

On May 3, 1989, the Court ordered published for comment several proposals regarding the mediation rule, MCR 2.403, and the offer of judgment rule, MCR 2.405. See 68 Michigan Bar Journal 558 (June, 1989). The January 3, 1990, order [effective March 31, 1990] adopts several of those changes, some with modifications. Other proposed amendments to MCR 2.403(H)(1), (I)(2), and (J), giving trial courts greater flexibility in the use of mediation fees, increasing penalties for late filing of mediation documents with each day that they are late, and requiring attorneys and unrepresented parties to attend mediation sessions, remain under consideration.

MCR 2.403(G)(1) and (I)(1) are amended to lengthen the time for giving notice of the mediation hearing and for submitting mediation summaries.

There is a minor change in MCR 2.403(H)(1) to give courts flexibility in setting the time when mediation fees are to be paid.

New MCR 2.403(H)(5) covers the refunding of fees when the mediation hearing is not held.

There are three minor amendments to MCR 2.403(I)(1). First, the language is changed to direct the parties to "file," rather than "submit," mediation documents. Second, the amended rule refers to a mediation "summary" rather than "summary or brief." The summary must include both the party's factual and legal arguments. Third, there is a change in the language regarding the filing of a proof of service of mediation documents. There is a corresponding change in subrule (I)(2), making the failure to serve opposing counsel grounds for imposing the late filing penalty.

In MCR 2.403(I)(2), new language provides that attorneys may not charge late filing penalties to their clients unless the clients have agreed to be responsible for the penalties.

MCR 2.403(L)(1) is amended to provide that the failure to file an acceptance or rejection is considered a rejection, as had been the case under former GCR 1963, 316.6(h)(1).

The revision of MCR 2.403(M) would clarify that the entry of a judgment following acceptance of an award disposes of the entire case, even if the case includes equitable claims on which the mediation panel is not permitted to make an award.

There are several changes in MCR 2.403(O)(6) to clarify what costs are recoverable.

In MCR 2.403(O)(8) there is new language setting the time within which a party must seek to recover costs under the mediation rule.

Staff Comment to 1991 Amendment

The July 2, 1991, amendment of MCR 2.403(O) adds a new subrule (9), in light of the decision in *Shay v JohnKAL, Inc*, 437 Mich 394, 471 NW2d 551 (decided July 2, 1991).

Staff Comment to 1995 Amendment

Former subrule 2.403(A)(3) is deleted [effective February 1, 1995]. The mediation for probate proceedings is covered in MCR 5.403. Mediation for civil actions in probate court remains under this rule. See MCR 5.101(C).

Staff Comment to February, 1997 Amendment

The November 6, 1996, amendment of MCR 2.403, relates to statutory changes made by 1995 PA 161 and 1995 PA 249.

The amendment of MCR 2.403 adds a new subrule (O)(10) to the mediation rule. It requires the adjusting of verdicts for relative fault as required by MCL 600.6304.

Staff Comment to October, 1997 Amendment

The order of May 8, 1997, postpones the effective date of the earlier amendment of MCR 2.403, affecting mediation procedure, to October 1, 1997. The order of May 8, 1997, adjusts MCR 2.403(K) and (N) in light of the repeal of MCR 4.003. The text of MCR 2.403 is the same as that adopted in the Court's March 5, 1997, order dealing with those rules.

Staff Comment to 2000 Amendment

The May 8, 2000, amendments [effective August 1, 2000] are based on the recommendations of the Michigan Supreme Court Dispute Resolution Task Force, which were published for comment on May 10, 1999 [see 459 Mich 1251], and were the subject of a series of public hearings across the state.

The Task Force report, issued in January 1999, and its Addendum report, issued in January 2000 after receipt of comments, should be consulted for the background and details of the amendments. Basically, the changes are as follows: The amendments of MCR 2.403, 2.404, 2.405, 2.501, 2.502 and 2.503 are mainly to change terminology, replacing "mediation," as used in current MCR 2.403, with the term "case evaluation." "Mediation" will be used to describe the facilitative process established in MCR 2.411, in keeping with the generally accepted usage of the term.

Staff Comment to 2009 Amendment

The amendment of MCR 2.112 clarifies that the subrule provisions apply to actions based on tort or another legal theory seeking damages for personal injury, property damage, or wrongful death to which MCL 600.2957 and MCL 600.6304 apply, and more closely parallels the statutory provisions on which it is based. A similar change has been made in MCR 2.403(O)(10), which was also based on MCL 600.6304.

Staff Comment to April, 2011 Amendment

The amendments of MCR 2.403, 2.411, and 3.216, and the adoption of new MCR 2.412 consolidate provisions related to mediation confidentiality into one rule and expand the number of exceptions to mediation confidentiality.

Staff Comment to December, 2011 Amendment

The amendments of MCR 2.403, 2.404, 2.410, 2.411, and 2.412 revise court rules relating to mediation and case evaluation largely as recommended by the Dispute Resolution Rules Committee convened by the State Court Administrative Office. The amendment of MCR 3.216 reflects amendments to provisions that appear in MCR 2.411 that also appear in MCR 3.216.

Staff Comment to 2014 Amendment

The amendments of MCR 2.403(O)(8), MCR 2.405(D)(6), and MCR 2.625(F)(2) add language that references a motion for rehearing or reconsideration (consistent with the Court of Appeals opinion in *MEEMIC Ins Co v DTE Energy Co*, 292 Mich App 278 [2011]) to the list of motions that toll the period of time in which a party may file a request for case-evaluation sanctions.

Staff Comment to January, 2016 Amendment

The amendments of MCR 2.403(O) allow a reasonable attorney fee to be included in a request for costs by attorneys who represent themselves or who are employed by a party to the case for services provided after case evaluation is rejected.

Staff Comment to March, 2016 Amendment

These amendments update cross-references that changed after the rule was adopted and make other nonsubstantive revisions.

Staff Comment to 2019 Amendment

The amendments of Rules 1.109, 2.102, 2.104, 2.106, 2.107, 2.117, 2.119, 2.403, 2.503, 2.506, 2.508, 2.518, 2.602, 2.603, 2.621, 3.101, 3.104, 3.203, 3.205, 3.210, 3.302, 3.607, 3.613, 3.614, 3.705, 3.801, 3.802, 3.805, 3.806, 4.201, 4.202, 4.303, 4.306, 5.001, 5.104, 5.105, 5.107, 5.108, 5.113, 5.117, 5.118, 5.119, 5.120, 5.125, 5.126, 5.132, 5.162, 5.202, 5.203, 5.205, 5.302, 5.304, 5.307, 5.308, 5.309, 5.310, 5.311, 5.313, 5.402, 5.404, 5.405, 5.409, 5.501, and 5.784 and addition of Rule 3.618 of the Michigan Court Rules are an expected progression necessary for design and implementation of the statewide electronic-filing system. These particular amendments will assist in implementing the goals of the project.

Rule 2.404   Selection of Case Evaluation Panels

(A) Case Evaluator Selection Plans.

(1) *Requirement.* Each trial court that submits cases to case evaluation under MCR 2.403 shall adopt by local administrative order a plan to maintain a list of persons available to serve as case evaluators and to assign case evaluators from the list to panels. The plan must be in writing and available to the public in the ADR clerk's office.

(2) *Alternative Plans.*

(a) A plan adopted by a district or probate court may use the list of case evaluators and appointment procedure of the circuit court for the circuit in which the court is located.

(b) Courts in adjoining circuits or districts may jointly adopt and administer a case evaluation plan.

(c) If it is not feasible for a court to adopt its own plan because of the low volume of cases to be submitted or because of inadequate numbers of available case evaluators, the court may enter into an agreement with a neighboring court to refer cases for case evaluation under the other court's system. The agreement may provide for payment by the referring court to cover the cost of administering case evaluation. However, fees and costs may not be assessed against the parties to actions evaluated except as provided by MCR 2.403.

(d) Other alternative plans must be submitted as local court rules under MCR 8.112(A).

(B) Lists of Case Evaluators.

(1) *Application.* An eligible person desiring to serve as a case evaluator may apply to the ADR clerk to be placed on the list of case evaluators. Application forms shall be available in the office of the ADR clerk. The form shall include an optional section identifying the applicant's gender and racial/ethnic background. The form shall include a certification that

(a) the case evaluator meets the requirements for service under the court's selection plan, and

(b) the case evaluator will not discriminate against parties, attorneys, or other case evaluators on the basis of race, ethnic origin, gender, or other protected personal characteristic.

(2) *Eligibility.* To be eligible to serve as a case evaluator, a person must meet the qualifications provided by this subrule.

(a) The applicant must have been a practicing lawyer for at least 5 years and be a member in good standing of the State Bar of Michigan. The plan may not require membership in any other organization as a qualification for service as a case evaluator.

(b) An applicant must reside, maintain an office, or have an active practice in the jurisdiction for which the list of case evaluators is compiled.

(c) An applicant must demonstrate that a substantial portion of the applicant's practice for the last 5 years has been devoted to civil litigation matters, including investigation, discovery, motion practice, case evaluation, settlement, trial preparation, and/or trial.

(d) If separate sublists are maintained for specific types of cases, the applicant must have had an active practice in the practice area for which the case evaluator is listed for at least the last 3 years.

If there are insufficient numbers of potential case evaluators meeting the qualifications stated in this rule, the plan may provide for consideration of alternative qualifications.

(3) *Review of Applications.* The plan shall provide for a person or committee to review applications annually, or more frequently if appropriate, and compile one or more lists of qualified case evaluators. Persons meeting the qualifications specified in this rule shall be placed on the list of approved case evaluators. Selections shall be made without regard to race, ethnic origin, or gender.

(a) If an individual performs this review function, the person must be an employee of the court.

(b) If a committee performs this review function, the following provisions apply.

(i) The committee must have at least three members.

(ii) The selection of committee members shall be designed to assure that the goals stated in subrule (D)(2) will be met.

(iii) A person may not serve on the committee more than 3 years in any 9 year period.

(c) Applicants who are not placed on the case evaluator list or lists shall be notified of that decision. The plan shall provide a procedure by which such an applicant may seek reconsideration of the decision by some other person or committee. The plan need not provide for a hearing of any kind as part of the reconsideration process. Documents considered in the initial review process shall be retained for at least the period of time during which the applicant can seek reconsideration of the original decision.

(4) *Specialized Lists.* If the number and qualifications of available case evaluators makes it practicable to do so, the ADR clerk shall maintain

(a) separate lists for various types of cases, and,

(b) where appropriate for the type of cases, separate sublists of case evaluators who primarily represent plaintiffs, primarily represent defendants, and neutral case evaluators whose practices are not identifiable as representing primarily plaintiffs or defendants.

(5) *Reapplication.* Persons shall be placed on the list of case evaluators for a fixed period of time, not to exceed seven years, and must reapply at the end of that time in the manner directed by the court.

(6) *Availability of Lists.* The list of case evaluators must be available to the public in the ADR clerk's office.

(7) *Removal from List.* The plan must include a procedure for removal from the list of case evaluators who have demonstrated incompetency, bias, made themselves consistently unavailable to serve as a case evaluator, or for other just cause.

(8) The court may require case evaluators to attend orientation or training sessions or provide written materials explaining the case evaluation process and the operation of the court's case evaluation program. However, case evaluators may not be charged any fees or costs for such programs or materials.

(C) Assignments to Panels.

(1) *Method of Assignment.* The ADR clerk shall assign case evaluators to panels in a random or rotating manner that assures as nearly as possible that each case evaluator on a list or sublist is assigned approximately the same number of cases over a period of time. If a substitute case evaluator must be assigned, the same or similar assignment procedure shall be used to select the substitute. The ADR clerk shall maintain records of service of case evaluators on panels and shall make those records available on request.

(2) *Assignment from Sublists.* If sublists of plaintiff, defense, and neutral case evaluators are maintained for a particular type of case, the panel shall include one case evaluator who primarily represents plaintiffs, one case evaluator who primarily represents defendants, and one neutral case evaluator. If a judge is assigned to a panel as permitted by MCR 2.403(D)(3), the judge shall serve as the neutral case evaluator if sublists are maintained for that class of cases.

(3) *Special Panels.* On stipulation of the parties, the court may appoint a panel selected by the parties. In such a case, the qualification requirements of subrule (B)(2) do not apply, and the parties may agree to modification of the procedures for conduct of case evaluation. Nothing in this rule or MCR 2.403

precludes parties from stipulating to other ADR procedures that may aid in resolution of the case.

(D) Supervision of Selection Process.

(1) The chief judge shall exercise general supervision over the implementation of this rule and shall review the operation of the court's case evaluation plan at least annually to assure compliance with this rule. In the event of noncompliance, the court shall take such action as is needed. This action may include recruiting persons to serve as case evaluators or changing the court's case evaluation plan.

(2) In implementing the selection plan, the court, court employees, and attorneys involved in the procedure shall take all steps necessary to assure that as far as reasonably possible the list of case evaluators fairly reflects the racial, ethnic, and gender diversity of the members of the state bar in the jurisdiction for which the list is compiled who are eligible to serve as case evaluators.

[Adopted May 8, 1997, effective October 1, 1997, 454 Mich. Amended May 9, 2000, effective August 1, 2000, 462 Mich; December 21, 2011, effective May 1, 2012, 490 Mich.]

Comments

Staff Comment to 1997 Adoption

The May 8, 1997, order repeals MCR 4.003, which governed removal of cases from circuit to district court, effective July 1, 1997. This reinstates the February 28, 1997, repeal of the rule, which was suspended on March 13, 1997.

In addition, the order postpones the effective date of earlier amendments of MCR 2.403, 2.405, and 3.216, and new MCR 2.404, affecting mediation procedure, to October 1, 1997. The order also makes adjustments in MCR 2.403(K) and (N) in light of the repeal of MCR 4.003. The text of MCR 2.403, 2.404, 2.405 and 3.216 is the same as that adopted in the Court's March 5, 1997, order dealing with those rules.

Staff Comment to 2000 Amendment

The May 8, 2000, amendments [effective August 1, 2000] are based on the recommendations of the Michigan Supreme Court Dispute Resolution Task Force, which were published for comment on May 10, 1999 [see 459 Mich 1251], and were the subject of a series of public hearings across the state.

The Task Force report, issued in January 1999, and its Addendum report, issued in January 2000 after receipt of comments, should be consulted for the background and details of the amendments. Basically, the changes are as follows:

The amendments of MCR 2.403, 2.404, 2.405, 2.501, 2.502 and 2.503 are mainly to change terminology, replacing "mediation," as used in current MCR 2.403, with the term "case evaluation." "Mediation" will be used to describe the facilitative process established in MCR 2.411, in keeping with the generally accepted usage of the term.

MCR 2.401 is amended to direct consideration of alternative dispute resolution processes at scheduling and pretrial conferences.

New MCR 2.410 has general provisions governing referral of cases to alternative dispute resolution processes. Local courts wishing to use ADR techniques are to adopt ADR plans within the framework provided by the rule.

The one ADR process that is specifically established by the rules is mediation under new MCR 2.411. Among other things, the rule establishes general standards for mediator qualifications, and procedures for selection of mediators.

MCR 3.216, the domestic relations mediation rule, is substantially revised, to be more comparable to the mediation process in MCR 2.411.

MCR 5.143, regarding use of alternative dispute resolution processes in probate court, is amended to conform to the other rule changes.

Staff Comment to 2011 Amendment

The amendments of MCR 2.403, 2.404, 2.410, 2.411, and 2.412 revise court rules relating to mediation and case evaluation largely as recommended by the Dispute Resolution Rules Committee convened by the State Court Administrative Office. The amendment of MCR 3.216 reflects amendments to provisions that appear in MCR 2.411 that also appear in MCR 3.216.

Rule 2.405   Offers to Stipulate to Entry of Judgment

(A) Definitions. As used in this rule:

(1) "Offer" means a written notification to an adverse party of the offeror's willingness to stipulate to the entry of a judgment in a sum certain, which is deemed to include all costs and interest then accrued. If a party has made more than one offer, the most recent offer controls for the purposes of this rule.

(2) "Counteroffer" means a written reply to an offer, served within 21 days after service of the offer, in which a party rejects an offer of the adverse party and makes his or her own offer.

(3) "Average offer" means the sum of an offer and a counteroffer, divided by two. If no counteroffer is made, the offer shall be used as the average offer.

(4) "Verdict" includes,

    (a) a jury verdict,

    (b) a judgment by the court after a nonjury trial,

    (c) a judgment entered as a result of a ruling on a motion after rejection of the offer of judgment.

(5) "Adjusted verdict" means the verdict plus interest and costs from the filing of the complaint through the date of the offer.

(6) "Actual costs" means the costs and fees taxable in a civil action and a reasonable attorney fee for services necessitated by the failure to stipulate to the entry of judgment.

(B) Offer. Until 28 days before trial, a party may serve on the adverse party a written offer to stipulate to the entry of a judgment for the whole or part of the claim, including interest and costs then accrued.

(C) Acceptance or Rejection of Offer.

(1) To accept, the adverse party, within 21 days after service of the offer, must serve on the other parties a written notice of agreement to stipulate to the entry of the judgment offered, and file the offer, the notice of acceptance, and proof of service of the notice with the court. The court shall enter a judgment according to the terms of the stipulation.

(2) An offer is rejected if the offeree

    (a) expressly rejects it in writing, or

    (b) does not accept it as provided by subrule (C)(1).

A rejection does not preclude a later offer by either party.

(3) A counteroffer may be accepted or rejected in the same manner as an offer.

(D) Imposition of Costs Following Rejection of Offer. If an offer is rejected, costs are payable as follows:

(1) If the adjusted verdict is more favorable to the offeror than the average offer, the offeree must pay to the offeror the offeror's actual costs incurred in the prosecution or defense of the action.

(2) If the adjusted verdict is more favorable to the offeree than the average offer, the offeror must pay to the offeree the offeree's actual costs incurred in the prosecution or defense of the action. However, an offeree who has not made a counteroffer may not recover actual costs unless the offer was made less than 42 days before trial.

(3) The court shall determine the actual costs incurred. The court may, in the interest of justice, refuse to award an attorney fee under this rule.

(4) Evidence of an offer is admissible only in a proceeding to determine costs.

(5) Proceedings under this rule do not affect a contract or relationship between a party and his or her attorney.

(6) A request for costs under this subrule must be filed and served within 28 days after the entry of the judgment or entry of an order denying a timely motion

    (i) for a new trial,

    (ii) to set aside the judgment, or

    (iii) for rehearing or reconsideration.

(E) Relationship to Case Evaluation. Costs may not be awarded under this rule in a case that has been submitted to case evaluation under MCR 2.403 unless the case evaluation award was not unanimous.

[Adopted effective March 1, 1985. Amended December 21, 1989, effective March 31, 1990, 434 Mich; May 8, 1997, effective October 1, 1997, 454 Mich; May 9, 2000, effective August 1, 2000, 462 Mich; October 2, 2013, effective January 1, 2014, 495 Mich.]

Comments

Staff Comment to 1985 Adoption

MCR 2.405 substantially revises the offer of judgment procedure found in GCR 1963, 519, under which only a party defending against a claim could invoke the procedure. Under MCR 2.405 either the claimant or the defending party may do so. Additional details regarding the procedure are added.

A party may offer to stipulate to entry of judgment in a specified amount. If an offer is accepted, judgment will be entered for that amount; if rejected, the case proceeds in the usual fashion. A party who has failed to accept an opposing party's offer of judgment may be subjected to payment of the opposing party's costs necessitated by the failure to accept if the verdict is less favorable to the rejecting party than the rejected offer. If each side has made an offer, the average of the two becomes the triggering value for determination of potential liability for costs.

As with the mediation rule, in determining whether a verdict has been more or less favorable to a party, it is to be adjusted by adding interest and costs. Compare MCR 2.403(O)(2), with subrule (A)(5).

The court has discretion not to include an attorney fee in the award of costs. See subrule (D)(3).

Finally, subrule (E) explains the relationship of this rule to mediation. In a case in which both procedures have been used, the cost provisions of the rule under which the later rejection occurred will be used.

Staff Comment to 1989 Amendment

On May 3, 1989, the Court ordered published for comment several proposals regarding the offer of judgment rule, MCR 2.405. See 432 Mich 1233-1235; 68 Mich B J 558 (June, 1989). The January 3, 1990, order adopts several of those changes, some with modifications.

New language is added to MCR 2.405(A)(2) to specify when a counteroffer must be served.

In MCR 2.405(D) there is new language setting the time within which a party must seek to recover costs under the offer of judgment rule.

The amendment to MCR 2.405(E) modifies the relationship between the cost provisions of the mediation and offer of judgment rules.

Staff Comment to 1997 Amendment

The order of May 8, 1997, postpones the effective date of the earlier amendment of MCR 2.405, affecting mediation procedure, to October 1, 1997. The text of MCR 2.405 is the same as that adopted in the Court's March 5, 1997, order dealing with those rules.

Staff Comment to 2000 Amendment

The amendment is based on the recommendations of the Michigan Supreme Court Dispute Resolution Task Force, which was published for comment on May 10, 1999, see 459 Mich 1251, and was the subject of a series of public hearings across the state.

The Task Force report, issued in January 1999, and its addendum report, issued in January 2000 after receipt of comments, should be consulted for the background and details of the amendment. Basically, the change is as follows:

The amendment of MCR 2.405 is mainly to change terminology, replacing 'mediation,' as used in current MCR 2.403, with the term 'case evaluation'.

'Mediation' will be used to describe the facilitative process established in MCR 2.411, in keeping with the generally accepted usage of the term.

Staff Comment to 2014 Amendment

The amendments of MCR 2.403(O)(8), MCR 2.405(D)(6), and MCR 2.625(F)(2) add language that references a motion for rehearing or reconsideration (consistent with the Court of Appeals opinion in *MEEMIC Ins Co v DTE Energy Co*, 292 Mich App 278 [2011]) to the list of motions that toll the period of time in which a party may file a request for case-evaluation sanctions.

Rule 2.406   Use of Facsimile Communication Equipment

(A) Definition. "Facsimile communication equipment" means a machine that transmits and reproduces graphic matter (as printing or still pictures) by means of signals sent over telephone lines.

(B) Use. Courts may permit the filing of pleadings, motions, affidavits, opinions, orders, or other documents by the use of facsimile communication equipment. Except as provided by MCR 2.002, a clerk shall not permit the filing of any document for which a filing fee is required unless the full amount of the filing fee is paid or deposited in advance with the clerk.

(C) Paper. All filings must be on good quality 8 1/2 by 11-inch paper, and the print must be no smaller than 12-point type. These requirements do not apply to attachments and exhibits, but parties are encouraged to reduce or enlarge such documents to 8 1/2 by 11 inches, if practical.

(D) Fees. In addition to fees required by statute, courts may impose fees for facsimile filings in accordance with the schedule that is established by the State Court Administrative Office for that purpose.

(E) Number of Pages. Courts may establish a maximum number of pages that may be sent at one time.

(F) Hours. Documents received during the regular business hours of the court will be deemed filed on that business day. Documents received after regular business hours and on weekends or designated court holidays will be deemed filed on the next business day. A document is considered filed if the transmission begins during regular business hours, as verified by the court, and the entire document is received.

(G) Originals. Documents filed by facsimile communication equipment shall be considered original documents. The filing party shall retain the documents that were transmitted by facsimile communication equipment.

(H) Signature. For purposes of MCR 1.109(E), a signature includes a signature transmitted by facsimile communication equipment.

[Adopted September 30, 2003, effective January 1, 2004, 469 Mich. Amended August 30, 2018, effective September 1, 2018, 502 Mich.]

Comments

Staff Comment to 2004 Adoption

The September 30, 2003, adoption of MCR 2.406, effective January 1, 2004, was proposed by the Michigan Judges Association to establish a uniform practice statewide for those courts that choose to allow the filing of documents by facsimile communication equipment. Coincident with the adoption of the new court rule, all similar local court rules were rescinded, along with Supreme Court Administrative Orders Nos. 1990-9 and 1994-2.

Staff Comment to 2018 Amendment

These amendments update cross-references in the rules, and are intended to reflect changes that are necessary as a result of the Court's recent e-Filing rules amendments.

Rule 2.407   Videoconferencing

(A) Definitions. In this subchapter:

(1) "Participants" include, but are not limited to, parties, counsel, and subpoenaed witnesses, but do not include the general public.

(2) "Videoconferencing" means the use of an interactive technology that sends video, voice, and data signals over a transmission circuit so that two or more individuals or groups can communicate with each other simultaneously using video codecs, monitors, cameras, audio microphones, and audio speakers.

(B) Application.

(1) Subject to standards published by the State Court Administrative Office and the criteria set forth in subsection (C), a court may, at the request of any participant, or sua sponte, allow the use of videoconferencing technology by any participant in any court-scheduled civil proceeding.

(2) Subject to State Court Administrative Office standards, courts may determine the manner and extent of the use of videoconferencing technology.

(3) This rule does not supersede a participant's ability to participate by telephonic means under MCR 2.402.

(C) Criteria for Videoconferencing. In determining in a particular case whether to permit the use of videoconferencing technology and the manner of proceeding with videoconferencing, the court shall consider the following factors:

(1) The capabilities of the court's videoconferencing equipment.

(2) Whether any undue prejudice would result.

(3) The convenience of the parties and the proposed witness, and the cost of producing the witness in person in relation to the importance of the offered testimony.

(4) Whether the procedure would allow for full and effective cross-examination, especially when the cross-examination would involve documents or other exhibits.

(5) Whether the dignity, solemnity, and decorum of the courtroom would tend to impress upon the witness the duty to testify truthfully.

(6) Whether a physical liberty or other fundamental interest is at stake in the proceeding.

(7) Whether the court is satisfied that it can sufficiently control the proceedings at the remote location so as to effectively extend the courtroom to the remote location.

(8) Whether the use of videoconferencing technology presents the person at a remote location in a diminished or distorted sense that negatively reflects upon the individual at the remote location to persons present in the courtroom.

(9) Whether the use of videoconferencing technology diminishes or detracts from the dignity, solemnity, and formality of the proceeding and undermines the integrity, fairness, or effectiveness of the proceeding.

(10) Whether the person appearing by videoconferencing technology presents a significant security risk to transport and be present physically in the courtroom.

(11) Whether the parties or witness(es) have waived personal appearance or stipulated to videoconferencing.

(12) The proximity of the videoconferencing request date to the proposed appearance date.

(13) Any other factors that the court may determine to be relevant.

(D) Request for Videoconferencing.

(1) A participant who requests the use of videoconferencing technology shall ensure that the equipment available at the remote location meets the technical and operational standards established by the State Court Administrative Office.

(2) A participant who requests the use of videoconferencing technology must provide the court with the videoconference dialing information and the participant's contact information in advance of the court date when videoconferencing technology will be used.

(3) There is no motion fee for requests submitted under this rule.

(E) Objections. The court shall rule on an objection to the use of videoconferencing under the factors set forth under subsection C.

(F) Mechanics of Videoconferencing. The use of any videoconferencing technology must be conducted in accordance with standards published by the State Court Administrative Office. All proceedings at which videoconferencing technology is used must be recorded verbatim by the court with the exception of hearings that are not required to be recorded by law.

[Adopted November 26, 2014, effective January 1, 2015, 497 Mich.]

Comments

Staff Comment to 2015 Adoption

The new court rule allows courts to use videoconferencing in civil court proceedings (including domestic relations proceedings) upon request of a participant or sua sponte by the court, subject to specified criteria and standards published by the State Court Administrative Office (SCAO). Amendments of MCR 3.210 and MCR 3.215 provide cross references to the new court rule. Adoption of MCR 2.407 does not affect MCR 3.904, MCR 5.738a, and MCR 6.006. In addition, as relevant to the rule amendments in this order, Administrative Order No. 2014–25, also issued today, requires SCAO to adopt videoconferencing standards, and requires courts to comply with those standards.

Rule 2.410.   Alternative Dispute Resolution

(A) Scope and Applicability of Rule; Definitions.

(1) All civil cases are subject to alternative dispute resolution processes unless otherwise provided by statute or court rule.

(2) For the purposes of this rule, alternative dispute resolution (ADR) means any process designed to resolve a legal dispute in the place of court adjudication, and includes settlement conferences ordered under MCR 2.401; case evaluation under MCR 2.403; mediation under MCR 2.411; domestic relations mediation under MCR 3.216; child protection mediation under MCR 3.970; and other procedures provided by local court rule or ordered on stipulation of the parties.

(B) ADR Plan.

(1) Each trial court that submits cases to ADR processes under this rule shall adopt an ADR plan by local administrative order. The plan must be in writing and available to the public in the ADR clerk's office.

(2) At a minimum, the ADR plan must:

(a) designate an ADR clerk, who may be the clerk of the court, the court administrator, the assignment clerk, or some other person;

(b) if the court refers cases to mediation under MCR 2.411, specify how the list of persons available to serve as mediators will be maintained and the system by which mediators will be assigned from the list under MCR 2.411(B)(3);

(c) include provisions for disseminating information about the operation of the court's ADR program to litigants and the public; and

(d) specify how access to ADR processes will be provided for indigent persons. If a party qualifies for waiver of filing fees under MCR 2.002 or the court determines on other grounds that the party is unable to pay the full cost of an ADR provider's services, and free or low-cost dispute resolution services are not available, the court shall not order that party to participate in an ADR process.

(3) The plan may also provide for referral relationships with local dispute resolution centers, including those affiliated with the Community Dispute Resolution Program. In establishing a referral relationship with centers or programs, courts, at a minimum, shall take into consideration factors that include whether parties are represented by counsel, the number and complexity of issues in dispute, the jurisdictional amount of the cases to be referred, and the ability of the parties to pay for dispute resolution services. The plan must preserve the right of parties to stipulate to the selection of their own mediator under MCR 2.411(B)(1).

(4) Courts in adjoining circuits or districts may jointly adopt and administer an ADR plan.

(C) Order for ADR.

(1) At any time, after consultation with the parties, the court may order that a case be submitted to an appropriate ADR process. More than one such order may be entered in a case.

(2) Unless the specific rule under which the case is referred provides otherwise, in addition to other provisions the court considers appropriate, the order shall

(a) specify, or make provision for selection of, the ADR provider;

(b) provide time limits for initiation and completion of the ADR process; and

(c) make provision for the payment of the ADR provider.

(3) The order may require attendance at ADR proceedings as provided in subrule (D).

(D) Attendance at ADR Proceedings.

(1) *Appearance of Counsel.* The attorneys attending an ADR proceeding shall be thoroughly familiar with the case and have the authority necessary to fully participate in the proceeding. The court may direct that the attorneys who intend to try the case attend ADR proceedings.

(2) *Presence of Parties.* The court may direct that the parties to the action, agents of parties, representatives of lienholders, representatives of insurance carriers, or other persons:

(a) be present at the ADR proceeding or be immediately available at the time of the proceeding; and

(b) have information and authority adequate for responsible and effective participation in the conference for all purposes, including settlement.

The court's order may specify whether the availability is to be in person or by telephone.

(3) *Failure to Attend.*

(a) Failure of a party or the party's attorney or other representative to attend a scheduled ADR proceeding, as directed by the court, may constitute a default to which MCR 2.603 is applicable or a ground for dismissal under MCR 2.504(B).

(b) The court shall excuse a failure to attend an ADR proceeding, and shall enter a just order other than one of default or dismissal, if the court finds that

(i) entry of an order of default or dismissal would cause manifest injustice; or

(ii) the failure to attend was not due to the culpable negligence of the party or the party's attorney.

The court may condition the order on the payment by the offending party or attorney of reasonable expenses as provided in MCR 2.313(B)(2).

(E) Objections to ADR. Within 14 days after entry of an order referring a case to an ADR process, a party may move to set aside or modify the order. A timely motion must be decided before the case is submitted to the ADR process.

(F) Supervision of ADR Plan. The chief judge shall exercise general supervision over the implementation of this rule and shall review the operation of the court's ADR plan at least annually to assure compliance with this rule. In the event of noncompliance, the court shall take such action as is needed. This action may include recruiting persons to serve as ADR providers or changing the court's ADR plan.

[Statement by Kelly, J., appears in 467 Mich.]

[Adopted May 9, 2000, effective August 1, 2000, 462 Mich. Amended January 31, 2003, effective May 1, 2003, 467 Mich; December 21, 2011, effective May 1, 2012, 490 Mich; March 28, 2018, effective May 1, 2018, 501 Mich.]

Comments

Staff Comment to 2000 Adoption

New MCR 2.410 is based on the recommendations of the Michigan Supreme Court Dispute Resolution Task Force, which was published for comment on May 10, 1999, see 459 Mich 1251, and was the subject of a series of public hearings across the state.

The Task Force report, issued in January 1999, and its addendum report, issued in January 2000 after receipt of comments, should be consulted for the background and details of the amendment. Basically, the change is as follows:

New MCR 2.410 has general provisions governing referral of cases to alternative dispute resolution processes. Local courts wishing to use ADR techniques are to adopt ADR plans within the framework provided by the rule.

Staff Comment to 2003 Amendment

MCR 2.401(F) and (G), MCR 2.410(D)(2) and (3), MCR 2.506(A), and MCR 7.213(A) were amended January 31, 2003, effective May 1, 2003. Before the amendments, each of these subrules included a requirement that someone with "authority to settle" (or similar language) attend the type of proceeding described in each subrule. The amendments substituted the more flexible requirement that the person attending the proceeding have "information and authority adequate for responsible and effective participation" in settlement discussions.

The 2003 amendments of MCR 2.401(G) and MCR 2.410(D)(3) de-emphasized the use of defaults as sanctions for a party's failure to comply fully with an order. The amended rules allow entry of a default, but tilt in favor of less drastic sanctions.

Staff Comment to 2011 Amendment

The amendments of MCR 2.403, 2.404, 2.410, 2.411, and 2.412 revise court rules relating to mediation and case evaluation largely as recommended by the Dispute Resolution Rules Committee convened by the State Court Administrative Office. The amendment of MCR 3.216 reflects amendments to provisions that appear in MCR 2.411 that also appear in MCR 3.216.

Staff Comment to 2018 Amendment

The amendments of MCR 2.410 and MCR 2.411 and adoption of the new MCR 3.970 provide explicit authority for judges to order mediation in child protection proceedings.

Rule 2.411.   Mediation

(A) Scope and Applicability of Rule; Definitions.

(1) This rule applies to cases that the court refers to mediation as provided in MCR 2.410. MCR 3.216 governs mediation of domestic relations cases. MCR 3.970 governs mediation in child protective proceedings.

(2) "Mediation" is a process in which a neutral third party facilitates communication between parties, assists in identifying issues, and helps explore solutions to promote a mutually acceptable settlement. A mediator has no authoritative decision-making power.

(B) Selection of Mediator.

(1) The parties may stipulate to the selection of a mediator. A mediator selected by agreement of the parties need not meet the qualifications set forth in subrule (F). The court must appoint a mediator stipulated to by the parties, provided the mediator is willing to serve within a period that would not interfere with the court's scheduling of the case for trial.

(2) If the order referring the case to mediation does not specify a mediator, the order shall set the date by which the parties are to have conferred on the selection of a mediator. If the parties do not advise the ADR clerk of the mediator agreed upon by that date, the court shall appoint one as provided in subrule (B)(3).

(3) The procedure for selecting a mediator from the approved list of mediators must be established by local ADR plan adopted under MCR 2.410(B). The ADR clerk shall assign mediators in a rotational manner that assures as nearly as possible that each mediator on the list is assigned approximately the same number of cases over a period of time. If a substitute mediator must be assigned, the same or similar assignment procedure shall be used to select the substitute.

(4) The court shall not appoint, recommend, direct, or otherwise influence a party's or attorney's selection of a mediator except as provided pursuant to this rule. The court may recommend or advise parties on the selection of a mediator only upon request of all parties by stipulation in writing or orally on the record.

(5) The rule for disqualification of a mediator is the same as that provided in MCR 2.003 for the disqualification of a judge. The mediator must promptly disclose any potential basis for disqualification.

(C) Scheduling and Conduct of Mediation.

(1) *Scheduling.* The order referring the case for mediation shall specify the time within which the mediation is to be completed. The ADR clerk shall send a copy of the order to each party and the mediator selected. Upon receipt of the court's order, the mediator shall promptly confer with the parties to schedule mediation in accordance with the order. Factors that may be considered in arranging the process may

include the need for limited discovery before mediation, the number of parties and issues, and the necessity for multiple sessions. The mediator may direct the parties to submit in advance, or bring to the mediation, documents or summaries providing information about the case.

(2) *Conduct of Mediation.* The mediator shall meet with counsel and the parties, explain the mediation process, and then proceed with the process. The mediator shall discuss with the parties and counsel, if any, the facts and issues involved. The mediation will continue until a settlement is reached, the mediator determines that a settlement is not likely to be reached, the end of the first mediation session, or until a time agreed to by the parties. Additional sessions may be held as long as it appears that the process may result in settlement of the case.

(3) *Completion of Mediation.* Within 7 days after the completion of the ADR process, the mediator shall so advise the court, stating only the date of completion of the process, who participated in the mediation, whether settlement was reached, and whether further ADR proceedings are contemplated.

(4) *Settlement.* If the case is settled through mediation, within 21 days the attorneys shall prepare and submit to the court the appropriate documents to conclude the case.

(5) Confidentiality in the mediation process is governed by MCR 2.412.

(D) Fees.

(1) A mediator is entitled to reasonable compensation commensurate with the mediator's experience and usual charges for services performed.

(2) The costs of mediation shall be divided between the parties on a pro-rata basis unless otherwise agreed by the parties or ordered by the court. The mediator's fee shall be paid no later than

(a) 42 days after the mediation process is concluded, or

(b) the entry of judgment, or

(c) the dismissal of the action,

whichever occurs first.

(3) If acceptable to the mediator, the court may order an arrangement for the payment of the mediator's fee other than that provided in subrule (D)(2).

(4) The mediator's fee is deemed a cost of the action, and the court may make an appropriate order to enforce the payment of the fee.

(5) If a party objects to the total fee of the mediator, the matter may be scheduled before the trial judge for determination of the reasonableness of the fee.

(E) List of Mediators.

(1) *Application.* To appear on a roster, an applicant, which may be an individual or organization may apply to the ADR clerk to be placed on the court's list of mediators. Application forms shall be available in the office of the ADR clerk.

(a) The form shall include a certification that

(i) the applicant meets the requirements for service under the court's selection plan;

(ii) the applicant will not discriminate against parties or attorneys on the basis of race, ethnic origin, gender, or other protected personal characteristic; and

(iii) the applicant will comply with the court's ADR plan, orders of the court regarding cases submitted to mediation, and the standards of conduct adopted by the State Court Administrator under subrule (G).

(b) The applicant shall indicate on the form the applicant's rate for providing mediation services.

(c) The form shall include an optional section identifying the applicant's gender and racial/ethnic background.

(d) An applicant Community Dispute Resolution Program center must select only mediators who meet the qualifications of this rule or training requirements established by the State Court Administrator to mediate cases ordered by the court.

(2) *Review of Applications.* The court's ADR plan shall provide for a person or committee to review applications annually, or more frequently if appropriate, and compile a list of qualified mediators.

(a) Applicants meeting the qualifications specified in this rule shall be placed on the list of approved mediators. Approved mediators shall be placed on the list for a fixed period, not to exceed seven years, and must reapply at the end of that time in the manner directed by the court.

(b) Selections shall be made without regard to race, ethnic origin, or gender. Residency or principal place of business may not be a qualification.

(c) The approved list and the applications of approved mediators, except for the optional section identifying the applicant's gender and racial/ethnic background, shall be available to the public in the office of the ADR clerk.

(d) An applicant may attach a résumé or biographical information to the application.

(3) *Rejection; Reconsideration.* Applicants who are not placed on the list shall be notified of that decision. Within 21 days of notification of the decision to reject an application, the applicant may seek reconsideration of the ADR clerk's decision by the Chief Judge. The court does not need to provide a hearing. Documents considered in the initial review process shall be retained for at least the period during which the applicant can seek reconsideration of the original decision.

(4) *Removal from List.* The ADR clerk may remove from the list mediators who have demonstrated incompetence, bias, made themselves consistently unavailable to serve as a mediator, or for other just cause. Within 21 days of notification of the decision to remove a mediator from the list, the mediator may seek reconsideration of the ADR clerk's decision by the Chief Judge. The court does not need to provide a hearing.

(F) Qualification of Mediators.

(1) *Small Claims Mediation.* District courts may develop individual plans to establish qualifications for persons serving as mediators in small claims cases.

(2) *General Civil Mediation.* To be eligible to serve as a general civil mediator, a person must meet the following minimum qualifications:

(a) Complete a training program approved by the State Court Administrator providing the generally accepted components of mediation skills;

(b) Have one or more of the following:

(i) Juris doctor degree or graduate degree in conflict resolution; or

(ii) 40 hours of mediation experience over two years, including mediation, co-mediation, observation, and role-playing in the context of mediation.

(c) Upon completion of the training required under subrule (F)(2)(a), observe two general civil mediation proceedings conducted by an approved mediator, and conduct one general civil mediation to conclusion under the supervision and observation of an approved mediator.

(3) An applicant who has specialized experience or training, but does not meet the specific requirements of subrule (F)(2), may apply to the ADR clerk for special approval. The ADR clerk shall make the determination on the basis of criteria provided by the State Court Administrator. Service as a case evaluator under MCR 2.403 does not constitute a qualification for serving as a mediator under this section.

(4) Approved mediators are required to obtain 8 hours of advanced mediation training during each 2–year period. Failure to submit documentation establishing compliance is ground for removal from the list under subrule(E)(4).

(5) Additional qualifications may not be imposed upon mediators.

(G) Standards of Conduct for Mediators. The State Court Administrator shall develop and approve standards of conduct for mediators designed to promote honesty, integrity, and impartiality in providing court-connected dispute resolution services. These standards shall be made a part of all training and educational requirements for court-connected programs, shall be provided to all mediators involved in court-connected programs, and shall be available to the public.

(H) Mediation of Discovery Disputes. The parties may stipulate to or the court may order the mediation of discovery disputes (unless precluded by MCR 3.216[C][3]). The discovery mediator may by agreement of the parties be the same mediator otherwise selected under subrule (B). All other provisions of this rule shall apply to a discovery mediator except:

(1) The order under subrule (C)(1) will specify the scope of issues or motions referred to the discovery mediator, or whether the mediator is appointed on an ongoing basis.

(2) The mediation sessions will be conducted as determined by the mediator, with or without parties, in any manner deemed reasonable and consistent with these rules and any court order.

(3) The court may specify that discovery disputes must first be submitted to the mediator before being filed as a motion unless there is a need for expedited attention by the court. In such cases, the moving party shall certify in the motion that it is filed only after failure to resolve the dispute through mediation or due to a need for immediate attention by the court.

(4) In cases involving complex issues of ESI, the court may appoint an expert under MRE 706. By stipulation of the parties, the court may also designate the expert as a discovery mediator of ESI issues under this rule, in which case the parties

should address in the order appointing the mediator whether the restrictions of MCR 2.411(C)(3) and 2.412(D) should be modified to expand the scope of permissible communications with the court.

[Adopted May 9, 2000, effective August 1, 2000, 462 Mich. Amended April 5, 2011, effective September 1, 2011, 489 Mich; December 21, 2011, effective May 1, 2012, 490 Mich; March 28, 2018, effective May 1, 2018, 501 Mich; June 19, 2019, effective January 1, 2020, 503 Mich.]

Comments

Staff Comment to 2000 Adoption

The May 8, 2000, amendments [effective August 1, 2000] are based on the recommendations of the Michigan Supreme Court Dispute Resolution Task Force, which were published for comment on May 10, 1999 [see 459 Mich 1251], and were the subject of a series of public hearings across the state.

The Task Force report, issued in January 1999, and its Addendum report, issued in January 2000 after receipt of comments, should be consulted for the background and details of the amendments. Basically, the changes are as follows:

The amendments of MCR 2.403, 2.404, 2.405, 2.501, 2.502 and 2.503 are mainly to change terminology, replacing "mediation," as used in current MCR 2.403, with the term "case evaluation." "Mediation" will be used to describe the facilitative process established in MCR 2.411, in keeping with the generally accepted usage of the term.

MCR 2.401 is amended to direct consideration of alternative dispute resolution processes at scheduling and pretrial conferences.

New MCR 2.410 has general provisions governing referral of cases to alternative dispute resolution processes. Local courts wishing to use ADR techniques are to adopt ADR plans within the framework provided by the rule.

The one ADR process that is specifically established by the rules is mediation under new MCR 2.411. Among other things, the rule establishes general standards for mediator qualifications, and procedures for selection of mediators.

MCR 3.216, the domestic relations mediation rule, is substantially revised, to be more comparable to the mediation process in MCR 2.411.

MCR 5.143, regarding use of alternative dispute resolution processes in probate court, is amended to conform to the other rule changes.

Staff Comment to April, 2011 Amendment

The amendments of MCR 2.403, 2.411, and 3.216, and the adoption of new MCR 2.412 consolidate provisions related to mediation confidentiality into one rule and expand the number of exceptions to mediation confidentiality.

Staff Comment to December, 2011 Amendment

The amendments of MCR 2.403, 2.404, 2.410, 2.411, and 2.412 revise court rules relating to mediation and case evaluation largely as recommended by the Dispute Resolution Rules Committee convened by the State Court Administrative Office. The amendment of MCR 3.216 reflects amendments to provisions that appear in MCR 2.411 that also appear in MCR 3.216.

Staff Comment to 2018 Amendment

The amendments of MCR 2.410 and MCR 2.411 and adoption of the new MCR 3.970 provide explicit authority for judges to order mediation in child protection proceedings.

Staff Comment to 2020 Amendment

These amendments are based on a proposal created by a special committee of the State Bar of Michigan and approved for submission to the Court by the Bar's Representative Assembly. The rules require mandatory discovery disclosure in many cases, adopt a presumptive limit on interrogatories (20 in most cases, but 35 in domestic relations proceedings) and limit a deposition to 7 hours. The amendments also update the rules to more specifically address issues related to electronically stored information, and encourage early action on discovery issues during the discovery period.

The amendment of MCR 2.309(A)(2) sets a presumptive limit of twenty interrogatories for each separately represented party. Several commenters suggested that the term "discrete subpart" be more explicitly defined. But the rule's reference to "a discrete subpart" is intended to draw guidance from federal courts construing FR Civ P 30(a)(1). Generally, subparts are not separately counted if they are logically or factually subsumed within and necessarily related to the primary question. In upholding the limit, parties and courts should also pragmatically balance the overall goals of discovery and the admonition of MCR 1.105. Further, the intent of the provision at MCR 2.301(B)(4) is to ensure that parties responding to discovery requests have the full time period to do so as provided for under these rules prior to the expiration of the discovery period.

Rule 2.412   Mediation Communications; Confidentiality and Disclosure

(A) Scope. This rule applies to cases that the court refers to mediation as defined and conducted under MCR 2.411 and MCR 3.216.

(B) Definitions.

(1) "Mediator" means an individual who conducts a mediation.

(2) "Mediation communications" include statements whether oral or in a record, verbal or nonverbal, that occur during the mediation process or are made for purposes of retaining a mediator or for considering, initiating, preparing for, conducting, participating in, continuing, adjourning, concluding, or reconvening a mediation.

(3) "Mediation party" means a person who or entity that participates in a mediation and whose agreement is necessary to resolve the dispute.

(4) "Mediation participant" means a mediation party, a nonparty, an attorney for a party, or a mediator who participates in or is present at a mediation.

(5) "Protected individual" is used as defined in the Estates and Protected Individuals Code, MCL 700.1106(x).

(6) "Vulnerable" is used as defined in the Social Welfare Act, MCL 400.11(f).

(C) Confidentiality. Mediation communications are confidential. They are not subject to discovery, are not admissible in a proceeding, and may not be disclosed to anyone other than mediation participants except as provided in subrule (D).

(D) Exceptions to Confidentiality. Mediation communications may be disclosed under the following circumstances:

(1) All mediation parties agree in writing to disclosure.

(2) A statute or court rule requires disclosure.

(3) The mediation communication is in the mediator's report under MCR 2.411(C)(3) or MCR 3.216(H)(6).

(4) The disclosure is necessary for a court to resolve disputes about the mediator's fee.

(5) The disclosure is necessary for a court to consider issues about a party's failure to attend under MCR 2.410(D)(3).

(6) The disclosure is made during a mediation session that is open or is required by law to be open to the public.

(7) Court personnel reasonably require disclosure to administer and evaluate the mediation program.

(8) The mediation communication is

(a) a threat to inflict bodily injury or commit a crime,

(b) a statement of a plan to inflict bodily injury or commit a crime, or

(c) is used to plan a crime, attempt to commit or commit a crime, or conceal a crime.

(9) The disclosure

(a) Involves a claim of abuse or neglect of a child, a protected individual, or a vulnerable adult; and

(b) Is included in a report about such a claim or sought or offered to prove or disprove such a claim; and

(i) Is made to a governmental agency or law enforcement official responsible for the protection against such conduct, or

(ii) Is made in any subsequent or related proceeding based on the disclosure under subrule (D)(9)(b)(i).

(10) The disclosure is included in a report of professional misconduct filed against a mediation participant or is sought or offered to prove or disprove misconduct allegations in the attorney disciplinary process.

(11) The mediation communication occurs in a case out of which a claim of malpractice arises and the disclosure is sought or offered to prove or disprove a claim of malpractice against a mediation participant.

(12) The disclosure is in a proceeding to enforce, rescind, reform, or avoid liability on a document signed by the mediation parties or acknowledged by the parties on an audio or video recording that arose out of mediation, if the court finds, after an in camera hearing, that the party seeking discovery or the proponent of the evidence has shown

(a) that the evidence is not otherwise available, and

(b) that the need for the evidence substantially outweighs the interest in protecting confidentiality.

(E) Scope of Disclosure When Permitted; Limitation on Confidentiality.

(1) If a mediation communication may be disclosed under subrule (D), only that portion of the communication necessary for the application of the exception may be disclosed.

(2) Disclosure of a mediation communication under subrule (D) does not render the mediation communication subject to disclosure for another purpose.

(3) Evidence or information that is otherwise admissible or subject to discovery does not become inadmissible or protected from discovery solely by reason of its disclosure or use in a mediation.

[Adopted April 5, 2011, effective September 1, 2011, 489 Mich. Amended December 21, 2011, effective May 1, 2012, 490 Mich. Amended effective August 14, 2019, 503 Mich.]

Comments

Staff Comment to 2011 Adoption

The amendments of MCR 2.403, 2.411, and 3.216, and the adoption of new MCR 2.412 consolidate provisions related to mediation confidentiality into one rule and expand the number of exceptions to mediation confidentiality.

Staff Comment to 2012 Amendment

The amendments of MCR 2.403, 2.404, 2.410, 2.411, and 2.412 revise court rules relating to mediation and case evaluation largely as recommended by the Dispute Resolution Rules Committee convened by the State Court Administrative Office. The amendment of MCR 3.216 reflects amendments to provisions that appear in MCR 2.411 that also appear in MCR 3.216.

Staff Comment to 2019 Amendment

These amendments update cross-references and make other nonsubstantive revisions to clarify the rules.

Rule 2.420 Settlements and Judgments for Minors and Legally Incapacitated Individuals

(A) Applicability. This rule governs the procedure to be followed for the entry of a consent judgment, a settlement, or a dismissal pursuant to settlement in an action brought for a minor or a legally incapacitated individual person by a next friend, guardian, or conservator or where a minor or a legally incapacitated individual is to receive a distribution from a wrongful death claim. Before an action is commenced, the settlement of a claim on behalf of a minor or a legally incapacitated individual is governed by the Estates and Protected Individuals Code.

(B) Procedure. In actions covered by this rule, a proposed consent judgment, settlement, or dismissal pursuant to settlement must be brought before the judge to whom the action is assigned, and the judge shall pass on the fairness of the proposal.

(1) If the claim is for damages because of personal injury to the minor or legally incapacitated individual,

(a) the minor or legally incapacitated individual shall appear in court personally to allow the judge an opportunity to observe the nature of the injury unless, for good cause, the judge excuses the minor's or legally incapacitated individual's presence, and

(b) the judge may require medical testimony, by deposition or in court, if not satisfied of the extent of the injury.

(2) If the next friend, guardian, or conservator is a person who has made a claim in the same action and will share in the settlement or judgment of the minor or legally incapacitated individual, then a guardian ad litem for the minor or legally incapacitated individual must be appointed by the judge before whom the action is pending to approve the settlement or judgment.

(3) If a guardian or conservator for the minor or legally incapacitated individual has been appointed by a probate court the terms of the proposed settlement or judgment may be approved by the court in which the action is pending upon a finding that the payment arrangement is in the best interests of the minor or legally incapacitated individual, but no judgment or dismissal may enter until the court receives written verification from the probate court, on a form substantially in the form approved by the state court administrator, that it has passed on the sufficiency of the bond and the bond, if any, has been filed with the probate court.

(4) The following additional provisions apply to settlements for minors.

(a) If the settlement or judgment requires payment of more than $5,000 to the minor either immediately, or if the settlement or judgment is payable in installments that exceed $5,000 in any single year during minority, a conservator must be appointed by the probate court before the entry of the judgment or dismissal. The judgment or dismissal must require that payment be made payable to the minor's conservator on behalf of the minor. The court shall not enter the judgment or dismissal until it receives written verification, on a form substantially in the form approved by the state court administrator, that the probate court has passed on the sufficiency of the bond of the conservator.

(b) If the settlement or judgment does not require payment of more than $5,000 to the minor in any single year, the money may be paid in accordance with the provisions of MCL 700.5102.

(5) If a settlement or judgment provides for the creation of a trust for the minor or legally incapacitated individual, the circuit court shall determine the amount to be paid to the trust, but the trust shall not be funded without prior approval of the

trust by the probate court pursuant to notice to all interested persons and a hearing.

[Adopted effective March 1, 1985. Amended February 24, 1998, effective May 1, 1998, 456 Mich; July 12, 2001, effective January 1, 2002, 464 Mich; October 3, 2006, effective January 1, 2007, 477 Mich.]

Comments

Staff Comment to 1985 Adoption

MCR 2.420 is a new rule based on third circuit local court rule 6.7. It creates procedures for approval of a consent judgment or dismissal pursuant to settlement in an action brought on behalf of a minor.

The rule has two additional features designed to clarify the relative authority of the probate court and the court in which the action is pending. Subrule (A) provides that before an action is commenced, the settlement of the claim is governed by the Revised Probate Code. Second, subrule (B)(2) provides that after an action has been commenced, the settlement is to be approved by the court in which the action is pending. In that circumstance the only role of the probate court is to consider the sufficiency of the bond filed by the conservator, if one has been appointed.

Staff Comment to 1998 Amendment

The May 1998 amendment of MCR 2.420 was based on a recommendation from the Michigan Judges Association to resolve the potential conflict that arises when a spouse serves as guardian or conservator for an incompetent person and settles a personal-injury lawsuit with a consortium claim. In such a circumstance, the rule requires that a guardian *ad litem* be appointed. A like change was made with regard to the settlement of lawsuits involving minors.

Staff Comment to 2002 Amendment

In evaluating whether the payment arrangement of a structured settlement is in the best interests of a minor or legally incapacitated individual, the court should consider the age and life expectancy and current and anticipated financial needs of the minor or individual, any income and estate tax implications, any impact on eligibility for government benefits and the present value of the proposed payment arrangement.

Staff Comment to 2006 Amendment

The amendment of MCR 2.420 clarifies the requirement that the payment of proceeds may be made only to a conservator on behalf of a legally incapacitated adult or a minor entitled to more than $5,000 in any one year during minority.

SUBCHAPTER 2.500   TRIALS; SUBPOENAS; JURIES

Rule 2.501   Scheduling Trials; Court Calendars

(A) Scheduling Conferences or Trial.

(1) Unless the further processing of the action is already governed by a scheduling order under MCR 2.401(B)(2), the court shall

(a) schedule a pretrial conference under MCR 2.401,

(b) schedule the action for an alternative dispute resolution process,

(c) schedule the action for trial, or

(d) enter another appropriate order to facilitate preparation of the action for trial.

(2) A court may adopt a trial calendar or other method for scheduling trials without the request of a party.

(B) Expedited Trials.

(1) On its own initiative, the motion of a party, or the stipulations of all parties, the court may shorten the time in which an action will be scheduled for trial, subject to the notice provisions of subrule (C).

(2) In scheduling trials, the court shall give precedence to actions involving a contest over the custody of minor children and to other actions afforded precedence by statute or court rule.

(C) Notice of Trial.
Attorneys and parties must be given 28 days' notice of trial assignments, unless

(1) a rule or statute provides otherwise as to a particular type of action,

(2) the adjournment is of a previously scheduled trial, or

(3) the court otherwise directs for good cause.

Notice may be given orally if the party is before the court when the matter is scheduled, or by mailing or delivering copies of the notice or calendar to attorneys of record and to any party who appears on his or her own behalf.

(D) Attorney Scheduling Conflicts.

(1) The court and counsel shall make every attempt to avoid conflicts in the scheduling of trials.

(2) When conflicts in scheduled trial dates do occur, it is the responsibility of counsel to notify the court as soon as the potential conflict becomes evident. In such cases, the courts and counsel involved shall make every attempt to resolve the conflict in an equitable manner, with due regard for the priorities and time constraints provided by statute and court rule. When counsel cannot resolve conflicts through consultation with the individual courts, the judges shall consult directly to resolve the conflict.

(3) Except where a statute, court rule, or other special circumstance dictates otherwise, priority for trial shall be given to the case in which the pending trial date was set first.

[Adopted effective March 1, 1985. Amended June 11, 1991, effective October 1, 1991, 437 Mich; May 9, 2000, effective August 1, 2000, 462 Mich.]

Comments

Staff Comment to 1985 Adoption

MCR 2.501 governs the matter of scheduling actions for trial, as did GCR 1963, 501.

Under subrule (A), following the completion of discovery the court must either schedule the case for trial, for a pretrial conference, or for mediation.

Subrule (B) expressly allows expediting trial on motion or stipulation or when an action is given precedence by statute or court rule.

As to the notice provision, unlike GCR 1963, 501.4, subrule (C) would not permit published notice of the trial calendar to substitute for individual notice, although, of course, a court could publish notice in addition to giving individual notice. The rule specifies that the parties are entitled to 28 days' notice of trial assignment, although for good cause the court may shorten the time.

The [March 1, 1985] amendment of MCR 2.501(C)(2) makes clear that parties need not be given 28 days' notice of trial assignment when a previously scheduled trial is being adjourned.

Staff Comment to 1991 Amendment

There are two changes [effective October 1, 1991] in MCR 2.501. Subrule (A) is modified in light of the related changes regarding scheduling in MCR 2.301 and 2.401. Second, subrule (D) is added covering attorney schedule conflicts.

Staff Comment to 2000 Amendment

The amendment is based on the recommendations of the Michigan Supreme Court Dispute Resolution Task Force, which was published for comment on May 10, 1999, see 459 Mich 1251, and was the subject of a series of public hearings across the state.

The Task Force report, issued in January 1999, and its addendum report, issued in January 2000 after receipt of comments, should be consulted for the background and details of the amendment. Basically, the change is as follows:

The amendment of MCR 2.501 is mainly to change terminology, replacing "mediation," as used in current MCR 2.403, with the term "case evaluation."

"Mediation" will be used to describe the facilitative process established in MCR 2.411, in keeping with the generally accepted usage of the term.

Rule 2.502   Dismissal for Lack of Progress

(A) Notice of Proposed Dismissal.

(1) On motion of a party or on its own initiative, the court may order that an action in which no steps or proceedings appear to have been taken within 91 days be dismissed for lack of progress unless the parties show that progress is being made or that the lack of progress is not attributable to the party seeking affirmative relief.

(2) A notice of proposed dismissal may not be sent with regard to a case

(a) in which a scheduling order has been entered under MCR 2.401(B)(2) and the times for completion of the scheduled events have not expired,

(b) which is set for a conference, an alternative dispute resolution process, hearing, or trial.

(3) The notice shall be given in the manner provided in MCR 2.501(C) for notice of trial.

(B) Action by Court.

(1) If a party does not make the required showing, the court may direct the clerk to dismiss the action for lack of progress. Such a dismissal is without prejudice unless the court specifies otherwise.

(2) If an action is not dismissed under this rule, the court shall enter orders to facilitate the prompt and just disposition of the action.

(C) Reinstatement of Dismissed Action. On motion for good cause, the court may reinstate an action dismissed for lack of progress on terms the court deems just. On reinstating an action, the court shall enter orders to facilitate the prompt and just disposition of the action.

[Adopted effective March 1, 1985. Amended June 11, 1991, effective October 1, 1991, 437 Mich; May 9, 2000, effective August 1, 2000, 462 Mich; June 10, 2003, effective September 1, 2003, 468 Mich.]

Comments

Staff Comment to 1985 Adoption

MCR 2.502 deals with the subject of dismissal for lack of progress, which was covered by GCR 1963, 501.3. Subrule (A) retains the shorter time limit in district court than in circuit court (182 days versus 1 year). Compare GCR 1963, 501.3, with DCR 501.3. The parties are given notice in the same manner as provided by MCR 2.501(C) for notices of trial.

Subrule (B)(1) adds language expressly providing that a dismissal under this rule is without prejudice unless the court specifies otherwise.

Subrule (B)(2) provides that an action may not be dismissed for lack of progress before the time for completion of discovery or if it is set for trial or pretrial conference.

Subrule (C) adds an express provision allowing reinstatement of an action that has been dismissed for lack of progress.

Staff Comment to 1991 Amendment

The rule governing dismissals for lack of progress, MCR 2.502, is restructured [effective October 1, 1991], and the time period that triggers the sending of a notice is reduced from one year (182 days in district court) to 91 days.

Staff Comment to 2000 Amendment

The May 8, 2000, amendments [effective August 1, 2000] are based on the recommendations of the Michigan Supreme Court Dispute Resolution Task Force, which were published for comment on May 10, 1999 [see 459 Mich 1251], and were the subject of a series of public hearings across the state.

The Task Force report, issued in January 1999, and its addendum report, issued in January 2000 after receipt of comments, should be consulted for the background and details of the amendment. Basically, the change is as follows:

The amendment of MCR 2.502 is mainly to change terminology, replacing 'mediation,' as used in current MCR 2.403, with the term 'case evaluation.' 'Mediation' will be used to describe the facilitative process established in MCR 2.411, in keeping with the generally accepted usage of the term.

Staff Comment to 2003 Amendment

The June 10, 2003, amendment of MCR 2.502(A)(1), effective September 1, 2003, expressly allows a party to move for dismissal of an action for lack of progress. Previously, the rule stated only that the court may notify parties of a potential dismissal when there has been a lack of progress.

Rule 2.503   Adjournments

(A) Applicability. This rule applies to adjournments of trials, alternative dispute resolution processes, pretrial conferences, and all motion hearings.

(B) Motion or Stipulation for Adjournment.

(1) Unless the court allows otherwise, a request for an adjournment must be by motion or stipulation made in writing or orally in open court and is based on good cause.

(2) A motion or stipulation for adjournment must state

(a) which party is requesting the adjournment,

(b) the reason for it, and

(c) whether other adjournments have been granted in the proceeding and, if so, the number granted.

(3) The entitlement of a motion or stipulation for adjournment must specify whether it is the first or a later request, e.g., "Plaintiff's Request for Third Adjournment."

(C) Absence of Witness or Evidence.

(1) A motion to adjourn a proceeding because of the unavailability of a witness or evidence must be made as soon as possible after ascertaining the facts.

(2) An adjournment may be granted on the ground of unavailability of a witness or evidence only if the court finds that the evidence is material and that diligent efforts have been made to produce the witness or evidence.

(3) If the testimony or the evidence would be admissible in the proceeding, and the adverse party stipulates in writing or on the record that it is to be considered as actually given in the proceeding, there may be no adjournment unless the court deems an adjournment necessary.

(D) Order for Adjournment; Costs and Conditions.

(1) In its discretion the court may grant an adjournment to promote the cause of justice. An adjournment may be entered by order of the court either in writing or on the record in open court, and the order must state the reason for the adjournment.

(2) In granting an adjournment, the court may impose costs and conditions. When an adjournment is granted conditioned on payment of costs, the costs may be taxed summarily to be paid on demand of the adverse party or the adverse party's attorney, and the adjournment may be vacated if nonpayment is shown by written statement verified under MCR 1.109(D)(3).

(E) Rescheduling.

(1) Except as provided in subrule (E)(2), at the time the proceeding is adjourned under this rule, or as soon thereafter as possible, the proceeding must be rescheduled for a specific date and time.

(2) A court may place the matter on a specified list of actions or other matters which will automatically reappear before the court on the first available date.

(F) Death or Change of Status of Attorney. If the court finds that an attorney

(1) has died or is physically or mentally unable to continue to act as an attorney for a party,

(2) has been disbarred,

(3) has been suspended,

(4) has been placed on inactive status, or

(5) has resigned from active membership in the bar,

the court shall adjourn a proceeding in which the attorney was acting for a party. The party is entitled to 28 days' notice that he or she must obtain a substitute attorney or advise the court in writing that the party intends to appear on his or her own behalf. See MCR 9.119.

[Adopted effective March 1, 1985. Amended May 9, 2000, effective August 1, 2000, 462 Mich; March 20, 2019, effective May 1, 2019, 502 Mich.]

Comments

Staff Comment to 1985 Adoption

MCR 2.503 is based on GCR 1963, 503. The term "continuance" is changed to "adjournment" throughout.

Subrule (A) is a new provision making clear that the adjournment procedure applies to pretrial conferences, mediations, and motion hearings, as well as to trials.

Subrule (D)(1) specifies that when it grants an adjournment, the court is to do so either in writing or on the record, stating the reasons for granting the adjournment.

Subrule (E) is new, requiring rescheduling when a case is adjourned, or as soon thereafter as possible.

The [March 1, 1985] amendment of MCR 2.503(E) reorganizes the section to make clear that the only exception to the requirement of rescheduling to a specific date is the provision of subrule (E)(2)—placement of the matter on a specified list of actions that appear automatically on the next available date. The court is permitted to delay the rescheduling briefly (for example, to ascertain available dates), but a specific date and time must be set.

Subrule (F) includes the provisions found in GCR 1963, 909 regarding adjournment on the death or disability of an attorney for a party.

Staff Comment to 2000 Amendment

The May 8, 2000, amendments [effective August 1, 2000] are based on the recommendations of the Michigan Supreme Court Dispute Resolution Task Force, which were published for comment on May 10, 1999 [see 459 Mich 1251], and were the subject of a series of public hearings across the state.

The Task Force report, issued in January 1999, and its Addendum report, issued in January 2000 after receipt of comments, should be consulted for the background and details of the amendments. Basically, the changes are as follows:

The amendments of MCR 2.403, 2.404, 2.405, 2.501, 2.502 and 2.503 are mainly to change terminology, replacing "mediation," as used in current MCR 2.403, with the term "case evaluation." "Mediation" will be used to describe the facilitative process established in MCR 2.411, in keeping with the generally accepted usage of the term.

MCR 2.401 is amended to direct consideration of alternative dispute resolution processes at scheduling and pretrial conferences.

New MCR 2.410 has general provisions governing referral of cases to alternative dispute resolution processes. Local courts wishing to use ADR techniques are to adopt ADR plans within the framework provided by the rule.

The one ADR process that is specifically established by the rules is mediation under new MCR 2.411. Among other things, the rule establishes general standards for mediator qualifications, and procedures for selection of mediators.

MCR 3.216, the domestic relations mediation rule, is substantially revised, to be more comparable to the mediation process in MCR 2.411.

MCR 5.143, regarding use of alternative dispute resolution processes in probate court, is amended to conform to the other rule changes.

Staff Comment to 2019 Amendment

The amendments of Rules 1.109, 2.102, 2.104, 2.106, 2.107, 2.117, 2.119, 2.403, 2.503, 2.506, 2.508, 2.518, 2.602, 2.603, 2.621, 3.101, 3.104, 3.203, 3.205, 3.210, 3.302, 3.607, 3.613, 3.614, 3.705, 3.801, 3.802, 3.805, 3.806, 4.201, 4.202, 4.303, 4.306, 5.001, 5.104, 5.105, 5.107, 5.108, 5.113, 5.117, 5.118, 5.119, 5.120, 5.125, 5.126, 5.132, 5.162, 5.202, 5.203, 5.205, 5.302, 5.304, 5.307, 5.308, 5.309, 5.310, 5.311, 5.313, 5.402, 5.404,

5.405, 5.409, 5.501, and 5.784 and addition of Rule 3.618 of the Michigan Court Rules are an expected progression necessary for design and implementation of the statewide electronic-filing system. These particular amendments will assist in implementing the goals of the project.

Rule 2.504   Dismissal of Actions

(A) Voluntary Dismissal; Effect.

(1) *By Plaintiff; by Stipulation.* Subject to the provisions of MCR 2.420 and MCR 3.501(E), an action may be dismissed by the plaintiff without an order of the court and on the payment of costs

(a) by filing a notice of dismissal before service by the adverse party of an answer or of a motion under MCR 2.116, whichever first occurs; or

(b) by filing a stipulation of dismissal signed by all the parties.

Unless otherwise stated in the notice of dismissal or stipulation, the dismissal is without prejudice, except that a dismissal under subrule (A)(1)(a) operates as an adjudication on the merits when filed by a plaintiff who has previously dismissed an action in any court based on or including the same claim.

(2) *By Order of Court.* Except as provided in subrule (A)(1), an action may not be dismissed at the plaintiff's request except by order of the court on terms and conditions the court deems proper.

(a) If a defendant has pleaded a counterclaim before being served with the plaintiff's motion to dismiss, the court shall not dismiss the action over the defendant's objection unless the counterclaim can remain pending for independent adjudication by the court.

(b) Unless the order specifies otherwise, a dismissal under subrule (A)(2) is without prejudice.

(B) Involuntary Dismissal; Effect.

(1) If a party fails to comply with these rules or a court order, upon motion by an opposing party, or sua sponte, the court may enter a default against the noncomplying party or a dismissal of the noncomplying party's action or claims.

(2) In an action, claim, or hearing tried without a jury, after the presentation of the plaintiff's evidence, the court, on its own initiative, may dismiss, or the defendant, without waiving the defendant's right to offer evidence if the motion is not granted, may move for dismissal on the ground that on the facts and the law, the plaintiff has no right to relief. The court may then determine the facts and render judgment against the plaintiff, or may decline to render judgment until the close of all the evidence. If the court renders judgment on the merits against the plaintiff, the court shall make findings as provided in MCR 2.517.

(3) Unless the court otherwise specifies in its order for dismissal, a dismissal under this subrule or a dismissal not provided for in this rule, other than a dismissal for lack of jurisdiction or for failure to join a party under MCR 2.205, operates as an adjudication on the merits.

(C) Dismissal of Counterclaim, Cross-Claim, or Third-Party Claim. This rule applies to the dismissal of a counterclaim, cross-claim, or third-party claim. A voluntary dismissal by the claimant alone, pursuant to subrule (A)(1), must be made before service by the adverse party of a responsive pleading or a motion under MCR 2.116, or, if no pleading or motion is filed, before the introduction of evidence at the trial.

(D) Costs of Previously Dismissed Action. If a plaintiff who has once dismissed an action in any court commences an action based on or including the same claim against the same defendant, the court may order the payment of such costs of the action previously dismissed as it deems proper and may stay proceedings until the plaintiff has complied with the order.

(E) Dismissal for Failure to Serve Defendant. An action may be dismissed as to a defendant under MCR 2.102(E).
[Adopted effective March 1, 1985. Amended June 17, 2008, effective September 1, 2008, 481 Mich.]

Comments

Staff Comment to 1985 Adoption

MCR 2.504 is based on GCR 1963, 504.

Subrule (B)(3) is made consistent with FR Civ P 41(b): Dismissals for failure to join a necessary party under MCR 2.205 are added to the category of dismissals that do not operate as an adjudication on the merits.

Staff Comment to 2008 Amendment

This amendment allows a court, on motion of any party or sua sponte, to enter a default or dismiss a party's action or claim for failure to comply with the rules or a court order. The amendment also allows the court to dismiss on its own initiative an action in which the plaintiff, on the law and the facts presented, is not entitled to relief, and makes the rule applicable to claims and hearings in addition to actions.

Rule 2.505 Consolidation; Separate Trials

(A) Consolidation. When actions involving a substantial and controlling common question of law or fact are pending before the court, it may

(1) order a joint hearing or trial of any or all the matters in issue in the actions;

(2) order the actions consolidated; and

(3) enter orders concerning the proceedings to avoid unnecessary costs or delay.

(B) Separate Trials. For convenience or to avoid prejudice, or when separate trials will be conducive to expedition and economy, the court may order a separate trial of one or more claims, cross-claims, counterclaims, third-party claims, or issues.
[Adopted effective March 1, 1985.]

Comments

Staff Comment to 1985 Adoption

MCR 2.505 is based on GCR 1963, 505.

In subrule (B), an additional ground is added for ordering separate trials—where separate trials would be conducive to expedition and economy.

Rule 2.506. Subpoena; Order to Attend

(A) Attendance of Party or Witness.

(1) The court in which a matter is pending may by order or subpoena command a party or witness to appear for the purpose of testifying in open court on a date and time certain and from time to time and day to day thereafter until excused by the court, and/or to produce documents, or other portable tangible things. A request for documents or tangible things under this rule must comply with MCR 2.302(B) and any scheduling order. A person or entity subpoenaed under this rule may file written objections to the request for documents before the designated time for appearance; such objections

shall be adjudicated under subrule (H). This subrule does not apply to discovery subpoenas (MCR 2.305) or requests for documents to a party where discovery is available (MCR 2.310). A copy of any subpoena for documents or tangible things shall be provided to the opposing party or his/her counsel.

(2) A subpoena may specify the form or forms in which ESI is to be produced, subject to objection. If the subpoena does not so specify, the person responding to the subpoena must produce the information in a form or forms in which the person ordinarily maintains it, or in a form or forms that are reasonably usable. A person producing ESI need only produce the same information in one form.

(3) A person responding to a subpoena need not provide discovery of ESI from sources that the person identifies as not reasonably accessible because of undue burden or cost. In a hearing or submission under subrule (H), the person responding to the subpoena must show that the information sought is not reasonably accessible because of undue burden or cost. If that showing is made, the court may nonetheless order discovery from such sources if the requesting party shows good cause, considering the limitations of MCR 2.302(C). The court may specify conditions for such discovery, including who bears the cost.

(4) The court may require a party and a representative of an insurance carrier for a party with information and authority adequate for responsible and effective participation in settlement discussions to be present or immediately available at trial.

(5) A subpoena may be issued only in accordance with this rule or MCR 2.305, 2.621(C), 9.112(D), 9.115(I)(1), or 9.212.

(B) Authorized Signatures.

(1) A subpoena signed by an attorney of record in the action or by the clerk of the court in which the matter is pending has the force and effect of an order signed by the judge of that court.

(2) For the purpose of this subrule, an authorized signature includes but is not limited to signatures written by hand, printed, stamped, typewritten, engraved, photographed, lithographed, or executed under MCR 1.109(E)(4).

(C) Notice to Witness of Required Attendance.

(1) The signer of a subpoena must issue it for service on the witness sufficiently in advance of the trial or hearing to give the witness reasonable notice of the date and time the witness is to appear. Unless the court orders otherwise, the subpoena must be served at least 2 days before the appearance or 14 days before the appearance when documents are requested.

(2) The party having the subpoena issued must take reasonable steps to keep the witness informed of adjournments of the scheduled trial or hearing.

(3) If the served witness notifies the party that it is impossible for the witness to be present in court as directed, the party must either excuse the witness from attendance at that time or notify the witness that a special hearing may be held to adjudicate the issue.

(D) Form of Subpoena. A subpoena must:

(1) be entitled in the name of the People of the State of Michigan;

(2) be imprinted with the seal of the Supreme Court of Michigan;

(3) have typed or printed on it the name of the court in which the matter is pending;

(4) state the place where the trial or hearing is scheduled;

(5) state the title of the action in which the person is expected to testify;

(6) state the file number assigned by the court; and

(7) state that failure to obey the commands of the subpoena or reasonable directions of the signer as to time and place to appear may subject the person to whom it is directed to penalties for contempt of court.

The state court administrator shall develop and approve a subpoena form for statewide use.

(E) Refusal of Witness to Attend or to Testify; Contempt.

(1) If a person fails to comply with a subpoena served in accordance with this rule or with a notice under subrule (C)(2), the failure may be considered a contempt of court by the court in which the action is pending.

(2) If a person refuses to be sworn or to testify regarding a matter not privileged after being ordered to do so by the court, the refusal may be considered a contempt of court.

(F) Failure of Party to Attend. If a party or an officer, director, or managing agent of a party fails to attend or produce documents or other tangible evidence pursuant to a subpoena or an order to attend without having served written objections, the court may:

(1) stay further proceedings until the order is obeyed;

(2) tax costs to the other party or parties to the action;

(3) strike all or a part of the pleadings of that party;

(4) refuse to allow that party to support or oppose designated claims and defenses;

(5) dismiss the action or any part of it; or

(6) enter judgment by default against that party.

(G) Service of Subpoena and Order to Attend; Fees.

(1) A subpoena may be served anywhere in Michigan in the manner provided by MCR 2.105. The fee for attendance and mileage provided by law must be tendered to the person on whom the subpoena is served at the time of service. Tender must be made in cash, by money order, by cashier's check, or by a check drawn on the account of an attorney of record in the action or the attorney's authorized agent.

(2) A subpoena may also be served by mailing to a witness a copy of the subpoena and a postage-paid card acknowledging service and addressed to the party requesting service. The fees for attendance and mileage provided by law are to be given to the witness after the witness appears at the court, and the acknowledgment card must so indicate. If the card is not returned, the subpoena must be served in the manner provided in subrule (G)(1).

(3) A subpoena or order to attend directed to the Michigan Department of Corrections, Michigan Department of Health and Human Services, Michigan State Police Forensic Laboratory, other accredited forensic laboratory, law enforcement, or other governmental agency may be served by electronic transmission, including by facsimile or over a computer network, provided there is a memorandum of understanding between the parties indicating the contact person, the method of transmission, and the e-mail or facsimile number where the subpoena or order to attend should be sent. A confirmation correspondence must be received from the recipient within 2 business days after email or facsimile service is complete, and the confirmation correspondence shall be filed with the court. If no confirmation correspondence is provided within 2 business days after email or facsimile transmission, the subpoena must be served in the manner provided in subrule (G)(1).

(4) A subpoena or order to attend directed to a party, or to an officer, director, or managing agent of a party, may be served in the manner provided by MCR 2.107, and fees and mileage need not be paid.

(H) Hearing on Subpoena or Order to Attend.

(1) A person served with a subpoena or order to attend under this rule may appear before the court in person or by writing to explain why the person should not be compelled to comply with the subpoena, order to attend, or directions of the party having it issued.

(2) The court may direct that a special hearing be held to adjudicate the issue.

(3) For good cause with or without a hearing, the court may excuse a witness from compliance with a subpoena, the directions of the party having it issued, or an order to attend.

(4) A person must comply with the command of a subpoena unless relieved by order of the court or written direction of the person who had the subpoena issued except that any obligation to produce documents, if timely written objections are served, is stayed pending resolution under this subrule.

(5) Any party may move to quash or modify a subpoena by motion under MCR 2.302(C) filed before the time specified in the subpoena, and serve same upon the nonparty, in which case the non-party's obligation to respond is stayed until the motion is resolved.

(I) Subpoena for Production of Hospital Medical Records.

(1) Except as provided in subrule (I)(5), a hospital may comply with a subpoena calling for production of medical records belonging to the hospital in the manner provided in this subrule. This subrule does not apply to X-ray films or to other portions of a medical record that are not susceptible to photostatic reproduction.

(a) The hospital may deliver or mail to the clerk of the court in which the action is pending, without cost to the parties, a complete and accurate copy of the original record.

(b) The copy of the record must be accompanied by a sworn certificate, in the form approved by the state court administrator, signed by the medical record librarian or another authorized official of the hospital, verifying that it is a complete and accurate reproduction of the original record.

(c) The envelope or other container in which the record is delivered to the court shall be clearly marked to identify its contents. If the hospital wishes the record returned when it is no longer needed in the action, that fact must be stated on the container, and, with the record, the hospital must provide the clerk with a self-addressed, stamped envelope that the clerk may use to return the record.

(d) The hospital shall promptly notify the attorney for the party who caused the subpoena to be issued that the documents involved have been delivered or mailed to the court in accordance with subrule (I)(1).

(2) The clerk shall keep the copies sealed in the container in which they were supplied by the hospital. The container shall be clearly marked to identify the contents, the name of the patient, and the title and number of the action. The container shall not be opened except at the direction of the court.

(3) If the hospital has requested that the record be returned, the clerk shall return the record to the hospital when 42 days have passed after a final order terminating the action, unless an appeal has been taken. In the event of an appeal, the record shall be returned when 42 days have passed after a final order terminating the appeal. If the hospital did not request that the record be returned as provided in subrule (I)(1)(c), the clerk may destroy the record after the time provided in this subrule.

(4) The admissibility of the contents of medical records produced under this rule or under MCR 2.314 is not affected or altered by these procedures and remains subject to the same objections as if the original records were personally produced by the custodian at the trial or hearing.

(5) A party may have a subpoena issued directing that an original record of a person be produced at the trial or hearing by the custodian of the record. The subpoena must specifically state that the original records, not copies, are required. A party may also require, by subpoena, the attendance of the custodian without the records.

[Adopted effective March 1, 1985. Amended effective September 4, 1985, 422 Mich. Amended June 11, 1991, effective October 1, 1991, 437 Mich; September 22, 1998, effective December 1, 1998, 459 Mich; January 31, 2003, effective May 1, 2003, 467 Mich; December 16, 2008, effective January 1, 2009, 482 Mich; September 23, 2015, effective January 1, 2016, 498 Mich; March 20, 2019, effective May 1, 2019, 502 Mich; June 19, 2019, effective January 1, 2020, 503 Mich.]

Comments

Staff Comment to 1985 Adoption

MCR 2.506 substantially revises the provisions of GCR 1963, 506 governing subpoenas and orders to attend.

Subrule (A) permits issuance of a subpoena that commands the witness to appear at a specified day and time and also from day to day thereafter until excused. Subrule (C) requires the party who had the subpoena issued to keep the witness informed of adjournments.

Subrule (A)(2) includes a new provision based on former third circuit local rule 13.1 permitting the trial court to require a party and the representative of an insurance carrier to be present or immediately available at trial or a settlement conference.

Subrule (B) permits the attorney of record in an action to sign a subpoena with the same force as if it were issued by the clerk, as was required under GCR 1963, 506.2.

Subrule (C)(1) requires the party having the subpoena issued to have it served on the witness a reasonable time before the witness is to appear. It specifies that, unless the court otherwise orders, at least 2 days' notice is required.

Subrule (D) specifies in greater detail than did former GCR 1963, 506.4 the information that must be included in the subpoena. It also directs the state court administrator to develop and approve a subpoena form for statewide use.

Subrule (F) modifies the provisions of former GCR 1963, 506.6(2) to make the sanctions available against a party also applicable if an officer, director, or managing agent of the party fails to appear in response to a subpoena or order to attend.

Subrule (G) provides more detail regarding the manner of service of subpoenas and orders to attend than did the corresponding GCR 1963, 506.5. When directed to a party (or officer, director, or managing agent), the subpoena or order may be served in the manner provided by MCR 2.107.

In addition, new subrule (G)(2) permits the service of subpoenas by mail, accompanied by a postage-paid card acknowledging service. This provision was formerly found only in the district court rules regarding criminal cases and civil infractions. See DCR 506.5(b).

Subrule (H) creates a procedure for a hearing on a witness's objection to a subpoena or order.

The [March 1, 1985] amendment of MCR 2.506 adds a new subrule (I) covering the subject of subpoenaing hospital medical records for trial. It carries forward a simplified version of former GCR 1963, 506.7, and incorporates language previously found in MCR 2.314(F).

Staff Comment to 1985 Amendment

The [September 4, 1985] amendment of MCR 2.506(B) permits the "signing" of subpoenas by methods other than a handwritten signature.

Staff Comment to 1991 Amendment

Language regarding requiring the presence of parties at trial is deleted from MCR 2.506 [effective October 1, 1991]. That subject is now covered by MCR 2.401(F).

Staff Comment to 1998 Amendment

The December 1, 1998 [effective date], amendments of Rules 2.305, 2.310, and 2.506 were suggested by the Representative Assembly of the State Bar of Michigan. The changes made clear that nonparty records-only discovery subpoenas are authorized. The normal procedure for noticing a deposition applies to records-only subpoenas, and the procedure in MCR 2.310 still pertains to requests to a nonparty for entry on land or production of items for testing or sampling. The time for responding to a document subpoena or a document request under Rule 2.305(B)(1) was changed from seven to fourteen days. The time for responding under Rule 2.310(C)(2) was changed from twenty-eight to fourteen days. The amendments also made nonsubstantive changes to clarify and simplify language.

Staff Comment to 2003 Amendment

MCR 2.401(F) and (G), MCR 2.410(D)(2) and (3), MCR 2.506(A), and MCR 7.213(A) were amended January 31, 2003, effective May 1, 2003. Before the amendments, each of these subrules included a requirement that someone with "authority to settle" (or similar language) attend the type of proceeding described in each subrule. The amendments substituted the more flexible requirement that the person attending the proceeding have "information and authority adequate for responsible and effective participation" in settlement discussions.

The 2003 amendments of MCR 2.401(G) and MCR 2.410(D)(3) de-emphasized the use of defaults as sanctions for a party's failure to comply fully with an order. The amended rules allow entry of a default, but tilt in favor of less drastic sanctions.

Staff Comment to 2008 Amendment

These amendments update Michigan's discovery rules as they relate to electronically stored information. The provisions of the proposal at MCR 2.302(B)(6) and MCR 2.506(A)(3) allow the court to shift the cost of discovery to the requesting party if discovery is requested from sources that are not reasonably accessible, and prohibit sanctions if information is lost or destroyed as a result of a good-faith, routine record destruction policy or "litigation hold" procedures. The "safe harbor" provision provided in MCR 2.302(B)(5) and in MCR 2.313 applies when information is lost or destroyed under a routine electronic information system, if the operation of the system was performed in good faith. Good faith may be shown by a party's actions to attempt to preserve information as part of a "litigation hold" that would otherwise have been lost or destroyed under an electronic information system.

The new language of MCR 2.302 and MCR 2.506 also allows parties to determine the format in which the information should be produced, and how to handle a situation in which protected information is inadvertently produced.

Staff Comment to 2016 Amendment

The amendment of MCR 2.506(G)(3) allows electronic or facsimile transmission of subpoenas to attend when the subpoenas are directed to specific identified departments or agencies and when there is a memorandum of understanding between the parties as described by the amendment; the revision also would require a confirmation to be received within 2 business days after email or facsimile transmission of the subpoena. If no confirmation is provided, the subpoena must be served in the traditional manner.

Staff Comment to 2019 Amendment

The amendments of Rules 1.109, 2.102, 2.104, 2.106, 2.107, 2.117, 2.119, 2.403, 2.503, 2.506, 2.508, 2.518, 2.602, 2.603, 2.621, 3.101, 3.104, 3.203, 3.205, 3.210, 3.302, 3.607, 3.613, 3.614, 3.705, 3.801, 3.802, 3.805, 3.806, 4.201, 4.202, 4.303, 4.306, 5.001, 5.104, 5.105, 5.107, 5.108, 5.113, 5.117, 5.118, 5.119, 5.120, 5.125, 5.126, 5.132, 5.162, 5.202, 5.203, 5.205, 5.302, 5.304, 5.307, 5.308, 5.309, 5.310, 5.311, 5.313, 5.402, 5.404,

5.405, 5.409, 5.501, and 5.784 and addition of Rule 3.618 of the Michigan Court Rules are an expected progression necessary for design and implementation of the statewide electronic-filing system. These particular amendments will assist in implementing the goals of the project.

Staff Comment to 2020 Amendment

These amendments are based on a proposal created by a special committee of the State Bar of Michigan and approved for submission to the Court by the Bar's Representative Assembly. The rules require mandatory discovery disclosure in many cases, adopt a presumptive limit on interrogatories (20 in most cases, but 35 in domestic relations proceedings) and limit a deposition to 7 hours. The amendments also update the rules to more specifically address issues related to electronically stored information, and encourage early action on discovery issues during the discovery period.

The amendment of MCR 2.309(A)(2) sets a presumptive limit of twenty interrogatories for each separately represented party. Several commenters suggested that the term "discrete subpart" be more explicitly defined. But the rule's reference to "a discrete subpart" is intended to draw guidance from federal courts construing FR Civ P 30(a)(1). Generally, subparts are not separately counted if they are logically or factually subsumed within and necessarily related to the primary question. In upholding the limit, parties and courts should also pragmatically balance the overall goals of discovery and the admonition of MCR 1.105. Further, the intent of the provision at MCR 2.301(B)(4) is to ensure that parties responding to discovery requests have the full time period to do so as provided for under these rules prior to the expiration of the discovery period.

Rule 2.507   Conduct of Trials

(A) Opening Statements. Before the introduction of evidence, the attorney for the party who is to commence the evidence must make a full and fair statement of that party's case and the facts the party intends to prove. Immediately thereafter or immediately before the introduction of evidence by the adverse party, the attorney for the adverse party must make a like statement. Opening statements may be waived with the consent of the court and the opposing attorney.

(B) Opening the Evidence. Unless otherwise ordered by the court, the plaintiff must first present the evidence in support of the plaintiff's case. However, the defendant must first present the evidence in support of his or her case, if

(1) the defendant's answer has admitted facts and allegations of the plaintiff's complaint to the extent that, in the absence of further statement on the defendant's behalf, judgment should be entered on the pleadings for the plaintiff, and

(2) the defendant has asserted a defense on which the defendant has the burden of proof, either as a counterclaim or as an affirmative defense.

(C) Examination and Cross-Examination of Witnesses. Unless otherwise ordered by the court, no more than one attorney for a party may examine or cross-examine a witness.

(D) Court View. On application of either party or on its own initiative, the court sitting as trier of fact without a jury may view property or a place where a material event occurred.

(E) Final Arguments. After the close of all the evidence, the parties may rest their cases with or without final arguments. The party who commenced the evidence is entitled to open the argument and, if the opposing party makes an argument, to make a rebuttal argument not beyond the issues raised in the preceding arguments.

(F) Time Allowed for Opening Statements and Final Arguments. The court may limit the time allowed each party for opening statements and final arguments. It shall give the parties adequate time for argument, having due regard for the complexity of the action, and may make separate time allowances for co-parties whose interests are adverse.

(G) Agreements to Be in Writing. An agreement or consent between the parties or their attorneys respecting the proceedings in an action is not binding unless it was made in open court, or unless evidence of the agreement is in writing, subscribed by the party against whom the agreement is offered or by that party's attorney.

[Adopted effective March 1, 1985. Amended February 23, 2006, effective May 1, 2006, 474 Mich; April 5, 2011, effective September 1, 2011, 489 Mich. Amended effective September 11, 2013, 495 Mich. Amended October 22, 2014, effective January 1, 2015, 497 Mich.]

Comments

Staff Comment to 1985 Adoption

MCR 2.507 is based on GCR 1963, 507. GCR 1963, 507.4 (parties as witnesses) and 507.5 (exceptions unnecessary) are omitted.

Subrule (D) adds provisions regarding appointment of an interpreter.

Staff Comment to 2006 Amendment

The amendments of MCR 2.507(G), 4.201(F)(5), and 4.202(H)(3) reflect amendments of MCL 600.2529 and 600.5756 by 1993 PA 189.

Staff Comment to 2011 Amendment

The amendment of MCR 2.507 was submitted to the Court to clarify that oral agreements not made in open court or in writing to settle a case will not be enforceable. Like an agreement subject to the statute of frauds, agreements to settle a case would be required to be made in open court or be submitted in writing to be binding.

Supreme Court Comment to 2013 Amendment

The Michigan Supreme Court embraces the goal of providing access to all the courts of this State. This includes interpreter services for persons with Limited English Proficiency (LEP), to ensure that they have meaningful access to our courts.

The rules we adopt today provide court-appointed foreign language interpreters for truly needy LEP persons to support their access to justice, while not compelling taxpayers to bear the burden for LEP persons who can afford to pay for this service.

Our rules provide for court interpreters without cost to indigent LEP persons. If a party is financially able to pay for interpretation costs, the court may order the party to reimburse the court at the conclusion of the case or court proceeding. Moreover, our rules provide additional protection by allowing the trial judge to provide a court interpreter without cost to any LEP party, based on the judge's finding that assessing costs for the interpreter would limit that person's access to court.

Some history is in order. In August 2010, under the leadership of then–Chief Justice Marilyn Kelly, the Supreme Court convened a steering committee of judges and court administrators to develop proposals addressing access to court services for LEP individuals. The steering committee produced a court rule proposal specifying the procedures for appointment of an interpreter in Michigan's trial courts, as well as creating a structure for certifying various levels of interpreters, and creating a board to produce recommended requirements for interpreters and handle any misconduct claims.

Since February 2011, the Court has also worked cooperatively with the United States Department of Justice to improve the ability of LEP persons to access Michigan's courts. The Court's staff has communicated regularly with the Department, sharing numerous versions of the proposed court rules, exchanging ideas for the hiring and training of interpreters, and devising new and innovative ways to provide interpreter services at low or reduced costs. The Justice Department, through its administrative investigation function, has identified areas for improvement in individual trial courts across the state.

As a result of the dedicated work of the LEP committee, as well as the helpful and productive discussions with the Justice Department, the Court has fashioned a rule that reasonably accommodates access to the courts for LEP individuals with limited resources, and provides additional protection by allowing the trial judge to make a fact-based individualized determination whether assessment of costs would limit an LEP person's access to the court. This is a truly "flexible and fact-dependent standard." 67 *Fed. Reg.* 41459 (June 18, 2002). In fact, the rule is an individualized assessment that balances the four factors of (1) the number or proportion of LEP persons eligible to be served or likely to be encountered in court; (2) the frequency with which LEP individuals come into contact with the courts; (3) the nature and importance of the court system in people's lives; and (4) the resources available and costs. *Id.* The rules the Court has adopted strike the balance between ensuring meaningful access while not imposing undue burdens on Michigan's local courts. *Id.*

The Court has adopted a rule that focuses on the critical legal requirement: *meaningful access*. Under Rule 1.111(B)(1), a court is required to provide an interpreter for a party or witness if the court determines one is needed for either the party or the witness to meaningfully participate. LEP services are provided to all who have a need for them, and, under the rule, only parties who are able to pay for them are subject to reimbursement at the conclusion of the matter. In determining whether a party has the ability to reimburse for interpreter services, the court will impose costs only if the party has income above 125% of the federal poverty level *and* the court finds assessment of the interpreter costs would not unreasonably impede the person's ability to pursue or defend a claim. In other words, Rules 1.111(A)(4) and (B)(1) ensure that there will be no chilling effect on the LEP person's opportunity to pursue or defend a legal action.

Further, the rule we adopt is a frank acknowledgement that our trial courts—and indeed, our State's economy—are under severe financial stress and cannot, without explicit legal authority, be required to provide, at taxpayer expense, interpreter services for all LEP persons regardless of their means.

We will conduct appropriate educational programs with state court judges, administrators, and stakeholders as we work to implement this significant change in Michigan's procedure for appointment of foreign language interpreters.

Staff Comment to 2015 Amendment

This amendment allows a court view when a court is sitting as trier of fact instead of a jury. The provision, which had been included in former MCR 2.513, was eliminated with the adoption of various jury reform proposals in 2011.

Rule 2.508　Jury Trial of Right

(A) Right Preserved. The right of trial by jury as declared by the constitution must be preserved to the parties inviolate.

(B) Demand for Jury.

(1) A party may demand a trial by jury of an issue as to which there is a right to trial by jury by filing a written demand for a jury trial within 28 days after the filing of the answer or a timely reply. The demand for jury must be filed as a separate document. The jury fee provided by law must be paid at the time the demand is filed.

(2) If a party appealing to the circuit court from a municipal court desires a trial by jury of an issue triable of right, demand for jury must be included in the claim of appeal. If another party desires trial by jury of an issue triable of right, the demand must be included in the party's notice of appearance.

(3)(a) If a case is entirely removed from circuit court to district court, or is entirely removed or transferred from district court to circuit court, a timely demand for a trial by jury in the court from which the case is removed or transferred remains effective in the court to which the case is removed or transferred. If a case is entirely removed or transferred from district court to circuit court, and if the amount paid to the district court for the jury fee is less than the circuit court jury fee, then the party requesting the jury shall pay the difference to the circuit court. If a case is entirely removed from circuit court to district court, no additional jury fee is to be paid to the district court nor is there to be a refund of any amount by which the circuit court jury fee exceeds the district court jury fee.

(b) If part of a case is removed from circuit court to district court, or part of a case is removed or transferred from district court to circuit court, but a portion of the case remains in the court from which the case is removed or transferred, then a demand for a trial by jury in the court from which the case is removed or transferred is not effective in the court to which the case is removed or transferred. A party who seeks a trial by jury in the court to which the case is partially removed or transferred must file a written demand for a trial by jury within 21 days of the removal or transfer order, and must pay the jury fee provided by law,

even if the jury fee was paid in the court from which the case is removed or transferred.

(c) The absence of a timely demand for a trial by jury in the court from which a case is entirely or partially removed or transferred does not preclude filing a demand for a trial by jury in the court to which the case is removed or transferred. A party who seeks a trial by jury in the court to which the case is removed or transferred must file a written demand for a trial by jury within 21 days of the removal or transfer order, and must pay the jury fee provided by law.

(d) A party who is added to a case after it has been removed or transferred may demand trial by jury in accordance with paragraph (B)(1).

(C) Specifications of Issues.

(1) In a demand for jury trial, a party may specify the issues the party wishes so tried; otherwise, the party is deemed to have demanded trial by jury of all the issues so triable.

(2) If a party has demanded trial by jury of only some of the issues, another party, within 14 days after service of a copy of the demand or within less time as the court may order, may serve a demand for trial by jury of another or all of the issues of fact in the action.

(D) Waiver; Withdrawal.

(1) A party who fails to file a demand or pay the jury fee as required by this rule waives trial by jury.

(2) Waiver of trial by jury is not revoked by an amendment of a pleading asserting only a claim or defense arising out of the conduct, transaction, or occurrence stated, or attempted to be stated, in the original pleading.

(3) A demand for trial by jury may not be withdrawn without the consent, expressed in writing or on the record, of the parties or their attorneys.

[Adopted effective March 1, 1985. Amended December 6, 1994, effective January 1, 1995, 447 Mich; March 20, 2019, effective May 1, 2019, 502 Mich.]

Comments

Staff Comment to 1985 Adoption

MCR 2.508 is based on GCR 1963, 508, and DCR 508.

The [March 1, 1985] amendment of MCR 2.508(B)(1) requires that the jury fee be paid at the time the jury demand is filed.

Staff Comment to 1995 Amendment

MCR 2.508(B)(3) took effect in 1995, as did an amendment of MCR 4.002(C). These changes were to address the procedural issue that arose in *Adamski v Cole*, 197 Mich App 124, 494 NW2d 794 (1992), *lv den* 445 Mich 863 (1994).

Staff Comment to 2019 Amendment

The amendments of Rules 1.109, 2.102, 2.104, 2.106, 2.107, 2.117, 2.119, 2.403, 2.503, 2.506, 2.508, 2.518, 2.602, 2.603, 2.621, 3.101, 3.104, 3.203, 3.205, 3.210, 3.302, 3.607, 3.613, 3.614, 3.705, 3.801, 3.802, 3.805, 3.806, 4.201, 4.202, 4.303, 4.306, 5.001, 5.104, 5.105, 5.107, 5.108, 5.113, 5.117, 5.118, 5.119, 5.120, 5.125, 5.126, 5.132, 5.162, 5.202, 5.203, 5.205, 5.302, 5.304, 5.307, 5.308, 5.309, 5.310, 5.311, 5.313, 5.402, 5.404, 5.405, 5.409, 5.501, and 5.784 and addition of Rule 3.618 of the Michigan Court Rules are an expected progression necessary for design and implementation of the statewide electronic-filing system. These particular amendments will assist in implementing the goals of the project.

Rule 2.509　Trial by Jury or by Court

(A) By Jury. If a jury has been demanded as provided in MCR 2.508, the action or appeal must be designated in the court records as a jury action. The trial of all issues so demanded must be by jury unless

(1) the parties agree otherwise by stipulation in writing or on the record, or

(2) the court on motion or on its own initiative finds that there is no right to trial by jury of some or all of those issues.

(B) By Court. Issues for which a trial by jury has not been demanded as provided in MCR 2.508 will be tried by the court. In the absence of a demand for a jury trial of an issue as to which a jury demand might have been made of right, the court in its discretion may order a trial by jury of any or all issues.

(C) Sequence of Trial. In an action in which some issues are to be tried by jury and others by the court, or in which a number of claims, cross-claims, defenses, counterclaims, or third-party claims involve a common issue, the court may determine the sequence of trial of the issues, preserving the constitutional right to trial by jury according to the basic nature of every issue for which a demand for jury trial has been made under MCR 2.508.

(D) Advisory Jury and Trial by Consent. In appeals to circuit court from a municipal court and in actions involving issues not triable of right by a jury because of the basic nature of the issue, the court on motion or on its own initiative may

(1) try the issues with an advisory jury; or

(2) with the consent of all parties, order a trial with a jury whose verdict has the same effect as if trial by jury had been a matter of right.

[Adopted effective March 1, 1985.]

Comments

Staff Comment to 1985 Adoption

MCR 2.509 is substantially the same as GCR 1963, 509.

Rule 2.510   Juror Personal History Questionnaire

(A) Form. The state court administrator shall adopt a juror personal history questionnaire.

(B) Completion of Questionnaire.

(1) The court clerk or the jury board, as directed by the chief judge, shall supply each juror drawn for jury service with a questionnaire in the form adopted pursuant to subrule (A). The court clerk or the jury board shall direct the juror to complete the questionnaire before the juror is called for service.

(2) Refusal to answer the questions on the questionnaire, or answering the questionnaire falsely, is contempt of court.

(C) Return of the Questionnaire.

(1) On completion, the questionnaire shall be returned to the court clerk or the jury board, as designated under subrule (B)(1). The only persons allowed to examine the questionnaire are:

   (a) the judges of the court;

   (b) the court clerk and deputy clerks;

   (c) parties to actions in which the juror is called to serve and their attorneys; and

   (d) persons authorized access by court rule or by court order.

(2) The attorneys must be given a reasonable opportunity to examine the questionnaires before being called on to challenge for cause.

   (a) The State Court Administrator shall develop model procedures for providing attorneys and parties reasonable access to juror questionnaires.

   (b) Each court shall select and implement one of these procedures by local administrative order adopted pursuant to MCR 8.112(B). If the State Court Administrator determines that, given the circumstances existing in an individual court, the procedure selected does not provide reasonable access, the State Court Administrator may direct the court to implement one of the other model procedures.

   (c) If the procedure selected allows attorneys or parties to receive copies of juror questionnaires, an attorney or party may not release them to any person who would not be entitled to examine them under subrule (C)(1).

(3) The questionnaires must be maintained for 3 years from the time they are returned. They may be created and maintained in any medium authorized by court rules pursuant to MCR 1.109.

(D) Summoning Jurors for Court Attendance. The court clerk, the court administrator, the sheriff, or the jury board, as designated by the chief judge, shall summon jurors for court attendance at the time and in the manner directed by the chief judge. For a juror's first required court appearance, service must be by written notice addressed to the juror at the juror's residence as shown by the records of the clerk or jury board. The notice may be by ordinary mail or by personal service. For later service, notice may be in the manner directed by the court. The person giving notice to jurors shall keep a record of the notice and make a return if directed by the court. The return is presumptive evidence of the fact of service.

(E) Special Provision Pursuant to MCL 600.1324. If a city located in more than one county is entirely within a single district of the district court, jurors shall be selected for court attendance at that district from a list that includes the names and addresses of jurors from the entire city, regardless of the county where the juror resides or the county where the cause of action arose.

[Adopted effective March 1, 1985. Amended March 12, 1987, effective April 1, 1987, 428 Mich; July 13, 2005, effective January 1, 2006, 473 Mich; May 28, 2008, effective September 1, 2008, 481 Mich; January 29, 2014, effective May 1, 2014, 495 Mich.]

Comments

Staff Comment to 1985 Adoption

MCR 2.510 corresponds to GCR 1963, 510.

The form of jury questionnaire is deleted from the rule, and a jury questionnaire form will be approved by the state court administrator. See subrule (A).

Staff Comment to 1987 Amendment

The [April 1, 1987] amendment to MCR 2.510(C)(2) provides for development of model procedures for providing access to juror personal history questionnaires. Corresponding Administrative Order 1987-1 requires courts to select and implement one of the model plans within two months after the State Court Administrator issues them.

Staff Comment to 2005 Amendment

On March 12, 2002, the Court appointed the Committee on the Rules of Criminal Procedure to review the rules to determine whether any of the provisions should be revised. The committee issued its report on June 16, 2003, recommending numerous amendments to existing rules, plus some new rules. A public hearing on the committee's recommendations was held May 27, 2004.

The Court adopted the committee's recommendations with respect to the amendments of Rules 2.511, 6.102, 6.104, 6.107, 6.112, 6.303, 6.304, 6.310, 6.311,

6.402, 6.412, 6.414, 6.419, 6.420, 6.427, 6.615, and 6.620, and the adoption of a new Rule 6.428.

The Court also adopted, with modifications, recommendations made by the committee and staff to amend other rules. Rule 2.510 was amended to conform to the newly enacted 2004 PA 12 (MCL 600.1332). The Court modified the committee's recommendation concerning Rule 6.001 to include a reference to 6.102 and to limit the application of 6.445 to subrules (A) through (G). The Court adopted the committee's recommendation with regard to Rule 6.004, except that the requirement that "whenever the defendant's constitutional right to a speedy trial is violated, the defendant is entitled to dismissal of the charge with prejudice" was retained and inserted into 6.004(A).

Staff Comment to 2008 Amendment

The amendment of MCR 2.510(E) was added by the Court pursuant to MCL 600.1324. Subrule (E) requires that, in a district court district comprised of a city located in two or more counties, jurors must be selected for court attendance at that district from a list that includes the names and addresses of jurors from the entire city. The rule is applicable to both civil and criminal cases pursuant to MCR 6.412(A).

Staff Comment to 2014 Amendment

The amendments of MCR 2.510 allow courts to authorize prospective jurors to complete and return questionnaires electronically, and allow courts to create and maintain them electronically (i.e., in any medium authorized by court rules pursuant to MCR 1.109). The change also deletes language in MCR 2.510(D) to clarify that the chief judge is responsible for initiation of the court's policies for summoning prospective jurors.

Rule 2.511   Impaneling the Jury

(A) Selection of Jurors.

(1) Persons who have not been discharged or excused as prospective jurors by the court are subject to selection for the action or actions to be tried during their term of service as provided by law.

(2) In an action that is to be tried before a jury, the names or corresponding numbers of the prospective jurors shall be deposited in a container, and the prospective jurors must be selected for examination by a random blind draw from the container.

(3) The court may provide for random selection of prospective jurors for examination from less than all of the prospective jurors not discharged or excused.

(4) Prospective jurors may be selected by any other fair and impartial method directed by the court or agreed to by the parties.

(B) Alternate Jurors. The court may direct that 7 or more jurors be impaneled to sit. After the instructions to the jury have been given and the action is ready to be submitted, unless the parties have stipulated that all the jurors may deliberate, the names of the jurors must be placed in a container and names drawn to reduce the number of jurors to 6, who shall constitute the jury. The court may retain the alternate jurors during deliberations. If the court does so, it shall instruct the alternate jurors not to discuss the case with any other person until the jury completes its deliberations and is discharged. If an alternate juror replaces a juror after the jury retires to consider its verdict, the court shall instruct the jury to begin its deliberations anew.

(C) Examination of Jurors; Discharge of Unqualified Juror. The court may conduct the examination of prospective jurors or may permit the attorneys to do so. When the court finds that a person in attendance at court as a juror is not qualified to serve as a juror, the court shall discharge him or her from further attendance and service as a juror.

(D) Challenges for Cause. The parties may challenge jurors for cause, and the court shall rule on each challenge. A juror challenged for cause may be directed to answer questions pertinent to the inquiry. It is grounds for a challenge for cause that the person:

(1) is not qualified to be a juror;

(2) is biased for or against a party or attorney;

(3) shows a state of mind that will prevent the person from rendering a just verdict, or has formed a positive opinion on the facts of the case or on what the outcome should be;

(4) has opinions or conscientious scruples that would improperly influence the person's verdict;

(5) has been subpoenaed as a witness in the action;

(6) has already sat on a trial of the same issue;

(7) has served as a grand or petit juror in a criminal case based on the same transaction;

(8) is related within the ninth degree (civil law) of consanguinity or affinity to one of the parties or attorneys;

(9) is the guardian, conservator, ward, landlord, tenant, employer, employee, partner, or client of a party or attorney;

(10) is or has been a party adverse to the challenging party or attorney in a civil action, or has complained of or has been accused by that party in a criminal prosecution;

(11) has a financial interest other than that of a taxpayer in the outcome of the action;

(12) is interested in a question like the issue to be tried.

Exemption from jury service is the privilege of the person exempt, not a ground for challenge.

(E) Peremptory Challenges.

(1) A juror peremptorily challenged is excused without cause.

(2) Each party may peremptorily challenge three jurors. Two or more parties on the same side are considered a single party for purposes of peremptory challenges. However, when multiple parties having adverse interests are aligned on the same side, three peremptory challenges are allowed to each party represented by a different attorney, and the court may allow the opposite side a total number of peremptory challenges not exceeding the total number of peremptory challenges allowed to the multiple parties.

(3) Peremptory challenges must be exercised in the following manner:

(a) First the plaintiff and then the defendant may exercise one or more peremptory challenges until each party successively waives further peremptory challenges or all the challenges have been exercised, at which point jury selection is complete.

(b) A "pass" is not counted as a challenge but is a waiver of further challenge to the panel as constituted at that time.

(c) If a party has exhausted all peremptory challenges and another party has remaining challenges, that party may continue to exercise their remaining peremptory challenges until such challenges are exhausted.

(F) Discrimination in the Selection Process.

(1) No person shall be subjected to discrimination during voir dire on the basis of race, color, religion, national origin, or sex.

(2) Discrimination during voir dire on the basis of race, color, religion, national origin, or sex for the purpose of achieving what the court believes to be a balanced, proportionate, or representative jury in terms of these characteristics shall not constitute an excuse or justification for a violation of this subsection.

(G) Replacement of Challenged Jurors. After the jurors have been seated in the jurors' box and a challenge for cause is sustained or a peremptory challenge or challenges exercised, another juror or other jurors must be selected and examined. Such jurors are subject to challenge as are previously seated jurors.

(H) Oath of Jurors; Instruction Regarding Prohibited Actions.

(1) The jury must be sworn by the clerk substantially as follows:

"Each of you do solemnly swear (or affirm) that, in this action now before the court, you will justly decide the questions submitted to you, that, unless you are discharged by the court from further deliberation, you will render a true verdict, and that you will render your verdict only on the evidence introduced and in accordance with the instructions of the court, so help you God."

(2) The court shall instruct the jurors that until their jury service is concluded, they shall not

(a) discuss the case with others, including other jurors, except as otherwise authorized by the court;

(b) read or listen to any news reports about the case;

(c) use a computer, cellular phone, or other electronic device with communication capabilities while in attendance at trial or during deliberation. These devices may be used during breaks or recesses but may not be used to obtain or disclose information prohibited in subsection (d) below;

(d) use a computer, cellular phone, or other electronic device with communication capabilities, or any other method, to obtain or disclose information about the case when they are not in court. As used in this subsection, information about the case includes, but is not limited to, the following:

(i) information about a party, witness, attorney, or court officer;

(ii) news accounts of the case;

(iii) information collected through juror research on any topics raised or testimony offered by any witness;

(iv) information collected through juror research on any other topic the juror might think would be helpful in deciding the case.

[Adopted effective March 1, 1985. Amended June 26, 2001, effective September 1, 2001, 464 Mich; July 13, 2005, effective January 1, 2006, 473 Mich; November 23, 2005, effective January 1, 2006, 474 Mich; June 30, 2009, effective September 1, 2009, 484 Mich; October 6, 2011, effective January 1, 2012, 490 Mich.]

Comments

Staff Comment to 1985 Adoption

MCR 2.511 corresponds to GCR 1963, 511.

Subrule (A) removes some of the detail of GCR 1963, 511.1. It preserves the principle of random selection of jurors from those available.

The language regarding alternate jurors in subrule (B) is modified to be consistent with the provision found in MCR 2.512(A)(3), allowing the parties to stipulate that all of the jurors impaneled (including alternates) may deliberate.

Subrule (D) deletes language (from GCR 1963, 511.4) that had restricted challenges for cause by requiring that they be made after the jurors have been questioned. It may be possible to excuse some jurors in advance based on the questionnaires.

Subrule (E) differs from GCR 1963, 511.5 in that the later provision said that peremptory challenges are to be made after all challenges for cause are completed. Peremptory challenges may be exercised at a time when only the jurors who have been selected from the panel and seated in the jury box have been questioned so as to permit challenges for cause. If a juror is peremptorily challenged and a new one called from the panel and questioned, the parties should be able to challenge that juror for cause.

Subrule (E)(3) makes clear that while a "pass" is not counted as a challenge, it does constitute a waiver of further challenge to the jury panel as then constituted. If the other parties also pass, jury selection is complete.

The oath of the jurors in subrule (G) is taken from PCR 511.7.

The provisions of GCR 1963, 511 and DCR 511 that were specifically applicable to criminal cases have been moved to chapter 6. See MCR 6.102, 6.202.

Staff Comment to 2001 Amendment

The June 26, 2001 amendments of MCR 2.511(B), MCR 6.411, and MCR 6.620(A), effective September 1, 2001, were based on a proposal from the Michigan Judges Association. Consistent with the December 1999 amendment of the Federal Rules of Criminal Procedure for the United States District Courts, the amendments allow courts to retain alternate jurors during deliberations.

Staff Comment to July, 2006 Amendment

On March 12, 2002, the Court appointed the Committee on the Rules of Criminal Procedure to review the rules to determine whether any of the provisions should be revised. The committee issued its report on June 16, 2003, recommending numerous amendments to existing rules, plus some new rules. A public hearing on the committee's recommendations was held May 27, 2004.

The Court adopted the committee's recommendations with respect to the amendments of Rules 2.511, 6.102, 6.104, 6.107, 6.112, 6.303, 6.304, 6.310, 6.311, 6.402, 6.412, 6.414, 6.419, 6.420, 6.427, 6.615, and 6.620, and the adoption of a new Rule 6.428.

Staff Comment to December, 2006 Amendment

The amendment of MCR 2.511(F) is new language that states that discrimination on the basis of race, color, religion, national origin, or sex during the selection process of a jury is prohibited even in cases where the purpose would be to achieve balanced representation. Former subrules (F) and (G) are relettered as (G) and (H).

Staff Comment to 2009 Amendment

This amendment requires judges to instruct jurors that they are prohibited from using computers or cell phones at trial or during deliberation, and are prohibited from using a computer or other electronic device or any other method to obtain or disclose information about the case when they are not in the courtroom. The instruction shall be given when the jury is empaneled.

The amendment prohibits jurors from reading about or listening to news reports about the case and prohibits discussion among jurors until deliberation. The prohibition on juror discussion does not apply to courts participating in the jury reform pilot project, which specifically allows jurors to discuss a case before the close of evidence.

Staff Comment to 2011 Amendment

Because MCL 600.1337 requires a court to discharge an unqualified juror regardless whether a party challenges the juror for cause, the amendment of MCR 2.511 clarifies that the discharge must be made when the court learns that the juror is not qualified to serve.

Rule 2.512 Instructions to Jury

(A) Request for Instructions.

(1) At a time the court reasonably directs, the parties must file written requests that the court instruct the jury on the law as stated in the requests. In the absence of a direction from the court, a party may file a written request for jury instructions at or before the close of the evidence.

(2) In addition to requests for instructions submitted under subrule (A)(1), after the close of the evidence, each party shall submit in writing to the court a statement of the issues and may

submit the party's theory of the case regarding each issue. The statement must be concise, be narrative in form, and set forth as issues only those disputed propositions of fact that are supported by the evidence. The theory may include those claims supported by the evidence or admitted.

(3) A copy of the requested instructions must be served on the adverse parties in accordance with MCR 2.107.

(4) The court shall inform the attorneys of its proposed action on the requests before their arguments to the jury.

(5) The court need not give the statements of issues or theories of the case in the form submitted if the court presents to the jury the material substance of the issues and theories of each party.

(B) Instructing the Jury.

(1) At any time during the trial, the court may, with or without request, instruct the jury on a point of law if the instruction will materially aid the jury in understanding the proceedings and arriving at a just verdict.

(2) Before or after arguments or at both times, as the court elects, the court shall instruct the jury on the applicable law, the issues presented by the case, and, if a party requests as provided in subrule (A)(2), that party's theory of the case.

(C) Objections. A party may assign as error the giving of or the failure to give an instruction only if the party objects on the record before the jury retires to consider the verdict (or, in the case of instructions given after deliberations have begun, before the jury resumes deliberations), stating specifically the matter to which the party objects and the grounds for the objection. Opportunity must be given to make the objection out of the hearing of the jury.

(D) Model Civil Jury Instructions and Model Criminal Jury Instructions.

(1) The Committee on Model Civil Jury Instructions and the Committee on Model Criminal Jury Instructions appointed by the Supreme Court have the authority to adopt model jury instructions and to amend or repeal those instructions approved by the predecessor committee. Before adopting, amending, or repealing an instruction, each committee shall publish notice of the committee's intent, together with the text of the instruction to be adopted, or the amendment to be made, or a reference to the instruction to be repealed, in the manner provided in MCR 1.201. The notice shall specify the time and manner for commenting on the proposal. If the committee finds it necessary to take immediate action, the committee may adopt a new instruction or revision while the public comment period is pending. The committee shall thereafter publish notice of its final action on the proposed change, including, if appropriate, the effective date of the adoption, amendment, or repeal. A model jury instruction does not have the force and effect of a court rule.

(2) Pertinent portions of the instructions approved by the Committee on Model Civil Jury Instructions or the Committee on Model Criminal Jury Instructions or a predecessor committee must be given in each action in which jury instructions are given if

(a) they are applicable,

(b) they accurately state the applicable law, and

(c) they are requested by a party.

(3) Whenever a committee recommends that no instruction be given on a particular matter, the court shall not give an instruction unless it specifically finds for reasons stated on the record that

(a) the instruction is necessary to state the applicable law accurately, and

(b) the matter is not adequately covered by other pertinent model civil jury instructions.

(4) This subrule does not limit the power of the court to give additional instructions on applicable law not covered by the model instructions. Additional instructions, when given, must be patterned as nearly as practicable after the style of the model instructions and must be concise, understandable, conversational, unslanted, and nonargumentative.

[Adopted effective March 1, 1985. Amended June 21, 2000, effective September 1, 2000, 462 Mich; June 29, 2011, effective September 1, 2011, 489 Mich; October 30, 2013, effective March 1, 2014, 495 Mich.]

Comments

Staff Comment to 1985 Adoption

MCR 2.512 corresponds to GCR 1963, 512. The language of GCR 1963, 512.1 that was specifically applicable to criminal cases is omitted.

Subrule (A)(3) is a new provision expressly allowing the parties to stipulate that all of the jurors impaneled (including alternates) may deliberate.

Staff Comment to 2000 Amendment

The June 21, 2000 amendment, effective September 1, 2000, changed MCR 2.512(B)(1) to read the same as MCR 6.420(A), as recommended by the Michigan Judges Association.

Staff Comment to 2011 Amendment

The amendments in this order reflect the Court's approval of many of the jury reform principles tested in the Court's two-year jury reform pilot project that ended in December 2010. Under this order, jury practices for both civil and criminal proceedings are generally incorporated in a new MCR 2.513. The Court will review the efficacy of these amendments in 2014.

Staff Comment to 2014 Amendment

The Court has determined that the function of adopting, amending, and repealing model criminal jury instructions should be structured similar to that for model civil jury instructions. As part of that structural change, this amendment requires trial courts to use model jury instructions in criminal cases under the same circumstances in which they are used in civil cases, i.e., if the instructions are applicable, accurately state the applicable law, and are requested by a party.

Rule 2.513   Conduct of Jury Trial

(A) Preliminary Instructions. After the jury is sworn and before evidence is taken, the court shall orally provide the jury with pretrial instructions reasonably likely to assist in its consideration of the case. Such instructions, at a minimum, shall communicate the duties of the jury, trial procedure, and the law applicable to the case as are reasonably necessary to enable the jury to understand the proceedings and the evidence. The jury also shall be orally instructed about the elements of all civil claims or all charged offenses, as well as the legal presumptions and burdens of proof. The court shall also provide each juror with a written copy of such instructions. MCR 2.512(D)(2) does not apply to such preliminary instructions.

(B) Court's Responsibility. The trial court must control the proceedings during trial, limit the evidence and arguments to relevant and proper matters, and take appropriate steps to ensure that the jurors will not be exposed to information or influences that might affect their ability to render an impartial verdict on the evidence presented in court. The court may not communicate with the jury or any juror pertaining to the case without notifying the parties and permitting them to be present. The court must ensure that all communications pertaining to the case between the court and the jury or any juror are made a part of the record.

(C) Opening Statements. Unless the parties and the court agree otherwise, the plaintiff or the prosecutor, before presenting evidence, must make a full and fair statement of the case and the facts the plaintiff or the prosecutor intends to prove. Immediately thereafter, or immediately before presenting evidence, the defendant may make a similar statement. The court may impose reasonable time limits on the opening statements.

(D) Interim Commentary. Each party may, in the court's discretion, present interim commentary at appropriate junctures of the trial.

(E) Reference Documents. The court may authorize or require counsel in civil and criminal cases to provide the jurors with a reference document or notebook, the contents of which should include, but which is not limited to, a list of witnesses, relevant statutory provisions, and, in cases where the interpretation of a document is at issue, copies of the relevant document. The court and the parties may supplement the reference document during trial with copies of the preliminary jury instructions, admitted exhibits, and other admissible information to assist jurors in their deliberations.

(F) Deposition Summaries. Where it appears likely that the contents of a deposition will be read to the jury, the court should encourage the parties to prepare concise, written summaries of depositions for reading at trial in lieu of the full deposition. Where a summary is prepared, the opposing party shall have the opportunity to object to its contents. Copies of the summaries should be provided to the jurors before they are read.

(G) Scheduling Expert Testimony. In a civil action, the court may, in its discretion, craft a procedure for the presentation of all expert testimony to assist the jurors in performing their duties. Such procedures may include, but are not limited to:

(1) Scheduling the presentation of the parties' expert witnesses sequentially; or

(2) allowing the opposing experts to be present during the other's testimony and to aid counsel in formulating questions to be asked of the testifying expert on cross-examination.

(H) Note Taking by Jurors. The court may permit the jurors to take notes regarding the evidence presented in court. If the court permits note taking, it must instruct the jurors that they need not take notes, and they should not permit note taking to interfere with their attentiveness. If the court allows jurors to take notes, jurors must be allowed to refer to their notes during deliberations, but the court must instruct the jurors to keep their notes confidential except as to other jurors during deliberations. The court shall ensure that all juror notes are collected and destroyed when the trial is concluded.

(I) Juror Questions. The court may permit the jurors to ask questions of witnesses. If the court permits jurors to ask questions, it must employ a procedure that ensures that such questions are addressed to the witnesses by the court itself, that inappropriate questions are not asked, and that the parties have an opportunity outside the hearing of the jury to object to the questions. The court shall inform the jurors of the procedures to be followed for submitting questions to witnesses.

(J) Jury View. On motion of either party, on its own initiative, or at the request of the jury, the court may order a jury view of property or of a place where a material event occurred. The parties are entitled to be present at the jury view, provided, however, that in a criminal case, the court may preclude a defendant from attending a jury view in the interests of safety and security. During the view, no person, other than an officer designated by the court, may speak to the jury concerning the subject connected with the trial. Any such communication must be recorded in some fashion.

(K) Juror Discussion. In a civil case, after informing the jurors that they are not to decide the case until they have heard all the evidence, instructions of law, and arguments of counsel, the court may instruct the jurors that they are permitted to discuss the evidence among themselves in the jury room during trial recesses. The jurors should be instructed that such discussions may only take place when all jurors are present and that such discussions must be clearly understood as tentative pending final presentation of all evidence, instructions, and argument.

(L) Closing Arguments. After the close of all the evidence, the parties may make closing arguments. The plaintiff or the prosecutor is entitled to make the first closing argument. If the defendant makes an argument, the plaintiff or the prosecutor may offer a rebuttal limited to the issues raised in the defendant's argument. The court may impose reasonable time limits on the closing arguments.

(M) Summing up the Evidence. After the close of the evidence and arguments of counsel, the court may fairly and impartially sum up the evidence if it also instructs the jury that it is to determine for itself the weight of the evidence and the credit to be given to the witnesses and that jurors are not bound by the court's summation. The court shall not comment on the credibility of witnesses or state a conclusion on the ultimate issue of fact before the jury.

(N) Final Instructions to the Jury.

(1) Before closing arguments, the court must give the parties a reasonable opportunity to submit written requests for jury instructions. Each party must serve a copy of the written requests on all other parties. The court must inform the parties of its proposed action on the requests before their closing arguments. After closing arguments are made or waived, the court must orally instruct the jury as required and appropriate, but at the discretion of the court, and on notice to the parties, the court may orally instruct the jury before the parties make closing arguments. After jury deliberations begin, the court may give additional instructions that are appropriate.

(2) *Solicit Questions about Final Instructions.* As part of the final jury instructions, the court shall advise the jury that it may submit in a sealed envelope given to the bailiff any written questions about the jury instructions that arise during deliberations. After orally delivering the final jury instructions, the court shall invite the jurors to ask any questions in order to clarify the instructions before they retire to deliberate.

If questions arise, the court and the parties shall convene, in the courtroom or by other agreed-upon means. The question shall be read into the record, and the attorneys shall offer comments on an appropriate response. The court may, in its discretion, provide the jury with a specific response to the jury's question, but the court shall respond to all questions asked, even if the response consists of a directive for the jury to continue its deliberations.

(3) *Copies of Final Instructions.* The court shall provide a written copy of the final jury instructions to take into the jury room for deliberation. Upon request by any juror, the court may provide additional copies as necessary. The court, in its discretion, also may provide the jury with a copy of electronically recorded instructions.

(4) *Clarifying or Amplifying Final Instructions.* When it appears that a deliberating jury has reached an impasse, or is otherwise in need of assistance, the court may invite the jurors to list the issues that divide or confuse them in the event that the judge can be of assistance in clarifying or amplifying the final instructions.

(O) Materials in the Jury Room. The court shall permit the jurors, on retiring to deliberate, to take into the jury room their notes and final instructions. The court may permit the jurors to take into the jury room the reference document, if one has been prepared, as well as any exhibits and writings admitted into evidence.

(P) Provide Testimony or Evidence. If, after beginning deliberation, the jury requests a review of certain testimony or evidence that has not been allowed into the jury room under subrule (O), the court must exercise its discretion to ensure fairness and to refuse unreasonable requests, but it may not refuse a reasonable request. The court may make a video or audio recording of witness testimony, or prepare an immediate transcript of such testimony, and such tape or transcript, or other testimony or evidence, may be made available to the jury for its consideration. The court may order the jury to deliberate further without the requested review, as long as the possibility of having the testimony or evidence reviewed at a later time is not foreclosed.

[Adopted effective March 1, 1985. Amended June 29, 2011, effective September 1, 2011, 489 Mich; March 13, 2019, effective May 1, 2019, 502 Mich.]

Comments

Staff Comment to 1985 Adoption

MCR 2.513 corresponds to GCR 1963, 513.

New subrule (B) is added, making clear that the judge trying a case without a jury may also view property or a place where a material event occurred.

Staff Comment to 2011 Amendment

The amendments in this order reflect the Court's approval of many of the jury reform principles tested in the Court's two-year jury reform pilot project that ended in December 2010. Under this order, jury practices for both civil and criminal proceedings are generally incorporated in a new MCR 2.513. The Court will review the efficacy of these amendments in 2014.

Staff Comment to 2019 Amendment

The amendment of MCR 2.513 explicitly provides that a court must orally recite its preliminary and final jury instructions for the jury (in addition to providing them in writing). The amendment clarifies that even though a juror is entitled to a written set of instructions, the judge must still orally instruct the jury. This amendment conforms the rule to the opinion issued by the Court in *People v Traver.*

Rule 2.514   Rendering Verdict

(A) Majority Verdict; Stipulations Regarding Number of Jurors and Verdict. The parties may stipulate in writing or on the record that

(1) the jury will consist of any number less than 6,

(2) a verdict or a finding of a stated majority of the jurors will be taken as the verdict or finding of the jury, or

(3) if more than 6 jurors were impaneled, all the jurors may deliberate.

Except as provided in MCR 5.740(C), in the absence of such stipulation, a verdict in a civil action tried by 6 jurors will be received when 5 jurors agree.

(B) Return; Poll.

(1) The jury must return its verdict in open court.

(2) A party may require a poll to be taken by the court asking each juror if it is his or her verdict.

(3) If the number of jurors agreeing is less than required, the jury must be sent back for further deliberation; otherwise, the verdict is complete, and the court shall discharge the jury.

(C) Discharge From Action; New Jury. The court may discharge a jury from the action:

(1) because of an accident or calamity requiring it;

(2) by consent of all the parties;

(3) whenever an adjournment or mistrial is declared;

(4) whenever the jurors have deliberated and it appears that they cannot agree.

The court may order another jury to be drawn, and the same proceedings may be had before the new jury as might have been had before the jury that was discharged.

(D) Responsibility of Officers.

(1) All court officers, including trial attorneys, must attend during the trial of an action until the verdict of the jury is announced.

(2) A trial attorney may, on request, be released by the court from further attendance, or the attorney may designate an associate or other attorney to act for him or her during the deliberations of the jury.

[Adopted effective March 1, 1985. Amended June 29, 2011, effective September 1, 2011, 489 Mich.]

Comments

Staff Comment to 1985 Adoption

MCR 2.514 is substantially the same as GCR 1963, 514.

Staff Comment to 2011 Amendment

The amendments in this order reflect the Court's approval of many of the jury reform principles tested in the Court's two-year jury reform pilot project that ended in December 2010. Under this order, jury practices for both civil and criminal proceedings are generally incorporated in a new MCR 2.513. The Court will review the efficacy of these amendments in 2014.

Rule 2.515   Special Verdicts

(A) Use of Special Verdicts; Form. The court may require the jury to return a special verdict in the form of a written finding on each issue of fact, rather than a general verdict. If a special verdict is required, the court shall, in advance of argument and in the absence of the jury, advise the attorneys of this fact and, on the record or in writing, settle the form of the verdict. The court may submit to the jury:

(1) written questions that may be answered categorically and briefly;

(2) written forms of the several special findings that might properly be made under the pleadings and evidence; or

(3) the issues by another method, and require the written findings it deems most appropriate.

The court shall give to the jury the necessary explanation and instruction concerning the matter submitted to enable the jury to make its findings on each issue.

(B) Judgment. After a special verdict is returned, the court shall enter judgment in accordance with the jury's findings.

(C) Failure to Submit Question; Waiver; Findings by Court. If the court omits from the special verdict form an issue of fact raised by the pleadings or the evidence, a party waives the right to a trial by jury of the issue omitted unless the party demands its submission to the jury before it retires for deliberations. The court may make a finding with respect to an issue omitted without a demand. If the court fails to do so, it is deemed to have made a finding in accord with the judgment on the special verdict.

[Adopted effective March 1, 1985. Amended June 29, 2011, effective September 1, 2011, 489 Mich.]

Comments

Staff Comment to 1985 Adoption

MCR 2.515 includes the part of GCR 1963, 515.1 that dealt with motions for a directed verdict. The remaining provisions of GCR 1963, 515 are relocated in the post-trial subchapter. See MCR 2.610.

Staff Comment to 2011 Amendment

The amendments in this order reflect the Court's approval of many of the jury reform principles tested in the Court's two-year jury reform pilot project that ended in December 2010. Under this order, jury practices for both civil and criminal proceedings are generally incorporated in a new MCR 2.513. The Court will review the efficacy of these amendments in 2014.

Rule 2.516   Motion for Directed Verdict

A party may move for a directed verdict at the close of the evidence offered by an opponent. The motion must state specific grounds in support of the motion. If the motion is not granted, the moving party may offer evidence without having reserved the right to do so, as if the motion had not been made. A motion for a directed verdict that is not granted is not a waiver of trial by jury, even though all parties to the action have moved for directed verdicts.

[Adopted effective March 1, 1985. Amended March 16, 1989, effective June 1, 1989, 432 Mich; June 2, 1998, effective September 1, 1998, 457 Mich; December 18, 2001, effective May 1, 2002, 465 Mich; June 29, 2011, effective September 1, 2011, 489 Mich.]

Comments

Staff Comment to 1985 Adoption

MCR 2.516 corresponds to GCR 1963, 516. The rule is reorganized and, in addition, has several substantive changes.

The provision on "preliminary" instructions, previously found in GCR 1963, 516.3, is modified in subrule (B)(1). The trial court is directed to give instructions after the selection of the jury and before taking of evidence. These instructions could include instructions on the law applicable to the case in much the same form as the traditional closing instructions.

The [March 1, 1985] amendment of MCR 2.516(B)(1) excepts preliminary instructions from the requirement that Standard Jury Instructions be given when applicable and requested.

Subrule (C) makes the provisions of GCR 1963, 516.2 regarding objections to instructions applicable to all instructions. The special provisions regarding objections to preliminary instructions (failure to give such instructions cannot be assigned as error, GCR 1963, 516.3) and additional instructions (objection to be made in motion for new trial, GCR 1963, 516.4) are omitted.

In subrule (B)(5), in addition to the authority to submit full or partial sets of written instructions to the jury as had been provided by GCR 1963, 516.1, a trial court may provide the jury with a full or partial (on stipulation) set of electronically recorded instructions.

The [March 1, 1985] amendment of MCR 2.516(D)(1) corrects an inadvertent failure to carry forward the 1980 amendment of GCR 1963, 516.6(1) regarding the operation of the Standard Jury Instruction Committee.

Former GCR 1963, 516.5, regarding condemnation proceedings, is omitted. Under MCL 213.62(1), jury procedure in condemnation cases is governed by the same rules as are other civil actions.

Staff Comment to 1989 Amendment

The 1989 amendment of MCR 2.516(B)(3) permits the court to elect to instruct the jury prior to final arguments, after final arguments, or at both times. The previous rule provided that instructions were to follow final arguments.

Staff Comment to 1998 Amendment

The June 1998 amendment of MCR 2.516(B)(5)(c), effective September 1, 1998, was suggested by the Michigan Judges Association. The amendment allows the trial court to provide the jury with a partial set of instructions if the jury asks for clarification or restatement of a particular instruction or instructions. Previously, a partial set of instructions could be provided only if the parties agreed. The amendment also added to MCR 2.516 (B)(5) the final sentence in MCR 6.414(G), to ensure that all instructions are made a part of the record.

Staff Comment to 2002 Amendment

The December 18, 2001 amendment of subrule (D), effective May 1, 2002, is consistent with the Supreme Court's adoption of Administrative Order 2001–6, which established the membership and terms for the new Committee on Model Civil Jury Instructions.

Staff Comment to 2011 Amendment

The amendments in this order reflect the Court's approval of many of the jury reform principles tested in the Court's two-year jury reform pilot project that ended in December 2010. Under this order, jury practices for both civil and criminal proceedings are generally incorporated in a new MCR 2.513. The Court will review the efficacy of these amendments in 2014.

Rule 2.517   Findings by Court

(A) Requirements.

(1) In actions tried on the facts without a jury or with an advisory jury, the court shall find the facts specially, state separately its conclusions of law, and direct entry of the appropriate judgment.

(2) Brief, definite, and pertinent findings and conclusions on the contested matters are sufficient, without over elaboration of detail or particularization of facts.

(3) The court may state the findings and conclusions on the record or include them in a written opinion.

(4) Findings of fact and conclusions of law are unnecessary in decisions on motions unless findings are required by a particular rule. See, e.g., MCR 2.504(B).

(5) The clerk shall notify the attorneys for the parties of the findings of the court.

(6) Requests for findings are not necessary for purposes of review.

(7) No exception need be taken to a finding or decision.

(B) Amendment. On motion of a party made within 21 days after entry of judgment, the court may amend its findings or make additional findings, and may amend the judgment accordingly. The motion may be made with a motion for new trial pursuant to MCR 2.611. When findings of fact are made in an action tried by the court without a jury, the question of the sufficiency of the evidence to support the findings may thereafter be raised whether the party raising the question has objected to the findings or has moved to amend them or for judgment.

[Adopted effective March 1, 1985.]

Comments

Staff Comment to 1985 Adoption

MCR 2.517 corresponds to GCR 1963, 517.

Subrule (A)(3) makes clear that the judge may either write an opinion setting forth the findings or may state them on the record.

The language of GCR 1963, 517.1 that findings are not to be set aside unless clearly erroneous is moved to MCR 2.613.

Rule 2.518   Receipt and Return or Disposal of Exhibits

(A) Receipt of Exhibits. Except as otherwise required by statute or court rule, materials that are intended to be used as evidence at or during a trial shall not be filed with the clerk of the court, but shall be submitted to the judge for introduction into evidence as exhibits. Exhibits introduced into evidence at or during court proceedings shall be received and maintained as provided by Michigan Supreme Court trial court records management standards. As defined in MCR 1.109, exhibits received and accepted into evidence under this rule are not court records.

(B) Return or Disposal of Exhibits. At the conclusion of a trial or hearing, the court shall direct the parties to retrieve the exhibits submitted by them except that any weapons and drugs shall be returned to the confiscating agency for proper disposition. If the exhibits are not retrieved by the parties as directed within 56 days after conclusion of the trial or hearing, the court may properly dispose of the exhibits without notice to the parties.

(C) Confidentiality. If the court retains discovery materials filed pursuant to MCR 1.109(D) or an exhibit submitted pursuant to this rule after a hearing or trial and the material is confidential as provided by law, court rule, or court order pursuant to MCR 8.119(I), the court must continue to maintain the material in a confidential manner.

[Adopted effective November 30, 1999, 461 Mich. Amended October 31, 2012, effective January 1, 2013, 493 Mich; August 30, 2018, effective September 1, 2018, 502 Mich; March 20, 2019, effective May 1, 2019, 502 Mich.]

Comments

Staff Comment to 1999 Adoption

The amendments of MCR 2.113, 5.113, 5.901, 7.210, 8.105, 8.110, 8.116, 8.203, 8.205, and 8.302 [effective November 30, 1999] and the addition of MCR 2.518 and 8.119 [effective November 30, 1999] are to accommodate statewide records standards applicable to all courts and all clerks of the courts as developed and recommended by the Michigan Trial Court Case File Management Standards Committee.

Staff Comment to 2013 Amendment

The amendments of these rules update the rules making them less "paper" focused and reflecting the use of electronic technology in the way courts process court records. The amendments also clarify and delineate the types of records and other materials maintained by a court, and clarify how access is provided.

Staff Comment to 2018 Amendment

These amendments update cross-references in the rules, and are intended to reflect changes that are necessary as a result of the Court's recent e-Filing rules amendments.

Staff Comment to 2019 Amendment

The amendments of Rules 1.109, 2.102, 2.104, 2.106, 2.107, 2.117, 2.119, 2.403, 2.503, 2.506, 2.508, 2.518, 2.602, 2.603, 2.621, 3.101, 3.104, 3.203, 3.205, 3.210, 3.302, 3.607, 3.613, 3.614, 3.705, 3.801, 3.802, 3.805, 3.806, 4.201, 4.202, 4.303, 4.306, 5.001, 5.104, 5.105, 5.107, 5.108, 5.113, 5.117, 5.118, 5.119, 5.120, 5.125, 5.126, 5.132, 5.162, 5.202, 5.203, 5.205, 5.302, 5.304, 5.307, 5.308, 5.309, 5.310, 5.311, 5.313, 5.402, 5.404, 5.405, 5.409, 5.501, and 5.784 and addition of Rule 3.618 of the Michigan Court Rules are an expected progression necessary for design and implementation of the statewide electronic-filing system. These particular amendments will assist in implementing the goals of the project.

SUBCHAPTER 2.600   JUDGMENTS AND ORDERS; POSTJUDGMENT PROCEEDINGS

Rule 2.601   Judgments

(A) Relief Available. Except as provided in subrule (B), every final judgment may grant the relief to which the party in whose favor it is rendered is entitled, even if the party has not demanded that relief in his or her pleadings.

(B) Default Judgment. A judgment by default may not be different in kind from, nor exceed in amount, the relief demanded in the pleading, unless notice has been given pursuant to MCR 2.603(B)(1).

[Adopted effective March 1, 1985.]

Comments

Staff Comment to 1985 Adoption

MCR 2.601 includes the provisions previously found in GCR 1963, 518.3. The portions of that rule regarding judgments in actions involving multiple claims and parties are relocated in a separate rule (MCR 2.604). The references to decrees and exceptions found in GCR 1963, 518.1 and 518.4 are deleted.

In subrule (A) the word "shall" is changed to "may", authorizing but not requiring the granting of relief in excess of that demanded.

Subrule (B) adds a reference to the procedure for giving notice of a request for a default judgment found in MCR 2.603(B)(1).

Rule 2.602   Entry of Judgments and Orders

(A) Signing; Statement; Date of Entry.

(1) Except as provided in this rule and in MCR 2.603, all judgments and orders must be in writing, signed by the court, and dated with the date they are signed.

(2) The date of signing an order or judgment is the date of entry.

(3) Each judgment must state, immediately preceding the judge's signature, whether it resolves the last pending claim and closes the case. Such a statement must also appear on any other order that disposes of the last pending claim and closes the case.

(4) Where electronic filing is implemented, judgments and orders must be issued under the seal of the court.

(B) Procedure of Entry of Judgments and Orders. An order or judgment shall be entered by one of the following methods:

(1) The court may sign the judgment or order at the time it grants the relief provided by the judgment or order.

(2) The court shall sign the judgment or order when its form is approved by all the parties and if, in the court's determination, it comports with the court's decision.

(3) Within 7 days after the granting of the judgment or order, or later if the court allows, a party may serve a copy of

the proposed judgment or order on the other parties, with a notice to them that it will be submitted to the court for signing if no written objections to its accuracy or completeness are filed with the court clerk within 7 days after service of the notice. The party must file with the court clerk the notice and proof of service along with the proposed judgment or order.

(a) If no written objections are filed within 7 days of the date of service of the notice, the judge shall sign the judgment or order if, in the court's determination, it comports with the court's decision. If the proposed judgment or order does not comport with the decision, the court shall direct the clerk to notify the parties to appear before the court on a specified date for settlement of the matter.

(b) Objections regarding the accuracy or completeness of the judgment or order must state with specificity the inaccuracy or omission.

(c) The party filing the objections must serve them on all parties as required by MCR 2.107, together with a notice of hearing and an alternative proposed judgment or order.

(d) The court must schedule the hearing upon filing of the first objection, and the party filing the objection must serve the notice of hearing under subrule (B)(3)(c). Other parties to the action may file objections with the court through the end of the 7–day period. The court must schedule a hearing for all objections within 14 days after the first objection is filed or as soon as is practical afterward.

(4) A party may prepare a proposed judgment or order and notice it for settlement before the court. Pursuant to MCR 2.119(G)(3)(b), a motion fee may not be charged.

(C) Conditional Dismissal. The court may enter a consent order for conditional dismissal under the following conditions:

(1) A consent order for conditional dismissal shall be signed and approved by all parties and shall clearly state the terms for reinstatement of the case and entry of judgment.

(2) If the breaching party defaults on the terms of the settlement agreement as provided for in the conditional dismissal order, the non-defaulting party may seek entry of an order for reinstatement of the case and entry of judgment.

(a) To obtain an order for reinstatement of the case and entry of judgment, the non-defaulting party shall file with the court an affidavit stating that the breaching party defaulted on the terms of the settlement agreement.

(b) The non-defaulting party shall serve a copy of an affidavit of non-compliance on the breaching party at its current address listed in the court records and file proof of service with the court.

(c) If the order for conditional dismissal states that judgment may be entered without notice or further process, the court shall enter the proposed judgment upon determining the conditions for entry of judgment in the conditional dismissal order are satisfied.

(d) If the order for conditional dismissal does not provide for immediate entry of judgment, the affidavit shall be accompanied by a notice to the breaching party that an order for reinstatement and for entry of judgment is being submitted to the court for entry if no written objections to its accuracy or completeness are filed with the court clerk within 14 days after service of the notice. Unless an objection is filed within 14 days after service of the notice, an order for

reinstatement of the case and entry of judgment shall be signed by the court and entered.

(i) An objection must be verified and state with specificity the reasons that an order for reinstatement of the case and entry of judgment should not enter.

(ii) If an objection is filed, the court shall set a hearing and serve notice of that hearing to all parties.

(iii) This 14–day notice provision may be waived in cases filed pursuant to MCR 4.201 if such waiver is acknowledged in writing.

(3) For the purposes of any statute of limitation, an action conditionally dismissed under this rule is deemed to have been initiated on the date the original complaint was properly filed.

(4) All parties to a conditional dismissal bear the affirmative duty to inform the court with jurisdiction over that case of any change of address until the terms of the settlement agreement have been satisfied.

(D) Placement in Case File. The signed judgment or order must be placed in the case file.

(E) Service.

(1) The party securing the signing of the judgment or order shall serve a copy, within 7 days after it has been signed, on all other parties, and file proof of service with the court clerk.

(2) If a judgment for reimbursement to the state for the value of game or protected animals is entered pursuant to MCL 324.40119 or for the value of fish is entered pursuant to MCL 324.48740, the clerk shall provide a copy of the judgment to the Department of Natural Resources. The judgment may be enforced as a civil judgment.

[Adopted effective March 1, 1985. Amended effective December 1, 1998; January 1, 2002. Amended February 23, 2006, effective May 1, 2006, 474 Mich; February 28, 2018, effective May 1, 2018, 501 Mich; March 20, 2019, effective May 1, 2019, 502 Mich.]

Comments

Staff Comment to 1985 Adoption

MCR 2.602 corresponds to GCR 1963, 522.

The language of subrule (A) is modified to require that the judgment or order be dated the date it is signed by the judge, prohibiting the backdating of judgments and orders.

Under GCR 1963, 522.1(1), a judgment or order approved as to form by all parties could only be entered by the court within the 10 days after the decision. Subrule (B)(2) deletes the 10-day limitation.

Subrule (B)(3) slightly modifies former GCR 1963, 522.1(2), which provided a procedure for entry of an order by serving a copy of a proposed order. The court may allow such a proposed order to be served after the time specified in the rule (7 days). Further, the rule specifies the event that begins the time within which the opposing party can object—service of the proposed order.

GCR 1963, 522.3 regarding the clerk's recording of proceedings in a "journal" are omitted. The rules governing the records to be kept by the clerk are placed in the administrative rules chapter. See MCR 8.105, 8.203.

Subrule (D)(2) is taken from DCR 522.1, covering certain Game Law violations.

Staff Comment to 1998 Amendment

The December 1, 1998 amendment of MCR 2.602(A) requires that all judgments designate whether they resolve the last pending claim and close a case. The requirement also pertains to other orders that dispose of all pending claims and close a case, *i.e.*, an order that does not decide the merits of a last pending claim but rather dismisses the claim for reasons such as lack of jurisdiction or a discovery violation. The goal of the amendment, which stemmed from a proposal of the Michigan Judges Association, is to facilitate docket management.

Staff Comment to 2002 Amendment

The September 12, 2001 amendment of MCR 2.602(B)(3), effective January 1, 2002, was based on a recommendation from the Michigan Judges Association to eliminate delay and unnecessary work caused by nonspecific and meaningless objections. The amendment shifted some of the burden of going forward from the proponent of the order to the objector and clarified the objection procedure.

Staff Comment to 2006 Amendment

The amendment of MCR 2.602(D)(2) provides current statutory references to the Natural Resources and Environmental Protection Act, MCL 324.101 *et seq.*

Staff Comment to 2018 Amendment

The amendment of MCR 2.602 provides procedural rules regarding entry of consent orders for conditional dismissal.

Staff Comment to 2019 Amendment

The amendments of Rules 1.109, 2.102, 2.104, 2.106, 2.107, 2.117, 2.119, 2.403, 2.503, 2.506, 2.508, 2.518, 2.602, 2.603, 2.621, 3.101, 3.104, 3.203, 3.205, 3.210, 3.302, 3.607, 3.613, 3.614, 3.705, 3.801, 3.802, 3.805, 3.806, 4.201, 4.202, 4.303, 4.306, 5.001, 5.104, 5.105, 5.107, 5.108, 5.113, 5.117, 5.118, 5.119, 5.120, 5.125, 5.126, 5.132, 5.162, 5.202, 5.203, 5.205, 5.302, 5.304, 5.307, 5.308, 5.309, 5.310, 5.311, 5.313, 5.402, 5.404, 5.405, 5.409, 5.501, and 5.784 and addition of Rule 3.618 of the Michigan Court Rules are an expected progression necessary for design and implementation of the statewide electronic-filing system. These particular amendments will assist in implementing the goals of the project.

Rule 2.603   Default and Default Judgment

(A) Entry of Default; Notice; Effect.

(1) If a party against whom a judgment for affirmative relief is sought has failed to plead or otherwise defend as provided by these rules, and that fact is verified in the manner prescribed by MCR 1.109(D)(3) and filed with the court in the request for default, the clerk must enter the default of that party.

(2) Notice that the default has been entered must be sent to all parties who have appeared and to the defaulted party. If the defaulted party has not appeared, the notice to the defaulted party may be served by personal service, by ordinary first-class mail at his or her last known address or the place of service, or as otherwise directed by the court.

The notice must be sent by the party who sought entry of the default. Proof of service and a copy of the notice must be filed with the court.

(3) After the default of a party has been entered, that party may not proceed with the action until the default has been set aside by the court in accordance with subrule (D) or MCR 2.612.

(B) Default Judgment.

(1) *Notice of Request for Default Judgment.*

(a) A party requesting a default judgment must give notice of the request to the defaulted party, if

(i) the party against whom the default judgment is sought has appeared in the action;

(ii) the request for entry of a default judgment seeks relief different in kind from, or greater in amount than, that stated in the pleadings; or

(iii) the pleadings do not state a specific amount demanded.

(b) The notice required by this subrule must be served at least 7 days before entry of the requested default judgment.

(c) If the defaulted party has appeared, the notice may be given in the manner provided by MCR 2.107. If the defaulted party has not appeared, the notice may be served by personal service, by ordinary first-class mail at the defaulted party's last known address or the place of service, or as otherwise directed by the court.

(d) If the default is entered for failure to appear for a scheduled trial, notice under this subrule is not required.

(2) *Default Judgment Entered by Clerk.* On written request of the plaintiff verified under MCR 1.109(D)(3) as to the amount due, the clerk may sign and enter a default judgment for that amount and costs against the defendant, if

(a) the plaintiff's claim against a defendant is for a sum certain or for a sum that can by computation be made certain;

(b) the default was entered because the defendant failed to appear;

(c) the defaulted defendant is not an infant or incompetent person; and

(d) the damages amount requested is not greater than the amount stated in the complaint.

(3) *Default Judgment Entered by Court.* In all other cases, the party entitled to a default judgment must file a motion that asks the court to enter the default judgment.

(a) A default judgment may not be entered against a minor or an incompetent person unless the person is represented in the action by a conservator, guardian ad litem, or other representative.

(b) If, in order for the court to enter a default judgment or to carry it into effect, it is necessary to

(i) take an account,

(ii) determine the amount of damages,

(iii) establish the truth of an allegation by evidence, or

(iv) investigate any other matter,

the court may conduct hearings or order references it deems necessary and proper, and shall accord a right of trial by jury to the parties to the extent required by the constitution.

(4) *Notice of Entry of Default Judgment.* The party who sought entry of the default judgment must promptly serve all parties with the default judgment. The default judgment shall be mailed to the defendant's last known address or the address of the place of service. Proof of service must be filed with the court.

(C) Nonmilitary Affidavit. Nonmilitary affidavits required by law must be filed before judgment is entered in actions in which the defendant has failed to appear.

(D) Setting Aside Default or Default Judgment.

(1) A motion to set aside a default or a default judgment, except when grounded on lack of jurisdiction over the defendant, shall be granted only if good cause is shown and a statement of facts showing a meritorious defense, verified in the manner prescribed by MCR 1.109(D)(3), is filed.

(2) Except as provided in MCR 2.612, if personal service was made on the party against whom the default was taken, the default, and default judgment if one has been entered, may be set aside only if the motion is filed

(a) before entry of a default judgment, or

(b) if a default judgment has been entered, within 21 days after the default judgment was entered.

(3) In addition, the court may set aside a default and a default judgment in accordance with MCR 2.612.

(4) An order setting aside the default or default judgment must be conditioned on the defaulted party paying the taxable costs incurred by the other party in reliance on the default or default judgment, except as prescribed in MCR 2.625(D). The order may also impose other conditions the court deems proper, including a reasonable attorney fee.

(E) Application to Parties Other Than Plaintiff. The provisions of this rule apply whether the party entitled to the default judgment is a plaintiff or a party who pleaded a cross-claim or counterclaim. In all cases a default judgment is subject to the limitations of MCR 2.601(B).

[Adopted effective March 1, 1985. Amended November 17, 1994, effective January 1, 1995, 447 Mich; October 5, 2004, effective January 1, 2005, 471 Mich; May 28, 2008, effective September 1, 2008, 481 Mich; October 3, 2012, effective January 1, 2013, 493 Mich; March 20, 2019, effective May 1, 2019, 502 Mich.]

Comments

Staff Comment to 1985 Adoption

MCR 2.603 corresponds to GCR 1963, 520 and DCR 520.

Subrule (A)(2) retains the distinction between circuit and district court practice regarding notice of the entry of default. In the district court, the clerk sends the notice (see DCR 520.1); in all other courts, the party who sought entry of the default does so (see GCR 1963, 520.1). In addition, a defaulted party—even one who has not filed an appearance—is to be given notice of the entry of default. This notice may be mailed to the defaulted defendant's last known address or the place of service.

Similarly, subrule (B)(1) requires the sending of notice to the defaulted party if the request for judgment seeks relief of a different kind or a greater amount than that stated in the pleadings. See MCR 2.601(B).

The provisions of subrules (B)(2) and (3), regarding entry of default judgment by the clerk and by the court, are substantially the same as the provisions of both GCR 1963, 520.2 and DCR 520.2(1) and (2) (although the requirement of notice to a defaulted defendant who has appeared is moved to subrule [B][1]).

Subrule (B)(4) adopts the district court rule (DCR 520.2[3]) requiring that the clerk give notice to all parties (including the defendant in default) of the entry of the default judgment.

Subrule (D) changes the time within which a defendant who was actually served must move to set aside a default judgment on grounds other than those provided in MCR 2.612. Under GCR 1963, 520.4 the motion was required to be filed before entry of judgment or within 4 months after entry of the default, whichever was later. Under subrule (D)(2), the motion must be filed before entry of judgment or, if judgment has been entered, within 21 days after entry of the default. If the motion is not filed within this time, the party must proceed under MCR 2.612.

The form of default found in GCR 1963, 520.7 is omitted.

Staff Comment to 1995 Amendment

The November 1994 amendment of paragraph (D) [effective January 1, 1995] clarified that attorney fees may be included among the taxable costs upon which an order setting aside a default must be conditioned. The Court of Appeals held to the contrary in *Webb v Watts (On Remand)*, 194 Mich App 529 (1992). The Supreme Court vacated the judgment of the Court of Appeals and dismissed the appeal in *Webb* for lack of a proper party defendant. 443 Mich 862 (1993).

Staff Comment to 2005 Amendment

The October 5, 2004, amendment, effective January 1, 2005, of MCR 2.603 clarified some ambiguities created by the former rule's inconsistent usage of "default," "default judgment," and some related terms. See, e.g., *ISB Sales v Dave's Cakes*, 258 Mich App 520 (2003).

Staff Comment to 2008 Amendment

This amendment eliminates the requirement to file for the cancellation of a note or writing indicating written evidence of indebtedness when applying to the clerk for a default judgment.

Staff Comment to 2013 Amendment

The amendment of MCR 2.603 clarifies that a court clerk may enter a default judgment if the requested damages are less than the amount claimed in the original complaint, to reflect payments that may have been made or otherwise credited.

Staff Comment to 2019 Amendment

The amendments of Rules 1.109, 2.102, 2.104, 2.106, 2.107, 2.117, 2.119, 2.403, 2.503, 2.506, 2.508, 2.518, 2.602, 2.603, 2.621, 3.101, 3.104, 3.203, 3.205, 3.210, 3.302,

3.607, 3.613, 3.614, 3.705, 3.801, 3.802, 3.805, 3.806, 4.201, 4.202, 4.303, 4.306, 5.001, 5.104, 5.105, 5.107, 5.108, 5.113, 5.117, 5.118, 5.119, 5.120, 5.125, 5.126, 5.132, 5.162, 5.202, 5.203, 5.205, 5.302, 5.304, 5.307, 5.308, 5.309, 5.310, 5.311, 5.313, 5.402, 5.404, 5.405, 5.409, 5.501, and 5.784 and addition of Rule 3.618 of the Michigan Court Rules are an expected progression necessary for design and implementation of the statewide electronic-filing system. These particular amendments will assist in implementing the goals of the project.

Rule 2.604 Judgment in Actions Involving Multiple Claims or Multiple Parties

(A) Except as provided in subrule (B), an order or other form of decision adjudicating fewer than all the claims, or the rights and liabilities of fewer than all the parties, does not terminate the action as to any of the claims or parties, and the order is subject to revision before entry of final judgment adjudicating all the claims and the rights and liabilities of all the parties. Such an order or other form of decision is not appealable as of right before entry of final judgment. A party may file an application for leave to appeal from such an order.

(B) In receivership and similar actions, the court may direct that an order entered before adjudication of all of the claims and rights and liabilities of all the parties constitutes a final order on an express determination that there is no just reason for delay.

[Adopted effective March 1, 1985. Amended May 16, 1995, effective July 1, 1995, 448 Mich. Amended effective September 19, 1995, 450 Mich.]

Comments

Staff Comment to 1985 Adoption

MCR 2.604 contains the provisions regarding judgments in actions involving multiple claims or parties previously found in GCR 1963, 518.2.

Staff Comment to July, 1995 Amendment

The amendment of MCR 2.604 eliminates the procedure under which a trial court could direct entry of final judgment on an order disposing of fewer than all the claims or parties, permitting an immediate appeal of right from such orders.

Staff Comment to September, 1995 Amendment

The September 19, 1995, amendment of MCR 2.604 permits a trial court to direct entry of final judgment on an order disposing of fewer than all the claims or parties in receivership and similar actions.

Rule 2.605 Declaratory Judgments

(A) Power to Enter Declaratory Judgment.

(1) In a case of actual controversy within its jurisdiction, a Michigan court of record may declare the rights and other legal relations of an interested party seeking a declaratory judgment, whether or not other relief is or could be sought or granted.

(2) For the purpose of this rule, an action is considered within the jurisdiction of a court if the court would have jurisdiction of an action on the same claim or claims in which the plaintiff sought relief other than a declaratory judgment.

(B) Procedure. The procedure for obtaining declaratory relief is in accordance with these rules, and the right to trial by jury may be demanded under the circumstances and in the manner provided in the constitution, statutes, and court rules of the State of Michigan.

(C) Other Adequate Remedy. The existence of another adequate remedy does not preclude a judgment for declaratory relief in an appropriate case.

(D) Hearing. The court may order a speedy hearing of an action for declaratory relief and may advance it on the calendar.

(E) Effect; Review. Declaratory judgments have the force and effect of, and are reviewable as, final judgments.

(F) Other Relief. Further necessary or proper relief based on a declaratory judgment may be granted, after reasonable notice and hearing, against a party whose rights have been determined by the declaratory judgment.

[Adopted effective March 1, 1985.]

Comments

Staff Comment to 1985 Adoption

MCR 2.605 is comparable to GCR 1963, 521. The District Court Rules did not include such a provision.

Additional language is included in subrule (A) expressly stating that while any court of record has the power to enter a declaratory judgment, it may do so only in a case of which it otherwise would have jurisdiction.

Rule 2.610   Motion for Judgment Notwithstanding the Verdict

(A) Motion.

(1) Within 21 days after entry of judgment, a party may move to have the verdict and judgment set aside, and to have judgment entered in the moving party's favor. The motion may be joined with a motion for a new trial, or a new trial may be requested in the alternative.

(2) If a verdict was not returned, a party may move for judgment within 21 days after the jury is discharged.

(3) A motion to set aside or otherwise nullify a verdict or a motion for a new trial is deemed to include a motion for judgment notwithstanding the verdict as an alternative.

(B) Ruling.

(1) If a verdict was returned, the court may allow the judgment to stand or may reopen the judgment and either order a new trial or direct the entry of judgment as requested in the motion.

(2) If a verdict was not returned, the court may direct the entry of judgment as requested in the motion or order a new trial.

(3) In ruling on a motion under this rule, the court must give a concise statement of the reasons for the ruling, either in a signed order or opinion filed in the action, or on the record.

(C) Conditional Ruling on Motion for New Trial.

(1) If the motion for judgment notwithstanding the verdict under subrule (A) is granted, the court shall also conditionally rule on any motion for a new trial, determining whether it should be granted if the judgment is vacated or reversed, and shall specify the grounds for granting or denying the motion for a new trial.

(2) A conditional ruling under this subrule has the following effects:

(a) If the motion for a new trial is conditionally granted, that ruling does not affect the finality of the judgment.

(b) If the motion for a new trial is conditionally granted and the judgment is reversed on appeal, the new trial proceeds unless the appellate court orders otherwise.

(c) If the motion for a new trial is conditionally denied, on appeal the appellee may assert error in that denial. If the judgment is reversed on appeal, subsequent proceedings are in accordance with the order of the appellate court.

(D) Motion for New Trial After Ruling. The party whose verdict has been set aside on a motion for judgment notwith-

standing the verdict may serve and file a motion for a new trial pursuant to MCR 2.611 within 14 days after entry of judgment. A party who fails to move for a new trial as provided in this subrule has waived the right to move for a new trial.

(E) Appeal After Denial of Motion.

(1) If the motion for judgment notwithstanding the verdict is denied, the party who prevailed on that motion may, as appellee, assert grounds entitling that party to a new trial if the appellate court concludes that the trial court erred in denying the motion for judgment notwithstanding the verdict.

(2) If the appellate court reverses the judgment, nothing in this rule precludes it from determining that the appellee is entitled to a new trial, or from directing the trial court to determine whether a new trial should be granted.

[Adopted effective March 1, 1985.]

Comments

Staff Comment to 1985 Adoption

MCR 2.610 is based on GCR 1963, 515.2, 515.3, and 812.8, concerning motions for judgment notwithstanding the verdict.

Subrule (A) does not include the requirement of GCR 1963, 515.2 that a party move for directed verdict as a condition of the right to move for judgment notwithstanding the verdict.

Rule 2.611   New Trials; Amendment of Judgments

(A) Grounds.

(1) A new trial may be granted to all or some of the parties, on all or some of the issues, whenever their substantial rights are materially affected, for any of the following reasons:

(a) Irregularity in the proceedings of the court, jury, or prevailing party, or an order of the court or abuse of discretion which denied the moving party a fair trial.

(b) Misconduct of the jury or of the prevailing party.

(c) Excessive or inadequate damages appearing to have been influenced by passion or prejudice.

(d) A verdict clearly or grossly inadequate or excessive.

(e) A verdict or decision against the great weight of the evidence or contrary to law.

(f) Material evidence, newly discovered, which could not with reasonable diligence have been discovered and produced at trial.

(g) Error of law occurring in the proceedings, or mistake of fact by the court.

(h) A ground listed in MCR 2.612 warranting a new trial.

(2) On a motion for a new trial in an action tried without a jury, the court may

(a) set aside the judgment if one has been entered,

(b) take additional testimony,

(c) amend findings of fact and conclusions of law, or

(d) make new findings and conclusions and direct the entry of a new judgment.

(B) Time for Motion. A motion for a new trial made under this rule or a motion to alter or amend a judgment must be filed and served within 21 days after entry of the judgment.

(C) On Initiative of Court. Within 21 days after entry of a judgment, the court on its own initiative may order a new trial for a reason for which it might have granted a new trial on motion of a party. The order must specify the grounds on which it is based.

(D) Affidavits.

(1) If the facts stated in the motion for a new trial or to amend the judgment do not appear on the record of the action, the motion must be supported by affidavit, which must be filed and served with the motion.

(2) The opposing party has 21 days after service within which to file and serve opposing affidavits. The period may be extended by the parties by written stipulation for 21 additional days, or may be extended or shortened by the court for good cause shown.

(3) The court may permit reply affidavits and may call and examine witnesses.

(E) Remittitur and Additur.

(1) If the court finds that the only error in the trial is the inadequacy or excessiveness of the verdict, it may deny a motion for new trial on condition that within 14 days the nonmoving party consent in writing to the entry of judgment in an amount found by the court to be the lowest (if the verdict was inadequate) or highest (if the verdict was excessive) amount the evidence will support.

(2) If the moving party appeals, the agreement in no way prejudices the nonmoving party's argument on appeal that the original verdict was correct. If the nonmoving party prevails, the original verdict may be reinstated by the appellate court.

(F) Ruling on Motion. In ruling on a motion for a new trial or a motion to amend the judgment, the court shall give a concise statement of the reasons for the ruling, either in an order or opinion filed in the action or on the record.

(G) Notice of Decision. The clerk must notify the parties of the decision on the motion for a new trial, unless the decision is made on the record while the parties are present.

[Adopted effective March 1, 1985.]

Comments

Staff Comment to 1985 Adoption

MCR 2.611 is substantially the same as GCR 1963, 527.

Rule 2.612   Relief from Judgment or Order

(A) Clerical Mistakes.

(1) Clerical mistakes in judgments, orders, or other parts of the record and errors arising from oversight or omission may be corrected by the court at any time on its own initiative or on motion of a party and after notice, if the court orders it.

(2) If a claim of appeal is filed or an appellate court grants leave to appeal, the trial court may correct errors as provided in MCR 7.208(A) and (C).

(B) Defendant Not Personally Notified. A defendant over whom personal jurisdiction was necessary and acquired, but who did not in fact have knowledge of the pendency of the action, may enter an appearance within 1 year after final judgment, and if the defendant shows reason justifying relief from the judgment and innocent third persons will not be prejudiced, the court may relieve the defendant from the judgment, order, or proceedings for which personal jurisdiction was necessary, on payment of costs or on conditions the court deems just.

(C) Grounds for Relief From Judgment.

(1) On motion and on just terms, the court may relieve a party or the legal representative of a party from a final judgment, order, or proceeding on the following grounds:

(a) Mistake, inadvertence, surprise, or excusable neglect.

(b) Newly discovered evidence which by due diligence could not have been discovered in time to move for a new trial under MCR 2.611(B).

(c) Fraud (intrinsic or extrinsic), misrepresentation, or other misconduct of an adverse party.

(d) The judgment is void.

(e) The judgment has been satisfied, released, or discharged; a prior judgment on which it is based has been reversed or otherwise vacated; or it is no longer equitable that the judgment should have prospective application.

(f) Any other reason justifying relief from the operation of the judgment.

(2) The motion must be made within a reasonable time, and, for the grounds stated in subrules (C)(1)(a), (b), and (c), within one year after the judgment, order, or proceeding was entered or taken. Except as provided in MCR 2.614(A)(1), a motion under this subrule does not affect the finality of a judgment or suspend its operation.

(3) This subrule does not limit the power of a court to entertain an independent action to relieve a party from a judgment, order, or proceeding; to grant relief to a defendant not actually personally notified as provided in subrule (B); or to set aside a judgment for fraud on the court.

(4) The procedure for obtaining any relief from a judgment shall be by motion as prescribed in these rules or by an independent action. Relief may not be sought or obtained by the writs of coram nobis, coram vobis, audita querela, bills of review, or bills in the nature of a bill of review.

[Adopted effective March 1, 1985. Amended February 23, 2006, effective May 1, 2006, 474 Mich. Amended effective September 28, 2011, 490 Mich. Amended September 18, 2019, effective January 1, 2020, 503 Mich.]

Comments

Staff Comment to 1985 Adoption

MCR 2.612 is comparable to GCR 1963, 528.

Subrule (A)(2) refers to MCR 7.208, which changes the time when the trial court's authority to correct the record ends after an appeal is taken. The trial court may do so until the record is sent to the appellate court. However, after a claim of appeal is filed or the appellate court has granted leave to appeal, notice to the parties is required before such a correction is made.

In subrule (B) the word "conditions" is substituted for "creditors" used in GCR 1963, 528.2.

Staff Comment to 2006 Amendment

The amendment of MCR 2.612(A)(2), 3.802(B)(1), 5.313(F), and 9.113(B)(2), effective May 1, 2006, reflect numbering changes in other rules.

Staff Comment to 2011 Amendment

The above noted changes are minor revisions of the rules that have been recommended to the Court to correct cross references and to reflect other technical changes.

Staff Comment to 2020 Amendment

The amendment of MCR 2.612 clarifies that writs of coram nobis, coram vobis, audita querela, and bills of review and bills in the nature of a bill of review remain abolished. This language was eliminated when the court rules were rewritten in 1985, but in light of occasional attempts to file these types of writs, it is deemed helpful to clarify that they are abolished.

Rule 2.613   Limitations on Corrections of Error

(A) Harmless Error. An error in the admission or the exclusion of evidence, an error in a ruling or order, or an error or defect in anything done or omitted by the court or by the parties is not ground for granting a new trial, for setting aside a verdict, or for vacating, modifying, or otherwise disturbing a judgment or order, unless refusal to take this action appears to the court inconsistent with substantial justice.

(B) Correction of Error by Other Judges. A judgment or order may be set aside or vacated, and a proceeding under a judgment or order may be stayed, only by the judge who entered the judgment or order, unless that judge is absent or unable to act. If the judge who entered the judgment or order is absent or unable to act, an order vacating or setting aside the judgment or order or staying proceedings under the judgment or order may be entered by a judge otherwise empowered to rule in the matter.

(C) Review of Findings by Trial Court. Findings of fact by the trial court may not be set aside unless clearly erroneous. In the application of this principle, regard shall be given to the special opportunity of the trial court to judge the credibility of the witnesses who appeared before it.

[Adopted effective March 1, 1985.]

Comments

Staff Comment to 1985 Adoption

MCR 2.613 includes the provisions of GCR 1963, 529, and the language from GCR 1963, 517.1 that the trial court's findings are not to be set aside unless clearly erroneous.

Rule 2.614.   Stay of Proceedings to Enforce Judgment

(A) Automatic Stay; Exceptions: Injunctions, Receiverships, and Family Litigation.

(1) Except as provided in this rule, execution may not issue on a judgment and proceedings may not be taken for its enforcement until 21 days after a final judgment (as defined in MCR 7.202[6]) is entered in the case. If a motion for new trial, a motion for rehearing or reconsideration, or a motion for other relief from judgment is filed and served within 21 days after entry of the judgment or within further time the trial court has allowed for good cause during that 21-day period, execution may not issue on the judgment and proceedings may not be taken for its enforcement until the expiration of 21 days after the entry of the order deciding the motion, unless otherwise ordered by the court on motion for good cause. Nothing in this rule prohibits the court from enjoining the transfer or disposition of property during the 21-day period.

(2) The following orders may be enforced immediately after entry unless the court orders otherwise on motion for good cause:

(a) A temporary restraining order.

(b) A preliminary injunction.

(c) Injunctive relief included in a final judgment.

(d) An interlocutory order in a receivership action.

(e) In a domestic relations action, an order before judgment concerning the custody, control, and management of property; for temporary alimony; or for support or custody of minor children and expenses.

(3) Subrule (C) governs the suspending, modifying, restoring, or granting of an injunction during the pendency of an appeal.

(B) Stay on Motion for Relief From Judgment. In its discretion and on proper conditions for the security of the adverse party, the court may stay the execution of, or proceedings to enforce, a judgment pending the disposition of a motion for relief from a judgment or order under MCR 2.612.

(C) Injunction Pending Appeal. If an appeal is taken from an interlocutory or final judgment granting, dissolving, or denying an injunction, the court may suspend, modify, restore, or grant an injunction during the pendency of the appeal on terms as to bond or otherwise that are proper for the security of the adverse party's rights.

(D) Stay on Appeal. Stay on appeal is governed by MCR 7.108, 7.209, and 7.305(I). If a party appeals a trial court's denial of the party's claim of governmental immunity, the party's appeal operates as an automatic stay of any and all proceedings in the case until the issue of the party's status is finally decided.

(E) Stay in Favor of Governmental Party. In an action or proceeding in which the state, an authorized state officer, a corporate body in charge of a state institution, or a municipal corporation, is a party, bond may not be required of that party as a prerequisite to taking an appeal or making an order staying proceedings.

(F) Power of Appellate Court Not Limited. This rule does not limit the power of the Court of Appeals or the Supreme Court to

(1) stay proceedings during the pendency of an appeal before them;

(2) suspend, modify, restore, or grant an injunction during the pendency of the appeal; or

(3) enter an order appropriate to preserve the status quo or effectiveness of the judgment to be entered.

(G) Stay of Judgment on Multiple Claims. When a court has ordered a final judgment on some, but not all, of the claims presented in the action under the conditions stated in MCR 2.604(B), the court may

(1) stay enforcement of the judgment until the entry of a later judgment or judgments, and

(2) prescribe conditions necessary to secure the benefit of the judgment to the party in whose favor it was entered.

[Adopted effective March 1, 1985. Amended effective September 19, 1995, 450 Mich. Amended May 30, 2008, effective September 1, 2008, 481 Mich; January 20, 2009, effective May 1, 2009, 483 Mich. Amended effective September 5, 2013, 495 Mich. Amended October 21, 2015, effective January 1, 2016, 498 Mich. Amended effective March 9, 2016, 499 Mich; December 14, 2016, 500 Mich; March 21, 2018, 501 Mich.]

Comments

Staff Comment to 1985 Adoption

MCR 2.614 is based on GCR 1963, 530.

Language is added to subrule (A)(1) to make clear that the trial court has the authority to enjoin the transfer of property during the automatic stay.

In subrule (A)(2) final injunctive orders are added to the list of orders which are not automatically stayed during the time for taking an appeal of right.

The provisions of GCR 1963, 530.4 regarding stays on appeal are replaced with a cross-reference to the appropriate provisions in the rules governing appeals. See subrule (D).

The references to the granting of a stay of proceedings by a single judge of the Court of Appeals or the Supreme Court, found in GCR 1963, 530.6, are omitted. See subrule (F).

Staff Comment to 1995 Amendment

The amendments of MCR 2.116(J)(1), 2.119(F)(1), 2.204(A)(4), and 2.614(G) correct cross-references to MCR 2.604 that were no longer correct after MCR 2.604 was amended on May 16, 1995, and further amended on September 19, 1995.

Staff Comment to 2008 Amendment

This amendment imposes an automatic stay of any and all proceedings in a case in which a party files a claim of appeal of a denial by the trial court of the party's claim of governmental immunity. No order is necessary for the stay to operate.

Staff Comment to 2009 Amendment

The amendments of MCR 2.614 conform to recent amendments of MCR 2.119, MCR 7.204, and MCR 7.205, adopted May 28, 2008, which clarified that a party seeking leave to appeal in the Court of Appeals has 21 days after the entry of an order deciding a motion for new trial, a motion for rehearing or reconsideration, or a motion for other relief from the order or judgment appealed to file a claim or appeal or an application for leave to appeal, if the motion is filed within the initial 21-day appeal period, or within further time the trial court has allowed for good cause during that 21-day period.

Staff Comment to 2013 Amendment

These amendments reflect changes that correct minor technical errors that have occurred in drafting or the changes respond to recent adopted rule revisions, which occasionally inadvertently create incorrect cross-references in other rules.

Staff Comment to March, 2016 Amendment

These amendments update cross-references that changed after the rule was adopted and make other nonsubstantive revisions.

Staff Comment to December, 2016 Amendment

These amendments relate to stay bonds. The amendments of MCR 7.209 are modeled on the recent revisions of MCR 7.108, the circuit court appeals rule, and provide that filing a bond automatically stays enforcement of a money judgment or order. The amendments further clarify that the provision for obtaining a stay of a money judgment by filing a bond under MCR 7.209(E)(2)(a) does not apply to domestic relations matters, in which a stay must be ordered by the trial court. The amendment of MCR 2.614 coordinates with the amendment of MCR 7.209 and clarifies that execution may not issue until 21 days after a *final* judgment enters in a case.

Staff Comment to 2018 Amendment

These amendments update cross-references and make other nonsubstantive revisions to clarify the rules. The amendment of MCR 6.110(B)(1) addresses an inadvertent omission from the last amendment of this rule that was intended to be shown in overstrike. Accordingly, the current rule does not match the published version. Striking the clause "for good cause shown" will provide consistency with other published versions of the rule and with the statute, MCL 766.7, which allows a magistrate to adjourn a preliminary examination with the consent of the parties without the need for good cause to be shown.

Rule 2.615   Enforcement of Tribal Judgments

(A) The judgments, decrees, orders, warrants, subpoenas, records, and other judicial acts of a tribal court of a federally recognized Indian tribe are recognized, and have the same effect and are subject to the same procedures, defenses, and proceedings as judgments, decrees, orders, warrants, subpoenas, records, and other judicial acts of any court of record in this state, subject to the provisions of this rule.

(B) The recognition described in subrule (A) applies only if the tribe or tribal court

(1) enacts an ordinance, court rule, or other binding measure that obligates the tribal court to enforce the judgments, decrees, orders, warrants, subpoenas, records, and judicial acts of the courts of this state, and

(2) transmits the ordinance, court rule or other measure to the State Court Administrative Office. The State Court Administrative Office shall make available to state courts the material received pursuant to paragraph (B)(1).

(C) A judgment, decree, order, warrant, subpoena, record, or other judicial act of a tribal court of a federally recognized Indian tribe that has taken the actions described in subrule (B) is presumed to be valid. To overcome that presumption, an objecting party must demonstrate that

(1) the tribal court lacked personal or subject-matter jurisdiction, or

(2) the judgment, decree, order, warrant, subpoena, record, or other judicial act of the tribal court

(a) was obtained by fraud, duress, or coercion,

(b) was obtained without fair notice or a fair hearing,

(c) is repugnant to the public policy of the State of Michigan, or

(d) is not final under the laws and procedures of the tribal court.

(D) This rule does not apply to judgments or orders that federal law requires be given full faith and credit.

[Adopted May 14, 1996, effective July 1, 1996, 451 Mich.]

Comments

Staff Comment to 1996 Adoption

The 1996 amendment of MCR 2.112(G) and (J) and the 1996 promulgation of MCR 2.615 were prompted by proposals from the Indian Tribal Court/State Trial Court Forum and from the State Bar of Michigan. The adopted rules reflect a synthesis of those sources, of a corresponding rule of the North Dakota Supreme Court, and of the model rules generated by the Michigan Indian Judicial Association.

Rule 2.620   Satisfaction of Judgment

A judgment may be shown satisfied of record in whole or in part by:

(1) filing with the clerk a satisfaction signed and acknowledged by the party or parties in whose favor the judgment was rendered, or their attorneys of record;

(2) payment to the clerk of the judgment, interest, and costs, if it is a money judgment only; or

(3) filing a motion for entry of an order that the judgment has been satisfied.

The court shall hear proofs to determine whether the order should be entered.

The clerk must, in each instance, indicate in the court records that the judgment is satisfied in whole or in part.

[Adopted effective March 1, 1985.]

Comments

Staff Comment to 1985 Adoption

MCR 2.620 is substantially the same as GCR 1963, 524.

Rule 2.621   Proceedings Supplementary to Judgment

(A) Relief Under These Rules. When a party to a civil action obtains a money judgment, that party may, by motion in that action or by a separate civil action:

(1) obtain the relief formerly obtainable by a creditor's bill;

(2) obtain relief supplementary to judgment under MCL 600.6101–600.6143 and

(3) obtain other relief in aid of execution authorized by statute or court rule.

(B) Pleading.

(1) If the motion or complaint seeks to reach an equitable interest of a debtor, it must be verified, and

(a) state the amount due the creditor on the judgment, over and above all just claims of the debtor by way of setoff or otherwise, and

(b) show that the debtor has equitable interests exceeding $100 in value.

(2) The judgment creditor may obtain relief under MCL 600.6110, and discovery under subchapter 2.300 of these rules.

(C) Subpoenas and Orders. A subpoena or order to enjoin the transfer of assets pursuant to MCL 600.6119 must be served under MCR 2.105. The subpoena must specify the amount claimed by the judgment creditor. The court shall endorse its approval of the issuance of the subpoena on the original subpoena, which must be filed in the action. The subrule does not apply to subpoenas for ordinary witnesses.

(D) Order Directing Delivery of Property or Money.

(1) When a court orders the payment of money or delivery of personal property to an officer who has possession of the writ of execution, the order may be entered on notice the court deems just, or without notice.

(2) If a receiver has been appointed, or a receivership has been extended to the supplementary proceeding, the order may direct the payment of money or delivery of property to the receiver.

(E) Receivers. When necessary to protect the rights of a judgment creditor, the court may, under MCR 2.622, appoint a receiver in a proceeding under subrule (A)(2), pending the determination of the proceeding.

(F) Violation of Injunction. The court may punish for contempt a person who violates the restraining provision of an order or subpoena or, if the person is not the judgment debtor, may enter judgment against the person in the amount of the unpaid portion of the judgment and costs allowed by law or these rules or in the amount of the value of the property transferred, whichever is less.

(G) New Proceeding. If there has been a prior supplementary proceeding with respect to the same judgment against the party, whether the judgment debtor or another person, further proceedings may be commenced against that party only by leave of court. Leave may be granted on ex parte motion of the judgment creditor, but only on a finding by the court, based on affidavit of the judgment creditor or another person having personal knowledge of the facts, other than the attorney of the judgment creditor. The affidavit must state that

(1) there is reason to believe that the party against whom the proceeding is sought to be commenced has property or income the creditor is entitled to reach, or, if a third party, is indebted to the judgment debtor;

(2) the existence of the property, income, or indebtedness was not known to the judgment creditor during the pendency of a prior supplementary proceeding; and

(3) the additional supplementary proceeding is sought in good faith to discover assets and not to harass the judgment debtor or third party.

(H) Appeal; Procedure; Bonds. A final order entered in a supplementary proceeding may be appealed in the usual manner. The appeal is governed by the provisions of chapter 7 of these rules except as modified by this subrule.

(1) The appellant must give a bond to the effect that he or she will pay all costs and damages that may be awarded against him or her on the appeal. If the appeal is by the judgment creditor, the amount of the bond may not exceed $200, and subrules (H)(2)–(4) do not apply. If the appeal is by a party other than the judgment creditor, subrules (H)(2)–(4) apply.

(2) If the order appealed from is for the payment of money or the delivery of property, the bond of the appellant must be in an amount at least double the amount of the money or property ordered to be paid or delivered. The bond must be on the condition that if the order appealed from is affirmed in whole or in part the appellant will

(a) pay the amount directed to be paid or deliver the property in as good condition as it is at the time of the appeal, and

(b) pay all damages and costs that may be awarded against the appellant.

(3) If the order appealed from directs the assignment or delivery of documents by the appellant, the documents must be delivered to the clerk of the court in which the proceeding is pending or placed in the hands of an officer or receiver, as the judge who entered the order directs, to await the appeal, subject to the order of the appellate courts.

(4) If the order appealed from directs the sale of real estate of the appellant or delivery of possession by the appellant, the appeal bond must also provide that during the possession of the property by the appellant, or any person holding under the appellant, he or she will not commit or suffer any waste of the property, and that if the order is affirmed he or she will pay the value of the use of the property from the time of appeal until the delivery of possession.

[Adopted effective March 1, 1985. Amended March 26, 2014, effective May 1, 2014, 495 Mich; March 20, 2019, effective May 1, 2019, 502 Mich.]

Comments

Staff Comment to 1985 Adoption

MCR 2.621 is substantially the same as GCR 1963, 741.

Subrule (C) allows subpoenas and orders under the rule to be served by any of the methods specified in MCR 2.105. Compare GCR 1963, 741.3, which did not allow substituted service under GCR 1963, 105.2.

Staff Comment to 2014 Amendment

The amendments of MCR 2.621 and MCR 2.622 were submitted to the Michigan Supreme Court on behalf of the "Receivership Committee" (a committee created because of a need identified by the Debtor/Creditor Rights Committee of the Business Law Section of the State Bar of Michigan) to expand and update the rules regarding receivership proceedings.

Staff Comment to 2019 Amendment

The amendments of Rules 1.109, 2.102, 2.104, 2.106, 2.107, 2.117, 2.119, 2.403, 2.503, 2.506, 2.508, 2.518, 2.602, 2.603, 2.621, 3.101, 3.104, 3.203, 3.205, 3.210, 3.302, 3.607, 3.613, 3.614, 3.705, 3.801, 3.802, 3.805, 3.806, 4.201, 4.202, 4.303, 4.306, 5.001, 5.104, 5.105, 5.107, 5.108, 5.113, 5.117, 5.118, 5.119, 5.120, 5.125, 5.126, 5.132, 5.162, 5.202, 5.203, 5.205, 5.302, 5.304, 5.307, 5.308, 5.309, 5.310, 5.311, 5.313, 5.402, 5.404, 5.405, 5.409, 5.501, and 5.784 and addition of Rule 3.618 of the Michigan Court Rules are an expected progression necessary for design and implementation of the statewide electronic-filing system. These particular amendments will assist in implementing the goals of the project.

Rule 2.622.   Receivers

(A) Appointment of Receiver. Upon the motion of a party or on its own initiative, and for good cause shown, the court may appoint a receiver as provided by law. A receiver appointed under this section is a fiduciary for the benefit of all persons appearing in the action or proceeding. For purposes of this rule, "receivership estate" means the entity, person, or property subject to the receivership.

(B) Selection of Receiver. If the court determines there is good cause to appoint a receiver, the court shall select the receiver in accordance with this subrule. Every receiver selected by the court must have sufficient competence, qualifications, and experience to administer the receivership estate.

(1) *Stipulated Receiver or No Objection Raised.* The moving party may request, or the parties may stipulate to, the selection of a receiver. The moving party shall describe how the nominated receiver meets the requirement in subsection (B) that a receiver selected by the court have sufficient competence, qualifications, and experience to administer the receivership estate, considering the factors listed in subsection (B)(5). If the nonmoving party does not file an objection to the moving party's nominated receiver within 14 days after the petition or motion is served, or if the parties stipulate to the selection of a receiver, the court shall appoint the receiver nominated by the party or parties, unless the court finds that a different receiver should be appointed.

(2) *Receiver Appointed Sua Sponte.* If the court appoints a receiver on its own initiative, any party may file objection to the selected receiver and submit an alternative nominee for appointment as receiver within 14 days after the order appointing the receiver is served. The objecting party shall describe how the alternative nominee meets the requirement in subsection (B) that a receiver selected by the court have sufficient competence, qualifications, and experience to administer the receivership estate, considering the factors listed in subsection (B)(5).

(3) *Reduction in Time to Object.* The court, for good cause shown, may in its discretion, with or without motion or notice, order the period for objection to the selected receiver reduced.

(4) *Objections.* The party filing an objection must serve it on all parties as required by MCR 2.107, together with a notice of hearing.

(5) If a party objects under subsection (B)(2) or the court makes an initial determination that a different receiver should be appointed than the receiver nominated by a party under subsection (B)(1), the court shall state its rationale for selecting a particular receiver after considering the following factors:

(a) experience in the operation and/or liquidation of the type of assets to be administered;

(b) relevant business, legal and receivership knowledge, if any;

(c) ability to obtain the required bonding if more than a nominal bond is required;

(d) any objections to any receiver considered for appointment;

(e) whether the receiver considered for appointment is disqualified under subrule (B)(6); and

(f) any other factor the court deems appropriate.

(6) Except as otherwise provided by law or by subrule (B)(7), a person or entity may not serve as a receiver or in any other professional capacity representing or assisting the receiver, if such person or entity:

(a) is a creditor or a holder of an equity security of the receivership estate:

(b) is or was an investment banker for any outstanding security of the receivership estate;

(c) has been, within three years before the date of the appointment of a receiver, an investment banker for a security of the receivership estate, or an attorney for such an investment banker, in connection with the offer, sale, or issuance of a security of the receivership estate;

(d) is or was, within two years before the date of the appointment of a receiver, a director, an officer, or an employee of the receivership estate or of an investment banker specified in subrule (b) or (c) of this section, unless the court finds the appointment is in the best interest of the receivership estate and that there is no actual conflict of interest by reason of the employment;

(e) has an interest materially adverse to the interest of any class of creditors or equity security holders by reason of any direct or indirect relationship to, connection with, or interest in the receivership estate or an investment banker specified in subrule (b) or (c) of this section, or for any other reason;

(f) has or represents an interest adverse to the receivership estate or stands in any relation to the subject of the action or proceeding that would tend to interfere with the impartial discharge of duties as an officer of the court.

(g) has, at any time within five years before the date of the appointment of a receiver, represented or been employed by the receivership estate or any secured creditor of the receivership estate as an attorney, accountant, appraiser, or in any other professional capacity and the court finds an actual conflict of interest by reason of the representation or employment;

(h) is an "insider" as defined by MCL 566.31(h);

(i) represents or is employed by a creditor of the receivership estate and, on objection of an interested party, the court finds an actual conflict of interest by reason of the representation or employment; or

(j) has a relationship to the action or proceeding that will interfere with the impartial discharge of the receiver's duties.

(7) Any person who has represented or has been employed by the receivership estate is eligible to serve for a specified limited purpose, if the court determines such employment or appointment is in the best interest of the receivership estate and if such professional does not represent or hold an interest materially adverse to the receivership estate.

(C) Order of Appointment. The order of appointment shall include provisions related to the following:

(1) bonding amounts and requirements as provided in subrule (G);

(2) identification of real and personal property of the receivership estate;

(3) procedures and standards related to the reasonable compensation of the receiver as provided in subrule (F);

(4) reports required to be produced and filed by the receiver, including the final report and accounting;

(5) a description of the duties, authority and powers of the receiver;

(6) a listing of property to be surrendered to the receiver; and

(7) any other provision the court deems appropriate.

(D) Duties.

(1) Within 7 days after entry of the order of appointment, the receiver shall file an acceptance of receivership with the court. The acceptance shall be served on all parties to the action.

(2) Unless otherwise ordered, within 28 days after the filing of the acceptance of appointment, the receiver shall provide notice of entry of the order of appointment to any person or entity having a recorded interest in all or any part of the receivership estate.

(3) The receiver shall file with the court an inventory of the property of the receivership estate within 35 days after entry of the order of appointment, unless an inventory has already been filed.

(4) The receiver shall account for all receipts, disbursements and distributions of money and property of the receivership estate.

(5) If there are sufficient funds to make a distribution to a class of creditors, the receiver may request that each creditor in the class of all creditors file a written proof of claim with the court. The receiver may contest the allowance of any claim.

(6) The receiver shall furnish information concerning the receivership estate and its administration as reasonably requested by any party to the action or proceeding.

(7) The receiver shall file with the court a final written report and final accounting of the administration of the receivership estate.

(E) Powers.

(1) Except as otherwise provided by law or by the order of appointment, a receiver has general power to sue for and collect all debts, demands, and rents of the receivership estate, and to compromise or settle claims.

(2) A receiver may liquidate the personal property of the receivership estate into money. By separate order of the court, a receiver may sell real property of the receivership estate.

(3) A receiver may pay the ordinary expenses of the receivership but may not distribute the funds in the receivership estate to a party to the action without an order of the court.

(4) A receiver may only be discharged on order of the court.

(F) Compensation and Expenses of Receiver.

(1) A receiver shall be entitled to reasonable compensation for services rendered to the receivership estate.

(2) The order appointing a receiver shall specify:

(a) the source and method of compensation of the receiver;

(b) that interim compensation may be paid to the receiver after notice to all parties to the action or proceeding and opportunity to object as provided in subsection (5);

(c) that all compensation of the receiver is subject to final review and approval of the court.

(3) All approved fees and expenses incurred by a receiver, including fees and expenses for persons or entities retained by the receiver, shall be paid or reimbursed as provided in the order appointing the receiver.

(4) The receiver shall file with the court an application for payment of fees and the original notice of the request. The notice shall provide that fees and expenses will be deemed approved if no written objection is filed with the court within 7 days after service of the notice. The receiver shall serve the notice and a copy of the application on all parties to the action or proceedings, and file a proof of service with the court.

(5) The application by a receiver, for interim or final payment of fees and expenses, shall include:

(a) A description in reasonable detail of the services rendered, time expended, and expenses incurred;

(b) The amount of compensation and expenses requested;

(c) The amount of any compensation and expenses previously paid to the receiver;

(d) The amount of any compensation and expenses received by the receiver from or to be paid by any source other than the receivership estate;

(e) A description in reasonable detail of any agreement or understanding for a division or sharing of compensation between the person rendering the services and any other person except as permitted in subpart (6).

If written objections are filed or if, in the court's determination, the application for compensation requires a hearing, the court shall schedule a hearing and notify all parties of the scheduled hearing.

(6) A receiver or person performing services for a receiver shall not, in any form or manner, share or agree to share compensation for services rendered to the receivership estate with any person other than a firm member, partner, employer, or regular associate of the person rendering the services except as authorized by order of the court.

(G) Bond. In setting an appropriate bond for the receiver, the court may consider factors including but not limited to:

(1) The value of the receivership estate, if known;

(2) The amount of cash or cash equivalents expected to be received into the receivership estate;

(3) The amount of assets in the receivership estate on deposit in insured financial institutions or invested in U.S. Treasury obligations;

(4) Whether the assets in the receivership estate cannot be sold without further order of the court;

(5) If the receiver is an entity, whether the receiver has sufficient assets or acceptable errors and omissions insurance to cover any potential losses or liabilities of the receivership estate;

(6) The extent to which any secured creditor is undersecured;

(7) Whether the receivership estate is a single parcel of real estate involving few trade creditors; and

(8) Whether the parties have agreed to a nominal bond.

(H) Intervention. An interested person or entity may move to intervene. Any motion to intervene shall comply with MCR 2.209.

(I) Removal of Receiver. After notice and hearing, the court may remove any receiver for good cause shown.

[Adopted effective March 1, 1985. Amended March 26, 2014, effective May 1, 2014, 495 Mich. Amended effective March 21, 2018, 501 Mich.]

Comments

Staff Comment to 1985 Adoption

MCR 2.622 is substantially the same as GCR 1963, 742.

Subrule (D) adds language expressly authorizing the court to allocate expenses among multiple creditors.

Staff Comment to 2014 Amendment

The amendments of MCR 2.621 and MCR 2.622 were submitted to the Michigan Supreme Court on behalf of the "Receivership Committee" (a committee created because of a need identified by the Debtor/Creditor Rights Committee of the Business Law Section of the State Bar of Michigan) to expand and update the rules regarding receivership proceedings.

Staff Comment to 2018 Amendment

These amendments update cross-references and make other nonsubstantive revisions to clarify the rules. The amendment of MCR 6.110(B)(1) addresses an inadvertent omission from the last amendment of this rule that was intended to be shown in overstrike. Accordingly, the current rule does not match the published version. Striking the clause "for good cause shown" will provide consistency with other published versions of the rule and with the statute, MCL 766.7, which allows a magistrate to adjourn a preliminary examination with the consent of the parties without the need for good cause to be shown.

Rule 2.625. Taxation of Costs

(A) Right to Costs.

(1) *In General.* Costs will be allowed to the prevailing party in an action, unless prohibited by statute or by these rules or unless the court directs otherwise, for reasons stated in writing and filed in the action.

(2) *Frivolous Claims and Defenses.* In an action filed on or after October 1, 1986, if the court finds on motion of a party that an action or defense was frivolous, costs shall be awarded as provided by MCL 600.2591.

(B) Rules for Determining Prevailing Party.

(1) *Actions With Several Judgments.* If separate judgments are entered under MCR 2.116 or 2.505(A) and the plaintiff prevails in one judgment in an amount and under circumstances which would entitle the plaintiff to costs, he or she is deemed the prevailing party. Costs common to more than one judgment may be allowed only once.

(2) *Actions With Several Issues or Counts.* In an action involving several issues or counts that state different causes of action or different defenses, the party prevailing on each issue or count may be allowed costs for that issue or count. If there is a single cause of action alleged, the party who prevails on the entire record is deemed the prevailing party.

(3) *Actions With Several Defendants.* If there are several defendants in one action, and judgment for or dismissal of one or more of them is entered, those defendants are deemed prevailing parties, even though the plaintiff ultimately prevails over the remaining defendants.

(4) *Costs on Review in Circuit Court.* An appellant in the circuit court who improves his or her position on appeal is deemed the prevailing party.

(C) Costs in Certain Trivial Actions. In an action brought for damages in contract or tort in which the plaintiff recovers less than $100 (unless the recovery is reduced below $100 by a counterclaim), the plaintiff may recover costs no greater than the amount of damages.

(D) Costs When Default or Default Judgment Set Aside. The following provisions apply to an order setting aside a default or a default judgment:

(1) If personal jurisdiction was acquired over the defendant, the order must be conditioned on the defendant's paying or securing payment to the party seeking affirmative relief the taxable costs incurred in procuring the default or the default judgment and acting in reliance on it;

(2) If jurisdiction was acquired by publication, the order may be conditioned on the defendant's paying or securing payment to the party seeking affirmative relief all or a part of the costs as the court may direct;

(3) If jurisdiction was in fact not acquired, costs may not be imposed.

(E) Costs in Garnishment Proceedings Brought Pursuant to 3.101(M). Costs in garnishment proceedings to resolve the dispute between a plaintiff and a garnishee regarding the garnishee's liability are allowed as in civil actions. Costs may be awarded to the garnishee defendant as follows:

(1) The court may award the garnishee defendant as costs against the plaintiff reasonable attorney fees and other necessary expenses the garnishee defendant incurred in filing the disclosure, if the issue of the garnishee defendant's liability to the principal defendant is not brought to trial.

(2) The court may award the garnishee defendant, against the plaintiff, the total costs of the garnishee defendant's defense, including all necessary expenses and reasonable attorney fees, if the issue of the garnishee defendant's liability to the principal defendant is tried and

   (a) the garnishee defendant is held liable in a sum no greater than that admitted in disclosure, or

   (b) the plaintiff fails to recover judgment against the principal defendant.

In either (a) or (b), the garnishee defendant may withhold from the amount due the principal defendant the sum awarded for costs, and is chargeable only for the balance.

(F) Procedure for Taxing Costs at the Time of Judgment.

(1) Costs may be taxed by the court on signing the judgment, or may be taxed by the clerk as provided in this subrule.

(2) When costs are to be taxed by the clerk, the party entitled to costs must present to the clerk, within 28 days after the judgment is signed, or within 28 days after entry of an order denying a motion for new trial, a motion to set aside the judgment, a motion for rehearing or reconsideration, or a motion for other postjudgment relief except a motion under MCR 2.612(C),

   (a) a bill of costs conforming to subrule (G),

   (b) a copy of the bill of costs for each other party, and

   (c) a list of the names and addresses of the attorneys for each party or of parties not represented by attorneys.

In addition, the party presenting the bill of costs shall immediately serve a copy of the bill and any accompanying affidavits on the other parties. Failure to present a bill of costs within the time prescribed constitutes a waiver of the right to costs.

(3) Within 14 days after service of the bill of costs, another party may file objections to it, accompanied by affidavits if appropriate. After the time for filing objections, the clerk must promptly examine the bill and any objections or affidavits submitted and allow only those items that appear to be correct, striking all charges for services that in the clerk's judgment were not necessary. The clerk shall notify the parties in the manner provided in MCR 2.107.

(4) The action of the clerk is reviewable by the court on motion of any affected party filed within 7 days from the date that notice of the taxing of costs was sent, but on review only those affidavits or objections that were presented to the clerk may be considered by the court.

(G) Bill of Costs; Supporting Affidavits.

(1) Each item claimed in the bill of costs, except fees of officers for services rendered, must be specified particularly.

(2) The bill of costs must be verified and must contain a statement that

(a) each item of cost or disbursement claimed is correct and has been necessarily incurred in the action, and

(b) the services for which fees have been charged were actually performed.

(3) If witness fees are claimed, an affidavit in support of the bill of costs must state the distance traveled and the days actually attended. If fees are claimed for a party as a witness, the affidavit must state that the party actually testified as a witness on the days listed.

(H) Taxation of Fees on Settlement. Unless otherwise specified a settlement is deemed to include the payment of any costs that might have been taxable.

(I) Special Costs or Damages.

(1) In an action in which the plaintiff's claim is reduced by a counterclaim, or another fact appears that would entitle either party to costs, to multiple costs, or to special damages for delay or otherwise, the court shall, on the application of either party, have that fact entered in the records of the court. A taxing officer may receive no evidence of the matter other than a certified copy of the court records or the certificate of the judge who entered the judgment.

(2) Whenever multiple costs are awarded to a party, they belong to the party. Officers, witnesses, jurors, or other persons claiming fees for services rendered in the action are entitled only to the amount prescribed by law.

(3) A judgment for multiple damages under a statute entitles the prevailing party to single costs only, except as otherwise specially provided by statute or by these rules.

(J) Costs in Headlee Amendment Suits. A plaintiff who prevails in an action brought pursuant to Const 1963, art 9, § 32 shall receive from the defendant the costs incurred by the plaintiff in maintaining the action as authorized by MCL 600.308a(1) and (6). Costs include a reasonable attorney fee.

(K) Procedure for Taxing Costs and Fees After Judgment.

(1) A judgment creditor considered a prevailing party to the action under subrule (B) may recover from the judgment debtor(s) the taxable costs and fees expended after a judgment is entered, including all taxable filing fees, service fees, certification fees, and any other costs, fees, and disbursements associated with postjudgment actions as allowed by MCL 600.2405.

(2) Until the judgment is satisfied, the judgment debtor may serve on the judgment creditor a request to review postjudgment taxable costs and fees.

(a) Within 28 days of receipt from a judgment debtor of a request to review postjudgment taxable costs and fees, the judgment creditor shall file with the court a memorandum of postjudgment taxable costs and fees and serve the same upon the judgment debtor. A memorandum of postjudgment taxable costs and fees shall include an itemized list of postjudgment taxable costs and fees. The memorandum must be verified by oath under MCR 1.109(D)(3).

(b) Within 28 days after receiving the memorandum of postjudgment taxable costs and fees from the judgment creditor, the judgment debtor may file a motion to review postjudgment taxable costs and fees. Upon receipt of a timely motion, the court shall review the memorandum filed by the judgment creditor and issue an order allowing or disallowing the postjudgment costs and fees. The review may be conducted at a hearing at the court's discretion. If the court disallows the postjudgment costs and fees or otherwise amends them in favor of the judgment debtor, the court may order the judgment creditor to deduct from the judgment balance the amount of the motion fee paid by the judgment debtor under this rule.

(c) The judgment creditor shall deduct any costs or fees disallowed by the court within 28 days after receipt of an order from the court disallowing the same.

(d) Any error in adding costs or fees to the judgment balance by the judgment creditor or its attorney is not actionable unless there is an affirmative finding by the court that the costs and fees were added in bad faith.

[Adopted effective March 1, 1985. Amended December 11, 1986, effective December 12, 1986, 426 Mich; April 3, 2001, effective July 1, 2001, 463 Mich; November 10, 2011, effective January 1, 2012, 490 Mich; October 2, 2013, effective January 1, 2014, 495 Mich; September 27, 2017, effective May 1, 2018, 501 Mich; August 30, 2018, effective September 1, 2018, 502 Mich.]

Comments

Staff Comment to 1985 Adoption

MCR 2.625 is comparable to GCR 1963, 526.

Subrule (C) would make the provision of GCR 1963, 526.6, limiting the availability of costs when less than $100 is recovered, applicable to all courts. Compare DCR 526.6.

Subrule (D)(3) slightly modifies the language previously found in GCR 1963, 526.8(3). The former provision said that if jurisdiction had not been acquired over the defendant, an order setting aside the default judgment was to be "without condition" as to costs. The new rule provides that in such a circumstance costs may not be imposed.

Subrule (F) includes several modifications regarding the taxing of costs by the clerk. The party submitting the bill of costs is to provide a copy for each other party, along with the addresses of their attorneys (or of parties not represented by attorneys). Subrule (F)(2) expressly requires service of the bill of costs. Subrule (F)(3) adds specific requirements that the clerk examine objections or affidavits that have been submitted and that the clerk notify the parties of the taxing of costs. In subrule (F)(4) the time for seeking review of the clerk's action by the court is modified. The time begins to run not from the date of taxing of costs, but from the date notice of the taxing was sent. Compare GCR 1963, 526.10(3).

The [March 1, 1985] amendment of MCR 2.625(F)(3) clarifies the time within which objections to a proposed bill of costs may be filed. The opposing party has 14 days within which to serve objections, and the clerk is to examine the bill promptly thereafter.

Subrule (H) is new, and provides that when a claim is settled, the settlement is deemed to include the payment of all taxable costs.

The language in subrule (I)(1) is modified to make clear that when the clerk taxes the costs, the notice is to be given by the party entitled to costs, not by the clerk.

The provisions found in GCR 1963, 526.7 and 526.14, regarding summary judgment and bond costs, are omitted. Those matters are covered by MCR 2.116(F) and by statute. See MCL 600.2405, 600.2441(2).

Staff Comment to 2001 Amendment

The April 3, 2001 amendment of MCR 2.625(F)(2), effective July 1, 2001, expanded the categories of postjudgment motions that extend the initial 28–day deadline for presenting a bill of costs. An exception is a motion under MCR 2.612(C), which does not extend the deadline.

Staff Comment to 2011 Amendment

The existing fact-specific pleading requirements in MCR 2.112(M) are retained and expanded to promote earlier consideration whether facts must be established in the case. The amendments of MCR 2.625 clarify that costs, including reasonable attorney fees, are recoverable in a Headlee action. The amendment of MCR 7.206(D)(3) allows parties to utilize electronic filing in Headlee cases, as well as other extraordinary writs or original actions filed in the Court of Appeals. The amendments of MCR 7.206 create a new specific subsection (7.206[E]) regarding the procedure for filing a Headlee action as an original proceeding in the Court of Appeals. The amendment of MCR 7.213 is intended to clarify that Headlee actions are considered priority matters in the Court of Appeals.

Staff Comment to 2014 Amendment

The amendments of MCR 2.403(O)(8), MCR 2.405(D)(6), and MCR 2.625(F)(2) add language that references a motion for rehearing or reconsideration (consistent with the Court of Appeals opinion in *MEEMIC Ins Co v DTE Energy Co*, 292 Mich App 278 [2011]) to the list of motions that toll the period of time in which a party may file a request for case-evaluation sanctions.

Staff Comment to 2017 Amendment

The amendments of MCR 2.625 and 3.101, submitted by the Michigan Creditor's Bar Association, address recent amendments of MCL 600.4012, clarify the authority and process for recovering postjudgment costs, and provide clearer procedure for garnishment proceedings.

Staff Comment to 2018 Amendment

These amendments update cross-references in the rules, and are intended to reflect changes that are necessary as a result of the Court's recent e-Filing rules amendments.

Rule 2.626 Attorney Fees

An award of attorney fees may include an award for the time and labor of any legal assistant who contributed nonclerical, legal support under the supervision of an attorney, provided the legal assistant meets the criteria set forth in Article 1, § 6 of the Bylaws of the State Bar of Michigan.

[Adopted October 24, 2000, effective January 1, 2001, 463 Mich.]

Comments

Staff Comment to 2000 Adoption

The October 24, 2000, adoption of MCR 2.626, effective January 1, 2001, was based on a proposal from the Representative Assembly of the State Bar of Michigan, in response to *Joerger v Gordon Food Service Inc*, 224 Mich App 167 (1997).

Rule 2.630 Disability of Judge

If, after a verdict is returned or findings of fact and conclusions of law are filed, the judge before whom an action has been tried is unable to perform the duties prescribed by these rules because of death, illness, or other disability, another judge regularly sitting in or assigned to the court in which the action was tried may perform those duties. However, if the substitute judge is not satisfied that he or she can do so, the substitute judge may grant a new trial.

[Adopted effective March 1, 1985.]

Comments

Staff Comment to 1985 Adoption

MCR 2.630 is substantially the same as GCR 1963, 531.

CHAPTER 3.   SPECIAL PROCEEDINGS AND ACTIONS
Effective March 1, 1985

SUBCHAPTER 3.000   GENERAL PROVISIONS

Rule 3.001   Applicability and Scope

The rules in this chapter apply in circuit court and in other courts as provided by law or by these rules. Except as otherwise provided in this chapter and law, proceedings under this chapter are governed by the Michigan Court Rules. [Adopted effective March 1, 1985. Amended October 31, 2012, effective January 1, 2013, 493 Mich.]

Comments

Staff Comment to 1985 Adoption

MCR 3.001 is new.

The rules in chapter 3 govern various special proceedings that were provided for by the General Court Rules, generally in the GCR 1963, 700 series. Some of these proceedings are available only in circuit court; others can be brought in other courts, at least in some circumstances.

Staff Comment to 2013 Amendment

The amendments of these rules update the rules making them less "paper" focused and reflecting the use of electronic technology in the way courts process court records. The amendments also clarify and delineate the types of records and other materials maintained by a court, and clarify how access is provided.

Rule 3.002   Indian Children

For purposes of applying the Indian Child Welfare Act, 25 USC 1901 *et seq.*, and the Michigan Indian Family Preservation Act, MCL 712B.1 *et seq.* to proceedings under the Juvenile Code, the Adoption Code, and the Estates and Protected Individuals Code, the following definitions taken from MCL 712B.3 and MCL 712B.7 shall apply.

(1) "Active efforts" means actions to provide remedial services and rehabilitative programs designed to prevent the breakup of the Indian family and to reunify the child with the Indian family. Active efforts require more than a referral to a service without actively engaging the Indian child and family. Active efforts include reasonable efforts as required by title IV–E of the social security act, 42 USC 670 to 679c, and also include doing or addressing all of the following:

(a) Engaging the Indian child, child's parents, tribe, extended family members, and individual Indian caregivers through the utilization of culturally appropriate services and in collaboration with the parent or child's Indian tribes and Indian social services agencies.

(b) Identifying appropriate services and helping the parents to overcome barriers to compliance with those services.

(c) Conducting or causing to be conducted a diligent search for extended family members for placement.

(d) Requesting representatives designated by the Indian child's tribe with substantial knowledge of the prevailing social and cultural standards and child rearing practice within the tribal community to evaluate the circumstances of the Indian child's family and to assist in developing a case plan that uses the resources of the Indian tribe and Indian community, including traditional and customary support, actions, and services, to address those circumstances.

(e) Completing a comprehensive assessment of the situation of the Indian child's family, including a determination of the likelihood of protecting the Indian child's health, safety, and welfare effectively in the Indian child's home.

(f) Identifying, notifying, and inviting representatives of the Indian child's tribe to participate in all aspects of the Indian child custody proceeding at the earliest possible point in the proceeding and actively soliciting the tribe's advice throughout the proceeding.

(g) Notifying and consulting with extended family members of the Indian child, including extended family members who were identified by the Indian child's tribe or parents, to identify and to provide family structure and support for the Indian child, to assure cultural connections, and to serve as placement resources for the Indian child.

(h) Making arrangements to provide natural and family interaction in the most natural setting that can ensure the Indian child's safety, as appropriate to the goals of the Indian child's permanency plan, including, when requested by the tribe, arrangements for transportation and other assistance to enable family members to participate in that interaction.

(i) Offering and employing all available family preservation strategies and requesting the involvement of the Indian child's tribe to identify those strategies and to ensure that those strategies are culturally appropriate to the Indian child's tribe.

(j) Identifying community resources offering housing, financial, and transportation assistance and in-home support services, in-home intensive treatment services, community support services, and specialized services for members of the Indian child's family with special needs, and providing information about those resources to the Indian child's family, and actively assisting the Indian child's family or offering active assistance in accessing those resources.

(k) Monitoring client progress and client participation in services.

(*l*) Providing a consideration of alternative ways of addressing the needs of the Indian child's family, if services do not exist or if existing services are not available to the family.

(2) "Child custody proceeding" shall mean and include

(a) "foster-care placement," which shall mean any action removing an Indian child from his or her parent or Indian custodian for temporary placement in a foster home or institution or the home of a guardian or conservator where the parent or Indian custodian cannot have the child returned upon demand, but where parental rights have not been terminated,

(b) "termination of parental rights," which shall mean any action resulting in the termination of the parent-child relationship,

(c) "preadoptive placement," which shall mean the temporary placement of an Indian child in a foster home or institution after the termination of parental rights, but before or in lieu of adoptive placement, and

(d) "adoptive placement," which shall mean the permanent placement of an Indian child for adoption, including any action resulting in a final decree of adoption.

Such term or terms shall not include a placement based upon an act that, if committed by an adult, would be deemed a crime or upon an award, in a divorce proceeding, of custody to one of the parents.

(3) "Court" means the family division of circuit court or the probate court.

(4) "Culturally appropriate services" means services that enhance an Indian child's and family's relationship to, identification, and connection with the Indian child's tribe. Culturally appropriate services should provide the opportunity to practice the teachings, beliefs, customs, and ceremonies of the Indian child's tribe so those may be incorporated into the Indian child's daily life, as well as services that address the issues that have brought the child and family to the attention of the department that are consistent with the tribe's beliefs about child rearing, child development, and family wellness. Culturally appropriate services may involve tribal representatives, extended family members, tribal elders, spiritual and cultural advisors, tribal social services, individual Indian caregivers, medicine men or women, and natural healers. If the Indian child's tribe establishes a different definition of culturally appropriate services, the court shall follow the tribe's definition.

(5) "Department" means the department of human services or any successor department or agency.

(6) "Exclusive jurisdiction" shall mean that an Indian tribe has jurisdiction exclusive as to any state over any child custody proceeding as defined above involving an Indian child who resides or is domiciled within the reservation of such tribe, except where such jurisdiction is otherwise vested in the state by existing federal law. Where an Indian child is a ward of a tribal court, the Indian tribe retains exclusive jurisdiction, regardless of the residence or domicile or subsequent change in his or her residence or domicile.

(7) "Extended family member" shall be as defined by the law or custom of the Indian child's tribe or, in the absence of such law or custom, shall be a person who has reached the age of 18 years and who is the Indian child's grandparent, aunt or uncle, brother or sister, brother-in-law or sister-in-law, niece or nephew, first or second cousin, or stepparent and includes the term "relative" as that term is defined in MCL 712A.13a(1)(j).

(8) "Foster home or institution" means a child caring institution as that term is defined in section 1 of 1973 PA 116, MCL 722.111.

(9) "Guardian" means a person who has qualified as a guardian of a minor under a parental or spousal nomination or a court order issued under section 19a or 19c of chapter XIIA, section 5204 or 5205 of the estates and protected individuals code, 1998 PA 386, MCL 700.5204 and 700.5205, or sections 600 to 644 of the mental health code, 1974 PA 258, MCL 330.1600 to 330.1644. Guardian may also include a person appointed by a tribal court under tribal code or custom. Guardian does not include a guardian ad litem.

(10) "Guardian ad litem" means an individual whom the court appoints to assist the court in determining the child's best interests. A guardian ad litem does not need to be an attorney.

(11) "Indian" means any member of any Indian tribe, band, nation, or other organized group or community of Indians recognized as eligible for the services provided to Indians by the secretary because of their status as Indians, including any Alaska native village as defined in section 1602(c) of the Alaska native claims settlement act, 43 USC 1602.

(12) "Indian child" means any unmarried person who is under age 18 and is either

(a) a member of an Indian tribe, or

(b) is eligible for membership in an Indian tribe as determined by that Indian tribe.

(13) "Indian child's tribe" means

(a) the Indian tribe in which an Indian child is a member or eligible for membership, or

(b) in the case of an Indian child who is a member of or eligible for membership in more than one tribe, the Indian tribe with which the Indian child has the most significant contacts.

(14) "Indian child welfare act" means the Indian child welfare act of 1978, 25 USC 1901 to 1963.

(15) "Indian custodian" means any Indian person who has custody of an Indian child under tribal law or custom or under state law, or to whom temporary physical care, custody, and control have been transferred by the child's parent.

(16) "Indian organization" means any group, association, partnership, corporation, or other legal entity owned or controlled by Indians, or a majority of whose members are Indians.

(17) "Indian tribe" means any Indian tribe, band, nation, or other organized group or community of Indians recognized as eligible for the services provided to Indians by the Secretary because of their status as Indians, including any Alaska Native village as defined in section 43 USC 1602(c).

(18) "Lawyer-guardian ad litem" means an attorney appointed under MCL 712B.21 to represent the child with the powers and duties as set forth in MCL 712A.17d. The provisions of MCL 712A.17d also apply to a lawyer-guardian ad litem appointed for the purposes of MIFPA under each of the following:

(a) MCL 700.5213 and 700.5219,

(b) MCL 722.24, and

(c) MCL 722.630.

(19) "Official tribal representative" means an individual who is designated by the Indian child's tribe to represent the tribe in a court overseeing a child custody proceeding. An official tribal representative does not need to be an attorney.

(20) "Parent" means any biological parent or parents of an Indian child or any Indian person who has lawfully adopted an Indian child, including adoptions under tribal law or custom. It does not include the putative father if paternity has not been acknowledged or established.

(21) "Reservation" means Indian country as defined in section 18 USC 1151 and any lands not covered under such section, for which title is either held by the United States in trust for the benefit of any Indian tribe or individual or held by

any Indian tribe or individual subject to a restriction by the United States against alienation.

(22) "Secretary" means the Secretary of the Interior.

(23) "Tribal court" means a court with jurisdiction over child custody proceedings and that is either a Court of Indian Offenses, a court established and operated under the code or custom of an Indian tribe, or any other administrative body of a tribe that is vested with authority over child custody proceedings.

(24) "Ward of tribal court" means a child over whom an Indian tribe exercises authority by official action in tribal court or by the governing body of the tribe.

[Adopted February 2, 2010, effective May 1, 2010, 485 Mich. Amended effective March 20, 2013, 493 Mich; March 9, 2016, 499 Mich.]

Comments

Staff Comment to 2010 Adoption

These amendments incorporate provisions of the Indian Child Welfare Act into specific provisions within various rules relating to child protective proceedings and juvenile status offenses. The language is designed to make the rules reflect a more integrated approach to addressing issues specific to Indian children.

MCR 3.002(1)(c) defines "preadoptive placement" to mean the "temporary placement of an Indian child in a foster home or institution after the termination of parental rights, but before or in lieu of adoptive placement, and ..." The phrase "in lieu of adoptive placement" is not intended to mean that it is permissible to leave a child in foster care indefinitely, in violation of MCL 712A.19b(6) or (7) or 45 CFR 1355.20, 45 CFR 1356.21, or 45 CFR 1356.50. Rather, it addresses situations where the parental rights to a child have been terminated and there is no permanency plan for adoption of the child. One example is when the child has been placed with a juvenile guardian and the guardianship is subsequently revoked. In this situation, jurisdiction over the child pursuant to MCL 712A.2(b) will be reinstated and the child is placed in foster care.

MCR 3.002(1): The definition of "child custody proceeding" is intended to apply the Indian Child Welfare Act to delinquency proceedings if an "Indian child" is charged with a so-called status offense in violation of MCL 712A.2(a)(2)–(4) or (d). Delinquency proceedings involving an Indian child charged with any other non-status offense are generally not subject to the Indian Child Welfare Act; however, if the initial investigation or subsequent review of a non-status delinquency case reveals that the Indian child involved suffers from child abuse or neglect, a separate child protective proceeding may be initiated, which would be subject to the Indian Child Welfare Act.

The amendment of MCR 3.905(C)(1) states that a court shall consider guidelines established by the Bureau of Indian Affairs (BIA) in determining whether good cause not to transfer exists (Guidelines for State Courts; Indian Child Custody Proceedings, 44 Fed Reg No 228, 67590–67592, C.2–C.4. [November 26, 1979]). Some examples of good cause are that the Indian tribe does not have a tribal court or that the Indian child is over 12 years old and objects to the transfer. For additional examples of good cause and relevant case law, see the BIA guidelines cited above and A Practical Guide to the Indian Child Welfare Act. (Native American Rights Fund, A Practical Guide to the Indian Child Welfare Act [Boulder, CO: Native American Rights Fund, 2007], 7.15 and 7.16, p 60.)

Staff Comment to 2013 Amendment

This proposal incorporates provisions of the newly enacted Michigan Indian Family Preservation Act into specific provisions within various rules relating to child protective proceedings and juvenile status offenses.

Staff Comment to 2016 Amendment

These amendments update cross-references that changed after the rule was adopted and make other nonsubstantive revisions.

SUBCHAPTER 3.100   DEBTOR–CREDITOR

Rule 3.101. Garnishment after Judgment

(A) **Definitions.** In this rule,

(1) "plaintiff" refers to any judgment creditor,

(2) "defendant" refers to any judgment debtor,

(3) "garnishee" refers to the garnishee defendant,

(4) "periodic payments" includes but is not limited to, wages, salary, commissions, bonuses, and other income paid to the defendant during the period of the writ; land contract payments; rent; and other periodic debt or contract payments. Interest payments and other payments listed in MCL 600.4012(14)(a)–(d) are not periodic payments.

(B) **Postjudgment Garnishments.**

(1) Periodic garnishments are garnishments of periodic payments, as provided in this rule.

(a) Unless otherwise ordered by the court, a writ of periodic garnishment served on a garnishee who is obligated to make periodic payments to the defendant is effective until the first to occur of the following events:

(i) the amount withheld pursuant to the writ equals the amount of the unpaid judgment, interest, and costs stated in the verified statement in support of the writ; however, if the plaintiff has sent a statement to the garnishee in accordance with MCL 600.4012(5)(a), the balance on which may include additional interest and costs, the periodic garnishment is effective until the balance on the most recent statement is withheld or

(ii) the plaintiff files and serves on the defendant and the garnishee a notice that the amount withheld exceeds the remaining unpaid judgment, interest, and costs, or that the judgment has otherwise been satisfied.

(b) The plaintiff may not obtain the issuance of a second writ of garnishment on a garnishee who is obligated to make periodic payments to the defendant while a prior writ served on that garnishee remains in effect relating to the same judgment.

(c) If a writ of periodic garnishment is served on a garnishee who is obligated to make periodic payments to the defendant while another order that has priority under MCL 600.4012(2) is in effect, or if a writ or order with higher priority is served on the garnishee while another writ is in effect, the garnishee is not obligated to withhold payments pursuant to the lower priority writ until the higher priority writ ceases to be effective under subrule (B)(1)(a). However, in the case of garnishment of earnings, the garnishee shall withhold pursuant to the lower priority writ to the extent that the amount being withheld pursuant to the higher priority order is less than the maximum that could be withheld by law pursuant to the lower priority writ (see, e.g., 15 USC 1673). Upon the expiration of the higher priority writ, the lower priority one becomes effective until it ceases to be effective under subrule (B)(1)(a). The garnishee shall notify the plaintiff of receipt of any higher priority writ or order and provide the information required by subrule (H)(2)(c).

(2) Nonperiodic garnishments are garnishments of property or obligations other than periodic payments.

(C) **Forms.** The state court administrator shall publish approved forms for use in garnishment proceedings. Separate forms shall be used for periodic and nonperiodic garnishments.

The verified statement, writ, and disclosure filed in garnishment proceedings must be substantially in the form approved by the state court administrator.

(D) Request for and Issuance of Writ. The clerk of the court that entered the judgment shall review the request. The clerk shall issue a writ of garnishment if the writ appears to be correct, complies with these rules and the Michigan statutes, and if the plaintiff, or someone on the plaintiff's behalf, makes and files a statement verified in the manner provided in MCR 1.109(D)(3) stating:

(1) that a judgment has been entered against the defendant and remains unsatisfied;

(2) the amount of the judgment; the total amount of the postjudgment interest accrued to date; the total amount of the postjudgment costs accrued to date, which may include the costs associated with filing the current writ of garnishment; the total amount of the postjudgment payments made to date, and the amount of the unsatisfied judgment now due (including interest and costs), which may include the costs associated with filing the current writ of garnishment;

(3) that the person signing the verified statement knows or has good reason to believe that

(a) a named person has control of property belonging to the defendant,

(b) a named person is indebted to the defendant, or

(c) a named person is obligated to make periodic payments to the defendant.

(E) Writ of Garnishment.

(1) The writ of garnishment must have attached or must include a copy of the verified statement requesting issuance of the writ, and must include information that will permit the garnishee to identify the defendant, such as the defendant's address, social security number, employee identification number, federal tax identification number, employer number, or account number, if known.

(2) Upon issuance of the writ, it shall be served upon the garnishee as provided in subrule (F)(1). The writ shall include the date on which it was issued and the last day by which it must be served to be valid, which is 182 days after it was issued.

(3) The writ shall direct the garnishee to:

(a) serve a copy of the writ on the defendant as provided in subrule (F)(2);

(b) within 14 days after the service of the writ, file with the court clerk a verified disclosure indicating the garnishee's liability (as specified in subrule [G][1]) to the defendant and mail or deliver a copy to the plaintiff and the defendant;

(c) deliver no tangible or intangible property to the defendant, unless allowed by statute or court rule;

(d) pay no obligation to the defendant, unless allowed by statute or court rule; and

(e) in the discretion of the court and in accordance with subrule (J), order the garnishee either to

(i) make all payments directly to the plaintiff or

(ii) send the funds to the court in the manner specified in the writ.

(4) The writ shall direct the defendant to refrain from disposing of

(a) any negotiable instrument representing a debt of the garnishee (except the earnings of the defendant), or

(b) any negotiable instrument of title representing property in which the defendant claims an interest held in the possession or control of the garnishee.

(5) The writ shall inform the defendant that unless the defendant files objections within 14 days after the service of the writ on the defendant or as otherwise provided under MCL 600.4012,

(a) without further notice the property or debt held pursuant to the garnishment may be applied to the satisfaction of the plaintiff's judgment, and

(b) periodic payments due to the defendant may be withheld until the judgment is satisfied and in the discretion of the court paid directly to the plaintiff.

(6) The writ shall direct the plaintiff to serve the garnishee as provided in subrule (F)(1), and to file a proof of service.

(F) Service of Writ.

(1) The plaintiff shall serve the writ of garnishment, a copy of the writ for the defendant, the disclosure form, and any applicable fees, on the garnishee within 182 days after the date the writ was issued in the manner provided for the service of a summons and complaint in MCR 2.105.

(2) The garnishee shall within 7 days after being served with the writ deliver a copy of the writ to the defendant or mail a copy to the defendant at the defendant's last known address by first class mail.

(G) Liability of Garnishee.

(1) Subject to the provisions of the garnishment statute and any setoff permitted by law or these rules, the garnishee is liable for

(a) all tangible or intangible property belonging to the defendant in the garnishee's possession or control when the writ is served on the garnishee, unless the property is represented by a negotiable document of title held by a bona fide purchaser for value other than the defendant;

(b) all negotiable documents of title and all goods represented by negotiable documents of title belonging to the defendant if the documents of title are in the garnishee's possession when the writ is served on the garnishee;

(c) all corporate share certificates belonging to the defendant in the garnishee's possession or control when the writ is served on the garnishee;

(d) all debts, whether or not due, owing by the garnishee to the defendant when the writ is served on the garnishee, except for debts evidenced by negotiable instruments or representing the earnings of the defendant;

(e) all debts owing by the garnishee evidenced by negotiable instruments held or owned by the defendant when the writ of garnishment is served on the defendant, as long as the instruments are brought before the court before their negotiation to a bona fide purchaser for value;

(f) the portion of the defendant's earnings that are not protected from garnishment by law (see, e.g., 15 USC 1673) as provided in subrule (B);

(g) all judgments in favor of the defendant against the garnishee in force when the writ is served on the garnishee;

(h) all tangible or intangible property of the defendant that, when the writ is served on the garnishee, the garnishee holds by conveyance, transfer, or title that is void as to creditors of the defendant, whether or not the defendant could maintain an action against the garnishee to recover the property; and

(i) the value of all tangible or intangible property of the defendant that, before the writ is served on the garnishee, the garnishee received or held by conveyance, transfer, or title that was void as to creditors of the defendant, but that the garnishee no longer held at the time the writ was served, whether or not the defendant could maintain an action against the garnishee for the value of the property.

(2) The garnishee is liable for no more than the amount of the unpaid judgment, interest, and costs as stated in the verified statement requesting the writ of garnishment unless a statement is sent to the garnishee in accordance with MCL 600.4012(5)(a), in which case the garnishee is liable for the amount of the remaining judgment balance as provided in the most recent statement. Property or debts exceeding that amount may be delivered or paid to the defendant notwithstanding the garnishment.

(H) Disclosure. The garnishee shall file with the court and deliver to the plaintiff and defendant, a verified disclosure within 14 days after being served with the writ.

(1) *Nonperiodic Garnishments.*

(a) If indebted to the defendant, the garnishee shall file a disclosure revealing the garnishee's liability to the defendant as specified in subrule (G)(1) and claiming any setoff that the garnishee would have against the defendant, except for claims for unliquidated damages for wrongs or injuries.

(b) If not indebted to the defendant, the garnishee shall file a disclosure so indicating.

(c) If the garnishee is indebted to the defendant, but claims that withholding is exempt under MCR 3.101(I)(6), the garnishee shall indicate on the disclosure the specific exemption. If the garnishee is indebted, but claims that withholding is exempt for some reason other than those set forth in MCR 3.101(I)(6), the garnishee shall indicate on the disclosure the basis for its claim of exemption and cite the legal authority for the exemption.

(2) *Periodic Garnishments.*

(a) If not obligated to make periodic payments to the defendant, the disclosure shall so indicate, and the garnishment shall be considered to have expired.

(b) If obligated to make periodic payments to the defendant, the disclosure shall indicate the nature and frequency of the garnishee's obligation. The information must be disclosed even if money is not owing at the time of the service of the writ.

(c) If a writ or order with a higher priority is in effect, in the disclosure the garnishee shall specify the court that issued the writ or order, the file number of the case in which it was issued, the date it was issued, and the date it was served.

(I) Withholding. This subrule applies only if the garnishee is indebted to or obligated to make periodic payments to the defendant.

(1) Except as otherwise provided in this subrule, the writ shall be effective as to obligations owed and property held by the garnishee as of the time the writ is served on the garnishee.

(2) In the case of periodic earnings, withholding shall commence according to the following provisions:

(a) For garnishees with weekly, biweekly, or semimonthly pay periods, withholding shall commence with the first full pay period after the writ was served.

(b) For garnishees with monthly pay periods, if the writ is served on the garnishee within the first 14 days of the pay period, withholding shall commence on the date the writ is served. If the writ is served on the garnishee on or after the 15th day of the pay period, withholding shall commence the first full pay period after the writ was served.

(3) In the case of periodic earnings, withholding shall cease when the periodic garnishment becomes no longer effective under subrule (B)(1).

(4) At the time that a periodic payment is withheld, the garnishee shall provide the following information to the plaintiff and defendant:

(a) the name of the parties;

(b) the case number;

(c) the date and amount withheld;

(d) the balance due on the writ.

The information shall also be provided to the court if funds are sent to the court.

(5) If funds have not been withheld because a higher priority writ or order was in effect, and the higher priority writ ceases to be effective before the lower priority writ ceases to be effective, the garnishee shall begin withholding pursuant to the lower priority writ as of the date that the higher priority writ ceases to be effective.

(6) A bank or other financial institution, as garnishee, shall not withhold exempt funds of the debtor from an account into which only exempt funds are directly deposited and where such funds are clearly identifiable upon deposit as exempt Social Security benefits, Supplemental Security Income benefits, Railroad Retirement benefits, Black Lung benefits, or Veterans Assistance benefits.

(J) Payment.

(1) After 28 days from the date of the service of the writ on the garnishee, the garnishee shall transmit all withheld funds to the plaintiff or the court as directed by the court pursuant to subrule (E)(3)(e) unless notified that objections have been filed.

(2) For periodic garnishments, all future payments shall be paid as they become due as directed by the court pursuant to subrule (E)(3)(e) until the garnishment ceases to be effective under subrule (B)(1).

(3) Upon receipt of proceeds from the writ, the court shall forward such proceeds to the plaintiff.

(4) Payment to the plaintiff may not exceed the amount of the unpaid judgment, interest, and costs stated in the verified statement requesting the writ of garnishment; however, if the plaintiff has sent a statement to the garnishee in accordance with MCL 600.4012(5)(a), the balance on which may include additional interest and costs, the garnishee shall pay to the plaintiff the amount provided in the most recent statement.

(5) In the case of earnings, the garnishee shall maintain a record of all payment calculations and shall make such information available for review by the plaintiff, the defendant, or the court, upon request.

(6) For periodic garnishments, within 14 days after the writ ceases to be effective under subrule (B)(1) or after the garnishee is no longer obligated to make periodic payments, the garnishee shall file with the court and mail or deliver to the plaintiff and the defendant, a final statement of the total amount paid on the writ. If the garnishee is the defendant's employer, the statement is to be filed within 14 days after the writ ceases to be effective, regardless of changes in employment status during the time that the writ was in effect. The statement shall include the following information:

(a) the names of the parties and the court in which the case is pending;

(b) the case number;

(c) the date of the statement;

(d) the total amount withheld.

(7) If the disclosure states that the garnishee holds property other than money belonging to the defendant, the plaintiff must proceed by motion (with notice to the defendant and the garnishee) to seek an appropriate order regarding application of the property to satisfaction of the judgment. If there are no pending objections to the garnishment, and the plaintiff has not filed such a motion within 56 days after the filing of the disclosure, the garnishment is dissolved and the garnishee may release the property to the defendant.

(K) Objections.

(1) Objections shall be filed with the court within 14 days of the date of service of the writ on the defendant or within 14 days of the date of the most recent statement sent to the defendant pursuant to MCL 600.4012(5)(a). Objections may be filed after the time provided in this subrule but do not suspend payment pursuant to subrule (J) unless ordered by the court. Objections may only be based on defects in or the invalidity of the garnishment proceeding itself or the balance provided on the statement sent pursuant to MCL 600.4012(5)(a), and may not be used to challenge the validity of the judgment previously entered.

(2) Objections shall be based on one or more of the following:

(a) the funds or property are exempt from garnishment by law;

(b) garnishment is precluded by the pendency of bankruptcy proceedings;

(c) garnishment is barred by an installment payment order;

(d) garnishment is precluded because the maximum amount permitted by law is being withheld pursuant to a higher priority garnishment or order;

(e) the judgment has been paid;

(f) the garnishment was not properly issued or is otherwise invalid;

(g) the balance on the statement sent pursuant to MCL 600.4012(5)(a) is incorrect.

(3) Within 7 days of the filing of objections, notice of the date of hearing on the objections shall be sent to the plaintiff, the defendant, and the garnishee. The hearing date shall be within 21 days of the date the objections are filed. In district court, notice shall be sent by the court. In circuit and probate court, notice shall be sent by the objecting party.

(4) The court shall notify the plaintiff, the defendant, and the garnishee of the court's decision.

(L) Steps After Disclosure; Third Parties; Interpleader; Discovery.

(1) Within 14 days after service of the disclosure, the plaintiff may serve the garnishee with written interrogatories or notice the deposition of the garnishee. The answers to the interrogatories or the deposition testimony becomes part of the disclosure.

(2) If the garnishee's disclosure declares that a named person other than the defendant and the plaintiff claims all or part of the disclosed indebtedness or property, the court may order that the claimant be added as a defendant in the garnishment action under MCR 2.207. The garnishee may proceed under MCR 3.603 as in interpleader actions, and other claimants may move to intervene under MCR 2.209.

(3) The discovery rules apply to garnishment proceedings.

(4) The filing of a disclosure, the filing of answers to interrogatories, or the personal appearance by or on behalf of the garnishee at a deposition does not waive the garnishee's right to question the court's jurisdiction, the validity of the proceeding, or the plaintiff's right to judgment.

(M) Determination of Garnishee's Liability.

(1) If there is a dispute regarding the garnishee's liability or if another person claims an interest in the garnishee's property or obligation, the issue shall be tried in the same manner as other civil actions.

(2) The verified statement acts as the plaintiff's complaint against the garnishee, and the disclosure serves as the answer. The facts stated in the disclosure must be accepted as true unless the plaintiff has served interrogatories or noticed a deposition within the time allowed by subrule (L)(1) or another party has filed a pleading or motion denying the accuracy of the disclosure. Except as the facts stated in the verified statement are admitted by the disclosure, they are denied. Admissions have the effect of admissions in responsive pleadings. The defendant and other claimants added under subrule (L)(2) may plead their claims and defenses as in other civil actions. The garnishee's liability to the plaintiff shall be tried on the issues thus framed.

(3) Even if the amount of the garnishee's liability is disputed, the plaintiff may move for judgment against the garnishee to the extent of the admissions in the disclosure. The general motion practice rules govern notice (including notice to the garnishee and the defendant) and hearing on the motion.

(4) The issues between the plaintiff and the garnishee will be tried by the court unless a party files a demand for a jury trial within 7 days after the filing of the disclosure, answers to interrogatories, or deposition transcript, whichever is filed last. The defendant or a third party waives any right to a jury trial unless a demand for a jury is filed with the pleading stating the claim.

(5) On the trial of the garnishee's liability, the plaintiff may offer the record of the garnishment proceeding and other

evidence. The garnishee may offer evidence not controverting the disclosure, or in the discretion of the court, may show error or mistakes in the disclosure.

(6) If the court determines that the garnishee is indebted to the defendant, but the time for payment has not arrived, a judgment may not be entered until after the time of maturity stated in the verdict or finding.

(N) Orders for Installment Payments.

(1) An order for installment payments under MCL 600.6201 *et seq.* suspends the effectiveness of a writ of garnishment of periodic payments for work and labor performed by the defendant from the time the order is served on the garnishee. An order for installment payments does not suspend the effectiveness of a writ of garnishment of nonperiodic payments or of an income tax refund or credit.

(2) If an order terminating the installment payment order is entered and served on the garnishee, the writ again becomes effective and retains its priority and remains in force as if the installment payment order had never been entered.

(O) Judgment and Execution.

(1) Judgment may be entered against the garnishee for the payment of money or the delivery of specific property as the facts warrant. A money judgment against the garnishee may not be entered in an amount greater than the amount of the unpaid judgment, interest, and costs as stated in the verified statement requesting the writ of garnishment. Judgment for specific property may be enforced only to the extent necessary to satisfy the judgment against the defendant.

(2) The judgment against the garnishee discharges the garnishee from all demands by the defendant for the money paid or property delivered in satisfaction of the judgment. If the garnishee is sued by the defendant for anything done under the provisions of these garnishment rules, the garnishee may introduce as evidence the judgment and the satisfaction.

(3) If the garnishee is chargeable for specific property that the garnishee holds for or is bound to deliver to the defendant, judgment may be entered and execution issued against the interest of the defendant in the property for no more than is necessary to satisfy the judgment against the defendant. The garnishee must deliver the property to the officer serving the execution, who shall sell, apply, and account as in other executions.

(4) If the garnishee is found to be under contract for the delivery of specific property to the defendant, judgment may be entered and execution issued against the interest of the defendant in the property for no more than is necessary to satisfy the judgment against the defendant. The garnishee must deliver the property to the officer serving the execution according to the terms of the contract. The officer shall sell, apply, and account as in ordinary execution.

(5) If the garnishee is chargeable for specific property and refuses to expose it so that execution may be levied on it, the court may order the garnishee to show cause why general execution should not issue against the garnishee. Unless sufficient cause is shown to the contrary, the court may order that an execution be issued against the garnishee in an amount not to exceed twice the value of the specifically chargeable property.

(6) The court may issue execution against the defendant for the full amount due the plaintiff on the judgment against the defendant. Execution against the garnishee may not be ordered by separate writ, but must always be ordered by endorsement on or by incorporation within the writ of execution against the defendant. The court may order additional execution to satisfy the plaintiff's judgment as justice requires.

(7) Satisfaction of all or part of the judgment against the garnishee constitutes satisfaction of a judgment to the same extent against the defendant.

(P) Appeals. A judgment or order in a garnishment proceeding may be set aside or appealed in the same manner and with the same effect as judgments or orders in other civil actions.

(Q) Receivership.

(1) If on disclosure or trial of a garnishee's liability, it appears that when the writ was served the garnishee possessed,

    (a) a written promise for the payment of money or the delivery of property belonging to the defendant, or

    (b) personal property belonging to the defendant,

the court may order the garnishee to deliver it to a person appointed as receiver.

(2) The receiver must

    (a) collect the written promise for payment of money or for the delivery of property and apply the proceeds on any judgment in favor of the plaintiff against the garnishee and pay any surplus to the garnishee, and

    (b) dispose of the property in an amount greater than any encumbrance on it can be obtained, and after paying the amount of the encumbrance, apply the balance to the plaintiff's judgment against the garnishee and pay any surplus to the garnishee.

(3) If the garnishee refuses to comply with the delivery order, the garnishee is liable for the amount of the written promise for the payment of money, the value of the promise for the delivery of property, or the value of the defendant's interest in the encumbered personal property. The facts of the refusal and the valuation must be included in the receiver's report to the court.

(4) The receiver shall report all actions pertaining to the promise or property to the court. The report must include a description and valuation of any property, with the valuation to be ascertained by appraisal on oath or in a manner the court may direct.

(R) Costs and Fees.

(1) Costs and fees are as provided by law or these rules.

(2) Within 28 days after receipt of the disclosure filed pursuant to subrule (H) by a garnishee of a periodic garnishment disclosing that it does not employ the defendant and is not otherwise liable for periodic payments, or from a garnishee of a nonperiodic garnishment disclosing that it does not hold property subject to garnishment and the defendant is not indebted to the garnishee, the plaintiff shall deduct any costs associated with that garnishment that may have been added to the judgment balance pursuant to MCR 2.625(K), unless the court otherwise directs.

(S) Failure to Disclose or to Do Other Acts; Default; Contempt.

(1) For garnishments filed under MCR 3.101(B)(2) (nonperiodic):

(a) If the garnishee fails to disclose or do a required act within the time limit imposed, a default may be taken as in other civil actions. A default judgment against a garnishee may not exceed the amount of the garnishee's liability as provided in subrule (G)(2).

(b) If the garnishee fails to comply with the court order, the garnishee may be adjudged in contempt of court.

(2) For garnishments filed under MCR 3.101(B)(1) (periodic): MCL 600.4012(6)–(10) governs default, default judgments, and motions to set aside default judgments for periodic garnishments.

(3) The court may impose costs on a garnishee whose default or contempt results in expense to other parties. Costs imposed shall include reasonable attorney fees and shall not be less than $100.

(4) This rule shall not apply to nonperiodic garnishments filed for an income tax refund or credit.

(T) Judicial Discretion. On motion the court may by order extend the time for:

(1) the garnishee's disclosure;

(2) the plaintiff's filing of written interrogatories;

(3) the plaintiff's filing of a demand for oral examination of the garnishee;

(4) the garnishee's answer to written interrogatories;

(5) the garnishee's appearance for oral examination; and

(6) the demand for jury trial.

The order must be filed with the court and served on the other parties.

[Adopted effective March 1, 1985. Amended October 26, 1993, effective April 1, 1994, 444 Mich; May 14, 1997, effective September 1, 1997, 454 Mich; May 19, 2009, effective September 1, 2009, 483 Mich; September 9, 2009, effective January 1, 2010, 485 Mich. Amended effective October 24, 2012, 493 Mich; June 5, 2013, 494 Mich. Amended September 23, 2015, effective October 1, 2015, 498 Mich. Amended effective March 9, 2016, 499 Mich. Amended September 20, 2017, effective May 1, 2018, 501 Mich; August 30, 2018, effective September 1, 2018, 502 Mich; March 20, 2019, effective May 1, 2019, 502 Mich.]

Comments

Staff Comment to 1994 Amendment

The October 26, 1993, amendment of MCR 3.101, effective April 1, 1994, makes a number of changes in the rule governing garnishment after judgment. In addition to changes in terminology and reorganization, the amendment makes significant adjustments in garnishment procedure, particularly regarding garnishments of periodic payments under 1991 PA 67.

The statute recognizes several levels of priority among garnishments and similar orders. Under subrule (B)(1)(c), the amendment clarifies that even if a higher priority writ or order is in effect, the lower priority one may nonetheless be given effect if the amount being withheld pursuant to the higher priority writ or order is less than the maximum that could be withheld by law.

As under the former rule, the State Court Administrator is to publish forms for use in garnishment proceedings. Under subrule (C) as amended, separate forms are to be used for periodic and nonperiodic garnishments.

Under the former rule, it was implicit that a writ of periodic garnishment had to be served within 91 days after it was issued, since that was the latest date that it could expire. The rule contained no provision for expiration of a nonperiodic writ. The amendment sets the same 91 days for nonperiodic garnishments, corresponding to the 91–day life of a summons. MCR 2.102(D). The writ form is to include the last day by which it must be served to be valid. See subrule (E)(2).

The amendment adjusts the time limits within which various actions must be taken. The garnishee is to serve a copy of the writ on the defendant within 7 days after the garnishee was served. Subrule (F)(2). The garnishee's disclosure must be filed and served within 14 days after the garnishee was served with the writ. Subrule (H). The defendant has 14 days after being served to file objections. Subrule (K)(1). Subrule (K) lists the grounds on which objections may be made, and provides that the objections may not be used as a challenge to the validity of the previously entered judgment. If objections are filed, within 7 days the court is to send notice of a date of hearing on the objections, with the hearing to be scheduled within 21 days of the date the objections were filed. Subrule (K)(3).

The amendment significantly modifies the former rule regarding the withholding of periodic payment of earnings, and as to payment by the garnishee to the court or the plaintiff. Under subrule (I)(2), withholding of earnings commences with the first full pay period after the writ was served as to garnishees with weekly, biweekly, or semimonthly pay periods. As to garnishees with monthly pay periods, if the writ is served within the first 14 days of a pay period, withholding commences on the date the writ is served. If service is after the 14th day of the pay period, withholding commences with the first full pay period after service. There are corresponding provisions regarding cessation of withholding in subrule (I)(3). As to weekly, biweekly, and semimonthly pay periods, withholding ceases at the end of the last full pay period before the expiration of the writ. As to monthly pay periods, withholding ceases at the expiration of the writ. Thus, the only circumstances in which a garnishee must compute the amount to be withheld for less than a full pay period is in the case of monthly pay periods.

Subrule (J) covers payment by the garnishee. Under the former rule, the garnishee had the option of sending withheld funds to the court or retaining them until receiving an order to pay. The amended rule requires the garnishee to hold the funds and, if not notified of objections to the garnishment within 28 days, to send the withheld amount to either the court or the plaintiff (or plaintiff's attorney) as specified in the writ. Under subrule (E)(3)(e), in issuing the writ, the court will include a direction as to whom payment is to be made. As to periodic garnishments, as successive payments become due, the garnishee is to make payment as directed by the writ. The garnishee would not be required to file an additional disclosure, but only to provide a statement with each payment including the information specified in subrule (I)(4), which is to be sent to the plaintiff and the defendant, and, if the funds are sent to the court, to the court as well. Within 14 days after the expiration of the writ, the garnishee is to file a final statement containing the information specified in subrule (J)(6).

In situations where the garnishee holds property belonging to the defendant, the garnishee is not to transfer the property until the court enters an order on motion by the plaintiff. If the plaintiff does not seek such an order within 56 days after filing of the disclosure, the garnishment is dissolved, and the garnishee may release the property. Subrule (J)(7).

Former MCR 3.101(S), regarding the procedure when the state is garnishee, is deleted by the amendment.

Staff Comment to 1997 Amendment

May 14, 1997, amendments [effective September 1, 1997] of the rules governing garnishment and installment payment orders are based on suggestions received from several sources following the major revisions of the garnishment rule effective April 1, 1994.

The amendment of MCR 3.101(A)(4) [effective September 1, 1997] modifies the definition of "periodic payments" in light of uncertainties caused by the current rule and the amendment of MCL 600.4012(4).

The amendment of MCR 3.101(K)(3) [effective September 1, 1997] requires the moving party, rather than the court, to send the notice of hearing on objections to garnishment in circuit and probate court actions.

The change in MCR 3.101(N) relates to installment payment orders under MCL 600.6201 et seq.

The remaining amendments to MCR 3.101 are technical corrections in terminology and cross references.

Staff Comment to May, 2009 Amendment

The amendments of MCR 3.101 add language to protect exempt funds from garnishment and require financial institutions to provide authority stating why certain funds are exempt.

Staff Comment to September, 2009 Amendment

The amendments of MCR 2.112 impose specific pleading requirements for a case that is a consumer debt action under the Michigan collection practices act, which will provide defendants with relevant information regarding the alleged debt. The amendments of MCR 3.101 require those who seek a garnishment to provide specific information regarding the interest and costs related to the judgment.

Staff Comment to 2012 Amendment

The amendments of MCR 3.101 are adopted to reflect recent statutory changes enacted in MCL 600.4012(1) in which the effective period for a periodic garnishment of wages, salary, and other earnings was extended from 91 days to 182 days. The amendments of MCR 3.101(B) and (E) change the effective period for *all* periodic garnishments to 182 days. (The amendments do not limit the 182–day effective period to periodic garnishments that only involve wages, salary, and other earnings.)

Staff Comment to 2013 Amendment

The Court retains the amendment of MCR 3.101, which extended the effective period for a writ of garnishment. This order further adopts a similar conforming amendment of MCR 3.101(F).

Staff Comment to 2015 Amendment

The amendments of MCR 3.101 eliminate subrule (B)(1)(a)(ii) and make other coordinating changes to reflect statutory revisions in 2015 PA 14 and 15.

Staff Comment to 2016 Amendment

These amendments update cross-references that changed after the rule was adopted and make other nonsubstantive revisions.

Staff Comment to 2017 Amendment

The amendments of MCR 2.625 and 3.101, submitted by the Michigan Creditor's Bar Association, address recent amendments of MCL 600.4012, clarify the authority and process for recovering postjudgment costs, and provide clearer procedure for garnishment proceedings.

Staff Comment to 2018 Amendment

These amendments update cross-references in the rules, and are intended to reflect changes that are necessary as a result of the Court's recent e-Filing rules amendments.

Staff Comment to 2019 Amendment

The amendments of Rules 1.109, 2.102, 2.104, 2.106, 2.107, 2.117, 2.119, 2.403, 2.503, 2.506, 2.508, 2.518, 2.602, 2.603, 2.621, 3.101, 3.104, 3.203, 3.205, 3.210, 3.302, 3.607, 3.613, 3.614, 3.705, 3.801, 3.802, 3.805, 3.806, 4.201, 4.202, 4.303, 4.306, 5.001, 5.104, 5.105, 5.107, 5.108, 5.113, 5.117, 5.118, 5.119, 5.120, 5.125, 5.132, 5.162, 5.202, 5.203, 5.205, 5.302, 5.304, 5.307, 5.308, 5.309, 5.310, 5.311, 5.313, 5.402, 5.404, 5.405, 5.409, 5.501, and 5.784 and addition of Rule 3.618 of the Michigan Court Rules are an expected progression necessary for design and implementation of the statewide electronic-filing system. These particular amendments will assist in implementing the goals of the project.

Rule 3.102   Garnishment Before Judgment

(A) Availability of Prejudgment Garnishment.

(1) After commencing an action on a contract, the plaintiff may obtain a prejudgment writ of garnishment under the circumstances and by the procedures provided in this rule.

(2) Except as provided in subrule (A)(3), a prejudgment garnishment may not be used

(a) unless the defendant is subject to the jurisdiction of the court under chapter 7 of the Revised Judicature Act, MCL 600.701 *et seq.*;

(b) to garnish a defendant's earnings; or

(c) to garnish property held or an obligation owed by the state or a governmental unit of the state.

(3) This rule also applies to a prejudgment garnishment in an action brought to enforce a foreign judgment. However, the following provisions apply:

(a) The defendant need not be subject to the court's jurisdiction;

(b) The request for garnishment must show that

(i) the defendant is indebted to the plaintiff on a foreign judgment in a stated amount in excess of all setoffs;

(ii) the defendant is not subject to the jurisdiction of the state, or that after diligent effort the plaintiff cannot serve the defendant with process; and

(iii) the person making the request knows or has good reason to believe that a named person

(A) has control of property belonging to the defendant, or

(B) is indebted to the defendant.

(c) Subrule (H) does not apply.

(B) Request for Garnishment. After commencing an action, the plaintiff may seek a writ of garnishment by filing an ex parte motion supported by a verified statement setting forth specific facts showing that:

(1) the defendant is indebted to the plaintiff on a contract in a stated amount in excess of all setoffs;

(2) the defendant is subject to the jurisdiction of the state;

(3) after diligent effort the plaintiff cannot serve the defendant with process; and

(4) the person signing the statement knows or has good reason to believe that a named person

(a) has control of property belonging to the defendant, or

(b) is indebted to the defendant.

On a finding that the writ is available under this rule and that the verified statement states a sufficient basis for issuance of the writ, the judge to whom the action is assigned may issue the writ.

(C) Writ of Garnishment. The writ of garnishment must have attached or include a copy of the verified statement, and must:

(1) direct the garnishee to:

(a) file with the court clerk within 14 days after the service of the writ on him or her a verified disclosure indicating his or her liability (as specified in subrule [E]) to the defendant;

(b) deliver no tangible or intangible property to the defendant, unless allowed by statute or court rule;

(c) pay no obligation to the defendant, unless allowed by statute or court rule; and

(d) promptly provide the defendant with a copy of the writ and verified statement by personal delivery or by first class mail directed to the defendant's last known address;

(2) direct the defendant to refrain from disposing of any negotiable instrument representing a debt of the garnishee or of any negotiable instrument of title representing property in which he or she claims an interest held in the possession or control of the garnishee;

(3) inform the defendant that unless the defendant files objections within 14 days after service of the writ on the defendant, or appears and submits to the jurisdiction of the court, an order may enter requiring the garnishee to deliver the garnished property or pay the obligation to be applied to the satisfaction of the plaintiff's claim; and

(4) command the process server to serve the writ and to file a proof of service.

(D) Service of Writ. MCR 3.101(F) applies to prejudgment garnishment.

(E) Liability of Garnishee. MCR 3.101(G) applies to prejudgment garnishment except that the earnings of the defendant may not be garnished before judgment.

(F) Disclosure. The garnishee shall file and serve a disclosure as provided in MCR 3.101(H).

(G) Payment or Deposit Into Court. MCR 3.101(I) and (J) apply to prejudgment garnishment, except that payment may not be made to the plaintiff until after entry of judgment, as provided in subrule (I).

(H) Objection; Dissolution of Prejudgment Garnishment. Objections to and dissolution of a prejudgment garnishment are governed by MCR 3.101(K) and MCR 3.103(H).

(I) Proceedings After Judgment.

(1) If the garnishment remains in effect until entry of judgment in favor of the plaintiff against the defendant, the garnished property or obligation may be applied to the satisfaction of the judgment in the manner provided in MCR 3.101(I), (J), (M), and (O).

(2) MCR 3.101(P) and (Q) and MCR 3.103(I)(2) apply to prejudgment garnishment.

(J) Costs and Fees; Default; Contempt; Judicial Discretion. MCR 3.101(R), (S), and (T) apply to prejudgment garnishment.

[Adopted effective March 1, 1985. Amended May 14, 1997, effective September 1, 1997, 454 Mich.]

Comments

Staff Comment to 1985 Adoption

MCR 3.102 contains the provisions of the garnishment rules regarding prejudgment garnishment procedure. Given the language of the Michigan prejudgment garnishment statute, MCL 600.4011(3), and the United States Supreme Court decision in *Shaffer v Heitner*, 433 U.S. 186, 97 S.Ct. 2569, 53 L.Ed.2d 683 (1977), prejudgment garnishment has a very limited role.

Subrules (A)(2)(b) and (c) prohibit prejudgment garnishment of the earnings of a defendant or of obligations owed by a governmental entity. See MCL 600.4011(4), (5).

Subrule (A)(3) modifies the rule as to "prejudgment" garnishment in an action brought on a foreign judgment. Such actions are not subject to the same jurisdictional problems as other prejudgment garnishments. See *Shaffer v Heitner*, supra, 433 U.S. 210–211, fn. 36.

In subrule (B)(2), the requirement that the defendant be subject to the jurisdiction of the state is added. See *Shaffer v Heitner*, supra. In addition, the judge, rather than the clerk, must issue the prejudgment writ of garnishment.

The provisions of subrule (C) regarding the writ of garnishment are virtually identical to the comparable provisions regarding a postjudgment writ of garnishment. See the note following MCR 3.101.

Most of the remainder of the rule makes various provisions of the postjudgment garnishment (MCR 3.101) and attachment (MCR 3.103) rules applicable to prejudgment garnishment procedure.

Staff Comment to 1997 Amendment

May 14, 1997, amendments [effective September 1, 1997] of the rules governing garnishment and installment payment orders are based on suggestions received from several sources following the major revisions of the garnishment rule effective April 1, 1994.

The amendments of MCR 3.102 are technical corrections in terminology and cross references.

Rule 3.103   Attachment

(A) Availability of Writ. After commencing an action, the plaintiff may obtain a writ of attachment under the circumstances and by the procedures provided in this rule. Except in an action brought on a foreign judgment, attachment may not be used unless the defendant is subject to the jurisdiction of the court under chapter 7 of the Revised Judicature Act. MCL 600.701 *et seq.*

(B) Motion for Writ.

(1) The plaintiff may seek a writ of attachment by filing an ex parte motion supported by an affidavit setting forth specific facts showing that

(a) at the time of the execution of the affidavit the defendant is indebted to the plaintiff in a stated amount on a contract in excess of all setoffs,

(b) the defendant is subject to the judicial jurisdiction of the state, and

(c) after diligent effort the plaintiff cannot serve the defendant with process.

In an action brought on a tort claim or a foreign judgment, subrules (B)(2) and (3), respectively, apply.

(2) In a tort action the following provisions apply:

(a) Instead of the allegations required by subrule (B)(1)(a), the affidavit in support of the motion must describe the injury claimed and state that the affiant in good faith believes that the defendant is liable to the plaintiff in a stated amount. The other requirements of subrule (B)(1) apply.

(b) If the writ is issued the court shall specify the amount or value of property to be attached.

(3) In an action brought on a foreign judgment, instead of the allegations required by subrule (B)(1), the affidavit in support of the motion must show that

(a) the defendant is indebted to the plaintiff on a foreign judgment in a stated amount in excess of all setoffs,

(b) the defendant is not subject to the jurisdiction of the state or that after diligent effort the plaintiff cannot serve the defendant with process.

(C) Issuance of Writ.

(1) On a finding that the writ is available under this rule and that the affidavit states a sufficient basis for issuance of the writ, the judge to whom the action is assigned may issue the writ.

(2) The judge's order shall specify what further steps, if any, must be taken by the plaintiff to notify the defendant of the action and the attachment.

(D) Contents of Writ. The writ of attachment must command the sheriff or other officer to whom it is directed

(1) to attach so much of the defendant's real and personal property not exempt from execution as is necessary to satisfy the plaintiff's demand and costs, and

(2) to keep the property in a secure place to satisfy any judgment that may be recovered by the plaintiff in the action until further order of the court.

(E) Execution of Writ; Subsequent Attachments.

(1) The sheriff or other officer to whom a writ of attachment is directed shall execute the writ by seizing and holding so much of the defendant's property not exempt from execution, wherever found within the county, as is necessary to satisfy the plaintiff's demand and costs. If insufficient property is seized, then the officer shall seize other property of the defendant not exempt from execution, wherever found within Michigan, as is necessary when added to that already seized, to satisfy the plaintiff's demand and costs. The property seized must be inventoried by the officer and appraised by two disinterested residents of the county in which the property was seized. After being sworn under oath to make a true appraisal, the apprais-

ers shall make and sign an appraisal. The inventory and appraisal must be filed and a copy served on the parties under MCR 2.107.

(2) In subsequent attachments of the same property while in the hands of the officer, the original inventory and appraisal satisfy the requirement of subrule (E)(1).

(F) Attachment of Realty; Stock.

(1) The officer may seize an interest in real estate by depositing a certified copy of the writ of attachment, including a description of the land affected, with the register of deeds for the county in which the land is located. It is not necessary that the officer enter on the land or be within view of it.

(2) Shares of stock or the interest of a stockholder in a domestic corporation must be seized in the manner provided for the seizure of that property on execution.

(G) Animals or Perishable Property; Sale; Distribution of Proceeds.

(1) When any of the property attached consists of animals or perishable property, the court may order the property sold and the money from the sale brought into court, to await the order of the court.

(2) After the order for a sale is entered, the officer having the property shall advertise and sell it in the manner that personal property of like character is required to be advertised and sold on execution. The officer shall deposit the proceeds with the clerk of the court in which the action is pending.

(3) If the plaintiff recovers judgment, the court may order the money paid to the plaintiff. If the judgment is entered against the plaintiff or the suit is dismissed or the attachment is dissolved, the court shall order the money paid to the defendant or other person entitled to it.

(H) Dissolution of Attachment.

(1) Except in an action brought on a foreign judgment, if the defendant submits to the jurisdiction of the court, the court shall dissolve the attachment.

(2) A person who owns, possesses, or has an interest in attached property may move at any time to dissolve the attachment. The defendant may move to dissolve the attachment without submitting to the jurisdiction of the court.

(a) When a motion for dissolution of attachment is filed, the court shall enter an order setting a time and place for hearing the motion, and may issue subpoenas to compel witnesses to attend.

(b) The plaintiff must be served with notice under MCR 2.107 at least 3 days before the hearing unless the court's order prescribes a different notice requirement.

(c) At the hearing, the proofs are heard in the same manner as in a nonjury trial. If the court decides that the defendant was not subject to the jurisdiction of the state or that the property was not subject to or was exempt from attachment, it shall dissolve the attachment and restore the property to the defendant, and the attachment may be dissolved for any other sufficient reason. The court may order the losing party to pay the costs of the dissolution proceeding.

(3) If the action is dismissed or judgment is entered for the defendant, the attachment is dissolved.

(I) Satisfaction of Judgment.

(1) If the attachment remains in effect until the entry of judgment against the defendant, the attached property may be applied to the satisfaction of the judgment, including interest and costs, in the same manner as in the case of an execution.

(2) If the court does not acquire personal jurisdiction over the defendant, either by service or by the defendant's appearance, a judgment against the defendant is not binding beyond the value of the attached property.

[Adopted effective March 1, 1985.]

Comments

Staff Comment to 1985 Adoption

MCR 3.103 covers attachment, and corresponds to GCR 1963, 735. The changes in this rule are similar to those in the prejudgment garnishment provisions. The attachment statute, MCL 600.4001, and United States Supreme Court decisions have similarly limited the availability of attachment.

Subrule (B) is changed to require that the defendant be subject to the jurisdiction of the state, and to require the judge, rather than the clerk, to issue the writ. However, this jurisdictional requirement does not apply in an action brought on a foreign judgment.

Subrule (B)(2) covers special requirements regarding tort actions, in which the amount of damages are likely to be uncertain. Compare GCR 1963, 735.4.

One of the conditions for the issuance of the writ is that the plaintiff had exercised diligent efforts to serve the defendant. Subrule (B)(1)(c). Accordingly, rather than simply requiring that the writ be served on the defendant (see GCR 1963, 735.7[1]), subrule (B)(5) requires the judge to specify what further steps must be taken to notify the defendant of the action and the application. Similarly, in subrules (D) and (E), as in subrule (B)(5), service requirements are omitted, since the very issuance of the writ depends on a showing that the defendant cannot be served.

The provisions of GCR 1963, 735.10, 735.11, and 735.12 are deleted.

Subrule (H) differs from the corresponding provision (GCR 1963, 735.13) in several respects. Subrule (H)(1) dissolves the attachment if the defendant submits to jurisdiction. Under subrule (H)(2) the defendant may move to dissolve the attachment without submitting to the court's jurisdiction. Subrule (H)(3) makes clear that the attachment is dissolved if the action is dismissed or judgment is entered for the defendant.

Subrule (I) is new and contains provisions consistent with the attachment statute regarding satisfaction of a judgment against the defendant.

Rule 3.104   Installment Payment Orders

(A) Motion for Installment Payment Order. A party against whom a money judgment has been entered may move for entry of an order permitting the judgment to be paid in installments in accordance with MCL 600.6201 *et seq.* A copy of the motion must be served on the plaintiff by the party who filed the objection.

(B) Consideration of Motion. The motion will be granted without further hearing unless the plaintiff files, and serves on the defendant, written objections within 14 days after the service date of the defendant's motion. If objections are filed, the clerk must promptly present the motion and objections to the court. The court will decide the motion based on the documents filed or notify the parties that a hearing will be required. Unless the court schedules the hearing, the moving party is responsible for noticing the motion for hearing.

(C) Failure to Comply with Installment Order. If the defendant fails to make payments pursuant to the order for installment payments, the plaintiff may file and serve on the defendant a motion to set aside the order for installment payments. Unless a hearing is requested within 14 days after service of the motion, the order to set aside the order for installment payments will be entered.

(D) Request After Failure to Comply with Previous Order. If the defendant moves for an order for installment payments within 91 days after a previous installment order has been set aside, unless good cause is shown the court shall assess costs against the defendant as a condition of entry of the new order.

[Adopted effective March 1, 1985. Amended May 14, 1997, effective September 1, 1997, 454 Mich; March 20, 2019, effective May 1, 2019, 502 Mich.]

Comments

Staff Comment to 1985 Adoption

MCR 3.104 corresponds to GCR 1963, 523. Most of the substantive provisions are omitted and replaced with a reference to the statutory procedures for installment judgments.

Staff Comment to 1997 Amendment

May 14, 1997, amendments [effective September 1, 1997] of the rules governing garnishment and installment payment orders are based on suggestions received from several sources following the major revisions of the garnishment rule effective April 1, 1994.

The changes in MCR 3.104 relate to installment payment orders under MCL 600.6201 et seq.; MSA 27A.6201 et seq.

Staff Comment to 2019 Amendment

The amendments of Rules 1.109, 2.102, 2.104, 2.106, 2.107, 2.117, 2.119, 2.403, 2.503, 2.506, 2.508, 2.518, 2.602, 2.603, 2.621, 3.101, 3.104, 3.203, 3.205, 3.210, 3.302, 3.607, 3.613, 3.614, 3.705, 3.801, 3.802, 3.805, 3.806, 4.201, 4.202, 4.303, 4.306, 5.001, 5.104, 5.105, 5.107, 5.108, 5.113, 5.117, 5.118, 5.119, 5.120, 5.125, 5.126, 5.132, 5.162, 5.202, 5.203, 5.205, 5.302, 5.304, 5.307, 5.308, 5.309, 5.310, 5.311, 5.313, 5.402, 5.404, 5.405, 5.409, 5.501, and 5.784 and addition of Rule 3.618 of the Michigan Court Rules are an expected progression necessary for design and implementation of the statewide electronic-filing system. These particular amendments will assist in implementing the goals of the project.

Rule 3.105   Claim and Delivery

(A) Nature of Action; Replevin. Claim and delivery is a civil action to recover

(1) possession of goods or chattels which have been unlawfully taken or unlawfully detained, and

(2) damages sustained by the unlawful taking or unlawful detention.

A statutory reference to the action of replevin is to be construed as a reference to the action of claim and delivery.

(B) Rules Applicable. A claim and delivery action is governed by the rules applicable to other civil actions, except as provided in MCL 600.2920, and this rule.

(C) Complaint; Joinder of Claims; Interim Payments. A claim and delivery complaint must:

(1) specifically describe the property claimed;

(2) state the value of the property claimed (which will be used only to set the amount of bond and not as an admission of value);

(3) state if the property claimed is an independent piece of property or a portion of divisible property of uniform kind, quality, and value; and

(4) specifically describe the nature of the claim and the basis for the judgment requested.

If the action is based on a security agreement, a claim for the debt may be joined as a separate count in the complaint. If the plaintiff, while the action is pending, receives interim payments equal to the amount originally claimed, the action must be dismissed.

(D) Answer. An answer to a claim and delivery complaint may concede the claim for possession and yet contest any other claim.

(E) Possession Pending Final Judgment.

(1) *Motion for Possession Pending Final Judgment.* After the complaint is filed, the plaintiff may file a verified motion requesting possession pending final judgment. The motion must

(a) describe the property to be seized, and

(b) state sufficient facts to show that the property described will be damaged, destroyed, concealed, disposed of, or used so as to substantially impair its value, before final judgment unless the property is taken into custody by court order.

(2) *Court Order Pending Hearing.* After a motion for possession pending final judgment is filed, the court, if good cause is shown, must order the defendant to

(a) refrain from damaging, destroying, concealing, disposing of, or using so as to substantially impair its value, the property until further order of the court; and

(b) appear before the court at a specified time to answer the motion.

(3) *Hearing on Motion for Possession Pending Final Judgment.*

(a) At least 7 days before a hearing on a motion filed under this subrule, the defendant must be served with

(i) a copy of the motion; and

(ii) an order entered under subrule (E)(2).

(b) At the hearing, each party may present proofs. To obtain possession before judgment, the plaintiff must establish

(i) that the plaintiff's right to possession is probably valid; and

(ii) that the property will be damaged, destroyed, concealed, disposed of, or used so as to substantially impair its value, before trial.

(c) Adjournment. A court may not

(i) grant an adjournment of this hearing on the basis that a defendant has not yet answered the complaint or the motion filed under this subrule; or

(ii) allow a hearing on this motion if the hearing date has been adjourned more than 56 days with the assent of the plaintiff, unless the plaintiff files a new motion which includes recitations of any payments made by the defendant after the original motion was filed.

(4) *Order for Custody Pending Final Judgment.* After proofs have been taken on the plaintiff's motion for possession pending final judgment, the court may order whatever relief the evidence requires. This includes:

(a) denying the motion;

(b) leaving the defendant in possession of the property and restraining the defendant from damaging, destroying, concealing, or disposing of the property. The court may condition the defendant's continued possession by requiring the defendant to

(i) furnish a penalty bond, payable to the plaintiff, of not less than $100 and at least twice the value of the property stated in the complaint; and

(ii) agree that he or she will surrender the property to the person adjudged entitled to possession and will pay any money that may be recovered against him or her in the action;

(c) ordering the sheriff or court officer to seize the property within 21 days and either hold it or deliver it to the plaintiff. The court may condition the plaintiff's possession by requiring the plaintiff to

(i) furnish a penalty bond payable to the defendant, and to the sheriff or court officer, of not less than $100 and at least twice the value of the property stated in the complaint; and

(ii) agree that he or she will surrender the property to the person adjudged entitled to possession, diligently prosecute the suit to final judgment, and pay any money that may be recovered against him or her in the action.

A bond required in a claim and delivery action must be approved by and filed with the court within the time the order provides.

(F) Seizure. A copy of an order issued under subrule (E)(4)(c) must be delivered to the sheriff or court officer, who must

(1) seize the property described in the order;

(2) serve a copy of the order on the defendant, under MCR 2.107; and

(3) file a return with the court showing seizure and service.

(G) Custody; Delivery. After seizing the property, the sheriff or court officer shall keep it in a secure place and deliver it in accordance with the court order. The sheriff or court officer is entitled to receive the lawful fees for seizing the property and the necessary expenses for seizing and keeping it.

(H) Judgment.

(1) The judgment must determine

(a) the party entitled to possession of the property,

(b) the value of the property,

(c) the amount of any unpaid debt, and

(d) any damages to be awarded.

(2) If the property is not in the possession of the party who is entitled to possession, a judgment must order the property to be immediately delivered to that party.

(3) If the action is tried on the merits, the value of the property and the damages are determined by the trier of fact.

(4) If the defendant has been deprived of the property by a prejudgment order and the main action is dismissed, the defendant may apply to the court for default judgment under MCR 2.603.

(5) If the plaintiff takes a default judgment, the value of the property and the damages are determined under MCR 2.603. A defendant who appeared at a show-cause proceeding is deemed to have filed an appearance.

(6) The party adjudged entitled to possession of the property described may elect to take judgment for the value of the property instead of possession. The judgment value may not exceed the unpaid debt, if any, secured by such property.

(7) The liability of a surety on a bond given under this rule may be determined on motion under MCR 3.604.

(I) Costs. Costs may be taxed in the discretion of the court. Costs may include the cost of a bond required by the court, and the costs of seizing and keeping the property.

(J) Execution.

(1) The execution issued on a judgment in a claim and delivery action must command the sheriff or court officer

(a) to levy the prevailing party's damages and costs on the property of the opposite party, as in other executions against property; and

(b) if the property described in the judgment is found in the possession of the defendant, to seize the property described in the judgment and deliver it to the prevailing party; or, if the property is not found in the possession of the defendant, to levy the value of it. The value may not exceed the total of the unpaid debt, costs, and damages.

(2) Execution may not issue on a judgment in a claim and delivery action if more than 28 days have passed from the signing of the judgment, unless

(a) the plaintiff files a motion for execution which must include, if money has been paid on the judgment, the amount paid and the conditions under which it was accepted; and

(b) a hearing is held after the defendant has been given notice and an opportunity to appear.

[Adopted effective March 1, 1985.]

Comments

Staff Comment to 1985 Adoption

MCR 3.105 is substantially the same as GCR 1963, 757.

Rule 3.106. Procedures Regarding Orders for the Seizure of Property and Orders of Eviction

(A) Scope of Rule. This rule applies to orders for the seizure of property and orders of eviction.

(B) Persons Who May Seize Property or Conduct Evictions. The persons who may seize property or conduct evictions are those persons named in MCR 2.103(B), and they are subject to the provisions of this rule unless a provision or a statute specifies otherwise.

(1) A court may provide that property shall be seized and evictions conducted only by

(a) court officers and bailiffs serving that court;

(b) sheriffs and deputy sheriffs;

(c) officers of the Department of State Police in an action in which the state is a party; and

(d) police officers of an incorporated city or village in an action in which the city or village is a party.

(2) Each court must post, in a public place at the court, a list of those persons who are serving as court officers or bailiffs. The court must provide the State Court Administrative Office with a copy of the list and a copy of each court officer's bond required under subsection (D)(1), and must notify the State Court Administrative Office of any changes.

(C) Appointment of Court Officers. Court officers may be appointed by a court for a term not to exceed 2 years.

(1) The appointment shall be made by the chief judge. Two or more chief judges may jointly appoint court officers for their respective courts.

(2) The appointing court must specify the nature of the court officer's employment relationship at the time of appointment.

(3) The appointing court must maintain a copy of each court officer's application, as required by the State Court Administrative Office.

(4) The State Court Administrative Office shall develop a procedure for the appointment and supervision of court officers, including a model application form. Considerations shall include, but are not limited to, an applicant's character, experience, and references.

(D) Conditions of Service as a Court Officer or Bailiff. Court officers and bailiffs must

(1) post a surety bond pursuant to MCR 8.204;

(2) provide the names and addresses of all financial institutions in which they deposit funds obtained under this rule, and the respective account numbers; and

(3) provide the names and addresses of those persons who regularly provide services to them in the seizure of property or evictions.

(E) Forms. The State Court Administrative Office shall publish forms approved for use with regard to the procedures described in this rule.

(F) Procedures Generally.

(1) All persons specified in MCR 2.103(B) must carry and display identification authorized by the court or the agency that they serve.

(2) A copy of the order for seizure of property or eviction shall be served on the defendant or the defendant's agent, or left or posted on the premises in a conspicuous place. If property is seized from any other location, a copy of the order shall be mailed to the defendant's last known address.

(G) Procedures Regarding Orders for Seizure of Property.

(1) Orders for seizure of property shall be issued pursuant to statute and endorsed upon receipt.

(2) No funds may be collected pursuant to an order for seizure of property prior to service under subrule (F)(2).

(3) An inventory and receipt shall be prepared upon seizure of property or payment of funds.

(a) The original shall be filed with the court within 7 days of the seizure or payment.

(b) A copy shall be

(i) provided to the parties or their respective attorneys or agents and posted on the premises in a conspicuous place; if the property is seized from any other location, a copy shall be mailed to the nonprevailing party's last known address, and

(ii) retained by the person who seized the property.

(4) Property seized shall be disposed of according to law.

(5) Within 21 days, and as directed by the court, any money that is received shall be paid to the court or deposited in a trust account for payment to the prevailing party or that party's attorney.

(6) Costs allowed by statute shall be paid according to law.

(a) Copies of all bills and receipts for service shall be retained for one year by the person serving the order.

(b) Statutory collection fees shall be paid in proportion to the amount received.

(c) There shall be no payment except as provided by law.

(7) Within 14 days after the expiration of the order or satisfaction of judgment, whichever is first, the following shall be filed with the court and a copy provided to the prevailing party or that party's attorney:

(a) a report summarizing collection activities, including an accounting of all money or property collected,

(b) a report that collection activities will continue pursuant to statute, if applicable, or

(c) a report that no collection activity occurred.

(H) Procedures Regarding Orders of Eviction. Copies of all bills and receipts for services shall be retained by the person serving the order for one year.

[Adopted September 12, 2001, effective May 1, 2002, 465 Mich. Amended September 18, 2019, effective January 1, 2020, 503 Mich.]

Comments

Staff Comment to 2002 Adoption

The September 12, 2001 addition of MCR 3.106, effective May 1, 2002, was recommended by an ad hoc committee of judges, court administrators, court clerks, attorneys, and court officers. The rule incorporated existing practice while protecting against abuses. The September 12, 2001 amendments of MCR 4.201 and 4.202, effective May 1, 2002, made changes consistent with new MCR 3.106.

Staff Comment to 2020 Amendment

The amendment of MCR 3.106 requires trial courts to provide a copy of each court officer's bond to SCAO along with the list of court officers.

Rule 3.110 Stockholders' Liability Proceedings

(A) Scope of Rule. This rule applies to actions brought under MCL 600.2909.

(B) When Action May Be Brought. An action against stockholders in which it is claimed that they are individually liable for debts of a corporation may not be brought until:

(1) a judgment has been recovered against the corporation for the indebtedness;

(2) an execution on the judgment has been issued to the county in which the corporation has its principal office or carries on its business; and

(3) the execution has been returned unsatisfied in whole or in part.

(C) Order for List of Stockholders. When the conditions set out in subrule (B) are met, the plaintiff may apply to the court that entered the judgment to order a list of stockholders. The court shall enter an order to be served on the secretary or other proper officer of the corporation, requiring the officer, within the time provided in the order, to file a statement under oath listing the names and addresses of all persons who appear by the corporation books to have been, or who the officer has reason to believe were, stockholders when the debt accrued, and the amount of stock held by each of them.

(D) Commencement of Action; Complaint. An action against the stockholders to impose personal liability on them for the debt of the corporation may be commenced and carried on as other civil actions under these rules. The complaint must, among other things, state:

(1) that the plaintiff has obtained a judgment against the corporation and the amount;

(2) that execution has been issued and returned unsatisfied in whole or in part, and the amount remaining unpaid;

(3) that the persons named as defendants are the persons listed in the statement filed by the officer of the corporation under subrule (C);

(4) the amount of stock held by each defendant, or that the plaintiff could not, with reasonable diligence, ascertain the amounts;

(5) the consideration received by the corporation for the debt on which judgment was rendered;

(6) a request for judgment against the stockholders in favor of the plaintiff for the amount alleged to be due from the corporation.

(E) Judgment Against Corporation as Evidence. At the trial the judgment against the corporation and the amount remaining unpaid are prima facie evidence of the amount due to the plaintiff but are not evidence that the debt on which the judgment was rendered is one for which the defendants are personally liable.

(F) Entry of Judgment Against Defendant. If a defendant admits the facts set forth in the complaint or defaults by failing to answer, or if the issues are determined against the defendant, judgment may be entered against him or her for the amount of the judgment against the corporation remaining unpaid, on proof that the debt is one for which that defendant is personally liable as a stockholder.

(G) Order of Apportionment; Execution. After judgment has been entered against all or some of the defendants, the court may apportion among these defendants the sum for which they have been adjudged liable pro rata according to the stock held by each. If any defendant fails to pay the amount apportioned against that defendant within 21 days, execution may issue as in other civil actions.

(H) Reapportionment. If execution is returned unsatisfied in whole or in part against any of the defendants as to whom apportionment has been made, the court has the power and the duty on application by the plaintiff to reapportion the sum remaining uncollected on the basis of subrule (G) among the remaining defendants adjudged liable. Execution may issue for the collection of these amounts.

(I) Contribution Among Stockholders. A stockholder who has been compelled to pay more than his or her pro rata share of the debts of the corporation, according to the amount of stock held, is entitled to contribution from other stockholders who are also liable for the debt and who have not paid their portions.

[Adopted effective March 1, 1985.]

Comments

Staff Comment to 1985 Adoption

MCR 3.110 is comparable to GCR 1963, 775.

Subrule (A) is modified to limit the application of the rule to actions under MCL 600.2909.

The language of present GCR 1963, 775.1, creating an exception for labor claims, is deleted because of the repeal of the statute on which that provision was based. See former MCL 600.2908.

SUBCHAPTER 3.200 DOMESTIC RELATIONS ACTIONS

Rule 3.201. Applicability of Rules

(A) Subchapter 3.200 Applies To:

(1) actions for divorce, separate maintenance, the annulment of marriage, the affirmation of marriage, paternity, support under MCL 552.451 *et seq.*, or MCL 722.1 *et seq.*, the custody of minors or parenting time under MCL 722.21 *et seq.* or MCL 722.1101 *et seq.*

(2) an expedited proceeding to determine paternity or child support under MCL 722.1491 *et seq.*, or to register a foreign judgment or order under MCL 552.2101 *et seq.* or MCL 722.1101 *et seq.*, and to

(3) proceedings that are ancillary or subsequent to the actions listed in subrules (A)(1) and (A)(2) and that relate to

(a) the custody of minors,

(b) parenting time with minors, or

(c) the support of minors and spouses or former spouses.

(B) As used in this subchapter with regard to child support, the terms "minor" or "child" may include children who have reached the age of majority, in the circumstances where the legislature has so provided.

(C) Except as otherwise provided in this subchapter, practice and procedure in domestic relations actions is governed by other applicable provisions of the Michigan Court Rules, except the number of interrogatories set forth in MCR 2.309(A)(2) shall be thirty-five.

(D) When used in this subchapter, unless the context otherwise indicates:

(1) "Case" means an action commenced in the family division of the circuit court by filing one of the following case initiating documents:

(a) an original complaint;

(b) transfer of an action from another court or tribunal;

(c) a foreign judgment or order;

(d) a petition under MCR 3.222(C);

(e) filing a consent judgment under MCR 3.223;

(f) a complaint and notice under MCR 3.230; or

(g) a request for entry of a consent agreement and a consent judgment or order under MCR 3.230.

(2) "File" means the repository for collection of the pleadings and other documents and materials related to a case. A file may include more than one case involving a family.

(3) "Jurisdiction" means the authority of the court to hear cases and make decisions and enter orders on cases.

(4) "Case initiating document" includes a statement, letter, or other document filed in lieu of a complaint to open a case and request relief under the Summary Support and Paternity Act, MCL 722.1491 *et seq.*, or to register a foreign judgment or order under the Uniform Interstate Family Support Act, MCL 552.2101 *et seq.* or the Uniform Child Custody Jurisdiction Enforcement Act, MCL 722.1101 *et seq.*

[Adopted January 28, 1993, effective May 1, 1993, 441 Mich. Amended August 11, 1997, effective September 1, 1997, 456 Mich; September 11, 2002, effective January 1, 2003, 467 Mich; September 20, 2018, effective April 1, 2019, 502 Mich; June 19, 2019, effective January 1, 2020, 503 Mich; September 18, 2019, effective January 1, 2020, 503 Mich.]

Comments

Staff Comment to 1993 Adoption

The revised rule [effective May 1, 1993] is similar to former Rule 3.201. The major difference is that the revised rule makes specific mention of additional types of domestic relations actions, such as paternity, injunctive relief under MCL 600.2950, family support under MCL 552.451 *et seq.*, the custody of minors under MCL 722.21 *et seq.*, and visitation with minors under MCL 722.27b.

Staff Comment to 1997 Amendment

The amendment of MCR 3.201 is designed to implement the statutes providing for the issuance of personal protection orders. See MCL 600.2950, MCL 600.2950a.

Staff Comment to 2002 Amendment

The September 11, 2002, amendments of MCR 3.201 and 3.204, effective January 1, 2003, are based on proposals by the Family Division Joint Rules Committee. New MCR 3.201(D) defines several terms, and new MCR 3.204(D) states the authority of the court to appoint a guardian ad litem for a minor child in a case in which child custody is disputed.

Staff Comment to 2019 Amendment

The amendments of MCR 3.201, 3.210, and 3.211 and addition of MCR 3.222 and 3.223 integrate the collaborative law process designed under the Uniform Collaborative Law Act (159 PA 2014; MCL 691.1331–691.1354) into the state's trial court system for practical use, and add a similar process for parties not represented by counsel who seek to submit a consent judgment.

Staff Comment to First January, 2020 Amendment

These amendments are based on a proposal created by a special committee of the State Bar of Michigan and approved for submission to the Court by the Bar's Representative Assembly. The rules require mandatory discovery disclosure in many cases, adopt a presumptive limit on interrogatories (20 in most cases, but 35 in domestic relations proceedings) and limit a deposition to 7 hours. The amendments also update the rules to more specifically address issues related to electronically stored information, and encourage early action on discovery issues during the discovery period.

The amendment of MCR 2.309(A)(2) sets a presumptive limit of twenty interrogatories for each separately represented party. Several commenters suggested that the term "discrete subpart" be more explicitly defined. But the rule's reference to "a discrete subpart" is intended to draw guidance from federal courts construing FR Civ P 30(a)(1). Generally, subparts are not separately counted if they are logically or factually subsumed within and necessarily related to the primary question. In upholding the limit, parties and courts should also pragmatically balance the overall goals of discovery and the admonition of MCR 1.105. Further, the intent of the provision at MCR 2.301(B)(4) is to ensure that parties responding to discovery requests have the full time period to do so as provided for under these rules prior to the expiration of the discovery period.

Staff Comment to Second January, 2020 Amendment

The amendment of MCR 3.201 and addition of MCR 3.230 provides procedural rules to incorporate the Summary Support and Paternity Act (366 PA 2014; MCL 722.1491, *et seq.*) to establish a parent's paternity or support obligation through a summary action.

Rule 3.202 Capacity to Sue

(A) Minors and Incompetent Persons. Except as provided in subrule (B), minors and incompetent persons may sue and be sued as provided in MCR 2.201.

(B) Emancipated Minors. An emancipated minor may sue and be sued in the minor's own name, as provided in MCL 722.4e(1)(b).

[Adopted January 28, 1993, effective May 1, 1993, 441 Mich.]

Comments

Staff Comment to 1993 Adoption

The revised rule [effective May 1, 1993] is similar to former Rule 3.202.

Rule 3.203. Service of Notice and Court Documents in Domestic Relations Cases

(A) Manner of Service. Unless otherwise required by court rule or statute, the summons and complaint must be served pursuant to MCR 2.105. In cases in which the court retains jurisdiction

(1) notice must be provided as set forth in the statute requiring the notice. Unless otherwise required by court rule or statute, service by mail shall be to a party's last known mailing address, and

(2) court documents and notice for which the statute or court rule does not specify the manner of service must be served as provided in MCR 2.107, except that service by mail shall be to a party's last known mailing address.

(3) *Alternative Electronic Service.* A party or an attorney may file an agreement with the friend of the court to authorize the friend of the court to serve notices and court papers on the party or attorney in accordance with MCR 2.107(C)(4).

(B) Place of Service; After Entry of Judgment or Order. When a domestic relations judgment or order requires the parties to inform the friend of the court office of any changes in their mailing address, a party's last known mailing address means the most recent address

(1) that the party provided in writing to the friend of the court office, or

(2) set forth in the most recent judgment or order entered in the case, or

(3) the address established by the friend of the court office pursuant to subrule (D).

(C) Place of Service; Before Entry of Judgment or Order. After a summons and complaint has been filed and served on a party, but before entry of a judgment or order that requires the parties to inform the friend of the court of any changes in their mailing address, the last known mailing address is the most recent address

(1) set forth in the pleadings, or

(2) that a party provides in writing to the friend of the court office.

(D) Administrative Change of Address. The friend of the court office may change a party's address administratively pursuant to the policy established by the state court administrator for that purpose when:

(1) a party's address changes in another friend of the court office pursuant to these rules, or

(2) notices and court documents are returned to the friend of the court office as undeliverable or the friend of the court determines that a federal automated database has determined that mail is not deliverable to the party's listed address.

(E) Service on Nonparties. Notice to a nonparty must be provided as set forth in the statute requiring the notice. Absent statutory direction, the notice may be provided by regular mail. Absent statutory direction, court documents initiating an action against nonparties to enforce a notice must be served in the same manner as a summons and complaint pursuant to MCR 2.105.

(F) Confidential Addresses. When a court order makes a party's address confidential, the party shall provide an alternative address for service of notice and court documents.

(G) Notice to Friend of the Court. Except where electronic filing is implemented, if a child of the parties or a child born during the marriage is under the age of 18, or if a party is pregnant, or if child support or spousal support is requested, the parties must provide the friend of the court with a copy of all pleadings and other documents filed in the action. The copy must be marked "friend of the court" and submitted to the court clerk at the time of filing. The court clerk must send the copy to the friend of the court. Where electronic filing is implemented, the court and the friend of the court shall determine the manner in which the court will make pleadings and other documents filed in the action available to the friend of the court. The court and friend of the court shall not require the parties to provide paper copies of electronically filed pleadings.

(H) Notice to Prosecuting Attorney. In an action for divorce or separate maintenance in which a child of the parties or a child born during the marriage is under the age of 18, or if a party is pregnant, the plaintiff must serve a copy of the summons and complaint on the prosecuting attorney when required by law.

(I) Notice to Attorneys.

(1) Copies of notices required to be given to the parties also must be sent to the attorneys of record.

(2) The notice requirement of this subrule remains in effect until 21 days after judgment is entered or until postjudgment matters are concluded, whichever is later.

(J) Service of Informational Pamphlet. If a child of the parties or a child born during the marriage is under the age of 18, or if a party is pregnant, or if child support or spousal support is requested, the plaintiff must serve with the complaint a copy of the friend of the court informational pamphlet required by MCL 552.505(1)(c). The proof of service must state that service of the informational pamphlet has been made.

[Adopted January 28, 1993, effective May 1, 1993, 441 Mich. Amended July 22, 2003, effective January 1, 2004, 469 Mich; June 21, 2017 effective September 1, 2017, 500 Mich. Amended effective March 21, 2018, 501 Mich. Amended August 30, 2018, effective September 1, 2018, 502 Mich; March 20, 2019, effective May 1, 2019, 502 Mich. Amended effective August 14, 2019, 503 Mich.]

Comments

Staff Comment to 1993 Adoption

Former Rule 3.203 has been revised substantially [effective May 1, 1993]. Parts of former subrule 3.203(C) have been moved to Rule 3.207. The provision that governs service on the prosecuting attorney has been changed to require submittal of a designated copy of pleadings and other papers at the time of filing. To insure that litigants receive the friend of the court informational pamphlet, a subrule has been added to require proof of service of the pamphlet.

Staff Comment to 2003 Amendment

The July 22, 2003, amendment of MCR 3.203, effective January 1, 2004 clarified how notice required by statute or court rule is to be provided when the statute or court rule does not specify.

Staff Comment to 2017 Amendment

The amendments of MCR 3.203 allow the friend of the court to use automated databases such as the United States Postal Services' National Change of Address database to identify outdated addresses and update them to correct addresses. The amendments allow a party or a party's attorney to agree to receive notices and other court papers from the friend of the court electronically. The amendments move the requirement to provide notices to attorneys of record from MCR 3.208.

Staff Comment to March, 2018 Amendment

These amendments update cross-references and make other nonsubstantive revisions to clarify the rules. The amendment of MCR 6.110(B)(1) addresses an inadvertent omission from the last amendment of this rule that was intended to be shown in overstrike. Accordingly, the current rule does not match the published version. Striking the clause "for good cause shown" will provide consistency with other published versions of the rule and with the statute, MCL 766.7, which allows a magistrate to adjourn a preliminary examination with the consent of the parties without the need for good cause to be shown.

Staff Comment to September, 2018 Amendment

These amendments update cross-references in the rules, and are intended to reflect changes that are necessary as a result of the Court's recent e-Filing rules amendments.

Staff Comment to May, 2019 Amendment

The amendments of Rules 1.109, 2.102, 2.104, 2.106, 2.107, 2.117, 2.119, 2.403, 2.503, 2.506, 2.508, 2.518, 2.602, 2.603, 2.621, 3.101, 3.104, 3.203, 3.205, 3.210, 3.302, 3.607, 3.613, 3.614, 3.705, 3.801, 3.802, 3.805, 3.806, 4.201, 4.202, 4.303, 4.306, 5.001, 5.104, 5.105, 5.107, 5.108, 5.113, 5.117, 5.118, 5.119, 5.120, 5.125, 5.126, 5.132, 5.162, 5.202, 5.203, 5.205, 5.302, 5.304, 5.307, 5.308, 5.309, 5.310, 5.311, 5.313, 5.402, 5.404, 5.405, 5.409, 5.501, and 5.784 and addition of Rule 3.618 of the Michigan Court Rules are an expected progression necessary for design and implementation of the statewide electronic-filing system. These particular amendments will assist in implementing the goals of the project.

Staff Comment to August, 2019 Amendment

These amendments update cross-references and make other nonsubstantive revisions to clarify the rules.

Rule 3.204   Proceedings Affecting Children

(A) Unless the court orders otherwise for good cause, if a circuit court action involving child support, custody, or parenting time is pending, or if the circuit court has continuing jurisdiction over such matters because of a prior action:

(1) A new action concerning support, custody or parenting time of the same child must be filed as a motion in the earlier action if the relief sought would have been available in the original cause of action. If the relief sought was not available in the original action, the new action must be filed as a new complaint.

(2) A new action for the support, custody, or parenting time of a different child of the same parents must be filed in the same county as the prior action if the circuit court for that county has jurisdiction over the new action and the new case must be assigned to the same judge to whom the previous action was assigned.

(3) Whenever possible, all actions involving the custody, parenting time, and support of children of the same parents shall be administered together. Unless the court finds that good cause exists not to do so, when the court enters a final order in a new action involving a new child of those parents, the order shall consolidate the provisions for custody, parenting time, and support for both that child and any children named in previous actions over which the court has jurisdiction involving the same parents. The order must reference the other cases and state that it supersedes the custody, parenting time, and

support provisions of the orders entered previously in those cases. In the new action, the court may modify custody, parenting time, and support provisions in preexisting orders involving another child or children of the same parents, provided that the modification is supported by evidence presented in the new case and both parents have had an opportunity to be heard concerning the proposed modifications.

(B) When more than one circuit court action involving support, custody, or parenting time of a child is pending, or more than one circuit court has continuing jurisdiction over those matters because of prior actions, a complaint for the support, custody, or parenting time of a different child of the same parents must be filed in whichever circuit court has jurisdiction to decide the new action. If more than one of the previously involved circuit courts would have jurisdiction to decide the new action, or if the action might be filed in more than one county within a circuit:

(1) The new action must be filed in the same county as a prior action involving the parents' separate maintenance, divorce, or annulment.

(2) If no prior action involves separate maintenance, divorce, or annulment, the new action must be filed:

(a) in the county of the circuit court that has issued a judgment affecting the majority of the parents' children in common, or

(b) if no circuit court for a county has issued a judgment affecting a majority of the parents' children in common, then in the county of the circuit court that has issued the most recent judgment affecting a child of the same parents.

(C) The court may enter an order that consolidates the custody, parenting time, and support provisions of multiple orders administratively when:

(1) the cases involve different children of the same parents but all other parties are the same, or

(2) more than one action involves the same child and parents.

The order must reference the other cases and state that it supersedes the custody, parenting time, and support provisions of the orders in those cases.

(D) In a case involving a dispute regarding the custody of a minor child, the court may, on motion of a party or on its own initiative, for good cause shown, appoint a guardian ad litem to represent the child and assess the costs and reasonable fees against the parties involved in full or in part.

[Adopted January 28, 1993, effective May 1, 1993, 441 Mich. Amended September 11, 2002, effective January 1, 2003, 467 Mich; May 28, 2008, effective September 1, 2008, 481 Mich; May 24, 2012, effective September 1, 2012, 491 Mich.]

Comments

Staff Comment to 1993 Adoption

This rule is new [effective May 1, 1993]. Subrule (A) clarifies the proper jurisdiction for original actions under the Child Custody Act, and subrule (B) makes clear that a subsequent action for support, custody, or visitation must be brought as an ancillary proceeding if a court has continuing jurisdiction because of a prior action. Where there is an existing or pending support obligation, subrule (C) requires that new actions for support be assigned to the same judge to whom the prior case is assigned.

Staff Comment to 2002 Amendment

The September 11, 2002, amendments of MCR 3.201 and 3.204, effective January 1, 2003, are based on proposals by the Family Division Joint Rules Committee. New MCR 3.201(D) defines several terms, and new MCR 3.204(D)

states the authority of the court to appoint a guardian ad litem for a minor child in a case in which child custody is disputed.

Staff Comment to 2008 Amendment

The amendments of MCR 3.204 consolidate multiple actions involving more than one child of the same parents in a single action so that all issues between the parents can be determined in a single action. The amendments also require multiple cases involving children of the same parents to be filed in the same county when possible to allow a single judge to consider all support, custody, and parenting time matters involving the same family. The amendment of MCR 3.204(A)(4) states that when the rule requires a supplemental pleading, all filing and judgment entry fees must be paid as if the action was filed separately.

Staff Comment to 2012 Amendment

The amendment of MCR 3.204 removes the requirement to file a new action as a supplemental complaint, which allows trial courts to consolidate cases in a way that is more compatible with trial court case management systems.

Rule 3.205 Prior and Subsequent Orders and Judgments Affecting Minors

(A) Jurisdiction. If an order or judgment has provided for continuing jurisdiction of a minor and proceedings are commenced in another Michigan court having separate jurisdictional grounds for an action affecting that minor, a waiver or transfer of jurisdiction is not required for the full and valid exercise of jurisdiction by the subsequent court.

(B) Notice to Prior Court, Friend of the Court, Juvenile Officer, and Prosecuting Attorney.

(1) As used in this rule, "appropriate official" means the friend of the court, juvenile officer, or prosecuting attorney, depending on the nature of the prior or subsequent court action and the court involved.

(2) If a minor is known to be subject to the prior continuing jurisdiction of a Michigan court, the plaintiff or other initiating party must send notice of proceedings in the subsequent court to

(a) the clerk or register of the prior court, and

(b) the appropriate official of the prior court.

(3) The notice must be sent at least 21 days before the date set for hearing. If the fact of continuing jurisdiction is not then known, notice must be sent immediately when it becomes known.

(4) The notice requirement of this subrule is not jurisdictional and does not preclude the subsequent court from entering interim orders before the expiration of the 21-day period, if required by the best interests of the minor.

(C) Prior Orders.

(1) Each provision of a prior order remains in effect until the provision is superseded, changed, or terminated by a subsequent order.

(2) A subsequent court must give due consideration to prior continuing orders of other courts, and may not enter orders contrary to or inconsistent with such orders, except as provided by law.

(D) Duties of Officials of Prior and Subsequent Courts.

(1) Upon receipt of the notice required by subrule (B), the appropriate official of the prior court

(a) must provide the subsequent court with copies of all relevant orders then in effect and copies of relevant records and reports, and

(b) may appear in person at proceedings in the subsequent court, as the welfare of the minor and the interests of justice require.

(2) Upon request of the prior court, the appropriate official of the subsequent court

(a) must notify the appropriate official of the prior court of all proceedings in the subsequent court, and

(b) must send copies of all orders entered in the subsequent court to the attention of the clerk or register and the appropriate official of the prior court.

(3) If a circuit court awards custody of a minor pursuant to MCL 722.26b, the clerk of the circuit court must send a copy of the judgment or order of disposition to the probate court that has prior or continuing jurisdiction of the minor as a result of the guardianship proceedings, regardless whether there is a request.

(4) Upon receipt of an order from the subsequent court, the appropriate official of the prior court must take the steps necessary to implement the order in the prior court.

[Adopted January 28, 1993, effective May 1, 1993, 441 Mich. Amended March 20, 2019, effective May 1, 2019, 502 Mich.]

Comments

Staff Comment to 1993 Adoption

Former Rule 3.205 has been rewritten [effective May 1, 1993] to clarify the relative responsibilities when two courts have asserted jurisdiction. The pleading requirement in former Rule 3.205 has been moved to Rule 3.206.

Staff Comment to 2019 Amendment

The amendments of Rules 1.109, 2.102, 2.104, 2.106, 2.107, 2.117, 2.119, 2.403, 2.503, 2.506, 2.508, 2.518, 2.602, 2.603, 2.621, 3.101, 3.104, 3.203, 3.205, 3.210, 3.302, 3.607, 3.613, 3.614, 3.705, 3.801, 3.802, 3.805, 3.806, 4.201, 4.202, 4.303, 4.306, 5.001, 5.104, 5.105, 5.107, 5.108, 5.113, 5.117, 5.118, 5.119, 5.120, 5.125, 5.126, 5.132, 5.162, 5.202, 5.203, 5.205, 5.302, 5.304, 5.307, 5.308, 5.309, 5.310, 5.311, 5.313, 5.402, 5.404, 5.405, 5.409, 5.501, and 5.784 and addition of Rule 3.618 of the Michigan Court Rules are an expected progression necessary for design and implementation of the statewide electronic-filing system. These particular amendments will assist in implementing the goals of the project.

Rule 3.206.   Initiating a Case

(A) Information in Case Initiating Document.

(1) The form, captioning, signing, and verifying of documents are prescribed in MCR 1.109(D) and (E).

(2) Except for matters considered confidential by statute or court rule, in all domestic relations actions, the complaint or other case initiating document must state

(a) the allegations required by applicable statutes;

(b) the residence information required by statute; and

(c) the complete names of any minors involved in the action, including all minor children of the parties and all minor children born during the marriage, and for complaints for divorce, the ages of all children born of the marriage.

(3) When any pending or resolved family division case exists that involves family members of the person(s) named in the case initiation document filed under subrule (2), the filing party must complete and file a case inventory listing those cases, if known. The case inventory is confidential, not subject to service requirements in MCR 3.203, and is available only to the party that filed it, the filing party's attorney, the court, and the friend of the court. The case inventory must be on a form approved by the State Court Administrative Office. This does not apply to outgoing requests to other states and incoming

registration actions filed under the Revised Uniform Reciprocal Enforcement of Support Act, MCL 780.151 *et seq.* and the Uniform Interstate Family Support Act, MCL 552.2101 *et seq.*

(4) In an action for divorce, separate maintenance, annulment of marriage, or affirmation of marriage, regardless of the contentions of the parties with respect to the existence or validity of the marriage, the complaint also must state

(a) the names of the parties before the marriage;

(b) whether there are minor children of the parties or minor children born during the marriage;

(c) whether a party is pregnant;

(d) the factual grounds for the action, except that in an action for divorce or separate maintenance the grounds must be stated in the statutory language, without further particulars; and

(e) whether there is property to be divided.

(5) A party who requests spousal support in an action for divorce, separate maintenance, annulment, affirmation of marriage, or spousal support, must allege facts sufficient to show a need for such support and that the other party is able to pay.

(6) A party who requests an order for personal protection or for the protection of property, including but not limited to restraining orders and injunctions against domestic violence, must allege facts sufficient to support the relief requested.

(B) In a case in which the custody or parenting time of a minor is to be determined or modified, the filing party shall file a Uniform Child Custody Jurisdiction Enforcement Act Affidavit, on a form approved by the State Court Administrative Office, as required by MCL 722.1209(1).

(C) Verified Statement and Verified Financial Information Form.

(1) *Verified Statement.* In an action involving a minor, or if child support or spousal support is requested, the party seeking relief must provide to the friend of the court a verified statement containing, at a minimum, personal identifying, financial, and health care coverage information of the parties and minor children. A copy of the Verified Statement must be served on the other party. The Verified Statement must be completed on a form approved by the State Court Administrative Office.

(2) *Verified Financial Information Form.* Unless waived in writing by the parties, or unless a settlement agreement or consent judgment of divorce or other final order disposing of the case has been signed by both parties at the time of filing, and except as set forth below, each party must serve a Verified Financial Information Form (as provided by SCAO) within 28 days following the date of service of defendant's initial responsive pleading. If a party is self-represented and his or her address is not disclosed due to domestic violence, the parties' Verified Financial Information forms will be exchanged at the first scheduled matter involving the parties or in another manner as specified by the court or stipulated to by the parties. A party who is a victim of domestic violence, sexual assault or stalking by another party to the case, may omit any information which might lead to the location of where the victim lives or works, or where a minor child may be found. Failing to provide this Verified Financial Information form may be addressed by the court or by motion consistent with MCR 2.313. The

Verified Financial Information form does not preclude other discovery. A proof of service must be filed when Verified Financial Information forms are served.

(3) The information in the Verified Statement and Verified Financial Information forms is confidential, and is not to be released other than to the court, the parties, or the attorneys for the parties, except on court order. For good cause, the addresses of a party and minors may be omitted from the copy of the Verified Statement and Verified Financial Information forms that are served on the other party. If a party excludes his or her address for good cause, that party shall either:

(a) submit to electronic filing and electronic service under MCR 1.109(G), or

(b) provide an alternative address where mail can be received.

(4) If any of the information required to be in the Verified Statement or Verified Financial Information forms is omitted, the party seeking relief must explain the reasons for the omission in those forms, or in a separate statement, verified under MCR 1.109(D)(3)(b) to be filed with the court by the due date of the form.

(5) A party who has served a Verified Financial Information form must supplement or correct its disclosure as ordered by the court or otherwise in a timely manner if the party learns that in some material respect the Verified Financial Information form is incomplete or incorrect, and if the additional or corrective information has not otherwise been made known to the other parties during the action or in writing.

(6) When the action is to establish paternity or child support and the pleadings are generated from Michigan's automated child support enforcement system, the party is not required to comply with subrule (C)(1) or (C)(2). However, the party may comply with subrule (C)(1) and (C)(2) to provide the other party an opportunity to supply any omissions or correct any inaccuracies.

(D) Attorney Fees and Expenses.

(1) A party may, at any time, request that the court order the other party to pay all or part of the attorney fees and expenses related to the action or a specific proceeding, including a post-judgment proceeding.

(2) A party who requests attorney fees and expenses must allege facts sufficient to show that:

(a) the party is unable to bear the expense of the action, including the expense of engaging in discovery appropriate for the matter, and that the other party is able to pay, or

(b) the attorney fees and expenses were incurred because the other party refused to comply with a previous court order, despite having the ability to comply, or engaged in discovery practices in violation of these rules.

[Adopted January 28, 1993, effective May 1, 1993, 441 Mich. Amended October 1, 1997, effective January 1, 1998, 456 Mich; September 11, 2002, effective January 1, 2003, 467 Mich; April 1, 2003, effective September 1, 2003, 468 Mich; May 30, 2018, effective September 1, 2018, 501 Mich. Amended effective September 11, 2019, 503 Mich. Amended June 19, 2019, effective January 1, 2020, 503 Mich; September 18, 2019, effective January 1, 2020, 503 Mich; November 13, 2019, effective January 1, 2020, 503 Mich.]

Comments

Staff Comment to 1993 Adoption

Former subrule 3.204(A) has been rewritten [effective May 1, 1993] as subrule 3.206(A) to clarify the pleading requirements for different types of domestic relations actions. Subrule (B) is similar to former subrule 3.204(B), except that the term "alimony" has been replaced by the term "spousal support," and there are several additions to the information that must be provided. For instance, it is now necessary to include in the verified statement the driver's license number and physical description of each party, any other names by which a party is known, and information about health care coverage. Also, the verified statement must now disclose the estimated weekly gross income of each party instead of the estimated after-tax income, and there must be a sworn affidavit identifying the reason for any omissions in the verified statement. Former subrule 3.204(C) has been eliminated; Rule 3.209 governs actions to be taken when parties reconcile. Subrule (C) governs attorney fees and expenses.

Staff Comment to 1998 Amendment

The amendment of MCR 3.206 relates to statutory changes made by 1996 PA 388, which created the family division of the circuit court. The amendment is effective January 1, 1998.

New MCR 3.206(A)(4) creates a requirement for identifying pending or prior family division actions involving members of the same family. References to that provision are included in MCR 5.931(B)(8), governing delinquency proceedings, and MCR 5.961(B)(7), governing child protective proceedings.

The amendment of Rule 3.206 of the Michigan Court Rules implements recent statutory changes that have created a family division of the circuit court. This amendment will remain in effect until further order of the court.

Staff Comment to 2002 Amendment

The September 11, 2002, amendments of MCR 3.206, 3.214, 3.705, 3.706, 3.708, 5.982, and 8.119, which were given immediate effect, are related to the group of domestic violence statutes enacted in December 2001 that took effect April 1, 2002.

The changes in MCR 3.206 and 3.214 are related to 2001 PA 195, which adopted the Uniform Child–Custody Jurisdiction and Enforcement Act, MCL 722.1101 et seq. There is also some nonsubstantive reorganization of MCR 3.214.

The amendment of MCR 3.705 implements the statutory provisions regarding the statement of reasons for granting or denying personal protection orders. See 2001 PA 196.

The amendment of MCR 3.706 incorporates the statutory provisions regarding enforceability of Michigan personal protection orders in other jurisdictions. See 2001 PA 200 and 201.

MCR 3.708 and 5.982 are amended to include foreign protection orders, which are made enforceable in Michigan by 2001 PA 197.

MCR 8.119(F) is amended to conform to 2001 PA 205, which directs that when a motion to seal court records involves allegations of domestic violence, the court is to consider the safety of the potential victim in ruling on the motion.

Note of January 22, 2003: By order dated September 11, 2002, this Court amended Rules 3.206, 3.214, 3.705, 3.706, 3.708, 5.982, and 8.119 of the Michigan Court Rules, effective immediately. 467 Mich xxvii-xxxi (No. 2, 2002). At the same time, the Court stated that it would consider at a future public hearing whether to retain the amendments, which relate to a group of statutes concerning domestic violence that were adopted in December 2001. Notice and an opportunity for comment at a public hearing having been provided, the amendments are retained.

Staff Comment to 2003 Amendment

The April 1, 2003, amendment of MCR 3.206(C), effective September 1, 2003, was suggested by the Michigan Judges Association to (1) reduce the number of hearings that occur because of a litigant's vindictive or wrongful behavior, (2) shift the costs associated with wrongful conduct to the party engaging in the improper behavior, (3) remove the ability of a vindictive litigant to apply financial pressure to the opposing party, (4) create a financial incentive for attorneys to accept a wronged party as a client, and (5) foster respect for court orders.

Staff Comment to 2018 Amendment

The amendments in this order are intended to begin moving trial courts toward a statewide uniform e-Filing process. In addition, the order moves existing language into MCR 1.109 as a way to, for the first time, include most filing requirements in one single rule, instead of scattered in various rules. The order largely mirrors the administrative orders that most e-Filing pilot projects have operated under, but contains some significant new provisions. For example, courts are required to maintain documents in an electronic document management system, and the electronic record is the official court record.

Staff Comment to 2019 Amendment

The amendments of MCR 1.109, 3.206, 3.931, and 3.961 enable family division courts to use the required case inventory form to administer cases while keeping the information confidential. This change is intended to prevent providing information that could affect the safety of domestic violence victims and their children.

Staff Comment to June, 2020 Amendment

These amendments are based on a proposal created by a special committee of the State Bar of Michigan and approved for submission to the Court by the Bar's Representative Assembly. The rules require mandatory discovery disclosure in many cases, adopt a presumptive limit on interrogatories (20 in most cases, but 35 in domestic relations proceedings) and limit a deposition to 7 hours. The amendments also update the rules to more specifically address issues related to electronically stored information, and encourage early action on discovery issues during the discovery period.

The amendment of MCR 2.309(A)(2) sets a presumptive limit of twenty interrogatories for each separately represented party. Several commenters suggested that the term "discrete subpart" be more explicitly defined. But the rule's reference to "a discrete subpart" is intended to draw guidance from federal courts construing FR Civ P 30(a)(1). Generally, subparts are not separately counted if they are logically or factually subsumed within and necessarily related to the primary question. In upholding the limit, parties and courts should also pragmatically balance the overall goals of discovery and the admonition of MCR 1.105. Further, the intent of the provision at MCR 2.301(B)(4) is to ensure that parties responding to discovery requests have the full time period to do so as provided for under these rules prior to the expiration of the discovery period.

Staff Comment to September, 2020 Amendment

The amendments of MCR 1.109, 2.107, 2.113, 2.116, 2.119, 2.222, 2.223, 2.225, 2.227, 3.206, 3.211, 3.212, 3.214, 3.303, 3.903, 3.921, 3.925, 3.926, 3.931, 3.933, 3.942, 3.950, 3.961, 3.971, 3.972, 4.002, 4.101, 4.201, 4.202, 4.302, 5.128, 5.302, 5.731, 6.101, 6.615, 8.105, and 8.119 and rescission of MCR 2.226 and 8.125 continue the process for design and implementation of the statewide electronic-filing system.

Staff Comment to November, 2020 Amendment

This amendment of MCR 3.206 combines and harmonizes two amendments issued in separate ADM files (ADM File No. 2002-37 and ADM File No. 2019-18) amending the same rule.

Rule 3.207 Ex Parte, Temporary, and Protective Orders

(A) Scope of Relief. The court may issue ex parte and temporary orders with regard to any matter within its jurisdiction, and may issue protective orders against domestic violence as provided in subchapter 3.700.

(B) Ex Parte Orders.

(1) Pending the entry of a temporary order, the court may enter an ex parte order if the court is satisfied by specific facts set forth in an affidavit or verified pleading that irreparable injury, loss, or damage will result from the delay required to effect notice, or that notice itself will precipitate adverse action before an order can be issued.

(2) The moving party must arrange for the service of true copies of the ex parte order on the friend of the court and the other party.

(3) An ex parte order is effective upon entry and enforceable upon service.

(4) An ex parte order remains in effect until modified or superseded by a temporary or final order.

(5) An ex parte order providing for child support, custody, or visitation pursuant to MCL 722.27a, must include the following notice:

"NOTICE:

"1. You may file a written objection to this order or a motion to modify or rescind this order. You must file the written objection or motion with the clerk of the court within 14 days after you were served with this order. You must serve a true copy of the objection or motion on the friend of the court and the party who obtained the order.

"2. If you file a written objection, the friend of the court must try to resolve the dispute. If the friend of the court cannot resolve the dispute and if you wish to bring the matter before the court without the assistance of counsel, the friend of the court must provide you with form pleadings and written instructions and must schedule a hearing with the court.

"3. The ex parte order will automatically become a temporary order if you do not file a written objection or motion to modify or rescind the ex parte order and a request for a hearing. Even if an objection is filed, the ex parte order will remain in effect and must be obeyed unless changed by a later court order."

(6) In all other cases, the ex parte order must state that it will automatically become a temporary order if the other party does not file a written objection or motion to modify or rescind the ex parte order and a request for a hearing. The written objection or motion and the request for a hearing must be filed with the clerk of the court, and a true copy provided to the friend of the court and the other party, within 14 days after the order is served.

(a) If there is a timely objection or motion and a request for a hearing, the hearing must be held within 21 days after the objection or motion and request are filed.

(b) A change that occurs after the hearing may be made retroactive to the date the ex parte order was entered.

(7) The provisions of MCR 3.310 apply to temporary restraining orders in domestic relations cases.

(C) Temporary Orders.

(1) A request for a temporary order may be made at any time during the pendency of the case by filing a verified motion that sets forth facts sufficient to support the relief requested.

(2) A temporary order may not be issued without a hearing, unless the parties agree otherwise or fail to file a written objection or motion as provided in subrules (B)(5) and (6).

(3) A temporary order may be modified at any time during the pendency of the case, following a hearing and upon a showing of good cause.

(4) A temporary order must state its effective date and whether its provisions may be modified retroactively by a subsequent order.

(5) A temporary order remains in effect until modified or until the entry of the final judgment or order.

(6) A temporary order not yet satisfied is vacated by the entry of the final judgment or order, unless specifically continued or preserved. This does not apply to support arrearages that have been assigned to the state, which are preserved unless specifically waived or reduced by the final judgment or order.

[Adopted January 28, 1993, effective May 1, 1993, 441 Mich. Amended January 23, 1996, effective April 1, 1996, 450 Mich; August 11, 1997, effective September 1, 1997, 456 Mich.]

Comments

Staff Comment to 1993 Adoption

Parts of revised Rule 3.207 [effective May 1, 1993] come from former Rule 3.206, but much of it is new. The revised rule clarifies and makes consistent existing practice. The terms "ex parte" and "temporary" are continued, but the term "interim" has been eliminated. "Hearing" in the context of subrule (C)(2) does not imply a full evidentiary hearing. Subrule (C)(3) permits modification of a temporary order on the basis of a showing of good cause, whereas former subrule 3.206(D)(3) permitted modification of a temporary order upon a change of circumstance. "Good cause" includes the prior entry of a temporary order without an evidentiary hearing. Subrule (D) emphasizes the availability of protective orders, as a matter of public concern and policy.

Staff Comment to 1996 Amendment

The 1996 amendment of MCR 3.207(B)(5) extended the mandatory notice provision in visitation cases to child support and custody cases. Other changes were made to reflect the November 1993 amendment of MCL 722.27a(13).

Staff Comment to 1997 Amendment

The amendment of MCR 3.207 is designed to implement the statutes providing for the issuance of personal protection orders. See MCL 600.2950, MCL 600.2950a.

Rule 3.208   Friend of the Court

(A) General. The friend of the court has the powers and duties prescribed by statute, including those duties in the Friend of the Court Act, MCL 552.501 *et seq.*, and the Support and Parenting Time Enforcement Act, MCL 552.601 *et seq.*

(B) Enforcement. The friend of the court is responsible for initiating proceedings to enforce an order or judgment for support, parenting time, or custody. The procedures in this subrule govern contempt proceedings under the Support and Parenting Time Enforcement Act. MCR 3.606 governs contempt proceedings under MCL 600.1701.

(1) If a party has failed to comply with an order or judgment, the friend of the court may move for an order to show cause why the party should not be held in contempt. Alternatively, in nonpayment of support cases and as allowed by the court, the friend of the court may schedule a hearing before a judge or referee for the party to show cause why the party should not be held in contempt.

(2) The order to show cause or the notice of the show cause hearing must be served personally, by ordinary mail at the party's last known address, or in another manner permitted by MCR 3.203.

(3) The notice of the show cause hearing shall comply with requirements for the form of a subpoena under MCR 2.506(D).

    (a) For the purpose of this subrule, an authorized signature is one that comports with MCR 1.109(E).

    (b) A notice under this subrule must state the amount past due and the source of information regarding the past due amount and act or failure to act that constitutes a violation of the court order. The state court administrator shall develop and approve a show cause hearing and notice form for statewide use. The show cause hearing and notice form may be combined in a single document.

    (c) A person must comply with the notice unless relieved by order of the court or written direction of the person who executed the notice.

(4) The show cause hearing may be held no sooner than seven days after the order or notice is served on the party. If service is by ordinary mail, the hearing may be held no sooner than nine days after the order or notice is mailed.

(5) The court may hold the show cause hearing without the friend of the court unless a party presents evidence that requires the court to receive further information from the friend of the court's records before making a decision. If the party fails to appear at the show cause hearing, the court may issue an order for arrest.

(6) The relief available under this rule is in addition to any other relief available by statute.

(7) The friend of the court may petition for an order of arrest at any time, if immediate action is necessary.

(C) Allocation and Distribution of Payments.

(1) Except as otherwise provided in this subrule, all payments shall be allocated and distributed as required by the guidelines established by the office of child support for that purpose.

(2) If the court determines that following the guidelines established by the office of child support would produce an unjust result in a particular case, the court may order that payments be made in a different manner. The order must include specific findings of fact that set forth the basis for the court's decision, and must direct the payer to designate with each payment the name of the payer and the payee, the case number, the amount, and the date of the order that allows the special payment.

(3) If a payer with multiple cases makes a payment directly to the friend of the court rather than through income withholding, the payment shall be allocated among all the cases unless the payer requests a different allocation in writing at the time of payment and provides the following information about each case for which payment is intended:

    (a) the name of the payer,

    (b) the name of the payee,

    (c) the case number, and

    (d) the amount designated for that case.

(D) Exceptions to Friend of the Court Enforcement. The friend of the court may inactivate its case and is not required to perform activities under the Friend of the Court Act, MCL 552.501 *et seq.*, and the Support and Parenting Time Enforcement Act, MCL 552.601 *et seq.*, when the case is no longer eligible for federal funding because a party fails or refuses to take action to allow the friend of the court's activities to receive federal funding or because the federal child support case is closed pursuant to Title IV, Part D of the Social Security Act, 42 USC 651 *et seq.*

[Adopted January 28, effective May 1, 1993, 441 Mich. Amended October 12, 2000, effective January 1, 2001, 463 Mich; October 23, 2000, effective January 1, 2001, 463 Mich. Amended effective April 3, 2001, 463 Mich. Amended June 21, 2017, effective September 1, 2017, 500 Mich; December 20, 2017, effective January 1, 2018, 501 Mich; August 30, 2018, effective September 1, 2018, 502 Mich.]

Comments

Staff Comment to 1993 Adoption

Former Rule 3.207 has been renumbered and modified [effective May 1, 1993] to eliminate provisions that have been superseded by statute and provisions that impose duties on the friend of the court that are impractical or unrealistic. Consistent with provisions of the federal child support enforcement program, subrule (C) prohibits the deduction of statutory fees from support money. The notice requirement in subrule (D) ends when the attorney's duty ends.

Staff Comment to January, 2001 Amendment

The amendment of MCR 3.208(C) on an interim basis [interim effect January 1, 2001] makes the court rule consistent with the requirements of the federal child support enforcement program, and establishes uniform allocation and distribution procedures among the various circuit courts.

Staff Comment to April, 2001 Amendment

The permanent adoption on April 3, 2001 of the interim amendments of MCR 3.208(C), which took effect January 1, 2001, kept the court rule consistent with the requirements of the federal child support enforcement program, and established uniform allocation and distribution procedures in the circuit courts.

Staff Comment to 2017 Amendment

The amendments of MCR 3.203 allow the friend of the court to use automated databases such as the United States Postal Services' National Change of Address database to identify outdated addresses and update them to correct addresses. The amendments allow a party or a party's attorney to agree to receive notices and other court papers from the friend of the court electronically. The amendments move the requirement to provide notices to attorneys of record from MCR 3.208.

Staff Comment to January, 2018 Amendment

The amendment of MCR 3.208 implements 2014 PA 378 permitting alternate procedures to set contempt proceedings to reduce the steps necessary to schedule a hearing. The amendments also clarify when the friend of the court must participate in a contempt hearing. In addition, the amendments implement 2014 PA 381 making the Office of Child Support responsible for determining allocation and distribution of child support payments, and allow the friend of the court to refrain from enforcing child support orders in situations in which it is inappropriate or unproductive for the friend of the court to continue to enforce child support orders.

Staff Comment to September, 2018 Amendment

These amendments update cross-references in the rules, and are intended to reflect changes that are necessary as a result of the Court's recent e-Filing rules amendments.

Rule 3.209.   Suspension of Enforcement and Dismissal

(A) Suspension of Enforcement.

(1) Because of a reconciliation or for any other reason, a party may file a motion to suspend the automatic enforcement of a support obligation by the friend of the court. Such a motion may be filed before or after the entry of a judgment.

(2) A support obligation cannot be suspended except by court order.

(B) Dismissal. Unless the order of dismissal specifies otherwise, dismissal of an action under MCR 2.502 or MCR 2.504 cancels past-due child support, except for that owed to the State of Michigan.

[Adopted January 28, 1993, effective May 1, 1993, 441 Mich.]

Comments

Staff Comment to 1993 Adoption

Subrule (A) of this new rule [effective May 1, 1993] takes into account recent statutory changes and clarifies the steps that a party may take to suspend automatic enforcement of a support obligation. Subrule (B) protects the interests of the state when an action is dismissed.

Rule 3.210.   Hearings and Trials

(A) In General.

(1) Proofs or testimony may not be taken in an action for divorce or separate maintenance until the expiration of the time prescribed by the applicable statute, except as otherwise provided by this rule.

(2) In cases of unusual hardship or compelling necessity, the court may, upon motion and proper showing, take testimony and render judgment at any time 60 days after commencing a case regardless of any stay.

(3) Testimony may be taken conditionally at any time for the purpose of perpetuating it.

(4) Testimony must be taken in person, except that the court may allow testimony to be taken by telephone in extraordinary circumstances, or under MCR 2.407.

(B) Default Cases.

(1) This subrule applies to the entry of a default and a default judgment in all cases governed by this subchapter.

(2) *Entry of Default.*

(a) A party may request the entry of a default of another party for failure to plead or otherwise defend by asserting facts setting forth proof of service and failure to plead or otherwise defend in a written request verified under MCR 1.109(D)(3). On filing of the request, the clerk must enter a default of the party.

(b) The party who requested entry of the default must provide prompt notice, as provided by MCR 3.203, to the defaulted party and all other parties and persons entitled to notice that the default has been entered, and file a proof of service.

(c) Except as provided under subrule (B)(2)(d), after the default of a party has been entered, that party may not proceed with the action until the default has been set aside by the court under subrule (B)(3).

(d) The court may permit a party in default to participate in discovery as provided in Subchapter 2.300, file motions, and participate in court proceedings, referee hearings, mediations, arbitrations, and other alternative dispute resolution proceedings. The court may impose conditions or limitations on the defaulted party's participation.

(e) A party in default must be served with the notice of default and a copy of every document later filed in the case as provided by MCR 3.203, and the person serving the notice or other document must file a proof of service with the court.

(3) *Setting Aside Default Before Entry of Default Judgment.* A motion to set aside a default, except when grounded on lack of jurisdiction over the defendant or subject matter, shall be granted only upon verified motion of the defaulted party showing good cause.

(4) *Notice of Hearing and Motion for Entry of Default Judgment.*

(a) A party moving for default judgment must schedule a hearing and serve the motion, notice of hearing, and a copy of the proposed judgment upon the defaulted party at least 14 days before the hearing on entry of the default judgment, and promptly file a proof of service when:

(i) the action involves entry of a judgment of divorce, separate maintenance, or annulment under subrule (B)(5)(a);

(ii) the proposed judgment involves a request for relief that is different from the relief requested in the complaint; or

(iii) the moving party does not have sufficient facts to complete the judgment or order without a judicial determination of the relief to which the party is entitled.

(b) If the action does not require a hearing under subrule (B)(4)(a) and if the relief can be determined based on information available to the moving party that is stated in or attached to the motion or complaint, the moving party for default judgment may either:

(i) schedule a hearing and serve the motion, notice of hearing, and a copy of the proposed judgment upon the defaulted party at least 14 days before the hearing on entry of the default judgment, and promptly file a proof of service, or

(ii) serve a verified motion for default judgment supporting the relief requested and a copy of the proposed judgment upon the defaulted party, along with a notice that it will be submitted to the court for signing if no written objections are filed with the court clerk within 14 days. If no written objections are filed within 14 days after filing, the moving party shall submit the judgment or order to the court for entry. If objections are filed, the moving party shall notice the entry of default judgment for hearing.

(c) Service under this subrule shall be made in the manner provided by MCR 3.203 or, as permitted by the court, in any manner reasonably calculated to give the defaulted party actual notice of the proceedings and an opportunity to be heard.

(d) If the default is entered for failure to appear for a scheduled trial or hearing, notice under this subrule is not required.

(5) *Entry of Default Judgment.*

(a) A judgment of divorce, separate maintenance, or annulment may not be entered as a matter of course on the default of a party because of failure to appear at the hearing or by consent, and the case must be heard in open court on proofs taken, except as otherwise provided by statute or court rule.

(b) Proofs for a default judgment may not be taken unless the proposed judgment has been given to the court. Nonmilitary affidavits required by law must be filed before a default judgment is entered in cases in which the defendant has failed to appear. A default judgment may not be entered against a minor or an incompetent person unless the person is represented in the action by a conservator or other representative, except as otherwise provided by law.

(c) The moving party may be required to present evidence sufficient to satisfy the court that the terms of the proposed judgment are in accordance with law. The court may consider relevant and material affidavits, testimony, documents, exhibits, or other evidence.

(d) In cases involving minor children, the court may take testimony and receive or consider relevant and material affidavits, testimony, documents, exhibits, or other evidence, as necessary, to make findings concerning the award of custody, parenting time, and support of the children.

(e) If the court does not approve the proposed judgment, the party who prepared it must, within 14 days, submit a modified judgment under MCR 2.602(B)(3), in conformity with the court's ruling, or as otherwise directed by the court.

(f) Upon entry of a default judgment and as provided by MCR 3.203, the moving party must serve a copy of the judgment as entered by the court on the defaulted party within 7 days after it has been entered, and promptly file a proof of service.

(6) *Setting Aside Default Judgment.*

(a) A motion to set aside a default judgment, except when grounded on lack of jurisdiction over the defendant, lack of subject matter jurisdiction, failure to serve the notice of default as required by subrule (B)(2)(b), or failure to serve the proposed default judgment and notice of hearing for the entry of the judgment under subrule (B)(4), shall be granted only if the motion is filed within 21 days after the default judgment was entered and if good cause is shown.

(b) In addition, the court may set aside a default judgment or modify the terms of the judgment in accordance with statute or MCR 2.612.

(7) *Costs.* An order setting aside the default or default judgment must be conditioned on the defaulted party paying the taxable costs incurred by the other party in reliance on the default or default judgment, except as prescribed in MCR 2.625(D). The order may also impose other conditions, including imposition of a reasonable attorney fee.

(C) Custody of a Minor.

(1) When the custody of a minor is contested, a hearing on the matter must be held within 56 days

(a) after the court orders, or

(b) after the filing of notice that a custody hearing is requested,

unless both parties agree to mediation under MCL 552.513 and mediation is unsuccessful, in which event the hearing must be held within 56 days after the final mediation session.

(2) If a custody action is assigned to a probate judge pursuant to MCL 722.26b, a hearing on the matter must be held by the probate judge within 56 days after the case is assigned.

(3) The court must enter a decision within 28 days after the hearing.

(4) The notice required by this subrule may be filed as a separate document, or may be included in another paper filed in the action if the notice is mentioned in the caption.

(5) The court may interview the child privately to determine if the child is of sufficient age to express a preference regarding custody, and, if so, the reasonable preference of the child. The court shall focus the interview on these determinations, and the information received shall be applied only to the reasonable preference factor.

(6) If a report has been submitted by the friend of the court, the court must give the parties an opportunity to review the report and to file objections before a decision is entered.

(7) The court may extend for good cause the time within which a hearing must be held and a decision rendered under this subrule.

(8) In deciding whether an evidentiary hearing is necessary with regard to a postjudgment motion to change custody, the court must determine, by requiring an offer of proof or otherwise, whether there are contested factual issues that must be resolved in order for the court to make an informed decision on the motion.

(D) The court must make findings of fact as provided in MCR 2.517, except that

(1) findings of fact and conclusions of law are required on contested postjudgment motions to modify a final judgment or order, and

(2) the court may distribute pension, retirement, and other deferred compensation rights with a qualified domestic relations order, without first making a finding with regard to the value of those rights.

(E) Consent Judgment.

(1) At a hearing that involves entry of a judgment of divorce, separate maintenance, or annulment under subrule (B)(5)(a), or at any time for all other actions, any party may present to the court for entry a judgment approved as to form and content and signed by all parties and their attorneys of record.

(2) If the court determines that the proposed consent judgment is not in accordance with law, the parties shall submit a modified consent judgment in conformity with the court's ruling within 14 days, or as otherwise directed by the court.

(3) Upon entry of a consent judgment and as provided by MCR 3.203, the moving party must serve a copy of the judgment as entered by the court on all other parties within 7 days after it has been entered and promptly file a proof of service.

[Adopted January 28, 1993, effective May 1, 1993, 441 Mich. Amended April 3, 2001, effective July 1, 2001, 463 Mich; December 30, 2003, effective May 1, 2004, 469 Mich; August 26, 2014, effective January 1, 2015, 497 Mich; November 26, 2014, effective January 1, 2015, 497 Mich. Amended effective March 9, 2016, 499 Mich. Amended September 20, 2018, effective April 1, 2019, 502 Mich; March 20, 2019, effective May 1, 2019, 502 Mich.]

Comments

Staff Comment to 1993 Adoption

Subrule (A) [effective May 1, 1993] expands the authority of the court to render judgment in certain cases after 60 days, which reflects current practice and perceived public concern. It also expressly permits the taking of testimony by electronic means, but only in extraordinary circumstances. Subrule (C) is similar to former subrule 3.206(F), with the addition of a provision for timely hearing if mediation is unsuccessful, and a provision about custody actions pursuant to MCL 722.26b.

Staff Comment to 2001 Amendment

The April 3, 2001 amendment of Rule 3.210, effective July 1, 2001, was based on a recommendation from the Michigan Judges Association and made clear that, in deciding whether an evidentiary hearing is necessary, the court must first determine whether there are contested factual issues that must be resolved in order to make an informed decision.

Staff Comment to 2004 Amendment

Coincident with its order of partial affirmance and remand in *Molloy* v *Molloy*, 466 Mich 852 (2002), the Supreme Court opened an administrative file to examine the extent to which, and the procedures by which, *in camera* testimony may be taken from children in custody cases. The adoption of subrule (C)(5) on December 30, 2003, effective May 1, 2004, clarified that the interview is to focus on the child's custodial preference and that the information received may be applied only to that factor.

Staff Comment to First January 1, 2015 Amendment

The amendments of MCR 3.210 clarify default and default judgment procedures to be used in domestic relations cases. The amendments also allow parties to reach agreement on issues related to property division, custody, parenting time, and support, and enter a consent judgment on those issues if the court approves.

Staff Comment to Second January 1, 2015 Amendment

The new court rule allows courts to use videoconferencing in civil court proceedings (including domestic relations proceedings) upon request of a participant or sua sponte by the court, subject to specified criteria and standards published by the State Court Administrative Office (SCAO). Amendments of MCR 3.210 and MCR 3.215 provide cross references to the new court rule. Adoption of MCR 2.407 does not affect MCR 3.904, MCR 5.738a, and MCR 6.006. In addition, as relevant to the rule amendments in this order, Administrative Order No. 2014–25, also issued today, requires SCAO to adopt videoconferencing standards, and requires courts to comply with those standards.

Staff Comment to 2016 Amendment

These amendments update cross-references that changed after the rule was adopted and make other nonsubstantive revisions.

Staff Comment to April, 2019 Amendment

The amendments of MCR 3.201, 3.210, and 3.211 and addition of MCR 3.222 and 3.223 integrate the collaborative law process designed under the Uniform Collaborative Law Act (159 PA 2014; MCL 691.1331–691.1354) into the state's trial court system for practical use, and add a similar process for parties not represented by counsel who seek to submit a consent judgment.

Staff Comment to May, 2019 Amendment

The amendments of Rules 1.109, 2.102, 2.104, 2.106, 2.107, 2.117, 2.119, 2.403, 2.503, 2.506, 2.508, 2.518, 2.602, 2.603, 2.621, 3.101, 3.104, 3.203, 3.205, 3.210, 3.302, 3.607, 3.613, 3.614, 3.705, 3.801, 3.802, 3.805, 3.806, 4.201, 4.202, 4.303, 4.306, 5.001, 5.104, 5.105, 5.107, 5.108, 5.113, 5.117, 5.118, 5.119, 5.120, 5.125, 5.126, 5.132, 5.162, 5.202, 5.203, 5.205, 5.302, 5.304, 5.307, 5.308, 5.309, 5.310, 5.311, 5.313, 5.402, 5.404, 5.405, 5.409, 5.501, and 5.784 and addition of Rule 3.618 of the Michigan Court Rules are an expected progression necessary for design and implementation of the statewide electronic-filing system. These particular amendments will assist in implementing the goals of the project.

Rule 3.211. Judgments and Orders

(A) Each separate subject in a judgment or order must be set forth in a separate paragraph that is prefaced by an appropriate heading.

(B) A judgment of divorce, separate maintenance, or annulment must include

(1) the insurance provisions required by MCL 552.101;

(2) a determination of the rights of the parties in pension, annuity, and retirement benefits, as required by MCL 552.101(3);

(3) a determination of the property rights of the parties; and

(4) a provision reserving or denying spousal support, if spousal support is not granted; a judgment silent with regard to spousal support reserves it.

(C) A judgment or order awarding custody of a minor must provide that

(1) the domicile or residence of the minor may not be moved from Michigan without the approval of the judge who awarded custody or the judge's successor,

(2) the person awarded custody must promptly notify the friend of the court in writing when the minor is moved to another address, and

(3) a parent whose custody or parenting time of a child is governed by the order shall not change the legal residence of the child except in compliance with section 11 of the Child Custody Act, MCL 722.31.

(D) Uniform Support Orders

(1) Any provisions regarding child support or spousal support must be prepared on the latest version of the Uniform Support Order approved by the state court administrative office. This order must accompany any judgment or order affecting child support or spousal support, and both documents must be signed by the judge. If only child support or spousal support is ordered, then only the Uniform Support Order must be submitted to the court for entry. The Uniform Support Order shall govern if the terms of the judgment or order conflict with the Uniform Support Order.

(2) No judgment or order concerning a minor or a spouse shall be entered unless either:

(a) the final judgment or order incorporates by reference a Uniform Support Order, or

(b) the final judgment or order states that no Uniform Support Order is required because support is reserved or spousal support is not ordered.

(E) Unless otherwise ordered, all support arrearages owing to the state are preserved upon entry of a final order or judgment. Upon a showing of good cause and notice to the friend of the court, the prosecuting attorney, and other interested parties, the court may waive or reduce such arrearages.

(F) Entry of Judgment or Order

(1) Within 21 days after the court renders an opinion or the settlement agreement is placed on the record, the moving party must submit a judgment, order, or a motion to settle the judgment or order, unless the court has granted an extension.

(2) The party submitting the first temporary order awarding child custody, parenting time, or support and the party submitting any final proposed judgment awarding child custody, parenting time, or support must:

(a) serve the friend of the court office and, unless the court orders otherwise, all other parties, with a completed copy of the latest version of the state court administrative office's Domestic Relations Judgment Information form, and

(b) file a proof of service with the court certifying that the Domestic Relations Judgment Information form has been provided to the friend of the court office and, unless the court orders otherwise, to all other parties.

(3) If the court modifies the proposed judgment or order before signing it, the party submitting the judgment or order must, within 7 days, submit a new Domestic Relations Judgment Information form to the friend of the court if any of the information previously submitted changes as a result of the modification.

(4) Before it signs a judgment or order awarding child support or spousal support, the court must determine that:

(a) the party submitting the judgment or order has certified that the Domestic Relations Judgment Information form in subrule (F)(2) has been submitted to the friend of the court, and

(b) pursuant to subrule (D)(2) any judgment or order concerning a minor or a spouse is accompanied by a Uniform Support Order or explains why a Uniform Support Order is unnecessary.

(5) The Domestic Relations Judgment Information form must be submitted to the friend of the court in addition to the verified statement that is required by MCR 3.206(C).

(G) Friend of the Court Review. The court may require that the judgment or order be submitted to the friend of the court for review to determine that it contains the provisions required by subrules (C), (D), (E), and (F).

(H) Service of Judgment or Order.

(1) When a judgment or order is obtained for temporary or permanent spousal support, child support, or separate maintenance, the prevailing party must immediately deliver one copy to the court clerk. The court clerk must file it with the friend of the court.

(2) The party securing entry of a judgment or order that provides for child support or spousal support must serve a copy on the party ordered to pay the support, as provided in MCR 2.602(E)(1), even if that party is in default.

(3) The record of divorce and annulment required by MCL 333.2864 must be filed at the time of the filing of the judgment.

[Adopted January 28, 1993, effective May 1, 1993, 441 Mich. Amended November 8, 2005, effective January 1, 2006, 474 Mich; February 1, 2012, effective May 1, 2012, 490 Mich. Amended effective March 21, 2018, 501 Mich. Amended August 30, 2018, effective September 1, 2018, 502 Mich; September 20, 2018, effective April 1, 2019, 502 Mich; September 18, 2019, effective January 1, 2020, 503 Mich.]

Comments

Staff Comment to 1993 Adoption

Rule 3.211 [effective May 1, 1993] is a reorganization and expansion of former Rule 3.209, consistent with statutory provisions and the provisions of the Michigan Child Support Guidelines. Subrule (E) takes into account the statutory changes that provide for support beyond age 18 in certain circumstances. Subrules (F), (G) and (H) are new. Subrule (F) requires notice to the friend of the court, the prosecuting attorney, and other interested parties, as well as a showing of good cause, before arrearages owing to the state may be waived or reduced. The prosecutor is included, as legal representative of the state, to insure that the court is adequately advised of such arrearages. Subrule (G) requires the moving party to submit a judgment or order within 21 days after the court issues an opinion or the settlement agreement is put on the record. Subrule (H) provides for the review of judgments and orders by the friend of the court, at the option of the court. There is a new requirement in subrule (I) regarding the filing of the record of divorce and annulment. The term "alimony" has been replaced by the term "spousal support" throughout the rule.

Staff Comment to 2005 Amendment

In subrule (D), the amendment effective January 1, 2006, requires that all support orders be entered on a standard form drafted by the state court administrative office. The Supreme Court shall review and approve any changes made to the Uniform Support Order by the state court administrative office because of changes in state or federal law.

In relettered subrule (F), the 2005 amendment allows personal information concerning a party to be provided to the friend of the court in a document separate from the court order, which is a public document.

Staff Comment to 2012 Amendment

This amendment eliminates the requirement that the Supreme Court approve changes to the Uniform Support Order forms. Without explicit approval required by the Supreme Court, the forms will be updated like other forms that are revised on a regular basis within the State Court Administrative Office.

Staff Comment to March, 2018 Amendment

These amendments update cross-references and make other nonsubstantive revisions to clarify the rules. The amendment of MCR 6.110(B)(1) addresses an inadvertent omission from the last amendment of this rule that was intended to be shown in overstrike. Accordingly, the current rule does not match the published version. Striking the clause "for good cause shown" will provide consistency with other published versions of the rule and with the statute, MCL 766.7, which allows a magistrate to adjourn a preliminary examination with the consent of the parties without the need for good cause to be shown.

Staff Comment to September, 2018 Amendment

These amendments update cross-references in the rules, and are intended to reflect changes that are necessary as a result of the Court's recent e-Filing rules amendments.

Staff Comment to 2019 Amendment

The amendments of MCR 3.201, 3.210, and 3.211 and addition of MCR 3.222 and 3.223 integrate the collaborative law process designed under the Uniform Collaborative Law Act (159 PA 2014; MCL 691.1331–691.1354) into the state's trial court system for practical use, and add a similar process for parties not represented by counsel who seek to submit a consent judgment.

Staff Comment to 2020 Amendment

The amendments of MCR 1.109, 2.107, 2.113, 2.116, 2.119, 2.222, 2.223, 2.225, 2.227, 3.206, 3.211, 3.212, 3.214, 3.303, 3.903, 3.921, 3.925, 3.926, 3.931, 3.933, 3.942, 3.950, 3.961, 3.971, 3.972, 4.002, 4.101, 4.201, 4.202, 4.302, 5.128, 5.302, 5.731, 6.101, 6.615, 8.105, and 8.119 and rescission of MCR 2.226 and 8.125 continue the process for design and implementation of the statewide electronic-filing system.

Rule 3.212 Postjudgment Transfer of Domestic Relations Cases

(A) Motion.

(1) A party, court-ordered custodian, or friend of the court may move for the postjudgment transfer of a domestic relations action in accordance with this rule, or the court may transfer such an action on its own motion. A transfer includes a change of venue and a transfer of all friend of the court responsibilities. The court may enter a consent order transferring a postjudgment domestic relations action, provided the conditions under subrule (B) are met.

(2) The postjudgment transfer of an action initiated pursuant to MCL 780.151 *et seq.*, is controlled by MCR 3.214.

(B) Conditions.

(1) A motion filed by a party or court-ordered custodian may be granted only if all of the following conditions are met:

(a) the transfer of the action is requested on the basis of the residence and convenience of the parties, or other good cause consistent with the best interests of the child;

(b) neither party nor the court-ordered custodian has resided in the county of current jurisdiction for at least 6 months prior to the filing of the motion;

(c) at least one party or the court-ordered custodian has resided in the county to which the transfer is requested for at least 6 months prior to the filing of the motion; and

(d) the county to which the transfer is requested is not contiguous to the county of current jurisdiction.

(2) When the court or the friend of the court initiates a transfer, the conditions stated in subrule (B)(1) do not apply.

(C) Unless the court orders otherwise for good cause, if a friend of the court becomes aware of a more recent final judgment involving the same parties issued in a different county, the friend of the court must initiate a transfer of the older case to the county in which the new judgment was entered if neither of the parents, any of their children who are affected by the judgment in the older case, nor another party resides in the county in which the older case was filed.

(D) Order for Transfer; Case Records.

(1) The transferring court must enter all necessary orders pertaining to the certification and postjudgment transfer of the action to the receiving court.

(a) The court may not enter an order transferring until all pending matters in the case have been resolved.

(b) The court must order the party who moved for the transfer to pay the applicable statutory filing fee directly to the receiving court unless fees have been waived in accordance with MCR 2.002.

(c) If the parties stipulate to the transfer of a case, they must share equally the cost of transfer unless the court orders otherwise.

(d) The court may also order one or both of the parties or the court-ordered custodian to pay past-due fees and costs under subrule (D)(4). Until all filing fees and court-ordered past-due fees and costs are paid, no further action in the case shall occur in the transferring court unless the moving party first demonstrates good cause and that substantial harm will occur absent the transferring court's immediate consideration.

(e) If the court or the friend of the court initiates the transfer, the statutory filing fee is waived.

(2) Except as otherwise ordered under subrule (D)(4), the transferring court must serve the order on the parties and send a copy to the receiving court. The clerk of the court and the friend of the court each must prepare the court's case records and the friend of the court's case records for transfer in accordance with the orders entered under subrule (1) and the Michigan Trial Court Records Management Standards and send them to the receiving court by a secure method.

(3) The receiving court shall temporarily suspend payment of the filing fee and open a case pending payment of the filing fee as ordered by the transferring court. The receiving court must notify the party of the new case number in the receiving court, the amount due, and the due date.

(4) The court may order that any past-due fees and costs be paid to the transferring friend of the court office at the time of transfer. If the court orders payment of past-due fees and costs, the order must state that the court will not send the order to the receiving court under subrule (1) and the records will not be transferred under subrule (2) until the past-due fees and costs are paid. If the past-due fees and costs are not paid within 28 days of entry, the transfer order becomes void.

(E) Payment of Filing Fee After Transfer. The party that moved for transfer must pay to the receiving court within 28 days of the due date provided under subrule (D)(3) the applicable filing fee as ordered by the transferring court. No further action in the case shall occur in the receiving court until the filing fee is paid unless the moving party first demonstrates good cause and that substantial harm will occur absent the receiving court's immediate consideration. If the fee is not paid to the receiving court within 28 days of the due date, the receiving court must order the case transferred back to the transferring court.

(F) Upon completion of the transfer, the transferee friend of the court must review the case and determine whether the case contains orders specific to the transferring court or county. The friend of the court must take such action as is necessary, which may include obtaining ex parte orders to transfer court- or county-specific actions to the transferee court.

[Adopted January 28, 1993, effective May 1, 1993, 441 Mich. Amended May 28, 2008, effective September 1, 2008, 481 Mich; September 18, 2019, effective January 1, 2020, 503 Mich.]

Comments

Staff Comment to 1993 Adoption

Former Rule 3.213 has been changed [effective May 1, 1993] to provide for the transfer of a case at the initiation of the court or the friend of the court, in the event that the court or the friend of the court is disqualified or for other reason believes that a transfer is necessary. Subrule (D) clarifies that the filing fee is to accompany the physical transfer of a case.

Staff Comment to 2008 Amendment

The amendments of MCR 3.212 require the friend of the court to transfer cases to allow a court to consolidate multiple cases involving different children of the same parents in a single court so that all issues between the parents could be determined in a single action. The amendments also allow the transferee friend of the court to take ex parte action to obtain orders to change county-specific orders to the transferee county or circuit.

Staff Comment to 2020 Amendment

The amendments of MCR 1.109, 2.107, 2.113, 2.116, 2.119, 2.222, 2.223, 2.225, 2.227, 3.206, 3.211, 3.212, 3.214, 3.303, 3.903, 3.921, 3.925, 3.926, 3.931, 3.933, 3.942, 3.950, 3.961, 3.971, 3.972, 4.002, 4.101, 4.201, 4.202, 4.302, 5.128, 5.302, 5.731, 6.101, 6.615, 8.105, and 8.119 and rescission of MCR 2.226 and 8.125 continue the process for design and implementation of the statewide electronic-filing system.

Rule 3.213 Postjudgment Motions and Enforcement

Postjudgment motions in domestic relations actions are governed by MCR 2.119.

[Adopted January 28, 1993, effective May 1, 1993, 441 Mich.]

Comments

Staff Comment to 1993 Adoption

This is a new rule [effective May 1, 1993]. There previously was no specific rule for postjudgment motions in domestic relations cases.

Rule 3.214. Actions Under Uniform Acts

(A) Governing Rules. Actions under the Revised Uniform Reciprocal Enforcement of Support Act (RURESA), MCL 780.151 *et seq.*, the Uniform Interstate Family Support Act (UIFSA), MCL 552.2101 *et seq.*, and the Uniform Child–Custody Jurisdiction and Enforcement Act (UCCJEA), MCL 722.1101 *et seq.*, are governed by the rules applicable to other civil actions, except as otherwise provided by those acts and this rule.

(B) RURESA Actions.

(1) *Definition.* As used in this subrule, "support order" is defined by MCL 780.153b(8).

(2) *Transfer; Initiating and Responding RURESA Cases.*

(a) If a Michigan court initiates a RURESA action and there exists in another Michigan court a prior valid support order, the initiating court must transfer to that other court any RURESA order entered in a responding state. The initiating court must inform the responding court of the transfer.

(b) If a court in another state initiates a RURESA action and there exists in Michigan a prior valid support order, the responsive proceeding should be commenced in the court that issued the prior valid support order. If the responsive proceeding is commenced erroneously in any other Michigan court and a RURESA order enters, that court, upon learning of the error, must transfer the RURESA order to the court that issued the prior valid support order. The transferring court must inform the initiating court of the transfer.

(c) A court ordering a transfer must send to the court that issued the prior valid support order all pertinent records. The clerk of the court and the friend of the court office must prepare the court and friend of the court records for transfer in accordance with the transfer order and the Michigan Trial Court Records Management Standards. The records must be sent to the court that issued the prior valid support order by a secure method within one business day of the date of the transfer order.

(d) The friend of the court office that issued the prior valid support order must receive and disburse immediately all payments made by the obligor or sent by a responding state.

(C) Sending Notices in UIFSA Cases. The friend of the court office shall send all notices and copies of orders required to be sent by the tribunal under MCL 552.2101 *et seq.*

(D) Registration of Child Custody Determinations Under UCCJEA. The procedure for registration and enforcement of a child custody determination by the court of another state is as provided in MCL 722.1304. There is no fee for the registration of such a determination.

[Adopted January 28, 1993, effective May 1, 1993, 441 Mich. Amended May 20, 1997, effective June 1, 1997, 454 Mich; September 11, 2002, effective January 1, 2003, 467 Mich. Amended effective March 21, 2018, 501 Mich. Amended September 18, 2019, effective January 1, 2020, 503 Mich.]

Comments

Staff Comment to 1993 Adoption

The revised rule [effective May 1, 1993] is essentially the same as former Rule 3.210.

Staff Comment to 1997 Amendment

The May 20, 1997 amendment of MCR 3.214 [effective June 1, 1997] was made to provide for the implementation of the Uniform Interstate Family Support Act, which became effective June 1, 1997. This Act was adopted so that Michigan would be in compliance with the federal Personal Responsibility and Work Opportunity Act of 1996.

The amendment makes it clear that the circuit court friend of the court office is responsible for sending various notices required by the Uniform Interstate Family Support Act.

Staff Comment to 2002 Amendment

The September 11, 2002, amendments of MCR 3.206, 3.214, 3.705, 3.706, 3.708, 5.982, and 8.119, which were given immediate effect, are related to the group of domestic violence statutes enacted in December 2001 that took effect April 1, 2002.

The changes in MCR 3.206 and 3.214 are related to 2001 PA 195, which adopted the Uniform Child–Custody Jurisdiction and Enforcement Act, MCL 722.1101 *et seq.* There is also some nonsubstantive reorganization of MCR 3.214.

The amendment of MCR 3.705 implements the statutory provisions regarding the statement of reasons for granting or denying personal protection orders. See 2001 PA 196.

The amendment of MCR 3.706 incorporates the statutory provisions regarding enforceability of Michigan personal protection orders in other jurisdictions. See 2001 PA 200 and 201.

MCR 3.708 and 5.982 are amended to include foreign protection orders, which are made enforceable in Michigan by 2001 PA 197.

MCR 8.119(F) is amended to conform to 2001 PA 205, which directs that when a motion to seal court records involves allegations of domestic violence, the court is to consider the safety of the potential victim in ruling on the motion.

Staff Comment to 2018 Amendment

These amendments update cross-references and make other nonsubstantive revisions to clarify the rules. The amendment of MCR 6.110(B)(1) addresses an inadvertent omission from the last amendment of this rule that was intended to be shown in overstrike. Accordingly, the current rule does not match the published version. Striking the clause "for good cause shown" will provide consistency with other published versions of the rule and with the statute, MCL 766.7, which allows a magistrate to adjourn a preliminary examination with the consent of the parties without the need for good cause to be shown.

Staff Comment to 2020 Amendment

The amendments of MCR 1.109, 2.107, 2.113, 2.116, 2.119, 2.222, 2.223, 2.225, 2.227, 3.206, 3.211, 3.212, 3.214, 3.303, 3.903, 3.921, 3.925, 3.926, 3.931, 3.933, 3.942, 3.950, 3.961, 3.971, 3.972, 4.002, 4.101, 4.201, 4.202, 4.302, 5.128, 5.302, 5.731, 6.101, 6.615, 8.105, and 8.119 and rescission of MCR 2.226 and 8.125 continue the process for design and implementation of the statewide electronic-filing system.

Rule 3.215 Domestic Relations Referees

(A) Qualifications of Referees. A referee appointed pursuant to MCL 552.507(1) must be a member in good standing of the State Bar of Michigan. A non-attorney friend of the court who was serving as a referee when this rule took effect on May 1, 1993, may continue to serve.

(B) Referrals to the Referee.

(1) The chief judge may, by administrative order, direct that specified types of domestic relations motions be heard initially by a referee.

(2) To the extent allowed by law, the judge to whom a domestic relations action is assigned may refer other motions in that action to a referee

(a) on written stipulation of the parties,

(b) on a party's motion, or

(c) on the judge's own initiative.

(3) In domestic relations matters, the judge to whom an action is assigned, or the chief judge by administrative order, may authorize referees to conduct settlement conferences and, subject to judicial review, scheduling conferences.

(C) Scheduling of the Referee Hearing.

(1) Within 14 days after receiving a motion referred under subrule (B)(1) or (B)(2), the referee must arrange for service of a notice scheduling a referee hearing on the attorneys for the parties, or on the parties if they are not represented by counsel. The notice of hearing must clearly state that the matter will be heard by a referee.

(2) The referee may adjourn a hearing for good cause without preparing a recommendation for an order, except that if the adjournment is subject to any terms or conditions, the referee may only prepare a recommendation for an adjournment order to be signed by a judge.

(D) Conduct of Referee Hearings.

(1) The Michigan Rules of Evidence apply to referee hearings.

(2) A referee must provide the parties with notice of the right to request a judicial hearing by giving

(a) oral notice during the hearing, and

(b) written notice in the recommendation for an order.

(3) Testimony must be taken in person, except that a referee may allow testimony to be taken by telephone for good cause, or under MCR 2.407.

(4) An electronic or stenographic record must be kept of all hearings.

(a) The parties must be allowed to make contemporaneous copies of the record if the referee's recording equipment can make multiple copies simultaneously and if the parties supply the recording media. A recording made under this rule may be used solely to assist the parties during the proceeding recorded or, at the discretion of the trial judge, in any judicial hearing following an objection to the referee's recommended order; it may not be used publicly.

(b) If ordered by the court, or if stipulated by the parties, the referee must provide a transcript, verified by oath, of each hearing held. The cost of preparing a transcript must be apportioned equally between the parties, unless otherwise ordered by the court.

(c) At least 7 days before the judicial hearing, a party who intends to offer evidence from the record of the referee hearing must provide notice to the court and each other party. If a stenographic transcript is necessary, except as provided in subrule (4)(b), the party offering the evidence must pay for the transcript.

(d) If the court on its own motion uses the record of the referee hearing to limit the judicial hearing under subrule (F), the court must make the record available to the parties and must allow the parties to file supplemental objections within 7 days of the date the record is provided to the parties. Following the judicial hearing, the court may assess the costs of preparing a transcript of the referee hearing to one or more of the parties. This subrule does not apply when a party requests the court to limit the judicial hearing under subrule (F) or when the court orders a transcript to resolve a dispute concerning what occurred at the referee hearing.

(E) Posthearing Procedures.

(1) Within 21 days after a hearing, the referee must either make a statement of findings on the record or submit a written, signed report containing a summary of testimony and a statement of findings. In either event, the referee must make a recommendation for an order and arrange for it to be submitted to the court and the attorneys for the parties, or the parties if they are not represented by counsel. A proof of service must be filed with the court.

(a) The referee must find facts specially and state separately the law the referee applied. Brief, definite, and pertinent findings and conclusions on the contested matters are sufficient, without overelaboration of detail or particularization of facts.

(b) The referee's recommended order must include:

(i) a signature line for the court to indicate its approval of the referee's recommended order;

(ii) notice that if the recommended order is approved by the court and no written objection is filed with the court clerk within 21 days after the recommended order is served, the recommended order will become the final order;

(iii) notice advising the parties of any interim effect the recommended order may have; and

(iv) prominent notice of all available methods for obtaining a judicial hearing.

(c) If the court approves the referee's recommended order, the recommended order must be served within 7 days of approval, or within 3 days of approval if the recommended order is given interim effect, and a proof of service must be filed with the court. If the recommendation is approved by the court and no written objection is filed with the court clerk within 21 days after service, the recommended order will become a final order.

(2) If the hearing concerns income withholding, the referee must arrange for a recommended order to be submitted to the court forthwith. If the recommended order is approved by the court, it must be given immediate effect pursuant to MCL 552.607(4).

(3) The recommended order may be prepared using any of the following methods:

(a) the referee may draft a recommended order;

(b) the referee may approve a proposed recommended order prepared by a party and submitted to the referee at the conclusion of the referee hearing;

(c) within 7 days of the date of the referee's findings, a party may draft a proposed recommended order and have it approved by all the parties and the referee; or

(d) within 7 days after the conclusion of the referee hearing, a party may serve a copy of a proposed recommended order on all other parties with a notice to them that it will be submitted to the referee for approval if no written objections to its accuracy or completeness are filed with the court clerk within 7 days after service of the notice. The party must file with the court clerk the original of the proposed recommended order and proof of its service on the other parties.

(i) If no written objections are filed within 7 days, the clerk shall submit the proposed recommended order to the referee for approval. If the referee does not approve the proposed recommended order, the referee may notify the parties to appear on a specified date for settlement of the matter.

(ii) To object to the accuracy or completeness of a proposed recommended order, the party must within 7 days after service of the proposed order, file written objections with the court clerk that state with specificity the inaccuracy or omission in the proposed recommended order, and serve the objections on all parties as required by MCR 2.107, together with a notice of hearing and an alternative proposed recommended order. Upon conclusion of the hearing, the referee shall sign the appropriate recommended order.

(4) A party may obtain a judicial hearing on any matter that has been the subject of a referee hearing and that resulted in a statement of findings and a recommended order by filing a written objection and notice of hearing within 21 days after the referee's recommendation for an order is served on the attorneys for the parties, or the parties if they are not represented by counsel. The objection must include a clear and concise statement of the specific findings or application of law to which an objection is made. Objections regarding the accuracy or completeness of the recommendation must state with specificity the inaccuracy or omission.

(5) The party who requests a judicial hearing must serve the objection and notice of hearing on the opposing party or counsel in the manner provided in MCR 2.119(C).

(6) A circuit court may, by local administrative order, establish additional methods for obtaining a judicial hearing.

(7) The court may hear a party's objection to the referee's recommendation for an order on the same day as the referee hearing, provided that the notice scheduling the referee hearing advises the parties that a same-day judicial hearing will be available and the parties have the option of refusing a same-day hearing if they have not yet decided whether they will object to the referee's recommendation for an order.

(8) The parties may waive their right to object to the referee's recommendation for an order by consenting in writing to the immediate entry of the recommended order.

(F) Judicial Hearings.

(1) The judicial hearing must be held within 21 days after the written objection is filed, unless the time is extended by the court for good cause.

(2) To the extent allowed by law, the court may conduct the judicial hearing by review of the record of the referee hearing, but the court must allow the parties to present live evidence at the judicial hearing. The court may, in its discretion:

(a) prohibit a party from presenting evidence on findings of fact to which no objection was filed;

(b) determine that the referee's finding was conclusive as to a fact to which no objection was filed;

(c) prohibit a party from introducing new evidence or calling new witnesses unless there is an adequate showing that the evidence was not available at the referee hearing;

(d) impose any other reasonable restrictions and conditions to conserve the resources of the parties and the court.

(3) If the court determines that an objection is frivolous or has been interposed for the purpose of delay, the court may assess reasonable costs and attorney fees.

(G) Interim Effect for Referee's Recommendation for an Order.

(1) Except as limited by subrules (G)(2) and (G)(3), the court may, by an administrative order or by an order in the case, provide that the referee's recommended order will take effect on an interim basis pending a judicial hearing. The court must provide notice that the referee's recommended order will be an interim order by including that notice under a separate heading in the referee's recommended order, or by an order adopting the referee's recommended order as an interim order.

(2) The court may not give interim effect to a referee's recommendation for any of the following orders:

(a) An order for incarceration;

(b) An order for forfeiture of any property;

(c) An order imposing costs, fines, or other sanctions.

(3) The court may not, by administrative order, give interim effect to a referee's recommendation for the following types of orders:

(a) An order under subrule (G)(2);

(b) An order that changes a child's custody;

(c) An order that changes a child's domicile;

(d) An order that would render subsequent judicial consideration of the matter moot.

[Adopted January 28, 1993, effective May 1, 1993, 441 Mich. Amended February 1, 2005, effective May 1, 2005, 472 Mich; October 25, 2005, effective January 1, 2006, 474 Mich; November 26, 2014, effective January 1, 2015, 497 Mich.]

Comments

Staff Comment to 1993 Adoption

There have been discrepancies among the circuits regarding domestic relations referees. This new rule [effective May 1, 1993] brings consistency to the system. Subrule (A) provides that referees must be members of the state bar. A grandfather clause permits a nonlawyer friend of the court to continue to serve as referee. Subrules (B) and (C) provide for timely scheduling and notice. Subrule (D) clarifies that an electronic or stenographic record of referee hearings is required, and permits a referee to take testimony by electronic means, in extraordinary circumstances. Subrule (E) explains procedures for requesting a judicial hearing. Subrule (F) provides that the judicial hearing may be based solely on the record of the referee hearing, if the parties consent.

Staff Comment to February, 2005 Amendment

The February 1, 2005, effective May 1, 2005, amendments implement 2004 PA 210, which redefines "de novo hearings" and allows trial courts to give interim effect to a referee's recommended order pending a hearing de novo pursuant to Michigan Court Rules.

Staff Comment to October, 2006 Amendment

These amendments, effective January 1, 2006, establish how the record of a referee hearing will be provided to parties and establish a procedure for a referee to submit a recommended order. MCR 3.215(D)(4)(a) tracks the language of MCR 8.109(B).

Staff Comment to 2015 Amendment

The new court rule allows courts to use videoconferencing in civil court proceedings (including domestic relations proceedings) upon request of a participant or sua sponte by the court, subject to specified criteria and standards published by the State Court Administrative Office (SCAO). Amendments of MCR 3.210 and MCR 3.215 provide cross references to the new court rule. Adoption of MCR 2.407 does not affect MCR 3.904, MCR 5.738a, and MCR 6.006. In addition, as relevant to the rule amendments in this order, Administrative Order No. 2014–25, also issued today, requires SCAO to adopt videoconferencing standards, and requires courts to comply with those standards.

Rule 3.216   Domestic Relations Mediation

(A) Scope and Applicability of Rule, Definitions.

(1) All domestic relations cases, as defined in MCL 552.502(m), and actions for divorce and separate maintenance that involve the distribution of property are subject to mediation under this rule, unless otherwise provided by statute or court rule.

(2) Domestic relations mediation is a nonbinding process in which a neutral third party facilitates communication between parties to promote settlement. If the parties so request, and the mediator agrees to do so, the mediator may provide a written recommendation for settlement of any issues that remain unresolved at the conclusion of a mediation proceeding. This procedure, known as evaluative mediation, is governed by subrule (I).

(3) This rule does not restrict the Friend of the Court from enforcing custody, parenting time, and support orders.

(4) The court may order, on stipulation of the parties, the use of other settlement procedures.

(B) Mediation Plan.
Each trial court that submits domestic relations cases to mediation under this rule shall include in its alternative dispute resolution plan adopted under MCR 2.410(B) provisions governing selection of domestic relations mediators, and for providing parties with information about mediation in the family division as soon as reasonably practical.

(C) Referral to Mediation.

(1) On written stipulation of the parties, on written motion of a party, or on the court's initiative, the court may submit to mediation by written order any contested issue in a domestic relations case, including postjudgment matters.

(2) The court may not submit contested issues to evaluative mediation unless all parties so request.

(3) Unless a court first conducts a hearing to determine whether mediation is appropriate, the court shall not submit a contested issue in a domestic relations action, including postjudgment proceedings, if the parties are subject to a personal protection order or are involved in a child abuse and neglect proceeding. The court may order mediation without a hearing if a protected party requests mediation.

(D) Objections to Referral to Mediation.

(1) To object to mediation, a party must file a written motion to remove the case from mediation and a notice of hearing of the motion, and serve a copy on the attorneys of record within 14 days after receiving notice of the order assigning the action to mediation. The motion must be set for hearing within 14 days after it is filed, unless the hearing is adjourned by agreement of counsel or unless the court orders otherwise.

(2) A timely motion must be heard before the case is mediated.

(3) Cases may be exempt from mediation on the basis of the following:

(a) child abuse or neglect;

(b) domestic abuse, unless attorneys for both parties will be present at the mediation session;

(c) inability of one or both parties to negotiate for themselves at the mediation, unless attorneys for both parties will be present at the mediation session;

(d) reason to believe that one or both parties' health or safety would be endangered by mediation; or

(e) for other good cause shown.

(E) Selection of Mediator.

(1) Domestic relations mediation will be conducted by a mediator selected as provided in this subrule.

(2) The parties may stipulate to the selection of a mediator. A mediator selected by agreement of the parties need not meet the qualifications set forth in subrule (G). The court must appoint a mediator stipulated to by the parties, provided the mediator is willing to serve within a period that would not interfere with the court's scheduling of the case for trial.

(3) If the parties have not stipulated to a mediator:

(a) the parties must indicate whether they prefer a mediator who is willing to conduct evaluative mediation. Failure to indicate a preference will be treated as not requesting evaluative mediation.

(b) The ADR clerk will assign a mediator from the list of qualified mediators maintained under subrule (F). The assignment shall be made on a rotational basis, except that if the parties have requested evaluative mediation, only a mediator who is willing to provide an evaluation may be assigned.

(4) The court shall not appoint, recommend, direct, or otherwise influence a party's or attorney's selection of a mediator except as provided pursuant to this rule. The court may recommend or advise parties on the selection of a mediator only upon request of all parties by stipulation in writing or orally on the record.

(5) The rule for disqualification of a mediator is the same as that provided in MCR 2.003 for the disqualification of a judge. The mediator must promptly disclose any potential basis for disqualification.

(F) List of Mediators.

(1) *Application.* To appear on a roster, an applicant, which may be an individual or organization, may apply to the ADR clerk to be placed on the court's list of mediators. Application forms shall be available in the office of the ADR clerk.

(a) The form shall include a certification that

(i) the applicant meets the requirements for service under the court's selection plan;

(ii) the applicant will not discriminate against parties or attorneys on the basis of race, ethnic origin, gender, or other protected personal characteristic; and

(iii) the applicant will comply with the court's ADR plan, orders of the court regarding cases submitted to mediation, and the standards of conduct adopted by the State Court Administrator under subrule (K).

(b) The applicant shall indicate on the form whether the applicant is willing to offer evaluative mediation, and the applicant's rate for providing mediation services.

(c) The form shall include an optional section identifying the applicant's gender and racial/ethnic background; however, this section shall not be made available to the public.

(2) *Review of Applications.* The court's ADR plan shall provide for a person or committee to review applications annually, or more frequently if appropriate, and compile a list of qualified mediators.

(a) Applicants meeting the qualifications specified in this rule shall be placed on the list of approved mediators. Approved mediators shall be placed on the list for a fixed period of time, not to exceed seven years, and must reapply at the end of that time in the manner directed by the court.

(b) Selections shall be made without regard to race, ethnic origin, or gender. Residency or principal place of business may not be a qualification.

(c) The approved list and the applications of approved mediators, except for the optional section identifying the applicant's gender and racial/ethnic background, shall be available to the public in the office of the ADR clerk.

(d) An applicant may attach a résumé or biographical information to the application.

(e) An applicant Community Dispute Resolution Program center must select only mediators who meet the qualifications of this rule or training requirements established by the State Court Administrator to mediate cases ordered by the court.

(3) *Rejection; Reconsideration.* Applicants who are not placed on the list shall be notified of that decision. Within 21 days of notification of the decision to reject an application, the applicant may seek reconsideration of the ADR clerk's decision by the presiding judge of the family division. The court does not need to provide a hearing. Documents considered in the initial review process shall be retained for at least the period during which the applicant can seek reconsideration of the original decision.

(4) *Removal from List.* The ADR clerk may remove from the list mediators who have demonstrated incompetence, bias, made themselves consistently unavailable to serve as a mediator, or for other just cause. Within 21 days of notification of the decision to remove a mediator from the list, the mediator may seek reconsideration of the ADR clerk's decision by the presiding judge of the family division. The court does not need to provide a hearing.

(G) Qualification of Mediators.

(1) To be eligible to serve as a domestic relations mediator under this rule, an applicant must meet the following minimum qualifications:

(a) The applicant must

(i) be a licensed attorney, a licensed or limited licensed psychologist, a licensed professional counselor, or a licensed marriage and family therapist;

(ii) have a master's degree in counseling, social work, or marriage and family therapy;

(iii) have a graduate degree in a behavioral science; or

(iv) have 5 years experience in family counseling.

(b) The applicant must have completed a training program approved by the State Court Administrator providing the generally accepted components of domestic relations mediation skills.

(c) Upon completion of the training required under subrule (G)(1)(b), the applicant must observe two domestic relations mediation proceedings conducted by an approved mediator, and conduct one domestic relations mediation to conclusion under the supervision and observation of an approved mediator.

(2) An applicant who has specialized experience or training, but does not meet the specific requirements of subrule (G)(1), may apply to the ADR clerk for special approval. The ADR clerk shall make the determination on the basis of criteria provided by the State Court Administrator.

(3) Approved mediators are required to obtain 8 hours of advanced mediation training during each 2–year period. Failure to submit documentation establishing compliance is grounds for removal from the list under subrule (F)(4).

(4) Additional qualifications may not be imposed upon mediators.

(H) Mediation Procedure.

(1) The mediator must schedule a mediation session within a reasonable time at a location accessible by the parties.

(2) The mediator must make reasonable inquiry as to whether either party has a history of a coercive or violent relationship with the other party. Throughout the mediation process, the mediator must make reasonable efforts to screen for the presence of coercion or violence that would make mediation physically or emotionally unsafe for any participant or that would impede achieving a voluntary and safe resolution of issues. A reasonable inquiry includes the use of the domestic violence screening protocol for mediators provided by the state court administrative office as directed by the supreme court.

(3) A mediator may require that no later than 3 business days before the mediation session, each party submit to the mediator, and serve on the opposing party, a mediation summary that provides the following information, where relevant:

(a) the facts and circumstances of the case;

(b) the issues in dispute;

(c) a description of the marital assets and their estimated value, where such information is appropriate and reasonably ascertainable;

(d) the income and expenses of the parties;

(e) a proposed settlement; and

(f) such documentary evidence as may be available to substantiate information contained in the summary.

Failure to submit these materials to the mediator within the designated time may subject the offending party to sanctions imposed by the court.

(4) The parties must attend the mediation session in person unless excused by the mediator.

(5) Except for legal counsel, the parties may not bring other persons to the mediation session, whether expert or lay witnesses, unless permission is first obtained from the mediator, after notice to opposing counsel. If the mediator believes it

would be helpful to the settlement of the case, the mediator may request information or assistance from third persons at the time of the mediation session.

(6) The mediator shall discuss with the parties and counsel, if any, the facts and issues involved. The mediation will continue until a settlement is reached, the mediator determines that a settlement is not likely to be reached, the end of the first mediation session, or until a time agreed to by the parties.

(7) Within 7 days of the completion of mediation, the mediator shall so advise the court, stating only the date of completion of the process, who participated in the mediation, whether settlement was reached, and whether further ADR proceedings are contemplated. If an evaluation will be made under subrule (I), the mediator may delay reporting to the court until completion of the evaluation process.

(8) If a settlement is reached as a result of the mediation, to be binding, the terms of that settlement must be reduced to a signed writing by the parties or acknowledged by the parties on an audio or video recording. After a settlement has been reached, the parties shall take steps necessary to enter judgment as in the case of other settlements.

(9) Confidentiality in the mediation process is governed by MCR 2.412.

(I) Evaluative Mediation.

(1) This subrule applies if the parties requested evaluative mediation, or if they do so at the conclusion of mediation and the mediator is willing to provide an evaluation.

(2) If a settlement is not reached during mediation, the mediator, within a reasonable period after the conclusion of mediation shall prepare a written report to the parties setting forth the mediator's proposed recommendation for settlement purposes only. The mediator's recommendation shall be submitted to the parties of record only and may not be submitted or made available to the court.

(3) If both parties accept the mediator's recommendation in full, the attorneys shall proceed to have a judgment entered in conformity with the recommendation.

(4) If the mediator's recommendation is not accepted in full by both parties and the parties are unable to reach an agreement as to the remaining contested issues, mediator shall report to the court under subrule (H)(6), and the case shall proceed toward trial.

(5) A court may not impose sanctions against either party for rejecting the mediator's recommendation. The court may not inquire and neither the parties nor the mediator may inform the court of the identity of the party or parties who rejected the mediator's recommendation.

(6) The mediator's report and recommendation may not be read by the court and may not be admitted into evidence or relied upon by the court as evidence of any of the information contained in it without the consent of both parties. The court shall not request the parties' consent to read the mediator's recommendation.

(J) Fees.

(1) A mediator is entitled to reasonable compensation based on an hourly rate commensurate with the mediator's experience and usual charges for services performed.

(2) Before mediation, the parties shall agree in writing that each shall pay one-half of the mediator's fee no later than:

(a) 42 days after the mediation process is concluded or the service of the mediator's report and recommendation under subrule (I)(2), or

(b) the entry of judgment, or

(c) the dismissal of the action,

whichever occurs first. If the court finds that some other allocation of fees is appropriate, given the economic circumstances of the parties, the court may order that one of the parties pay more than one-half of the fee.

(3) If acceptable to the mediator, the court may order an arrangement for the payment of the mediator's fee other than that provided in subrule (J)(2).

(4) The mediator's fee is deemed a cost of the action, and the court may make an appropriate judgment under MCL 552.13(1) to enforce the payment of the fee.

(5) In the event either party objects to the total fee of the mediator, the matter may be scheduled before the trial judge for determination of the reasonableness of the fee.

(K) Standards of Conduct. The State Court Administrator shall develop and approve standards of conduct for domestic relations mediators designed to promote honesty, integrity, and impartiality in providing court-connected dispute resolution services. These standards shall be made a part of all training and educational requirements for court-connected programs, shall be provided to all mediators involved in court-connected programs, and shall be available to the public.

[Adopted January 28, 1993, effective May 1, 1993, 441 Mich. Amended May 8, 1997, effective October 1, 1997, 454 Mich; May 9, 2000, effective August 1, 2000, 462; March 14, 2007, effective May 1, 2007, 477 Mich; April 5, 2011, effective September 1, 2011, 489 Mich; December 21, 2011, effective May 1, 2012, 490 Mich. Amended effective September 5, 2013, 495 Mich. Amended October 1, 2014, effective January 1, 2015, 497 Mich; May 24, 2017, effective September 1, 2017, 500 Mich.]

Comments

Staff Comment to 1993 Adoption

Former MCR 3.211 was approved by the Supreme Court effective October 1, 1987, for a one-year period. Local rules and administrative orders relating to domestic relations mediation were suspended in the interim. The Court extended the rule on July 8, 1988, until further order. Pending a full review, the rule again has been extended, as renumbered [effective May 1, 1993], with only minor changes for grammar and style, until further order of the Court.

Staff Comment to 1997 Amendment

The May 8, 1997 [effective October 1, 1997], order repeals MCR 4.003, which governed removal of cases from circuit to district court, effective July 1, 1997. This reinstates the February 28, 1997, repeal of the rule, which was suspended on March 13, 1997.

In addition, the order of May 8, 1997, postpones the effective date of earlier amendments of MCR 3.216, affecting mediation procedure, to October 1, 1997. The text of MCR 3.216 is the same as that adopted in the Court's March 5, 1997, order dealing with those rules.

Staff Comment to 2000 Amendment

The amendment is based on the recommendations of the Michigan Supreme Court Dispute Resolution Task Force, which was published for comment on May 10, 1999, see 459 Mich 1251, and was the subject of a series of public hearings across the state.

The Task Force report, issued in January 1999, and its addendum report, issued in January 2000 after receipt of comments, should be consulted for the background and details of the amendment. Basically, the change is as follows:

MCR 3.216, the domestic relations mediation rule, is substantially revised, to be more comparable to the mediation process in MCR 2.411.

Staff Comment to 2007 Amendment

This amendment corrects a reference to a relettered provision of MCL 552.502, the Friend of the Court Act.

Staff Comment to April, 2011 Amendment

The amendments of MCR 2.403, 2.411, and 3.216, and the adoption of new MCR 2.412 consolidate provisions related to mediation confidentiality into one rule and expand the number of exceptions to mediation confidentiality.

Staff Comment to December, 2011 Amendment

The amendments of MCR 2.403, 2.404, 2.410, 2.411, and 2.412 revise court rules relating to mediation and case evaluation largely as recommended by the Dispute Resolution Rules Committee convened by the State Court Administrative Office. The amendment of MCR 3.216 reflects amendments to provisions that appear in MCR 2.411 that also appear in MCR 3.216.

Staff Comment to 2013 Amendment

These amendments reflect changes that correct minor technical errors that have occurred in drafting or the changes respond to recent adopted rule revisions, which occasionally inadvertently create incorrect cross-references in other rules.

Staff Comment to 2015 Amendment

The amendment clarifies that distribution of property in divorce or separate maintenance actions is subject to domestic relations mediation.

Staff Comment to 2017 Amendment

The amendments of MCR 3.216 update the rule to be consistent with 2016 PA 93, which allows a court to order mediation if a protected party requests it and requires a mediator to screen for the presence of domestic violence throughout the process.

Rule 3.217   Actions Under the Paternity Act

(A) Governing Law. Procedure in actions under the Paternity Act, MCL 722.711 *et seq.* is governed by the rules applicable to other civil actions except as otherwise provided by this rule and the act.

(B) Blood or Tissue Typing Tests. A petition for blood or tissue typing tests under MCL 722.716 must be filed at or before the pretrial conference or, if a pretrial conference is not held, within the time specified by the court. Failure to timely petition waives the right to such tests, unless the court, in the interest of justice, permits a petition at a later time.

(C) Advice Regarding Right to an Attorney.

(1) The summons issued under MCL 722.714 must include a form advising the alleged father of the right to an attorney as described in subrule (C)(2), and the procedure for requesting the appointment of an attorney. The form must be served with the summons and the complaint, and the proof of service must so indicate.

(2) If the alleged father appears in court following the issuance of a summons under MCL 722.714, the court must personally advise him that he is entitled to the assistance of an attorney, and that the court will appoint an attorney at public expense, at his request, if he is financially unable to retain an attorney of his choice.

(3) If the alleged father indicates that he wants to proceed without an attorney, the record must affirmatively show that he was given the advice required by subrule (C)(2) and that he waived the right to counsel.

(4) If the alleged father does not appear in court following the issuance of a summons under MCL 722.714, subrule (C)(3) does not apply.

(D) Visitation Rights of Noncustodial Parent.

(1) On the petition of either party, the court may provide in the order of filiation for such reasonable visitation by the noncustodial parent as the court deems justified and in the best interests of the child.

(2) Absent a petition from either party, the right of reasonable visitation is reserved.

[Adopted January 28, 1993, effective May 1, 1993, 441 Mich. Amended effective December 23, 2003, 469 Mich.]

Comments

Staff Comment to 1993 Adoption

The revised rule [effective May 1, 1993] is similar to former Rule 3.212. Because of statutory changes, subrule (D) has been modified to eliminate the provision for appearance following issuance of a summons.

Staff Comment to 2003 Amendment

The December 23, 2003 amendment of MCR 3.217 deleted subrule (B), which provided for jury trials in paternity actions. It conformed the rule to MCL 722.715(1), which was amended by 1998 PA 113 to eliminate jury trials in such cases.

Rule 3.218   Friend of the Court Records; Access

(A) General. Friend of the court records are not subject to a subpoena issued under these Michigan Court Rules. Unless another rule specifically provides for the protection or release of friend of the court records, this rule governs. When used in this subrule, unless the context indicates otherwise,

(1) "records" means any case-specific information the friend of the court office maintains in any media;

(2) "access" means inspection of records, obtaining copies of records upon receipt of payment for costs of reproduction, and oral transmission by staff of information contained in friend of the court records;

(3) "confidential information" means

(a) staff notes;

(b) any confidential information from the Department of Human Services child protective services unit or information included in any reports to protective services from a friend of the court office;

(c) records from alternative dispute resolution processes, including the confidentiality of mediation records as defined in MCR 2.412;

(d) communications from minors;

(e) friend of the court grievances filed by the opposing party and the responses;

(f) any information when a court order prohibits its release;

(g) except as provided in MCR 3.219, any information for which a privilege could be claimed, or that was provided by a governmental agency subject to the express written condition that it remain confidential; and

(h) all information classified as confidential by the laws and regulations of title IV, part D of the Social Security Act, 42 USC 651 *et seq.*

(4) Reference to an agency, office, officer, or capacity includes an employee or contractor working within that agency or office, or an employee or caseworker acting on behalf of that office or working in the capacity referred to.

(5) "Governmental agency" means any entity exercising constitutional, legislative, executive, or judicial authority, when providing benefits or services.

(B) A friend of the court office must provide access to nonconfidential records to the following:

(1) A party; third–party custodian; guardian or conservator; guardian ad litem or counsel for a minor; lawyer–guardian ad litem; an attorney of record; and the personal representative of the estate of a party.

The friend of the court may honor a request from a person identified in this paragraph to release information to a governmental agency providing services to that individual, or before which an application for services is pending.

(2) An officer in the Judge Advocate General's office in any branch of the United States military, if the request is made on behalf of a service member on active duty otherwise identified in this subrule.

(C) Unless the release is otherwise prohibited by law, a friend of the court office must provide access to all nonconfidential and confidential records to the following:

(1) Other agencies and individuals as necessary for the friend of the court to implement the state's plan under Title IV, Part D of the Social Security Act, 42 USC 651 *et seq.* or as required by the court, state law, or regulation that is consistent with this state's IV–D plan.

(2) The Department of Human Services, as necessary to report suspected abuse or neglect or to allow the Department of Human Services to investigate or provide services to a party or child in the case.

(3) Other agencies that provide services under Title IV, part D of the Social Security Act, 42 USC 651 *et seq.*

(4) Auditors from state and federal agencies, as required to perform their audit functions with respect to a friend of the court matter.

(5) Corrections, parole, or probation officers, when, in the opinion of the friend of the court, access would assist the office in enforcing a provision of a custody, parenting time, or support order.

(6) Michigan law enforcement personnel who are conducting a civil or criminal investigation related directly to a friend of the court matter, and to federal law enforcement officers pursuant to a federal subpoena in a criminal or civil investigation.

(D) A citizen advisory committee established under the Friend of the Court Act, MCL 552.501 *et seq.*

(1) shall be given access to a grievance filed with the friend of the court, and to information related to the case, other than confidential information.

(2) may be given access to confidential information related to a grievance if the court so orders, upon demonstration by the committee that the information is necessary to the performance of its duties and that the release will not impair the rights of a party or the well-being of a child involved in the case.

When a citizen advisory committee requests information that may be confidential, the friend of the court shall notify the parties of the request and that they have 14 days from the date the notice was mailed to file a written response with the court.

If the court grants access to the information, it may impose such terms and conditions as it determines are appropriate to protect the rights of a party of the well-being of a child.

(E) A friend of the court office may refuse to provide access to a record in the friend of the court file if the friend of the court did not create or author the record. On those occasions,

the requestor may request access from the person or entity that created the record.

(F) Any person who is denied access to friend of the court records or confidential information may file a motion for an order of access with the judge assigned to the case or, if none, the chief judge.

(G) A court, by administrative order adopted pursuant to MCR 8.112(B), may make reasonable regulations necessary to protect friend of the court records and to prevent excessive and unreasonable interference with the discharge of friend of the court functions.

[Adopted January 28, 1993, effective May 1, 1993, 441 Mich. Amended December 8, 2000, effective April 1, 2001, 463 Mich; October 31, 2012, effective January 1, 2013, 493 Mich; November 27, 2013, effective January 1, 2014, 495 Mich.]

Comments

Staff Comment to 1993 Adoption

This new rule [effective May 1, 1993] insures that there will be reasonable access to friend of the court files.

Staff Comment to 2000 Amendment

The December 7, 2000 amendments of MCR 3.218, effective April 1, 2001, are consistent with changes made effective March 1, 1999, to the Child Custody Act, MCL 722.21 *et seq.*, and the Friend of the Court Act, MCL 552.501 *et seq.*

Staff Comment to 2013 Amendment

The amendments of these rules update the rules making them less "paper" focused and reflecting the use of electronic technology in the way courts process court records. The amendments also clarify and delineate the types of records and other materials maintained by a court, and clarify how access is provided.

Staff Comment to 2014 Amendment

These amendments reflect state and federal statutory and regulation revisions that have occurred in the last decade, and add specificity and detail to the existing language in MCR 3.218.

Rule 3.219 Dissemination of a Professional Report

If there is a dispute involving custody, visitation, or change of domicile, and the court uses a community resource to assist its determination, the court must assure that copies of the written findings and recommendations of the resource are provided to the friend of the court and to the attorneys of record for the parties, or the parties if they are not represented by counsel. The attorneys for the parties, or the parties if they are not represented by counsel, may file objections to the report before a decision is made.

[Adopted January 28, 1993, effective May 1, 1993, 441 Mich.]

Comments

Staff Comment to 1993 Adoption

This is a new rule [effective May 1, 1993]. It recognizes the circuit court's ability to use community resources in resolving disputes under the Child Custody Act.

Rule 3.221 Hearings on Support and Parenting Time Enforcement Act Bench Warrants

(A) Definitions.

(1) Unless the context indicates otherwise, the term "bond" means the performance bond required by MCL 552.631.

(2) The term "cash" means money or the equivalent of money, such as a money order, cashier's check, or negotiable check or a payment by debit or credit card, which equivalent is accepted as cash by the agency accepting the payment.

(3) Unless the context indicates otherwise, the term "person," when used in this rule, means a party who has been arrested on a bench warrant issued pursuant to MCL 552.631.

(B) Hearing on the Merits. The court shall hold a hearing in connection with the matter in which the warrant was issued within 21 days of the date of arrest. Except as provided in this rule, a person who does not post a bond, within 48 hours of arrest excluding weekends and holidays, shall be brought before the court that issued the warrant for further proceedings on the matter in which the warrant was issued. The hearing may be adjourned when necessary to give notice of the proceedings to another party or to receive additional evidence. In the event the hearing is adjourned, the court shall set terms of release under subrule (F). Failure to hold a hearing within 21 days will not deprive the court of jurisdiction to proceed.

(C) Bond Review Hearing. A person who has not posted a bond, and whose case cannot be heard as provided in subrule (B), must without unnecessary delay be brought before a judge, or referee for a review of the bond.

(D) Place of Bond Review Hearing. Except as otherwise provided in this subrule, a bond review hearing under subrule (E) must be held in the circuit court specified in the warrant. If a person is arrested in a circuit other than the one specified in the warrant, the arresting agency must make arrangements to assure that the person is promptly transported to the court specified in the warrant for a hearing in accordance with the provisions of this rule. If prompt transportation cannot be arranged, the bond review hearing must be held in the jurisdiction in which the individual is being held.

(E) Conduct of Bond Review Hearing. At the bond review hearing, the person must be advised of the purpose of the hearing on the merits and a determination must be made of what form of prehearing release is appropriate. A verbatim record must be made of the bond review hearing. Pending the hearing required under subrule (B), the person must be released on conditions under subrule (F).

(F) Conditional Release. The person must be released on condition that the person will appear for a hearing under subrule (B) and any other conditions that are appropriate to ensure that the person will appear as required for a hearing under subrule (B), including requiring the person to:

(1) make reports to a court agency as required by the court or the agency;

(2) comply with restrictions on personal associations, place of residence, place of employment, or travel;

(3) surrender driver's license or passport;

(4) comply with a specified curfew;

(5) continue or seek employment or participate in a work program;

(6) continue or begin an educational program;

(7) remain in the custody of a responsible member of the community who agrees to monitor the person and report any violation of any release condition to the court;

(8) post a bond as described in subrule (G).

In the event the person cannot satisfy a condition of release, the arresting agency must make arrangements with the authorities in the county of the court specified in the warrant to have the person promptly transported to that county for a hearing in accordance with the provisions of this rule.

(G) Performance Bond Modification. If it is determined for reasons stated on the record that the person's appearance cannot otherwise be assured, the person, in addition to any conditions described in subrule (F), may be required to post a bond at the person's option, executed:

(1) by the person, or by another who is not a licensed surety, and secured by a cash deposit for the full bond amount, or

(2) by a surety approved by the court.

(H) Decision; Statement of Reasons.

(1) In deciding what terms and conditions to impose under subrule (F), relevant information, including the following shall be considered:

(a) the person's record for reporting information to the friend of the court and complying with court orders;

(b) the person's record of appearance or nonappearance at court proceedings;

(c) the person's history of substance abuse or addiction;

(d) the amount of support owed;

(e) the person's employment status and history and financial history insofar as these factors relate to the ability to post bond;

(f) the availability of responsible members of the community who would vouch for or monitor the person;

(g) facts indicating the person's ties to the community, including family ties and relationships, and length of residence; and

(h) any other facts bearing on the risk of nonappearance.

(2) The reasons for requiring a bond under subrule (F), must be stated on the record. A finding on each of the enumerated factors is not necessary.

(3) Nothing in this rule may be construed to sanction the determination of prehearing release on the basis of race, religion, gender, economic status, or other impermissible criteria.

(I) Review; Modification of Release Decision.

(1) *Review.* A party seeking review of a release decision may file a motion in the court having appellate jurisdiction over the decision maker. If the decision was made by a referee, a party is entitled to a new hearing. Otherwise, the reviewing court may not stay, vacate, modify, or reverse the release decision except on finding an abuse of discretion.

(2) *Emergency Release.* If a person is ordered released from custody as a result of a court order or law requiring the release of prisoners to relieve jail conditions, the court ordering the release shall impose conditions of release in accordance with this rule to ensure the appearance of the individual as required. If such conditions of release are imposed, the court must inform the person of the conditions on the record or by furnishing to the person or the person's lawyer a copy of the release order setting forth the conditions.

(J) Termination of Release Order.

(1) After a bond is set pursuant to subrule (G), if the person appears for the hearing in subrule (B) the court must vacate the release order, discharge a third party who has posted the bond,

and return the cash posted in the full amount of a bond. At the court's discretion, an arrested person who has deposited money with the court may be required to forfeit all or a portion of the amount to pay support, fines, fees, costs, and sanctions.

(2) If the person fails to comply with any conditions of release, the court that issued the original bench warrant may issue a new bench warrant for the person's arrest and enter an order revoking the release order and declaring the bond, if any, forfeited.

(a) The court must mail notice of any revocation order immediately to the person at the person's last known address and, if forfeiture of bond has been ordered, to anyone who posted bond.

(b) If the person does not appear and surrender to the court within 28 days after the revocation date or does not within the period satisfy the court that there was compliance with the conditions of release or that compliance was impossible through no fault of the person, the court may continue the revocation order and enter judgment forfeiting the bond against the individual and anyone who posted bond for the entire amount of the bond and costs of the court proceedings and costs associated with the arrest.

(K) Plan for Remote Bond Review Hearings. In each county, the court with trial jurisdiction over friend of the court cases must adopt and file with the State Court Administrator a plan for conducting bond review hearings on bench warrants issued as a result of a show cause hearing when the person is arrested in another county and cannot be transported immediately. The plan shall provide for the use of available technology for a person's appearance and the transmission and presentation of evidence in hearings under this rule.

[Adopted January 28, 2003, effective August 1, 2003, 469 Mich. Amended effective April 2, 2014, pending public comment, 495 Mich. Retained effective October 1, 2014, 497 Mich.]

Comments

Staff Comment to 2003 Adoption

MCR 3.221, which was adopted July 22, 2003, to be effective August 1, 2003, implemented 2002 PA 567 by establishing the procedure to be used when a child support payer is arrested pursuant to a bench warrant issued for failure to appear at a show cause proceeding for nonpayment of support. The public act amended MCL 552.602, 552.631, 552.633, and 552.635, effective June 1, 2003.

Staff Comment to 2014 Amendment

The amendments of MCR 3.221 strike the term "magistrate" from subsections (C) and (I) to clarify the rule because there is no statutory authority for district court magistrates to conduct bond review hearings on support and parenting time enforcement act bench warrants.

Rule 3.222.   Uniform Collaborative Law Act Process and Agreements

(A) Scope and Applicability of Rules. This rule and MCL 691.1331 *et seq.*, the Uniform Collaborative Law Act, govern collaborative law practice in domestic relations cases.

(1) *Definitions.* For purposes of this rule:

(a) "Collaborative matter" means a dispute, transaction, claim, problem, or issue for resolution, including a dispute, claim, or issue in a proceeding, that is described in a collaborative law participation agreement and arises under the family or domestic relations law of this state.

(b) "Collaborative law participation agreement" means an agreement by persons to participate in a collaborative law process.

(c) "Collaborative law process" means a procedure intended to resolve a collaborative matter without intervention by a court in which persons sign a collaborative law participation agreement and are represented by collaborative lawyers.

(d) "Party A" is the equivalent of a plaintiff and means the party responsible for filing and service requirements.

(e) "Party B" is the equivalent of a defendant and means the non-filing party.

(B) Commencing an Action Involving Parties in a Collaborative Law Process.

(1) Where the parties have entered into a collaborative law participation agreement and do not already have a pending domestic relations case, the parties shall proceed under subrule (C).

(2) Where a party has filed a domestic relations case with the court under MCR 2.102 and the parties subsequently sign a collaborative law participation agreement, the parties shall file notice of the signed agreement and a motion to stay proceedings on a form approved by the State Court Administrative Office.

(a) The court shall either stay the proceedings without a hearing or schedule a hearing on the notice within 28 days after the motion is filed. An initial order granting a stay shall be effective for 364 days from the date of filing of the motion. Upon stipulation of the parties, the court may extend the stay period.

(b) The court may require the parties and collaborative lawyers to file a status report on the collaborative law process. The status report shall be on a form approved by the State Court Administrative Office and shall include only information on whether the process is ongoing, concluded, or terminated. It shall not include a report, assessment, evaluation, recommendation, finding, or other communication regarding the matter.

(c) The parties shall promptly file notice with the court when a collaborative law process concludes or terminates. The notice shall be on a form approved by the State Court Administrative Office.

(i) The stay of the proceeding is lifted when the notice is filed. If the parties reached an agreement, they shall proceed under MCR 3.222(D).

(ii) If the parties have not filed notice before the stay expires, the court shall provide notice of intent to dismiss the case for lack of progress as prescribed by subrule (E). Before dismissing the proceeding, the court shall provide parties an opportunity to be heard.

(C) Establishing Jurisdiction and Starting the Statutory Waiting Period. At any time after a collaborative law participation agreement is signed, if the parties are not already under the court's jurisdiction, the parties may commence an action to submit to the court's jurisdiction.

(1) When the parties have concluded a collaborative law process and are requesting entry of a final judgment or final order, the parties shall file a petition to submit to court jurisdiction and request for entry of a final judgment or final

order on a form approved by the State Court Administrative Office.

(a) The petition shall be brought "In the Matter of" the names of Party A and Party B and the subject matter of the collaborative law agreement using the case type codes under MCR 8.117. The petition shall:

   (i) contain, at a minimum, the grounds for jurisdiction, the statutory grounds to enter the judgment or order, and a request to enter the judgment or order;

   (ii) comply with the provisions of MCR 2.113 and MCR 3.206(A) and (B);

   (iii) be signed by both parties;

   (iv) be accompanied by the proposed final judgment or proposed final order, that complies with MCR 3.211 and is signed by both parties;

   (v) be accompanied by a verified statement if required by MCR 3.206(C) and judgment information form if required by MCR 3.211(F); and

   (vi) under MCL 691.1345, be accompanied by domestic violence screening forms. The domestic violence screening form shall be limited to reporting personal protection actions, domestic violence criminal actions, and child protective actions involving the parties and shall be on a form approved by the State Court Administrative Office. Each party must complete a separate form.

The petition may also contain a request to waive the six-month statutory waiting period under MCL 552.9f.

(b) On the filing of the petition and request for entry of final judgment or final order and payment of the filing fees, the court clerk shall assign a case number and judge. The requirement to issue a summons under MCR 2.102(A) is not applicable. Unless requested by the parties on filing of a motion, the court clerk shall not schedule the matter until the conclusion of the statutory waiting period. The petition under this subrule serves as a complaint and answer and as an appearance of both attorneys, and starts the statutory waiting period(s) under MCL 552.9f.

(2) To commence an action at any time before the conclusion of the collaborative law process, the parties shall file a petition for court jurisdiction and declaration of intent to file a proposed final judgment or proposed final order on a form approved by the State Court Administrative Office.

(a) The petition shall be brought "In the Matter of" the names of Party A and Party B and shall state the type of action corresponding to the assigned case type code in MCR 8.117 (listed under Case File Management Standard [A][6]). The petition shall:

   (i) contain, at a minimum, the grounds for jurisdiction, the statutory grounds to enter the judgment or order, and a request to enter the judgment or order;

   (ii) comply with the provisions of MCR 2.113 and MCR 3.206(A) and (B);

   (iii) be signed by both parties;

   (iv) be accompanied by a verified statement if required by MCR 3.206(C), and

   (v) under MCL 691.1345, be accompanied by domestic violence screening forms. The domestic violence screening form shall be limited to reporting personal protection

actions, domestic violence criminal actions, and child protective actions involving the parties and shall be on a form approved by the State Court Administrative Office. Each party must complete a separate form.

The petition may also contain a request to waive the six-month statutory waiting period under MCL 552.9f.

(b) On the filing of the petition and payment of the filing fees, the court clerk shall assign a case number and judge. The requirement to issue a summons under MCR 2.102(A) is not applicable. Unless requested by the parties on filing of a motion, the court clerk shall not schedule the matter for a pretrial or settlement conference. The petition under this subrule serves as a complaint and answer and as an appearance of both attorneys and starts the statutory waiting period(s) under MCL 552.9f.

(c) At any time during the collaborative law process, the parties may request the court to issue, in addition to a final judgment or final order, any other order approving an agreement resulting from the process.

(d) Unless the collaborative law process has concluded, the parties shall file a status report with the court within 182 days of the filing date of the petition and again at 364 days. The status report shall be on a form approved by the State Court Administrative Office and shall include only information on whether the process is ongoing or concluded. It may not include a report, assessment, evaluation, recommendation, finding, or other communication regarding the matter.

(e) At the conclusion of the collaborative law process, the parties shall file a proposed final judgment or proposed final order that complies with MCR 3.211 and a judgment information form if required by MCR 3.211(F).

(D) Entry of Final Judgment or Final Order.

(1) At its discretion, the court may conduct a hearing before entering the final judgment or final order.

(2) The final judgment or final order shall be served in accordance with MCR 2.602(E).

(3) Nothing in this rule precludes the court from waiving the six-month statutory waiting period in accordance with MCL 552.9f.

(E) Dismissal.

(1) *Lack of Progress.* The clerk shall provide notice of intent to dismiss the case for lack of progress if:

   (a) the parties have not filed a notice that a collaborative law process has concluded or terminated before the expiration of a stay under subrule (B)(2)(c), or

   (b) the parties have not filed a proposed final judgment or proposed final order within 28 days after the statutory waiting period has expired.

(2) *Notice of Intent to Dismiss.* A notice of intent to dismiss the case for lack of progress shall be given in the manner provided in MCR 2.501(C) for notice of trial. The notice shall state that the case will be dismissed no sooner than 28 days after the date of the notice unless the parties do one of the following:

   (a) file a proposed final judgment or proposed final order under this rule,

(b) file a complaint under MCR 2.101, or

(c) request a hearing.

(3) *Other Dismissal.* A party may dismiss a collaborative law matter commenced under this rule at any time under MCR 2.504.

(F) Terminating the Collaborative Law Process. If a party files a complaint under MCL 691.1335(4)(b)(i), the clerk shall proceed on the complaint in accordance with MCR 2.102(A). The court shall dismiss the petition filed under subrule (C)(1) or (C)(2). Pursuant to MCL 691.1339, the attorneys in the collaborative law agreement are disqualified from representing either party in the new action.

[Adopted September 20, 2018, effective April 1, 2019, 502 Mich. Amended effective August 14, 2019, 503 Mich.]

Comments

Staff Comment to 2019 Adoption

The amendments of MCR 3.201, 3.210, and 3.211 and addition of MCR 3.222 and 3.223 integrate the collaborative law process designed under the Uniform Collaborative Law Act (159 PA 2014; MCL 691.1331–691.1354) into the state's trial court system for practical use, and add a similar process for parties not represented by counsel who seek to submit a consent judgment.

Staff Comment to 2019 Amendment

These amendments update cross-references and make other nonsubstantive revisions to clarify the rules.

Rule 3.223. Summary Proceeding for Entry of Consent Judgment or Order

(A) Scope and Applicability of Rules. This rule governs practice and procedure for entering a consent judgment or consent order as an original action.

(B) Definitions. For purposes of this rule:

(1) "Party A" is the equivalent of a plaintiff and means the party responsible for filing and service requirements.

(2) "Party B" is the equivalent of a defendant and means the non-filing party.

(C) Commencing an Action.

(1) The parties shall file a petition to submit to court jurisdiction and request for entry of a proposed consent judgment or proposed consent order on a form approved by the State Court Administrative Office.

(a) The petition shall be brought "In the Matter of" the names of Party A and Party B and the subject matter of the proposed consent judgment or proposed consent order using the case type codes under MCR 8.117. The petition shall:

(i) contain, at a minimum, the grounds for jurisdiction, the statutory grounds to enter the judgment or order, and a request to enter the judgment or order;

(ii) comply with the provisions of MCR 2.113 and MCR 3.206(A) and (B);

(iii) be signed by both parties;

(iv) be accompanied by the proposed consent judgment or consent order, that complies with MCR 3.211 and is signed by both parties;

(v) be accompanied by a verified statement if required by MCR 3.206(C) and a judgment information form if required by MCR 3.211(F); and

(vi) under MCL 691.1345, be accompanied by domestic violence screening forms. The domestic violence screening form shall be limited to reporting personal protection actions, domestic violence criminal actions, and child protective actions involving the parties and shall be on a form approved by the State Court Administrative Office. Each party must complete a separate form.

(b) The petition may contain a request to waive the six-month statutory waiting period under MCL 552.9f.

(2) The petition filed under subrule (1)(a) serves as a complaint and answer unless a party files an objection under subrule (5). It also serves as an appearance of the attorney who signs the petition.

(3) On the filing of the petition and request for entry of consent judgment or consent order and payment of the filing fees, the court clerk shall:

(a) assign a case number and judge, and shall issue a notice of the filing on a form approved by the State Court Administrative Office to be served by Party A as provided in MCR 2.103 and 2.105. The court clerk shall not issue a summons under MCR 2.102(A), and

(b) schedule a hearing date on the proposed consent judgment or consent order but shall not schedule the matter for any pretrial proceedings unless requested by the parties on filing of a motion. The hearing date may not be scheduled sooner than 60 days after the date of the notice of filing. Nothing in this rule precludes the court from waiving the six-month statutory waiting period in accordance with MCL 552.9f.

(4) The notice of the filing must be issued "In the name of the people of the State of Michigan," under the seal of the court that issued it. It must be directed to both parties and include:

(a) the name and address of the court,

(b) the names of the parties,

(c) the case number and name of assigned judge,

(d) the names, addresses, and bar numbers of any attorneys representing the parties,

(e) the date on which the notice of filing was issued,

(f) the date on which the proposed consent judgment or order will be heard by the court,

(g) a statement that if either party objects to this summary proceeding at any time before entry of the proposed consent judgment or consent order, the case will be dismissed, and

(h) a statement that the hearing on the proposed consent judgment or consent order will be held under MCR 3.210 at the conclusion of any applicable statutory waiting period.

(5) If either party objects to this summary proceeding any time before entry of the proposed consent judgment or proposed consent order, the court shall dismiss the case.

(6) At any time after the filing of the proposed consent judgment or proposed consent order, the parties may file stipulations and motions and the court may enter temporary orders.

(D) Entry of Final Consent Judgment or Consent Order. The court shall conduct a hearing on the proposed consent judgment or proposed consent order in accordance with MCR 3.210. Except when a consent judgment is derived through MCR 3.222, both petitioners shall be present for this hearing.

The final consent judgment or final consent order shall be served in accordance with MCR 2.602(D).

(E) Dismissal. A party may dismiss a matter commenced under this rule at any time under MCR 2.504 or as provided under subrule (C)(5).

[Adopted September 20, 2018, effective April 1, 2019, 502 Mich. Amended effective August 14, 2019, 503 Mich.]

Comments

Staff Comment to 2019 Adoption

The amendments of MCR 3.201, 3.210, and 3.211 and addition of MCR 3.222 and 3.223 integrate the collaborative law process designed under the Uniform Collaborative Law Act (159 PA 2014; MCL 691.1331–691.1354) into the state's trial court system for practical use, and add a similar process for parties not represented by counsel who seek to submit a consent judgment.

Staff Comment to 2019 Amendment

These amendments update cross-references and make other nonsubstantive revisions to clarify the rules.

Rule 3.224. Friend of the Court Alternative Dispute Resolution

(A) Friend of the Court Alternative Dispute Resolution Plan. The chief judge of each circuit court shall submit a friend of the court alternative dispute resolution (ADR) plan to the State Court Administrative Office (SCAO) for approval as a local administrative order. The plan shall:

(1) Require the use of the domestic violence screening protocol provided by the SCAO to identify domestic violence, the existence of a protection order as defined in MCL 552.513 between the parties or other protective order, child abuse or neglect, and other safety concerns. The plan shall provide a method to address those concerns.

(2) State the circumstances under which the friend of the court may exclude a case from friend of the court ADR under subrule (D)(2).

(3) Designate the matters each friend of the court ADR process will address, subject to subrule (C)(1).

(4) Designate which friend of the court ADR processes are used in prejudgment or postjudgment friend of the court domestic relations cases.

(5) Designate the manner in which the friend of the court will conduct each process.

(6) Specify how cases are referred to friend of the court ADR.

(7) Address how the court complies with the training, qualifications, and confidentiality provisions for friend of the court ADR processes established by the SCAO pursuant to subrule (J).

(8) Provide that attorneys of record will be allowed to attend, and participate in, all friend of the court ADR processes, or elect not to attend upon mutual agreement with opposing counsel and their client.

(9) Set forth any additional procedures, standards, training, qualifications, and confidentiality requirements of any other friend of the court ADR process the court uses other than those processes set forth in this rule.

(10) Provide that participants in a friend of the court ADR process may not record the proceeding.

(B) Definitions. When used in this rule, unless the context indicates otherwise:

(1) "Domestic violence" means the presence of coercion or violence that would make friend of the court ADR physically or emotionally unsafe for any participant, or that would impede the achievement of a voluntary and safe resolution of issues.

(2) "Friend of the court ADR" means a process established under MCL 552.513 by which the parties are assisted to voluntarily agree to resolve a dispute concerning child custody, parenting time, or support that arises from a domestic relations matter. Friend of the court ADR includes friend of the court mediation, and may include facilitative and information-gathering conferences, joint meetings, and other friend of the court alternative dispute resolution services.

(3) "Friend of the court facilitative and information-gathering conference" is a process in which a facilitator assists the parties in reaching an agreement. If the parties fail to reach an agreement, the facilitator may prepare a report and/or recommended order.

(4) "Friend of the court domestic relations mediation" means a process in which a neutral third party facilitates confidential communication between parties to explore solutions to settle custody and parenting time or support issues for friend of the court cases. Friend of the court domestic relations mediation is not governed by MCR 3.216, which relates to domestic relations mediation conducted without participation or supervision of the friend of the court.

(5) "Joint meeting" means a process in which a person discusses proposed solutions with the parties to a custody or parenting time complaint or an objection to a friend of the court support recommendation.

(6) "Protected party" means a person who has a personal protection order or other protective order against another party to the case or a person who, due to the presence of coercion or violence in a relationship with another party to the case, could be physically or emotionally unsafe.

(C) Friend of the Court ADR Referral.

(1) On written stipulation of the parties, on written motion of a party, or on the court's initiative, the court may order any contested custody, parenting time, or support issue in a domestic relations case, including postjudgment matters to the friend of the court mediation by written order.

(2) The court may, by an order or through its friend of the court ADR plan, provide that the parties are to meet with a person conducting ADR other than friend of the court domestic relations mediation concerning custody, parenting time, and support issues, unless otherwise provided by statute or court rule.

(D) Cases Exempt from Friend of the Court ADR.

(1) Parties who are, or have been, subject to a personal protection order or other protective order or who are involved in a past or present child abuse and neglect proceeding may not be referred to friend of the court ADR without a hearing to determine whether friend of the court ADR is appropriate. The court may order ADR if a protected party requests it without holding a hearing.

(2) The friend of the court may exempt cases from ADR by the friend of the court on the basis of the following:

(a) child abuse or neglect;

(b) domestic abuse, unless the protected party submits a written consent and the friend of the court takes additional precautions to ensure the safety of the protected party and court staff;

(c) inability of one or both parties to negotiate for themselves at the ADR, unless attorneys for both parties will be present at the ADR session;

(d) reason to believe that one or both parties' health or safety would be endangered by ADR; or

(e) for other good cause shown.

(3) The friend of the court shall notify the court when a friend of the court case has been exempted from friend of the court ADR.

(4) If the friend of the court exempts a case from ADR, a party may file a motion and schedule a hearing to request the court to order friend of the court ADR.

(E) Objections to Friend of the Court ADR.

(1) A party may object to ADR under this rule. An objection must be based on one or more of the factors in subrule (D)(2), and must allege facts in support of the objection.

(2) *Objection to Mediation:*

(a) To object to friend of the court domestic relations mediation, a party must file a written motion to remove the case from friend of the court mediation and a notice of hearing of the motion, and serve a copy on all parties or their attorneys of record within 14 days after receiving notice of the order. The motion must be set for hearing within 14 days after it is filed, unless the hearing is adjourned by agreement of counsel or the court orders otherwise.

(b) A timely motion must be heard before the case is mediated.

(3) *Objection to Friend of the Court Facilitative Information–Gathering Conference:*

(a) To object to a friend of the court facilitative and information-gathering conference, a party must include the objection within the pleading or postjudgment motion initiating the action, a responsive pleading or answer, or file the objection within 14 days of the date that the notice is sent to the party. All objections must be filed with the court.

(b) The objecting party must schedule the hearing, and serve a copy of the objection and notice of hearing on all parties and/or attorneys of record.

(c) If a party timely objects, the friend of the court shall not hold a facilitative and information-gathering conference unless the court orders a conference after motion and hearing or the objecting party withdraws the objection.

(4) *Objection to Joint Meetings:*

(a) To object to a joint meeting, the party must file a written objection with the friend of the court and provide a copy to all parties and their attorneys of record before the time scheduled for the joint meeting.

(b) If a party files an objection, the friend of the court shall not hold a joint meeting unless the court orders a joint meeting following a hearing on motion of a party or the objecting party withdraws the objection.

(F) Friend of the Court Facilitative and Information–Gathering Conference Procedure.

(1) A friend of the court facilitative and information-gathering conference shall use the following procedure:

(a) The conference may not begin until the friend of the court case has been screened for domestic violence using a screening protocol provided by the State Court Administrative Office as directed by the Supreme Court.

(b) If domestic violence is identified or suspected, the conference may not proceed unless the protected party submits a written consent and the friend of the court takes additional precautions to ensure the safety of court staff and the protected party. Throughout the facilitative and information-gathering conference process, the facilitator must make reasonable efforts to screen domestic violence that would make the conference physically or emotionally unsafe for any participant or that would impede achieving a voluntary and safe resolution of issues.

(c) At the beginning of the conference, the facilitator will advise the parties and their attorneys, if applicable, of the following:

(i) the purpose of the conference and how the facilitator will conduct the conference and submit an order or recommendation to the court under (F)(2)(a);

(ii) how information gathered during the conference will be used;

(iii) that statements made during the conference are not confidential and can be used in other court proceedings, and shall not be recorded; and

(iv) that the parties are expected to provide information as required by MCL 552.603 to the friend of the court and the consequences of not doing so.

(2) If the parties resolve all contested issues, the facilitator shall submit a report to the court as provided in subrule (I) and may provide a proposed order to the court setting forth the parties' agreements.

(a) If the parties do not resolve all contested issues at the conference or the parties agree to resolve all or some contested issues but do not sign the proposed order, the facilitator shall submit a report as provided in subrule (I) and may do one of the following:

(i) Prepare and forward a recommended order to the court within seven days from the date of the conference. The court may enter the recommended order if it approves the order and must serve it on all parties and attorneys of record within seven days after the date the court enters the order. Accompanying the order must be a notice that a party may object to the order by filing a written objection to the court within 21 days after the date of service, and by scheduling a hearing on the objection. If there is a timely objection, the hearing must be held within 21 days after the objection is filed. If a party objects, the order remains in effect pending a hearing on a party's objection unless the court orders otherwise.

(ii) Prepare and serve a recommended order on the parties within seven days from the date of the conference along with a notice that the recommended order will be presented to the court for entry unless a party objects by filing a written objection within 21 days after the date of service, and by scheduling a hearing on the objection. If neither party files a timely objection, the court may enter the order if it approves.

(iii) Submit a recommendation to the court for further action the court might take to help the parties resolve the remaining contested issues in the case, or alert the court there are contested issues that might require the court's immediate attention.

(b) A party may consent to entry of a recommended order by signing a copy of the order at the time of the conference or after receiving the recommended order. A party who consents to entry of the order waives the right to object to the order and must file a motion to set the order aside once it enters.

(c) Except for communications made during domestic violence screening under subrule (A)(1), (F)(1)(a), and (H)(1)(a), communications made during a friend of the court facilitative and information-gathering conference are not confidential and may be used in court proceedings.

(G) Friend of the Court Domestic Relations Mediation Procedure.

(1) Domestic relations mediation will be conducted by a mediator selected by the friend of the court.

(a) The mediation may not begin until the friend of the court case has been screened for domestic violence using a screening protocol provided by the State Court Administrative Office as directed by the Supreme Court.

(b) If domestic violence is identified or suspected, the mediation process may not continue unless the protected party submits a written consent and the friend of the court takes additional precautions to ensure the safety of the protected party and court staff. Throughout the mediation process, the mediator must make reasonable efforts to screen for the presence of coercion or violence that would make mediation physically or emotionally unsafe for any participant or that would impede achieving a voluntary and safe resolution of issues.

(c) At the beginning of the mediation, the mediator will advise the parties and their attorneys, if applicable, of the following:

(i) the purpose of mediation;

(ii) how the mediator will conduct mediation;

(iii) except as provided for in MCR 2.412(D)(8), statements made during the mediation process are confidential and cannot be used in court proceedings.

(d) If the parties reach an agreement, the mediator shall submit a proposed order and a report pursuant to subrule (I) within seven days.

(e) If the parties do not reach an agreement within seven days of the completion of mediation, the mediator shall so advise the court stating only the date of completion of the process, who participated in the mediation, whether settlement was reached, and whether additional friend of the court ADR proceedings are contemplated.

(2) With the exceptions provided for in MCR 2.412(D), communications during friend of the court domestic relations mediation process are confidential and cannot be used in court proceedings and cannot be recorded.

(H) Joint Meeting Procedure.

(1) Joint meetings shall be conducted as provided in this subrule:

(a) The joint meeting may not begin until the friend of the court case has been screened for domestic violence using a screening protocol provided by the State Court Administrative Office as directed by the Supreme Court.

(b) If domestic violence is identified or suspected, the meeting may not proceed unless the protected party submits a written consent and the friend of the court takes additional precautions to ensure the safety of the protected party and court staff. Throughout the joint meeting, the person conducting the joint meeting must make reasonable efforts to screen for the presence of coercion or violence that would make the joint meeting physically or emotionally unsafe for any participant or that would impede achieving a voluntary and safe resolution of issues.

(c) At the beginning of a joint meeting, the person conducting the meeting shall do the following:

(i) advise the parties that statements made during the joint meeting are not confidential and can be used in other court proceedings;

(ii) advise the parties that the purpose of the meeting is for the parties to reach an accommodation and how the person will conduct the meeting;

(iii) advise the parties that the person may recommend an order to the court to resolve the dispute; and

(iv) explain to the parties the information provided for in subrules (H)(1)(d)–(e).

(d) At the conclusion of a joint meeting, the person conducting the meeting shall submit a report within seven days pursuant to subrule (I) and may do one of the following:

(i) If the parties reach an accommodation, record the accommodation in writing and provide a copy to the parties and attorneys of record. If the accommodation modifies an order, the person must submit a proposed order to the court. If the court approves the order, the court shall enter it; or

(ii) Submit an order to the court stating the person's recommendation for resolving the dispute. The parties may consent by signing the recommended order and waiving the objection period in accordance with (H)(1)(e)(iii). If the court approves the order, the court shall enter it.

(e) If the person conducting the joint meeting submits a recommended order within seven days to the court, the friend of the court must serve the parties and attorneys of record a copy of the order and a notice that provides the following information:

(i) that the court may enter the recommended order resolving the dispute unless a party objects to the order within 21 days after the notice is sent;

(ii) when and where a written objection must be submitted;

(iii) that a party may waive the 21-day objection period by returning a signed copy of the recommended order; and

(iv) if a party files a written objection within the 21–day limit, the friend of the court office shall set a court hearing before a judge or referee to resolve the dispute. If a party fails to file a written objection within the 21–day limit, the office shall submit the proposed order to the court for entry if the court approves it.

(2) Except for communications made during domestic violence screening, communications made during a joint meeting are not confidential and may be used in other court proceedings and cannot be recorded.

(I) The SCAO shall develop forms for reports and orders that the friend of the court shall use in the ADR processes under this court rule.

(1) A report form for a proposed consent order shall contain sufficient information to allow the court to make an independent determination that the proposed order is in the child's best interest.

(2) When the parties do not resolve some or all of the issues in a facilitative and information-gathering conference or when the friend of the court submits a proposed order following a joint meeting, the report shall contain the parties' agreed-upon and disputed facts and issues.

(3) A report under this subrule is not a friend of the court report entitled to consideration under MRE 1101(b)(9). In any contested hearing, the court may use the report to:

(a) decide the contested matter to the extent the parties do not dispute the issues or facts in the report or to the extent that the contested issues and facts are not material to the court's decision; or

(b) if the parties dispute any issues or facts in the report, the court must make an independent determination based on evidence and testimony presented at the hearing or a subsequent hearing.

(4) The court may, on its own motion, order the friend of the court to conduct an investigation and provide a report under MCL 552.505(1)(G).

(J) Qualification of ADR Providers.

(1) The SCAO shall establish training and qualification requirements for persons conducting each type of ADR under this court rule.

(2) The SCAO shall also provide a process for waiving training and qualification requirements when:

(a) the trial court demonstrates a person who meets the requirements is not reasonably available and the court's proposed candidate has suitable qualifications equivalent to those established by the SCAO; or

(b) the person will complete the requirements within a reasonable time determined by the SCAO.

[Adopted July 24, 2019, effective January 1, 2020, 503 Mich.]

Comments

Staff Comment to 2020 Adoption

This proposal was developed by a workgroup facilitated by SCAO's Friend of the Court division to make more uniform the ADR processes used by Friend of the Court offices.

Rule 3.229. Filing Confidential Materials

(A) If a party or interested party files any of the following items with the court, the party shall identify the document as a confidential document and the items shall be served on the other parties in the case and maintained in a nonpublic file in accordance with subrule (B):

(1) verified statements and disclosure forms under MCR 3.206(B);

(2) child protective services reports;

(3) psychological evaluations;

(4) custody evaluations;

(5) medical, mental health, and academic records of a minor;

(6) any part of a confidential file under MCR 3.903(A)(3);

(7) any item designated as confidential or nonpublic by statute or court rule; and

(8) any other document which, in the court's discretion, should not be part of the public record.

(B) Any item filed and identified under subrule (A) is nonpublic and must be maintained separately from the legal file. The filer waives any claim of confidentiality to any item filed under subrule (A) that is not identified by the filer as confidential. The nonpublic file must be made available for any appellate review.

[Adopted June 19, 2019, effective January 1, 2020, 503 Mich. Amended December 27, 2019, effective January 1, 2020, 503 Mich.]

Comments

Staff Comment to 2020 Adoption

These amendments are based on a proposal created by a special committee of the State Bar of Michigan and approved for submission to the Court by the Bar's Representative Assembly. The rules require mandatory discovery disclosure in many cases, adopt a presumptive limit on interrogatories (20 in most cases, but 35 in domestic relations proceedings) and limit a deposition to 7 hours. The amendments also update the rules to more specifically address issues related to electronically stored information, and encourage early action on discovery issues during the discovery period.

The amendment of MCR 2.309(A)(2) sets a presumptive limit of twenty interrogatories for each separately represented party. Several commenters suggested that the term "discrete subpart" be more explicitly defined. But the rule's reference to "a discrete subpart" is intended to draw guidance from federal courts construing FR Civ P 30(a)(1). Generally, subparts are not separately counted if they are logically or factually subsumed within and necessarily related to the primary question. In upholding the limit, parties and courts should also pragmatically balance the overall goals of discovery and the admonition of MCR 1.105. Further, the intent of the provision at MCR 2.301(B)(4) is to ensure that parties responding to discovery requests have the full time period to do so as provided for under these rules prior to the expiration of the discovery period.

Staff Comment to 2020 Amendment

The amendment of MCR 3.229 requires the filer to identify nonpublic documents when they are submitted to the clerk, and stipulates that the filer waives any claim of confidentiality where such documents are filed without a designation of confidentiality. These amendments update the language originally adopted by the Court as part of the civil discovery rules proposal in ADM File No. 2018–19.

Rule 3.230. Actions Under the Summary Support and Paternity Act

(A) Scope and Applicability of Rules; Definitions.

(1) Procedure in actions under the Summary Support and Paternity Act, MCL 722.1491 *et seq.*, is governed by the rules applicable to other domestic relations actions, except as otherwise provided in this rule and the act.

(2) *Definitions.* For purposes of this rule

(a) "IV–D agency" means the agency in a county that provides support and paternity establishment services under MCL 722.1501.

(b) "Plaintiff" means

(i) The child's mother, father, or alleged father on whose behalf the IV–D agency files the action, or

(ii) The Michigan Department of Health and Human Services when the IV–D agency files an action on behalf of a child.

(c) "Expedited paternity action" means an action commenced to establish either paternity or paternity and support under MCL 722.1491 *et seq.*

(d) "Expedited support action" means an action commenced to establish a parent's support obligation under MCL 722.1499.

(B) Commencing an Action.

(1) A IV–D agency commences an expedited paternity or expedited support action by filing one of the following with the court:

(a) A complaint and notice, or

(b) A request to enter a consent agreement, and a consent judgment or order signed by the parties.

(2) Upon filing an action, the court clerk shall assign a case number and judge. The court clerk shall not issue a summons under MCR 2.102.

(3) A complaint, notice, and request for entry of a consent agreement used to initiate an action or set child support must be completed on forms approved by the State Court Administrative Office.

(4) *Complaint.* A complaint filed in an expedited action shall:

(a) comply with MCR 1.109, MCR 2.113, and MCR 3.206(A),

(b) be verified and signed by the mother or alleged father, or signed "on information and belief" by the IV–D agency,

(c) comply with MCR 2.201(E) if the plaintiff is a minor,

(d) state the relief being requested, and either

(i) comply with MCL 722.1495 and other applicable laws and rules if filed in an expedited paternity action, or

(ii) comply with MCL 722.1499 and other applicable laws and rules if filed in an expedited support action.

(5) *Notice.* A notice to initiate an expedited paternity or expedited support action shall be titled "In the name of the people of the state of Michigan," and shall be signed by the IV–D agency. The notice must be directed to the defendant and:

(a) comply with MCR 1.109(D);

(b) include the name, address, and phone number of the IV–D agency filing the action;

(c) state that written responses, agreements, and other actions must be filed with the court within 21 days after being served, and if the defendant fails to file a written response pursuant to statute or take other action within 21 days, an order or a judgment may be entered granting the relief requested in the complaint without further notice or hearing; and

(d) include an expiration date, which does not exceed 126 days after the date the action is filed.

(6) *Request to Enter Consent Agreement.* A request for entry of a consent judgment or order to initiate an expedited paternity or expedited support action shall:

(a) comply with MCR 1.109(D)(1),

(b) contain the grounds for jurisdiction, the statutory grounds to enter the judgment or order, and a request for entry of the judgment or order without further notice; and

(c) be signed by the parties and the IV–D agency.

(7) The requirement to submit a verified statement or disclosure form required under MCR 3.206(C) does not apply to an expedited paternity or expedited support action, unless otherwise directed by the court.

(C) Service.

(1) A complaint and notice filed under subrule (B)(1)(a) must be served on the parties by the IV–D agency in accordance with MCR 2.105, or in the alternative, may be served by mail in accordance with MCL 722.1495(4).

(2) Pursuant to MCL 722.1501(4)(c), a request to enter a consent judgment or order filed under subrule (B)(1)(b) is considered served at the time of filing, and a party's signature on the request to enter a consent agreement, judgment, or order acknowledges service.

(3) After a party has been served under subrule (C)(1) or (2), other court papers, orders, and notices shall be served in accordance with MCR 3.203.

(D) Dismissal as to Defendant Not Served.

(1) Upon expiration of the notice under subrule (B)(5)(d), the action is deemed dismissed without prejudice if the defendant has not been served with notice of the action unless the defendant has responded.

(2) A court shall set aside a dismissal of an action under this subrule without hearing upon showing by the IV–D agency within 28 days of the expiration of the notice that the defendant did in fact receive timely notice or had submitted to the court's jurisdiction before the dismissal.

(E) Setting Child Support.

(1) At the time that a complaint is filed, or any time after establishing paternity or a duty to support a child, the IV–D agency may provide notice setting a proposed support amount. The proposed support obligation shall be calculated by application of the Michigan Child Support Formula or a properly documented deviation from the amount calculated using the formula. The notice or an accompanying calculation results report must state the amounts calculated for support, the proposed effective date, and the facts and assumptions upon which the calculation is based.

(2) A notice and calculation report setting a child support amount shall be filed with the court and provided to the parties. The notice shall contain statements notifying the parties of all of the following:

(a) that objections and responses to the notice must be filed within 21 days from:

(i) the date of service, if the notice setting child support is served at the same time as the complaint and notice; or

(ii) the date of mailing or service, if the notice is served under MCR 3.203.

(b) a party may object to the proposed child support amount based on either a mistake in the facts or assumptions used to calculate support, or on an error in the calculation by filing an answer requesting a hearing on the proposed obligation;

(c) if no objection is filed, an order will be submitted to the court in the proposed amounts for entry without further notice or hearing;

(d) if an objection is filed, a hearing will be scheduled, unless the IV–D agency recalculates the amount and sends a new notice.

(3) If the IV–D agency receives information from a party after filing a notice setting a child support amount and before a support order is submitted for entry, the agency may recalculate support and issue a new notice and calculation report under this subrule proposing a corrected child support amount.

(F) Response.

(1) Within 21 days after being served with a notice under subrule (B) or a notice under subrule (E), a party must file a response with the court or take another action permitted by law or these rules. The party must serve copies of the response on the IV–D agency and the other party in accordance with MCR 3.203.

(2) The IV–D agency shall immediately forward to the court any response it receives from a party who has not filed the response with the court.

(3) A request to enter a consent agreement, or a consent judgment or order filed under subrule (B)(1)(b) does not require a response. A party may file an additional response or motion regarding issues not resolved by the agreement, consent judgment or order, or the other party filing an additional response.

(4) Within 14 days after the time permitted for responses under subrule (F)(1), if a party has filed a response, or pursuant to any matter left unresolved, the IV–D agency shall take one or more of the following actions:

(a) schedule genetic testing, if a party in an expedited paternity action requests genetic testing;

(b) schedule a hearing on any matters or relief proposed in a complaint or notice that are contested, and the IV–D agency may submit a proposed order or judgment that incorporates any proposed relief that was not contested; or

(c) submit a proposed judgment or order that incorporates any proposed relief that a party agrees to or that was not contested.

(G) Failure to Respond.

(1) Subrule MCR 3.210(B) does not apply to proceedings under this rule.

(2) If neither party in an action to establish paternity brought against an alleged father requests genetic tests and the defendant does not otherwise defend within 21 days after receiving notice, the IV–D agency may request entry of a judgment establishing defendant as the child's legal father by submitting a proposed judgment for entry.

(3) In an action to establish paternity brought by an alleged father against the child's mother, if the mother does not admit the alleged father's paternity, the court shall not determine paternity unless based on genetic test results.

(4) When a defendant does not respond or otherwise defend, the IV–D agency shall submit a proposed order that establishes the duty to support the child.

(5) If neither party files an objection to a notice setting a support amount within 21 days, the IV–D agency shall submit a support order in the recommended amounts to the court.

(6) Nonmilitary affidavits required by law must be filed before a judgment is entered in cases in which the defendant has failed to respond or appear.

(7) A judgment may not be entered against a minor or an incompetent person who has failed to respond or appear unless the person is assisted in the action by a conservator or other representative, except as otherwise provided by law.

(H) Judgments and Orders.

(1) The court may consider the complaints and other documents filed with the court, relevant and material affidavits, or other evidence when entering an order in an expedited paternity or support action.

(2) Entering Orders. The court may enter a proposed judgment or order submitted by the IV–D agency without hearing if the court is satisfied of all of the following:

(a) that the parties were given proper notice and opportunity to file a response,

(b) the statutory and rule requirements were met, and

(c) the terms of the judgment or order are in accordance with the law.

(3) The IV–D agency seeking entry of a proposed judgment or order must schedule a hearing and serve the motion, notice of hearing, and a copy of the proposed judgment or orders upon the parties at least 14 days before the hearing, and promptly file a proof of service when:

(a) the proposed judgment involves a request for relief that is different from the relief requested in the complaint; or

(b) the IV–D agency does not have sufficient facts to complete the judgment or order without a judicial determination of the relief to which the party is entitled.

(4) If the court determines that a proposed judgment or order is not in accordance with the law or that the court needs additional information to decide the matter, the court may direct the IV–D agency or the parties to do any of the following within 14 days:

(a) submit a modified proposed judgment or order in conformity with the court's ruling;

(b) file additional affidavits or other documents and notices, or

(c) schedule a hearing to present evidence sufficient to satisfy the court or to meet statutory requirements.

(5) A party may waive a statutory waiting period or further notice prior to entry of a consent judgment or order.

(6) If paternity of a child has not been established and a party or IV–D agency requests genetic testing, the court may order the parties and child to submit to genetic testing without a hearing.

(7) Upon entry of a judgment or order and as provided by MCR 3.203, the IV–D agency must serve a copy as entered by the court on all parties within 7 days after entry, and promptly file a proof of service.

[Adopted September 18, 2019, effective January 1, 2020, 503 Mich.]

Comments

Staff Comment to 2020 Adoption

The amendment of MCR 3.201 and addition of MCR 3.230 provides procedural rules to incorporate the Summary Support and Paternity Act (366 PA 2014; MCL 722.1491, *et seq.*) to establish a parent's paternity or support obligation through a summary action.

SUBCHAPTER 3.300   EXTRAORDINARY WRITS

Rule 3.301.   Extraordinary Writs in General

(A) Applicability and Scope of Rules.

(1) A civil action or appropriate motion in a pending action may be brought to obtain

(a) superintending control,

(b) habeas corpus,

(c) mandamus, or

(d) quo warranto.

Unless a particular rule or statute specifically provides otherwise, an original action may not be commenced in the Supreme Court or the Court of Appeals if the circuit court would have jurisdiction of an action seeking that relief.

(2) These special rules govern the procedure for seeking the writs or relief formerly obtained by the writs, whether the right to relief is created by statute or common law. If the right to relief is created by statute, the limitations on relief in the statute apply, as well as the limitations on relief in these rules.

(3) The general rules of procedure apply except as otherwise provided in this subchapter.

(B) Joinder of Claims. More than one kind of writ may be sought in an action either as an independent claim or as an alternative claim. Subject to MCR 2.203, other claims may be joined in an action for a writ or writs.

(C) Process; Service of Writs. Process must be issued and served as in other civil actions. However, if a writ, order, or order to show cause is issued before service of process, then service of the writ, order, or order to show cause in the manner prescribed in MCR 2.105, accompanied by a copy of the complaint, makes service of other process unnecessary.

(D) Assignment for Trial. Actions brought under these special rules may be given precedence under MCR 2.501(B).

(E) Records. The action taken on applications for writs or orders to show cause must be noted in court records in the same manner as actions taken in other civil actions.

(F) No Automatic Stay. The automatic stay provisions of MCR 2.614(A) do not apply to judgments in actions brought under this subchapter.

(G) Procedure Where Relief Is Sought in Supreme Court or Court of Appeals.

(1) MCR 7.306 applies to original proceedings brought in the Supreme Court to obtain relief under this subchapter.

(2) MCR 7.206 applies to original proceedings brought in the Court of Appeals to obtain relief under this subchapter.

[Adopted effective March 1, 1985. Amended effective March 21, 2018, 501 Mich.]

Comments

Staff Comment to 1985 Adoption

MCR 3.301 is comparable to GCR 1963, 710.

The amendment of MCR 3.301(A)(1) [entered January 25, 1985, effective March 1, 1985] adds language comparable to that found in GCR 1963, 710.1(3), providing that original actions are not to be brought in the Supreme Court or Court of Appeals if the circuit court would have jurisdiction. The provision of GCR 1963, 710.5 regarding pretrial conferences is omitted.

GCR 1963, 710.7, regarding the procedures to be followed in the Court of Appeals, is replaced with cross-references to the provisions of chapter 7 governing original proceedings in the Supreme Court and the Court of Appeals.

Staff Comment to 2018 Amendment

These amendments update cross-references and make other nonsubstantive revisions to clarify the rules. The amendment of MCR 6.110(B)(1) addresses an inadvertent omission from the last amendment of this rule that was intended to be shown in overstrike. Accordingly, the current rule does not match the published version. Striking the clause "for good cause shown" will provide consistency with other published versions of the rule and with the statute, MCL 766.7, which allows a magistrate to adjourn a preliminary examination with the consent of the parties without the need for good cause to be shown.

Rule 3.302.   Superintending Control

(A) Scope. A superintending control order enforces the superintending control power of a court over lower courts or tribunals.

(B) Policy Concerning Use. If another adequate remedy is available to the party seeking the order, a complaint for superintending control may not be filed. See subrule (D)(2), and MCR 7.101(A)(2), and 7.306(A).

(C) Writs Superseded. A superintending control order replaces the writs of certiorari and prohibition and the writ of mandamus when directed to a lower court or tribunal.

(D) Jurisdiction.

(1) The Supreme Court, the Court of Appeals, and the circuit court have jurisdiction to issue superintending control orders to lower courts or tribunals.

(2) When an appeal in the Supreme Court, the Court of Appeals, or the circuit court is available, that method of review must be used. If superintending control is sought and an appeal is available, the complaint for superintending control must be dismissed.

(E) Procedure for Superintending Control in Circuit Court.

(1) *Complaint.* A person seeking superintending control in the circuit court must file a complaint with the court. Only the plaintiff's name may appear in the title of the action (for example, *In re Smith*). The plaintiff must serve a copy of the complaint on the court or tribunal over which superintending control is sought. If the superintending control action arises out of a particular action, a copy of the complaint must also be

served on each other party to the proceeding in that court or tribunal.

(2) *Answer.* Anyone served under subrule (E)(1) may file an answer within 21 days after the complaint is served.

(3) *Issuance of Order; Dismissal.*

(a) After the filing of a complaint and answer or, if no answer is filed, after expiration of the time for filing an answer, the court may

(i) issue an order to show cause why the order requested should not be issued,

(ii) issue the order requested, or

(iii) dismiss the complaint.

(b) If a need for immediate action is shown, the court may enter an order before an answer is filed.

(c) The court may require in an order to show cause that additional records and documents be filed.

(d) An order to show cause must specify the date for hearing the complaint.

[Adopted effective March 1, 1985. Amended effective May 7, 2014, 495 Mich; March 21, 2018, 501 Mich. Amended March 20, 2019, effective May 1, 2019, 502 Mich.]

Comments

Staff Comment to 1985 Adoption

MCR 3.302 is substantially the same as GCR 1963, 711.

Subrule (D) is modified (from GCR 1963, 711.4) to take account of the superintending control and appellate jurisdiction of the Recorder's Court of the City of Detroit. See MCL 725.10b; MCL 770.3(1)(c).

Staff Comment to 2014 Amendment

These amendments reflect changes that correct minor technical errors that have occurred in drafting or the changes respond to recent adopted rule revisions, which occasionally inadvertently create incorrect cross-references in other rules.

Staff Comment to 2018 Amendment

These amendments update cross-references and make other nonsubstantive revisions to clarify the rules. The amendment of MCR 6.110(B)(1) addresses an inadvertent omission from the last amendment of this rule that was intended to be shown in overstrike. Accordingly, the current rule does not match the published version. Striking the clause "for good cause shown" will provide consistency with other published versions of the rule and with the statute, MCL 766.7, which allows a magistrate to adjourn a preliminary examination with the consent of the parties without the need for good cause to be shown.

Staff Comment to 2019 Amendment

The amendments of Rules 1.109, 2.102, 2.104, 2.106, 2.107, 2.117, 2.119, 2.403, 2.503, 2.506, 2.508, 2.518, 2.602, 2.603, 2.621, 3.101, 3.104, 3.203, 3.205, 3.210, 3.302, 3.607, 3.613, 3.614, 3.705, 3.801, 3.802, 3.805, 3.806, 4.201, 4.202, 4.303, 4.306, 5.001, 5.104, 5.105, 5.107, 5.108, 5.113, 5.117, 5.118, 5.119, 5.120, 5.125, 5.126, 5.132, 5.162, 5.202, 5.203, 5.205, 5.302, 5.304, 5.307, 5.308, 5.309, 5.310, 5.311, 5.313, 5.402, 5.404, 5.405, 5.409, 5.501, and 5.784 and addition of Rule 3.618 of the Michigan Court Rules are an expected progression necessary for design and implementation of the statewide electronic-filing system. These particular amendments will assist in implementing the goals of the project.

Rule 3.303. Habeas Corpus to Inquire into Cause of Detention

(A) Jurisdiction and Venue; Persons Detained on Criminal Charges.

(1) An action for habeas corpus to inquire into the cause of detention of a person may be brought in any court of record except the probate court.

(2) The action must be brought in the county in which the prisoner is detained. If it is shown that there is no judge in that county empowered and available to issue the writ or that

the judicial circuit for that county has refused to issue the writ, the action may be brought in the Court of Appeals.

(3) A prisoner detained in a county jail for a criminal charge, who has not been sentenced to detention by a court of competent jurisdiction, may be removed from detention by a writ of habeas corpus to inquire into the cause of detention only if the writ is issued by the court in which the prisoner would next appear if the criminal process against the prisoner continued, or by the judicial circuit for the county in which the prisoner is detained. This subrule does not limit the power of the Court of Appeals or Supreme Court to issue the writ.

(B) Who May Bring. An action for habeas corpus may be brought by the prisoner or by another person on the prisoner's behalf.

(C) Complaint. The complaint must state:

(1) that the person on whose behalf the writ is applied for (the prisoner) is restrained of his or her liberty;

(2) the name, if known, or the description of the prisoner;

(3) the name, if known, or the description of the officer or person by whom the prisoner is restrained;

(4) the place of restraint, if known;

(5) that the action for habeas corpus by or on behalf of the prisoner is not prohibited;

(6) the cause or pretense of the restraint, according to the plaintiff's best knowledge and belief; and

(7) why the restraint is illegal.

(D) Issuance of the Writ or Order to Show Cause.

(1) On the filing of the complaint, the court may issue

(a) a writ of habeas corpus directed to the person having custody of the prisoner, or that person's superior, ordering him or her to bring the prisoner before the court forthwith; or

(b) an order to show cause why the writ should not be issued,

unless it appears that the prisoner is not entitled to relief.

(2) On the showing required by MCL 600.4337, the court may issue a warrant in lieu of habeas corpus.

(3) Duplicate original writs may be issued.

(E) Certification of Record. When proceedings in another court or agency are pertinent to a determination of the issue raised in a habeas corpus action, the court may order the transcript of the record and proceedings certified to the court within a specified time. The order must identify the records to be certified with sufficient specificity to allow them to be located.

(F) Issuance Without Application or Before Filing.

(1) A judge of a court of record, except the probate court, may issue a writ of habeas corpus or order to show cause if

(a) the judge learns that a person within the judge's jurisdiction is illegally restrained, or

(b) an application is presented to the judge before or after normal court hours.

(2) If the prisoner is being held on criminal charges, the writ or order may only be issued by a judge of a court authorized to issue a writ of habeas corpus under subrule (A)(3).

(3) If a complaint is presented to a judge under the provisions of subrule (F)(1)(b), it need not be filed with the court before the issuance of a writ of habeas corpus. The complaint must subsequently be filed with the court whether or not the writ is granted.

(G) Endorsement of Allowance of Writ. Every writ issued must be endorsed with a certificate of its allowance and the date of the allowance. The endorsement must be signed by the judge issuing the writ, or, if the writ is issued by a panel of more than 1 judge, by a judge of the court.

(H) Form of Writ. A writ of habeas corpus must be substantially in the form approved by the state court administrator.

(I) Service of Writ.

(1) *Person to Be Served.* The writ or order to show cause must be served on the defendant in the manner prescribed in MCR 2.105. If the defendant cannot be found, or if the defendant does not have the prisoner in custody, the writ or order to show cause may be served on anyone having the prisoner in custody or that person's superior, in the manner and with the same effect as if that person had been made a defendant in the action.

(2) *Tender of Fees.* If the Attorney General or a prosecuting attorney brings the action, or if a judge issues the writ on his or her own initiative, there is no fee. In other actions, to make the service of a writ of habeas corpus effective, the person making service must give the fee provided by law or this rule to the person having custody of the prisoner or to that person's superior.

(a) If the prisoner is in the custody of a sheriff, coroner, constable, or marshal, the fee is that allowed by law to a sheriff for bringing up a prisoner.

(b) If the prisoner is in the custody of another person, the fee is that, if any, allowed by the court issuing the writ, not exceeding the fee allowed by law to a sheriff for similar services.

(J) Sufficiency of Writ. The writ or order to show cause may not be disobeyed because of a defect in form. The writ or order to show cause is sufficient if the prisoner is designated by name, if known, or by a description sufficient to permit identification. The writ or order may designate the person to whom it is directed as the person having custody of the prisoner. Anyone served with the writ or order is deemed the person to whom it is directed and is considered a defendant in the action.

(K) Time for Answer and Hearing.

(1) If the writ is to be answered and the hearing held on a specified day and hour, the answer must be made and the prisoner produced at the time and place specified in the writ.

(2) If an order to show cause is issued, it must be answered as provided in subrule (N), and the hearing must be held at the time and place specified in the order.

(L) Notice of Hearing Before Discharge.

(1) When the answer states that the prisoner is in custody on process under which another person has an interest in continuing the custody, an order of discharge may not be issued unless the interested person or that person's attorney has had at least 4 days' notice of the time and place of the hearing.

(2) When the answer states that the prisoner is detained on a criminal charge, the prisoner may not be discharged until sufficient notice of the time and place of the hearing is given to the prosecuting attorney of the county within which the prisoner is detained or, if there is no prosecuting attorney within the county, to the Attorney General.

(M) Habeas Corpus to Obtain Custody of Child.

(1) A complaint seeking a writ of habeas corpus to inquire into a child's custody must be presented to the judicial circuit for the county in which the child resides or is found.

(2) An order to show cause, not a writ of habeas corpus, must be issued initially if the action is brought by a parent, foster parent, or other relative of the child, to obtain custody of a child under the age of 16 years from a parent, foster parent, or other relative of the child. The court may direct the friend of the court to investigate the circumstances of the child's custody.

(N) Answer.

(1) *Contents of Answer; Contempt.* The defendant or person served must obey the writ or order to show cause or show good cause for not doing so, and must answer the writ or order to show cause within the time allowed. Failure to file an answer is contempt. The answer must state plainly and unequivocally

(a) whether the defendant then has, or at any time has had, the prisoner under his or her control and, if so, the reason; and

(b) if the prisoner has been transferred, to whom, when the transfer was made, and the reason or authority for the transfer.

(2) *Attachments.* If the prisoner is detained because of a writ, warrant, or other written authority, a copy must be attached to the answer, and the original must be produced at the hearing. If an order under subrule (E) requires it, the answer must be accompanied by the certified transcript of the record and proceedings.

(3) *Verification.* The answer must be signed by the person answering, and, except when the person is a sworn public officer and answers in his or her official capacity, it must be verified by oath.

(O) Answer May Be Controverted. In a reply or at a hearing, the plaintiff or the prisoner may controvert the answer under oath, to show either that the restraint is unlawful or that the prisoner is entitled to discharge.

(P) Prisoner; When Bailed. Because a habeas corpus action must be decided promptly with no more than the brief delay provided by subrule (Q)(2), release of a prisoner on bail will not normally be considered until after determination that legal cause exists for the detention. Thereafter, if the prisoner is entitled to bail, the court issuing the writ or order may set bail.

(Q) Hearing and Judgment.

(1) The court shall proceed promptly to hear the matter in a summary manner and enter judgment.

(2) In response to the writ of habeas corpus or order to show cause, the defendant may request adjournment of the hearing. Adjournment may be granted only for the brief delay necessary to permit the defendant

(a) to prepare a written answer (unless waived by the plaintiff); or

(b) to present to the court or judge issuing the writ or order testimonial or documentary evidence to establish the cause of detention at the time for answer.

(3) In the defendant's presence, the court shall inform the prisoner that he or she has the right to an attorney and the right to remain silent.

(4) From the time the prisoner is produced in response to the writ or order until judgment is entered, the judge who issued the writ or order has custody of the prisoner and shall make certain that the prisoner's full constitutional rights are protected.

(5) The hearing on the return to a writ of habeas corpus or an order to show cause must be recorded verbatim, unless a court reporter or recorder is not available. If the hearing is conducted without a verbatim record being made, as soon as possible the judge shall prepare and certify a narrative written report. The original report is part of the official record in the action, and copies must be sent forthwith to the parties or their attorneys.

(6) If the prisoner is restrained because of mental disease, the court shall consider the question of the prisoner's mental condition at the time of the hearing, rather than merely the legality of the original detention.

[Adopted effective March 1, 1985. Amended September 18, 2019, effective January 1, 2020, 503 Mich.]

Comments

Staff Comment to 1985 Adoption

MCR 3.303 is comparable to GCR 1963, 712.

Subrule (A)(1) is rewritten to remove the authority of a single judge of the Court of Appeals to entertain an action for habeas corpus. The rule does not list the courts in which the action may be brought, as did GCR 1963, 712.1(1), but rather provides that it may be brought in any court of record except the probate court. See MCL 600.4304.

Subrule (A)(2) is revised. If there is no judge in the county empowered and available to issue the writ, or the circuit court of a county has refused to issue it, the action can be brought in the Court of Appeals, rather than in an adjoining county as was provided in GCR 1963, 712.1(2).

Subrule (A)(3) is revised with regard to prisoners detained pending criminal proceedings. In addition to the circuit court in that county, the court in which the prisoner would next appear if the criminal process continued (e.g., the Recorder's Court of the City of Detroit or the district court) may do so.

Subrule (B) is a new provision explicitly stating that the action may be brought on behalf of a prisoner by another person. See MCL 600.4307.

Subrule (C) omits the requirement of GCR 1963, 712.3(2) that a copy of the warrant or process by which the prisoner is being held be attached to the complaint.

Subrule (D)(2) limits the circumstances in which a warrant in lieu of habeas corpus may be issued by citing the controlling statute.

Subrule (F) adds additional detail as to the procedure when a writ of habeas corpus is sought after court hours or when a judge issues the writ without a complaint being filed. Compare GCR 1963, 712.7.

Subrule (M), regarding habeas corpus to obtain custody of a child, limits the bringing of such actions to the circuit court. Compare GCR 1963, 712.14.

The form for a writ of habeas corpus, found in GCR 1963, 712.9, is omitted. Such forms will be approved by the state court administrator.

Staff Comment to 2020 Amendment

The amendments of MCR 1.109, 2.107, 2.113, 2.116, 2.119, 2.222, 2.223, 2.225, 2.227, 3.206, 3.211, 3.212, 3.214, 3.303, 3.903, 3.921, 3.925, 3.926, 3.931, 3.933, 3.942, 3.950, 3.961, 3.971, 3.972, 4.002, 4.101, 4.201, 4.202, 4.302, 5.128, 5.302, 5.731, 6.101, 6.615, 8.105, and 8.119 and rescission of MCR 2.226 and 8.125 continue the process for design and implementation of the statewide electronic-filing system.

Rule 3.304   Habeas Corpus to Bring Prisoner to Testify or for Prosecution

(A) Jurisdiction; When Available. A court of record may issue a writ of habeas corpus directing that a prisoner in a jail or prison in Michigan be brought to testify

(1) on the court's own initiative; or

(2) on the ex parte motion of a party in an action before a court or an officer or body authorized to examine witnesses.

A writ of habeas corpus may also be issued to bring a prisoner to court for prosecution. Subrules (C)–(G) apply to such a writ.

(B) Contents of Motion. The motion must be verified by the party and must state

(1) the title and nature of the action in which the testimony of the prisoner is desired; and

(2) that the testimony of the prisoner is relevant and necessary to the party in that proceeding.

(C) Direction to Surrender Custody for Transportation. The writ may direct that the prisoner be placed in the custody of a designated officer for transportation to the place where the hearing or trial is to be held, rather than requiring the custodian to bring the prisoner to that place.

(D) Form of Writ. A writ of habeas corpus to produce a prisoner to testify or for prosecution must be substantially in the form approved by the state court administrator.

(E) Answer and Hearing. If the prisoner is produced or delivered to the custody of a designated officer as ordered, the person served with the writ need not answer the writ, and a hearing on the writ is unnecessary.

(F) Remand. When a prisoner is brought on a writ of habeas corpus to testify or for prosecution, the prisoner must be returned to the original custodian after testifying or prosecution.

(G) Applicability of Other Rules. MCR 3.303(G), (I), (J), and (K)(1) apply to habeas corpus to produce a prisoner to testify or for prosecution.

[Adopted effective March 1, 1985.]

Comments

Staff Comment to 1985 Adoption

MCR 3.304 corresponds to GCR 1963, 713. The rule is expanded to allow its procedures to be used to bring a prisoner for prosecution as well as to testify.

Subrule (B)(2) modifies the provisions of GCR 1963, 713.2(2) by eliminating the requirement that the verified motion state that the party's attorney has advised that the witness is necessary.

Subrule (C) provides that the writ may direct that the prisoner be placed in the custody of a designated officer for transportation to the hearing, rather than requiring the custodian to transport the prisoner.

Rule 3.305.   Mandamus

(A) Jurisdiction.

(1) An action for mandamus against a state officer may be brought in the Court of Appeals or the Court of Claims.

(2) All other actions for mandamus must be brought in the circuit court unless a statute or rule requires or allows the action to be brought in another court.

(B) Venue.

(1) The general venue statutes and rules apply to actions for mandamus unless a specific statute or rule contains a special venue provision.

(2) In addition to any other county in which venue is proper, an action for mandamus against a state officer may be brought in Ingham County.

(C) Order to Show Cause. On ex parte motion and a showing of the necessity for immediate action, the court may issue an order to show cause. The motion may be made in the complaint. The court shall indicate in the order when the defendant must answer the order.

(D) Answer. If necessity for immediate action is not shown, and the action is not dismissed, the defendant must answer the complaint as in an ordinary civil action.

(E) Exhibits. A party may attach to the pleadings, as exhibits, certified or authenticated copies of record evidence on which the party relies.

(F) Hearings in Circuit Court. The court may hear the matter or may allow the issues to be tried by a jury.

(G) Writ Contained in Judgment. If the judgment awards a writ of mandamus, the writ may be contained in the judgment in the form of an order, and a separate writ need not be issued or served.

[Adopted effective March 1, 1985. Amended effective March 21, 2018, 501 Mich.]

Comments

Staff Comment to 1985 Adoption

MCR 3.305 is comparable to GCR 1963, 714.

Subrule (A)(1) permits actions against state officers to be brought in either the Court of Appeals or the circuit court. See MCL 600.4401.

In subrule (A)(2) the list of other categories of mandamus defendants is replaced with a reference to "all other" mandamus actions. Compare GCR 1963, 714.1(2).

The venue provisions of subrule (B) are new.

Staff Comment to 2018 Amendment

These amendments update cross-references and make other nonsubstantive revisions to clarify the rules. The amendment of MCR 6.110(B)(1) addresses an inadvertent omission from the last amendment of this rule that was intended to be shown in overstrike. Accordingly, the current rule does not match the published version. Striking the clause "for good cause shown" will provide consistency with other published versions of the rule and with the statute, MCL 766.7, which allows a magistrate to adjourn a preliminary examination with the consent of the parties without the need for good cause to be shown.

Rule 3.306 Quo Warranto

(A) Jurisdiction.

(1) An action for quo warranto against a person who usurps, intrudes into, or unlawfully holds or exercises a state office, or against a state officer who does or suffers an act that by law works a forfeiture of the office, must be brought in the Court of Appeals.

(2) All other actions for quo warranto must be brought in the circuit court.

(B) Parties.

(1) *Actions by Attorney General.* An action for quo warranto is to be brought by the Attorney General when the action is against:

(a) a person specified in subrule (A)(1);

(b) a person who usurps, intrudes into, or wrongfully holds or exercises an office in a public corporation created by this state's authority;

(c) an association, or number of persons, acting as a corporation in Michigan without being legally incorporated;

(d) a corporation that is in violation of a provision of the act or acts creating, offering, or renewing the corporation;

(e) a corporation that has violated the provisions of a law under which the corporation forfeits its charter by misuse;

(f) a corporation that has forfeited its privileges and franchises by nonuse;

(g) a corporation that has committed or omitted acts that amount to a surrender of its corporate rights, privileges, and franchises, or has exercised a franchise or privilege not conferred on it by law.

(2) *Actions by Prosecutor or Citizen.* Other actions for quo warranto may be brought by the prosecuting attorney of the proper county, without leave of court, or by a citizen of the county by special leave of the court.

(3) *Application to Attorney General.*

(a) A person may apply to the Attorney General to have the Attorney General bring an action specified in subrule (B)(1). The Attorney General may require the person to give security to indemnify the state against all costs and expenses of the action. The person making the application, and any other person having the proper interest, may be joined as parties plaintiff.

(b) If, on proper application and offer of security, the Attorney General refuses to bring the action, the person may apply to the appropriate court for leave to bring the action himself or herself.

(C) Person Alleged to Be Entitled to Office. If the action is brought against the defendant for usurping an office, the complaint may name the person rightfully entitled to the office, with an allegation of his or her right to it, and that person may be made a party.

(D) Venue. The general venue statutes and rules apply to actions for quo warranto, unless a specific statute or rule contains a special venue provision applicable to an action for quo warranto.

(E) Hearing. The court may hear the matter or may allow the issues to be tried by a jury.

[Adopted effective March 1, 1985.]

Comments

Staff Comment to 1985 Adoption

MCR 3.306 is comparable to GCR 1963, 715.

The venue provisions are stated in somewhat more detail in subrule (D) than in GCR 1963, 715.4.

Rule 3.310 Injunctions

(A) Preliminary Injunctions.

(1) Except as otherwise provided by statute or these rules, an injunction may not be granted before a hearing on a motion for a preliminary injunction or on an order to show cause why a preliminary injunction should not be issued.

(2) Before or after the commencement of the hearing on a motion for a preliminary injunction, the court may order the

trial of the action on the merits to be advanced and consolidated with the hearing on the motion. Even when consolidation is not ordered, evidence received at the hearing for a preliminary injunction that would be admissible at the trial on the merits becomes part of the trial record and need not be repeated at the trial. This provision may not be used to deny the parties any rights they may have to trial by jury.

(3) A motion for a preliminary injunction must be filed and noticed for hearing in compliance with the rules governing other motions unless the court orders otherwise on a showing of good cause.

(4) At the hearing on an order to show cause why a preliminary injunction should not issue, the party seeking injunctive relief has the burden of establishing that a preliminary injunction should be issued, whether or not a temporary restraining order has been issued.

(5) If a preliminary injunction is granted, the court shall promptly schedule a pretrial conference. The trial of the action on the merits must be held within 6 months after the injunction is granted, unless good cause is shown or the parties stipulate to a longer period. The court shall issue its decision on the merits within 56 days after the trial is completed.

(B) Temporary Restraining Orders.

(1) A temporary restraining order may be granted without written or oral notice to the adverse party or the adverse party's attorney only if

    (a) it clearly appears from specific facts shown by affidavit or by a verified complaint that immediate and irreparable injury, loss, or damage will result to the applicant from the delay required to effect notice or from the risk that notice will itself precipitate adverse action before an order can be issued;

    (b) the applicant's attorney certifies to the court in writing the efforts, if any, that have been made to give the notice and the reasons supporting the claim that notice should not be required; and

    (c) a permanent record or memorandum is made of any nonwritten evidence, argument, or other representations made in support of the application.

(2) A temporary restraining order granted without notice must:

    (a) be endorsed with the date and time of issuance;

    (b) describe the injury and state why it is irreparable and why the order was granted without notice;

    (c) except in domestic relations actions, set a date for hearing at the earliest possible time on the motion for a preliminary injunction or order to show cause why a preliminary injunction should not be issued.

(3) Except in domestic relations actions, a temporary restraining order granted without notice expires by its terms within such time after entry, not to exceed 14 days, as the court sets unless within the time so fixed the order, for good cause shown, is extended for a like period or unless the party against whom the order is directed consents that it may be extended for a longer period. The reasons for the extension must be stated on the record or in a document filed in the action.

(4) A temporary restraining order granted without notice must be filed forthwith in the clerk's office and entered in the court records.

(5) A motion to dissolve a temporary restraining order granted without notice takes precedence over all matters except older matters of the same character, and may be heard on 24 hours' notice. For good cause shown, the court may order the motion heard on shorter notice. The court may set the time for the hearing at the time the restraining order is granted, without waiting for the filing of a motion to dissolve it, and may order that the hearing on a motion to dissolve a restraining order granted without notice be consolidated with the hearing on a motion for a preliminary injunction or an order to show cause why a preliminary injunction should not be issued. At a hearing on a motion to dissolve a restraining order granted without notice, the burden of justifying continuation of the order is on the applicant for the restraining order whether or not the hearing has been consolidated with a hearing on a motion for a preliminary injunction or an order to show cause.

(C) Form and Scope of Injunction. An order granting an injunction or restraining order

(1) must set forth the reasons for its issuance;

(2) must be specific in terms;

(3) must describe in reasonable detail, and not by reference to the complaint or other document, the acts restrained; and

(4) is binding only on the parties to the action, their officers, agents, servants, employees, and attorneys, and on those persons in active concert or participation with them who receive actual notice of the order by personal service or otherwise.

(D) Security.

(1) Before granting a preliminary injunction or temporary restraining order, the court may require the applicant to give security, in the amount the court deems proper, for the payment of costs and damages that may be incurred or suffered by a party who is found to have been wrongfully enjoined or restrained.

(2) Security is not required of the state or of a Michigan county or municipal corporation or its officer or agency acting in an official capacity. As to other parties, if security is not required the order must state the reason.

(3) If the party enjoined deems the security insufficient and has had no prior opportunity to be heard, the party may object to the sufficiency of the surety in the manner provided in MCR 3.604(E). The procedures provided in MCR 3.604(F) apply to the objection.

(4) When a bond is required before the issuance of an injunction or temporary restraining order, the bond must be filed with the clerk before the sealing and delivery of the injunction or restraining order.

(E) Stay of Action. An injunction or temporary restraining order may not be granted in one action to stay proceedings in another action pending in another court if the relief requested could be sought in the other pending action.

(F) Denial of Application. When an application for a preliminary injunction or temporary restraining order is denied, but an order is not signed, an endorsement of the denial must be made on the complaint or affidavit, and the complaint or affidavit filed.

(G) Later Application After Denial of Injunction.

(1) If a circuit judge has denied an application for an injunction or temporary restraining order, in whole or in part, or has granted it conditionally or on terms, later application for the same purpose and in relation to the same matter may not be made to another circuit judge.

(2) If an order is entered on an application in violation of subrule (G)(1), it is void and must be revoked by the judge who entered it, on due proof of the facts. A person making the later application contrary to this rule is subject to punishment for contempt.

(H) Motion for Injunction in Pending Actions.
An injunction may also be granted before or in connection with final judgment on a motion filed after an action is commenced.

(I) Application to Special Actions.
This rule applies to a special statutory action for an injunction only to the extent that it does not conflict with special procedures prescribed by the statute or the rules governing the special action.

[Adopted effective March 1, 1985. Amended March 12, 2002, effective September 1, 2002, 465 Mich.]

Comments

Staff Comment to 1985 Adoption

MCR 3.310 is a substantial revision of GCR 1963, 718. In general, the rule makes Michigan practice much more like that under FR Civ P 65.

The rule adopts the terminology used in the federal rule, distinguishing between temporary restraining orders, which are entered without notice, and preliminary injunctions, which are granted with notice and after hearing.

Subrule (A)(2) adopts the principle of FR Civ P 65(a)(2), which permits the trial of the action to be consolidated with the hearing on the motion for preliminary injunction.

New subrules (A)(3) and (4) emphasize that at a hearing on a motion for a preliminary injunction or on an order to show cause, the burden of proof is on the party seeking the injunction, even though a temporary restraining order may have been issued. Subrule (B)(5) includes a related provision: At a hearing on a motion to dissolve a temporary restraining order granted without notice, the party seeking continuation of the restraining order has the burden of proving that he or she is entitled to that relief.

Subrule (B)(1)(a) makes it a ground for a temporary restraining order that there is a risk that notice itself will precipitate adverse action before an order can be entered.

Subrule (B)(1)(c) requires that a record be kept of any evidence, argument, or representations made to the court in support of an application for a temporary restraining order.

Subrule (B)(2)(c) requires that a temporary restraining order set a date for hearing on the question of issuance of a preliminary injunction. This is consistent with FR Civ P 65(b). Domestic relations actions are excepted from that provision.

Subrule (B)(3) adopts the formulation of FR Civ P 65(b) that a temporary restraining order expires automatically after a specified time (14 days in subrule [B][3]) unless the court extends it for good cause or on the consent of the enjoined party. Again, domestic relations actions are excepted.

Although there is some reorganization, subrules (C)–(I) essentially carry forward the provisions of GCR 1963, 718.3–718.11.

Staff Comment to 2002 Amendment

The March 12, 2002 amendments of Rules 3.310, 7.208, and 7.213, effective September 1, 2002, require trial courts to expeditiously decide actions in which preliminary injunctions have been granted, and allow them to proceed even if the Court of Appeals has granted interlocutory leave to appeal. Similarly, if the Court of Appeals grants leave to review entry of a preliminary injunction on an interlocutory basis, that Court is required to give priority to resolution of the appeal. See *Michigan Coalition of State Employee Unions v Michigan Civil Service Comm*, 465 Mich 212, 214, n 1 (2001).

SUBCHAPTER 3.400   PROCEEDINGS INVOLVING REAL PROPERTY

Rule 3.401   Partition

(A) Matters to Be Determined by Court. On the hearing of an action or proceeding for partition, the court shall determine

(1) whether the premises can be partitioned without great prejudice to the parties;

(2) the value of the use of the premises and of improvements made to the premises; and

(3) other matters the court considers pertinent.

(B) Partition or Sale in Lieu of Partition. If the court determines that the premises can be partitioned, MCR 3.402 governs further proceedings. If the court determines that the premises cannot be partitioned without undue prejudice to the owners, it may order the premises sold in lieu of partition under MCR 3.403.

(C) Joinder of Lienholders. A creditor having a lien on all or part of the premises, by judgment, mortgage, or otherwise, need not be made a party to the partition proceedings. However, the plaintiff may join every creditor having a specific lien on the undivided interest or estate of a party. If the creditors are made parties, the complaint must state the nature of every lien or encumbrance.

[Adopted effective March 1, 1985.]

Comments

Staff Comment to 1985 Adoption

MCR 3.401, 3.402, and 3.403 cover the same subject matter as GCR 1963, 748, 749, 750, and 751. There is some reorganization, with the general provisions being placed in MCR 3.401, the procedure for partitioning in 3.402, and the procedure for sale in lieu of partition in 3.403.

MCR 3.401 includes the substance of GCR 1963, 748 and 751, as well as a new subrule (B), which refers to the other two partition rules.

Rule 3.402   Partition Procedure

(A) Determination of Parties' Interests. In ordering partition the court shall determine the rights and interests of the parties in the premises, and describe parts or shares that are to remain undivided for owners whose interests are unknown or not ascertained.

(B) Appointment of Partition Commissioner.

(1) The court shall appoint a disinterested person as partition commissioner to make the partition according to the court's determination of the rights and interests of the parties. If the parties agree, three commissioners may be appointed who shall meet together to perform their duties and act by majority vote.

(2) The partition commissioner must be sworn before an officer authorized to administer oaths to honestly and impartially partition the property as directed by the court. The oath must be filed with the clerk of the court.

(3) If the partition commissioner dies, resigns, or neglects to serve, the court may appoint a replacement.

(C) Proceedings Before Partition Commissioner.

(1) The partition commissioner

(a) may apply to the court for instructions;

(b) must give notice of the meeting to consider the problems of the partition to the parties so that they may be heard if they wish to be; and

(c) may take evidence at the meeting concerning the problems of partition.

(2) The partition commissioner shall divide the premises and allot the respective shares according to the terms in the court's judgment or separate order, and shall designate the several shares and portions by reference to a plat or survey prepared by a land surveyor or engineer licensed by the state.

(3) The partition commissioner must report to the court, specifying the procedures followed, describing the land divided and the shares allotted to each party, and listing the commissioner's charges. The parties shall not be present during the preparation of the report or during the deliberations of a panel of three commissioners. A copy of the report must be sent to each party who has appeared in the action.

(D) Setting Aside, Modification, or Confirmation of Partition Commissioner's Report.

(1) The court may modify or set aside the report and may refer the action to either the same or a newly appointed partition commissioner as often as necessary.

(2) On confirming the report, the court shall enter a judgment binding and conclusive on:

(a) all parties named in the action who

(i) have an interest in the partitioned premises as owners in fee or tenants for years,

(ii) are entitled to the reversion, remainder, or inheritance of the premises after the termination of a particular estate in the premises,

(iii) are or will become entitled to a beneficial interest in the premises, or

(iv) have an interest in an undivided share of the premises as tenants for years, for life, or in dower;

(b) the legal representatives of the parties listed in subrule (D)(2)(a);

(c) all persons interested in the premises who were unknown at the time the action was commenced and were given sufficient notice either by publication or personally; and

(d) all other persons claiming from any of the above parties or persons.

(3) The judgment and partition do not affect persons who have claims as tenants in dower or for life to the entire premises subject to the partition; nor do they preclude a person, except those specified in subrule (D)(2), from claiming title to the premises in question or from controverting the title or interest of the parties among whom the partition was made.

(4) An authenticated copy of the report, the judgment confirming it, and any incorporated surveys may be recorded with the register of deeds of the county in which the land is located. Copies of subdivision plats already of record need not be recorded.

(E) Expenses and Costs. The court may order that the expenses and costs, including attorney fees, be paid by the parties in accordance with their respective rights and equities in the premises. An order requiring a party to pay expenses and costs may be enforced in the same manner as a judgment.

(F) Setting Off of Interests in Special Cases.

(1) The court may by order set off the interest that belonged to a deceased party, without subdivision, to those claiming under that party when it is expedient to do so. Those legally entitled under or through the deceased party must be mentioned by name in the judgment.

(2) If the original parties in interest were fully known, but death, legal proceedings, or other operation of law has caused uncertainty about the identity of the present parties in interest, the interests originally owned by known parties but now owned by unknown persons may be separated as provided in this rule, instead of being left undivided. The division and judgment operate to convey the title to the persons claiming under the known party, according to their legal rights.

(3) If an interest in the premises belongs to known or unknown parties who have not appeared in the action, the court shall order partition of the ascertained interests of the known parties who have appeared in the action. The residue of the premises remains for the parties whose interests have not been ascertained, subject to future division.

[Adopted effective March 1, 1985.]

Comments

Staff Comment to 1985 Adoption

MCR 3.402 is comparable to GCR 1963, 749.

Subrule (B)(1) changes the current provision of GCR 1963, 749.1, by permitting appointment of only a single partition commissioner. Compare MCL 700.208, which provides for only one commissioner in partition proceedings in probate court.

In subrule (C)(2) the requirements for the description of the shares of the premises are stated in terms of a plat or survey, rather than the language of GCR 1963, 749.2(2), which spoke of "posts, stones, or other permanent monuments".

New subrule (D)(4) adds a requirement that a copy of the report and the judgment confirming it may be recorded with the register of deeds.

Subrule (E) simplifies the language of GCR 1963, 749.4 regarding expenses and costs.

Rule 3.403   Sale of Premises and Division of Proceeds as Substitute for Partition

(A) Order of Sale.

(1) If a party has a dower interest or life estate in all or a part of the premises at the time of the order for sale, the court shall determine whether, under all the circumstances and with regard for the interests of all the parties, that interest should be excepted from the sale or be sold with the premises. If the court orders that the sale include that party's interest, the sale conveys that interest.

(2) In the order of sale the court shall designate:

(a) which premises are to be sold;

(b) whether the premises are to be sold in separate parcels or together;

(c) whether there is a minimum price at which the premises may be sold;

(d) the terms of credit to be allowed and the security to be required; and

(e) how much of the proceeds will be invested, as required by this rule, for the benefit of unknown owners, infants, parties outside Michigan, and parties who have dower interests or life estates.

(B) Specific Procedures and Requirements of Sale.

(1) The person appointed by the court to conduct the sale shall give notice of the sale, including the terms. Notice must be given in the same manner as required by MCL 600.6052.

(2) Neither the person conducting the sale nor anyone acting in his or her behalf may directly or indirectly purchase or be interested in the purchase of the premises sold. The conservator of a minor or legally incapacitated individual may not purchase or be interested in the purchase of lands that are the subject of the proceedings, except for the benefit of the ward. Sales made contrary to this provision are voidable, except as provided by MCL 700.5421.

(3) The part of the price for which credit is allowed must be secured at interest by a mortgage of the premises sold, a note of the purchaser, and other security the court prescribes.

(a) The person conducting the sale may take separate mortgages and other securities in the name of the clerk of the court and the clerk's successors for the shares of the purchase money the court directs to be invested, and in the name of a known owner, 18 years of age or older, who desires to have his or her share so invested.

(b) When the sale is confirmed, the person conducting the sale must deliver the mortgages and other securities to the clerk of the court, or to the known owners whose shares are invested.

(4) After completing the sale, the person conducting the sale shall file a report with the court, stating

(a) the name of each purchaser,

(b) a description of the parcels of land sold to each purchaser, and

(c) the price paid for each parcel.

A copy of the report must be sent to each party who has appeared in the action.

(5) If the court confirms the sale, it shall enter an order authorizing and directing the person conducting the sale to execute conveyances pursuant to the sale.

(6) Conveyances executed according to these rules shall be recorded in the county where the land is located. These conveyances are a bar against

(a) all interested persons who were made parties to the proceedings;

(b) all unknown parties who were ordered to appear and answer by proper publication or personal service of notice;

(c) all persons claiming through parties listed in subrules (B)(6)(a) and (b);

(d) all persons who have specific liens on an undivided share or interest in the premises, if they were made parties to the proceedings.

(7) If the court confirms the sale, and the successful bidder fails to purchase under the terms of the sale, the court may order that the premises be resold at that bidder's risk. That bidder is liable to pay the amount of his or her bid minus the amount received on resale.

(C) Costs and Expenses of the Proceeding. The person conducting the sale shall deduct the costs and expenses of the

proceeding, including the plaintiff's reasonable attorney fees as determined by the court, from the proceeds of the sale and pay them to the plaintiff or the plaintiff's attorney.

(D) Distribution of Proceeds of Sale.

(1) When premises that include a dower interest or life estate are sold, the owner of the dower interest or life estate shall be compensated as provided in this subrule.

(a) Unless the owner consents to the alternative compensation provided in subrule (D)(1)(b), the court shall order that the following amount be invested in interest-bearing accounts insured by an agency of the United States government, with the interest paid annually for life to the owner of the dower interest or life estate:

(i) in the case of a dower interest, one-third of the proceeds of the sale of the premises or of the undivided share of the premises on which the claim of dower existed, after deduction of the owner's share of the expenses of the proceeding;

(ii) in the case of a life estate, the entire proceeds of the sale of the premises, or undivided share of the premises in which the life estate existed, after deduction of the proportion of the owner's share of the expenses of the proceeding.

If the owner of the dower interest or life estate is unknown, the court shall order the protection of the person's rights in the same manner, as far as possible, as if he or she were known and had appeared.

(b) If, before the person conducting the sale files the report of sale, the owner of the dower interest or life estate consents, the court shall direct that the owner be paid an amount that, on the principles of law applicable to annuities, is reasonable compensation for the interest or estate. To be effective the consent must be by a written instrument witnessed and acknowledged in the manner required to make a deed eligible for recording.

(2) If there are encumbrances on the estate or interest in the premises of a party to the proceeding, the person conducting the sale must pay to the clerk the portion of the proceeds attributable to the sale of that estate or interest, after deducting the share of the costs, charges, and expenses for which it is liable. The party who owned that estate or interest may apply to the court for payment of his or her claim out of these proceeds. The application must be accompanied by

(a) an affidavit stating the amount due on each encumbrance and the name and address of the owner of each encumbrance, as far as known; and

(b) proof by affidavit that notice was served on each owner of an encumbrance, in the manner prescribed in MCR 2.107.

The court shall hear the proofs, determine the rights of the parties, and direct who must pay the costs of the trial.

After ascertaining the amount of existing encumbrances, the court shall order the distribution of the money held by the clerk among the creditors having encumbrances, according to their priority. When paying an encumbrance the clerk must procure satisfaction of the encumbrance, acknowledged in the form required by law, and must record the satisfaction of the encumbrance. The clerk may pay the expenses of these services out of the portion of the money in court that belongs to the party by whom the encumbrance was payable.

The proceedings under this subrule to ascertain and settle the amounts of encumbrances do not affect other parties to the proceedings for partition and do not delay the payment to a party whose estate in the premises is not subject to an encumbrance or the investing of the money for the benefit of such a person.

(3) The proceeds of a sale, after deducting the costs, must be divided among the parties whose rights and interests have been sold, in proportion to their respective rights in the premises.

(a) The shares of the parties who are 18 years of age or older must be paid to them or to their legal representatives (or brought into court for their use) by the person conducting the sale.

(b) The court may direct that the share of a minor or a legally incapacitated individual be paid to his or her conservator or be invested in interest-bearing accounts insured by an agency of the United States government in the name and for the benefit of the minor or legally incapacitated individual.

(c) If a party whose interest has been sold is absent from the state and has no legal representative in the state or is not known or named in the proceedings, the court shall direct that his or her share be invested in interest-bearing accounts insured by the United States government for the party's benefit until claimed.

(4) The court may require that before receiving a share of the proceeds of a sale a party give a note to secure refund of the share, with interest, if the party is later found not entitled to it.

(5) When the court directs that security be given or investments be made, or the person conducting the sale takes security on the sale of real estate, the bonds, notes, and investments must be taken in the name of the clerk of the court and the clerk's successors in office, unless provision is made to take them in the name of a known owner.

The clerk must hold them and deliver them to his or her successor, and must receive the interest and principal as they become due and apply or reinvest them, as the court directs. The clerk shall annually give to the court a written, sworn account of the money received and the disposition of it.

A security, bond, note, mortgage, or other evidence of the investment may not be discharged, transferred, or impaired by an act of the clerk without the order of the court. A person interested in an investment, with the leave of the court, may prosecute it in the name of the existing clerk, and an action is not abated by the death, removal from office, or resignation of the clerk to whom the instruments were executed or the clerk's successors.

[Adopted effective March 1, 1985. Amended December 18, 2001, effective May 1, 2002, 465 Mich.]

Comments

Staff Comment to 1985 Adoption

MCR 3.403 is comparable to GCR 1963, 750.

The language of subrule (B)(2) is modified from that in GCR 1963, 750.3(2) in accordance with the terms of the Revised Probate Code.

Subrule (B)(7) deletes the language found in GCR 1963, 750.3(7) that entitled a defaulting purchaser to the amount by which the proceeds of the resale exceeds his or her bid.

In subrule (D)(3), the terminology is changed to conform to the Revised Probate Code. Compare GCR 1963, 750.5(4).

The provisions of GCR 1963, 750.5(6) regarding investment of the proceeds of sale by the clerk are modified in subrule (D). The clerk's authority to invest in mortgages is deleted and replaced with a provision that the proceeds are to be invested in accounts insured by an agency of the United States government.

Staff Comment to 2002 Amendment

The December 18, 2001 amendments, effective May 1, 2002, updated various rules in light of the Estates and Protected Individuals Code (EPIC), MCL 700.1101 *et seq.*, and revisions made to EPIC by 2000 PA 312, 313, and 469.

Rule 3.410   Foreclosure of Mortgages and Land Contracts

(A) Rules Applicable. Except as prescribed in this rule, the general rules of procedure apply to actions to foreclose mortgages and land contracts.

(B) Pleading.

(1) A plaintiff seeking foreclosure or satisfaction of a mortgage on real estate or a land contract must state in the complaint whether an action has ever been brought to recover all or part of the debt secured by the mortgage or land contract and whether part of the debt has been collected or paid.

(2) In a complaint for foreclosure or satisfaction of a mortgage or a land contract, it is not necessary to set out in detail the rights and interests of the defendants who are purchasers of, or who have liens on, the premises, subsequent to the recording of the mortgage or land contract. It is sufficient for the plaintiff, after setting out his or her own interest in the premises, to state generally that the defendants have or claim some interest in the premises as subsequent purchasers, encumbrancers, or otherwise.

(C) Time for Sale. A sale under a judgment of foreclosure may not be ordered on less than 42 days' notice. Publication may not begin until the time set by the judgment for payment has expired, and

(1) until 6 months after an action to foreclose a mortgage is begun;

(2) until 3 months after an action to foreclose a land contract is begun.

(D) Disposition of Surplus. When there is money remaining from a foreclosure sale after paying the amount due the plaintiff, a party to the action may move for the disposition of the surplus in accordance with the rights of the parties entitled to it.

(E) Administration of Mortgage Trusts in Equity.

(1) Proceedings of the kind described in MCL 600.3170 are governed by the procedures prescribed by MCL 451.401–451.405, except as modified by this subrule.

(2) A bond, other obligation, or beneficial interest held by or for the benefit of the mortgagor or the mortgagor's successor in estate, or subject to an agreement or option by which the mortgagor or the mortgagor's successor in estate may acquire it or an interest in it, may not be considered in determining a majority of such obligations or beneficial interests, either as part of the majority or as part of the whole number of which the majority is required.

[Adopted effective March 1, 1985.]

Comments

Staff Comment to 1985 Adoption

MCR 3.410 is comparable to GCR 1963, 745.

Most of the procedures regarding foreclosure of mortgage trusts, found in GCR 1963, 745.5, are deleted and replaced in subrule (E) with a reference to statutory procedures.

Rule 3.411   Civil Action to Determine Interests in Land

(A) This rule applies to actions to determine interests in land under MCL 600.2932. It does not apply to summary proceedings to recover possession of premises under MCL 600.5701–600.5759.

(B) Complaint.

(1) The complaint must describe the land in question with reasonable certainty by stating

(a) the section, township, and range of the premises;

(b) the number of the block and lot of the premises; or

(c) another description of the premises sufficiently clear so that the premises may be identified.

(2) The complaint must allege

(a) the interest the plaintiff claims in the premises;

(b) the interest the defendant claims in the premises; and

(c) the facts establishing the superiority of the plaintiff's claim.

(C) Written Evidence of Title to Be Referred to in Pleadings.

(1) Written evidence of title may not be introduced at trial unless it has been sufficiently referred to in the pleadings in accordance with this rule.

(2) The plaintiff must attach to the complaint, and the defendant must attach to the answer, a statement of the title on which the pleader relies, showing from whom the title was obtained and the page and book where it appears of record.

(3) Within a reasonable time after demand for it, a party must furnish to the adverse party a copy of an unrecorded conveyance on which he or she relies or give a satisfactory reason for not doing so.

(4) References to title may be amended or made more specific in accordance with the general rules regarding amendments and motions for more definite statement.

(D) Findings as to Rights in and Title to Premises.

(1) After evidence has been taken, the court shall make findings determining the disputed rights in and title to the premises.

(2) If a party not in possession of the premises is found to have had a right to possession at the time the action was commenced, but that right expired before the trial, that party must prove the damages sustained because the premises were wrongfully withheld, and the court shall enter judgment in the amount proved.

(E) Claim for Reasonable Value of Use of Premises.

(1) Within 28 days after the finding of title, the party found to have title to the premises may file a claim against the party who withheld possession of the premises for the reasonable value of the use of the premises during the period the premises were withheld, beginning 6 years before the action was commenced.

(2) The court shall hear evidence and make findings, determining the value of the use of the premises.

(a) The findings must be based on the value of the use of the premises in their condition at the time the withholding party, or those through whom that party claims, first went into possession. The use of the buildings or improvements put on the land by the party who withheld possession may not be considered.

(b) The findings must be based on the general value of the use of the premises, not on a peculiar value the use of the premises had to the party who withheld possession or might have had to the party who had title.

(F) Claim for Value of Buildings Erected and Improvements Made on Premises.

(1) Within 28 days after the finding of title, a party may file a claim against the party found to have title to the premises for the amount that the present value of the premises has been increased by the erection of buildings or the making of improvements by the party making the claim or those through whom he or she claims.

(2) The court shall hear evidence as to the value of the buildings erected and the improvements made on the premises, and the value the premises would have if they had not been improved or built upon. The court shall determine the amount the premises would be worth at the time of the claim had the premises not been improved, and the amount the value of the premises was increased at the time of the claim by the buildings erected and improvements made.

(3) The party claiming the value of the improvements may not recover their value if they were made in bad faith.

(G) Election by Party in Title.

(1) The person found to have title to the premises may elect to abandon them to the party claiming the value of the improvements and to take a judgment against that party for the value the premises would have had at the time of the trial if they had not been improved. The election must be filed with the court within 28 days after the findings on the claim for improvements. The judgment for the value of the premises is a lien against the premises.

(2) If the person found to have title does not elect to abandon the premises under subrule (G)(1), the judgment will provide that he or she recover the premises and pay the value of the improvements to the clerk of the court within the time set in the judgment.

(a) The person found to have title must pay the amount, plus accrued interest, before taking possession of the premises under the judgment, if that person is not already in possession.

(b) If the person found to have title fails to pay the amount of the judgment and the accrued interest within the time set in the judgment, he or she is deemed to have abandoned all claim of title to the premises to the parties in whose favor the judgment for the value of the improvements runs.

(H) Judgment Binding Only on Parties to Action. Except for title acquired by adverse possession, the judgment determining a claim to title, equitable title, right to possession, or other interests in lands under this rule, determines only the rights and interests of the known and unknown persons who are parties to the action, and of persons claiming through those parties by title accruing after the commencement of the action.

(I) Possession Under Judgment Not to Be Affected by Vacation of Judgment Alone. When the judgment in an action under these rules determines that a party is entitled to possession of the premises in dispute, that party's right to possession is not affected by vacation of the judgment and the granting of a new trial, until a contrary judgment is rendered as a result of the new trial.

[Adopted effective March 1, 1985. Amended May 22, 2007, effective September 1, 2007, 478 Mich.]

Comments

Staff Comment to 1985 Adoption

MCR 3.411 is comparable to GCR 1963, 754.

New subrule (A) states the applicability of the rule.

Subrule (G)(1) states more specifically than did GCR 1963, 754.6(1) the manner in which the party found to have title may exercise the election to abandon the premises and take a judgment for the value of the premises before improvement.

Staff Comment to 2007 Amendment

This amendment clarifies that MCR 3.411(H), under which a judgment determining an interest in land is effective only as to the parties to the action, does not apply to an action in which title was determined under the principle of adverse possession. Under longstanding Michigan caselaw, interests in land acquired by adverse possession are effective against all the world, not just those individuals who are parties to the action. See, for example, *Lawson v Bishop*, 212 Mich 691 (1920), and *Gorte v Dep't of Transportation*, 202 Mich App 161 (1993).

Rule 3.412   Construction Liens

In an action to enforce a lien under MCL 570.1101 *et seq.*, or other similar law, if the plaintiff has joined others holding liens or others have filed notice of intention to claim liens against the same property, it is not necessary for the plaintiff to answer the counterclaim or cross-claim of another lien claimant, nor for the other lien claimants to answer the plaintiff's complaint or the cross-claim of another lien claimant, unless one of them disputes the validity or amount of the lien sought to be enforced. If no issue has been raised between lien claimants as to the validity or amount of a lien, the action is ready for hearing when at issue between the lien claimants and the owners, part owners, or lessees of the property.

[Adopted effective March 1, 1985.]

Comments

Staff Comment 1985 Adoption

MCR 3.412 is substantially the same as GCR 1963, 793. The current statute uses the term "construction" lien, rather than "mechanics'" lien. See MCL 570.1101.

SUBCHAPTER 3.500   REPRESENTATIVE ACTIONS

Rule 3.501   Class Actions

(A) Nature of Class Action.

(1) One or more members of a class may sue or be sued as representative parties on behalf of all members in a class action only if:

(a) the class is so numerous that joinder of all members is impracticable;

(b) there are questions of law or fact common to the members of the class that predominate over questions affecting only individual members;

(c) the claims or defenses of the representative parties are typical of the claims or defenses of the class;

(d) the representative parties will fairly and adequately assert and protect the interests of the class; and

(e) the maintenance of the action as a class action will be superior to other available methods of adjudication in promoting the convenient administration of justice.

(2) In determining whether the maintenance of the action as a class action will be superior to other available methods of adjudication in promoting the convenient administration of justice, the court shall consider among other matters the following factors:

(a) whether the prosecution of separate actions by or against individual members of the class would create a risk of

(i) inconsistent or varying adjudications with respect to individual members of the class that would confront the party opposing the class with incompatible standards of conduct; or

(ii) adjudications with respect to individual members of the class that would as a practical matter be dispositive of the interests of other members not parties to the adjudications or substantially impair or impede their ability to protect their interests;

(b) whether final equitable or declaratory relief might be appropriate with respect to the class;

(c) whether the action will be manageable as a class action;

(d) whether in view of the complexity of the issues or the expense of litigation the separate claims of individual class members are insufficient in amount to support separate actions;

(e) whether it is probable that the amount which may be recovered by individual class members will be large enough in relation to the expense and effort of administering the action to justify a class action; and

(f) whether members of the class have a significant interest in controlling the prosecution or defense of separate actions.

(3) Class members shall have the right to be excluded from the action in the manner provided in this rule, subject to the authority of the court to order them made parties to the action pursuant to other applicable court rules.

(4) Class members have the right to intervene in the action, subject to the authority of the court to regulate the orderly course of the action.

(5) An action for a penalty or minimum amount of recovery without regard to actual damages imposed or authorized by statute may not be maintained as a class action unless the statute specifically authorizes its recovery in a class action.

(B) Procedure for Certification of Class Action.

(1) *Motion.*

(a) Within 91 days after the filing of a complaint that includes class action allegations, the plaintiff must move for certification that the action may be maintained as a class action.

(b) The time for filing the motion may be extended by order on stipulation of the parties or on motion for cause shown.

(2) *Effect of Failure to File Motion.* If the plaintiff fails to file a certification motion within the time allowed by subrule (B)(1), the defendant may file a notice of the failure. On the filing of such a notice, the class action allegations are deemed stricken, and the action continues by or against the named parties alone. The class action allegations may be reinstated only if the plaintiff shows that the failure was due to excusable neglect.

(3) *Action by Court.*

(a) Except on motion for good cause, the court shall not proceed with consideration of the motion to certify until service of the summons and complaint on all named defendants or until the expiration of any unserved summons under MCR 2.102(D).

(b) The court may allow the action to be maintained as a class action, may deny the motion, or may order that a ruling be postponed pending discovery or other preliminary procedures.

(c) In an order certifying a class action, the court shall set forth a description of the class.

(d) When appropriate the court may order that

(i) the action be maintained as a class action limited to particular issues or forms of relief, or

(ii) a proposed class be divided into separate classes with each treated as a class for purposes of certifying, denying certification, or revoking a certification.

(e) If certification is denied or revoked, the action shall continue by or against the named parties alone.

(C) Notice to Class Members.

(1) *Notice Requirement.* Notice shall be given as provided in this subrule to persons who are included in a class action by certification or amendment of a prior certification, and to persons who were included in a class action by a prior certification but who are to be excluded from the class by amendment or revocation of the certification.

(2) *Proposals Regarding Notice.* The plaintiff shall include in the motion for certification a proposal regarding notice covering the matters that must be determined by the court under subrule (C)(3). In lieu of such a proposal, the plaintiff may state reasons why a determination of these matters cannot then be made and offer a proposal as to when such a determination should be made. Such a proposal must also be included in a motion to revoke or amend certification.

(3) *Action by Court.* As soon as practicable, the court shall determine how, when, by whom, and to whom the notice shall be given; the content of the notice; and to whom the response to the notice is to be sent. The court may postpone the notice determination until after the parties have had an opportunity for discovery, which the court may limit to matters relevant to the notice determination.

(4) *Manner of Giving Notice.*

(a) Reasonable notice of the action shall be given to the class in such manner as the court directs.

(b) The court may require individual written notice to all members who can be identified with reasonable effort. In lieu of or in addition to individual notice, the court may require notice to be given through another method reasonably calculated to reach the members of the class. Such methods may include using publication in a newspaper or magazine; broadcasting on television or radio; posting; or distribution through a trade or professional association, union, or public interest group.

(c) In determining the manner of notice, the court shall consider, among other factors,

(i) the extent and nature of the class,

(ii) the relief requested,

(iii) the cost of notifying the members,

(iv) the resources of the plaintiff, and

(v) the possible prejudice to be suffered by members of the class or by others if notice is not received.

(5) *Content of Notice.* The notice shall include:

(a) a general description of the action, including the relief sought, and the names and addresses of the representative parties;

(b) a statement of the right of a member of the class to be excluded from the action by submitting an election to be excluded, including the manner and time for exercising the election;

(c) a description of possible financial consequences for the class;

(d) a general description of any counterclaim or notice of intent to assert a counterclaim by or against members of the class, including the relief sought;

(e) a statement that the judgment, whether favorable or not, will bind all members of the class who are not excluded from the action;

(f) a statement that any member of the class may intervene in the action;

(g) the address of counsel to whom inquiries may be directed; and

(h) other information the court deems appropriate.

(6) *Cost of Notice.*

(a) The plaintiff shall bear the expense of the notification required by subrule (C)(1). The court may require the defendant to cooperate in the notice process, but any additional costs incurred by the defendant in doing so shall be paid by the plaintiff.

(b) Upon termination of the action, the court may allow as taxable costs the expenses of notification incurred by the prevailing party.

(c) Subrules (C)(6)(a) and (b) shall not apply when a statute provides for a different allocation of the cost of notice in a particular class of actions.

(7) *Additional Notices.* In addition to the notice required by subrule (C)(1), during the course of the action the court may require that notice of any other matter be given in such manner as the court directs to some or all of the members of the class.

(D) Judgment.

(1) The judgment shall describe the parties bound.

(2) A judgment entered before certification of a class binds only the named parties.

(3) A motion for judgment (including partial judgment) under MCR 2.116 may be filed and decided before the decision on the question of class certification. A judgment entered before certification in favor of a named party does not preclude that party from representing the class in the action if that is otherwise appropriate.

(4) A complaint that does not include class action allegations may not be amended to include such allegations after the granting of judgment or partial judgment under MCR 2.116.

(5) A judgment entered in an action certified as a class action binds all members of the class who have not submitted an election to be excluded, except as otherwise directed by the court.

(E) Dismissal or Compromise. An action certified as a class action may not be dismissed or compromised without the approval of the court, and notice of the proposed dismissal or compromise shall be given to the class in such manner as the court directs.

(F) Statute of Limitations.

(1) The statute of limitations is tolled as to all persons within the class described in the complaint on the commencement of an action asserting a class action.

(2) The statute of limitations resumes running against class members other than representative parties and intervenors:

(a) on the filing of a notice of the plaintiff's failure to move for class certification under subrule (B)(2);

(b) 28 days after notice has been made under subrule (C)(1) of the entry, amendment, or revocation of an order of certification eliminating the person from the class;

(c) on entry of an order denying certification of the action as a class action;

(d) on submission of an election to be excluded;

(e) on final disposition of the action.

(3) If the circumstance that brought about the resumption of the running of the statute is superseded by a further order of the trial court, by reversal on appeal, or otherwise, the statute of limitations shall be deemed to have been tolled continuously from the commencement of the action.

(G) Discovery. Representative parties and intervenors are subject to discovery in the same manner as parties in other civil actions. Other class members are subject to discovery in the same manner as persons who are not parties, and may be required to submit to discovery procedures applicable to parties to the extent ordered by the court.

(H) Counterclaims.

(1) *Right to File Counterclaims.* A party to a class action may file counterclaims as in any other action, including counterclaims by or against a class or an individual class member.

(2) *Notice of Intent to File Counterclaims.* The defendant may file notice of intent to assert counterclaims against absent class members before notice of certification is given under subrule (C)(1), identifying or describing the persons against

whom counterclaims may be filed and describing the nature of the counterclaims.

(3) *Time to File.* A counterclaim against a class member other than a representative party must be filed and served within 56 days after the class member intervenes or submits a claim for distribution of a share of any award recovered in the action, whichever is earlier, or within such further time as the court allows.

(4) *Notice to Class Members.* If the notice of certification given under subrule (C)(1) did not notify potential class members of the counterclaim, each class member against whom a counterclaim is asserted shall be permitted to elect to be excluded from the action. Notice of this right shall be served with the counterclaim.

(5) *Control of Action.* The court shall take such steps as are necessary to prevent the pendency of counterclaims from making the action unmanageable as a class action. Such steps include but are not limited to severing counterclaims for separate trial under MCR 2.505(B) or ordering that consideration of the counterclaims be deferred until after determination of the issue of the defendant's liability, at which time the court may hear the counterclaims, remove them to a lower court, change venue, dismiss them without prejudice, or take other appropriate action.

(I) Defendant Classes.

(1) An action that seeks to recover money from individual members of a defendant class may not be maintained as a class action.

(2) A representative of a defendant class, other than a public body or a public officer, may decline to defend the action in a representative capacity unless the court finds that the convenient administration of justice otherwise requires.

[Adopted effective March 1, 1985.]

Comments

Staff Comment to 1985 Adoption

MCR 3.501 is substantially the same as GCR 1963, 208.

Rule 3.502 Secondary Action by Shareholders

(A) Pleading. In an action brought by one or more shareholders in an incorporated or unincorporated association because the association has refused or failed to enforce rights which may properly be asserted by it, the complaint shall set forth under oath and with particularity the efforts of the plaintiff to secure from the managing directors or trustees the action the plaintiff desires and the reasons for the failure to obtain such action, or the reasons for not making such an effort.

(B) Security. At any stage of an action under this subrule the court may require such security and impose such terms as shall fairly and adequately protect the interests of the class or association in whose behalf the action is brought or defended.

(C) Notice. The court may order that notice be given, in the manner and to the persons it directs,

(1) of the right of absent persons to appear and present claims and defenses;

(2) of the pendency of the action;

(3) of a proposed settlement;

(4) of entry of judgment; or

(5) of any other proceedings in the action.

(D) Inadequate Representation. Whenever the representation appears to the court inadequate to protect the interests of absent persons who may be bound by the judgment, the court may at any time prior to judgment order an amendment of the pleadings to eliminate references to representation of absent persons, and the court shall enter judgment in such form as to affect only the parties to the action and those adequately represented.

[Adopted effective March 1, 1985.]

Comments

Staff Comment to 1985 Adoption

MCR 3.502 is substantially the same as GCR 1963, 211.1.

Rule 3.503   Action by Fiduciary

(A) Court Order. When a proceeding is instituted by a fiduciary seeking instruction or authorization with respect to

fiduciary duties or the trust property, and it appears that it is impracticable to bring all of the beneficiaries before the court, the court shall enter an order:

(1) setting forth the form of and manner for giving notice of the proceedings to the beneficiaries, and

(2) selecting representatives of the beneficiaries to act as representatives of the class.

(B) Notice. The contents of the notice shall fairly state the purpose of the proceedings and shall specify the time and place of hearing. Where an applicable statute provides for notice, the court may dispense with other notice.

[Adopted effective March 1, 1985.]

Comments

Staff Comment to 1985 Adoption

MCR 3.503 is substantially the same as GCR 1963, 211.2.

SUBCHAPTER 3.600   MISCELLANEOUS PROCEEDINGS

Rule 3.601   Public Nuisances

(A) Procedure to Abate Public Nuisance. Actions to abate public nuisances are governed by the general rules of procedure and evidence applicable to nonjury actions, except as provided by the statutes covering public nuisances and by this rule.

(B) Default; Hearing; Notice and Time. If a defendant fails to answer within the time provided, his or her default may be taken. On answer of a defendant or entry of a defendant's default, a party other than a defendant in default may notice the action for hearing on 7 days' notice. Hearings in actions under this rule take precedence over actions that are not entitled to priority by statute or rule and may be held at the time they are noticed without further pretrial proceedings.

(C) Motions; Hearing. Motions by the defendant filed and served with the answer are heard on the day of the hearing of the action.

(D) Entry of Order or Judgment; Preliminary Injunction.

(1) On the day noticed for hearing, the court shall hear and determine the disputed issues and enter a proper order and judgment.

(2) If the hearing is adjourned at the defendant's request, and the court is satisfied by affidavit or otherwise that the allegations in the complaint are true and that the plaintiff is entitled to relief, an injunction as requested may be granted, to be binding until further order.

(3) If service is not obtained on all of the defendants named in the complaint, the court has jurisdiction to hear the action and enter a proper order of abatement and judgment against those defendants who have been served. The order and judgment may not adversely affect the interests of the defendants who have not been served.

(E) Temporary Restraining Order. If a preliminary injunction is requested in the complaint and the court is satisfied by affidavit or otherwise that the material allegations are true, and that the plaintiff is entitled to relief, it may issue a temporary restraining order in accordance with MCR 3.310(B), restraining the defendant from conducting, maintaining, and

permitting the continuance of the nuisance and from removing or permitting the removal of the liquor, furniture, fixtures, vehicles, or other things used in the maintenance of the nuisance, until the final hearing and determination on the complaint or further order.

(F) Substitution for Complaining Party. The court may substitute the Attorney General or prosecuting attorney for the complaining party and direct the substituted officer to prosecute the action to judgment.

(G) Further Orders of Court. The court may enter other orders consistent with equity and not inconsistent with the provisions of the statute and this rule.

[Adopted effective March 1, 1985.]

Comments

Staff Comment to 1985 Adoption

MCR 3.601 is comparable to GCR 1963, 782.

The provision of GCR 1963, 782.2 regarding service of process is deleted. The same methods of service would be available under MCR 2.105.

Subrule (B) modifies the language of GCR 1963, 782.3 to make clear that any party not in default may notice the action for hearing.

Subrule (D)(3) modifies the language of GCR 1963, 782.4 to make clear that an order or judgment may not adversely affect the interests of defendants who have not been served.

In subrule (E), an additional requirement for the issuance of a temporary restraining order is added: Not only must the court be satisfied that the allegations are true, but also it must find that those allegations justify the relief sought. The rule also incorporates the provisions of MCR 3.310 regarding temporary restraining orders.

In several places, the word "shall" is changed to "may" to emphasize the judge's discretion in entering orders. See subrules (D)(2) and (E).

Rule 3.602.   Arbitration

(A) Applicability of Rule. Courts shall have all powers described in MCL 691.1681 *et seq.*, or reasonably related thereto, for arbitrations governed by that statute. The remainder of this rule applies to all other forms of arbitration, in the absence of contradictory provisions in the arbitration agreement or limitations imposed by statute, including MCL 691.1683(2).

(B) Proceedings Regarding Arbitration

(1) A request for an order to compel or to stay arbitration or for another order under this rule must be by motion, which shall be heard in the manner and on the notice provided by these rules for motions. If there is not a pending action between the parties, the party seeking the requested relief must first file a complaint as in other civil actions.

(2) On motion of a party showing an agreement to arbitrate and the opposing party's refusal to arbitrate, the court may order the parties to proceed with arbitration and to take other steps necessary to carry out the arbitration agreement. If the opposing party denies the existence of an agreement to arbitrate, the court shall summarily determine the issues and may order arbitration or deny the motion.

(3) On motion, the court may stay an arbitration proceeding commenced or threatened on a showing that there is no agreement to arbitrate. If there is a substantial and good-faith dispute, the court shall summarily try the issue and may enter a stay or direct the parties to proceed to arbitration.

(4) A motion to compel arbitration may not be denied on the ground that the claim sought to be arbitrated lacks merit or is not filed in good faith, or because fault or grounds for the claim have not been shown.

(C) Action Involving Issues Subject to Arbitration; Stay. Subject to MCR 3.310(E), an action or proceeding involving an issue subject to arbitration must be stayed if an order for arbitration or motion for such an order has been made under this rule. If the issue subject to arbitration is severable, the stay may be limited to that issue. If a motion for an order compelling arbitration is made in the action or proceeding in which the issue is raised, an order for arbitration must include a stay.

(D) Hearing; Time; Place; Adjournment.

(1) The arbitrator shall set the time and place for the hearing, and may adjourn it as necessary.

(2) On a party's request for good cause, the arbitrator may postpone the hearing to a time not later than the day set for rendering the award.

(E) Oath of Arbitrator and Witnesses.

(1) Before hearing testimony, the arbitrator must be sworn to hear and fairly consider the matters submitted and to make a just award according to his or her best understanding.

(2) The arbitrator has the power to administer oaths to the witnesses.

(F) Discovery and Subpoenas.

(1) The court may enforce a subpoena or discovery-related order for the attendance of a witness in this state and for the production of records and other evidence issued by an arbitrator in connection with an arbitration proceeding in another state on conditions determined by the court so as to make the arbitration proceeding fair, expeditious, and cost effective.

(2) A subpoena or discovery-related order issued by an arbitrator in another state shall be served in the manner provided by law for service of subpoenas in a civil action in this state and, on motion to the court by a party to the arbitration proceeding or the arbitrator, enforced in the manner provided by law for enforcement of subpoenas in a civil action in this state.

(3) On a party's request, the arbitrator may permit the taking of a deposition, for use as evidence, of a witness who cannot be subpoenaed or is unable to attend the hearing. The arbitrator may designate the manner of and the terms for taking the deposition.

(G) Representation by Attorney. A party has the right to be represented by an attorney at a proceeding or hearing under this rule. A waiver of the right before the proceeding or hearing is ineffective.

(H) Award by Majority; Absence of Arbitrator. If the arbitration is by a panel of arbitrators, the hearing shall be conducted by all of them, but a majority may decide any question and render a final award unless the concurrence of all of the arbitrators is expressly required by the agreement to submit to arbitration. If, during the course of the hearing, an arbitrator ceases to act for any reason, the remaining arbitrator or arbitrators may continue with the hearing and determine the controversy.

(I) Award; Confirmation by Court. A party may move for confirmation of an arbitration award within one year after the award was rendered. The court may confirm the award, unless it is vacated, corrected, or modified, or a decision is postponed, as provided in this rule.

(J) Vacating Award.

(1) A request for an order to vacate an arbitration award under this rule must be made by motion. If there is not a pending action between the parties, the party seeking the requested relief must first file a complaint as in other civil actions. A complaint or motion to vacate an arbitration award must be filed no later than 21 days after the date of the arbitration award.

(2) On motion of a party, the court shall vacate an award if:

(a) the award was procured by corruption, fraud, or other undue means;

(b) there was evident partiality by an arbitrator appointed as a neutral, corruption of an arbitrator, or misconduct prejudicing a party's rights;

(c) the arbitrator exceeded his or her powers; or

(d) the arbitrator refused to postpone the hearing on a showing of sufficient cause, refused to hear evidence material to the controversy, or otherwise conducted the hearing to prejudice substantially a party's rights.

The fact that the relief could not or would not be granted by a court of law or equity is not ground for vacating or refusing to confirm the award.

(3) A motion to vacate an award must be filed within 91 days after the date of the award. However, if the motion is predicated on corruption, fraud, or other undue means, it must be filed within 21 days after the grounds are known or should have been known. A motion to vacate an award in a domestic relations case must be filed within 21 days after the date of the award.

(4) In vacating the award, the court may order a rehearing before a new arbitrator chosen as provided in the agreement, or, if there is no such provision, by the court. If the award is vacated on grounds stated in subrule (J)(2)(c) or (d), the court may order a rehearing before the arbitrator who made the award. The time within which the agreement requires the

award to be made is applicable to the rehearing and commences from the date of the order.

(5) If the motion to vacate is denied and there is no motion to modify or correct the award pending, the court shall confirm the award.

(K) Modification or Correction of Award.

(1) A request for an order to modify or correct an arbitration award under this rule must be made by motion. If there is not a pending action between the parties, the party seeking the requested relief must first file a complaint as in other civil actions. A complaint to correct or modify an arbitration award must be filed no later than 21 days after the date of the arbitration award.

(2) On motion made within 91 days after the date of the award, the court shall modify or correct the award if:

(a) there is an evident miscalculation of figures or an evident mistake in the description of a person, a thing, or property referred to in the award;

(b) the arbitrator has awarded on a matter not submitted to the arbitrator, and the award may be corrected without affecting the merits of the decision on the issues submitted; or

(c) the award is imperfect in a matter of form, not affecting the merits of the controversy.

(3) If the motion is granted, the court shall modify and correct the award to effect its intent and shall confirm the award as modified and corrected. Otherwise, the court shall confirm the award as made.

(4) A motion to modify or correct an award may be joined in the alternative with a motion to vacate the award.

(L) Judgment. The court shall render judgment giving effect to the award as corrected, confirmed, or modified. The judgment has the same force and effect, and may be enforced in the same manner, as other judgments.

(M) Costs. The costs of the proceedings may be taxed as in civil actions, and, if provision for the fees and expenses of the arbitrator has not been made in the award, the court may allow compensation for the arbitrator's services as it deems just. The arbitrator's compensation is a taxable cost in the action.

(N) Appeals. Appeals may be taken as from orders or judgments in other civil actions.

[Adopted effective March 1, 1985. Amended February 23, 2006, effective May 1, 2006, 474 Mich. Amended effective June 15, 2006, 475 Mich; January 1, 2007, 470 Mich. Amended October 2, 2007, effective January 1, 2008, 479 Mich; June 4, 2014, effective September 1, 2014, 496 Mich. Amended effective March 21, 2018, 501 Mich.]

Comments

Staff Comment to 1985 Adoption

MCR 3.602 is comparable to GCR 1963, 769.

Subrule (A) clarifies the applicability of the arbitration rule to arbitrations under the medical malpractice provisions of MCL 600.5040–600.5065.

Subrule (B)(1) requires that a request to invoke court jurisdiction in an arbitration matter is to be made by filing a civil action, unless the matter arises in a pending action, in which case a motion may be used.

The references to the "judgment roll" in GCR 1963, 769.13(1) are omitted from subrule (L).

Subrule (M) modifies the provision on fees and costs. GCR 1963, 769.12 referred to costs provided by law in the case of references. However, the relevant statute had been repealed.

Staff Comment to February, 2006 Amendment

MCR 3.602(A) is amended and subrules (I)–(N) of 3.602 are deleted because 1993 PA 78 repealed MCL 600.5040–600.5065.

Staff Comment to June, 2006 Amendment

Subrules (I)–(N), which were deleted in error in the order dated February 23, 2006, are reinstated.

Staff Comment to 2007 Amendment

The amendments eliminate the term "application," and substitute the word "motion" or "complaint," depending upon whether there is a pending action. "Application" is not a defined term within the Michigan Court Rules or in the arbitration act, MCL 600.5025.

The revisions also clarify that a complaint to stay or compel arbitration, or to vacate, modify, or correct an award must first be filed, and then a motion, consistent with the spirit of MCR 3.602(B)(1), must be filed. They also set timing deadlines consistent with the time frame allowed under the federal arbitration act, 9 USC 1 *et seq.*, by requiring that a motion to vacate, modify, or correct an award be filed within 91 days. However, for domestic relations cases, and for motions that claim an award is based on corruption, fraud, or other undue means, the current 21-day filing period applies for motions to vacate an arbitration award.

Staff Comment to 2014 Amendment

The amendments of MCR 3.602 apply to all other forms of arbitration that are not described in the newly adopted Revised Uniform Arbitration Act, MCL 691.1681 *et seq.*

Staff Comment to 2018 Amendment

These amendments update cross-references and make other nonsubstantive revisions to clarify the rules. The amendment of MCR 6.110(B)(1) addresses an inadvertent omission from the last amendment of this rule that was intended to be shown in overstrike. Accordingly, the current rule does not match the published version. Striking the clause "for good cause shown" will provide consistency with other published versions of the rule and with the statute, MCL 766.7, which allows a magistrate to adjourn a preliminary examination with the consent of the parties without the need for good cause to be shown.

Rule 3.603   Interpleader

(A) Availability.

(1) Persons having claims against the plaintiff may be joined as defendants and required to interplead when their claims are such that the plaintiff is or may be exposed to double or multiple liability. It is not a ground for objection to the joinder that the claims of the several claimants or the titles on which their claims depend do not have a common origin or are not identical, but are adverse to and independent of one another, or that the plaintiff denies liability to any or all of the claimants in whole or in part.

(2) A defendant exposed to liability as described in subrule (A)(1), may obtain interpleader by counterclaim or cross-claim. A claimant not already before the court may be joined as defendant, as provided in MCR 2.207 or MCR 2.209.

(3) If one or more actions concerning the subject matter of the interpleader action have already been filed, the interpleader action must be filed in the court where the first action was filed.

(B) Procedure.

(1) The court may order the property or the amount of money as to which the plaintiff admits liability to be deposited with the court or otherwise preserved, or to be secured by a bond in an amount sufficient to assure payment of the liability admitted.

(2) The court may thereafter enjoin the parties before it from commencing or prosecuting another action regarding the subject matter of the interpleader action.

(3) On hearing, the court may order the plaintiff discharged from liability as to property deposited or secured before determining the rights of the claimants.

(C) Rule Not Exclusive. The provisions of this rule supplement and do not in any way limit the joinder of parties permitted by MCR 2.206.

(D) Disposition of Earlier Action. If another action concerning the subject matter of the interpleader action has previously been filed, the court in which the earlier action was filed may:

(1) transfer the action, entirely or in part, to the court in which the interpleader action is pending,

(2) hold the action entirely or partially in abeyance, pending resolution of the interpleader action,

(3) dismiss the action, entirely or in part, or

(4) upon a showing of good cause, proceed with the action, explaining on the record the basis of the decision to proceed.

(E) Actual Costs. The court may award actual costs to an interpleader plaintiff. For the purposes of this rule, actual costs are those costs taxable in any civil action, and a reasonable attorney fee as determined by the trial court.

(1) The court may order that the plaintiff's actual costs of filing the interpleader request, tendering the disputed property to the court, and participating in the case as a disinterested stakeholder be paid from the disputed property or by another party.

(2) If the plaintiff incurs actual costs other than those described in subrule (1) due to another party's unreasonable litigation posture, the court may order that the other party pay those additional actual costs.

(3) An award made pursuant to this rule may not include reimbursement for the actual costs of asserting the plaintiff's own claim to the disputed property, or of supporting or opposing another party's claim.

[Adopted effective March 1, 1985. Amended September 17, 1996, effective December 1, 1996, 453 Mich; August 1, 2002, effective January 1, 2003, 467 Mich.]

Comments

Staff Comment to 1985 Adoption

MCR 3.603 is comparable to GCR 1963, 210.

Staff Comment to 1996 Amendment

The 1996 amendment of MCR 3.603 added paragraph (A)(3) and subrule (D). These changes were made to address the situation discussed in *Marsh v Foremost Ins Co*, 451 Mich 62; 544 NW2d 646 (1996).

Staff Comment to 2002 Amendment

The August 1, 2002, amendment, effective January 1, 2003, added subrule (E). It authorizes courts to award actual costs, including a reasonable attorney fee, to an interpleader plaintiff. Depending on the circumstances, the court may order that the money be paid either from the disputed property or by another party. See *Terra Energy, Ltd v Michigan*, 241 Mich App 393 (2000), lv den 463 Mich 994 (2001).

Rule 3.604　Bonds

(A) Scope of Rule. This rule applies to bonds given under the Michigan Court Rules and the Revised Judicature Act, unless a rule or statute clearly indicates that a different procedure is to be followed.

(B) Submission to Jurisdiction of Court by Surety. A surety on a bond or undertaking given under the Michigan Court Rules or the Revised Judicature Act submits to the jurisdiction of the court and consents that further proceedings affecting the surety's liability on the bond or undertaking may be conducted under this rule.

(C) Death of Party; Substitution of Surety. If the only plaintiff or the only defendant dies during the pendency of an action, in addition to the parties substituted under MCR 2.202, each surety on a bond given by the deceased party shall be made a party to the action, on notice to the surety in the manner prescribed in MCR 2.107.

(D) Affidavit of Surety; Notice of Bond.

(1) A surety on a bond, except for a surety company authorized to do business in Michigan, must execute an affidavit that he or she has pecuniary responsibility and attach the affidavit to the bond.

(2) In alleging pecuniary responsibility, a surety must affirm that he or she owns assets not exempt from execution having a fair market value exceeding his or her liabilities by at least twice the amount of the bond.

(3) A copy of a bond and the accompanying affidavit must be promptly served on the party for whose benefit it is given in the manner prescribed in MCR 2.107. Proof of service must be filed promptly with the court in which the bond has been filed.

(4) In an action alleging medical malpractice filed on or after October 1, 1986, notice of the filing of security for costs or the affidavit in lieu of such security, required by MCL 600.2912d, 600.2912e, shall be given as provided in MCR 2.109(B).

(E) Objections to Surety. A party for whose benefit a bond is given may, within 7 days after receipt of a copy of the bond, serve on the officer taking the bond and the party giving the bond a notice that the party objects to the sufficiency of the surety. Failure to do so waives all objections to the surety.

(F) Hearing on Objections to Surety. Notice of objection to a surety must be filed as a motion for hearing on objections to the bond.

(1) On demand of the objecting party, the surety must appear at the hearing of the motion and be subject to examination as to the surety's pecuniary responsibility or the validity of the execution of the bond.

(2) After the hearing, the court may approve or reject the bond as filed or require an amended, substitute, or additional bond, as the circumstances warrant.

(3) In an appeal to the circuit court from a lower court or tribunal, an objection to the surety is heard in the circuit court.

(G) Surety Company Bond. A surety company certified by the Commissioner of Insurance as authorized to do business in Michigan may act as surety on a bond.

(H) Assignment or Delivery of Bond. If the condition of a bond is broken, or the circumstances require, the court shall direct the delivery or assignment of the bond for prosecution to the person for whose benefit it was given. Proceedings to enforce the bond may be taken in the action pursuant to subrule (I).

(I) Judgment Against Surety.

(1) *Judgment on Motion.* In an action in which a bond or other security has been posted, judgment may be entered directly against the surety or the security on motion without the necessity of an independent action on a showing that the condition has occurred giving rise to the liability on the bond or to the forfeiture of the security.

(2) *Notice.* Notice of the hearing on the motion for judgment must be given to the surety or the owner of the security in the manner prescribed in MCR 2.107. The notice may be mailed to the address stated in the bond or stated when the security was furnished unless the surety or owner has given notice of a change of address.

(3) *Restitution.* If in later proceedings in the action, on appeal or otherwise, it is determined that the surety is not liable or that the security should not have been forfeited, the court may order restitution of money paid or security forfeited.

(J) Application to Another Judge After Supersedeas Refused.

(1) If a circuit judge has denied an application for supersedeas in whole or in part, or has granted it conditionally or on terms, a later application for the same purpose and in the same matter may not be made to another circuit judge if the first judge is available.

(2) If an order is entered contrary to the provisions of subrule (J)(1), it is void and must be revoked by the judge who entered it, on proof of the facts. A person making a later application contrary to this rule is subject to punishment for contempt.

(K) Cash or Securities Bond. The furnishing of a cash or securities bond under MCL 600.2631 is deemed compliance with these rules.

(L) Stay of Proceedings Without Bond. If a party required to give a bond under these rules for supersedeas, appeal, or otherwise is unable to give the bond by reason of poverty, the court may, on proof of the inability, limit or eliminate the requirement for surety on the bond on appropriate conditions and for a reasonable time.

[Adopted effective March 1, 1985. Amended December 11, 1986, effective December 12, 1986, 426 Mich.]

Comments

Staff Comment to 1985 Adoption

MCR 3.604 brings together the various provisions regarding bonds found in GCR 1963, 525 and 763.

Subrule (B) does not include the language of GCR 1963, 763.1 making the clerk the surety's agent for service of papers.

Subrule (J)(1) omits the language of GCR 1963, 736.9(1), which referred to persons other than a judge authorized to grant bonds.

Rule 3.605 Collection of Penalties, Fines, Forfeitures, and Forfeited Recognizances

(A) Definition. The term "penalty," as used in this rule, includes fines, forfeitures, and forfeited recognizances, unless otherwise provided in this rule.

(B) Parties. The civil action for a pecuniary penalty incurred for the violation of an ordinance of a city or village must be brought in the name of the city or village. Other actions to recover penalties must be brought in the name of the people of the State of Michigan.

(C) Judgment on Penalty. In an action against a party liable for a penalty, judgment may be rendered directly against the party and in favor of the other party on motion and showing that the condition has occurred giving rise to the penalty. This subrule does not apply to forfeited civil recognizances under MCR 3.604 or to forfeited criminal recognizances under MCL 765.28.

(D) Remission of Penalty. An application for the remission of a penalty, including a bond forfeiture, may be made to the judge who imposed the penalty or ordered the forfeiture. The application may not be heard until reasonable notice has been given to the prosecuting attorney (or municipal attorney) and he or she has had an opportunity to examine the matter and prepare to resist the application. The application may not be granted without payment of the costs and expenses incurred in the proceedings for the collection of the penalty, unless waived by the court.

(E) Duty of Clerk When Fine Without Order for Commitment; Duty of Prosecutor. When a fine is imposed by a court on a person, without an order for the immediate commitment of the person until the fine is paid, the clerk of the court shall deliver a copy of the order imposing the fine to the prosecuting attorney of the county in which the court is held, or the municipal attorney in the case of a fine that is payable to a municipality. The prosecuting attorney (or municipal attorney) shall obtain execution to collect the fine.

[Adopted effective March 1, 1985. Amended May 25, 2016, effective September 1, 2016, 499 Mich.]

Comments

Staff Comment to 1985 Adoption

MCR 3.605 is comparable to GCR 1963, 772.

In subrules (D) and (E), the references to the "prosecuting attorney" are changed to references to prosecuting attorney "or municipal attorney" to take account of the application of the rule to the district court. See DCR 772.4.

Staff Comment to 2016 Amendment

The amendments of MCR 3.605, 3.606, 3.928, 3.944, 3.956, 6.001, 6.425, 6.445, 6.610, and 6.933 were submitted by the Michigan State Planning Body for the Delivery of Legal Services to the Poor. The rule revisions are intended to provide clarity and guidance to courts regarding what courts would be required to do before incarcerating a defendant for failure to pay.

Rule 3.606 Contempts Outside Immediate Presence of Court

(A) Initiation of Proceeding. For a contempt committed outside the immediate view and presence of the court, on a proper showing on ex parte motion supported by affidavits, the court shall either

(1) order the accused person to show cause, at a reasonable time specified in the order, why that person should not be punished for the alleged misconduct; or

(2) issue a bench warrant for the arrest of the person.

(B) Writ of Habeas Corpus. A writ of habeas corpus to bring up a prisoner to testify may be used to bring before the court a person charged with misconduct under this rule. The court may enter an appropriate order for the disposition of the person.

(C) Bond for Appearance.

(1) The court may allow the giving of a bond in lieu of arrest, prescribing in the bench warrant the penalty of the bond and the return day for the defendant.

(2) The defendant is discharged from arrest on executing and delivering to the arresting officer a bond

(a) in the penalty endorsed on the bench warrant to the officer and the officer's successors,

(b) with two sufficient sureties, and

(c) with a condition that the defendant appear on the return day and await the order and judgment of the court.

(3) *Return of Bond.* On returning a bench warrant, the officer executing it must return the bond of the defendant, if one was taken. The bond must be filed with the bench warrant.

(D) Assignment of Bond; Damages. The court may order assignment of the bond to an aggrieved party who is authorized by the court to prosecute the bond under MCR 3.604(H). The measure of the damages to be assessed in an action on the bond is the extent of the loss or injury sustained by the aggrieved party because of the misconduct for which the order for arrest was issued, and that party's costs and expenses in securing the order. The remainder of the penalty of the bond is paid into the treasury of the county in which the bond was taken, to the credit of the general fund.

(E) Prosecution on Bond by Attorney General or Prosecutor. If the court does not order an assignment as provided in (D), it shall order the breach prosecuted by the Attorney General or by the prosecuting attorney for the county in which the bond was taken, under MCR 3.604. The penalty recovered is to be paid into the treasury of the county in which the bond was taken, to the credit of the general fund.

(F) The court shall not sentence a person to a term of incarceration for nonpayment unless the court has complied with the provisions of MCR 6.425(E)(3). Proceedings to which the Child Support and Parenting Time Enforcement Act, MCL 552.602 *et seq.*, applies are subject to the requirements of that act.

[Adopted effective March 1, 1985. Amended May 25, 2016, effective September 1, 2016, 499 Mich.]

Comments

Staff Comment to 1985 Adoption

MCR 3.606 is substantially the same as GCR 1963, 760.

Staff Comment to 2016 Amendment

The amendments of MCR 3.605, 3.606, 3.928, 3.944, 3.956, 6.001, 6.425, 6.445, 6.610, and 6.933 were submitted by the Michigan State Planning Body for the Delivery of Legal Services to the Poor. The rule revisions are intended to provide clarity and guidance to courts regarding what courts would be required to do before incarcerating a defendant for failure to pay.

Rule 3.607 Proceedings to Restore Lost Records or Documents in Courts of Record

(A) Application for Order. When a record or paper relating to an action or proceeding pending or determined in a Michigan court of record is lost, a person having an interest in its recovery may apply to the court having jurisdiction of the action or the record for an order that a duplicate of the lost record or paper be prepared and filed in the court.

(B) Manner of Proceeding; Notice to Interested Parties. The party making the application must show to the satisfaction of the court that the record or paper once existed and has been lost, without the fault or connivance, directly or indirectly, of the applicant. On that showing, the court shall direct the manner of proceeding to replace the lost item, and the notice to be given to parties interested in the application.

(C) Witnesses; Interrogatories. The court before which the application is pending may issue subpoenas for and compel the attendance of witnesses, or may compel witnesses to submit to examination on interrogatories and to establish facts relevant to the proceeding.

(D) Order; Effect of Duplicate. If the court is satisfied that the record or paper proposed as a substitute for the lost one exhibits all the material facts of the original, the court shall enter an order providing that the substitute record or paper be filed or recorded with the officer who had custody of the original. During the continuance of the loss, the substituted record or paper has the same effect in all respects and in all places as the original.

[Adopted effective March 1, 1985. Amended March 20, 2019, effective May 1, 2019, 502 Mich.]

Comments

Staff Comment to 1985 Adoption

MCR 3.607 is substantially the same as GCR 1963, 766.

Staff Comment to 2019 Amendment

The amendments of Rules 1.109, 2.102, 2.104, 2.106, 2.107, 2.117, 2.119, 2.403, 2.503, 2.506, 2.508, 2.518, 2.602, 2.603, 2.621, 3.101, 3.104, 3.203, 3.205, 3.210, 3.302, 3.607, 3.613, 3.614, 3.705, 3.801, 3.802, 3.805, 3.806, 4.201, 4.202, 4.303, 4.306, 5.001, 5.104, 5.105, 5.107, 5.108, 5.113, 5.117, 5.118, 5.119, 5.120, 5.125, 5.126, 5.132, 5.162, 5.202, 5.203, 5.205, 5.302, 5.304, 5.307, 5.308, 5.309, 5.310, 5.311, 5.313, 5.402, 5.404, 5.405, 5.409, 5.501, and 5.784 and addition of Rule 3.618 of the Michigan Court Rules are an expected progression necessary for design and implementation of the statewide electronic-filing system. These particular amendments will assist in implementing the goals of the project.

Rule 3.611 Voluntary Dissolution of Corporations

(A) Scope; Rules Applicable. This rule governs actions to dissolve corporations brought under MCL 600.3501. The general rules of procedure apply to these actions, except as provided in this rule and in MCL 600.3501–600.3515.

(B) Contents of Complaint; Statements Attached. A complaint seeking voluntary dissolution of a corporation must state why the plaintiff desires a dissolution of the corporation, and there must be attached:

(1) an inventory of all the corporation's property;

(2) a statement of all encumbrances on the corporation's property;

(3) an account of the corporation's capital stock, specifying the names of the stockholders, their addresses, if known, the number of shares belonging to each, the amount paid in on the shares, and the amount still due on them;

(4) an account of all the corporation's creditors and the contracts entered into by the corporation that may not have been fully satisfied and canceled, specifying:

(a) the address of each creditor and of every known person with whom the contracts were made, if known, and if not known, that fact to be stated;

(b) the amount owing to each creditor;

(c) the nature of each debt, demand, or obligation; and

(d) the basis of and consideration for each debt, demand, or obligation; and

(5) the affidavit of the plaintiff that the facts stated in the complaint, accounts, inventories, and statements are complete and true, so far as the plaintiff knows or has the means of knowing.

(C) Notice of Action. Process may be served as in other actions, or, on the filing of the complaint, the court may order all persons interested in the corporation to show cause why the corporation should not be dissolved, at a time and place to be specified in the order, but at least 28 days after the date of the order. Notice of the contents of the order must be served by mail on all creditors and stockholders at least 28 days before the hearing date, and must be published once each week for 3 successive weeks in a newspaper designated by the court.

(D) Hearing. At a hearing ordered under subrule (C), the court shall hear the allegations and proofs of the parties and take testimony relating to the property, debts, credits, engagements, and condition of the corporation. After the hearing, the court may dismiss the action, order the corporation dissolved, appoint a receiver, schedule further proceedings, or enter another appropriate order.

(E) Suits by Receiver. An action may be brought by the receiver in his or her own name and may be continued by the receiver's successor or co-receiver. An action commenced by or against the corporation before the filing of the complaint for dissolution is not abated by the complaint or by the judgment of dissolution, but may be prosecuted or defended by the receiver. The court in which an action is pending may on motion order substitution of parties or enter another necessary order.

[Adopted effective March 1, 1985.]

Comments

Staff Comment to 1985 Adoption

MCR 3.611 is comparable to GCR 1963, 778. New subrule (A) specifies the applicability of the rule.

Rule 3.612 Winding up of Corporation Whose Term or Charter has Expired

(A) Scope; Rules Applicable. This rule applies to actions under MCL 450.1801 *et seq.* The general rules of procedure apply to these actions, except as provided in this rule and in MCL 450.1801 *et seq.*

(B) Contents of Complaint. The complaint must include:

(1) the nature of the plaintiff's interest in the corporation or its property, the date of organization of the corporation, the title and the date of approval of the special act under which the corporation is organized, if appropriate, and the term of corporate existence;

(2) whether any of the corporation's stockholders are unknown to the plaintiff;

(3) that the complaint is filed on behalf of the plaintiff and all other persons interested in the property of the corporation as stockholders, creditors, or otherwise who may choose to join as parties plaintiff and share the expense of the action;

(4) an incorporation by reference of the statements required by subrule (C);

(5) other appropriate allegations; and

(6) a demand for appropriate relief, which may include that the affairs of the corporation be wound up and its assets disposed of and distributed and that a receiver of its property be appointed.

(C) Statements Attached to Complaint. The complaint must have attached:

(1) a copy of the corporation's articles of incorporation, if they are on file with the Department of Commerce, and, if the corporation is organized by special act, a copy of the act;

(2) a statement of the corporation's assets, so far as known to the plaintiff;

(3) a statement of the amount of capital stock and of the amount paid in, as far as known, from the last report of the corporation on file with the Department of Commerce or, if none has been filed, from the articles of incorporation on file with the Department of Commerce, or the special legislative act organizing the corporation;

(4) if the corporation's stock records are accessible to the plaintiff, a list of the stockholders' names and addresses and the number of shares held by each, insofar as shown in the records;

(5) a statement of all encumbrances on the corporation's property, and all claims against the corporation, and the names and addresses of the encumbrancers and claimants, so far as known to the plaintiff; and

(6) a statement of the corporation's debts, the names and addresses of the creditors, and the nature of the consideration for each debt, so far as known to the plaintiff.

(D) Parties Defendant. The corporation must be made a defendant. All persons claiming encumbrances on the property may be made defendants. It is not necessary to make a stockholder or creditor of the corporation a defendant.

(E) Process and Order for Appearance; Publication.

(1) Process must be issued and served as in other civil actions or, on the filing of the complaint, the court may order the appearance and answer of the corporation, its stockholders, and creditors at least 28 days after the date of the order.

(2) The order for appearance must be published in the manner prescribed in MCR 2.106.

(3) When proof of the publication is filed and the time specified in the order for the appearance of the corporation, stockholders, and creditors has expired, an order may be entered taking the complaint as confessed by those who have not appeared.

(F) Appearance by Defendants.

(1) Within the time the order for appearance sets, the following persons may appear and defend the suit as the corporation might have:

(a) a stockholder in the corporation while it existed and who still retains rights in its property by owning stock;

(b) an assignee, purchaser, heir, devisee, or personal representative of a stockholder; or

(c) a creditor of the corporation, whose claim is not barred by the statute of limitations.

(2) All persons so appearing must defend in the name of the corporation.

(3) If a person other than the corporation has been named as a defendant in the complaint, that person must be served with process as in other civil actions.

(G) Subsequent Proceedings. So far as applicable, the procedures established in MCR 3.611 govern hearings and later proceedings in an action under this rule.

(H) Continuation of Proceeding for Benefit of Stockholder or Creditor. If the plaintiff fails to establish that he or she is a stockholder or creditor of the corporation, the action may be continued by another stockholder or creditor who has appeared in the action.

[Adopted effective March 1, 1985. Amended effective September 28, 2011, 490 Mich.]

Comments

Staff Comment to 1985 Adoption

MCR 3.612 is comparable to GCR 1963, 779.

New subrule (A) states the applicability of the rule.

There are changes in terminology to take account of statutory changes regarding corporate filings. Compare, for example, subrules (C)(1) and (3) with GCR 1963, 779.2(1) and (3).

Staff Comment to 2011 Amendment

The above noted changes are minor revisions of the rules that have been recommended to the Court to correct cross references and to reflect other technical changes.

Rule 3.613   Change of Name

(A) Published Notice, Contents. A published notice of a proceeding to change a name shall include the name of the petitioner; the current name of the subject of the petition; the proposed name; and the time, date and place of the hearing.

(B) Minor's Signature. A petition for a change of name by a minor need not be signed in the presence of a judge. However, the separate written consent that must be signed by a minor 14 years of age or older shall be signed in the presence of the judge.

(C) Notice to Noncustodial Parent. Service on a noncustodial parent of a minor who is the subject of a petition for change of name shall be made in the following manner.

(1) *Address Known.* If the noncustodial parent's address or whereabouts is known, that parent shall be served with a copy of the petition and a notice of hearing at least 14 days before the hearing in a manner prescribed by MCR 2.107(C).

(2) *Address Unknown.* If the noncustodial parent's address or whereabouts is not known and cannot be ascertained after diligent inquiry, that parent shall be served with a notice of hearing by publishing in a newspaper and filing a proof of service as provided by MCR 2.106(F) and (G). The notice must be published one time at least 14 days before the date of the hearing, must include the name of the noncustodial parent and a statement that the result of the hearing may be to bar or affect the noncustodial parent's interest in the matter, and that publication must be in the county where the court is located unless a different county is specified by statute, court rule, or order of the court. A notice published under this subrule need not set out the contents of the petition if it contains the information required under subrule (A). A single publication may be used to notify the general public and the noncustodial parent whose address cannot be ascertained if the notice contains the noncustodial parent's name.

(D) Consultation With Minor, Presumption. A child 7 years of age and under is presumed not of sufficient age to be consulted concerning a preference on change of name.

(E) Confidential Records. In cases where the court orders that records are to be confidential and that no publication is to take place, records are to be maintained in a sealed envelope marked confidential and placed in a private file. Except as otherwise ordered by the court, only the original petitioner may gain access to confidential files, and no information relating to a confidential record, including whether the record exists, shall be accessible to the general public.

[Formerly Rule 5.781, adopted February 6, 1991, effective April 1, 1991, 437 Mich. Renumbered Rule 3.613 and amended, December 18, 2001, effective May 1, 2002, 456 Mich. Amended September 23, 2015, effective January 1, 2016, 498 Mich; March 20, 2019, effective May 1, 2019, 502 Mich.]

Comments

Staff Comment to 2002 Renumber and Amendment

The amendment and renumbering of MCR 5.750–5.756 and 5.781–5.783 as MCR 3.800–3.806 and 3.613–3.615, effective May 1, 2002, were proposed by the Family Division Joint Rules Committee. The statute creating the family division of circuit court gave it jurisdiction of a number of types of proceedings formerly heard in the probate court. See MCL 600.1021. The amendments move the rules governing adoptions, change of name, Parental Rights Restoration Act proceedings, and proceedings regarding persons who pose health threats to others, from Chapter 5, which contains probate court provisions, to Chapter 3. In addition, there are several modifications of the rules. The change-of-name rule will use the circuit court publication procedure. MCR 3.613(C)(2). A provision on confidentiality of records is added to the change-of-name rule. MCR 3.613(E). New subrule MCR 3.614(C) will specify the interested parties in a petition for treatment of infectious disease. (File No. 99–55.)

Staff Comment to 2016 Amendment

The amendments of MCR 3.613 provide clarification that distinguish a written consent from a petition for a name change, and reflect the statutory requirement that the written consent be signed by the minor in the presence of the judge.

Staff Comment to 2019 Amendment

The amendments of Rules 1.109, 2.102, 2.104, 2.106, 2.107, 2.117, 2.119, 2.403, 2.503, 2.506, 2.508, 2.518, 2.602, 2.603, 2.621, 3.101, 3.104, 3.203, 3.205, 3.210, 3.302, 3.607, 3.613, 3.614, 3.705, 3.801, 3.802, 3.805, 3.806, 4.201, 4.202, 4.303, 4.306, 5.001, 5.104, 5.105, 5.107, 5.108, 5.113, 5.117, 5.118, 5.119, 5.120, 5.125, 5.126, 5.132, 5.162, 5.202, 5.203, 5.205, 5.302, 5.304, 5.307, 5.308, 5.309, 5.310, 5.311, 5.313, 5.402, 5.404, 5.405, 5.409, 5.501, and 5.784 and addition of Rule 3.618 of the Michigan Court Rules are an expected progression necessary for design and implementation of the statewide electronic-filing system. These particular amendments will assist in implementing the goals of the project.

Rule 3.614   Health Threats to Others

(A) Public Health Code, Application. Except as modified by this rule, proceedings relating to carriers of contagious diseases who pose threats to the health of others under part 52 of the public health code [1] are governed by the rules generally applicable to civil proceedings.

(B) Service of Documents. The moving party is responsible for service when service is required.

(C) Interested Parties. The interested parties in a petition for treatment of infectious disease are the petitioner and the respondent.

(D) Commitment Review Panel.

(1) *Appointment.* On receipt of a petition for treatment of infectious disease which requests that the individual be committed to an appropriate facility, the Court shall forthwith appoint a Commitment Review Panel from a list of physicians prepared by the Department of Public Health.

(2) *Respondent's Choice of Physician.* On motion of the respondent requesting that a specific physician be appointed to the Commitment Review Panel, the Court shall appoint the physician so requested, unless the physician refuses. If the individual is unable to pay such physician, the court shall pay such physician a reasonable fee comparable with fees paid to other court appointed experts. On appointment of the requested physician, the Court shall discharge one of the initially appointed physicians.

(3) The Commitment Review Panel shall make written recommendations to the Court prior to the date of hearing on the petition. The recommendations shall be substantially in a form approved by the State Court Administrator.

(E) Commitment to Facility.

(1) *Renewal of Order of Commitment.* A motion for continuing commitment shall be filed at least 14 days prior to the expiration of the order of commitment. The motion shall be made by the director of the commitment facility or the director's designee. The court shall conduct a hearing on the motion prior to the expiration of the existing order of commitment. Notice shall be given as on the initial petition and to the local department of public health. The court shall reconvene the respondent's Commitment Review Panel. At the hearing, the petitioner must show good cause for continued commitment in the facility. No order of commitment shall exceed 6 months in length.

(2) *Reevaluation at Request of Respondent.* Once within any six-month period or more often by leave of the court, an individual committed to a facility for treatment of an infectious disease may file in the court a petition for a new Commitment Review Panel recommendation on whether the patient's commitment should be terminated. Within 14 days after receipt of the report of the reconvened Commitment Review Panel, the court shall review the panel's report and enter an order. The court may modify, continue or terminate its order of commitment without a hearing.

[Formerly Rule 5.782, adopted April 1, 1991, effective July 1, 1991, 437 Mich. Renumbered Rule 3.614 and amended, December 18, 2001, effective May 1, 2002, 465 Mich. Amended March 20, 2019, effective May 1, 2019, 502 Mich.]

¹ M.C.L.A. § 333.5201 *et seq.*

Comments

Staff Comment to 2002 Renumber and Amendment

The amendment and renumbering of MCR 5.750–5.756 and 5.781–5.783 as MCR 3.800–3.806 and 3.613–3.615, effective May 1, 2002, were proposed by the Family Division Joint Rules Committee. The statute creating the family division of circuit court gave it jurisdiction of a number of types of proceedings formerly heard in the probate court. See MCL 600.1021. The amendments move the rules governing adoptions, change of name, Parental Rights Restoration Act proceedings, and proceedings regarding persons who pose health threats to others, from Chapter 5, which contains probate court provisions, to Chapter 3. In addition, there are several modifications of the rules. The change-of-name rule will use the circuit court publication procedure. MCR 3.613(C)(2). A provision on confidentiality of records is added to the change-of-name rule. MCR 3.613(E). New subrule MCR 3.614(C) will specify the interested parties in a petition for treatment of infectious disease. (File No. 99–55.)

Staff Comment to 2019 Amendment

The amendments of Rules 1.109, 2.102, 2.104, 2.106, 2.107, 2.117, 2.119, 2.403, 2.503, 2.506, 2.508, 2.518, 2.602, 2.603, 2.621, 3.101, 3.104, 3.203, 3.205, 3.210, 3.302, 3.607, 3.613, 3.614, 3.705, 3.801, 3.802, 3.805, 3.806, 4.201, 4.202, 4.303, 4.306, 5.001, 5.104, 5.105, 5.107, 5.108, 5.113, 5.117, 5.118, 5.119, 5.120, 5.125, 5.126, 5.132, 5.162, 5.202, 5.203, 5.205, 5.302, 5.304, 5.307, 5.308, 5.309, 5.310, 5.311, 5.313, 5.402, 5.404, 5.405, 5.409, 5.501, and 5.784 and addition of Rule 3.618 of the Michigan Court Rules are an expected progression necessary for design and implementation of the statewide electronic-filing system. These particular amendments will assist in implementing the goals of the project.

Rule 3.615   Parental Rights Restoration Act Proceedings

(A) Applicable Rules. A proceeding by a minor to obtain a waiver of parental consent for an abortion shall be governed by the rules applicable to civil proceedings except as modified by this rule.

(B) Confidentiality, Use of Initials, Private File, Reopening.

(1) The court shall assure the confidentiality of the file, the assistance given the minor by court personnel, and the proceedings.

(2) If requested by the minor, the title of the proceeding shall be by initials or some other means of assuring confidentiality. At the time the petition is filed, the minor shall file a Confidential Information Sheet listing the minor's name, date of birth, permanent residence, title to be used in the proceeding and the method by which the minor may be reached during the pendency of the proceeding. The Confidential Information Sheet and all other documents containing identifying information shall be sealed in an envelope marked confidential on which the case number has been written and placed in a private file. Confidential information shall not be entered into a computer file.

(3) The court shall maintain only one file of all papers for each case. The file shall be inspected only by the judge, specifically authorized court personnel, the minor, her attorney, her next friend, the guardian ad litem, and any other person authorized by the minor. After the proceedings are completed, the file may be opened only by order of the court for good cause shown and only for a purpose specified in the order of the court.

(4) The file of a completed case shall not be destroyed until two years after the minor has reached the age of majority. The court shall not microfilm or otherwise copy the file.

(C) Advice of Rights, Method of Contact.

(1) If a minor seeking a waiver of parental consent makes first contact with the court by personal visit to the court, the court shall provide a written notice of rights and forms for a petition for waiver of parental consent, a confidential information sheet, and a request for appointment of an attorney, each substantially in the form approved by the state court administrator.

(2) If a minor seeking a waiver of parental consent makes first contact with the court by telephone, the court shall tell the minor that she can receive a notice of rights and forms for a petition, a confidential information sheet, and a request for appointment of an attorney by coming to the court or that the court will mail such forms to the minor. If the minor requests that the court mail the forms, the court shall mail the forms within 24 hours of the telephone contact to an address specified by the minor.

(3) Any person on personal visit to the court shall be given, on request, a copy of the notice of rights or any other form.

(D) Assistance With Preparation of Petition. On request of the minor or next friend, the court shall provide the minor with assistance in preparing and filing of a petition, confidential information sheet and request for appointment of an attorney, each substantially in the form approved by the state court administrator.

(E) Next Friend. If the minor proceeds through a next friend, the petitioner shall certify that the next friend is not disqualified by statute and that the next friend is an adult. The next friend may act on behalf of the minor without prior appointment of the court and is not responsible for the costs of the action.

(F) Attorney, Request, Appointment, Duties.

(1) At the request of the minor or next friend before or after filing the petition, the court shall immediately appoint an attorney to represent the minor. The request shall be in writing in substantially the form approved by the state court administrator. Except for good cause stated on the record, the court shall appoint an attorney selected by the minor if the minor has secured the attorney's agreement to represent her or the attorney has previously indicated to the court a willingness to be appointed.

(2) If it deems necessary, the court may appoint an attorney to represent the minor at any time.

(3) The minor shall contact the court appointed attorney within 24 hours of such appointment. The court shall advise the minor of this requirement.

(4) If an attorney is appointed to represent a minor prior to filing a petition, the attorney shall consult with the minor within 48 hours of appointment.

(G) Guardian ad Litem, Appointment, Duties.

(1) *Request of Minor.* The court shall immediately appoint a guardian ad litem to represent the minor at the request of the minor or next friend before or after filing the petition.

(2) *Appointment on Court's Motion.*

(a) At any time if it deems necessary, the court may appoint a guardian ad litem to assist the court.

(b) The guardian ad litem may obtain information by contacting the minor and other persons with the consent of the minor, provided the confidentiality of the proceedings is not violated.

(H) Filing Petition, Setting Hearing, Notice of Hearing.

(1) The petition shall be filed in person by the minor, attorney or next friend.

(2) The court shall set a time and place for a hearing and notify the filer at the time the petition is filed. The court shall give notice of the hearing only to the minor, the minor's attorney, next friend and guardian ad litem. Notice of hearing may be oral or written and may be given at any time prior to the hearing. The hearing may be scheduled to commence immediately if the minor and her attorney, if any, are ready to proceed.

(3) Insofar as practical, at the minor's request the hearing shall be scheduled at a time and place that will not interfere with the minor's school attendance.

(I) Venue, Transfer. Venue is in the county of the minor's residence or where the minor is found at the time of the filing of the petition. Transfer of venue properly laid shall not be made without consent of the minor.

(J) Hearing.

(1) *Burden and Standard of Proof.* The petitioner has the burden of proof by preponderance of the evidence and must establish the statutory criteria at a hearing.

(2) *Closed Hearing.* The hearing shall be closed to the public. The court shall limit attendance at the hearing to the minor, the minor's attorney, the next friend, the guardian ad litem, persons who are called to testify by the minor or with the minor's consent, necessary court personnel and one support

person who would not be disqualified as a next friend by MCL 722.902(d).

(3) All relevant and material evidence may be received.

(4) The hearing may be conducted informally in the chambers of a judge.

(5) The hearing shall commence and be concluded within 72 hours, excluding Sundays and holidays, of the filing of the petition, unless the minor consents to an adjournment. The order of the court shall be issued within 48 hours, excluding Sundays and holidays, of the conclusion of the hearing.

(K) Order.

(1) *Order Granting Waiver, Duration, Effect.* If the petition is granted, the court immediately shall provide the minor with two certified copies of the order granting waiver of parental consent. The order shall be valid for 90 days from the date of entry. Nothing in the order shall require or permit an abortion that is otherwise prohibited by law.

(2) *Order Denying Waiver, Notice of Appeal, Appointment of Counsel, Preparation of Transcript.* If the order denies relief, the court shall endorse the time and date on the order. The order shall be served on the minor's attorney or, if none, the minor along with

(a) a unified appellate document substantially in the form approved by the state court administrator which may be used as notice of appeal, claim of appeal, request for appointment of an attorney and order of transcript, and

(b) a notice that, if the minor desires to appeal, the minor must file the notice of appeal with the court within 24 hours.

(3) *Appeal.*

(a) Upon receipt of a timely notice of appeal, the court must appoint counsel and order that the transcript be prepared immediately and two copies filed within 72 hours. If the minor was represented by counsel in the court proceedings, the court must reappoint the same attorney unless there is good cause for a different appointment. As soon as the transcript is filed, the court shall forward the file to the Court of Appeals.

(b) Time for Filing Notice.

(1) If the order was entered at the conclusion of the hearing or at any other time when the minor's attorney or, if none, the minor was in attendance at court, the minor must file the notice of appeal within 24 hours of the date and time stamped on the order, or

(2) If the order was entered at any other time, the minor must file the notice of appeal within 24 hours of the time when the order was received by the minor's attorney or, if none, the minor.

(c) If a court in which a document is to be filed is closed for business at the end of a filing period, the document will be filed on a timely basis if filed during the morning of the next day when the court is open for business.

(d) Perfection of Appeal. The minor's attorney must perfect the appeal by filing in the Court of Appeals a claim of appeal and a copy of the order denying waiver. The appeal must be perfected within 72 hours, excluding Sundays and holidays, of the filing of the notice of appeal.

(e) *Brief.* The minor's attorney shall file at the time of perfecting appeal five copies of the brief on appeal. The brief need not contain citations to the transcript.

(f) *Oral Argument.* There will be no oral argument, unless ordered by the Court of Appeals.

[Formerly Rule 5.783, adopted March 28, 1991, effective April 1, 1991, 437 Mich. Renumbered Rule 3.615 and amended, December 18, 2001, effective May 1, 2002, 465 Mich.]

Comments

Staff Comment to 2002 Renumber and Amendment

The amendment and renumbering of MCR 5.750–5.756 and 5.781–5.783 as MCR 3.800–3.806 and 3.613–3.615, effective May 1, 2002, were proposed by the Family Division Joint Rules Committee. The statute creating the family division of circuit court gave it jurisdiction of a number of types of proceedings formerly heard in the probate court. See MCL 600.1021. The amendments move the rules governing adoptions, change of name, Parental Rights Restoration Act proceedings, and proceedings regarding persons who pose health threats to others, from Chapter 5, which contains probate court provisions, to Chapter 3. In addition, there are several modifications of the rules. The change-of-name rule will use the circuit court publication procedure. MCR 3.613(C)(2). A provision on confidentiality of records is added to the change-of-name rule. MCR 3.613(E). New subrule MCR 3.614(C) will specify the interested parties in a petition for treatment of infectious disease. (File No. 99–55.)

Rule 3.616. Proceeding to Determine Continuation of Voluntary Foster Care Services

(A) Scope of Rule. This rule governs review of all voluntary foster care agreements made pursuant to article II of the Young Adult Voluntary Foster Care Act, MCL 400.645 through MCL 400.663.

(B) Jurisdiction. Upon the filing of a petition under this rule, the family division of the circuit court has jurisdiction to review an agreement for the voluntary extension of foster care services after age 18.

(C) Court File. Upon the filing of a petition under subrule (E), the court shall open a file using the appropriate case classification code as referenced in MCR 8.117. The file shall be closed following the issuance of the court's determination under subrule (F).

(D) Form. The petition and the judicial determination shall be prepared on forms approved by the state court administrator.

(E) Ex Parte Petition; Filing, Contents, Service. Within 150 days after the signing of a voluntary foster care agreement, the Department of Human Services shall file with the family division of the circuit court, in the county where the youth resides, an ex parte petition requesting the court's determination that continuing in voluntary foster care is in the youth's best interests.

(1) *Contents of Petition.* The petition shall contain

(a) the youth's name, date of birth, race, gender, and current address;

(b) the name, date of birth, and residence address of the youth's parents or legal custodian (if parental rights have not been terminated);

(c) the name and address of the youth's foster parent or parents;

(d) a statement that the youth has been notified of the right to request a hearing regarding continuing in foster care;

(e) a showing that jurisdiction of a court over the youth's child protective proceeding has been terminated, including the name of the court and the date jurisdiction was terminated; and

(f) any other information the Department of Human Services, parent or legal custodian, youth, or foster parent wants the court to consider.

(2) *Supporting Documents.* The petition shall be accompanied by a written report prepared pursuant to MCL 400.655 and a copy of the signed voluntary foster care agreement.

(3) *Service.* The Department of Human Services shall serve the petition on

(a) the youth; and

(b) the foster parent or parents, if any.

(F) Judicial Determination. The court shall review the petition, report, and voluntary foster care agreement filed pursuant to subrule (E), and then make a determination whether continuing in voluntary foster care is in the best interests of the youth.

(1) *Written Order; Time.* The court shall issue an order that includes its determination and individualized findings that support its determination. The findings shall be based on the Department of Human Services' written report and other information filed with the court. The order must be signed and dated within 21 days of the filing of the petition.

(2) *Service.* The court shall serve the order on

(a) the Department of Human Services;

(b) the youth; and

(c) the foster parent or parents, if any.

(G) Confidential File. The Department of Human Services and the youth are entitled to access to the records contained in the file, but otherwise, the file is confidential.

[Adopted February 1, 2012, effective April 1, 2012, 490 Mich. Amended effective May 24, 2012, 491 Mich. Amended February 6, 2013, effective May 1, 2013, 493 Mich. Amended effective March 21, 2018, 501 Mich.]

Comments

Staff Comment to 2012 Adoption

New MCR 3.616 implements the judicial action requirements of 2011 PA 225, the Young Adult Voluntary Foster Care Act, MCL 400.641 *et seq.*

This Court adopted the new rule to become effective April 1, 2012, to coincide with implementation of the Department of Human Services' new program to provide continuing voluntary foster care for youth between the ages of 18 and 21, which will begin operating on April 1, 2012. Having this new court rule in place will enable Michigan to receive federal Title IV–E funding for that program.

By this same order, the Court is inviting public comment to allow interested persons an opportunity to comment and to provide an opportunity to be heard at a future public hearing. This will allow the Court to consider amending the rule in response to any comments that it receives.

Staff Comment to 2012 Amendment

The amendment inserts reference to the youth's race, which would make the rule consistent with MCL 400.655(a). In addition, the requirement in subsection (f) is deleted because that information already must be included in the report provided in subsection (E)(2).

Staff Comment to 2013 Amendment

The amendments of MCR 3.616 provide that the files of adult foster care youth are confidential, but may be accessed by the youth and by DHS. The amendment eliminates the requirement that the petition and order be served on the previous court in which the youth's child protection case was disposed because the case is no longer active. This order also corrects numbering of subsection (F)(2)(i)–(iv) so that the subsections are labeled with letters (a)–(c).

Staff Comment to 2018 Amendment

These amendments update cross-references and make other nonsubstantive revisions to clarify the rules. The amendment of MCR 6.110(B)(1) addresses an inadvertent omission from the last amendment of this rule that was intended to be shown in overstrike. Accordingly, the current rule does not match the published version. Striking the clause "for good cause shown" will provide consistency with other published versions of the rule and with the statute, MCL 766.7, which allows a magistrate to adjourn a preliminary examination with the consent of the parties without the need for good cause to be shown.

Rule 3.617. Delayed Registration of Birth

The entire record for delayed registration of birth is confidential. Except as otherwise ordered by the court, only the legal parent or parents and the child may gain access to the confidential file, and no information relating to a confidential record, including whether the record exists, shall be accessible to the general public.

[Adopted effective September 23, 2015, 498 Mich. Amended effective March 21, 2018, 501 Mich.]

Comments

Staff Comment to 2015 Adoption

This new rule, MCR 3.617, requires adoption files of foreign-born children who are adopted by a parent who is a resident of this state to be retained as confidential records (as are the adoption records that are governed by MCL 710.67 and MCL 710.68).

Staff Comment to 2018 Amendment

These amendments update cross-references and make other nonsubstantive revisions to clarify the rules. The amendment of MCR 6.110(B)(1) addresses an inadvertent omission from the last amendment of this rule that was intended to be shown in overstrike. Accordingly, the current rule does not match the published version. Striking the clause "for good cause shown" will provide consistency with other published versions of the rule and with the statute, MCL 766.7, which allows a magistrate to adjourn a preliminary examination with the consent of the parties without the need for good cause to be shown.

Rule 3.618. Emancipation of Minor

(A) Interested Persons. The persons interested in a petition for emancipation of a minor are

(1) the minor,

(2) parents of the minor,

(3) the affiant on an affidavit supporting emancipation, and

(4) any guardian or conservator.

(B) Summons.

(1) A summons in an emancipation proceeding must be served on an interested person at least 14 days before the date of hearing unless the interested person has waived his or her right to service.

(2) The summons must direct the person to whom it is addressed to appear at a time and place specified by the court and must identify the nature of hearing.

(C) Manner of Serving Summons and Petition.

(1) Except as provided in subrule (C)(2), a summons and petition for emancipation must be served by personal service.

(2) If service of the summons and petition cannot be made under subrule (C)(1) because the whereabouts of an interested person could not be ascertained after diligent inquiry, the petitioner must file proof of the efforts made to locate the interested person in a statement verified under MCR 1.109(D)(3). If the court finds, on reviewing the statement, that a reasonable attempt was made, the court may issue an ex parte order directing another manner of service reasonably calculat-

ed to give notice of the proceedings, including notice by publication under subrule (3).

(3) *Service by Publication.*

(a) Requirements. A notice of hearing or other notice required to be made by publication must be published in a newspaper as defined by MCR 2.106(F) at least one time 21 days before the date of hearing. Publication shall be in the county in which the court is located.

(b) Contents of Notice. The published notice must include the name of the individual to whom the notice is given, a statement describing the nature of the hearing, and a statement that the hearing may affect the individual's interest in the matter. If an interested person has once been served by publication, notice is only required on an interested person whose address is known or becomes known during the proceedings.

(c) Service of Notice. A copy of the notice shall be mailed to the individual to whom the notice is given at his or her last known address. If the last known address of the individual cannot be ascertained after diligent inquiry, mailing a copy of the notice is not required.

(d) Proof of service under this subrule shall be made according to MCR 2.106(G).

(D) Time of Service.

(1) A summons shall be personally served at least 14 days before hearing on a petition of emancipation, except as allowed under subrule (C)(2).

(2) If the summons is served by registered mail, it must be sent at least 21 days before hearing if the interested person to be served resides in Michigan, or at least 28 days before hearing if the interested person to be served resides outside of Michigan.

(E) Other Service. The clerk of the court shall serve an order issued by the court. If notice of the petition and hearing was given to an interested person by publication, a copy of an order issued by the court need not be served on that interested person.

(F) Proof of Service

(1) *Summons and Petition.* Proof of service of the summons and petition must be made in the manner provided in MCR 2.104(A).

(2) *Other Documents.* Proof of service of other documents permitted or required to be served under this rule must be made in the manner provided in MCR 2.107(D).

[Adopted March 20, 2019, effective May 1, 2019, 502 Mich.]

Comments

Staff Comment to 2019 Adoption

The amendments of Rules 1.109, 2.102, 2.104, 2.106, 2.107, 2.117, 2.119, 2.403, 2.503, 2.506, 2.508, 2.518, 2.602, 2.603, 2.621, 3.101, 3.104, 3.203, 3.205, 3.210, 3.302, 3.607, 3.613, 3.614, 3.705, 3.801, 3.802, 3.805, 3.806, 4.201, 4.202, 4.303, 4.306, 5.001, 5.104, 5.105, 5.107, 5.108, 5.113, 5.117, 5.118, 5.119, 5.120, 5.125, 5.126, 5.132, 5.162, 5.202, 5.203, 5.205, 5.302, 5.304, 5.307, 5.308, 5.309, 5.310, 5.311, 5.313, 5.402, 5.404, 5.405, 5.409, 5.501, and 5.784 and addition of Rule 3.618 of the Michigan Court Rules are an expected progression necessary for design and implementation of the statewide electronic-filing system. These particular amendments will assist in implementing the goals of the project.

SUBCHAPTER 3.700   PERSONAL PROTECTION PROCEEDINGS

Rule 3.701   Applicability of Rules; Forms

(A) Scope. Except as provided by this subchapter and the provisions of MCL 600.2950 and 600.2950a, actions for personal protection for relief against domestic violence or stalking are governed by the Michigan Court Rules. Procedure related to personal protection orders against adults is governed by this subchapter. Procedure related to personal protection orders against minors is governed by subchapter 3.900, except as provided in MCR 3.981.

(B) Forms. The state court administrator shall approve forms for use in personal protection act proceedings. The forms shall be made available for public distribution by the clerk of the circuit court.

[Adopted August 11, 1997, effective September 1, 1997, 456 Mich. Amended December 22, 1999, effective January 10, 2000, 461 Mich; June 1, 2001, effective September 1, 2001, 464 Mich; February 4, 2003, effective May 1, 2003, 467 Mich.]

Comments

Staff Comment to 1997 Adoption

The amendments of MCR 3.201, 3.207, and 8.117 and addition of subchapter 3.700 [effective September 1, 1997], are designed to implement the statutes providing for the issuance of personal protection orders. See MCL 600.2950, MCL 600.2950a.

Staff Comment to 1999 Amendment

These rules [effective January 10, 2000] clarify the procedure applicable to the new minor personal protection orders ("minor PPOs") created in 1998 PA 474–477, which went into effect March 1, 1999. Because the new statutes do not make clear whether existing PPO procedural rules apply or rules for Juvenile Code proceedings apply, these rules are promulgated to assure consistency in the processing of minor PPOs in Michigan's Circuit Court Family Divisions. Immediate adoption has been ordered to provide needed procedural guidance for courts already facing minor PPO cases.

Staff Comment to 2001 Amendment

The June 1, 2001 amendments of MCR 3.701, MCR 3.702, 3.703, 3.704, 3.706, 3.707, and 3.708, effective September 1, 2001, are designed, in part, to clarify the court rule provisions adopted effective September 1, 1997. 456 Mich clxxxiv (1997).

Staff Comment to 2003 Amendment

The amendment of MCR 3.301(A) [sic] changes the cross-reference to the subchapter governing juvenile proceedings.

Rule 3.702   Definitions

When used in this subchapter, unless the context otherwise indicates:

(1) "personal protection order" means a protection order as described under MCL 600.2950 and 600.2950a;

(2) "petition" refers to a pleading for commencing an independent action for personal protection and is not considered a motion as defined in MCR 2.119;

(3) "petitioner" refers to the party seeking protection;

(4) "respondent" refers to the party to be restrained;

(5) "existing action" means an action in this court or any other court in which both the petitioner and the respondent are parties; existing actions include, but are not limited to, pending and completed domestic relations actions, criminal actions, other actions for personal protection orders.

(6) "minor" means a person under the age of 18.

(7) "minor personal protection order" means a personal protection order issued by a court against a minor and under jurisdiction granted by MCL 712A.2(h).

[Adopted August 11, 1997, effective September 1, 1997, 456 Mich. Amended December 22, 1999, effective January 10, 2000, 461 Mich; June 1, 2001, effective September 1, 2001, 464 Mich.]

Comments

Staff Comment to 1997 Adoption

MCR 3.702 is designed to implement the statutes providing for the issuance of personal protection orders. See MCL 600.2950; MSA 27A.2950, MCL 600.2950a; MSA 27A.2950(1).

Staff Comment to 1999 Amendment

This rule clarifies the procedure applicable to the minor personal protection orders ("minor PPO's") created in 1998 PA 474–477, which went into effect March 1, 1999. Because the new statutes did not make clear whether existing PPO procedural rules applied or rules for Juvenile Code proceedings applied, this rule was promulgated to assure consistency in the processing of minor PPO's in Michigan's Circuit Court Family Divisions. Immediate adoption was ordered to provide needed procedural guidance for courts already facing minor PPO cases.

Staff Comment to 2001 Amendment

The June 1, 2001 amendments of MCR 3.701, MCR 3.702, 3.703, 3.704, 3.706, 3.707, and 3.708, effective September 1, 2001, are designed, in part, to clarify the court rule provisions adopted effective September 1, 1997. 456 Mich clxxxiv (1997).

Rule 3.703   Commencing a Personal Protection Action

(A) Filing. A personal protection action is an independent action commenced by filing a petition with a court. There are no fees for filing a personal protection action and no summons is issued. A personal protection action may not be commenced by filing a motion in an existing case or by joining a claim to an action.

(B) Petition in General. The petition must

(1) be in writing;

(2) state with particularity the facts on which it is based;

(3) state the relief sought and the conduct to be restrained;

(4) state whether an ex parte order is being sought;

(5) state whether a personal protection order action involving the same parties has been commenced in another jurisdiction; and

(6) be signed by the party or attorney as provided in MCR 1.109(E). The petitioner may omit his or her residence address from the documents filed with the court, but must provide the court with a mailing address.

(C) Petition Against a Minor. In addition to the requirements outlined in (B), a petition against a minor must list:

(1) the minor's name, address, and either age or date of birth; and

(2) if known or can be easily ascertained, the names and addresses of the minor's parent or parents, guardian, or custodian.

(D) Other Pending Actions; Order, Judgments.

(1) The petition must specify whether there are any other pending actions in this or any other court, or orders or judgments already entered by this or any other court affecting

the parties, including the name of the court and the case number, if known.

(a) If the petition is filed in the same court as a pending action or where an order or judgment has already been entered by that court affecting the parties, it shall be assigned to the same judge.

(b) If there are pending actions in another court or orders or judgments already entered by another court affecting the parties, the court should contact the court where the pending actions were filed or orders or judgments were entered, if practicable, to determine any relevant information.

(2) If the prior action resulted in an order providing for continuing jurisdiction of a minor, and the new action requests relief with regard to the minor, the court must comply with MCR 3.205.

(E) Venue.

(1) If the respondent is an adult, the petitioner may file a personal protection action in any county in Michigan regardless of residency.

(2) If the respondent is a minor, the petitioner may file a personal protection order in either the petitioner's or respondent's county of residence. If the respondent does not live in this state, venue for the action is proper in the petitioner's county of residence.

(F) Minor or Legally Incapacitated Individual as Petitioner.

(1) If the petitioner is a minor or a legally incapacitated individual, the petitioner shall proceed through a next friend. The petitioner shall certify that the next friend is not disqualified by statute and that the next friend is an adult.

(2) Unless the court determines appointment is necessary, the next friend may act on behalf of the minor or legally incapacitated person without appointment. However, the court shall appoint a next friend if the minor is less than 14 years of age. The next friend is not responsible for the costs of the action.

(G) Request for Ex Parte Order.

If the petition requests an ex parte order, the petition must set forth specific facts showing that immediate and irreparable injury, loss, or damage will result to the petitioner from the delay required to effect notice or from the risk that notice will itself precipitate adverse action before an order can be issued.

[Adopted August 11, 1997, effective September 1, 1997, 456 Mich. Amended December 22, 1999, effective January 10, 2000, 461 Mich; June 1, 2001, effective September 1, 2001, 464 Mich; August 30, 2018, effective September 1, 2018, 502 Mich.]

Comments

Staff Comment to 1997 Adoption

MCR 3.703 is designed to implement the statutes providing for the issuance of personal protection orders. See MCL 600.2950 and MCL 600.2950a.

Staff Comment to 2000 Amendment

This rule clarifies the procedure applicable to the minor personal protection orders ("minor PPOs") created in 1998 PA 474-477, which went into effect March 1, 1999. Because the new statutes did not make clear whether existing PPO procedural rules applied or rules for Juvenile Code proceedings applied, this rule was promulgated to assure consistency in the processing of minor PPOs in Michigan's Circuit Court Family Divisions. Immediate adoption was ordered to provide needed procedural guidance for courts already facing minor PPO cases.

Staff Comment to 2001 Amendment

The June 1, 2001 amendments of MCR 3.701, MCR 3.702, 3.703, 3.704, 3.706, 3.707, and 3.708, effective September 1, 2001, are designed, in part, to clarify the court rule provisions adopted effective September 1, 1997. 456 Mich clxxxiv (1997).

Staff Comment to 2018 Amendment

These amendments update cross-references in the rules, and are intended to reflect changes that are necessary as a result of the Court's recent e-Filing rules amendments.

Rule 3.704　Dismissal

Except as specified in MCR 3.705(A)(5) and (B), an action for a personal protection order may only be dismissed upon motion by the petitioner prior to the issuance of an order. There is no fee for such a motion.

[Adopted August 11, 1997, effective September 1, 1997, 456 Mich. Amended June 1, 2001, effective September 1, 2001, 464 Mich.]

Comments

Staff Comment to 1997 Adoption

MCR 3.704 is designed to implement the statutes providing for the issuance of personal protection orders. See MCL 600.2950 and MCL 600.2950a.

Staff Comment to 2001 Amendment

The amendment of MCR 3.704 is designed, in part, to clarify the court rule provisions adopted effective September 1, 1997. 456 Mich clxxxiv (1997).

Rule 3.705　Issuance of Personal Protection Orders

(A) Ex Parte Orders.

(1) The court must rule on a request for an ex parte order within one business day of the filing date of the petition.

(2) If it clearly appears from specific facts shown by verified complaint, written petition, or affidavit that the petitioner is entitled to the relief sought, an ex parte order shall be granted if immediate and irreparable injury, loss, or damage will result from the delay required to effectuate notice or that the notice will itself precipitate adverse action before a personal protection order can be issued. In a proceeding under MCL 600.2950a, the court must state in writing the specific reasons for issuance of the order. A permanent record or memorandum must be made of any nonwritten evidence, argument or other representations made in support of issuance of an ex parte order.

(3) An ex parte order is valid for not less than 182 days, and must state its expiration date.

(4) If an ex parte order is entered, the petitioner shall serve the petition and order as provided in MCR 3.706(D). However, failure to make service does not affect the order's validity or effectiveness.

(5) If the court refuses to grant an ex parte order, it shall state the reasons in writing and shall advise the petitioner of the right to request a hearing as provided in subrule (B). If the petitioner does not request a hearing within 21 days of entry of the order, the order denying the petition is final. The court shall not be required to give such notice if the court determines after interviewing the petitioner that the petitioner's claims are sufficiently without merit that the action should be dismissed without a hearing.

(B) Hearings.

(1) The court shall schedule a hearing as soon as possible in the following instances, unless it determines after interviewing the petitioner that the claims are sufficiently without merit that the action should be dismissed without a hearing:

(a) the petition does not request an ex parte order; or

(b) the court refuses to enter an ex parte order and the petitioner subsequently requests a hearing.

(2) The petitioner shall serve on the respondent notice of the hearing along with the petition as provided in MCR 2.105(A). If the respondent is a minor, and the whereabouts of the respondent's parent or parents, guardian, or custodian is known, the petitioner shall also in the same manner serve notice of the hearing and the petition on the respondent's parent or parents, guardian, or custodian. One day before the hearing on a petition seeking a PPO under MCL 600.2950 or MCL 600.2950a(1) is deemed sufficient notice. Two days before the hearing on a petition seeking a PPO under MCL 600.2950a(2) is deemed sufficient notice.

(3) The hearing shall be held on the record. In accordance with MCR 2.407, the court may allow the use of videoconferencing technology by any participant as defined in MCR 2.407(A)(1).

(4) The petitioner must attend the hearing. If the petitioner fails to attend the hearing, the court may adjourn and reschedule the hearing or dismiss the petition.

(5) If the respondent fails to appear at a hearing on the petition and the court determines the petitioner made diligent attempts to serve the respondent, whether the respondent was served or not, the order may be entered without further notice to the respondent if the court determines that the petitioner is entitled to relief.

(6) At the conclusion of the hearing the court must state the reasons for granting or denying a personal protection order on the record and enter an appropriate order. In addition, the court must state the reasons for denying a personal protection order in writing, and, in a proceeding under MCL 600.2950a, the court must state in writing the specific reasons for issuance of the order.

(C) Pursuant to 18 USC 2265(d)(3), a court is prohibited from making available to the public on the Internet any information regarding the registration of, filing of a petition for, or issuance of an order under this rule if such publication would be likely to publicly reveal the identity or location of the party protected under the order.

[Adopted August 11, 1997, effective September 1, 1997, 456 Mich. Amended December 22, 1999, effective January 10, 2000, 461 Mich; September 11, 2002, effective January 1, 2003, 467 Mich; February 1, 2011, effective February 1, 2011, 488 Mich; June 4, 2014, effective September 1, 2014, 496 Mich; September 21, 2016, effective January 1, 2017, 500 Mich; March 20, 2019, effective May 1, 2019, 502 Mich.]

Comments

Staff Comment to 1997 Adoption

MCR 3.705 is designed to implement the statutes providing for the issuance of personal protection orders. See MCL 600.2950 and MCL 600.2950a.

Staff Comment to 1999 Amendment

This rule clarifies the procedure applicable to the minor personal protection orders ("minor PPOs") created in 1998 PA 474-477, which went into effect March 1, 1999. Because the new statutes did not make clear whether existing PPO procedural rules applied or rules for Juvenile Code proceedings applied, this rule was promulgated to assure consistency in the processing of minor PPOs in Michigan's Circuit Court Family Divisions. Immediate adoption was ordered to provide needed procedural guidance for courts already facing minor PPO cases.

Staff Comment to 2002 Amendment

The September 11, 2002, amendments of MCR 3.206, 3.214, 3.705, 3.706, 3.708, 5.982, and 8.119, which were given immediate effect, are related to the group of domestic violence statutes enacted in December 2001 that took effect April 1, 2002.

The changes in MCR 3.206 and 3.214 are related to 2001 PA 195, which adopted the Uniform Child-Custody Jurisdiction and Enforcement Act, MCL 722.1101 et seq. There is also some nonsubstantive reorganization of MCR 3.214.

The amendment of MCR 3.705 implements the statutory provisions regarding the statement of reasons for granting or denying personal protection orders. See 2001 PA 196.

The amendment of MCR 3.706 incorporates the statutory provisions regarding enforceability of Michigan personal protection orders in other jurisdictions. See 2001 PA 200 and 201.

MCR 3.708 and 5.982 are amended to include foreign protection orders, which are made enforceable in Michigan by 2001 PA 197.

MCR 8.119(F) is amended to conform to 2001 PA 205, which directs that when a motion to seal court records involves allegations of domestic violence, the court is to consider the safety of the potential victim in ruling on the motion.

Staff Comment to 2011 Amendment

This amendment, submitted to the Court by the State Bar of Michigan Domestic Violence Committee, amends MCR 3.705 to allow sufficient time for a respondent to file a written motion and offer of proof at least 24 hours before a hearing as required by statute. MCL 600.2950a(4) requires that a respondent who wants to introduce evidence covered by the rape shield provision of MCL 750.520j submit a notice and offer of proof at least 24 hours before the hearing. Before adoption of this amendment, the rule's one-day notice of hearing requirement would not have provided the respondent 24 hours within which to submit the offer of proof, so the SBM Domestic Violence Committee recommended that the rule be amended to change the time provision regarding notice of hearing for a sexual assault PPO to two days instead of one day.

Staff Comment to 2014 Amendment

The amendment of MCR 3.705(C) prohibits publication of information on the Internet that could reveal the identity or location of the protected party.

Staff Comment to 2017 Amendment

These amendments permit courts to expand the use of videoconferencing technology in many court proceedings, and clarify the proceedings at which videoconferencing technology may be used.

Staff Comment to 2019 Amendment

The amendments of Rules 1.109, 2.102, 2.104, 2.106, 2.107, 2.117, 2.119, 2.403, 2.503, 2.506, 2.508, 2.518, 2.602, 2.603, 2.621, 3.101, 3.104, 3.203, 3.205, 3.210, 3.302, 3.607, 3.613, 3.614, 3.705, 3.801, 3.802, 3.805, 3.806, 4.201, 4.202, 4.303, 4.306, 5.001, 5.104, 5.105, 5.107, 5.108, 5.113, 5.117, 5.118, 5.120, 5.125, 5.126, 5.132, 5.162, 5.202, 5.203, 5.205, 5.302, 5.304, 5.307, 5.308, 5.309, 5.310, 5.311, 5.313, 5.402, 5.404, 5.405, 5.409, 5.501, and 5.784 and addition of Rule 3.618 of the Michigan Court Rules are an expected progression necessary for design and implementation of the statewide electronic-filing system. These particular amendments will assist in implementing the goals of the project.

Rule 3.706. Orders

(A) Form and Scope of Order. An order granting a personal protection order must include the following:

(1) A statement that the personal protection order has been entered, listing the type or types of conduct enjoined.

(2) A statement that the personal protection order is effective when signed by the judge and is immediately enforceable anywhere in Michigan, and that, after service, the personal protection order may be enforced by another state, an Indian tribe, or a territory of the United States.

(3) A statement that violation of the personal protection order will subject the individual restrained or enjoined to either of the following:

(a) If the respondent is 17 years of age or more, immediate arrest and, if the respondent is found guilty of criminal contempt, imprisonment for not more than 93 days and may be fined not more than $500; or

(b) If the respondent is less than 17 years of age, immediate apprehension and, if the respondent is found in contempt, the dispositional alternatives listed in MCL 712A.18.

(4) An expiration date stated clearly on the face of the order.

(5) A statement that the personal protection order is enforceable anywhere in Michigan by any law enforcement agency, and that if the respondent violates the personal protection order in another jurisdiction, the respondent is subject to the enforcement procedures and penalties of the jurisdiction in which the violation occurred.

(6) Identification of the law enforcement agency, designated by the court to enter the personal protection order into the law enforcement information network.

(7) For ex parte orders, a statement that, within 14 days after being served with or receiving actual notice of the order, the individual restrained or enjoined may file a motion to modify or terminate the personal protection order and a request for a hearing, and that motion forms and filing instructions are available from the clerk of the court.

(B) Mutual Orders Prohibited. A personal protection order may not be made mutual.

(C) Existing Custody and Parenting Time Orders.

(1) *Contact With Court Having Prior Jurisdiction.* The court issuing a personal protection order must contact the court having jurisdiction over the parenting time or custody matter as provided in MCR 3.205, and where practicable, the judge should consult with that court, as contemplated in MCR 3.205(C)(2), regarding the impact upon custody and parenting time rights before issuing the personal protection order.

(2) *Conditions Modifying Custody and Parenting Time Provisions.* If the respondent's custody or parenting time rights will be adversely affected by the personal protection order, the issuing court shall determine whether conditions should be specified in the order which would accommodate the respondent's rights or whether the situation is such that the safety of the petitioner and minor children would be compromised by such conditions.

(3) *Effect of Personal Protection Order.* A personal protection order takes precedence over any existing custody or parenting time order until the personal protection order has expired, or the court having jurisdiction over the custody or parenting time order modifies the custody or parenting time order to accommodate the conditions of the personal protection order.

(a) If the respondent or petitioner wants the existing custody or parenting time order modified, the respondent or petitioner must file a motion with the court having jurisdiction of the custody or parenting time order and request a hearing. The hearing must be held within 21 days after the motion is filed.

(b) Proceedings to modify custody and parenting time orders are subject to subchapter 3.200.

(D) Service. The petitioner shall serve the order on the respondent as provided in MCR 2.105(A). If the respondent is a minor, and the whereabouts of the respondent's parent or parents, guardian, or custodian is known, the petitioner shall also in the same manner serve the order on the respondent's parent or parents, guardian, or custodian. On an appropriate showing, the court may allow service in another manner as

provided in MCR 2.105(I). Failure to serve the order does not affect its validity or effectiveness.

(E) Oral Notice. If oral notice of the order is made by a law enforcement officer as described in MCL 600.2950(22) or 600.2950a(22), proof of the notification must be filed with the court by the law enforcement officer.

[Adopted August 11, 1997, effective September 1, 1997, 456 Mich. Amended December 22, 1999, effective January 10, 2000, 460 Mich; June 1, 2001, effective September 1, 2001, 464 Mich; September 11, 2002, effective January 1, 2003, 467 Mich. Amended effective March 21, 2018, 501 Mich.]

Comments

Staff Comment to 1997 Adoption

MCR 3.706 is designed to implement the statutes providing for the issuance of personal protection orders. See MCL 600.2950 and MCL 600.2950a.

Staff Comment to 1999 Amendment

This rule clarifies the procedure applicable to the minor personal protection orders ("minor PPOs") created in 1998 PA 474-477, which went into effect March 1, 1999. Because the new statutes did not make clear whether existing PPO procedural rules applied or rules for Juvenile Code proceedings applied, this rule was promulgated to assure consistency in the processing of minor PPOs in Michigan's Circuit Court Family Divisions. Immediate adoption was ordered to provide needed procedural guidance for courts already facing minor PPO cases.

Staff Comment to 2001 Amendment

The amendment of MCR 3.706 is designed, in part, to clarify the court rule provisions adopted effective September 1, 1997. 456 Mich clxxxiv (1997).

Staff Comment to 2002 Amendment

The September 11, 2002, amendments of MCR 3.206, 3.214, 3.705, 3.706, 3.708, 5.982, and 8.119, which were given immediate effect, are related to the group of domestic violence statutes enacted in December 2001 that took effect April 1, 2002.

The changes in MCR 3.206 and 3.214 are related to 2001 PA 195, which adopted the Uniform Child–Custody Jurisdiction and Enforcement Act, MCL 722.1101 *et seq.* There is also some nonsubstantive reorganization of MCR 3.214.

The amendment of MCR 3.705 implements the statutory provisions regarding the statement of reasons for granting or denying personal protection orders. See 2001 PA 196.

The amendment of MCR 3.706 incorporates the statutory provisions regarding enforceability of Michigan personal protection orders in other jurisdictions. See 2001 PA 200 and 201.

MCR 3.708 and 5.982 are amended to include foreign protection orders, which are made enforceable in Michigan by 2001 PA 197.

MCR 8.119(F) is amended to conform to 2001 PA 205, which directs that when a motion to seal court records involves allegations of domestic violence, the court is to consider the safety of the potential victim in ruling on the motion.

Staff Comment to 2018 Amendment

These amendments update cross-references and make other nonsubstantive revisions to clarify the rules. The amendment of MCR 6.110(B)(1) addresses an inadvertent omission from the last amendment of this rule that was intended to be shown in overstrike. Accordingly, the current rule does not match the published version. Striking the clause "for good cause shown" will provide consistency with other published versions of the rule and with the statute, MCL 766.7, which allows a magistrate to adjourn a preliminary examination with the consent of the parties without the need for good cause to be shown.

Rule 3.707. Modification, Termination, or Extension of Order

(A) Modification or Termination.

(1) *Time for Filing and Service.*

(a) The petitioner may file a motion to modify or terminate the personal protection order and request a hearing at any time after the personal protection order is issued.

(b) The respondent may file a motion to modify or terminate an ex parte personal protection order or an ex parte order extending a personal protection order and request a hearing within 14 days after being served with, or receiving actual notice of, the order. Any motion otherwise to modify or terminate a personal protection order by the respondent requires a showing of good cause.

(c) The moving party shall serve the motion to modify or terminate the order and the notice of hearing at least 7 days before the hearing date as provided in MCR 2.105(A)(2) at the mailing address or addresses provided to the court. On an appropriate showing, the court may allow service in another manner as provided in MCR 2.105(I). If the moving party is a respondent who is issued a license to carry a concealed weapon and is required to carry a weapon as a condition of employment, a police officer certified by the Michigan law enforcement training council act of 1965, 1965 PA 203, MCL 28.601 to 28.616, a sheriff, a deputy sheriff or a member of the Michigan department of state police, a local corrections officer, department of corrections employee, or a federal law enforcement officer who carries a firearm during the normal course of employment, providing notice one day before the hearing is deemed as sufficient notice to the petitioner.

(2) *Hearing on the Motion.* The court must schedule and hold a hearing on a motion to modify or terminate a personal protection order within 14 days of the filing of the motion, except that if the respondent is a person described in MCL 600.2950(2) or 600.2950a(5), the court shall schedule the hearing on the motion within 5 days after the filing of the motion.

(3) *Notice of Modification or Termination.* If a personal protection order is modified or terminated, the clerk must immediately notify the law enforcement agency specified in the personal protection order of the change. A modified or terminated order must be served as provided in MCR 2.107.

(B) Extension of Order.

(1) *Time for Filing.* The petitioner may file an ex parte motion to extend the effectiveness of the order, without hearing, by requesting a new expiration date. The motion must be filed with the court that issued the personal protection order no later than 3 days before the order is to expire. The court must act on the motion within 3 days after it is filed. Failure to timely file a motion to extend the effectiveness of the order does not preclude the petitioner from commencing a new personal protection action regarding the same respondent, as provided in MCR 3.703.

(2) *Notice of Extension.* If the expiration date on a personal protection order is extended, an amended order must be entered. The clerk must immediately notify the law enforcement agency specified in the personal protection order of the change. The order must be served on the respondent as provided in MCR 2.107.

(C) Minors and Legally Incapacitated Individuals. Petitioners or respondents who are minors or legally incapacitated individuals must proceed through a next friend, as provided in MCR 3.703(F).

(D) Fees. There are no motion fees for modifying, terminating, or extending a personal protection order.

[Adopted August 11, 1997, effective September 1, 1997, 456 Mich. Amended December 22, 1999, effective January 10, 2000, 461 Mich; June 1, 2001, effective September 1, 2001, 464 Mich; October 6, 2011, effective January 1, 2012, 490 Mich. Amended effective March 21, 2018, 501 Mich.]

Comments

Staff Comment to 1997 Adoption

MCR 3.707 is designed to implement the statutes providing for the issuance of personal protection orders. See MCL 600.2950 and MCL 600.2950a.

Staff Comment to 1999 Amendment

This rule clarifies the procedure applicable to the minor personal protection orders ("minor PPOs") created in 1998 PA 474-477, which went into effect March 1, 1999. Because the new statutes did not make clear whether existing PPO procedural rules applied or rules for Juvenile Code proceedings applied, this rule was promulgated to assure consistency in the processing of minor PPOs in Michigan's Circuit Court Family Divisions. Immediate adoption was ordered to provide needed procedural guidance for courts already facing minor PPO cases.

Staff Comment to 2001 Amendment

The amendment of MCR 3.707 is designed, in part, to clarify the court rule provisions adopted effective September 1, 1997. 456 Mich clxxxiv (1997).

Staff Comment to 2011 Amendment

The amendment of MCR 3.707 clarifies that the right to bring a motion to modify or terminate a personal protection order within 14 days after the order enters applies to ex parte PPOs only, not those orders that enter following a full hearing. In addition, for a respondent to file a motion to modify or terminate a PPO more than 14 days after its issuance, this amendment requires the respondent to show good cause.

Staff Comment to 2018 Amendment

These amendments update cross-references and make other nonsubstantive revisions to clarify the rules. The amendment of MCR 6.110(B)(1) addresses an inadvertent omission from the last amendment of this rule that was intended to be shown in overstrike. Accordingly, the current rule does not match the published version. Striking the clause "for good cause shown" will provide consistency with other published versions of the rule and with the statute, MCL 766.7, which allows a magistrate to adjourn a preliminary examination with the consent of the parties without the need for good cause to be shown.

Rule 3.708. Contempt Proceedings for Violation of Personal Protection Orders

(A) In General.

(1) A personal protection order is enforceable under MCL 600.2950(23), (25), 600.2950a(23), (25), 764.15b, and 600.1701 et seq. For the purpose of this rule, "personal protection order" includes a foreign protection order enforceable in Michigan under MCL 600.2950*l*.

(2) Proceedings to enforce a minor personal protection order where the respondent is under 18 are governed by subchapter 3.900. Proceedings to enforce a personal protection order issued against an adult, or to enforce a minor personal protection order still in effect when the respondent is 18 or older, are governed by this rule.

(B) Motion to Show Cause.

(1) *Filing.* If the respondent violates the personal protection order, the petitioner may file a motion, supported by appropriate affidavit, to have the respondent found in contempt. There is no fee for such a motion. If the petitioner's motion and affidavit establish a basis for a finding of contempt, the court shall either:

(a) order the respondent to appear at a specified time to answer the contempt charge; or

(b) issue a bench warrant for the arrest of the respondent.

(2) *Service.* The petitioner shall serve the motion to show cause and the order on the respondent by personal service at least 7 days before the show cause hearing.

(C) Arrest.

(1) If the respondent is arrested for violation of a personal protection order as provided in MCL 764.15b(1), the court in

the county where the arrest is made shall proceed as provided in MCL 764.15b(2)-(5), except as provided in this rule.

(2) A contempt proceeding brought in a court other than the one that issued the personal protection order shall be entitled "In the Matter of Contempt of [Respondent]." The clerk shall provide a copy of any documents pertaining to the contempt proceeding to the court that issued the personal protection order.

(3) If it appears that a circuit judge will not be available within 24 hours after arrest, the respondent shall be taken, within that time, before a district court, which shall set bond and order the respondent to appear for arraignment before the family division of the circuit court in that county.

(D) Appearance or Arraignment; Advice to Respondent. At the respondent's first appearance before the circuit court, whether for arraignment under MCL 764.15b, enforcement under MCL 600.2950, 600.2950a, or 600.1701, or otherwise, the court must:

(1) advise the respondent of the alleged violation,

(2) advise the respondent of the right to contest the charge at a contempt hearing,

(3) advise the respondent that he or she is entitled to a lawyer's assistance at the hearing and, if the court determines it might sentence the respondent to jail, that the court will appoint a lawyer at public expense if the individual wants one and is financially unable to retain one,

(4) if requested and appropriate, appoint a lawyer,

(5) set a reasonable bond pending a hearing of the alleged violation,

(6) take a guilty plea as provided in subrule (E) or schedule a hearing as provided in subrule (F).

As long as the respondent is either present in the courtroom or has waived the right to be present, on motion of either party, the court may use telephonic, voice, or videoconferencing technology to take testimony from an expert witness or, upon a showing of good cause, any person at another location.

(E) Pleas of Guilty. The respondent may plead guilty to the violation. Before accepting a guilty plea, the court, speaking directly to the respondent and receiving the respondent's response, must

(1) advise the respondent that by pleading guilty the respondent is giving up the right to a contested hearing and, if the respondent is proceeding without legal representation, the right to a lawyer's assistance as set forth in subrule (D)(3),

(2) advise the respondent of the maximum possible jail sentence for the violation,

(3) ascertain that the plea is understandingly, voluntarily, and knowingly made, and

(4) establish factual support for a finding that the respondent is guilty of the alleged violation.

(F) Scheduling or Postponing Hearing. Following the respondent's appearance or arraignment, the court shall do the following:

(1) Set a date for the hearing at the earliest practicable time except as required under MCL 764.15b.

(a) The hearing of a respondent being held in custody for an alleged violation of a personal protection order must be held within 72 hours after the arrest, unless extended by the court on the motion of the arrested individual or the prosecuting attorney. The court must set a reasonable bond pending the hearing unless the court determines that release will not reasonably ensure the safety of the individuals named in the personal protection order.

(b) If a respondent is released on bond pending the hearing, the bond may include any condition specified in MCR 6.106(D) necessary to reasonably ensure the safety of the individuals named in the personal protection order, including continued compliance with the personal protection order. The release order shall also comply with MCL 765.6b.

(c) If the alleged violation is based on a criminal offense that is a basis for a separate criminal prosecution, upon motion of the prosecutor, the court may postpone the hearing for the outcome of that prosecution.

(2) Notify the prosecuting attorney of a criminal contempt proceeding.

(3) Notify the petitioner and his or her attorney, if any, of the contempt proceeding and direct the party to appear at the hearing and give evidence on the charge of contempt.

(G) Prosecution After Arrest. In a criminal contempt proceeding commenced under MCL 764.15b, the prosecuting attorney shall prosecute the proceeding unless the petitioner retains his or her own attorney for the criminal contempt proceeding.

(H) The Violation Hearing.

(1) *Jury.* There is no right to a jury trial.

(2) *Conduct of the Hearing.* The respondent has the right to be present at the hearing, to present evidence, and to examine and cross-examine witnesses. As long as the respondent is either present in the courtroom or has waived the right to be present, on motion of either party, and with the consent of the parties, the court may use telephonic, voice, or videoconferencing technology to take testimony from an expert witness or, upon a showing of good cause, any person at another location.

(3) *Evidence; Burden of Proof.* The rules of evidence apply to both criminal and civil contempt proceedings. The petitioner or the prosecuting attorney has the burden of proving the respondent's guilt of criminal contempt beyond a reasonable doubt and the respondent's guilt of civil contempt by clear and convincing evidence.

(4) *Judicial Findings.* At the conclusion of the hearing, the court must find the facts specially, state separately its conclusions of law, and direct entry of the appropriate judgment. The court must state its findings and conclusions on the record or in a written opinion made a part of the record.

(5) *Sentencing.*

(a) If the respondent pleads or is found guilty of criminal contempt, the court shall impose a sentence of incarceration for no more than 93 days and may impose a fine of not more than $500.00.

(b) If the respondent pleads or is found guilty of civil contempt, the court shall impose a fine or imprisonment as specified in MCL 600.1715 and 600.1721.

In addition to such a sentence, the court may impose other conditions to the personal protection order.

(I) Mechanics of Use. The use of videoconferencing technology under this rule must be in accordance with the standards established by the State Court Administrative Office. All proceedings at which videoconferencing technology is used must be recorded verbatim by the court.

[Adopted August 11, 1997, effective September 1, 1997, 456 Mich. Amended December 22, 1999, effective January 10, 2000, 461 Mich; June 1, 2001, effective September 1, 2001, 464 Mich; September 11, 2002, effective January 1, 2003, 467 Mich; February 4, 2003, effective May 1, 2003, 467 Mich; September 21, 2016, effective January 1, 2017, 500 Mich. Amended effective March 21, 2018, 501 Mich.]

Comments

Staff Comment to 1997 Adoption

MCR 3.708 is designed to implement the statutes providing for the issuance of personal protection orders. See MCL 600.2950 and MCL 600.2950a.

Staff Comment to 1999 Amendment

This rule clarifies the procedure applicable to the minor personal protection orders ("minor PPOs") created in 1998 PA 474-477, which went into effect March 1, 1999. Because the new statutes did not make clear whether existing PPO procedural rules applied or rules for Juvenile Code proceedings applied, this rule was promulgated to assure consistency in the processing of minor PPOs in Michigan's Circuit Court Family Divisions. Immediate adoption was ordered to provide needed procedural guidance for courts already facing minor PPO cases.

Staff Comment to 2001 Amendment

The amendment of MCR 3.708 is designed, in part, to clarify the court rule provisions adopted effective September 1, 1997. 456 Mich clxxxiv (1997).

Staff Comment to 2002 Amendment

The September 11, 2002, amendments of MCR 3.206, 3.214, 3.705, 3.706, 3.708, 5.982, and 8.119, which were given immediate effect, are related to the group of domestic violence statutes enacted in December 2001 that took effect April 1, 2002.

The changes in MCR 3.206 and 3.214 are related to 2001 PA 195, which adopted the Uniform Child–Custody Jurisdiction and Enforcement Act, MCL 722.1101 *et seq.* There is also some nonsubstantive reorganization of MCR 3.214.

The amendment of MCR 3.705 implements the statutory provisions regarding the statement of reasons for granting or denying personal protection orders. See 2001 PA 196.

The amendment of MCR 3.706 incorporates the statutory provisions regarding enforceability of Michigan personal protection orders in other jurisdictions. See 2001 PA 200 and 201.

MCR 3.708 and 5.982 are amended to include foreign protection orders, which are made enforceable in Michigan by 2001 PA 197.

MCR 8.119(F) is amended to conform to 2001 PA 205, which directs that when a motion to seal court records involves allegations of domestic violence, the court is to consider the safety of the potential victim in ruling on the motion.

Staff Comment to 2003 Amendment

The amendment of MCR 3.708(A)(2) changes the cross-reference to the subchapter governing juvenile proceedings.

Staff Comment to 2017 Amendment

These amendments permit courts to expand the use of videoconferencing technology in many court proceedings, and clarify the proceedings at which videoconferencing technology may be used.

Staff Comment to 2018 Amendment

These amendments update cross-references and make other nonsubstantive revisions to clarify the rules. The amendment of MCR 6.110(B)(1) addresses an inadvertent omission from the last amendment of this rule that was intended to be shown in overstrike. Accordingly, the current rule does not match the published version. Striking the clause "for good cause shown" will provide consistency with other published versions of the rule and with the statute, MCL 766.7, which allows a magistrate to adjourn a preliminary examination with the consent of the parties without the need for good cause to be shown.

Rule 3.709   Appeals

(A) Rules Applicable. Except as provided by this rule, appeals involving personal protection order matters must comply with subchapter 7.200. Appeals involving minor personal protection actions under the Juvenile Code must additionally comply with MCR 3.993.

(B) From Entry of Personal Protection Order.

(1) Either party has an appeal of right from

(a) an order granting or denying a personal protection order after a hearing under subrule 3.705(B)(6), or

(b) the ruling on respondent's first motion to rescind or modify the order if an ex parte order was entered.

(2) Appeals of all other orders are by leave to appeal.

(C) From Finding After Violation Hearing.

(1) The respondent has an appeal of right from a sentence for criminal contempt entered after a contested hearing.

(2) All other appeals concerning violation proceedings are by application for leave.

[Statement by Kelly, J., appears in 461 Mich.]

[Adopted August 11, 1997, effective September 1, 1997, 456 Mich. Amended December 22, 1999, effective January 10, 2000, 461 Mich; February 4, 2003, effective May 1, 2003, 467 Mich.]

Comments

Staff Comment to 1997 Adoption

MCR 3.709 is designed to implement the statutes providing for the issuance of personal protection orders. See MCL 600.2950 and MCL 600.2950a.

Staff Comment to 1999 Amendment

This rule clarifies the procedure applicable to the minor personal protection orders ("minor PPOs") created in 1998 PA 474-477, which went into effect March 1, 1999. Because the new statutes did not make clear whether existing PPO procedural rules applied or rules for Juvenile Code proceedings applied, this rule was promulgated to assure consistency in the processing of minor PPOs in Michigan's Circuit Court Family Divisions. Immediate adoption was ordered to provide needed procedural guidance for courts already facing minor PPO cases.

Staff Comment to 2003 Amendment

The amendment of MCR 3.709(A) changes the cross-reference to the subchapter governing juvenile proceedings.

SUBCHAPTER 3.800   ADOPTION

Rule 3.800   Applicable Rules; Interested Parties; Indian Child

(A) Generally. Except as modified by the rules in this chapter, adoption proceedings are governed by Michigan Court Rules.

(B) Interested Parties.

(1) The persons interested in various adoption proceedings, including proceedings involving an Indian child, are as provided by MCL 710.24a except as otherwise provided in subrules (2) and (3).

(2) If the court knows or has reason to know the adoptee is an Indian child, in addition to subrule (B)(1), the persons interested are the Indian child's tribe and the Indian custodian, if any, and, if the Indian child's parent or Indian custodian, or tribe, is unknown, the Secretary of the Interior.

(3) The interested persons in a petition to terminate the rights of the noncustodial parent pursuant to MCL 710.51(6) are:

(a) the petitioner;

(b) the adoptee, if over 14 years of age;

(c) the noncustodial parent; and

(d) if the court knows or has reason to know the adoptee is an Indian child, the Indian child's tribe and the Indian custodian, if any, and, if the Indian child's parent or Indian custodian, or tribe, is unknown, the Secretary of the Interior.

[Formerly Rule 5.750, adopted effective March 1, 1985. Renumbered Rule 3.800, amended December 18, 2001, effective May 1, 2002, 465 Mich. Amended February 4, 2003, effective May 1, 2003, 467 Mich; February 2, 2010, effective May 1, 2010, 485 Mich; October 31, 2012, effective January 1, 2013, 493 Mich. Amended effective March 20, 2013, 493 Mich. Amended June 4, 2014, effective September 1, 2014, 496 Mich. Amended effective August 14, 2019, 503 Mich.]

Comments

Staff Comment to 1985 Adoption

MCR 5.750 is substantially the same as PCR 750.

Staff Comment to 2002 Renumber and Amendment

The amendment and renumbering of MCR 5.750–5.756 and 5.781–5.783 as MCR 3.800–3.806 and 3.613–3.615, effective May 1, 2002, were proposed by the Family Division Joint Rules Committee. The statute creating the family division of circuit court gave it jurisdiction of a number of types of proceedings formerly heard in the probate court. See MCL 600.1021. The amendments move the rules governing adoptions, change of name, Parental Rights Restoration Act proceedings, and proceedings regarding persons who pose health threats to others, from Chapter 5, which contains probate court provisions, to Chapter 3. In addition, there are several modifications of the rules. The change-of-name rule will use the circuit court publication procedure. MCR 3.613(C)(2). A provision on confidentiality of records is added to the change-of-name rule. MCR 3.613(E). New subrule MCR 3.614(C) will specify the interested parties in a petition for treatment of infectious disease. (File No. 99–55.)

Staff Comment to 2003 Amendment

The amendment of MCR 3.800 moves the provision regarding the interested parties in adoption proceedings from MCR 5.125(C)(32) and makes nonsubstantive language changes.

Staff Comment to 2010 Amendment

These amendments incorporate provisions of the Indian Child Welfare Act into specific provisions within various rules relating to child protective proceedings and juvenile status offenses. The language is designed to make the rules reflect a more integrated approach to addressing issues specific to Indian children.

MCR 3.002(1)(c) defines "preadoptive placement" to mean the "temporary placement of an Indian child in a foster home or institution after the termination of parental rights, but before or in lieu of adoptive placement, and ..." The phrase "in lieu of adoptive placement" is not intended to mean that it is permissible to leave a child in foster care indefinitely, in violation of MCL 712A.19b(6) or (7) or 45 CFR 1355.20, 45 CFR 1356.21, or 45 CFR 1356.50. Rather, it addresses situations where the parental rights to a child have been terminated and there is no permanency plan for adoption of the child. One example is when the child has been placed with a juvenile guardian and the guardianship is subsequently revoked. In this situation, jurisdiction over the child pursuant to MCL 712A.2(b) will be reinstated and the child is placed in foster care.

MCR 3.002(1): The definition of "child custody proceeding" is intended to apply the Indian Child Welfare Act to delinquency proceedings if an "Indian child" is charged with a so-called status offense in violation of MCL 712A.2(a)(2)–(4) or (d). Delinquency proceedings involving an Indian child charged with any other non-status offense are generally not subject to the Indian Child Welfare Act; however, if the initial investigation or subsequent review of a non-status delinquency case reveals that the Indian child involved suffers from child abuse or neglect, a separate child protective proceeding may be initiated, which would be subject to the Indian Child Welfare Act.

The amendment of MCR 3.905(C)(1) states that a court shall consider guidelines established by the Bureau of Indian Affairs (BIA) in determining whether good cause not to transfer exists (Guidelines for State Courts; Indian Child Custody Proceedings, 44 Fed Reg No 228, 67590–67592, C.2–C.4. [November 26, 1979]). Some examples of good cause are that the Indian tribe does not have a tribal court or that the Indian child is over 12 years old and objects to the

transfer. For additional examples of good cause and relevant case law, see the BIA guidelines cited above and A Practical Guide to the Indian Child Welfare Act. (Native American Rights Fund, A Practical Guide to the Indian Child Welfare Act [Boulder, CO: Native American Rights Fund, 2007], 7.15 and 7.16, p 60.)

Staff Comment to January, 2013 Amendment

The amendments of these rules update the rules making them less "paper" focused and reflecting the use of electronic technology in the way courts process court records. The amendments also clarify and delineate the types of records and other materials maintained by a court, and clarify how access is provided.

Staff Comment to March, 2013 Amendment

This proposal incorporates provisions of the newly enacted Michigan Indian Family Preservation Act into specific provisions within various rules relating to child protective proceedings and juvenile status offenses.

Staff Comment to 2014 Amendment

These amendments incorporate provisions of the Michigan Indian Family Preservation Act and the Indian Child Welfare Act and reflect a more integrated approach to addressing issues specific to Indian children.

Staff Comment to 2019 Amendment

These amendments update cross-references and make other nonsubstantive revisions to clarify the rules.

Rule 3.801. Documents, Execution

(A) A waiver, affirmation, or disclaimer to be executed by the father of a child born out of wedlock may be executed any time after the conception of the child. If a putative father acknowledges paternity, he must receive notice of the hearing if the child is an Indian child.

(B) A release or consent is valid if executed in accordance with the law at the time of execution.

[Formerly Rule 5.751, adopted effective March 1, 1985. Amended June 17, 1997, effective September 1, 1997, 454 Mich. Renumbered Rule 3.801, and amended, December 18, 2001, effective May 1, 2002, 465 Mich. Amended June 4, 2014, effective September 1, 2014, 496 Mich; March 20, 2019, effective May 1, 2019, 502 Mich.]

Comments

Staff Comment to 1985 Adoption

MCR 5.751 is substantially the same as PCR 751.

Staff Comment to 1997 Amendment

Former subrule (A) is deleted as redundant in light of subchapter 5.100. Former subrule (B) is deleted because it is unnecessary. Subrule (C)(1) is deleted as covered in MCL 710.34. Subrule (C)(2) is deleted because it is not required by law. Former subrule (D)(1) is deleted because it dilutes the requirements of statute. The remaining portions of subrule (D) are redesignated as (A) and (B). Former subrule (E) is deleted.

Staff Comment to 2002 Renumber and Amendment

The amendment and renumbering of MCR 5.750–5.756 and 5.781–5.783 as MCR 3.800–3.806 and 3.613–3.615, effective May 1, 2002, were proposed by the Family Division Joint Rules Committee. The statute creating the family division of circuit court gave it jurisdiction of a number of types of proceedings formerly heard in the probate court. See MCL 600.1021. The amendments move the rules governing adoptions, change of name, Parental Rights Restoration Act proceedings, and proceedings regarding persons who pose health threats to others, from Chapter 5, which contains probate court provisions, to Chapter 3. In addition, there are several modifications of the rules. The change-of-name rule will use the circuit court publication procedure. MCR 3.613(C)(2). A provision on confidentiality of records is added to the change-of-name rule. MCR 3.613(E). New subrule MCR 3.614(C) will specify the interested parties in a petition for treatment of infectious disease. (File No. 99–55.)

Staff Comment to 2014 Amendment

These amendments incorporate provisions of the Michigan Indian Family Preservation Act and the Indian Child Welfare Act and reflect a more integrated approach to addressing issues specific to Indian children.

Staff Comment to 2019 Amendment

The amendments of Rules 1.109, 2.102, 2.104, 2.106, 2.107, 2.117, 2.119, 2.403, 2.503, 2.506, 2.508, 2.518, 2.602, 2.603, 2.621, 3.101, 3.104, 3.203, 3.205, 3.210, 3.302, 3.607, 3.613, 3.614, 3.705, 3.801, 3.802, 3.805, 3.806, 4.201, 4.202, 4.303, 4.306, 5.001,

5.104, 5.105, 5.107, 5.108, 5.113, 5.117, 5.118, 5.119, 5.120, 5.125, 5.126, 5.132, 5.162, 5.202, 5.203, 5.205, 5.302, 5.304, 5.307, 5.308, 5.309, 5.310, 5.311, 5.313, 5.402, 5.404, 5.405, 5.409, 5.501, and 5.784 and addition of Rule 3.618 of the Michigan Court Rules are an expected progression necessary for design and implementation of the statewide electronic-filing system. These particular amendments will assist in implementing the goals of the project.

Rule 3.802 Manner and Method of Service

(A) Service of Documents.

(1) A notice of intent to release or consent pursuant to MCL 710.34(1) may only be served by personal service by a peace officer or a person authorized by the court.

(2) Notice of a petition to identify a putative father and to determine or terminate his rights, or a petition to terminate the rights of a parent under MCL 710.51(6), must be served on the individual or the individual's attorney in the manner provided in:

(a) MCR 2.107(C)(1) or (2), or

(b) MCR 2.105(A)(2), but service is not made for purpose of this subrule until the individual or the individual's attorney receives the notice or petition.

(3) *Notice of Proceeding Concerning Indian Child.* If the court knows or has reason to know an Indian child is the subject of an adoption proceeding and an Indian tribe does not have exclusive jurisdiction as defined in MCR 3.002(6),

(a) in addition to any other service requirements, the petitioner shall notify the parent or Indian custodian and the Indian child's tribe, by personal service or by registered mail with return receipt requested and delivery restricted to the addressee, of the pending proceedings on a petition for adoption of the Indian child and of their right of intervention on a form approved by the State Court Administrative Office. If the identity or location of the parent or Indian custodian, or of the Indian child's tribe, cannot be determined, notice shall be given to the Secretary of the Interior by registered mail with return receipt requested.

(b) the court shall notify the parent or Indian custodian and the Indian child's tribe of all other hearings pertaining to the adoption proceeding as provided in this rule. If the identity or location of the parent or Indian custodian, or of the tribe, cannot be determined, notice of the hearings shall be given to the Secretary of the Interior. Such notice may be made by first-class mail.

(4) Except as provided in subrules (B) and (C), all other documents may be served by mail under MCR 2.107(C)(3), e-mail under MCR 2.107(C)(4), or electronic service under MCR 1.109(G)(6)(a).

(B) Service When Identity or Whereabouts of Father are Unascertainable

(1) If service cannot be made under subrule (A)(2) because the identity of the father of a child born out of wedlock or the whereabouts of the identified father has not been ascertained after diligent inquiry, the petitioner must file proof of the efforts made to identify or locate the father in a statement verified under MCR 1.109(D)(3). No further service is necessary before the hearing to identify the father and to determine or terminate his rights.

(2) At the hearing, the court shall take evidence concerning the attempt to identify or locate the father. If the court finds that a reasonable attempt was made, the court shall proceed under MCL 710.37(2). If the court finds that a reasonable attempt was not made, the court shall adjourn the hearing under MCL 710.36(7) and shall

(a) order a further attempt to identify or locate the father so that service can be made under subrule (A)(2)(a), or

(b) direct any manner of substituted service of the notice of hearing except service by publication.

(C) Service When Whereabouts of Parent are Unascertainable. If service of a petition to terminate the parental rights of a parent pursuant to MCL 710.51(6) cannot be made under subrule (A)(2) because the whereabouts of that parent have not been ascertained after diligent inquiry, the petitioner must file proof of the efforts made to locate that parent in a statement made under MCR 1.109(D)(3). If the court finds, on reviewing the statement, that service cannot be made because the whereabouts of the person have not been determined after reasonable efforts, the court may direct any manner of substituted service of the notice of hearing, including service by publication.

(D) Service by Publication.

(1) *Requirements.* A notice of hearing or other notice required to be made by publication must be published in a newspaper as defined by MCR 2.106(F) at least one time 21 days before the date of the hearing. Publication shall be in the county in which the court is located.

(2) *Contents of Notice.* The published notice must include the name of the individual to whom the notice is given, a statement describing the nature of the hearing, and a statement that the result of the hearing may affect the individual's interest in the matter, including possible termination of parental rights.

(3) *Service of Notice.* A copy of the notice shall be mailed to the individual to whom the notice is given at his or her last known address. If the last known address of the individual cannot be ascertained after diligent inquiry, mailing a copy of the notice is not required.

(4) Proof of service under this subrule shall be made according to MCR 2.106(G).

[Formerly Rule 5.752, adopted effective March 1, 1985. Amended June 17, 1997, effective September 1, 1997, 454 Mich. Renumbered Rule 3.802, and amended, December 18, 2001, effective May 1, 2002, 465 Mich. Amended February 23, 2006, effective May 1, 2006, 474 Mich; February 2, 2010, effective May 1, 2010, 485 Mich. Amended effective September 28, 2011, 490 Mich. Amended effective, pending public comment, March 20, 2013, 493 Mich. Amended June 4, 2014, effective September 1, 2014, 496 Mich; August 30, 2018, effective September 1, 2018, 502 Mich; March 20, 2019, effective May 1, 2019, 502 Mich; November 20, 2019, effective January 1, 2020, 503 Mich.]

Comments

Staff Comment to 1985 Adoption

MCR 5.752 corresponds to PCR 752.

Subrule (A)(1) limits the requirement of personal service to notices under MCL 710.34(1), as to which the statute requires personal service.

New subrule (C) creates a procedure for notice of a petition to terminate the parental rights of a noncustodial parent when that person's identity or whereabouts is unknown. If the court concludes that reasonable efforts have been made to locate the parent, it may direct an appropriate method of substituted service.

Staff Comment to 1997 Amendment

Subrule (A) is amended to add the requirement that the putative father and noncustodial parent must be served with certain papers by personal service or by certified mail, return receipt requested. Subrule (B) applies only to putative fathers described in MCL 710.39(1), while subrule (C) applies only to a noncustodial parent described in MCL 710.51. Subrule (C) is amended to more precisely delineate the criteria for the court's ruling.

Staff Comment to 2002 Renumber and Amendment

The amendment and renumbering of MCR 5.750–5.756 and 5.781–5.783 as MCR 3.800–3.806 and 3.613–3.615, effective May 1, 2002, were proposed by the Family Division Joint Rules Committee. The statute creating the family division of circuit court gave it jurisdiction of a number of types of proceedings formerly heard in the probate court. See MCL 600.1021. The amendments move the rules governing adoptions, change of name, Parental Rights Restoration Act proceedings, and proceedings regarding persons who pose health threats to others, from Chapter 5, which contains probate court provisions, to Chapter 3. In addition, there are several modifications of the rules. The change-of-name rule will use the circuit court publication procedure. MCR 3.613(C)(2). A provision on confidentiality of records is added to the change-of-name rule. MCR 3.613(E). New subrule MCR 3.614(C) will specify the interested parties in a petition for treatment of infectious disease. (File No. 99–55.)

Staff Comment to 2006 Amendment

The amendment of MCR 2.612(A)(2), 3.802(B)(1), 5.313(F), and 9.113(B)(2), effective May 1, 2006, reflect numbering changes in other rules.

Staff Comment to 2010 Amendment

These amendments incorporate provisions of the Indian Child Welfare Act into specific provisions within various rules relating to child protective proceedings and juvenile status offenses. The language is designed to make the rules reflect a more integrated approach to addressing issues specific to Indian children.

MCR 3.002(1)(c) defines "preadoptive placement" to mean the "temporary placement of an Indian child in a foster home or institution after the termination of parental rights, but before or in lieu of adoptive placement, and ..." The phrase "in lieu of adoptive placement" is not intended to mean that it is permissible to leave a child in foster care indefinitely, in violation of MCL 712A.19b(6) or (7) or 45 CFR 1355.20, 45 CFR 1356.21, or 45 CFR 1356.50. Rather, it addresses situations where the parental rights to a child have been terminated and there is no permanency plan for adoption of the child. One example is when the child has been placed with a juvenile guardian and the guardianship is subsequently revoked. In this situation, jurisdiction over the child pursuant to MCL 712A.2(b) will be reinstated and the child is placed in foster care.

MCR 3.002(1): The definition of "child custody proceeding" is intended to apply the Indian Child Welfare Act to delinquency proceedings if an "Indian child" is charged with a so-called status offense in violation of MCL 712A.2(a)(2)–(4) or (d). Delinquency proceedings involving an Indian child charged with any other non-status offense are generally not subject to the Indian Child Welfare Act; however, if the initial investigation or subsequent review of a non-status delinquency case reveals that the Indian child involved suffers from child abuse or neglect, a separate child protective proceeding may be initiated, which would be subject to the Indian Child Welfare Act.

The amendment of MCR 3.905(C)(1) states that a court shall consider guidelines established by the Bureau of Indian Affairs (BIA) in determining whether good cause not to transfer exists (Guidelines for State Courts; Indian Child Custody Proceedings, 44 Fed Reg No 228, 67590–67592, C.2–C.4. [November 26, 1979]). Some examples of good cause are that the Indian tribe does not have a tribal court or that the Indian child is over 12 years old and objects to the transfer. For additional examples of good cause and relevant case law, see the BIA guidelines cited above and A Practical Guide to the Indian Child Welfare Act. (Native American Rights Fund, A Practical Guide to the Indian Child Welfare Act [Boulder, CO: Native American Rights Fund, 2007], 7.15 and 7.16, p 60.)

Staff Comment to 2011 Amendment

The above noted changes are minor revisions of the rules that have been recommended to the Court to correct cross references and to reflect other technical changes.

Staff Comment to 2013 Amendment

This proposal incorporates provisions of the newly enacted Michigan Indian Family Preservation Act into specific provisions within various rules relating to child protective proceedings and juvenile status offenses.

Staff Comment to 2014 Amendment

These amendments incorporate provisions of the Michigan Indian Family Preservation Act and the Indian Child Welfare Act and reflect a more integrated approach to addressing issues specific to Indian children.

Staff Comment to 2018 Amendment

These amendments update cross-references in the rules, and are intended to reflect changes that are necessary as a result of the Court's recent e-Filing rules amendments.

Staff Comment to 2019 Amendment

The amendments of Rules 1.109, 2.102, 2.104, 2.106, 2.107, 2.117, 2.119, 2.403, 2.503, 2.506, 2.508, 2.518, 2.602, 2.603, 2.621, 3.101, 3.104, 3.203, 3.205, 3.210, 3.302, 3.607, 3.613, 3.614, 3.705, 3.801, 3.802, 3.805, 3.806, 4.201, 4.202, 4.303, 4.306, 5.001, 5.104, 5.105, 5.107, 5.108, 5.113, 5.117, 5.118, 5.119, 5.120, 5.125, 5.126, 5.132, 5.162, 5.202, 5.203, 5.205, 5.302, 5.304, 5.307, 5.308, 5.309, 5.310, 5.311, 5.313, 5.402, 5.404, 5.405, 5.409, 5.501, and 5.784 and addition of Rule 3.618 of the Michigan Court Rules are an expected progression necessary for design and implementation of the statewide electronic-filing system. These particular amendments will assist in implementing the goals of the project.

Staff Comment to 2020 Amendment

The amendment of MCR 3.802 eliminates references to the "noncustodial parent" to make the rule consistent with the statute (MCL 710.51) allowing stepparent adoption when the petitioning stepparent's spouse has joint legal custody, rather than requiring sole legal custody.

Rule 3.803   Financial Reports, Subsequent Orders

(A) Updated Accounting and Statements.

(1) The update of the accounting filed pursuant to MCL 710.54(8) may include by reference the total expenses itemized in the accounting required by MCL 710.54(7).

(2) Any verified statement filed pursuant to MCL 710.54(7) need not be filed again unless, at the time of the update required by MCL 710.54(8), any such statement does not reflect the facts at that time.

(B) Subsequent Orders.

(1) Only one order approving fees disclosed in the financial reports by MCL 710.54(7) need be entered, and it must be entered after the filing required by MCL 710.54(8).

(2) The order placing the child may be entered before the elapse of the 7–day period required by MCL 710.54(7).

(3) The final order of adoption may be entered before the elapse of the 21–day period required by MCL 710.54(8).
[Formerly Rule 5.783, adopted June 17, 1997, effective September 1, 1997, 454 Mich. Renumbered Rule 3.803, and amended, December 18, 2001, effective May 1, 2002, 465 Mich.]

Comments

Staff Comment to 1997 Adoption

This rule is new. Subrules (A) and (B) eliminate the potential for redundancies in the updating requirements of MCL 710.54(7) and (8). Subrules (B)(2) and (3) allow a court to reduce the time for review of the statutorily required documents.

Staff Comment to 2002 Renumber and Amendment

The amendment and renumbering of MCR 5.750–5.756 and 5.781–5.783 as MCR 3.800–3.806 and 3.613–3.615, effective May 1, 2002, were proposed by the Family Division Joint Rules Committee. The statute creating the family division of circuit court gave it jurisdiction of a number of types of proceedings formerly heard in the probate court. See MCL 600.1021. The amendments move the rules governing adoptions, change of name, Parental Rights Restoration Act proceedings, and proceedings regarding persons who pose health threats to others, from Chapter 5, which contains probate court provisions, to Chapter 3. In addition, there are several modifications of the rules. The change-of-name rule will use the circuit court publication procedure. MCR 3.613(C)(2). A provision on confidentiality of records is added to the change-of-name rule. MCR 3.613(E). New subrule MCR 3.614(C) will specify the interested parties in a petition for treatment of infectious disease. (File No. 99–55.)

Rule 3.804   Consent and Release

(A) Contents and Execution of Consent or Release; Indian Child. In addition to the requirements of MCL 710.29 or MCL 710.44, if a parent of an Indian child intends to voluntarily consent to adoptive placement or the termination of his or her parental rights for the express purpose of adoption pursuant to MCL 712B.13, the following requirements must be met:

(1) except in stepparent adoptions under MCL 710.23a(4), both parents must consent.

(2) to be valid, consent must be executed on a form approved by the State Court Administrative Office, in writing, recorded before a judge of a court of competent jurisdiction, and accompanied by the presiding judge's certificate that the terms and consequences of the consent were fully explained in detail and were fully understood by the parent. The court shall also certify that either the parent fully understood the explanation in English or that it was interpreted into a language that the parent understood. Any consent given before, or within 10 days after, the birth of the Indian child is not valid.

(3) the consent must contain the information prescribed by MCL 712B.13(2).

(4) in a direct placement, as defined in MCL 710.22(*o*), a consent by a parent shall be accompanied by a verified statement that complies with MCL 712B.13(6).

(B) Hearing on Consent to Adopt.

(1) The consent hearing required by MCL 710.44(1) must be promptly scheduled by the court after the court examines and approves the report of the investigation or foster family study filed pursuant to MCL 710.46. If an interested party has requested a consent hearing, the hearing shall be held within 7 days of the filing of the report or foster family study.

(2) A consent hearing involving an Indian child pursuant to MCL 712B.13 must be held in conjunction with either a consent to adopt, as required by MCL 710.44, or a release, as required by MCL 710.29. Notice of the hearing must be sent to the parties prescribed in MCR 3.800(B) in compliance with MCR 3.802(A)(3).

(3) *Use of Videoconferencing Technology.* Except for a consent hearing involving an Indian child pursuant to MCL 712B.13, the court may allow the use of videoconferencing technology under this subchapter in accordance with MCR 2.407.

(C) Notice of Child Support Obligation.

(1) Before executing a release, as part of the explanation of the parent's legal rights, the parent shall be informed that the obligation to support the child will continue until a court of competent jurisdiction modifies or terminates the obligation, an order of adoption is entered, or the child is emancipated by operation of law.

(2) Before executing the consent, as part of the explanation of the parent's legal rights, the parent shall be informed that the obligation to support the child will continue until a court of competent jurisdiction modifies or terminates the obligation, an order of adoption is entered, or the child is emancipated by operation of law.

(3) Failure to provide required notice under this subsection does not affect the obligation imposed by law or otherwise establish a remedy or cause of action on behalf of the parent.

(D) Withdrawal of Consent to Adopt Indian Child. A parent who executes a consent under MCL 712B.13 may withdraw that consent at any time before entry of a final order of adoption by filing a written demand requesting the return of the child. Once a demand is filed with the court, the court shall order the return of the child. Withdrawal of consent under MCL 712B.13 constitutes a withdrawal of a release executed under MCL 710.29 or a consent to adopt executed under MCL 710.44.

[Formerly Rule 5.754, adopted June 17, 1997, effective September 1, 1997, 454 Mich. Renumbered Rule 3.804, and amended, December 18, 2001, effective May 1, 2002, 465 Mich. Amended June 4, 2014, effective September 1, 2014, 496 Mich; November 2, 2016, effective January 1, 2017, 500 Mich; March 28, 2018, effective May 1, 2018, 501 Mich.]

Comments

Staff Comment to 1997 Adoption

This rule is new.

Staff Comment to 2002 Renumber and Amendment

The amendment and renumbering of MCR 5.750–5.756 and 5.781–5.783 as MCR 3.800–3.806 and 3.613–3.615, effective May 1, 2002, were proposed by the Family Division Joint Rules Committee. The statute creating the family division of circuit court gave it jurisdiction of a number of types of proceedings formerly heard in the probate court. See MCL 600.1021. The amendments move the rules governing adoptions, change of name, Parental Rights Restoration Act proceedings, and proceedings regarding persons who pose health threats to others, from Chapter 5, which contains probate court provisions, to Chapter 3. In addition, there are several modifications of the rules. The change-of-name rule will use the circuit court publication procedure. MCR 3.613(C)(2). A provision on confidentiality of records is added to the change-of-name rule. MCR 3.613(E). New subrule MCR 3.614(C) will specify the interested parties in a petition for treatment of infectious disease. (File No. 99–55.)

Staff Comment to 2014 Amendment

These amendments incorporate provisions of the Michigan Indian Family Preservation Act and the Indian Child Welfare Act and reflect a more integrated approach to addressing issues specific to Indian children.

Staff Comment to 2017 Amendment

This amendment permits courts to use videoconferencing technology in adoption consent/release hearings.

Staff Comment to 2018 Amendment

The amendments incorporate into both the rules concerning juvenile proceedings and adoption proceedings the requirement to notify parents that the termination of parental rights does not automatically terminate the obligation to provide support for a child. The amendments also make clear that failure to provide the notice would not affect the parent's obligation to continue to pay child support.

Rule 3.805 Temporary Placements, Time for Service of Notice of Hearing to Determine Disposition of Child

(A) Time for Service. Service of notice of hearing on a petition for disposition of a child under MCL 710.23e(1) must be served at least:

(1) 3 days before the date set for hearing for personal service under MCR 2.107(C)(1) or (2), e-mail service under MCR 2.107(C)(4), or electronic service under MCR 1.109(G)(6)(a); or

(2) 7 days before the date set for hearing when served by first-class mail under MCR 2.107(C)(3).

(B) Interested Party, Whereabouts Unknown. If the whereabouts of an interested party, other than the putative father who did not join in the temporary placement, is unknown, service on that interested party will be sufficient if service is attempted at the last known address of the interested party.

(C) Putative Father, Identity or Whereabouts Unknown. If the identity of the putative father is unknown or the whereabouts of a putative father who did not join in the temporary placement is unknown, he need not be served notice of the hearing.

[Formerly Rule 5.755, adopted June 17, 1997, effective September 1, 1997, 454 Mich. Renumbered Rule 3.805, and amended, December 18, 2001, effective May 1, 2002, 465 Mich. Amended March 20, 2019, effective May 1, 2019, 502 Mich.]

Comments

Staff Comment to 1997 Adoption

This rule is new. It deals with service of notice of the hearing mandated by MCL 710.23e(1).

Staff Comment to 2002 Renumbering and Amendment

The amendment and renumbering of MCR 5.750–5.756 and 5.781–5.783 as MCR 3.800–3.806 and 3.613–3.615, effective May 1, 2002, were proposed by the Family Division Joint Rules Committee. The statute creating the family division of circuit court gave it jurisdiction of a number of types of proceedings formerly heard in the probate court. See MCL 600.1021. The amendments move the rules governing adoptions, change of name, Parental Rights Restoration Act proceedings, and proceedings regarding persons who pose health threats to others, from Chapter 5, which contains probate court provisions, to Chapter 3. In addition, there are several modifications of the rules. The change-of-name rule will use the circuit court publication procedure. MCR 3.613(C)(2). A provision on confidentiality of records is added to the change-of-name rule. MCR 3.613(E). New subrule MCR 3.614(C) will specify the interested parties in a petition for treatment of infectious disease. (File No. 99–55.)

Staff Comment to 2019 Amendment

The amendments of Rules 1.109, 2.102, 2.104, 2.106, 2.107, 2.117, 2.119, 2.403, 2.503, 2.506, 2.508, 2.518, 2.602, 2.603, 2.621, 3.101, 3.104, 3.203, 3.205, 3.210, 3.302, 3.607, 3.613, 3.614, 3.705, 3.801, 3.802, 3.805, 3.806, 4.201, 4.202, 4.303, 4.306, 5.001, 5.104, 5.105, 5.107, 5.108, 5.113, 5.117, 5.118, 5.119, 5.120, 5.125, 5.126, 5.132, 5.162, 5.202, 5.203, 5.205, 5.302, 5.304, 5.307, 5.308, 5.309, 5.310, 5.311, 5.313, 5.402, 5.404, 5.405, 5.409, 5.501, and 5.784 and addition of Rule 3.618 of the Michigan Court Rules are an expected progression necessary for design and implementation of the statewide electronic-filing system. These particular amendments will assist in implementing the goals of the project.

Rule 3.806   Rehearings

(A) Filing, Notice and Response. A party may seek rehearing under MCL 710.64(1) by timely filing a petition stating the basis for rehearing. Immediately upon filing the petition, the petitioner must give all interested parties notice of its filing in accordance with MCR 3.802. Any interested party may file a response within 7 days of the date of service of notice on the interested party.

(B) Procedure for Determining Whether to Grant a Rehearing. The court must base a decision on whether to grant a rehearing on the record, the pleading filed, or a hearing on the petition. The court may grant a rehearing only for good cause. The reasons for its decision must be in writing or stated on the record.

(C) Procedure if Rehearing Granted. If the court grants a rehearing, the court may, after notice, take new evidence on the record. It may affirm, modify, or vacate its prior decision in whole or in part. The court must state the reasons for its action in writing or on the record.

(D) Stay. Pending a ruling on the petition for rehearing, the court may stay any order, or enter another order in the best interest of the minor.

[Formerly Rule 5.755, adopted effective March 1, 1985. Renumbered Rule 5.756, June 17, 1997, effective September 1, 1997, 454 Mich. Renumbered Rule 3.806, and amended, December 18, 2001, effective May 1, 2002, 465 Mich. Amended March 20, 2019, effective May 1, 2019, 502 Mich.]

Comments

Staff Comment to 1997 Renumbering

This rule has been redesignated from 5.755. It has been rewritten to provide more specific guidance.

Staff Comment to 2002 Renumbering and Amendment

The amendment and renumbering of MCR 5.750–5.756 and 5.781–5.783 as MCR 3.800–3.806 and 3.613–3.615, effective May 1, 2002, were proposed by the Family Division Joint Rules Committee. The statute creating the family division of circuit court gave it jurisdiction of a number of types of proceedings formerly heard in the probate court. See MCL 600.1021. The amendments move the rules governing adoptions, change of name, Parental Rights Restoration Act proceedings, and proceedings regarding persons who pose health threats to others, from Chapter 5, which contains probate court provisions, to Chapter 3. In addition, there are several modifications of the rules. The change-of-name rule will use the circuit court publication procedure. MCR 3.613(C)(2). A provision on confidentiality of records is added to the change-of-name rule. MCR 3.613(E). New subrule MCR 3.614(C) will specify the interested parties in a petition for treatment of infectious disease. (File No. 99–55.)

Staff Comment to 2019 Amendment

The amendments of Rules 1.109, 2.102, 2.104, 2.106, 2.107, 2.117, 2.119, 2.403, 2.503, 2.506, 2.508, 2.518, 2.602, 2.603, 2.621, 3.101, 3.104, 3.203, 3.205, 3.210, 3.302, 3.607, 3.613, 3.614, 3.705, 3.801, 3.802, 3.805, 3.806, 4.201, 4.202, 4.303, 4.306, 5.001, 5.104, 5.105, 5.107, 5.108, 5.113, 5.117, 5.118, 5.119, 5.120, 5.125, 5.126, 5.132, 5.162, 5.202, 5.203, 5.205, 5.302, 5.304, 5.307, 5.308, 5.309, 5.310, 5.311, 5.313, 5.402, 5.404, 5.405, 5.409, 5.501, and 5.784 and addition of Rule 3.618 of the Michigan Court Rules are an expected progression necessary for design and implementation of the statewide electronic-filing system. These particular amendments will assist in implementing the goals of the project.

Rule 3.807   Indian Child

(A) Definitions. If an Indian child, as defined by the Michigan Indian Family Preservation Act, MCL 712B.3, is the subject of an adoption proceeding, the definitions in MCR 3.002 shall control.

(B) Jurisdiction, Notice, Transfer, Intervention.

(1) If an Indian child is the subject of an adoption proceeding and an Indian tribe has exclusive jurisdiction as defined in MCR 3.002(6), the matter shall be dismissed.

(2) If an Indian child is the subject of an adoption proceeding and an Indian tribe does not have exclusive jurisdiction as defined in MCR 3.002(6), the court shall ensure that the petitioner has given notice of the proceedings to the persons prescribed in MCR 3.800(B) in accordance with MCR 3.802(A)(3).

(a) If either parent or the Indian custodian or the Indian child's tribe petitions the court to transfer the proceeding to the tribal court, the court shall transfer the case to the tribal court unless either parent objects to the transfer of the case to tribal court jurisdiction or the court finds good cause not to transfer. When the court makes a good-cause determination under MCL 712B.7, adequacy of the tribe, tribal court, or tribal social services shall not be considered. A court may determine that good cause not to transfer a case to tribal court exists only if the person opposing the transfer shows by clear and convincing evidence that either of the following applies:

(i) The Indian tribe does not have a tribal court.

(ii) The requirement of the parties or witnesses to present evidence in tribal court would cause undue hardship to those parties or witnesses that the Indian tribe is unable to mitigate.

(b) The court shall not dismiss the matter until the transfer has been accepted by the tribal court.

(c) If the tribal court declines transfer, the Michigan Indian Family Preservation Act applies, as do the provisions of these rules that pertain to an Indian child (see MCL 712B.3 and MCL 712B.5).

(d) A petition to transfer may be made at any time in accordance with MCL 712B.7(3).

(3) The Indian custodian of the child, the Indian child's tribe, and the Indian child have a right to intervene at any point in the proceeding pursuant to MCL 712B.7(6).

(C) Record of Tribal Affiliation. Upon application by an Indian individual who has reached the age of 18 and who was the subject of an adoption placement, the court that entered the final decree shall inform such individual of the tribal affiliation, if any, of the individual's biological parents and provide such other information as may be necessary to protect any rights flowing from the individual's tribal relationship. (25 USC 1917.)

[Adopted February 2, 2010, effective May 1, 2010, 485 Mich. Amended March 22, 2011, effective March 22, 2011, 489 Mich. Amended effective, pending public comment, March 20, 2013, 493 Mich. Amended effective September 5, 2013, 495 Mich. Amended June 4, 2014, effective September 1, 2014, 496 Mich.]

Comments

Staff Comment to 2010 Adoption

These amendments incorporate provisions of the Indian Child Welfare Act into specific provisions within various rules relating to child protective proceedings and juvenile status offenses. The language is designed to make the rules reflect a more integrated approach to addressing issues specific to Indian children.

MCR 3.002(1)(c) defines "preadoptive placement" to mean the "temporary placement of an Indian child in a foster home or institution after the termination of parental rights, but before or in lieu of adoptive placement, and . . ." The phrase "in lieu of adoptive placement" is not intended to mean that it is permissible to leave a child in foster care indefinitely, in violation of MCL 712A.19b(6) or (7) or 45 CFR 1355.20, 45 CFR 1356.21, or 45 CFR 1356.50. Rather, it addresses situations where the parental rights to a child have been terminated and there is no permanency plan for adoption of the child. One example is when the child has been placed with a juvenile guardian and the guardianship is subsequently revoked. In this situation, jurisdiction over the child pursuant to MCL 712A.2(b) will be reinstated and the child is placed in foster care.

MCR 3.002(1): The definition of "child custody proceeding" is intended to apply the Indian Child Welfare Act to delinquency proceedings if an "Indian child" is charged with a so-called status offense in violation of MCL 712A.2(a)(2)–(4) or (d). Delinquency proceedings involving an Indian child charged with any other non-status offense are generally not subject to the Indian Child Welfare Act; however, if the initial investigation or subsequent review of a non-status delinquency case reveals that the Indian child involved suffers from child abuse or neglect, a separate child protective proceeding may be initiated, which would be subject to the Indian Child Welfare Act.

The amendment of MCR 3.905(C)(1) states that a court shall consider guidelines established by the Bureau of Indian Affairs (BIA) in determining whether good cause not to transfer exists (Guidelines for State Courts; Indian Child Custody Proceedings, 44 Fed Reg No 228, 67590–67592, C.2–C.4. [November 26, 1979]). Some examples of good cause are that the Indian tribe does not have a tribal court or that the Indian child is over 12 years old and objects to the transfer. For additional examples of good cause and relevant case law, see the BIA guidelines cited above and A Practical Guide to the Indian Child Welfare Act. (Native American Rights Fund, A Practical Guide to the Indian Child Welfare Act [Boulder, CO: Native American Rights Fund, 2007], 7.15 and 7.16, p 60.)

Staff Comment to 2011 Amendment

The amendments of MCR 3.807, 3.921, and 5.402 have been made to clarify former language and to correct cross references.

Staff Comment to March, 2013 Amendment

This proposal incorporates provisions of the newly enacted Michigan Indian Family Preservation Act into specific provisions within various rules relating to child protective proceedings and juvenile status offenses.

Staff Comment to September, 2013 Amendment

These amendments reflect changes that correct minor technical errors that have occurred in drafting or the changes respond to recent adopted rule revisions, which occasionally inadvertently create incorrect cross-references in other rules.

Staff Comment to 2014 Amendment

These amendments incorporate provisions of the Michigan Indian Family Preservation Act and the Indian Child Welfare Act and reflect a more integrated approach to addressing issues specific to Indian children.

Rule 3.808.   Finalizing Adoption; Findings of Court

Before entering a final order of adoption, the trial court shall determine that the adoptee is not the subject of any pending proceedings on rehearing or reconsideration, or on appeal from a decision to terminate parental rights. The trial court shall make the following findings on the record:

That any appeal of the decision to terminate parental rights has reached disposition; that no appeal, application for leave to appeal, or motion for rehearing or reconsideration is pending; and that the time for all appellate proceedings in this matter has expired.

[Adopted March 28, 2018, effective May 1, 2018, 501 Mich.]

Comments

Staff Comment to 2018 Adoption

The addition of MCR 3.808 is consistent with § 56 of the Michigan Adoption Code, MCL 710.56. This new rule arises out of *In re JK*, 468 Mich 202 (2003), and *In re Jackson*, 498 Mich 943 (2015), which involved cases where a final order of adoption was entered despite pending appellate proceedings involving the adoptee children. Although the Michigan Court of Appeals has adopted a policy to suppress in its register of actions and online case search tool the names of children (and parents) who are the subject of appeals from proceedings involving the termination of parental rights, this information remains open to the public. Therefore, in order to make the determination required of this new rule, a trial court may contact the clerk of the Michigan Court of Appeals, the Michigan Supreme Court, or any other court where proceedings may be pending.

Rule 3.809.   Notice Following Involuntary Termination of Parental Rights

(A) If the parental rights of a parent whose identity and whereabouts are known are involuntarily terminated, the court shall notify the parent, either orally or in a writing, that the obligation to support the child will continue until a court of competent jurisdiction modifies or terminates the obligation, an order of adoption is entered, or the child is emancipated by operation of law.

(B) If the whereabouts of a parent are unknown, the notice required by subsection (A) may be provided in a notice of hearing provided pursuant to MCR 3.802(C).

(C) Failure to provide required notice under this subsection does not affect the obligation imposed by law or otherwise establish a remedy or cause of action on behalf of the parent.

[Adopted March 28, 2018, effective May 1, 2018, 501 Mich.]

Comments

Staff Comment to 2018 Adoption

The amendments incorporate into both the rules concerning juvenile proceedings and adoption proceedings the requirement to notify parents that the termination of parental rights does not automatically terminate the obligation to provide support for a child. The amendments also make clear that failure to provide the notice would not affect the parent's obligation to continue to pay child support.

Rule 3.810.   Transcripts for Purposes of Appeal

In an appeal following the involuntary termination of parental rights, if the court finds that the respondent is financially unable to pay for the preparation of transcripts for appeal, the court must order transcripts prepared at public expense.

[Adopted March 28, 2018, effective May 1, 2018, 501 Mich.]

Comments

Staff Comment to 2018 Adoption

This new rule requires a court to provide a respondent whose rights are involuntarily terminated under the Adoption Code with transcripts for the purposes of appeal if respondent is unable to pay for their preparation, similar to the requirement in MCR 3.977(J)(3) for respondents whose rights are terminated under the Juvenile Code.

SUBCHAPTER 3.900   PROCEEDINGS INVOLVING JUVENILES

Rule 3.901   Applicability of Rules

(A) Scope.

(1) The rules in this subchapter, in subchapter 1.100, and in subchapter 8.100 govern practice and procedure in the family division of the circuit court in all cases filed under the Juvenile Code.

(2) Other Michigan Court Rules apply to juvenile cases in the family division of the circuit court only when this subchapter specifically provides.

(3) The Michigan Rules of Evidence, except with regard to privileges, do not apply to proceedings under this subchapter, except where a rule in this subchapter specifically so provides. MCL 722.631 governs privileges in child protective proceedings.

(B) Application. Unless the context otherwise indicates:

(1) MCR 3.901–3.930, and 3.991–3.993 apply to delinquency proceedings and child protective proceedings;

(2) MCR 3.931–3.950 apply only to delinquency proceedings;

(3) MCR 3.951–3.956 apply only to designated proceedings;

(4) MCR 3.961–3.979 apply only to child protective proceedings;

(5) MCR 3.981–3.989 apply only to minor personal protection order proceedings.

[Adopted February 4, 2003, effective May 1, 2003, 467 Mich. Amended September 30, 2008, effective January 1, 2009, 482 Mich; April 14, 2009, effective July 1, 2009, 483 Mich; February 2, 2010, effective May 1, 2010, 485 Mich; October 31, 2012, effective January 1, 2013, 493 Mich; May 30, 2018, effective September 1, 2018, 501 Mich.]

Comments

Staff Comment to 2003 Adoption

MCR 3.901 corresponds to former Rule 5.901. References to the rules applicable to various types of proceedings are changed to reflect the addition of new rules. New subrule (a)(3) restates the principle found in MRE 1101(b)(7) regarding the applicability of the rules of evidence to juvenile cases, and referring to the statute abrogating privileges in certain juvenile proceedings.

Staff Comment to 2008 Amendment

These amendments allow the court to return or destroy exhibits within 56 days of the completion of the trial or hearing in a juvenile proceeding. In addition, the court must maintain confidential documents that are admitted as exhibits in accordance with MCR 3.903(A)(3).

Staff Comment to 2009 Amendment

The amendments of Rules 3.901, 3.903, 3.921, 3.965, 3.975, 3.976, 3.977, and 3.978, and new rule 3.979 of the Michigan Court Rules reflect the enactment of 2008 PA 199–203.

Staff Comment to 2010 Amendment

These amendments incorporate provisions of the Indian Child Welfare Act into specific provisions within various rules relating to child protective proceedings and juvenile status offenses. The language is designed to make the rules reflect a more integrated approach to addressing issues specific to Indian children. MCR 3.002(1)(c) defines "preadoptive placement" to mean the "temporary placement of an Indian child in a foster home or institution after the termination of parental rights, but before or in lieu of adoptive placement, and . . ." The phrase "in lieu of adoptive placement" is not intended to mean that it is permissible to leave a child in foster care indefinitely, in violation of MCL 712A.19b(6) or (7) or 45 CFR 1355.20, 45 CFR 1356.21, or 45 CFR 1356.50. Rather, it addresses situations where the parental rights to a child have been terminated and there is no permanency plan for adoption of the child. One example is when the child has been placed with a juvenile guardian and the guardianship is subsequently revoked. In this situation, jurisdiction over the child pursuant to MCL 712A.2(b) will be reinstated and the child is placed in foster care.

MCR 3.002(1): The definition of "child custody proceeding" is intended to apply the Indian Child Welfare Act to delinquency proceedings if an "Indian child" is charged with a so-called status offense in violation of MCL 712A.2(a)(2)–(4) or (d). Delinquency proceedings involving an Indian child charged with any other non-status offense are generally not subject to the Indian Child Welfare Act; however, if the initial investigation or subsequent review of a non-status delinquency case reveals that the Indian child involved suffers from child abuse or neglect, a separate child protective proceeding may be initiated, which would be subject to the Indian Child Welfare Act.

The amendment of MCR 3.905(C)(1) states that a court shall consider guidelines established by the Bureau of Indian Affairs (BIA) in determining whether good cause not to transfer exists (Guidelines for State Courts; Indian Child Custody Proceedings, 44 Fed Reg No 228, 67590–67592, C.2–C.4. [November 26, 1979]). Some examples of good cause are that the Indian tribe does not have a tribal court or that the Indian child is over 12 years old and objects to the transfer. For additional examples of good cause and relevant case law, see the BIA guidelines cited above and A Practical Guide to the Indian Child Welfare Act. (Native American Rights Fund, A Practical Guide to the Indian Child Welfare Act [Boulder, CO: Native American Rights Fund, 2007], 7.15 and 7.16, p 60.)

Staff Comment to 2013 Amendment

The amendments of these rules update the rules making them less "paper" focused and reflecting the use of electronic technology in the way courts process court records. The amendments also clarify and delineate the types of records and other materials maintained by a court, and clarify how access is provided.

Staff Comment to 2018 Amendment

The amendments in this order are intended to begin moving trial courts toward a statewide uniform e-Filing process. In addition, the order moves existing language into MCR 1.109 as a way to, for the first time, include most filing requirements in one single rule, instead of scattered in various rules. The order largely mirrors the administrative orders that most e-Filing pilot projects have operated under, but contains some significant new provisions. For example, courts are required to maintain documents in an electronic document management system, and the electronic record is the official court record.

Rule 3.902   Construction

(A) In General. The rules are to be construed to secure fairness, flexibility, and simplicity. The court shall proceed in a manner that safeguards the rights and proper interests of the parties. Limitations on corrections of error are governed by MCR 2.613.

(B) Philosophy. The rules must be interpreted and applied in keeping with the philosophy expressed in the Juvenile Code. The court shall ensure that each minor coming within the jurisdiction of the court shall:

(1) receive the care, guidance, and control, preferably in the minor's own home, that is conducive to the minor's welfare and the best interests of the public; and

(2) when removed from parental control, be placed in care as nearly as possible equivalent to the care that the minor's parents should have given the minor.

[Adopted February 4, 2003, effective May 1, 2003, 467 Mich.]

Comments

Staff Comment to 2003 Adoption

MCR 3.902 is unchanged from former Rule 5.902.

Rule 3.903. Definitions

(A) General Definitions. When used in this subchapter, unless the context otherwise indicates:

(1) "Case" means an action initiated in the family division of the circuit court by:

(a) submission of an original complaint, petition, or citation;

(b) acceptance of transfer of an action from another court or tribunal; or

(c) filing or registration of a foreign judgment or order.

(2) "Child protective proceeding" means a proceeding concerning an offense against a child.

(3) "Confidential file" means

(a) that part of a file made confidential by statute or court rule, including, but not limited to,

(i) the diversion record of a minor pursuant to the Juvenile Diversion Act, MCL 722.821 *et seq.*;

(ii) the separate statement about known victims of juvenile offenses, as required by the Crime Victim's Rights Act, MCL 780.751 *et seq.*;

(iii) the testimony taken during a closed proceeding pursuant to MCR 3.925(A)(2) and MCL 712A.17(7);

(iv) the dispositional reports pursuant to MCR 3.943(C)(3) and 3.973(E)(4);

(v) biometric data required to be maintained pursuant to MCL 28.243;

(vi) reports of sexually motivated crimes, MCL 28.247;

(vii) test results of those charged with certain sexual offenses or substance abuse offenses, MCL 333.5129;

(b) the contents of a social file maintained by the court, including materials such as:

(i) youth and family record fact sheet;

(ii) social study;

(iii) reports (such as dispositional, investigative, laboratory, medical, observation, psychological, psychiatric, progress, treatment, school, and police reports);

(iv) Department of Human Services records;

(v) correspondence;

(vi) victim statements;

(vii) information regarding the identity or location of a foster parent, preadoptive parent, or relative caregiver.

(4) "Court" means the family division of the circuit court.

(5) "Delinquency proceeding" means a proceeding concerning an offense by a juvenile, as defined in MCR 3.903(B)(3).

(6) "Designated proceeding" means a proceeding in which the prosecuting attorney has designated, or has requested the court to designate, the case for trial in the family division of the circuit court in the same manner as an adult.

(7) "Father" means:

(a) A man married to the mother at any time from a minor's conception to the minor's birth, unless a court has determined, after notice and a hearing, that the minor was conceived or born during the marriage, but is not the issue of the marriage;

(b) A man who legally adopts the minor;

(c) A man who by order of filiation or by judgment of paternity is judicially determined to be the father of the minor;

(d) A man judicially determined to have parental rights; or

(e) A man whose paternity is established by the completion and filing of an acknowledgment of parentage in accordance with the provisions of the Acknowledgment of Parentage Act, MCL 722.1001 *et seq.*, or a previously applicable procedure. For an acknowledgment under the Acknowledgment of Parentage Act, the man and mother must each sign the acknowledgment of parentage before a notary public appointed in this state. The acknowledgment shall be filed at either the time of birth or another time during the child's lifetime with the state registrar.

(8) "File" means a repository for collection of the pleadings and other documents and materials related to a case.

(9) An authorized petition is deemed "filed" when it is delivered to, and accepted by, the clerk of the court.

(10) "Formal calendar" means judicial proceedings other than a delinquency proceeding on the consent calendar, a preliminary inquiry, or a preliminary hearing of a delinquency or child protective proceeding.

(11) "Guardian" means a person appointed as guardian of a child by a Michigan court pursuant to MCL 700.5204 or 700.5205, by a court of another state under a comparable statutory provision, or by parental or testamentary appointment as provided in MCL 700.5202, or a juvenile guardian appointed pursuant to MCL 712A.19a or MCL 712A.19c.

(12) "Juvenile Code" means 1944 (1st Ex Sess) PA 54, MCL 712A.1 *et seq.*, as amended.

(13) "Juvenile Guardian" means a person appointed guardian of a child by a Michigan court pursuant to MCL 712A.19a or MCL 712a.19c. A juvenile guardianship is distinct from a guardianship authorized under the Estates and Protected Individuals Code.

(14) "Legal Custodian" means an adult who has been given legal custody of a minor by order of a circuit court in Michigan or a comparable court of another state or who possesses a valid power of attorney given pursuant to MCL 700.5103 or a comparable statute of another state. It also includes the term "Indian custodian" as defined in MCR 3.002(15).

(15) "Legally admissible evidence" means evidence admissible under the Michigan Rules of Evidence.

(16) "Minor" means a person under the age of 18, and may include a person of age 18 or older over whom the court has continuing jurisdiction pursuant to MCL 712A.2a.

(17) "Officer" means a government official with the power to arrest or any other person designated and directed by the court to apprehend, detain, or place a minor.

(18) "Parent" means the mother, the father as defined in MCR 3.903(A)(7), or both, of the minor. It also includes the term "parent" as defined in MCR 3.002(20).

(19) "Party" includes the

    (a) petitioner and juvenile in a delinquency proceeding;

    (b) petitioner, child, respondent, and parent, guardian, or legal custodian in a protective proceeding.

(20) "Petition" means a complaint or other written allegation, verified in the manner provided in MCR 1.109(D)(3), that a parent, guardian, nonparent adult, or legal custodian has harmed or failed to properly care for a child, or that a juvenile has committed an offense.

(21) "Petition authorized to be filed" refers to written permission given by the court to file the petition among the court's public records as permitted by MCR 3.925. Until a petition is authorized, it must be filed with the clerk and maintained as a nonpublic record, accessible only by the court and parties. After authorization, a petition and any associated records may be made nonpublic only as permitted by rule or statute.

(22) "Petitioner" means the person or agency who requests the court to take action.

(23) "Preliminary inquiry" means informal review by the court to determine appropriate action on a petition.

(24) "Putative father" means a man who is alleged to be the biological father of a child who has no father as defined in MCR 3.903(A)(7).

(25) "Records" are as defined in MCR 1.109 and MCR 8.119 and include, but are not limited to, pleadings, complaints, citations, motions, authorized and unauthorized petitions, notices, memoranda, briefs, exhibits, available transcripts, findings of the court, registers of action, consent calendar case plans, and court orders.

(26) "Register of actions" means the case history of all cases, as defined in subrule (A)(1), maintained in accordance with Michigan Supreme Court Case File Management Standards. See MCR 8.119(D)(1)(a).

(27) "Trial" means the fact-finding adjudication of an authorized petition to determine if the minor comes within the jurisdiction of the court. "Trial" also means a specific adjudication of a parent's unfitness to determine whether the parent is subject to the dispositional authority of the court.

(B) Delinquency Proceedings. When used in delinquency proceedings, unless the context otherwise indicates:

(1) "Detention" means court-ordered removal of a juvenile from the custody of a parent, guardian, or legal custodian, pending trial, disposition, commitment, or further order.

(2) "Juvenile" means a minor alleged or found to be within the jurisdiction of the court for having committed an offense.

(3) "Offense by a juvenile" means an act that violates a criminal statute, a criminal ordinance, a traffic law, or a provision of MCL 712A.2(a) or (d).

(4) "Prosecuting attorney" means the prosecuting attorney for a county, an assistant prosecuting attorney for a county, the attorney general, the deputy attorney general, an assistant attorney general, a special prosecuting attorney, and, in connection with the prosecution of an ordinance violation, an attorney for the political subdivision or governmental entity that enacted the ordinance, charter, rule, or regulation upon which the ordinance violation is based.

(C) Child Protective Proceedings. When used in child protective proceedings, unless the context otherwise indicates:

(1) "Agency" means a public or private organization, institution, or facility responsible pursuant to court order or contractual arrangement for the care and supervision of a child.

(2) "Amended petition" means a petition filed to correct or add information to an original petition as defined in subrule (A)(21) before it is adjudicated.

(3) "Child" means a minor alleged or found to be within the jurisdiction of the court pursuant to MCL 712A.2(b).

(4) "Contrary to the welfare of the child" includes, but is not limited to, situations in which the child's life, physical health, or mental well-being is unreasonably placed at risk.

(5) "Foster care" means 24-hour a day substitute care for children placed away from their parents, guardians, or legal custodians, and for whom the court has given the Department of Human Services placement and care responsibility, including, but not limited to,

    (a) care provided to a child in a foster family home, foster family group home, or child caring institution licensed or approved under MCL 722.111 *et seq.*, or

    (b) care provided to a child in a relative's home pursuant to an order of the court.

(6) "Lawyer-guardian ad litem" means that term as defined in MCL 712A.13a(1)(g).

(7) "Nonparent adult" means a person who is 18 years of age or older and who, regardless of the person's domicile, meets all the following criteria in relation to a child over whom the court takes jurisdiction under this chapter:

    (a) has substantial and regular contact with the child,

    (b) has a close personal relationship with the child's parent or with a person responsible for the child's health or welfare, and

    (c) is not the child's parent or a person otherwise related to the child by blood or affinity to the third degree.

(8) "Nonrespondent parent" means a parent who is not named as a respondent in a petition filed under MCL 712A.2(b).

(9) "Offense against a child" means an act or omission by a parent, guardian, nonparent adult, or legal custodian asserted as grounds for bringing the child within the jurisdiction of the court pursuant to the Juvenile Code.

(10) "Placement" means court-approved transfer of physical custody of a child to foster care, a shelter home, a hospital, or a private treatment agency.

(11) "Prosecutor" or "prosecuting attorney" means the prosecuting attorney of the county in which the court has its principal office or an assistant to the prosecuting attorney.

(12) Except as provided in MCR 3.977(B), "respondent" means the parent, guardian, legal custodian, or nonparent adult who is alleged to have committed an offense against a child.

(13) "Supplemental petition" means:

    (a) a written allegation, verified in the manner provided in MCR 1.109(D)(3), that a parent, for whom a petition was authorized, has committed an additional offense since the adjudication of the petition, or

(b) a written allegation, verified in the manner provided in MCR 1.109(D)(3), that a nonrespondent parent is being added as an additional respondent in a case in which an original petition has been authorized and adjudicated against the other parent under MCR 3.971 or MCR 3.972, or

(c) a written allegation, verified in the manner provided in MCR 1.109(D)(3), that requests the court terminate parental rights of a parent or parents under MCR 3.977(F) or MCR 3.977(H).

(D) Designated Proceedings.

(1) "Arraignment" means the first hearing in a designated case at which

(a) the juvenile is informed of the allegations, the juvenile's rights, and the potential consequences of the proceeding;

(b) the matter is set for a probable cause or designation hearing; and,

(c) if the juvenile is in custody or custody is requested pending trial, a decision is made regarding custody pursuant to MCR 3.935(C).

(2) "Court-designated case" means a case in which the court, pursuant to a request by the prosecuting attorney, has decided according to the factors set forth in MCR 3.952(C)(3) that the juvenile is to be tried in the family division of circuit court in the same manner as an adult for an offense other than a specified juvenile violation.

(3) "Designated case" means either a prosecutor-designated case or a court–designated case.

(4) "Designation hearing" means a hearing on the prosecuting attorney's request that the court designate the case for trial in the same manner as an adult in the family division of circuit court.

(5) "Preliminary examination" means a hearing at which the court determines whether there is probable cause to believe that the specified juvenile violation or alleged offense occurred and whether there is probable cause to believe that the juvenile committed the specified juvenile violation or alleged offense.

(6) "Prosecutor-designated case" means a case in which the prosecuting attorney has endorsed a petition charging a juvenile with a specified juvenile violation with the designation that the juvenile is to be tried in the same manner as an adult in the family division of the circuit court.

(7) "Sentencing" means the imposition of any sanction on a juvenile that could be imposed on an adult convicted of the offense for which the juvenile was convicted or the decision to delay the imposition of such a sanction.

(8) "Specified juvenile violation" means any offense, attempted offense, conspiracy to commit an offense, or solicitation to commit an offense, as enumerated in MCL 712A.2d, that would constitute:

(a) burning of a dwelling house, MCL 750.72;

(b) assault with intent to commit murder, MCL 750.83;

(c) assault with intent to maim, MCL 750.86;

(d) assault with intent to rob while armed, MCL 750.89;

(e) attempted murder, MCL 750.91;

(f) first-degree murder, MCL 750.316;

(g) second-degree murder, MCL 750.317;

(h) kidnapping, MCL 750.349;

(i) first-degree criminal sexual conduct, MCL 750.520b;

(j) armed robbery, MCL 750.529;

(k) carjacking, MCL 750.529a;

(*l*) robbery of a bank, safe, or vault, MCL 750.531;

(m) possession, manufacture, or delivery of, or possession with intent to manufacture or deliver, 650 grams (1,000 grams beginning March 1, 2003) or more of any schedule 1 or 2 controlled substance, MCL 333.7401, 333.7403;

(n) assault with intent to do great bodily harm less than murder, MCL 750.84, if armed with a dangerous weapon as defined by MCL 712A.2d(9)(b);

(*o*) first-degree home invasion, MCL 750.110a(2), if armed with a dangerous weapon as defined by MCL 712A.2d(9)(b);

(p) escape or attempted escape from a medium-security or high-security facility operated by the Department of Human Services or a high-security facility operated by a private agency under contract with the Department of Human Services, MCL 750.186a;

(q) any lesser-included offense of an offense described in subrules (a)—(p), if the petition alleged that the juvenile committed an offense described in subrules (a)—(p); or

(r) any offense arising out of the same transaction as an offense described in subrules (a)—(p), if the petition alleged that the juvenile committed an offense described in subrules (a)—(p).

(9) "Tried in the same manner as an adult" means a trial in which the juvenile is afforded all the legal and procedural protections that an adult would be given if charged with the same offense in a court of general criminal jurisdiction.

(E) Minor Personal Protection Order Proceedings. When used in minor personal protection order proceedings, unless the context otherwise indicates:

(1) "Minor personal protection order" means a personal protection order issued by a court against a minor under jurisdiction granted by MCL 712A.2(h).

(2) "Original petitioner" means the person who originally petitioned for the minor personal protection order.

(3) "Prosecutor" or "prosecuting attorney" means the prosecuting attorney of the county in which the court has its principal office or an assistant to the prosecuting attorney.

(F) Michigan Indian Family Preservation Act. If an Indian child, as defined by the Michigan Indian Family Preservation Act, MCL 712B.1 *et seq.*, is the subject of a protective proceeding or is charged with a status offense in violation of MCL 712A.2(a)(2)–(4) or (d), the definitions in MCR 3.002 shall control.

[Adopted February 4, 2003, effective May 1, 2003, 467 Mich. Amended April 30, 2003, effective May 1, 2003, 467 Mich; September 30, 2008, effective January 1, 2009, 482 Mich; April 14, 2009, effective July 1, 2009, 483 Mich; February 2, 2010, effective May 1, 2010, 485 Mich. Amended effective September 28, 2011, 490 Mich. Amended October 31, 2012, effective January 1, 2013, 493 Mich. Amended effective, pending public comment, March 20, 2013, 493 Mich. Amended effective September 5, 2013, 495 Mich. Amended effective, pending public comment, March 25, 2015, 497 Mich. Amended effective September 23, 2015, 498 Mich; December 14, 2016, 500 Mich. Amended May 24, 2017, effective September 1, 2017, 500 Mich; March 28, 2018, effective May 1, 2018, 501 Mich; August 30, 2018, effective September 1, 2018, 502 Mich. Amended effective August 14, 2019, 503 Mich. Amended September 18, 2019, effective January 1, 2020, 503 Mich.]

Comments

Staff Comment to 2003 Adoption

MCR 3.903 corresponds to former Rule 5.903. The amendments add several new definitions, including definitions of "case" [subrule (A)(1)]; "file" [subrule (A)(8)]; "guardian" [subrule (A)(11)]; "legal custodian" [subrule (A)(13)]; "legally admissible evidence" [subrule(A)(14)]; "putative father" [subrule (A)(23)]; "contrary to the welfare of the child" [subrule (C)(3)]; "lawyer-guardian ad litem" [subrule (C)(5)]; "non-parent adult"[subrule (C)(6)]; "prosecutor" [subrule (E)(3)].

Other provisions are modified. Among those changes are the following:

The separate definition of "child born out of wedlock" in former Rule 5.903 (A)(1) is deleted, with the substance of that provision being included in subrule (A)(7).

The definition of "confidential file" is rewritten to include the concept of the "social file." See subrule (A)(3).

In subrule (A)(4), and elsewhere throughout the rules, references to "juvenile court" are eliminated. Compare former Rule 5.903(A)(8).

Subrule (A)(5) adds a reference to the provision defining an offense by a juvenile.

In subrule (A)(7), changes are made in the definition of "father" to conform to statutory amendments. See MCL 333.2824, 333.21532, 722.1001 *et seq.* Former Rule 5.903(A)(4)(c) is deleted. While the presence of a man's name on the minor's birth certificate is a good indication that he is the father, it does not in itself create parental rights, which arise from the other listed circumstances, such as marriage to the mother, acknowledgment of parentage under the 722.1001 *et seq.*, or court order.

In subrule (A)(17), the definition of "parent" is shortened to include only the mother and father of the child. In a number of other rules, "parent, guardian, or legal custodian" is used where the former rules used "parent."

The definition of "party" in subrule (A)(18) is modified to include all respondents, which would include nonparent adults. See MCL 712A.2(b)(2); 712A.6b.

In subrule (B)(1), the definition of "detention" is limited to court ordered removal of the juvenile from the parent or custodian.

The definition of "major offense" is deleted from former Rule 5.903(B)(3). The substance of the definition is included in MCR 3.935(D)(1)(b), the only place where that term was used.

The definition of "reportable juvenile offense" in former MCR 5.903(B)(6) is deleted in light of statutory changes. See MCL 28.243, as amended by 2001 PA 187. Related changes are made elsewhere in the rules in which that term was used. See MCR 3.903(A)(3), 3.925(F), 3.936, and 3.945(B)(1).

The definition of "concerned person" is deleted from former Rule 5.903(C)(3). That term is used in only one other place in the rules, where it is separately defined. See MCR 3.977(A)(2)(d).

Additional details are added to the definition of "foster care" in subrule (C)(4).

The definition of "placement" in subrule (C)(8) is modified so as not to limit the term to removal from the parental home.

Staff Comment to 2003 Amendment

The April 30, 2003, order makes corrections to a number of the rules governing proceedings regarding juveniles that had been adopted on February 4, 2003. The changes are effective May 1, corresponding to the effective date of the February 4 amendments. In addition to these changes, a number of corrections of punctuation and capitalization and changes in the Notes that accompanied the rules have been made and will appear in the published version of the rules.

The amendments of MCR 3.903(D)(8)(m), 6.903(H)(16), 6.931(E)(3), and 6.933(C)(1) conform the rules to 2002 PA 665, which changed the amounts of controlled substances required for certain violations. See MCL 333.7401(2)(a)(i), 333.7403(2)(a)(i). MCR 3.933(C)(1) is also modified in light of *People v Valentin*, 457 Mich 1 (1998).

The amendment of MCR 3.935(B)(1) corrects the inadvertent omission of references to guardians and legal custodians.

The amendments of MCR 3.922(E)(1)(c), 3.943(A), 3.945(A)(1), 3.965(E)(1), and 3.972(C)(2)(c) correct minor errors in wording.

The amendment of MCR 3.977(G) deletes the word "hearing" in the reference to progress reviews. Under MCR 3.974(A)(1), progress reviews do not require hearings.

The amendment of MCR 3.980(B) and (C) revise the provisions on removal of American Indian children from the home to clarify the distinction between emergency removals and removals after hearing.

The amendments of MCR 3.982(A), 6.903(I)–(L) and 6.937(A) correct cross-reference, citation and numbering errors.

Staff Comment to 2008 Amendment

The amendments clarify that information regarding the identity or location of a foster parent, preadoptive parent, or relative caregiver is part of the confidential file and, therefore, a proof of service that includes identifying or location information regarding those parties must also be maintained in the confidential file. In addition, the amendments change references in the rule from Family Independence Agency to Department of Human Services.

Staff Comment to 2009 Amendment

The amendments of Rules 3.901, 3.903, 3.921, 3.965, 3.975, 3.976, 3.977, and 3.978, and new rule 3.979 of the Michigan Court Rules reflect the enactment of 2008 PA 199–203.

Staff Comment to 2010 Amendment

These amendments incorporate provisions of the Indian Child Welfare Act into specific provisions within various rules relating to child protective proceedings and juvenile status offenses. The language is designed to make the rules reflect a more integrated approach to addressing issues specific to Indian children.

MCR 3.002(1)(c) defines "preadoptive placement" to mean the "temporary placement of an Indian child in a foster home or institution after the termination of parental rights, but before or in lieu of adoptive placement, and " The phrase "in lieu of adoptive placement" is not intended to mean that it is permissible to leave a child in foster care indefinitely, in violation of MCL 712A.19b(6) or (7) or 45 CFR 1355.20, 45 CFR 1356.21, or 45 CFR 1356.50. Rather, it addresses situations where the parental rights to a child have been terminated and there is no permanency plan for adoption of the child. One example is when the child has been placed with a juvenile guardian and the guardianship is subsequently revoked. In this situation, jurisdiction over the child pursuant to MCL 712A.2(b) will be reinstated and the child is placed in foster care.

MCR 3.002(1): The definition of "child custody proceeding" is intended to apply the Indian Child Welfare Act to delinquency proceedings if an "Indian child" is charged with a so-called status offense in violation of MCL 712A.2(a)(2)–(4) or (d). Delinquency proceedings involving an Indian child charged with any other non-status offense are generally not subject to the Indian Child Welfare Act; however, if the initial investigation or subsequent review of a non-status delinquency case reveals that the Indian child involved suffers from child abuse or neglect, a separate child protective proceeding may be initiated, which would be subject to the Indian Child Welfare Act.

The amendment of MCR 3.905(C)(1) states that a court shall consider guidelines established by the Bureau of Indian Affairs (BIA) in determining whether good cause not to transfer exists (Guidelines for State Courts; Indian Child Custody Proceedings, 44 Fed Reg No 228, 67590–67592, C.2–C.4. [November 26, 1979]). Some examples of good cause are that the Indian tribe does not have a tribal court or that the Indian child is over 12 years old and objects to the transfer. For additional examples of good cause and relevant case law, see the BIA guidelines cited above and A Practical Guide to the Indian Child Welfare Act. (Native American Rights Fund, A Practical Guide to the Indian Child Welfare Act [Boulder, CO: Native American Rights Fund, 2007], 7.15 and 7.16, p 60.)

Staff Comment to 2011 Amendment

The above noted changes are minor revisions of the rules that have been recommended to the Court to correct cross references and to reflect other technical changes.

Staff Comment to January, 2013 Amendment

The amendments of these rules update the rules making them less "paper" focused and reflecting the use of electronic technology in the way courts process court records. The amendments also clarify and delineate the types of records and other materials maintained by a court, and clarify how access is provided.

Staff Comment to March, 2013 Amendment

This proposal incorporates provisions of the newly enacted Michigan Indian Family Preservation Act into specific provisions within various rules relating to child protective proceedings and juvenile status offenses.

Staff Comment to September, 2013 Amendment

These amendments reflect changes that correct minor technical errors that have occurred in drafting or the changes respond to recent adopted rule revisions, which occasionally inadvertently create incorrect cross-references in other rules.

Staff Comment to March, 2015 Amendment

The amendments of MCR 3.903, 3.920, 3.961, and 3.965 were prompted by the Michigan Supreme Court's decision in *In re Sanders*, 495 Mich 394 (2014), to provide clarification and procedural provisions consistent with the Court's holding in that case.

Staff Comment to September, 2015 Amendment

The Court retained the amendments of MCR 3.903, 3.920, 3.961, and 3.965 that became effective on March 25, 2015, and were prompted by the Michigan

Supreme Court's decision in *In re Sanders*, 495 Mich 394 (2014), to provide clarification and procedural provisions with regard to a nonrespondent parent and adjudication that is consistent with the Court's holding. The Court further amended MCR 3.961(C)(3), effective immediately, to require the court to proceed against each respondent parent in accordance with MCR 3.971 or MCR 3.972 if *either* the amended *or supplemental* petition is authorized.

Staff Comment to 2016 Amendment

These amendments update cross-references and make other nonsubstantive revisions to clarify the rules.

Staff Comment to 2017 Amendment

The amendments of MCR 3.903, 3.932, and 3.936 clarify the procedures used for consent calendar proceedings in juvenile delinquency cases, consistent with the recent enactment of 2016 PA 185.

Staff Comment to May, 2018 Amendment

The amendment of MCR 3.903 removes the requirement that juvenile guardianship information be maintained in a nonpublic manner. This change resolves the conflict between the child protective proceeding social file (which is considered nonpublic) and the juvenile guardianship file (which is public), and makes the rule consistent with current court practices.

Staff Comment to September, 2018 Amendment

These amendments update cross-references in the rules, and are intended to reflect changes that are necessary as a result of the Court's recent e-Filing rules amendments.

Staff Comment to 2019 Amendment

These amendments update cross-references and make other nonsubstantive revisions to clarify the rules.

Staff Comment to 2020 Amendment

The amendments of MCR 1.109, 2.107, 2.113, 2.116, 2.119, 2.222, 2.223, 2.225, 2.227, 3.206, 3.211, 3.212, 3.214, 3.303, 3.903, 3.921, 3.925, 3.926, 3.931, 3.933, 3.942, 3.950, 3.961, 3.971, 3.972, 4.002, 4.101, 4.201, 4.202, 4.302, 5.128, 5.302, 5.731, 6.101, 6.615, 8.105, and 8.119 and rescission of MCR 2.226 and 8.125 continue the process for design and implementation of the statewide electronic-filing system.

Rule 3.904   Use of Videoconferencing Technology

(A) Delinquency, Designated, and Personal Protection Violation Proceedings. Courts may use videoconferencing technology in delinquency, designated, and personal protection violation proceedings as follows.

(1) *Juvenile in the Courtroom or at a Separate Location.* Videoconferencing technology may be used between a courtroom and a facility when conducting preliminary hearings under MCR 3.935(A)(1), preliminary examinations under MCR 3.953 and MCR 3.985, postdispositional progress reviews, and dispositional hearings where the court does not order a more restrictive placement or more restrictive treatment.

(2) *Juvenile in the Courtroom–Other Proceedings.* Except as otherwise provided in this rule, as long as the juvenile is either present in the courtroom or has waived the right to be present, on motion of either party showing good cause, the court may use videoconferencing technology to take testimony from an expert witness or a person at another location in any delinquency, designated, or personal protection violation proceeding under this subchapter. If the proceeding is a trial, the court may use videoconferencing technology with the consent of the parties. A party who does not consent to the use of videoconferencing technology to take testimony from a person at trial shall not be required to articulate any reason for not consenting.

(B) Child Protective and Juvenile Guardianship Proceedings.

(1) Except as provided in subrule (B)(2), courts may allow the use of videoconferencing technology by any participant, as defined in MCR 2.407(A)(1), in any proceeding.

(2) As long as the respondent is either present in the courtroom or has waived the right to be present, on motion of either party showing good cause, the court may use videoconferencing technology to take testimony from an expert witness or any person at another location in the following proceedings:

(a) removal hearings under MCR 3.967 and evidentiary hearings; and

(b) termination of parental rights proceedings under MCR 3.977 and trials, with the consent of the parties. A party who does not consent to the use of videoconferencing technology to take testimony from a person at trial shall not be required to articulate any reason for not consenting.

(C) Mechanics of Use. The use of videoconferencing technology under this rule must be in accordance with the standards established by the State Court Administrative Office. All proceedings at which videoconferencing technology is used must be recorded verbatim by the court.

[Adopted February 14, 2007, effective May 1, 2007, 477 Mich. Corrected July 18, 2007, effective May 1, 2007, 477 Mich. Amended September 21, 2016, effective January 1, 2017, 500 Mich.]

Comments

Staff Comment to 2007 Adoption

Rule 3.904, effective May 1, 2007, allows courts to use interactive video technology during the specified delinquency and child protective proceedings, if the court does not order more restrictive placement or treatment.

Staff Comment to 2017 Amendment

These amendments permit courts to expand the use of videoconferencing technology in many court proceedings, and clarify the proceedings at which videoconferencing technology may be used.

Rule 3.905   Indian Children; Jurisdiction, Notice, Transfer, Intervention

(A) If an Indian child is the subject of a protective proceeding or is charged with a status offense in violation of MCL 712A.2(a)(2)–(4) or (d), and if an Indian tribe has exclusive jurisdiction as defined in MCR 3.002(6), and the matter is not before the state court as a result of emergency removal pursuant to MCL 712B.7(2), the matter shall be dismissed.

(B) If an Indian child is the subject of a protective proceeding or is charged with a status offense in violation of MCL 712A.2(a)(2)–(4) or (d), and if an Indian tribe has exclusive jurisdiction as defined in MCR 3.002(6), and the matter is before the state court as a result of emergency removal pursuant to MCL 712B.7(2), and either the tribe notifies the state court that it is exercising its jurisdiction, or the emergency no longer exists, then the state court shall dismiss the matter.

(C) If an Indian child is the subject of a protective proceeding or is charged with a status offense in violation of MCL 712A.2(a)(2)–(4) or (d) and an Indian tribe does not have exclusive jurisdiction as defined in MCR 3.002(6), the court shall ensure that the petitioner has given notice of the proceedings to the persons described in MCR 3.921 in accordance with MCR 3.920(C).

(1) If either parent or the Indian custodian or the Indian child's tribe petitions the court to transfer the proceeding to the tribal court, the court shall transfer the case to the tribal court unless either parent objects to the transfer of the case to tribal court jurisdiction or the court finds good cause not to transfer. When the court makes a good-cause determination under this

section, adequacy of the tribe, tribal court, or tribal social services shall not be considered. A court may determine that good cause not to transfer a case to tribal court exists only if the person opposing the transfer shows by clear and convincing evidence that either of the following applies:

    (a) The Indian tribe does not have a tribal court.

    (b) The requirement of the parties or witnesses to present evidence in tribal court would cause undue hardship to those parties or witnesses that the Indian tribe is unable to mitigate.

    (2) The court shall not dismiss the matter until the transfer has been accepted by the tribal court.

    (3) If the tribal court declines transfer, the Michigan Indian Family Preservation Act applies to the continued proceeding in state court, as do the provisions of these rules that pertain to an Indian child. See MCL 712B.3 and MCL 712B.5.

    (4) A petition to transfer may be made at any time in accordance with MCL 712B.7(3).

    (D) The Indian custodian of the child, the Indian child's tribe and the Indian child have a right to intervene at any point in the proceeding pursuant to MCL 712B.7(6).

[Adopted February 2, 2010, effective May 1, 2010, 485 Mich. Amended effective, pending public comment, March 20, 2013, 493 Mich. Amended effective September 5, 2013, 495 Mich.]

Comments

Staff Comment to 2010 Adoption

These amendments incorporate provisions of the Indian Child Welfare Act into specific provisions within various rules relating to child protective proceedings and juvenile status offenses. The language is designed to make the rules reflect a more integrated approach to addressing issues specific to Indian children.

MCR 3.002(1)(c) defines "preadoptive placement" to mean the "temporary placement of an Indian child in a foster home or institution after the termination of parental rights, but before or in lieu of adoptive placement, and . . ." The phrase "in lieu of adoptive placement" is not intended to mean that it is permissible to leave a child in foster care indefinitely, in violation of MCL 712A.19b(6) or (7) or 45 CFR 1355.20, 45 CFR 1356.21, or 45 CFR 1356.50. Rather, it addresses situations where the parental rights to a child have been terminated and there is no permanency plan for adoption of the child. One example is when the child has been placed with a juvenile guardian and the guardianship is subsequently revoked. In this situation, jurisdiction over the child pursuant to MCL 712A.2(b) will be reinstated and the child is placed in foster care.

MCR 3.002(1): The definition of "child custody proceeding" is intended to apply the Indian Child Welfare Act to delinquency proceedings if an "Indian child" is charged with a so-called status offense in violation of MCL 712A.2(a)(2)–(4) or (d). Delinquency proceedings involving an Indian child charged with any other non-status offense are generally not subject to the Indian Child Welfare Act; however, if the initial investigation or subsequent review of a non-status delinquency case reveals that the Indian child involved suffers from child abuse or neglect, a separate child protective proceeding may be initiated, which would be subject to the Indian Child Welfare Act.

The amendment of MCR 3.905(C)(1) states that a court shall consider guidelines established by the Bureau of Indian Affairs (BIA) in determining whether good cause not to transfer exists (Guidelines for State Courts; Indian Child Custody Proceedings, 44 Fed Reg No 228, 67590–67592, C.2–C.4. [November 26, 1979]). Some examples of good cause are that the Indian tribe does not have a tribal court or that the Indian child is over 12 years old and objects to the transfer. For additional examples of good cause and relevant case law, see the BIA guidelines cited above and A Practical Guide to the Indian Child Welfare Act. (Native American Rights Fund, A Practical Guide to the Indian Child Welfare Act [Boulder, CO: Native American Rights Fund, 2007], 7.15 and 7.16, p 60.)

Staff Comment to March, 2013 Amendment

This proposal incorporates provisions of the newly enacted Michigan Indian Family Preservation Act into specific provisions within various rules relating to child protective proceedings and juvenile status offenses.

Staff Comment to September, 2013 Amendment

These amendments reflect changes that correct minor technical errors that have occurred in drafting or the changes respond to recent adopted rule revisions, which occasionally inadvertently create incorrect cross-references in other rules.

Rule 3.911.   Jury

    (A) Right. The right to a jury in a juvenile proceeding exists only at the trial.

    (B) Jury Demand. A party who is entitled to a trial by jury may demand a jury by filing a written demand with the court within:

    (1) 14 days after the court gives notice of the right to jury trial, or

    (2) 14 days after an appearance by an attorney or lawyer-guardian ad litem, whichever is later, but no later than 21 days before trial.

    The court may excuse a late filing in the interest of justice.

    (C) Jury Procedure. Jury procedure in juvenile cases is governed by MCR 2.508–2.516, except as provided in this subrule.

    (1) In a delinquency proceeding,

      (a) each party is entitled to 5 peremptory challenges, and

      (b) the verdict must be unanimous.

    (2) In a child protective proceeding,

      (a) each party is entitled to 5 peremptory challenges, with the child considered a separate party, and

      (b) a verdict in a case tried by 6 jurors will be received when 5 jurors agree.

    (3) Two or more parties on the same side, other than a child in a child protective proceeding, are considered a single party for the purpose of peremptory challenges.

      (a) When two or more parties are aligned on the same side and have adverse interests, the court shall allow each such party represented by a different attorney 3 peremptory challenges.

      (b) When multiple parties are allowed more than 5 peremptory challenges under this subrule, the court may allow the opposite side a total number of peremptory challenges not to exceed the number allowed to the multiple parties.

    (4) In a designated case, jury procedure is governed by MCR 6.401–6.420.

[Adopted February 4, 2003, effective May 1, 2003, 467 Mich.]

Comments

Staff Comment to 2003 Adoption

MCR 3.911 corresponds to former Rule 5.911. The time for making a jury demand is increased from 7 days before trial to 21 days. See subrule (B)(2).

Rule 3.912.   Judge

    (A) Judge Required. A judge must preside at:

    (1) a jury trial;

    (2) a waiver proceeding under MCR 3.950;

    (3) the preliminary examination, trial, and sentencing in a designated case;

    (4) a proceeding on the issuance, modification, or termination of a minor personal protection order.

    (B) Right; Demand. The parties have the right to a judge at a hearing on the formal calendar. A party may demand that a judge rather than a referee preside at a nonjury trial by filing a written demand with the court within:

(1) 14 days after the court gives notice of the right to a judge, or

(2) 14 days after an appearance by an attorney or lawyer-guardian ad litem, whichever is later, but no later than 21 days before trial.

The court may excuse a late filing in the interest of justice.

(C) Designated Cases.

(1) The judge who presides at the preliminary examination may not preside at the trial of the same designated case unless a determination of probable cause is waived. The judge who presides at a preliminary examination may accept a plea in the designated case.

(2) The juvenile has the right to demand that the same judge who accepted the plea or presided at the trial of a designated case preside at sentencing or delayed imposition of sentence, but not at a juvenile disposition of the designated case.

(D) Disqualification of Judge. The disqualification of a judge is governed by MCR 2.003.

[Adopted February 4, 2003, effective May 1, 2003, 467 Mich.]

Comments

Staff Comment to 2003 Adoption

MCR 3.912 corresponds to former Rule 5.912. The time for making a judge demand is increased from 7 days before trial to 21 days. See subrule (B)(2). In addition, there is some reorganization of the provisions.

Rule 3.913.   Referees

(A) Assignment of Matters to Referees.

(1) *General.* Subject to the limitations in subrule (A)(2), the court may assign a referee to conduct a preliminary inquiry or to preside at a hearing other than those specified in MCR 3.912(A) and to make recommended findings and conclusions.

(2) *Attorney and Nonattorney Referees.*

(a) Delinquency Proceedings. Except as otherwise provided by MCL 712A.10, only a person licensed to practice law in Michigan may serve as a referee at a delinquency proceeding other than a preliminary inquiry or preliminary hearing, if the juvenile is before the court under MCL 712A.2(a)(1).

(b) Child Protective Proceedings. Only a person licensed to practice law in Michigan may serve as a referee at a child protective proceeding other than a preliminary inquiry, preliminary hearing, a progress review under MCR 3.974(A) or (B), or an emergency removal hearing under MCR 3.974(C). In addition, either an attorney or a nonattorney referee may issue an ex parte placement order under MCR 3.963(B).

(c) Designated Cases. Only a referee licensed to practice law in Michigan may preside at a hearing to designate a case or to amend a petition to designate a case and to make recommended findings and conclusions.

(d) Minor Personal Protection Actions. A nonattorney referee may preside at a preliminary hearing for enforcement of a minor personal protection order. Only a referee licensed to practice law in Michigan may preside at any other hearing for the enforcement of a minor personal protection order and make recommended findings and conclusions.

(B) Duration of Assignment. Unless a party has demanded trial by jury or by a judge pursuant to MCR 3.911 or 3.912, a referee may conduct the trial and further proceedings through disposition.

(C) Advice of Right to Review of Referee's Recommendations. During a hearing held by a referee, the referee must inform the parties of the right to file a request for review of the referee's recommended findings and conclusions as provided in MCR 3.991(B).

[Adopted February 4, 2003, effective May 1, 2003, 467 Mich. Amended June 5, 2013, effective September 1, 2013, 494 Mich. Amended effective March 9, 2016, 499 Mich.]

Comments

Staff Comment to 2003 Adoption

MCR 3.913 corresponds to former Rule 5.913. The main changes are in organization.

Staff Comment to 2013 Amendment

The changes of MCR 3.913, 3.963, 3.965, and 3.974 incorporate the statutory changes enacted in 2012 Public Act 163.

Staff Comment to 2016 Amendment

These amendments update cross-references that changed after the rule was adopted and make other nonsubstantive revisions.

Rule 3.914   Prosecuting Attorney

(A) General. On request of the court, the prosecuting attorney shall review the petition for legal sufficiency and shall appear at any child protective proceeding or any delinquency proceeding.

(B) Delinquency Proceedings.

(1) *Petition Approval.* Only the prosecuting attorney may request the court to take jurisdiction of a juvenile under MCL 712A.2(a)(1).

(2) *Appearance.* The prosecuting attorney shall participate in every delinquency proceeding under MCL 712A.2(a)(1) that requires a hearing and the taking of testimony.

(C) Child Protective Proceedings.

(1) *Legal Consultant to Agency.* On request of the Michigan Family Independence Agency or of an agent under contract with the agency, the prosecuting attorney shall serve as a legal consultant to the agency or agent at all stages of a child protective proceeding.

(2) *Retention of Counsel.* In a child protective proceeding, the agency may retain legal representation of its choice when the prosecuting attorney does not appear on behalf of the agency or an agent under contract with the agency.

(D) Designated Proceedings.

(1) *Specified Juvenile Violation.* In a case in which the petition alleges a specified juvenile violation, only the prosecuting attorney may designate the case, or request leave to amend a petition to designate the case, for trial of the juvenile in the same manner as an adult.

(2) *Other Offenses.* In a case in which the petition alleges an offense other than the specified juvenile violation, only the prosecuting attorney may request the court to designate the case for trial of the juvenile in the same manner as an adult.

(E) Minor Personal Protection Orders. The prosecuting attorney shall prosecute criminal contempt proceedings as provided in MCR 3.987(B).

[Adopted February 4, 2003, effective May 1, 2003, 467 Mich.]

Rule 3.915   Assistance of Attorney

(A) Delinquency Proceedings.

(1) *Advice.* If the juvenile is not represented by an attorney, the court shall advise the juvenile of the right to the assistance of an attorney at each stage of the proceedings on the formal calendar, including trial, plea of admission, and disposition.

(2) *Appointment of an Attorney.* The court shall appoint an attorney to represent the juvenile in a delinquency proceeding if:

(a) the parent, guardian, or legal custodian refuses or fails to appear and participate in the proceedings;

(b) the parent, guardian, or legal custodian is the complainant or victim;

(c) the juvenile and those responsible for the support of the juvenile are found financially unable to retain an attorney, and the juvenile does not waive an attorney;

(d) those responsible for the support of the juvenile refuse or neglect to retain an attorney for the juvenile, and the juvenile does not waive an attorney; or

(e) the court determines that the best interests of the juvenile or the public require appointment.

(3) *Waiver of Attorney.* The juvenile may waive the right to the assistance of an attorney except where a parent, guardian, legal custodian, or guardian ad litem objects or when the appointment is based on subrule (A)(2)(e). The waiver by a juvenile must be made in open court to the judge or referee, who must find and place on the record that the waiver was voluntarily and understandingly made.

(B) Child Protective Proceedings.

(1) *Respondent.*

(a) Advice and Right to Counsel. At respondent's first court appearance, the court shall advise the respondent of the right to retain an attorney to represent the respondent at any hearing conducted pursuant to these rules and that

(i) the respondent has the right to a court appointed attorney at any hearing conducted pursuant to these rules, including the preliminary hearing, if the respondent is financially unable to retain an attorney, and,

(ii) if the respondent is not represented by an attorney, the respondent may request a court-appointed attorney at any later hearing.

(b) Appointment of an Attorney. The court shall appoint an attorney to represent the respondent at any hearing, including the preliminary hearing, conducted pursuant to these rules if

(i) the respondent requests appointment of an attorney, and

(ii) it appears to the court, following an examination of the record, through written financial statements, or otherwise, that the respondent is financially unable to retain an attorney.

(c) The respondent may waive the right to the assistance of an attorney, except that the court shall not accept the waiver by a respondent who is a minor when a parent, guardian, legal custodian, or guardian ad litem objects to the waiver.

(2) *Child.*

(a) The court must appoint a lawyer-guardian ad litem to represent the child at every hearing, including the preliminary hearing. The child may not waive the assistance of a lawyer-guardian ad litem. The duties of the lawyer-guardian ad litem are as provided by MCL 712A.17d. At each hearing, the court shall inquire whether the lawyer-guardian ad litem has met or had contact with the child, as required by the court or MCL 712A.17d(1)(d) and if the lawyer–guardian ad litem has not met or had contact with the child, the court shall require the lawyer-guardian ad litem to state, on the record, the reasons for failing to do so.

(b) If a conflict arises between the lawyer-guardian ad litem and the child regarding the child's best interests, the court may appoint an attorney to represent the child's stated interests.

(C) Appearance. The appearance of an attorney is governed by MCR 2.117(B).

(D) Duration.

(1) An attorney retained by a party may withdraw only on order of the court.

(2) An attorney or lawyer-guardian ad litem appointed by the court to represent a party shall serve until discharged by the court. The court may permit another attorney to temporarily substitute for the child's lawyer-guardian ad litem at a hearing, if that would prevent the hearing from being adjourned, or for other good cause. Such a substitute attorney must be familiar with the case and, for hearings other than a preliminary hearing or emergency removal hearing, must review the agency case file and consult with the foster parents and caseworker before the hearing unless the child's lawyer-guardian ad litem has done so and communicated that information to the substitute attorney. The court shall inquire on the record whether the attorneys have complied with the requirements of this subrule.

(E) Costs. When an attorney is appointed for a party under this rule, the court may enter an order assessing costs of the representation against the party or against a person responsible for the support of that party, which order may be enforced as provided by law.

[Adopted effective May 1, 2003, 467 Mich. Amended effective amended February 25, 2004, 469 Mich. Amended October 24, 2006, effective January 1, 2007, 477 Mich; October 6, 2011, effective January 1, 2012, 490 Mich.]

Staff Comment to 2004 Amendment

The February 25, 2004, amendments of MCR 3.915, 3.965, 3.975, 3.976 and 3.977, effective immediately, are based on recommendations from the Family Independence Agency and Supreme Court Adoption Work Group.

The amendment of MCR 3.915(B)(2)(a) is designed to enforce the statutory requirement in MCL 712A.17d that lawyers-guardians ad litem for children meet with their clients before each hearing.

The amendment of MCR 3.915(D)(2) addresses the substitution of lawyers-guardians ad litem.

The amendments of MCR 3.965(B)(13) and (E) require the court to ask parents, guardians, or legal custodians to identify relatives who might be available to care for the child. The amendment to subsection (E) also requires the court to ask parents, guardians, or legal custodians to identify the child's treating physician in certain circumstances. See MCL 712A.18f(6).

The amendments of MCR 3.975(B) and MCR 3.976(C) require the court to notify interested parties that they may provide input at dispositional review and permanency planning hearings.

The amendments of MCR 3.976(B)(3) and (E)(2) encourage early holding of permanency planning hearings and early filing of petitions for termination of parental rights, where appropriate.

MCR 3.977(C)(2) is a new provision that requires courts to give child welfare cases priority in scheduling.

Staff Comment to 2006 Amendment

The amendment of MCR 3.915 corresponds with the January 3, 2005, amendments of MCL 712A.17d enacted in 2004 PA 475 requiring the lawyer-guardian ad litem to "meet with or observe the child," and authorizing the court to allow alternative means of contact with the child if good cause is shown on the record. Other changes in MCR 3.915 are stylistic changes of the rule's language.

Staff Comment to 2011 Amendment

The amendment of MCR 3.915 clarifies that counsel should be appointed for a parent even at the preliminary hearing of a child protective proceeding.

Rule 3.916   Guardian Ad Litem

(A) General. The court may appoint a guardian ad litem for a party if the court finds that the welfare of the party requires it.

(B) Appearance. The appearance of a guardian ad litem must be in writing and in a manner and form designated by the court. The appearance shall contain a statement regarding the existence of any interest that the guardian ad litem holds in relation to the minor, the minor's family, or any other person in the proceeding before the court or in other matters.

(C) Access to Information. The appearance entitles the guardian ad litem to be furnished copies of all petitions, motions, and orders filed or entered, and to consult with the attorney of the party for whom the guardian ad litem has been appointed.

(D) Costs. The court may assess the cost of providing a guardian ad litem against the party or a person responsible for the support of the party, and may enforce the order of reimbursement as provided by law.

[Adopted February 4, 2003, effective May 1, 2003, 467 Mich.]

Comments

Staff Comment to 2003 Adoption

MCR 3.916 corresponds to former Rule 5.916. Minor changes only.

Rule 3.917   Court Appointed Special Advocate

(A) General. The court may, upon entry of an appropriate order, appoint a volunteer special advocate to assess and make recommendations to the court concerning the best interests of the child in any matter pending in the family division.

(B) Qualifications. All court appointed special advocates shall receive appropriate screening.

(C) Duties. Each court appointed special advocate shall maintain regular contact with the child, investigate the background of the case, gather information regarding the child's status, provide written reports to the court and all parties before each hearing, and appear at all hearings when required by the court.

(D) Term of Appointment. A court appointed special advocate shall serve until discharged by the court.

(E) Access to Information. Upon appointment by the court, the special advocate may be given access to all information, confidential or otherwise, contained in the court file if the court so orders. The special advocate shall consult with the child's lawyer-guardian ad litem.

[Adopted February 4, 2003, effective May 1, 2003, 467 Mich.]

Comments

Staff Comment to 2003 Adoption

MCR 3.917 is a new rule defining the role of court appointed special advocates, which some courts have appointed in individual cases.

Rule 3.920   Service of Process

(A) General.

(1) Unless a party must be summoned as provided in subrule (B), a party shall be given notice of a juvenile proceeding in any manner authorized by the rules in this subchapter.

(2) MCR 2.004 applies in juvenile proceedings involving incarcerated parties.

(B) Summons.

(1) *In General.* A summons may be issued and served on a party before any juvenile proceeding.

(2) *When Required.* Except as otherwise provided in these rules, the court shall direct the service of a summons in the following circumstances:

(a) In a delinquency proceeding, a summons must be served on the parent or parents, guardian, or legal custodian having physical custody of the juvenile, directing them to appear with the juvenile for trial. The juvenile must also be served with a summons to appear for trial. A parent without physical custody must be notified by service as provided in subrule (D), unless the whereabouts of the parent remain unknown after a diligent inquiry.

(b) In a child protective proceeding, a summons must be served on any respondent and any nonrespondent parent. A summons may be served on a person having physical custody of the child directing such person to appear with the child for hearing. A guardian or legal custodian who is not a respondent must be served with notice of hearing in the manner provided by subrule (D).

(c) In a personal protection order enforcement proceeding involving a minor respondent, a summons must be served on the minor. A summons must also be served on the parent or parents, guardian, or legal custodian, unless their whereabouts remain unknown after a diligent inquiry.

(3) *Content.* The summons must direct the person to whom it is addressed to appear at a time and place specified by the court and must:

(a) identify the nature of hearing;

(b) explain the right to an attorney and the right to trial by judge or jury, including, where appropriate, that there is no right to a jury at a termination hearing;

(c) if the summons is for a child protective proceeding, include a notice that the hearings could result in termination of parental rights; and

(d) have a copy of the petition attached.

(4) *Manner of Serving Summons.*

(a) Except as provided in subrule (B)(4)(b), a summons required under subrule (B)(2) must be served by delivering the summons to the party personally.

(b) If the court finds, on the basis of testimony or a motion and affidavit, that personal service of the summons is impracticable or cannot be achieved, the court may by ex parte order direct that it be served in any manner reasonably calculated to give notice of the proceedings and an opportunity to be heard, including publication.

(c) If personal service of a summons is not required, the court may direct that it be served in a manner reasonably calculated to provide notice.

(5) *Time of Service.*

(a) A summons shall be personally served at least:

(i) 14 days before hearing on a petition that seeks to terminate parental rights or a permanency planning hearing,

(ii) 7 days before trial or a child protective dispositional review hearing, or

(iii) 3 days before any other hearing.

(b) If the summons is served by registered mail, it must be sent at least 7 days earlier than subrule (a) requires for personal service of a summons if the party to be served resides in Michigan, or 14 days earlier than required by subrule (a) if the party to be served resides outside Michigan.

(c) If service is by publication, the published notice must appear in a newspaper in the county where the party resides, if known, and, if not, in the county where the action is pending. The published notice need not include the petition itself. The notice must be published at least once 21 days before a hearing specified in subrule (a)(i), 14 days before trial or a hearing specified in subrule (a)(ii), or 7 days before any other hearing.

(C) Notice of Proceeding Concerning Indian Child. If the court knows or has reason to know an Indian child is the subject of a protective proceeding or is charged with a status offense in violation of MCL 712A.2(a)(2)–(4) or (d) and an Indian tribe does not have exclusive jurisdiction as defined in MCR 3.002(6):

(1) in addition to any other service requirements, the petitioner shall notify the parent or Indian custodian and the Indian child's tribe by registered mail with return receipt requested of the pending proceedings on a petition filed under MCR 3.931 or MCR 3.961 and of their right of intervention on a form approved by the State Court Administrative Office. If the identity or location of the parent or Indian custodian, or of the tribe, cannot be determined, notice shall be given to the Secretary of the Interior by registered mail with return receipt requested. Subsequent notices shall be served in accordance

with this subrule for proceedings under MCR 3.967 and MCR 3.977.

(2) the court shall notify the parent or Indian custodian and the Indian child's tribe of all hearings other than those specified in subrule (1) as provided in subrule (D). If the identity or location of the parent or Indian custodian or the tribe cannot be determined, notice of the hearings shall be given to the Secretary of the Interior. Such notice may be by first-class mail.

(D) Notice of Hearing.

(1) *General.* Notice of a hearing must be given in writing or on the record at least 7 days before the hearing except as provided in subrules (D)(2) and (D)(3), or as otherwise provided in the rules.

(2) *Preliminary Hearing; Emergency Removal Hearing.*

(a) When a juvenile is detained, notice of the preliminary hearing must be given to the juvenile and to the parent of the juvenile as soon as the hearing is scheduled. The notice may be in person, in writing, on the record, or by telephone.

(b) When a child is placed outside the home, notice of the preliminary hearing or an emergency removal hearing under MCR 3.974(C)(3) must be given to the parent of the child as soon as the hearing is scheduled. The notice may be in person, in writing, on the record, or by telephone.

(3) *Permanency Planning Hearing; Termination Proceedings.*

(a) Notice of a permanency planning hearing must be given in writing at least 14 days before the hearing.

(b) Notice of a hearing on a petition requesting termination of parental rights in a child protective proceeding must be given in writing at least 14 days before the hearing.

(4) *Failure to Appear.* When a party fails to appear in response to a notice of hearing, the court may order the party's appearance by summons or subpoena.

(E) Subpoenas.

(1) The attorney for a party or the court on its own motion may cause a subpoena to be served upon a person whose testimony or appearance is desired.

(2) It is not necessary to tender advance fees to the person served a subpoena in order to compel attendance.

(3) Except as otherwise stated in this subrule, service of a subpoena is governed by MCR 2.506.

(F) Waiver of Notice and Service. A person may waive notice of hearing or service of process. The waiver shall be in writing. When a party waives service of a summons required by subrule (B), the party must be provided the advice required by subrule (B)(3).

(G) Subsequent Notices. After a party's first appearance before the court, subsequent notice of proceedings and pleadings shall be served on that party or, if the party has an attorney, on the attorney for the party as provided in subrule (D), except that a summons must be served for trial or termination hearing as provided in subrule (B).

(H) Notice Defects. The appearance and participation of a party at a hearing is a waiver by that party of defects in service with respect to that hearing unless objections regarding the specific defect are placed on the record. If a party appears or participates without an attorney, the court shall advise the party that the appearance and participation waives notice defects and of the party's right to seek an attorney.

(I) Proof of Service.

(1) *Summons.* Proof of service of a summons must be made in the manner provided in MCR 2.104(A).

(2) *Other Papers.* Proof of service of other papers permitted or required to be served under these rules must be made in the manner provided in MCR 2.107(D).

(3) *Publication.* If the manner of service used involves publication, proof of service must be made in the manner provided in MCR 2.106(G)(1), and (G)(3) if the publication is accompanied by a mailing.

(4) *Content.* The proof of service must identify the papers served. A proof of service for papers served on a foster parent, preadoptive parent, or relative caregiver shall be maintained in the confidential social file as identified in MCR 3.903(A)(3)(b)(vii).

(5) *Failure to File.* Failure to file proof of service does not affect the validity of the service.

[Adopted February 4, 2003, effective May 1, 2003, 467 Mich. Amended September 30, 2008, effective January 1, 2009, 482 Mich; February 2, 2010, effective May 1, 2010, 485 Mich. Amended effective September 28, 2011, 490 Mich. Amended effective March 20, 2013, pending public comment, 493 Mich. Amended effective September 5, 2013, 495 Mich. Amended effective, pending public comment, March 25, 2015, 497 Mich. Amended effective September 23, 2015, 498 Mich; March 9, 2016, 499 Mich.]

Comments

Staff Comment to 2003 Adoption

MCR 3.920 corresponds to former Rule 5.920.

New subrule (A)(2) cross-references the recently adopted notice provision applicable to incarcerated parties. See MCR 2.004.

The provisions on service of the summons in delinquency and child protective proceedings are rewritten. A new provision on the service of a summons in personal protection order cases is added in subrule (B)(2)(c).

The provisions of subrule (B)(4) covering substitute service are revised, deleting references to registered or certified mail and allowing the court to direct service in any manner reasonably calculated to give notice.

Subrule (F), regarding subsequent notices, is modified in light of *In re Atkins*, 237 Mich App 249 (1999).

New subrule (G) covers waiver of notice defects by appearance at a hearing.

New subrule (H) adds provisions governing proof of service.

Staff Comment to 2008 Amendment

The amendments clarify that information regarding the identity or location of a foster parent, preadoptive parent, or relative caregiver is part of the confidential file and, therefore, a proof of service that includes identifying or location information regarding those parties must also be maintained in the confidential file. In addition, the amendments change references in the rule from Family Independence Agency to Department of Human Services.

Staff Comment to 2010 Amendment

These amendments incorporate provisions of the Indian Child Welfare Act into specific provisions within various rules relating to child protective proceedings and juvenile status offenses. The language is designed to make the rules reflect a more integrated approach to addressing issues specific to Indian children.

MCR 3.002(1)(c) defines "preadoptive placement" to mean the "temporary placement of an Indian child in a foster home or institution after the termination of parental rights, but before or in lieu of adoptive placement, and . . ." The phrase "in lieu of adoptive placement" is not intended to mean that it is permissible to leave a child in foster care indefinitely, in violation of MCL 712A.19b(6) or (7) or 45 CFR 1355.20, 45 CFR 1356.21, or 45 CFR 1356.50. Rather, it addresses situations where the parental rights to a child have been terminated and there is no permanency plan for adoption of the child. One example is when the child has been placed with a juvenile guardian and the guardianship is subsequently revoked. In this situation, jurisdiction over the child pursuant to MCL 712A.2(b) will be reinstated and the child is placed in foster care.

MCR 3.002(1): The definition of "child custody proceeding" is intended to apply the Indian Child Welfare Act to delinquency proceedings if an "Indian child" is charged with a so-called status offense in violation of MCL 712A.2(a)(2)–(4) or (d). Delinquency proceedings involving an Indian child charged with any other non-status offense are generally not subject to the Indian Child Welfare Act; however, if the initial investigation or subsequent review of a non-status delinquency case reveals that the Indian child involved suffers from child abuse or neglect, a separate child protective proceeding may be initiated, which would be subject to the Indian Child Welfare Act.

The amendment of MCR 3.905(C)(1) states that a court shall consider guidelines established by the Bureau of Indian Affairs (BIA) in determining whether good cause not to transfer exists (Guidelines for State Courts; Indian Child Custody Proceedings, 44 Fed Reg No 228, 67590–67592, C.2–C.4. [November 26, 1979]). Some examples of good cause are that the Indian tribe does not have a tribal court or that the Indian child is over 12 years old and objects to the transfer. For additional examples of good cause and relevant case law, see the BIA guidelines cited above and A Practical Guide to the Indian Child Welfare Act. (Native American Rights Fund, A Practical Guide to the Indian Child Welfare Act [Boulder, CO: Native American Rights Fund, 2007], 7.15 and 7.16, p 60.)

Staff Comment to 2011 Amendment

The above noted changes are minor revisions of the rules that have been recommended to the Court to correct cross references and to reflect other technical changes.

Staff Comment to March, 2013 Amendment

This proposal incorporates provisions of the newly enacted Michigan Indian Family Preservation Act into specific provisions within various rules relating to child protective proceedings and juvenile status offenses.

Staff Comment to September, 2013 Amendment

These amendments reflect changes that correct minor technical errors that have occurred in drafting or the changes respond to recent adopted rule revisions, which occasionally inadvertently create incorrect cross-references in other rules.

Staff Comment to March, 2015 Amendment

The amendments of MCR 3.903, 3.920, 3.961, and 3.965 were prompted by the Michigan Supreme Court's decision in *In re Sanders*, 495 Mich 394 (2014), to provide clarification and procedural provisions consistent with the Court's holding in that case.

Staff Comment to September, 2015 Amendment

The Court retained the amendments of MCR 3.903, 3.920, 3.961, and 3.965 that became effective on March 25, 2015, and were prompted by the Michigan Supreme Court's decision in *In re Sanders*, 495 Mich 394 (2014), to provide clarification and procedural provisions with regard to a nonrespondent parent and adjudication that is consistent with the Court's holding. The Court further amended MCR 3.961(C)(3), effective immediately, to require the court to proceed against each respondent parent in accordance with MCR 3.971 or MCR 3.972 if *either* the amended *or supplemental* petition is authorized.

Staff Comment to 2016 Amendment

These amendments update cross-references that changed after the rule was adopted and make other nonsubstantive revisions.

Rule 3.921   Persons Entitled to Notice

(A) Delinquency Proceedings.

(1) *General.* In a delinquency proceeding, the court must notify the following persons of each hearing except as provided in subrule (A)(3):

(a) the juvenile,

(b) the custodial parents, guardian, or legal custodian of the juvenile,

(c) the noncustodial parent who has requested notice at a hearing or in writing,

(d) the guardian ad litem or lawyer-guardian ad litem of a juvenile appointed pursuant to these rules,

(e) the attorney retained or appointed to represent the juvenile,

(f) the prosecuting attorney, and

(g) in accordance with the notice provisions of MCR 3.905, if the juvenile is charged with a status offense in violation of MCL 712A.2(a)(2)–(4) or (d) and if the court knows or has reason to know the juvenile is an Indian child:

    (i) the juvenile's tribe and, if the tribe is unknown, the Secretary of the Interior, and

    (ii) the juvenile's parents or Indian custodian, and if unknown, the Secretary of the Interior.

(2) *Notice to the Petitioner.* The petitioner must be notified of the first hearing on the petition.

(3) *Parent Without Physical Custody.* A parent of the minor whose parental rights over the minor have not been terminated at the time the minor comes to court, must be notified of the first hearing on the formal calendar, unless the whereabouts of the parent are unknown.

(B) Protective Proceedings.

(1) *General.* In a child protective proceeding, except as provided in subrules (B)(2) and (3), the court shall ensure that the following persons are notified of each hearing:

(a) the respondent,

(b) the attorney for the respondent,

(c) the lawyer-guardian ad litem for the child,

(d) subject to subrule (D), the parents, guardian, or legal custodian, if any, other than the respondent,

(e) the petitioner,

(f) a party's guardian ad litem appointed pursuant to these rules,

(g) the foster parents, preadoptive parents, and relative caregivers of a child in foster care under the responsibility of the state,

(h) in accordance with the notice provisions of MCR 3.905, if the court knows or has reason to know the child is an Indian child:

    (i) the child's tribe and, if the tribe is unknown, the Secretary of the Interior, and

    (ii) the child's parents or Indian custodian, and if unknown, the Secretary of the Interior, and

(i) any other person the court may direct to be notified.

(2) *Dispositional Review Hearings and Permanency Planning Hearings.* Before a dispositional review hearing or a permanency planning hearing, the court shall ensure that the following persons are notified in writing of each hearing:

(a) the agency responsible for the care and supervision of the child,

(b) the person or institution having court-ordered custody of the child,

(c) the parents of the child, subject to subrule (D), and the attorney for the respondent parent, unless parental rights have been terminated,

(d) the guardian or legal custodian of the child, if any,

(e) the guardian ad litem for the child,

(f) the lawyer-guardian ad litem for the child,

(g) the attorneys for each party,

(h) the prosecuting attorney if the prosecuting attorney has appeared in the case,

(i) the child, if 11 years old or older,

(j) if the court knows or has reason to know the child is an Indian child, the child's tribe,

(k) the foster parents, preadoptive parents, and relative caregivers of a child in foster care under the responsibility of the state,

(l) if the court knows or has reason to know the child is an Indian child and the parents, guardian, legal custodian, or tribe are unknown, to the Secretary of Interior, and

(m) any other person the court may direct to be notified.

(3) *Termination of Parental Rights.* Written notice of a hearing to determine if the parental rights to a child shall be terminated must be given to those appropriate persons or entities listed in subrule (B)(2), except that if the court knows or has reason to know the child is an Indian child, notice shall be given in accordance with MCR 3.920(C)(1).

(C) Juvenile Guardianships. In a juvenile guardianship, the following persons shall be entitled to notice:

(1) the child, if 11 years old or older;

(2) the Department of Human Services;

(3) the parents of the child, unless parental rights over the child have been terminated;

(4) the juvenile guardian or proposed juvenile guardian;

(5) any court that previously had jurisdiction over the child in a child protective proceeding, if different than the court that entered an order authorizing a juvenile guardianship;

(6) the attorneys for any party;

(7) the prosecuting attorney, if the prosecuting attorney has appeared in the case;

(8) if the court knows or has reason to know the child is an Indian child, the child's tribe, Indian custodian, or if the tribe is unknown, the Secretary of the Interior;

(9) the Michigan Children's Institute superintendent; and

(10) any other person the court may direct to be notified.

(D) Putative Fathers. If, at any time during the pendency of a proceeding, the court determines that the minor has no father as defined in MCR 3.903(A)(7), the court may, in its discretion, take appropriate action as described in this subrule.

(1) The court may take initial testimony on the tentative identity and address of the natural father. If the court finds probable cause to believe that an identifiable person is the natural father of the minor, the court shall direct that notice be served on that person in any manner reasonably calculated to provide notice to the putative father, including publication if his whereabouts remain unknown after diligent inquiry. Any notice by publication must not include the name of the putative father. If the court finds that the identity of the natural father is unknown, the court must direct that the unknown father be given notice by publication. The notice must include the following information:

(a) if known, the name of the child, the name of the child's mother, and the date and place of birth of the child;

(b) that a petition has been filed with the court;

(c) the time and place of hearing at which the natural father is to appear to express his interest, if any, in the minor; and

(d) a statement that failure to attend the hearing will constitute a denial of interest in the minor, a waiver of notice for all subsequent hearings, a waiver of a right to appointment of an attorney, and could result in termination of any parental rights.

(2) After notice to the putative father as provided in subrule (D)(1), the court may conduct a hearing and determine, as appropriate, that:

(a) the putative father has been served in a manner that the court finds to be reasonably calculated to provide notice to the putative father.

(b) a preponderance of the evidence establishes that the putative father is the natural father of the minor and justice requires that he be allowed 14 days to establish his relationship according to MCR 3.903(A)(7). The court may extend the time for good cause shown.

(c) there is probable cause to believe that another identifiable person is the natural father of the minor. If so, the court shall proceed with respect to the other person in accord with subrule (D).

(d) after diligent inquiry, the identity of the natural father cannot be determined. If so, the court may proceed without further notice and without appointing an attorney for the unidentified person.

(3) The court may find that the natural father waives all rights to further notice, including the right to notice of termination of parental rights, and the right to an attorney if

(a) he fails to appear after proper notice, or

(b) he appears, but fails to establish paternity within the time set by the court.

(E) Failure to Appear; Notice by Publication. When persons whose whereabouts are unknown fail to appear in response to notice by publication or otherwise, the court need not give further notice by publication of subsequent hearings, except a hearing on the termination of parental rights.

[Adopted February 4, 2003, effective May 1, 2003, 467 Mich. Amended March 7, 2007, effective May 1, 2007, 477 Mich; April 14, 2009, effective July 1, 2009, 483 Mich; February 2, 2010, effective May 1, 2010, 485 Mich; March 22, 2011, effective March 22, 2011, 489 Mich. Amended effective September 28, 2011, 490 Mich; March 20, 2013, 493 Mich; August 14, 2019, 503 Mich. Amended September 18, 2019, effective January 1, 2020, 503 Mich.]

Comments

Staff Comment to 2003 Adoption

MCR 3.921 corresponds to former Rule 5.921.

In subrule (A), the provisions regarding persons to be notified in delinquency proceedings are reorganized, and the prosecuting attorney is added.

The changes in subrule (B) regarding child protective proceedings are largely in terminology, consistent with other proposed changes.

The provisions regarding notice to putative fathers in subrule (C) are rewritten.

Staff Comment to 2007 Amendment

This amendment adds a requirement mandated by 42 USC 629h that for states receiving federal Court Improvement Program grants, a court rule must be in effect ensuring that foster parents, preadoptive parents, and relative caregivers are notified of any proceedings relating to the child. Form JC 45 will be amended to allow courts to instruct the Department of Human Services to provide notice to the listed individuals, and to require the Department of Human Services to inform courts that it has notified the required parties.

Staff Comment to 2009 Amendment

The amendments of Rules 3.901, 3.903, 3.921, 3.965, 3.975, 3.976, 3.977, and 3.978, and new rule 3.979 of the Michigan Court Rules reflect the enactment of 2008 PA 199–203.

Staff Comment to 2010 Amendment

The amendments of Rules 3.901, 3.903, 3.921, 3.965, 3.975, 3.976, 3.977, and 3.978, and new rule 3.979 of the Michigan Court Rules reflect the enactment of 2008 PA 199–203.

These amendments incorporate provisions of the Indian Child Welfare Act into specific provisions within various rules relating to child protective proceedings and juvenile status offenses. The language is designed to make the rules reflect a more integrated approach to addressing issues specific to Indian children.

MCR 3.002(1)(c) defines "preadoptive placement" to mean the "temporary placement of an Indian child in a foster home or institution after the termination of parental rights, but before or in lieu of adoptive placement, and ..." The phrase "in lieu of adoptive placement" is not intended to mean that it is permissible to leave a child in foster care indefinitely, in violation of MCL 712A.19b(6) or (7) or 45 CFR 1355.20, 45 CFR 1356.21, or 45 CFR 1356.50. Rather, it addresses situations where the parental rights to a child have been terminated and there is no permanency plan for adoption of the child. One example is when the child has been placed with a juvenile guardian and the guardianship is subsequently revoked. In this situation, jurisdiction over the child pursuant to MCL 712A.2(b) will be reinstated and the child is placed in foster care.

MCR 3.002(1): The definition of "child custody proceeding" is intended to apply the Indian Child Welfare Act to delinquency proceedings if an "Indian child" is charged with a so-called status offense in violation of MCL 712A.2(a)(2)–(4) or (d). Delinquency proceedings involving an Indian child charged with any other non-status offense are generally not subject to the Indian Child Welfare Act; however, if the initial investigation or subsequent review of a non-status delinquency case reveals that the Indian child involved suffers from child abuse or neglect, a separate child protective proceeding may be initiated, which would be subject to the Indian Child Welfare Act.

The amendment of MCR 3.905(C)(1) states that a court shall consider guidelines established by the Bureau of Indian Affairs (BIA) in determining whether good cause not to transfer exists (Guidelines for State Courts; Indian Child Custody Proceedings, 44 Fed Reg No 228, 67590–67592, C.2–C.4. [November 26, 1979]). Some examples of good cause are that the Indian tribe does not have a tribal court or that the Indian child is over 12 years old and objects to the transfer. For additional examples of good cause and relevant case law, see the BIA guidelines cited above and A Practical Guide to the Indian Child Welfare Act. (Native American Rights Fund, A Practical Guide to the Indian Child Welfare Act [Boulder, CO: Native American Rights Fund, 2007], 7.15 and 7.16, p 60.)

Staff Comment to March, 2011 Amendment

The amendments of MCR 3.807, 3.921, and 5.402 have been made to clarify former language and to correct cross references.

Staff Comment to September, 2011 Amendment

The above noted changes are minor revisions of the rules that have been recommended to the Court to correct cross references and to reflect other technical changes.

Staff Comment to 2013 Amendment

This proposal incorporates provisions of the newly enacted Michigan Indian Family Preservation Act into specific provisions within various rules relating to child protective proceedings and juvenile status offenses.

Staff Comment to 2019 Amendment

These amendments update cross-references and make other nonsubstantive revisions to clarify the rules.

Staff Comment to 2020 Amendment

The amendments of MCR 1.109, 2.107, 2.113, 2.116, 2.119, 2.222, 2.223, 2.225, 2.227, 3.206, 3.211, 3.212, 3.214, 3.303, 3.903, 3.921, 3.925, 3.926, 3.931, 3.933, 3.942, 3.950, 3.961, 3.971, 3.972, 4.002, 4.101, 4.201, 4.202, 4.302, 5.128, 5.302, 5.731, 6.101, 6.615, 8.105, and 8.119 and rescission of MCR 2.226 and 8.125 continue the process for design and implementation of the statewide electronic-filing system.

Rule 3.922. Pretrial Procedures in Delinquency and Child Protection Proceedings

(A) Discovery.

(1) The following materials are discoverable as of right in all proceedings and shall be produced no less than 21 days before trial, even without a discovery request:

(a) all written or recorded statements and notes of statements made by the juvenile or respondent that are in possession or control of petitioner or a law enforcement agency, including oral statements if they have been reduced to writing;

(b) all written or recorded statements made by any person with knowledge of the events in possession or control of petitioner or a law enforcement agency, including, but not limited to, police reports, allegations of neglect and/or abuse included on a complaint submitted to Child Protective Services, and Child Protective Services investigation reports, except that the identity of the reporting person shall be protected in accordance with MCL 722.625;

(c) the names of all prospective witnesses;

(d) a list of all prospective exhibits;

(e) a list of all physical or tangible objects that are prospective evidence that are in the possession or control of petitioner or a law enforcement agency;

(f) the results of all scientific, medical, psychiatric, psychological, or other expert tests, experiments, or evaluations, including the reports or findings of all experts, that are relevant to the subject matter of the petition;

(g) the results of any lineups or showups, including written reports or lineup sheets;

(h) all search warrants issued in connection with the matter, including applications for such warrants, affidavits, and returns or inventories;

(i) any written, video, or recorded statement that pertains to the case and made by a witness whom the party may call at trial;

(j) the curriculum vitáe of an expert the party may call at trial and either a report prepared by the expert containing, or a written description of, the substance of the proposed testimony of the expert, the expert's opinion, and the underlying bases of that opinion; and

(k) any criminal record that the party may use at trial to impeach a witness.

(2) On motion of a party, the court may permit discovery of any other materials and evidence, including untimely requested materials and evidence that would have been discoverable of right under subrule (A)(1) if timely requested. Absent manifest injustice, no motion for discovery will be granted unless the moving party has requested and has not been provided the materials or evidence sought through an order of discovery.

(3) Depositions may only be taken as authorized by the court.

(4) Failure to comply with subrules (A)(1) and (A)(2) may result in such sanctions in keeping with those assessable under MCR 2.313.

(B) Discovery and Disclosure in Delinquency Matters.

(1) In delinquency matters, in addition to disclosures required by provisions of law and as required or allowed by subrule (A)(1)–(3), a party shall provide all other parties the following, which are discoverable as of right and, even without a discovery request, shall be produced no less than 21 days before trial:

(a) a description or list of criminal convictions, known to the respondent's attorney or prosecuting attorney, of any witness whom the party may call at trial;

(b) any exculpatory information or evidence known to the prosecuting attorney;

(c) any written or recorded statements, including electronically recorded statements, by a defendant, codefendant, or accomplice pertaining to the case even if that person is not a prospective witness at trial; and

(d) any plea agreement, grant of immunity, or other agreement for testimony in connection with the case.

(2) In delinquency matters, notwithstanding any other provision of this rule, there is no right to have disclosed or to discover information or evidence that is protected by constitution, statute, or privilege, including information or evidence protected by a respondent's right against self-incrimination, except as provided in subrule (B)(3).

(3) In delinquency matters, if a respondent demonstrates a good-faith belief, grounded in articulable fact, that there is a reasonable probability that records protected by privilege are likely to contain material information necessary to the defense, the court shall conduct an in camera inspection of the records.

(a) If the privilege is absolute, and the privilege holder refuses to waive the privilege to permit an in camera inspection, the court shall suppress or strike the privilege holder's testimony.

(b) If the court is satisfied, following an in camera inspection, that the records reveal evidence necessary to the defense, the court shall direct that such evidence as is necessary to the defense be made available to respondent's counsel. If the privilege is absolute and the privilege holder refuses to waive the privilege to permit disclosure, the court shall suppress or strike the privilege holder's testimony.

(c) Regardless of whether the court determines that the records should be made available to the respondent, the court shall make findings sufficient to facilitate meaningful appellate review.

(d) The court shall seal and preserve the records for review in the event of an appeal:

(i) by the respondent, on an interlocutory basis or following conviction, if the court determines that the records should not be made available to the defense or

(ii) by the prosecution, on an interlocutory basis, if the court determines that the records should be made available to the defense.

(e) Records disclosed under this rule shall remain in the exclusive custody of counsel for the parties, shall be used only for the limited purpose approved by the court, and shall be subject to such other terms and conditions as the court may provide.

(f) Excision. When some parts of material or information are discoverable and other parts are not discoverable, the party must disclose the discoverable parts and may excise the remainder. The party must inform the other party that nondiscoverable information has been excised and withheld. On motion, the court must conduct a hearing in camera to determine whether the reasons for excision are justifiable. If the court upholds the excision, it must seal and preserve the record of the hearing for review in the event of an appeal.

(4) At delinquency dispositions, reviews, designation hearings, hearings on alleged violation of court orders or probation, and detention hearings, the following shall be provided to the respondent, respondent's counsel, and the prosecuting attorney no less than seven (7) days before the hearing:

(a) assessments and evaluations to be considered by the court during the hearing;

(b) documents including but not limited to police reports, witnesses statements, reports prepared by probation officers, reports prepared by intake officers, and reports prepared by placement/detention staff to be considered by the court during the hearing; and

(c) predisposition reports and documentation regarding recommendations in the report including but not limited to documents regarding restitution.

(5) Failure to comply with subrules (B)(1) and (B)(4) may result in sanctions in keeping with those assessable under MCR 2.313.

(C) Notice of Defenses; Rebuttal.

(1) Within 21 days after the juvenile has been given notice of the date of trial, but no later than 7 days before the trial date, the juvenile or the juvenile's attorney must file a written notice with the court and prosecuting attorney of the intent to rely on a defense of alibi or insanity. The notice shall include a list of the names and addresses of defense witnesses.

(2) Within 7 days after receipt of notice, but no later than 2 days before the trial date, the prosecutor shall provide written notice to the court and defense of an intent to offer rebuttal to the above-listed defenses. The notice shall include names and addresses of rebuttal witnesses.

(3) Failure to comply with subrules (1) and (2) may result in the sanctions set forth in MCL 768.21.

(D) Motion Practice. Motion practice in juvenile proceedings is governed by MCR 2.119.

(E) Pretrial Conference. The court may direct the parties to appear at a pretrial conference. The scope and effect of a pretrial conference are governed by MCR 2.401, except as otherwise provided in or inconsistent with the rules of this subchapter.

(F) Notice of Intent.

(1) Within 21 days after the parties have been given notice of the date of trial, but no later than 7 days before the trial date, the proponent must file with the court, and serve all parties, written notice of the intent to:

(a) use a support person, including the identity of the support person, the relationship to the witness, and the anticipated location of the support person during the hearing.

(b) request special arrangements for a closed courtroom or for restricting the view of the respondent/defendant from the witness or other special arrangements allowed under law and ordered by the court.

(c) use a videotaped deposition as permitted by law.

(d) admit out-of-court hearsay statements under MCR 3.972(C)(2), including the identity of the persons to whom a statement was made, the circumstances leading to the statement, and the statement to be admitted.

(2) Within 7 days after receipt or notice, but no later than 2 days before the trial date, the nonproponent parties must provide written notice to the court of an intent to offer rebuttal testimony or evidence in opposition to the request and must include the identity of the witnesses to be called.

(3) The court may shorten the time periods provided in subrule (E) if good cause is shown.

[Adopted February 4, 2003, effective May 1, 2003, 467 Mich. Amended April 30, 2003, effective May 1, 2003, 467 Mich; June 19, 2019, effective January 1, 2020, 503 Mich.]

Comments

Staff Comment to 2003 Adoption

MCR 3.922 corresponds to former Rule 5.922.

Several changes are made in the discovery provisions.

In subrule (A)(1), the language regarding listing of exhibits, tangible objects, and the results of tests or experiments is modified.

New subrule (A)(3) expressly provides that depositions may be taken only with court authorization.

New subrule (A)(4) provides that failure to comply with discovery provisions subjects a party to MCR 2.313 sanctions.

In subrule (B)(1), the references to the defenses of diminished capacity and mental illness negating an element of the alleged offense are deleted in light of *People v Carpenter*, 464 Mich 223 (2001).

In subrule (C), the special provision on the time for filing motions to suppress is deleted.

A new subrule (E) is added requiring parties to give notice of intent to request certain procedures, including use of a "support person," special arrangements for a closed courtroom or restricted view of a witness, use of a video-taped deposition, or admission of hearsay. See MCL 712A.17b; MCR 3.972(C)(2).

Staff Comment to 2003 Amendment

The April 30, 2003, order makes corrections to a number of the rules governing proceedings regarding juveniles that had been adopted on February 4, 2003. The changes are effective May 1, corresponding to the effective date of the February 4 amendments. In addition to these changes, a number of corrections of punctuation and capitalization and changes in the Notes that accompanied the rules have been made and will appear in the published version of the rules.

The amendments of MCR 3.903(D)(8)(m), 6.903(H)(16), 6.931(E)(3), and 6.933(C)(1) conform the rules to 2002 PA 665, which changed the amounts of controlled substances required for certain violations. See MCL 333.7401(2)(a)(i), 333.7403(2)(a)(i). MCR 3.933(C)(1) is also modified in light of *People v Valentin*, 457 Mich 1 (1998).

The amendment of MCR 3.935(B)(1) corrects the inadvertent omission of references to guardians and legal custodians.

The amendments of MCR 3.922(E)(1)(c), 3.943(A), 3.945(A)(1), 3.965(E)(1), and 3.972(C)(2)(c) correct minor errors in wording.

The amendment of MCR 3.977(G) deletes the word "hearing" in the reference to progress reviews. Under MCR 3.974(A)(1), progress reviews do not require hearings.

The amendment of MCR 3.980(B) and (C) revise the provisions on removal of American Indian children from the home to clarify the distinction between emergency removals and removals after hearing.

The amendments of MCR 3.982(A), 6.903(I)–(L) and 6.937(A) correct cross-reference, citation and numbering errors.

Staff Comment to 2020 Amendment

These amendments are based on a proposal created by a special committee of the State Bar of Michigan and approved for submission to the Court by the Bar's Representative Assembly. The rules require mandatory discovery disclosure in many cases, adopt a presumptive limit on interrogatories (20 in most cases, but 35 in domestic relations proceedings) and limit a deposition to 7 hours. The amendments also update the rules to more specifically address issues related to electronically stored information, and encourage early action on discovery issues during the discovery period.

The amendment of MCR 2.309(A)(2) sets a presumptive limit of twenty interrogatories for each separately represented party. Several commenters suggested that the term "discrete subpart" be more explicitly defined. But the rule's reference to "a discrete subpart" is intended to draw guidance from federal courts construing FR Civ P 30(a)(1). Generally, subparts are not separately counted if they are logically or factually subsumed within and necessarily related to the primary question. In upholding the limit, parties and courts should also pragmatically balance the overall goals of discovery and the admonition of MCR 1.105. Further, the intent of the provision at MCR 2.301(B)(4) is to ensure that parties responding to discovery requests have the full time period to do so as provided for under these rules prior to the expiration of the discovery period.

Rule 3.923   Miscellaneous Procedures

(A) Additional Evidence. If at any time the court believes that the evidence has not been fully developed, it may:

(1) examine a witness,

(2) call a witness, or

(3) adjourn the matter before the court, and

   (a) cause service of process on additional witnesses, or

   (b) order production of other evidence.

(B) Examination or Evaluation. The court may order that a minor or a parent, guardian, or legal custodian be examined or evaluated by a physician, dentist, psychologist, or psychiatrist.

(C) Biometric Data and Photographing. A juvenile must have biometric data collected when required by law. The court may permit the collection of biometric data or photographing, or both, of a minor concerning whom a petition has been filed. Biometric data and photographs must be placed in the confidential files, capable of being located and destroyed on court order.

(D) Lineup. If a complaint or petition is filed against a juvenile alleging violation of a criminal law or ordinance, the court may, at the request of the prosecuting attorney, order the juvenile to appear at a place and time designated by the court for identification by another person, including a corporeal lineup pursuant to MCL 712A.32. If the court orders the juvenile to appear for such an identification procedure, the court must notify the juvenile and the juvenile's parent, guardian or legal custodian that the juvenile has the right to consult with an attorney and have an attorney present during the identification procedure and that if the juvenile and the juvenile's parent, guardian or legal custodian cannot afford an attorney, the court will appoint an attorney for the juvenile if requested on the record or in writing by the juvenile or the juvenile's parent, guardian or legal custodian.

(E) Electronic Equipment; Support Person. The court may allow the use of videoconferencing technology, speaker telephone, or other similar electronic equipment to facilitate hearings or to protect the parties. The court may allow the use of videotaped statements and depositions, anatomical dolls, or support persons, and may take other measures to protect the child witness as authorized by MCL 712A.17b.

(F) Impartial Questioner. The court may appoint an impartial person to address questions to a child witness at a hearing as the court directs.

(G) Adjournments. Adjournments of trials or hearings in child protective proceedings should be granted only

(1) for good cause,

(2) after taking into consideration the best interests of the child, and

(3) for as short a period of time as necessary.

[Adopted February 4, 2003, effective May 1, 2003, 467 Mich. Amended effective December 14, 2016, 500 Mich; August 14, 2019, 503 Mich..]

Comments

Staff Comment to 2003 Adoption

MCR 3.923 corresponds to former Rule 5.923.

Subrule (C) specifically provides that fingerprinting must be done as required by law. See, e.g., MCL 712A.11(5) and 712A.18(10). In addition, it adjusts the language giving the court discretion to require fingerprinting and photographing

of a minor, applying that principle to juveniles concerning whom a petition has been filed, rather than to those who are in court custody, as in former Rule 5.923(C).

Former MCR 5.923(F) allowed the judge to appoint a psychologist or psychiatrist to question a child witness. MCR 3.923(F) allows anyone to be designated as such a questioner.

The adjournment provisions of subrule (G) are simplified, giving the judge more flexibility, and deleting the motion requirement.

Staff Comment to 2016 Amendment

These amendments update cross-references and make other nonsubstantive revisions to clarify the rules.

Staff Comment to 2019 Amendment

These amendments update cross-references and make other nonsubstantive revisions to clarify the rules.

Rule 3.924   Information Furnished on Request by Court

Persons or agencies providing testimony, reports, or other information at the request of the court, including otherwise confidential information, records, or reports that are relevant and material to the proceedings following authorization of a petition, are immune from any subsequent legal action with respect to furnishing the information to the court.

[Adopted February 4, 2003, effective May 1, 2003, 467 Mich.]

Comments

Staff Comment to 2003 Adoption

MCR 3.924 corresponds to former Rule 5.924. The provision on immunity for persons providing information to the court is modified to expressly encompass otherwise confidential information.

Rule 3.925   Open Proceedings; Judgments and Orders; Records Confidentiality; Destruction of Court Records; Setting Aside Adjudications

(A) Open Proceedings.

(1) *General.* Except as provided in subrule (A)(2), juvenile proceedings on the formal calendar and preliminary hearings shall be open to the public.

(2) *Closed Proceedings; Criteria.* The court, on motion of a party or a victim, may close the proceedings to the public during the testimony of a child or during the testimony of the victim to protect the welfare of either. In making such a determination, the court shall consider the nature of the proceedings; the age, maturity, and preference of the witness; and, if the witness is a child, the preference of a parent, guardian, or legal custodian that the proceedings be open or closed. The court may not close the proceedings to the public during the testimony of the juvenile if jurisdiction is requested under MCL 712A.2(a)(1).

(B) Record of Proceedings. A record of all hearings must be made. All proceedings on the formal calendar must be recorded by stenographic recording or by mechanical or electronic recording as provided by statute or MCR 8.108. A plea of admission or no contest, including any agreement with or objection to the plea, must be recorded.

(C) Judgments and Orders. The form and signing of judgments are governed by MCR 2.602(A)(1) and (2). Judgments and orders may be served on a person by first-class mail to the person's last known address, by e-mail under MCR 2.107(C)(4), or electronic service under MCR 1.109(G)(6)(a).

(D) Public Access to Case File Records; Confidential File.

(1) *General.* Except as otherwise required by MCR 3.903(A)(21), case file records maintained under Chapter XIIA of the Probate Code, MCL 712A.1 *et seq.*, other than confidential files, must be open to the general public.

(2) *Confidential Files.* Confidential files are defined in MCR 3.903(A)(3) and include the social case file and those records in the legal case file made confidential by statute, court rule, or court order. Only persons who are found by the court to have a legitimate interest may be allowed access to the confidential files. In determining whether a person has a legitimate interest, the court shall consider the nature of the proceedings, the welfare and safety of the public, the interest of the minor, and any restriction imposed by state or federal law.

(E) Retention and Destruction of Court Records. The court shall destroy its case files and other court records only as prescribed by the records retention and disposal schedule established under MCR 8.119(K). Destruction of a case record does not negate, rescind, or set aside an adjudication.

(F) Setting Aside Adjudications and Convictions.

(1) *Adjudications.* The setting aside of juvenile adjudications is governed by MCL 712A.18e.

(2) *Convictions.* The court may only set aside a conviction as provided by MCL 780.621 *et seq.*

(G) Access to Juvenile Offense Record of Convicted Adults. When the juvenile offense record of an adult convicted of a crime is made available to the appropriate agency, as provided in MCL 791.228(1), the record must state whether, with regard to each adjudication, the juvenile had an attorney or voluntarily waived an attorney.

[Adopted February 4, 2003, effective May 1, 2003, 467 Mich. Amended December 6, 2005, effective January 1, 2006, 474 Mich; February 6, 2013, effective May 1, 2013, 493 Mich. Amended effective September 5, 2013, 495 Mich; May 7, 2014, 495 Mich. Amended May 25, 2016, effective January 1, 2017, 499 Mich; September 18, 2019, effective January 1, 2020, 503 Mich.]

Comments

Staff Comment to 2003 Adoption

MCR 3.925 corresponds to former Rule 5.925.

Subrule (B) regarding the recording of hearings is modified in light of MCL 712A.17(1), and to provide that a plea of admission (and any agreement with or objection to the plea) must be recorded.

Subrule (C) incorporates the circuit court rule regarding signing of judgments and orders, MCR 2.602(A), in place of the current provision, which refers to Subchapter 5.600. Judgments and orders may be served by first-class mail to the person's last known address.

The provision on confidentiality of files in subrule (D)(2) adds an explicit recognition of restrictions imposed by law.

Subrule (E) regarding destruction of files and records is substantially rewritten.

The provisions regarding setting aside adjudications are placed in a separate subrule (F), and simplified by referring to the governing statute, MCL 712A.18e.

Staff Comment to 2005 Amendment

The December 6, 2005, amendment of MCR 3.925(E)(2)(c) requires that the records and files of all juvenile offenses be destroyed when the person becomes 30 years old, except for the register of actions. The rule previously required that the records and files of certain adjudicated juvenile offenses be retained permanently.

Staff Comment to May, 2013 Amendment

The amendments of MCR 3.925 clarify the rules and procedures for retention and destruction of various records in juvenile cases.

Staff Comment to September, 2013 Amendment

These amendments reflect changes that correct minor technical errors that have occurred in drafting or the changes respond to recent adopted rule revisions, which occasionally inadvertently create incorrect cross-references in other rules.

Staff Comment to 2014 Amendment

These amendments reflect changes that correct minor technical errors that have occurred in drafting or the changes respond to recent adopted rule revisions, which occasionally inadvertently create incorrect cross-references in other rules.

Staff Comment to 2017 Amendment

The amendments of MCR 3.925, 8.119, and 8.302 and the adoption of MCR 5.133 are an expected progression in the development of policies and procedures that standardize management of court records and provide a uniform basis for developing parameters on the use of technology in creating, accessing, routing, maintaining, and disposing of court records. These particular amendments will assist in implementing the goals of 2013 PA 199 and 201 and improving the policies and procedures adopted by the Court in 2012 under Administrative File No. 2006–47.

Staff Comment to 2020 Amendment

The amendments of MCR 1.109, 2.107, 2.113, 2.116, 2.119, 2.222, 2.223, 2.225, 2.227, 3.206, 3.211, 3.212, 3.214, 3.303, 3.903, 3.921, 3.925, 3.926, 3.931, 3.933, 3.942, 3.950, 3.961, 3.971, 3.972, 4.002, 4.101, 4.201, 4.202, 4.302, 5.128, 5.302, 5.731, 6.101, 6.615, 8.105, and 8.119 and rescission of MCR 2.226 and 8.125 continue the process for design and implementation of the statewide electronic-filing system.

Rule 3.926 Transfer of Jurisdiction; Change of Venue

(A) Definition. As used in MCL 712A.2, a child is "found within the county" in which the offense against the child occurred, in which the offense committed by the juvenile occurred, or in which the minor is physically present.

(B) Transfer to County of Residence. When a minor is brought before the family division of the circuit court in a county other than that in which the minor resides, the court may request transfer of the case to the court in the county of residence before trial. The court shall not order transfer of the case until the court to which the case is to be transferred has granted the request to accept the transfer.

(1) If both parents reside in the same county, or if the child resides in the county with a parent who has been awarded legal custody, a guardian, a legal custodian, or the child's sole legal parent, that county will be presumed to be the county of residence.

(2) In circumstances other than those enumerated in subsection (1) of this section, the court shall consider the following factors in determining the child's county of residence:

(a) The county of residence of the parent or parents, guardian, or legal custodian.

(b) Whether the child has ever lived in the county, and, if so, for how long.

(c) Whether either parent has moved to another county since the inception of the case.

(d) Whether the child is subject to the prior continuing jurisdiction of another court.

(e) Whether a court has entered an order placing the child in the county for the purpose of adoption.

(f) Whether the child has expressed an intention to reside in the county.

(g) Any other factor the court considers relevant.

(3) If the child has been placed in a county by court order or by placement by a public or private agency, the child shall not be considered a resident of the county in which he or she has been placed, unless the child has been placed for the purpose of adoption.

(C) Costs. When a court other than the court in a county in which the minor resides orders disposition, it will be responsible for any costs incurred in connection with such order unless

(1) the court in the county in which the minor resides agrees to pay the costs of such disposition, or

(2) the minor is made a state ward pursuant to the Youth Rehabilitation Services Act, MCL 803.301 *et seq.*, and the county of residence withholds consent to a transfer of the case.

(D) Change of Venue; Grounds. The court, on motion by a party, may order a case to be heard before a court in another county:

(1) for the convenience of the parties and witnesses, provided that a judge of the other court agrees to hear the case; or

(2) when an impartial trial cannot be had where the case is pending.

All costs of the proceeding in another county are to be borne by the court ordering the change of venue.

(E) Bifurcated Proceeding. If the judge of the transferring court and the judge of the receiving court agree, the case may be bifurcated to permit adjudication in the transferring court and disposition in the receiving court. The case may be returned to the receiving court immediately after the transferring court enters its order of adjudication.

(F) Transfer of Records.

(1) The transferring court must enter all necessary orders pertaining to the certification and transfer of the action to the receiving court. Where the courts have agreed to bifurcate the proceedings, the court adjudicating the case shall send any supplemented pleadings and other records to the court entering the disposition in the case.

(2) The clerk of the court must prepare the case records for transfer in accordance with the orders entered under subrule (1) and the Michigan Trial Court Records Management Standards and send them to the receiving court by a secure method.

(G) Designated Cases. Designated cases are to be filed in the county in which the offense is alleged to have occurred. Other than a change of venue for the purpose of trial, a designated case may not be transferred to any other county, except, after conviction, a designated case may be transferred to the juvenile's county of residence for entry of a juvenile disposition only. Sentencing of a juvenile, including delayed imposition of sentence, may only be done in the county in which the offense occurred.

[Adopted February 4, 2003, effective May 1, 2003, 467 Mich. Amended September 18, 2019, effective January 1, 2020, 503 Mich.]

Comments

Staff Comment to 2003 Adoption

MCR 3.926 corresponds to former Rule 5.926.

Details are added to subrule (B) regarding the county to which a case may be transferred.

New subrule (E) covers the subject of bifurcating proceedings, allowing adjudication in one county and disposition in another. See MCL 712A.2(D). Language regarding transfer of records is included in subrule (F).

Staff Comment to 2020 Amendment

The amendments of MCR 1.109, 2.107, 2.113, 2.116, 2.119, 2.222, 2.223, 2.225, 2.227, 3.206, 3.211, 3.212, 3.214, 3.303, 3.903, 3.921, 3.925, 3.926, 3.931, 3.933, 3.942, 3.950, 3.961, 3.971, 3.972, 4.002, 4.101, 4.201, 4.202, 4.302, 5.128, 5.302, 5.731, 6.101, 6.615, 8.105, and 8.119 and rescission of MCR 2.226 and 8.125 continue the process for design and implementation of the statewide electronic-filing system.

Rule 3.927   Prior Court Orders

In a juvenile proceeding involving a minor who is subject to a prior order of another Michigan court, the manner of notice to the other court and the authority of the family division of the circuit court to proceed are governed by MCR 3.205.

[Adopted February 4, 2003, effective May 1, 2003, 467 Mich.]

Comments

Staff Comment to 2003 Adoption

MCR 3.927 corresponds to former Rule 5.927.

Rule 3.928   Contempt of Court

(A) Power. The court has the authority to hold persons in contempt of court as provided by MCL 600.1701 and 712A.26. A parent, guardian, or legal custodian of a juvenile who is within the court's jurisdiction and who fails to attend a hearing as required is subject to the contempt power as provided in MCL 712A.6a.

(B) Procedure. Contempt of court proceedings are governed by MCL 600.1711, 600.1715, and MCR 3.606. MCR 3.982–3.989 govern proceedings against a minor for contempt of a minor personal protection order.

(C) Contempt by Juvenile. A juvenile under court jurisdiction who is convicted of criminal contempt of court, and who was at least 17 years of age when the contempt was committed, may be sentenced to up to 93 days in the county jail as a disposition for the contempt. Juveniles sentenced under this subrule need not be lodged separately and apart from adult prisoners. Younger juveniles found in contempt of court are subject to a juvenile disposition under these rules.

(D) Determination of Ability to Pay. A juvenile and/or parent shall not be detained or incarcerated for the nonpayment of court-ordered financial obligations as ordered by the court, unless the court determines that the juvenile and/or parent has the resources to pay and has not made a good-faith effort to do so.

[Adopted February 4, 2003, effective May 1, 2003, 467 Mich. Amended effective May 6, 2008, 480 Mich. Amended May 25, 2016, effective September 1, 2016, 499 Mich.]

Comments

Staff Comment to 2003 Adoption

MCR 3.928 corresponds to former Rule 5.928. The rule is largely rewritten, and incorporates additional statutory (MCL 600.1701 *et seq.*) and court rule (MCR 3.606, 3.982–3.989) provisions. New subrule (C) covers contempt by the juvenile.

Staff Comment to 2008 Amendment

This amendment changes the current maximum penalty from 30 days in jail for contempt to 93 days in jail for contempt of court to conform to MCL 600.1715.

Staff Comment to 2016 Amendment

The amendments of MCR 3.605, 3.606, 3.928, 3.944, 3.956, 6.001, 6.425, 6.445, 6.610, and 6.933 were submitted by the Michigan State Planning Body for the Delivery of Legal Services to the Poor. The rule revisions are intended to provide clarity and guidance to courts regarding what courts would be required to do before incarcerating a defendant for failure to pay.

Rule 3.929   Use of Facsimile Communication Equipment

The parties may file records, as defined in MCR 3.903(A)(25), by the use of facsimile communication equipment. Filing of records by the use of facsimile communication equipment in juvenile proceedings is governed by MCR 2.406.

[Adopted October 3, 2006, effective January 1, 2007, 477 Mich. Amended effective September 28, 2011, 490 Mich.]

Comments

Staff Comment to 2007 Adoption

New Rule 3.929 states that filing records by facsimile communication equipment is allowed in juvenile proceedings. MCR 3.903(A)(24) defines the term "records," and MCR 2.406 governs the filing of records by facsimile communication equipment.

Staff Comment to 2011 Amendment

The above noted changes are minor revisions of the rules that have been recommended to the Court to correct cross references and to reflect other technical changes.

Rule 3.930   Receipt and Return or Disposal of Exhibits in Juvenile Proceedings

(A) Receipt of Exhibits. Except as otherwise required by statute or court rule, materials that are intended to be used as evidence at or during a trial shall not be filed with the clerk of the court, but shall be submitted to the judge for introduction into evidence as exhibits. Exhibits introduced into evidence at or during court proceedings shall be received and maintained as provided by the Michigan Supreme Court trial court case file management standards. As defined in MCR 1.109, exhibits received and accepted into evidence under this rule are not court records.

(B) Return or Disposal of Exhibits. At the conclusion of a trial or hearing, the court shall direct the parties to retrieve the exhibits submitted by them except that any weapons and drugs shall be returned to the confiscating agency for proper disposition. If the exhibits are not retrieved by the parties as directed within 56 days after conclusion of the trial or hearing, the court may properly dispose of the exhibits without notice to the parties.

(C) Confidentiality. If the court retains discovery materials filed pursuant to MCR 1.109(D) or an exhibit submitted pursuant to this rule after a hearing or trial and the material is confidential as provided by MCR 3.903(A)(3) or order of the court pursuant to MCR 8.119(I), the court must continue to maintain the material in a confidential manner.

[Adopted September 30, 2008, effective January 1, 2009, 482 Mich. Amended October 31, 2012, effective January 1, 2013, 493 Mich; August 30, 2018, effective September 1, 2018, 502 Mich.]

Comments

Staff Comment to 2008 Adoption

These amendments allow the court to return or destroy exhibits within 56 days of the completion of the trial or hearing in a juvenile proceeding. In addition, the court must maintain confidential documents that are admitted as exhibits in accordance with MCR 3.903(A)(3).

Staff Comment to 2013 Amendment

The amendments of these rules update the rules making them less "paper" focused and reflecting the use of electronic technology in the way courts process court records. The amendments also clarify and delineate the types of records and other materials maintained by a court, and clarify how access is provided.

Staff Comment to 2018 Amendment

These amendments update cross-references in the rules, and are intended to reflect changes that are necessary as a result of the Court's recent e-Filing rules amendments.

Rule 3.931.   Initiating Delinquency Proceedings

(A) Commencement of Proceeding. Any request for court action against a juvenile must be by written petition. The form, captioning, signing, and verifying of documents are prescribed in MCR 1.109(D) and (E). When any pending or resolved family division case exists that involves family members of the person(s) named in the petition filed under subrule (B), the petitioner must complete and file a case inventory listing those cases, if known. The case inventory is confidential, not subject to service requirements in MCR 3.203, and is available only to the party that filed it, the filing party's attorney, the court, and the friend of the court. The case inventory must be on a form approved by the State Court Administrative Office.

(B) Content of Petition. A petition must contain the following information:

(1) the juvenile's name, address, and date of birth, if known;

(2) the names and addresses, if known, of

  (a) the juvenile's mother and father,

  (b) the guardian, legal custodian, or person having custody of the juvenile, if other than a mother or father,

  (c) the nearest known relative of the juvenile, if no parent, guardian, or legal custodian can be found, and

  (d) the juvenile's membership or eligibility for membership in an Indian tribe, if any, and the identity of the tribe.

(3) sufficient allegations that, if true, would constitute an offense by the juvenile;

(4) a citation to the section of the Juvenile Code relied upon for jurisdiction;

(5) a citation to the federal, state, or local law or ordinance allegedly violated by the juvenile;

(6) the court action requested; and

(7) if applicable, the notice required by MCL 257.732(8), and the juvenile's Michigan driver's license number.

(C) Citation or Appearance Ticket.

(1) A citation or appearance ticket may be used to initiate a delinquency proceeding if the charges against the juvenile are limited to violations of the Michigan Vehicle Code, or of a provision of an ordinance substantially corresponding to any provision of that law, as provided by MCL 712A.2b.

(2) The citation or appearance ticket shall be treated by the court as if it were a petition, except that it may not serve as a basis for pretrial detention.

(D) Motor Vehicle Violations; Failure to Appear. If the juvenile is a Michigan resident and fails to appear or otherwise to respond to any matter pending relative to a motor vehicle violation, the court

(1) must initiate the procedure required by MCL 257.321a for the failure to answer a citation, and

(2) may issue an order to apprehend the juvenile after a petition is filed with the court.

[Adopted February 4, 2003, effective May 1, 2003, 467 Mich. Amended February 2, 2010, effective May 1, 2010, 485 Mich. Amended effective August 24, 2012, 492 Mich. Amended May 30, 2018, effective September 1, 2018, 501 Mich. Amended effective September 11, 2019. Amended September 18, 2019, effective January 1, 2020, 503 Mich.]

Comments

Staff Comment to 2003 Adoption

MCR 3.931 corresponds to former Rule 5.931. Subrule (C), covering use of a citation or appearance ticket, is rewritten to be more consistent with the governing statutes. MCL 712A.12b, 764.9c.

Staff Comment to 2010 Amendment

These amendments incorporate provisions of the Indian Child Welfare Act into specific provisions within various rules relating to child protective proceedings and juvenile status offenses. The language is designed to make the rules reflect a more integrated approach to addressing issues specific to Indian children.

MCR 3.002(1)(c) defines "preadoptive placement" to mean the "temporary placement of an Indian child in a foster home or institution after the termination of parental rights, but before or in lieu of adoptive placement, and . . ." The phrase "in lieu of adoptive placement" is not intended to mean that it is permissible to leave a child in foster care indefinitely, in violation of MCL 712A.19b(6) or (7) or 45 CFR 1355.20, 45 CFR 1356.21, or 45 CFR 1356.50. Rather, it addresses situations where the parental rights to a child have been terminated and there is no permanency plan for adoption of the child. One example is when the child has been placed with a juvenile guardian and the guardianship is subsequently revoked. In this situation, jurisdiction over the child pursuant to MCL 712A.2(b) will be reinstated and the child is placed in foster care.

MCR 3.002(1): The definition of "child custody proceeding" is intended to apply the Indian Child Welfare Act to delinquency proceedings if an "Indian child" is charged with a so-called status offense in violation of MCL 712A.2(a)(2)–(4) or (d). Delinquency proceedings involving an Indian child charged with any other non-status offense are generally not subject to the Indian Child Welfare Act; however, if the initial investigation or subsequent review of a non-status delinquency case reveals that the Indian child involved suffers from child abuse or neglect, a separate child protective proceeding may be initiated, which would be subject to the Indian Child Welfare Act.

The amendment of MCR 3.905(C)(1) states that a court shall consider guidelines established by the Bureau of Indian Affairs (BIA) in determining whether good cause not to transfer exists (Guidelines for State Courts; Indian Child Custody Proceedings, 44 Fed Reg No 228, 67590–67592, C.2–C.4. [November 26, 1979]). Some examples of good cause are that the Indian tribe does not have a tribal court or that the Indian child is over 12 years old and objects to the transfer. For additional examples of good cause and relevant case law, see the BIA guidelines cited above and A Practical Guide to the Indian Child Welfare Act. (Native American Rights Fund, A Practical Guide to the Indian Child Welfare Act [Boulder, CO: Native American Rights Fund, 2007], 7.15 and 7.16, p 60.)

Staff Comment to 2012 Amendment

These amendments reflect changes to correct minor technical errors that have occurred in drafting or to respond to recent adopted rule revisions, which occasionally inadvertently create incorrect cross-references in other rules.

Staff Comment to 2018 Amendment

The amendments in this order are intended to begin moving trial courts toward a statewide uniform e-Filing process. In addition, the order moves existing language into MCR 1.109 as a way to, for the first time, include most filing requirements in one single rule, instead of scattered in various rules. The order largely mirrors the administrative orders that most e-Filing pilot projects have operated under, but contains some significant new provisions. For example, courts are required to maintain documents in an electronic document management system, and the electronic record is the official court record.

Staff Comment to 2019 Amendment

The amendments of MCR 1.109, 3.206, 3.931, and 3.961 enable family division courts to use the required case inventory form to administer cases while keeping the information confidential. This change is intended to prevent providing information that could affect the safety of domestic violence victims and their children.

Staff Comment to 2020 Amendment

The amendments of MCR 1.109, 2.107, 2.113, 2.116, 2.119, 2.222, 2.223, 2.225, 2.227, 3.206, 3.211, 3.212, 3.214, 3.303, 3.903, 3.921, 3.925, 3.926, 3.931, 3.933, 3.942, 3.950, 3.961, 3.971, 3.972, 4.002, 4.101, 4.201, 4.202, 4.302, 5.128, 5.302, 5.731, 6.101, 6.615, 8.105, and 8.119 and rescission of MCR 2.226 and 8.125 continue the process for design and implementation of the statewide electronic-filing system.

Rule 3.932   Summary Initial Proceedings

(A) Preliminary Inquiry. When a petition is not accompanied by a request for detention of the juvenile, the court may conduct a preliminary inquiry. Except in cases involving offenses enumerated in the Crime Victim's Rights Act, MCL 780.781(1)(g), the preliminary inquiry need not be conducted on the record. The court may, in the interest of the juvenile and the public:

(1) deny authorization of the petition;

(2) refer the matter to a public or private agency providing available services pursuant to the Juvenile Diversion Act, MCL 722.821 *et seq.*;

(3) direct that the juvenile and the parent, guardian, or legal custodian be notified to appear for further informal inquiry on the petition;

(4) proceed on the consent calendar as provided in subrule (C); or

(5) place the matter on the formal calendar as provided in subrule (D).

(B) Offenses Listed in the Crime Victim's Rights Act. A case involving the alleged commission of an offense listed in the Crime Victim's Rights Act, MCL 780.781(1)(g), may only be removed from the adjudicative process upon compliance with the procedures set forth in that act. See MCL 780.786b.

(C) Consent Calendar.

(1) If the court determines that formal jurisdiction should not be acquired over the juvenile, the court may proceed with the case on the consent calendar. A case transferred to the consent calendar shall be transferred before disposition but may occur any time after receiving a petition, citation, or appearance ticket. Upon transfer, the clerk of the court shall make the case nonpublic.

(2) A case shall not be placed on the consent calendar unless the juvenile and the parent, guardian, or legal custodian and the prosecutor, agree to have the case placed on the consent calendar. A case involving the alleged commission of an offense as that term is defined in section 31 of the Crime Victim's Rights Act, MCL 780.781 et seq., shall only be placed on the consent calendar upon compliance with procedures set forth in MCL 780.786b.

(3) *Biometric Data.* Except as otherwise required by law, a juvenile shall not have biometric data collected unless the court has authorized the petition. If the court authorizes the petition and the juvenile is alleged to have committed an offense that requires the juvenile to have biometric data collected according to law, the court shall ensure the juvenile has biometric data collected before placing the case on consent calendar under subrule (C)(1).

(4) *Victim Notice.* After a case is placed on consent calendar, the prosecutor shall provide the victim notice as required by article 2 of the Crime Victim's Rights act, MCL 780.781 to 780.802.

(5) *Conference.* After placing a matter on the consent calendar, the court shall conduct a consent calendar case conference with the juvenile, the juvenile's attorney, if any, and the juvenile's parent, guardian, or legal custodian. The prosecutor and victim may, but need not, be present. At the conference, the court shall discuss the allegations with the juvenile and issue a written consent calendar case plan in accordance with MCL 712A.2f(7).

(6) *Case Plan.* The case plan is not an order of the court, but shall be included as part of the case record. If the court

determines the juvenile has violated the terms of the case plan, it may transfer the case to the formal calendar in accordance with subrule (C)(9).

(7) *Disposition.* The court shall not enter an order of disposition in a case while it is on the consent calendar.

(8) *Access to Consent Calendar Case Records.* Records of consent calendar proceedings shall be nonpublic. Access to consent calendar case records is governed by MCL 712A.2f(5).

(9) *Transfer to Formal Calendar.* If it appears to the court at any time that proceeding on the consent calendar is not in the best interest of either the juvenile or the public, the court may transfer the case from the consent calendar to the formal calendar. The court shall proceed with the case where court proceedings left off before the case was placed on the consent calendar.

(a) If the original petition was not authorized before being placed on the consent calendar, the court may, without hearing, transfer the case from the consent calendar to the formal calendar on the charges contained in the original petition to determine whether the petition should be authorized.

(b) If the original petition was authorized before being placed on the consent calendar, the court shall conduct a hearing on the record before transferring the case to the formal calendar. At the hearing, the court shall:

(i) Advise the juvenile that any statements made during the consent calendar proceedings cannot be used against the juvenile at a trial on the same charge.

(ii) Allow the juvenile and the juvenile's attorney, if any, the opportunity to address the court and state on the record why the case should not be transferred to the formal calendar.

(10) *Closing the Case.* Upon a judicial determination that the juvenile has completed the terms of the consent calendar case plan, the court shall report the successful completion to the juvenile and the Department of State Police. The report to the Department of State police shall be in a form prescribed by the Department of State Police.

(11) *Record Retention.* The case records shall only be destroyed in accordance with the approved record retention and disposal schedule established by the State Court Administrative Office.

(D) Formal Calendar. The court may authorize a petition to be filed and docketed on the formal calendar if it appears to the court that formal court action is in the best interest of the juvenile and the public. The court shall not authorize an original petition under MCL 712A.2(a)(1), unless the prosecuting attorney has approved submitting the petition to the court. At any time before disposition, the court may transfer the matter to the consent calendar.

[Adopted February 4, 2003, effective May 1, 2003, 467 Mich. Amended October 13, 2009, effective May 1, 2010, 485 Mich; May 22, 2013, effective September 1, 2013, 494 Mich. Amended effective September 5, 2013, 495 Mich. Amended May 24, 2017, effective September 1, 2017, 500 Mich. Amended effective August 14, 2019, 503 Mich.]

Comments

Staff Comment to 2003 Adoption

MCR 3.932 corresponds to former Rule 5.932.

Several provisions are modified in recognition of the requirements of the Crime Victim's Rights Act, MCL 780.751 *et seq.*

The provisions governing proceedings on the consent calendar are substantially rewritten. See subrule (C).

Staff Comment to 2009 Amendment

The amendment of MCR 3.932 requires a court to enter a plea for violations of the Michigan Vehicle Code, and requires a court to report to the Secretary of State violations of the Michigan Vehicle Code that are handled on the court's consent calendar.

Staff Comment to September 1, 2013 Amendment

The amendments require the prosecutor's consent to placing a juvenile on the consent calendar and prohibit the court from considering on the consent calendar an offense that includes an "assaultive crime" as defined in the Juvenile Diversion Act.

Staff Comment to September 5, 2013 Amendment

These amendments reflect changes that correct minor technical errors that have occurred in drafting or the changes respond to recent adopted rule revisions, which occasionally inadvertently create incorrect cross-references in other rules.

Staff Comment to 2017 Amendment

The amendments of MCR 3.903, 3.932, and 3.936 clarify the procedures used for consent calendar proceedings in juvenile delinquency cases, consistent with the recent enactment of 2016 PA 185.

Staff Comment to 2019 Amendment

These amendments update cross-references and make other nonsubstantive revisions to clarify the rules.

Rule 3.933   Acquiring Physical Control of Juvenile

(A) Custody Without Court Order. When an officer apprehends a juvenile for an offense without a court order and does not warn and release the juvenile, does not refer the juvenile to a diversion program, and does not have authorization from the prosecuting attorney to file a complaint and warrant charging the juvenile with an offense as though an adult pursuant to MCL 764.1f, the officer may:

(1) issue a citation or ticket to appear at a date and time to be set by the court and release the juvenile;

(2) accept a written promise of the parent, guardian, or legal custodian to bring the juvenile to court, if requested, at a date and time to be set by the court, and release the juvenile to the parent, guardian, or legal custodian; or

(3) take the juvenile into custody and request the prosecutor to file a petition, if:

(a) the officer has reason to believe that because of the nature of the offense, the interest of the juvenile or the interest of the public would not be protected by release of the juvenile, or

(b) a parent, guardian, or legal custodian cannot be located or has refused to take custody of the juvenile.

(B) Custody With Court Order. When a petition is presented to the court, and probable cause exists to believe that a juvenile has committed an offense, the court may issue an order to apprehend the juvenile. The order may include authorization to

(1) enter specified premises as required to bring the juvenile before the court, and

(2) detain the juvenile pending preliminary hearing.

(C) Notification of Court. The officer who apprehends a juvenile must immediately contact the court when:

(1) the officer detains the juvenile,

(2) the officer is unable to reach a parent, guardian, or legal custodian who will appear promptly to accept custody of the juvenile, or

(3) the parent, guardian, or legal custodian will not agree to bring the juvenile to court as provided in subrule (A)(2).

(D) Separate Custody of Juvenile. While awaiting arrival of the parent, guardian, or legal custodian, appearance before the court, or otherwise, the juvenile must be maintained separately from adult prisoners to prevent any verbal, visual, or physical contact with an adult prisoner.

[Adopted February 4, 2003, effective May 1, 2003, 467 Mich. Amended September 18, 2019, effective January 1, 2020, 503 Mich.]

Comments

Staff Comment to 2003 Adoption

MCR 3.933 corresponds to former Rule 5.933.

Staff Comment to 2020 Amendment

The amendments of MCR 1.109, 2.107, 2.113, 2.116, 2.119, 2.222, 2.223, 2.225, 2.227, 3.206, 3.211, 3.212, 3.214, 3.303, 3.903, 3.921, 3.925, 3.926, 3.931, 3.933, 3.942, 3.950, 3.961, 3.971, 3.972, 4.002, 4.101, 4.201, 4.202, 4.302, 5.128, 5.302, 5.731, 6.101, 6.615, 8.105, and 8.119 and rescission of MCR 2.226 and 8.125 continue the process for design and implementation of the statewide electronic-filing system.

Rule 3.934　Arranging Court Appearance; Detained Juvenile

(A) General. Unless the prosecuting attorney has authorized a complaint and warrant charging the juvenile with an offense as though an adult pursuant to MCL 764.1f, when a juvenile is apprehended and not released, the officer shall:

(1) forthwith take the juvenile

(a) before the court for a preliminary hearing, or

(b) to a place designated by the court pending the scheduling of a preliminary hearing;

(2) ensure that the petition is prepared and presented to the court;

(3) notify the parent, guardian, or legal custodian of the detaining of the juvenile and of the need for the presence of the parent, guardian, or legal custodian at the preliminary hearing;

(4) prepare a custody statement for submission to the court including:

(a) the grounds for and the time and location of detention, and

(b) the names of persons notified and the times of notification, or the reason for failure to notify.

(B) Temporary Detention; Court Not Open.

(1) *Grounds.* A juvenile apprehended without court order when the court is not open may be detained pending preliminary hearing if the offense or the juvenile meets a circumstance set forth in MCR 3.935(D)(1), or if no parent, guardian, or legal custodian can be located.

(2) *Designated Court Person.* The court must designate a judge, referee, or other person who may be contacted by the officer taking a juvenile into custody when the court is not open. In each county there must be a designated facility open at all times at which an officer may obtain the name of the person to be contacted for permission to detain the juvenile pending preliminary hearing.

[Adopted February 4, 2003, effective May 1, 2003, 467 Mich.]

Comments

Staff Comment to 2003 Adoption

MCR 3.934 corresponds to former Rule 5.934.

Rule 3.935　Preliminary Hearing

(A) Time.

(1) *Commencement.* The preliminary hearing must commence no later than 24 hours after the juvenile has been taken into court custody, excluding Sundays and holidays, as defined by MCR 8.110(D)(2), or the juvenile must be released.

(2) *General Adjournment.* The court may adjourn the hearing for up to 14 days:

(a) to secure the attendance of the juvenile's parent, guardian, or legal custodian or of a witness, or

(b) for other good cause shown.

(3) *Special Adjournment; Specified Juvenile Violation.* This subrule applies to a juvenile accused of an offense that allegedly was committed between the juvenile's 14th and 17th birthdays and that would constitute a specified juvenile violation listed in MCL 712A.2(a)(1).

(a) On a request of a prosecuting attorney who has approved the submission of a petition with the court, conditioned on the opportunity to withdraw it within 5 days if the prosecuting attorney authorizes the filing of a complaint and warrant with a magistrate, the court shall comply with subrules (i)–(iii).

(i) The court shall adjourn the preliminary hearing for up to 5 days to give the prosecuting attorney the opportunity to determine whether to authorize the filing of a criminal complaint and warrant charging the juvenile with an offense as though an adult pursuant to MCL 764.1f, instead of unconditionally approving the filing of a petition with the court.

(ii) The court, during the special adjournment under subrule 3(a), must defer a decision regarding whether to authorize the filing of the petition.

(iii) The court, during the special adjournment under subrule (3)(a), must release the juvenile pursuant to MCR 3.935(E) or detain the juvenile pursuant to MCR 3.935(D).

(b) If, at the resumption of the preliminary hearing following special adjournment, the prosecuting attorney has not authorized the filing with a magistrate of a criminal complaint and warrant on the charge concerning the juvenile, approval of the petition by the prosecuting attorney shall no longer be deemed conditional and the court shall proceed with the preliminary hearing and decide whether to authorize the petition to be filed.

(c) This rule does not preclude the prosecuting attorney from moving for a waiver of jurisdiction over the juvenile under MCR 3.950.

(B) Procedure.

(1) The court shall determine whether the parent, guardian, or legal custodian has been notified and is present. The preliminary hearing may be conducted without a parent, guardian, or legal custodian present, provided a guardian ad litem or attorney appears with the juvenile.

(2) The court shall read the allegations in the petition.

(3) The court shall determine whether the petition should be dismissed, whether the matter should be referred to alternate services pursuant to the Juvenile Diversion Act, MCL 722.821 *et seq.*, whether the matter should be heard on the consent calendar as provided by MCR 3.932(C), or whether to continue the preliminary hearing.

(4) If the hearing is to continue, the court shall advise the juvenile on the record in plain language of:

(a) the right to an attorney pursuant to MCR 3.915(A)(1);

(b) the right to trial by judge or jury on the allegations in the petition and that a referee may be assigned to hear the case unless demand for a jury or judge is filed pursuant to MCR 3.911 or 3.912; and

(c) the privilege against self-incrimination and that any statement by the juvenile may be used against the juvenile.

(5) If the charge is a status offense in violation of MCL 712A.2(a)(2)–(4) or (d), the court must inquire if the juvenile or a parent is a member of an Indian tribe. If the court knows or has reason to know the child is an Indian child, the court must determine the identity of the tribe and comply with MCR 3.905 before proceeding with the hearing.

(6) The juvenile must be allowed an opportunity to deny or otherwise plead to the allegations.

(7) Unless the preliminary hearing is adjourned, the court must decide whether to authorize the petition to be filed pursuant to MCR 3.932(D). If it authorizes the filing of the petition, the court must:

(a) determine if biometric data must be taken as provided by MCL 712A.11(5) and MCR 3.936; and

(b) determine if the juvenile should be released, with or without conditions, or detained, as provided in subrules (C)–(F).

(8) The juvenile may be detained pending the completion of the preliminary hearing if the conditions for detention under subrule (D) are established.

(C) Determination Whether to Release or Detain.

(1) *Factors.* In determining whether the juvenile is to be released, with or without conditions, or detained, the court shall consider the following factors:

(a) the juvenile's family ties and relationships,

(b) the juvenile's prior delinquency record,

(c) the juvenile's record of appearance or nonappearance at court proceedings,

(d) the violent nature of the alleged offense,

(e) the juvenile's prior history of committing acts that resulted in bodily injury to others,

(f) the juvenile's character and mental condition,

(g) the court's ability to supervise the juvenile if placed with a parent or relative, and

(h) any other factor indicating the juvenile's ties to the community, the risk of nonappearance, and the danger to the juvenile or the public if the juvenile is released.

(2) *Findings.* The court must state the reasons for its decision to grant or deny release on the record or in a written memorandum. The court's statement need not include a finding on each of the enumerated factors.

(D) Detention.

(1) *Conditions for Detention.* A juvenile may be ordered detained or continued in detention if the court finds probable cause to believe the juvenile committed the offense, and that one or more of the following circumstances are present:

(a) the offense alleged is so serious that release would endanger the public safety;

(b) the juvenile is charged with an offense that would be a felony if committed by an adult and will likely commit another offense pending trial, if released, and

(i) another petition is pending against the juvenile,

(ii) the juvenile is on probation, or

(iii) the juvenile has a prior adjudication, but is not under the court's jurisdiction at the time of apprehension;

(c) there is a substantial likelihood that if the juvenile is released to the parent, guardian, or legal custodian, with or without conditions, the juvenile will fail to appear at the next court proceeding;

(d) the home conditions of the juvenile make detention necessary;

(e) the juvenile has run away from home;

(f) the juvenile has failed to remain in a detention facility or nonsecure facility or placement in violation of a valid court order; or

(g) pretrial detention is otherwise specifically authorized by law.

(2) *Waiver.* A juvenile may waive the probable cause determination required by subrule (1) only if the juvenile is represented by an attorney.

(3) *Evidence; Findings.* The juvenile may contest the sufficiency of evidence by cross-examination of witnesses, presentation of defense witnesses, or by other evidence. The court shall permit the use of subpoena power to secure attendance of defense witnesses. The Michigan Rules of Evidence do not apply, other than those with respect to privileges.

(4) *Type of Detention.* The detained juvenile must be placed in the least restrictive environment that will meet the needs of the juvenile and the public, and that will conform to the requirements of MCL 712A.15 and 712A.16.

(E) Release; Conditions.

(1) The court may release a juvenile to a parent pending the resumption of the preliminary hearing, pending trial, or until further order without conditions, or, if the court determines that release with conditions is necessary to reasonably ensure the appearance of the juvenile as required or to reasonably ensure the safety of the public, the court may, in its discretion, order that the release of the juvenile be on the condition or combination of conditions that the court determines to be appropriate, including, but not limited to:

(a) that the juvenile will not commit any offense while released,

(b) that the juvenile will not use alcohol or any controlled substance or tobacco product,

(c) that the juvenile will participate in a substance abuse assessment, testing, or treatment program,

(d) that the juvenile will participate in a treatment program for a physical or mental condition,

(e) that the juvenile will comply with restrictions on personal associations or place of residence,

(f) that the juvenile will comply with a specified curfew,

(g) that the juvenile will maintain appropriate behavior and attendance at an educational program, and

(h) that the juvenile's driver's license or passport will be surrendered.

(2) *Violation of Conditions of Release.* If a juvenile is alleged to have violated the conditions set by the court, the court may order the juvenile apprehended and detained immediately. The court may then modify the conditions or revoke the juvenile's release status after providing the juvenile an opportunity to be heard on the issue of the violation of conditions of release.

(F) Bail. In addition to any other conditions of release, the court may require a parent, guardian, or legal custodian to post bail.

(1) *Cash or Surety Bond.* The court may require a parent, guardian, or legal custodian to post a surety bond or cash in the full amount of the bail, at the option of the parent, guardian, or legal custodian. A surety bond must be written by a person or company licensed to write surety bonds in Michigan. Except as otherwise provided by this rule, MCR 3.604 applies to bonds posted under this rule.

(2) *Option to Deposit Cash or 10 Percent of Bail.* Unless the court requires a surety bond or cash in the full amount of the bail as provided in subrule (F)(1), the court shall advise the parent, guardian, or legal custodian of the option to satisfy the monetary requirement of bail by:

(a) posting either cash or a surety bond in the full amount of bail set by the court or a surety bond written by a person or company licensed to write surety bonds in Michigan, or

(b) depositing with the register, clerk, or cashier of the court currency equal to 10 percent of the bail, but at least $10.

(3) *Revocation or Modification.* The court may modify or revoke the bail for good cause after providing the parties notice and an opportunity to be heard.

(4) *Return of Bail.* If the conditions of bail are met, the court shall discharge any surety.

(a) If disposition imposes reimbursement or costs, the bail money posted by the parent must first be applied to the amount of reimbursement and costs, and the balance, if any, returned.

(b) If the juvenile is discharged from all obligations in the case, the court shall return the cash posted, or return 90 percent and retain 10 percent if the amount posted represented 10 percent of the bail.

(5) *Forfeiture.* If the conditions of bail are not met, the court may issue a writ for the apprehension of the juvenile and enter an order declaring the bail money, if any, forfeited.

(a) The court must immediately mail notice of the forfeiture order to the parent at the last known address and to any surety.

(b) If the juvenile does not appear and surrender to the court within 28 days from the forfeiture date, or does not within the period satisfy the court that the juvenile is not at fault, the court may enter judgment against the parent and surety, if any, for the entire amount of the bail and, when allowed, costs of the court proceedings.

[Adopted February 4, 2003, effective May 1, 2003, 467 Mich. Amended April 30, 2003, effective May 1, 2003, 467 Mich; February 2, 2010, effective May 1, 2010, 485 Mich. Amended effective March 20, 2013, 493 Mich; August 14, 2019, 503 Mich.]

Comments

Staff Comment to 2003 Adoption

MCR 3.935 corresponds to former Rule 5.935.

The changes in subrules (A) and (B) are in terminology and organization.

The provisions on pretrial detention and release are substantially rewritten. See subrules (C)–(F). A new list of conditions that may be imposed on release are included in subrule (E)(1).

Staff Comment to 2003 Amendment

The April 30, 2003, order makes corrections to a number of the rules governing proceedings regarding juveniles that had been adopted on February 4, 2003. The changes are effective May 1, corresponding to the effective date of the February 4 amendments. In addition to these changes, a number of corrections of punctuation and capitalization and changes in the Notes that accompanied the rules have been made and will appear in the published version of the rules.

The amendments of MCR 3.903(D)(8)(m), 6.903(H)(16), 6.931(E)(3), and 6.933(C)(1) conform the rules to 2002 PA 665, which changed the amounts of controlled substances required for certain violations. See MCL 333.7401(2)(a)(i), 333.7403(2)(a)(i). MCR 3.933(C)(1) is also modified in light of *People v Valentin*, 457 Mich 1 (1998).

The amendment of MCR 3.935(B)(1) corrects the inadvertent omission of references to guardians and legal custodians.

The amendments of MCR 3.922(E)(1)(c), 3.943(A), 3.945(A)(1), 3.965(E)(1), and 3.972(C)(2)(c) correct minor errors in wording.

The amendment of MCR 3.977(G) deletes the word "hearing" in the reference to progress reviews. Under MCR 3.974(A)(1), progress reviews do not require hearings.

The amendment of MCR 3.980(B) and (C) revise the provisions on removal of American Indian children from the home to clarify the distinction between emergency removals and removals after hearing.

The amendments of MCR 3.982(A), 6.903(I)–(L) and 6.937(A) correct cross-reference, citation and numbering errors.

Staff Comment to 2010 Amendment

These amendments incorporate provisions of the Indian Child Welfare Act into specific provisions within various rules relating to child protective proceedings and juvenile status offenses. The language is designed to make the rules reflect a more integrated approach to addressing issues specific to Indian children.

MCR 3.002(1)(c) defines "preadoptive placement" to mean the "temporary placement of an Indian child in a foster home or institution after the termination of parental rights, but before or in lieu of adoptive placement, and …" The phrase "in lieu of adoptive placement" is not intended to mean that it is permissible to leave a child in foster care indefinitely, in violation of MCL 712A.19b(6) or (7) or 45 CFR 1355.20, 45 CFR 1356.21, or 45 CFR 1356.50. Rather, it addresses situations where the parental rights to a child have been terminated and there is no permanency plan for adoption of the child. One example is when the child has been placed with a juvenile guardian and the guardianship is subsequently revoked. In this situation, jurisdiction over the child pursuant to MCL 712A.2(b) will be reinstated and the child is placed in foster care.

MCR 3.002(1): The definition of "child custody proceeding" is intended to apply the Indian Child Welfare Act to delinquency proceedings if an "Indian child" is charged with a so-called status offense in violation of MCL 712A.2(a)(2)–(4) or (d). Delinquency proceedings involving an Indian child charged with any other non-status offense are generally not subject to the Indian Child Welfare Act; however, if the initial investigation or subsequent review of a non-status delinquency case reveals that the Indian child involved suffers from child abuse or neglect, a separate child protective proceeding may be initiated, which would be subject to the Indian Child Welfare Act.

The amendment of MCR 3.905(C)(1) states that a court shall consider guidelines established by the Bureau of Indian Affairs (BIA) in determining whether good cause not to transfer exists (Guidelines for State Courts; Indian

Child Custody Proceedings, 44 Fed Reg No 228, 67590–67592, C.2–C.4. [November 26, 1979]). Some examples of good cause are that the Indian tribe does not have a tribal court or that the Indian child is over 12 years old and objects to the transfer. For additional examples of good cause and relevant case law, see the BIA guidelines cited above and A Practical Guide to the Indian Child Welfare Act. (Native American Rights Fund, A Practical Guide to the Indian Child Welfare Act [Boulder, CO: Native American Rights Fund, 2007], 7.15 and 7.16, p 60.)

Staff Comment to 2013 Amendment

This proposal incorporates provisions of the newly enacted Michigan Indian Family Preservation Act into specific provisions within various rules relating to child protective proceedings and juvenile status offenses.

Staff Comment to 2019 Amendment

These amendments update cross-references and make other nonsubstantive revisions to clarify the rules.

Rule 3.936. Biometric Data

(A) **General.** The court must permit the collection of biometric data of a juvenile pursuant to MCL 712A.11(5) and 712A.18(10), and as provided in this rule. Notice of biometric data collection retained by the court is confidential.

(B) **Order for Biometric Data.** At the time that the court authorizes the filing of a petition alleging a juvenile offense and before the court enters an order of disposition on a juvenile offense or places the case on consent calendar, the court shall examine the confidential files and verify that the juvenile has had biometric data collected. If it appears to the court that the juvenile has not had biometric data collected, the court must:

(1) direct the juvenile to go to the law enforcement agency involved in the apprehension of the juvenile, or to the sheriff's department, so biometric data may be taken; or

(2) issue an order to the sheriff's department to apprehend the juvenile and to take the biometric data of the juvenile.

(C) **Notice of Disposition.** The court shall notify the Department of State Police in writing:

(1) of any juvenile who had had biometric data collected for a juvenile offense and who was found not to be within the jurisdiction of the court under MCL 712A.2(a)(1); or

(2) that the court took jurisdiction of a juvenile under MCL 712A.2(a)(1), who had biometric data collected for a juvenile offense, specifying the offense, the method of adjudication, and the disposition ordered.

(D) **Order for Destruction of Biometric Data.** The court, on motion filed pursuant to MCL 28.243(8), shall issue an order directing the Department of State Police, or other official holding the information, to destroy the biometric data and arrest card of the juvenile pertaining to the offense, other than an offense as listed in MCL 28.243(12), when a juvenile has had biometric data collected for a juvenile offense and no petition on the offense is submitted to the court, the court does not authorize the petition, or the court has neither placed the case on consent calendar nor taken jurisdiction of the juvenile under MCL 712A.2(a)(1).

[Adopted February 4, 2003, effective May 1, 2003, 467 Mich. Amended September 9, 2009, effective January 1, 2010, 485 Mich; May 24, 2017, effective September 1, 2017, 500 Mich. Amended effective August 14, 2019, 503 Mich.]

Comments

Staff Comment to 2003 Adoption

MCR 3.936 corresponds to former Rule 5.936. There are a few adjustments to conform to statutory changes made by 2001 PA 187, amending MCL 28.241 *et seq.*

Staff Comment to 2009 Amendment

The amendment of MCR 3.936 eliminates the reference to the return of juvenile fingerprints, and instead, requires the destruction of fingerprints, which more closely follows the statutory authority in MCL 28.243.

Staff Comment to 2017 Amendment

The amendments of MCR 3.903, 3.932, and 3.936 clarify the procedures used for consent calendar proceedings in juvenile delinquency cases, consistent with the recent enactment of 2016 PA 185.

Staff Comment to 2019 Amendment

These amendments update cross-references and make other nonsubstantive revisions to clarify the rules.

Rule 3.939   Case Transferred from District Court Pursuant to Subchapter 6.900

(A) **General Procedure.** Except as provided in subrule (B), the court shall hear and dispose of a case transferred pursuant to MCL 766.14 in the same manner as if the case had been commenced in the family division of circuit court. A petition that has been approved by the prosecuting attorney must be submitted to the court.

(B) **Probable Cause Finding of Magistrate.** The court may use the probable cause finding of the magistrate made at the preliminary examination to satisfy the probable cause requirement of MCR 3.935(D)(1).

[Adopted February 4, 2003, effective May 1, 2003, 467 Mich.]

Comments

Staff Comment to 2003 Adoption

MCR 3.939 corresponds to former Rule 5.939.

Rule 3.941   Pleas of Admission or No Contest

(A) **Capacity.** A juvenile may offer a plea of admission or of no contest to an offense with the consent of the court. The court shall not accept a plea to an offense unless the court is satisfied that the plea is accurate, voluntary, and understanding.

(B) **Conditional Pleas.** The court may accept a plea of admission or of no contest conditioned on preservation of an issue for appellate review.

(C) **Plea Procedure.** Before accepting a plea of admission or of no contest, the court must personally address the juvenile and must comply with subrules (1)–(4).

(1) *An Understanding Plea.* The court shall tell the juvenile:

(a) the name of the offense charged,

(b) the possible dispositions,

(c) that if the plea is accepted, the juvenile will not have a trial of any kind, so the juvenile gives up the rights that would be present at trial, including the right:

(i) to trial by jury,

(ii) to trial by the judge if the juvenile does not want trial by jury,

(iii) to be presumed innocent until proven guilty,

(iv) to have the petitioner or prosecutor prove guilt beyond a reasonable doubt,

(v) to have witnesses against the juvenile appear at the trial,

(vi) to question the witnesses against the juvenile,

(vii) to have the court order any witnesses for the juvenile's defense to appear at the trial,

(viii) to remain silent and not have that silence used against the juvenile, and

(ix) to testify at trial, if the juvenile wants to testify.

(2) *A Voluntary Plea.*

(a) The court shall confirm any plea agreement on the record.

(b) The court shall ask the juvenile if any promises have been made beyond those in a plea agreement or whether anyone has threatened the juvenile.

(3) *An Accurate Plea.* The court may not accept a plea of admission or of no contest without establishing support for a finding that the juvenile committed the offense:

(a) either by questioning the juvenile or by other means when the plea is a plea of admission, or

(b) by means other than questioning the juvenile when the juvenile pleads no contest. The court shall also state why a plea of no contest is appropriate.

(4) *Support for Plea.* The court shall inquire of the parent, guardian, legal custodian, or guardian ad litem, if present, whether there is any reason why the court should not accept the plea tendered by the juvenile.

(D) Plea Withdrawal. The court may take a plea of admission or of no contest under advisement. Before the court accepts the plea, the juvenile may withdraw the plea offer by right. After the court accepts the plea, the court has discretion to allow the juvenile to withdraw a plea.

[Adopted February 4, 2003, effective May 1, 2003, 467 Mich.]

Comments

Staff Comment to 2003 Adoption

MCR 3.941 corresponds to former Rule 5.941.

The language requiring that the parent's or guardian ad litem's agreement or objection to a plea be on the record is deleted from this rule, but is included in MCR 3.925(B).

Rule 3.942   Trial

(A) Time. In all cases the trial must be held within 6 months after the authorization of the petition, unless adjourned for good cause. If the juvenile is detained, the trial has not started within 63 days after the juvenile is taken into custody, and the delay in starting the trial is not attributable to the defense, the court must immediately order the juvenile released pending trial without requiring that bail be posted, unless the juvenile is being detained on another matter.

(B) Preliminary Matters.

(1) The court shall determine whether all parties are present.

(a) The juvenile has the right to be present at the trial with an attorney, parent, guardian, legal custodian, or guardian ad litem, if any.

(b) The court may proceed in the absence of a parent, guardian, or legal custodian who was properly notified to appear.

(c) The victim has the right to be present at trial as provided by MCL 780.789.

(2) The court shall read the allegations contained in the petition, unless waived.

(3) The court shall inform the juvenile of the right to the assistance of an attorney pursuant to MCR 3.915 unless an attorney appears representing the juvenile. If the juvenile requests to proceed without the assistance of an attorney, the court must advise the juvenile of the dangers and disadvantages of self-representation and make sure the juvenile is literate and competent to conduct the defense.

(C) Evidence; Standard of Proof. The Michigan Rules of Evidence and the standard of proof beyond a reasonable doubt apply at trial.

(D) Verdict. In a delinquency proceeding, the verdict must be guilty or not guilty of either the offense charged or a lesser included offense.

[Adopted February 4, 2003, effective May 1, 2003, 467 Mich. Amended September 18, 2019, effective January 1, 2020, 503 Mich.]

Comments

Staff Comment to 2003 Adoption

MCR 3.942 corresponds to former Rule 5.942.

New subrule (D) expressly provides that in a delinquency case, the verdict may be on the charged offense or a lesser included one.

Staff Comment to 2020 Amendment

The amendments of MCR 1.109, 2.107, 2.113, 2.116, 2.119, 2.222, 2.223, 2.225, 2.227, 3.206, 3.211, 3.212, 3.214, 3.303, 3.903, 3.921, 3.925, 3.926, 3.931, 3.933, 3.942, 3.950, 3.961, 3.971, 3.972, 4.002, 4.101, 4.201, 4.202, 4.302, 5.128, 5.302, 5.731, 6.101, 6.615, 8.105, and 8.119 and rescission of MCR 2.226 and 8.125 continue the process for design and implementation of the statewide electronic-filing system.

Rule 3.943   Dispositional Hearing

(A) General. A dispositional hearing is conducted to determine what measures the court will take with respect to a juvenile and, when applicable, any other person, once the court has determined following trial or plea that the juvenile has committed an offense.

(B) Time. The interval between the plea of admission or trial and disposition, if any, is within the court's discretion. When the juvenile is detained, the interval may not be more than 35 days, except for good cause.

(C) Evidence.

(1) The Michigan Rules of Evidence, other than those with respect to privileges, do not apply at dispositional hearings. All relevant and material evidence, including oral and written reports, may be received by the court and may be relied upon to the extent of its probative value, even though such evidence may not be admissible at trial.

(2) The juvenile, or the juvenile's attorney, and the petitioner shall be afforded an opportunity to examine and controvert written reports so received and, in the court's discretion, may be allowed to cross-examine individuals making reports when those individuals are reasonably available.

(3) No assertion of an evidentiary privilege, other than the privilege between attorney and client, shall prevent the receipt and use, at a dispositional hearing, of materials prepared pursuant to a court-ordered examination, interview, or course of treatment.

(D) Presence of Juvenile and Victim.

(1) The juvenile may be excused from part of the dispositional hearing for good cause shown, but must be present when the disposition is announced.

(2) The victim has the right to be present at the dispositional hearing and to make an impact statement as provided by the Crime Victim's Rights Act, MCL 780.751 *et seq.*

(E) Dispositions.

(1) If the juvenile has been found to have committed an offense, the court may enter an order of disposition as provided by MCL 712A.18.

(2) In making second and subsequent dispositions in delinquency cases, the court must consider imposing increasingly severe sanctions, which may include imposing additional conditions of probation; extending the term of probation; imposing additional costs; ordering a juvenile who has been residing at home into an out-of-home placement; ordering a more restrictive placement; ordering state wardship for a child who has not previously been a state ward; or any other conditions deemed appropriate by the court. Waiver of jurisdiction to adult criminal court, either by authorization of a warrant or by judicial waiver, is not considered a sanction for the purpose of this rule.

(3) Before a juvenile is placed in an institution outside the state of Michigan as a disposition, the court must find that:

(a) institutional care is in the best interests of the juvenile,

(b) equivalent facilities to meet the juvenile's needs are not available within Michigan, and

(c) the placement will not cause undue hardship.

(4) The court shall not enter an order of disposition for a juvenile offense until the court verifies that the juvenile has had biometric data collected. If the juvenile has not been fingerprinted, the court shall proceed as provided by MCR 3.936.

(5) If the court enters an order pursuant to the Crime Victim's Rights Act, MCL 780.751 *et seq.*, the court shall only order the payment of one assessment at any dispositional hearing, regardless of the number of offenses.

(6) The court shall prepare and forward to the Secretary of State an abstract of its findings at such times and for such offenses as are required by law.

(7) Mandatory Detention for Use of a Firearm.

(a) In addition to any other disposition, a juvenile, other than a juvenile sentenced in the same manner as an adult under MCL 712A.18(1)(m), shall be committed under MCL 712A.18(1)(e) to a detention facility for a specified period of time if all the following circumstances exist:

(i) the juvenile is under the jurisdiction of the court under MCL 712A.2(a)(1),

(ii) the juvenile was found to have violated a law of this state or of the United States or a criminal municipal ordinance, and

(iii) the juvenile was found to have used a firearm during the offense.

(b) The length of the commitment to a detention facility shall not exceed the length of the sentence that could have been imposed if the juvenile had been sentenced as an adult.

(c) "Firearm" means any weapon from which a dangerous projectile may be propelled by using explosives, gas, or air as a means of propulsion, except any smoothbore rifle or hand gun designed and manufactured exclusively for propelling BB's not exceeding .177 caliber by means of spring, gas, or air.

[Adopted February 4, 2003, effective May 1, 2003, 467 Mich. Amended April 30, 2003, effective May 1, 2003, 467 Mich. Amended effective December 14, 2016, 500 Mich; August 14, 2019, 503 Mich.]

Comments

Staff Comment to 2003 Adoption

MCR 3.943 corresponds to former Rule 5.943.

Subrule (A) is modified to make clear that a dispositional hearing takes place only after a finding that the juvenile has committed an offense.

Subrule (C)(1) specifies that the rules of evidence do not apply in dispositional phase proceedings, except those with respect to privileges.

The amendment of subrule (D) recognizes the right of the victim to present an impact statement.

New subrule (E)(2) directs the consideration of increasingly severe sanctions in second and subsequent dispositions.

New subrule (E)(5) provides that only one assessment under the Crime Victim's Rights Act is to be made regardless of the number of offenses.

New subrule (E)(6) specifically requires forwarding an abstract of findings to the Secretary of State as required by law.

Staff Comment to 2003 Amendment

The April 30, 2003, order makes corrections to a number of the rules governing proceedings regarding juveniles that had been adopted on February 4, 2003. The changes are effective May 1, corresponding to the effective date of the February 4 amendments. In addition to these changes, a number of corrections of punctuation and capitalization and changes in the Notes that accompanied the rules have been made and will appear in the published version of the rules.

The amendments of MCR 3.903(D)(8)(m), 6.903(H)(16), 6.931(E)(3), and 6.933(C)(1) conform the rules to 2002 PA 665, which changed the amounts of controlled substances required for certain violations. See MCL 333.7401(2)(a)(i), 333.7403(2)(a)(i). MCR 3.933(C)(1) is also modified in light of *People v Valentin*, 457 Mich 1 (1998).

The amendment of MCR 3.935(B)(1) corrects the inadvertent omission of references to guardians and legal custodians.

The amendments of MCR 3.922(E)(1)(c), 3.943(A), 3.945(A)(1), 3.965(E)(1), and 3.972(C)(2)(c) correct minor errors in wording.

The amendment of MCR 3.977(G) deletes the word "hearing" in the reference to progress reviews. Under MCR 3.974(A)(1), progress reviews do not require hearings.

The amendment of MCR 3.980(B) and (C) revise the provisions on removal of American Indian children from the home to clarify the distinction between emergency removals and removals after hearing.

The amendments of MCR 3.982(A), 6.903(I)–(L) and 6.937(A) correct cross-reference, citation and numbering errors.

Staff Comment to 2016 Amendment

These amendments update cross-references and make other nonsubstantive revisions to clarify the rules.

Staff Comment to 2019 Amendment

These amendments update cross-references and make other nonsubstantive revisions to clarify the rules.

Rule 3.944   Probation Violation

(A) Petition; Temporary Custody.

(1) Upon receipt of a sworn supplemental petition alleging that the juvenile has violated any condition of probation, the court may:

(a) direct that the juvenile be notified pursuant to MCR 3.920 to appear for a hearing on the alleged violation, which notice must include a copy of the probation violation petition and a notice of the juvenile's rights as provided in subrule (C)(1); or

(b) order that the juvenile be apprehended and brought to the court for a detention hearing, which must be commenced within 24 hours after the juvenile has been taken into court custody, excluding Sundays and holidays as defined in MCR 8.110(D)(2).

(2) When a juvenile is apprehended pursuant to court order as provided in subrule (A)(1)(b), the officer must:

(a) forthwith take the juvenile

(i) to the court for a detention hearing, or

(ii) to the place designated by the court pending the scheduling of a detention hearing; and

(b) notify the custodial parent, guardian, or legal custodian that the juvenile has been taken into custody, of the time and place of the detention hearing, if known, and of the need for the presence of the parent, guardian, or legal custodian at the detention hearing.

(B) Detention Hearing; Procedure. At the detention hearing:

(1) The court must determine whether a parent, guardian, or legal custodian has been notified and is present. If a parent, guardian, or legal custodian has been notified, but fails to appear, the detention hearing may be conducted without a parent, guardian, or legal custodian if a guardian ad litem or attorney appears with the juvenile.

(2) The court must provide the juvenile with a copy of the petition alleging probation violation.

(3) The court must read the petition to the juvenile, unless the attorney or juvenile waives the reading.

(4) The court must advise the juvenile of the juvenile's rights as provided in subrule (C)(1) and of the possible dispositions.

(5) The juvenile must be allowed an opportunity to deny or otherwise plead to the probation violation. If the juvenile wishes to admit the probation violation or plead no contest, the court must comply with subrule (D) before accepting the plea.

(a) If the juvenile admits the probation violation or pleads no contest, and the court accepts the plea, the court may modify the existing order of probation or may order any disposition available under MCL 712A.18 or MCL 712A.18a.

(b) If the juvenile denies the probation violation or remains silent, the court must schedule a probation violation hearing, which must commence within 42 days. The court may order the juvenile detained without bond pending the probation violation hearing if there is probable cause to believe the juvenile violated probation. If the hearing is not commenced within 42 days, and the delay in commencing the hearing is not attributable to the juvenile, the juvenile must be released pending hearing without requiring that bail be posted.

(C) Probation Violation Hearing.

(1) At the probation violation hearing, the juvenile has the following rights:

(a) the right to be present at the hearing,

(b) the right to an attorney pursuant to MCR 3.915(A)(1),

(c) the right to have the petitioner prove the probation violation by a preponderance of the evidence,

(d) the right to have the court order any witnesses to appear at the hearing,

(e) the right to question witnesses against the juvenile,

(f) the right to remain silent and not have that silence used against the juvenile, and

(g) the right to testify at the hearing, if the juvenile wants to testify.

(2) At the probation violation hearing, the Michigan Rules of Evidence do not apply, other than those with respect to privileges. There is no right to a jury.

(3) If it is alleged that the juvenile violated probation by having been found, pursuant to MCR 3.941 or MCR 3.942, to have committed an offense, the juvenile may then be found to have violated probation pursuant to this rule.

(D) Pleas of Admission or No Contest. If the juvenile wishes to admit the probation violation or plead no contest, before accepting the plea, the court must:

(1) tell the juvenile the nature of the alleged probation violation;

(2) tell the juvenile the possible dispositions;

(3) tell the juvenile that if the plea is accepted, the juvenile will not have a contested hearing of any kind, so the juvenile would give up the rights that the juvenile would have at a contested hearing, including the rights as provided in subrule (C)(1);

(4) confirm any plea agreement on the record;

(5) ask the juvenile if any promises have been made beyond those in the plea agreement and whether anyone has threatened the juvenile;

(6) establish support for a finding that the juvenile violated probation,

(a) by questioning the juvenile or by other means when the plea is a plea of admission, or

(b) by means other than questioning the juvenile when the juvenile pleads no contest. The court must also state why a plea of no contest is appropriate;

(7) inquire of the parent, guardian, legal custodian, or guardian ad litem whether there is any reason why the court should not accept the juvenile's plea. Agreement or objection by the parent, guardian, legal custodian, or guardian ad litem to a plea of admission or of no contest by a juvenile shall be placed on the record if the parent, guardian, legal custodian, or guardian ad litem is present; and

(8) determine that the plea is accurately, voluntarily and understandingly made.

(E) Disposition of Probation Violation; Reporting.

(1) If, after hearing, the court finds that a violation of probation has occurred, the court may modify the existing order of probation or order any disposition available under MCL 712A.18 or MCL 712A.18a.

(2) If, after hearing, the court finds that a violation of probation occurred on the basis of the juvenile having committed an offense, that finding must be recorded as a violation of probation only and not a finding that the juvenile committed the underlying offense. That finding must not be reported to the State Police or the Secretary of State as an adjudication or a disposition.

(F) Determination of Ability to Pay. A juvenile and/or parent shall not be detained or incarcerated for the nonpayment of court-ordered financial obligations as ordered by the court, unless the court determines that the juvenile and/or parent has the resources to pay and has not made a good-faith effort to do so.

[Adopted February 4, 2003, effective May 1, 2003, 467 Mich. Amended May 25, 2016, effective September 1, 2016, 499 Mich.]

Comments

Staff Comment to 2003 Adoption

The provisions of former Rule 5.944 are split into two rules, with MCR 3.944 covering probation violation, and new MCR 3.945 covering dispositional review. Former subrules 5.944(B)–(E) are relocated to MCR 3.945.

The probation violation provisions are much more detailed than those found in former Rule 5.944(A).

Subrule (A)(2) covers notice to the juvenile's parents after apprehension of the juvenile under a court order.

Subrule (B) sets up procedures for a hearing regarding detention pending disposition of the violation charges.

Subrule (C) adds details regarding the rights of the juvenile at the probation violation hearing and other procedural provisions, which are briefly stated in former Rule 5.944(A)(5).

New subrule (D) has detailed provisions regarding pleas of admission and no contest, which include the sort of advice that is given in other plea proceedings.

Staff Comment to 2016 Amendment

The amendments of MCR 3.605, 3.606, 3.928, 3.944, 3.956, 6.001, 6.425, 6.445, 6.610, and 6.933 were submitted by the Michigan State Planning Body for the Delivery of Legal Services to the Poor. The rule revisions are intended to provide clarity and guidance to courts regarding what courts would be required to do before incarcerating a defendant for failure to pay.

Rule 3.945   Dispositional Review

(A) Dispositional Review Hearings.

(1) *Generally.* The court must conduct periodic hearings to review the dispositional orders in delinquency cases in which the juvenile has been placed outside the home. Such review hearings must be conducted at intervals designated by the court, or may be requested at any time by a party or by a probation officer or caseworker. The victim has a right to make a statement at the hearing or submit a written statement for use at the hearing, or both. At a dispositional review hearing, the court may modify or amend the dispositional order or treatment plan to include any disposition permitted by MCL 712A.18 and MCL 712A.18a or as otherwise permitted by law. The Michigan Rules of Evidence, other than those with respect to privileges, do not apply.

(2) *Required Review Hearings.*

(a) If the juvenile is placed in out-of-home care, the court must hold dispositional review hearings no later than every 182 days after the initial disposition, as provided in MCL 712A.19(2).

(b) A review hearing is required before a juvenile is moved to a more physically restrictive type of placement, unless the court in its dispositional order has provided for a more physically restrictive type of placement. A review hearing is not required if the juvenile and a parent consent to the new placement in a writing filed with the court. A juvenile, who has been ordered placed in a juvenile facility, may be released only with the approval of the court.

(B) Hearing to Extend Jurisdiction.

(1) *When Required.* When a juvenile committed under MCL 712A.18(1)(e) for an offense specified in MCL 712A.18d remains under court jurisdiction after the juvenile's 18th birthday, the court must conduct a hearing to determine whether to extend the court's jurisdiction to age 21, pursuant to MCL 712A.18d.

(a) Time of Hearing. Unless adjourned for good cause, a commitment review hearing must be held as nearly as possible to, but before, the juvenile's 19th birthday.

(b) Notice of Hearing. Notice of the hearing must be given to the prosecuting attorney, the agency or the superintendent of the institution or facility to which the juvenile has been committed, the juvenile, and, if the address or whereabouts are known, the parent, guardian or legal custodian of the juvenile, at least 14 days before the hearing. The notice must clearly indicate that the court may extend jurisdiction over the juvenile until the juvenile reaches 21 years of age and must include advice to the juvenile and the parent, guardian, or legal custodian that the juvenile has the right to an attorney.

(2) *Appointment of Attorney.* The court must appoint an attorney to represent the juvenile at the hearing unless an attorney has been retained.

(3) *Evidence; Commitment Report.* The Michigan Rules of Evidence do not apply, other than those with respect to privileges. The institution, agency, or facility must prepare a report for use at the hearing to extend jurisdiction. The report must contain information required by MCL 803.225. The court must consider this information in determining whether to extend jurisdiction beyond the age of 19.

(4) *Burden of Proof; Findings.* The court must extend jurisdiction over the juvenile until the age of 21, unless the juvenile proves by a preponderance of the evidence that the juvenile has been rehabilitated and does not present a serious risk to public safety. In making the determination, the court must consider the following factors:

(a) the extent and nature of the juvenile's participation in education, counseling, or work programs;

(b) the juvenile's willingness to accept responsibility for prior behavior;

(c) the juvenile's behavior in the current placement;

(d) the juvenile's prior record, character, and physical and mental maturity;

(e) the juvenile's potential for violent conduct, as demonstrated by prior behavior;

(f) the recommendations of the institution, agency, or facility charged with the juvenile's care regarding the appropriateness of the juvenile's release or continued custody; and

(g) any other information the prosecuting attorney or the juvenile submits.

(C) Review of Extended Jurisdiction Cases.

(1) *Out–of–Home Care.* If the juvenile is placed outside the home, the court must hold a dispositional review hearing no later than every 182 days after the hearing to extend jurisdiction.

(2) *Periodic Review.* If the institution, agency, or facility to which the juvenile was committed believes that the juvenile has been rehabilitated and does not present a serious risk to public safety, the institution, agency, or facility may petition the court to conduct a review hearing at any time before the juvenile becomes 21 years of age.

(D) Juvenile on Conditional Release. The procedures set forth in MCR 3.944 apply to juveniles committed under MCL 712A.18 who have allegedly violated a condition of release after

being returned to the community on release from a public institution. The court need not conduct such a hearing when there will be an administrative hearing by the agency to which the juvenile is committed, provided the court has not retained jurisdiction.

[Adopted February 4, 2003, effective May 1, 2003, 467 Mich. Amended April 30, 2003, effective May 1, 2003, 467 Mich.]

Comments

Staff Comment to 2003 Adoption

MCR 3.945 is new, covering the post-disposition reviews and hearing procedures formerly found in subrules 5.944(B)–(E), with additional details.

Subrule (A) has general provisions directing review hearings in all delinquency cases in which the juvenile is placed outside the home, including specific time limits, and specifically requiring a hearing before the juvenile is moved to a more restrictive environment.

Subrule (B) deals with extension of the court's jurisdiction after a juvenile's 18th birthday, as permitted by MCL 712A.18D. The provision has more detail than former MCR 5.944(D)(3) on matters such as the time and notice of hearing, appointment of counsel, rules of evidence, and burden of proof, as well as the factors that are to be considered in making the decision. See MCL 712A.18D(1). The burden of proof is on the juvenile to prove both rehabilitation and that the juvenile does not present a serious risk to public safety. See MCL 712A.18d(2).

Subrule (C) covers review hearings in extended jurisdiction cases.

Staff Comment to 2003 Amendment

The April 30, 2003, order makes corrections to a number of the rules governing proceedings regarding juveniles that had been adopted on February 4, 2003. The changes are effective May 1, corresponding to the effective date of the February 4 amendments. In addition to these changes, a number of corrections of punctuation and capitalization and changes in the Notes that accompanied the rules have been made and will appear in the published version of the rules.

The amendments of MCR 3.903(D)(8)(m), 6.903(H)(16), 6.931(E)(3), and 6.933(C)(1) conform the rules to 2002 PA 665, which changed the amounts of controlled substances required for certain violations. See MCL 333.7401(2)(a)(i), 333.7403(2)(a)(i). MCR 3.933(C)(1) is also modified in light of *People v Valentin*, 457 Mich 1 (1998).

The amendment of MCR 3.935(B)(1) corrects the inadvertent omission of references to guardians and legal custodians.

The amendments of MCR 3.922(E)(1)(c), 3.943(A), 3.945(A)(1), 3.965(E)(1), and 3.972(C)(2)(c) correct minor errors in wording.

The amendment of MCR 3.977(G) deletes the word "hearing" in the reference to progress reviews. Under MCR 3.974(A)(1), progress reviews do not require hearings.

The amendment of MCR 3.980(B) and (C) revise the provisions on removal of American Indian children from the home to clarify the distinction between emergency removals and removals after hearing.

The amendments of MCR 3.982(A), 6.903(I)–(L) and 6.937(A) correct cross-reference, citation and numbering errors.

Rule 3.946 Post–Dispositional Secure Detention Pending Return to Placement

(A) If a juvenile who has been found to have committed an offense that would be a misdemeanor or a felony if committed by an adult has been placed out of the home by court order or by the Family Independence Agency, and the juvenile leaves such placement without authority, upon being apprehended the juvenile may be detained without the right to bail. Any detention must be authorized by the court.

(B) If a juvenile is placed in secure detention pursuant to this rule and no new petition is filed that would require a preliminary hearing pursuant to MCR 3.935, and no probation violation petition is filed, the court must conduct a detention hearing within 48 hours after the juvenile has been taken into custody, excluding Sundays and holidays as defined by MCR 8.110(D)(2).

(C) At the detention hearing the court must:

(1) assure that the custodial parent, guardian, or legal custodian has been notified, if that person's whereabouts are known,

(2) advise the juvenile of the right to be represented by an attorney,

(3) determine whether the juvenile should be released or should continue to be detained.

[Adopted February 4, 2003, effective May 1, 2003, 467 Mich.]

Comments

Staff Comment to 2003 Adoption

MCR 3.946 is a new provision dealing with a situation in which a juvenile has been placed out of home by court order or by the Family Independence Agency for having committed an offense that would be a crime if committed by an adult.

Subrule (A) provides that if the juvenile leaves that detention without authority, on apprehension the juvenile may be confined without the right to bail.

Under subrule (B), if no new petition is filed, the court is to hold a detention hearing within 48 hours.

Subrule (C) covers notice and the right to advice regarding representation by an attorney.

Rule 3.950 Waiver of Jurisdiction

(A) Authority. Only a judge assigned to hear cases in the family division of the circuit court of the county where the offense is alleged to have been committed may waive jurisdiction pursuant to MCL 712A.4.

(B) Definition. As used in this rule, "felony" means an offense punishable by imprisonment for more than one year or an offense designated by law as a felony.

(C) Motion by Prosecuting Attorney. A motion by the prosecuting attorney requesting that the family division waive its jurisdiction to a court of general criminal jurisdiction must be in writing and must clearly indicate the charges and that if the motion is granted the juvenile will be prosecuted as though an adult.

(1) A motion to waive jurisdiction of the juvenile must be filed within 14 days after the petition has been authorized to be filed. Absent a timely motion and good cause shown, the juvenile shall no longer be subject to waiver of jurisdiction on the charges.

(2) A copy of the motion seeking waiver must be personally served on the juvenile and the parent, guardian, or legal custodian of the juvenile, if their addresses or whereabouts are known or can be determined by the exercise of due diligence.

(D) Hearing Procedure. The waiver hearing consists of two phases. Notice of the date, time, and place of the hearings may be given either on the record directly to the juvenile or to the attorney for the juvenile, the prosecuting attorney, and all other parties, or in writing, served on each individual.

(1) *First Phase.* The first-phase hearing is to determine whether there is probable cause to believe that an offense has been committed that if committed by an adult would be a felony, and that there is probable cause to believe that the juvenile who is 14 years of age or older committed the offense.

(a) The probable cause hearing must be commenced within 28 days after the authorization of the petition unless adjourned for good cause.

(b) At the hearing, the prosecuting attorney has the burden to present legally admissible evidence to establish each element of the offense and to establish probable cause that the juvenile committed the offense.

(c) The court need not conduct the first phase of the waiver hearing, if:

(i) the court has found the requisite probable cause at a hearing under MCR 3.935(D)(1), provided that at the earlier hearing only legally admissible evidence was used to establish probable cause that the offense was committed and probable cause that the juvenile committed the offense; or

(ii) the juvenile, after being informed by the court on the record that the probable cause hearing is equivalent to and held in place of preliminary examination in district court, waives the hearing. The court must determine that the waiver of hearing is freely, voluntarily, and understandingly given and that the juvenile knows there will be no preliminary examination in district court if the court waives jurisdiction.

(2) *Second Phase.* If the court finds the requisite probable cause at the first-phase hearing, or if there is no hearing pursuant to subrule (D)(1)(c), the second-phase hearing shall be held to determine whether the interests of the juvenile and the public would best be served by granting the motion. However, if the juvenile has been previously subject to the general criminal jurisdiction of the circuit court under MCL 712A.4 or 600.606, the court shall waive jurisdiction of the juvenile to the court of general criminal jurisdiction without holding the second-phase hearing.

(a) The second-phase hearing must be commenced within 28 days after the conclusion of the first phase, or within 35 days after the authorization of the petition if there was no hearing under subrule (D)(1)(c), unless adjourned for good cause.

(b) The Michigan Rules of Evidence, other than those with respect to privileges, do not apply to the second phase of the waiver hearing.

(c) The prosecuting attorney has the burden of establishing by a preponderance of the evidence that the best interests of the juvenile and the public would be served by waiver.

(d) The court, in determining whether to waive the juvenile to the court having general criminal jurisdiction, shall consider and make findings on the following criteria, giving greater weight to the seriousness of the alleged offense and the juvenile's prior record of delinquency than to the other criteria:

(i) the seriousness of the alleged offense in terms of community protection, including, but not limited to, the existence of any aggravating factors recognized by the sentencing guidelines, the use of a firearm or other dangerous weapon, and the effect on any victim;

(ii) the culpability of the juvenile in committing the alleged offense, including, but not limited to, the level of the juvenile's participation in planning and carrying out the offense and the existence of any aggravating or mitigating factors recognized by the sentencing guidelines;

(iii) the juvenile's prior record of delinquency including, but not limited to, any record of detention, any police

record, any school record, or any other evidence indicating prior delinquent behavior;

(iv) the juvenile's programming history, including, but not limited to, the juvenile's past willingness to participate meaningfully in available programming;

(v) the adequacy of the punishment or programming available in the juvenile justice system;

(vi) the dispositional options available for the juvenile.

(e) In determining whether to waive the juvenile to the court having general criminal jurisdiction, the court may also consider any stipulation by the defense to a finding that the best interests of the juvenile and the public support a waiver.

(E) Grant of Waiver Motion.

(1) If the court determines that it is in the best interests of the juvenile and public to waive jurisdiction over the juvenile, the court must:

(a) Enter a written order granting the motion to waive jurisdiction and transferring the matter to the appropriate court having general criminal jurisdiction for arraignment of the juvenile on an information.

(b) Make findings of fact and conclusions of law forming the basis for entry of the waiver order. The findings and conclusions may be incorporated in a written opinion or stated on the record.

(c) Advise the juvenile, orally or in writing, that

(i) the juvenile is entitled to appellate review of the decision to waive jurisdiction,

(ii) the juvenile must seek review of the decision in the Court of Appeals within 21 days of the order to preserve the appeal of right, and

(iii) if the juvenile is financially unable to retain an attorney, the court will appoint one to represent the juvenile on appeal.

(d) The court shall send, without cost, a copy of the order and a copy of the written opinion or transcript of the court's findings and conclusions, to the court having general criminal jurisdiction.

(2) Upon the grant of a waiver motion, a juvenile must be transferred to the adult criminal justice system and is subject to the same procedures used for adult criminal defendants. Juveniles waived pursuant to this rule are not required to be kept separate and apart from adult prisoners.

(F) Denial of Waiver Motion. If the waiver motion is denied, the court shall make written findings or place them on the record. A transcript of the court's findings or, if a written opinion is prepared, a copy of the written opinion must be sent to the prosecuting attorney and the juvenile, or juvenile's attorney, upon request. If the juvenile is detained and the trial of the matter in the family division has not started within 28 days after entry of the order denying the waiver motion, and the delay is not attributable to the defense, the court shall forthwith order the juvenile released pending trial without requiring that bail be posted, unless the juvenile is being detained on another matter.

(G) Psychiatric Testimony.

(1) A psychiatrist, psychologist, or certified social worker who conducts a court-ordered examination for the purpose of a

waiver hearing may not testify at a subsequent criminal proceeding involving the juvenile without the juvenile's written consent.

(2) The juvenile's consent may only be given:

(a) in the presence of an attorney representing the juvenile or, if no attorney represents the juvenile, in the presence of a parent, guardian, or legal custodian;

(b) after the juvenile has had an opportunity to read the report of the psychiatrist, psychologist, or certified social worker; and

(c) after the waiver decision is rendered.

(3) Consent to testimony by the psychiatrist, psychologist, or certified social worker does not waive the juvenile's privilege against self-incrimination.

[Adopted February 4, 2003, effective May 1, 2003, 467 Mich. Amended September 18, 2019, effective January 1, 2020, 503 Mich.]

Comments

Staff Comment to 2003 Adoption

MCR 3.950 corresponds to former Rule 5.950.

New subrule (A) makes clear that only a judge assigned to the family division of circuit court may waive jurisdiction under MCL 712A.4.

Staff Comment to 2020 Amendment

The amendments of MCR 1.109, 2.107, 2.113, 2.116, 2.119, 2.222, 2.223, 2.225, 2.227, 3.206, 3.211, 3.212, 3.214, 3.303, 3.903, 3.921, 3.925, 3.926, 3.931, 3.933, 3.942, 3.950, 3.961, 3.971, 3.972, 4.002, 4.101, 4.201, 4.202, 4.302, 5.128, 5.302, 5.731, 6.101, 6.615, 8.105, and 8.119 and rescission of MCR 2.226 and 8.125 continue the process for design and implementation of the statewide electronic-filing system.

Rule 3.951   Initiating Designated Proceedings

(A) Prosecutor–Designated Cases. The procedures in this subrule apply if the prosecuting attorney submits a petition designating the case for trial in the same manner as an adult.

(1) *Time for Arraignment.*

(a) If the juvenile is in custody or custody is requested, the arraignment must commence no later than 24 hours after the juvenile has been taken into court custody, excluding Sundays and holidays as defined by MCR 8.110(D)(2), or the juvenile must be released. The court may adjourn the arraignment for up to 7 days to secure the attendance of the juvenile's parent, guardian, or legal custodian or of a witness, or for other good cause shown.

(b) If the juvenile is not in custody and custody is not requested, the juvenile must be brought before the court for an arraignment as soon as the juvenile's attendance can be secured.

(2) *Procedure.*

(a) The court shall determine whether the juvenile's parent, guardian, or legal custodian has been notified and is present. The arraignment may be conducted without a parent, guardian, or legal custodian, provided a guardian ad litem or attorney appears with the juvenile.

(b) The court shall read the allegations in the petition and advise the juvenile on the record in plain language:

(i) of the right to an attorney pursuant to MCR 3.915(A)(1);

(ii) of the right to trial by judge or jury on the allegations in the petition;

(iii) of the right to remain silent and that any statement made by the juvenile may be used against the juvenile;

(iv) of the right to have a preliminary examination within 14 days;

(v) that the case has been designated for trial in the same manner as an adult and, if the prosecuting attorney proves that there is probable cause to believe an offense was committed and there is probable cause to believe that the juvenile committed the offense, the juvenile will be afforded all the rights of an adult charged with the same crime and that upon conviction the juvenile may be sentenced as an adult; and

(vi) of the maximum possible prison sentence and any mandatory minimum sentence required by law.

(c) Unless the arraignment is adjourned, the court must decide whether to authorize the petition to be filed. If it authorizes the filing of the petition, the court must:

(i) determine if biometric data must be taken as provided by MCR 3.936;

(ii) schedule a preliminary examination within 14 days before a judge other than the judge who would conduct the trial;

(iii) if the juvenile is in custody or custody is requested, determine whether to detain or release the juvenile as provided in MCR 3.935(C).

(d) If the juvenile is in custody or custody is requested, the juvenile may be detained pending the completion of the arraignment if it appears to the court that one of the circumstances in MCR 3.935(D)(1) is present.

(3) *Amendment of Petition.* If a petition submitted by the prosecuting attorney alleging a specified juvenile violation did not include a designation of the case for trial as an adult:

(a) The prosecuting attorney may, by right, amend the petition to designate the case during the preliminary hearing.

(b) The prosecuting attorney may request leave of the court to amend the petition to designate the case no later than the pretrial hearing or, if there is no pretrial hearing, at least 21 days before trial, absent good cause for further delay. The court may permit the prosecuting attorney to amend the petition to designate the case as the interests of justice require.

(B) Court–Designated Cases. The procedures in this subrule apply if the prosecuting attorney submits a petition charging an offense other than a specified juvenile violation and requests the court to designate the case for trial in the same manner as an adult.

(1) *Time for Arraignment.*

(a) If the juvenile is in custody or custody is requested, the arraignment must commence no later than 24 hours after the juvenile has been taken into court custody, excluding Sundays and holidays as defined by MCR 8.110(D)(2), or the juvenile must be released. The court may adjourn the arraignment for up to 7 days to secure the attendance of the juvenile's parent, guardian, or legal custodian or of a witness, or for other good cause shown.

(b) If the juvenile is not in custody and custody is not requested, the juvenile must be brought before the court for an arraignment as soon as the juvenile's attendance can be secured.

(2) *Procedure.*

(a) The court shall determine whether the juvenile's parent, guardian, or legal custodian has been notified and is present. The arraignment may be conducted without a parent, guardian, or legal custodian, provided a guardian ad litem or attorney appears with the juvenile.

(b) The court shall read the allegations in the petition, and advise the juvenile on the record in plain language:

(i) of the right to an attorney pursuant to MCR 3.915(A)(1);

(ii) of the right to trial by judge or jury on the allegations in the petition;

(iii) of the right to remain silent and that any statement made by the juvenile may be used against the juvenile;

(iv) of the right to have a designation hearing within 14 days;

(v) of the right to have a preliminary examination within 14 days after the case is designated if the juvenile is charged with a felony or offense for which an adult could be imprisoned for more than one year;

(vi) that if the case is designated by the court for trial in the same manner as an adult and, if a preliminary examination is required by law, the prosecuting attorney proves that there is probable cause to believe that an offense was committed and there is probable cause to believe that the juvenile committed the offense, the juvenile will be afforded all the rights of an adult charged with the same crime and that upon conviction the juvenile may be sentenced as an adult;

(vii) of the maximum possible prison sentence and any mandatory minimum sentence required by law.

(c) Unless the arraignment is adjourned, the court must decide whether to authorize the petition to be filed. If it authorizes the filing of the petition, the court must:

(i) determine if biometric data must be taken as provided by MCR 3.936;

(ii) schedule a designation hearing within 14 days;

(iii) if the juvenile is in custody or custody is requested, determine whether to detain or release the juvenile as provided in MCR 3.935(C).

(d) If the juvenile is in custody or custody is requested, the juvenile may be detained pending the completion of the arraignment if it appears to the court that one of the circumstances in MCR 3.935(D)(1) is present.

(3) *Amendment of Petition.* If a petition submitted by the prosecuting attorney alleging an offense other than a specified juvenile violation did not include a request that the court designate the case for trial as an adult:

(a) The prosecuting attorney may, by right, amend the petition to request the court to designate the case during the preliminary hearing.

(b) The prosecuting attorney may request leave of the court to amend the petition to request the court to designate the case no later than the pretrial hearing or, if there is no pretrial hearing, at least 21 days before trial, absent good cause for further delay. The court may permit the prosecut-

ing attorney to amend the petition to request the court to designate the case as the interests of justice require.

[Adopted February 4, 2003, effective May 1, 2003, 467 Mich. Amended effective December 17, 2003, 467 Mich; August 14, 2019, 503 Mich.]

Comments

Staff Comment to 2003 Adoption

MCR 3.951 corresponds to former Rule 5.951. The rule is reorganized to eliminate unnecessary repetition, but is not changed in substance.

Staff Comment to 2003 Amendment

The December 17, 2003, amendment of MCR 3.951(B)(2)(c) corrected an inadvertent error in the rule as adopted effective May 1, 2003. The amendment returned the provision to the substance of former MCR 5.951, allowing referees to conduct designation hearings under MCR 3.951(B).

Staff Comment to 2019 Amendment

These amendments update cross-references and make other nonsubstantive revisions to clarify the rules.

Rule 3.952 Designation Hearing

(A) Time. The designation hearing shall be commenced within 14 days after the arraignment, unless adjourned for good cause.

(B) Notice.

(1) A copy of the petition or a copy of the petition and separate written request for court designation must be personally served on the juvenile and the juvenile's parent, guardian, or legal custodian, if the address or whereabouts of the juvenile's parent, guardian, or custodian is known or can be determined by the exercise of due diligence.

(2) Notice of the date, time, and place of the designation hearing must be given to the juvenile, the juvenile's parent, guardian, or legal custodian, the attorney for the juvenile, if any, and the prosecuting attorney. The notice may be given either orally on the record or in writing, served on each individual by mail, or given in another manner reasonably calculated to provide notice.

(C) Hearing Procedure.

(1) *Evidence.* The Michigan Rules of Evidence, other than those with respect to privileges, do not apply.

(2) *Burden of Proof.* The prosecuting attorney has the burden of proving by a preponderance of the evidence that the best interests of the juvenile and the public would be served by designation.

(3) *Factors to be Considered.* In determining whether to designate the case for trial in the same manner as an adult, the court must consider all the following factors, giving greater weight to the seriousness of the alleged offense and the juvenile's prior delinquency record than to the other factors:

(a) the seriousness of the alleged offense in terms of community protection, including, but not limited to, the existence of any aggravating factors recognized by the sentencing guidelines, the use of a firearm or other dangerous weapon, and the effect on any victim;

(b) the culpability of the juvenile in committing the alleged offense, including, but not limited to, the level of the juvenile's participation in planning and carrying out the offense and the existence of any aggravating or mitigating factors recognized by the sentencing guidelines;

(c) the juvenile's prior record of delinquency, including, but not limited to, any record of detention, any police record, any school record, or any other evidence indicating prior delinquent behavior;

(d) the juvenile's programming history, including, but not limited to, the juvenile's past willingness to participate meaningfully in available programming;

(e) the adequacy of the punishment or programming available in the juvenile justice system; and

(f) the dispositional options available for the juvenile.

(D) Grant of Request for Court Designation.

(1) If the court determines that it is in the best interests of the juvenile and the public that the juvenile be tried in the same manner as an adult in the family division of the circuit court, the court must:

(a) Enter a written order granting the request for court designation and

(i) schedule a preliminary examination within 14 days if the juvenile is charged with a felony or an offense for which an adult could be imprisoned for more than one year, or

(ii) schedule the matter for trial or pretrial hearing if the juvenile is charged with a misdemeanor.

(b) Make findings of fact and conclusions of law forming the basis for entry of the order designating the petition. The findings and conclusions may be incorporated in a written opinion or stated on the record.

(E) Denial of Request for Designation. If the request for court designation is denied, the court shall make written findings or place them on the record. Further proceedings shall be conducted pursuant to MCR 3.941–3.944.

[Adopted February 4, 2003, effective May 1, 2003, 467 Mich.]

Comments

Staff Comment to 2003 Adoption

MCR 3.952 corresponds to former Rule 5.952.

Rule 3.953   Preliminary Examination in Designated Cases

(A) Requirement. A preliminary examination must be held only in designated cases in which the juvenile is alleged to have committed a felony or an offense for which an adult could be imprisoned for more than one year.

(B) Waiver. The juvenile may waive the preliminary examination if the juvenile is represented by an attorney and the waiver is made and signed by the juvenile in open court. The judge shall find and place on the record that the waiver was freely, understandingly, and voluntarily given.

(C) Combined Hearing. The preliminary examination may be combined with a designation hearing provided that the Michigan Rules of Evidence, except as otherwise provided by law, apply only to the preliminary examination phase of the combined hearing.

(D) Time. The preliminary examination must commence within 14 days of the arraignment in a prosecutor-designated case or within 14 days after court-ordered designation of a petition, unless the preliminary examination was combined with the designation hearing.

(E) Procedure. The preliminary examination must be conducted in accordance with MCR 6.110.

(F) Findings.

(1) If the court finds there is probable cause to believe that the alleged offense was committed and probable cause to believe the juvenile committed the offense, the court may schedule the matter for trial or a pretrial hearing.

(2) If the court does not find there is probable cause to believe that the alleged offense was committed or does not find there is probable cause to believe the juvenile committed the offense, the court shall dismiss the petition, unless the court finds there is probable cause to believe that a lesser included offense was committed and probable cause to believe the juvenile committed that offense.

(3) If the court finds there is probable cause to believe that a lesser included offense was committed and probable cause to believe the juvenile committed that offense, the court may, as provided in MCR 3.952, further determine whether the case should be designated as a case in which the juvenile should be tried in the same manner as an adult. If the court designates the case following the determination of probable cause under this subrule, the court may schedule the matter for trial or a pretrial hearing.

(G) Confinement. If the court has designated the case and finds probable cause to believe that a felony or an offense for which an adult could be imprisoned for more than one year has been committed and probable cause to believe that the juvenile committed the offense, the judge may confine the juvenile in the county jail pending trial. If the juvenile is under 17 years of age, the juvenile may be confined in jail only if the juvenile can be separated by sight and sound from adult prisoners and if the sheriff has approved the confinement.

[Adopted February 4, 2003, effective May 1, 2003, 467 Mich.]

Comments

Staff Comment to 2003 Adoption

MCR 3.953 corresponds to former Rule 5.953.

Rule 3.954   Trial of Designated Cases

Trials of designated cases are governed by subchapter 6.400, except for MCR 6.402(A). The court may not accept a waiver of trial by jury until after the juvenile has been offered an opportunity to consult with a lawyer. Pleas in designated cases are governed by subchapter 6.300.

[Adopted February 4, 2003, effective May 1, 2003, 467 Mich.]

Comments

Staff Comment to 2003 Adoption

MCR 3.954 corresponds to former Rule 5.954.

Subchapter 6.300 is made applicable to pleas in designated cases.

Rule 3.955   Sentencing or Disposition in Designated Cases

(A) Determining Whether to Sentence or Impose Disposition. If a juvenile is convicted under MCL 712A.2d, sentencing or disposition shall be made as provided in MCL 712A.18(1)(m) and the Crime Victim's Rights Act, MCL 780.751 *et seq.*, if applicable. In deciding whether to enter an order of disposition, or impose or delay imposition of sentence, the court shall consider all the following factors, giving greater weight to the seriousness of the offense and the juvenile's prior record:

(1) the seriousness of the alleged offense in terms of community protection, including but not limited to, the existence of any aggravating factors recognized by the sentencing guidelines,

the use of a firearm or other dangerous weapon, and the effect on any victim;

(2) the culpability of the juvenile in committing the alleged offense, including, but not limited to, the level of the juvenile's participation in planning and carrying out the offense and the existence of any aggravating or mitigating factors recognized by the sentencing guidelines;

(3) the juvenile's prior record of delinquency including, but not limited to, any record of detention, any police record, any school record, or any other evidence indicating prior delinquent behavior;

(4) the juvenile's programming history, including, but not limited to, the juvenile's past willingness to participate meaningfully in available programming;

(5) the adequacy of the punishment or programming available in the juvenile justice system; and

(6) the dispositional options available for the juvenile.

The court also shall give the juvenile, the juvenile's lawyer, the prosecutor, and the victim an opportunity to advise the court of any circumstances they believe the court should consider in deciding whether to enter an order of disposition or to impose or delay imposition of sentence.

(B) Burden of Proof. The court shall enter an order of disposition unless the court determines that the best interests of the public would be served by sentencing the juvenile as an adult. The prosecuting attorney has the burden of proving by a preponderance of the evidence that, on the basis of the criteria in subrule (A), it would be in the best interests of the public to sentence the juvenile as an adult.

(C) Sentencing. If the court determines that the juvenile should be sentenced as an adult, either initially or following a delayed imposition of sentence, the sentencing hearing shall be held in accordance with the procedures set forth in MCR 6.425.

(D) Delayed Imposition of Sentence. If the court determines that the juvenile should be sentenced as an adult, the court may, in its discretion, enter an order of disposition delaying imposition of sentence and placing the juvenile on probation on such terms and conditions as it considers appropriate, including ordering any disposition under MCL 712A.18. A delayed sentence may be imposed in accordance with MCR 3.956.

(E) Disposition Hearing. If the court does not determine that the juvenile should be sentenced as an adult, the court shall hold a dispositional hearing and comply with the procedures set forth in MCR 3.943.

[Adopted February 4, 2003, effective May 1, 2003, 467 Mich. Amended effective July 17, 2003, 467 Mich; October 1, 2003, 467 Mich; December 14, 2016, 500 Mich.]

Comments

Staff Comment to 2003 Adoption

MCR 3.955 corresponds to former Rule 5.955.

A reference to the Crime Victim's Rights Act, MCL 780.751 *et seq.*, is added in subrule (A).

Staff Comment to July, 2003 Amendment

The July 17, 2003 amendment of MCR 3.955 is explained in *People v Petty*, 469 Mich _____ (2003) [469 Mich 108, 665 N.W.2d 443].

Staff Comment to October, 2003 Amendment

The September 30, 2003, amendment of MCR 3.955, effective October 1, 2003, modified the last paragraph of subrule (A) by substituting the words "juvenile" and "juvenile's lawyer" for the words "defendant" and "defendant's lawyer."

Staff Comment to 2016 Amendment

These amendments update cross-references and make other nonsubstantive revisions to clarify the rules.

Rule 3.956 Review Hearings; Probation Violation

(A) Review Hearings in Delayed Imposition of Sentence Cases.

(1) *When Required.* If the court entered an order of disposition delaying imposition of sentence, the court shall conduct a review hearing to determine whether the juvenile has been rehabilitated and whether the juvenile presents a serious risk to public safety.

(a) Time of Hearing.

(i) Annual Review. The court shall conduct an annual review of the probation, including, but not limited to, the services being provided to the juvenile, the juvenile's placement, and the juvenile's progress in placement. In conducting the review, the court must examine any report prepared under MCL 803.223, and any report prepared by the officer or agency supervising probation. The court may order changes in the juvenile's probation on the basis of the review including, but not limited to, imposition of sentence.

(ii) Review on Request of Institution or Agency. If an institution or agency to which the juvenile was committed believes that the juvenile has been rehabilitated and does not present a serious risk to public safety, the institution or agency may petition the court to conduct a review hearing at any time before the juvenile becomes 19 years of age or, if the court has extended jurisdiction, any time before the juvenile becomes 21 years of age.

(iii) Mandatory Review. The court shall schedule a review hearing to be held within 42 days before the juvenile attains the age of 19, unless adjourned for good cause.

(iv) Final Review. The court shall conduct a final review of the juvenile's probation not less than 91 days before the end of the probation period.

(b) Notice of Hearing. Notice of the hearing must be given at least 14 days before the hearing to

(i) the prosecuting attorney;

(ii) the agency or the superintendent of the institution or facility to which the juvenile has been committed;

(iii) the juvenile; and

(iv) if the address or whereabouts are known, the parent, guardian, or legal custodian of the juvenile.

The notice must clearly indicate that the court may extend jurisdiction over the juvenile or impose sentence and must advise the juvenile and the parent, guardian, or legal custodian of the juvenile that the juvenile has a right to an attorney.

(2) *Appointment of Attorney.* The court must appoint an attorney to represent the juvenile unless an attorney has been retained. The court may assess the cost of providing an attorney as costs against the juvenile or those responsible for the juvenile's support, or both, if the persons to be assessed are financially able to comply.

(3) *Evidence; Commitment Report.* The court may consider the commitment report prepared as provided in MCL 803.225 and any report prepared upon the court's order by the officer or agency supervising probation.

(4) *Burden of Proof; Findings.*

(a) Before the court may continue jurisdiction over the juvenile or impose sentence, the prosecuting attorney must demonstrate by a preponderance of the evidence that the juvenile has not been rehabilitated or that the juvenile presents a serious risk to public safety. The Michigan Rules of Evidence, other than those with respect to privileges, do not apply. In making the determination, the court must consider the following factors:

(i) the extent and nature of the juvenile's participation in education, counseling, or work programs;

(ii) the juvenile's willingness to accept responsibility for prior behavior;

(iii) the juvenile's behavior in the current placement;

(iv) the juvenile's prior record, character, and physical and mental maturity;

(v) the juvenile's potential for violent conduct as demonstrated by prior behavior;

(vi) the recommendation of the institution, agency, or facility charged with the juvenile's care for the juvenile's release or continued custody;

(vii) any other information the prosecuting attorney or the juvenile submit.

(b) Before the court may impose a sentence at the final review hearing, the court must determine that the best interests of the public would be served by the imposition of a sentence provided by law for an adult offender. In making the determination, the court must consider the following factors, in addition to the criteria specified in subrule (4)(a):

(i) the effect of treatment on the juvenile's rehabilitation;

(ii) whether the juvenile is likely to be dangerous to the public if released;

(iii) the best interests of the public welfare and the protection of public security.

(5) *Sentencing Credit.* If a sentence of imprisonment is imposed, the juvenile shall receive credit for the time served on probation.

(B) Violation of Probation in Delayed Imposition of Sentence Cases.

(1) *Subsequent Conviction.* If a juvenile placed on probation under an order of disposition delaying imposition of sentence is found by the court to have violated probation by being convicted of a felony or a misdemeanor punishable by imprisonment for more than 1 year, or adjudicated as responsible for an offense that if committed by an adult would be a felony or a misdemeanor punishable by imprisonment for more than 1 year, the court shall revoke probation and sentence the juvenile to imprisonment for a term that does not exceed the penalty that could have been imposed for the offense for which the juvenile was originally convicted and placed on probation.

(2) *Other Violations of Probation.* If a juvenile placed on probation under an order of disposition delaying imposition of sentence is found by the court to have violated probation other

than as provided in subrule (B)(1), the court may impose sentence or may order any of the following for the juvenile:

(a) A change in placement.

(b) Community service.

(c) Substance abuse counseling.

(d) Mental health counseling.

(e) Participation in a vocational-technical program.

(f) Incarceration in the county jail for not more than 30 days if the present county jail facility would meet all requirements under federal law and regulations for housing juveniles, and if the court has consulted with the sheriff to determine when the sentence will begin to ensure that space will be available for the juvenile. If the juvenile is under 17 years of age, the juvenile must be placed in a room or ward out of sight and sound from adult prisoners.

(g) Other participation or performance as the court considers necessary.

(3) *Hearing.* The probation violation hearing must be conducted pursuant to MCR 3.944(C).

(4) *Sentencing Credit.* If a sentence of imprisonment is imposed, the juvenile must receive credit for the time served on probation.

(C) Determination of Ability to Pay. A juvenile and/or parent shall not be detained or incarcerated for the nonpayment of court-ordered financial obligations as ordered by the court, unless the court determines that the juvenile and/or parent has the resources to pay and has not made a good-faith effort to do so.

[Adopted February 4, 2003, effective May 1, 2003, 467 Mich. Amended May 25, 2016, effective September 1, 2016, 499 Mich.]

Comments

Staff Comment to 2003 Adoption

MCR 3.956 corresponds to former Rule 5.956.

Staff Comment to 2016 Amendment

The amendments of MCR 3.605, 3.606, 3.928, 3.944, 3.956, 6.001, 6.425, 6.445, 6.610, and 6.933 were submitted by the Michigan State Planning Body for the Delivery of Legal Services to the Poor. The rule revisions are intended to provide clarity and guidance to courts regarding what courts would be required to do before incarcerating a defendant for failure to pay.

Rule 3.961. Initiating Child Protective Proceedings

(A) Form. Absent exigent circumstances, a request for court action to protect a child must be in the form of a petition. The form, captioning, signing, and verifying of documents are prescribed in MCR 1.109(D) and (E). When any pending or resolved family division case exists that involves family members of the person(s) named in the petition filed under subrule (B), the petitioner must complete and file a case inventory listing those cases, if known. The case inventory is confidential, not subject to service requirements in MCR 3.203, and is available only to the party that filed it, the filing party's attorney, the court, and the friend of the court. The case inventory must be on a form approved by the State Court Administrative Office.

(B) Content of Petition. A petition must contain the following information, if known:

(1) The child's name, address, and date of birth.

(2) The names and addresses of:

(a) the child's mother and father,

(b) the parent, guardian, legal custodian, or person who has custody of the child, if other than a mother or father, and

(c) the nearest known relative of the child, if no parent, guardian, or legal custodian can be found.

(3) The essential facts that constitute an offense against the child under the Juvenile Code.

(4) A citation to the section of the Juvenile Code relied on for jurisdiction.

(5) The child's membership or eligibility for membership in an Indian tribe, if any, and the identity of the tribe.

(6) The type of relief requested. A request for removal of the child or a parent or for termination of parental rights at the initial disposition must be specifically stated. If the petition requests removal of an Indian child or if an Indian child was taken into protective custody pursuant to MCR 3.963 as a result of an emergency, the petition must specifically describe:

(a) the active efforts as defined in MCR 3.002, that have been made to provide remedial services and rehabilitative programs designed to prevent the breakup of the Indian family; and

(b) documentation, including attempts, to identify the child's tribe.

(C) Amended and Supplemental Petitions.

(1) If a nonrespondent parent is being added as an additional respondent to a petition that has been authorized by the court under MCR 3.962 or MCR 3.965 against the first respondent parent, and the first respondent parent has not made a plea under MCR 3.971 or a trial has not been conducted under MCR 3.972, the allegations against the second respondent shall be filed in an amended petition.

(2) If a nonrespondent parent is being added as an additional respondent in a case in which a petition has been authorized under MCR 3.962 or MCR 3.965, and adjudicated by plea under MCR 3.971 or by trial under MCR 3.972, the allegations against the second respondent shall be filed in a supplemental petition.

(3) If either an amended or supplemental petition is not accompanied by a request for placement of the child or the child is not in protective or temporary custody, the court shall conduct a preliminary inquiry to determine the appropriate action to be taken on a petition. If either the amended or supplemental petition contains a request for removal, the court shall conduct a preliminary hearing to determine the appropriate action to be taken on the petition consistent with MCR 3.965(B). If either the amended or supplemental petition is authorized, the court shall proceed against each respondent parent in accordance with MCR 3.971 or MCR 3.972.

[Adopted February 4, 2003, effective May 1, 2003, 467 Mich. Amended February 2, 2010, effective May 1, 2010, 485 Mich. Amended effective, pending public comment, March 20, 2013, 493 Mich; March 25, 2015, 497 Mich. Amended effective September 23, 2015, 498 Mich. Amended May 30, 2018, effective September 1, 2018, 501 Mich. Amended effective September 11, 2019, 503 Mich. Amended September 18, 2019, effective January 1, 2020, 503 Mich.]

Comments

Staff Comment to 2003 Adoption

MCR 3.961 corresponds to former Rule 5.961.

Subrule (B)(6) requires that a request for removal of a child or parent, or for termination of parental rights, be specifically stated in the petition.

Staff Comment to 2010 Amendment

These amendments incorporate provisions of the Indian Child Welfare Act into specific provisions within various rules relating to child protective proceedings and juvenile status offenses. The language is designed to make the rules reflect a more integrated approach to addressing issues specific to Indian children.

MCR 3.002(1)(c) defines "preadoptive placement" to mean the "temporary placement of an Indian child in a foster home or institution after the termination of parental rights, but before or in lieu of adoptive placement, and ..." The phrase "in lieu of adoptive placement" is not intended to mean that it is permissible to leave a child in foster care indefinitely, in violation of MCL 712A.19b(6) or (7) or 45 CFR 1355.20, 45 CFR 1356.21, or 45 CFR 1356.50. Rather, it addresses situations where the parental rights to a child have been terminated and there is no permanency plan for adoption of the child. One example is when the child has been placed with a juvenile guardian and the guardianship is subsequently revoked. In this situation, jurisdiction over the child pursuant to MCL 712A.2(b) will be reinstated and the child is placed in foster care.

MCR 3.002(1): The definition of "child custody proceeding" is intended to apply the Indian Child Welfare Act to delinquency proceedings if an "Indian child" is charged with a so-called status offense in violation of MCL 712A.2(a)(2)–(4) or (d). Delinquency proceedings involving an Indian child charged with any other non-status offense are generally not subject to the Indian Child Welfare Act; however, if the initial investigation or subsequent review of a non-status delinquency case reveals that the Indian child involved suffers from child abuse or neglect, a separate child protective proceeding may be initiated, which would be subject to the Indian Child Welfare Act.

The amendment of MCR 3.905(C)(1) states that a court shall consider guidelines established by the Bureau of Indian Affairs (BIA) in determining whether good cause not to transfer exists (Guidelines for State Courts; Indian Child Custody Proceedings, 44 Fed Reg No 228, 67590–67592, C.2–C.4. [November 26, 1979]). Some examples of good cause are that the Indian tribe does not have a tribal court or that the Indian child is over 12 years old and objects to the transfer. For additional examples of good cause and relevant case law, see the BIA guidelines cited above and A Practical Guide to the Indian Child Welfare Act. (Native American Rights Fund, A Practical Guide to the Indian Child Welfare Act [Boulder, CO: Native American Rights Fund, 2007], 7.15 and 7.16, p 60.)

Staff Comment to 2013 Amendment

This proposal incorporates provisions of the newly enacted Michigan Indian Family Preservation Act into specific provisions within various rules relating to child protective proceedings and juvenile status offenses.

Staff Comment to March, 2015 Amendment

The amendments of MCR 3.903, 3.920, 3.961, and 3.965 were prompted by the Michigan Supreme Court's decision in *In re Sanders*, 495 Mich 394 (2014), to provide clarification and procedural provisions consistent with the Court's holding in that case.

Staff Comment to September, 2015 Amendment

The Court retained the amendments of MCR 3.903, 3.920, 3.961, and 3.965 that became effective on March 25, 2015, and were prompted by the Michigan Supreme Court's decision in *In re Sanders*, 495 Mich 394 (2014), to provide clarification and procedural provisions with regard to a nonrespondent parent and adjudication that is consistent with the Court's holding. The Court further amended MCR 3.961(C)(3), effective immediately, to require the court to proceed against each respondent parent in accordance with MCR 3.971 or MCR 3.972 if *either* the amended *or supplemental* petition is authorized.

Staff Comment to 2018 Amendment

The amendments in this order are intended to begin moving trial courts toward a statewide uniform e-Filing process. In addition, the order moves existing language into MCR 1.109 as a way to, for the first time, include most filing requirements in one single rule, instead of scattered in various rules. The order largely mirrors the administrative orders that most e-Filing pilot projects have operated under, but contains some significant new provisions. For example, courts are required to maintain documents in an electronic document management system, and the electronic record is the official court record.

Staff Comment to 2019 Amendment

The amendments of MCR 1.109, 3.206, 3.931, and 3.961 enable family division courts to use the required case inventory form to administer cases while keeping the information confidential. This change is intended to prevent providing information that could affect the safety of domestic violence victims and their children.

Staff Comment to 2020 Amendment

The amendments of MCR 1.109, 2.107, 2.113, 2.116, 2.119, 2.222, 2.223, 2.225, 2.227, 3.206, 3.211, 3.212, 3.214, 3.303, 3.903, 3.921, 3.925, 3.926, 3.931, 3.933, 3.942,

3.950, 3.961, 3.971, 3.972, 4.002, 4.101, 4.201, 4.202, 4.302, 5.128, 5.302, 5.731, 6.101, 6.615, 8.105, and 8.119 and rescission of MCR 2.226 and 8.125 continue the process for design and implementation of the statewide electronic-filing system.

Rule 3.962   Preliminary Inquiry

(A) Purpose. When a petition is not accompanied by a request for placement of the child and the child is not in temporary custody, the court may conduct a preliminary inquiry to determine the appropriate action to be taken on a petition.

(B) Action by Court. A preliminary inquiry need not be conducted on the record or in the presence of the parties. At the preliminary inquiry, the court may:

(1) Deny authorization of the petition.

(2) Refer the matter to alternative services.

(3) Authorize the filing of the petition if it contains the information required by MCR 3.961(B), and there is probable cause to believe that one or more of the allegations is true. For the purpose of this subrule, probable cause may be established with such information and in such a manner as the court deems sufficient.

[Adopted February 4, 2003, effective May 1, 2003, 467 Mich.]

Comments

Staff Comment to 2003 Adoption

MCR 3.962 corresponds to former Rule 5.962.

Subrule (B) provides that the preliminary inquiry need not be conducted on the record or in the presence of the parties.

Rule 3.963.   Acquiring Physical Custody of Child

(A) Taking Custody Without Court Order.

(1) An officer may without court order remove a child from the child's surroundings and take the child into protective custody if, after investigation, the officer has reasonable grounds to believe that a child is at substantial risk of harm or is in surroundings that present an imminent risk of harm and the child's immediate removal from those surroundings is necessary to protect the child's health and safety. If the child is an Indian child who resides or is domiciled on a reservation, but is temporarily located off the reservation, the officer may take the child into protective custody only when necessary to prevent imminent physical damage or harm to the child.

(2) An officer who takes a child into protective custody under this rule shall immediately notify the Department of Human Services. While awaiting the arrival of the Department of Human Services, the child shall not be held in a detention facility.

(3) If a child taken into protective custody under this subrule is not released, the Department of Human Services shall immediately contact the designated judge or referee as provided in subrule (D) to seek an ex parte court order for placement of the child pursuant to subrule (B)(4).

(B) Court–Ordered Custody.

(1) *Order to Take Child into Protective Custody.* The court may issue a written order, electronically or otherwise, authorizing a child protective services worker, an officer, or other person deemed suitable by the court to immediately take a child into protective custody when, after presentment of a petition or affidavit of facts to the court, the court has reasonable cause to

believe that all the following conditions exist, together with specific findings of fact:

(a) The child is at substantial risk of harm or is in surroundings that present an imminent risk of harm and the child's immediate removal from those surroundings is necessary to protect the child's health and safety. If the child is an Indian child who resides or is domiciled on a reservation, but is temporarily located off the reservation, the child is subject to the exclusive jurisdiction of the tribal court. However, the state court may enter an order for protective custody of that child when it is necessary to prevent imminent physical damage or harm to the child.

(b) The circumstances warrant issuing an order pending a hearing in accordance with:

(i) MCR 3.965 for a child who is not yet under the jurisdiction of the court, or

(ii) MCR 3.974(C) for a child who is already under the jurisdiction of the court under MCR 3.971 or 3.972.

(c) Consistent with the circumstances, reasonable efforts were made to prevent or eliminate the need for removal of the child.

(d) No remedy other than protective custody is reasonably available to protect the child.

(e) Continuing to reside in the home is contrary to the child's welfare.

(2) The court may include in such an order authorization to enter specified premises to remove the child.

(3) The court shall inquire whether a member of the child's immediate or extended family is available to take custody of the child pending a preliminary hearing, or an emergency removal hearing if the court already has jurisdiction over the child under MCR 3.971 or MCR 3.972, whether there has been a central registry clearance, and whether a criminal history check has been initiated.

(4) *Ex parte Placement Order.* If an officer has taken a child into protective custody without court order under subsection (A), or if the Department of Human Services is requesting the court grant it protective custody and placement authority, the Department of Human Services shall present to the court a petition or affidavit of facts and request a written ex parte placement order. If a judge finds all the factors in subrule (B)(1)(a)–(e) are present, the judge may issue a placement order; if a referee finds all the factors in subrule (B)(1)(a)–(e) are present, the referee may issue an interim placement order pending a preliminary hearing. The written order shall contain specific findings of fact. It shall be communicated, electronically or otherwise, to the Department of Human Services.

(C) Arranging for Court Appearance. An officer or other person who takes a child into protective custody must:

(1) immediately attempt to notify the child's parent, guardian, or legal custodian of the protective custody;

(2) inform the parent, guardian, or legal custodian of the date, time, and place of the preliminary or emergency removal hearing scheduled by the court;

(3) immediately bring the child to the court for preliminary hearing, or immediately contact the court for instructions regarding placement pending preliminary hearing;

(4) if the court is not open, DHS must contact the person designated under subrule (D) for permission to place the child pending the hearing;

(5) ensure that the petition is prepared and submitted to the court;

(6) file a custody statement with the court that includes:

(a) a specific and detailed account of the circumstances that led to the emergency removal, and

(b) the names of persons notified and the times of notification or the reason for failure to notify.

(D) Designated Court Contact.

(1) When the Department of Human Services seeks a placement order for a child in protective custody under subrule (A) or (B), DHS shall contact a judge or referee designated by the court for that purpose.

(2) If the court is closed, the designated judge or referee may issue an ex parte order for placement upon receipt, electronically or otherwise, of a petition or affidavit of facts. The order must be communicated in writing, electronically or otherwise, to the appropriate county DHS office and filed with the court the next business day.

[Adopted February 4, 2003, effective May 1, 2003, 467 Mich. Amended October 24, 2006, effective January 1, 2007, 477 Mich; May 31, 2007, effective September 1, 2007, 478 Mich; February 2, 2010, effective May 1, 2010, 485 Mich. Amended effective, pending public comment, March 20, 2013, 493 Mich. Amended June 5, 2013, effective September 1, 2013, 494 Mich; May 27, 2015, effective September 1, 2015, 498 Mich. Amended effective August 14, 2019, 503 Mich.]

Comments

Staff Comment to 2003 Adoption

MCR 3.963 corresponds to former Rule 5.963.

The revisions substitute "protective" for "temporary" custody.

Subrule (B)(2) adds a requirement that there be a showing that continuation of the child's residence in the home would be contrary to the child's welfare. This is related to federal statutes and implementing regulations. See 45 CFR 1356.21(c), (d).

Staff Comment to 2006 Amendment

The amendment of MCR 3.963(B)(1) reflects the reality that Family Division judges or referees are not always presented with a petition when a request is made to remove a child from the home. In emergency circumstances, a police officer or social worker may seek the court's permission to remove a child from a home, but will not have an opportunity to draft a petition before seeking the child's removal. Other changes require orders authorizing the removal of a child to be in writing. The amendment also clarifies that the court should make a "reasonable efforts" finding at the child's removal, or within 60 days of the child's removal under MCR 3.965, or make a finding that "reasonable efforts" are not required. [Revision from order dated May 31, 2007.]

Staff Comment to 2010 Amendment

These amendments incorporate provisions of the Indian Child Welfare Act into specific provisions within various rules relating to child protective proceedings and juvenile status offenses. The language is designed to make the rules reflect a more integrated approach to addressing issues specific to Indian children.

MCR 3.002(1)(c) defines "preadoptive placement" to mean the "temporary placement of an Indian child in a foster home or institution after the termination of parental rights, but before or in lieu of adoptive placement, and ..." The phrase "in lieu of adoptive placement" is not intended to mean that it is permissible to leave a child in foster care indefinitely, in violation of MCL 712A.19b(6) or (7) or 45 CFR 1355.20, 45 CFR 1356.21, or 45 CFR 1356.50. Rather, it addresses situations where the parental rights to a child have been terminated and there is no permanency plan for adoption of the child. One example is when the child has been placed with a juvenile guardian and the guardianship is subsequently revoked. In this situation, jurisdiction over the child pursuant to MCL 712A.2(b) will be reinstated and the child is placed in foster care.

MCR 3.002(1): The definition of "child custody proceeding" is intended to apply the Indian Child Welfare Act to delinquency proceedings if an "Indian child" is

charged with a so-called status offense in violation of MCL 712A.2(a)(2)–(4) or (d). Delinquency proceedings involving an Indian child charged with any other non-status offense are generally not subject to the Indian Child Welfare Act; however, if the initial investigation or subsequent review of a non-status delinquency case reveals that the Indian child involved suffers from child abuse or neglect, a separate child protective proceeding may be initiated, which would be subject to the Indian Child Welfare Act.

The amendment of MCR 3.905(C)(1) states that a court shall consider guidelines established by the Bureau of Indian Affairs (BIA) in determining whether good cause not to transfer exists (Guidelines for State Courts; Indian Child Custody Proceedings, 44 Fed Reg No 228, 67590–67592, C.2–C.4. [November 26, 1979]). Some examples of good cause are that the Indian tribe does not have a tribal court or that the Indian child is over 12 years old and objects to the transfer. For additional examples of good cause and relevant case law, see the BIA guidelines cited above and A Practical Guide to the Indian Child Welfare Act (Native American Rights Fund, A Practical Guide to the Indian Child Welfare Act [Boulder, CO: Native American Rights Fund, 2007], 7.15 and 7.16, p 60.)

Staff Comment to March, 2013 Amendment

This proposal incorporates provisions of the newly enacted Michigan Indian Family Preservation Act into specific provisions within various rules relating to child protective proceedings and juvenile status offenses.

Staff Comment to September, 2013 Amendment

The changes of MCR 3.913, 3.963, 3.965, and 3.974 incorporate the statutory changes enacted in 2012 Public Act 163.

Staff Comment to 2015 Amendment

The amendments of MCR 3.963, 3.966, and 3.974 provide clarity regarding procedures to be followed when an emergency removal of a child has occurred but a dispositional hearing has not been held.

Staff Comment to 2019 Amendment

These amendments update cross-references and make other nonsubstantive revisions to clarify the rules.

Rule 3.965. Preliminary Hearing

(A) Time for Preliminary Hearing.

(1) *Child in Protective Custody.* The preliminary hearing must commence no later than 24 hours after the child has been taken into protective custody, excluding Sundays and holidays, as defined by MCR 8.110(D)(2), unless adjourned for good cause shown, or the child must be released.

(2) *Severely Physically Injured or Sexually Abused Child.* When the Department of Human Services submits a petition in cases in which the child has been severely physically injured, as that term is defined in MCL 722.628(3)(c), or sexually abused, and subrule (A)(1) does not apply, the preliminary hearing must commence no later than 24 hours after the agency submits a petition or on the next business day following the submission of the petition.

(B) Procedure.

(1) The court must determine if the parent, guardian, or legal custodian has been notified, and if the lawyer-guardian ad litem for the child is present. The preliminary hearing may be adjourned for the purpose of securing the appearance of an attorney, parent, guardian, or legal custodian or may be conducted in the absence of the parent, guardian, or legal custodian if notice has been given or if the court finds that a reasonable attempt to give notice was made.

(2) The court must inquire if the child or either parent is a member of an Indian tribe. If the court knows or has reason to know the child is an Indian child, the court must determine the identity of the child's tribe and, if the child was taken into protective custody pursuant to MCR 3.963(A) or the petition requests removal of the child, follow the procedures set forth in MCR 3.967. If necessary, the court may adjourn the preliminary hearing pending the conclusion of the removal hearing. A

removal hearing may be held in conjunction with the preliminary hearing if all necessary parties have been notified as required by MCR 3.905, there are no objections by the parties to do so, and at least one qualified expert witness is present to provide testimony.

(3) The child's lawyer-guardian ad litem must be present to represent the child at the preliminary hearing. The court may make temporary orders for the protection of the child pending the appearance of an attorney or pending the completion of the preliminary hearing. The court must direct that the lawyer-guardian ad litem for the child receive a copy of the petition.

(4) If the respondent is present, the court must assure that the respondent has a copy of the petition. The court must read the allegations in the petition in open court, unless waived.

(5) The court shall determine if the petition should be dismissed or the matter referred to alternate services. If the court so determines the court must release the child. Otherwise, the court must continue the hearing.

(6) The court must advise the respondent of the right to the assistance of an attorney at the preliminary hearing and any subsequent hearing pursuant to MCR 3.915(B)(1)(a).

(7) The court must advise the respondent of the right to trial on the allegations in the petition and that the trial may be before a referee unless a demand for a jury or judge is filed pursuant to MCR 3.911 or 3.912.

(8) The court must advise a nonrespondent parent of his or her right to seek placement of his or her children in his or her home.

(9) The court shall allow the respondent an opportunity to deny or admit the allegations and make a statement of explanation.

(10) The court must inquire whether the child is subject to the continuing jurisdiction of another court and, if so, which court.

(11) The court may adjourn the hearing for up to 14 days to secure the attendance of witnesses or for other good cause shown. If the court knows or has reason to know the child is an Indian, the court may adjourn the hearing for up to 21 days to ensure proper notice to the tribe or Secretary of the Interior as required by MCR 3.920(C)(1). If the preliminary hearing is adjourned, the court may make temporary orders for the placement of the child when necessary to assure the immediate safety of the child, pending the completion of the preliminary hearing and subject to subrule (C), and as applicable, MCR 3.967.

(12) Unless the preliminary hearing is adjourned, the court must decide whether to authorize the filing of the petition and, if authorized, whether the child should remain in the home, be returned home, or be placed in foster care pending trial. The court may authorize the filing of the petition upon a showing of probable cause, unless waived, that one or more of the allegations in the petition are true and fall within MCL 712A.2(b). The Michigan Rules of Evidence do not apply, other than those with respect to privileges, except to the extent that such privileges are abrogated by MCL 722.631.

(13) If the court authorizes the filing of the petition, the court:

(a) may release the child to a parent, guardian, or legal custodian and may order such reasonable terms and conditions believed necessary to protect the physical health or mental well-being of the child; or

(b) may order placement of the child after making the determinations specified in subrule (C), if those determinations have not previously been made. If the child is an Indian child, the child must be placed in descending order of preference with:

(i) a member of the child's extended family,

(ii) a foster home licensed, approved, or specified by the child's tribe,

(iii) an Indian foster family licensed or approved by the department,

(iv) an institution for children approved by an Indian tribe or operated by an Indian organization that has a program suitable to meet the child's needs.

The court may order another placement for good cause shown in accordance with MCL 712B.23(3)–(5). If the Indian child's tribe has established a different order of preference than the order prescribed above, placement shall follow that tribe's order of preference as long as the placement is the least restrictive setting appropriate to the particular needs of the child, as provided in MCL 712B.23(6). The standards to be applied in meeting the preference requirements above shall be the prevailing social and cultural standards of the Indian community in which the parent or extended family resides or with which the parent or extended family members maintain social and cultural ties.

(14) The court must inquire of the parent, guardian, or legal custodian regarding the identity of relatives of the child who might be available to provide care. If the father of the child has not been identified, the court must inquire of the mother regarding the identity and whereabouts of the father.

(15) If the court orders removal of the child from a parent's care or custody, the court shall advise the parent, guardian, or legal custodian of the right to appeal that action.

(C) Pretrial Placement.

(1) *Placement; Proofs.* If the child was not released under subrule (B), the court shall receive evidence, unless waived, to establish that the criteria for placement set forth in subrule 3.965(C)(2) are present. The respondent shall be given an opportunity to cross-examine witnesses, to subpoena witnesses, and to offer proofs to counter the admitted evidence.

(2) *Criteria.* The court may order placement of the child into foster case if the court finds all of the following:

(a) Custody of the child with the parent presents a substantial risk of harm to the child's life, physical health, or mental well-being.

(b) No provision of service or other arrangement except removal of the child is reasonably available to adequately safeguard the child from the risk as described in subrule (a).

(c) Continuing the child's residence in the home is contrary to the child's welfare.

(d) Consistent with the circumstances, reasonable efforts were made to prevent or eliminate the need for removal of the child.

(e) Conditions of child custody away from the parent are adequate to safeguard the child's health and welfare.

(3) *Contrary to the Welfare Findings.* Contrary to the welfare findings must be made. If placement is ordered, the court must make a statement of findings, in writing or on the record, explicitly including the finding that it is contrary to the welfare of the child to remain at home and the reasons supporting that finding. If the "contrary to the welfare of the child" finding is placed on the record and not in a written statement of findings, it must be capable of being transcribed. The findings may be made on the basis of hearsay evidence that possesses adequate indicia of trustworthiness. If continuing the child's residence in the home is contrary to the welfare of the child, the court shall not return the child to the home, but shall order the child placed in the most family-like setting available consistent with the child's needs.

(4) *Reasonable Efforts Findings.* Reasonable efforts findings must be made. In making the reasonable efforts determination under this subrule, the child's health and safety must be of paramount concern to the court. When the court has placed a child with someone other than the custodial parent, guardian, or legal custodian, the court must determine whether reasonable efforts to prevent the removal of the child have been made or that reasonable efforts to prevent removal are not required. The court must make this determination at the earliest possible time, but no later than 60 days from the date of removal, and must state the factual basis for the determination in the court order. Nunc pro tunc orders or affidavits are not acceptable. Reasonable efforts to prevent a child's removal from the home are not required if a court of competent jurisdiction has determined that

(a) the parent has subjected the child to aggravated circumstances as listed in sections 18(1) and (2) of the Child Protection Law, MCL 722.638(1) and (2); or

(b) the parent has been convicted of 1 or more of the following:

(i) murder of another child of the parent,

(ii) voluntary manslaughter of another child of the parent,

(iii) aiding or abetting, attempting, conspiring, or soliciting to commit such a murder or such a voluntary manslaughter, or

(iv) a felony assault that results in serious bodily injury to the child or another child of the parent; or

(c) parental rights of the parent with respect to a sibling have been terminated involuntarily; or

(d) the parent is required to register under the Sex Offender Registration Act.

(5) *Record Checks; Home Study.* If the child has been placed in a relative's home,

(a) the court may order the Family Independence Agency to report the results of a criminal record check and central registry clearance of the residents of the home to the court before, or within 7 days after, the placement, and

(b) the court must order the Family Independence Agency to perform a home study with a copy to be submitted to the court not more than 30 days after the placement.

(6) *No Right to Bail.* No one has the right to post bail in a protective proceeding for the release of a child in the custody of the court.

(7) *Parenting Time or Visitation.*

(a) Unless the court suspends parenting time pursuant to MCL 712A.19b(4), or unless the child has a guardian or legal custodian, the court must permit each parent frequent parenting time with a child in placement unless parenting time, even if supervised, may be harmful to the child.

(b) If the child was living with a guardian or legal custodian, the court must determine what, if any, visitation will be permitted with the guardian or legal custodian.

(8) *Medical Information.* Unless the court has previously ordered the release of medical information, the order placing the child in foster care must include:

(a) an order that the child's parent, guardian, or legal custodian provide the supervising agency with the name and address of each of the child's medical providers, and

(b) an order that each of the child's medical providers release the child's medical records.

(D) Advice; Initial Service Plan. If placement is ordered, the court must, orally or in writing, inform the parties:

(1) that the agency designated to care and supervise the child will prepare an initial service plan no later than 30 days after the placement;

(2) that participation in the initial service plan is voluntary unless otherwise ordered by the court;

(3) that the general elements of an initial service plan include:

(a) the background of the child and the family,

(b) an evaluation of the experiences and problems of the child,

(c) a projection of the expected length of stay in foster care, and

(d) an identification of specific goals and projected time frames for meeting the goals;

(4) that, on motion of a party, the court will review the initial service plan and may modify the plan if it is in the best interests of the child; and

(5) that the case may be reviewed for concurrent planning.

The court shall direct the agency to identify, locate, and consult with relatives to determine if placement with a relative would be in the child's best interests, as required by MCL 722.954a(2). In a case to which MCL 712A.18f(6) applies, the court shall require the agency to provide the name and address of the child's attending physician of record or primary care physician.

[Adopted February 4, 2003, effective May 1, 2003, 467 Mich. Amended effective May 1, 2003, 467 Mich; February 25, 2004, 469 Mich. Amended October 24, 2006, effective January 1, 2007, 477 Mich; May 31, 2007, effective September 1, 2007, 478 Mich; April 14, 2009, effective July 1, 2009, 483 Mich; February 2, 2010, effective May 1, 2010, 485 Mich. Amended effective March 20, 2013, 493 Mich. Amended June 5, 2013, effective September 1, 2013, 494 Mich. Amended effective September 5, 2013, 495 Mich; October 2, 2013, 495 Mich; March 25, 2015, 497 Mich; September 23, 2015, 498 Mich; March 9, 2016, 499 Mich; June 12, 2019, 503 Mich.]

Comments

Staff Comment to 2003 Adoption

MCR 3.965 corresponds to former Rule 5.965.

A new subrule (A)(2) is added, providing that in the case of a petition involving a child who has been severely physically injured or sexually abused, the preliminary hearing must begin no later than 24 hours after submission of the petition, or the next business day.

Subrule (B), regarding procedure at the hearing, is substantially rewritten. Subrule (B)(1) permits the hearing to go forward in the absence of the parent, guardian, or legal custodian if notice has been given or if a reasonable attempt to do so was made.

Other provisions include requirements that a copy of the petition be provided to various persons [subrules (B)(2)–(3)]; that inquiries be made regarding whether the child is subject to the jurisdiction of another court and about American Indian tribe membership [subrules (B)(8)–(9)]; and providing for temporary orders for placement of the child where the hearing is adjourned [Subrule (10)].

Subrule (B)(11) provides that the Rules of Evidence do not apply, except those regarding privileges. However, the privilege provision is qualified by incorporation of MCL 722.631, which abrogates certain privileges.

Subrule (B)(12) provides that if a court authorizes the petition, it may order the child released to the parent, guardian, or legal custodian or, on making appropriate findings, the court may order placement of the child.

Subrules (D) and (C) are substantially rewritten. A number of the changes are designed to comply with the requirements of 42 USC 671, and associated regulations. 45 CFR 1356.21.

Subrule (C)(2) would add a requirement that if the child is removed from the home, the child is to be placed in the most family-like setting available, consistent with the child's needs. See MCL 712A.13a(10).

Subrule (C)(4) provides for a criminal record check and central registry clearance, as well as a Family Independence Agency home study, if the child is placed in a relative's home.

Subrule (C)(6)(b) provides for visitation with a guardian or legal custodian with whom the child has been living.

Subrule (C)(7) requires that an order placing a child in foster care direct the child's parent or custodian to provide the agency with the name and address of the child's medical providers, and the order is to direct the providers to release medical records.

New subrule (D) includes a number of provisions regarding the determination whether reasonable efforts have been made to avoid removing the child from the home. Exceptions are created where the parent has subjected the child to certain aggravating circumstances listed in MCL 712A.19b(3)(k) or committed certain serious crimes.

Staff Comment to 2003 Amendment

The April 30, 2003, order makes corrections to a number of the rules governing proceedings regarding juveniles that had been adopted on February 4, 2003. The changes are effective May 1, corresponding to the effective date of the February 4 amendments. In addition to these changes, a number of corrections of punctuation and capitalization and changes in the Notes that accompanied the rules have been made and will appear in the published version of the rules.

The amendments of MCR 3.903(D)(8)(m), 6.903(H)(16), 6.931(E)(3), and 6.933(C)(1) conform the rules to 2002 PA 665, which changed the amounts of controlled substances required for certain violations. See MCL 333.7401(2)(a)(i), 333.7403(2)(a)(i). MCR 3.933(C)(1) is also modified in light of *People v Valentin*, 457 Mich 1 (1998).

The amendment of MCR 3.935(B)(1) corrects the inadvertent omission of references to guardians and legal custodians.

The amendments of MCR 3.922(E)(1)(c), 3.943(A), 3.945(A)(1), 3.965(E)(1), and 3.972(C)(2)(c) correct minor errors in wording.

The amendment of MCR 3.977(G) deletes the word "hearing" in the reference to progress reviews. Under MCR 3.974(A)(1), progress reviews do not require hearings.

The amendment of MCR 3.980(B) and (C) revise the provisions on removal of American Indian children from the home to clarify the distinction between emergency removals and removals after hearing.

The amendments of MCR 3.982(A), 6.903(I)–(L) and 6.937(A) correct cross-reference, citation and numbering errors.

Staff Comment to 2004 Amendment

The February 25, 2004, amendments of MCR 3.915, 3.965, 3.975, 3.976 and 3.977, effective immediately, are based on recommendations from the Family Independence Agency and Supreme Court Adoption Work Group.

The amendment of MCR 3.915(B)(2)(a) is designed to enforce the statutory requirement in MCL 712A.17d that lawyers-guardians ad litem for children meet with their clients before each hearing.

The amendment of MCR 3.915(D)(2) addresses the substitution of lawyers-guardians ad litem.

The amendments of MCR 3.965 (B)(13) and (E) require the court to ask parents, guardians, or legal custodians to identify relatives who might be available to care for the child. The amendment to subsection (E) also requires the court to ask parents, guardians, or legal custodians to identify the child's treating physician in certain circumstances. See MCL 712A.18f(6).

The amendments of MCR 3.975(B) and MCR 3.976(C) require the court to notify interested parties that they may provide input at dispositional review and permanency planning hearings.

The amendments of MCR 3.976(B)(3) and (E)(2) encourage early holding of permanency planning hearings and early filing of petitions for termination of parental rights, where appropriate.

MCR 3.977(C)(2) is a new provision that requires courts to give child welfare cases priority in scheduling.

Staff Comment to 2006 Amendment

The amendment of MCR 3.965(B)(11) more accurately reflects the decisions made at the preliminary hearing in Family Division courts and discourages the practice of the court's placing a child in a specific foster care facility. "Foster care" is defined in MCR 3.903(C)(4) as including placement with a relative and specifies that the court has given the Family Independence Agency (now the Department of Human Services) placement and care responsibility.

The amendments of MCR 3.965(C)(3) require the court to make not only a "contrary to the welfare" finding, but also to include the reasons for that finding.

The amendments of MCR 3.965(D)(2) conform the rule language to that of the recent amendments of the "reasonable efforts" language in MCL 712A.19a, as amended by 2004 PA 473, and make its language consistent with the proposed "reasonable efforts" language in MCR 3.976(B)(1). The amendments add language to clarify that a court can determine that reasonable efforts to prevent removal have been made or can determine that reasonable efforts to prevent removal are not required due to aggravated circumstances. [Revision from order dated May 31, 2007.]

Staff Comment to 2007 Amendment

An additional amendment of MCR 3.965(D)(2)(b)(iii) mirrors the provision in the federal Social Security Act at 42 USC 671(a)(15)(D)(ii)(III), which was suggested in a letter from the Department of Health and Human Services. For the full text of the letter, please see the staff comment of MCR 3.976.

Staff Comment to 2009 Amendment

The amendments of Rules 3.901, 3.903, 3.921, 3.965, 3.975, 3.976, 3.977, and 3.978, and new rule 3.979 of the Michigan Court Rules reflect the enactment of 2008 PA 199–203.

Staff Comment to 2010 Amendment

These amendments incorporate provisions of the Indian Child Welfare Act into specific provisions within various rules relating to child protective proceedings and juvenile status offenses. The language is designed to make the rules reflect a more integrated approach to addressing issues specific to Indian children.

MCR 3.002(1)(c) defines "preadoptive placement" to mean the "temporary placement of an Indian child in a foster home or institution after the termination of parental rights, but before or in lieu of adoptive placement, and . . ." The phrase "in lieu of adoptive placement" is not intended to mean that it is permissible to leave a child in foster care indefinitely, in violation of MCL 712A.19b(6) or (7) or 45 CFR 1355.20, 45 CFR 1356.21, or 45 CFR 1356.50. Rather, it addresses situations where the parental rights to a child have been terminated and there is no permanency plan for adoption of the child. One example is when the child has been placed with a juvenile guardian and the guardianship is subsequently revoked. In this situation, jurisdiction over the child pursuant to MCL 712A.2(b) will be reinstated and the child is placed in foster care.

MCR 3.002(1): The definition of "child custody proceeding" is intended to apply the Indian Child Welfare Act to delinquency proceedings if an "Indian child" is charged with a so-called status offense in violation of MCL 712A.2(a)(2)–(4) or (d). Delinquency proceedings involving an Indian child charged with any other non-status offense are generally not subject to the Indian Child Welfare Act; however, if the initial investigation or subsequent review of a non-status delinquency case reveals that the Indian child involved suffers from child abuse or neglect, a separate child protective proceeding may be initiated, which would be subject to the Indian Child Welfare Act.

The amendment of MCR 3.905(C)(1) states that a court shall consider guidelines established by the Bureau of Indian Affairs (BIA) in determining whether good cause not to transfer exists (Guidelines for State Courts; Indian Child Custody Proceedings, 44 Fed Reg No 228, 67590–67592, C.2–C.4. [November 26, 1979]). Some examples of good cause are that the Indian tribe does not have a tribal court or that the Indian child is over 12 years old and objects to the transfer. For additional examples of good cause and relevant case law, see the BIA guidelines cited above and A Practical Guide to the Indian Child Welfare Act.

(Native American Rights Fund, A Practical Guide to the Indian Child Welfare Act [Boulder, CO: Native American Rights Fund, 2007], 7.15 and 7.16, p 60.)

Staff Comment to March, 2013 Amendment

This proposal incorporates provisions of the newly enacted Michigan Indian Family Preservation Act into specific provisions within various rules relating to child protective proceedings and juvenile status offenses.

Staff Comment to September 1, 2013 Amendment

The changes of MCR 3.913, 3.963, 3.965, and 3.974 incorporate the statutory changes enacted in 2012 Public Act 163.

Staff Comment to September 5, 2013 Amendment

These amendments reflect changes that correct minor technical errors that have occurred in drafting or the changes respond to recent adopted rule revisions, which occasionally inadvertently create incorrect cross-references in other rules.

Staff Comment to October, 2013 Amendment

The amendment of MCR 3.965 allows a slightly longer adjournment period in cases that involve Indian children to accommodate the statutory provisions that require notice to be provided at least ten days before the hearing.

Staff Comment to March, 2015 Amendment

The amendments of MCR 3.903, 3.920, 3.961, and 3.965 were prompted by the Michigan Supreme Court's decision in *In re Sanders*, 495 Mich 394 (2014), to provide clarification and procedural provisions consistent with the Court's holding in that case.

Staff Comment to September, 2015 Amendment

The Court retained the amendments of MCR 3.903, 3.920, 3.961, and 3.965 that became effective on March 25, 2015, and were prompted by the Michigan Supreme Court's decision in *In re Sanders*, 495 Mich 394 (2014), to provide clarification and procedural provisions with regard to a nonrespondent parent and adjudication that is consistent with the Court's holding. The Court further amended MCR 3.961(C)(3), effective immediately, to require the court to proceed against each respondent parent in accordance with MCR 3.971 or MCR 3.972 if *either* the amended *or supplemental* petition is authorized.

Staff Comment to 2016 Amendment

These amendments update cross-references that changed after the rule was adopted and make other nonsubstantive revisions.

Staff Comment to 2019 Amendment

The amendments of MCR 3.965, 3.971, 3.972, 3.973, and 3.993 incorporate a requirement for a trial court to notify a respondent in a child protection proceeding of the right to appeal following a child's removal from the home and the initial dispositional order, and that failure to do so may bar respondent from later challenging the court's assumption of jurisdiction.

Rule 3.966 Other Placement Review Proceedings

(A) Review of Placement Order and Initial Service Plan.

(1) On motion of a party, the court must review the placement order or the initial service plan, and may modify the order and plan if it is in the best interest of the child. If removal from the parent, guardian, or legal custodian is requested, at the hearing on the motion, the court shall follow the placement procedures in MCR 3.965(B) and (C).

(2) If the child is removed from the home and disposition is not completed, the court shall conduct a dispositional hearing in accordance with MCR 3.973.

(B) Petitions to Review Placement Decisions by Supervising Agency.

(1) *General.* The court may review placement decisions when all of the following apply:

(a) a child has been removed from the home;

(b) the supervising agency has made a placement decision after identifying, locating, and consulting with relatives to determine placement with a fit and appropriate relative who would meet the child's developmental, emotional, and physical needs as an alternative to nonrelative foster care;

(c) the supervising agency has provided written notice of the placement decision;

(d) a person receiving notice has disagreed with the placement decision and has given the child's lawyer-guardian ad litem written notice of the disagreement within 5 days of the date on which the person receives notice; and

(e) the child's lawyer-guardian ad litem determines the decision is not in the child's best interest.

(2) *Petition for Review.* If the criteria in subrule (1) are met, within 14 days after the date of the agency's written placement decision, the child's lawyer-guardian ad litem must file a petition for review.

(3) *Hearing on Petition.* The court must commence a review hearing on the record within 7 days of the filing of the petition.

(C) Disputes Between Agency and Foster Care Review Board Regarding Change In Placement.

(1) *General.* The court must conduct a hearing upon notice from the Foster Care Review Board that, after an investigation, it disagrees with a proposed change in placement by the agency of a child who is not a permanent ward of the Michigan Children's Institute.

(2) *Procedure.*

(a) Time. The court must set the hearing no sooner than 7 days and no later than 14 days after receipt of the notice from the Foster Care Review Board that there is a disagreement regarding a placement change.

(b) Notice. The court must provide notice of the hearing date to the foster parents, each interested party, and the prosecuting attorney if the prosecuting attorney has appeared in the case.

(c) Evidence. The court may hear testimony from the agency and any other interested party. The court may consider any other evidence bearing upon the proposed change in placement. The Rules of Evidence do not apply to a hearing under this rule.

(d) Findings. The court must order the continuation or restoration of placement unless the court finds that the proposed change in placement is in the child's best interests.

[Adopted February 4, 2003, effective May 1, 2003, 467 Mich. Amended October 24, 2006, effective January 1, 2007, 477 Mich; May 27, 2015, effective September 1, 2015, 498 Mich.]

Comments

Staff Comment to 2003 Adoption

MCR 3.966 is new. However, subrule (A) includes the provisions of former Rule 5.965(C)(8).

Subrule (B) sets forth a procedure for review of placement decisions by the supervising agency. The review is initiated by the child's lawyer-guardian ad litem when certain conditions are met.

New subrule (C) governs resolution of disputes between an agency and the Foster Care Review Board regarding changes in placement.

Staff Comment to 2006 Amendment

The amendments of MCR 3.966 delete the term "custody order," and add the requirement from 2004 PA 477 that a review hearing occur within 182 days of a child's removal from the home.

Staff Comment to 2015 Amendment

The amendments of MCR 3.963, 3.966, and 3.974 provide clarity regarding procedures to be followed when an emergency removal of a child has occurred but a dispositional hearing has not been held.

Rule 3.967　Removal Hearing for Indian Child

(A) Child in Protective Custody. If an Indian child is taken into protective custody pursuant to MCR 3.963(A) or (B) or MCR 3.974, a removal hearing must be completed within 14 days after removal from a parent or Indian custodian unless that parent or Indian custodian has requested an additional 20 days for the hearing pursuant to MCL 712B.9(2) or the court adjourns the hearing pursuant to MCR 3.923(G). Absent extraordinary circumstances that make additional delay unavoidable, temporary emergency custody shall not be continued for more than 45 days.

(B) Child Not in Protective Custody. If an Indian child has not been taken into protective custody and the petition requests removal of that child, a removal hearing must be conducted before the court may enter an order removing the Indian child from the parent or Indian custodian.

(C) Notice of the removal hearing must be sent to the parties prescribed in MCR 3.921 in compliance with MCR 3.920(C)(1).

(D) Evidence. An Indian child may be removed from a parent or Indian custodian, or, for an Indian child already taken into protective custody pursuant to MCR 3.963 or MCR 3.974(B), remain removed from a parent or Indian custodian pending further proceedings, only upon clear and convincing evidence, including the testimony of at least one qualified expert witness, as described in MCL 712B.17, who has knowledge about the child-rearing practices of the Indian child's tribe, that active efforts as defined in MCR 3.002 have been made to provide remedial services and rehabilitative programs designed to prevent the breakup of the Indian family, that these efforts have proved unsuccessful, and that continued custody of the child by the parent or Indian custodian is likely to result in serious emotional or physical damage to the child. The active efforts must take into account the prevailing social and cultural conditions and way of life of the Indian child's tribe.

(E) A removal hearing may be combined with any other hearing.

(F) The Indian child, if removed from home, must be placed in descending order of preference with:

(1) a member of the child's extended family,

(2) a foster home licensed, approved, or specified by the child's tribe,

(3) an Indian foster family licensed or approved by department,

(4) an institution for children approved by an Indian tribe or operated by an Indian organization that has a program suitable to meet the child's needs.

The court may order another placement for good cause shown in accordance with MCL 712B.23(3)–(5). If the Indian child's tribe has established a different order of preference than the order prescribed in subrule (F), placement shall follow that tribe's order of preference as long as the placement is the least restrictive setting appropriate to the particular needs of the child, as provided in MCL 712B.23(6).

The standards to be applied in meeting the preference requirements above shall be the prevailing social and cultural standards of the Indian community in which the parent or extended family resides or with which the parent or extended family members maintain social and cultural ties.

[Adopted February 2, 2010, effective May 1, 2010, 485 Mich. Amended effective, pending public comment, March 20, 2013, 493 Mich. Amended effective September 5, 2013, 495 Mich.]

Comments

Staff Comment to 2010 Adoption

These amendments incorporate provisions of the Indian Child Welfare Act into specific provisions within various rules relating to child protective proceedings and juvenile status offenses. The language is designed to make the rules reflect a more integrated approach to addressing issues specific to Indian children.

MCR 3.002(1)(c) defines "preadoptive placement" to mean the "temporary placement of an Indian child in a foster home or institution after the termination of parental rights, but before or in lieu of adoptive placement, and ..." The phrase "in lieu of adoptive placement" is not intended to mean that it is permissible to leave a child in foster care indefinitely, in violation of MCL 712A.19b(6) or (7) or 45 CFR 1355.20, 45 CFR 1356.21, or 45 CFR 1356.50. Rather, it addresses situations where the parental rights to a child have been terminated and there is no permanency plan for adoption of the child. One example is when the child has been placed with a juvenile guardian and the guardianship is subsequently revoked. In this situation, jurisdiction over the child pursuant to MCL 712A.2(b) will be reinstated and the child is placed in foster care.

MCR 3.002(1): The definition of "child custody proceeding" is intended to apply the Indian Child Welfare Act to delinquency proceedings if an "Indian child" is charged with a so-called status offense in violation of MCL 712A.2(a)(2)–(4) or (d). Delinquency proceedings involving an Indian child charged with any other non-status offense are generally not subject to the Indian Child Welfare Act; however, if the initial investigation or subsequent review of a non-status delinquency case reveals that the Indian child involved suffers from child abuse or neglect, a separate child protective proceeding may be initiated, which would be subject to the Indian Child Welfare Act.

The amendment of MCR 3.905(C)(1) states that a court shall consider guidelines established by the Bureau of Indian Affairs (BIA) in determining whether good cause not to transfer exists (Guidelines for State Courts; Indian Child Custody Proceedings, 44 Fed Reg No 228, 67590–67592, C.2–C.4. [November 26, 1979]). Some examples of good cause are that the Indian tribe does not have a tribal court or that the Indian child is over 12 years old and objects to the transfer. For additional examples of good cause and relevant case law, see the BIA guidelines cited above and A Practical Guide to the Indian Child Welfare Act. (Native American Rights Fund, A Practical Guide to the Indian Child Welfare Act [Boulder, CO: Native American Rights Fund, 2007], 7.15 and 7.16, p 60.)

Staff Comment to March, 2013 Amendment

This proposal incorporates provisions of the newly enacted Michigan Indian Family Preservation Act into specific provisions within various rules relating to child protective proceedings and juvenile status offenses.

Staff Comment to September, 2013 Amendment

These amendments reflect changes that correct minor technical errors that have occurred in drafting or the changes respond to recent adopted rule revisions, which occasionally inadvertently create incorrect cross-references in other rules.

Rule 3.970.　Child Protection Mediation

(A) Scope and Applicability of Rule; Definitions.

(1) This rule applies to the mediation of child protective proceedings.

(2) "Mediation" includes dispute resolution processes in which a neutral third party facilitates communication between parties, assists in identifying issues, and helps explore solutions to promote a mutually acceptable settlement. A mediator or facilitator has no authoritative decision-making power.

(B) ADR Plan. Each trial court that submits child protective proceedings to mediation processes under this rule shall either incorporate the process into its current ADR plan, or if the court does not have an approved ADR plan, adopt an ADR plan by local administrative order under MCR 2.410(B).

(C) Order for Mediation.

(1) At any stage in the proceedings, after consultation with the parties, the court may order that a case be submitted to mediation.

(2) Unless a court first conducts a hearing to determine whether mediation is appropriate, the court shall not refer a case to mediation if the parties are subject to a personal protection order or other protective order. The court may order mediation without a hearing if a protected party requests mediation.

(3) In addition to other provisions the court considers appropriate, the order shall:

(a) specify, or make provision for selection of, the mediation provider;

(b) provide time limits for initiation and completion of the mediation process.

The court shall not order a party to pay a fee for mediation services.

(4) The order may require attendance at mediation proceedings as provided in subrule (E).

(D) Objections to Mediation. A party may orally object to an order to mediate or in writing. Cases may be exempt from mediation on the basis of the following:

(1) Domestic abuse, unless attorneys for both parties will be present at the mediation session;

(2) Inability of one or both parties to negotiate for themselves at the mediation, unless attorneys for both parties will be present at the mediation session;

(3) Reason to believe that one or both parties' health or safety would be endangered by mediation;

(4) A showing that the parties have made significant efforts to resolve the issues such that mediation is likely to be unsuccessful; or

(5) For other good cause shown.

(E) Attendance at Mediation Proceedings.

(1) *Attendance of Counsel.* The court may direct that the attorneys representing the parties attend mediation proceedings. If the attorney representing a party is unable to attend, another attorney associated with the representing attorney may attend, but must be familiar with the case.

(2) *Presence of Parties.* The court may direct that the parties to the action and other persons:

(a) be present at the mediation proceeding or be immediately available by some other means at the time of the proceeding; and

(b) have information and authority adequate for responsible and effective participation in the proceeding for all purposes.

The court's order may specify whether the availability is to be in person or by other means.

(3) Except for legal counsel, the parties may not bring other persons to the mediation session unless permission is first obtained from the mediator, after notice to opposing counsel.

(4) *Failure to appear.* The failure of a party to appear in accordance with this rule may be considered a contempt of court.

(F) Selection of the Mediator.

(1) The parties may stipulate to the selection of a mediator. A mediator selected by agreement of the parties need not meet the qualifications set forth in subrule (H). The court must appoint a mediator stipulated to by the parties, provided the mediator is willing to serve within a period that would not interfere with the court's scheduling of the case. If the parties do not stipulate to a particular mediator, the court may select a Community Dispute Resolution Program (CDRP) center or other mediator who meets the requirements of subrule (H).

(2) The rule for disqualification of a mediator is the same as that provided in MCR 2.003 for the disqualification of a judge. The mediator must promptly disclose any potential basis for disqualification.

(G) Scheduling and Mediation Process.

(1) *Scheduling.* The order referring the case for mediation shall specify the time within which the mediation is to be completed. A copy of the order shall be sent to each party, the CDRP center or the mediator selected. Upon receipt of the court's order, the CDRP center or mediator shall promptly confer with the parties to schedule mediation in accordance with the order. The mediator may direct the parties to submit in advance, or bring to the mediation, documents or summaries providing information about the case.

(2) The mediator must make reasonable inquiry as to whether either party has a history of a coercive or violent relationship with the other party. Throughout the mediation process, the mediator must make reasonable efforts to screen for the presence of coercion or violence that would make mediation physically or emotionally unsafe for any participant or that would impede achieving a voluntary and safe resolution of issues. A reasonable inquiry includes the use of the domestic violence screening protocol for mediators provided by the State Court Administrative Office as directed by the Supreme Court.

(3) *Mediation Process.* The mediator shall discuss with the parties and counsel, if any, the facts and issues involved. Mediation participants may ask to meet separately with the mediator throughout the mediation process. The mediation will continue until: an agreement is reached, the mediator determines that an agreement is not likely to be reached, the end of the first mediation session, or until a time agreed to by the parties. Additional sessions may be held as long as it appears to the mediator that the process may result in an agreement.

(4) Following their attendance at a mediation session, a party may withdraw from mediation without penalty at any time.

(5) *Completion of Mediation.* Within two days after the completion of the mediation process, the CDRP center or the mediator shall so advise the court, stating only: the date of completion of the process, who appeared at the mediation, whether an agreement was reached, and whether further mediation proceedings are contemplated. If an agreement was reached, the CDRP center or the mediator shall submit the agreement to the court within 14 days of the completion of mediation.

(6) Agreements reached in mediation are not binding unless the terms are incorporated in an order of the court or placed on the record and the court complies with MCR 3.971.

(7) *Confidentiality.* Confidentiality in the mediation process is governed by MCR 2.412. However, previously uninvestigat-

ed allegations of abuse or neglect identified during the mediation process are not confidential and may be disclosed. The mediator shall advise the parties, orally and in writing, of the rules regarding confidentiality under MCR 2.412 and MCL 722.631.

(H) Qualification of Mediators.

(1) To be eligible to serve as a mediator in child protection cases, a person must meet the following minimum qualifications:

(a) Complete a general civil or domestic relations mediation training program approved by the State Court Administrator providing the generally accepted components of mediation skills;

(b) Have one or more of the following:

(i) Juris doctor degree, graduate degree in conflict resolution or a behavioral science, or 5 years of experience in the child protection field; or

(ii) 40 hours of mediation experience over two years, including mediation, co-mediation, observation, and role-playing in the context of mediation.

(c) Upon completion of the training required under subrule (H)(1)(a), observe two general civil or domestic relations mediation proceedings conducted by an approved mediator, and conduct one general civil or domestic relations mediation to conclusion under the supervision and observation of an approved mediator.

(d) Complete a 15–hour advanced training program on child protection mediation practice and an 8–hour training program on domestic violence screening approved by the State Court Administrator.

(2) Approved mediators are required to complete 8 hours of advanced mediation training during each 2–year period.

(3) Additional requirements may not be imposed upon mediators.

[Adopted March 28, 2018, effective May 1, 2018, 501 Mich.]

Comments

Staff Comment to 2018 Adoption

The amendments of MCR 2.410 and MCR 2.411 and adoption of the new MCR 3.970 provide explicit authority for judges to order mediation in child protection proceedings.

Rule 3.971. Pleas of Admission or No Contest

(A) General. A respondent may make a plea of admission or of no contest to the original allegations in the petition. The court has discretion to allow a respondent to enter a plea of admission or a plea of no contest to an amended petition. The plea may be taken at any time after the authorization of the petition, provided that the petitioner and the attorney for the child have been notified of a plea offer to an amended petition and have been given the opportunity to object before the plea is accepted.

(B) Advice of Rights and Possible Disposition. Before accepting a plea of admission or plea of no contest, the court must advise the respondent on the record or in a writing that is made a part of the file:

(1) of the allegations in the petition;

(2) of the right to an attorney, if respondent is without an attorney;

(3) that, if the court accepts the plea, the respondent will give up the rights to

(a) trial by a judge or trial by a jury,

(b) have the petitioner prove the allegations in the petition by a preponderance of the evidence,

(c) have witnesses against the respondent appear and testify under oath at the trial,

(d) cross-examine witnesses, and

(e) have the court subpoena any witnesses the respondent believes could give testimony in the respondent's favor;

(4) of the consequences of the plea, including that the plea can later be used as evidence in a proceeding to terminate parental rights if the respondent is a parent.

(5) if parental rights are subsequently terminated, the obligation to support the child will continue until a court of competent jurisdiction modifies or terminates the obligation, an order of adoption is entered, or the child is emancipated by operation of law. Failure to provide required notice under this subsection does not affect the obligation imposed by law or otherwise establish a remedy or cause of action on behalf of the parent;

(6) that appellate review is available to challenge a court's initial order of disposition following adjudication, and such a challenge can include any issues leading to the disposition, including any errors in the adjudicatory process;

(7) that an indigent respondent is entitled to appointment of an attorney to represent the respondent on appeal of the initial dispositional order and to preparation of relevant transcripts; and

(8) the respondent may be barred from challenging the assumption of jurisdiction in an appeal from the order terminating parental rights if they do not timely file an appeal of the initial dispositional order under MCR 3.993(A)(1), 3.993(A)(2), or a delayed appeal under MCR 3.993(C).

(C) Right to Appellate Review. The respondent may challenge the assumption of jurisdiction in an appeal from the order terminating respondent's parental rights if the respondent's parental rights are terminated at the initial dispositional hearing pursuant to MCR 3.977(E). In addition, the respondent may challenge the assumption of jurisdiction in an appeal from the order terminating respondent's parental rights if the court fails to properly advise the respondent of their right to appeal pursuant to subrule (B)(6)–(8).

(D) Voluntary, Accurate Plea.

(1) *Voluntary Plea.* The court shall not accept a plea of admission or of no contest without satisfying itself that the plea is knowingly, understandingly, and voluntarily made.

(2) *Accurate Plea.* The court shall not accept a plea of admission or of no contest without establishing support for a finding that one or more of the statutory grounds alleged in the petition are true, preferably by questioning the respondent unless the offer is to plead no contest. If the plea is no contest, the court shall not question the respondent, but, by some other means, shall obtain support for a finding that one or more of the

258

statutory grounds alleged in the petition are true. The court shall state why a plea of no contest is appropriate.

[Adopted February 4, 2003, effective May 1, 2003, 467 Mich. Amended March 28, 2018, effective May 1, 2018, 501 Mich. Amended effective June 12, 2019, 503 Mich. Amended September 18, 2019, effective January 1, 2020, 503 Mich.]

Comments

Staff Comment to 2003 Adoption

MCR 3.971 corresponds to former Rule 5.971.

Subrule (B)(4) provides that a plea may be used as evidence in a proceeding to terminate parental rights only if the respondent is a parent.

Subrule (C)(2) is modified to refer to a finding that the statutory grounds alleged in the petition are true, rather than to a finding that the child is within the jurisdiction of the court.

Staff Comment to 2018 Amendment

The amendments incorporate into both the rules concerning juvenile proceedings and adoption proceedings the requirement to notify parents that the termination of parental rights does not automatically terminate the obligation to provide support for a child. The amendments also make clear that failure to provide the notice would not affect the parent's obligation to continue to pay child support.

Staff Comment to 2019 Amendment

The amendments of MCR 3.965, 3.971, 3.972, 3.973, and 3.993 incorporate a requirement for a trial court to notify a respondent in a child protection proceeding of the right to appeal following a child's removal from the home and the initial dispositional order, and that failure to do so may bar respondent from later challenging the court's assumption of jurisdiction.

Staff Comment to 2020 Amendment

The amendments of MCR 1.109, 2.107, 2.113, 2.116, 2.119, 2.222, 2.223, 2.225, 2.227, 3.206, 3.211, 3.212, 3.214, 3.303, 3.903, 3.921, 3.925, 3.926, 3.931, 3.933, 3.942, 3.950, 3.961, 3.971, 3.972, 4.002, 4.101, 4.201, 4.202, 4.302, 5.128, 5.302, 5.731, 6.101, 6.615, 8.105, and 8.119 and rescission of MCR 2.226 and 8.125 continue the process for design and implementation of the statewide electronic-filing system.

Rule 3.972   Trial

(A) Time. If the child is not in placement, the trial must be held within 6 months after the authorization of the petition unless adjourned for good cause under MCR 3.923(G). If the child is in placement, the trial must commence as soon as possible, but not later than 63 days after the child is removed from the home unless the trial is postponed:

(1) on stipulation of the parties for good cause;

(2) because process cannot be completed; or

(3) because the court finds that the testimony of a presently unavailable witness is needed.

When trial is postponed pursuant to subrule (2) or (3), the court shall release the child to the parent, guardian, or legal custodian unless the court finds that releasing the child to the custody of the parent, guardian, or legal custodian will likely result in physical harm or serious emotional damage to the child.

If the child has been removed from the home, a review hearing must be held within 182 days of the date of the child's removal from the home, even if the trial has not been completed before the expiration of that 182–day period.

(B) Preliminary Proceedings.

(1) The court shall determine that the proper parties are present. The respondent has the right to be present, but the court may proceed in the absence of the respondent provided notice has been served on the respondent. The child may be excused as the court determines the child's interests require.

(2) The court shall read the allegations in the petition, unless waived.

(C) Evidentiary Matters.

(1) *Evidence; Standard of Proof.* Except as otherwise provided in these rules, the rules of evidence for a civil proceeding and the standard of proof by a preponderance of evidence apply at the trial, notwithstanding that the petition contains a request to terminate parental rights.

(2) *Child's Statement.* Any statement made by a child under 10 years of age or an incapacitated individual under 18 years of age with a developmental disability as defined in MCL 330.1100a(25) regarding an act of child abuse, child neglect, sexual abuse, or sexual exploitation, as defined in MCL 722.622 (g), (k), (z), or (aa), performed with or on the child by another person may be admitted into evidence through the testimony of a person who heard the child make the statement as provided in this subrule.

(a) A statement describing such conduct may be admitted regardless of whether the child is available to testify or not, and is substantive evidence of the act or omission if the court has found, in a hearing held before trial, that the circumstances surrounding the giving of the statement provide adequate indicia of trustworthiness. This statement may be received by the court in lieu of or in addition to the child's testimony.

(b) If the child has testified, a statement denying such conduct may be used for impeachment purposes as permitted by the rules of evidence.

(c) If the child has not testified, a statement denying such conduct may be admitted to impeach a statement admitted under subrule (2)(a) if the court has found, in a hearing held before trial, that the circumstances surrounding the giving of the statement denying the conduct provide adequate indicia of trustworthiness.

(D) Recommendation by Lawyer–Guardian ad Litem. At the conclusion of the proofs, the lawyer-guardian ad litem for the child may make a recommendation to the finder of fact regarding whether one or more of the statutory grounds alleged in the petition have been proven.

(E) Verdict. In a child protective proceeding, the verdict must be whether one or more of the statutory grounds alleged in the petition have been proven.

(F) Respondent's Rights Following Trial and Possible Disposition. If the trial results in a verdict that one or more statutory grounds for jurisdiction has been proven, the court shall advise the respondent orally or in writing that:

(1) appellate review is available to challenge a court's assumption of jurisdiction in an appeal of the initial order of disposition,

(2) that an indigent respondent is entitled to appointment of an attorney to represent the respondent on appeal and to preparation of relevant transcripts, and

(3) the respondent may be barred from challenging the assumption of jurisdiction if they do not timely file an appeal under MCR 3.993(A)(1), 3.993(A)(2), or a delayed appeal under MCR 3.993(C).

(G) Right to Appellate Review. The respondent may challenge the assumption of jurisdiction in an appeal from the order terminating respondent's parental rights if the respondent's parental rights are terminated at the initial dispositional hearing pursuant to MCR 3.977(E). In addition, the respondent may challenge the assumption of jurisdiction in an appeal from the order terminating respondent's parental rights if the court fails to properly advise the respondent of their right to appeal pursuant to subrule (F)(1)–(3).

[Adopted February 4, 2003, effective May 1, 2003, 467 Mich. Amended April 30, 2003, effective May 1, 2003, 467 Mich; October 24, 2006, effective January 1, 2007, 477 Mich; November 7, 2006, effective January 1, 2007, 477 Mich; July 3, 2007, effective September 1, 2007, 478 Mich. Amended effective March 9, 2016, 499 Mich; June 12, 2019, 503 Mich; August 14, 2019, 503 Mich. Amended September 18, 2019, effective January 1, 2020, 503 Mich.]

Comments

Staff Comment to 2003 Adoption

MCR 3.972 corresponds to former Rule 5.972.

Subrule (A) would expressly authorize adjournment of a trial for good cause in accordance with MCR 5.932(G).

Subrule (C) revises the provisions governing use of hearsay regarding statements by a child under 10 years of age. The provision is made applicable to an incapacitated individual under 18 years of age with a developmental disability. New subrules (2) and (3) permit use of hearsay denying abuse or neglect for impeachment.

New subrule (D) would permit the lawyer-guardian ad litem for the child to make a recommendation regarding whether the statutory grounds alleged have been proven.

New subrule (E) specifies that the verdict is to address whether one or more of the statutory grounds alleged in the petition has been proven.

Staff Comment to 2003 Amendment

The April 30, 2003, order makes corrections to a number of the rules governing proceedings regarding juveniles that had been adopted on February 4, 2003. The changes are effective May 1, corresponding to the effective date of the February 4 amendments. In addition to these changes, a number of corrections of punctuation and capitalization and changes in the Notes that accompanied the rules have been made and will appear in the published version of the rules.

The amendments of MCR 3.903(D)(8)(m), 6.903(H)(16), 6.931(E)(3), and 6.933(C)(1) conform the rules to 2002 PA 665, which changed the amounts of controlled substances required for certain violations. See MCL 333.7401(2)(a)(i), 333.7403(2)(a)(i). MCR 3.933(C)(1) is also modified in light of *People v Valentin*, 457 Mich 1 (1998).

The amendment of MCR 3.935(B)(1) corrects the inadvertent omission of references to guardians and legal custodians.

The amendments of MCR 3.922(E)(1)(c), 3.943(A), 3.945(A)(1), 3.965(E)(1), and 3.972(C)(2)(c) correct minor errors in wording.

The amendment of MCR 3.977(G) deletes the word "hearing" in the reference to progress reviews. Under MCR 3.974(A)(1), progress reviews do not require hearings.

The amendment of MCR 3.980(B) and (C) revise the provisions on removal of American Indian children from the home to clarify the distinction between emergency removals and removals after hearing.

The amendments of MCR 3.982(A), 6.903(I)–(L) and 6.937(A) correct cross-reference, citation and numbering errors.

Staff Comment to October, 2006 Amendment

The amendments of MCR 3.972 conform the rule language to the requirements of the Adoption and Safe Families Act and foster compliance with the timing requirements of that act, thereby helping to increase the possibility that children in foster care will receive federal funding. The amendments require that a review hearing be held within 182 days of a child's removal from the home, even if the trial in the proceeding has not been completed. [Revision from order dated May 31, 2007.]

Staff Comment to November, 2006 Amendment

This amendment of MCR 3.972(C)(2) allows testimony of the child to be admitted in a child protective proceeding trial if the statement is offered by a person who heard the child make the statement.

Staff Comment to S2007 Amendment

These amendments correct references that were changed as a result of statutory amendments made in 2002 to the Child Protection Law, as well as 2005 amendments of the Mental Health Code.

Staff Comment to 2016 Amendment

These amendments update cross-references that changed after the rule was adopted and make other nonsubstantive revisions.

Staff Comment to June, 2019 Amendment

The amendments of MCR 3.965, 3.971, 3.972, 3.973, and 3.993 incorporate a requirement for a trial court to notify a respondent in a child protection proceeding of the right to appeal following a child's removal from the home and the initial dispositional order, and that failure to do so may bar respondent from later challenging the court's assumption of jurisdiction.

Staff Comment to August, 2019 Amendment

These amendments update cross-references and make other nonsubstantive revisions to clarify the rules.

Staff Comment to 2020 Amendment

The amendments of MCR 1.109, 2.107, 2.113, 2.116, 2.119, 2.222, 2.223, 2.225, 2.227, 3.206, 3.211, 3.212, 3.214, 3.303, 3.903, 3.921, 3.925, 3.926, 3.931, 3.933, 3.942, 3.950, 3.961, 3.971, 3.972, 4.002, 4.101, 4.201, 4.202, 4.302, 5.128, 5.302, 5.731, 6.101, 6.615, 8.105, and 8.119 and rescission of MCR 2.226 and 8.125 continue the process for design and implementation of the statewide electronic-filing system.

Rule 3.973.   Dispositional Hearing

(A) Purpose. A dispositional hearing is conducted to determine what measures the court will take with respect to a child properly within its jurisdiction and, when applicable, against any adult, once the court has determined following trial, plea of admission, or plea of no contest that one or more of the statutory grounds alleged in the petition are true.

(B) Notice. Unless the dispositional hearing is held immediately after the trial, notice of hearing may be given by scheduling it on the record in the presence of the parties or in accordance with MCR 3.920.

(C) Time. The interval, if any, between the trial and the dispositional hearing is within the discretion of the court. When the child is in placement, the interval may not be more than 28 days, except for good cause.

(D) Presence of Parties.

(1) The child may be excused from the dispositional hearing as the interests of the child require.

(2) The respondent has the right to be present or may appear through an attorney.

(3) The court may proceed in the absence of parties provided that proper notice has been given.

(E) Evidence; Reports.

(1) The Michigan Rules of Evidence do not apply at the initial dispositional hearing, other than those with respect to privileges. However, as provided by MCL 722.631, no assertion of an evidentiary privilege, other than the privilege between attorney and client, shall prevent the receipt and use, at the dispositional phase, of materials prepared pursuant to a court-ordered examination, interview, or course of treatment.

(2) All relevant and material evidence, including oral and written reports, may be received and may be relied on to the extent of its probative value. The court shall consider the case service plan and any written or oral information concerning the child from the child's parent, guardian, legal custodian, foster parent, child caring institution, or relative with whom the child is placed. If the agency responsible for the care and supervision of the child recommends not placing the child with the parent, guardian, or legal custodian, the agency shall report in writing what efforts were made to prevent removal, or to rectify conditions that caused removal, of the child from the home.

(3) The parties shall be given an opportunity to examine and controvert written reports so received and may be allowed to cross-examine individuals making the reports when those individuals are reasonably available.

(4) Written reports, other than those portions made confidential by law, case service plans, and court orders, including all updates and revisions, shall be available to the foster parent, child caring institution, or relative with whom the child is placed. The foster parents, child caring institution, or relative with whom the child is placed shall not have the right to cross-examine individuals making such reports or the right to controvert such reports beyond the making of a written or oral statement concerning the child as provided in subrule (E)(2).

(5) Reports in the Agency's case file, including but not limited to case services plans, treatment plans, substance abuse evaluations, psychological evaluations, therapists' reports, drug and alcohol screening results, contracted service provider reports, and parenting time logs shall be provided to the court and parties no less than seven (7) days before the hearing.

(6) The court, upon receipt of a local foster care review board's report, shall include the report in the court's confidential social file. The court shall ensure that all parties have had the opportunity to review the report and file objections before a dispositional order, dispositional review order, or permanency planning order is entered. The court may at its discretion include recommendations from the report in its orders.

(F) Dispositional Orders.

(1) The court shall enter an order of disposition as provided in the Juvenile Code and these rules.

(2) The court shall not enter an order of disposition until it has examined the case service plan as provided in MCL 712A.18f. The court may order compliance with all or part of the case service plan and may enter such orders as it considers necessary in the interest of the child.

(3) The court, on consideration of the written report prepared by the agency responsible for the care and supervision of the child pursuant to MCL 712A.18f(1), shall, when appropriate, include a statement in the order of disposition as to whether reasonable efforts were made:

(a) to prevent the child's removal from home, or

(b) to rectify the conditions that caused the child to be removed from the child's home.

(4) *Medical Information.* Unless the court has previously ordered the release of medical information, the order placing the child in foster care must include the following:

(a) an order that the child's parent, guardian, or legal custodian provide the supervising agency with the name and address of each of the child's medical providers, and

(b) an order that each of the child's medical providers release the child's medical records.

(5) *Child Support.* The court may include an order requiring one or both of the child's parents to pay child support. All child support orders entered under this subrule must comply with MCL 552.605 and MCR 3.211(D).

(G) Respondent's Rights Upon Entry of Dispositional Order. When the court enters an initial order of disposition following adjudication the court shall advise the respondent orally or in writing:

(1) that at any time while the court retains jurisdiction over the minor, the respondent may challenge the continuing exercise of that jurisdiction by filing a motion for rehearing, MCL 712A.21 or MCR 3.992, or by filing an application for leave to appeal with the Michigan Court of Appeals,

(2) that appellate review is available to challenge both an initial order of disposition following adjudication and any order removing a child from a parent's care and custody,

(3) that an indigent respondent is entitled to appointment of an attorney to represent the respondent on any appeal as of right and to preparation of relevant transcripts, and

(4) the respondent may be barred from challenging the assumption of jurisdiction or the removal of the minor from a parent's care and custody in an appeal from the order terminating parental rights if they do not timely file an appeal under MCR 3.993(A)(1), 3.993(A)(2), or a delayed appeal under MCR 3.993(C).

(H) Right to Appellate Review. The respondent may challenge the assumption of jurisdiction in an appeal from the order terminating respondent's parental rights if the respondent's parental rights are terminated at the initial dispositional hearing pursuant to MCR 3.977(E). In addition, the respondent may challenge the assumption of jurisdiction in an appeal from the order terminating respondent's parental rights if the court fails to properly advise the respondent of their right to appeal pursuant to subrule (G)(2)-(4).

(I) Subsequent Review. When the court does not terminate jurisdiction upon entering its dispositional order, it must:

(1) follow the review procedures in MCR 3.975 for a child in placement, or

(2) review the progress of a child at home pursuant to the procedures of MCR 3.974(A).

(J) Allegations of Additional Abuse or Neglect.

(1) Proceedings on a supplemental petition seeking termination of parental rights on the basis of allegations of additional abuse or neglect, as defined in MCL 722.622(f) and (j), of a child who is under the jurisdiction of the court are governed by MCR 3.977.

(2) Where there is no request for termination of parental rights, proceedings regarding allegations of additional abuse or neglect, as defined in MCL 722.622(f) and (j), of a child who is under the jurisdiction of the court, including those made under MCL 712A.19(1), are governed by MCR 3.974 for a child who is at home or MCR 3.975 for a child who is in foster care.

[Adopted February 4, 2003, effective May 1, 2003, 467 Mich. Amended effective October 15, 2003, 467 Mich. Amended May 30, 2006, effective July 1, 2006, 475 Mich; October 24, 2006, effective January 1, 2007, 477 Mich; July 3, 2007, effective September 1, 2007, 478 Mich; September 21, 2010, effective January 1, 2011, 487 Mich. Amended effective June 12, 2019, 503 Mich. Amended June 19, 2019, effective January 1, 2020, 503 Mich.]

Comments

Staff Comment to 2003 Adoption

MCR 3.973 corresponds to subrule (A) of former Rule 5.973. The remaining provisions of former Rule 5.973 are relocated to new MCR 3.974 [subrules (D)–(E)], 3.975 [subrule (B)], and 3.976 [subrule (C)].

Like former MCL 5.973(A)(3), subrule (C)(1) would permit the child to be excused from the dispositional hearing, but would remove the condition that the child's guardian ad litem or attorney be present. However the presence of the lawyer-guardian ad litem is required by other provisions. See MCL 712A.17d(1)(g); MCR 3.915(B)(2).

The provision of subrules (E)(1) regarding the Michigan Rules of Evidence is modified to say that they do not apply at the *initial* dispositional hearing. Language regarding privileges is also added.

New subrule (F)(4) would provide for release of medical information in connection with an order placing a child in foster care.

New subrules (G) and (H) deal with subsequent review and supplemental petitions alleging additional abuse and neglect.

Staff Comment to 2003 Amendment

The October 15, 2003, amendment of MCR 3.973(E)(4) corrected the misdesignation of the subrule referred to in the text.

Staff Comment to 2006 Amendment

The amendment provides that the court may enter a child support order at the dispositional hearing and that it must use the Michigan Child Support Formula as required by statute and the Uniform Support Order required by court rule in establishing the child support order.

Staff Comment to January, 2007 Amendment

The amendment of MCR 3.973(C), reducing the time for holding a dispositional hearing from 35 to 28 days, conforms the time for resolving an abuse and neglect case to the mandatory federal time lines for ensuring that a child removed from the home receives federal foster care funding. Although federal law does not require that a dispositional hearing be held within a certain period, adding this requirement will encourage courts to complete disposition within 91 days, which then prompts scheduling of a dispositional review hearing 91 days later, and ensure compliance with the federal requirement to complete a review hearing within 182 days of the child's removal from the home.

Staff Comment to September, 2007 Amendment

These amendments correct references that were changed as a result of statutory amendments made in 2002 to the Child Protection Law, as well as 2005 amendments of the Mental Health Code.

Staff Comment to 2011 Amendment

The amendments of MCR 3.973, 3.975, and 3.976 require a court to maintain a local foster care review board report in the court's confidential social file, and ensure that all parties have had the opportunity to review the report before the court enters a dispositional order, dispositional review order, or permanency planning order. Courts also may include recommendations from the report in their orders under the new language.

Staff Comment to 2019 Amendment

The amendments of MCR 3.965, 3.971, 3.972, 3.973, and 3.993 incorporate a requirement for a trial court to notify a respondent in a child protection proceeding of the right to appeal following a child's removal from the home and the initial dispositional order, and that failure to do so may bar respondent from later challenging the court's assumption of jurisdiction.

Staff Comment to 2020 Amendment

These amendments are based on a proposal created by a special committee of the State Bar of Michigan and approved for submission to the Court by the Bar's Representative Assembly. The rules require mandatory discovery disclosure in many cases, adopt a presumptive limit on interrogatories (20 in most cases, but 35 in domestic relations proceedings) and limit a deposition to 7 hours. The amendments also update the rules to more specifically address issues related to electronically stored information, and encourage early action on discovery issues during the discovery period.

The amendment of MCR 2.309(A)(2) sets a presumptive limit of twenty interrogatories for each separately represented party. Several commenters suggested that the term "discrete subpart" be more explicitly defined. But the rule's reference to "a discrete subpart" is intended to draw guidance from federal courts construing FR Civ P 30(a)(1). Generally, subparts are not separately counted if they are logically or factually subsumed within and necessarily related to the primary question. In upholding the limit, parties and courts should also pragmatically balance the overall goals of discovery and the admonition of MCR 1.105. Further, the intent of the provision at MCR 2.301(B)(4) is to ensure that parties responding to discovery requests have the full time period to do so as provided for under these rules prior to the expiration of the discovery period.

Rule 3.974   Procedures for Child at Home; Petition Authorized

(A) Review of Child's Progress.

(1) *General.* The court shall periodically review the progress of a child not in foster care over whom it has taken jurisdiction.

(2) *Time.* If the child was never removed from the home, the progress of the child must be reviewed no later than 182 days from the date the petition was authorized and no later than 91 days after that for the first year that the child is subject to the jurisdiction of the court. After that first year, a review hearing shall be held no later than 182 days from the immediately preceding review hearing before the end of the first year and no later than every 182 days from each preceding hearing until the court terminates its jurisdiction. The review shall occur no later than 182 days after the child returns home when the child is no longer in foster care. If the child was removed from the home and subsequently returned home, review hearings shall be held in accordance with MCR 3.975.

(3) *Change of Placement.* Except as provided in subrule (C), the court may not order a change in the placement of a child without a hearing. If the child for whom the court has authorized a petition remains at home or has otherwise returned home from foster care, and it comes to the court's attention at a review hearing held pursuant to subrule (A)(2), or as otherwise provided in this rule, that the child should be removed from the home, the court may order the placement of the child. If the court orders the child to be placed out of the home following a review hearing held pursuant to subrule (A)(2), the parent must be present and the court shall comply with the placement provisions in MCR 3.965(C). If the parent is not present, the court shall proceed under subrule (C) before it may order removal. If the child is an Indian child, in addition to a hearing held in accordance with this rule, the court must also conduct a removal hearing in accordance with MCR 3.967 before it may order the placement of the Indian child.

(B) Hearing on Petition for Out-of-Home Placement.

(1) *Preadjudication.* If a child for whom a petition has been authorized under MCR 3.962 or MCR 3.965 is not yet under the jurisdiction of the court and an amended petition has been filed to remove the child from the home, the court shall conduct a hearing on the petition in accordance with MCR 3.965.

(2) *Postadjudication.* If a child is under the jurisdiction of the court and a supplemental petition has been filed to remove the child from the home, the court shall conduct a hearing on the petition. The court shall ensure that the parties are given notice of the hearing as provided in MCR 3.920 and MCR 3.921. Unless the child remains in the home, the court shall comply with the placement provisions in MCR 3.965(C) and must make a written determination that the criteria for placement listed in MCR 3.965(C)(2) are satisfied. If the court orders that the child be placed out of the home, the court shall proceed under subrule (D).

(C) Emergency Removal; Protective Custody.

(1) *General.* If a child, for whom the court has authorized an original petition remains at home or is returned home following a hearing pursuant to the rules in this subchapter, the court may order the child to be taken into protective custody pending an emergency removal hearing pursuant to the conditions listed in MCR 3.963(B)(1) and upon receipt, electronically or otherwise, of a petition or affidavit of fact. If the child is an Indian child and the child resides or is domiciled within a reservation, but is temporarily located off the reservation, the court may order the child to be taken into protective custody only when necessary to prevent imminent physical damage or harm to the child.

(2) *Notice.* The court shall ensure that the parties are given notice of the emergency removal hearing as provided in MCR 3.920 and MCR 3.921.

(3) *Emergency Removal Hearing.* If the court orders the child to be taken into protective custody under MCR 3.963, the court must conduct an emergency removal hearing no later than 24 hours after the child has been taken into custody, excluding Sundays and holidays as defined in MCR 8.110(D)(2). If the child is an Indian child, the court must also conduct a removal hearing in accordance with MCR 3.967 in order for the child to remain removed from a parent or Indian custodian.

(a) Preadjudication. If a child for whom a petition has been authorized under MCR 3.962 or MCR 3.965 is not yet under the jurisdiction of the court, the emergency removal hearing shall be conducted in the manner provided by MCR 3.965.

(b) Postadjudication. If a child is under the jurisdiction of the court, unless the child is returned to the parent pending disposition or dispositional review, the court shall comply with the placement provisions in MCR 3.965(C) and must make a written determination that the criteria for placement listed in MCR 3.965(C)(2) are satisfied. The parent, guardian, or legal custodian from whom the child was removed must be given an opportunity to state why the child should not be removed from, or should be returned to, the custody of the parent, guardian, or legal custodian.

The respondent parent, guardian, or legal custodian from whom the child is removed must receive a written statement of the reasons for removal and be advised of the following rights at a hearing to be held under subrule (D):

(i) to be represented by an attorney at the hearing;

(ii) to contest the continuing placement at the hearing within 14 days; and

(iii) to use compulsory process to obtain witnesses for the hearing.

(D) Procedure Following Postadjudication Out-of-Home Placement. If the child is in placement under subrule (B)(2) or (C)(3)(b), the court shall proceed as follows:

(1) If the court has not held a dispositional hearing under MCR 3.973, the court shall conduct the dispositional hearing within 28 days after the child is placed by the court, except for good cause shown.

(2) If the court has already held a dispositional hearing under MCR 3.973, a dispositional review hearing must commence no later than 14 days after the child is placed by the court, except for good cause shown. The dispositional review hearing may be combined with the removal hearing for an Indian child prescribed by MCR 3.967. The dispositional review hearing must be conducted in accordance with the procedures and rules of evidence applicable to a dispositional hearing.

[Adopted February 4, 2003, effective May 1, 2003, 467 Mich. Amended October 24, 2006, effective January 1, 2007, 477 Mich; February 2, 2010, effective May 1, 2010, 485 Mich. Amended effective, pending public comment, March 20, 2013, 493 Mich. Amended June 5, 2013, effective September 1, 2013, 494 Mich; May 27, 2015, effective September 1, 2015, 498 Mich.]

Comments

Staff Comment to 2003 Adoption

New MCR 3.974 corresponds to subrules (D) and (E) of former Rule 5.973.

The provisions of former Rule 5.974, governing termination of parental rights, are relocated to new MCR 3.977 and 3.978.

Subrule (A)(1) makes clear that the court's progress review does not require a hearing.

Subrule (B) permits removal of the child to protect the child's health, safety, or welfare pending an emergency removal hearing. At such a hearing, a written determination of the criteria for placement is required.

Staff Comment to 2006 Amendment

The amendment of MCR 3.974(A)(2) conforms the review hearing time lines to recent statutory amendments of MCL 712A.19 as implemented by 2004 PA 477. It also requires courts to hold a hearing to conduct a review, which will generate an order with appropriate findings and determinations.

Staff Comment to 2010 Amendment

These amendments incorporate provisions of the Indian Child Welfare Act into specific provisions within various rules relating to child protective proceedings and juvenile status offenses. The language is designed to make the rules reflect a more integrated approach to addressing issues specific to Indian children.

MCR 3.002(1)(c) defines "preadoptive placement" to mean the "temporary placement of an Indian child in a foster home or institution after the termination of parental rights, but before or in lieu of adoptive placement, and ..." The phrase "in lieu of adoptive placement" is not intended to mean that it is permissible to leave a child in foster care indefinitely, in violation of MCL 712A.19b(6) or (7) or 45 CFR 1355.20, 45 CFR 1356.21, or 45 CFR 1356.50. Rather, it addresses situations where the parental rights to a child have been terminated and there is no permanency plan for adoption of the child. One example is when the child has been placed with a juvenile guardian and the guardianship is subsequently revoked. In this situation, jurisdiction over the child pursuant to MCL 712A.2(b) will be reinstated and the child is placed in foster care.

MCR 3.002(1): The definition of "child custody proceeding" is intended to apply the Indian Child Welfare Act to delinquency proceedings if an "Indian child" is charged with a so-called status offense in violation of MCL 712A.2(a)(2)–(4) or (d). Delinquency proceedings involving an Indian child charged with any other non-status offense are generally not subject to the Indian Child Welfare Act; however, if the initial investigation or subsequent review of a non-status delinquency case reveals that the Indian child involved suffers from child abuse or neglect, a separate child protective proceeding may be initiated, which would be subject to the Indian Child Welfare Act.

The amendment of MCR 3.905(C)(1) states that a court shall consider guidelines established by the Bureau of Indian Affairs (BIA) in determining whether good cause not to transfer exists (Guidelines for State Courts; Indian Child Custody Proceedings, 44 Fed Reg No 228, 67590–67592, C.2–C.4. [November 26, 1979]). Some examples of good cause are that the Indian tribe does not have a tribal court or that the Indian child is over 12 years old and objects to the transfer. For additional examples of good cause and relevant case law, see the BIA guidelines cited above and A Practical Guide to the Indian Child Welfare Act. (Native American Rights Fund, A Practical Guide to the Indian Child Welfare Act [Boulder, CO: Native American Rights Fund, 2007], 7.15 and 7.16, p 60.)

Staff Comment to March, 2013 Amendment

This proposal incorporates provisions of the newly enacted Michigan Indian Family Preservation Act into specific provisions within various rules relating to child protective proceedings and juvenile status offenses.

Staff Comment to September, 2013 Amendment

The changes of MCR 3.913, 3.963, 3.965, and 3.974 incorporate the statutory changes enacted in 2012 Public Act 163.

Staff Comment to 2015 Amendment

The amendments of MCR 3.963, 3.966, and 3.974 provide clarity regarding procedures to be followed when an emergency removal of a child has occurred but a dispositional hearing has not been held.

Rule 3.975. Post–Dispositional Procedures: Child in Foster Care

(A) Dispositional Review Hearings. A dispositional review hearing is conducted to permit court review of the progress made to comply with any order of disposition and with the case service plan prepared pursuant to MCL 712A.18f and court evaluation of the continued need and appropriateness for the child to be in foster care.

(B) Notice. The court shall ensure that written notice of a dispositional review hearing is given to the appropriate persons in accordance with MCR 3.920 and MCR 3.921(B)(2). The notice must inform the parties of their opportunity to participate in the hearing and that any information they wish to provide should be submitted in advance to the court, the agency, the lawyer-guardian ad litem for the child, or an attorney for one of the parties.

(C) Time. The court must conduct dispositional review hearings at intervals as follows, as long as the child remains in foster care:

(1) not more than 182 days after the child's removal from his or her home and no later than every 91 days after that for the first year that the child is subject to the jurisdiction of the court. After the first year that the child has been removed from his or her home and is subject to the jurisdiction of the court, a review hearing shall be held not more than 182 days from the immediately preceding review hearing before the end of that first year and no later than every 182 days from each preceding review hearing thereafter until the case is dismissed; or

(2) if a child is under the care and supervision of the agency and is either placed with a relative and the placement is intended to be permanent or is in a permanent foster family agreement, not more than 182 days after the child has been removed from his or her home and no later than 182 days after that so long as the child is subject to the jurisdiction of the court, the Michigan Children's Institute, or other agency as provided in MCR 3.976(E)(3).

A review hearing under this subrule shall not be canceled or delayed beyond the number of days required in this subrule, regardless of whether a petition to terminate parental rights or another matter is pending.

(D) Early Review Option. At the initial dispositional hearing and at every regularly scheduled dispositional review hearing, the court must decide whether it will conduct the next dispositional review hearing before what would otherwise be the next regularly scheduled dispositional review hearing as provided in subrule (C). In deciding whether to shorten the interval between review hearings, the court shall, among other factors, consider:

(1) the ability and motivation of the parent, guardian, or legal custodian to make changes needed to provide the child a suitable home environment;

(2) the reasonable likelihood that the child will be ready to return home earlier than the next scheduled dispositional review hearing.

(E) Procedure. Dispositional review hearings must be conducted in accordance with the procedures and rules of evidence applicable to the initial dispositional hearing. The Agency shall provide to all parties all reports in its case file, including but not limited to initial and updated case service plans, treatment plans, psychological evaluations, psychiatric evaluations, substance abuse evaluations, drug and alcohol screens, therapists' reports, contracted service provider reports, and parenting time logs. The reports shall be provided to the parties at least seven (7) days before the hearing. The reports that are filed with the court must be offered into evidence. The court shall consider any written or oral informa-

tion concerning the child from the child's parent, guardian, legal custodian, foster parent, child caring institution, or relative with whom a child is placed, in addition to any other relevant and material evidence at the hearing. The court, on request of a party or on its own motion, may accelerate the hearing to consider any element of a case service plan. The court, upon receipt of a local foster care review board's report, shall include the report in the court's confidential social file. The court shall ensure that all parties have had the opportunity to review the report and file objections before a dispositional order, dispositional review order, or permanency planning order is entered. The court may at its discretion include recommendations from the report in its orders.

(F) Criteria.

(1) *Review of Case Service Plan.* The court, in reviewing the progress toward compliance with the case service plan, must consider:

(a) the services provided or offered to the child and parent, guardian, or legal custodian of the child;

(b) whether the parent, guardian, or legal custodian has benefited from the services provided or offered;

(c) the extent of parenting time or visitation, including a determination regarding the reasons either was not frequent or never occurred;

(d) the extent to which the parent, guardian, or legal custodian complied with each provision of the case service plan, prior court orders, and any agreement between the parent, guardian, or legal custodian and the agency;

(e) any likely harm to the child if the child continues to be separated from his or her parent, guardian, or custodian;

(f) any likely harm to the child if the child is returned to the parent, guardian, or legal custodian; and

(g) if the child is an Indian child, whether the child's placement remains appropriate and complies with MCR 3.967(F).

(2) *Progress Toward Returning Child Home.* The court must decide the extent of the progress made toward alleviating or mitigating conditions that caused the child to be, and to remain, in foster care. The court shall also review the concurrent plan, if applicable.

(G) Dispositional Review Orders. The court, following a dispositional review hearing, may:

(1) order the return of the child home,

(2) change the placement of the child,

(3) modify the dispositional order,

(4) modify any part of the case service plan,

(5) enter a new dispositional order, or

(6) continue the prior dispositional order.

(H) Returning Child Home Without Dispositional Review Hearing. Unless notice is waived, if not less than 7 days written notice is given to all parties before the return of a child to the home, and if no party requests a hearing within the 7 days, the court may issue an order without a hearing permitting the agency to return the child home.

[Adopted February 4, 2003, effective May 1, 2003, 467 Mich. Amended effective February 25, 2004, 469 Mich. Amended October 24, 2006, effective January 1, 2007, 477 Mich; April 14, 2009, effective July 1, 2009, 483 Mich; February 2, 2010, effective May 1, 2010, 485 Mich; September 21, 2010, effective January 1, 2011, 487 Mich; June 19, 2019, effective January 1, 2020, 503 Mich.]

Comments

Staff Comment to 2003 Adoption

New MCR 3.975 corresponds to subrule (B) of former Rule 5.973.

Subrule (C) adjusts the times for dispositional review hearings to coordinate with the modified provisions on permanency planning hearings in new MCR 5.976 and recent amendments of MCL 712A.19a, 712A.19c.

In subrule (G), two new options for orders following a dispositional review hearing are added.

Staff Comment to 2004 Amendment

The February 25, 2004, amendments of MCR 3.915, 3.965, 3.975, 3.976 and 3.977, effective immediately, are based on recommendations from the Family Independence Agency and Supreme Court Adoption Work Group.

The amendment of MCR 3.915(B)(2)(a) is designed to enforce the statutory requirement in MCL 712A.17d that lawyers-guardians ad litem for children meet with their clients before each hearing.

The amendment of MCR 3.915(D)(2) addresses the substitution of lawyers-guardians ad litem.

The amendments of MCR 3.965 (B)(13) and (E) require the court to ask parents, guardians, or legal custodians to identify relatives who might be available to care for the child. The amendment to subsection (E) also requires the court to ask parents, guardians, or legal custodians to identify the child's treating physician in certain circumstances. See MCL 712A.18f(6).

The amendments of MCR 3.975(B) and MCR 3.976(C) require the court to notify interested parties that they may provide input at dispositional review and permanency planning hearings.

The amendments of MCR 3.976(B)(3) and (E)(2) encourage early holding of permanency planning hearings and early filing of petitions for termination of parental rights, where appropriate.

MCR 3.977(C)(2) is a new provision that requires courts to give child welfare cases priority in scheduling.

Staff Comment to 2007 Amendment

The amendment of MCR 3.975 conforms the review hearing time lines to statutory amendments of MCL 712A.19 as implemented by 2004 PA 477.

Staff Comment to 2009 Amendment

The amendments of Rules 3.901, 3.903, 3.921, 3.965, 3.975, 3.976, 3.977, and 3.978, and new rule 3.979 of the Michigan Court Rules reflect the enactment of 2008 PA 199–203.

Staff Comment to February, 2010 Amendment

These amendments incorporate provisions of the Indian Child Welfare Act into specific provisions within various rules relating to child protective proceedings and juvenile status offenses. The language is designed to make the rules reflect a more integrated approach to addressing issues specific to Indian children.

MCR 3.002(1)(c) defines "preadoptive placement" to mean the "temporary placement of an Indian child in a foster home or institution after the termination of parental rights, but before or in lieu of adoptive placement, and ..." The phrase "in lieu of adoptive placement" is not intended to mean that it is permissible to leave a child in foster care indefinitely, in violation of MCL 712A.19b(6) or (7) or 45 CFR 1355.20, 45 CFR 1356.21, or 45 CFR 1356.50. Rather, it addresses situations where the parental rights to a child have been terminated and there is no permanency plan for adoption of the child. One example is when the child has been placed with a juvenile guardian and the guardianship is subsequently revoked. In this situation, jurisdiction over the child pursuant to MCL 712A.2(b) will be reinstated and the child is placed in foster care.

MCR 3.002(1): The definition of "child custody proceeding" is intended to apply the Indian Child Welfare Act to delinquency proceedings if an "Indian child" is charged with a so-called status offense in violation of MCL 712A.2(a)(2)–(4) or (d). Delinquency proceedings involving an Indian child charged with any other non-status offense are generally not subject to the Indian Child Welfare Act; however, if the initial investigation or subsequent review of a non-status delinquency case reveals that the Indian child involved suffers from child abuse or neglect, a separate child protective proceeding may be initiated, which would be subject to the Indian Child Welfare Act.

The amendment of MCR 3.905(C)(1) states that a court shall consider guidelines established by the Bureau of Indian Affairs (BIA) in determining whether good cause not to transfer exists (Guidelines for State Courts; Indian Child Custody Proceedings, 44 Fed Reg No 228, 67590–67592, C.2–C.4. [November 26, 1979]). Some examples of good cause are that the Indian tribe does not have a tribal court or that the Indian child is over 12 years old and objects to the transfer. For additional examples of good cause and relevant case law, see the BIA guidelines cited above and A Practical Guide to the Indian Child Welfare Act. (Native American Rights Fund, A Practical Guide to the Indian Child Welfare Act [Boulder, CO: Native American Rights Fund, 2007], 7.15 and 7.16, p 60.)

Staff Comment to 2011 Amendment

The amendments of MCR 3.973, 3.975, and 3.976 require a court to maintain a local foster care review board report in the court's confidential social file, and ensure that all parties have had the opportunity to review the report before the court enters a dispositional order, dispositional review order, or permanency planning order. Courts also may include recommendations from the report in their orders under the new language.

Staff Comment to 2020 Amendment

These amendments are based on a proposal created by a special committee of the State Bar of Michigan and approved for submission to the Court by the Bar's Representative Assembly. The rules require mandatory discovery disclosure in many cases, adopt a presumptive limit on interrogatories (20 in most cases, but 35 in domestic relations proceedings) and limit a deposition to 7 hours. The amendments also update the rules to more specifically address issues related to electronically stored information, and encourage early action on discovery issues during the discovery period.

The amendment of MCR 2.309(A)(2) sets a presumptive limit of twenty interrogatories for each separately represented party. Several commenters suggested that the term "discrete subpart" be more explicitly defined. But the rule's reference to "a discrete subpart" is intended to draw guidance from federal courts construing FR Civ P 30(a)(1). Generally, subparts are not separately counted if they are logically or factually subsumed within and necessarily related to the primary question. In upholding the limit, parties and courts should also pragmatically balance the overall goals of discovery and the admonition of MCR 1.105. Further, the intent of the provision at MCR 2.301(B)(4) is to ensure that parties responding to discovery requests have the full time period to do so as provided for under these rules prior to the expiration of the discovery period.

Rule 3.976. Permanency Planning Hearings

(A) Permanency Plan. At or before each permanency planning hearing, the court must determine whether the agency has made reasonable efforts to finalize the permanency plan. At the hearing, the court must review the permanency plan for a child in foster care. The court must determine whether and, if applicable, when:

(1) the child may be returned to the parent, guardian, or legal custodian;

(2) a petition to terminate parental rights should be filed;

(3) the child may be placed in a legal guardianship;

(4) the child may be permanently placed with a fit and willing relative; or

(5) the child may be placed in another planned permanent living arrangement, but only in those cases where the agency has documented to the court a compelling reason for determining that it would not be in the best interests of the child to follow one of the options listed in subrules (1)–(4).

(B) Time.

(1) An initial permanency planning hearing must be held within 28 days after a judicial determination that reasonable efforts to reunite the family or to prevent removal are not required given one of the following circumstances:

(a) There has been a judicial determination that the child's parent has subjected the child to aggravated circumstances as listed in sections 18(1) and (2) of the Child Protection Law, 1975 PA 238, MCL 722.638.

(b) The parent has been convicted of one of the following:

(i) murder of another child of the parent;

(ii) voluntary manslaughter of another child of the parent;

(iii) aiding or abetting, attempting, conspiring, or soliciting to commit such a murder or such a voluntary manslaughter; or

(iv) a felony assault that results in serious bodily injury to the child or another child of the parent.

(c) The parent has had rights to one of the child's siblings involuntarily terminated.

(2) If subrule (1) does not apply, the court must conduct an initial permanency planning hearing no later than 12 months after the child's removal from the home, regardless of whether any supplemental petitions are pending in the case.

(3) *Requirement of Annual Permanency Planning Hearings.* During the continuation of foster care, the court must hold permanency planning hearings beginning no later than 12 months after the initial permanency planning hearing. The interval between permanency planning hearings is within the discretion of the court as appropriate to the circumstances of the case, but must not exceed 12 months. The court may combine the permanency planning hearing with a review hearing.

(4) The judicial determination to finalize the court-approved permanency plan must be made within the time limits prescribed in subsections (1)–(3).

(C) **Notice.** The parties entitled to participate in a permanency planning hearing include the:

(1) parents of the child, if the parent's parental rights have not been terminated,

(2) child, if the child is of an appropriate age to participate,

(3) guardian,

(4) legal custodian,

(5) foster parents,

(6) preadoptive parents,

(7) relative caregivers, and

(8) if the child is an Indian child, the child's tribe.

Written notice of a permanency planning hearing must be given as provided in MCR 3.920 and MCR 3.921(B)(2). The notice must include a brief statement of the purpose of the hearing, and must include a notice that the hearing may result in further proceedings to terminate parental rights. The notice must inform the parties of their opportunity to participate in the hearing and that any information they wish to provide should be submitted in advance to the court, the agency, the lawyer-guardian ad litem for the child, or an attorney for one of the parties.

(D) **Hearing Procedure; Evidence.**

(1) *Procedure.* Each permanency planning hearing must be conducted by a judge or a referee. Paper reviews, ex parte hearings, stipulated orders, or other actions that are not open to the participation of (a) the parents of the child, unless parental rights have been terminated; (b) the child, if of

appropriate age; and (c) foster parents or preadoptive parents, if any, are not permanency planning hearings.

(2) *Evidence.* The Michigan Rules of Evidence do not apply, other than those with respect to privileges, except to the extent such privileges are abrogated by MCL 722.631. At the permanency planning hearing all relevant and material evidence, including oral and written reports, may be received by the court and may be relied upon to the extent of its probative value. The court must consider any written or oral information concerning the child from the child's parent, guardian, custodian, foster parent, child caring institution, or relative with whom the child is placed, in addition to any other evidence offered at the hearing. The court shall obtain the child's views regarding the permanency plan in a manner appropriate to the child's age. The parties must be afforded an opportunity to examine and controvert written reports received and may be allowed to cross-examine individuals who made the reports when those individuals are reasonably available.

(3) The court, upon receipt of a local foster care review board's report, shall include the report in the court's confidential social file. The court shall ensure that all parties have had the opportunity to review the report and file objections before a dispositional order, dispositional review order, or permanency planning order is entered. The court may at its discretion include recommendations from the report in its orders.

(4) Written reports in the Agency case file, including but not limited to case service plans, treatment plans, substance abuse evaluations, psychological evaluations, therapists' reports, drug and alcohol screens, contracted service provider reports, and parenting time logs, shall be provided to the court and parties no less than seven (7) days before the hearing.

(E) **Determinations; Permanency Options.**

(1) In the case of a child who will not be returned home, the court shall consider in-state and out-of-state placement options. In the case of a child placed out of state, the court shall determine whether the out-of-state placement continues to be appropriate and in the child's best interests. The court shall ensure that the agency is providing appropriate services to assist a child who will transition from foster care to independent living.

(2) *Determining Whether to Return Child Home.* At the conclusion of a permanency planning hearing, the court must order the child returned home unless it determines that the return would cause a substantial risk of harm to the life, the physical health, or the mental well-being of the child. Failure to substantially comply with the case service plan is evidence that the return of the child to the parent may cause a substantial risk of harm to the child's life, physical health, or mental well-being. In addition, the court shall consider any condition or circumstance of the child that may be evidence that a return to the parent would cause a substantial risk of harm to the child's life, physical health, or mental well-being.

(3) *Continuing Foster Care Pending Determination on Termination of Parental Rights.* If the court determines at a permanency planning hearing that the child should not be returned home, it may order the agency to initiate proceedings to terminate parental rights. Except as otherwise provided in this subsection, if the child has been in foster care under the responsibility of the state for 15 of the most recent 22 months,

the court shall order the agency to initiate proceedings to terminate parental rights. If the court orders the agency to initiate proceedings to terminate parental rights, the order must specify the date, or the time within which the petition must be filed. In either case, the petition must be filed no later than 28 days after the date the permanency planning hearing is concluded. The court is not required to order the agency to initiate proceedings to terminate parental rights if one or more of the following apply:

(a) The child is being cared for by relatives.

(b) The case service plan documents a compelling reason for determining that filing a petition to terminate parental rights would not be in the best interests of the child. A compelling reason not to file a petition to terminate parental rights includes, but is not limited to, any of the following:

(i) Adoption is not the appropriate permanency goal for the child.

(ii) No grounds to file a petition to terminate parental rights exist.

(iii) The child is an unaccompanied refugee minor as defined in 45 CFR 400.111.

(iv) There are international legal obligations or compelling foreign policy reasons that preclude terminating parental rights.

(c) The state has not provided the child's family, during the period set in the case service plan, with the services the state considers necessary for the child's safe return to his or her home, if reasonable efforts to reunify the family are required.

If the court does not require the agency to initiate proceedings to terminate parental rights under this provision, the court shall state on the record the reason or reasons for its decision.

(4) *Other Permanency Plans.* If the court does not return the child to the parent, guardian, or legal custodian and if the agency demonstrates that termination of parental rights is not in the best interests of the child, the court may

(a) continue the placement of the child in foster care for a limited period to be set by the court while the agency continues to make reasonable efforts to finalize the court-approved permanency plan for the child,

(b) place the child with a fit and willing relative,

(c) upon a showing of compelling reasons, place the child in an alternative planned permanent living arrangement, or

(d) appoint a juvenile guardian for the child pursuant to MCL 712A.19a and MCR 3.979.

The court must articulate the factual basis for its determination in the court order adopting the permanency plan.

[Adopted February 4, 2003, effective May 1, 2003, 467 Mich. Amended effective February 25, 2004, 469 Mich. Amended October 24, 2006, effective January 1, 2007, 477 Mich; May 31, 2007, effective September 1, 2007, 478 Mich; April 14, 2009, effective July 1, 2009, 483 Mich; February 2, 2010, effective May 1, 2010, 485 Mich; September 21, 2010, effective January 1, 2011, 487 Mich; February 6, 2013, effective May 1, 2013, 493 Mich; June 19, 2019, effective January 1, 2020, 503 Mich.]

Comments

Staff Comment to 2003 Adoption

New MCR 3.976 corresponds to subrule (C) of former Rule 5.973. A number of the changes in its provisions regarding permanency planning hearings are designed to comply with federal statutes and regulations. See, *e.g.*, 45 CFR 1356.21(b)(2).

Subrule (B) substantially modifies the provisions regarding the time for permanency planning hearings. See 45 CFR 1356.21(b)(3); MCL 712A.19a(2). It also includes language based on MCL 722.954b(1) to emphasize that extensions of the hearing date beyond the one-year period are not to be granted because of a change in agency staff.

Subrule (D)(1) makes clear that certain kinds of reviews are not considered permanency planning hearings. See 45 CFR 1355.20(a).

The language changes in subrules (E)(2) and (3) is based on MCL 712A.19a(7) and (8).

Staff Comment to 2004 Amendment

The February 25, 2004, amendments of MCR 3.915, 3.965, 3.975, 3.976 and 3.977, effective immediately, are based on recommendations from the Family Independence Agency and Supreme Court Adoption Work Group.

The amendment of MCR 3.915(B)(2)(a) is designed to enforce the statutory requirement in MCL 712A.17d that lawyers-guardians ad litem for children meet with their clients before each hearing.

The amendment of MCR 3.915(D)(2) addresses the substitution of lawyers-guardians ad litem.

The amendments of MCR 3.965 (B)(13) and (E) require the court to ask parents, guardians, or legal custodians to identify relatives who might be available to care for the child. The amendment to subsection (E) also requires the court to ask parents, guardians, or legal custodians to identify the child's treating physician in certain circumstances. See MCL 712A.18f(6).

The amendments of MCR 3.975(B) and MCR 3.976(C) require the court to notify interested parties that they may provide input at dispositional review and permanency planning hearings.

The amendments of MCR 3.976(B)(3) and (E)(2) encourage early holding of permanency planning hearings and early filing of petitions for termination of parental rights, where appropriate.

MCR 3.977(C)(2) is a new provision that requires courts to give child welfare cases priority in scheduling.

Staff Comment to January, 2007 Amendment

The amendments of MCR 3.976(B)(1) track amendments of MCL 712A.19a of the Juvenile Code as adopted by 2004 PA 473. The change of the phrase "one year" to "12 months" in subrules (B)(2) and (3) conforms the rule's language to that used in the Juvenile Code and to the other Family Division rules that generally mention time limits in terms of months rather than years. The additional language in subrule (2) and new subrule (4) ensures that the permanency planning hearing is completed within the time limitations required by the Adoption and Safe Families Act (ASFA), 42 USC 675(C). Compliance with ASFA is necessary for a child placed in foster care to receive federal funds. 42 USC 672. Amendments of MCR 3.975(C) clarify, in compliance with federal regulations, the specific parties that are entitled to participate in permanency planning hearings. Amendments of MCR 3.976(E)(1) clarify the kinds of placement decisions courts must make in order to comply with the Children's Bureau's interpretation of ASFA regarding qualifying placements for federal foster care funds.

Staff Comment to September, 2007 Amendment

The amendment of MCR 3.976(B)(1)(a) deletes a phrase ("guardian, custodian, or nonparent adult") to make the rule more consistent with the federal statute that requires a permanency planning hearing to be held if the court finds that reasonable efforts to prevent removal or reunite the family are not required because the parent (as opposed to the guardian, custodian, or nonparent adult) has subjected the child to aggravated circumstances.

The amendment of MCR 3.976(B)(1)(b)(iii), which is identical to a change made in MCR 3.965(D)(2)(b)(iii), mirrors the provision in the federal Social Security Act at 42 USC 671(a)(15)(D)(ii)(III), as pointed out by the Department of Health and Human Services.

Staff Comment to 2009 Amendment

The amendments of Rules 3.901, 3.903, 3.921, 3.965, 3.975, 3.976, 3.977, and 3.978, and new rule 3.979 of the Michigan Court Rules reflect the enactment of 2008 PA 199–203.

Staff Comment to 2010 Amendment

These amendments incorporate provisions of the Indian Child Welfare Act into specific provisions within various rules relating to child protective proceedings and juvenile status offenses. The language is designed to make the rules reflect a more integrated approach to addressing issues specific to Indian children. MCR 3.002(1)(c) defines "preadoptive placement" to mean the "temporary placement of an Indian child in a foster home or institution after the termination of parental rights, but before or in lieu of adoptive placement, and ..." The phrase "in lieu of adoptive placement" is not intended to mean that it is permissible to leave a child in foster care indefinitely, in violation of MCL 712A.19b(6) or (7) or 45 CFR 1355.20, 45 CFR 1356.21, or 45 CFR 1356.50. Rather, it addresses situations where the parental rights to a child have been terminated and there is no permanency plan for adoption of the child. One example is when the child has been placed with a juvenile guardian and the guardianship is subsequently revoked. In this situation, jurisdiction over the child pursuant to MCL 712A.2(b) will be reinstated and the child is placed in foster care.

MCR 3.002(1): The definition of "child custody proceeding" is intended to apply the Indian Child Welfare Act to delinquency proceedings if an "Indian child" is charged with a so-called status offense in violation of MCL 712A.2(a)(2)–(4) or (d). Delinquency proceedings involving an Indian child charged with any other non-status offense are generally not subject to the Indian Child Welfare Act; however, if the initial investigation or subsequent review of a non-status delinquency case reveals that the Indian child involved suffers from child abuse or neglect, a separate child protective proceeding may be initiated, which would be subject to the Indian Child Welfare Act.

The amendment of MCR 3.905(C)(1) states that a court shall consider guidelines established by the Bureau of Indian Affairs (BIA) in determining whether good cause not to transfer exists (Guidelines for State Courts; Indian Child Custody Proceedings, 44 Fed Reg No 228, 67590–67592, C.2–C.4. [November 26, 1979]). Some examples of good cause are that the Indian tribe does not have a tribal court or that the Indian child is over 12 years old and objects to the transfer. For additional examples of good cause and relevant case law, see the BIA guidelines cited above and A Practical Guide to the Indian Child Welfare Act. (Native American Rights Fund, A Practical Guide to the Indian Child Welfare Act [Boulder, CO: Native American Rights Fund, 2007], 7.15 and 7.16, p 60.)

Staff Comment to 2011 Amendment

The amendments of MCR 3.973, 3.975, and 3.976 require a court to maintain a local foster care review board report in the court's confidential social file, and ensure that all parties have had the opportunity to review the report before the court enters a dispositional order, dispositional review order, or permanency planning order. Courts also may include recommendations from the report in their orders under the new language.

Staff Comment to 2013 Amendment

The amendment of MCR 3.976 requires a court to indicate on the record the reason that no petition for termination of parental rights need be filed, thus providing a record to future auditors who review the state's foster care program that the court explicitly chose the option.

Staff Comment to 2020 Amendment

These amendments are based on a proposal created by a special committee of the State Bar of Michigan and approved for submission to the Court by the Bar's Representative Assembly. The rules require mandatory discovery disclosure in many cases, adopt a presumptive limit on interrogatories (20 in most cases, but 35 in domestic relations proceedings) and limit a deposition to 7 hours. The amendments also update the rules to more specifically address issues related to electronically stored information, and encourage early action on discovery issues during the discovery period.

The amendment of MCR 2.309(A)(2) sets a presumptive limit of twenty interrogatories for each separately represented party. Several commenters suggested that the term "discrete subpart" be more explicitly defined. But the rule's reference to "a discrete subpart" is intended to draw guidance from federal courts construing FR Civ P 30(a)(1). Generally, subparts are not separately counted if they are logically or factually subsumed within and necessarily related to the primary question. In upholding the limit, parties and courts should also pragmatically balance the overall goals of discovery and the admonition of MCR 1.105. Further, the intent of the provision at MCR 2.301(B)(4) is to ensure that parties responding to discovery requests have the full time period to do so as provided for under these rules prior to the expiration of the discovery period.

Rule 3.977. Termination of Parental Rights

(A) General.

(1) This rule applies to all proceedings in which termination of parental rights is sought. Proceedings for termination of parental rights involving an Indian child, are governed by 25 USC 1912 in addition to this rule.

(2) Parental rights of the respondent over the child may not be terminated unless termination was requested in an original, amended, or supplemental petition by:

(a) the agency,

(b) the child,

(c) the guardian, legal custodian, or representative of the child,

(d) a concerned person as defined in MCL 712A.19b(6),

(e) the state children's ombudsman, or

(f) the prosecuting attorney, without regard to whether the prosecuting attorney is representing or acting as a legal consultant to the agency or any other party.

(3) The burden of proof is on the party seeking by court order to terminate the rights of the respondent over the child. There is no right to a jury determination.

(B) Definition. When used in this rule, unless the context otherwise indicates, "respondent" includes

(1) the natural or adoptive mother of the child;

(2) the father of the child as defined by MCR 3.903(A)(7).

"Respondent" does not include other persons to whom legal custody has been given by court order, persons who are acting in the place of the mother or father, or other persons responsible for the control, care, and welfare of the child.

(C) Notice; Priority.

(1) Notice must be given as provided in MCR 3.920 and MCR 3.921(B)(3).

(2) Hearings on petitions seeking termination of parental rights shall be given the highest possible priority consistent with the orderly conduct of the court's caseload.

(D) Suspension of Parenting Time. If a petition to terminate parental rights to a child is filed, the court may suspend parenting time for a parent who is a subject of the petition.

(E) Termination of Parental Rights at the Initial Disposition. The court shall order termination of the parental rights of a respondent at the initial dispositional hearing held pursuant to MCR 3.973, and shall order that additional efforts for reunification of the child with the respondent shall not be made, if

(1) the original, or amended, petition contains a request for termination;

(2) at the trial or plea proceedings, the trier of fact finds by a preponderance of the evidence that one or more of the grounds for assumption of jurisdiction over the child under MCL 712A.2(b) have been established;

(3) at the initial disposition hearing, the court finds on the basis of clear and convincing legally admissible evidence that had been introduced at the trial or plea proceedings, or that is introduced at the dispositional hearing, that one or more facts alleged in the petition:

(a) are true, and

(b) establish grounds for termination of parental rights under MCL 712A.19b(3)(a), (b), (d), (e), (f), (g), (h), (i), (j), (k), (*l*), or (m);

(4) termination of parental rights is in the child's best interests.

(F) Termination of Parental Rights on the Basis of Different Circumstances. The court may take action on a supplemental petition that seeks to terminate the parental rights of a respondent over a child already within the jurisdiction of the court on the basis of one or more circumstances new or different from the offense that led the court to take jurisdiction.

(1) The court must order termination of the parental rights of a respondent, and must order that additional efforts for reunification of the child with the respondent must not be made, if

(a) the supplemental petition for termination of parental rights contains a request for termination;

(b) at the hearing on the supplemental petition, the court finds on the basis of clear and convincing legally admissible evidence that one or more of the facts alleged in the supplemental petition:

(i) are true; and

(ii) come within MCL 712A.19b(3)(a), (b), (c)(ii), (d), (e), (f), (g), (i), (j), (k), (l), or (m); and

(c) termination of parental rights is in the child's best interests.

(2) *Discovery and Time for Disclosures and Hearing on Petition.* Parties shall make disclosures as detailed in MCR 3.922(A) at least 21 days prior to the termination hearing and have rights to discovery consistent with that rule. The hearing on a supplemental petition for termination of parental rights under this subrule shall be held within 42 days after the filing of the supplemental petition. The court may, for good cause shown, extend the period for an additional 21 days.

(G) Termination of Parental Rights; Indian Child. In addition to the required findings in this rule, the parental rights of a parent of an Indian child must not be terminated unless:

(1) the court is satisfied that active efforts as defined in MCR 3.002 have been made to provide remedial service and rehabilitative programs designed to prevent the breakup of the Indian family and that these efforts have proved unsuccessful, and

(2) the court finds evidence beyond a reasonable doubt, including testimony of at least one qualified expert witness as described in MCL 712B.17, that parental rights should be terminated because continued custody of the child by the parent or Indian custodian will likely result in serious emotional or physical damage to the child.

(H) Termination of Parental Rights; Other. If the parental rights of a respondent over the child were not terminated pursuant to subrule (E) at the initial dispositional hearing or pursuant to subrule (F) at a hearing on a supplemental petition on the basis of different circumstances, and the child is within the jurisdiction of the court, the court must, if the child is in foster care, or may, if the child is not in foster care, following a dispositional review hearing under MCR 3.975, a progress review under MCR 3.974, or a permanency planning hearing under MCR 3.976, take action on a supplemental petition that seeks to terminate the parental rights of a respondent over the child on the basis of one or more grounds listed in MCL 712A.19b(3).

(1) *Time.*

(a) Filing Petition. The supplemental petition for termination of parental rights may be filed at any time after the initial dispositional review hearing, progress review, or permanency planning hearing, whichever occurs first.

(b) Hearing on Petition. The hearing on a supplemental petition for termination of parental rights under this subrule must be held within 42 days after the filing of the supplemental petition. The court may, for good cause shown, extend the period for an additional 21 days.

(2) *Evidence.* The Michigan Rules of Evidence do not apply, other than those with respect to privileges, except to the extent such privileges are abrogated by MCL 722.631. At the hearing all relevant and material evidence, including oral and written reports, may be received by the court and may be relied upon to the extent of its probative value. The parties must be afforded an opportunity to examine and controvert written reports received by the court and shall be allowed to cross-examine individuals who made the reports when those individuals are reasonably available.

(3) *Order.* The court must order termination of the parental rights of a respondent and must order that additional efforts for reunification of the child with the respondent must not be made, if the court finds

(a) on the basis of clear and convincing evidence admitted pursuant to subrule (H)(2) that one or more facts alleged in the petition:

(i) are true; and

(ii) come within MCL 712A.19b(3).

(b) that termination of parental rights is in the child's best interests.

(I) Findings.

(1) *General.* The court shall state on the record or in writing its findings of fact and conclusions of law. Brief, definite, and pertinent findings and conclusions on contested matters are sufficient. If the court does not issue a decision on the record following hearing, it shall file its decision within 28 days after the taking of final proofs, but no later than 70 days after the commencement of the hearing to terminate parental rights.

(2) *Denial of Termination.* If the court finds that the parental rights of respondent should not be terminated, the court must make findings of fact and conclusions of law.

(3) *Order of Termination.* An order terminating parental rights under the Juvenile Code may not be entered unless the court makes findings of fact, states its conclusions of law, and includes the statutory basis for the order.

(J) Respondent's Rights Following Termination.

(1) *Advice.* Immediately after entry of an order terminating parental rights, the court shall advise the respondent parent orally or in writing that:

(a) The respondent is entitled to appellate review of the order.

(b) If the respondent is financially unable to provide an attorney to perfect an appeal, the court will appoint an attorney and furnish the attorney with the complete transcript and record of all proceedings.

(c) A request for the assistance of an attorney must be made within 14 days after notice of the order is given or an order is entered denying a timely filed postjudgment motion. The court must then give a form to the respondent with the instructions (to be repeated on the form) that if the respondent desires the appointment of an attorney, the form must be returned to the court within the required period (to be stated on the form).

(d) The respondent has the right to file a denial of release of identifying information, a revocation of a denial of release, and to keep current the respondent's name and address as provided in MCL 710.27.

(e) The respondent's obligation to support the child will continue until a court of competent jurisdiction modifies or terminates the obligation, an order of adoption is entered, or the child is emancipated by operation of law. Failure to provide required notice under this subsection does not affect the obligation imposed by law or otherwise establish a remedy or cause of action on behalf of the parent.

(2) *Appointment of Attorney.*

(a) If a request is timely filed and the court finds that the respondent is financially unable to provide an attorney, the court shall appoint an attorney within 14 days after the respondent's request is filed. The chief judge of the court shall bear primary responsibility for ensuring that the appointment is made within the deadline stated in this rule.

(b) In a case involving the termination of parental rights, the order described in (J)(2) and (3) must be entered on a form approved by the State Court Administrator's Office, entitled "Claim of Appeal and Order Appointing Counsel," and the court must immediately send to the Court of Appeals a copy of the Claim of Appeal and Order Appointing Counsel, a copy of the judgment or order being appealed, and a copy of the complete register of actions in the case. The court must also file in the Court of Appeals proof of having made service of the Claim of Appeal and Order Appointing Counsel on the respondent(s), appointed counsel for the respondent(s), the court reporter(s)/recorder(s), petitioner, the prosecuting attorney, the lawyer-guardian ad litem for the child(ren) under MCL 712A.13a(1)(f), and the guardian ad litem or attorney (if any) for the child(ren). Entry of the order by the trial court pursuant to this subrule constitutes a timely filed claim of appeal for the purposes of MCR 7.204.

(3) *Transcripts.* If the court finds that the respondent is financially unable to pay for the preparation of transcripts for appeal, the court must order the complete transcripts of all proceedings prepared at public expense.

(K) Review Standard. The clearly erroneous standard shall be used in reviewing the court's findings on appeal from an order terminating parental rights.

[Adopted February 4, 2003, effective May 1, 2003, 467 Mich. Amended effective February 25, 2004. Amended February 3, 2004, effective May 1, 2004, 469 Mich. Amended effective February 25, 2004, 469 Mich. Amended April 14, 2009, effective July 1, 2009, 483 Mich; February 2, 2010, effective May 1, 2010, 485 Mich. Amended effective August 24, 2012, 492 Mich. Amended effective, pending public comment, March 20, 2013, 493 Mich. Amended effective September 5, 2013, 495 Mich; May 7, 2014, 495 Mich. Amended March 28, 2018, effective May 1, 2018, 501 Mich. Amended effective August 14, 2019, 503 Mich. Amended June 12, 2019, effective January 1, 2020, 503 Mich.]

Comments

Staff Comment to 2003 Adoption

MCR 3.977 corresponds to former Rule 5.974.

Subrule (A)(1) is amended to make clear that with regard to termination of parental rights involving an Indian child, in addition to satisfying the federal standard, state grounds for termination must be established. There is a corresponding change in MCR 3.980(D).

New subrule (D) automatically suspends the parenting time of a parent as to whom a petition to terminate parental rights is filed. The court can reinstate parenting time on an appropriate showing. See MCL 712A.19b(4).

Subrule (E) more specifically states the grounds on which termination of parental rights may be ordered at the first dispositional hearing.

Subrule (F), regarding termination of parental rights on a supplemental petition alleging different circumstances, is modified to more closely correspond to the procedures applicable to the initial termination hearing.

Subrule (G) is modified to reflect case law holding that the provisions of the rule and MCL 712A.19b(1) apply both where the child is in foster care and where the child is not in foster care. See *In re Marin*, 198 Mich App 560 (1993).

Subrule (G)(1) clarifies that a supplemental petition for termination of parental rights may be filed at any time after the initial dispositional review hearing, progress review, or permanency planning hearing.

Subrule (G)(2) includes a provision regarding the applicability of the Rules of Evidence, similar to that found in a number of the other rules.

Subrule (G)(3) parallels the standard of proof provisions of subrules (E) and (F). Even though the grounds for terminating parental rights are established, the court is not to order termination if there is clear and convincing evidence that termination is not in the best interests of the child. See *In re Trejo Minors*, 462 Mich 341, 354–356 (2000).

Staff Comment to 2003 Amendment

The April 30, 2003, order makes corrections to a number of the rules governing proceedings regarding juveniles that had been adopted on February 4, 2003. The changes are effective May 1, corresponding to the effective date of the February 4 amendments. In addition to these changes, a number of corrections of punctuation and capitalization and changes in the Notes that accompanied the rules have been made and will appear in the published version of the rules.

The amendments of MCR 3.903(D)(8)(m), 6.903(H)(16), 6.931(E)(3), and 6.933(C)(1) conform the rules to 2002 PA 665, which changed the amounts of controlled substances required for certain violations. See MCL 333.7401(2)(a)(i), 333.7403(2)(a)(i). MCR 3.933(C)(1) is also modified in light of *People v Valentin*, 457 Mich 1 (1998).

The amendment of MCR 3.935(B)(1) corrects the inadvertent omission of references to guardians and legal custodians.

The amendments of MCR 3.922(E)(1)(c), 3.943(A), 3.945(A)(1), 3.965(E)(1), and 3.972(C)(2)(c) correct minor errors in wording.

The amendment of MCR 3.977(G) deletes the word "hearing" in the reference to progress reviews. Under MCR 3.974(A)(1), progress reviews do not require hearings.

The amendment of MCR 3.980(B) and (C) revise the provisions on removal of American Indian children from the home to clarify the distinction between emergency removals and removals after hearing.

The amendments of MCR 3.982(A), 6.903(I)–(L) and 6.937(A) correct cross-reference, citation and numbering errors.

Staff Comment to February 3, 2004 Amendment

The February 3, 2004, amendments to MCR 3.977(I), effective May 1, 2004, accomplish the following: (1) shorten the deadline for requesting the appointment of counsel following entry of orders terminating parental rights; (2) impose a new deadline for entry of the order appointing counsel in such cases; (3) impose primary responsibility on the chief judge of the court to ensure that the appointment is timely made; and (4) require the appointment of counsel and the transcript order to be contained on a form that functions as the claim of appeal.

Subrule (I)(2)(b) is a new rule that provides that the order appointing appellate counsel also serves as a claim of appeal in cases where the respondent makes a timely request for appellate counsel. The subrule further directs the State Court Administrative Office to approve a form for use by the trial courts that will act as a combination order of appointment, transcript order, and claim of appeal.

The amendment to MCR 7.204(A)(1) shortens the time for requesting the appointment of appellate counsel in appeals from orders terminating parental rights. This new deadline conforms to the amendments to MCR 3.977(I).

Staff Comment to February 25, 2004 Amendment

The February 25, 2004, amendments of MCR 3.915, 3.965, 3.975, 3.976 and 3.977, effective immediately, are based on recommendations from the Family Independence Agency and Supreme Court Adoption Work Group.

The amendment of MCR 3.915(B)(2)(a) is designed to enforce the statutory requirement in MCL 712A.17d that lawyers-guardians ad litem for children meet with their clients before each hearing.

The amendment of MCR 3.915(D)(2) addresses the substitution of lawyers-guardians ad litem.

The amendments of MCR 3.965(B)(13) and (E) require the court to ask parents, guardians, or legal custodians to identify relatives who might be available to care for the child. The amendment to subsection (E) also requires the court to ask parents, guardians, or legal custodians to identify the child's treating physician in certain circumstances. See MCL 712A.18f(6).

The amendments of MCR 3.975(B) and MCR 3.976(C) require the court to notify interested parties that they may provide input at dispositional review and permanency planning hearings.

The amendments of MCR 3.976(B)(3) and (E)(2) encourage early holding of permanency planning hearings and early filing of petitions for termination of parental rights, where appropriate.

MCR 3.977(C)(2) is a new provision that requires courts to give child welfare cases priority in scheduling.

Staff Comment to 2009 Amendment

The amendments of Rules 3.901, 3.903, 3.921, 3.965, 3.975, 3.976, 3.977, and 3.978, and new rule 3.979 of the Michigan Court Rules reflect the enactment of 2008 PA 199–203.

Staff Comment to 2010 Amendment

These amendments incorporate provisions of the Indian Child Welfare Act into specific provisions within various rules relating to child protective proceedings and juvenile status offenses. The language is designed to make the rules reflect a more integrated approach to addressing issues specific to Indian children.

MCR 3.002(1)(c) defines "preadoptive placement" to mean the "temporary placement of an Indian child in a foster home or institution after the termination of parental rights, but before or in lieu of adoptive placement, and . . ." The phrase "in lieu of adoptive placement" is not intended to mean that it is permissible to leave a child in foster care indefinitely, in violation of MCL 712A.19b(6) or (7) or 45 CFR 1355.20, 45 CFR 1356.21, or 45 CFR 1356.50. Rather, it addresses situations where the parental rights to a child have been terminated and there is no permanency plan for adoption of the child. One example is when the child has been placed with a juvenile guardian and the guardianship is subsequently revoked. In this situation, jurisdiction over the child pursuant to MCL 712A.2(b) will be reinstated and the child is placed in foster care.

MCR 3.002(1): The definition of "child custody proceeding" is intended to apply the Indian Child Welfare Act to delinquency proceedings if an "Indian child" is charged with a so-called status offense in violation of MCL 712A.2(a)(2)–(4) or (d). Delinquency proceedings involving an Indian child charged with any other non-status offense are generally not subject to the Indian Child Welfare Act; however, if the initial investigation or subsequent review of a non-status delinquency case reveals that the Indian child involved suffers from child abuse or neglect, a separate child protective proceeding may be initiated, which would be subject to the Indian Child Welfare Act.

The amendment of MCR 3.905(C)(1) states that a court shall consider guidelines established by the Bureau of Indian Affairs (BIA) in determining whether good cause not to transfer exists (Guidelines for State Courts; Indian Child Custody Proceedings, 44 Fed Reg No 228, 67590–67592, C.2–C.4. [November 26, 1979]). Some examples of good cause are that the Indian tribe does not have a tribal court or that the Indian child is over 12 years old and objects to the transfer. For additional examples of good cause and relevant case law, see the BIA guidelines cited above and A Practical Guide to the Indian Child Welfare Act. (Native American Rights Fund, A Practical Guide to the Indian Child Welfare Act [Boulder, CO: Native American Rights Fund, 2007], 7.15 and 7.16, p 60.)

Staff Comment to 2012 Amendment

These amendments reflect changes to correct minor technical errors that have occurred in drafting or to respond to recent adopted rule revisions, which occasionally inadvertently create incorrect cross-references in other rules.

Staff Comment to March, 2013 Amendment

This proposal incorporates provisions of the newly enacted Michigan Indian Family Preservation Act into specific provisions within various rules relating to child protective proceedings and juvenile status offenses.

Staff Comment to September, 2013 Amendment

These amendments reflect changes that correct minor technical errors that have occurred in drafting or the changes respond to recent adopted rule revisions, which occasionally inadvertently create incorrect cross-references in other rules.

Staff Comment to 2014 Amendment

These amendments reflect changes that correct minor technical errors that have occurred in drafting or the changes respond to recent adopted rule revisions, which occasionally inadvertently create incorrect cross-references in other rules.

Staff Comment to First May 1, 2018 Amendment

The amendments of MCR 3.977(J) were submitted by the Court of Appeals, and require the production of the complete transcript in appeals from termination of parental rights proceedings when counsel is appointed by the court. The

amendments codify existing practice in many courts, and the Court of Appeals believes they promote proper consideration of appeal issues and eliminate unnecessary delays to the appellate process. Note that the proposal published for comment also contained a similar revision of MCR 6.425. That concept is included with other substantive changes as part of ADM File No. 2014-36 at MCR 6.425(G)(1)(f) and will be incorporated in the order that issues in that file.

Staff Comment to Second May 1, 2018 Amendment

The amendments incorporate into both the rules concerning juvenile proceedings and adoption proceedings the requirement to notify parents that the termination of parental rights does not automatically terminate the obligation to provide support for a child. The amendments also make clear that failure to provide the notice would not affect the parent's obligation to continue to pay child support.

Staff Comment to 2019 Amendment

These amendments update cross-references and make other nonsubstantive revisions to clarify the rules.

Staff Comment to 2020 Amendment

These amendments are based on a proposal created by a special committee of the State Bar of Michigan and approved for submission to the Court by the Bar's Representative Assembly. The rules require mandatory discovery disclosure in many cases, adopt a presumptive limit on interrogatories (20 in most cases, but 35 in domestic relations proceedings) and limit a deposition to 7 hours. The amendments also update the rules to more specifically address issues related to electronically stored information, and encourage early action on discovery issues during the discovery period.

The amendment of MCR 2.309(A)(2) sets a presumptive limit of twenty interrogatories for each separately represented party. Several commenters suggested that the term "discrete subpart" be more explicitly defined. But the rule's reference to "a discrete subpart" is intended to draw guidance from federal courts construing FR Civ P 30(a)(1). Generally, subparts are not separately counted if they are logically or factually subsumed within and necessarily related to the primary question. In upholding the limit, parties and courts should also pragmatically balance the overall goals of discovery and the admonition of MCR 1.105. Further, the intent of the provision at MCR 2.301(B)(4) is to ensure that parties responding to discovery requests have the full time period to do so as provided for under these rules prior to the expiration of the discovery period.

Rule 3.978   Post-Termination Review Hearings

(A) Review Hearing Requirement. If a child remains in foster care following the termination of parental rights to the child, the court must conduct a hearing not more than 91 days after the termination of parental rights and not later than every 91 days after that hearing for the first year following the termination of parental rights to the child. At the post-termination review hearing, the court shall review the child's placement in foster care and the progress toward the child's adoption or other permanent placement, as long as the child is subject to the jurisdiction, control, or supervision of the court, or of the Michigan Children's Institute or other agency. If the child is residing in another permanent planned living arrangement or is placed with a fit and willing relative and the child's placement is intended to be permanent, the court must conduct a hearing not more than 182 days from the preceding review hearing.

(B) Notice; Right to be Heard. The foster parents (if any) of a child and any preadoptive parents or relative providing care to the child must be provided with notice of and an opportunity to be heard at each hearing.

(C) Findings. The court must make findings on whether reasonable efforts have been made to establish permanent placement for the child, and may enter such orders as it considers necessary in the best interests of the child, including appointment of a juvenile guardian pursuant to MCL 712A.19c and MCR 3.979.

(D) Termination of Jurisdiction. The jurisdiction of the court in the child protective proceeding may terminate when a court of competent jurisdiction enters an order:

(1) terminating the rights of the entity with legal custody and enters an order placing the child for adoption, or

(2) appointing a juvenile guardian under MCR 3.979 after conducting a review hearing under subsection (A) of this rule.

[Adopted February 4, 2003, effective May 1, 2003, 467 Mich. Amended October 24, 2006, effective January 1, 2007, 477 Mich; April 14, 2009, effective July 1, 2009, 483 Mich.]

Comments

Staff Comment to 2003 Adoption

MCR 3.978 corresponds to former Rule 5.974(J), governing review hearings after termination of parental rights. The provision is modified to conform to the shortened time limit provided by statute. See MCL 712A.19c. It also excludes from review hearings cases in which a child has been placed under permanent foster family agreement, or placed with a relative and the placement is intended to be permanent. See MCL 712A.19(4) details are added regarding the conduct of the hearing.

Staff Comment to 2006 Amendment

The amendment of MCR 3.978(A) clarifies a misconception created by the existing language of the subrule. Because the current language appears to create an exception for relative placements and permanent foster care arrangements, courts often failed to hold the requisite post-termination review hearings in such situations. The amendment makes it clear to Family Division courts that they are required to hold post-termination review hearings even in cases in which the child is placed with a relative or in a long-term foster care setting. The phrase "permanent planned living arrangement" replaces the reference to "permanent foster family agreement." The substituted phrase comports with the Children's Bureau's interpretation of ASFA regarding qualifying permanent placements for receipt of federal foster care funds.

Staff Comment to 2009 Amendment

The amendments of Rules 3.901, 3.903, 3.921, 3.965, 3.975, 3.976, 3.977, and 3.978, and new rule 3.979 of the Michigan Court Rules reflect the enactment of 2008 PA 199–203.

Rule 3.979   Juvenile Guardianships

(A) Appointment of Juvenile Guardian; Process. If the court determines at a posttermination review hearing or a permanency planning hearing that it is in the child's best interests, the court may appoint a juvenile guardian for the child pursuant to MCL 712A.19a or MCL 712A.19c.

(1) Under MCR 3.979(A), the court shall order the Department of Human Services to:

(a) conduct a criminal record check and central registry clearance of the residents of the home and submit the results to the court within 7 days; and

(b) perform a home study with a copy to be submitted to the court within 28 days, unless a home study has been performed within the immediately preceding 365 days, in which case a copy of that home study shall be submitted to the court.

(2) If a child for whom a juvenile guardianship is proposed is in foster care, the court shall continue the child's placement and order the information required above about the proposed juvenile guardian. If the information required above has already been provided to the court, the court may issue an order appointing the proposed juvenile guardian pursuant to subrule (B).

(3) If the parental rights over a child who is the subject of a proposed juvenile guardianship have been terminated, the court shall not appoint a guardian without the written consent of the Michigan Children's Institute (MCI) superintendent. The court may order the Department of Human Services to seek the consent of the MCI superintendent. The consent must be filed with the court no later than 28 days after the permanency planning hearing or the posttermination review hearing, or such longer time as the court may allow for good cause shown.

(a) If a person denied consent believes that the decision to withhold consent by the MCI superintendent is arbitrary or capricious, the person may file a motion with the court within 56 days of receipt of the decision to deny consent. A motion under this subsection shall contain information regarding both of the following:

(i) the specific steps taken by the person or agency to obtain the consent required and the results, if any, and

(ii) the specific reasons why the person or agency believes that the decision to withhold consent was arbitrary or capricious.

(b) If a motion is filed alleging that the MCI superintendent's failure to consent was arbitrary or capricious, the court shall set a hearing date and ensure that notice is provided to the MCI superintendent and all parties entitled to notice under MCR 3.921.

(c) If a hearing is held and the court finds by clear and convincing evidence that the decision to withhold consent was arbitrary or capricious, the court may approve the guardianship without the consent of the MCI superintendent.

The court shall determine the continuing necessity and appropriateness of the child's placement.

(B) Order Appointing Juvenile Guardian. After receiving the information ordered by the court under subsection (A)(1), and after finding that appointment of a juvenile guardian is in the child's best interests, the court may enter an order appointing a juvenile guardian. The order appointing a juvenile guardian shall be on a form approved by the state court administrator. Within 7 days of receiving the information, the court shall enter an order appointing a juvenile guardian or schedule the matter for a hearing. A separate order shall be entered for each child.

(1) *Acceptance of Appointment.* A juvenile guardian appointed by the court shall file an acceptance of appointment with the court on a form approved by the state court administrator. The acceptance shall state, at a minimum, that the juvenile guardian accepts the appointment, submits to personal jurisdiction of the court, will not delegate the juvenile guardian's authority, and will perform required duties.

(2) *Letters of Authority.* On the filing of the acceptance of appointment, the court shall issue letters of authority on a form approved by the state court administrator. Any restriction or limitation of the powers of the juvenile guardian must be set forth in the letters of authority, including but not limited to, not moving the domicile of the child from the state of Michigan without court approval.

(3) *Certification.* Certification of the letters of authority and a statement that on a given date the letters are in full force and effect may appear on the face of copies furnished to the juvenile guardian or interested persons.

(4) *Notice.* Notice of a proceeding relating to the juvenile guardianship shall be delivered or mailed to the juvenile guardian by first-class mail at the juvenile guardian's address

as listed in the court records and to his or her address as then known to the petitioner. Any notice mailed first class by the court to the juvenile guardian's last address on file shall be considered notice to the juvenile guardian.

(C) Court Jurisdiction; Review Hearings; Lawyer–Guardian ad Litem.

(1) *Jurisdiction.*

(a) Except as otherwise provided in this rule, the court's jurisdiction over a juvenile guardianship shall continue until terminated by court order. The court's jurisdiction over a juvenile under section 2(b) of the Juvenile Code, MCL 712A.2(b), and the jurisdiction of the MCI under section 3 of 1935 PA 220, MCL 400.203, shall be terminated after the court appoints a juvenile guardian under this section and conducts a review hearing pursuant to MCR 3.975 when parental rights to the child have not been terminated, or a review hearing pursuant to MCR 3.978 when parental rights to the child have been terminated.

(b) Unless terminated by court order, the court's jurisdiction over a juvenile guardianship ordered under MCL 712A.19a or MCL 712A.19c for a youth 16 years of age or older shall continue until 120 days after the youth's eighteenth birthday. Upon notice by the Department of Health and Human Services that extended guardianship assistance beyond age 18 will be provided to a youth pursuant to MCL 400.665, the court shall retain jurisdiction over the guardianship until that youth no longer receives extended guardianship assistance.

(2) *Review Hearings.* The review hearing following appointment of the juvenile guardian must be conducted within 91 days of the most recent review hearing if it has been one year or less from the date the child was last removed from the home, or within 182 days of the most recent review hearing if it has been more than one year from the date the child was last removed from the home.

(3) *Lawyer–Guardian ad Litem.* The appointment of the lawyer-guardian ad litem in the child protective proceeding terminates upon entry of the order terminating the court's jurisdiction pursuant to MCL 712A.2(b). At any time after a juvenile guardian is appointed, the court may reappoint the lawyer-guardian ad litem or may appoint a new lawyer-guardian ad litem if the court is satisfied that such action is warranted. A lawyer-guardian ad litem appointed under this subrule is subject to the provisions of MCL 712A.17d.

(D) Court Responsibilities.

(1) *Annual Reviews.*

(a) Review on Condition of Child. The court shall conduct an annual review of a juvenile guardianship as to the condition of the child until the child's eighteenth birthday. The review shall be commenced within 63 days after the anniversary date of the appointment of the guardian. The court may conduct a review of a juvenile guardianship at any time it deems necessary. If the report by the juvenile guardian has not been filed as required by subrule (E)(1), the court shall take appropriate action.

(b) Review on Extended Guardianship Assistance. If, under subrule (C)(1)(b), the Department of Health and Human Services has notified the court that extended guardianship assistance has been provided to a youth pursuant to

MCL 400.665, the court shall conduct an annual review hearing at least once every 12 months thereafter to determine that the guardianship meets the criteria under MCL 400.667. The duty to conduct an annual review hearing on extended guardianship assistance shall discontinue when the youth is no longer eligible for extended guardianship assistance. Notice of the hearing under this subrule shall be sent to the guardian and the youth as provided in MCR 3.920(D)(1).

(i) The hearing conducted under this subrule may be adjourned up to 28 days for good cause shown.

(ii) If requested by the court, the guardian must provide proof at the review hearing that the youth is in compliance with the criteria of MCL 400.667.

(iii) Following a review hearing under this subrule, the court shall issue an order to support its determination and serve the order on the Department of Health and Human Services, the guardian, and the youth.

(c) Termination of Juvenile Guardianship. Upon receipt of notice from the Department of Health and Human Services that it will not continue extended guardianship assistance, the court shall immediately terminate the juvenile guardianship.

(2) *Investigation.* The court shall appoint the Department of Human Services or another person to conduct an investigation of the juvenile guardianship of a child when deemed appropriate by the court or upon petition by the Department of Human Services or an interested person. The investigator shall file a written report with the court within 28 days of such appointment and shall serve it on the other interested parties listed in MCR 3.921(C). The report shall include a recommendation regarding whether the juvenile guardianship should continue or be modified and whether a hearing should be scheduled. If the report recommends modification, the report shall state the nature of the modification.

(3) *Judicial Action.* After informal review of the report provided in subrule (D)(2), the court shall enter an order denying the modification or set a date for a hearing to be held within 28 days.

(4) Upon notice of a child's death the court shall enter an order of discharge. The court may schedule a hearing on the matter before entering an order of discharge.

(E) Duties and Authority of Guardian Appointed to Juvenile Guardianship. A juvenile guardianship approved under these rules is authorized by the Juvenile Code and is distinct from a guardianship authorized under the Estates and Protected Individuals Code. A juvenile guardian has all the powers and duties of a guardian set forth under section 5215 of the Estates and Protected Individuals Code.

(1) *Report of Juvenile Guardian.* A juvenile guardian shall file a written report annually within 56 days after the anniversary of appointment and at other times as the court may order. Reports must be on a form approved by the state court administrator. The juvenile guardian must serve the report on the persons listed in MCR 3.921.

(2) *Petition for Conservator.* At the time of appointing a juvenile guardian or during the period of the juvenile guardianship, the court shall determine whether there would be sufficient assets under the control of the juvenile guardian to

require a conservatorship. If so, the court shall order the juvenile guardian to petition the probate court for a conservator pursuant to MCL 700.5401 *et seq.*

(3) *Address of Juvenile Guardian.* The juvenile guardian must keep the court informed in writing within 7 days of any change in the juvenile guardian's address.

(4) The juvenile guardian shall provide the court and interested persons with written notice within 14 days of the child's death.

(F) Revocation or Termination of Guardianship.

(1) *Motion or Petition.*

(a) Revocation of Juvenile Guardianship. The court shall, on its own motion or upon petition from the Department of Human Services or the child's lawyer-guardian ad litem, hold a hearing to determine whether a juvenile guardianship established under this section shall be revoked.

(b) Termination of Juvenile Guardian and Appointment of Successor. A juvenile guardian or other interested person may petition the court for permission to terminate the guardianship. A petition may include a request for appointment of a successor juvenile guardian.

(2) *Hearing.* If a petition for revocation or termination is filed with the court, the court shall hold a hearing within 28 days to determine whether to grant the petition to revoke or terminate the juvenile guardianship. The court may order temporary removal of the child under MCR 3.963 to protect the health, safety, or welfare of the child, pending the revocation or termination hearing. If the court orders removal of the child from the juvenile guardian to protect the child's health, safety, or welfare, the court must proceed under MCR 3.974(B).

(3) *Investigation and Report.* In preparation for the revocation or termination hearing, the court shall order the Department of Human Services to perform an investigation and file a written report of the investigation. The report shall be filed with the court no later than 7 days before the hearing. The report shall include the reasons for terminating a juvenile guardianship or revoking a juvenile guardianship, and a recommendation regarding temporary placement, if necessary.

(4) *Notice.* The court shall ensure that interested persons are given notice of the hearing as provided in MCR 3.920 and MCR 3.921. The court may proceed in the absence of interested persons provided that proper notice has been given. The notice must inform the interested persons of their opportunity to participate in the hearing and that any information they wish to provide should be submitted in advance to the court, the agency, the lawyer-guardian ad litem for the child, and an attorney for one of the parties.

(5) *Action Following Motion or Petition to Revoke Juvenile Guardianship.* After notice and a hearing on a petition to revoke the juvenile guardianship, if the court finds by a preponderance of evidence that continuation of the juvenile guardianship is not in the child's best interests, and upon finding that it is contrary to the welfare of the child to be placed in or remain in the juvenile guardian's home and that reasonable efforts were made to prevent removal, the court shall revoke the juvenile guardianship. The court shall enter an order revoking the juvenile guardianship and placing the child under the care and supervision of the Department of Human Services on a form approved by the state court administrator.

Jurisdiction over the child under MCL 712A.2(b) is reinstated under the previous child protective proceeding upon entry of the order revoking the juvenile guardianship.

(6) *Action Following Petition to Terminate Appointment of Juvenile Guardian.* After notice and a hearing on a petition to terminate the appointment of a juvenile guardian, if the court finds it is in the child's best interests to terminate the appointment and if there is:

(a) no successor, the court shall proceed according to subrule (F)(5); or

(b) a successor, the court shall terminate the appointment of the juvenile guardian and proceed with an investigation and appointment of a successor juvenile guardian in accordance with the requirements of this rule, and the court's jurisdiction over the juvenile guardianship shall continue. An order terminating a juvenile guardianship and appointing a successor juvenile guardian shall be entered on a form approved by the state court administrator.

(7) *Dispositional Review Hearing.* The court shall hold a dispositional review hearing pursuant to MCR 3.973 or MCR 3.978 within 42 days of revocation of a juvenile guardianship. The Department of Human Services shall prepare a case service plan and file it with the court no later than 7 days before the hearing. Subsequent postdispositional review hearings shall be scheduled in conformity with MCR 3.974 and MCR 3.975.

[Adopted April 14, 2009, effective July 1, 2009, 483 Mich. Amended effective September 28, 2011, 490 Mich. Amended October 3, 2012, effective January 1, 2013, 493 Mich; May 25, 2016, effective September 1, 2016, 499 Mich. Amended effective December 14, 2016, 500 Mich.]

Comments

Staff Comment to 2009 Adoption

The amendments of Rules 3.901, 3.903, 3.921, 3.965, 3.975, 3.976, 3.977, and 3.978, and new rule 3.979 of the Michigan Court Rules reflect the enactment of 2008 PA 199–203.

Staff Comment to 2011 Amendment

The above noted changes are minor revisions of the rules that have been recommended to the Court to correct cross references and to reflect other technical changes.

Staff Comment to 2013 Amendment

The amendment of MCR 3.979 implements the judicial action requirements of 2011 PA 225 and 2011 PA 229 by: (1) acknowledging court jurisdiction over guardianships for which the Department of Human Services will continue providing subsidies after the wards reach age 18; and (2) requiring that the supervising courts conduct annual review hearings and make appropriate findings. Adoption of the amendment enables Michigan to receive federal Title IV–E funding for the post–18 guardianship program.

Staff Comment to September, 2016 Amendment

The amendment of MCR 3.979 requires a court to maintain jurisdiction over a juvenile guardianship for 120 days after the juvenile's 18th birthday in cases where DHHS is making an eligibility determination for extended guardianship assistance. The revisions of MCR 3.979 also reflect recent amendments of the Young Adult Voluntary Foster Care Act (MCL 400.669) and the Juvenile Code (MCL 712A.2a).

Staff Comment to December, 2016 Amendment

These amendments update cross-references and make other nonsubstantive revisions to clarify the rules.

Rule 3.981 Minor Personal Protection Orders; Issuance; Modification; Recision; Appeal

Procedure for the issuance, dismissal, modification, or recision of minor personal protection orders is governed by subchapter 3.700. Procedure in appeals related to minor personal protection orders is governed by MCR 3.709 and MCR 3.993.

[Adopted February 4, 2003, effective May 1, 2003, 467 Mich.]

Comments

Staff Comment to 2003 Adoption

MCR 3.981 corresponds to former Rule 5.981.

Rule 3.982. Enforcement of Minor Personal Protection Orders

(A) In General. A minor personal protection order is enforceable under MCL 600.2950(22), (25), 600.2950a(22), (25), 764.15b, and 600.1701 et seq. For the purpose of MCR 3.981–3.989, "minor personal protection order" includes a foreign protection order against a minor respondent enforceable in Michigan under MCL 600.2950*l*.

(B) Procedure. Unless indicated otherwise in these rules, contempt proceedings for the enforcement of minor personal protection orders where the respondent is under 18 years of age are governed by MCR 3.982–3.989.

(C) Form of Proceeding. A contempt proceeding brought in a court other than the one that issued the minor personal protection order shall be entitled "In the Matter of Contempt of [Respondent], a minor". The clerk shall provide a copy of the contempt proceeding to the court that issued the minor personal protection order.

[Adopted February 4, 2003, effective May 1, 2003, 467 Mich. Amended April 30, 2003, effective May 1, 2003, 467 Mich. Amended effective March 21, 2018, 501 Mich.]

Comments

Staff Comment to 2003 Adoption

MCR 3.982 corresponds to former Rule 5.982.

Current subrule (C), concerning supplemental petitions, is deleted. The substance of those provisions is included in MCR 5.983(A).

Staff Comment to 2003 Amendment

The April 30, 2003, order makes corrections to a number of the rules governing proceedings regarding juveniles that had been adopted on February 4, 2003. The changes are effective May 1, corresponding to the effective date of the February 4 amendments. In addition to these changes, a number of corrections of punctuation and capitalization and changes in the Notes that accompanied the rules have been made and will appear in the published version of the rules.

The amendments of MCR 3.903(D)(8)(m), 6.903(H)(16), 6.931(E)(3), and 6.933(C)(1) conform the rules to 2002 PA 665, which changed the amounts of controlled substances required for certain violations. See MCL 333.7401(2)(a)(i), 333.7403(2)(a)(i). MCR 3.933(C)(1) is also modified in light of *People v Valentin*, 457 Mich 1 (1998).

The amendment of MCR 3.935(B)(1) corrects the inadvertent omission of references to guardians and legal custodians.

The amendments of MCR 3.922(E)(1)(c), 3.943(A), 3.945(A)(1), 3.965(E)(1), and 3.972(C)(2)(c) correct minor errors in wording.

The amendment of MCR 3.977(G) deletes the word "hearing" in the reference to progress reviews. Under MCR 3.974(A)(1), progress reviews do not require hearings.

The amendment of MCR 3.980(B) and (C) revise the provisions on removal of American Indian children from the home to clarify the distinction between emergency removals and removals after hearing.

The amendments of MCR 3.982(A), 6.903(I)–(L) and 6.937(A) correct cross-reference, citation and numbering errors.

Staff Comment to 2018 Amendment

These amendments update cross-references and make other nonsubstantive revisions to clarify the rules. The amendment of MCR 6.110(B)(1) addresses an inadvertent omission from the last amendment of this rule that was intended to be shown in overstrike. Accordingly, the current rule does not match the published version. Striking the clause "for good cause shown" will provide consistency with

other published versions of the rule and with the statute, MCL 766.7, which allows a magistrate to adjourn a preliminary examination with the consent of the parties without the need for good cause to be shown.

Rule 3.983 Initiation of Contempt Proceedings by Supplemental Petition

(A) Filing. If a respondent allegedly violates a minor personal protection order, the original petitioner, a law enforcement officer, a prosecuting attorney, a probation officer, or a caseworker may submit a supplemental petition in writing to have the respondent found in contempt. The supplemental petition must contain a specific description of the facts constituting a violation of the personal protection order. There is no fee for such a petition.

(B) Scheduling. Upon receiving the supplemental petition, the court must either:

(1) set a date for a preliminary hearing on the supplemental petition, to be held as soon as practicable, and issue a summons to appear; or

(2) issue an order authorizing a peace officer or other person designated by the court to apprehend the respondent.

(C) Service. If the court sets a date for a preliminary hearing, the petitioner shall serve the supplemental petition and summons on the respondent and, if the relevant addresses are known or are ascertainable upon diligent inquiry, on the respondent's parent or parents, guardian, or custodian. Service must be in the manner provided by MCR 3.920 at least 7 days before the preliminary hearing.

(D) Order to Apprehend.

(1) A court order to apprehend the respondent may include authorization to:

(a) enter specified premises as required to bring the minor before the court, and

(b) detain the minor pending preliminary hearing if it appears there is a substantial likelihood of retaliation or continued violation.

(2) Upon apprehending a minor respondent under a court order, the officer shall comply with MCR 3.984(B) and (C).

[Adopted February 4, 2003, effective May 1, 2003, 467 Mich.]

Comments

Staff Comment to 2003 Adoption

MCR 3.983 corresponds to former Rule 5.983.

The changes in subrule (A) are the result of adding provisions from former Rule 5.982(C) regarding supplemental petitions.

Subrule (B) adds a requirement of diligent search for the address of the minor's parent, guardian, or custodian.

Rule 3.984 Apprehension of Alleged Violator

(A) Apprehension; Release to Parent, Guardian, or Custodian. When an officer apprehends a minor for violation of a minor personal protection order without a court order for apprehension and does not warn and release the minor, the officer may accept a written promise of the minor's parent, guardian, or custodian to bring the minor to court, and release the minor to the parent, guardian, or custodian.

(B) Custody; Detention. When an officer apprehends a minor in relation to a minor personal protection order pursuant to a court order that specifies that the minor is to be brought directly to court; or when an officer apprehends a minor for an alleged violation of a minor personal protection order without a court order, and either the officer has failed to obtain a written promise from the minor's parent, guardian, or custodian to bring the minor to court, or it appears to the officer that there is a substantial likelihood of retaliation or violation by the minor, the officer shall immediately do the following:

(1) If the whereabouts of the minor's parent or parents, guardian, or custodian is known, inform the minor's parent or parents, guardian, or custodian of the minor's apprehension and of the minor's whereabouts and of the need for the parent or parents, guardian, or custodian to be present at the preliminary hearing;

(2) Take the minor

(a) before the court for a preliminary hearing, or

(b) to a place designated by the court pending the scheduling of a preliminary hearing;

(3) Prepare a custody statement for submission to the court including:

(a) the grounds for and the time and location of detention, and

(b) the names of persons notified and the times of notification, or the reason for failure to notify; and

(4) Ensure that a supplemental petition is prepared and filed with the court.

(C) Separate Custody. While awaiting arrival of the parent, guardian, or custodian, appearance before the court, or otherwise, a minor under 17 years of age must be maintained separately from adult prisoners to prevent any verbal, visual, or physical contact with an adult prisoner.

(D) Designated Court Person. The court must designate a judge, referee or other person who may be contacted by the officer taking a minor under 17 into custody when the court is not open. In each county there must be a designated facility open at all times at which an officer may obtain the name of the person to be contacted for permission to detain the minor pending preliminary hearing.

(E) Out-of-County Violation. Subject to MCR 3.985(H), if a minor is apprehended for violation of a minor personal protection order in a jurisdiction other than the jurisdiction where the minor personal protection order was issued, the apprehending jurisdiction may notify the issuing jurisdiction that it may request that the respondent be returned to the issuing jurisdiction for enforcement proceedings.

[Adopted February 4, 2003, effective May 1, 2003, 467 Mich.]

Comments

Staff Comment to 2003 Adoption

MCR 3.984 corresponds to former Rule 5.984.

Rule 3.985   Preliminary Hearing

(A) Time.

(1) *Commencement.* If the respondent was apprehended or arrested for violation of a minor personal protection order or was apprehended or arrested under a court order, and the respondent is taken into court custody or is jailed, the preliminary hearing must commence no later than 24 hours after the minor was apprehended or arrested, excluding Sundays and holidays, as defined in MCR 8.110(D)(2), or the minor

must be released. Otherwise, the preliminary hearing must commence as soon as practicable after the apprehension or arrest, or the submission of a supplemental petition.

(2) *General Adjournment.* The court may adjourn the hearing for up to 14 days:

(a) to secure the attendance of witnesses or the minor's parent, guardian, or custodian, or

(b) for other good cause shown.

(B) Procedure.

(1) The court shall determine whether the parent, guardian, or custodian has been notified and is present. The preliminary hearing may be conducted without a parent, guardian, or custodian provided a guardian ad litem or attorney appears with the minor.

(2) Unless waived by the respondent, the court shall read the allegations in the supplemental petition, and ensure that the respondent has received written notice of the alleged violation.

(3) Immediately after the reading of the allegations, the court shall advise the respondent on the record in plain language of the rights to:

(a) contest the allegations at a violation hearing;

(b) an attorney at every stage in the proceedings, and, if the court determines it might sentence the respondent to jail or place the respondent in secure detention, the fact that the court will appoint an attorney at public expense if the respondent wants one and is financially unable to retain one;

(c) a nonjury trial and that a referee may be assigned to hear the case unless demand for a judge is filed pursuant to MCR 3.912;

(d) have witnesses against the respondent appear at a violation hearing and to question the witnesses;

(e) have the court order any witnesses for the respondent's defense to appear at the hearing; and

(f) remain silent and to not have that silence used against the respondent, and that any statement by the respondent may be used against the respondent.

(4) The court must decide whether to authorize the filing of the supplemental petition and proceed formally, or to dismiss the supplemental petition.

(5) The respondent must be allowed an opportunity to deny or otherwise plead to the allegations. If the respondent wishes to enter a plea of admission or of nolo contendere, the court shall follow MCR 3.986.

(6) If the court authorizes the filing of the supplemental petition, the court must:

(a) set a date and time for the violation hearing, or, if the court accepts a plea of admission or no contest, either enter a dispositional order or set the matter for dispositional hearing; and

(b) either release the respondent pursuant to subrule (E) or order detention of the respondent as provided in subrule (F).

(C) Notification. Following the preliminary hearing, if the respondent denies the allegations in the supplemental petition, the court must:

(1) notify the prosecuting attorney of the scheduled violation hearing;

(2) notify the respondent, respondent's attorney, if any, and respondent's parents, guardian, or custodian of the scheduled violation hearing and direct the parties to appear at the hearing and give evidence on the charge of contempt.

Notice of hearing must be given by personal service or ordinary mail at least 7 days before the violation hearing, unless the respondent is detained, in which case notice of hearing must be served at least 24 hours before the hearing.

(D) Failure to Appear. If the respondent was notified of the preliminary hearing and fails to appear for the preliminary hearing, the court may issue an order in accordance with MCR 3.983(D) authorizing a peace officer or other person designated by the court to apprehend the respondent.

(1) If the respondent is under 17 years of age, the court may order the respondent detained pending a hearing on the apprehension order; if the court releases the respondent it may set bond for the respondent's appearance at the violation hearing.

(2) If the respondent is 17 years of age, the court may order the respondent confined to jail pending a hearing on the apprehension order. If the court releases the respondent it must set bond for the respondent's appearance at the violation hearing.

(E) Release of Respondent.

(1) Subject to the conditions set forth in subrule (F), the respondent may be released, with conditions, to a parent, guardian, or custodian pending the resumption of the preliminary hearing or pending the violation hearing after the court considers available information on

(a) family ties and relationships,

(b) the minor's prior juvenile delinquency or minor personal protection order record, if any,

(c) the minor's record of appearance or nonappearance at court proceedings,

(d) the violent nature of the alleged violation,

(e) the minor's prior history of committing acts that resulted in bodily injury to others,

(f) the minor's character and mental condition,

(g) the court's ability to supervise the minor if placed with a parent or relative,

(h) the likelihood of retaliation or violation of the order by the respondent, and

(i) any other factors indicating the minor's ties to the community, the risk of nonappearance, and the danger to the respondent or the original petitioner if the respondent is released.

(2) Bail procedure is governed by MCR 3.935(F).

(F) Detention Pending Violation Hearing.

(1) *Conditions.* A minor shall not be removed from the parent, guardian, or custodian pending violation hearing or further court order unless:

(a) probable cause exists to believe the minor violated the minor personal protection order; and

(b) at the preliminary hearing the court finds one or more of the following circumstances to be present:

(i) there is a substantial likelihood of retaliation or continued violation by the minor who allegedly violated the minor personal protection order;

(ii) there is a substantial likelihood that if the minor is released to the parent, with or without conditions, the minor will fail to appear at the next court proceeding; or

(iii) detention pending violation hearing is otherwise specifically authorized by law.

(2) *Waiver.* A minor respondent in custody may waive the probable cause phase of a detention determination only if the minor is represented by an attorney.

(3) *Evidence; Findings.* At the preliminary hearing the minor respondent may contest the sufficiency of evidence to support detention by cross-examination of witnesses, presentation of defense witnesses, or by other evidence. The court shall permit the use of subpoena power to secure attendance of defense witnesses. A finding of probable cause under subrule (F)(1)(a) may be based on hearsay evidence which possesses adequate guarantees of trustworthiness.

(4) *Type of Detention.* The detained minor must be placed in the least restrictive environment that will meet the needs of the minor and the public, and conforms to the requirements of MCL 712A.15 and 712A.16.

(G) Findings. At the preliminary hearing the court must state the reasons for its decision to release or detain the minor on the record or in a written memorandum.

(H) Out-of-County Violation. When a minor is apprehended for violation of a minor personal protection order in a jurisdiction other than the one that issued the personal protection order, and the apprehending jurisdiction conducts the preliminary hearing, if it has not already done so, the apprehending jurisdiction must immediately notify the issuing jurisdiction that the latter may request that the respondent be returned to the issuing jurisdiction for enforcement proceedings.

[Adopted February 4, 2003, effective May 1, 2003, 467 Mich.]

Comments

Staff Comment to 2003 Adoption

MCR 3.985 corresponds to former Rule 5.985.

Rule 3.986   Pleas of Admission or No Contest

(A) Capacity. A minor may offer a plea of admission or of no contest to the violation of a minor personal protection order with the consent of the court. The court shall not accept a plea to a violation unless the court is satisfied that the plea is accurate, voluntary, and understanding.

(B) Qualified Pleas. The court may accept a plea of admission or of no contest conditioned on preservation of an issue for appellate review.

(C) Support of Plea by Parent, Guardian, Custodian. The court shall inquire of the parents, guardian, custodian, or guardian ad litem whether there is any reason the court should not accept the plea tendered by the minor. Agreement or objection by the parent, guardian, custodian, or guardian ad litem to a plea of admission or of no contest by a minor must be placed on the record if that person is present.

(D) Plea Withdrawal. The court may take a plea of admission or of no contest under advisement. Before the court accepts the plea, the minor may withdraw the plea offer by right. After the court accepts a plea, the court has discretion to allow the minor to withdraw the plea.

[Adopted February 4, 2003, effective May 1, 2003, 467 Mich.]

Comments

Staff Comment to 2003 Adoption

MCR 3.986 corresponds to former Rule 5.986.

Rule 3.987   Violation Hearing

(A) Time. Upon completion of the preliminary hearing the court shall set a date and time for the violation hearing if the respondent denies the allegations in the supplemental petition. The violation hearing must be held within 72 hours of apprehension, excluding Sundays and holidays, as defined in MCR 8.110(D)(2), if the respondent is detained. If the respondent is not detained the hearing must be held within 21 days.

(B) Prosecution After Apprehension. If a criminal contempt proceeding is commenced under MCL 764.15b, the prosecuting attorney shall prosecute the proceeding unless the petitioner retains an attorney to prosecute the criminal contempt proceeding. If the prosecuting attorney determines that the personal protection order was not violated or that it would not be in the interest of justice to prosecute the criminal contempt violation, the prosecuting attorney need not prosecute the proceeding.

(C) Preliminary Matters.

(1) The court must determine whether the appropriate parties have been notified and are present.

   (a) The respondent has the right to be present at the violation hearing along with parents, guardian, or custodian, and guardian ad litem and attorney.

   (b) The court may proceed in the absence of a parent properly noticed to appear, provided the respondent is represented by an attorney.

   (c) The original petitioner has the right to be present at the violation hearing.

(2) The court must read the allegations contained in the supplemental petition, unless waived.

(3) Unless an attorney appears with the minor, the court must inform the minor of the right to the assistance of an attorney and that, if the court determines that it might sentence the respondent to jail or place the respondent in secure detention, the court will appoint an attorney at public expense if the respondent wants one and is financially unable to retain one. If the juvenile requests to proceed without the assistance of an attorney, the court must advise the minor of the dangers and disadvantages of self-representation and determine whether the minor is literate and competent to conduct the defense.

(D) Jury. There is no right to a jury trial.

(E) Conduct of the Hearing. The respondent has the right to be present at the hearing, to present evidence, and to examine and cross-examine witnesses.

(F) Evidence; Burden of Proof. The rules of evidence apply to both criminal and civil contempt proceedings. The petitioner or the prosecuting attorney has the burden of proving the respondent's guilt of criminal contempt beyond a reasonable doubt and the respondent's guilt of civil contempt by a preponderance of the evidence.

(G) Judicial Findings. At the conclusion of the hearing, the court must make specific findings of fact, state separately its conclusions of law, and direct entry of the appropriate judgment. The court must state its findings and conclusions on the record or in a written opinion made a part of the record.

[Adopted February 4, 2003, effective May 1, 2003, 467 Mich.]

Comments

Staff Comment to 2003 Adoption

MCR 3.987 corresponds to former Rule 5.987.

Rule 3.988   Dispositional Hearing

(A) Time. The time interval between the entry of judgment finding a violation of a minor personal protection order and disposition, if any, is within the court's discretion, but may not be more than 35 days. When the minor is detained, the interval may not be more than 14 days, except for good cause.

(B) Presence of Respondent and Petitioner.

(1) The respondent may be excused from part of the dispositional hearing for good cause, but the respondent must be present when the disposition is announced.

(2) The petitioner has the right to be present at the dispositional hearing.

(C) Evidence.

(1) At the dispositional hearing all relevant and material evidence, including oral and written reports, may be received by the court and may be relied on to the extent of its probative value, even though such evidence may not be admissible at the violation hearing.

(2) The respondent, or the respondent's attorney, and the petitioner shall be afforded an opportunity to examine and controvert written reports so received and, in the court's discretion, may be allowed to cross-examine individuals making reports when such individuals are reasonably available.

(3) No assertion of an evidentiary privilege, other than the privilege between attorney and client, shall prevent the receipt and use, at the dispositional phase, of materials prepared pursuant to a court-ordered examination, interview, or course of treatment.

(D) Dispositions.

(1) If a minor respondent at least 17 years of age pleads or is found guilty of criminal contempt, the court may impose a sentence of incarceration of up to 93 days and may impose a fine of not more than $500.

(2) If a minor respondent pleads or is found guilty of civil contempt, the court shall

   (a) impose a fine or imprisonment as specified in MCL 600.1715 and 600.1721, if the respondent is at least 17 years of age.

   (b) subject the respondent to the dispositional alternatives listed in MCL 712A.18, if the respondent is under 17 years of age.

(3) In addition to the sentence, the court may impose other conditions to the minor personal protection order.

[Adopted February 4, 2003, effective May 1, 2003, 467 Mich.]

Comments

Staff Comment to 2003 Adoption

MCR 3.988 corresponds to former Rule 5.988.

Rule 3.989   Supplemental Dispositions

When it is alleged that a minor placed on probation for the violation of a minor personal protection order has violated a condition of probation, the court shall follow the procedures for supplemental disposition as provided in MCR 3.944.

[Adopted February 4, 2003, effective May 1, 2003, 467 Mich.]

Comments

Staff Comment to 2003 Adoption

MCR 3.989 corresponds to former Rule 5.989.

Rule 3.991   Review of Referee Recommendations

(A) General.

(1) Before signing an order based on a referee's recommended findings and conclusions, a judge of the court shall review the recommendations if requested by a party in the manner provided by subrule (B).

(2) If no such request is filed within the time provided by subrule (B)(3), the court may enter an order in accordance with the referee's recommendations.

(3) Nothing in this rule prohibits a judge from reviewing a referee's recommendation before the expiration of the time for requesting review and entering an appropriate order.

(4) After the entry of an order under subrule (A)(3), a request for review may not be filed. Reconsideration of the order is by motion for rehearing under MCR 3.992.

(B) Form of Request; Time. A party's request for review of a referee's recommendation must:

(1) be in writing,

(2) state the grounds for review,

(3) be filed with the court within 7 days after the conclusion of the inquiry or hearing or within 7 days after the issuance of the referee's written recommendations, whichever is later, and

(4) be served on the interested parties by the person requesting review at the time of filing the request for review with the court. A proof of service must be filed.

(C) Response. A party may file a written response within 7 days after the filing of the request for review.

(D) Prompt Review; No Party Appearance Required. Absent good cause for delay, the judge shall consider the request within 21 days after it is filed if the minor is in placement or detention. The judge need not schedule a hearing to rule on a request for review of a referee's recommendations.

(E) Review Standard. The judge must enter an order adopting the referee's recommendation unless:

(1) the judge would have reached a different result had he or she heard the case; or

(2) the referee committed a clear error of law, which

(a) likely would have affected the outcome, or

(b) cannot otherwise be considered harmless.

(F) Remedy. The judge may adopt, modify, or deny the recommendation of the referee, in whole or in part, on the basis of the record and the memorandums prepared, or may conduct a hearing, whichever the court in its discretion finds appropriate for the case.

(G) Stay. The court may stay any order or grant bail to a detained juvenile, pending its decision on review of the referee's recommendation.

[Adopted February 4, 2003, effective May 1, 2003, 467 Mich.]

Comments

Staff Comment to 2003 Adoption

MCR 3.991 corresponds to former Rule 5.991.

Subrule (A) is amended to provide for entry of an order based on the referee's recommendation if no request for review is filed within 7 days. However, the court has the option of reviewing the recommendation and entering an appropriate order earlier. Once the court has entered an order, the review procedure is no longer available, and a party must file a motion for rehearing under MCR 3.992.

New subrule (B)(4) is added, explicitly requiring service of the request for review on interested parties.

New subrule (C) sets the time for a party to file a written response to a request for review.

The review standard of subrule (E) is modified to refer to adopting the referee's recommendation, rather than denial of the request for review.

Rule 3.992   Rehearings; New Trial

(A) Time and Grounds. Except for the case of a juvenile tried as an adult in the family division of the circuit court for a criminal offense, and except for a case in which parental rights are terminated, a party may seek a rehearing or new trial by filing a written motion stating the basis for the relief sought within 21 days after the date of the order resulting from the hearing or trial. In a case that involves termination of parental rights, a motion for new trial, rehearing, reconsideration, or other postjudgment relief shall be filed within 14 days after the date of the order terminating parental rights. The court may entertain an untimely motion for good cause shown. A motion will not be considered unless it presents a matter not previously presented to the court, or presented, but not previously considered by the court, which, if true, would cause the court to reconsider the case.

(B) Notice. All parties must be given notice of the motion in accordance with Rule 3.920.

(C) Response by Parties. Any response by parties must be in writing and filed with the court and served on the opposing parties within 7 days after notice of the motion.

(D) Procedure. The judge may affirm, modify, or vacate the decision previously made in whole or in part, on the basis of the record, the memoranda prepared, or a hearing on the motion, whichever the court in its discretion finds appropriate for the case.

(E) Hearings. The court need not hold a hearing before ruling on a motion. Any hearing conducted shall be in accordance with the rules for dispositional hearings and, at the discretion of the court, may be assigned to the person who conducted the hearing. The court shall state the reasons for its decision on the motion on the record or in writing.

(F) Stay. The court may stay any order, or grant bail to a detained juvenile, pending a ruling on the motion.

[Adopted February 4, 2003, effective May 1, 2003, 467 Mich. Amended effective May 7, 2014, 495 Mich.]

Comments

Staff Comment to 2003 Adoption

MCR 3.992 corresponds to former Rule 5.992.

In subrule (A), the language regarding the time for requesting a new trial or rehearing is modified to refer to the date of the order resulting from the hearing.

Staff Comment to 2014 Amendment

These amendments reflect changes that correct minor technical errors that have occurred in drafting or the changes respond to recent adopted rule revisions, which occasionally inadvertently create incorrect cross-references in other rules.

Rule 3.993 Appeals

(A) The following orders are appealable to the Court of Appeals by right:

(1) any order removing a child from a parent's care and custody,

(2) an initial order of disposition following adjudication in a child protective proceeding,

(3) an order of disposition placing a minor under the supervision of the court in a delinquency proceedings,

(4) an order terminating parental rights,

(5) any order required by law to be appealed to the Court of Appeals,

(6) any order involving an Indian child that is subject to potential invalidation under § 39 of the Michigan Indian Family Preservation Act, MCL 712B.1 *et seq.* or § 1914 of the Indian Child Welfare Act, 25 USC 1901 *et seq.*, which includes, but is not limited to, an order regarding:

(a) recognition of the jurisdiction of a tribal court pursuant to MCL 712B.7, MCL 712B.29, or 25 USC 1911;

(b) transfer to tribal court pursuant to MCL 712B.7 or 25 USC 1911;

(c) intervention pursuant to MCL 712B.7 or 25 USC 1911;

(d) extension of full faith and credit to public acts, records, and judicial proceedings of an Indian tribe pursuant to MCL 712B.7 or 25 USC 1911;

(e) removal of a child from the home, placement into foster care, or continuance of an out-of-home placement pursuant to MCL 712B.9, MCL 712B.15, MCL 712B.25, MCL 712B.29, or 25 USC 1912;

(f) termination of parental rights pursuant to MCL 712B.9, MCL 712B.15, or 25 USC 1912;

(g) appointment of counsel pursuant to MCL 712B.21 or 25 USC 1912;

(h) examination of reports pursuant to MCL 712B.11 or 25 USC 1912;

(i) voluntary consent to or withdrawal of a voluntary consent to a foster care placement or to a termination of parental right pursuant to MCL 712B.13, MCL 712B.25, MCL 712B.27, or 25 USC 1913;

(j) foster care, pre-adoptive, or adoptive placement of an Indian child pursuant to MCL 712B.23; and

(7) any final order.

In any appeal as of right, an indigent respondent is entitled to appointment of an attorney to represent the respondent on appeal and to preparation of relevant transcripts.

(B) All orders not listed in subrule (A) are appealable to the Court of appeals by leave.

(C) Procedure; Delayed Appeals.

(1) *Applicable Rules.* Except as modified by this rule, chapter 7 of the Michigan Court Rules governs appeals from the family division of the circuit court.

(2) *Delayed Appeals; Termination of Parental Rights.* The Court of Appeals may not grant an application for leave to appeal an order of the family division of the circuit court terminating parental rights if filed more than 63 days after entry of an order of judgment on the merits, or if filed more than 63 days after entry of an order denying reconsideration or rehearing.

[Adopted February 4, 2003, effective May 1, 2003, 467 Mich. Amended March 13, 2019, effective May 1, 2019, 502 Mich. Amended effective June 12, 2019, 503 Mich.]

Comments

Staff Comment to 2003 Adoption

MCR 3.993 corresponds to former Rule 5.993.

Former subrule 5.933(C)(2), which required the use of a minor's initials in published opinions, is deleted.

Staff Comment to May, 2019 Amendment

The amendment of MCR 3.993, recommended by the State Bar of Michigan, establishes a list of specific orders that can be appealed by right regarding an Indian child subject to a child protective proceeding.

Staff Comment to June, 2019 Amendment

The amendments of MCR 3.965, 3.971, 3.972, 3.973, and 3.993 incorporate a requirement for a trial court to notify a respondent in a child protection proceeding of the right to appeal following a child's removal from the home and the initial dispositional order, and that failure to do so may bar respondent from later challenging the court's assumption of jurisdiction.

CHAPTER 4. DISTRICT COURT
Effective March 1, 1985

SUBCHAPTER 4.000   GENERAL PROVISIONS

Rule 4.001   Applicability

The rules in this chapter apply to the specific types of proceedings within the jurisdiction of the district and municipal courts. Except as otherwise provided in this chapter, proceedings under this chapter are governed by Michigan Court Rules.

[Adopted effective March 1, 1985. Amended October 31, 2012, effective January 1, 2013, 493 Mich.]

Comments

Staff Comment to 1985 Adoption

MCR 4.001 is a new provision indicating the applicability of the rules in chapter 4. The chapter title refers only to the district court; however, the few remaining municipal courts are subject to the same rules because MCL 600.6502 provides that absent some provision to the contrary, the municipal courts are governed by the rules and statutes applicable to the district court.

Staff Comment to 2013 Amendment

The amendments of these rules update the rules making them less "paper" focused and reflecting the use of electronic technology in the way courts process court records. The amendments also clarify and delineate the types of records and other materials maintained by a court, and clarify how access is provided.

Rule 4.002   Transfer of Actions from District Court to Circuit Court

(A) Counterclaim or Cross–Claim in Excess of Jurisdiction.

(1) If a defendant asserts a counterclaim or cross-claim seeking relief of an amount or nature beyond the jurisdiction or power of the district court in which the action is pending, and accompanies the notice of the claim with a statement verified in the manner prescribed by MCR 1.109(D)(3) indicating that the defendant is justly entitled to the relief demanded, the clerk shall record the pleadings and present them to the judge to whom the action is assigned. The judge shall either order the action transferred to the circuit court to which appeal of the action would ordinarily lie or inform the defendant that transfer will not be ordered without a motion and notice to the other parties.

(2) Transfer of summary proceedings to recover possession of premises are governed under MCR 4.201(G)(2) and 4.202(I)(4) and subrules (C) and (D) of this rule.

(B) Change in Conditions.

(1) A party may, at any time, file a motion with the district court in which an action is pending, requesting that the action be transferred to circuit court. The motion must be supported by a statement verified in the manner prescribed by MCR 1.109(D)(3) indicating that

(a) due to a change in condition or circumstance, or

(b) due to facts not known by the party at the time the action was commenced,

the party wishes to seek relief of an amount or nature that is beyond the jurisdiction or power of the court to grant.

(2) If the district court finds that the party filing the motion may be entitled to the relief the party now seeks to claim and that the delay in making the claim is excusable, the court shall order the action transferred to the circuit court to which an appeal of the action would ordinarily lie.

(C) Order for Transfer; Case Records.

(1) The district court must enter all necessary orders pertaining to the certification and transfer of the action to the circuit court. The district court must order the moving party to pay the applicable statutory filing fee directly to the circuit court, unless fees have been waived in accordance with MCR 2.002.

(2) The district court may also order the party seeking transfer to pay the opposing parties the costs they have reasonably incurred up to that time that would not have been incurred if the action had originally been brought in circuit court.

(3) The district court must serve the order on the parties and send a copy to the circuit court. The clerk of the district court must prepare the case records for transfer in accordance with the orders entered under subrule (1) and the Michigan Trial Court Records Management Standards and send them to the receiving court by a secure method.

(4) The circuit court shall temporarily suspend payment of the filing fee and open a case pending payment of the filing fee and costs as ordered by the district court. The circuit court must notify the moving party of the new case number in the circuit court, the amount due, and the due date.

(5) After transfer, no further proceedings may be conducted in the district court, and the action shall proceed in the circuit court. The circuit court may order further pleadings and set the time when they must be filed.

(D) Payment of Filing and Jury Fees After Transfer; Payment of Costs.

(1) The party that moved for transfer must pay to the circuit court within 28 days of the date of the transfer order the applicable filing fee as ordered by the district court. No further action may be had in the case until payment is made. If the fee is not paid to the circuit court within 28 days of the date of the transfer order, the circuit court will either dismiss the counterclaim or cross-claim or order the case transferred back to the district court.

(2) If the jury fee has been paid, the clerk of the district court must forward it to the clerk of the circuit court to which the action is transferred as soon as possible after the case records have been transferred. If the amount paid to the district court for the jury fee is less than the circuit court jury fee, then the party requesting the jury shall pay the difference to the circuit court.

(3) If the court ordered payment of costs, the moving party must pay them to the opposing parties within 28 days of the

281

date of the transfer order. If the costs are not paid within 28 days of the date of entry, the circuit court will either dismiss the counterclaim or cross-claim and/or order the case transferred back to the district court to proceed on the original claim.

[Adopted effective March 1, 1985. Amended December 6, 1994, effective January 1, 1995, 447 Mich; September 18, 2019, effective January 1, 2020, 503 Mich.]

Comments

Staff Comment to 1985 Adoption

MCR 4.002 is based on DCR 203.5 and GCR 1963, 704. The rule uses the term "transfer" to distinguish the procedure from the statutory "removal" from the circuit to the district court under MCL 600.641.

Subrule (A) is changed to make clear that only the court may transfer the case. The clerk is to present the counterclaim or cross-claim and the affidavit to the judge to whom the case is assigned, and the judge shall either order the case transferred or inform the defendant that a motion is required.

New subrule (A)(2) is added excepting from the operation of this rule transfer of summary proceedings to recover possession of premises. The rules governing those proceedings include their own transfer provisions. MCR 4.201(G)(2), 4.202(I)(4).

Subrule (B) is new. It would permit transfer of a case on a motion of any party, including the plaintiff, if changed conditions or facts not known at the time the action was commenced justify relief beyond the jurisdiction or power of the court in which the case is pending. The court may order transfer on findings that the moving party may be entitled to the relief sought and that the delay in seeking the relief was excusable.

Subrule (C) slightly modifies the cost provisions previously found in DCR 203.5(2). The party seeking transfer need pay only the opposing party's costs that would not have been incurred had the action originally been brought in the circuit court.

The [March 1, 1985] amendment of MCR 4.002(C) provides that if the jury fee has been paid in the district court before transfer of the action to circuit court, the fee is to be forwarded to the circuit court by the clerk.

Subrule (E) also includes provisions previously found in GCR 1963, 704. However, the circuit court is not required to order further pleadings after transfer, but may do so.

Staff Comment to 1995 Amendment

MCR 2.508(B)(3) took effect in 1995, as did an amendment of MCR 4.002(C). These changes were to address the procedural issue that arose in *Adamski v Cole*, 197 Mich App 124; 494 NW2d 794 (1992), lv den 445 Mich 863 (1994).

Staff Comment to 2020 Amendment

The amendments of MCR 1.109, 2.107, 2.113, 2.116, 2.119, 2.222, 2.223, 2.225, 2.227, 3.206, 3.211, 3.212, 3.214, 3.303, 3.903, 3.921, 3.925, 3.926, 3.931, 3.933, 3.942, 3.950, 3.961, 3.971, 3.972, 4.002, 4.101, 4.201, 4.202, 4.302, 5.128, 5.302, 5.731, 6.101, 6.615, 8.105, and 8.119 and rescission of MCR 2.226 and 8.125 continue the process for design and implementation of the statewide electronic-filing system.

Rule 4.003. Removal of Actions from Circuit Court to District Court [Repealed effective July 1, 1997]

Comments

Staff Comment to 1997 Repeal

The May 8, 1997, order repeals MCR 4.003, which governed removal of cases from circuit to district court, effective July 1, 1997. This reinstates the February 28, 1997, repeal of the rule, which was suspended on March 13, 1997.

In addition, the order postpones the effective date of earlier amendments of MCR 2.403, 2.405, and 3.216, and new MCR 2.404, affecting mediation procedure, to October 1, 1997. The order also makes adjustments in MCR 2.403(K) and (N) in light of the repeal of MCR 4.003. The text of MCR 2.403, 2.404, 2.405 and 3.216 is the same as that adopted in the Court's March 5, 1997, order dealing with those rules.

SUBCHAPTER 4.100   CIVIL INFRACTION ACTIONS

Rule 4.101 Civil Infraction Actions

(A) Citation; Complaint; Summons; Warrant.

(1) Except as otherwise provided by court rule or statute, a civil infraction action may be initiated by a law enforcement officer serving a written citation on the alleged violator, and filing the citation in the district court. The citation serves as the complaint in a civil infraction action and may be prepared electronically or on paper. The citation must be signed by the officer in accordance with MCR 1.109(E)(4); if a citation is prepared electronically and filed with a court as data, the name of the officer that is associated with issuance of the citation satisfies this requirement.

　　(a) If the infraction is a parking violation, the action may be initiated by an authorized person placing a citation securely on the vehicle or mailing a citation to the registered owner of the vehicle.

　　(b) If the infraction is a municipal civil infraction, the action may be initiated by an authorized local official serving a written citation on the alleged violator. If the infraction involves the use or occupancy of land or a building or other structure, service may be accomplished by posting the citation at the site and sending a copy to the owner by first-class mail.

(2) A violation alleged on a citation may not be amended except by the prosecuting official or a police officer for the plaintiff.

(3) The citation serves as a summons to command

　　(a) the initial appearance of the defendant; and

　　(b) a response from the defendant as to his or her responsibility for the alleged violation.

(4) A warrant may not be issued for a civil infraction unless permitted by statute.

(B) Appearances; Failure to Appear; Default Judgment.

(1) Depending on the nature of the violation and on the procedure appropriate to the violation, a defendant may appear in person, by representation, or by mail.

(2) A defendant may not appear by making a telephone call to the court, but a defendant may telephone the court to obtain a date to appear.

(3) A clerk of the court may enter a default after certifying, on a form to be furnished by the court, that the defendant has not made a scheduled appearance, or has not answered a citation within the time allowed by statute.

(4) If a defendant fails to appear or otherwise to respond to any matter pending relative to a civil infraction action, the court:

　　(a) must enter a default against the defendant;

　　(b) must make a determination of responsibility, if the complaint is sufficient;

　　(c) must impose a sanction by entering a default judgment;

　　(d) must send the defendant a notice of the entry of the default judgment and the sanctions imposed; and

　　(e) may retain the driver's license of a nonresident as permitted by statute, if the court has received that license pursuant to statute. The court need not retain the license past its expiration date.

(5) If a defendant fails to appear or otherwise to respond to any matter pending relative to a traffic civil infraction, the court

(a) must notify the secretary of state of the entry of the default judgment, as required by MCL 257.732, and

(b) must initiate the procedures required by MCL 257.321a.

(6) If a defendant fails to appear or otherwise to respond to any matter pending relative to a state civil infraction, the court must initiate the procedures required by MCL 257.321a.

(C) Appearance by Police Officer at Informal Hearing.

(1) If a defendant requests an informal hearing, the court shall schedule an informal hearing and notify the police officer who issued the citation to appear at the informal hearing.

(2) The attendance of the officer at the hearing may not be waived.

Except when the court is notified before the commencement of a hearing of an emergency preventing an on-duty officer from appearing, failure of the police officer to appear as required by this rule shall result in a dismissal of the case without prejudice.

(D) Motion to Set Aside Default Judgment.

(1) A defendant may move to set aside a default judgment within 14 days after the court sends notice of the judgment to the defendant. The motion

(a) may be informal,

(b) may be either written or presented to the court in person,

(c) must explain the reason for the nonappearance of the defendant,

(d) must state that the defendant wants to offer a defense to or an explanation of the complaint, and

(e) must be accompanied by a cash bond equal to the fine and costs due at the time the motion is filed.

(2) For good cause, the court may

(a) set aside the default and direct that a hearing on the complaint take place, or

(b) schedule a hearing on the motion to set aside the default judgment.

(3) A defendant who does not file this motion on time may use the procedure set forth in MCR 2.603(D).

(E) Response.

(1) Except as provided in subrule (4), an admission without explanation may be offered to and accepted by

(a) a district judge;

(b) a district court magistrate as authorized by the chief judge, the presiding judge, or the only judge of the district; or

(c) other district court personnel, as authorized by a judge of the district.

(2) Except as provided in subrule (4), an admission with explanation may be written or offered orally to a judge or district court magistrate, as authorized by the district judge.

(3) Except as provided in subrule (4), a denial of responsibility must be made by the defendant appearing at a time set either by the citation or as the result of a communication with the court.

(4) If the violation is a trailway municipal civil infraction, and there has been damage to property or a vehicle has been impounded, the defendant's response must be made at a formal hearing.

(F) Contested Actions; Notice; Defaults.

(1) An informal hearing will be held unless

(a) a party expressly requests a formal hearing, or

(b) the violation is a trailway municipal civil infraction which requires a formal hearing pursuant to MCL 600.8717(4).

(2) The provisions of MCR 2.501(C) regarding the length of notice of trial assignment do not apply in civil infraction actions.

(3) A defendant who obtains a hearing date other than the date specified in the citation, but who does not appear to explain or contest responsibility, is in default, and the procedures established by subrules (B)(4)-(6) apply.

(4) For any hearing held under this subchapter, in accordance with MCR 2.407, the court may allow the use of videoconferencing technology by any participant as defined in MCR 2.407(A)(1).

(G) Postdetermination Orders; Sanctions, Fines, and Costs; Schedules.

(1) A court may not increase a scheduled civil fine because the defendant has requested a hearing.

(2) Upon a finding of responsibility in a traffic civil infraction action, the court:

(a) must inform the secretary of state of the finding, as required by MCL 257.732; and

(b) must initiate the procedures required by MCL 257.321a, if the defendant fails to pay a fine or to comply with an order or judgment of the court.

(3) Upon a finding of responsibility in a state civil infraction action, the court must initiate the procedures required by MCL 257.321a(1), if the defendant fails to pay a fine or to comply with an order or judgment of the court.

(4) The court may waive fines, costs and fees, pursuant to statute or court rule, or to correct clerical error.

(H) Appeal; Bond.

(1) An appeal following a formal hearing is a matter of right. Except as otherwise provided in this rule, the appeal is governed by subchapter 7.100.

(a) A defendant who appeals must post with the district court, at the time the appeal is taken, a bond equal to the fine and costs imposed. A defendant who has paid the fine and costs is not required to post a bond.

(b) If a defendant who has posted a bond fails to comply with the requirements of MCR 7.104(D), the appeal may be considered abandoned, and the district court may dismiss the appeal on 14 days' notice to the parties pursuant to MCR 7.113. The court clerk must promptly notify the circuit court of a dismissal and the circuit court shall dismiss the claim of appeal. If the appeal is dismissed or the judgment is affirmed, the district court may apply the bond to the fine and costs.

(c) A plaintiff's appeal must be asserted by the prosecuting authority of the political unit that provided the plaintiff's attorney for the formal hearing. A bond is not required.

(2) An appeal following an informal hearing is a matter of right, and must be asserted in writing, within 7 days after the decision, on a form to be provided by the court. The appeal will result in a de novo formal hearing.

(a) A defendant who appeals must post a bond as provided in subrule (1)(a). If a defendant who has posted a bond defaults by failing to appear at the formal hearing, or if the appeal is dismissed or the judgment is affirmed, the bond may be applied to the fine and costs.

(b) A plaintiff's appeal must be asserted by the prosecuting authority of the political unit that is responsible for providing the plaintiff's attorney for the formal hearing. A bond is not required.

(3) There is no appeal of right from an admission of responsibility. However, within 14 days after the admission, a defendant may file with the district court a written request to withdraw the admission, and must post a bond as provided in subrule (1)(a). If the court grants the request, the case will be scheduled for either a formal hearing or an informal hearing, as ordered by the court. If the court denies the request, the bond may be applied to the fine and costs.

[Adopted effective March 1, 1985. Amended March 23, 1989, effective June 1, 1989, 432 Mich; April 27, 1989, effective July 1, 1989, 432 Mich; April 24, 1997, effective September 2, 1997, 454 Mich; October 18, 2005, effective January 1, 2006, 474 Mich; December 13, 2005, effective January 1, 2006, 474 Mich. Amended effective August 24, 2012, 492 Mich. Amended September 21, 2016, effective January 1, 2017, 500 Mich; September 18, 2019, effective January 1, 2020, 503 Mich.]

Comments

Staff Comment to 1985 Adoption

MCR 4.101 is based on DCR 2011. There is some reorganization and several slight modifications.

In subrule (A)(4), the prohibition on issuing a warrant for a civil infraction is qualified where issuance of a warrant is permitted by statute.

Under DCR 2011.3(A)(3), in order to enter a default, the clerk was required to certify that the defendant had not answered the citation. Subrule (B)(3)(b) adds the words "within the time allowed by statute".

In subrule (E)(1) the reference to a "sworn" complaint is removed. Under MCL 257.727c(3), the citation is treated as sworn to if it includes the declaration provided by that statute.

The [March 1, 1985] amendment of MCR 4.101(E) excepts civil infraction actions from the requirement of MCR 2.501(C) that the parties be given at least 28 days' notice of trial.

Subrule (G)(2) provides that if a defendant who has posted a bond to appeal fails to appear at the formal hearing, the bond may be applied to the fine and costs imposed.

Staff Comment to June, 1989 Amendment

The March 23, 1989 [amendment to MCR 4.101, effective June 1, 1989, makes] several changes in the procedures for appealing to the circuit court.

MCR 4.101(G)(4) is amended to clarify the bond requirement when a defendant appeals to circuit court in a civil infraction action.

Staff Comment to July, 1989 Amendment

The May 3, 1989 amendments to MCR 4.101(B) and (F), 4.102(B) and 8.105(G) [effective July 1, 1989], suggested by the Task Force on Reporting Traffic-Related Offenses, are intended to implement recent statutory changes.

Staff Comment to 1997 Amendment

The September 1997 amendments of MCR 4.101, 4.401, and 6.615, and the addition of MCR 8.125, [effective September 2, 1997] were adopted at the request of the Michigan District Judges Association because of recent statutory changes that created new categories of civil infractions, and the availability of electronic filing. In addition, the amendment of MCR 4.401(G) was made to clarify the procedure for challenging a civil infraction judgment.

Staff Comment to October, 2006 Amendment

The amendment of MCR 4.101(A)(2) limits amendment of a violation on a citation filed with the court to the prosecuting official. The deletion of former subsection (A)(3) conforms to a change in MCR 6.615(A)(3), which takes effect January 1, 2006. The new subsection (C) requires the court to schedule an informal hearing when requested by the defendant, and notify the officer who issued the citation to appear, prohibits waiver of the presence of the officer at an informal hearing, and establishes procedures if the police officer fails to appear for a hearing. The amendment of relettered (F)(1) makes this section consistent with changes of MCR 6.615(D)(1), which take effect January 1, 2006.

Staff Comment to December, 2006 Amendment

The amendment of MCR 4.101(A)(2) clarifies that those who may amend the violation on a citation are the prosecuting attorney or attorney for the political subdivision, the officer who issued the citation, or another police officer for the plaintiff.

Staff Comment to 2012 Amendment

These amendments reflect changes to correct minor technical errors that have occurred in drafting or to respond to recent adopted rule revisions, which occasionally inadvertently create incorrect cross-references in other rules.

Staff Comment to 2017 Amendment

These amendments permit courts to expand the use of videoconferencing technology in many court proceedings, and clarify the proceedings at which videoconferencing technology may be used.

Staff Comment to 2020 Amendment

The amendments of MCR 1.109, 2.107, 2.113, 2.116, 2.119, 2.222, 2.223, 2.225, 2.227, 3.206, 3.211, 3.212, 3.214, 3.303, 3.903, 3.921, 3.925, 3.926, 3.931, 3.933, 3.942, 3.950, 3.961, 3.971, 3.972, 4.002, 4.101, 4.201, 4.202, 4.302, 5.128, 5.302, 5.731, 6.101, 6.615, 8.105, and 8.119 and rescission of MCR 2.226 and 8.125 continue the process for design and implementation of the statewide electronic-filing system.

SUBCHAPTER 4.200　LANDLORD–TENANT PROCEEDINGS; LAND CONTRACT FORFEITURE

Rule 4.201　Summary Proceedings to Recover Possession of Premises

(A) Applicable Rules; Forms. Except as provided by this rule and MCL 600.5701 *et seq.*, a summary proceeding to recover possession of premises from a person in possession as described in MCL 600.5714 is governed by the Michigan Court Rules. Forms available for public distribution at the court clerk's office may be used in the proceeding.

(B) Complaint.

(1) *In General.* The complaint must

(a) comply with the general pleading requirements;

(b) have attached to it a copy of any written instrument on which occupancy was or is based;

(c) have attached to it copies of any notice to quit and any demand for possession (the copies must show when and how they were served);

(d) describe the premises or the defendant's holding if it is less than the entire premises; and

(e) show the plaintiff's right to possession and indicate why the defendant's possession is improper or unauthorized.

(2) *Jury Demand.* If the plaintiff wants a jury trial, the demand must be made on a form approved by the State Court

Administrative Office and filed along with the complaint. The jury trial fee must be paid when the demand is filed.

(3) *Specific Requirements.*

(a) If rent or other money is due and unpaid, the complaint must show

(i) the rental period and rate;

(ii) the amount due and unpaid when the complaint was filed; and

(iii) the date or dates the payments became due.

(b) If the tenancy involves housing operated by or under the rules of a governmental unit, the complaint must contain specific reference to the rules or law establishing the basis for ending the tenancy.

(c) If the tenancy is of residential premises, the complaint must allege that the lessor or licensor has performed his or her covenants to keep the premises fit for the use intended and in reasonable repair during the term of the lease or license, unless the parties to the lease or license have modified those obligations.

(d) If possession is claimed for a serious and continuing health hazard or for extensive and continuing physical injury to the premises pursuant to MCL 600.5714(1)(d), the complaint must

(i) describe the nature and the seriousness or extent of the condition on which the complaint is based, and

(ii) state the period of time for which the property owner has been aware of the condition.

(e) If possession is sought for trespass pursuant to MCL 600.5714(1)(f), the complaint must describe, when known by the plaintiff, the conditions under which possession was unlawfully taken or is unlawfully held and allege that no lawful tenancy of the premises has existed between the parties since defendant took possession.

(C) Summons.

(1) The summons must comply with MCR 2.102, except that it must command the defendant to appear for trial in accord with MCL 600.5735(2), unless by local court rule the provisions of MCL 600.5735(4) have been made applicable.

(2) The summons must also include the following advice to the defendant:

(a) The defendant has the right to employ an attorney to assist in answering the complaint and in preparing defenses.

(b) If the defendant does not have an attorney but does have money to retain one, he or she might locate an attorney through the State Bar of Michigan or a local lawyer referral service.

(c) If the defendant does not have an attorney and cannot pay for legal help, he or she might qualify for assistance through a local legal aid office.

(d) The defendant has a right to a jury trial which will be lost unless it is demanded in the first defense response, written or oral. The jury trial fee must be paid when the demand is made, unless payment of fees is waived under MCR 2.002.

(D) Service of Process. A copy of the summons and complaint and all attachments must be served on the defendant by mail. Unless the court does the mailing and keeps a record,

the plaintiff must perfect the mail service by attaching a postal receipt to the proof of service. In addition to mailing, the defendant must be served in one of the following ways:

(1) By a method provided in MCR 2.105;

(2) By delivering the documents at the premises to a member of the defendant's household who is

(a) of suitable age,

(b) informed of the contents, and

(c) asked to deliver the documents to the defendant; or

(3) After diligent attempts at personal service have been made, by securely attaching the documents to the main entrance of the tenant's dwelling unit. A return of service made under this subrule must list the attempts at personal service. Service under this subrule is effective only if a return of service is filed showing that, after diligent attempts, personal service could not be made. An officer who files proof that service was made under this subrule is entitled to the regular personal service fee.

(E) Recording. All landlord-tenant summary proceedings conducted in open court must be recorded by stenographic or mechanical means, and only a reporter or recorder certified under MCR 8.108(G) may file a transcript of the record in a Michigan court.

(F) Appearance and Answer; Default.

(1) *Appearance and Answer.* The defendant or the defendant's attorney must appear and answer the complaint by the date on the summons. Appearance and answer may be made as follows:

(a) By filing a written answer or a motion under MCR 2.115 or 2.116 and serving a copy on the plaintiff or the plaintiff's attorney. If proof of the service is not filed before the hearing, the defendant or the defendant's attorney may attest to service on the record.

(b) By orally answering each allegation in the complaint at the hearing. The answers must be recorded.

(2) *Right to an Attorney.* If either party appears in person without an attorney, the court must inform that party of the right to retain an attorney. The court must also inform the party about legal aid assistance when it is available.

(3) *Jury Demand.* If the defendant wants a jury trial, he or she must demand it in the first response, written or oral. The jury trial fee must be paid when the demand is made.

(4) *Default.*

(a) If the defendant fails to appear, the court, on the plaintiff's motion, may enter a default and may hear the plaintiff's proofs in support of judgment. If satisfied that the complaint is accurate, the court must enter a default judgment under MCL 600.5741, and in accord with subrule (K). The default judgment must be mailed to the defendant by the court clerk and must inform the defendant that (if applicable)

(i) he or she may be evicted from the premises;

(ii) he or she may be liable for a money judgment.

(b) If the plaintiff fails to appear, a default judgment as to costs under MCL 600.5747 may be entered.

(c) If a party fails to appear, the court may adjourn the hearing for up to 7 days. If the hearing is adjourned, the court must mail notice of the new date to the party who failed to appear.

(5) *Use of Videoconferencing Technology.* For any hearing held under this subchapter, in accordance with MCR 2.407, the court may allow the use of videoconferencing technology by any participant as defined in MCR 2.407(A)(1).

(G) Claims and Counterclaims.

(1) *Joinder.*

(a) A party may join:

(i) A money claim or counterclaim described by MCL 600.5739. A money claim must be separately stated in the complaint. A money counterclaim must be labeled and separately stated in a written answer.

(ii) A claim or counterclaim for equitable relief.

(b) Unless service of process under MCR 2.105 was made on the defendant, a money claim must be

(i) dismissed without prejudice, or

(ii) adjourned until service of process is complete

if the defendant does not appear or file an answer to the complaint.

(c) A court with a territorial jurisdiction which has a population of more than 1,000,000 may provide, by local rule, that a money claim or counterclaim must be tried separately from a claim for possession unless joinder is allowed by leave of the court pursuant to subrule (G)(1)(e).

(d) If trial of a money claim or counterclaim

(i) might substantially delay trial of the possession claim, or

(ii) requires that the premises be returned before damages can be determined, the court must adjourn the trial of the money claim or counterclaim to a date no later than 28 days after the time expires for issuing an order of eviction. A party may file and serve supplemental pleadings no later than 7 days before trial, except by leave of the court.

(e) If adjudication of a money counterclaim will affect the amount the defendant must pay to prevent issuance of an order of eviction, that counterclaim must be tried at the same time as the claim for possession, subrules (G)(1)(c) and (d) notwithstanding, unless it appears to the court that the counterclaim is without merit.

(2) *Removal.*

(a) A summary proceedings action need not be removed from the court in which it is filed because an equitable defense or counterclaim is interposed.

(b) If a money claim or counterclaim exceeding the court's jurisdiction is introduced, the court, on motion of either party or on its own initiative, shall order, in accordance with the procedures in MCR 4.002, removal of that portion of the action to the circuit court, if the money claim or counterclaim is sufficiently shown to exceed the court's jurisdictional limit.

(H) Interim Orders. On motion of either party, or by stipulation, for good cause, a court may issue such interim orders as are necessary, including, but not limited to the following:

(1) *Injunctions.* The interim order may award injunctive relief

(a) to prevent the person in possession from damaging the property; or

(b) to prevent the person seeking possession from rendering the premises untenantable or from suffering the premises to remain untenantable.

(2) *Escrow Orders.*

(a) If trial is adjourned more than 7 days and the plaintiff shows a clear need for protection, the court may order the defendant to pay a reasonable rent for the premises from the date the escrow order is entered, including a pro rata amount per day between the date of the order and the next date rent ordinarily would be due. In determining a reasonable rent, the court should consider evidence offered concerning the condition of the premises or other relevant factors. The order must provide that:

(i) payments be made to the court clerk within 7 days of the date of entry of the order, and thereafter within 7 days of the date or dates each month when rent would ordinarily be due, until the right to possession is determined;

(ii) the plaintiff must not interfere with the obligation of the defendant to comply with the escrow order; and

(iii) if the defendant does not comply with the order, the defendant waives the right to a jury trial only as to the possession issue, and the plaintiff is entitled to an immediate trial within 14 days which may be by jury if a party requests it and if, in the court's discretion, the court's schedule permits it. The 14-day limit need not be rigidly adhered to if the plaintiff is responsible for a delay.

(b) Only the court may order the disbursement of money collected under an escrow order. The court must consider the defendant's defenses. If trial was postponed to permit the premises to be repaired, the court may condition disbursement by requiring that the repairs be completed by a certain time. Otherwise, the court may condition disbursement as justice requires.

(I) Consent Judgment When Party Is Not Represented. The following procedures apply to consent judgments and orders entered when either party is not represented by an attorney.

(1) The judgment or order may not be enforced until 3 regular court business days have elapsed after the judgment or order was entered. The judge shall review, in court, a proposed consent judgment or order with the parties, and shall notify them of the delay required by this subrule at the time the terms of the consent judgment or order are placed on the record.

(2) A party who was not represented by an attorney at the time of the consent proceedings may move to set aside the consent judgment or order within the 3-day period. Such a motion stays the judgment or order until the court decides the motion or dismisses it after notice to the moving party.

(3) The court shall set aside a consent judgment or order on a satisfactory showing that the moving party misunderstood the basis for, or the rights which were being relinquished in, the judgment or order.

(J) Trial.

(1) *Time.* When the defendant appears, the court may try the action, or, if good cause is shown, may adjourn trial up to 56

days. If the court adjourns trial for more than 7 days, an escrow order may be entered pursuant to subrule (H)(2). The parties may adjourn trial by stipulation in writing or on the record, subject to the approval of the court.

(2) *Pretrial Action.* At trial, the court must first decide pretrial motions and determine if there is a triable issue. If there is no triable issue, the court must enter judgment.

(3) *Government Reports.* If the defendant claims that the plaintiff failed to comply with an ordinance or statute, the court may admit an authenticated copy of any relevant government employee's report filed with a government agency. Objections to the report affect the weight given it, not its admissibility.

(4) *Payment or Acceptance of Money.* The payment or the acceptance of money by a party before trial does not necessarily prevent or delay the proceedings.

(K) Judgment.

(1) *Requirements.* A judgment for the plaintiff must

    (a) comply with MCL 600.5741;

    (b) state when and under what conditions, if any, an order of eviction will issue;

    (c) separately state possession and money awards; and

    (d) advise the defendant of the right to appeal or file a postjudgment motion within 10 days.

If the judgment is in favor of the defendant, it must comply with MCL 600.5747.

(2) *Injunctions.* The judgment may award injunctive relief

    (a) to prevent the person in possession from damaging the property; or

    (b) to prevent the person seeking possession from rendering the premises untenantable, or from suffering the premises to remain untenantable.

(3) *Partial Payment.* The judgment may provide that acceptance of partial payment of an amount due under the judgment will not prevent issuance of an order of eviction.

(4) *Costs.* Only those costs permitted by MCL 600.5759 may be awarded.

(5) *Notice.* The court must mail or deliver a copy of the judgment to the parties. The time period for applying for the order of eviction does not begin to run until the judgment is mailed or delivered.

(L) Order of Eviction.

(1) *Request.* When the time stated in the judgment expires, a party awarded possession may apply for an order of eviction. The application must:

    (a) be written;

    (b) be verified by a person having knowledge of the facts stated;

    (c) if any money has been paid after entry of the judgment, show the conditions under which it was accepted; and

    (d) state whether the party awarded judgment has complied with its terms.

(2) *Issuance of Order of Eviction and Delivery of Order.* Subject to the provisions of subrule (L)(4), the order of eviction shall be delivered to the person serving the order for service within 7 days after the order is filed.

(3) *Issuance Immediately on Judgment.* The court may issue an order immediately on entering judgment if

    (a) the court is convinced the statutory requirements are satisfied, and

    (b) the defendant was given notice, before the judgment of a request for immediate issuance of the order.

The court may condition the order to protect the defendant's interest.

(4) *Limitations on Time for Issuance and Execution.* Unless a hearing is held after the defendant has been given notice and an opportunity to appear, an order of eviction may not

    (a) be issued later than 56 days after judgment is entered,

    (b) be executed later than 56 days after it is issued.

(5) *Acceptance of Partial Payment.* An order of eviction may not be issued if any part of the amount due under the judgment has been paid, unless

    (a) a hearing is held after the defendant has been given notice and an opportunity to appear, or

    (b) the judgment provides that acceptance of partial payment of the amount due under the judgment will not prevent issuance of an order of eviction.

(M) Postjudgment Motions. Except as provided in MCR 2.612, any postjudgment motion must be filed no later than 10 days after judgment enters.

(1) If the motion challenges a judgment for possession, the court may not grant a stay unless

    (a) the motion is accompanied by an escrow deposit of 1 month's rent, or

    (b) the court is satisfied that there are grounds for relief under MCR 2.612(C), and issues an order that waives payment of the escrow; such an order may be ex parte.

If a stay is granted, a hearing shall be held within 14 days after it is issued.

(2) If the judgment does not include an award of possession, the filing of the motion stays proceedings, but the plaintiff may move for an order requiring a bond to secure the stay. If the initial escrow deposit is believed inadequate, the plaintiff may apply for continuing adequate escrow payments in accord with subrule (H)(2). The filing of a postjudgment motion together with a bond, bond order, or escrow deposit stays all proceedings, including an order of eviction issued but not executed.

(3) If a motion is filed to set aside a default money judgment, except when grounded on lack of jurisdiction over the defendant, the court may not grant the motion unless

    (a) the motion is accompanied by an affidavit of facts showing a meritorious defense, and

    (b) good cause is shown.

(N) Appeals From Possessory Judgments.

(1) *Rules Applicable.* Except as provided by this rule, appeals must comply with MCR 7.101 through 7.115.

(2) *Time.* An appeal of right must be filed within 10 days after the entry of judgment.

(3) *Stay of Order of Eviction.*

    (a) Unless a stay is ordered by the trial court, an order of eviction must issue as provided in subrule (L).

(b) The filing of a claim of appeal together with a bond or escrow order of the court stays all proceedings, including an order of eviction issued but not executed.

(4) *Appeal Bond; Escrow.*

(a) A plaintiff who appeals must file a bond providing that if the plaintiff loses he or she will pay the appeal costs.

(b) A defendant who appeals must file a bond providing that if the defendant loses, he or she will pay

(i) the appeal costs,

(ii) the amount due stated in the judgment, and

(iii) damages from the time of forcible entry, the detainer, the notice to quit, or the demand for possession.

The court may waive the bond requirement of subrule (N)(4)(b)(i) on the grounds stated in MCR 2.002(C) or (D).

(c) If the plaintiff won a possession judgment, the court shall enter an escrow order under subrule (H)(2) and require the defendant to make payments while the appeal is pending. This escrow order may not be retroactive as to arrearages preceding the date of the post-trial escrow order unless there was a pretrial escrow order entered under subrule (H)(2), in which case the total escrow amount may include the amount accrued between the time of the original escrow order and the filing of the appeal.

(d) If it is established that an appellant cannot obtain sureties or make a sufficient cash deposit, the court must permit the appellant to comply with an escrow order.

(O) Objections to Fees Covered by Statute for Orders of Eviction. Objections shall be by motion. The fee to be paid shall be reasonable in light of all the circumstances. In determining the reasonableness of a fee, the court shall consider all issues bearing on reasonableness, including but not limited to

(1) the time of travel to the premises,

(2) the time necessary to execute the order,

(3) the amount and weight of the personal property removed from the premises,

(4) who removed the personal property from the premises,

(5) the distance that the personal property was moved from the premises, and

(6) the actual expenses incurred in executing the order of eviction.

[Adopted effective March 1, 1985. Amended September 12, 2001, effective May 1, 2002, 465 Mich; February 23, 2006, effective May 1, 2006, 474 Mich; January 20, 2009, effective May 1, 2009, 483 Mich. Amended effective August 24, 2012, 492 Mich; September 5, 2013, 495 Mich. Amended February 4, 2015, effective May 1, 2015, 497 Mich; September 21, 2016, effective January 1, 2017, 500 Mich; March 20, 2019, effective May 1, 2019, 502 Mich. Amended effective May 1, 2019, 502 Mich. Amended September 18, 2019, effective January 1, 2020, 503 Mich.]

Comments

Staff Comment to 1985 Adoption

MCR 4.201 is based on DCR 754. There are several minor changes.

DCR 754.2(8) required that the complaint include certain additional information when the housing involved is operated by a local governmental unit. Subrule (B)(2)(b) deletes the limitation to local units, and also covers housing operated under the rules of a governmental unit as well as housing operated by the governmental unit.

In subrule (C)(2)(d), regarding payment of the jury fee, a cross-reference is added to MCR 2.002, governing waiver or suspension of fees for indigent persons.

Subrule (K)(5) permits the court to deliver a copy of the judgment to the parties rather than to mail it. Compare DCR 754.11(e).

Subrule (L)(4) modifies the language of DCR 754.12(c)(3) by adding an exception to the requirement that there must be a hearing before issuance of a writ of restitution when there has been partial payment of the amount due under the judgment. A hearing is not required if the judgment includes the provision permitted by subrule (K)(3)—that partial payment does not prevent the issuance of a writ of restitution.

Staff Comment to 2002 Amendment

The September 12, 2001 addition of MCR 3.106, effective May 1, 2002, was recommended by an ad hoc committee of judges, court administrators, court clerks, attorneys, and court officers. The rule incorporated existing practice while protecting against abuses. The September 12, 2001 amendments of MCR 4.201 and 4.202, effective May 1, 2002, made changes consistent with new MCR 3.106.

Staff Comment to 2006 Amendment

The amendments of MCR 2.507(G), 4.201(F)(5), and 4.202(H)(3) reflect amendments of MCL 600.2529 and 600.5756 by 1993 PA 189.

Staff Comment to 2009 Amendment

The amendment of MCR 4.201(G)(1)(b) clarifies that service of process for purposes of a money claim is sufficient if completed pursuant to MCR 2.105; otherwise, if the defendant does not appear or file an answer to the complaint, a money claim must be dismissed without prejudice, or adjourned until service of process is complete.

These amendments reflect changes to correct minor technical errors that have occurred in drafting or to respond to recent adopted rule revisions, which occasionally inadvertently create incorrect cross-references in other rules.

Staff Comment to 2012 Amendment

These amendments reflect changes to correct minor technical errors that have occurred in drafting or to respond to recent adopted rule revisions, which occasionally inadvertently create incorrect cross-references in other rules.

Staff Comment to 2013 Amendment

These amendments reflect changes that correct minor technical errors that have occurred in drafting or the changes respond to recent adopted rule revisions, which occasionally inadvertently create incorrect cross-references in other rules.

Staff Comment to 2015 Amendment

This amendment of MCR 4.201 clarifies that a motion to set aside a default money judgment in a landlord/tenant case must be accompanied by an affidavit of facts showing a meritorious defense, and good cause must be shown. This is the standard for setting aside a default judgment under MCR 2.603(D)(1).

Staff Comment to 2017 Amendment

These amendments permit courts to expand the use of videoconferencing technology in many court proceedings, and clarify the proceedings at which videoconferencing technology may be used.

Staff Comment to First May, 2019 Amendment

The amendments of Rules 1.109, 2.102, 2.104, 2.106, 2.107, 2.117, 2.119, 2.403, 2.503, 2.506, 2.508, 2.518, 2.602, 2.603, 2.621, 3.101, 3.104, 3.203, 3.205, 3.210, 3.302, 3.607, 3.613, 3.614, 3.705, 3.801, 3.802, 3.805, 3.806, 4.201, 4.202, 4.303, 4.306, 5.001, 5.104, 5.105, 5.107, 5.108, 5.113, 5.117, 5.118, 5.119, 5.120, 5.125, 5.126, 5.132, 5.162, 5.202, 5.203, 5.205, 5.302, 5.304, 5.307, 5.308, 5.309, 5.310, 5.311, 5.313, 5.402, 5.404, 5.405, 5.409, 5.501, and 5.784 and addition of Rule 3.618 of the Michigan Court Rules are an expected progression necessary for design and implementation of the statewide electronic-filing system. These particular amendments will assist in implementing the goals of the project.

Staff Comment to Second May, 2019 Amendment

The amendments in this order include only the nonsubstantive changes of MCR 4.201 that were incorporated in the order that entered on March 20, 2019. In response to concerns raised by numerous commenters that the new rule would make it difficult to ensure defendants were served timely with the summons and complaint, the rule now will remain largely unchanged for further discussion and input, with an expectation that this issue and others will be addressed in a future set of proposed court rule revisions.

Staff Comment to 2020 Amendment

The amendments of MCR 1.109, 2.107, 2.113, 2.116, 2.119, 2.222, 2.223, 2.225, 2.227, 3.206, 3.211, 3.212, 3.214, 3.303, 3.903, 3.921, 3.925, 3.926, 3.931, 3.933, 3.942, 3.950, 3.961, 3.971, 3.972, 4.002, 4.101, 4.201, 4.202, 4.302, 5.128, 5.302, 5.731, 6.101, 6.615, 8.105, and 8.119 and rescission of MCR 2.226 and 8.125 continue the process for design and implementation of the statewide electronic-filing system.

Rule 4.202 Summary Proceedings; Land Contract Forfeiture

(A) Applicable Rules. Except as provided by this rule and MCL 600.5701 *et seq.*, a summary proceeding to recover possession of premises after forfeiture of an executory contract for the purchase of premises as described in MCL 600.5726 is governed by the Michigan Court Rules.

(B) Jurisdiction.

(1) *Status of Premises.* The proceeding may be brought when the premises are vacant or are in the possession of

(a) the vendee,

(b) a party to the contract,

(c) an assignee of the contract, or

(d) a third party.

(2) *Powers of Court.* The court may do all things necessary to hear and resolve the proceeding, including but not limited to

(a) hearing and deciding all issues,

(b) ordering joinder of additional parties,

(c) ordering or permitting amendments or additional pleadings, and

(d) making and enforcing writs and orders.

(C) Necessary Parties. The plaintiff must join as defendants

(1) the vendee named in the contract,

(2) any person known to the plaintiff to be claiming an interest in the premises under the contract, and

(3) any person in possession of the premises, unless that party has been released from liability.

(D) Complaint. The complaint must:

(1) comply with the general pleading requirements;

(2) allege

(a) the original selling price,

(b) the principal balance due, and

(c) the amount in arrears under the contract;

(3) state with particularity any other material breach claimed as a basis for forfeiture; and

(4) have attached to it a copy of the notice of forfeiture, showing when and how it was served on each named defendant.

(E) Summons. The summons must comply with MCR 2.102 and MCL 600.5735, and command the defendant to appear and answer or take other action permitted by law within the time permitted by statute after service of the summons on the defendant.

(F) Service of Process. The defendant must be served with a copy of the complaint and summons under MCR 2.105.

(G) Recording. All executory contract summary proceedings conducted in open court must be recorded by stenographic or mechanical means, and only a reporter or recorder certified under MCR 8.108(G) may file a transcript of the record in a Michigan court.

(H) Answer; Default.

(1) *Answer.* The answer must comply with general pleading requirements and allege those matters on which the defendant intends to rely to defeat the claim or any part of it.

(2) *Default.*

(a) If the defendant fails to appear, the court, on the plaintiff's motion, may enter a default and may hear the plaintiff's proofs in support of judgment. If satisfied that the complaint is accurate, the court must enter a default judgment under MCL 600.5741, and in accord with subrule (J). The plaintiff must mail the default judgment to the defendant and file a proof of service with the court. The default judgment must inform the defendant that (if applicable)

(i) he or she may be evicted from the premises;

(ii) he or she may be liable for a money judgment.

(b) If the plaintiff fails to appear, a default and judgment as to costs under MCL 600.5747 may be entered.

(c) If a party fails to appear, the court may adjourn the hearing for up to 7 days. If the hearing is adjourned, the court must mail notice of the new date to the party who failed to appear.

(3) *Use of Videoconferencing Technology.* For any hearing held under this subchapter, in accordance with MCR 2.407, the court may allow the use of videoconferencing technology by any participant as defined in MCR 2.407(A)(1).

(I) Joinder; Removal.

(1) A party may join a claim or counterclaim for equitable relief or a money claim or counterclaim described by MCL 600.5739. A money claim must be separately stated in the complaint. A money counterclaim must be labeled and separately stated in a written answer. If such a joinder is made, the court may order separate summary disposition of the claim for possession, as described by MCL 600.5739.

(2) A court with a territorial jurisdiction which has a population of more than 1,000,000 may provide, by local rule, that a money claim or counterclaim must be tried separately from a claim for possession unless joinder is allowed by leave of the court pursuant to subrule (I)(3).

(3) If adjudication of a money counterclaim will affect the amount the defendant must pay to prevent the issuance of a writ of restitution, the counterclaim must be tried at the same time as the claim for possession, subrules (I)(1) and (2) notwithstanding, unless it appears to the court that the counterclaim is without merit.

(4) If a money claim or counterclaim exceeding the court's jurisdiction is introduced, the court, on motion of either party or on its own initiative, shall order, in accordance with the procedures in MCR 4.002, removal of that portion of the action, if the money claim or counterclaim is sufficiently shown to exceed the court's jurisdictional limit.

(J) Judgment. The judgment

(1) must comply with MCL 600.5741;

(2) must state when, and under what conditions, if any, a writ of restitution will issue;

(3) must state that an appeal or postjudgment motion to challenge the judgment may be filed within 10 days;

(4) may contain such other terms and conditions as the nature of the action and the rights of the parties require; and

(5) *Notice.* The plaintiff must mail or deliver a copy of the judgment to the parties. The time period for applying for the order of eviction does not begin to run until the judgment is mailed or delivered.

(K) Order of Eviction.

(1) *Request.* When the time stated in the judgment expires, a party awarded possession may apply for an order of eviction. The application must:

(a) be written;

(b) be verified by a person having knowledge of the facts stated;

(c) if any money due under the judgment has been paid, show the conditions under which it was accepted; and

(d) state whether the party awarded judgment has complied with its terms.

(2) *Hearing Required if Part of Judgment Has Been Paid.* An order of eviction may not be issued if any part of the amount due under the judgment has been paid unless a hearing has been held after the defendant has been given notice and an opportunity to appear.

(L) Appeal. Except as provided by this rule or by law, the rules applicable to other appeals to circuit court (see MCR 7.101–7.115) apply to appeals from judgments in land contract forfeiture cases. However, in such cases the time limit for filing a claim of appeal under MCR 7.104(A) is 10 days.

[Adopted effective March 1, 1985. Amended September 12, 2001, effective May 1, 2002, 465 Mich; February 23, 2006, effective May 1, 2006, 474 Mich. Amended effective August 24, 2012, 492 Mich. Amended September 21, 2016, effective January 1, 2017, 500 Mich; March 20, 2019, effective May 1, 2019, 502 Mich; September 18, 2019, effective January 1, 2020, 503 Mich.]

Comments

Staff Comment to 1985 Adoption

MCR 4.202 is substantially the same as DCR 755.

Subrule (J)(5) permits the court to deliver a copy of the judgment to the parties as a substitute for mailing.

The [March 1, 1985] amendment of MCR 4.202 adds a new subrule (L) expressly incorporating the rules applicable to other appeals from district to circuit court (MCR 7.101–7.103), except that the time for taking an appeal of a land contract forfeiture judgment is 10 days.

Staff Comment to 2002 Amendment

The September 12, 2001 addition of MCR 3.106, effective May 1, 2002, was recommended by an ad hoc committee of judges, court administrators, court clerks, attorneys, and court officers. The rule incorporated existing practice while protecting against abuses. The September 12, 2001 amendments of MCR 4.201 and 4.202, effective May 1, 2002, made changes consistent with new MCR 3.106.

Staff Comment to 2006 Amendment

The amendments of MCR 2.507(G), 4.201(F)(5), and 4.202(H)(3) reflect amendments of MCL 600.2529 and 600.5756 by 1993 PA 189.

Staff Comment to 2012 Amendment

These amendments reflect changes to correct minor technical errors that have occurred in drafting or to respond to recent adopted rule revisions, which occasionally inadvertently create incorrect cross-references in other rules.

Staff Comment to 2017 Amendment

These amendments permit courts to expand the use of videoconferencing technology in many court proceedings, and clarify the proceedings at which videoconferencing technology may be used.

Staff Comment to 2019 Amendment

The amendments of Rules 1.109, 2.102, 2.104, 2.106, 2.107, 2.117, 2.119, 2.403, 2.503, 2.506, 2.508, 2.518, 2.602, 2.603, 2.621, 3.101, 3.104, 3.203, 3.205, 3.210, 3.302, 3.607, 3.613, 3.614, 3.705, 3.801, 3.802, 3.805, 3.806, 4.201, 4.202, 4.303, 4.306, 5.001, 5.104, 5.105, 5.107, 5.108, 5.113, 5.117, 5.118, 5.119, 5.120, 5.125, 5.126, 5.132, 5.162, 5.202, 5.203, 5.205, 5.302, 5.304, 5.307, 5.308, 5.309, 5.310, 5.311, 5.313, 5.402, 5.404, 5.405, 5.409, 5.501, and 5.784 and addition of Rule 3.618 of the Michigan Court Rules are an expected progression necessary for design and implementation of the statewide electronic-filing system. These particular amendments will assist in implementing the goals of the project.

Staff Comment to 2020 Amendment

The amendments of MCR 1.109, 2.107, 2.113, 2.116, 2.119, 2.222, 2.223, 2.225, 2.227, 3.206, 3.211, 3.212, 3.214, 3.303, 3.903, 3.921, 3.925, 3.926, 3.931, 3.933, 3.942, 3.950, 3.961, 3.971, 3.972, 4.002, 4.101, 4.201, 4.202, 4.302, 5.128, 5.302, 5.731, 6.101, 6.615, 8.105, and 8.119 and rescission of MCR 2.226 and 8.125 continue the process for design and implementation of the statewide electronic-filing system.

SUBCHAPTER 4.300   SMALL CLAIMS ACTIONS

Rule 4.301   Applicability of Rules

Actions in a small claims division are governed by the procedural provisions of Chapter 84 of the Revised Judicature Act, MCL 600.8401 *et seq.*, and by this subchapter of the rules. After judgment, other applicable Michigan Court Rules govern actions that were brought in a small claims division.

[Adopted effective March 1, 1985.]

Comments

Staff Comment to 1985 Adoption

MCR 4.301 is comparable to DCR 5001. The substance of DCR 4005.10 is added, making clear that after entry of judgment the rules applicable to other actions apply to actions that were brought in the small claims division.

The amendment of MCR 4.301 [entered January 25, 1985, effective March 1, 1985] modifies the reference to the small claims chapter of the Revised Judicature Act, to be consistent with 1984 PA 278, which was effective January 1, 1985.

Rule 4.302   Statement of Claim

(A) Contents. The statement of the claim must be in an affidavit in substantially the form approved by the state court administrator. Affidavit forms shall be available at the clerk's office. The nature and amount of the claim must be stated in concise, nontechnical language, and the affidavit must state the date or dates when the claim arose. The form, captioning, signing, and verifying of documents are prescribed in MCR 1.109(D) and (E).

(B) Affidavit; Signature.

(1) If the plaintiff is an individual, the affidavit must be signed by the plaintiff, or the plaintiff's guardian, conservator, or next friend.

(2) If the plaintiff is a sole proprietorship, a partnership, or a corporation, the affidavit must be signed by a person authorized to file the claim by MCL 600.8407(3).

(C) Names.

(1) The affidavit must state the full and correct name of the plaintiff and whether the plaintiff is a corporation or a partnership. If the plaintiff was acting under an assumed name when the claim arose, the assumed name must be given.

(2) The defendant may be identified as permitted by MCL 600.8426, or as is proper in other civil actions.

(D) Claims in Excess of Statutory Limitation. If the amount of the plaintiff's claim exceeds the statutory limitation, the actual amount of the claim must be stated. The claim must state that by commencing the action the plaintiff waives any claim to the excess over the statutory limitation, and that the amount equal to the statutory limitation, exclusive of costs, is claimed by the action. A judgment on the claim is a bar to a later action in any court to recover the excess.

[Adopted effective March 1, 1985. Amended May 30, 2018, effective September 1, 2018, 501 Mich; September 18, 2019, effective January 1, 2020, 503 Mich.]

Comments

Staff Comment to 1985 Adoption

MCR 4.302 is comparable to DCR 5002.

Under subrule (A) affidavit forms are to be available at the clerk's office. See MCL 600.8403.

Subrule (B)(2) modifies the provisions of DCR 5002.2 to take account of the 1978 amendment of MCL 600.8407(3), as to who may sign the complaint on behalf of certain parties.

Subrule (C) is changed (from DCR 5002.3) to refer to the statute applicable to the names of the parties.

Staff Comment to 2018 Amendment

The amendments in this order are intended to begin moving trial courts toward a statewide uniform e-Filing process. In addition, the order moves existing language into MCR 1.109 as a way to, for the first time, include most filing requirements in one single rule, instead of scattered in various rules. The order largely mirrors the administrative orders that most e-Filing pilot projects have operated under, but contains some significant new provisions. For example, courts are required to maintain documents in an electronic document management system, and the electronic record is the official court record.

Staff Comment to 2020 Amendment

The amendments of MCR 1.109, 2.107, 2.113, 2.116, 2.119, 2.222, 2.223, 2.225, 2.227, 3.206, 3.211, 3.212, 3.214, 3.303, 3.903, 3.921, 3.925, 3.926, 3.931, 3.933, 3.942, 3.950, 3.961, 3.971, 3.972, 4.002, 4.101, 4.201, 4.202, 4.302, 5.128, 5.302, 5.731, 6.101, 6.615, 8.105, and 8.119 and rescission of MCR 2.226 and 8.125 continue the process for design and implementation of the statewide electronic-filing system.

Rule 4.303 Notice

(A) Contents. The notice to the defendant must meet the requirements of MCL 600.8404. The court clerk shall notify the plaintiff to appear at the time and place specified with the books, papers, and witnesses necessary to prove the claim, and that if the plaintiff fails to appear, the claim will be dismissed.

(B) Certified Mail. If the defendant is a corporation or a partnership, the certified mail described in MCL 600.8405 need not be deliverable to the addressee only, but may be deliverable to and signed for by an agent of the addressee.

(C) Notice Not Served. If it appears that notice was not received by the defendant at least 7 days before the appearance date and the defendant does not appear, the clerk must, at the plaintiff's request, issue further notice without additional cost to the plaintiff, setting the hearing for a future date. The further notice may be served as provided in MCR 2.105.

[Adopted effective March 1, 1985. Amended March 20, 2019, effective May 1, 2019, 502 Mich.]

Comments

Staff Comment to 1985 Adoption

MCR 4.303 is comparable to DCR 5003.

Unlike DCR 5003.1, subrule (A) does not include the provision regarding notice that the defendant may arrange terms of payment. That requirement was included in the 1978 amendment of MCL 600.8404, which is incorporated in subrule (A).

Staff Comment to 2019 Amendment

The amendments of Rules 1.109, 2.102, 2.104, 2.106, 2.107, 2.117, 2.119, 2.403, 2.503, 2.506, 2.508, 2.518, 2.602, 2.603, 2.621, 3.101, 3.104, 3.203, 3.205, 3.210, 3.302, 3.607, 3.613, 3.614, 3.705, 3.801, 3.802, 3.805, 3.806, 4.201, 4.202, 4.303, 4.306, 5.001, 5.104, 5.105, 5.107, 5.108, 5.113, 5.117, 5.118, 5.119, 5.120, 5.125, 5.126, 5.132, 5.162, 5.202, 5.203, 5.205, 5.302, 5.304, 5.307, 5.308, 5.309, 5.310, 5.311, 5.313, 5.402, 5.404,

5.405, 5.409, 5.501, and 5.784 and addition of Rule 3.618 of the Michigan Court Rules are an expected progression necessary for design and implementation of the statewide electronic-filing system. These particular amendments will assist in implementing the goals of the project.

Rule 4.304 Conduct of Trial

(A) Appearance. If the parties appear, the court shall hear the claim as provided in MCL 600.8411. In accordance with MCR 2.407, the court may allow the use of videoconferencing technology by any participant as defined in MCR 2.407(A)(1). The trial may be adjourned to a later date for good cause.

(B) Nonappearance.

(1) If a defendant fails to appear, judgment may be entered by default if the claim is liquidated, or on the ex parte proofs the court requires if the claim is unliquidated.

(2) If the plaintiff fails to appear, the claim may be dismissed for want of prosecution, the defendant may proceed to trial on the merits, or the action may be adjourned, as the court directs.

(3) If all parties fail to appear, the claim may be dismissed for want of prosecution or the court may order another disposition, as justice requires.

[Adopted effective March 1, 1985. Amended September 21, 2016, effective January 1, 2017, 500 Mich.]

Comments

Staff Comment to 1985 Adoption

MCR 4.304 is substantially the same as DCR 5004.

Staff Comment to 2017 Amendment

These amendments permit courts to expand the use of videoconferencing technology in many court proceedings, and clarify the proceedings at which videoconferencing technology may be used.

Rule 4.305 Judgments

(A) Entry of Judgments. A judgment must be entered at the time of the entry of the court's findings, and must contain the payment and stay provisions required by MCL 600.8410(2).

(B) Modification; Vacation. A judgment of the small claims division may be modified or vacated in the same manner as judgments in other civil actions, except that an appeal may not be taken.

(C) Garnishment. A writ of garnishment may not be issued to enforce the judgment until the expiration of 21 days after it was entered. If a judgment had been ordered to be paid by installments, an affidavit for a writ of garnishment must so state and must state that the order has been set aside or vacated.

[Adopted effective March 1, 1985.]

Comments

Staff Comment to 1985 Adoption

MCR 4.305 is comparable to DCR 5005.

The provisions of DCR 5005.2 regarding installment payments are omitted. Language is added to subrule (A) to incorporate the 1978 statutory amendment regarding installment payments and stays. MCL 600.8410(2).

Language is added to subrule (B) to make clear that, while the district court may modify a judgment as in other actions, an appeal is not available.

The garnishment provisions of subrule (C) are modified with the addition of a prohibition on garnishment for 21 days after entry of the judgment. In a sense, this corresponds to the automatic stay provisions of other civil actions. See MCR 2.614(A).

Rule 4.306   Removal to Trial Court

(A) Demand. A party may demand that the action be removed from the small claims division to the trial court for further proceedings by

(1) signing a written demand for removal and filing it with the clerk at or before the time set for hearing; or

(2) appearing before the court at the time and place set for hearing and demanding removal.

(B) Order; Fee. On receiving a demand for removal, the court shall, by a written order filed in the action, direct removal to the trial court for further proceedings.

(1) The order must direct a defendant to file a written answer and serve it as provided in MCR 2.107 within 14 days after the date of the order.

(2) The party demanding removal must promptly serve the order on the opposing party and file proof of service with the court.

(3) There is no fee for the removal, order, or mailing.

(C) Motion for More Definite Statement. After removal, the affidavit is deemed to be a sufficient statement of the plaintiff's claim unless a defendant, within the time permitted for answer, files a motion for a more definite statement.

(1) The motion must state the information sought and must be supported by an affidavit that the defendant

(a) does not have the information and cannot secure it with the exercise of reasonable diligence, and

(b) is unable to answer the plaintiff's claim without it.

(2) The court may decide the motion without a hearing on just and reasonable terms or may direct that a hearing be held after notice to both parties at a time set by the court.

(3) If the plaintiff fails to file a more definite statement after having been ordered to do so, the clerk shall dismiss the claim for want of prosecution.

(D) Default. On removal, if the defendant fails to file an answer or motion within the time permitted, the clerk shall enter the default of the defendant. MCR 2.603 governs further proceedings.

(E) Procedure After Removal. Except as provided in this rule, further proceedings in actions removed to the trial court are governed by the rules applicable to other civil actions.
[Adopted effective March 1, 1985. Amended March 20, 2019, effective May 1, 2019, 502 Mich.]

Comments

Staff Comment to 1985 Adoption

MCR 4.306 is comparable to DCR 5006.

Subrule (C)(2) allows the denial, as well as the granting, of a motion for a more definite statement without a hearing. Compare DCR 5006.3. This is consistent with the general motion practice rule. See MCR 2.119(E)(3).

Subrule (E) modifies the language of DCR 5006.5. After removal to the trial court, all provisions governing other cases in district court apply, not only those applicable to trials.

Staff Comment to 2019 Amendment

The amendments of Rules 1.109, 2.102, 2.104, 2.106, 2.107, 2.117, 2.119, 2.403, 2.503, 2.506, 2.508, 2.518, 2.602, 2.603, 2.621, 3.101, 3.104, 3.203, 3.205, 3.210, 3.302, 3.607, 3.613, 3.614, 3.705, 3.801, 3.802, 3.805, 3.806, 4.201, 4.202, 4.303, 4.306, 5.001, 5.104, 5.105, 5.107, 5.108, 5.113, 5.117, 5.118, 5.119, 5.120, 5.125, 5.126, 5.132, 5.162, 5.202, 5.203, 5.205, 5.302, 5.304, 5.307, 5.308, 5.309, 5.310, 5.311, 5.313, 5.402, 5.404, 5.405, 5.409, 5.501, and 5.784 and addition of Rule 3.618 of the Michigan Court Rules are an expected progression necessary for design and implementation of the statewide electronic-filing system. These particular amendments will assist in implementing the goals of the project.

SUBCHAPTER 4.400   MAGISTRATES

Rule 4.401   District Court Magistrates

(A) Procedure. Proceedings involving district court magistrates must be in accordance with relevant statutes and rules.

(B) Duties. Notwithstanding statutory provisions to the contrary, district court magistrates exercise only those duties expressly authorized by the chief judge of the district or division.

(C) Control of Magisterial Action. An action taken by a district court magistrate may be superseded, without formal appeal, by order of a district judge in the district in which the magistrate serves.

(D) Appeals. Appeals of right may be taken from a decision of the district court magistrate to the district court in the district in which the magistrate serves by filing a written claim of appeal in substantially the form provided by MCR 7.104 within 7 days of the entry of the decision of the magistrate. No fee is required on the filing of the appeal, except as otherwise provided by statute or court rule. The action is heard de novo by the district court.

(E) A district court magistrate may use videoconferencing technology in accordance with MCR 2.407 and MCR 6.006.
[Adopted effective March 1, 1985. Amended April 24, 1997, effective September 2, 1997, 454 Mich; November 26, 2001, effective January 1, 2002, 465 Mich. Amended effective August 24, 2012, 492 Mich. Amended September 21, 2016, effective January 1, 2017, 500 Mich.]

Comments

Staff Comment to 1985 Adoption

MCR 4.401 includes the provisions of DCR 3001.1–3001.4. The remaining provisions of DCR 3001, covering administrative matters, are placed in MCR 8.205.

Staff Comment to 1997 Amendment

The September 1997 amendment of MCR 4.401 was adopted at the request of the Michigan District Judges Association because of recent statutory changes that created new categories of civil infractions, and the availability of electronic filing.

Staff Comment to 2002 Amendment

The amendment of MCR 4.401(D) recognized numbering changes in other rules and the elimination of the "parallel citation" requirement from the Michigan Uniform System of Citation (Supreme Court AO 2001-5).

Staff Comment to 2012 Amendment

These amendments reflect changes to correct minor technical errors that have occurred in drafting or to respond to recent adopted rule revisions, which occasionally inadvertently create incorrect cross-references in other rules.

Staff Comment to 2017 Amendment

These amendments permit courts to expand the use of videoconferencing technology in many court proceedings, and clarify the proceedings at which videoconferencing technology may be used.

CHAPTER 5.   PROBATE COURT
Effective March 1, 1985

SUBCHAPTER 5.000   GENERAL PROVISIONS

Rule 5.001   Applicability

(A) Applicability of Rules. Procedure in probate court is governed by the general rules set forth in chapter one and by the rules applicable to other civil proceedings set forth in chapter two, except as modified by the rules in this chapter.

(B) Terminology.

(1) References to the "clerk" in the Michigan Court Rules also apply to the register in probate court proceedings.

(2) References to "pleadings" in the Michigan Court Rules also apply to petitions, objections, and claims in probate court proceedings.

[Adopted July 12, 2001, effective January 1, 2002, 464 Mich. Amended March 20, 2019, effective May 1, 2019, 502 Mich.]

Comments

Staff Comment to 2019 Amendment

The amendments of Rules 1.109, 2.102, 2.104, 2.106, 2.107, 2.117, 2.119, 2.403, 2.503, 2.506, 2.508, 2.518, 2.602, 2.603, 2.621, 3.101, 3.104, 3.203, 3.205, 3.210, 3.302, 3.607, 3.613, 3.614, 3.705, 3.801, 3.802, 3.805, 3.806, 4.201, 4.202, 4.303, 4.306, 5.001, 5.104, 5.105, 5.107, 5.108, 5.113, 5.117, 5.118, 5.119, 5.120, 5.125, 5.126, 5.132, 5.162, 5.202, 5.203, 5.205, 5.302, 5.304, 5.307, 5.308, 5.309, 5.310, 5.311, 5.313, 5.402, 5.404, 5.405, 5.409, 5.501, and 5.784 and addition of Rule 3.618 of the Michigan Court Rules are an expected progression necessary for design and implementation of the statewide electronic-filing system. These particular amendments will assist in implementing the goals of the project.

SUBCHAPTER 5.100   GENERAL RULES OF PLEADING AND PRACTICE

Rule 5.101   Form and Commencement of Action; Confidential Records

(A) Form of Action. There are two forms of action, a "proceeding" and a "civil action."

(B) Commencement of Proceeding. A proceeding is commenced by filing an application or a petition with the court.

(C) Civil Actions, Commencement, Governing Rules. The following actions must be titled civil actions and commenced by filing a complaint and are governed by the rules applicable to civil actions in circuit court:

(1) Any action against another filed by a fiduciary or trustee.

(2) Any action filed by a claimant after notice that the claim has been disallowed.

(D) Records are public except as otherwise indicated in court rule and statute.

[Adopted July 12, 2001, effective January 1, 2002, 464 Mich. Amended effective August 24, 2012, 492 Mich. Amended October 31, 2012, effective January 1, 2013, 493 Mich.]

Comments

Staff Comment to 2012 Amendment

These amendments reflect changes to correct minor technical errors that have occurred in drafting or to respond to recent adopted rule revisions, which occasionally inadvertently create incorrect cross-references in other rules.

Staff Comment to 2013 Amendment

The amendments of these rules update the rules making them less "paper" focused and reflecting the use of electronic technology in the way courts process court records. The amendments also clarify and delineate the types of records and other materials maintained by a court, and clarify how access is provided.

Rule 5.102   Notice of Hearing

A petitioner, fiduciary, or other moving party must cause to be prepared, served, and filed, a notice of hearing for all matters requiring notification of interested persons. It must state the time and date, the place, and the nature of the hearing. Hearings must be noticed for and held at times previously approved by the court.

[Adopted July 12, 2001, effective January 1, 2002, 464 Mich.]

Rule 5.103   Who May Serve

(A) Qualifications. Service may be made by any adult or emancipated minor, including an interested person.

(B) Service in a Governmental Institution. Personal service on a person in a governmental institution, hospital, or home must be made by the person in charge of the institution or a person designated by that person.

[Adopted July 12, 2001, effective January 1, 2002, 464 Mich.]

Rule 5.104   Proof of Service; Waiver and Consent; Unopposed Petition

(A) Proof of Service.

(1) Whenever service is required by statute or court rule, a proof of service must be filed promptly and before a hearing to which the document relates. If the document does not involve a hearing, a proof of service must be filed with the document. The proof of service must include a description of the documents served, the date of service, the manner and method of service, and the person or persons served.

(2) Except as otherwise provided by rule, proof of service of a document required or permitted to be served may be by

(a) including it at the end of the notice of hearing or other documents being filed with the court, or;

(b) a written statement by the individual who served the notice of hearing or other documents, verified under MCR 1.109(D)(3).

(3) Subrule (A)(1) notwithstanding, in decedent estates, no proof of service need be filed in connection with informal proceedings or unsupervised administration unless required by court rule.

(4) In unsupervised administration of a trust, subrule (A)(1) notwithstanding, no proof of service need be filed unless required by court rule.

(B) Waiver and Consent.

(1) *Waiver.* The right to notice of hearing may be waived. The waiver must

(a) be stated on the record at the hearing, or

(b) be in a writing, which is dated and signed by the interested person or someone authorized to consent on the interested person's behalf and specifies the hearing to which it applies.

(2) *Consent.* The relief requested in an application, petition, or motion may be granted by consent. An interested person who consents to an application, petition, or motion does not have to be served with or waive notice of hearing on the application, petition, or motion. The consent must

(a) be stated on the record at the hearing, or

(b) be in a writing which is dated and signed by the interested person or someone authorized to consent on the interested person's behalf and must contain a statement that the person signing has received a copy of the application, petition, or motion.

(3) *Who May Waive and Consent.* A waiver and a consent may be made

(a) by a legally competent interested person;

(b) by a person designated in these rules as eligible to be served on behalf of an interested person who is a legally disabled person; or

(c) on behalf of an interested person whether competent or legally disabled, by an attorney who has previously filed a written appearance.

However, a guardian, conservator, or trustee cannot waive or consent with regard to petitions, motions, accounts, or reports made by that person as guardian, conservator, or trustee.

(4) *Order.* If all interested persons have consented, the order may be entered immediately.

(C) Unopposed Petition. If a petition is unopposed at the time set for the hearing, the court may either grant the petition on the basis of the recitations in the petition or conduct a hearing. However, an order determining heirs based on an uncontested petition to determine heirs may only be entered on the basis of testimony or a completed SCAO–approved testimony identifying heirs form verified under MCR 1.109(D)(3). An order granting a petition to appoint a guardian may only be entered on the basis of testimony at a hearing.

[Adopted July 12, 2001, effective January 1, 2002, 464 Mich. Amended December 18, 2001, effective May 1, 2002, 465 Mich; August 30, 2018, effective September 1, 2018, 502 Mich; March 20, 2019, effective May 1, 2019, 502 Mich.]

Comments

Staff Comment to 2002 Adoption

Subrule (A)(3) is new [effective January 1, 2002]. It indicates that proofs of service are not required in unsupervised administration except where a rule specifically requires it. See, for instance, MCR 5.309(C)(3). The last clause of subrule (B)(4) is deleted. See MCR 5.308(B)(1). New subrule (C) creates a procedure for granting unopposed petitions without a hearing.

Staff Comment to 2002 Amendment

The December 18, 2001 amendments, effective May 1, 2002, updated various rules in light of the Estates and Protected Individuals Code (EPIC), MCL 700.1101 *et seq.*, and revisions made to EPIC by 2000 PA 312, 313, and 469.

Staff Comment to 2018 Amendment

These amendments update cross-references in the rules, and are intended to reflect changes that are necessary as a result of the Court's recent e-Filing rules amendments.

Staff Comment to 2019 Amendment

The amendments of Rules 1.109, 2.102, 2.104, 2.106, 2.107, 2.117, 2.119, 2.403, 2.503, 2.506, 2.508, 2.518, 2.602, 2.603, 2.621, 3.101, 3.104, 3.203, 3.205, 3.210, 3.302, 3.607, 3.613, 3.614, 3.705, 3.801, 3.802, 3.805, 3.806, 4.201, 4.202, 4.303, 4.306, 5.001, 5.104, 5.105, 5.107, 5.108, 5.113, 5.117, 5.118, 5.119, 5.120, 5.125, 5.126, 5.132, 5.162, 5.202, 5.203, 5.205, 5.302, 5.304, 5.307, 5.308, 5.309, 5.310, 5.311, 5.313, 5.402, 5.404, 5.405, 5.409, 5.501, and 5.784 and addition of Rule 3.618 of the Michigan Court Rules are an expected progression necessary for design and implementation of the statewide electronic-filing system. These particular amendments will assist in implementing the goals of the project.

Rule 5.105   Manner and Method of Service

(A) Manner of Service.

(1) Service on an interested person may be by personal service within or without the State of Michigan.

(2) Unless another method of service is required by statute, court rule, or special order of a probate court, service may be made:

(a) to the current address of an interested person by registered, certified, or ordinary first-class mail, or

(b) by electronic service in accordance with MCR 1.109(G)(6)(a).

Foreign consul and the Attorney General may be served by mail or by electronic service in accordance with MCR 1.109(G)(6)(a).

(3) An interested person whose address or whereabouts is not known may be served by publication, if a declaration of intent to give notice by publication, verified under MCR 1.109(D)(3) is filed with the court. The declaration must set forth facts asserting that the address or whereabouts of the interested person could not be ascertained on diligent inquiry. Except in proceedings seeking a determination of a presumption of death based on absence pursuant to MCL 700.1208(2), after an interested person has once been served by publication, notice is only required on an interested person whose address is known or becomes known during the proceedings.

(4) The court, for good cause on ex parte petition, may direct the manner of service if

(a) no statute or court rule provides for the manner of service on an interested person, or

(b) service cannot otherwise reasonably be made.

(B) Method of Service.

(1) *Personal Service.*

(a) On an Attorney. Personal service of a document on an attorney must be made by

(i) handing it to the attorney personally;

(ii) leaving it at the attorney's office with a clerk or with some person in charge or, if no one is in charge or present, by leaving it in some conspicuous place there, or by electronically delivering a facsimile to the attorney's office;

(iii) if the office is closed or the attorney has no office, by leaving it at the attorney's usual residence with some person of suitable age and discretion residing there; or

(iv) sending the document by registered mail or certified mail, return receipt requested, and delivery restricted to the addressee; but service is not made for purpose of this subrule until the attorney receives the document.

(b) On Other Individuals. Personal service of a document on an individual other than an attorney must be made by

(i) handing it to the individual personally;

(ii) leaving it at the person's usual residence with some person of suitable age and discretion residing there; or

(iii) sending the document by registered mail or certified mail, return receipt requested, and delivery restricted to the addressee; but service is not made for purpose of this subrule until the individual receives the document.

(c) On Persons Other Than Individuals. Service on an interested person other than an individual must be made in the manner provided in MCR 2.105(C)-(G).

(2) *Mailing.* Mailing of a copy under this rule means enclosing it in a sealed envelope with first-class postage fully prepaid, addressed to the person to be served, and depositing the envelope and its contents in the United States mail. Service by mail is complete at the time of mailing.

(3) *Publication.* Service by publication must be made in the manner provided in MCR 5.106.

(4) *E-mail.* Unless otherwise limited or provided by this court rule or MCR 1.109(G)(6)(a)(ii), parties to a civil action or interested persons to a proceeding may agree to service by e-mail in the manner provided in and governed by MCR 2.107(C)(4).

(5) *Electronic Service.* Electronic service of a document shall be made in accordance with MCR 1.109(G)(6)(a) when required.

(C) Petitioner, Service Not Required. For service of notice of hearing on a petition, the petitioner, although otherwise an interested person, is presumed to have waived notice and consented to the petition, unless the petition expressly indicates that the petitioner does not waive notice and does not consent to the granting of the requested prayers without a hearing. Although a petitioner or a fiduciary may in fact be an interested person, the petitioner need not indicate, either by written waiver or proof of service, that the petitioner has received a copy of any document required by these rules to be served on interested persons.

(D) Service on Persons Under Legal Disability or Otherwise Legally Represented. In a guardianship or conservatorship proceeding, a petition or notice of hearing asking for an order that affects the ward or protected individual must be served on that ward or protected individual if he or she is 14 years of age or older. In all other circumstances, service on an interested person under legal disability or otherwise legally represented must be made on the following:

(1) The guardian of an adult, conservator, or guardian ad litem of a minor or other legally incapacitated individual, except with respect to:

(a) a petition for commitment or

(b) a petition, account, inventory, or report made as the guardian, conservator, or guardian ad litem.

(2) The trustee of a trust with respect to a beneficiary of the trust, except that the trustee may not be served on behalf of the beneficiary on petitions, accounts, or reports made by the trustee as trustee or as personal representative of the settlor's estate.

(3) The guardian ad litem of any person, including an unascertained or unborn person, except as otherwise provided in subrule (D)(1).

(4) A parent of a minor with whom the minor resides, provided the interest of the parent in the outcome of the hearing is not in conflict with the interest of the minor and provided the parent has filed an appearance on behalf of the minor.

(5) The attorney for an interested person who has filed a written appearance in the proceeding. If the appearance is in the name of the office of the United States attorney, the counsel for the Veterans' Administration, the Attorney General, the prosecuting attorney, or the county or municipal corporation counsel, by a specifically designated attorney, service must be directed to the attention of the designated attorney at the address stated in the written appearance.

(6) The agent of an interested person under an unrevoked power of attorney filed with the court. A power of attorney is deemed unrevoked until written revocation is filed or it is revoked by operation of law.

For purposes of service, an emancipated minor without a guardian or conservator is not deemed to be under legal disability.

(E) Service on Beneficiaries of Future Interests. A notice that must be served on unborn or unascertained interested persons not represented by a fiduciary or guardian ad litem is considered served on the unborn or unascertained interested persons if it is served as provided in this subrule.

(1) If an interest is limited to persons in being and the same interest is further limited to the happening of a future event to unascertained or unborn persons, notice and documents must be served on the persons to whom the interest is first limited.

(2) If an interest is limited to persons whose existence as a class is conditioned on some future event, notice and documents must be served on the persons in being who would comprise the class if the required event had taken place immediately before the time when the documents are served.

(3) If a case is not covered by subrule (E)(1) or (2), notice and documents must be served on all known persons whose interests are substantially identical to those of the unascertained or unborn interested persons.

[Adopted July 12, 2001, effective January 1, 2002, 464 Mich. Amended January 14, 2009, effective May 1, 2009, 483 Mich; February 2, 2010, effective April 1, 2010, 485 Mich; August 30, 2018, effective September 1, 2018, 502 Mich. Amended March 20, 2019, effective May 1, 2019, 502 Mich.]

Comments

Staff Comment to 2001 Adoption

Notice of a petition to appoint a guardian or conservator must be served on the prospective ward or individual to be protected [effective January 1, 2002]. In addition, MCL 700.5219(2) and 700.5405(2) require service on a minor ward or a protected individual of petitions or orders after the fiduciary's appointment. However, the fiduciary may be served on behalf of these individuals under MCR 2.105(B)(3) in a civil action or a proceeding other than the protective proceeding relating to that individual.

Staff Comment to 2009 Amendment

These amendments were adopted primarily as a result of submissions by the Michigan Probate Judges Association and the State Bar of Michigan's Probate and Estate Planning Section. This was a joint effort to increase the oversight of guardianship and conservatorship proceedings, as well as to improve other procedures in probate court.

Staff Comment to 2010 Amendment

These changes, submitted by the Probate and Estate Planning Council of the State Bar of Michigan and the Michigan Probate Judges Association, have been designed so that the rules conform to recently-enacted statutory changes creating the Michigan Trust Code. The amendments correct and insert cross-references to the applicable statutory provisions, and make other technical changes. In addition, new MCR 5.208 incorporates the notice requirements for both decedent estates and trusts currently contained in MCR 5.306 and MCR 5.503, and replaces those rules.

Staff Comment to 2018 Amendment

These amendments update cross-references in the rules, and are intended to reflect changes that are necessary as a result of the Court's recent e-Filing rules amendments.

Staff Comment to 2019 Amendment

The amendments of Rules 1.109, 2.102, 2.104, 2.106, 2.107, 2.117, 2.119, 2.403, 2.503, 2.506, 2.508, 2.518, 2.602, 2.603, 2.621, 3.101, 3.104, 3.203, 3.205, 3.210, 3.302, 3.607, 3.613, 3.614, 3.705, 3.801, 3.802, 3.805, 3.806, 4.201, 4.202, 4.303, 4.306, 5.001, 5.104, 5.105, 5.107, 5.108, 5.113, 5.117, 5.118, 5.119, 5.120, 5.125, 5.126, 5.132, 5.162, 5.202, 5.203, 5.205, 5.302, 5.304, 5.307, 5.308, 5.309, 5.310, 5.311, 5.313, 5.402, 5.404, 5.405, 5.409, 5.501, and 5.784 and addition of Rule 3.618 of the Michigan Court Rules are an expected progression necessary for design and implementation of the statewide electronic-filing system. These particular amendments will assist in implementing the goals of the project.

Rule 5.106 Publication of Notice of Hearing

(A) Requirements. A notice of hearing or other notice required to be made by publication must be published in a newspaper as defined by MCR 2.106(F) one time at least 14 days before the date of the hearing, except that publication of a notice seeking a determination of a presumption of death based on absence pursuant to MCL 700.1208(2) must be made once a month for 4 consecutive months before the hearing.

(B) Contents of Published Notice. If notice is given to a person by publication because the person's address or whereabouts is not known and cannot be ascertained after diligent inquiry, the published notice must include the name of the person to whom the notice is given and a statement that the result of the hearing may be to bar or affect the person's interest in the matter.

(C) Affidavit of Publication. The person who orders the publication must cause to be filed with the court a copy of the publication notice and the publisher's affidavit stating

(1) the facts that establish the qualifications of the newspaper, and

(2) the date or dates the notice was published.

(D) Service of Notice. A copy of the notice:

(1) must be mailed to an interested person at his or her last known address if the person's present address is not known and cannot be ascertained by diligent inquiry;

(2) need not be mailed to an interested person if an address cannot be ascertained by diligent inquiry.

(E) Location of Publication. Publication must be in the county where the court is located unless a different county is specified by statute, court rule, or order of the court.

[Adopted July 12, 2001, effective January 1, 2002, 464 Mich.]

Comments

Staff Comment to 2001 Adoption

An example of the other notice referred to in subrule (A) [effective January 1, 2002] is found in MCR 5.309(C)(2).

Rule 5.107. Other Documents Required to be Served

(A) Other Documents to be Served. The person filing a petition, an application, a completed SCAO–approved testimony identifying heirs form, a completed SCAO–approved supplemental testimony identifying heirs form, a motion or objection, a response, an instrument offered or admitted to probate, an accounting, or a sworn closing statement with the court must serve a copy of that document on interested persons. The person who obtains an order from the court must serve a copy of the order on interested persons.

(B) Exceptions.

(1) Service of the papers listed in subrule (A) is not required to be made on an interested person whose address or whereabouts, on diligent inquiry, is unknown, or on an unascertained or unborn person. The court may excuse service on an interested person for good cause.

(2) Service is not required for a small estate filed under MCL 700.3982.

[Adopted July 12, 2001, effective January 1, 2002, 464 Mich. Amended March 20, 2019, effective May 1, 2019, 502 Mich.]

Comments

Staff Comment to 2019 Amendment

The amendments of Rules 1.109, 2.102, 2.104, 2.106, 2.107, 2.117, 2.119, 2.403, 2.503, 2.506, 2.508, 2.518, 2.602, 2.603, 2.621, 3.101, 3.104, 3.203, 3.205, 3.210, 3.302, 3.607, 3.613, 3.614, 3.705, 3.801, 3.802, 3.805, 3.806, 4.201, 4.202, 4.303, 4.306, 5.001, 5.104, 5.105, 5.107, 5.108, 5.113, 5.117, 5.119, 5.120, 5.125, 5.126, 5.132, 5.162, 5.202, 5.203, 5.205, 5.302, 5.304, 5.307, 5.308, 5.309, 5.310, 5.311, 5.313, 5.402, 5.404, 5.405, 5.409, 5.501, and 5.784 and addition of Rule 3.618 of the Michigan Court Rules are an expected progression necessary for design and implementation of the statewide electronic-filing system. These particular amendments will assist in implementing the goals of the project.

Rule 5.108 Time of Service

(A) Personal. Personal service of a petition or motion must be made at least 7 days before the date set for hearing, or an adjourned date, unless a different period is provided or permitted by court rule. This subrule applies regardless of conflicting statutory provisions.

(B) Mail.

(1) *Petition or Motion.* Service by mail of a petition or motion must be made at least 14 days before the date set for hearing, or an adjourned date.

(2) *Application by a Guardian or Conservator Appointed in Another State.*

(a) A court may appoint a temporary guardian or conservator without a hearing pursuant to MCL 700.5202a, MCL 700.5301a, or MCL 700.5433.

(b) If a court appoints a temporary guardian or conservator pursuant to MCL 700.5202a, MCL 700.5301a or MCL 700.5433, the temporary guardian or conservator must, not later than 14 days after the appointment, serve notice of the appointment by mail to all interested persons.

(C) Electronic Service. Electronic service made under MCR 1.109(G)(6)(a) must be made at least 7 days before the date set for hearing or an adjourned date.

(D) Exception: Foreign Consul. This rule does not affect the manner and time for service on foreign consul provided by law.

(E) Computation of Time. MCR 1.108 governs computation of time in probate proceedings.

(F) Responses. A written response or objection may be served at any time before the hearing or at a time set by the court.

[Adopted July 12, 2001, effective January 1, 2002, 464 Mich. Amended October 1, 2014, effective January 1, 2015, 497 Mich; March 20, 2019, effective May 1, 2019, 502 Mich.]

Comment

Staff Comment to 2015 Amendment

These Chapter 5 rule amendments, submitted to the Court by the Probate and Estate Planning Section of the State Bar of Michigan, comport to recent legislation regarding guardianships and conservatorships.

Staff Comment to 2019 Amendment

The amendments of Rules 1.109, 2.102, 2.104, 2.106, 2.107, 2.117, 2.119, 2.403, 2.503, 2.506, 2.508, 2.518, 2.602, 2.603, 2.621, 3.101, 3.104, 3.203, 3.205, 3.210, 3.302, 3.607, 3.613, 3.614, 3.705, 3.801, 3.802, 3.805, 3.806, 4.201, 4.202, 4.303, 4.306, 5.001, 5.104, 5.105, 5.107, 5.108, 5.113, 5.117, 5.118, 5.119, 5.120, 5.125, 5.126, 5.132, 5.162, 5.202, 5.203, 5.205, 5.302, 5.304, 5.307, 5.308, 5.309, 5.310, 5.311, 5.313, 5.402, 5.404, 5.405, 5.409, 5.501, and 5.784 and addition of Rule 3.618 of the Michigan Court Rules are an expected progression necessary for design and implementation of the statewide electronic-filing system. These particular amendments will assist in implementing the goals of the project.

Rule 5.109   Notice of Guardianship Proceedings Concerning Indian Child

If an Indian child is the subject of a guardianship proceeding and an Indian tribe does not have exclusive jurisdiction as defined in MCR 3.002(2):

(1) in addition to any other service requirements, the petitioner shall notify the parent or Indian custodian and the Indian child's tribe, by personal service or by registered mail with return receipt requested and delivery restricted to the addressee, of the pending proceedings on a petition to establish guardianship over the Indian child and of their right of intervention on a form approved by the State Court Administrative Office. If the identity or location of the parent or Indian custodian, or of the Indian child's tribe, cannot be determined, notice shall be given to the Secretary of the Interior by registered mail with return receipt requested. If a petition is filed with the court that subsequently identifies the minor as an Indian child after a guardianship has been established, notice of that petition must be served in accordance with this subrule.

(2) the court shall notify the parent or Indian custodian and the Indian child's tribe of all other hearings pertaining to the guardianship proceeding as provided in MCR 5.105. If the identity or location of the parent or Indian custodian, or of the Indian child's tribe, cannot be determined, notice of the hearings shall be given to the Secretary of the Interior. Such notice may be made by first-class mail.

[Adopted February 2, 2010, effective May 1, 2010, 485 Mich. Amended June 4, 2014, effective September 1, 2014, 496 Mich.]

Comment

Staff Comment to 2010 Adoption

These amendments incorporate provisions of the Indian Child Welfare Act into specific provisions within various rules relating to child protective proceedings and juvenile status offenses. The language is designed to make the rules reflect a more integrated approach to addressing issues specific to Indian children.

MCR 3.002(1)(c) defines "preadoptive placement" to mean the "temporary placement of an Indian child in a foster home or institution after the termination of parental rights, but before or in lieu of adoptive placement, and . . ." The phrase "in lieu of adoptive placement" is not intended to mean that it is permissible to leave a child in foster care indefinitely, in violation of MCL

712A.19b(6) or (7) or 45 CFR 1355.20, 45 CFR 1356.21, or 45 CFR 1356.50. Rather, it addresses situations where the parental rights to a child have been terminated and there is no permanency plan for adoption of the child. One example is when the child has been placed with a juvenile guardian and the guardianship is subsequently revoked. In this situation, jurisdiction over the child pursuant to MCL 712A.2(b) will be reinstated and the child is placed in foster care.

MCR 3.002(1): The definition of "child custody proceeding" is intended to apply the Indian Child Welfare Act to delinquency proceedings if an "Indian child" is charged with a so-called status offense in violation of MCL 712A.2(a)(2)–(4) or (d). Delinquency proceedings involving an Indian child charged with any other non-status offense are generally not subject to the Indian Child Welfare Act; however, if the initial investigation or subsequent review of a non-status delinquency case reveals that the Indian child involved suffers from child abuse or neglect, a separate child protective proceeding may be initiated, which would be subject to the Indian Child Welfare Act.

The amendment of MCR 3.905(C)(1) states that a court shall consider guidelines established by the Bureau of Indian Affairs (BIA) in determining whether good cause not to transfer exists (Guidelines for State Courts; Indian Child Custody Proceedings, 44 Fed Reg No 228, 67590–67592, C.2–C.4. [November 26, 1979]). Some examples of good cause are that the Indian tribe does not have a tribal court or that the Indian child is over 12 years old and objects to the transfer. For additional examples of good cause and relevant case law, see the BIA guidelines cited above and A Practical Guide to the Indian Child Welfare Act (Native American Rights Fund, A Practical Guide to the Indian Child Welfare Act [Boulder, CO: Native American Rights Fund, 2007], 7.15 and 7.16, p 60.)

Staff Comment to 2014 Amendment

These amendments incorporate provisions of the Michigan Indian Family Preservation Act and the Indian Child Welfare Act and reflect a more integrated approach to addressing issues specific to Indian children.

Rule 5.112   Prior Proceedings Affecting the Person of a Minor

Proceedings affecting the person of a minor subject to the prior continuing jurisdiction of another court of record are governed by MCR 3.205, including the requirement that petitions in such proceedings must contain allegations with respect to the prior proceedings.

[Adopted July 12, 2001, effective January 1, 2002, 464 Mich.]

Rule 5.113.   Form, Captioning, Signing, and Verifying of Documents

(A) Forms of Documents Generally. The form, captioning, signing, and verifying of documents are prescribed in MCR 1.109(D) and (E). If the State Court Administrative Office has approved a form for a particular purpose, it must be used when preparing that particular document for filing with the court. An application, petition, inventory, accounting, proof of claim, or proof of service must be verified in accordance with MCR 1.109(D)(3).

(B) Contents of Petitions.

(1) A petition must include allegations and representations sufficient to justify the relief sought and must:

(a) identify the petitioner, and the petitioner's interest in proceedings, and qualification to petition;

(b) include allegations as to residence, domicile, or property situs essential to establishing court jurisdiction;

(c) identify and incorporate, directly or by reference, any documents to be admitted, construed, or interpreted;

(d) include any additional allegations required by law or court rule;

(e) except when ex parte relief is sought, include a current list of interested persons, indicate the existence and form of incapacity of any of them, the mailing addresses of the persons or their representatives, the nature of representation and the need, if any, for special representation.

(2) The petition may incorporate by reference documents and lists of interested persons previously filed with the court if changes in the papers or lists are set forth in the incorporating petition.

(C) Filing by Registered Mail. Except as otherwise stated in this subrule, any document required by law to be filed in or delivered to the court by registered mail may be filed in accordance with MCR 1.109(G)(6)(a). Deliveries of wills or codicils must be delivered in accordance with MCL 700.2515 and 700.2516.

(D) Filing Additional Documents. The court in its discretion may receive for filing a document not required to be filed.
[Adopted July 12, 2001, effective January 1, 2002, 464 Mich. Amended December 18, 2001, effective May 1, 2002, 465 Mich; October 31, 2012, effective January 1, 2013, 493 Mich; May 30, 2018, effective September 1, 2018, 501 Mich; March 20, 2019, effective May 1, 2019, 502 Mich.]

Comments

Staff Comment to 2002 Adoption

Former subrule (C) is deleted because the matter is covered in MCR 8.119(C). New subrule (C) [effective April 1, 2000] allows a person otherwise required to file a document with the court by registered mail, to use certified mail, return receipt requested. New subrule (D) gives the court discretion to regulate the practice of filing papers in addition to those required to be filed.

Staff Comment to 2002 Amendment

The December 18, 2001 amendments, effective May 1, 2002, updated various rules in light of the Estates and Protected Individuals Code (EPIC), MCL 700.1101 et seq., and revisions made to EPIC by 2000 PA 312, 313, and 469.

Staff Comment to 2013 Amendment

The amendments of these rules update the rules making them less "paper" focused and reflecting the use of electronic technology in the way courts process court records. The amendments also clarify and delineate the types of records and other materials maintained by a court, and clarify how access is provided.

Staff Comment to 2018 Amendment

The amendments in this order are intended to begin moving trial courts toward a statewide uniform e-Filing process. In addition, the order moves existing language into MCR 1.109 as a way to, for the first time, include most filing requirements in one single rule, instead of scattered in various rules. The order largely mirrors the administrative orders that most e-Filing pilot projects have operated under, but contains some significant new provisions. For example, courts are required to maintain documents in an electronic document management system, and the electronic record is the official court record.

Staff Comment to 2019 Amendment

The amendments of Rules 1.109, 2.102, 2.104, 2.106, 2.107, 2.117, 2.119, 2.403, 2.503, 2.506, 2.508, 2.518, 2.602, 2.603, 2.621, 3.101, 3.104, 3.203, 3.205, 3.210, 3.302, 3.607, 3.613, 3.614, 3.705, 3.801, 3.802, 3.805, 3.806, 4.201, 4.202, 4.303, 4.306, 5.001, 5.104, 5.105, 5.107, 5.108, 5.113, 5.117, 5.118, 5.119, 5.120, 5.125, 5.126, 5.132, 5.162, 5.202, 5.203, 5.205, 5.302, 5.304, 5.307, 5.308, 5.309, 5.310, 5.311, 5.313, 5.402, 5.404, 5.405, 5.409, 5.501, and 5.784 and addition of Rule 3.618 of the Michigan Court Rules are an expected progression necessary for design and implementation of the statewide electronic-filing system. These particular amendments will assist in implementing the goals of the project.

Rule 5.114. Signing and Authentication of Papers [Repealed effective September 1, 2018.]

Rule 5.117   Appearance by Attorneys

(A) Representation of Fiduciary. An attorney filing an appearance on behalf of a fiduciary shall represent the fiduciary.

(B) Appearance.

(1) *In General.* An attorney may generally appear by an act indicating that the attorney represents an interested person in

the proceeding. A limited appearance may be made by an attorney for an interested person in a civil action or a proceeding as provided in MCR 2.117(B)(2)(c), except that any reference to parties of record in MCR 2.117(B)(2)(c) shall instead refer to interested persons. An appearance by an attorney for an interested person is deemed an appearance by the interested person. Unless a particular rule indicates otherwise, any act required to be performed by an interested person may be performed by the attorney representing the interested person.

(2) *Notice of Appearance.* If an appearance is made in a manner not involving the filing of a document served with the court or if the appearance is made by filing a document which is not served on the interested persons, the attorney must promptly file a written appearance and serve it on the interested persons whose addresses are known or who are authorized users of the electronic filing system under MCR 1.109(G)(6)(a) and on the fiduciary.

(3) *Appearance by Law Firm.*

(a) A pleading, appearance, motion, or other document filed by a law firm on behalf of a client is deemed the appearance of the individual attorney first filing a document in the action. All notices required by these rules may be served on that individual. That attorney's appearance continues until an order of substitution or withdrawal is entered. This subrule is not intended to prohibit other attorneys in the law firm from appearing in the action on behalf of the client.

(b) The appearance of an attorney is deemed to be the appearance of every member of the law firm. Any attorney in the firm may be required by the court to conduct a court-ordered conference or trial if it is within the scope of the appearance.

(C) Duration of Appearance by Attorney.

(1) *In General.* Unless otherwise stated in the appearance or ordered by the court, an attorney's appearance applies only in the court in which it is made or to which the action is transferred and only for the proceeding in which it is filed.

(2) *Appearance on Behalf of Fiduciary.* An appearance on behalf of a fiduciary applies until the proceedings are completed, the client is discharged, or an order terminating the appearance is entered.

(3) *Termination of Appearance on Behalf of a Personal Representative.* In unsupervised administration, the probate register may enter an order terminating an appearance on behalf of a personal representative if the personal representative consents in writing to the termination.

(4) *Other Appearance.* An appearance on behalf of a client other than a fiduciary applies until a final order is entered disposing of all claims by or against the client, or an order terminating the appearance is entered.

(5) *Limited Scope Appearances.* Notwithstanding other provisions in this section, limited appearances under MCR 2.117(B)(2)(c) may be terminated in accordance with MCR 2.117(C)(3), except that any reference to parties of record in MCR 2.117(B)(2)(c) shall instead refer to interested persons.

(6) *Substitution of Attorneys.* In the case of a substitution of attorneys, the court in a supervised administration or the probate register in an unsupervised administration may enter

an order permitting the substitution without prior notice to the interested persons or fiduciary. If the order is entered, the substituted attorney must give notice of the substitution to all interested persons and the fiduciary.

(D) Right to Determination of Compensation. An attorney whose services are terminated retains the right to have compensation determined before the proceeding is closed.

[Adopted July 12, 2001, effective January 1, 2002, 464 Mich. Amended March 20, 2019, effective May 1, 2019, 502 Mich; November 20, 2019, effective January 1, 2020, 503 Mich.]

Comments

Staff Comment to 2019 Amendment

The amendments of Rules 1.109, 2.102, 2.104, 2.106, 2.107, 2.117, 2.119, 2.403, 2.503, 2.506, 2.508, 2.518, 2.602, 2.603, 2.621, 3.101, 3.104, 3.203, 3.205, 3.210, 3.302, 3.607, 3.613, 3.614, 3.705, 3.801, 3.802, 3.805, 3.806, 4.201, 4.202, 4.303, 4.306, 5.001, 5.104, 5.105, 5.107, 5.108, 5.113, 5.117, 5.118, 5.119, 5.120, 5.125, 5.126, 5.132, 5.162, 5.202, 5.203, 5.205, 5.302, 5.304, 5.307, 5.308, 5.309, 5.310, 5.311, 5.313, 5.402, 5.404, 5.405, 5.409, 5.501, and 5.784 and addition of Rule 3.618 of the Michigan Court Rules are an expected progression necessary for design and implementation of the statewide electronic-filing system. These particular amendments will assist in implementing the goals of the project.

Staff Comment to 2020 Amendment

The amendment of MCR 5.117 clarifies that the rules authorizing limited scope representation are explicitly applicable to civil cases and proceedings in probate court.

Rule 5.118. Amending or Supplementing Documents

(A) Documents Subject to Hearing. A person who has filed a document that is subject to a hearing may amend or supplement the document

(1) before a hearing if notice is given pursuant to these rules, or

(2) at the hearing without new notice of hearing if the court determines that material prejudice would not result to the substantial rights of the person to whom the notice should have been directed.

(B) Documents Not Subject to Hearing. A person who has filed a document that is not subject to a hearing may amend or supplement the document if service is made pursuant to these rules.

[Adopted July 12, 2001, effective January 1, 2002, 464 Mich. Amended March 20, 2019, effective May 1, 2019, 502 Mich.]

Comments

Staff Comment to 2019 Amendment

The amendments of Rules 1.109, 2.102, 2.104, 2.106, 2.107, 2.117, 2.119, 2.403, 2.503, 2.506, 2.508, 2.518, 2.602, 2.603, 2.621, 3.101, 3.104, 3.203, 3.205, 3.210, 3.302, 3.607, 3.613, 3.614, 3.705, 3.801, 3.802, 3.805, 3.806, 4.201, 4.202, 4.303, 4.306, 5.001, 5.104, 5.105, 5.107, 5.108, 5.113, 5.117, 5.118, 5.119, 5.120, 5.125, 5.126, 5.132, 5.162, 5.202, 5.203, 5.205, 5.302, 5.304, 5.307, 5.308, 5.309, 5.310, 5.311, 5.313, 5.402, 5.404, 5.405, 5.409, 5.501, and 5.784 and addition of Rule 3.618 of the Michigan Court Rules are an expected progression necessary for design and implementation of the statewide electronic-filing system. These particular amendments will assist in implementing the goals of the project.

Rule 5.119 Additional Petitions; Objections; Hearing Practices

(A) Right to Hearing, New Matter. An interested person may, within the period allowed by law or these rules, file a petition and obtain a hearing with respect to the petition. The petitioner must serve copies of the petition and notice of hearing on the fiduciary and other interested persons whose addresses are known or who are authorized users of the electronic filing system under MCR 1.109(G)(6)(a).

(B) Objection to Pending Matter. An interested person may object to a pending petition orally at the hearing or by filing and serving a document which conforms with MCR 1.109(D) and MCR 5.113. The court may adjourn a hearing based on an oral objection and require that a proper written objection be filed and served.

(C) Adjournment. A petition that is not heard on the day for which it is noticed, in the absence of a special order, stands adjourned from day to day or until a day certain.

(D) Briefs; Argument. The court may require that briefs of law and fact and proposed orders be filed as a condition precedent to oral argument. The court may limit oral argument.

[Adopted July 12, 2001, effective January 1, 2002, 464 Mich. Amended August 30, 2018, effective September 1, 2018, 502 Mich; March 20, 2019, effective May 1, 2019, 502 Mich.]

Comments

Staff Comment to 2018 Amendment

These amendments update cross-references in the rules, and are intended to reflect changes that are necessary as a result of the Court's recent e-Filing rules amendments.

Staff Comment to 2019 Amendment

The amendments of Rules 1.109, 2.102, 2.104, 2.106, 2.107, 2.117, 2.119, 2.403, 2.503, 2.506, 2.508, 2.518, 2.602, 2.603, 2.621, 3.101, 3.104, 3.203, 3.205, 3.210, 3.302, 3.607, 3.613, 3.614, 3.705, 3.801, 3.802, 3.805, 3.806, 4.201, 4.202, 4.303, 4.306, 5.001, 5.104, 5.105, 5.107, 5.108, 5.113, 5.117, 5.118, 5.119, 5.120, 5.125, 5.126, 5.132, 5.162, 5.202, 5.203, 5.205, 5.302, 5.304, 5.307, 5.308, 5.309, 5.310, 5.311, 5.313, 5.402, 5.404, 5.405, 5.409, 5.501, and 5.784 and addition of Rule 3.618 of the Michigan Court Rules are an expected progression necessary for design and implementation of the statewide electronic-filing system. These particular amendments will assist in implementing the goals of the project.

Rule 5.120 Action by Fiduciary in Contested Matter; Notice to Interested Persons; Failure to Intervene

The fiduciary represents the interested persons in a contested matter. The fiduciary must give notice to all interested persons whose addresses are known or who are authorized users of the electronic filing system under MCR 1.109(G)(6)(a) that a contested matter has been commenced and must keep such interested persons reasonably informed of the fiduciary's actions concerning the matter. The fiduciary must inform the interested persons that they may file a petition to intervene in the matter and that failure to intervene shall result in their being bound by the actions of the fiduciary. The interested person shall be bound by the actions of the fiduciary after such notice and until the interested person notifies the fiduciary that the interested person has filed with the court a petition to intervene.

[Adopted July 12, 2001, effective January 1, 2002, 464 Mich. Amended March 20, 2019, effective May 1, 2019, 502 Mich.]

Comments

Staff Comment to 2019 Amendment

The amendments of Rules 1.109, 2.102, 2.104, 2.106, 2.107, 2.117, 2.119, 2.403, 2.503, 2.506, 2.508, 2.518, 2.602, 2.603, 2.621, 3.101, 3.104, 3.203, 3.205, 3.210, 3.302, 3.607, 3.613, 3.614, 3.705, 3.801, 3.802, 3.805, 3.806, 4.201, 4.202, 4.303, 4.306, 5.001, 5.104, 5.105, 5.107, 5.108, 5.113, 5.117, 5.118, 5.119, 5.120, 5.125, 5.126, 5.132, 5.162, 5.202, 5.203, 5.205, 5.302, 5.304, 5.307, 5.308, 5.309, 5.310, 5.311, 5.313, 5.402, 5.404, 5.405, 5.409, 5.501, and 5.784 and addition of Rule 3.618 of the Michigan Court Rules are an expected progression necessary for design and implementation of the statewide electronic-filing system. These particular amendments will assist in implementing the goals of the project.

Rule 5.121 Guardian Ad Litem; Visitor

(A) Appointment.

(1) *Guardian Ad Litem.* The court shall appoint a guardian ad litem when required by law. If it deems necessary, the court may appoint a guardian ad litem to appear for and represent the interests of any person in any proceeding. The court shall state the purpose of the appointment in the order of appointment. The order may be entered with or without notice.

(2) *Visitor.* The court may appoint a visitor when authorized by law.

(B) Revocation. If it deems necessary, the court may revoke the appointment and appoint another guardian ad litem or visitor.

(C) Duties. Before the date set for hearing, the guardian ad litem or visitor shall conduct an investigation and shall make a report in open court or file a written report of the investigation and recommendations. The guardian ad litem or visitor need not appear personally at the hearing unless required by law or directed by the court. Any written report must be filed with the court at least 24 hours before the hearing or such other time specified by the court.

(D) Evidence.

(1) *Reports, Admission Into Evidence.* Oral and written reports of a guardian ad litem or visitor may be received by the court and may be relied on to the extent of their probative value, even though such evidence may not be admissible under the Michigan Rules of Evidence.

(2) *Reports, Review and Cross–Examination.*

(a) Any interested person shall be afforded an opportunity to examine and controvert reports received into evidence.

(b) The person who is the subject of a report received under subrule (D)(1) shall be permitted to cross-examine the individual making the report if the person requests such an opportunity.

(c) Other interested persons may cross-examine the individual making a report on the contents of the report, if the individual is reasonably available. The court may limit cross-examination for good cause.

(E) Attorney–Client Privilege.

(1) *During Appointment of Guardian Ad Litem.* When the guardian ad litem appointed to represent the interest of a person is an attorney, that appointment does not create an attorney-client relationship. Communications between that person and the guardian ad litem are not subject to the attorney-client privilege. The guardian ad litem must inform the person whose interests are represented of this lack of privilege as soon as practicable after appointment. The guardian ad litem may report or testify about any communication with the person whose interests are represented.

(2) *Later Appointment as Attorney.* If the appointment of the guardian ad litem is terminated and the same individual is appointed attorney, the appointment as attorney creates an attorney-client relationship. The attorney-client privilege re-

lates back to the date of the appointment of the guardian ad litem.

[Adopted July 12, 2001, effective January 1, 2002, 464 Mich.]

Comments

Staff Comment to 2001 Adoption

This rule was MCR 5.201. Subrule (C) is amended by adding a requirement that a guardian ad litem file any written report with the court 24 hours before a hearing. This will provide the court and interested persons with some notice of the contents of the report. Any more notice would often be impractical. The 24 hour provision contains an exception that the court might specify another time for filing a report in an emergency.

Rule 5.125. Interested Persons Defined

(A) Special Persons. In addition to persons named in subrule (C) with respect to specific proceedings, the following persons must be served:

(1) The Attorney General must be served if required by law or court rule. The Attorney General must be served in the specific proceedings enumerated in subrule (C) when the decedent is not survived by any known heirs, or the protected person has no known presumptive heirs.

(2) A foreign consul must be served if required by MCL 700.1401(4) or court rule. An attorney who has filed an appearance for a foreign consul must be served when required by subrule (A)(5).

(3) On a petition for the appointment of a guardian or conservator of a person on whose account benefits are payable by the Veterans' Administration, the Administrator of Veterans' Affairs must be served through the administrator's Michigan district counsel.

(4) A guardian, conservator, or guardian ad litem of a person must be served with notice of proceedings as to which the represented person is an interested person, except as provided by MCR 5.105(D)(1).

(5) An attorney who has filed an appearance must be served notice of proceedings concerning which the attorney's client is an interested person.

(6) A special fiduciary appointed under MCL 700.1309.

(7) A person who filed a demand for notice under MCL 700.3205 or a request for notice under MCL 700.5104 if the demand or request has not been withdrawn, expired, or terminated by court order.

(8) In a guardianship proceeding for a minor, if the minor is an Indian child as defined by the Michigan Indian Family Preservation Act, MCL 712B.1 *et seq.*, the minor's tribe and the Indian custodian, if any, and, if the Indian child's parent or Indian custodian or tribe is unknown, the Secretary of the Interior.

(B) Special Conditions for Interested Persons.

(1) *Claimant.* Only a claimant who has properly presented a claim and whose claim has not been disallowed and remains unpaid need be notified of specific proceedings under subrule (C).

(2) *Devisee.* Only a devisee whose devise remains unsatisfied, or a trust beneficiary whose beneficial interest remains unsatisfied, need be notified of specific proceedings under subrule (C).

(3) *Trust as Devisee.* If either a trust or a trustee is a devisee, the trustee is the interested person. If no trustee has qualified, the interested persons are the qualified trust beneficiaries described in MCL 700.7103(g)(i) and the nominated trustee, if any.

(4) *Father of a Child Born out of Wedlock.* Except as otherwise provided by law, the natural father of a child born out of wedlock need not be served notice of proceedings in which the child's parents are interested persons unless his paternity has been determined in a manner provided by law.

(5) *Decedent as Interested Person.* If a decedent is an interested person, the personal representative of the decedent's estate is the interested person. If there is no personal representative, the interested persons are the known heirs of the estate of the decedent, and the known devisees. If there are no known heirs, the Attorney General must receive notice.

(C) Specific Proceedings. Subject to subrules (A) and (B) and MCR 5.105(E), the following provisions apply. When a single petition requests multiple forms of relief, the petitioner must give notice to all persons interested in each type of relief:

(1) The persons interested in an application or a petition to probate a will are the

   (a) devisees,

   (b) nominated trustee and qualified trust beneficiaries described in MCL 700.7103(g)(i) of a trust created under the will,

   (c) heirs,

   (d) nominated personal representative, and

   (e) trustee of a revocable trust described in MCL 700.7605(1).

(2) The persons interested in an application or a petition to appoint a personal representative, other than a special personal representative, of an intestate estate are the

   (a) heirs,

   (b) nominated personal representative, and

   (c) trustee of a revocable trust described in MCL 700.7605(1).

(3) The persons interested in a petition to determine the heirs of a decedent are the presumptive heirs.

(4) The persons interested in a petition of surety for discharge from further liability are the

   (a) principal on the bond,

   (b) co-surety,

   (c) devisees of a testate estate,

   (d) heirs of an intestate estate,

   (e) qualified trust beneficiaries, as referred to in MCL 700.7103(g)(i),

   (f) protected person and presumptive heirs of the protected person in a conservatorship, and

   (g) claimants.

(5) The persons interested in a proceeding for spouse's allowance are the

   (a) devisees of a testate estate,

   (b) heirs of an intestate estate,

   (c) claimants,

   (d) spouse, and

   (e) the personal representative, if the spouse is not the personal representative.

(6) The persons interested in a proceeding for examination or approval of an account of a fiduciary are:

   (a) for a testate estate, the devisees under the will (and if one of the devisees is a trustee or a trust, the persons referred to in MCR 5.125[B][3]),

   (b) for an intestate estate, the heirs,

   (c) for a conservatorship, the protected individual (if he or she is 14 years of age or older), the presumptive heirs of the protected individual, and the guardian ad litem, if any,

   (d) for a final conservatorship or guardianship account following the death of the protected person, the personal representative, if one has been appointed,

   (e) for a guardianship, the ward (if he or she is 14 years of age or older), the presumptive heirs of the ward, and the guardian ad litem, if any,

   (f) for a revocable trust, the settlor (and if the petitioner has a reasonable basis to believe the settlor is an incapacitated individual, those persons who are entitled to be reasonably informed, as referred to in MCL 700.7603[2]), the current trustee, and any other person named in the terms of the trust to receive either an account or a notice of such a proceeding, including a trust director,

   (g) for an irrevocable trust, the current trustee, the qualified trust beneficiaries, as defined in MCL 700.7103(g), and any other person named in the terms of the trust to receive either an account or a notice of such a proceeding, including a trust director,

   (h) in all matters described in this subsection (6), any person whose interests would be adversely affected by the relief requested, including a claimant or an insurer or surety who might be subject to financial obligations as the result of the approval of the account.

(7) The persons interested in a proceeding for partial distribution of the estate of a decedent are the

   (a) devisees of a testate estate entitled to share in the residue,

   (b) heirs of an intestate estate,

   (c) claimants, and

   (d) any other person whose unsatisfied interests in the estate may be affected by such assignment.

(8) The persons interested in a petition for an order of complete estate settlement under MCL 700.3952 or a petition for discharge under MCR 5.311(B)(3) are the

   (a) devisees of a testate estate,

   (b) heirs unless there has been an adjudication that decedent died testate,

   (c) claimants, and

   (d) such other persons whose interests are affected by the relief requested.

(9) The persons interested in a proceeding for an estate settlement order pursuant to MCL 700.3953 are the

   (a) personal representative,

   (b) devisees,

(c) claimants, and

(d) such other persons whose interests are affected by the relief requested.

(10) The persons interested in a proceeding for assignment and distribution of the share of an absent apparent heir or devisee in the estate of a decedent are the

(a) devisees of the will of the decedent,

(b) heirs of the decedent if the decedent did not leave a will,

(c) devisees of the will of the absent person, and

(d) presumptive heirs of the absent person.

(11) The persons interested in a petition for supervised administration after an estate has been commenced are the

(a) devisees, unless the court has previously found decedent died intestate,

(b) heirs, unless the court has previously found decedent died testate,

(c) personal representative, and

(d) claimants.

(12) The persons interested in an independent request for adjudication under MCL 700.3415 and a petition for an interim order under MCL 700.3505 are the

(a) personal representative, and

(b) other persons who will be affected by the adjudication.

(13) The persons interested in a petition for settlement of a wrongful-death action or distribution of wrongful-death proceeds are the

(a) heirs of the decedent,

(b) other persons who may be entitled to distribution of wrongful-death proceeds, and

(c) claimants whose interests are affected.

(14) The persons interested in a will contest settlement proceeding are the

(a) heirs of the decedent and

(b) devisees affected by settlement.

(15) The persons interested in a partition proceeding where the property has not been assigned to a trust under the will are the

(a) heirs in an intestate estate or

(b) devisees affected by partition.

(16) The persons interested in a partition proceeding where the property has been assigned to a trust under the will are the

(a) trustee and

(b) beneficiaries affected by the partition.

(17) The persons interested in a petition to establish the cause and date of death in an accident or disaster case under MCL 700.1208 are the heirs of the presumed decedent.

(18) The persons interested in a proceeding under the Mental Health Code that may result in an individual receiving involuntary mental health treatment or judicial admission of an individual with a developmental disability to a center are the

(a) individual,

(b) individual's attorney,

(c) petitioner,

(d) prosecuting attorney or petitioner's attorney,

(e) director of any hospital or center to which the individual has been admitted,

(f) the individual's spouse, if the spouse's whereabouts are known,

(g) the individual's guardian, if any,

(h) in a proceeding for judicial admission to a center, the community mental health program, and

(i) such other relatives or persons as the court may determine.

(19) The persons interested in a proceeding under the Mental Health Code in a petition for appointment of a guardian of an individual with a developmental disability are the

(a) individual,

(b) individual's attorney,

(c) petitioner,

(d) individual's presumptive heirs,

(e) preparer of the report or another appropriate person who performed an evaluation,

(f) director of any facility where the individual may be residing,

(g) individual's guardian ad litem, if appointed, and

(h) such other persons as the court may determine.

(20) The persons interested in an application for appointment of a guardian of a minor by a guardian appointed in another state and in a petition for appointment of a guardian of a minor are

(a) the minor, if 14 years of age or older;

(b) if known by the petitioner or applicant, each person who had the principal care and custody of the minor during the 63 days preceding the filing of the petition or application;

(c) the parents of the minor or, if neither of them is living, any grandparents and the adult presumptive heirs of the minor;

(d) the nominated guardian, and

(e) if known by the petitioner or applicant, a guardian or conservator appointed by a court in another state to make decisions regarding the person of a minor.

(21) The persons interested in the acceptance of parental appointment of the guardian of a minor under MCL 700.5202 are

(a) the minor, if 14 years of age or older,

(b) the person having the minor's care, and

(c) each grandparent and the adult presumptive heirs of the minor.

(22) The persons interested in a 7-day notice of acceptance of appointment as guardian of an incapacitated individual under MCL 700.5301 are the

(a) incapacitated individual,

(b) person having the care of the incapacitated individual, and

(c) presumptive heirs of the incapacitated individual.

(23) The persons interested in an application for appointment of a guardian of an incapacitated individual by a guardian

appointed in another state or in a petition for appointment of a guardian of an alleged incapacitated individual are

(a) the alleged incapacitated individual or the incapacitated individual,

(b) if known, a person named as attorney in fact under a durable power of attorney,

(c) the alleged incapacitated individual's spouse or the incapacitated individual's spouse,

(d) the alleged incapacitated individual's adult children and the individual's parents or the incapacitated individual's adult children and parents,

(e) if no spouse, adult child, or parent is living, the presumptive heirs of the individual,

(f) the person who has the care and custody of the alleged incapacitated individual or of the incapacitated individual,

(g) the nominated guardian, and

(h) if known by the petitioner or applicant, a guardian or conservator appointed by a court in another state to have care and control of the incapacitated individual.

(24) The persons interested in receiving a copy of the report of a guardian of a minor, or of a legally incapacitated individual, on the condition of a ward are:

(a) the ward, if 14 years of age or older;

(b) the person who has principal care and custody of the ward, if other than the guardian;

(c) for an adult guardianship, the spouse and adult children or, if no adult children are living, the presumptive heirs of the individual; and

(d) for a minor guardianship, the parents of the minor or, if neither of them is living, any grandparents and the adult presumptive heirs of the minor.

(25) The persons interested in an application for appointment of a conservator for a protected individual by a conservator appointed in another state or for the petition for the appointment of a conservator or for a protective order are:

(a) the individual to be protected if 14 years of age or older,

(b) the presumptive heirs of the individual to be protected,

(c) if known, a person named as attorney in fact under a durable power of attorney,

(d) the nominated conservator,

(e) a governmental agency paying benefits to the individual to be protected or before which an application for benefits is pending, and

(f) if known by the petitioner or applicant, a guardian or conservator appointed by a court in another state to manage the protected individual's finances.

(26) The persons interested in a petition for the modification or termination of a guardianship or conservatorship or for the removal of a guardian or a conservator are

(a) those interested in a petition for appointment under subrule (C)(20), (22), (23), or (25) as the case may be, and

(b) the guardian or conservator.

(27) The persons interested in a petition by a conservator for instructions or approval of sale of real estate or other assets are

(a) the protected individual and

(b) those persons listed in subrule (C)(25) who will be affected by the instructions or order.

(28) The persons interested in receiving a copy of an inventory or account of a conservator or of a guardian are:

(a) the protected individual or ward, if he or she is 14 years of age or older,

(b) the presumptive heirs of the protected individual or ward,

(c) the claimants,

(d) the guardian ad litem, and

(e) the personal representative, if any.

(29) The persons interested in a petition for approval of a trust under MCR 2.420 are

(a) the protected individual if 14 years of age or older,

(b) the presumptive heirs of the protected individual,

(c) if there is no conservator, a person named as attorney in fact under a durable power of attorney,

(d) the nominated trustee, and

(e) a governmental agency paying benefits to the individual to be protected or before which an application for benefits is pending.

(30) Interested persons for any proceeding concerning a durable power of attorney for health care are

(a) the patient,

(b) the patient's advocate,

(c) the patient's spouse,

(d) the patient's adult children,

(e) the patient's parents if the patient has no adult children,

(f) if the patient has no spouse, adult children, or parents, the patient's minor children, or, if there are none, the presumptive heirs whose addresses are known,

(g) the patient's guardian and conservator, if any, and

(h) the patient's guardian ad litem.

(31) Persons interested in a proceeding to require, hear, or settle an accounting of an agent under a power of attorney are

(a) the principal,

(b) the attorney in fact or agent,

(c) any fiduciary of the principal,

(d) the principal's guardian ad litem or attorney, if any, and

(e) the principal's presumptive heirs.

(32) Subject to the provisions of Part 3 of Article VII of the Estates and Protected Individuals Code, the persons interested in the modification or termination of a noncharitable irrevocable trust are:

(a) the qualified trust beneficiaries affected by the relief requested,

(b) the settlor,

(c) if the petitioner has a reasonable basis to believe the settlor is an incapacitated individual, the settlor's representative, as referred to in MCL 700.7411(6);

(d) the trust director, if any, as referred to in MCL 700.7103(m),

(e) the current trustee, and

(f) any other person named in the terms of the trust to receive notice of such a proceeding.

(33) Subject to the provisions of Part 3 of Article VII of the Estates and Protected Individuals Code, the persons interested in a proceeding affecting a trust other than those already covered by subrules (C)(6), (C)(29), and (C)(32) are:

(a) the qualified trust beneficiaries affected by the relief requested,

(b) the holder of a power of appointment affected by the relief requested,

(c) the current trustee,

(d) in a proceeding to appoint a trustee, the proposed trustee,

(e) the trust director, if any, as referred to in MCL 700.7103(m),

(f) the settlor of a revocable trust, and

(g) if the petitioner has a reasonable basis to believe the settlor is an incapacitated individual, those persons who are entitled to be reasonably informed, as referred to in MCL 700.7603(2).

(D) The court shall make a specific determination of the interested persons if they are not defined by statute or court rule.

(E) In the interest of justice, the court may require additional persons be served.

[Adopted July 12, 2001, effective January 1, 2002, 464 Mich. Amended December 18, 2001, effective May 1, 2002, 465 Mich; February 4, 2003, effective May 1, 2003, 467 Mich; July 1, 2004, effective September 1, 2004, 470 Mich. Amended effective January 8, 2008, 480 Mich; May 28, 2008, 481 Mich. Amended January 14, 2009, effective May 1, 2009, 483 Mich; February 2, 2010, effective April 1, 2010, 485 Mich; February 2, 2010, effective May 1, 2010, 485 Mich. Amended effective September 28, 2011, 490 Mich; May 7, 2014, 495 Mich. Amended June 4, 2014, effective September 1, 2014, 496 Mich; October 1, 2014, effective January 1, 2015, 497 Mich; May 23, 2018, effective September 1, 2018, 501 Mich; March 20, 2019, effective May 1, 2019, 502 Mich. Amended effective August 14, 2019, 503 Mich.]

Comments

Staff Comment to 2001 Adoption

This rule was MCR 5.205. The proceedings described in subrules (C)(27), (28), and (30) have been transferred to the exclusive jurisdiction of the family division of the circuit court. However, the subrules are left in place temporarily until development of rules for family division.

Staff Comment to 2002 Amendment

The December 18, 2001 amendments, effective May 1, 2002, updated various rules in light of the Estates and Protected Individuals Code (EPIC), MCL 700.1101 *et seq.*, and revisions made to EPIC by 2000 PA 312, 313, and 469.

Staff Comment to 2003 Amendment

The amendments of MCR 5.125(C) delete provisions listing interested parties in petitions for treatment of infectious disease and adoption proceedings, which are now within the jurisdiction of the family division of the circuit court. The substance of those provisions is included in MCR 3.615 and 3.800.

Staff Comment to 2004 Amendment

The July 1, 2004, amendment of MCR 5.125, effective September 1, 2004, added persons and entities such as insurers and sureties whose interests would be adversely affected to the list of interested persons who must receive notice of a proceeding for an examination of an account of a fiduciary.

Staff Comment to January, 2008 Amendment

The amendment of MCR 5.125 conforms the rule to language in MCL 700.5311 by clarifying that parents are interested persons entitled to notice in a petition for the appointment of a guardian of an alleged incapacitated individual, regardless of whether the alleged incapacitated individual has living adult children.

Staff Comment to May, 2008 Amendment

By this order, the Court retains the amendment of MCR 5.125 that conforms the rule to language in MCL 700.5311 by clarifying that parents are interested persons entitled to notice in a petition for appointment of a guardian for an alleged incapacitated individual, and further clarifies that only adult children are entitled to notice under this rule and the statute.

Staff Comment to 2009 Amendment

These amendments were adopted primarily as a result of submissions by the Michigan Probate Judges Association and the State Bar of Michigan's Probate and Estate Planning Section. This was a joint effort to increase the oversight of guardianship and conservatorship proceedings, as well as to improve other procedures in probate court.

Staff Comment to April, 2010 Amendment

These changes, submitted by the Probate and Estate Planning Council of the State Bar of Michigan and the Michigan Probate Judges Association, have been designed so that the rules conform to recently-enacted statutory changes creating the Michigan Trust Code. The amendments correct and insert cross-references to the applicable statutory provisions, and make other technical changes. In addition, new MCR 5.208 incorporates the notice requirements for both decedent estates and trusts currently contained in MCR 5.306 and MCR 5.503, and replaces those rules.

Staff Comment to May, 2010 Amendment

These amendments incorporate provisions of the Indian Child Welfare Act into specific provisions within various rules relating to child protective proceedings and juvenile status offenses. The language is designed to make the rules reflect a more integrated approach to addressing issues specific to Indian children.

MCR 3.002(1)(c) defines "preadoptive placement" to mean the "temporary placement of an Indian child in a foster home or institution after the termination of parental rights, but before or in lieu of adoptive placement, and . . ." The phrase "in lieu of adoptive placement" is not intended to mean that it is permissible to leave a child in foster care indefinitely, in violation of MCL 712A.19b(6) or (7) or 45 CFR 1355.20, 45 CFR 1356.21, or 45 CFR 1356.50. Rather, it addresses situations where the parental rights to a child have been terminated and there is no permanency plan for adoption of the child. One example is when the child has been placed with a juvenile guardian and the guardianship is subsequently revoked. In this situation, jurisdiction over the child pursuant to MCL 712A.2(b) will be reinstated and the child is placed in foster care.

MCR 3.002(1): The definition of "child custody proceeding" is intended to apply the Indian Child Welfare Act to delinquency proceedings if an "Indian child" is charged with a so-called status offense in violation of MCL 712A.2(a)(2)–(4) or (d). Delinquency proceedings involving an Indian child charged with any other non-status offense are generally not subject to the Indian Child Welfare Act; however, if the initial investigation or subsequent review of a non-status delinquency case reveals that the Indian child involved suffers from child abuse or neglect, a separate child protective proceeding may be initiated, which would be subject to the Indian Child Welfare Act.

The amendment of MCR 3.905(C)(1) states that a court shall consider guidelines established by the Bureau of Indian Affairs (BIA) in determining whether good cause not to transfer exists (Guidelines for State Courts; Indian Child Custody Proceedings, 44 Fed Reg No 228, 67590–67592, C.2–C.4. [November 26, 1979]). Some examples of good cause are that the Indian tribe does not have a tribal court or that the Indian child is over 12 years old and objects to the transfer. For additional examples of good cause and relevant case law, see the BIA guidelines cited above and A Practical Guide to the Indian Child Welfare Act. (Native American Rights Fund, A Practical Guide to the Indian Child Welfare Act [Boulder, CO: Native American Rights Fund, 2007], 7.15 and 7.16, p 60.)

Staff Comment to 2011 Amendment

The above noted changes are minor revisions of the rules that have been recommended to the Court to correct cross references and to reflect other technical changes.

Staff Comment to May, 2014 Amendment

These amendments reflect changes that correct minor technical errors that have occurred in drafting or the changes respond to recent adopted rule revisions, which occasionally inadvertently create incorrect cross-references in other rules.

Staff Comment to September, 2014 Amendment

These amendments incorporate provisions of the Michigan Indian Family Preservation Act and the Indian Child Welfare Act and reflect a more integrated approach to addressing issues specific to Indian children.

Staff Comment to 2015 Amendment

These Chapter 5 rule amendments, submitted to the Court by the Probate and Estate Planning Section of the State Bar of Michigan, comport to recent legislation regarding guardianships and conservatorships.

Staff Comment to 2018 Amendment

The amendment of MCR 5.125(C)(22) ensures that minor children of an alleged legally incapacitated person receive notice of a petition as presumptive heirs. The amendment of MCR 5.125(C)(23) was submitted by the Representative Assembly of the State Bar of Michigan, and clarifies the definition of persons interested in receiving a copy of a guardianship report for a minor, as referenced by MCL 700.5215, and expressly distinguishes between adult and minor guardianships.

Staff Comment to May, 2019 Amendment

The amendments of Rules 1.109, 2.102, 2.104, 2.106, 2.107, 2.117, 2.119, 2.403, 2.503, 2.506, 2.508, 2.518, 2.602, 2.603, 2.621, 3.101, 3.104, 3.203, 3.205, 3.210, 3.302, 3.607, 3.613, 3.614, 3.705, 3.801, 3.802, 3.805, 3.806, 4.201, 4.202, 4.303, 4.306, 5.001, 5.104, 5.105, 5.107, 5.108, 5.113, 5.117, 5.118, 5.119, 5.120, 5.125, 5.126, 5.132, 5.162, 5.202, 5.203, 5.205, 5.302, 5.304, 5.307, 5.308, 5.309, 5.310, 5.311, 5.313, 5.402, 5.404, 5.405, 5.409, 5.501, and 5.784 and addition of Rule 3.618 of the Michigan Court Rules are an expected progression necessary for design and implementation of the statewide electronic-filing system. These particular amendments will assist in implementing the goals of the project.

Staff Comment to August, 2019 Amendment

These amendments update cross-references and make other nonsubstantive revisions to clarify the rules.

Rule 5.126   Demand or Request for Notice

(A) Applicability. For purposes of this rule "demand" means a demand or request. This rule governs the procedures to be followed regarding a person who files a demand for notice pursuant to MCL 700.3205 or MCL 700.5104. This person under both sections is referred to as a "demandant."

(B) Procedure.

(1) *Obligation to Provide Notice or Copies of Documents.* Except in small estates under MCL 700.3982 and MCL 700.3983, the person responsible for serving a document in a decedent estate, guardianship, or conservatorship in which a demand for notice is filed is responsible for providing copies of any orders and filings pertaining to the proceeding in which the demandant has requested notification. If no proceeding is pending at the time the demand is filed, the court must notify the petitioner or applicant at the time of filing that a demand for notice has been filed and of the responsibility to provide notice to the demandant.

(2) *Rights and Obligations of Demandant.*

(a) The demandant must serve on interested persons a copy of a demand for notice filed after a proceeding has been commenced.

(b) Unless the demand for notice is limited to a specified class of documents, the demandant is entitled to receive copies of all orders and filings subsequent to the filing of the demand. The copies must be served on the demandant through the electronic filing system if the demandant is an authorized user under MCR 1.109(G)(6)(a), but if not, mailed to the address specified in the demand. If the copies are undeliverable, no further copies of documents need be provided to the demandant.

(C) Termination, Withdrawal.

(1) *Termination on Disqualification of Demandant.* The fiduciary or an interested person may petition the court to determine that a person who filed a demand for notice does not meet the requirements of statute or court rule to receive notification. The court on its own motion may require the

demandant to show cause why the demand should not be stricken.

(2) *Expiration of Demand When no Proceeding is Opened.* If a proceeding is not opened, the demand expires three years from the date the demand is filed.

(3) *Withdrawal.* The demandant may withdraw the demand at any time by communicating the withdrawal in writing to the fiduciary and to the court. If withdrawn, the demandant shall not continue to be served with documents in the case.

[Adopted July 12, 2001, effective January 1, 2002, 464 Mich; March 20, 2019, effective May 1, 2019, 502 Mich.]

Comments

Staff Comment to 2001 Adoption

This rule is new. It deals with the demand for notice in MCL 700.3205 and the request for notice in MCL 700.5104.

Staff Comment to 2019 Amendment

The amendments of Rules 1.109, 2.102, 2.104, 2.106, 2.107, 2.117, 2.119, 2.403, 2.503, 2.506, 2.508, 2.518, 2.602, 2.603, 2.621, 3.101, 3.104, 3.203, 3.205, 3.210, 3.302, 3.607, 3.613, 3.614, 3.705, 3.801, 3.802, 3.805, 3.806, 4.201, 4.202, 4.303, 4.306, 5.001, 5.104, 5.105, 5.107, 5.108, 5.113, 5.117, 5.118, 5.119, 5.120, 5.125, 5.126, 5.132, 5.162, 5.202, 5.203, 5.205, 5.302, 5.304, 5.307, 5.308, 5.309, 5.310, 5.311, 5.313, 5.402, 5.404, 5.405, 5.409, 5.501, and 5.784 and addition of Rule 3.618 of the Michigan Court Rules are an expected progression necessary for design and implementation of the statewide electronic-filing system. These particular amendments will assist in implementing the goals of the project.

Rule 5.127   Venue of Certain Actions

(A) Defendant Found Incompetent to Stand Trial. When a criminal defendant is found mentally incompetent to stand trial and is referred to the probate court for admission to a treating facility,

(1) if the defendant is a Michigan resident, venue is proper in the county where the defendant resides;

(2) if the defendant is not a Michigan resident, venue is proper in the county of the referring criminal court.

(B) Guardian of Property of Nonresident with a Developmental Disability. If an individual with a developmental disability is a nonresident of Michigan and needs a guardian for Michigan property under the Mental Health Code, venue is proper in the probate court of the county where any of the property is located.

(C) Guardian of Individual With a Developmental Disability Who is in a Facility. If venue for a proceeding to appoint a guardian for an individual with a developmental disability who is in a facility is questioned, and it appears that the convenience of the individual with a developmental disability or guardian would not be served by proceeding in the county where the individual with a developmental disability was found, venue is proper in the county where the individual with a developmental disability most likely would reside if not disabled. In making its decision, the court shall consider the situs of the property of the individual with a developmental disability and the residence of relatives or others who have provided care.

[Adopted July 12, 2001, effective January 1, 2002, 464 Mich.]

Comments

Staff Comment to 2001 Adoption

This rule was MCR 5.220.

Rule 5.128.   Change of Venue

Reasons for Change. On petition by an interested person or on the court's own initiative, the venue of a proceeding may be changed to another county by court order for the convenience of the parties and witnesses, for convenience of the attorneys, or if an impartial trial cannot be had in the county where the action is pending. Procedure for change of venue is governed by MCR 2.222 and MCR 2.223 except that a court must also transfer the original of an unadmitted will or a certified copy of an admitted will.

[Adopted July 12, 2001, effective January 1, 2002, 464 Mich. Amended effective September 28, 2011, 490 Mich. Amended September 18, 2019, effective January 1, 2020, 503 Mich.]

Comments

Staff Comment to 2001 Adoption

This rule was MCR 5.221.

Staff Comment to 2011 Amendment

The above noted changes are minor revisions of the rules that have been recommended to the Court to correct cross references and to reflect other technical changes.

Staff Comment to 2020 Amendment

The amendments of MCR 1.109, 2.107, 2.113, 2.116, 2.119, 2.222, 2.223, 2.225, 2.227, 3.206, 3.211, 3.212, 3.214, 3.303, 3.903, 3.921, 3.925, 3.926, 3.931, 3.933, 3.942, 3.950, 3.961, 3.971, 3.972, 4.002, 4.101, 4.201, 4.202, 4.302, 5.128, 5.302, 5.731, 6.101, 6.615, 8.105, and 8.119 and rescission of MCR 2.226 and 8.125 continue the process for design and implementation of the statewide electronic-filing system.

Rule 5.131.   Discovery Generally

(A) Civil Actions. Discovery for civil actions in probate court is governed by subchapter 2.300.

(B) Proceedings.

(1) *Discovery in General.* With the exception of mandatory initial disclosures under MCR 2.302(A), the discovery rules in subchapter 2.300 apply in probate proceedings, and, except as otherwise ordered by the court, any interested person in a probate proceeding is considered a party for the purpose of applying discovery rules.

(2) *Mandatory Initial Disclosure.*

(a) Demand or Objection. Mandatory disclosures under MCR 2.302(A) are required in probate proceedings if, by the time of the first hearing on the petition initiating the proceeding:

(i) an interested person other than the petitioner files a demand for mandatory initial disclosure and properly serves the demand on all interested persons or

(ii) an interested person objects to or otherwise contests the petition, in writing or orally, properly serves any written objection or response on all interested persons, and the judge determines mandatory initial disclosure is appropriate.

When mandatory initial disclosures are required through demand or objection, and except as otherwise ordered by the court, such disclosures must be made by the petitioner and any demandant or objecting interested person.

(b) Court Order. At any time, on its own motion or on a motion filed by an interested person, the court may require:

(i) mandatory disclosures and designate those interested persons who must make disclosures or

(ii) in a proceeding with some parties already making disclosures, an additional interested person or persons to make disclosures.

(c) Time for Initial Disclosures.

(i) The petitioner must serve initial disclosures within 14 days after the first hearing on the petition subject to a demand or objection.

(ii) The demandant or objecting interested person must serve initial disclosures within the later of 14 days after the petitioner's disclosures are due or 28 days after the demand or objection is filed.

(iii) When mandatory disclosures are ordered pursuant to MCR 5.131(B)(2)(b)(ii), an interested person's disclosures are due within 21 days after the court's order.

(3) *Scope of Discovery in Probate Proceedings.* Discovery in a probate proceeding is limited to matters raised in any petitions or objections pending before the court.

[Adopted July 12, 2001, effective January 1, 2002, 464 Mich. Amended June 19, 2019, effective January 1, 2020, 503 Mich.]

Comments

Staff Comment to 2002 Adoption

This rule was MCR 5.301. New subrule (B) clarifies that discovery in a probate proceeding is not available for the subject matter of a prospective civil action before the filing of such an action.

Staff Comment to 2020 Amendment

These amendments are based on a proposal created by a special committee of the State Bar of Michigan and approved for submission to the Court by the Bar's Representative Assembly. The rules require mandatory discovery disclosure in many cases, adopt a presumptive limit on interrogatories (20 in most cases, but 35 in domestic relations proceedings) and limit a deposition to 7 hours. The amendments also update the rules to more specifically address issues related to electronically stored information, and encourage early action on discovery issues during the discovery period.

The amendment of MCR 2.309(A)(2) sets a presumptive limit of twenty interrogatories for each separately represented party. Several commenters suggested that the term "discrete subpart" be more explicitly defined. But the rule's reference to "a discrete subpart" is intended to draw guidance from federal courts construing FR Civ P 30(a)(1). Generally, subparts are not separately counted if they are logically or factually subsumed within and necessarily related to the primary question. In upholding the limit, parties and courts should also pragmatically balance the overall goals of discovery and the admonition of MCR 1.105. Further, the intent of the provision at MCR 2.301(B)(4) is to ensure that parties responding to discovery requests have the full time period to do so as provided for under these rules prior to the expiration of the discovery period.

Rule 5.132.   Proof of Wills

(A) Deposition of Witness to Will. If no written objection has been filed to the admission to probate of a document purporting to be the will of a decedent, the deposition of a witness to the will or of other witnesses competent to testify at a proceeding for the probate of the will may be taken and filed without notice. However, the deposition is not admissible in evidence if at the hearing on the petition for probate of the will an interested person who was not given notice of the taking of the deposition as provided by MCR 2.306(B) objects to its use.

(B) Use of Copy of Will. When proof of a will is required and a deposition is to be taken, a copy of the original will or other document reproduced in accordance with the Records Reproduction Act, MCL 24.401 *et seq.* may be used at the deposition.

[Adopted July 12, 2001, effective January 1, 2002, 464 Mich; March 20, 2019, effective May 1, 2019, 502 Mich.]

Comments

Staff Comment to 2001 Adoption

This rule was MCR 5.302.

Staff Comment to 2019 Amendment

The amendments of Rules 1.109, 2.102, 2.104, 2.106, 2.107, 2.117, 2.119, 2.403, 2.503, 2.506, 2.508, 2.518, 2.602, 2.603, 2.621, 3.101, 3.104, 3.203, 3.205, 3.210, 3.302, 3.607, 3.613, 3.614, 3.705, 3.801, 3.802, 3.805, 3.806, 4.201, 4.202, 4.303, 4.306, 5.001, 5.104, 5.105, 5.107, 5.108, 5.113, 5.117, 5.118, 5.119, 5.120, 5.125, 5.126, 5.132, 5.162, 5.202, 5.203, 5.205, 5.302, 5.304, 5.307, 5.308, 5.309, 5.310, 5.311, 5.313, 5.402, 5.404, 5.405, 5.409, 5.501, and addition of Rule 3.618 of the Michigan Court Rules are an expected progression necessary for design and implementation of the statewide electronic-filing system. These particular amendments will assist in implementing the goals of the project.

Rule 5.133   Opening Wills Originally Filed for Safekeeping

If a will filed for safekeeping under MCL 700.2515 remains unopened 100 years after the date it was filed with a court, the will shall be opened by the probate register and maintained in accordance with MCR 8.302. Upon opening, the will shall be considered a will delivered after the death of the testator and shall be retained for the period prescribed in the record retention and disposal schedule established under MCR 8.119(K).

[Adopted May 25, 2016, effective January 1, 2017, 499 Mich.]

Comments

Staff Comment to 2016 Adoption

The amendments of MCR 3.925, 8.119, and 8.302 and the adoption of MCR 5.133 are an expected progression in the development of policies and procedures that standardize management of court records and provide a uniform basis for developing parameters on the use of technology in creating, accessing, routing, maintaining, and disposing of court records. These particular amendments will assist in implementing the goals of 2013 PA 199 and 201 and improving the policies and procedures adopted by the Court in 2012 under Administrative File No. 2006-47.

Rule 5.140   Use of Videoconferencing Technology

(A) Except as otherwise prescribed by this rule, upon request of any participant or sua sponte, the court may allow the use of videoconferencing technology under this chapter in accordance with MCR 2.407.

(B) In a mental health proceeding, if the subject of the petition wants to be physically present, the court must allow the individual to be present unless the court excludes or waives the physical presence of the subject pursuant to MCL 330.1455. This does not apply to proceedings concerning a person originally committed as a result of MCL 330.2050.

(C) In a proceeding concerning a conservatorship, guardianship, or protected individual, if the subject of the petition wants to be physically present, the court must allow the individual to be present. The right to be present for the subject of a minor guardianship applies only to a minor 14 years of age or older.

(D) The court may not use videoconferencing technology for a consent hearing required to be held pursuant to the Michigan Indian Family Preservation Act and MCR 5.404(B).

(E) Mechanics of Use. The use of videoconferencing technology under this chapter must be in accordance with the standards established by the State Court Administrative Office. All proceedings at which videoconferencing technology is used must be recorded verbatim by the court.

[Adopted September 21, 2016, effective January 1, 2017, 500 Mich. Amended December 14, 2016 effective January 1, 2017, 500 Mich.]

Comments

Staff Comment to 2016 Adoption

These amendments permit courts to expand the use of videoconferencing technology in many court proceedings, and clarify the proceedings at which videoconferencing technology may be used.

Staff Comment to 2016 Amendment

These amendments update cross-references and make other nonsubstantive revisions to clarify the rules.

Rule 5.141   Pretrial Procedures; Conferences; Scheduling Orders

The procedures of MCR 2.401 shall apply in a contested proceeding.

[Adopted July 12, 2001, effective January 1, 2002, 464 Mich.]

Comments

Staff Comment to 2001 Adoption

This rule was MCR 5.401.

Rule 5.142   Pretrial Motions in Contested Proceedings

In a contested proceeding, pretrial motions are governed by the rules that are applicable in civil actions in circuit court.

[Adopted July 12, 2001, effective January 1, 2002, 464 Mich.]

Comments

Staff Comment to 2001 Adoption

This rule was MCR 5.402.

Rule 5.143   Alternative Dispute Resolution

(A) The court may submit to mediation, case evaluation, or other alternative dispute resolution process one or more requests for relief in any contested proceeding. MCR 2.410 applies to the extent possible.

(B) If a dispute is submitted to case evaluation, MCR 2.403 and 2.404 shall apply to the extent feasible, except that sanctions must not be awarded unless the subject matter of the case evaluation involves money damages or division of property.

[Adopted July 12, 2001, effective January 1, 2002, 464 Mich.]

Rule 5.144.   Administratively Closed File

(A) Administrative Closing. The court may administratively close a file

(1) for failure to file a notice of continuing administration as provided by MCL 700.3951(3) or

(2) for other reasons as provided by MCR 5.203(D) or, after notice and hearing, upon a finding of good cause.

In a conservatorship, the court may administratively close a file only when there are insufficient assets in the estate to employ a successor or special fiduciary, or after notice and hearing upon a finding of good cause.

(B) Reopening Administratively Closed Estate. Upon petition by an interested person, with or without notice as the court directs, the court may order an administratively closed estate reopened. The court may appoint the previously appointed fiduciary, a successor fiduciary, a special fiduciary, or a special personal representative, or the court may order completion of the administration without appointing a fiduciary. In a decedent estate, the court may order supervised administration if it finds that supervised administration is necessary under the circumstances.

[Adopted July 12, 2001, effective January 1, 2002, 464 Mich. Amended effective November 15, 2005, 474 Mich; March 21, 2018, 501 Mich.]

Comments

Staff Comment to 2001 Adoption

This rule is new.

Staff Comment to 2005 Amendment

The amendments of MCR 5.144, 5.203, 5.207, 5.302, 5.307, 5.404, and 5.409, effective immediately, were developed as a result of the state court administrative office's statewide conservatorship case review prompted by the Performance Audit of Selected Probate Court Conservatorship Cases by the Michigan Office of the Auditor General and the State Bar of Michigan Probate and Estate Planning Section's Uniformity of Practice Committee's survey of probate court practices. The amendment of MCR 5.144(A)(2) eliminates the ability to close a conservatorship estate because of suspension of a fiduciary unless there are insufficient funds available to hire a special fiduciary, or after notice and hearing and a finding of good cause. The amendment of MCR 5.203(D) adds the financial institution and guardian ad litem to the list required to receive notice when a fiduciary is suspended. The amendment of MCR 5.207(A) allows for better court oversight when real property is sold. The amendment of MCR 5.302(A) requires that a copy of a death certificate be attached to the petition or application when commencing a decedent estate. In the event that the death certificate is not available, the petitioner may provide alternative documentation. The amendment of MCR 5.307(A) allows for the deduction of secured loans when calculating the inventory fee due. The amendment of MCR 5.404(A) creates a new subsection that requires the use of a SCAO approved social history form when one is required to be filed with a petition for guardianship of a minor. The amendment of MCR 5.409(B)(2) requires that joint property belonging to the protected person be listed on the inventory along with the type of ownership. The amendment of MCR 5.409(C)(1) clarifies that the fiduciary must serve the account on the interested persons and file the proof of service with the court. The amendment of MCR 5.409(C)(4) provides the process for filing a proof of restricted account and annual verification of funds on deposit with the court. The amendment of MCR 5.409(C)(5) adds the requirement to present a financial institution statement to the court when filing the annual account. The amendment of MCR 5.409(C)(6) requires the court to either review or allow the account annually and to hold a hearing on the accounts at least once every three years.

Staff Comment to 2018 Amendment

These amendments update cross-references and make other nonsubstantive revisions to clarify the rules. The amendment of MCR 6.110(B)(1) addresses an inadvertent omission from the last amendment of this rule that was intended to be shown in overstrike. Accordingly, the current rule does not match the published version. Striking the clause "for good cause shown" will provide consistency with other published versions of the rule and with the statute, MCL 766.7, which allows a magistrate to adjourn a preliminary examination with the consent of the parties without the need for good cause to be shown.

Rule 5.151   Jury Trial, Applicable Rules

Jury trials in probate proceedings shall be governed by MCR 2.508 through 2.516 except as modified by this subchapter or MCR 5.740 for mental health proceedings.

[Adopted July 12, 2001, effective January 1, 2002, 464 Mich. Amended February 4, 2003, effective May 1, 2003, 467 Mich.]

Comments

Staff Comment to 2001 Adoption

This rule was MCR 5.501.

Staff Comment to 2003 Amendment

The amendment of MCR 5.151 deletes the reference to Juvenile proceedings, which are no longer within the jurisdiction of the probate court.

Rule 5.158   Jury Trial of Right in Contested Proceedings

(A) Demand. A party may demand a trial by jury of an issue for which there is a right to trial by jury by filing in a manner provided by these rules a written demand for a jury trial within 28 days after an issue is contested. However, if trial is conducted within 28 days of the issue being joined, the jury demand must be filed at least 4 days before trial. A party who was not served with notice of the hearing at least 7 days before the hearing or trial may demand a jury trial at any time before the time set for the hearing. The court may adjourn the hearing in order to impanel the jury. A party may include the demand in a pleading if notice of the demand is included in the caption of the pleading. The jury fee provided by law must be paid at the time the demand is filed.

(B) Waiver. A party who fails to file a demand or pay the jury fee as required by this rule waives trial by jury. A jury is waived if trial or hearing is commenced without a demand being filed.

[Adopted July 12, 2001, effective January 1, 2002, 464 Mich.]

Comments

Staff Comment to 2001 Adoption

This rule was MCR 5.508. It covers how a party with a right to a jury trial may exercise that right. It does not purport to grant a right to a jury trial where none exists otherwise. Any such right is limited to a participant at the trial.

Rule 5.162   Form and Signing of Judgments and Orders

(A) Form of Judgments and Orders. A proposed judgment or order must be prepared in accordance with MCR 2.602(A) and MCR 1.109(D)(2).

(B) Procedure for Entry of Judgments and Orders. In a contested matter, the procedure for entry of judgments and orders is as provided in MCR 2.602(B).

[Adopted July 12, 2001, effective January 1, 2002, 464 Mich; March 20, 2019, effective May 1, 2019, 502 Mich.]

Comments

Staff Comment to 2001 Adoption

This rule was MCR 5.602.

Staff Comment to 2019 Amendment

The amendments of Rules 1.109, 2.102, 2.104, 2.106, 2.107, 2.117, 2.119, 2.403, 2.503, 2.506, 2.508, 2.518, 2.602, 2.603, 2.621, 3.101, 3.104, 3.203, 3.205, 3.210, 3.302, 3.607, 3.613, 3.614, 3.705, 3.801, 3.802, 3.805, 3.806, 4.201, 4.202, 4.303, 4.306, 5.001, 5.104, 5.105, 5.107, 5.108, 5.113, 5.117, 5.118, 5.119, 5.120, 5.125, 5.126, 5.132, 5.162, 5.202, 5.203, 5.205, 5.302, 5.304, 5.307, 5.308, 5.309, 5.310, 5.311, 5.313, 5.402, 5.404, 5.405, 5.409, 5.501, and 5.784 and addition of Rule 3.618 of the Michigan Court Rules are an expected progression necessary for design and implementation of the statewide electronic-filing system. These particular amendments will assist in implementing the goals of the project.

SUBCHAPTER 5.200   PROVISIONS COMMON TO MULTIPLE TYPES OF FIDUCIARIES

Rule 5.201   Applicability

Except for MCR 5.204 and MCR 5.208, which apply in part to trustees and trusts, rules in this subchapter contain requirements applicable to all fiduciaries except trustees and apply to all estates except trusts.

[Adopted July 12, 2001, effective January 1, 2002, 464 Mich. Amended February 2, 2010, effective April 1, 2010, 485 Mich.]

Staff Comment to 2001 Adoption

This rule is new. It addresses the matters formerly covered in MCR 5.715. The use of the term fiduciary in this subchapter differs from that in the Estates and Protected Individuals Code by excluding trustee. That exclusion is only for convenience of this subchapter which does not apply to trusts or trustees.

Staff Comment to 2010 Amendment

These changes, submitted by the Probate and Estate Planning Council of the State Bar of Michigan and the Michigan Probate Judges Association, have been designed so that the rules conform to recently-enacted statutory changes creating the Michigan Trust Code. The amendments correct and insert cross-references to the applicable statutory provisions, and make other technical changes. In addition, new MCR 5.208 incorporates the notice requirements for both decedent estates and trusts currently contained in MCR 5.306 and MCR 5.503, and replaces those rules.

Rule 5.202   Letters of Authority

(A) Issuance.   Letters of authority shall be issued after the appointment and qualification of the fiduciary. If bond is ordered, the letters shall be issued after proof of bond has been filed with the court, unless otherwise ordered. Unless ordered by the court, letters of authority will not have an expiration date.

(B) Restrictions and Limitations.   The court may restrict or limit the powers of a fiduciary. The restrictions and limitations imposed must appear on the letters of authority. The court may modify or remove the restrictions and limitations with or without a hearing.

(C) Certification.   A certification of the letters of authority and a statement that on a given date the letters are in full force and effect may appear on the face of copies furnished to the fiduciary or interested persons.

[Adopted July 12, 2001, effective January 1, 2002, 464 Mich. Amended December 18, 2001, effective May 1, 2002, 465 Mich; March 20, 2019, effective May 1, 2019, 502 Mich.]

Staff Comment to 2001 Adoption

This rule was MCR 5.716. Former subrule (B) is deleted because the subject matter is covered in MCL 700.3951. The remaining subrules are redesignated. The register may not impose restrictions in the letters of authority. One of the restrictions imposed by the court may be a limit on the length of time that the letters are effective. These rules use only the term "letters of authority" but the Estates and Protected Individuals Code uses other terms. See MCL 700.3504 and MCL 700.7504.

Staff Comment to 2002 Amendment

The December 18, 2001 amendments, effective May 1, 2002, updated various rules in light of the Estates and Protected Individuals Code (EPIC), MCL 700.1101 *et seq.*, and revisions made to EPIC by 2000 PA 312, 313, and 469.

Staff Comment to 2019 Amendment

The amendments of Rules 1.109, 2.102, 2.104, 2.106, 2.107, 2.117, 2.119, 2.403, 2.503, 2.506, 2.508, 2.518, 2.602, 2.603, 2.621, 3.101, 3.104, 3.203, 3.205, 3.210, 3.302, 3.607, 3.613, 3.614, 3.705, 3.801, 3.802, 3.805, 3.806, 4.201, 4.202, 4.303, 4.306, 5.001, 5.104, 5.105, 5.107, 5.108, 5.113, 5.117, 5.118, 5.119, 5.120, 5.125, 5.126, 5.132, 5.162, 5.202, 5.203, 5.205, 5.302, 5.304, 5.307, 5.308, 5.309, 5.310, 5.311, 5.313, 5.402, 5.404, 5.405, 5.409, 5.501, and 5.784 and addition of Rule 3.618 of the Michigan Court Rules are an expected progression necessary for design and implementation of the statewide electronic-filing system. These particular amendments will assist in implementing the goals of the project.

Rule 5.203   Follow–Up Procedures

Except in the instance of a personal representative who fails to timely comply with the requirements of MCL 700.3951(1), if it appears to the court that the fiduciary is not properly administering the estate, the court shall proceed as follows:

(A) Notice of Deficiency.   The court must notify the fiduciary, the attorney for the fiduciary, if any, and each of the sureties for the fiduciary of the nature of the deficiency, together with a notice to correct the deficiency within 28 days, or, in the alternative, to appear before the court or an officer designated by it at a time specified within 28 days for a conference concerning the deficiency. Service of the notice of deficiency is complete on mailing to the last known address of the fiduciary or when served under MCR 1.109(G)(6)(a).

(B) Conference, Memorandum.   If a conference is held, the court must prepare a written memorandum setting forth the date of the conference, the persons present, and any steps required to be taken to correct the deficiency. The steps must be taken within the time set by the court but not to exceed 28 days from the date of the conference. A copy of the memorandum must be given to those present at the conference. If the fiduciary is not present at the conference, a copy of the memorandum must be mailed to the last known address of the fiduciary or served on the fiduciary under MCR 1.109(G)(6)(a).

(C) Extension of Time.   For good cause, the court may extend the time for performance of required duties for a further reasonable period or periods, but any extended period may not exceed 28 days and shall only be extended to a day certain. The total period as extended may not exceed 56 days.

(D) Suspension of Fiduciary, Appointment of Special Fiduciary.   If the fiduciary fails to perform the duties required within the time allowed, the court may do any of the following: suspend the powers of the dilatory fiduciary, appoint a special fiduciary, and close the estate administration. If the court suspends the powers of the dilatory fiduciary or closes the estate administration, the court must notify the dilatory fiduciary, the attorney of record for the dilatory fiduciary, the sureties on any bond of the dilatory fiduciary that has been filed, any financial institution listed on the most recent inventory or account where the fiduciary has deposited funds, any currently serving guardian ad litem, and the interested persons at their addresses shown in the court file. This rule does not preclude contempt proceedings as provided by law.

(E) Reports on the Status of Estates.   The chief judge of each probate court must file with the state court administrator, on forms provided by the state court administrative office, any reports on the status of estates required by the state court administrator.

[Adopted July 12, 2001, effective January 1, 2002, 464 Mich. Amended effective November 15, 2005, 474 Mich. Amended March 20, 2019, effective May 1, 2019, 502 Mich.]

Staff Comment to 2001 Adoption

This rule was MCR 5.717. It applies to any potential improper administration of an estate, except for a failure to timely file a notice of continuing administration which is covered by MCL 700.3951.

Staff Comment to 2005 Amendment

The amendments of MCR 5.144, 5.203, 5.207, 5.302, 5.307, 5.404, and 5.409, effective immediately, were developed as a result of the state court administrative office's statewide conservatorship case review prompted by the Performance Audit of Selected Probate Court Conservatorship Cases by the Michigan Office of the Auditor General and the State Bar of Michigan Probate and Estate Planning Section's Uniformity of Practice Committee's survey of probate court practices. The amendment of MCR 5.144(A)(2) eliminates the ability to close a conservatorship estate because of suspension of a fiduciary unless there are insufficient funds available to hire a special fiduciary, or after notice and hearing and a finding of good cause. The amendment of MCR 5.203(D) adds the financial institution and guardian ad litem to the list required to receive notice when a fiduciary is suspended. The amendment of MCR 5.207(A) allows for better court oversight when real property is sold. The amendment of MCR 5.302(A) requires that a copy of a death certificate be attached to the petition or application when commencing a decedent estate. In the event that the death certificate is not available, the petitioner may provide alternative documentation. The amendment of MCR 5.307(A) allows for the deduction of secured loans when calculating the inventory fee due. The amendment of MCR 5.404(A) creates a new subsection that requires the use of a SCAO approved social history form when one is required to be filed with a petition for guardianship of a minor. The amendment of MCR 5.409(B)(2) requires that joint property belonging to the protected person be listed on the inventory along with the type of ownership. The amendment of MCR 5.409(C)(1) clarifies that the fiduciary must serve the account on the interested persons and file the proof of service with the court. The amendment of MCR 5.409(C)(4) provides the process for filing a proof of restricted account and annual verification of funds on deposit with the court. The amendment of MCR 5.409(C)(5) adds the requirement to present a financial institution statement to the court when filing the annual account. The amendment of MCR 5.409(C)(6) requires the court to either review or allow the account annually and to hold a hearing on the accounts at least once every three years.

Staff Comment to 2019 Amendment

The amendments of Rules 1.109, 2.102, 2.104, 2.106, 2.107, 2.117, 2.119, 2.403, 2.503, 2.506, 2.508, 2.518, 2.602, 2.603, 2.621, 3.101, 3.104, 3.203, 3.205, 3.210, 3.302, 3.607, 3.613, 3.614, 3.705, 3.801, 3.802, 3.805, 3.806, 4.201, 4.202, 4.303, 4.306, 5.001, 5.104, 5.105, 5.107, 5.108, 5.113, 5.117, 5.118, 5.119, 5.120, 5.125, 5.126, 5.132, 5.162, 5.202, 5.203, 5.205, 5.302, 5.304, 5.307, 5.308, 5.309, 5.310, 5.311, 5.313, 5.402, 5.404, 5.405, 5.409, 5.501, and 5.784 and addition of Rule 3.618 of the Michigan Court Rules are an expected progression necessary for design and implementation of the statewide electronic-filing system. These particular amendments will assist in implementing the goals of the project.

Rule 5.204   Appointment of Special Fiduciary

(A) Appointment. The court may appoint a special fiduciary or enjoin a person subject to the court's jurisdiction under MCL 700.1309 on its own initiative, on the notice it directs, or without notice in its discretion.

(B) Duties and Powers. The special fiduciary has all the duties and powers specified in the order of the court appointing the special fiduciary. Appointment of a special fiduciary suspends the powers of the general fiduciary unless the order of appointment provides otherwise. The appointment may be for a specified time and the special fiduciary is an interested person for all purposes in the proceeding until the appointment terminates.

[Adopted July 12, 2001, effective January 1, 2002, 464 Mich.]

Comments

Staff Comment to 2001 Adoption

This rule was MCR 5.718. It is amended to give the court maximum flexibility to use a special fiduciary to respond to reports of problems concerning a general fiduciary. See MCL 700.1309. This rule does not apply to a special personal representative under MCL 700.3614.

Rule 5.205   Address of Fiduciary

A fiduciary must keep the court and the interested persons informed in writing within 7 days of any change in the fiduciary's address even if the fiduciary is an authorized user of the electronic filing system. Any notice served on the fiduciary by the court to the last address on file or under MCR 1.109(G)(6)(a) shall be notice to the fiduciary.

[Adopted July 12, 2001, effective January 1, 2002, 464 Mich. Amended March 20, 2019, effective May 1, 2019, 502 Mich.]

Comments

Staff Comment to 2001 Adoption

This rule is new. The substance was formerly in MCR 5.707(B).

Staff Comment to 2019 Amendment

The amendments of Rules 1.109, 2.102, 2.104, 2.106, 2.107, 2.117, 2.119, 2.403, 2.503, 2.506, 2.508, 2.518, 2.602, 2.603, 2.621, 3.101, 3.104, 3.203, 3.205, 3.210, 3.302, 3.607, 3.613, 3.614, 3.705, 3.801, 3.802, 3.805, 3.806, 4.201, 4.202, 4.303, 4.306, 5.001, 5.104, 5.105, 5.107, 5.108, 5.113, 5.117, 5.118, 5.119, 5.120, 5.125, 5.126, 5.132, 5.162, 5.202, 5.203, 5.205, 5.302, 5.304, 5.307, 5.308, 5.309, 5.310, 5.311, 5.313, 5.402, 5.404, 5.405, 5.409, 5.501, and 5.784 and addition of Rule 3.618 of the Michigan Court Rules are an expected progression necessary for design and implementation of the statewide electronic-filing system. These particular amendments will assist in implementing the goals of the project.

Rule 5.206   Duty to Complete Administration

A fiduciary and an attorney for a fiduciary must take all actions reasonably necessary to regularly administer an estate and close administration of an estate. If the fiduciary or the attorney fails to take such actions, the court may act to regularly close the estate and assess costs against the fiduciary or attorney personally.

[Adopted July 12, 2001, effective January 1, 2002, 464 Mich. Amended January 14, 2009, effective May 1, 2009, 483 Mich.]

Comments

Staff Comment to 2001 Adoption

This rule is new.

Staff Comment to 2009 Amendment

These amendments were adopted primarily as a result of submissions by the Michigan Probate Judges Association and the State Bar of Michigan's Probate and Estate Planning Section. This was a joint effort to increase the oversight of guardianship and conservatorship proceedings, as well as to improve other procedures in probate court.

Rule 5.207   Sale of Real Estate

(A) Petition. Any petition to approve the sale of real estate must contain the following:

(1) the terms and purpose of the sale,

(2) the legal description of the property,

(3) the financial condition of the estate before the sale, and

(4) an appended copy of the most recent assessor statement or tax statement showing the state equalized value of the property. If the court is not satisfied that the evidence provides the fair market value, a written appraisal may be ordered.

(B) Bond. The court may require a bond before approving a sale of real estate in an amount sufficient to protect the estate.

[Adopted July 12, 2001, effective January 1, 2002, 464 Mich. Amended effective November 15, 2005, 474 Mich. Amended October 11, 2007, effective January 1, 2008, 479 Mich.]

Comments

Staff Comment to 2001 Adoption

This rule is new. Interested persons to be served notice of hearing on a sale of real estate are listed in MCR 5.125(C)(12) and (26) for decedent estates and conservatorships, respectively.

Staff Comment to 2005 Amendment

The amendments of MCR 5.144, 5.203, 5.207, 5.302, 5.307, 5.404, and 5.409, effective immediately, were developed as a result of the state court administrative office's statewide conservatorship case review prompted by the Performance Audit of Selected Probate Court Conservatorship Cases by the Michigan Office of the Auditor General and the State Bar of Michigan Probate and Estate Planning Section's Uniformity of Practice Committee's survey of probate court practices. The amendment of MCR 5.144(A)(2) eliminates the ability to close a conservatorship estate because of suspension of a fiduciary unless there are insufficient funds available to hire a special fiduciary, or after notice and hearing and a finding of good cause. The amendment of MCR 5.203(D) adds the financial institution and guardian ad litem to the list required to receive notice when a fiduciary is suspended. The amendment of MCR 5.207(A) allows for better court oversight when real property is sold. The amendment of MCR 5.302(A) requires that a copy of a death certificate be attached to the petition or application when commencing a decedent estate. In the event that the death certificate is not available, the petitioner may provide alternative documentation. The amendment of MCR 5.307(A) allows for the deduction of secured loans when calculating the inventory fee due. The amendment of MCR 5.404(A) creates a new subsection that requires the use of a SCAO approved social history form when one is required to be filed with a petition for guardianship of a minor. The amendment of MCR 5.409(B)(2) requires that joint property belonging to the protected person be listed on the inventory along with the type of ownership. The amendment of MCR 5.409(C)(1) clarifies that the fiduciary must serve the account on the interested persons and file the proof of service with the court. The amendment of MCR 5.409(C)(4) provides the process for filing a proof of restricted account and annual verification of funds on deposit with the court. The amendment of MCR 5.409(C)(5) adds the requirement to present a financial institution statement to the court when filing the annual account. The amendment of MCR 5.409(C)(6) requires the court to either review or allow the account annually and to hold a hearing on the accounts at least once every three years.

Staff Comment to 2007 Amendment

These amendments were proposed by the Probate and Estate Planning Section of the State Bar of Michigan, and are intended to address and clarify practice issues within the amended rules. The amendment of MCR 5.207(A)(4) provides the alternative of including a tax statement to show the state equalized value of property. The amendments of MCR 5.307(B) and MCR 5.409(B)(3) require the name and address of each financial institution be added to the inventory, and requires that the institution's main address or branch used most frequently by the filer be identified. The amendment of MCR 5.409(C)(1) requires any account filed with the court to comply with relevant court rules. The amendment of MCR 5.409(C)(4) extends the time in which to file proof of a minor's assets in a restricted account from 14 to 28 days. The amendment of MCR 5.409(C)(5) allows the option of filing an annual verification of funds on deposit or presenting a copy of a financial institution statement with an annual account.

Rule 5.208 Notice to Creditors, Presentment of Claims

(A) Publication of Notice to Creditors; Contents. Unless the notice has already been given, the personal representative must publish, and a special personal representative may publish, in a newspaper, as defined by MCR 2.106(F), in a county in which a resident decedent was domiciled or in which the proceeding as to a nonresident was initiated, a notice to creditors as provided in MCL 700.3801. The notice must include:

(1) The name, and, if known, the date of death, and date of birth of the decedent;

(2) The name and address of the personal representative;

(3) The name and address of the court where proceedings are filed; and

(4) A statement that claims will be forever barred unless presented to the personal representative, or to both the court and the personal representative within 4 months after the publication of the notice.

(B) Notice to Known Creditors and Trustee. A personal representative who has published notice must cause a copy of the published notice or a similar notice to be served personally or by mail on each known creditor of the estate and to the trustee of a trust of which the decedent is settlor, as defined in MCL 700.7605(1). Notice need not be served on the trustee if the personal representative is the trustee.

(1) Within the time limits prescribed by law, the personal representative must cause a copy of the published notice or a similar notice to be served personally or by mail on each creditor of the estate whose identity at the time of publication or during the 4 months following publication is known to, or can be reasonably ascertained by, the personal representative.

(2) If, at the time of the publication, the address of a creditor is unknown and cannot be ascertained after diligent inquiry, the name of the creditor must be included in the published notice.

(C) Publication of Notice to Creditors and Known Creditors by Trustee. A notice that must be published under MCL 700.7608 must include:

(1) The name, and, if known, date of death, and date of birth of the trust's deceased settlor;

(2) The trust's name or other designation;

(3) The date the trust was established;

(4) The name and address of each trustee serving at the time of or as a result of the settlor's death;

(5) The name and address of the trustee's attorney, if any and must be served on known creditors as provided in subrule (B) above.

(D) No Notice to Creditors. No notice need be given to creditors in the following situations:

(1) The decedent or settlor has been dead for more than 3 years;

(2) Notice need not be given to a creditor whose claim has been presented or paid;

(3) For a personal representative:

(a) The estate has no assets;

(b) The estate qualifies and is administered under MCL 700.3982, MCL 700.3983, or MCL 700.3987;

(c) Notice has previously been given under MCL 700.7608 in the county where the decedent was domiciled in Michigan.

(4) For a trustee, the costs of administration equal or exceed the value of the trust estate.

(E) Presentment of Claims. A claim shall be presented to the personal representative or trustee by mailing or delivering the claim to the personal representative or trustee, or the attorney for the personal representative or trustee, or, in the case of an estate, by filing the claim with the court and mailing or delivering a copy of the claim to the personal representative.

(F) A claim is considered presented

(1) on mailing, if addressed to the personal representative or trustee, or the attorney for the personal representative or trustee, or

(2) in all other cases, when received by the personal representative, or trustee or the attorney for the personal representative or trustee or in the case of an estate when filed with the court.

[Adopted February 2, 2010, effective April 1, 2010, 485 Mich. Amended May 17, 2011, effective September 1, 2011, 489 Mich. Amended effective September 5, 2013, 495 Mich. Amended October 1, 2014, effective January 1, 2015, 497 Mich.]

Comments

Staff Comment to 2010 Adoption

These changes, submitted by the Probate and Estate Planning Council of the State Bar of Michigan and the Michigan Probate Judges Association, have been designed so that the rules conform to recently-enacted statutory changes creating the Michigan Trust Code. The amendments correct and insert cross-references to the applicable statutory provisions, and make other technical changes. In addition, new MCR 5.208 incorporates the notice requirements for both decedent estates and trusts currently contained in MCR 5.306 and MCR 5.503, and replaces those rules.

Staff Comment to 2011 Amendment

The amendment of MCR 5.208 removes the requirement to list a decedent's last known address on the Notice to Creditors form.

Staff Comment to 2013 Amendment

These amendments reflect changes that correct minor technical errors that have occurred in drafting or the changes respond to recent adopted rule revisions, which occasionally inadvertently create incorrect cross-references in other rules.

Staff Comment to 2015 Amendment

These Chapter 5 rule amendments, submitted to the Court by the Probate and Estate Planning Section of the State Bar of Michigan, comport to recent legislation regarding guardianships and conservatorships.

SUBCHAPTER 5.300   PROCEEDINGS IN DECEDENT ESTATES

Rule 5.301   Applicability

The rules in this subchapter apply to decedent estate proceedings other than proceedings provided by law for small estates under MCL 700.3982.

[Adopted July 12, 2001, effective January 1, 2002, 464 Mich.]

Comments

Staff Comment to 2001 Adoption

This rule was MCR 5.701. Former subrule (B) is deleted because the term "temporary personal representative" has been replaced in the Estates and Protected Individuals Code (EPIC) by "special personal representative". The code defines special personal representative. MCL 700.1107(e).

Rule 5.302   Commencement of Decedent Estates

(A) Methods of Commencement. A decedent estate may be commenced by filing an application for an informal proceeding or a petition for a formal testacy proceeding. A request for supervised administration may be made in a petition for a formal testacy proceeding.

(1) When filing either an application or petition to commence a decedent estate, a copy of the death certificate must be attached. If the death certificate is not available, the petitioner may provide alternative documentation of the decedent's death.

(2) Where electronic filing is implemented, if the application or petition to commence a decedent estate indicates that there is a will, it is available, and that it is not already in the court's possession, an exact copy of the will and any codicils must be attached to the application or petition. Within 14 days of the filing of the application or petition, the original will and any codicils must be filed with the court or the case will be dismissed without notice and hearing. Notice of a dismissal for failure to file the original will and any codicils shall be served on the petitioner and any interested persons in a manner provided under MCR 5.105(B).

(3) The court is prohibited from requiring additional documentation, such as information about the proposed or appointed personal representative.

(B) Testimony Identifying Heirs Form. At least one completed SCAO–approved testimony identifying heirs and devisees form must be submitted with the application or petition that commences proceedings. A testimony identifying heirs form must be verified under MCR 1.109(D)(3).

(C) Preservation of Testimony. If a hearing is held, proofs included as part of the record are deemed preserved for further administration purposes.

(D) Petition by Parent of Minor. In the interest of justice, the court may allow a custodial parent who has filed an appearance to file a petition to commence proceedings in a decedent estate on behalf of a minor child where the child is an interested person in the estate.

[Adopted July 12, 2001, effective January 1, 2002, 464 Mich. Amended December 18, 2001, effective May 1, 2002, 465 Mich. Amended effective November 15, 2005, 474 Mich. Amended October 11, 2007, effective January 1, 2008, 479 Mich; January 14, 2009, effective May 1, 2009, 483 Mich; March 20, 2019, effective May 1, 2019, 502 Mich; September 18, 2019, effective January 1, 2020, 503 Mich.]

Comments

Staff Comment to 2001 Adoption

This rule is new. It incorporates part of former MCR 5.702(A). See MCL 700.3301 for commencing an informal proceeding by application and MCL 700.3401 for commencing a formal testacy proceeding by petition. Provision for multiple requests in one petition are found in MCL 700.3107(1)(b) and 700.3502(1). For matters covered by former MCR 5.702(B), see MCL 700.3614–700.3618. The term "informal proceedings" is defined in MCL 700.1105(b). These rules use the term "formal proceeding" to refer to both a formal testacy proceeding defined in MCL 700.3401 and an independent request to the court authorized by MCL 700.3415.

Staff Comment to 2002 Amendment

The December 18, 2001 amendments, effective May 1, 2002, updated various rules in light of the Estates and Protected Individuals Code (EPIC), MCL 700.1101 *et seq.*, and revisions made to EPIC by 2000 PA 312, 313, and 469.

Staff Comment to 2005 Amendment

The amendments of MCR 5.144, 5.203, 5.207, 5.302, 5.307, 5.404, and 5.409, effective immediately, were developed as a result of the state court administrative office's statewide conservatorship case review prompted by the Performance Audit of Selected Probate Court Conservatorship Cases by the Michigan Office of the Auditor General and the State Bar of Michigan Probate and Estate Planning Section's Uniformity of Practice Committee's survey of probate court practices. The amendment of MCR 5.144(A)(2) eliminates the ability to close a conservatorship estate because of suspension of a fiduciary unless there are insufficient funds available to hire a special fiduciary, or after notice and hearing and a finding of good cause. The amendment of MCR 5.203(D) adds the financial institution and guardian ad litem to the list required to receive notice when a fiduciary is suspended. The amendment of MCR 5.207(A) allows for better court oversight when real property is sold. The amendment of MCR 5.302(A) requires that a copy of a death certificate be attached to the petition or application when commencing a decedent estate. In the event that the death certificate is not available, the petitioner may provide alternative documentation. The amendment of MCR 5.307(A) allows for the deduction of secured loans when calculating the inventory fee due. The amendment of MCR 5.404(A) creates a new subsection that requires the use of a SCAO approved social history form when one is required to be filed with a petition for guardianship of a minor. The amendment of MCR 5.409(B)(2) requires that joint property belonging to the protected person be listed on the inventory along with the type of ownership. The amendment of MCR 5.409(C)(1) clarifies that the fiduciary must serve the account on the interested persons and file the proof of service with the court. The amendment of MCR 5.409(C)(4) provides the process for filing a proof of restricted account and annual verification of funds on deposit with the court. The amendment of MCR 5.409(C)(5) adds the requirement to present a financial institution statement to the court when filing the annual account. The amendment of MCR 5.409(C)(6) requires the court to either review or allow the account annually and to hold a hearing on the accounts at least once every three years.

Staff Comment to 2007 Amendment

These amendments were proposed by the Probate and Estate Planning Section of the State Bar of Michigan, and are intended to address and clarify practice issues within the amended rules. The amendment of MCR 5.207(A)(4) provides the alternative of including a tax statement to show the state equalized value of property. The amendments of MCR 5.307(B) and 5.409(B)(3) require the name and address of each financial institution be added to the inventory, and requires that the institution's main address or branch used most frequently by the filer be identified. The amendment of MCR 5.409(C)(1) requires any account filed with the court to comply with relevant court rules. The amendment of MCR 5.409(C)(4) extends the time in which to file proof of a minor's assets in a restricted account from 14 to 28 days. The amendment of MCR 5.409(C)(5) allows the option of filing an annual verification of funds on deposit or presenting a copy of a financial institution statement with an annual account.

Staff Comment to 2009 Amendment

These amendments were adopted primarily as a result of submissions by the Michigan Probate Judges Association and the State Bar of Michigan's Probate and Estate Planning Section. This was a joint effort to increase the oversight of guardianship and conservatorship proceedings, as well as to improve other procedures in probate court.

Staff Comment to 2019 Amendment

The amendments of Rules 1.109, 2.102, 2.104, 2.106, 2.107, 2.117, 2.119, 2.403, 2.503, 2.506, 2.508, 2.518, 2.602, 2.603, 2.621, 3.101, 3.104, 3.203, 3.205, 3.210, 3.302, 3.607, 3.613, 3.614, 3.705, 3.801, 3.802, 3.805, 3.806, 4.201, 4.202, 4.303, 4.306, 5.001, 5.104, 5.105, 5.107, 5.108, 5.113, 5.117, 5.118, 5.119, 5.120, 5.125, 5.126, 5.132, 5.162, 5.202, 5.203, 5.205, 5.302, 5.304, 5.307, 5.308, 5.309, 5.310, 5.311, 5.313, 5.402, 5.404, 5.405, 5.409, 5.501, and 5.784 and addition of Rule 3.618 of the Michigan Court Rules are an expected progression necessary for design and implementation of the statewide electronic-filing system. These particular amendments will assist in implementing the goals of the project.

Staff Comment to 2020 Amendment

The amendments of MCR 1.109, 2.107, 2.113, 2.116, 2.119, 2.222, 2.223, 2.225, 2.227, 3.206, 3.211, 3.212, 3.214, 3.303, 3.903, 3.921, 3.925, 3.926, 3.931, 3.933, 3.942, 3.950, 3.961, 3.971, 3.972, 4.002, 4.101, 4.201, 4.202, 4.302, 5.128, 5.302, 5.731, 6.101, 6.615, 8.105, and 8.119 and rescission of MCR 2.226 and 8.125 continue the process for design and implementation of the statewide electronic-filing system.

Rule 5.304   Notice of Appointment

(A) Notice of Appointment. The personal representative must, not later than 14 days after appointment, serve notice of appointment by personal service or by first-class mail as provided in MCL 700.3705 and the agreement and notice relating to attorney fees required by MCR 5.313(D). No notice of appointment need be served if the person serving as personal representative is the only person to whom notice must be given.

(B) Publication of Notice. If the address or identity of a person who is to receive notice of appointment is not known and cannot be ascertained with reasonable diligence, the notice of appointment must be published one time in a newspaper, as defined in MCR 2.106(F), in the county in which a resident decedent was domiciled or in the county in which the proceedings with respect to a nonresident were initiated. The published notice of appointment is sufficient if it includes:

(1) statements that estate proceedings have been commenced, giving the name and address of the court, and, if applicable, that a will has been admitted to probate,

(2) the name of any interested person whose name is known but whose address cannot be ascertained after diligent inquiry, and a statement that the result of the administration may be to bar or affect that person's interest in the estate, and

(3) the name and address of the person appointed personal representative, and the name and address of the court.

(C) Prior Publication. After an interested person has once been served by publication, notice of appointment is only required if that person's address is known or becomes known during the proceedings or the person registers as an authorized user of the electronic filing system under MCR 1.109(G)(6)(a).

[Adopted July 12, 2001, effective January 1, 2002, 464 Mich. Amended March 20, 2019, effective May 1, 2019, 502 Mich.]

Comments

Staff Comment to 2001 Adoption

This rule is new. It and the two succeeding rules deal with all the notices that a personal representative must give at the commencement of administration, in addition to notice of hearing. Subrule (C) limits the requirement to serve an interested person by publication to the first such notice. Thus, the publication required under subrule (B) will not have to be made in formal proceedings if the notice of the petition for formal testacy or appointment proceedings was already published.

Staff Comment to 2019 Amendment

The amendments of Rules 1.109, 2.102, 2.104, 2.106, 2.107, 2.117, 2.119, 2.403, 2.503, 2.506, 2.508, 2.518, 2.602, 2.603, 2.621, 3.101, 3.104, 3.203, 3.205, 3.210, 3.302, 3.607, 3.613, 3.614, 3.705, 3.801, 3.802, 3.805, 3.806, 4.201, 4.202, 4.303, 4.306, 5.001, 5.104, 5.105, 5.107, 5.108, 5.113, 5.117, 5.118, 5.119, 5.120, 5.125, 5.126, 5.132, 5.162, 5.202, 5.203, 5.205, 5.302, 5.304, 5.307, 5.308, 5.309, 5.310, 5.311, 5.313, 5.402, 5.404, 5.405, 5.409, 5.501, and 5.784 and addition of Rule 3.618 of the Michigan Court Rules are an expected progression necessary for design and implementation of the statewide electronic-filing system. These particular amendments will assist in implementing the goals of the project.

Rule 5.305   Notice to Spouse; Election

(A) Notice to Spouse. In the estate of a decedent who was domiciled in the state of Michigan at the time of death, the personal representative, except a special personal representative, must serve notice of the rights of election under part 2 of article II of the Estates and Protected Individuals Code, including the time for making the election and the rights to exempt property and allowances under part 4 of article II of the code, on the surviving spouse of the decedent within 28 days after the personal representative's appointment. An election as provided in subrule (C) may be filed in lieu of the notice. No notice need be given if the surviving spouse is the personal representative or one of several personal representatives or if there is a waiver under MCL 700.2205.

(B) Proof of Service. The personal representative is not required to file a proof of service of the notice of the rights of election.

(C) Spouse's Election. If the surviving spouse exercises the right of election, the spouse must serve a copy of the election on the personal representative personally or by mail. The election must be made within 63 days after the date for presentment of claims or within 63 days after the service of the inventory upon the surviving spouse, whichever is later. The election may be filed with the court.

(D) Assignment of Dower. A petition for the assignment of dower under MCL 558.1–558.29 must include:

(1) a full and accurate description of the land in Michigan owned by a deceased husband and of which he died seized, from which the petitioner asks to have the dower assigned;

(2) the name, age, and address of the widow and the names and addresses of the other heirs;

(3) the date on which the husband died and his domicile on the date of his death; and

(4) the fact that the widow's right to dower has not been barred and that she or some other person interested in the land wishes it set apart.

If there is a minor or other person other than the widow under legal disability having no legal guardian or conservator, there may not be a hearing on the petition until after the appointment of a guardian ad litem for such person.

[Adopted July 12, 2001, effective January 1, 2002, 464 Mich.]

Comments

Staff Comment to 2001 Adoption

This rule is new. The topic was treated in former MCR 5.707(A)(2). See MCL 700.3705(5) on the duty of the personal representative to provide the notice and MCL 700.2202 on the time and manner for making the election. Subrule (B) overrides MCL 700.2202(4). Subrule (D) was former MCR 5.707(C).

Rule 5.307   Requirements Applicable to All Decedent Estates

(A) Inventory Fee. Within 91 days of the date of the letters of authority, the personal representative must submit to the court the information necessary for computation of the probate inventory fee. The inventory fee must be paid no later than the filing of the petition for an order of complete estate settlement under MCL 700.3952, the petition for settlement order under MCL 700.3953, or the sworn statement under MCL 700.3954, or one year after appointment, whichever is earlier.

(B) Notice of Continued Administration. If unable to complete estate administration within one year of the original personal representative's appointment, the personal representative must file with the court and serve on all interested persons a notice that the estate remains under administration, specifying the reason for the continuation of administration. The notice must be served within 28 days of the first anniversary of appointment and all subsequent anniversaries during which the administration remains uncompleted.

(C) Notice to Personal Representative. At the time of appointment, the court must provide the personal representative with written notice of information to be provided to the court. The notice should be substantially in the following form or in the form specified by MCR 5.310(E), if applicable:

"Inventory Information: Within 91 days of the date of the letters of authority, you must submit to the court the information necessary for computation of the probate inventory fee. You must also provide the name and address of each financial institution listed on your inventory at the time the inventory is presented to the court. The address for a financial institution shall be either that of the institution's main headquarters or the branch used most frequently by the personal representative.

"Change of Address: You must keep the court and all interested persons informed in writing within 7 days of any change in your address that you have provided for service."

"Notice of Continued Administration: If you are unable to complete the administration of the estate within one year of the original personal representative's appointment, you must file with the court and all interested persons a notice that the estate remains under administration, specifying the reason for the continuation of the administration. You must give this notice within 28 days of the first anniversary of the original appointment and all subsequent anniversaries during which the administration remains uncompleted."

"Duty to Complete Administration of Estate: You must complete the administration of the estate and file appropriate closing documents with the court. Failure to do so may result in personal assessment of costs."

(D) Claim by Personal Representative. A claim by a personal representative against the estate for an obligation that arose before the death of the decedent shall only be allowed in a formal proceeding by order of the court.

(E) Requiring or Filing of Additional Documents. Except in formal proceedings and supervised administration, the court may not require the filing of any documents other than those required to be filed by statute or court rule. However, additional documents may be filed under MCR 5.113(D).
[Adopted July 12, 2001, effective January 1, 2002, 464 Mich. Amended December 18, 2001, effective May 1, 2002, 465 Mich. Amended effective November 15, 2005, 474 Mich; March 20, 2007, 477 Mich. Amended May 22, 2007, effective September 1, 2007, 478 Mich; October 11, 2007, effective January 1, 2008, 479 Mich; January 1, 2009, effective May 1, 2009, 483 Mich; March 20, 2019, effective May 1, 2019, 502 Mich.]

Comments

Staff Comment to 2001 Adoption

This rule is new. It deals with matters addressed in former MCR 5.707, but it is substantially changed to comply with the new provisions of the Estates and Protected Individuals Code. Since the normal process occurs without court supervision or monitoring, most of the provisions of the former rule have been omitted or moved to the rules on supervised administration or formal proceedings. Former MCR 5.707(C) on assignment of dower has been moved to MCR 5.305(D). Subrule (C) supersedes the notice and objection procedure of MCL 700.3804(3).

Staff Comment to 2002 Amendment

The December 18, 2001 amendments, effective May 1, 2002, updated various rules in light of the Estates and Protected Individuals Code (EPIC), MCL 700.1101 *et seq.*, and revisions made to EPIC by 2000 PA 312, 313, and 469.

Staff Comment to 2005 Amendment

The amendments of MCR 5.144, 5.203, 5.207, 5.302, 5.307, 5.404, and 5.409, effective immediately, were developed as a result of the state court administrative office's statewide conservatorship case review prompted by the Performance Audit of Selected Probate Court Conservatorship Cases by the Michigan Office of the Auditor General and the State Bar of Michigan Probate and Estate Planning Section's Uniformity of Practice Committee's survey of probate court practices. The amendment of MCR 5.144(A)(2) eliminates the ability to close a conservatorship estate because of suspension of a fiduciary unless there are insufficient funds available to hire a special fiduciary, or after notice and hearing and a finding of good cause. The amendment of MCR 5.203(D) adds the financial institution and guardian ad litem to the list required to receive notice when a fiduciary is suspended. The amendment of MCR 5.207(A) allows for better court oversight when real property is sold. The amendment of MCR 5.302(A) requires that a copy of a death certificate be attached to the petition or application when commencing a decedent estate. In the event that the death certificate is not available, the petitioner may provide alternative documentation. The amendment of MCR 5.307(A) allows for the deduction of secured loans when calculating the inventory fee due. The amendment of MCR 5.404(A) creates a new subsection that requires the use of a SCAO approved social history form when one is required to be filed with a petition for guardianship of a minor. The amendment of MCR 5.409(B)(2) requires that joint property belonging to the protected person be listed on the inventory along with the type of ownership. The amendment of MCR 5.409(C)(1) clarifies that the fiduciary must serve the account on the interested persons and file the proof of service with the court. The amendment of MCR 5.409(C)(4) provides the process for filing a proof of restricted account and annual verification of funds on deposit with the court. The amendment of MCR 5.409(C)(5) adds the requirement to present a financial institution statement to the court when filing the annual account. The amendment of MCR 5.409(C)(6) requires the court to either review or allow the account annually and to hold a hearing on the accounts at least once every three years.

Staff Comment to March, 2007 Amendment

The amendments of MCR 5.307(B) and 5.310(E) conform to language in MCL 700.3951 by clarifying that a Notice of Continued Administration is tracked from the date of the appointment of the original personal representative, including a special personal representative.

Staff Comment to May, 2007 Amendment

The amendment of MCR 5.307 eliminates the requirement to reduce the value of property by the amount of secured loans for purposes of determining the inventory fee. This amendment conforms the court rule to the requirement for setting the inventory fee in § 871 of the Revised Judicature Act, MCL 600.871, as expressed in *Wolfe–Haddad Estate v Oakland Co*, 272 Mich App 323 (2006).

Staff Comment to October, 2007 Amendment

These amendments were proposed by the Probate and Estate Planning Section of the State Bar of Michigan, and are intended to address and clarify practice issues within the amended rules. The amendment of MCR 5.207(A)(4) provides the alternative of including a tax statement to show the state equalized value of property. The amendments of MCR 5.307(B) and MCR 5.409(B)(3) require the name and address of each financial institution be added to the inventory, and requires that the institution's main address or branch used most frequently by the filer be identified. The amendment of MCR 5.409(C)(1) requires any account filed with the court to comply with relevant court rules. The amendment of MCR 5.409(C)(4) extends the time in which to file proof of a minor's assets in a restricted account from 14 to 28 days. The amendment of MCR 5.409(C)(5) allows the option of filing an annual verification of funds on deposit or presenting a copy of a financial institution statement with an annual account.

Staff Comment to 2009 Amendment

These amendments were adopted primarily as a result of submissions by the Michigan Probate Judges Association and the State Bar of Michigan's Probate and Estate Planning Section. This was a joint effort to increase the oversight of guardianship and conservatorship proceedings, as well as to improve other procedures in probate court.

Staff Comment to 2019 Amendment

The amendments of Rules 1.109, 2.102, 2.104, 2.106, 2.107, 2.117, 2.119, 2.403, 2.503, 2.506, 2.508, 2.518, 2.602, 2.603, 2.621, 3.101, 3.104, 3.203, 3.205, 3.210, 3.302, 3.607, 3.613, 3.614, 3.705, 3.801, 3.802, 3.805, 3.806, 4.201, 4.202, 4.303, 4.306, 5.001, 5.104, 5.105, 5.107, 5.108, 5.113, 5.117, 5.118, 5.119, 5.120, 5.125, 5.126, 5.132, 5.162, 5.202, 5.203, 5.205, 5.302, 5.304, 5.307, 5.308, 5.309, 5.310, 5.311, 5.313, 5.402, 5.404, 5.405, 5.409, 5.501, and 5.784 and addition of Rule 3.618 of the Michigan Court Rules are an expected progression necessary for design and implementation of the statewide electronic-filing system. These particular amendments will assist in implementing the goals of the project.

Rule 5.308   Formal Proceedings

(A) Accounts. Any account filed with the court must be in the form required by MCR 5.310(C)(2)(c).

(B) Determination of Heirs.

(1) *Determination During Estate Administration.* Every petition for formal probate of a will or for adjudication of intestacy shall include a request for a determination of heirs unless heirs were previously determined. Determination of heirs is also required whenever supervised administration is requested. No other petition for a formal proceeding, including a petition to appoint a personal representative which does not request formal probate of a will or adjudication of intestacy, need contain a request for determination of heirs. The personal representative or an interested person may at any time file a petition for determination of heirs. Heirs may only be determined in a formal hearing.

(2) *Determination Without Estate Administration.*

(a) Petition and Testimony Identifying Heirs Form. Any person may initiate a formal proceeding to determine intestacy and heirs without appointment of a personal representative by filing a petition and a completed SCAO–approved testimony identifying heirs form sufficient to establish the domicile of the decedent at the time of death and the identity of the interested persons. A testimony identifying heirs form must be verified under MCR 1.109(D)(3).

(b) Notice, Publication. The petitioner must serve notice of hearing on all interested persons. If an interested person's address or whereabouts is not known, the petitioner shall serve notice on that person by publication as provided in MCR 5.105(A)(3). The court may require other publication if it deems necessary.

(c) Order. If notice and proofs are sufficient, the court must enter an order determining the date of death, the domicile of the decedent at the time of death, whether the decedent died intestate, and the names of the heirs.

(d) Closing File. If there are no further requests for relief and no appeal, the court may close its file.

[Adopted July 12, 2001, effective January 1, 2002, 464 Mich. Amended December 18, 2001, effective May 1, 2002, 465 Mich; March 20, 2019, effective May 1, 2019, 502 Mich.]

Comments

Staff Comment to 2001 Adoption

This rule is new. Subrule (B) deals with the matter covered by former MCR 5.708. Subrule (B)(1) summarizes the requirements of the Estates and Protected Individuals Code on when a petition for formal proceedings must include a request for determination of heirs. Subrule (B)(2) changes the provisions of the previous rule in light of the revision in the statutory authorization for a court to determine heirs without further proceedings, now found at MCL 700.3106 and 700.3402(2)(c).

Staff Comment to 2002 Amendment

The December 18, 2001 amendments, effective May 1, 2002, updated various rules in light of the Estates and Protected Individuals Code (EPIC), MCL 700.1101 *et seq.*, and revisions made to EPIC by 2000 PA 312, 313, and 469.

Staff Comment to 2019 Amendment

The amendments of Rules 1.109, 2.102, 2.104, 2.106, 2.107, 2.117, 2.119, 2.403, 2.503, 2.506, 2.508, 2.518, 2.602, 2.603, 2.621, 3.101, 3.104, 3.203, 3.205, 3.210, 3.302, 3.607, 3.613, 3.614, 3.705, 3.801, 3.802, 3.805, 3.806, 4.201, 4.202, 4.303, 4.306, 5.001, 5.104, 5.105, 5.107, 5.108, 5.113, 5.117, 5.118, 5.120, 5.125, 5.126, 5.132, 5.162, 5.202, 5.203, 5.205, 5.302, 5.304, 5.307, 5.308, 5.309, 5.310, 5.311, 5.313, 5.402, 5.405, 5.409, 5.501, and 5.784 and addition of Rule 3.618 of the Michigan Court Rules are an expected progression necessary for design and implementation of the statewide electronic-filing system. These particular amendments will assist in implementing the goals of the project.

Rule 5.309   Informal Proceedings

(A) Denial of Application. If the probate register denies the application for informal probate or informal appointment, the applicant may file a petition for a formal proceeding, which may include a request for supervised administration.

(B) Effect of Form of Administration in Another State or Country. The fact that any particular form of administration has been initiated in the estate of a decedent in another state or country does not preclude any other form of proceedings with respect to that decedent in Michigan without regard to the form of the proceeding in the other state or country.

(C) Notice of Intent to Seek Informal Appointment as Personal Representative.

(1) A person who desires to be appointed personal representative in informal proceedings must serve notice of intent to seek appointment and a copy of the application on each person having a prior or equal right to appointment who does not renounce this right in writing before the appointment is made.

(2) Service of notice of intent to seek appointment and a copy of the application must be made at least 14 days by mail or 7 days by personal service before appointment as personal representative. If the address of one or more of the persons having a prior or equal right to appointment is unknown and cannot be ascertained after diligent inquiry, notice of the intent to file the application must be published pursuant to MCR 5.106 at least 14 days prior to the appointment, but a copy of the application need not be published.

(3) Proof of service must be filed with the court along with the application for informal appointment as personal representative.

(D) Publication. If the address of an heir, devisee, or other interested person entitled to the information on the informal probate under MCL 700.3306 is unknown and cannot be ascertained after diligent inquiry, the information in MCL 700.3306(2) must be provided by publication pursuant to MCR 5.106. Publication of notice under this rule is not required if a personal representative has been appointed and provided notice under MCR 5.304.

[Adopted July 12, 2001, effective January 1, 2002, 464 Mich. Amended January 14, 2009, effective May 1, 2009, 483 Mich; March 20, 2019, effective May 1, 2019, 502 Mich.]

Comments

Staff Comment to 2001 Adoption

This rule is new. Subrule (B) allows use of any of the various forms of proceedings or administration–informal or formal, unsupervised or supervised–in this state without regard to the form which may have been used in another state or country in the administration of the estate of the same decedent. Subrule (C) deals with the notice of intent requirement of MCL 700.3310. See also MCL 700.1401.

Staff Comment to 2009 Amendment

These amendments were adopted primarily as a result of submissions by the Michigan Probate Judges Association and the State Bar of Michigan's Probate and Estate Planning Section. This was a joint effort to increase the oversight of guardianship and conservatorship proceedings, as well as to improve other procedures in probate court.

Staff Comment to 2019 Amendment

The amendments of Rules 1.109, 2.102, 2.104, 2.106, 2.107, 2.117, 2.119, 2.403, 2.503, 2.506, 2.508, 2.518, 2.602, 2.603, 2.621, 3.101, 3.104, 3.203, 3.205, 3.210, 3.302, 3.607, 3.613, 3.614, 3.705, 3.801, 3.802, 3.805, 3.806, 4.201, 4.202, 4.303, 4.306, 5.001, 5.104, 5.105, 5.107, 5.108, 5.113, 5.117, 5.118, 5.119, 5.120, 5.125, 5.126, 5.132, 5.162, 5.202, 5.203, 5.205, 5.302, 5.304, 5.307, 5.308, 5.309, 5.310, 5.311, 5.313, 5.402, 5.404, 5.405, 5.409, 5.501, and 5.784 and addition of Rule 3.618 of the Michigan Court Rules are an expected progression necessary for design and implementation of the statewide electronic-filing system. These particular amendments will assist in implementing the goals of the project.

Rule 5.310   Supervised Administration

(A) Applicability. The other rules applicable to decedent estates apply to supervised administration unless they conflict with this rule.

(B) Commencement of Supervised Administration. A request for supervised administration in a decedent estate may be made in the petition for formal testacy and appointment proceedings. A petition for formal testacy and appointment proceedings including a request for supervised administration may be filed at any time during the estate proceedings if testacy has not previously been adjudicated. If testacy and appointment have been previously adjudicated, a separate petition for supervised administration may be filed at any time during administration of the estate. Whenever supervised administration is requested, the court must determine heirs unless heirs were previously determined, even if supervised administration is denied.

(C) Filing Documents With the Court. The personal representative must file the following additional documents with the court and serve copies on the interested persons:

(1) *Inventory.* The personal representative must file an inventory as prescribed by MCR 5.307(A).

(2) *Accountings.*

(a) Time for Filing. Unless the court designates a shorter period, the personal representative must file accountings within 56 days after the end of the accounting period. A final account must be filed when the estate is ready for closing or on removal of a personal representative. The court may order an interim accounting at any time the court deems necessary.

(b) Accounting Period. The accounting period ends on the anniversary date of the issuance of the letters of authority or, if applicable, on the anniversary date of the close of the last period covered by an accounting. The personal representative may elect to change the accounting period so that it ends on a different date. If the personal representative elects to make such a change, the first accounting period thereafter shall not be more than a year. A notice of the change must be filed with the court.

(c) Contents. All accountings must be itemized, showing in detail receipts and disbursements during the accounting period, unless itemization is waived by all interested persons. A written description of services performed must be included or appended regarding compensation sought by a personal representative. This description need not be duplicated in the order. The accounting must include notice that (i) objections concerning the accounting must be brought to the court's attention by an interested person because the court does not normally review the accounting without an objection; (ii) interested persons have a right to review proofs of income and disbursements at a time reasonably convenient to the personal representative and the interested person; (iii) interested persons may object to all or part of an accounting by filing an objection with the court before allowance of the accounting; and (iv) if an objection is filed and not otherwise resolved, the court will hear and determine the objection.

(d) Proof of Income and Disbursements. After filing and before the allowance of an accounting, the personal representative must make proofs of income and disbursements reasonably available for examination by any interested person who requests to see them or as required by the court. An interested person, with or without examination of the proofs of income and disbursements, may file an objection to an accounting with the court. If an interested person files an objection without examining the proofs and the court concludes that such an examination would help resolve the objection, the court may order the interested person to examine the proofs before the court hears the objection.

(e) Deferral of Hearings on Accountings. Hearing on each accounting may be deferred in the discretion of the court. The court in any case at any time may require a hearing on an accounting with or without a request by an interested person.

(3) Notice of appointment.

(4) Fees notice pursuant to MCR 5.313.

(5) Notice to spouse.

(6) Affidavit of any required publication.

(7) Such other documents as are ordered by the court.

(D) Tax Information. The personal representative must file with the court

(1) in the case of a decedent dying before October 1, 1993, proof that all Michigan inheritance taxes have been paid or

(2) in the case of an estate of a decedent dying after September 30, 1993, either

(a) if a federal estate tax return was required to be filed for the decedent, proof from the Michigan Department of Treasury that all Michigan estate taxes have been paid, or

(b) if no federal estate tax return was required to be filed for the decedent, a statement that no Michigan estate tax is due.

(E) Notice to Personal Representative. When supervised administration is ordered, the court must serve a written notice of duties on the personal representative. The notice must be substantially as follows:

"Inventories: You are required to file an inventory of the assets of the estate within 91 days of the date of your letters of authority or as ordered by the court. The inventory must list in reasonable detail all the property owned by the decedent at the time of death, indicating, for each listed item, the fair market value at the time of decedent's death and the type and amount of any encumbrance. If the value of any item has been obtained through an appraiser, the inventory should include the appraiser's name and address with the item or items appraised by that appraiser.

"Accountings: You are required to file annually, or more often if the court directs, a complete itemized accounting of your administration of the estate, showing in detail all the receipts and disbursements and the property remaining in your hands together with the form of the property. When the estate is ready for closing, you are required to file a final accounting and an itemized and complete list of all properties remaining. Subsequent annual and final accountings must be filed within 56 days after the close of the accounting period.

"Change of Address: You are required to keep the court and interested persons informed in writing within 7 days of any change in your address that you have provided for service.

"Notice of Continued Administration: If you are unable to complete the administration of the estate within one year of the original personal representative's appointment, you must file with the court and all interested persons a notice that the estate remains under administration, specifying the reason for the continuation of the administration. You must give this notice within 28 days of the first anniversary of the original appointment and all subsequent anniversaries during which the administration remains uncompleted.

"Duty to Complete Administration of Estate: You must complete the administration of the estate and file appropriate closing documents with the court. Failure to do so may result in personal assessment of costs."

(F) Changing from Supervised to Unsupervised Administration. At any time during supervised administration, any interested person or the personal representative may petition the court to terminate supervision of administration. The court may terminate supervision unless the court finds that proceeding with supervision is necessary under the circumstances. Termination of supervision does not discharge the personal representative.

(G) Approval of compensation of an attorney must be sought pursuant to MCR 5.313.

(H) Order of Complete Estate Settlement. An estate being administered in supervised administration must be closed

under MCL 700.3952, using the procedures specified in MCR 5.311(B)(1).

[Adopted July 12, 2001, effective January 1, 2002, 464 Mich. Amended December 18, 2001, effective May 1, 2002, 465 Mich. Amended effective March 20, 2007, 477 Mich. Amended March 20, 2019, effective May 1, 2019, 502 Mich.]

Comments

Staff Comment to 2001 Adoption

This rule is new, but the contents are modeled on the former provisions of MCR 5.707. Papers required to be served on interested persons are subject to MCR 5.104. Requirements regarding the inventory are in MCL 700.3706 and MCL 700.3707. Requirements regarding accountings are in MCL 700.3703(4). Subrule (C) lists only those papers not required to be filed by some other rule or statute. The reader should not rely on subrule (C) as a complete list of papers which the personal representative must file with the court. Subrule (F) is modeled on former MCR 5.709(H) and permits moving from supervised administration to unsupervised administration. Determination of whether continuing supervision is necessary should be guided by MCL 700.3502(2) and (3).

Staff Comment to 2002 Amendment

The December 18, 2001 amendments, effective May 1, 2002, updated various rules in light of the Estates and Protected Individuals Code (EPIC), MCL 700.1101 *et seq.*, and revisions made to EPIC by 2000 PA 312, 313, and 469.

Staff Comment to 2007 Amendment

The amendments of MCR 5.307(B) and 5.310(E) conform to language in MCL 700.3951 by clarifying that a Notice of Continued Administration is tracked from the date of the appointment of the original personal representative, including a special personal representative.

Staff Comment to 2019 Amendment

The amendments of Rules 1.109, 2.102, 2.104, 2.106, 2.107, 2.117, 2.119, 2.403, 2.503, 2.506, 2.508, 2.518, 2.602, 2.603, 2.621, 3.101, 3.104, 3.203, 3.205, 3.210, 3.302, 3.607, 3.613, 3.614, 3.705, 3.801, 3.802, 3.805, 3.806, 4.201, 4.202, 4.303, 4.306, 5.001, 5.104, 5.105, 5.107, 5.108, 5.113, 5.117, 5.118, 5.119, 5.120, 5.125, 5.126, 5.132, 5.162, 5.202, 5.203, 5.205, 5.302, 5.304, 5.307, 5.308, 5.309, 5.310, 5.311, 5.313, 5.402, 5.404, 5.405, 5.409, 5.501, and 5.784 and addition of Rule 3.618 of the Michigan Court Rules are an expected progression necessary for design and implementation of the statewide electronic-filing system. These particular amendments will assist in implementing the goals of the project.

Rule 5.311   Closing Estate

(A) Closing by Sworn Statement. In unsupervised administration, a personal representative may close an estate by filing a sworn closing statement under MCL 700.3954 or 700.3988.

(B) Formal Proceedings.

(1) *Requirements for Order of Complete Estate Settlement under MCL 700.3952.* An estate being administered in supervised administration must be closed by an order for complete estate settlement under MCL 700.3952. All other estates may be closed under that provision. A petition for complete estate settlement must state the relief requested. If the petitioner requests a determination of testacy, the petitioner must comply with the requirements of the statute and court rules dealing with a determination of testacy in a formal proceeding.

(2) *Requirements for Settlement Order under MCL 700.3953.* A personal representative or a devisee may file a petition for a settlement order under MCL 700.3953; only in an estate being administered under a will admitted to probate in an informal proceeding. The petition may not contain a request for a determination of the decedent testacy status in a formal proceeding.

(3) *Discharge.* A personal representative may petition for discharge from liability with notice to the interested persons. A personal representative who files such a petition with the court must also file the documents described in MCR 5.310(C) and (D), as applicable, proofs of service of those documents that are required to be served on interested persons, and such other

documents as the court may require. The court may order the personal representative discharged if the court is satisfied that the personal representative has properly administered the estate.

(4) *Other Requests for Relief.* With respect to other requests for relief, the petitioner must file appropriate documents to support the request for relief.

(5) *Order.* If the estate administration is completed, the order entered under MCL 700.3952 or MCL 700.3953 shall, in addition to any other relief, terminate the personal representative's authority and close the estate.

(C) Closing of Reopened Estate. After completion of the reopened estate administration, the personal representative shall proceed to close the estate by filing a petition under MCL 700.3952 or MCL 700.3953 or a supplemental closing statement under MCL 700.3954. If a supplemental closing statement is filed, the personal representative must serve a copy on each interested person. If an objection is not filed within 28 days, the personal representative is entitled to receive a supplemental certificate of completion.

[Adopted July 12, 2001, effective January 1, 2002, 464 Mich. Amended March 20, 2019, effective May 1, 2019, 502 Mich.]

Comments

Staff Comment to 2001 Adoption

This rule is new. Use of a sworn statement to close an estate is limited to situations specified in MCL 700.3954 and MCL 700.3988.

Staff Comment to 2019 Amendment

The amendments of Rules 1.109, 2.102, 2.104, 2.106, 2.107, 2.117, 2.119, 2.403, 2.503, 2.506, 2.508, 2.518, 2.602, 2.603, 2.621, 3.101, 3.104, 3.203, 3.205, 3.210, 3.302, 3.607, 3.613, 3.614, 3.705, 3.801, 3.802, 3.805, 3.806, 4.201, 4.202, 4.303, 4.306, 5.001, 5.104, 5.105, 5.107, 5.108, 5.113, 5.117, 5.118, 5.119, 5.120, 5.125, 5.126, 5.132, 5.162, 5.202, 5.203, 5.205, 5.302, 5.304, 5.307, 5.308, 5.309, 5.310, 5.311, 5.313, 5.402, 5.404, 5.405, 5.409, 5.501, and 5.784 and addition of Rule 3.618 of the Michigan Court Rules are an expected progression necessary for design and implementation of the statewide electronic-filing system. These particular amendments will assist in implementing the goals of the project.

Rule 5.312　Reopening Decedent Estate

(A) Reopening by Application. If there is good cause to reopen a previously administered estate, other than an estate that was terminated in supervised administration, any interested person may apply to the register to reopen the estate and appoint the former personal representative or another person who has priority. For good cause and without notice, the register may reopen the estate, appoint the former personal representative or a person who has priority, and issue letters of authority with a specified termination date.

(B) Reopening by Petition. The previously appointed personal representative or an interested person may file a petition with the court to reopen the estate and appoint a personal representative under MCL 700.3959.

(C) Calculation of Due Dates. For purposes of determining when the inventory fee calculation, the inventory filing, the inventory fee payment, and the notice of continued administration are due, a reopened decedent estate is to be treated as a new case.

[Adopted July 12, 2001, effective January 1, 2002, 464 Mich. Amended December 18, 2001, effective May 1, 2002, 465 Mich.]

Comments

Staff Comment to 2001 Adoption

This rule is new. It is adapted from former MCR 5.709(J). It deals with reopening an estate after administration has been closed. Note that in estates closed by closing statement under MCL 700.3954, the appointment of the personal representative continues for one year. In such estates, the personal representative would have authority to act during that period without being reappointed. There is no restriction, other than with regard to supervised administration, against using informal proceedings to reopen an estate that had been closed by order.

Staff Comment to 2002 Amendment

The December 18, 2001 amendments, effective May 1, 2002, updated various rules in light of the Estates and Protected Individuals Code (EPIC), MCL 700.1101 *et seq.*, and revisions made to EPIC by 2000 PA 312, 313, and 469.

Rule 5.313　Compensation of Attorneys

(A) Reasonable Fees and Costs. An attorney is entitled to receive reasonable compensation for legal services rendered on behalf of a personal representative, and to reimbursement for costs incurred in rendering those services. In determining the reasonableness of fees, the court must consider the factors listed in MRPC 1.5(a). The court may also take into account the failure to comply with this rule.

(B) Written Fee Agreement. At the commencement of the representation, the attorney and the personal representative or the proposed personal representative must enter into a written fee agreement signed by them. A copy of the agreement must be provided to the personal representative.

(C) Records. Regardless of the fee agreement, every attorney who represents a personal representative must maintain time records for services that must reflect the following information: the identity of the person performing the services, the date the services are performed, the amount of time expended in performing the services, and a brief description of the services.

(D) Notice to Interested Persons. Within 14 days after the appointment of a personal representative or the retention of an attorney by a personal representative, whichever is later, the personal representative must serve on the interested persons whose interests will be affected by the payment of attorney fees, a notice on a form approved by the State Court Administrator and a copy of the written fee agreement. The notice must state:

(1) the anticipated frequency of payment,

(2) that the person is entitled to a copy of each statement for services or costs upon request,

(3) that the person may object to the fees at any time prior to the allowance of fees by the court,

(4) that an objection may be made in writing or at a hearing and that a written objection must be filed with the court and a copy served on the personal representative or attorney.

(E) Payment of Fees. A personal representative may make, and an attorney may accept, payments for services and costs, on a periodic basis without prior court approval if prior to the time of payment

(1) the attorney and personal representative have entered a written fee agreement;

(2) copies of the fee agreement and the notice required by subrule (D) have been sent to all interested persons who are affected;

(3) a statement for services and costs (containing the information required by subrule (C) has been sent to the personal representative and each interested person who has requested a copy of such statement; and

(4) no written, unresolved objection to the fees, current or past, has been served on the attorney and personal representative.

In all other instances, attorney fees must be approved by the court prior to payment. Costs may be paid without prior court approval. Attorney fees and costs paid without prior court approval remain subject to review by the court.

(F) Claims for compensation, Required Information. Except when the compensation is consented to by all the parties affected, the personal representative must append to an accounting, petition, or motion in which compensation is claimed a statement containing the information required by subrule (C).

(G) Contingent Fee Agreements under MCR 8.121. Subrules (C), (E), and (F) of this rule do not apply to a contingent fee agreement between a personal representative and an attorney under MCR 8.121.

[Adopted July 12, 2001, effective January 1, 2002, 464 Mich. Amended February 23, 2006, effective May 1, 2006, 474 Mich; March 20, 2019, effective May 1, 2019, 502 Mich.]

Comments

Staff Comment to 2001 Adoption

This rule was MCR 8.303. It is amended to limit its applicability to attorneys representing personal representatives and to reflect changes in practice and terminology by the Estates and Protected Individuals Code, MCL 700.1101 *et seq.* The rule is not intended to dictate the terms of a fee agreement. It requires that any fee be reasonable and fairly disclosed to the personal representative and interested persons.

Staff Comment to 2006 Amendment

The amendment of MCR 2.612(A)(2), 3.802(B)(1), 5.313(F), and 9.113(B)(2), effective May 1, 2006, reflect numbering changes in other rules.

Staff Comment to 2019 Amendment

The amendments of Rules 1.109, 2.102, 2.104, 2.106, 2.107, 2.117, 2.119, 2.403, 2.503, 2.506, 2.508, 2.518, 2.602, 2.603, 2.621, 3.101, 3.104, 3.203, 3.205, 3.210, 3.302, 3.607, 3.613, 3.614, 3.705, 3.801, 3.802, 3.805, 3.806, 4.201, 4.202, 4.303, 4.306, 5.001, 5.104, 5.105, 5.107, 5.108, 5.113, 5.117, 5.118, 5.119, 5.120, 5.125, 5.126, 5.132, 5.162, 5.202, 5.203, 5.205, 5.302, 5.304, 5.307, 5.308, 5.309, 5.310, 5.311, 5.313, 5.402, 5.404, 5.405, 5.409, 5.501, and 5.784 and addition of Rule 3.618 of the Michigan Court Rules are an expected progression necessary for design and implementation of the statewide electronic-filing system. These particular amendments will assist in implementing the goals of the project.

SUBCHAPTER 5.400   GUARDIANSHIP, CONSERVATORSHIP, AND PROTECTIVE ORDER PROCEEDINGS

Rule 5.401   General Provisions

This subchapter governs guardianships, conservatorships, and protective order proceedings. The other rules in chapter 5 also apply to these proceedings unless they conflict with rules in this subchapter. Except as modified in this subchapter, proceedings for guardianships of adults and minors, conservatorships, and protective orders shall be in accordance with the Estates and Protected Individuals Code, 1998 PA 386 and, where applicable, the Michigan Indian Family Preservation Act, MCL 712B.1 *et seq.*, the Indian Child Welfare Act, 25 USC 1901 *et seq.*, or the Mental Health Code, 1974 PA 258, as amended.

[Adopted July 12, 2001, effective January 1, 2002, 464 Mich. Amended June 4, 2014, effective September 1, 2014, 496 Mich.]

Comments

Staff Comment to 2001 Adoption

This rule was MCR 5.761.

Staff Comment to 2014 Amendment

These amendments incorporate provisions of the Michigan Indian Family Preservation Act and the Indian Child Welfare Act and reflect a more integrated approach to addressing issues specific to Indian children.

Rule 5.402   Common Provisions

(A) Petition; Multiple Prayers. A petition for the appointment of a guardian or a conservator or for a protective order may contain multiple prayers for relief.

(B) Petition by Minor. A petition and a nomination for the appointment of a guardian or conservator of a minor may be executed and made by a minor 14 years of age or older.

(C) Responsibility for Giving Notice; Manner of Service. The petitioner is responsible for giving notice of hearing. Regardless of statutory provisions, an interested person may be served the notice by mail, personal service, or when necessary, publication. However, if the person who is the subject of the petition is 14 years of age or older, notice of the initial hearing must be served on the person personally unless another method of service is specifically permitted in the circumstances.

(D) Letters of Authority. After entering an order appointing a fiduciary, the court must issue letters of authority after an acceptance of appointment is filed, and if ordered, the filing of the fiduciary's bond. The letters of authority shall be issued on a form approved by the state court administrator. Any restriction or limitation of the powers of a guardian or conservator must be set forth in the letters of authority.

(E) Indian Child; Definitions, Jurisdiction, Notice, Transfer, Intervention.

(1) If an Indian child, as defined by the Michigan Indian Family Preservation Act, is the subject of a guardianship proceeding, the definitions in MCR 3.002 shall control.

(2) If an Indian child is the subject of a petition to establish guardianship of a minor and an Indian tribe has exclusive jurisdiction as defined in MCR 3.002(6), the matter shall be dismissed.

(3) If an Indian child is the subject of a petition to establish guardianship of a minor and an Indian tribe does not have exclusive jurisdiction as defined in MCR 3.002(6), the court shall ensure that the petitioner has given notice of the proceedings to the persons prescribed in MCR 5.125(A)(8) and (C)(20) in accordance with MCR 5.109(1).

(a) If either parent or the Indian custodian or the Indian child's tribe petitions the court to transfer the proceeding to the tribal court, the court shall transfer the case to the tribal court unless either parent objects to the transfer of the case to tribal court jurisdiction or the court finds good cause not to transfer. When the court makes a good-cause determination under MCL 712B.7, adequacy of the tribe, tribal court, or tribal social services shall not be considered. A court may determine that good cause not to transfer a case to tribal court exists only if the person opposing the transfer shows by clear and convincing evidence that either of the following applies:

(i) The Indian tribe does not have a tribal court.

(ii) The requirement of the parties or witnesses to present evidence in tribal court would cause undue hardship to those parties or witnesses that the Indian tribe is unable to mitigate.

(b) The court shall not dismiss the matter until the transfer has been accepted by the tribal court.

(c) If the tribal court declines transfer, the Michigan Indian Family Preservation Act applies, as do the provisions of these rules that pertain to an Indian child (see MCL 712B.3 and MCL 712B.5).

(d) A petition to transfer may be made at any time in accordance with MCL 712B.7(3).

(4) The Indian custodian of the child, the Indian child's tribe, and the Indian child have a right to intervene at any point in the proceeding pursuant to MCL 712B.7(6).

(5) If the court discovers a child may be an Indian child after a guardianship is ordered, the court shall do all of the following:

(a) schedule a hearing to be conducted in accordance with MCR 5.404(C) and MCR 5.404(F).

(b) enter an order for an investigation in accordance with MCR 5.404(A)(2). The order shall be on a form approved by the State Court Administrative Office and shall require the guardian to cooperate in the investigation. The court shall mail a copy of the order to the persons prescribed in MCR 5.125(A)(8), (C)(20), and (C)(26) by first-class mail.

(c) provide notice of the guardianship and the hearing scheduled in subrule (5)(a) and the potential applicability of the Indian Child Welfare Act and the Michigan Indian Family Preservation Act on a form approved by the State Court Administrative Office to the persons prescribed in MCR 5.125(A)(8), (C)(20), and (C)(26) in accordance with MCR 5.109(1). A copy of the notice shall be served on the guardian.

[Adopted July 12, 2001, effective January 1, 2002, 464 Mich. Amended February 2, 2010, effective May, 1, 2010, 485 Mich; March 22, 2011, effective March 22, 2011, 489 Mich. Amended effective, pending public comment, March 20, 2013, 493 Mich. Amended June 4, 2014, effective September 1, 2014, 496 Mich. Amended effective September 23, 2015, 498 Mich. Amended March 20, 2019, effective May 1, 2019, 502 Mich. Amended effective August 14, 2019, 503 Mich.]

Comments

Staff Comment to 2001 Adoption

This rule was MCR 5.762. MCR 5.104(C) excludes a petition to appoint a guardian from the unopposed petition procedure of that subrule.

Staff Comment to 2010 Amendment

These amendments incorporate provisions of the Indian Child Welfare Act into specific provisions within various rules relating to child protective proceedings and juvenile status offenses. The language is designed to make the rules reflect a more integrated approach to addressing issues specific to Indian children.

MCR 3.002(1)(c) defines "preadoptive placement" to mean the "temporary placement of an Indian child in a foster home or institution after the termination of parental rights, but before or in lieu of adoptive placement, and . . ." The phrase "in lieu of adoptive placement" is not intended to mean that it is permissible to leave a child in foster care indefinitely, in violation of MCL 712A.19b(6) or (7) or 45 CFR 1355.20, 45 CFR 1356.21, or 45 CFR 1356.50. Rather, it addresses situations where the parental rights to a child have been terminated and there is no permanency plan for adoption of the child. One example is when the child has been placed with a juvenile guardian and the guardianship is subsequently revoked. In this situation, jurisdiction over the

child pursuant to MCL 712A.2(b) will be reinstated and the child is placed in foster care.

MCR 3.002(1): The definition of "child custody proceeding" is intended to apply the Indian Child Welfare Act to delinquency proceedings if an "Indian child" is charged with a so-called status offense in violation of MCL 712A.2(a)(2)–(4) or (d). Delinquency proceedings involving an Indian child charged with any other non-status offense are generally not subject to the Indian Child Welfare Act; however, if the initial investigation or subsequent review of a non-status delinquency case reveals that the Indian child involved suffers from child abuse or neglect, a separate child protective proceeding may be initiated, which would be subject to the Indian Child Welfare Act.

The amendment of MCR 3.905(C)(1) states that a court shall consider guidelines established by the Bureau of Indian Affairs (BIA) in determining whether good cause not to transfer exists (Guidelines for State Courts; Indian Child Custody Proceedings, 44 Fed Reg No 228, 67590–67592, C.2–C.4. [November 26, 1979]). Some examples of good cause are that the Indian tribe does not have a tribal court or that the Indian child is over 12 years old and objects to the transfer. For additional examples of good cause and relevant case law, see the BIA guidelines cited above and A Practical Guide to the Indian Child Welfare Act. (Native American Rights Fund, A Practical Guide to the Indian Child Welfare Act [Boulder, CO: Native American Rights Fund, 2007], 7.15 and 7.16, p 60.)

Staff Comment to 2011 Amendment

The amendments of MCR 3.807, 3.921, and 5.402 have been made to clarify former language and to correct cross references.

Staff Comment to 2013 Amendment

This proposal incorporates provisions of the newly enacted Michigan Indian Family Preservation Act into specific provisions within various rules relating to child protective proceedings and juvenile status offenses.

Staff Comment to 2014 Amendment

These amendments incorporate provisions of the Michigan Indian Family Preservation Act and the Indian Child Welfare Act and reflect a more integrated approach to addressing issues specific to Indian children.

Staff Comment to 2015 Amendment

The amendment of MCR 5.402(E)(5)(a) requires a court that discovers a child of an ordered guardianship may be an Indian child to schedule a hearing in accordance with MCR 5.404(C) and MCR 5.404(F), the amendment of MCR 5.402(E)(5)(b) requires the court to enter an order for investigation in accordance with MCR 5.404(A)(2), and the amendment of MCR 5.402(E)(5)(c) requires notice of the hearing scheduled in subrule (5)(a) to be provided to the persons prescribed.

Staff Comment to May, 2019 Amendment

The amendments of Rules 1.109, 2.102, 2.104, 2.106, 2.107, 2.117, 2.119, 2.403, 2.503, 2.506, 2.508, 2.518, 2.602, 2.603, 2.621, 3.101, 3.104, 3.203, 3.205, 3.210, 3.302, 3.607, 3.613, 3.614, 3.705, 3.801, 3.802, 3.805, 3.806, 4.201, 4.202, 4.303, 4.306, 5.001, 5.104, 5.105, 5.107, 5.108, 5.113, 5.117, 5.118, 5.119, 5.120, 5.125, 5.126, 5.132, 5.162, 5.202, 5.203, 5.205, 5.302, 5.304, 5.307, 5.308, 5.309, 5.310, 5.311, 5.313, 5.402, 5.404, 5.405, 5.409, 5.501, and 5.784 and addition of Rule 3.618 of the Michigan Court Rules are an expected progression necessary for design and implementation of the statewide electronic-filing system. These particular amendments will assist in implementing the goals of the project.

Staff Comment to August, 2019 Amendment

These amendments update cross-references and make other nonsubstantive revisions to clarify the rules.

Rule 5.403   Proceedings on Temporary Guardianship

(A) Limitation. The court may appoint a temporary guardian in the course of a proceeding for permanent guardianship or pursuant to an application to appoint a guardian serving in another state to serve as guardian in this state.

(B) Notice of Hearing, Minor. For good cause stated on the record and included in the order, the court may shorten the period for notice of hearing or may dispense with notice of a hearing for the appointment of a temporary guardian of a minor, except that the minor shall always receive notice if the minor is 14 years of age or older. If a temporary guardian is appointed following an ex parte hearing in a case in which the notice period was shortened or eliminated, the court shall send notice of the appointment to all interested persons. The notice shall inform the interested persons about their right to object to the appointment, the process for objecting, and the date of the next hearing, if any. If an interested person objects to the appointment of a temporary guardian following an ex parte hearing in a case in which the notice period was shortened or eliminated, the court shall hold a hearing on the objection within 14 days from the date the objection is filed.

(C) Temporary Guardian for Incapacitated Individual Where no Current Appointment; Guardian Ad Litem. A petition for a temporary guardian for an alleged incapacitated individual shall specify in detail the emergency situation requiring the temporary guardianship. For the purpose of an emergency hearing, the court shall appoint a guardian ad litem unless such appointment would cause delay and the alleged incapacitated individual would likely suffer serious harm if immediate action is not taken. The duties of the guardian ad litem are to visit the alleged incapacitated individual, report to the court and take such other action as directed by the court. The requirement of MCL 700.5312(1) that the court hold the fully noticed hearing within 28 days applies only when the court grants temporary relief.

(D) Temporary Guardian for Minor.

(1) *Before Appointment of Guardian.* If necessary during proceedings for the appointment of a guardian for a minor, the court may appoint a temporary guardian after a hearing at which testimony is taken. The petition for a temporary guardian shall specify in detail the conditions requiring a temporary guardianship. Where a petition for appointment of a limited guardian has been filed, the court, before the appointment of a temporary guardian, shall take into consideration the limited guardianship placement plan in determining the powers and duties of the parties during the temporary guardianship.

(2) *When Guardian Previously Appointed.* If it comes to the attention of the court that a guardian of a minor is not properly performing the duties of a guardian, the court, after a hearing at which testimony is taken, may appoint a temporary guardian for a period not to exceed 6 months. The temporary guardian shall have the authority of the previously appointed guardian whose powers are suspended during the term of the temporary guardianship. The temporary guardian shall determine whether a petition to remove the guardian should be filed. If such a petition is not filed, the temporary guardian shall report to court with recommendations for action that the court should take in order to protect the minor upon expiration of the term of the temporary guardian. The report shall be filed within 1 month of the date of the expiration of the temporary guardianship.

[Adopted July 12, 2001, effective January 1, 2002, 464 Mich. Amended December 5, 2006, effective January 1, 2007, 477 Mich; January 14, 2009, effective May 1, 2009, 483 Mich; October 1, 2014, effective January 1, 2015, 497 Mich.]

Comments

Staff Comment to 2001 Adoption

This rule was MCR 5.763.

Staff Comment to 2006 Amendment

The amendment of MCR 5.403(B) requires the court to state on the record and in the order the reasons for shortening or eliminating notice of hearing for the appointment of a temporary guardian of a minor. It also requires the court to serve interested persons with notice that a temporary guardian has been appointed for a minor, if the appointment followed an ex parte hearing for which the notice period was shortened or eliminated. The new rule provisions allow interested persons to object to entry of the order and have a hearing on the matter within 14 days.

Staff Comment to 2009 Amendment

These amendments were adopted primarily as a result of submissions by the Michigan Probate Judges Association and the State Bar of Michigan's Probate and Estate Planning Section. This was a joint effort to increase the oversight of guardianship and conservatorship proceedings, as well as to improve other procedures in probate court.

Staff Comment to 2015 Amendment

These Chapter 5 rule amendments, submitted to the Court by the Probate and Estate Planning Section of the State Bar of Michigan, comport to recent legislation regarding guardianships and conservatorships.

Rule 5.404 Guardianship of Minor

(A) Petition for Guardianship of Minor.

(1) *Petition.* A petition for guardianship of a minor shall be filed on a form approved by the State Court Administrative Office. The petitioner shall state in the petition whether or not the minor is an Indian child or whether that fact is unknown. The petitioner shall document all efforts made to determine a child's membership or eligibility for membership in an Indian tribe and shall provide them, upon request, to the court, Indian tribe, Indian child, Indian child's lawyer-guardian ad litem, parent, or Indian custodian.

(2) *Investigation.* Upon the filing of a petition, the court may appoint a guardian ad litem to represent the interests of a minor and may order the Department of Health and Human Services or a court employee or agent to conduct an investigation of the proposed guardianship and file a written report of the investigation in accordance with MCL 700.5204(1). If the petition involves an Indian child, the report shall contain the information required in MCL 712B.25(1). The report shall be filed with the court and served no later than 7 days before the hearing on the petition. If the petition for guardianship states that it is unknown whether the minor is an Indian child, the investigation shall include an inquiry into Indian tribal membership.

(3) *Guardianship of an Indian Child.* If the petition involves an Indian child and both parents intend to execute a consent pursuant to MCL 712B.13 and these rules, the court shall proceed under subrule (B). If the petition involves an Indian child and a consent will not be executed pursuant to MCL 712B.13 and these rules, the petitioner shall state in the petition what active efforts were made to provide remedial services and rehabilitative programs designed to prevent the breakup of the Indian family as defined in MCR 3.002(1). The court shall proceed under subrule (C).

(4) *Social History.* The petitioner must file a social history before a hearing is held on a petition for guardianship of a minor and shall do so on a form approved by the State Court Administrative Office. The social history for minor guardianship is confidential, and it is not to be released, except on order of the court, to the parties or the attorneys for the parties.

(5) *Limited Guardianship of the Child of a Minor.* On the filing of a petition for appointment of a limited guardian for a child whose parent is an unemancipated minor, the court shall appoint a guardian ad litem to represent the minor parent. A limited guardianship placement plan is not binding on the minor parent until consented to by the guardian ad litem.

(B) Voluntary Consent to Guardianship of an Indian Child. A voluntary consent to guardianship of an Indian child must be executed by both parents or the Indian custodian.

(1) *Form of Consent.* To be valid, the consent must contain the information prescribed by MCL 712B.13(2) and be executed on a form approved by the State Court Administrative Office, in writing, recorded before a judge of a court of competent jurisdiction, and accompanied by the presiding judge's certificate that the terms and consequences of the consent were fully explained in detail and were fully understood by the parent or Indian custodian. The court shall also certify that either the parent or Indian custodian fully understood the explanation in English or that it was interpreted into a language that the parent or Indian custodian understood. Any consent given before, or within 10 days after, the birth of the Indian child is not valid. The court may not use videoconferencing technology for the consent hearing required to be held under the Michigan Indian Family Preservation Act and this subrule.

(2) *Hearing.* The court must conduct a hearing on a petition for voluntary guardianship of an Indian child in accordance with this rule before the court may enter an order appointing a guardian. Notice of the hearing on the petition must be sent to the persons prescribed in MCR 5.125(A)(8) and (C)(20) in compliance with MCR 5.109(1). At the hearing on the petition, the court shall determine:

(a) if the tribe has exclusive jurisdiction as defined in MCR 3.002(6). The court shall comply with MCR 5.402(E)(2).

(b) that a valid consent has been executed by both parents or the Indian custodian as required by MCL 712B.13 and this subrule.

(c) if it is in the Indian child's best interest to appoint a guardian.

(d) if a lawyer-guardian ad litem should be appointed to represent the Indian child.

(3) *Withdrawal of Consent.* A consent may be withdrawn at any time by sending written notice to the court substantially in compliance with a form approved by the State Court Administrative Office. Upon receipt of the notice, the court shall immediately enter an ex parte order terminating the guardianship and returning the Indian child to the parent or Indian custodian except, if both parents executed a consent, both parents must withdraw their consent or the court must conduct a hearing within 21 days to determine whether to terminate the guardianship.

(C) Involuntary Guardianship of an Indian Child.

(1) *Hearing.* The court must conduct a hearing on a petition for involuntary guardianship of an Indian child in accordance with this rule before the court may enter an order appointing a guardian. Notice of the hearing must be sent to the persons prescribed in MCR 5.125(A)(8) and (C)(20) in compliance with MCR 5.109(1). At the hearing on the petition, the court shall determine:

(a) if the tribe has exclusive jurisdiction as defined in MCR 3.002(6). The court shall comply with MCR 5.402(E)(2).

(b) if the placement with the guardian meets the placement requirements in subrule (C)(2) and (3).

(c) if it is in the Indian child's best interest to appoint a guardian.

(d) if a lawyer-guardian ad litem should be appointed to represent the Indian child.

(e) whether or not each parent wants to consent to the guardianship if consents were not filed with the petition. If each parent wants to consent to the guardianship, the court shall proceed in accordance with subrule (B).

(2) *Placement.* An Indian child shall be placed in the least restrictive setting that most approximates a family and in which his or her special needs, if any, may be met. The child shall be placed within reasonable proximity to his or her home, taking into account any special needs of the child. Absent good cause to the contrary, the placement of an Indian child must be in descending order of preference with:

(a) a member of the child's extended family,

(b) a foster home licensed, approved, or specified by the child's tribe,

(c) an Indian foster family licensed or approved by the Department of Human Services,

(d) an institution for children approved by an Indian tribe or operated by an Indian organization that has a program suitable to meet the child's needs.

The standards to be applied in meeting the preference requirements above shall be the prevailing social and cultural standards of the Indian community in which the parent or extended family resides or with which the parent or extended family members maintain social and cultural ties.

(3) *Deviating from Placement.* The court may order another placement for good cause shown in accordance with MCL 712B.23(3)–(5) and 25 USC 1915(c). If the Indian child's tribe has established a different order of preference than the order prescribed in subrule (C)(2), placement shall follow that tribe's order of preference as long as the placement is the least restrictive setting appropriate to the particular needs of the child, as provided in MCL 712B.23(6). Where appropriate, the preference of the Indian child or parent shall be considered.

(D) Hearing. If the petition for guardianship of a minor does not indicate that the minor is an Indian child as defined in MCR 3.002(12), the court must inquire if the child or either parent is a member of an Indian tribe. If the child is a member or if a parent is a member and the child is eligible for membership in the tribe, the court shall either dismiss the petition or allow the petitioner to comply with MCR 5.404(A)(1).

(E) Limited Guardianship Placement Plans and Court-Structured Plans.

(1) All limited guardianship placement plans and court-structured plans shall at least include provisions concerning all of the following:

(a) visitation and contact with the minor by the parent or parents sufficient to maintain a parent and child relationship;

(b) the duration of the guardianship;

(c) financial support for the minor; and

(d) in a limited guardianship, the reason why the parent or parents are requesting the court to appoint a limited guardian for the minor.

(2) All limited guardianship placement plans and court-structured plans may include the following:

(a) a schedule of services to be followed by the parent or parents, child, and guardian and

(b) any other provisions that the court deems necessary for the welfare of the child.

(3) *Modification of Placement Plan.*

(a) The parties to a limited guardianship placement plan may file a proposed modification of the plan without filing a petition. The proposed modification shall be substantially in the form approved by the state court administrator.

(b) The court shall examine the proposed modified plan and take further action under subrules (c) and (d) within 14 days after the filing of the proposed modified plan.

(c) If the court approves the proposed modified plan, the court shall endorse the modified plan and notify the interested persons of its approval.

(d) If the court does not approve the modification, the court either shall set the proposed modification plan for a hearing or notify the parties of the objections of the court and that they may schedule a hearing or submit another proposed modified plan.

(F) Evidence.

(1) *Involuntary Guardianship of an Indian Child.* If a petition for guardianship involves an Indian child and the petition was not accompanied by a consent executed pursuant to MCL 712B.13 and these rules, the court may remove the Indian child from a parent or Indian custodian and place that child with a guardian only upon clear and convincing evidence that:

(a) active efforts have been made to provide remedial services and rehabilitative programs designed to prevent the breakup of the Indian family,

(b) these efforts have proved unsuccessful, and

(c) continued custody of the child by the parent or Indian custodian is likely to result in serious emotional or physical damage to the child.

The evidence shall include the testimony of at least one qualified expert witness, as described in MCL 712B.17, who has knowledge about the child-rearing practices of the Indian child's tribe. The active efforts must take into account the prevailing social and cultural conditions and way of life of the Indian child's tribe. If the petitioner cannot show active efforts have been made, the court shall dismiss the petition and may refer the petitioner to the Department of Human Services for child protective services or to the tribe for services.

(2) *Reports, Admission into Evidence.* At any hearing concerning a guardianship of a minor, all relevant and material evidence, including written reports, may be received by the court and may be relied on to the extent of their probative value, even though such evidence may not be admissible under the Michigan Rules of Evidence.

(3) *Written Reports, Review and Cross–Examination.* Interested persons shall be afforded an opportunity to examine and controvert written reports so received and, in the court's discretion, may be allowed to cross-examine individuals making reports when such individuals are reasonably available.

(4) *Privilege, Abrogation.* No assertion of an evidentiary privilege, other than the privilege between attorney and client, shall prevent the receipt and use of materials prepared pursuant to a court-ordered examination, interview, or course of treatment.

(G) Review of Guardianship for Minor.

(1) *Periodic Review.* The court shall conduct a review of a guardianship of a minor annually in each case where the minor is under age 6 as of the anniversary of the qualification of the guardian. The review shall be commenced within 63 days after the anniversary date of the qualification of the guardian. The court may at any time conduct a review of a guardianship as it deems necessary.

(2) *Investigation.* The court shall appoint the Department of Human Services or any other person to conduct an investigation of the guardianship of a minor. The investigator shall file a written report with the court within 28 days after such appointment. The report shall include a recommendation regarding whether the guardianship should be continued or modified and whether a hearing should be scheduled. If the report recommends modification, the report shall state the nature of the modification.

(3) *Judicial Action.* After informal review of the report, the court shall enter an order continuing the guardianship or set a date for a hearing to be held within 28 days. If a hearing is set, an attorney may be appointed to represent the minor.

(H) Termination of Guardianship.

(1) *Necessity of Order.* A guardianship may terminate without order of the court on the minor's death, adoption, marriage, or attainment of majority or in accordance with subrule (H)(6). No full, testamentary, or limited guardianship shall otherwise terminate without an order of the court.

(2) *Continuation of Guardianship.* When a court has continued a guardianship for a period not exceeding one year, the court shall hold the final hearing not less than 28 days before the expiration of the period of continuance.

(3) *Petition for Family Division of Circuit Court to Take Jurisdiction.* If the court appoints an attorney or the Department of Human Services to investigate whether to file a petition with the family division of circuit court to take jurisdiction of the minor, the attorney or Department of Human Services shall, within 21 days, report to the court that a petition has been filed or why a petition has not been filed.

(a) If a petition is not filed with the family division, the court shall take such further action as is warranted, except the guardianship may not be continued for more than one year after the hearing on the petition to terminate.

(b) If a petition is filed with the family division, the guardianship shall terminate when the family division authorizes the petition under MCL 712A.11, unless the family division determines that continuation of such guardianship pending disposition is necessary for the well-being of the child.

(4) *Resignation of Limited Guardian.* A petition by a limited guardian to resign shall be treated as a petition for termination of the limited guardianship. The parents or the sole parent with the right to custody may file a petition for a new limited guardianship. If the court does not approve the new limited guardianship or if no petition is filed, the court may proceed in the manner for termination of a guardianship under

section 5209 or 5219 of the Estates and Protected Individuals Code, MCL 700.5209 or MCL 700.5219.

(5) *Petition for Termination by a Party Other Than a Parent.* If a petition for termination is filed by a party other than a parent or Indian custodian, the court may proceed in the manner for termination of a guardianship under section 5209 of the Estates and Protected Individuals Code, MCL 700.5209.

(6) *Voluntary Consent Guardianship.* The guardianship of an Indian child established pursuant to subrule (C) shall be terminated in accordance with subrule (B)(3).

[Adopted July 12, 2001, effective January 1, 2002, 464 Mich. Amended December 18, 2001, effective May 1, 2002, 465 Mich. Amended effective November 15, 2005, 474 Mich. Amended February 2, 2010, effective May 1, 2010, 485 Mich; June 4, 2014, effective September 1, 2014, 496 Mich. Amended effective March 9, 2016, 499 Mich. Amended September 21, 2016, effective January 1, 2017, 500 Mich; March 20, 2019, effective May 1, 2019, 502 Mich. Amended effective August 14, 2019, 503 Mich.]

Comments

Staff Comment to 2001 Adoption

This rule was MCR 5.764.

Staff Comment to 2002 Amendment

The December 18, 2001 amendments, effective May 1, 2002, updated various rules in light of the Estates and Protected Individuals Code (EPIC), MCL 700.1101 *et seq.*, and revisions made to EPIC by 2000 PA 312, 313, and 469.

Staff Comment to 2005 Amendment

The amendments of MCR 5.144, 5.203, 5.207, 5.302, 5.307, 5.404, and 5.409, effective immediately, were developed as a result of the state court administrative office's statewide conservatorship case review prompted by the Performance Audit of Selected Probate Court Conservatorship Cases by the Michigan Office of the Auditor General and the State Bar of Michigan Probate and Estate Planning Section's Uniformity of Practice Committee's survey of probate court practices. The amendment of MCR 5.144(A)(2) eliminates the ability to close a conservatorship estate because of suspension of a fiduciary unless there are insufficient funds available to hire a special fiduciary, or after notice and hearing and a finding of good cause. The amendment of MCR 5.203(D) adds the financial institution and guardian ad litem to the list required to receive notice when a fiduciary is suspended. The amendment of MCR 5.207(A) allows for better court oversight when real property is sold. The amendment of MCR 5.302(A) requires that a copy of a death certificate be attached to the petition or application when commencing a decedent estate. In the event that the death certificate is not available, the petitioner may provide alternative documentation. The amendment of MCR 5.307(A) allows for the deduction of secured loans when calculating the inventory fee due. The amendment of MCR 5.404(A) creates a new subsection that requires the use of a SCAO approved social history form when one is required to be filed with a petition for guardianship of a minor. The amendment of MCR 5.409(B)(2) requires that joint property belonging to the protected person be listed on the inventory along with the type of ownership. The amendment of MCR 5.409(C)(1) clarifies that the fiduciary must serve the account on the interested persons and file the proof of service with the court. The amendment of MCR 5.409(C)(4) provides the process for filing a proof of restricted account and annual verification of funds on deposit with the court. The amendment of MCR 5.409(C)(5) adds the requirement to present a financial institution statement to the court when filing the annual account. The amendment of MCR 5.409(C)(6) requires the court to either review or allow the account annually and to hold a hearing on the accounts at least once every three years.

Staff Comment to 2010 Amendment

These amendments incorporate provisions of the Indian Child Welfare Act into specific provisions within various rules relating to child protective proceedings and juvenile status offenses. The language is designed to make the rules reflect a more integrated approach to addressing issues specific to Indian children.

MCR 3.002(1)(c) defines "preadoptive placement" to mean the "temporary placement of an Indian child in a foster home or institution after the termination of parental rights, but before or in lieu of adoptive placement, and ..." The phrase "in lieu of adoptive placement" is not intended to mean that it is permissible to leave a child in foster care indefinitely, in violation of MCL 712A.19b(6) or (7) or 45 CFR 1355.20, 45 CFR 1356.21, or 45 CFR 1356.50. Rather, it addresses situations where the parental rights to a child have been terminated and there is no permanency plan for adoption of the child. One example is when the child has been placed with a juvenile guardian and the

guardianship is subsequently revoked. In this situation, jurisdiction over the child pursuant to MCL 712A.2(b) will be reinstated and the child is placed in foster care.

MCR 3.002(1): The definition of "child custody proceeding" is intended to apply the Indian Child Welfare Act to delinquency proceedings if an "Indian child" is charged with a so-called status offense in violation of MCL 712A.2(a)(2)–(4) or (d). Delinquency proceedings involving an Indian child charged with any other non-status offense are generally not subject to the Indian Child Welfare Act; however, if the initial investigation or subsequent review of a non-status delinquency case reveals that the Indian child involved suffers from child abuse or neglect, a separate child protective proceeding may be initiated, which would be subject to the Indian Child Welfare Act.

The amendment of MCR 3.905(C)(1) states that a court shall consider guidelines established by the Bureau of Indian Affairs (BIA) in determining whether good cause not to transfer exists (Guidelines for State Courts; Indian Child Custody Proceedings, 44 Fed Reg No 228, 67590–67592, C.2–C.4. [November 26, 1979]). Some examples of good cause are that the Indian tribe does not have a tribal court or that the Indian child is over 12 years old and objects to the transfer. For additional examples of good cause and relevant case law, see the BIA guidelines cited above and A Practical Guide to the Indian Child Welfare Act. (Native American Rights Fund, A Practical Guide to the Indian Child Welfare Act [Boulder, CO: Native American Rights Fund, 2007], 7.15 and 7.16, p 60.)

Staff Comment to 2014 Amendment

These amendments incorporate provisions of the Michigan Indian Family Preservation Act and the Indian Child Welfare Act and reflect a more integrated approach to addressing issues specific to Indian children.

Staff Comment to 2016 Amendment

These amendments update cross-references that changed after the rule was adopted and make other nonsubstantive revisions.

Staff Comment to 2017 Amendment

These amendments permit courts to expand the use of videoconferencing technology in many court proceedings, and clarify the proceedings at which videoconferencing technology may be used.

Staff Comment to May, 2019 Amendment

The amendments of Rules 1.109, 2.102, 2.104, 2.106, 2.107, 2.117, 2.119, 2.403, 2.503, 2.506, 2.508, 2.518, 2.602, 2.603, 2.621, 3.101, 3.104, 3.203, 3.205, 3.210, 3.302, 3.607, 3.613, 3.614, 3.705, 3.801, 3.802, 3.805, 3.806, 4.201, 4.202, 4.303, 4.306, 5.001, 5.104, 5.105, 5.107, 5.108, 5.113, 5.117, 5.118, 5.119, 5.120, 5.125, 5.126, 5.132, 5.162, 5.202, 5.203, 5.205, 5.302, 5.304, 5.307, 5.308, 5.309, 5.310, 5.311, 5.313, 5.402, 5.404, 5.405, 5.409, 5.501, and 5.784 and addition of Rule 3.618 of the Michigan Court Rules are an expected progression necessary for design and implementation of the statewide electronic-filing system. These particular amendments will assist in implementing the goals of the project.

Staff Comment to August, 2019 Amendment

These amendments update cross-references and make other nonsubstantive revisions to clarify the rules.

Rule 5.405   Proceedings on Guardianship of Incapacitated Individual

(A) Examination by Physician or Mental Health Professional.

(1) *Admission of Report.* The court may receive into evidence without testimony a written report of a physician or mental health professional who examined an individual alleged to be incapacitated, provided that a copy of the report is filed with the court five days before the hearing and that the report is on the form required by the state court administrator. A party offering a report must promptly inform the parties that the report is filed and available. The court may issue on its own initiative, or any party may secure, a subpoena to compel the preparer of the report to testify.

(2) *Abrogation of Privilege.* A report ordered by the court may be used in guardianship proceedings without regard to any privilege. Any privilege regarding a report made as part of an independent evaluation at the request of a respondent is waived if the respondent seeks to have the report considered in the proceedings.

(3) *Determination of Fee.* As a condition of receiving payment, the physician or mental health professional shall submit an itemized statement of services and expenses for approval. In reviewing a statement, the court shall consider the time required for examination, evaluation, preparation of reports and court appearances; the examiner's experience and training; and the local fee for similar services.

(B) Hearings at Site Other Than Courtroom. When hearings are not held in the courtroom where the court ordinarily sits, the court shall ensure a quiet and dignified setting that permits an undisturbed proceeding and inspires the participants' confidence in the integrity of the judicial process.

(C) Guardian of Incapacitated Individual Appointed by Will or Other Writing.

(1) *Appointment.* A guardian appointed by will or other writing under MCL 700.5301 may qualify after the death or adjudicated incapacity of a parent or spouse who had been the guardian of an incapacitated individual by filing an acceptance of appointment with the court that has jurisdiction over the guardianship. Unless the court finds the person unsuitable or incompetent for the trust, the court shall issue to the nominated guardian letters of guardianship equivalent to those that had been issued to the deceased guardian.

(2) *Notice, Revocation.* The testamentary guardian shall notify the court in which the testamentary instrument has been or will be filed of the appointment as guardian. The probating court shall notify the court having jurisdiction over the guardianship if the will is denied probate, and the court having the guardianship jurisdiction shall immediately revoke the letters of guardianship.

[Adopted July 12, 2001, effective January 1, 2002, 464 Mich. Amended March 20, 2019, effective May 1, 2019, 502 Mich.]

Comments

Staff Comment to 2001 Adoption

This rule was MCR 5.765. Subrule (C) is changed to reflect the nomination of a guardian by a writing other than a will in MCL 700.5301. If there is a difference between the court designated by the rule for filing the acceptance of appointment and that designated by the statute, the nominated guardian should file in both courts.

Staff Comment to 2019 Amendment

The amendments of Rules 1.109, 2.102, 2.104, 2.106, 2.107, 2.117, 2.119, 2.403, 2.503, 2.506, 2.508, 2.518, 2.602, 2.603, 2.621, 3.101, 3.104, 3.203, 3.205, 3.210, 3.302, 3.607, 3.613, 3.614, 3.705, 3.801, 3.802, 3.805, 3.806, 4.201, 4.202, 4.303, 4.306, 5.001, 5.104, 5.105, 5.107, 5.108, 5.113, 5.117, 5.118, 5.119, 5.120, 5.125, 5.126, 5.132, 5.162, 5.202, 5.203, 5.205, 5.302, 5.304, 5.307, 5.308, 5.309, 5.310, 5.311, 5.313, 5.402, 5.404, 5.405, 5.409, 5.501, and 5.784 and addition of Rule 3.618 of the Michigan Court Rules are an expected progression necessary for design and implementation of the statewide electronic-filing system. These particular amendments will assist in implementing the goals of the project.

Rule 5.406 Testamentary Guardian of Individual with Developmental Disabilities

(A) Appointment. If the court has not appointed a standby guardian, a testamentary guardian may qualify after the death of a parent who had been the guardian of an individual with developmental disabilities by filing an acceptance of appointment with the court that appointed the deceased parent as guardian. If the nominated person is to act as guardian of the estate of the ward, the guardian should also file a bond in the amount last required of the deceased guardian. Unless the court finds the person unsuitable or incompetent for the appointment, the court shall issue to the testamentary guardian

letters of authority equivalent to those that had been issued to the deceased guardian.

(B) Notice, Revocation. The testamentary guardian must notify the court in which the testamentary instrument has been or will be filed of the appointment as guardian. The probating court shall notify the court having jurisdiction over the guardianship if the will is denied probate, and the court having the guardianship jurisdiction shall immediately revoke the letters of authority.

[Adopted July 12, 2001, effective January 1, 2002, 464 Mich.]

Comments

Staff Comment to 2001 Adoption

This rule was MCR 5.766.

Rule 5.407 Conservatorship; Settlements

A conservator may not enter into a settlement in any court on behalf of the protected person if the conservator will share in the settlement unless a guardian ad litem has been appointed to represent the protected person's interest and has consented to such settlement in writing or on the record or the court approves the settlement over any objection.

[Adopted July 12, 2001, effective January 1, 2002, 464 Mich. Amended December 18, 2001, effective May 1, 2002, 465 Mich.]

Comments

Staff Comment to 2001 Adoption

This rule was MCR 5.767.

Staff Comment to 2002 Amendment

The December 18, 2001 amendments, effective May 1, 2002, updated various rules in light of the Estates and Protected Individuals Code (EPIC), MCL 700.1101 *et seq.*, and revisions made to EPIC by 2000 PA 312, 313, and 469.

Rule 5.408 Review and Modification of Guardianships of Legally Incapacitated Individuals

(A) Periodic Review of Guardianship.

(1) *Periodic Review.* The court shall commence a review of a guardianship of a legally incapacitated individual not later than 1 year after the appointment of the guardian and not later than every 3 years thereafter.

(2) *Investigation.* The court shall appoint a person to investigate the guardianship and report to the court by a date set by the court. The person appointed must visit the legally incapacitated individual or include in the report to the court an explanation why a visit was not practical. The report shall include a recommendation on whether the guardianship should be modified.

(3) *Judicial Action.* After informal review of the report, the court shall enter an order continuing the guardianship, or enter an order appointing an attorney to represent the legally incapacitated individual for the purpose of filing a petition for modification of guardianship. In either case, the court shall send a copy of the report and the order to the legally incapacitated individual and the guardian.

(4) *Petition for Modification.* If an attorney is appointed under subrule (A)(3), the attorney shall file proper pleadings with the court within 14 days of the date of appointment.

(B) Petition for Modification; Appointment of Attorney or Guardian Ad Litem.

(1) *Petition by Legally Incapacitated Individual.* If a petition for modification or written request for modification comes from the legally incapacitated individual and that individual does not have an attorney, the court shall immediately appoint an attorney.

(2) *Petition by Person Other Than Legally Incapacitated Individual.* If a petition for modification or written request for modification comes from some other party, the court shall appoint a guardian ad litem. If the guardian ad litem ascertains that the legally incapacitated individual contests the relief requested, the court shall appoint an attorney for the legally incapacitated individual and terminate the appointment of the guardian ad litem.

[Adopted July 12, 2001, effective January 1, 2002, 464 Mich.]

Comments

Staff Comment to 2001 Adoption

This rule was MCR 5.768.

Rule 5.409 Report of Guardian; Inventories and Accounts of Conservators

(A) Reports. A guardian shall file a written report annually within 56 days after the anniversary of appointment and at other times as the court may order. Reports must be in the form approved by the state court administrator. The guardian must serve the report on the persons listed in MCR 5.125(C)(24).

(B) Inventories.

(1) *Guardian.* At the time of appointing a guardian, the court shall determine whether there would be sufficient assets under the control of the guardian to require the guardian to file an inventory. If the court determines that there are sufficient assets, the court shall order the guardian to file an inventory.

(2) *Filing and Service.* Within 56 days after appointment, a conservator or, if ordered to do so, a guardian shall file with the court a verified inventory of the estate of the protected person, serve copies on the persons required by law or court rule to be served, and file proof of service with the court.

(3) *Contents.* The guardian or conservator must provide the name and address of each financial institution listed on the inventory. The address for a financial institution shall be either that of the institution's main headquarters or the branch used most frequently by the guardian or conservator. Property that the protected individual owns jointly or in common with others must be listed on the inventory along with the type of ownership and value.

(C) Accounts.

(1) *Filing, Service.* A conservator must file an annual account unless ordered not to by the court. A guardian must file an annual account if ordered by the court. The provisions of the court rules apply to any account that is filed with the court, even if the account was not required by court order. The account must be served on interested persons, and proof of service must be filed with the court. The copy of the account served on interested persons must include a notice that any objections to the account should be filed with the court and noticed for hearing. When required, an accounting must be filed within 56 days after the end of the accounting period.

(2) *Accounting Period.* The accounting period ends on the anniversary date of the issuance of the letters of authority, unless the conservator selects another accounting period or unless the court orders otherwise. If the conservator selects another accounting period, notice of that selection shall be filed with the court. The accounting period may be a calendar year or a fiscal year ending on the last day of a month. The conservator may use the same accounting period as that used for income tax reporting, and the first accounting period may be less than a year but not longer than a year.

(3) *Hearing.* On filing, the account may be set for hearing or the hearing may be deferred to a later time.

(4) *Exception, Conservatorship of Minor.* Unless otherwise ordered by the court, no accounting is required in a minor conservatorship where the assets are restricted or in a conservatorship where no assets have been received by the conservator. If the assets are ordered to be placed in a restricted account, proof of the restricted account must be filed with the court within 28 days of the conservator's qualification or as otherwise ordered by the court. The conservator must file with the court an annual verification of funds on deposit with a copy of the corresponding financial institution statement attached.

(5) *Contents.* The accounting is subject to the provisions of MCR 5.310(C)(2)(c) and (d), except that references to a personal representative shall be to a conservator. A copy of the corresponding financial institution statement or a verification of funds on deposit must be filed with the court, either of which must reflect the value of all liquid assets held by a financial institution dated within 30 days after the end of the accounting period, unless waived by the court for good cause.

(6) *Periodic Review.* The court shall either review or allow accounts annually, unless no account is required under MCR 5.409(C)(1) or (C)(4). Accounts shall be set for hearing to determine whether they will be allowed at least once every three years.

(D) Service and Notice. A copy of the account must be served on the interested persons as provided by these rules. Notice of hearing to approve the account must be served on interested persons as provided in subchapter 5.100 of these rules.

(E) Procedures. The procedures prescribed in MCR 5.203, 5.204 and 5.310(E) apply to guardianship and conservatorship proceedings, except that references to a personal representative shall be to a guardian or conservator, as the situation dictates.

(F) Death of Ward. If an individual who is subject to a guardianship or conservatorship dies, the guardian or conservator must give written notification to the court within 14 days of the individual's date of death. If accounts are required to be filed with the court, a final account must be filed within 56 days of the date of death.

[Adopted July 12, 2001, effective January 1, 2002, 464 Mich. Amended December 18, 2001, effective May 1, 2002, 465 Mich. Amended effective November 15, 2005, 474 Mich. Amended October 11, 2007, effective January 1, 2008, 479 Mich; March 20, 2019, effective May 1, 2019, 502 Mich.]

Comments

Staff Comment to 2001 Adoption

This rule was MCR 5.769. Subrule (C) is amended to reflect that MCL 700.5418 requires annual accounting. Two exceptions are added in subrule (C)(4) for situations where no purpose would be served by an accounting. New subrule (C)(6) [effective January 1, 2002] requires court review of accounts no less often than once every three years. The scope of the review is not defined, so as to allow the court flexibility in choosing among methods such as staff review, appointment of a guardian ad litem and other methods which may be appropriate for specific files. However, minimum levels of review should be consistent with standards to be set by the State Court Administrator.

Staff Comment to 2002 Amendment

The December 18, 2001 amendments, effective May 1, 2002, updated various rules in light of the Estates and Protected Individuals Code (EPIC), MCL 700.1101 *et seq.*, and revisions made to EPIC by 2000 PA 312, 313, and 469.

Staff Comment to 2005 Amendment

The amendments of MCR 5.144, 5.203, 5.207, 5.302, 5.307, 5.404, and 5.409, effective immediately, were developed as a result of the state court administrative office's statewide conservatorship case review prompted by the Performance Audit of Selected Probate Court Conservatorship Cases by the Michigan Office of the Auditor General and the State Bar of Michigan Probate and Estate Planning Section's Uniformity of Practice Committee's survey of probate court practices. The amendment of MCR 5.144(A)(2) eliminates the ability to close a conservatorship estate because of suspension of a fiduciary unless there are insufficient funds available to hire a special fiduciary, or after notice and hearing and a finding of good cause. The amendment of MCR 5.203(D) adds the financial institution and guardian ad litem to the list required to receive notice when a fiduciary is suspended. The amendment of MCR 5.207(A) allows for better court oversight when real property is sold. The amendment of MCR 5.302(A) requires that a copy of a death certificate be attached to the petition or application when commencing a decedent estate. In the event that the death certificate is not available, the petitioner may provide alternative documentation. The amendment of MCR 5.307(A) allows for the deduction of secured loans when calculating the inventory fee due. The amendment of MCR 5.404(A) creates a new subsection that requires the use of a SCAO approved social history form when one is required to be filed with a petition for guardianship of a minor. The amendment of MCR 5.409(B)(2) requires that joint property belonging to the protected person be listed on the inventory along with the type of ownership. The amendment of MCR 5.409(C)(1) clarifies that the fiduciary must serve the account on the interested persons and file the proof of service with the court. The amendment of MCR 5.409(C)(4) provides the process for filing a proof of restricted account and annual verification of funds on deposit with the court. The amendment of MCR 5.409(C)(5) adds the requirement to present a financial institution statement to the court when filing the annual account. The amendment of MCR 5.409(C)(6) requires the court to either review or allow the account annually and to hold a hearing on the accounts at least once every three years.

Staff Comment to 2007 Amendment

These amendments were proposed by the Probate and Estate Planning Section of the State Bar of Michigan, and are intended to address and clarify practice issues within the amended rules. The amendment of MCR 5.207(A)(4) provides the alternative of including a tax statement to show the state equalized value of property. The amendments of MCR 5.307(B) and MCR 5.409(B)(3) require the name and address of each financial institution be added to the inventory, and requires that the institution's main address or branch used most frequently by the filer be identified. The amendment of MCR 5.409(C)(1) requires any account filed with the court to comply with relevant court rules. The amendment of MCR 5.409(C)(4) extends the time in which to file proof of a minor's assets in a restricted account from 14 to 28 days. The amendment of MCR 5.409(C)(5) allows the option of filing an annual verification of funds on deposit or presenting a copy of a financial institution statement with an annual account.

Staff Comment to 2019 Amendment

The amendments of Rules 1.109, 2.102, 2.104, 2.106, 2.107, 2.117, 2.119, 2.403, 2.503, 2.506, 2.508, 2.518, 2.602, 2.603, 2.621, 3.101, 3.104, 3.203, 3.205, 3.210, 3.302, 3.607, 3.613, 3.614, 3.705, 3.801, 3.802, 3.805, 3.806, 4.201, 4.202, 4.303, 4.306, 5.001, 5.104, 5.105, 5.107, 5.108, 5.113, 5.117, 5.118, 5.119, 5.120, 5.125, 5.126, 5.132, 5.162, 5.202, 5.203, 5.205, 5.302, 5.304, 5.307, 5.308, 5.309, 5.310, 5.311, 5.313, 5.402, 5.404, 5.405, 5.409, 5.501, and 5.784 and addition of Rule 3.618 of the Michigan Court Rules are an expected progression necessary for design and implementation of the statewide electronic-filing system. These particular amendments will assist in implementing the goals of the project.

Rule 5.411 Bond of Conservator

In all conservatorships in which there are unrestricted assets, the court may require a bond in the amount the court finds necessary to protect the estate or as required by statute. No bond shall be required of trust companies organized under the laws of Michigan or of banks with trust powers unless the court orders that a bond be required.

[Adopted January 14, 2009, effective May 1, 2009, 483 Mich.]

Comments

Staff Comment to 2009 Adoption

These amendments were adopted primarily as a result of submissions by the Michigan Probate Judges Association and the State Bar of Michigan's Probate and Estate Planning Section. This was a joint effort to increase the oversight of guardianship and conservatorship proceedings, as well as to improve other procedures in probate court.

SUBCHAPTER 5.500   TRUST PROCEEDINGS

Rule 5.501   Trust Proceedings in General

(A) Applicability. This subchapter applies to all trusts as defined in MCL 700.1107(n), including a trust established under a will and a trust created by court order or a separate document.

(B) Unsupervised Administration of Trusts. Unless an interested person invokes court jurisdiction, the administration of a trust shall proceed expeditiously, consistent with the terms of the trust, free of judicial intervention and without court order, approval, or other court action. Neither registration nor a proceeding concerning a trust results in continued supervisory proceedings.

(C) Commencement of Trust Proceedings. A proceeding concerning a trust is commenced by filing a petition in the court. Registration of the trust is not required for filing a petition.

(D) Appointment of Trustee not Named in Creating Document. An interested person may petition the court for appointment of a trustee when there is a vacancy in a trusteeship. The court may issue an order appointing as trustee the person nominated in the petition or another person.

The order must state whether the trustee must file a bond or sign and file an acceptance.

(E) Qualification of Trustee. A trustee appointed by an order of the court, nominated as a trustee in a will that has been admitted to probate shall qualify by signing and filing an acceptance indicating the nominee's willingness to serve. The trustee must serve the acceptance and order, if any, on the then known qualified trust beneficiaries described in MCL 700.7103(g)(i) and, in the case of a testamentary trustee, on the personal representative of the decedent estate, if one has been appointed. No letters of trusteeship shall be issued by the court. The trustee or the attorney for the trustee may establish the trustee's incumbency by executing an affidavit to that effect, identifying the trustee and the trust and indicating that any required bond has been filed with the court and is in force.

(F) Transitional Rule. A trustee of a trust under the jurisdiction of the court before April 1, 2000, may request an order of the court closing court supervision and the file. On request by the trustee or on its own initiative, the court may order the closing of supervision of the trust and close the file.

The trustee must give notice of the order to all current trust beneficiaries. Closing supervision does not preclude any interested trust beneficiary from later petitioning the court for supervision. Without regard to whether the court file is closed, all letters of authority for existing trusts are canceled as of April 1, 2000, and the trustee's incumbency may be established in the manner provided in subrule (E).

[Adopted July 12, 2001, effective January 1, 2002, 464 Mich. Amended December 18, 2001, effective May 1, 2002, 465 Mich; February 2, 2010, effective April 1, 2010, 485 Mich; March 20, 2019, effective May 1, 2019, 502 Mich.]

Comments

Staff Comment to 2001 Adoption

This rule is new. The Estates and Protected Individuals Code provides that courts do not generally supervise trusts. MCL 700.7201(2). Subrule (F) applies to trusts under court supervision as of April 1, 2000, including those under former MCR 5.722(E).

Staff Comment to 2002 Amendment

The December 18, 2001 amendments, effective May 1, 2002, updated various rules in light of the Estates and Protected Individuals Code (EPIC), MCL 700.1101 *et seq.*, and revisions made to EPIC by 2000 PA 312, 313, and 469.

Staff Comment to 2010 Amendment

These changes, submitted by the Probate and Estate Planning Council of the State Bar of Michigan and the Michigan Probate Judges Association, have been designed so that the rules conform to recently-enacted statutory changes creating the Michigan Trust Code. The amendments correct and insert cross-references to the applicable statutory provisions, and make other technical changes. In addition, new MCR 5.208 incorporates the notice requirements for both decedent estates and trusts currently contained in MCR 5.306 and MCR 5.503, and replaces those rules.

Staff Comment to 2019 Amendment

The amendments of Rules 1.109, 2.102, 2.104, 2.106, 2.107, 2.117, 2.119, 2.403, 2.503, 2.506, 2.508, 2.518, 2.602, 2.603, 2.621, 3.101, 3.104, 3.203, 3.205, 3.210, 3.302, 3.607, 3.613, 3.614, 3.705, 3.801, 3.802, 3.805, 3.806, 4.201, 4.202, 4.303, 4.306, 5.001, 5.104, 5.105, 5.107, 5.108, 5.113, 5.117, 5.118, 5.119, 5.120, 5.125, 5.126, 5.132, 5.162, 5.202, 5.203, 5.205, 5.302, 5.304, 5.307, 5.308, 5.309, 5.310, 5.311, 5.313, 5.402, 5.404, 5.405, 5.409, 5.501, and 5.784 and addition of Rule 3.618 of the Michigan Court Rules are an expected progression necessary for design and implementation of the statewide electronic-filing system. These particular amendments will assist in implementing the goals of the project.

Rule 5.502 Supervision of Trusts

If, during a trust proceeding, the court orders supervision of the trust, the court shall specify the terms of the supervision.

[Adopted July 12, 2001, effective January 1, 2002, 464 Mich.]

Comments

Staff Comment to 2001 Adoption

This rule is new.

SUBCHAPTER 5.730   MENTAL HEALTH RULES

Rule 5.730 Mental Health Code; Application

Except as modified by this subchapter, civil admission and discharge proceedings under the Mental Health Code are governed by the rules generally applicable to probate court.

[Adopted effective March 1, 1985. Amended June 17, 1997, effective September 1, 1997, 454 Mich.]

Comments

Staff Comment to 1985 Adoption

MCR 5.730 is substantially the same as PCR 730.

Rule 5.731. Access to Records

Case records filed with the court under the mental health code are public except as otherwise indicated in court rule or statute.

[Adopted October 31, 2012, effective January 1, 2013, 492 Mich. Amended September 18, 2019, effective January 1, 2020, 503 Mich.]

Comments

Staff Comment to 2013 Adoption

The amendments of these rules update the rules making them less "paper" focused and reflecting the use of electronic technology in the way courts process court records. The amendments also clarify and delineate the types of records and other materials maintained by a court, and clarify how access is provided.

Staff Comment to 2020 Amendment

The amendments of MCR 1.109, 2.107, 2.113, 2.116, 2.119, 2.222, 2.223, 2.225, 2.227, 3.206, 3.211, 3.212, 3.214, 3.303, 3.903, 3.921, 3.925, 3.926, 3.931, 3.933, 3.942, 3.950, 3.961, 3.971, 3.972, 4.002, 4.101, 4.201, 4.202, 4.302, 5.128, 5.302, 5.731, 6.101, 6.615, 8.105, and 8.119 and rescission of MCR 2.226 and 8.125 continue the process for design and implementation of the statewide electronic-filing system.

Rule 5.732 Attorneys

(A) Continuing Appointment of Attorney. The attorney of record must represent the individual in all probate court proceedings under the Mental Health Code until the attorney is discharged by court order or another attorney has filed an appearance on the individual's behalf.

(B) Duties. The attorney must serve as an advocate for the individual's preferred position. If the individual does not express a preference, the attorney must advocate for the position that the attorney believes is in the individual's best interest.

(C) Waiver; Appointment of Guardian Ad Litem. The individual may waive an attorney only in open court and after consultation with an attorney. The court may not accept the waiver if it appears that the waiver is not voluntarily and understandingly made. If an attorney is waived, the court may appoint a guardian ad litem for the individual.

[Adopted effective March 1, 1985. Amended June 17, 1997, effective September 1, 1997, 454 Mich.]

Comments

Staff Comment to 1985 Adoption

MCR 5.732 is substantially the same as PCR 732.

Staff Comment to 1997 Amendment

Subrule (B)(1) is struck because the topic is covered by § 455(2) of the Mental Health Code, MCL 330.1455(2). Subrule (B) is further amended to require the attorney to advocate for the disposition that is in the individual's best interest, if the individual does not express a preference for a disposition. Former subrule (C) is deleted as no longer necessary. Former subrule (D) is redesignated as (C).

Rule 5.733 Appointment of Independent Examiner; Determination of Fees and Expenses

(A) Appointment. When an indigent individual requests an independent clinical evaluation, the court must appoint the physician, psychiatrist, or licensed psychologist chosen by the individual, unless the person chosen refuses to examine the individual or the requested appointment would require unreasonable expense.

(B) Determination of Fee. In its order of appointment, a court must direct the independent examiner to submit an itemized statement of services and expenses for approval. In reviewing a fee, the court must consider:

(1) the time required for examination, evaluation, preparation of reports, and court appearances;

(2) the examiner's experience and training; and

(3) the local fee for similar services.

[Adopted effective March 1, 1985. Amended June 17, 1997, effective September 1, 1997, 454 Mich.]

Comments

Staff Comment to 1985 Adoption

MCR 5.733 is based on PCR 733.

Language is added in subrule (A) to allow an adjournment of up to 7 days when the demand for an independent medical examination is made less than 7 days before the hearing.

Staff Comment to 1997 Amendment

The final sentence of subrule (A) has been deleted. See MCL 330.1462, as amended by 1995 PA 290.

Rule 5.734   Service of Papers; Notice of Subsequent Petitions; Time for Service

(A) Service of Papers. When required by the Mental Health Code, the court must have the necessary papers served. The individual must be served personally. The individual's attorney also must be served.

(B) Notice of Subsequent Petitions. The court must serve a copy of a petition for the second or continuing order of involuntary mental health treatment or petition for discharge and the notice of hearing on all persons required to be served with notice of hearing on the initial petition or application for hospitalization.

(C) Time for Service.

(1) A notice of hearing must be served on the individual and the individual's attorney

(a) at least 2 days before the time of a hearing that is scheduled by the court to be held within 7 days or less; or

(b) at least 5 days before the time scheduled for other hearings.

(2) A notice of hearing must be served on other interested parties

(a) by personal service, at least 2 days before the time of a hearing that is scheduled by the court to be held within 7 days or less; or

(b) by personal service or by mail, at least 5 days before the time scheduled for other hearings.

The court may permit service of a notice of hearing on the individual, the individual's attorney, or other interested parties within a shorter period of time with the consent of the individual and the individual's attorney.

[Adopted effective March 1, 1985. Amended June 17, 1997, effective September 1, 1997, 454 Mich.]

Comments

Staff Comment to 1985 Adoption

MCR 5.734 is substantially the same as PCR 734.

Staff Comment to 1997 Amendment

Former subrule (C) is struck as redundant to subchapter 5.100. Former subrule (D) is redesignated as (C).

Rule 5.735   Adjournment

A hearing may be adjourned only for good cause. The reason for an adjournment must be submitted in writing to the court and to the opposing attorney or stated on the record. [Adopted effective March 1, 1985.]

Comments

Staff Comment to 1985 Adoption

MCR 5.735 is substantially the same as PCR 735.

Rule 5.737   Waiver of Rights

Unless a statute or court rule requires that a waiver be made by the individual personally and on the record, a waiver may be in writing signed by the individual, witnessed by the individual's attorney, and filed with the court.

[Adopted effective March 1, 1985. Amended June 17, 1997, effective September 1, 1997, 454 Mich.]

Comments

Staff Comment to 1985 Adoption

MCR 5.737 corresponds to PCR 737, although it is written from a different perspective. The former rule said that where a statute or rule requires a specific waiver, the respondent is to waive the rights personally and on the record. MCR 5.737 says that unless a particular provision requires a special kind of waiver, rights can be waived in a writing signed by the respondent and witnessed by the respondent's attorney.

Rule 5.738   Conditions at Hearings

(A) Hearings at Hospitals. When hearings are not held in the courtroom where the court ordinarily sits, the court shall ensure a quiet and dignified setting that permits an undisturbed proceeding and inspires the participants' confidence in the integrity of the judicial process.

(B) Clothing. The individual may attend a hearing in personal clothing.

(C) Restraints at Hearing. At a court hearing, the individual may not be handcuffed or otherwise restrained, except

(1) on the prior approval of the court, based on the individual's immediate past conduct indicating the individual is reasonably likely to try to escape or to inflict physical harm on himself or herself or others; or

(2) after an incident occurring during transportation in which the individual has attempted to escape or inflict physical harm on himself or herself or others.

[Adopted effective March 1, 1985. Amended June 17, 1997, effective September 1, 1997, 454 Mich.]

Comments

Staff Comment to 1985 Adoption

MCR 5.738 is substantially the same as PCR 738.

Rule 5.738a   Use of Interactive Video Technology [Repealed effective January 1, 2017.]

Comments

Staff Comment to 2017 Repeal

MCR 5.738a was repealed effective January 1, 2017 by order of the Michigan Supreme Court dated September 21, 2016, 500 Mich.

Rule 5.740   Jury Trial

(A) Persons Permitted to Demand Jury Trial. Notwithstanding MCR 5.158(A), only an individual alleged to be in need of involuntary mental health treatment or an individual with mental retardation alleged to meet the criteria for judicial admission may demand a jury trial in a civil admission proceeding.

(B) Time for Demand. An individual may demand a jury trial any time before testimony is received at the hearing for which the jury is sought.

(C) Verdict in Commitment Proceedings. In proceedings involving possible commitment to a hospital or facility under the Mental Health Code, or to a correctional or training facility under the juvenile code, the jury's verdict must be unanimous.

(D) Fee. A jury fee is not required from a party demanding a jury trial under the Mental Health Code.

[Adopted effective March 1, 1985. Amended December 1, 1994, effective February 1, 1995, 447 Mich; June 17, 1997, effective September 1, 1997, 454 Mich; December 18, 2001, effective May 1, 2002, 465 Mich.]

Comments

Staff Comment to 1985 Adoption

MCR 5.740 is substantially the same as PCR 740.

Staff Comment to 1995 Amendment

Subrule (C) is former MCR 5.512. New subrule (D) is taken from former MCR 5.508(A)(4).

Staff Comment to 1997 Amendment

The last sentence in subrule (B) has been deleted. See MCL 330.1462, as amended by 1995 PA 290.

Staff Comment to 2002 Amendment

The December 18, 2001 amendments, effective May 1, 2002, updated various rules in light of the Estates and Protected Individuals Code (EPIC), MCL 700.1101 *et seq.*, and revisions made to EPIC by 2000 PA 312, 313, and 469.

Rule 5.741 Inquiry Into Adequacy of Treatment

(A) Written Report or Testimony Required. Before ordering a course of involuntary mental health treatment or of care and treatment at a center, the court must receive a written report or oral testimony describing the type and extent of treatment that will be provided to the individual and the appropriateness and adequacy of this treatment.

(B) Use of Written Report; Notice. The court may receive a written report in evidence without accompanying testimony if a copy is filed with the court before the hearing. At the time of filing the report with the court, the preparer of the report must promptly provide the individual's attorney with a copy of the report. The attorney may subpoena the preparer of the report to testify.

[Adopted effective March 1, 1985. Amended June 17, 1997, effective September 1, 1997, 454 Mich.]

Comments

Staff Comment to 1985 Adoption

MCR 5.741 is substantially the same as PCR 741.

Staff Comment to 1997 Amendment

Subrule (B) is amended [effective September 1, 1997] to require the preparer of the report to serve it on the individual's attorney. Subrule (C) is deleted.

Rule 5.743 Appeal by Individual Receiving Involuntary Mental Health Treatment Who is Returned to Hospital After Authorized Leave

(A) Applicability. This rule applies to an individual receiving involuntary mental health treatment who has been returned to a hospital following an authorized leave.

(B) Notifications. When an individual receiving involuntary mental health treatment has been returned to a hospital from an authorized leave in excess of 10 days, the director of the hospital must, within 24 hours, notify the court of the return and notify the individual of the right to appeal the return and have a hearing to determine the appeal. The court must notify the individual's attorney or appoint a new attorney to consult with the individual and determine whether the individual desires a hearing.

(C) Request and Time for Hearing. An individual who wishes to appeal must request a hearing in writing within 7 days of the notice to the individual under subrule (B). The court must schedule a requested hearing to be held within 7 days of the court's receipt of the request.

(D) Reports Filed With Court. At least 3 days before the hearing, the director of the hospital must deliver to the court, the individual, and the individual's attorney, copies of a clinical certificate and a current alternative treatment report.

(E) Conduct of Hearing. At the hearing, the director of the hospital must show that the individual requires treatment in a hospital. The clinical certificate may be admitted in evidence without accompanying testimony by the preparer. However, the individual's attorney may subpoena the preparer of the clinical certificate to testify.

(F) Order After Hearing. If the court finds that the individual requires treatment at a hospital, it must dismiss the appeal and order the individual returned to the hospital. If the court finds that the director lacked an adequate basis for concluding that the individual requires further treatment in the hospital, it must do one of the following:

(1) order the individual returned to authorized leave status; or

(2) order treatment through an alternative to hospitalization

(a) (if the individual was under an order of hospitalization of up to 60 days), for a period not to exceed the difference between 90 days and the combined time the individual has been hospitalized and on authorized leave status, or

(b) (if the individual was under an order of hospitalization of up to 90 days or under a continuing order), for a period not to exceed the difference between 1 year and the combined time the individual has been hospitalized and on authorized leave status.

[Adopted effective March 1, 1985. Amended June 17, 1997, effective September 1, 1997, 454 Mich.]

Comments

Staff Comment to 1985 Adoption

MCR 5.743 is substantially the same as PCR 743.

Staff Comment to 1997 Amendment

Some terminology is changed throughout the rule to reflect current statutory usage. New subrule (A) specifies the topic of the rule. Subrule (C), formerly (B), is rewritten for clarity. Subrule (D), formerly (C), is modified to require that the court be provided with available, current information for its review of the decision to return the individual to the hospital. Subrules (E) and (F) are modified to eliminate the suggestion that appeal rehears the decision to require involuntary mental health treatment including hospitalization. The appeal only reviews the return of the individual to the hospital for up to the remainder of the period previously authorized. Former subrule (E)(4) is deleted because it referred to individuals with mental retardation, now under MCR 5.743a and 5.743b. Former subrule (F) is deleted because voluntary admissions are no longer subject to return procedures under § 408 of the Mental Health Code, MCL 330.1408.

Rule 5.743a   Appeal by Administratively Admitted Individual Returned to Center After Authorized Leave

(A) Applicability. This rule applies to an individual with a developmental disability who was admitted to a center by an administrative admission and who has been returned to a center following an authorized leave.

(B) Notifications. When an administratively admitted individual has been returned to a center from an authorized leave in excess of 10 days, the director of the center must, within 24 hours, notify the court of the return and notify the individual of the right to appeal the return. The court must notify the individual's guardian, if any, and the parents of an individual who is a minor of the return and the right to appeal the return and have a hearing to determine the appeal.

(C) Request for Hearing. An individual who wishes to appeal that individual's return must request a hearing in writing within 7 days of the notice to the individual under subrule (B). If the individual is less than 13 years of age, the request may be made by the individual's parent or guardian. The court must schedule a requested hearing to be held within 7 days of the court's receipt of the request.

(D) Statement Filed With Court. At least 3 days before the hearing, the director of the center must deliver to the court, the individual, the individual's parents or guardian, if applicable, and the individual's attorney a statement setting forth:

(1) the reason for the individual's return to the center;

(2) the reason the individual is believed to need care and treatment at the center; and

(3) the plan for further care and treatment.

(E) Conduct of Hearing. The hearing shall proceed as provided in § 511(4) of the Mental Health Code, MCL 330.1511. At the hearing, the director of the center must show that the individual needs care and treatment at the center and that no alternative to the care and treatment provided at the center is available and adequate to meet the individual's needs.

(F) Order After Hearing. If the court finds the individual requires care and treatment at the center, it must dismiss the appeal and order the individual to remain at the center. If the court finds the director did not sustain the burden of proof, it must order the individual returned to authorized leave status. [Adopted June 17, 1997, effective September 1, 1997, 454 Mich.]

Comments

Staff Comment to 1997 Adoption

This rule is new. See § 537 of the Mental Health Code, MCL 330.1537.

Rule 5.743b   Appeal by Judicially Admitted Individual Returned to Center After Authorized Leave

(A) Applicability. This rule applies to an individual with mental retardation who has been admitted to a center by judicial order, and who has been on authorized leave for a continuous period of less than 1 year.

(B) Notifications. When a judicially admitted individual has been returned to a center from an authorized leave in excess of 10 days, the director of the center must, within 24 hours, notify the court of the return and notify the individual of the right to appeal the return and have a hearing to determine the appeal. The court must notify the individual's attorney or appoint a new attorney to consult with the individual and to determine whether the individual desires a hearing.

(C) Request for Hearing. An individual who wishes to appeal the return must request a hearing in writing within 7 days of the notice to the individual under subrule (B). The court must schedule a requested hearing to be held within 7 days of the court's receipt of the request.

(D) Statement Filed With Court. At least 3 days before the hearing, the director of the center must deliver to the court, the individual, and the individual's attorney a statement setting forth:

(1) the reason for the individual's return to the center;

(2) the reason the individual is believed to need care and treatment at the center; and

(3) the plan for further care and treatment.

(E) Report. The court may order an examination of the individual and the preparation and filing with the court of a report that contains such information as the court deems necessary.

(F) Conduct of Hearing. The court shall proceed as provided in § 511(4) of the Mental Health Code, MCL 330.1511(4). At the hearing, the director of the center must show that the individual needs care and treatment at the center, and that no alternative to the care and treatment provided at the center is available and adequate to meet the individual's needs.

(G) Order After Hearing. If the court finds the individual requires care and treatment at the center, it must dismiss the appeal and order the individual to remain at the center. If the court finds the director did not sustain the burden of proof, it must do one of the following:

(1) order the individual returned to authorized leave status; or

(2) order the individual to undergo a program of care and treatment for up to one year as an alternative to remaining at the center.

[Adopted June 17, 1997, effective September 1, 1997, 454 Mich.]

Comments

Staff Comment to 1997 Adoption

This rule is new. See MCL 330.1537.

Rule 5.744.   Proceedings Regarding Hospitalization Without a Hearing

(A) Scope of Rule. This rule applies to any proceeding involving an individual hospitalized without a hearing as ordered by a court or a psychiatrist and the rights of that individual.

(B) Notification. A notification requesting an order of hospitalization or a notification requesting a change in an alternative treatment program, a notice of noncompliance, or a notice of hospitalization as ordered by a psychiatrist, must be in writing.

(C) Service of Papers. If the court enters a new or modified order without a hearing, the court must serve the individual with a copy of that order. If the order includes hospitalization, the court must also serve the individual with notice of the right to object and demand a hearing.

(D) Objection; Scheduling Hearing. An individual hospitalized without a hearing, either by order of the court or by a psychiatrist's order, may file an objection to the order not later than 7 days after receipt of notice of the right to object. The court must schedule a hearing to be held within 10 days after receiving the objection.

(E) Conduct of Hearing. A hearing convened under this rule is without a jury. At the hearing the party seeking hospitalization of the individual must present evidence that hospitalization is necessary.

[Adopted effective March 1, 1985. Amended June 1, 1997, effective September 1, 1997, 454 Mich; October 3, 2006, effective January 1, 2007, 477 Mich.]

Comments

Staff Comment to 1985 Adoption

MCR 5.744 is substantially the same as PCR 744.

Staff Comment to 1997 Amendment

This rule has been substantially rewritten to reflect the changes in §§ 475 and 475a of the Mental Health Code, MCL 330.1475 and 300.1475a, that only provide a right to a hearing when the individual is placed in a hospital, not when there is a change in alternate treatment programs. The psychiatrist's order mentioned in subrule (D) is the order of hospitalization found in MCL 330.1474a.

Staff Comment to 2006 Amendment

The amendment of MCR 5.744 expands the scope of the rule to more accurately reflect the procedures delineated in MCL 330.1474, 330.1474a, 330.1475, and 330.1475a.

Rule 5.744a Proceedings Regarding an Individual Subject to Judicial Admission Who is Transferred to a Center from Alternative Setting

(A) Applicability. This rule applies to an individual with mental retardation under court order to undergo a program of care and treatment as an alternative to admission to a center.

(B) Immediate Transfer. After the court receives written notification concerning the need to transfer a judicially admitted individual receiving alternative care and treatment, the court may direct the filing of additional information and may do one of the following:

(1) modify its original order and direct the individual's transfer to another program of alternative care and treatment for the remainder of the 1–year period;

(2) enter a new order directing the individual's admission to either

    (a) a center recommended by the community mental health services program; or

    (b) a licensed hospital requested by the individual or the individual's family if private funds are to be used; or

(3) set a date for a hearing.

(C) Investigation Report. On receipt of notification, the court must promptly obtain from the community mental health services program or other appropriate agency a report stating

(1) the reason for concern about the adequacy of the care and treatment being received at the time of the notification;

(2) the continued suitability of that care and treatment; and

(3) the adequacy of care and treatment available at another alternative or at a center or licensed hospital.

(D) Service of Papers. If the court enters a new order without a hearing, it must serve the interested parties with a copy of that order and a copy of the investigation report when it becomes available. If the order includes transfer of the individual to a center, the court must also serve the interested parties with written notification of the individual's right to object and demand a hearing.

(E) Hearing. If within 7 days of service under subrule (D) the court receives a written objection from the individual or the individual's attorney, guardian, or presumptive heir, the court must schedule a hearing to be held within 10 days of the court's receipt of the objection.

(F) Conduct of Hearing. A hearing convened under this rule is without a jury. At the hearing, the person seeking transfer of the individual to a center must present evidence that the individual had not complied with the applicable order or that the order is not sufficient to prevent the individual from inflicting harm or injuries on himself, herself or others. The evidence must support a finding that transfer to another alternative, a center or a licensed hospital is necessary.

(G) Order After Hearing. The court may affirm or rescind the order issued under subrule (B), order a new program of care and treatment, or order discharge. The court may not place the individual in a center without inquiring into the adequacy of care and treatment for that individual at that center.

[Adopted June 1, 1997, effective September 1, 1997, 454 Mich.]

Comments

Staff Comment to 1997 Adoption

This rule is new. See MCL 330.1519(4).

Rule 5.745 Multiple Proceedings

(A) New Proceedings Not Prohibited. The admission of an individual under the Mental Health Code may not be invalidated because the individual is already subject to a court order as a result of a prior admission proceeding.

(B) Procedure. On being informed that an individual is subject to a previous court order, the court must:

(1) if it was the court issuing the previous order, dismiss the new proceeding and determine the proper disposition of the individual under its previous order or vacate the previous order and proceed under the new petition; or

(2) if the previous order was issued by another court, continue the new proceeding and issue an appropriate order. After entry of the order, the court with the new proceeding must consult with the court with the prior proceeding to determine if the best interests of the individual will be served by changing venue of the prior proceeding to the county where the new proceeding has been initiated. If not, the court with the new proceeding must transfer the matter to the other court.

(C) Disposition. The court may treat a petition or certificate filed in connection with the more recent proceeding as "notification" under MCR 5.743 or 5.744 and proceed with disposition under those rules.

[Adopted effective March 1, 1985. Amended June 17, 1997, effective September 1, 1997, 454 Mich.]

Comments

Staff Comment to 1985 Adoption

MCR 5.745 is substantially the same as PCR 745.

Staff Comment to 1997 Amendment

Subrule (B) is modified [effective September 1, 1997] to make clear that the preference is for the matter to proceed with the court already familiar with the patient, unless it is in the best interest of the patient for a new court to start a new proceeding.

Rule 5.746 Placement of Individual with a Developmental Disability in a Facility

(A) Petition for Authorization. If placement in a facility of an individual with a developmental disability has not been authorized or if permission is sought for authorization to place the individual in a more restrictive setting than previously ordered, a guardian of the individual must petition the court for authorization to place the individual in a facility or in a more restricted setting.

(B) Order. If the court grants the petition for authorization, it may order that:

(1) the guardian may execute an application for the individual's administrative admission to a specific center;

(2) the guardian may request the individual's temporary admission to a center for a period not to exceed 30 days for each admission; or

(3) the guardian may place the individual in a specific facility or class of facility as defined in MCL 330.1600.

(C) Notice of Hearing. Notice of hearing on a petition for authorization to place an individual must be given to those persons required to be served with notice of hearing for the appointment of a guardian.

[Adopted effective March 1, 1985. Amended June 17, 1997, effective September 1, 1997, 454 Mich.]

Comments

Staff Comment to 1985 Adoption

MCR 5.746 is substantially the same as PCR 746.

Staff Comment to 1997 Amendment

This rule refers to the initial authorization for a guardian to place in any facility an individual with a developmental disability, MCL 330.1623 and a modification of that authorization, MCL 330.1637. Subrule (C) refers to the notice required by MCL 330.1614. Provisions of the former rule which duplicate statutory requirements have been removed.

Rule 5.747 Petition for Discharge of Individual

At a hearing on a petition for discharge of an individual, the burden is on the person who seeks to prevent discharge to show that the individual is a person requiring treatment.

[Adopted effective March 1, 1985. Amended June 17, 1997, effective September 1, 1997, 454 Mich.]

Comments

Staff Comment to 1985 Adoption

MCR 5.747 is a new rule, covering the burden of proof with regard to petitions seeking discharge of a patient. See MCL 330.1484, 330.1485. The burden is on the person seeking to prevent discharge. See *In re Wagstaff,* 93 MichApp 755 (1979).

Rule 5.748 Transitional Provision on Termination of Indefinite Orders of Hospitalization

If on March 27, 1996, any individual is subject to any order that may result in the individual's hospitalization for a period beyond March 27, 1997, a petition for a determination that the individual continues to require involuntary mental health treatment must be filed on or before the time set for the second periodic review after March 27, 1996. The petition may be for involuntary health treatment for a period of not more than one year. This rule expires on March 28, 1997.

[Adopted May 7, 1996, effective June 1, 1996, 451 Mich.]

Comments

Staff Comment to 1996 Adoption

This new provision deals with the effect of §§ 469 and 472 of the Mental Health Code, MCL 330.1469 and MCL 330.1472, which limit the term of orders of involuntary treatment to one year. The treatment options are described in §§ 469(11) and 472(3), MCL 330.1469(11) and MCL 330.1472(3).

SUBCHAPTER 5.780 MISCELLANEOUS PROCEEDINGS

Rule 5.784 Proceedings on a Durable Power of Attorney for Health Care or Mental Health Treatment

(A) Petition, Who Shall File. The petition concerning a durable power of attorney for health care or mental health treatment must be filed by any interested party or the patient's attending physician.

(B) Venue. Venue for any proceeding concerning a durable power of attorney for health care or mental health treatment is proper in the county in which the patient resides or the county where the patient is found.

(C) Notice of Hearing, Service, Manner and Time.

(1) *Manner of Service.* If the address of an interested party is known or can be learned by diligent inquiry, notice must be by mail or personal service, but service by mail must be supplemented by facsimile, electronic mail, or telephone contact within the period for timely service when the hearing is an expedited hearing or a hearing on the initial determination regarding whether the patient is unable to participate in medical or mental health treatment decisions.

(2) *Waiving Service.* At an expedited hearing or a hearing on an initial determination regarding whether the patient is unable to participate in medical or mental health treatment decisions, the court may dispense with notice of the hearing on those interested parties who could not be contacted after diligent effort by the petitioner.

(3) *Time of Service.* Notice of hearing must be served at least 2 days before the time of a hearing on an initial determination regarding whether the patient is unable to participate in medical or mental health treatment decisions. Notice of an expedited hearing must be served at such time as directed by the court. Notice of other hearings must be served at such time as directed by MCR 5.108.

(D) Hearings.

(1) *Time.* Hearings on a petition for an initial determination regarding whether a patient is unable to participate in a medical or mental health treatment decision must be held within 7 days of the filing of the petition. The court may order an expedited hearing on any petition concerning a durable power of attorney for health care or mental health treatment

decisions on a showing of good cause to expedite the proceedings. A showing of good cause to expedite proceedings may be made ex parte.

(2) *Trial.* Disputes concerning durable powers of attorney for health care or mental health treatment decisions are tried by the court without a jury.

(3) *Proof.* The petitioner has the burden of proof by a preponderance of evidence on all contested issues except that the standard is by clear and convincing evidence on an issue whether a patient has authorized the patient advocate under a durable power of attorney for health care to decide to withhold or withdraw treatment, which decision could or would result in the patient's death, or authorized the patient advocate under a durable power of attorney for mental health treatment to seek the forced administration of medication or hospitalization.

(4) *Privilege, Waiver.* The physician-patient privilege must not be asserted.

(E) Temporary Relief. On a sufficient showing of need, the court may issue a temporary restraining order pursuant to MCR 3.310 pending a hearing on any petition concerning a durable power of attorney for health care or mental health treatment. MCR 5.784 retained 5.31.05.

[Adopted January 16, 1992, effective April 1, 1992, 439 Mich. Amended effective March 8, 2005, 472 Mich. Amended March 20, 2019, effective May 1, 2019, 502 Mich.]

Comments

Staff Comment to 1992 Adoption

The rule addresses proceedings under § 496 of the Revised Probate Code, MCL 700.496.

Staff Comment to 2005 Amendment

Public Acts 532, 551-557, and 559 of 2004, effective January 3, 2005, authorize a durable power of attorney for mental health treatment decisions. The amendments of MCR 5.784 broaden the rule to cover proceedings concerning durable powers of attorney for mental health treatment.

Staff Comment to 2019 Amendment

The amendments of Rules 1.109, 2.102, 2.104, 2.106, 2.107, 2.117, 2.119, 2.403, 2.503, 2.506, 2.508, 2.518, 2.602, 2.603, 2.621, 3.101, 3.104, 3.203, 3.205, 3.210, 3.302, 3.607, 3.613, 3.614, 3.705, 3.801, 3.802, 3.805, 3.806, 4.201, 4.202, 4.303, 4.306, 5.001, 5.104, 5.105, 5.107, 5.108, 5.113, 5.117, 5.118, 5.119, 5.120, 5.125, 5.126, 5.132, 5.162, 5.202, 5.203, 5.205, 5.302, 5.304, 5.307, 5.308, 5.309, 5.310, 5.311, 5.313, 5.402, 5.404, 5.405, 5.409, 5.501, and 5.784 and addition of Rule 3.618 of the Michigan Court Rules are an expected progression necessary for design and implementation of the statewide electronic-filing system. These particular amendments will assist in implementing the goals of the project.

SUBCHAPTER 5.800   APPEALS

Rule 5.801   Appeals to Court of Appeals

(A) Appeal of Right. A party or an interested person aggrieved by a final order of the probate court may appeal as a matter of right as provided by this rule.

Orders appealable of right to the Court of Appeals are defined as and limited to the following:

(1) a final order, as defined in MCR 7.202(6)(a), affecting the rights or interests of a party to a civil action commenced in the probate court under MCR 5.101(C);

(2) a final order affecting the rights or interests of an interested person in a proceeding involving a decedent estate, the estate of a person who has disappeared or is missing, a conservatorship or other protective proceeding, the estate of an individual with developmental disabilities, or an inter vivos trust or a trust created under a will. These are defined as and limited to orders resolving the following matters:

(a) appointing or removing a fiduciary or trust director as defined in MCL 700.7103(m), or denying such an appointment or removal;

(b) admitting or denying to probate of a will, codicil, or other testamentary instrument;

(c) determining the validity of a governing instrument as defined in MCL 700.1104(m);

(d) interpreting or construing a governing instrument as defined in MCL 700.1104(m);

(e) approving or denying a settlement relating to a governing instrument as defined in MCL 700.1104(m);

(f) reforming, terminating, or modifying or denying the reformation, termination or modification of a trust;

(g) granting or denying a petition to consolidate or divide trusts;

(h) discharging or denying the discharge of a surety on a bond from further liability;

(i) allowing, disallowing, or denying a claim;

(j) assigning, selling, leasing, or encumbering any of the assets of an estate or trust;

(k) authorizing or denying the continuation of a business;

(*l*) determining special allowances in a decedent's estate such as a homestead allowance, an exempt property allowance, or a family allowance;

(m) authorizing or denying rights of election;

(n) determining heirs, devisees, or beneficiaries;

(o) determining title to or rights or interests in property;

(p) authorizing or denying partition of property;

(q) authorizing or denying specific performance;

(r) ascertaining survivorship of parties;

(s) granting or denying a petition to bar a mentally incompetent or minor wife from dower in the property of her living husband;

(t) granting or denying a petition to determine *cy pres;*

(u) directing or denying the making or repayment of distributions;

(v) determining or denying a constructive trust;

(w) determining or denying an oral contract relating to a will;

(x) allowing or disallowing an account, fees, or administration expenses;

(y) surcharging or refusing to surcharge a fiduciary or trust director as referred to in MCL 700.7103(m);

(z) determining or directing payment or apportionment of taxes;

(aa) distributing proceeds recovered for wrongful death under MCL 600.2922;

(bb) assigning residue;

(cc) granting or denying a petition for instructions;

(dd) authorizing disclaimers;

(ee) allowing or disallowing a trustee to change the principal place of a trust's administration;

(ff) adoption assistance determinations pursuant to MCL 400.115k;

(3) a final order affecting the rights and interests of an adult or a minor in a guardianship proceeding under the Estates and Protected Individuals Code;

(4) a final order affecting the rights or interests of a person under the Mental Health Code;

(5) an order entered in a probate proceeding, other than a civil action commenced in a probate court, that otherwise affects with finality the rights or interests of a party or an interested person in the subject matter; or

(6) other appeals as provided by law.

(B) Appeal by Leave. All orders of the probate court not listed in subrule (A) are appealable to the Court of Appeals by leave of that court.

[Adopted July 12, 2001, effective January 1, 2002, 464 Mich. Amended February 2, 2010, effective April 1, 2010, 485 Mich. Amended effective June 21, 2017, 500 Mich; August 14, 2019, 503 Mich.]

Comments

Staff Comment to 2010 Amendment

These changes, submitted by the Probate and Estate Planning Council of the State Bar of Michigan and the Michigan Probate Judges Association, have been designed so that the rules conform to recently-enacted statutory changes creating the Michigan Trust Code. The amendments correct and insert cross-references to the applicable statutory provisions, and make other technical changes. In addition, new MCR 5.208 incorporates the notice requirements for both decedent estates and trusts currently contained in MCR 5.306 and MCR 5.503, and replaces those rules.

Staff Comment to 2017 Amendment

These amendments conform to recent statutory changes that require all appeals from probate court to be heard in the Court of Appeals, instead of the bifurcated system that previously required some probate appeals to be heard in the Court of Appeals and some to be heard in the local circuit court. The amendments also establish priority status for appeals in guardianship and involuntary mental health treatment cases, similar to child custody cases.

Staff Comment to 2019 Amendment

These amendments update cross-references and make other nonsubstantive revisions to clarify the rules.

Rule 5.802 Appellate Procedure; Stays Pending Appeal

(A) Procedure. Except as modified by this subchapter, chapter 7 of these rules governs appeals from the probate court.

(B) Record.

(1) An appeal from the probate court is on the papers filed and a written transcript of the proceedings in the probate court or on a record settled and agreed to by the parties and approved by the court.

(2) The probate register may transmit certified copies of the necessary documents and papers in the file if the original papers are needed for further proceedings in the probate court. The parties shall not be required to pay for the copies as costs or otherwise.

(C) Stays Pending Appeals. An order removing or appointing a fiduciary; appointing a special personal representative or a special fiduciary; granting a new trial or rehearing; granting an allowance to the spouse or children of a decedent; granting permission to sue on a fiduciary's bond; or suspending a fiduciary and appointing a special fiduciary, is not stayed pending appeal unless ordered by the court on motion for good cause.

[Adopted July 12, 2001, effective January 1, 2002, 464 Mich. Amended February 2, 2010, effective April 1, 2010, 485 Mich. Amended effective June 21, 2017, 500 Mich.]

Comments

Staff Comment to 2010 Amendment

These changes, submitted by the Probate and Estate Planning Council of the State Bar of Michigan and the Michigan Probate Judges Association, have been designed so that the rules conform to recently-enacted statutory changes creating the Michigan Trust Code. The amendments correct and insert cross-references to the applicable statutory provisions, and make other technical changes. In addition, new MCR 5.208 incorporates the notice requirements for both decedent estates and trusts currently contained in MCR 5.306 and MCR 5.503, and replaces those rules.

Staff Comment to 2017 Amendment

These amendments conform to recent statutory changes that require all appeals from probate court to be heard in the Court of Appeals, instead of the bifurcated system that previously required some probate appeals to be heard in the Court of Appeals and some to be heard in the local circuit court. The amendments also establish priority status for appeals in guardianship and involuntary mental health treatment cases, similar to child custody cases.

SUBCHAPTER 5.900 PROCEEDINGS INVOLVING JUVENILES [DELETED]

Rules 5.901 to 5.993. [Deleted effective May 1, 2003]

Comments

Staff Comment to 2003 Deletion

The amendments are based on proposals submitted by the Family Division Joint Rules Committee appointed by the Supreme Court. They include revision of most of the rules in subchapter 5.900, which governs procedure in cases formerly heard in the juvenile division of probate court, and in subchapter 6.900, which covers criminal cases brought against juveniles, as well as several new

rules. The revised rules from subchapter 5.900 are relocated to subchapter 3.900, in recognition of the transfer of jurisdiction of such matters to the family division of the circuit court. See MCL 600.1001 *et seq.*

In addition, a related order is being entered concurrently. It amends a number of miscellaneous rules in other chapters and the Michigan Rules of Evidence to correct references to the juvenile provisions.

This Comment and the Notes following the individual rules are published only for the benefit of the bench and bar and are not an authoritative construction by the Court.

CHAPTER 6.   CRIMINAL PROCEDURE
Effective March 1, 1985

SUBCHAPTER 6.000   GENERAL PROVISIONS

Rule 6.001.   Scope; Applicability of Civil Rules; Superseded Rule and Statutes

(A) Felony Cases. The rules in subchapters 6.000–6.500 govern matters of procedure in criminal cases cognizable in the circuit courts and in courts of equivalent criminal jurisdiction.

(B) Misdemeanor Cases. MCR 6.001–6.004, 6.005(B) and (C), 6.006, 6.101, 6.102(D) and (F), 6.103, 6.104(A), 6.106, 6.125, 6.202, 6.425(E)(3), 6.427, 6.430, 6.435, 6.440, 6.445(A)–(G), and the rules in subchapter 6.600 govern matters of procedure in criminal cases cognizable in the district courts.

(C) Juvenile Cases. The rules in subchapter 6.900 govern matters of procedure in the district courts and in circuit courts and courts of equivalent criminal jurisdiction in cases involving juveniles against whom the prosecutor has authorized the filing of a criminal complaint as provided in MCL 764.1f.

(D) Civil Rules Applicable. The provisions of the rules of civil procedure apply to cases governed by this chapter, except

(1) as otherwise provided by rule or statute,

(2) when it clearly appears that they apply to civil actions only,

(3) when a statute or court rule provides a like or different procedure, or

(4) with regard to limited appearances and notices of limited appearance.

Depositions and other discovery proceedings under subchapter 2.300 may not be taken for the purposes of discovery in cases governed by this chapter. The provisions of MCR 2.501(C) regarding the length of notice of trial assignment do not apply in cases governed by this chapter.

(E) Rules and Statutes Superseded. The rules in this chapter supersede all prior court rules in this chapter and any statutory procedure pertaining to and inconsistent with a procedure provided by a rule in this chapter.

[Adopted effective October 1, 1989. Amended October 25, 1990, effective January 1, 1991, 436 Mich; July 13, 2005, effective January 1, 2006, 473 Mich; December 14, 2005, effective January 1, 2006, 474 Mich; January 23, 2007, effective May 1, 2007, 477 Mich; September 19, 2012, effective January 1, 2013, 493 Mich; October 1, 2014, effective January 1, 2015, 497 Mich; May 25, 2016, effective September 1, 2016, 499 Mich; September 20, 2017, effective January 1, 2018, 501 Mich; May 30, 2018, effective September 1, 2018, 501 Mich; May 22, 2019, effective September 1, 2019, 502 Mich.]

Comments

Staff Comment to 1989 Adoption

MCR 6.001 is a new rule but includes a modified version of former 6.001 pertaining to the applicability of the rules of civil procedure.

Although the rules that have been developed and incorporated in this chapter are relatively comprehensive, criminal procedure is such a diverse and pervasive area of the law that a substantial portion of criminal procedure will continue to be regulated by statutes, the civil court rules, and case-law prescribed procedures. Subrules (D) and (E) provide standards for identifying what civil rule and statutory procedures will continue to be applicable.

Furthermore, although the rules in this chapter attempt to comply with state and federal constitutional requirements, they avoid, to the extent that it is practical, codification of constitutional requirements and standards. As with the other Michigan court rules, constitutional requirements apply independently of these rules and, in the event of any conflict, prevail over the requirements of these rules.

Subrule (A) identifies the subchapters in which the rules governing procedure in felony cases will be found.

Subrule (B) similarly identifies the subchapters in which the rules governing procedure in misdemeanor cases will be found.

With one exception, the former rules in this chapter applicable to misdemeanor proceedings in district court have been amended with new numbers for placement in the appropriate subchapters. Former 6.201, entitled "Criminal Procedure Generally," has been renumbered 6.610. Former 6.202, entitled "Impaneling The Jury," has been renumbered 6.620. Former 6.205, entitled "Other Rules Applicable," has not been renumbered, but rather, its provisions have been incorporated in the instant subrule. Consequently, it has been superseded.

One other change pertinent to this subrule is noteworthy. MCR 4.102, entitled "Misdemeanor Cases," has been retitled "Misdemeanor Traffic Cases," and renumbered 6.615 for placement with the other misdemeanor rules.

Subrule (C) designates subchapter 6.900 as the subchapter in which will be found the rules governing criminal prosecution of juveniles as provided in MCL 764.1f.

Subrule (D) is a slightly modified version of former 6.001. This subrule makes the provisions of the rules of civil procedure applicable generally in criminal cases and then sets forth exceptions. The only substantive modification this subrule makes is in the exception described in subrule (D)(3). The former rule described this exception as "when a statute or court rule provides a different procedure." In this subrule language has been added so this exception now provides: "when a statute or court provides a *like* or different procedure." This change reflects that the rules of criminal procedure that have been adopted now set forth procedures not only that are "different," but also, similar or identical to the procedures set forth in the civil rules. Since the rules in this chapter govern criminal procedure, it follows that civil rules providing "like" procedures should no longer be applicable. Likewise, it follows that statutes prescribing criminal procedures take precedence over, and should render inapplicable, civil rules providing like procedures.

Subrule (E) declares that all of the prior rules in this chapter not readopted in this version of the rules are superseded. It also declares that the rules supersede certain undetermined statutory procedures and sets forth a test for determining what those statutory procedures are. A statutory procedure is superseded if it "pertain[s] to and is inconsistent with a procedure provided by a rule in this chapter." Some superseded statutory procedures are discussed in the commentary to the rules. See, for example, 6.402 setting forth an oral waiver of jury trial procedure that supersedes the statutory procedure having the added requirement of a written waiver. Like the court rule the statutory procedure pertains to waiver of jury trial. It is inconsistent with the court rule procedure because, if applicable, it would render invalid waivers complying with the court rule requirements.

Staff Comment to 1991 Amendment

The [January 1, 1991] amendment of MCR 6.001(B) makes the probation revocation procedure set forth in MCR 6.445 applicable to all probation revocation proceedings in district court regardless of the seriousness of the misdemeanor conviction that led to probation. The proposal for such an amendment of this subrule was submitted by the Michigan District Judges Association.

Staff Comment to July, 2006 Amendment

On March 12, 2002, the Court appointed the Committee on the Rules of Criminal Procedure to review the rules to determine whether any of the provisions should be revised. The committee issued its report on June 16, 2003, recommending numerous amendments to existing rules, plus some new rules. A public hearing on the committee's recommendations was held May 27, 2004.

The Court adopted the committee's recommendations with respect to the amendments of Rules 2.511, 6.102, 6.104, 6.107, 6.112, 6.303, 6.304, 6.310, 6.311,

6.402, 6.412, 6.414, 6.419, 6.420, 6.427, 6.615, and 6.620, and the adoption of a new Rule 6.428.

The Court also adopted, with modifications, recommendations made by the committee and staff to amend other rules. Rule 2.510 was amended to conform to the newly enacted 2004 PA 12 (MCL 600.1332). The Court modified the committee's recommendation concerning Rule 6.001 to include a reference to 6.102 and to limit the application of 6.445 to subrules (A) through (G). The Court adopted the committee's recommendation with regard to Rule 6.004, except that the requirement that "whenever the defendant's constitutional right to a speedy trial is violated, the defendant is entitled to dismissal of the charge with prejudice" was retained and inserted into 6.004(A).

Staff Comment to December, 2006 Amendment

The amendment of MCR 6.001 corrects a drafting error in the Court's order of July 13, 2005.

Staff Comment to 2007 Amendment

The amendment of Rule 6.001 makes subrules 6.005(B) and (C) applicable to misdemeanor cases. Subrules 6.005(B) and (C) set forth the factors to be used by the court in determining whether a criminal defendant is indigent and, if a defendant is able to pay part of the cost of a lawyer, allow the court to require the defendant to contribute to the cost of providing a lawyer and establish a plan for collecting the contribution.

Staff Comment to 2013 Amendment

The revision of MCR 6.001 provides a cross reference to MCR 6.202, a new rule adopted in this order. MCR 6.202 incorporates a "notice and demand" procedure into the Michigan Court Rules with regard to forensic reports. Under the rule, a party could seek to admit a forensic report as evidence if notice requirements are met and no objection is filed. If a party objects to admission of the report, the analyst would be required to testify.

Staff Comment to 2015 Amendment

The amendment of MCR 6.001(B) includes additional rules and subrules that are found in Chapter 6 that govern procedural issues relevant to criminal cases falling under the jurisdiction of district courts.

Staff Comment to 2016 Amendment

The amendments of MCR 3.605, 3.606, 3.928, 3.944, 3.956, 6.001, 6.425, 6.445, 6.610, and 6.933 were submitted by the Michigan State Planning Body for the Delivery of Legal Services to the Poor. The rule revisions are intended to provide clarity and guidance to courts regarding what courts would be required to do before incarcerating a defendant for failure to pay.

Staff Comment to January, 2018 Amendment

The amendments of Rules 1.0, 1.2, 4.2, and 4.3 of the Michigan Rules of Professional Conduct and Rules 2.107, 2.117, and 6.001 of the Michigan Court Rules were submitted to the Court by the State Bar of Michigan Representative Assembly. The rules are intended to provide guidance for attorneys and clients who prefer to engage in a limited scope representation. The rules allow for such an agreement "preferably in writing," and enable an attorney to file a notice of LSR with the court when the representation is undertaken as well as a termination notice when the representation has ended. The rules also explicitly allow attorneys to provide document preparation services for a self-represented litigant without having to file an appearance with the court.

Staff Comment to September, 2018 Amendment

The amendments in this order are intended to begin moving trial courts toward a statewide uniform e-Filing process. In addition, the order moves existing language into MCR 1.109 as a way to, for the first time, include most filing requirements in one single rule, instead of scattered in various rules. The order largely mirrors the administrative orders that most e-Filing pilot projects have operated under, but contains some significant new provisions. For example, courts are required to maintain documents in an electronic document management system, and the electronic record is the official court record.

Staff Comment to 2019 Amendment

The amendments more explicitly require restitution to be ordered at the time of sentencing as required by statute, and establish a procedure for modifying restitution amounts.

Rule 6.002   Purpose and Construction

These rules are intended to promote a just determination of every criminal proceeding. They are to be construed to secure simplicity in procedure, fairness in administration, and the elimination of unjustifiable expense and delay.

[Adopted effective October 1, 1989.]

Comments

Staff Comment to 1989 Adoption

MCR 6.002 is a new rule patterned after Federal Rules of Criminal Procedure, Rule 2.

Rule 6.003   Definitions

For purposes of subchapters 6.000–6.800:

(1) "Party" includes the lawyer representing the party.

(2) "Defendant's lawyer" includes a self-represented defendant proceeding without a lawyer.

(3) "Prosecutor" includes any lawyer prosecuting the case.

(4) "Court" or "judicial officer" includes a judge, a magistrate, or a district court magistrate authorized in accordance with the law to perform the functions of a magistrate.

(5) "Court clerk" includes a deputy clerk.

(6) "Court reporter" includes a court recorder.

[Adopted effective October 1, 1989.]

Comments

Staff Comment to 1989 Adoption

MCR 6.003 is a new rule. The scope rule, 6.001, makes the definitions in this rule applicable to the rules found in Subchapters 6.000–6.800.

Subrule (4), which defines a "court" or "judicial officer," recognizes a statutory distinction between a "magistrate" and a "district court magistrate" set forth in MCL 761.1(f). The "functions of a magistrate" that a district court magistrate may be authorized to perform are set forth in MCL 600.8501 *et seq.*, and subject to MCR 4.401(B).

Rule 6.004   Speedy Trial

(A) Right to Speedy Trial. The defendant and the people are entitled to a speedy trial and to a speedy resolution of all matters before the court. Whenever the defendant's constitutional right to a speedy trial is violated, the defendant is entitled to dismissal of the charge with prejudice.

(B) Priorities in Scheduling Criminal Cases. The trial court has the responsibility to establish and control a trial calendar. In assigning cases to the calendar, and insofar as it is practicable,

(1) the trial of criminal cases must be given preference over the trial of civil cases, and

(2) the trial of defendants in custody and of defendants whose pretrial liberty presents unusual risks must be given preference over other criminal cases.

(C) Delay in Felony and Misdemeanor Cases; Recognizance Release. In a felony case in which the defendant has been incarcerated for a period of 180 days or more to answer for the same crime or a crime based on the same conduct or arising from the same criminal episode, or in a misdemeanor case in which the defendant has been incarcerated for a period of 28 days or more to answer for the same crime or a crime based on the same conduct or arising from the same criminal episode, the defendant must be released on personal recognizance, unless the court finds by clear and convincing evidence that the defendant is likely either to fail to appear for future proceedings or to present a danger to any other person or the community. In computing the 28–day and 180–day periods, the court is to exclude

(1) periods of delay resulting from other proceedings concerning the defendant, including but not limited to competency and criminal responsibility proceedings, pretrial motions, interlocutory appeals, and the trial of other charges,

(2) the period of delay during which the defendant is not competent to stand trial,

(3) the period of delay resulting from an adjournment requested or consented to by the defendant's lawyer,

(4) the period of delay resulting from an adjournment requested by the prosecutor, but only if the prosecutor demonstrates on the record either

(a) the unavailability, despite the exercise of due diligence, of material evidence that the prosecutor has reasonable cause to believe will be available at a later date; or

(b) exceptional circumstances justifying the need for more time to prepare the state's case,

(5) a reasonable period of delay when the defendant is joined for trial with a codefendant as to whom the time for trial has not run, but only if good cause exists for not granting the defendant a severance so as to enable trial within the time limits applicable, and

(6) any other periods of delay that in the court's judgment are justified by good cause, but not including delay caused by docket congestion.

(D) Untried Charges Against State Prisoner.

(1) *The 180–Day Rule.* Except for crimes exempted by MCL 780.131(2), the inmate shall be brought to trial within 180 days after the department of corrections causes to be delivered to the prosecuting attorney of the county in which the warrant, indictment, information, or complaint is pending written notice of the place of imprisonment of the inmate and a request for final disposition of the warrant, indictment, information, or complaint. The request shall be accompanied by a statement setting forth the term of commitment under which the prisoner is being held, the time already served, the time remaining to be served on the sentence, the amount of good time or disciplinary credits earned, the time of parole eligibility of the prisoner, and any decisions of the parole board relating to the prisoner. The written notice and statement shall be delivered by certified mail.

(2) *Remedy.* In the event that action is not commenced on the matter for which request for disposition was made as required in subsection (1), no court of this state shall any longer have jurisdiction thereof, nor shall the untried warrant, indictment, information, or complaint be of any further force or effect, and the court shall enter an order dismissing the same with prejudice.

[Adopted effective October 1, 1989. Amended July 13, 2005, effective January 1, 2006, 473 Mich.]

Comments

Staff Comment to 1989 Adoption

MCR 6.004 is a modified version of the former speedy trial rule, 6.109.

Subrule (A) is not new. It restates the dual entitlements to speedy trial described in the speedy trial statute, MCL 768.1. Former 6.109(A), pertaining to scheduling of criminal cases, made reference to these entitlements in more general language ("the right of the accused to a speedy trial and the interest of the public in prompt disposition of criminal cases"). Of course, in addition to the statutory right to a speedy trial, the defendant has a constitutional right. See Const 1963, art 1, § 20; US Const, Am VI.

Subrule (B) is a stylistically improved version of former 6.109(A) except for its first sentence, which is based on the first sentence of former 6.109(C). Former 6.109(C), describing the Chief Judge's duty to report delays of trials, and former

6.109(D), describing the State Court Administrator's duty to investigate the delays reported, have been removed from this rule and from this chapter and reincorporated respectively in 8.110(E), the "chief judge rule," and 8.103, the "state court administrator rule."

Subrule (C) is a stylistically improved version of former 6.109(B) except for two substantive changes.

Subrule (C)(3) is based on former 6.109(B)(2), but eliminates the latter's requirements for the defendant's concurrence "on the record" and after "he or she has been advised by the court of his or her right to a speedy trial and the effect of concurrence."

Subrule (C)(4)(b) substitutes a more restrictive standard ("exceptional circumstances justifying the need for more time to prepare the state's case") for exclusion of delay resulting from an adjournment requested by the prosecutor in place of the standard of former 6.109(B)(3)(b) ("the adjournment is granted for good cause on the record to allow the prosecutor additional time to prepare the state's case"). The new standard is based on 2 ABA Standards for Criminal Justice (2d ed), Standard 12–2.3(d)(ii) ("additional time is justified because of the exceptional circumstances of the case").

Subrule (D) is new. It incorporates the requirements of the statutory 180–day rule set forth in MCL 780.131 *et seq.* As the rule reflects, a statutory amendment has exempted from the requirements of the 180–day rule certain criminal offenses (those committed by an inmate of a state correctional facility "while incarcerated in the correctional facility" or "after the inmate has escaped from the correctional facility and before he or she has been returned to the custody of the Department of Corrections"). 1988 PA 400. MCL 780.131(2).

Subrule (D) incorporates the court's interpretation of the 180–day rule statute in *People v Hendershot,* 357 Mich 300 (1959) (construing the statute as requiring "good faith action" on the part of the prosecutor within the 180–day period to ready the case for trial) and, with one significant exception, the rules adopted by the Court in *People v Hill,* 402 Mich 272 (1978), to effectuate the purpose of the statute. *Hill* held that the 180–day period begins to run not only from when the prosecutor "knows or should know" that a charge is pending against the state prison inmate, but also from when "the Department of Corrections knows or should know" of such a charge. The statutory remedy of dismissal was held applicable in both situations. Subrule (D) modifies *Hill* by changing the remedy, when the 180–day rule is violated due to "lack of notice from the Department of Corrections," from dismissal to "sentence credit for the period of delay."

Staff Comment to 2005 Amendment

On March 12, 2002, the Court appointed the Committee on the Rules of Criminal Procedure to review the rules to determine whether any of the provisions should be revised. The committee issued its report on June 16, 2003, recommending numerous amendments to existing rules, plus some new rules. A public hearing on the committee's recommendations was held May 27, 2004.

The Court adopted the committee's recommendations with respect to the amendments of Rules 2.511, 6.102, 6.104, 6.107, 6.112, 6.303, 6.304, 6.310, 6.311, 6.402, 6.412, 6.414, 6.419, 6.420, 6.427, 6.615, and 6.620, and the adoption of a new Rule 6.428.

The Court also adopted, with modifications, recommendations made by the committee and staff to amend other rules. Rule 2.510 was amended to conform to the newly enacted 2004 PA 12 (MCL 600.1332). The Court modified the committee's recommendation concerning Rule 6.001 to include a reference to 6.102 and to limit the application of 6.445 to subrules (A) through (G). The Court adopted the committee's recommendation with regard to Rule 6.004, except that the requirement that "whenever the defendant's constitutional right to a speedy trial is violated, the defendant is entitled to dismissal of the charge with prejudice" was retained and inserted into 6.004(A).

Rule 6.005   Right To Assistance of Lawyer; Advice; Appointment for Indigents; Waiver; Joint Representation; Grand Jury Proceedings

(A) Advice of Right. At the arraignment on the warrant or complaint, the court must advise the defendant

(1) of entitlement to a lawyer's assistance at all subsequent court proceedings, and

(2) that the court will appoint a lawyer at public expense if the defendant wants one and is financially unable to retain one.

The court must question the defendant to determine whether the defendant wants a lawyer and, if so, whether the defendant is financially unable to retain one.

(B) Questioning Defendant About Indigency. If the defendant requests a lawyer and claims financial inability to retain one, the court must determine whether the defendant is indigent. The determination of indigency must be guided by the following factors:

(1) present employment, earning capacity and living expenses;

(2) outstanding debts and liabilities, secured and unsecured;

(3) whether the defendant has qualified for and is receiving any form of public assistance;

(4) availability and convertibility, without undue financial hardship to the defendant and the defendant's dependents, of any personal or real property owned; and

(5) any other circumstances that would impair the ability to pay a lawyer's fee as would ordinarily be required to retain competent counsel.

The ability to post bond for pretrial release does not make the defendant ineligible for appointment of a lawyer.

(C) Partial Indigency. If a defendant is able to pay part of the cost of a lawyer, the court may require contribution to the cost of providing a lawyer and may establish a plan for collecting the contribution.

(D) Appointment or Waiver of a Lawyer. If the court determines that the defendant is financially unable to retain a lawyer, it must promptly appoint a lawyer and promptly notify the lawyer of the appointment. The court may not permit the defendant to make an initial waiver of the right to be represented by a lawyer without first

(1) advising the defendant of the charge, the maximum possible prison sentence for the offense, any mandatory minimum sentence required by law, and the risk involved in self-representation, and

(2) offering the defendant the opportunity to consult with a retained lawyer or, if the defendant is indigent, the opportunity to consult with an appointed lawyer.

(E) Advice at Subsequent Proceedings. If a defendant has waived the assistance of a lawyer, the record of each subsequent proceeding (e.g., preliminary examination, arraignment, proceedings leading to possible revocation of youthful trainee status, hearings, trial or sentencing) need show only that the court advised the defendant of the continuing right to a lawyer's assistance (at public expense if the defendant is indigent) and that the defendant waived that right. Before the court begins such proceedings,

(1) the defendant must reaffirm that a lawyer's assistance is not wanted; or

(2) if the defendant requests a lawyer and is financially unable to retain one, the court must appoint one; or

(3) if the defendant wants to retain a lawyer and has the financial ability to do so, the court must allow the defendant a reasonable opportunity to retain one.

The court may refuse to adjourn a proceeding to appoint counsel or allow a defendant to retain counsel if an adjournment would significantly prejudice the prosecution, and the defendant has not been reasonably diligent in seeking counsel.

(F) Multiple Representation. When two or more indigent defendants are jointly charged with an offense or offenses or their cases are otherwise joined, the court must appoint separate lawyers unassociated in the practice of law for each defendant. Whenever two or more defendants who have been jointly charged or whose cases have been joined are represented by the same retained lawyer or lawyers associated in the practice of law, the court must inquire into the potential for a conflict of interest that might jeopardize the right of each defendant to the undivided loyalty of the lawyer. The court may not permit the joint representation unless:

(1) the lawyer or lawyers state on the record the reasons for believing that joint representation in all probability will not cause a conflict of interests;

(2) the defendants state on the record after the court's inquiry and the lawyer's statement, that they desire to proceed with the same lawyer; and

(3) the court finds on the record that joint representation in all probability will not cause a conflict of interest and states its reasons for the finding.

(G) Unanticipated Conflict of Interest. If, in a case of joint representation, a conflict of interest arises at any time, including trial, the lawyer must immediately inform the court. If the court agrees that a conflict has arisen, it must afford one or more of the defendants the opportunity to retain separate lawyers. The court should on its own initiative inquire into any potential conflict that becomes apparent, and take such action as the interests of justice require.

(H) Scope of Trial Lawyer's Responsibilities. The responsibilities of the trial lawyer who represents the defendant include

(1) representing the defendant in all trial court proceedings through initial sentencing,

(2) filing of interlocutory appeals the lawyer deems appropriate, and

(3) responding to any preconviction appeals by the prosecutor. The defendant's lawyer must either:

    (i) file a substantive brief in response to the prosecutor's interlocutory application for leave to appeal, or

    (ii) notify the Court of Appeals that the lawyer will not be filing a brief in response to the application.

(4) Unless an appellate lawyer has been appointed or retained, or if retained trial counsel withdraws, the trial lawyer who represents the defendant is responsible for filing postconviction motions the lawyer deems appropriate, including motions for new trial, for a directed verdict of acquittal, to withdraw plea, or for resentencing.

(5) when an appellate lawyer has been appointed or retained, promptly making the defendant's file, including all discovery material obtained, available for copying upon request of that lawyer. The trial lawyer must retain the materials in the defendant's file for at least five years after the case is disposed in the trial court.

(I) Assistance of Lawyer at Grand Jury Proceedings.

(1) A witness called before a grand jury or a grand juror is entitled to have a lawyer present in the hearing room while the witness gives testimony. A witness may not refuse to appear for reasons of unavailability of the lawyer for that witness.

Except as otherwise provided by law, the lawyer may not participate in the proceedings other than to advise the witness.

(2) The prosecutor assisting the grand jury is responsible for ensuring that a witness is informed of the right to a lawyer's assistance during examination by written notice accompanying the subpoena to the witness and by personal advice immediately before the examination. The notice must include language informing the witness that if the witness is financially unable to retain a lawyer, the chief judge in the circuit court in which the grand jury is convened will on request appoint one for the witness at public expense.

[Adopted effective October 1, 1989. Amended October 23, 1995, effective January 1, 1996, 450 Mich; December 13, 2002, effective January 1, 2004, 467 Mich; July 13, 2005, effective January 1, 2006, 473 Mich; May 17, 2011, effective September 1, 2011, 489 Mich; February 1, 2012, effective May 1, 2012, 490 Mich.]

Comments

Staff Comment to 1989 Adoption

MCR 6.005 is a modified version of former 6.101(C).

Subrule (A) is a stylistically improved version of former 6.101(C)(1). The title of the "arraignment on the complaint *and* warrant" found in former 6.101(C)(1) has been changed in subrule (A) to "arraignment on the warrant *or* complaint" corresponding to the title of Rule 6.104 and its recognition that an arraignment on a complaint without the issuance of a warrant is statutorily authorized. See MCL 764.1c.

Subrule (B) is new. It incorporates the indigency standard and criteria set forth in Administrative Order No. 1972–4, 387 Mich xxx (1972). The last sentence of this subrule is based on 1 ABA Standards for Criminal Justice (2d ed), Standard 5–6.1 ("[c]ounsel should not be denied merely . . . because bond has been or can be posted").

Subrule (C) is new. It is based on 1 ABA Standards for Criminal Justice (2d ed), Standard 5–6.2 ("[t]he ability to pay part of the cost of adequate representation should not preclude eligibility"). This subrule pertains to contribution and should not be construed as authorizing subsequent reimbursement.

The first sentence of subrule (D), dealing with appointment, is a modified version of the first sentence of former 6.101(C)(2) (requiring the appointment to be made "promptly"), adding the requirement that the court "promptly notify the lawyer of the appointment." The remainder of subrule (D) pertains to the defendant's *initial* waiver of the right to be represented by a lawyer and addresses the defendant's constitutional right to self-representation. See *Faretta v California*, 422 US 806; 95 SCt 2525; 45 LEd2d 562 (1975). The requirements of subrules (1) and (2) are intended to ensure that the defendant's decision to waive the right to representation and to proceed without a lawyer is an informed and voluntary one. Subrule (2) does not require that the defendant actually consult with a lawyer, but rather, that the defendant be "offer[ed] . . . the opportunity" to consult with one.

Subrule (E) is a stylistically improved version of former 6.101(C)(3).

Subrule (F) substantially changes former 6.101(C)(4). The former rule permitted joint representation regardless of whether the lawyer was appointed or retained. The rule as changed requires the appointment of "separate lawyers unassociated in the practice of law" for each defendant. This change avoids conflict of interest problems that arose despite the procedure set forth in the former rule (and repeated in this rule as to retained counsel) to protect against such problems. The latter procedure is kept in retained counsel cases in recognition of a defendant's right to choose joint representation, at least where no conflict of interest is apparent.

Subrule (G) is a slightly modified version of the last part of former 6.101(C)(4). The former rule required a lawyer representing joined defendants to immediately inform the court of a conflict of interest that "occurs during trial." The modified rule expands the lawyer's duty by requiring the lawyer to immediately inform the court of a conflict of interest that "arises at any time, including trial." This expansion recognizes that a conflict of interest may arise before, during, or after trial. Furthermore, the duty of the court to inquire into potential conflicts is now directive ("should") rather than permissive ("may").

Subrule (H) expands the scope of an appointed trial lawyer's responsibilities set forth in former 6.101(C)(2). The former rule made no reference to an appointed trial attorney's ability to file "postconviction motions the lawyer deems appropriate." Clearly, there are circumstances when it is more appropriate for the trial attorney to seek postconviction relief for his client than to await the appointment of appellate counsel. Under the scheme of the rules, however, a defendant should have only one appointed lawyer representing him at any time, and consequently,

the appointment of appellate counsel should act as an end to the responsibilities of the trial attorney under the appointment order.

The language change in subrule (3) is significant. Former 6.101(C)(2)(c) authorized the appointed attorney to "respond to prosecutor appeals to the Court of Appeals, either interlocutory or as of right." The substituted language in subrule (H)(3) gives the appointed trial lawyer responsibility for "responding to any preconviction appeals by the prosecutor." This latter language indicates that the appointed lawyer is responsible for responding to any appeals by the prosecutor, whether by leave or by right, that are "preconviction." This would include a prosecutor's appeal taken from the trial court grant of a defense motion resulting in a new trial. The language of the former rule, making the appointed trial lawyer responsible for any appeals by the prosecutor "as of right," is now too broad in light of the statutory amendment that has expanded the prosecutor's right to appeal to include postconviction appeals. 1988 PA 66, MCL 770.12.

Subrule (I) is new.

Subrule (J) repeats, with minor stylistic changes, former 6.107(C), dealing with the right of a witness to the assistance of a lawyer at grand jury proceedings.

Staff Comment to 1996 Amendment

The 1996 amendment of MCR 6.005(D) emphasized that the advice in subrules (D)(1) and (D)(2) pertains only to the defendant's *initial* waiver of the right to the assistance of a lawyer. The amendment of subrule (E) clarified that when a defendant has waived the assistance of a lawyer, the record of subsequent proceedings need only show that the court advised the defendant of the continuing right to a lawyer's assistance, and that the defendant waived that right.

Staff Comment to 2004 Amendment

MCR 8.123 was adopted on December 13, 2002, effective January 1, 2004. Subrule (B) requires trial courts to standardize their procedures for selecting and compensating appointed counsel. Subrule (D) requires the courts to maintain records of appointments and compensation. Subrule (E) requires that the records be public records.

Staff Comment to 2005 Amendment

On March 12, 2002, the Court appointed the Committee on the Rules of Criminal Procedure to review the rules to determine whether any of the provisions should be revised. The committee issued its report on June 16, 2003, recommending numerous amendments to existing rules, plus some new rules. A public hearing on the committee's recommendations was held May 27, 2004.

The Court adopted the committee's recommendations with respect to the amendments of Rules 2.511, 6.102, 6.104, 6.107, 6.112, 6.303, 6.304, 6.310, 6.311, 6.402, 6.412, 6.414, 6.419, 6.420, 6.427, 6.615, and 6.620, and the adoption of a new Rule 6.428.

The Court also adopted, with modifications, recommendations made by the committee and staff to amend other rules. Rule 2.510 was amended to conform to the newly enacted 2004 PA 12 (MCL 600.1332). The Court modified the committee's recommendation concerning Rule 6.001 to include a reference to 6.102 and to limit the application of 6.445 to subrules (A) through (G). The Court adopted the committee's recommendation with regard to Rule 6.004, except that the requirement that "whenever the defendant's constitutional right to a speedy trial is violated, the defendant is entitled to dismissal of the charge with prejudice" was retained and inserted into 6.004(A).

The Court adopted the committee's recommendations with regard to Rule 6.005 with the exception of the committee's recommendation that there be a ban on the joint representation of multiple defendants in all cases.

Staff Comment to 2011 Amendment

The amendment of MCR 6.005(H) revises the rule to clarify that appointed and retained defense counsel in a criminal proceeding either must file a substantive response to a prosecutor's application for interlocutory appeal or notify the Court of Appeals that the lawyer intends not to submit a pleading.

Staff Comment to 2012 Amendment

This amendment clarifies that trial counsel is required to make a defendant's file available to an appellate lawyer, and is required to retain the file for at least five years after disposition of the case in the trial court. This file was prompted by reports of appellate counsel having difficulty obtaining trial materials (especially video or audio materials that were not transcribed as part of the transcript). The five-year period mirrors the five-year retention period contained in MRPC 1.15(b)(2).

Rule 6.006. Video and Audio Proceedings

(A) Defendant in the Courtroom or at a Separate Location. District and circuit courts may use two-way interactive video technology to conduct the following proceedings between a courtroom and a prison, jail, or other location: initial arraignments on the warrant or complaint, probable cause conferences, arraignments on the information, pretrial conferences, pleas, sentencings for misdemeanor offenses, show cause hearings, waivers and adjournments of extradition, referrals for forensic determination of competency, waivers adjournments of preliminary examinations, and hearings on postjudgment motions to amend restitution.

(B) Defendant in the Courtroom—Preliminary Examinations. As long as the defendant is either present in the courtroom or has waived the right to be present, on motion of either party, district courts may use telephonic, voice, or video conferencing, including two-way interactive video technology, to take testimony from an expert witness or, upon a showing of good cause, any person at another location in a preliminary examination.

(C) Defendant in the Courtroom—Other Proceedings. As long as the defendant is either present in the courtroom or has waived the right to be present, upon a showing of good cause, district and circuit courts may use videoconferencing technology to take testimony from a person at another location in the following proceedings:

(1) evidentiary hearings, competency hearings, sentencings, probation revocation proceedings, and proceedings to revoke a sentence that does not entail an adjudication of guilt, such as youthful trainee status;

(2) with the consent of the parties, trials. A party who does not consent to the use of videoconferencing technology to take testimony from a person at trial shall not be required to articulate any reason for not consenting.

(D) Mechanics of Use. The use of telephonic, voice, video conferencing, or two-way interactive video technology, must be in accordance with any requirements and guidelines established by the State Court Administrative Office, and all proceedings at which such technology is used must be recorded verbatim by the court.

[Adopted July 13, 2005, effective January 1, 2006, 473 Mich. Amended December 14, 2005, effective January 1, 2006, 474 Mich; December 22, 2014, effective January 1, 2015, 497 Mich. Amended effective May 27, 2015, 498 Mich. Amended September 21, 2016, effective January 1, 2017, 500 Mich; May 22, 2019, effective September 1, 2019, 502 Mich.]

Comments

Staff Comment to 2005 Adoption

On March 12, 2002, the Court appointed the Committee on the Rules of Criminal Procedure to review the rules to determine whether any of the provisions should be revised. The committee issued its report on June 16, 2003, recommending numerous amendments to existing rules, plus some new rules. A public hearing on the committee's recommendations was held May 27, 2004.

The Court did follow the committee's recommendation that a new Rule 6.006, Video and Audio Proceedings, be adopted and included in the rule most of the committee's recommendations. However, the Court did limit the application of the rule at trial to situations where the parties have consented to the taking of testimony of a witness by use of two-way interactive video technology. The Court also modified the committee's recommendation concerning such testimony at preliminary examinations to conform to the newly enacted 2004 PA 20 (MCL 766.11a).

Staff Comment to 2005 Amendment

On July 13, 2005, the Court issued an order adding MCR 6.006(A) as recommended by the Committee on the Rules of Criminal Procedure. The amendment of MCR 6.006(A) clarifies the Court's order of July 13, 2005, that the rule is also applicable if the defendant is in the courtroom. The amendment also makes the language of the rule consistent with other rules.

Staff Comment to January, 2015 Amendment

The amendments of MCR 6.006, 6.104, 6.110, and 6.111 and adoption of new Rule 6.108 create procedural rules for conducting probable cause conferences and amend current provisions of the preliminary examination court rules to coordinate with 2014 PA 123 and 124.

Staff Comment to May, 2015 Amendment

The Court retained the amendments that became effective January 1, 2015, and adopted additional amendments of MCR 6.108 and MCR 6.110 to provide further clarification as suggested in comment letters received by the court.

Staff Comment to 2017 Amendment

These amendments permit courts to expand the use of videoconferencing technology in many court proceedings, and clarify the proceedings at which videoconferencing technology may be used.

Staff Comment to 2019 Amendment

The amendments more explicitly require restitution to be ordered at the time of sentencing as required by statute, and establish a procedure for modifying restitution amounts.

Rule 6.007 Confidential Records

Records are public except as otherwise indicated in court rule or statute.

[Adopted October 31, 2012, effective January 1, 2013, 493 Mich.]

Comments

Staff Comment to 2013 Adoption

The amendments of these rules update the rules making them less "paper" focused and reflecting the use of electronic technology in the way courts process court records. The amendments also clarify and delineate the types of records and other materials maintained by a court, and clarify how access is provided.

Rule 6.008. Criminal Jurisdiction

(A) District Court. The district court has jurisdiction over all misdemeanors and all felonies through the preliminary examination and until the entry of an order to bind the defendant over to the circuit court.

(B) Circuit Court. The circuit court has jurisdiction over all felonies from the bindover from the district court unless otherwise provided by law. The failure of the court to properly document the bindover decision shall not deprive the circuit court of jurisdiction. A party challenging a bindover decision must do so before any plea of guilty or no contest, or before trial.

(C) Pleas and Verdicts in Circuit Court. The circuit court retains jurisdiction over any case in which a plea is entered or a verdict rendered to a charge that would normally be cognizable in the district court.

(D) Sentencing Misdemeanors in Circuit Court. The circuit court shall sentence all defendants bound over to circuit court on a felony that either plead guilty to, or are found guilty of, a misdemeanor.

(E) Concurrent Jurisdiction. As part of a concurrent jurisdiction plan, the circuit court and district court may enter into an agreement for district court probation officers to prepare the presentence investigation report and supervise on probation defendants who either plead guilty to, or are found guilty of, a misdemeanor in circuit court. The case remains under the jurisdiction of the circuit court.

[Adopted September 20, 2017, effective January 1, 2018, 501 Mich.]

Comment

Staff Comment to 2018 Adoption

The addition of Rule 6.008 establishes procedures for a circuit court to follow if a defendant bound over to circuit court on a felony either pleads guilty to, or is convicted of, a misdemeanor in circuit court. Remand to district court would remain a possibility in certain limited circumstances, including where the evidence is insufficient to support the bindover, *People v Miklovich*, 375 Mich 536, 539; 134 NW2d 720 (1965); *People v Salazar*, 124 Mich App 249, 251–252; 333 NW2d 567 (1983), or where there was a defect in the waiver of the right to a preliminary examination, *People v Reedy*, 151 Mich App 143, 147; 390 NW2d 215 (1986);

People v Skowronek, 57 Mich App 110, 113; 226 NW2d 74 (1975), or where the prosecutor adds a new charge on which the defendant did not have a preliminary examination, *People v Bercheny*, 387 Mich 431, 434; 196 NW2d 767 (1972), adopting the opinion in *People v Davis*, 29 Mich App 443, 463; 185 NW2d 609 (1971), aff'd *People v Bercheny*, 387 Mich 431 (1972). See also MCR 6.110(H).

SUBCHAPTER 6.100   PRELIMINARY PROCEEDINGS

Rule 6.101.   Complaint

(A) Definition and Form. A complaint is a written accusation that a named or described person has committed a specified criminal offense. The complaint must include the substance of the accusation against the accused and the name and statutory citation of the offense. At the time of filing, specified case initiation information shall be provided in the form and manner approved by the State Court Administrative Office.

(B) Signature and Oath. The complaint must be signed and verified under MCR 1.109(D)(3). Any requirement of law that a complaint filed with the court must be sworn is met by this verification.

(C) Prosecutor's Approval or Posting of Security. A complaint may not be filed without a prosecutor's written approval endorsed on the complaint or attached to it, or unless security for costs is filed with the court.

[Adopted effective October 1, 1989. Amended May 30, 2018, effective September 1, 2018, 501 Mich; September 18, 2019, effective January 1, 2020, 503 Mich.]

Comments

Staff Comment to 1989 Adoption

MCR 6.101 is a new rule. Subrules (A) and (B) state the statutory requirements for a complaint set forth in MCL 764.1a(1) and MCL 764.1d. Additionally, subrule (A) incorporates, for efficiency purposes, the requirement that the complaint include "the name and statutory citation of the offense." Subrule (C) implements the statutory provisions of MCL 764.1(1), including the procedure permitting a private citizen to file a complaint when "security for costs is filed with the magistrate."

Like the cited statutes, this rule does not apply to prosecutions arising as a result of grand jury proceedings. See *People v O'Hara*, 278 Mich 281, 293 (1936).

Staff Comment to 2018 Amendment

The amendments in this order are intended to begin moving trial courts toward a statewide uniform e-Filing process. In addition, the order moves existing language into MCR 1.109 as a way to, for the first time, include most filing requirements in one single rule, instead of scattered in various rules. The order largely mirrors the administrative orders that most e-Filing pilot projects have operated under, but contains some significant new provisions. For example, courts are required to maintain documents in an electronic document management system, and the electronic record is the official court record.

Staff Comment to 2020 Amendment

The amendments of MCR 1.109, 2.107, 2.113, 2.116, 2.119, 2.222, 2.223, 2.225, 2.227, 3.206, 3.211, 3.212, 3.214, 3.303, 3.903, 3.921, 3.925, 3.926, 3.931, 3.933, 3.942, 3.950, 3.961, 3.971, 3.972, 4.002, 4.101, 4.201, 4.202, 4.302, 5.128, 5.302, 5.731, 6.101, 6.615, 8.105, and 8.119 and rescission of MCR 2.226 and 8.125 continue the process for design and implementation of the statewide electronic-filing system.

Rule 6.102   Arrest on a Warrant

(A) Issuance of Warrant. A court must issue an arrest warrant, or a summons in accordance with MCR 6.103, if presented with a proper complaint and if the court finds probable cause to believe that the accused committed the alleged offense.

(B) Probable Cause Determination. A finding of probable cause may be based on hearsay evidence and rely on factual allegations in the complaint, affidavits from the complainant or others, the testimony of a sworn witness adequately preserved to permit review, or any combination of these sources.

(C) Contents of Warrant; Court's Subscription. A warrant must

(1) contain the accused's name, if known, or an identifying name or description;

(2) describe the offense charged in the complaint;

(3) command a peace officer or other person authorized by law to arrest and bring the accused before a judicial officer of the judicial district in which the offense allegedly was committed or some other designated court; and

(4) be signed by the court.

(D) Warrant Specification of Interim Bail. Where permitted by law, the court may specify on the warrant the bail that an accused may post to obtain release before arraignment on the warrant and, if the court deems it appropriate, include as a bail condition that the arrest of the accused occur on or before a specified date or within a specified period of time after issuance of the warrant.

(E) Execution and Return of Warrant. Only a peace officer or other person authorized by law may execute an arrest warrant. On execution or attempted execution of the warrant, the officer must make a return on the warrant and deliver it to the court before which the arrested person is to be taken.

(F) Release on Interim Bail. If an accused has been arrested pursuant to a warrant that includes an interim bail provision, the accused must either be arraigned promptly or released pursuant to the interim bail provision. The accused may obtain release by posting the bail on the warrant and by submitting a recognizance to appear before a specified court at a specified date and time, provided that

(1) the accused is arrested prior to the expiration date, if any, of the bail provision;

(2) the accused is arrested in the county in which the warrant was issued, or in which the accused resides or is employed, and the accused is not wanted on another charge;

(3) the accused is not under the influence of liquor or controlled substance; and

(4) the condition of the accused or the circumstances at the time of arrest do not otherwise suggest a need for judicial review of the original specification of bail.

[Adopted effective October 1, 1989. Amended July 13, 2005, effective January 1, 2006, 473 Mich.]

Comments

Staff Comment to 1989 Adoption

MCR 6.102 is a new rule.

Subrule (A) states the requirements for issuance of a warrant set forth in MCL 764.1a except that it substitutes "probable cause" for "reasonable cause." These terms are viewed as equivalent, with "probable cause" being preferable because it is a familiar and recognized standard.

Subrule (B) is consistent with the requirements of MCL 764.1a(2). Additionally, this subrule imposes the requirement that any sworn testimony relied on in making the probable cause determination be "adequately preserved to permit review." An objective of this subrule is to ensure that there is a reviewable record in the event that the probable cause determination is subsequently challenged. Accordingly, if any oral testimony is relied on, it must be preserved adequately in some fashion to permit a review of its sufficiency to support the probable cause determination. An electronically recorded or verbatim written record obviously satisfies this requirement. A written or recorded oral summary of the testimony sufficiently contemporaneous to be reliable, and certified as accurate by the judicial officer, may also satisfy this requirement.

Subrule (C) sets forth the requirements of MCL 764.1b.

Subrule (D) sets forth a new procedure. It authorizes in felony cases the specification on the warrant of interim bail similar to the procedure currently authorized by statute in misdemeanor cases. See MCL 780.582 and MCL 780.585. Subrule (D) further authorizes the court, in its discretion, to include an expiration date for the interim bail provision. This option permits the court to set a cut-off date, beyond which release may not be obtained, to prevent the release of a person who may be avoiding arrest. However, setting of an expiration date may also defeat the purpose of the interim bail provision if it is too short or is used in cases where the arrest of the defendant is sought solely in a passive fashion such as awaiting the defendant's stop for a traffic offense.

Subrule (E) implements MCL 764.1b.

Subrule (F) is new and sets forth a procedure applicable when an accused is arrested on a warrant containing an interim bail provision. The arresting agency has the option of either releasing the accused on the interim bail or immediately taking the accused to be arraigned if the arraignment can be conducted promptly. This subrule also lists conditions that must be met in order for an accused to be eligible for release on interim bail. Subrule (2) requires that the accused be arrested in the county in which the warrant was issued or in which the accused resides or is employed. The purpose of this limitation is to preclude the availability of interim bail to a person who may be avoiding arrest. Subrule (3) does not preclude interim bail release of an accused who was under the influence of liquor at the time of arrest but who is no longer in that condition. Subrule (4) is a catch-all provision and should be applied in good faith. Implicit in subrule (F) is the condition that the accused be satisfactorily identified as the person named in the warrant. Additionally, the rule does not preclude the police agency from requiring the accused to submit to photographing and fingerprinting before being released.

Staff Comment to 2005 Amendment

On March 12, 2002, the Court appointed the Committee on the Rules of Criminal Procedure to review the rules to determine whether any of the provisions should be revised. The committee issued its report on June 16, 2003, recommending numerous amendments to existing rules, plus some new rules. A public hearing on the committee's recommendations was held May 27, 2004.

The Court adopted the committee's recommendations with respect to the amendments of Rules 2.511, 6.102, 6.104, 6.107, 6.112, 6.303, 6.304, 6.310, 6.311, 6.402, 6.412, 6.414, 6.419, 6.420, 6.427, 6.615, and 6.620, and the adoption of a new Rule 6.428.

The Court also adopted, with modifications, recommendations made by the committee and staff to amend other rules. Rule 2.510 was amended to conform to the newly enacted 2004 PA 12 (MCL 600.1332). The Court modified the committee's recommendation concerning Rule 6.001 to include a reference to 6.102 and to limit the application of 6.445 to subrules (A) through (G). The Court adopted the committee's recommendation with regard to Rule 6.004, except that the requirement that "whenever the defendant's constitutional right to a speedy trial is violated, the defendant is entitled to dismissal of the charge with prejudice" was retained and inserted into 6.004(A).

Rule 6.103   Summons Instead of Arrest

(A) Issuance of Summons. If the prosecutor so requests, the court may issue a summons instead of an arrest warrant. If an accused fails to appear in response to a summons, the court, on request, must issue an arrest warrant.

(B) Form. A summons must contain the same information as an arrest warrant, except that it should summon the accused to appear before a designated court at a stated time and place.

(C) Service and Return of Summons. A summons may be served by

(1) delivering a copy to the named individual; or

(2) leaving a copy with a person of suitable age and discretion at the individual's home or usual place of abode; or

(3) mailing a copy to the individual's last known address.

Service should be made promptly to give the accused adequate notice of the appearance date. The person serving the summons must make a return to the court before which the person is summoned to appear.

[Adopted effective October 1, 1989.]

Comments

Staff Comment to 1989 Adoption

MCR 6.103 is a new rule based on Federal Rule of Criminal Procedure 4. Subrule (A) is a variation of Federal Rule 4(a), which provides in part:

"Upon the request of the attorney for the government a summons instead of a warrant shall issue."

Under subrule (A) a summons may not be issued except on the request of the prosecutor, but the court retains the discretion ("may") to decline the request and issue an arrest warrant instead. The second sentence of subrule (A) also varies from the federal rule, which provides:

"If a defendant fails to appear in response to the summons, a warrant shall issue."

Under subrule (A) issuance of the arrest warrant for failure to appear in response to a summons is not automatic, and is required only on the request of the prosecutor. A prosecutor's "request" made under this rule should be in writing.

Subrule (B) is based on Federal Rule 4(c)(2).

Subrule (C) is based on provisions in Federal Rule 4(d)(3) and (4).

Rule 6.104   Arraignment on the Warrant or Complaint

(A) Arraignment Without Unnecessary Delay. Unless released beforehand, an arrested person must be taken without unnecessary delay before a court for arraignment in accordance with the provisions of this rule, or must be arraigned without unnecessary delay by use of two-way interactive video technology in accordance with MCR 6.006(A).

(B) Place of Arraignment. An accused arrested pursuant to a warrant must be taken to a court specified in the warrant. An accused arrested without a warrant must be taken to a court in the judicial district in which the offense allegedly occurred. If the arrest occurs outside the county in which these courts are located, the arresting agency must make arrangements with the authorities in the demanding county to have the accused promptly transported to the latter county for arraignment in accordance with the provisions of this rule. If prompt transportation cannot be arranged, the accused must be taken without unnecessary delay before the nearest available court for preliminary appearance in accordance with subrule (C). In the alternative, the provisions of this subrule may be satisfied by use of two-way interactive video technology in accordance with MCR 6.006(A).

(C) Preliminary Appearance Outside County of Offense. When, under subrule (B), an accused is taken before a court outside the county of the alleged offense either in person or by way of two-way interactive video technology, the court must advise the accused of the rights specified in subrule (E)(2) and determine what form of pretrial release, if any, is appropriate. To be released, the accused must submit a recognizance for appearance within the next 14 days before a court specified in the arrest warrant or, in a case involving an arrest without a warrant, before either a court in the judicial district in which the offense allegedly occurred or some other court designated by that court. The court must certify the recognizance and have it delivered or sent without delay to the appropriate court. If the accused is not released, the arresting agency must arrange prompt transportation to the judicial district of the offense. In all cases, the arraignment is then to continue under subrule (D), if applicable, and subrule (E) either in the judicial district of the alleged offense or in such court as otherwise is designated.

(D) Arrest Without Warrant. If an accused is arrested without a warrant, a complaint complying with MCR 6.101 must be filed at or before the time of arraignment. On receiving the complaint and on finding probable cause, the court must either issue a warrant or endorse the complaint as provided in MCL 764.1c. Arraignment of the accused may then proceed in accordance with subrule (E).

(E) Arraignment Procedure; Judicial Responsibilities. The court at the arraignment must

(1) inform the accused of the nature of the offense charged, and its maximum possible prison sentence and any mandatory minimum sentence required by law;

(2) if the accused is not represented by a lawyer at the arraignment, advise the accused that

(a) the accused has a right to remain silent,

(b) anything the accused says orally or in writing can be used against the accused in court,

(c) the accused has a right to have a lawyer present during any questioning consented to, and

(d) if the accused does not have the money to hire a lawyer, the court will appoint a lawyer for the accused;

(3) advise the accused of the right to a lawyer at all subsequent court proceedings and, if appropriate, appoint a lawyer;

(4) set a date for a probable cause conference not less than 7 days or more than 14 days after the date of the arraignment and set a date for preliminary examination not less than 5 days or more than 7 days after the date of the probable cause conference;

(5) determine what form of pretrial release, if any, is appropriate; and

(6) ensure that the accused has had biometric data collected as required by law.

The court may not question the accused about the alleged offense or request that the accused enter a plea.

(F) Arraignment Procedure; Recording. A verbatim record must be made of the arraignment.

(G) Plan for Judicial Availability. In each county, the court with trial jurisdiction over felony cases must adopt and file with the state court administrator a plan for judicial availability. The plan shall

(1) make a judicial officer available for arraignments each day of the year, or

(2) make a judicial officer available for setting bail for every person arrested for commission of a felony each day of the year conditioned upon

(a) the judicial officer being presented a proper complaint and finding probable cause pursuant to MCR 6.102(A), and

(b) the judicial officer having available information to set bail.

This portion of the plan must provide that the judicial officer shall order the arresting officials to arrange prompt transportation of any accused unable to post bond to the judicial district of the offense for arraignment not later than the next regular business day.

[Adopted effective October 1, 1989. Amended October 1, 1989, effective April 1, 1990; February 19, 1990, effective April 1, 1990; August 3, 1994, effective October 1, 1994, 446 Mich; July 13, 2005, effective January 1, 2006, 473 Mich; December 22, 2014, effective January 1, 2015, 497 Mich. Amended effective May 27, 2015, 498 Mich; August 14, 2019, 503 Mich.]

Comments

Staff Comment to 1989 Adoption

MCR 6.104 is a new rule.

Subrule (A) implements the requirement for prompt arraignment of a person arrested with a warrant, MCL 764.26, or without a warrant, MCL 764.13. The rule recognizes, however, that prompt arraignment is not required if an arrested person is "released beforehand." This may occur as a result of outright release of an arrested person by the police agency because of the decision not to file a complaint, or because the defendant was released on a secured or unsecured recognizance issued by a judge or magistrate in lieu of prompt arraignment. When a delay becomes "unnecessary" and what its effect is on the admissibility of evidence are left to case law. See, for example, *People v Cipriano*, 431 Mich 315 (1988).

Subrule (B) makes some modifications in existing law. With regard to an accused arrested *without a warrant* in the county in which an alleged offense occurred, it implements the requirement of MCL 764.13 that the accused be taken "before a magistrate of the judicial district in which the offense is charged to have been committed." With regard to an accused arrested *with a warrant* in the county in which the alleged offense occurred, the rule requires that the accused be taken before "a court specified in the warrant." MCR 6.102(C) permits the warrant to command a peace officer to bring the accused before a magistrate of the judicial district in which the offense is charged to have been committed "or some other designated court." These latter quoted provisions accommodate the requirement for prompt arraignments, including weekends, by allowing specification in the warrant of another court, such as one shared by the judicial districts for the purpose of conducting weekend or nonbusiness-hour arraignments. This does not imply, however, that an accused arrested without a warrant may not be taken before a court that is not in the judicial district in which the offense occurred but that is authorized to conduct weekend or nonbusiness-hour arraignments for that court.

The remainder of the procedure described in this subrule, setting forth responsibilities pertaining to an accused arrested in a county outside the one in which the offense occurred, is new. The rule provides that on the arrest of an accused in such a county, the arresting agency "must make arrangements with the authorities in the demanding county" to have the accused promptly transported to that county for arraignment as required by this rule. This does not imply that it is the arresting agency's responsibility to transport the accused to the demanding county if the authorities in the demanding county refuse to provide such transportation. In such a situation, the arresting agency has the option of itself providing the transportation or taking the accused to a local court for a "preliminary appearance" as provided in subrule (C).

Subrule (C) sets forth the procedure that the local court must follow in conducting a preliminary appearance occurring outside the county of the offense and the duty of the arresting agency if the accused is not released as a result of that appearance. At that appearance the court's duty is solely to advise the unrepresented accused of *Miranda* rights and decide if the accused may be released on a secured or unsecured recognizance to appear "within the next 14 days" before a court in the judicial district in which the offense occurred. The recognizance promptly must be delivered or mailed to the appropriate court. If the accused is not released, the arresting agency has no option other than to "arrange prompt transportation" of the accused to the judicial district of the offense. Accordingly, if the police agency in the demanding county still declines to provide prompt transportation of the accused, that responsibility will fall on the arresting agency.

Subrule (D) repeats the procedure set forth in MCL 764.1c. The rule's substitution of the terminology "probable cause" for the statutory terminology "reasonable cause" does not indicate a substantive difference.

Subrule (E) sets forth the arraignment procedure that must be followed by a court authorized to perform the arraignment of the accused. The procedure has some requirements extending beyond current practice. Requiring the arraigning court to give *Miranda* rights to an unrepresented accused is new and addresses Fifth and Sixth Amendment concerns. Subrule (E)(6) implements a statutory requirement for the arraigning court to ensure that the accused has been fingerprinted. MCL 764.29. The last sentence of subrule (E) prohibits the court from questioning the accused "about the alleged offense" but does not preclude other questioning pertinent to the court's performance of its arraignment functions.

Subrule (F) is new but does not state a new requirement.

Staff Comment to 1990 Amendment

The February 9, 1990 amendment of MCR 6.104(G) [effective April 1, 1990] is a slightly altered version of a proposal made by the Michigan District Judges Association.

Staff Comment to 1994 Amendment

In 1994, MCR 6.104(E)(4) and MCR 6.907(C)(2) were amended to reflect the change made by 1994 PA 167, which extended from 12 to 14 days the period within which a preliminary examination must be conducted. MCL 766.4. A similar change was also made in MCR 6.445(C), concerning the timing of a probation revocation hearing.

Staff Comment to 2005 Amendment

On March 12, 2002, the Court appointed the Committee on the Rules of Criminal Procedure to review the rules to determine whether any of the provisions should be revised. The committee issued its report on June 16, 2003, recommending numerous amendments to existing rules, plus some new rules. A public hearing on the committee's recommendations was held May 27, 2004.

The Court adopted the committee's recommendations with respect to the amendments of Rules 2.511, 6.102, 6.104, 6.107, 6.112, 6.303, 6.304, 6.310, 6.311, 6.402, 6.412, 6.414, 6.419, 6.420, 6.427, 6.615, and 6.620, and the adoption of a new Rule 6.428.

Staff Comment to January, 2015 Amendment

The amendments of MCR 6.006, 6.104, 6.110, and 6.111 and adoption of new Rule 6.108 create procedural rules for conducting probable cause conferences and amend current provisions of the preliminary examination court rules to coordinate with 2014 PA 123 and 124.

Staff Comment to May, 2015 Amendment

The Court retained the amendments that became effective January 1, 2015, and adopted additional amendments of MCR 6.108 and MCR 6.110 to provide further clarification as suggested in comment letters received by the court.

Staff Comment to 2019 Amendment

These amendments update cross-references and make other nonsubstantive revisions to clarify the rules.

Rule 6.106   Pretrial Release

(A) In General. At the defendant's arraignment on the complaint and/or warrant, unless an order in accordance with this rule was issued beforehand, the court must order that, pending trial, the defendant be

(1) held in custody as provided in subrule (B);

(2) released on personal recognizance or an unsecured appearance bond; or

(3) released conditionally, with or without money bail (ten percent, cash or surety).

(B) Pretrial Release/Custody Order Under Const 1963, Art 1, § 15.

(1) The court may deny pretrial release to

(a) a defendant charged with

(i) murder or treason, or

(ii) committing a violent felony and

[A]   at the time of the commission of the violent felony, the defendant was on probation, parole, or released pending trial for another violent felony, or

[B]   during the 15 years preceding the commission of the violent felony, the defendant had been convicted of 2 or more violent felonies under the laws of this state or

substantially similar laws of the United States or another state arising out of separate incidents, if the court finds that proof of the defendant's guilt is evident or the presumption great;

(b) a defendant charged with criminal sexual conduct in the first degree, armed robbery, or kidnapping with the intent to extort money or other valuable thing thereby, if the court finds that proof of the defendant's guilt is evident or the presumption great, unless the court finds by clear and convincing evidence that the defendant is not likely to flee or present a danger to any other person.

(2) A "violent felony" within the meaning of subrule (B)(1) is a felony, an element of which involves a violent act or threat of a violent act against any other person.

(3) If the court determines as provided in subrule (B)(1) that the defendant may not be released, the court must order the defendant held in custody for a period not to exceed 90 days after the date of the order, excluding delays attributable to the defense, within which trial must begin or the court must immediately schedule a hearing and set the amount of bail.

(4) The court must state the reasons for an order of custody on the record and on a form approved by the State Court Administrator's Office entitled "Custody Order." The completed form must be placed in the court file.

(5) The court may, in its custody order, place conditions on the defendant, including but not limited to restricting or prohibiting defendant's contact with any other named person or persons, if the court determines the conditions are reasonably necessary to maintain the integrity of the judicial proceedings or are reasonably necessary for the protection of one or more named persons. If an order under this paragraph is in conflict with another court order, the most restrictive provisions of the orders shall take precedence until the conflict is resolved.

(6) Nothing in this rule limits the ability of a jail to impose restrictions on detainee contact as an appropriate means of furthering penological goals.

(C) Release on Personal Recognizance. If the defendant is not ordered held in custody pursuant to subrule (B), the court must order the pretrial release of the defendant on personal recognizance, or on an unsecured appearance bond, subject to the conditions that the defendant will appear as required, will not leave the state without permission of the court, and will not commit any crime while released, unless the court determines that such release will not reasonably ensure the appearance of the defendant as required, or that such release will present a danger to the public.

(D) Conditional Release. If the court determines that the release described in subrule (C) will not reasonably ensure the appearance of the defendant as required, or will not reasonably ensure the safety of the public, the court may order the pretrial release of the defendant on the condition or combination of conditions that the court determines are appropriate including

(1) that the defendant will appear as required, will not leave the state without permission of the court, and will not commit any crime while released, and

(2) subject to any condition or conditions the court determines are reasonably necessary to ensure the appearance of the defendant as required and the safety of the public, which may include requiring the defendant to

(a) make reports to a court agency as are specified by the court or the agency;

(b) not use alcohol or illicitly use any controlled substance;

(c) participate in a substance abuse testing or monitoring program;

(d) participate in a specified treatment program for any physical or mental condition, including substance abuse;

(e) comply with restrictions on personal associations, place of residence, place of employment, or travel;

(f) surrender driver's license or passport;

(g) comply with a specified curfew;

(h) continue to seek employment;

(i) continue or begin an educational program;

(j) remain in the custody of a responsible member of the community who agrees to monitor the defendant and report any violation of any release condition to the court;

(k) not possess a firearm or other dangerous weapon;

(*l*) not enter specified premises or areas and not assault, beat, molest or wound a named person or persons;

(m) comply with any condition limiting or prohibiting contact with any other named person or persons. If an order under this paragraph limiting or prohibiting contact with any other named person or persons is in conflict with another court order, the most restrictive provision of the orders shall take precedence until the conflict is resolved. The court may make this condition effective immediately on entry of a pretrial release order and while defendant remains in custody if the court determines it is reasonably necessary to maintain the integrity of the judicial proceeding or it is reasonably necessary for the protection of one or more named persons.

(n) satisfy any injunctive order made a condition of release; or

(*o*) comply with any other condition, including the requirement of money bail as described in subrule (E), reasonably necessary to ensure the defendant's appearance as required and the safety of the public.

(E) Money Bail. If the court determines for reasons it states on the record that the defendant's appearance or the protection of the public cannot otherwise be assured, money bail, with or without conditions described in subrule (D), may be required.

(1) The court may require the defendant to

(a) post, at the defendant's option,

(i) a surety bond that is executed by a surety approved by the court in an amount equal to ¼ of the full bail amount, or

(ii) bail that is executed by the defendant, or by another who is not a surety approved by the court, and secured by

[A] a cash deposit, or its equivalent, for the full bail amount, or

[B] a cash deposit of 10 percent of the full bail amount, or, with the court's consent,

[C] designated real property; or

(b) post, at the defendant's option,

(i) a surety bond that is executed by a surety approved by the court in an amount equal to the full bail amount, or

(ii) bail that is executed by the defendant, or by another who is not a surety approved by the court, and secured by

[A] a cash deposit, or its equivalent, for the full bail amount, or, with the court's consent,

[B] designated real property.

(2) The court may require satisfactory proof of value and interest in property if the court consents to the posting of a bond secured by designated real property.

(F) Decision; Statement of Reasons.

(1) In deciding which release to use and what terms and conditions to impose, the court is to consider relevant information, including

(a) defendant's prior criminal record, including juvenile offenses;

(b) defendant's record of appearance or nonappearance at court proceedings or flight to avoid prosecution;

(c) defendant's history of substance abuse or addiction;

(d) defendant's mental condition, including character and reputation for dangerousness;

(e) the seriousness of the offense charged, the presence or absence of threats, and the probability of conviction and likely sentence;

(f) defendant's employment status and history and financial history insofar as these factors relate to the ability to post money bail;

(g) the availability of responsible members of the community who would vouch for or monitor the defendant;

(h) facts indicating the defendant's ties to the community, including family ties and relationships, and length of residence, and

(i) any other facts bearing on the risk of nonappearance or danger to the public.

(2) If the court orders the defendant held in custody pursuant to subrule (B) or released on conditions in subrule (D) that include money bail, the court must state the reasons for its decision on the record. The court need not make a finding on each of the enumerated factors.

(3) Nothing in subrules (C) through (F) may be construed to sanction pretrial detention nor to sanction the determination of pretrial release on the basis of race, religion, gender, economic status, or other impermissible criteria.

(G) Custody Hearing.

(1) *Entitlement to Hearing.* A court having jurisdiction of a defendant may conduct a custody hearing if the defendant is being held in custody pursuant to subrule (B) and a custody hearing is requested by either the defendant or the prosecutor. The purpose of the hearing is to permit the parties to litigate all of the issues relevant to challenging or supporting a custody decision pursuant to subrule (B).

(2) *Hearing Procedure.*

(a) At the custody hearing, the defendant is entitled to be present and to be represented by a lawyer, and the defendant and the prosecutor are entitled to present witnesses and evidence, to proffer information, and to cross-examine each other's witnesses.

(b) The rules of evidence, except those pertaining to privilege, are not applicable. Unless the court makes the findings required to enter an order under subrule (B)(1), the defendant must be ordered released under subrule (C) or (D). A verbatim record of the hearing must be made.

(H) Appeals; Modification of Release Decision.

(1) *Appeals.* A party seeking review of a release decision may file a motion in the court having appellate jurisdiction over the court that made the release decision. There is no fee for filing the motion. The reviewing court may not stay, vacate, modify, or reverse the release decision except on finding an abuse of discretion.

(2) *Modification of Release Decision.*

(a) Prior to Arraignment on the Information. Prior to the defendant's arraignment on the information, any court before which proceedings against the defendant are pending may, on the motion of a party or its own initiative and on finding that there is a substantial reason for doing so, modify a prior release decision or reopen a prior custody hearing.

(b) Arraignment on Information and Afterwards. At the defendant's arraignment on the information and afterwards, the court having jurisdiction of the defendant may, on the motion of a party or its own initiative, make a de novo determination and modify a prior release decision or reopen a prior custody hearing.

(c) Burden of Going Forward. The party seeking modification of a release decision has the burden of going forward.

(3) *Emergency Release.* If a defendant being held in pretrial custody under this rule is ordered released from custody as a result of a court order or law requiring the release of prisoners to relieve jail conditions, the court ordering the defendant's release may, if appropriate, impose conditions of release in accordance with this rule to ensure the appearance of the defendant as required and to protect the public. If such conditions of release are imposed, the court must inform the defendant of the conditions on the record or by furnishing to the defendant or the defendant's lawyer a copy of the release order setting forth the conditions.

(I) Termination of Release Order.

(1) If the conditions of the release order are met and the defendant is discharged from all obligations in the case, the court must vacate the release order, discharge anyone who has posted bail or bond, and return the cash (or its equivalent) posted in the full amount of the bail, or, if there has been a deposit of 10 percent of the full bail amount, return 90 percent of the deposited money and retain 10 percent.

(2) If the defendant has failed to comply with the conditions of release, the court may issue a warrant for the arrest of the defendant and enter an order revoking the release order and declaring the bail money deposited or the surety bond, if any, forfeited.

(a) The court must mail notice of any revocation order immediately to the defendant at the defendant's last known address and, if forfeiture of bail or bond has been ordered, to anyone who posted bail or bond.

(b) If the defendant does not appear and surrender to the court within 28 days after the revocation date, the court may continue the revocation order and enter judgment for the state or local unit of government against the defendant and anyone who posted bail or bond for an amount not to exceed the full amount of the bail, and costs of the court proceedings, or if a surety bond was posted, an amount not to exceed the full amount of the surety bond. If the amount of a forfeited surety bond is less than the full amount of the bail, the defendant shall continue to be liable to the court for the difference, unless otherwise ordered by the court. If the defendant does not within that period satisfy the court that there was compliance with the conditions of release other than appearance or that compliance was impossible through no fault of the defendant, the court may continue the revocation order and enter judgment for the state or local unit of government against the defendant alone for an amount not to exceed the full amount of the bond, and costs of the court proceedings.

(c) The 10 percent bail deposit made under subrule (E)(1)(a)(ii)[B] must be applied to the costs and, if any remains, to the balance of the judgment. The amount applied to the judgment must be transferred to the county treasury for a circuit court case, to the treasuries of the governments contributing to the district control unit for a district court case, or to the treasury of the appropriate municipal government for a municipal court case. The balance of the judgment may be enforced and collected as a judgment entered in a civil case.

(3) If money was deposited on a bail or bond executed by the defendant, the money must be first applied to the amount of any fine, costs, or statutory assessments imposed and any balance returned, subject to subrule (I)(1).

[Adopted effective October 1, 1989. Amended March 12, 1992, March 23, 1992, and May 21, 1992, effective June 1, 1992, 439 Mich; July 13, 2005, effective January 1, 2006, 473 Mich; May 22, 2007, effective September 1, 2007, 478 Mich; September 23, 2015, effective January 1, 2016, 498 Mich.]

Comments

Staff Comment to 1989 Adoption

MCR 6.106 repeats former MCR 6.110. A court-appointed committee is developing a proposed revision of this rule.

Staff Comment to 1992 Amendment

Revised MCR 6.106 [effective June 1, 1992] is based on a proposed revision of the pretrial release rule submitted by a committee appointed by the Court to study the need for updating the former rule. The revised rule contains many of the changes recommended by the committee to improve the pretrial release procedure, and modifications made by the Court after consideration of comments received following publication.

The May 21, 1992 amendments of revised MCR 6.106, which is to take effect on June 1, 1992, make several technical changes.

Staff Comment to 2005 Amendment

On March 12, 2002, the Court appointed the Committee on the Rules of Criminal Procedure to review the rules to determine whether any of the provisions should be revised. The committee issued its report on June 16, 2003, recommending numerous amendments to existing rules, plus some new rules. A public hearing on the committee's recommendations was held May 27, 2004.

The Court adopted the committee's recommendations with respect to the amendments of Rules 2.511, 6.102, 6.104, 6.107, 6.112, 6.303, 6.304, 6.310, 6.311, 6.402, 6.412, 6.414, 6.419, 6.420, 6.427, 6.615, and 6.620, and the adoption of a new Rule 6.428.

Staff had recommended that a new 6.106(D)(2)(m) be adopted. The Court modified the recommendation to clarify that "the most restrictive provision of each order shall take precedence over the other court order until the conflict is resolved." Rules 6.106(E) and 6.106(I) were amended to conform to the newly enacted 2004 PA 167 (MCL 765.6) and 2004 PA 332 (MCL 765.28).

Staff Comment to 2007 Amendment

This amendment clarifies that bail agents are liable only for the appearance of a defendant, and not for compliance with conditions imposed on a defendant by the court as part of a conditional release pursuant to MCR 6.106. The amendment also clarifies that a court may continue the revocation order and enter judgment against a defendant for failure to comply with the conditions of release or failure to satisfy the court that compliance with those conditions was impossible, regardless of whether the defendant failed to appear.

The amendment also prohibits a court from entering a judgment that includes the costs of the proceeding against a surety. MCL 765.28 limits judgment against the surety to an amount not more than the full amount of the surety bond.

Staff Comment to 2016 Amendment

The amendment of MCR 6.106 clarifies that a court would determine issues concerning defendant's pretrial release, if any, at the time of defendant's arraignment on the complaint and/or warrant.

The amendments of MCR 6.106(B) and (D) clarify that courts are permitted to exercise their inherent power to order conditions, including but not limited to those conditions that restrict or prohibit a pretrial defendant's contact with any named person to be effective immediately, even while defendant remains in custody. These conditions are allowed in a custody order when the protective restriction or prohibition is reasonably necessary to maintain the integrity of the judicial proceedings or is reasonably necessary for the protection of one or more named persons.

Rule 6.107   Grand Jury Proceedings

(A) Right to Grand Jury Records. Whenever an indictment is returned by a grand jury or a grand juror, the person accused in the indictment is entitled to the part of the record, including a transcript of the part of the testimony of all witnesses appearing before the grand jury or grand juror, that touches on the guilt or innocence of the accused of the charge contained in the indictment.

(B) Procedure to Obtain Records.

(1) To obtain the part of the record and transcripts specified in subrule (A), a motion must be addressed to the chief judge of the circuit court in the county in which the grand jury issuing the indictment was convened.

(2) The motion must be filed within 14 days after arraignment on the indictment or at a reasonable time thereafter as the court may permit on a showing of good cause and a finding that the interests of justice will be served.

(3) On receipt of the motion, the chief judge shall order the entire record and transcript of testimony taken before the grand jury to be delivered to the chief judge by the person having custody of it for an in-camera inspection by the chief judge.

(4) Following the in-camera inspection, the chief judge shall certify the parts of the record, including the testimony of all grand jury witnesses that touches on the guilt or innocence of the accused, as being all of the evidence bearing on that issue contained in the record, and have two copies of it prepared, one to be delivered to the attorney for the accused, or to the accused if not represented by an attorney, and one to the attorney charged with the responsibility for prosecuting the indictment.

(5) The chief judge shall then have the record and transcript of all testimony of grand jury witnesses returned to the person from whom it was received for disposition according to law.

[Adopted effective October 1, 1989. Amended July 13, 2005, effective January 1, 2006, 473 Mich.]

Comments

Staff Comment to 1989 Adoption

MCR 6.107(A) and (B), governing the right to obtain and procedure for obtaining grand jury records, are unchanged from the former rule. Former MCR 6.107(C), which covered the right to counsel at grand jury proceedings, is relocated to MCR 6.005(J).

Staff Comment to 2005 Amendment

On March 12, 2002, the Court appointed the Committee on the Rules of Criminal Procedure to review the rules to determine whether any of the provisions should be revised. The committee issued its report on June 16, 2003, recommending numerous amendments to existing rules, plus some new rules. A public hearing on the committee's recommendations was held May 27, 2004.

The Court adopted the committee's recommendations with respect to the amendments of Rules 2.511, 6.102, 6.104, 6.107, 6.112, 6.303, 6.304, 6.310, 6.311, 6.402, 6.412, 6.414, 6.419, 6.420, 6.427, 6.615, and 6.620, and the adoption of a new Rule 6.428.

Rule 6.108   The Probable Cause Conference

(A) Right to a Probable Cause Conference. The state and the defendant are entitled to a probable cause conference, unless waived by both parties. If the probable cause conference is waived, the parties shall provide written notice to the court and indicate whether the parties will be conducting a preliminary examination, waiving the examination, or entering a plea.

(B) A district court magistrate may conduct probable cause conferences when authorized to do so by the chief district judge and may conduct all matters allowed at the probable cause conference, except taking pleas and imposing sentences unless permitted by statute to take pleas or impose sentences.

(C) The probable cause conference shall include discussions regarding a possible plea agreement and other pretrial matters, including bail and bond modification.

(D) The district court judge must be available during the probable cause conference to take pleas, consider requests for modification of bond, and if requested by the prosecutor, take the testimony of a victim.

(E) The probable cause conference for codefendants who are arraigned at least 72 hours before the probable cause conference shall be consolidated and only one joint probable cause conference shall be held unless the prosecuting attorney consents to the severance, a defendant seeks severance by motion and it is granted, or one of the defendants is unavailable and does not appear at the hearing.

[Adopted December 22, 2014, effective January 1, 2015, 497 Mich. Amended effective May 27, 2015, 498 Mich.]

Comments

Staff Comment to January, 2015 Adoption

The amendments of MCR 6.006, 6.104, 6.110, and 6.111 and adoption of new Rule 6.108 create procedural rules for conducting probable cause conferences and amend current provisions of the preliminary examination court rules to coordinate with 2014 PA 123 and 124.

Staff Comment to May, 2015 Amendment

The Court retained the amendments that became effective January 1, 2015, and adopted additional amendments of MCR 6.108 and MCR 6.110 to provide further clarification as suggested in comment letters received by the Court.

Rule 6.110.   The Preliminary Examination

(A) Right to Preliminary Examination. Where a preliminary examination is permitted by law, the people and the defendant are entitled to a prompt preliminary examination. The defendant may waive the preliminary examination with the consent of the prosecuting attorney. Upon waiver of the preliminary examination, the court must bind the defendant over for trial on the charge set forth in the complaint or any amended complaint. The preliminary examination for codefendants shall be consolidated and only one joint preliminary examination shall be held unless the prosecuting attorney consents to the severance, a defendant seeks severance by motion and it is granted, or one of the defendants is unavailable and does not appear at the hearing.

(B) Time of Examination; Remedy.

(1) Unless adjourned by the court, the preliminary examination must be held on the date specified by the court at the arraignment on the warrant or complaint. If the parties consent, the court may adjourn the preliminary examination for a reasonable time. If a party objects, the court may not adjourn a preliminary examination unless it makes a finding on the record of good cause shown for the adjournment. A violation of this subrule is deemed to be harmless error unless the defendant demonstrates actual prejudice.

(2) Upon the request of the prosecuting attorney, the preliminary examination shall commence immediately at the date and time set for the probable cause conference for the sole purpose of taking and preserving the testimony of the victim, if the victim is present, as long as the defendant is either present in the courtroom or has waived the right to be present. If victim testimony is taken as provided under this rule, the preliminary examination will be continued at the date originally set for that event.

(C) Conduct of Examination. A verbatim record must be made of the preliminary examination. Each party may subpoena witnesses, offer proofs, and examine and cross-examine witnesses at the preliminary examination. The court must conduct the examination in accordance with the Michigan Rules of Evidence.

(D) Exclusionary Rules.

(1) The court shall allow the prosecutor and defendant to subpoena and call witnesses from whom hearsay testimony was introduced on a satisfactory showing that live testimony will be relevant.

(2) If, during the preliminary examination, the court determines that evidence being offered is excludable, it must, on motion or objection, exclude the evidence. If, however, there has been a preliminary showing that the evidence is admissible, the court need not hold a separate evidentiary hearing on the question of whether the evidence should be excluded. The decision to admit or exclude evidence, with or without an evidentiary hearing, does not preclude a party from moving for and obtaining a determination of the question in the trial court on the basis of

(a) a prior evidentiary hearing, or

(b) a prior evidentiary hearing supplemented with a hearing before the trial court, or

(c) if there was no prior evidentiary hearing, a new evidentiary hearing.

(E) Probable Cause Finding. If, after considering the evidence, the court determines that probable cause exists to believe both that an offense not cognizable by the district court has been committed and that the defendant committed it, the court must bind the defendant over for trial. If the court finds probable cause to believe that the defendant has committed an offense cognizable by the district court, it must proceed thereafter as if the defendant initially had been charged with that offense.

(F) Discharge of Defendant. No Finding of Probable Cause. If, after considering the evidence, the court determines that probable cause does not exist to believe either that an offense has been committed or that the defendant committed it, the court must discharge the defendant without prejudice to the prosecutor initiating a subsequent prosecution for the same offense or reduce the charge to an offense that is not a felony. Except as provided in MCR 8.111(C), the subsequent preliminary examination must be held before the same judicial officer and the prosecutor must present additional evidence to support the charge.

(G) Return of Examination. Immediately on concluding the examination, the court must certify and transmit to the court before which the defendant is bound to appear the prosecutor's authorization for a warrant application, the complaint, a copy of the register of actions, the examination return, and any recognizances received.

(H) Motion to Dismiss. If, on proper motion, the trial court finds a violation of subrule (C), (D), (E), or (F), it must either dismiss the information or remand the case to the district court for further proceedings.

(I) Scheduling the Arraignment. Unless the trial court does the scheduling of the arraignment on the information, the district court must do so in accordance with the administrative orders of the trial court.

[Adopted effective October 1, 1989. Amended July 13, 2005, effective January 1, 2006, 473 Mich; December 22, 2014, effective January 1, 2015, 497 Mich. Amended effective May 27, 2015, 498 Mich; May 27, 2015, 498 Mich; March 21, 2018, 501 Mich.]

Comments

Staff Comment to 1989 Adoption

MCR 6.110 is a new rule except for subrule (A).

The first sentence of subrule (A) revises the language of former MCR 6.108, by more closely following the language of the statutory description of the right of the state and the defendant to "a prompt examination" found in MCL 766.1. The remainder of this subrule is new. The defendant's right to a preliminary examination following the filing of a complaint, and the waiver procedure found in the second sentence of subrule (A), are set forth in MCL 767.42. The defendant's right to a preliminary examination following indictment by a grand jury was recognized in *People v Duncan*, 388 Mich 489 (1972).

Subrule (B)(1) implements the statutory 12–day rule set forth in MCL 766.4 and the statutory adjournment procedure set forth in MCL 766.7 as interpreted in *People v Crawford*, 429 Mich 151 (1987).

Subrule (B)(2) incorporates with minor revisions the procedural remedy adopted in *Crawford*, 429 Mich 161–162, for violations of the 12–day rule or of the statutory adjournment procedure. This rule varies from *Crawford* by changing from 20 to 21 days the time after the filing of the information in which a motion to dismiss may be filed, and by expressly prohibiting the defendant from seeking postconviction relief on the basis of a violation of subrule (B)(1).

Subrule (C) implements existing law. MCL 766.11, MCL 766.12. See MCL 600.2167 expressly authorizing admission at a preliminary examination of a report made by a state technician.

Subrule (D) reflects existing law and practice.

Subrules (E) and (F) implement MCL 766.13. Although the language the rules use in describing the bind-over and discharge standards is different than that used in the statute, no substantive difference is intended. The other provisions in these subrules are also consistent with existing law.

Subrule (G) is consistent with the procedure set forth in MCL 766.15.

Subrule (H) is consistent with current practice. This subrule does not address, and leaves to case law, what effect a violation of these rules or an error in ruling on a motion filed in the trial court may have when raised following conviction.

Subrule (I) reflects current practice.

Staff Comment to 2005 Amendment

On March 12, 2002, the Court appointed the Committee on the Rules of Criminal Procedure to review the rules to determine whether any of the provisions should be revised. The committee issued its report on June 16, 2003, recommending numerous amendments to existing rules, plus some new rules. A public hearing on the committee's recommendations was held May 27, 2004.

The Court adopted the committee's recommendations with respect to the amendments of Rules 2.511, 6.102, 6.104, 6.107, 6.112, 6.303, 6.304, 6.310, 6.311, 6.402, 6.412, 6.414, 6.419, 6.420, 6.427, 6.615, and 6.620, and the adoption of a new Rule 6.428.

The Court also adopted, with modifications, recommendations made by the committee and staff to amend other rules. Rule 2.510 was amended to conform to the newly enacted 2004 PA 12 (MCL 600.1332). The Court modified the committee's recommendation concerning Rule 6.001 to include a reference to 6.102 and to limit the application of 6.445 to subrules (A) through (G). The Court adopted the committee's recommendation with regard to Rule 6.004, except that the requirement that "whenever the defendant's constitutional right to a speedy trial is violated, the defendant is entitled to dismissal of the charge with prejudice" was retained and inserted into 6.004(A).

The Court modified the committee's recommendation with regard to Rule 6.110 to eliminate the conflict with MCL 766.7. The Court did not adopt the committee's recommendations to amend 6.110(C) and (D).

Staff Comment to January, 2015 Amendment

The amendments of MCR 6.006, 6.104, 6.110, and 6.111 and adoption of new Rule 6.108 create procedural rules for conducting probable cause conferences and amend current provisions of the preliminary examination court rules to coordinate with 2014 PA 123 and 124.

Staff Comment to May, 2015 Amendment

The Court retained the amendments that became effective January 1, 2015, and adopted additional amendments of MCR 6.108 and MCR 6.110 to provide further clarification as suggested in comment letters received by the Court.

Staff Comment to 2018 Amendment

These amendments update cross-references and make other nonsubstantive revisions to clarify the rules. The amendment of MCR 6.110(B)(1) addresses an inadvertent omission from the last amendment of this rule that was intended to be shown in overstrike. Accordingly, the current rule does not match the published version. Striking the clause "for good cause shown" will provide consistency with other published versions of the rule and with the statute, MCL 766.7, which allows a magistrate to adjourn a preliminary examination with the consent of the parties without the need for good cause to be shown.

Rule 6.111   Circuit Court Arraignment in District Court

(A) The circuit court arraignment may be conducted by a district judge in criminal cases cognizable in the circuit court immediately after the bindover of the defendant. A district court judge shall take a felony plea as provided by court rule if a plea agreement is reached between the parties. Following a plea, the case shall be transferred to the circuit court where the circuit judge shall preside over further proceedings, including sentencing. The circuit court judge's name shall be available to the litigants before the plea is taken.

(B) Arraignments conducted pursuant to this rule shall be conducted in conformity with MCR 6.113.

(C) Pleas taken pursuant to this rule shall be taken in conformity with MCR 6.301, 6.302, 6.303, and 6.304, as applicable, and, once taken, shall be governed by MCR 6.310.

[Adopted July 13, 2005, effective January 1, 2006, 473 Mich. Amended December 22, 2014, effective January 1, 2015, 497 Mich. Amended effective May 27, 2015, 498 Mich.]

Comments

Staff Comment to 2005 Adoption

On March 12, 2002, the Court appointed the Committee on the Rules of Criminal Procedure to review the rules to determine whether any of the provisions should be revised. The committee issued its report on June 16, 2003, recommending numerous amendments to existing rules, plus some new rules. A public hearing on the committee's recommendations was held May 27, 2004.

The Court adopted the committee's recommendations with respect to the amendments of Rules 2.511, 6.102, 6.104, 6.107, 6.112, 6.303, 6.304, 6.310, 6.311, 6.402, 6.412, 6.414, 6.419, 6.420, 6.427, 6.615, and 6.620, and the adoption of a new Rule 6.428.

The Court also adopted, with modifications, recommendations made by the committee and staff to amend other rules. Rule 2.510 was amended to conform to the newly enacted 2004 PA 12 (MCL 600.1332). The Court modified the committee's recommendation concerning Rule 6.001 to include a reference to 6.102 and to limit the application of 6.445 to subrules (A) through (G). The Court adopted the committee's recommendation with regard to Rule 6.004, except that the requirement that "whenever the defendant's constitutional right to a speedy trial is violated, the defendant is entitled to dismissal of the charge with prejudice" was retained and inserted into 6.004(A).

The committee recommended that the Court adopt a new Rule 6.111, permitting a plea of guilty or nolo contendere to be taken by a district judge in criminal cases cognizable in the circuit court after bindover immediately following the conclusion or waiver of a preliminary examination, with the consent of the defendant, defense attorney, and prosecutor. The Court accepted and expanded upon the committee's recommendation by adopting a new Rule 6.111, Circuit Court Arraignment in District Court. In addition to allowing the district judge to conduct an arraignment and accept a plea of guilty or nolo contendere in such cases, the new rule also permits pleas of not guilty, guilty but mentally ill, or not guilty by reason of insanity. The rule also requires that such arraignment be conducted in conformity with Rule 6.113.

Staff Comment to January, 2015 Amendment

The amendments of MCR 6.006, 6.104, 6.110, and 6.111 and adoption of new Rule 6.108 create procedural rules for conducting probable cause conferences and amend current provisions of the preliminary examination court rules to coordinate with 2014 PA 123 and 124.

Staff Comment to May, 2015 Amendment

The Court retained the amendments that became effective January 1, 2015, and adopted additional amendments of MCR 6.108 and MCR 6.110 to provide further clarification as suggested in comment letters received by the court.

Rule 6.112   The Information or Indictment

(A) Informations and Indictments; Similar Treatment. Except as otherwise provided in these rules or elsewhere, the law and rules that apply to informations and prosecutions on informations apply to indictments and prosecutions on indictments.

(B) Use of Information or Indictment. A prosecution must be based on an information or an indictment. Unless the defendant is a fugitive from justice, the prosecutor may not file an information until the defendant has had or waives a preliminary examination. An indictment is returned and filed without a preliminary examination. When this occurs, the indictment shall commence judicial proceedings.

(C) Time of Filing Information or Indictment. The prosecutor must file the information or indictment on or before the date set for the arraignment.

(D) Information; Nature and Contents; Attachments. The information must set forth the substance of the accusation against the defendant and the name, statutory citation, and penalty of the offense allegedly committed. If applicable, the information must also set forth the notice required by MCL 767.45, and the defendant's Michigan driver's license number. To the extent possible, the information should specify the time and place of the alleged offense. Allegations relating to conduct, the method of committing the offense, mental state, and the consequences of conduct may be stated in the alternative. A list of all witnesses known to the prosecutor who may be called at trial and all res gestae witnesses known to the prosecutor or investigating law enforcement officers must be attached to the information. A prosecutor must sign the information.

(E) Bill of Particulars. The court, on motion, may order the prosecutor to provide the defendant a bill of particulars describing the essential facts of the alleged offense.

(F) Notice of Intent to Seek Enhanced Sentence. A notice of intent to seek an enhanced sentence pursuant to MCL 769.13 must list the prior convictions that may be relied upon for purposes of sentence enhancement. The notice must be filed within 21 days after the defendant's arraignment on the information charging the underlying offense or, if arraignment is waived or eliminated as allowed under MCR 6.113(E), within 21 days after the filing of the information charging the underlying offense.

(G) Harmless Error. Absent a timely objection and a showing of prejudice, a court may not dismiss an information or reverse a conviction because of an untimely filing or because of an incorrectly cited statute or a variance between the information and proof regarding time, place, the manner in which the offense was committed, or other factual detail relating to the alleged offense.

(H) Amendment of Information or Notice of Intent to Seek Enhanced Sentence. The court before, during, or after trial may permit the prosecutor to amend the information or the notice of intent to seek enhanced sentence unless the proposed amendment would unfairly surprise or prejudice the defendant. On motion, the court must strike unnecessary allegations from the information.

[Adopted effective October 1, 1989. Amended effective October 3, 2000, 463 Mich. Amended July 13, 2005, effective January 1, 2006, 473 Mich. Amended effective April 23, 2014, 495 Mich; October 1, 2014, 497 Mich. Amended September 21, 2016, effective January 1, 2017, 500 Mich.]

Comments

Staff Comment to 1989 Adoption

MCR 6.112 is new.

Subrules (A) and (B) implement existing law. See MCL 767.1, MCL 767.2 and MCL 767.42.

Subrule (C) sets forth a new requirement. It mandates that the information be filed on or before the date set for the arraignment. This represents a change from the past practice under which it was permissible for an information to be filed after the date set for the arraignment.

The second sentence of subrule (C) merely restates the rule announced in *People v Shelton,* 412 Mich 565 (1982).

Subrule (D) implements existing law. See MCL 767.45, MCL 767.44, MCL 767.51, MCL 767.40, and MCL 767.40a(1).

Subrule (E) reflects current law and practice. See MCL 767.44 and MCL 767.51.

Subrule (F) sets forth a harmless error rule consistent with current law. See MCL 767.45, MCL 767.51, and MCL 767.76.

Subrule (G) implements existing law. MCL 767.76. What type of amendment may or may not "unfairly surprise or prejudice the defendant" is left to case law.

Staff Comment to 2000 Amendment

The October 3, 2000, amendment of MCR 6.112 made the court rule consistent with MCL 769.13.

Staff Comment to 2005 Amendment

On March 12, 2002, the Court appointed the Committee on the Rules of Criminal Procedure to review the rules to determine whether any of the provisions should be revised. The committee issued its report on June 16, 2003, recommending numerous amendments to existing rules, plus some new rules. A public hearing on the committee's recommendations was held May 27, 2004.

The Court adopted the committee's recommendations with respect to the amendments of Rules 2.511, 6.102, 6.104, 6.107, 6.112, 6.303, 6.304, 6.310, 6.311,

6.402, 6.412, 6.414, 6.419, 6.420, 6.427, 6.615, and 6.620, and the adoption of a new Rule 6.428.

Staff Comment to 2014 Amendment

These amendments clarify how a prosecutor's notice of enhanced sentence required under MCL 769.13(1) is to be provided in courts in which arraignment has been eliminated under MCR 6.113(E).

Staff Comment to 2017 Amendment

The amendments of MCR 6.112 clarify the procedure for amending a notice of intent to seek an enhanced sentence by requiring such amendment to be approved by the court, and eliminate the provision that makes the harmless-error standard inapplicable when a notice of intent to seek an enhanced sentence is not filed timely.

Rule 6.113 The Arraignment on the Indictment or Information

(A) Time of Conducting. Unless the defendant waives arraignment or the court for good cause orders a delay, or as otherwise permitted by these rules, the court with trial jurisdiction must arraign the defendant on the scheduled date. The court may hold the arraignment before the preliminary examination transcript has been prepared and filed. Unless the defendant demonstrates actual prejudice, failure to hold the arraignment on the scheduled date is to be deemed harmless error.

(B) Arraignment Procedure. The prosecutor must give a copy of the information to the defendant before the defendant is asked to plead. Unless waived by the defendant, the court must either state to the defendant the substance of the charge contained in the information or require the information to be read to the defendant. If the defendant has waived legal representation, the court must advise the defendant of the pleading options. If the defendant offers a plea other than not guilty, the court must proceed in accordance with the rules in subchapter 6.300. Otherwise, the court must enter a plea of not guilty on the record. A verbatim record must be made of the arraignment.

(C) Waiver. A defendant represented by a lawyer may, as a matter of right, enter a plea of not guilty or stand mute without arraignment by filing, at or before the time set for the arraignment, a written statement signed by the defendant and the defendant's lawyer acknowledging that the defendant has received a copy of the information, has read or had it read or explained, understands the substance of the charge, waives arraignment in open court, and pleads not guilty to the charge or stands mute.

(D) Preliminary Examination Transcript. The court reporter shall transcribe and file the record of the preliminary examination if such is demanded or ordered pursuant to MCL 766.15.

(E) Elimination of Arraignments. A circuit court may submit to the State Court Administrator pursuant to MCR 8.112(B) a local administrative order that eliminates arraignment for a defendant represented by an attorney, provided other arrangements are made to give the defendant a copy of the information and any notice of intent to seek an enhanced sentence, as provided in MCR 6.112(F).

[Adopted effective October 1, 1989. Amended July 13, 2005, effective January 1, 2006, 473 Mich. Amended effective April 23, 2014, 495 Mich; October 1, 2014, 497 Mich.]

Comments

Staff Comment to 1989 Adoption

MCR 6.113 is new, except for subrules (B) and (C).

Subrule (A) corresponds to current practice. The procedure for scheduling of the arraignment date is set forth in MCR 6.110(I).

Subrule (B) incorporates a revised version of former MCR 6.101(D)(1). The former rule required the indictment or information to "be read to the defendant unless expressly waived by the defendant or his or her attorney." Subrule (B) gives the court the option of stating to the defendant "the substance of the charge contained in the information" in lieu of having it read to the defendant. This subrule also sets forth the subsequent procedure that must be followed at the arraignment of eliciting the defendant's plea. If the defendant is proceeding in propria persona, the court must advise the defendant of the pleading options. Those options are set forth in MCR 6.301.

Subrule (C) repeats former rule 6.101(D)(2) with stylistic changes.

Subrule (D) sets forth a procedure that differs from the statutory procedure set forth in MCL 766.15(2), (3). The statute permits a party to file a written request for the preparation and filing of a preliminary examination transcript "if filed within 2 weeks following the arraignment on the information or indictment." Subrule (D) provides that if at the time of the arraignment the transcript has not been requested and the parties are unable to agree either that it will not be needed or to postpone their decision to a later date (for example, because of plea negotiations), the court must order the transcript prepared. The objective of this requirement is to accelerate necessary transcript preparation and not to have unnecessary transcripts prepared. Accordingly, proper implementation of this rule to avoid waste requires the parties and the court at the arraignment to resolve whether the transcript is needed or whether that decision should be postponed to a later date when that need can be determined. The subrule further provides that the court may specify in its order how the reporter's fees will be paid. If the order is the result of a request or demand by a nonindigent defendant, the order should provide for the reporter's fees to be paid by the defendant. If the order is based on the demand or request of the prosecutor, or on the court's own initiative, the appropriate funding unit may be specified.

Staff Comment to 2005 Amendment

On March 12, 2002, the Court appointed the Committee on the Rules of Criminal Procedure to review the rules to determine whether any of the provisions should be revised. The committee issued its report on June 16, 2003, recommending numerous amendments to existing rules, plus some new rules. A public hearing on the committee's recommendations was held May 27, 2004.

The Court adopted the committee's recommendations with respect to the amendments of Rules 2.511, 6.102, 6.104, 6.107, 6.112, 6.303, 6.304, 6.310, 6.311, 6.402, 6.412, 6.414, 6.419, 6.420, 6.427, 6.615, and 6.620, and the adoption of a new Rule 6.428.

The committee recommended that the Court adopt a new Rule 6.111, permitting a plea of guilty or nolo contendere to be taken by a district judge in criminal cases cognizable in the circuit court after bindover immediately following the conclusion or waiver of a preliminary examination, with the consent of the defendant, defense attorney, and prosecutor. The Court accepted and expanded upon the committee's recommendation by adopting a new Rule 6.111, Circuit Court Arraignment in District Court. In addition to allowing the district judge to conduct an arraignment and accept a plea of guilty or nolo contendere in such cases, the new rule also permits pleas of not guilty, guilty but mentally ill, or not guilty by reason of insanity. The rule also requires that such arraignment be conducted in conformity with Rule 6.113.

The Court did not adopt the committee's recommendations to strike the current 6.113(D), but instead amended the rule to incorporate the language of MCL 766.15. The committee's recommendation for a new 6.113(D) was instead adopted as a new 6.113(E).

Staff Comment to 2014 Amendment

These amendments clarify how a prosecutor's notice of enhanced sentence required under MCL 769.13(1) is to be provided in courts in which arraignment has been eliminated under MCR 6.113(E).

Rule 6.120   Joinder and Severance; Single Defendant

(A) Charging Joinder. The prosecuting attorney may file an information or indictment that charges a single defendant with any two or more offenses. Each offense must be stated in a separate count. Two or more informations or indictments against a single defendant may be consolidated for a single trial.

(B) Postcharging Permissive Joinder or Severance. On its own initiative, the motion of a party, or the stipulation of all parties, except as provided in subrule (C), the court may join offenses charged in two or more informations or indictments against a single defendant, or sever offenses charged in a single information or indictment against a single defendant, when appropriate to promote fairness to the parties and a fair determination of the defendant's guilt or innocence of each offense.

(1) Joinder is appropriate if the offenses are related. For purposes of this rule, offenses are related if they are based on

    (a) the same conduct or transaction, or

    (b) a series of connected acts, or

    (c) a series of acts constituting parts of a single scheme or plan.

(2) Other relevant factors include the timeliness of the motion, the drain on the parties' resources, the potential for confusion or prejudice stemming from either the number of charges or the complexity or nature of the evidence, the potential for harassment, the convenience of witnesses, and the parties' readiness for trial.

(3) If the court acts on its own initiative, it must provide the parties an opportunity to be heard.

(C) Right of Severance; Unrelated Offenses. On the defendant's motion, the court must sever for separate trials offenses that are not related as defined in subrule (B)(1).

[Adopted effective October 1, 1989. Amended July 13, 2005, effective January 1, 2006, 473 Mich.]

Comments

Staff Comment to 1989 Adoption

MCR 6.120 is a new rule. It sets forth the procedure for joining or severing charges against a single defendant.

Subrule (A) is patterned after 2 ABA Standards for Criminal Justice (2d ed), Standard 13–2.1, and permits joinder in the charging instrument of charges, related or unrelated, against a single defendant. This provision is consistent with Michigan law. See *People v Tobey*, 401 Mich 141 (1977), and *People v Thompson*, 410 Mich 66 (1980). This subrule does not address the issue of joinder of charges that may be required because of double jeopardy considerations. See, for example, *People v White*, 390 Mich 245 (1973).

Subrule (B) pertains to the defendant's unqualified right to severance of unrelated offenses. This provision varies from ABA Standard 13–3.1 which entitles both the defendant *and the prosecutor* to severance of unrelated offenses.

The standard in subrule (B), defining when two offenses "are related," is derived from ABA Standard 13–1.2, and a predecessor standard, ABA Project on Minimum Standards for Criminal Justice, Standards Relating to Joinder and Severance (Approved Draft, 1968), Standard 1.1. Elaboration on this standard may be found in *People v Tobey*, 401 Mich 141 (1977).

Subrule (C) relates to the procedure for joining or severing charges other than those that have been severed pursuant to the defendant's right to severance under subrule (B). On the motion of either party, the court may allow the joinder or severance of charges on determining that the joinder or severance "is appropriate to promote fairness to the parties *and* a fair determination of the defendant's guilt or innocence of each offense." This standard combines "fairness to the parties" with ABA Standard 13–3.1(b)(i). Some of the factors relevant to the two prongs of this standard are listed in this rule. The rule further permits the court to "sever" offenses on its own initiative, but subject to the considerations of this rule if there is an objection. This subrule does not address constitutional considerations (e.g., double jeopardy), which independently may require or preclude joinder or severance depending on the circumstances.

Staff Comment to 2005 Amendment

The amendments, effective January 1, 2006, of the rule reflect the recommendations of the Committee on the Rules of Criminal Procedure as requested by the Court in *People v Nutt*, 469 Mich 565 (2004).

Rule 6.121 Joinder and Severance; Multiple Defendants

(A) Permissive Joinder. An information or indictment may charge two or more defendants with the same offense. It may charge two or more defendants with two or more offenses when

(1) each defendant is charged with accountability for each offense, or

(2) the offenses are related as defined in MCR 6.120(B).

When more than one offense is alleged, each offense must be stated in a separate count. Two or more informations or indictments against different defendants may be consolidated for a single trial whenever the defendants could be charged in the same information or indictment under this rule.

(B) Right of Severance; Unrelated Offenses. On a defendant's motion, the court must sever offenses that are not related as defined in MCR 6.120(B).

(C) Right of Severance; Related Offenses. On a defendant's motion, the court must sever the trial of defendants on related offenses on a showing that severance is necessary to avoid prejudice to substantial rights of the defendant.

(D) Discretionary Severance. On the motion of any party, the court may sever the trial of defendants on the ground that severance is appropriate to promote fairness to the parties and a fair determination of the guilt or innocence of one or more of the defendants. Relevant factors include the timeliness of the motion, the drain on the parties' resources, the potential for confusion or prejudice stemming from either the number of defendants or the complexity or nature of the evidence, the convenience of witnesses, and the parties' readiness for trial.

[Adopted effective October 1, 1989.]

Comments

Staff Comment to 1989 Adoption

MCR 6.121 is a new rule. It sets forth procedure for joining or severing the cases of multiple defendants.

Subrule (A) relates to the permissive joinder of the charges against two or more defendants either as a result of being placed in the same charging instrument or as a result of consolidation of the defendants' cases for trial. A joinder of cases for trial may be based on a prosecution or defense motion. The standard for permitting joinder is patterned after 2 ABA Standards for Criminal Justice (2d ed), Standard 13–2.2(a).

Subrule (B) incorporates by reference a defendant's right to severance of unrelated offenses as provided in MCR 6.120(B). The effect of such a severance in multiple defendant cases will depend on the circumstances.

Subrule (C) sets forth a defendant's entitlement to a separate trial, if not obtainable pursuant to subrule (B), on a showing that it "is necessary to avoid prejudice to substantial rights of the defendant." This standard is taken from *People v Schram*, 378 Mich 145, 156 (1966), and *People v Carroll*, 396 Mich 408, 414 (1976). It is said to reflect a strong policy in favor of joint trials set forth in MCL 768.5; and found in case law. The right of a defendant to a fair trial and other substantial rights, however, may necessitate severance. See, for example, *People v Hurst*, 396 Mich 1, 4 (1976), stating that a defendant is entitled to a separate trial if it appears that a codefendant "may testify to exculpate himself and incriminate the defendant seeking a separate trial."

Subrule (D) is similar to MCR 6.120(C) but pertains only to severance. It provides that "any party" may invoke the court's discretion to grant separate trials on the ground that it will "promote fairness to the parties and a fair determination of the guilt or innocence of one or more of the defendants." Like MCR 6.120(C), this rule does not address constitutional considerations, such as double jeopardy, that may in some cases preclude severance.

Rule 6.125 Mental Competency Hearing

(A) Applicable Provisions. Except as provided in these rules, a mental competency hearing in a criminal case is governed by MCL 330.2020 *et seq.*

(B) Time and Form of Motion. The issue of the defendant's competence to stand trial or to participate in other criminal proceedings may be raised at any time during the proceedings against the defendant. The issue may be raised by the court before which such proceedings are pending or being held, or by motion of a party. Unless the issue of defendant's competence arises during the course of proceedings, a motion raising the issue of defendant's competence must be in writing. If the competency issue arises during the course of proceedings, the court may adjourn the proceeding or, if the proceeding is defendant's trial, the court may, consonant with double jeopardy considerations, declare a mistrial.

(C) Order for Examination.

(1) On a showing that the defendant may be incompetent to stand trial, the court must order the defendant to undergo an examination by a certified or licensed examiner of the center for forensic psychiatry or other facility officially certified by the department of mental health to perform examinations relating to the issue of competence to stand trial.

(2) The defendant must appear for the examination as required by the court.

(3) If the defendant is held in detention pending trial, the examination may be performed in the place of detention or the defendant may be transported by the sheriff to the diagnostic facility for examination.

(4) The court may order commitment to a diagnostic facility for examination if the defendant fails to appear for the examination as required or if commitment is necessary for the performance of the examination.

(5) The defendant must be released from the facility on completion of the examination and, if (3) is applicable, returned to the place of detention.

(D) Independent Examination. On a showing of good cause by either party, the court may order an independent examination of the defendant relating to the issue of competence to stand trial.

(E) Hearing. A competency hearing must be held within 5 days of receipt of the report required by MCL 330.2028 or on conclusion of the proceedings then before the court, whichever is sooner, unless the court, on a showing of good cause, grants an adjournment.

(F) Motions; Testimony.

(1) A motion made while a defendant is incompetent to stand trial must be heard and decided if the presence of the defendant is not essential for a fair hearing and decision on the motion.

(2) Testimony may be presented on a pretrial defense motion if the defendant's presence could not assist the defense.

[Adopted effective October 1, 1989.]

Comments

Staff Comment to 1989 Adoption

With three exceptions, MCR 6.125 is a stylistically revised version of former MCR 6.106.

Subrule (B) dealing with when and how the issue of defendant's competence may be raised is substantially expanded to allow the issue to be raised "at any time during the proceedings against the defendant," thus including proceedings in the district court, or subsequent to trial, such as sentencing. Furthermore, it may be raised by *any* court before which such proceedings "are pending or being held." The party's motion raising this issue must be in writing unless the issue manifests itself during the course of court proceedings, in which event the court, on its own initiative or on the motion of a party, may adjourn the proceedings and issue an order for examination under this rule. Of course, if the competency issue arises during the course of the defendant's trial, double jeopardy considerations must be accommodated.

In addition to the foregoing expansion in subrule (B), this rule incorporates a new provision in subrule (D) giving the trial court discretion, "on a showing of good cause by either party," to order an independent examination of the defendant's competency to stand trial. Because of a presumption that the Center for Forensic Psychiatry or other facility officially certified by the Department of Mental Health will properly perform their functions, "good cause" justifying an independent competency examination should arise only in exceptional cases.

The only other substantive change in this rule is in subrule (E), which changes the provision in the former rule requiring the competency hearing to be held within 7 days of receipt of the psychiatric report, to 5 days. This change has been made to make the court rule consistent with the statute, MCL 330.2030, which mandates the competency hearing to be held "within 5 days" of receipt of the psychiatric report or at the conclusion of the proceedings then before the court, "whichever is sooner."

SUBCHAPTER 6.200 DISCOVERY

Rule 6.201 Discovery

(A) Mandatory Disclosure. In addition to disclosures required by provisions of law other than MCL 767.94a, a party upon request must provide all other parties:

(1) the names and addresses of all lay and expert witnesses whom the party may call at trial; in the alternative, a party may provide the name of the witness and make the witness available to the other party for interview; the witness list may be amended without leave of the court no later than 28 days before trial;

(2) any written or recorded statement, including electronically recorded statements, pertaining to the case by a lay witness whom the party may call at trial, except that a defendant is not obliged to provide the defendant's own statement;

(3) the curriculum vitae of an expert the party may call at trial and either a report by the expert or a written description of the substance of the proposed testimony of the expert, the expert's opinion, and the underlying basis of that opinion;

(4) any criminal record that the party may use at trial to impeach a witness;

(5) a description or list of criminal convictions, known to the defense attorney or prosecuting attorney, of any witness whom the party may call at trial; and

(6) a description of and an opportunity to inspect any tangible physical evidence that the party may introduce at trial, including any document, photograph, or other paper, with copies to be provided on request. A party may request a hearing regarding any question of costs of reproduction, including the cost of providing copies of electronically recorded statements. On good cause shown, the court may order that a party be given the opportunity to test without destruction any tangible physical evidence.

(B) Discovery of Information Known to the Prosecuting Attorney. Upon request, the prosecuting attorney must provide each defendant:

(1) any exculpatory information or evidence known to the prosecuting attorney;

(2) any police report and interrogation records concerning the case, except so much of a report as concerns a continuing investigation;

(3) any written or recorded statements, including electronically recorded statements, by a defendant, codefendant, or accomplice pertaining to the case, even if that person is not a prospective witness at trial;

(4) any affidavit, warrant, and return pertaining to a search or seizure in connection with the case; and

(5) any plea agreement, grant of immunity, or other agreement for testimony in connection with the case.

(C) Prohibited Discovery.

(1) Notwithstanding any other provision of this rule, there is no right to discover information or evidence that is protected from disclosure by constitution, statute, or privilege, including information or evidence protected by a defendant's right against self-incrimination, except as provided in subrule (2).

(2) If a defendant demonstrates a good-faith belief, grounded in articulable fact, that there is a reasonable probability that records protected by privilege are likely to contain material information necessary to the defense, the trial court shall conduct an in camera inspection of the records.

(a) If the privilege is absolute, and the privilege holder refuses to waive the privilege to permit an in camera inspection, the trial court shall suppress or strike the privilege holder's testimony.

(b) If the court is satisfied, following an in camera inspection, that the records reveal evidence necessary to the defense, the court shall direct that such evidence as is necessary to the defense be made available to defense counsel. If the privilege is absolute and the privilege holder refuses to waive the privilege to permit disclosure, the trial court shall suppress or strike the privilege holder's testimony.

(c) Regardless of whether the court determines that the records should be made available to the defense, the court shall make findings sufficient to facilitate meaningful appellate review.

(d) The court shall seal and preserve the records for review in the event of an appeal

(i) by the defendant, on an interlocutory basis or following conviction, if the court determines that the records should not be made available to the defense, or

(ii) by the prosecution, on an interlocutory basis, if the court determines that the records should be made available to the defense.

(e) Records disclosed under this rule shall remain in the exclusive custody of counsel for the parties, shall be used only for the limited purpose approved by the court, and shall be subject to such other terms and conditions as the court may provide.

(D) Excision. When some parts of material or information are discoverable and other parts are not discoverable, the party must disclose the discoverable parts and may excise the remainder. The party must inform the other party that nondiscoverable information has been excised and withheld. On motion, the court must conduct a hearing in camera to determine whether the reasons for excision are justifiable. If the court upholds the excision, it must seal and preserve the record of the hearing for review in the event of an appeal.

(E) Protective Orders. On motion and a showing of good cause, the court may enter an appropriate protective order. In considering whether good cause exists, the court shall consider the parties' interests in a fair trial; the risk to any person of harm, undue annoyance, intimidation, embarrassment, or threats; the risk that evidence will be fabricated; and the need for secrecy regarding the identity of informants or other law enforcement matters. On motion, with notice to the other party, the court may permit the showing of good cause for a protective order to be made in camera. If the court grants a protective order, it must seal and preserve the record of the hearing for review in the event of an appeal.

(F) Timing of Discovery. Unless otherwise ordered by the court, the prosecuting attorney must comply with the requirements of this rule within 21 days of a request under this rule and a defendant must comply with the requirements of this rule within 21 days of a request under this rule.

(G) Copies. Except as ordered by the court on good cause shown, a party's obligation to provide a photograph or paper of any kind is satisfied by providing a clear copy.

(H) Continuing Duty to Disclose. If at any time a party discovers additional information or material subject to disclosure under this rule, the party, without further request, must promptly notify the other party.

(I) Modification. On good cause shown, the court may order a modification of the requirements and prohibitions of this rule.

(J) Violation. If a party fails to comply with this rule, the court, in its discretion, may order the party to provide the discovery or permit the inspection of materials not previously disclosed, grant a continuance, prohibit the party from introducing in evidence the material not disclosed, or enter such other order as it deems just under the circumstances. Parties are encouraged to bring questions of noncompliance before the court at the earliest opportunity. Willful violation by counsel of an applicable discovery rule or an order issued pursuant thereto may subject counsel to appropriate sanctions by the court. An order of the court under this section is reviewable only for abuse of discretion.

(K) Except as otherwise provided in MCR 2.302(B)(6), electronic materials are to be treated in the same manner as nonelectronic materials under this rule. Nothing in this rule shall be construed to conflict with MCL 600.2163a.

[Adopted effective January 1, 1995. Amended November 16, 1994, effective January 1, 1995, 447 Mich; May 7, 1996, effective July 1, 1996, 451 Mich; September 29, 1997, effective January 1, 1998, 456 Mich; July 13, 2005, effective January 1, 2006, 473 Mich; September 21, 2010, effective January 1, 2011, 487 Mich.]

Comments

Staff Comment to 1995 Adoption

MCR 6.201 took effect January 1, 1995. It followed the Court's decision in *People v Lemcool*, 445 Mich 491; 518 NW2d 437 (1994) and the enactment of 1994 PA 113, MCL 767.94a. Pursuant to Administrative Order 1994–10, discovery in criminal cases is governed by this court rule, and not by MCL 767.94a.

Staff Comment to 1996 Amendment

Consistent with *People v Stanaway*, 446 Mich 643 (1994), the addition of subrule (C)(2) in 1996 provided for the in-camera inspection of confidential records protected by privilege, and subsequent appellate review.

Staff Comment to 1998 Amendment

The January 1, 1998 amendment of MCR 6.201 added subrule (H), at the recommendation of the Michigan Judges Association, and redesignated former subrules (H) and (I) to be (I) and (J), respectively. New subrule (H) imposes a continuing obligation of disclosure similar to the obligation that exists in civil cases.

Staff Comment to 2005 Amendment

On March 12, 2002, the Court appointed the Committee on the Rules of Criminal Procedure to review the rules to determine whether any of the provisions should be revised. The committee issued its report on June 16, 2003, recommending numerous amendments to existing rules, plus some new rules. A public hearing on the committee's recommendations was held May 27, 2004.

The Court adopted the committee's recommendations with respect to the amendments of Rules 2.511, 6.102, 6.104, 6.107, 6.112, 6.303, 6.304, 6.310, 6.311, 6.402, 6.412, 6.414, 6.419, 6.420, 6.427, 6.615, and 6.620, and the adoption of a new Rule 6.428.

The Court also adopted, with modifications, recommendations made by the committee and staff to amend other rules. Rule 2.510 was amended to conform to the newly enacted 2004 PA 12 (MCL 600.1332). The Court modified the committee's recommendation concerning Rule 6.001 to include a reference to 6.102 and to limit the application of 6.445 to subrules (A) through (G). The Court adopted the committee's recommendation with regard to Rule 6.004, except that the requirement that "whenever the defendant's constitutional right to a speedy trial is violated, the defendant is entitled to dismissal of the charge with prejudice" was retained and inserted into 6.004(A).

The Court adopted most of the committee and staff recommendations concerning Rule 6.201, except that the Court did not strike the language "except so much of a report as concerns a continuing investigation" in Rule 6.201(B)(2).

Staff Comment to 2010 Amendment

This amendment specifically incorporates electronically recorded statements into the materials that must be provided to other parties in a criminal proceeding, although the judge may specify the conditions for discovery as allowed under MCR 2.302(B)(6).

Rule 6.202 Disclosure of Forensic Laboratory Report and Certificate; Applicability; Admissibility of Report and Certificate; Extension of Time; Adjournment

(A) This rule shall apply to criminal trials in the district and circuit courts.

(B) Disclosure. Upon receipt of a forensic laboratory report and certificate, if applicable, by the examining expert, the prosecutor shall serve a copy of the laboratory report and certificate on the opposing party's attorney or party, if not represented by an attorney, within 14 days after receipt of the laboratory report and certificate. A proof of service of the report and certificate, if applicable, on the opposing party's attorney or party, if not represented by an attorney, shall be filed with the court.

(C) Notice and Demand.

(1) *Notice.* If a party intends to offer the report described in subsection (B) as evidence at trial, the party's attorney or party, if not represented by an attorney, shall provide the opposing party's attorney or party, if not represented by an attorney, with notice of that fact in writing. If the prosecuting attorney intends to offer the report as evidence at trial, notice to the defendant's attorney or the defendant, if not represented by an attorney, shall be included with the report. If the

defendant intends to offer the report as evidence at trial, notice to the prosecuting attorney shall be provided within 14 days after receipt of the report. Except as provided in subrule (C)(2), the report and certification, if applicable, is admissible in evidence to the same effect as if the person who performed the analysis or examination had personally testified.

(2) *Demand.* Upon receipt of a copy of the laboratory report and certificate, if applicable, the opposing party's attorney or party, if not represented by an attorney, may file a written objection to the use of the laboratory report and certificate. The written objection shall be filed with the court in which the matter is pending, and shall be served on the opposing party's attorney or party, if not represented by an attorney, within 14 days of receipt of the notice. If a written objection is filed, the report and certificate are not admissible under subrule (C)(1). If no objection is made to the use of the laboratory report and certificate within the time allowed by this section, the report and certificate are admissible in evidence as provided in subrule (C)(1).

(3) For good cause the court shall extend the time period of filing a written objection.

(4) *Adjournment.* Compliance with this court rule shall be good cause for an adjournment of the trial.

(D) Certification. Except as otherwise provided, the analyst who conducts the analysis on the forensic sample and signs the report shall complete a certificate on which the analyst shall state (i) that he or she is qualified by education, training, and experience to perform the analysis, (ii) the name and location of the laboratory where the analysis was performed, (iii) that performing the analysis is part of his or her regular duties, and (iv) that the tests were performed under industry-approved procedures or standards and the report accurately reflects the analyst's findings and opinions regarding the results of those tests or analysis. A report submitted by an analyst who is employed by a laboratory that is accredited by a national or international accreditation entity that substantially meets the certification requirements described above may provide proof of the laboratory's accreditation certificate in lieu of a separate certificate.

[Adopted September 19, 2012, effective January 1, 2013, 493 Mich.]

Comments

Staff Comment to 2013 Adoption

The revision of MCR 6.001 provides a cross reference to MCR 6.202, a new rule adopted in this order. MCR 6.202 incorporates a "notice and demand" procedure into the Michigan Court Rules with regard to forensic reports. Under the rule, a party could seek to admit a forensic report as evidence if notice requirements are met and no objection is filed. If a party objects to admission of the report, the analyst would be required to testify.

SUBCHAPTER 6.300   PLEAS

Rule 6.301   Available Pleas

(A) Possible Pleas. Subject to the rules in this subchapter, a defendant may plead not guilty, guilty, nolo contendere, guilty but mentally ill, or not guilty by reason of insanity. If the defendant refuses to plead or stands mute, or the court, pursuant to the rules, refuses to accept the defendant's plea, the court must enter a not guilty plea on the record. A plea of not guilty places in issue every material allegation in the information and permits the defendant to raise any defense not otherwise waived.

(B) Pleas That Require the Court's Consent. A defendant may enter a plea of nolo contendere only with the consent of the court.

(C) Pleas That Require the Consent of the Court and the Prosecutor. A defendant may enter the following pleas only with the consent of the court and the prosecutor:

(1) A defendant who has asserted an insanity defense may enter a plea of guilty but mentally ill or a plea of not guilty by reason of insanity. Before such a plea may be entered, the defendant must comply with the examination required by law.

(2) A defendant may enter a conditional plea of guilty, nolo contendere, guilty but mentally ill, or not guilty by reason of insanity. A conditional plea preserves for appeal a specified pretrial ruling or rulings notwithstanding the plea-based judgment and entitles the defendant to withdraw the plea if a specified pretrial ruling is overturned on appeal. The ruling or rulings as to which the defendant reserves the right to appeal must be specified orally on the record or in a writing made a part of the record. The appeal is by application for leave to appeal only.

(D) Pleas to Lesser Charges. The court may not accept a plea to an offense other than the one charged without the consent of the prosecutor.

[Adopted effective October 1, 1989. Amended effective December 30, 1994, 455 Mich.]

Comments

Staff Comment to 1989 Adoption

MCR 6.301 is a new rule, but incorporates elements of former 6.101.

Subrule (A) describes the various pleas available to a defendant under the rules in this subchapter. In addition to the pleas of not guilty, guilty, and nolo contendere described in the former rule, the rules in this subchapter add the pleas of guilty but mentally ill and not guilty by reason of insanity. A plea of guilty but mentally ill was created by statute. MCL 768.36(2). A plea of not guilty by reason of insanity is created by these rules. See subrule (C)(1) and 6.304. The second sentence of subrule (A) is a modified version of former 6.101(E)(1). It allows a court to refuse to accept a defendant's plea, but only "pursuant to the rules." The quoted phrase refers to pleas that can be refused (1) because they require the court's consent [pleas in nolo contendere and the pleas described in subrule (C)] or (2) because they fail to comply with a requirement of the rules in this subchapter. The last sentence of subrule (A) is a stylistically revised version of former 6.101(E)(2).

Subrule (B) is a modification of a provision in former 6.101(F). The former rule provided that the court's consent was required before a defendant would be permitted to plead guilty or nolo contendere. Subrule (B) has deleted the requirement for the court's consent to a plea of guilty. The consent provision in the former rule has been construed as giving the trial court the discretion to refuse to accept a guilty plea because of disagreement with the plea bargain agreed to by the prosecutor and the defendant. See *People v Ott*, 144 Mich App 76 (1985). Accordingly, deletion of the consent provision indicates that the trial court may not refuse to accept a guilty plea based solely on disagreement with the wisdom of the plea, of the charge, or of the plea bargain, unless the bargain is conditioned on the court's agreement to some provision, such as sentence disposition. See 6.302(C)(3). As is noted in subrule (A), however, the court may refuse to accept a plea based on noncompliance with a requirement in these rules.

As indicated, subrule (B) retains the discretion of the court, subject to the requirements of these rules, to accept or reject a plea of nolo contendere. Rule 6.302(D)(2)(a) requires the court to state on the record "why a plea of nolo contendere is appropriate."

Subrule (C) is new. It describes two categories of pleas requiring the consent of both the court and the prosecutor. Subrule (C)(1) describes the pleas of guilty but mentally ill and not guilty by reason of insanity. A plea of guilty but mentally ill was created by statute, MCL 768.36(2), and is now implemented in these rules. See subrule (A) above and 6.303. The statute conditions entry of such a plea on the consent of the prosecutor and the trial court, and on the defendant having asserted a defense of insanity and having complied with the examination requirements of the insanity defense statute. MCL 768.20a.

The plea of not guilty by reason of insanity is new and is recognized for the first time in these rules. See subrule (A) above and 6.304. Not guilty by reason of insanity has existed however, as a defense assertable at trial. In cases in which prosecutors chose not to contest this defense, the practice was followed by which the parties, with the court's consent, agreed to entry of a judgment of not guilty by reason of insanity following a pro forma bench trial. The rules take advantage of the benefits of this past practice while providing a structured plea procedure allowing elimination of an unnecessary pro forma trial.

Subrule (C)(2) incorporates and expands the conditional plea procedure authorized in *People v Reid*, 420 Mich 326 (1984), by which a defendant, with the agreement of the prosecutor and the court, may enter a plea of guilty while preserving, for appeal purposes, a challenge to a pretrial ruling that might otherwise be waived by the plea. This subrule expands the availability of the conditional plea procedure to the other forms of plea available under these rules. It also permits a conditional plea to be used to preserve challenges to one or more pretrial rulings and places no limitation on the type of ruling that may be preserved. Consistent with *Reid*, however, it requires that the defendant be permitted to withdraw the plea if any ruling preserved by this procedure is overturned on appeal. Furthermore, the subrule requires that any challenged ruling being preserved for appeal be "specified orally on the record or in a writing made a part of the record." The availability of this procedure, however, should not be construed as precluding a defendant from raising on appeal issues that are not waived by entry of a plea. The question of what issues are not waived by a plea is addressed by case law. See, for example, *People v New*, 427 Mich 482 (1986).

Subrule (D) is new and sets forth the settled principle stated in *Genesee Prosecutor v Genesee Circuit Judge*, 391 Mich 115 (1974).

Staff Comment to 1994 Amendment

The December 30, 1994 amendments of MCR 6.301, 6.302, 6.311, 6.425, 7.203, 7.204 and 7.205 modified procedure regarding appeals in criminal cases in light of the amendment of Const 1963, art 1, § 20 at the November 1994 general election and the legislation implementing the constitutional amendment. Changes will remain in effect until April 1, 1995 and will be reconsidered by the Court in light of comments received and any further legislation.

Rule 6.302. Pleas of Guilty and Nolo Contendere

(A) Plea Requirements. The court may not accept a plea of guilty or nolo contendere unless it is convinced that the plea is understanding, voluntary, and accurate. Before accepting a plea of guilty or nolo contendere, the court must place the defendant or defendants under oath and personally carry out subrules (B)–(E).

(B) An Understanding Plea. Speaking directly to the defendant or defendants, the court must advise the defendant or defendants of the following and determine that each defendant understands:

(1) the name of the offense to which the defendant is pleading; the court is not obliged to explain the elements of the offense, or possible defenses;

(2) the maximum possible prison sentence for the offense and any mandatory minimum sentence required by law, including a requirement for mandatory lifetime electronic monitoring under MCL 750.520b or 750.520c;

(3) if the plea is accepted, the defendant will not have a trial of any kind, and so gives up the rights the defendant would have at a trial, including the right:

(a) to be tried by a jury;

(b) to be presumed innocent until proved guilty;

(c) to have the prosecutor prove beyond a reasonable doubt that the defendant is guilty;

(d) to have the witnesses against the defendant appear at the trial;

(e) to question the witnesses against the defendant;

(f) to have the court order any witnesses the defendant has for the defense to appear at the trial;

(g) to remain silent during the trial;

(h) to not have that silence used against the defendant; and

(i) to testify at the trial if the defendant wants to testify.

(4) if the plea is accepted, the defendant will be giving up any claim that the plea was the result of promises or threats that were not disclosed to the court at the plea proceeding, or that it was not the defendant's own choice to enter the plea;

(5) if the plea is accepted, the defendant may be giving up the right to appeal issues that would otherwise be appealable if she or he were convicted at trial. Further, any appeal from the conviction and sentence pursuant to the plea will be by application for leave to appeal and not by right;

The requirements of subrules (B)(3) and (B)(5) may be satisfied by a writing on a form approved by the State Court Administrative Office. If a court uses a writing, the court shall address the defendant and obtain from the defendant orally on the record a statement that the rights were read and understood and a waiver of those rights. The waiver may be obtained without repeating the individual rights.

(C) A Voluntary Plea.

(1) The court must ask the prosecutor and the defendant's lawyer whether they have made a plea agreement. If they have made a plea agreement, which may include an agreement to a sentence to a specific term or within a specific range, the agreement must be stated on the record or reduced to writing and signed by the parties. The parties may memorialize their agreement on a form substantially approved by the SCAO. The written agreement shall be made part of the case file.

(2) If there is a plea agreement, the court must ask the prosecutor or the defendant's lawyer what the terms of the agreement are and confirm the terms of the agreement with the other lawyer and the defendant.

(3) If there is a plea agreement and its terms provide for the defendant's plea to be made in exchange for a sentence to a specified term or within a specified range or a prosecutorial sentence recommendation, the court may

(a) reject the agreement; or

(b) accept the agreement after having considered the presentence report, in which event it must sentence the defendant to a specified term or within a specified range as agreed to; or

(c) accept the agreement without having considered the presentence report; or

(d) take the plea agreement under advisement.

If the court accepts the agreement without having considered the presentence report or takes the plea agreement under advisement, it must explain to the defendant that the court is not bound to follow an agreement to a sentence for a specified term or within a specified range or a recommendation agreed to by the prosecutor, and that if the court chooses not to follow an agreement to a sentence for a specified term or within a specified range, the defendant will be allowed to withdraw from the plea agreement. A judge's decision not to follow the sentence recommendation does not entitle the defendant to withdraw the defendant's plea.

(4) The court must ask the defendant:

(a) (if there is no plea agreement) whether anyone has promised the defendant anything, or (if there is a plea agreement) whether anyone has promised anything beyond what is in the plea agreement;

(b) whether anyone has threatened the defendant; and

(c) whether it is the defendant's own choice to plead guilty.

(D) An Accurate Plea.

(1) If the defendant pleads guilty, the court, by questioning the defendant, must establish support for a finding that the defendant is guilty of the offense charged or the offense to which the defendant is pleading.

(2) If the defendant pleads nolo contendere, the court may not question the defendant about participation in the crime. The court must:

(a) state why a plea of nolo contendere is appropriate; and

(b) hold a hearing, unless there has been one, that establishes support for a finding that the defendant is guilty of the offense charged or the offense to which the defendant is pleading.

(E) Additional Inquiries. On completing the colloquy with the defendant, the court must ask the prosecutor and the defendant's lawyer whether either is aware of any promises, threats, or inducements other than those already disclosed on the record, and whether the court has complied with subrules (B)–(D). If it appears to the court that it has failed to comply with subrules (B)–(D), the court may not accept the defendant's plea until the deficiency is corrected.

(F) Plea Under Advisement; Plea Record. The court may take the plea under advisement. A verbatim record must be made of the plea proceeding.

[Adopted effective October 1, 1989. Amended effective December 30, 1994; March 1, 1995; June 30, 1995. Amended effective October 15, 1995, 450 Mich; August 15, 1996, 450 Mich; September 1, 1997, 452 Mich. Amended March 28, 2000, effective April 1, 2000, 461 Mich; April 23, 2002, effective September 1, 2002, 466 Mich. Amended effective July 13, 2005, 473 Mich. Amended December 14, 2005, effective January 1, 2006, 474 Mich. Amended effective June 20, 2012, 491 Mich. Amended September 18, 2013, effective January 1, 2014, 495 Mich; September 20, 2018, effective January 1, 2019, 502 Mich.]

Comments

Staff Comment to 1989 Adoption

With a few modifications, MCR 6.302 repeats former 6.101(F)(1)–(6).

The first sentence of subrule (A) repeats former 6.101(5) except that it limits the applicability of this rule to a plea of guilty or nolo contendere. Pertinent provisions of this rule, however, are incorporated by reference in the rules applicable to the plea of guilty but mentally ill, 6.303, and the plea of not guilty by reason of insanity, 6.304. The second sentence of subrule (A) repeats a provision in former 6.101(F).

Subrule (B) is a stylistically improved version of former 6.101(F)(1) and incorporates two substantive changes.

Subrule (B)(2) enlarges former 6.101(F)(1)(b) (requiring the court to advise the defendant of "the maximum possible prison sentence for the offense") by adding the requirement that the court also advise the defendant of "any mandatory minimum sentence required by law."

Subrule (B)(3)(b) changes the advice required by former 6.101(F)(1)(c)(ii) ("to trial by the court if the defendant does not want trial by a jury") to reflect that the consent of the prosecutor and the court is also required. This change corresponds to the legislative amendment conditioning the defendant's statutory right to a bench trial on obtaining the consent of the prosecutor and the court. 1988 PA 89, MCL 763.3. See 6.401.

Subrules (C)(1) and (2) repeat former 6.101(F)(2)(a) and (b).

Subrule (C)(3) is new. It incorporates and clarifies the sentence-bargaining procedures set forth in *People v Killebrew*, 416 Mich 189, 206–212 (1982). Subrule (3)(b) recognizes that frequently trial courts have access to a presentence report at the time of the plea proceeding and are in a position to make a final acceptance of the agreement. In such a case the court is bound to comply with the sentence agreement, be it for a specific disposition or recommended disposition. If the court does not have a presentence report or chooses not to consider it at that time, the court's options are to accept the agreement conditionally, (3)(c), or take the plea agreement under advisement, (3)(d). A conditionally accepted agreement is binding on the defendant unless the court chooses not to follow the sentence disposition or recommendation. If, however, the court takes a plea agreement under advisement, the plea is not accepted and the defendant has the right under 6.310(A) to withdraw the plea "until the court accepts it on the record." If the court accepts the agreement conditionally or takes the plea agreement under advisement, it must inform the defendant that the court is not bound to follow the sentence agreement, but that the defendant will be allowed to withdraw the plea in the event that the court does not follow it.

Subrule (C)(4) repeats, with stylistic changes, former 6.101(F)(2)(c).

Subrule (D) repeats, with stylistic changes, the procedure for establishing the factual basis for the plea set forth in former 6.101(F)(3).

Subrule (E) is a stylistically revised version of former 6.101(F)(4)(a). Former 6.101(F)(4)(b), requiring the court to state whether it has agreed to any plea or sentence bargaining, has been eliminated from this subrule because it is now covered in subrule (C)(3).

The first sentence of subrule (F) repeats the provision in former 6.101(F)(6). The last sentence of subrule (F) repeats the record requirement found in former 6.101(H).

Staff Comment to 1994 Amendment

The December 30, 1994 amendments of MCR 6.301, 6.302, 6.311, 6.425, 7.203, 7.204 and 7.205 modified procedure regarding appeals in criminal cases in light of the amendment of Const 1963, art 1, § 20 at the November 1994 general election and the legislation implementing the constitutional amendment. Changes will remain in effect until April 1, 1995 and will be reconsidered by the Court in light of comments received and any further legislation.

Staff Comment to 1995 Amendment

The 1995 amendment of MCR 6.302(A) [effective March 1, 1995] requires the court to place a defendant under oath before accepting a plea of guilty or nolo contendere. The amendment of subrule (B) requires the court to inform the defendant that, by pleading guilty or nolo contendere, the defendant gives up any claim that the plea was the result of promises or threats that were not disclosed to the court at the plea proceeding, or that it was not the defendant's own choice to enter the plea. The amendment of subrule (E) requires the court to inquire whether either the prosecutor or the defendant's lawyer is aware of any promises, threats, or inducements other than those already disclosed on the record.

Staff Comment to 2000 Amendment

The March 28, 2000 amendment of Rules 6.302, 6.425, and 6.615, and the adoption of new Rule 6.625, were made in light of 1999 PA 200, MCL 770.3a, and were effective as to pleas taken on or after April 1, 2000.

Staff Comment to 2002 Amendment

The April 23, 2002 amendment of MCR 6.302(B), effective September 1, 2002, shortens the advice given at plea proceedings regarding an "understanding plea" by eliminating the requirement that the court list the circumstances in which it has discretion to appoint counsel at public expense. That advice remains in MCR 6.425(E)(2)(c).

Staff Comment to July, 2006 Amendment

On March 12, 2002, the Court appointed the Committee on the Rules of Criminal Procedure to review the rules to determine whether any of the provisions should be revised. The committee issued its report on June 16, 2003, recommending numerous amendments of MCR 6.302 and 6.725. The committee did not recommend any amendments of MCR 6.625. A public hearing on the committee's recommendation was held May 27, 2004.

The Court adopted most of the committee's recommendations regarding Rule 6.302, and modified the rule to conform to the ruling of the United States Supreme Court in *Halbert v Michigan*, 545 US ___; 2005 WL 1469183 (June 23, 2005).

The Court adopted many of the committee's recommendations concerning MCR 6.425, however, the Court eliminated the requirement that "[n]ot later than the date of sentencing, the court must complete a sentencing information report on a form to be prescribed by and returned to the state court administrator" in MCR 6.425(D). The Court also modified the language of the rule to incorporate the Court's holding in *People v Babcock*, 469 Mich 247 (2003) and to conform to the ruling in *Halbert*.

The Court did not follow the committee's recommendation that MCR 6.625 not be amended, but instead modified the rule to conform to the ruling in *Halbert*.

Staff Comment to December, 2006 Aendment

The amendment of MCR 6.302(B) was recommended by the Committee on the Rules of Criminal Procedure after the Court issued its order of July 13, 2005. It clarifies that, in addition to the trial rights the defendant gives up if the plea is accepted, the defendant may also be advised in writing that any appeal from the conviction and sentence pursuant to the plea will be by application for leave to appeal and not by right.

Staff Comment to 2012 Amendment

This amendment codifies the holding of the recently released opinion in *People v Cole*, 491 Mich ___ (2012), in which this Court held that a trial court must advise a defendant who is subject to lifetime electronic monitoring requirement of that part of the sentence during the plea proceeding.

Staff Comment to 2014 Amendment

The amendments of MCR 6.302 and MCR 6.310 eliminate the ability of a defendant to withdraw a plea if the defendant and prosecutor agree that the prosecutor will recommend a particular sentence, but the court chooses to impose a sentence greater than that recommended by the prosecutor. Further, the amendment clarifies that a defendant's misconduct that occurs between the time the plea is accepted and the defendant's sentencing may result in a forfeiture of the defendant's right to withdraw a plea in either a *Cobbs* or *Killebrew* case. In addition, the amendments require that a plea agreement (which may include a sentence agreement) must be stated on the record or reduced to writing. A form developed to accommodate this writing is available on the Court's website. The amendments also include various technical changes to reflect that a sentence agreement includes a sentence for a specific term or a sentence within a specific range.

Staff Comment to 2019 Amendment

The amendment of MCR 6.302 requires a trial court judge to advise a defendant that if a plea is accepted, the defendant will give up the right to appeal issues that might have been available after the conclusion of a trial. Such an advisement would prompt further discussions between counsel and defendant, if necessary.

Rule 6.303   Plea of Guilty but Mentally Ill

Before accepting a plea of guilty but mentally ill, the court must comply with the requirements of MCR 6.302. In addition to establishing a factual basis for the plea pursuant to MCR 6.302(D)(1) or (D)(2)(b), the court must examine the psychiatric reports prepared and hold a hearing that establishes support for a finding that the defendant was mentally ill, at the time of the offense to which the plea is entered. The reports must be made a part of the record.

[Adopted effective October 1, 1989. Amended July 13, 2005, effective January 1, 2006, 473 Mich.]

Comments
Staff Comment to 1989 Adoption

MCR 6.303 is a new rule. The availability of the plea of guilty but mentally ill is noted in 6.301(A). The statutory authorization for the plea is found in MCL 768.36(2). The statute sets forth some procedural prerequisites to the plea, including that the defendant have asserted the defense of insanity and undergone psychiatric examination as provided in the insanity defense statute. These requirements are incorporated in 6.301(C)(1). Additionally, before acceptance of the plea, the court is required to examine the psychiatric reports and hold a hearing to establish that the defendant was mentally ill at the time of the offense. In *People v Booth*, 414 Mich 343 (1982), the Court determined that the latter statutory procedure was intended as an adjunct to the traditional plea procedure. Accordingly, it fashioned a procedure combining the court rule plea procedure relating to the issue of criminal liability and the statutory procedure relating to the issue of mental illness.

The rule is consistent with the procedure adopted in *Booth*. The court must comply with the requirements of the guilty plea rule, including the advice

requirements and establishing a factual basis for the criminal liability either by direct questioning as provided in 6.302(D)(1), or the nolo contendere procedure provided in (D)(2)(b). Additionally, as to the issue of mental illness, the court must follow the statutory requirements of examining the psychiatric reports prepared and holding a hearing to establish that the defendant was mentally ill, "but not insane," at the time of the offense. Of course, "hearing" implies that the parties are entitled to present evidence at the hearing. The court rule also incorporates the statutory requirement for the psychiatric reports to be made a part of the record.

Staff Comment to 2005 Amendment

On March 12, 2002, the Court appointed the Committee on the Rules of Criminal Procedure to review the rules to determine whether any of the provisions should be revised. The committee issued its report on June 16, 2003, recommending numerous amendments to existing rules, plus some new rules. A public hearing on the committee's recommendations was held May 27, 2004.

The Court adopted the committee's recommendations with respect to the amendments of Rules 2.511, 6.102, 6.104, 6.107, 6.112, 6.303, 6.304, 6.310, 6.311, 6.402, 6.412, 6.414, 6.419, 6.420, 6.427, 6.615, and 6.620, and the adoption of a new Rule 6.428.

Rule 6.304   Plea of Not Guilty by Reason of Insanity

(A) Advice to Defendant. Before accepting a plea of not guilty by reason of insanity, the court must comply with the requirements of MCR 6.302 except that subrule (C) of this rule, rather than MCR 6.302(D), governs the manner of determining the accuracy of the plea.

(B) Additional Advice Required. After complying with the applicable requirements of MCR 6.302, the court must advise the defendant, and determine whether the defendant understands, that the plea will result in the defendant's commitment for diagnostic examination at the center for forensic psychiatry for up to 60 days, and that after the examination, the probate court may order the defendant to be committed for an indefinite period of time.

(C) Factual Basis. Before accepting a plea of not guilty by reason of insanity, the court must examine the psychiatric reports prepared and hold a hearing that establishes support for findings that

(1) the defendant committed the acts charged, and

(2) that, by a preponderance of the evidence, the defendant was legally insane at the time of the offense.

(D) Report of Plea. After accepting the defendant's plea, the court must forward to the center for forensic psychiatry a full report, in the form of a settled record, of the facts concerning the crime to which the defendant pleaded and the defendant's mental state at the time of the crime.

[Adopted effective October 1, 1989. Amended July 13, 2005, effective January 1, 2006, 473 Mich.]

Comments
Staff Comment to 1989 Adoption

MCR 6.304 is a new rule. It sets forth the procedure for the new plea of not guilty by reason of insanity. It is similar to the procedure in 6.303 providing for a plea of guilty but mentally ill. It incorporates additional procedural steps, however, requiring additional advice because of the consequences of the plea, and a hearing and reporting procedure corresponding to the statutory requirements relating to a person acquitted of criminal charges by reason of insanity MCL 330.2050. The statute requires a person acquitted of criminal charges by reason of insanity to be committed to the center for forensic psychiatry for a period not to exceed 60 days. It further requires the court to forward to the center "a full report, in the form of a settled record, of the facts concerning the crime which the patient was found to have committed but of which he was acquitted by reason of insanity." This latter requirement necessitates a more elaborate fact finding than is required to establish a factual basis for a guilty plea or a plea of guilty but mentally ill.

Subrule (A) requires the trial court to comply with the requirements of the guilty plea rule, 6.302, except that the factual basis for the plea is to be governed by the procedures set forth in subrule (C).

Subrule (B) requires the court to give the defendant additional advice concerning the unique consequences of this plea to ensure that the defendant's plea is made voluntarily and understandingly. The court must advise the defendant that the plea will result in the defendant's commitment for a diagnostic examination that may last up to 60 days and that afterwards the defendant may be committed for an indefinite period of time.

The procedure for establishing a factual basis for this plea differs from the other plea procedures because of the greater likelihood that the defendant will not be able to supply a factual basis establishing that the crime was committed, and also because of the more elaborate report requirement that the court is statutorily required to make to the center for forensic psychiatry. This does not preclude the court, however, from considering statements and testimony elicited from the defendant or from relying on other information admitted during the course of the hearing. Additionally, the court must consider the psychiatric reports prepared and such other evidence presented at the hearing that establishes a reasonable doubt concerning the defendant's sanity at the time of the offense.

Subrule (D) implements the statutory reporting requirement applicable to a person acquitted by reason of insanity. Since the plea procedure has the same effect as an acquittal following a trial, the same subsequent examination and commitment procedure must be followed.

Staff Comment to 2005 Amendment

On March 12, 2002, the Court appointed the Committee on the Rules of Criminal Procedure to review the rules to determine whether any of the provisions should be revised. The committee issued its report on June 16, 2003, recommending numerous amendments to existing rules, plus some new rules. A public hearing on the committee's recommendations was held May 27, 2004.

The Court adopted the committee's recommendations with respect to the amendments of Rules 2.511, 6.102, 6.104, 6.107, 6.112, 6.303, 6.304, 6.310, 6.311, 6.402, 6.412, 6.414, 6.419, 6.420, 6.427, 6.615, and 6.620, and the adoption of a new Rule 6.428.

Rule 6.310. Withdrawal or Vacation of Plea

(A) Withdrawal Before Acceptance. The defendant has a right to withdraw any plea until the court accepts it on the record.

(B) Withdrawal After Acceptance but Before Sentence. Except as provided in subsection (3), after acceptance but before sentence,

(1) a plea may be withdrawn on the defendant's motion or with the defendant's consent, only in the interest of justice, and may not be withdrawn if withdrawal of the plea would substantially prejudice the prosecutor because of reliance on the plea. If the defendant's motion is based on an error in the plea proceeding, the court must permit the defendant to withdraw the plea if it would be required by subrule (C).

(2) the defendant is entitled to withdraw the plea if

(a) the plea involves an agreement for a sentence for a specified term or within a specified range, and the court states that it is unable to follow the agreement; the trial court shall then state the sentence it intends to impose, and provide the defendant the opportunity to affirm or withdraw the plea; or

(b) the plea involves a statement by the court that it will sentence to a specified term or within a specified range, and the court states that it is unable to sentence as stated; the trial court shall provide the defendant the opportunity to affirm or withdraw the plea, but shall not state the sentence it intends to impose.

(3) Except as allowed by the trial court for good cause, a defendant is not entitled to withdraw a plea under subsection (2)(a) or (2)(b) if the defendant commits misconduct after the plea is accepted but before sentencing. For purposes of this rule, misconduct is defined to include, but is not limited to: absconding or failing to appear for sentencing, violating terms of conditions on bond or the terms of any sentencing or plea agreement, or otherwise failing to comply with an order of the court pending sentencing.

(C) Motion to Withdraw Plea After Sentence.

(1) The defendant may file a motion to withdraw the plea within 6 months after sentence or within the time provided by subrule (C)(2).

(2) If 6 months have elapsed since sentencing, the defendant may file a motion to withdraw the plea if:

(a) the defendant has filed a request for the appointment of counsel pursuant to MCR 6.425(G)(1) within the 6-month period,

(b) the defendant or defendant's lawyer, if one is appointed, has ordered the appropriate transcripts within 28 days of service of the order granting or denying the request for counsel or substitute counsel, unless the transcript has already been filed or has been ordered by the court under MCR 6.425(G), and

(c) the motion to withdraw the plea is filed in accordance with the provisions of this subrule within 42 days after the filing of the transcript. If the transcript was filed before the order appointing counsel or substitute counsel, or the order denying the appointment of counsel, the 42-day period runs from the date of that order.

(3) Thereafter, the defendant may seek relief only in accordance with the procedure set forth in subchapter 6.500.

(4) If the trial court determines that there was an error in the plea proceeding that would entitle the defendant to have the plea set aside, the court must give the advice or make the inquiries necessary to rectify the error and then give the defendant the opportunity to elect to allow the plea and sentence to stand or to withdraw the plea. If the defendant elects to allow the plea and sentence to stand, the additional advice given and inquiries made become part of the plea proceeding for the purposes of further proceedings, including appeals.

(5) If a motion to withdraw plea is received by the court after the expiration of the periods set forth above, and if the appellant is an inmate in the custody of the Michigan Department of Corrections and has submitted the motion as a pro se party, the motion shall be deemed presented for filing on the date of deposit of the motion in the outgoing mail at the correctional institution in which the inmate is housed. Timely filing may be shown by a sworn statement filed with the motion, which must set forth the date of deposit and state that first-class postage has been prepaid. The exception applies to cases in which a plea was accepted on or after the effective date of this amendment. This exception also applies to an inmate housed in a penal institution in another state or in a federal penal institution who seeks to withdraw a plea in a Michigan court.

(D) Preservation of Issues. A defendant convicted on the basis of a plea may not raise on appeal any claim of noncompliance with the requirements of the rules in this subchapter, or any other claim that the plea was not an understanding, voluntary, or accurate one, unless the defendant has moved to withdraw the plea in the trial court, raising as a basis for withdrawal the claim sought to be raised on appeal.

(E) Vacation of Plea on Prosecutor's Motion. On the prosecutor's motion, the court may vacate a plea if the defendant has failed to comply with the terms of a plea agreement.

[Adopted effective October 1, 1989. Amended July 13, 2005, effective January 1, 2006, 473 Mich; September 18, 2013, effective January 1, 2014, 495 Mich; April 19, 2018, effective May 1, 2018, 501 Mich; May 23, 2018, effective September 1, 2018, 501 Mich; August 30, 2018, effective September 1, 2018, 502 Mich.]

Comments

Staff Comment to 1989 Adoption

With the exception of subrule (A), MCR 6.310 substantially modifies prior rules and law.

Subrule (A) is a modified version of Rule 6.101(F)(6)(a). The rule states the defendant's right to withdraw "any plea" until it is accepted on the record. The terminology "any plea" is used to make it clear that this rule applies to any of the forms of plea described in these rules.

Subrule (B) sets forth the procedure for withdrawing a plea after it has been accepted but before the sentence has been imposed. The former rule, 6.101(F)(6)(b), did not place any limits on the court's discretion to set aside an accepted plea ("the court may set it aside"). Case law indicated that the trial judge's discretion "should be exercised with great liberality" when the defendant's request was made before sentencing. *People v Zaleski*, 375 Mich 71, 79 (1965). Subrule (B) states a new standard. It permits the court to allow a plea to be withdrawn before sentencing if it is "in the interest of justice" *and* if withdrawal of the plea would not "substantially prejudice the prosecutor because of reliance on the plea." The new standard has similarities to Federal Rule of Criminal Procedure 32(d) ("upon a showing by the defendant of any fair and just reason") and ABA Standard, 14–2.1(a) ("for any fair and just reason unless the prosecution has been substantially prejudiced by reliance upon the defendant's plea.").

The foregoing portion of subrule (B) pertains to discretionary withdrawals of pleas. The last portion of subrule (B) deals with withdrawals that are not discretionary, but rather, mandatory because of a defect in the plea or the plea proceeding entitling the defendant to withdraw the plea regardless of whether the motion is made before or after sentencing. The latter bases for withdrawal are discussed in 6.311(B).

Subrule (C) is a new rule authorizing the court to vacate a plea before sentencing on the basis of the prosecutor's motion and showing that the defendant has failed to comply with the terms of a plea agreement. Because the trial court's authority is discretionary ("may vacate"), the court is not required to vacate a plea if it finds that the breach was insignificant.

Staff Comment to 2005 Amendment

On March 12, 2002, the Court appointed the Committee on the Rules of Criminal Procedure to review the rules to determine whether any of the provisions should be revised. The committee issued its report on June 16, 2003, recommending numerous amendments to existing rules, plus some new rules. A public hearing on the committee's recommendations was held May 27, 2004.

The Court adopted the committee's recommendations with respect to the amendments of Rules 2.511, 6.102, 6.104, 6.107, 6.112, 6.303, 6.304, 6.310, 6.311, 6.402, 6.412, 6.414, 6.419, 6.420, 6.427, 6.615, and 6.620, and the adoption of a new Rule 6.428.

Staff Comment to 2014 Amendment

The amendments of MCR 6.302 and MCR 6.310 eliminate the ability of a defendant to withdraw a plea if the defendant and prosecutor agree that the prosecutor will recommend a particular sentence, but the court chooses to impose a sentence greater than that recommended by the prosecutor. Further, the amendment clarifies that a defendant's misconduct that occurs between the time the plea is accepted and the defendant's sentencing may result in a forfeiture of the defendant's right to withdraw a plea in either a *Cobbs* or *Killebrew* case. In addition, the amendments require that a plea agreement (which may include a sentence agreement) must be stated on the record or reduced to writing. A form developed to accommodate this writing is available on the Court's website. The amendments also include various technical changes to reflect that a sentence agreement includes a sentence for a specific term or a sentence within a specific range.

Staff Comment to May, 2018 Amendment

The amendments, submitted by SADO, are intended to clarify practices and provide protections for criminal defendants represented by assigned appellate counsel. The amendments allow an additional 42 days to file post-judgment motions in certain circumstances, and where delay is due to the trial court, clarify in the amendment of MCR 7.205 that in certain circumstances, substitute appellate counsel may file a delayed application for leave to appeal within 42 days of appointment (even if later than six months after sentencing), add language to MCR 7.211 to guide parties and courts if relief is granted in the trial court, and change the procedure for seeking permission to file a brief longer than 50 pages in length.

Staff Comment to First September, 2018 Amendment

The amendments of MCR 6.310, 6.429, and 6.431 establish a "prison-mailbox" rule for post-sentencing motions to withdraw plea, motions to correct an invalid sentence, and motions for new trial, filed by *in pro per* defendants in the custody of the Department of Corrections.

Staff Comment to Second September, 2018 Amendment

These amendments update cross-references in the rules, and are intended to reflect changes that are necessary as a result of the Court's recent e-Filing rules amendments.

Rule 6.312 Effect of Withdrawal or Vacation of Plea

If a plea is withdrawn by the defendant or vacated by the trial court or an appellate court, the case may proceed to trial on any charges that had been brought or that could have been brought against the defendant if the plea had not been entered.

[Adopted effective October 1, 1989.]

Comments

Staff Comment to 1989 Adoption

MCR 6.312 is a modified version of former 6.101(F)(7)(d). *People v McMiller*, 389 Mich 425 (1973), and *People v Thornton*, 403 Mich 389 (1978), held that when a plea-based conviction was reversed on appeal or set aside by the trial court for violation of plea-taking rules, the defendant could not be reprosecuted on a higher charge arising out of the same transaction. Former MCR 6.101(F)(7)(d) removed that prohibition as to pleas set aside by the trial court. The new provision allows prosecution on higher charges regardless of whether the plea is withdrawn by the defendant or vacated by the trial court or an appellate court.

SUBCHAPTER 6.400   TRIALS

Rule 6.401 Right to Trial by Jury or by the Court

The defendant has the right to be tried by a jury, or may, with the consent of the prosecutor and approval by the court, elect to waive that right and be tried before the court without a jury.

[Adopted effective October 1, 1989.]

Comments

Staff Comment to 1989 Adoption

MCR 6.401 is a new rule. It states the statutory right of a defendant to elect waiver of a jury trial in favor of trial by the court. A 1988 legislative amendment has conditioned the defendant's right by requiring "the consent of the prosecutor and approval by the court." 1988 PA 89, MCL 763.3.

Rule 6.402 Waiver of Jury Trial by the Defendant

(A) Time of Waiver. The court may not accept a waiver of trial by jury until after the defendant has been arraigned or has waived an arraignment on the information, or, in a court where arraignment on the information has been eliminated under MCR 6.113(E), after the defendant has otherwise been provided with a copy of the information, and has been offered an opportunity to consult with a lawyer.

(B) Waiver and Record Requirements. Before accepting a waiver, the court must advise the defendant in open court of the constitutional right to trial by jury. The court must also ascertain, by addressing the defendant personally, that the defendant understands the right and that the defendant voluntarily chooses to give up that right and to be tried by the court. A verbatim record must be made of the waiver proceeding.
[Adopted effective October 1, 1989. Amended July 13, 2005, effective January 1, 2006, 473 Mich.]

Comments

Staff Comment to 1989 Adoption

MCR 6.402 is a new rule. It sets forth a procedure for waiver of jury trial that differs substantially from the requirements set forth in MCL 763.3 and the procedure implementing those requirements adopted in *People v Pasley*, 419 Mich 297 (1984).

Subrule (A) is consistent with the requirements of subsection (2) of the statute, permitting the waiver "after the defendant has been arraigned and has had the opportunity to consult with legal counsel." The rule uses the terminology "*offered* an opportunity to consult with a lawyer" to clarify that actual consultation with a lawyer is not required so long as a defendant has been offered the opportunity and declined it.

The waiver procedure set forth in subrule (B) differs from the statute and the procedure adopted in *Pasley* because it eliminates the written waiver requirement and replaces it with an oral waiver procedure consistent with the waiver procedure applicable at plea proceedings. See 6.302(B)(3). The statutory procedure is superseded by the court rule procedure. See 6.001(E).

Staff Comment to 2005 Amendment

On March 12, 2002, the Court appointed the Committee on the Rules of Criminal Procedure to review the rules to determine whether any of the provisions should be revised. The committee issued its report on June 16, 2003, recommending numerous amendments to existing rules, plus some new rules. A public hearing on the committee's recommendations was held May 27, 2004.

The Court adopted the committee's recommendations with respect to the amendments of Rules 2.511, 6.102, 6.104, 6.107, 6.112, 6.303, 6.304, 6.310, 6.311, 6.402, 6.412, 6.414, 6.419, 6.420, 6.427, 6.615, and 6.620, and the adoption of a new Rule 6.428.

Rule 6.403   Trial by the Judge in Waiver Cases

When trial by jury has been waived, the court with jurisdiction must proceed with the trial. The court must find the facts specially, state separately its conclusions of law, and direct entry of the appropriate judgment. The court must state its findings and conclusions on the record or in a written opinion made a part of the record.
[Adopted effective October 1, 1989.]

Comments

Staff Comment to 1989 Adoption

MCR 6.403 is a new rule, but incorporates existing law. The first sentence of the rule describes the judge's duty set forth in MCL 763.4. The second sentence incorporates the special fact finding requirements of MCR 2.517(A)(1), made applicable to criminal cases by *People v Jackson*, 390 Mich 621, 627 (1973). Since this rule adopts an existing rule, it also implicitly incorporates the existing body of decisional law beginning with *Jackson* addressing issues such as the sufficiency of fact findings and the appropriate remedy when findings are insufficient.

The applicability of special fact finding at bench trials, however, should not be construed as implying that it is not required in relation to other evidentiary hearings at which the court must decide a contested factual issue. See, for example, *People v LaBate*, 122 MichApp 644 (1983), holding the special fact-finding requirement applicable at an entrapment hearing.

Rule 6.410   Jury Trial; Number of Jurors; Unanimous Verdict

(A) Number of Jurors. Except as provided in this rule, a jury that decides a case must consist of 12 jurors. At any time before a verdict is returned, the parties may stipulate with the court's consent to have the case decided by a jury consisting of a specified number of jurors less than 12. On being informed of the parties' willingness to stipulate, the court must personally advise the defendant of the right to have the case decided by a jury consisting of 12 jurors. By addressing the defendant personally, the court must ascertain that the defendant understands the right and that the defendant voluntarily chooses to give up that right as provided in the stipulation. If the court finds that the requirements for a valid waiver have been satisfied, the court may accept the stipulation. Even if the requirements for a valid waiver have been satisfied, the court may, in the interest of justice, refuse to accept a stipulation, but it must state its reasons for doing so on the record. The stipulation and procedure described in this subrule must take place in open court and a verbatim record must be made.

(B) Unanimous Verdicts. A jury verdict must be unanimous.
[Adopted effective October 1, 1989. Amended December 15, 1994, effective March 1, 1995, 447 Mich.]

Comments

Staff Comment to 1989 Adoption

MCR 6.410 is a new rule. Its provisions modify and change existing law.

Subrule (A) sets forth a procedure by which a defendant charged with a felony may waive the constitutional right to have the case decided by twelve jurors. See Const 1963, art 1, § 20. Waiver of this right was held permissible in *Attorney General v Montgomery*, 275 Mich 504 (1936), and a waiver procedure was subsequently incorporated in former GCR 1963, 512.1, allowing the parties to stipulate orally or in writing to a jury of less than twelve. This provision, however, was deleted from MCR 2.512 as part of a general excision of criminal provisions from the civil rules.

Subrule (A) recognizes that a defendant may waive the right to trial by twelve jurors. To ensure, however, that the waiver is voluntary and not the product of coercion, the rule restricts the availability of stipulation and waiver until after the jury is impaneled. Additionally, the subrule sets forth a stipulation and oral waiver procedure to ensure that the waiver is an informed and voluntary one. The rule permits the court, however, to decline to accept the stipulation if the court determines, and states the reasons why, it is not in the interest of justice.

GCR 1963, 512.1 also authorized the parties in a criminal case to stipulate to a less than unanimous verdict. In *People v Miller*, 121 Mich App 691 (1982), it was held that under existing law a defendant may waive the constitutional right to a unanimous jury verdict. Subrule (B) changes the law by mandating that a jury verdict in a criminal case governed by these rules be unanimous. This mandate implicitly prohibits a stipulation or waiver to a less than unanimous verdict.

Staff Comment to 1994 Amendment

Consistent with *People v Champion*, 442 Mich 874 (1993), the March 1995 amendment of subrule (A) permits the parties to stipulate, with the court's consent and at any time before a verdict is returned, to proceed with fewer than 12 jurors.

Rule 6.411   Additional Jurors

The court may impanel more than 12 jurors. If more than the number of jurors required to decide the case are left on the jury before deliberations are to begin, the names of the jurors must be placed in a container and names drawn from it to reduce the number of jurors to the number required to decide the case. The court may retain the alternate jurors during deliberations. If the court does so, it shall instruct the alternate jurors not to discuss the case with any other person until the jury completes its deliberations and is discharged. If an alternate juror replaces a juror after the jury retires to consider its verdict, the court shall instruct the jury to begin its deliberations anew.
[Adopted effective October 1, 1989. Amended June 26, 2001, effective September 1, 2001, 465 Mich.]

Comments

Staff Comment to 1989 Adoption

MCR 6.411 restates former 6.102(A), permitting the impaneling of more than 12 jurors, but with a modification providing for the number of jurors to be reduced prior to deliberations to the number "required to decide the case." This modification accommodates the possibility that there has been a stipulation to a jury of less than twelve as provided in Rule 6.410(A).

Staff Comment to 2001 Amendment

The June 26, 2001 amendments of MCR 2.511(B), MCR 6.411, and MCR 6.620(A), effective September 1, 2001, were based on a proposal from the Michigan Judges Association. Consistent with the December 1999 amendment of the Federal Rules of Criminal Procedure for the United States District Courts, the amendments allow courts to retain alternate jurors during deliberations.

Rule 6.412   Selection of the Jury

(A) Selecting and Impaneling the Jury. Except as otherwise provided by the rules in this subchapter, MCR 2.510 and 2.511 govern the procedure for selecting and impaneling the jury.

(B) Instructions and Oath Before Selection. Before beginning the jury selection process, the court should give the prospective jurors appropriate preliminary instructions and must have them sworn.

(C) Voir Dire of Prospective Jurors.

(1) *Scope and Purpose.* The scope of voir dire examination of prospective jurors is within the discretion of the court. It should be conducted for the purposes of discovering grounds for challenges for cause and of gaining knowledge to facilitate an intelligent exercise of peremptory challenges. The court should confine the examination to these purposes and prevent abuse of the examination process.

(2) *Conduct of the Examination.* The court may conduct the examination of prospective jurors or permit the lawyers to do so. If the court conducts the examination, it may permit the lawyers to supplement the examination by direct questioning or by submitting questions for the court to ask. On its own initiative or on the motion of a party, the court may provide for a prospective juror or jurors to be questioned out of the presence of the other jurors.

(D) Challenges for Cause.

(1) *Grounds.* A prospective juror is subject to challenge for cause on any ground set forth in MCR 2.511(D) or for any other reason recognized by law.

(2) *Procedure.* If, after the examination of any juror, the court finds that a ground for challenging a juror for cause is present, the court on its own initiative should, or on motion of either party must, excuse the juror from the panel.

(E) Peremptory Challenges.

(1) *Challenges by Right.* Each defendant is entitled to 5 peremptory challenges unless an offense charged is punishable by life imprisonment, in which case a defendant being tried alone is entitled to 12 peremptory challenges, 2 defendants being tried jointly are each entitled to 10 peremptory challenges, 3 defendants being tried jointly are each entitled to 9 peremptory challenges, 4 defendants being tried jointly are each entitled to 8 peremptory challenges, and 5 or more defendants being tried jointly are each entitled to 7 peremptory challenges. The prosecutor is entitled to the same number of peremptory challenges as a defendant being tried alone, or, in the case of jointly tried defendants, the total number of peremptory challenges to which all the defendants are entitled.

(2) *Additional Challenges.* On a showing of good cause, the court may grant one or more of the parties an increased number of peremptory challenges. The additional challenges granted by the court need not be equal for each party.

(F) Oath After Selection. After the jury is selected and before trial begins, the court must have the jurors sworn.
[Adopted effective October 1, 1989. Amended July 13, 2005, effective January 1, 2006, 473 Mich.]

Comments

Staff Comment to 1989 Adoption

MCR 6.412 is a new rule.

Subrule (A) incorporates by reference the jury selection procedure set forth in the civil rules.

Subrule (B) is consistent with existing practice. Appropriate preliminary instructions and an appropriate oath may be found in the Michigan Criminal Jury Instructions.

The provisions in subrule (C)(1) pertaining to voir dire of perspective jurors reflects existing law. See *People v Harrell*, 398 Mich 384, 388 (1976). The provision in the last sentence of subrule (C)(1) is new and states the trial court's responsibility to confine voir dire examination to its proper purposes.

The provisions in subrule (C)(2) are consistent with existing law. See *Harrell*, supra. The "or" in the first sentence is used in its conjunctive sense, indicating that voir dire examination may be conducted by the court, by the lawyers, or by both.

Subrule (D)(1) is consistent with existing law and incorporates by reference the grounds for challenge for cause set forth in MCR 2.511(D). Subrule (D)(2) also reflects the existing law. It provides, however, that the court's duty to discharge a juror for cause sua sponte is directive ("should") rather than mandatory or permissive.

Subrule (E)(1) substantially changes existing law. By statute, MCL 768.13, and pursuant to former 6.102(B), every defendant charged with a capital offense was entitled to 20 peremptory challenges, whether tried separately or jointly, and the prosecutor was entitled to 15 peremptory challenges for each defendant. Subrule (B) reduces the entitlement to peremptory challenges in such cases to 12 for individually charged defendants, and a progressively reduced number for each defendant in multiple defendant cases to a minimum of seven challenges per defendant. Subrule (B) also changes the prosecutor's entitlement to peremptory challenges by making it equal to the total number of peremptory challenges available to the defendants in a case. The peremptory challenge entitlement applicable in noncapital cases is unchanged. See former 6.102(B) and MCL 768.12.

Subrule (E)(2) is a new provision that gives the court discretion, "on a showing of good cause," to allow a party or the parties additional peremptory challenges. It is based on 3 ABA Standards for Criminal Justice (2d ed), Standard 15–2.6(a), which indicates that such additional challenges should be allowed "when special circumstances justify doing so."

Subrule (F) is consistent with current practice. The Michigan Criminal Jury Instructions set forth an appropriate oath and appropriate jury instructions.

Staff Comment to 2005 Amendment

On March 12, 2002, the Court appointed the Committee on the Rules of Criminal Procedure to review the rules to determine whether any of the provisions should be revised. The committee issued its report on June 16, 2003, recommending numerous amendments to existing rules, plus some new rules. A public hearing on the committee's recommendations was held May 27, 2004.

The Court adopted the committee's recommendations with respect to the amendments of Rules 2.511, 6.102, 6.104, 6.107, 6.112, 6.303, 6.304, 6.310, 6.311, 6.402, 6.412, 6.414, 6.419, 6.420, 6.427, 6.615, and 6.620, and the adoption of a new Rule 6.428.

Rule 6.416   Presentation of Evidence

Subject to the rules in this chapter and to the Michigan rules of evidence, each party has discretion in deciding what witnesses and evidence to present.

[Adopted effective October 1, 1989.]

Comments

Staff Comment to 1989 Adoption

MCR 6.416 is a new rule. It is consistent with a 1986 legislative amendment abrogating the prosecutor's duty to endorse and produce res gestae witnesses. See 1986 PA 46, MCL 767.40. Although this rule gives each party the right to decide what witnesses and evidence to present, that right is made subject to the requirements of the rules of criminal procedure and the Michigan Rules of Evidence.

Rule 6.417. Mistrial

Before ordering a mistrial, the court must, on the record, give each defendant and the prosecutor an opportunity to comment on the propriety of the order, to state whether that party consents or objects, and to suggest alternatives.

[Adopted May 23, 2018, effective September 1, 2018, 501 Mich.]

Comments

Staff Comment to 2018 Adoption

This new rule, based on FR Crim P 26.3, requires a trial court to provide parties an opportunity to comment on a proposed order of mistrial, to state their consent or objection, or suggest alternatives. The rule was pursued following the Court's consideration of *People v Howard*, docket 153651.

Rule 6.419 Motion for Directed Verdict of Acquittal

(A) Before Submission to the Jury. After the prosecutor has rested the prosecution's case-in-chief or after the close of all the evidence, the court on the defendant's motion must direct a verdict of acquittal on any charged offense for which the evidence is insufficient to sustain a conviction. The court may on its own consider whether the evidence is insufficient to sustain a conviction. If the court denies a motion for a judgment of acquittal at the close of the government's evidence, the defendant may offer evidence without having reserved the right to do so.

(B) Reserving Decision. The court may reserve decision on the motion, proceed with the trial (where the motion is made before the close of all the evidence), submit the case to the jury, and decide the motion either before the jury returns a verdict or after it returns a verdict of guilty or is discharged without having returned a verdict. If the court reserves decision, it must decide the motion on the basis of the evidence at the time the ruling was reserved.

(C) After Jury Verdict. After a jury verdict, the defendant may file an original or renewed motion for directed verdict of acquittal in the same manner as provided by MCR 6.431(A) for filing a motion for a new trial.

(D) Bench Trial. In an action tried without a jury, after the prosecutor has rested the prosecution's case-in-chief, the defendant, without waiving the right to offer evidence if the motion is not granted, may move for acquittal on the ground that a reasonable doubt exists. The court may then determine the facts and render a verdict of acquittal, or may decline to render judgment until the close of all the evidence. If the court renders a verdict of acquittal, the court shall make findings of fact.

(E) Conditional New Trial Ruling. If the court grants a directed verdict of acquittal after the jury has returned a guilty verdict, it must also conditionally rule on any motion for a new trial by determining whether it would grant the motion if the directed verdict of acquittal is vacated or reversed.

(F) Explanation of Rulings on Record. The court must state orally on the record or in a written ruling made a part of the record its reasons for granting or denying a motion for a directed verdict of acquittal and for conditionally granting or denying a motion for a new trial.

[Adopted effective October 1, 1989. Amended July 13, 2005, effective January 1, 2006, 473 Mich; May 2, 2013, effective September 1, 2013, 493 Mich.]

Comments

Staff Comment to 1989 Adoption

MCR 6.419 is a new rule.

Subrule (A) is based on 3 ABA Standards for Criminal Justice (2d ed), Standard 15–3.5(b) and is consistent with existing practice except for the provision prohibiting the court from reserving decision on a defense motion for directed verdict made at the close of the prosecution's proofs. This rule does not state the standard of proof that the court must apply in determining the sufficiency of the evidence. The standard is constitutional and it is therefore left to case law. See *People v Hampton*, 407 Mich 354 (1979).

Subrule (B) pertains to motions for directed verdict of acquittal made after the jury verdict. It incorporates by reference the same postconviction procedures that a defendant may use to move for a new trial. This rule does not impose any time limits on a motion for directed verdict of acquittal in the event that the jury does not reach a verdict and is discharged.

Subrule (C) is derived from MCR 2.610(C), which requires the court to rule conditionally on any motion for new trial in the event that it grants a motion for judgment notwithstanding the verdict.

Subrule (D) is derived from the provisions in MCR 2.610(B)(3) and (C)(1) requiring the court to place on the record the reasons for its rulings.

Staff Comment to 2005 Amendment

On March 12, 2002, the Court appointed the Committee on the Rules of Criminal Procedure to review the rules to determine whether any of the provisions should be revised. The committee issued its report on June 16, 2003, recommending numerous amendments to existing rules, plus some new rules. A public hearing on the committee's recommendations was held May 27, 2004.

The Court adopted the committee's recommendations with respect to the amendments of Rules 2.511, 6.102, 6.104, 6.107, 6.112, 6.303, 6.304, 6.310, 6.311, 6.402, 6.412, 6.414, 6.419, 6.420, 6.427, 6.615, and 6.620, and the adoption of a new Rule 6.428.

Staff Comment to 2013 Amendment

New subrules (A) and (B) are modeled on FR Crim P 29. As with the 1994 Amendments to FR Crim P 29, this amendment should remove the dilemma in cases in which the trial court would feel pressured to make an immediate, and possibly erroneous, decision or violate the former version of the rule by reserving judgment on the motion. The stakes in this area are unusually high because double jeopardy precludes appellate review of a trial court's decision to grant a motion for directed verdict of acquittal before the jury reaches a verdict. See, e.g., *Evans v Michigan*, __ US __; 133 S Ct 1069; 185 L Ed 2d 124 (2013). Allowing the court to reserve judgment until after the jury returns a verdict mitigates double jeopardy concerns because "reversal would result in reinstatement of the jury verdict of guilt, not a new trial." *Id.*, 133 S Ct at 1081 n 9, citing *United States v Wilson*, 420 US 332; 95 S Ct 1013; 43 L Ed 2d 232 (1975).

Rule 6.420 Verdict

(A) Return. The jury must return its verdict in open court.

(B) Several Defendants. If two or more defendants are jointly on trial, the jury at any time during its deliberations may return a verdict with respect to any defendant as to whom it has agreed. If the jury cannot reach a verdict with respect to any other defendant, the court may declare a mistrial as to that defendant.

(C) Several Counts. If a defendant is charged with two or more counts, and the court determines that the jury is deadlocked so that a mistrial must be declared, the court may inquire of the jury whether it has reached a unanimous verdict on any of the counts charged, and, if so, may accept the jury's verdict on that count or counts.

(D) Poll of Jury. Before the jury is discharged, the court on its own initiative may, or on the motion of a party must, have each juror polled in open court as to whether the verdict announced is that juror's verdict. If polling discloses the jurors are not in agreement, the court may (1) discontinue the poll and order the jury to retire for further deliberations, or (2) either (a) with the defendant's consent, or (b) after determining that the jury is deadlocked or that some other manifest necessity exists, declare a mistrial and discharge the jury.

[Adopted effective October 1, 1989. Amended July 13, 2005, effective January 1, 2006, 473 Mich.]

Comments

Staff Comment to 1989 Adoption

MCR 6.420 is a new rule.

Subrules (A) and (B) are consistent with existing practice and are based on Federal Rules of Criminal Procedure 31(a) and (b).

Subrule (C) is consistent with the jury polling procedure set forth in MCR 2.512, but is modified to address constitutional concerns applicable in criminal jury trials. See *People v Hall*, 396 Mich 650, 654–655 (1976).

The option in subrule (C) permitting the court to "discontinue the poll and order the jury to retire for further deliberations" requires the court to cut off the polling as soon as disagreement is disclosed. The court should not allow the polling to continue because of its potentially coercive effect. Nor, for the same reason, should the court question the jury to determine where the jury stands numerically. See *People v Wilson*, 390 Mich 689 (1973).

Staff Comment to 2005 Amendment

On March 12, 2002, the Court appointed the Committee on the Rules of Criminal Procedure to review the rules to determine whether any of the provisions should be revised. The committee issued its report on June 16, 2003, recommending numerous amendments to existing rules, plus some new rules. A public hearing on the committee's recommendations was held May 27, 2004.

The Court adopted the committee's recommendations with respect to the amendments of Rules 2.511, 6.102, 6.104, 6.107, 6.112, 6.303, 6.304, 6.310, 6.311, 6.402, 6.412, 6.414, 6.419, 6.420, 6.427, 6.615, and 6.620, and the adoption of a new Rule 6.428.

Rule 6.425. Sentencing; Appointment of Appellate Counsel

(A) Presentence Report; Contents.

(1) Prior to sentencing, the probation officer must investigate the defendant's background and character, verify material information, and report in writing the results of the investigation to the court. The report must be succinct and, depending on the circumstances, include:

(a) a description of the defendant's prior criminal convictions and juvenile adjudications,

(b) a complete description of the offense and the circumstances surrounding it,

(c) a brief description of the defendant's vocational background and work history, including military record and present employment status,

(d) a brief social history of the defendant, including marital status, financial status, length of residence in the community, educational background, and other pertinent data,

(e) the defendant's medical history, substance abuse history, if any, and, if indicated, a current psychological or psychiatric report,

(f) information concerning the financial, social, psychological, or physical harm suffered by any victim of the offense, including the restitution needs of the victim,

(g) if provided and requested by the victim, a written victim's impact statement as provided by law,

(h) any statement the defendant wishes to make,

(i) a statement prepared by the prosecutor on the applicability of any consecutive sentencing provision,

(j) an evaluation of and prognosis for the defendant's adjustment in the community based on factual information in the report,

(k) a specific recommendation for disposition, and

(*l*) any other information that may aid the court in sentencing.

(2) A presentence investigation report shall not include any address or telephone number for the home, workplace, school, or place of worship of any victim or witness, or a family member of any victim or witness, unless an address is used to identify the place of the crime or to impose conditions of release from custody that are necessary for the protection of a named individual. Upon request, any other address or telephone number that would reveal the location of a victim or witness or a family member of a victim or witness shall be exempted from disclosure unless an address is used to identify the place of the crime or to impose conditions of release from custody that are necessary for the protection of a named individual.

(3) Regardless of the sentence imposed, the court must have a copy of the presentence report and of any psychiatric report sent to the Department of Corrections. If the defendant is sentenced to prison, the copies must be sent with the commitment papers.

(B) Presentence Report; Disclosure Before Sentencing. The court must provide copies of the presentence report to the prosecutor, and the defendant's lawyer, or the defendant if not represented by a lawyer, at a reasonable time, but not less than two business days, before the day of sentencing. The prosecutor and the defendant's lawyer, or the defendant if not represented by a lawyer, may retain a copy of the report or an amended report. If the presentence report is not made available to the prosecutor and the defendant's lawyer, or the defendant if not represented by a lawyer, at least two business days before the day of sentencing, the prosecutor and the defendant's lawyer, or the defendant if not represented by a lawyer, shall be entitled, on oral motion, to an adjournment of the day of sentencing to enable the moving party to review the presentence report and to prepare any necessary corrections, additions, or deletions to present to the court. The court may exempt from disclosure information or diagnostic opinion that might seriously disrupt a program of rehabilitation and sources of information that have been obtained on a promise of confidentiality. When part of the report is not disclosed, the court must inform the parties that information has not been disclosed and state on the record the reasons for nondisclosure. To the extent it can do so without defeating the purpose of nondisclosure, the court also must provide the parties with a written or oral summary of the nondisclosed information and give them an opportunity to comment on it. The court must have the information exempted from disclosure specifically noted in the report. The court's decision to exempt part of the report from disclosure is subject to appellate review.

(C) Presentence Report; Disclosure After Sentencing. After sentencing, the court, on written request, must provide the prosecutor, the defendant's lawyer, or the defendant not represented by a lawyer, with a copy of the presentence report and any attachments to it. The court must exempt from disclosure any information the sentencing court exempted from disclosure pursuant to subrule (B).

(D) Sentencing Guidelines. The court must use the sentencing guidelines, as provided by law. Proposed scoring of the guidelines shall accompany the presentence report.

(E) Sentencing Procedure.

(1) The court must sentence the defendant within a reasonably prompt time after the plea or verdict unless the court delays sentencing as provided by law. At sentencing, the court must, on the record:

(a) determine that the defendant, the defendant's lawyer, and the prosecutor have had an opportunity to read and discuss the presentence report,

(b) give each party an opportunity to explain, or challenge the accuracy or relevancy of, any information in the presentence report, and resolve any challenges in accordance with the procedure set forth in subrule (E)(2),

(c) give the defendant, the defendant's lawyer, the prosecutor, and the victim an opportunity to advise the court of any circumstances they believe the court should consider in imposing sentence,

(d) state the sentence being imposed, including the minimum and maximum sentence if applicable, together with any credit for time served to which the defendant is entitled,

(e) if the sentence imposed is not within the guidelines range, articulate the reasons justifying that specific departure, and

(f) order the dollar amount of restitution that the defendant must pay to make full restitution as required by law to any victim of the defendant's course of conduct that gives rise to the conviction, or to that victim's estate.

(2) *Resolution of Challenges.*

(a) If any information in the presentence report is challenged, the court must allow the parties to be heard regarding the challenge, and make a finding with respect to the challenge or determine that a finding is unnecessary because it will not take the challenged information into account in sentencing. If the court finds merit in the challenge or determines that it will not take the challenged information into account in sentencing, it must direct the probation officer to

(i) correct or delete the challenged information in the report, whichever is appropriate, and

(ii) provide defendant's lawyer with an opportunity to review the corrected report before it is sent to the Department of Corrections.

(b) Any dispute as to the proper amount or type of restitution shall be resolved by the court by a preponderance of the evidence. The burden of demonstrating the amount of the loss sustained by a victim as a result of the offense shall be on the prosecuting attorney.

(3) *Incarceration for Nonpayment.*

(a) The court shall not sentence a defendant to a term of incarceration, nor revoke probation, for failure to comply with an order to pay money unless the court finds, on the record, that the defendant is able to comply with the order without manifest hardship and that the defendant has not made a good-faith effort to comply with the order.

(b) Payment Alternatives. If the court finds that the defendant is unable to comply with an order to pay money without manifest hardship, the court may impose a payment alternative, such as a payment plan, modification of any existing payment plan, or waiver of part or all of the amount of money owed to the extent permitted by law.

(c) Determining Manifest Hardship. The court shall consider the following criteria in determining manifest hardship:

(i) Defendant's employment status and history.

(ii) Defendant's employability and earning ability.

(iii) The willfulness of the defendant's failure to pay.

(iv) Defendant's financial resources.

(v) Defendant's basic living expenses including but not limited to food, shelter, clothing, necessary medical expenses, or child support.

(vi) Any other special circumstances that may have bearing on the defendant's ability to pay.

(F) Advice Concerning the Right to Appeal; Appointment of Counsel.

(1) In a case involving a conviction following a trial, immediately after imposing sentence, the court must advise the defendant, on the record, that

(a) the defendant is entitled to appellate review of the conviction and sentence,

(b) if the defendant is financially unable to retain a lawyer, the court will appoint a lawyer to represent the defendant on appeal, and

(c) the request for a lawyer must be filed within 42 days after sentencing.

(2) In a case involving a conviction following a plea of guilty or nolo contendere, immediately after imposing sentence, the court must advise the defendant, on the record, that

(a) the defendant is entitled to file an application for leave to appeal,

(b) if the defendant is financially unable to retain a lawyer, the court will appoint a lawyer to represent the defendant on appeal, and

(c) the request for a lawyer must be filed within 42 days after sentencing.

(3) The court also must give the defendant a request for counsel form containing an instruction informing the defendant that the form must be completed and filed within 42 days after sentencing if the defendant wants the court to appoint a lawyer. The court must give the defendant an opportunity to tender a completed request for counsel form at sentencing if the defendant wishes to do so.

(4) A request for counsel must be deemed filed on the date on which it is received by the court or the Michigan Appellate Assigned Counsel System (MAACS), whichever is earlier.

(5) When imposing sentence in a case in which sentencing guidelines enacted in 1998 PA 317, MCL 777.1 et seq., are applicable, if the court imposes a minimum sentence that is longer or more severe than the range provided by the sentencing guidelines, the court must advise the defendant on the record and in writing that the defendant may seek appellate review of the sentence, by right if the conviction followed trial or by application if the conviction entered by plea, on the

ground that it is longer or more severe than the range provided by the sentencing guidelines.

(G) Appointment of Lawyer and Preparation of Transcript; Scope of Appellate Lawyer's Responsibilities.

(1) *Appointment of Lawyer and Preparation of Transcript.*

(a) All requests for the appointment of appellate counsel must be granted or denied on forms approved by the State Court Administrative Office and provided by MAACS.

(b) Within 7 days after receiving a defendant's request for a lawyer, or within 7 days after the disposition of a postjudgment motion if one is filed, the trial court must submit the request, the judgment of sentence, the register of actions, and any additional requested information to MAACS under procedures approved by the Appellate Defender Commission for the preparation of an appropriate order granting or denying the request. The court must notify MAACS if it intends to deny the request for counsel.

(c) Within 7 days after receiving a request and related information from the trial court, MAACS must provide the court with a proposed order appointing appellate counsel or denying the appointment of appellate counsel. A proposed appointment order must name the State Appellate Defender Office (SADO) or an approved private attorney who is willing to accept an appointment for the appeal.

(d) Within 7 days after receiving a proposed order from MAACS, the trial court must rule on the request for a lawyer. If the defendant is indigent, the court must enter an order appointing a lawyer if the request for a lawyer is filed within 42 days after entry of the judgment of sentence or, if applicable, within the time for filing an appeal of right. The court should liberally grant an untimely request as long as the defendant may file an application for leave to appeal. A denial of counsel must include a statement of reasons.

(e) In a case involving a conviction following a trial, if the defendant's request for a lawyer was filed within the time for filing a claim of appeal, the order must be entered on an approved form entitled "Claim of Appeal and Appointment of Counsel." Entry of the order by the trial court pursuant to this subrule constitutes a timely filed claim of appeal for the purposes of MCR 7.204.

(f) An appointment order must direct the court reporter to prepare and file, within the time limits specified in MCR 7.210, the full transcript of all proceedings, and provide for the payment of the reporter's fees.

(g) The trial court must serve MAACS with a copy of its order granting or denying a request for a lawyer. Unless MAACS has agreed to provide the order to any of the following, the trial court must also serve a copy of its order on the defendant, defense counsel, the prosecutor, and, if the order includes transcripts, the court reporter(s)/recorder(s). If the order is in the form of a Claim of Appeal and Appointment of Counsel, the court must also serve the Court of Appeals with a copy of the order and the judgment being appealed.

(2) *Scope of Appellate Lawyer's Responsibilities.* The responsibilities of the appellate lawyer appointed to represent the defendant include representing the defendant

(a) in available postconviction proceedings in the trial court the lawyer deems appropriate,

(b) in postconviction proceedings in the Court of Appeals,

(c) in available proceedings in the trial court the lawyer deems appropriate under MCR 7.208(B) or 7.211(C)(1), and

(d) as appellee in relation to any postconviction appeal taken by the prosecutor.

[Adopted effective October 1, 1989. Amended effective July 1, 1994, 445 Mich; December 30, 1994, 447 Mich; May 6, 1998, 457 Mich. Amended December 15, 1998, effective January 1, 1999, 459 Mich; March 28, 2000, effective April 1, 2000, 461 Mich; February 1, 2005, effective May 1, 2005, 472 Mich. Amended effective July 13, 2005, 473 Mich. Amended December 14, 2005, effective January 1, 2006, 474 Mich; February 5, 2010, effective May 1, 2010, 485 Mich; July 1, 2010, effective July 1, 2010, 486 Mich; December 29, 2010, effective January 1, 2011, 487 Mich; May 25, 2016, effective September 1, 2016, 499 Mich; March 28, 2018, effective May 1, 2018, 501 Mich; May 15, 2019, effective September 1, 2019, 502 Mich; May 22, 2019, effective September 1, 2019, 502 Mich.]

Comments

Staff Comment to 1989 Adoption

MCR 6.425 is a new rule but incorporates elements of former 6.101.

Subrule (A) is based on MCL 771.14 which sets forth the duties of a probation officer in relation to preparation of presentence reports and prescribes the contents of such reports. This subrule expands the content requirements by including information relevant to sentencing traditionally included in presentence reports. The content of the victim's impact statement described in subrule (A)(7) is set forth in MCL 780.763. The last paragraph of the subrule implements the statutory requirement set forth in MCL 771.14(7).

Subrule (B) is a stylistically revised version of former 6.101(K) except for three substantive modifications. The provision in the former rule requiring the court to give the parties an opportunity to review the presentence report "prior to sentencing" has been modified in this subrule to require the review opportunity to be given "at a reasonable time before the day of sentencing." This rule also modifies the portion of the rule setting forth the procedure for withholding disclosure of confidential or sensitive information in the presentence report. The rule adds the requirements that (1) "[t]o the extent it can do so without defeating the purpose of nondisclosure, the court also must provide the parties with a written or oral summary of the nondisclosed information and give them an opportunity to comment on it," and (2) the "court must have the information exempted from disclosure specifically noted in the report." The procedure requiring, if feasible, the summarizing of nondisclosed information is new. The procedure of specifically noting in the report information withheld from disclosure is not new, but rather, reflects the statutory requirement set forth in MCL 771.14(3).

Subrule (C) is based on, but substantially modifies the procedure set forth in former 6.101(K) for furnishing, after sentencing, a copy of the presentence report to the parties. The former rule required the court to furnish a copy of the report to the parties "[o]n the filing of the defendant's first claim of appeal or application for leave to appeal." Subrule (C) deletes the precondition that a claim of appeal or application be filed and replaces it with the simple requirement of a written request made "after sentencing." A party's right to obtain a copy of the presentence report should not be conditioned on the existence of an appeal since a common objective of obtaining a copy of the report is to determine whether it discloses a ground for appeal. For the same reason, language in the former rule requiring provision of a copy of the report to "the defendant if proceeding without an attorney" has been replaced with "the defendant not represented by a lawyer." This latter language describes an unrepresented defendant who has not yet filed any sort of appeal. A defendant who has filed an appeal and is proceeding in propria persona falls within the definition of "defendant's lawyer." See 6.003(2).

Subrule (D)(1) is new. It incorporates the requirements and procedure for use of the Sentencing Guidelines set forth in Supreme Court administrative orders. The reference to "applicable Sentencing Guidelines" reflects that the guidelines have gone through revisions and that the duty to apply refers to the guidelines version applicable at the time the defendant was sentenced. The language describing the procedure that must be followed is taken verbatim from Administrative Order No. 1988–4.

Subrule (D)(2), setting forth the sentencing procedure, is a substantially modified version of former 6.101(G). It contains a new provision requiring the court to sentence the defendant "within a reasonably prompt time after the plea or verdict unless the court delays sentencing as provided by law." Reasonably prompt sentencing is consistent with existing practice and its inclusion in the rule does not indicate a change in procedure. This provision also takes into account, however, that statutory provisions may authorize the court to delay sentencing. See, for example, MCL 771.1 authorizing in certain cases the court to delay sentencing for a period of up to one year.

Subrule (D)(2)(a) is new but is consistent with current practice and implements the requirement in subrule (B) for the parties to be given an opportunity to review the presentence report before sentencing.

Subrule (D)(2)(b) is new to this rule, but incorporates the requirement in former 6.101(K) for the parties to "be given an opportunity at the time of sentencing to explain or controvert any factual representations in the presentence report."

Subrules (D)(2)(c) and (d) are stylistically revised versions of former 6.101(G)(2) and (3).

Subrule (D)(2)(e) is new and incorporates the articulation requirement adopted in *People v Coles,* 417 Mich 523, 549 (1983).

Subrule (D)(2)(f) is new and implements a requirement in the Crime Victim's Rights Act. MCL 780.766. See also Const 1963, art 1, § 24.

The provision found in former 6.101(G) declaring that a failure to comply with the provisions of that subrule "shall require resentencing" has been deleted from this subrule. Whether failure to comply with a provision in this subrule will entitle a defendant to resentencing depends on the nature of the noncompliance and must be determined by reference to past case law or on an individual case basis.

Subrule (D)(3) is new but sets forth a procedure consistent with the requirements of MCL 771.14(5) and the procedure prescribed in *People v Fleming,* 428 Mich 408, 418 (1987). The procedural requirements of the rule, however, are expanded to require that when, as a result of a challenge, information in the presentence report is deleted or corrected, the defendant's lawyer must be given "an opportunity to review the corrected report before it is sent to the Department of Corrections."

Subrule (E), concerning appellate rights advice at sentencing, is a modified version of former 6.101(J)(1).

Subrule (E)(1) requires the court to advise the defendant of the right to appellate review of both the "conviction and sentence." The advice in the former rule referred to the right to appellate review of the "conviction," but made no mention of the sentence.

Subrule (E)(2) deletes the advice required by the former rule relating to furnishing the appointed lawyer with portions of the transcript and record required to perfect an appeal. There is no need for reference to this right in light of the provisions in these rules fully setting forth the defendant's rights to transcript and record.

Subrule (E)(3) requires the defendant to be advised that the request for an appellate lawyer must be made within 42 days of sentencing. The former rule provided that the request must be made within 56 days.

The last paragraph of subrule (E) is a stylistically revised version of the provision in the former rule requiring the defendant to be provided with a request for counsel form containing pertinent instructions. This provision implements MCL 771.14(7).

Subrule (F) is new but incorporates elements of former 6.101(J)(2).

Subrule (F)(1)(a) sets forth a new requirement for the court to rule on a defendant's request for appellate lawyer "within 14 days after receiving it," unless there is a postjudgment motion pending, in which event the ruling must be made after, but within 14 days of, the disposition of the motion. This provision avoids delay in the appointment of an appellate lawyer, but also avoids dual representation and appointment of an appellate lawyer that may not be necessary if the court grants the defendant relief pursuant to a pending postconviction motion.

Subrule (F)(1)(b) is new but is consistent with general practice. The policy view underlying this provision is that every defendant should have one appeal, either by right or by leave, and it should be with legal representation, particularly in cases that may have arguable appellate issues or involve conviction of a serious offense. In certain cases, the filing of a postjudgment motion will result in the time for requesting appellate counsel [42 days after entry of judgment, see MCR 6.425(E)] expiring while the defendant still has the right to file a claim of appeal [42 days after decision on the motion, MCR 7.204(A)(2)(3)]. In that situation, the court must appoint counsel (assuming the defendant is indigent) if the request is filed while an appeal of right is available.

Subrule (F)(1)(c) is a substantially revised version of former 6.101(J)(2)(a). The rule parallels the like rule pertaining to the "responsibilities" of an appointed trial lawyer, 6.005(H). This subrule reflects the various types of postconviction proceedings available under the scheme of the rules. Subrule (F)(1)(c)(i) refers to "available postconviction proceedings in the trial court" because such proceedings are not available to an appointed appellate lawyer if the appointment order acted as a claim of appeal. See subrule (F)(3). In that event the lawyer may only use the procedures set forth in 7.208(B) or 7.211(C)(1). See, for example, 6.429(B)(2). A lawyer appointed after the claim of appeal period has expired, however, may file a postconviction motion in the trial court before filing an application for leave to appeal. See, for example, 6.429(B)(3). Likewise, a lawyer appointed without a claim of appeal having been filed may not proceed under 7.208(B). Accordingly, subrule (iii) also includes the modifier "available."

Regardless of whether the appointment order acted as a claim of appeal, the appointed lawyer is responsible for representing a defendant in postconviction proceedings in the Court of Appeals (ii) and as appellee in relation to any postconviction appeal taken by the prosecutor (iv). This latter provision reflects the legislatively enlarged right of the prosecutor to appeal by right, and the corresponding responsibility of the appointed appellate lawyer to respond to any appeals, including applications to the Supreme Court, taken by the prosecutor.

Subrules (i) and (iii) recognize that the decision to proceed in the trial court prior to an appeal is within the lawyer's discretion ("the lawyer deems appropriate").

Subrule (F)(2) is a substantially revised version of former 6.101(J)(2) and (3). The appointment order, regardless of whether it also acts as a claim of appeal pursuant to subrule (F)(3), must include directions to the court reporter to prepare and file the trial or plea transcript, the sentencing transcript and whatever other transcripts of recorded proceedings, not previously transcribed, that the court or parties request. The former rule merely provided for the order to authorize the reporter to prepare transcripts requested by the attorney. This new provision will substantially accelerate the preparation of necessary transcripts.

The appointment order must also provide for payment of the reporter's fees. A copy of the order must be served "promptly" on the parties, the court reporter, and the Michigan Appellate Assigned Counsel System. This rule applies only to an order appointing a lawyer to represent a defendant on an appeal of right or by leave.

Subrule (F)(3) is a new rule. It is designed to substantially accelerate the commencement of appeals by having the appointment order also act as a claim of appeal in cases in which the defendant's request for a lawyer was timely, or, if not timely, was made within the time for filing a timely claim of appeal. The subrule further provides that the State Court Administrator's Office is to approve a form for use by the trial courts that will act as a combination order of appointment and claim of appeal. The completed form and a copy of the judgment being appealed from must be sent "immediately" to the Court of Appeals. Copies of the order must also be served as provided in subrule (F)(2) and a proof of such service filed in the Court of Appeals. The last sentence of this rule clarifies that entry of the order by the trial court pursuant to this subrule constitutes the filing of a claim of appeal for jurisdictional purposes under MCR 7.204. The defense need not file anything further in the Court of Appeals to perfect the filing of the claim. Any defects in the filings in the Court of Appeals required by this subrule must be corrected by the trial court but do not affect the validity of the claim of appeal, effectively filed on entry of the appointment order.

Staff Comment to July, 1994 Amendment

The May 2, 1994 amendment of subrule (F)(2)(a)(i), effective July 1, 1994, was based on a proposal from the Michigan Judges Association. The amendment specifies that the court reporter shall not be directed to transcribe the jury voir dire unless certain conditions are met.

Staff Comment to December, 1994 Amendment

The December 30, 1994 amendments of MCR 6.301, 6.302, 6.311, 6.425, 7.203, 7.204 and 7.205 modified procedure regarding appeals in criminal cases in light of the amendment of Const 1963, art 1, § 20 at the November 1994 general election and the legislation implementing the constitutional amendment. Changes will remain in effect until April 1, 1995 and will be reconsidered by the Court in light of comments received and any further legislation.

Staff Comment to May, 1998 Amendment

The May 6, 1998, amendment [effective May 6, 1998] of subrule F(2)(a)(i) removed the limitations on transcription of the jury voir dire that took effect July 1, 1994.

Staff Comment to September, 1999 Amendment

MCR 6.425(D)(1) was amended in 1998 [effective January 1, 1999] in response to the enactment of the sentencing guidelines. 1998 PA 317, MCL 777.1 *et seq.*

Staff Comment to December, 1998 Amendment

MCR 6.425(E)(4) was added in 1998 [effective January 1, 1999] in response to the enactment of the sentencing guidelines. See MCL 769.34(7), as amended by 1998 PA 317.

Staff Comment to 2000 Amendment

The March 28, 2000 amendment of Rules 6.302, 6.425, and 6.615, and the adoption of new Rule 6.625, were made in light of 1999 PA 200, MCL 770.3a, and were effective as to pleas taken on or after April 1, 2000.

Staff Comment to February, 2005 Amendment

The February 1, 2005, effective May 1, 2005, amendments were recommended by the Court of Appeals Record Production Work Group.

The amendment of MCR 6.425(F) expedites the ordering of additional transcripts in criminal appeals that have been requested by appointed counsel by requiring trial courts to order additional transcripts within 14 days after receiving a timely request.

Although the rules contain no specific deadline within which counsel is required to order additional transcripts, the Court of Appeals has always applied a 28-day guideline to ensure that appellate attorneys are quickly reviewing their orders of appointment to determine whether additional transcripts are necessary. Court of Appeals Internal Operating Procedure 7.204(C)(2) states that appointed counsel should review the order shortly after appointment to confirm that all necessary transcripts were ordered. The same concept is stated in IOP 7.210(B)(1)-1. The 28-day guideline is stated in IOP 7.210(B)(l)-2.

The amendment of MCR 7.210(B)(3)(a) enhances an attorney's ability to discover and order missing transcripts in all appeals by requiring the court reporter or recorder to specifically articulate on the certificate for each proceeding requested: the estimated length of the transcript ordered and the identity of the court reporter or recorder responsible for the transcript if it is not the individual filing the certificate.

The amendment of MCR 8.119(D)(1)(c) expedites the ordering of transcripts in all appeals by requiring the circuit court's register of actions to include a notation as to whether a hearing was held on the record, and the name and certification number of the court reporter or recorder responsible for transcribing the hearing. The subrule is also divided for the ease of the reader.

Staff Comment to July, 2005 Amendment

On March 12, 2002, the Court appointed the Committee on the Rules of Criminal Procedure to review the rules to determine whether any of the provisions should be revised. The committee issued its report on June 16, 2003, recommending numerous amendments of MCR 6.302 and 6.725. The committee did not recommend any amendments of MCR 6.625. A public hearing on the committee's recommendation was held May 27, 2004.

The Court adopted most of the committee's recommendations regarding Rule 6.302, and modified the rule to conform to the ruling of the United States Supreme Court in *Halbert v Michigan*, 545 US ___; 2005 WL 1469183 (June 23, 2005).

The Court adopted many of the committee's recommendations concerning MCR 6.425, however, the Court eliminated the requirement that "[n]ot later than the date of sentencing, the court must complete a sentencing information report on a form to be prescribed by and returned to the state court administrator" in MCR 6.425(D). The Court also modified the language of the rule to incorporate the Court's holding in *People v Babcock*, 469 Mich 247 (2003) and to conform to the ruling in *Halbert*.

The Court did not follow the committee's recommendation that MCR 6.625 not be amended, but instead modified the rule to conform to the ruling in *Halbert*.

Staff Comment to Deember, 2005 Amendment

The amendment of MCR 6.425 was made to more accurately reflect the holding of the United States Supreme Court in *Halbert v Michigan*, 545 US 605; 205 WL 1469183 (June 23, 2005).

Staff Comment to February, 2010 Amendment

The amendments of Rules 6.425 and 6.610 of the Michigan Court Rules were submitted by the Representative Assembly of the State Bar of Michigan. The amendments increase the time within which a court is required to provide copies of the presentence report to the prosecutor, the defendant's lawyer, or the defendant if not represented by a lawyer, to at least two business days before the day of sentencing. If the report is not made available at least two days before sentencing, the prosecutor or defendant's lawyer, or the defendant, when not represented by a lawyer, is entitled to an adjournment to prepare any necessary corrections, additions, or deletions to present to the court. The revisions of these rules also prohibit the inclusion of specific information in the report about the victim or witness, and require that the court instruct those who review the report that they are precluded from making a copy of the report and must return their copy to the court before or at the defendant's sentencing. The confidentiality provision is based on MCL 791.229.

Staff Comment to July, 2010 Amendment

By order dated February 5, 2010, the Court adopted various amendments of MCR 6.425 and MCR 6.610 to require prosecutors and defendants to have access to the presentence investigation report at least two days before sentencing and allow adjournment if the parties do not receive the report in that time, to ensure the confidentiality of the PSI report, and to limit the victim or witness information that may be included in a PSI report. Following entry of the February order and shortly after its May 1, 2010, effective date, the Court considered the matter further, specifically with regard to mandatory confidentiality provisions that not only represented a significant change in current practice, but, also, underscored a fundamental tension between the explicit provisions of MCL 791.229, which describes who may have a copy of the report and for what purposes, and subsequent caselaw, which has expanded access of PSI reports in certain circumstances. In light of this tension, the Court has invited interested associations that oppose the language as adopted by the Court to approach the Legislature to resolve the conflict. However, if legislation on this subject is not enacted and effective by the end of this calendar year, an amendment to allow prosecutors, defense counsel, and defendants to retain a copy of the presentence investigation report will automatically go into effect on January 1, 2011.

Staff Comment to December, 2010 Amendment

This order codifies statutory changes enacted as 2010 PA 247 and 2010 PA 248.

Staff Comment to 2016 Amendment

The amendments of MCR 3.605, 3.606, 3.928, 3.944, 3.956, 6.001, 6.425, 6.445, 6.610, and 6.933 were submitted by the Michigan State Planning Body for the Delivery of Legal Services to the Poor. The rule revisions are intended to provide clarity and guidance to courts regarding what courts would be required to do before incarcerating a defendant for failure to pay.

Staff Comment to 2018 Amendment

The amendments of MCR 6.425(G) reflect recent changes to the appellate counsel assignment process by extending and segmenting the timeframe for courts to respond to appointment requests, requiring judges to provide a statement of reason when appellate counsel is denied, encouraging courts to liberally grant untimely requests for appellate counsel in guilty plea cases, requiring the filing of all lower court transcripts as part of an order appointing counsel, and clarifying MAACS' assumption of the trial court's service obligations.

Staff Comment to (May 15), September, 2019 Amendment

The amendment of MCR 6.425 makes the rule consistent that requests for counsel must be completed and filed with the court or submitted to MAACS within 42 days after sentencing and allows defendants the opportunity to tender a completed form at sentencing. It also removes the requirement for a sentencing judge to articulate substantial and compelling reasons to deviate from the guidelines range, pursuant to *People v Lockridge*, 498 Mich 358; 870 NW2d 502 (2015).

Staff Comment to (May 22), September, 2019 Amendment

The amendments more explicitly require restitution to be ordered at the time of sentencing as required by statute, and establish a procedure for modifying restitution amounts.

Rule 6.427. Judgment

Within 7 days after sentencing, the court must date and sign a written judgment of sentence that includes:

(1) the title and file number of the case;

(2) the defendant's name;

(3) the crime for which the defendant was convicted;

(4) the defendant's plea;

(5) the name of the defendant's attorney if one appeared;

(6) the jury's verdict or the finding of guilt by the court;

(7) the term of the sentence;

(8) the place of detention;

(9) the conditions incident to the sentence;

(10) whether the conviction is reportable to the Secretary of State pursuant to statute, and, if so, the defendant's Michigan driver's license number; and

(11) the dollar amount of restitution that the defendant is ordered to pay.

If the defendant was found not guilty or for any other reason is entitled to be discharged, the court must enter judgment accordingly. The date a judgment is signed is its entry date.
[Adopted effective October 1, 1989. Amended July 13, 2005, effective January 1, 2006, 473 Mich; May 22, 2019, effective September 1, 2019, 502 Mich.]

Comments

Staff Comment to 1989 Adoption

MCR 6.427 restates the former judgment rule, 6.103, and adds two provisions. Subrule (10) is added to accommodate the recording and reporting requirements set forth in MCL 257.732. The second addition is the penultimate sentence in the rule, which reflects that entry of judgment is also required in the event that the defendant is entitled to discharge.

Staff Comment to 2005 Amendment

On March 12, 2002, the Court appointed the Committee on the Rules of Criminal Procedure to review the rules to determine whether any of the provisions should be revised. The committee issued its report on June 16, 2003, recommending numerous amendments to existing rules, plus some new rules. A public hearing on the committee's recommendations was held May 27, 2004.

The Court adopted the committee's recommendations with respect to the amendments of Rules 2.511, 6.102, 6.104, 6.107, 6.112, 6.303, 6.304, 6.310, 6.311, 6.402, 6.412, 6.414, 6.419, 6.420, 6.427, 6.615, and 6.620, and the adoption of a new Rule 6.428.

Staff Comment to 2019 Amendment

The amendments more explicitly require restitution to be ordered at the time of sentencing as required by statute, and establish a procedure for modifying restitution amounts.

Rule 6.428   Reissuance of Judgment

If the defendant did not appeal within the time allowed by MCR 7.204(A)(2) and demonstrates that the attorney or attorneys retained or appointed to represent the defendant on direct appeal from the judgment either disregarded the defendant's instruction to perfect a timely appeal of right, or otherwise failed to provide effective assistance, and, but for counsel's deficient performance, the defendant would have perfected a timely appeal of right, the trial court shall issue an order restarting the time in which to file an appeal of right. [Adopted July 13, 2005, effective January 1, 2006, 473 Mich.]

Comments

Staff Comment to 2005 Adoption

On March 12, 2002, the Court appointed the Committee on the Rules of Criminal Procedure to review the rules to determine whether any of the provisions should be revised. The committee issued its report on June 16, 2003, recommending numerous amendments to existing rules, plus some new rules. A public hearing on the committee's recommendations was held May 27, 2004.

The Court adopted the committee's recommendations with respect to the amendments of Rules 2.511, 6.102, 6.104, 6.107, 6.112, 6.303, 6.304, 6.310, 6.311, 6.402, 6.412, 6.414, 6.419, 6.420, 6.427, 6.615, and 6.620, and the adoption of a new Rule 6.428.

Rule 6.429.   Correction and Appeal of Sentence

(A) Authority to Modify Sentence. The court may correct an invalid sentence, on its own initiative after giving the parties an opportunity to be heard, or on motion by either party. But the court may not modify a valid sentence after it has been imposed except as provided by law. Any correction of an invalid sentence on the court's own initiative must occur within 6 months of the entry of the judgment of conviction and sentence.

(B) Time for Filing Motion.

(1) A motion to correct an invalid sentence may be filed before the filing of a timely claim of appeal.

(2) If a claim of appeal has been filed, a motion to correct an invalid sentence may only be filed in accordance with the procedure set forth in MCR 7.208(B) or the remand procedure set forth in MCR 7.211(C)(1).

(3) If the defendant may only appeal by leave or fails to file a timely claim of appeal, a motion to correct an invalid sentence may be filed:

(a) within 6 months of entry of the judgment of conviction and sentence, or,

(b) if 6 months have elapsed since entry of the judgment of conviction and sentence, the defendant may file a motion to correct an invalid sentence if:

(i) the defendant has filed a request for the appointment of counsel pursuant to MCR 6.425(G)(1) within the 6-month period,

(ii) The defendant or defendant's lawyer, if one is appointed, has ordered the appropriate transcripts within 28 days of service of the order granting or denying the request for counsel or substitute counsel, unless the transcript has already been filed or has been ordered by the court under MCR 6.425(G), and

(iii) The motion to correct invalid sentence is filed in accordance with the provisions of this subrule within 42 days after the filing of the transcript. If the transcript was filed before the order appointing counsel or substitute counsel, or the order or denying the appointment of counsel, the 42-day period runs from the date of that order.

(4) If the defendant is no longer entitled to appeal by right or by leave, the defendant may seek relief pursuant to the procedure set forth in subchapter 6.500.

(5) If a motion to correct an invalid sentence is received by the court after the expiration of the periods set forth above, and if the appellant is an inmate in the custody of the Michigan Department of Corrections and has submitted the motion as a pro se party, the motion shall be deemed presented for filing on the date of deposit of the motion in the outgoing mail at the correctional institution in which the inmate is housed. Timely filing may be shown by a sworn statement filed with the motion, which must set forth the date of deposit and state that first-class postage has been prepaid. The exception applies to cases in which a judgment of conviction and sentence is entered on or after the effective date of this amendment. This exception also applies to an inmate housed in a penal institution in another state or in a federal penal institution who seeks to correct an invalid sentence in a Michigan court.

(C) Preservation of Issues Concerning Sentencing Guidelines Scoring and Information Considered in Sentencing. A party shall not raise on appeal an issue challenging the scoring of the sentencing guidelines or challenging the accuracy of information relied upon in determining a sentence that is within the appropriate guidelines sentence range unless the party has raised the issue at sentencing, in a proper motion for resentencing, or in a proper motion to remand filed in the court of appeals. [Adopted effective October 1, 1989. Amended January 26, 1996, effective April 1, 1996, 450 Mich. Amended effective June 29, 2004, 470 Mich. Amended July 13, 2005, effective January 1, 2006, 473 Mich; April 19, 2018, effective May 1, 2018, 501 Mich; May 23, 2018, effective September 1, 2018, 501 Mich; August 30, 2018, effective September 1, 2018, 502 Mich.]

Comments

Staff Comment to 1989 Adoption

MCR 6.429 is a new rule.

Subrule (A) states the settled principle in this jurisdiction that the trial court may not modify a valid sentence after it has been imposed. See *People v Barfield*, 411 Mich 700 (1981). The Legislature, however, has authorized trial courts to modify some types of sentences. See, for example, MCL 801.257 authorizing trial courts to reduce the sentence of jail inmates by one-quarter for good conduct.

Although the trial court may not modify a valid sentence, it may correct an invalid sentence after it has been imposed. See *People v Whalen*, 412 Mich 166 (1981). Invalid sentence refers to any error or defect in the sentence or sentencing procedure that entitles a defendant to be resentenced or to have the sentence changed.

Subrule (B) sets the times within which a motion for resentencing may be filed.

Subrule (B)(1) sets the basic time at 42 days after the entry of the judgment. Such a timely motion extends the time for filing a claim of appeal. See MCR 7.204(A)(2)(d). The remaining subrules follow the filing of later motions that do not have the effect of extending the time for taking an appeal of right.

Under subrule (B)(2), if a claim of appeal has been filed, typically as a result of the appointment of appellate counsel [see MCR 6.425(F)(3)], the motion must be made in the manner provided in MCR 7.208(B) or by seeking an order of the Court of Appeals remanding the case to the trial court under MCR 7.211(C)(1).

Subrule (B)(3) provides that if a defendant fails to file a timely claim of appeal, the motion for resentencing may be filed at any time before expiration of the time for filing an application for leave to appeal.

Finally, under subrule (B)(4), a defendant who is not entitled to appeal by right or by leave, either because the defendant has had an appeal or because the 18–month time limit has expired [see MCR 7.205(F)(3)], may only seek relief under the procedure provided by Subchapter 6.500.

The rules governing motions for judgment of acquittal [MCR 6.419(B)], to withdraw a plea [MCR 6.311(A)], and for new trial [MCR 6.431(A)], have similar time limits.

Subrule (C) incorporates the issue preservation requirement adopted in *People v Walker*, 428 Mich 261, 266 (1987), for challenges to Sentencing Guidelines scoring. The rule provides that a defendant who wishes to challenge the scoring of Sentencing Guidelines must make the challenge in the trial court before raising it on the defendant's initial appeal, whether that appeal is by right or by leave. The rule further sets forth the various methods by which the defendant may raise the issue in the trial court.

Staff Comment to 1996 Amendment

The amendment of MCR 6.429(C) modifies the rule governing preservation of issues regarding sentence guideline scoring and presentence report information. Such challenges must be made at or before sentencing unless the party demonstrates that the challenge was brought as soon as the inaccuracy could reasonably have been discovered.

Staff Comment to 2004 Amendment

The June 29, 2004 amendment of MCR 6.429(C), effective immediately, conformed the rule to MCL 769.34(10) by incorporating the statutory language.

Staff Comment to 2005 Amendment

On March 12, 2002, the Court appointed the Committee on the Rules of Criminal Procedure to review the rules to determine whether any of the provisions should be revised. The committee issued its report on June 16, 2003, recommending numerous amendments to existing rules, plus some new rules. A public hearing on the committee's recommendations was held May 27, 2004.

The Court adopted the committee's recommendations with respect to the amendments of Rules 2.511, 6.102, 6.104, 6.107, 6.112, 6.303, 6.304, 6.310, 6.311, 6.402, 6.412, 6.414, 6.419, 6.420, 6.427, 6.615, and 6.620, and the adoption of a new Rule 6.428.

The Court also adopted, with modifications, recommendations made by the committee and staff to amend other rules. Rule 2.510 was amended to conform to the newly enacted 2004 PA 12 (MCL 600.1332). The Court modified the committee's recommendation concerning Rule 6.001 to include a reference to 6.102 and to limit the application of 6.445 to subrules (A) through (G). The Court adopted the committee's recommendation with regard to Rule 6.004, except that the requirement that "whenever the defendant's constitutional right to a speedy trial is violated, the defendant is entitled to dismissal of the charge with prejudice" was retained and inserted into 6.004(A).

Rules 6.429 and 6.431 were amended to provide that if the defendant may only appeal by leave or fails to file a timely claim of appeal, a motion to correct an invalid sentence or a motion for a new trial may be filed within 6 months of entry of the judgment of conviction and sentence.

Staff Comment to First May, 2018 Amendment

The amendments, submitted by SADO, are intended to clarify practices and provide protections for criminal defendants represented by assigned appellate counsel. The amendments allow an additional 42 days to file post-judgment motions in certain circumstances, and where delay is due to the trial court, clarify in the amendment of MCR 7.205 that in certain circumstances, substitute appellate counsel may file a delayed application for leave to appeal within 42 days of appointment (even if later than six months after sentencing), add language to MCR 7.211 to guide parties and courts if relief is granted in the trial court, and

change the procedure for seeking permission to file a brief longer than 50 pages in length.

Staff Comment to Second May, 2018 Amendment

The amendments of MCR 6.310, 6.429, and 6.431 establish a "prison-mailbox" rule for post-sentencing motions to withdraw plea, motions to correct an invalid sentence, and motions for new trial, filed by *in pro per* defendants in the custody of the Department of Corrections.

Staff Comment to First September, 2018 Amendment

This amendment provides trial courts with authority to *sua sponte* address erroneous judgments of sentence, following the Court's recent consideration of the issue in *People v Comer*, 500 Mich 278 (2017). The amendment requires any such correction initiated by the court to occur within six months after entry of the judgment of conviction and sentence.

Staff Comment to Second September, 2018 Amendment

These amendments update cross-references in the rules, and are intended to reflect changes that are necessary as a result of the Court's recent e-Filing rules amendments.

Rule 6.430. Postjudgment Motion to Amend Restitution

(A) The court may amend an order of restitution entered under this section on a motion filed by the prosecuting attorney, the victim, or the defendant based upon new or updated information related to the injury, damages, or loss for which the restitution was ordered.

(B) Filing. The moving party must file the motion and a copy of the motion with the clerk of the court in which the defendant was convicted and sentenced. Upon receipt of a motion, the clerk shall file it under the same case number as the original conviction. If an appeal is pending when the motion is filed, the moving party must serve a copy on the appellate court.

(C) Service and Notice of Hearing. If the defendant is the moving party, he/she shall serve a copy of the motion and notice of its filing on the prosecuting attorney and the prosecutor shall then serve a copy of the motion and notice upon the victim. If the prosecutor is the moving party, he/she shall serve a copy of the motion and notice of its filing on the defendant and the victim. If the victim is the moving party, he/she shall serve a copy of the motion and notice of its filing on the defendant and the prosecutor. The home address, home telephone number, work address, and work telephone number of the victim, if included on a motion to amend restitution, is nonpublic. The non-moving party is permitted but not required to respond. Any response to the motion shall comply with the time for service of the response as provided in MCR 2.119(C)(2). The court shall provide written notice of hearing on the motion to the defendant and prosecutor. The prosecutor shall then serve notice of hearing upon the victim.

(D) Appearance. As permitted by MCR 6.006(A), the court may allow the defendant to appear by two-way interactive video technology to conduct the proceeding between a courtroom and a prison, jail, or other location.

(E) Ruling. The court, in writing, shall enter an appropriate order disposing of the motion and, if the motion is granted, enter an order amending the restitution. If an appeal was pending when the motion was filed, the moving party must provide a copy of the order to the appellate court.

(F) Appeal. An appeal from this subsection is processed as provided by MCR 7.100 *et seq.*, and 7.200 *et seq.*

[Adopted May 22, 2019, effective September 1, 2019, 502 Mich.]

Staff Comment to 2019 Adoption

The amendments more explicitly require restitution to be ordered at the time of sentencing as required by statute, and establish a procedure for modifying restitution amounts.

Rule 6.431.   New Trial

(A) Time for Making Motion.

(1) A motion for a new trial may be filed before the filing of a timely claim of appeal.

(2) If a claim of appeal has been filed, a motion for a new trial may only be filed in accordance with the procedure set forth in MCR 7.208(B) or the remand procedure set forth in MCR 7.211(C)(1).

(3) If the defendant may only appeal by leave or fails to file a timely claim of appeal, a motion for a new trial may be filed:

(a) within 6 months of entry of the judgment of conviction and sentence, or

(b) If 6 months have elapsed since entry of the judgment of conviction and sentence, the defendant may file a motion for new trial if:

(i) the defendant has filed a request for the appointment of counsel pursuant to MCR 6.425(G)(1) within the 6–month period,

(ii) the defendant or defendant's lawyer, if one is appointed, has ordered the appropriate transcripts within 28 days of service of the order granting or denying the request for counsel or substitute counsel, unless the transcript has already been filed or has been ordered by the court under MCR 6.425(G), and

(iii) the motion for a new trial is filed in accordance with the provisions of this subrule within 42 days after the filing of the transcript. If the transcript was filed before the order appointing counsel or substitute counsel, or the order denying the appointment of counsel, the 42–day period runs from the date of that order.

(4) If the defendant is no longer entitled to appeal by right or by leave, the defendant may seek relief pursuant to the procedure set forth in subchapter 6.500.

(5) If a motion for new trial is received by the court after the expiration of the periods set forth above, and if the appellant is an inmate in the custody of the Michigan Department of Corrections and has submitted the motion as a pro se party, the motion shall be deemed presented for filing on the date of deposit of the motion in the outgoing mail at the correctional institution in which the inmate is housed. Timely filing may be shown by a sworn statement filed with the motion, which must set forth the date of deposit and state that first-class postage has been prepaid. The exception applies to cases in which the trial court rendered its decision on or after the effective date of this amendment. This exception also applies to an inmate housed in a penal institution in another state or in a federal penal institution who seeks a new trial in a Michigan court.

(B) Reasons for Granting.

On the defendant's motion, the court may order a new trial on any ground that would support appellate reversal of the conviction or because it believes that the verdict has resulted in a miscarriage of justice. The court must state its reasons for granting or denying a new trial orally on the record or in a written ruling made a part of the record.

(C) Trial Without Jury.

If the court tried the case without a jury, it may, on granting a new trial and with the defendant's consent, vacate any judgment it has entered, take additional testimony, amend its findings of fact and conclusions of law, and order the entry of a new judgment.

(D) Inclusion of Motion for Judgment of Acquittal.

The court must consider a motion for a new trial challenging the weight or sufficiency of the evidence as including a motion for a directed verdict of acquittal.

[Adopted effective October 1, 1989. Amended July 13, 2005, effective January 1, 2006, 473 Mich; April 19, 2018, effective May 1, 2018, 501 Mich; May 23, 2018, effective September 1, 2018, 501 Mich; August 30, 2018, effective September 1, 2018, 502 Mich.]

Staff Comment to 1989 Adoption

MCR 6.431 is a new rule.

Subrule (A) sets the time limits within which a motion for new trial may be filed.

Subrule (A)(1) sets the basic time at 42 days after the entry of judgment. Such a timely motion extends the time for filing the claim of appeal. See MCR 7.204(A)(2)(d). The remaining subrules follow the filing of later motions that do not have the effect of extending the time for taking an appeal of right.

Under subrule (A)(2), if a claim of appeal has been filed, typically as a result of the appointment of appellate counsel [see MCR 6.425(F)(3)], the motion must be made in the manner provided in MCR 7.208(B) or by seeking an order of the Court of Appeals remanding the case to the trial court under MCR 7.211(C)(1).

Subrule (A)(3) provides that if a defendant fails to file a timely claim of appeal, the motion to withdraw the plea may be filed at any time before expiration of the time for filing an application for leave to appeal.

Finally, under subrule (A)(4), a defendant who is not entitled to appeal by right or by leave, either because the defendant has had an appeal or because the 18–month time limit has expired [see MCR 7.205(F)(3)], may only seek relief under the procedure provided by Subchapter 6.500.

The rules governing motions for judgment of acquittal [MCR 6.419(B)], to withdraw a plea [MCR 6.311(A)], and for resentencing [MCR 6.429(B)], have similar time limits.

Subrule (B) substantially modifies the statutory standards for granting a new trial set forth in MCL 770.1 and applied by the courts. See *People v Hampton*, 407 Mich 354, 372–373 (1979). The statute provides that the trial court may grant a new trial (1) "for any cause for which by law a new trial may be granted," or (2) "when it appears to the court that justice has not been done." Although the court rule repeats in stylistically revised language the first standard, it substitutes a new second standard: "Because [the trial court] believes the verdict has resulted in a miscarriage of justice." What substantive difference, if any, exists between the new standard and the former standard is left to be addressed by case law.

Subrule (C) incorporates the provisions in MCR 2.611(A)(2) and adds a condition found in the Uniform Rules of Criminal Procedure, Rule 552(a), requiring "the defendant's consent."

Subrule (D) is derived from MCR 2.610(A)(3), which requires a motion for new trial to be "deemed to include a motion for judgment notwithstanding the verdict as an alternative." Subrule (D), however, limits its own applicability to a motion for new trial "challenging the weight or sufficiency of the evidence." When making findings pursuant to this rule the trial court should clearly distinguish on the record and in its order its disposition of the two motions. See 6.419(D).

Staff Comment to 2005 Amendment

On March 12, 2002, the Court appointed the Committee on the Rules of Criminal Procedure to review the rules to determine whether any of the provisions should be revised. The committee issued its report on June 16, 2003, recommending numerous amendments to existing rules, plus some new rules. A public hearing on the committee's recommendations was held May 27, 2004.

The Court adopted the committee's recommendations with respect to the amendments of Rules 2.511, 6.102, 6.104, 6.107, 6.112, 6.303, 6.304, 6.310, 6.311, 6.402, 6.412, 6.414, 6.419, 6.420, 6.427, 6.615, and 6.620, and the adoption of a new Rule 6.428.

The Court also adopted, with modifications, recommendations made by the committee and staff to amend other rules. Rule 2.510 was amended to conform to the newly enacted 2004 PA 12 (MCL 600.1332). The Court modified the committee's recommendation concerning Rule 6.001 to include a reference to 6.102 and to limit the application of 6.445 to subrules (A) through (G). The Court adopted the committee's recommendation with regard to Rule 6.004, except that the requirement that "whenever the defendant's constitutional right to a speedy trial is violated, the defendant is entitled to dismissal of the charge with prejudice" was retained and inserted into 6.004(A).

Rules 6.429 and 6.431 were amended to provide that if the defendant may only appeal by leave or fails to file a timely claim of appeal, a motion to correct an invalid sentence or a motion for a new trial may be filed within 6 months of entry of the judgment of conviction and sentence.

Staff Comment to May, 2018 Amendment

The amendments, submitted by SADO, are intended to clarify practices and provide protections for criminal defendants represented by assigned appellate counsel. The amendments allow an additional 42 days to file post-judgment motions in certain circumstances, and where delay is due to the trial court, clarify in the amendment of MCR 7.205 that in certain circumstances, substitute appellate counsel may file a delayed application for leave to appeal within 42 days of appointment (even if later than six months after sentencing), add language to MCR 7.211 to guide parties and courts if relief is granted in the trial court, and change the procedure for seeking permission to file a brief longer than 50 pages in length.

Staff Comment to First September, 2018 Amendment

The amendments of MCR 6.310, 6.429, and 6.431 establish a "prison-mailbox" rule for post-sentencing motions to withdraw plea, motions to correct an invalid sentence, and motions for new trial, filed by *in pro per* defendants in the custody of the Department of Corrections.

Staff Comment to Second September, 2018 Amendment

These amendments update cross-references in the rules, and are intended to reflect changes that are necessary as a result of the Court's recent e-Filing rules amendments.

Rule 6.433   Documents for Postconviction Proceedings; Indigent Defendant

(A) Appeals of Right. An indigent defendant may file a written request with the sentencing court for specified court documents or transcripts, indicating that they are required to pursue an appeal of right. The court must order the clerk to provide the defendant with copies of documents without cost to the defendant, and, unless the transcript has already been ordered as provided in MCR 6.425(G), must order the preparation of the transcript.

(B) Appeals by Leave. An indigent defendant who may file an application for leave to appeal may obtain copies of transcripts and other documents as provided in this subrule.

(1) The defendant must make a written request to the sentencing court for specified documents or transcripts indicating that they are required to prepare an application for leave to appeal.

(2) If the requested materials have been filed with the court and not provided previously to the defendant, the court clerk must provide a copy to the defendant. If the requested materials have been provided previously to the defendant, on defendant's showing of good cause to the court, the clerk must provide the defendant with another copy.

(3) If the request includes the transcript of a proceeding that has not been transcribed, the court must order the materials transcribed and filed with court. After the transcript has been prepared, court clerk must provide a copy to the defendant.

(C) Other Postconviction Proceedings. An indigent defendant who is not eligible to file an appeal of right or an application for leave to appeal may obtain records and documents as provided in this subrule.

(1) The defendant must make a written request to the sentencing court for specific court documents or transcripts indicating that the materials are required to pursue postconviction remedies in a state or federal court and are not otherwise available to the defendant.

(2) If the documents or transcripts have been filed with the court and not provided previously to the defendant, the clerk must provide the defendant with copies of such materials without cost to the defendant. If the requested materials have been provided previously to the defendant, on defendant's showing of good cause to the court, the clerk must provide the defendant with another copy.

(3) The court may order the transcription of additional proceedings if it finds that there is good cause for doing so. After such a transcript has been prepared, the clerk must provide a copy to the defendant.

(4) Nothing in this rule precludes the court from ordering materials to be supplied to the defendant in a proceeding under subchapter 6.500.

[Adopted effective October 1, 1989. Amended May 2, 1994, effective July 1, 1994, 445 Mich. Amended effective May 6, 1998, 459 Mich. Amended March 15, 2007, effective May 1, 2007, 477 Mich; May 18, 2010, effective September 1, 2010, 486 Mich; August 30, 2018, effective September 1, 2018, 502 Mich.]

Comments

Staff Comment to 1989 Adoption

MCR 6.433 covers the subject of providing copies of court documents and transcripts to indigent defendants for use on appeal or in other postconviction proceedings. It covers the subject in more detail than the corresponding provision of the former rule, MCR 6.101(L). The new rule is structured around the various types of postconviction procedures available.

Subrule (A) deals with the provision of documents for use in appeals of right. At this stage, the defendant has the broadest right of access to free copies of documents and transcripts.

Subrule (B) deals with a defendant who is eligible to file an application for leave to appeal—i.e., a defendant who has not previously appealed of right or sought leave to appeal and as to whom the 18–month time limit on applications has not expired. See MCR 7.205(F)(3). Such a defendant is entitled to copies of materials that have not been previously furnished to the defendant. As to materials that have been previously furnished, the defendant must show good cause to be entitled to a new copy. If proceedings have not been transcribed, the court is to order preparation of the transcript.

Subrule (C) deals with defendants who are not eligible to appeal by right or to apply for leave to appeal. Such defendants have more restricted rights to documents. There is a threshold requirement that the documents are not otherwise available to the defendant. If that standard is met, documents or transcripts that had been filed with the court are to be supplied to the defendant. The court has discretion as to whether to order transcription of additional proceedings on a finding of good cause.

Staff Comment to 1994 Amendment

The May 2, 1994 amendment, which added subrule (D), effective July 1, 1994, was based on a proposal from the Michigan Judges Association. The amendment specifies that the court shall not order the transcript of the jury voir dire unless certain conditions are met.

Staff Comment to 1998 Amendment

The May 6, 1998, deletion of subrule D removed the limitations on transcription of the jury voir dire that took effect July 1, 1994.

Staff Comment to 2007 Amendment

These changes reflect relettered provisions of MCR 6.425.

Staff Comment to 2010 Amendment

This amendment inserts a "good cause" provision into MCR 6.433(C) to require a defendant in postconviction proceedings to show good cause to obtain a second set of court documents. Th is amendment mirrors the good-cause provision in MCR 6.433(B)(2) for appeals by leave.

Staff Comment to 2018 Amendment

These amendments update cross-references in the rules, and are intended to reflect changes that are necessary as a result of the Court's recent e-Filing rules amendments.

Rule 6.435   Correcting Mistakes

(A) Clerical Mistakes. Clerical mistakes in judgments, orders, or other parts of the record and errors arising from oversight or omission may be corrected by the court at any time on its own initiative or on motion of a party, and after notice if the court orders it.

(B) Substantive Mistakes. After giving the parties an opportunity to be heard, and provided it has not yet entered judgment in the case, the court may reconsider and modify, correct, or rescind any order it concludes was erroneous.

(C) Correction of Record. If a dispute arises as to whether the record accurately reflects what occurred in the trial court, the court, after giving the parties the opportunity to be heard, must resolve the dispute and, if necessary, order the record to be corrected.

(D) Correction During Appeal. If a claim of appeal has been filed or leave to appeal granted in the case, corrections under this rule are subject to MCR 7.208(A) and (B).

[Adopted effective October 1, 1989.]

Comments

Staff Comment to 1989 Adoption

MCR 6.435 is a new rule that combines former court rule provisions with a new provision.

Subrule (A) repeats verbatim the civil clerical mistakes rule, MCR 2.612(A)(1). Under this rule the court may correct an inadvertent error or omission in the record, or in an order or judgment. The correction can be made by the court at any time subject to the limitation in subrule (D) pertaining to cases on appeal. The court, in its discretion, may give the parties prior notice.

Subrule (B) is new and pertains to mistakes relating not to the accuracy of the record, but rather, to the correctness of the conclusions and decisions reflected in the record. Substantive mistake refers to a conclusion or decision that is erroneous because it was based on a mistaken belief in the facts or the applicable law. Unlike clerical mistakes under subrule (A), the court's ability to correct substantive mistakes pursuant to subrule (B) ends with the entry of the judgment. See 6.427. This limitation does not, however, prohibit a party aggrieved by a substantive mistake from obtaining relief by using available postconviction procedures.

The following examples illustrate the distinction between the two foregoing provisions. A prison sentence entered on a judgment that is erroneous because the judge misspoke or the clerk made a typing error is correctable under subrule (A). A prison sentence entered on a judgment that is erroneous because the judge relied on mistaken facts (for example, confused codefendants) or made a mistake of law (for example, unintentionally imposed a sentence in violation of the *Tanner* rule) is a substantive mistake and is correctable by the judge under subrule (B) until the judge signs the judgment, but not afterwards. In the latter event, however, the defendant may obtain relief by filing a postconviction motion. See 6.429.

Subrule (C) is consistent with MCR 7.208(B)(2) but it is patterned stylistically after Federal Rule of Appellate Procedure 10(e).

Subrule (D) repeats the limitation in MCR 2.612(A)(2) applicable to corrections under subrule (A) when a case is on appeal but expands it to reflect that this limitation is applicable as well to corrections of the record under subrule (C). See 7.208(B).

Rule 6.440   Disability of Judge

(A) During Jury Trial. If, by reason of death, sickness, or other disability, the judge before whom a jury trial has commenced is unable to continue with the trial, another judge regularly sitting in or assigned to the court, on certification of having become familiar with the record of the trial, may proceed with and complete the trial.

(B) During Bench Trial. If a judge becomes disabled during a trial without a jury, another judge may be substituted for the disabled judge, but only if

(1) both parties consent in writing to the substitution, and

(2) the judge certifies having become familiar with the record of the trial, including the testimony previously given.

(C) After Verdict. If, after a verdict is returned or findings of fact and conclusions of law are filed, the trial judge because of disability becomes unable to perform the remaining duties the court must perform, another judge regularly sitting in or assigned to the court may perform those duties; but if that judge is not satisfied of an ability to perform those duties because of not having presided at the trial or determines that it is appropriate for any other reason, the judge may grant the defendant a new trial.

[Adopted effective October 1, 1989.]

Comments

Staff Comment to 1989 Adoption

MCR 6.440 is a new rule.

Subrule (A) is based on Federal Rule of Criminal Procedure 25(a) and substantially changes existing law. Under MCR 2.630 substitution of a judge due to disability in a jury trial case is limited to "after a verdict is returned." Under subrule (A), substitution is permissible during a jury trial provided the substitute judge has certified "having become familiar with the record of the trial."

Subrule (B) is based on Rule 741(e) of the Uniform Rules of Criminal Procedure and likewise substantially changes existing law. Substitution of a judge presiding over a bench trial is limited by MCR 2.630 to after the "findings of fact and conclusions of law are filed." Under subrule (B) substitution is permissible during a bench trial if the parties give their consent in writing *and* if the substitute judge has certified "having become familiar with the record of the trial, including the testimony previously given."

Subrule (C) is a modified version of MCR 2.630 that adds a provision from Federal Rule of Criminal Procedure 25(b) allowing a substitute judge to grant a new trial not only if the judge is not satisfied of having the ability to perform the remaining duties, but also if the judge determines that a new trial is "appropriate for any other reason."

Rule 6.445   Probation Revocation

(A) Issuance of Summons; Warrant. On finding probable cause to believe that a probationer has violated a condition of probation, the court may

(1) issue a summons in accordance with MCR 6.103(B) and (C) for the probationer to appear for arraignment on the alleged violation, or

(2) issue a warrant for the arrest of the probationer.

An arrested probationer must promptly be brought before the court for arraignment on the alleged violation.

(B) Arraignment on the Charge. At the arraignment on the alleged probation violation, the court must

(1) ensure that the probationer receives written notice of the alleged violation,

(2) advise the probationer that

(a) the probationer has a right to contest the charge at a hearing, and

(b) the probationer is entitled to a lawyer's assistance at the hearing and at all subsequent court proceedings, and that the court will appoint a lawyer at public expense if the probationer wants one and is financially unable to retain one,

(3) if requested and appropriate, appoint a lawyer,

(4) determine what form of release, if any, is appropriate, and

(5) subject to subrule (C), set a reasonably prompt hearing date or postpone the hearing.

(C) Scheduling or Postponement of Hearing. The hearing of a probationer being held in custody for an alleged probation violation must be held within 14 days after the arraignment or the court must order the probationer released from that custody pending the hearing. If the alleged violation is based on a criminal offense that is a basis for a separate criminal prosecution, the court may postpone the hearing for the outcome of that prosecution.

(D) Continuing Duty to Advise of Right to Assistance of Lawyer. Even though a probationer charged with probation violation has waived the assistance of a lawyer, at each subsequent proceeding the court must comply with the advice and waiver procedure in MCR 6.005(E).

(E) The Violation Hearing.

(1) *Conduct of the Hearing.* The evidence against the probationer must be disclosed to the probationer. The probationer has the right to be present at the hearing, to present evidence, and to examine and cross-examine witnesses. The court may consider only evidence that is relevant to the violation alleged, but it need not apply the rules of evidence except those pertaining to privileges. The state has the burden of proving a violation by a preponderance of the evidence.

(2) *Judicial Findings.* At the conclusion of the hearing, the court must make findings in accordance with MCR 6.403.

(F) Pleas of Guilty. The probationer may, at the arraignment or afterward, plead guilty to the violation. Before accepting a guilty plea, the court, speaking directly to the probationer and receiving the probationer's response, must

(1) advise the probationer that by pleading guilty the probationer is giving up the right to a contested hearing and, if the probationer is proceeding without legal representation, the right to a lawyer's assistance as set forth in subrule (B)(2)(b),

(2) advise the probationer of the maximum possible jail or prison sentence for the offense,

(3) ascertain that the plea is understandingly, voluntarily, and accurately made, and

(4) establish factual support for a finding that the probationer is guilty of the alleged violation.

(G) Sentencing. If the court finds that the probationer has violated a condition of probation, or if the probationer pleads guilty to a violation, the court may continue probation, modify the conditions of probation, extend the probation period, or revoke probation and impose a sentence of incarceration. The court may not sentence the probationer to prison without having considered a current presentence report and may not sentence the probationer to prison or jail (including for failing to pay fines, costs, restitution, and other financial obligations imposed by the court) without having complied with the provisions set forth in MCR 6.425(B) and (E).

(H) Review.

(1) In a case involving a sentence of incarceration under subrule (G), the court must advise the probationer on the record, immediately after imposing sentence, that

(a) the probationer has a right to appeal, if the underlying conviction occurred as a result of a trial, or

(b) the probationer is entitled to file an application for leave to appeal, if the underlying conviction was the result of a plea of guilty or nolo contendere.

(2) In a case that involves a sentence other than incarceration under subrule (G), the court must advise the probationer on the record, immediately after imposing sentence, that the probationer is entitled to file an application for leave to appeal.

[Adopted effective October 1, 1989. Amended August 3, 1994, effective October 1, 1994, 446 Mich; September 1998, effective January 1, 1999, 459 Mich; February 1, 2005, effective May 1, 2005, 472 Mich. Amended effective July 13, 2005, 473 Mich. Amended May 22, 2007, effective September 1, 2007, 478 Mich; May 25, 2016, effective September 1, 2016, 499 Mich. Amended effective December 14, 2016, 500 Mich.]

Comments

Staff Comment to 1989 Adoption

MCR 6.445 is a stylistically improved version of the former probation revocation rule, 6.111, but incorporates a number of substantive changes.

Subrule (A)(1) substitutes an expanded summons option. The former rule, 6.111(A)(1)(a), restricted the use of summons to an alleged probation violation "other than a criminal offense." The expanded option in subrule (A)(1) gives the court discretion to issue a summons for any alleged probation violation. This is similar to the summons option in 6.103, available when a defendant is charged with a felony. Unlike that summons procedure, however, issuance of a summons under this rule is not conditioned on being requested by the prosecutor. It is, however, required to comply with the form requirements of 6.103(B) and the service and return provisions of 6.103(C).

Subrule (B) is a substantially revised version of former 6.111(B), conforming more closely with the procedure and advice provisions in the arraignment rule, 6.104. The requirement for the court to advise a probationer of the ability to ask for bail in former 6.111(B)(2) is replaced with the provision in subrule (B)(4) requiring only that the court make a bail decision. The requirement to advise the probationer that the court will set a date for a hearing in former 6.111(B)(4) is replaced with the provision in subrule (B)(5) requiring the court to set a reasonably prompt hearing date. The requirement to advise the probationer of the right to be released from custody if the revocation hearing is not held within fourteen days is replaced with the provision in subrule (C) requiring the hearing of a probationer in custody to be held within twelve days or the court must order the probationer released. The change from fourteen to twelve days in this latter provision is made to be consistent with the twelve-day rule for preliminary examinations on which this provision is based.

Subrule (C) is new but incorporates stylistically revised versions of the provisions in former 6.111(B)(5) (discussed above) and in former (D)(2), allowing postponement of the hearing to await the outcome of the criminal prosecution on which a probation violation may be based.

Subrule (D) incorporates by reference the continuing advice requirement relating to legal representation set forth in 6.005(E) rather than repeating it verbatim as did former 6.111(C).

Subrule (E) is a stylistically revised version of the former revocation hearing rule, 6.111(D). Additionally, subrule (E)(1) adds a new provision consistent with existing law recognizing that, in addition to relevance, the only other limitation on the evidence that the court may consider at the hearing is that it conform with the admissibility requirements of privilege law.

Subrule (E)(2) makes a modification by referring to the special fact-finding requirements of 6.403 in place of the reference in former 6.111(D)(4) to the like provision in the civil rules, MCR 2.517(A).

Subrule (F) is a stylistically revised version of former 6.111(E). The only significant change is in language in subrule (F)(2) which substitutes "maximum possible jail or prison sentence" for the former language "maximum possible sentence." This change clarifies that this advice requirement pertains only to maximum possible incarceration and not to other consequences such as maximum possible fine. Additionally, the term "jail" is added to accommodate the use of the procedure in this rule in misdemeanor cases.

Subrule (G) is a stylistically revised version of former 6.111(F). Additionally, this subrule expands the court's duties, when imposing a "prison sentence," to conforming with the presentence report disclosure procedure, 6.425(B), sentencing procedure, 6.425(D)(2), and presentence report challenge procedure, 6.425(D)(3), applicable to felony sentencing.

Subrule (H) is a stylistically improved version of former 6.111(G).

Staff Comment to 1994 Amendment

In 1994, MCR 6.104(E)(4) and MCR 6.907(C)(2) were amended to reflect the change made by 1994 PA 167, which extended from 12 to 14 days the period within which a preliminary examination must be conducted. MCL 766.4. A similar change was also made in MCR 6.445(C), concerning the timing of a probation revocation hearing.

Staff Comment to 1998 Amendment

The September 1998 amendment of MCR 6.445(H), effective January 1, 1999, was proposed by the Michigan Judges Association, in light of the 1994 amendment of Const 1963, art 1, § 20, and the related amendment of MCR 6.425.

Staff Comment to Februar, 2005 Amendment

The February 1, 2005, effective May 1, 2005, amendment of MCR 6.445(H), effective May 1, 2005, requires a sentencing judge to advise a probationer whose probation is revoked that the probationer is entitled to appeal by right if the probationer's underlying conviction resulted from a trial. Where the underlying conviction resulted from a plea of guilty or nolo contendere, the probationer would be entitled to file an application for leave to appeal.

Staff Comment to July, 2005 Amendment

On March 12, 2002, the Court appointed the Committee on the Rules of Criminal Procedure to review the rules to determine whether any of the provisions should be revised. The committee issued its report on June 16, 2003, recommending numerous amendments of MCR 6.302 and 6.725. The committee did not recommend any amendments of MCR 6.625. A public hearing on the committee's recommendation was held May 27, 2004.

The Court adopted most of the committee's recommendations regarding Rule 6.302, and modified the rule to conform to the ruling of the United States Supreme Court in *Halbert v Michigan*, 545 US 605; 2005 WL 1469183 (June 23, 2005).

The Court adopted many of the committee's recommendations concerning MCR 6.425, however, the Court eliminated the requirement that "[n]ot later than the

date of sentencing, the court must complete a sentencing information report on a form to be prescribed by and returned to the state court administrator" in MCR 6.425(D). The Court also modified the language of the rule to incorporate the Court's holding in *People v Babcock*, 469 Mich 247 (2003) and to conform to the ruling in *Halbert*.

The Court did not follow the committee's recommendation that MCR 6.625 not be amended, but instead modified the rule to conform to the ruling in *Halbert*.

Staff Comment to 2007 Amendment

The amendment of the rule creates uniformity between MCR 6.302, which deals with the requirements for pleas of guilty and nolo contendere to criminal offenses, and MCR 6.445, which deals with the requirements for pleas of guilty to probation-revocation violations.

Staff Comment to September, 2016 Amendment

The amendments of MCR 3.605, 3.606, 3.928, 3.944, 3.956, 6.001, 6.425, 6.445, 6.610, and 6.933 were submitted by the Michigan State Planning Body for the Delivery of Legal Services to the Poor. The rule revisions are intended to provide clarity and guidance to courts regarding what courts would be required to do before incarcerating a defendant for failure to pay.

Staff Comment to December, 2016 Amendment

These amendments update cross-references and make other nonsubstantive revisions to clarify the rules.

SUBCHAPTER 6.500   POSTAPPEAL RELIEF

Rule 6.501. Scope of Subchapter

Unless otherwise specified by these rules, a judgment of conviction and sentence entered by the circuit court not subject to appellate review under subchapters 7.200 or 7.300 may be reviewed only in accordance with the provisions of this subchapter.

[Adopted effective October 1, 1989. Amended effective May 7, 2014, 495 Mich.]

Comments

Staff Comment to 1989 Adoption

New Subchapter 6.500 establishes a procedure for postappeal proceedings challenging criminal convictions. It provides the exclusive means to challenge convictions in Michigan courts for a defendant who has had an appeal by right or by leave, who has unsuccessfully sought leave to appeal, or who is unable to file an application for leave to appeal to the Court of Appeals because 18 months have elapsed since the judgment. See MCR 7.205(F)(3). The rules are similar in structure to the federal rules governing proceedings under 28 USC 2255, though there are a number of differences in substance and language.

Staff Comment to 2014 Amendment

These amendments reflect changes that correct minor technical errors that have occurred in drafting or the changes respond to recent adopted rule revisions, which occasionally inadvertently create incorrect cross-references in other rules.

Rule 6.502   Motion for Relief from Judgment

(A) Nature of Motion. The request for relief under this subchapter must be in the form of a motion to set aside or modify the judgment. The motion must specify all of the grounds for relief which are available to the defendant and of which the defendant has, or by the exercise of due diligence, should have knowledge.

(B) Limitations on Motion. A motion may seek relief from one judgment only. If the defendant desires to challenge the validity of additional judgments, the defendant must do so by separate motions. For the purpose of this rule, multiple convictions resulting from a single trial or plea proceeding shall be treated as a single judgment.

(C) Form of Motion. The motion may not be noticed for hearing, and must be typed or legibly handwritten and include a verification by the defendant or defendant's lawyer in accor-

dance with MCR 1.109(D)(3). Except as otherwise ordered by the court, the combined length of the motion and any memorandum of law in support may not exceed 50 pages double-spaced, exclusive of attachments and exhibits. If the court enters an order increasing the page limit for the motion, the same order shall indicate that the page limit for the prosecutor's response provided for in MCR 6.506(A) is increased by the same amount. The motion must be substantially in the form approved by the State Court Administrative Office, and must include:

(1) The name of the defendant;

(2) The name of the court in which the defendant was convicted and the file number of the defendant's case;

(3) The place where the defendant is confined, or, if not confined, the defendant's current address;

(4) The offenses for which the defendant was convicted and sentenced;

(5) The date on which the defendant was sentenced;

(6) Whether the defendant was convicted by a jury, by a judge without jury, or on a plea of guilty, guilty but mentally ill, or nolo contendere;

(7) The sentence imposed (probation, fine, and/or imprisonment), the length of the sentence imposed, and whether the defendant is now serving that sentence;

(8) The name of the judge who presided at trial and imposed sentence;

(9) The court, title, and file number of any proceeding (including appeals and federal court proceedings) instituted by the defendant to obtain relief from conviction or sentence, specifying whether a proceeding is pending or has been completed;

(10) The name of each lawyer who represented the defendant at any time after arrest, and the stage of the case at which each represented the defendant;

(11) The relief requested;

(12) The grounds for the relief requested;

(13) The facts supporting each ground, stated in summary form;

(14) Whether any of the grounds for the relief requested were raised before; if so, at what stage of the case, and, if not, the reasons they were not raised;

(15) Whether the defendant requests the appointment of counsel, and, if so, information necessary for the court to determine whether the defendant is entitled to appointment of counsel at public expense.

Upon request, the clerk of each court with trial level jurisdiction over felony cases shall make available blank motion forms without charge to any person desiring to file such a motion.

(D) Return of Insufficient Motion. If a motion is not submitted on a form approved by the State Court Administrative Office, or does not substantially comply with the requirements of these rules, the court shall either direct that it be returned to the defendant with a statement of the reasons for its return, along with the appropriate form, or adjudicate the motion under the provisions of these rules. The clerk of the court shall retain a copy of the motion.

(E) Attachments to Motion. The defendant may attach to the motion any affidavit, document, or evidence to support the relief requested.

(F) Amendment and Supplementation of Motion. The court may permit the defendant to amend or supplement the motion at any time.

(G) Successive Motions.

(1) Except as provided in subrule (G)(2), regardless of whether a defendant has previously filed a motion for relief from judgment, after August 1, 1995, one and only one motion for relief from judgment may be filed with regard to a conviction. The court shall return without filing any successive motions for relief from judgment. A defendant may not appeal the denial or rejection of a successive motion.

(2) A defendant may file a second or subsequent motion based on a retroactive change in law that occurred after the first motion for relief from judgment or a claim of new evidence that was not discovered before the first such motion. The clerk shall refer a successive motion that asserts that one of these exceptions is applicable to the judge to whom the case is assigned for a determination whether the motion is within one of the exceptions.

The court may waive the provisions of this rule if it concludes that there is a significant possibility that the defendant is innocent of the crime.

(3) For purposes of subrule (G)(2), "new evidence" includes new scientific evidence. This includes, but is not limited to, shifts in science entailing changes:

(a) in a field of scientific knowledge, including shifts in scientific consensus;

(b) in a testifying expert's own scientific knowledge and opinions; or

(c) in a scientific method on which the relevant scientific evidence at trial was based.

[Adopted effective October 1, 1989. Amended June 2, 1995, effective August 1, 1995, 449 Mich; June 26, 2006, effective September 1, 2006, 475 Mich; August 30, 2018, effective September 1, 2018, 502 Mich; September 24, 2018, effective January 1, 2019, 502 Mich.]

Comments

Staff Comment to 1989 Adoption

The defendant initiates proceedings under Subchapter 6.500 by filing a motion for relief from judgment. The motion is to list all grounds for relief of which defendant has knowledge or with reasonable diligence should have knowledge. The motion is to be limited to a single judgment, although multiple convictions resulting from a single trial or plea proceeding are treated as if they were a single judgment and may be included in the same motion. Subrule (C) spells out the required contents of the motion, which is to be in substantially the form approved by the State Court Administrator. The defendant is permitted to attach affidavits, evidentiary material, or a memorandum of law to the motion. If the motion does not comply with the requirements of the rule, the court may direct that it be returned to the defendant with a statement of the reasons for its rejection.

Staff Comment to 1995 Amendment

New MCR 6.502(G) limits criminal defendants to filing one motion for relief from judgment with respect to a conviction, except where the motion is based on a retroactive change in the law or on newly discovered evidence.

Staff Comment to 2006 Amendment

On March 12, 2002, the Court appointed the Committee on the Rules of Criminal Procedure to review the rules to determine whether any of the provisions should be revised. The committee issued its report on June 16, 2003, recommending numerous amendments of existing rules, plus some new rules. A public hearing on the committee's recommendations was held May 27, 2004.

The Court adopted the committee's recommendations with respect to the amendments of Rules 6.503 and 6.504.

With regard to Rules 6.502 and 6.506, the Court adopted a 50–page limitation rather than the 25–page limitation recommended by the committee. The Court did not adopt the committee's recommendation that the successive motion limitation of Rule 6.502(G) be eliminated; however, the Court did adopt remaining amendments of Rules 6.502 and 6.506 as recommended by the committee.

Instead of adopting the committee's recommendations regarding amendments of Rule 6.509, the Court adopted alternative language similar to language recommended by the Court of Appeals.

The Court did not adopt the committee's recommendation to amend Rules 6.501 and 6.508.

Staff Comment to 2018 Amendment

These amendments update cross-references in the rules, and are intended to reflect changes that are necessary as a result of the Court's recent e-Filing rules amendments.

Staff Comment to 2019 Amendment

The amendments make several substantive changes in MCR 6.502 regarding postjudgment relief from judgment motions. First, the new language in MCR 6.502(G)(2) inserts a discretionary "actual innocence" waiver provision similar to that in MCR 6.508(D)(3). Further, MCR 6.502(G)(3) is added to clarify that shifts in science are included in the definition of "new evidence" for purposes of the exemption from the successive motion limitation. Finally, new language is added to MRPC 3.8 to require certain actions by a prosecutor who knows of new, credible, and material evidence creating a reasonable likelihood that defendant is innocent of the crime for which defendant was convicted, or who knows of clear and convincing evidence that shows defendant is innocent of the crime. The additional language of MRPC 3.8 is taken largely from the ABA Model Rules of Professional Conduct 3.8, and includes the "safe harbor" provision as a separate provision of the rule (as opposed to being part of the comments as in the model rule).

Rule 6.503 Filing and Service of Motion

(A) Filing; Copies.

(1) A defendant seeking relief under this subchapter must file a motion, and a copy of the motion with the clerk of the court in which the defendant was convicted and sentenced.

(2) Upon receipt of a motion, the clerk shall file it under the same number as the original conviction.

(B) Service. The defendant shall serve a copy of the motion and notice of its filing on the prosecuting attorney. Unless so ordered by the court as provided in this subchapter, the filing and service of the motion does not require a response by the prosecutor.

[Adopted effective October 1, 1989. Amended June 26, 2006, effective September 1, 2006, 475 Mich.]

Comments

Staff Comment to 1989 Adoption

The defendant is to file the original and two copies of the motion with the court, and the clerk will serve it on the prosecuting attorney. The prosecutor is not required to respond unless directed by the court.

Staff Comment to 2006 Amendment

For comments concerning the June 26, 2006 amendment effective September 1, 2006, see the Staff Comment to 2006 Amendments under Rule 6.502.

Rule 6.504　Assignment; Preliminary Consideration by Judge; Summary Denial

(A) Assignment to Judge. The motion shall be presented to the judge to whom the case was assigned at the time of the defendant's conviction. If the appropriate judge is not available, the motion must be assigned to another judge in accordance with the court's procedure for the reassignment of cases. The chief judge may reassign cases in order to correct docket control problems arising from the requirements of this rule.

(B) Initial Consideration by Court.

(1) The court shall promptly examine the motion, together with all the files, records, transcripts, and correspondence relating to the judgment under attack. The court may request that the prosecutor provide copies of transcripts, briefs, or other records.

(2) If it plainly appears from the face of the materials described in subrule (B)(1) that the defendant is not entitled to relief, the court shall deny the motion without directing further proceedings. The order must include a concise statement of the reasons for the denial. The clerk shall serve a copy of the order on the defendant and the prosecutor. The court may dismiss some requests for relief or grounds for relief while directing a response or further proceedings with respect to other specified grounds.

(3) If the motion is summarily dismissed under subrule (B)(2), the defendant may move for reconsideration of the dismissal within 21 days after the clerk serves the order. The motion must concisely state why the court's decision was based on a clear error and that a different decision must result from correction of the error. A motion which merely presents the same matters that were considered by the court will not be granted.

(4) If the entire motion is not dismissed under subrule (B)(2), the court shall order the prosecuting attorney to file a response as provided in MCR 6.506, and shall conduct further proceedings as provided in MCR 6.505–6.508.

[Adopted effective October 1, 1989. Amended June 26, 2006, effective September 1, 2006, 475 Mich.]

Comments

Staff Comment to 1989 Adoption

The motion is to be assigned to the judge to whom the case was assigned at the time of the conviction. The usual procedures for using a substitute judge are to be followed where that judge is not available. The judge is to examine the motion together with the court's records regarding the case. The court may request that the prosecutor provide copies of other materials.

The court may summarily dismiss the motion if it "plainly appears" from the materials that the defendant is not entitled to relief. The provision outlining the grounds for relief is found in MCR 6.508(D). The "plainly appears" standard is taken from the corresponding federal rule implementing 28 USC 2255. Rule 4 of the Rules Governing Proceedings in the United States District Courts Under § 2255 of Title 28, United States Code. The court can summarily dismiss some claims, while directing further proceedings on others. Subrule (B)(3) provides a procedure by which the defendant may request reconsideration of a summary dismissal.

If the entire motion is not summarily dismissed, the court is to direct the prosecutor to file a response and to conduct further proceedings.

Staff Comment to 2006 Amendment

For comments concerning the June 26, 2006 amendment effective September 1, 2006, see the Staff Comment to 2006 Amendments under Rule 6.502.

Rule 6.505　Right to Legal Assistance

(A) Appointment of Counsel. If the defendant has requested appointment of counsel, and the court has determined that the defendant is indigent, the court may appoint counsel for the defendant at any time during the proceedings under this subchapter. Counsel must be appointed if the court directs that oral argument or an evidentiary hearing be held.

(B) Opportunity to Supplement the Motion. If the court appoints counsel to represent the defendant, it shall afford counsel 56 days to amend or supplement the motion. The court may extend the time on a showing that a necessary transcript or record is not available to counsel.

[Adopted effective October 1, 1989.]

Comments

Staff Comment to 1989 Adoption

The matter of appointment of counsel for a defendant is covered by MCR 6.505. The court may appoint counsel at any time, and is required to do so if it directs that oral argument or an evidentiary hearing be held. If counsel is appointed, the court is to allow counsel time to amend or supplement the motion.

Rule 6.506　Response by Prosecutor

(A) Contents of Response. On direction of the court pursuant to MCR 6.504(B)(4), the prosecutor shall respond in writing to the allegations in the motion. The trial court shall allow the prosecutor a minimum of 56 days to respond. If the response refers to transcripts or briefs that are not in the court's file, the prosecutor shall submit copies of those items with the response. Except as otherwise ordered by the court, the response shall not exceed 50 pages double-spaced, exclusive of attachments and exhibits.

(B) Filing and Service. The prosecutor shall file the response and one copy with the clerk of the court and serve one copy on the defendant.

[Adopted effective October 1, 1989. Amended June 26, 2006, effective September 1, 2006, 475 Mich.]

Comments

Staff Comment to 1989 Adoption

If the court does not summarily dismiss the motion under MCR 6.504, it is to direct the prosecutor to file a response. MCR 6.506 has several provisions regarding filing and service of the response. The prosecutor is to supply copies of transcripts or briefs to which the response refers that are not in the court's file.

Staff Comment to 2006 Amendment

For comments concerning the June 26, 2006 amendment effective September 1, 2006, see the Staff Comment to 2006 Amendments under Rule 6.502.

Rule 6.507 Expansion of Record

(A) Order to Expand Record. If the court does not deny the motion pursuant to MCR 6.504(B)(2), it may direct the parties to expand the record by including any additional materials it deems relevant to the decision on the merits of the motion. The expanded record may include letters, affidavits, documents, exhibits, and answers under oath to interrogatories propounded by the court.

(B) Submission to Opposing Party. Whenever a party submits items to expand the record, the party shall serve copies of the items to the opposing party. The court shall afford the opposing party an opportunity to admit or deny the correctness of the items.

(C) Authentication. The court may require the authentication of any item submitted under this rule.

[Adopted effective October 1, 1989.]

Comments

Staff Comment to 1989 Adoption

The court is given considerable discretion in the matter of expanding the record if further information is necessary to decide the motion.

Rule 6.508. Procedure; Evidentiary Hearing; Determination

(A) Procedure Generally. If the rules in this subchapter do not prescribe the applicable procedure, the court may proceed in any lawful manner. The court may apply the rules applicable to civil or criminal proceedings, as it deems appropriate.

(B) Decision Without Evidentiary Hearing. After reviewing the motion and response, the record, and the expanded record, if any, the court shall determine whether an evidentiary hearing is required. If the court decides that an evidentiary hearing is not required, it may rule on the motion or, in its discretion, afford the parties an opportunity for oral argument.

(C) Evidentiary Hearing. If the court decides that an evidentiary hearing is required, it shall schedule and conduct the hearing as promptly as practicable. At the hearing, the rules of evidence other than those with respect to privilege do not apply. The court shall assure that a verbatim record is made of the hearing.

(D) Entitlement to Relief. The defendant has the burden of establishing entitlement to the relief requested. The court may not grant relief to the defendant if the motion

(1) seeks relief from a judgment of conviction and sentence that still is subject to challenge on appeal pursuant to subchapter 7.200 or subchapter 7.300;

(2) alleges grounds for relief which were decided against the defendant in a prior appeal or proceeding under this subchapter, unless the defendant establishes that a retroactive change in the law has undermined the prior decision;

(3) alleges grounds for relief, other than jurisdictional defects, which could have been raised on appeal from the conviction and sentence or in a prior motion under this subchapter, unless the defendant demonstrates

(a) good cause for failure to raise such grounds on appeal or in the prior motion, and

(b) actual prejudice from the alleged irregularities that support the claim for relief. As used in this subrule, "actual prejudice" means that,

(i) in a conviction following a trial,

(A) but for the alleged error, the defendant would have had a reasonably likely chance of acquittal; or

(B) where the defendant rejected a plea based on incorrect information from the trial court or ineffective assistance of counsel, it is reasonably likely that

(1) the prosecutor would not have withdrawn any plea offer;

(2) the defendant and the trial court would have accepted the plea but for the improper advice; and

(3) the conviction or sentence, or both, under the plea's terms would have been less severe than under the judgment and sentence that in fact were imposed.

(ii) in a conviction entered on a plea of guilty, guilty but mentally ill, or nolo contendere, the defect in the proceedings was such that it renders the plea an involuntary one to a degree that it would be manifestly unjust to allow the conviction to stand;

(iii) in any case, the irregularity was so offensive to the maintenance of a sound judicial process that the conviction should not be allowed to stand regardless of its effect on the outcome of the case;

(iv) in the case of a challenge to the sentence, the sentence is invalid.

The court may waive the "good cause" requirement of subrule (D)(3)(a) if it concludes that there is a significant possibility that the defendant is innocent of the crime.

(E) Ruling. The court, either orally or in writing, shall set forth in the record its findings of fact and its conclusions of law, and enter an appropriate order disposing of the motion.

[Adopted effective October 1, 1989. Amended September 18, 2019, effective January 1, 2020, 503 Mich.]

Comments

Staff Comment to 1989 Adoption

Most of the provisions on governing hearings and decision on the motion are found in MCR 6.508. Where no particular provision of Subchapter 6.500 prescribes a procedure, the court has discretion to select appropriate procedures. The court is to determine whether the case can be decided on the motion and response, the court records, and the expanded record, if any. If it decides that an evidentiary hearing is not required, it is to rule on the motion, with or without hearing oral argument. If an evidentiary hearing is ordered, the rules of evidence, other than those with respect to privilege, do not apply. Compare MRE 1101(b)(3). A verbatim record is to be made of any evidentiary hearing.

MCR 6.508(D) covers the standard for entitlement to relief. There are three basic provisions.

First, the motion is to be denied if it seeks relief from a conviction that is still subject to challenge on appeal.

Second, if the issues raised were previously decided against the defendant in an appeal or a proceeding under Subchapter 6.500, relief is to be denied unless there has been a retroactive change in the law that undermines the prior decision.

Third, relief is not to be granted where the defendant could have raised the issue in a prior appeal or motion under Subchapter 6.500, unless defendant demonstrates both good cause for failure to raise the issue previously and actual prejudice from the alleged error. These standards are based on several decisions of the United States Supreme Court. See *Wainright v Sykes*, 433 US 72; 97 S Ct 2497; 53 L Ed 2d 594 (1977) (habeas corpus action by state prisoner); *United States v Frady*, 456 US 152; 102 S Ct 1584; 71 L Ed 2d 816 (1982) (under 28 USC 2255).

Actual prejudice is defined in subrule (D)(3)(b). In the case of a trial, it means that but for the error the defendant would have had a reasonably likely chance of acquittal. In the case of a plea-based conviction, the defect must be such that the plea is rendered involuntary to a degree that it would be manifestly unjust to allow the conviction to stand. In any case, actual prejudice can be shown if the irregularity was so offensive to the maintenance of a sound judicial process that the conviction should not be allowed to stand regardless of its effect on the outcome of the case. Finally, where the challenge is to the sentence, actual prejudice requires that the sentence be invalid.

The court is allowed to waive the good cause requirement if it concludes that there is a significant possibility that the defendant is innocent.

The court is to make findings of fact and conclusions of law either in writing or orally on the record, followed by entry of an appropriate order.

Staff Comment 2020 Amendment

The amendment of MCR 6.508 enables a defendant to show actual prejudice in a motion for relief for judgment where defendant rejected a plea based on incorrect information from the trial court or ineffective assistance of counsel, and it was reasonably likely the defendant and court would have accepted the plea (which would have been less severe than the judgment or sentence issued after trial) but for the improper advice.

Rule 6.509 Appeal

(A) Availability of Appeal. Appeals from decisions under this subchapter are by application for leave to appeal to the Court of Appeals pursuant to MCR 7.205. The 6–month time limit provided by MCR 7.205(G)(3), runs from the decision under this subchapter. Nothing in this subchapter shall be construed as extending the time to appeal from the original judgment.

(B) Responsibility of Appointed Counsel. If the trial court has appointed counsel for the defendant during the proceeding, that appointment authorizes the attorney to represent the defendant in connection with an application for leave to appeal to the Court of Appeals.

(C) Responsibility of the Prosecutor. If the prosecutor has not filed a response to the defendant's application for leave to appeal in the appellate court, the prosecutor must file an appellee's brief if the appellate court grants the defendant's application for leave to appeal. The prosecutor must file an appellee's brief within 56 days after an order directing a response pursuant to subrule (D).

(D) Responsibility of the Appellate Court. If the appellate court grants the defendant's application for leave to appeal and the prosecutor has not filed a response in the appellate court, the appellate court must direct the prosecutor to file an appellee's brief, and give the prosecutor the opportunity to file an appellee's brief pursuant to subrule (C), before granting further relief to the defendant.

[Adopted effective October 1, 1989. Amended June 2, 1995, effective November 1, 1995, 449 Mich; June 26, 2006, effective September 1, 2006, 475 Mich. Amended effective September 28, 2011, 490 Mich; May 7, 2014, 495 Mich.]

Comments

Staff Comment to 1989 Adoption

Appeals from decisions under Subchapter 6.500 are by application for leave to appeal to the Court of Appeals. The rule does not extend the time to appeal from the original judgment. If the trial court appointed counsel for the defendant during the proceeding, that appointment authorizes the attorney to represent the defendant in connection with an application for leave to appeal to the Court of Appeals.

Staff Comment to 1995 Amendment

In MCR 6.509(A), the reference to the time for filing an application for leave to appeal is changed to 12 months to conform to the March 3, 1995, amendment of MCR 7.205(F)(3).

Staff Comment to 2006 Amendment

For comments concerning the June 26, 2006 amendment effective September 1, 2006, see the Staff Comment to 2006 Amendments under Rule 6.502.

Staff Comment to 2011 Amendment

The above noted changes are minor revisions of the rules that have been recommended to the Court to correct cross references and to reflect other technical changes.

Staff Comment to 2014 Amendment

These amendments reflect changes that correct minor technical errors that have occurred in drafting or the changes respond to recent adopted rule revisions, which occasionally inadvertently create incorrect cross-references in other rules.

SUBCHAPTER 6.600 CRIMINAL PROCEDURE IN DISTRICT COURT

Rule 6.610. Criminal Procedure Generally

(A) Precedence. Criminal cases have precedence over civil actions.

(B) Pretrial. The court, on its own initiative or on motion of either party, may direct the prosecutor and the defendant, and, if represented, the defendant's attorney to appear for a pretrial conference. The court may require collateral matters and pretrial motions to be filed and argued no later than this conference.

(C) Record. Unless a writing is permitted, a verbatim record of the proceedings before a court under subrules (D)–(F) must be made.

(D) Arraignment; District Court Offenses.

(1) Whenever a defendant is arraigned on an offense over which the district court has jurisdiction, the defendant must be informed of

(a) the name of the offense;

(b) the maximum sentence permitted by law; and

(c) the defendant's right

(i) to the assistance of an attorney and to a trial;

(ii) (if subrule [D][2] applies) to an appointed attorney; and

(iii) to a trial by jury, when required by law.

The information may be given in a writing that is made a part of the file or by the court on the record.

(2) An indigent defendant has a right to an appointed attorney whenever the offense charged requires on conviction a minimum term in jail or the court determines it might sentence to a term of incarceration, even if suspended.

If an indigent defendant is without an attorney and has not waived the right to an appointed attorney, the court may not sentence the defendant to jail or to a suspended jail sentence.

(3) The right to the assistance of an attorney, to an appointed attorney, or to a trial by jury is not waived unless the defendant

(a) has been informed of the right; and

(b) has waived it in a writing that is made a part of the file or orally on the record.

(4) The court may allow a defendant to enter a plea of not guilty or to stand mute without formal arraignment by filing a written statement signed by the defendant and any defense attorney of record, reciting the general nature of the charge,

the maximum possible sentence, the rights of the defendant at arraignment, and the plea to be entered. The court may require that an appropriate bond be executed and filed and appropriate and reasonable sureties posted or continued as a condition precedent to allowing the defendant to be arraigned without personally appearing before the court.

(E) Pleas of Guilty and Nolo Contendere. Before accepting a plea of guilty or nolo contendere, the court shall in all cases comply with this rule.

(1) The court shall determine that the plea is understanding, voluntary, and accurate. In determining the accuracy of the plea,

(a) if the defendant pleads guilty, the court, by questioning the defendant, shall establish support for a finding that defendant is guilty of the offense charged or the offense to which the defendant is pleading, or

(b) if the defendant pleads nolo contendere, the court shall not question the defendant about the defendant's participation in the crime, but shall make the determination on the basis of other available information.

(2) The court shall inform the defendant of the right to the assistance of an attorney. If the offense charged requires on conviction a minimum term in jail, the court shall inform the defendant that if the defendant is indigent the defendant has the right to an appointed attorney. The court shall also give such advice if it determines that it might sentence to a term of incarceration, even if suspended.

(3) The court shall advise the defendant of the following:

(a) the mandatory minimum jail sentence, if any, and the maximum possible penalty for the offense,

(b) that if the plea is accepted the defendant will not have a trial of any kind and that the defendant gives up the following rights that the defendant would have at trial:

(i) the right to have witnesses called for the defendant's defense at trial,

(ii) the right to cross-examine all witnesses called against the defendant,

(iii) the right to testify or to remain silent without an inference being drawn from said silence,

(iv) the presumption of innocence and the requirement that the defendant's guilt be proven beyond a reasonable doubt.

(4) A defendant or defendants may be informed of the trial rights listed in subrule (3)(b) as follows:

(a) on the record,

(b) in a writing made part of the file, or

(c) in a writing referred to on the record.

Except as provided in subrule (E)(7), if the court uses a writing pursuant to subrule (E)(4)(b) or (c), the court shall address the defendant and obtain from the defendant orally on the record a statement that the rights were read and understood and a waiver of those rights. The waiver may be obtained without repeating the individual rights.

(5) The court shall make the plea agreement a part of the record and determine that the parties agree on all the terms of that agreement. The court shall accept, reject or indicate on what basis it accepts the plea.

(6) The court must ask the defendant:

(a) (if there is no plea agreement) whether anyone has promised the defendant anything, or (if there is a plea agreement) whether anyone has promised anything beyond what is in the plea agreement;

(b) whether anyone has threatened the defendant; and

(c) whether it is the defendant's own choice to plead guilty.

(7) A plea of guilty or nolo contendere in writing is permissible without a personal appearance of the defendant and without support for a finding that defendant is guilty of the offense charged or the offense to which the defendant is pleading if

(a) the court decides that the combination of the circumstances and the range of possible sentences makes the situation proper for a plea of guilty or nolo contendere;

(b) the defendant acknowledges guilt or nolo contendere, in a writing to be placed in the district court file, and waives in writing the rights enumerated in subrule (3)(b); and

(c) the court is satisfied that the waiver is voluntary.

A "writing" includes digital communications, transmitted through electronic means, which are capable of being stored and printed.

(8) The following provisions apply where a defendant seeks to challenge the plea.

(a) A defendant may not challenge a plea on appeal unless the defendant moved in the trial court to withdraw the plea for noncompliance with these rules. Such a motion may be made either before or after sentence has been imposed. After imposition of sentence, the defendant may file a motion to withdraw the plea within the time for filing an application for leave to appeal under MCR 7.105(G)(2).

(b) If the trial court determines that a deviation affecting substantial rights occurred, it shall correct the deviation and give the defendant the option of permitting the plea to stand or of withdrawing the plea. If the trial court determines either a deviation did not occur, or that the deviation did not affect substantial rights, it may permit the defendant to withdraw the plea only if it does not cause substantial prejudice to the people because of reliance on the plea.

(c) If a deviation is corrected, any appeal will be on the whole record including the subsequent advice and inquiries.

(9) The State Court Administrator shall develop and approve forms to be used under subrules (E)(4)(b) and (c) and (E)(7)(b).

(F) Sentencing.

(1) For sentencing, the court shall:

(a) require the presence of the defendant's attorney, unless the defendant does not have one or has waived the attorney's presence;

(b) provide copies of the presentence report (if a presentence report was prepared) to the prosecutor and the defendant's lawyer, or the defendant if not represented by a lawyer, at a reasonable time, but not less than two business days before the day of sentencing. The prosecutor and the defendant's lawyer, or the defendant if not represented by a lawyer, may retain a copy of the report or an amended report. If the presentence report is not made available to the prosecutor and the defendant's lawyer, or the defendant if not represented by a lawyer, at least two business days before the day of sentencing, the prosecutor and the defendant's lawyer, or the defendant if not represented by a lawyer, shall be entitled, on oral motion, to an adjournment to enable the moving party to review the presentence report and to prepare any necessary corrections, additions or deletions to present to the court, or otherwise advise the court of circumstances the prosecutor or defendant believes should be considered in imposing sentence. A presentence investigation report shall not include any address or telephone number for the home, workplace, school, or place of worship of any victim or witness, or a family member of any victim or witness, unless an address is used to identify the place of the crime or to impose conditions of release from custody that are necessary for the protection of a named individual. Upon request, any other address or telephone number that would reveal the location of a victim or witness or a family member of a victim or witness shall be exempted from disclosure unless an address is used to identify the place of the crime or to impose conditions of release from custody that are necessary for the protection of a named individual.

(c) inform the defendant of credit to be given for time served, if any.

(d) order the dollar amount of restitution that the defendant must pay to make full restitution as required by law to any victim of the defendant's course of conduct that gives rise to the conviction, or to that victim's estate. Any dispute as to the proper amount or type of restitution shall be resolved by the court by a preponderance of the evidence. The burden of demonstrating the amount of the loss sustained by a victim as a result of the offense shall be on the prosecuting attorney.

(2) The court shall not sentence a defendant to a term of incarceration for nonpayment unless the court has complied with the provisions of MCR 6.425(E)(3).

(3) Unless a defendant who is entitled to appointed counsel is represented by an attorney or has waived the right to an attorney, a subsequent charge or sentence may not be enhanced because of this conviction and the defendant may not be incarcerated for violating probation or any other condition imposed in connection with this conviction.

(4) Immediately after imposing a sentence of incarceration, even if suspended, the court must advise the defendant, on the record or in writing, that:

(a) if the defendant wishes to file an appeal and is financially unable to retain a lawyer, the court will appoint a lawyer to represent the defendant on appeal, and

(b) the request for a lawyer must be made within 14 days after sentencing.

(G) Motion for New Trial. A motion for a new trial must be filed within 21 days after the entry of judgment. However, if an appeal has not been taken, a delayed motion may be filed within the time for filing an application for leave to appeal.

(H) Arraignment; Offenses Not Cognizable by the District Court. In a prosecution in which a defendant is charged with a felony or a misdemeanor not cognizable by the district court, the court shall

(1) inform the defendant of the nature of the charge;

(2) inform the defendant of

(a) the right to a preliminary examination;

(b) the right to an attorney, if the defendant is not represented by an attorney at the arraignment;

(c) the right to have an attorney appointed at public expense if the defendant is indigent; and

(d) the right to consideration of pretrial release.

If a defendant not represented by an attorney waives the preliminary examination, the court shall ascertain that the waiver is freely, understandingly, and voluntarily given before accepting it.

[Adopted effective October 1, 1989. Amended July 20, 1999, effective October 1, 1999, 460 Mich; June 13, 2000, effective September 1, 2000, 462 Mich; December 21, 2000, effective April 1, 2001, 463 Mich; July 13, 2005, effective January 1, 2006, 473 Mich; January 23, 2007, effective May 1, 2007, 477 Mich; February 5, effective May 1, 2010, 485 Mich; July 1, 2010, effective July 1, 2010, 486 Mich; December 29, 2010, effective January 1, 2011, 487 Mich. Amended effective August 24, 2012, 492 Mich; March 9, 2016, 499 Mich. Amended May 25, 2016, effective September 1, 2016, 499 Mich; May 23, 2018, effective September 1, 2018, 501 Mich; May 22, 2019, effective September 1, 2019, 502 Mich.]

Comments

Staff Comment to 1989 Adoption

MCR 6.610 contains the provisions formerly found in MCR 6.201.

Staff Comment to 1999 Amendment

The July 1999 amendment of subrules (D) and (E), effective October 1, 1999, was based on a recommendation from the Prosecuting Attorneys Association of Michigan, in light of statutory changes effected by 1998 PA 341, 1998 PA 342, and 1998 PA 350.

Staff Comment to 2000 Amendment

The amendment of MCR 6.610(E)(7) [effective September 1, 2000] establishes time limits for moving to withdraw pleas in district court criminal cases, comparable to those in circuit court cases. See MCR 6.311. New MCR 6.610(H) sets time limits for filing a motion for a new trial in district court criminal cases.

The amendment of MCR 7.103(B)(6) [effective September 1, 2000] places a 6–month time limit on applications for leave to appeal to circuit court, corresponding to the 12–month limit applicable in appeals to the Court of Appeals. See MCR 7.205(F)(3). As to judgments entered before the effective date of the amendment, the 6–month period specified in MCR 7.103(B)(6) begins on the effective date, September 1, 2000.

Staff Comment to 2001 Amendment

The December 21, 2000 amendment of subrules (D)(2) and (E)(2), effective April 1, 2001, was recommended by the Prosecuting Attorneys Association of Michigan, in light of the holding in *People v Reichenbach*, 459 Mich 109, 120 (1998), that, under both the United States and the Michigan Constitutions, a defendant accused of a misdemeanor is entitled to appointed trial counsel only if "actually imprisoned."

Staff Comment to 2006 Amendment

On March 12, 2002, the Court appointed the Committee on the Rules of Criminal Procedure to review the rules to determine whether any of the provisions should be revised. The committee issued its report on June 16, 2003, recommending numerous amendments to existing rules, plus some new rules. A public hearing on the committee's recommendations was held May 27, 2004.

The Court adopted the committee's recommendations with respect to the amendments of Rules 2.511, 6.102, 6.104, 6.107, 6.112, 6.303, 6.304, 6.310, 6.311, 6.402, 6.412, 6.414, 6.419, 6.420, 6.427, 6.615, and 6.620, and the adoption of a new Rule 6.428.

The committee's recommendation that Rule 6.610 be amended was adopted, except for committee's proposal to add a new 6.610(F) providing for discovery in district court.

Staff Comment to 2007 Amendment

The amendment of Rule 6.610 ensures that indigent defendants who are convicted in district court and sentenced to terms of incarceration, are aware of their right to counsel pursuant to *Halbert v Michigan*, 545 US 605 (2005), and *Shelton v Alabama*, 535 US 654 (2002). The amendment requires that after imposing a sentence of incarceration, even if suspended, the court must advise the defendant that if the defendant wishes to file an appeal and is financially unable to retain a lawyer, the court will appoint a lawyer to represent the defendant on appeal if the request for a lawyer is made within 14 days after sentencing.

Staff Comment to May, 2010 Amendment

The amendments of Rules 6.425 and 6.610 of the Michigan Court Rules were submitted by the Representative Assembly of the State Bar of Michigan. The amendments increase the time within which a court is required to provide copies of the presentence report to the prosecutor, the defendant's lawyer, or the defendant if not represented by a lawyer, to at least two business days before the day of sentencing. If the report is not made available at least two days before sentencing, the prosecutor or defendant's lawyer, or the defendant, when not represented by a lawyer, is entitled to an adjournment to prepare any necessary corrections, additions, or deletions to present to the court. The revisions of these rules also prohibit the inclusion of specific information in the report about the victim or witness, and require that the court instruct those who review the report that they are precluded from making a copy of the report and must return their copy to the court before or at the defendant's sentencing. The confidentiality provision is based on MCL 791.229.

Staff Comment to July, 2010 Amendment

By order dated February 5, 2010, the Court adopted various amendments of MCR 6.425 and MCR 6.610 to require prosecutors and defendants to have access to the presentence investigation report at least two days before sentencing and allow adjournment if the parties do not receive the report in that time, to ensure the confidentiality of the PSI report, and to limit the victim or witness information that may be included in a PSI report. Following entry of the February order and shortly after its May 1, 2010, effective date, the Court considered the matter further, specifically with regard to mandatory confidentiality provisions that not only represented a significant change in current practice, but, also, underscored a fundamental tension between the explicit provisions of MCL 791. 229, which describes who may have a copy of the report and for what purposes, and subsequent caselaw, which has expanded access of PSI reports in certain circumstances. In light of this tension, the Court has invited interested associations that oppose the language as adopted by the Court to approach the Legislature to resolve the conflict. However, if legislation on this subject is not enacted and effective by the end of this calendar year, an amendment to allow prosecutors, defense counsel, and defendants to retain a copy of the presentence investigation report will automatically go into effect on January 1, 2011.

Staff Comment to 2011 Amendment

This order codifies statutory changes enacted as 2010 PA 247 and 2010 PA 248.

Staff Comment to 2012 Amendment

These amendments reflect changes to correct minor technical errors that have occurred in drafting or to respond to recent adopted rule revisions, which occasionally inadvertently create incorrect cross-references in other rules.

Staff Comment to March, 2016 Amendment

These amendments update cross-references that changed after the rule was adopted and make other nonsubstantive revisions.

Staff Comment to September, 2016 Amendment

The amendments of MCR 3.605, 3.606, 3.928, 3.944, 3.956, 6.001, 6.425, 6.445, 6.610, and 6.933 were submitted by the Michigan State Planning Body for the Delivery of Legal Services to the Poor. The rule revisions are intended to provide clarity and guidance to courts regarding what courts would be required to do before incarcerating a defendant for failure to pay.

Staff Comment to 2018 Amendment

The amendment of MCR 6.610 eliminates an arguable conflict by exempting pleas taken under subsection (E)(7) from the requirements of subsection (E)(4), and clarifies what constitutes a "writing" by incorporating digital communications.

Staff Comment to 2019 Amendment

The amendments more explicitly require restitution to be ordered at the time of sentencing as required by statute, and establish a procedure for modifying restitution amounts.

Rule 6.615 Misdemeanor Traffic Cases

(A) Citation; Complaint; Summons; Warrant.

(1) A misdemeanor traffic case may be initiated by one of the following procedures:

(a) Service of a written citation by a law enforcement officer on the defendant, and the filing of the citation in the district court. The citation may be prepared electronically or on paper. The citation must be signed by the officer in accordance with MCR 1.109(E)(4); if a citation is prepared electronically and filed with a court as data, the name of the officer that is associated with issuance of the citation satisfies this requirement.

(b) The filing of a sworn complaint in the district court and the issuance of an arrest warrant. A citation may serve as the sworn complaint and as the basis for a misdemeanor warrant.

(c) Other special procedures authorized by statute.

(2) The citation serves as a summons to command

(a) the initial appearance of the defendant; and

(b) a response from the defendant as to his or her guilt of the violation alleged.

(B) Appearances; Failure to Appear. If a defendant fails to appear or otherwise to respond to any matter pending relative to a misdemeanor traffic citation, the court shall proceed as provided in this subrule.

(1) If the defendant is a Michigan resident, the court

(a) must initiate the procedures required by MCL 257.321a for the failure to answer a citation; and

(b) may issue a warrant for the defendant's arrest.

(2) If the defendant is not a Michigan resident,

(a) the court may mail a notice to appear to the defendant at the address in the citation;

(b) the court may issue a warrant for the defendant's arrest; and

(c) if the court has received the driver's license of a nonresident, pursuant to statute, it may retain the license as allowed by statute. The court need not retain the license past its expiration date.

(C) Arraignment. An arraignment in a misdemeanor traffic case may be conducted by

(1) a judge of the district, or

(2) a district court magistrate as authorized by statute and by the judges of the district.

(D) Contested Cases. A misdemeanor traffic case must be conducted in compliance with the constitutional and statutory procedures and safeguards applicable to misdemeanors cognizable by the district court.

[Adopted effective October 1, 1989. Amended April 4, 1997, effective September 2, 1997, 454 Mich; March 28, 2000, effective April 1, 2000, 461 Mich; July 13, 2005, effective January 1, 2006, 473 Mich; September 18, 2019, effective January 1, 2020, 503 Mich.]

Comments

Staff Comment to 1989 Adoption

MCR 6.615 is the rule governing misdemeanor traffic cases, formerly found in MCR 4.102.

Staff Comment to 1997 Amendment

The September 1997 amendment of MCR 6.615 was adopted at the request of the Michigan District Judges Association because of recent statutory changes that created new categories of civil infractions, and the availability of electronic filing.

Staff Comment to 2000 Amendment

The amendment of rule 6.615 was made in light of 1999 PA 200, MCL 770.3a and was effective as to pleas taken on or after April 1, 2000.

Staff Comment to 2005 Amendment

On March 12, 2002, the Court appointed the Committee on the Rules of Criminal Procedure to review the rules to determine whether any of the provisions should be revised. The committee issued its report on June 16, 2003, recommending numerous amendments to existing rules, plus some new rules. A public hearing on the committee's recommendations was held May 27, 2004.

The Court adopted the committee's recommendations with respect to the amendments of Rules 2.511, 6.102, 6.104, 6.107, 6.112, 6.303, 6.304, 6.310, 6.311, 6.402, 6.412, 6.414, 6.419, 6.420, 6.427, 6.615, and 6.620, and the adoption of a new Rule 6.428.

Staff Comment to 2020 Amendment

The amendments of MCR 1.109, 2.107, 2.113, 2.116, 2.119, 2.222, 2.223, 2.225, 2.227, 3.206, 3.211, 3.212, 3.214, 3.303, 3.903, 3.921, 3.925, 3.926, 3.931, 3.933, 3.942, 3.950, 3.961, 3.971, 3.972, 4.002, 4.101, 4.201, 4.202, 4.302, 5.128, 5.302, 5.731, 6.101, 6.615, 8.105, and 8.119 and rescission of MCR 2.226 and 8.125 continue the process for design and implementation of the statewide electronic-filing system.

Rule 6.620   Impaneling the Jury

(A) Alternate Jurors. The court may direct that 7 or more jurors be impaneled to sit in a criminal case. After the instructions to the jury have been given and the case submitted, the names of the jurors must be placed in a container and names drawn to reduce the number of jurors to 6, who shall constitute the jury. The court may retain the alternate jurors during deliberations. If the court does so, it shall instruct the alternate jurors not to discuss the case with any other person until the jury completes its deliberations and is discharged. If an alternate juror replaces a juror after the jury retires to consider its verdict, the court shall instruct the jury to begin its deliberations anew.

(B) Peremptory Challenges.

(1) Each defendant is entitled to three peremptory challenges. The prosecutor is entitled to the same number of peremptory challenges as a defendant being tried alone, or, in the case of jointly tried defendants, the total number of peremptory challenges to which all the defendants are entitled.

(2) *Additional Challenges.* On a showing of good cause, the court may grant one or more of the parties an increased number of peremptory challenges. The additional challenges granted by the court need not be equal for each party.

[Adopted effective October 1, 1989. Amended June 26, 2001, effective September 1, 2001, 465 Mich; July 13, 2005, effective January 1, 2006, 473 Mich.]

Comments

Staff Comment to 1989 Adoption

MCR 6.620 contains the jury selection procedures formerly found in 6.202.

Staff Comment to 2001 Amendment

The amendment was based on a proposal from the Michigan Judges Association. Consistent with the December 1999 amendment of the Federal Rules of Criminal Procedure for the United States District Courts, the amendment allows courts to retain alternate jurors during deliberations.

Staff Comment to 2005 Amendment

On March 12, 2002, the Court appointed the Committee on the Rules of Criminal Procedure to review the rules to determine whether any of the provisions should be revised. The committee issued its report on June 16, 2003, recommending numerous amendments to existing rules, plus some new rules. A public hearing on the committee's recommendations was held May 27, 2004.

The Court adopted the committee's recommendations with respect to the amendments of Rules 2.511, 6.102, 6.104, 6.107, 6.112, 6.303, 6.304, 6.310, 6.311, 6.402, 6.412, 6.414, 6.419, 6.420, 6.427, 6.615, and 6.620, and the adoption of a new Rule 6.428.

Rule 6.625   Appeal; Appointment of Appellate Counsel

(A) An appeal from a misdemeanor case is governed by subchapter 7.100.

(B) If the court imposed a sentence of incarceration, even if suspended, and the defendant is indigent, the court must enter an order appointing a lawyer if, within 14 days after sentencing, the defendant files a request for a lawyer or makes a request on the record. Unless there is a postjudgment motion pending, the court must rule on a defendant's request for a lawyer within 14 days after receiving it. If there is a postjudgment motion pending, the court must rule on the request after the court's disposition of the pending motion and within 14 days after that disposition. If a lawyer is appointed, the 21 days for taking an appeal pursuant to MCR 7.104(A)(3) and MCR 7.105(A)(3) shall commence on the day of the appointment.

[Adopted March 28, 2000, effective April 1, 2000, 461 Mich. Amended effective July 13, 2005, 473 Mich. Amended January 23, 2007, effective May 1, 2007, 477 Mich. Amended effective August 24, 2012, 492 Mich.]

Comments

Staff Comment to 2000 Adoption

The adoption of rule 6.625 was made in light of 1999 PA 200, MCL 770.3a, and was effective as to pleas taken on or after April 1, 2000.

Staff Comment to 2005 Amendment

On March 12, 2002, the Court appointed the Committee on the Rules of Criminal Procedure to review the rules to determine whether any of the provisions should be revised. The committee issued its report on June 16, 2003, recommending numerous amendments of MCR 6.302 and 6.725. The committee did not recommend any amendments of MCR 6.625. A public hearing on the committee's recommendation was held May 27, 2004.

The Court adopted most of the committee's recommendations regarding Rule 6.302, and modified the rule to conform to the ruling of the United States Supreme Court in *Halbert v Michigan*, 545 US 605; 2005 WL 1469183 (June 23, 2005).

The Court adopted many of the committee's recommendations concerning MCR 6.425, however, the Court eliminated the requirement that "[n]ot later than the date of sentencing, the court must complete a sentencing information report on a form to be prescribed by and returned to the state court administrator" in MCR 6.425(D). The Court also modified the language of the rule to incorporate the Court's holding in *People v Babcock*, 469 Mich 247 (2003) and to conform to the ruling in *Halbert*.

The Court did not follow the committee's recommendation that MCR 6.625 not be amended, but instead modified the rule to conform to the ruling in *Halbert*.

Staff Comment to 2007 Amendment

The amendment of Rule 6.625 requires the court to enter an order appointing a lawyer to represent an indigent defendant on appeal from a conviction in district court if the court imposed a sentence of incarceration, even if suspended, and the defendant requests a lawyer within 14 days after sentencing. If there is a postjudgment motion pending, the court must rule on the request for counsel within 14 days after the disposition of the postjudgment motion. The amendment also provides that if a lawyer is appointed, the 21 days for taking an appeal pursuant to subrules 7.101(B)(1) and 7.103(B)(1) shall commence on the day of the appointment.

Staff Comment to 2012 Amendment

These amendments reflect changes to correct minor technical errors that have occurred in drafting or to respond to recent adopted rule revisions, which occasionally inadvertently create incorrect cross-references in other rules.

SUBCHAPTER 6.900   RULES APPLICABLE TO JUVENILES CHARGED WITH SPECIFIED OFFENSES SUBJECT TO THE JURISDICTION OF THE CIRCUIT OR DISTRICT COURT

Rule 6.901   Applicability

(A) Precedence. The rules in this subchapter take precedence over, but are not exclusive of, the rules of procedure applicable to criminal actions against adult offenders.

(B) Scope. The rules apply to criminal proceedings in the district court and the circuit court concerning a juvenile against whom the prosecuting attorney has authorized the filing of a criminal complaint charging a specified juvenile violation instead of approving the filing of a petition in the family division of the circuit court. The rules do not apply to a person charged solely with an offense in which the family division has waived jurisdiction pursuant to MCL 712A.4.

(C) Video and Audio Proceedings. The courts may use telephonic, voice, or videoconferencing technology under this subchapter as prescribed by MCR 6.006.

[Adopted effective October 1, 1989. Amended February 4, 2003, effective May 1, 2003, 467 Mich; September 21, 2016, effective January 1, 2017, 500 Mich.]

Comments

Staff Comment to 2003 Amendment

The changes in MCR 6.901 (B) conform the terminology to statutory amendments, MCL 712A.2(a)(1), 764.1f(2), and the elimination of the Recorder's Court for the city of Detroit. See MCL 600.9931.

Staff Comment to 2017 Amendment

These amendments permit courts to expand the use of videoconferencing technology in many court proceedings; and clarify the proceedings at which videoconferencing technology may be used.

Rule 6.903   Definitions

When used in this subchapter, unless the context otherwise indicates:

(A) "Commitment review hearing" includes a hearing as required by MCL 769.1 to decide whether the jurisdiction of the court shall continue over a juvenile who was placed on juvenile probation and committed to state wardship.

(B) "Commitment review report" means a report on a juvenile committed to state wardship for use at a commitment review hearing prepared by the Family Independence Agency pursuant to MCL 803.225 (§ 5 of the Juvenile Facilities Act).

(C) "Court" means the circuit court as provided in MCL 600.606, but does not include the family division of the circuit court.

(D) "Family division" means the family division of the circuit court.

(E) "Juvenile" means a person 14 years of age or older, who is subject to the jurisdiction of the court for having allegedly committed a specified juvenile violation on or after the person's 14th birthday and before the person's 17th birthday.

(F) "Juvenile sentencing hearing" means a hearing conducted by the court following a criminal conviction to determine whether the best interests of the juvenile and of the public would be served:

(1) by retaining jurisdiction over the juvenile, placing the juvenile on juvenile probation, and committing the juvenile to a state institution or agency as a state ward, as provided in MCL 769.1; or

(2) by imposing sentence as provided by law for an adult offender.

(G) "Juvenile facility" means an institution or facility operated by the juvenile division of the circuit court, a state institution or agency described in the Youth Rehabilitation Services Act, MCL 803.301 *et seq.*, or a county facility or institution operated as an agency of the county other than a facility designed or used to incarcerate adults.

(H) "Specified Juvenile Violation" means one or more of the following offenses allegedly committed by a juvenile in which the prosecuting attorney has authorized the filing of a criminal complaint and warrant instead of proceeding in the family division of the circuit court:

(1) burning a dwelling house, MCL 750.72;

(2) assault with intent to commit murder, MCL 750.83;

(3) assault with intent to maim, MCL 750.86;

(4) assault with intent to rob while armed, MCL 750.89;

(5) attempted murder, MCL 750.91;

(6) first-degree murder, MCL 750.316;

(7) second-degree murder, MCL 750.317;

(8) kidnapping MCL 750.349;

(9) first-degree criminal sexual conduct, MCL 750.520b;

(10) armed robbery, MCL 750.529;

(11) carjacking, MCL 750.529a;

(12) bank, safe, or vault robbery, MCL 750.531;

(13) assault with intent to do great bodily harm, MCL 750.84, if armed with a dangerous weapon;

(14) first-degree home invasion, MCL 750.110a(2), if armed with a dangerous weapon;

(15) escape or attempted escape from a medium-security or high-security juvenile facility operated by the Family Independence Agency, or a high-security facility operated by a private agency under contract with the Family Independence Agency, MCL 750.186a;

(16) possession of [MCL 333.7403(2)(a)(i)] or manufacture, delivery, or possession with intent to manufacture or deliver of 650 grams (1,000 grams beginning March 1, 2003) or more of a schedule 1 or 2 controlled substance [MCL 333.7401(2)(a)(i)];

(17) any attempt, MCL 750.92; solicitation, MCL 750.157b; or conspiracy, MCL 750.157a; to commit any of the offenses listed in subrules (1)–(16);

(18) any lesser-included offense of an offense listed in subrules (1)–(17) if the juvenile is charged with a specified juvenile violation;

(19) any other violation arising out of the same transaction if the juvenile is charged with one of the offenses listed in subrules (1)–(17).

(I) "Dangerous Weapon" means one of the following:

(1) a loaded or unloaded firearm, whether operable or inoperable;

(2) a knife, stabbing instrument, brass knuckles, blackjack, club, or other object specifically designed or customarily carried or possessed for use as a weapon;

(3) an object that is likely to cause death or bodily injury when used as a weapon and that is used as a weapon, or carried or possessed for use as a weapon;

(4) an object or device that is used or fashioned in a manner leading a person to believe the object or device is an object or device described in subrules (1)–(3).

(J) "Magistrate" means a judge of the district court or a municipal court as defined in MCL 761.1(f).

(K) "Progress report" means the report on a juvenile in state wardship prepared by the Family Independence Agency for the court as required by MCL 803.223 (§ 3 of the Juvenile Facilities Act) and by these rules.

(L) "Social report" means the written report on a juvenile for use at the juvenile sentencing hearing prepared by the Family Independence Agency as required by MCL 803.224 (§ 4 of the Juvenile Facilities Act).

(M) "State wardship" means care and control of a juvenile until the juvenile's 21st birthday by an institution or agency within or under the supervision of the Family Independence Agency as provided in the Youth Rehabilitation Services Act, MCL 803.301 *et seq.*, while the juvenile remains under the jurisdiction of the court on the basis of a court order of juvenile probation and commitment as provided in MCL 769.1.

[Adopted effective October 1, 1989. Amended February 4, 2003, effective May 1, 2003, 467 Mich.]

Comments

Staff Comment to 2003 Amendment

The amendments of MCR 6.903 adjust several definitions to conform to statutory changes abolishing the Recorder's Court for the city of Detroit; creating the family division of the circuit court; reducing the age of juveniles subject to the provisions to 14 years; and defining "specified juvenile violations" and "dangerous weapon." See, *e.g.*, MCL 712A.2(a)(1); 764.1f; 600.606; 600.1001; 600.9931.

The April 30, 2003, order makes corrections to a number of the rules governing proceedings regarding juveniles that had been adopted on February 4, 2003. The changes are effective May 1, corresponding to the effective date of the February 4 amendments. In addition to these changes, a number of corrections of punctuation and capitalization and changes in the Notes that accompanied the rules have been made and will appear in the published version of the rules.

The amendments of MCR 3.903(D)(8)(m), 6.903(H)(16), 6.931(E)(3), and 6.933(C)(1) conform the rules to 2002 PA 665, which changed the amounts of controlled substances required for certain violations. See MCL 333.7401(2)(a)(i), 333.7403(2)(a)(i). MCR 3.933(C)(1) is also modified in light of *People v Valentin*, 457 Mich 1 (1998).

The amendment of MCR 3.935(B)(1) corrects the inadvertent omission of references to guardians and legal custodians.

The amendments of MCR 3.922(E)(1)(c), 3.943(A), 3.945(A)(1), 3.965(E)(1), and 3.972(C)(2)(c) correct minor errors in wording.

The amendment of MCR 3.977(G) deletes the word "hearing" in the reference to progress reviews. Under MCR 3.974(A)(1), progress reviews do not require hearings.

The amendment of MCR 3.980(B) and (C) revise the provisions on removal of American Indian children from the home to clarify the distinction between emergency removals and removals after hearing.

The amendments of MCR 3.982(A), 6.903(I)–(L) and 6.937(A) correct cross-reference, citation and numbering errors.

Rule 6.905   Assistance of Attorney

(A) Advice of Right. If the juvenile is not represented by an attorney, the magistrate or court shall advise the juvenile at each stage of the criminal proceedings of the right to the assistance of an attorney. If the juvenile has waived the right to an attorney, the court at later proceedings must reaffirm that the juvenile continues to not want an attorney.

(B) Court–Appointed Attorney. Unless the juvenile has a retained attorney, or has waived the right to an attorney, the magistrate or the court must appoint an attorney to represent the juvenile.

(C) Waiver of Attorney. The magistrate or court may permit a juvenile to waive representation by an attorney if:

(1) an attorney is appointed to give the juvenile advice on the question of waiver;

(2) the magistrate or the court finds that the juvenile is literate and is competent to conduct a defense;

(3) the magistrate or the court advises the juvenile of the dangers and of the disadvantages of self-representation;

(4) the magistrate or the court finds on the record that the waiver is voluntarily and understandingly made; and

(5) the court appoints standby counsel to assist the juvenile at trial and at the juvenile sentencing hearing.

(D) Cost. The court may assess cost of legal representation, or part thereof, against the juvenile or against a person responsible for the support of the juvenile, or both. The order assessing cost shall not be binding on a person responsible for the support of the juvenile unless an opportunity for a hearing has been given and until a copy of the order is served on the person, personally or by first class mail to the person's last known address.

[Adopted effective October 1, 1989. Amended February 4, 2003, effective May 1, 2003, 467 Mich.]

Comments

Staff Comment to 2003 Amendment

MCR 6.905 is unchanged from the current rule.

Rule 6.907   Arraignment on Complaint and Warrant

(A) Time. When the prosecuting attorney authorizes the filing of a complaint and warrant charging a juvenile with a specified juvenile violation instead of approving the filing of a petition in the family division of the circuit court, the juvenile in custody must be taken to the magistrate for arraignment on the charge. The prosecuting attorney must make a good-faith effort to notify the parent of the juvenile of the arraignment. The juvenile must be released if arraignment has not commenced:

(1) within 24 hours of the arrest of the juvenile; or

(2) within 24 hours after the prosecuting attorney authorized the complaint and warrant during special adjournment pursuant to MCR 3.935(A)(3), provided the juvenile is being detained in a juvenile facility.

(B) Temporary Detention Pending Arraignment. If the prosecuting attorney has authorized the filing of a complaint and warrant charging a specified juvenile violation instead of approving the filing of a petition in the family division of the circuit court, a juvenile may, following apprehension, be detained pending arraignment:

(1) in a juvenile facility operated by the county;

(2) in a regional juvenile detention facility operated by the state; or

(3) in a facility operated by the family division of the circuit court with the consent of the family division or an order of a court as defined in MCR 6.903(C).

If no juvenile facility is reasonably available and if it is apparent that the juvenile may not otherwise be safely detained, the magistrate may, without a hearing, authorize that the juvenile be lodged pending arraignment in a facility used to incarcerate adults. The juvenile must be kept separate from adult prisoners as required by law.

(C) Procedure. At the arraignment on the complaint and warrant:

(1) The magistrate shall determine whether a parent, guardian, or an adult relative of the juvenile is present. Arraignment may be conducted without the presence of a parent, guardian, or adult relative provided the magistrate appoints an attorney to appear at arraignment with the juvenile or provided an attorney has been retained and appears with the juvenile.

(2) The magistrate shall set a date for the juvenile's preliminary examination within the next 14 days, less time given and used by the prosecuting attorney under special adjournment pursuant to MCR 3.935(A)(3), up to three days' credit. The magistrate shall inform the juvenile and the parent, guardian, or adult relative of the juvenile, if present, of the preliminary examination date. If a parent, guardian, or an adult relative is not present at the arraignment, the court shall direct the attorney for the juvenile to advise a parent or guardian of the juvenile of the scheduled preliminary examination.

[Adopted effective October 1, 1989. Amended August 3, 1994, effective October 1, 1994, 446 Mich; February 4, 2003, effective May 1, 2003, 467 Mich. Amended effective August 24, 2012, 492 Mich.]

Comments

Staff Comment to 1994 Amendment

In 1994, MCR 6.104(E)(4) and MCR 6.907(C)(2) were amended to reflect the change made by 1994 PA 167, which extended from 12 to 14 days the period within which a preliminary examination must be conducted. MCL 766.4. A similar change was also made in MCR 6.445(C), concerning the timing of a probation revocation hearing.

Staff Comment to 2003 Amendment

The changes in MCR 6.907 conform the terminology to statutory amendments defining "specified juvenile violation." See MCL 712A.2(a)(1); 764.1f; 600.606.

Staff Comment to 2012 Amendment

These amendments reflect changes to correct minor technical errors that have occurred in drafting or to respond to recent adopted rule revisions, which occasionally inadvertently create incorrect cross-references in other rules.

Rule 6.909 Releasing or Detaining Juveniles before Trial or Sentencing

(A) Bail; Detention.

(1) *Bail.* Except as provided in subrule (2) the magistrate or court must advise the juvenile of a right to bail as provided for an adult accused. The magistrate or the court may order a juvenile released to a parent or guardian on the basis of any lawful condition, including that bail be posted.

(2) *Detention Without Bail.* If the proof is evident or if the presumption is great that the juvenile committed the offense, the magistrate or the court may deny bail:

(a) to a juvenile charged with first-degree murder, second-degree murder, or

(b) to a juvenile charged with first-degree criminal sexual conduct, or armed robbery,

(i) who is likely to flee, or

(ii) who clearly presents a danger to others.

(B) Place of Confinement.

(1) *Juvenile Facility.* Except as provided in subrule (B)(2) and in MCR 6.907(B), a juvenile charged with a crime and not released must be placed in a juvenile facility while awaiting trial and, if necessary, sentencing, rather than being placed in a jail or similar facility designed and used to incarcerate adult prisoners.

(2) *Jailing of Juveniles; Restricted.* On motion of a prosecuting attorney or a superintendent of a juvenile facility in which the juvenile is detained, the magistrate or court may order the juvenile confined in a jail or similar facility designed and used to incarcerate adult prisoners upon a showing that

(a) the juvenile's habits or conduct are considered a menace to other juveniles; or

(b) the juvenile may not otherwise be safely detained in a juvenile facility.

(3) *Family Division Operated Facility.* The juvenile shall not be placed in an institution operated by the family division of the circuit court except with the consent of the family division or on order of a court as defined in MCR 6.903(C).

(4) *Separate Custody of Juvenile.* The juvenile in custody or detention must be maintained separately from the adult prisoners or adult accused as required by MCL 764.27a.

(C) Speedy Trial. Within 7 days of the filing of a motion, the court shall release a juvenile who has remained in detention while awaiting trial for more than 91 days to answer for the specified juvenile violation unless the trial has commenced. In computing the 91–day period, the court is to exclude delays as provided in MCR 6.004(C)(1)–(6) and the time required to conduct the hearing on the motion.

[Adopted effective October 1, 1989. Amended February 4, 2003, effective May 1, 2003, 467 Mich.]

Comments

Staff Comment to 2003 Amendment

The changes in MCR 6.909 conform the terminology to statutory amendments defining "specified juvenile violation." See MCL 712A.2(a)(1); 764.1f; 600.606.

Rule 6.911 Preliminary Examination

(A) Waiver. The juvenile may waive a preliminary examination if the juvenile is represented by an attorney and the waiver is made and signed by the juvenile in open court. The magistrate shall find and place on the record that the waiver was freely, understandingly, and voluntarily given.

(B) Transfer to Family Division of Circuit Court. If the magistrate, following preliminary examination, finds that there is no probable cause to believe that a specified juvenile violation occurred or that there is no probable cause to believe that the juvenile committed the specified juvenile violation, but that some other offense occurred that if committed by an adult would constitute a crime, and that there is probable cause to believe that the juvenile committed that offense, the magistrate shall transfer the matter to the family division of the circuit court in the county where the offense is alleged to have been committed for further proceedings. If the court transfers the matter to the family division, a transcript of the preliminary examination shall be sent to the family division without charge upon request.

[Adopted effective October 1, 1989. Amended February 4, 2003, effective May 1, 2003, 467 Mich.]

Comments

Staff Comment to 2003 Amendment

The changes in MCR 6.911 conform the terminology to statutory amendments defining "specified juvenile violation." See MCL 712A.2(a)(1); 764.1f; 600.606.

Rule 6.931 Juvenile Sentencing Hearing

(A) General. If the juvenile has been convicted of an offense listed in MCL 769.1(1)(a)–(*l*), the court must sentence the juvenile in the same manner as an adult. Unless a juvenile is required to be sentenced in the same manner as an adult, a judge of a court having jurisdiction over a juvenile shall conduct a juvenile sentencing hearing unless the hearing is waived as provided in subrule (B). At the conclusion of the juvenile sentencing hearing, the court shall determine whether to impose a sentence against the juvenile as though an adult offender or whether to place the juvenile on juvenile probation and commit the juvenile to state wardship pursuant to MCL 769.1b.

(B) No Juvenile Sentencing Hearing; Consent. The court need not conduct a juvenile sentencing hearing if the prosecuting attorney, the juvenile, and the attorney for the juvenile, consent that it is not in the best interest of the public to sentence the juvenile as though an adult offender. If the juvenile sentence hearing is waived, the court shall not impose a sentence as provided by law for an adult offender. The court must place the juvenile on juvenile probation and commit the juvenile to state wardship.

(C) Notice of Juvenile Sentencing Hearing Following Verdict. If a juvenile sentencing hearing is required, the prosecuting attorney, the juvenile, and the attorney for the juvenile must be advised on the record immediately following conviction of the juvenile by a guilty plea or verdict of guilty that a hearing will be conducted at sentencing, unless waived, to determine whether to sentence the juvenile as an adult or to place the juvenile on juvenile probation and commit the juvenile to state wardship as though a delinquent. The court may announce the scheduled date of the hearing. On request, the court shall notify the victim of the juvenile sentencing hearing.

(D) Review of Reports. The court must give the prosecuting attorney, the juvenile, and the attorney for the juvenile, an opportunity to review the presentence report and the social report before the juvenile sentencing hearing. The court may exempt information from the reports as provided in MCL 771.14 and 771.14a.

(E) Juvenile Sentencing Hearing Procedure.

(1) *Evidence.* At the juvenile sentencing hearing all relevant and material evidence may be received by the court and relied upon to the extent of its probative value, even though such evidence may not be admissible at trial. The rules of evidence do not apply. The court shall receive and consider the presentence report prepared by the probation officer and the social report prepared by the Family Independence Agency.

(2) *Standard of Proof.* The court must sentence the juvenile in the same manner as an adult unless the court determines by a preponderance of the evidence, except as provided in subrule

(3)(c), that the best interests of the public would be served by placing the juvenile on probation and committing the juvenile to state wardship.

(3) *Alternative Sentences For Juveniles Convicted of Certain Controlled Substance Offenses.* If a juvenile is convicted of a violation or conspiracy to commit a violation of MCL 333.7403(2)(a)(i), the court shall determine whether the best interests of the public would be served by:

(a) imposing the sentence provided by law for an adult offender;

(b) placing the individual on probation and committing the individual to a state institution or agency as provided in MCL 769.1(3); or

(c) imposing a sentence of imprisonment for any term of years, but not less than 25 years, if the court determines by clear and convincing evidence that such a sentence would serve the best interests of the public.

In making its determination, the court shall use the criteria set forth in subrule (4).

(4) *Criteria.* The court shall consider the following criteria in determining whether to sentence the juvenile as though an adult offender or whether to place the juvenile on juvenile probation and commit the juvenile to state wardship, giving more weight to the seriousness of the alleged offense and the juvenile's prior record of delinquency:

(a) the seriousness of the alleged offense in terms of community protection, including, but not limited to, the existence of any aggravating factors recognized by the sentencing guidelines, the use of a firearm or other dangerous weapon, and the impact on any victim;

(b) the culpability of the juvenile in committing the alleged offense, including, but not limited to, the level of the juvenile's participation in planning and carrying out the offense and the existence of any aggravating or mitigating factors recognized by the sentencing guidelines;

(c) the juvenile's prior record of delinquency, including, but not limited to, any record of detention, any police record, any school record, or any other evidence indicating prior delinquent behavior;

(d) the juvenile's programming history, including, but not limited to, the juvenile's past willingness to participate meaningfully in available programming;

(e) the adequacy of the punishment or programming available in the juvenile justice system; and

(f) the dispositional options available for the juvenile.

(5) *Findings.* The court must make findings of fact and conclusions of law forming the basis for the juvenile probation and commitment decision or the decision to sentence the juvenile as though an adult offender. The findings and conclusions may be incorporated in a written opinion or stated on the record.

(F) Postjudgment Procedure; Juvenile Probation and Commitment to State Wardship. If the court retains jurisdiction over the juvenile, places the juvenile on juvenile probation, and commits the juvenile to state wardship, the court shall comply with subrules (1)–(11):

(1) The court shall enter a judgment that includes a provision for reimbursement by the juvenile or those responsible for the

juvenile's support, or both, for the cost of care and services pursuant to MCL 769.1(7). An order assessing such cost against a person responsible for the support of the juvenile shall not be binding on the person, unless an opportunity for a hearing has been given and until a copy of the order is served on the person, personally or by first class mail to the person's last known address.

(2) The court shall advise the juvenile at sentencing that if the juvenile, while on juvenile probation, is convicted of a felony or a misdemeanor punishable by more than one year's imprisonment, the court must revoke juvenile probation and sentence the juvenile to a term of years in prison not to exceed the penalty that might have been imposed for the offense for which the juvenile was originally convicted.

(3) The court shall assure that the juvenile receives a copy of the social report.

(4) The court shall send a copy of the order and a copy of the written opinion or transcript of the findings and conclusions of law to the Family Independence Agency.

(5) The court shall not place the juvenile on deferred sentencing, as provided in MCL 771.1(2).

(6) The court shall not place the juvenile on life probation for conviction of a controlled substance violation, as set forth in MCL 771.1(4).

(7) The five-year limit on the term of probation for an adult felony offender shall not apply.

(8) The court shall not require as a condition of juvenile probation that the juvenile report to a department of corrections probation officer.

(9) The court shall not, as a condition of juvenile probation, impose jail time against the juvenile except as provided in MCR 6.933(B)(2).

(10) The court shall not commit the juvenile to the Department of Corrections for failing to comply with a restitution order.

(11) The court shall not place the juvenile in a Department of Corrections camp for one year, as otherwise provided in MCL 771.3a(1).

[Adopted effective October 1, 1989. Amended September 29, 1993, effective December 1, 1993, 444 Mich; February 4, 2003, effective May 1, 2003, 467 Mich.]

Comments

Staff Comment to 1993 Amendment

The 1993 amendment of MCR 6.931(A) clarified that a sentencing hearing is to take place when a juvenile is convicted (unless the hearing is waived), without regard to whether the conviction enters by plea or following a trial.

Staff Comment to 2003 Amendment

MCR 6.931(A) is modified to conform to the statute regarding offenses for which a juvenile must be sentenced in the same manner as an adult, MCL 769.1(1), and provides for a juvenile sentencing hearing in other cases.

In subrule (E)(2), the standard of proof at the juvenile sentencing hearing is established. The juvenile must be sentenced as an adult unless the court determines that the best interests of the public would be served by placing the juvenile on probation and committing the juvenile to state wardship.

Subrule (E)(3) contains provisions regarding alternate sentences for juveniles convicted of offenses involving 650 grams or more of controlled substances.

Subrule (E)(4) revises the criteria that the court is to consider in deciding whether to impose an adult or juvenile sentence.

The April 30, 2003, order makes corrections to a number of the rules governing proceedings regarding juveniles that had been adopted on February 4, 2003. The changes are effective May 1, corresponding to the effective date of the February 4

amendments. In addition to these changes, a number of corrections of punctuation and capitalization and changes in the Notes that accompanied the rules have been made and will appear in the published version of the rules.

The amendments of MCR 3.903(D)(8)(m), 6.903(H)(16), 6.931(E)(3), and 6.933(C)(1) conform the rules to 2002 PA 665, which changed the amounts of controlled substances required for certain violations. See MCL 333.7401(2)(a)(i), 333.7403(2)(a)(i). MCR 3.933(C)(1) is also modified in light of *People v Valentin,* 457 Mich 1 (1998).

The amendment of MCR 3.935(B)(1) corrects the inadvertent omission of references to guardians and legal custodians.

The amendments of MCR 3.922(E)(1)(c), 3.943(A), 3.945(A)(1), 3.965(E)(1), and 3.972(C)(2)(c) correct minor errors in wording.

The amendment of MCR 3.977(G) deletes the word "hearing" in the reference to progress reviews. Under MCR 3.974(A)(1), progress reviews do not require hearings.

The amendment of MCR 3.980(B) and (C) revise the provisions on removal of American Indian children from the home to clarify the distinction between emergency removals and removals after hearing.

The amendments of MCR 3.982(A), 6.903(I)–(L) and 6.937(A) correct cross-reference, citation and numbering errors.

Rule 6.933   Juvenile Probation Revocation

(A) General Procedure. When a juvenile, who was placed on juvenile probation and committed to an institution as a state ward, is alleged to have violated juvenile probation, the court shall proceed as provided in MCR 6.445(A)–(F).

(B) Disposition In General.

(1) *Certain Criminal Offense Violations.*

(a) If the court finds that the juvenile has violated juvenile probation by being convicted of a felony or a misdemeanor punishable by more than one year's imprisonment, the court must revoke the probation of the juvenile and order the juvenile committed to the Department of Corrections for a term of years not to exceed the penalty that could have been imposed for the offense that led to the probation. The court in imposing sentence shall grant credit against the sentence as required by law.

(b) The court may not revoke probation and impose sentence under subrule (B)(1) unless at the original sentencing the court gave the advice, as required by MCR 6.931(F)(2), that subsequent conviction of a felony or a misdemeanor punishable by more than one year's imprisonment would result in the revocation of juvenile probation and in the imposition of a sentence of imprisonment.

(2) *Other Violations.* If the court finds that the juvenile has violated juvenile probation, other than as provided in subrule (B)(1), the court may order the juvenile committed to the department of corrections as provided in subrule (B)(1), or may order the juvenile continued on juvenile probation and under state wardship, and may order any of the following:

(a) a change of placement,

(b) restitution,

(c) community service,

(d) substance abuse counseling,

(e) mental health counseling,

(f) participation in a vocational-technical education program,

(g) incarceration in a county jail for not more than 30 days, and

(h) any other participation or performance as the court considers necessary.

If the court determines to place the juvenile in jail for up to 30 days, and the juvenile is under 17 years of age, the juvenile must be placed separately from adult prisoners as required by law.

(3) If the court revokes juvenile probation pursuant to subrule (B)(1), the court must receive an updated presentence report and comply with MCR 6.445(G) before it imposes a prison sentence on the juvenile.

(C) Disposition Regarding Specific Underlying Offenses.

(1) *Controlled Substance Violation Punishable by Mandatory Nonparolable Life Sentence For Adults.* A juvenile who was placed on probation and committed to state wardship for manufacture, delivery, or possession with the intent to deliver 650 grams (1,000 grams beginning March 1, 2003) or more of a controlled substance, MCL 333.7401(2)(a)(i), may be resentenced only to a term of years following mandatory revocation of probation for commission of a subsequent felony or a misdemeanor punishable by more than one year of imprisonment.

(2) *First–Degree Murder.* A juvenile convicted of first-degree murder who violates juvenile probation by being convicted of a felony or a misdemeanor punishable by more than one year's imprisonment may only be sentenced to a term of years, not to nonparolable life.

(D) Review. The juvenile may appeal as of right from the imposition of a sentence of incarceration after a finding of juvenile probation violation.

(E) Determination of Ability to Pay. A juvenile and/or parent shall not be detained or incarcerated for the nonpayment of court-ordered financial obligations as ordered by the court, unless the court determines that the juvenile and/or parent has the resources to pay and has not made a good-faith effort to do so.

[Adopted effective October 1, 1989. Amended February 4, 2003, effective May 1, 2003, 467 Mich; May 25, 2016, effective September 1, 2016, 499 Mich.]

Comments

Staff Comment to 2003 Amendment

New MCR 6.933(B)(1) specifies the consequences of failure to give certain advice to the juvenile at the original sentencing regarding probation violation.

Subrule (B)(2) is modified to conform to MCL 771.7(2).

New subrule (C) limits the sentencing options following probation violation in cases in which the underlying offense was first-degree murder or involved 650 grams [now 1,000 grams] or more of a controlled substance.

The April 30, 2003, order makes corrections to a number of the rules governing proceedings regarding juveniles that had been adopted on February 4, 2003. The changes are effective May 1, corresponding to the effective date of the February 4 amendments. In addition to these changes, a number of corrections of punctuation and capitalization and changes in the Notes that accompanied the rules have been made and will appear in the published version of the rules.

The amendments of MCR 3.903(D)(8)(m), 6.903(H)(16), 6.931(E)(3), and 6.933(C)(1) conform the rules to 2002 PA 665, which changed the amounts of controlled substances required for certain violations. See MCL 333.7401(2)(a)(i), 333.7403(2)(a)(i). MCR 3.933(C)(1) is also modified in light of *People v Valentin*, 457 Mich 1 (1998).

The amendment of MCR 3.935(B)(1) corrects the inadvertent omission of references to guardians and legal custodians.

The amendments of MCR 3.922(E)(1)(c), 3.943(A), 3.945(A)(1), 3.965(E)(1), and 3.972(C)(2)(c) correct minor errors in wording.

The amendment of MCR 3.977(G) deletes the word "hearing" in the reference to progress reviews. Under MCR 3.974(A)(1), progress reviews do not require hearings.

The amendment of MCR 3.980(B) and (C) revise the provisions on removal of American Indian children from the home to clarify the distinction between emergency removals and removals after hearing.

The amendments of MCR 3.982(A), 6.903(I)–(L) and 6.937(A) correct cross-reference, citation and numbering errors.

Staff Comment to 2016 Amendment

The amendments of MCR 3.605, 3.606, 3.928, 3.944, 3.956, 6.001, 6.425, 6.445, 6.610, and 6.933 were submitted by the Michigan State Planning Body for the Delivery of Legal Services to the Poor. The rule revisions are intended to provide clarity and guidance to courts regarding what courts would be required to do before incarcerating a defendant for failure to pay.

Rule 6.935   Progress Review of Court–Committed Juveniles

(A) General. When a juvenile is placed on probation and committed to a state institution or agency, the court retains jurisdiction over the juvenile while the juvenile is on probation and committed to that state institution or agency. The court shall review the progress of a juvenile it has placed on juvenile probation and committed to state wardship.

(B) Time.

(1) *Semiannual Progress Reviews.* The court must conduct a progress review no later than 182 days after the entry of the order placing the juvenile on juvenile probation and committing the juvenile to state wardship. A review shall be made semiannually thereafter as long as the juvenile remains in state wardship.

(2) *Annual Review.* The court shall conduct an annual review of the services being provided to the juvenile, the juvenile's placement, and the juvenile's progress in that placement.

(C) Progress Review Report. In conducting these reviews, the court shall examine the progress review report prepared by the Family Independence Agency, covering placement and services being provided the juvenile and the progress of the juvenile, and the court shall also examine the juvenile's annual report prepared under MCL 803.223 (§ 3 of the Juvenile Facilities Act). The court may order changes in the juvenile's placement or treatment plan including, but not limited to, committing the juvenile to the jurisdiction of the Department of Corrections, on the basis of the review.

(D) Hearings for Progress and Annual Reviews. Unless the court orders a more restrictive placement or treatment plan, there shall be no requirement that the court hold a hearing when conducting a progress review for a court-committed juvenile pursuant to MCR 6.935(B). However, the court may not order a more physically restrictive change in the level of placement of the juvenile or order more restrictive treatment absent a hearing as provided in MCR 6.937.

[Adopted effective October 1, 1989. Amended February 4, 2003, effective May 1, 2003, 467 Mich.]

Comments

Staff Comment to 2003 Amendment

The amendments of MCR 6.935 add details regarding the reviews to be conducted for juveniles who have been placed on juvenile probation and committed to state wardship.

Rule 6.937   Commitment Review Hearing

(A) Required Hearing Before Age 19 for Court–Committed Juveniles. The court shall schedule and hold, unless adjourned for good cause, a commitment review hearing as nearly as possible to, but before, the juvenile's 19th birthday.

(1) *Notice.* The Family Independence Agency or agency, facility, or institution to which the juvenile is committed, shall advise the court at least 91 days before the juvenile attains age 19 of the need to schedule a commitment review hearing. Notice of the hearing must be given to the prosecuting attorney, the agency or the superintendent of the facility to which the juvenile has been committed, the juvenile, and the parent of the juvenile if the parent's address or whereabouts are known, at least 14 days before the hearing. Notice must clearly indicate that the court may extend jurisdiction over the juvenile until the age of 21. The notice shall include advice to the juvenile and the parent of the juvenile that the juvenile has the right to an attorney.

(2) *Appointment of an Attorney.* The court must appoint an attorney to represent the juvenile at the hearing unless an attorney has been retained or is waived pursuant to MCR 6.905(C).

(3) *Reports.* The state institution or agency charged with the care of the juvenile must prepare a commitment report as required by MCL 769.1b(4) and 803.225(1). The commitment report must contain all of the following, as required by MCL 803.225(1)(a)–(d):

(a) the services and programs currently being utilized by, or offered to, the juvenile and the juvenile's participation in those services and programs;

(b) where the juvenile currently resides and the juvenile's behavior in the current placement;

(c) the juvenile's efforts toward rehabilitation; and

(d) recommendations for the juvenile's release or continued custody.

The report created pursuant to MCL 803.223 for the purpose of annual reviews may be combined with a commitment review report.

(4) *Findings; Criteria.* Before the court continues the jurisdiction over the juvenile until the age of 21, the prosecutor must demonstrate by a preponderance of the evidence that the juvenile has not been rehabilitated or that the juvenile presents a serious risk to public safety. The rules of evidence do not apply. In making the determination, the court must consider the following factors:

(a) the extent and nature of the juvenile's participation in education, counseling, or work programs;

(b) the juvenile's willingness to accept responsibility for prior behavior;

(c) the juvenile's behavior in the current placement;

(d) the prior record and character of the juvenile and physical and mental maturity;

(e) the juvenile's potential for violent conduct as demonstrated by prior behavior;

(f) the recommendations of the state institution or agency charged with the juvenile's care for the juvenile's release or continued custody; and

(g) other information the prosecuting attorney or the juvenile may submit.

(B) **Other Commitment Review Hearings.** The court, on motion of the institution, agency, or facility to which the juvenile is committed, may release a juvenile at any time upon a showing by a preponderance of evidence that the juvenile has been rehabilitated and is not a risk to public safety. The notice provision in subrule (A), other than the requirement that the court clearly indicate that it may extend jurisdiction over the juvenile until the age of 21, and the criteria in subrule (A) shall apply. The rules of evidence shall not apply. The court must appoint an attorney to represent the juvenile at the hearing unless an attorney has been retained or the right to counsel waived. The court, upon notice and opportunity to be heard as provided in this rule, may also move the juvenile to a more restrictive placement or treatment program.

[Adopted effective October 1, 1989. Amended February 4, 2003, effective May 1, 2003, 467 Mich.]

Comments

Staff Comment to 2003 Amendment

The April 30, 2003, order makes corrections to a number of the rules governing proceedings regarding juveniles that had been adopted on February 4, 2003. The changes are effective May 1, corresponding to the effective date of the February 4 amendments. In addition to these changes, a number of corrections of punctuation and capitalization and changes in the Notes that accompanied the rules have been made and will appear in the published version of the rules.

The amendment of MCR 6.937(A) emphasizes that the review hearing is to be held as close as possible to, but before, the juvenile's 19th birthday.

New subrule (A)(3) mandates the preparation of a commitment report under the Juvenile Facilities Act containing specified information. See MCL 803.225; MCL 769.1b(4).

The amendments of MCR 3.903(D)(8)(m), 6.903(H)(16), 6.931(E)(3), and 6.933(C)(1) conform the rules to 2002 PA 665, which changed the amounts of controlled substances required for certain violations. See MCL 333.7401(2)(a)(i), 333.7403(2)(a)(i). MCR 3.933(C)(1) is also modified in light of *People v Valentin*, 457 Mich 1 (1998).

The amendment of MCR 3.935(B)(1) corrects the inadvertent omission of references to guardians and legal custodians.

The amendments of MCR 3.922(E)(1)(c), 3.943(A), 3.945(A)(1), 3.965(E)(1), and 3.972(C)(2)(c) correct minor errors in wording.

The amendment of MCR 3.977(G) deletes the word "hearing" in the reference to progress reviews. Under MCR 3.974(A)(1), progress reviews do not require hearings.

The amendment of MCR 3.980(B) and (C) revise the provisions on removal of American Indian children from the home to clarify the distinction between emergency removals and removals after hearing.

The amendments of MCR 3.982(A), 6.903(I)–(L) and 6.937(A) correct cross-reference, citation and numbering errors.

Rule 6.938 Final Review Hearings

(A) **General.** The court must conduct a final review of the juvenile's probation and commitment not less than 3 months before the end of the period that the juvenile is on probation and committed to the state institution or agency. If the court determines at this review that the best interests of the public would be served by imposing any other sentence provided by law for an adult offender, the court may impose that sentence.

(B) **Notice Requirements.** Not less than 14 days before a final review hearing is to be conducted, the prosecuting attorney, juvenile, and, if addresses are known, the juvenile's parents or guardian must be notified. The notice must state that the court may impose a sentence upon the juvenile and must advise the juvenile and the juvenile's parent or guardian of the right to legal counsel.

(C) **Appointment of Counsel.** If an attorney has not been retained or appointed to represent the juvenile, the court must appoint an attorney and may assess the cost of providing an attorney as costs against the juvenile or those responsible for the juvenile's support, or both, if the persons to be assessed are financially able to comply.

(D) Criteria. In determining whether the best interests of the public would be served by imposing sentence, the court shall consider the following:

(1) the extent and nature of the juvenile's participation in education, counseling, or work programs;

(2) the juvenile's willingness to accept responsibility for prior behavior;

(3) the juvenile's behavior in the current placement;

(4) the prior record and character of the juvenile and the juvenile's physical and mental maturity;

(5) the juvenile's potential for violent conduct as demonstrated by prior behavior;

(6) the recommendations of the state institution or agency charged with the juvenile's care for the juvenile's release or continued custody;

(7) the effect of treatment on the juvenile's rehabilitation;

(8) whether the juvenile is likely to be dangerous to the public if released;

(9) the best interests of the public welfare and the protection of public security; and

(10) other information the prosecuting attorney or juvenile may submit.

(E) Credit for Time Served on Probation. If a sentence is imposed, the juvenile must receive credit for the period of time served on probation and committed to a state agency or institution.

[Adopted February 4, 2003, effective May 1, 2003, 467 Mich.]

Comments

Staff Comment to 2003 Adoption

New MCR 6.938 implements MCL 769.1b(5)–(6), providing for a final review hearing preceding the end of the period for which the juvenile is on probation and committed to state wardship. At the hearing, the court is to determine, using criteria drawn from MCL 769.1b(1), whether to sentence the juvenile as though an adult.

CHAPTER 7. APPELLATE RULES

Effective March 1, 1985

SUBCHAPTER 7.100   APPEALS TO CIRCUIT COURT

Rule 7.101   Scope of Rules

(A) Scope of Rules. The rules in this subchapter govern appeals to the circuit court.

(B) Rules Do Not Affect Jurisdiction. These rules do not restrict or enlarge the appellate jurisdiction of the circuit court.

[Adopted effective March 1, 1985. Amended March 23, 1989, effective June 1, 1989, 432 Mich; June 25, 1996, effective August 1, 1996, 451 Mich; December 18, 2001, effective May 1, 2002, 465 Mich; May 30, 2008, effective September 1, 2008, 481 Mich; February 2, 2010, effective May 1, 2010, 485 Mich; December 8, 2011, effective May 1, 2012, 490 Mich.]

Comments

Staff Comment to 1985 Adoption

MCR 7.101 is based on GCR 1963, 701.

In subrule (A)(1) a reference to the Recorder's Court of the City of Detroit is added in view of that court's jurisdiction over certain appeals. See MCL 770.3(1)(c).

The provisions regarding appeal bonds are revised from the corresponding provisions of GCR 1963, 701.5(a)(1) and 701.8. Subrule (C)(2) covers the bond which is required in order to take an appeal, and subrule (H) covers the subject of bond to stay enforcement of a trial court decision. Separate provisions regarding appeals from probate court and of civil infraction actions are added.

The reference to GCR 1963, 120 (which deals with waiver of fees and costs) in GCR 1963, 701.8(a)(2) is replaced with references to the provision regarding excusing bond requirements, MCR 3.604(L). See subrules (C)(2)(a) and (H)(1)(b)(ii).

Subrule (G) corresponds to GCR 1963, 701.7. Language is added to make clear that an appellant's performance of required acts after the specified time, but before an order dismissing the appeal, does not necessarily prevent dismissal.

Subrule (H)(5) is a new provision explicitly covering the possibility that the request for a stay may be made in the circuit court. It is similar to MCR 7.209(D), which deals with the authority of the Court of Appeals with regard to bonds and stays in appeals to that court.

Subrule (J) is new. It covers the authority of the circuit court to dismiss an appeal, a point that was briefly mentioned in GCR 1963, 701.13(b).

Under subrule (K) oral argument may be requested on the title page of a brief, as in the Court of Appeals. See MCR 7.212(C)(1).

New subrules (O) and (P) cover taxation of costs and imposition of penalties for vexatious appeals. The latter provision is similar to the rules applicable to the Court of Appeals (MCR 7.216[C]) and the Supreme Court (7.315[D]).

Staff Comment to 1989 Amendment

The March 23, 1989, amendments to MCR 7.101 [effective June 1, 1989] make several changes in the procedures for appealing to the circuit court.

The requirement of filing a copy of the judgment or order appealed from with the claim of appeal is deleted.

The requirement of filing a copy of the claim of appeal with the trial court is moved to subrule (C)(2)(a), and language is added to that subrule requiring that a copy of the judgment or order appealed from also be filed at that time.

In order to remove a potential conflict with subrule (C)(3), subrule (C)(2) is amended to provide that the acts it requires must be performed no later than the filing of the claim of appeal, rather than within the time allowed for filing the claim.

Language is added in subrule (C)(2)(b) to make clear that the bond is to be filed in the trial court.

Subrule (C)(3) is amended to delete language that appeared to require a second filing of the claim of appeal.

Subrule (G) is amended to authorize the trial court to dismiss the appeal for failure to perform the acts required by subrule (C)(2).

Staff Comment to 1996 Amendment

The June 25, 1996, amendment of MCR 7.101(B)(1), governing the time for filing an appeal of right in the circuit court, makes the rule consistent with the corresponding provision regarding appeals to the Court of Appeals, MCR 7.204(A)(1), by providing that timely motions for rehearing or reconsideration extend the time for taking an appeal.

Staff Comment to 2002 Amendment

The December 18, 2001 amendments, effective May 1, 2002, updated various rules in light of the Estates and Protected Individuals Code (EPIC), MCL 700.1101 *et seq.*, and revisions made to EPIC by 2000 PA 312, 313, and 469.

Staff Comment to 2008 Amendment

This amendment imposes an automatic stay of any and all proceedings in a case in which a party files a claim of appeal of a denial by the trial court of the party's claim of governmental immunity. No order is necessary for the stay to operate.

Staff Comment to 2010 Amendment

This amendment clarifies that briefs filed in cases that involve an appeal to a circuit court from a district court or an appeal of a decision by a state administrative agency, board, or commission may not exceed 50 pages in length, similar to the length restriction in cases filed in the Court of Appeals.

Staff Comment to 2011 Amendment

These rules reflect a total rewrite of the rules relating to appeals to circuit court, and are modeled on the rules of the Court of Appeals.

Rule 7.102   Definitions

For purposes of this subchapter:

(1) "agency" means any governmental entity other than a "trial court," the decisions of which are subject to appellate review in the circuit court;

(2) "appeal" means judicial review by the circuit court of a judgment, order, or decision of a "trial court" or "agency," even if the statute or constitutional provision authorizing circuit court appellate review uses a term other than "appeal." "Appeal" does not include actions commenced under the Freedom of Information Act, MCL 15.231 *et seq.*, proceedings described in MCR 3.302 through MCR 3.306, and motions filed under MCR 6.110(H);

(3) "appeal fee" means the fee required to be paid to the circuit court upon filing an appeal and any fee required to be paid to the "trial court" or "agency" in conjunction with the appeal;

(4) "clerk" means clerk of the court;

(5) "court" means the circuit court;

(6) "date of filing" means the date of receipt of a document by the "clerk";

(7) "entry" is as defined in MCR 7.204(A);

(8) "final judgment" or "final order" is as defined in MCR 7.202(6); and

(9) "trial court" means the district or municipal court from which the "appeal" is taken.

[Adopted effective March 1, 1985. Amended December 8, 2011, effective May 1, 2012, 490 Mich. Amended effective June 21, 2017, 500 Mich.]

Comments

Staff Comment to 1985 Adoption

MCR 7.102 is substantially the same as GCR 1963, 702.

Staff Comment to 2011 Amendment

These rules reflect a total rewrite of the rules relating to appeals to circuit court, and are modeled on the rules of the Court of Appeals.

Staff Comment to 2017 Amendment

These amendments conform to recent statutory changes that require all appeals from probate court to be heard in the Court of Appeals, instead of the bifurcated system that previously required some probate appeals to be heard in the Court of Appeals and some to be heard in the local circuit court. The amendments also establish priority status for appeals in guardianship and involuntary mental health treatment cases, similar to child custody cases.

Rule 7.103 Appellate Jurisdiction of the Circuit Court

(A) Appeal of Right. The circuit court has jurisdiction of an appeal of right filed by an aggrieved party from the following:

(1) a final judgment or final order of a district or municipal court, except a judgment based on a plea of guilty or nolo contendere;

(2) a final order or decision of an agency governed by the Administrative Procedures Act, MCL 24.201 *et seq.*; and

(3) a final order or decision of an agency from which an appeal of right to the circuit court is provided by law.

(B) Appeal by Leave. The circuit court may grant leave to appeal from:

(1) a judgment or order of a trial court when

(a) no appeal of right exists, or

(b) an appeal of right could have been taken but was not timely filed;

(2) a final order or decision of an agency from which an appeal by leave to the circuit court is provided by law;

(3) an interlocutory order or decision of an agency if an appeal of right would have been available for a final order or decision and if waiting to appeal of right would not be an adequate remedy;

(4) a final order or decision of an agency if an appeal of right was not timely filed and a statute authorizes a late appeal; and

(5) a decision of the Michigan Parole Board to grant parole.

[Adopted effective March 1, 1985. Amended June 13, 2000, effective September 1, 2000, 462 Mich; January 23, 2007, effective May 1, 2007, 477 Mich; December 8, 2011, effective May 1, 2012, 490 Mich. Amended effective June 21, 2017, 500 Mich.]

Comments

Staff Comment to 1985 Adoption

MCR 7.103 is comparable to GCR 1963, 703.

As in the corresponding rules applicable to the Court of Appeals (MCR 7.205[E]) and the Supreme Court (MCR 7.302[C][3]), subrule (B)(6) does not refer to an affidavit of "nonculpable negligence" (see GCR 1963, 703.2[f]), but rather says that the affidavit must explain the delay and that the appellate court may consider the length of and reason for the delay in deciding whether to grant the application.

Subrule (C) states in more detail than did GCR 1963, 703.3 what actions must be taken after leave to appeal is granted, and when.

Staff Comment to 2000 Amendment

The amendment of MCR 7.103(B)(6) [effective September 1, 2000] places a 6-month time limit on applications for leave to appeal to circuit court, corresponding to the 12-month limit applicable in appeals to the Court of Appeals. See MCR 7.205(F)(3). As to judgments entered before the effective date of the amendment, the 6-month period specified in MCR 7.103(B)(6) begins on the effective date, September 1, 2000.

Staff Comment to 2007 Amendment

The amendment of Rule 7.103 is a technical amendment necessitated by the amendment of Rule 6.625.

Staff Comment to 2011 Amendment

These rules reflect a total rewrite of the rules relating to appeals to circuit court, and are modeled on the rules of the Court of Appeals.

Staff Comment to 2017 Amendment

These amendments conform to recent statutory changes that require all appeals from probate court to be heard in the Court of Appeals, instead of the bifurcated system that previously required some probate appeals to be heard in the Court of Appeals and some to be heard in the local circuit court. The amendments also establish priority status for appeals in guardianship and involuntary mental health treatment cases, similar to child custody cases.

Rule 7.104 Filing Appeal of Right

(A) Time Requirements. The time limit for an appeal of right is jurisdictional. See MCR 7.103(A). Time is computed as provided in MCR 1.108. An appeal of right to the circuit court must be taken within:

(1) 21 days or the time allowed by statute after entry of the judgment, order, or decision appealed, or

(2) 21 days after the entry of an order denying a motion for new trial, a motion for rehearing or reconsideration, or a motion for other relief from the judgment, order, or decision, if the motion was filed within:

(a) the initial 21–day period, or

(b) further time the trial court or agency may have allowed during that 21–day period.

(3) If a criminal defendant requests appointment of an attorney within 21 days after entry of the judgment of sentence, an appeal of right must be taken within 21 days after entry of an order:

(a) appointing or denying the appointment of an attorney, or

(b) denying a timely filed motion described in subrule (2).

(B) Manner of Filing. To vest the circuit court with jurisdiction in an appeal of right, an appellant must file with the clerk of the circuit court within the time for taking an appeal:

(1) the claim of appeal, and

(2) the circuit court's appeal fee, unless the appellant is indigent.

(C) Claim of Appeal.

(1) *Form.*

(a) The caption of a claim of appeal shall comply with MCR 1.109(D)(1).

(b) In an appeal from a trial court, the claim of appeal should name the parties in the same order as they appear in the trial court, with the added designation "appellant" or "appellee."

(2) *Content.* The claim should state:

"[*name of appellant(s)*] claim[s] an appeal from the [*judgment or order*] entered on [*date*] in the [*name of trial court*] by [*name of judge*]."

(3) *Signature.* The appellant or the appellant's attorney must date and sign the claim of appeal.

(D) Other Documents. The appellant shall file the following documents with the claim of appeal:

(1) a copy of the judgment, order, or decision appealed;

(2) a copy of the certificate of the court reporter or recorder or a statement that the transcript has been ordered, pursuant to MCR 7.109(B)(3)(a). If there is nothing to be transcribed, the appellant must file a statement so indicating;

(3) in an agency appeal, a copy of a written request or order for a certified copy of the record to be sent to the circuit court;

(4) if the appellant has filed a bond, a true copy of the bond;

(5) proof that money, property, or documents have been delivered or deposited as required by law;

(6) a copy of the register of actions, if any;

(7) proof that the appeal fee of the trial court or agency has been tendered;

(8) anything else required by law to be filed; and

(9) proof that a copy of the claim of appeal and other documents required by this subrule were served on all parties, the trial court or agency, and any other person or officer entitled by law to notice of the appeal.

(E) Service Requirements in Trial Court or Agency. Within the time for taking the appeal, the appellant shall serve on the trial court or agency from which the appeal is taken:

(1) a copy of the claim of appeal;

(2) any fee required by law;

(3) any bond required by law as a condition for taking the appeal;

(4) in an agency appeal, a copy of a written request for a certified copy of the record to be sent to the circuit court; and

(5) unless there is nothing to be transcribed, the certificate of the court reporter or recorder or a statement that the transcript has been ordered and payment for it made or secured. If a statement is filed, the certificate of the court reporter or recorder must be filed within 7 days after a transcript is ordered by a party or the court.

(F) Appearance. Within 14 days after being served with the claim of appeal, the appellee shall file an appearance in the circuit court identifying the individual appellate attorneys. An appellee who does not file an appearance is not entitled to notice of further proceedings.

[Adopted effective March 1, 1985. Amended January 19, 1996, effective April 1, 1996, 450 Mich; February 29, 2000, effective March 10, 2000, 461 Mich; December 8, 2011, effective May 1, 2012, 490 Mich. Amended effective August 24, 2012, 492 Mich. Amended August 30, 2018, effective September 1, 2018, 502 Mich.]

Comments

Staff Comment to 1985 Adoption

MCR 7.104 is substantially the same as GCR 1963, 706.

Staff Comment to 1996 Amendment

The 1996 addition of MCR 7.104(D) was recommended by the State Bar of Michigan, in light of the passage of 1992 PA 22, which established a procedure by which prosecutors and victims may appeal a decision of the parole board. MCL 791.234(7).

Staff Comment to 2000 Amendment

The February 29, 2000 amendment of MCR 7.104(D), effective March 10, 2000, eliminated the references to an appeal of a parole decision by a prisoner. A prisoner's right to appeal such a decision was eliminated by the Legislature in 1999 PA 191, amending MCL 791.234.

Staff Comment to 2011 Amendment

These rules reflect a total rewrite of the rules relating to appeals to circuit court, and are modeled on the rules of the Court of Appeals.

Staff Comment to 2012 Amendment

These amendments reflect changes to correct minor technical errors that have occurred in drafting or to respond to recent adopted rule revisions, which occasionally inadvertently create incorrect cross-references in other rules.

Staff Comment to 2018 Amendment

These amendments update cross-references in the rules, and are intended to reflect changes that are necessary as a result of the Court's recent e-Filing rules amendments.

Rule 7.105. Application for Leave to Appeal

(A) Time Requirements. An application for leave to appeal must be filed with the clerk of the circuit court within:

(1) 21 days or the time allowed by statute after entry of the judgment, order, or decision appealed, or

(2) 21 days after the entry of an order denying a motion for new trial, a motion for rehearing or reconsideration, or a motion for other relief from the judgment, order, or decision if the motion was filed within:

(a) the initial 21–day period, or

(b) such further time as the trial court or agency may have allowed during that 21–day period.

(3) If a criminal defendant, who has pled guilty or nolo contendere, requests appointment of an attorney within 21 days after entry of the judgment of sentence, an application must be filed within 21 days after entry of an order:

(a) appointing or denying the appointment of an attorney, or

(b) denying a timely filed motion described in subrule (2).

(B) Manner of Filing. To apply for leave to appeal, the appellant must file:

(1) a signed application for leave to appeal:

(a) stating the date and nature of the judgment, order, or decision appealed;

(b) concisely reciting the appellant's allegations of error and the relief sought;

(c) setting forth a concise argument in support of the appellant's position on each issue that conforms with MCR 7.212(C); and

(d) if the order appealed is interlocutory, setting forth facts showing how the appellant would suffer substantial harm by awaiting final judgment before taking an appeal;

(2) a copy of the judgment, order, or decision appealed and the opinion or findings of the trial court or agency;

(3) if the appeal is from a trial court, a copy of the register of actions;

(4) if the appeal is from an agency, a copy of the written request or order for a certified copy of the record to be sent to the circuit court;

(5) unless waived by stipulation of the parties or trial court order, a copy of certain transcripts as follows:

(a) in an appeal relating to an evidentiary hearing in a civil or criminal case, the transcript of the evidentiary hearing, including the opinion or findings of the court that conducted the hearing;

(b) in an appeal challenging jury instructions, the transcript of the entire charge to the jury;

(c) in an appeal from a judgment in a criminal case entered pursuant to a plea of guilty or nolo contendere, the transcripts of the plea and sentence;

(d) in an appeal from an order granting or denying a new trial, the portion of the transcript permitting the circuit court to determine whether the trial court's decision on the motion was for a legally recognized reason based on arguable support in the record;

(e) in an appeal raising a sentencing issue, the transcript of the sentencing proceeding and the transcript of any hearing on a motion related to sentencing;

(f) in an appeal raising any other issue, the portion of the transcript substantiating the existence of the issue, objections or lack thereof, arguments of counsel, and any comment or ruling of the trial judge; or

(g) if the transcript is not yet available, the appellant must file a copy of the certificate of the court reporter or recorder or a statement that a transcript has been ordered, in which case the certificate of the court reporter or recorder must be filed within 7 days after a transcript is ordered by a party or the court. If there is nothing to be transcribed, the appellant must file a statement so indicating within 7 days after the transcript is ordered;

(6) proof that a copy of the application was served on all other parties and that a notice of the filing of the application was filed with the trial court or agency. If service cannot be reasonably accomplished, the appellant may ask the circuit court to prescribe service under MCR 2.107(E); and

(7) the circuit court's appeal fee, unless the appellant is indigent.

(C) Answer. Any other party in the case may file, within 21 days of service of the application:

(1) a signed answer to the application conforming to MCR 7.212(D), and

(2) proof that a copy was served on all other parties.

(D) Reply. Within 7 days after service of the answer, the appellant may file a reply brief that conforms to MCR 7.212.

(E) Decision.

(1) There is no oral argument unless directed by the court.

(2) Absent good cause, the court shall decide the application within 35 days of the filing date.

(3) The court may grant or deny leave to appeal or grant other relief. The court shall promptly serve a copy of the order on the parties and the trial court or agency.

(4) If an application is granted, MCR 7.104 governs further proceedings, except that:

(a) the filing of a claim of appeal is not required,

(b) the appellant must complete the acts required by MCR 7.104(D) and (E) within 7 days after the entry of the order granting leave to appeal, and

(c) an appellee may file a claim of cross appeal within 14 days after service of the order granting leave to appeal.

(5) Unless otherwise ordered, the appeal is limited to the issues raised in the application.

(F) Immediate Consideration. When an appellant requires a decision on an application in fewer than 35 days, the appellant must file a motion for immediate consideration concisely stating why an immediate decision is required.

(G) Late Appeal.

(1) When an appeal of right or an application for leave was not timely filed, the appellant may file an application as prescribed under subrule (B) accompanied by a statement of facts explaining the delay. The answer may challenge the claimed reasons for the delay. The circuit court may consider the length of and the reasons for the delay in deciding whether to grant the application.

(2) A late application may not be filed more than 6 months after entry of:

(a) the order, judgment, or decision appealed;

(b) an order denying a motion for a new trial, a motion for rehearing or reconsideration, or a motion for other relief from the judgment, order, or decision, if the motion was timely filed; or

(c) an order denying a motion for new trial under MCR 6.610(G) or a motion to withdraw a plea under MCR 6.610(E)(8).

[Adopted effective March 1, 1985. Amended January 25, 1985, effective March 1, 1985, 421 Mich. Amended effective March 19, 1985, 421 Mich. Amended February 2, 2010, effective May 1, 2010, 485 Mich.; February 25, 2010, effective May 1, 2010, 485 Mich; December 8, 2011, effective May 1, 2012, 490 Mich. Amended effective August 24, 2012, 492 Mich. Amended October 2, 2013, effective January 1, 2014, 495 Mich.]

Comments

Staff Comment to 1985 Adoption

MCR 7.105 corresponds to GCR 1963, 705, which was effective February 1, 1984. There are several modifications.

Under GCR 1963, 705.3(1)(b), the agency whose decision was being reviewed was the respondent on appeal. That is changed in subrule (C)(1)(b). The person who seeks to sustain the agency decision is the respondent. The rule contemplates that there may be no such person in a particular case, and explains the way the caption should be arranged in that situation.

Subrules (D) and (K) permit service of papers by any manner permitted in MCR 2.107. This is in contrast to GCR 1963, 705.4 and 705.11, which required mailing.

Subrule (I) adds additional detail, not found in GCR 1963, 705.9, concerning the procedure for taking additional evidence. The request to take additional evidence, before either the court or the agency, must be included in or filed with the petition for review. The appellant is required to notice the request for hearing in the same manner as provided for notice of motions. If the taking of additional evidence is ordered, further proceedings on appeal are stayed until the completion of the taking of the evidence.

In subrule (J) the grounds for motions to dismiss and to affirm are adjusted to conform to the corresponding provisions regarding motions in the Court of Appeals. See MCR 7.211(C)(2) and (3). Compare GCR 1963, 705.10 and 817.5(2). In addition, under subrule (J)(3)(b) it is a ground for affirmance that the petitioner did not timely or properly raise an issue only if the petitioner was required to raise the matter at an earlier stage. Compare GCR 1963, 705.10(2)(c).

Subrule (K) adds a provision governing the filing of reply briefs. The petitioner has 14 days after the service of the appellee's brief to do so.

Staff Comment to 1985 Amendment

The amendment of MCR 7.105(K)(1) [effective March 1, 1985] adds a reference to the statute (MCL 24.304[2]) that sets the time within which the administrative agency record is to be transferred to the circuit court for use in the appeal.

The March 19, 1985, amendments of MCR 7.105 clarify the status of the agency in appeals from certain administrative agency decisions. Under subrule (C)(1)(b), the agency may become a respondent by filing an appearance. Under subrule (G), when the petitioner seeks a stay, the agency is deemed a respondent whether or not it has filed an appearance.

Staff Comment to First February, 2010 Amendment

This amendment clarifies that briefs filed in cases that involve an appeal to a circuit court from a district court or an appeal of a decision by a state administrative agency, board, or commission may not exceed 50 pages in length, similar to the length restriction in cases filed in the Court of Appeals.

Staff Comment to Second February, 2010 Amendment

These amendments create a prison mailbox rule, which allow a claim of appeal or application for leave to appeal to be deemed presented for filing when a prison inmate acting pro se places the legal documents in the prison's outgoing mail. The rule applies to appeals from administrative agencies, appeals from circuit court (both claims of appeal and applications for leave to appeal), and appeals from decisions of the Court of Appeals to the Supreme Court.

Staff Comment to 2011 Amendment

These rules reflect a total rewrite of the rules relating to appeals to circuit court, and are modeled on the rules of the Court of Appeals.

Staff Comment to 2012 Amendment

These amendments reflect changes to correct minor technical errors that have occurred in drafting or to respond to recent adopted rule revisions, which occasionally inadvertently create incorrect cross-references in other rules.

Staff Comment to 2014 Amendment

These amendments permit the filing of a reply brief in support of an application for leave to appeal in the circuit court and the Court of Appeals, and following the filing of a claim of appeal in the circuit court.

Rule 7.106 Cross Appeals

(A) Right of Cross Appeal.

(1) Any appellee may file a cross appeal when:

(a) an appeal of right is filed, or

(b) the circuit court grants leave to appeal.

(2) If there is more than one plaintiff or defendant in a civil action and one party appeals, any other party may file a cross appeal against all or any of the other parties as well as against the party who first appealed. If the cross appeal operates against a party not affected by the first appeal or in a manner different from the first appeal, that party may file a further cross appeal.

(B) Time Requirements. A cross appeal must be filed with the clerk of the circuit court within 14 days after the claim of appeal is served on the cross appellant or the order granting leave to appeal is entered.

(C) Manner of Filing. To file a cross appeal, the cross appellant must file:

(1) a claim of cross appeal in the form required by MCR 7.104(C);

(2) any required fee;

(3) a copy of the judgment, order, or decision from which the cross appeal is taken; and

(4) proof that a copy of the claim of cross appeal was served on all parties.

(D) Additional Requirements. The cross appellant must perform the steps required by MCR 7.104(D) and (E) unless compliance with this subrule would duplicate the appellant's filing of the same document. The cross appellant is not required to order a transcript or file a court reporter's certificate, unless the initial appeal is dismissed.

(E) Dismissed Appeal. If the initial appeal is dismissed, the cross appeal may continue. If there is a transcript to be produced and the certificate of the court reporter or recorder has not been filed, the cross appellant must file the certificate within 14 days after the order dismissing the appeal. If there is nothing to be transcribed, the cross appellant must file a

statement so indicating within 14 days after the order dismissing the appeal.

(F) Delayed Cross Appeal. A party seeking leave to take a delayed cross appeal must proceed under MCR 7.105(F).

[Adopted December 8, 2011, effective May 1, 2012, 490 Mich.]

Comments

Staff Comment to 2012 Adoption

These rules reflect a total rewrite of the rules relating to appeals to circuit court, and are modeled on the rules of the Court of Appeals.

Rule 7.107. Authority of Trial Court or Agency

After a claim of appeal is filed or leave to appeal is granted, jurisdiction vests in the circuit court. The trial court or agency may not set aside or amend the judgment, order, or decision appealed except by circuit court order or as otherwise provided by law. In all other respects, the authority of the trial court or agency is governed by MCR 7.208(C) through (J).

[Adopted December 8, 2011, effective May 1, 2012, 490 Mich. Amended effective March 21, 2018, 501 Mich.]

Comments

Staff Comment to 2012 Adoption

These rules reflect a total rewrite of the rules relating to appeals to circuit court, and are modeled on the rules of the Court of Appeals.

Staff Comment to 2018 Amendment

These amendments update cross-references and make other nonsubstantive revisions to clarify the rules. The amendment of MCR 6.110(B)(1) addresses an inadvertent omission from the last amendment of this rule that was intended to be shown in overstrike. Accordingly, the current rule does not match the published version. Striking the clause "for good cause shown" will provide consistency with other published versions of the rule and with the statute, MCL 766.7, which allows a magistrate to adjourn a preliminary examination with the consent of the parties without the need for good cause to be shown.

Rule 7.108. Stay of Proceedings; Bond; Review

(A) General Provisions.

(1) A motion for bond or a stay pending appeal may not be filed in the circuit court unless such a motion was decided by the trial court. The motion must include a copy of the trial court's opinion and order and a copy of the transcript of the hearing, unless its production has been waived.

(2) Except as otherwise provided by rule or law, the circuit court may amend the amount of bond, order an additional or different bond and set the amount, or require different or additional sureties. The circuit court may also remand a bond matter to the trial court. The circuit court may grant a stay of proceedings in the trial court or stay the effect or enforcement of any judgment or order of a trial court on terms the circuit court deems just.

(B) Civil Actions.

(1) *Automatic Stay.* Unless otherwise provided by rule, statute, or court order, an execution may not issue and proceedings may not be taken to enforce an order or judgment until expiration of the time for taking an appeal of right.

(2) *Effect of Appeal.* An appeal does not stay execution unless:

(a) the appellant files a bond in an amount not less than 1–1/4 times the amount of the judgment or order being enforced, including any costs, interest, attorney fees, and sanctions assessed to date of filing the bond. When the bond is filed, the judgment or order shall automatically be stayed pending entry of a final order under MCR 7.108(B)(4)(c) to stay enforcement of the judgment even though objections to the bond or surety may be filed, or

(b) the trial court grants a stay with or without bond under MCR 3.604(L), MCR 7.209(E)(2)(b), or MCL 600.2605. The stay order must conform to any condition expressly required by the statute authorizing review.

(3) *Bond Form and Content.* The bond must:

(a) recite the names and designations of the parties and the judge in the trial court; identify the parties for whom and against whom judgment was entered; and state the amount of the judgment, including any costs, interest, attorney fees, and sanctions assessed;

(b) contain the promises and conditions that the appellant will:

(i) diligently file and prosecute the appeal to decision taken from the judgment or order stayed, and will perform and satisfy the judgment or order stayed if it is not set aside or reversed;

(ii) perform or satisfy the judgment or order stayed if the appeal is dismissed;

(iii) pay and satisfy any judgment or order entered and any costs assessed against the principal on the bond in the circuit court, Court of Appeals, or Supreme Court; and

(iv) do any other act which is expressly required in the statute authorizing appeal or ordered by the court;

(c) be executed by the appellant along with one or more sufficient sureties as required by MCR 3.604; and

(d) include the conditions provided in MCR 4.201(N)(4) if the appeal is from a judgment for the possession of land.

(4) *Notice of Bond; Objections; Stay Orders.*

(a) A copy of a bond and any accompanying power of attorney or affidavit must be promptly served on all parties in the manner prescribed in MCR 2.107. At the same time, the party seeking the stay shall file a proposed stay order pursuant to MCR 2.602(B)(3). Proof of service must be filed promptly with the trial court in which the bond has been filed.

(b) Objections shall be filed and served within 7 days after service of the notice of bond. Objections to the amount of the bond are governed by MCR 2.602(B)(3). Objections to the surety are governed by MCR 3.604(E).

(c) If no timely objections to the bond, surety, or stay order are filed, the trial court shall promptly enter the order staying enforcement of the judgment or order pending all appeals. Unless otherwise ordered, the stay shall continue until jurisdiction is again vested in the trial court or until further order of an appellate court.

(d) Any stay order must be promptly served on all parties in the manner prescribed in MCR 2.107. Proof of service must be filed promptly with the trial court.

(e) All hearings under this rule may be held by telephone conference as provided in MCR 2.402.

(5) For good cause shown, the trial court may set the amount of the bond in a greater or lesser amount adequate to protect the interests of the parties.

(6) A bond may be secured under MCL 600.2631.

(7) If an execution has issued, it is suspended by giving notice of filing of the bond to the officer holding the execution.

(C) Criminal Cases.

(1) *Immediate Effect.* A criminal judgment may be executed immediately even though the time for taking an appeal has not elapsed. The granting of bond and its amount are within the discretion of the trial court, subject to the applicable laws and rules on bonds pending appeals in criminal cases.

(2) *Bond Form and Content.* If a bond is granted, the defendant must promise in writing:

(a) to prosecute the appeal to decision;

(b) if the sentence is one of incarceration, to surrender immediately to the county sheriff or as otherwise directed, if the judgment of sentence is affirmed on appeal or if the appeal is dismissed;

(c) if the sentence is other than one of incarceration, to perform and comply with the judgment of sentence if it is affirmed on appeal or if the appeal is dismissed;

(d) to appear in the trial court if the case is remanded for retrial or further proceedings or if a conviction is reversed and retrial is allowed;

(e) to remain in Michigan unless the court gives written approval to leave;

(f) to notify the trial court clerk in writing of a change of address; and

(g) to comply with any other conditions imposed by law or the court.

(3) *Notice of Bond; Objections.* A criminal defendant filing a bond after conviction shall give notice to the prosecuting attorney of the time and place the bond will be filed. The bond is subject to the objection procedure provided in MCR 3.604.

(D) Civil Infractions. An appeal bond and stay in a civil infraction proceeding is governed by MCR 4.101(H)(1).

[Adopted December 8, 2011, effective May 1, 2012, 490 Mich. Amended effective August 24, 2012, 492 Mich; June 21, 2017, 500 Mich; March 21, 2018, 501 Mich.]

Comments

Staff Comment to 2012 Adoption

These rules reflect a total rewrite of the rules relating to appeals to circuit court, and are modeled on the rules of the Court of Appeals.

Staff Comment to 2012 Amendment

These amendments reflect changes to correct minor technical errors that have occurred in drafting or to respond to recent adopted rule revisions, which occasionally inadvertently create incorrect cross-references in other rules.

Staff Comment to 2017 Amendment

These amendments conform to recent statutory changes that require all appeals from probate court to be heard in the Court of Appeals, instead of the bifurcated system that previously required some probate appeals to be heard in the Court of Appeals and some to be heard in the local circuit court. The amendments also establish priority status for appeals in guardianship and involuntary mental health treatment cases, similar to child custody cases.

Staff Comment to 2018 Amendment

These amendments update cross-references and make other nonsubstantive revisions to clarify the rules. The amendment of MCR 6.110(B)(1) addresses an inadvertent omission from the last amendment of this rule that was intended to be shown in overstrike. Accordingly, the current rule does not match the published version. Striking the clause "for good cause shown" will provide consistency with other published versions of the rule and with the statute, MCL 766.7, which allows a magistrate to adjourn a preliminary examination with the consent of the parties without the need for good cause to be shown.

Rule 7.109   Record on Appeal

(A) Content of Record.   Appeals to the circuit court are heard on the original record.

(1) *Appeal From Trial Court.*   The record is as defined in MCR 7.210(A)(1).

(2) *Appeal From Agency.*   The record is as defined in MCR 7.210(A)(2).

(3) *Excluded Evidence.*   The record on appeal must include the substance of the excluded evidence or the transcript of proceedings in the trial court or agency excluding it.   Excluded exhibits must be maintained by the party offering them.

(4) *Stipulations.*   The parties may stipulate in writing regarding any matters relevant to the trial court or agency record if the stipulation is made a part of the record on appeal and sent to the circuit court.

(B) Transcript.

(1) *Appellant's Duties; Orders; Stipulations.*

(a) The appellant is responsible for securing the filing of the transcript as provided in this rule.   Unless otherwise provided by circuit court order or this subrule, the appellant shall order the full transcript of testimony and other proceedings in the trial court or agency.   Under MCR 7.104(D)(2), a party must serve a copy of any request for transcript preparation on the opposing party and file a copy with the circuit court.

(b) On the appellant's motion, with notice to the appellee, the trial court or agency may order that no transcript or some portion less than the full transcript be included in the record on appeal.   The motion must be filed within the time required for filing an appeal, and, if the motion is granted, the appellee may file any portions of the transcript omitted by the appellant.

(c) The parties may stipulate that no transcript or some portion less than the full transcript be filed.

(d) The parties may agree on a statement of facts without procuring the transcript and the statement signed by the parties may be filed with the trial court or agency and sent as the record of testimony in the action.

(2) *Transcript Unavailable.*   When a transcript of the proceedings in the trial court or agency cannot be obtained, the appellant shall file a settled statement of facts using the procedure in MCR 7.210(B)(2) unless a statute provides otherwise.

(3) *Duties of Court Reporter or Recorder.*

(a) Certificate.   Within 7 days after a transcript is ordered by a party or the court, the court reporter or recorder shall furnish a certificate stating that the transcript has been ordered and payment for it made or secured and that it will be filed as soon as possible or has already been filed.

(b) Time for Filing.

(i) The court reporter or recorder shall file the transcript in the trial court or agency within:

[A] 14 days after a transcript is ordered by a party or the court for an application for leave to appeal from an order granting or denying a motion to suppress evidence in a criminal case;

[B] 28 days after a transcript is ordered by a party or the court in an appeal of a criminal conviction based on a plea of guilty, guilty but mentally ill, or nolo contendere or an appeal from the dismissal or reduction of a felony charge following a preliminary examination; or

[C] 56 days after a transcript is ordered by a party or the court in all other cases.

(ii) The circuit court may extend or shorten these time limits in an appeal pending in the court on motion filed by the court reporter or recorder or a party.

(c) Copies.   Additional copies of the transcripts required by the appellant may be ordered from the court reporter or recorder.   Photocopies of the transcript furnished by the court reporter or recorder may also be made.

(d) Form of Transcript.   The transcript must be prepared in the form provided by MCR 7.210(B)(3)(d).

(e) Notice.   Immediately after the transcript is filed, the court reporter or recorder shall notify the circuit court and all parties that it has been filed and file in the circuit court an affidavit of mailing of notice to the parties.

(f) Discipline.   A court reporter or recorder failing to comply with the requirements of these rules is subject to disciplinary action, including punishment for contempt of court.

(g) Responsibility When More Than One Reporter or Recorder.   In a case in which portions of the transcript must be prepared by more than one reporter or recorder, the person who recorded the beginning of the proceeding is responsible for ascertaining that the entire transcript has been prepared, filing it, and giving the notice required by subrule (B)(3)(e), unless the court has designated another person.

(C) Exhibits.   Unless otherwise ordered by the circuit court, trial court, or agency, the offering parties shall maintain exhibits in their possession.

(D) Reproduction of Records.   The trial court or agency shall procure copies of file contents as provided in MCR 7.210(D).

(E) Record on Motion.   If, before the complete record on appeal is sent to the circuit court, a party files a motion that requires the circuit court to have the record, the trial court or agency shall, on request of a party or the circuit court, send the circuit court the documents needed.

(F) Service of the Record.   Within 14 days after the transcript is filed with the trial court or agency, the appellant shall serve a copy of the entire record on appeal, including the transcripts and exhibits in his or her possession, on each appellee.   However, copies of documents the appellee already possesses need not be served.   On request, the appellant shall make available to the appellee exhibits incapable of being copied.   Proof that the record was served must be promptly filed with the circuit court and the trial court or agency.   If the filing of a transcript has been excused as provided in subrule (B), the record shall be served within 14 days after the filing of the transcript substitute.

(G) Transmission of Record.

(1) Within 14 days after the complete transcript has been filed or a certified copy of the record has been requested, the

trial court or agency shall promptly send the record to the circuit court, except for those things omitted by written stipulation of the parties. The trial court may order removal of exhibits, if any, from the record. Weapons, drugs, or money are not to be sent unless requested by the circuit court. The trial court or agency shall append a certificate identifying the name of the case, listing the papers with reasonable definiteness, and indicating that the required fees have been paid and any required bond filed. The record transmitted shall include:

(a) a register of actions in the case;

(b) any exhibits on file;

(c) all documents and papers from the court file;

(d) all transcripts;

(e) all opinions, findings, and orders of the trial court or agency; and

(f) the order or judgment appealed.

(2) Transcripts and all other documents which are part of the record on appeal must be attached in one or more file folders or other suitable hard-surfaced binders showing the name of the trial court or agency, the title of the case, and the file number.

(3) The circuit court must immediately send written notice to the parties when the record is filed in the circuit court.

(H) Return of Record. After deciding the appeal, the circuit court shall promptly send the original record with a certified copy of its order and any written opinion

(1) to the clerk of the Court of Appeals if a timely application for leave to appeal is filed in the Court of Appeals, or

(2) to the clerk of the trial court or agency from which the record was received if no timely application for leave to appeal is filed in the Court of Appeals.

(I) Notice of Return of Record. The trial court or agency clerk shall promptly notify all parties of the return of the record.

[Adopted December 8, 2011, effective May 1, 2012, 490 Mich. Amended effective June 21, 2017, 500 Mich.]

Comments

Staff Comment to 2012 Adoption

These rules reflect a total rewrite of the rules relating to appeals to circuit court, and are modeled on the rules of the Court of Appeals.

Staff Comment to 2017 Amendment

These amendments conform to recent statutory changes that require all appeals from probate court to be heard in the Court of Appeals, instead of the bifurcated system that previously required some probate appeals to be heard in the Court of Appeals and some to be heard in the local circuit court. The amendments also establish priority status for appeals in guardianship and involuntary mental health treatment cases, similar to child custody cases.

Rule 7.110   Motions in Circuit Court Appeals

Motion practice in a circuit court appeal is governed by MCR 2.119. Motions may include special motions identified in MCR 7.211(C). Absent good cause, the court shall decide motions within 28 days after the hearing date.

[Adopted December 8, 2011, effective May 1, 2012, 490 Mich.]

Comments

Staff Comment to 2012 Adoption

These rules reflect a total rewrite of the rules relating to appeals to circuit court, and are modeled on the rules of the Court of Appeals.

Rule 7.111   Briefs

(A) Time for Filing and Service.

(1) *Appellant's Brief.*

(a) Within 28 days after the circuit court provides written notice under MCR 7.109(G)(3) that the record on appeal is filed with the circuit court, the appellant must file a brief conforming to MCR 7.212(C) and serve it on all other parties to the appeal. The time may be extended for 14 days by stipulation and order. The circuit court may extend the time on motion. The filing of a motion does not stay the time for filing a brief.

(b) If an appellant does not file a brief within the time provided by subrule (A)(1)(a), the appeal may be considered abandoned, and the circuit court may dismiss the appeal on 14 days' notice to the parties. Compliance with subrule (A)(1)(a) after notice is sent does not preclude a dismissal of the appeal unless the appellant shows a reasonable excuse for the late filing.

(2) *Appellee's Brief.* Within 21 days after the appellant's brief is served on the appellee, the appellee may file a brief. The brief must conform to MCR 7.212(D) and must be served on all other parties to the appeal. The time may be extended for 14 days by stipulation and order. The circuit court may extend the time on motion. The filing of the motion does not stay the time for filing a brief.

(3) Within 14 days after the appellee's brief is served on appellant, the appellant may file a reply brief. The brief must conform to MCR 7.212(G) and must be served on all other parties to the appeal.

(4) *Briefs in Cross Appeals.* The filing and service of briefs by a cross appellant and a cross appellee are governed by subrules (A)(1)–(3).

(5) *Earlier Filing and Service.* For good cause shown, the circuit court may grant a motion to shorten the time for filing and serving briefs.

(6) *Late Filing.* Any party failing to timely file and serve a brief under these rules forfeits oral argument. For good cause shown, the court may grant a motion to reinstate oral argument.

(B) Length and Form of Briefs. The appellant's brief must comply with MCR 7.212(B) and (C), and the appellee's brief must comply with MCR 7.212(B) and (D).

(C) Request for Oral Argument. A party filing a timely brief is entitled to oral argument by writing "ORAL ARGUMENT REQUESTED" in capital letters or boldface type on the title page of the brief.

(D) Nonconforming Briefs. If, on its own initiative or on a party's motion, the circuit court concludes that a brief does not substantially comply with the requirements in this rule, it may order the party filing the brief to correct the deficiencies within a specified time or it may strike the nonconforming brief.

[Adopted December 8, 2011, effective May 1, 2012, 490 Mich. Amended October 2, 2013, effective January 1, 2014, 495 Mich.]

Comments

Staff Comment to 2012 Adoption

These rules reflect a total rewrite of the rules relating to appeals to circuit court, and are modeled on the rules of the Court of Appeals.

Staff Comment to 2014 Amendment

These amendments permit the filing of a reply brief in support of an application for leave to appeal in the circuit court and the Court of Appeals, and following the filing of a claim of appeal in the circuit court.

Rule 7.112   Miscellaneous Relief

In addition to its general appellate powers, the circuit court may grant relief as provided in MCR 7.216.

[Adopted December 8, 2011, effective May 1, 2012, 490 Mich.]

Comments

Staff Comment to 2012 Adoption

These rules reflect a total rewrite of the rules relating to appeals to circuit court, and are modeled on the rules of the Court of Appeals.

Rule 7.113   Dismissal

(A) Involuntary Dismissal.

(1) *Dismissal.* If the appellant fails to pursue the appeal in conformity with the court rules, the circuit court will notify the parties that the appeal shall be dismissed unless the deficiency is remedied within 14 days after service of the notice.

(2) *Reinstatement.* Within 14 days after the date of the dismissal order, the appellant may move for reinstatement by showing mistake, inadvertence, or excusable neglect.

(B) Voluntary Dismissal. In all cases where the parties file a signed stipulation agreeing to dismiss the appeal or the appellant files an unopposed motion to withdraw the appeal, the circuit court shall enter an order of dismissal.

(C) Notice of Dismissal. Immediately upon entry, a copy of an order dismissing an appeal must be sent to the parties and the trial court or agency.

[Adopted December 8, 2011, effective May 1, 2012, 490 Mich.]

Comments

Staff Comment to 2012 Adoption

These rules reflect a total rewrite of the rules relating to appeals to circuit court, and are modeled on the rules of the Court of Appeals.

Rule 7.114   Oral Argument; Decision and Effect of Judgment, Reconsideration

(A) Oral Argument. If requested in accord with MCR 7.111(C), the court shall schedule oral argument unless it concludes that the briefs and record adequately present the facts and legal arguments, and the court's deliberation would not be significantly aided by oral argument.

(B) Decision. The circuit court shall decide the appeal by oral or written opinion and issue an order. The court's order is its judgment.

(C) Effect of Judgment. Unless otherwise ordered by the circuit court or the Court of Appeals, a judgment is effective after expiration of the period for filing a timely application for leave to appeal or, if such an application is filed, after the Court of Appeals decides the case. Enforcement is to be obtained in the trial court or agency after the record is returned as provided in MCR 7.109(H).

(D) Reconsideration. A motion for reconsideration is governed by MCR 2.119(F).

[Adopted December 8, 2011, effective May 1, 2012, 490 Mich.]

Comments

Staff Comment to 2012 Adoption

These rules reflect a total rewrite of the rules relating to appeals to circuit court, and are modeled on the rules of the Court of Appeals.

Rule 7.115   Taxation of Costs, Fees

(A) Right to Costs. Except as the circuit court otherwise directs, the prevailing party in a civil case is entitled to costs.

(B) Time for Filing. Within 28 days after the dispositive order, opinion, or order denying rehearing is mailed, the prevailing party may file a certified or verified bill of costs with the clerk and serve a copy on all other parties. Each item claimed in the bill must be specified. Failure to file a bill of costs within the time prescribed waives the right to costs.

(C) Objections. Any other party may file objections to the bill of costs with the clerk within 7 days after a copy of the bill is served. The objecting party must serve a copy of the objections on the prevailing party and file proof of that service.

(D) Taxation. The clerk will promptly verify the bill and tax those costs available.

(E) Review. The action by the clerk will be reviewed by the circuit court on motion of either party filed within 7 days from the date of taxation, but on review only those affidavits or objections that were previously filed with the clerk may be considered by the court.

(F) Taxable Costs and Fees. A prevailing party may tax only the reasonable costs and fees incurred in the appeal, including:

(1) printing of briefs, or if briefs were typewritten, a charge of $1 per original page;

(2) obtaining any stay bond;

(3) the transcript and necessary copies of it;

(4) documents required for the record on appeal;

(5) fees paid to the clerk or to the trial court clerk incident to the appeal;

(6) taxable costs and fees allowed by law in appeals under MCL 600.2441;

(7) the additional costs incurred when a party to an appeal under the Administrative Procedures Act unreasonably refused to stipulate to shortening the record as provided in MCL 24.304(2); and

(8) other expenses taxable under applicable court rules or statutes.

[Adopted December 8, 2011, effective May 1, 2012, 490 Mich.]

Comments

Staff Comment to 2012 Adoption

These rules reflect a total rewrite of the rules relating to appeals to circuit court, and are modeled on the rules of the Court of Appeals.

Rule 7.116   Appeals under the Michigan Employment Security Act

(A) Scope. This rule governs appeals to the circuit court under the Michigan Employment Security Act, MCL 421.1 *et seq.* Unless this rule provides otherwise, MCR 7.101 through 7.115 apply.

(B) Time Requirements. An appeal of right from an order or decision of the Michigan Compensation Appellate Commission must be taken within 30 days after the mailing of the commission's decision.

(C) Manner of Filing. Except as provided in subrule (B), the claim of appeal shall conform with MCR 7.104 and must include statements of jurisdiction and venue. In addition, proof that the claim of appeal was served on the Michigan Compensation Appellate Commission and all interested parties must be filed in the circuit court. The unemployment agency is a party to any appeal under MCL 421.38(3), but the Michigan Compensation Appellate Commission is not a party to the appeal.

(D) Venue. Venue is determined under MCL 421.38(1).

(E) Appearance of Appellee. Within 14 days after service of the claim of appeal, the appellee must file an appearance in the circuit court.

(F) Record on Appeal. Within 42 days after the claim of appeal is served on the Michigan Compensation Appellate Commission, or within further time as the circuit court allows, the Michigan Compensation Appellate Commission must transmit to the clerk of the circuit court a certified copy of the record of proceedings before the administrative law judge and the Michigan Compensation Appellate Commission. The Michigan Compensation Appellate Commission must notify the parties that the record was transmitted.

(G) Standard of Review and Decision on Appeal. Under MCL 421.38, the circuit court may reverse an order or decision of the Michigan Compensation Appellate Commission only if it finds that the order or decision is contrary to law or is not supported by competent, material, and substantial evidence on the whole record. In all other respects, MCR 7.114 applies.

[Adopted December 8, 2011, effective May 1, 2012, 490 Mich. Amended effective August 24, 2012, 492 Mich.]

Comments

Staff Comment to 2012 Adoption

These rules reflect a total rewrite of the rules relating to appeals to circuit court, and are modeled on the rules of the Court of Appeals.

Staff Comment to 2012 Amendment

These amendments reflect changes to correct minor technical errors that have occurred in drafting or to respond to recent adopted rule revisions, which occasionally inadvertently create incorrect cross-references in other rules.

Rule 7.117   Appeals from the Michigan Civil Service Commission

(A) Scope. This rule governs appeals to the circuit court from the Michigan Civil Service Commission. Unless this rule provides otherwise, MCR 7.101 through 7.115 apply.

(B) Procedure. An appeal from a decision of the Michigan Civil Service Commission must comply with MCR 7.119.

(C) Commission as Party. An appeal challenging any decision, rule, or regulation of the Michigan Civil Service Commission must name the commission as a party and must serve the commission at the Office of the State Personnel Director in Lansing, Michigan.

[Adopted December 8, 2011, effective May 1, 2012, 490 Mich.]

Comments

Staff Comment to 2012 Adoption

These rules reflect a total rewrite of the rules relating to appeals to circuit court, and are modeled on the rules of the Court of Appeals.

Rule 7.118   Appeals from the Michigan Parole Board

(A) Scope. This rule governs appeals to the circuit court from the Michigan Parole Board. Unless this rule provides otherwise, MCR 7.101 through 7.115 apply.

(B) No Appeal of Right. There is no appeal of right from a decision of the parole board.

(C) Access to Reports and Guidelines. Upon request, the prosecutor, the victim, and the prisoner shall receive the parole eligibility report, any prior parole eligibility reports that are mentioned in the parole board's decision, and any parole guidelines that support the action taken.

(D) Application for Leave to Appeal.

(1) *Parties.*

(a) Only the prosecutor or a victim may file an application for leave to appeal.

(b) The prisoner shall be the appellee.

(c) The parole board may move to intervene as an appellee.

(2) *Time Requirements.* An application for leave to appeal must be filed within 28 days after the parole board mails a notice of action granting parole and a copy of any written opinion to the prosecutor and the victim, if the victim requested notification under MCL 780.771.

(3) *Manner of Filing.* An application for leave must comply with MCR 7.105, must include statements of jurisdiction and venue, and must be served on the parole board and the prisoner. If the victim seeks leave, the prosecutor must be served. If the prosecutor seeks leave, the victim must be served if the victim requested notification under MCL 780.771.

(a) Service on the parole board, the victim, or the prosecutor must be accomplished by certified mail, return receipt requested, in compliance with MCR 2.105(A)(2).

(b) Service on a prisoner incarcerated in a state correctional facility must be accomplished by serving the application for leave on the warden or administrator, along with the form approved by the State Court Administrative Office for personal service on a prisoner. Otherwise, service must be accomplished by certified mail, return receipt requested, as described in MCR 2.103(C) and MCR 2.104(A)(2) or in compliance with MCR 2.105(A)(2). In addition to the pleadings, service on the prisoner must also include a notice in a form approved by the State Court Administrative Office advising the prisoner that:

(i) the prisoner may respond to the application for leave to appeal through retained counsel or in propria persona, although no response is required, and

(ii) if an order of parole is issued under MCL 791.236 before the completion of appellate proceedings, a stay may be granted in the manner provided by MCR 7.108, except that no bond is required.

(c) Proof of service must be promptly filed with the clerk of the circuit court and must include a copy of the return receipt and, in the case of the prisoner, a copy of the certificate of service executed by the appropriate prison official.

(4) *Venue.* An application for leave to appeal a decision of the parole board may only be filed in the circuit court of the sentencing county under MCL 791.234(11).

(E) Late Application. A late application for leave to appeal may be filed under MCR 7.105(F).

(F) Stay of Order of Parole.

(1) An order of parole issued under MCL 791.236 shall not be executed until 28 days after the mailing of the notice of action.

(2) If an order is issued under MCL 791.235 before completion of appellate proceedings, a stay may be granted in the manner provided by MCR 7.108, except that no bond is required.

(G) Decision to Grant Leave to Appeal.

(1) The circuit court shall make its determination within 28 days after the application for leave to appeal is filed.

(2) If the court does not make its determination within 28 days, the court shall enter an order to produce the prisoner before the court for a show cause hearing to determine whether the prisoner shall be released on parole pending disposition of the appeal.

(H) Procedure After Leave to Appeal Granted. If leave to appeal is granted, MCR 7.105(D)(4) applies along with the following:

(1) *Record on Appeal.*

(a) The record on appeal shall consist of the prisoner's central office file at the Department of Corrections and any other documents considered by the parole board in reaching its decision.

(b) Within 14 days after being served with an order granting leave to appeal, the parole board shall send copies of the record to the circuit court and the other parties. In all other respects, the record on appeal shall be processed in compliance with MCR 7.109.

(c) The expense of preparing and serving the record on appeal may be taxed as costs to a nonprevailing appellant, except that expenses may not be taxed to an indigent party.

(2) *Briefs.* Briefs must comply with MCR 7.111, except:

(a) the appellant's brief is due 28 days after the record is served on the parties, and

(b) the appellee's brief, if filed, is due 21 days after the appellant's brief is served on the appellee.

(3) *Burden of Proof.* The appellant has the burden of establishing that the decision of the parole board was

(a) in violation of the Michigan Constitution, a statute, an administrative rule, or a written agency regulation that is exempted from promulgation pursuant to MCL 24.207, or

(b) a clear abuse of discretion.

(4) *Remand to the Parole Board.* On motion by a party or on the court's own motion, the court may remand the matter to the parole board for an explanation of its decision.

(a) The parole board shall hear and decide the matter within 28 days of the date of the order, unless the board determines that an adjournment is necessary to obtain evidence or there is other good cause for an adjournment.

(b) The time for filing briefs on appeal under subrule (H)(2) is tolled while the matter is pending on remand.

(I) Subsequent Appeal to the Court of Appeals. An appeal of a circuit court decision is by emergency application for leave to appeal to the Court of Appeals under MCR 7.205(F), and the Court of Appeals shall expedite the matter.

(J) Parole Board Responsibility After Reversal or Remand.

(1) If a decision of the parole board is reversed or remanded, the board shall review the matter and take action consistent with the circuit court's decision within 28 days.

(2) If the circuit court order requires the board to undertake further review of the file or to reevaluate its prior decision, the board shall provide the parties with an opportunity to be heard.

(3) An appeal to the Court of Appeals does not affect the board's jurisdiction to act under this subsection.

[Adopted December 8, 2011, effective May 1, 2012, 490 Mich. Amended effective August 24, 2012, 492 Mich; March 9, 2016, 499 Mich.]

Comments

Staff Comment to 2012 Adoption

These rules reflect a total rewrite of the rules relating to appeals to circuit court, and are modeled on the rules of the Court of Appeals.

Staff Comment to 2012 Amendment

These amendments reflect changes to correct minor technical errors that have occurred in drafting or to respond to recent adopted rule revisions, which occasionally inadvertently create incorrect cross-references in other rules.

Staff Comment to 2016 Amendment

These amendments update cross-references that changed after the rule was adopted and make other nonsubstantive revisions.

Rule 7.119   Appeals from Agencies Governed by the Administrative Procedures Act

(A) Scope. This rule governs an appeal to the circuit court from an agency decision where MCL 24.201 *et seq.* applies. Unless this rule provides otherwise, MCR 7.101 through MCR 7.115 apply.

(B) Appeal of Right.

(1) *Time Requirements.* Judicial review of a final decision or order shall be by filing a claim of appeal in the circuit court within 60 days after the date of mailing of the notice of the agency's final decision or order. If a rehearing before the agency is timely requested, then the claim of appeal must be filed within 60 days after delivery or mailing of the notice of the agency's decision or order on rehearing, as provided in the statute or constitutional provision authorizing appellate review.

(2) *Manner of Filing.*

(a) Claim of Appeal—Form. The claim of appeal shall conform with the requirements of MCR 7.104(C)(1), except that:

(i) the party aggrieved by the agency decision is the appellant and is listed first in the caption; and

(ii) the party seeking to sustain the agency's decision is the appellee; or

(iii) if there is no appellee, then the caption may read "In re [*name of appellant or other identification of the subject of the appeal*]," followed by the designation of the appellant. Except where otherwise provided by law, the agency or another party to the case may become an appellee by filing an appearance within 21 days after service of the claim of appeal.

(b) Claim of Appeal—Content. The claim of appeal must:

(i) state "[*Name of appellant*] claims an appeal from the decision entered on [*date*] by [*name of the agency*]," and

(ii) include concise statements of the following:

[A] the statute, rule, or other authority enabling the agency to conduct the proceedings;

[B] the statute or constitutional provision authorizing appellate review of the agency's decision or order in the circuit court; and

[C] the facts on which venue is based under MCL 24.303(1).

(c) Signature. The claim of appeal must be signed as stated in MCR 7.104(C)(3).

(d) Other Documents. In addition to the claim of appeal, the appellant shall also comply with MCR 7.104(D).

(e) Filing Requirements in the Agency. The appellant must comply with MCR 7.104(E).

(f) Service. In addition to the service requirements found in MCR 7.104(D)(9), the appellant must also serve the Attorney General.

(3) *Appearance.* The appellee shall file an appearance that complies with MCR 7.104(F) within 14 days after service of the claim of appeal.

(C) Application for Interlocutory Appeal. A preliminary procedural or intermediate agency action or ruling is not immediately reviewable, except that a court may grant interlocutory appeal of a preliminary, procedural, or intermediate decision by an agency only on a showing that review of the final decision would not be an adequate remedy.

(1) *Time Requirements.* An application for interlocutory appeal must be filed with the court within 14 days of the decision.

(2) *Manner of Filing.* In addition to the requirements of MCR 7.105(B), the application must:

(a) include a jurisdictional statement citing:

(i) the statute, rule, or other authority enabling the agency to conduct proceedings, and

(ii) the statute or constitutional provision authorizing appellate review of the agency's decision or order in the circuit court;

(b) include a statement of venue with supporting facts;

(c) set forth why review of the agency's final decision will not be an adequate remedy; and

(d) state the relief sought.

(3) *Answer.* An appellee may file an answer to an application for interlocutory appeal under MCR 7.105(C). The circuit court may require the filing of an answer.

(4) *If Application is Granted.* If the application is granted, the appeal proceeds in the same manner as an appeal of right.

(D) Late Appeal. The appellant may file an application for late appeal if permitted by statute.

(1) *Time Requirements.* Unless inconsistent with the statute authorizing the appeal, the application must be filed within six months after entry of the agency decision or order.

(2) *Manner of Filing.* In addition to the requirements of MCR 7.105(B), the application must include:

(a) a statement citing the statute authorizing a late appeal;

(b) a statement of facts explaining the delay; and

(c) statements of jurisdiction and venue complying with subrules (C)(2)(a) and (b).

(3) *Answer.* An appellee may file an answer to the application for late appeal under MCR 7.105(C). The circuit court may require the filing of an answer.

(4) *If Application is Granted.* If the application is granted, the appeal proceeds in the same manner as an appeal of right.

(E) Stay of Enforcement. The filing of an appeal does not stay enforcement of the agency's decision or order.

(1) A party may file a motion seeking a stay in the circuit court.

(2) For purposes of this subrule, the agency is entitled to notice even if it has not filed an appearance in the appeal.

(3) The court may order a stay on appropriate terms and conditions if it finds that:

(a) the moving party will suffer irreparable injury if a stay is not granted;

(b) the moving party made a strong showing that it is likely to prevail on the merits;

(c) the public interest will not be harmed if a stay is granted; and

(d) the harm to the moving party in the absence of a stay outweighs the harm to the other parties to the proceedings if a stay is granted.

(4) If the motion for stay is granted, the circuit court may set appropriate terms and conditions for the posting of a bond

(a) in the amount required by any applicable statute authorizing the appeal, or

(b) in an amount and with sureties that the circuit court deems adequate to protect the public and the parties when there are no statutory instructions.

(5) *Temporary Stay.*

(a) The circuit court may grant a temporary stay of enforcement without written notice only if

(i) it clearly appears from facts alleged in the motion that immediate and irreparable injury will result if a stay is not entered before a hearing, and

(ii) the moving party certifies to the court in writing that it made reasonable efforts to contact the other parties and agency, but was unsuccessful.

(b) A temporary stay may be granted by the court until a hearing can be held. A hearing on a motion to dissolve a temporary stay will be heard on 24 hours' notice, or less on order of the court for good cause shown, and takes precedence over all matters except previously filed matters of the same character.

(F) Stipulations. The parties may stipulate regarding any issue on appeal or any part of the record on appeal if the stipulation is embodied in an order entered by the court.

(G) Additional Evidence. A motion to present proofs of alleged irregularity in procedure before the agency, or to allow the taking of additional evidence before the agency, is timely only if it is filed with or included with the claim of appeal or application. The appellant shall promptly notice the motion for decision. If the court orders the taking of additional evidence, the time for filing briefs is stayed until the taking of the evidence is completed.

(H) Decision. The court may affirm, reverse, remand, or modify the decision of the agency and may grant further relief as appropriate based on the record, findings, and conclusions.

(1) If the agency's decision or order is not supported by competent, material, and substantial evidence on the whole record, the court shall specifically identify the finding or findings that lack support.

(2) If the agency's decision or order violates the Constitution or a statute, is affected by a material error of law, or is affected by an unlawful procedure resulting in material prejudice to a party, the court shall specifically identify the agency's conclusions of law that are being reversed.

[Adopted December 8, 2011, effective May 1, 2012, 490 Mich. Amended effective August 24, 2012, 492 Mich.]

Comments

Staff Comment to 2012 Adoption

These rules reflect a total rewrite of the rules relating to appeals to circuit court, and are modeled on the rules of the Court of Appeals.

Staff Comment to 2012 Amendment

These amendments reflect changes to correct minor technical errors that have occurred in drafting or to respond to recent adopted rule revisions, which occasionally inadvertently create incorrect cross-references in other rules.

Rule 7.120 Licensing Appeals under the Michigan Vehicle Code

(A) Scope. This rule governs appeals to the circuit court under the Michigan Vehicle Code, MCL 257.1 *et seq.*, from a final determination by the Secretary of State pertaining to an operator's license, a chauffeur's license, a vehicle group designation, or an endorsement. Unless this rule provides otherwise, MCR 7.101 through 7.115 apply.

(B) Appeal of Right.

(1) *Time Requirements.* The time for filing an appeal of right is governed by MCL 257.323(1).

(2) *Manner of Filing.*

(a) Claim of Appeal—Form. The claim of appeal shall conform to the requirements of MCR 7.104(C)(1), except that the party aggrieved by the Secretary of State's determination is the appellant.

(b) Claim of Appeal—Content. The claim of appeal must:

(i) state the appellant's full name, current address, birth date, and driver's license number;

(ii) state "[*name of appellant*] claims an appeal from the decision on [*date*] by the Secretary of State"; and

(iii) include concise statements of the following:

[A] the nature of any determination by the Secretary of State;

[B] the statute authorizing the Secretary of State's determination;

[C] the subsection of MCL 257.323 under which the appeal is taken; and

[D] the facts on which venue is based.

(c) Signature. The claim of appeal must be signed as stated in MCR 7.104(C)(3).

(d) Other Documents. The appellant must attach as exhibits accompanying the claim of appeal:

(i) a copy of the Secretary of State's determination, and

(ii) any affidavits supporting the claim of appeal.

(e) Service. The appellant shall serve the claim of appeal on all parties.

(3) *Appearance.* The appellee shall file an appearance within 14 days that complies with MCR 7.104(F).

(C) Application for Late Appeal.

(1) *Time Requirements.* An application for late appeal must be filed within the time set forth in MCL 257.323(1).

(2) *Manner of Filing.* In addition to the requirements of MCR 7.105(B), the application must comply with MCR 7.120(B)(2)(b) and must include a statement showing good cause for the delay.

(3) *Answer.* An appellee may file an answer to the application for late appeal under MCR 7.105(C). The circuit court may require the filing of an answer.

(4) *If Application is Granted.* If the application is granted, the appeal proceeds in the same manner as an appeal of right.

(D) Stay of Enforcement. The filing of a claim of appeal or an application for late appeal does not stay enforcement of the Secretary of State's decision or order. The appellant may file for a stay of enforcement under MCL 257.323a. The appellant shall serve a copy of the order granting or denying the stay on the Secretary of State. The Secretary of State may file a motion challenging the stay.

(E) Stipulations. The parties may stipulate regarding any issue on appeal or any part of the record on appeal if the stipulation is embodied in an order entered by the court.

(F) Proceedings Under MCL 257.323(3).

(1) *Briefs.* The court may require briefs and may enter an order setting a briefing schedule. Unless otherwise ordered, briefs must comply with MCR 7.111.

(2) *Hearing.* The court shall schedule a hearing under MCL 257.323(2). During the hearing, the court may take testimony and examine all the facts and circumstances relating to the denial, suspension, or restriction of the person's license under MCL 257.303(1)(d), MCL 257.320, MCL 257.904(10), MCL 257.904(11), MCL 257.310d, or for a first violation of MCL 257.625f.

(3) *Decision.* For denials, suspensions, or restrictions of the person's license under MCL 257.303(1)(d), MCL 257.320, MCL 257.904(10), MCL 257.904(11), MCL 257.310d, or for a first violation of MCL 257.625f, the circuit court may affirm, modify, or set aside the restriction, suspension, or denial. The circuit court, however, shall not order the Secretary of State to issue a restricted or unrestricted chauffeur's license that would permit the person to drive a commercial motor vehicle that hauls hazardous materials.

(4) *Appellant's Responsibility After Decision.* Pursuant to MCL 257.323(3), the appellant shall file a certified copy of the circuit court's order with the Secretary of State's office in Lansing within 7 days after entry of the order for denials, suspensions, or restrictions of the person's license arising under

405

MCL 257.303(1)(d), MCL 257.320, MCL 257.904(10), MCL 257.904(11), MCL 257.310d, or for a first violation of MCL 257.625f.

(G) Proceedings Under MCL 257.323(4).

(1) *Briefs.* Unless otherwise ordered, the parties must file briefs complying with MCR 7.111.

(2) *Oral Argument.* If requested in accord with MCR 7.111(C), the court shall schedule oral argument unless it concludes that the briefs and record adequately present the facts and legal arguments, and the court's deliberation would not be significantly aided by oral argument.

(3) *Decision.* The court shall confine its consideration to a review of the record prepared under MCL 257.322, MCL 257.625f, or MCL 257.204a for statutory legal issues and shall not grant restricted driving privileges. The court shall set aside the Secretary of State's determination only if the appellant's substantial rights have been prejudiced because the determination is:

(a) in violation of the Constitution of the United States, the Michigan Constitution, or a statute;

(b) in excess of the Secretary of State's statutory authority or jurisdiction;

(c) made upon unlawful procedure that results in material prejudice to the appellant;

(d) not supported by competent, material, and substantial evidence on the whole record;

(e) arbitrary, capricious, or clearly an abuse or unwarranted exercise of discretion; or

(f) affected by other substantial and material error of law.

[Adopted December 8, 2011, effective May 1, 2012, 490 Mich.]

Comments

Staff Comment to 2012 Adoption

These rules reflect a total rewrite of the rules relating to appeals to circuit court, and are modeled on the rules of the Court of Appeals.

Rule 7.121 Concealed Pistol License Appeals

(A) Scope. This rule governs appeals to the circuit court under MCL 28.425d. Unless this rule provides otherwise, MCR 7.101 through MCR 7.114 apply.

(B) Suspensions and Revocations. Failure of the county clerk to reinstate a concealed pistol license under MCL 28.428(2) or (6) shall be considered a failure to issue a license under MCL 28.425d unless otherwise noted by statute.

(C) Appeal of Right.

(1) *Time Requirements.* Time requirements are governed by MCR 7.104(A).

(2) *Manner of Filing.*

(a) Claim of Appeal—Form. The claim of appeal shall conform with the requirements of MCR 7.104(C)(1), except that:

(i) the license applicant or licensee is the appellant, and

(ii) the county clerk, department of state police, or entity taking the fingerprints may be the appellee.

(b) Claim of Appeal—Content. The claim of appeal must state whether the appellant is appealing a statutory disqualification, failure to issue a receipt, or failure to issue a

concealed pistol license, and the facts on which venue is based.

(c) Signature. The claim of appeal must be signed as stated in MCR 7.104(C)(3).

(d) Service. The appellant shall serve the claim of appeal on all parties.

(e) Request for Certified Record. Within the time for filing a claim of appeal, the appellant shall send a written request to the county clerk to send a certified copy of the record to the circuit court.

(3) *Appearance.* The appellee shall file an appearance that complies with MCR 7.104(F) within 14 days after service of the claim of appeal.

(4) *Briefs.* Unless otherwise ordered, the parties must file briefs complying with MCR 7.111.

(5) *Oral Argument.* If requested in accord with MCR 7.111(C), the court shall hold oral argument within 14 days after the appellee's brief was filed or due. The court may dispense with oral argument under MCR 7.114(A).

(D) Notice of Decision. The circuit court shall serve the parties with a copy of its order resolving the appeal.

[Adopted December 8, 2011, effective May 1, 2012, 490 Mich. Amended effective August 24, 2012, 492 Mich. Amended May 24, 2017, effective September 1, 2017, 500 Mich.]

Comments

Staff Comment to 2012 Adoption

These rules reflect a total rewrite of the rules relating to appeals to circuit court, and are modeled on the rules of the Court of Appeals.

Staff Comment to 2012 Amendment

These amendments reflect changes to correct minor technical errors that have occurred in drafting or to respond to recent adopted rule revisions, which occasionally inadvertently create incorrect cross-references in other rules.

Staff Comment to 2017 Amendment

The amendments of MCR 7.121 update the court rules to incorporate statutory changes enacted in 2015 PA 3 and 207.

Rule 7.122 Appeals from Zoning Ordinance Determinations

(A) Scope.

(1) This rule governs appeals to the circuit court from a determination under a zoning ordinance by any officer, agency, board, commission, or zoning board of appeals, and by any legislative body of a city, village, township, or county authorized to enact zoning ordinances. Unless this rule provides otherwise, MCR 7.101 through MCR 7.115 apply. This rule does not apply to legislative decisions of a city, village, township, or county, such as the adoption of or amendment to a zoning ordinance.

(2) This rule does not restrict the right of a party to bring a complaint for relief relating to a determination under a zoning ordinance. A party may seek a stay of enforcement under MCR 7.123(E).

(3) An appeal under this section is an appeal of right.

(B) Time Requirements. An appeal under this rule must be filed within the time prescribed by the statute applicable to the appeal. If no time is specified in the applicable statute, the appeal must be filed within 30 days after the certification of the minutes of the board or commission from which the appeal is taken or within 30 days after the board or commission issued its decision in writing, whichever deadline comes first.

(C) Manner of Filing.

(1) *Claim of Appeal—Form.* The claim of appeal shall conform to the requirements of MCR 7.104(C)(1), except that:

(a) the party aggrieved by the determination shall be designated the appellant; and

(b) the city, village, township, or county under whose ordinance the determination was made shall be designated the "appellee," except that when a city, village, township, county, or an officer or entity authorized to appeal on its behalf, appeals a determination as an aggrieved party, then the appellee(s) shall be designated as the board, commission, or other entity that made the determination and the party that prevailed before the board, commission, or other entity that made the determination.

(2) *Claim of Appeal—Content.* The claim of appeal must:

(a) state "[*Name of appellant*] claims an appeal from the decision on [*date*] by [*name of the officer or entity*]"; and

(b) include concise statements of the following:

(i) the nature of the determination by the officer or entity;

(ii) the statute authorizing the officer or entity's proceedings and determination;

(iii) the statute or constitutional provision under which the appeal is taken;

(iv) the facts on which venue is based;

(v) the grounds on which relief is sought, stated in as many separate paragraphs as there are separate grounds alleged; and

(vi) the relief sought.

(3) *Signature.* The claim of appeal must be signed as stated in MCR 7.104(C)(3).

(4) *Other Documents.* The appellant must attach to the claim of appeal a copy of the order and/or minutes of the officer or entity from which the appeal is taken or must indicate that there is no such document to attach.

(5) *Service.* Upon filing the claim of appeal, the appellant, shall serve a copy of the claim of appeal and all attachments upon the clerk of the city, village, township, or county as well as the board, commission, or other entity that made a determination that is the subject of the appeal. Service shall be in the manner provided in MCR 2.107, and appellant shall promptly file a proof of service with the court.

(D) Bond. An appellant shall not be required to post a bond unless so ordered by the court.

(E) Record on Appeal; Transmittal of the Record.

(1) The record includes the original or a copy certified by the city, village, township, or county clerk of the application, all documents and material submitted by any person or entity with respect to the application, the minutes of all proceedings, and any determination of the officer or entity.

(2) Within 28 days after service of the claim of appeal, the clerk of the city, village, township, or county from which the appeal is taken must file the record with the court.

(3) If the record is not available within 28 days after service of the claim of appeal, the clerk of the city, village, township, or county from which the appeal is taken shall notify the court of the estimated date of transmittal of the record.

(4) If the clerk of the city, village, township, or county postpones transmittal of the record or transmittal is otherwise delayed, the court may on motion or its own initiative exercise superintending control over the clerk to prevent delay.

(5) The clerk of the city, village, township, or county from which the appeal is taken must notify the appellant and appellee of the transmittal of the record to the court.

(6) Motions regarding the contents of the record or to prepare a transcript of proceedings before the officer or entity must be filed within 21 days after transmission of the record to the court.

(F) Briefs. Unless otherwise ordered, the parties must file briefs complying with MCR 7.111.

(G) Decision.

(1) *Appeals Under MCL 125.3606.*

(a) In an appeal from a city, village, township, or county board of zoning appeals, the court shall apply the standard of review under MCL 125.3606(1).

(b) If the court finds the record inadequate to review the decision or finds that additional material evidence exists that with good reason was not presented, the court shall order further zoning board of appeals proceedings on conditions that the court considers proper. The zoning board of appeals may modify the findings and decision as a result of the new proceedings or may affirm the original decision. The supplementary record and decision shall be filed with the court.

(c) The court may affirm, reverse, or modify the decision of the board of appeals.

(2) *Other Appeals.* In an appeal from a final determination under a zoning ordinance where no right of appeal to a zoning board of appeals exists, the court shall determine whether the decision was authorized by law and the findings were supported by competent, material, and substantial evidence on the whole record.

(H) Notice of Decision. The court shall serve the parties with a copy of its order resolving the appeal.

[Adopted December 8, 2011, effective May 1, 2012, 490 Mich.]

Comments

Staff Comment to 2012 Adoption

These rules reflect a total rewrite of the rules relating to appeals to circuit court, and are modeled on the rules of the Court of Appeals.

Rule 7.123 Appeals from Agencies Not Governed by Another Rule

(A) Scope. This rule governs an appeal to the circuit court from an agency decision that is not governed by another rule in this subchapter. Unless this rule provides otherwise, MCR 7.101 through 7.115 apply.

(B) Appeal of Right.

(1) *Time Requirements.* Time requirements are governed by MCR 7.104(A).

(2) *Manner of Filing.*

(a) Claim of Appeal—Form. The claim of appeal shall conform to the requirements of MCR 7.119(B)(2)(a).

(b) Claim of Appeal—Content. The claim of appeal must:

(i) state "[*Name of appellant*] claims an appeal from the decision on [*date*] by [*name of the agency*]," and

(ii) include concise statements of the following:

[A] the nature of the proceedings before the agency;

[B] citation to the statute, rule, or other authority enabling the agency to conduct the proceedings;

[C] citation to the statute or constitutional provision authorizing appellate review of the agency's decision or order in the circuit court; and

[D] the facts on which venue is based.

(c) Signature. The claim of appeal must be signed as stated in MCR 7.104(C)(3).

(d) Other Documents. The appellant must also comply with MCR 7.104(D).

(e) Filing Requirements in the Agency. The appellant must comply with MCR 7.104(E).

(f) Service. The appellant must comply with MCR 7.104(D)(7).

(3) *Appearance.* The appellee shall file an appearance that complies with MCR 7.104(F) within 14 days after service of the claim of appeal.

(C) Application for Leave to Appeal or for Interlocutory Appeal.

(1) *Time Requirements.* An application must comply with MCR 7.105(A).

(2) *Manner of Filing.* An application must comply with MCR 7.105 and MCR 7.123(B)(2)(b)(ii). An application for interlocutory appeal shall also state why review of the agency's final decision will not be an adequate remedy.

(3) *Answer.* An appellee may file an answer to an application that complies with MCR 7.105(C). The circuit court may require the filing of an answer.

(4) *If Application is Granted.* If the application is granted, the appeal proceeds as an appeal of right.

(D) Late Appeal. The appellant may file an application for late appeal if permitted by statute.

(1) *Time Requirements.* Unless inconsistent with the statute authorizing late appeal, the application must be filed within six months after entry of the agency decision or order.

(2) *Manner of Filing.* In addition to the requirements of MCR 7.105(B), the application must include:

(a) a statement citing the statute authorizing a late appeal;

(b) a statement of facts explaining the delay; and

(c) statements of jurisdiction and venue complying with MCR 7.123(B)(2)(b)(ii).

(3) *Answer.* An appellee may file an answer to the application for late appeal under MCR 7.105(C). The circuit court may require the filing of an answer.

(4) *If Application is Granted.* If the application is granted, the appeal proceeds in the same manner as an appeal of right.

(E) Stay of Enforcement. The filing of an appeal or an application for leave to appeal does not stay enforcement of the agency's decision or order.

(1) A party may file a motion seeking a stay in the circuit court.

(2) For purposes of this subrule, the agency is entitled to notice even if it has not filed an appearance in the appeal.

(3) The court may order a stay on appropriate terms and conditions if it finds that:

(a) the moving party will suffer irreparable injury if a stay is not granted;

(b) the moving party made a strong showing that it is likely to prevail on the merits;

(c) the public interest will not be harmed if a stay is granted; and

(d) the harm to the moving party in the absence of a stay outweighs the harm to the other parties to the proceedings if a stay is granted.

(4) If the motion for stay is granted, the circuit court may set appropriate terms and conditions for the posting of a bond:

(a) in the amount required by any applicable statute authorizing the appeal, or

(b) in an amount and with sureties that the circuit court deems adequate to protect the public and the parties when there are no statutory instructions.

(5) *Temporary Stay.*

(a) The circuit court may grant a temporary stay of enforcement without written notice only if

(i) it clearly appears from facts alleged in the motion that immediate and irreparable injury will result if a stay is not entered before a hearing, and

(ii) the moving party certifies to the court in writing that it made reasonable efforts to contact the other parties and agency, but was unsuccessful.

(b) A temporary stay may be granted by the court until a hearing can be held. A hearing on a motion to dissolve a temporary stay will be heard on 24 hours' notice, or less on order of the court for good cause shown, and takes precedence over all matters except previously filed matters of the same character.

(F) Stipulations. The parties may stipulate regarding any issue on appeal or any part of the record on appeal if the stipulation is embodied in an order entered by the court.

(G) Decision. The court may affirm, reverse, remand, or modify the decision of the agency and may grant further relief as appropriate based on the record, findings, and conclusions.

(1) If the agency's decision or order is not supported by competent, material, and substantial evidence on the whole record, the court shall specifically identify the finding or findings that lack support.

(2) If the agency's decision or order violates the Constitution or a statute, is affected by a material error of law, or is affected by an unlawful procedure resulting in material prejudice to a party, the court shall specifically identify the agency's conclusions of law that are being reversed.

[Adopted November 8, 2011, effective May 1, 2012, 490 Mich. Amended effective August 24, 2012, 492 Mich.]

Comments
Staff Comment to 2012 Adoption

These rules reflect a total rewrite of the rules relating to appeals to circuit court, and are modeled on the rules of the Court of Appeals.

Staff Comment to 2012 Amendment

These amendments reflect changes to correct minor technical errors that have occurred in drafting or to respond to recent adopted rule revisions, which occasionally inadvertently create incorrect cross-references in other rules.

SUBCHAPTER 7.200   COURT OF APPEALS

Rule 7.201.   Organization and Operation of Court of Appeals

(A) Chief Judge and Chief Judge Pro Tempore.

(1) The Supreme Court shall select a judge of the Court of Appeals to serve as chief judge. No later than October 1 of each odd-numbered year, the Court of Appeals may submit the names of no fewer than two judges whom the judges of that court recommend for selection as chief judge.

(2) The chief judge shall select a chief judge pro tempore, who shall fulfill such functions as the chief judge assigns.

(3) The chief judge and chief judge pro tempore shall serve a two-year term beginning on January 1 of each even-numbered year, provided that the chief judge serves at the pleasure of the Supreme Court and the chief judge pro tempore serves at the pleasure of the chief judge.

(B) Court of Appeals Clerk; Place of Filing Papers; Fees.

(1) The court shall appoint a chief clerk who is subject to the requirements imposed on the Supreme Court clerk in MCR 7.301(C). The clerk's office must be located in Lansing and be operated under the court's direction. With the court's approval, the clerk may appoint assistant and deputy clerks.

(2) Papers to be filed with the court or the clerk must be filed in the clerk's office in Lansing or with a deputy clerk in Detroit, Troy, or Grand Rapids. Fees paid to a deputy clerk must be forwarded to the clerk's office in Lansing. Claims of appeal, applications, motions, and complaints need not be accepted for filing until all required documents have been filed and the requisite fees have been paid.

(3) If a case is accepted for filing without all of the required documents, transcripts, or fees, the appellant, or the plaintiff in an original action under MCR 7.206, must supply the missing items within 21 days after the date of the clerk's notice of deficiency. The chief judge or another designated judge may dismiss the appeal and assess costs if the deficiency is not remedied within that time.

(C) Sessions of Court. There are 9 regular sessions of the court each year. Except as otherwise required for the efficient administration of the court, each session begins on the first Tuesday during the months of October through June. Each session continues for the number of days necessary to conclude the hearing of cases scheduled for argument. The chief judge may order a special session.

(D) Panels. The court shall sit to hear cases in panels of 3 judges. The decision of a majority of the judges of a panel in attendance at the hearing is the decision of the court. Except as modified by the Supreme Court, a decision of the court is final. The judges must be rotated so that each judge sits with every other judge with equal frequency, consistent with the efficient administration of the court's business. The Supreme Court may assign persons to act as temporary judges of the court, under the constitution and statutes. Only one temporary judge may sit on a 3-judge panel.

(E) Assignments and Presiding Judge. Before the calendar for each session is prepared, the chief judge shall assign the judges to each panel and the cases to be heard by them and designate one of them as presiding judge. A presiding judge presides at a hearing and performs other functions the court or the Supreme Court by rule or special order directs. The chief judge may assign a motion or any other matter to any panel.

(F) Place of Hearing. The court shall sit in Detroit, Lansing, Grand Rapids, and Marquette, or another place the chief judge designates. A calendar case will be assigned for hearing in the city nearest to the court or tribunal from which the appeal was taken or as the parties stipulate, except as otherwise required for the efficient administration of the court's business.

(G) Judicial Conferences. At least once a year and at other times the chief judge finds necessary, the judges shall meet to consider proposals to amend the rules of the court, improve the administration of justice, including the operations of the court, and transact any business which properly comes before them.

(H) Approval of Expenses. The state court administrator shall approve the expenses for operation of the court and the expense accounts of the judges, including attendance at a judicial conference. The state court administrator shall prepare a budget for the court.

[Adopted effective March 1, 1985. Amended October 19, 1989, effective January 1, 1992, 433 Mich; December 15, 1993, effective February 1, 1994, 444 Mich. Amended effective September 13, 1995, 450 Mich; November 6, 1996, 453 Mich. Amended June 2, 1999, effective September 1, 1999, 459 Mich. Amended effective January 4, 2005, 471 Mich; March 21, 2018, 501 Mich.]

Comments

Staff Comment to 1985 Adoption

MCR 7.201 is comparable to GCR 1963, 800.

Staff Comment to 1994 Amendment

MCR 7.201(B)(3) [effective February 1, 1994] is a new provision. It specifies the time for completing a filing and allows the chief judge to dismiss a case or assess costs if a deficiency is not remedied within that time.

Staff Comment to 1995 Amendment

In 1995, MCR 7.201(A) was amended to provide that the Supreme Court would appoint the Chief Judge of the Court of Appeals. As indicated in its 1995 order, the Supreme Court took this step 'to facilitate the Court's exercise of its constitutional responsibility to administer and superintend the courts of this state' and to "enhance the Supreme Court's ability to implement sound policies statewide, and assure a greater degree of responsiveness to the leadership that the constitution requires this Court to exercise."

Staff Comment to 1999 Amendment

MCR 7.201(B) permits the Chief Judge, or another designated judge, acting alone, to enter certain orders when a party does not proceed in accordance with the rules.

Staff Comment to 2005 Amendment

The amendment of MCR 7.201(B)(2) replaces the reference to Southfield with a reference to Troy. This amendment corresponds with the Court of Appeals November 29, 2004, relocation of its Southfield office to Troy.

Staff Comment to 2018 Amendment

These amendments update cross-references and make other nonsubstantive revisions to clarify the rules. The amendment of MCR 6.110(B)(1) addresses an inadvertent omission from the last amendment of this rule that was intended to be shown in overstrike. Accordingly, the current rule does not match the published version. Striking the clause "for good cause shown" will provide consistency with other published versions of the rule and with the statute, MCL 766.7, which allows a magistrate to adjourn a preliminary examination with the consent of the parties without the need for good cause to be shown.

Rule 7.202.   Definitions

For purposes of this subchapter:

(1) "clerk" means the Court of Appeals clerk, unless otherwise stated;

(2) "date of filing" means the date of receipt of a document by a court clerk;

(3) "entry fee" means the fee required by law or, in lieu of that fee, a motion to waive fees or a copy of an order appointing an attorney;

(4) "filing" means the delivery of a document to a court clerk and the receipt and acceptance of the document by the clerk with the intent to enter it in the record of the court;

(5) "custody case" means a domestic relations case in which the custody of a minor child is an issue, an adoption case, or a case in which the family division of circuit court has entered an order terminating parental rights or an order of disposition removing a child from the child's home;

(6) "final judgment" or "final order" means:

(a) In a civil case,

(i) the first judgment or order that disposes of all the claims and adjudicates the rights and liabilities of all the parties, including such an order entered after reversal of an earlier final judgment or order;

(ii) an order designated as final under MCR 2.604(B);

(iii) in a domestic relations action, a postjudgment order that, as to a minor, grants or denies a motion to change legal custody, physical custody, or domicile,

(iv) a postjudgment order awarding or denying attorney fees and costs under MCR 2.403, 2.405, 2.625 or other law or court rule,

(v) an order denying governmental immunity to a governmental party, including a governmental agency, official, or employee under MCR 2.116(C)(7) or an order denying a motion for summary disposition under MCR 2.116(C)(10) based on a claim of governmental immunity;

(b) In a criminal case,

(i) an order dismissing the case;

(ii) the original sentence imposed following conviction;

(iii) a sentence imposed following the granting of a motion for resentencing;

(iv) a sentence imposed, or order entered, by the trial court following a remand from an appellate court in a prior appeal of right; or

(v) a sentence imposed following revocation of probation.

[Adopted effective March 1, 1985. Amended October 19, 1995, effective January 1, 1996, 450 Mich; June 2, 1999, effective September 1, 1999, 459 Mich; December 13, 2000, effective April 1, 2001, 463 Mich. Amended effective September 1, 2002, 466 Mich. Amended February 3, 2004, effective May 1, 2004, 469 Mich; March 14, 2007, effective May 1, 2007, 477 Mich; September 30, 2008, effective January 1, 2009, 482 Mich; September 20, 2018, effective January 1, 2019, 502 Mich.]

Comments

Staff Comment to 1985 Adoption

MCR 7.202 is a new provision defining several terms used in the Court of Appeals subchapter.

Staff Comment to 1996 Amendment

The October 19, 1995, amendment of MCR 7.202 [effective January 1, 1996] adds a definition of "final judgment" or "final order". The principal effect would be to eliminate appeals of right from certain postjudgment orders.

Staff Comment to 1999 Amendment

Former MCR 7.202(6)-The definition of "signed" was deleted from the rule.

Staff Comment to 2000 Amendment

The amendment of MCR 7.202(7)(b)(iv) makes certain orders entered by the trial court on remand from an appellate court appealable by right.

Staff Comment to 2002 Amendment

The June 4, 2002, amendments of MCR 7.202, 7.203, and 7.209, effective September 1, 2002, involve orders appealable by right to the Court of Appeals.

The provisions concerning custody orders in domestic relations cases and orders regarding attorney fees and costs are moved from MCR 7.203(A)(3) and (4) to MCR 7.202(7)(a)(iii) and (iv). There is also a change in the language regarding fees and costs, to refer to "postjudgment" orders.

New MCR 7.202(7)(a)(v) includes as "final" an order denying immunity to a governmental defendant, as is provided in many jurisdictions. See, *e.g.*, *Mitchell v Forsyth*, 472 US 511; 105 S Ct 2806; 86 L Ed 2d 411 (1985).

Language is added to MCR 7.203(A) to make clear that an appeal from an order described in MCR 7.202(7)(a)(iii)–(v) is limited to the portion of the order regarding which there is an appeal of right. In addition, obsolete references to the recorder's court are deleted from that subrule.

New MCR 7.209(E)(4) provides for a stay with respect to a governmental party who takes an appeal of right from an order denying immunity.

Staff Comment to 2004 Amendment

The February 3, 2004, amendment of MCR 7.202, 7.204, 7.205, and 7.212, effective May 1, 2004, was adopted on the basis of a recommendation from a work group appointed by the Court of Appeals. The amendments clarify the definition of "entry" of an order for jurisdictional purposes at the Court of Appeals.

Staff Comment to 2007 Amendment

This change reflects the fact that after court reorganization accomplished pursuant to MCL 600.1001 *et seq.*, cases involving the termination of parental rights are handled by the family division of circuit court, and not by the juvenile division of probate court.

Staff Comment to 2008 Amendment

This amendment clarifies that motions for summary disposition that involve claims of governmental immunity based on MCR 2.116(C)(7) and (C)(10) that are denied are appealable by right in the Court of Appeals. This language addresses the jurisdictional issue that arose in the cases of *Newton v Michigan State Police*, 263 Mich App 251 (2004), and *Walsh v Taylor*, 263 Mich App 618 (2004).

Staff Comment to 2019 Amendment

The amendment of MCR 7.202 clarifies what constitutes a final postjudgment order in a domestic relations case for purposes of appeal by right. This issue was raised in *Marik v Marik*, docket 154549.

Rule 7.203   Jurisdiction of the Court of Appeals

(A) Appeal of Right. The court has jurisdiction of an appeal of right filed by an aggrieved party from the following:

(1) A final judgment or final order of the circuit court, or court of claims, as defined in MCR 7.202(6), except a judgment or order of the circuit court

(a) on appeal from any other court or tribunal;

(b) in a criminal case in which the conviction is based on a plea of guilty or nolo contendere;

An appeal from an order described in MCR 7.202(6)(a)(iii)–(v) is limited to the portion of the order with respect to which there is an appeal of right.

(2) A judgment or order of a court or tribunal from which appeal of right to the Court of Appeals has been established by law or court rule.

(B) Appeal by Leave. The court may grant leave to appeal from:

(1) a judgment or order of the circuit court and court of claims that is not a final judgment appealable of right;

(2) a final judgment entered by the circuit court on appeal from any other court;

(3) a final order of an administrative agency or tribunal which by law is appealable to or reviewable by the Court of Appeals or the Supreme Court;

(4) any other judgment or order appealable to the Court of Appeals by law or rule;

(5) any judgment or order when an appeal of right could have been taken but was not timely filed.

(C) Extraordinary Writs, Original Actions, and Enforcement Actions. The court may entertain an action for:

(1) superintending control over a lower court or a tribunal immediately below it arising out of an action or proceeding which, when concluded, would result in an order appealable to the Court of Appeals;

(2) mandamus against a state officer (see MCL 600.4401);

(3) habeas corpus (see MCL 600.4304);

(4) quo warranto involving a state office or officer;

(5) any original action required by law to be filed in the Court of Appeals or Supreme Court;

(6) any action to enforce a final order of an administrative tribunal or agency required by law to be filed in the Court of Appeals or Supreme Court.

(D) Other Appeals and Proceedings. The court has jurisdiction over any other appeal or action established by law. An order concerning the assignment of a case to the business court under MCL 600.8301 *et seq.* shall not be appealed to the Court of Appeals.

(E) Appeals by Prosecution. Appeals by the prosecution in criminal cases are governed by MCL 770.12, except as provided by MCL 770.3.

(F) Dismissal.

(1) Except when a motion to dismiss has been filed, the chief judge or another designated judge may, acting alone, dismiss an appeal or original proceeding for lack of jurisdiction.

(2) The appellant or plaintiff may file a motion for reconsideration within 21 days after the date of the order of dismissal. The motion shall be submitted to a panel of 3 judges. No entry fee is required for a motion filed under this subrule.

(3) The clerk will not accept for filing a motion for reconsideration of an order issued by a 3–judge panel that denies a motion for reconsideration filed under subrule (2).

[Adopted effective March 1, 1985. Amended March 30, 1989, effective October 1, 1989, 432 Mich; December 15, 1993, effective February 1, 1994, 444 Mich. Amended effective December 27, 1994. Amended October 19, 1995, effective January 1, 1996, 450 Mich; amended June 2, 1999, effective September 1, 1999, 459 Mich; November 30, 1999, 461 Mich. Amended December 22, 1999, effective February 1, 2000, 461 Mich. Amended effective September 11, 2001, 465 Mich. Amended June 4, 2002, effective September 1, 2002, 466 Mich; January 22, 2003, effective May 1, 2003, 467 Mich. Amended effective October 5, 2004, 471 Mich. Amended December 21, 2005, effective January 1, 2006, 474 Mich; June 5, 2013, effective September 1, 2013, 494 Mich. Amended effective May 7, 2014, 495 Mich; December 14, 2016, 500 Mich.]

Comments

Staff Comment to 1985 Adoption

MCR 7.203 is drawn from GCR 1963, 801, 806.1, 806.2, and 816.2(2). The provisions of the former rules are rewritten, although their substance is not changed.

In subrule (B)(2) a reference to cases that were appealed to the Recorder's Court of the City of Detroit is added, in view of that court's appellate jurisdiction over the 36th District Court. MCL 770.3(1)(c).

The [March 1, 1985] amendment of MCR 7.203(B)(2) corrects an inadvertent addition of the words "or tribunal" at the end of the subrule, which describes the class of cases appealable to the Court of Appeals by leave. This makes the rule consistent with GCR 1963, 806.2(4).

Subrule (B)(3) is new. It limits review of agency decisions to final orders, a principle that had previously been expressed in appellate decisions.

The 18–month time limit on filing an application for leave to appeal in a civil action (see GCR 1963, 806.2) is placed in MCR 7.205(F).

Staff Comment to 1989 Amendment

The [October 1, 1989] amendment of MCR 7.203(E) incorporates the statute governing appeals by the prosecutor. The circumstances in which such appeals can be taken was considerably expanded by 1988 PA 66.

Staff Comment to February, 1994 Amendment

The change in MCR 7.203(A)(1) [effective February 1, 1994] eliminates appeals of right as to certain types of judgments or orders. An appeal from a lower court judgment after review of an agency decision will be by leave only. In domestic relations cases, the only postjudgment orders that will be appealable by right are those involving the custody of minors.

Staff Comment to December, 1994 Amendment

The December 30, 1994 amendments of MCR 6.301, 6.302, 6.311, 6.425, 7.203, 7.204 and 7.205 modified procedure regarding appeals in criminal cases in light of the amendment of Const 1963, art 1, § 20 at the November 1994 general election and the legislation implementing the constitutional amendment. Changes will remain in effect until April 1, 1995 and will be reconsidered by the Court in light of comments received and any further legislation.

Staff Comment to 1996 Amendment

New MCR 7.203(A)(3) retains an exception, formerly found in MCR 7.203(A)(1), for postjudgment orders in divorce and paternity actions that affect the custody of a minor. MCR 7.203(A)(2) is amended to make clear that appeals of right exist where so provided by court rule, as well as by statute. See, e.g., MCR 5.801(B); MCR 5.993(A).

Staff Comment to September, 1999 Amendment

New MCR 7.203(F) permits the chief judge, or another designated judge, acting alone, to dismiss an appeal or original proceeding for lack of jurisdiction, and creates a procedure for the appellant or plaintiff to seek reconsideration of that decision.

Staff Comment to November, 1999 Amendment

The amendment of MCR 7.203(A)(1) is explained in *Allied Electric Supply Co, Inc v Tenaglia*, 461 Mich 285, 290; 602 NW2d 572 (1999).

Staff Comment to December, 1999 Amendment

The amendment to MCR 7.203 deals with the issue regarding the relationship of appeals and orders awarding or denying attorney fees and costs.

MCR 7.203(A) is amended to make orders awarding or denying sanctions appealable by right.

Staff Comment to 2001 Amendment

The September 11, 2001, amendment of subrule (A)(3) clarified that the provision applies to all domestic relations actions, not just to divorce and paternity actions.

The amendment of MCR 7.203(E) incorporates the statute governing appeals by the prosecutor. The circumstances in which such appeals can be taken was considerably expanded by 1988 PA 66.

Staff Comment to 2002 Amendment

The June 4, 2002, amendments of MCR 7.202, 7.203, and 7.209, effective September 1, 2002, involve orders appealable by right to the Court of Appeals.

The provisions concerning custody orders in domestic relations cases and orders regarding attorney fees and costs are moved from MCR 7.203(A)(3) and (4) to MCR 7.202(7)(a)(iii) and (iv). There is also a change in the language regarding fees and costs, to refer to "postjudgment" orders.

New MCR 7.202(7)(a)(v) includes as "final" an order denying immunity to a governmental defendant, as is provided in many jurisdictions. See, *e.g.*, *Mitchell v Forsyth*, 472 US 511; 105 S Ct 2806; 86 L Ed 2d 411 (1985).

Language is added to MCR 7.203(A) to make clear that an appeal from an order described in MCR 7.202(7)(a)(iii)–(v) is limited to the portion of the order regarding which there is an appeal of right. In addition, obsolete references to the recorder's court are deleted from that subrule.

New MCR 7.209(E)(4) provides for a stay with respect to a governmental party who takes an appeal of right from an order denying immunity.

Staff Comment to 2003 Amendment

The January 22, 2003, amendment of MCR 7.211(B), effective May 1, 2003, clarifies the deadline for answering a substantive motion when there also is a motion for immediate consideration of that motion.

The January 22, 2003, amendment of MCR 7.215(H), effective May 1, 2003, details how the Court of Appeals carries out the notification duties assigned to it by the 2000 PA 503 amendments of the Crime Victims Rights Act, MCL 780.751 *et seq.*

The January 22, 2003, amendment of MCR 7.215(I) (4), effective May 1, 2003, added the provision that the Court of Appeals clerk will not accept untimely motions for reconsideration. The same amendment order changed the title of a motion for "rehearing" to "reconsideration" in several other MCR Subchapter 7.200 rules.

Staff Comment to 2004 Amendment

New subrule MCR 7.203(G) implements the Court of Appeals expedited summary disposition docket. Subrule (G) alerts litigants involved in appeals from orders disposing of summary disposition motions that they are to follow the procedures set forth in the administrative order.

Staff Comment to 2005 Amendment

The amendments of MCR 7.203(A) and 7.209(D), effective January 1, 2006, recognize numbering changes in MCR 7.202.

Staff Comment to 2013 Amendment

Under 2012 PA 333, an order by a court in which a case is assigned to a business court is not subject to appeal by right or leave in the Court of Appeals. That prohibition is codified in MCR 7.203(D). Note that the decision to assign a case to a business court is appealable to the court's chief judge under the amendment of MCR 2.112 adopted in ADM File No. 2012–36.

Staff Comment to 2014 Amendment

These amendments reflect changes that correct minor technical errors that have occurred in drafting or the changes respond to recent adopted rule revisions, which occasionally inadvertently create incorrect cross-references in other rules.

Staff Comment to 2016 Amendment

These amendments update cross-references and make other nonsubstantive revisions to clarify the rules.

Rule 7.204. Filing Appeal of Right; Appearance

(A) Time Requirements. The time limit for an appeal of right is jurisdictional. See MCR 7.203(A). The provisions of MCR 1.108 regarding computation of time apply. For purposes of subrules (A)(1) and (A)(2), "entry" means the date a judgment or order is signed, or the date that data entry of the judgment or order is accomplished in the issuing tribunal's register of actions.

(1) An appeal of right in a civil action must be taken within

(a) 21 days after entry of the judgment or order appealed from;

(b) 21 days after the entry of an order deciding a motion for new trial, a motion for rehearing or reconsideration, or a motion for other relief from the order or judgment appealed, if the motion was filed within the initial 21–day appeal period or within further time the trial court has allowed for good cause during that 21–day period;

(c) 14 days after entry of an order of the family division of the circuit court terminating parental rights under the Juvenile Code, or entry of an order denying a motion for new trial, rehearing, reconsideration, or other postjudgment relief from an order terminating parental rights, if the motion was filed within the initial 14–day appeal period or within further time the trial court may have allowed during that period; or

(d) another time provided by law.

If a party in a civil action is entitled to the appointment of an attorney and requests the appointment within 14 days after the final judgment or order, the 14–day period for the taking of an appeal or the filing of a postjudgment motion begins to run from the entry of an order appointing or denying the appointment of an attorney. If a timely postjudgment motion is filed before a request for appellate counsel, the party may request counsel within 14 days after the decision on the motion.

(2) An appeal of right in a criminal case must be taken

(a) in accordance with MCR 6.425(G)(1);

(b) within 42 days after entry of an order denying a timely motion for the appointment of a lawyer pursuant to MCR 6.425(G)(1);

(c) within 42 days after entry of the judgment or order appealed from; or

(d) within 42 days after the entry of an order denying a motion for a new trial, for directed verdict of acquittal, or to correct an invalid sentence, if the motion was filed within the time provided in MCR 6.419(C), 6.429(B), or 6.431(A), as the case may be.

(e) If a claim of appeal is received by the court after the expiration of the periods set forth above, and if the appellant is an inmate in the custody of the Michigan Department of Corrections and has submitted the claim as a pro se party, the claim shall be deemed presented for filing on the date of deposit of the claim in the outgoing mail at the correctional institution in which the inmate is housed. Timely filing may be shown by a sworn statement, which must set forth the date of deposit and state that first-class postage has been prepaid. The exception applies to claims of appeal from decisions or orders rendered on or after March 1, 2010. This exception also applies to an inmate housed in a penal institution in another state or in a federal penal institution who seeks to appeal in a Michigan court.

A motion for rehearing or reconsideration of a motion mentioned in subrules (A)(1)(b) or (A)(2)(d) does not extend the time for filing a claim of appeal, unless the motion for rehearing or reconsideration was itself filed within the 21- or 42–day period.

(3) Where service of the judgment or order on appellant was delayed beyond the time stated in MCR 2.602, the claim of appeal must be accompanied by an affidavit setting forth facts

showing that the service was beyond the time stated in MCR 2.602. Appellee may file an opposing affidavit within 14 days after being served with the claim of appeal and affidavit. If the Court of Appeals finds that service of the judgment or order was delayed beyond the time stated in MCR 2.602 and the claim of appeal was filed within 14 days after service of the judgment or order, the claim of appeal will be deemed timely.

(B) Manner of Filing. To vest the Court of Appeals with jurisdiction in an appeal of right, an appellant shall file with the clerk within the time for taking an appeal

(1) the claim of appeal, and

(2) the entry fee.

(C) Other Documents. With the claim of appeal, the appellant shall file the following documents with the clerk:

(1) a copy of the judgment or order appealed from;

(2) a copy of the certificate of the court reporter or recorder filed under subrule (E)(4), a statement by the attorney that the transcript has been ordered (in which case the certificate of the court reporter or recorder must be filed as soon as possible thereafter), or a statement by the attorney that there is no record to be transcribed;

(3) proof that a copy of the claim of appeal was served on all other parties in the case and on any other person or officer entitled by rule or law to notice of the appeal;

(4) if the appellant has filed a bond, a true copy of the bond;

(5) a copy of the register of actions of the lower court, tribunal, or agency; and

(6) a jurisdictional checklist on a form provided by the clerk's office.

(D) Form of Claim of Appeal.

(1) A claim of appeal is entitled "In the Court of Appeals." The parties are named in the same order as they appear in the trial court, with the added designation "appellant" or "appellee" as appropriate. The claim must be substantially in the following form:

[*Name of appellant*], [*plaintiff or defendant*], claims an appeal from the [*judgment or order*] entered [*date of judgment or order or date sentence imposed*] in the [*name of court or tribunal from which the appeal is taken*] by [*name of judge or officer who entered the judgment, order, or sentence*].

(2) The claim of appeal must be dated and signed, and must list the appropriate business address and telephone number under the signature.

(3) If the case involves

(a) a contest as to the custody of a minor child,

(b) a case involving an adult or minor guardianship under the Estates and Protected Individuals Code or under the Mental Health Code or an involuntary mental health treatment case under the Mental Health Code, or

(c) a ruling that a provision of the Michigan Constitution, a Michigan statute, a rule or regulation included in the Michigan Administrative Code, or any other action of the legislative or executive branch of state government is invalid,

that fact must be stated in capital letters on the claim of appeal. In an appeal specified in subrule (D)(3)(c), the Court of

Appeals shall give expedited consideration to the appeal, and, if the state or an officer or agency of the state is not a party to the appeal, the Court of Appeals shall send copies of the claim of appeal and the judgment or order appealed from to the Attorney General.

(E) Trial Court Filing Requirements. Within the time for taking the appeal, the appellant shall file in the court or the tribunal from which the appeal is taken

(1) a copy of the claim of appeal;

(2) any fee required by law;

(3) any bond required by law as a condition for taking the appeal; and

(4) unless there is no record to be transcribed, the certificate of the court reporter or recorder stating that a transcript has been ordered and payment for it made or secured, and that it will be filed as soon as possible or has already been filed.

(F) Other Requirements. Within the time for taking the appeal, the appellant shall also

(1) make any delivery or deposit of money, property, or documents, and do any other act required by the statute authorizing the appeal, and file with the clerk an affidavit or other evidence of compliance;

(2) serve on all other parties in the case and on any other person or officer entitled by rule or law to notice of the appeal a copy of the claim of appeal and a copy of any bond filed under subrule (C)(4).

(G) Appearance. Within 14 days after being served with the claim of appeal, the appellee shall file an appearance (identifying the individual attorneys of record) in the Court of Appeals and in the court or tribunal from which the appeal is taken. An appellee who does not file a timely appearance is not entitled to notice of further proceedings until an appearance is filed.

(H) Docketing Statement. In all civil appeals, within 28 days after the claim of appeal is filed, the appellant must file two copies of a docketing statement with the clerk of the Court of Appeals and serve a copy on the opposing parties.

(1) *Contents.* The docketing statement must contain the information required from time to time by the Court of Appeals through the office of the Chief Clerk on forms provided by the Clerk's office and must set forth:

(a) the nature of the proceeding;

(b) the date of entry of the judgment or order sought to be reviewed as defined in MCR 7.204(A) or MCR 7.205(A), and whether the appeal was timely filed and is within the court's jurisdiction;

(c) a concise, accurate summary of all facts material to consideration of the issues presented, but transcripts are not required at this stage;

(d) the issues presented by the appeal, including a concise summary of how they arose and how they were preserved in the trial court. General conclusory statements such as, "the judgment of the trial court is not supported by the law or the facts," will not be accepted;

(e) a reference to all related or prior appeals, and the appropriate citation, if any.

(2) *Amendment.* The Court of Appeals may, upon motion and good cause shown, allow for the amendment of the docketing statement.

(3) *Cross Appeals.* A party who files a cross appeal shall file a docketing statement in accordance with this rule within 28 days after filing the cross appeal.

(4) *Dismissal.* If the appellant fails to file a timely docketing statement, the chief judge may dismiss the appeal pursuant to MCR 7.217.

[Adopted effective March 1, 1985. Amended August 23, 1989, effective October 1, 1989, 432 Mich; December 15, 1993, effective February 1, 1994, 444 Mich; January 28, 1994, effective February 1, 1994, 444 Mich. Amended effective December 30, 1994, 447 Mich. Amended February 23, 1995, effective May 1, 1995, 448 Mich; April 30, 1996, effective September 1, 1997, 454 Mich; June 2, 1998, effective September 1, 1998, 457 Mich. Amended effective November 30, 1999, 461 Mich. Amended May 17, 2002, effective September 1, 2002, 466 Mich; February 3, 2004, effective May 1, 2004, 469 Mich; March 30, 2004, effective May 1, 2004, 469 Mich. Amended effective November 2, 2004, 471 Mich. Amended February 23, 2006, effective May 1, 2006, 474 Mich; March 15, 2007, effective May 1, 2007, 477 Mich; May 28, 2008, effective September 1, 2008, 481 Mich; February 25, 2010, effective May 1, 2010, 485 Mich. Amended effective June 21, 2017, 500 Mich; March 21, 2018, 501 Mich. Amended August 30, 2018, effective September 1, 2018, 502 Mich.]

Comments

Staff Comment to 1985 Adoption

MCR 7.204 is based on GCR 1963, 802.1, 803.1, 803.5, 804.1, and 805. The rule brings together the various provisions on the filing of an appeal of right.

The [March 1, 1985] amendments of MCR 6.101(F)(7)(e) and 7.204(A)(3) have the effect of allowing a criminal defendant to file a motion for resentencing in the trial court before filing a claim of appeal. If the defendant does so, the time for taking an appeal of right runs from the denial of the motion.

Under GCR 1963, 805(3) the appellant was required to file a copy of the court reporter or recorder's certificate that the transcript had been ordered. GCR 1963, 812.3(1); MCR 7.210(B)(3)(a). Subrule (C)(2) permits as a substitute a statement by the attorney that the transcript has been ordered. In certain circumstances the time required to obtain the certificate itself might delay the taking of an appeal. However, the certificate must be filed as soon as possible thereafter.

Subrule (C)(4) adds a requirement that if a bond was filed a copy of it must be filed in the Court of Appeals with the claim of appeal. A copy must be served on the other parties under subrule (F)(2).

Subrule (G) adds a new requirement that the appellee file an appearance in the Court of Appeals. Under MCR 2.117(C)(1), an appearance by an attorney in the trial court continues only until the entry of final judgment and through the time for taking an appeal of a party. Thus, a timely claim of appeal could be served on the attorney for a party. However, the trial court appearance will have expired by the time the appellant's brief is to be served.

The provisions of GCR 1963, 803.6, which halved the time for filing a claim of appeal (among other steps) in certain cases, are omitted.

The checklist of steps on appeal formerly found in GCR 1963, 823 is omitted.

Staff Comment to 1989 Amendment

There are three changes [under the October 1, 1989 amendment] in MCR 7.204(A). The last paragraph of MCR 7.204(A)(1) is amended to adjust the relationship between the times for taking an appeal of right and for requesting appointment of counsel in those situations in which a civil litigant is entitled to such an appointment. Under the prior rule, a party could lose an appeal of right where a post-trial motion was filed but counsel was not requested until more than 21 days after the judgment.

The provisions of subrule (A)(2) on the taking of an appeal of right in criminal cases are modified to take account of the revised procedures in MCR 6.425(E) and (F). The basic time for taking an appeal, or for requesting counsel, is shortened from 56 to 42 days. Former subrule (A)(3), which created a separate procedure in guilty plea cases, is eliminated.

A new concluding paragraph of MCR 7.204(A) is added to make clear that a series of postjudgment motions cannot indefinitely extend the time for taking an appeal. Only motions filed within 21 days after the judgment in civil cases, and 42 days in criminal cases, extend the time for taking an appeal.

Staff Comment to February, 1994 Amendment

MCR 7.204(H) is a new provision [adopted December 15, 1993, effective February 1, 1994]. It requires that a docketing statement be filed in all appeals.

The January 28, 1994 amendment of MCR 7.204(H) [effective February 1, 1994] makes it clear that the requirement that a docketing statement be filed applies only in appeals of civil cases. The Supreme Court is considering, as a separate matter, whether to impose such a requirement in appeals of criminal cases.

Staff Comment to December, 1994 Amendment

The December 30, 1994 amendments of MCR 6.301, 6.302, 6.311, 6.425, 7.203, 7.204 and 7.205 modified procedure regarding appeals in criminal cases in light of the amendment of Const 1963, art 1, § 20 at the November 1994 general election and the legislation implementing the constitutional amendment. Changes will remain in effect until April 1, 1995 and will be reconsidered by the Court in light of comments received and any further legislation.

Staff Comment to 1995 Amendment

MCR 7.204(C)(5) is amended to require a copy of the docket or calendar entries in all appeals of right.

Staff Comment to 1997 Amendment

There are two changes in MCR 7.204(H) regarding the docketing statement that must be filed in the Court of Appeals. Two copies would be required, and the Court of Appeals would be authorized to require that additional information be included on the docketing statement form.

Staff Comment to 1998 Amendment

MCR 7.204(C) requires a jurisdictional checklist to be filed with the claim of appeal.

Staff Comment to 1999 Amendment

The amendment of MCR 7.204(A) is explained in Allied Electric Supply Co, Inc v Tenaglia, 461 Mich 285, 290; 602 NW2d 572 (1999).

Staff Comment to 2002 Amendment

The May 17, 2002, amendments of MCR 7.204, 7.212, 7.213, 7.215, and 7.302, which are effective September 1, 2002, relate to appeals in which a Michigan constitutional provision, statute, regulation, or other governmental action has been held to be invalid.

The amendment of MCR 7.204(D)(3) requires that the claim of appeal identify cases involving such a ruling, and directs the Court of Appeals to give expedited treatment to such appeals and to send copies of the claim of appeal and the order appealed from to the Attorney General if the state is not a party.

Staff Comment to February, 2004 Amendment

The February 3, 2004, amendment of MCR 7.202, 7.204, 7.205, and 7.212, effective May 1, 2004, was adopted on the basis of a recommendation from a work group appointed by the Court of Appeals. The amendments [in subrule (A), adding the third sentence to the introductory paragraph, and adding new paragraph (3)] clarify the definition of "entry" of an order for jurisdictional purposes at the Court of Appeals.

The February 3, 2004, amendments to MCR 3.977(I), effective May 1, 2004, accomplish the following: (1) shorten the deadline for requesting the appointment of counsel following entry of orders terminating parental rights; (2) impose a new deadline for entry of the order appointing counsel in such cases; (3) impose primary responsibility on the chief judge of the court to ensure that the appointment is timely made; and (4) require the appointment of counsel and the transcript order to be contained on a form that functions as the claim of appeal.

Subrule (I)(2)(b) is a new rule that provides that the order appointing appellate counsel also serves as a claim of appeal in cases where the respondent makes a timely request for appellate counsel. The subrule further directs the State Court Administrative Office to approve a form for use by the trial courts that will act as a combination order of appointment, transcript order, and claim of appeal.

The amendment to MCR 7.204(A)(1) shortens the time for requesting the appointment of appellate counsel in appeals from orders terminating parental rights. This new deadline conforms to the amendments to MCR 3.977(I).

Staff Comment to April, 2004 Amendment

The March 30, 2004, amendment of Rule 7.204(A)(1)(c), which was given immediate effect, shortened the deadline for filing claims of appeal in retained appeals from orders terminating parental rights or denying timely filed postconviction motions. The purpose of this amendment was to conform the deadline for filing claims of appeal in appeals with retained counsel to the recently adopted 14-day deadline in appeals with appointed counsel from orders terminating parental rights.

Staff Comment to Third May 1, 2004 Amendment

The order of April 2, 2004, is designed to make the effective date of changes of MCR 7.204 coincide with effective dates of earlier amendments of the Rules.

The order of April 2, 2004, referenced above, provided: "On order of the Court, the order amending Rule 7.204 of the Michigan Court Rules, entered March 30, 2004, is modified to change the effective date of the amendment of Rule 7.204 of the Michigan Court Rules to May 1, 2004."

Staff Comment to November, 2004 Amendment

The amendment of MCR 7.204(A)(1)(c) clarifies that the 14-day time limit for seeking an appeal from an order terminating parental rights or entry of an order denying postjudgment relief from an order terminating parental rights is limited to appeals from orders entered under the Juvenile Code. This limitation is consistent with MCL 710.65, which provides a 21-day limit for appeals from orders entered under the Adoption Code.

Staff Comment to 2006 Amendment

The amendment of MCR 7.204(C)(5) makes the terminology consistent with current usage. See MCR 8.119(D)(1)(c). The amendment also clarifies the distinction between the lower court register of actions and the Court of Appeals docketing statement referred to in MCR 7.204(H) and 7.205(D)(3).

Staff Comment to 2007 Amendment

These changes reflect relettered provisions of MCR 6.425.

Staff Comment to 2008 Amendment

The amendments of MCR 7.204 and MCR 7.205 clarify that a party who seeks to appeal to the Court of Appeals has 21 days after the entry of an order deciding a motion for new trial, a motion for rehearing or reconsideration, or a motion for other relief from the order or judgment appealed to file a claim of appeal or an application for leave to appeal, if the motion is filed within the initial 21-day appeal period. The amendments also limit the ability of the trial court to extend the 21-day period under MCR 7.204(A)(1)(b), MCR 7.205(A)(2), and MCR 7.205(F)(3)(b) to situations in which good cause is shown.

For consistency with the amendments of MCR 7.204 and MCR 7.205, and to eliminate a conflict between MCR 2.119(F)(1) and MCR 7.204(A)(1)(b), the time limit for filing a motion for rehearing or reconsideration in the trial court under MCR 2.119(F)(1) is increased from 14 to 21 days.

Staff Comment to 2010 Amendment

These amendments create a prison mailbox rule, which allow a claim of appeal or application for leave to appeal to be deemed presented for filing when a prison inmate acting pro se places the legal documents in the prison's outgoing mail. The rule applies to appeals from administrative agencies, appeals from circuit court (both claims of appeal and applications for leave to appeal), and appeals from decisions of the Court of Appeals to the Supreme Court.

Staff Comment to 2017 Amendment

These amendments conform to recent statutory changes that require all appeals from probate court to be heard in the Court of Appeals, instead of the bifurcated system that previously required some probate appeals to be heard in the Court of Appeals and some to be heard in the local circuit court. The amendments also establish priority status for appeals in guardianship and involuntary mental health treatment cases, similar to child custody cases.

Staff Comment to March, 2018 Amendment

These amendments update cross-references and make other nonsubstantive revisions to clarify the rules. The amendment of MCR 6.110(B)(1) addresses an inadvertent omission from the last amendment of this rule that was intended to be shown in overstrike. Accordingly, the current rule does not match the published version. Striking the clause "for good cause shown" will provide consistency with other published versions of the rule and with the statute, MCL 766.7, which allows a magistrate to adjourn a preliminary examination with the consent of the parties without the need for good cause to be shown.

Staff Comment to September, 2018 Amendment

These amendments update cross-references in the rules, and are intended to reflect changes that are necessary as a result of the Court's recent e-Filing rules amendments.

Rule 7.205.   Application for Leave to Appeal

(A) Time Requirements. An application for leave to appeal must be filed within

(1) 21 days after entry of the judgment or order to be appealed from or within other time as allowed by law or rule; or

(2) 21 days after entry of an order deciding a motion for new trial, a motion for rehearing or reconsideration, or a motion for other relief from the order or judgment appealed, if the motion

was filed within the initial 21-day appeal period or within further time the trial court has allowed for good cause during that 21-day period.

For purposes of subrules (A)(1) and (A)(2), "entry" means the date a judgment or order is signed, or the date that data entry of the judgment or order is accomplished in the issuing tribunal's register of actions.

(3) If an application for leave to appeal in a criminal case is received by the court after the expiration of the periods set forth above or the period set forth in MCR 7.205(G), and if the appellant is an inmate in the custody of the Michigan Department of Corrections and has submitted the application as a pro se party, the application shall be deemed presented for filing on the date of deposit of the application in the outgoing mail at the correctional institution in which the inmate is housed. Timely filing may be shown by a sworn statement, which must set forth the date of deposit and state that first-class postage has been prepaid. The exception applies to applications for leave to appeal from decisions or orders rendered on or after March 1, 2010. This exception also applies to an inmate housed in a penal institution in another state or in a federal penal institution who seeks to appeal in a Michigan court.

(B) Manner of Filing. To apply for leave to appeal, the appellant shall file with the clerk:

(1) 5 copies of an application for leave to appeal (one signed), stating the date and nature of the judgment or order appealed from; concisely reciting the appellant's allegations of error and the relief sought; setting forth a concise argument, conforming to MCR 7.212(C), in support of the appellant's position on each issue; and, if the order appealed from is interlocutory, setting forth facts showing how the appellant would suffer substantial harm by awaiting final judgment before taking an appeal;

(2) 5 copies of the judgment or order appealed from, of the register of actions of the lower court, tribunal, or agency, of the opinion or findings of the lower court, tribunal, or agency, and of any opinion or findings reviewed by the lower court, tribunal, or agency.

(3) if the appeal is from an administrative tribunal or agency, or from a circuit court on review of an administrative tribunal or agency, evidence that the tribunal or agency has been requested to send its record to the Court of Appeals;

(4) 1 copy of certain transcripts, as follows:

(a) in an appeal relating to the evidence presented at an evidentiary hearing in a civil or criminal case, the transcript of the evidentiary hearing, including the opinion or findings of the court which conducted the hearing;

(b) in an appeal from the circuit court after an appeal from another court, the transcript of proceedings in the court reviewed by the circuit court;

(c) in an appeal challenging jury instructions, the transcript of the entire charge to the jury;

(d) in an appeal from a judgment in a criminal case entered pursuant to a plea of guilty or nolo contendere, the transcripts of the plea and sentence;

(e) in an appeal from an order granting or denying a new trial, such portion of the transcript of the trial as, in relation to the issues raised, permits the court to determine whether the trial court's decision on the motion was for a legally recognized reason and based on arguable support in the record;

   (f) in an appeal raising a sentencing issue, the transcript of the sentencing proceeding and the transcript of any hearing on a motion relating to sentencing;

   (g) in an appeal raising any other issue, such portion of the transcript as substantiates the existence of the issue, objections or lack thereof, arguments of counsel, and any comment or ruling of the trial judge.

If the transcript is not yet available, or if there is no record to be transcribed, the appellant shall file a copy of the certificate of the court reporter or recorder or a statement by the appellant's attorney as provided in MCR 7.204(C)(2). The appellant must file the transcript with the Court of Appeals as soon as it is available.

   (5) proof that a copy of the filed documents was served on all other parties; and

   (6) the entry fee.

(C) Answer. Any other party in the case may file with the clerk, within 21 days of service of the application,

   (1) 5 copies of an answer to the application (one signed) conforming to MCR 7.212(D), except that transcript page references are not required unless a transcript has been filed; and

   (2) proof that a copy was served on the appellant and any other appellee.

(D) Reply. A reply brief may be filed as provided by MCR 7.212(G).

(E) Decision.

   (1) *There is No Oral Argument.* The application is decided on the documents filed and, in an appeal from an administrative tribunal or agency, the certified record.

   (2) The court may grant or deny the application; enter a final decision; grant other relief; request additional material from the record; or require a certified concise statement of proceedings and facts from the court, tribunal, or agency whose order is being appealed. The clerk shall enter the court's order and mail copies to the parties.

   (3) If an application is granted, the case proceeds as an appeal of right, except that the filing of a claim of appeal is not required and the time limits for the filing of a cross appeal and for the taking of the other steps in the appeal, including the filing of the docketing statement (28 days), and the filing of the court reporter's or recorder's certificate if the transcript has not been filed (14 days), run from the date the order granting leave is certified.

   (4) Unless otherwise ordered, the appeal is limited to the issues raised in the application and supporting brief.

(F) Emergency Appeal.

   (1) If the order appealed requires acts or will have consequences within 56 days of the date the application is filed, appellant shall alert the clerk of that fact by prominent notice on the cover sheet or first page of the application, including the date by which action is required.

   (2) When an appellant requires a hearing on an application in less than 21 days, the appellant shall file and serve a motion for immediate consideration, concisely stating facts showing why an immediate hearing is required. A notice of hearing of the application and motion or a transcript is not required. An answer may be filed within the time the court directs. If a copy of the application and of the motion for immediate consideration are personally served under MCR 2.107(C)(1) or (2), the application may be submitted to the court immediately on filing. If mail service is used, it may not be submitted until the first Tuesday 7 days after the date of service, unless the party served acknowledges receipt. In all other respects, submission, decision, and further proceedings are as provided in subrule (E).

   (3) Where the trial court makes a decision on the admissibility of evidence and the prosecutor or the defendant files an interlocutory application for leave to appeal seeking to reverse that decision, the trial court shall stay proceedings pending resolution of the application in the Court of Appeals, unless the trial court makes findings that the evidence is clearly cumulative or that an appeal is frivolous because legal precedent is clearly against the party's position. The appealing party must pursue the appeal as expeditiously as practicable, and the Court of Appeals shall consider the matter under the same priority as that granted to an interlocutory criminal appeal under MCR 7.213(C)(1). If the application for leave to appeal is filed by the prosecutor and the defendant is incarcerated, the defendant may request that the trial court reconsider whether pretrial release is appropriate.

(G) Late Appeal.

   (1) When an appeal of right was not timely filed or was dismissed for lack of jurisdiction, or when an application for leave was not timely filed, the appellant may file an application as prescribed in subrule (B), file 5 copies of a statement of facts explaining the delay, and serve 1 copy on all other parties. The answer may challenge the claimed reasons for delay. The court may consider the length of and the reasons for delay in deciding whether to grant the application. In all other respects, submission, decision, and further proceedings are as provided in subrule (E).

   (2) In a criminal case, the defendant may not file an application for leave to appeal from a judgment of conviction and sentence if the defendant has previously taken an appeal from that judgment by right or leave granted or has sought leave to appeal that was denied.

   (3) Except as provided in subrules (G)(4) and (G)(5), leave to appeal may not be granted if an application for leave to appeal is filed more than 6 months after the later of:

   (a) entry of a final judgment or other order that could have been the subject of an appeal of right under MCR 7.203(A), but if a motion described in MCR 7.204(A)(1)(b) was filed within the time prescribed in that rule, then the 6 months are counted from the time of entry of the order denying that motion; or

   (b) entry of the order or judgment to be appealed from, but if a motion for new trial, a motion for rehearing or reconsideration, or a motion for other relief from the order or judgment appealed was filed within the initial 21–day appeal period or within further time the trial court has allowed for good cause during that 21–day period, then the 6 months are counted from the entry of the order deciding the motion.

(4) The limitation provided in subrule (G)(3) does not apply to an application for leave to appeal by a criminal defendant if the defendant files an application for leave to appeal within 21 days after the trial court decides a motion for a new trial, for directed verdict of acquittal, to withdraw a plea, or to correct an invalid sentence, if the motion was filed within the time provided in MCR 6.310(C), MCR 6.419(C), MCR 6.429(B), and MCR 6.431(A), or if

(a) the defendant has filed a delayed request for the appointment of counsel pursuant to MCR 6.425(G)(1) within the 6–month period,

(b) the defendant or defendant's lawyer, if one is appointed, has ordered the appropriate transcripts within 28 days of service of the order granting or denying the delayed request for counsel or for substitute counsel, unless the transcript has already been filed or has been ordered by the court under MCR 6.425(G), and

(c) the application for leave to appeal is filed in accordance with the provisions of this rule within 42 days after the filing of the transcript. If the transcript was filed before the order appointing counsel, or substitute counsel, or the order denying the appointment of counsel, the 42–day period runs from the date of that order.

A motion for rehearing or reconsideration of a motion mentioned in subrule (G)(4) does not extend the time for filing an application for leave to appeal, unless the motion for rehearing or reconsideration was itself filed within 21 days after the trial court decides the motion mentioned in subrule (G)(4), and the application for leave to appeal is filed within 21 days after the court decides the motion for rehearing or reconsideration.

A defendant who seeks to rely on one of the exceptions in subrule (G)(4) must file with the application for leave to appeal an affidavit stating the relevant docket entries, a copy of the register of actions of the lower court, tribunal, or agency, or other documentation showing that the application is filed within the time allowed.

(5) Notwithstanding the 6–month limitation period otherwise provided in subrule (G)(3), leave to appeal may be granted if a party's claim of appeal is dismissed for lack of jurisdiction within 21 days before the expiration of the 6–month limitation period, or at any time after the 6–month limitation period has expired, and the party files a late application for leave to appeal from the same lower court judgment or order within 21 days of the dismissal of the claim of appeal or within 21 days of denial of a timely filed motion for reconsideration. A party filing a late application in reliance on this provision must note the dismissal of the prior claim of appeal in the statement of facts explaining the delay.

(6) The time limit for late appeals from orders terminating parental rights is 63 days, as provided by MCR 3.993(C)(2).

(H) Certified Concise Statement.

(1) When the Court of Appeals requires a certified concise statement of proceedings and facts, the appellant shall, within 7 days after the order requiring the certified concise statement is certified, serve on all other parties a copy of a proposed concise statement of proceedings and facts, describing the course of proceedings and the facts pertinent to the issues raised in the application, and notice of hearing with the date, time, and place for settlement of the concise statement.

(2) Hearing on the proposed concise statement must be within 14 days after the proposed concise statement and notice is served on the other parties.

(3) Objections to the proposed concise statement must be filed in writing with the trial court and served on the appellant and any other appellee before the time set for settlement.

(4) The trial court shall promptly settle objections to the proposed concise statement and may correct it or add matters of record necessary to present the issues properly. When a court's discretionary act is being reviewed, the trial court may add to the statement its reasons for the act. Within 7 days after the settlement hearing, the trial court shall certify the proposed or a corrected concise statement of proceedings and facts as fairly presenting the factual basis for the questions to be reviewed as directed by the Court of Appeals. Immediately after certification, the trial court shall send the certified concise statement to the Court of Appeals clerk and serve a copy on each party.

[Adopted effective March 1, 1985. Amended December 23, 1987, effective January 1, 1988, 429 Mich; August 23, 1989, effective October 1, 1989, 432 Mich; December 15, 1993, effective February 1, 1994, 444 Mich; December 30, 1994, effective December 27, 1994, 447 Mich; March 7, 1996, effective April 1, 1996, 450 Mich; April 30, 1997, effective September 1, 1997, 454 Mich; June 2, 1998, effective September 1, 1998, 457 Mich; April 23, 2002, effective September 1, 2002, 466 Mich; June 26, 2003, effective September 1, 2003; February 3, 2004, effective May 1, 2004, 469 Mich; October 18, 2005, effective January 1, 2006, 474 Mich; February 23, 2006, effective May 1, 2006, 474 Mich; March 28, 2006, effective May 1, 2006, 474 Mich; May 28, 2008, effective September 1, 2008, 481 Mich; March 10, 2009, effective May 1, 2009, 483 Mich; February 25, 2010, effective May 1, 2010, 485 Mich; June 2, 2011, effective September 1, 2011, 489 Mich; December 8, 2011, effective January 1, 2012, 490 Mich; October 2, 2013, effective January 1, 2014, 495 Mich. Amended effective May 7, 2014, 495 Mich; March 9, 2016, 499 Mich; June 21, 2017, 500 Mich; March 21, 2018, 501 Mich. Amended April 19, 2018, effective May 1, 2018, 501 Mich; August 30, 2018, effective September 1, 2018, 502 Mich.]

Comments

Staff Comment to 1985 Adoption

MCR 7.205 is based on GCR 1963, 803.2–803.4 and 806.2–806.7.

Throughout the rule 5 copies of the application and related documents are required, rather than 4 as under GCR 1963, 806.3(4).

GCR 1963, 806.3 required that a concise statement of the proceedings and facts be filed with every timely application. That provision is not included in the new rule. Such a statement is necessary only if the Court of Appeals directs that it be prepared. See subrule (G).

The rule omits the language in GCR 1963, 806.3(1)(a) that required the Court of Appeals to "pay particular attention" to certain grounds for appeal.

Subrule (B) requires additional papers to be filed with the application in certain cases. In appeals from administrative tribunals, proof must be submitted that the tribunal record has been requested. Subrule (B)(4). Transcripts are required in certain appeals. Subrule (B)(5). A certificate of the probate court must be filed when required by law (see MCL 600.863[3]). Subrule (B)(6).

Both subrule (D), covering decision by the Court of Appeals, and subrule (E), governing emergency appeals, include more detailed procedures than the corresponding rules, GCR 1963, 806.7 and 806.5.

The [March 1, 1985] amendment of MCR 7.205(D) subdivides the provision into several paragraphs, and sets 14 days after a Court of Appeals order granting leave to appeal as the time within which the court reporter's or recorder's certificate regarding the transcript must be filed.

Subrule (F), governing late appeals, does not require an affidavit showing that the delay was not due to "culpable negligence". See GCR 1963, 806.4(2). Rather, the affidavit is only required to explain the delay, and the court will consider the length of and reasons for the delay in reaching its decision.

Most of the special provisions of GCR 1963, 806.6 regarding appeals from administrative tribunals are omitted.

Staff Comment to 1989 Amendment

There are several significant changes in MCR 7.205(F) [under the October 1, 1989 amendment]. First, subrule (F)(2) is added, limiting a criminal defendant to a single appeal. Thereafter, the defendant must utilize the procedure established in Subchapter 6.500.

Second, the 18–month time limit on applications for leave to appeal, formerly applicable only to civil cases, is extended to criminal cases. However, under subrule (F)(4), if a criminal defendant initiates the process by requesting counsel within the 18–month period, and the subsequent steps regarding ordering the transcript and filing the application are taken within specified time limits, the 18–month limitation does not apply. A criminal defendant who seeks to rely on those exceptions must document the facts that make the application a timely one.

Staff Comment to February, 1994 Amendment

MCR 7.205(B) and (C) have been changed [effective February 1, 1994] to require that the application for leave to appeal and the answer to the application include the parties' arguments. Separate briefs no longer will be filed.

Staff Comment to December, 1994 Amendment

The December 30, 1994 amendments of MCR 6.301, 6.302, 6.311, 6.425, 7.203, 7.204 and 7.205 modified procedure regarding appeals in criminal cases in light of the amendment of Const 1963, art 1, § 20 at the November 1994 general election and the legislation implementing the constitutional amendment. Changes will remain in effect until April 1, 1995 and will be reconsidered by the Court in light of comments received and any further legislation.

Staff Comment to 1995 Amendment

The amendment of MCR 7.205(F) shortens the limitation on filing late appeals from 18 to 12 months. This amendment is effective November 1, 1995.

Staff Comment to 1996 Amendment

The amendments of MCR 7.205(B)(2) and (3) [effective April 1, 1996] require the filing of additional materials with applications for leave to appeal in certain cases.

On January 26, 1996, MCR 7.205(B)(4) was amended [effective April 1, 1996] to require the filing of transcripts with applications for leave to appeal in additional circumstances. The March 7, 1996, order [effective April 1, 1996] clarifies that if the transcript is not yet available, a court reporter's or recorder's certificate or attorney's statement may be filed, comparable to the procedure in appeals of right. See MCR 7.204(C)(2).

Staff Comment to 1997 Amendment

The amendment of MCR 7.205(E) [effective September 1, 1997] requires an appellant to notify the clerk if the order appealed from requires action or will have consequences within 56 days of the filing of the application.

Staff Comment to 1998 Amendment

MCR 7.205(B) and (C) eliminate the filing of a notice of hearing, instead specifying the time for response.

Staff Comment to 2002 Amendment

The April 23, 2002, amendment of subrule (F)(3), effective September 1, 2002, broadens the instances in which a late application for leave to appeal can be filed in the Court of Appeals.

Staff Comment to 2003 Amendment

The June 6, 2003, amendments of MCR 7.205, 7.210, 7.215, 7.302, and 7.316, which are effective September 1, 2003, deal with the time for filing applications for leave to appeal to the Supreme Court.

The amendments of MCR 7.302(C)(1), (2), and (4) set time limits of 56 days in criminal cases and 42 days in civil ones, but with a 28–day time limit for appeals from orders terminating parental rights, in recognition of the adverse consequences of delay on the children involved in such cases. Late applications will not be accepted. MCR 7.302(C)(3), 7.316(B).

The amendment of MCR 7.302(D)(2) provides a 28–day time limit for filing applications for leave to appeal as cross-appellant.

There are also nonsubstantive changes in several rules governing procedure in the Court of Appeals. In MCR 7.205(F)(5), a reference is added to MCR 3.993(C)(2) (formerly MCR 5.993[C][1]), which sets the time limit for late applications in parental-rights-termination cases. The language of MCR 7.210 and 7.215 is adjusted to conform to the changes in the Supreme Court rules.

Staff Comment to 2004 Amendment

The February 3, 2004, amendment of MCR 7.202, 7.204, 7.205, and 7.212, effective May 1, 2004, was adopted on the basis of a recommendation from a work group appointed by the Court of Appeals. The amendments clarify the definition of "entry" of an order for jurisdictional purposes at the Court of Appeals.

Staff Comment to 2005 Amendment

The October 18, 2005, amendment of MCR 7.205 reflects recently approved amendments of MCR 6.310, MCR 6.425, MCR 6.429, and MCR 6.431.

Staff Comment to February, 2006 Amendment

The amendment of MCR 7.204(C)(5) makes the terminology consistent with current usage. See MCR 8.119(D)(1)(c). The amendment also clarifies the distinction between the lower court register of actions and the Court of Appeals docketing statement referred to in MCR 7.204(H) and 7.205(D)(3).

Staff Comment to March, 2006 Amendment

The amendment corrects the opening sentence of subrule (F)(4).

Staff Comment to 2008 Amendment

The amendments of MCR 7.204 and MCR 7.205 clarify that a party who seeks to appeal to the Court of Appeals has 21 days after the entry of an order deciding a motion for new trial, a motion for rehearing or reconsideration, or a motion for other relief from the order or judgment appealed to file a claim of appeal or an application for leave to appeal, if the motion is filed within the initial 21–day appeal period. The amendments also limit the ability of the trial court to extend the 21–day period under MCR 7.204(A)(1)(b), MCR 7.205(A)(2), and MCR 7.205(F)(3)(b) to situations in which good cause is shown.

For consistency with the amendments of MCR 7.204 and MCR 7.205, and to eliminate a conflict between MCR 2.119(F)(1) and MCR 7.204(A)(1)(b), the time limit for filing a motion for rehearing or reconsideration in the trial court under MCR 2.119(F)(1) is increased from 14 to 21 days.

Staff Comment to 2009 Amendment

The amendment of MCR 7.205(F)(5) allows a party to file a late application for leave to appeal after the 12–month limitation period in MCR 7.205(F)(3) if the party's claim of appeal was dismissed for lack of jurisdiction within 21 days before the 12–month period expires or after it expires. A party must file its late application for leave to appeal within 21 days of dismissal of the claim of appeal or within 21 days of denial of a timely filed motion for reconsideration.

Staff Comment to 2010 Amendment

These amendments create a prison mailbox rule, which allow a claim of appeal or application for leave to appeal to be deemed presented for filing when a prison inmate acting pro se places the legal documents in the prison's outgoing mail. The rule applies to appeals from administrative agencies, appeals from circuit court (both claims of appeal and applications for leave to appeal), and appeals from decisions of the Court of Appeals to the Supreme Court.

Staff Comment to June, 2011 Amendment

The amendment of MCR 7.205 reduces the late appeal period from 12 months to 6 months.

Staff Comment to December, 2011 Amendment

This amendment addresses the situation that arose in *People v Richmond*, 486 Mich 29 (2010), in which a prosecutor's dismissal of a case following a trial court's suppression of evidence in the case resulted in a finding that the appeal of the suppression order was moot. Under the amendment above, a party could pursue an interlocutory appeal of a trial court suppression order and in most cases would be entitled to a stay in the case.

Staff Comment to January, 2014 Amendment

These amendments permit the filing of a reply brief in support of an application for leave to appeal in the circuit court and the Court of Appeals, and following the filing of a claim of appeal in the circuit court.

Staff Comment to May, 2014 Amendment

These amendments reflect changes that correct minor technical errors that have occurred in drafting or the changes respond to recent adopted rule revisions, which occasionally inadvertently create incorrect cross-references in other rules.

Staff Comment to 2016 Amendment

These amendments update cross-references that changed after the rule was adopted and make other nonsubstantive revisions.

Staff Comment to 2017 Amendment

These amendments conform to recent statutory changes that require all appeals from probate court to be heard in the Court of Appeals, instead of the bifurcated system that previously required some probate appeals to be heard in the Court of Appeals and some to be heard in the local circuit court. The amendments also establish priority status for appeals in guardianship and involuntary mental health treatment cases, similar to child custody cases.

Staff Comment to March, 2018 Amendment

These amendments update cross-references and make other nonsubstantive revisions to clarify the rules. The amendment of MCR 6.110(B)(1) addresses an inadvertent omission from the last amendment of this rule that was intended to be shown in overstrike. Accordingly, the current rule does not match the published version. Striking the clause "for good cause shown" will provide consistency with other published versions of the rule and with the statute, MCL 766.7, which allows a magistrate to adjourn a preliminary examination with the consent of the parties without the need for good cause to be shown.

Staff Comment to May, 2018 Amendment

The amendments, submitted by SADO, are intended to clarify practices and provide protections for criminal defendants represented by assigned appellate counsel. The amendments allow an additional 42 days to file post-judgment motions in certain circumstances, and where delay is due to the trial court, clarify in the amendment of MCR 7.205 that in certain circumstances, substitute appellate counsel may file a delayed application for leave to appeal within 42 days of appointment (even if later than six months after sentencing), add language to MCR 7.211 to guide parties and courts if relief is granted in the trial court, and change the procedure for seeking permission to file a brief longer than 50 pages in length.

Staff Comment to September, 2018 Amendment

These amendments update cross-references in the rules, and are intended to reflect changes that are necessary as a result of the Court's recent e-Filing rules amendments.

Rule 7.206 Extraordinary Writs, Original Actions, and Enforcement Actions

(A) General Rules of Pleading. Except as otherwise provided in this rule, the general rules of pleading apply as nearly as practicable. See MCR 1.109 and 2.111–2.113.

(B) Superintending Control, Mandamus, and Habeas Corpus. To the extent that they do not conflict with this rule, the rules in subchapter 3.300 apply to actions for superintending control, mandamus, and habeas corpus.

(C) Quo Warranto. In a quo warranto action, the Attorney General also must be served with a copy of each pleading and document filed in the Court of Appeals. The Attorney General has the right to intervene as a party on either side.

(D) Actions for Extraordinary Writs and Original Actions.

(1) *Filing of Complaint.* To commence an original action, the plaintiff shall file with the clerk:

(a) 5 copies of a complaint (1 signed), which may have copies of supporting documents or affidavits attached to each copy;

(b) 5 copies of a supporting brief (1 signed) conforming to MCR 7.212(C) to the extent possible;

(c) proof that a copy of each of the filed documents was served on every named defendant and, in a superintending control action, on any other party involved in the case which gave rise to the complaint for superintending control; and

(d) the entry fee.

(2) *Answer.* The defendant or any other interested party must file with the clerk within 21 days of service of the complaint and any supporting documents or affidavits:

(a) 5 copies of an answer to the complaint (1 signed), which may have copies of supporting documents or affidavits attached to each copy;

(b) 5 copies of an opposing brief (1 signed) conforming to MCR 7.212(D) to the extent possible; and

(c) proof that a copy of each of the filed documents was served on the plaintiff and any other interested party.

(3) *Electronic Filing.* The parties may file all pleadings and other papers permitted by this rule electronically with the Court of Appeals. All electronically filed documents must be in PDF digital format, while appendices and other nonoriginal filings may be scanned. All electronic filings must be submitted in accordance with the instructions set forth on the website of the Michigan Court of Appeals. Pro se parties may file pleadings and other papers in paper form.

(4) *Preliminary Hearing.* There is no oral argument on preliminary hearing of a complaint. The court may deny relief, grant peremptory relief, or allow the parties to proceed to full hearing on the merits in the same manner as an appeal of right either with or without referral to a judicial circuit or tribunal or agency for the taking of proofs and report of factual findings. If the case is ordered to proceed to full hearing, the time for filing a brief by the plaintiff begins to run from the date the order allowing the case to proceed is certified or the date the transcript or report of factual findings on referral is filed, whichever is later. The plaintiff's brief must conform to MCR 7.212(C). An opposing brief must conform to MCR 7.212(D). In a habeas corpus proceeding, the prisoner need not be brought before the Court of Appeals.

(E) Actions to Enforce the Headlee Amendment, Pursuant to Const 1963, art 9, § 32.

(1) *Filing of Complaint.* To commence an action pursuant to Const 1963, art 9, § 32, the plaintiff shall file with the clerk:

(a) 5 copies of the complaint (1 signed), which conforms with the special pleading requirements of MCR 2.112(M) and indicates, inter alia, whether there are any factual questions that are anticipated to require resolution by the court and whether the plaintiff(s) anticipate(s) the need for discovery and the development of a factual record;

(b) 5 copies of a supporting brief (1 signed) conforming to MCR 7.212(C) to the extent possible;

(c) proof that a copy of each of the filed documents was served on every named defendant and the office of the attorney general; and

(d) the entry fee.

(2) *Answer.* The named defendant(s) shall file with the clerk within 21 days of service of the complaint:

(a) 5 copies of an answer to the complaint (1 signed), which conforms with the special pleading requirements of MCR 2.112(M) and indicates, inter alia, whether there are any factual questions that are anticipated to require resolution by the court and whether the named defendant(s) anticipate(s) the need for discovery and the development of a factual record;

(b) 5 copies of a supporting brief (1 signed) conforming to MCR 7.212(C) to the extent possible;

(c) proof that a copy of each of the filed documents was served on every named plaintiff.

(3) *Subsequent proceedings.* Following receipt of the answer:

(a) the chief clerk shall promptly select a panel of the court by random draw and assign that panel to commence proceedings in the suit; and

(b) the panel of the court may deny relief or grant peremptory relief without oral argument; or

(c) if the panel of the court determines that the issues framed in the parties' pleadings and supporting briefs solely present jurisprudentially significant questions of law, the panel shall direct that the suit proceed to a full hearing on the merits in the same manner as an appeal as of right and notify the parties of the date for the filing of supplemental briefs, if such briefs are determined to be necessary, and of the date for oral argument, which shall be on an expedited basis; or

(d) if the panel of the court determines that the issues framed in the parties' pleadings and supplemental briefs present factual questions for resolution, the panel shall refer the suit to a judicial circuit for the purposes of holding pretrial proceedings, conducting a hearing to receive evidence and arguments of law, and issuing a written report for the panel setting forth proposed findings of fact and conclusions of law. The proceedings before the circuit court shall proceed as expeditiously as due consideration of the circuit court's docket, facts and issues of law requires. Following the receipt of the report from the circuit court, the panel shall notify counsel for the parties of the schedule for filing briefs in response to the circuit court's report and of the date for oral argument, which shall be on an expedited basis.

(F) Enforcement of Administrative Tribunal or Agency Orders.

(1) *Complaint.* To obtain enforcement of a final order of an administrative tribunal or agency, the plaintiff shall file with the clerk within the time limit provided by law:

(a) 5 copies of a complaint (one signed) concisely stating the basis for relief and the relief sought;

(b) 5 copies of the order sought to be enforced;

(c) 5 copies of a supporting brief (one signed) which conforms to MCR 7.212(C) to the extent possible;

(d) a notice of preliminary hearing on the complaint on the first Tuesday at least 21 days after the complaint and supporting documents are served on the defendant, the agency (unless the agency is the plaintiff), and any other interested party;

(e) proof that a copy of each of the filed documents was served on the defendant, the agency (unless the agency is the plaintiff), and any other interested party;

(f) the certified tribunal or agency record or evidence the plaintiff has requested that the certified record be sent to the Court of Appeals; and

(g) the entry fee.

(2) *Answer.* The defendant must file, and any other interested party may file, with the clerk before the date of the preliminary hearing:

(a) 5 copies of an answer to the complaint (one signed);

(b) 5 copies of an opposing brief (one signed) conforming to MCR 7.212(D) to the extent possible; and

(c) proof that a copy of each of the filed documents was served on the plaintiff, the agency, and any other interested party.

(3) *Preliminary Hearing.* There is no oral argument on preliminary hearing of a complaint. The court may deny relief, grant peremptory relief, or allow the parties to proceed to full hearing on the merits in the same manner as an appeal of right. If the case is ordered to proceed to full hearing, the time for filing of a brief by the plaintiff begins to run from the date the clerk certifies the order allowing the case to proceed. The plaintiff's brief must conform to MCR 7.212(C). An opposing brief must conform to MCR 7.212(D). The case is heard on the certified record transmitted by the tribunal or agency. MCR 7.210(A)(2), regarding the content of the record, applies.

[Adopted effective March 1, 1985. Amended June 2, 1998, effective September 1, 1998, 457 Mich; November 27, 2007, effective January 1, 2008, 480 Mich; November 10, 2011, effective January 1, 2012, 490 Mich; August 30, 2018, effective September 1, 2018, 502 Mich.]

Comments

Staff Comment to 1985 Adoption

MCR 7.206 corresponds to GCR 1963, 816.2(2). The provisions are rewritten to more precisely prescribe the procedures to be followed.

Five copies of the complaint and other papers are required, rather than four.

The rule incorporates the pleading rules of chapter 2 (see subrule [A]), and the provisions generally governing extraordinary writs in subchapter 3.300 (see subrule [B]).

Subrule (E) is a new provision covering actions to enforce orders of administrative agencies, where statutes provide for such proceedings. E.g., MCL 423.23(d) (enforcement of decisions of the Michigan Employment Relations Commission).

Staff Comment to 1998 Amendment

MCR 7.206(D) eliminates the filing of a notice of hearing, instead specifying the time for response.

Staff Comment to 2007 Amendment

For the comments of the order amending this rule issued November 27, 2007, effective January 1, 2008, see the 2007 comments under MCR 2.112.

Staff Comment to 2011 Amendment

The existing fact-specific pleading requirements in MCR 2.112(M) are retained and expanded to promote earlier consideration whether facts must be established in the case. The amendments of MCR 2.625 clarify that costs, including reasonable attorney fees, are recoverable in a Headlee action. The amendment of MCR 7.206(D)(3) allows parties to utilize electronic filing in Headlee cases, as well as other extraordinary writs or original actions filed in the Court of Appeals. The amendments of MCR 7.206 create a new specific subsection (7.206[E]) regarding the procedure for filing a Headlee action as an original proceeding in the Court of Appeals. The amendment of MCR 7.213 is intended to clarify that Headlee actions are considered priority matters in the Court of Appeals.

Staff Comment to 2018 Amendment

These amendments update cross-references in the rules, and are intended to reflect changes that are necessary as a result of the Court's recent e-Filing rules amendments.

Rule 7.207   Cross Appeals

(A) Right of Cross Appeal.

(1) When an appeal of right is filed or the court grants leave to appeal any appellee may file a cross appeal.

(2) If there is more than 1 party plaintiff or defendant in a civil action and 1 party appeals, any other party, whether on the same or opposite side as the party first appealing, may file a cross appeal against all or any of the other parties to the case as well as against the party who first appealed. If the cross appeal operates against a party not affected by the first appeal or in a manner different from the first appeal, that party may file a further cross appeal as if the cross appeal affecting that party had been the first appeal.

(B) Manner of Filing. To file a cross appeal, the cross appellant shall file with the clerk a claim of cross appeal in the form required by MCR 7.204(D) and the entry fee

(1) within 21 days after the claim of appeal is filed with the Court of Appeals or served on the cross appellant, whichever is later, if the first appeal was of right; or

(2) within 21 days after the clerk certifies the order granting leave to appeal, if the appeal was initiated by application for leave to appeal.

The cross appellant shall file proof that a copy of the claim of cross appeal was served on the cross appellee and any other party in the case. A copy of the judgment or order from which the cross appeal is taken must be filed with the claim.

(C) Additional Requirements. The cross appellant shall perform the steps required by MCR 7.204(E) and (F), except that the cross appellant is not required to order a transcript or file a court reporter's or recorder's certificate unless the initial appeal is abandoned or dismissed. Otherwise the cross appeal proceeds in the same manner as an ordinary appeal.

(D) Abandonment or Dismissal of Appeal. If the appellant abandons the initial appeal or the court dismisses it, the cross appeal may nevertheless be prosecuted to its conclusion. Within 21 days after the clerk certifies the order dismissing the initial appeal, if there is a record to be transcribed, the cross appellant shall file a certificate of the court reporter or recorder that a transcript has been ordered and payment for it made or secured and will be filed as soon as possible or has already been filed.

(E) Delayed Cross Appeal. A party seeking leave to take a delayed cross appeal shall proceed under MCR 7.205.

[Adopted effective March 1, 1985. Amended September 15, 1998, effective November 1, 1998, 459 Mich.]

Comments

Staff Comment to 1985 Adoption

MCR 7.207 corresponds to GCR 1963, 807. The rule is rewritten but retains most of the substance of the former rule.

The principal change is the extension of the right to cross appeal to criminal cases. Compare subrule (A)(1) with GCR 1963, 807.1.

New subrule (E) expressly provides for delayed cross appeal, directing the cross appellant to proceed under MCR 7.205, the rule governing applications for leave to appeal.

Staff Comment to 1998 Amendment

The September 15, 1998 amendment of MCR 7.207(B), effective November 1, 1998, provided, consistent with *Hall* v *Stewart*, 454 Mich 903 (1997), that a claim of cross appeal is timely if filed within 21 days after a claim of appeal is filed or the claim is served on the cross appellant, whichever is later, if the first appeal was of right.

Rule 7.208 Authority of Court or Tribunal Appealed From

(A) Limitations. After a claim of appeal is filed or leave to appeal is granted, the trial court or tribunal may not set aside or amend the judgment or order appealed from except

(1) by order of the Court of Appeals,

(2) by stipulation of the parties,

(3) after a decision on the merits in an action in which a preliminary injunction was granted, or

(4) as otherwise provided by law.

In a criminal case, the filing of the claim of appeal does not preclude the trial court from granting a timely motion under subrule (B).

(B) Postjudgment Motions in Criminal Cases.

(1) No later than 56 days after the commencement of the time for filing the defendant-appellant's brief as provided by MCR 7.212(A)(1)(a)(iii), the defendant may file in the trial court a motion for a new trial, for judgment of acquittal, to withdraw a plea, or to correct an invalid sentence.

(2) A copy of the motion must be filed with the Court of Appeals and served on the prosecuting attorney.

(3) The trial court shall hear and decide the motion within 28 days of filing, unless the court determines that an adjournment is necessary to secure evidence needed for the decision on the motion or that there is other good cause for an adjournment.

(4) Within 28 days of the trial court's decision, the court reporter or recorder must file with the trial court clerk the transcript of any hearing held.

(5) If the motion is granted in whole or in part,

(a) the defendant must file the appellant's brief or a notice of withdrawal of the appeal within 42 days after the trial court's decision or after the filing of the transcript of any hearing held, whichever is later;

(b) the prosecuting attorney may file a cross appeal in the manner provided by MCR 7.207 within 21 days after the trial court's decision. If the defendant has withdrawn the appeal before the prosecuting attorney has filed a cross appeal, the prosecuting attorney may file a claim of appeal or an application for leave to appeal within the 21–day period.

(6) If the motion is denied, defendant-appellant's brief must be filed within 42 days after the decision by the trial court, or the filing of the transcript of any trial court hearing, whichever is later.

(C) Correction of Defects. Except as otherwise provided by rule and until the record is filed in the Court of Appeals, the trial court or tribunal has jurisdiction

(1) to grant further time to do, properly perform, or correct any act in the trial court or tribunal in connection with the appeal that was omitted or insufficiently done, other than to extend the time for filing a claim of appeal or for paying the entry fee or to allow delayed appeal;

(2) to correct any part of the record to be transmitted to the Court of Appeals, but only after notice to the parties and an opportunity for a hearing on the proposed correction.

After the record is filed in the Court of Appeals, the trial court may correct the record only with leave of the Court of Appeals.

(D) Probate Actions. The probate court retains continuing jurisdiction to decide other matters pertaining to the proceeding from which an appeal was filed.

(E) Supervision of Property. When an appeal is filed while property is being held for conservation or management under the order or judgment of the trial court, that court retains jurisdiction over the property pending the outcome of the appeal, except as the Court of Appeals otherwise orders.

(F) Temporary Orders. A trial court order entered before final judgment concerning custody, control, and management of property; temporary alimony, support or custody of a minor child, or expenses in a domestic relations action; or a preliminary injunction, remains in effect and is enforceable in the trial court, pending interlocutory appeal, except as the trial court or the Court of Appeals may otherwise order.

(G) Stays and Bonds. The trial court retains authority over stay and bond matters, except as the Court of Appeals otherwise orders.

(H) Matters Pertaining to Appointment of Attorney. Throughout the pendency of an appeal involving an indigent person, the trial court retains authority to appoint, remove, or replace an attorney except as the Court of Appeals otherwise orders.

(I) Acts by Other Judges. Whenever the trial judge who has heard a case dies, resigns, or vacates office, or is unable to perform any act necessary to an appeal of a case within the time prescribed by law or these rules, another judge of the same court, or if another judge of that court is unavailable, another judge assigned by the state court administrator, may perform the acts necessary to the review process. Whenever a case is heard by a judge assigned from another court, the judicial acts necessary in the preparation of a record for appeal may be performed, with consent of the parties, by a judge of the court in which the case was heard.

(J) Attorney Fees and Costs. The trial court may rule on requests for costs or attorney fees under MCR 2.403, 2.405, 2.625 or other law or court rule, unless the Court of Appeals orders otherwise.

[Adopted effective March 1, 1985. Amended August 23, 1989, effective October 1, 1989, 432 Mich; March 15, 1996, effective April 1, 1996, 450 Mich; December 22, 1999, effective February 1, 2000, 461 Mich; March 12, 2002, effective September 1, 2002, 465 Mich. Amended effective September 28, 2011, 490 Mich; June 21, 2017, 500 Mich.]

Comments

Staff Comment to 1985 Adoption

MCR 7.208 is based on GCR 1963, 802 and 812.9.

Subrule (B)(2) gives the court or tribunal from which the appeal is taken the authority to correct the record, after notice to the parties and opportunity for hearing, until the record is sent to the Court of Appeals.

Subrules (E) and (F) explicitly state the authority of the trial court to deal with stays, bonds, and matters relating to attorneys appointed for indigent persons.

Staff Comment to 1989 Amendment

[Under the October 1, 1989 amendment,] MCR 7.208(B) creates a new procedure under which a criminal defendant-appellant may file postjudgment motions in the trial court notwithstanding the fact that the Court of Appeals has jurisdiction of the case because the order appointing appellate counsel serves as the claim of appeal. See MCR 6.425(F)(3). Unlike motions to remand under MCR 7.211(C)(1), leave of the Court of Appeals is not required to take advantage of this procedure. The defendant-appellant may take advantage of this procedure by filing a motion in the trial court within 28 days after the period for filing the appellant's brief has begun to run. The rule sets forth the time limits for processing such a motion in the trial court and for further proceedings in the Court of Appeals following various possible dispositions of the motion by the trial court.

Staff Comment to 1996 Amendment

The March 15, 1996, amendment of MCR 7.208(B)(1) [effective April 1, 1996] extends the time during which a criminal defendant may file postjudgment motions in the trial court, despite the fact that the Court of Appeals has jurisdiction of the case, from 28 days after the commencement of the time for filing the defendant-appellant's brief to 56 days.

Staff Comment to 1999 Amendment

The amendment to MCR 7.208 deals with the issue regarding the relationship of appeals and orders awarding or denying attorney fees and costs.

The amendment concerns the authority of the trial court to rule on requests for sanctions when an appeal has been taken. See Co-Jo, Inc v Strand, 226 Mich App 108; 572 NW2d 251 (1997). New MCR 7.208(I) provides that the trial court has the authority to rule on such requests despite the pendency of an appeal.

Staff Comment to 2002 Amendment

The March 12, 2002 amendments of Rules 3.310, 7.208, and 7.213, effective September 1, 2002, require trial courts to expeditiously decide actions in which preliminary injunctions have been granted, and allow them to proceed even if the Court of Appeals has granted interlocutory leave to appeal. Similarly, if the Court of Appeals grants leave to review entry of a preliminary injunction on an interlocutory basis, that Court is required to give priority to resolution of the appeal. See *Michigan Coalition of State Employee Unions* v *Michigan Civil Service Comm*, 465 Mich 212, 214, n 1 (2001).

Staff Comment to 2011 Amendment

The above noted changes are minor revisions of the rules that have been recommended to the Court to correct cross references and to reflect other technical changes.

Staff Comment to 2017 Amendment

These amendments conform to recent statutory changes that require all appeals from probate court to be heard in the Court of Appeals, instead of the bifurcated system that previously required some probate appeals to be heard in the Court of Appeals and some to be heard in the local circuit court. The amendments also establish priority status for appeals in guardianship and involuntary mental health treatment cases, similar to child custody cases.

Rule 7.209.   Bond; Stay of Proceedings

(A) Effect of Appeal; Prerequisites.

(1) Except for an automatic stay pursuant to MCR 2.614 or MCL 600.867, or except as otherwise provided under this rule, an appeal does not stay the effect or enforceability of a judgment or order of a trial court unless the trial court or the Court of Appeals otherwise orders. An automatic stay under MCR 2.614(D) operates to stay any and all proceedings in a cause in which a party has appealed a trial court's denial of the party's claim of governmental immunity.

(2) A motion for bond or for a stay pending appeal may not be filed in the Court of Appeals unless such a motion was decided by the trial court.

(3) A motion for bond or a stay pending appeal filed in the Court of Appeals must include a copy of the trial court's opinion and order, and a copy of the transcript of the hearing on the motion in the trial court.

(B) Responsibility for Setting Amount of Bond in Trial Court.

(1) *Civil Actions and Probate Proceedings.* Unless determined by law, or as otherwise provided by this rule, the dollar amount of a stay or appeal bond in a civil action or probate proceeding must be set by the trial court in an amount adequate to protect the opposite party.

(2) *Criminal Cases.* In a criminal case the granting of bond pending appeal and the amount of it are within the discretion of the trial court, subject to applicable law and rules. Bond must be sufficient to guarantee the appearance of the defendant. Unless bond pending appeal is allowed and a bond is filed with the trial court, a criminal judgment may be executed immediately, even though the time for taking an appeal has not elapsed.

(C) Amendment of Bond. On motion, the trial court may order an additional or different bond, set the amount, and approve or require different sureties.

(D) Review by Court of Appeals. Except as otherwise provided by rule or law, on motion filed in a case pending before it, the Court of Appeals may amend the amount of bond set by the trial court, order an additional or different bond and set the amount, or require different or additional sureties. The Court of Appeals may also refer a bond or bail matter to the court from which the appeal is taken. The Court of Appeals may grant a stay of proceedings in the trial court or stay of effect or enforcement of any judgment or order of a trial court on the terms it deems just.

(E) Stay of Proceedings by Trial Court.

(1) Unless otherwise provided by rule, statute, or court order, an execution may not issue and proceedings may not be taken to enforce an order or judgment until expiration of the time for taking an appeal of right.

(2) An appeal does not stay execution unless:

(a) Except in a domestic relations matter, the party seeking to stay a money judgment files with the court a bond in compliance with MCR 3.604 in an amount not less than 110% of the judgment or order being enforced, including any costs, interest, attorney fees, and sanctions assessed to the date of filing the bond, with the party in whose favor the judgment or order was entered as the obligee, by which the party promises to

(i) perform and satisfy the judgment or order stayed if it is not set aside or reversed, and

(ii) prosecute to completion any appeal subsequently taken from the judgment or order stayed and perform and satisfy the judgment or order entered by the Court of Appeals or Supreme Court; or

(b) The trial court grants a stay with or without bond, or with a reduced bond, as justice requires or as otherwise provided by statute (see MCL 500.3036).

(3) The court may order, on stipulation or otherwise, other forms of security in lieu of the bond in subsection (E)(2)(a), including but not limited to an irrevocable letter of credit.

(4) When the bond is filed under subsection (E)(2)(a), the judgment or order shall automatically be stayed pending entry of a final order under subsection (G).

(5) If a stay bond filed under this subrule substantially meets the requirements of subrule (F), it will be a sufficient bond to stay proceedings pending disposition of an appeal subsequently filed.

(6) The stay order must conform to any condition expressly required by the statute authorizing review.

(7) If a government party files a claim of appeal from an order described in MCR 7.202(6)(a)(v), the proceedings shall be stayed during the pendency of the appeal, unless the Court of Appeals directs otherwise.

(F) Conditions of Stay Bond.

(1) *Civil Actions and Probate Proceedings.* In a bond filed for stay pending appeal in a civil action or probate proceeding, the appellant shall promise in writing:

(a) to prosecute the appeal to decision;

(b) to perform or satisfy a judgment or order of the Court of Appeals or the Supreme Court;

(c) to perform or satisfy the judgment or order appealed from, if the appeal is dismissed;

(d) in an action involving the possession of land or judgment for foreclosure of a mortgage or land contract, to pay the appellee the damages which may result from the stay of proceedings; and

(e) to do any other act which is expressly required in the statute authorizing appeal.

(2) *Criminal Cases.* A criminal defendant for whom bond pending appeal is allowed after conviction shall promise in writing:

(a) to prosecute the appeal to decision;

(b) if the sentence is one of incarceration, to surrender himself or herself to the sheriff of the county in which he or she was convicted or other custodial authority if the sentence is affirmed on appeal or if the appeal is dismissed;

(c) if the judgment or order appealed is other than a sentence of incarceration, to perform and comply with the order of the trial court if it is affirmed on appeal or if the appeal is dismissed;

(d) to appear in the trial court if the case is remanded for retrial or further proceedings or if a conviction is reversed and retrial is allowed;

(e) to remain in Michigan unless the court gives written approval to leave; and

(f) to notify the trial court clerk of a change of address.

(G) Sureties and Filing of Bond; Service of Bond; Objections; Stay Orders. Except as otherwise specifically provided in this rule, MCR 3.604 applies. A bond must be filed with the clerk of the court that entered the order or judgment to be stayed.

(1) *Civil Actions and Probate Proceedings.*

(a) A copy of a bond and any accompanying power of attorney or affidavit must be promptly served on all parties in the manner prescribed in MCR 2.107. At the same time, the party seeking the stay shall file a proposed stay order pursuant to MCR 2.602(B)(3). Proof of service must be filed promptly with the trial court in which the bond has been filed.

(b) Objections shall be filed and served within 7 days after service of the bond. Objections to the amount of the bond are governed by MCR 2.602(B)(3). Objections to the surety are governed by MCR 3.604(E).

(c) If no timely objections to the bond, surety, or stay order are filed, the trial court shall promptly enter the order staying enforcement of the judgment or order pending all appeals. The stay shall continue until otherwise ordered by the trial court or an appellate court.

(d) Any stay order must be promptly served on all parties in the manner prescribed in MCR 2.107. Proof of service must be filed promptly with the trial court.

(e) All hearings under this rule may be held by telephone conference as provided in MCR 2.402.

(f) For good cause shown, the trial court may set the amount of the bond in a greater or lesser amount adequate to protect the interests of the parties.

(g) A bond may be secured under MCL 600.2631.

(2) *Criminal Cases.* A criminal defendant filing a bond after conviction shall give notice to the county prosecuting attorney of the time and place the bond will be filed. The bond is subject to the objection procedure provided in MCR 3.604.

(H) Stay of Execution.

(1) If a bond is filed before execution issues, and notice is given to the officer having authority to issue execution, execution is stayed. If the bond is filed after the issuance but before execution, and notice is given to the officer holding it, execution is suspended.

(2) The Court of Appeals may stay or terminate a stay of any order or judgment of a lower court or tribunal on just terms.

(3) When the amount of the judgment is more than $1000 over the insurance policy coverage or surety obligation, then the policy or obligation does not qualify to stay execution under MCL 500.3036 on the portion of the judgment in excess of the policy or bond limits. Stay pending appeal may be achieved by complying with that statute and by filing a bond in an additional amount adequate to protect the opposite party or by obtaining a trial court or Court of Appeals order waiving the additional bond.

(4) A statute exempting a municipality or other governmental agency from filing a bond to stay execution supersedes the requirements of this rule.

(I) Ex Parte Stay. Whenever an ex parte stay of proceedings is necessary to allow a motion in either the trial court or the Court of Appeals, the court before which the motion will be heard may grant an ex parte stay for that purpose. Service of a copy of the order, with a copy of the motion, any affidavits on which the motion is based, and notice of hearing on the motion, shall operate as a stay of proceedings until the court rules on the motion unless the court supersedes or sets aside the order in the interim. Proceedings may not be stayed for longer than necessary to enable the party to make the motion according to the practice of the court, and if made, until the decision of the court.

[Adopted effective March 1, 1985. Amended December 15, 1993, effective February 1, 1994, 444 Mich; June 4, 2002, effective September 1, 2002, 466 Mich; December 21, 2005, effective January 1, 2006, 474 Mich; May 30, 2008, effective September 1, 2008, 481 Mich; October 21, 2015, effective January 1, 2016, 498 Mich. Comments amended effective December 14, 2016. Amended effective June 21, 2017, 500 Mich; March 21, 2018, 501 Mich.]

Comments

Staff Comment to 1985 Adoption

MCR 7.209 is based on GCR 1963, 808. The provisions are rewritten, but retain the substance of the former rule.

Subrule (F) lists the required conditions of a stay bond in criminal cases in more detail than GCR 1963, 808.1–808.2.

In subrule (H)(3) the language regarding a stay when the judgment exceeds the amount of insurance coverage is modified to more closely conform to the applicable statute. MCL 500.3036.

Subrule (H)(4) adds a new provision recognizing the exemption of certain governmental units from bond requirements. See also MCR 2.614(E).

Staff Comment to 1994 Amendment

MCR 7.209(A) has been amended [effective February 1, 1994] to require that a motion for bond or stay first be decided by the trial court.

Staff Comment to 2002 Amendment

The June 4, 2002, amendments of MCR 7.202, 7.203, and 7.209, effective September 1, 2002, involve orders appealable by right to the Court of Appeals.

The provisions concerning custody orders in domestic relations cases and orders regarding attorney fees and costs are moved from MCR 7.203(A)(3) and (4) to MCR 7.202(7)(a)(iii) and (iv). There is also a change in the language regarding fees and costs, to refer to "postjudgment" orders.

New MCR 7.202(7)(a)(v) includes as "final" an order denying immunity to a governmental defendant, as is provided in many jurisdictions. See, *e.g., Mitchell v Forsyth*, 472 US 511; 105 S Ct 2806; 86 L Ed 2d 411 (1985).

Language is added to MCR 7.203(A) to make clear that an appeal from an order described in MCR 7.202(7)(a)(iii)–(v) is limited to the portion of the order regarding which there is an appeal of right. In addition, obsolete references to the recorder's court are deleted from that subrule.

New MCR 7.209(E)(4) provides for a stay with respect to a governmental party who takes an appeal of right from an order denying immunity.

Staff Comment to 2005 Amendment

The amendments of MCR 7.203(A) and 7.209(D), effective January 1, 2006, recognize numbering changes in MCR 7.202.

Staff Comment to 2008 Amendment

This amendment imposes an automatic stay of any and all proceedings in a case in which a party files a claim of appeal of a denial by the trial court of the party's claim of governmental immunity. No order is necessary for the stay to operate.

Staff Comment to January, 2016 Amendment

These amendments relate to stay bonds. The amendments of MCR 7.209 are modeled on the recent revisions of MCR 7.108, the circuit court appeals rule, and provide that filing a bond automatically stays enforcement of a money judgment or order. The amendments further clarify that the provision for obtaining a stay of a money judgment by filing a bond under MCR 7.209(E)(2)(a) does not apply to domestic relations matters, in which a stay must be ordered by the trial court. The amendment of MCR 2.614 coordinates with the amendment of MCR 7.209 and clarifies that execution may not issue until 21 days after a *final* judgment enters in a case.

Staff Comment to December, 2016 Amendment

These amendments update cross-references and make other nonsubstantive revisions to clarify the rules.

Staff Comment to 2017 Amendment

These amendments conform to recent statutory changes that require all appeals from probate court to be heard in the Court of Appeals, instead of the bifurcated system that previously required some probate appeals to be heard in the Court of Appeals and some to be heard in the local circuit court. The amendments also establish priority status for appeals in guardianship and involuntary mental health treatment cases, similar to child custody cases.

Staff Comment to 2018 Amendment

These amendments update cross-references and make other nonsubstantive revisions to clarify the rules. The amendment of MCR 6.110(B)(1) addresses an inadvertent omission from the last amendment of this rule that was intended to be shown in overstrike. Accordingly, the current rule does not match the published version. Striking the clause "for good cause shown" will provide consistency with other published versions of the rule and with the statute, MCL 766.7, which allows a magistrate to adjourn a preliminary examination with the consent of the parties without the need for good cause to be shown.

Rule 7.210. Record on Appeal

(A) Content of Record. Appeals to the Court of Appeals are heard on the original record.

(1) *Appeal From Court.* In an appeal from a lower court, the record consists of the original papers filed in that court or a certified copy, the transcript of any testimony or other proceedings in the case appealed, and the exhibits introduced. In an appeal from probate court in an estate or trust proceeding, an adult or minor guardianship proceeding under the Estates and Protected Individuals Code, or a proceeding under the Mental Health code, only the order appealed from and those petitions, opinions, and other documents pertaining to it need be included.

(2) *Appeal From Tribunal or Agency.* In an appeal from an administrative tribunal or agency, the record includes all documents, files, pleadings, testimony, and opinions and orders of the tribunal, agency, or officer (or a certified copy), except those summarized or omitted in whole or in part by stipulation of the parties. Testimony not transcribed when the certified record is sent for consideration of an application for leave to appeal, and not omitted by stipulation of the parties, must be filed and sent to the court as promptly as possible.

(3) *Excluded Evidence.* The substance or transcript of excluded evidence offered at a trial and the proceedings at the trial in relation to it must be included as part of the record on appeal.

(4) *Stipulations.* The parties in any appeal to the Court of Appeals may stipulate in writing regarding any matters relevant to the lower court or tribunal or agency record if the stipulation is made a part of the record on appeal and sent to the Court of Appeals.

(B) Transcript.

(1) *Appellant's Duties; Orders; Stipulations.*

(a) The appellant is responsible for securing the filing of the transcript as provided in this rule. Except in cases governed by MCR 3.977(J)(3) or MCR 6.425(G), or as otherwise provided by Court of Appeals order or the remainder of this subrule, the appellant shall order from the court reporter or recorder the full transcript of testimony and other proceedings in the trial court or tribunal. Once an appeal is filed in the Court of Appeals, a party must serve a copy of any request for transcript preparation on opposing counsel and file a copy with the Court of Appeals.

(b) In an appeal from probate court in an estate or trust proceeding, an adult or minor guardianship proceeding under the Estates and Protected Individuals Code, or a proceeding under the Mental Health code, only that portion of the transcript concerning the order appealed from need be filed. The appellee may file additional portions of the transcript.

(c) On the appellant's motion, with notice to the appellee, the trial court or tribunal may order that some portion less than the full transcript (or no transcript at all) be included in the record on appeal. The motion must be filed within the time required for filing an appeal, and, if the motion is granted, the appellee may file any portions of the transcript omitted by the appellant. The filing of the motion extends the time for filing the court reporter's or recorder's certificate until 7 days after entry of the trial court's or tribunal's order on the motion.

(d) The parties may stipulate that some portion less than the full transcript (or none) be filed.

(e) The parties may agree on a statement of facts without procuring the transcript and the statement signed by the parties may be filed with the trial court or tribunal clerk and sent as the record of testimony in the action.

(2) *Transcript Unavailable.* When a transcript of the proceedings in the trial court or tribunal cannot be obtained from the court reporter or recorder, the appellant shall take the following steps to settle the record and to cause the filing of a certified settled statement of facts to serve as a substitute for the transcript.

(a) No later than 56 days after the filing of the available transcripts, or 28 days after the filing of the available transcripts in a child custody case or interlocutory criminal appeal, or, if no transcripts are available, within 14 days after filing the claim of appeal, the appellant shall file with the trial court or tribunal clerk, and serve on each appellee, a motion to settle the record and, where reasonably possible, a proposed statement of facts. A proposed statement of facts must concisely set forth the substance of the testimony, or the oral proceedings before the trial court or tribunal if no testimony was taken, in sufficient detail to provide for appellate review.

(b) Except as otherwise provided, the appellant shall notice the motion to settle the record for hearing before the trial court or tribunal to be held within 21 days of the filing of the motion. If it is not the typical practice of a tribunal to conduct hearings, the motion to settle the record must be filed with the tribunal for consideration by the tribunal within 21 days of the filing of the motion. The motion shall be filed and served at least 14 days before the date noticed for hearing or consideration to settle the record. If appellant filed a proposed statement of facts with the motion, appellee must file and serve on the appellant and other appellees an amendment or objection to the proposed statement of facts in the trial court or tribunal at least 7 days before the time set for the settlement hearing or consideration. The trial court may adopt and file the appellant's proposed statement of facts as the certified settled statement of facts.

(c) The trial court or tribunal shall settle any controversy and certify a settled statement of facts as an accurate, fair, and complete statement of the proceedings before it. The certified settled statement of facts must concisely set forth the substance of the testimony, or the oral proceedings before the trial court or tribunal if no testimony was taken, in sufficient detail to provide for appellate review.

(d) The appellant shall file the settled statement of facts and the certifying order with the trial court or tribunal clerk and Court of Appeals.

(3) *Duties of Court Reporter or Recorder.*

(a) Certificate. Within 7 days after a transcript is ordered by a party or the court, the court reporter or recorder shall furnish a certificate stating:

(i) that the transcript has been ordered, that payment for the transcript has been made or secured, that it will be filed as soon as possible or has already been filed, and the estimated number of pages for each of the proceedings requested;

(ii) as to each proceeding requested, whether the court reporter or recorder filing the certificate recorded the proceeding; and if not,

(iii) the name and certification number of the court reporter or recorder responsible for the transcript of that proceeding.

(b) Time for Filing. The court reporter or recorder shall give precedence to transcripts necessary for interlocutory criminal appeals and custody cases. The court reporter or recorder shall file the transcript with the trial court or tribunal clerk within

(i) 14 days after it is ordered for an application for leave to appeal from an order granting or denying a motion to suppress evidence in a criminal case;

(ii) 28 days after it is ordered in an appeal of a criminal conviction based on a plea of guilty, guilty but mentally ill, or nolo contendere;

(iii) 42 days after it is ordered in any other interlocutory criminal appeal or custody case;

(iv) 91 days after it is ordered in other cases.

The Court of Appeals may extend or shorten these time limits in an appeal pending in the court on motion filed by the court reporter or recorder or a party.

(c) Copies. Additional copies of the transcripts required by the appellant may be ordered from the court reporter or recorder or photocopies may be made of the transcript furnished by the court reporter or recorder.

(d) Form of Transcript. The transcript must be filed in one or more volumes under a hard-surfaced or other suitable cover, stating the title of the action, and prefaced by a table of contents showing the subject matter of the transcript with page references to the significant parts of the trial or proceedings, including the testimony of each witness by name, the arguments of the attorneys, and the jury instructions. The pages of the transcript must be consecutively numbered on the bottom of each page. Transcripts filed with the court must contain only a single transcript page per document page, not multiple pages combined on a single document page.

(e) Notice. Immediately after the transcript is filed, the court reporter or recorder shall notify the Court of Appeals and all parties that it has been filed and file in the Court of Appeals an affidavit of mailing of notice to the parties.

(f) Discipline. A court reporter or recorder failing to comply with the requirements of these rules is subject to disciplinary action by the courts, including punishment for contempt of court, on the court's own initiative or motion of a party.

(g) Responsibility When More Than One Reporter or Recorder. In a case in which portions of the transcript must be prepared by more than one reporter or recorder, unless the court has designated another person, the person who recorded the beginning of the proceeding is responsible for ascertaining that the entire transcript has been prepared, filing it, and giving the notice required by subrule (B)(3)(e).

(C) Exhibits. Within 21 days after the claim of appeal is filed, a party possessing any exhibits offered in evidence, whether admitted or not, shall file them with the trial court or tribunal clerk, unless by stipulation of the parties or order of the trial court or tribunal they are not to be sent, or copies, summaries, or excerpts are to be sent. Xerographic copies of exhibits may be filed in lieu of originals unless the trial court or tribunal orders otherwise. When the record is returned to the trial court or tribunal, the trial court or tribunal clerk shall return the exhibits to the parties who filed them.

(D) Reproduction of Records. Where facilities for the copying or reproduction of records are available to the clerk of the court or tribunal whose action is to be reviewed, the clerk, on a party's request and on deposit of the estimated cost or security for the cost, shall procure for the party as promptly as possible and at the cost to the clerk the requested number of copies of documents, transcripts, and exhibits on file.

(E) Record on Motion. If, before the time the complete record on appeal is sent to the Court of Appeals, a party files a motion that requires the Court of Appeals to have the record, the trial court or tribunal clerk shall, on request of a party or the Court of Appeals, send the Court of Appeals the documents needed.

(F) Service of Record. Within 21 days after the transcript is filed with the trial court clerk, the appellant shall serve a copy of the entire record on appeal, including the transcript and exhibits, on each appellee. However, copies of documents the appellee already possesses need not be served. Proof that the record was served must be promptly filed with the Court of Appeals and the trial court or tribunal clerk. If the filing of a transcript has been excused as provided in subrule (B), the record is to be served within 21 days after the filing of the transcript substitute.

(G) Transmission of Record. Within 21 days after the briefs have been filed or the time for filing the appellee's brief has expired, or when the court requests, the trial court or tribunal clerk shall send to the Court of Appeals the record on appeal in the case pending on appeal, except for those things omitted by written stipulation of the parties. Weapons, drugs, or money are not to be sent unless the Court of Appeals requests. The trial court or tribunal clerk shall append a certificate identifying the name of the case and the papers with reasonable definiteness and shall include as part of the record:

(1) a register of actions in the case;

(2) all opinions, findings, and orders of the court or tribunal; and

(3) the order or judgment appealed from.

Transcripts and all other documents which are part of the record on appeal must be attached in one or more file folders or other suitable hard-surfaced binders showing the name of the trial court or tribunal, the title of the case, and the file number.

(H) Return of Record. After the Court of Appeals disposes of an appeal, the Court of Appeals shall promptly send the original record, together with a certified copy of the opinion, judgment, or order entered by the Court of Appeals

(1) to the Clerk of the Supreme Court if an application for leave to appeal is filed in the Supreme Court, or

(2) to the clerk of the court or tribunal from which it was received when

(a) the period for an application for leave to appeal to the Supreme Court has expired without the filing of an application, and

(b) there is pending in the Court of Appeals no

(i) timely motion for reconsideration,

(ii) timely petition for a special panel under MCR 7.215(I), or

(iii) timely request by a judge of the Court of Appeals for a special panel under MCR 7.215(I),

and the period for such a timely motion, petition, or request has expired.

(I) Notice by Trial Court or Tribunal Clerk. The trial court or tribunal clerk shall promptly notify all parties of the return of the record in order that they may take the appropriate action in the trial court or tribunal under the Court of Appeals mandate.

[Adopted effective March 1, 1985. Amended March 30, 1989, effective October 1, 1989, 432 Mich. Amended effective November 30, 1990, 437 Mich. Amended May 2, 1994, effective July 1, 1994, 445 Mich; January 26, 1996, effective April 1, 1996, 450 Mich; September 27, 1996, effective January 1, 1997, 453 Mich. Amended effective October 21, 1997, 457 Mich; May 6, 1998, 457 Mich; November 30, 1999, 461 Mich. Amended November 26, 2001, effective January 1, 2002, 465 Mich; January 22, 2003, effective May 1, 2003, 467 Mich; June 6, 2003, effective September 1, 2003, 468 Mich; February 1, 2005, effective May 1, 2005, 472 Mich; October 3, 2006, effective January 1, 2007, 477 Mich; March 15, 2007, effective May 1, 2007, 477 Mich. Amended effective September 28, 2011, 490 Mich. Amended April 4, 2012, effective May 1, 2012, 491 Mich. Amended effective June 21, 2017, 500 Mich. Amended August 30, 2018, effective September 1, 2018, 502 Mich. Amended effective August 14, 2019, 503 Mich.]

Comments

Staff Comment to 1985 Adoption

MCR 7.210 is based on GCR 1963, 809, 811, 812, and 815.1(2). The provisions are rewritten and are more detailed than the former rules, although the substance is basically the same.

Under subrules (A)(1) and (B)(1)(a), in an appeal from a probate court estate or trust proceeding, only the papers and the portion of the transcript that are relevant to the order appealed from are required.

GCR 1963, 812.3(1) said that a court reporter who fails to file a transcript as required by the rule was subject to punishment for contempt. This provision is modified slightly in subrule (B)(3)(f), which says that the court reporter is subject to discipline for any failure to comply with the duties imposed by the rules.

Subrule (B)(3)(g) is a new provision dealing with the situation in which more than one court reporter or recorder took the testimony in a case. Unless the court designates another person, the reporter or recorder who records the beginning of the proceeding is responsible for ascertaining that the transcript has been prepared, filing it, and giving the required notices. This is consistent with the general rule covering court reporters and recorders, MCR 8.108(B)(2).

Under subrule (H) certain types of exhibits are not to be sent to the Court of Appeals unless that court requests them.

GCR 1963, 812.8 is omitted. Similar provisions are included in MCR 2.610(C)–(E).

Staff Comment to 1989 Amendment

There are three changes [under the October 1, 1989 amendment] in MCR 7.210. MCR 7.210(B)(1)(a) is amended to clarify the relative duties of the appellant and the court reporter with regard to the ordering and filing of transcripts.

In MCR 7.210(B)(3)(b)(iv) the time limit on filing of transcripts in trial cases is reduced from 91 days to 56.

The amendment of MCR 7.210(H) sets 21 days as the time within which the trial court or tribunal clerk is to send the record on appeal to the Court of Appeals after the transcript is filed.

Staff Comment to 1990 Amendment

The [November 30,] 1990 amendment of MCR 7.210(I) permits the Court of Appeals to retain the lower court records until the completion of proceedings under Administrative Order 1990–6.

Staff Comment to 1994 Amendment

The May 2, 1994 amendment of subrule (B)(1)(a), effective July 1, 1994, was based on a proposal from the Michigan Judges Association. The amendment recognizes a change in Rule 6.433 regarding the transcribing of the jury voir dire.

Staff Comment to April, 1996 Amendment

The amendment of MCR 7.210(B)(3)(d) allows transcripts to be prepared with up to four reduced pages of transcript appearing on a single page.

Staff Comment to September, 1996 Amendment

The September 27, 1996, amendment of MCR 7.210(B)(3)(b)(iv) [effective as to transcripts ordered on or after January 1, 1997, but before November 1, 1997] lengthens the time within which the court reporter or recorder must file the transcript in most appeals from 56 to 91 days, which was the time limit before the October 1, 1989, amendment of the rule. The shortened time limits for filing transcripts in appeals from decisions on motions to suppress evidence in criminal cases, appeals of plea-based criminal convictions, other interlocutory criminal appeals, and appeals in custody cases are not affected. The Court will reexamine the need for the increase in time for filing transcripts before November 1, 1997.

Staff Comment to 1997 Amendment

The October 21, 1997, order extends indefinitely the September 27, 1996, amendment of MCR 7.210(B)(3)(b)(iv), which lengthened the time within which the court reporter or recorder must file the transcript in most appeals from 56 to 91 days.

Staff Comment to 1999 Amendment

The amendment of MCR 7.210 is to accommodate statewide records standards applicable to all courts and all clerks of the courts as developed and recommended by the Michigan Trial Court Case File Management Standards Committee.

Staff Comment to 2002 Amendment

The amendment of MCR 7.210(H) recognized numbering changes in other rules and the elimination of the 'parallel citation' requirement from the Michigan Uniform System of Citation (Supreme Court AO 2001-5).

Staff Comment to January, 2003 Amendment

The January 22, 2003, amendment of MCR 7.211(B), effective May 1, 2003, clarifies the deadline for answering a substantive motion when there also is a motion for immediate consideration of that motion.

The January 22, 2003, amendment of MCR 7.215(H), effective May 1, 2003, details how the Court of Appeals carries out the notification duties assigned to it by the 2000 PA 503 amendments of the Crime Victims Rights Act, MCL 780.751 et seq.

The January 22, 2003, amendment of MCR 7.215(I)(4), effective May 1, 2003, added the provision that the Court of Appeals clerk will not accept untimely motions for reconsideration. The same amendment order changed the title of a motion for "rehearing" to "reconsideration" in several other MCR Subchapter 7.200 rules.

Staff Comment to June, 2003 Amendment

The June 6, 2003, amendments of MCR 7.205, 7.210, 7.215, 7.302, and 7.316, which are effective September 1, 2003, deal with the time for filing applications for leave to appeal to the Supreme Court.

The amendments of MCR 7.302(C)(1), (2), and (4) set time limits of 56 days in criminal cases and 42 days in civil ones, but with a 28–day time limit for appeals from orders terminating parental rights, in recognition of the adverse consequences of delay on the children involved in such cases. Late applications will not be accepted. MCR 7.302(C)(3), 7.316(B).

The amendment of MCR 7.302(D)(2) provides a 28–day time limit for filing applications for leave to appeal as cross-appellant.

There are also nonsubstantive changes in several rules governing procedure in the Court of Appeals. In MCR 7.205(F)(5), a reference is added to MCR 3.993(C)(2) (formerly MCR 5.993[C][1]), which sets the time limit for late applications in parental-rights-termination cases. The language of MCR 7.210 and 7.215 is adjusted to conform to the changes in the Supreme Court rules.

Staff Comment to 2005 Amendment

The February 1, 2005, effective May 1, 2005, amendments were recommended by the Court of Appeals Record Production Work Group.

The amendment of MCR 6.425(F) expedites the ordering of additional transcripts in criminal appeals that have been requested by appointed counsel by requiring trial courts to order additional transcripts within 14 days after receiving a timely request.

Although the rules contain no specific deadline within which counsel is required to order additional transcripts, the Court of Appeals has always applied a 28-day guideline to ensure that appellate attorneys are quickly reviewing their orders of appointment to determine whether additional transcripts are necessary. Court of Appeals Internal Operating Procedure 7.204(C)(2) states that appointed counsel should review the order shortly after appointment to confirm that all necessary transcripts were ordered. The same concept is stated in IOP 7.210(B)(1)-1. The 28-day guideline is stated in IOP 7.210(B)(l)-2.

The amendment of MCR 7.210(B)(3)(a) enhances an attorney's ability to discover and order missing transcripts in all appeals by requiring the court reporter or recorder to specifically articulate on the certificate for each proceeding requested: the estimated length of the transcript ordered and the identity of the court reporter or recorder responsible for the transcript if it is not the individual filing the certificate.

The amendment of MCR 8.119(D)(1)(c) expedites the ordering of transcripts in all appeals by requiring the circuit court's register of actions to include a notation as to whether a hearing was held on the record, and the name and certification number of the court reporter or recorder responsible for transcribing the hearing. The subrule is also divided for the ease of the reader.

Staff Comment to 2006 Amendment

The amendment of MCR 7.210 resolves a conflict between this rule, which generally requires production of the full transcript of testimony and other proceedings in the trial court or tribunal for appeal, and MCR 3.977(I)(1)(b), which allows the trial court to furnish only the portions of the transcript and record the attorney requires to appeal. See, also, Administrative Memorandum 2004–02.

Staff Comment to 2007 Amendment

These changes reflect relettered provisions of MCR 6.425.

Staff Comment to 2011 Amendment

The above noted changes are minor revisions of the rules that have been recommended to the Court to correct cross references and to reflect other technical changes.

Staff Comment to 2012 Amendment

The amendments of MCR 7.210 and MCR 7.212 extend the time period in which parties may request that a court settle a record for which a transcript is not available and clarify the procedure for doing so.

Staff Comment to 2017 Amendment

These amendments conform to recent statutory changes that require all appeals from probate court to be heard in the Court of Appeals, instead of the bifurcated system that previously required some probate appeals to be heard in the Court of Appeals and some to be heard in the local circuit court. The amendments also establish priority status for appeals in guardianship and involuntary mental health treatment cases, similar to child custody cases.

Staff Comment to 2018 Amendment

These amendments update cross-references in the rules, and are intended to reflect changes that are necessary as a result of the Court's recent e-Filing rules amendments.

Staff Comment to 2019 Amendment

These amendments update cross-references and make other nonsubstantive revisions to clarify the rules.

Rule 7.211. Motions in Court of Appeals

(A) Manner of Making Motion. A motion is made in the Court of Appeals by filing:

(1) 5 copies of a motion (one signed) stating briefly but distinctly the facts and the grounds on which it is based and the relief requested;

(2) the entry fee;

(3) for a motion to dismiss, to affirm, or for peremptory reversal, 5 copies of a supporting brief. A supporting brief may be filed with any other motion. A brief must conform to MCR 7.212(C) as nearly as possible, except that page references to a transcript are not required unless the transcript is relevant to the issue raised in the motion. A brief in conformance with MCR 7.212(C) is not required in support of a motion to affirm when the appellant argues that:

(a) the trial court's findings of fact are clearly erroneous;

(b) the trial court erred in applying established law;

(c) the trial court abused its discretion; or

(d) a sentence which is within the sentencing guidelines is invalid.

Instead of a brief in support of a motion to affirm in such a circumstance, the movant may append those portions of the transcript that are pertinent to the issues raised in the motion; in that case, the motion must include a summary of the movant's position;

(4) a motion for immediate consideration if the party desires a hearing on a date earlier than the applicable date set forth in subrules (B)(2)(a)-(e);

(5) proof that a copy of the motion, the motion for immediate consideration if one has been filed, and any other supporting papers were served on all other parties to the appeal.

(B) Answer.

(1) A party to an appeal may answer a motion by filing:

(a) 5 copies of an answer (one signed); and

(b) proof that a copy of the answer and any other opposing papers were served on all other parties to the appeal.

(2) Subject to subrule (3), the answer must be filed within

(a) 21 days after the motion is served on the other parties, for a motion to dismiss, to remand, or to affirm;

(b) 35 days after the motion is served on the appellee, if the motion is for peremptory reversal;

(c) 56 days after the motion is served on the defendant, for a motion to withdraw as the appointed appellate attorney;

(d) 14 days after the motion is served on the other parties, for a motion for reconsideration of an opinion or an order, to stay proceedings in the trial court, to strike a full or partial pleading on appeal, to file an amicus brief, to hold an appeal in abeyance, or to reinstate an appeal after dismissal under MCR 7.217(D);

(e) 7 days after the motion is served on the other parties, for all other motions.

If a motion for immediate consideration has been filed, all answers to all affected motions must be filed within 7 days if the motions for immediate consideration was served by mail, or within such time as the Court of Appeals directs. See subrule (C)(6).

(3) In its discretion, the Court of Appeals may dispose of the following motions before the answer period has expired: motion to extend time to order or file transcripts, to extend time to file a brief or other appellate pleading, to substitute one attorney for another, for oral argument when the right to oral argument was not otherwise preserved as described in MCR 7.212, or for an out-of-state attorney to appear and practice in Michigan.

(4) Five copies of an opposing brief may be filed. A brief must conform to MCR 7.212(D) as nearly as possible, except that page references to a transcript are not required unless the transcript is relevant to the issue raised in the motion.

(C) Special Motions. If the record on appeal has not been sent to the Court of Appeals, except as provided in subrule (C)(6), the party making a special motion shall request the clerk of the trial court or tribunal to send the record to the Court of Appeals. A copy of the request must be filed with the motion.

(1) *Motion to Remand.*

(a) Within the time provided for filing the appellant's brief, the appellant may move to remand to the trial court. The motion must identify an issue sought to be reviewed on appeal and show

(i) that the issue is one that is of record and that must be initially decided by the trial court; or

(ii) that development of a factual record is required for appellate consideration of the issue.

A motion under this subrule must be supported by affidavit or offer of proof regarding the facts to be established at a hearing.

(b) A timely motion must be granted if it is accompanied by a certificate from the trial court that it will grant a motion for new trial.

(c) In a case tried without a jury, the appellant need not file a motion for remand or a motion for new trial to challenge the great weight of the evidence in order to preserve the issue for appeal.

(d) If a motion to remand is granted, further proceedings in the Court of Appeals are stayed until completion of the proceedings in the trial court pursuant to the remand, unless the Court of Appeals orders otherwise.

(e) If the trial court grants the appellant relief in whole or in part,

(i) Unless the Court of Appeals orders otherwise, appellant must file the brief on appeal or notice of withdrawal of appeal within 21 days after the trial court's decision or after the filing of the transcript of any hearing held, whichever is later.

(ii) The appellee may file a cross appeal in the manner provided by MCR 7.207 within 21 days after the trial court's decision. If the appellant has withdrawn the appeal before the appellee has filed a cross appeal, the appellee may file a claim of appeal or an application for leave to appeal within the 21 day period.

(f) If the trial court denies the appellant's request for relief, appellant's brief must be filed within 21 days after the decision by the trial court, or the filing of the transcript of any trial court hearing, whichever is later.

(2) *Motion to Dismiss.* An appellee may file a motion to dismiss an appeal any time before it is placed on a session calendar on the ground that

(a) the appeal is not within the Court of Appeals jurisdiction;

(b) the appeal was not filed or pursued in conformity with the rules; or

(c) the appeal is moot.

(3) *Motion to Affirm.* After the appellant's brief has been filed, an appellee may file a motion to affirm the order or judgment appealed from on the ground that

(a) it is manifest that the questions sought to be reviewed are so unsubstantial as to need no argument or formal submission; or

(b) the questions sought to be reviewed were not timely or properly raised.

The decision to grant a motion to affirm must be unanimous. An order denying a motion to affirm may identify the judge or judges who would have granted it but for the unanimity requirement of this subrule.

(4) *Motion for Peremptory Reversal.* The appellant may file a motion for peremptory reversal on the ground that reversible error is so manifest that an immediate reversal of the judgment or order appealed from should be granted without formal argument or submission. The decision to grant a motion for peremptory reversal must be unanimous. An order denying a motion for peremptory reversal may identify the judge or judges who would have granted it but for the unanimity requirement of this subrule.

(5) *Motion to Withdraw.* A court-appointed appellate attorney for an indigent appellant may file a motion to withdraw if the attorney determines, after a conscientious and thorough review of the trial court record, that the appeal is wholly frivolous.

(a) A motion to withdraw is made by filing:

(i) 5 copies of a motion to withdraw (one signed) which identifies any points the appellant seeks to assert and any other matters that the attorney has considered as a basis for appeal;

(ii) 5 copies of a brief conforming to MCR 7.212(C), which refers to anything in the record that might arguably support the appeal, contains relevant record references, and cites and deals with those authorities which appear to bear on the points in question;

(iii) proof that copies of the motion, brief in support, and notice that the motion may result in the conviction or trial court judgment being affirmed were served on the appellant by certified mail; and

(iv) proof that a copy of the motion only and not the brief was served the appellee.

(b) If the appeal is available only by leave of the court, the motion shall be filed within 56 days after the transcript is filed or within the deadline for filing a late application for leave to appeal, whichever comes first. The filing of such a motion, with the accompanying brief required by MCR 7.211(C)(5)(a)(ii), shall be treated as the filing of an application for leave to appeal on behalf of the appellant.

(c) The motion to withdraw and supporting papers will be submitted to the court for decision on the first Tuesday

(i) 28 days after the appellant is served in appeals from orders of the family division of the circuit court terminating parental rights under the Juvenile Code, or

(ii) 56 days after the appellant is served in all other appeals.

The appellant may file with the court an answer and brief in which he or she may make any comments and raise any points that he or she chooses concerning the appeal and the attorney's motion. The appellant must file proof that a copy of the answer was served on his or her attorney.

(d) If the court finds that the appeal is wholly frivolous, it may grant the motion and affirm the conviction or trial court judgment in appeals by right or deny leave to appeal in appeals by leave. If the court affirms the conviction or trial court judgment or denies leave to appeal, the appellant's attorney shall mail to the appellant a copy of the transcript within 14 days after the order affirming is certified and file proof of that service. If the court finds any legal point arguable on its merits, it may deny the motion and order the court appointed attorney to proceed in support of the appeal or grant the motion and order the appointment of substitute appellate counsel to proceed in support of the appeal.

(6) *Motion for Immediate Consideration.* A party may file a motion for immediate consideration to expedite hearing on another motion. The motion must state facts showing why immediate consideration is required. If a copy of the motion for immediate consideration and a copy of the motion of which immediate consideration is sought are personally served under MCR 2.107(C)(1) or (2), the motions may be submitted to the court immediately on filing. If mail service is used, motions may not be submitted until the first Tuesday 7 days after the date of service, unless the party served acknowledges receipt. The trial court or tribunal record need not be requested unless it is required as to the motion of which immediate consideration is sought.

(7) *Confession of Error by Prosecutor.* In a criminal case, if the prosecutor concurs in the relief requested by the defendant, the prosecutor shall file a confession of error so indicating, which may state reasons why concurrence in the relief requested is appropriate. The confession of error shall be submitted to one judge pursuant to MCR 7.211(E). If the judge approves the confession of error, the judge shall enter an order or opinion granting the relief. If the judge rejects the confession of error, the case shall be submitted for decision through the ordinary processes of the court, and the confession of error shall be submitted to the panel assigned to decide the case.

(8) *Vexatious Proceedings.* A party's request for damages or other disciplinary action under MCR 7.216(C) must be contained in a motion filed under this rule. A request that is contained in any other pleading, including a brief filed under MCR 7.212, will not constitute a motion under this rule. A

party may file a motion for damages or other disciplinary action under MCR 7.216(C) at any time within 21 days after the date of the order or opinion that disposes of the matter that is asserted to have been vexatious.

(9) *Motion to Seal Court of Appeals File in Whole or in Part.*

(a) Trial court files that have been sealed in whole or in part by a trial court order will remain sealed while in the possession of the Court of Appeals. Public requests to view such trial court files will be referred to the trial court.

(b) Materials that are subject to a protective order entered under MCR 2.302(C) may be submitted for inclusion in the Court of Appeals file in sealed form if they are accompanied by a copy of the protective order. A party objecting to such sealed submissions may file an appropriate motion in the Court of Appeals.

(c) Except as otherwise provided by statute or court rule, the procedure for sealing a Court of Appeals file is governed by MCR 8.119(I). Materials that are subject to a motion to seal a Court of Appeals file in whole or in part shall be held under seal pending the court's disposition of the motion.

(d) Any party or interested person may file an answer in response to a motion to seal a Court of Appeals file within 7 days after the motion is served on the other parties, or within 7 days after the motion is filed in the Court of Appeals, whichever is later.

(e) An order granting a motion shall include a finding of good cause, as defined by MCR 8.119(I)(2), and a finding that there is no less restrictive means to adequately and effectively protect the specific interest asserted.

(f) An order granting or denying a motion to seal a Court of Appeals file in whole or in part may be challenged by any person at any time during the pendency of an appeal.

(D) Submission of Motions. Motions in the Court of Appeals are submitted on Tuesday of each week. There is no oral argument on motions, unless ordered by the court.

(E) Decision on Motions.

(1) Except as provided in subrule (E)(2), orders may be entered only on the concurrence of the majority of the judges to whom the motion has been assigned.

(2) The chief judge or another designated judge may, acting alone, enter an order disposing of an administrative motion. Administrative motions include, but are not limited to:

(a) a motion to consolidate;

(b) a motion to extend the time to file a transcript or brief;

(c) a motion to strike a nonconforming brief;

(d) a motion for oral argument in a case that has not yet been placed on a session calendar;

(e) a motion to adjourn the hearing date of an application, complaint, or motion;

(f) a motion to dismiss a criminal appeal on the grounds that the defendant has absconded;

(g) a motion to file an amicus curiae brief;

(h) a motion to allow an out-of-state attorney to appear and practice.

[Adopted effective March 1, 1985. Amended March 30, 1989, effective October 1, 1989, 432 Mich; February 23, 1995, effective May 1, 1995, 448 Mich. Amended effective June 2, 1995, 449 Mich; August 1, 1995, 449 Mich. Amended January 26, 1996, effective April 1, 1996, 450 Mich; April 30, 1997, effective September 1, 1997, 454 Mich; June 2, 1998, effective September 1, 1998, 457 Mich; January 22, 2003, effective May 1, 2003, 467 Mich; July 9, 2003, effective September 1, 2003, 468 Mich. Amended effective December 17, 2003, 469 Mich. Amended June 28, 2005, effective September 1, 2005, 472 Mich; January 31, 2006, effective May 1, 2006, 474 Mich; October 17, 2006, effective January 1, 2007, 477 Mich; May 18, 2010, effective September 1, 2010, 486 Mich. Amended effective May 7, 2014, 495 Mich. Amended May 27, 2015, effective September 1, 2015, 498 Mich; September 20, 2017, effective January 1, 2018, 501 Mich; April 19, 2018, effective May 1, 2018, 501 Mich.]

Comments

Staff Comment to 1985 Adoption

MCR 7.211 is based on GCR 1963, 817. The provisions of the former rule are rewritten, but their substance is retained. A number of new provisions are added.

The rule requires that 5 copies of the motion and related documents be filed, rather than 4 as under GCR 1963, 817.1.

Subrule (A)(5) modifies the time periods for notice of submission of motions. Compare GCR 1963, 817.2 and 817.5(4).

Subrule (B) is a new provision covering the manner of responding to a motion.

Under subrule (C)(1), if a motion to remand is granted, proceedings in the Court of Appeals are stayed pending the proceedings on remand. In general, under MCR 7.212(A)(5), the filing of a motion does not stay the time for filing briefs.

Subrule (C) also includes several new provisions covering particular motions: motions for peremptory reversal (C)(4); motions to withdraw by appointed attorneys for indigent persons (C)(5); and motions for immediate consideration of other motions (C)(6).

Staff Comment to 1989 Amendment

There are several changes [under the October 1, 1989 amendment] in MCR 7.211. In MCR 7.211(A)(5)(b) the time within which the appellee may respond to a motion for peremptory reversal is lengthened from 21 to 35 days.

There are two changes in MCR 7.211(C)(1), the rule covering motions to remand. First, the language is modified with regard to the showing that must be made by the moving party. An affidavit or offer of proof is required. Second, language is added setting the time within which the appellant's brief is due following proceedings on remand at 42 days, unless the Court of Appeals sets another time.

Staff Comment to May, 1995 Amendment

There are several amendments of MCR 7.211 [effective May 1, 1995]. Under subrule (A), the brief requirement is changed for certain motions to affirm. Subrule (C)(1) is reorganized. New subrule (C)(1)(b) eliminates the need for a motion to remand to preserve a great weight of evidence issue in nonjury cases. Under subrule (C)(1)(c), the time for filing the appellant's brief after completion of the proceedings on remand is shortened from 42 to 21 days.

Staff Comment to June, 1995 Amendment

MCR 7.211(A)(5)(d) and (e) are amended [effective June 2, 1995] in light of the March 3, 1995, amendment of MCR 7.215(H) [effective May 1, 1995; see MCR 7.215(G) effective August 1, 1995], regarding motions for rehearing.

Staff Comment to August, 1995 Amendment

The amendment of MCR 7.211(C)(1) [effective August 1, 1995] revises the rule governing motions to remand, deleting the direction that the Court of Appeals "must" grant such motions under certain circumstances, thus giving the Court greater discretion in ruling on such motions.

Staff Comment to 1996 Amendment

New MCR 7.211(C)(7) provides a procedure for handling confessions of error by prosecutors in criminal cases.

Staff Comment to 1997 Amendment

The amendments of MCR 7.211(C)(3) and (4) [effective September 1, 1997] require orders granting motions to affirm or for peremptory reversal to be unanimous.

Staff Comment to 1998 Amendment

MCR 7.211(A) and (B) eliminate the filing of a notice of hearing, instead specifying the time for response.

MCR 7.211(A)(2) eliminates the requirement of filing affidavits with motions.

MCR 7.211(B)(2)(a) (former [A][5][a]) adds motions to remand to the list of motions for which the notice period for submission is 21 days.

Staff Comment to May, 2003 Amendment

The January 22, 2003, amendment of MCR 7.211(B), effective May 1, 2003, clarifies the deadline for answering a substantive motion when there also is a motion for immediate consideration of that motion.

The January 22, 2003, amendment of MCR 7.215(H), effective May 1, 2003, details how the Court of Appeals carries out the notification duties assigned to it by the 2000 PA 503 amendments of the Crime Victims Rights Act, MCL 780.751 *et seq.*

The January 22, 2003, amendment of MCR 7.215(I) (4), effective May 1, 2003, added the provision that the Court of Appeals clerk will not accept untimely motions for reconsideration. The same amendment order changed the title of a motion for "rehearing" to "reconsideration" in several other MCR Subchapter 7.200 rules.

Staff Comment to September, 2003 Amendment

The July 9, 2003, addition of MCR 7.211(C)(8), effective September 1, 2003, requires a separate motion to request damages or other disciplinary action for vexatious proceedings. To assure jurisdiction to consider the issue and to provide finality to the appeal, such a motion must be filed within 21 days after the date of the order or opinion that disposes of the matter that is asserted to have been vexatious. If the assertion concerns the entire appeal, the motion must be filed within 21 days of the date of the order or opinion that disposes of the entire appeal. If the assertion concerns a specific motion or motions filed by an opposing party, the motion for damages must be filed within 21 days of the date of the order disposing of the underlying motion or motions.

Staff Comment to December, 2003 Amendment

The December 17, 2003, amendments of MCR 7.211(C)(5)(a) brought the rule into conformity with the 1998 amendments of subrules (A) and (B), which eliminated the filing of a notice of hearing, instead specifying the time for a response. Subrule (C)(5)(a)(iii) and the "notice of hearing" language in subrule (C)(5)(a)(iv) were deleted, and former subrules (C)(5)(a)(iv) and (v) were redesignated subrules (C)(5)(a)(iii) and (iv), respectively. The December 17, 2003, amendment of MCR 7.213(A)(3) conformed that subrule to the May 1, 2003, amendment of MCR 7.215 by changing the cross-reference from former subrule (I) to subrule (J).

Staff Comment to 2005 Amendment

The September 1, 2005, amendment of MCR 7.211(C) creates new subrule (9) to clarify the procedure for motions to seal Court of Appeals files and to unseal previously sealed files. The rule incorporates by reference the procedures for sealing files in the trial courts set forth in MCR 8.119(F). The amendment also contains additional language unique to cases pending in the Court of Appeals.

Staff Comment to January, 2006 Amendment

The amendment clarifies that where claims that are the subject of motions for remand require development of facts not of record, the motion must be supported by affidavit or offer of proof regarding the facts to be established at a hearing.

Staff Comment to October, 2006 Amendment

The amendment of subrule (B) extends the time to answer certain motions from 7 to 14 days, and establishes a new category of motions that can be decided in less than 7 days without delaying submission until the answer period has expired. The amendment also clarifies that answers to motions for immediate consideration and any motions affected by such a motion are to be filed within 7 days if the motion for immediate consideration was served by mail or within such time as the Court directs in light of the circumstances of the case.

The amendment of subrule (C) reduces from 56 days to 28 days the deadline for submission of a motion to withdraw as appointed counsel in an appeal from an order terminating parental rights. The 56–day deadline is retained for all other appeals

Staff Comment to 2010 Amendment

These amendments of MCR 7.211, 7.313, and 8.119 clarify that materials filed with a trial court, with the Court of Appeals, or with the Supreme Court that relate to a motion to seal a record are nonpublic until the court disposes of the motion.

Staff Comment to 2014 Amendment

These amendments reflect changes that correct minor technical errors that have occurred in drafting or the changes respond to recent adopted rule revisions, which occasionally inadvertently create incorrect cross-references in other rules.

Staff Comment to 2015 Amendment

The amendment of MCR 7.211(C)(1)(c) clarifies that an appellant, in a case tried without a jury, is not required to file a motion for remand or a motion for a new trial to challenge the great weight of the evidence to preserve the issue for appeal.

Staff Comment to January, 2018 Amendment

The amendments of MCR 7.211 allow motions to withdraw for frivolous appeal in cases that proceed by leave to be heard in the Court of Appeals. This alternative to the proposal published for comment was recommended to the Court by the Michigan Appellate Assigned Counsel System, and supported by the Court of Appeals.

Staff Comment to May, 2018 Amendment

The amendments, submitted by SADO, are intended to clarify practices and provide protections for criminal defendants represented by assigned appellate counsel. The amendments allow an additional 42 days to file post-judgment motions in certain circumstances, and where delay is due to the trial court, clarify in the amendment of MCR 7.205 that in certain circumstances, substitute appellate counsel may file a delayed application for leave to appeal within 42 days of appointment (even if later than six months after sentencing), add language to MCR 7.211 to guide parties and courts if relief is granted in the trial court, and change the procedure for seeking permission to file a brief longer than 50 pages in length.

Rule 7.212.   Briefs

(A) Time for Filing and Service.

(1) *Appellant's Brief.*

(a) Filing. The appellant shall file 5 typewritten, xerographic, or printed copies of a brief with the Court of Appeals within

(i) 28 days after the claim of appeal is filed, the order granting leave is certified, the transcript is filed with the trial court, or a settled statement of facts and certifying order is filed with the trial court or tribunal, whichever is later, in a child custody case, adult or minor guardianship case under the Estates and Protected Individuals Code or under the Mental Health Code, involuntary mental health treatment cases under the Mental Health Code, or an interlocutory criminal appeal. This time may be extended only by the Court of Appeals on motion; or

(ii) the time provided by MCR 7.208(B)(5)(a), 7.208(B)(6), or 7.211(C)(1), in a case in which one of those rules applies; or

(iii) 56 days after the claim of appeal is filed, the order granting leave is certified, the transcript is filed with the trial court or tribunal, or a settled statement of facts and certifying order is filed with the trial court or tribunal, whichever is later, in all other cases. In a criminal case in which substitute counsel is appointed for the defendant, the time runs from the date substitute counsel is appointed, the transcript is filed, or a settled statement of facts and certifying order is filed, whichever is later. The parties may extend the time within which the brief must be filed for 28 days by signed stipulation filed with the Court of Appeals. The Court of Appeals may extend the time on motion.

(b) Service. Within the time for filing the appellant's brief, 1 copy must be served on all other parties to the appeal and proof of that service filed with the Court of Appeals and served with the brief.

(2) *Appellee's Brief.*

(a) Filing. The appellee shall file 5 typewritten, xerographic, or printed copies of a brief with the Court of Appeals within

(i) 21 days after the appellant's brief is served on the appellee, in an interlocutory criminal appeal, adult or minor guardianship case under the Estates and Protected Individuals Code or under the Mental Health Code, involuntary mental health treatment cases under the Mental Health Code, or a child custody case. This time may be extended only by the Court of Appeals on motion;

(ii) 35 days after the appellant's brief is served on the appellee, in all other cases. The parties may extend this time for 28 days by signed stipulation filed with the Court of Appeals. The Court of Appeals may extend the time on motion.

(b) Service. Within the time for filing the appellee's brief, 1 copy must be served on all other parties to the appeal and proof of that service must be filed with the Court of Appeals.

(3) *Earlier Filing and Service.* The time for filing and serving the appellant's or the appellee's brief may be shortened by order of the Court of Appeals on motion showing good cause.

(4) *Late Filing.* Any party failing to timely file and serve a brief required by this rule forfeits the right to oral argument.

(5) *Motions.* The filing of a motion does not stay the time for filing a brief.

(B) Length and Form of Briefs. Except as permitted by order of the Court of Appeals, and except as provided in subrule (G), briefs are limited to 50 pages double-spaced, exclusive of tables, indexes, and appendixes. Quotations and footnotes may be single-spaced. At least one-inch margins must be used, and printing shall not be smaller than 12–point type. A motion for leave to file a brief in excess of the page limitations of this subrule must be filed by the due date of the brief and shall accompany the proposed brief. Such motions are disfavored and will be granted only for extraordinary and compelling reasons. If the motion is denied, the movant shall file a conforming brief within 21 days after the date of the order deciding the motion.

(C) Appellant's Brief; Contents. The appellant's brief must contain, in the following order:

(1) A title page, stating the full title of the case and in capital letters or boldface type "ORAL ARGUMENT REQUESTED" or "ORAL ARGUMENT NOT REQUESTED." If the appeal involves a ruling that a provision of the Michigan Constitution, a Michigan statute, a rule or regulation included in the Michigan Administrative Code, or any other action of the legislative or executive branch of state government is invalid, the title page must include the following in capital letters or boldface type:

"THE APPEAL INVOLVES A RULING THAT A PROVISION OF THE CONSTITUTION, A STATUTE, RULE OR REGULATION, OR OTHER STATE GOVERNMENTAL ACTION IS INVALID";

(2) A table of contents, listing the subject headings of the brief, including the principal points of argument, in the order of presentation, with the numbers of the pages where they appear in the brief;

(3) An index of authorities, listing in alphabetical order all case authorities cited, with the complete citations including the years of decision, and all other authorities cited, with the numbers of the pages where they appear in the brief;

(4) A statement of the basis of jurisdiction of the Court of Appeals.

(a) The statement concerning appellate jurisdiction must identify the statute, court rule, or court decision believed to confer jurisdiction on the Court of Appeals and the following information:

(i) the date of signing the judgment or order, or the date of data entry of the judgment or order in the issuing tribunal's register of actions, as applicable to confer jurisdiction on the Court of Appeals under MCR 7.204 or MCR 7.205.

(ii) the filing date of any motion claimed to toll the time within which to appeal, the disposition of such a motion, and the date of entry of the order disposing of it;

(iii) in cases where appellate counsel is appointed, the date the request for appointment of appellate counsel was filed;

(iv) in cases where appellate counsel is retained or the party is proceeding in propria persona, the filing date of the claim of appeal or the date of the order granting leave to appeal or leave to proceed under MCR 7.206.

(b) If the order sought to be reviewed adjudicates fewer than all the claims, or the rights and liabilities of fewer than all the parties, the statement must provide enough information to enable the court to determine whether there is jurisdiction.

(5) A statement of questions involved, stating concisely and without repetition the questions involved in the appeal. Each question must be expressed and numbered separately and be followed by the trial court's answer to it or the statement that the trial court failed to answer it and the appellant's answer to it. When possible, each answer must be given as "Yes" or "No";

(6) A statement of facts that must be a clear, concise, and chronological narrative. All material facts, both favorable and unfavorable, must be fairly stated without argument or bias. The statement must contain, with specific page references to the transcript, the pleadings, or other document or paper filed with the trial court,

(a) the nature of the action;

(b) the character of pleadings and proceedings;

(c) the substance of proof in sufficient detail to make it intelligible, indicating the facts that are in controversy and those that are not;

(d) the dates of important instruments and events;

(e) the rulings and orders of the trial court;

(f) the verdict and judgment; and

(g) any other matters necessary to an understanding of the controversy and the questions involved;

(7) The arguments, each portion of which must be prefaced by the principal point stated in capital letters or boldface type. As to each issue, the argument must include a statement of the applicable standard or standards of review and supporting authorities, and must comply with the provisions of MCR

7.215(C) regarding citation of unpublished Court of Appeals opinions. Facts stated must be supported by specific page references to the transcript, the pleadings, or other document or paper filed with the trial court. Page references to the transcript, the pleadings, or other document or paper filed with the trial court must also be given to show whether the issue was preserved for appeal by appropriate objection or by other means. If determination of the issues presented requires the study of a constitution, statute, ordinance, administrative rule, court rule, rule of evidence, judgment, order, written instrument, or document, or relevant part thereof, this material must be reproduced in the brief or in an addendum to the brief. If an argument is presented concerning the sentence imposed in a criminal case, the appellant's attorney must send a copy of the presentence report to the court at the time the brief is filed;

(8) The relief, stating in a distinct, concluding section the order or judgment requested;

(9) A signature; and

(10) A separately filed appendix, only as provided in section (J) of this rule.

(D) Appellee's Brief; Contents.

(1) Except as otherwise provided in this subrule, the appellee's brief must conform to subrule (C).

(2) The appellee must state whether the jurisdictional summary and the standard or standards of review stated in the appellant's brief are complete and correct. If they are not, the appellee must provide a complete jurisdictional summary and a counterstatement of the standard or standards of review, and supporting authorities.

(3) Unless under the headings "Statement of Questions Involved" and "Statement of Facts" the appellee accepts the appellant's statements, the appellee shall include:

(a) a counter-statement of questions involved, stating the appellee's version of the questions involved; and

(b) a counter-statement of facts, pointing out the inaccuracies and deficiencies in the appellant's statement of facts without repeating that statement and with specific page references to the transcript, the pleadings, or other document or paper filed with the trial court, to support the appellee's assertions.

(E) Briefs in Cross Appeals. The filing and service of briefs by a cross appellant and a cross appellee are governed by subrules (A)–(D).

(F) Supplemental Authority. Without leave of court, a party may file an original and four copies of a one-page communication, titled "supplemental authority," to call the court's attention to new authority released after the party filed its brief. Such a communication,

(1) may not raise new issues;

(2) may only discuss how the new authority applies to the case, and may not repeat arguments or authorities contained in the party's brief;

(3) may not cite unpublished opinions.

(G) Reply Briefs. An appellant or a cross-appellant may reply to the brief of an appellee or cross-appellee within 21 days after service of the brief of the appellee or cross-appellee. Reply briefs must be confined to rebuttal of the arguments in the appellee's or cross-appellee's brief and must be limited to 10 pages, exclusive of tables, indexes, and appendices, and must include a table of contents and an index of authorities. No additional or supplemental briefs may be filed except as provided by subrule (F) or by leave of the Court.

(H) Amicus Curiae.

(1) An amicus curiae brief may be filed only on motion granted by the Court of Appeals. The motion must be filed within 21 days after the appellee's brief is filed. If the motion is granted, the order will state the date by which the brief must be filed.

(2) The brief is limited to the issues raised by the parties. An amicus curiae may not participate in oral argument except by court order.

(3) Except for briefs presented on behalf of amicus curiae listed in MCR 7.312 (H)(2), a brief filed under this rule shall indicate whether counsel for a party authored the brief in whole or in part and whether such counsel or a party made a monetary contribution intended to fund the preparation or submission of the brief, and shall identify every person other than the amicus curiae, its members, or its counsel, who made such a monetary contribution. The disclosure shall be made in the first footnote on the first page of text.

(I) Nonconforming Briefs. If, on its own initiative or on a party's motion, the court concludes that a brief does not substantially comply with the requirements in this rule, it may order the party who filed the brief to file a supplemental brief within a specified time correcting the deficiencies, or it may strike the nonconforming brief.

(J) Appendix.

(1) In all civil cases (except those pertaining to child protection proceedings, including termination of parental rights, and non-criminal delinquency proceedings under chapter XIIA of the Probate Code and adoptions under chapter X), and in all appeals from administrative agencies, except those described in section (J)(5) of this rule, the appellant shall file and serve an appendix. The appellant's appendix shall contain a table of contents and copies of the following documents if they exist:

(a) The judgment or order(s) appealed from, including any written opinion, memorandum, findings of fact and conclusions of law stated on the record, in conjunction with the judgment or order(s) appealed from;

(b) A copy of the trial court docket sheet;

(c) The relevant pages of any transcripts cited in support of the appellant's position on appeal. Where appropriate, the appellant may attach pages preceding and succeeding the page cited if helpful to provide context to the citation. If a complete trial, deposition, or administrative transcript is filed, the index to such transcript must be included. Only non-compressed (one sheet to a page) transcripts may be filed;

(d) If a jury instruction is challenged, a copy of the instruction, any portion of the transcript containing a discussion of the instruction, and any relevant request for the instruction; and

(e) Any other exhibit, pleading, or other evidence that was submitted to the trial court and that is relevant and necessary for the Court to consider in deciding the appeal. Briefs submitted in the trial court are not required to be included in the appendix unless they pertain to a contested preservation issue.

For material that is subject to an existing protective order, or for evidence that is not subject to such an order, but which contains information that is confidential or privileged, the procedures of MCR 7.211(C)(9) apply.

(2) The appellee shall file and serve an appendix with its responsive brief only if the appellant's appendix does not contain all the information set forth in section (J)(1) of this rule. The appellee's appendix shall not contain any of the documents contained in the appellant's appendix, but shall only contain additional information described in section (J)(1) that is relevant and necessary to the determination of the issues raised in the appeal.

(3) Each volume of any appendix shall contain no more than 250 pages. The table of contents shall identify each document with reasonable definiteness, and indicate the volume and page of the appendix where the document is located. The cover to the appendix shall indicate in bold type whether it is the "Appellant's Appendix" or "Appellee's Appendix."

(a) For a paper appendix, each document shall also be tabbed. A paper appendix shall be bound separate from the brief. Five copies of the paper appendix shall be filed with the court.

(b) If an appendix is to be filed electronically, it must be filed as an independent .pdf file or a series of independent .pdf files. The table of contents for electronically filed appendixes shall contain bookmarks, linking to each document in the appendix.

(4) In cases involving more than one appellant or appellee, including cases consolidated for appeal, to avoid duplication each side shall, where practicable, file a joint rather than separate appendixes.

(5) This subsection does not apply to appeals arising from the Michigan Public Service Commission (in which the record is available on the Commission's e-docket) or the Michigan Tax Tribunal (in which the record is available on the Tribunal's tax docket lookup page). In those cases, the parties shall cite to the document number and relevant pages.

[Adopted effective March 1, 1985. Amended September 10, 1997, effective December 1, 1987, 429 Mich; March 30, 1989, effective October 1, 1989, 423 Mich; May 22, 1991, effective August 1, 1991, 437 Mich; October 26, 1993, effective January 1, 1994, 444 Mich; February 23, 1995, effective May 1, 1995, 448 Mich; May 16, 1995, effective July 1, 1995, 448 Mich; January 26, 1996, effective April 1, 1996, 450 Mich; April 30, 1997, effective September 1, 1997, 454 Mich; June 2, 1998, effective September 1, 1998, 457 Mich; June 2, 1999, effective September 1, 1999, 459 Mich; November 26, 2001, effective January 1, 2002, 456 Mich; May 17, 2002, effective September 1, 2002, 465 Mich; February 3, 2004, effective May 1, 2004, 469 Mich; April 4, 2012, effective May 1, 2012, 491 Mich; March 23, 2016, effective May 1, 2016, 499 Mich. Amended effective June 21, 2017, 500 Mich. Amended April 19, 2018, effective May 1, 2018, 501 Mich; June 14, 2018, effective September 1, 2018, 501 Mich; April 3, 2019, effective May 1, 2019, 502 Mich.]

Comments

Staff Comment to 1985 Adoption

MCR 7.212 is based on GCR 1963, 813, 814, and 815. The provisions are reorganized and rewritten, but retain most of the substance of the former rules.

Subrules (A)(1) and (2) set shorter time limits for filing briefs in child custody cases and interlocutory criminal appeals than for briefs in other appeals.

Subrule (A)(5) is a new provision explicitly stating that the filing of a motion does not stay the time for filing a brief.

Subrule (B) sets a 50–page limit on the length of briefs.

Subrule (C)(3) requires parallel citations of Michigan statutes. Compare GCR 1963, 813.1.

Subrules (F) and (G) are new provisions covering supplemental and amicus curiae briefs.

Subrule (H) is a new provision regarding the striking of nonconforming briefs.

Staff Comment to 1987 Amendment

The [December 1, 1987] amendment of MCR 7.212(C)(6) has the same purpose as Rules 21.1(f) and 34.1(f) of the Rules of the United States Supreme Court, and Rule 28(f) of the Federal Rules of Appellate Procedure.

Staff Comment to 1989 Amendment

There are a number of relatively minor changes in MCR 7.212 [under the October 1, 1989 amendment]. There are two changes in MCR 7.212(A)(1)(a) with regard to the time for filing the appellant's brief. First, new subrule (a)(ii) refers to MCR 7.208(B) and 7.211(C)(1), which include time limits for filing an appellant's brief in certain circumstances. Second, new language is added in subrule (a)(iii) to make clear that where substitute counsel is appointed in a criminal case, the time for filing the brief runs from the date substitute counsel is appointed, or from the time the transcript is filed if the substitution of counsel was made before the transcript was completed.

There are two minor changes in the language of MCR 7.212(B) regarding lengths of briefs. Appendices are added to the list of items that are excluded in determining the length. Second, single spacing of footnotes is expressly permitted.

MCR 7.212(H) is amended to provide that in the case of a nonconforming brief, the Court of Appeals is given the option of ordering the party to file a supplemental brief curing the deficiencies as an alternative to striking the brief.

Staff Comment to 1991 Amendment

In order to assist the Court of Appeals and the Supreme Court in deciding appeals in which sentencing issues are raised, the 1991 amendment of MCR 7.212(C)(6) requires a party who raises a sentencing issue to submit a copy of the presentence report. Because the copy is sent to the court for its review (not "filed" with the court), it is not included in the appellate court's public file.

Staff Comment to 1994 Amendment

The 1993 addition of MCR 7.212(G) and the accompanying change in MCR 7.212(B) [both effective January 1, 1994] were to provide direction regarding the filing of reply briefs in the Court of Appeals. Former subrules (G) and (H) were redesignated (H) and (I) when the 1993 amendment became effective [on January 1, 1994].

Staff Comment to May, 1995 Amendment

The amendment of MCR 7.212(C) [effective May 1, 1995] requires the appellant's brief to include a jurisdictional statement and to state the standard of review applicable to each issue raised. Subrule (D) requires the appellee to respond as to those matters.

Staff Comment to July, 1995 Amendment

The amendment of MCR 7.212(B) [effective July 1, 1995] adds requirements regarding margins and type size for briefs in the Court of Appeals.

Staff Comment to 1996 Amendment

The amendment of MCR 7.212(C)(7) requires page references to the record showing preservation of issues.

The amendment of MCR 7.212(F) revises the rule regarding supplemental briefs. Without leave of the Court, a party may file a one-page document citing the new authority and indicating how it applies to the case. Other supplemental briefs may only be filed with leave of the Court on motion.

Staff Comment to 1997 Amendment

The amendment of MCR 7.212(C)(4) [effective September 1, 1997] requires that the jurisdictional statement in a brief filed in the Court of Appeals include information about the date of the request for appointment of counsel, if applicable.

Under the amendment of MCR 7.212(H) [effective September 1, 1997], a motion for leave to file an amicus curiae brief may be filed up to 21 days after the appellee's brief. Amicus briefs are expressly limited to the issues raised by the parties.

Staff Comment to 1998 Amendment

MCR 7.212(B) requires a party to obtain advance permission to file a brief in excess of the page limit set by the rule.

Staff Comment to 1999 Amendment

MCR 7.212(C) and (D) clarify the requirement of specific page references to the record in appellate briefs.

Staff Comment to January, 2002 Amendment

The November 26, 2001 amendments of MCR 4.401(D), 7.210(H), 7.212(C), 7.213(A), and 7.302(C), effective January 1, 2002, recognized numbering changes in other rules and the elimination of the "parallel citation" requirement from the Michigan Uniform System of Citation (Supreme Court AO 2001-5).

Staff Comment to September, 2002 Amendment

The May 17, 2002, amendments of MCR 7.204, 7.212, 7.213, 7.215, and 7.302, which are effective September 1, 2002, relate to appeals in which a Michigan constitutional provision, statute, regulation, or other governmental action has been held to be invalid.

The amendment of MCR 7.212(C)(1) requires identification of such cases on the title page of the brief on appeal.

Staff Comment to 2004 Amendment

The February 3, 2004, amendment of MCR 7.202, 7.204, 7.205, and 7.212, effective May 1, 2004, was adopted on the basis of a recommendation from a work group appointed by the Court of Appeals. The amendments clarify the definition of "entry" of an order for jurisdictional purposes at the Court of Appeals.

Staff Comment to 2012 Amendment

The amendments of MCR 7.210 and MCR 7.212 extend the time period in which parties may request that a court settle a record for which a transcript is not available and clarify the procedure for doing so.

Staff Comment to 2016 Amendment

An unpublished opinion may be cited, for example, if there is no published authority on a given legal proposition or if it is necessary to demonstrate a conflict in interpretation of the law. The changes in MCR 2.119 and MCR 7.212 provide cross-references to MCR 7.215(C).

Staff Comment to 2017 Amendment

These amendments conform to recent statutory changes that require all appeals from probate court to be heard in the Court of Appeals, instead of the bifurcated system that previously required some probate appeals to be heard in the Court of Appeals and some to be heard in the local circuit court. The amendments also establish priority status for appeals in guardianship and involuntary mental health treatment cases, similar to child custody cases.

Staff Comment to May, 2018 Amendment

The amendments, submitted by SADO, are intended to clarify practices and provide protections for criminal defendants represented by assigned appellate counsel. The amendments allow an additional 42 days to file post-judgment motions in certain circumstances, and where delay is due to the trial court, clarify in the amendment of MCR 7.205 that in certain circumstances, substitute appellate counsel may file a delayed application for leave to appeal within 42 days of appointment (even if later than six months after sentencing), add language to MCR 7.211 to guide parties and courts if relief is granted in the trial court, and change the procedure for seeking permission to file a brief longer than 50 pages in length.

Staff Comment to September, 2018 Amendment

The amendment of MCR 7.212 requires an appellant to file an appendix with specific documents when filing the appellant's and/or appellee's principal brief or responsive brief. The amendment is intended to identify for practitioners the key portions of the record that the Court deems necessary for thorough and efficient review of the issues on appeal.

Staff Comment to 2019 Amendment

The amendments of MCR 7.212 and 7.312 require amicus briefs to indicate certain information regarding the preparation of the brief and disclosure of monetary contributions. The amendments are similar to Supreme Court Rule 37.6.

Rule 7.213   Calendar Cases

(A) Mediation in Calendar Cases.

(1) *Selection for Mediation.*

(a) At any time during the pendency of an appeal before the Court of Appeals, the chief judge or another designated judge may order an appeal submitted to mediation. When a case is selected for mediation, participation is mandatory; however, the chief judge or another designated judge may remove the case on finding that mediation would be inappropriate. Appeals of domestic relations actions and protection matters are excluded from mediation under this rule.

(b) To identify cases for mediation, the Court of Appeals will review civil appeals to determine if mediation would be of assistance to the court or the parties. At any time, a party to a pending civil appeal may file a written request that the appeal be submitted to mediation. Such a request may be made without formal motion and shall be confidential.

(c) A party to a case that has been selected for mediation may file a request to have the case removed from mediation. Such a request may be made without formal motion and shall be confidential. If the request to remove is premised on a desire to avoid the cost of mediation, it is not necessary to demonstrate an inability to pay such costs.

(d) The submission of an appeal to mediation will not toll any filing deadlines in the appeal unless the court orders otherwise.

(2) *Mediation Procedure.*

(a) Mediation shall be conducted by a mediator selected by stipulation of the parties or designated by the court. A mediator designated by the court shall be an attorney, licensed in Michigan, who has met the qualifications of mediators provided in MCR 2.411(F).

(b) Mediation shall consider the possibility of settlement, the simplification of the issues, and any other matters that the mediator determines may aid in the handling or disposition of the appeal.

(c) The order referring the case to mediation shall specify the time within which the mediation is to be completed. Within 7 days after the time stated in the order, the mediator shall file a notice with the clerk stating only the date of completion of mediation, who participated in the mediation, whether settlement was reached, and whether any further mediation is warranted.

(d) If mediation results in full or partial settlement of the case, the parties shall file, within 21 days after the filing of the notice by the mediator, a stipulation to dismiss (in full or in part) pursuant to MCR 7.218(B).

(e) The mediator may charge a reasonable fee, which shall be divided between and borne equally by the parties unless otherwise agreed and paid by the parties directly to the mediator. If a party does not agree upon the fee requested by the mediator, upon motion of the party, the chief judge or another designated judge shall set a reasonable fee. In all other respects, mediator fees shall be governed by MCR 2.411(D).

(f) The statements and comments made during mediation are confidential as provided in MCR 2.412 and may not be disclosed in the notice filed by the mediator under (A)(2)(c) of this rule or by the participants in briefs or in argument.

(g) Upon failure by a party or attorney to comply with a provision of this rule or the order submitting the case to mediation, the chief judge or another designated judge may assess reasonable expenses, including attorney's fees, caused by the failure, may assess all or a portion of appellate costs, or may dismiss the appeal.

(3) *Selection of Mediator.*

(a) Except as otherwise provided in this rule, the selection of a mediator shall be governed by MCR 2.411(B).

(b) Within the time provided in the order referring a case to mediation, the parties may stipulate to the selection of a mediator. Such stipulation shall be filed with the clerk of the court. If the parties do not file a stipulation agreeing to a mediator within the time provided, the court shall appoint a mediator from the roster of approved mediators maintained by the circuit court in which the case originated.

(B) Notice of Calendar Cases. After the briefs of both parties have been filed, or after the expiration of the time for filing the appellee's brief, the clerk shall notify the parties that the case will be submitted as a "calendar case" at the next available session of the court.

(C) Priority on Calendar. The priority of cases on the session calendar is in accordance with the initial filing dates of the cases, except that precedence shall be given to:

(1) interlocutory criminal appeals;

(2) child custody cases, guardianship cases under the Estates and Protected Individuals Code and under the Mental Health Code, and involuntary mental health treatment cases under the Mental Health Code;

(3) interlocutory appeals from the grant of a preliminary injunction;

(4) appeals from all cases involving election issues, including, but not limited to, recall elections and petition disputes;

(5) appeals of decisions holding that a provision of the Michigan Constitution, a Michigan statute, a rule or regulation included in the Michigan Administrative Code, or any other action of the legislative or executive branch of state government is invalid; and

(6) actions brought under Const 1963, art 9, §§ 29–34 (Headlee actions); and

(7) cases that the court orders expedited.

(D) Arrangement of Calendar. Twenty-one days before the first day of the session, the clerk shall mail to all parties in each calendar case notice of the designated panel, location, day, and order in which the cases will be called.

(E) Adjournment. A change may not be made in the session calendar, except by order of the court on its own initiative or in response to timely motions filed by the parties. A calendar case will not be withdrawn after being placed on the session calendar, except on a showing of extreme emergency.
[Adopted effective March 1, 1985. Amended February 23, 1995, effective May 1, 1995, 448 Mich; November 25, 1997, effective January 1, 1998, 456 Mich; October 23, 2001, effective January 1, 2002, 465 Mich; May 17, 2002, effective September 1, 2002, 465 Mich; January 31 2003, effective May 1, 2003, 467 Mich. Amended effective December 17, 2003, 469 Mich; February 23, 2006, 474 Mich. Amended November 10, 2011, effective January 1, 2012, 490 Mich. Amended effective September 21, 2016, 500 Mich; January 25, 2017, 500 Mich; June 21, 2017, 500 Mich.]

Comments

Staff Comment to 1985 Adoption

MCR 7.213 is taken from GCR 1963, 816. Two parts of the former rule are moved to other rules: Most of 816.2 is placed in MCR 7.206, and 816.5 is 7.216(C).

Subrule (B) has additional language expressly requiring that interlocutory criminal appeals and child custody cases be given priority in scheduling.

Staff Comment to 1995 Amendment

New MCR 7.213(A) allows the Court of Appeals to order pre-argument conferences in appropriate cases.

Staff Comment to 1997 Amendment

The January 1, 1998 amendment of MCR 7.213 modifies the procedure for pre-argument conferences in the Court of Appeals. Ordinarily, the conference will be conducted by a judge or attorney selected by the Court of Appeals. However, the parties may agree to an alternative procedure using a special moderator.

Staff Comment to January, 2002 Amendment

The amendments of MCR 7.213(A) and (C), effective January 1, 2002, were requested by the Court of Appeals. The term "mediator" was substituted for the term "moderator" in subrule (A), to be consistent with other recent rule changes governing case facilitation and mediation. In addition, subrule (A) was amended to allow the court to require the attendance of client representatives with settlement authority at pre-argument settlement conferences. (File No. 01–13.) The amendment of subrule (C) required that cases be placed on the session calendar in the order in which they are filed. (File No. 01–08.)

The November 26, 2001, amendment of MCR 7.213(A) recognized numbering changes in other rules and the elimination of the 'parallel citation' requirement from the Michigan Uniform System of Citation (Supreme Court AO 2001-5).

Staff Comment to September, 2002 Amendment

The March 12, 2002 amendments of Rules 3.310, 7.208, and 7.213, effective September 1, 2002, require trial courts to expeditiously decide actions in which preliminary injunctions have been granted, and allow them to proceed even if the Court of Appeals has granted interlocutory leave to appeal. Similarly, if the Court of Appeals grants leave to review entry of a preliminary injunction on an interlocutory basis, that Court is required to give priority to resolution of the appeal. See *Michigan Coalition of State Employee Unions* v *Michigan Civil Service Comm*, 465 Mich 212, 214, n 1 (2001).

The May 17, 2002, amendments of MCR 7.204, 7.212, 7.213, 7.215, and 7.302, which are effective September 1, 2002, relate to appeals in which a Michigan constitutional provision, statute, regulation, or other governmental action has been held to be invalid.

Language is added to MCR 7.213(C) directing that such cases be given precedence in placement on the Court of Appeals session calendar. The subrule as amended includes language previously added by an amendment dated March 12, 2002, also to be effective September 1, 2002, regarding orders granting preliminary injunctions.

Staff Comment to May, 2003 Amendment

MCR 2.401(F) and (G), MCR 2.410(D)(2) and (3), MCR 2.506(A), and MCR 7.213(A) were amended January 31, 2003, effective May 1, 2003. Before the amendments, each of these subrules included a requirement that someone with "authority to settle" (or similar language) attend the type of proceeding described in each subrule. The amendments substituted the more flexible requirement that the person attending the proceeding have "information and authority adequate for responsible and effective participation" in settlement discussions.

The 2003 amendments of MCR 2.401(G) and MCR 2.410(D)(3) de-emphasized the use of defaults as sanctions for a party's failure to comply fully with an order. The amended rules allow entry of a default, but tilt in favor of less drastic sanctions.

Staff Comment to December, 2003 Amendment

The December 17, 2003, amendments of MCR 7.211(C)(5)(a) brought the rule into conformity with the 1998 amendments of subrules (A) and (B), which eliminated the filing of a notice of hearing, instead specifying the time for a response. Subrule (C)(5)(a)(iii) and the "notice of hearing" language in subrule (C)(5)(a)(iv) were deleted, and former subrules (C)(5)(a)(iv) and (v) were redesignated subrules (C)(5)(a)(iii) and (iv), respectively. The December 17, 2003, amendment of MCR 7.213(A)(3) conformed that subrule to the May 1, 2003, amendment of MCR 7.215 by changing the cross-reference from former subrule (I) to subrule (J).

Staff Comment to 2006 Amendment

The amendment of Rule 7.213(C), effective immediately, of the Michigan Court Rules would require the Court of Appeals to give priority to appeals involving election cases.

Staff Comment to 2011 Amendment

The existing fact-specific pleading requirements in MCR 2.112(M) are retained and expanded to promote earlier consideration whether facts must be established in the case. The amendments of MCR 2.625 clarify that costs, including reasonable attorney fees, are recoverable in a Headlee action. The amendment of MCR 7.206(D)(3) allows parties to utilize electronic filing in Headlee cases, as well as other extraordinary writs or original actions filed in the Court of Appeals. The amendments of MCR 7.206 create a new specific subsection (7.206[E]) regarding the procedure for filing a Headlee action as an original proceeding in the Court of Appeals. The amendment of MCR 7.213 is intended to clarify that Headlee actions are considered priority matters in the Court of Appeals.

Staff Comment to 2016 Amendment

This proposal, submitted by the Michigan Court of Appeals, would make permanent the mediation pilot project that has been operating under authority of Administrative Order No. 2015–8 since October 2015. The proposed amendments have been adopted with immediate effect to enable the mediation program to continue during the comment period.

Staff Comment to January, 2017 Amendment

The Court retained the amendments previously adopted in this file, and included a new clarifying provision at the suggestion of several commenters that domestic relations actions and protection matters are excluded from the mediation program.

Staff Comment to June, 2017 Amendment

These amendments conform to recent statutory changes that require all appeals from probate court to be heard in the Court of Appeals, instead of the bifurcated system that previously required some probate appeals to be heard in the Court of Appeals and some to be heard in the local circuit court. The amendments also establish priority status for appeals in guardianship and involuntary mental health treatment cases, similar to child custody cases.

Rule 7.214   Argument of Calendar Cases

(A) Request for Argument. Oral argument of a calendar case is not permitted, except on order of the court, unless a party has stated on the title page of his or her brief in capital letters or boldface type "ORAL ARGUMENT REQUESTED." The failure of a party to properly request oral argument or to timely file and serve a brief waives the right to oral argument. If neither party is entitled to oral argument, the clerk will list the case as submitted on briefs.

(B) Length of Argument. In a calendar case the time allowed for argument is 30 minutes for each side. When only one side is represented, only 15 minutes is allowed to that side. The time for argument may be extended by the court on motion filed at least 21 days before the session begins, or by the presiding judge during argument.

(C) Call for Argument. The court, on each day of the session, will call the cases for argument in the order they appear on the session calendar as arranged.

(D) Submission on Briefs. A case may be submitted on briefs by stipulation at any time.

(E) Decision Without Oral Argument. Cases may be assigned to panels of judges for appropriate review and disposition without oral argument as provided in this subrule.

(1) If, as a result of review under this rule, the panel unanimously concludes that

(a) the dispositive issue or issues have been recently authoritatively decided;

(b) the briefs and record adequately present the facts and legal arguments, and the court's deliberation would not be significantly aided by oral argument; or

(c) the appeal is without merit;

the panel may enter without oral argument an appropriate order or opinion dismissing the appeal, affirming, reversing, or vacating the judgment or order appealed from, or remanding the case for additional proceedings.

(2) Any party's brief may include, at the conclusion of the brief, a statement setting forth the reasons why oral argument should be heard.

[Adoptive effective March 1, 1985. Amended July 11, 1991, effective August 1, 1991, 437 Mich.]

Comments

Staff Comment to 1985 Adoption

MCR 7.214 is based on GCR 1963, 819 and 815.3. It retains the substance of the former rules, except that the rehearing provisions of GCR 1963, 819.3 are moved to MCR 7.215(H).

Rule 7.215.   Opinions, Orders, Judgments, and Final Process for Court of Appeals

(A) Opinions of Court. An opinion must be written and bear the writer's name or the label "per curiam" or "memorandum" opinion. An opinion of the court that bears the writer's name shall be published by the Supreme Court reporter of decisions. A memorandum opinion shall not be published. A per curiam opinion shall not be published unless one of the judges deciding the case directs the reporter to do so at the time it is filed with the clerk. A copy of an opinion to be published must be delivered to the reporter no later than when it is filed with the clerk. The reporter is responsible for having those opinions published as are opinions of the Supreme Court, but in separate volumes containing opinions of the Court of Appeals only, in a form and under a contract approved by the Supreme Court. An opinion not designated for publication shall be deemed "unpublished."

(B) Standards for Publication. A court opinion must be published if it:

(1) establishes a new rule of law;

(2) construes as a matter of first impression a provision of a constitution, statute, regulation, ordinance, or court rule;

(3) alters, modifies, or reverses an existing rule of law;

(4) reaffirms a principle of law or construction of a constitution, statute, regulation, ordinance, or court rule not applied in a reported decision since November 1, 1990;

(5) involves a legal issue of significant public interest;

(6) criticizes existing law; or [1]

(7) resolves a conflict among unpublished Court of Appeals opinions brought to the Court's attention; or

(8) decides an appeal from a lower court order ruling that a provision of the Michigan Constitution, a Michigan statute, a rule or regulation included in the Michigan Administrative Code, or any other action of the legislative or executive branch of state government is invalid.

(C) Precedent of Opinions.

(1) An unpublished opinion is not precedentially binding under the rule of stare decisis. Unpublished opinions should not be cited for propositions of law for which there is published authority. If a party cites an unpublished opinion, the party shall explain the reason for citing it and how it is relevant to the issues presented. A party who cites an unpublished opinion must provide a copy of the opinion to the court and to opposing parties with the brief or other paper in which the citation appears.

(2) A published opinion of the Court of Appeals has precedential effect under the rule of stare decisis. The filing of an application for leave to appeal to the Supreme Court or a Supreme Court order granting leave to appeal does not diminish the precedential effect of a published opinion of the Court of Appeals.

(D) Requesting Publication.

(1) Any party may request publication of an authored or per curiam opinion not designated for publication by

(a) filing with the clerk 4 copies of a letter stating why the opinion should be published, and

(b) mailing a copy to each party to the appeal not joining in the request.

Such a request must be filed within 21 days after release of the unpublished opinion or, if a timely motion for rehearing is filed, within 21 days after the denial of the motion.

(2) Any party served with a copy of the request may file a response within 14 days in the same manner as provided in subrule (D)(1).

(3) Promptly after the expiration of the time provided in subrule (D)(2), the clerk shall submit the request, and any response that has been received, to the panel that filed the opinion. Within 21 days after submission of the request, the panel shall decide whether to direct that the opinion be published. The opinion shall be published only if the panel unanimously so directs. Failure of the panel to act within 21 days shall be treated as a denial of the request.

(4) The Court of Appeals shall not direct publication if the Supreme Court has denied an application for leave to appeal under MCR 7.305.

(E) Judgment.

(1) When the Court of Appeals disposes of an original action or an appeal, whether taken as of right, by leave granted, or by order in lieu of leave being granted, its opinion or order is its judgment. An order denying leave to appeal is not deemed to dispose of an appeal.

(2) The clerk shall send a certified copy of the opinion or order, with the date of filing stamped on it, to each party and, in an appeal, to the court or tribunal from which the appeal was received. In criminal cases, the clerk shall provide an additional copy of any opinion or order disposing of an appeal or of any order denying leave to appeal to the defendant's lawyer, which the lawyer must promptly send to the defendant. An opinion or order is notice of the entry of judgment of the Court of Appeals.

(F) Execution and Enforcement.

(1) *Routine Issuance.* Unless otherwise ordered by the Court of Appeals or the Supreme Court or as otherwise provided by these rules,

(a) the Court of Appeals judgment is effective after the expiration of the time for filing an application for leave to appeal to the Supreme Court, or, if such an application is filed, after the disposition of the case by the Supreme Court;

(b) execution on the Court of Appeals judgment is to be obtained or enforcement proceedings had in the trial court or tribunal after the record has been returned (by the clerk under MCR 7.210[H] or by the Supreme Court clerk under MCR 7.310) with a certified copy of the court's judgment or, if a record was not transmitted to the Court of Appeals, after the time specified for return of the record had it been transmitted.

(2) *Exceptional Issuance.* The court may order that a judgment described in subrule (E) has immediate effect. The order does not prevent the filing of a motion for rehearing, but the filing of the motion does not stay execution or enforcement.

(G) Entry, Issuance, Execution on, and Enforcement of All Other Orders. An order other than one described in

subrule (E) is entered on the date of filing. The clerk must promptly send a certified copy to each party and to the trial court or tribunal. Unless otherwise stated, an order is effective on the date it is entered.

(H) Certain Dispositive Orders and Opinions in Criminal Cases; Expedited Notice to Prosecutor. In a criminal case, if the prosecuting attorney files a notice of a victim's request for information and proof that copies of the notice were served on the other parties to the appeal, then, coincident with issuing an order or opinion that reverses a conviction, vacates a sentence, remands a case to the trial court for a new trial, or denies the prosecuting attorney's appeal, the clerk of the court must electronically transmit a copy of the order or opinion to the prosecuting attorney at a facsimile number or electronic mail address provided by the prosecuting attorney in the notice.

(I) Reconsideration.

(1) A motion for reconsideration may be filed within 21 days after the date of the order or the date stamped on an opinion. The motion shall include all facts, arguments, and citations to authorities in a single document and shall not exceed 10 double-spaced pages. A copy of the order or opinion of which reconsideration is sought must be included with the motion. Motions for reconsideration are subject to the restrictions contained in MCR 2.119(F)(3).

(2) A party may answer a motion for reconsideration within 14 days after the motion is served on the party. An answer to a motion for reconsideration shall be a single document and shall not exceed 7 double-spaced pages.

(3) The clerk will not accept for filing a motion for reconsideration of an order denying a motion for reconsideration.

(4) The clerk will not accept for filing a late motion for reconsideration.

(J) Resolution of Conflicts in Court of Appeals Decisions.

(1) *Precedential Effect of Published Decisions.* A panel of the Court of Appeals must follow the rule of law established by a prior published decision of the Court of Appeals issued on or after November 1, 1990, that has not been reversed or modified by the Supreme Court, or by a special panel of the Court of Appeals as provided in this rule.

(2) *Conflicting Opinion.* A panel that follows a prior published decision only because it is required to do so by subrule (1) must so indicate in the text of its opinion, citing this rule and explaining its disagreement with the prior decision. The panel's opinion must be published in the official reports of opinions of the Court of Appeals.

(3) *Convening of Special Panel.*

(a) Poll of Judges. Except as provided in subrule (3)(b), within 28 days after release of the opinion indicating disagreement with a prior decision as provided in subrule (2), the chief judge must poll the judges of the Court of Appeals to determine whether the particular question is both outcome determinative and warrants convening a special panel to rehear the case for the purpose of resolving the conflict that would have been created but for the provisions of subrule (1). Special panels may be convened to consider outcome-determinative questions only.

(b) Effect of Pending Supreme Court Appeal. No poll shall be conducted and a special panel shall not be convened if, at the time the judges are required to be polled, the Supreme Court has granted leave to appeal in the controlling case.

(c) *Order.* Immediately following the poll, an order reflecting the result must be entered. The chief clerk of the Court of Appeals must provide a copy of the order to the Clerk of the Supreme Court. The order must be published in the official reports of opinions of the Court of Appeals.

(4) *Composition of Panel.* A special panel convened pursuant to this rule consists of 7 judges of the Court of Appeals selected by lot, except that judges who participated in either the controlling decision or the opinion in the case at bar may not be selected.

(5) *Consideration of Case by Panel.* An order directing the convening of a special panel must vacate only that portion of the prior opinion in the case at bar addressing the particular question that would have been decided differently but for the provisions of subrule (1). The special panel shall limit its review to resolving the conflict that would have been created but for the provisions of subrule (1) and applying its decision to the case at bar. The parties are permitted to file supplemental briefs, and are entitled to oral argument before the special panel unless the panel unanimously agrees to dispense with oral argument. The special panel shall return to the original panel for further consideration any remaining, unresolved issues, as the case may require.

(6) *Decision.* The decision of the special panel must be by published opinion or order and is binding on all panels of the Court of Appeals unless reversed or modified by the Supreme Court.

(7) *Reconsideration; Appeal.* There is no appeal from the decision of the Court of Appeals as to whether to convene a special panel. As to the decision in the case at bar, the time limits for moving for rehearing or for filing an application for leave to appeal to the Supreme Court run from the date of the order declining to convene a special panel or, if a special panel is convened, from the date of the decision of the special panel, except that, if the case is returned to the original panel for further consideration in accordance with subrule (5), the time limits shall run from the date of the original panel's decision, after return from the special panel. If a motion for reconsideration is filed, it shall be submitted to the special panel, which, if appropriate, may refer some or all of the issues presented to the original panel.

[Adopted effective March 1, 1985. Amended February 26, 1987, effective April 1, 1987, 428 Mich. Amended effective October 7, 1987, 429 Mich. Amended March 30, 1989, effective October 1, 1989, 432 Mich; August 28, 1991, effective November 1, 1991, 438 Mich; February 23, 1995, effective May 1, 1995, 448 Mich; June 2, 1995, effective August 1, 1995, 449 Mich; April 30, 1997, effective September 1, 1997, 454 Mich; June 2, 1998, effective September 1, 1998, 457 Mich; June 2, 1999, effective September 1, 1999, 459 Mich; December 13, 2000, effective April 1, 2001, 463 Mich; May 17, 2002, effective September 1, 2002, 466 Mich; January 22, 2003, effective May 1, 2003, 467 Mich; June 6, 2003, effective September 1, 2003, 468 Mich. Amended effective August 24, 2012, 492 Mich. Amended March 23, 2016, effective May 1, 2016, 499 Mich. Amended effective March 21, 2018, 501 Mich; August 14, 2019, 503 Mich.]

1 So in original.

Comments

Staff Comment to 1985 Adoption

MCR 7.215 is based on GCR 1963, 819.4 and 821.

Subrules (B), (C), and (D) are new, covering the standards for publication of opinions, the precedential force of unpublished opinions, and the procedure by which a party can request publication.

Subrule (E) makes the Court of Appeals opinion the judgment of the court, unlike GCR 1963, 821.2.

Subrule (F) explicitly covers the matter of the enforcement of the decisions of the Court of Appeals, a matter that was left to inference under GCR 1963, 821.3. Enforcement is to be had in the trial court after the record has been returned from the Court of Appeals. See MCR 7.210(I).

Subrule (G) is a new provision covering the issuance and effective date of orders.

The rehearing provisions of subrule (H) are taken from GCR 1963, 819.4. Request for rehearing is by motion, to which MCR 7.211 would apply. The new rule explicitly provides for motions for rehearing as to orders as well as of decisions by opinion.

Staff Comment to 1987 Amendment

The [October 7, 1987] addition of MCR 7.215(C)(2) is a change from the prior rule as stated in *People v Phillips,* 416 Mich 63, 74–75; 330 NW2d 366 (1982).

Staff Comment to 1989 Amendment

The [October 1, 1989] amendment of MCR 7.215(C)(1) requires a party who cites an unpublished Court of Appeals decision to serve copies of the decision on the court and the opposing parties.

Changes are also made in subrules (E)–(G) with the object of treating orders which dispose of an appeal as the equivalent of an opinion for the purpose of determining when they can be enforced. Such an opinion or order is to be enforced in the trial court after the return of the record by the appellate courts (or, if a record was not transmitted, when it would have been returned had it been transmitted). Other orders are effective immediately, unless the Court of Appeals orders otherwise. An order denying leave to appeal is not considered to dispose of an appeal.

There are also several other minor changes. The Court of Appeals clerk is to send a criminal defense lawyer an extra copy of the opinion or order, including an order denying leave to appeal, which the attorney is to send to the defendant. Under former Administrative Order No. 1983–7, copies were required only of orders and opinions that disposed of an appeal.

Staff Comment to 1991 Amendment

The August 28, 1991 amendment of MCR 7.215(F) [effective November 1, 1991] clarifies the matter of the effective date of Court of Appeals judgments.

Staff Comment to May, 1995 Amendment

The amendment of MCR 7.215(H) clarifies the procedure regarding motions for rehearing.

Staff Comment to August, 1995 Amendment

The amendment of MCR 7.215 eliminates the procedure under which persons may request publication of Court of Appeals decisions that were originally designated as not for publication. Also, subrule (A) is modified to require that a decision to publish a per curiam or memorandum opinion must be made by a majority of the panel rather than by a single judge.

Staff Comment to 1997 Amendment

The provisions of Administrative Order 1994–4, dealing with Court of Appeals conflict resolution panels, are incorporated into the court rules as new MCR 7.215(H). Also, such panels are authorized to dispense with oral argument (by unanimous vote), and their decisions must be published in Michigan Appeals Reports.

Staff Comment to 1998 Amendment

MCR 7.215(G)(1) requires a copy of the order with a motion for rehearing of the order.

Staff Comment to 1999 Amendment

MCR 7.215(H) modifies several provisions in the rule governing resolution of conflicts in Court of Appeals decisions.

Staff Comment to 2000 Amendment

The amendment to MCR 7.215(A) permits a single judge of the Court of Appeals panel to designate an opinion for publication.

New MCR 7.215(D) re-establishes a procedure under which a party may request publication of a Court of Appeals opinion that was not initially designated for publication. The former provision was deleted in 1995.

Staff Comment to 2002 Amendment

The May 17, 2002, amendments of MCR 7.204, 7.212, 7.213, 7.215, and 7.302, which are effective September 1, 2002, relate to appeals in which a Michigan constitutional provision, statute, regulation, or other governmental action has been held to be invalid.

New MCR 7.215(B)(8) would add decisions in such cases to the list of those in which the Court of Appeals is required to publish its decisions.

Staff Comment to May, 2003 Amendment

The January 22, 2003, amendment of MCR 7.211(B), effective May 1, 2003, clarifies the deadline for answering a substantive motion when there also is a motion for immediate consideration of that motion.

The January 22, 2003, amendment of MCR 7.215(H), effective May 1, 2003, details how the Court of Appeals carries out the notification duties assigned to it by the 2000 PA 503 amendments of the Crime Victims Rights Act, MCL 780.751 *et seq.*

The January 22, 2003, amendment of MCR 7.215(I)(4), effective May 1, 2003, added the provision that the Court of Appeals clerk will not accept untimely motions for reconsideration. The same amendment order changed the title of a motion for "rehearing" to "reconsideration" in several other MCR Subchapter 7.200 rules.

Staff Comment to September, 2003 Amendment

The June 6, 2003, amendments of MCR 7.205, 7.210, 7.215, 7.302, and 7.316, which are effective September 1, 2003, deal with the time for filing applications for leave to appeal to the Supreme Court.

The amendments of MCR 7.302(C)(1), (2), and (4) set time limits of 56 days in criminal cases and 42 days in civil ones, but with a 28-day time limit for appeals from orders terminating parental rights, in recognition of the adverse consequences of delay on the children involved in such cases. Late applications will not be accepted. MCR 7.302(C)(3), 7.316(B).

The amendment of MCR 7.302(D)(2) provides a 28-day time limit for filing applications for leave to appeal as cross-appellant.

There are also nonsubstantive changes in several rules governing procedure in the Court of Appeals. In MCR 7.205(F)(5), a reference is added to MCR 3.993(C)(2) (formerly MCR 5.993[C][1]), which sets the time limit for late applications in parental-rights-termination cases. The language of MCR 7.210 and 7.215 is adjusted to conform to the changes in the Supreme Court rules.

Staff Comment to 2012 Amendment

These amendments reflect changes to correct minor technical errors that have occurred in drafting or to respond to recent adopted rule revisions, which occasionally inadvertently create incorrect cross-references in other rules.

Staff Comment to 2016 Amendment

An unpublished opinion may be cited, for example, if there is no published authority on a given legal proposition or if it is necessary to demonstrate a conflict in interpretation of the law. The changes in MCR 2.119 and MCR 7.212 provide cross-references to MCR 7.215(C).

Staff Comment to 2018 Amendment

These amendments update cross-references and make other nonsubstantive revisions to clarify the rules. The amendment of MCR 6.110(B)(1) addresses an inadvertent omission from the last amendment of this rule that was intended to be shown in overstrike. Accordingly, the current rule does not match the published version. Striking the clause "for good cause shown" will provide consistency with other published versions of the rule and with the statute, MCL 766.7, which allows a magistrate to adjourn a preliminary examination with the consent of the parties without the need for good cause to be shown.

Staff Comment to 2019 Amendment

These amendments update cross-references and make other nonsubstantive revisions to clarify the rules.

Rule 7.216   Miscellaneous Relief

(A) Relief Obtainable. The Court of Appeals may, at any time, in addition to its general powers, in its discretion, and on the terms it deems just:

(1) exercise any or all of the powers of amendment of the trial court or tribunal;

(2) allow substitution, addition, or deletion of parties or allow parties to be rearranged as appellants or appellees, on reasonable notice;

(3) permit amendment or additions to the grounds for appeal;

(4) permit amendments, corrections, or additions to the transcript or record;

(5) remand the case to allow additional evidence to be taken;

(6) draw inferences of fact;

(7) enter any judgment or order or grant further or different relief as the case may require;

(8) if a judgment notwithstanding the verdict is set aside on appeal, grant a new trial or other relief as necessary;

(9) direct the parties as to how to proceed in any case pending before it;

(10) dismiss an appeal or an original proceeding for lack of jurisdiction or failure of the appellant or the plaintiff to pursue the case in conformity with the rules.

(B) Allowing Act After Expiration of Time. When any nonjurisdictional act is required to be done within a designated time, the Court of Appeals may permit it to be done after expiration of the period on motion showing that there was good cause for delay or that it was not due to the culpable negligence of the party or attorney.

(C) Vexatious Proceedings.

(1) The Court of Appeals may, on its own initiative or on the motion of any party filed under MCR 7.211(C)(8), assess actual and punitive damages or take other disciplinary action when it determines that an appeal or any of the proceedings in an appeal was vexatious because

(a) the appeal was taken for purposes of hindrance or delay or without any reasonable basis for belief that there was a meritorious issue to be determined on appeal; or

(b) a pleading, motion, argument, brief, document, record filed in the case or any testimony presented in the case was grossly lacking in the requirements of propriety, violated court rules, or grossly disregarded the requirements of a fair presentation of the issues to the court.

(2) Damages may not exceed actual damages and expenses incurred by the opposing party because of the vexatious appeal or proceeding, including reasonable attorney fees, and punitive damages in an added amount not exceeding the actual damages. The court may remand the case to the trial court or tribunal for a determination of actual damages.

[Adopted effective March 1, 1985. Amended July 9, 2003, effective September 1, 2003, 468 Mich.]

Comments

Staff Comment to 1985 Adoption

MCR 7.216 is based on GCR 1963, 816.5 and 820.

Subrule (A)(10) expressly authorizes the Court of Appeals to dismiss a case for lack of jurisdiction or for failure of the appellant or plaintiff to pursue the case in conformity with the rules.

Subrule (C) modifies the limitations on damages that may be imposed for vexatious proceedings. The punitive aspect of damages is measured by the adverse party's expenses, rather than the amount of the judgment in the trial court. Compare GCR 1963, 816.5.

The [March 1, 1985] amendment of MCR 7.216(C)(1) modifies the language regarding imposition of sanctions for vexatious appellate proceedings. First, references to dismissal of the appeal are deleted. That subject is covered by MCR 7.216(A)(7) and (10). Second, the limitation that a motion for costs could be brought only before a case is placed on a session calendar is deleted.

Staff Comment to 2003 Amendment

The July 9, 2003, amendment of MCR 7.216(C)(1), effective September 1, 2003, was consistent with the addition of MCR 7.211(C)(8), on that same date.

Rule 7.217 Involuntary Dismissal of Cases

(A) Dismissal. If the appellant, or the plaintiff in an original action under MCR 7.206, fails to order a transcript, file a brief, or comply with court rules, the clerk will notify the parties that the appeal may be dismissed for want of prosecution unless the deficiency is remedied within 21 days after the date of the clerk's notice of deficiency. If the deficiency is not remedied within that time, the chief judge or another designated judge may dismiss the appeal for want of prosecution.

(B) Notice. A copy of an order dismissing an appeal for want of prosecution will be sent to the parties and the court or tribunal from which the appeal originated.

(C) Other Action. In all instances of failure to prosecute an appeal to hearing as required, the chief judge or another designated judge may take such other action as is deemed appropriate.

(D) Reinstatement.

(1) Within 21 days after the date of the clerk's notice of dismissal pursuant to this rule, the appellant or plaintiff may seek relief from dismissal by showing mistake, inadvertence, or excusable neglect.

(2) The chief judge of the Court of Appeals will decide all untimely motions for reinstatement of an appeal.

[Adopted effective March 1, 1985. Amended December 15, 1993, effective February 1, 1994, 444 Mich; June 2, 1999, effective September 1, 1999, 459 Mich; June 17, 2003, effective September 1, 2003, 468 Mich. Amended effective October 19, 2004, 471 Mich; March 8, 2005, 472 Mich.]

Comments

Staff Comment to 1994 Amendment

MCR 7.217 [as amended effective February 1, 1994] is a new provision that simplifies the current procedure for dismissing no-progress cases.

Staff Comment to 1999 Amendment

MCR 7.217(A) and (C) permit the Chief Judge, or another designated judge, acting alone, to enter certain orders when a party does not proceed in accordance with the rules.

Staff Comment to 2003 Amendment

The June 17, 2003, amendment of MCR 7.217(D), effective September 1, 2003, reduced from 56 to 21 days the time for seeking relief from an involuntary dismissal of an appeal by the Court of Appeals. This change corresponds to the 21 days allowed appointed counsel to move under MCR 7.215(I) for reconsideration of an order involuntarily remanding a case to the trial court for the appointment of substitute counsel. See Court of Appeals IOP 7.217(C) and IOP 7.217(D).

Staff Comment to 2004 Amendment

The amendment of MCR 7.217(D) prohibits the Court of Appeals clerk from accepting untimely motions for reinstatement of an appeal that is involuntarily dismissed for want of prosecution. The amendment makes the rule consistent with MCR 7.215(I)(4), which prohibits the acceptance of a late motion for reconsideration.

Staff Comment to 2005 Amendment

The March 8, 2005, amendment of MCR 7.217(D)(2) requires the chief judge of the Court of Appeals to decide all untimely motions for reinstatement of an appeal that is involuntarily dismissed for want of prosecution.

Rule 7.218 Voluntary Dismissal

(A) Dismissal by Appellant. In all cases where the appellant or plaintiff in an original action under MCR 7.206 files an unopposed motion to withdraw the appeal, the clerk will enter an order of dismissal.

(B) Stipulation to Dismiss. The parties to a case in the Court of Appeals may file with the clerk a signed stipulation agreeing to dismissal of an appeal or an action brought under MCR 7.206. On payment of all fees, the clerk will enter an order dismissing the appeal or the action under MCR 7.206, except that class actions or cases submitted on a session calendar may not be dismissed except by order of the Court of Appeals.

[Adopted effective March 1, 1985. Amended February 23, 1995, effective May 1, 1995, 448 Mich.]

Comments

Staff Comment to 1985 Adoption

MCR 7.218 is based on GCR 1963, 809.

The rule includes the parts of GCR 1963, 809 that dealt with stipulations to dismiss. The clerk will not automatically dismiss a case that has been submitted on a session calendar; an order of the court is required.

The parts of GCR 1963, 809 that dealt with stipulations regarding the record are placed in MCR 7.210(A)(4).

Staff Comment to 1995 Amendment

MCR 7.218 allows dismissal of an appeal if the appellant's motion to withdraw the appeal is unopposed.

Rule 7.219 Taxation of Costs; Fees

(A) Right to Costs. Except as the Court of Appeals otherwise directs, the prevailing party in a civil case is entitled to costs.

(B) Time for Filing. Within 28 days after the dispositive order, opinion, or order denying reconsideration is mailed, the prevailing party may file a certified or verified bill of costs with the clerk and serve a copy on all other parties. Each item claimed in the bill must be specified. Failure to file a bill of costs within the time prescribed waives the right to costs.

(C) Objections. Any other party may file objections to the bill of costs with the clerk within 7 days after a copy of the bill is served. The objecting party must serve a copy of the objections on the prevailing party and file proof of that service.

(D) Taxation. The clerk will promptly verify the bill and tax those costs allowable.

(E) Review. The action by the clerk will be reviewed by the Court of Appeals on motion of either party filed within 7 days from the date of taxation, but on review only those affidavits or objections which were previously filed with the clerk may be considered by the court.

(F) Costs Taxable. A prevailing party may tax only the reasonable costs incurred in the Court of Appeals, including:

(1) printing of briefs, or if briefs were typewritten, a charge of $1 per original page;

(2) any appeal or stay bond;

(3) the transcript and necessary copies of it;

(4) documents required for the record on appeal;

(5) fees paid to the clerk or to the trial court clerk incident to the appeal;

(6) taxable costs allowed by law in appeals to the Supreme Court (MCL 600.2441); and

(7) other expenses taxable under applicable court rules.

(G) Fees Paid to Clerk. The clerk shall collect the following fees, which may be taxed as costs:

(1) the fee required by law for a claim of appeal, application for leave to appeal, application for delayed appeal, original complaint, or motion;

(2) 50¢ per page for a certified copy of a paper from a public record;

(3) $5 for certified docket entries;

(4) $1 per document for certification of a copy presented to the clerk; and

(5) 50¢ per page for a copy of an opinion; however, one copy must be given without charge to each party in a case.

A person who is unable to pay a filing fee may ask the court to waive the fee by filing a motion and an affidavit disclosing the reason for the inability.

(H) Rule Applicable. Except as provided in this rule, MCR 2.625 applies generally to taxation of costs in the Court of Appeals.

(I) Violation of Rules. The Court of Appeals may impose costs on a party or an attorney when in its discretion they should be assessed for violation of these rules.

[Adopted effective March 1, 1985. Amended January 22, 2003, effective May 1, 2003, 467 Mich.]

Comments

Staff Comment to 1985 Adoption

MCR 7.219 is based on GCR 1963, 822.

Subrules (F) and (G) carry forward the provisions of GCR 1963, 822.2 and 822.3 regarding the fees and expenses that may be collected and taxed. The fee for a copy of a Court of Appeals opinion is changed to 50¢ per page, to conform with MCL 600.321(4).

New subrules (A)–(E) provide the procedure for taxation of costs, formerly covered by reference to the rule governing taxation of costs in trial courts. See GCR 1963, 822.1.

Subrule (I) adds explicit authorization for the Court of Appeals to impose costs on a party or attorney for violation of the rules.

Staff Comment to 2003 Amendment

The January 22, 2003, amendment of MCR 7.211(B), effective May 1, 2003, clarifies the deadline for answering a substantive motion when there also is a motion for immediate consideration of that motion.

The January 22, 2003, amendment of MCR 7.215(H), effective May 1, 2003, details how the Court of Appeals carries out the notification duties assigned to it by the 2000 PA 503 amendments of the Crime Victims Rights Act, MCL 780.751 *et seq.*

The January 22, 2003, amendment of MCR 7.215(I)(4), effective May 1, 2003, added the provision that the Court of Appeals clerk will not accept untimely motions for reconsideration. The same amendment order changed the title of a motion for "rehearing" to "reconsideration" in several other MCR Subchapter 7.200 rules.

SUBCHAPTER 7.300 SUPREME COURT

Rule 7.301. Organization and Operation of Supreme Court

(A) Chief Justice. At the first meeting of the Supreme Court in each odd-numbered year, the justices shall select by majority vote one among them to serve as Chief Justice.

(B) Term and Sessions. The annual term of the Court begins on August 1 and ends on July 31. Except as provided in MCR 7.313(E), the end of a term has no effect on pending cases. Oral arguments are generally scheduled at sessions in October, November, December, January, March, April, and May. The Court will only schedule cases for argument in September, February, June, July, or August pursuant to an order on the Court's own initiative or upon a showing of special cause by a moving party.

(C) Supreme Court Clerk

(1) *Appointment; General Provisions.* The Supreme Court will appoint a clerk who shall keep the clerk's office in Lansing under the direction of the Court. Where the term "clerk" appears in this subchapter without modification, it means the Supreme Court clerk. The clerk may not practice law other than as clerk while serving as clerk.

(2) *Duties.* The clerk shall perform the following duties:

(a) Furnish bond before taking office. The bond must be in favor of the people of the state and in the penal sum of $10,000, approved by the Chief Justice and filed with the Secretary of State, and conditioned on the faithful performance of the clerk's official duties. The fee for the bond is a Court expense.

(b) Collect the fees provided for by statute or court rule.

(c) Deposit monthly with the State Treasurer the fees collected, securing and filing a receipt for them.

(d) Provide for the recording of Supreme Court proceedings as the Court directs.

(e) Care for and maintain custody of all records, seals, books, and papers pertaining to the clerk's office and filed or deposited there.

(f) Return the original record as provided in MCR 7.310(B) after an appeal has been decided by the Court.

(D) Deputy Supreme Court Clerks. The Supreme Court may appoint deputy Supreme Court clerks. A deputy clerk shall carry out the duties assigned by the clerk and perform the duties of the clerk if the clerk is absent or unable to act.

(E) Reporter of Decisions. The Supreme Court will appoint a reporter of decisions. The reporter shall:

(1) prepare the decisions, including concurring and dissenting opinions, of the Supreme Court for publication;

(2) write a brief statement of the facts of each case and headnotes containing the points made;

(3) ensure that opinions are published in advance sheets as soon as practicable; and

(4) ensure that bound volumes are printed as soon as practicable after the last opinion included in a volume is issued.

The reasons for denying leave to appeal, as required by Const 1963, art 6, § 6 and filed in the clerk's office, are not to be published and are not to be regarded as precedent.

(F) Supreme Court Crier. The Supreme Court will appoint a court crier. The court crier shall

(1) have charge of the Supreme Court courtroom and the offices and other rooms assigned to the Supreme Court justices; and

(2) have the power to serve an order, process, or writ issued by the Supreme Court; collect the fee for that service allowed

by law to sheriffs; and deposit monthly with the State Treasurer all the fees collected, securing a receipt for them.
[Adopted May 27, 2015, effective September 1, 2015, 498 Mich. Amended September 27, 2017, effective January 1, 2018, 501 Mich.]

Comments

Staff Comment to 2015 Adoption

These new rules of the Michigan Supreme Court were designed to more closely follow the style of rules used in the Court of Appeals, thereby making practice and procedure more similar in the two courts.

Staff Comment to 2017 Amendment

The amendment of MCR 7.300 *et seq.* would clarify certain practices and procedures in the Supreme Court, especially as they pertain to electronic filing by parties and electronic notification of the Court's opinions and orders, as well as require only the signed originals of documents to be filed in hard copy.

Rule 7.302. Electronic Filing, Service, and Notification

(A) Electronic Filing. Documents may be filed electronically in lieu of submitting paper copies unless specifically required by court order.

(B) Electronic Service. A document that is electronically filed may be served electronically on registered users of the e-filing system at their registered email addresses.

(C) Electronic Notification. The clerk may electronically transmit or provide electronic access to Court notices, orders, opinions, and other communications to the parties, attorneys, the Court of Appeals, and the trial court or tribunal.
[Adopted September 27, 2017, effective January 1, 2018, 501 Mich.]

Comment

Staff Comment to 2018 Adoption

The amendment of MCR 7.300 *et seq.* would clarify certain practices and procedures in the Supreme Court, especially as they pertain to electronic filing by parties and electronic notification of the Court's opinions and orders, as well as require only the signed originals of documents to be filed in hard copy.

Rule 7.303   Jurisdiction of the Supreme Court

(A) Mandatory Review. The Supreme Court shall review a Judicial Tenure Commission order recommending discipline, removal, retirement, or suspension (see MCR 9.223 to 9.226).

(B) Discretionary Review. The Supreme Court may

(1) review by appeal a case pending in the Court of Appeals or after decision by the Court of Appeals (see MCR 7.305);

(2) review by appeal a final order of the Attorney Discipline Board (see MCR 9.122);

(3) issue an advisory opinion (see Const 1963, art 3, § 8 and MCR 7.308(B));

(4) respond to a certified question (see MCR 7.308(A));

(5) exercise superintending control over a lower court or tribunal (see MCR 7.306);

(6) exercise other jurisdiction as provided by the constitution or by law.
[Adopted May 27, 2015, effective September 1, 2015, 498 Mich.]

Comments

Staff Comment to 2015 Adoption

These new rules of the Michigan Supreme Court were designed to more closely follow the style of rules used in the Court of Appeals, thereby making practice and procedure more similar in the two courts.

Rule 7.305.   Application for Leave to Appeal

(A) What to File. To apply for leave to appeal, a party must file:

(1) 1 signed copy of an application for leave to appeal prepared in conformity with MCR 7.212(B) and consisting of the following:

(a) a statement identifying the judgment or order appealed and the date of its entry;

(b) the questions presented for review related in concise terms to the facts of the case;

(c) a table of contents and index of authorities conforming to MCR 7.212(C)(2) and (3);

(d) a concise statement of the material proceedings and facts conforming to MCR 7.212(C)(6);

(e) a concise argument, conforming to MCR 7.212(C)(7), in support of the appellant's position on each of the stated questions and establishing a ground for the application as required by subrule (B); and

(f) a statement of the relief sought.

(2) 1 copy of any opinion, findings, or judgment of the trial court or tribunal relevant to the question as to which leave to appeal is sought and 1 copy of the opinion or order of the Court of Appeals, unless review of a pending case is being sought;

(3) proof that a copy of the application was served on all other parties, and that a notice of the filing of the application was served on the clerks of the Court of Appeals and the trial court or tribunal; and

(4) the fee provided by MCR 7.319(C)(1).

(B) Grounds. The application must show that

(1) the issue involves a substantial question about the validity of a legislative act;

(2) the issue has significant public interest and the case is one by or against the state or one of its agencies or subdivisions or by or against an officer of the state or one of its agencies or subdivisions in the officer's official capacity;

(3) the issue involves a legal principle of major significance to the state's jurisprudence;

(4) in an appeal before a decision of the Court of Appeals,

(a) delay in final adjudication is likely to cause substantial harm, or

(b) the appeal is from a ruling that a provision of the Michigan Constitution, a Michigan statute, a rule or regulation included in the Michigan Administrative Code, or any other action of the legislative or executive branches of state government is invalid;

(5) in an appeal of a decision of the Court of Appeals,

(a) the decision is clearly erroneous and will cause material injustice, or

(b) the decision conflicts with a Supreme Court decision or another decision of the Court of Appeals; or

(6) in an appeal from the Attorney Discipline Board, the decision is clearly erroneous and will cause material injustice.

(C) When to File.

(1) *Bypass Application.* In an appeal before the Court of Appeals decision, the application must be filed within 42 days after:

(a) a claim of appeal is filed in the Court of Appeals;

(b) an application for leave to appeal is filed in the Court of Appeals; or

(c) an original action is filed in the Court of Appeals.

(2) *Application After Court of Appeals Decision.* Except as provided in subrule (C)(4), the application must be filed within 28 days in termination of parental rights cases, within 42 days in other civil cases, or within 56 days in criminal cases, after:

(a) the Court of Appeals order or opinion resolving an appeal or original action, including an order denying an application for leave to appeal,

(b) the Court of Appeals order or opinion remanding the case to the lower court or Tribunal for further proceedings while retaining jurisdiction,

(c) the Court of Appeals order denying a timely filed motion for reconsideration, or

(d) the Court of Appeals order granting a motion to publish an opinion that was originally released as unpublished.

(3) *Interlocutory Application from the Court of Appeals.* Except as provided in subrules (C)(1) and (C)(2), the application must be filed within 28 days after a Court of Appeals order that does not resolve the appeal or original action, including an order granting an application for leave to appeal.

(4) *Attorney Discipline Board Decision.* In an appeal from an order of discipline or dismissal entered by the Attorney Discipline Board, the application must be filed within the time provided in MCR 9.122(A)(1).

(5) *Late Application, Exception.* Late applications will not be accepted except as allowed under this subrule. If an application for leave to appeal in a criminal case is not received within the time periods provided in subrules (C)(1) or (2), and the appellant is an inmate in the custody of the Michigan Department of Corrections and has submitted the application as a pro se party, the application shall be deemed presented for filing on the date of deposit of the application in the outgoing mail at the correctional institution in which the inmate is housed. Timely filing may be shown by a sworn statement, which must set forth the date of deposit and state that first-class postage was prepaid. The exception applies to applications from decisions of the Court of Appeals rendered on or after March 1, 2010. This exception also applies to an inmate housed in a federal or other state correctional institution who is acting pro se in a criminal appeal from a Michigan court.

(6) *Decisions Remanding for Further Proceedings.* If the decision of the Court of Appeals remands the case to a lower court for further proceedings, an application for leave to appeal may be filed within 28 days in termination of parental rights cases, 42 days in other civil cases, and 56 days in criminal cases, after the date of

(a) the Court of Appeals order or opinion remanding the case,

(b) the Court of Appeals order denying a timely filed motion for reconsideration of a decision remanding the case, or

(c) the Court of Appeals order or opinion disposing of the case following the remand procedure, in which case an application may be made on all issues raised initially in the Court of Appeals, as well as those related to the remand proceedings.

(7) *Effect of Appeal on Decision Remanding Case.* If a party appeals a decision that remands for further proceedings as provided in subrule (C)(6)(a), the following provisions apply:

(a) If the Court of Appeals decision is a judgment under MCR 7.215(E)(1), an application for leave to appeal stays proceedings on remand unless the Court of Appeals or the Supreme Court orders otherwise.

(b) If the Court of Appeals decision is an order other than a judgment under MCR 7.215(E)(1), the proceedings on remand are not stayed by an application for leave to appeal unless so ordered by the Court of Appeals or the Supreme Court.

(8) *Orders Denying Motions to Remand.* If the Court of Appeals has denied a motion to remand, the appellant may raise issues relating to that denial in an application for leave to appeal the decision on the merits.

(D) Answer. A responding party may file 1 signed copy of an answer within 28 days after service of the application. The party must file proof that a copy of the answer was served on all other parties.

(E) Reply. The appellant may file 1 signed copy of a reply within 21 days after service of the answer, along with proof of its service on all other parties. The reply must:

(1) contain only a rebuttal of the arguments in the answer;

(2) include a table of contents and an index of authorities; and

(3) be no longer than 10 pages, exclusive of tables, indexes, and appendixes.

(F) Nonconforming Pleading. On its own initiative or on a party's motion, the Court may order a party who filed a pleading that does not substantially comply with the requirements of this rule to file a conforming pleading within a specified time or else it may strike the nonconforming pleading. The submission to the clerk of a nonconforming pleading does not satisfy the time limitation for filing the pleading if it has not been corrected within the specified time.

(G) Submission and Argument. Applications for leave to appeal may be submitted for a decision after the reply brief has been filed or the time for filing such has expired, whichever occurs first. There is no oral argument on an application for leave to appeal unless ordered by the Court under subrule (H)(1).

(H) Decision.

(1) *Possible Court Actions.* The Court may grant or deny the application for leave to appeal, enter a final decision, direct argument on the application, or issue a peremptory order. The clerk shall issue the order entered and provide either a paper copy or access to an electronic version to each party and to the Court of Appeals clerk.

(2) *Appeal Before Court of Appeals Decision.* If leave to appeal is granted before a decision of the Court of Appeals, the

appeal is thereafter pending in the Supreme Court only, and subchapter 7.300 applies.

(3) *Appeal After Court of Appeals Decision.* If leave to appeal is denied after a decision of the Court of Appeals, the Court of Appeals decision becomes the final adjudication and may be enforced in accordance with its terms. If leave to appeal is granted, jurisdiction over the case is vested in the Supreme Court, and subchapter 7.300 applies.

(4) *Issues on Appeal.*

(a) Unless otherwise ordered by the Court, an appeal shall be limited to the issues raised in the application for leave to appeal.

(b) On motion of any party establishing good cause, the Court may grant a request to add additional issues not raised in the application for leave to appeal or not identified in the order granting leave to appeal. Permission to brief and argue additional issues does not extend the time for filing the brief and appendixes.

(I) Stay of Proceedings. MCR 7.209 applies to appeals in the Supreme Court. When a stay bond has been filed on appeal to the Court of Appeals under MCR 7.209 or a stay has been entered or takes effect pursuant to MCR 7.209(E)(7), it operates to stay proceedings pending disposition of the appeal in the Supreme Court unless otherwise ordered by the Supreme Court or the Court of Appeals.

[Adopted May 27, 2015, effective September 1, 2015, 498 Mich. Amended September 27, 2017, effective January 1, 2018, 501 Mich. Amended effective March 21, 2018, 501 Mich; August 14, 2019, 503 Mich.]

Comments

Staff Comment to 2015 Adoption

These new rules of the Michigan Supreme Court were designed to more closely follow the style of rules used in the Court of Appeals, thereby making practice and procedure more similar in the two courts.

Staff Comment to January, 2018 Amendment

The amendment of MCR 7.300 *et seq.* would clarify certain practices and procedures in the Supreme Court, especially as they pertain to electronic filing by parties and electronic notification of the Court's opinions and orders, as well as require only the signed originals of documents to be filed in hard copy.

Staff Comment to March, 2018 Amendment

These amendments update cross-references and make other nonsubstantive revisions to clarify the rules. The amendment of MCR 6.110(B)(1) addresses an inadvertent omission from the last amendment of this rule that was intended to be shown in overstrike. Accordingly, the current rule does not match the published version. Striking the clause "for good cause shown" will provide consistency with other published versions of the rule and with the statute, MCL 766.7, which allows a magistrate to adjourn a preliminary examination with the consent of the parties without the need for good cause to be shown.

Staff Comment to 2019 Amendment

These amendments update cross-references and make other nonsubstantive revisions to clarify the rules.

Rule 7.306. Original Proceedings

(A) When Available. A complaint may be filed to invoke the Supreme Court's superintending control power:

(1) over a lower court or tribunal, including the Attorney Discipline Board, when an application for leave to appeal could not have been filed under MCR 7.305, or

(2) over the Board of Law Examiners or the Attorney Grievance Commission.

When a dispute regarding court operations arises between judges within a court that would give rise to a complaint under this rule, the judges shall participate in mediation as provided through the State Court Administrator's Office before filing such a complaint. The mediation shall be conducted in compliance with MCR 2.411(C)(2).

(B) What to File. To initiate an original proceeding, a plaintiff must file with the clerk:

(1) 1 signed copy of a complaint prepared in conformity with MCR 7.212(B) and entitled, for example,

> "[*Plaintiff*] v [*Court of Appeals, Board of Law Examiners, Attorney Discipline Board, or Attorney Grievance Commission*]."

The clerk shall retitle a complaint that is named differently.

(2) 1 signed copy of a brief conforming as nearly as possible to MCR 7.212(B) and (C);

(3) proof that the complaint and brief were served on the defendant, and, for a complaint filed against the Attorney Discipline Board or Attorney Grievance Commission, on the respondent in the underlying discipline matter; and

(4) the fee provided by MCR 7.319(C)(1).

Copies of relevant documents, record evidence, or supporting affidavits may be attached as exhibits to the complaint.

(C) Answer. The defendant must file the following with the clerk within 28 days after service of the complaint:

(1) 1 signed copy of an answer in conformity with MCR 7.212(B) and (D). The grievance administrator's answer to a complaint against the Attorney Grievance Commission must show the investigatory steps taken and any other pertinent information.

(2) Proof that a copy of the answer was served on the plaintiff.

(D) Brief by Respondent in Action Against Attorney Grievance Commission or Attorney Discipline Board. A respondent in an action against the Attorney Grievance Commission or Attorney Discipline Board may file a response brief with the clerk within 28 days after service of the complaint, and a proof that a copy of the response brief was served on plaintiff and defendant. A response brief filed under this subsection shall conform to MCR 7.212(B) and (D).

(E) Reply Brief. 1 signed copy of a reply brief may be filed as provided in MCR 7.305(E).

(F) Actions Against Attorney Grievance Commission; Confidentiality. The clerk shall keep the file in an action against the Attorney Grievance Commission or the grievance administrator confidential and not open to the public if it appears that the complaint relates to matters that are confidential under MCR 9.126. In the answer to a complaint, the grievance administrator shall certify to the clerk whether the matters involved in the action are deemed confidential under MCR 9.126. The protection provided in MCR 9.126 continues unless and until the Court orders otherwise.

(G) Nonconforming Pleading. On its own initiative or on a party's motion, the Court may order a party who filed a pleading that does not substantially comply with the requirements of this rule to file a conforming pleading within a specified time or else it may strike the nonconforming pleading. The submission to the clerk of a nonconforming pleading does not satisfy the time limitation for filing the pleading if it has not been corrected within the specified time.

(H) Submission and Argument. Original proceedings may be submitted for a decision after service of the reply brief or the time for filing a reply brief has expired, whichever occurs first. There is no oral argument on an original complaint unless ordered by the Court.

(I) Decision. The Court may set the case for argument as on leave granted, grant or deny the relief requested, or provide other relief that it deems appropriate, including an order to show cause why the relief sought in the complaint should not be granted.

[Adopted May 27, 2015, effective September 1, 2015, 498 Mich. Amended May 25, 2016, effective September 1, 2016, 499 Mich; May 24, 2017, effective September 1, 2017, 500 Mich.; September 27, 2017, effective January 1, 2018, 501 Mich. Amended effective March 21, 2018, 501 Mich.]

Comments

Staff Comment to 2015 Adoption

These new rules of the Michigan Supreme Court were designed to more closely follow the style of rules used in the Court of Appeals, thereby making practice and procedure more similar in the two courts.

Staff Comment to 2016 Amendment

The amendments of MCR 7.306 expressly authorize a respondent attorney to file a brief in actions of superintending control when the complainant objects to a dismissal by the AGC or ADB; the amendments also require the party filing for superintending control to serve copies of the complaint and brief on the respondent and allow 21 days for respondent attorney to submit a brief, with copies to be served on the plaintiff and defendant.

Staff Comment to 2017 Amendment

Under the amendment of MCR 7.306, judges in an intra-court dispute are required to submit to mediation before filing a complaint for superintending control in the Supreme Court under this rule.

Staff Comment to January, 2018 Amendment

The amendment of MCR 7.300 *et seq.* would clarify certain practices and procedures in the Supreme Court, especially as they pertain to electronic filing by parties and electronic notification of the Court's opinions and orders, as well as require only the signed originals of documents to be filed in hard copy.

Staff Comment to March, 2018 Amendment

These amendments update cross-references and make other nonsubstantive revisions to clarify the rules. The amendment of MCR 6.110(B)(1) addresses an inadvertent omission from the last amendment of this rule that was intended to be shown in overstrike. Accordingly, the current rule does not match the published version. Striking the clause "for good cause shown" will provide consistency with other published versions of the rule and with the statute, MCL 766.7, which allows a magistrate to adjourn a preliminary examination with the consent of the parties without the need for good cause to be shown.

Rule 7.307   Cross–Appeal

(A) Filing. An application for leave to appeal as a cross-appellant may be filed with the clerk within 28 days after service of the application for leave to appeal. The cross-appellant's application must comply with the requirements of MCR 7.305(A). A late application to cross-appeal will not be accepted.

(B) Alternative Arguments; New or Different Relief. A party is not required to file a cross-appeal to advance alternative arguments in support of the judgment or order appealed. A cross-appeal is required to seek new or different relief than that provided by the judgment or order appealed.

[Adopted May 27, 2015, effective September 1, 2015, 498 Mich. Amended September 27, 2017, effective January 1, 2018, 501 Mich.]

Comments

Staff Comment to 2015 Adoption

These new rules of the Michigan Supreme Court were designed to more closely follow the style of rules used in the Court of Appeals, thereby making practice and procedure more similar in the two courts.

Staff Comment to 2017 Amendment

The amendment of MCR 7.300 *et seq.* would clarify certain practices and procedures in the Supreme Court, especially as they pertain to electronic filing by parties and electronic notification of the Court's opinions and orders, as well as require only the signed originals of documents to be filed in hard copy.

Rule 7.308   Certified Questions and Advisory Opinions

(A) Certified Questions

(1) *From Michigan Courts.*

(a) Whenever a trial court or tribunal from which an appeal may be taken to the Court of Appeals or to the Supreme Court has pending before it an action or proceeding involving a controlling question of public law, and the question is of such public moment as to require an early determination according to executive message of the governor addressed to the Supreme Court, the Court may authorize the court or tribunal to certify the question to the Court with a statement of the facts sufficient to make clear the application of the question. Further proceedings relative to the case are stayed to the extent ordered by the court or tribunal, pending receipt of a decision of the Supreme Court.

(b) If any question is not properly stated or if sufficient facts are not given, the Court may require a further and better statement of the question or of the facts.

(c) The Court shall render its decision on a certified question in the ordinary form of an opinion, to be published with other opinions of the Court.

(d) After the decision of the Court has been sent, the lower court or tribunal will proceed with or dispose of the case in accordance with the Court's answer.

(2) *From Other Courts.*

(a) When a federal court, another state's appellate court, or a tribal court considers a question that Michigan law may resolve and that is not controlled by Michigan Supreme Court precedent, the court may on its own initiative or that of an interested party certify the question to the Court.

(b) A certificate may be prepared by stipulation or at the certifying court's direction, and must contain

(i) the case title;

(ii) a factual statement; and

(iii) the question to be answered.

The presiding judge must sign it, and the clerk of the federal, other state, or tribal court must certify it.

(3) *Briefing.* The parties to the underlying proceeding shall submit briefs in conformity with MCR 7.312 that include a request for oral argument on the title page of the pleading, if oral argument is desired. Unless the Court directs a different time or procedure for filing, or the parties file a written stipulation agreeing to a different schedule;

(a) the brief and appendixes of the appellant, or the plaintiff if the underlying proceeding was not an appeal, are due within 35 days after the certificate is filed with the Court;

(b) the brief and appendixes of an appellee, or a defendant if the underlying proceeding was not an appeal, are due within 28 days after service of the appellant's brief; and

(c) a reply brief is due within 21 days after service of the last timely filed appellee's or defendant's brief.

Joint or individual appendixes may be filed in conformity with MCR 7.312(D).

(4) *Submission and Argument.* A certified question may be submitted for a decision after receipt of the question and after the reply is filed or the time for filing the reply has passed, whichever occurs first. There is no oral argument on a certified question unless ordered by the Court.

(5) *Decision.* The Supreme Court may deny the request for a certified question by order, issue a peremptory order, or render a decision in the ordinary form of an opinion to be published with other opinions of the Court. The clerk shall send a paper copy or provide electronic notice of the Court's decision to the certifying court.

(6) *Costs.* The Supreme Court shall divide costs equally among the parties, subject to redistribution by the certifying court.

(B) Advisory Opinion

(1) *Form of Request.* A request for an advisory opinion by either house of the legislature or the governor pursuant to Const 1963, art 3, § 8 may be in the form of a letter that includes a copy or verbatim statement of the enacted legislation and identifies the specific questions to be answered by the Court. One signed copy of the request and one set of supporting documents are to be filed with the Court.

(2) *Briefing.* The governor, any member of the house or senate, and the attorney general may file briefs in support of or opposition to the enacted legislation within 28 days after the request for an advisory opinion is filed. Interested parties may file amicus curiae briefs on motion granted by the Court. The party shall file 1 signed copy of the brief that conforms as nearly as possible to MCR 7.312.

(3) *Submission and Argument.* Advisory opinions may be submitted for a decision after the brief in support of the advisory opinion request has been filed. There is no oral argument on a request for an advisory opinion unless ordered by the Court.

(4) *Decision.* The Supreme Court may deny the request for an advisory opinion by order, issue a peremptory order, or render a decision in the ordinary form of an opinion to be published with other opinions of the Court.

[Adopted May 27, 2015, effective September 1, 2015, 498 Mich. Amended September 27, 2017, effective January 1, 2018, 501 Mich. Amended effective August 14, 2019, 503 Mich.]

Comments

Staff Comment to 2015 Adoption

These new rules of the Michigan Supreme Court were designed to more closely follow the style of rules used in the Court of Appeals, thereby making practice and procedure more similar in the two courts.

Staff Comment to 2017 Amendment

The amendment of MCR 7.300 et seq. would clarify certain practices and procedures in the Supreme Court, especially as they pertain to electronic filing by parties and electronic notification of the Court's opinions and orders, as well as require only the signed originals of documents to be filed in hard copy.

Staff Comment to 2019 Amendment

These amendments update cross-references and make other nonsubstantive revisions to clarify the rules.

Rule 7.310.   Record on Appeals

(A) Transmission of Record. An appeal is heard on the original papers, which constitute the record on appeal. When requested by the Supreme Court clerk to do so, the Court of Appeals clerk or the lower court clerk shall send to the Supreme Court clerk all papers or electronic documents on file in the Court of Appeals or the lower court, certified by the clerk. For an appeal originating from an administrative board, office, or tribunal, the record on appeal is the certified record filed with the Court of Appeals clerk and the papers or electronic documents filed with the Court of Appeals clerk.

(B) Return of Record. After final adjudication or other disposition of an appeal, the Supreme Court clerk shall return the original record to the Court of Appeals clerk, to the clerk of the trial court or tribunal in which the record was made, or to the clerk of the court to which the case has been remanded for further proceedings. Thereafter, the clerk of the lower court or tribunal to which the original record has been sent shall promptly notify the attorneys of the receipt of the record. The Supreme Court clerk shall provide a certified copy of the order or judgment entered by the Supreme Court to the Court of Appeals clerk and to the clerk of the trial court or tribunal from which the appeal was taken.

(C) Stipulations. The parties may stipulate in writing regarding any matter constituting the basis for an application for leave to appeal or regarding any matter relevant to a part of the record on appeal.

[Adopted May 27, 2015, effective September 1, 2015, 498 Mich. Amended September 27, 2017, effective January 1, 2018, 501 Mich.]

Comments

Staff Comment to 2015 Adoption

These new rules of the Michigan Supreme Court were designed to more closely follow the style of rules used in the Court of Appeals, thereby making practice and procedure more similar in the two courts.

Staff Comment to 2017 Amendment

The amendment of MCR 7.300 et seq. would clarify certain practices and procedures in the Supreme Court, especially as they pertain to electronic filing by parties and electronic notification of the Court's opinions and orders, as well as require only the signed originals of documents to be filed in hard copy.

Rule 7.311   Motions in Supreme Court

(A) What to File. To have a motion heard, a party must file with the clerk:

(1) 1 signed copy of a motion and supporting papers, except as otherwise provided in this rule, stating briefly but distinctly the grounds on which the motion is based and the relief requested and including an affidavit supporting any allegations of fact in the motion;

(2) proof that the motion and supporting papers were served on each opposing party; and

(3) the fee provided by MCR 7.319(C)(2) or (3).

(B) Submission and Argument. Motions are submitted for decisions on Tuesday of each week at least 14 days after they are filed, but administrative orders (e.g., on motions to extend time for filing a pleading, to file an amicus brief, to appear and practice, to exceed the page limit) may be entered earlier to advance the efficient administration of the Court. There is no oral argument on a motion unless ordered by the Court.

(C) Answer. An opposing party may file 1 signed copy of an answer at any time before an order is entered on the motion.

(D) Motion to Seal File. Except as otherwise provided by statute or court rule, the procedure for sealing a Supreme Court file is governed by MCR 8.119(I). Materials that are subject to a motion to seal a file in whole or in part shall be held under seal pending the Court's disposition of the motion.

(E) Motion for Immediate Consideration or to Expedite Proceedings. A party may move for immediate consideration of a motion or to expedite any proceeding before the Court. The motion or an accompanying affidavit must identify the manner of service of the motion on the other parties and explain why immediate consideration of the motion or expedited scheduling of the proceeding is necessary. If the motion is granted, the Court will schedule an earlier hearing or render an earlier decision on the matter.

(F) Motion for Rehearing.

(1) To move for rehearing, a party must file within 21 days after the opinion was filed:

   (a) 1 signed copy of a motion for rehearing; and

   (b) proof that a copy was served on each party.

The motion for rehearing must include reasons why the Court should modify its opinion. Motions for rehearing are subject to the restrictions contained in MCR 2.119(F)(3).

(2) Unless otherwise ordered by the Court, the timely filing of a motion for rehearing postpones issuance of the Court's judgment order until the motion is either denied by the Court or, if granted, until at least 21 days after the filing of the Court's decision on rehearing.

(3) Any party or amicus curiae that participated in the case may answer a motion for rehearing within 14 days after it is served by filing

   (a) 1 copy of the answer; and

   (b) proof that a copy was served on all other parties.

(4) Unless ordered by the Court, there is no oral argument on a motion for rehearing.

(5) The clerk shall refuse to accept for filing a late-filed motion for rehearing or a motion for reconsideration of an order denying a motion for rehearing.

(G) Motion for Reconsideration. To move for reconsideration of a court order, a party must file the items required by subrule (A) within 21 days after the date of certification of the order. The motion shall include all facts, arguments, and citations to authorities in a single document and shall not exceed 10 double-spaced pages. A copy of the order for which reconsideration is sought must be included with the motion. Motions for reconsideration are subject to the restrictions contained in MCR 2.119(F)(3). The clerk shall refuse to accept for filing a late-filed motion or a motion for reconsideration of an order denying a motion for reconsideration. The filing of a motion for reconsideration does not stay the effect of the order addressed in the motion.

[Adopted May 27, 2015, effective September 1, 2015, 498 Mich. Amended September 27, 2017, effective January 1, 2018, 501 Mich.]

Comments

Staff Comment to 2015 Adoption

These new rules of the Michigan Supreme Court were designed to more closely follow the style of rules used in the Court of Appeals, thereby making practice and procedure more similar in the two courts.

Staff Comment to 2017 Amendment

The amendment of MCR 7.300 *et seq.* would clarify certain practices and procedures in the Supreme Court, especially as they pertain to electronic filing by parties and electronic notification of the Court's opinions and orders, as well as require only the signed originals of documents to be filed in hard copy.

Rule 7.312. Briefs and Appendixes in Calendar Cases

(A) Form and Length. Briefs in calendar cases must be prepared in conformity with MCR 7.212(B), (C), (D), and (G) as to form and length. Briefs shall be printed on only the front side of the page of good quality, white unglazed paper by any printing, duplicating, or copying process that provides a clear image. Typewritten, handwritten, or carbon copy pages may be used so long as the printing is legible.

(B) Citation of Record; Summary of Arguments.

(1) A party's statement of facts or counterstatement of facts shall provide the appendix page numbers of the transcript pages, pleadings, or other documents being cited or referred to.

(2) If the argument of any one issue in a brief exceeds 20 pages, a summary of the argument must be included. The summary must be a succinct, accurate, and clear condensation of the argument actually made in the body of the brief and may not be a mere repetition of the headings under which the argument is arranged.

(C) Cover. A brief must have a suitable cover of heavy paper. The cover page must follow this general form:

IN THE SUPREME COURT

APPEAL FROM THE [COURT OR TRIBUNAL APPEALED FROM]

[JUDGE OR PRESIDING OFFICER]

[Name of Party] _____,

Plaintiff–[Appellant or Appellee],

                              MSC No.   [leave blank]

v   COA No. _____

                              Trial Ct No. _____

[Name of Party] _____,

Defendant–[Appellant or Appellee].

Brief on Appeal—[Appellant or Appellee]

ORAL ARGUMENT [REQUESTED/NOT REQUESTED]

_____

Attorney for [PL or DF]–[AT or AE]

[Business Address]

_____

_____

_____

(D) Appendixes.

(1) *Form.* Appendixes must be prepared in conformity with MCR 7.212(B), and shall be similarly endorsed as briefs under MCR 7.312(C) but designated as an appendix. Appendixes must be printed on both sides of the page and, if they

encompass more than 20 sheets of paper, must also be submitted on electronic storage media in a file format that can be opened, read, and printed by the Court.

(2) *Appellant's Appendix.* An appendix filed by the appellant must be entitled "Appellant's Appendix," must be separately bound, and numbered separately from the brief with the letter "a" following each page number (e.g., 1a, 2a, 3a). Each page of the appendix must include a header that briefly describes the character of the document, such as the names of witnesses for testimonial evidence or the nature of the documents for record evidence. The appendix must include a table of contents and, when applicable, must contain:

(a) the relevant docket entries of the trial court or tribunal and the Court of Appeals arranged in a single column;

(b) the trial court judgment, order, or decision in question and the Court of Appeals opinion or order being appealed;

(c) any relevant finding or opinion of the trial court;

(d) any relevant portions of the pleadings or other parts of the record; and

(e) any relevant portions of the transcript, including the complete jury instructions if an issue is raised regarding a jury instruction.

The items listed in subrules (D)(2)(a) to (e) must be presented in chronological order.

(3) *Joint Appendix.*

(a) The parties may stipulate to use a joint appendix, so designated, containing the matters that are deemed necessary to fairly decide the questions involved. A joint appendix shall meet the requirements of subrule (D)(2) and shall be separately bound and served with the appellant's brief.

(b) The stipulation to use a joint appendix may provide that either party may file, as a supplemental appendix, any additional portion of the record not covered by the joint appendix.

(4) *Appellee's Appendix.* An appendix, entitled "Appellee's Appendix," may be filed. The appellee's appendix must comply with the provisions of subrule (D)(2) and be numbered separately from the brief with the letter "b" following each page number (e.g., 1b, 2b, 3b). Materials included in the appellant's appendix or joint appendix may not be repeated in the appellee's appendix, except to clarify the subject matter involved.

(E) Time for Filing. Unless the Court directs a different time for filing,

(1) the appellant's brief and appendixes, if any, are due within 56 days after the leave to appeal is granted;

(2) the appellee's brief and appendixes, if any, are due within 35 days after the appellant's brief is served on the appellee; and

(3) the reply brief is due within 21 days after the appellee's brief is served on the appellant.

(F) What to File. Each party shall:

(1) file 1 signed copy of a brief and 1 set of appendixes with the clerk;

(2) serve 2 copies on each attorney who has appeared in the case for a separate party or group of parties and on each party who has appeared in person;

(3) serve 1 copy on the Attorney General in a criminal case or in a case in which the state is a named or interested party; and

(4) file a proof of service with the clerk.

(G) Cross–Appeal Briefs. The filing and service of cross-appeal briefs are governed by subrule (F). An appellee/cross-appellant may file a combined brief for the primary appeal and the cross-appeal within 35 days after service of the appellant's brief in the primary appeal. An appellant/cross-appellee may file a combined reply brief for the primary appeal and a responsive brief for the cross-appeal within 35 days after service of the cross-appellant's brief. A reply to the cross-appeal may be filed within 21 days after service of the responsive brief.

(H) Amicus Curiae Briefs and Argument.

(1) An amicus curiae brief may be filed only on motion granted by the Court except as provided in subsection (2).

(2) A motion for leave to file an amicus curiae brief is not required if the brief is presented by the Attorney General on behalf of the people of the state of Michigan, the state of Michigan, or an agency or official of the state of Michigan; on behalf of any political subdivision of the state when submitted by its authorized legal officer, its authorized agent, or an association representing a political subdivision; or on behalf of the Prosecuting Attorneys Association of Michigan or the Criminal Defense Attorneys of Michigan.

(3) An amicus curiae brief must conform to subrules (A), (B), (C) and (F), and must be filed within 21 days after the brief of the appellee has been filed or the time for filing such brief has expired, or at any other time the Court directs.

(4) Except for briefs presented on behalf of amicus curiae listed in subrule (H)(2), a brief filed under this rule shall indicate whether counsel for a party authored the brief in whole or in part and whether such counsel or a party made a monetary contribution intended to fund the preparation or submission of the brief, and shall identify every person other than the amicus curiae, its members, or its counsel, who made such a monetary contribution. The disclosure shall be made in the first footnote on the first page of text.

(5) An amicus curiae may not participate in oral argument except by Court order.

(I) Supplemental Authority. A party may file 1 signed copy of a supplemental authority in conformity with MCR 7.212(F).

(J) Extending or Shortening Time; Failure to File; Forfeiture of Oral Argument.

(1) The time provided for filing and serving the briefs and appendixes may be shortened or extended by order of the Court on its own initiative or on motion of a party.

(2) If the appellant fails to file the brief and appendixes within the time required, the Court may dismiss the case and award costs to the appellee or affirm the judgment or order appealed.

(3) A party filing a brief late forfeits the right to oral argument.

[Adopted May 27, 2015, effective September 1, 2015, 498 Mich. Amended effective December 14, 2016, 500 Mich. Amended September 27, 2017, effective January 1, 2018, 501 Mich; April 3, 2019, effective May 1, 2019, 502 Mich.]

Comments

Staff Comment to 2015 Adoption

These new rules of the Michigan Supreme Court were designed to more closely follow the style of rules used in the Court of Appeals, thereby making practice and procedure more similar in the two courts.

Staff Comment to 2016 Amendment

These amendments update cross-references and make other nonsubstantive revisions to clarify the rules.

Staff Comment to 2017 Amendment

The amendment of MCR 7.300 *et seq.* would clarify certain practices and procedures in the Supreme Court, especially as they pertain to electronic filing by parties and electronic notification of the Court's opinions and orders, as well as require only the signed originals of documents to be filed in hard copy.

Staff Comment to 2019 Amendment

The amendments of MCR 7.212 and 7.312 require amicus briefs to indicate certain information regarding the preparation of the brief and disclosure of monetary contributions. The amendments are similar to Supreme Court Rule 37.6.

Rule 7.313.   Supreme Court Calendar

(A) Definition. A case in which leave to appeal has been granted, or a case initiated in the Supreme Court that the Court determines will be argued at a monthly session, is termed a "calendar case."

(B) Notice of Hearing; Request for Oral Argument.

(1) After the briefs of both parties have been filed or the time for filing the appellant's reply brief has expired, the clerk shall notify the parties that the calendar cases and the cases to be argued on the application under MCR 7.305(H)(1) will be heard at a monthly session of the Supreme Court not less than 35 days after the date of the notice. The Court may direct that a case be scheduled for argument at a future monthly session with expedited briefing times or may shorten the 35–day notice period on its own initiative or on motion of a party.

(2) Except on order of the Court, a party who has not specifically requested oral argument on the title page of its brief or has forfeited argument by not timely filing its brief is not entitled to oral argument unless it files a motion for oral argument at least 21 days before the first day of the monthly session. If neither party is entitled to oral argument, the clerk will list the case as submitted on briefs. The Court may direct that a case be submitted on briefs without oral argument even when a party would otherwise be entitled to oral argument.

(C) Arrangement of Calendar. At least 21 days before the first day of the monthly session, the clerk will place cases on the session calendar and arrange the order in which they are to be heard. The cases will be called and heard in that order except as provided in subrule (D).

(D) Rearrangement of Calendar; Adjournment. At least 21 days before the first day of a session, the parties may stipulate to have a case specially placed on the calendar, grouped to suit the convenience of the attorneys, or placed at the beginning or end of the call. After that time, changes to the session calendar may be requested only by motion, not by stipulation of the parties. A motion to adjourn a case from the call after the schedule is released will be granted only by order upon a showing of good cause with an explanation of why the motion could not have been filed sooner. Costs payable to the Court may be imposed on the moving party for a late-filed motion to adjourn.

(E) Reargument of Undecided Calendar Cases. When a calendar case remains undecided at the end of the term in which it was argued, the parties may file supplemental briefs. In addition, by directive of the Court or upon a party's written request within 14 days after the beginning of the new term, the clerk shall schedule the case for reargument. This subrule does not apply to a case argued on the application for leave to appeal under MCR 7.305(H)(1).

[Adopted May 27, 2015, effective September 1, 2015, 498 Mich. Amended September 27, 2017, effective January 1, 2018, 501 Mich.]

Comments

Staff Comment to 2015 Adoption

These new rules of the Michigan Supreme Court were designed to more closely follow the style of rules used in the Court of Appeals, thereby making practice and procedure more similar in the two courts.

Staff Comment to 2017 Amendment

The amendment of MCR 7.300 *et seq.* would clarify certain practices and procedures in the Supreme Court, especially as they pertain to electronic filing by parties and electronic notification of the Court's opinions and orders, as well as require only the signed originals of documents to be filed in hard copy.

Rule 7.314   Call and Argument of Cases

(A) Call; Notice of Argument; Adjournment From Call. The Court, on the first day of each monthly session, will call the cases for argument in the order they stand on the calendar as arranged in accordance with MCR 7.313(C), and proceed from day to day during the session in the same order. A case may not be adjourned after being placed on the call, except on a showing of extreme emergency. A case may be submitted on briefs by stipulation at any time.

(B) Argument.

(1) In a calendar case in which both sides are entitled to oral argument, the time allowed for argument is 30 minutes for each side unless the Court orders otherwise. When only one side is scheduled for oral argument, 15 minutes is allowed unless the Court orders otherwise.

(2) In a case being argued on the application for leave to appeal under MCR 7.305(H)(1), each side that is entitled to oral argument is allowed 15 minutes to argue unless the Court orders otherwise.

The time for argument may be extended by Court order on motion of a party filed at least 14 days before the session begins or by the Chief Justice during the argument.

[Adopted May 27, 2015, effective September 1, 2015, 498 Mich.]

Comments

Staff Comment to 2015 Adoption

These new rules of the Michigan Supreme Court were designed to more closely follow the style of rules used in the Court of Appeals, thereby making practice and procedure more similar in the two courts.

Rule 7.315.   Opinions, Orders, and Judgments

(A) Opinions of Court. An opinion must be written and bear the authoring justice's name or the label "Per Curiam" or "Memorandum Opinion." Each justice deciding a case must sign an opinion. Except for affirmance of action by a lower court or tribunal by even division of the justices, a decision of the Court must be made by concurrence of a majority of the justices voting.

(B) Filing and Publication. The Court shall file a signed opinion with the clerk, who shall stamp the date of filing on it.

The reporter of decisions is responsible for having the opinions printed in a form and under a contract approved by the Court in accordance with MCR 7.301(E).

(C) Orders or Judgments Pursuant to Opinions.

(1) *Entry.* The clerk shall enter an order or judgment pursuant to an opinion as of the date the opinion is filed with the clerk.

(2) *Routine Issuance.*

(a) If a motion for rehearing is not timely filed under MCR 7.311(F)(1), the clerk shall send a certified copy of the order or judgment to the Court of Appeals with its file, and to the trial court or tribunal that tried the case with its record, not less than 21 days or more than 28 days after entry of the order or judgment.

(b) If a motion for rehearing is timely filed, the clerk shall fulfill the responsibilities under subrule (C)(2)(a) promptly after the Court denies the motion or, if the motion is granted, enter a new order or judgment after the Court's decision on rehearing.

(3) *Exceptional Issuance.* The Court may direct the clerk to dispense with the time requirement of subrule (C)(2)(a) and issue the order or judgment when its opinion is filed. An order or judgment issued under this subrule does not preclude the filing of a motion for rehearing, but the filing of a motion does not stay execution or enforcement.

(4) *Execution or Enforcement.* Unless otherwise ordered by the Court, an order or judgment is effective when it is issued under subrule (C)(2)(a) or (b) or (C)(3), and enforcement is to be obtained in the trial court.

(D) Entry, Issuance, Execution, and Enforcement of Other Orders and Judgments. An order or judgment, other than those by opinion under subrule (C), is entered on the date of filing. Unless otherwise stated, an order or judgment is effective the date it is entered. The clerk must promptly send a copy or provide electronic notification of the order or judgment to each party, the Court of Appeals, and the trial court or tribunal. A motion may not be decided or an order entered by the Court unless all required documents have been filed and the requisite fees have been paid.

[Adopted May 27, 2015, effective September 1, 2015, 498 Mich. Amended September 27, 2017, effective January 1, 2018, 501 Mich.]

Comments

Staff Comment to 2015 Adoption

These new rules of the Michigan Supreme Court were designed to more closely follow the style of rules used in the Court of Appeals, thereby making practice and procedure more similar in the two courts.

Staff Comment to 2018 Amendment

The amendment of MCR 7.300 *et seq.* would clarify certain practices and procedures in the Supreme Court, especially as they pertain to electronic filing by parties and electronic notification of the Court's opinions and orders, as well as require only the signed originals of documents to be filed in hard copy.

Rule 7.316. Miscellaneous Relief

(A) Relief Obtainable. While a matter is pending in the Supreme Court, the Court may, at any time, in addition to its general powers

(1) exercise any or all of the powers of amendment of the lower court or tribunal;

(2) on reasonable notice as it may require, allow substitution of parties by reason of marriage, death, bankruptcy, assignment, or any other cause; allow new parties to be added or parties to be dropped; or allow parties to be rearranged as appellants or appellees;

(3) permit the reasons or grounds of appeal to be amended or new grounds to be added;

(4) permit the transcript or record to be amended by correcting errors or adding matters that should have been included;

(5) adjourn the case until further evidence is taken and brought before it;

(6) draw inferences of fact;

(7) enter any judgment or order that ought to have been entered, and enter other and further orders and grant relief as the case may require;

(8) if a judgment notwithstanding the verdict is set aside on appeal, grant a new trial or other relief; or

(9) *Order an Appeal Submitted to Mediation.* The mediator shall file a status report with this Court within the time specified in the order. If mediation results in full or partial settlement of the case, the parties shall file, within 21 days after the filing of the notice by the mediator, a stipulation to dismiss (in full or in part) with this Court pursuant to MCR 7.318.

(B) Allowing Act After Expiration of Time. When, under the practice relating to appeals or stay of proceedings, a nonjurisdictional act is required to be done within a designated time, the Court may at any time, on motion and notice, permit it to be done after the expiration of the period on a showing that there was good cause for the delay or that it was not due to the culpable negligence of the party or attorney. The Court will not accept for filing a motion to file a late application for leave to appeal under MCR 7.305(C), a late application for leave to cross-appeal under MCR 7.307(A), a late motion for rehearing under MCR 7.311(F), or a late motion for reconsideration under MCR 7.311(G).

(C) Vexatious Proceedings; Vexatious Litigator.

(1) The Court may, on its own initiative or the motion of any party filed before a case is placed on a session calendar, dismiss an appeal, assess actual and punitive damages, or take other disciplinary action when it determines that an appeal or original proceeding was vexatious because

(a) the matter was filed for purposes of hindrance or delay or is not reasonably well-grounded in fact or warranted by existing law or a good-faith argument for the extension, modification, or reversal of existing law; or

(b) a pleading, motion, argument, brief, document, or record filed in the case or any testimony presented in the case was grossly lacking in the requirements of propriety, violated court rules, or grossly disregarded the requirements of a fair presentation of the issues to the Court.

(2) Damages may not exceed actual damages and expenses incurred by the opposing party because of the vexatious appeal or proceeding, including reasonable attorney fees, and punitive damages in an added amount not exceeding the actual damages. The Court may remand the case to the trial court or tribunal for a determination of actual damages.

(3) *Vexatious Litigator.* If a party habitually, persistently, and without reasonable cause engages in vexatious conduct under subrule (C)(1), the Court may, on its own initiative or on motion of another party, find the party to be a vexatious litigator and impose filing restrictions on the party. The restrictions may include prohibiting the party from continuing or instituting legal proceedings in the Court without first obtaining leave, prohibiting the filing of actions in the Court without the filing fee or security for costs required by MCR 7.209 or MCR 7.319, or other restriction the Court deems just.

[Adopted May 27, 2015, effective September 1, 2015, 498 Mich. Amended May 21, 2017, effective September 1, 2017, 500 Mich; September 27, 2017, effective January 1, 2018, 501 Mich.]

Comments

Staff Comment to 2015 Adoption

These new rules of the Michigan Supreme Court were designed to more closely follow the style of rules used in the Court of Appeals, thereby making practice and procedure more similar in the two courts.

Staff Comment to 2017 Amendment

The amendment of MCR 7.316 explicitly provides that the Supreme Court may order an appeal to mediation.

Staff Comment to 2018 Amendment

The amendment of MCR 7.300 *et seq.* would clarify certain practices and procedures in the Supreme Court, especially as they pertain to electronic filing by parties and electronic notification of the Court's opinions and orders, as well as require only the signed originals of documents to be filed in hard copy.

Rule 7.317.   Involuntary Dismissal; No Progress

(A) Designation. If an appellant's brief has not been timely filed under MCR 7.312(E)(1) or within the time period granted by an order extending the time for filing the brief, or if the appellant fails to pay the filing fee or pursue the case in substantial conformity with the rules, the case shall be designated as one in which no progress has been made.

(B) Notice; Dismissal. When a case is designated as one in which no progress is made, the clerk shall mail or provide electronic notice to each party notice that, unless the appellant's brief that conforms with the rules is filed within 21 days or a motion is filed seeking further extension upon a showing of good cause, the case will be dismissed. An administrative order dismissing an action under this rule will be sent or made electronically accessible to the parties and the lower court or tribunal from which the action arose.

(C) Reinstatement. Within 21 days of the dismissal order, the appellant may seek reinstatement of the action by paying the filing fee or by filing a conforming brief along with a motion showing mistake, inadvertence, or excusable neglect. The clerk shall not accept a late-filed motion to reinstate.

(D) Dismissal for Lack of Jurisdiction. The Court may dismiss an appeal, application, or an original proceeding for lack of jurisdiction at any time.

[Adopted May 27, 2015, effective September 1, 2015, 498 Mich. Amended September 27, 2017, effective January 1, 2018, 501 Mich.]

Comments

Staff Comment to 2015 Adoption

These new rules of the Michigan Supreme Court were designed to more closely follow the style of rules used in the Court of Appeals, thereby making practice and procedure more similar in the two courts.

Staff Comment to 2018 Amendment

The amendment of MCR 7.300 *et seq.* would clarify certain practices and procedures in the Supreme Court, especially as they pertain to electronic filing by

parties and electronic notification of the Court's opinions and orders, as well as require only the signed originals of documents to be filed in hard copy.

Rule 7.318.   Voluntary Dismissal

The parties may file with the clerk a stipulation agreeing to the administrative dismissal by the Chief Justice of an application for leave to appeal, an appeal, or an original proceeding in which leave has not been granted or argument has not been directed on the application. The Court may deny the stipulation in a matter scheduled, or to be scheduled, for oral argument if it concludes that the matter should be decided notwithstanding the stipulation. Costs payable to the Court may be imposed on the parties in the order granting the stipulated dismissal if the case has been scheduled for oral argument and the stipulation is received less than 21 days before the first day of the monthly session.

[Adopted May 27, 2015, effective September 1, 2015, 498 Mich. Amended September 27, 2017, effective January 1, 2018, 501 Mich.]

Comments

Staff Comment to 2015 Adoption

These new rules of the Michigan Supreme Court were designed to more closely follow the style of rules used in the Court of Appeals, thereby making practice and procedure more similar in the two courts.

Staff Comment to 2017 Amendment

The amendment of MCR 7.300 *et seq.* would clarify certain practices and procedures in the Supreme Court, especially as they pertain to electronic filing by parties and electronic notification of the Court's opinions and orders, as well as require only the signed originals of documents to be filed in hard copy.

Rule 7.319   Taxation of Costs;   Fees

(A) Rules Applicable. The procedure for taxation of costs in the Supreme Court is as provided in MCR 7.219.

(B) Expenses Taxable. Unless the Court otherwise orders, a prevailing party may tax only the reasonable costs incurred in the Supreme Court, including an amount not to exceed $2 per original page for the necessary expense of printing the briefs and appendixes required by these rules.

(C) Fees Paid to Clerk. The Clerk shall collect the following fees, which may be taxed as costs when costs are allowed by the Court:

(1) $375 for an application for leave to appeal or an original action;

(2) $150 for a motion for immediate consideration or a motion to expedite appeal, except that a prosecuting attorney is exempt from paying a fee under this subdivision in an appeal arising out of a criminal proceeding if the defendant is represented by a court-appointed lawyer;

(3) $75 for all other motions;

(4) 50 cents per page for a certified copy of a paper from a public record or a copy of an opinion;

(5) $5 for certified docket entries; and

(6) $1 for certification of a copy presented to the clerk.

A party who is unable to pay a filing fee may ask the Court to waive the fee by filing a motion and an affidavit disclosing the reason for that inability. There is no fee for filing the motion but, if the motion is denied, the party must pay the fee for the underlying filing.

(D) Violation of Rules. The Supreme Court may impose costs on a party or an attorney when in its discretion they should be assessed for violation of these rules.

[Adopted May 27, 2015, effective September 1, 2015, 498 Mich. Amended September 27, 2017, effective January 1, 2018, 501 Mich.]

Comments

Staff Comment to 2015 Adoption

These new rules of the Michigan Supreme Court were designed to more closely follow the style of rules used in the Court of Appeals, thereby making practice and procedure more similar in the two courts.

Staff Comment to 2018 Amendment

The amendment of MCR 7.300 *et seq.* would clarify certain practices and procedures in the Supreme Court, especially as they pertain to electronic filing by parties and electronic notification of the Court's opinions and orders, as well as require only the signed originals of documents to be filed in hard copy

CHAPTER 8. ADMINISTRATIVE RULES OF COURT
Effective March 1, 1985

SUBCHAPTER 8.100 GENERAL ADMINISTRATIVE ORDERS

Rule 8.101 Applicability of Administrative Rules

The administrative rules of subchapter 8.100 apply to all courts established by the constitution and laws of Michigan, unless a rule otherwise provides.

[Adopted effective March 1, 1985.]

Comments

Staff Comment to 1985 Adoption

MCR 8.101 is substantially the same as GCR 1963, 934.

Rule 8.103 State Court Administrator

The state court administrator, under the Supreme Court's supervision and direction, shall:

(1) supervise and examine the administrative methods and systems employed in the offices of the courts, including the offices of the clerks and other officers, and make recommendations to the Supreme Court for the improvement of the administration of the courts;

(2) examine the status of court calendars, determine the need for assistance to a court, and report to the Supreme Court;

(3) on receipt of the quarterly reports as provided in MCR 8.110(C)(5), investigate each case in an effort to determine the reason for delays, recommend actions to eliminate delays, and recommend further actions to expedite process to insure speedy trials of criminal cases;

(4) recommend to the Supreme Court the assignment of judges where courts are in need of assistance and carry out the direction of the Supreme Court as to the assignment of judges;

(5) collect and compile statistical and other data, make reports of the business transacted by the courts, and transmit the reports to the Supreme Court so that the statistics and other data may be used in taking proper action in the administration of justice;

(6) prepare and submit budget estimates of state appropriations necessary for the maintenance and operation of the judicial system;

(7) obtain reports from courts, and the judges, clerks, and other officers of the courts, in accordance with rules adopted by the Supreme Court on cases and other judicial business conducted or pending in the courts, and report on them to the Supreme Court;

(8) recommend to the Supreme Court policies for the improvement of the judicial system;

(9) approve and publish forms as required by these rules, and such other recommended forms as the administrator deems advisable; and

(10) attend to other matters assigned by the Supreme Court.

[Adopted effective March 1, 1985. Amended August 23, 1989, effective October 1, 1989; March 28, 1991, effective June 1, 1991, 437 Mich; March 24, 1998, effective April 1, 1998, 456 Mich; January 23, 2007, effective May 1, 2007, 477 Mich; March 14, 2007, effective May 1, 2007, 477 Mich.]

Comments

Staff Comment to 1985 Adoption

MCR 8.103 is comparable to GCR 1963, 901.1.

New item (8) in the list of duties is based on DCR 4005.11 and PCR 901.2. Throughout the rules, the forms previously included in the General Court Rules have been deleted. The state court administrator is directed to approve forms.

Staff Comment to 1989 Amendment

MCR 8.103 has been amended [effective October 1, 1989] by the addition of a new item (3) incorporating a provision previously located in the former speedy trial rule, MCR 6.109(D). Former items (3)–(9) have been redesignated (4)–(10), but are otherwise unchanged.

Staff Comment to 1991 Amendment

The amendments to MCR 8.103 and 8.109 effective June 1, 1991, authorize the state court administrator to approve equipment for video or audio recording of trial court proceedings and require courts to use only approved equipment if such recordings are used to make the official record of proceedings.

Staff Comment to 1998 Amendment

The amendment of MCR 8.103 makes technical changes necessary in light of statutory amendments and corrects cross-references.

The amendment of MCR 8.103 makes changes in cross-references necessitated by earlier amendments. Some published versions of the rules already include several of these corrections.

Staff Comment to January, 2007 Amendment

These changes clarify that certified electronic operators do not have the authority to prepare transcripts. The amendments also increase the late renewal fee to $100, and remove references to approval by the state court administrator of recording devices, requiring instead that recording systems meet SCAO-approved standards.

Staff Comment to March, 2007 Amendment

This change is required as a result of a previous amendment of MCR 8.110, dated September 12, 2006, in ADM File No. 2004–42, requiring that the Delay in Criminal Proceedings Report be submitted quarterly instead of monthly.

Rule 8.104 Judicial Meetings

(A) Meetings to Be Called by State Court Administrator. The state court administrator, under the Supreme Court's supervision and direction, may call

(1) an annual statewide meeting of the circuit, recorder's, and Court of Appeals judges;

(2) an annual statewide meeting of the probate judges;

(3) an annual statewide meeting of the district judges; and

(4) additional statewide or regional meetings of judges as may be desirable.

(B) Presiding Officer. The Chief Justice of the Supreme Court or another person designated by the Chief Justice shall preside at judicial meetings called by the state court administrator.

(C) Secretary. The state court administrator or deputy administrator acts as secretary at judicial meetings called by the state court administrator.

(D) Purposes. At the meetings, the judges are to

(1) study the organization, rules, methods of procedure, and practice of the judicial system in general;

(2) study the problems of administration confronting the courts and judicial system in general; and

(3) make recommendations for

(a) modifying or ameliorating existing conditions,

(b) harmonizing and improving laws, and

(c) amending the rules and statutes relating to practice and procedure.

[Adopted effective March 1, 1985.]

Comments

Staff Comment to 1985 Adoption

MCR 8.104 is based on GCR 1963, 901.2.

In subrule (A)(1) a provision is added for the statewide annual meeting of the district judges.

Subrules (B) and (C) designate the presiding officer and secretary of the judicial meetings.

Rule 8.105   General Duties of Clerks

(A) Office Hours. The office of the clerk of every court of record must be open, and the clerk or deputy clerk must be in attendance, during business hours on all days except Saturdays, Sundays, and legal holidays, and at other times that the court is in session.

(B) Court Records and Reporting Duties. The clerk of every circuit court shall maintain court records and make reports as prescribed by MCR 8.119.

(C) Notice of Judgments, Orders, and Opinions. The court clerk must deliver, in the manner provided in MCR 2.107, a copy of the judgment, final order, written opinion, or findings entered in a civil action to the attorney or party who sought the order, judgment, opinion or findings. Except where e-Filing is implemented, if the attorney or party does not provide at least one copy when filing a proposed order or judgment, the clerk, when complying with this subrule, may charge the reproduction fee authorized by the court's local administrative order under MCR 8.119(H)(2).

(D) Filing of Assurance of Discontinuance Under MCL 445.870. The clerk of every judicial circuit shall, without charge, receive and file an assurance of discontinuance accepted by the Attorney General under MCL 445.870.

[Adopted effective March 1, 1985. Amended June 16, 1988, effective October 1, 1988, 430 Mich; April 27, 1989, effective July 1, 1989, 432 Mich; October 3, 1991, effective January 1, 1992, 439 Mich. Amended effective November 30, 1999, 461 Mich. Amended September 18, 2019, effective January 1, 2020, 503 Mich.]

Comments

Staff Comment to 1985 Adoption

MCR 8.105 corresponds to GCR 1963, 907.

The provisions of GCR 1963, 907.3 and 907.4 are placed in MCR 8.106 with the other provisions covering money paid into court.

The language of subrule (A) modifies GCR 1963, 907(1) by eliminating the requirement that the clerk be present during business hours on Saturday, except when the court is in session.

The [March 1, 1985] amendment of MCR 8.105(D) adds additional language, based on GCR 502.2, requiring the clerk to retain the original of certain judgments and orders.

Subrule (E) omits the reference found in GCR 1963, 907(7) to MCL 445.801 *et seq.*, because that statute has been repealed.

GCR 1963, 907(6) is omitted. It required the clerk to give notice to federal district courts when the circuit court had disbarred, suspended, or reinstated an attorney.

Staff Comment to 1989 Amendment

This amendment, suggested by the Task Force on Reporting Traffic-Related Offenses, is intended to implement recent statutory changes.

Staff Comment to 1991 Amendment

The 1991 amendment added a subrule to govern the sealing of records. It was based on rules in effect in other jurisdictions, notably New York and Texas. The subrule recognizes the presumption that court records are to be open to the general public, and that the sealing of court records is a matter of public concern. The intent of the rule is to insure consistency and confidence in the way in which such matters are handled.

Staff Comment to 1999 Amendment

The amendment of MCR 8.105 is to accommodate statewide records standards applicable to all courts and all clerks of the courts as developed and recommended by the Michigan Trial Court Case File Management Standards Committee.

Staff Comment to 2020 Amendment

The amendments of MCR 1.109, 2.107, 2.113, 2.116, 2.119, 2.222, 2.223, 2.225, 2.227, 3.206, 3.211, 3.212, 3.214, 3.303, 3.903, 3.921, 3.925, 3.926, 3.931, 3.933, 3.942, 3.950, 3.961, 3.971, 3.972, 4.002, 4.101, 4.201, 4.202, 4.302, 5.128, 5.302, 5.731, 6.101, 6.615, 8.105, and 8.119 and rescission of MCR 2.226 and 8.125 continue the process for design and implementation of the statewide electronic-filing system.

Rule 8.106   Money Paid into Court

(A) When Court Order Required. Except as otherwise provided by law or when the money is in the form of cash bonds, the clerk may not perform services in handling money under MCL 600.2529(1)(f) without a signed order of the court.

(B) Disposition of Interest Earned. If the clerk deposits money in an interest-bearing account, the clerk retains as a fee one-tenth of the interest earned, but not more than $100 each year or part of the year. The fee must be deposited in the county general fund, as required by law. The balance of the interest earned and the principal must be disbursed to the persons entitled to the balance.

(C) Accounts; Records. The accounts of the clerk with the banks in which the money is directed to be deposited must be kept in a single trust fund, with the designation of the rights in the fund appearing on the court's records.

(D) Orders to Pay Out Funds. Orders on the banks for the payment of money out of court are made payable to the order of the person entitled to the money or of that person's duly authorized attorney, and must specify in what action or on what account the money is to be paid out, and the time when the judgment or order authorizing the payment was made.

(E) NSF Checks. A court may assess costs for reasonable expenses incurred for checks returned to the court due to insufficient funds.

[Adopted effective March 1, 1985. Amended effective October 18, 1990, 436 Mich.]

Comments

Staff Comment to 1985 Adoption

MCR 8.106 includes the provisions of GCR 1963, 533 and 907(3) and (4).

Staff Comment to 1990 Amendment

The [October 18,] 1990 amendment added MCR 8.106(E), which permits a court to assess costs when checks are returned because of nonsufficient funds.

Rule 8.107   Statement by Trial Judge as to Matters Undecided

(A) Time. Matters under submission to a judge or judicial officer should be promptly determined. Short deadlines should be set for presentation of briefs and affidavits and for production of transcripts. Decisions, when possible, should be made from the bench or within a few days of submission; otherwise a decision should be rendered no later than 35 days after submission. For the purpose of this rule, the time of submission is the time the last argument or presentation in the matter was made, or the expiration of the time allowed for filing the last brief or production of transcripts, as the case may be.

(B) Report as to Matters Undecided. On the first business day of January, April, July, and October of each year, every trial judge shall file a certified statement with the chief judge in the form prescribed by the state court administrator. The statement shall provide information on all matters pending during the reporting period that were not decided within 56 days from submission. The judge shall state the reason that a decision was not made within 56 days. A report is required regardless of whether there is any case to report. The chief judge shall sign and file, or electronically submit, the statement with the state court administrator.

[Adopted effective March 1, 1985. Amended October 25, 2006, effective January 1, 2006, 474 Mich.]

Comments

Staff Comment to 1985 Adoption

MCR 8.107 is based on GCR 1963, 910. The form of the report is deleted from the rule and will be prescribed by the state court administrator.

Staff Comment to 2006 Amendment

New MCR 8.107(A) requires a judge to decide matters promptly after submission. MCR 8.107(B) requires a judge to submit quarterly reports that include information on all matters pending during the reporting period that were not decided within 56 days of submission.

The amendments of MCR 8.110(C) require monthly reports to the state court administrator in felony cases where there has been a delay of more than 154 days between the order binding a defendant over to circuit court and adjudication in felony cases, or a delay of more than 91 days between a defendant's first appearance on the warrant and complaint, or citation, and adjudication in misdemeanor cases and local ordinance violations that carry criminal penalties.

Rule 8.108   Court Reporters and Recorders

(A) Scope of Rule. This rule prescribes the duties of court reporters and recorders, the procedure for certifying them, the effect of noncertification, objections to certification, and display requirements.

(B) Attendance at Court; Taking Testimony.

(1) The court reporter or recorder shall attend the court sessions under the direction of the court and take a verbatim record of the following:

(a) the voir dire of prospective jurors;

(b) the testimony;

(c) the charge to the jury;

(d) in a jury trial, the opening statements and final arguments;

(e) the reasons given by the court for granting or refusing any motion made by a party during the course of a trial; and

(f) opinions and orders dictated by the court and other matters as may be prescribed by the court.

This subrule does not apply to actions tried in the small claims division of the district court or in the municipal courts. In the probate court proceedings, the reporter or recorder shall take a verbatim record of proceedings as required by law and chapter 5 of these rules.

(2) The court reporter or recorder who begins to record a case shall take the record of the entire case unless he or she shows good cause for failure to do so or is otherwise excused by the court.

(C) Records Kept. All records, as defined in MCR 8.119(F) and regardless of format, that are created and kept by the court reporter or recorder belong to the court, must remain in the physical possession of the court, and are subject to access in accordance with MCR 8.119(H). The court reporter or recorder who takes the testimony on the trial or the hearing of any case shall prefix the record of the testimony of each witness with the full name of the witness and the date and time testimony was taken. At the conclusion of the trial of the case the reporter or recorder shall secure all of the records and properly entitle them on the outside, and shall safely keep them in the court according to the Michigan Trial Court Case File Management Standards. If the court reporter or recorder needs access to the records for purposes of transcribing off-site, the reporter or recorder may take only a reproduction of the original recording, which must be returned to the court upon filing of the transcript.

(D) Transfer of Records; Inspection. If the court reporter or recorder dies, resigns, is removed from office, or leaves the state, records he or she created and kept in each case pursuant to subrule (C) must be transferred to the clerk of the court in which the case was tried. The clerk shall safely keep the records in accordance with the Michigan Trial Court Case File Management Standards and MCR 8.119(F). On order of the court, a transcript shall be made from the records and filed as a part of the public record in the case.

(E) Furnishing Transcript. The court reporter or recorder shall furnish without delay, in legible English, a transcript of the records taken by him or her (or any part thereof) to any party on request. The reporter or recorder is entitled to receive the compensation prescribed in the statute on fees from the person who makes the request.

(F) Filing Transcript.

(1) On order of the trial court, the court reporter or recorder shall make and file in the clerk's office a transcript of his or her records, in legible English, of any civil or criminal case (or any part thereof) without expense to either party; the transcript is a part of the records in the case.

(2) Except when otherwise provided by contract, the court reporter or recorder shall receive from the appropriate governmental unit the compensation specified in the statute on fees for a transcript ordered by a court.

(G) Certification.

(1) *Certification Requirement.*

(a) Only reporters, recorders, or voice writers certified pursuant to this subrule may record or prepare transcripts of proceedings held in Michigan courts or of depositions taken in Michigan pursuant to these rules. This rule applies to the preparation of transcripts of videotaped courtroom proceedings or videotaped or audiotaped depositions, but not to the recording of such proceedings or depositions by means of videotaping. An operator holding a CEO certification under subrule (G)(7)(b) may record proceedings, but may not prepare transcripts.

(b) Proceedings held pursuant to MCR 6.102 or 6.104 need not be recorded by persons certified under this rule; however, transcripts of such proceedings must be prepared by court reporters, recorders, or voice writers certified pursuant to this rule.

(c) An indigent party who is represented by a nonprofit legal aid program providing free civil legal services to the indigent may use persons who are not certified pursuant to this rule to transcribe and file depositions taken by videotaping or audiotaping. Such depositions shall be otherwise prepared and certified in accordance with this rule.

(d) Any person who acts in the capacity of a court reporter or recorder shall not maintain an action in the courts of this state for the collection of compensation for the performance of an act for which certification is required by this rule without alleging and proving that the person was certified under this rule at the time of the performance of the act. "Person" refers to both individuals and the entity or entities for which a court reporter or recorder performs services.

(e) Any other court rule notwithstanding, an objection to the status of a court reporter's or recorder's certification or lack thereof must be placed on the record at the outset of the court proceeding or deposition or that objection is waived. If the objection is waived, the use of transcripts of the court proceeding or deposition for any purpose provided in these rules shall be allowed.

(f) Prior to the beginning of any deposition taken under these rules, the court reporter or recorder must display to all counsel initially present, and to each other person attending the deposition who is not represented by counsel, proof that the reporter or recorder has been certified as required by this rule. Proof of such certification, by certification number, shall also be displayed on the title page and certificate page of each court and deposition transcript and on the stationery and business cards, if any, of each court reporter or recorder required to be certified by this rule.

(2) *Court Reporting and Recording Board of Review.*

(a) The Supreme Court shall appoint a Court Reporting and Recording Board of Review, composed of

(i) a Court of Appeals judge, to be the chairperson;

(ii) a circuit judge;

(iii) a probate judge;

(iv) a district judge;

(v) a court reporter who is an employee of a Michigan court;

(vi) a court recorder who is an employee of a Michigan court;

(vii) a court reporter who is not an employee of a Michigan court;

(viii) a court recorder who is not an employee of a Michigan court; and,

(ix) an attorney.

(b) Appointments to the board shall be for terms of 4 years. A board member may be reappointed to a new term.

Initial appointments may be of different lengths so that no more than 3 terms expire in the same year. The Supreme Court may remove a member at any time.

(c) If a position on the board becomes vacant because of death, resignation, or removal, or because a member is no longer employed in the capacity in which he or she was appointed, the board shall notify the Supreme Court Clerk and the Court shall appoint a successor to serve the remainder of the term.

(d) The state court administrator shall assign a staff person to serve as board secretary.

(3) *Certification by Testing.*

(a) The board shall approve administration of an examination to be offered at least twice each year testing knowledge and speed, and, as to a recorder, operator, or voice writer, familiarity with basic logging techniques and minor repair and maintenance procedures. The board shall determine the passing score.

(b) In order to be eligible for registration for an examination, an applicant must

(i) be at least 18 years of age,

(ii) be a high school graduate, and

(iii) not have been under sentence for a felony for a period of two years.

(c) In addition, an applicant for the certified shorthand reporter examination must have satisfactorily completed a post-high school approved, accredited, or recognized course of study in court reporting and submit documentation of same prior to testing.

(d) An applicant for the CER/CSMR/CEO examination must have satisfactorily completed a post-high school board-approved workshop or course of study, or other board-approved curriculum and submit documentation of same prior to testing.

(e) All CERs/CSMRs/CEOs who are fully certified by December 31, 2005, are exempt from the requirements of subparagraph (d).

(f) The certification fee is $60.

(4) *Reciprocal Certification.* A reporter, recorder, operator, or voice writer certified in another state may apply to the board for certification based on the certification already obtained.

(5) *Temporary Certification.* A new reporter, recorder, operator, or voice writer may receive one temporary certification to enable him or her to work until the results of the next test are released. If the person does not take the test, the temporary certification may not be extended unless good cause is shown. If the person takes the test and fails, the board may extend the temporary certification.

(6) *Renewal, Review, and Revocation of Certification.*

(a) Certifications under this rule must be renewed annually. The fee for renewal is $30. Renewal applications must be filed by August 1. A renewal application filed after that date must be accompanied by an additional late fee of $100. The board may require certified reporters, recorders, operators, and voice writers to submit, as a condition of renewal, such information as the board reasonably deems necessary to determine that the reporter, recorder, operator, or voice writer has used his or her reporting or recording skills during the preceding year.

(b) The board must review the certification of a reporter, recorder, operator, or voice writer who has not used his or her skills in the preceding year, and shall determine whether the certification of such a reporter, recorder, operator, or voice writer may be renewed without the necessity of a certification test.

(c) The board may review the certification of a reporter, recorder, operator, or voice writer and may impose sanctions, including revoking the certification, for good cause after a hearing before the board.

(d) If, after a reporter's, recorder's, operator's, or voice writer's certification is revoked or voided by the board and the reporter, recorder, operator, or voice writer applies to take the certification examination and passes, the board may issue a conditional certification for a prescribed period imposing restrictions or conditions that must be met for continued certification. At the end of the conditional period, an unconditional certification may be issued.

(7) *Designations.* The board shall assign an identification number to each person certified. A court reporter, recorder, operator, or voice writer must place the identification number assigned on his or her communications with the courts, including certificates, motions, affidavits, and transcripts. The board will use the following certification designations:

(a) certified electronic recorder (CER);

(b) certified electronic operator (CEO);

(c) certified shorthand reporter (CSR);

(d) certified voice writer/stenomask reporter (CSMR).

The designations are to be used only by reporters, recorders, operators, or voice writers certified by the board. A reporter, recorder, operator, or voice writer may be given more than one designation by passing different tests.

[Adopted effective March 1, 1985. Amended January 22, 1987, effective April 1, 1987, 428 Mich; March 1, 1990, effective April 1, 1990, 434 Mich; March 28, 1991, effective June 1, 1991, 437 Mich. Amended effective January 28, 1997, 454 Mich. Amended January 28, 1997, effective January 1, 1998, 454 Mich; October 10, 2005, effective January 1, 2006, 474 Mich; January 23, 2007, effective May 1, 2007, 477 Mich; October 31, 2012 effective January 1, 2013, 493 Mich. Amended effective December 14, 2016, 500 Mich.]

Comments

Staff Comment to 1985 Adoption

MCR 8.108 is comparable to GCR 1963, 915.

In subrule (B) language is added excepting actions tried in the small claims division of the district court and in the municipal courts, and providing that probate court proceedings must be recorded as provided by law and the rules in chapter 5. See MCL 600.859.

Subrule (D) modifies GCR 1963, 915.4 by providing that the transfer of a court reporter's records in certain circumstances is to the court clerk, rather than the county clerk.

The temporary provisions for "grandfather" certification of reporters and recorders with more than one year of experience on June 1, 1979, are omitted. See GCR 1963, 915.7(c).

In subrule (G)(7) language from Administrative Order 1977–3 is incorporated, requiring court reporters and recorders to use the identification number assigned by the Court Reporting and Recording Board of Review.

Staff Comment to 1987 Amendment

The January 27, 1987, amendments to MCR 8.108(G) are effective April 1, 1987. The principal changes are as follows:

1. Specifying that only certified reporters and recorders may record and file transcripts of proceedings in Michigan courts. Subrule (G)(1).

2. Expanding the membership of the Board of Review from 5 to 9 persons. Subrule (G)(2)(a).

3. Providing a fixed term for board members and establishing procedures for filling vacancies. Subrule (G)(2)(b) and (c).

4. Modifying the provisions regarding testing by permitting administration of more than 2 tests per year; setting minimum educational and other qualifications for persons seeking to register for a test; and raising the registration fee from $25 to $50. Subrule (G)(3).

5. Establishing a $20 fee for the annual renewal of a certification, and permitting the board to require submission of certain information as a condition of renewal. Subrule (G)(6)(a).

6. Authorizing the board to impose sanctions other than revocation of certification. Subrule (G)(6)(c).

7. Adding a new type of certification—certified electronic operator. Subrule (G)(7)(b). Persons with that certification may record proceedings but may not prepare or file transcripts. Subrule (G)(1).

Staff Comment to 1990 Amendment

The March 1, 1990, amendment of MCR 8.108, effective April 1, 1990, makes two changes. First, new subrule (F)(1)(b) is added, creating an exception to the requirement that only certified reporters or recorders may record proceedings in Michigan courts. The certification requirement will not apply to proceedings in district court under MCR 6.102 and 6.104. It is anticipated that many such proceedings will be conducted at locations other than the normal court facilities and during non-business hours. Requiring the presence of a certified reporter or recorder at all such proceedings might be difficult in some jurisdictions. However, any transcripts of such proceedings must be prepared by a certified reporter or recorder.

Second, the fee for renewal of the certification is raised from $20 to $25.

Another proposal published for comment in 1989, which would extend the certification requirement to persons who record and file depositions, remains under consideration. See 68 Michigan Bar Journal, 567 (June 1989).

Staff Comment to 1991 Amendment

MCR 8.108(G) is amended to change the fees for court reporter and recorder certification and renewal to $60 and $30, respectively, effective June 1, 1991.

Staff Comment to 1997 Amendment

The January 28, 1997, amendment of MCR 8.108(G)(3) eliminates the requirement of Michigan residency for eligibility to take the court reporter/recorder certification tests. This change is related to the amendment of MCR 8.108(G)(1), effective January 1, 1998, to provide that only certified reporters and recorders may record and prepare transcripts of depositions taken in Michigan pursuant to the Michigan Court Rules. The amendment also establishes a penalty for late filing of certification renewal applications.

Staff Comment to 1998 Amendment

The January 28, 1997, amendment of MCR 8.108(G)(1) [effective as to depositions taken on or after January 1, 1998] provides that only reporters and recorders certified by the Court Reporting and Recording Board of Review may record and prepare transcripts of depositions taken in Michigan pursuant to the Michigan Court Rules. The requirement does not apply to the videotaping of depositions, however.

Staff Comment to 2005 Amendment

The amendment of MCR 8.108(G) as recommended by the Michigan Court Reporting and Recording Board of Review, expands the rule's coverage to include operators and voice writers and mandates completion of a board-approved course as a condition for certification of court recorders, operators, and voice writers.

Staff Comment to 2007 Amendment

These changes clarify that certified electronic operators do not have the authority to prepare transcripts. The amendments also increase the late renewal fee to $100, and remove references to approval by the state court administrator of recording devices, requiring instead that recording systems meet SCAO-approved standards.

Staff Comment to 2013 Amendment

The amendments of these rules update the rules making them less "paper" focused and reflecting the use of electronic technology in the way courts process court records. The amendments also clarify and delineate the types of records and other materials maintained by a court, and clarify how access is provided.

Staff Comment to 2016 Amendment

These amendments update cross-references and make other nonsubstantive revisions to clarify the rules.

Rule 8.109   Mechanical Recording of Court Proceedings

(A) Official Record. Trial courts are authorized to use audio and video recording equipment for making a record of court proceedings. If a trial court uses audio or video recording equipment for making the record of court proceedings, it shall use only recording equipment that meet the standards as published by the State Court Administrative Office (i.e., the Standards for Digital Video Recording Systems, the Standards for Digital Audio Recording Systems), or analog equipment that the State Court Administrative Office has approved for use.

(B) Operating Standards. Trial courts that use audio or video recording equipment, whether digital or analog, must adhere to the audio and video recording operating standards published by the State Court Administrative Office.

(C) Other Recordings. On motion of an attorney or of a party appearing on his or her own behalf, a court may permit audio recording of a part or all of a proceeding and may permit photographic recording of visual exhibits. The court may regulate the manner of audio or photographic recording so that it does not disrupt the proceeding. An audio or photographic recording made under this rule may be used solely to assist in the prosecution or defense during the proceeding recorded; it may not be used publicly.

[Adopted effective March 1, 1985. Amended March 28, 1991, effective June 1, 1991, 437 Mich; January 23, 2007, effective May 1, 2007, 477 Mich; January 29, 2014, effective May 1, 2014, 495 Mich.]

Comments

Staff Comment to 1985 Adoption

MCR 8.109 is substantially the same as GCR 1963, 917.

Staff Comment to 1991 Amendment

The amendment of MCR 8.109, effective June 1, 1991, authorizes the state court administrator to approve equipment for video or audio recording of trial court proceedings and requires courts to use only approved equipment if such recordings are used to make the official record of proceedings.

Staff Comment to 2007 Amendment

These changes clarify that certified electronic operators do not have the authority to prepare transcripts. The amendments also increase the late renewal fee to $100, and remove references to approval by the state court administrator of recording devices, requiring instead that recording systems meet SCAO–approved standards.

Staff Comment to 2014 Amendment

The amendments of MCR 8.109 provide explicit authority for courts to use audio and video recording equipment to make a record of court proceedings and require that trial courts using recording equipment follow the standards for recording proceedings that are published by the State Court Administrative Office.

Rule 8.110.   Chief Judge Rule

(A) Applicability. This rule applies to all trial courts: i.e., the judicial circuits of the circuit court, the districts of the district court, the probate court in each county or a probate district established by law, and the municipal courts.

(B) Chief Judge, Chief Judge Pro Tempore, and Presiding Judges of Divisions.

(1) The Supreme Court shall select a judge to serve as chief judge of each trial court. Any judge seeking appointment as chief judge shall complete and submit an application for chief judge on the form available on SCAO's website. The application will describe the criteria for selection of chief judges.

SCAO will also provide an opportunity for any judge or judges to provide information to the Court (which will be kept confidential) regarding the selection of a particular person as chief judge. When SCAO is considering whether to consolidate a specific group of courts under the supervision of a single chief judge, SCAO shall inform and seek input from those courts. SCAO may seek additional information as needed from any court or judge during the appointment process, and will give respectful consideration to all applicants and to any information it receives.

(2) Unless a chief judge pro tempore or presiding judge is named by the Supreme Court, the chief judge shall select a chief judge pro tempore and a presiding judge of any division of the trial court. The chief judge pro tempore and any presiding judges shall fulfill such functions as the chief judge assigns.

(3) The chief judge, chief judge pro tempore, and any presiding judges shall serve a two-year term beginning on January 1 of each even-numbered year, provided that the chief judge serves at the pleasure of the Supreme Court and the chief judge pro tempore and any presiding judges serve at the pleasure of the chief judge. A chief judge shall attend training as required by the State Court Administrator.

(4) The Supreme Court may appoint a judge of another court to serve as chief judge of a trial court.

(a) Apart from the duties of a chief judge described under this rule, the chief probate judge has various obligations imposed by statute. If the chief judge of a probate court is not a probate judge, the senior probate judge shall serve as the chief probate judge in meeting the statutory obligations of a chief probate judge.

(b) The senior probate judge is the judge with the longest service as a probate judge. If two judges have the same number of years of service, the judge who received the highest number of votes in the first election is the senior probate judge.

(C) Duties and Powers of Chief Judge.

(1) A chief judge shall act in conformity with the Michigan Court Rules, administrative orders of the Supreme Court, and local court rules, and should freely solicit the advice and suggestions of the other judges of his or her bench and geographic jurisdiction. If a local court management council has adopted the by-laws described in AO 1998–5 the chief judge shall exercise the authority and responsibilities under this rule in conformity with the provisions of AO 1998–5.

(2) As the presiding officer of the court, a chief judge shall:

(a) call and preside over meetings of the court;

(b) appoint committees of the court;

(c) initiate policies concerning the court's internal operations and its position on external matters affecting the court;

(d) meet regularly with all chief judges whose courts are wholly or partially within the same county;

(e) represent the court in its relations with the Supreme Court, other courts, other agencies of government, the bar, the general public, and the news media, and in ceremonial functions;

(f) counsel and assist other judges in the performance of their responsibilities; and

(g) cooperate with all investigations conducted by the Judicial Tenure Commission.

(3) As director of the administration of the court, a chief judge shall have administrative superintending power and control over the judges of the court and all court personnel with authority and responsibility to:

(a) supervise caseload management and monitor disposition of the judicial work of the court;

(b) direct the apportionment and assignment of the business of the court, subject to the provisions of MCR 8.111;

(c) determine the hours of the court and the judges; coordinate and determine the number of judges and court personnel required to be present at any one time to perform necessary judicial administrative work of the court, and require their presence to perform that work;

(d) supervise the performance of all court personnel, with authority to hire, discipline, or discharge such personnel, with the exception of a judge's secretary and law clerk, if any;

(e) coordinate judicial and personnel vacations and absences, subject to the provisions of subrule (D);

(f) supervise court finances, including financial planning, the preparation and presentation of budgets, and financial reporting;

(g) request assignments of visiting judges and direct the assignment of matters to the visiting judges;

(h) effect compliance by the court with all applicable court rules and provisions of the law; and

(i) perform any act or duty or enter any order necessarily incidental to carrying out the purposes of this rule.

(4) If a judge does not timely dispose of his or her assigned judicial work or fails or refuses to comply with an order or directive from the chief judge made under this rule, the chief judge shall report the facts to the state court administrator who will, under the Supreme Court's direction, initiate whatever corrective action is necessary.

(5) A chief judge may relieve the judge from presiding over some or all of the judge's docket with approval of the state court administrator.

(6) The chief judge of the court in which criminal proceedings are pending shall have filed with the state court administrator a quarterly report listing the following cases in a format prescribed by the state court administrator:

(a) in felony cases in which there has been a delay of more than 301 days between the order binding the defendant over to circuit court and adjudication;

(b) misdemeanor cases and cases involving local ordinance violations that have criminal penalties in which there has been a delay of more than 126 days between the date of the defendant's first appearance on the warrant and complaint or citation and adjudication;

(c) in computing the 126-day and 301-day periods, the court shall exclude periods of delay

(1) between the time a preadjudication warrant is issued and a defendant is arraigned;

(2) between the time a defendant is referred for evaluation to determine whether he or she is competent to stand trial and the receipt of the report; or

(3) during the time a defendant is deemed incompetent to stand trial.

(4) during the time an order is in effect that stays the disposition or proceedings of the case pending interlocutory appellate review.

(7) A chief judge may delegate administrative duties to a trial court administrator or others.

(8) Where a court rule or statute does not already require it, the chief judge may, by administrative order, direct the clerk of the court to provide litigants and attorneys with copies of forms approved by the state court administrator. In addition, except when a court rule or statute specifies that the court or clerk of the court must provide certain forms without charge, the administrative order may allow the clerk to provide the forms at the cost of reproduction to the clerk.

(9) The delegation of such authority to a chief judge does not in any way limit the Supreme Court's authority to exercise "general superintending control over all courts" under Const 1963, art 6, § 4.

(D) Court Hours; Court Holidays; Judicial Absences.

(1) *Court Hours.* The chief judge shall enter an administrative order under MCR 8.112(B) establishing the court's hours.

(2) *Court Holidays; Local Modification.*

(a) The following holidays are to be observed by all state courts, except those courts which have adopted modifying administrative orders pursuant to MCR 8.112(B):

New Year's Day, January 1;

Martin Luther King, Jr., Day, the third Monday in January in conjunction with the federal holiday;

Presidents' Day, the third Monday in February;

Memorial Day, the last Monday in May;

Independence Day, July 4;

Labor Day, the first Monday in September;

Veterans' Day, November 11;

Thanksgiving Day, the fourth Thursday in November;

Friday after Thanksgiving;

Christmas Eve, December 24;

Christmas Day, December 25;

New Year's Eve, December 31;

(b) When New Year's Day, Independence Day, Veterans' Day, or Christmas Day falls on Saturday, the preceding Friday shall be a holiday. When New Year's Day, Independence Day, Veterans' Day, or Christmas Day falls on Sunday, the following Monday shall be a holiday. When Christmas Eve or New Year's Eve falls on Friday, the preceding Thursday shall be a holiday. When Christmas Eve or New Year's Eve falls on Saturday or Sunday, the preceding Friday shall be a holiday.

(c) Courts are encouraged to promulgate a modifying administrative order if appropriate to accommodate or achieve uniformity with the holiday practices of local governmental units regarding local public employees.

(d) With the prior approval of the chief judge, a judge may continue a trial in progress or dispose of judicial matters on any of the listed holidays if he or she finds it to be necessary.

(e) Any action taken by a court on February 12, Lincoln's birthday, or on the second Monday in October, Columbus Day, shall be valid.

(3) *Judicial Vacation Standard.* A judge may take an annual vacation leave of 20 days with the approval of the chief judge to ensure docket coordination and coverage. A judge may take an additional 10 days of annual vacation leave with the approval of the chief judge. A maximum of 15 days of annual vacation unused due to workload constraints may be carried into the next calendar year, if approved by the chief judge. Vacation days do not include:

(a) attendance at Michigan judicial conferences;

(b) attendance, with the chief judge's approval, at educational meetings or seminars;

(c) attendance, with the chief judge's approval, at meetings of judicial committees or committees substantially related to judicial administration of justice;

(d) absence due to illness; or

(e) administrative leave, with the chief judge's approval.

(4) *Judicial Education Leave Standard.* A judge is expected to take judicial education leave of 2 weeks every 3 years to participate in continuing legal education and training at Michigan judicial training programs and nationally recognized judicial education programs, including graduate and refresher courses. Judicial education leave does not include judicial conferences for which attendance is required. The use of judicial education leave approved by the chief judge does not affect a judge's annual leave.

(5) *Judicial Professional Leave Standard.* Judges are encouraged, as part of their regular judicial responsibilities, to participate in professional meetings and conferences that advance the administration of justice or the public's understanding of the judicial system; to serve on commissions and committees of state and national organizations that contribute to the improvement of the law or that advance the interests of the judicial system; and to serve on Supreme Court-appointed or in-house assignments or committees. The use of judicial professional leave approved by the chief judge does not affect a judge's annual leave or education leave.

(6) *Approval of Judicial Absences.* A judge may not be absent from the court without the chief judge's prior approval, except for personal illness. In making the decision on a request to approve a vacation or other absence, the chief judge shall consider, among other factors, the pending caseload of the judge involved. The chief judge shall withhold approval of vacation, judicial education, or judicial professional leave that conforms to these standards only if withholding approval is necessary to ensure the orderly conduct of judicial business. The chief judge shall maintain records of absences to be available at the request of the Supreme Court.

[Adopted effective March 1, 1985. Amended June 27, 1998, effective October 1, 1988, 430 Mich; August 23, 1989, effective October 1, 1989, 432 Mich. Amended effective January 8, 1993, 441 Mich; September 13, 1995, 450 Mich; August 18, 1997, 456 Mich. Amended March 24, 1998, effective April 1, 1998, 456 Mich; February 23, 1999, effective March 1, 1999, 459 Mich. Amended effective November 30, 1999, 461 Mich. Amended October 25, 2005, effective January 1, 2006; February 23, 2006, effective May 1, 2006, 474 Mich; July 20, 2006, effective September 1, 2006, 475 Mich. Amended effective September 12, 2006, 477 Mich. Amended February 1, 2011, effective May 1, 2011, 488 Mich; June 5, 2013, effective September 1, 2013, 494 Mich; December 5, 2018, effective January 1, 2019, 502 Mich; December 18, 2019, effective January 1, 2020, 503 Mich.]

Comments

Staff Comment to 1985 Adoption

MCR 8.110 is based on GCR 1963, 925.

Subrule (F)(2) specifies court holidays, subject to the option of local courts to modify them by local administrative order. The list was formerly found in Administrative Order 1981–1.

The [March 1, 1985] amendment of MCR 8.110(F)(2)(a) changes the designation of Martin Luther King, Jr., Day to conform to the date set by federal statute.

In subrules (G)(1)(a) and (H)(2), the temporary provisions regarding the terms of office of the executive chief judge and the joint executive committee of the third circuit and recorder's courts have been deleted.

Staff Comment to 1988 Amendment

The 1988 amendment allows local flexibility in meeting the needs of pro per litigants and others for approved forms.

Staff Comment to 1989 Amendment

MCR 8.110 has been amended [effective October 1, 1989] by the addition of a new subrule (E)(5) incorporating a provision previously located in the former speedy trial rule, MCR 6.109(C). Former subrules (E)(5) and (6) have been redesignated (E)(6) and (7), but are otherwise unchanged.

Staff Comment to 1993 Amendment

The January 8, 1993, amendment to MCR 8.110(F) makes Christmas Eve and New Year's Eve holidays regardless of the day of the week on which they fall, and specifies when the holidays are to be observed when those days fall on Friday, Saturday, or Sunday.

Staff Comment to 1995 Amendment

In 1995, MCR 7.201(A) was amended to provide that the Supreme Court would appoint the Chief Judge of the Court of Appeals. In 1995, the Supreme Court also consolidated MCR 8.110(B), (C), and (D) into a new MCR 8.110(B), which likewise provided that the chief judges of the trial courts would be appointed by the Supreme Court. MCR 8.110(G) and (H) were repealed. MCR 8.110 was also amended to require chief judges to meet regularly with other chief judges whose courts are wholly or partially in the same county. As indicated in its 1995 order, the Supreme Court took these steps "to facilitate the Court's exercise of its constitutional responsibility to administer and superintend the courts of this state" and to "enhance the Supreme Court's ability to implement sound policies statewide, and assure a greater degree of responsiveness to the leadership that the constitution requires this Court to exercise."

Staff Comment to 1998 Amendment

The amendment of MCR 8.110 makes technical changes necessary in light of statutory amendments and corrects cross-references.

The amendment of MCR 8.110 makes changes in cross-references necessitated by earlier amendments. Some published versions of the rules already include several of these corrections.

Staff Comment to March, 1999 Amendment

The 1999 amendment to MCR 8.110(A) [effective March 1, 1999] eliminates the reference to the Recorder's Court, which was merged with the Third Circuit Court in Wayne County by 1996 Public Act 374, effective October 1, 1997.

In addition, MCR 8.110(D) was amended, effective March 1, 1999, by renumbering MCR 8.110(D)(4) as MCR 8.110(D)(6), amending MCR 8.110(D)(3), and adding new subrules MCR 8.110(D)(4) & (5) to provide standards for judicial leave and for the responsibilities of chief judges for approval of judicial leave.

Staff Comment to November, 1999 Amendment

The amendment of MCR 8.110 is to accommodate statewide records standards applicable to all courts and all clerks of the courts as developed and recommended by the Michigan Trial Court Case File Management Standards Committee.

Staff Comment to 2005 Amendment

New MCR 8.107(A) requires a judge to decide matters promptly after submission. MCR 8.107(B) requires a judge to submit quarterly reports that include information on all matters pending during the reporting period that were not decided within 56 days of submission.

The amendments of MCR 8.110(C) require monthly reports to the state court administrator in felony cases where there has been a delay of more than 154 days between the order binding a defendant over to circuit court and adjudication in felony cases, or a delay of more than 91 days between a defendant's first appearance on the warrant and complaint, or citation, and adjudication in misdemeanor cases and local ordinance violations that carry criminal penalties.

Staff Comment to May, 2006 Amendment

The amendment of MCR 8.110(C)(1), effective May 1, 2006, changes references to AO 1997–6, which was rescinded and replaced by AO 1998–5.

Staff Comment to July, 2006 Amendment

The amendment of MCR 8.110(B)(1) changed the requirement that recommendations for chief judge be submitted no later than October 1 of each odd-numbered year to September 1.

Staff Comment to September, 2006 Amendment

The amendments modify the reporting requirements for the Delay in Criminal Proceedings Report to reflect the 100 percent disposition periods incorporated in Administrative Order No. 2003–7, to make the reporting quarterly instead of monthly, and to eliminate the need to give a reason for delay.

Staff Comment to 2011 Amendment

The amendment of MCR 8.110(C)(5)(c)(4) excludes cases that are stayed during an interlocutory appeal from being included in the group of cases delayed beyond the time guidelines that are required to be reported by the chief judge to the State Court Administrator.

Staff Comment to 2013 Amendment

The amendment of MCR 8.110 updates the rule to reflect today's emphasis on collaboration and local sharing of resources, and the revisions also clarify who is required to fulfill the statutory "chief" probate judge obligations.

Staff Comment to 2018 Amendment

The amendment of MCR 8.110 explicitly provides that a chief judge, with approval of the state court administrator, may relieve a judge from presiding over some or all of the judge's caseload. The delegation of such authority to a chief judge does not in any way limit the Supreme Court's authority to exercise "general superintending control over all courts" under Const 1963, art 6, § 4.

Staff Comment to 2020 Amendment

The amendments of this rule expand and clarify the chief judge selection process, modify the judicial vacation standard as it relates to the number of carryover days and when they may be used, and allow the State Court Administrator to require a chief judge to attend training.

Rule 8.111   Assignment of Cases

(A) Application. The rule applies to all courts defined in subrule 8.110(A), regardless whether the court is acting in the capacity of a trial court or an appellate court.

(B) Assignment. All cases must be assigned by lot, unless a different system has been adopted by local court administrative order under the provisions of subrule 8.112. Assignment will occur at the time the case is filed or before a contested hearing or uncontested dispositional hearing in the case, as the chief judge directs. Civil actions must be assigned within appropriate categories determined by the chief judge. The chief judge may receive fewer assignments in order to perform the duties of chief judge.

(C) Reassignment.

(1) If a judge is disqualified or for other good cause cannot undertake an assigned case, the chief judge may reassign it to another judge by a written order stating the reason. To the extent feasible, the alternate judge should be selected by lot. The chief judge shall file the order with the trial court clerk and have the clerk notify the attorneys of record. The chief judge may also designate a judge to act temporarily until a case is reassigned or during a temporary absence of a judge to whom a case has been assigned.

(2) If a judge is reassigned under a concurrent jurisdiction plan or a family court plan, the successor judge will be assigned all cases filed after the date of reassignment, any pending matters, and postjudgment matters that relate to disposed cases. The chief judge shall submit a local administrative order under MCR 8.112 identifying the revised caseload distribution.

(D) Actions Arising Out of Same Transaction or Occurrence. Subject to subrule 8.111(C),

(1) if one of two or more actions arising out of the same transaction or occurrence has been assigned to a judge, the other action or actions must be assigned to that judge;

(2) if an action arises out of the same transaction or occurrence as a civil action previously dismissed or transferred, the action must be assigned to the judge to whom the earlier action was assigned;

(3) the attorney for the party bringing the other action under subrule (1) or the new action under subrule (2) shall notify the clerk of the fact in writing in the manner prescribed in MCR 1.109(D)(2). An attorney who knowingly fails to do so is subject to disciplinary action.

(4) the chief judge may reassign cases, other than those encompassed by subrule 8.111(D)(1), in order to correct docket control problems resulting from the requirements of this rule.

[Adopted effective March 1, 1985. Amended April 13, 1989, effective July 1, 1989, 432 Mich; March 24, 1998, effective April 1, 1998, 456 Mich; June 5, 2013, effective September 1, 2013, 494 Mich; January 29, 2014, effective May 1, 2014, 495 Mich; August 30, 2018, effective September 1, 2018, 502 Mich. Amended effective August 14, 2019, 503 Mich.]

Comments

Staff Comment to 1985 Adoption

MCR 8.111 is substantially the same as GCR 1963, 926.

Subrule (D)(2) adds an additional circumstance in which an action must be assigned to the judge to whom a previous action involving the same subject matter had been assigned—when the previous action has been transferred to another court.

Staff Comment to 1989 Amendment

The [July 1, 1989] amendment to MCR 8.111 authorizes the chief judge to reassign cases where necessary to correct any workload imbalance resulting from the rule's requirements.

Staff Comment to 1998 Amendment

The amendment of MCR 8.111 makes technical changes necessary in light of statutory amendments and corrects cross-references.

The amendment of MCR 8.111 makes changes in cross-references necessitated by earlier amendments. Some published versions of the rules already include several of these corrections.

Staff Comment to 2013 Amendment

The amendment of MCR 8.111 clarifies that reassignment under a concurrent jurisdiction plan or family court plan is effective on the date of the reassignment, and the successor judge will handle not only the new cases that are filed in that court, but also will preside over any matters then pending and postjudgment matters that arise. A court will be required to submit a local administrative order to the State Court Administrative Office describing the revised caseload distribution when a reassignment occurs.

Staff Comment to 2014 Amendment

This amendment of MCR 8.111 clarifies that the rule applies regardless whether a court is acting in the capacity of a trial court or an appellate court, such as a circuit court considering an appeal of a district court or probate court determination.

Staff Comment to 2018 Amendment

These amendments update cross-references in the rules, and are intended to reflect changes that are necessary as a result of the Court's recent e-Filing rules amendments.

Staff Comment to 2019 Amendment

These amendments update cross-references and make other nonsubstantive revisions to clarify the rules.

Rule 8.112   Local Court Rules; Administrative Orders

(A) Local Court Rules.

(1) A trial court may adopt rules regulating practice in that court if the rules are not in conflict with these rules and regulate matters not covered by these rules.

(2) If a practice of a trial court is not specifically authorized by these rules, and

(a) reasonably depends on attorneys or litigants being informed of the practice for its effectiveness, or

(b) requires an attorney or litigant to do some act in relation to practice before that court, the practice, before enforcement, must be adopted by the court as a local court rule and approved by the Supreme Court.

(3) Unless a trial court finds that immediate action is required, it must give reasonable notice and an opportunity to comment on a proposed local court rule to the members of the bar in the affected judicial circuit, district, or county. The court shall send the rule and comments received to the Supreme Court clerk.

(4) If possible, the number of a local court rule supplementing an area covered by these rules must correspond with the numbering of these rules and bear the prefix LCR. For example, a local rule supplementing MCR 2.301 should be numbered LCR 2.301.

(B) Administrative Orders.

(1) A trial court may issue an administrative order governing only internal court management.

(2) Administrative orders must be sequentially numbered during the calendar year of their issuance. E.g., Recorder's Court Administrative Order Nos. 1984–1, 1984–2.

(3) Before its effective date, an administrative order must be sent to the state court administrator. If the state court administrator directs, a trial court shall stay the effective date of an administrative order or shall revoke it. A trial court may submit such an order to the Supreme Court as a local court rule.

[Adopted effective March 1, 1985.]

Comments

Staff Comment to 1985 Adoption

MCR 8.112 is substantially the same as GCR 1963, 927.

Rule 8.113   Requests for Investigation of Courts

(A) Submission of Request. A request for investigation of a court may be submitted to the state court administrator.

(B) Action by State Court Administrator. The state court administrator may

(1) attempt to informally resolve the dispute,

(2) inform the complainant that an investigation pursuant to this rule is not appropriate under the circumstances,

(3) direct the complainant to the Judicial Tenure Commission or the Attorney Grievance Commission,

(4) request an investigation by the Judicial Tenure Commission or the Attorney Grievance Commission,

(5) refer a matter to the Supreme Court for possible exercise of the Supreme Court's power of superintending control over the judiciary, or

(6) take any other appropriate action.

(C) Cooperation With Inquiry. Judges, court employees, and members of the bar shall cooperate with the state court administrator on request for assistance in inquiries pursuant to this rule.

(D) Review Prohibited; Action Without Prejudice to Other Proceedings. There is no appeal from or review of any action taken by the state court administrator under this rule, but nothing in this rule limits the right of any person to request an investigation by the Judicial Tenure Commission or the Attorney Grievance Commission or to file an action for superintending control in an appropriate court.

[Adopted effective March 1, 1985.]

Comments

Staff Comment to 1985 Adoption

MCR 8.113 substantially revises the provisions of GCR 1963, 930, regarding superintendence of the judiciary.

The new rule provides for informal inquiries by the state court administrator. The formal procedures in GCR 1963, 930 were superseded to a large degree by the creation of the Judicial Tenure Commission and the related provisions under GCR 1963, 932. See subchapter 9.200.

Rule 8.115   Courtroom Decorum; Policy Regarding Use of Cell Phones or Other Portable Electronic Communication Devices

(A) Display of Flags. The flags of the United States and of the State of Michigan must be displayed in a conspicuous place adjacent to the bench at all times when court is in session.

(B) Judicial Robe. When acting in his or her official capacity in the courtroom, a judge shall wear a black robe.

(C) Establishment of a Policy Regarding Portable Electronic Communication Devices.

(1) A facility that contains a courtroom may determine use of electronic equipment in nonjudicial areas of the facility.

(2) The chief judge may establish a policy regarding the use of cell phones or other portable electronic communication devices within the court, except that no photographs may be taken of any jurors or witnesses, and no photographs may be taken inside any courtroom without permission of the court. The policy regarding the use of cell phones or other portable electronic communication devices shall be posted in a conspicuous location outside and inside each courtroom. Failure to comply with this section or with the policy established by the chief judge may result in a fine, including confiscation of the device, incarceration, or both for contempt of court.

[Adopted effective March 1, 1985. Amended August 25, 2009, effective September 1, 2009, 485 Mich.]

Comments

Staff Comment to 1985 Adoption

MCR 8.115 is substantially the same as GCR 1963, 916.

Staff Comment to 2009 Amendment

This rule authorizes a court's chief judge to establish a policy for the use of cell phones and other portable electronic devices in courtrooms, and requires that the policy be posted in a conspicuous location in each courtroom. The amendment also acknowledges that the policy for cell phone and electronic device usage in nonjudicial areas may be set by the operators of the facility in which courtrooms are located. No photographs may be taken of jurors and witnesses, and no photographs are allowed without the judge's permission. Failure to comply with the judge's policy may result in a fine (including confiscation of the device), incarceration, or both for contempt of court.

Rule 8.116 Sessions of Court

(A) Opening Court; Recesses. A definite time must be set for all court sessions, and the judge shall promptly open a session. Recesses shall be taken regularly, but should be short, and court must resume on time.

(B) Participants to Be Punctual. Persons having business with a court must be in court and ready to begin at the opening of the session, and must otherwise be punctual for all court business.

(C) Staggered Scheduling. A judge shall stagger the docket schedule so that an attorney or party may be heard within a time reasonably close to the scheduled time, and, except for good cause, the docket shall be called in order.

(D) Access to Court Proceedings.

(1) Except as otherwise provided by statute or court rule, a court may not limit access by the public to a court proceeding unless

(a) a party has filed a written motion that identifies the specific interest to be protected, or the court *sua sponte* has identified a specific interest to be protected, and the court determines that the interest outweighs the right of access;

(b) the denial of access is narrowly tailored to accommodate the interest to be protected, and there is no less restrictive means to adequately and effectively protect the interest; and

(c) the court states on the record the specific reasons for the decision to limit access to the proceeding.

(2) Any person may file a motion to set aside an order that limits access to a court proceeding under this rule, or an objection to entry of such an order. MCR 2.119 governs the proceedings on such a motion or objection. If the court denies the motion or objection, the moving or objecting person may file an application for leave to appeal in the same manner as a party to the action.

(3) Whenever the court enters an order limiting access to a proceeding that otherwise would be public, the court must forward a copy of the order to the State Court Administrative Office.

[Adopted effective March 1, 1985. Amended January 29, 1987, effective April 1, 1987, 428 Mich. Amended effective November 30, 1999, 461 Mich. Amended January 22, 2003, effective May 1, 2003, 467 Mich.]

Comments

Staff Comment to 1985 Adoption

MCR 8.116 is a new rule based on former Genesee circuit local court rule 18, covering the conduct of sessions of court.

Staff Comment to 1987 Amendment

The [April 1, 1987] amendment provides for a procedure to challenge either a request to limit access of the public to court proceedings or records of the proceedings that are otherwise public, or an order which has entered accomplishing such a purpose.

Staff Comment to 1999 Amendment

The amendment of MCR 8.116 is to accommodate statewide records standards applicable to all courts and all clerks of the courts as developed and recommended by the Michigan Trial Court Case File Management Standards Committee.

Staff Comment to 2003 Amendment

The January 22, 2003, amendment of MCR 8.116, effective May 1, 2003, is based on a recommendation from the Michigan Press Association and is similar to the "sealed record rules" found in MCR 8.119(F).

Rule 8.117. Case Classification Codes

Use of Case–Type Code. As required by MCR 1.109(D)(1)(b)(iii), the person filing a case initiating document must assign one case-type code from a list provided by the State Court Administrator according to the principal subject matter of the action (not the nature of the proceedings), and shall provide this code with other case initiation information required by MCR 1.109(D)(2). The case code must be included in the caption of all other documents filed in the case. *

[Adopted effective March 1, 1985. Amended January 22, 1987, effective March 1, 1987, 428 Mich; April 6, 1987, effective June 1, 1987, 428 Mich; March 25, 1998, effective July 1, 1988, 430 Mich; March 23, 1989, effective March 30, 1989, 432 Mich; April 11, 1991, effective May 1, 1991, 437 Mich; November 13, 1991, effective January 1, 1992, 439 Mich; June 18, 1992, effective September 1, 1992, 440 Mich; December 3, 1992, effective February, 1, 1993, August 26, 1994, effective September 12, 1994, 446 Mich; July 13, 1995, effective September 1, 1995, 449 Mich; May 20, 1997, effective June 1, 1997, 454 Mich. Amended effective September 1, 1997; May 20, 1999, 456 Mich; May 23, 2000, 462 Mich. Amended May 30, 2018, effective September 1, 2018, 501 Mich.]

* Publisher's Note: *For a list of Case-Type Codes, please reference the "Case File Management Standards" found in the Michigan Court Rules, preceding Chapter 1.*

Comments

Staff Comment to 1985 Adoption

MCR 8.117 incorporates the case information control system most recently adopted in Administrative Order 1983–5. The rule covering the captioning of pleadings, MCR 2.113(C)(1)(d), requires the use of the case-type codes.

The [March 1, 1985] amendment of MCR 8.117 modifies the list of case-type codes, adding codes applicable to district and probate court.

Staff Comment to 1989 Amendment

[The March 30, 1989, amendment added (25) and (26) to subrule (D).] These two case-type codes were added to this list in response to 1988 PA 490 and 1988 PA 403.

Staff Comment to 1991 Amendment

The [May 1,] 1991 amendments of MCR 8.117(B)(3) and (C)(1) were made at the suggestion of the Negligence Law Section Council of the State Bar. The amendments of (B)(4) and (D) were made at the suggestion of the State Court Administrative Office.

Staff Comment to 1992 Amendment

The November 13, 1991 amendments to MCR 8.117(C) [effective January 1, 1992] were made at the suggestion of the Michigan District Judges Association and the State Court Administrative Office in response to 1991 PA 93, 1991 PA 95, 1991 PA 98 and 1991 PA 99.

Staff Comment to 1994 Amendment

The August 26, 1994 amendment changes several case classification code subrules in light of 1994 PA 12.

Staff Comment to June, 1997 Amendment

May 20, 1997, these amendments [effective June 1, 1997] are made to provide for the implementation of the Uniform Interstate Family Support Act, which is effective June 1, 1997. This Act was adopted so that Michigan would be in compliance with the federal Personal Responsibility and Work Opportunity Act of 1996.

The amendment provides new case classification codes for actions filed pursuant to the Uniform Interstate Family Support Act.

Staff Comment to September, 1997 Amendment

MCR 8.117 is designed to implement the statutes providing for the issuance of personal protection orders. See MCL 600.2950, MCL 600.2950a.

Staff Comment to 2000 Amendment

These amendments [effective May 23, 2000] are made to allow for flexibility in making changes to case classification codes. Case classification codes are used principally for administrative purposes by trial courts and the State Court Administrator for collecting management information regarding case and for identifying the administrative processing of cases.

The notice requirements of MCR 1.201 were dispensed with in order that several changes in case classification codes required with the implementation of the Estates and Protected Individuals Code, MCL 700.1101 *et seq.* could be implemented immediately by the State Court Administrator. The Estates and Protected Individuals Code became effective April 1, 2000. This matter will be included on the Court's future public hearing agenda for the purpose of receiving comments.

The State Court Administrator will incorporate case classification codes in the Case File Management Standards maintained by that office. The State Court Administrator will publish a revised case classification code schedule immediately, and will periodically publish case classification codes for the benefit of the public and the bar.

Staff Comment to 2018 Amendment

The amendments in this order are intended to begin moving trial courts toward a statewide uniform e-Filing process. In addition, the order moves existing language into MCR 1.109 as a way to, for the first time, include most filing requirements in one single rule, instead of scattered in various rules. The order largely mirrors the administrative orders that most e-Filing pilot projects have operated under, but contains some significant new provisions. For example, courts are required to maintain documents in an electronic document management system, and the electronic record is the official court record.

Rule 8.119. Court Records and Reports; Duties of Clerks

Rule 8.119 effective until December 31, 2020. See following Rule 8.119, effective January 1, 2021.

(A) Applicability. This rule applies to all records in every trial court. For purposes of this rule, records are as defined in MCR 1.109, MCR 3.218, MCR 3.903, and MCR 8.119(D)–(G).

(B) Records Standards. Trial courts shall comply with the records standards in this rule, MCR 1.109, and as prescribed by the Michigan Supreme Court.

(C) Filing of Documents and Other Materials. The clerk of the court shall process and maintain documents filed with the court as prescribed by Michigan Court Rules and the Michigan Trial Court Records Management Standards and all filed documents must be file stamped in accordance with these standards. The clerk of the court may only reject documents that do not comply with MCR 1.109(D)(1) and (2), are not signed in accordance with MCR 1.109(E), or are not accompanied by a required filing fee or a request for fee waiver, unless already waived or suspended by court order.

(D) Records Kept by the Clerk of the Court. The clerk of the court shall maintain the following case records in accordance with the Michigan Trial Court Records Management Standards. Documents and other materials made nonpublic or confidential by court rule, statute, or order of the court pursuant to subrule (I) must be designated accordingly and maintained to allow only authorized access. In the event of transfer or appeal of a case, every rule, statute, or order of the court under subrule (I) that makes a document or other materials in that case nonpublic or confidential applies uniformly to every court in Michigan, irrespective of the court in which the document or other materials were originally filed.

(1) *Case History and Case Files.* The clerk shall maintain records of each case consisting of case history (known as a register of actions) and, except for civil infractions, a case file in such form and style as may be prescribed by the State Court Administrative Office. Each case shall be assigned a case number on receipt of a case initiating document. The case number shall comply with MCR 1.109(D)(1)(b)(iii). In addition to the case number, a separate petition number shall be assigned to each petition filed under the juvenile code, MCL 712A.1 *et seq.*, as required under MCR 1.109(D)(1)(d). The case number (and petition number if applicable) shall be recorded in the court's automated case management system

and on the case file. The records shall include the following characteristics:

(a) Case History. The clerk shall create and maintain a case history of each case, known as a register of actions, in the court's automated case management system. The automated case management system shall be capable of chronologically displaying the case history for each case and shall also be capable of searching a case by number or party name (previously known as numerical and alphabetical indices) and displaying the case number, date of filing, names of parties, and names of any attorneys of record. The case history shall contain both pre- and post-judgment information and shall, at a minimum, consist of the data elements prescribed in the Michigan Trial Court Records Management Standards. Each entry shall be brief, but shall show the nature of each item filed, each order or judgment of the court, and the returns showing execution. Each entry shall be dated with not only the date of filing, but with the date of entry and shall indicate the person recording the action.

(b) Case File. The clerk of the court shall maintain a file of each action, bearing the case number assigned to it, for all pleadings, process, written opinions and findings, orders, and judgments filed in the action, and any other materials prescribed by court rule, statute, or court order to be filed with the clerk of the court. If case file records are maintained separately from the case files, the clerk shall maintain them as prescribed by the Michigan Trial Court Records Management Standards.

(2) *Calendars.* The clerk may maintain calendars of actions. A calendar is a schedule of cases ready for court action that identifies times and places of activity.

(3) *Abolished Records.*

(a) Journals. Except for recording marriages, journals shall not be maintained.

(b) Dockets. Case history replaces a docket. Wherever these rules or applicable statutes require entries on a docket, those entries shall be entered in the court's automated case management system.

(4) *Official Court Record.* There is only one official court record, regardless whether original or suitable-duplicate and regardless of the medium. Suitable–duplicate is defined in the Michigan Trial Court Records Management Standards. Documents electronically filed with the court or generated electronically by the court are original records and are the official court record. A paper printout of any electronically filed or generated document is a copy and is a nonrecord for purposes of records retention and disposal.

(E) Other Case Records. The clerk or other persons designated by the chief judge of the court shall maintain in the manner prescribed by these rules, other materials filed with or handled by the court for purposes of case processing, including but not limited to wills filed for safekeeping, case evaluations, exhibit logs, presentence reports, probation files, problem-solving court treatment files, financial statements for collections, and friend of the court records.

(F) Court Recordings, Log Notes, Jury Seating Charts, and Media. Court recordings, log notes, jury seating charts, and all other records such as tapes, backup tapes, discs, and any other medium used or created in the making of a record of proceedings and kept pursuant to MCR 8.108 are court records and are subject to access in accordance with subrule (H)(2)(b).

(G) Other Court Records. All court records not included in subrules (D), (E), and (F) are considered administrative and fiscal records or nonrecord materials and are not subject to public access under subrule (H). These records are defined in the approved records retention and disposal schedule for trial courts.

(H) Access to Records. Except as otherwise provided in subrule (F), only case records as defined in subrule (D) are public records, subject to access in accordance with these rules. The clerk shall not permit any case record to be taken from the court without the order of the court. A court may provide access to the public case history information through a publicly accessible website, and business court opinions may be made available as part of an indexed list as required under MCL 600.8039; however, all other public information in its case files may be provided through electronic means only upon request. The court may provide access to any case record that is not available in paper or digital image, as defined by MCR 1.109(B), if it can reasonably accommodate the request. Any materials filed with the court pursuant to MCR 1.109(D), in a medium for which the court does not have the means to readily access and reproduce those materials, may be made available for public inspection using court equipment only. The court is not required to provide the means to access or reproduce the contents of those materials if the means is not already available.

(1) Unless access to a case record or information contained in a record as defined in subrule (D) is restricted by statute, court rule, or an order entered pursuant to subrule (I), any person may inspect that record and may obtain copies as provided in subrule (J). In accordance with subrule (J), the court may collect a fee for the cost of providing copies.

(2) Every court shall adopt an administrative order pursuant to MCR 8.112(B) to

(a) make reasonable regulations necessary to protect its public records and prevent excessive and unreasonable interference with the discharge of its functions;

(b) establish a policy for whether to provide access for records defined in subrule (F) and if access is to be provided, outline the procedure for accessing those records;

(c) specify the reasonable cost of reproduction of records provided under subrule (J); and

(d) specify the process for determining costs under subrule (J).

(I) Sealed Records.

(1) Except as otherwise provided by statute or court rule, a court may not enter an order that seals courts records, in whole or in part, in any action or proceeding, unless

(a) a party has filed a written motion that identifies the specific interest to be protected,

(b) the court has made a finding of good cause, in writing or on the record, which specifies the grounds for the order, and

(c) there is no less restrictive means to adequately and effectively protect the specific interest asserted.

(2) In determining whether good cause has been shown, the court must consider,

(a) the interests of the parties, including, where there is an allegation of domestic violence, the safety of the alleged or potential victim of the domestic violence, and

(b) the interest of the public.

(3) The court must provide any interested person the opportunity to be heard concerning the sealing of the records.

(4) Materials that are subject to a motion to seal a record in whole or in part must be made nonpublic temporarily pending the court's disposition of the motion.

(5) For purposes of this rule, "court records" includes all documents and records of any nature that are filed with or maintained by the clerk in connection with the action.

(6) A court may not seal a court order or opinion, including an order or opinion that disposes of a motion to seal the record.

(7) Whenever the court grants a motion to seal a court record, in whole or in part, the court must forward a copy of the order to the Clerk of the Supreme Court and to the State Court Administrative Office.

(8) Nothing in this rule is intended to limit the court's authority to issue protective orders pursuant to MCR 2.302(C) without a motion to seal or require that a protective order issued under MCR 2.302(C) be filed with the Clerk of the Supreme Court and the State Court Administrative Office. A protective order issued under MCR 2.302(C) may authorize parties to file materials under seal in accordance with the provisions of the protective order without the necessity of filing a motion to seal under this rule.

(9) Any person may file a motion to set aside an order that disposes of a motion to seal the record, to unseal a document filed under seal pursuant to MCR 2.302(C), or an objection to entry of a proposed order. MCR 2.119 governs the proceedings on such a motion or objection. If the court denies a motion to set aside the order or enters the order after objection is filed, the moving or objecting person may file an application for leave to appeal in the same manner as a party to the action. See MCR 8.116(D).

(J) Access and Reproduction Fees.

(1) A court may not charge a fee to access public case history information or to retrieve or inspect a case document irrespective of the medium in which the case record is retained, the manner in which access to the case record is provided (including whether a record is retained onsite or offsite), and the technology used to create, store, retrieve, reproduce, and maintain the case record.

(2) A court may charge a reproduction fee for a document pursuant to MCL 600.1988, except when required by law or court rule to provide a copy without charge to a person or other entity.

(3) The court may provide access to its public case records in any medium authorized by the records reproduction act, 1992 PA 116; MCL 24.401 to 24.403.

(4) Reproduction of a case document means the act of producing a copy of that document through any medium authorized by the records reproduction act, 1992 PA 116; MCL 24.401 to 24.403.

(a) A court may charge only for the actual cost of labor and supplies and the actual use of the system, including printing from a public terminal, to reproduce a case document and not the cost associated with the purchase and maintenance of any system or technology used to store, retrieve, and reproduce the document.

(b) If a person wishes to obtain copies of documents in a file, the clerk shall provide copies upon receipt of the actual cost of reproduction.

(c) Except as otherwise directed by statute or court rule, a standard fee may be established, pursuant to (H)(2), for providing copies of documents on file.

(5) A court is not required to create a new record out of its existing records. A new record means the compilation of information into a format that does not currently exist or that cannot be generated electronically using predefined formats available through a court's case management system. Providing access to documents or furnishing copies of documents in an existing file does not constitute creation of a new record, even when the output appears in a format different than the format of the original record or document because the output is the result of predefined formats.

(a) A court may create a new record or compilation of records pertaining to case files or case-related information on request, provided that the record created or compiled does not disclose information that would otherwise be confidential or restricted by statute, court rule, or an order entered pursuant to subrule (I).

(b) A court may charge only for the actual cost of labor and supplies and the actual use of the system to develop, generate, and validate the accuracy of a new record and not the cost associated with the purchase and maintenance of any system or technology used to store, retrieve, and reproduce the information or documents for creating a new record.

(c) If a court creates a new record, the clerk shall provide access to the new record upon receipt of the actual cost of creating the record.

(K) Retention Periods and Disposal of Court Records. For purposes of retention, the records of the trial courts include: (1) administrative and fiscal records, (2) case file and other case records, (3) court recordings, log notes, jury seating charts, and recording media, and (4) nonrecord material. The records of the trial courts shall be retained in the medium prescribed by MCR 1.109. The records of a trial court may not be disposed of except as authorized by the records retention and disposal schedule and upon order by the chief judge of that court. Before disposing of records subject to the order, the court shall first transfer to the Archives of Michigan any records specified as such in the Michigan trial courts approved records retention and disposal schedule. An order disposing of court records shall comply with the retention periods established by the State Court Administrative Office and approved by the state court administrator, Attorney General, State Administrative Board, Archives of Michigan, and Records Management Services of the Department of Management and Budget, in accordance with MCL 399.811.

(L) Reporting Duties.

(1) The clerk of every court shall submit reports and records as required by statute and court rule.

(2) The clerk of every court shall submit reports or provide records as required by the State Court Administrative Office, without costs.

[Adopted effective November 30, 1999, 461 Mich. Amended effective September 11, 2002, 467 Mich. Amended February 1, 2005, effective May 1, 2005, 472 Mich; May 18, 2010, effective September 1, 2010, 486 Mich. Amended effective September 28, 2011, 490 Mich. Amended October 31, 2012, effective January 1, 2013, 493 Mich; June 5, 2013, effective September 1, 2013, 494 Mich; May 25, 2016, effective January 1, 2017, 499 Mich; May 16, 2018, effective September 1, 2018, 501 Mich; May 30, 2018, effective September 1, 2018, 501 Mich; September 18, 2019, effective January 1, 2020, 503 Mich.]

Rule 8.119. Court Records and Reports; Duties of Clerks

Rule 8.119 effective January 1, 2021. See previous Rule 8.119, effective until December 31, 2020.

(A) Applicability. This rule applies to all records in every trial court. For purposes of this rule, records are as defined in MCR 1.109, MCR 3.218, MCR 3.903, and MCR 8.119(D)–(G).

(B) Records Standards. Trial courts shall comply with the records standards in this rule, MCR 1.109, and as prescribed by the Michigan Supreme Court.

(C) Filing of Documents and Other Materials. The clerk of the court shall process and maintain documents filed with the court as prescribed by Michigan Court Rules and the Michigan Trial Court Records Management Standards and all filed documents must be file stamped in accordance with these standards. The clerk of the court may only reject documents that do not comply with MCR 1.109(D)(1) and (2), are not signed in accordance with MCR 1.109(E), or are not accompanied by a required filing fee or a request for fee waiver, unless already waived or suspended by court order.

(D) Records Kept by the Clerk of the Court. The clerk of the court shall maintain the following case records in accordance with the Michigan Trial Court Records Management Standards. Documents and other materials made nonpublic or confidential by court rule, statute, or order of the court pursuant to subrule (I) must be designated accordingly and maintained to allow only authorized access. In the event of transfer or appeal of a case, every rule, statute, or order of the court under subrule (I) that makes a document or other materials in that case nonpublic or confidential applies uniformly to every court in Michigan, irrespective of the court in which the document or other materials were originally filed.

(1) *Case History and Case Files.* The clerk shall maintain records of each case consisting of case history (known as a register of actions) and, except for civil infractions, a case file in such form and style as may be prescribed by the State Court Administrative Office. Each case shall be assigned a case number on receipt of a case initiating document. The case number shall comply with MCR 1.109(D)(1)(b)(iii). In addition to the case number, a separate petition number shall be assigned to each petition filed under the juvenile code, MCL 712A.1 *et seq.*, as required under MCR 1.109(D)(1)(d). The case number (and petition number if applicable) shall be recorded in the court's automated case management system and on the case file. The records shall include the following characteristics:

(a) Case History. The clerk shall create and maintain a case history of each case, known as a register of actions, in the court's automated case management system. The automated case management system shall be capable of chronologically displaying the case history for each case and shall also be capable of searching a case by number or party name (previously known as numerical and alphabetical indices) and displaying the case number, date of filing, names of parties, and names of any attorneys of record. The case history shall contain both pre- and post-judgment information and shall, at a minimum, consist of the data elements prescribed in the Michigan Trial Court Records Management Standards. Each entry shall be brief, but shall show the nature of each item filed, each order or judgment of the court, and the returns showing execution. Each entry shall be dated with not only the date of filing, but with the date of entry and shall indicate the person recording the action. Protected personal identifying information entered into the court's case management system as required by MCR 1.109(D)(9)(d) shall be maintained for the purposes for which it was collected and for which its use is authorized by federal or state law or court rule; however, it shall not be included or displayed as case history, including when transferred to the Archives of Michigan pursuant to law.

(b) Case File. The clerk of the court shall maintain a file of each action, bearing the case number assigned to it, for all pleadings, process, written opinions and findings, orders, and judgments filed in the action, and any other materials prescribed by court rule, statute, or court order to be filed with the clerk of the court. If case file records are maintained separately from the case files, the clerk shall maintain them as prescribed by the Michigan Trial Court Records Management Standards.

(2) *Calendars.* The clerk may maintain calendars of actions. A calendar is a schedule of cases ready for court action that identifies times and places of activity.

(3) *Abolished Records.*

(a) Journals. Except for recording marriages, journals shall not be maintained.

(b) Dockets. Case history replaces a docket. Wherever these rules or applicable statutes require entries on a docket, those entries shall be entered in the court's automated case management system.

(4) *Official Court Record.* There is only one official court record, regardless whether original or suitable-duplicate and regardless of the medium. Suitable–duplicate is defined in the Michigan Trial Court Records Management Standards. Documents electronically filed with the court or generated electronically by the court are original records and are the official court record. A paper printout of any electronically filed or generated document is a copy and is a nonrecord for purposes of records retention and disposal.

(E) Other Case Records. The clerk or other persons designated by the chief judge of the court shall maintain in the manner prescribed by these rules, other materials filed with or handled by the court for purposes of case processing, including but not limited to wills filed for safekeeping, case evaluations, exhibit logs, presentence reports, probation files, problem-solving court treatment files, financial statements for collections, and friend of the court records.

(F) Court Recordings, Log Notes, Jury Seating Charts, and Media. Court recordings, log notes, jury seating charts,

and all other records such as tapes, backup tapes, discs, and any other medium used or created in the making of a record of proceedings and kept pursuant to MCR 8.108 are court records and are subject to access in accordance with subrule (H)(2)(b).

(G) Other Court Records. All court records not included in subrules (D), (E), and (F) are considered administrative and fiscal records or nonrecord materials and are not subject to public access under subrule (H). These records are defined in the approved records retention and disposal schedule for trial courts.

(H) Access to Records. Except as otherwise provided in subrule (F), only case records as defined in subrule (D) are public records, subject to access in accordance with these rules. The clerk shall not permit any case record to be taken from the court without the order of the court. A court may provide access to the public case history information through a publicly accessible website, and business court opinions may be made available as part of an indexed list as required under MCL 600.8039. If a request is made for a public record that is maintained electronically, the court is required to provide a means for access to that record; however, the documents cannot be provided through a publicly accessible website if protected personal identifying information has not been redacted from those documents. The court may provide access to any case record that is not available in paper or digital image, as defined by MCR 1.109(B), if it can reasonably accommodate the request. Any materials filed with the court pursuant to MCR 1.109(D), in a medium for which the court does not have the means to readily access and reproduce those materials, may be made available for public inspection using court equipment only. The court is not required to provide the means to access or reproduce the contents of those materials if the means is not already available.

(1) Unless access to a case record or information contained in a record as defined in subrule (D) is restricted by statute, court rule, or an order entered pursuant to subrule (I), any person may inspect that record and may obtain copies as provided in subrule (J). In accordance with subrule (J), the court may collect a fee for the cost of providing copies.

(2) Every court shall adopt an administrative order pursuant to MCR 8.112(B) to

(a) make reasonable regulations necessary to protect its public records and prevent excessive and unreasonable interference with the discharge of its functions;

(b) establish a policy for whether to provide access for records defined in subrule (F) and if access is to be provided, outline the procedure for accessing those records;

(c) specify the reasonable cost of reproduction of records provided under subrule (J); and

(d) specify the process for determining costs under subrule (J).

(I) Sealed Records.

(1) Except as otherwise provided by statute or court rule, a court may not enter an order that seals courts records, in whole or in part, in any action or proceeding, unless

(a) a party has filed a written motion that identifies the specific interest to be protected,

(b) the court has made a finding of good cause, in writing or on the record, which specifies the grounds for the order, and

(c) there is no less restrictive means to adequately and effectively protect the specific interest asserted.

(2) In determining whether good cause has been shown, the court must consider,

(a) the interests of the parties, including, where there is an allegation of domestic violence, the safety of the alleged or potential victim of the domestic violence, and

(b) the interest of the public.

(3) The court must provide any interested person the opportunity to be heard concerning the sealing of the records.

(4) Materials that are subject to a motion to seal a record in whole or in part must be made nonpublic temporarily pending the court's disposition of the motion.

(5) For purposes of this rule, "court records" includes all documents and records of any nature that are filed with or maintained by the clerk in connection with the action.

(6) A court may not seal a court order or opinion, including an order or opinion that disposes of a motion to seal the record.

(7) Whenever the court grants a motion to seal a court record, in whole or in part, the court must forward a copy of the order to the Clerk of the Supreme Court and to the State Court Administrative Office.

(8) Nothing in this rule is intended to limit the court's authority to issue protective orders pursuant to MCR 2.302(C) without a motion to seal or require that a protective order issued under MCR 2.302(C) be filed with the Clerk of the Supreme Court and the State Court Administrative Office. A protective order issued under MCR 2.302(C) may authorize parties to file materials under seal in accordance with the provisions of the protective order without the necessity of filing a motion to seal under this rule.

(9) Any person may file a motion to set aside an order that disposes of a motion to seal the record, to unseal a document filed under seal pursuant to MCR 2.302(C), or an objection to entry of a proposed order. MCR 2.119 governs the proceedings on such a motion or objection. If the court denies a motion to set aside the order or enters the order after objection is filed, the moving or objecting person may file an application for leave to appeal in the same manner as a party to the action. See MCR 8.116(D).

(J) Access and Reproduction Fees.

(1) A court may not charge a fee to access public case history information or to retrieve or inspect a case document irrespective of the medium in which the case record is retained, the manner in which access to the case record is provided (including whether a record is retained onsite or offsite), and the technology used to create, store, reproduce, and maintain the case record.

(2) A court may charge a reproduction fee for a document pursuant to MCL 600.1988, except when required by law or court rule to provide a copy without charge to a person or other entity.

(3) The court may provide access to its public case records in any medium authorized by the records reproduction act, 1992 PA 116; MCL 24.401 to 24.403.

(4) Reproduction of a case document means the act of producing a copy of that document through any medium authorized by the records reproduction act, 1992 PA 116; MCL 24.401 to 24.403.

(a) A court may charge only for the actual cost of labor and supplies and the actual use of the system, including printing from a public terminal, to reproduce a case document and not the cost associated with the purchase and maintenance of any system or technology used to store, retrieve, and reproduce the document.

(b) If a person wishes to obtain copies of documents in a file, the clerk shall provide copies upon receipt of the actual cost of reproduction.

(c) Except as otherwise directed by statute or court rule, a standard fee may be established, pursuant to (H)(2), for providing copies of documents on file.

(5) A court is not required to create a new record out of its existing records. A new record means the compilation of information into a format that does not currently exist or that cannot be generated electronically using predefined formats available through a court's case management system. Providing access to documents or furnishing copies of documents in an existing file does not constitute creation of a new record, even when the output appears in a format different than the format of the original record or document because the output is the result of predefined formats.

(a) A court may create a new record or compilation of records pertaining to case files or case-related information on request, provided that the record created or compiled does not disclose information that would otherwise be confidential or restricted by statute, court rule, or an order entered pursuant to subrule (I).

(b) A court may charge only for the actual cost of labor and supplies and the actual use of the system to develop, generate, and validate the accuracy of a new record and not the cost associated with the purchase and maintenance of any system or technology used to store, retrieve, and reproduce the information or documents for creating a new record.

(c) If a court creates a new record, the clerk shall provide access to the new record upon receipt of the actual cost of creating the record.

(K) Retention Periods and Disposal of Court Records. For purposes of retention, the records of the trial courts include: (1) administrative and fiscal records, (2) case file and other case records, (3) court recordings, log notes, jury seating charts, and recording media, and (4) nonrecord material. The records of the trial courts shall be retained in the medium prescribed by MCR 1.109. The records of a trial court may not be disposed of except as authorized by the records retention and disposal schedule and upon order by the chief judge of that court. Before disposing of records subject to the order, the court shall first transfer to the Archives of Michigan any records specified as such in the Michigan trial courts approved records retention and disposal schedule. An order disposing of court records shall comply with the retention periods established by the State Court Administrative Office and approved by the state court administrator, Attorney General, State Administrative Board, Archives of Michigan, and Records Management Services of the Department of Management and Budget, in accordance with MCL 399.811.

(L) Reporting Duties.

(1) The clerk of every court shall submit reports and records as required by statute and court rule.

(2) The clerk of every court shall submit reports or provide records as required by the State Court Administrative Office, without costs.

[Adopted effective November 30, 1999, 461 Mich. Amended effective September 11, 2002, 467 Mich. Amended February 1, 2005, effective May 1, 2005, 472 Mich; May 18, 2010, effective September 1, 2010, 486 Mich. Amended effective September 28, 2011, 490 Mich. Amended October 31, 2012, effective January 1, 2013, 493 Mich; June 5, 2013, effective September 1, 2013, 494 Mich; May 25, 2016, effective January 1, 2017, 499 Mich; May 16, 2018, effective September 1, 2018, 501 Mich; May 30, 2018, effective September 1, 2018, 501 Mich; September 18, 2019, effective January 1, 2020, 503 Mich; May 22, 2019, effective January 1, 2021, 502 Mich.]

Comments

Staff Comment to 1999 Adoption

The adoption of MCR 8.119 is to accommodate statewide records standards applicable to all courts and all clerks of the courts as developed and recommended by the Michigan Trial Court Case File Management Standards Committee.

Staff Comment to 2002 Amendment

The September 11, 2002, amendments of MCR 3.206, 3.214, 3.705, 3.706, 3.708, 5.982, and 8.119, which were given immediate effect, are related to the group of domestic violence statutes enacted in December 2001 that took effect April 1, 2002.

MCR 8.119(F) is amended to conform to 2001 PA 205, which directs that when a motion to seal court records involves allegations of domestic violence, the court is to consider the safety of the potential victim in ruling on the motion.

Staff Comment to 2005 Amendment

The February 1, 2005, effective May 1, 2005, amendments were recommended by the Court of Appeals Record Production Work Group.

The amendment of MCR 8.119(D)(1)(c) expedites the ordering of transcripts in all appeals by requiring the circuit court's register of actions to include a notation as to whether a hearing was held on the record, and the name and certification number of the court reporter or recorder responsible for transcribing the hearing. The subrule is also divided for the ease of the reader.

Staff Comment to 2010 Amendment

These amendments of MCR 7.211, 7.313, and 8.119 clarify that materials filed with a trial court, with the Court of Appeals, or with the Supreme Court that relate to a motion to seal a record are nonpublic until the court disposes of the motion.

Staff Comment to 2011 Amendment

The above noted changes are minor revisions of the rules that have been recommended to the Court to correct cross references and to reflect other technical changes.

Staff Comment to January, 2013 Amendment

The amendments of these rules update the rules making them less "paper" focused and reflecting the use of electronic technology in the way courts process court records. The amendments also clarify and delineate the types of records and other materials maintained by a court, and clarify how access is provided.

Staff Comment to September, 2013 Amendment

The amendments of MCR 2.112 provide a means to identify business court cases and the placement of those matters on the business court docket. The amendment of MCR 8.119 allows business court opinions to be published.

Staff Comment to 2017 Amendment

The amendments of MCR 3.925, 8.119, and 8.302 and the adoption of MCR 5.133 are an expected progression in the development of policies and procedures that standardize management of court records and provide a uniform basis for developing parameters on the use of technology in creating, accessing, routing, maintaining, and disposing of court records. These particular amendments will assist in implementing the goals of 2013 PA 199 and 201 and improving the

policies and procedures adopted by the Court in 2012 under Administrative File No. 2006–47.

Staff Comment to First September, 2018 Amendment

The amendment of MCR 8.119 clarifies the procedure for sealing files and better accommodates protective orders issued under MCR 2.302 by clarifying that a protective order may authorize parties to file materials without also filing a motion to seal.

Staff Comment to Second September, 2018 Amendment

The amendments in this order are intended to begin moving trial courts toward a statewide uniform e-Filing process. In addition, the order moves existing language into MCR 1.109 as a way to, for the first time, include most filing requirements in one single rule, instead of scattered in various rules. The order largely mirrors the administrative orders that most e-Filing pilot projects have operated under, but contains some significant new provisions. For example, courts are required to maintain documents in an electronic document management system, and the electronic record is the official court record.

Staff Comment to 2020 Amendment

The amendments of MCR 1.109, 2.107, 2.113, 2.116, 2.119, 2.222, 2.223, 2.225, 2.227, 3.206, 3.211, 3.212, 3.214, 3.303, 3.903, 3.921, 3.925, 3.926, 3.931, 3.933, 3.942, 3.950, 3.961, 3.971, 3.972, 4.002, 4.101, 4.201, 4.202, 4.302, 5.128, 5.302, 5.731, 6.101, 6.615, 8.105, and 8.119 and rescission of MCR 2.226 and 8.125 continue the process for design and implementation of the statewide electronic-filing system.

Staff Comment to 2021 Amendment

The amendments make certain personal identifying information nonpublic and clarify the process regarding redaction.

Rule 8.120   Law Students and Recent Graduates; Participation in Legal Aid Clinics, Defender Offices, and Legal Training Programs

(A) Legal Aid Clinics; Defender Offices. Effective legal service for each person in Michigan, regardless of that person's ability to pay, is important to the directly affected person, to our court system, and to the whole citizenry. Law students and recent law graduates, under supervision by a member of the state bar, may staff public and nonprofit defender offices, and legal aid clinics that are organized under a city or county bar association or an accredited law school or for the primary purpose of providing free legal services to indigent persons.

(B) Legal Training Programs. Law students and recent law graduates may participate in legal training programs organized in the offices of county prosecuting attorneys, county corporation counsel, city attorneys, the Attorney Grievance Commission, and the Attorney General.

(C) Eligible Students. A student in a law school approved by the American Bar Association who has received a passing grade in law school courses and has completed the first year is eligible to participate in a clinic or program listed in subrules (A) and (B) if the student meets the academic and moral standards established by the dean of that school. For the purpose of this rule, a "recent law graduate" is a person who has graduated from law school within the last year. The student or graduate must certify in writing that he or she has read and is familiar with the Michigan Rules of Professional Conduct and the Michigan Court Rules, and shall take an oath which is reasonably equivalent to the Michigan Lawyer's Oath in requiring at a minimum the promise to: (a) support the Constitution of the United States; (b) support the Constitution of the State of Michigan; (c) maintain the respect due to courts of justice and judicial officers; (d) never seek to mislead a judge or jury by any artifice or false statement of fact or law; (e) maintain the confidence and preserve inviolate the secrets of the client; (f) abstain from all offensive personality; (g) advance no fact prejudicial to the honor or reputation of a party or witness, unless required by the justice of the cause; and (h) in all other respects conduct himself or herself personally and professionally in conformity with the high standards of conduct imposed upon members of the state bar of Michigan.

(D) Scope; Procedure.

(1) A member of the legal aid clinic, in representing an indigent person, Is authorized to advise the person and to negotiate and appear on the person's behalf in all Michigan courts except the Supreme Court. Except as otherwise provided in this rule, the indigent person that will be assisted by the student must consent in writing to the representation. In a situation in which a law student provides short-term, limited-scope legal advice by telephone in the context of a clinical program intended to assist indigent persons offered as part of a law school curriculum, the clinic patron shall be informed that:

(a) the advice provided may be rendered by a law student, and

(b) by proceeding to the consultation following notification that the advice may be provided by a law student, the clinic patron consents to such representation.

(2) Representation must be conducted under the supervision of a state bar member. Supervision by a state bar member includes the duty to examine and sign all pleadings filed. It does not require the state bar member to be present

(a) while a law student or graduate is advising an indigent person or negotiating on the person's behalf, or

(b) during a courtroom appearance of a law student or graduate, except

(i) during an appellate argument or

(ii) in a criminal or juvenile case exposing the client to a penalty of imprisonment.

The supervising attorney shall assume all personal professional responsibility for the student's or graduate's work, and should consider purchasing professional liability insurance to cover the practice of such student or graduate.

(3) A law student or graduate may not appear in a case in a Michigan court without the approval of the judge or a majority of the panel of judges to which the case is assigned. If the judge or a majority of the panel grants approval, the judge or a majority of the panel may suspend the proceedings at any stage if the judge or a majority of the panel determines that the representation by the law student or graduate

(a) is professionally inadequate, and

(b) substantial justice requires suspension.

In the Court of Appeals, a request for a law student or graduate to appear at oral argument must be submitted by motion to the panel that will hear the case. The panel may deny the request or establish restrictions or other parameters for the representation on a case-by-case basis.

(4) A law student or graduate serving in a prosecutor's, county corporation counsel's, city attorney's, Attorney Grievance Commission's, or Attorney General's program may be authorized to perform comparable functions and duties assigned by the prosecuting attorney, county attorney, city attorney, Attorney Grievance Commission attorney, or Attorney General, except that

(a) the law student or graduate is subject to the conditions and restrictions of this rule; and

(b) the law student or graduate may not be appointed as an assistant prosecutor, assistant corporation counsel, assistant city attorney, assistant Attorney Grievance Commission attorney, or assistant Attorney General.

[Adopted effective March 1, 1985. Amended effective May 17, 1993, 442 Mich. Amended June 21, 2000, effective September 1, 2000, 462 Mich; November 16, 2010, effective January 1, 2011, 487 Mich; December 29, 2010, effective January 1, 2011, 487 Mich; April 19, 2011, effective September 1, 2011, 489 Mich.]

Comments

Staff Comment to 1985 Adoption

MCR 8.120 is based on GCR 1963, 921.

Subrule (A) allows recent law graduates to work not only in training programs organized by prosecuting attorneys or city attorneys, but also in legal aid clinics. Compare GCR 1963, 921.1. Subrule (B) defines a "recent law graduate" as a person who has graduated from law school within the last year.

Staff Comment to 1993 Amendment

The only change in the rule [under the May 17, 1993 amendment] is to include references to "county corporation counsel" in appropriate places in the rule.

Staff Comment to 2000 Amendment

The June 21, 2000 amendment of MCR 8.120, effective September 1, 2000, restructured the rule to specifically mention public and nonprofit defender organizations, and to recognize that not all clinics that provide free legal services to indigent persons are funded under the Legal Services Corporation Act, 42 USC 2996, et seq. The amendment also added legal training programs sponsored by the Attorney General to the list of programs in which eligible law school students and recent law school graduates may participate.

Staff Comment to First November, 2010 Amendment

Under this amendment, a law student or recent law graduate who is a member of a legal aid clinic is eligible to appear on behalf of a client in the Court of Appeals. The appearance would require the same protections that now exist, i.e., supervision by a licensed attorney who signs all pleadings, and approval by a majority of the judges of the assigned panel. In addition, the amendments require that an indigent person indicate in writing that he or she consents to the representation by the student, and the student must certify that he or she is familiar with the Michigan Rules of Professional Conduct and the Michigan Court Rules. The amendments further state that the supervising attorney shall assume personal professional liability for the student's or graduate's work, and require students and recent graduates to take an oath similar to the one taken by licensed attorneys. The Court will review the effects of this rule in two years.

Staff Comment to Second December, 2010 Amendment

The amendment of MCR 8.120 further revises the order that was dated November 16, 2010 (effective January 1, 2011), by providing that clinic patrons must be informed that if they are seeking advice as part of a short-term "hotline-type" situation, It may be a law student providing the counsel, and that by proceeding to the consultation following that notification, the clinic patron consents to such representation.

Staff Comment to 2011 Amendment

This proposal contains various amendments of the attorney discipline rules recommended by the Attorney Grievance Commission, which also were thoroughly reviewed by a State Bar of Michigan workgroup at the request of the Court.

Rule 8.121 Contingent Fees in Claims or Actions for Personal Injury, Wrongful Death, and No-Fault Benefits

(A) Allowable Contingent Fee Agreements. In any claim or action for personal injury or wrongful death based upon the alleged conduct of another or for no-fault benefits, in which an attorney enters into an agreement, expressed or implied, whereby the attorney's compensation is dependent or contingent in whole or in part upon successful prosecution or settlement or upon the amount of recovery, the receipt, retention, or sharing by such attorney, pursuant to agreement or otherwise, of compensation which is equal to or less than the fee stated in subrule (B) is deemed to be fair and reasonable.

The receipt, retention, or sharing of compensation which is in excess of such a fee shall be deemed to be the charging of a "clearly excessive fee" in violation of MRPC 1.5(a), unless such fee is received as a result of an award of attorney fees payable pursuant to MCL 500.3148, or other award or sanction made pursuant to statute, court rule, or the common law.

(B) Maximum Fee. The maximum allowable fee for the claims and actions referred to in subrule (A) is one-third of the amount recovered.

(C) Computation.

(1) The amount referred to in subrule (B) shall be computed on the net sum recovered after deducting from the amount recovered all disbursements properly chargeable to the enforcement of the claim or prosecution of the action. In computing the fee, the costs as taxed and any interest included in or upon the amount of a judgment shall be deemed part of the amount recovered.

(2) In the case of a settlement payable in installments, the amount referred to in subrule (B) shall be computed using the present value of the future payments.

(a) If an annuity contract will be used to fund the future payments, "present value" is the actual cost of purchasing the annuity contract. The attorney for the defendant must disclose to the court and the parties the amount paid for the annuity contract, after any rebates or other discounts.

(b) If the defendant will make the future payments directly, "present value" is the amount that an entity of the same financial standing as the defendant would pay for an annuity contract. The court may appoint an independent expert to certify the "present value" as defined in this paragraph. The court may base its findings on the expert's testimony or affidavit.

(D) Agreements for Lower Fees. An attorney may enter into contingent fee arrangements calling for less compensation than that allowed by subrule (B).

(E) Advice to Client. An attorney must advise a client, before entering into a contingent fee arrangement, that attorneys may be employed under other fee arrangements in which the attorney is compensated for the reasonable value of the services performed, such as on an hourly or per diem basis. The method of compensation used by an individual attorney remains the attorney's option, and this rule does not require an attorney to accept compensation in a manner other than that chosen by the attorney.

(F) Agreements to Be in Writing. Contingent fee arrangements made by an attorney with a client must be in writing and a copy provided to the client.

(G) Applicability. This rule does not apply to agreements reduced to writing before May 3, 1975. The one-third provision of subrule (B) applies to contingent fee agreements entered into after July 9, 1981. Earlier agreements are subject to the rule in effect at the time the agreement was made.

[Adopted effective March 1, 1985. Amended February 5, 1998, effective April 1, 1998, 456 Mich; October 8, 2002, effective January 1, 2003, 467 Mich; April 5, 2011, effective September 1, 2011, 489 Mich.]

Comments

Staff Comment to 1985 Adoption

MCR 8.121 is based on GCR 1963, 928.

Subrule (C) adds a provision regarding computation of the maximum fee when the settlement is payable in installments. The computation is to be made using the present value of the future payments.

Staff Comment to 1998 Amendment

The amendment of subrule A adopted February 5, 1998, and effective April 1, 1998, replaced an obsolete cross reference with an updated cross reference to MRPC 1.5(a).

Staff Comment to 2002 Amendment

The October 8, 2002 amendment of MCR 8.121(C), effective January 1, 2003, defines the term "present value" as it is used to calculate a contingent attorney fee when the recovery includes a "structured settlement," a settlement that calls for future installment payments. The amendment was based on a proposal submitted by a special committee of the Civil Division of the Wayne Circuit Court.

Staff Comment to 2011 Amendment

The amendment of MCR 8.121 extends the rule to contingent fee agreements in no-fault cases, except for attorney fees or other sanction awarded pursuant to statute or other authority.

Rule 8.122   Claims by Clients against Attorneys

Attorneys are officers of Michigan's one court of justice and are subject to the summary jurisdiction of the court. The circuit court of the county in which an attorney resides or maintains an office has jurisdiction, on verified written complaint of a client, and after reasonable notice and hearing, to enter an order for the payment of money or for the performance of an act by the attorney which law and justice may require. All courts have like jurisdiction over similar complaints regarding matters arising from actions or proceedings in those courts.

[Adopted effective March 1, 1985.]

Comments

Staff Comment to 1985 Adoption

MCR 8.122 is substantially the same as GCR 1963, 908.

Rule 8.123.   Counsel Appointments; Procedure and Records [Repealed effective September 18, 2019]

Rule 8.125.   Electronic Filing of Citation [Repealed effective January 1, 2020]

Rule 8.126   Temporary Admission to the Bar

(A) Temporary Admission. Except as otherwise provided in this rule, an out of state attorney may seek temporary admission as determined by this subsection. Any person who is licensed to practice law in another state or territory, or in the District of Columbia, of the United States of America, or in any foreign country, and who is not disbarred or suspended in any jurisdiction, and who is eligible to practice in at least one jurisdiction, may be permitted to appear and practice in a specific case in a court, before an administrative tribunal or agency, or in a specific arbitration proceeding in this state when associated with and on motion of an active member of the State Bar of Michigan who appears of record in the case. An out-of-state attorney may be temporarily admitted to practice under this rule in no more than five cases in a 365–day period. Permission to appear and practice is within the discretion of the court, administrative tribunal or agency, or arbitrator and may be revoked at any time for misconduct. For purposes of this rule, an out-of-state attorney is one who is licensed to practice law in another state or territory, or in the District of Columbia, of the United States of America, or in a foreign country and who is not a member of the State Bar of Michigan.

(1) *Procedure.*

(a) Motion. An attorney seeking temporary admission must be associated with a Michigan attorney. The Michigan attorney with whom the out-of-state attorney is associated shall file with the court or administrative tribunal or agency, or arbitrator an appearance and a motion that seeks permission for the temporary admission of the out-of-state attorney. The motion shall be supported by a current certificate of good standing issued by a jurisdiction where the out-of-state attorney is licensed and eligible to practice, the document supplied by the State Bar of Michigan showing that the required fee has been paid and an affidavit of the out-of-state attorney seeking temporary admission, which affidavit shall verify

(i) the jurisdictions in which the attorney is or has been licensed or has sought licensure;

(ii) the jurisdiction where the attorney is presently eligible to practice;

(iii) that the attorney is not disbarred, or suspended in any jurisdiction, and is not the subject of any pending disciplinary action, and that the attorney is licensed and is in good standing in all jurisdictions where licensed; and

(iv) that he or she is familiar with the Michigan Rules of Professional Conduct, Michigan Court Rules, and the Michigan Rules of Evidence.

The out-of-state attorney must attach to the affidavit copies of any disciplinary dispositions. The motion shall include an attestation of the Michigan attorney that the attorney has read the out-of-state attorney's affidavit, has made a reasonable inquiry concerning the averments made therein, believes the out-of-state attorney's representations are true, and agrees to ensure that the procedures of this rule are followed. The motion shall also include the addresses and e-mail addresses of both attorneys.

(b) Fee. In each case in which an out-of-state attorney seeks temporary admission in Michigan, the out-of-state attorney must pay a fee equal to the discipline and client-protection portions of a bar member's annual dues. The fee must be paid electronically to the State Bar of Michigan, in conjunction with submission of an electronic copy of the motion, the certificate of good standing and the affidavit to the State Bar of Michigan, pursuant to procedures established by the State Bar of Michigan. Upon receipt of the fee remitted electronically, confirmation of payment will issue electronically to the out-of-state attorney through the State Bar of Michigan's automated process.

Within seven days after receipt of the copy of the motion and fee, the State Bar of Michigan must notify the court, administrative tribunal or agency, or arbitrator and both attorneys whether the out-of-state attorney has been granted permission to appear temporarily in Michigan within the past 365 days, and, if so, the number of such appearances. The notification will be issued electronically, pursuant to the procedures established by the State Bar of Michigan. No order or other writing granting permission to appear in a case shall be entered by a court, administrative tribunal or agency, or arbitrator until the notification is received from the State Bar of Michigan.

The State Bar of Michigan shall retain the discipline portion of the fee for administration of the request for temporary admission and disciplinary oversight and allocate the client-protection portion to the Client Protection Fund. If a request for investigation is filed with the grievance administrator against an attorney while temporarily admitted to practice in Michigan, the entire amount of the administration fee paid by that attorney for the case in which the allegations of misconduct arose would be transferred to the disciplinary system.

(c) Order. Following notification by the State Bar of Michigan, if the out-of-state attorney has been granted permission to appear temporarily in fewer than 5 cases within the past 365 days, the court, administrative tribunal or agency, or arbitrator may enter an order granting permission to the out-of-state attorney to appear temporarily in a case. If an order or other writing granting permission is entered, the Michigan attorney shall submit an electronic copy of the order or writing to the State Bar of Michigan within seven days.

(d) By seeking permission to appear under this rule, an out-of-state attorney consents to the jurisdiction of Michigan's attorney disciplinary system.

(B) Waiver. An applicant is not required to associate with local counsel, limited to the number of appearances to practice, or required to pay the fee to the State Bar of Michigan, if the applicant establishes to the satisfaction of the court in which the attorney seeks to appear that:

(1) the applicant appears for the limited purpose of participating in a child custody proceeding as defined by MCL 712B.3(b) in a Michigan court pursuant to the Michigan Indian Family Preservation Act, MCL 712B.1 *et seq.*; and

(2) the applicant represents an Indian tribe as defined by MCL 712B.3; and

(3) the applicant presents an affidavit from the Indian child's tribe asserting the tribe's intent to intervene and participate in the state court proceeding, and averring the child's membership or eligibility for membership under tribal law; and

(4) the applicant presents an affidavit that verifies:

(a) the jurisdictions in which the attorney is or has been licensed or has sought licensure;

(b) the jurisdiction where the attorney is presently eligible to practice;

(c) that the attorney is not disbarred, or suspended in any jurisdiction, is not the subject of any pending disciplinary action, and that the attorney is licensed and is in good standing in all jurisdictions where licensed; and

(d) that he or she is familiar with the Michigan Rules of Professional Conduct, Michigan Court Rules, and the Michigan Rules of Evidence.

(5) If the court in which the attorney seeks to appear is satisfied that the out of state attorney has met the requirements in this subrule, the court shall enter an order authorizing the out of state attorney's temporary admission.

[Adopted June 27, 2008, effective September 1, 2008, 481 Mich. Amended April 5, 2011, effective September 1, 2011, 489 Mich; February 3, 2016, effective May 1, 2016, 499 Mich; March 9, 2016, effective May 1, 2016, 499 Mich; May 24, 2017, effective September 1, 2017, 500 Mich.]

Comments

Staff Comment to 2008 Adoption

The adoption of MCR 8.126 and the amendments of MCR 9. 108 and Rule 15 of the Rules Concerning the State Bar of Michigan apply to out-of-state attorneys who seek temporary admission to the bar on or after September 1, 2008. They allow an out-of-state attorney to be authorized to appear temporarily (also known as pro hac vice appearance) in no more than five cases within a 365-day period. Because misconduct will subject the out-of-state attorney to disciplinary action in Michigan, a fee equal to the discipline and client-protection fund portions of a bar member's annual dues is imposed. The fee is required to be paid only once in each fiscal year of the State Bar of Michigan for which the attorney seeks admission. The Attorney Grievance Commission is required to keep a record of all such temporary appearances ordered by Michigan courts and administrative tribunals and agencies, and the attorney discipline system is entitled to receipt of the discipline portion of the fee paid in applying for the temporary admission. The Client Protection Fund is entitled to receipt of the portion of the fee representing the client protection fund fee. The State Bar of Michigan will apprise the Attorney Grievance Commission of any fees paid for temporary admissions.

The Court plans to review these rules again within two years of their effective dates in light of the information gathered by the Attorney Grievance Commission.

Staff Comment to 2011 Amendment

Michigan's pro hac vice rule, MCR 8.126, has been in place since 2008, and these changes reflect revisions to update the rule that were adopted at the request of the AGC and the State Bar of Michigan. The revisions include a requirement that the fee be charged for each request for pro hac vice admission, that the court that grants the motion send a copy of the order to the AGC (instead of requiring that the Michigan attorney send the copy to the AGC), that the rule specifically include an attorney's temporary admission for arbitration proceedings, and that the fee be required to be paid before an order enters.

Staff Comment to March, 2016 Amendment

These amendments update cross-references that changed after the rule was adopted and make other nonsubstantive revisions.

Staff Comment to May, 2016 Amendment

These rule revisions combine and transfer the ministerial functions of processing the payment and monitoring the number of cases for which an out-of-state attorney is temporarily admitted in Michigan to the State Bar of Michigan. In addition, the Michigan attorney associated with the out-of-state attorney is required to submit a copy of the order granting permission to the out-of-state attorney to the state bar for purposes of monitoring.

Staff Comment to 2017 Amendment

The amendment of MCR 8.126, submitted by the Michigan Tribal State Federal Judicial Forum, waives fees and other requirements for out of state attorneys who seek temporary admission in Michigan. The exemption from certain requirements applies only in cases in which the attorney desires to represent an Indian tribe intervening in a child custody proceeding.

Rule 8.127. Foreign Language Board of Review and Regulation of Foreign Language Interpreters

(A) Foreign Language Board of Review.

(1) The Supreme Court shall appoint a Foreign Language Board of Review, which shall include:

(a) a circuit judge;

(b) a probate judge;

(c) a district judge;

(d) a court administrator;

(e) a fully-certified foreign language interpreter who practices regularly in Michigan courts;

(f) an advocate representing the interests of the limited English proficiency populations in Michigan;

(g) a prosecuting attorney in good standing and with experience using interpreters in the courtroom;

(h) a criminal defense attorney in good standing and with experience using interpreters in the courtroom;

(i) a family law attorney in good standing and with experience using interpreters in the courtroom.

(2) Appointments to the board shall be for terms of three years. A board member may be appointed to no more than two full terms. Initial appointments may be of different lengths so that no more than three terms expire in the same year. The Supreme Court may remove a member at any time.

(3) If a position on the board becomes vacant because of death, resignation, or removal, or because a member is no longer employed in the capacity in which he or she was appointed, the board shall notify the state court administrator who will recommend a successor to the Supreme Court to serve the remainder of the term.

(4) The state court administrator shall assign a staff person to serve as executive secretary to the board.

(B) Responsibilities of Foreign Language Board of Review. The Foreign Language Board of Review has the following responsibilities:

(1) The board shall recommend to the state court administrator a Michigan Code of Professional Responsibility for Court Interpreters, which the state court administrator may adopt in full, in part, or in a modified form. The Code shall govern the conduct of Michigan court interpreters.

(2) The board must review a complaint that the State Court Administrative Office schedules before it pursuant to subrule (D). The board must review the complaint and any response and hear from the interpreter and any witnesses at a meeting of the board. The board shall determine what, if any, action it will take, which may include revoking certification, prohibiting the interpreter from obtaining certification, suspending the interpreter from participating in court proceedings, placing the interpreter on probation, imposing any fines authorized by law, and placing any remedial conditions on the interpreter.

(3) *Interpreter Certification Requirements.* The board shall recommend requirements for interpreters to the state court administrator that the state court administrator may adopt in full, in part, or in a modified form concerning the following:

(a) requirements for certifying interpreters as defined in MCR 1.111(A)(4). At a minimum, those requirements must include that the applicant is at least 18 years of age and not under sentence for a felony for at least two years and that the interpreter attends an orientation program for new interpreters.

(b) requirements for interpreters to be qualified as defined in MCR 1.111(A)(6).

(c) requirements under which an interpreter certified in another state or in the federal courts may apply for certification based on the certification already obtained. The certification must be a permanent or regular certification and not a temporary or restricted certification.

(d) requirements for interpreters as defined in MCR 1.111(A)(4) to maintain their certification.

(e) requirements for entities that provide interpretation services by telecommunications equipment to be qualified as defined in MCR 1.111(A)(6).

(C) Interpreter Registration.

(1) Interpreters who meet the requirements of MCR 1.111(A)(4) and MCR 1.111(A)(6)(a) and (b) must register with

the State Court Administrative Office and renew their registration before October 1 of each year in order to maintain their status. The fee for registration is $60. The fee for renewal is $30. The renewal application shall include a statement showing that the applicant has used interpreting skills during the 12 months preceding registration. Effective 2019, renewal applications must be filed or postmarked on or before September 1. Any application filed or postmarked after that date must be accompanied by a late fee of $100. Any late registration made after December 31 or any application that does not demonstrate efforts to maintain proficiency shall require board approval.

(2) Entities that employ a certified foreign language interpreter as defined in MCR 1.111(A)(4), or a qualified foreign language interpreter as defined in MCR 1.111(A)(6) must also register with the State Court Administrative Office and pay the registration fee and renewal fees.

(D) Interpreter Misconduct or Incompetence.

(1) An interpreter, trial court judge, or attorney who becomes aware of misconduct on the part of an interpreter committed in the course of a trial or other court proceeding that violates the Michigan Code of Professional Responsibility for Court Interpreters must report details of the misconduct to the State Court Administrative Office.

(2) Any person may file a complaint in writing on a form provided by the State Court Administrative Office. The complaint shall describe in detail the incident and the alleged incompetence, misconduct, or omission. The State Court Administrative Office may dismiss the complaint if it is plainly frivolous, insufficiently clear, or alleges conduct that does not violate this rule. If the complaint is not dismissed, the State Court Administrative Office shall send the complaint to the interpreter by regular mail or electronically at the address on file with the office.

(3) The interpreter shall answer the complaint within 28 days after the date the complaint is sent. The answer shall admit, deny, or further explain each allegation in the complaint. If the interpreter fails to answer, the allegations in the complaint are considered true and correct.

(4) The State Court Administrative Office may review records and interview the complainant, the interpreter, and witnesses, or set the matter for a hearing before the Foreign Language Board of Review. Before setting the matter for a hearing, the State Court Administrative Office may propose a resolution to which the interpreter may stipulate.

(5) If the complaint is not resolved by stipulation, the State Court Administrative Office shall notify the Foreign Language Board of Review, which shall hold a hearing. The State Court Administrative Office shall send notice of the date, time, and place of the hearing to the interpreter by regular mail or electronically. The hearing shall be closed to the public. A record of the proceedings shall be maintained but shall not be public.

(6) The interpreter may attend all of the hearings except the board's deliberations. The interpreter may be represented by counsel and shall be permitted to make a statement, obtain testimony from the complainant and witnesses, and comment on the claims and evidence.

(7) The State Court Administrative Office shall maintain a record of all interpreters who are sanctioned for incompetence or misconduct. If the interpreter is certified in Michigan under MCR 1.111(A)(5) because of certification pursuant to another state or federal test, the state court administrator shall report the findings and any sanctions to the certification authority in the other jurisdiction.

(8) This subrule shall not be construed to:

(a) restrict an aggrieved person from seeking to enforce this rule in the proceeding, including an appeal; or

(b) require exhaustion of administrative remedies.

(9) The State Court Administrative Office shall make complaint forms readily available and shall also provide complaint forms in such languages as determined by the State Court Administrative Office.

(10) Entities that employ interpreters are subject to the same requirements and procedures established by this subrule.

[Adopted effective September 11, 2013, 495 Mich. Amended effective May 7, 2014, 495 Mich. Amended May 22, 2019, effective September 1, 2019, 502 Mich.]

Comments

Staff Comment to 2014 Amendment

These amendments reflect changes that correct minor technical errors that have occurred in drafting or the changes respond to recent adopted rule revisions, which occasionally inadvertently create incorrect cross-references in other rules.

Staff Comment to 2019 Amendment

The amendments of MCR 1.111 and 8.127 require additional testing for qualified interpreters and include a minor revision in the timing for recertification applications. The amendments, proposed by the Foreign Language Board of Review, promote greater confidence that a qualified foreign language interpreter is proficient in the language and reduce the possibility that renewals are delayed.

SUBCHAPTER 8.200   ADMINISTRATIVE RULES APPLICABLE IN DISTRICT COURT

Rule 8.201 Allocation of Costs in Third–Class Districts

(A) Duties of Clerks of Each Third-Class Control Unit Having a Clerk.

(1) On the last day of March, June, September, and December of each year, the clerk of each third-class control unit having a clerk (see MCL 600.8281) shall determine the total number of civil and criminal cases filed during the preceding three months in the district and each political subdivision of the district under subrule (B). These figures are the total number of cases entered and commenced in that district and each political subdivision.

(2) The clerk shall determine the total cost of maintaining, financing, and operating the district court within the district.

(3) The clerk shall determine the proper share of the costs to be borne by each political subdivision by use of the following formula: (the number of cases entered and commenced in each political subdivision divided by the total number of cases entered and commenced in the district) multiplied by the total cost of maintaining, financing, and operating the district court.

(4) The clerk shall determine the proper share of the salary of the court reporter or recorder under MCL 600.8621(1) by use of the following formula: (the number of cases entered and commenced in each political subdivision divided by the total number of cases entered and commenced in the district) multiplied by the total salary of the court reporter or recorder.

(5) The clerk shall certify the figures determined under subrules (A)(3) and (4) to the treasurer of each political subdivision in the district. Payment by each political subdivision of any unpaid portion of its certified share of the cost and salaries is then due.

(B) Determination of Cases Entered and Commenced.

(1) *In the District.* The total number of cases entered and commenced in the district is the total number of civil and criminal cases filed in the district for the time period in question, excepting those cases not attributable to a specific political subdivision under subrules (B)(2)(b) and (B)(3)(b).

(2) *In Each Political Subdivision Having a District Court Clerk.* The total number of cases entered and commenced in each political subdivision having a district court clerk is the total number of civil and criminal cases filed in the political subdivision for the time period in question, excepting those cases involving a filing plaintiff and one or more defendants whose residences are outside the political subdivision where filed.

(a) Cases in which a filing plaintiff and one or more defendants reside in the same political subdivision are deemed to have been entered and commenced in that political subdivision, even though filed elsewhere for purposes of MCL 600.8104.

(b) Cases in which the filing plaintiff and one or more defendants reside outside the political subdivision where the case was filed, but none of the defendants resides in the same political subdivision as the plaintiff, are to be disregarded for purposes of this rule and MCL 600.8104.

(3) *In Each Political Subdivision Having No District Court Clerk.*

(a) The total number of cases entered and commenced for the time period in question in each political subdivision having no district court clerk is the total number of civil and criminal cases in which the filing plaintiff and one or more defendants reside in the political subdivision, no matter where the case is filed.

(b) If more than one political subdivision qualifies under subrule (B)(3)(a), all are credited with one case for purposes of this rule and MCL 600.8104.

[Adopted effective March 1, 1985.]

Comments

Staff Comment to 1985 Adoption

MCR 8.201 is substantially the same as DCR 4003.

Rule 8.202   Payment of Assigned Attorneys and Transcript Costs

(A) Misdemeanor Cases. The political subdivision or subdivisions responsible for maintaining, financing, and operating the appointing court are responsible for paying assigned attorneys, regardless of whether the defendant is charged with violating a state law or an ordinance, and regardless of whether

a fine or costs are actually assessed. If a county board of commissioners has taken or takes formal action to relieve cities or townships of part or all of the cost of paying assigned attorneys, that formal action shall control the payment of assigned attorneys in that county.

(B) Appeals. If an indigent defendant appealing to circuit court from a district or municipal court conviction is entitled to an assigned attorney or a transcript, the cost shall be paid by the same political subdivision or divisions that were responsible for or would have been responsible for paying an assigned attorney under subrule (A).

[Adopted effective March 1, 1985.]

Comments

Staff Comment to 1985 Adoption

MCR 8.202 incorporates the provisions of Administrative Orders 1975–6 and 1975–7 regarding payment of assigned counsel costs in district court.

Rule 8.203   Records and Entries Kept by Clerk

The clerk of every district court shall maintain court records and make reports as prescribed by MCR 8.119.

[Adopted effective March 1, 1985. Amended effective November 30, 1999.]

Comments

Staff Comment to 1985 Adoption

MCR 8.203 is substantially the same as DCR 4002.

Staff Comment to 1999 Amendment

The amendment of MCR 8.203 is to accommodate statewide records standards applicable to all courts and all clerks of the courts as developed and recommended by the Michigan Trial Court Case File Management Standards Committee.

Rule 8.204   Bonds for Clerks, Deputies, Magistrates, and Official Process Servers

All clerks, deputy clerks, magistrates, and official process servers of the district court must file with the chief judge a bond approved by the chief judge in a penal sum determined by the state court administrator, conditioned that the officer will

(1) perform the duties as clerk, deputy clerk, magistrate, or process server of that court; and

(2) account for and pay over all money which may be received by the officer to the person or persons lawfully entitled.

The bonds must be in favor of the court and the state.

[Adopted effective March 1, 1985.]

Comments

Staff Comment to 1985 Adoption

MCR 8.204 is based on DCR 4005.1.

The amount of the required bonds will be set by the state court administrator, rather than by the rule.

Rule 8.205   Magistrates

The court shall provide the name, address, and telephone number of each magistrate to the clerk of the district court for the district in which the magistrate serves.

[Adopted effective March 1, 1985. Amended effective November 30, 1999, 461 Mich.]

Comments

Staff Comment to 1985 Adoption

MCR 8.205 is based on DCR 3001.5.

The form of the magistrate's report is deleted and will be prescribed by the state court administrator.

Subrule (B) is a new provision emphasizing that the district court provide the name, address, and telephone number of each magistrate to the clerk of the district court.

Staff Comment to 1999 Amendment

The amendment of MCR 8.205 is to accommodate statewide records standards applicable to all courts and all clerks of the courts as developed and recommended by the Michigan Trial Court Case File Management Standards Committee.

SUBCHAPTER 8.300   ADMINISTRATIVE RULES APPLICABLE IN PROBATE COURT

Rule 8.301   Powers of Register of Probate, Deputy Registers, and Clerks

(A) Judicial Responsibility. The judges of probate are responsible for the direction and supervision of the registers of probate, deputy registers of probate, probate clerks, and other personnel employed by the court to assist in the work of the court.

(B) Entry of Order Specifying Authority.

(1) To the extent authorized by the chief judge of a probate court by a general order, the probate register, the deputy probate register, the clerks of the probate court, and other court employees designated in the order, have the authority, until the further order of the court, to do all acts required of the probate judge except judicial acts in a contested matter and acts forbidden by law to be performed by the probate register.

(2) The order of the chief judge may refer to the power

(a) to set the time and place for hearings in all matters; take acknowledgments; administer oaths; sign notices to fiduciaries, attorneys, and sureties; sign citations and subpoenas; conduct conferences with fiduciaries required to ensure prompt administration of estates; and take testimony as provided by law or court rule; and

(b) to sign or by device indicate the name of a judge to all orders and letters of authority of the court, with the same force and effect as though the judge had signed them. In all such cases, the register or the designated deputy must place his or her initials under the name of the judge.

(C) Statutory Authority. In addition to the powers which may be granted by order of the chief judge, the probate registers and deputy registers have the authority granted by statute and may take acknowledgments to the same extent as a notary public.

[Adopted effective March 1, 1985. Amended December 1, 1994, effective February 1, 1995, 447 Mich; February 23, 2006, effective May 1, 2006, 474 Mich.]

Comments

Staff Comment to 1985 Adoption

MCR 8.301 is substantially the same as PCR 907.

Staff Comment to 1995 Amendment

Former MCR 5.602(B) is incorporated into subrule (B)(2)(b).

Staff Comment to 2006 Amendment

The amendment of MCR 8.301(B)(2)(a) is made to conform to the definition of court in MCL 710.22 and to the provision in 710. 46, which provides that the family division of the circuit court shall direct a full investigation upon the filing of an adoption petition.

Rule 8.302   Records and Entries Kept by Clerk

The clerk of every probate court shall maintain court records and make reports as prescribed by MCR 8.119. In addition, any unsealed testamentary document filed with the probate court must be safeguarded by reproducing the document in a format authorized by the Records Reproduction Act (MCL 24.401 *et seq.*) and maintaining it in accordance with the Michigan Trial Court Case File Management Standards.

[Adopted effective March 1, 1985. Amended effective November 30, 1999, 461 Mich. Amended May 25, 2016, effective January 1, 2017, 499 Mich.]

Comments

Staff Comment to 1985 Adoption

MCR 8.302 includes the portions of PCR 917.1 that cover the recording, copying, and filing of papers.

Staff Comment to 1999 Amendment

The amendment of MCR 8.302 is to accommodate statewide records standards applicable to all courts and all clerks of the courts as developed and recommended by the Michigan Trial Court Case File Management Standards Committee.

Staff Comment to 2017 Amendment

The amendments of MCR 3.925, 8.119, and 8.302 and the adoption of MCR 5.133 are an expected progression in the development of policies and procedures that standardize management of court records and provide a uniform basis for developing parameters on the use of technology in creating, accessing, routing, maintaining, and disposing of court records. These particular amendments will assist in implementing the goals of 2013 PA 199 and 201 and improving the policies and procedures adopted by the Court in 2012 under Administrative File No. 2006-47.

CHAPTER 9. PROFESSIONAL DISCIPLINARY PROCEEDINGS

Effective March 1, 1985

SUBCHAPTER 9.100 ATTORNEY GRIEVANCE COMMISSION; ATTORNEY DISCIPLINE BOARD

Rule 9.101 Definitions

As used in subchapter 9.100:

(1) "board" means the Attorney Discipline Board;

(2) "commission" means the Attorney Grievance Commission;

(3) "administrator" means the grievance administrator;

(4) "investigator" means a person specially designated by the administrator to assist him or her in the investigation of alleged misconduct or requested reinstatement;

(5) "attorney" or "lawyer" means a person regularly licensed, specially admitted, permitted to practice law in Michigan on a temporary or other limited basis, or who is otherwise subject to the disciplinary authority of Michigan pursuant to order or rule of the Supreme Court;

(6) "respondent" means an attorney named in a request for investigation or complaint, or proceedings for reciprocal discipline, based on a judgment of conviction, or transfers to inactive status under MCR 9.121;

(7) "request for investigation" means the first step in bringing alleged misconduct to the administrator's attention;

(8) "complaint" means the formal charge prepared by the administrator and filed with the board;

(9) "review" means examination by the board of a hearing panel's order on petition by the administrator, complainant, or respondent;

(10) "appeal" means judicial re-examination by the Supreme Court of the board's final order on petition by the administrator, complainant, or respondent;

(11) "grievance" means alleged misconduct;

(12) "investigation" means fact finding on alleged misconduct under the administrator's direction.

(13) "disbarment" means revocation of the license to practice law.

(14) "complainant" means a person who signs a request for investigation.

(15) "disability inactive status" means inactive status to which a lawyer has been transferred pursuant to MCR 9.121 or a similar rule of another jurisdiction.

(16) "disciplinary proceeding" means a proceeding commenced under this subchapter seeking the imposition of discipline for misconduct.

[Adopted effective March 1, 1985. Amended March 19, 1987, effective June 1, 1987, 428 Mich; April 19, 2011, effective September 1, 2011, 489 Mich.]

Comments

Staff Comment to 1985 Adoption

MCR 9.101 is substantially the same as GCR 1963, 950.

Staff Comment to 2011 Amendment

This proposal contains various amendments of the attorney discipline rules recommended by the Attorney Grievance Commission, which also were thoroughly reviewed by a State Bar of Michigan workgroup at the request of the Court.

Rule 9.102 Construction; Severability

(A) Construction. Subchapter 9.100 is to be liberally construed for the protection of the public, the courts, and the legal profession and applies to all pending matters of misconduct and reinstatement and to all future proceedings, even though the alleged misconduct occurred before the effective date of subchapter 9.100. Procedures must be as expeditious as possible.

(B) Severability. If a court finds a portion of subchapter 9.100 or its application to a person or circumstances invalid, the invalidity does not affect the remaining portions or other applications. To this end the rules are severable.

[Adopted effective March 1, 1985.]

Comments

Staff Comment to 1985 Adoption

MCR 9.102 includes the provisions of GCR 1963, 951.1 and 951.3.

GCR 1963, 951.2, concerning the application of masculine or singular words to the feminine or plural, is omitted. The singular/plural point is covered by MCR 1.107.

Rule 9.103 Standards of Conduct for Attorneys

(A) General Principles. The license to practice law in Michigan is, among other things, a continuing proclamation by the Supreme Court that the holder is fit to be entrusted with professional and judicial matters and to aid in the administration of justice as an attorney and counselor and as an officer of the court. It is the duty of every attorney to conduct himself or herself at all times in conformity with standards imposed on members of the bar as a condition of the privilege to practice law. These standards include, but are not limited to, the rules of professional responsibility and the rules of judicial conduct that are adopted by the Supreme Court.

(B) Duty to Assist Public to Request Investigation. An attorney shall assist a member of the public to communicate to the administrator, in appropriate form, a request for investigation of a member of the bar. An attorney shall not charge or collect a fee in connection with answering a request for investigation unless he or she is acting as counsel for a respondent in connection with a disciplinary investigation or proceeding.

(C) Duty to Assist Administrator. An attorney other than a respondent or respondent's attorney shall cooperate with the administrator in the investigation, prosecution, and disposition of a request for investigation or proceeding under this subchapter.

[Adopted effective March 1, 1985. Amended April 19, 2011, effective September 1, 2011, 489 Mich.]

Comments

Staff Comment to 1985 Adoption

MCR 9.103 is substantially the same as GCR 1963, 952.

Staff Comment to 2011 Amendment

This proposal contains various amendments of the attorney discipline rules recommended by the Attorney Grievance Commission, which also were thoroughly reviewed by a State Bar of Michigan workgroup at the request of the Court.

Rule 9.104 Grounds for Discipline in General

The following acts or omissions by an attorney, individually or in concert with another person, are misconduct and grounds for discipline, whether or not occurring in the course of an attorney-client relationship:

(1) conduct prejudicial to the proper administration of justice;

(2) conduct that exposes the legal profession or the courts to obloquy, contempt, censure, or reproach;

(3) conduct that is contrary to justice, ethics, honesty, or good morals;

(4) conduct that violates the standards or rules of professional conduct adopted by the Supreme Court;

(5) conduct that violates a criminal law of a state or of the United States, an ordinance, or tribal law pursuant to MCR 2.615;

(6) knowing misrepresentation of any facts or circumstances surrounding a request for investigation or complaint;

(7) failure to answer a request for investigation or complaint in conformity with MCR 9.113 and 9.115(D);

(8) contempt of the board or a hearing panel;

(9) violation of an order of discipline; or

(10) entering into an agreement or attempting to obtain an agreement, that:

(a) the professional misconduct or the terms of a settlement of a claim for professional misconduct shall not be reported to the administrator;

(b) the plaintiff shall withdraw a request for investigation or shall not cooperate with the investigation or prosecution of misconduct by the administrator; or

(c) the record of any civil action for professional misconduct shall be sealed from review by the administrator.

[Adopted effective March 1, 1985. Amended March 19, 1987, effective June 17, 1987, 428 Mich. Amended effective July 30, 2001, 465 Mich. Amended April 19, 2011, effective September 1, 2011, 489 Mich.]

Comments

Staff Comment to 1985 Adoption

MCR 9.104 is substantially the same as GCR 1963, 953.

Staff Comment to 1987 Amendment

The [June 1, 1987] amendment to MCR 9.104(6) extends the subrule to cover requests for investigation in the same manner as formal complaints.

The [June 1, 1987] amendments to the final paragraph give foreign adjudications of misconduct full faith and credit by recognizing them as conclusive proof of misconduct. The additional language is taken from the American Bar Association Standards for Lawyer Discipline and Disability Proceedings, Standard No. 10.2.

Staff Comment to 2001 Amendment

The July 30, 2001 amendment of MRPC 8.1 expressly precluded bar applicants from engaging in the unauthorized practice of law, and stated an applicant's continuing obligation to update the affidavit of personal history. The structure of MCR 9.104 was changed for greater clarity.

Staff Comment to 2011 Amendment

This proposal contains various amendments of the attorney discipline rules recommended by the Attorney Grievance Commission, which also were thoroughly reviewed by a State Bar of Michigan workgroup at the request of the Court.

Rule 9.105 Purpose and Funding of Disciplinary Proceedings

(A) **Purpose.** Discipline for misconduct is not intended as punishment for wrongdoing, but for the protection of the public, the courts, and the legal profession. The fact that certain misconduct has remained unchallenged when done by others or when done at other times or has not been earlier made the subject of disciplinary proceedings is not an excuse.

(B) **Funding.** The legal profession, through the State Bar of Michigan, is responsible for the reasonable and necessary expenses of the board, the commission, and the administrator, as determined by the Supreme Court.

[Adopted effective March 1, 1985. Amended effective July 27, 1990, 435 Mich. Amended July 30, 1993, effective October 1, 1993, 443 Mich. Amended effective November 21, 1995, 450 Mich; April 19, 2011, effective September 1, 2011, 489 Mich.]

Comments

Staff Comment to 1985 Adoption

MCR 9.105 is substantially the same as GCR 1963, 954.

Staff Comment to 1990 Amendment

The [July 27,] 1990 amendment prevents potential conflicts of interest by disqualifying from practice before the disciplinary agencies those attorneys (and their associates) who make decisions about the level of State Bar funding for the AGC and ADB.

Staff Comment to 1993 Amendment

The July 30, 1993, amendments of MCR 9.105, 9.108, and 9.110 [effective October 1, 1993] provide that the Supreme Court, rather than the State Bar Board of Commissioners will approve the budgets of the Attorney Grievance Commission and the Attorney Discipline Board. This change had been recommended by the State Bar Representative Assembly.

Staff Comment to 1995 Amendment

The 1995 amendment eliminated language that precluded lawyers associated in the practice of law with members of the State Bar Board of Commissioners from representing respondents in attorney disciplinary proceedings. The commissioners themselves still are prohibited from such representation, however.

Staff Comment to 2011 Amendment

This proposal contains various amendments of the attorney discipline rules recommended by the Attorney Grievance Commission, which also were thoroughly reviewed by a State Bar of Michigan workgroup at the request of the Court.

Rule 9.106 Types of Discipline; Minimum Discipline

Misconduct is grounds for:

(1) disbarment of an attorney from the practice of law in Michigan;

(2) suspension of the license to practice law in Michigan for a specified term, not less than 30 days, with such additional conditions relevant to the established misconduct as a hearing panel, the board, or the Supreme Court may impose, and, if the term exceeds 179 days, until the further order of a hearing panel, the board, or the Supreme Court;

(3) reprimand with such conditions relevant to the established misconduct as a hearing panel, the board, or the Supreme Court may impose;

(4) probation ordered by a hearing panel, the board, or the Supreme Court under MCR 9.121(C); or

(5) requiring restitution, in an amount set by a hearing panel, the board, or the Supreme Court, as a condition of an order of discipline.

[Adopted effective March 1, 1985. Amended March 19, 1987, effective June 1, 1987, 428 Mich; April 19, 2011, effective September 1, 2011, 489 Mich.]

Comments

Staff Comment to 1985 Adoption

MCR 9.106 is substantially the same as GCR 1963, 955.

Staff Comment to 1987 Amendment

The [June 1, 1987] expansion of MCR 9.106(2) and (3) will allow the adjudicative bodies greater discretion to impose temporary restrictions or requirements such as continuing legal education, reformation of law office operations, personal counseling, and other conditions relevant to the established misconduct and the causes thereof. These conditions would be in addition to the restrictions already mandated in the case of a suspension.

[Effective June 1, 1987] Amended MCR 9.106(2) provides that all suspensions must be for a period of at least 30 days.

[Effective June 1, 1987] Amended MCR 9.106(6) conforms the rule to the present practice under which the commission, rather than the administrator, exercises the power to admonish. It also details the admonishment procedure.

Staff Comment to 2011 Amendment

This proposal contains various amendments of the attorney discipline rules recommended by the Attorney Grievance Commission, which also were thoroughly reviewed by a State Bar of Michigan workgroup at the request of the Court.

Rule 9.107 Rules Exclusive on Discipline

(A) Proceedings for Discipline. Subchapter 9.100 governs the procedure to discipline attorneys. A proceeding under subchapter 9.100 is subject to the superintending control of the Supreme Court. An investigation or proceeding may not be held invalid because of a nonprejudicial irregularity or an error not resulting in a miscarriage of justice.

(B) Local Bar Associations. A local bar association may not conduct a separate proceeding to discipline an attorney.

[Adopted effective March 1, 1985. Amended April 19, 2011, effective September 1, 2011, 489 Mich.]

Comments

Staff Comment to 1985 Adoption

MCR 9.107 is substantially the same as GCR 1963, 956.

Staff Comment to 2011 Amendment

This proposal contains various amendments of the attorney discipline rules recommended by the Attorney Grievance Commission, which also were thoroughly reviewed by a State Bar of Michigan workgroup at the request of the Court.

Rule 9.108 Attorney Grievance Commission

(A) Authority of Commission. The Attorney Grievance Commission is the prosecution arm of the Supreme Court for discharge of its constitutional responsibility to supervise and discipline Michigan attorneys and those temporarily admitted to practice under MCR 8.126 or otherwise subject to the disciplinary authority of the Supreme Court.

(B) Composition. The commission consists of 3 laypersons and 6 attorneys appointed by the Supreme Court. The members serve 3–year terms. A member may not serve more than 2 full terms.

(C) Chairperson and Vice–Chairperson. The Supreme Court shall designate from among the members of the commission a chairperson and a vice-chairperson who shall serve 1–year terms in those offices. The commencement and termination dates for the 1–year terms shall coincide appropriately with the 3–year membership terms of those officers and the other commission members. The Supreme Court may reappoint these officers for additional terms and may remove these officers prior to the expiration of a term. An officer appointed to fill a mid-term vacancy shall serve the remainder of that term and may be reappointed to serve up to 2 more full terms.

(D) Internal Rules.

(1) The commission must elect annually from among its membership a secretary to keep the minutes of the commission's meetings and issue the required notices.

(2) Five members constitute a quorum. The commission acts by majority vote of the members participating in the meeting.

(3) The commission must meet monthly at a time and place the chairperson designates. Notice of a regular monthly meeting is not required.

(4) A special meeting may be called by the chairperson or by petition of 3 commission members on 7 days' written notice. The notice may be waived in writing or by attending the meeting. Special meetings may be conducted through electronic means.

(E) Powers and Duties. The commission has the power and duty to:

(1) recommend attorneys to the Supreme Court for appointment as administrator and deputy administrator;

(2) supervise the investigation of attorney misconduct, including requests for investigation of and complaints against attorneys;

(3) supervise the administrator;

(4) when prompt action is required, seek an injunction from the Supreme Court enjoining an attorney's misconduct or enjoining an attorney from engaging in the practice of law, even if a disciplinary proceeding concerning that conduct is not pending before the board;

(5) annually propose a budget for the commission and the administrator's office, including compensation, and submit it to the Supreme Court for approval;

(6) submit to the Supreme Court proposed changes in these rules; and

(7) perform other duties provided in these rules.

[Adopted effective March 1, 1985. Amended effective July 27, 1990, 435 Mich; September 14, 1990. Amended December 18, 1990, effective February 1, 1991, 437 Mich; July 30, 1993, effective October 1, 1993, 443 Mich; March 30, 1995, effective July 1, 1995, 448 Mich; October 8, 2002, effective January 1, 2003, 467 Mich; June 27, 2008, effective September 1, 2008, 481 Mich; April 19, 2011, effective September 1, 2011, 489 Mich; February 3, 2016, effective May 1, 2016, 499 Mich; May 24, 2017, effective September 1, 2017, 500 Mich.]

Comments

Staff Comment to 1985 Adoption

MCR 9.108 is substantially the same as GCR 1963, 957.

Staff Comment to July, 1990 Amendment

The [July 27,] 1990 amendments effected the following changes: (1) The Supreme Court will select the commission members who serve as chairperson and vice-chairperson; previously, the commission elected those officers. (2) Although appointed for one-year terms, the chairperson and vice-chairperson will serve at the pleasure of the Supreme Court and may be removed from office prior to the expiration of a term. (3) The Supreme Court will select the grievance administrator and the deputy administrator, but the commission will retain an advisory role in the selection process.

Staff Comment to September, 1990 Amendment

The [September 14, 1990] court rule change provides that all members of the Attorney Grievance Commission are to be appointed by the Michigan Supreme Court. The membership is increased from seven to nine members. Of the nine members, three are to be laypersons and six are to be attorneys. Five members will constitute a quorum.

Staff Comment to 1991 Amendment

The 1991 amendment added subrule (E)(7), requiring an annual report to the Supreme Court.

Staff Comment to 1993 Amendment

The July 30, 1993, amendments of MCR 9.105, 9.108, and 9.110 [effective October 1, 1993] provide that the Supreme Court, rather than the State Bar Board of Commissioners will approve the budgets of the Attorney Grievance Commission and the Attorney Discipline Board. This change had been recommended by the State Bar Representative Assembly.

Staff Comment to 1995 Amendment

The 1995 amendment of paragraph (E) requires the Attorney Grievance Commission to submit quarterly reports to the Supreme Court. The commission previously was required to submit annual reports.

Staff Comment to 2003 Amendment

The October 8, 2002 amendments of MCR 9.108(E)(7) and 9.110(E)(8), effective January 1, 2003, require at least quarterly reports from the Attorney Discipline Board and the Attorney Grievance Commission and a joint annual report that summarizes activities of both agencies.

Staff Comment to 2008 Amendment

The adoption of MCR 8.126 and the amendments of MCR 9.108 and Rule 15 of the Rules Concerning the State Bar of Michigan apply to out-of-state attorneys who seek temporary admission to the bar on or after September 1, 2008. They allow an out-of-state attorney to be authorized to appear temporarily (also known as pro hac vice appearance) in no more than five cases within a 365–day period. Because misconduct will subject the out-of-state attorney to disciplinary action in Michigan, a fee equal to the discipline and client-protection fund portions of a bar member's annual dues is imposed. The fee is required to be paid only once in each fiscal year of the State Bar of Michigan for which the attorney seeks admission. The Attorney Grievance Commission is required to keep a record of all such temporary appearances ordered by Michigan courts and administrative tribunals and agencies, and the attorney discipline system is entitled to receipt of the discipline portion of the fee paid in applying for the temporary admission. The Client Protection Fund is entitled to receipt of the portion of the fee representing the client protection fund fee. The State Bar of Michigan will apprise the Attorney Grievance Commission of any fees paid for temporary admissions.

The Court plans to review these rules again within two years of their effective dates in light of the information gathered by the Attorney Grievance Commission.

Staff Comment to 2011 Amendment

This proposal contains various amendments of the attorney discipline rules recommended by the Attorney Grievance Commission, which also were thoroughly reviewed by a State Bar of Michigan workgroup at the request of the Court.

Staff Comment to 2016 Amendment

These rule revisions combine and transfer the ministerial functions of processing the payment and monitoring the number of cases for which an out-of-state attorney is temporarily admitted in Michigan to the State Bar of Michigan. In addition, the Michigan attorney associated with the out-of-state attorney is required to submit a copy of the order granting permission to the out-of-state attorney to the state bar for purposes of monitoring.

Staff Comment to 2017 Amendment

The amendment of MCR 9.108 clarifies that the Court has the authority to enjoin an attorney from practicing law, at the request of the Attorney Grievance Commission.

Rule 9.109   Grievance Administrator

(A) Appointment. The administrator and the deputy administrator must be attorneys. The commission may recom-

mend one or more candidates for appointment as administrator and deputy administrator. The Supreme Court shall appoint the administrator and the deputy administrator, may terminate their appointments at any time with or without cause, and shall determine their salaries and the other terms and conditions of their employment.

(B) Powers and Duties. The administrator has the power and duty to:

(1) employ or retain attorneys, investigators, and staff with the approval of the commission;

(2) supervise the attorneys, investigators, and staff;

(3) assist the public in preparing requests for investigation;

(4) maintain the commission records created as a result of these rules;

(5) investigate alleged misconduct of attorneys, including initiating an investigation in his or her own name if necessary;

(6) prosecute complaints the commission authorizes;

(7) prosecute or defend reviews and appeals as the commission authorizes;

(8) report to the Supreme Court at least quarterly regarding the commission's activities, and to submit a joint annual report with the board that summarizes the activities of both agencies during the past year; and

(9) perform other duties provided in these rules or assigned by the commission.

(C) Legal Counsel for the Administrator.

(1) The administrator may appoint and retain volunteer legal counsel needed to prosecute proceedings under these rules.

(2) Legal counsel may

(a) commence proceedings under this subchapter;

(b) present evidence relating to disciplinary and court proceedings;

(c) prepare and file arguments and briefs;

(d) inform the administrator about the progress of cases assigned; and

(e) perform other duties assigned by the administrator.

[Adopted effective March 1, 1985. Amended effective July 27, 1990, 435 Mich. Amended April 19, 2011, effective September 1, 2011, 489 Mich.]

Comments

Staff Comment to 1985 Adoption

MCR 9.109 is substantially the same as GCR 1963, 958.

Staff Comment to 1990 Amendment

The [July 27,] 1990 amendment shifted the responsibility for hiring the administrator and the deputy administrator from the Attorney Grievance Commission to the Supreme Court. The AGC retains an advisory role in the process.

Staff Comment to 2011 Amendment

This proposal contains various amendments of the attorney discipline rules recommended by the Attorney Grievance Commission, which also were thoroughly reviewed by a State Bar of Michigan workgroup at the request of the Court.

Rule 9.110   Attorney Discipline Board

(A) Authority of Board. The Attorney Discipline Board is the adjudicative arm of the Supreme Court for discharge of its exclusive constitutional responsibility to supervise and discipline Michigan attorneys and those temporarily admitted to practice under MCR 8.126 or otherwise subject to the disciplinary authority of the Supreme Court.

(B) Composition. The board consists of 6 attorneys and 3 laypersons appointed by the Supreme Court. The members serve 3–year terms. A member may not serve more than 2 full terms.

(C) Chairperson and Vice–Chairperson. The Supreme Court shall designate from among the members of the board a chairperson and a vice-chairperson who shall serve 1–year terms in those offices. The commencement and termination dates of the 1–year terms shall coincide appropriately with the 3–year board terms of those officers and the other board members. The Supreme Court may reappoint these officers for additional terms and may remove an officer prior to the expiration of a term. An officer appointed to fill a midterm vacancy shall serve the remainder of that term and may be reappointed to serve two full terms.

(D) Internal Rules.

(1) The board must elect annually from among its membership a secretary to supervise the keeping of the minutes of the board's meetings and the issuance of the required notices.

(2) *Five Members Constitute a Quorum.* The board acts by a majority vote of the members present.

(3) The board shall meet monthly as often as necessary to maintain a current docket, but no less than every 2 months, at a time and place the chairperson designates.

(4) A special meeting may be called by the chairperson or by petition of 3 board members on 7 days' written notice. The notice may be waived in writing or by attending the meeting.

(E) Powers and Duties. The board has the power and duty to:

(1) appoint an attorney to serve as its general counsel and executive director;

(2) appoint hearing panels, masters, monitors and mentors;

(3) assign a proceeding under this subchapter to a hearing panel or to a master, except that a proceeding for reinstatement under MCR 9.124 may not be assigned to a master;

(4) on request of the respondent, the administrator, or the complainant, review a final order of discipline or dismissal by a hearing panel;

(5) on leave granted by the board, review a nonfinal order of a hearing panel;

(6) discipline and reinstate attorneys under these rules and exercise continuing jurisdiction over orders of discipline and reinstatement;

(7) file with the Supreme Court clerk its orders of suspension, disbarment, and reinstatement;

(8) annually propose a budget for the board and submit it to the Supreme Court for approval;

(9) report to the Supreme Court at least quarterly regarding its activities, and to submit a joint annual report with the Attorney Grievance Commission that summarizes the activities of both agencies during the past year; and

(10) submit to the Supreme Court proposed changes in these rules.

[Adopted effective March 1, 1985. Amended December 18, 1990, effective February 1, 1991, 437 Mich; May 30, 1991, effective June 3, 1991, 437 Mich; July 30, 1993, effective October 1, 1993, 443 Mich; January 4, 1994, effective March 1, 1994, 444 Mich; October 8, 2002, effective January 1, 2003, 467 Mich; April 19, 2011, effective September 1, 2011, 489 Mich.]

Comments

Staff Comment to 1985 Adoption

MCR 9.110 is substantially the same as GCR 1963, 959.

Staff Comment to February, 1991 Amendment

The [February 1,] 1991 amendment added subrule (D)(8), requiring an annual report to the Supreme Court.

Staff Comment to June, 1991 Amendment

Pursuant to the amendment of June 3, 1991, the Supreme Court will appoint all members of the Attorney Discipline Board as vacancies occur.

Staff Comment to 1993 Amendment

The July 30, 1993, amendments of MCR 9.105, 9.108, and 9.110 [effective October 1, 1993] provide that the Supreme Court, rather than the State Bar Board of Commissioners will approve the budgets of the Attorney Grievance Commission and the Attorney Discipline Board. This change had been recommended by the State Bar Representative Assembly.

The amendment [to subrule (B) effective October 1, 1993] increases the composition of the Attorney Discipline Board. Per the amendment the Board now consists of 6 attorneys and 3 laypersons.

Staff Comment to 1994 Amendment

The March 1, 1994 amendments provided for Supreme Court appointment of the board's officers (new subrule [C] and related changes elsewhere); revised the responsibilities of the board's secretary (subrule [E][1]); and clarified the procedures for assigning cases and taking appeals from hearing panel decisions (subrules [E][3] and [4]).

Staff Comment to 2003 Amendment

The October 8, 2002 amendments of MCR 9.108(E)(7) and 9.110(E)(8), effective January 1, 2003, require at least quarterly reports from the Attorney Discipline Board and the Attorney Grievance Commission and a joint annual report that summarizes activities of both agencies.

Staff Comment to 2011 Amendment

This proposal contains various amendments of the attorney discipline rules recommended by the Attorney Grievance Commission, which also were thoroughly reviewed by a State Bar of Michigan workgroup at the request of the Court.

Rule 9.111   Hearing Panels

(A) Composition; Quorum. The board must establish hearing panels from a list of volunteer lawyers maintained by its executive director. The board must annually appoint 3 attorneys to each hearing panel and must fill a vacancy as it occurs. Following appointment, the board may designate the panel's chairperson, vice-chairperson, and secretary. Thereafter, a hearing panel may elect a chairperson, vice-chairperson, and secretary. A hearing panel must convene at the time and place designated by its chairperson or by the board. Two members constitute a quorum. A hearing panel acts by a majority vote. If a panel is unable to reach a majority decision, the matter shall be referred to the board for reassignment to a new panel.

(B) Hearing Panelists or Masters; Discipline.

(1) An attorney shall not be appointed as a hearing panelist or master if he or she:

(a) has ever been the subject of an order that imposes discipline, or

(b) has been admonished or placed on contractual probation within the preceding 5 years.

(2) A hearing panelist or master who becomes the subject of an order imposing discipline, an admonition, or placement on contractual probation shall be removed from the roster of hearing panelists. A hearing panelist or master who becomes the subject of a formal discipline proceeding shall be removed from consideration of any pending matter; shall be placed on the ADB's roster of inactive panelists; and shall not be assigned to a panel until the formal discipline proceeding has been resolved. A hearing panelist or master who becomes the subject of an otherwise confidential request for investigation must disclose that investigation to the parties in the matter before the panelist or master, or must disqualify himself or herself from participation in the matter.

(C) Powers and Duties. A hearing panel shall do the following:

(1) Schedule a public hearing on a proceeding under this subchapter assigned to it within 56 days after the proceeding is commenced or after the date that notice of the reinstatement is published, except that a proceeding for reciprocal discipline shall be governed by MCR 9.120. A hearing must be concluded within 91 days after it is begun, unless the board grants an extension for good cause.

(2) Receive evidence and make written findings of fact.

(3) Discipline and reinstate attorneys or dismiss a complaint by order under these rules and exercise continuing jurisdiction over its orders of discipline and reinstatement.

(4) Report its actions to the board within 35 days of the later of the filing of the transcript or the closing of the record, unless extended by the board chairperson.

(5) Perform other duties provided in these rules.

[Adopted effective March 1, 1985. Amended January 4, 1994, effective March 1, 1994, 444 Mich; April 19, 2011, effective September 1, 2011, 489 Mich.]

Comments

Staff Comment to 1985 Adoption

MCR 9.111 is substantially the same as GCR 1963, 960.

Staff Comment to 1994 Amendment

The March 1, 1994 amendments to subrule (A) modified the procedures for choosing hearing panel officers and specified the procedure to be followed if a hearing panel is unable to reach a majority decision.

Staff Comment to 2011 Amendment

This proposal contains various amendments of the attorney discipline rules recommended by the Attorney Grievance Commission, which also were thoroughly reviewed by a State Bar of Michigan workgroup at the request of the Court.

Rule 9.112   Requests for Investigation

(A) Availability to Public. The administrator shall furnish a form for a request for investigation to a person who alleges misconduct against an attorney. Use of the form is not required for filing a request for investigation.

(B) Form of Request. A request for investigation of alleged misconduct must

(1) be in writing;

(2) describe the alleged misconduct, including the approximate time and place of it;

(3) be signed by the complainant; and

(4) be filed with the administrator.

(C) Handling by Administrator.

(1) *Request for Investigation of Attorney.* After a preliminary review, the administrator shall either

(a) notify the complainant and the respondent that the allegations of the request for investigation are inadequate, incomplete, or insufficient to warrant the further attention of the commission; or

(b) serve a copy of the request for investigation on the respondent by ordinary mail at the respondent's address on file with the state bar as required by Rule 2 of the Supreme Court Rules Concerning the State Bar of Michigan. Service is effective at the time of mailing, and nondelivery does not affect the validity of service. If a respondent has not filed an answer, no formal complaint shall be filed with the board unless the administrator has served the request for investigation by registered or certified mail return receipt requested.

(2) *Request for Investigation of Judge.* The administrator shall forward to the Judicial Tenure Commission a request for investigation of a judge, even if the request arises from the judge's conduct before he or she became a judge or from conduct unconnected with his or her judicial office. MCR 9.116 thereafter governs.

(3) *Request for Investigation of Member or Employee of Commission or Board, or the Relative of Member or Employee of Commission or Board.* Except as modified by MCR 9.131, MCR 9.104–9.130 apply to a request for investigation of an attorney who is a member of or is employed by the board or the commission, or who is a relative of a member or employee of the board or commission.

"Relative" includes spouse, child, parent, brother, sister, grandparent, grandchild, first cousin, uncle, aunt, niece, nephew, brother-in-law, sister-in-law, daughter-in-law, son-in-law, mother-in-law, and father-in-law, whether natural, adopted, step or foster. The term also includes same-sex or different-sex individuals who have a relationship of a romantic, intimate, committed, or dating nature.

(D) Subpoenas.

(1) After the request for investigation has been served on the respondent, the commission may issue subpoenas to require the appearance of a witness or the production of documents or other tangible things concerning matters then under investigation. Upon request filed with the board, the board chairperson may quash or modify the subpoena if compliance would be unreasonable or oppressive. Documents or other tangible things so produced may be retained by the grievance administrator, copied, or may be subjected to nondestructive testing. Subpoenas shall be returnable before the administrator or a person designated by the administrator.

(2) A person who without just cause, after being commanded by a subpoena, fails or refuses to appear or give evidence, to be sworn or affirmed, or to answer a proper question after being ordered to do so is in contempt. The administrator may initiate a contempt proceeding before the board chairperson or his or her designee, or under MCR 3.606 in the circuit court for the county where the act or refusal to act occurred. In the event of a finding of contempt by the respondent, the respondent's license to practice law may be suspended until he or she complies with the order of the board chairperson or his or her designee.

(3) A subpoena issued pursuant to this subrule and certified by the commission chairperson shall be sufficient authorization for taking a deposition or seeking the production of evidence outside the State of Michigan. If the deponent or the person possessing the subpoenaed evidence will not comply voluntarily, the proponent of the subpoena may utilize MCR 2.305(D) or any similar provision in a statute or court rule of Michigan or of the state, territory, or country where the deponent or possessor resides or is present.

(4) Upon receipt of a subpoena certified to be duly issued under the rules or laws of another lawyer disciplinary or admissions jurisdiction, the administrator may issue a subpoena directing a person domiciled or found within the state of Michigan to give testimony and/or produce documents or other things for use in the other lawyer disciplinary proceedings as directed in the subpoena of the other jurisdiction. The practice and procedure applicable to subpoenas issued under this subdivision shall be that of the other jurisdiction, except that:

(a) the testimony or production shall be only in the county where the person resides or is employed, or as otherwise fixed by the grievance administrator for good cause shown; and,

(b) compliance with any subpoena issued pursuant to this subdivision and contempt for failure in this respect shall be sought as elsewhere provided in this subchapter.

[Adopted effective March 1, 1985. Amended March 19, 1987, effective June 1, 1987, 428 Mich; December 18, 1990, effective February 1, 1991, 437 Mich. Amended effective January 29, 1992, 439 Mich. Amended January 4, 1994, effective March 1, 1994, 444 Mich; April 19, 2011, effective September 1, 2011, 489 Mich; May 23, 2018, effective September 1, 2018, 501 Mich.]

Comments

Staff Comment to 1985 Adoption

MCR 9.112 is substantially the same as GCR 1963, 961.

Staff Comment to 1987 Amendment

The [June 1, 1987] change in MCR 9.112(A) codifies an Attorney Discipline Board decision.

Staff Comment to 1991 Amendment

The [February 1,] 1991 amendment added to subrule (C)(1)(a) the requirement that the respondent attorney be given notice of the request for investigation even if the request is rejected at the preliminary investigation stage.

Staff Comment to 1992 Amendment

The amendment effective January 29, 1992 added subrule (D) dealing with subpoenas. Many of the provisions formerly appeared in MCR 9.114. The amendment also specified when investigative subpoenas may be issued and authorized the nondestructive testing of subpoenaed items.

Staff Comment to 1994 Amendment

The March 1, 1994 amendment added subrule (D)(3), which states that a subpoena issued by the AGC authorizes the holder to seek the assistance of courts in other states to compel attendance at a deposition or the production of tangible evidence.

Staff Comment to 2011 Amendment

This proposal contains various amendments of the attorney discipline rules recommended by the Attorney Grievance Commission, which also were thoroughly reviewed by a State Bar of Michigan workgroup at the request of the Court.

Staff Comment to 2018 Amendment

The amendments of MCR 9.112 and MCR 9.131 provide that relatives of AGC or ADB members or employees are subject to the same procedure for review of allegations of misconduct as the Board or Commission member or employee. This change comports with recent Supreme Court practice. These amendments are intended to address any perceived conflict of interest that may exist if the procedures in MCR 9.112 were to be used to review a request for investigation of the relative of a member or employee of the Attorney Grievance Commission or Attorney Discipline Board.

Rule 9.113   Answer by Respondent

(A) Answer. Within 21 days after being served with a request for investigation under MCR 9.112(C)(1)(b) or such further time as permitted by the administrator, the respondent shall file with the administrator a written answer signed by respondent in duplicate fully and fairly disclosing all the facts and circumstances pertaining to the alleged misconduct. Misrepresentation in the answer is grounds for discipline. Respondent's signature constitutes verification that he or she has read the document. The administrator shall provide a copy of the answer and any supporting documents, or documents related to a refusal to answer under MCR 9.113(B)(1), to the person who filed the request for investigation. If the administrator determines that there is cause for not disclosing some or all of the answer or documents supporting the answer, then the administrator need not provide those portions of the answer or the supporting documents to the person who filed the request for investigation.

(B) Refusal or Failure to Answer.

(1) A respondent may refuse to answer a request for investigation on expressed constitutional or professional grounds.

(2) The failure of a respondent to answer within the time period required under these rules other than as permitted in subrule (B)(1), or as further permitted by the administrator is misconduct. See MCR 9.104(A)(7).

(3) If a respondent refuses to answer under subrule (B)(1), the refusal may be submitted under seal to a hearing panel for adjudication. If a panel finds that the refusal was not proper, it shall direct the attorney to answer the request for investigation within 21 days after its order.

(C) Attorney–Client Privilege. A person who files a request for investigation of an attorney irrevocably waives any attorney-client privilege that he or she may have as to matters relating to the request for the purposes of the commission's investigation.

(D) Representation by Attorney. The respondent may be represented by an attorney.

[Adopted effective March 1, 1985. Amended March 19, 1987, effective June 1, 1987, 428 Mich; December 18, 1990, effective February 1, 1991, 437 Mich; February 23, 2006, effective May 1, 2006, 474 Mich; April 19, 2011, effective September 1, 2011, 489 Mich; October 3, 2012, effective January 1, 2013, 493 Mich.]

Comments

Staff Comment to 1985 Adoption

MCR 9.113 corresponds to GCR 1963, 962.

Subrule (C) is a new provision regarding waiver of the attorney-client privilege.

Staff Comment to 1987 Amendment

The [June 1, 1987] addition to MCR 9.113(A) clarifies the requirement that answers to requests for investigation must be in writing.

[Effective June 1, 1987] MCR 9.114(A)(2) has been moved and renumbered MCR 9.113(B)(3) because it more properly belongs in this rule. The submission to a hearing panel is permissive rather than mandatory since, in most cases, the administrator will not contest the propriety of respondent's exercise of a privilege, and submission to a hearing panel in such circumstances would be unnecessary.

Staff Comment to 1991 Amendment

The [February 1,] 1991 amendment to subrule (A) added the requirement that the complainant be given copies of the respondent's answer and any supporting documents.

Staff Comment to 2006 Amendment

The amendment of MCR 2.612(A)(2), 3.802(B)(1), 5.313(F), and 9.113(B)(2), effective May 1, 2006, reflect numbering changes in other rules.

Staff Comment to 2011 Amendment

This proposal contains various amendments of the attorney discipline rules recommended by the Attorney Grievance Commission, which also were thoroughly reviewed by a State Bar of Michigan workgroup at the request of the Court.

Staff Comment to 2013 Amendment

The amendment of MCR 9.113(A) clarifies that the grievance administrator has the discretion to withhold all or part of respondent's answer and any supporting documents from the person who filed the request for investigation.

Rule 9.114   Action by Administrator or Commission after Answer

(A) Action After Investigation. After an answer is filed or the time for filing an answer has expired, the administrator may

(1) dismiss the request for investigation and notify the complainant and the respondent of the reasons for the dismissal,

(2) conduct further investigation. Upon completion of the investigation, the grievance administrator shall refer the matter to the commission for its review. The commission may direct that a complaint be filed, that the file be closed, that the respondent be admonished or placed on contractual probation with the respondent's consent, or

(3) close a file administratively where warranted under the circumstances.

(B) Admonition. With a respondent's consent, a respondent may be admonished by the commission without filing a complaint. An admonition does not constitute discipline and shall be confidential except as provided by this rule, MCR 9.115(J)(3) and by MCR 9.126(D)(4).

(1) The administrator shall notify the respondent of the provisions of this rule by ordinary mail at the respondent's address on file with the state bar as required by Rule 2 of the Supreme Court Rules Concerning the State Bar of Michigan, or as otherwise directed by respondent.

(2) The respondent may, within 21 days of service of the admonition or such additional time as permitted by the administrator, notify the commission in writing that respondent objects to the admonition. Upon timely receipt of the written objection, the commission shall vacate the admonition and either dismiss the request for investigation or authorize the filing of a complaint. Failure of a respondent to object constitutes an acceptance.

(C) Contractual Probation. For purposes of this subrule, "contractual probation" means the placement of a consenting respondent on probation by the commission, without the filing of formal charges. Contractual probation does not constitute discipline, and shall be confidential under MCR 9.126 except as provided by MCR 9.115(J)(3).

(1) If the commission finds that the alleged misconduct, if proven, would not result in disbarment or a substantial suspension of a respondent's license to practice law, the commission may defer disposition of the matter and place the respondent on contractual probation for a period not to exceed three years, provided the following criteria are met:

(a) the misconduct is significantly related to a respondent's substance abuse problem, or mental or physical infirmity or disability,

(b) the terms and conditions of the contractual probation, which shall include an appropriate period of treatment, are agreed upon by the commission and the respondent, and

(c) the commission determines that contractual probation is appropriate and in the best interests of the public, the courts, the legal profession, and the respondent.

(2) A contractual probation may include one or more of these requirements:

(a) Periodic alcohol or drug testing.

(b) Attendance at support-group or comparable meetings.

(c) Professional counseling on a regular basis.

(d) An initial written diagnosis and prognosis by the provider followed by quarterly verification of treatment by the provider as agreed upon by the commission and the respondent. The provider shall notify the commission of any failure to adhere to the treatment plan.

(3) The respondent is responsible for any costs associated with the contractual probation and related treatment.

(4) Upon written notice to the respondent and an opportunity to file written objections, the commission may terminate the contractual probation and file disciplinary proceedings or take other appropriate action based on the misconduct, if

(a) the respondent fails to satisfactorily complete the terms and conditions of the contractual probation, or

(b) the commission concludes that the respondent has committed other misconduct that warrants the filing of a formal complaint.

(5) The placing of a respondent on contractual probation shall constitute a final disposition that entitles the complainant to notice in accordance with MCR 9.114(D), and to file an action in accordance with MCR 9.122(A)(2).

(D) Assistance of Law Enforcement Agencies. The administrator may request a law enforcement office to assist in an investigation by furnishing all available information about the respondent. Law enforcement officers are requested to comply promptly with each request.

(E) Assistance of Courts. If the grievance administrator determines that a nonpublic court file exists, including files on expunged convictions, and that it is relevant to a pending investigation concerning a respondent attorney, the administrator may request that a court release to the Attorney Grievance Commission the nonpublic court file. Courts are requested to comply promptly with each request.

(F) Report by Administrator. The administrator shall inform the complainant and, if the respondent answered, the respondent, of the final disposition of every request for investigation.

(G) Retention of Records. All files and records relating to allegations of misconduct by an attorney must be retained by the commission for the lifetime of the attorney, except as follows:

(1) Where 3 years have passed from the conclusion of formal disciplinary action or the issuance of an admonishment, nonessential documents may be discarded.

(2) The administrator may destroy the files or records relating to a closed or dismissed request for investigation after 3 years have elapsed from the date of dismissal or closing.

(3) If no request for investigation was pending when the files or records were created or acquired, and no related request for investigation was filed subsequently, the administrator may destroy the files or records after 1 year has elapsed from the date when they were created or acquired by the commission.
[Adopted effective March 1, 1985. Amended March 19, 1987, effective June 1, 1987, 428 Mich. Amended effective September 27, 1990; January 29, 1992, 439 Mich; September 1, 1995, 450 Mich. Amended October 19, 1995, effective December 1, 1995, 450 Mich; March 24, 1998, effective April 1, 1998, 456 Mich; July 1, 2003, effective September 1, 2003, 468 Mich; April 19, 2011, effective September 1, 2011, 489 Mich.]

Comments

Staff Comment to 1985 Adoption

MCR 9.114 is substantially the same as GCR 1963, 963.

Staff Comment to 1987 Amendment

The [June 1, 1987] change in MCR 9.114(A) transfers the power to admonish from the grievance administrator to the grievance commission, in conformity with present practice and amended MCR 9.106(6). The last sentence of MCR 9.114(A) has been moved to MCR 9.113(B)(3). New subrule MCR 9.114(C)(2) provides for enforcement of the subpoena in the same manner as provided for hearing panel subpoenas in MCR 9.115(I)(2).

Staff Comment to 1990 Amendment

The [July 27,] 1990 amendment to subrule (E) modified the rules regarding the retention of commission records.

Staff Comment to 1992 Amendment

The amendment effective January 29, 1992 moved former subrule (C) [with changes] to MCR 9.112.

Staff Comment to September, 1995 Amendment

The 1995 amendment of MCR 9.114 permits the commission to defer disposition of a discipline matter and place a consenting respondent on contractual probation for up to two years, provided the alleged misconduct is significantly related to substance abuse and, if proven, would not result in a substantial suspension or revocation of the respondent's license to practice law.

Staff Comment to December, 1995 Amendment

The 1995 amendment of MCR 9.114(A) authorizes the Grievance Administrator to dismiss a request for investigation after an answer is filed, without referring the matter to the Attorney Grievance Commission.

Staff Comment to 1998 Amendment

The amendment of MCR 9.114 makes technical changes necessary in light of statutory amendments and corrects cross-references.

The amendment of MCR 9.114 makes changes in cross-references necessitated by earlier amendments. Some published versions of the rules already include several of these corrections.

Staff Comment to 2003 Amendment

The July 1, 2003, amendments of MCR 7.304, 9.114, and 9.122, effective September 1, 2003, clarified that a complaint for mandamus is inappropriate in instances where a party really is asking the Supreme Court to exercise its power of superintending control over the Board of Law Examiners, the Attorney Discipline Board, or the Attorney Grievance Commission.

Staff Comment to 2011 Amendment

This proposal contains various amendments of the attorney discipline rules recommended by the Attorney Grievance Commission, which also were thoroughly reviewed by a State Bar of Michigan workgroup at the request of the Court.

Rule 9.115   Hearing Panel Procedure

(A) Rules Applicable. Except as otherwise provided in these rules, the rules governing practice and procedure in a nonjury civil action apply to a proceeding before a hearing panel. Pleadings must conform as nearly as practicable to the requirements of subchapter 2.100. The original of the formal complaint and all other pleadings must be filed with the board.

The formal complaint must be served on the respondent. All other pleadings must be served on the opposing party and each member of the hearing panel. Proof of service of the formal complaint may be filed at any time prior to the date of the hearing. Proof of service of all other pleadings must be filed with the original pleadings.

(B) Complaint. Except as provided by MCR 9.120, a complaint setting forth the facts of the alleged misconduct begins proceedings before a hearing panel. The administrator shall prepare the complaint, file it with the board, and serve it on the respondent and a respondent's employer. The unwillingness of a complainant to proceed, or a settlement between the complainant and the respondent, does not itself affect the right of the administrator to proceed.

(C) Service. Service of the complaint and a default must be made by personal service or by registered or certified mail addressed to the person at the person's last known address. An attorney's last known address is the address on file with the state bar as required by Rule 2 of the Supreme Court Rules Concerning the State Bar of Michigan. A respondent's attorney of record must also be served, but service may be made under MCR 2.107. Service is effective at the time of mailing, and nondelivery does not affect the validity of the service.

(D) Answer.

(1) A respondent must serve and file a signed answer or take other action permitted by law or these rules within 21 days after being served with the complaint in the manner provided in MCR 9.115(C). A signature constitutes verification that the respondent has read the answer or other response.

(2) A default, with the same effect as a default in a civil action, may enter against a respondent who fails within the time permitted to file an answer admitting, denying, or explaining the complaint, or asserting the grounds for failing to do so.

(E) Representation by Attorney. The respondent may be represented by an attorney, who must enter an appearance, which has the same effect as an appearance under MCR 2.117.

(F) Prehearing Procedure.

(1) *Extensions.* If good cause is shown, the hearing panel chairperson may grant one extension of time per party for filing pleadings and may grant one adjournment per party. Additional requests may be granted by the board chairperson if good cause is shown. Pending criminal or civil litigation of substantial similarity to the allegations of the complaint is not necessarily grounds for an adjournment.

(2) *Motion to Disqualify.*

(a) Within 14 days after an answer has been filed or the time for filing the answer has expired, each member of the hearing panel shall disclose in a writing filed with the board any information that the member believes could be grounds for disqualification under the guidelines of MCR 2.003(C), including pending requests for investigation filed against the member. The duty to disclose shall be a continuing one. The board shall serve a copy of the disclosure on each party and each panel member.

(b) A motion to disqualify must be filed within 14 days after the moving party discovers the ground for disqualification. If the discovery is made within 14 days of the hearing date, the motion must be made forthwith. If a motion is not timely filed, untimeliness is a factor in deciding whether the motion should be granted. All known grounds for disqualification must be included at the time the motion is filed. An affidavit must accompany the motion. The board chairperson shall decide the motion under the guidelines of MCR 2.003.

(c) The board must assign a substitute for a disqualified member of a hearing panel. If all are disqualified, the board must reassign the complaint to another panel.

(3) *Amendment of Pleadings.* The administrator and the respondent each may amend a pleading once as a matter of course within 14 days after being served with a responsive pleading by the opposing party, or within 15 days after serving the pleading if it does not require a responsive pleading. Otherwise, a party may amend a pleading only by leave granted by the hearing panel chairperson or with the written consent of the adverse party.

(4) *Discovery.* Pretrial or discovery proceedings are not permitted, except as follows:

(a) Within 21 days after the service of a formal complaint, a party may demand in writing that documentary evidence that is to be introduced at the hearing by the opposing party be made available for inspection or copying. Within 14 days after service of a written demand, the documents shall be made available, provided that the administrator need not comply prior to the filing of the respondent's answer; in such case, the administrator shall comply with the written demand within 14 days after the filing of the respondent's answer. The respondent shall comply with the written demand within 14 days, except that the respondent need not comply until the time for filing an answer to the formal complaint has expired. Any other documentary evidence to be introduced at the hearing by either party shall be supplied to the other party no later than 14 days prior to the hearing. Any documentary evidence not so supplied shall be excluded from the hearing except for good cause shown.

(i) Within 21 days after the service of a formal complaint, a party may demand in writing that the opposing party supply written notification of the name and address of any person to be called as a witness at the hearing. Within 14 days after the service of a written demand, the notification shall be supplied. However, the administrator need not comply prior to the filing of the respondent's answer to the formal complaint; in such cases, the administrator shall comply with the written demand within 14 days of the filing of the respondent's answer to the formal complaint. The respondent shall comply with the written demand within 14 days, except that the respondent need not comply until the time for filing an answer to the formal complaint has expired. Except for good cause shown, a party who is required to give said notification must give supplemental notice to the adverse party within 7 days after any additional witness has been identified, and must give the supplemental notice immediately if the additional witness is identified less than 14 days before a scheduled hearing.

(ii) Within 21 days following the filing of an answer, the administrator and respondent shall exchange the names and addresses of all persons having knowledge of relevant facts and comply with reasonable requests for (1) nonprivi-leged information and evidence relevant to the charges against the respondent, and (2) other material upon good cause shown to the chair of the hearing panel.

(b) A deposition may be taken of a witness who lives outside the state or is physically unable to attend the hearing. For good cause shown, the hearing panel may allow the parties to depose other witnesses.

(c) The hearing panel may order a prehearing conference held before a panel member to obtain admissions or otherwise narrow the issues presented by the pleadings.

If a party fails to comply with subrule (F)(4)(a), the hearing panel or the board may, on motion and showing of material prejudice as a result of the failure, impose one or more of the sanctions set forth in MCR 2.313(B)(2)(a)–(c).

(5) *Discipline by Consent.*

(a) In exchange for a stated form of discipline and on the condition that the plea or admission is accepted by the commission and the hearing panel, a respondent may offer to

(i) plead no contest or to admit all or some of the facts and misconduct alleged in the complaint or otherwise agreed to by the parties or

(ii) stipulate to facts and misconduct in a proceeding filed under subchapter 9.100 not initiated by a formal complaint.

The respondent's offer shall first be submitted to the commission. If an agreement is reached with the commission, the administrator and the respondent shall file with the board and the hearing panel a stipulation for a consent order of discipline. At the time of the filing, the administrator shall serve a copy of the stipulation upon the complainant.

(b) The stipulation shall include:

(i) admissions, which may be contained in an answer to the complaint, or a plea of no contest to facts sufficient to enable the hearing panel to determine the nature of the misconduct and conclude that the discipline proposed is appropriate in light of the identified misconduct;

(ii) citation to the applicable American Bar Association Standards for Imposing Lawyer Sanctions; and

(iii) disclosure of prior discipline.

Admonishments and contractual probations shall be filed separately and kept confidential until the hearing panel accepts the stipulation under this rule.

(c) Upon filing of a stipulation for a consent order of discipline, the hearing panel may:

(i) approve the stipulation and file a report and enter a final order of discipline; or

(ii) communicate with the administrator and the respondent about any concerns it may have regarding the stipulation. Before rejecting a stipulation, a hearing panel shall advise the parties that it is considering rejecting a stipulation and the basis for the rejection. The hearing panel shall provide an opportunity, at a status conference or comparable proceeding, for the parties to offer additional information in support of the stipulation.

(d) If a hearing panel rejects a stipulation, the hearing panel shall advise the parties in writing of its reason or reasons for rejecting the stipulation and allow the parties an opportunity to submit an amended stipulation.

(e) If a hearing panel rejects an amended stipulation, or if no amended stipulation is filed within 21 days after rejection of the initial stipulation, the matter shall be reassigned to a different hearing panel. Upon reassignment to a different hearing panel,

(i) the stipulation and any amended stipulation shall be deemed withdrawn,

(ii) statements and stipulations made in connection with the stipulation and any amended stipulation shall be inadmissible in disciplinary proceedings against the respondent and not binding on either party, and

(iii) the newly assigned hearing panel shall conduct a hearing.

(G) Hearing Time and Place; Notice. The board or the chairperson of the hearing panel shall set the time and place for a hearing. Notice of a hearing must be served by the board or the chairperson of the hearing panel on the administrator, the respondent, the complainant, and any attorney of record at least 21 days before the initial hearing. Unless the board or the chairperson of the hearing panel otherwise directs, the hearing must be in the county in which the respondent has or last had an office or residence. If the hearing panel fails to convene or complete its hearing within a reasonable time, the board may reassign the complaint to another panel or to a master. A party may file a motion for a change of venue. The motion must be filed with the board and shall be decided by the board chairperson, in part, on the basis of the guidelines in MCR 2.221. Notwithstanding MRE 615, there shall be a presumption that a complainant is entitled to be present during a hearing, which may only be overcome upon a finding by the panel, supported by facts that are particular to the proceeding, that testimony by the complainant is likely to be materially affected by exposure to other testimony at the hearing.

(H) Respondent's Appearance. The respondent shall personally appear at the hearing, unless excused by the panel, and is subject to cross-examination as an opposite party under MCL 600.2161.

(1) Where satisfactory proofs are entered into the record that a respondent possessed actual notice of the proceedings, but who still failed to appear, a panel shall suspend him or her effective 7 days from the date of entry of the order and until further order of the panel or the board.

(2) If the respondent, or the respondent's attorney on his or her behalf, claims physical or mental incapacity as a reason for the respondent's failure to appear before a hearing panel or the board, the panel or the board on its own initiative may, effective immediately, suspend the respondent from the practice of law until further order of the panel or board. The order of suspension must be filed and served as other orders of discipline.

(I) Hearing; Contempt.

(1) A hearing panel may issue subpoenas (including subpoenas for production of documents and other tangible things), cause testimony to be taken under oath, and rule on the admissibility of evidence under the Michigan Rules of Evidence. The oath or affirmation may be administered by a panel member. A subpoena must be issued in the name and under the seal of the board. It must be signed by a panel or board member, by the administrator, or by the respondent or the respondent's attorney. A subpoenaed witness must be paid the same fee and mileage as a witness subpoenaed to testify in the circuit court. Parties must notify their own witnesses of the date, time, and place of the hearing.

(2) A person who without just cause fails or refuses to appear and give evidence as commanded by a subpoena, to be sworn or affirmed, or to answer a proper question after he or she has been ordered to do so, is in contempt. The administrator may initiate a contempt proceeding under MCR 3.606 in the circuit court for the county where the act or refusal to act occurred.

(3) Upon a showing of good cause by a party, a panel may permit a witness to testify by telephonic, voice, or video conferencing.

(J) Decision.

(1) The hearing panel must file a report on its decisions regarding the misconduct charges and, if applicable, the resulting discipline. The report must include a certified transcript, a summary of the evidence, pleadings, exhibits and briefs, and findings of fact. The discipline section of the report must also include a summary of all previous misconduct for which the respondent was disciplined, admonished, or placed on contractual probation.

(2) Upon a finding of misconduct, the hearing panel shall conduct a separate sanction hearing to determine the appropriate discipline. The sanction hearing shall be conducted as soon after the finding of misconduct as is practicable and may be held immediately following the panel's ruling that misconduct has been established.

(3) If the hearing panel finds that the charge of misconduct is established by a preponderance of the evidence, it must enter an order of discipline. The order shall take effect 21 days after it is served on the respondent unless the panel finds good cause for the order to take effect on a different date, in which event the panel's decision must explain the reasons for ordering a different effective date. The discipline ordered may be concurrent or consecutive to other discipline. In determining the discipline to be imposed, any and all relevant evidence of aggravation or mitigation shall be admissible, including, but not limited to, records of the board, previous admonitions and orders of discipline, and the previous placement of the respondent on contractual probation.

(4) If the hearing panel finds that the charge of misconduct is not established by a preponderance of the evidence, it must enter an order dismissing the complaint.

(5) The report and order must be signed by the panel chairperson and filed with the board and the administrator. A copy must be served on the parties as required by these rules.

(K) Stay of Discipline. If a discipline order is a suspension of 179 days or less, a stay of the discipline order will automatically issue on the timely filing by the respondent of a petition for review and a petition for a stay of the discipline. If the discipline ordered is more severe than a suspension of 179 days, the respondent may petition the board for a stay pending review of the discipline order. Once granted, a stay remains effective until the further order of the board.

(L) Enforcement. The administrator shall take the necessary steps to enforce a discipline order after it is effective.

(M) Resignation by Respondent; Admission of Charges. An attorney's resignation may not be accepted while a request for investigation or a complaint is pending, except pursuant to an order of disbarment.

[Adopted effective March 1, 1985. Amended March 19, 1987, effective June 1, 1987, 428 Mich; January 4, 1994, effective March 1, 1994, 444 Mich; June 8, 1995, effective September 1, 1995, 449 Mich; December 9, 1997, effective April 1, 1998, 456 Mich; April 19, 2011, effective September 1, 2011, 489 Mich. Amended effective January 25, 2017, 500 Mich.]

Comments

Staff Comment to 1985 Adoption

MCR 9.115 is substantially the same as GCR 1963, 964.

Staff Comment to 1987 Amendment

[Effective June 1, 1987] MCR 9.115(A) specifies service and filing requirements, and adds a requirement that hearing panel members be served with copies of the pleadings.

MCR 9.115(B) is amended [effective June 1, 1987] to acknowledge the different procedure employed in MCR 9.120 (attorney convicted of a crime). Additionally, deletion of the phrase "14 days later" incorporates an intervening amendment to former GCR 1963, 964.2, the predecessor of this rule.

MCR 9.115(F)(4)(a) and (b) are amended [effective June 1, 1987] to provide for reciprocal discovery.

MCR 9.115(G) is amended [effective June 1, 1987] to provide for service of notices of hearing on the grievance administrator and the attorneys of record. It also authorizes the board to refer a complaint to a master if the hearing panel fails to act within a reasonable time.

MCR 9.115(J) is amended [effective June 1, 1987] to provide for a bifurcated hearing procedure. The first phase determines misconduct if any; the second phase determines the discipline. Subrule (J)(3) provides that prior discipline orders or admonishments, if any, should be considered by a hearing panel in the assessment of discipline.

MCR 9.115(K) is amended [effective June 1, 1987] to conform with MCR 9.122(C). Both rules will now provide for an automatic stay pending appeal when the discipline order imposes a suspension of less than 180 days. This rule governs appeals to the board. MCR 9.122(C) governs appeals to the Supreme Court.

MCR 9.115(M) is amended [effective June 1, 1987] to eliminate past uncertainty regarding the effect of a resignation while charges were still pending.

Staff Comment to 1994 Amendment

The March 1, 1994 amendments: (1) authorized the chairperson of the hearing panel to act on behalf of the panel, and the chairperson of the board to act on behalf of the board, in ruling on requests for extensions (subrule [F][1]); (2) required hearing panelists to make advance written disclosures of possible grounds for their disqualification (subrule [F][2]); (3) allowed pleadings to be amended once as a matter of right and subsequently by leave granted or if the opposing party consents (subrule [F][3]); (4) expanded the authority for taking depositions (subrule [F][4]); (5) required that an offer of consent discipline be approved by the commission before being submitted to a hearing panel (subrule [F][5]); (6) allowed a party to move for a change of venue (subrule [G]); (7) allowed a hearing panel to submit a single report covering its findings on both misconduct and discipline (subrule [J][1]); (8) allowed the hearing panel to begin the hearing on discipline immediately after announcing its findings regarding misconduct (subrule [J][2]); (9) allowed the hearing panel to specify that its discipline order shall take effect either earlier or later than the otherwise presumed 21 days after the order is entered (subrule [J][3]); (10) required the respondent to petition for a stay pending review even in situations where the stay will be granted automatically if it is requested (subrule [K]).

Staff Comment to 1995 Amendment

The 1995 amendment of MCR 9.115(J) permits a hearing panel, when determining discipline, to consider a respondent's previous placement on contractual probation under the 1995 amendment of MCR 9.114.

Staff Comment to 1997 Amendment

The 1997 amendment of the rule, which took effect April 1, 1998, added a second paragraph to MCR 9.115(F)(4)(b). The change, which was recommended by the State Bar of Michigan, permits reciprocal discovery of witness statements in lawyer discipline proceedings.

Staff Comment to 2011 Amendment

This proposal contains various amendments of the attorney discipline rules recommended by the Attorney Grievance Commission, which also were thoroughly reviewed by a State Bar of Michigan workgroup at the request of the Court.

Staff Comment to 2017 Amendment

The amendment of MCR 9.115(F)(5) clarifies that a hearing panel may allow parties to submit an amended stipulation. If a hearing panel rejects an amended stipulation, the matter would be referred to a different hearing panel to conduct a hearing. This language was submitted jointly by the Attorney Grievance Commission and Attorney Discipline Board.

Rule 9.116   Judges; Former Judges

(A) Judges. The administrator or commission may not take action against an incumbent judge, except that this rule does not prohibit an action by the administrator or commission against:

(1) a magistrate or referee for misconduct unrelated to judicial functions, whether before or during the period when the person serves as a magistrate or referee; or

(2) a visiting judge as provided in MCR 9.203(E). If the Judicial Tenure Commission receives a request for investigation of a magistrate or referee or visiting judge arising from the practice of law, the Judicial Tenure Commission shall refer the matter to the administrator or commission for investigation in the first instance. If the administrator or the commission dismisses the request for investigation referred by the Judicial Tenure Commission, or a request for investigation of a magistrate, referee or visiting judge submitted directly to the commission by a complainant, the administrator or commission shall notify the Judicial Tenure Commission, which may take action as it deems appropriate.

(B) Former Judges. The administrator or commission may take action against a former judge for conduct resulting in removal as a judge, and for any conduct which was not the subject of a disposition by the Judicial Tenure Commission or by the Court. The administrator or commission may not take action against a former judge for conduct where the court imposed a sanction less than removal or the Judicial Tenure Commission has taken any action under MCR 9.207(B)(1)–(5).

(C) Judicial Tenure Commission Record. The record of the Judicial Tenure Commission proceeding is admissible at a hearing involving a former judge. The administrator or the respondent may introduce additional evidence.

[Adopted effective March 1, 1985. Amended March 19, 1987, effective June 1, 1987, 428 Mich; November 7, 1994, effective January 1, 1995, 447 Mich; April 19, 2011, effective September 1, 2011, 489 Mich.]

Comments

Staff Comment to 1985 Adoption

MCR 9.116 is substantially the same as GCR 1963, 965.

Staff Comment to 1987 Amendment

[Effective June 1, 1987] MCR 9.116(D) is amended, and MCR 9.116(E) is added to clarify the present practice.

Staff Comment to 1995 Amendment

Subrule (A) took effect in 1995. It permits the Attorney Grievance Commission to proceed against a lawyer who is a magistrate or referee and who is charged with misconduct unrelated to the duties of a magistrate or referee, without waiting for the Judicial Tenure Commission to make a recommendation. In such a case, subrule (A) also has the effect of removing the ceiling on discipline stated in subrule (E).

Staff Comment to 2011 Amendment

This proposal contains various amendments of the attorney discipline rules recommended by the Attorney Grievance Commission, which also were thoroughly reviewed by a State Bar of Michigan workgroup at the request of the Court.

Rule 9.117   Hearing Procedure Before Master

If the board assigns a complaint to a master, the master shall hold a public hearing on the complaint and receive evidence. To the extent that MCR 9.115 may be applied, it governs procedure before a master. After the hearing, the master shall prepare a report containing

(1) a brief statement of the proceedings,

(2) findings of fact, and

(3) conclusions of law.

The master shall file the report with a hearing panel designated by the board and serve a copy on the administrator and the respondent. Within 14 days after the report is filed, the administrator or the respondent may file objections to the report and a supporting brief. The panel must determine if the record supports the findings of fact and conclusions of law and impose discipline, if warranted. Further proceedings are governed by MCR 9.118.

[Adopted effective March 1, 1985.]

Comments

Staff Comment to 1985 Adoption

MCR 9.117 is substantially the same as GCR 1963, 966.

Rule 9.118   Review of Order of Hearing Panel

(A) Review of Order; Time.

(1) The administrator, the complainant, or the respondent may petition the board in writing to review the order of a hearing panel filed under MCR 9.113(B), 9.115, 9.116, 9.120, 9.121 or 9.124. The board may grant review of a nonfinal order and decide such interlocutory matters without a hearing. A petition for review must set forth the reasons and the grounds on which review is sought and must be filed with the board within 21 days after the order is served. The petitioner must serve copies of the petition and the accompanying documents on the other party and the complainant and file a proof of service with the board.

(2) A cross-petition for review may be filed within 21 days after the petition for review is served on the cross-petitioner. The cross-petition must be served on the other party and the complainant, and a proof of service must be filed with the board.

(3) A delayed petition for review may be considered by the board chairperson under the guidelines of MCR 7.205(G). If a petition for review is filed more than 12 months after the order of the hearing panel is entered, the petition may not be granted.

(B) Order to Show Cause.

If a petition for review is timely filed or a delayed petition for review is accepted for filing, the board shall issue an order to show cause, at a date and time specified, why the order of the hearing panel should not be affirmed. The order shall establish a briefing schedule for all parties and may require that an answer to the petition or cross-petition be filed. An opposing party may file an answer even if the order does not require one. The board must serve the order to show cause on the administrator, respondent, and complainant at least 21 days before the hearing. Failure to comply with the order to show cause, including, but not limited to, a requirement for briefs, may be grounds for dismissal of a petition for review. Dismissal of a petition for review shall not affect the validity of a cross-petition for review.

(C) Hearing.

(1) A hearing on the order to show cause must be heard by a sub-board of at least 3 board members assigned by the chairperson. The board must make a final decision on consideration of the whole record, including a transcript of the presentation made to the sub-board and the sub-board's recommendation. The respondent shall appear personally at the review hearing unless excused by the board. Failure to appear may result in denial of any relief sought by the respondent, or any other action allowable under MCR 9.118(D).

(2) If the board believes that additional testimony should be taken, it may refer the case to a hearing panel or a master. The panel or the master shall then take the additional testimony and shall make a supplemental report, including a transcript of the additional testimony, pleadings, exhibits, and briefs with the board. Notice of the filing of the supplemental report and a copy of the report must be served as an original report and order of a hearing panel.

(D) Decision.

After the hearing on the order to show cause, the board may affirm, amend, reverse, or nullify the order of the hearing panel in whole or in part or order other discipline. A discipline order is not effective until 28 days after it is served on the respondent unless the board finds good cause for the order to take effect earlier.

(E) Motion for Reconsideration; Stay.

A motion for reconsideration may be filed at any time before the board's order takes effect. An answer to a motion for reconsideration may be filed. If the discipline order is a suspension for 179 days or less, a stay of the discipline order will automatically issue on the timely filing by the respondent of a motion for reconsideration. If the discipline is greater than a 179-day suspension, the respondent may petition for a stay. If the board grants a stay, the stay remains effective for 28 days after the board enters its order granting or denying reconsideration.

(F) Filing Orders.

The board must file a copy of its discipline order with the Supreme Court clerk and the clerk of the county where the respondent resides and where his or her office is located. The order must be served on all parties. If the respondent requests it in writing, a dismissal order must be similarly filed and served.

[Adopted effective March 1, 1985. Amended March 19, 1987, effective June 1, 1987, 428 Mich; January 4, 1994, effective March 1, 1994, 444 Mich; October 3, 2000, effective January 1, 2001, 463 Mich. Amended effective October 14, 2003, 469 Mich. Amended April 19, 2011, effective September 1, 2011, 489 Mich. Amended effective March 9, 2016, 499 Mich.]

Comments

Staff Comment to 1985 Adoption

MCR 9.118 is substantially the same as GCR 1963, 967.

Staff Comment to 1987 Amendment

MCR 9.118(A)(3) is added [effective June 1, 1987] to codify existing practice regarding delayed petitions. New subrule (A)(2) provides for cross-petitions.

MCR 9.118(B) is amended [effective June 1, 1987] to provide for dismissal of petitions for review that are not timely prosecuted.

MCR 9.118(C) is amended [effective June 1, 1987] to require a respondent to appear at a review hearing. This is a codification of language now routinely included in board orders to show cause.

MCR 9.118(D) is amended [effective June 1, 1987] to codify present practice allowing motions for reconsideration and provide that the board may stay an order of discipline while it considers a motion for reconsideration. See also MCR 9.122(A)(1).

Staff Comment to 1994 Amendment

The March 1, 1994 amendments: (1) listed in subrule (A)(1) the orders that are appealable to the board; (2) in subrule (A)(1), added a requirement that a copy of the petition for review be served on the person who filed the request for investigation; (3) added to subrule (A)(2) a requirement that the cross-petition for review be served on the other interested parties; (4) in subrule (A)(3), authorized the board's chairperson, rather than the full board, to make the decision on whether to accept a delayed petition for review; (5) added to subrule (B) provisions for a briefing schedule; (6) moved the reconsideration and stay provisions from subrule (D) to a new subrule (E) and added language clarifying that merely filing a motion for reconsideration does not automatically stay the board's order.

Staff Comment to 2000 Amendment

The October 3, 2000 amendment of MCR 9.118(A)(3), effective January 1, 2001, made the 12–month period specified in MCR 7.205(F)(3) applicable to delayed petitions for review of hearing panel orders. Cf. *Grievance Admin v Underwood*, 462 Mich 188 (2000).

Staff Comment to 2003 Amendment

The October 14, 2003 amendments of MCR 7.302, 9.118, and 9.122, effective immediately, adjusted the time limits for filing appeals from Attorney Discipline Board orders of discipline or dismissal, setting the time at 28 days. Adjustments were necessary in light of the amendment of MCR 7.302, effective September 1, 2003, which changed the times for filing other appeals to the Supreme Court.

Staff Comment to 2011 Amendment

This proposal contains various amendments of the attorney discipline rules recommended by the Attorney Grievance Commission, which also were thoroughly reviewed by a State Bar of Michigan workgroup at the request of the Court.

Staff Comment to 2016 Amendment

These amendments update cross-references that changed after the rule was adopted and make other nonsubstantive revisions.

Rule 9.119 Conduct of Disbarred, Suspended, or Inactive Attorneys

(A) Notification to Clients. An attorney who has resigned under Rule 3 of the Rules Concerning the State Bar of Michigan, or been disbarred, or suspended, or who is transferred to inactive status pursuant to MCR 9.121, or who is suspended for nondisciplinary reasons pursuant to Rule 4 of the Supreme Court Rules Concerning the State Bar of Michigan, shall, within 7 days of the effective date of the order of discipline, resignation, the transfer to inactive status or the nondisciplinary suspension, notify all his or her active clients, in writing, by registered or certified mail, return receipt requested, of the following:

(1) the nature and duration of the discipline imposed, the transfer to inactive status, or the nondisciplinary suspension, or the resignation;

(2) the effective date of such discipline, transfer to inactive status, or nondisciplinary suspension, or resignation;

(3) the attorney's inability to act as an attorney after the effective date of such discipline, transfer to inactive status, nondisciplinary suspension, or resignation;

(4) the location and identity of the custodian of the clients' files and records, which will be made available to them or to substitute counsel;

(5) that the clients may wish to seek legal advice and counsel elsewhere; provided that, if the disbarred, suspended, inactive, or resigned attorney was a member of a law firm, the firm may continue to represent each client with the client's express written consent;

(6) the address to which all correspondence to the attorney may be addressed.

(B) Conduct in Litigated Matters. In addition to the requirements of subsection (A) of this rule, the affected attorney must, by the effective date of the order of disbarment, suspension, transfer to inactive status, or resignation, in every matter in which the attorney is representing a client in litigation, file with the tribunal and all parties a notice of the attorney's disqualification from the practice of law. The affected attorney shall either file a motion to withdraw from the representation, or, with the client's knowledge and consent, a substitution of counsel.

(C) Filing of Proof of Compliance. Within 14 days after the effective date of the order of disbarment, suspension, or transfer to inactive status, pursuant to MCR 9.121, or resignation the disbarred, suspended, inactive, or resigned attorney shall file with the administrator and the board an affidavit showing full compliance with this rule. The affidavit must include as an appendix copies of the disclosure notices and mailing receipts required under subrules (A) and (B) of this rule. The affidavit must set forth any claim by the affected attorney that he or she does not have active clients at the time of the effective date of the change in status. A disbarred, suspended, inactive, or resigned attorney shall keep and maintain records of the various steps taken under this rule so that, in any subsequent proceeding instituted by or against him or her, proof of compliance with this rule and with the disbarment or suspension order will be available.

(D) Conduct After Entry of Order Prior to Effective Date. A disbarred or suspended attorney, after entry of the order of disbarment or suspension and prior to its effective date, shall not accept any new retainer or engagement as attorney for another in any new case or legal matter of any nature, unless specifically authorized by the board chairperson upon a showing of good cause and a finding that it is not contrary to the interests of the public and profession. However, during the period between the entry of the order and its effective date, the suspended or disbarred attorney may complete, on behalf of any existing client, all matters that were pending on the entry date.

(E) Conduct After Effective Date of Order. An attorney who is disbarred, suspended, transferred to inactive status pursuant to MCR 9.121, or who resigns is, during the period of disbarment, suspension, or inactivity, or from and after the date of resignation, forbidden from:

(1) practicing law in any form;

(2) having contact either in person, by telephone, or by electronic means, with clients or potential clients of a lawyer or law firm either as a paralegal, law clerk, legal assistant, or lawyer;

(3) appearing as an attorney before any court, judge, justice, board, commission, or other public authority; and

(4) holding himself or herself out as an attorney by any means.

(F) Compensation of Disbarred, Suspended, Resigned, or Inactive Attorney. An attorney who has been disbarred or suspended, has resigned, or who is transferred to inactive status pursuant to MCR 9.121 may not share in any legal fees for legal services performed by another attorney during the period of disqualification from the practice of law. A disbarred, suspended, resigned, or inactive attorney may be compensated on a quantum meruit basis for legal services rendered and expenses paid by him or her prior to the effective date of the disbarment, suspension, resignation, or transfer to inactive status.

(G) Receivership.

(1) *Attorney with a Firm.* If an attorney who is a member of a firm is disbarred, suspended, is transferred to inactive status pursuant to MCR 9.121, or resigns his or her license to practice law, the firm may continue to represent each client with the client's express written consent. Copies of the signed consents shall be maintained with the client file.

(2) *Attorney Practicing Alone.* If an attorney is transferred to inactive status, resigns, or is disbarred or suspended and fails to give notice under the rule, or disappears, is imprisoned, or dies, and there is no partner, executor or other responsible person capable of conducting the attorney's affairs, the administrator may ask the chief judge in the judicial circuit in which the attorney maintained his or her practice to appoint a person to act as a receiver with necessary powers, including:

(a) to obtain and inventory the attorney's files;

(b) to take any action necessary to protect the interests of the attorney and the attorney's clients;

(c) to change the address at which the attorney's mail is delivered and to open the mail; or

(d) to secure (garner) the lawyer's bank accounts.

The person appointed is analogous to a receiver operating under the direction of the circuit court.

(3) *Confidentiality.* The person appointed may not disclose to any third parties any information protected by MRPC 1.6 without the client's written consent.

(4) *Publication of Notice.* Upon receipt of notification from the receiver, the state bar shall publish in the Michigan Bar Journal notice of the receivership, including the name and address of the subject attorney, and the name, address, and telephone number of the receiver.

[Adopted effective March 1, 1985. Amended March 19, 1987, effective June 1, 1987, 428 Mich; April 19, 2011, effective September 1, 2011, 489 Mich.]

Comments

Staff Comment to 1987 Amendment

The new MCR 9.119 [effective June 1, 1987] is a complete revision of the present [former] rule.

Staff Comment to 2011 Amendment

This proposal contains various amendments of the attorney discipline rules recommended by the Attorney Grievance Commission, which also were thoroughly reviewed by a State Bar of Michigan workgroup at the request of the Court.

Rule 9.120 Conviction of Criminal Offense; Reciprocal Discipline

(A) Notification of the Grievance Administrator and the Attorney Discipline Board.

(1) When a lawyer is convicted of a crime, the lawyer, the prosecutor or other authority who prosecuted the lawyer, and the defense attorney who represented the lawyer must notify the grievance administrator and the board of the conviction. This notice must be given in writing within 14 days after the conviction.

(2) A lawyer who has been the subject of an order of discipline or transferred to inactive status by any court of record or any body authorized by law or by rule of court to conduct disciplinary proceedings against attorneys, of the United States, or of any state or territory of the United States or of the District of Columbia, or who has resigned from the bar or roster of attorneys in lieu of discipline by, or during the pendency of, discipline proceedings before such court or body shall inform the grievance administrator and board of entry of such order, transfer, or resignation within 14 days of the entry of the order, transfer, or resignation.

(B) Criminal Conviction.

(1) On conviction of a felony, an attorney is automatically suspended until the effective date of an order filed by a hearing panel under MCR 9.115(J). A conviction occurs upon the return of a verdict of guilty or upon the acceptance of a plea of guilty or nolo contendere. The board may, on the attorney's motion, set aside the automatic suspension when it appears consistent with the maintenance of the integrity and honor of the profession, the protection of the public, and the interests of justice. The board must set aside the automatic suspension if the felony conviction is vacated, reversed, or otherwise set aside for any reason by the trial court or an appellate court.

(2) In a disciplinary proceeding instituted against an attorney based on the attorney's conviction of a criminal offense, a certified copy of the judgment of conviction is conclusive proof of the commission of the criminal offense.

(3) The administrator may file with the board a judgment of conviction showing that an attorney has violated a criminal law of a state or of the United States, an ordinance, or tribal law pursuant to MCR 2.615. The board shall then order the attorney to show cause why a final order of discipline should not be entered, and the board shall refer the proceeding to a hearing panel for hearing. At the hearing, questions as to the validity of the conviction, alleged trial errors, and the availability of appellate remedies shall not be considered. After the hearing, the panel shall issue an order under MCR 9.115(J).

(4) On a pardon the board may, and on a reversal of the conviction the board must, by order filed and served under MCR 9.118(F), vacate the order of discipline. The attorney's name must be returned to the roster of Michigan attorneys and counselors at law, but the administrator may nevertheless proceed against the respondent for misconduct which had led to the criminal charge.

(C) Reciprocal Discipline.

(1) A certified copy of a final adjudication by any court of record or any body authorized by law or by rule of court to conduct disciplinary proceedings against attorneys by any state or territory of the United States or of the District of Columbia, a United States court, or a federal administrative agency, determining that an attorney, whether or not admitted in that jurisdiction, has committed misconduct or has been transferred to disability inactive status, shall establish conclusively the misconduct or the disability for purposes of a proceeding under subchapter 9.100 of these rules and comparable discipline or transfer shall be imposed in the Michigan proceeding unless the respondent was not afforded due process of law in the course of the original proceedings, the imposition of comparable discipline or transfer in Michigan would be clearly inappropriate, or the reason for the original transfer to disability inactive status no longer exists.

(2) Upon the filing by the grievance administrator of a certified copy of final adjudication described in paragraph

(C)(1) with the board, the board shall issue an order directed to the lawyer and the administrator:

(a) attaching a copy of the order from the other jurisdiction; and

(b) directing, that, within 21 days from service of the order, the lawyer and administrator shall inform the board (i) of any objection to the imposition of comparable discipline or disability inactive status in Michigan based on the grounds set forth in paragraph (C)(1) of this rule, and (ii) whether a hearing is requested.

(3) Upon receipt of an objection to the imposition of comparable discipline or disability inactive status raising one or more of the issues identified in paragraph (C)(1) of this rule, the board shall assign the matter to a hearing panel for disposition. The opposing party shall have 21 days to reply to an objection. If a hearing is requested, and the hearing panel grants the request, the hearing shall be held in accordance with the procedures set forth in MCR 9.115 except as otherwise provided in this rule.

(4) Papers filed under this rule shall conform as nearly as practicable to the requirements of subchapter 2.100 and shall be filed with the board and served on the opposing party and each member of the hearing panel once assigned.

(5) The burden is on the party seeking to avoid the imposition of comparable discipline or transfer to disability inactive status to demonstrate that it is not appropriate for one or more of the grounds set forth in paragraph (C)(1). "Comparable" discipline does not mean that the dates of a period of disqualification from practice in this state must coincide with the dates of the period of disqualification, if any, in the original jurisdiction.

(6) If the 21–day period discussed in paragraph (C)(2)(b) has expired without objection by either party, the respondent is in default, with the same effect as a default in a civil action, and the board shall impose comparable discipline or transfer to disability inactive status unless it appears that one of the grounds set forth in paragraph (C)(1) of this rule requires a different result, in which case the board shall schedule a hearing in accord with paragraph (3) of this rule. An order entered pursuant to this subparagraph may be set aside if the requirements of MCR 2.603(D) are established.

(7) In the event the discipline or transfer to disability inactive status imposed in the original jurisdiction is stayed, any reciprocal discipline imposed in Michigan shall be deferred until the stay expires.

[Adopted effective March 1, 1985. Amended March 19, 1987, effective June 1, 1987, 428 Mich; October 22, 1991, effective January 1, 1992, 439 Mich; January 17, 1992, effective March 1, 1992, 439 Mich; April 19, 2011, effective September 1, 2011, 489 Mich.]

Comments

Staff Comment to 1985 Adoption

MCR 9.120 is substantially the same as GCR 1963, 969.

Staff Comment to 1987 Amendment

The [June 1, 1987] amendment deletes the often overlooked requirement that the convicted attorney report the conviction to the grievance administrator. See former subrule (A)(1).

The [June 1, 1987] amendment to subrule (A)(3) limits the issues to be considered by the hearing panel. The panel is not to relitigate issues that have been or will be litigated in the criminal trial court or the appellate courts.

Staff Comment to 1991 Amendment

The 1991 amendment restored, in subrule (A), the requirement that criminal convictions be reported to the grievance authorities. See now-repealed GCR 1963, 969.1(a) and the originally enacted language of MCR 9.120(A)(1). The 1991 amendment redesignated former subrules (A) and (B) as subrules (B) and (C), respectively.

Staff Comment to 1992 Amendment

The [March 1,] 1992 amendment directed that the notice of conviction, which was required to be sent to the Grievance Administrator, must also be sent to the Attorney Discipline Board.

Staff Comment to 2011 Amendment

This proposal contains various amendments of the attorney discipline rules recommended by the Attorney Grievance Commission, which also were thoroughly reviewed by a State Bar of Michigan workgroup at the request of the Court.

Rule 9.121 Attorney Declared to be Incompetent or Alleged to be Incapacitated or Asserting Impaired Ability

(A) Adjudication by Court. If an attorney has been judicially declared incompetent or involuntarily committed on the grounds of incompetency or disability, the board, on proper proof of the fact, must enter an order effective immediately transferring the attorney to inactive status for an indefinite period and until further order of the board.

(B) Allegations of Incompetency or Incapacity.

(1) If it is alleged in a complaint by the administrator that an attorney is incapacitated to continue the practice of law because of mental or physical infirmity or disability or because of addiction to drugs or intoxicants, a hearing panel shall take action necessary to determine whether the attorney is incapacitated.

(a) Examination.

(i) Upon a showing of good cause that a mental or physical condition is the basis of respondent's incompetency or incapacity as alleged in a complaint by the administrator, a hearing panel may order respondent to submit to one or more medical examination(s) or psychological examination(s) that are relevant to a condition of respondent shown to be in controversy.

(ii) If testing is ordered, the administrator and respondent may stipulate to the expert(s) who will conduct the examination(s), prepare a report within 28 days of the conclusion of the examination(s), and provide a copy of said report to both parties. The content of a report prepared by an expert(s) pursuant to this paragraph is admissible into evidence in the proceedings, subject to relevancy objections.

(iii) If the administrator and/or respondent hire their own expert(s) to conduct the examination(s), the expert(s) will conduct the examination(s), prepare a report within 28 days of the conclusion of the examination(s), and provide a copy of said report to both parties. A report prepared pursuant to this paragraph is only admissible as substantive evidence upon stipulation by both parties. The respondent will be responsible for the expenses incurred by retaining his or her examiner.

(iv) On its own motion or on the motion of either party, the hearing panel may appoint an expert of its own selection to conduct the necessary examination(s). The expert so appointed will conduct the examination(s), prepare a report within 28 days of the conclusion of the examination(s), and provide a copy of said report to both parties. The content of a report prepared by an expert(s) pursuant to this paragraph is admissible into evidence in the proceedings unless, within 14 days of delivery of the report, a party objects, in which case either party may subpoena the expert(s) to testify at the hearing at that party's expense.

(b) Expert's Report. The expert's report as required by paragraph (a) shall include:

(i) the expert's resume or curriculum vitae;

(ii) a statement of facts, and a list of the tests that were administered and the test results;

(iii) a diagnosis, prognosis, a statement of limitations on the opinion because of the scope of the examination or testing, and recommendation for treatment, if any; and

(iv) no physician-patient privilege shall apply under this rule.

(2) The hearing panel shall provide notice to the attorney of the proceedings. Upon the request of a party, or on its own motion, and following a finding of good cause, a panel may recommend the appointment of counsel by the board to represent the respondent if he or she is without representation.

(3) If, after a hearing, the hearing panel concludes that the attorney is incapacitated from continuing to practice law, it shall enter an order transferring him or her to inactive status for an indefinite period and until further order of the board.

(4) Pending disciplinary proceedings against the attorney must be held in abeyance.

(5) Proceedings conducted under this subrule are subject to review by the board as provided in MCR 9.118.

(C) Assertion of Impaired Ability; Probation.

(1) If, in response to a formal complaint filed under subrule 9.115(B), the respondent asserts in mitigation and thereafter demonstrates by a preponderance of the evidence that

(a) during the period when the conduct that is the subject of the complaint occurred, his or her ability to practice law competently was materially impaired by physical or mental disability or by drug or alcohol addiction,

(b) the impairment was the cause of or substantially contributed to that conduct,

(c) the cause of the impairment is susceptible to treatment, and

(d) he or she in good faith intends to undergo treatment, and submits a detailed plan for such treatment, the hearing panel, the board, or the Supreme Court may enter an order placing the respondent on probation for a specific period not to exceed 3 years if it specifically finds that an order of probation is not contrary to the public interest.

(2) If the respondent alleges impairment by physical or mental disability or by drug or alcohol addiction pursuant to subrule (C)(1), the hearing panel may order the respondent to submit to a physical or mental examination in accord with the procedure set forth in MCR 9.121(B)(1)(a). The panel may direct that the expense of the examination be paid by the respondent. A respondent who fails or refuses to comply with an examination order, or refuses to undergo an examination requested by the administrator, shall not be eligible for probation.

(3) The probation order

(a) must specify the treatment the respondent is to undergo,

(b) may require the respondent to practice law only under the direct supervision of other attorneys, or

(c) may include any other terms the evidence shows are likely to eliminate the impairment without subjecting the respondent's clients or the public to a substantial risk of harm because the respondent is permitted to continue to practice law during the probation period.

(4) A respondent may be placed on probation for up to 3 years. The probation order expires on the date specified in it unless the administrator petitions for, and the hearing panel, board, or court grants, an extension. An extension may not exceed 3 years. A probation order may be dissolved if the respondent demonstrates that the impairment giving rise to the probation order has been removed and that the probation order has been fully complied with, but only one motion to accelerate dissolution of a probation order may be filed during the probation period.

(5) On proof that a respondent has violated a probation order, he or she may be suspended or disbarred.

(D) Publication of Change in Status. The board must publish in the Michigan Bar Journal a notice of transfer to inactive status. A copy of the notice and the order must be filed and served under MCR 9.118.

(E) Reinstatement. An attorney transferred to inactive status under this rule may not resume active status until reinstated by the board's order and, if inactive 3 years or more, recertified by the Board of Law Examiners. The attorney may petition for reinstatement to active status once a year or at shorter intervals as the board may direct. A petition for reinstatement must be granted by a panel on a showing by clear and convincing evidence that the attorney's disability has been removed and that he or she is fit to resume the practice of law. A panel may take the action necessary to determine whether the attorney's disability has been removed, including an examination of the attorney conducted in accord with the procedure set forth in MCR 9.121(B)(1)(a). The panel may direct that the expense of the examination be paid by the attorney. If an attorney was transferred to inactive status under subrule 9.121(A) and subsequently has been judicially declared to be competent, a panel may dispense with further evidence that the disability has been removed and may order reinstatement to active status on terms it finds proper and advisable, including recertification.

(F) Waiver of Privilege. By filing a petition for reinstatement to active status under this rule, the attorney waives the doctor-patient privilege with respect to treatment during the period of his or her disability. The attorney shall disclose the name of every psychiatrist, psychologist, physician, and hospital or other institution by whom or in which the attorney has been examined or treated since the transfer to inactive status. The attorney shall furnish to a panel written consent for each to divulge whatever information and records are requested by the panel's medical or psychological experts.

[Adopted effective March 1, 1985. Amended March 19, 1987, effective June 1, 1987, 428 Mich; January 4, 1994, effective March 1, 1994, 444 Mich; April 19, 2011, effective September 1, 2011, 489 Mich.]

Comments

Staff Comment to 1985 Adoption

MCR 9.121 is substantially the same as GCR 1963, 970.

Staff Comment to 1987 Amendment

[Effective June 1, 1987] Subrule (C)(2) provides for examination of the respondent by an independent expert selected by the hearing panel or the board.

Staff Comment to 1994 Amendment

The March 1, 1994 amendment to subrule (C)(2) made the examination by an independent expert appointed by the hearing panel discretionary, rather than mandatory. The amendment also added the language that denies eligibility for probation if the respondent refuses to undergo an examination by a physician selected by the grievance administrator.

Staff Comment to 2011 Amendment

This proposal contains various amendments of the attorney discipline rules recommended by the Attorney Grievance Commission, which also were thoroughly reviewed by a State Bar of Michigan workgroup at the request of the Court.

Rule 9.122. Review by Supreme Court

(A) Kinds Available; Time for Filing.

(1) A party aggrieved, including the complainant, by a final order entered by the board on review under MCR 9.118, may apply for leave to appeal to the Supreme Court under MCR 7.305 within 28 days after the order is entered. If a motion for reconsideration is filed before the board's order takes effect, the application for leave to appeal to the Supreme Court may be filed within 28 days after the board enters its order granting or denying reconsideration.

(2) If a request for investigation has been dismissed under MCR 9.112(C)(1)(a) or 9.114(A), a party aggrieved by the dismissal may file a complaint in the Supreme Court under MCR 7.306 within 182 days after the date of the letter notifying the party of the dismissal.

(B) Rules Applicable. Except as modified by this rule, subchapter 7.300 governs an appeal.

(C) Stay of Order. If the discipline order is a suspension of 179 days or less, a stay of the order will automatically issue on the timely filing of an appeal by the respondent. The stay remains effective for 21 days following the conclusion of the appeal or further order of the Supreme Court. The respondent may petition the Supreme Court for a stay pending appeal of other orders of the board.

(D) Record on Appeal. The original papers constitute the record on appeal. The board shall certify the original record and file it with the Supreme Court promptly after the briefs of the parties have been filed. The record must include a list of docket entries, a transcript of testimony taken, and all pleadings, exhibits, briefs, findings of fact, and orders in the proceeding. If the record contains material protected, the protection continues unless otherwise ordered by the Supreme Court.

(E) Disposition. The Supreme Court may make any order it deems appropriate, including dismissing the appeal. The parties may stipulate to dismiss the appeal with prejudice.

[Adopted effective March 1, 1985. Amended March 19, 1987, effective June 1, 1987, 428 Mich; July 1, 2003, effective September 1, 2003, 468 Mich. Amended effective October 14, 2003, 469 Mich. Amended April 19, 2011, effective September 1, 2011, 489 Mich. Amended effective December 14, 2016, 500 Mich. Amended May 23, 2018, effective September 1, 2018, 501 Mich.]

Comments

Staff Comment to 1985 Adoption

MCR 9.122 is substantially the same as GCR 1963, 971.

Staff Comment to 1987 Amendment

[Effective June 1, 1987] Amended MCR 9.122(A)(1) eliminates uncertainty by stating that the filing of a motion for reconsideration extends the deadline for filing an application for leave to appeal to the Supreme Court. See also MCR 9.118(D).

Staff Comment to September, 2003 Amendment

The July 1, 2003, amendments of MCR 7.304, 9.114, and 9.122, effective September 1, 2003, clarified that a complaint for mandamus is inappropriate in instances where a party really is asking the Supreme Court to exercise its power of superintending control over the Board of Law Examiners, the Attorney Discipline Board, or the Attorney Grievance Commission.

Staff Comment to October, 2003 Amendment

The October 14, 2003 amendments of MCR 7.302, 9.118, and 9.122, effective immediately, adjusted the time limits for filing appeals from Attorney Discipline Board orders of discipline or dismissal, setting the time at 28 days. Adjustments were necessary in light of the amendment of MCR 7.302, effective September 1, 2003, which changed the times for filing other appeals to the Supreme Court.

Staff Comment to 2011 Amendment

This proposal contains various amendments of the attorney discipline rules recommended by the Attorney Grievance Commission, which also were thoroughly reviewed by a State Bar of Michigan workgroup at the request of the Court.

Staff Comment to 2016 Amendment

These amendments update cross-references and make other nonsubstantive revisions to clarify the rules.

Staff Comment to 2018 Amendment

The amendment of MCR 9.122 establishes a 182–day time period within which a grievant may file a complaint in the Supreme Court after the Attorney Grievance Commission has dismissed a request for investigation.

Rule 9.123 Eligibility for Reinstatement

(A) Suspension, 179 Days or Less. An attorney whose license has been suspended for 179 days or less pursuant to disciplinary proceedings may be reinstated in accordance with this rule. The attorney may file, not sooner than 7 days before the last day of the suspension, with the board and serve on the administrator an affidavit showing that the attorney has fully complied with all requirements of the suspension order. The affidavit must contain a statement that the attorney will continue to comply with the suspension order until the attorney is reinstated. A materially false statement contained in the affidavit is a basis for an action by the administrator and additional discipline. Within 7 days after the filing of the affidavit, the administrator may file with the board and serve on the attorney an objection to reinstatement based on the attorney's failure to demonstrate compliance with the suspension order. If the administrator files an objection, an order of reinstatement will be issued only if the objection is withdrawn or a hearing panel makes a determination that the attorney has complied with the suspension order. An objection which cannot be resolved without the adjudication of a disputed issue of fact shall be promptly referred to a hearing panel for decision on an expedited basis. If the administrator does not file an objection and the board is not otherwise apprised of a basis to conclude that the attorney has failed to comply with the suspension order, the board must promptly issue an order of reinstatement. The order must be filed and served under MCR 9.118(F).

(B) Disbarment or Suspension More Than 179 Days. An attorney whose license to practice law has been revoked or suspended for more than 179 days is not eligible for reinstatement until the attorney has petitioned for reinstatement under

MCR 9.124 and has established by clear and convincing evidence that:

(1) he or she desires in good faith to be restored to the privilege of practicing law in Michigan;

(2) the term of the suspension ordered has elapsed or 5 years have elapsed since his or her disbarment or resignation;

(3) he or she has not practiced or attempted to practice law contrary to the requirement of his or her suspension or disbarment;

(4) he or she has complied fully with the order of discipline;

(5) his or her conduct since the order of discipline has been exemplary and above reproach;

(6) he or she has a proper understanding of and attitude toward the standards that are imposed on members of the bar and will conduct himself or herself in conformity with those standards;

(7) taking into account all of the attorney's past conduct, including the nature of the misconduct which led to the revocation or suspension, he or she nevertheless can safely be recommended to the public, the courts, and the legal profession as a person fit to be consulted by others and to represent them and otherwise act in matters of trust and confidence, and in general to aid in the administration of justice as a member of the bar and as an officer of the court;

(8) he or she is in compliance with the requirements of subrule (C), if applicable; and

(9) he or she has reimbursed the client security fund of the State Bar of Michigan or has agreed to an arrangement satisfactory to the fund to reimburse the fund for any money paid from the fund as a result of his or her conduct. Failure to fully reimburse as agreed is ground for vacating an order of reinstatement.

(C) Reinstatement After Three Years. An attorney who, as a result of disciplinary proceedings, resigns, is disbarred, or is suspended for any period of time, and who does not practice law for 3 years or more, whether as the result of the period of discipline or voluntarily, must be recertified by the Board of Law Examiners before the attorney may be reinstated to the practice of law.

(D) Petition for Reinstatement; Filing Limitations.

(1) Except as provided in subrule (D)(3), an attorney whose license to practice law has been suspended may not file a petition for reinstatement earlier than 56 days before the term of suspension ordered has fully elapsed.

(2) An attorney whose license to practice law has been revoked or who has resigned may not file a petition for reinstatement until 5 years have elapsed since the attorney's resignation or disbarment.

(3) An attorney whose license to practice law has been suspended because of conviction of a felony for which a term of incarceration was imposed may not file a petition for reinstatement until six months after completion of the sentence, including any period of parole.

(4) An attorney who has been disbarred or suspended and who has been denied reinstatement may not file a new petition for reinstatement until at least 1 year from the effective date of the most recent hearing panel order granting or denying reinstatement.

(E) Abatement or Modification of Conditions of Discipline or Reinstatement. When a condition has been imposed in an order of discipline or in an order of reinstatement, the attorney may request an order of abatement discharging the lawyer from the obligation to comply with the condition, or an order modifying the condition. The attorney may so request either before or with the attorney's affidavit of compliance under MCR 9.123(A) or petition for reinstatement under MCR 9.123(B). The request may be granted only if the attorney shows by clear and convincing evidence that a timely, good-faith effort has been made to meet the condition but it is impractical to fulfill the condition.

[Adopted effective March 1, 1985. Amended January 4, 1994, effective March 1, 1994, 444 Mich. Amended effective September 15, 1994, 447 Mich. Amended April 30, 1996, effective July 1, 1996, 451 Mich; December 1, 1999, effective February 1, 2000, 461 Mich; April 19, 2011, effective September 1, 2011, 489 Mich; November 20, 2019, effective January 1, 2020, 503 Mich.]

Comments

Staff Comment to 1985 Adoption

MCR 9.123 is substantially the same as GCR 1963, 972.

Staff Comment to March, 1994 Amendment

The March 1, 1994 amendments: (1) increased the automatic reinstatement eligibility threshold in subrules (A) and (B) from 119 to 179 days; and (2) added new subrule (D), which specifies the earliest dates at which attorneys may petition for reinstatement.

The amendments to subrules (A) and (B) apply only to discipline orders issued after the amendment's effective date.

Staff Comment to 1996 Amendment

The July 1, 1996, amendment of subrule (B)(7) allows the Attorney Discipline Board to consider all an attorney's past conduct when deciding whether to grant reinstatement.

Staff Comment to 1999 Amendment

The December 1, 1999 amendment of Rule 9.123(D), effective February 1, 2000, precludes a lawyer whose license to practice law has been suspended because of a felony conviction from petitioning for reinstatement until six months after completion of any sentence of incarceration, including any term of parole. The word "parole" indicates that the lawyer was in the custody of the Michigan Department of Corrections. The rule also applies, however, to persons who were incarcerated in other jurisdictions under similar circumstances, regardless of the terminology employed.

Staff Comment to 2011 Amendment

This proposal contains various amendments of the attorney discipline rules recommended by the Attorney Grievance Commission, which also were thoroughly reviewed by a State Bar of Michigan workgroup at the request of the Court.

Staff Comment to 2020 Amendment

The amendment of MCR 9.123 updates the attorney discipline process for reinstatement of short-term suspensions and allows for abatement or modification of a condition in certain circumstances.

Rule 9.124   Procedure for Reinstatement

(A) Filing of Petition. An attorney petitioning for reinstatement shall file the original petition for reinstatement with the Supreme Court clerk and a copy with the board and the commission.

(B) Petitioner's Responsibilities.

(1) Separately from the petition for reinstatement, the petitioner must serve only upon the administrator a personal history affidavit. The affidavit is to become part of the administrator's investigative file and may not be disclosed to the public except under the provisions of MCR 9.126. The affidavit must contain the following information:

(a) every residence address since the date of disqualification from the practice of law;

(b) employment history since the time of disqualification, including the nature of employment, the name and address of every employer, the duration of such employment, and the name of the petitioner's immediate supervisor at each place of employment; if requested by the grievance administrator, the petitioner must provide authorization to obtain a copy of the petitioner's personnel file from the employer;

(c) a copy of a current driver's license;

(d) any continuing legal education in which the petitioner participated during the period of disqualification from the practice of law;

(e) bank account statements, from the date of disqualification until the filing of the petition for reinstatement, for each and every bank account in which petitioner is named in any capacity;

(f) copies of the petitioner's personal and business federal, state, and local tax returns from the date of disqualification until the filing of the petition for reinstatement, and if the petitioner owes outstanding income taxes, interest, and penalties, the petitioner must provide a current statement from the taxation authority of the current amount due; if requested by the grievance administrator, the petitioner must provide a waiver granting the grievance administrator authority to obtain information from the tax authority;

(g) any and all professional or occupational licenses obtained or maintained during the period of disqualification and whether any were suspended or revoked;

(h) any and all names used by petitioner since the time of disqualification;

(i) petitioner's place and date of birth;

(j) petitioner's social security number;

(k) whether, since the time of disqualification, petitioner was a party or a witness in any civil case, and the title, docket number, and court in which the case occurred;

(l) whether the petitioner was a party to any civil case, including the title, docket number, and court in which such case was filed; the petitioner must provide copies of the complaints and any dispositional orders or judgments, including settlement agreements, in such cases;

(m) whether the petitioner was a defendant or a witness in any criminal case, and the title, docket number, and court in which such case was filed; the petitioner must provide copies of the indictments or complaints and any dispositional orders or judgments of conviction in cases in which the petitioner was a defendant;

(n) whether the petitioner was subject to treatment or counseling for mental or emotional impairments, or for substance abuse or gambling addictions since the time of disqualification; if so, the petitioner must provide a current statement from the petitioner's service provider setting forth an evaluative conclusion regarding the petitioner's impairment(s), the petitioner's treatment records, and prognosis for recovery.

(2) The petitioner must, contemporaneously with the filing of the petition for reinstatement and service on the administrator of the personal history affidavit, remit

(a) to the administrator the fee for publication of a reinstatement notice in the Michigan Bar Journal.

(b) to the board the basic administrative costs required under MCR 9.128(B)(1)

(i) an administrative cost of $750 where the discipline imposed was a suspension of less than 3 years;

(ii) an administrative cost of $1,500 where the discipline imposed was a suspension of 3 years or more or disbarment.

(3) If the petition is facially sufficient and the petitioner has provided proof of service of the personal history affidavit upon the administrator and paid the publication fee required by subrule (B)(2), the board shall assign the petition to a hearing panel. Otherwise, the board may dismiss the petition without prejudice, on its own motion or the motion of the administrator.

(4) A petitioner who files the petition before the term of suspension ordered has fully elapsed must file an updated petition and serve upon the administrator an updated personal history affidavit within 14 days after the term of suspension ordered has fully elapsed. All petitioners remain under a continuing obligation to provide updated information bearing upon the petition or the personal history affidavit.

(5) The petitioner must cooperate fully in the investigation by the administrator into the petitioner's eligibility for reinstatement by promptly providing any information requested. If requested, the petitioner must participate in a recorded interview and answer fully and fairly under oath all questions about eligibility for reinstatement.

(C) Administrator's Responsibilities.

(1) Within 14 days after the commission receives its copy of the petition for reinstatement, the administrator shall submit to the Michigan Bar Journal for publication a notice briefly describing the nature and date of the discipline, the misconduct for which the petitioner was disciplined, and the matters required to be proved for reinstatement.

(2) The administrator shall investigate the petitioner's eligibility for reinstatement before a hearing on it, report the findings in writing to the board and the hearing panel within 56 days of the date the board assigns the petition to the hearing panel, and serve a copy on the petitioner.

(a) For good cause, the hearing panel may allow the administrator to file the report at a later date, but in no event later than 7 days before the hearing.

(b) The report must summarize the facts of all previous misconduct and the available evidence bearing on the petitioner's eligibility for reinstatement. The report is part of the record but does not restrict the parties in the presentation of additional relevant evidence at the hearing. Any evidence omitted from the report or received by the administrator after the filing of the report must be disclosed promptly to the hearing panel and to the opposing party.

(D) Hearing on Petition. A reinstatement hearing may not be held earlier than 28 days after the administrator files the investigative report with the hearing panel unless the hearing panel has extended the deadline for filing the report. The proceeding on a petition for reinstatement must conform as nearly as practicable to a hearing on a complaint. The petitioner shall appear personally before the hearing panel for cross-examination by the administrator and the hearing panel and answer fully and fairly under oath all questions regarding eligibility for reinstatement. The administrator and the petitioner may call witnesses or introduce evidence bearing upon the petitioner's eligibility for reinstatement. The hearing panel must enter an order granting or denying reinstatement and make a written report signed by the chairperson, including a transcript of the testimony taken, pleadings, exhibits and briefs, and its findings of fact. A reinstatement order may grant reinstatement subject to conditions that are relevant to the established misconduct or otherwise necessary to insure the integrity of the profession, to protect the public, and to serve the interests of justice. The report and order must be filed and served under MCR 9.118(F).

(E) Review. Review is available under the rules governing review of other hearing panel orders.

[Adopted effective March 1, 1985. Amended January 4, 1994, effective March 1, 1994, 444 Mich. Amended effective November 2, 2004, 471 Mich. Amended November 10, 2005, effective January 1, 2006, 474 Mich; April 19, 2011, effective September 1, 2011, 489 Mich.]

Comments

Staff Comment to 1985 Adoption

MCR 9.124 is substantially the same as GCR 1963, 973.

Staff Comment to 1994 Amendment

The March 1, 1994 amendments: (1) clarified the subrule (A) procedures for filing a reinstatement petition; (2) added new subrule (B); (3) in subrule (C), clarified the grievance administrator's responsibilities in reinstatement proceedings and shortened the time that the administrator has to prepare the investigative report; and (4) in subrule (D), authorized conditional reinstatements and codified the existing practice under which the administrator is allowed to call witnesses and present evidence bearing on the petitioner's eligibility for reinstatement.

Staff Comment to 2004 Amendment

The amendments of MCR 9.124(B)(1) require a petitioner for reinstatement to file a personal history affidavit only with the grievance administrator and prevent its disclosure to the public except as provided by MCR 9.126. The amendment of MCR 9.124(B)(2) clarifies that a petition for reinstatement must be accompanied by both a publication fee and administrative costs imposed by MCR 9.128(B)(1). The amendment of MCR 9.126(C) clarifies that a personal history affidavit filed pursuant to MCR 9.124(B)(1) is a confidential document and is not open to the public.

Staff Comment to 2005 Amendment

The amendment of MCR 9.124(B)(1) expands the information a petitioner for reinstatement is required to include in or attach to the petitioner's personal history affidavit. The amendment of subrule (b) adds a requirement that the petitioner, at the grievance administrator's request, provide authorization for the grievance administrator to obtain a copy of the petitioner's personnel file regarding any employment held since the time of disqualification. The amendment of subrule (f) requires a petitioner to attach copies of petitioner's tax returns from the date of disqualification to the date of the petition for reinstatement. The amendment of subrule (l) adds a requirement that a petitioner provide copies of any civil complaints and judgments or dispositional orders with respect to any resolution of a civil complaint involving the petitioner. According to the amendment of subrule (m), a petitioner is required to provide copies of criminal complaints and dispositional orders or judgments of conviction for any criminal case in which the petitioner was a defendant. Subrule (n) requires a petitioner to state on his or her personal history affidavit whether, since the date of disqualification, the petitioner received treatment for mental or emotional impairments or substance abuse or gambling addictions. The amendment of MCR 9.124(C) simply codifies what already occurs in hearings on petitions for reinstatement and appeals from decisions following those hearings.

Staff Comment to 2011 Amendment

This proposal contains various amendments of the attorney discipline rules recommended by the Attorney Grievance Commission, which also were thoroughly reviewed by a State Bar of Michigan workgroup at the request of the Court.

Rule 9.125   Immunity

A person is absolutely immune from suit for statements and communications transmitted solely to the administrator, the commission, or the commission staff, or given in an investigation or proceeding on alleged misconduct or reinstatement. The administrator, legal counsel, investigators, members of hearing panels, masters, receivers appointed under MCR 9.119(G), voluntary investigators, fee arbitrators, mentors, practice monitors, the commission, the board, and their staffs are absolutely immune from suit for conduct arising out of the performance of their duties.

A medical or psychological expert who administers testing or provides a report pursuant to MCR 9.114(C) or MCR 9.121 is absolutely immune from suit for statements and communications transmitted solely to the administrator, the commission, or the commission staff, or given in an investigation or formal disciplinary proceeding.

[Adopted effective March 1, 1985. Amended March 19, 1987, effective June 1, 1987, 428 Mich; April 19, 2011, effective September 1, 2011, 489 Mich.]

Comments

Staff Comment to 1985 Adoption

MCR 9.125 is substantially the same as GCR 1963, 974.

Staff Comment to 1987 Amendment

The [June 1, 1987] amendments to MCR 9.125 provide for absolute immunity for complainants, disciplinary officials and staff acting within the scope of their duties. The rule is patterned after the Standards for Lawyer Discipline and Disability Proceedings promulgated by the American Bar Association.

Staff Comment to 2011 Amendment

This proposal contains various amendments of the attorney discipline rules recommended by the Attorney Grievance Commission, which also were thoroughly reviewed by a State Bar of Michigan workgroup at the request of the Court.

Rule 9.126   Open Hearings; Privileged, Confidential Files and Records

(A) Investigations. Except as provided in these rules, investigations by the administrator or the staff are privileged from disclosure, confidential, and may not be made public. At the respondent's option, final disposition of a request for investigation not resulting in formal charges may be made public. In addition, any interested person may inspect the request for investigation and the respondent's answer thereto if a disciplinary proceeding has been filed.

(B) Hearings. Hearings before a hearing panel and the board must be open to the public, but not their deliberations.

(C) Papers. Formal pleadings, reports, findings, recommendations, discipline, reprimands, transcripts, and orders resulting from hearings must be open to the public. A personal history affidavit filed pursuant to MCR 9.124(B)(1) is a confidential document that is not open to the public. This subrule does not apply to a request for a disclosure authorization submitted to the board or the Supreme Court pursuant to subrules (D)(8) or (E)(8).

(D) Other Records. Other files and records of the board, the commission, the administrator, legal counsel, hearing panels and their members, and the staff of each may not be examined by or disclosed to anyone except

(1) the commission,

(2) the administrator,

(3) the respondent as provided under MCR 9.115(F)(4),

(4) members of hearing panels or the board,

(5) authorized employees,

(6) the Supreme Court, or

(7) other persons who are expressly authorized by the board or the Supreme Court.

If a disclosure is made to the Supreme Court, the board, or a hearing panel, the information must also be disclosed to the respondent, except as it relates to an investigation, unless the court otherwise orders.

(E) Other Information. Notwithstanding any prohibition against disclosure set forth in this rule or elsewhere, the commission shall disclose the substance of information concerning attorney or judicial misconduct to the Judicial Tenure Commission, upon request. The commission also may make such disclosure to the Judicial Tenure Commission, absent a request, and to:

(1) the State Bar of Michigan Client Protection Fund,

(2) the State Bar of Michigan:

(a) Committee on Judicial Qualifications;

(b) Lawyers and Judges Assistance Program;

(c) District and Standing Committees on Character and Fitness; or

(d) Unauthorized Practice of Law Committee,

(3) any court-authorized attorney disciplinary or admissions agency, including any federal district court or federal disciplinary agency considering the licensing of attorneys in its jurisdiction,

(4) the Michigan Appellate Assigned Counsel System,

(5) any Michigan court considering the appointment of a lawyer in a pending matter as house counsel, or a standing appointment,

(6) a lawyer representing the respondent in an unrelated disciplinary investigation or proceeding;

(7) law enforcement agencies; or

(8) other persons who are expressly authorized by the board or the Supreme Court.

[Adopted effective March 1, 1985. Amended March 19, 1987, effective June 1, 1987, 428 Mich; December 18, 1990, effective February 1, 1991, 437 Mich. Amended effective March 18, 1992, 439 Mich. Amended September 22, 1998, effective December 1, 1998, 459 Mich. Amended effective November 2, 2004, 471 Mich. Amended April 19, 2011, effective September 1, 2011, 489 Mich. Amended effective December 14, 2016, 500 Mich.]

Comments

Staff Comment to 1985 Adoption

MCR 9.126 is substantially the same as GCR 1963, 975.

Staff Comment to 1991 Amendment

The [February 1,] 1991 amendment added subrule (E)(5), providing that the Attorney Discipline Board or the Supreme Court may authorize the Attorney Grievance Commission to release "information" about misconduct to persons other than those listed in subrules (E)(1)–(4). Subrule (D) already contained a similar provision regarding "files and records". The 1991 amendment also added subrule (F) and the second sentence of subrule (C).

Staff Comment to 1992 Amendment

The March 18, 1992 amendment to subrule (A) added the provision for public access to the request for investigation and the answer to it in situations where a formal complaint has been filed. The amendment applies to cases in which requests for investigation (which later result in the filing of formal complaints) are filed after the effective date of the rule amendment.

Staff Comment to 1998 Amendment

The December 1, 1998 amendment of MCR 9.126 and 9.222 made mandatory the disclosure of information, upon request, between the Attorney Grievance Commission and the Judicial Tenure Commission. The amendment of State Bar Rule 15, § 1 authorized the State Bar's Committee on Character and Fitness to disclose to the Attorney Grievance Commission information concerning the bar application of a disciplined lawyer who is requesting reinstatement to the practice of law. Under the amendment, the lawyer must be notified of the request, and the hearing panel must determine the relevancy of the information before permitting it to be used in a public document or proceeding.

Staff Comment to 2004 Amendment

The amendments of MCR 9.124(B)(1) require a petitioner for reinstatement to file a personal history affidavit only with the grievance administrator and prevent its disclosure to the public except as provided by MCR 9.126. The amendment of MCR 9.124(B)(2) clarifies that a petition for reinstatement must be accompanied by both a publication fee and administrative costs imposed by MCR 9.128(B)(1). The amendment of MCR 9.126(C) clarifies that a personal history affidavit filed pursuant to MCR 9.124(B)(1) is a confidential document and is not open to the public.

Staff Comment to 2011 Amendment

This proposal contains various amendments of the attorney discipline rules recommended by the Attorney Grievance Commission, which also were thoroughly reviewed by a State Bar of Michigan workgroup at the request of the Court.

Staff Comment to 2016 Amendment

These amendments update cross-references and make other nonsubstantive revisions to clarify the rules.

Rule 9.127   Enforcement

(A) Interim Suspension. The Supreme Court, the board, or a hearing panel may order the interim suspension of a respondent who fails to comply with its lawful order. The suspension shall remain in effect until the respondent complies with the order or no longer has the power to comply. If the respondent is ultimately disciplined, the respondent shall not receive credit against the disciplinary suspension or disbarment for any time of suspension under this rule. All orders of hearing panels under this rule shall be reviewable immediately under MCR 9.118. All orders of the board under this rule shall be appealable immediately under MCR 9.122. The reviewing authority may issue a stay pending review or appeal.

(B) Contempt. The administrator may enforce a discipline order or an order granting or denying reinstatement by proceeding against a respondent for contempt of court. The proceeding must conform to MCR 3.606. The petition must be filed by the administrator in the circuit court in the county in which the alleged contempt took place, or in which the respondent resides, or has or had an office. Enforcement proceedings under this rule do not bar the imposition of additional discipline upon the basis of the same noncompliance with the discipline order.

[Adopted effective March 1, 1985. Amended effective June 1, 1987.]

Comments

Staff Comment to 1985 Adoption

MCR 9.127 is substantially the same as GCR 1963, 976.

Staff Comment to 1987 Amendment

New subrule (A) [effective June 1, 1987] provides a vehicle for prompt enforcement of preliminary orders, e.g., orders requiring a psychiatric examination.

Amended subrule (B) [effective June 1, 1987] codifies the current rule that the administrator is not compelled to make an election of remedies in enforcing an order of discipline.

Rule 9.128   Costs

(A) Generally. The hearing panel and the board, in an order of discipline or an order granting or denying reinstatement, must include a provision directing the payment of costs within a specified period of time. Under exceptional circumstances, the board may grant a motion to reduce administrative costs assessed under this rule, but may not reduce the assessment for actual expenses. Reimbursement must be a condition in a reinstatement order.

(B) Amount and Nature of Costs Assessed. The costs assessed under these rules shall include both basic administrative costs and disciplinary expenses actually incurred by the board, the commission, a master, or a panel for the expenses of that investigation, hearing, review and appeal, if any.

(1) *Basic Administrative Costs:*

(a) for discipline by consent pursuant to MCR 9.115(F)(5), $750;

(b) for all other orders imposing discipline, $1,500;

(c) with the filing of a petition for reinstatement as set forth in MCR 9.124(B)(2)(b)(i) and (ii);

(2) *Actual Expenses.* Within 14 days of the conclusion of a proceeding before a panel or a written request from the board, whichever is later, the grievance administrator shall file with the board an itemized statement of the commission's expenses allocable to the hearing, including expenses incurred during the grievance administrator's investigation. Copies shall be served upon the respondent and the panel. An itemized statement of the expenses of the board, the commission, and the panel, including the expenses of a master, shall be a part of the report in all matters of discipline and reinstatement.

(C) Certification of Nonpayment. If the respondent fails to pay the costs within the time prescribed, the board shall serve a certified notice of the nonpayment upon the respondent. Copies must be served on the administrator and the State Bar of Michigan. Commencing on the date a certified report of nonpayment is filed, interest on the unpaid fees and costs shall accrue thereafter at the rates applicable to civil judgments.

(D) Automatic Suspension for Nonpayment. The respondent will be suspended automatically, effective 7 days from the mailing of the certified notice of nonpayment, and until the respondent pays the costs assessed or the board approves a suitable plan for payment. The board shall file a notice of suspension with the clerk of the Supreme Court and the State Bar of Michigan. A copy must be served on the respondent and the administrator. A respondent who is suspended for nonpayment of costs under this rule is required to comply with the requirements imposed by MCR 9.119 on suspended attorneys.

(E) Reinstatement. A respondent who has been automatically suspended under this rule and later pays the costs or obtains approval of a payment plan, and is otherwise eligible, may seek automatic reinstatement pursuant to MCR 9.123(A) even if the suspension under this rule exceeded 179 days. However, a respondent who is suspended under this rule and, as a result, does not practice law in Michigan for 3 years or more, must be recertified by the Board of Law Examiners before the respondent may be reinstated.

[Adopted effective March 1, 1985. Amended March 1, 1987, effective June 1, 1987, 428 Mich; January 4, 1994, effective March 1, 1994, 444 Mich. Amended effective November 16, 1994, 447 Mich. Amended July 29, 2002, effective September 1, 2002, 467 Mich; October 8, 2002, effective January 1, 2003, 467 Mich; April 19, 2011, effective September 1, 2011, 489 Mich.]

Comments

Staff Comment to 1985 Adoption

MCR 9.128 is substantially the same as GCR 1963, 977.

Staff Comment to 1987 Amendment

The [June 1, 1987] amendment provides for automatic suspension in cases where a respondent fails to pay costs. This is designed to avoid the current cumbersome procedures requiring an entirely new proceeding. It is similar to the practices in other jurisdictions.

Staff Comment to March, 1994 Amendment

The March 1, 1994 amendments: (1) divided MCR 9.128 into two subrules; (2) clarified the rules regarding a disciplined or reinstated attorney's obligation to reimburse the State Bar for the expenses of the disciplinary proceedings; (3) provided for the accrual of interest on delinquent reimbursement obligations; and (4) added the requirement that an attorney who is suspended under this rule for more than three years must be recertified by the Board of Law Examiners.

Staff Comment to November, 1994 Amendment

The [November 16,] 1994 amendment of MCR 9.128(A) added the sentence "An attorney who is suspended for nonpayment of costs under this rule is required to comply with the requirements imposed by MCR 9.119 on suspended attorneys." The amendment reflected the Supreme Court's holding in *Grievance Administrator v Floyd*, 447 Mich 422; 523 NW2d 227 (1994).

Staff Comment to 2002 Amendment

The July 29, 2002 amendment of MCR 9.128 was suggested by the Attorney Grievance Commission and the Attorney Discipline Board. It allocates a greater share of the cost of operating the discipline system to those who are disciplined. Among other changes, the new provisions permit an assessment for basic administrative costs as well as actual expenses, and expressly include investigative costs in actual expenses.

Staff Comment to 2011 Amendment

This proposal contains various amendments of the attorney discipline rules recommended by the Attorney Grievance Commission, which also were thoroughly reviewed by a State Bar of Michigan workgroup at the request of the Court.

Rule 9.129   Expenses; Reimbursement

The state bar must reimburse each investigator, legal counsel, hearing panel member, board member, master, and commission member for the actual and necessary expenses the board, commission, or administrator certifies as incurred as a result of these rules.

[Adopted effective March 1, 1985. Amended April 19, 2011, effective September 1, 2011, 489 Mich.]

Comments

Staff Comment to 1985 Adoption

MCR 9.129 is substantially the same as GCR 1963, 978.

Staff Comment to 2011 Amendment

This proposal contains various amendments of the attorney discipline rules recommended by the Attorney Grievance Commission, which also were thoroughly reviewed by a State Bar of Michigan workgroup at the request of the Court.

Rule 9.130   MCR 8.122 Cases; Arbitration; Discipline; Filing Complaint by Administrator

(A) Arbitration. On written agreement between an attorney and his or her client, the administrator or an attorney the administrator assigns may arbitrate a dispute and enter an award in accordance with the arbitration laws. Except as otherwise provided by this subrule, the arbitration is governed by MCR 3.602. The award and a motion for entry of an order or judgment must be filed in the court having jurisdiction under MCR 8.122. If the award recommends discipline of the attorney, it must also be treated as a request for investigation.

(B) Complaint. If the administrator finds that the filing of a complaint in the appropriate court under MCR 8.122 will be a hardship to the client and that the client may have a meritorious claim, the administrator may file the complaint on behalf of the client and prosecute it to completion without cost to the client.

[Adopted effective March 1, 1985. Amended June 21, 2000, effective September 1, 2000, 462 Mich; April 19, 2011, effective September 1, 2011, 489 Mich.]

Comments

Staff Comment to 1985 Adoption

MCR 9.130 is substantially the same as GCR 1963, 979.

Staff Comment to 2000 Amendment

The June 21, 2000 amendment of subrule 9.130(B), effective September 1, 2000, clarified that arbitration of attorney-discipline matters is governed by MCR 3.602, except as otherwise provided by subrule 9.130(B).

Staff Comment to 2011 Amendment

This proposal contains various amendments of the attorney discipline rules recommended by the Attorney Grievance Commission, which also were thoroughly reviewed by a State Bar of Michigan workgroup at the request of the Court.

Rule 9.131. Investigation of Member or Employee of Board or Commission, or Relative of Member or Employee of Board or Commission; Investigation of Attorney Representing Respondent or Witness; Representation by Member or Employee of Board or Commission

(A) Investigation of Commission Member or Employee, or Relative of Member or Employee of Commission. If the request is for investigation of an attorney who is a member or employee of the commission, or a relative of a member or employee of the commission, the following provisions apply:

(1) The administrator shall serve a copy of the request for investigation on the respondent by ordinary mail. Within 21 days after service, the respondent shall file with the administrator an answer to the request for investigation conforming to MCR 9.113. The administrator shall send a copy of the answer to the complainant.

(2) After the answer is filed or the time for answer has expired, the administrator shall send copies of the request for investigation and the answer to the Supreme Court clerk.

(3) The Supreme Court shall review the request for investigation and the answer and shall either dismiss the request for investigation or appoint volunteer legal counsel to investigate the matter.

(4) If, after conducting the investigation, appointed counsel determines that the request for investigation does not warrant the filing of a formal complaint, he or she shall file a report setting out the reasons for that conclusion with the administrator, who shall send a copy of the report to the Supreme Court clerk, the respondent, and the complainant. Review of a decision not to file a formal complaint is limited to a proceeding under MCR 9.122(A)(2). If appointed counsel determines not to file a complaint, the administrator shall close and maintain the file under MCR 9.114(E). MCR 9.126(A) governs the release of information regarding the investigation.

(5) If, after conducting the investigation, appointed counsel determines that the request for investigation warrants the filing of a formal complaint, he or she shall prepare and file a complaint with the board under MCR 9.115(B).

(6) Further proceedings are as in other cases except that the complaint will be prosecuted by appointed counsel rather than by the administrator.

If the request is for investigation of the administrator, the term "administrator" in this rule means a member of the commission or some other employee of the commission designated by the chairperson.

"Relative" includes spouse, child, parent, brother, sister, grandparent, grandchild, first cousin, uncle, aunt, niece, nephew, brother-in-law, sister-in-law, daughter-in-law, son-in-law, mother-in-law, and father-in-law, whether natural, adopted, step or foster. The term also includes same-sex or different-sex individuals who have a relationship of a romantic, intimate, committed, or dating nature.

(B) Investigation of Board Member or Employee or Relative of Board Member or Employee. Before the filing of a formal complaint, the procedures regarding a request for investigation of a member or employee of the board or relative of a member or employee of the board, are the same as in other cases. Thereafter, the following provisions apply:

(1) The administrator shall file the formal complaint with the board and send a copy to the Supreme Court clerk.

(2) The chief justice shall appoint a hearing panel and may appoint a master to conduct the hearing. The hearing procedure is as provided in MCR 9.115, 9.117, or 9.120, as is appropriate, except that no matters shall be submitted to the board. Procedural matters ordinarily within the authority of the board shall be decided by the hearing panel, except that a motion to disqualify a member of the panel shall be decided by the chief justice.

(3) The order of the hearing panel is effective 21 days after it is filed and served as required by MCR 9.115(J), and shall be treated as a final order of the board. The administrator shall send a copy of the order to the Supreme Court clerk.

(4) *MCR 9.118 Does Not Apply.* Review of the hearing panel decision is by the Supreme Court as provided by MCR 9.122.

"Relative" includes spouse, child, parent, brother, sister, grandparent, grandchild, first cousin, uncle, aunt, niece, nephew, brother-in-law, sister-in-law, daughter-in-law, son-in-law, mother-in-law, and father-in-law, whether natural, adopted, step or foster. The term also includes same-sex or different-sex individuals who have a relationship of a romantic, intimate, committed, or dating nature.

(C) Investigation of Attorney Representing a Respondent or Witness in Proceedings Before Board or Commission.

(1) *Request by a Former Client.* A request for investigation filed by an attorney or witness against his or her counsel for alleged misconduct occurring in a disciplinary investigation or proceeding, shall be treated under the procedures set forth in MCR 9.112.

(2) *Request by Person Other Than Former Client.* If a person other than the attorney's former client requests an investigation for alleged misconduct committed during the

course of that attorney's representation of a respondent or a witness in proceedings before the board or the commission, the procedures in subrule (A) shall be followed. A request for investigation that alleges misconduct of this type may be filed only by the chairperson of the commission, and only if the commission passes a resolution authorizing the filing by the chairperson.

(D) Representation by Commission or Board Member or Employee. A member or employee of the Attorney Grievance Commission or the Attorney Discipline Board and its hearing panels may not represent a respondent in proceedings before the commission, the board, or the Judicial Tenure Commission, including preliminary discussions with employees of the respective commission or board prior to the filing of a request for investigation.

[Adopted effective March 1, 1985. Amended September 5, 1991, effective October 1, 1991, 438 Mich; April 23, 1996, effective July 1, 1996, 451 Mich; April 19, 2011, effective September 1, 2011, 489 Mich; May 23, 2018, effective September 1, 2018, 501 Mich.]

Comments

Staff Comment to 1985 Adoption

MCR 9.131 is substantially the same as GCR 1963, 980.

Staff Comment to 1991 Amendment

The amendment of October 1, 1991 added subrule (C), creating a special procedure for cases in which it is alleged that an attorney acted improperly while representing a respondent or a witness in proceedings before the board or the commission.

Staff Comment to 1996 Amendment

The amendment of MCR 9.131, effective July 1, 1996, precluded members and employees of the Attorney Grievance Commission and the Attorney Discipline Board and its hearing panels from representing a respondent in proceedings before either of those bodies or the Judicial Tenure Commission.

Staff Comment to 2011 Amendment

This proposal contains various amendments of the attorney discipline rules recommended by the Attorney Grievance Commission, which also were thoroughly reviewed by a State Bar of Michigan workgroup at the request of the Court.

Staff Comment to 2018 Amendment

The amendments of MCR 9.112 and MCR 9.131 provide that relatives of AGC or ADB members or employees are subject to the same procedure for review of allegations of misconduct as the Board or Commission member or employee. This change comports with recent Supreme Court practice. These amendments are intended to address any perceived conflict of interest that may exist if the procedures in MCR 9.112 were to be used to review a request for investigation of the relative of a member or employee of the Attorney Grievance Commission or Attorney Discipline Board.

SUBCHAPTER 9.200   JUDICIAL TENURE COMMISSION

Rule 9.200.   Construction

An independent and honorable judiciary being indispensable to justice in our society, subchapter 9.200 shall be construed to preserve the integrity of the judicial system, to enhance public confidence in that system, and to protect the public, the courts, and the rights of the judges who are governed by these rules in the most expeditious manner that is practicable and fair.

[Adopted effective January 21, 2003, 467 Mich. Rescinded and readopted April 11, 2019, effective September 1, 2019, 502 Mich.]

Comments

Staff Comment to 2019 Readoption

This new version of MCR 9.200 *et seq.* reflects a reorganization suggested by the Judicial Tenure Commission, and includes various technical changes to update and modernize the rules.

Rule 9.201.   Definitions

As used in this chapter, unless the context or subject matter otherwise requires

(A) "commission" means the Judicial Tenure Commission.

(B) "judge" means:

(1) a person who is serving as a judge or justice of any court of the judicial branch of state or local government by virtue of election, appointment, or assignment;

(2) a magistrate or a referee of any such court; or

(3) a person who formerly held such office if a request for investigation was filed during the person's term of office. If the person is no longer a judge and the alleged misconduct relates to the person's actions as a judge, it is not necessary that the request for investigation be filed during the former judge's term of office; nothing in this paragraph deprives the Attorney Grievance Commission of its authority to proceed against a former judge.

(C) "respondent" is a judge against whom a request for investigation has been filed.

(D) "chairperson" is the commission chairperson and includes the acting chairperson.

(E) "master" means one or more judges or former judges appointed by the Supreme Court at the commission's request to hold hearings on a complaint against a respondent.

(F) "disciplinary counsel" is the commission's executive director or other attorney appointed by the commission to act as the prosecutor in negotiating settlements, presenting evidence at the hearing on the complaint, and in proceedings in the Supreme Court other than litigating a recommendation on a complaint made after a hearing before the commission.

(G) "commission counsel" is the attorney appointed by the commission to provide it with counsel whenever the commission appoints the executive director as disciplinary counsel, including acting in proceedings in the Supreme Court. The disciplinary counsel may not serve as the commission counsel in the same case.

(H) "request for investigation" is an allegation of judicial misconduct, physical or mental disability, or other circumstance that the commission may undertake to investigate under Const 1963, art 6, § 30, and MCR 9.220.

(I) "complaint" is a written document issued at the direction of the commission, alleging specific charges of misconduct in office, mental or physical disability, or some other ground that warrants action under Const 1963, art 6, § 30.

[Adopted effective March 1, 1985. Amended effective January 21, 2003, 467 Mich. Rescinded and readopted April 11, 2019, amended effective September 1, 2019, 502 Mich.]

Comments

Staff Comment to 1985 Adoption

MCR 9.201 is substantially the same as GCR 1963, 932.3.

Staff Comment to 2019 Readoption

This new version of MCR 9.200 *et seq.* reflects a reorganization suggested by the Judicial Tenure Commission, and includes various technical changes to update and modernize the rules.

Rule 9.202. Standards of Judicial Conduct

(A) Responsibility of Judge. A judge is personally responsible for the judge's own behavior and for the proper conduct and administration of the court in which the judge presides.

(B) Grounds for Action. A judge is subject to censure, suspension with or without pay, retirement, or removal for conviction of a felony, physical or mental disability that prevents the performance of judicial duties, misconduct in office, persistent failure to perform judicial duties, habitual intemperance, or conduct that is clearly prejudicial to the administration of justice. In addition to any other sanction imposed, a judge may be ordered to pay the costs, fees, and expenses incurred by the commission in prosecuting the complaint only if the judge engaged in conduct involving fraud, deceit, or intentional misrepresentation, or if the judge made misleading statements to the commission, the commission's investigators, the master, or the Supreme Court.

(1) Misconduct in office includes, but is not limited to:

(a) persistent incompetence in the performance of judicial duties;

(b) persistent neglect in the timely performance of judicial duties;

(c) persistent failure to treat persons fairly and courteously;

(d) treatment of a person unfairly or discourteously because of the person's race, gender, or other protected personal characteristic;

(e) misuse of judicial office for personal advantage or gain, or for the advantage or gain of another; and

(f) failure to cooperate with a reasonable request made by the commission in its investigation of a respondent.

(2) Conduct in violation of the Code of Judicial Conduct or the Rules of Professional Conduct may constitute a ground for action with regard to a judge, whether the conduct occurred before or after the respondent became a judge or was related to judicial office.

(3) In deciding whether action with regard to a judge is warranted, the commission shall consider all the circumstances, including but not limited to the age of the allegations and the possibility of unfair prejudice to the judge because of the staleness of the allegations or unreasonable delay in pursuing the matter and whether respondent has corrected the behavior. [Formerly Rule 9.205, adopted effective March 1, 1985. Amended effective May 5, 1987, 428 Mich. Amended July 16, 1993, effective October 1, 1993, 443 Mich. Amended effective January 21, 2003, 467 Mich. Amended December 14, 2005, effective January 1, 2006, 474 Mich. Renumbered Rule 9.202, rescinded and readopted April 11, 2019, amended effective September 1, 2019, 502 Mich.]

Comments

Staff Comment to 1985 Adoption

MCR 9.205 corresponds to GCR 1963, 932.4.

New subrule (B) expressly states that misconduct in office or incapacity is grounds for discipline.

Staff Comment to 1987 Amendment

The 1987 amendment to MCR 9.205 is designed to permit greater flexibility in responding to the problems caused by a judge's disability.

Staff Comment to 1993 Amendment

The explanation of the 1993 amendment is found in the opening paragraphs of the Court's July 16, 1993 order, reported at 443 Mich xxiii (1993).

Staff Comment to 2005 Amendment

The amendment of Rule 9.205 allows the Judicial Tenure Commission to recommend and this Court to order that a disciplined judge pay the costs, fees, and expenses incurred by the commission in prosecuting the complaint of judicial misconduct when the judge has engaged in conduct involving fraud, deceit, intentional misrepresentation, or misleading statements to the commission, the commission's investigators, the master, or the Supreme Court. Cf. *In re Noecker,* 472 Mich 1 (2005).

Staff Comment to 2019 Readoption and Renumbering

This new version of MCR 9.200 *et seq.* reflects a reorganization suggested by the Judicial Tenure Commission, and includes various technical changes to update and modernize the rules.

Rule 9.210. Judicial Tenure Commission; Organization

(A) Appointment of Commissioners. As provided by Const 1963, art 6, § 30, the Judicial Tenure Commission consists of 9 persons. The commissioners selected by the judges shall be chosen by vote conducted by the state court administrator. The commissioners selected by the state bar members shall be chosen by vote conducted by the State Bar of Michigan. Both elections must be conducted in accordance with nomination and election procedures approved by the Supreme Court. Immediately after a commissioner's selection, the selecting authority shall notify the Supreme Court and the Judicial Tenure Commission.

(B) Term of Office. A commissioner's term of office shall be 3 years. To achieve staggered terms, the following terms shall expire in consecutive years:

(1) one of the appointments of the Governor, the judge of a court of limited jurisdiction, and one of the attorneys selected by the state bar;

(2) the other appointment of the Governor, the probate judge, and the other attorney selected by the state bar;

(3) the Court of Appeals judge, the circuit judge, and the judge selected by the state bar.

(C) Oath of Office. The following oath shall be administered to all members of the Judicial Tenure Commission:

"I do solemnly swear (or affirm) that I will support the Constitution of the United States and the Constitution of this state, and that I will faithfully discharge the duties of the office of Judicial Tenure Commission member according to the best of my ability."

(D) Vacancy.

(1) A vacancy in the office of a commissioner occurs:

(a) when a commissioner resigns or is incapable of serving as a member of the commission;

(b) when a judge who is a member of the commission no longer holds the office held when selected;

(c) when an attorney selected by state bar members is no longer entitled to practice in the courts of this state; and

(d) when an appointee of the Governor becomes an attorney.

The commission shall notify the appointing authority of a vacancy.

(2) Vacancies must be filled by selection of a successor in the same manner required for the selection of the predecessor. The commissioner selected shall hold office for the unexpired term of the predecessor. Vacancies must be filled within 3 months after the vacancy occurs. If a vacancy occurs after the selection of a new commissioner but before that commissioner's term officially begins, the commissioner-elect shall fill that vacancy and serve the remainder of the unexpired term.

(3) A member may resign by submitting a resignation in writing to the commission, which must certify the vacancy to the selecting authority.

(E) Commission Expenses.

(1) The commission's budget must be submitted to the Supreme Court for approval.

(2) The commission's expenses must be included in and paid from the appropriation for the Supreme Court.

(3) A commissioner may not receive compensation for services but shall be paid reasonable and necessary expenses.

(F) Quorum and Chairperson.

(1) At its first meeting in odd-numbered years, the commission shall elect from among its members a chairperson, a vice-chairperson, and a secretary, each to serve 2 years. The vice-chairperson shall act as chairperson when the chairperson is absent. If both are absent, the members present may select one among them to act as temporary chairperson.

(2) A quorum for the transaction of business by the commission is 5.

(3) The vote of a majority of the members constitutes the adoption or rejection of a motion or resolution before the commission. The chairperson is entitled to cast a vote as a commissioner.

(4) Regular meetings at which no public hearing is scheduled may be held in person, by telephone, or by teleconference, provided that the telephone or teleconference method is a secure connection.

(G) Meetings of Commission. Meetings must be held at the call of the chairperson or the executive director, or upon the written request of 3 commission members.

(H) Commission Staff.

(1) The commission shall employ an executive director or equivalent person or persons, and such other staff members as the commission concludes are warranted, to perform the duties that the commission directs, subject to the availability of funds under its budget.

(2) The executive director, other disciplinary counsel, or any other person who is involved in the investigation or prosecution of a respondent

(a) shall not be present or participate in any manner in the decision of the commission to file a complaint, or during the deliberations of the commission to recommend action by the Supreme Court with regard to that respondent, and

(b) shall have no substantive ex parte communication with the commission regarding a complaint that the commission has authorized.

(3) Commission employees are exempt from the operation of Const 1963, art 11, § 5, as are employees of courts of record.

[Formerly Rule 9.202, adopted effective March 1, 1985. Amended effective January 21, 2003, 467 Mich. Renumbered Rule 9.210, rescinded and readopted April 11, 2019, amended effective September 1, 2019, 502 Mich.]

Comments

Staff Comment to 1985 Adoption

MCR 9.202 corresponds to GCR 1963, 932.1.

Subrule (B) rewords GCR 1963, 932.1(2), but achieves the same effect as rules 932.1(2) and 932.28 (which set the starting date for the terms of the first members of the commission).

Subrule (E)(3) is based on rule 2 of the Administrative Rules of the Judicial Tenure Commission.

Staff Comment to 2019 Readoption and Renumbering

This new version of MCR 9.200 *et seq.* reflects a reorganization suggested by the Judicial Tenure Commission, and includes various technical changes to update and modernize the rules.

Rule 9.211. Judicial Tenure Commission; Powers; Review

(A) Authority of Commission. The commission has all the powers provided for under Const 1963, art 6, § 30, and further powers provided by Supreme Court rule. Proceedings before the commission or a master are governed by these rules. The commission may adopt and publish internal operating procedures for its internal operation and the administration of its proceedings that do not conflict with this subchapter and shall submit them to the Supreme Court for approval.

(B) Review as an Appellate Court. The commission may not function as an appellate court to review the decision of a court or to exercise superintending or administrative control of a court, but may examine decisions incident to a request for investigation of judicial misconduct, disability, or other circumstance that the commission may undertake to investigate under Const 1963, art 6, § 30, and MCR 9.220. An erroneous decision by a judge made in good faith and with due diligence is not judicial misconduct.

(C) Control of Commission Action. Proceedings under these rules are subject to the direct and exclusive superintending control of the Supreme Court. No other court has jurisdiction to restrict, control, or review the orders of the master or the commission.

(D) Errors and Irregularities. An investigation or proceeding under this subchapter may not be held invalid by reason of a nonprejudicial irregularity or for an error not resulting in a miscarriage of justice.

(E) Jurisdiction Over Visiting Judges. Notwithstanding MCR 9.116(B), the Attorney Grievance Commission may take action immediately with regard to a visiting judge who currently holds no other judicial office if the allegations pertain to professional or personal activities unrelated to the judge's activities as a judge.

[Formerly Rule 9.203, adopted effective March 1, 1985. Amended effective August 30, 1990. Amended March 24, 1998, effective April 1, 1998, 456 Mich. Amended effective January 21, 2003, 467 Mich. Renumbered Rule 9.211, rescinded and readopted April 11, 2019, amended effective September 1, 2019, 502 Mich.]

Comments

Staff Comment to 1985 Adoption

MCR 9.203 corresponds to GCR 1963, 932.2.

Subrule (B) is based on rule 1 of the Administrative Rules of the Judicial Tenure Commission.

Staff Comment to 1990 Amendment

New subrule (E) [effective August 30, 1990] resolves a potential jurisdictional conflict between the Judicial Tenure Commission and the Attorney Grievance Commission. See and compare MCR 9.116(A). The new subrule makes it clear that the AGC is free to investigate allegations of nonjudicial misconduct by a visiting judge. The AGC would continue to defer to the JTC pursuant to MCR 9.116(A) if the allegations involve judicial misconduct. But see *In the Matter of Probert*, 411 Mich 210 (1981).

Staff Comment to 1998 Amendment

The amendment of MCR 9.203 makes technical changes necessary in light of statutory amendments and corrects cross-references.

The amendment of MCR 9.203 makes changes in cross-references necessitated by earlier amendments. Some published versions of the rules already include several of these corrections.

Staff Comment to 2019 Readoption and Renumbering

This new version of MCR 9.200 *et seq.* reflects a reorganization suggested by the Judicial Tenure Commission, and includes various technical changes to update and modernize the rules.

Rule 9.212.   Disqualification of Commission Member of Employee

(A) Disqualification From Participation. A judge who is a member of the commission or a justice of the Supreme Court is disqualified from participating in that capacity in proceedings involving the judge's or justice's own actions or for any reason set forth in MCR 2.003(C).

(B) Disqualification from Representation. A member or employee of the commission may not represent

(1) a respondent in proceedings before the commission, including preliminary discussions with employees of the commission before the filing of a request for investigation; or

(2) a judge in proceedings before the Attorney Grievance Commission, or the Attorney Discipline Board and its hearing panels, as to any matter that was pending before the Judicial Tenure Commission during the member's or the employee's tenure with the commission.

The law firm of an attorney member of the commission may not represent a respondent in proceedings before the commission, including preliminary discussions with employees of the commission before the filing of a request for investigation.

[Formerly Rule 9.204, adopted effective March 1, 1985. Amended April 23, 1996, effective July 1, 1996, 451 Mich. Amended effective January 21, 2003, 467 Mich. Renumbered Rule 9.212, rescinded and readopted April 11, 2019, amended effective September 1, 2019, 502, Mich.]

Comments

Staff Comment to 1985 Adoption

MCR 9.204 is substantially the same as GCR 1963, 932.5.

Staff Comment to 1996 Amendment

The amendment of MCR 9.204, effective July 1, 1996, precluded members and employees of the Judicial Tenure Commission from representing (1) a respondent in proceedings before the Judicial Tenure Commission, and (2) a judge or former judge in proceedings before the Attorney Grievance Commission, or the Attorney Discipline Board and its hearing panels, as to matters pending before the Judicial Tenure Commission during the member's or employee's tenure with the Judicial Tenure Commission.

Staff Comment to 2019 Readoption and Renumbering

This new version of MCR 9.200 *et seq.* reflects a reorganization suggested by the Judicial Tenure Commission, and includes various technical changes to update and modernize the rules.

Rule 9.220.   Preliminary Investigation

(A) Request for Investigation. A request for investigation of a judge must be made in writing and verified on oath of the grievant. The commission also is authorized to act on its own initiative or at the request of the Supreme Court, the Chief Justice, the state court administrator, or the Attorney Grievance Commission.

(B) Investigation. Upon receiving a request for investigation that is not clearly unfounded or frivolous, the commission shall direct that an investigation be conducted to determine whether a complaint should be filed and a hearing held.

(C) Adjourned Investigation. If a request for investigation is filed less than 90 days before an election in which the respondent is a candidate, and the request is not dismissed forthwith as clearly unfounded or frivolous, the commission shall postpone its investigation until after the election unless two-thirds of the commission members present or participating by telephone or teleconference determine that the public interest and the interests of justice require otherwise.

(D) Physical or Mental Examination. In the course of an investigation where a respondent's physical or mental condition is at issue, the commission may require the respondent to submit to a physical or mental examination. Failure of the respondent to submit to the examination may constitute judicial misconduct. MCR 2.311(B) is applicable to the examination.

(E) Expediting Matters. When the integrity of the judicial system requires, the Supreme Court may direct that the commission expedite its consideration of any investigation, and may set a deadline for the commission to submit any recommendation to the Court, notwithstanding any other provision in this subchapter.

[Formerly Rule 9.207, adopted effective March 1, 1985. Amended effective January 21, 2003, 467 Mich. Amended March 20, 2007, effective May 1, 2007, 477 Mich. Amended effective March 21, 2018, 501 Mich. Renumbered Rule 9.220, rescinded and readopted April 11, 2019, amended effective September 1, 2019, 502 Mich.]

Comments

Staff Comment to 1985 Adoption

MCR 9.207 corresponds to GCR 1963, 932.7.

Subrule (A) is taken from rule 3 of the Administrative Rules of the Judicial Tenure Commission.

Subrule (F) is taken from rule 4 of the Administrative Rules of the Judicial Tenure Commission.

Staff Comment to 2007 Amendment

This amendment allows a judge admonished by the Judicial Tenure Commission to request review of the admonishment by the Supreme Court. The amendment in subsection B adds a letter designation and descriptive heading to the provision relating to adjournments granted for requests for investigation filed within 90 days of an election in which the respondent is a candidate.

Staff Comment to 2018 Amendment

These amendments update cross-references and make other nonsubstantive revisions to clarify the rules. The amendment of MCR 6.110(B)(1) addresses an inadvertent omission from the last amendment of this rule that was intended to be shown in overstrike. Accordingly, the current rule does not match the published version. Striking the clause "for good cause shown" will provide consistency with other published versions of the rule and with the statute, MCL 766.7, which allows a magistrate to adjourn a preliminary examination with the consent of the parties without the need for good cause to be shown.

Staff Comment to 2019 Readoption and Renumbering

This new version of MCR 9.200 *et seq.* reflects a reorganization suggested by the Judicial Tenure Commission, and includes various technical changes to update and modernize the rules.

Rule 9.221.   Evidence

(A) Taking of Evidence During Investigation. The commission may take evidence before it or an individual member of the commission, or before the executive director or other member of the staff for purposes of the investigation.

(B) The commission may request that a respondent comment on any aspect of an investigation. The respondent shall have 21 days from the date of the request for comments to provide a response. The executive director may extend the response time for an additional 21 days. Any further request for additional time may only be granted by the commission or its chairperson for good cause shown. The respondent must sign the response, and that signature shall serve as the respondent's attestation as to the veracity of the respondent's response.

(C) Issuance of Subpoenas. The commission may issue subpoenas for the attendance of witnesses to provide statements or produce documents or other tangible evidence exclusively for consideration by the commission and its staff during the investigation. Before the filing of a complaint, the entitlement appearing on the subpoena shall not disclose the name of a respondent under investigation.

(D) Sanctions for Contempt; Disobedience by Respondent.

(1) Contempt proceedings against a nonparty for failure to obey a subpoena issued pursuant to this rule may be brought pursuant to MCR 2.506(E) in the circuit court for the county in which the individual resides, where the individual is found, where the contempt occurred, or where the hearing is to be held.

(2) If a respondent disobeys a subpoena or other lawful order of the commission or the master, whether before or during the hearing, the commission or the master may order such sanctions as are just, including, but not limited to, those set forth in MCR 2.313(B)(2)(a)–(e).

(E) Cooperation With Investigation. A judge, clerk, court employee, member of the bar, or other officer of a court must comply with a reasonable request made by the commission in its investigation. Failure to cooperate may be considered judicial misconduct or attorney misconduct. No court may charge the Judicial Tenure Commission for copying costs or certification costs, whether under MCL 600.2546 or otherwise, unless the Michigan Supreme Court specifically so authorizes.
[Formerly Rule 9.208, adopted effective March 1, 1985. Amended effective January 21, 2003, 467 Mich. Amended May 28, 2008, effective September 1, 2008, 481 Mich. Renumbered Rule 9.221, rescinded and readopted April 11, 2019, amended effective September 1, 2019, 502 Mich.]

Comments

Staff Comment to 1985 Adoption

MCR 9.208 corresponds to GCR 1963, 932.8. The provisions are reorganized without changing the substance of the rule.

Staff Comment to 2008 Amendment

These amendments require that all parties to a Judicial Tenure Commission proceeding that is scheduled for a public hearing exchange material in their possession that they intend to introduce as evidence at the hearing. The amendments also require the parties to give supplemental notice of any additional material within 5 days after having been identified, and at least 10 days before a scheduled hearing.

Staff Comment to 2019 Readoption and Renumbering

This new version of MCR 9.200 *et seq.* reflects a reorganization suggested by the Judicial Tenure Commission, and includes various technical changes to update and modernize the rules.

Rule 9.222.   Further Investigation; The "28–Day Letter"

(A) Before filing a complaint, the commission must give written notice to the respondent who is the subject of a request for investigation. The purpose of the notice is to afford the respondent an opportunity to apprise the commission, in writing within 28 days, of such matters as the respondent may choose, including information about the factual aspects of the allegations and other relevant issues. The notice shall specify the allegations and may include the date of the conduct, the location where the conduct occurred, and the name of the case or identification of the court proceeding relating to the conduct. The respondent shall sign the response and that signature shall serve as the respondent's attestation as to the veracity of the respondent's response.

(1) For good cause shown, the commission or its chairperson may grant a reasonable extension of the 28–day period.

(2) The Supreme Court may shorten the time periods prescribed in this and other provisions of this subchapter at its own initiative or at the request of the commission.

(B) In the commission's discretion, it may issue a "28–day letter" without having first requested the respondent's comments pursuant to MCR 9.221(B).

(C) The commission may continue to investigate until it issues a complaint, at which point the disciplinary counsel may continue investigating as needed.

(D) If a respondent requests in response to a written notice from the commission under this rule, the commission may offer the respondent an opportunity to appear informally before the commission to present such information as the respondent may choose, including information about the factual aspects of the allegations and other relevant issues.
[Formerly Rule 9.207, adopted effective March 1, 1985. Amended effective January 21, 2003, 467 Mich. Amended March 20, 2007, effective May 1, 2007, 477 Mich. Amended effective March 21, 2018, 501 Mich. Renumbered Rule 9.222, rescinded and readopted April 11, 2019, amended effective September 1, 2019, 502 Mich.]

Comments

Staff Comment to 1985 Adoption

MCR 9.207 corresponds to GCR 1963, 932.7.

Subrule (A) is taken from rule 3 of the Administrative Rules of the Judicial Tenure Commission.

Subrule (F) is taken from rule 4 of the Administrative Rules of the Judicial Tenure Commission.

Staff Comment to 2007 Amendment

This amendment allows a judge admonished by the Judicial Tenure Commission to request review of the admonishment by the Supreme Court. The amendment in subsection B adds a letter designation and descriptive heading to the provision relating to adjournments granted for requests for investigation filed within 90 days of an election in which the respondent is a candidate.

Staff Comment to 2018 Amendment

These amendments update cross-references and make other nonsubstantive revisions to clarify the rules. The amendment of MCR 6.110(B)(1) addresses an inadvertent omission from the last amendment of this rule that was intended to be shown in overstrike. Accordingly, the current rule does not match the published version. Striking the clause "for good cause shown" will provide consistency with other published versions of the rule and with the statute, MCL 766.7, which allows a magistrate to adjourn a preliminary examination with the consent of the parties without the need for good cause to be shown.

Staff Comment to 2019 Readoption and Renumbering

This new version of MCR 9.200 *et seq.* reflects a reorganization suggested by the Judicial Tenure Commission, and includes various technical changes to update and modernize the rules.

Rule 9.223.   Conclusion of Investigation;   Notice

(A) If the commission determines at any time in the investigation that there are insufficient grounds to warrant filing a complaint, the commission may:

(1) dismiss the matter;

(2) dismiss the matter with a letter of explanation or caution that addresses the respondent's conduct;

(3) dismiss the matter with or without a letter of explanation or caution that addresses the respondent's conduct contingent upon the satisfaction of conditions imposed by the commission, which may include a period of monitoring;

(4) admonish the respondent; or

(5) recommend to the Supreme Court private censure, with a statement of reasons.

(B) Notice to Respondent. Before taking action under subrule (A)(2)–(5), the commission must first have given written notice to the respondent of the nature of the allegations in the request for investigation and afforded the respondent a reasonable opportunity to respond in writing, pursuant to MCR 9.221(B), MCR 9.222(A), or both.

(C) On final disposition of a request for investigation without the filing of a complaint, the commission shall give written notice of the disposition to the respondent who was the subject of the request. The commission also shall provide written notice to the grievant that the matter has been resolved without the filing of a complaint.

[Formerly Rule 9.207, adopted effective March 1, 1985. Amended effective January 21, 2003, 467 Mich. Amended March 20, 2007, effective May 1, 2007, 477 Mich. Amended effective March 21, 2018, 501 Mich. Renumbered Rule 9.222, rescinded and readopted April 11, 2019, amended effective September 1, 2019, 502 Mich.]

Comments

Staff Comment to 1985 Adoption

MCR 9.207 corresponds to GCR 1963, 932.7.

Subrule (A) is taken from rule 3 of the Administrative Rules of the Judicial Tenure Commission.

Subrule (F) is taken from rule 4 of the Administrative Rules of the Judicial Tenure Commission.

Staff Comment to 2007 Amendment

This amendment allows a judge admonished by the Judicial Tenure Commission to request review of the admonishment by the Supreme Court. The amendment in subsection B adds a letter designation and descriptive heading to the provision relating to adjournments granted for requests for investigation filed within 90 days of an election in which the respondent is a candidate.

Staff Comment to 2018 Amendment

These amendments update cross-references and make other nonsubstantive revisions to clarify the rules. The amendment of MCR 6.110(B)(1) addresses an inadvertent omission from the last amendment of this rule that was intended to be shown in overstrike. Accordingly, the current rule does not match the published version. Striking the clause "for good cause shown" will provide consistency with other published versions of the rule and with the statute, MCL 766.7, which allows a magistrate to adjourn a preliminary examination with the consent of the parties without the need for good cause to be shown.

Staff Comment to 2019 Readoption and Renumbering

This new version of MCR 9.200 *et seq.* reflects a reorganization suggested by the Judicial Tenure Commission, and includes various technical changes to update and modernize the rules.

Rule 9.224.   Complaint

(A) Upon determining that there is sufficient evidence to believe that the respondent under investigation has engaged in misconduct, the commission may issue a complaint against that respondent.

(B) If the commission issues a complaint, it shall appoint the executive director or another attorney to act as disciplinary counsel. If the executive director assumes the role of disciplinary counsel, the commission shall appoint outside counsel to act as commission counsel. If the commission appoints outside counsel to act as disciplinary counsel, the executive director shall serve as commission counsel.

(C) Upon issuing a complaint, the commission shall petition the Court for the appointment of a master.

[Adopted April 11, 2019, effective September 1, 2019, 502 Mich.]

Comments

Staff Comment to 2019 Adoption

This new version of MCR 9.200 *et seq.* reflects a reorganization suggested by the Judicial Tenure Commission, and includes various technical changes to update and modernize the rules.

Rule 9.225.   Interim Suspension

(A) Petition.

(1) With the filing of a complaint, the commission may petition the Supreme Court for an order suspending a respondent from acting as a judge until final adjudication of the complaint.

(2) In extraordinary circumstances, the commission may petition the Supreme Court for an order suspending a respondent from acting as a judge in response to a request for investigation, pending a decision by the commission regarding the filing of a complaint. In such a circumstance, the documents filed with the Court must be kept under seal unless the petition is granted. Conviction of a felony is grounds for automatic interim suspension, with or without pay, pending action by the commission. If the respondent is suspended without pay, the respondent's pay shall be held in escrow pending the final resolution of disciplinary proceedings.

Whenever a petition for interim suspension is granted, the processing of the case shall be expedited in the commission and in the Supreme Court. The commission shall set forth in the petition an approximate date for submitting a final recommendation to the Court.

(3) Notwithstanding any other provision of this rule, in a matter in which a respondent poses a substantial threat of serious harm to the public or to the administration of justice, the commission may petition the Supreme Court for an order suspending a respondent from acting as a judge without pay in response to a request for investigation, pending a decision by the commission regarding the issuance of a complaint. The respondent's pay shall be held in escrow pending the final resolution of disciplinary proceedings.

Whenever a petition for interim suspension is granted, the processing of the case shall be expedited in the commission and in the Supreme Court. The commission shall set forth in the petition an approximate date for submitting a final recommendation to the Court.

(B) Contents; Affidavit or Transcript. The petition must be accompanied by a sworn affidavit or court transcript and state facts in support of the allegations and the assertion that immediate suspension is necessary for the proper administration of justice.

(C) Service; Answer. A copy of the petition and supporting documents must be served on the respondent, who may file an answer to the petition within 14 days after service of the petition, unless the commission has filed a motion for immediate consideration. The commission must be served with a copy of the answer.

[Formerly Rule 9.219, adopted effective March 1, 1985. Amended effective January 21, 2003, 467 Mich. Renumbered Rule 9.225, rescinded and readopted April 11, 2019, amended effective September 1, 2019, 502 Mich.]

Comments

Staff Comment to 1985 Adoption

MCR 9.219 is substantially the same as GCR 1963, 932.19.

Staff Comment to 2019 Readoption and Renumbering

This new version of MCR 9.200 *et seq.* reflects a reorganization suggested by the Judicial Tenure Commission, and includes various technical changes to update and modernize the rules.

Rule 9.230. Pleadings

Other than motions, the complaint and answer are the only pleadings allowed.

(A) Complaint.

(1) *Filing; Service.* A complaint may not be issued before the completion of a preliminary investigation. Upon concluding that there is sufficient evidence to warrant the issuance of a complaint, the commission shall direct the executive director or equivalent staff member to do the following:

(a) enter the complaint in the commission docket, which is a public record;

(b) retain the complaint in the commission office; and

(c) promptly serve a copy of the complaint on the respondent.

(2) *Form of Complaint.* A complaint must be entitled:

"Complaint Against ___, Judge. No. ___."

A complaint must be in form similar to a complaint filed in a civil action in the circuit court.

(B) Answer.

(1) *Filing.* Within 14 days after service of the complaint, the respondent must file with the commission the original and 9 copies of an answer verified by the respondent.

(2) *Form.* The answer must be in form similar to an answer in a civil action in the circuit court and must contain a full and fair disclosure of all facts and circumstances pertaining to the allegations regarding the respondent. Willful concealment, misrepresentation, or failure to file an answer and disclosure are additional grounds for disciplinary action under the complaint.

(3) Affirmative defenses, including the defense of laches, must be asserted in the answer or they will not be considered.

[Formerly Rule 9.209, adopted effective March 1, 1985. Amended effective January 21, 2003, 467 Mich. Renumbered Rule 9.230, rescinded and readopted April 11, 2019, amended effective September 1, 2019, 502 Mich.]

Comments

Staff Comment to 1985 Adoption

MCR 9.209 is substantially the same as GCR 1963, 932.9.

Staff Comment to 2019 Readoption and Renumbering

This new version of MCR 9.200 *et seq.* reflects a reorganization suggested by the Judicial Tenure Commission, and includes various technical changes to update and modernize the rules.

Rule 9.231. Appointment of Master

(A) The Supreme Court shall appoint a master to conduct the hearing within a reasonable period of the date of the petition and shall establish a date for completion of the hearing procedure.

(B) The master shall set a time and a place for the hearing and shall notify the respondent and the examiner at least 28 days in advance. The master shall rule on all motions and other procedural matters incident to the complaint, answer, and hearing. Recommendations on dispositive motions shall not be announced until the conclusion of the hearing, except that the master may refer to the commission on an interlocutory basis a recommendation regarding a dispositive motion.

(C) The master may conduct one or more pretrial conferences, and may order a prehearing conference to obtain admissions or otherwise narrow the issues presented by the pleadings.

(D) Unless the parties agree to waive them, closing arguments at the hearing before the master shall be oral and take place upon conclusion of the presentation of evidence. The master may not adjourn or postpone closing arguments for the preparation of a transcript or the submission of proposed findings of fact.

(E) MCR 2.003(B) shall govern all matters concerning the disqualification of a master.

[Formerly Rule 9.210, adopted effective March 1, 1985. Amended effective January 21, 2003, 467 Mich. Renumbered Rule 9.231, rescinded and readopted April 11, 2019, amended effective September 1, 2019, 502 Mich.]

Comments

Staff Comment to 1985 Adoption

MCR 9.210 corresponds to GCR 1963, 932.10.

Subrule (C) is taken from rule 5 of the Administrative Rules of the Judicial Tenure Commission.

Staff Comment to 2019 Readoption and Renumbering

This new version of MCR 9.200 *et seq.* reflects a reorganization suggested by the Judicial Tenure Commission, and includes various technical changes to update and modernize the rules.

Rule 9.232. Discovery

(A) Pretrial or discovery proceedings are not permitted, except as follows:

(1) At least 21 days before a scheduled public hearing,

(a) the parties shall provide to one another, in writing, the names and addresses of all persons whom they intend to call at the hearing, a copy of all statements and affidavits given by those persons, and any material in their possession that they intend to introduce as evidence at the hearing, and

(b) the disciplinary counsel or executive director shall provide to the respondent copies of all exculpatory material in its possession.

(2) The parties shall give supplemental notice to one another within 5 days after any additional witness or material has been identified and at least 10 days before a scheduled hearing.

(B) A deposition may be taken of a witness who is living outside the state or who is unable to attend a hearing, or otherwise as allowed for good cause shown.

(C) If a party fails to comply with subrules (A) or (B), the master may, on motion and showing of material prejudice as a result of the failure, impose one or more of the sanctions set forth in MCR 2.313(B)(2)(a)–(e).

[Formerly Rule 9.208, adopted effective March 1, 1985. Amended effective January 21, 2003, 467 Mich. Amended May 28, 2008, effective September 1, 2008, 481 Mich. Renumbered Rule 9.232, rescinded and readopted April 11, 2019, amended effective September 1, 2019, 502 Mich.]

Comments

Staff Comment to 1985 Adoption

MCR 9.208 corresponds to GCR 1963, 932.8. The provisions are reorganized without changing the substance of the rule.

Staff Comment to 2008 Amendment

These amendments require that all parties to a Judicial Tenure Commission proceeding that is scheduled for a public hearing exchange material in their possession that they intend to introduce as evidence at the hearing. The amendments also require the parties to give supplemental notice of any additional material within 5 days after having been identified, and at least 10 days before a scheduled hearing.

Staff Comment to 2019 Readoption and Renumbering

This new version of MCR 9.200 *et seq.* reflects a reorganization suggested by the Judicial Tenure Commission, and includes various technical changes to update and modernize the rules.

Rule 9.233. Public Hearing

(A) Procedure. The public hearing must conform as nearly as possible to the rules of procedure and evidence governing the trial of civil actions in the circuit court. A respondent is entitled to be represented by an attorney. Disciplinary counsel shall present the evidence in support of the charges set forth in the complaint and at all times shall have the burden of proving the allegations by a preponderance of the evidence. Any employee, officer, or agent of the respondent's court, law enforcement officer, public officer or employee, or attorney who testifies as a witness in the hearing, whether called by the disciplinary counsel or by the respondent, is subject to cross-examination by either party as an opposite party under MCL 600.2161.

(B) Effect of Failure to Comply.

(1) If the respondent is in default for not having filed a timely answer or fails to attend the proceedings without being excused by the master, the commission, or the court, the allegations set forth in the complaint shall be deemed admitted, taken as true, and may form the basis for the master to make findings of fact.

(2) The respondent's failure to testify in his or her own behalf or to submit to a medical examination requested by the commission or the master may be considered as an evidentiary fact, unless the failure was due to circumstances unrelated to the facts in issue at the hearing.

(C) Record. The proceedings at the hearing must be recorded by stenographic or mechanical means. If the master declines to admit evidence, a separate record shall be made so

that the commission and/or the court may consider that evidence and determine whether to include it in the record.

[Formerly Rule 9.211, adopted effective March 1, 1985. Amended effective January 21, 2003, 467 Mich. Renumbered Rule 9.233, rescinded and readopted April 11, 2019, amended effective September 1, 2019, 502 Mich.]

Comments

Staff Comment to 1985 Adoption

MCR 9.211 is substantially the same as GCR 1963, 932.11.

Staff Comment to 2019 Readoption and Renumbering

This new version of MCR 9.200 *et seq.* reflects a reorganization suggested by the Judicial Tenure Commission, and includes various technical changes to update and modernize the rules.

Rule 9.234. Subpoenas

(A) Issuance of Subpoenas. The attorneys may issue subpoenas for the attendance of witnesses or the production of documents or other tangible evidence.

(B) Sanctions for Contempt; Disobedience by Respondent.

(1) Contempt proceedings against a nonparty for failure to obey a subpoena issued pursuant to this rule may be brought pursuant to MCR 2.506(E) in the circuit court for the county in which the individual resides, in which the individual is found, in which the contempt occurred, or in which the hearing is to be held.

(2) If a respondent disobeys a subpoena or other lawful order of the commission or the master, whether before or during the hearing, the commission or the master may order such sanctions as are just, including, but not limited to, those set forth in MCR 2.313(B)(2)(a)–(e).

[Formerly Rule 9.212, adopted effective March 1, 1985. Amended effective January 21, 2003, 467 Mich. Renumbered Rule 9.234, rescinded and readopted April 11, 2019, amended effective September 1, 2019, 502 Mich.]

Comments

Staff Comment to 1985 Adoption

MCR 9.212 is substantially the same as GCR 1963, 932.12.

Staff Comment to 2019 Readoption and Renumbering

This new version of MCR 9.200 *et seq.* reflects a reorganization suggested by the Judicial Tenure Commission, and includes various technical changes to update and modernize the rules.

Rule 9.235. Amendments of Complaint or Answer

The master, before the conclusion of the hearing, or the commission, before its determination, may allow or require amendments of the complaint or the answer. The complaint may be amended to conform to the proofs or to set forth additional facts, whether occurring before or after the commencement of the hearing. If an amendment is made, the respondent must be given reasonable time to answer the amendment and to prepare and present a defense against the matters charged in the amendment. A "28-day letter" is not required to amend a complaint.

[Formerly Rule 9.213, adopted effective March 1, 1985. Amended effective January 21, 2003, 467 Mich. Renumbered Rule 9.235, rescinded and readopted April 11, 2019, amended effective September 1, 2019, 502 Mich.]

Comments

Staff Comment to 1985 Adoption

MCR 9.213 is substantially the same as GCR 1963, 932.13.

Staff Comment to 2019 Readoption and Renumbering

This new version of MCR 9.200 *et seq.* reflects a reorganization suggested by the Judicial Tenure Commission, and includes various technical changes to update and modernize the rules.

Rule 9.236.   Report of Master

The court reporter shall prepare a transcript of the proceedings conducted before the master within 21 days of the conclusion of the hearing, filing the original with the commission, and serving copies on the respondent (or the respondent's attorney) and disciplinary counsel, by e-mail. Within 21 days after a transcript of the proceedings is provided, the master shall prepare and transmit to the commission a report that contains a brief statement of the proceedings and findings of fact and conclusions of law with respect to the issues presented by the complaint and the answer. On receiving the report, the commission must promptly send a copy to the respondent, unless the master has already done so.

[Formerly Rule 9.214, adopted effective March 1, 1985. Amended effective January 21, 2003, 467 Mich. Renumbered Rule 9.236, rescinded and readopted April 11, 2019, amended effective September 1, 2019, 502 Mich.]

Comments

Staff Comment to 1985 Adoption

MCR 9.214 is substantially the same as GCR 1963, 932.14.

Staff Comment to 2019 Readoption and Renumbering

This new version of MCR 9.200 *et seq.* reflects a reorganization suggested by the Judicial Tenure Commission, and includes various technical changes to update and modernize the rules.

Rule 9.240.   Objections to Report of Master

Within 28 days after the master's report is mailed to the respondent, disciplinary counsel or the respondent may file with the commission an original and 9 copies of a brief in support of or in opposition to all or part of the master's report. The briefs must include a discussion of possible sanctions and, except as otherwise permitted by the commission, are limited to 50 pages in length. A copy of the brief must be served on the opposite party, who shall have 14 days to respond.

[Formerly Rule 9.215, adopted effective March 1, 1985. Amended effective January 21, 2003, 467 Mich. Renumbered Rule 9.240, rescinded and readopted April 11, 2019, amended effective September 1, 2019, 502 Mich.]

Comments

Staff Comment to 1985 Adoption

MCR 9.215 is substantially the same as GCR 1963, 932.15.

Staff Comment to 2019 Readoption and Renumbering

This new version of MCR 9.200 *et seq.* reflects a reorganization suggested by the Judicial Tenure Commission, and includes various technical changes to update and modernize the rules.

Rule 9.241.   Appearance Before Commission

When the hearing before the master has concluded, the commission shall set a date for hearing objections to the report. Both the respondent and the disciplinary counsel may present oral argument at the hearing before the commission.

[Formerly Rule 9.216, adopted effective March 1, 1985. Amended effective January 21, 2003, 467 Mich; January 11, 2005, 471 Mich. Renumbered Rule 9.241, rescinded and readopted April 11, 2019, amended effective September 1, 2019, 502 Mich.]

Comments

Staff Comment to 1985 Adoption

MCR 9.216 is substantially the same as GCR 1963, 932.16.

Staff Comment to 2005 Amendment

The amendment of MCR 9.216 imposes a 50-page limit for briefs filed with the Judicial Tenure Commission. It reflects the page limit that the Commission currently imposes for briefs filed in Judicial Tenure Commission proceedings.

Staff Comment to 2019 Readoption and Renumbering

This new version of MCR 9.200 *et seq.* reflects a reorganization suggested by the Judicial Tenure Commission, and includes various technical changes to update and modernize the rules.

Rule 9.242.   Extension of Time

For good cause shown, the commission or its chairperson may extend for periods not to exceed 28 days the time for the filing of an answer, for the commencement of a hearing before the commission, for the filing of the master's report, and for the filing of a statement of objections to the report of a master.

[Formerly Rule 9.217, adopted effective March 1, 1985. Amended effective January 21, 2003, 467 Mich. Renumbered Rule 9.242, rescinded and readopted April 11, 2019, amended effective September 1, 2019, 502 Mich.]

Comments

Staff Comment to 1985 Adoption

MCR 9.217 is substantially the same as GCR 1963, 932.17.

Staff Comment to 2019 Readoption and Renumbering

This new version of MCR 9.200 *et seq.* reflects a reorganization suggested by the Judicial Tenure Commission, and includes various technical changes to update and modernize the rules.

Rule 9.243.   Hearing Additional Evidence

The commission may order a hearing before itself or the master for the taking of additional evidence at any time while the complaint is pending before it. The order must set the time and place of hearing and indicate the matters about which evidence is to be taken. A copy of the order must be sent to the respondent at least 14 days before the hearing.

[Formerly Rule 9.218, adopted effective March 1, 1985. Amended effective January 21, 2003, 467 Mich. Renumbered Rule 9.244, rescinded and readopted April 11, 2019, effective September 1, 2019, 502 Mich.]

Comments

Staff Comment to 1985 Adoption

MCR 9.218 is substantially the same as GCR 1963, 932.18.

Staff Comment to 2019 Readoption and Renumbering

This new version of MCR 9.200 *et seq.* reflects a reorganization suggested by the Judicial Tenure Commission, and includes various technical changes to update and modernize the rules.

Rule 9.244.   Commission Decision

(A) Majority Decision.

(1) The affirmative vote of 5 commission members who have considered the report of the master and any objections, and who were present at an oral hearing provided for in MCR 9.241, or have read the transcript of that hearing, is required for a recommendation of action with regard to a respondent. A commissioner may file a written dissent.

(2) It is not necessary that a majority agree on the specific conduct that warrants a recommendation of action with regard to a respondent, or on the specific action that is warranted, only that there was some conduct that warrants such a recommendation.

(B) Record of Decision.

(1) The commission must make written findings of fact and conclusions of law along with its recommendations for action with respect to the issues of fact and law in the proceedings, but

may adopt the findings of the master, in whole or in part, by reference. The commission's report must include a list of all respondent's prior disciplinary actions under MCR 9.223(A)(2)–(5) or MCR 9.224 and must include an acknowledgment that the commission has included its consideration of any prior discipline in the commission's recommended action. The list of previous disciplinary actions shall be submitted under seal and will be retained in a nonpublic manner. Disclosure of any prior disciplinary action will occur only if the information is relevant to any recommendation or imposed sanction.

(2) The commission shall undertake to ensure that the action it is recommending in individual cases is reasonably proportionate to the conduct of the respondent and reasonably equivalent to the action that has been taken previously in equivalent cases.

[Formerly Rule 9.220, adopted effective March 1, 1985. Amended effective January 21, 2003, 467 Mich. Renumbered Rule 9.244, rescinded and readopted April 11, 2019, amended effective September 1, 2019, 502 Mich.]

Comments

Staff Comment to 1985 Adoption

MCR 9.220 is substantially the same as GCR 1963, 932.20.

Staff Comment to 2019 Readoption and Renumbering

This new version of MCR 9.200 *et seq.* reflects a reorganization suggested by the Judicial Tenure Commission, and includes various technical changes to update and modernize the rules.

Rule 9.245.   Consent Agreements

(A) Consent Agreements. At any time, the respondent and the disciplinary counsel (or the executive director acting as the putative disciplinary counsel) may enter into confidential negotiations. A consent agreement may

(1) include stipulated facts and an agreement as to the sanction; or

(2) include just the stipulated facts, with no agreement as to the sanction.

The parties may present a signed consent agreement to the commission, which shall review the matter and decide whether to accept it. If the consent agreement is filed under subsection (1), the parties do not file briefs and the matter is not set on the docket for argument following the commission's decision, unless otherwise directed by the Court. If the consent agreement is filed under subsection (2), the matter proceeds pursuant to MCR 9.250 and MCR 9.251.

(B) Commission Action. If the commission agrees to the terms set forth in the consent agreement in subsection (1), the commission shall issue a decision and recommendation as if there had been a master's report filed. If the commission agrees to the terms set forth in the consent agreement in subsection (2), the stipulated facts serve in lieu of a master's report and the matter then proceeds to a hearing before the commission, with the briefing schedule and an appearance before the commission, as set forth in MCR 9.240 and MCR 9.241. The time for filing a brief before the commission in matters filed under subsection (2) shall start with the filing of the consent agreement. A copy of the consent agreement shall be attached to the commission's decision. The commission's recommendation must include its rationale for accepting the consent agreement as well as a list of all respondent's prior disciplinary actions under MCR 9.223(A)(2)–(5) or MCR 9.224 and must include an acknowledgment that the commission has included its consideration of any prior discipline in the commis-

sion's recommended action. The list of previous disciplinary actions shall be submitted under seal and will be retained in a nonpublic manner. Disclosure of any prior disciplinary action will occur only if the information is relevant to any recommendation or imposed sanction.

(C) Prior or Pending Discipline Actions. As part of a proposed consent agreement, the parties shall submit a list of all pending or previous disciplinary action taken against the respondent, sufficient information to understand the context of the individual circumstances, and the disposition of each incident. For purposes of this rule, "disciplinary actions" include any disposition other than a dismissal under MCR 9.223(A)(1), including nonsanctions under MCR 9.223(A)(2)–(5). The parties also shall include information about actions initiated against the respondent in proceedings other than disciplinary actions, including court cases for superintending control, criminal proceedings, internal discipline actions, or any other allegations of judicial misconduct. The list of previous disciplinary actions shall be submitted under seal and will be retained in a nonpublic manner. Disclosure of any prior disciplinary action will occur only if the information is relevant to any recommendation or imposed sanction.

(D) Action With Respondent's Consent. With the consent of the respondent and the commission, the Supreme Court may impose a sanction or take other action at any stage of the proceedings under these rules.

(E) Confidentiality. A consent agreement submitted to the commission shall not be made public until after the commission has accepted its terms and the Court has approved it.

[Adopted April 11, 2019, effective September 1, 2019, 502 Mich.]

Comments

Staff Comment to 2019 Adoption

This new version of MCR 9.200 *et seq.* reflects a reorganization suggested by the Judicial Tenure Commission, and includes various technical changes to update and modernize the rules.

Rule 9.250.   Filing and Service of Documents after Commission's Decision

(A) Within 21 days after issuing its decision and recommendation, the commission must file in the Supreme Court:

(1) the original record arranged in chronological order and indexed and certified;

(2) one copy of the order; and

(3) a proof of service on the respondent.

(B) The commission must serve the respondent with:

(1) notice of the filing under MCR 9.250(A)(1);

(2) 2 copies of the order;

(3) 2 copies of the index to the original record; and

(4) a copy of a portion of the original record not submitted by or previously furnished to the respondent.

If the commission files electronically, then the applicable court rules governing electronic filing apply.

[Formerly Rule 9.223, adopted effective March 1, 1985. Amended effective January 21, 2003, 467 Mich. Amended January 10, 2006, effective May 1, 2006, 474 Mich. Amended effective March 21, 2018, 501 Mich. Renumbered Rule 9.250, rescinded and readopted April 11, 2019, amended effective September 1, 2019, 502 Mich.]

Comments

Staff Comment to 1985 Adoption

MCR 9.223 is substantially the same as GCR 1963, 932.23.

Staff Comment to 2006 Amendment

The amendment of MCR 9.223 eliminates the requirement that the Judicial Tenure Commission file an appendix with its recommendation for discipline against a judge.

Staff Comment to 2018 Amendment

These amendments update cross-references and make other nonsubstantive revisions to clarify the rules. The amendment of MCR 6.110(B)(1) addresses an inadvertent omission from the last amendment of this rule that was intended to be shown in overstrike. Accordingly, the current rule does not match the published version. Striking the clause "for good cause shown" will provide consistency with other published versions of the rule and with the statute, MCL 766.7, which allows a magistrate to adjourn a preliminary examination with the consent of the parties without the need for good cause to be shown.

Staff Comment to 2019 Readoption and Renumbering

This new version of MCR 9.200 *et seq.* reflects a reorganization suggested by the Judicial Tenure Commission, and includes various technical changes to update and modernize the rules.

Rule 9.251. Review by Supreme Court

(A) Petition by Respondent. Within 28 days after being served, a respondent may file in the Supreme Court one copy of

(1) a petition to reject or modify the commission's recommendation, which must:

    (a) be based on the record,

    (b) specify the grounds relied on,

    (c) be verified, and

    (d) include a brief in support; and

(2) an appendix presenting portions of the record that the respondent believes necessary to fairly judge the issues.

The respondent must serve the commission with one copy of the petition and one copy of the appendix and file proof of that service. If the respondent files electronically, then the applicable rules governing electronic filing apply.

(B) Role of Commission Counsel and Disciplinary Counsel. If a respondent submits a petition under subsection (A), commission counsel shall appear on behalf of the commission, submit the brief of the commission under subrule (C), and shall advocate only for the position recommended by the commission. Filing of documents with the commission shall be deemed service on commission counsel. Disciplinary counsel's involvement in the case is ended, unless the matter is remanded for further proceedings before the commission or master.

(C) Brief of Commission. Within 21 days after respondent's petition is served, the commission must file

(1) one copy of a reply brief, and

(2) proof that the respondent was served with one copy of the brief.

The commission may file one copy of an appendix containing portions of the record not included in the respondent's appendix that the commission believes necessary to fairly judge the issues. If the disciplinary counsel files electronically, then the applicable rules governing electronic filing apply.

(D) Review in Absence of Petition by Respondent. If the respondent does not file a petition, the Supreme Court will review the commission's recommendation on the record file.

The Supreme Court may order that briefs be filed or arguments be presented.

(E) Form of Briefs. A brief filed under this subrule is to be similar to a brief filed in an appeal to the Supreme Court.

(F) Additional Evidence. The Supreme Court may, if cause is shown, order that further evidence be taken and added to the original record.

(G) Submission. The clerk will place the case on a session calendar under MCR 7.313. Oral argument may be requested.

[Formerly Rule 9.224, adopted effective March 1, 1985. Amended effective January 21, 2003, 467 Mich. Amended January 10, 2006, effective May 1, 2006, 474 Mich. Amended effective March 9, 2016, 499 Mich; March 21, 2018, 501 Mich. Renumbered Rule 9.251, rescinded and readopted April 11, 2019, amended effective September 1, 2019, 502 Mich.]

Comments

Staff Comment to 1985 Adoption

MCR 9.224 is substantially the same as GCR 1963, 932.24.

Staff Comment to 2006 Amendment

The amendment of MCR 9.224(A) requires the respondent judge to file an appendix if the respondent files a petition to reject or modify the commission's decision. The amendment of 9.224(B) allows the Judicial Tenure Commission to file a supplemental appendix with its brief in response to a respondent judge's petition.

Staff Comment to 2016 Amendment

These amendments update cross-references that changed after the rule was adopted and make other nonsubstantive revisions.

Staff Comment to 2018 Amendment

These amendments update cross-references and make other nonsubstantive revisions to clarify the rules. The amendment of MCR 6.110(B)(1) addresses an inadvertent omission from the last amendment of this rule that was intended to be shown in overstrike. Accordingly, the current rule does not match the published version. Striking the clause "for good cause shown" will provide consistency with other published versions of the rule and with the statute, MCL 766.7, which allows a magistrate to adjourn a preliminary examination with the consent of the parties without the need for good cause to be shown.

Staff Comment to 2019 Readoption and Renumbering

This new version of MCR 9.200 *et seq.* reflects a reorganization suggested by the Judicial Tenure Commission, and includes various technical changes to update and modernize the rules.

Rule 9.252. Decision by Supreme Court

(A) The Supreme Court shall review the record of the proceedings and file a written opinion and judgment, which may accept or reject the recommendations of the commission or modify the recommendations by imposing a greater, lesser, or entirely different sanction. When appropriate, the Court may remand the matter to the commission for further proceedings, findings, or explication.

(B) If the commission issues a decision based on a consent agreement between the respondent and the disciplinary counsel under subrule 9.245(A)(1) and the Court determines to impose a greater, lesser, or entirely different sanction, the respondent shall be afforded the opportunity to withdraw the consent and the matter shall be remanded to the commission for further proceedings.

[Formerly Rule 9.225, adopted effective March 1, 1985. Amended effective January 21, 2003, 467 Mich. Renumbered Rule 9.252, rescinded and readopted April 11, 2019, amended effective September 1, 2019, 502 Mich.]

Comments

Staff Comment to 1985 Adoption

MCR 9.225 is substantially the same as GCR 1963, 932.25.

Staff Comment to 2019 Readoption and Renumbering

This new version of MCR 9.200 *et seq.* reflects a reorganization suggested by the Judicial Tenure Commission, and includes various technical changes to update and modernize the rules.

Rule 9.253.   Motion for Rehearing

Unless the Supreme Court directs otherwise, the respondent may file a motion for rehearing within 14 days after the filing of the decision. If the Supreme Court directs in the decision that a motion for rehearing may not be filed, the decision is final on filing.

[Formerly Rule 9.226, adopted effective March 1, 1985. Amended effective January 21, 2003, 467 Mich. Renumbered Rule 9.253, rescinded and readopted April 11, 2019, effective September 1, 2019, 502 Mich.]

Comments

Staff Comment to 1985 Adoption

MCR 9.226 is substantially the same as GCR 1963, 932.26.

Staff Comment to 2019 Readoption and Renumbering

This new version of MCR 9.200 *et seq.* reflects a reorganization suggested by the Judicial Tenure Commission, and includes various technical changes to update and modernize the rules.

Rule 9.260.   Service

(A) Respondent. When provision is made under these rules for serving a complaint or other document on a respondent, the service must be made in person or by registered or certified mail or through an overnight delivery service to the respondent's judicial office or last known residence. If an attorney has appeared for a respondent, service may be on the attorney in lieu of service on the respondent.

(B) Commission. Service on the commission must be made by personal delivery or by registered or certified mail or through an overnight delivery service to the executive director at the commission's office.

(C) Disciplinary Counsel. Service on the disciplinary counsel must be made by personal delivery or by registered or certified mail or through an overnight delivery service to the disciplinary counsel at that individual's address on record with the state bar.

(D) Alternative Service. The respondent, the respondent's attorney, the executive director, disciplinary counsel, and/or commission counsel may serve one another via e-mail with a paper copy being sent via regular mail to the individual's address on record with the state bar.

[Formerly Rule 9.206, adopted effective March 1, 1985. Amended effective January 21, 2003, 467 Mich. Renumbered Rule 9.260, rescinded and readopted April 11, 2019, amended effective September 1, 2019, 502 Mich.]

Comments

Staff Comment to 1985 Adoption

MCR 9.206 is substantially the same as GCR 1963, 932.6.

Staff Comment to 2019 Readoption and Renumbering

This new version of MCR 9.200 *et seq.* reflects a reorganization suggested by the Judicial Tenure Commission, and includes various technical changes to update and modernize the rules.

Rule 9.261.   Confidentiality; Disclosure

(A) Scope of Rule. Except as provided in this rule, all papers filed with the commission and all proceedings before it are confidential in nature and are absolutely privileged from disclosure by the commission or its staff, including former members and employees, in any other matter, including but not limited to civil, criminal, legislative, or administrative proceed-

ings. All the commission's investigative files and commission-generated documents are likewise confidential and privileged from disclosure. Nothing in this rule prohibits the respondent from making statements regarding the respondent's conduct.

(B) Before Filing a Complaint.

(1) Before a complaint is filed, neither a commissioner nor a member of the commission staff may disclose the existence or contents of an investigation, testimony taken, or papers filed in it, except as needed for investigative purposes.

(2) The commission may at any time make public statements as to matters pending before it on its determination by a majority vote that it is in the public interest to do so, limited to statements

   (a) that there is an investigation pending,

   (b) that the investigation is complete and there is insufficient evidence for the commission to file a complaint, or

   (c) with the consent of the respondent, that the investigation is complete and some specified disciplinary action has been taken.

(C) Discretionary Waiver of Confidentiality or Privilege. The commission may waive the confidentiality or privilege protections if:

(1) the respondent waives, in writing, the right to confidentiality or privilege;

(2) the grievant waives, in writing, the right to confidentiality or privilege;

(3) the witness whose statement, testimony, or other evidentiary item will be disclosed waives, in writing, the right to confidentiality or privilege; and

(4) a majority of the commission determines that the public interest will be served by doing so.

(D) After Filing of Complaint

(1) When the commission issues a complaint, the following shall not be confidential or privileged:

   (a) the complaint and all subsequent pleadings filed with the commission or master, all stipulations entered, all findings of fact made by the master or commission, and all reports of the master or commission; however, all papers filed with and proceedings before the commission during the period preceding the issuance of a complaint remain confidential and privileged except where offered into evidence in a formal hearing; and

   (b) the formal hearing before the master or commission, and the public hearing provided for in MCR 9.241.

(2) This subrule neither limits nor expands a respondent's right to discovery under MCR 9.232.

(3) The confidentiality or privilege of any otherwise nonpublic disciplinary action is waived in any proceeding on a concurrent or subsequent complaint.

(E) Disclosure to Grievant. Upon completion of an investigation or proceeding on a complaint, the commission shall disclose to the grievant that the commission

(1) has found no basis for action against the respondent or determined not to proceed further in the matter,

(2) has taken an appropriate corrective action, the nature of which shall not be disclosed, or

(3) has recommended that the respondent be publicly censured, suspended, removed, or retired from office.

(F) Public Safety Exception. When the commission receives information concerning a threat to the safety of any person or persons, information concerning such person may be provided to the person threatened, to persons or organizations responsible for the safety of the person threatened, and to law enforcement or any appropriate prosecutorial agency.

(G) Disclosure to State Court Administrator.

(1) The commission may refer to the state court administrator requests for investigation and other communications received by the commission concerning the conduct of a judge if, in the opinion of the commission, the communications are properly within the scope of the duties of the administrator. The commission may provide the administrator with files, records, investigations, and reports of the commission relating to the matter. Such a referral does not preclude action by the commission if the judge's conduct is of such a nature as to constitute grounds for action by the commission or cannot be adequately resolved or corrected by action of the administrator.

(2) The commission may disclose to the administrator, upon request, the substance of files and records of the commission concerning a former judge who has been or may be assigned judicial duties by the administrator; a copy of the information disclosed must be furnished to the judge.

(H) Disclosure to Attorney Grievance Commission. Notwithstanding the prohibition against disclosure in this rule, the commission shall disclose information concerning a judge's misconduct in office, mental or physical disability, or some other ground that warrants commission action under Const 1963, art 6, § 30, to the Attorney Grievance Commission upon request. Absent a request, the commission may make such disclosure to the Attorney Grievance Commission. In the event of a dispute concerning the release of information, either the Attorney Grievance Commission or the Judicial Tenure Commission may petition the Supreme Court for an order resolving the dispute.

(I) Disclosure to Chief Judge. Notwithstanding the prohibition against disclosure in this rule, and except for those situations that involve a dismissal with explanation, the commission shall notify the chief judge of a court when the commission has taken action under MCR 9.223(A)(2)–(5) involving a magistrate or referee of that court. Upon the chief judge's request, the referee or magistrate shall provide the chief judge with a copy of the commission's written notice of disposition.

[Formerly Rule 9.221, adopted effective March 1, 1985. Amended effective January 21, 2003, 467 Mich; June 8, 2005, 472 Mich. Amended October 2, 2013, effective January 1, 2014, 495 Mich. Renumbered Rule 9.261, rescinded and readopted April 11, 2019, amended effective September 1, 2019, 502 Mich.]

Comments

Staff Comment to 1985 Adoption

MCR 9.221 is substantially the same as GCR 1963, 932.21.

Staff Comment to 2005 Amendment

New subrule (A) explains that Judicial Tenure Commission proceedings and investigative files are confidential and privileged from disclosure. The subrule addresses the ruling in *Lawrence v Van Aken*, 316 F Supp 2d 547 (WD Mich, 2004), which required the commission to disclose its investigative files because the language of MCR 9.221 did not render the files "privileged" from disclosure.

Subrule (B) clarifies that, before it files a formal complaint, the commission is limited in the type of information it can divulge regarding an investigation. New

subrule (C) allows the commission to waive confidentiality of its records, in certain specified circumstances, and divulge information related to an investigation. New subrule (D) clarifies when the commission can reveal information about an investigation after the commission files a formal complaint.

New subrule (E) specifies the instances in which the commission can disclose information about the investigation to the grievant. New subrule (F) creates a "public safety exception" to the rule prohibiting disclosure. This exception authorizes the commission to disclose threats against a person to the person whose safety is threatened. Subrule (H) allows either the Judicial Tenure Commission or the Attorney Grievance Commission to ask the Supreme Court to resolve a dispute regarding the disclosure of the commission's investigatory records.

Staff Comment to 2014 Amendment

The amendment of MCR 9.221 adds a new subrule (I) that requires the Judicial Tenure Commission to notify a court's chief judge if a referee or magistrate is subject to a corrective action that does not rise to the level of a formal complaint, including a letter of caution, a conditional dismissal, an admonishment, or a recommendation for private censure. The new requirement does not apply to a dismissal with explanation.

Staff Comment to 2019 Readoption and Renumbering

This new version of MCR 9.200 *et seq.* reflects a reorganization suggested by the Judicial Tenure Commission, and includes various technical changes to update and modernize the rules.

Rule 9.262.   Record Retention

The commission shall develop a record-retention policy, which shall include a description of the materials that are to be stored, a list of the time for which specific materials must be maintained, and procedures for the disposal of records.

[Formerly Rule 9.222, adopted effective March 1, 1985. Amended September 22, 1998, effective December 1, 1998, 459 Mich. Amended effective January 21, 2003, 467 Mich. Renumbered Rule 9.262, rescinded and readopted April 11, 2019, effective September 1, 2019, 502 Mich.]

Comments

Staff Comment to 1985 Adoption

MCR 9.222 is substantially the same as GCR 1963, 932.22.

Staff Comment to 1998 Amendment

The December 1, 1998 amendment of MCR 9.126 and 9.222 made mandatory the disclosure of information, upon request, between the Attorney Grievance Commission and the Judicial Tenure Commission. The amendment of State Bar Rule 15, § 1 authorized the State Bar's Committee on Character and Fitness to disclose to the Attorney Grievance Commission information concerning the bar application of a disciplined lawyer who is requesting reinstatement to the practice of law. Under the amendment, the lawyer must be notified of the request, and the hearing panel must determine the relevancy of the information before permitting it to be used in a public document or proceeding.

Staff Comment to 2019 Readoption and Renumbering

This new version of MCR 9.200 *et seq.* reflects a reorganization suggested by the Judicial Tenure Commission, and includes various technical changes to update and modernize the rules.

Rule 9.263.   Immunity

A person is absolutely immune from civil suit for statements and communications transmitted solely to the commission, its employees, or its agents, or given in an investigation or proceeding on allegations regarding a respondent, and no civil action predicated upon the statements or communications may be instituted against a grievant, a witness, or his or her counsel. Members of the commission and their employees and agents, masters, disciplinary counsel, and commission counsel are absolutely immune from civil suit for all conduct in the course of their official duties.

[Formerly Rule 9.227, adopted July 10, 1995, effective September 1, 1995, 449 Mich. Amended effective January 21, 2003, 467 Mich. Amended March 27, 2007, effective May 1, 2007, 477 Mich. Renumbered Rule 9.263, rescinded and readopted April 11, 2019, amended effective September 1, 2019, 502 Mich.]

Comments

Staff Comment to 1995 Adoption

MCR 9.227 is based on the proposed revision of the Michigan Code of Judicial Conduct submitted by the State Bar Representative Assembly. See 442 Mich 1216 (1993). It is effective September 1, 1995.

Staff Comment to 2007 Amendment

This proposal extends immunity from civil suit for statements or communications made to agents of the Judicial Tenure Commission, and adds agents to the individuals who are immune from civil suit for conduct in the course of their official duties with the commission.

Staff Comment to 2019 Readoption and Renumbering

This new version of MCR 9.200 *et seq.* reflects a reorganization suggested by the Judicial Tenure Commission, and includes various technical changes to update and modernize the rules.

Rule 9.264. Ethics Materials and Programs

The commission shall work with other groups and organizations, including the State Bar of Michigan, to develop educational materials and programs that are designed to assist judges in maintaining an awareness and understanding of their ethical obligations.

[Formerly Rule 9.228, adopted effective January 21, 2003, 467 Mich. Renumbered Rule 9.264, rescinded and readopted April 11, 2019, effective September 1, 2019, 502 Mich.]

Comments

Staff Comment to 2019 Readoption and Renumbering

This new version of MCR 9.200 *et seq.* reflects a reorganization suggested by the Judicial Tenure Commission, and includes various technical changes to update and modernize the rules.

INDEX TO
MICHIGAN COURT RULES OF 1985

APPEARANCES—Cont'd

Bond, in lieu of arrest, contempt outside immediate presence of court, **Rule 3.606**

Civil infractions, **Rule 4.101**

Corporations, winding up, expiration of term or charter, **Rule 3.612**

Domestic relations actions,
  Collaborative law process, **Rule 3.222**
  Consent judgments and decrees, **Rule 3.223**

Failure to appear, default judgment, **Rule 2.603**

Judicial tenure commission, investigations and investigators, **Rule 9.222**
  Masters, objections, **Rule 9.241**

Juvenile Delinquents and Dependents, this index

Lack of progress, notice, dismissal and nonsuit, **Rule 2.502**

Land contract forfeiture, **Rule 4.202**

Landlord and tenant, summary proceedings, recovering possession of premises, **Rule 4.201**

Law students or recent graduates, **Rule 8.120**

Motions, contested motions, **Rule 2.119**

Orders of court, contests, **Rule 2.506**

Parties, this index

Peace officers, infractions, **Rule 4.101**

Probate proceedings, attorneys, **Rule 5.117**

Restitution, amendments, **Rule 6.430**

Subpoenas, contests, **Rule 2.506**

Traffic rules and regulations, misdemeanors, **Rule 6.615**

APPENDIX

Appeal and Review, this index

APPLICATION OF RULES

See specific index headings

APPLICATIONS

See specific index headings

APPOINTMENTS

See specific index headings

APPRAISAL AND APPRAISERS

Attachment, seized property, **Rule 3.103**

ARBITRATION AND AWARD

See, also,
  Alternative Dispute Resolution, generally, this index
  Mediation, generally, this index

Generally, **Rule 3.602**

Agreement to arbitrate, summary judgment, bar of claim, **Rule 2.116**

Attorneys, clients, complaints, **Rule 9.130**

Case evaluation, **Rules 2.403, 2.404**

ARGUMENT AND CONDUCT OF COUNSEL

Generally, **Rule 2.507**

Closing arguments, trial, **Rule 2.507**

Final arguments, trial, **Rule 2.507**
  Reporting, **Rule 8.108**

Judicial tenure commission, investigations and investigators, masters, **Rules 9.231, 9.241**

Opening statements. Trial, this index

Oral argument,
  Appeal and Review, this index
  Motions, contested motions, **Rule 2.119**

ARGUMENT AND CONDUCT OF COUNSEL—Cont'd

Probate proceedings, **Rule 5.117**

ARRAIGNMENT

Generally, **Rules 6.101, 6.104, 6.610**

Advisements, right to counsel, **Rule 6.101**

Availability plan, judicial personnel, **Rule 6.104**

Circuit courts, crimes and offenses, district courts, **Rule 6.111**

Indictment or information, **Rule 6.113**

Juvenile proceedings, life offenses, **Rule 6.907**

Preliminary examination, scheduling, **Rule 6.110**

Pretrial release, **Rule 6.106**

Probation, revocation, **Rule 6.445**

Traffic offenses, misdemeanors, **Rule 6.615**

ARREST

Bail, generally, this index

Bench warrants, contempt outside immediate presence of court, **Rule 3.606**

Contempt, outside immediate presence of court, **Rule 3.606**

Domestic relations, failure to comply, **Rule 3.208**

Personal protection orders, violations, contempt, **Rule 3.708**

Warrants, **Rule 6.102**
  Civil infractions, **Rule 4.101**
  Contempt, outside immediate presence of court, **Rule 3.606**
  Probation violation, **Rule 6.445**
  Traffic rules and regulations, misdemeanors, **Rule 6.615**

ASSIGNMENT OF CASES

Generally, **Rule 8.111**

Case evaluation, panels, **Rule 2.404**

ASSIGNMENTS

Bonds (officers and fiduciaries), **Rule 3.604**
  Contempt outside immediate presence of court, **Rule 3.606**

Probate Proceedings, this index

Summary judgment, bar of claim, **Rule 2.116**

ASSOCIATIONS AND SOCIETIES

Depositions,
  Oral examinations, **Rule 2.306**
  Subpoenas, **Rule 2.305**
  Written questions, **Rule 2.307**

Parties, names, **Rule 2.201**

Pleading, legal existence, **Rule 2.112**

Quo warranto, **Rule 3.306**

Secondary action by shareholders, **Rule 3.502**

Service of process, **Rule 2.105**

ASSUMED NAMES

Capacity to sue or be sued, **Rule 2.201**

ASSUMPTION OF RISK

Pleadings, affirmative defenses, **Rule 2.111**

ATTACHMENT

Generally, **Rule 3.103**

Service of process, **Rule 2.103**

ATTENDANCE OF WITNESSES

Subpoenas, generally, this index

CONTINUING EDUCATION
Protective proceedings for children and minors, mediators, **Rule 3.970**

CONTINUING LEGAL EDUCATION
Judges, **Rule 8.110**

CONTRACTS
Attorneys, contractual probation, **Rule 9.114**
Case classification codes, **Rule 8.117**
Corporations, accounting, voluntary dissolution, **Rule 3.611**
Domestic relations actions,
   Alternative electronic service, **Rule 3.203**
   Collaborative law process, **Rule 3.222**
Garnishment,
   Postjudgment garnishment, **Rule 3.101**
   Prejudgment garnishment, **Rule 3.102**
Land Contracts, generally, this index
Plea agreements, criminal proceedings, **Rules 6.302, 6.610**
Service of process, alternative electronic service, **Rule 2.107**

CONTRIBUTION
Shares and shareholders, liability proceedings, **Rule 3.110**

CONTRIBUTORY NEGLIGENCE
Pleadings, affirmative defenses, **Rule 2.111**

CONTROLLED SUBSTANCES
Forfeitures, case classification codes, **Rule 8.117**

CONVERSION
Documents, electronic filing and service, **Rule 1.109**

CONVEYANCES
Deeds and Conveyances, generally, this index

CONVICTION OF CRIME
Attorneys, discipline, **Rule 9.120**

COPIES
See specific index headings

CORPORATIONS
Complaints,
   Shareholders liability proceedings, **Rule 3.110**
   Voluntary dissolution, **Rule 3.611**
   Winding up, expiration of term or charter, **Rule 3.612**
Debtors and creditors,
   Accounting, voluntary dissolution, **Rule 3.611**
   Shares and shareholders, liability proceedings, **Rule 3.110**
Depositions,
   Failure to provide or permit discovery, **Rule 2.313**
   Oral examinations, **Rule 2.306**
   Subpoenas, **Rule 2.305**
   Written questions, **Rule 2.307**
Dissolution, voluntary dissolution, **Rule 3.611**
Indebtedness, shareholders liability proceedings, **Rule 3.110**
Parties, suing in corporate name, **Rule 2.201**
Partnerships, generally, this index
Personal liability, stockholders, **Rule 3.110**
Quo warranto, **Rule 3.306**

CORPORATIONS—Cont'd
Receivers and receivership, actions and proceedings, case classification codes, **Rule 8.117**
Secondary action by shareholders, **Rule 3.502**
Service of process, **Rule 2.105**
Shares and Shareholders, generally, this index
Small claims actions, affidavits, signatures, **Rule 4.302**
Subpoenas, depositions, **Rule 2.305**
Voluntary dissolution, **Rule 3.611**
Winding up, expiration of term or charter, **Rule 3.612**

CORRECTIONAL INSTITUTIONS
Case classification codes, **Rule 8.117**
Children and minors, actions and proceedings, **Rule 2.004**
Depositions on oral examination, prisoners, **Rule 2.306**
Domestic relations actions, telecommunications, **Rule 2.004**
Habeas corpus,
   Bringing prisoner to testify or for prosecution, **Rule 3.304**
   Inquiring into cause of detention, **Rule 3.303**
Orders of court, children and minors, telecommunications, **Rule 2.004**
Pro se litigants,
   New trial, motions, **Rule 6.431**
   Pleas, withdrawal, vacation, **Rule 6.310**
   Sentence and punishment, correction, **Rule 6.429**

COSTS
   Generally, **Rule 2.625**
Adjournments, **Rule 2.503**
Affidavits,
   Bill of costs, **Rule 2.625**
   Waiver, **Rule 2.002**
Alternative dispute resolution, case evaluation, rejection, **Rule 2.403**
Appeal and Review, this index
Application of rules, waiver, **Rule 2.002**
Applications, waiver, **Rule 2.002**
Arbitration and award, **Rule 3.602**
Attachment, **Rule 3.103**
Attorneys, this index
Bail, forfeitures, failure to comply with conditions, **Rule 6.106**
Bill of costs, **Rule 2.625**
Case evaluation, rejection, **Rule 2.403**
Certificates and certification, waiver, **Rule 2.002**
Change of venue, **Rules 2.222, 2.223**
   Joinder of parties, bad faith, **Rule 2.225**
Claim and delivery, **Rule 3.105**
Class actions, notice, **Rule 3.501**
Commencement of actions, previously dismissed actions, **Rule 2.504**
Communications equipment, hearings, pretrial or status conferences, **Rule 2.402**
Compromise and settlement, **Rule 2.625**
Confidential or privileged information, waiver, **Rule 2.002**
Criminal proceedings, bail, use, payment, **Rule 6.106**
De novo review, waiver, orders of court, **Rule 2.002**
Default judgment, setting aside, **Rules 2.603, 2.625**
Denial, waiver, orders of court, **Rule 2.002**

DISCOVERY—Cont'd

Electronic data—Cont'd

Requests, **Rule 2.310**

Entry on property,

Failure to provide or permit discovery, **Rule 2.313**

Inspection and other purposes, **Rule 2.310**

Subpoenas, **Rule 2.305**

Evasive answers, **Rule 2.313**

Exemptions, initial disclosures, **Rule 2.302**

Exhibits, use at trial, **Rule 2.302**

Experts, **Rule 2.302**

Failure to identify, sanctions, **Rule 2.313**

Failure to provide or permit, **Rule 2.313**

Filing, **Rule 2.302**

Effect, **Rule 1.109**

Final pretrial conference, **Rule 2.401**

Forms, initial disclosures, **Rule 2.302**

Garnishment, after judgment, **Rule 3.101**

General rules, **Rule 2.302**

Identity and location of persons having knowledge, supplementation of responses, **Rule 2.302**

Inadmissible evidence, **Rule 2.302**

Incomplete answers, **Rule 2.313**

Initial disclosures, **Rule 2.302**

Availability, **Rule 2.301**

Failure to provide or permit, **Rule 2.313**

Probate proceedings, **Rule 5.131**

Removal, destruction, **Rule 2.316**

Inspection and inspectors,

Entry on land, **Rule 2.310**

Failure to provide or permit discovery, **Rule 2.313**

Subpoenas, **Rule 2.305**

Insurance agreements, **Rule 2.302**

Interrogatories, generally, this index

Joinder, parties, initial disclosures, **Rule 2.302**

Judgment creditors, supplementary proceedings, **Rule 2.621**

Judicial tenure commission, investigations and investigators, masters, **Rule 9.232**

Juvenile Delinquents and Dependents, this index

Mandatory initial disclosures, **Rule 2.302**

Mediation, **Rule 2.411**

Confidential or privileged information, **Rule 2.412**

Medical examinations, **Rule 2.311**

Medical records or information, **Rule 2.314**

Mental examinations, **Rule 2.311**

Motions, order compelling discovery, **Rule 2.313**

No fault cases, initial disclosures, **Rule 2.302**

Nonparties, subpoenas, failure to provide or permit, **Rule 2.313**

Objections, removal or destruction, **Rule 2.316**

Orders of court,

Compelling, **Rule 2.313**

Final pretrial conference, **Rule 2.401**

Mediation, **Rule 2.411**

Plans and specifications, **Rule 2.401**

Procedure, **Rule 2.302**

Removal or destruction, **Rule 2.316**

Scheduling orders, **Rule 2.401**

Personal injuries, initial disclosures, **Rule 2.302**

DISCOVERY—Cont'd

Physical examinations, **Rule 2.311**

Order for completion, **Rule 2.401**

Plans and specifications, **Rule 2.401**

Pretrial conference, **Rule 2.401**

Prior statements, **Rule 2.302**

Privileged records, criminal proceedings, **Rule 6.201**

Probate proceedings, **Rule 5.131**

Production of Documents and Things, generally, this index

Protective Orders, this index

Protective Proceedings for Children and Minors, this index

Psychiatric examinations, **Rule 2.311**

Records and recordation. Electronic data, generally, ante

Removal of materials, **Rule 2.316**

Requests for admissions. Admissions, this index

Sanctions, **Rule 2.302**

Criminal proceedings, **Rule 6.201**

Failure to provide or permit, **Rule 2.313**

Judicial tenure commission, investigations and investigators, **Rule 9.232**

Pretrial conferences, lack of diligence, **Rule 2.401**

Scope, **Rules 2.301, 2.302**

Probate proceedings, **Rule 5.131**

Sequence, **Rules 2.301, 2.302**

Service, **Rule 2.302**

Signatures, **Rule 2.302**

Statements previously made, **Rule 2.302**

Stipulations,

Destruction or removal of discovery material, **Rule 2.316**

District courts, permitting before entry of judgment, **Rule 2.302**

Mediation, **Rule 2.411**

Procedure, **Rule 2.302**

Time, completion, **Rule 2.301**

Striking, failure to sign, **Rule 2.302**

Supplementary proceedings, **Rule 2.621**

Supplementation of responses, **Rule 2.302**

Failure, sanctions, **Rule 2.313**

Termination of parental rights, **Rule 3.977**

Time, **Rule 2.302**

Completion, **Rule 2.301**

Criminal proceedings, **Rule 6.201**

Initial disclosures, **Rule 2.302**

Trial preparation materials, **Rule 2.302**

Video depositions, **Rule 2.315**

DISCRETIONARY REVIEW

Supreme court, **Rule 7.303**

DISCRIMINATION

Jury, selection of jurors, **Rule 2.511**

Labor and employment, case classification codes, **Rule 8.117**

DISEASES

Case classification codes, **Rule 8.117**

Health threats to others, commitment, **Rule 3.614**

DISMISSAL AND NONSUIT

Generally, **Rule 2.504**

Affidavits, conditional dismissal, reinstatement, entry of judgment, **Rule 2.602**

IDENTITY AND IDENTIFICATION—Cont'd
Requests for admissions, captions, **Rule 2.312**

ILLNESS
Attorneys, adjournment of proceedings, **Rule 2.503**
Diseases, generally, this index
Judges, substitute judge, **Rule 2.630**

IMMUNITIES
Privileges and Immunities, generally, this index

IMPROVEMENTS
Quiet title actions, claim for value of improvements made, **Rule 3.411**

INACTIVE STATUS
Attorneys, this index

INCAPACITATED PERSONS
Guardians of Incapacitated Persons, generally, this index
Personal protection orders, petitions, **Rule 3.703**

INCOMPETENT PERSONS
Attorneys, **Rule 9.121**
Capacity to sue, domestic relations actions, **Rule 3.202**
Compromise and settlement, **Rule 2.420**
Criminal defendants, proceedings for admission to treating facility, venue, **Rule 5.127**
Default judgment, entry, **Rule 2.603**
Guardian Ad Litem, generally, this index
Intellectual and Developmental Disabilities, generally, this index
Mental Health, generally, this index
Next Friend, generally, this index
Party to action, **Rule 2.201**
Probate proceedings, service, **Rule 5.105**
Sale of premises and division of proceeds, substitute for partition, **Rule 3.403**
Temporary guardian, guardian ad litem appointment, **Rule 5.403**

INCRIMINATION
Self incrimination, juvenile proceedings, preliminary hearings, rights, **Rule 3.935**

INCUMBRANCES
Liens and Incumbrances, generally, this index

INDEPENDENT EXAMINERS
Mental health, civil admission and discharge proceedings, **Rule 5.733**

INDIANS
Indigenous Peoples, generally, this index

INDICTMENT AND INFORMATION
Generally, **Rule 6.112**
Arraignment, **Rules 6.101, 6.113**
Dismissal and nonsuit, preliminary examination, violations, **Rule 6.110**
Returning indictment by grand jury, **Rule 6.107**

INDIGENOUS PEOPLES
Adoption,
Appeal and review, appeal as of right, **Rule 3.993**
Consent, **Rule 3.804**

INDIGENOUS PEOPLES—Cont'd
Adoption—Cont'd
Jurisdiction, **Rule 3.807**
Service, **Rule 3.802**
Termination of parental rights, **Rule 3.002**
Appeal and review, orders of court, appeal as of right, **Rule 3.993**
Audio or video recordings, videoconferencing, limitations, **Rules 5.140, 5.404**
Certified questions, supreme court, **Rule 7.308**
Children and minors,
Adoption, generally, ante
Appeal and review, appeal as of right, **Rule 3.993**
Attorneys, temporary admission, **Rule 8.126**
Custody proceedings, **Rule 3.002**
Protective proceedings for children and minors, generally, post
Consent,
Adoption, **Rule 3.804**
Guardian and ward, **Rule 5.404**
Custody,
Actions and proceedings, **Rule 3.002**
Attorneys, temporary admission, **Rule 8.126**
Foster care, appeal as of right, **Rule 3.993**
Full faith and credit, appeal and review, appeal as of right, **Rule 3.993**
Guardian and ward, **Rule 5.404**
Courts, powers and duties, **Rule 5.402**
Notice, **Rule 5.109**
Videoconferencing, limitations, **Rule 5.140**
Hearings,
Consent, adoption, **Rule 3.804**
Guardian and ward, **Rules 5.402, 5.404**
Videoconferencing, limitations, **Rules 5.140, 5.404**
Intervention, appeal and review, appeal as of right, **Rule 3.993**
Investigations and investigators, guardian and ward, **Rule 5.402**
Judgments, enforcement of tribal judgments, **Rule 2.615**
Juvenile delinquents and dependents, **Rule 3.002**
Appeal and review, **Rule 3.993**
Emergency removal, **Rule 3.974**
Placement, hearings, **Rule 3.974**
Preliminary hearings, notice to tribe, **Rule 3.935**
Service of process, **Rule 3.920**
Notice,
Guardian and ward, **Rules 5.109, 5.402**
Support, adoption, termination of parental rights, **Rules 3.804, 3.971, 3.977**
Orders of court,
Appeal and review, appeal as of right, **Rule 3.993**
Personal protection orders, enforcement, **Rule 3.706**
Pleading, tribal law or judgments, **Rule 2.112**
Protective proceedings for children and minors,
Child custody proceedings, **Rule 3.002**
Hearings, **Rule 3.967**
Member of tribe or band, notice, **Rule 3.965**
Removal of child and taking into temporary custody, **Rule 3.967**
Status offenses, **Rule 3.905**

JUVENILE DELINQUENTS AND DEPENDENTS
—Cont'd
Transfers—Cont'd
Life offenses, **Rule 6.911**
Waiver of jurisdiction, **Rule 3.950**
Trial, **Rule 3.942**
Designated cases, **Rule 3.954**
Jury, **Rule 3.911**
Judge presiding, **Rule 3.912**
Venue, **Rule 3.926**
Verdict, jury verdict, **Rule 3.911**
Victims of crime, presence, **Rules 3.942, 3.943**
Video recordings, statements, child witnesses, **Rule 3.923**
Videoconferencing, **Rules 2.004, 3.904, 3.923, 6.901**
Visitation, child in placement, **Rule 3.965**
Voluntary plea, **Rule 3.941**
Volunteers, court appointed special advocates, **Rule 3.917**
Waiver,
Jurisdiction, prosecution as adult, **Rule 3.950**
Notice, hearings, **Rule 3.920**
Preliminary examination, designated cases, **Rule 3.953**
Preliminary hearings, life offenses, **Rule 6.911**
Probable cause, detention determination, **Rule 3.935**
Right to attorney, life offenses, **Rule 6.905**
Weapons, firearm use during offense, mandatory detention, **Rule 3.943**
Withdrawal, pleas, **Rule 3.941**
Witnesses,
Discovery, **Rule 3.922**
Privileges and immunities, furnishing information on request of court, **Rule 3.924**
Protection of child witness, **Rule 3.923**
Videoconferencing, **Rules 2.004, 3.904, 3.923, 6.901**
Waiver of jurisdiction, prosecution as adult, **Rule 3.950**

LABOR AND EMPLOYMENT
Civil service, **Rules 7.104, 7.117**
Discrimination, case classification codes, **Rule 8.117**
Employment Security, generally, this index
Garnishment, generally, this index
Judicial tenure commission, **Rule 9.210**

LABOR DISPUTES
Case classification codes, **Rule 8.117**

LAND
Real Estate, generally, this index

LAND CONTRACTS
Case classification codes, **Rule 8.117**
Forfeiture, **Rules 3.410, 4.202**
Appeals, conditions of appeal bond, **Rule 7.209**
Garnishment, **Rule 3.101**

LAND SURVEYORS
Entry on land, discovery, **Rule 2.310**

LANDLORD AND TENANT
Case classification codes, **Rule 8.117**
Forcible Entry and Detainer, generally, this index
Summary proceedings, recovering possession of premises, **Rule 4.201**

LANGUAGE
Interpreters, trial, **Rule 2.507**

LAW CLERKS
Judges, disqualification, **Rule 2.003**

LAW ENFORCEMENT OFFICERS
Appearances, infractions, **Rule 4.101**

LAW EXAMINERS BOARD
Supreme court, superintending control power, **Rule 7.306**

LAW STUDENTS
Legal aid clinics, **Rule 8.120**

LAWS
Ordinances, generally, this index
Statutes, generally, this index

LAWYERS
Attorneys, generally, this index

LEASE OF GOODS
Receivers in supplementary proceedings, **Rule 2.622**

LEAVE OF ABSENCE
Judges, educational leave, **Rule 8.110**

LEAVE TO APPEAL
Appeal and Review, this index

LEGAL AID CLINICS
Generally, **Rule 8.120**

LEGAL HOLIDAYS
Holidays, generally, this index

LEGAL SERVICES PROGRAMS
Costs, waiver, eligibility, **Rule 2.002**

LETTERS OF AUTHORITY
Conservators and Conservatorship, this index
Guardian and Ward, this index
Probate proceedings, **Rule 5.202**

LETTERS ROGATORY
Depositions, foreign countries, taking, **Rule 2.304**

LIABILITY
Case evaluation, rejection, costs, **Rule 2.403**

LICENSES AND PERMITS
Affirmative defenses, pleadings, **Rule 2.111**
Attorneys,
Revocation or suspension, misconduct, **Rule 9.106**
Standards of conduct, **Rule 9.103**
Drivers licenses. Motor Vehicles, this index
Weapons, concealed weapons, appeal and review, **Rule 7.121**

LIENS AND INCUMBRANCES
Construction liens, **Rule 3.412**
Corporations,
Statement, voluntary dissolution, **Rule 3.611**
Winding up, expiration of term or charter, **Rule 3.612**
Joinder of lienholders, partition, **Rule 3.401**
Mechanics liens, **Rule 3.412**
Mortgages, generally, this index
Partition, joinder of lienholders, **Rule 3.401**
Quiet title actions, **Rule 3.411**

MENTAL HEALTH—Cont'd

Civil admission and discharge proceedings—Cont'd

  Transfer from alternative treatment, **Rule 5.744a**

  Waiver of rights, **Rule 5.737**

    Right to attorney, **Rule 5.732**

Commitment,

  Diagnostic facility, mental competency hearings, criminal proceedings, **Rule 6.106**

  Incompetent criminal defendants, venue, **Rule 5.127**

  Jury verdict, **Rule 5.740**

Competency to stand trial, **Rule 6.125**

Confidential or privileged information, records and recordation, **Rule 5.731**

Crimes and offenses,

  Guilty pleas, **Rule 6.303**

  Incompetent to stand trial, proceeding for admission to treating facility, venue, **Rule 5.127**

  Mental competency hearings, **Rules 6.106, 6.125**

  Not guilty pleas, **Rule 6.304**

Default judgment, entry, **Rule 2.603**

Depositions on oral examination, **Rule 2.306**

Developmental disability. Intellectual and Developmental Disabilities, generally, this index

Disclosure, records and recordation, **Rule 5.731**

Durable power of attorney, treatment, **Rule 5.784**

Evidence. Civil admission and discharge proceedings, ante

Fees, jury trial, **Rule 5.740**

Forms, civil admission and discharge proceedings, appeal and review, claim of appeal, **Rule 7.204**

Guardian Ad Litem, generally, this index

Guilty pleas, crimes and offenses, **Rule 6.303**

Hearings,

  Civil admission and discharge proceedings, ante

  Videoconferencing, **Rule 5.140**

Indefinite hospitalization orders, termination, transition rule, **Rule 5.748**

Jury, fees, **Rule 5.740**

Mental competency hearing, criminal proceedings, **Rule 6.106**

Not guilty pleas, crimes and offenses, **Rule 6.304**

Notice. Civil admission and discharge proceedings, ante

Party to action, **Rule 2.201**

Petitions,

  Admission to hospital, interested persons, **Rule 5.125**

  Civil admission and discharge proceedings, ante

  Continuing involuntary care, **Rule 5.748**

Pleas, crimes and offenses,

  Guilty pleas, **Rule 6.303**

  Not guilty pleas, **Rule 6.304**

Power of attorney, durable power of attorney, treatment, **Rule 5.784**

Priorities and preferences, appeal and review, calendar cases, **Rule 7.213**

Probate proceedings, service, **Rule 5.105**

Records and recordation,

  Appeal and review, record on appeal, **Rule 7.210**

  Confidential or privileged information, **Rule 5.731**

Reports. Civil admission and discharge proceedings, ante

Sale of premises and division of proceeds, substitute for partition, **Rule 3.403**

Summary judgment, barring of claim, **Rule 2.116**

MENTAL HEALTH—Cont'd

Transcripts, appeal and review, **Rule 7.210**

Treatment and care, durable power of attorney, **Rule 5.784**

Videoconferencing, hearings, **Rule 5.140**

Witnesses, videoconferencing, **Rule 5.140**

MERGER AND CONSOLIDATION

Chief judges and justices, **Rule 8.110**

MICHIGAN, STATE OF

State, generally, this index

MILEAGE

Subpoenas, **Rule 2.506**

MINORS

Children and Minors, generally, this index

MISCONDUCT

Arbitration, vacating award, **Rule 3.602**

Attorneys, this index

MISDEMEANORS

Crimes and Offenses, generally, this index

MISREPRESENTATION

Fraud, generally, this index

MISTAKES

Errors, generally, this index

MISTRIAL

Crimes and offenses, orders of court, requirements, **Rule 6.417**

Jury, discharge, **Rule 2.514**

  Criminal proceedings, **Rule 6.420**

Mental incompetency of defendant, **Rule 6.125**

MODEL CIVIL JURY INSTRUCTIONS

Generally, **Rule 2.512**

MONEY

Appeal and review, contributions, amicus curiae, briefs, disclosure, **Rules 7.212, 7.312**

Bail, **Rule 6.106**

Restitution, orders of court, **Rules 6.425, 6.427, 6.610**

MONOPOLIES AND UNFAIR TRADE

Case classification codes, **Rule 8.117**

MORTGAGES

Foreclosure, **Rule 3.410**

  Appeal, conditions of bond, **Rule 7.209**

  Case classification codes, **Rule 8.117**

Partition, joinder of lienholders, **Rule 3.401**

Sale of premises and division of proceeds, substitute for partition, **Rule 3.403**

MOTIONS

Generally, **Rule 2.119**

Access, proceedings, limitation, **Rule 8.116**

Acquittal, directed verdicts, **Rule 6.419**

Adjournments, **Rule 2.503**

Appeal and Review, this index

Arbitration, **Rule 3.602**

Attachment, **Rule 3.103**

Attorney fees, contested motion, failure to appear or respond, **Rule 2.119**

MOTIONS—Cont'd

Uncontested orders, **Rule 2.119**

Unpublished opinions, briefs, citations, **Rules 2.119, 7.215**

Vexatious litigators, supreme court, powers and duties, **Rule 7.316**

View by jury, **Rule 2.513**

MOTOR VEHICLE INSURANCE

No fault cases, discovery, initial disclosures, **Rule 2.302**

MOTOR VEHICLES

Appeal and review, licenses and permits, **Rule 7.120**

Case classification codes, **Rule 8.117**

Drivers licenses,

Numbers and numbering, filing, limitations, **Rule 1.109**

Traffic offenses, nonresidents,

Civil infractions, **Rule 4.101**

Misdemeanors, **Rule 6.615**

Traffic Rules and Regulations, generally, this index

MULTIPLE LIABILITY

Interpleader, **Rule 3.603**

MULTIPLE PARTIES

Parties, this index

MUNICIPAL CHARTERS

Pleadings, identification, **Rule 2.112**

MUNICIPAL CIVIL INFRACTIONS

Citations, **Rule 4.101**

MUNICIPAL COURTS

Generally, **Rule 4.001 et seq.**

Administrative orders, **Rule 8.112**

Appeal and review, appeals from municipal courts, **Rule 7.102**

Application of rules, **Rule 4.001**

Assignment of cases, **Rule 8.111**

Chief judges, **Rule 8.110**

Local court rules, **Rule 8.112**

MUNICIPALITIES

Appeal bonds, exemption, **Rule 7.209**

Ordinances, generally, this index

Party to action, bond, prerequisite to taking appeal or making order stating proceedings, **Rule 2.614**

Service of process, **Rule 2.105**

NAMES

Assumed names, capacity to sue or be sued, **Rule 2.201**

Captions, **Rule 1.109**

Change of name, **Rule 3.613**

Case classification codes, **Rule 8.117**

Magistrates, **Rule 8.205**

Small claims actions, affidavits, **Rule 4.302**

NATIONAL IDENTIFICATION NUMBERS

Personal identifying information, filing, limitations, **Rule 1.109**

NATIONAL ORIGIN

Discrimination, generally, this index

NATIVE AMERICANS

Indigenous Peoples, generally, this index

NECESSARY PARTIES

Joinder, **Rule 2.205**

NEGLIGENCE

Affirmative defenses, pleadings, **Rule 2.111**

Case classification codes, **Rule 8.117**

Personal Injuries, generally, this index

Pleadings, affirmative defenses, **Rule 2.111**

NEGOTIABLE INSTRUMENTS

Garnishment, **Rule 3.101**

Insufficient funds checks, costs, **Rule 8.106**

Sale of premises and division of proceeds, substitute for partition, **Rule 3.403**

NEW TRIAL

Generally, **Rule 2.611**

Appeal and Review, this index

Child protective proceedings, **Rule 3.992**

Conditional ruling, motion for new trial and judgment notwithstanding verdict, **Rule 2.610**

Criminal proceedings, motions, **Rules 6.431, 6.610**

Directed verdict of acquittal, **Rule 6.419**

Disability of judge, **Rules 2.630, 6.440**

Grounds, **Rule 2.611**

Harmless error, **Rule 2.613**

Judgment notwithstanding verdict, setting aside on appeal, **Rules 7.216, 7.316**

Juvenile proceedings, **Rule 3.992**

Motions, **Rules 2.611, 7.211**

Criminal proceedings, **Rules 6.431, 6.610**

Joining with motion for judgment notwithstanding verdict, **Rule 2.610**

Stay of proceedings to enforce judgment, **Rule 2.614**

Quiet title actions, affecting right to possession, **Rule 3.411**

Remand, generally, this index

Time, criminal proceedings, motions, **Rule 6.431**

Waiver, right to move, following judgment notwithstanding verdict, **Rule 2.610**

NEWLY DISCOVERED EVIDENCE

New trial, grounds, **Rule 2.611**

Relief from judgment or order, **Rule 2.612**

NEWSPAPERS

See, also, Publication, generally, this index

Service of process, publication, **Rule 2.106**

NEXT FRIEND

Generally, **Rule 2.201**

Abortion, waiver of parental consent, **Rule 3.615**

Domestic relations actions, capacity of minor to sue, **Rule 3.202**

Personal protection orders, petitions on behalf of minors or incapacitated persons, **Rule 3.703**

NO CONTEST PLEA

Nolo Contendere Plea, generally, this index

NO FAULT CASES

Discovery, initial disclosures, **Rule 2.302**

NOLO CONTENDERE PLEA

Generally, **Rules 2.111, 6.101, 6.302, 6.610**

RULES OF EVIDENCE

Effective March 1, 1978

Adopting Order

On order of the Court, the notice requirements of GCR 1963, 933 having been complied with, and changes made after considering the comments received, the following new MRE 101–1102 were adopted January 5, 1978, to be effective March 1, 1978.

In adopting these rules, the Court should not be understood as foreclosing consideration of a challenge to the wisdom, validity or meaning of a rule when a question is brought to the Court judicially or by a proposal for a change in a rule. See, e.g., *Meek v Centre County Banking Co,* 268 US 426; 45 S Ct 560; 69 L Ed 1028 (1925), and *Mississippi Publishing Corp v Murphree,* 326 US 438; 66 S Ct 242; 90 L Ed 185 (1946). While these rules are binding on Michigan courts, the Court does not intend to preclude evidentiary objection in the trial court based on a challenge to the wisdom, validity or meaning of a rule and development of a separate record so as to properly present the challenge for review by this Court.

As of 1995, the Michigan Court Rules, Michigan Rules of Professional Conduct, Michigan Code of Judicial Conduct, and other codes produced by the Michigan Supreme Court were all phrased in gender-neutral language. However, the Michigan Rules of Evidence retained the masculine pronouns found in the original Federal Rules of Evidence, from which the Michigan rules were adapted. The Rules of the Board of Law Examiners also retained masculine pronouns. The 1995 amendments rephrased the Michigan Rules of Evidence and the Rules of the Board of Law Examiners in gender-neutral language. No substantive change was made.

[Adopted effective March 1, 1978.]

Rule 101.   Scope

These rules govern proceedings in the courts of this state to the extent and with the exceptions stated in Rule 1101.   A statutory rule of evidence not in conflict with these rules or other rules adopted by the Supreme Court is effective until superseded by rule or decision of the Supreme Court.

[Adopted effective March 1, 1978.]

Comments

Staff Comment to 1978 Adoption

The first sentence of Michigan Rule of Evidence (MRE) 101 is identical with Rule 101 as recommended by the National Conference of Commissioners on Uniform State Laws in its Uniform Rules of Evidence (1974) and is similar to Rule 101 of the Federal Rules of Evidence.   The second sentence of MRE 101 has no equivalent in the Federal Rules of Evidence or the Uniform Rules of Evidence; it is similar to GCR 1963, 16.

Rule 102.   Purpose

These rules are intended to secure fairness in administration, elimination of unjustifiable expense and delay, and promotion of growth and development of the law of evidence to the end that the truth may be ascertained and proceedings justly determined.

[Adopted effective March 1, 1978.]

Comments

Staff Comment to 1978 Adoption

MRE 102 is identical with Rule 102 of the Federal Rules of Evidence, except that the words "are intended" are substituted for the words "shall be construed."

Rule 103.   Rulings on Evidence

(a) **Effect of Erroneous Ruling.**   Error may not be predicated upon a ruling which admits or excludes evidence unless a substantial right of the party is affected, and

(1) *Objection.*   In case the ruling is one admitting evidence, a timely objection or motion to strike appears of record, stating the specific ground of objection, if the specific ground was not apparent from the context; or

(2) *Offer of Proof.*   In case the ruling is one excluding evidence, the substance of the evidence was made known to the court by offer or was apparent from the context within which questions were asked.

Once the court makes a definitive ruling on the record admitting or excluding evidence, either at or before trial, a party need not renew an objection or offer of proof to preserve a claim of error for appeal.

(b) **Record of Offer and Ruling.**   The court may add any other or further statement which shows the character of the evidence, the form in which it was offered, the objection made, and the ruling thereon.   It may direct the making of an offer in question and answer form.

(c) **Hearing of Jury.**   In jury cases, proceedings shall be conducted, to the extent practicable, so as to prevent inadmissible evidence from being suggested to the jury by any means, such as making statements or offers of proof or asking questions in the hearing of the jury.

(d) **Plain Error.**   Nothing in this rule precludes taking notice of plain errors affecting substantial rights although they were not brought to the attention of the court.

[Adopted effective March 1, 1978.   Amended October 23, 2001, effective January 1, 2002, 465 Mich.]

Comments

Staff Comment to 1978 Adoption

MRE 103 is identical with Rule 103 of the Federal Rules of Evidence.

Staff Comment to 2001 Amendment

The October 23, 2001 amendment of MRE 103(a), effective January 1, 2002, is identical to the amendment of FRE 103(a) that took effect on December 1, 2000. The added language says that a party need not make repetitive objections or offers of proof after the court has made a "definitive ruling".

Rule 104.   Preliminary Questions

(a) **Questions of Admissibility Generally.**   Preliminary questions concerning the qualification of a person to be a witness, the existence of a privilege, or the admissibility of evidence shall be determined by the court, subject to the provisions of subdivision (b).   In making its determination it is not bound by the Rules of Evidence except those with respect to privileges.

(b) **Relevancy Conditioned on Fact.**   When the relevancy of evidence depends upon the fulfillment of a condition of fact, the court shall admit it upon, or subject to, the introduction of evidence sufficient to support a finding of the fulfillment of the condition.

(c) **Hearing of Jury.**   Hearings on the admissibility of confessions shall in all cases be conducted out of the hearing of the jury.   Hearings on other preliminary matters shall be so conducted when the interests of justice require, or when an accused is a witness, and so requests.

(d) **Testimony by Accused.**   The accused does not, by testifying upon a preliminary matter, become subject to cross-examination as to other issues in the case.

(e) **Weight and Credibility.**   This rule does not limit the right of a party to introduce before the jury evidence relevant to weight or credibility.

[Adopted effective March 1, 1978.   Amended May 1, 1985, effective June 1, 1995, 448 Mich.]

Comments

Staff Comment to 1978 Adoption

MRE 104 is identical with Rule 104 of the Federal Rules of Evidence.

Rule 105.   Limited Admissibility

When evidence which is admissible as to one party or for one purpose but not admissible as to another party or for another purpose is admitted, the court, upon request, shall restrict the evidence to its proper scope and instruct the jury accordingly.

[Adopted effective March 1, 1978.]

Comments

Staff Comment to 1978 Adoption

MRE 105 is identical with Rule 105 of the Federal Rules of Evidence.

Rule 106.   Remainder of or Related Writings or Recorded Statements

When a writing or recorded statement or part thereof is introduced by a party, an adverse party may require the introduction at that time of any other part or any other writing or recorded statement which ought in fairness to be considered contemporaneously with it.

[Adopted effective March 1, 1978.   Amended May 1, 1995, effective June 1, 1995, 448 Mich.]

Comments

Staff Comment to 1978 Adoption

MRE 106 is identical with Rule 106 of the Federal Rules of Evidence.

Rule 201. Judicial Notice of Adjudicative Facts

(a) **Scope of Rule.** This rule governs only judicial notice of adjudicative facts, and does not preclude judicial notice of legislative facts.

(b) **Kinds of Facts.** A judicially noticed fact must be one not subject to reasonable dispute in that it is either (1) generally known within the territorial jurisdiction of the trial court or (2) capable of accurate and ready determination by resort to sources whose accuracy cannot reasonably be questioned.

(c) **When Discretionary.** A court may take judicial notice, whether requested or not, and may require a party to supply necessary information.

(d) **Opportunity to Be Heard.** A party is entitled upon timely request to an opportunity to be heard as to the propriety of taking judicial notice and the tenor of the matter noticed. In the absence of prior notification, the request may be made after judicial notice has been taken.

(e) **Time of Taking Notice.** Judicial notice may be taken at any stage of the proceeding.

(f) **Instructing Jury.** In a civil action or proceeding, the court shall instruct the jury to accept as conclusive any fact judicially noticed. In a criminal case, the court shall instruct the jury that it may, but is not required to, accept as conclusive any fact judicially noticed.

[Adopted effective March 1, 1978.]

Comments

Staff Comment to 1978 Adoption

MRE 201 is identical with Rule 201 of the Federal Rules of Evidence except that the phrase "and does not preclude judicial notice of legislative facts" is added to MRE 201(a); the phrase "and may require a party to supply necessary information" is added to MRE 201(c); and Rule 201(d) of the Federal Rules of Evidence is omitted and the subsequent subdivisions of the rule relettered accordingly. Federal Rule 201(d), which is omitted, reads as follows: "(d) When mandatory. A court shall take judicial notice if requested by a party and supplied with the necessary information."

Rule 202. Judicial Notice of Law

(a) **When Discretionary.** A court may take judicial notice without request by a party of (1) the common law, constitutions, and public statutes in force in every state, territory, and jurisdiction of the United States; (2) private acts and resolutions of the Congress of the United States and of the Legislature of Michigan, and ordinances and regulations of governmental subdivisions or agencies of Michigan; and (3) the laws of foreign countries.

(b) **When Conditionally Mandatory.** A court shall take judicial notice of each matter specified in paragraph (a) of this rule if a party requests it and (1) furnishes the court sufficient information to enable it properly to comply with the request and (2) has given each adverse party such notice as the court may require to enable the adverse party to prepare to meet the request.

[Adopted effective March 1, 1978.]

Comments

Staff Comment to 1978 Adoption

MRE 202 has no equivalent in the Federal Rules of Evidence. It is derived in part from Rule 9 as recommended by the National Conference of Commissioners on Uniform State Laws in its Uniform Rules of Evidence (1953).

Rule 301. Presumptions in Civil Actions and Proceedings

In all civil actions and proceedings not otherwise provided for by statute or by these rules, a presumption imposes on the party against whom it is directed the burden of going forward with evidence to rebut or meet the presumption, but does not shift to such party the burden of proof in the sense of the risk of nonpersuasion, which remains throughout the trial upon the party on whom it was originally cast.

[Adopted effective March 1, 1978.]

Comments

Staff Comment to 1978 Adoption

MRE 301 is identical with Rule 301 of the Federal Rules of Evidence except that MRE 301 employs the phrase "by statute" in place of the Federal Rules phrase "by Act of Congress."

Rule 302. Presumptions in Criminal Cases

(a) **Scope.** In criminal cases, presumptions against an accused, recognized at common law or created by statute, including statutory provisions that certain facts are prima facie evidence of other facts or of guilt, are governed by this rule.

(b) **Instructing the Jury.** Whenever the existence of a presumed fact against an accused is submitted to the jury, the court shall instruct the jury that it may, but need not, infer the existence of the presumed fact from the basic facts and that the prosecution still bears the burden of proof beyond a reasonable doubt of all the elements of the offense.

[Adopted effective March 1, 1978.]

Comments

Staff Comment to 1978 Adoption

MRE 302(a) is similar to Rule 303(a) as recommended by the National Conference of Commissioners on Uniform State Laws in its Uniform Rules of Evidence (1974). MRE 302(b) is a modified version of Rule 303(c) of the Uniform Rules of Evidence.

Rule 401. Definition of "Relevant Evidence"

"Relevant evidence" means evidence having any tendency to make the existence of any fact that is of consequence to the determination of the action more probable or less probable than it would be without the evidence.

[Adopted effective March 1, 1978.]

Comments

Staff Comment to 1978 Adoption

MRE 401 is identical with Rule 401 of the Federal Rules of Evidence.

Rule 402. Relevant Evidence Generally Admissible; Irrelevant Evidence Inadmissible

All relevant evidence is admissible, except as otherwise provided by the Constitution of the United States, the Constitution of the State of Michigan, these rules, or other rules adopted by the Supreme Court. Evidence which is not relevant is not admissible.

[Adopted effective March 1, 1978.]

Staff Comment to 1978 Adoption

MRE 402 is patterned after Rule 402 of the Federal Rules of Evidence, with modifications necessary to accommodate application to the Michigan courts.

Rule 403. Exclusion of Relevant Evidence on Grounds of Prejudice, Confusion, or Waste of Time

Although relevant, evidence may be excluded if its probative value is substantially outweighed by the danger of unfair prejudice, confusion of the issues, or misleading the jury, or by considerations of undue delay, waste of time, or needless presentation of cumulative evidence.
[Adopted effective March 1, 1978.]

Comments

Staff Comment to 1978 Adoption

MRE 403 is identical with Rule 403 of the Federal Rules of Evidence.

Rule 404. Character Evidence Not Admissible to Prove Conduct; Exceptions; Other Crimes

(a) **Character Evidence Generally.** Evidence of a person's character or a trait of character is not admissible for the purpose of proving action in conformity therewith on a particular occasion, except:

(1) *Character of Accused.* Evidence of a pertinent trait of character offered by an accused, or by the prosecution to rebut the same; or if evidence of a trait of character of the alleged victim of the crime is offered by the accused and admitted under subdivision (a)(2), evidence of a trait of character for aggression of the accused offered by the prosecution;

(2) *Character of Alleged Victim of Homicide.* When self-defense is an issue in a charge of homicide, evidence of a trait of character for aggression of the alleged victim of the crime offered by an accused, or evidence offered by the prosecution to rebut the same, or evidence of a character trait of peacefulness of the alleged victim offered by the prosecution in a charge of homicide to rebut evidence that the alleged victim was the first aggressor;

(3) *Character of Alleged Victim of Sexual Conduct Crime.* In a prosecution for criminal sexual conduct, evidence of the alleged victim's past sexual conduct with the defendant and evidence of specific instances of sexual activity showing the source or origin of semen, pregnancy, or disease;

(4) *Character of Witness.* Evidence of the character of a witness, as provided in Rules 607, 608, and 609.

(b) **Other Crimes, Wrongs, or Acts.**

(1) Evidence of other crimes, wrongs, or acts is not admissible to prove the character of a person in order to show action in conformity therewith. It may, however, be admissible for other purposes, such as proof of motive, opportunity, intent, preparation, scheme, plan, or system in doing an act, knowledge, identity, or absence of mistake or accident when the same is material, whether such other crimes, wrongs, or acts are contemporaneous with, or prior or subsequent to the conduct at issue in the case.

(2) The prosecution in a criminal case shall provide written notice at least 14 days in advance of trial, or orally on the record later if the court excuses pretrial notice on good cause shown, of the general nature of any such evidence it intends to introduce at trial and the rationale, whether or not mentioned in subparagraph (b)(1), for admitting the evidence. If necessary to a determination of the admissibility of the evidence under this rule, the defendant shall be required to state the theory or theories of defense, limited only by the defendant's privilege against self-incrimination.

[Adopted effective March 1, 1978. Amended December 17, 1990, effective March 1, 1991, 437 Mich. Amended effective June 24, 1994, 445 Mich. Amended November 10, 1994, effective January 1, 1995, 447 Mich; May 1, 1995, effective June 1, 1995, 448 Mich; May 21, 2001, effective September 1, 2001, 464 Mich; October 11, 2017, effective January 1, 2018, 501 Mich.]

Comments

Staff Comment to 1978 Adoption

MRE 404(a) is identical with Rule 404(a) of the Federal Rules of Evidence except for the addition of MRE 404(a)(3), and language changes incident thereto, regarding evidence of the character of the victim in a case charging criminal sexual conduct. MRE 404(b) is identical with Rule 404(b) of the Federal Rules of Evidence except that the word "plan" is replaced by the phrase "scheme, plan, or system in doing an act," and there is added the phrase "when the same is material, whether such other crime, wrongs, or acts are contemporaneous with, or prior or subsequent to the crime charged."

Staff Comment to 1991 Amendment

The amendment deleted "the crime charged" and substituted "the conduct at issue in the case" in subrule (b). The rule applies in civil cases even though it is used more often in criminal cases.

Staff Comment to 1994 Amendment

The June 24, 1994 amendment codifies *People* v *VanderVliet*, 444 Mich 52, 89 (1993).

Staff Comment to 1995 Amendment

The January 1, 1995 amendment added the requirement that the prosecution specify its rationale for admitting the evidence.

Staff Comment to 2001 Amendment

The September 1, 2001 amendment of subrule (a)(1) allows the prosecution to introduce evidence of the defendant's aggressive character if the defendant has introduced similar evidence about the alleged victim to support a self-defense theory. This change is similar to an amendment to FRE 404(a)(1) that became effective on December 1, 2000.

The September 1, 2001 amendment of subrule (a)(2) limits the accused's use of evidence of the alleged victim's character to a character trait for aggression in a homicide case in which self-defense is an issue. These limitations mark differences between the Michigan and Federal versions of subrule (a)(2).

The September 1, 2001 amendments of subrules (a)(2) and (3) substituted "alleged victim" for "victim." The change conforms MRE 404(a) to FRE 404(a) as amended effective December 1, 2000.

Staff Comment to 2018 Amendment

The amendments of MRE 404(b) require written notice to be provided at least 14 days before trial, or orally on the record later if the court finds there is good cause. This notice requirement replaces the former language that required only "reasonable notice in advance of trial, or during trial if the court excuses pretrial notice on good cause shown." The amendment is not intended to discourage oral notice provided earlier than 14 days in advance of trial, so long as such notice is then confirmed in writing as provided in the rule.

Rule 405. Methods of Proving Character

(a) **Reputation or Opinion.** In all cases in which evidence of character or a trait of character of a person is admissible, proof may be made by testimony as to reputation or by testimony in the form of an opinion. On cross-examination, inquiry is allowable into reports of relevant specific instances of conduct.

(b) **Specific Instances of Conduct.** In cases in which character or a trait of character of a person is an essential element of a charge, claim, or defense, proof may also be made of specific instances of that person's conduct.

[Adopted effective March 1, 1978. Amended December 17, 1990, effective March 1, 1991, 437 Mich; May 1, 1995, effective June 1, 1995, 448 Mich.]

Comments

Staff Comment to 1978 Adoption

MRE 405 is identical with Rule 405 of the Federal Rules of Evidence except that the phrase "or by testimony in the form of an opinion" is omitted from the first sentence of MRE 405(a), with a corresponding change in the caption; and the second sentence of MRE 405(a) is changed to limit inquiry on cross-examination to "reports of" relevant specific instances of conduct.

Staff Comment to 1991 Amendment

The 1991 amendment conformed MRE 405 to its federal counterpart by adding "or by testimony in the form of an opinion" to the first sentence in subrule (a). See also the 1991 amendment to MRE 608.

Rule 406. Habit; Routine Practice

Evidence of the habit of a person or of the routine practice of an organization, whether corroborated or not and regardless of the presence of eyewitnesses, is relevant to prove that the conduct of the person or organization on a particular occasion was in conformity with the habit or routine practice.

[Adopted effective March 1, 1978.]

Comments

Staff Comment to 1978 Adoption

MRE 406 is identical with Rule 406 of the Federal Rules of Evidence.

Rule 407. Subsequent Remedial Measures

When, after an event, measures are taken which, if taken previously, would have made the event less likely to occur, evidence of the subsequent measures is not admissible to prove negligence or culpable conduct in connection with the event. This rule does not require the exclusion of evidence of subsequent measures when offered for another purpose, such as proving ownership, control, or feasibility of precautionary measures, if controverted, or impeachment.

[Adopted effective March 1, 1978.]

Comments

Staff Comment to 1978 Adoption

MRE 407 is identical with Rule 407 of the Federal Rules of Evidence.

Rule 408. Compromise and Offers to Compromise

Evidence of (1) furnishing or offering or promising to furnish, or (2) accepting or offering or promising to accept, a valuable consideration in compromising or attempting to compromise a claim which was disputed as to either validity or amount, is not admissible to prove liability for or invalidity of the claim or its amount. Evidence of conduct or statements made in compromise negotiations is likewise not admissible. This rule does not require the exclusion of any evidence otherwise discoverable merely because it is presented in the course of compromise negotiations. This rule also does not require exclusion when the evidence is offered for another purpose, such as proving bias or prejudice of a witness, negativing a contention of undue delay, or proving an effort to obstruct a criminal investigation or prosecution.

[Adopted effective March 1, 1978.]

Comments

Staff Comment to 1978 Adoption

MRE 408 is identical with Rule 408 of the Federal Rules of Evidence.

Rule 409. Payment of Medical and Similar Expenses

Evidence of furnishing or offering or promising to pay medical, hospital, or similar expenses occasioned by an injury is not admissible to prove liability for the injury.

[Adopted effective March 1, 1978.]

Comments

Staff Comment to 1978 Adoption

MRE 409 is identical with Rule 409 of the Federal Rules of Evidence.

Rule 410. Inadmissibility of Pleas, Plea Discussions, and Related Statements

Except as otherwise provided in this rule, evidence of the following is not, in any civil or criminal proceeding, admissible against the defendant who made the plea or was a participant in the plea discussions:

(1) A plea of guilty which was later withdrawn;

(2) A plea of nolo contendere, except that, to the extent that evidence of a guilty plea would be admissible, evidence of a plea of nolo contendere to a criminal charge may be admitted in a civil proceeding to support a defense against a claim asserted by the person who entered the plea;

(3) Any statement made in the course of any proceedings under MCR 6.302 or comparable state or federal procedure regarding either of the foregoing pleas; or

(4) Any statement made in the course of plea discussions with an attorney for the prosecuting authority which do not result in a plea of guilty or which result in a plea of guilty later withdrawn.

However, such a statement is admissible (i) in any proceeding wherein another statement made in the course of the same plea or plea discussions has been introduced and the statement ought in fairness be considered contemporaneously with it, or (ii) in a criminal proceeding for perjury or false statement if the statement was made by the defendant under oath, on the record and in the presence of counsel.

[Adopted effective March 1, 1978. Amended July 18, 1991, effective October 1, 1991, 437 Mich.]

Comments

Staff Comment to 1978 Adoption

MRE 410 is identical with Rule 410 of the Federal Rules of Evidence and Rule 11(e)(6) of the Federal Rules of Criminal Procedure except that the concluding phrase "if the statement was made by the defendant under oath, on the record, and in the presence of counsel" is omitted from MRE 410.

Staff Comment to 1991 Amendment

For the most part, the October 1, 1991 amendments conformed MRE 410 to the current version of its federal counterpart. The conforming changes included the placement of the commas around the phrase "in any civil or criminal proceeding." That clarified the rule's original intent as explained in *Lichon v American Universal Ins Co,* 435 Mich 408 (1990). However, the exception in subrule (2), which exception has no federal counterpart, altered one of the holdings in *Lichon* by allowing evidence of a nolo contendere plea in certain circumstances. See also MRE 803(22), which was amended concurrently.

Rule 411.   Liability Insurance

Evidence that a person was or was not insured against liability is not admissible upon the issue whether the person acted negligently or otherwise wrongfully. This rule does not require the exclusion of evidence of insurance against liability when offered for another purpose, such as proof of agency, ownership, or control, if controverted, or bias or prejudice of a witness.

[Adopted effective March 1, 1978. Amended May 1, 1995, effective June 1, 1995, 448 Mich.]

Comments

Staff Comment to 1978 Adoption

MRE 411 is identical with Rule 411 of the Federal Rules of Evidence except that the words "if controverted" in the second sentence are added.

Rule 501.   Privilege; General Rule

Privilege is governed by the common law, except as modified by statute or court rule.

[Adopted effective March 1, 1978.]

Comments

Staff Comment to 1978 Adoption

MRE 501 is derived in part from GCR 1963, 601.

Rule 601.   Witnesses; General Rule of Competency

Unless the court finds after questioning a person that the person does not have sufficient physical or mental capacity or sense of obligation to testify truthfully and understandably, every person is competent to be a witness except as otherwise provided in these rules.

[Adopted effective March 1, 1978. Amended May 1, 1995, effective June 1, 1995, 448 Mich.]

Comments

Staff Comment to 1978 Adoption

MRE 601 is identical with Rule 601 as recommended by the National Conference of Commissioners on Uniform State Laws in its Uniform Rules of Evidence (1974) and with the United States Supreme Court version of Rule 601 of the Federal Rules of Evidence, except for the addition of the introductory clause, "[u]nless the court finds after questioning a person that he does not have sufficient physical or mental capacity or sense of obligation to testify truthfully and understandably."

Rule 602.   Lack of Personal Knowledge

A witness may not testify to a matter unless evidence is introduced sufficient to support a finding that the witness has personal knowledge of the matter. Evidence to prove personal knowledge may, but need not, consist of the witness' own testimony. This rule is subject to the provisions of Rule 703, relating to opinion testimony by expert witnesses.

[Adopted effective March 1, 1978. Amended May 1, 1995, effective June 1, 1995, 448 Mich.]

Comments

Staff Comment to 1978 Adoption

MRE 602 is identical with Rule 602 of the Federal Rules of Evidence.

Rule 603.   Oath or Affirmation

Before testifying, every witness shall be required to declare that the witness will testify truthfully, by oath or affirmation administered in a form calculated to awaken the witness' conscience and impress the witness' mind with the duty to do so.

[Adopted effective March 1, 1978. Amended May 1, 1995, effective June 1, 1995, 448 Mich.]

Comments

Staff Comment to 1978 Adoption

MRE 603 is identical with Rule 603 of the Federal Rules of Evidence.

Rule 604.   Interpreters

An interpreter is subject to the provisions of these rules relating to qualification as an expert and the administration of an oath or affirmation to make a true translation.

[Adopted effective March 1, 1978. Amended May 1, 1995, effective June 1, 1995, 448 Mich.]

Comments

Staff Comment to 1978 Adoption

MRE 604 is identical with Rule 604 of the Federal Rules of Evidence.

Rule 605.   Competency of Judge as Witness

The judge presiding at the trial may not testify in that trial as a witness. No objection need be made in order to preserve the point.

[Adopted effective March 1, 1978.]

Comments

Staff Comment to 1978 Adoption

MRE 605 is identical with Rule 605 of the Federal Rules of Evidence.

Rule 606.   Competency of Juror as Witness

(a) At the trial. A member of the jury may not testify as a witness before that jury in the trial of the case in which the juror is sitting. No objection need be made in order to preserve the point.

(b) Inquiry into validity of verdict or indictment. Upon an inquiry into the validity of a verdict or indictment, a juror may not testify as to any matter or statement occurring during the course of the jury's deliberations or to the effect of anything upon that or any other juror's mind or emotions as influencing the juror to assent to or dissent from the verdict or indictment or concerning the juror's mental processes in connection therewith. But a juror may testify about (1) whether extraneous prejudicial information was improperly brought to the jury's attention, (2) whether any outside influence was improperly brought to bear upon any juror, or (3) whether there was a mistake in entering the verdict onto the verdict form. A juror's affidavit or evidence of any statement by the juror may not be received on a matter about which the juror would be precluded from testifying.

[Adopted effective March 1, 1978. Amended May 1, 1995, effective June 1, 1995, 448 Mich; December 22, 2011, effective January 1, 2012, 490 Mich.]

Comments

Staff Comment to 1978 Adoption

MRE 606 is similar to Rule 606(a) of the Federal Rules of Evidence. MRE 606 differs from Federal Rule 606(a) in providing that as to the error committed by permitting a juror to testify as a witness, "[n]o objection need be made in order to preserve the point."

Staff Comment to 2011 Amendment

The amendment of MRE 606 makes Michigan's rule more consistent with FRE 606, and clarifies the types of information a juror may testify to if an inquiry is made into a verdict or indictment.

Rule 607. Who May Impeach

The credibility of a witness may be attacked by any party, including the party calling the witness.

[Adopted effective March 1, 1978. Amended December 17, 1990, effective March 1, 1991, 437 Mich; May 1, 1995, effective June 1, 1995, 448 Mich.]

Comments

Staff Comment to 1978 Adoption

[Former] MRE 607 differ[ed] from Rule 607 of the Federal Rules of Evidence, which reads: "The credibility of a witness may be attacked by any party, including the party calling him."

Staff Comment to 1991 Amendment

The 1991 amendment conformed MRE 607 to its federal counterpart by eliminating the restrictions on a party impeaching its own witness.

Rule 608. Evidence of Character and Conduct of Witness

(a) Opinion and Reputation Evidence of Character. The credibility of a witness may be attacked or supported by evidence in the form of opinion or reputation, but subject to these limitations: (1) the evidence may refer only to character for truthfulness or untruthfulness, and (2) evidence of truthful character is admissible only after the character of the witness for truthfulness has been attacked by opinion or reputation evidence or otherwise.

(b) Specific Instances of Conduct. Specific instances of the conduct of a witness, for the purpose of attacking or supporting the witness' credibility, other than conviction of crime as provided in Rule 609, may not be proved by extrinsic evidence. They may, however, in the discretion of the court, if probative of truthfulness or untruthfulness, be inquired into on cross-examination of the witness (1) concerning the witness' character for truthfulness or untruthfulness, or (2) concerning the character for truthfulness or untruthfulness of another witness as to which character the witness being cross-examined has testified.

The giving of testimony, whether by an accused or by any other witness, does not operate as a waiver of the accused's or the witness' privilege against self-incrimination when examined with respect to matters which relate only to credibility.

[Adopted effective March 1, 1978. Amended December 17, 1990, effective March 1, 1991, 437 Mich; May 1, 1995, effective June 1, 1995, 448 Mich.]

Comments

Staff Comment to 1978 Adoption

MRE 608 is identical with Rule 608 of the Federal Rules of Evidence except that the first clause of Federal Rule 608(a) provides that the credibility of a witness may be attacked or supported by "evidence *in the form of opinion or* reputation"; and the last clause of Federal Rule 608(a) reads, "attacked by *opinion or* reputation evidence or otherwise." (Emphasis supplied.) In addition, the caption is modified to reflect the elimination of opinion as a means of proving character.

Staff Comment to 1991 Amendment

The 1991 amendment conformed MRE 608(a) to its federal counterpart by adding language that permits opinion testimony. See also the 1991 amendment to MRE 405.

Rule 609. Impeachment by Evidence of Conviction of Crime

(a) General Rule. For the purpose of attacking the credibility of a witness, evidence that the witness has been convicted of a crime shall not be admitted unless the evidence has been elicited from the witness or established by public record during cross-examination, and

(1) the crime contained an element of dishonesty or false statement, or

(2) the crime contained an element of theft, and

(A) the crime was punishable by imprisonment in excess of one year or death under the law under which the witness was convicted, and

(B) the court determines that the evidence has significant probative value on the issue of credibility and, if the witness is the defendant in a criminal trial, the court further determines that the probative value of the evidence outweighs its prejudicial effect.

(b) Determining Probative Value and Prejudicial Effect. For purposes of the probative value determination required by subrule (a)(2)(B), the court shall consider only the age of the conviction and the degree to which a conviction of the crime is indicative of veracity. If a determination of prejudicial effect is required, the court shall consider only the conviction's similarity to the charged offense and the possible effects on the decisional process if admitting the evidence causes the defendant to elect not to testify. The court must articulate, on the record, the analysis of each factor.

(c) Time Limit. Evidence of a conviction under this rule is not admissible if a period of more than ten years has elapsed since the date of the conviction or of the release of the witness from the confinement imposed for that conviction, whichever is the later date.

(d) Effect of Pardon, Annulment, or Certificate of Rehabilitation. Evidence of a conviction is not admissible under this rule if (1) the conviction has been the subject of a pardon, annulment, certificate of rehabilitation, or other equivalent procedure based on a finding of the rehabilitation of the person convicted, and that person has not been convicted of a subsequent crime which was punishable by death or imprisonment in excess of one year, or (2) the conviction has been the subject of a pardon, annulment, or other equivalent procedure based on a finding of innocence.

(e) Juvenile Adjudications. Evidence of juvenile adjudications is generally not admissible under this rule, except in subsequent cases against the same child in the juvenile division of a probate court. The court may, however, in a criminal case or a juvenile proceeding against the child allow evidence of a juvenile adjudication of a witness other than the accused if conviction of the offense would be admissible to attack the credibility of an adult and the court is satisfied that admission is necessary for a fair determination of the case or proceeding.

(f) Pendency of Appeal. The pendency of an appeal therefrom does not render evidence of a conviction inadmissible. Evidence of the pendency of an appeal is admissible.

[Adopted effective March 1, 1978. Amended effective May 14, 1980, 408 Mich; March 1, 1988, 429 Mich.]

Comments

Staff Comment to 1978 Adoption

MRE 609(a) is a modified version of Rule 609(a) of the Federal Rules of Evidence, differing from the Federal Rule by inserting the word "theft" before the phrase "dishonesty or false statement," and by requiring a determination by the court that "the probative value of admitting this evidence on the issue of credibility outweighs its prejudicial effect" as a condition of admissibility as to *all* convictions used for impeachment. MRE 609(b) is identical with Rule 609(b) of the Federal Rules of Evidence except for omission from the first sentence of the phrase "unless the court determines, in the interests of justice, that the probative value of the conviction supported by specific facts and circumstances substantially outweighs its prejudicial effect" and the omission of the entire second sentence. Subdivisions (c), (d) and (e) are identical with the equivalent provisions of Rule 609 of the Federal Rules of Evidence. A "pardon" within the meaning of MRE 609(c) would not include, for example, a pardon granted solely to avoid deportation.

Staff Comment to 1988 Amendment

MRE 609(a) and (b) were amended by *People* v *Allen*, 429 Mich 558 (1988), effective March 1, 1988. The *Allen* amendments use a bright-line test to automatically determine the admissibility of most prior convictions. Theft convictions, which are neither automatically admitted nor automatically excluded by the bright-lines, are tested by additional criteria.

Subdivision (c) is similar to, and subdivisions (d), (e) and (f) are virtually identical with the equivalent provisions of Rule 609 of the Federal Rules of Evidence. A "pardon" within the meaning of MRE 609(d) would not include, for example, a pardon granted solely to avoid deportation.

Rule 610. Religious Beliefs or Opinions

Evidence of the beliefs or opinions of a witness on matters of religion is not admissible for the purpose of showing that by reason of their nature the witness' credibility is impaired or enhanced.

[Adopted effective March 1, 1978. Amended May 1, 1995, effective June 1, 1995, 448 Mich.]

Comments

Staff Comment to 1978 Adoption

MRE 610 is identical with Rule 610 of the Federal Rules of Evidence.

Rule 611. Mode and Order of Interrogation and Presentation

(a) Control by Court. The court shall exercise reasonable control over the mode and order of interrogating witnesses and presenting evidence so as to (1) make the interrogation and presentation effective for the ascertainment of the truth, (2) avoid needless consumption of time, and (3) protect witnesses from harassment or undue embarrassment.

(b) Appearance of Parties and Witnesses. The court shall exercise reasonable control over the appearance of parties and witnesses so as to (1) ensure that the demeanor of such persons may be observed and assessed by the fact-finder and (2) ensure the accurate identification of such persons.

(c) Scope of Cross-Examination. A witness may be cross-examined on any matter relevant to any issue in the case, including credibility. The judge may limit cross-examination with respect to matters not testified to on direct examination.

(d) Leading Questions.

(1) Leading questions should not be used on the direct examination of a witness except as may be necessary to develop the witness' testimony.

(2) Ordinarily leading questions should be permitted on cross-examination.

(3) When a party calls a hostile witness, an adverse party or a witness identified with an adverse party, interrogation may be by leading questions. It is not necessary to declare the intent to ask leading questions before the questioning begins or before the questioning moves beyond preliminary inquiries.

[Adopted effective March 1, 1978. Amended July 18, 1991, effective October 1, 1991, 437 Mich; August 25, 2009, effective September 1, 2009, 484 Mich.]

Comments

Staff Comment to 1978 Adoption

MRE 611(a) and (c) are identical with Rule 611(a) and (c) of the Federal Rules of Evidence. MRE 611(b) is inconsistent with Federal Rule 611(b), which provides: "Cross-examination should be limited to the subject matter of the direct examination and matters affecting the credibility of the witness. The court may, in the exercise of discretion, permit inquiry into additional matters as if on direct examination."

After a witness has been examined under the procedure of the last sentence of MRE 611(c), the opposing party should be permitted to ask leading questions only as to those matters covered on the direct examination of the witness; leading questions should not be permitted as to new matters.

Staff Comment to 1991 Amendment

The October 1, 1991 amendment added subrule (c)(3). That subrule permits attorneys who call adverse witnesses to begin asking leading questions at any point even if they have not declared in advance their intent to do so. Cf. *Mally v Excelsior Wrapper Co*, 181 Mich 568 (1914), and *Ferguson v Gonyaw*, 64 Mich App 685, 688–692 (1975), *lv den* 396 Mich 817 (1976). However, this right still is subject to the trial judge's authority to "exercise reasonable control over the mode and order of interrogating . . . ." Subrule (a).

Staff Comment to 2009 Amendment

This amendment explicitly states that a judge shall establish reasonable standards regarding the appearance of parties and witnesses to evaluate the demeanor of those individuals and to ensure accurate identification.

Rule 612. Writing or Object Used to Refresh Memory

(a) While Testifying. If, while testifying, a witness uses a writing or object to refresh memory, an adverse party is entitled to have the writing or object produced at the trial, hearing, or deposition in which the witness is testifying.

(b) Before Testifying. If, before testifying, a witness uses a writing or object to refresh memory for the purpose of testifying and the court in its discretion determines that the interests of justice so require, an adverse party is entitled to have the writing or object produced, if practicable, at the trial, hearing, or deposition in which the witness is testifying.

(c) Terms and Conditions of Production and Use. A party entitled to have a writing or object produced under this rule is entitled to inspect it, to cross-examine the witness thereon, and to introduce in evidence, for their bearing on credibility only unless otherwise admissible under these rules for another purpose, those portions which relate to the testimony of the witness. If production of the writing or object at the trial, hearing, or deposition is impracticable, the court may order it made available for inspection. If it is claimed that the writing or object contains matters not related to the subject matter of the testimony the court shall examine the writing or object in camera, excise any portions not so related, and order delivery of the remainder to the party entitled thereto. Any portion withheld over objections shall be preserved and made available to the appellate court in the event of an appeal. If a writing or object is not produced, made available for inspection, or delivered pursuant to order under this rule, the court shall make any order justice requires, except that in criminal cases when the prosecution elects not to comply, the order shall be one striking the testimony or, if the court in its discretion determines that the interests of justice so require, declaring a mistrial.

[Adopted effective March 1, 1978. Amended December 17, 1990, effective March 1, 1991, 437 Mich; May 1, 1995, effective June 1, 1995, 448 Mich.]

Comments

Staff Comment to 1978 Adoption

MRE 612 is identical with Rule 612 as recommended by the National Conference of Commissioners on Uniform State Laws in its Uniform Rules of Evidence (1974). MRE 612 is similar in some respects to Rule 612 of the Federal Rules of Evidence.

Staff Comment to 1991 Amendment

The 1991 amendment added "for their bearing on credibility only unless otherwise admissible under these rules for another purpose" in subrule (c).

Rule 613. Prior Statements of Witnesses

(a) Examining Witness Concerning Prior Statement. In examining a witness concerning a prior statement made by the witness, whether written or not, the statement need not be shown nor its contents disclosed to the witness at that time, but on request it shall be shown or disclosed to opposing counsel and the witness.

(b) Extrinsic Evidence of Prior Inconsistent Statement of Witness. Extrinsic evidence of a prior inconsistent statement by a witness is not admissible unless the witness is afforded an opportunity to explain or deny the same and the opposite party is afforded an opportunity to interrogate the witness thereon, or the interests of justice otherwise require. This provision does not apply to admissions of a party-opponent as defined in Rule 801(d)(2).

[Adopted effective March 1, 1978. Amended December 17, 1990, effective March 1, 1991, 437 Mich; May 1, 1995, effective June 1, 1995, 448 Mich.]

Comments

Staff Comment to 1978 Adoption

MRE 613(a) is inconsistent with Rule 613(a) of the Federal Rules of Evidence, which provides: "In examining a witness concerning a prior statement made by him, whether written or not, the statement need not be shown nor its contents disclosed to him at that time, but on request the same shall be shown or disclosed to opposing counsel." MRE 613(b) is identical with Federal Rule 613(b).

Staff Comment to 1991 Amendment

The 1991 amendment modified the provision in subrule (a), which required that a witness always be shown a copy of the witness former statement before being questioned about the statement. The amendment requires only that the statement be disclosed "on request." The rule remains more restrictive than its federal counterpart.

Rule 614. Calling and Interrogation of Witnesses by Court

(a) Calling by Court. The court may, on its own motion or at the suggestion of a party, call witnesses, and all parties are entitled to cross-examine witnesses thus called.

(b) Interrogation by Court. The court may interrogate witnesses, whether called by itself or by a party.

(c) Objections. Objections to the calling of witnesses by the court or to interrogation by it may be made at the time or at the next available opportunity when the jury is not present.

[Adopted effective March 1, 1978.]

Comments

Staff Comment to 1978 Adoption

MRE 614 is identical with Rule 614 of the Federal Rules of Evidence.

Rule 615. Exclusion of Witnesses

At the request of a party the court may order witnesses excluded so that they cannot hear the testimony of other witnesses, and it may make the order of its own motion. This rule does not authorize exclusion of (1) a party who is a natural person, or (2) an officer or employee of a party which is not a natural person designated as its representative by its attorney,

or (3) a person whose presence is shown by a party to be essential to the presentation of the party's cause.

[Adopted effective March 1, 1978. Amended May 1, 1995, effective June 1, 1995, 448 Mich.]

Comments

Staff Comment to 1978 Adoption

MRE 615 is identical with Rule 615 of the Federal Rules of Evidence, except that the word "may" is substituted for the word "shall" in the first clause of the first sentence.

Rule 701. Opinion Testimony by Lay Witnesses

If the witness is not testifying as an expert, the witness' testimony in the form of opinions or inferences is limited to those opinions or inferences which are (a) rationally based on the perception of the witness and (b) helpful to a clear understanding of the witness' testimony or the determination of a fact in issue.

[Adopted effective March 1, 1978. Amended May 1, 1995, effective June 1, 1995, 448 Mich.]

Comments

Staff Comment to 1978 Adoption

MRE 701 is identical with Rule 701 of the Federal Rules of Evidence.

Rule 702. Testimony by Experts

If the court determines that scientific, technical, or other specialized knowledge will assist the trier of fact to understand the evidence or to determine a fact in issue, a witness qualified as an expert by knowledge, skill, experience, training, or education may testify thereto in the form of an opinion or otherwise if (1) the testimony is based on sufficient facts or data, (2) the testimony is the product of reliable principles and methods, and (3) the witness has applied the principles and methods reliably to the facts of the case.

[Adopted effective March 1, 1978. Amended July 22, 2003, effective January 1, 2004, 469 Mich.]

Comments

Staff Comment to 1978 Adoption

MRE 702 is identical with Rule 702 of the Federal Rules of Evidence except for the addition after the word "If" of the phrase "the court determines that recognized."

Staff Comment to 2004 Amendment

The July 22, 2003, amendment of MRE 702, effective January 1, 2004, conforms the Michigan rule to Rule 702 of the Federal Rules of Evidence, as amended effective December 1, 2000, except that the Michigan rule retains the words "the court determines that" after the word "If" at the outset of the rule. The new language requires trial judges to act as gatekeepers who must exclude unreliable expert testimony. See *Daubert v Merrell Dow Pharmaceuticals, Inc*, 509 US 579; 113 S Ct 2786; 125 L Ed 2d 469 (1993), and *Kumho Tire Co, Ltd v Carmichael*, 526 US 137; 119 S Ct 1167; 143 L Ed 2d 238 (1999). The retained words emphasize the centrality of the court's gatekeeping role in excluding unproven expert theories and methodologies from jury consideration.

Rule 703. Bases of Opinion Testimony by Experts

The facts or data in the particular case upon which an expert bases an opinion or inference shall be in evidence. This rule does not restrict the discretion of the court to receive expert opinion testimony subject to the condition that the factual bases of the opinion be admitted in evidence hereafter.

[Adopted effective March 1, 1978. Amended May 1, 1995, effective June 1, 1995, 448 Mich; March 25, 2003, effective September 1, 2003, 468 Mich.]

Staff Comment to 1978 Adoption

MRE 703 is inconsistent with Rule 703 of the Federal Rules of Evidence, which provides: "The facts or data in the particular case upon which an expert bases an opinion or inference may be those perceived by or made known to him at or before the hearing. If of a type reasonably relied upon by experts in the particular field in forming opinions or inferences upon the subject, the facts or data need not be admissible in evidence."

Staff Comment to 2003 Amendment

The March 25, 2003, amendments of MRE 703 and 1101, effective September 1, 2003, were recommended by the Advisory Committee on the Michigan Rules of Evidence appointed by the Supreme Court. (See January 28, 2003, follow-up report from Honorable William J. Giovan, advisory committee chair, at http://www.courts.michigan.gov/supremecourt/Resources/Administrative/index.htm.) The modification of MRE 703 corrects a common misreading of the rule by allowing an expert's opinion only if that opinion is based exclusively on evidence that has been introduced into evidence in some way other than through the expert's hearsay testimony. New MRE 1101(b)(9) allows a trial judge to consider a friend of the court report prepared pursuant to MCL 552.505(1)(d) or (e), which "may include reports and evaluations by outside persons or agencies if requested by the parties or the court." New MRE 1101(b)(10) allows probate judges who are conducting preliminary mental health hearings to consider expert opinions that otherwise would be excluded by MRE 703 because the opinions are based on hearsay information.

Rule 704.   Opinion on Ultimate Issue

Testimony in the form of an opinion or inference otherwise admissible is not objectionable because it embraces an ultimate issue to be decided by the trier of fact.

[Adopted effective March 1, 1978.]

Comments

Staff Comment to 1978 Adoption

MRE 704 is identical with Rule 704 of the Federal Rules of Evidence.

Rule 705.   Disclosure of Facts or Data Underlying Expert Opinion

The expert may testify in terms of opinion or inference and give reasons therefor without prior disclosure of the underlying facts or data, unless the court requires otherwise. The expert may in any event be required to disclose the underlying facts or data on cross-examination.

[Adopted effective March 1, 1978. Amended May 1, 1995, effective June 1, 1995, 448 Mich.]

Comments

Staff Comment to 1978 Adoption

MRE 705 is identical with Rule 705 of the Federal Rules of Evidence.

Rule 706.   Court–Appointed Experts

(a) Appointment. The court may on its own motion or on the motion of any party enter an order to show cause why expert witnesses should not be appointed, and may request the parties to submit nominations. The court may appoint any expert witnesses agreed upon by the parties, and may appoint expert witnesses of its own selection. An expert witness shall not be appointed by the court unless the witness consents to act. A witness so appointed shall be informed of the witness' duties by the court in writing, a copy of which shall be filed with the clerk, or at a conference in which the parties shall have opportunity to participate. A witness so appointed shall advise the parties of the witness' findings, if any; the witness' deposition may be taken by any party; and the witness may be called to testify by the court or any party. The witness shall be subject to cross-examination by each party, including a party calling the witness.

(b) Compensation. Expert witnesses so appointed are entitled to reasonable compensation in whatever sum the court may allow. The compensation thus fixed is payable from funds which may be provided by law in criminal cases and civil actions and proceedings involving just compensation under the Fifth Amendment. In other civil actions and proceedings the compensation shall be paid by the parties in such proportion and at such time as the court directs, and thereafter charged in like manner as other costs.

(c) Disclosure of Appointment. In the exercise of its discretion, the court may authorize disclosure to the jury of the fact that the court appointed the expert witness.

(d) Parties' Experts of Own Selection. Nothing in this rule limits the parties in calling expert witnesses of their own selection.

[Adopted effective March 1, 1978. Amended May 1, 1995, effective June 1, 1995, 437 Mich.]

Comments

Staff Comment to 1978 Adoption

MRE 706 is identical with Rule 706 of the Federal Rules of Evidence.

Rule 707.   Use of Learned Treatises for Impeachment

To the extent called to the attention of an expert witness upon cross-examination, statements contained in published treatises, periodicals, or pamphlets on a subject of history, medicine, or other science or art, established as a reliable authority by the testimony or admission of the witness or by other expert testimony or by judicial notice, are admissible for impeachment purposes only. If admitted, the statements may be read into evidence but may not be received as exhibits.

[Adopted effective March 1, 1978. Amended December 17, 1990, effective March 1, 1991, 437 Mich.]

Comments

Staff Comment to 1978 Adoption

MRE 707 is taken from Rule 803(18) of the Federal Rules of Evidence but with the addition of the phrase "are admissible for impeachment purposes only."

Staff Comment to 1991 Amendment

The 1991 amendment deleted "or relied upon by him in direct examination" from the first sentence. It also added the entire final sentence. Compare and contrast Federal Rule of Evidence 803(18) from which MRE 707 is derived.

Rule 801.   Hearsay; Definitions

The following definitions apply under this article:

(a) Statement. A "statement" is (1) an oral or written assertion or (2) nonverbal conduct of a person, if it is intended by the person as an assertion.

(b) Declarant. A "declarant" is a person who makes a statement.

(c) Hearsay. "Hearsay" is a statement, other than the one made by the declarant while testifying at the trial or hearing, offered in evidence to prove the truth of the matter asserted.

(d) Statements Which Are Not Hearsay. A statement is not hearsay if—

(1) *Prior Statement of Witness.* The declarant testifies at the trial or hearing and is subject to cross-examination concern-

ing the statement, and the statement is (A) inconsistent with the declarant's testimony, and was given under oath subject to the penalty of perjury at a trial, hearing, or other proceeding, or in a deposition, or (B) consistent with the declarant's testimony and is offered to rebut an express or implied charge against the declarant of recent fabrication or improper influence or motive, or (C) one of identification of a person made after perceiving the person; or

(2) *Admission by Party-Opponent.* The statement is offered against a party and is (A) the party's own statement, in either an individual or a representative capacity, except statements made in connection with a guilty plea to a misdemeanor motor vehicle violation or an admission of responsibility for a civil infraction under laws pertaining to motor vehicles, or (B) a statement of which the party has manifested an adoption or belief in its truth, or (C) a statement by a person authorized by the party to make a statement concerning the subject, or (D) a statement by the party's agent or servant concerning a matter within the scope of the agency or employment, made during the existence of the relationship, or (E) a statement by a coconspirator of a party during the course and in furtherance of the conspiracy on independent proof of the conspiracy.

[Adopted effective March 1, 1978. Amended December 17, 1990, effective March 1, 1991, 437 Mich; May 1, 1995, effective June 1, 1995, 448 Mich.]

Comments

Staff Comment to 1978 Adoption

MRE 801(a), (b) and (c) are identical with Rule 801(a), (b) and (c) of the Federal Rules of Evidence. MRE 801(d) is identical with Federal Rule 801(d) except for:

(1) The omission of (1)(A) and (B), which read: "(A) inconsistent with his testimony, or (B) consistent with his testimony and is offered to rebut an express or implied charge against him of recent fabrication or improper influence or motive";

(2) The addition in (2)(A) of the phrase: "except statements made in connection with a guilty plea to a misdemeanor motor vehicle violation";

(3) The addition in (2)(B) of the phrase: "subject to the rule announced in *People v Bobo*, 390 Mich 355 [212 N.W.2d 190] (1973)"; and

(4) The addition in (2)(E) of the phrase: "on independent proof of the conspiracy."

Staff Comment to 1991 Amendment

The 1991 amendments added subrules (d)(1)(A) and (B), and deleted from subrule (d)(2)(B) the citation to *People v Bobo*, 390 Mich 355 (1973). These changes conformed the rule to its federal counterpart.

In subrule (d)(2)(A), the 1991 amendments added the language that recognizes the decriminalization of most traffic offenses.

Rule 802. Hearsay Rule

Hearsay is not admissible except as provided by these rules.

[Adopted effective March 1, 1978.]

Comments

Staff Comment to 1978 Adoption

MRE 802 is similar to Rule 802 of the Federal Rules of Evidence and Rule 802 as recommended by the National Conference of Commissioners on Uniform State Laws in its Uniform Rules of Evidence (1974).

Rule 803. Hearsay Exceptions; Availability of Declarant Immaterial

The following are not excluded by the hearsay rule, even though the declarant is available as a witness:

(1) Present Sense Impression. A statement describing or explaining an event or condition made while the declarant was perceiving the event or condition, or immediately thereafter.

(2) Excited Utterance. A statement relating to a startling event or condition made while the declarant was under the stress of excitement caused by the event or condition.

(3) Then Existing Mental, Emotional, or Physical Condition. A statement of the declarant's then existing state of mind, emotion, sensation, or physical condition (such as intent, plan, motive, design, mental feeling, pain, and bodily health), but not including a statement of memory or belief to prove the fact remembered or believed unless it relates to the execution, revocation, identification, or terms of declarant's will.

(4) Statements Made for Purposes of Medical Treatment or Medical Diagnosis in Connection With Treatment. Statements made for purposes of medical treatment or medical diagnosis in connection with treatment and describing medical history, or past or present symptoms, pain, or sensations, or the inception or general character of the cause or external source thereof insofar as reasonably necessary to such diagnosis and treatment.

(5) Recorded Recollection. A memorandum or record concerning a matter about which a witness once had knowledge but now has insufficient recollection to enable the witness to testify fully and accurately, shown to have been made or adopted by the witness when the matter was fresh in the witness' memory and to reflect that knowledge correctly. If admitted, the memorandum or record may be read into evidence but may not itself be received as an exhibit unless offered by an adverse party.

(6) Records of Regularly Conducted Activity. A memorandum, report, record, or data compilation, in any form, of acts, transactions, occurrences, events, conditions, opinions, or diagnoses, made at or near the time by, or from information transmitted by, a person with knowledge, if kept in the course of a regularly conducted business activity, and if it was the regular practice of that business activity to make the memorandum, report, record, or data compilation, all as shown by the testimony of the custodian or other qualified witness, or by certification that complies with a rule promulgated by the supreme court or a statute permitting certification, unless the source of information or the method or circumstances of preparation indicate lack of trustworthiness. The term "business" as used in this paragraph includes business, institution, association, profession, occupation, and calling of every kind, whether or not conducted for profit.

(7) Absence of Entry in Records Kept in Accordance With the Provisions of Paragraph (6). Evidence that a matter is not included in the memoranda, reports, records, or data compilations, in any form, kept in accordance with the provisions of paragraph (6), to prove the nonoccurrence or nonexistence of the matter, if the matter was of a kind of which a memorandum, report, record, or data compilation was regularly made and preserved, unless the sources of information or other circumstances indicate lack of trustworthiness.

(8) Public Records and Reports. Records, reports, statements, or data compilations, in any form, of public offices or agencies, setting forth (A) the activities of the office or agency, or (B) matters observed pursuant to duty imposed by law as to which matters there was a duty to report, excluding, however, in criminal cases matters observed by police officers and other law enforcement personnel, and subject to the limitations of MCL 257.624.

(9) Records of Vital Statistics. Records or data compilations, in any form, of births, fetal deaths, deaths, or marriages, if the report thereof was made to a public office pursuant to requirements of law.

(10) Absence of Public Record or Entry. To prove the absence of a record, report, statement, or data compilation, in any form, or the nonoccurrence or nonexistence of a matter of which a record, report, statement, or data compilation, in any form, was regularly made and preserved by a public office or agency, evidence in the form of a certification in accordance with Rule 902, or testimony, that diligent search failed to disclose the record, report, statement, or data compilation, or entry.

(11) Records of Religious Organizations. Statements of births, marriages, divorces, deaths, legitimacy, ancestry, relationship by blood or marriage, or other similar facts of personal or family history, contained in a regularly kept record of a religious organization.

(12) Marriage, Baptismal, and Similar Certificates. Statements of fact contained in a certificate that the maker performed a marriage or other ceremony or administered a sacrament, made by a member of the clergy, public official, or other person authorized by the rules or practices of a religious organization or by law to perform the act certified, and purporting to have been issued at the time of the act or within a reasonable time thereafter.

(13) Family Records. Statements of fact concerning personal or family history contained in family Bibles, genealogies, charts, engravings on rings, inscriptions on family portraits, engravings on urns, crypts, or tombstones, or the like.

(14) Records of Documents Affecting an Interest in Property. The record of a document purporting to establish or affect an interest in property, as proof of the content of the original recorded document and its execution and delivery by each person by whom it purports to have been executed, if the record is a record of a public office and an applicable statute authorizes the recording of documents of that kind in that office.

(15) Statements in Documents Affecting an Interest in Property. A statement contained in a document purporting to establish or affect an interest in property if the matter stated was relevant to the purpose of the document, unless dealings with the property since the document was made have been inconsistent with the truth of the statement or the·purport of the document.

(16) Statements in Ancient Documents. Statements in a document in existence twenty years or more the authenticity of which is established.

(17) Market Reports, Commercial Publications. Market quotations, tabulations, lists, directories, or other published compilations, generally used and relied upon by the public or by persons in particular occupations.

(18) Deposition Testimony of an Expert. Testimony given as a witness in a deposition taken in compliance with law in the course of the same proceeding if the court finds that the deponent is an expert witness and if the deponent is not a party to the proceeding.

(19) Reputation Concerning Personal or Family History. Reputation among members of a person's family by blood, adoption, or marriage, or among a person's associates, or in the community, concerning a person's birth, adoption, marriage, divorce, death, legitimacy, relationship by blood, adoption, or marriage, ancestry, or other similar fact of personal or family history.

(20) Reputation Concerning Boundaries or General History. Reputation in a community, arising before the controversy, as to boundaries of or customs affecting lands in the community, and reputation as to events of general history important to the community or state or nation in which located.

(21) Reputation as to Character. Reputation of a person's character among associates or in the community.

(22) Judgment of Previous Conviction. Evidence of a final judgment, entered after a trial or upon a plea of guilty (or upon a plea of nolo contendere if evidence of the plea is not excluded by MRE 410), adjudging a person guilty of a crime punishable by death or imprisonment in excess of one year, to prove any fact essential to sustain the judgment, but not including, when offered by the state in a criminal prosecution for purposes other than impeachment, judgments against persons other than the accused. The pendency of an appeal may be shown but does not affect admissibility.

(23) Judgment as to Personal, Family, or General History, or Boundaries. Judgments as proof of matters of personal, family or general history, or boundaries, essential to the judgment, if the same would be provable by evidence of reputation.

(24) Other Exceptions. A statement not specifically covered by any of the foregoing exceptions but having equivalent circumstantial guarantees of trustworthiness, if the court determines that (A) the statement is offered as evidence of a material fact, (B) the statement is more probative on the point for which it is offered than any other evidence that the proponent can procure through reasonable efforts, and (C) the general purposes of these rules and the interests of justice will best be served by admission of the statement into evidence. However, a statement may not be admitted under this exception unless the proponent of the statement makes known to the adverse party, sufficiently in advance of the trial or hearing to provide the adverse party with a fair opportunity to prepare to meet it, the proponent's intention to offer the statement and the particulars of it, including the name and address of the declarant.

[Adopted effective March 1, 1978. Amended December 17, 1990, effective March 1, 1991, 437 Mich; July 18, 1991, effective October 1, 1991, 437 Mich; May 1, 1995, effective June 1, 1995, 448 Mich; January 19, 1996, effective April 1, 1996, 450 Mich; May 21, 2001, effective September 1, 2001, 464 Mich.]

Comments

Staff Comment to 1978 Adoption

MRE 803 is identical with Rule 803 of the Federal Rules of Evidence except:

(1) MRE 803(4) is less broad than Federal Rule 803(4), which reads as follows: *"Statements for purposes of medical diagnosis or treatment.* Statements made for purposes of medical diagnosis or treatment and describing medical history, or past or present symptoms, pain, or sensation, or the inception or general character of the cause or external source thereof insofar as reasonably pertinent to diagnosis or treatment."

(2) MRE 803(6) is identical with Federal Rule 803(6) except that the phrase "acts, events, conditions, opinions, or diagnosis" is replaced by the phrase "acts, transactions, occurrences, or events."

(3) MRE 803(8) is identical with Federal Rule 803(8) except for the addition to clause (B) of the phrase "and subject to the limitations of MCL 257.624, and the deletion of the following language: "or (C) in civil actions and proceedings and

against the Government in criminal cases, factual findings resulting from an investigation made pursuant to authority granted by law, unless the sources of information or other circumstances indicate lack of trustworthiness."

(4) MRE 803(18) has no parallel in the Federal Rules. It is consistent with GCR 1963, 302.4(3)[1].

(5) MRE 803(22) is identical with Federal Rule 803(22) except that the word "state" is substituted for "Government".

(6) The Michigan Rules of Evidence contain no catch-all hearsay exception such as found in Federal Rule 803(24).

Staff Comment to March, 1991 Amendment

The [March 1,] 1991 amendment conformed subrule (6) to its federal counterpart by adding the words "conditions, opinions, or diagnoses."

Staff Comment to October, 1991 Amendment

The October 1, 1991 amendment to MRE 803(22) altered one of the holdings in *Lichon v American Universal Insurance Co,* 435 Mich 408 (1990), by allowing, in narrowly defined circumstances, evidence of a conviction obtained on a plea of nolo contendere. See also MRE 410(2), which was added concurrently.

Staff Comment to 1996 Amendment

The 1996 adoption of MRE 803(24) and MRE 804(b)(6) incorporated into the Michigan Rules of Evidence the residual or "catch-all" exceptions to the hearsay rule that are part of the Federal Rules of Evidence.

Staff Comment to 2001 Amendment

The September 1, 2001 amendment of MRE 803(6) allows properly authenticated records to be introduced into evidence without requiring the records' custodian to appear and testify to their authenticity. See also MRE 902(11), which was added at the same time.

Rule 803A. Hearsay Exception; Child's Statement About Sexual Act

A statement describing an incident that included a sexual act performed with or on the declarant by the defendant or an accomplice is admissible to the extent that it corroborates testimony given by the declarant during the same proceeding, provided:

(1) the declarant was under the age of ten when the statement was made;

(2) the statement is shown to have been spontaneous and without indication of manufacture;

(3) either the declarant made the statement immediately after the incident or any delay is excusable as having been caused by fear or other equally effective circumstance; and

(4) the statement is introduced through the testimony of someone other than the declarant.

If the declarant made more than one corroborative statement about the incident, only the first is admissible under this rule.

A statement may not be admitted under this rule unless the proponent of the statement makes known to the adverse party the intent to offer the statement, and the particulars of the statement, sufficiently in advance of the trial or hearing to provide the adverse party with a fair opportunity to prepare to meet the statement.

This rule applies in criminal and delinquency proceedings only.

[Adopted December 17, 1990, effective March 1, 1991, 437 Mich.]

Comments

Staff Comment to 1991 Adoption

New MRE 803A reinstates the Michigan common law hearsay exception known as the tender years rule. See *People v Baker,* 251 Mich 322 (1930). Cf. *People v Kreiner,* 415 Mich 372 (1982).

Rule 804. Hearsay Exceptions; Declarant Unavailable

(a) Definition of Unavailability. "Unavailability as a witness" includes situations in which the declarant—

(1) is exempted by ruling of the court on the ground of privilege from testifying concerning the subject matter of the declarant's statement; or

(2) persists in refusing to testify concerning the subject matter of the declarant's statement despite an order of the court to do so; or

(3) has a lack of memory of the subject matter of the declarant's statement; or

(4) is unable to be present or to testify at the hearing because of death or then existing physical or mental illness or infirmity; or

(5) is absent from the hearing and the proponent of a statement has been unable to procure the declarant's attendance (or in the case of a hearsay exception under subdivision (b)(2), (3), or (4), the declarant's attendance or testimony) by process or other reasonable means, and in a criminal case, due diligence is shown.

A declarant is not unavailable as a witness if exemption, refusal, claim of lack of memory, inability, or absence is due to the procurement or wrongdoing of the proponent of a statement for the purpose of preventing the witness from attending or testifying.

(b) Hearsay Exceptions. The following are not excluded by the hearsay rule if the declarant is unavailable as a witness:

(1) *Former Testimony.* Testimony given as a witness at another hearing of the same or a different proceeding, if the party against whom the testimony is now offered, or, in a civil action or proceeding, a predecessor in interest, had an opportunity and similar motive to develop the testimony by direct, cross, or redirect examination.

(2) *Statement Under Belief of Impending Death.* In a prosecution for homicide or in a civil action or proceeding, a statement made by a declarant while believing that the declarant's death was imminent, concerning the cause or circumstances of what the declarant believed to be impending death.

(3) *Statement Against Interest.* A statement which was at the time of its making so far contrary to the declarant's pecuniary or proprietary interest, or so far tended to subject the declarant to civil or criminal liability, or to render invalid a claim by the declarant against another, that a reasonable person in the declarant's position would not have made the statement unless believing it to be true. A statement tending to expose the declarant to criminal liability and offered to exculpate the accused is not admissible unless corroborating circumstances clearly indicate the trustworthiness of the statement.

(4) *Statement of Personal or Family History.*

(A) A statement concerning the declarant's own birth, adoption, marriage, divorce, legitimacy, relationship by blood, adoption, or marriage, ancestry, or other similar fact of personal or family history, even though declarant had no means of acquiring personal knowledge of the matter stated; or

(B) a statement concerning the foregoing matters, and death also, of another person, if the declarant was related to the other by blood, adoption, or marriage or was so intimately associated with the other's family as to be likely to have accurate information concerning the matter declared.

(5) *Deposition Testimony.* Testimony given as a witness in a deposition taken in compliance with law in the course of the same or another proceeding, if the party against whom the testimony is now offered, or, in a civil action or proceeding, a predecessor in interest, had an opportunity and similar motive to develop the testimony by direct, cross, or redirect examination.

For purposes of this subsection only, "unavailability of a witness" also includes situations in which:

(A) The witness is at a greater distance than 100 miles from the place of trial or hearing, or is out of the United States, unless it appears that the absence of the witness was procured by the party offering the deposition; or

(B) On motion and notice, such exceptional circumstances exist as to make it desirable, in the interests of justice, and with due regard to the importance of presenting the testimony of witnesses orally in open court, to allow the deposition to be used.

(6) *Statement by Declarant Made Unavailable by Opponent.* A statement offered against a party that has engaged in or encouraged wrongdoing that was intended to, and did, procure the unavailability of the declarant as a witness.

(7) *Other Exceptions.* A statement not specifically covered by any of the foregoing exceptions but having equivalent circumstantial guarantees of trustworthiness, if the court determines that (A) the statement is offered as evidence of a material fact, (B) the statement is more probative on the point for which it is offered than any other evidence that the proponent can procure through reasonable efforts, and (C) the general purposes of these rules and the interests of justice will best be served by admission of the statement into evidence. However, a statement may not be admitted under this exception unless the proponent of the statement makes known to the adverse party, sufficiently in advance of the trial or hearing to provide the adverse party with a fair opportunity to prepare to meet it, the proponent's intention to offer the statement and the particulars of it, including the name and address of the declarant.

[Adopted effective March 1, 1978. Amended July 24, 1989, effective December 1, 1989, 432 Mich; May 1, 1995, effective June 1, 1995, 448 Mich; January 19, 1996, effective April 1, 1996, 450 Mich; May 21, 2001, effective September 1, 2001, 464 Mich.]

Comments

Staff Comment to 1978 Adoption

MRE 804 is identical with Rule 804 of the Federal Rules of Evidence except:

(1) MRE 804(a)(3) is identical with Federal Rule 804(a)(3) except that the word "has" is substituted for the phrase "testifies to."

(2) MRE 804(a)(5) is identical with Federal Rule 804(a)(5) except for the addition of the phrase: "and in a criminal case, due diligence is shown."

(3) MRE 804(b)(3) is identical with Federal Rule 804(b)(3) except that the phrase "reasonable person" is substituted for the phrase "reasonable man."

(4) The Michigan Rules of Evidence contain no catch-all hearsay exception such as found in Federal Rule 804(b)(5).

Staff Comment to 1989 Amendment

The new subrule (b)(5) defines several hearsay exceptions for deposition testimony. The new subrule combines a part of former subrule (b)(1) with parts of former MCR 2.308(A), which has been amended concurrently.

Staff Comment to 1996 Amendment

The 1996 adoption of MRE 803(24) and MRE 804(b)(6) incorporated into the Michigan Rules of Evidence the residual or "catch-all" exceptions to the hearsay rule that are part of the Federal Rules of Evidence.

Staff Comment to 2001 Amendment

MRE 804(b)(6) was added effective September 1, 2001. It is almost identical to FRE 804(b)(6), which was added to the federal rules effective 12/01/97. The new subrule creates a hearsay exception for prior statements by a witness who has become unavailable due to wrongful acts committed or encouraged by the party against whom the statement is to be introduced.

Rule 805. Hearsay Within Hearsay

Hearsay included within hearsay is not excluded under the hearsay rule if each part of the combined statements conforms with an exception to the hearsay rule provided in these rules.

[Adopted effective March 1, 1978.]

Comments

Staff Comment to 1978 Adoption

MRE 805 is identical with Rule 805 of the Federal Rules of Evidence.

Rule 806. Attacking and Supporting Credibility of Declarant

When a hearsay statement, or a statement defined in Rule 801(d)(2)(C), (D), or (E), has been admitted in evidence, the credibility of the declarant may be attacked, and if attacked may be supported, by any evidence which would be admissible for those purposes if declarant had testified as a witness. Evidence of a statement or conduct by the declarant at any time, inconsistent with the declarant's hearsay statement, is not subject to any requirement that the declarant may have been afforded an opportunity to deny or explain. If the party against whom a hearsay statement has been admitted calls the declarant as a witness, the party is entitled to examine the declarant on the statement as if under cross-examination.

[Adopted effective March 1, 1978. Amended May 1, 1995, effective June 1, 1995, 448 Mich.]

Comments

Staff Comment to 1978 Adoption

MRE 806 is identical with Rule 806 of the Federal Rules of Evidence.

Rule 901. Requirement of Authentication or Identification

(a) **General Provision.** The requirement of authentication or identification as a condition precedent to admissibility is satisfied by evidence sufficient to support a finding that the matter in question is what its proponent claims.

(b) **Illustrations.** By way of illustration only, and not by way of limitation, the following are examples of authentication or identification conforming with the requirements of this rule:

(1) *Testimony of Witness With Knowledge.* Testimony that a matter is what it is claimed to be.

(2) *Nonexpert Opinion on Handwriting.* Nonexpert opinion as to the genuineness of handwriting, based upon familiarity not acquired for purposes of the litigation.

(3) *Comparison by Trier or Expert Witness.* Comparison by the trier of fact or by expert witnesses with specimens which have been authenticated.

(4) *Distinctive Characteristics and the Like.* Appearance, contents, substance, internal patterns, or other distinctive characteristics, taken in conjunction with circumstances.

(5) *Voice Identification.* Identification of a voice, whether heard firsthand or through mechanical or electronic transmission or recording, by opinion based upon hearing the voice at any time under circumstances connecting it with the alleged speaker.

(6) *Telephone Conversations.* Telephone conversations, by evidence that a call was made to the number assigned at the time by the telephone company to a particular person or business, if (A) in the case of a person, circumstances, including self-identification, show the person answering to be the one called, or (B) in the case of a business, the call was made to a place of business and the conversation related to business reasonably transacted over the telephone.

(7) *Public Records or Reports.* Evidence that a writing authorized by law to be recorded or filed and in fact recorded or filed in a public office, or a purported public record, report, statement, or data compilation, in any form, is from the public office where items of this nature are kept.

(8) *Ancient Documents or Data Compilation.* Evidence that a document or data compilation, in any form, (A) is in such condition as to create no suspicion concerning its authenticity, (B) was in a place where it, if authentic, would likely be, and (C) has been in existence 20 years or more at the time it is offered.

(9) *Process or System.* Evidence describing a process or system used to produce a result and showing that the process or system produces an accurate result.

(10) *Methods Provided by Statute or Rule.* Any method of authentication or identification provided by the Supreme Court of Michigan or by a Michigan statute.

[Adopted effective March 1, 1978.]

Comments

Staff Comment to 1978 Adoption

MRE 901(a) and (b)(1) through (9) are identical with Rule 901(a) and (b)(1) through (9) of the Federal Rules of Evidence. MRE 901(b)(10) is a modified version of Rule 901(b)(10) of the Federal Rules of Evidence. Nothing contained in MRE 901(b)(5) authorizes the admission of voiceprint evidence.

Rule 902. Self–Authentication

Extrinsic evidence of authenticity as a condition precedent to admissibility is not required with respect to the following:

(1) **Domestic Public Documents Under Seal.** A document bearing a seal purporting to be that of the United States, or of any state, district, commonwealth, territory, or insular possession thereof, or the Panama Canal Zone, or the Trust Territory of the Pacific Islands, or of a political subdivision, department, officer, or agency thereof, and a signature purporting to be an attestation or execution.

(2) **Domestic Public Documents Not Under Seal.** A document purporting to bear the signature in the official capacity of an officer or employee of any entity included in paragraph (1) hereof, having no seal, if a public officer having a seal and having official duties in the district or political subdivision of the officer or employee certifies under seal that

the signer has the official capacity and that the signature is genuine.

(3) **Foreign Public Documents.** A document purporting to be executed or attested in an official capacity by a person authorized by the laws of a foreign country to make the execution or attestation, and accompanied by a final certification as to the genuineness of the signature and official position (A) of the executing or attesting person, or (B) of any foreign official whose certificate of genuineness of signature and official position relates to the execution or attestation or is in a chain of certificates of genuineness of signature and official position relating to the execution or attestation. A final certification may be made by a secretary of embassy or legation, consul general, consul, vice consul, or consular agent of the United States, or a diplomatic or consular official of the foreign country assigned or accredited to the United States. If reasonable opportunity has been given to all parties to investigate the authenticity and accuracy of official documents, the court may, for good cause shown, order that they be treated as presumptively authentic without final certification or permit them to be evidenced by an attested summary with or without final certification.

(4) **Certified Copies of Public Records.** A copy of an official record or report or entry therein, or of a document authorized by law to be recorded or filed and actually recorded or filed in a public office, including data compilations in any form, certified as correct by the custodian or other person authorized to make the certification, by certificate complying with paragraph (1), (2), or (3) or complying with any law of the United States or of this state.

(5) **Official Publications.** Books, pamphlets, or other publications purporting to be issued by public authority.

(6) **Newspapers and Periodicals.** Printed materials purporting to be newspapers or periodicals.

(7) **Trade Inscriptions and the Like.** Inscriptions, signs, tags, or labels purporting to have been affixed in the course of business and indicating ownership, control, or origin.

(8) **Acknowledged Documents.** Documents accompanied by a certificate of acknowledgment executed in the manner provided by law by a notary public or other officer authorized by law to take acknowledgments.

(9) **Commercial Paper and Related Documents.** Commercial paper, signatures thereon, and documents relating thereto to the extent provided by general commercial law.

(10) **Presumptions Created by Law.** Any signature, document, or other matter declared by any law of the United States or of this state to be presumptively or prima facie genuine or authentic.

(11) **Certified Records of Regularly Conducted Activity.** The original or a duplicate of a record, whether domestic or foreign, of regularly conducted business activity that would be admissible under rule 803(6), if accompanied by a written declaration under oath by its custodian or other qualified person certifying that

(A) The record was made at or near the time of the occurrence of the matters set forth by, or from information transmitted by, a person with knowledge of those matters;

(B) The record was kept in the course of the regularly conducted business activity; and

(C) It was the regular practice of the business activity to make the record.

A party intending to offer a record into evidence under this paragraph must provide written notice of that intention to all adverse parties, and must make the record and declaration available for inspection sufficiently in advance of their offer into evidence to provide an adverse party with a fair opportunity to challenge them.

[Adopted effective March 1, 1978. Amended effective June 1, 1995, 448 Mich; September 1, 2001, 464 Mich.]

Comments

Staff Comment to 1978 Adoption

MRE 902 is identical with Rule 902 of the Federal Rules of Evidence, except that MRE 902(4) and (10) are identical with Rules 902(4) and (10), respectively, as recommended by the National Conference of Commissioners on Uniform State Laws in its Uniform Rules of Evidence (1974).

Staff Comment to 2001 Amendment

MRE 902(11) was added effective September 1, 2001. Together with a concurrently adopted amendment of MRE 803(6), it allows a written certification of business records to substitute for a court appearance and testimony by the records' custodian. The advance notice provision provides the opposing party a fair opportunity to challenge the certification.

Rule 903.   Subscribing Witness' Testimony Unnecessary

The testimony of a subscribing witness is not necessary to authenticate a writing unless required by the laws of the jurisdiction whose laws govern the validity of the writing.

[Adopted effective March 1, 1978.]

Comments

Staff Comment to 1978 Adoption

MRE 903 is identical with Rule 903 of the Federal Rules of Evidence.

Rule 1001.   Contents of Writings, Recordings, and Photographs; Definitions

For purposes of this article the following definitions are applicable:

(1) **Writings and Recordings.** "Writings" and "recordings" consist of letters, words, or numbers, or their equivalent, set down by handwriting, typewriting, printing, photostating, photographing, magnetic impulse, mechanical or electronic recording, or other form of data compilation.

(2) **Photographs.** "Photographs" include still photographs, X-ray films, video tapes, and motion pictures.

(3) **Original.** An "original" of a writing or recording is the writing or recording itself or any counterpart intended to have the same effect by a person executing or issuing it. An "original" of a photograph includes the negative or any print therefrom. If data are stored in a computer or similar device, any printout or other output readable by sight, shown to reflect the data accurately, is an "original."

(4) **Duplicate.** A "duplicate" is a counterpart produced by the same impression as the original, or from the same matrix, or by means of photography, including enlargements and miniatures, or by mechanical or electronic re-recording, or by chemical reproduction, or by other equivalent techniques, which accurately reproduces the original.

[Adopted effective March 1, 1978.]

Comments

Staff Comment to 1978 Adoption

MRE 1001 is identical with Rule 1001 of the Federal Rules of Evidence except for the insertion of a comma after the word "techniques" in MRE 1001(4).

Rule 1002.   Requirement of Original

To prove the content of a writing, recording, or photograph, the original writing, recording, or photograph is required, except as otherwise provided in these rules or by statute.

[Adopted effective March 1, 1978.]

Comments

Staff Comment to 1978 Adoption

MRE 1002 is identical with Rule 1002 as recommended by the National Conference of Commissioners on Uniform State Laws in its Uniform Rules of Evidence (1974). MRE 1002 is similar to Rule 1002 of the Federal Rules of Evidence.

Rule 1003.   Admissibility of Duplicates

A duplicate is admissible to the same extent as an original unless (1) a genuine question is raised as to the authenticity of the original or (2) in the circumstances it would be unfair to admit the duplicate in lieu of the original.

[Adopted effective March 1, 1978.]

Comments

Staff Comment to 1978 Adoption

MRE 1003 is identical with Rule 1003 of the Federal Rules of Evidence.

Rule 1004.   Admissibility of Other Evidence of Contents

The original is not required, and other evidence of the contents of a writing, recording, or photograph is admissible if—

(1) **Originals Lost or Destroyed.** All originals are lost or have been destroyed, unless the proponent lost or destroyed them in bad faith; or

(2) **Original Not Obtainable.** No original can be obtained by any available judicial process or procedure; or

(3) **Original in Possession of Opponent.** At a time when an original was under the control of the party against whom offered, that party was put on notice, by the pleadings or otherwise, that the contents would be a subject of proof at the hearing, and that party does not produce the original at the hearing; or

(4) **Collateral Matters.** The writing, recording, or photograph is not closely related to a controlling issue.

[Adopted effective March 1, 1978. Amended May 1, 1995, effective June 1, 1995, 448 Mich.]

Comments

Staff Comment to 1978 Adoption

MRE 1004 is identical with Rule 1004 of the Federal Rules of Evidence.

Rule 1005.   Public Records

The contents of an official record, or of a document authorized to be recorded or filed and actually recorded or filed, including data compilations in any form, if otherwise admissible,

may be proved by copy, certified as correct in accordance with Rule 902 or testified to be correct by a witness who has compared it with the original. If a copy which complies with the foregoing cannot be obtained by the exercise of reasonable diligence, then other evidence of the contents may be given.
[Adopted effective March 1, 1978.]

Comments

Staff Comment to 1978 Adoption

MRE 1005 is identical with Rule 1005 of the Federal Rules of Evidence.

Rule 1006. Summaries

The contents of voluminous writings, recordings, or photographs which cannot conveniently be examined in court may be presented in the form of a chart, summary, or calculation. The originals, or duplicates, shall be made available for examination or copying, or both, by other parties at reasonable time and place. The court may order that they be produced in court.
[Adopted effective March 1, 1978.]

Comments

Staff Comment to 1978 Adoption

MRE 1006 is identical with Rule 1006 of the Federal Rules of Evidence.

Rule 1007. Testimony or Written Admission of a Party

Contents of writings, recordings, or photographs may be proved by the testimony or deposition of the party against whom offered or by that party's written admission, without accounting for the nonproduction of the original.
[Adopted effective March 1, 1978. Amended May 1, 1995, effective June 1, 1995, 448 Mich.]

Comments

Staff Comment to 1978 Adoption

MRE 1007 is identical with Rule 1007 of the Federal Rules of Evidence.

Rule 1008. Functions of Court and Jury

When the admissibility of other evidence of contents of writings, recordings, or photographs under these rules depends upon the fulfillment of a condition of fact, the question whether the condition has been fulfilled is ordinarily for the court to determine in accordance with the provisions of Rule 104. However, when an issue is raised (a) whether the asserted writing ever existed, or (b) whether another writing, recording, or photograph produced at the trial is the original, or (c) whether other evidence of contents correctly reflects the contents, the issue is for the trier of fact to determine as in the case of other issues of fact.
[Adopted effective March 1, 1978.]

Comments

Staff Comment to 1978 Adoption

MRE 1008 is identical with Rule 1008 of the Federal Rules of Evidence.

Rule 1101. Applicability

(a) Rules Applicable. Except as otherwise provided in subdivision (b), these rules apply to all actions and proceedings in the courts of this state.

(b) Rules Inapplicable. The rules other than those with respect to privileges do not apply in the following situations and proceedings:

(1) *Preliminary Questions of Fact.* The determination of questions of fact preliminary to admissibility of evidence when the issue is to be determined by the court under Rule 104(a).

(2) *Grand Jury.* Proceedings before grand juries.

(3) *Miscellaneous Proceedings.* Proceedings for extradition or rendition; sentencing, or granting or revoking probation; issuance of warrants for arrest, criminal summonses, and search warrants; and proceedings with respect to release on bail or otherwise.

(4) *Contempt Proceedings.* Contempt proceedings in which the court may act summarily.

(5) *Small Claims.* Small claims division of the district court.

(6) *In Camera Custody Hearings.* In camera proceedings in child custody matters to determine a child's custodial preference.

(7) *Proceedings Involving Juveniles.* Proceedings in the family division of the circuit court wherever MCR subchapter 3.900 states that the Michigan Rules of Evidence do not apply.

(8) *Preliminary Examinations.* At preliminary examinations in criminal cases, hearsay is admissible to prove, with regard to property, the ownership, authority to use, value, possession and entry.

(9) *Domestic Relations Matters.* The court's consideration of a report or recommendation submitted by the friend of the court pursuant to MCL 552.505(1)(g) or (h).

(10) *Mental Health Hearings.* In hearings under Chapters 4, 4A, 5, and 6 of the Mental Health Code, MCL 330.1400 *et seq.*, the court may consider hearsay data that are part of the basis for the opinion presented by a testifying mental health expert.
[Adopted effective March 1, 1978. Amended December 17, 1990, effective March 1, 1991, 437 Mich. Amended effective May 14, 2001, 464 Mich. Amended February 4, 2003, effective May 1, 2003, 467 Mich; March 25, 2003, effective September 1, 2003, 468 Mich.]

Comments

Staff Comment to 1978 Adoption

MRE 1101 is identical with Rule 1101 as recommended by the National Conference of Commissioners on Uniform State Laws in its Uniform Rules of Evidence (1974) except that in MRE 1101(b)(3) the words "[preliminary examination] detention hearing in criminal cases" are deleted, and MRE 1101(b)(5) is added, there being no equivalent in the Uniform Rule.

Staff Comment to 1991 Amendment

In subrule (b)(5), the 1991 amendments deleted an obsolete reference to a court that no longer exists. The amendments also added the present subrules (b)(6) and (7).

Staff Comment to 2001 Amendment

MRE 1101(8) was added effective May 14, 2001. In property crime cases, it allows the use of hearsay to prove certain elements of property crimes at the preliminary examination.

Staff Comment to February, 2003 Amendment

The amendment of MRE 1101(7) changes the references to the subchapter governing juvenile proceedings.

Staff Comment to September, 2003 Amendment

The March 25, 2003, amendments of MRE 703 and 1101, effective September 1, 2003, were recommended by the Advisory Committee on the Michigan Rules of Evidence appointed by the Supreme Court. (See January 28, 2003, follow-up report from Honorable William J. Giovan, advisory committee chair, at http://www.courts.michigan.gov/supremecourt/Resources/Administrative/index.htm.)

The modification of MRE 703 corrects a common misreading of the rule by allowing an expert's opinion only if that opinion is based exclusively on evidence that has been introduced into evidence in some way other than through the expert's hearsay testimony. New MRE 1101(b)(9) allows a trial judge to consider a friend of the court report prepared pursuant to MCL 552.505(1)(d) or (e), which "may include reports and evaluations by outside persons or agencies if requested by the parties or the court." New MRE 1101(b)(10) allows probate judges who are conducting preliminary mental health hearings to consider expert opinions that otherwise would be excluded by MRE 703 because the opinions are based on hearsay information.

Rule 1102.   Title

These rules are named the Michigan Rules of Evidence and may be cited as MRE.

The notes following the individual rules were drafted by the chair and the reporter of the committee which drafted the proposed rules of evidence for the benefit of the bench and bar and are not authoritative constructions by the Court.

[Adopted effective March 1, 1978.   Amended May 1, 1995, effective June 1, 1995, 448 Mich.]

INDEX TO
MICHIGAN RULES OF EVIDENCE

643

EXTRADITION
Application of rules, **Evid. Rule 1101**

FALSE SWEARING
Perjury, generally, this index

FAMILY
Blood or marriage, records of religious organizations, hearsay exception, **Evid. Rule 803**
Portraits, statements concerning inscriptions, hearsay exception, **Evid. Rule 803**

FAMILY DIVISION
Circuit courts, children and minors, **Evid. Rule 1101**

FAMILY HISTORY OR RECORDS
Hearsay, this index

FEDERAL AGENCIES
Documents, self authentication, **Evid. Rule 902**

FEDERAL GOVERNMENT
United States, generally, this index

FELONIES
Crimes and Offenses, generally, this index

FETAL DEATHS
Records and recordation, hearsay exception, **Evid. Rule 803**

FINES AND PENALTIES
Sentence and punishment. Crimes and Offenses, this index

FOREIGN DIPLOMATIC AND CONSULAR OFFICERS
Certificates and certification, genuineness, foreign public documents, **Evid. Rule 902**

FOREIGN DOCUMENTS
Certificates and certification, genuineness, **Evid. Rule 902**

GENEALOGIES
Personal or family history, hearsay exception, **Evid. Rule 803**

GOOD MORAL CHARACTER
Character and Reputation, generally, this index

GOVERNMENTAL AGENCIES
Documents, self authentication, **Evid. Rule 902**

GRAND JURY
Proceedings, **Evid. Rule 1101**

GRAVEYARDS
Monuments and memorials, engravings, hearsay exceptions, **Evid. Rule 803**

GUILTY PLEA
Crimes and Offenses, this index

HABIT
Relevant evidence, **Evid. Rule 406**

HANDWRITING
Writings, generally, this index

HARASSMENT
Witnesses, interrogation, **Evid. Rule 611**

HEALTH AND SANITATION
Hearsay exceptions, statements respecting, **Evid. Rule 803**

HEARINGS
Judicial notice, adjudicative facts, **Evid. Rule 201**
Jury, this index

HEARSAY
Generally, **Evid. Rule 802**
Absence and absentees,
    Declarant unavailable, exception, **Evid. Rule 804**
    Records and recordation, exception, **Evid. Rule 803**
Admission, party opponent, **Evid. Rule 801**
Adoption,
    Character and reputation, exception, **Evid. Rule 803**
    Statement of declarant concerning, exception, **Evid. Rule 804**
Agent or servant, **Evid. Rule 801**
Ancestry, records of religious organizations, exception, **Evid. Rule 803**
Attacking or supporting, credibility, **Evid. Rule 806**
Availability of declarant immaterial, **Evid. Rule 803**
Baptismal certificates, exception, **Evid. Rule 803**
Births,
    Records and recordation, exception, **Evid. Rule 803**
    Statement of declarant concerning, exception, **Evid. Rule 804**
Bodily health, statements respecting, exception, **Evid. Rule 803**
Boundaries, character and reputation, exception, **Evid. Rule 803**
Certificates, marriage, baptismal, exception, **Evid. Rule 803**
Character and reputation, exception, **Evid. Rule 803**
Children and minors, sexual acts, **Evid. Rule 803a**
Commercial publications, exception, **Evid. Rule 803**
Criminal liability, exculpatory evidence, admissibility, exception, **Evid. Rule 804**
Cross examination, **Evid. Rule 806**
Death,
    Declarant unavailable, exception, **Evid. Rule 804**
    Records and recordation, exception, **Evid. Rule 803**
    Statement under belief of impending death, exception, **Evid. Rule 804**
Declarant unavailable, exception, **Evid. Rule 804**
Definitions, **Evid. Rule 801**
Depositions, exception, **Evid. Rule 804**
Design, exception, **Evid. Rule 803**
Divorce,
    Records and recordation, exception, **Evid. Rule 803**
    Statement of declarant concerning, exception, **Evid. Rule 804**
Emotional condition, exception, **Evid. Rule 803**
Engravings, rings, urns, crypts or tombstones, statements concerning, exception, **Evid. Rule 803**
Exceptions, **Evid. Rule 803**
Excited utterance, exception, **Evid. Rule 803**
Family bibles, personal or family history, exception, **Evid. Rule 803**
Family history or records,
    Character and reputation, exception, **Evid. Rule 803**

ADMINISTRATIVE ORDERS OF THE SUPREME COURT

2012–4. Adoption of Concurrent Jurisdiction Plan for the 48th Circuit Court, the 57th District Court, and Allegan County Probate Court.

2012–5. Adoption of Administrative Order (Implementation of Trial Court Performance Measures).

2012–6. Adoption of Concurrent Jurisdiction Plan for the 37th Circuit Court, the 10th District Court, and the Calhoun County Probate Court.

2012–7. Adoption of Administrative Order (to Allow State Court Administrative Office to Authorize a Judicial Officer's Appearance by Video Communication Equipment).

2013–1. Adoption of Concurrent Jurisdiction Plan for the 18th Circuit Court, the 74th District Court, and the Bay County Probate Court.

2013–2. Adoption of Concurrent Jurisdiction Plan for the 14th Circuit Court, the 60th District Court, and the Muskegon County Probate Court.

2013–3. Adoption of Concurrent Joseph County Probate Court.

2013–4. Adoption of Concurrent Jurisdiction Plan for the 56th Circuit Court, the 56–a District Court, and the Eaton County Probate Court.

2013–5. Adoption of Concurrent Jurisdiction Plan for the 54th Circuit Court, the 71–B District Court, and the Tuscola County Probate Court.

2013–6. Implementation of Business Court Standards.

2013–7. Adoption of Concurrent Jurisdiction Plan for the 38th Circuit Court, the 1st District Court, and the Monroe County Probate Court.

2013–8. Trial Court Requirements for Providing Meaningful Access to the Court for Limited English Proficient Persons.

2013–9. Adoption of Concurrent Jurisdiction Plan for the 40th Circuit Court, the 71–a District Court, and the Lapeer County Probate Court.

2013–10. Adoption of Concurrent Jurisdiction Plan for the 44th Circuit Court, the 53rd District Court, and the Livingston County Probate Court.

2013–11. Adoption of Concurrent Jurisdiction Plan for the 1st Circuit Court, the 2–B District Court, and the Hillsdale County Probate Court.

2013–12. Revised Caseflow Management Guidelines and Rescission of Administrative Order No. 2011–3.

2013–13. Creation of Committee on Model Criminal Jury Instructions.

2013–14. Adoption of Concurrent Jurisdiction Plan for the 20th Circuit Court, the 58th District Court, and the Ottawa County Probate Court.

2013–15. Adoption of Concurrent Clair County Probate Court.

2013–16. Adoption of Concurrent Jurisdiction Plan for the 25th Circuit Court, the 96th District Court, and the Marquette County Probate Court.

2014–1. Adoption of Concurrent Jurisdiction Plan for the 15th Circuit Court, the 3–a District

Court, and the Branch County Probate Court.

2014–2. Adoption of Concurrent Jurisdiction Plan for the 9th Circuit Court, the 8th District Court, and the Kalamazoo County Probate Court.

2014–3. Adoption of Concurrent Jurisdiction Plan for the 29th Circuit Court, the 65A and 65B District Courts, and the Clinton County and Gratiot County Probate Courts.

2014–4. Adoption of Concurrent Jurisdiction Plan for the 30th Circuit Court, the 54A, 54B, and 55th District Courts, and the Ingham County Probate Court.

2014–5. Order Creating the Task Force on the Role of the State Bar of Michigan.

2014–6. Adoption of Concurrent Jurisdiction Plan for the 43rd Circuit Court, the 4th District Court, and the Cass County Probate Court.

2014–7. Adoption of Concurrent Jurisdiction Plan for the 42nd Circuit Court, the 75th District Court, and the Midland County Probate Court.

2014–8. Adoption of Concurrent Jurisdiction Plan for the 27th Circuit Court, the 78th District Court, and the Newaygo County and Oceana County Probate Courts.

2014–9. Adoption of Concurrent Jurisdiction Plan for the 24th Circuit Court, the 73A District Court, and the Sanilac County Probate Court.

2014–10. Adoption of Concurrent Jurisdiction Plan for the 6th Circuit Court and the Oakland County Probate Court.

2014–11. Adjustment of Discipline Portion of State Bar of Michigan Dues.

2014–12. Order Creating the Michigan Tribal State Federal Judicial Forum.

2014–13. Automated Income Tax Garnishment Pilot Project in 36th District Court.

2014–14. Adoption of Concurrent Jurisdiction Plan for the 47th Circuit Court, the 94th District Court, and the Delta County Probate Court.

2014–15. Adoption of Concurrent Jurisdiction Plan for the 16th Circuit Court, the 42nd District Court, and the Macomb County Probate Court.

2014–16. Adoption of Concurrent Jurisdiction Plan for the 32nd Circuit Court, the 98th District Court, and the Gogebic and Ontonagon County Probate Courts.

2014–17. Adoption of Concurrent Jurisdiction Plan for the 4th Circuit Court, the 12th District Court, and the Jackson County Probate Court.

2014–18. Merger of the State Appellate Defender Office (SADO) and Michigan Appellate Assigned Counsel System (MAACS).

2014–19. Reporting Requirements of the 36th District Court [Terminated Effective December 21, 2016.].

2014–20. Adoption of Concurrent Jurisdiction Plan for the 35th Circuit Court, the 66th District Court, and the Shiawassee County Probate Court.

2014–21.	Adoption of Concurrent Jurisdiction Plan for the 18th District Court and the 29th District Court.
2014–22.	Rescission of Administrative Order No. 2006–3 (Michigan Uniform System of Citation).
2014–23.	E–Filing System for the Michigan Supreme Court and the Michigan Court of Appeals.
2014–23.	E–Filing System for the Michigan Supreme Court and the Michigan Court of Appeals.
2014–24.	Extension of Expiration Date for E–Filing Pilot Project in Oakland Circuit Court, Family Division.
2014–25.	Establishment of Videoconferencing Standards.
2015–1.	Authorization of Pilot Project for Summary Jury Trials in the 16th Circuit Court and for Pilot Projects Testing Summary Jury Trials in Other Courts Approved by the Michigan Supreme Court.
2015–2.	Adoption of Concurrent Jurisdiction Plan for the 52nd Circuit Court, the 73B District Court, and the Huron County Probate Court.
2015–3.	Establishment of Michigan Trial Court Standards and Guidelines for Websites and Social Media.
2015–4.	Authorization for Use of GarnIT in the 36th, 46th, and 47th District Courts.
2015–5.	Adoption of Administrative Order Requiring Trial Courts to Comply with Certain ADA - Related Practices.
2015–6.	Adoption of Concurrent Jurisdiction Plan for the 23rd Circuit Court, the 81st District Court, and the Alcona, Arenac, Iosco, and Oscoda County Probate Courts.
2015–7.	Adoption of Concurrent Jurisdiction Plan for the 26th Circuit Court, the 88th District Court, and the Montmorency County Probate Court.
2015–8.	Authorization of Pilot Project to Study Feasibility and Effectiveness of Mediation in the Court of Appeals.
2015–9.	Authorization of a One–Year Pilot Project Related to the SADO/MAACS Merger.
2015–10.	Adoption of Concurrent Jurisdiction Plan for the 51st Circuit Court, the 79th District Court, and the Mason County Probate Court.
2016–1.	Authorizes the 7th Circuit Court to Require Parties and Attorneys to Submit Pleadings in Electronic Format in Personal Injury or Other Civil Cases Arising from Allegations of Lead or Other Contaminants in Flint Water.
2016–2.	Regulations Governing a System for Appointment of Counsel for Indigent Defendants in Criminal Cases and Minimum Standards for Indigent Criminal Defense Services.
2016–3.	Prisoner Electronic Filing Program with the Michigan Supreme Court and the Michigan Department of Corrections.
2016–4.	Adoption of Administrative Order to Expedite Disposition of Pending Probate Appeals in Circuit Court.
2016–5.	Adoption of New Antinepotism Policy and Rescission of AO No. 1996–11.
2017–1.	Adjustment of Discipline Portion of State Bar of Michigan Dues.
2017–2.	Adoption of Concurrent Jurisdiction (Plan for the 19th Circuit Court, the 85th District Court, and the Benzie and Manistee County Probate Courts).
2017–3.	Merger of the State Appellate Defender Office (SADO) and Michigan Appellate Assigned Counsel System (MAACS).
2018–1.	Adoption of Concurrent Jurisdiction Plan for the 34th Circuit Court, the 82nd District Court, the Ogemaw and Roscommon County Probate Courts.
2018–2.	Adoption of Concurrent Jurisdiction Plan for the 8th Circuit Court, the 64th District Court, the Ionia and Montcalm County Probate Courts.
2019–1.	Establishment of Court Security Committees.
2019–2.	Trial Court Requirements for Providing Meaningful Access to the Court for Mandated Electronic Filers.
2019–3.	Concurrent Jurisdiction Plan for the 41st Circuit Court.
2019–4.	Electronic Filing in the 3rd, 6th, 13th, 16th, and 20th Circuit Courts.
2019–5.	Concurrent Jurisdiction Plan for the 17th Circuit Court and the Kent County Probate Court.
2019–6.	Briefs Formatted for Optimized Reading on Electronic Displays.

Order 1968–2. Judicial Tenure Commission

Directed to State Bar of Michigan:

The State Bar shall publish in its journal a notice to all members that they may nominate judges and practicing attorneys who are not judges from among whom the membership will elect one judge and two attorneys as members of the judicial tenure commission. Nominating petitions, available at the State Bar office, will require the signature of 50 attorneys in good standing, and must be filed with the State Bar by a determined deadline (i.e., 30 days after publication).

In the event two nominations for each position are not received by the petition method, the board of commissioners shall thereupon nominate up to that number.

Within 10 days after the nomination of candidates therefor, the State Bar shall cause to be mailed to each member a ballot containing the names of the nominees divided into two categories,

(1) all judges nominated,

(2) all nonjudges nominated,

and space for write-in candidates.

The ballots shall be returned to the office of the State Bar of Michigan on or before (a date certain). Five tellers selected by the board of commissioners shall meet at the office of the State Bar on (a date certain), to tally the ballots. The judge receiving the highest number of votes, and the two nonjudges receiving the highest number of votes shall be declared elected.

[Adopted effective November 19, 1968, 381 Mich.]

Order 1969–4. Sexual Psychopaths

It appearing upon repeal of P.A.1939, No. 165, that jurisdiction to hear petitions to test the recovery of persons committed as criminal sexual psychopaths under the provisions of said act remains unresolved, that proceedings in various courts wherein relief has been sought have been dismissed with the result that a situation has continued for several months wherein the proper forum for reviewing the propriety of continued custody of persons committed under the provisions of said law remains in question, that protection of the basic rights of such persons and the uninterrupted administration of justice requires designation of a proper forum for hearing said matters until such time as the legislature shall provide clarification, now therefore, pursuant to the provisions of Constitution 1963, art. 6, § 13, and P.A.1961, No. 236, § 601, the revised judicature act.

It is ordered, that until such time as there is further legislative clarification of jurisdiction of proceedings for testing recovery of persons committed under the provisions of said P.A.1939, No. 165, as amended, jurisdiction shall continue and proceedings shall be conducted in accordance with the provisions of section 7 of said act, C.L.1948, § 780.507, as amended by P.A.1952, No. 58 (Stat.Ann.1954 Rev. § 28.967[7])

This order shall constitute a rule of the Supreme Court within Constitution 1963, art. 6, § 13, and shall be effective as of August 1, 1968, the date of effect of the repeal of P.A.1939, No. 165, as amended.

[Adopted effective October 20, 1969, 382 Mich. Rescinded by order, June 4, 2004, 470 Mich. Readopted by order, September 14, 2004, 471 Mich.]

Comments

Staff Comment to June, 2004 Order

Administrative Order No. 1969–4 was originally adopted to provide individuals who previously had been adjudicated as criminal sexual psychopaths with a proper forum for reviewing the propriety of their continued custody. The statutes dealing with the commitment of an individual as a criminal sexual psychopath have been repealed. There are no longer any individuals confined in state institutions because of their status as criminal sexual psychopaths, and, therefore, Administrative Order No. 1969–4 is obsolete and rescinded.

Staff Comment to September, 2004 Order

The Court was informed erroneously that there are no longer individuals confined in state institutions because of their status as criminal sexual psychopaths and, therefore, Administrative Order No. 1969–4 was obsolete and should be rescinded. The Court has since learned that, in fact, there are two individuals still confined by the Michigan Department of Community Health as criminal sexual psychopaths. Administrative Order No. 1969–4 is not obsolete and the rescission order that was entered on June 4, 2004, is vacated and Administrative Order No. 1969–4 is reinstated.

Order 1972–1. Judicial Assignments— Probate Courts

It is ordered that the assignment of a judge to serve as a judge of the probate court of a county in which he was not elected or appointed as a probate judge shall be made only by order of this Court or through the Court Administrator, and no judge shall so serve unless assigned in conformity herewith. This shall not apply to a judge of the circuit court for such county as provided for by M.C.L.A. 701.11.

It is further ordered that this order be given immediate effect.

[Adopted effective January 10, 1972, 386 Mich.]

Order 1972–2. Assignment of Counsel in the Recorder's Court

It appearing to the Court that the Defender's Office of the Legal Aid and Defender Association of Detroit is a nonprofit organization providing counsel to indigent defendants in the Wayne Circuit Court and the Recorder's Court of the City of Detroit, and that such method of providing counsel to indigent defendants should be encouraged for the efficient administration of criminal justice; and

It further appearing that assignments from Recorder's Court have been irregular, sometimes involving too many such assignments and sometimes too few;

Now, therefore, IT IS ORDERED that, from the date of this order until the further order of this Court, the Presiding Judge of Recorder's Court of the City of Detroit shall assign as counsel, on a weekly basis, the Defender's Office of the Legal Aid and Defender Association of Detroit in twenty-five per cent of all cases wherein counsel are appointed for indigent defendants.

[Adopted effective May 11, 1972, 387 Mich. Amended by Order 1997–5, effective July 25, 1997, 455 Mich.]

Order 1973–1. Legal Assistance for Litigants in the Landlord–Tenant Division of the Common Pleas Court

It appearing to the Court that there is sufficient necessity to furnish legal aid, on a case-to-case basis, to litigants in summary proceeding actions commenced in the Landlord-Tenant Division of Common Pleas Court and that existing standards of indigency preclude eligibility of said litigants for legal assistance, now therefore it is Ordered, effective from date of this order until further order of the Court, that all parties in summary proceeding actions who cannot afford an attorney in the proceedings shall be eligible for legal assistance from the legal aid clinics in the nature and manner administered under GCR 1963, 921; Provided however, that no plaintiff shall qualify for said services if he has a monetary interest in more than one income unit of real property.

[Adopted effective January 12, 1973, 389 Mich.]

Order 1977–1. Standard Criminal Jury Instructions

Proposed GCR and DCR 516.8, which would direct the use of the Standard Criminal Jury Instructions under certain conditions, were published in the State Bar Journal in April, 1976, for comment by the bench and bar. Comments have been received from proponents and opponents of the concept of pattern instructions. The intelligent concerns expressed by both sides have caused the Court to conclude that it would be provident to observe and evaluate actual trial use of the instructions over a substantial period before making the decision regarding implementation of use of the instructions by court rule.

Accordingly all members of the bench and bar are urged to use the instructions. Such use, particularly in the manner proposed in the rules published in the April 1976 Bar Journal, would provide a basis for communicating to the Court advantages or disadvantages encountered in their use. Comments based on such use are invited immediately, and on a continuing basis. It is the intention of the Court to readdress the question of implementation of the Standard Criminal Jury Instructions by court rule after approximately one year's experience has been obtained.

[Adopted effective January 6, 1977, 399 Mich.]

Order 1978–4. Public Communication by Lawyers

A lawyer may on behalf of himself, his partner or associate, or any other lawyer affiliated with him or his firm, use or participate in the use of any form of public communication that is not false, fraudulent, misleading, or deceptive. Except for DR 2–103 and DR 2–104, disciplinary rules in conflict with this order are suspended for a period of one year.

[Adopted effective March 15, 1978. Amended by Order 1979–3, effective February 2, 1979. Amended by Order 1979–7, effective August 31, 1979.]

Order 1978–5. Standard Criminal Jury Instructions

To assist the Supreme Court in evaluating the Standard Criminal Jury Instructions, every trial judge is requested during the four-month period beginning August 1, 1978, at the conclusion of every criminal case tried to a jury, to dictate to the court reporter a statement (outside the presence of the jury, counsel and the parties) of the offense or offenses covered by the instructions; the extent to which he used the Standard Criminal Jury Instructions; if he did not use them, why he did not; and any additional comments he may care to make to assist the Supreme Court in evaluating those instructions and in considering whether they should be made obligatory in the sense that the Standard Civil Jury Instructions are generally required to be given. The statement is not considered part of the record on appeal. The court reporter shall forward the statement to Donald Ubell, Chief Commissioner of the Supreme Court, within two weeks after the judge instructs the jury.

[Entered June 2, 1978, 420 Mich.]

Order 1979–4. Fingerprinting of Applicants for Admission to Bar

On order of the Court, pursuant to the power of superintending control, Const.1963, art. VI, § 4, and MCL 600.904; MSA 27A.904, empowering the Court to provide for the organization, government and membership of the State Bar of Michigan, and to adopt rules and regulations concerning the conduct and activities of the State Bar of Michigan and the investigation and examination of applicants for admission to the bar, the Board of Law Examiners is ORDERED forthwith to require that any applicant for admission to the State Bar of Michigan by examination be fingerprinted to enable the State Bar Committee on Character and Fitness to determine whether the applicant has a record of criminal convictions in jurisdictions other than Michigan. The Board of Law Examiners and the State Bar Committee on Character and Fitness are authorized to exchange fingerprint data with the Federal Bureau of Investigation, Identification Division.

[Adopted effective March 8, 1979, 406 Mich.]

Order 1981–6. Expedited Appellate Consideration of Orders Terminating Parental Rights

Directed to the clerk of the court of appeals and the clerk of this Court:

On order of the Court, it appearing that there is a need to expedite consideration of appeals terminating parental rights under the juvenile code, the clerk of the court of appeals and of this Court are directed to give priority to such appeals in scheduling them for submission to their respective courts.

[Adopted effective November 4, 1981, 412 Mich.]

Order 1981–7. Regulations Governing a System for Appointment of Appellate Counsel for Indigents in Criminal Cases and Minimum Standards for Indigent Criminal Appellate Defense Services. [Superseded effective November 15, 2017, 501 Mich.]

Order 1983–2. Construction, Remodeling, or Renovation of Court Facilities

The Court has received and reviewed the recommendation of the Courthouse Study Advisory Committee which urges the adoption of the Guidelines contained in Volume I of *The Michigan Courthouse Study*, pp. 53–171. The Court finds that the Guidelines reflect sound principles of court facility planning and design, application of which can greatly improve the functioning of Michigan's courts.

Accordingly, all courts and communities planning for and carrying out either construction, remodeling, or renovation of court facilities are urged to use the Guidelines.

[Adopted effective March 2, 1983, 413 Mich.]

Order 1983–7. Additional Copy of Order or Opinion in Criminal Case

On order of the Court, effective immediately, the Clerk of the Court of Appeals is directed to provide an additional copy of any order or opinion disposing of an appeal in a criminal case to the defendant's lawyer if the defendant was represented by counsel. Counsel shall thereupon forward the additional copy to the defendant.

[Adopted effective October 7, 1983, 417 Mich.]

Order 1985–3. Appellate Assigned Counsel: Rules and Standards. [Superseded effective November 15, 2017, 501 Mich.]

Order 1985–5. Juvenile Court Standards and Administrative Guidelines for the Care of Children

Pursuant to Administrative Order No. 1985–5, this Court adopted the *Juvenile Court Standards and Administrative Guidelines for the Care of Children,* as amended by Administrative Order No. 1988–3. We now order that the *Juvenile Court Standards and Administrative Guidelines* continue in effect, as modified below, until the further order of this Court:

I. Court administrators, supervisory personnel, county juvenile officers, probation officers, caseworkers, and personnel of court-operated child care facilities shall meet the following minimum standards in order to qualify for employment, unless the state court administrator grants an exception under I(G). *Desired standards are those preferred qualifications that extend beyond minimal standards but are not required to perform the job function.*

These standards shall apply only to new staff hired by the juvenile court on or after the effective date of these standards. A court employee who is currently in a position that was approved under regulations that preceded the implementation of these standards shall be deemed qualified for that position. A court-appointed person hired after the effective date of these standards shall meet the minimum qualification of these standards for that position.

A. *Court Administrator/Director.* The person in the juvenile court who is directly responsible to the chief or presiding probate judge and who is delegated administrative responsibilities for the operation of the court.

A court administrator, at the time of appointment, shall possess the following qualifications:

1. Education and Experience

a. Desired Standards

(1) Master's degree in social sciences, business or public administration, education, criminal justice, a related field that qualifies the person to manage or supervise the delivery of juvenile services, or a law degree with a minimum of four years of supervisory experience with juvenile court staff.

b. Minimum Standards

(1) Master's degree in social sciences, business or public administration, education, criminal justice, a related field that qualifies the person to manage or supervise the delivery of juvenile services, or a law degree with a minimum of one year of experience working with juvenile court staff or related human service field.

(2) A bachelor's degree in those same areas and two years of supervisory experience working with juvenile court staff or related human services field. (Courts with only one level of supervision may use two years of casework experience in lieu of supervisory experience.)

c. Knowledge, Skills and Abilities.

1. Knowledge of the juvenile justice system and overall children's services programs.

2. Knowledge of supervisory responsibilities and techniques.

3. Knowledge of the principles of administrative management.

4. Knowledge of programs and services provided by governmental agencies and the private sector.

5. Knowledge of the principles and methods concerned with personal and social problem solving.

6. Knowledge of the factors concerned in delinquency, neglect and abuse of children.

7. Knowledge of labor relations and personnel practices.

8. Ability to develop budgetary matters.

9. Ability to organize, direct and monitor service delivery work units and coordinate activities with other sections or agencies.

10. Ability to supervise professional and support staff, evaluate staff performance and assist in staff training.

11. Ability to develop policy and procedural materials and funding proposals.

12. Ability to analyze program data and recommend policy and procedural changes and program objectives.

13. Ability to interpret and effectively communicate administrative and professional policies and procedures to staff, governmental agencies, community organizations, advisory committees and the public.

14. Ability to speak and write effectively.

B. *Supervisory Personnel.* Those directly responsible for ongoing supervision of professional and support staff providing direct services to children, youth, and their families.

A supervisor, at the time of appointment, shall possess the following qualifications:

1. Education and Experience

a. Desired Standards

(1) Master's degree in social work, education, a human service field, or a related field that qualifies the person to manage or supervise the delivery of juvenile services, with one year of professional experience in juvenile court work.

b. Minimum Standards

(1) A bachelor's degree in social sciences, education, a human service field, or a related field that qualifies the person to manage or supervise the delivery of juvenile services, with two years of professional experience with a juvenile court staff or in a child welfare agency.

c. Knowledge, Skills and Abilities.

1. Knowledge of supervisory responsibilities and techniques.

2. Knowledge of principles, practices and techniques of child welfare work.

3. Knowledge of family dynamics and the effects of social conditions on family functioning.

4. Knowledge of factors concerned in delinquency, abuse and neglect of children.

5. Knowledge of principles and methods concerned with personal and social problem solving.

6. Knowledge of the juvenile justice system and overall children's services programs including related laws.

7. Knowledge of labor relations and personnel practices.

8. Knowledge of organizations, functions and treatment programs for children.

9. Ability to supervise professional and support staff, evaluate staff performance and assist in staff training.

10. Ability to speak and write effectively.

11. Ability to develop child welfare programs with community organizations.

12. Ability to apply social casework methods to child welfare services.

13. Ability to interpret and effectively communicate administrative and professional policies and procedures to staff, governmental agencies, community organizations, advisory committees and the public.

C. *Direct Services: Probation Officers/Casework Staff.*
The professional staff who work directly with children and their families and other relevant individuals and who are primarily responsible for the development, implementation and review of plans for children, youth and their families.

Each county shall provide for a minimum of one delinquency probation officer/casework staff person (but exclusive of clinical staff and detention home personnel) for every 6,000 (or major fraction thereof) children under 19 years of age in the county.

A probation officer/caseworker, at the time of appointment, shall possess the following qualifications:

1. Education and Experience

   a. Desired Standards

    (1) Bachelor's degree in social work, criminal justice, education, behavioral sciences, or a related field that qualifies the person to manage or supervise the delivery of juvenile services, with two years of casework experience in juvenile court or a related child welfare agency and must complete the Michigan Judicial Institute certification training for juvenile court staff within two years after date of employment.

   b. Minimum Standards

    (1) Bachelor's degree in social sciences, education, a related human service field, or a related field that qualifies the person to manage or supervise the delivery of juvenile services, and must complete the Michigan Judicial Institute certification training for juvenile court staff within two years after date of employment.

   c. Knowledge, Skills and Abilities.

    1. Knowledge of the principles and methods concerned with personal and social problem solving.

    2. Knowledge of factors concerned in delinquency, neglect and abuse of children.

    3. Knowledge of family dynamics and the effects of social conditions on family functioning.

    4. Knowledge of the juvenile justice system and children's services programs.

    5. Knowledge of the principles, procedures and techniques of child welfare work.

    6. Ability to apply social casework methods to child welfare services.

    7. Ability to develop child welfare programs with community organizations.

    8. Ability to relate effectively to the public and individuals on their caseload.

    9. Ability to speak and write effectively.

D. *Administrator of County Child Care Facility.* The person responsible to the chief or presiding probate judge or to the juvenile court administrator and to whom is delegated overall administrative responsibility for the day-to-day operation of county child care facilities operated by the court.

The administrator, at the time of appointment, shall possess the following qualifications:

1. Education and Experience

   a. Desired Standards

    (1) Master's degree in social work, sociology, psychology, guidance and counseling, education, business administration, criminal justice, public administration, or a related field that qualifies the person to manage or supervise the delivery of juvenile services, and two years of supervisory experience in a juvenile court, public or private child care facility.

   b. Minimum Standards

    (1) Same as above with a minimum of one year of supervisory experience in a juvenile court, public or private child care facility.

    (2) Bachelor's degree in social science, education, human service field, or a related field that qualifies the person to manage or supervise the delivery of juvenile services, and two years of experience in a juvenile court, public or private child care facility.

   c. Knowledge, Skills and Abilities.

    1. Knowledge of supervisory responsibilities and techniques.

    2. Knowledge of principles and methods concerned with personal and social problem solving.

    3. Knowledge of factors concerned in delinquency, neglect and abuse of children.

    4. Knowledge of family dynamics and effects of social conditions on family functioning.

    5. Knowledge of the juvenile justice system and children's services programs.

    6. Knowledge of child welfare organizations, functions and treatment programs relevant to residential care of children.

    7. Knowledge of group treatment modalities.

    8. Knowledge of labor relations, personnel policies and practices.

    9. Ability to organize, direct and monitor service delivery work units and coordinate activities with other sections or agencies.

    10. Ability to direct, monitor and coordinate several functions of a residential program.

    11. Ability to supervise professional and support staff, evaluate staff performance, and assist in staff training.

    12. Ability to analyze program data and recommend policy and procedural changes and program objectives.

    13. Ability to analyze personal and social data and apply rehabilitative principles within the facility.

    14. Ability to interpret and effectively communicate administrative and professional policies and procedures to staff, governmental agencies, community organizations, advisory committees, and the public.

    15. Ability to speak and write effectively.

E. *Child Care Staff Supervisor.* The child care supervisor is directly responsible for supervision of child care workers in the facility.

The child care supervisor, at the time of appointment, shall possess the following qualifications:

1. Education and Experience

   a. Desired Standards

(1) Bachelor's degree in social work, psychology, sociology, education, criminal justice,related human services field, or a related field that qualifies the person to manage or supervise the delivery of juvenile services, with two years of experience with a juvenile court or a public or private child care agency.

b. Minimum Standards

(1) Two years of college in a human services or education field or a related field that qualifies the person to manage or supervise the delivery of juvenile services, and two years of work experience in a child care institution.

c. Knowledge, Skills and Abilities.

1. Knowledge of supervisory responsibilities and techniques.

2. Knowledge of the principles and methods concerned with personal and social problem solving.

3. Knowledge of factors concerned in delinquency, abuse and neglect of children.

4. Knowledge of family dynamics and the effects of social conditions on family functioning.

5. Knowledge of the juvenile justice system and children's services.

6. Knowledge of group treatment modalities.

7. Ability to supervise staff, evaluate staff performance and assist in staff training activities.

8. Ability to analyze personal and social data and apply rehabilitation principles in a practice setting.

9. Ability to interpret administrative and professional policies and procedures to staff.

10. Ability to apply social casework methods to child welfare activity.

11. Ability to speak and write effectively.

12. Basic knowledge of first aid and CPR training.

13. Knowledge of labor relations and personnel practices.

F. *Child Care Worker.* The person who provides direct care of children in the facility.

A child care worker, at the time of appointment, shall possess the following qualifications:

1. Education and Experience

a. Desired Standards

(1) Bachelor's degree in social sciences, human services, or a related field, that qualifies the person to work with juveniles.

b. Minimum Standards

(1) A high school diploma or its equivalent.

c. Knowledge, Skills and Abilities.

1. Knowledge of appropriate conduct and manners.

2. Knowledge of potential facility management problems including behavior problems, food services.

3. Knowledge of potential behavior problems of children and youth.

4. Ability to provide role model for residents.

5. Ability to gain the respect, confidence and cooperation of children and youth.

6. Ability to teach children personal hygiene, proper conduct and household work.

7. Ability to understand and relate to problem children in a positive manner.

8. Ability to comprehend and follow oral and written directions.

9. Basic knowledge of first aid and CPR training within six months after date of employment.

G. *Exceptions.* The state court administrator may authorize a court to hire an employee who does not meet the educational requirements established in these standards if the court provides a reasonable period within which the candidate must meet the educational standards.

H. A bachelor's degree or other post-secondary degree is a degree from a college or university that is accredited by an accrediting body of the Council for Higher Education Accreditation.

II. Contents of Juvenile Court Case Records.

A. *Purpose.* A complete case record serves a range of purposes including, but not limited to, the following:

1. Provides an information base for planning and the delivery of services to a youth and family.

2. Provides documentation from which the worker can make appropriate recommendations for placement and services.

3. Provides an information base to assist in transfer of cases between workers and agencies.

B. *Case Record Contents for Youth Under Court Jurisdiction Placed in Their Own Home.* A separate case record shall be maintained for each youth or family under court supervision. Records shall be maintained in a uniform and organized manner and shall be protected against destruction (except as provided by court rule) and damage and shall be stored in a manner that safeguards confidentiality.

1. Records shall be typed or legibly handwritten and shall include as a minimum the following:

a. A report of the original complaint and/or petition and an appropriate social study.

b. Copies of orders of the court regarding the child and family.

c. Individual case plans with time frames where appropriate.

d. Youth Record Fact Sheet containing the following information: child's full name; date and place of birth; sex; religion of parents and child; parents' full names including mother's maiden name; address, dates and place of marriage or divorce; if deceased, date, place and cause of death; names, addresses and birth dates of other children in the family; names and addresses of near relatives; appropriate medical records.

e. Dates of casework visits or contact with child and family. Summary reports of child's progress under care, *completed at least semi-annually.*

f. School reports, including grades, progress reports, and social and psychological reports if available and appropriate.

g. Reports of psychological tests or psychiatric examinations and follow-up treatment, if available.

h. Family financial report where appropriate.

i. Discharge summary and order for discharge.

j. Correspondence.

C. *Case Record Contents for Youth Under Court Jurisdiction in Out-of-Home Placement.* Case records for youth in *out-of-home placements* shall include the *same items as indicated for youth placed in their own home* with the following additions:

1. Individual *Case Plans* shall, where appropriate, include:

a. Description of type and appropriateness of the placement.

b. Action steps and goals expected to be accomplished by the agency.

c. Action steps and goals expected to be accomplished by the parents.

d. Action steps and goals expected to be accomplished by the child.

e. Action steps and goals expected to be accomplished by the court worker.

f. Plan for assuring proper care (supervision; review).

g. Plan for regular and frequent visitation between child and parents unless such visits, even if supervised, would not be in the best interest of the child.

h. Time frames for accomplishing elements of the case plan.

2. Record of youth's placements. Name of place, beginning and ending dates of residence.

3. Documentation of emergency medical care authorization.

4. Health Record, which includes:

a. Medical history

b. Documentation of current and prior immunizations

c. Dental information

5. Medicaid approval.

6. Governmental benefits and parental support information.

7. Foster care termination summary or residential agency summary.

[Adopted effective April 30, 1985, 422 Mich. Amended by Order 1988–3, effective April 29, 1988, 430 Mich. Amended May 19, 2009, effective September 1, 2009, 483 Mich.]

Comments

Staff Comment to 2009 Amendment

These amendments expand the eligible education categories prospective employees (including administrators, supervisory personnel, county juvenile officers, probation officers, caseworkers, and personnel of court-operated child care facilities) must meet to be considered for employment. In addition, the amendments allow the state court administrator to waive the employment standards if the court provides a reasonable period within which the candidate must meet the education standards, and establish minimum accreditation requirements.

Order 1987–1. Providing Access to Juror Personal History Questionnaires

This Court has amended MCR 2.510(C)(2), effective April 1, 1987, to direct the State Court Administrator to develop model procedures for providing attorneys and parties access to juror personal history questionnaires. Individual courts are directed to select and implement one of these procedures within two months after the State Court Administrator notifies the courts of the issuance of the model procedures.

[Adopted effective February 3, 1987, 428 Mich.]

Order 1988–3. Juvenile Court Standards and Administrative Guidelines for the Care of Children [See Order 1985-5, entered April 29, 1988.]

Order 1988–4. Sentencing Guidelines

Administrative Order 1985–2, 420 Mich lxii, and Administrative Order 1984–1, 418 Mich lxxx, are rescinded as of October 1, 1988. The Sentencing Guidelines Advisory Committee is authorized to issue the second edition of the sentencing guidelines, to be effective October 1, 1988. Until further order of the Court, every judge of the circuit court must thereafter use the second edition of the sentencing guidelines when imposing a sentence for an offense that is included in the guidelines.

Whenever a judge of the circuit court determines that a minimum sentence outside the recommended minimum range should be imposed, the judge may do so. When such a sentence is imposed, the judge must explain on the record the aspects of the case that have persuaded the judge to impose a sentence outside the recommended minimum range.

[Adopted effective June 7, 1988, 430 Mich. Rescinded by Order 1998–4, effective January 1, 1999. Amended effective July 13, 2005, 473 Mich.]

Comments

Staff Comment to 2005 Amendment

The amendment of MCR 6.425(D), effective immediately, eliminated the requirement that the sentencing court complete a sentencing information report. Given this amendment of MCR 6.425(D), and because the judge is required to explain any departure on the record, the requirement that the judge complete a sentencing information report was also stricken from this administrative order. References to the Recorder's Court of the City of Detroit and the Sentencing Guidelines Advisory Committee were also stricken because they no longer exist.

Order 1989–1. Film or Electronic Media Coverage of Court Proceedings

The following guidelines shall apply to film or electronic media coverage of proceedings in Michigan courts:

1. Definitions.

(a) "Film or electronic media coverage" means any recording or broadcasting of court proceedings by the media using television, radio, photographic, or recording equipment.

(b) "Media" or "media agency" means any person or organization engaging in news gathering or reporting and includes any newspaper, radio or television station or network, news service, magazine, trade paper, professional journal, or other news reporting or news gathering agency.

(c) "Judge" means the judge presiding over a proceeding in the trial court, the presiding judge of a panel in the Court of Appeals, or the Chief Justice of the Supreme Court.

2. Limitations.

(a) *In the Trial Courts.*

(i) Film or electronic media coverage shall be allowed upon request in all court proceedings. Requests by representatives of media agencies for such coverage must be made in writing to the clerk of the particular court not less than three business days before the proceeding is scheduled to begin. A judge has the discretion to honor a request that does not comply with the requirements of this subsection. The court shall provide that the parties be notified of a request for film or electronic media coverage.

(ii) A judge may terminate, suspend, limit, or exclude film or electronic media coverage at any time upon a finding, made and articulated on the record in the exercise of discretion, that the fair administration of justice requires such action, or that rules established under this order or additional rules imposed by the judge have been violated. The judge has sole discretion to exclude coverage of certain witnesses, including but not limited to the victims of sex crimes and their families, police informants, undercover agents, and relocated witnesses.

(iii) Film or electronic media coverage of the jurors or the jury selection process shall not be permitted.

(iv) A trial judge's decision to terminate, suspend, limit, or exclude film or electronic media coverage is not appealable, by right or by leave.

(b) *In the Court of Appeals and the Supreme Court.*

(i) Film or electronic media coverage shall be allowed upon request in all court proceedings except for good cause as determined under MCR 8.116(D)(1). Requests by representatives of media agencies for such coverage must be made in writing to the clerk of the particular court not less than three business days before the proceeding is scheduled to begin. A judge has the discretion to honor a request that does not comply with the requirements of this subsection. The court shall provide that the parties be notified of a request for film or electronic media coverage.

(ii) A judge may terminate, suspend, limit, or exclude film or electronic media coverage at any time upon a finding, made and articulated on the record, that good cause requires such action or that rules established under this order or additional rules imposed by the judge have been violated. If a court makes such a finding, it must issue an order that states with particularity the reasons for termination, suspension, limitation, or exclusion of film or electronic media coverage.

(iii) If a judge of the Court of Appeals terminates, suspends, limits, or excludes film or electronic media coverage, the person who requested permission to film or otherwise provide for electronic media coverage may appeal that decision to the Chief Judge of the Court of Appeals. If the Chief Judge affirms the judge's decision, the requester may appeal by leave to the Supreme Court.

3. **Judicial Authority.** Nothing in these guidelines shall be construed as altering the authority of the Chief Justice, the Chief Judge of the Court of Appeals, trial court chief judges, or trial judges to control proceedings in their courtrooms, and to ensure decorum and prevent distractions and to ensure the fair administration of justice in the pending cause.

4. **Equipment and Personnel.** Unless the judge orders otherwise, the following rules apply:

(a) Not more than two videotape or television cameras, operated by not more than one person each, shall be permitted in any courtroom.

(b) Not more than two still photographers, utilizing not more than two still cameras each with not more than two lenses for each camera, and related necessary equipment, shall be permitted in any courtroom.

(c) Not more than one audio system for radio and/or television recording purposes shall be permitted in any courtroom. If such an audio system is permanently in place in the courtroom, pickup shall be made from that system; if it is not, microphones and wires shall be placed as unobtrusively as possible.

(d) Media agency representatives shall make their own pooling arrangements without calling upon the court to mediate any dispute relating to those arrangements. In the absence of media agency agreement on procedures, personnel, and equipment, the judge shall not permit the use of film or electronic media coverage.

5. **Sound and Light Criteria.**

(a) Only television, photographic, and audio equipment which does not produce distracting sound or light shall be utilized to cover judicial proceedings. Courtroom lighting shall be supplemented only if the judge grants permission.

(b) Only still camera equipment which does not produce distracting sound or light shall be employed to cover judicial proceedings. No artificial lighting device of any kind shall be employed with a still camera.

(c) Media agency personnel must demonstrate in advance, to the satisfaction of the judge, that the equipment proposed for utilization will not detract from the proceedings.

6. **Location of Equipment and Personnel.**

(a) Television camera equipment and attendant personnel shall be positioned in such locations in the courtroom as shall be designated by the judge. Audio and video tape recording and amplification equipment which is not a component of a camera or microphone shall be located in a designated area remote from the courtroom.

(b) Still camera photographers shall be positioned in such locations in the courtroom as shall be designated by the judge. Still camera photographers shall assume fixed positions within the designated areas and shall not move about in any way that would detract from the proceedings.

(c) Photographic or audio equipment may be placed in, moved about in, or removed from, the courtroom only during a recess. Camera film and lenses may be changed in the courtroom only during a recess.

(d) Representatives of the media agencies are invited to submit suggested equipment positions to the judge for consideration.

7. **Conferences.** There shall be no audio pickup, broadcast or video closeup of conferences between an attorney and client, between co-counsel, between counsel and the judge held at the bench at trial, or between judges in an appellate proceeding.

8. Conduct of Media Agency Personnel. Persons assigned by media agencies to operate within the courtroom shall dress and deport themselves in ways that will not detract from the proceedings.

9. Nonexclusivity. These guidelines shall not preclude coverage of any judicial proceeding by news reporters or other persons who are employing more traditional means, such as taking notes or drawing pictures.

[Adopted effective January 13, 1989, 432 Mich. Amended December 5, 2012, effective January 1, 2013, 493 Mich.]

Comments

Staff Comment to 2013 Amendment

The amendment of Administrative Order No. 1989–1 adds new language to clarify and expand the standards that allow film or electronic media coverage of court proceedings in the Court of Appeals and the Supreme Court.

Order 1989–3. In Re the Appointment of Appellate Assigned Counsel. [Superseded effective November 15, 2017, 501 Mich.]

Order 1989–4. Use of Facsimile Communication Equipment in Mental Health Proceedings

On order of the Court, the probate courts for the Counties of Calhoun, Kalamazoo and Oceana are authorized until further order of this Court, to conduct an experimental program which will utilize facsimile communication equipment to transmit petitions, physicians' certificates and other supporting documents from the Kalamazoo Regional Psychiatric Hospital for filing in the aforementioned courts. In all cases, the court will consider the documents filed when they are received by the facsimile equipment, and the court will initiate all notices so that the hearings are held within the time frames required by the Mental Health Code and Rules.

The facsimile documents shall be file-stamped when received and treated like an original, until the original documents are received by mail. If the original is not received within five days, the facsimile documents shall be copied on ordinary paper.

When the original documents are received by mail, the court shall file-stamp the originals with the date they were received and place them in the court file. A statement shall also be placed in the file, itemizing the documents received by facsimile, and indicating the date received. After comparing the facsimile documents with the original documents, the facsimile documents and any copies thereof shall be discarded.

The State Court Administrative Office shall provide assistance in the implementation of the pilot project and shall conduct an evaluation of the experimental program after the individual courts submit a report on the pilot project within 15 days after June 30, 1990. The pilot courts shall cooperate with the State Court Administrative Office.

[Adopted effective November 22, 1989.]

Order 1990–2. Interest on Lawyer Trust Accounts

On order of the Court, Administrative Order No. 1987–3 is VACATED and this order replaces it. The provisions of this order are adopted February 21, 1990, effective immediately.

1. Lawyer Trust Account Program. The Board of Trustees of the Michigan State Bar Foundation has been designated and has agreed to organize and administer the Lawyer Trust Account Program.

2. Powers and Duties.

(A) The Board shall have general supervisory authority over the administration of the Lawyer Trust Account Program.

(B) The Board shall receive funds from lawyers' interest-bearing trust accounts established in accordance with MRPC 1.15 of the Code [Rules] of Professional Conduct and shall make appropriate temporary investments of such funds pending disbursement of them.

(C) The Board shall, by grants and appropriations it deems appropriate, disburse funds as follows:

[*Publisher's Note: See, now, Administrative Order 1997–9.*]

(D) The Board shall maintain proper books and records of all Program receipts and disbursements and shall have them audited annually by a certified public accountant. The Board shall annually within 90 days after the close of its fiscal year cause to be presented an audited financial statement of its Program receipts and expenditures for the year. The statement shall be filed with the clerk of this Court and shall be published in the next available issue of the Michigan Bar Journal.

(E) The Board shall monitor the operation of the Lawyer Trust Account Program, propose to this Court changes in this order or in MRPC 1.15, and may, subject to approval by this Court, adopt and publish such instructions or guidelines not inconsistent with this order which it deems necessary to administer the Lawyer Trust Account Program.

3. Executive Director.

(A) The Board may appoint an executive director of the Lawyer Trust Account Program to serve on a full- or part-time basis at the pleasure of the Board. The executive director shall be paid such compensation as is fixed by the Board.

(B) The executive director shall be responsible and accountable to the Board for the proper administration of this Program.

(C) The executive director may employ persons or contract for services as the Board may approve.

4. Compensation and Expenses of the Board.

(A) The President and other members of the Board shall administer the Lawyer Trust Account Program without compensation, but shall be paid their reasonable and necessary expenses incurred in the performance of their duties.

(B) All expenses of the operation of the Lawyer Trust Account Program shall be paid from funds which the Board receives from the Program.

(C) The Board may borrow from the State Bar of Michigan or a commercial lender monies needed to finance the operation of the Lawyer Trust Account Program from the time it is constituted until the Program becomes operational. Any sum so borrowed shall be repaid, together with interest at prevailing market rates, as promptly as the initial receipts from the Program permit.

5. Disposition of Funds Upon Dissolution. If the Program or its administration by the Michigan State Bar Foundation is discontinued, any Program funds then on hand shall be transferred in accordance with the order of this Court terminating the Program or its administration by the Michigan State Bar Foundation.

[Adopted effective February 21, 1990.]

Order 1990–3. In Re Recommendations of the Task Force on Gender Issues in the Courts and the Task Force on Racial/Ethnic Issues in the Courts

In September, 1987, the Michigan Supreme Court appointed two nineteen-member task forces to examine the court system and to recommend changes to assure equal treatment for men and women, free from race or gender bias. The task forces were the Task Force on Racial/Ethnic Issues in the Courts and the Task Force on Gender Issues in the Courts.

The task forces submitted their final reports to this Court in December, 1989. They made a total of 167 recommendations for eliminating bias in the courtroom and among court personnel, in professional organizations, and in legal education. Many of these proposals can be implemented fairly quickly. Others will require long-range planning. All merit serious consideration.

This Court is in the process of reviewing all of the recommendations in order to determine the appropriate steps to be taken. We are persuaded upon preliminary examination that several of the proposals ought to be acted upon immediately. Therefore, we direct:

That judges, employees of the judicial system, attorneys and other court officers commit themselves to the elimination of racial, ethnic and gender discrimination in the Michigan judicial system;

That the State Bar of Michigan review the process for this Court's appointment of members of the Board of Commissioners of the State Bar and recommend to this Court whether the process should be changed in order to assure full participation by women and minority lawyers;

That the State Bar of Michigan make recommendations to this Court with regard to the proposals by the task forces that the Rules of Professional Conduct and the Code of Judicial Conduct be amended to specifically prohibit sexual harassment and invidious discrimination;

That members of the State Bar of Michigan support the Michigan Minority Demonstration Project and the American Bar Association Minority Demonstration Project; and

That the Michigan Judicial Institute continue its efforts to eliminate gender and racial/ethnic bias in the court environment through the education of judges, court administrators and others.

This Court is committed to assuring the fair and equal application of the rule of law for all persons in the Michigan court system. To that end, we support the principles that underlie the 167 recommendations that have been made. We are indebted to the thirty-eight men and women who gave of their time and talents to serve on the two task forces, and commend them for their dedication.

[Adopted effective June 12, 1990.]

Order 1990–8. Use of Facsimile Communication Equipment in Mental Health Proceedings

Until further order of the court, the probate courts in the Kalamazoo Regional Psychiatric Hospital catchment area are authorized to utilize facsimile communication equipment to transmit petitions, physician's certificates and other supporting documents from the Kalamazoo Regional Psychiatric Hospital for filing in the courts.

Participation by the probate courts listed below shall be subject to the discretion of the Chief Judge of the probate court and with the approval of the State Court Administrator.

The probate courts in the Kalamazoo Regional Psychiatric Hospital catchment area are located in the following counties: Allegan, Barry, Benzie, Berrien, Calhoun, Cass, Gratiot, Ionia, Kalamazoo, Kent, Lake, Manistee, Mason, Mecosta, Montcalm, Muskegon, Newaygo, Oceana, Osceola, Ottawa, St. Joseph, and Van Buren.

In all cases, the court will consider the documents filed when they are received by the facsimile equipment, and the court will initiate all notices so that the hearings are held within the time frames required by the Mental Health Code and Rules.

The facsimile documents shall be file-stamped when received and treated like an original, until the original documents are received by mail. If the original is not received within five days, the facsimile documents shall be copied on ordinary paper.

When the original documents are received by mail, the court shall file-stamp the originals with the date they were received and place them in the court file. A statement shall also be placed in the file, itemizing the documents received by facsimile and indicating the date received. After comparing the facsimile documents with the original documents, the facsimile documents and any copies thereof shall be discarded.

The State Court Administrative Office shall assist in the implementation of the use of facsimile equipment in mental health proceedings for those courts electing to participate.

The State Court Administrative Office shall review the pilot projects after the participating courts submit a report within 15 days after November 1, 1991.

[Adopted effective October 22, 1990.]

Order 1991–1. Use of Facsimile Communication Equipment in Mental Health Proceedings

Until further order of the court,[1] all Michigan probate courts are authorized to utilize facsimile communication equipment to transmit petitions, physician's certificates and other supporting documents from the state regional psychiatric hospitals for filing in the courts.

Participation by Michigan probate courts shall be subject to the discretion of the Chief Judge of the probate court and with the approval of the State Court Administrator.

In all cases, the probate court will consider the documents filed when they are received by the facsimile equipment, and the probate court will initiate all notices so that the hearings are held within the time frames required by the Mental Health Code[2] and Court Rules.

The facsimile documents shall be file-stamped when received and treated like originals, until the original documents are received by mail. If the originals are not received within five days, the facsimile documents shall be copied on ordinary paper.

When the original documents are received by mail, the probate court shall file-stamp the originals with the date they are received and place them in the court file. A statement shall also be placed in the file itemizing the documents received by facsimile and indicating the date received. After comparing the facsimile documents with the original documents, the facsimile documents and any copies thereof shall be discarded.

The State Court Administrative Office shall assist in the implementation of the use of facsimile equipment in mental health proceedings for those courts electing to participate.

The State Court Administrative Office shall review the pilot project after the participating courts submit a report within 15 days after January 1, 1992.

[Adopted effective April 10, 1991.]

1 See Administrative Order 1992–3, entered April 3, 1992.

2 M.C.L.A. § 330.1001 *et seq.*

Order 1991–7. Election Procedures for Judicial Members of the Judicial Tenure Commission

Administrative Order 1980–3 is hereby RESCINDED, and the following procedure is established for the election of judicial members of the Judicial Tenure Commission.

Each year in which the term of a commissioner selected by the judges of the courts of this state expires, the state court administrator shall send a notice to all judges eligible to vote for the commissioner position to be filled that they may nominate judges to fill the position. The notice, with a nominating petition, shall be mailed before July 17, with the instruction that, to be valid, nominating petitions must be filed at the office of the administrator in Lansing before September 1.

For a judge to be nominated petitions must be signed by at least ten judges eligible to vote for the nominee, except that a judge of the Court of Appeals may be nominated by petitions signed by five judges of that court. The administrator shall determine the validity of each nomination.

Before September 20, the administrator shall mail a ballot to every judge eligible to vote. A ballot will not be counted unless marked and returned in a sealed envelope addressed to the office of the administrator in Lansing with a postmark of not later than October 20.

In the event there is only one nominee, a ballot will not be mailed, and the nominee will be declared elected. The state court administrator will certify the declared election to the Chief Justice of the Supreme Court, Supreme Court Clerk and Executive Director of the Judicial Tenure Commission before December 15.

The administrator or designee, and three tellers appointed by the administrator, shall canvass the ballots and certify the count to the Supreme Court Clerk before November 1. The nominee receiving the highest number of votes will be declared elected. If there is a tie vote, the administrator shall mail a second ballot, consisting of those nominees receiving the highest count, by November 1. The second ballot must be marked and returned in a sealed envelope addressed to the office of the administrator in Lansing with a postmark of not later than November 30. The four tellers shall canvass these second ballots and, if a tie vote still results, they shall determine the successful nominee by lot. They shall certify the count or the result of the selection by lot to the Supreme Court Clerk before December 15.

If a vacancy occurs or is impending, the Judicial Tenure Commission shall notify the administrator promptly. The procedure set forth above shall be followed, except that time limits may be shortened to insure that the election occurs within 90 days, and the dates set forth above shall not be applicable.

[Adopted effective July 29, 1991.]

Order 1992–2. Court of Appeals Docketing Statement

On order of the Court, the Court of Appeals is authorized to require appellants in that Court to file a docketing statement in appeals of right. The Court of Appeals will supply the docketing statement form after the appeal has been filed. This requirement will govern appeals of right filed after April 1, 1992.

[Adopted January 22, 1992, effective April 1, 1992, 439 Mich.]

Order 1992–6. Temporary Judges on Court of Appeals Panels

On the order of the Court, Administrative Order No. 1991–9 is amended to read as follows:

For the purpose of addressing the serious problem of the volume of cases presently awaiting disposition in the Court of Appeals, it is hereby ordered that the provision of MCR 7.201(D) which requires that only one temporary judge may sit on a three-judge panel is suspended. This suspension is for the limited purpose of permitting the assignment of panels of former judges of the Court of Appeals and former justices of the Supreme Court. In all other respects the aforementioned provision of MCR 7.201(D) shall remain in effect. The suspension of MCR 7.201(D) for the limited purpose which is provided for in this order shall be effective until September 30, 1993.

[Adopted effective September 29, 1992.]

Order 1993–2. Silicone Gel Implant Product Liability Litigation

On order of the Court, it appearing that a large number of actions have been filed alleging personal injuries due to silicone gel implant devices, and that coordination of pretrial proceedings in those cases will promote the economical and expeditious resolution of that litigation, pursuant to Const 1963, art 6, § 4, we direct all state courts to follow the procedures set forth in this administrative order.

1. This order applies to all pending and future personal injury silicone gel implant product liability actions pending or to be filed in Michigan courts other than the Third Judicial Circuit. For the purposes of this order, "silicone gel implant product liability actions" include all cases in which it is alleged that a party has suffered personal injury or economic loss caused by any silicone gel implant, regardless of the theory of recovery. Until the transfer of the action under paragraph 2 of this order, the parties to such an action shall include the words "Implant Case" on the top right-hand corner of the first page of any papers subsequently filed in this action.

2. Each court in which a silicone gel implant product liability action is pending shall enter an order changing venue of

the action to the Third Judicial Circuit within 14 days of the date of this order. Upon the filing of a new silicone gel implant product liability action, the court shall enter an order changing venue to the Third Judicial Circuit within 14 days after the action is filed. The court shall send a copy of the order to the State Court Administrator. A party who objects to the transfer of an action under this paragraph may raise the objection by filing a motion in the Third Judicial Circuit. Such a motion must be filed within 14 days after the transfer of the action. Nothing in this order shall be construed as a finding that venue is proper in Wayne County.

3. Proceedings in each action transferred under this order shall be conducted in accordance with the Initial Case Management Order entered in Third Circuit Civil Action Number 93–302061 NP on February 8, 1993, and such further orders as may be entered by the Third Judicial Circuit. The Third Judicial Circuit shall cooperate with the State Court Administrator in monitoring the proceedings in the actions. Orders entered by the court in which the action was originally filed that are inconsistent with orders entered by the Third Judicial Circuit are superseded.

4. After the close of discovery, the Third Judicial Circuit shall conduct a settlement conference or conferences. If settlement is not reached as to all claims, the Third Judicial Circuit shall enter an order changing venue to the court in which the action was originally filed, or if appropriate to some other court, for further proceedings. A copy of the order shall be sent to the State Court Administrator.

5. Depositions taken in *In Re: Silicone Gel Breast Implants Products Liability Litigation* (MDL–926), Master File No. CV 92–P–10000–S (N.D.Ala) [hereinafter MDL], may be used in any actions governed by Third Judicial Circuit case management orders as provided in this paragraph notwithstanding that they were not taken in these actions. Such depositions may be used against a party in a Michigan state court action who is not also a party in an MDL proceeding only if the party proposing to use the MDL deposition gives written notice of that intention. The notice shall specifically designate the portions of the MDL deposition to be used and the noticing party must provide a transcript of the testimony being offered and a copy of the videotape of the deposition, if any, to the party against whom the deposition is proposed to be offered. That party may file a motion for further examination of the MDL witness, specifying the subjects as to which further examination is sought. If the motion is granted, the further deposition of the MDL witness may cover only those subjects designated in the order. The judge of the Third Judicial Circuit shall specify the times within which notices and motions under this paragraph may be filed.

6. If discovery proceedings have been conducted in an action prior to a transfer under this order, those discovery materials remain part of the record in the action in which they were produced, and may be used in further proceedings where otherwise appropriate notwithstanding the transfer under this rule. The materials are not part of the record in other cases governed by Third Judicial Circuit case management orders.

7. MCR 2.222, MCR 2.223, and MCR 2.224 do not apply to changes of venue pursuant to this order.

[Adopted effective March 31, 1993, 442 Mich.]

Order 1994–6. Reductions in Trial Court Budgets by Funding Units

On order of the Court, it appearing that a number of court funding units have reduced their original appropriations for the courts for the current fiscal year, this Administrative Order, applicable to all trial courts as defined in MCR 8.110(A), is adopted effective September 16, 1994.

1. If a court is notified by its funding unit of a reduction of the original appropriation for the court for the current fiscal year, the court shall immediately file a copy of that notice with the State Court Administrative Office.

2. Within 10 days after filing the notice, the chief judge must provide the following to the State Court Administrative Office Regional Administrator:

a. A copy of the court's original budget.

b. A copy of a revised budget in light of the reduced appropriation.

c. A statement of the amount of the reduction in court revenue by source, and a statement of anticipated revenues for the remainder of this fiscal year by source.

d. A budget reduction plan to reduce court operations in light of anticipated reductions in revenue, and an impact statement describing,

  i. Any anticipated reduction in the trial court work force that would be required.

  ii. Any anticipated reduction in court hours that would be required.

  iii. Any anticipated reductions in revenues that are anticipated, by source and by recipient.

  iv. The impact on other entities that would occur, including at a minimum potential service reductions, work flow backlogs, and revenue shortfalls. Other entities to be reviewed should include, at a minimum, the youth home (if any), the local jail, the prosecuting attorney (county and municipal), local law enforcement agencies, community mental health agencies, and county clerk's office.

  v. The schedule to be used for implementing reductions and for distributing notices to employees, other agencies, etc., and the date funds are estimated to be depleted under the revised budget plan.

e. An emergency services plan which outlines what services are essential and must be provided by the court. The emergency services plan should consider services which at a minimum will preserve rights guaranteed by the Michigan and U.S. Constitutions, and those guaranteed by statute.

If a copy of such a notice of reduction of appropriation has already been sent to the State Court Administrative Office, the additional information required by this section must be provided within 10 days of the effective date of this order. The State Court Administrative Office may grant an extension of time in its sole discretion.

3. After reviewing the revised budget and impact statement a designee of the State Court Administrator shall meet with the chief judge to discuss implementation of the plan and any anticipated need for assistance from other courts to assure provision of emergency services. Thereafter, the implementation of the plan shall begin immediately.

4. The State Court Administrative Office shall monitor the implementation of the plan. The chief judge shall notify the SCAO when budgeted funds are anticipated to be depleted and the date the emergency services plan filed pursuant to this Order will be implemented.

5. The State Court Administrator shall re-assign sitting judges as necessary to ensure as nearly as possible the maximum use of judicial resources in light of reduced operations, and to assist in the provision of emergency services to affected trial courts.

6. The procedures set forth in Administrative Order 1985–6 are not affected by this order and must be followed before the court may institute litigation against the funding unit.

[Adopted September 9, 1994, effective September 16, 1994, 447 Mich.]

Order 1994–8. Allocation of Funds from Lawyer Trust Account Program

On order of the Court, effective October 4, 1994, until further order of the Court, Administrative Order 1990–2 is MODI-FIED so as to provide that the funds to be distributed by the Board of Trustees of the Michigan State Bar Foundation shall be disbursed as follows: [1]

1. 50 percent of the net proceeds of the Lawyer Trust Account Program to support the delivery of civil legal services to the poor;

2. 20 percent of the net proceeds of the Lawyer Trust Account Program for criminal indigent services and other purposes which the Supreme Court deems appropriate;

3. 15 percent of the net proceeds of the Lawyer Trust Account Program to support programs to promote improvements in the administration of justice;

4. 10 percent of the net proceeds of the Lawyer Trust Account Program to support implementation, within the judiciary, of the recommendations of the Task Force on Gender Issues in the Courts and the Task Force on Racial/Ethnic Issues in the Courts; and

5. 5 percent of the net proceeds of the Lawyer Trust Account Program to support the activities of the Michigan Supreme Court Historical Society.

Administrative Order 1991–10 is rescinded.

[Adopted effective October 4, 1994. Amended effective October 13, 1994, 447 Mich.]

[1] See, now, Administrative Order 1997–9.

Order 1994–9. Suspension of Interest on Delinquent Costs Imposed in Attorney Discipline Proceedings

The Attorney Discipline Board has proposed that a 60–day period be provided during which interest would not be assessed on costs paid by suspended or disbarred attorneys who are in default on their obligations to pay costs in connection with discipline proceedings. On order of the Court, we AUTHOR-IZE the Attorney Discipline Board to notify persons delinquent in payment of costs that interest will not be assessed if the costs are paid within 60 days of the date of the notice.

[Adopted effective November 16, 1994, 447 Mich.]

Order 1994–10. Discovery in Criminal Cases

On May 4, 1994, the Governor signed House Bill 4227, concerning discovery by the prosecution of certain information known to the defendant in a criminal case. 1994 PA 113, MCL 767.94a; MSA 28.1023(194a). On November 16, 1994, this Court promulgated MCR 6.201, which is a comprehensive treatment of the subject of discovery in criminal cases.

On order of the Court, effective January 1, 1995, discovery in criminal cases heard in the courts of this state is governed by MCR 6.201 and not by MCL 767.94a; MSA 28.1023(194a). Const 1963, art 6, § 5; MCR 1.104.

[Adopted November 16, 1994, effective January 1, 1995, 447 Mich.]

Order 1994–11. Summary Jury Trial

On order of the Court, the provisions of Administrative Order No. 1988–2, regarding a summary jury trial procedure, are continued in effect until June 30, 1995.

Order 1995–1. Temporary Judges on Court of Appeals Panels

On order of the Court, the terms and conditions of Administrative Order No. 1992–6 are continued in effect until October 1, 1995. This Court will, in the near future, appoint a committee to examine the continuing need for use of judges, other than sitting Court of Appeals judges, to assist the Court of Appeals in processing its caseload. The committee will be asked to report its findings to this Court no later than June 1, 1995.

Order 1995–3. Summary Jury Trial

On order of the Court, the provisions of Administrative Order No. 1988–2, regarding a summary jury trial procedure, are continued in effect until June 30, 1997.

Order 1995–4. Temporary Judges on Court of Appeals Panels

On order of the Court, the terms and conditions of Administrative Order No. 1992–6 are continued in effect until December 31, 1995.

Order 1995–5. Reciprocal Visiting Judge Assignments for Judges of the Third Judicial Circuit and Recorder's Court of the City of Detroit

On order of the Court, Administrative Order No. 1986–1 is rescinded, effective immediately. In addition, Joint Administrative Order No. 1986–1 for the Third Judicial Circuit Court and the Recorder's Court for the City of Detroit and Joint Local Court Rule 6.102 for the Third Judicial Circuit and Recorder's Court for the City of Detroit are vacated effective immediately.

Order 1995–6. Temporary Judges on Court of Appeals Panels

On order of the Court, the terms and conditions of Administrative Order No. 1992–6 are extended until March 31, 1996.

Order 1996–3. Temporary Judges on Court of Appeals Panels

On order of the Court, the terms and conditions of Administrative Order No. 1992–6 are extended until September 30, 1996.

RILEY, J., would not extend the terms and conditions of Administrative Order No. 1992–6.

Order 1996–4   Resolution of Conflicts in Court of Appeals Decisions

On order of the Court, the terms and conditions of Administrative Order 1994–4 [1] are continued in effect until the further order of this Court.

[Adopted effective April 23, 1996, 451 Mich.]

[1] Administrative Order 1994–4, was repealed effective September 1, 1997. The provisions of Administrative Order 1994–4 were incorporated into MCR 7.215(H). The Staff Comment to the 1997 Repeal of Administrative Order 1994–4, states: "The provisions of Administrative Order 1994–4, dealing with Court of Appeals conflict resolution panels, are incorporated into the court rules as new MCR 7.215(H). Also, such panels are authorized to dispense with oral argument (by unanimous vote), and their decisions must be published in Michigan Appeals Reports."

Order 1996–8   Election of Members of the State Bar Board of Commissioners and the Representative Assembly

On order of the Court, for the purpose of the 1996 election of members of the State Bar Board of Commissioners and the Representative Assembly, the deadlines expressed in State Bar Rules 5, § 4 and 6, § 4 are extended as follows: Petitions are to be filed by May 31, 1996; ballots are to be mailed to everyone entitled to vote by June 17, 1996; ballots are to be returned bearing a postmark date not later than July 1, 1996. This administrative order governs the 1996 election only.

Order 1996–10   Temporary Judges on Court of Appeals Panels

On order of the Court, the terms and conditions of Administrative Order No. 1992–6 are extended until March 31, 1997.

Order 1997–2   Suspension of License to Practice Law

On order of the Court, in light of 1996 PA 236, [1] 1996 PA 238 [2] and 1996 PA 239, [3] we authorize circuit courts to issue suspensions of licenses to practice law subject to the conditions specified in the above-mentioned legislative enactments. The order shall be effective upon entry by the circuit court. The Office of the Friend of the Court shall send a copy of the suspension order or rescission of a prior suspension order to the Clerk of the Supreme Court, the State Court Administrative Office, the State Bar of Michigan, the Attorney Grievance Commission, and the Attorney Discipline Board.

[Adopted effective April 1, 1997, 454 Mich.]

[1] See M.C.L.A. § 338.3431 et seq.

[2] See M.C.L.A. § 600.909.

[3] See M.C.L.A. §§ 552.602, 552.603, 552.552.607a, 552.623, 552.628, 552.629, 552.630, 552.633, 552.635, 552.644, and 552.645.

Order 1997–4   Appointment of Executive Chief Judge for Third Circuit Court and Recorder's Court; Establishment of Executive Committee

On order of the Court, it appearing that the administration of justice would be served by the appointment of an Executive Chief Judge to oversee the administration of the Third Circuit Court and Recorder's Court in order to facilitate the orderly transition to a single court; it is ORDERED that the Honor-able Michael F. Sapala is appointed as Executive Chief Judge of the Third Circuit and Recorder's Courts, effective immediately.

The Executive Chief Judge of the Third Circuit Court and Recorder's Court has all of the responsibility and authority of chief judge pursuant to Michigan Court Rule 8.110 and as otherwise indicated in the Michigan Court Rules.

The Chief Judge of the Recorder's Court and Chief Judge of the Third Circuit Court shall continue to have responsibility for docket management, facilities and security, day to day management of personnel, budget and purchasing activity, and other responsibilities delegated by the Executive Chief Judge.

It is further ORDERED, that effective October 1, 1997, the Honorable Michael F. Sapala shall be the Chief Judge of the Third Circuit Court.

It is further ORDERED, effective immediately, that an Executive Committee of the Third Circuit Court and Recorder's Court is established to provide assistance to the Executive Chief Judge in developing administrative policy. The Chief Justice shall appoint members of the Executive Committee from the benches of the Third Circuit Court and Recorder's Court. Effective October 1, 1997, and until further order of this Court, the Executive Committee shall serve the Third Circuit Court, and shall provide assistance to the Chief Judge of the Third Circuit Court.

[Adopted effective June 4, 1997, 454 Mich.]

Comments

Staff Comment to 1997 Adoption

This order has been entered by the Court in anticipation of the merger of the Third Circuit Court and Recorder's Court as mandated by 1996 PA 374, which will take place effective 10-01-97. The appointment of an Executive Chief Judge is designed to facilitate planning for the merger and to assure a consistent approach to policy issues affecting both courts which will have an impact on the administration of the Third Circuit Court after 10-01-97.

Order 1997-5.   Defenders - Third Circuit Court [Repealed effective September 18, 2019]

Order 1997–7   Establishment of Child Support Coordinating Council

Note: *For later history, see Administrative Order 2002–1 which reconstituted the Council. Administrative Order 2002–1 was later rescinded by Administrative Order 2011–2.*

On order of the Court, the following order is effective immediately.

As part of its adjudication of domestic relations and juvenile cases, the judicial branch of government plays an integral role in the delivery of programs affecting Michigan's families, including those involving child support. Recognizing the importance of the judiciary's role in family matters, this Court has previously directed the issuance of requirements and guidelines for the implementation and operation of the family division of the circuit court.

The Court recognizes the importance of meeting its unique responsibilities toward Michigan's families in the most effective manner. Therefore, the Judiciary seeks to complement its independent adjudicative authority with the ability to provide seamless and cost effective service to the public through greater direct coordination with the executive branch of government concerning programs affecting families. To that end, we now direct, in partnership with the executive branch of government, that an interbranch council be formed to provide coordination regarding Michigan's child support program.

It is therefore ordered, concurrent with the Executive Order issued today by Governor John Engler, that the Child Support Coordinating Council is established.

The Council is advisory in nature and is charged with the following responsibilities:

1. To establish statewide program goals and objectives for the child support program.

2. To review and recommend child support program policy.

3. To share information on program issues.

4. To analyze and recommend state positions on pending and proposed changes in court rules and federal and state legislation.

The Council shall consist of ten (10) members, five (5) appointed by the Governor, one of whom shall be the Director of the Office of Child Support in the Family Independence Agency, and five (5) appointed by the Chief Justice, one of whom shall be the State Court Administrator. The Director of the Child Support Enforcement System shall be an ex-officio member.

The term of appointment is two years, except that of those first appointed, two appointees of the Governor and three appointees of the Chief Justice shall be appointed to a term of one year. Reappointment is at the discretion of the respective appointing authorities.

Chairmanship of the Council shall rotate in alternate calendar years. The Director of the Office of Child Support shall serve as chairperson in even-numbered years and the State Court Administrator shall serve as chairperson in odd-numbered years. When not serving as Chair of the Council, the Director or Administrator shall serve as Vice–Chair of the Council.

The Council shall meet quarterly or more frequently as the Council deems necessary. The Chair shall organize the time and location of meetings and facilitate the conduct of the meetings. The Chair will develop an agenda for each meeting to which the Vice–Chair may contribute.

By-laws for the operation of the Council shall be developed and approved by the membership.

Policy changes due to federal or state law changes will be brought to the Council by either the Office of Child Support or by the State Court Administrative Office or submitted to the Chair or Vice–Chair from other sources. The Council shall develop a format for presentation and discussion of issues which shall include an opportunity for issues to be raised through information sharing during regular meetings or to be placed on the agenda through the Chair or the Vice–Chair.

In developing recommendations or in drafting proposed legislation or rules, the members may seek comment where appropriate through a process determined by the members.

If the Council cannot reach agreement on an issue requiring its recommendation, the alternative positions shall be documented in writing for decision by the Governor and Chief Justice.

[Adopted effective October 23, 1997, 450 Mich.]

Order 1997–8   Establishment of Court Data Standards

In order to ensure effective administration of trial court information systems and facilitate the efficient exchange of trial court case information, IT IS ORDERED that the State Court Administrator establish court data standards. Chief judges shall take necessary action to ensure their courts' information systems comply with data standards established by the State Court Administrator.

The State Court Administrator shall provide reasonable time frames for compliance with court data standards. Not less than two years will be provided for compliance with data standards initially established pursuant to this order.

[Adopted effective November 12, 1997, 465 Mich.]

Order 1997–9   Allocation of Funds from Lawyer Trust Account Program

On order of the Court, effective November 14, 1997, until further order of the Court, Administrative Order 1994–8, which modified Administrative Order 1990–2, is modified so as to provide that the funds to be distributed by the Board of Trustees of the Michigan State Bar Foundation shall be disbursed as follows:

1. Seventy percent of the net proceeds of the Lawyer Trust Account Program to support the delivery of civil legal services to the poor;

2. Fifteen percent of the net proceeds of the Lawyer Trust Account Program to support programs to promote improvements in the administration of justice;

3. Ten percent of the proceeds of the Lawyer Trust Account Program to support implementation, within the judiciary, of the recommendations of the Task Force on Gender Issues in the Courts and the Task Force on Racial/Ethnic Issues in the Courts; and

4. Five percent of the net proceeds of the Lawyer Trust Account Program to support the activities of the Michigan Supreme Court Historical Society.

[Adopted effective November 14, 1997, 456 Mich.]

Order 1997–10   Allocation of Funds from Lawyer Trust Account Program

See Administrative Order No. 2006-8 for provisions supplemental to this order.

On order of the Court, the following order is effective February 1, 1998. The Court invites public comment on ways in which the objectives of the policy expressed in this order—an informed public and an accountable judicial branch—might be achieved most effectively and efficiently, consistent with the exercise of the constitutional responsibilities of the judicial branch. Comments should be sent to the Supreme Court Clerk by January 31, 1998.

(A) Scope, Coverage, and Definitions.

(1) This order does not apply to the adjudicative function of the judicial branch. It neither broadens nor restricts the availability of information relating to a court's adjudicative records.

(2) Solely as used in this order:

(a) "Adjudicative record" means any writing of any nature, and information in any form, that is filed with a court in connection with a matter to be adjudicated, and any writing prepared in the performance of an adjudicative function of the judicial branch.

(b) "Administrative function" means the nonfinancial, managerial work that a court does, outside the context of any particular case.

(c) "Administrative record" means a writing, other than a financial record or an employee record, prepared in the performance of an administrative function of the judicial branch.

(d) "Employee record" means information concerning an employee of the Supreme Court, State Court Administrative Office, Michigan Judicial Institute, and Board of Law Examiners.

(e) "Financial record" means the proposed budget, enacted budget, judicial salary information, and annual revenues and expenditures of a court.

(f) "Judge" means a justice of the Supreme Court or a judge of the Court of Appeals, circuit court, probate court, district court, or municipal court.

(g) "Person" means any individual or entity, except an individual incarcerated in a local, state, or federal correctional facility of any kind.

(h) "Supreme Court administrative agency" means the State Court Administrative Office, the Office of the Clerk, the Office of the Chief Justice, the Supreme Court Finance Department, and the Public Information Office.

(B) Access to Information Regarding Supreme Court Administrative, Financial, and Employee Records.

(1) Upon a written request that describes an administrative record, an employee record, or a financial record sufficiently to enable the Supreme Court administrative agency to find the record, a person has a right to examine, copy, or receive copies of the record, except as provided in this order.

(2) Requests for an administrative or employee record of a Supreme Court administrative agency must be directed to the administrative agency or to the Public Information Office. Requests for a financial record must be directed to the Supreme Court Finance Department. An administrative record, employee record, or financial record must be available for examination during regular business hours.

(3) A Supreme Court administrative agency may make reasonable rules to protect its records and to prevent unreasonable interference with its functions.

(4) This order does not require the creation of a new administrative record, employee record, or financial record.

(5) A reasonable fee may be charged for providing a copy of an administrative record, employee record, or financial record. The fee must be limited to the actual marginal cost of providing the copy, including materials and the time required to find the record and delete any exempt material. A person requesting voluminous records may be required to submit a deposit representing no more than half the estimated fee.

(6) A copyrighted administrative record is a public record that may not be re-published without proper authorization.

(7) The following are exempt from disclosure:

(a) Personal information if public disclosure would be an unwarranted invasion of an individual's privacy. Such information includes, but is not limited to:

(i) The home address, home telephone number, social security account number, financial institution record, electronic transfer fund number, deferred compensation, savings bonds, W–2 and W–4 forms, and any court-enforced judgment of a judge or employee.

(ii) The benefit selection of a judge or employee.

(iii) Detail in a telephone bill, including the telephone number and name of the person or entity called.

(iv) Telephone logs and messages.

(v) Unemployment compensation records and worker's disability compensation records.

(b) Information that would endanger the safety or well-being of an individual.

(c) Information that, if disclosed, would undermine the discharge of a constitutional or statutory responsibility.

(d) Records or information exempted from disclosure by a statutory or common law privilege.

(e) An administrative record or financial record that is to a substantial degree advisory in nature and preliminary to a final administrative decision, rather than to a substantial degree factual in nature.

(f) Investigative records compiled by the State Court Administrative Office pursuant to MCR 8.113.

(g) An administrative record or financial record relating to recommendations for appointments to court positions, court-sponsored committees, or evaluation of persons for appointment to court positions or court-sponsored committees.

(h) Trade secrets, bids, or other commercial information if public disclosure would give or deny a commercial benefit to an individual or commercial entity.

(i) Examination materials that would affect the integrity of a testing process.

(j) Material exempt from disclosure under MCL 15.243; MSA 4.1801(13).

(k) The identity of judges assigned to or participating in the preparation of a written decision or opinion.

(*l*) Correspondence between individuals and judges. Such correspondence may be made accessible to the public by the sender or the recipient, unless the subject matter of the correspondence is otherwise protected from disclosure.

(m) Reports filed pursuant to MCR 8.110(C)(5), and information compiled by the Supreme Court exclusively for purposes of evaluating judicial and court performance, pursuant to MCL 600.238; MSA 27A.238. Such information shall be made accessible to the public as directed by separate administrative order.

(n) An administrative record, employee record, or financial record in draft form.

(*o*) The work product of an attorney or law clerk employed by or representing the judicial branch in the regular course of business or representation of the judicial branch.

(p) Correspondence with the Judicial Tenure Commission regarding any judge or judicial officer, or materials received from the Judicial Tenure Commission regarding any judge or judicial officer.

(q) Correspondence with the Attorney Grievance Commission or Attorney Discipline Board regarding any attorney, judge, or judicial officer, or materials received from the Attorney Grievance Commission or Attorney Discipline Board regarding any attorney, judge, or judicial officer.

(8) A request for a record may be denied if the custodian of the record determines that:

(a) compliance with the request would create an undue financial burden on court operations because of the amount of equipment, materials, staff time, or other resources required to satisfy the request.

(b) compliance with the request would substantially interfere with the constitutionally or statutorily mandated functions of the court.

(c) the request is made for the purpose of harassing or substantially interfering with the routine operations of the court.

(d) the request is submitted within one month following the date of the denial of a substantially identical request by the same requester, denied under substantially identical rules and circumstances.

(9) A person's request to examine, copy, or receive copies of an administrative record, employee record, or financial record must be granted, granted in part and denied in part, or denied, as promptly as practicable. A request must include sufficient information to reasonably identify what is being sought. The person requesting the information shall not be required to have detailed information about the court's filing system or procedures to submit a request. A Supreme Court administrative agency may require that a request be made in writing if the request is complex or involves a large number of records. Upon request, a partial or complete denial must be accompanied by a written explanation. A partial or complete denial is not subject to an appeal.

(10) Employee records are not open to public access, except for the following information:

(a) The full name of the employee.

(b) The date of employment.

(c) The current and previous job titles and descriptions within the judicial branch, and effective dates of employment for previous employment within the judicial branch.

(d) The name, location, and telephone number of the court or agency of the employee.

(e) The name of the employee's current supervisor.

(f) Any information authorized by the employee to be released to the public or to a named individual, unless otherwise prohibited by law.

(g) The current salary of the employee. A request for salary information pursuant to this order must be in writing. The individual who provides the information must immediately notify the employee that a request for salary information has been made, and that the information has been provided.

(11) The design and operation of all future automated record management systems must incorporate processing features and procedures that maximize the availability of administrative records or financial records maintained electronically. Automated systems development policies must require the identification and segregation of confidential data elements from database sections that are accessible to the public. Whenever feasible, any major enhancements or upgrades to existing systems are to include modifications that segregate confidential information from publicly accessed databases.

[Adopted December 9, 1997, effective February 1, 1998, 456 Mich. Amended March 14, 2007, effective May 1, 2007, 477 Mich.]

Comments

Staff Comment to 2007 Amendment

This amendment corrects an incorrect reference.

Order 1997–11   Access to Judicial Branch Administrative Decisionmaking

On order of the Court, the following order is effective February 1, 1998. The Court invites public comment on ways in which the objectives of the policy expressed in this order—an informed public and an accountable judicial branch—might be achieved most effectively and efficiently, consistent with the exercise of the constitutional responsibilities of the judicial branch. Comments should be sent to the Supreme Court Clerk by January 31, 1998.

(A) Scope, Coverage, and Definitions. This order neither broadens nor restricts the extent to which court proceedings are conducted in public.

(B) Supreme Court Administrative Public Hearings.

(1) At least three times annually the Supreme Court will conduct an administrative public hearing on rules or administrative orders significantly affecting the delivery of justice proposed for adoption or amendment. An agenda of an administrative public hearing will be published not less than 28 days before the hearing in the manner most likely to come to the attention of interested persons. Public notice of any amendments to the agenda after publication will be made in the most effective manner practicable under the circumstances. Persons who notify the clerk of the Supreme Court in writing not less than 7 days before the hearing of their desire to address the Court at the hearing will be afforded the opportunity to do so.

(2) Unless immediate action is required, the adoption or amendment of rules or administrative orders that will significantly affect the administration of justice will be preceded by an administrative public hearing under subsection (1). If no public hearing has been held before a rule is adopted or amended, the matter will be placed on the agenda of the next public hearing, at which time the Supreme Court will hear public comment regarding whether the rule should be retained or amended.

(3) The adoption or amendment of a court rule or administrative order by the Supreme Court shall be by a recorded vote, and shall be available upon request from the Supreme Court Clerk.

(C) State Court Administrative Office; Administrative Public Hearings.

(1) Task forces, commissions, and working groups created at the direction of the Supreme Court and convened to advise the State Court Administrative Office and the Michigan Supreme Court on matters significantly affecting the delivery of justice must provide an opportunity for public attendance at one or more meetings.

(2) Notice of a meeting that is open to the public pursuant to this order must be provided in a manner reasonably likely to come to the attention of interested persons.

(3) A meeting held pursuant to this section must be held at a reasonably convenient time and in a handicap accessible setting.

(4) Persons interested in making a public comment at a meeting held pursuant to this section must be afforded the opportunity for public comment to the extent practicable. If the business of the meeting precludes the opportunity for public comment by any person wishing to comment, the person must be allowed to speak at a subsequent meeting or, if no future meeting will be held, be given the opportunity to have a written public comment recorded in the minutes and distributed to members of the task force, commission, or working group.

[Adopted December 9, 1997, effective February 1, 1998, 456 Mich.]

Order 1998–1   Reassignment of Circuit Court Actions to District Judges

In 1996 PA 374 the Legislature repealed former MCL 600.641; MSA 27A.641, which authorized the removal of actions from circuit court to district court on the ground that the amount of damages sustained may be less than the jurisdictional limitation as to the amount in controversy applicable to the district court. In accordance with that legislation, we repealed former MCR 4.003, the court rule implementing that procedure. It appearing that some courts have been improperly using transfers of actions under MCR 2.227 as a substitute for the former removal procedure, and that some procedure for utilizing district judges to try actions filed in circuit court would promote the efficient administration of justice, we adopt this administrative order, effective immediately, to apply to actions filed after January 1, 1997.

A circuit court may not transfer an action to district court under MCR 2.227 based on the amount in controversy unless: (1) The parties stipulate to the transfer and to an appropriate amendment of the complaint, see MCR 2.111(B)(2); or (2) From the allegations of the complaint, it appears to a legal certainty that the amount in controversy is not greater than the applicable jurisdictional limit of the district court.

Circuit courts and the district courts within their geographic jurisdictions are strongly urged to enter into agreements, to be implemented by joint local administrative orders, to provide that certain actions pending in circuit court will be reassigned to district judges for further proceedings. An action designated for such reassignment shall remain pending as a circuit court action, and the circuit court shall request the State Court Administrator assign the district judge to the circuit court for the purpose of conducting proceedings. Such administrative orders may specify the categories of cases that are appropriate or inappropriate for such reassignment, and shall include a procedure for resolution of disputes between circuit and district courts as to whether a case was properly reassigned to a district judge.

Because this order was entered without having been considered at a public hearing under Administrative Order 1997–11, the question whether to retain or amend the order will be placed on the agenda for the next administrative public hearing, currently scheduled for September 24, 1998.

[Adopted effective June 16, 1998, 456 Mich. Amended effective November 7, 2006, 477 Mich.]

Comments

Staff Comment to 2006 Amendment

This order deletes the requirement in Administrative Order No. 1998–1 for courts to report to the State Court Administrative Office when a case is transferred from circuit court to district court. That requirement was originally adopted to monitor the transfer of cases from circuit court to district court, following the repeal of a statute authorizing the practice. The transfer of cases under MCR 2.227 has been working smoothly and without incident, and no further statewide monitoring is necessary.

Order 1998–3   Family Division of the Circuit Court; Support Payments

The family division of the circuit court is responsible for the receipt and disbursement of child and spousal support payments. Those transactions require substantial public resources in order to ensure that the funds are properly receipted and disbursed on a timely basis for the benefit of those who receive the funds.

Michigan circuit courts have an exemplary record for the rapid and efficient receipt and disbursement of support payments. The implementation of electronic funds transfer processes for receipt and disbursement of funds provides the opportunity for more timely processing of support payments, and the opportunity for reducing the cost of such transactions. Furthermore, it is apparent that the implementation of electronic funds transfers for support payments will facilitate the implementation of central distribution processes required by the federal Personal Responsibility and Work Opportunity Act of 1996.[1]

Therefore, it is ordered that circuit courts, in receiving and disbursing support payments, shall use electronic funds transfer to the fullest extent possible.

In implementing electronic funds transfers, circuit courts will follow guidelines established by the State Court Administrator for that purpose.

[Adopted effective November 24, 1998, 459 Mich.]

[1] Pub.L. 104–193. See United States Code Annotated Tables for classification.

Order 1998–4   Sentencing Guidelines

On order of the Court, Administrative Order 1998–2, 459 Mich CLxxiii (1998), is vacated.

The sentencing guidelines promulgated by the Supreme Court in Administrative Order 1988–4, 430 Mich ci (1988), are rescinded, effective January 1, 1999, for all cases in which the offense is committed on or after January 1, 1999. The sentencing guidelines promulgated in Administrative Order 1988–4, as governed by the appellate case law concerning those guidelines, remain in effect for applicable offenses committed before January 1, 1999.[1]

[Adopted December 15, 1998, effective January 1, 1999, 459 Mich.]

[1] For current Sentencing Guidelines, see M.C.L.A. § 777.1 *et seq.* A Sentencing Guidelines Manual is available from the publisher.

Order 1998–5   Chief Judge Responsibilities; Local Intergovernmental Relations

I. Applicability. This Administrative Order applies to all trial courts as defined in MCR 8.110(A).

II. Court Budgeting. If the local funding unit requests that a proposed court budget be submitted in line-item detail, the chief judge must comply with the request. If a court budget has been appropriated in line-item detail, without prior approval of the funding unit, a court may not transfer between line-item accounts to: (a) create new personnel positions or to supplement existing wage scales or benefits, except to implement across the board increases that were granted to employees of the funding unit after the adoption of the court's budget at the same rate, or (b) reclassify an employee to a higher level of an existing category. A chief judge may not enter into a multiple-year commitment concerning any personnel economic issue unless: (1) the funding unit agrees, or (2) the agreement does not exceed the percentage increase or the duration of a multiple-year contract that the funding unit has negotiated for its employees. Courts must notify the funding unit or a local court management council of transfers between lines within 10 business days of the transfer. The requirements shall not be construed to restrict implementation of collective bargaining agreements.

III. Funding Disputes; Mediation and Legal Action. If, after the local funding unit has made its appropriations (including, for purposes of this section, amendments of existing appropriations or enforcement of existing appropriations), a court concludes that the funds provided for its operations by its local funding unit are insufficient to enable the court to properly perform its duties and that legal action is necessary, the procedures set forth in this order must be followed.

1. The chief judge of the court shall notify the State Court Administrator that a dispute exists regarding court funding that the court and the local funding unit have been unable to resolve. The notice must be accompanied by a written communication indicating that the chief judge of the court has approved the commencement of legal proceedings. With the notice, the court must supply the State Court Administrator with all facts relevant to the funding dispute. The State Court Administrator must attempt to aid the court and the local funding unit to resolve the dispute. If requested by the court and the local funding unit, the State Court Administrator must appoint a person or entity to serve as mediator within five business days. Any mediation that occurs as a result of the appointment of a mediator under this paragraph is intended to be the mediation referred to in MCL 141.438(6) and (8) and MCL 141.436(9).

2. If the court concludes that a civil action to compel funding is necessary, a civil action may be commenced by the chief judge, consistent with MCL 141.436 and MCL 141.438, if applicable.[1] If not applicable, a civil action may be commenced by the court, and the State Court Administrator is authorized to assign a disinterested judge to preside over the action.

3. Chief judges or representatives of funding units may request the assistance of the State Court Administrative Office to mediate situations involving potential disputes at any time, before differences escalate to the level of a formal funding dispute.

IV. Local Court Management Council Option. Where a local court management council has been created by a funding unit, the chief judge of a trial court for which the council operates as a local court management council, or the chief judge's designee, may serve as a member of the council. Unless the local court management council adopts the bylaws described below, without the agreement of the chief judge, the council serves solely in an advisory role with respect to decisions concerning trial court management otherwise reserved exclusively to the chief judge of the trial court pursuant to court order and administrative order of the Supreme Court.

A chief judge, or the chief judge's designee, must serve as a member of a council whose nonjudicial members agree to the adoption of the following bylaws:

1) Council membership includes the chief judge of each court for which the council operates as a local court management council.

2) Funding unit membership does not exceed judicial membership by more than one vote. Funding unit membership is determined by the local funding unit; judicial membership is determined by the chief judge or chief judges. Judicial membership may not be an even number.

3) Any action of the council requires an affirmative vote by a majority of the funding unit representatives on the council and a majority vote of the judicial representatives on the council.

4) Once a council has been formed, dissolution of the council requires the majority vote of the funding unit representatives and the judicial representatives of the council.

5) Meetings of the council must comply with the Open Meetings Act.[2] Records of the council are subject to the Freedom of Information Act.[3]

If such bylaws have been adopted, a chief judge shall implement any personnel policies agreed upon by the council concerning compensation, fringe benefits, and pensions of court employees, and shall not take any action inconsistent with policies of the local court management council concerning those matters. Management policies concerning the following are to be established by the chief judge, but must be consistent with the written employment policies of the local funding unit except to the extent that conformity with those policies would impair the operation of the court: holidays, leave, work schedules, discipline, grievance process, probation, classification, personnel records, and employee compensation for closure of court business due to weather conditions.

As a member of a local court management council that has adopted the bylaws described above, a chief judge or the chief judge's designee must not act in a manner that frustrates or impedes the collective bargaining process. If an impasse occurs in a local court management council concerning issues affecting the collective bargaining process, the chief judge or judges of the council must immediately notify the State Court Administrator, who will initiate action to aid the local court management council in resolving the impasse.

It is expected that before and during the collective bargaining process, the local court management council will agree on bargaining strategy and a proposed dollar value for personnel costs. Should a local court management council fail to agree on strategy or be unable to develop an offer for presentation to employees for response, the chief judge must notify the State

Court Administrator. The State Court Administrator must work to break the impasse and cause to be developed for presentation to employees a series of proposals on which negotiations must be held.

V. Participation by Funding Unit in Negotiating Process. If a court does not have a local court management council, the chief judge, in establishing personnel policies concerning compensation, fringe benefits, pensions, holidays, or leave, must consult regularly with the local funding unit and must permit a representative of the local funding unit to attend and participate in negotiating sessions with court employees, if desired by the local funding unit. The chief judge shall inform the funding unit at least 72 hours in advance of any negotiating session. The chief judge may permit the funding unit to act on the chief judge's behalf as negotiating agent.

VI. Consistency with Funding Unit Personnel Policies. To the extent possible, consistent with the effective operation of the court, the chief judge must adopt personnel policies consistent with the written employment policies of the local funding unit. Effective operation of the court to best serve the public in multicounty circuits and districts, and in third class district courts with multiple funding units may require a single, uniform personnel policy that does not wholly conform with specific personnel policies of any of the court's funding units.

1. *Unscheduled Court Closing Due to Weather Emergency.* If a chief judge opts to close a court and dismiss court employees because of a weather emergency, the dismissed court employees must use accumulated leave time or take unpaid leave if the funding unit has employees in the same facility who are not dismissed by the funding unit. If a collective bargaining agreement with court staff does not allow the use of accumulated leave time or unpaid leave in the event of court closure due to weather conditions, the chief judge shall not close the court unless the funding unit also dismisses its employees working at the same facility as the court.

Within 90 days of the issuance of this order, a chief judge shall develop and submit to the State Court Administrative Office a local administrative order detailing the process for unscheduled court closing in the event of bad weather. In preparing the order, the chief judge shall consult with the court's funding unit. The policy must be consistent with any collective bargaining agreements in effect for employees working in the court.

2. *Court Staff Hours.* The standard working hours of court staff, including when they begin and end work, shall be consistent with the standard working hours of the funding unit. Any deviation from the standard working hours of the funding unit must be reflected in a local administrative order, as required by the chief judge rule, and be submitted for review and comment to the funding unit before it is submitted to the SCAO for approval.

VII. Training Programs. The Supreme Court will direct the development and implementation of ongoing training seminars of judges and funding unit representatives on judicial/legislative relations, court budgeting, expenditures, collective bargaining, and employee management issues.

VIII. Collective Bargaining. For purposes of collective bargaining pursuant to 1947 PA 336, a chief judge or a designee of the chief judge shall bargain and sign contracts with employees of the court. Notwithstanding the primary role of the chief judge concerning court personnel pursuant to MCR 8.110, to the extent that such action is consistent with the effective and efficient operation of the court, a chief judge of a trial court may designate a representative of a local funding unit or a local court management council to act on the court's behalf for purposes of collective bargaining pursuant to 1947 PA 336 only, and, as a member of a local court management council, may vote in the affirmative to designate a local court management council to act on the court's behalf for purposes of collective bargaining only.

IX. Effect on Existing Agreements. This order shall not be construed to impair existing collective bargaining agreements. Nothing in this order shall be construed to amend or abrogate agreements between chief judges and local funding units in effect on the date of this order. Any existing collective bargaining agreements that expire within 90 days may be extended for up to 12 months.

If the implementation of 1996 PA 374 pursuant to this order requires a transfer of court employees or a change of employers, all employees of the former court employer shall be transferred to, and appointed as employees of, the appropriate employer, subject to all rights and benefits they held with the former court employer. The employer shall assume and be bound by any existing collective bargaining agreement held by the former court employer and, except where the existing collective bargaining agreement may otherwise permit, shall retain the employees covered by that collective bargaining agreement. A transfer of court employees shall not adversely affect any existing rights and obligations contained in the existing collective bargaining agreement. An employee who is transferred shall not, by reason of the transfer, be placed in any worse position with respect to worker's compensation, pension, seniority, wages, sick leave, vacation, health and welfare insurance, or any other terms and conditions of employment that the employee enjoyed as an employee of the former court employer. The rights and benefits thus protected may be altered by a future collective bargaining agreement.

X. Requests for Assistance. The chief judge or a representative of the funding unit may request the assistance of the State Court Administrative Office to facilitate effective communication between the court and the funding unit.

[Adopted effective December 28, 1998, 459 Mich. Amended September 18, 2007, effective October 1, 2007, 480 Mich. Amended effective January 29, 2014, 495 Mich; June 4, 2014, 496 Mich.]

1 The statutory provisions referred to in this paragraph relate to funding disputes between courts and their county funding unit(s). Third class district courts and municipal courts are not subject to the referenced statutory provisions.

2 MCL 15.261 *et seq.*; MSA 4.1800(11) *et seq.*

3 MCL 15.231 *et seq.*; MSA 4.1801(1) *et seq.*

Staff Comment to January, 2014 Amendment

The amendments of Administrative Order No. 1998–5 modify the way county-funded courts pursue disputes over court funding. These modifications are adopted with immediate effect, but pending public comment and a future public hearing, in light of the recent enactment of 2013 PA 172.

Staff Comment to June, 2014 Amendment

The amendments of Administrative Order No. 1998–5 modify the way courts pursue disputes over court funding. These modifications were adopted following enactment of 2013 PA 172.

Order 1999–1 Assignment of Medical Support Enforcement Matters to the Third Circuit for Discovery Purposes

Administrative Order No. 1997–3 is rescinded. On order of the Court, it appears that the administration of justice would be served in matters pending in circuit courts relating to support of minor children; any sitting judge of the Third Circuit Court assigned to the family division of the Third Circuit Court may act in proceedings involving the financial and medical support of minor children in jurisdictions other than the Third Circuit Court according to the following procedures:

1. This order applies to all pending and future actions involving the enforcement of financial or medical support of minor children filed in jurisdictions other than the Third Circuit Court.

2. In actions where the circuit court, office of the friend of the court, requires the discovery of information relating to the availability of health or medical care insurance coverage to the parents of children subject to orders of support pending in that court, the chief circuit judge may refer those actions by writing or through electronic means to the Third Circuit Court Friend of the Court Office for assistance in the discovery of such information.

3. Upon acceptance of the referral under section 2 by the Chief Judge of the Third Circuit or his or her designee, a judge of the Family Division of the Third Circuit Court designated by the Chief Judge of the Third Circuit Court may issue appropriate orders in that action for the purpose of discovery of information related to the availability of medical or health care insurance to the parents of minor children who are the subjects of that action. The judge(s) so assigned may by subpoena or other lawful means require the production of information for that purpose through single orders which apply to all cases referred from all jurisdictions making referrals under section 2.

4. The State Court Administrative Office shall be responsible to oversee the administration of this order and shall report to the Supreme Court as needed regarding administration of this order.

[Adopted effective January 21, 1999, 459 Mich.]

Comments

Staff Comment to 1999 Amendment

This order is issued to facilitate the Medical Support Enforcement System Project, which is a cooperative effort of the Family Independence Agency and the judiciary. The intent of the program is to ensure that courts are able to effectively establish and enforce child support orders that include provision of health care coverage for minor children pursuant to MCL 552.452(5), 722.27(5), 722.3(6), and 722.717(6). The Supreme Court issued Administrative Order No. 1997–3 on a short term basis, and through this order provides for discovery of medical information through the Third Circuit Court until further order of the Court.

Order 1999–3 Discovery in Misdemeanor Cases

On order of the Court, in the case of *People v Sheldon*, 234 Mich App 68; 592 NW2d 121 (1999) (COA Docket No. 204254), the Court of Appeals ruled that MCR 6.201, which provides for discovery in criminal felony cases, also applies to criminal misdemeanor cases. That ruling was premised on an erroneous interpretation of our Administrative Order No. 1994–10. By virtue of this Administrative Order, we wish to inform the bench and bar that MCR 6.201 applies only to criminal felony cases. Administrative Order No. 1994–10 does not enlarge the scope of applicability of MCR 6.201. See MCR 6.001(A) and (B).

[Adopted effective April 30, 1999, 459 Mich.]

Order 1999–4 Establishment of Michigan Trial Court Case File Management Standards

This version of Order 1999-4 effective until December 31, 2020. See following version of Order 1999-4, effective January 1, 2021.

In order to improve the administration of justice; to improve the service to the public, other agencies, and the judiciary; to improve the performance and efficiency of Michigan trial court operations; and to enhance the trial courts' ability to preserve an accurate record of the trial courts' proceedings, decisions, orders, and judgments pursuant to statute and court rule, IT IS ORDERED that the State Court Administrator establish Michigan Trial Court Case File Management Standards and that trial courts conform to those standards. The State Court Administrative Office shall enforce the standards and assist courts in adopting practices to conform to those standards.

[Adopted effective November 30, 1999, 461 Mich.]

Order 1999–4 Establishment of Michigan Trial Court Records Management Standards

This version of Order 1999-4 effective January 1, 2021. See previous version of Order 1999-4, effective until December 31, 2020.

In order to improve the administration of justice; to improve the service to the public, other agencies, and the judiciary; to improve the performance and efficiency of Michigan trial court operations; to enhance the trial courts' ability to create and maintain an accurate record of the trial courts' proceedings, decisions, orders, and judgments pursuant to statute and court rule, it is ordered that the State Court Administrator establish Michigan Trial Court Records Management Standards for data, case records, and other court records and that trial courts conform to those standards. The State Court Administrative Office must enforce the standards and assist courts in adopting practices to conform to those standards.

Case records under MCR 8.119(D) must be made available electronically to the same extent they are available at the courthouse, provided that certain personal data identifiers are not available to the public. In order to protect privacy and address security concerns, it is ordered that protected personal identifying information, as defined in court rule, filed with the state courts of Michigan in any form or manner and for any purpose must be nonpublic. The State Court Administrative Office must establish standards and develop court forms that ensure all protected personal identifying information necessary to a given court case is provided to the court separately from filed documents except as otherwise required by law.

[Adopted effective November 30, 1999, 461 Mich. Amended May 22, 2019, effective January 1, 2021, 502 Mich.]

Order 2000–3 Video Proceedings (Circuit and District Courts)

On order of the Court, Administrative Orders 1990–1, 1991–2, 1992–1, and 1993–1 are rescinded.

[Adopted effective July 18, 2000, 462 Mich. Amended July 13, 2005, effective January 1, 2006, 473 Mich.]

Staff Comment to 2000 Adoption

Administrative Order 2000–3 [entered July 18, 2000] added waivers and adjournments of preliminary examinations and extradition hearings, and hearings on referrals for forensic determination of competency, to those proceedings for which interactive video technology may be used in the circuit and district courts.

Staff Comment to 2005 Amendment

Effective January 1, 2006, video and audio proceedings are governed by MCR 6.006.

Order 2000–5   In Re Microsoft Antitrust Litigation

On order of the Court, it appearing that a number of actions have been filed alleging violation of the Michigan Antitrust Reform Act (hereafter "MARA"[1]) by Microsoft Corporation, and that coordination of pretrial and trial proceedings in those cases will promote the economical and expeditious resolution of that litigation, pursuant to Const 1963, art 6, sec 4, we direct all state courts to follow the procedures set forth in this administrative order.

1. This order applies to all pending and future Microsoft MARA actions pending or to be filed in Michigan courts other than the Third Judicial Circuit, including any Microsoft MARA cases remanded by a federal court to a Michigan court other than the Third Judicial Circuit. For purposes of this order, "Microsoft MARA actions" include all cases in which it is alleged that a party has suffered harm due to violations of the MARA by Microsoft Corporation.

2. Any orders in place in Michigan courts staying proceedings in a Microsoft MARA action as a result of Administrative Order 2000–2 may now be rescinded. Administrative Order 2000–2 is RESCINDED.

3. Each court in which a Microsoft MARA action is pending shall enter an order changing venue of the action to the Third Judicial Circuit within 14 days of the date of this order. Upon the filing of a new Microsoft MARA action, the court shall enter an order changing venue to the Third Judicial Circuit within 14 days after the action is filed. The court shall send a copy of the order to the State Court Administrator. A party who objects to the transfer of an action under this paragraph may raise the objection by filing a motion in the Third Judicial Circuit. Such a motion must be filed within 14 days after the transfer of the action. Nothing in this order shall be construed as a finding that venue is proper in Wayne County.

4. Until the transfer of an action under paragraph 3, the parties to the action shall include the words "Microsoft MARA case" on the top right-hand corner of the first page of any papers subsequently filed in this action.

5. The Third Judicial Circuit shall cooperate with the State Court Administrator in monitoring the proceedings in the actions.

6. MCR 2.222 and MCR 2.223 do not apply to changes of venue pursuant to this order.

[Adopted effective August 8, 2000, 463 Mich.]

[1] M.C.L.A. § 445.771 et seq.; MSA 28.70(1) et seq.

Order 2000–1   Security Policies for Court Facilities

It appearing that the orderly administration of justice would be best served by prompt action, the following order is given immediate effect. The Court invites public comment regarding the merits of the order. Comments may be submitted in writing or electronically to the Supreme Court Clerk by *June 1, 2001*. P.O. Box 30052, Lansing, MI 48909, or MSC_clerk@jud. state.mi.us. When submitting a comment, please refer to File No. 01–15.

This matter will be considered by the Court at a public hearing to be held June 14, 2001, in Kalamazoo. Persons interested in addressing this issue at the hearing should notify the Clerk by *June 12, 2001*. Further information about the hearing will be posted on the Court's website, www. supremecourt.state.mi.us. When requesting time to speak at the hearing, please refer to File No. 01–15.

The issue of courthouse safety is important not only to the judicial employees of this state, but also to all those who are summoned to Michigan courtrooms or who visit for professional or personal reasons. Accordingly, the Supreme Court today issues the following declaration regarding the presence of weapons in court facilities.

It is ordered that weapons are not permitted in any courtroom, office, or other space used for official court business or by judicial employees unless the chief judge or other person designated by the chief judge has given prior approval consistent with the court's written policy.

Each court is directed to submit a written policy conforming with this order to the State Court Administrator for approval, as soon as is practicable. In developing a policy, courts are encouraged to collaborate with other entities in shared facilities and, where appropriate, to work with local funding units. Such a policy may be part of a general security program or it may be a separate plan.

[Adopted effective March 27, 2001, 463 Mich.]

Order 2001–2   Uniform Effective Dates for Court Rule Amendments

On the basis of a request from the Appellate Practice Section of the State Bar of Michigan, the Supreme Court published for comment a proposed amendment of Rule 1.201 of the Michigan Court Rules. File No. 00–11.463 Mich 1219 (No. 4, 2000). The matter also was on the agenda of the public hearing held March 29, 2001, in Lansing. The proposal provided that an amendment of the court rules would not take effect until at least two months after its adoption, and that the effective date would be either April 1 or October 1, absent the need for immediate action.

The Court understands the concerns expressed by those who submitted written comments and those who addressed this proposal at the public hearing. After careful consideration, however, the Court is persuaded that the best approach to more uniformity in the rulemaking process is not a court rule amendment, but rather an administrative order that provides for three effective dates during the year.

Accordingly, on ORDER of the Court, unless there is a need for immediate action, amendments of the Michigan Court Rules will take effect on January 1, May 1, or September 1.

[Adopted effective April 5, 2001, 463 Mich.]

Order 2001–3   Security Policy for the Michigan Supreme Court

Effective immediately, in accordance with Article 6, sections 1, 4, and 5 of the Michigan Constitution, and Administrative

Order 2001–1, the following policy is adopted for the Supreme Court.

IT IS ORDERED THAT

1. No weapons are allowed in the courtroom of the Supreme Court or in other facilities used for official business of the Court. This prohibition does not apply to security personnel of the Court in the performance of their official duties, or to law enforcement officers in the performance of their official duties, if the officer is in uniform (or otherwise properly identified) and is not a party to a matter then before the Court. The Chief Justice may authorize additional exceptions under appropriate circumstances.

2. All persons and objects are subject to screening by Court security personnel, for the purpose of keeping weapons from entering Court facilities.

3. Notice shall be posted that "No weapons are permitted in this Court facility."

4. Persons in violation of this order may be held in contempt of Court.

[Adopted effective May 25, 2001, 464 Mich.]

Order 2001–6   Committee on Model Civil Jury Instructions

Forty years ago, in response to a resolution of the Michigan Judicial Conference, the Supreme Court appointed a committee to prepare jury instructions for use in civil cases. In 1970, the Court amended former Rule 516 of the General Court Rules to authorize the use of these instructions by trial courts. Later that year, the Court approved general instructions and instructions governing personal injury actions. In 1975, at the request of the committee that had developed the instructions, the Court appointed a new Committee on Standard Jury Instructions to oversee the task of maintaining the accuracy of existing model instructions and developing new instructions. Five years later, the Court amended the court rules to give the committee express standing authority to propose and modify standard instructions.

The Court has reconstituted the Committee on Standard Jury Instructions from time to time to provide for new members and to make permanent the status of the committee's reporter. But the committee has until now operated without a defined structure and without a fixed number of members.

The Court is appreciative of the faithful and distinguished service that has been rendered over the years by members of the current and predecessor committees. Many of the present members have given long and selfless service, and their contributions have greatly enhanced the administration of justice. As part of an effort to regularize all the working groups that the Court has established, and to ensure continuity, we are persuaded that it now would be beneficial to develop a formal structure and membership for this committee. In addition, we are renaming the committee to clarify that the instructions apply to civil cases and that they are model instructions.

Therefore, on order of the Court, a new Committee on Model Civil Jury Instructions is established. The committee shall consist of 21 persons to be appointed by the Supreme Court. The Supreme Court will designate one member to serve as the chairperson of the committee. Generally members will be

appointed for three-year terms and may be reappointed for two additional terms. However, to facilitate the transition and the staggering of terms, some initial appointments will be for abbreviated terms and those appointees who are members of the current Committee on Standard Jury Instructions will not be eligible for reappointment.

Effective January 1, 2002, the following persons are appointed to the new Committee on Model Civil Jury Instructions:

For terms ending December 31, 2002

Honorable Susan D. Borman

Peter L. Dunlap

R. Emmet Hannick

Honorable Harold Hood

Honorable Robert M. Ransom

George T. Sinas

Sheldon J. Stark

For terms ending December 31, 2003

David C. Coey

Honorable Pat M. Donofrio

Honorable Bruce A. Newman

Honorable Wendy L. Potts

Michael B. Rizik, Jr.

Valerie P. Simmons

Susan H. Zitterman

For terms ending December 31, 2004

Thomas Blaske

Honorable William J. Giovan

Mark R. Granzotto

Maurice G. Jenkins

Steven W. Martineau

Honorable Susan Bieke Neilson

Mary Massaron Ross

Judge Hood is designated as chairperson for the duration of his term, after which Judge Giovan shall assume that position. Sharon M. Brown is appointed reporter for the committee.

It shall be the duty of the committee to ensure that the Model Civil Jury Instructions accurately state applicable law, and that the instructions are concise, understandable, conversational, unslanted, and not argumentative. In this regard, the committee shall have the authority to amend or repeal existing instructions and, when necessary, to adopt new instructions. Before doing so, the committee shall provide a text of the proposal to the secretary of the State Bar and the state court administrator, who shall give the notice specified in Rule 1.201 of the Michigan Court Rules. The notice shall state the time and method for commenting on the proposal. Following the comment period and any public hearing that the committee may hold on the matter, the committee shall provide notice of its decision in the same manner in which it provided notice of proposed instructions.

[Adopted effective December 18, 2001, 465 Mich.]

Order 2002–2   Facsimile Transmission of Documents in the Court of Appeals

On order of the Court, the Court of Appeals is authorized, beginning September 1, 2002, and until further order of the

Supreme Court, to accept the facsimile transmission of documents in the following circumstances:

(1) The Court of Appeals shall accept the filing of the following documents by facsimile (fax) transmission:

(a) answers to motions filed under MCR 7.211(B)(2)(e);

(b) answers to pleadings that were accompanied by a motion for immediate consideration under MCR 7.211(C)(6).

(2) The Court of Appeals may expand or restrict the other types of filings accepted by fax upon notice published in its Internal Operating Procedures.

(3) Allowable fax filings will be received by the Court of Appeals at any time. However, fax filings received on weekends, designated Court of Appeals holidays, or after 4:00 p.m. Eastern Time will be considered filed on the next business day. The time of receipt will be the time the cover sheet is received by the Court of Appeals, except if less than the entire document is received through no fault of the Court of Appeals or its facsimile equipment. If less than the entire document is received through no fault of the Court of Appeals or its facsimile equipment, there is no filing.

(4) A cover sheet provided by the Court of Appeals must accompany every transmission. The following information must be included on the cover sheet:

(a) case name and Court of Appeals docket number (or applicable case names and docket numbers of cases consolidated by the Court of Appeals to which the faxed filing applies);

(b) county of case origin;

(c) title of document being filed;

(d) name, attorney P-number (if applicable), telephone number, and fax number of the attorney or party sending the fax;

(e) if fees have not already been paid, the credit card number, expiration date, and authorized signature of the cardholder;

(f) number of pages in the transmission, including the cover sheet.

(5) All fax filings must be on 8½″ × 11″ paper, in at least 12–point type. Every page must be numbered consecutively, and the background and print must contrast sufficiently to be easily readable.

(6) The fax filing shall be considered the document filed in the Court of Appeals. The attorney or party filing the document shall retain the original document, to be produced only at the request of the Court of Appeals. No further copies should be mailed to the Court of Appeals unless requested.

(7) Attachments to a filing must be labeled in the format of "Attachment X" on the lower right-hand corner of either a separate page or the first page of the attachment.

(8) All other requirements of the court rules apply to fax filings, including the signature, page limitations, filing fees, and service on other parties.

(9) A service fee shall be charged for the receipt of each fax transmission in the amount published in the Internal Operating Procedures. Fax filings in multiple Court of Appeals docket numbers must be transmitted separately under separate cover sheets unless the cases have already been consolidated by the Court of Appeals.

(10) Service fees and filing fees must be paid, or permission to charge the fees to an authorized credit card must be allowed by the filing party on the cover sheet, at the same time the fax filing is sent. A credit card transaction must be approved by the issuing financial institution before the document will be accepted as filed by the Court of Appeals.

[Adopted April 23, 2002, effective September 1, 2002, 466 Mich.]

MCR 7.211(B)(2)(e) provides that answers to certain motions must be filed 7 days after the motions are served on the other parties. A filing made in person may be served by mail. When service is accomplished through mailing, it is complete "at the time of mailing." MCR 2.107(C)(3). In Michigan, where the mail process can consume two or three days of the seven-day response time, attorneys or parties who are located at a distance from a district office of the Clerk of the Court are disadvantaged in their ability to timely answer such motions.

This administrative order, adopted April 23, 2002, effective September 1, 2002, remedies this geographical disparity by permitting all parties or attorneys to make certain filings by fax. This administrative order will apply statewide, ensuring that all rights and responsibilities under it will affect each case and each filing in the same manner. Consistent with practice in the Court of Appeals under the court rules, it is *not* anticipated that service of the faxed filings on the other parties must be by facsimile. Service may be accomplished by any means that is otherwise acceptable under the court rules.

Order 2002–3   Family Violence Indicator (Family Division of Circuit Court and Probate Court)

On order of the Court, the need for immediate action having been found, the Court adopts the following requirements for friends of the court, to be effective upon implementation of an automated child support enforcement system within the Family Independence Agency, MCL 400.231 *et seq.*, and the availability of necessary programming. The provisions of this order will be considered further by the Court at a public hearing. Notice of future public hearings will be provided by the Court and posted at the Court's website, http://www.courts.michigan.gov/supremecourt.

The friends of the court shall adhere to the following rules in managing their files and records:

(1) When the Family Violence Indicator is set in the statewide automated child support enforcement system for an individual in an action, that individual's address shall be considered confidential under MCR 3.218(A)(3)(f).

(2) Friend of the court offices shall cause a Family Violence Indicator to be set in the statewide automated child support enforcement system on all the files and records in an action involving an individual when:

(a) a personal protection order has been entered protecting that individual,

(b) the friend of the court becomes aware of an order of any Michigan court that provides for confidentiality of the individual's address, or denies access to the individual's address,

(c) an individual files a sworn statement with the office setting forth specific incidents or threats of domestic violence or child abuse, or

(d) the friend of the court becomes aware that a determination has been made in another state that a disclosure risk comparable to any of the above risk indicators exists for the individual.

(3) When the Family Violence Indicator has been set for an individual in any action, the Family Violence Indicator shall be set in all other actions within the statewide automated child support enforcement system concerning that same individual.

(4) When the Family Violence Indicator has been set for a custodial parent in any action, the Family Violence Indicator shall also be set for all minors for which the individual is a custodial parent. When the Family Violence Indicator has been set for any minor in an action, the Family Violence Indicator shall also be set for the minor's custodian.

(5) The friend of the court office shall cause the Family Violence Indicator to be removed:

(a) by order of the circuit court,

(b) at the request of the protected party, when the protected party files a sworn statement with the office that the threats of violence or child abuse no longer exist, unless a protective order or other order of any Michigan court is in effect providing for confidentiality of an individual's address, or

(c) at the request of a state that had previously determined that a disclosure risk comparable to the risks in paragraph two existed for the individual.

(6) When the Family Violence Indicator has been removed for an individual in any action, the Family Violence Indicator that was set automatically for other persons and cases associated with that individual shall also be removed.

[Adopted May 2, 2002, effective September 1, 2002, 466 Mich.]

Comments

Staff Comment to 2002 Adoption

A copy of this order will be given to the secretary of the State Bar and to the State Court Administrator. Comments on this order may be sent to the Supreme Court clerk in writing or electronically by *August 1, 2002.* Clerk, P.O. Box 30052, Lansing, MI 48909, or MSC_clerk@jud.state.mi.us. When filing a comment, please refer to File No. 2002–07.

Order 2002–4   Cases Involving Children Absent from Court-Ordered Placement without Legal Permission

In Michigan, the family division of the circuit court is entrusted with protecting the welfare of children who are under its jurisdiction. This includes thousands of victims of abuse or neglect who are placed by court order in a variety of environments, such as foster care, to ensure their safety.

Recently, there have been reports of several hundred children in Michigan who are absent from court-ordered placements without permission from the court. In some situations, the child has run away. Other times, especially in the case of younger children, there has been an abduction, often by a family member. Regardless of the reason, there can be no justification for the unauthorized disappearance from court-ordered placement of even one child.

The Legislature has given the Family Independence Agency the responsibility of supervising children who are under court jurisdiction because of abuse or neglect. Any effort to locate children who are absent from court-ordered placements thus must include both the agency and the courts. Accordingly, on order of the Court, each circuit court must develop a plan for reviewing cases involving children who are absent from court-ordered placements without permission from the court. Such plans must include the establishment of a special docket or

other expedited process for review of such cases, either through the dispositional review hearings that are required by statute and court rule in all child-protective proceedings, or through formal status conferences or emergency status reviews. In addition, the plans should:

A. identify the judge who has responsibility for ensuring compliance with the plan;

B. address the coordination of the efforts of the Family Independence Agency and the court to locate absent children;

C. describe the process for reviewing such cases;

D. address any special problems that the court has identified;

E. describe the court's procedures for obtaining information regarding the whereabouts of absent children and for promptly scheduling hearings to determine their legal status; and

F. describe the court's procedures for giving priority to cases involving children ages 15 and younger, particularly if the child may have been abducted.

Each circuit court must submit a local administrative order to the State Court Administrative Office by February 1, 2003, describing its plan for reviewing cases involving children who are absent from court-ordered placements without permission from the court.

[Adopted effective November 19, 2002, 467 Mich.]

Order 2002–5   Differentiated Case Scheduling at the Court of Appeals

The Court of Appeals is engaged in a delay-reduction initiative, with the goal of disposing of 95 percent of its cases within 18 months of filing beginning in October 2003. To assist in reaching that goal, the Supreme Court orders that the Court of Appeals may give precedence on the session calendar under Rule 7.213(C) of the Michigan Court Rules to any appeals that the Court of Appeals determines are appropriate for differentiated case management. Specifically, the Court of Appeals may schedule such cases on the session calendar as soon as the time for filing the briefs has elapsed, the record has been received, and the matter has been prepared for submission in accordance with internal procedure.

This order is effective immediately and will remain in effect until December 31, 2003, at which time the Court will decide whether to amend Rule 7.213(C) on a permanent basis, consistent with this administrative order. In the meantime, the Court will further consider this interim order at a public hearing. The schedule of future public hearings will be posted on the Court's website, www.courts.mi.gov/supremecourt. Please refer to Administrative File No. 2002–44 in any correspondence or inquiry.

[Adopted effective December 23, 2002, 467 Mich.]

Order 2003–1   Concurrent Jurisdiction

Pursuant to MCL 600.401 *et seq.*, as added by 2002 PA 678, courts may establish a plan of concurrent jurisdiction, subject to certain conditions and limitations, within a county or judicial circuit. Subject to approval by the Supreme Court, a plan of concurrent jurisdiction may be adopted by a majority vote of judges of the participating trial courts.

The plan shall provide for the assignment of cases to judges of the participating courts as necessary to implement the plan. Plans must address both judicial and administrative changes to court operations, including but not limited to the allocation of judicial resources, court governance, budget and fiscal management, personnel, record keeping, facilities, and information systems.

If a plan of concurrent jurisdiction submitted to the Supreme Court includes an agreement as to the allocation of court revenue pursuant to MCL 600.408(4), it must be accompanied by a copy of approving resolutions from each of the affected local funding units.

A plan of concurrent jurisdiction may include a family court plan filed pursuant to MCL 600.1011, as amended by 2002 PA 682, and Administrative Order 2003–2.

In developing a plan, courts shall seek the input of all the affected judges, court staff, and other persons and entities that provide court services or are affected by the court's operations. The plan must be submitted to the local funding unit for a review of the plan's financial implications at least 30 days before it is submitted to the State Court Administrative Office. The funding unit may submit a letter to the chief judges that indicates agreement with the plan or that outlines any financial concerns that should be taken into consideration before the plan is adopted. The chief judges shall submit a copy of any such letter to the State Court Administrative Office when the concurrent jurisdiction plan is filed.

A plan of concurrent jurisdiction will not take effect until at least 90 days after it is approved by the Supreme Court. Each plan shall be submitted to the Supreme Court in the format specified by the State Court Administrative Office.
[Adopted January 28, 2003, effective May 1, 2003, 467 Mich.]

Order 2003–2 Family Court Plans

Pursuant to MCL 600.1011, as amended by 2002 PA 682, the chief circuit and chief probate judges in each judicial circuit shall enter into an agreement by July 1, 2003, that establishes a plan known as the "family court plan." The plan shall describe how the family division of the circuit court will operate in that circuit and how to coordinate and promote that which the Legislature has described as "more efficient and effective services to families and individuals."

In a probate court district that includes counties that are in different judicial circuits, the chief judge of each judicial circuit that includes such a probate court district and the chief probate judge shall enter into a family court plan for that circuit.

The chief circuit and chief probate judges shall file family court plans with the State Court Administrative Office no later than July 1, 2003. Chief circuit and chief probate judges shall seek the input of all the judges of the circuit and probate courts, staff of the circuit and probate courts, and other entities that provide services to families within that jurisdiction or that will be affected by the operation of the family division.

The county clerk must be afforded the opportunity to participate in the development of plans for the management of court records. The county clerk may submit a letter to the chief judge of the circuit court indicating either concurrence or disagreement with the plan for the management of court records. The chief judge shall submit a copy of the letter to the State Court Administrative Office when the family court plan is filed. Disagreements regarding the plans for the management of court records may be resolved through mediation at the direction of the Supreme Court.

A family court plan submitted for a judicial circuit shall be approved by the State Court Administrative Office for filing or returned to the chief circuit and chief probate judges for amendment in accordance with 2002 PA 682 and guidelines provided by the State Court Administrative Office.

A family court plan shall specifically identify all circuit and probate judges serving pursuant to the plan.

Any amendment to a family court plan must be filed with the State Court Administrative Office and accepted for filing before implementation of the amended provisions.

In any circuit court in which the chief circuit and chief probate judges are unable to agree upon a family court plan by July 1, 2003, the State Court Administrative Office will develop a family court plan for that circuit, subject to approval by the Supreme Court.

Administrative Order 1997–1 is rescinded.
[Adopted January 28, 2003, effective May 1, 2003, 467 Mich.]

Order 2003–3 Appointment of Counsel for Indigent Criminal Defendants

In cases in which the defendant may lack the financial means to retain counsel and the Supreme Court is granting leave to appeal, an inquiry into the defendant's financial status may be necessary. Where the Court orders such an inquiry, it shall proceed in the manner outlined in this administrative order, effective immediately.

The defendant must file, on a form developed by the State Court Administrative Office, an affidavit concerning present financial status. The affidavit must be filed in the circuit court from which the case is being appealed. The circuit court must provide the prosecuting attorney with a copy of the defendant's affidavit within 7 days. The prosecuting attorney may challenge the defendant's asserted lack of financial means to retain counsel by filing an appropriate motion with the circuit court within 14 days after the prosecuting attorney receives the copy of the affidavit. The circuit court may question the asserted lack of financial means on its own motion. If such a motion is filed by the prosecuting attorney or if the issue is raised by the circuit court *sua sponte*, the circuit court must conduct a hearing on the matter within 21 days after the motion is filed or the issue is raised. The prosecuting attorney, the defendant, and an attorney appointed by the circuit court to represent the defendant must appear at the hearing.

If such a motion is filed or if the issue is raised by the circuit court, the circuit court must determine whether the defendant lacks the financial means to retain counsel on the basis of (1) the defendant's present assets, employment, earning capacity, and living expenses; (2) the defendant's outstanding debts and liabilities, both secured and unsecured; (3) whether the defendant has qualified for, and is receiving, any form of public assistance; (4) the availability and convertibility, without undue financial hardship to the defendant or the defendant's family, of real or personal property owned by the defendant; (5) whether the defendant is incarcerated; and (6) any other circumstances that would affect the defendant's ability to pay the fee that ordinarily would be required to retain competent counsel. If the defendant's lack of financial means appears to be temporary, the circuit court may order that the defendant repay, on appropriate terms, the expense of appointed counsel.

If, after such a challenge or question, the circuit court determines that the defendant lacks the financial means to retain counsel, the circuit court must appoint counsel or continue the appointment of previously appointed counsel within 14 days after the hearing. If there has not been such a challenge or question, the circuit court must appoint counsel or continue the appointment of previously appointed counsel within 28 days after the defendant files an affidavit concerning present financial status. The circuit court must promptly forward to the Clerk of the Supreme Court a copy of the appointment order and must promptly provide counsel with any portion of the record that counsel requires.

If the defendant does not file an affidavit concerning present financial status or if the circuit court determines that the defendant does not lack the financial means to retain counsel, the circuit court must promptly notify the Clerk of this Court.

Administrative Order No. 1972–4, 387 Mich xxx (1972), is rescinded.

[Adopted effective April 1, 2003, 468 Mich.]

Comments

Staff Comment to 2003 Adoption

Administrative Order No. 2003–03 replaces Administrative Order No. 1972–4, 387 Mich xxx (1972), and simplifies the form of order used when the Supreme Court directs the appointment of counsel. Administrative Order No. 2003–03 is not intended as a substantive or procedural change in the process for appointment of appellate counsel in the Supreme Court.

Order 2003–5   Annual Dues Notice for the State Bar of Michigan

On order of the Court, the State Bar of Michigan shall include in the annual dues notice, beginning with the notice issued for fiscal year 2003–2004, a request for information regarding the following matters:

1. Other jurisdictions in which the member is or has been licensed to practice law, and whether the member has received any discipline in those jurisdictions.

2. The malpractice insurance covering the member.

3. Felony and misdemeanor convictions in any jurisdiction after the date the member received a license to practice law in any jurisdiction.

The member shall be required to provide the requested information and to verify that, to the best of the member's knowledge, the information is accurate.

On further order of the Court, the State Bar of Michigan also shall provide in the annual dues notice, beginning with the notice issued for fiscal year 2003–2004, an opportunity for members to make voluntary tax-deductible contributions of $5 or some other amount to benefit the Michigan Supreme Court Learning Center.

[Adopted effective August 6, 2003, 469 Mich.]

Order 2003–6   Case Management at the Court of Appeals

On March 11, 2003, the Supreme Court published for comment proposed amendments of several provisions of sub-

chapter 7.200 of the Michigan Court Rules that the Court of Appeals stated would aid its effort to dispose of 95 percent of its cases within 18 months of filing, beginning in October 2003. The proposals generated considerable comment both in writing and at the public hearing held on September 25, 2003.

Those who have participated in the significant debate concerning the processing of cases in the Court of Appeals, especially the Court of Appeals itself and the State Bar of Michigan, have proceeded with integrity and ultimate concern for the efficient and effective delivery of justice to the citizens of Michigan. We commend this cooperative approach and trust that such commitment will mark a continuing effort to improve our appellate system, even in this time of budgetary crisis.

Accordingly, on order of the Court, and building on the delay-reduction measures already implemented by the Court of Appeals, we direct the Court of Appeals to develop a plan for the management of civil cases that includes "just in time" briefing. In developing a plan that is in the best interests of the administration of justice and the participants in the appellate process, we encourage the Court of Appeals to continue to work with the State Bar of Michigan and other interested groups and individuals. The plan shall be submitted to this Court by February 1, 2004.

The amended proposal submitted by the Court of Appeals on August 29, 2003, remains under consideration and can be viewed in the list of proposed rule amendments at www.courts. michigan.gov/supremecourt/Resources/Administrative/index. htm.

[Adopted effective November 4, 2003, 469 Mich.]

Order 2004–1   State Bar of Michigan Activities

Administrative Order No. 1993–5 is rescinded, effective immediately.

I. Ideological Activities Generally. The State Bar of Michigan shall not, except as provided in this order, use the dues of its members to fund activities of an ideological nature that are not reasonably related to:

(A) the regulation and discipline of attorneys;

(B) the improvement of the functioning of the courts;

(C) the availability of legal services to society;

(D) the regulation of attorney trust accounts; and

(E) the regulation of the legal profession, including the education, the ethics, the competency, and the integrity of the profession.

The State Bar of Michigan shall permanently post on its website, and annually publish in the Michigan Bar Journal, a notice advising members of these limitations on the use of dues and the State Bar budget.

II. Activities Intended to Influence Legislation.

(A) The State Bar of Michigan may use the mandatory dues of all members to review and analyze pending legislation.

(B) The State Bar of Michigan may use the mandatory dues of all members to provide content-neutral technical assistance to legislators, provided that:

(1) a legislator requests the assistance;

(2) the executive director, in consultation with the president of the State Bar of Michigan, approves the request in a

letter to the legislator stating that providing technical assistance does not imply either support for or opposition to the legislation; and

(3) the executive director of the State Bar of Michigan annually prepares and publishes in the Michigan Bar Journal a report summarizing all technical assistance provided during the preceding year.

(C) No other activities intended to influence legislation may be funded with members' mandatory dues, unless the legislation in question is limited to matters within the scope of the ideological-activities requirements in Section I.

(D) Neither the State Bar of Michigan nor any person acting as its representative shall take any action to support or oppose legislation unless the position has been approved by a two-thirds vote of the Board of Commissioners or Representative Assembly taken after all members were advised, by notice posted on the State Bar website at least 2 weeks prior to the Board or Assembly meeting, that the proposed legislation might be discussed at the meeting. The posted notice shall include a brief summary of the legislation, a link to the text and status of the pending legislation on the Michigan Legislature website, and a statement that members may express their opinion to the State Bar of Michigan at the meeting, electronically, or by written or telephonic communication. The webpage on which the notice is posted shall provide an opportunity for members to respond electronically, and the comments of members who wish to have their comments made public shall be accessible on the same webpage.

(E) The results of all Board and Assembly votes on proposals to support or oppose legislation shall be posted on the State Bar website as soon as possible after the vote, and published in the next Michigan Bar Journal. When either body adopts a position on proposed legislation by a less-than-unanimous vote, a roll call vote shall be taken, and each commissioner's or assembly-person's vote shall be included in the published notice.

(F) Those sections of the State Bar of Michigan that are funded by the voluntary dues of their members are not subject to this order, and may engage in ideological activities on their own behalf. Whenever a section engages in ideological activities, it must include on the first page of each submission, before the text begins and in print larger than the statement's text, a disclosure indicating

(1) that the section is not the State Bar of Michigan but rather a section whose membership is voluntary,

(2) that the position expressed is that of the section only, and that the State Bar has no position on the matter, or, if the State Bar has a position on the matter, what that position is,

(3) the total membership of the section,

(4) the process used by the section to take an ideological position,

(5) the number of members in the decision- making body, and

(6) the number who voted in favor and opposed to the position.

If an ideological communication is made orally, the same information must be effectively communicated to the audience receiving the communication.

Although the bylaws of the State Bar of Michigan may not generally prohibit sections from engaging in ideological activity, for a violation of this Administrative Order or the State Bar of Michigan's bylaws, the State Bar of Michigan may revoke the authority of a section to engage in ideological activities, or to use State Bar facilities or personnel in any fashion, by a majority vote of the Board of Commissioners. If the Board determines a violation occurred, the section shall, at a minimum, withdraw its submission and communicate the withdrawal in the same manner as the original communication occurred to the extent possible. The communication shall be at the section's own cost and shall acknowledge that the position was unauthorized.

III. Challenges Regarding State Bar Activities.

(A) A member who claims that the State Bar of Michigan is funding ideological activity in violation of this order may file a challenge by giving written notice, by e-mail or regular mail, to the executive director.

(1) A challenge involving legislative advocacy must be filed with the State Bar by e-mail or regular mail within 60 days of the posting of notice of adoption of the challenged position on the State Bar of Michigan website; a challenge sent by regular mail must be postmarked on or before the last day of the month following the month in which notice of adoption of that legislative position is published in the Michigan Bar Journal pursuant to section II(E).

(2) A challenge involving ideological activity appearing in the annual budget of the State Bar of Michigan must be postmarked or e-mailed on or before October 20 following the publication of the budget funding the challenged activity.

(3) A challenge involving any other ideological activity must be postmarked or e-mailed on or before the last day of the month following the month in which disclosure of that ideological activity is published in the Michigan Bar Journal.

Failure to challenge within the time allotted shall constitute a waiver.

(B) After a written challenge has been received, the executive director shall place the item on the agenda of the next meeting of the Board of Commissioners, and shall make a report and recommendation to the Board concerning disposition of the challenge. In considering the challenge, the Board shall direct the executive director to take one or more of the following actions:

(1) dismiss the challenge, with explanation;

(2) discontinue the challenged activity;

(3) revoke the challenged position, and publicize the revocation in the same manner and to the same extent as the position was communicated;

(4) arrange for reimbursement to the challenger of a pro rata share of the cost of the challenged activity; and

(5) arrange for reimbursement of all members requesting a pro rata share of the cost of the challenged activity in the next dues billing.

(C) A challenger or the State Bar of Michigan may seek review by this Court as to whether the challenged activity violates the limitations on State Bar ideological activities set forth in this order, and as to the appropriate remedy for a violation.

(D) A summary of the challenges filed under this section during a legislative term and their disposition shall be posted on the State Bar's website.

IV. Other State Bar Activities. The State Bar of Michigan shall:

(A) annually publish in the Michigan Bar Journal a notice informing members that, upon request, their names will be removed from the mailing list that is used for commercial mailings, and

(B) annually publish in the Michigan Bar Journal a notice informing members of the Young Lawyers Section that, upon request, their membership in that section will be terminated.

[Adopted effective February 3, 2004.]

Comments

Staff Comment to 2004 Adoption

The February 3, 2004, amendment of Section I and the related changes in Section II are designed to ensure a higher degree of confidence that State Bar positions reflect consensus among the membership and to ensure the vitality of the Bar's mechanisms for soliciting, understanding, and representing the views of its members.

The changes in Section II(B)(2) and (3) are housekeeping measures that transfer the authority for approval of legislators' requests for technical assistance from the president of the State Bar to the executive director, in consultation with the president, and that gives the executive director sole authority over the publication responsibility.

The changes to Section II are designed to make the procedures for member challenges to State Bar advocacy more practical and effective. The State Bar has identified two problems with the current exception for the ideological activities of State Bar sections: a section viewpoint may not be reflective of the views of a segment of the profession, and the section may be communicating its views in such a way that they are mistakenly perceived to be the views of the Bar as a whole. Subsection (F) is intended to reinforce the requirements of the current bylaws and to pave the way toward correction of these problems.

The amendment of Section IV is a housekeeping measure that eliminates the funding provision for the Lawyers Auxiliary Law Day program, which does not fit with the other issues in the order. Law Day activities are not of an ideological nature, but are educational and designed to introduce students to the court system and to encourage greater public understanding of the legal system.

Order 2004–2 Approval of the Adoption of Concurrent Jurisdiction Plans for Barry, Berrien, Isabella, Lake, and Washtenaw Counties, and for the 46th Circuit Consisting of Crawford, Kalkaska, and Otsego Counties

Administrative Order No. 2003–1 and MCL 600.401 *et seq.* authorize Michigan trial courts to adopt concurrent jurisdiction plans within a county or judicial circuit, subject to approval of the Court.

The Court hereby approves adoption of concurrent jurisdiction plans for the following trial courts effective August 1, 2004:

BARRY COUNTY
5th Circuit Court
56B District Court
Barry County Probate Court
BERRIEN COUNTY
2nd Circuit Court
5th District Court
Berrien County Probate Court
ISABELLA COUNTY
21st Circuit Court
76th District Court
Isabella County Probate Court

LAKE COUNTY
51st Circuit Court
79th District Court
Lake County Probate Court
WASHTENAW COUNTY
22nd Circuit Court
14A, 14B, & 15th District Courts
Washtenaw County Probate Court
CRAWFORD, KALKASKA, AND OTSEGO COUNTIES
46th Circuit Court
87th District Court
Crawford County Probate Court
Kalkaska County Probate Court
Otsego County Probate Court

The plans shall remain on file with the state court administrator.

Amendments to concurrent jurisdiction plans may be implemented by local administrative order pursuant to MCR 8.112. Plan amendments shall conform to the requirements of Administrative Order No. 2003–1 and MCL 600.401 *et seq.*

The Court also rescinds Administrative Order Nos. 1993–3, 1996–1, 1996–2, 1996–5, 1996–6, 1996–7, 1996–9, and 1997–12, effective August 1, 2004.

[Adopted April 28, 2004, effective August 1, 2004, 470 Mich.]

Order 2004–4 Adoption of Concurrent Jurisdiction Plans for Genesee and Van Buren Counties

Administrative Order No. 2003–1 and MCL 600.401 *et seq.* authorize Michigan trial courts to adopt concurrent jurisdiction plans within a county or judicial circuit, subject to approval of the Court.

The Court hereby approves adoption of concurrent jurisdiction plans for the following trial courts effective October 1, 2004:

GENESEE COUNTY
7th Circuit Court
Genesee County Probate Court
67th District Court
68th District Court
VAN BUREN COUNTY
36th Circuit Court
Van Buren County Probate Court
7th District Court

The plans shall remain on file with the State Court Administrator.

Amendments to concurrent jurisdiction plans may be implemented by local administrative order pursuant to MCR 8.112. Plan amendments shall conform to the requirements of Administrative Order No. 2003–1 and MCL 600.401 *et seq.*

[Adopted June 22, 2004, effective October 1, 2004, 470 Mich. Amended effective September 16, 2015, 498 Mich.]

Order 2004–5 Expedited Summary Disposition Docket in the Court of Appeals [Original]

On order of the Court, notice of the proposed expedited docket and an opportunity for comment in writing and at a public hearing having been provided, and consideration having been given to the comments received, the following proposal is adopted for a two-year period, effective January 1, 2005.

1. Applicability. This administrative order applies to appeals filed on or after January 1, 2005, arising solely from orders granting or denying motions for summary disposition under MCR 2.116. These appeals are to be placed on an expedited appeal track under which they shall generally be briefed, argued, and disposed of within six months of filing. A motion to remove is required to divert such appeals to the standard appeal track.

2. Time Requirements. Appeals by right or by leave in cases covered by this order must be taken within the time stated in MCR 7.204 or MCR 7.205. Claims of cross-appeal must be filed within 14 days after the claim of appeal is filed with the Court of Appeals or served on the cross-appellant, whichever is later, or within 14 days after the clerk certifies the order granting leave to appeal.

3. Trial Court Orders on Motions for Summary Disposition. If the trial court concludes that summary disposition is warranted under MCR 2.116(C), the court shall render judgment without delay in an order that specifies the subsection of MCR 2.116(C) under which the judgment is entered.

4. Claim of Appeal—Form of Filing. With the following exceptions, a claim of appeal filed under this order shall conform in all respects with the requirements of MCR 7.204.

(A) A docketing statement will not be required as long as the case proceeds on the summary disposition track.

(B) When the claim of appeal is filed, it shall be accompanied by:

(1) evidence that the transcript of the hearing(s) on the motion for summary disposition has been ordered, or

(2) a statement that there is no record to transcribe, or

(3) a statement that the transcript has been waived.

Failure to file one of the above three documents with the claim of appeal will *not* toll subsequent filing deadlines for transcripts or briefs. Sustained failure to provide the required documentation may result in dismissal of the appeal under MCR 7.201(B)(3), as long as the Court of Appeals provides a minimum 7–day warning.

5. Application for Leave—Form of Filing. An application for leave to appeal filed under this administrative order shall conform in all pertinent respects with the requirements of MCR 7.205.

6. Claim of Cross–Appeal. A claim of cross-appeal filed under this administrative order shall conform in all pertinent respects with the requirements of MCR 7.207.

7. Removal from Summary Disposition Track. A party may file a motion to remove the case from the summary disposition track to the standard track.

(A) *Time to File.* Motions to remove by the appellant or the cross-appellant must be filed with the claim of appeal or claim of cross-appeal, respectively, or within 7 days after the date of certification of an order granting application for leave to appeal. Motions to remove by the appellee or cross-appellee must be filed no later than the time for filing of the appellee's brief.

(B) *Form.* Motions to remove shall concisely state the basis for removal, and must be in the form prescribed by the Court of Appeals. This form shall include a statement advising whether the appellee is expected to oppose the motion.

(C) *Answer.* An answer to a motion to remove must be filed within 7 days after service of the motion. The answer should state whether the appellee is expected to file a claim of cross-appeal.

(D) *Disposition.* Within 14 days after the filing of the motion to remove, the Court of Appeals shall issue an order disposing of the motion and setting the time for further filings in the case. The time for further filings in the case will commence on the date of certification of the order on the motion.

(E) *Docketing Statement.* If the case is removed from the summary disposition track, a docketing statement must be filed within 14 days after the date of certification of the order on the motion.

(F) The Court of Appeals may remove a case from the summary disposition track at any time, on its own motion, if it appears to the Court that the case is not an appropriate candidate for processing under this administrative order.

(G) *Effect of Removal.* If the Court of Appeals removes a case from the summary disposition track, the parties are entitled to file briefs in accordance with the time and page limitations set forth in MCR 7.212. The time for filing the briefs commences from the date of certification of the order removing the case from the summary disposition docket.

8. Transcript—Production for Purposes of Appeal.

(A) *Appellant.*

(1) The appellant may waive the transcript. See section 4(B)(3) above.

(2) If the appellant desires the transcript for the appeal, the appellant must order the transcript before or contemporaneously with the filing of the claim of appeal.

(3) If the transcript is not timely filed, the appellant must file one of the following motions with the Court of Appeals within 7 days after the transcript is due:

(a) a motion for an order for the court reporter or recorder to show cause, or

(b) a motion to extend time to file the transcript.

(4) The time for filing the appellant's brief will be tolled by the timely filing of one of the above motions. The order disposing of such motion shall state the time for filing the appellant's brief.

(5) If the ordered transcript is not timely filed, and if the appellant fails to file either of the above motions within the time prescribed, the time for filing the brief will commence on the date the transcript was due. In such event, the appellant's brief shall be filed within 56 days after the claim of appeal was filed or 28 days after certification of the order granting leave to appeal.

(B) *Appellee.*

(1) The appellee may order the transcript within 14 days after service of the claim of appeal and notice that the appellant has waived the transcript.

(2) The appellee's transcript order will not affect the time for filing the appellant's brief.

(3) If the transcript is not timely filed, the appellee must file one of the following motions with the Court of Appeals within 7 days after the transcript is due:

(a) a motion for an order for the court reporter or recorder to show cause, or

(b) a motion to extend the time to file the transcript.

(4) The time for filing the appellee's brief will be tolled by the timely filing of one of the above motions. The order disposing of such motion shall state the time for filing the appellee's brief.

(5) If the ordered transcript is not timely filed, and if the appellee fails to file either of the above motions within the time prescribed, the time for filing the brief will commence on the date the transcript was due.

(C) *Court Reporter.* The court reporter or recorder shall file the transcript with the trial court or tribunal within 28 days after it is ordered by either the appellant or the appellee. The court reporter or recorder shall conform in all other respects with the requirements of MCR 7.210.

(D) *Transcript Fee.* The court reporter or recorder shall be entitled to the sum of $3.00 per original page and 50 cents per page for each copy for transcripts ordered and timely filed in appeals processed under the expedited docket. If the court reporter or recorder does not timely file the transcript, the rate will remain $1.75 per original page and 30 cents per page for each transcript, as set by MCL 600.2543.

9. Briefs on Appeal.

(A) With the following exceptions, the parties' briefs shall conform to the requirements of MCR 7.212.

(B) *Time For Filing.*

(1) The appellant's brief shall be filed within 28 days after the claim of appeal is filed, the order granting leave is certified, or the timely ordered transcript is timely filed with the trial court, whichever is later, or as ordered by the Court. In appeals by leave, the appellant may rely on the application for leave to appeal rather than filing a separate brief by filing 5 copies of the application for leave to appeal with a cover letter indicating that the appellant is relying on the application in lieu of filing a brief on appeal.

(2) The appellee's brief shall be filed within 21 days after the appellant's brief is served on the appellee, or as ordered by the Court.

(3) Time for filing any party's brief may be extended for 14 days on motion for good cause shown. If the motion is filed by the appellant within the original 28–day brief filing period, the motion will toll the time for any sanctions for untimely briefs. A motion may include a statement from opposing counsel that counsel does not oppose the 14–day extension. A motion to extend the time for filing a brief will be submitted for disposition forthwith; opposing counsel need not file an answer.

(4) If the appellant's brief is not filed within 7 days after the date due, the Court of Appeals shall issue an order assessing costs and warning the appellant that the case will be dismissed if the brief is not filed within 14 days after the deadline. If the brief is not filed within that 14–day period, the Court of Appeals shall issue an order that dismisses the appeal and that may assess additional costs.

(C) *Length and Form.* Briefs filed under this administrative order are limited to 35 pages, double-spaced, exclusive of tables, indexes, and appendices.

(1) At the time each brief is filed, the filing party must provide the Court of Appeals with that party's trial court summary disposition motion or response, brief, and appendices. Failure to file these documents at the time of filing the appellant's brief will not extend the time to file the appellee's brief, however.

(2) The appellant may wish to include a copy of the transcript (if any) if it was completed after the lower court file was transmitted to the Court of Appeals.

(D) Reply briefs may be filed within 14 days of the filing of appellee's brief and are limited to 5 pages, double-spaced, exclusive of tables, indexes, and appendices.

10. Record on Appeal.
The Court of Appeals shall request the record on appeal from the trial court or tribunal clerk as soon as jurisdiction has been confirmed and material filing deficiencies have been corrected. The trial court or tribunal clerk shall transmit the record as directed in MCR 7.210(G).

11. Notice of Cases.
Within 7 days after the filing of the appellee's brief, or after the expiration of the time for filing the appellee's brief, the clerk shall notify the parties that the case will be submitted as a "calendar case" on the summary disposition track.

12. Decision of the Court.
The opinion or order of the panel shall be issued no later than 35 days after submission of the case to, or oral argument before, a panel of judges for final disposition.

This order will remain in effect for two years from the date of its implementation, during which time the Court of Appeals Delay Reduction Work Group will monitor the expedited docket program. If, at any time during that monitoring process, it becomes apparent to the work group that procedural aspects of the program need to be modified, the group is encouraged to seek authorization from this Court to implement modifications. The work group will provide this Court with written updates on the pilot program before the one-year and eighteen-month anniversaries of the program's implementation. At the end of the two-year pilot period, this Court will evaluate expedited processing of summary disposition appeals to determine whether the procedure will be discontinued, changed, or continued.
[Adopted October 5, 2004, effective January 1, 2005, 471 Mich.]

For text of Administrative Order as amended by the December 21, 2005, see Administrative Order No. 2004-5 (A1)

For text of Administrative Order as amended by the November 9, 2006, see Administrative Order No. 2004-5 (A2)

Comments

Staff Comment to 2005 Adoption

This is a new procedure requested by the Court of Appeals for the processing of appeals from orders granting or denying summary disposition. The new procedure applies to appeals filed after January 1, 2005. The procedure will be in effect for a two-year pilot period with ongoing monitoring by the delay reduction work group. That group will provide updates to the Court before the one-year and eighteen-month anniversaries of the pilot period. The group is authorized, during the two-year pilot period, to seek from the Court modification of the expedited docket procedures.

The transcript rate is authorized by statute. 2004 PA 328.

The Court of Appeals offered the following explanation of the expedited docket procedure:

The Court of Appeals estimates that summary disposition appeals make up about 50% of the Court's nonpriority civil cases. The procedure proposed by the Court's Case Management Work Group and announced in this administrative order is structured to facilitate disposition of eligible appeals within about 180 days after filing with the Court of Appeals. The work group's report can be accessed on the Court of Appeals website at http://courtofappeals.mijud.net/resources/specialproj.htm.

The procedure announced here is intended to apply to appeals arising solely from orders on motions for summary disposition. Orders that reference other issues between the parties will not be eligible for this track. If an eligible appeal is deemed to be inappropriate for the expedited docket, the Court can remove it, either on its own motion or on motion of one or both of the parties. Such motions must be in the form prescribed by the Court of Appeals. See http://courtofappeals.mijud.net/resources/forms.htm

The procedure encourages parties to evaluate whether a transcript of hearing(s) on the motion would be helpful on appeal. If little was stated on the record, or there is nothing to be gained from the transcript, it can be waived. In such cases, the appellant's brief (accompanied by the appellant's trial court motion, brief, and appendices) will be due within 28 days after filing the claim of appeal or entry of an order granting leave to appeal. If the transcript is ordered, it will be due within 28 days, with the appellant's brief due 28 days later. The appellee's brief (accompanied by its trial court motion, brief, and appendices) will be due 21 days from service of the appellant's brief. Motions to extend the time for filing briefs will be granted only on good cause shown and, generally, only for a maximum of 14 days. As a general matter, good cause will be limited to unexpected events that directly affect the ability to timely file the brief. When the motion is premised on work load considerations, at a minimum the completed, the case will be referred to the Court's research attorneys for an expedited review and it will then be submitted to a panel of judges for disposition.

Order 2004–5 (A1) Expedited Summary Disposition Docket in the Court of Appeals [Amendment]

For the indefinite suspension of the expedited summary disposition docket, see Administrative Order 2007–2.

Text of Administrative Order 2004-5 as amended by the December 21, 2005, order

Pursuant to Administrative Order No. 2004–5, this Court adopted an expedited summary disposition docket in the Court of Appeals to take effect on January 1, 2005, and to expire on December 31, 2006. We now order that the expedited summary disposition docket continue in effect, as modified *infra*, for a twelve–month period.

1. Applicability. This amended administrative order applies to appeals filed on or after January 1, 2006, arising solely from orders granting or denying motions for summary disposition under MCR 2.116. These appeals are to be placed on an expedited appeal track under which they shall generally be briefed, argued, and disposed of within six months of filing. A motion to remove is required to divert such appeals to the standard appeal track.

2. Time Requirements. Appeals by right or by leave in cases covered by this order must be taken within the time stated in MCR 7.204 or MCR 7.205. Claims of cross-appeal must be filed within 14 days after the claim of appeal is filed with the Court of Appeals or served on the cross-appellant, whichever is later, or within 14 days after the clerk certifies the order granting leave to appeal.

3. Trial Court Orders on Motions for Summary Disposition. If the trial court concludes that summary disposition is warranted under MCR 2.116(C), the court shall render judgment without delay in an order that specifies the subsection of MCR 2.116(C) under which the judgment is entered.

4. Claim of Appeal—Form of Filing. With the following exceptions, a claim of appeal filed under this order shall conform in all respects with the requirements of MCR 7.204.

(A) A docketing statement will not be required as long as the case proceeds on the summary disposition track.

(B) When the claim of appeal is filed, it shall be accompanied by:

(1) evidence that the transcript of the hearing(s) on the motion for summary disposition has been ordered, or

(2) a statement that there is no record to transcribe, or

(3) the stipulation of the parties that the transcript has been waived.

Failure to file one of the above three documents with the claim of appeal will *not* toll subsequent filing deadlines for transcripts or briefs. Sustained failure to provide the required documentation may result in dismissal of the appeal under MCR 7.201(B)(3), as long as the Court of Appeals provides a minimum 7–day warning.

5. Application for Leave—Form of Filing. An application for leave to appeal, or an answer to an application for leave to appeal, filed under this administrative order shall conform in all pertinent respects with the requirements of MCR 7.205. At the time an application or an answer is filed, the filing party must provide the Court of Appeals with 5 copies of that party's trial court summary disposition motion or response, brief, and appendices.

6. Claim of Cross–Appeal. Subject to the filing deadline contained in section 2, a claim of cross-appeal filed under this administrative order shall conform in all other pertinent respects with the requirements of MCR 7.207.

7. Removal from Summary Disposition Track. A party may file a motion to remove the case from the summary disposition track to the standard track.

(A) *Time to File.* A motion to remove may be filed by any party at any time. However, filing of the motion most closely in time to discovery of the basis for removal will maximize the likelihood that the motion will be granted.

(B) *Form.* Motions to remove shall concisely state the basis for removal, and must be in the form prescribed by the Court of Appeals. This form shall include a statement advising whether the appellee is expected to oppose the motion.

(C) *Answer.* An answer to a motion to remove must be filed within 7 days after service of the motion. If applicable, the answer should state whether the appellee is expected to file a claim of cross-appeal.

(D) *Disposition.* Within 14 days after the filing of the motion to remove, the Court of Appeals shall issue an order disposing of the motion and setting the time for further filings in the case. The time for further filings in the case will commence on the date of certification of the order on the motion.

(E) *Docketing Statement.* If the case is removed from the summary disposition track, a docketing statement must be filed within 14 days after the date of certification of the order on the motion.

(F) *Administrative Removal.* The Court of Appeals may remove a case from the summary disposition track at any time, on its own motion, if it appears to the Court that the case is not an appropriate candidate for processing under this administrative order.

(G) *Effect of Removal.* If the Court of Appeals removes a case from the summary disposition track, the order shall state whether, and the deadlines by which, the parties are entitled to file briefs in accordance with the time and page limitations set forth in MCR 7.212.

8. Transcript—Production for Purposes of Appeal.

(A) *Appellant.*

(1) The appellant must order the transcript of the hearing(s) on the motion for summary disposition before or contemporaneously with the filing of the claim of appeal or application for leave to appeal, unless there is no record to transcribe or all parties to the appeal stipulate that the transcript is unnecessary.

(2) Evidence that the transcript was ordered must be filed with the claim of appeal or application for leave to appeal. Appropriate evidence of the ordering includes (but is not limited to) the following:

(a) a letter to the specific court reporter requesting the specific hearing dates and enclosing any required deposit; or

(b) an "Appeal Transcript, Demand, Order and Acknowledgment" form, or

(c) a Court reporter or recorder's certificate.

(3) If the transcript is not timely filed, the appellant or an appellee may file an appropriate motion with the Court of Appeals at any time. Avoiding undue delay in filing the motion under the circumstances of the case, and concisely stating the specific basis for it, will maximize the likelihood that the motion will be granted.

(4) If an appropriate motion is filed, the order disposing of such motion shall state the time for filing any outstanding brief(s).

(5) Absent an order of the Court of Appeals that resets the time, and regardless of whether the ordered transcript is timely filed, the time for filing the appellant's brief will commence on the date the claim of appeal was filed or the order granting leave was certified. In such event, the appellant's brief shall be filed within 56 days after the claim of appeal was filed or 28 days after certification of the order granting leave to appeal. See section 9(B)(1).

(B) *Appellee.*

(1) If the transcript has been ordered by the appellant but is not filed by the time the appellant's brief is served on an appellee, the appellee may file an appropriate motion with the Court of Appeals. Avoiding undue delay in filing the motion under the circumstances of the case, and concisely stating the specific basis for it, will maximize the likelihood that the motion will be granted.

(2) If an appropriate motion is filed, the order shall state the time for filing any outstanding appellee briefs.

(C) *Court Reporter.* The court reporter or recorder shall file the transcript with the trial court or tribunal within 28 days after it is ordered by either the appellant or the appellee. The court reporter or recorder shall conform in all other respects with the requirements of MCR 7.210.

(D) *Transcript Fee.* The court reporter or recorder shall be entitled to the sum of $3.00 per original page and 50 cents per page for each copy for transcripts ordered in appeals processed under the expedited docket, if the transcript is filed within 28 days after it was ordered. If the court reporter or recorder does not file the transcript within 28 days after it was ordered, the rate will remain $1.75 per original page and 30 cents per page for each transcript, as set by MCL 600.2543.

9. Briefs on Appeal.

(A) With the following exceptions, the parties' briefs shall conform to the requirements of MCR 7.212.

(B) *Time For Filing.*

(1) In appeals by right, the appellant's brief shall be filed within 56 days after the claim of appeal is filed, or as ordered by the Court. In appeals by leave, the appellant's brief shall be filed within 28 days after the order granting leave is certified, or as ordered by the Court. In appeals by leave, the appellant may rely on the application for leave to appeal rather than filing a separate brief by timely filing 5 copies of the application for leave to appeal with a new cover page indicating that the appellant is relying on the application in lieu of filing a brief on appeal. The cover page should indicate whether oral argument is requested or is not requested. MCR 7.212(C)(1).

(2) The appellee's brief shall be filed within 28 days after the appellant's brief is served on the appellee, or as ordered by the Court. In appeals by leave, the appellee may rely on the answer to the application for leave to appeal rather than filing a separate brief by timely filing 5 copies of the answer to the application for leave to appeal with a new cover page indicating that the appellee is relying on the answer to the application in lieu of filing a brief on appeal. The cover page should indicate whether oral argument is requested or is not requested. MCR 7.212(C)(1) and (D)(1).

(3) Time for filing any party's brief may be extended for 14 days on motion for good cause shown, filed within the original brief-filing period. If the motion is filed by the appellant within the original brief-filing period, the motion will toll the time for any sanctions for untimely briefs. A motion may include a statement from opposing counsel that counsel does not oppose the 14–day extension. A motion to extend the time for filing a brief will be submitted for disposition forthwith; opposing counsel need not file an answer.

(4) If the appellant's brief is not filed within 7 days after the date due, the Court of Appeals shall issue an order assessing costs and warning the appellant that the case will be dismissed if the brief is not filed within 14 days after the deadline. If the brief is not filed within that 14–day period, the Court of Appeals shall issue an order that dismisses the appeal and that may assess additional costs.

(C) *Length and Form.* Briefs filed under this administrative order are limited to 35 pages, double-spaced, exclusive of tables, indexes, and appendices. At the time each brief is filed, the filing party must provide the Court of Appeals with that party's trial court summary disposition motion or response, brief, and appendices. Failure to file these documents at the time of filing the appellant's brief will not extend the time to file the appellee's brief, however. Provided such omission is noted appropriately in the appellee's brief, the appellee may omit these appendices if they were included with the appellant's brief.

(D) A reply brief may be filed within 14 days after the appellee's brief is served on the appellant, and is limited to 5 pages, double-spaced, exclusive of tables, indexes, and appendices.

10. Record on Appeal. The Court of Appeals shall request the record on appeal from the trial court or tribunal clerk 28 days after jurisdiction has been confirmed and material filing deficiencies have been corrected. The trial court or tribunal clerk shall transmit the record as directed in MCR 7.210(G).

11. Notice of Cases. Within 7 days after the filing of the appellee's brief, or after the expiration of the time for filing the appellee's brief, the clerk shall notify the parties that the case will be submitted as a "calendar case" on the summary disposition track.

12. Decision of the Court. The opinion or order of the panel shall be issued no later than 35 days after submission of the case to, or oral argument before, a panel of judges for final disposition.

This amended order will remain in effect until December 31, 2006, during which time the Court of Appeals Work Group will monitor the expedited docket program. If, at any time during that monitoring process, it becomes apparent to the work group that procedural aspects of the program need to be modified, the group is encouraged to seek authorization from this Court to implement modifications. The work group will provide this Court with written updates on the pilot program before the one-year and eighteen-month anniversaries of the program's implementation. At the end of the two-year pilot period, this Court will evaluate expedited processing of summary disposition appeals to determine whether the procedure will be discontinued, changed, or continued.

[Adopted October 5, 2004, effective January 1, 2005, 471 Mich. Amended effective December 21, 2005, 474 Mich.]

For text of Administrative Order prior to the December 21, 2005, see Administrative Order 2004-5.

For text of Administrative Order as amended by the November 9, 2006, see Administrative Order No. 2004-5 (A2).

Comments

Staff Comment to 2005 Amendment

The amendments require an appellant to order the transcripts or the preparation of transcripts may be waived by stipulation. Evidence of ordering the transcripts must be filed with the claim of appeal or application for leave to appeal. Provisions also are added to allow appropriate motions if ordered transcripts are not timely filed. If the transcript was not filed by the time the appellant's brief was served on multiple appellees, only one appellee needs to file an appropriate motion. The order on the motion will state the deadline for filing *any* outstanding briefs.

The amendments identify the trial court documents that must be appended to applications for leave to appeal and answers filed in response.

A party may file a motion to remove a case from the expedited summary disposition docket at any time, not just within a narrow time period. The amendments require the order of removal to state whether, and the deadlines by which, parties may file standard briefs.

The amendments provide that an appellant's brief will be due in 56 days from the claim of appeal or 28 days from the order granting leave to appeal. An appellee's brief will be due in 28 days from service of the appellant's brief.

The amendments allow an appellee to omit appendices if the documents were appended to the appellant's brief.

The amendments delete many filing deadlines for motion practice under the rule. Instead, pertinent provisions indicate that filing a motion most closely in time to discovery of the basis for it will maximize the likelihood that it will be granted.

Order 2004–5 (A2)   Expedited Summary Disposition Docket in the Court of Appeals [Second Amendment]

For the indefinite suspension of the expedited summary disposition docket, see Administrative Order 2007–2.

Text of Administrative Order 2004-5 as amended by the November 9, 2006, order

Pursuant to Administrative Order No. 2004–5, this Court adopted an expedited summary disposition docket in the Court of Appeals to take effect on January 1, 2005, and to expire on December 31, 2006. On December 21, 2005, Amended Administrative Order No. 2004–5 was adopted to take effect January 1, 2006. We now order that the expedited summary disposition docket continue in effect, as modified *infra*, for an additional one-year period to expire December 31, 2007.

Although the Court of Appeals has failed to meet the stated objectives for this pilot program during its existence, the Court is persuaded to approve the extension of the expedited summary disposition docket because the Court of Appeals Work Group (which consists of members of the Court of Appeals, Court of Appeals staff members, and members of the Appellate Practice Section) unanimously recommended the extension in anticipation that the newest recommended changes will permit the program to meet its goals. The Court of Appeals and members of the bar should not presume that this extension in any way signals the Court's intention to eventually make the program permanent, particularly if it does not meet its intended goal of reducing appellate delay in the Court of Appeals during this additional year of experimentation.

1. Applicability. This amended administrative order applies to appeals filed on or after January 1, 2007, arising solely from orders granting or denying motions for summary disposition under MCR 2.116. Unless otherwise removed by order of the Court of Appeals, these appeals shall be placed on an expedited appeal track under which they shall generally be briefed, argued, and disposed of within six months of filing. A motion to remove is required for a party to divert such appeals to the standard appeal track.

2. Time Requirements. Appeals by right or by leave in cases covered by this second amended order must be taken within the time stated in MCR 7.204 or MCR 7.205. Claims of cross-appeal must be filed within the time stated in MCR 7.207.

3. Trial Court Orders on Motions for Summary Disposition. If the trial court concludes that summary disposition is warranted under MCR 2.116(C), the court shall render judgment without delay in an order that specifies the subsection of MCR 2.116(C) under which the judgment is entered.

4. Claim of Appeal—Form of Filing. With the following exceptions, a claim of appeal filed under this order shall conform in all respects with the requirements of MCR 7.204.

(A) A docketing statement is not required unless the case is removed by order before the filing of the appellant's brief.

(B) When the claim of appeal is filed, it shall be accompanied by:

(1) evidence that the transcript of the hearing(s) on the motion for summary disposition has been ordered, or

(2) a statement that there is no record to transcribe, or

(3) the stipulation of the parties that the transcript has been waived.

Failure to file one of the above three documents with the claim of appeal will *not* toll subsequent filing deadlines for transcripts or briefs. Sustained failure to provide the required documentation may result in dismissal of the appeal under MCR 7.201(B)(3), as long as the Court of Appeals provides a minimum 7–day warning.

5. Application for Leave—Form of Filing. An application for leave to appeal, or an answer to an application for leave to appeal, filed under this second amended administrative order shall conform in all pertinent respects with the requirements of MCR 7.205. At the time an application or an answer is filed, the filing party must provide the Court of Appeals with 5 copies of that party's trial court summary disposition motion or response, brief, and appendices.

6. Claim of Cross–Appeal. A claim of cross-appeal filed under this second amended administrative order shall conform in all pertinent respects with the requirements of MCR 7.207. Upon the filing of a claim of cross-appeal in an appeal proceeding on the summary disposition track, the Court will remove the case from the track as provided in section 7, if it determines that the case is no longer appropriate for the track.

7. Removal from Summary Disposition Track. A party may file a motion, or the Court may act sua sponte, to remove a case from the summary disposition track to the standard track.

(A) *Time to File.* A motion to remove may be filed by any party at any time.

(B) *Form.* Motions to remove shall concisely state the basis for removal, and must be in the form prescribed by the Court of Appeals. Factors that weigh in favor of removal include:

(1) the length of one or more briefs exceeds 25 pages; removal of the case from the summary disposition track becomes more likely as the briefs approach the 35–page limit under section 9(C),

(2) the lower court record consists of more than 3 moderately sized files and more than 100 pages of transcripts from the relevant hearing(s) and deposition(s),

(3) there are more than four issues to be decided, and

(4) one or more of the issues are matters of first impression, including the first interpretation of a statute, or are factually or legally complex.

(C) *Fee.* No fee is required for a motion to remove from the summary disposition track.

(D) *Answer.* An answer to a motion to remove must be filed within 7 days after service of the motion.

(E) *Disposition.* Motions to remove shall be liberally granted. Within 14 days after the filing of the motion to remove, the Court of Appeals shall issue an order disposing of the motion and setting the time for further filings, if any, in the case. The time for further filings in the case will commence on the date of certification of the order on the motion.

(F) *Docketing Statement.* If the case is removed from the summary disposition track before the filing of the appellant's brief, a docketing statement must be filed within 14 days after the date of certification of the order on the motion.

(G) *Administrative Removal.* The Court of Appeals will remove a case from the summary disposition track, on its own motion, if it appears to the Court that the case is not an appropriate candidate for processing under this second amended administrative order. Such administrative removal may be made at any time, even after the parties' briefs are filed.

(H) *Effect of Removal.* If the Court of Appeals removes a case from the summary disposition track before the filing of the appellant's brief, the parties are entitled to file briefs in accordance with the time requirements and page limitations set forth in MCR 7.212. New or supplemental briefs shall not be permitted in cases removed from the summary disposition track after the filing of the parties' briefs except upon motion of a party and further order of the Court.

8. Transcript—Production for Purposes of Appeal.

(A) *Appellant.*

(1) The appellant must order the transcript of the hearing(s) on the motion for summary disposition before or contemporaneously with the filing of the claim of appeal or application for leave to appeal, unless there is no record to transcribe or all parties to the appeal stipulate that the transcript is unnecessary.

(2) Evidence that the transcript was ordered must be filed with the claim of appeal or application for leave to appeal. Appropriate evidence of the ordering includes (but is not limited to) the following:

(a) a letter to the specific court reporter requesting the specific hearing dates and enclosing any required deposit, or

(b) an "Appeal Transcript, Demand, Order and Acknowledgment" form, or

(c) a court reporter or recorder's certificate.

(3) If the transcript is not timely filed, the appellant or an appellee may file an appropriate motion with the Court of Appeals at any time. Avoiding undue delay in filing the motion under the circumstances of the case, and concisely stating the specific basis for it, will maximize the likelihood that the motion will be granted.

(4) If an appropriate motion is filed, the order disposing of such motion shall state the time for filing any outstanding brief(s).

(5) Absent an order of the Court of Appeals that resets the time, the appellant's brief will be due as provided in section 9(B)(1), regardless of whether the ordered transcript is timely filed.

(B) *Appellee.*

(1) If the transcript has been ordered by the appellant but is not filed by the time the appellant's brief is served on an appellee, the appellee may file an appropriate motion with the Court of Appeals. Avoiding undue delay in filing the motion under the circumstances of the case, and concisely stating the specific basis for it, will maximize the likelihood that the motion will be granted.

(2) If an appropriate motion is filed, the order shall state the time for filing any outstanding appellee briefs.

(C) *Court Reporter.* The court reporter or recorder shall file the transcript with the trial court or tribunal within 28 days after it is ordered by either the appellant or the appellee. The court reporter or recorder shall conform in all other respects with the requirements of MCR 7.210.

(D) *Transcript Fee.* The court reporter or recorder shall be entitled to the sum of $3.00 per original page and 50 cents per page for each copy for transcripts ordered in appeals processed under the expedited docket, if the transcript is filed within 28 days after it was ordered. If the court reporter or recorder does not file the transcript within 28 days after it was ordered, the rate will remain $1.75 per original page and 30 cents per page for each transcript, as set by MCL 600.2543.

9. Briefs on Appeal.

(A) With the following exceptions, the parties' briefs shall conform to the requirements of MCR 7.212.

(B) *Time For Filing.*

(1) In appeals by right, the appellant's brief shall be filed within 56 days after the claim of appeal is filed, or as ordered by the Court. In appeals by leave, the appellant's brief shall be filed within 28 days after the order granting leave is certified, or as ordered by the Court. In appeals by leave, the appellant may rely on the application for leave to appeal rather than filing a separate brief by timely filing 5 copies of the application for leave to appeal with a new cover page indicating that the appellant is relying on the application in lieu of filing a brief on appeal. The cover page should indicate whether oral argument is requested or is not requested. MCR 7.212(C)(1).

(2) The appellee's brief shall be filed within 28 days after the appellant's brief is served on the appellee, or as ordered by the Court. In appeals by leave, the appellee may rely on the answer to the application for leave to appeal rather than filing a separate brief by timely filing 5 copies of the answer to the application for leave to appeal with a new cover page indicating that the appellee is relying on the answer to the application in lieu of filing a brief on appeal. The cover page should indicate whether oral argument is requested or is not requested. MCR 7.212(C)(1) and (D)(1).

(3) Time for filing any party's brief may be extended for 14 days on motion for good cause shown. If the motion is filed by the appellant within the original brief-filing period, the motion will toll the time for any sanctions for untimely briefs. A motion may include a statement from opposing counsel that counsel does not oppose the 14–day extension. A motion to extend the time for filing a brief will be submitted for disposition forthwith; opposing counsel need not file an answer.

(4) If the appellant's brief is not filed within 7 days after the date due, the Court of Appeals shall issue an order assessing costs and warning the appellant that the case will be dismissed if the brief is not filed within 7 days after the clerk's certification of the order. If the brief is not filed within that 7–day period, the Court of Appeals shall issue an order that dismisses the appeal and that may assess additional costs.

(C) *Length and Form.* Briefs filed under this second amended administrative order are limited to 35 pages, double-spaced, exclusive of tables, indexes, and appendices. At the time each brief is filed, the filing party must provide the Court of Appeals with that party's trial court summary disposition motion or response, brief, and appendices. Failure to file these documents at the time of filing the appellant's brief will not extend the time to file the appellee's brief. If the appellant filed copies of the appellee's summary disposition response, brief, and appendices, the appellee may omit these documents provided that appellee notes the omission prominently on the title page of the appellee's brief.

(D) A reply brief may be filed within 14 days after the appellee's brief is served on the appellant, and is limited to 5 pages, double-spaced, exclusive of tables, indexes, and appendices.

10. Record on Appeal.
The Court of Appeals shall request the record on appeal from the trial court or tribunal clerk 28 days after jurisdiction has been confirmed and material filing deficiencies have been corrected. The trial court or tribunal clerk shall transmit the record as directed in MCR 7.210(G).

11. Notice of Cases.
Within 7 days after the filing of the appellee's brief, or after the expiration of the time for filing the appellee's brief, the clerk shall notify the parties that the case will be submitted as a "calendar case" on the summary disposition track.

12. Decision of the Court.
The opinion or order of the panel shall be issued no later than 35 days after submission of the case to, or oral argument before, a panel of judges for final disposition.

This amended order will remain in effect until December 31, 2007, during which time the Court of Appeals Work Group will monitor the expedited docket program. If, at any time during that monitoring process, it becomes apparent to the work group that procedural aspects of the program need to be modified, the group is encouraged to seek authorization from this Court to implement modifications. The work group will provide this Court with a written report by November 1, 2007, for this Court's use in evaluating expedited processing of summary disposition appeals to determine whether the procedure will be discontinued, changed, or continued.

[Adopted October 5, 2004, effective January 1, 2005, 471 Mich. Amended effective December 21, 2005, 474 Mich; November 9, 2006, 477 Mich.]

For text of the Administrative Order as entered October 5, 2004, effective January 1, 2005, see Administrative Order 2004-5.

For text of the Administrative Order as amended by the December 21, 2005, see Administrative Order 2004-5 (A1).

Comments

Staff Comment to 2006 Amendment

Staff Comment for second amended order: After 18 months' experience with the expedited track, the Case Management Work Group has reviewed Court data indicating that the expedited track has attracted substantially more filings than had been projected and that only 29 percent of the expedited track cases are being disposed within 180 days of filing. Court data also indicates that roughly 30 percent of the cases on the expedited track are quantifiably more difficult cases than the Work Group had anticipated would be filed on the track.

In the early months of the program, the Court made a significant effort to discourage parties and attorneys from filing motions to remove cases from the track. Further, although the original and amended administrative order authorized the Court to administratively remove cases from the track at any time, in fact the Court rarely exercised that authority because of a perception that it would be unfair to remove a case that the parties and attorneys had succeeded in briefing on the shortened timeline. These two policies undoubtedly led to the large number of nonroutine appeals that continued on the track from filing to disposition.

Now, in an effort to continue to provide practitioners and parties with a properly functioning expedited track for processing *routine* appeals from orders granting or denying summary disposition, the work group proposes to modify the track to facilitate motions to remove so that cases that are inappropriate for the track can be diverted to the standard track as easily as possible. Further, the Court also will more actively exercise its existing authority to remove cases that are too complex for expedited processing.

As standards for determining whether a case should be removed from the track, the second amended administrative order states that parties and practitioners should focus on markers such as:

• Brief Length—one or more of the briefs are more than 25 pages in length.

• Lower Court Record—there are more than one to three moderately sized lower court files and more than 100 pages of transcript from the relevant motion hearing(s) and deposition(s).

• Issues Raised on Appeal—there are more than four issues and one or more of the issues involve (i) matters of first impression, including the first-time construction of a Michigan statute or court rule, and (ii) complex facts or law. Additional issues may be allowed if they are merely separate factual challenges involving the same general area of law.

Further, the Court of Appeals notes that Case–Type Codes also offer some guidance in this area. Summary disposition appeals in cases that fall within one of the following case-type codes have often proven to be factually or legally complex, and thus may be inappropriate for the track: AA, AS, AW, CB, CD, CH, CL, CP, DE, MK, MM, MT, MZ, ND, NS, NZ, PZ, TI, and TV.

In more specific detail, the following changes are proposed in the second amended administrative order:

1. It will run for a period of 12 months from January 2007 through December 2007.

2. It will apply to cases filed on or after January 1, 2007. Note, however, that qualifying summary disposition applications for leave to appeal that are pending on January 1 can continue to be ordered onto the track by the panel if leave is granted.

3. The time for filing a claim of cross-appeal is changed from 14 days to 21 days to conform with MCR 7.207.

4. A motion to remove from the track may still be filed by any party, but no motion fee will be required. As noted above, the second amended administrative order recites specific criteria to be applied by parties and attorneys in making this request that are derived from case data gathered in the first 18 months of the experimental program. These criteria reflect quantifiable differences between routine and nonroutine appeals from orders on summary disposition motions. Parties and attorneys are urged to carefully apply these criteria so that nonroutine cases, which are inappropriate for expedited processing by the Court, are removed from the track as early as possible in each appeal.

5. Absent a party's motion to remove, the Court will exercise its administrative removal authority at any time, even if the determination cannot be made until after the parties have filed their briefs. This authority is essential to the Court's ability to manage the expedited track so that routine summary disposition appeals can be disposed within 180 days of filing.

6. The time for filing appellant's brief that was previously stated in section 8(A)(5), Transcript Production, has been replaced with a cross reference to the primary statement of time for filing in section 9(B)(1), concerning Briefs on Appeal.

7. Under the current administrative order, if appellant's brief is not filed within 7 days after the due date, and a warning order is issued under Sec. 9(B)(4), the order must direct that the brief be filed within 14 days of the original deadline, more than 7 days of which have already elapsed by operation of the provision. The proposed amendment will provide appellant with 7 days from the date of the order in which to file the brief and avoid dismissal.

8. Briefs filed under the second amended administrative order are still limited to 35 pages. However, the Court of Appeals notes that case data gathered in the first 18 months of the experimental program indicates that appellants' briefs in the bulk of the nonroutine summary disposition appeals exceeded an average of 20–21 pages in length. The most complex appeals averaged 35 pages. Thus, one of the removal factors listed in section 7(B) is that the length of one or both briefs exceeds 25 pages. In the Court's view, a case that cannot be briefed in 25 pages is *usually* not appropriate for continued placement on the track.

9. Briefs on appeal must be accompanied by the filing party's trial court summary disposition documents. Appellee can omit these appendices if they were filed by appellant, but appellee must note the basis for the omission on the title page of its brief.

Order 2004–6 Minimum Standards for Indigent Criminal Appellate Defense Services

On order of the Court, this is to advise that the Court has considered revised minimum standards for indigent criminal appellate defense services proposed by the Appellate Defender Commission pursuant to 1978 PA 620, MCL 780.711 to 780.719. The Court approves the standards with some revisions replacing those adopted in Administrative Order No. 1981–7, effective January 1, 2005.

PREAMBLE:

The Michigan Legislature in MCL 780.712(5) requires the Appellate Defender Commission to develop minimum standards to which all criminal appellate defense services shall conform. Pursuant to this mandate, these standards are intended to serve as guidelines to help counsel achieve the goal of effective appellate and postjudgment representation. Criminal appellants are not constitutionally entitled to counsel's adherence to these guidelines. Hence, counsel's failure to comply with any standard does not of itself constitute grounds for either a claim of ineffective assistance of counsel or a violation of the Michigan Rules of Professional Conduct, and no failure to comply with one or more of these standards shall, unless it is independently a violation of a rule of professional conduct, serve as the basis for a request for investigation with the Attorney Grievance Commission.

Standard 1. Counsel shall promptly examine the trial court record and register of actions to determine the proceedings, in addition to trial, plea, and sentencing, for which transcripts or other documentation may be useful or necessary, and, in consultation with the defendant and, if possible, trial counsel, determine whether any relevant proceedings have been omitted from the register of actions, following which counsel shall request preparation and filing of such additional pertinent transcripts and review all transcripts and lower court records relevant to the appeal. Although the trial court is responsible for ordering the record pursuant to MCR 6.425(F)(2), appellate counsel is nonetheless responsible for ensuring that all useful and necessary portions of the transcript are ordered.

Standard 2. Before filing the initial postconviction or appellate motion or brief and after reviewing the relevant transcripts and lower court records, counsel must consult with the defendant about the proposed issues to be raised on appeal and advise of any foreseeable benefits or risks in pursuing the appeal generally or any particular issue specifically. At counsel's discretion, such confidential consultation may occur during an interview with the defendant in person or through an attorney agent, by a comparable video alternative, or by such other reasonable means as counsel deems sufficient, in light of all the circumstances.

Standard 3. Counsel should raise those issues, recognizable by a practitioner familiar with criminal law and procedures on a current basis and who engages in diligent legal research, which offer reasonable prospects of meaningful postconviction or appellate relief, in a form that protects where possible the defendant's option to pursue collateral attacks in state or federal courts. If a potentially meritorious issue involves a matter not reflected in the trial court record, counsel should move for and conduct such evidentiary hearings as may be required.

Standard 4. When a defendant insists that a particular claim or claims be raised on appeal against the advice of counsel, counsel shall inform the defendant of the right to present the claim or claims *in propria persona*. Defendant's filing shall consist of one brief filed with or without an appropriate accompanying motion. Counsel shall also provide such procedural advice and clerical assistance as may be required to conform the defendant's filing for acceptability to the court. The defendant's filing *in propria persona* must be received by the Court of Appeals within 84 days after the appellant's brief is filed by the attorney, but if the case is noticed for submission within that 84–day period, the filing must be received no later than 7 days before the date of submission, or within the 84–day period, whichever is earlier. The 84–day deadline may be extended only by the Court of Appeals on counsel's motion, upon a showing of good cause for the failure to file defendant's pleading within the 84–day deadline.

Standard 5. An appeal may never be abandoned by counsel; an appeal may be dismissed on the basis of the defendant's informed consent, or counsel may seek withdrawal pursuant to *Anders v California*, 386 US 738; 87 S Ct 1396; 18 L Ed 2d 493 (1967), and related constitutional principles.

Standard 6. Counsel should request oral argument, and preserve the right to oral argument by timely filing the defendant's brief on appeal. Oral argument may be waived if counsel subsequently concludes that the defendant's rights will be adequately protected by submission of the appeal on the briefs alone.

Standard 7. Counsel must keep the defendant apprised of the status of the appeal and promptly forward copies of pleadings filed and opinions or orders issued by a court.

Standard 8. Upon final disposition of the case by the court, counsel shall promptly and accurately inform the defendant of the courses of action that may be pursued as a result of that disposition, and the scope of any further representation counsel may provide. If counsel's representation terminates, counsel shall cooperate promptly and fully with the defendant and any successor counsel in the transmission of records and information.

Standard 9. Upon acceptance of the assignment, counsel is prohibited from seeking or accepting fees from the defendant or any other source beyond those authorized by the appointing authority.

[Adopted October 5, 2004, effective January 1, 2005, 471 Mich.]

Comments

Staff Comment to 2005 Adoption

The Appellate Defender Commission submitted proposed revised standards for indigent criminal appellate defense services. The revised standards replace those adopted in Administrative Order No. 1981–7, effective January 1, 2005.

Standard 1 corresponds to former Standard 6 regarding counsel's obligation to review the lower court records and promptly request and review the transcripts. Standard 1 recognizes that pursuant to MCR 6.425(F)(2), the trial court bears the primary responsibility for ordering the record, but also highlights counsel's responsibility for ensuring that the trial court orders all useful and necessary portions of the transcript.

Standard 2 corresponds to former Standards 3 and 4, which related to counsel's obligation to consult with the client about the appellate issues and any foreseeable risks or benefits in pursuing the appeal. It clarifies that counsel generally should warn defendant not only of the risks and benefits of pursuing the appeal, but also the risks and benefits of pursuing a particular issue. This standard does not mandate a personal meeting with the defendant as did former Standard 3.

Standard 3 corresponds to former Standard 9, regarding counsel's duties to raise issues that offer reasonable prospects of meaningful postconviction relief and to former Standard 8, regarding counsel's obligation to move for and conduct any necessary evidentiary hearings.

Standard 4 corresponds to former Standard 11 regarding briefs filed by defendants *in propria persona*. This standard sets a deadline for the filing of such briefs of 84 days from the date that the attorney files the appellant's brief. The standard continues the requirement that appellate counsel provide the defendant with clerical assistance in filing the brief *in propria persona* and allows extensions of this deadline only upon a showing of good cause for the failure to file the defendant's brief within the 84–day deadline.

Standard 5 replaces former Standard 12 regarding dismissal of the appeal. It deletes the requirement for written consent and allows counsel to dismiss the appeal on the basis of the defendant's "informed consent." It also allows counsel to seek permission to withdraw where, in counsel's opinion, there are no meritorious appellate issues.

Standard 6 incorporates the principles articulated in former Standards 15 and 16 relating to counsel's obligation to timely file the defendant's pleadings and request and present an oral argument on the defendant's behalf.

Standard 7 is a more concise version of former Standard 17, but its provisions are essentially identical. Counsel is required to keep the defendant apprised of the appeal and send the defendant copies of pleadings and court orders or opinions.

Standard 8 incorporates the requirements of former Standards 18 and 19. It states that upon the court's final disposition of the case, counsel shall promptly and accurately inform the defendant of the courses of action that may be pursued and the scope of any further representation counsel may provide. If the Court of Appeals disposition terminates counsel's representation, counsel shall cooperate fully with the defendant or successor counsel in the transmission of records and information.

Standard 9 corresponds to former Standard 20, prohibiting appointed counsel from seeking or accepting fees from the defendant or any other source beyond those authorized by the appointing authority.

Order 2004–7 Adoption of Concurrent Jurisdiction Plans for the Third Circuit of Wayne County, the 19th District Court, the 29th District Court, and the 35th District Court

Administrative Order No. 2003-1 and MCL 600.401 *et seq.* authorize Michigan trial courts to adopt concurrent jurisdiction plans within a county or judicial circuit, subject to approval of the Court.

The Court hereby approves adoption of the following concurrent jurisdiction plans effective May 1, 2005:

Third Circuit of Wayne County and the 19th District Court

Third Circuit of Wayne County and the 29th District Court

Third Circuit of Wayne County and the 35th District Court

The plans shall remain on file with the State Court Administrator.

Amendments of concurrent jurisdiction plans may be implemented by local administrative order pursuant to MCR 8.112. Plan amendments shall conform to the requirements of Administrative Order No. 2003-1 and MCL 600.401 *et seq.*

[Adopted December 8, 2004, effective May 1, 2005, 471 Mich.]

Order 2005–1 Adoption of Concurrent Jurisdiction Plan for the 41st Circuit Court [Rescinded effective April 14, 2019]

Order 2005–2 Clarification of Time for Filing Postjudgment Motions

On July 13, 2005, this Court entered an order, effective January 1, 2006, that reduced the time from 12 months to 6 months for filing postjudgment motions pursuant to MCR 6.310(C) (motion to withdraw plea), 6.419(B) (motion for directed verdict of acquittal), 6.429(B) (motion to correct invalid sentence), and 6.431(A) (motion for new trial). This amendment is not applicable to cases where the order appointing appellate counsel was entered on or before December 31, 2005. In cases where the order appointing appellate counsel was entered on or before December 31, 2005, such postjudgment motions shall be filed within 12 months of the date of the order appointing appellate counsel.

[Adopted effective October 18, 2005, 474 Mich.]

Order 2005–3 Adoption of Concurrent Jurisdiction Plan for the 45th Circuit Court and the 3B District Court of St. Joseph County

Administrative Order No. 2003-1 and MCL 600.401 *et seq.* authorize Michigan trial courts to adopt concurrent jurisdiction plans within a county or judicial circuit, subject to approval of the Court.

The Court hereby approves adoption of the following concurrent jurisdiction plan effective March 1, 2006:

The 45th Circuit Court and the 3B District Court

The plans shall remain on file with the state court administrator.

Amendments of concurrent jurisdiction plans may be implemented by local administrative order pursuant to MCR 8.112. Plan amendments shall conform to the requirements of Administrative Order No. 2003-1 and MCL 600.401 *et seq.*

[Adopted November 30, 2005, effective March 1, 2006, 474 Mich.]

Order 2006–2 Privacy Policy and Access to Court Records

The Social Security Number Privacy Act, 2004 PA 454, requires all persons who, in the ordinary course of business, obtain one or more social security numbers, to create a privacy policy in order to ensure the confidentiality of social security numbers, prohibit unlawful disclosure of such numbers, limit access to information or documents containing social security numbers, provide for proper disposal of documents containing social security numbers, and establish penalties for violation of the privacy policy.

The management of documents within court files is the responsibility of the judiciary. In the regular course of business, courts are charged with the duty to maintain information contained within public documents that is itself non-public, based upon statute, court rule, or court order. In carrying out its responsibility to maintain these documents, the judiciary must balance the need for openness with the delicate issue of personal privacy. In an effort to prevent the illegal or unethical use of information found within court files, the following privacy policy is provided for all court records, effective March 1, 2006, and to be implemented prospectively.

Accordingly, on order of the Court,

A. The State Court Administrative Office is directed to assist trial courts in implementing this privacy policy and to update case file management standards established pursuant to this order.

B. Trial courts are directed to:

1. limit the collection and use of a social security number for party and court file identification purposes on cases filed on or after March 1, 2006, to the last 4 digits;

2. implement updated case file management standards for nonpublic records;

3. eliminate the collection of social security numbers for purposes other than those required or allowed by statute, court rule, court order, or collection activity when it is required for purposes of identification;

4. establish minimum penalties for court employees and custodians of the records who breach this privacy policy; and

5. cooperate with the State Court Administrative Office in implementing the privacy policy established pursuant to this order.

On further order of the Court, the following policies for access to court records are established.

Access to Public Court Records. Access to court records is governed by MCR 8.119 and the Case File Management Standards.

Access to Nonpublic Records

1. Maintenance of nonpublic records is governed by the NonPublic and Limited Access Court Records Chart and the Case File Management Standards.

2. The parties to a case are allowed to view nonpublic records within their court file unless otherwise provided by statute or court rule.

3. If a request is made by a member of the public to inspect or copy a nonpublic record or a record that does not exist, court staff shall state, "No public record exists."

Social Security Numbers and Nonpublic Records

1. The clerk of the court shall be allowed to maintain public files containing social security numbers on documents filed with the clerk subject to the requirements in this section.

2. No person shall file a document with the court that contains another person's social security number except when the number is required or allowed by statute, court rule, court order, or for purposes of collection activity when it is required for identification. A person who files a document with the court in violation of this directive is subject to punishment for contempt and is liable for costs and attorney fees related to protection of the social security number.

3. A person whose social security number is contained in a document filed with the clerk on or after March 1, 2006, may file a motion asking the court to direct the clerk to:

   a. redact the number on any document that does not require or allow a social security number pursuant to statute, court rule, court order, or for purposes of collection activity when it is required for identification; or

   b. file a document that requires or allows a social security number pursuant to statute, court rule, court order, or for purposes of collection activity when it is required for identification, in a separate nonpublic file.

The clerk shall comply with the court's order and file the request in the court file.

4. Dissemination of social security numbers is restricted to the purposes for which they were collected and for which their

use is authorized by federal or state law. Upon receiving a request for copies of a public document filed on or after March 1, 2006, that contains a social security number pursuant to statute, court rule, court order, or for purposes of collection activity when it is required for identification, a court shall provide a copy of the document after redacting all social security numbers on the copy. This requirement does not apply to requests for certified copies or true copies when required by law or for requests to view or inspect files. This requirement does not apply to those uses for which the social security number was provided.

Retention and Disposal of Nonpublic Records. Retention and disposal of nonpublic records and information shall be governed by General Schedule 16 and the Michigan Trial Court Case File Management Standards.

[Adopted February 10, 2006, effective March 1, 2006, 474 Mich.]

Order 2006–4   Adoption of Concurrent Jurisdiction Plan for the 28th Circuit Court and the 84th District Court of Wexford County

Administrative Order No. 2003–1 and MCL 600.401 *et seq.* authorize Michigan trial courts to adopt concurrent jurisdiction plans within a county or judicial circuit, subject to approval of the Court.

The Court hereby approves adoption of the following concurrent jurisdiction plan, effective August 1, 2006:

The 28th Circuit Court and the 84th District Court

The plan shall remain on file with the state court administrator.

Amendments of concurrent jurisdiction plans may be implemented by local administrative order pursuant to MCR 8.112. Plan amendments shall conform to the requirements of Administrative Order No. 2003–1 and MCL 600.401 *et seq.*

[Adopted April 5, 2006, effective August 1, 2006, 474 Mich.]

Order 2006–5   Adoption of the Michigan Child Support Formula as Juvenile Court Reimbursement Guideline

On order of the Court, notice of the proposed changes and an opportunity for comment in writing and at a public hearing having been provided, and consideration having been given to the comments received, the Court adopts the Michigan Child Support Formula Schedules Supplement from the Michigan Child Support Formula Manual to replace the July 30, 1990, Schedule of Payments in the Guideline for Court Ordered Reimbursement, effective July 1, 2006.

[Adopted May 30, 2006, effective July 1, 2006, 475 Mich.]

Order 2006–6   Prohibition on "Bundling" Cases

The Court has determined that trial courts should be precluded from "bundling" asbestos-related cases for settlement or trial. It is the opinion of the Court that each case should be decided on its own merits, and not in conjunction with other cases. Thus, no asbestos-related disease personal injury action shall be joined with any other such case for settlement or for any other purpose, with the exception of discovery. This order in no way precludes or diminishes the ability of a court to consolidate asbestos-related disease personal injury actions for discovery purposes only.

For purposes of this Administrative Order, "asbestos-related disease personal injury actions" include all cases in which it is alleged that a party has suffered personal injury caused by exposure to asbestos, regardless of the theory of recovery.

[Adopted effective August 9, 2006, 476 Mich.]

Comments

Staff Comment to 2006 Adoption

This Administrative Order prohibits the practice of "bundling," or joining, asbestos-related personal injury actions in order to maximize the number of cases settled. The order does not, however, preclude consolidation for discovery purposes.

The purpose of this order is to ensure that cases filed by plaintiffs who exhibit physical symptoms as a result of exposure to asbestos are settled or tried on the merits of that case alone. Bundling can result in seriously ill plaintiffs receiving less for their claim in settlement than they might otherwise have received if their case was not joined with another case or other cases.

The order is designed to preclude both the practice of settling cases in which plaintiffs with symptoms and plaintiffs without symptoms are settled together, as well as the practice of settling cases in which the plaintiffs are similarly situated (either with or without symptoms allegedly related to asbestos exposure.)

Staff Comment to 2007 Retention

On August 9, 2006, this Court adopted Administrative Order No. 2006–6, which prohibited the "bundling" of asbestos-related cases. 476 Mich xliv-li (2006). At the same time, the Court stated that it would accept comments on the administrative order until December 1, 2006. Notice and an opportunity for comment at a public hearing having been provided, the order is retained.

Order 2006–8   Deliberative Privilege and Case Discussions in the Supreme Court

The following administrative order, supplemental to the provisions of Administrative Order No. 1997–10, is effective immediately.

All correspondence, memoranda and discussions regarding cases or controversies are confidential. This obligation to honor confidentiality does not expire when a case is decided. The only exception to this obligation is that a Justice may disclose any unethical, improper or criminal conduct to the JTC or proper authority.

Adopted effective December 6, 2006, 477 Mich.

Order 2006–9   Adoption of Concurrent Jurisdiction Plan for the 28th Circuit Court, the 84th District Court, and the Probate Court of Missaukee County

Administrative Order No. 2003–1 and MCL 600.401 *et seq.* authorize Michigan trial courts to adopt concurrent jurisdiction plans within a county or judicial circuit, subject to approval of the Court.

The Court hereby approves the adoption of the following concurrent jurisdiction plan effective April 1, 2007:

The 28th Circuit Court, the 84th District Court, and the Probate Court of Missaukee County

The plan shall remain on file with the state court administrator.

Amendments to concurrent jurisdiction plans may be implemented by local administrative order pursuant to MCR 8.112. Plan amendments shall conform to the requirements of Administrative Order No. 2003–1 and MCL 600.401 *et seq.*

[Adopted December 27, 2006, effective April 1, 2007, 477 Mich.]

Order 2007–2 Expedited Summary Disposition Docket in the Court of Appeals

Pursuant to Administrative Order No. 2004–5, this Court adopted an expedited summary disposition docket in the Court of Appeals to take effect on January 1, 2005, and to expire on December 31, 2006. On December 21, 2005, Amended Administrative Order No. 2004–5 was adopted to take effect January 1, 2006, and to expire December 31, 2007. At the request of Chief Judge William C. Whitbeck, we now order that the expedited summary disposition docket be suspended indefinitely effective May 7, 2007.

The Court of Appeals has indicated that as of May 7, 2007, all cases currently on the expedited summary disposition track will no longer be considered on an expedited basis and will proceed on the standard track. If any party believes this shift would create a hardship or a significant inequity, a party may file a motion for appropriate relief in conformity with MCR 7.211. Parties to cases that were filed under the expedited summary disposition docket need not file a docketing statement, as is required for cases that were not filed under the expedited summary disposition docket. If transcripts in an expedited summary disposition case have been ordered and are completed by the court reporter within the time limits established in Administrative Order No. 2004–5, the court reporter is entitled to charge the premium rate per page.

[Adopted May 2, 2007, effective May 7, 2007, 477 Mich.]

Comments

Staff Comment to 2007 Adoption

The expedited summary disposition track was created at the request of the Court of Appeals to deal more quickly with cases that were appealed following a grant or denial of summary disposition by the trial court. It was intended to assess the question whether parties and the court could brief, argue, and dispose of cases within six months of filing. While parties generally have been able to meet the stricter briefing requirements under the program, the court's serious budget constraints have prevented it from meeting the expedited timelines, which the court believes places practitioners at a disadvantage. Rather than continue to be unable to comply with the time requirements of the expedited summary disposition track, the Court believes it is more advisable to suspend the operation of the expedited track indefinitely.

Order 2007–3 E–Filing in Oakland County [Rescinded effective October 23, 2019]

Comments

Staff Comment to 2013 Amendment

Administrative Order No. 2007–3 has been revised to allow a judge to require a paper copy in the limited circumstances in which the motion is dispositive or the motion with brief and attachments exceeds 40 pages in length.

Order 2007–4 Adoption of Concurrent Jurisdiction Plan for the 49th Circuit Court, the 77th District Court, and Probate District 18 of Mecosta and Osceola Counties

Administrative Order No. 2003–1 and MCL 600.401 *et seq.* authorize Michigan trial courts to adopt concurrent jurisdiction plans within a county or judicial circuit, subject to approval of the Court.

The Court hereby approves the adoption of the following concurrent jurisdiction plan, effective April 1, 2008:

The 49th Circuit Court, the 77th District Court, and Probate District 18 of Mecosta and Osceola Counties

The plan shall remain on file with the state court administrator.

Amendments to concurrent jurisdiction plans may be implemented by local administrative order pursuant to MCR 8.112. Plan amendments shall conform to the requirements of Administrative Order No. 2003–1 and MCL 600.401 *et seq.*

[Adopted December 18, 2007, effective April 1, 2008, 480 Mich.]

Order 2008–1 Pilot Project No. 1 17th Judicial Circuit Court (Expedited Process in the Resolution of the Low Conflict Docket of the Family Division)

On order of the Court, the 17th Judicial Circuit Court is authorized to implement a domestic relations pilot project. The pilot project will study the effectiveness of the use of pleadings that contain nonadversarial language, and the requirement that parents submit parenting time plans to encourage settlements and reduce postjudgment litigation.

The pilot project shall begin April 1, 2008, or as soon thereafter as is possible, and shall remain in effect until July 30, 2009, or until further order of this Court.

The 17th Judicial Circuit Court will track the degree of participation and the overall effectiveness of this pilot project and shall report to and provide information as requested by the State Court Administrative Office.

1. **Purpose of the Pilot Project.** The purpose of the pilot project is to study the effectiveness of the use of nonadversarial language in pleadings, judgments, and orders, and the effectiveness of a proposed provision for inclusion of parenting time plans, particularly in relation to the just, speedy, and economical determination of the actions involved in the pilot project and the reduction of postjudgment litigation. Except for matters related to the form of pleadings and orders, requirements for parenting time plans, and the use of nonadversarial language during the pilot project, the Michigan Court Rules govern all other aspects of the cases involved in the pilot project.

2. **Construction and Participation.**

(a) The 17th Judicial Circuit Court shall determine a method by local administrative order that creates a pool of pilot-project cases and also a pool of control-group cases. The local administrative order shall specify the cases to be included in the pilot project by one of the following methods: the date an action is filed, a specific number of consecutive cases or actions filed, or by the assigned judge.

(b) Participation also shall include postjudgment proceedings in qualifying cases that were included in the pilot pool.

(c) This is a mandatory project. A self-represented party is not excused from the project merely because the individual does not have counsel.

3. **Nonadversarial Terms.** The pilot project will incorporate the use of nonadversarial terms, such as "mother" or "parent" instead of "plaintiff" or "defendant." However, the use of nonadversarial language will not change the roles of parents as custodians for purposes of any state or federal law for which custody is required to be determined. Judgments and orders produced in the pilot project will clearly delineate how custody is to be determined for purposes of state and federal laws that require a person to be designated as a custodian.

4. Procedure. When an attorney or a pro se parent files a complaint with the clerk's office, and the clerk's office determines that the new case meets the requirements of the pilot project, that parent will be given two informational pamphlets explaining the purpose of the project, as well as two sets of instructions for a parenting time plan and two blank forms for proposed parenting time plans. Each of these documents must be approved by the State Court Administrative Office before they are distributed by the court to the parent.

The parent's attorney or the pro se parent seeking the divorce will be responsible for serving the informational pamphlet regarding parenting time instructions and the proposed parenting time plan on the other parent. The parent's attorney must ensure that his or her client receives the informational pamphlet containing the parenting time instructions and the proposed parenting time plan.

Each parent must complete the proposed parenting time plan and file it with the court within 28 days of filing his or her initial pleadings. The parents must also serve the other parent's attorney, or the other parent if that parent is not represented, and the friend of the court with a copy of the proposed parenting time plan.

5. Amendment. These processes may be amended upon the recommendation of the participating judges, approval of the chief judge, and authorization by the state court administrator.

6. Expiration. Unless otherwise directed by the Michigan Supreme Court, this pilot program shall continue until June 30, 2015.

Unless otherwise directed by the Michigan Supreme Court, this pilot program Shall continue until July 30, 2009.

Adopted effective April 8, 2008, 480 Mich.

Order 2008–2   Adoption of a Pilot Project to Study the Effects of the Jury Reform Proposal

On order of the Court, the judges listed below are authorized to implement a pilot project to study the effects of the jury-reform proposal that was published for comment by this Court in an order that entered July 11, 2006. The purposes of the pilot project are to determine whether, and in what way, the proposed jury-reform amendments support the goal of meaningful juror participation, and lead to greater confidence in the validity of the specific verdict and the overall jury system. In addition, the Court is interested in the effects of the proposed rules on court efficiency and the opinions of the attorneys and jurors who will operate under them. Courts that participate in the pilot project will operate under the following rules for the period of the pilot project, which will continue through December 31, 2010, or as otherwise ordered by the Court. At the Court's request, the participating courts will update the Court on the pilot program's status, and the judges' perceptions of the program's success. The Court anticipates that the pilot courts will apply these rules to the greatest extent possible as a way to test and assess all of the proposed ideas. The pilot project's success will be measured by the Court's evaluation of surveys that have been completed by the courts to determine the jurors', judges', and attorneys' responses to the various procedures being tested.

Participant judges include the following:

The Honorable Wendy L. Potts (6th Circuit Court)

The Honorable David Viviano (16th Circuit Court)

The Honorable Timothy G. Hicks (14th Circuit Court)

The Honorable Kenneth W. Schmidt and the Honorable William J. Caprathe (18th Circuit Court)

The Honorable Richard J. Celello (41st Circuit Court)

The Honorable Paul E. Stutesman (45th Circuit Court)

The Honorable Beth Gibson (92nd District Court)

The Honorable Peter J. Wadel (79th District Court)

The Honorable Donald L. Sanderson (2B District Court)

The Honorable Thomas P. Boyd (55th District Court)

The Honorable Richard W. May (90th District Court)

Rule 2.512   INSTRUCTIONS TO JURY

(A) Request for Instructions.

(1) At a time the court reasonably directs, the parties must file written requests that the court instruct the jury on the law as stated in the requests. In the absence of a direction from the court, a party may file a written request for jury instructions at or before the close of the evidence.

(2) In addition to requests for instructions submitted under subrule (A)(1), after the close of the evidence, each party shall submit in writing to the court a statement of the issues and may submit the party's theory of the case regarding each issue. The statement must be concise, be narrative in form, and set forth as issues only those disputed propositions of fact that are supported by the evidence. The theory may include those claims supported by the evidence or admitted.

(3) A copy of the requested instructions must be served on the adverse parties in accordance with MCR 2.107.

(4) The court shall inform the attorneys of its proposed action on the requests before their arguments to the jury.

(5) The court need not give the statements of issues or theories of the case in the form submitted if the court presents to the jury the material substance of the issues and theories of each party.

(B) Instructing the Jury.

(1) At any time during the trial, the court may, with or without request, instruct the jury on a point of law if the instruction will materially aid the jury in understanding the proceedings and arriving at a just verdict.

(2) Before or after arguments or at both times, as the court elects, the court shall instruct the jury on the applicable law, the issues presented by the case, and, if a party requests as provided in subrule (A)(2), that party's theory of the case.

(C) Objections. A party may assign as error the giving of or the failure to give an instruction only if the party objects on the record before the jury retires to consider the verdict (or, in the case of instructions given after deliberations have begun, before the jury resumes deliberations), stating specifically the matter to which the party objects and the grounds for the objection. Opportunity must be given to make the objection out of the hearing of the jury.

(D) Model Civil Jury Instructions.

(1) The Committee on Model Civil Jury Instructions appointed by the Supreme Court has the authority to adopt model civil jury instructions (M Civ JI) and to amend or repeal those instructions approved by the predecessor committee. Before

adopting, amending, or repealing an instruction, the committee shall publish notice of the committee's intent, together with the text of the instruction to be adopted, or the amendment to be made, or a reference to the instruction to be repealed, in the manner provided in MCR 1.201. The notice shall specify the time and manner for commenting on the proposal. The committee shall thereafter publish notice of its final action on the proposed change, including, if appropriate, the effective date of the adoption, amendment, or repeal. A model civil jury instruction does not have the force and effect of a court rule.

(2) Pertinent portions of the instructions approved by the Committee on Model Civil Jury Instructions or its predecessor committee must be given in each action in which jury instructions are given if

(a) they are applicable,

(b) they accurately state the applicable law, and

(c) they are requested by a party.

(3) Whenever the committee recommends that no instruction be given on a particular matter, the court shall not give an instruction unless it specifically finds for reasons stated on the record that

(a) the instruction is necessary to state the applicable law accurately, and

(b) the matter is not adequately covered by other pertinent model civil jury instructions.

(4) This subrule does not limit the power of the court to give additional instructions on applicable law not covered by the model instructions. Additional instructions, when given, must be patterned as nearly as practicable after the style of the model instructions and must be concise, understandable, conversational, unslanted, and nonargumentative.

Rule 2.513   CONDUCT OF JURY TRIAL

(A) Preliminary Instructions. After the jury is sworn and before evidence is taken, the court shall provide the jury with pretrial instructions reasonably likely to assist in its consideration of the case. Such instructions, at a minimum, shall communicate the duties of the jury, trial procedure, and the law applicable to the case as are reasonably necessary to enable the jury to understand the proceedings and the evidence. The jury also shall be instructed about the elements of all civil claims or all charged offenses, as well as the legal presumptions and burdens of proof. The court shall provide each juror with a copy of such instructions. MCR 2.512(D)(2) does not apply to such preliminary instructions.

(B) Court's Responsibility. The trial court must control the proceedings during trial, limit the evidence and arguments to relevant and proper matters, and take appropriate steps to ensure that the jurors will not be exposed to information or influences that might affect their ability to render an impartial verdict on the evidence presented in court. The court may not communicate with the jury or any juror pertaining to the case without notifying the parties and permitting them to be present. The court must ensure that all communications pertaining to the case between the court and the jury or any juror are made a part of the record.

(C) Opening Statements. Unless the parties and the court agree otherwise, the plaintiff or the prosecutor, before presenting evidence, must make a full and fair statement of the case and the facts the plaintiff or the prosecutor intends to prove. Immediately thereafter, or immediately before presenting evidence, the defendant may make a similar statement. The court may impose reasonable time limits on the opening statements.

(D) Interim Commentary. Each party may, in the court's discretion, present interim commentary at appropriate junctures of the trial.

(E) Reference Documents. The court must encourage counsel in civil and criminal cases to provide the jurors with a reference document or notebook, the contents of which should include, but which is not limited to, witness lists, relevant statutory provisions, and, in cases where the interpretation of a document is at issue, copies of the relevant document. The court and the parties may supplement the reference document during trial with copies of the preliminary jury instructions, admitted exhibits, and other appropriate information to assist jurors in their deliberations.

(F) Deposition Summaries. Where it appears likely that the contents of a deposition will be read to the jury, the court should encourage the parties to prepare concise, written summaries of depositions for reading at trial in lieu of the full deposition. Where a summary is prepared, the opposing party shall have the opportunity to object to its contents. Copies of the summaries should be provided to the jurors before they are read.

(G) Scheduling Expert Testimony. The court may, in its discretion, craft a procedure for the presentation of all expert testimony to assist the jurors in performing their duties. Such procedures may include, but are not limited to:

(1) Scheduling the presentation of the parties' expert witnesses sequentially; or

(2) allowing the opposing experts to be present during the other's testimony and to aid counsel in formulating questions to be asked of the testifying expert on cross-examination; or

(3) providing for a panel discussion by all experts on a subject after or in lieu of testifying. The panel discussion, moderated by a neutral expert or the trial judge, would allow the experts to question each other.

(H) Note Taking by Jurors. The court may permit the jurors to take notes regarding the evidence presented in court. If the court permits note taking, it must instruct the jurors that they need not take notes, and they should not permit note taking to interfere with their attentiveness. If the court allows jurors to take notes, jurors must be allowed to refer to their notes during deliberations, but the court must instruct the jurors to keep their notes confidential except as to other jurors during deliberations. The court shall ensure that all juror notes are collected and destroyed when the trial is concluded.

(I) Juror Questions. The court may permit the jurors to ask questions of witnesses. If the court permits jurors to ask questions, it must employ a procedure that ensures that such questions are addressed to the witnesses by the court itself, that inappropriate questions are not asked, and that the parties have an opportunity outside the hearing of the jury to object to the questions. The court shall inform the jurors of the procedures to be followed for submitting questions to witnesses.

(J) Jury View. On motion of either party, on its own initiative, or at the request of the jury, the court may order a jury view of property or of a place where a material event occurred. The parties are entitled to be present at the jury view. During the view, no person, other than an officer designated by the court, may speak to the jury concerning the subject connected with the trial. Any such communication must be recorded in some fashion.

(K) Juror Discussion. After informing the jurors that they are not to decide the case until they have heard all the evidence, instructions of law, and arguments of counsel, the court may instruct the jurors that they are permitted to discuss the evidence among themselves in the jury room during trial recesses. The jurors should be instructed that such discussions may only take place when all jurors are present and that such discussions must be clearly understood as tentative pending final presentation of all evidence, instructions, and argument.

(L) Closing Arguments. After the close of all the evidence, the parties may make closing arguments. The plaintiff or the prosecutor is entitled to make the first closing argument. If the defendant makes an argument, the plaintiff or the prosecutor may offer a rebuttal limited to the issues raised in the defendant's argument. The court may impose reasonable time limits on the closing arguments.

(M) Comment on the Evidence. After the close of the evidence and arguments of counsel, the court may fairly and impartially sum up the evidence and comment to the jury about the weight of the evidence, if it also instructs the jury that it is to determine for itself the weight of the evidence and the credit to be given to the witnesses and that jurors are not bound by the court's summation or comment. The court shall not comment on the credibility of witnesses or state a conclusion on the ultimate issue of fact before the jury.

(N) Final Instructions to the Jury.

(1) Before closing arguments, the court must give the parties a reasonable opportunity to submit written requests for jury instructions. Each party must serve a copy of the written requests on all other parties. The court must inform the parties of its proposed action on the requests before their closing arguments. After closing arguments are made or waived, the court must instruct the jury as required and appropriate, but at the discretion of the court, and on notice to the parties, the court may instruct the jury before the parties make closing arguments. After jury deliberations begin, the court may give additional instructions that are appropriate.

(2) *Solicit Questions about Final Instructions.* As part of the final jury instructions, the court shall advise the jury that it may submit in a sealed envelope given to the bailiff any written questions about the jury instructions that arise during deliberations. Upon concluding the final instructions, the court shall invite the jurors to ask any questions in order to clarify the instructions before they retire to deliberate.

If questions arise, the court and the parties shall convene, in the courtroom or by other agreed-upon means. The question shall be read into the record, and the attorneys shall offer comments on an appropriate response. The court may, in its discretion, provide the jury with a specific response to the jury's question, but the court shall respond to all questions asked, even if the response consists of a directive for the jury to continue its deliberations.

(3) *Copies of Final Instructions.* The court shall provide each juror with a written copy of the final jury instructions to take into the jury room for deliberation. The court, in its discretion, also may provide the jury with a copy of electronically recorded instructions.

(4) *Clarifying or Amplifying Final Instructions.* When it appears that a deliberating jury has reached an impasse, or is otherwise in need of assistance, the court may invite the jurors to list the issues that divide or confuse them in the event that the judge can be of assistance in clarifying or amplifying the final instructions.

(O) Materials in the Jury Room. The court shall permit the jurors, on retiring to deliberate, to take into the jury room their notes and final instructions. The court may permit the jurors to take into the jury room the reference document, if one has been prepared, as well as any exhibits and writings admitted into evidence.

(P) Provide Testimony or Evidence. If, after beginning deliberation, the jury requests a review of certain testimony or evidence that has not been allowed into the jury room under subrule (O), the court must exercise its discretion to ensure fairness and to refuse unreasonable requests, but it may not refuse a reasonable request. The court may make a video or audio recording of witness testimony, or prepare an immediate transcript of such testimony, and such tape or transcript, or other testimony or evidence, may be made available to the jury for its consideration. The court may order the jury to deliberate further without the requested review, as long as the possibility of having the testimony or evidence reviewed at a later time is not foreclosed.

Rule 2.514 RENDERING VERDICT

(A) Majority Verdict; Stipulations Regarding Number of Jurors and Verdict. The parties may stipulate in writing or on the record that

(1) the jury will consist of any number less than 6,

(2) a verdict or a finding of a stated majority of the jurors will be taken as the verdict or finding of the jury, or

(3) if more than 6 jurors were impaneled, all the jurors may deliberate.

Except as provided in MCR 5.740(C), in the absence of such stipulation, a verdict in a civil action tried by 6 jurors will be received when 5 jurors agree.

(B) Return; Poll.

(1) The jury must return its verdict in open court.

(2) A party may require a poll to be taken by the court asking each juror if it is his or her verdict.

(3) If the number of jurors agreeing is less than required, the jury must be sent back for further deliberation; otherwise, the verdict is complete, and the court shall discharge the jury.

(C) Discharge From Action; New Jury. The court may discharge a jury from the action:

(1) because of an accident or calamity requiring it;

(2) by consent of all the parties;

(3) whenever an adjournment or mistrial is declared;

(4) whenever the jurors have deliberated and it appears that they cannot agree.

The court may order another jury to be drawn, and the same proceedings may be had before the new jury as might have been had before the jury that was discharged.

(D) Responsibility of Officers.

(1) All court officers, including trial attorneys, must attend during the trial of an action until the verdict of the jury is announced.

(2) A trial attorney may, on request, be released by the court from further attendance, or the attorney may designate an associate or other attorney to act for him or her during the deliberations of the jury.

Rule 2.515   SPECIAL VERDICTS

(A) Use of Special Verdicts; Form. The court may require the jury to return a special verdict in the form of a written finding on each issue of fact, rather than a general verdict. If a special verdict is required, the court shall, in advance of argument and in the absence of the jury, advise the attorneys of this fact and, on the record or in writing, settle the form of the verdict. The court may submit to the jury:

(1) written questions that may be answered categorically and briefly;

(2) written forms of the several special findings that might properly be made under the pleadings and evidence; or

(3) the issues by another method, and require the written findings it deems most appropriate.

The court shall give to the jury the necessary explanation and instruction concerning the matter submitted to enable the jury to make its findings on each issue.

(B) Judgment. After a special verdict is returned, the court shall enter judgment in accordance with the jury's findings.

(C) Failure to Submit Question; Waiver; Findings by Court. If the court omits from the special verdict form an issue of fact raised by the pleadings or the evidence, a party waives the right to a trial by jury of the issue omitted unless the party demands its submission to the jury before it retires for deliberations. The court may make a finding with respect to an issue omitted without a demand. If the court fails to do so, it is deemed to have made a finding in accord with the judgment on the special verdict.

Rule 2.516   MOTION FOR DIRECTED VERDICT

A party may move for a directed verdict at the close of the evidence offered by an opponent. The motion must state specific grounds in support of the motion. If the motion is not granted, the moving party may offer evidence without having reserved the right to do so, as if the motion had not been made. A motion for a directed verdict that is not granted is not a waiver of trial by jury, even though all parties to the action have moved for directed verdicts.

[Adopted effective August 5, 2008, 482 Mich.]

Order 2009–2   Extension of Pilot Project No. 1 17th Circuit Court

On order of the Court, the provisions of the pilot project authorized in Administrative Order No. 2008–1, relating to the use of parenting time plans and nonadversarial language in domestic relations proceedings in the 17th Circuit Court, are continued in effect through February 28, 2011.

[Adopted effective January 14, 2009, 483 Mich.]

Order 2009–3   Adoption of Concurrent Jurisdiction Plan for the 53rd Circuit Court of Cheboygan and Presque Isle Counties and the Presque Isle County Probate Court

Administrative Order No. 2003–1 and MCL 600.401 *et seq.* authorize Michigan trial courts to adopt concurrent jurisdiction plans within a county or judicial circuit, subject to approval of the Court.

The Court hereby approves adoption of the following concurrent jurisdiction plan effective July 1, 2009:

● The 53rd Circuit Court of Cheboygan and Presque Isle Counties and the Presque Isle County Probate Court.

The plan shall remain on file with the state court administrator.

Amendments of concurrent jurisdiction plans may be implemented by local administrative order pursuant to MCR 8.112. Plan amendments shall conform to the requirements of Administrative Order No. 2003–1 and MCL 600.401 *et seq.*

[Adopted March 10, 2009, effective July 1, 2009, 483 Mich.]

Order 2009–4   E-Filing Pilot Project in the 42nd Circuit Court

On order of the Court, the 42nd Circuit Court is authorized to implement an electronic filing pilot project to study, in asbestos cases, the effectiveness of electronically filing court documents in lieu of traditional paper filings. The pilot project shall begin May 19, 2009, or as soon thereafter as is possible, and shall remain in effect until July 30, 2013, or further order of this Court. The 42nd Circuit Court acknowledges that certain rules regarding electronic filing have been published for comment by this Court. If this Court adopts electronic-filing rules during the pendency of this pilot project, the 42nd Circuit Court will, within 60 days of the effective date of the rules, comply with the requirements of those rules.

The 42nd Circuit Court will track the participation in and effectiveness of this pilot project and shall report to and provide such information upon request by the State Court Administrative Office.

1. Construction. The purpose of the pilot project is to study the effectiveness of electronically filing court documents in connection with the just, speedy, and economical determination of the actions involved in the pilot project. This court may exercise its discretion to grant necessary relief to avoid the consequences of error so as not to affect the substantial rights of the parties. The Michigan Court Rules govern all other aspects of the cases involved in the pilot project, except for matters related to electronically filing documents during the pilot project.

2. Definitions

(a) "Clerk" means the Midland County Clerk.

(b) "E-filing" means any court pleading, motion, brief, response, list, order, judgment, notice, or other document filed electronically pursuant to the pilot project.

(c) "LAO" means all local administrative orders governing the 42nd Circuit Court.

(d) "MCR" means the Michigan Court Rules.

(e) "Pilot project" means the initiative by the 42nd Circuit Court, the Clerk, and the Midland County Information Systems Department in conjunction with Wiznet, Inc., CherryLAN Systems, Inc., and under the supervision of the State Court Administrative Office. This e-filing application facilitates the electronic filing of pleadings, motions, briefs, responses, lists, orders, judgments, notices, and other documents.

(f) "Asbestos" means the matters that the pilot project will test and are described as all pending cases identified as an "NP" Case Type based in whole or in part on a claim of injury as a result of exposure to asbestos.

(g) "Technical malfunction" means any hardware, software, or other malfunction that prevents a user from timely filing a complete e-filing or sending or receiving service of an e-filing.

3. Participation in the Pilot Project

(a) Participation in the pilot project shall be mandatory in all pending "Asbestos" type cases. Participation shall be assigned following the filing and service of the initial complaint or other initial filing and assignment of the case to the participating judge.

(b) This is a mandatory e-filing project. It is presumed that all documents will be filed electronically. However, the court recognizes that circumstances may arise that will prevent one from e-filing. To ensure that all parties retain access to the courts, parties that demonstrate good cause will be permitted to file their documents with the clerk, who will then file the documents electronically. Among the factors that the 42nd Circuit Court will consider in determining whether good cause exists to excuse a party from mandatory e-filing are a party's access to the Internet and indigency. A self-represented party is not excused from the pilot project merely because the individual does not have counsel.

4. E-filings Submission, Acceptance, and Time of Service with the Court; Signature

(a) In an effort to facilitate uniform service within the scope of this pilot project, the 42nd Circuit Court strongly recommends electronic service.

(b) Program participants must submit e-filings pursuant to these rules and the pilot project's technical requirements. The clerk may, in accordance with MCR 8.119(C), reject documents submitted for filing that do not comply with MCR 2.113(C)(1), are not accompanied by the proper fees, do not conform to the technical requirements of this pilot project, or are otherwise submitted in violation of a statute, an MCR, an LAO, or the program rules.

(c) E-filings may be submitted to the court at any time, but shall only be reviewed and accepted for filing by the Office of the Clerk during the normal business hours of 8:00 a.m. to 4:30 p.m. E-filings submitted after business hours shall be deemed filed on the business day the e-filing is accepted (usually the next business day). The clerk shall process e-filings on a first-in, first-out basis.

(d) E-filings shall be treated as if they were hand-delivered to the court for all purposes under statute, the MCR, and the LAO.

(e) A pleading, document, or instrument e-filed or electronically served under this rule shall be deemed to have been signed by the judge, court clerk, attorney, party, or declarant.

(i) Signatures submitted electronically shall use the following form: /s/ *John L. Smith.*

(ii) A document that requires a signature under penalty of perjury is deemed signed by the declarant if, before filing, the declarant has signed a printed form of the document.

(iii) An e-filed document that requires a signature of a notary public is deemed signed by the notary public if, before filing, the notary public has signed a printed form of the document.

(f) The original of a sworn or verified document that is an e-filing (e.g., a verified pleading) or part of an e-filing (e.g., an affidavit, notarization, or bill of costs) must be maintained by the filing attorney and made available upon reasonable request of the court, the signatory, or opposing party.

(g) Proposed orders shall be submitted to the court in accordance with the provisions of the pilot project. The court and the clerk shall exchange the documents for review and signature pursuant to MCR 2.602(B).

(h) By electronically filing the document, the electronic filer affirms compliance with these rules.

5. Time for Service and Filing of Pleadings, Documents, and Motions; Judge's Copies; Hearings on Motions; Fees.

(a) All times for filing and serving e-filings shall be governed by the applicable statute, the MCR, and the LAO as if the e-filings were hand-delivered.

(b) The electronic submission of a motion and brief through this pilot project satisfies the requirements of filing a judge's copy under MCR 2.119(A)(2). A judge may require that one "courtesy copy" or "chambers copy" of any dispositive motion and all accompanying exhibits, as well as responses and replies, or any motion and brief in which the motion, brief, and attachments equal 40 pages or more be submitted directly to the judge's chamber in paper format. Any exhibits must be appropriately tabbed. Good practice requires that in appropriate cases, relevant portions of lengthy documents be highlighted. A printed copy of the e-filing transmission receipt must be attached to the front of the pleading. The requirement to provide a "courtesy copy" or "chambers copy" at a judge's request shall expire on May 22, 2018.

(c) Applicable fees, including e-filing fees and service fees, shall be paid electronically through procedures established by the clerk at the same time and in the same amount as required by statute, court rule, or administrative order.

(i) Each e-filing is subject to the following e-filing fees;

Type of Filing	Fee
EFO (e-filing only)	$5.00
EFS (e-filing with service)	$8.00
SO (service only)	$5.00

(ii) Users who use credit cards for payment are also responsible for a 3% user fee.

6. Service

(a) All parties shall provide the court and opposing parties with one e-mail address with the functionality required for the pilot project. All service shall originate from and be perfected upon this e-mail address.

(b) Unless otherwise agreed to by the court and the parties, all e-filings must be served electronically to the e-mail addresses of all parties. The subject matter line for the transmittal of document served by e-mail shall state: "Service of e-filing in case [insert caption of case]."

(c) The parties and the court may agree that, instead of e-mail service, e-filings may be served to the parties (but not the court) by facsimile or by traditional means. For those choosing to accept facsimile service:

    (i) the parties shall provide the court and the opposing parties with one facsimile number with appropriate functionality,

    (ii) the facsimile number shall serve as the number to which service may be made,

    (iii) the sender of the facsimile should obtain a confirmation of delivery, and

    (iv) parties shall comply with the requirements of MCR 2.406 on the use of facsimile communication equipment.

(d) Proof of service shall be submitted to the 42nd Circuit Court according to MCR 2.104 and this administrative order.

7. Format and Form of E-filing and Service

(a) A party may only e-file documents for one case in each transaction.

(b) All e-filings shall comply with MCR 1.109 and the technical requirements of the court's vendor.

(c) Any exhibit or attachment that is part of an e-filing must be clearly designated and identified as an exhibit or attachment.

(d) All e-filings, subject to subsection 6(c) above, shall be served on the parties in the same format and form as submitted to the court.

8. Pleadings, Motions, and Documents not to be E-filed.

The following documents shall not be e-filed during the pilot project and must be filed by the traditional methods provided in the MCR and the LAO:

(a) documents to be filed under seal (pursuant to court order),

(b) initiating documents, and

(c) documents for case evaluation proceedings.

9. Official Court Record; Certified Copies

(a) For purposes of this pilot project, e-filings are the official court record. An appellate record shall be certified in accordance with MCR 7.210(A)(1).

(b) Certified or true copies of e-filed documents shall be issued in the conventional manner by the clerk in compliance with the Michigan Trial Court Case File Management Standards.

(c) At the conclusion of the pilot project, if the program does not continue as a pilot project or in some other format, the clerk shall convert all e-filings to paper form in accordance with MCR 8.119(D)(1)(d). Participating attorneys shall provide reasonable assistance in constructing the paper record.

(d) At the conclusion of the pilot project, if the program continues as a pilot project or in another format, the clerk shall provide for record retention and public access in a manner consistent with the instructions of the Court and the court rules.

10. Court Notices, Orders, and Judgments.

At the court's discretion, the court may issue, file, and serve orders, judgments, and notices as e-filings. Pursuant to a stipulation and order, the parties may agree to accept service from the court via facsimile pursuant to the procedures set forth in Section 6(c) above.

11. Technical Malfunctions

(a) A party experiencing a technical malfunction with the party's equipment (such as format or conversion problems or inability to access the pilot sites), another party's equipment (such as an inoperable e-mail address), or an apparent technical malfunction of the court's pilot equipment, software, or server shall use reasonable efforts to timely file or receive service by traditional methods and shall provide prompt notice to the court and the parties of any such malfunction.

(b) If a technical malfunction has prevented a party from timely filing, responding to, or otherwise perfecting or receiving service of an e-filing, the affected party may petition the 42nd Circuit Court for relief. Such petition shall contain an adequate proof of the technical malfunction and set forth good cause for failure to use non-electronic means to timely file or serve a document. The court shall liberally consider proof of the technical malfunction and use its discretion in determining whether such relief is warranted.

12. Privacy Considerations

(a) With respect to any e-filing, the following requirements for personal information shall apply:

    (i) Social Security Numbers. Pursuant to Administrative Order No. 2006–2, full social security numbers shall not be included in e-filings. If an individual's social security number must be referenced in an e-filing, only the last four digits of that number may be used and the number specified in substantially the following format: XXX–XX–1234.

    (ii) Names of Minor Children. Unless named as a party, the identity of a minor child shall not be included in e-filings. If a nonparty minor child must be mentioned, only the initials of that child's name may be used.

    (iii) Dates of Birth. An individual's full birth date shall not be included in e-filings. If an individual's date of birth must be referenced in an e-filing, only the year may be used and the date specified in substantially the following format: XX/XX/1998.

    (iv) Financial Account Numbers. Full financial account numbers shall not be included in e-filings unless required by statute, court rule, or other authority. If a financial account number must be referenced in an e-filing, only the last four digits of these numbers may be used and the number specified in substantially the following format: XXXXX1234.

    (v) Driver's License Numbers and State–Issued Personal Identification Card Numbers. A person's full driver's license number and state-issued personal identification number shall not be included in e-filings. If an individual's driver's license number or state-issued personal identification card number must be referenced in an e-filing, only the last four digits of that number should be used and the number specified in substantially the following format: X–XXX–XXX–XX1–234.

(vi) Home Addresses. With the exception of a self-represented party, full home addresses shall not be included in e-filings. If an individual's home address must be referenced in an e-filing, only the city and state shall be used.

(b) Parties wishing to file a complete personal data identifier listed above may:

(i) Pursuant to and in accordance with the MCR and the LAO, file a motion to file a traditional paper version of the document under seal. The court, in granting the motion to file the document under seal, may still require that an e-filing that does not reveal the complete personal data identifier be filed for the public files, or

(ii) Pursuant to and in accordance with the applicable MCR and LAO, obtain a court order to file a traditional paper reference list under seal. The reference list shall contain the complete personal data identifiers and the redacted identifiers used in the e-filing. All references in the case to the redacted identifiers included in the reference list shall be construed to refer to the corresponding complete personal data identifiers. The reference list must be filed under seal, and may be amended as of right.

(c) Parties should exercise caution when filing papers that contain private or confidential information, including, but not limited to, the information covered above and listed below:

(i) Medical records, treatment and diagnosis;

(ii) Employment history;

(iii) Individual financial information;

(iv) Insurance information;

(v) Proprietary or trade secret information;

(vi) Information regarding an individual's cooperation with the government; and

(vii) Personal information regarding the victim of any criminal activity.

13. Records and Reports. Further, the 42nd Circuit Court shall file an annual report with the Supreme Court covering the project to date by January 1 of each year (or more frequently or on another date as specified by the Court) that outlines the following:

(a) Detailed financial data that show the total amount of money collected in fees for documents filed or served under the pilot project to date, the original projections for collections of fees, and whether the projections have been met or exceeded.

(b) Detailed financial information regarding the distribution or retention of collected fees, including the amount paid to Wiznet per document and in total for the subject period, the amount paid to CherryLAN in total for the subject period, the amount retained by the court per document and in total for the period, and whether the monies retained by the court are in a separate account or commingled with other monies.

(c) A detailed itemization of all costs attributed to the project to date and a statement of whether and when each cost will recur.

(d) A detailed itemization of all cost savings to the court whether by reduced personnel or otherwise and a statement of whether any cost savings to the court are reflected in the fee structure charged to the parties.

(e) Information regarding how the filing and service fees were calculated and whether it is anticipated that those fees will be necessary and continued after the conclusion of the pilot program.

(f) A statement of projections regarding anticipated e-filing and service-fee collections and expenditures for the upcoming periods.

14. Amendment. These rules may be amended upon the recommendation of the participating judges, the approval of the chief judge, and authorization by the state court administrator.

15. Expiration. Unless otherwise directed by the Michigan Supreme Court, this pilot project, requiring parties to electronically file documents in cases assigned to participating judges, shall continue until July 30, 2013.

[Adopted effective May 19, 2009, 483 Mich. Amended effective May 22, 2013, 494 Mich.]

Comments

Staff Comment to 2013 Amendment

Administrative Order No. 2009–4 has been revised to allow a judge to require a paper copy in the limited circumstances in which the motion is dispositive or the motion with brief and attachments exceeds 40 pages in length.

Order 2009–5   E-Filing Pilot Project in the 56th Circuit Court (Eaton County)

On order of the Court, the 56th Circuit Court is authorized to implement an Electronic Document Filing Project. The pilot project is established to study the effectiveness of electronically filing court documents in lieu of traditional paper filings. The pilot project shall begin as soon as possible after approval by the Court, and shall remain in effect until July 1, 2011, or further order of this Court. The 56th Circuit Court is aware that rules regarding electronic filing have been published for comment by this Court. If this Court adopts electronic-filing rules during the pendency of the 56th Circuit Electronic Document Filing Pilot Project, the 56th Circuit Court will, within 60 days of the effective date of the rules, comply with the requirements of those rules.

The 56th Circuit Court will track the participation and effectiveness of this pilot program and shall report to, and make such findings available to, the Michigan Supreme Court.

1. Construction. The purpose of the pilot program is to study the effectiveness of electronically filing court documents in connection with the just, speedy, and economical determination of the actions involved in the pilot program. The 56th Circuit Court may exercise its discretion to grant necessary relief to avoid the consequences of error so as not to affect the substantial rights of the parties. Except for matters related to electronically filing documents during the pilot program, the Michigan Court Rules govern all other aspects of the cases involved in the pilot program.

2. Definitions

a. "Clerk" means the Eaton County Clerk.

b. "E-filing" means any court pleading, motion, brief, response, list, order, judgment, notice, or other document filed electronically pursuant to the pilot program.

c. "LAO" means all local administrative orders governing the 56th Judicial Circuit Court.

d. "MCR" means Michigan Court Rules.

e. "Pilot program" means the initiative by the 56th Judicial Circuit Court, the Eaton County Clerk, the Eaton County Department of Information Services, and the Judicial Information Systems division of the State Court Administrative Office in conjunction with Wiznet, Inc. This e-filing application facilitates the electronic filing of pleadings, motions, briefs, responses, lists, orders, judgments, notices, and other documents. The Eaton County pilot program will begin testing with "C," "N," and circuit court domestic cases wherein the case suffix begins with a "D." The court intends this pilot program to include all circuit and family division judges, including the probate judge sitting by assignment in the family division of the circuit court. A judge may exempt a case or cases from the pilot program. The pilot program is expected to last approximately two years.

f. "Technical malfunction" means any hardware, software, or other malfunction that prevents a user from timely filing a complete e-filing or sending or receiving service of an e-filing.

g. "Filing Party" means any party or attorney representing a party who has registered to file pleadings or papers electronically in a particular matter.

3. Participation in the Pilot Program

a. Participation by parties and counsel in the pilot program will initially be voluntary to accommodate training. Commencing on a date certain to be set by the court approximately 90 days following the launch of the pilot program, all attorneys filing a new "DO" case shall be required to file all pleadings and papers therein electronically. On a date certain to be set by the court approximately 180 days following the initiation of mandatory "DO" filings, attorneys filing a new "DM" case shall be required to file all pleadings and papers therein electronically. Approximately 180 days following the initiation of mandatory "DM" filings, all attorneys filing a new civil case in circuit court wherein the suffix of the case starts with a "C" or an "N," and in all newly filed domestic matters not already required to be filed electronically wherein the suffix starts with a "D," all pleadings and papers filed therein shall be required to file electronically. Mandatory filings in an identified case type shall also include newly filed domestic post-disposition proceedings.

b. Parties not represented by counsel may voluntarily participate in the pilot program. An unrepresented party who initially chooses to voluntarily participate in this pilot program may withdraw from the program at any time by filing a hard copy of a paper or pleading pursuant to the Michigan Court Rules, at which time the Clerk shall create a paper file and maintain the paper file as outlined in § 4(d).

c. Pursuant to the schedule outlined in § 3(a), it is presumed that all documents will be filed electronically. However, the Court recognizes that circumstances may arise that would prevent an attorney or participating party from filing a document or documents electronically. To ensure that all parties retain access to the courts, parties that demonstrate good cause will be permitted to file a hard copy of their documents with the clerk, at which time the Clerk shall create a paper file and maintain the paper file as outlined in § 4(d).

d. A public access terminal will be available at the Eaton County Courthouse for those persons wishing to participate in the pilot program or to review electronically filed documents but without sufficient equipment to facilitate participation. The electronic filing system utilized for this pilot program limits access to those person who are parties in a matter to case files in which they have registered as a filing party. Those not a party to the case may access the case file by making a request to the Circuit Court Clerk, where proper protocol with regard to access to public and non-public files will be followed. Electronically retained documents may be printed and presented to the requester. A customary copy fee may be applied if the requestor seeks to retain the provided copy.

4. E-filings Submission, Acceptance, and Time of Service with the Court; Signature

a. In an effort to facilitate uniform service within the scope of this program, the 56th Circuit Court strongly recommends electronic service.

b. Program participants must submit e-filings pursuant to these rules and the pilot program's technical requirements. The clerk may, in accordance with MCR 8.119(C) reject documents submitted for filing that do not comply with MCR 2.113(C)(1), are not accompanied by the proper fees, do not conform to the technical requirements of this pilot program, or are otherwise submitted in violation of a statute, MCR, LAO, or program rules.

c. E-filings may be submitted to the court at any time, but shall only be reviewed and accepted for filing by the Eaton County Clerk's Office during normal business hours of 8:00 a.m. to 5:00 p.m. E-filings received by the clerk's office before midnight will be granted that day's date for filing purposes. For purposes of determining e-filing receipt time, the receipt time reflected on the clerk's computer will serve as the official time of receipt.

d. In any mandatory case, as outlined in § 3(a), wherein all parties are represented by counsel, and subject to § 3(c), the court shall create and maintain only an electronic file. In those instances where a party is originally represented by counsel who subsequently withdraws and the party desires to continue in pro per without participating in this pilot program, a paper file shall be created by the clerk with a notice that the file was originally created electronically, and any documents filed before the creation of the paper file will be maintained electronically. Subsequent electronically filed documents will be retained in electronic format and only the verification of receipt of an electronically filed document will be placed into the paper file. If the pro per litigant wishes to participate in the pilot program, the clerk shall maintain only an electronic file.

e. In any mandatory case as outlined in § 3(a) wherein some parties are represented by counsel and other parties are not, and at least one of those parties not represented by counsel does not desire to voluntarily participate in this pilot program, the clerk shall create a paper file. All pleadings and papers submitted electronically will be retained in electronic format and only the verification of receipt of an electronically filed document will be placed into the paper file. All paper filing will be retained in the paper file created by the clerk.

f. These rules apply to parties added or joined to an existing matter. If counsel represents the new party or parties, all papers filed by counsel must be done so in conformity with these rules. Sections 3(b), 4(d), and 4(e) set forth the respective rights and obligations of unrepresented parties. The clerk shall maintain its files in conformity with these rules.

g. E-filings shall be treated as if they were hand-delivered to the court for all purposes under statute, MCR, and LAO.

h. A pleading, document, or instrument e-filed or electronically served under this rule shall be deemed to have been signed by the judge, court clerk, attorney, party or declarant:

   i. Signatures submitted electronically shall use the following form: /s/ John L. Smith.

   ii. A document that requires a signature under the penalty of perjury is deemed signed by the declarant if, before filing, the declarant has signed a printed form of the document.

   iii. An e-filed document that requires a signature of a notary public is deemed signed by the notary public if, before filing, the notary public has signed a printed form of the document.

i. The original of a sworn or verified document that is an e-filing (e.g., a verified pleading) or part of an e-filing (e.g., an affidavit, notarization or bill of costs) must be maintained by the filing attorney and made available upon reasonable request of the court, the signatory or opposing party.

j. Proposed orders shall be processed by the court in accordance with the provisions of the pilot program. The clerk shall present the document to the court for review and signature pursuant to MCR 2.602(B).

k. By electronically filing the document, the electronic filer indicates compliance with these rules.

5. Time for Service and Filing of Pleadings, Documents and Motions; Judge's Copies; Hearings on Motions; Fees

a. All times for filing and serving e-filings shall be governed by applicable statute, MCR, and LAO, with the exception that e-filings received by the Clerk's Office before midnight will be granted that day's date for filing purposes, and electronic service sent before midnight will be deemed served on that business day.

b. The electronic submission of a motion and brief through this pilot program satisfies the requirements of filing a judge's copy under MCR 2.119(A)(2). Upon request of the court, the filing party shall promptly provide an electronic or paper judge's copy to chambers.

c. For documents filed electronically, applicable fees, including e-filing fees and service fees, shall be paid electronically through procedures established by the Eaton County Clerk's Office at the same time and in the same amount as required by statute, court rule, or administrative order.

   i. Each e-filing is subject to the following e-filing fees.

Type of Filing	Fee
EFO (e-filing only)	$5.00
EFS (e-filing with service)	$8.00
SO (service only)	$5.00

   ii. Users who use credit cards for payment may also be responsible for a user fee, as set by the Eaton County Clerk up to a maximum of 2% of the transaction amount.

d. User fees shall not be waived on the basis of indigency. Indigent litigants not represented by counsel may file hard copies of papers and pleadings.

6. Service

a. All attorneys, and parties appearing pro se, participating in this pilot program shall provide the court and counsel, where opposing counsel is present, with one e-mail address with the functionality required for the pilot program. All service on opposing counsel shall originate from and be perfected upon this e-mail address.

b. Unless otherwise agreed to by the court and the parties, all e-filings must be served electronically to the e-mail address of opposing counsel. The subject-matter line for the transmittal of document served by e-mail shall state: "Service of e-filing in case [insert caption of case]."

c. In matters where an attorney represents a party and the opposing side or sides are unrepresented, service by all parties shall be by traditional means, unless otherwise agreed to in writing.

d. The parties and the court may agree that, instead of e-mail service, e-filings may be served to the parties (but not the court) by facsimile or by traditional means. For those choosing to accept facsimile service:

   i. The parties shall provide the court and opposing parties with one facsimile number with appropriate functionality,

   ii. The facsimile number shall serve as the number to which service may be made,

   iii. The sender of the facsimile should obtain a confirmation of delivery, and

   iv. Parties shall comply with the requirements of MCR 2.406 on the use of facsimile communication equipment.

e. In mandatory situations, and those where one chooses to voluntarily participate in the pilot program, proof of service shall be submitted electronically to the 56th Circuit Court according to MCR 2.104 and these rules.

7. Format and Form of E-filing and Service

a. An attorney or party may only e-file documents for one case per transaction.

b. All e-filings shall comply with MCR 1.109 and the technical requirements of the court's vendor.

c. Any exhibit or attachment that is part of an e-filing must be clearly designated and identified as an exhibit or attachment.

d. All e-filings, subject to subsection 6(d), shall be served on the parties in the same format and form as submitted to the court.

8. Pleadings, Motions, and Documents not to be E-filed. Documents to be filed under seal (pursuant to court order) shall not be e-filed during the pilot program and must be filed by the traditional methods provided in the MCR. The obligation of the clerk in such an instance shall be governed by § 4 of this administrative order.

9. Official Court Record; Certified Copies

a. For purposes of this pilot program, e-filings are the official court record. An appellate record shall be certified in accordance with MCR 7.210(A)(1).

b. Certified or true copies of e-filed documents shall be issued in the conventional manner by the Eaton County Clerk's Office in compliance with the Michigan Trial Court Case File Management Standards.

c. At the conclusion of the pilot program, if the program does not continue as a pilot project or in some other format, the clerk shall convert all e-filings to paper form in accordance with MCR 8.119(D)(1)(d), unless electronic means of long-term retention is approved. Participating attorneys shall provide reasonable assistance in constructing the paper record.

d. At the conclusion of the pilot program, if the program continues as a pilot project or in another format, the clerk shall provide for record retention and public access in a manner consistent with the instructions of the court and court rules.

10. Court Notices, Orders, and Judgments. At the court's discretion, the court may issue, file, and serve orders, judgments, and notices as e-filings. Pursuant to stipulation and order, the parties may agree to accept service from the court via facsimile pursuant to the procedures set forth in Rule 6(c).

11. Technical Malfunctions

a. A party experiencing a technical malfunction with the party's equipment (such as PDF conversion problems or inability to access the pilot program sites), another party's equipment (such as an inoperable e-mail address), or an apparent technical malfunction of the court's pilot program equipment, software, or server shall use reasonable efforts to timely file or receive service by traditional methods and shall provide prompt notice to the court and the parties of any such malfunction.

b. If a technical malfunction has prevented a party from timely filing, responding to, or otherwise perfecting or receiving service of an e-filing, the affected party may petition the 56th Circuit Court for relief. Such petition shall contain an adequate proof of the technical malfunction and set forth good cause for failure to use non-electronic means to timely file or serve a document. The court shall liberally consider proof of the technical malfunction and use its discretion in determining whether such relief is warranted.

12. Privacy Considerations

a. With respect to any e-filing, the following requirements for personal information shall apply:

i. Social Security Numbers. Full social security numbers shall not be included in e-filings. If an individual's social security number must be referenced in an e-filing, only the last four digits of that number may be used and the number specified in substantially the following format: XXX–XX–1234.

ii. Names of Minor Children. Unless named as a party, the identity of minor children shall not be included in e-filings. If a non-party minor child must be mentioned, only the initials of that child's name may be used.

iii. Dates of Birth. An individual's full birth date shall not be included in e-filings. If an individual's date of birth must be referenced in an e-filing, only the year may be used and the date specified in substantially the following format: XX/XX/1998.

iv. Financial Account Numbers. Full financial account numbers shall not be included in e-filings unless required by statute, court rule, or other authority. If a financial account number must be referenced in an e-filing, only the last four digits of these numbers may be used and the number specified in substantially the following format: XXXXXX1234.

v. Driver's License Numbers and State–Issued Personal Identification Card Numbers. A person's full driver's license number and state-issued personal identification number shall not be included in e-filings. If an individual's driver's license number or state-issued personal identification card number must be referenced in an e-filing, only the last four digits of that number should be used and the number specified in substantially the following format: X–XXX–XXX–XX1–234.

vi. Home Addresses. With the exception of a self-represented party, full home addresses shall not be included in e-filings. If an individual's home address must be referenced in an e-filing, only the city and state should be used.

b. Parties wishing to file a complete personal data identifier listed above may:

i. Pursuant to, and in accordance with the MCR and administrative orders, file a motion seeking the court's permission to file a traditional paper version of the document under seal. The court may, in granting the motion to file the document under seal, still require that an e-filing that does not reveal the complete personal data identifier be filed for the public files.

or

ii. Pursuant to and in accordance with the applicable MCR and LAO, obtain a court order to file a traditional paper reference list under seal. The reference list shall contain the complete personal data identifiers and the redacted identifiers used in the e-filing. All references in the case to the redacted identifiers included in the reference list shall be construed to refer to the corresponding complete personal data identifiers. The reference list must be filed under seal, and may be amended as of right.

c. Parties should exercise caution when filing papers that contain private or confidential information, including, but not limited to, the information covered above and listed below:

i. Medical records, treatment, and diagnosis;

ii. Employment history;

iii. Individual financial information;

iv. Insurance information;

v. Proprietary or trade secret information;

vi. Information regarding an individual's cooperation with the government; and

vii. Personal information regarding the victim of any criminal activity.

13. Amendment. These rules may be amended upon the recommendation of the participating judges, the approval of the chief judge, and authorization by the state court administrator.

14. Expiration. Unless otherwise directed by the Michigan Supreme Court, this pilot program, requiring parties to electronically file documents in cases assigned to participating judges, shall continue until July 1, 2011, or further order of the 56th Circuit Court.

Adopted effective July 21, 2009, 484 Mich.

Order 2009–6　A Court Shall Submit a Local Administrative Order to SCAO When Appointing Magistrates and Referees

On order of the Court, effective January 1, 2010, a court shall submit local administrative orders to the State Court Administrative Office to identify individuals appointed as magistrates or referees in that court.

Courts are authorized by statute to appoint magistrates and referees to positions that allow those magistrates and referees to perform various functions. As the entity charged with supervision of the state's courts, it is essential that the State Court Administrative Office of the Michigan Supreme Court be aware of the identity of each of these appointed individuals. In addition, because the law with regard to magistrates allows the court that appoints the magistrate to establish the scope of the duties the magistrate will perform, and because immunity for the magistrate's actions extends only to those actions that are performed within the scope of the authority established by the court that appoints the magistrate, it is also essential that the Supreme Court be notified of the scope of authority granted by each court to its magistrate or magistrates. Further, the Michigan Court Rules grant courts the authority to determine the specific types of hearings and proceedings to be heard by referees, and this information should likewise be submitted to the State Court Administrative Office.

Accordingly, on order of the Court,

A.　Each court that appoints a magistrate or referee shall submit a local administrative order to the State Court Administrative Office that identifies an individual appointed as a magistrate or referee. The local administrative order shall include the name and contact information for the individual and the date the appointment is or was effective.

B.　Further, each court that appoints a magistrate or referee shall describe the scope of the authority conferred by the court on the magistrate or referee.

C.　It is the responsibility of a magistrate or referee to notify the State Court Administrative Office of changes in the individual's contact information during the course of the appointment.

[Adopted September 9, 2009, effective January 1, 2010, 485 Mich.]

Comments

Staff Comment to 2009 Adoption

Administrative Order No. 2009–6 requires a court to submit a local administrative order to the State Court Administrative Office regarding the identity of magistrates and referees, as well as a description of the scope of the authority of magistrates and referees. These requirements provide the State Court Administrative Office necessary information about who these individuals are and what functions they perform in the trial court. It is the magistrate's or referee's responsibility to update his or her contact information.

Order 2009–7　Adoption of a Pilot Project in the 46th District Court to Study the Effects of Proposed Rule 8.119 of the Michigan Court Rules

On August 11, 2009, the 46th District Court submitted a letter to the Court in which the 46th District Court proposed revision of MCR 8.119 to implement a process that would allow a court clerk to return to a litigant a document that the clerk has identified as nonconforming with the Michigan Court Rules, requirements contained in the Michigan statutes, or the Michigan Supreme Court records standards. Upon receipt of the returned document, the litigant would have several options: the litigant could correct the nonconformity identified by the clerk, submit documentation in support of the document, request the clerk to submit the paper as it was initially submitted for immediate review by the court, or withdraw the document. On order of the Court, the 46th District Court is authorized to implement a pilot project in its court to study the effects of proposed Rule 8.119, limited to cases that involve garnishments and consumer debt collections.

The purpose of the pilot project is to determine whether the proposed language represents a feasible and practical procedure for courts to follow in screening documents that are submitted for filing in cases that involve garnishments and consumer debt collections. The Court is interested in learning whether this procedure will increase efficiency within the court (including assessing Its effect on the clerk and the judges of the court), and determining what effect the procedure will have on litigants. The 46th District Court will operate under the following rule for the period of the pilot project, which will begin on the date this order enters and continue for one year or as otherwise ordered by the Court. The 46th District Court will provide a report to the Court within three months of the conclusion of the pilot project regarding the court's assessment of the feasibility of the procedure described below. In addition, litigants will have an opportunity to provide feedback on the pilot project through a survey to be included when documents are returned by clerks, and through polls conducted of those who participate in the judicial review procedure. The 46th District Court shall keep a list of litigants who request that the submitted document be reviewed by a judge.

[Adopted effective October 13, 2009, 485 Mich. Amended effective January 21, 2010, 485 Mich.]

Comments

Staff Comment to 2009 Adoption

Under this pilot project, the 46th District Court shall test its proposal to allow court clerks to return certain nonconforming papers submitted to the court in garnishment or consumer debt collections actions. If the clerk returns a paper as nonconforming, the litigant may respond by submitting supporting documentation, submitting an amended document, asking that the document be submitted to the court for immediate review, or withdrawing the paper. If, upon review, the judge disallows filing of the document, an order would enter disallowing the filing and would state the reason in the order.

Staff Comment to 2010 Amendment

Under this pilot project, the 46th District Court shall test its proposal to allow court clerks to return certain nonconforming papers submitted to the court in garnishment or consumer debt collections actions. If the clerk returns a paper as nonconforming, the litigant may respond by submitting supporting documentation, submitting an amended document, asking that the document be submitted to the court for immediate review, or withdrawing the paper. If, upon review, the judge disallows filing of the document, an order would enter disallowing the filing and would state the reason in the order.

Order 2010–1　Adoption of Administrative Order to Establish and Require Compliance with Court Collections Program and Reporting Requirements

On order of the Court, notice of the proposed changes and an opportunity for comment in writing and at a public hearing having been provided, and consideration having been given to the comments received, the following administrative order is adopted, effective May 1, 2010.

Enforcing court orders, including financial sanctions, is a responsibility of the courts that, if done effectively, enhances the courts' integrity and credibility while providing funds to assure victims are made whole and support law enforcement, libraries, the crime victim's rights fund, and local governments. In order to improve the enforcement and collection of court-ordered financial sanctions, it is ordered that the State Court Administrator establish court collections program requirements and that all circuit courts, circuit court family divisions, district courts, and municipal courts comply with those requirements. The State Court Administrative Office shall enforce the requirements and assist courts in adopting practices in compliance with those requirements.

In order to effectively monitor and measure the effect of collections programs, it is ordered that the State Court Administrator establish reporting requirements regarding outstanding receivables and collections efforts undertaken by courts, including establishment of the reporting format, method, and due dates. It is further ordered that all circuit courts, circuit court family divisions, district courts, and municipal courts comply with those requirements. The State Court Administrative Office shall facilitate compliance with and enforce the requirements.

[Adopted February 2, 2010, effective May 1, 2010, 485 Mich.]

Order 2010–2   Adoption of Concurrent Jurisdiction Plan for the 12th Circuit Court and the Baraga County Probate Court

Administrative Order No. 2003–1 and MCL 600.401 *et seq.* authorize Michigan trial courts to adopt concurrent jurisdiction plans within a county or judicial circuit, subject to approval of the Court.

The Court approves adoption of the following concurrent jurisdiction plan, effective July 1, 2010:

● The 12th Circuit Court and the Baraga County Probate Court

The plan shall remain on file with the state court administrator.

Amendments to concurrent jurisdiction plans may be implemented by local administrative order pursuant to MCR 8.112. Plan amendments shall conform to the requirements of Administrative Order No. 2003–1 and MCL 600.401 *et seq.*

[Adopted March 16, 2010, effective July 1, 2010, 485 Mich.]

Order 2010–3   E–Filing Project in Oakland Circuit Court, Family Division

On order of the Court, the Sixth Judicial Circuit Court, in consultation with the State Court Administrative Office (SCAO), developed this project to study the effectiveness of electronically filing court documents in connection with the just, speedy, and economical determination of Family Division actions in a mandatory electronic filing environment. By further order of the Court, the Sixth Circuit Court Family Division is authorized to continue its e-filing project during a transition period while the State Court Administrative Office prepares and implements a statewide e-filing system. In addition, it is anticipated that the Sixth Circuit Court Family Division, along with other court locations that participated as e-filing pilot courts, will be among the first group of courts that will connect with any statewide system for purposes of testing and early integration.

Participation in this program is mandatory for cases with a "DO" case code and assigned to program judge(s), and, effective immediately, will be gradually implemented for cases with a "DM" case code.

The Sixth Judicial Circuit Court will report to and provide information as requested by the State Court Administrative Office.

1. **Construction.** The purpose of the transition period for e-filing is to continue successful e-filing efforts in the Sixth Circuit Court Family Division and to coordinate with state efforts, through a vendor or otherwise, to build and operate a statewide system of e–filing. The Court may exercise its discretion to grant necessary relief to avoid the consequences of error so as not to affect the substantial rights of the parties. Except for matters related to electronically filing or service of documents during the transition period, the Michigan Rules of Court govern all other aspects of the cases involved in the project.

2. **Definitions.**

(a) "Clerk" means the Oakland County Clerk.

(b) "E-filing" means any court pleading, motion, brief, response, list, order, judgment, notice, or other document filed electronically pursuant to the project.

(c) "LAO" means all local administrative orders governing the Sixth Judicial Circuit Court.

(d) "MCR" means the Michigan Rules of Court.

(e) "Transition e-filing program" or "project" means the initiative by the Sixth Judicial Circuit Court, the Oakland County Clerk, and the Oakland County Department of Information Technology in conjunction with the court's vendor and under the supervision of the SCAO. This e-filing application facilitates the electronic filing of pleadings, motions, briefs, responses, lists, orders, judgments, notices, and other documents during the period after enactment of statutory authority to fund and operate a statewide electronic filing system. The vision is that all state courts in Michigan will eventually permit e-filing (with appropriate modifications and improvements). The Oakland County project will begin testing with two Circuit Court judges with "DO" type civil cases. "DM" type cases are also included in the scope of this project. The Court plans to expand the program to all Family Division judges who wish to participate.

(f) "Technical malfunction" means any hardware, software, or other malfunction that prevents a user from timely filing a complete e-filing or sending or receiving service of an e-filing.

(g) "Wiznet envelope" means an electronic submission that contains one or more Wiznet transactions.

(h) "Wiznet transaction" means the submission of one or more related documents which results in a single register of actions entry. A single register of actions entry is determined by the Clerk. E.g. a motion, brief, affidavit, notice of hearing, and proof of service for a single motion submitted at one time frequently constitutes a single register of actions entry.

3. **Participation in the Program.**

(a) Participation in the program shall be mandatory in all pending or newly filed "DO" type cases assigned to participating Circuit Court judges. Participation for new filings shall begin following the filing of the initial complaint or other initiating document, and assignment of the case to a participating judge. At the discretion of the e-filing judge, participation in the program may also include proceedings in post-disposition cases assigned to the judge.

In addition, this order authorizes e-filing for all "DM" cases. Recognizing the logistical challenges associated with implementing e-filing in "DM" cases, the Court authorizes the Family Division of the Sixth Circuit Court to gradually implement the program beginning with a limited number of cases assigned to a single judge and a single Friend of the Court referee team assigned to that judge. The Sixth Circuit Court may expand the scope of the program at any time to include additional judges and/or FOC referee teams without further authorization of the Court.

(b) This is a mandatory e-filing project. It is presumed that all documents will be filed electronically. However, the Court recognizes that circumstances will arise which prevent one from e-filing. To ensure that all parties retain access to the courts, parties that demonstrate good cause will be permitted to file their documents with the Clerk, who will then file the documents electronically. Among the factors that the Court will consider in determining whether good cause exists to excuse a party from mandatory e-filing are a party's access to the Internet and indigency. A self-represented party is not excused from the project merely because the individual does not have counsel.

4. E-filings Submission, Acceptance, and Time of Service with the Court; Signature.

(a) Program participants must submit e-filings pursuant to these rules and the program's technical requirements. The Clerk may, in accordance with MCR 8.119(C) reject documents submitted for filing that do not comply with MCR 2.113(C), are not accompanied by the proper fees, clearly violate AO 2006–2, do not conform to the technical requirements of this pilot project, or are otherwise submitted in violation of statute, court rule, administrative order, or program rules.

(b) E-filings may be submitted to the court at any time, but shall only be reviewed and accepted for filing by the Oakland County Clerk's Office during normal business hours of 8:00 a.m. to 4:30 p.m. E–filings submitted after business hours shall be deemed filed the business day the e-filing is accepted (usually the next business day). The Clerk shall process electronic submissions on a first in/ first out basis.

(c) E-filings shall be treated as if they were hand delivered to the court for all purposes under statute, court rule, and administrative order.

(d) A pleading, document, or instrument e-filed or electronically served under this rule shall be deemed to have been signed by the judge, court clerk, attorney, party, or declarant.

(i) Signatures submitted electronically shall use the following form: /s/ John L. Smith.

(ii) A document that requires a signature under the penalty of perjury is deemed signed by the declarant if, before filing, the declarant has signed a printed form of the document.

(iii) An e-filed document that requires a signature of a notary public is deemed signed by the notary public if, before filing, the notary public has signed a printed form of the document.

(e) The original of a sworn or verified document that is an e-filing (e.g., a verified pleading) or part of an e-filing (e.g., an affidavit, notarization, or bill of costs) must be maintained by the filing attorney or self represented litigant and made available upon reasonable request of the court, the signatory, or opposing party.

(f) Proposed orders shall be submitted to the court in accordance with the provisions of the pilot. The Court and Clerk shall exchange the documents for review and signature pursuant to MCR 2.602(B).

(g) By electronically filing the document, the electronic filer indicates compliance with these rules.

5. Time for Service and Filing of Pleadings, Documents, and Motions; Judge's Copies; Hearings on Motions; Fees.

(a) All times for filing and serving e-filings shall be governed by the applicable statute, court rule, and administrative order as if the e-filings were hand delivered. Where a praecipe is required by LCR 2.119(A), it must be submitted electronically to the Court through the epraecipe application at http://courts.oakgov.com/ePraecipe/.

(b) The electronic submission of a motion and brief through this program satisfies the requirements of filing a Judge's Copy under MCR 2.119(A)(2). A judge may require that one "courtesy copy" or "chambers copy" of any dispositive motion and all accompanying exhibits, as well as responses and replies, or any motion and brief in which the motion, brief, and attachments equal 40 pages or more be submitted directly to the judge's chamber in paper format. Any exhibits must be appropriately tabbed. Good practice requires that in appropriate cases, relevant portions of lengthy documents be highlighted. A printed copy of the e-filing transmission receipt must be attached to the front of the pleading. The requirement to provide a "courtesy copy" or "chambers copy" at a judge's request shall expire on May 22, 2018.

(c) Applicable fees, including e-file fees and service fees, shall be paid electronically through procedures established by the Oakland County Clerk's Office at the same time and in the same amount as required by statute, court rule, or administrative order.

6. Service.

(a) All parties shall register as a service contact with the court vendor's application which will provide the court and opposing parties with one email address with the functionality required for the program.

(b) It is highly recommended that all e-filings must be served electronically to the email addresses of all parties.

(c) The parties and court may agree that, instead of eservice, e-filings may be served to the parties (but not the court) as provided in MCR 2.107.

(d) For those choosing to accept facsimile service:

(i) the parties shall provide the court and opposing parties with one facsimile number with appropriate functionality,

(ii) the facsimile number shall serve as the number to which service may be made,

(iii) the sender of the facsimile should obtain a confirmation of delivery, and

(iv) parties shall comply with the requirements of MCR 2.406 on the use of facsimile communication equipment.

(e) Proof of Service shall be submitted to the Court according to MCR 2.104 and these rules.

7. Format and Form of E-filing and Service.

(a) A party may only e-file documents for one case per Wiznet envelope.

(b) A party may e-file multiple Wiznet transactions within a single Wiznet envelope, subject to subrule 7(a).

(c) All e-filings shall comply with MCR 1.109 and the technical requirements of the Court's vendor and, after implementation, the vendor implementing the statewide e-filing system.

(d) Any exhibit or attachment that is part of an e-filing must be clearly designated and identified as an exhibit or attachment.

(e) All e-filings, subject to subsection 6(c) above, shall be served on the parties in same format and form as submitted to the court.

8. Pleadings, Motions, and Documents not to be E-filed. The following documents shall not be e-filed during the Pilot program and must be filed by the traditional methods provided in the court rules and administrative orders:

(a) documents to be filed under seal (pursuant to court order), and

(b) initiating documents, and

(c) documents related to divorce proceedings that are not filed in the court file, such as a verified statement of divorce and judgment information forms.

9. Official Court Record; Certified Copies.

(a) For purposes of this program, the electronic version of all documents filed with the Court, with the exception of documents filed under seal [see 8(a) and MCR 8.119(F)] is the official court record. An appellate record shall be certified in accordance with MCR 7.210(A)(1).

(b) Certified or true copies of e-filed documents shall be issued in the conventional manner by the Oakland County Clerk's Office in compliance with the Michigan Trial Court Case File Management Standards.

(c) At the conclusion of the program, if the program does not continue in some other format, the clerk shall convert all e-filings to paper form in accordance with MCR 8.119(D)(1)(d). Participating attorneys shall provide reasonable assistance in constructing the paper record.

(d) At the conclusion of the program, the Court and Clerk shall provide for record retention and public access in a manner consistent with the instructions of the court and court rules.

10. Court Notices, Orders, and Judgments. The Court shall issue, file, and serve orders, judgments, and notices as e-filings. A party exempted from e-filing under this program shall be served in accordance with MCR 2.107(C).

11. Technical Malfunctions.

(a) A party experiencing a technical malfunction with the party's equipment (such as PDF conversion problems or inability to access the program sites), another party's equipment (such as an inoperable email address), or an apparent technical malfunction of the court's equipment, software or server shall use reasonable efforts to timely file or receive service as provided in these rules and shall provide prompt notice to the court and parties of any such malfunction.

(b) If a technical malfunction has prevented a party from timely filing, responding to, or otherwise perfecting or receiving service of an e-filing, the affected party may petition the Court for relief. Such petition shall contain an adequate proof of the technical malfunction and set forth good cause for failure to use non-electronic means to timely file or serve a document. The Court shall liberally consider proof of the technical malfunction and use its discretion in determining whether such relief is warranted.

12. Privacy Considerations.

(a) With respect to any e-filing, the following requirements for personal information shall apply:

1. Social Security Numbers. Pursuant to Administrative Order 2006–2, full social security numbers shall not be included in any e-filings. If an individual's social security number must be referenced in an e-filing, only the last four digits of that number may be used and the number specified in substantially the following format: XXX–XX–1234.

2. Names of Minor Children. Unless named as a party or otherwise required by statute, court rule, or administrative order, the identity of minor children shall not be included in any e-filings. If a non-party minor child must be mentioned, only the initials of that child's name may be used.

3. Dates of Birth. Except as required by statute, court rule, or administrative order, an individual's full birth date shall not be included in any e-filings. Subject to the above limitation, if an individual's date of birth is otherwise referenced in an e-filing, only the year may be used and the date specified in substantially the following format: XX/XX/1998.

4. Financial Account Numbers. Full Financial account numbers shall not be included in any e-filings unless required by statute, court rule, or other authority. If a financial account number must be referenced in an e-filing, only the last four digits of these numbers may be used and the number specified in substantially the following format: XXXXX1234.

5. Driver's License Numbers and State–Issued Personal Identification Card Numbers. A person's full Driver's license number and state-issued personal identification number shall not be included in any e-filings. If an individual's driver's license number or state-issued personal identification card number must be referenced in an e-filing, only the last four digits of that number should be used and the number specified in substantially the following format: X–XXX–XXX–XX1–234.

6. Home Addresses. With the exception of a self-represented party, full home addresses shall not be included in any e-filings. If an individual's home address must be referenced in an e-filing, only the city and state should be used. For a party whose address has been made confidential by court order pursuant to MCR 3.203(F), the alternative address shall be treated as specified above.

(b) Parties wishing to file a complete personal data identifier listed above may:

1. Pursuant to and in accordance with court rules and administrative orders, file a motion to file a traditional paper version of the document under seal. The Court may, in granting the motion to file the document under seal, still require that an e-filing that does not reveal the complete personal data identifier be filed for the public files.

OR

2. Pursuant to and in accordance with the applicable court rules and administrative orders, obtain a court order to file a traditional paper reference list under seal. The reference list shall contain the complete personal data identifiers and the redacted identifiers used in the e-filing. All references in the case to the redacted identifiers included in the reference list shall be construed to refer to the corresponding complete personal data identifiers. The reference list must be filed under seal, and may be amended as of right.

(c) Parties should exercise caution when filing papers that contain private or confidential information, including, but not limited to, the information covered above and listed below:

1. Medical records, treatment and diagnosis;

2. Employment history;

3. Individual financial information;

4. Insurance information;

5. Proprietary or trade secret information;

6. Information regarding an individual's cooperation with the government; and

7. Personal information regarding the victim of any criminal activity.

(d) These rules are designed to protect the private personal identifiers and information of individuals involved or referenced in actions before the Court. Nothing in these rules should be interpreted as authority for counsel or a self-represented litigant to deny discovery to the opposing party under the umbrella of complying with these rules.

13. Amendment. Procedural aspects of these rules may be amended upon the recommendation of the participating judges, the approval of the chief judge, and authorization by the State Court Administrator. Proposed substantive changes, including, for example, a proposed expansion of the program to permit additional case types and a proposed change in fees, must be submitted to the Supreme Court for approval.

14. Financial data. Detailed financial data as defined in Administrative Order No. 2009–1, including costs generated and savings realized under the terms of this e-filing project, shall be included in the Oakland Circuit Court's annual report for submission to this Court.

15. Expiration. This pilot program, requiring parties to electronically file documents in cases assigned to participating judges, shall continue until further order of this Court.

[Adopted March 16, 2010, effective March 16, 2010, 485 Mich. Amended effective October 20, 2011, 490 Mich; January 23, 2013, 493 Mich; May 22, 2013, 494 Mich; November 26, 2014, 497 Mich; June 17, 2015, 498 Mich; September 16, 2015, 498 Mich. Amended December 23, 2015, effective January 1, 2016, 498 Mich.]

Comments

Staff Comment to 2013 Amendment

Administrative Order No. 2010–3 has been revised to allow a judge to require a paper copy in the limited circumstances in which the motion is dispositive or the motion with brief and attachments exceeds 40 pages in length.

Order 2010–4 E–Filing Project in the 13th Judicial Circuit Court [Rescinded effective October 23, 2019]

Order 2010–5 29th Judicial Circuit Court Pilot Project No. 1 (Family Division Informal Docket for Low Conflict Domestic Relations Cases)

On order of the Court, the 29th Judicial Circuit Court is authorized to implement a domestic relations pilot project to test the effectiveness of an informal docket for selected domestic relations cases.

The pilot project shall begin September 1, 2010, or as soon as an evaluator has been selected to evaluate the project, and shall continue for three years, or until further order of this Court.

If this Court adopts generally applicable Michigan Court Rules for informal dockets during the pendency of the pilot project, the 29th Judicial Circuit Court must, within 60 days of the effective date of the adopted rules, modify its procedures to comply with those new rules.

The 29th Judicial Circuit Court must collect and provide statistics and other information to the State Court Administrative Office and its retained evaluator to assist in evaluating the effectiveness of the project.

1. Purpose of the Pilot Project. The purpose of the pilot project is to study the effectiveness of alternative, less formal procedures designed to help *pro se* domestic relations litigants use the judicial system more effectively, foster a cooperative ongoing relationship between the parties, and improve the court's processing of domestic relations cases.

2. Participation

(a) The 29th Judicial Circuit Court shall issue a local administrative order that specifies one of the following criteria for creating a pool of pilot project cases and a separate pool of comparison group cases: (i) selection based on *case filing dates*, (ii) selection of a *specific number of filed cases* that satisfy all the other project criteria, or (iii) selection by the *presiding judge*.

(b) The court shall select cases for participation as soon as possible after the filing and service of each complaint.

(c) This is a voluntary project. The court will not require parties to participate, but will offer the opportunity to all those who qualify.

3. Friend of the Court Settlement Conference. After service of the complaint, the answer to complaint, and the summons, the court will refer *pro se* parties to the Friend of the Court Office for a settlement conference and the subsequent preparation of a recommended order for custody, parenting time, and child support. During the conference, an FOC staff person will provide information about the pilot project and verify that the case meets all the selection criteria. Eligible parties who agree to participate must sign a consent form.

4. Hearings With the Assigned Family Division Judge. After the assignment clerk receives copies of both parties' consent forms, the clerk will schedule the parties for an initial hearing with the presiding judge within 30 days. If either party objects to the FOC settlement conference recommended order, the objection will be heard at the initial hearing, provided that the objecting party has filed a written statement of those reasons and sent copies to the other party, the judge's assignment clerk, the judge's office, and the Friend of the Court. During the initial hearing, the judge and the parties must discuss the following issues, as applicable to each case:

- Unresolved disputes.
- Possible evidence.
- Possible witnesses.
- The schedule for subsequent hearings. [1]
- Any property settlement agreements. If the parties have not yet agreed on the division of all the marital property, the court may grant an extension.
- The procedure for preparing and entering a judgment of divorce, including which party will prepare the judgment.

The Assigned Family Division Judge will explain the conference-style hearing to both parties at the initial hearing. Both parties must agree in court on the record to the use of the conference-style hearing. If the parties do not agree to use conference-style hearing, the parties may still participate in the informal docket project and use informal evidentiary rules and procedures

For pilot project cases, conference-style hearings will be conducted. Both parties and all witnesses will be sworn in. The hearings will be recorded. Either party may present evidence. Either party or the judge may ask questions.

If there is more than one unresolved issue, the judge will instruct the parties to discuss each issue individually and then facilitate the parties' discussions. Although parties will have an opportunity to question each other, the parties may ask only issue-clarifying questions. The judge may allow or reject each question.

All witnesses must testify in a similar manner. They may provide narrative testimony. The parties and the judge may question the witnesses. The judge may allow conversations between the parties and the witnesses.

If the court determines the case should be removed from the pilot project for any reason, the court will state the reasons on the record.

[Adopted July 13, 2010, effective September 1, 2010, 486 Mich.]

[1] At the initial settlement conference with the Friend of the Court, parties will receive motion forms, including a form to request removal of the domestic relations case from the project, and a judgment of divorce form.

Order 2010–6   E–Filing in the 16th Circuit Court (Macomb County) [Rescinded effective October 23, 2019]

Order 2011–1   E–Filing Project in the 3rd Circuit Court (Wayne County) [Rescinded effective October 23, 2019]

Order 2011–2   Rescission of Administrative Order No. 2002–1 (Dissolution of the Child Support Leadership Council)

On order of the Court, Administrative Order No. 2002–1 is rescinded, effective immediately.

[Adopted effective June 30, 2011, 489 Mich.]

Order 2011–4   E–Filing Rules for the 20th Circuit Court [Rescinded effective October 23, 2019]

Order 2011–6   E–Filing in Oakland County Probate Court

On order of the Court, the Oakland County Probate Court is authorized to continue its e-filing project during a transition period while the State Court Administrative Office prepares and implements a statewide e-filing system. The Oakland County Probate Court is aware that rules regarding electronic filing have been published for comment by this Court. If this Court adopts electronic-filing rules during the pendency of the Oakland County Probate Court Electronic Document Filing Pilot Project, the Oakland County Probate Court will, within 60 days of the effective date of the rules, comply with the requirements of those rules. In addition, it is anticipated that the Oakland County Probate Court, along with other court locations that participated as e-filing pilot courts, will be among the first group of courts that will connect with any statewide system for purposes of testing and early integration.

The Oakland County Probate Court will report to and provide information as requested by the State Court Administrative Office.

1. Construction. The purpose of the transition period for e-filing is to review and potentially recommence e-filing efforts in the Oakland County Probate Court and to coordinate with state efforts, through a vendor or otherwise, to build and operate a statewide system of e-filing . The Oakland County Probate Court may exercise its discretion to grant necessary relief to avoid the consequences of error so as not to affect the substantial rights of the parties. Except for matters related to electronically filing or service of documents during the transition period, the Michigan Rules of Court govern all other aspects of the cases involved in the program.

2. Definitions.

(a) "Register" means the Oakland County Probate Register.

(b) "E-filing" means any court pleading, motion, brief, response, list, order, judgment, notice, claims, inventories, accounts, reports, or other documents filed electronically pursuant to the program.

(c) "LAO" means all local administrative orders governing the Oakland County Probate Court.

(d) "MCR" means the Michigan Rules of Court.

(e) "Transition e-filing program" or "project" means the initiative by the Oakland County Probate Court in conjunction with the Oakland County Department of Information Technology, and in part with Tyler, Inc. (Wiznet), and under the supervision of the State Court Administrative Office. This e-filing application facilitates the electronic filing of pleadings, motions, briefs, responses, lists, orders, judgments, notices, claims, inventories, accounts, reports, and other documents during the period after enactment of statutory authority to fund and operate a statewide electronic filing system. The Oakland County program will begin testing with one probate judge with "DE", "DA," "TV," and "CZ" case types. The court plans to expand the program to all probate judges as soon as practicable.

(f) "Technical malfunction" means any hardware, software, or other malfunction that prevents a user from timely filing a complete e-filing or sending or receiving service of an e-filing.

(g) "Wiznet envelope" means an electronic submission that contains one or more Wiznet transactions.

(h) "Wiznet transaction" means the submission of one or more related documents which results in a single register of actions entry.

3. Participation in the Program.

(a) If the court recommences its efiling program, participation in the program shall be mandatory in all newly filed DE, DA, TV or CZ case types assigned to the participating probate judges. Participation shall begin following the filing of the initial petition, complaint or other initiating document, and assignment of the case to a participating judge pursuant to the court's LAO. At the discretion of the judge, participation may also include post-disposition proceedings in qualifying case types assigned to participating judges.

(b) This is a mandatory e-filing project. It is presumed that all documents will be filed electronically. However, the Court recognizes that circumstances may arise that will prevent a party from e-filing. To ensure that all parties retain access to the Courts, parties that demonstrate good cause will be permitted to file their documents with the register's office, who will then file the documents electronically. Among the factors that the Oakland County Probate Court will consider in determining whether good cause exists to excuse a party from mandatory e-filing are a party's access to the Internet and indigency. A self-represented party is not excused from the project merely because the individual does not have counsel.

4. E-filings Submission, Acceptance, and Time of Service with the Court; Signature.

(a) Program participants must submit e-filings pursuant to these rules and the program's technical requirements. The register may, in accordance with MCR 8.119(C), reject documents submitted for filing that do not comply with MCR 5.113 or MCR 2.113(C)(2), are not accompanied by the proper fees, clearly violate Administrative Order No. 2006–2, do not conform to the technical requirements of this project, or are otherwise submitted in violation of a statute, an MCR, an LAO, or the program rules.

(b) E-filings may be submitted to the court at any time, but shall only be reviewed and accepted for filing by the Oakland County Probate Court during the normal business hours of the register's office. E-filings submitted after business hours shall be deemed filed on the business day the e-filing is accepted for filing. The register's office shall process electronic submissions on a first-in, first-out basis.

(c) E-filings shall be treated as if they were hand delivered to the court for all purposes under statute, court rule, and administrative order.

(d) A pleading, document, or instrument e-filed or electronically served under this rule shall be deemed to have been signed by the judge, register, attorney, party, or declarant.

(i) Signatures submitted electronically shall be scanned copies of the actual signed document, or shall use the following form for the signature: /s/John L. Smith.

(ii) A document that requires a signature under the penalty of perjury, or is required to be signed by the fiduciary or trustee under MCR 5.114(A)(3), is deemed signed by the declarant or fiduciary if, before filing, the declarant or fiduciary has signed a printed form of the document.

(iii) An e-filed document that requires a signature of a notary public is deemed signed by the notary public if, before filing, the notary public has signed a printed form of the document.

(e) The original of a sworn or verified document that is an e-filing (e.g., a verified pleading) or part of an e-filing (e.g. an affidavit, notarization, or bill of costs) must be maintained by the filing attorney or self-represented litigant and made available upon reasonable request of the court, the signatory, or opposing party.

(f) Proposed orders shall be submitted to the court in accordance with the provisions of the pilot program. The court and the register shall exchange the documents for review and signature pursuant to MCR 2.602(B).

(g) By electronically filing the document, the electronic filer indicates compliance with these rules.

5. Time for Service and Filing of Pleadings, Documents, and Motions; Judge's Copies; Hearings on Motions; Fees.

(a) All times for filing and serving filings shall be governed by the applicable statute, the MCR and the LAO as if the e-filings were hand delivered.

(b) The electronic submission of a motion and brief through this program satisfies the requirements of filing a judge's copy where applicable under the MCR. A judge may require that one "courtesy copy" or "chambers copy" of any dispositive motion and all accompanying exhibits, as well as responses and replies, or any motion and brief in which the motion, brief, and attachments equal 40 pages or more be submitted directly to the judge's chamber in paper format. Any exhibits must be appropriately tabbed. Good practice requires that in appropriate cases, relevant portions of lengthy documents be highlighted. A printed copy of the e-filing transmission receipt must be attached to the front of the pleading. The requirement to provide a "courtesy copy" or "chambers copy" at a judge's request shall expire on May 22, 2018.

(c) Applicable fees, including e-filing fees and service fees, shall be paid electronically through procedures established by the Oakland County Probate Court at the same time and in the same amount as required by statute, court rule, or administrative order. Inventory fees shall be paid according to procedures established by the court.

6. Service.

(a) All parties shall register as a service contact with the Tyler (Wiznet) application which will provide the court and opposing parties with one e-mail address with the functionality required for the program. All service shall originate from and be perfected upon this e-mail address.

(b) Unless otherwise agreed to by the court and the parties, all e-filings must be served electronically to the e-mail address of all interested parties. The subject matter line for the transmittal of document served by e-mail shall state: "Service of e-filing in case [insert caption of case]."

(c) The parties and the court may agree that, instead of e-mail service, e-filings may be served to the parties (but not the court) by other appropriate means under the MCR. For those choosing to accept facsimile service:

(i) the parties shall provide the court and the opposing parties with one facsimile number with appropriate functionality,

(ii) the facsimile number shall serve as the number to which service may be made,

(iii) the sender of the facsimile should obtain a confirmation of delivery, and

(iv) parties shall comply with the requirements of the MCR on the use of facsimile communication equipment.

(d) The court reserves the right to serve parties by traditional means, including facsimile, when necessary to ensure appropriate service of notices, opinions and orders, and other official court documents.

(e) Proof of Service shall be submitted to the Oakland County Probate Court according to the MCR and these rules.

7. Format and Form of E–filing and Service.

(a) A party may only e-file documents for one case in each transaction.

(b) All e-filings shall comply with MCR 1.109 and the technical requirements of the court's vendor and, after implementation, the vendor implementing the statewide e-filing system.

(c) Any exhibit or attachment that is part of an e-filing must be clearly designated and identified as an exhibit or attachment.

(d) All e-filings, subject to subsection 6(c) above, shall be served on the parties in the same format and form as submitted to the court.

8. Pleadings, Motions, and Documents Not to Be E–Filed.
The following documents shall not be e-filed during the program and must be filed by the traditional methods provided in the MCR and the LAO:

(a) documents to be filed under seal (pursuant to court order),

(b) initiating documents,

(c) original documents which are required by statute to be filed with the court, such as wills submitted for probate. In such case, the document shall be e-filed using a copy of the document and the original shall be delivered to the court for filing within 14 days of the e-filing date,

(d) inventories that are being presented pursuant to MCL 700.3706,

(e) documents for case evaluation proceedings.

9. Official Court Record; Certified Copies.

(a) For purposes of this program, the electronic version of all documents filed with the Court, with the exception of documents filed under seal, is the official court record. An appellate record for the Court of Appeals shall be certified in accordance with MCR 7.210(A)(1).

(b) Certified copies of e-filed documents shall be issued in the conventional manner by the Oakland County Probate Register in compliance with the Michigan Trial Court Case File Management Standards.

(c) At the conclusion of the program, if the program does not continue in some other format, the register shall convert all e-filings to paper form in accordance with MCR 8.119(D)(1)(d). Participating attorneys shall provide reasonable assistance in constructing the paper record.

(d) At the conclusion of the program, the register shall provide for record retention and public access in a manner consistent with the instructions of the court and the court rules.

10. Court Notices, Orders, and Judgments.
At the court's discretion, the court and register may issue, file and serve orders, judgments, and notices as e-filings.

11. Technical Malfunctions.

(a) A party experiencing a technical malfunction with the party's equipment (such as Portable Document Format [PDF] conversion problems or inability to access the program sites), another party's equipment (such as an inoperable e-mail address), or an apparent technical malfunction of the court's equipment, software, or server shall use reasonable efforts to timely file or receive service by traditional methods and shall provide prompt notice to the court and the parties of any such malfunction.

(b) If a technical malfunction has prevented a party from timely filing, responding to, or otherwise perfecting or receiving service of an e-filing, the affected party may petition the Oakland County Probate Court for relief. Such petition shall contain an adequate proof of the technical malfunction and set forth good cause for failure to use non-electronic means to timely file or serve a document. The court shall liberally consider proof of the technical malfunction and use its discretion in determining whether such relief is warranted.

12. Privacy Considerations.

(a) Social Security Numbers. Pursuant to Administrative Order No. 2006–2, full social security numbers shall not be included in e-filings. If an individual's social security number must be referenced in an e-filing, only the last four digits of that number may be used and the number specified in substantially the following format: XXX–XX–1234.

(b) Parties should exercise caution when filing papers that contain private or confidential information, including, but not limited to, the information covered above and listed below:

1. Medical records, treatment and diagnosis;

2. Employment history;

3. Individual financial information;

4. Insurance information;

5. Proprietary or trade secret information;

6. Information regarding an individual's cooperation with the government; and

7. Personal information regarding the victim of any criminal activity.

13.
If the e-filing program is recommenced, the Oakland Probate Court shall file an annual report with the Supreme Court covering the project to date by January 1 of each year (or more frequently or on another date as specified by the Court) that outlines the following:

(a) Detailed financial data that show the total amount of money collected in fees for documents filed or served under the project to date, the original projections for collections of fees, and whether the projections have been met or exceeded.

(b) Detailed financial information regarding the distribution or retention of collected fees, including the amount paid to Tyler per document and in total for the subject period, the amount retained by the court per document and in total for the period, and whether the monies retained by the court are in a separate account or commingled with other monies.

(c) A detailed itemization of all costs attributed to the project to date and a statement of whether and when each cost will recur.

(d) A detailed itemization of all cost savings to the court whether by reduced personnel or otherwise and a statement of whether any cost savings to the court are reflected in the fee structure charged to the parties.

14. Amendment. Procedural aspects of these rules may be amended upon the recommendation of the participating judges, the approval of the chief judge, and authorization by the State Court Administrator. Proposed substantive changes, including, for example, a proposed expansion of the program to permit additional case types and a proposed change in fees, must be submitted to the Supreme Court for approval.

15. Expiration. This program, requiring parties to electronically file documents in cases assigned to participating judges, shall continue until further order of the Court.

[Adopted October 20, 2011, effective September 1, 2011, 490 Mich. Amended May 22, 2013, effective May 22, 2013, 494 Mich; December 23, 2015, effective January 1, 2016, 498 Mich.]

Comments

Staff Comment to 2013 Amendment

The revisions of Administrative Order No. 2011–6 regarding Oakland County Probate Court's e-filing project both extend the expiration date of the project until July 31, 2018, and revise paragraph 9(c) to delete the requirement that all e-filings must be converted to paper records at the conclusion of the pilot project. In addition, the order is updated to allow a judge to require a paper copy in the limited circumstances in which the motion is dispositive or the motion with brief and attachments exceeds 40 pages in length.

Order 2012–1 Adoption of Concurrent Jurisdiction Plan for the 10th Circuit Court, the 70th District Court and the Saginaw County Probate Court

Administrative Order No. 2003–1 and MCL 600.401 *et seq.* authorize Michigan trial courts to adopt concurrent jurisdiction plans within a county or judicial circuit, subject to approval of the Court.

The Court hereby approves adoption of the following concurrent jurisdiction plan effective August 1, 2012:

• The 10th Circuit Court, the 70th District Court, and the Saginaw County Probate Court

The plan shall remain on file with the state court administrator.

Amendments to concurrent jurisdiction plans may be implemented by local administrative order pursuant to MCR 8.112. Plan amendments shall conform to the requirements of Administrative Order No. 2003–1 and MCL 600.401 *et seq.*

[Adopted April 4, 2012, effective August 1, 2012, 491 Mich.]

Order 2012–2 Adoption of Concurrent Jurisdiction Plan for the 33rd Circuit Court, the 90th District Court, and Charlevoix/Emmet Probate District

Administrative Order No. 2003–1 and MCL 600.401 *et seq.* authorize Michigan trial courts to adopt concurrent jurisdiction plans within a county or judicial circuit, subject to approval of the Court.

The Court hereby approves adoption of the following concurrent jurisdiction plan effective January 1, 2013:

■ The 33rd Circuit Court, the 90th District Court, and Charlevoix/Emmet Probate District

The plan shall remain on file with the state court administrator.

Amendments to concurrent jurisdiction plans may be implemented by local administrative order pursuant to MCR 8.112. Plan amendments shall conform to the requirements of Administrative Order No. 2003–1 and MCL 600.401 *et seq.*

[Adopted September 19, 2012, effective January 1, 2013, 493 Mich.]

Order 2012–3 Adoption of Concurrent Jurisdiction Plan for the 57th Circuit Court, the 90th District Court, and Charlevoix/Emmet Probate District

Administrative Order No. 2003–1 and MCL 600.401 *et seq.* authorize Michigan trial courts to adopt concurrent jurisdiction plans within a county or judicial circuit, subject to approval of the Court.

The Court hereby approves adoption of the following concurrent jurisdiction plan effective January 1, 2013:

• The 57th Circuit Court, the 90th District Court, and Charlevoix/Emmet Probate District

The plan shall remain on file with the state court administrator.

Amendments to concurrent jurisdiction plans may be implemented by local administrative order pursuant to MCR 8.112. Plan amendments shall conform to the requirements of Administrative Order No. 2003–1 and MCL 600.401 *et seq.*

[Adopted September 19, 2012, effective January 1, 2013, 493 Mich.]

Order 2012–4 Adoption of Concurrent Jurisdiction Plan for the 48th Circuit Court, the 57th District Court, and Allegan County Probate Court

Administrative Order No. 2003–1 and MCL 600.401 *et seq.* authorize Michigan trial courts to adopt concurrent jurisdiction plans within a county or judicial circuit, subject to approval of the Court.

The Court hereby approves adoption of the following concurrent jurisdiction plan effective February 1, 2013:

• The 48th Circuit Court, the 57th District Court, and Allegan County Probate Court

The plan shall remain on file with the state court administrator.

Amendments to concurrent jurisdiction plans may be implemented by local administrative order pursuant to MCR 8.112. Plan amendments shall conform to the requirements of Administrative Order No. 2003–1 and MCL 600.401 *et seq.*

[Adopted October 24, 2012, effective February 1, 2013, 493 Mich.]

Order 2012–5   Adoption of Administrative Order (Implementation of Trial Court Performance Measures)

Performance measurement is a critical means to assess the services provided to the public and the processes used to deliver those services. Performance measurement can assist in assessing and recognizing areas within courts that are working well, and those that require attention and improvement.

Trial court performance measures are not a new concept. The National Center for State Courts first issued the 10 CourTools in 2005; in the 1990s, SCAO formed a task force, including judges and court administrators, to study how to measure a court's performance. In 2009, the state court administrator convened the Trial Court Performance Measures Committee, which piloted performance measures and offered recommendations. The committee stressed that all trial courts should embrace performance measures as an opportunity to provide high-quality public service in the most efficient way. Further, because transparency and accountability are integral elements of an efficient and effective judiciary, SCAO's standardized statewide performance measure reports should be readily available to the public.

In an effort to ensure continued improvement in the judiciary, the Court adopts this order.

A. The State Court Administrative Office is directed to:

1. Develop a plan for implementation of performance measures in all trial courts. The initial plan shall be submitted to the Supreme Court for approval, and the plan subsequently shall be periodically reviewed by the Court.

2. Assist trial courts in implementing and posting performance measures.

3. In conjunction with the Trial Court Performance Measures Committee, assess and report on the effectiveness of the performance measures and modify the measures as needed.

B. Trial courts are directed to:

1. Comply with the trial court performance measures plan developed by the State Court Administrative Office.

2. Report performance measure information to the State Court Administrative Office.

C. SCAO's standardized statewide performance measure reports shall be made available to the public on the Internet after approval by the Supreme Court.

[Adopted effective December 5, 2012, 493 Mich.]

Comments

Staff Comment to 2012 Adoption

This administrative order authorizes the implementation of performance measures in trial courts.

Order 2012–6   Adoption of Concurrent Jurisdiction Plan for the 37th Circuit Court, the 10th District Court, and the Calhoun County Probate Court

Administrative Order No. 2003–1 and MCL 600.401 *et seq.* authorize Michigan trial courts to adopt concurrent jurisdiction plans within a county or judicial circuit, subject to approval of the Court.

The Court hereby approves adoption of the following concurrent jurisdiction plan effective January 1, 2013, or as soon thereafter as possible:

● The 37th Circuit Court, the 10th District Court, and the Calhoun County Probate Court.

The plan shall remain on file with the state court administrator.

Amendments to concurrent jurisdiction plans may be implemented by local administrative order pursuant to MCR 8.112. Plan amendments shall conform to the requirements of Administrative Order No. 2003–1 and MCL 600.401 *et seq.*

[Adopted December 5, 2012, effective January 1, 2013, 493 Mich.]

Order 2012–7   Adoption of Administrative Order (to Allow State Court Administrative Office to Authorize a Judicial Officer's Appearance by Video Communication Equipment)

The State Court Administrative Office is authorized, until further order of this Court, to approve the use of two-way interactive video technology in the trial courts to allow judicial officers to preside remotely in any proceeding that may be conducted by two-way interactive technology or communication equipment without the consent of the parties under the Michigan Court Rules and statutes. Remote participation by judicial officers shall be limited to the following specific situations:

1) judicial assignments;

2) circuits and districts that are comprised of more than one county and would require a judicial officer to travel to a different courthouse within the circuit or district;

3) district court districts that have multiple court locations in which a judicial officer would have to travel to a different courthouse within the district;

4) a multiple district plan in which a district court magistrate would have to travel to a different district.

The judicial officer who presides remotely must be physically present in a courthouse located within his or her judicial circuit, district, or multiple district area.

For circuits or districts that are comprised of more than one county, each court that seeks permission to allow its judicial officers to preside by video communication equipment must submit a proposed local administrative order for approval by the State Court Administrator pursuant to MCR 8.112(B). The local administrative order must describe how the program will be implemented and the administrative procedures for each type of hearing for which two-way interactive video technology will be used. The State Court Administrative Office shall either approve the proposed local administrative order or return it to the chief judge for amendment in accordance with requirements and guidelines provided by the State Court Administrative Office.

For judicial assignments, the assignment order will allow remote participation by judges as long as the assigned judge is physically present in a courthouse located within the judge's judicial circuit or district. A local administrative order is not required for assignments.

For multiple district plans, the plan will allow remote participation by district court magistrates as long as the magistrate is physically present in a courthouse located within the multiple district area. No separate local administrative order is required.

The State Court Administrative Office shall assist courts in implementing the technology, and shall report periodically to this Court regarding its assessment of the program. Those courts using the technology shall provide statistics and otherwise cooperate with the State Court Administrative Office in monitoring the use of video communication equipment.

[Adopted December 5, 2012, effective January 1, 2013, 493 Mich.]

Comments

Staff Comment to 2013 Adoption

This administrative order allows the State Court Administrative Office to authorize a judge to preside using videoconferencing equipment in certain types of proceedings.

Order 2013–1 Adoption of Concurrent Jurisdiction Plan for the 18th Circuit Court, the 74th District Court, and the Bay County Probate Court

Administrative Order No. 2003–1 and MCL 600.401 *et seq.* authorize Michigan trial courts to adopt concurrent jurisdiction plans within a county or judicial circuit, subject to approval of the Court.

The Court hereby approves adoption of the following concurrent jurisdiction plan effective immediately:

● The 18th Circuit Court, the 74th District Court, and the Bay County Probate Court.

The plan shall remain on file with the state court administrator.

Amendments to concurrent jurisdiction plans may be implemented by local administrative order pursuant to MCR 8.112. Plan amendments shall conform to the requirements of Administrative Order No. 2003–1 and MCL 600.401 *et seq.*

[Adopted effective January 23, 2013, 493 Mich.]

Order 2013–2 Adoption of Concurrent Jurisdiction Plan for the 14th Circuit Court, the 60th District Court, and the Muskegon County Probate Court

Administrative Order No. 2003–1 and MCL 600.401 *et seq.* authorize Michigan trial courts to adopt concurrent jurisdiction plans within a county or judicial circuit, subject to approval of the Court.

The Court hereby approves adoption of the following concurrent jurisdiction plan effective immediately:

● The 14th Circuit Court, the 60th District Court, and the Muskegon County Probate Court.

The plan shall remain on file with the state court administrator.

Amendments to concurrent jurisdiction plans may be implemented by local administrative order pursuant to MCR 8.112. Plan amendments shall conform to the requirements of Administrative Order No. 2003–1 and MCL 600.401 *et seq.*

[Adopted effective January 23, 2013, 493 Mich.]

Order 2013–3 Adoption of Concurrent Jurisdiction Plan for the 45th Circuit Court, the 3–B District Court, and the St. Joseph County Probate Court

Administrative Order No. 2003–1 and MCL 600.401 *et seq.* authorize Michigan trial courts to adopt concurrent jurisdiction plans within a county or judicial circuit, subject to approval of the Court.

The Court hereby approves adoption of the following concurrent jurisdiction plan effective immediately:

● The 45th Circuit Court, the 3–B District Court, and the St. Joseph County Probate Court.

The plan shall remain on file with the state court administrator.

Amendments to concurrent jurisdiction plans may be implemented by local administrative order pursuant to MCR 8.112. Plan amendments shall conform to the requirements of Administrative Order No. 2003–1 and MCL 600.401 *et seq.*

[Adopted effective March 20, 2013, 493 Mich.]

Order 2013–4 Adoption of Concurrent Jurisdiction Plan for the 56th Circuit Court, the 56–A District Court, and the Eaton County Probate Court

Administrative Order No. 2003–1 and MCL 600.401 *et seq.* authorize Michigan trial courts to adopt concurrent jurisdiction plans within a county or judicial circuit, subject to approval of the Court.

The Court hereby approves adoption of the following concurrent jurisdiction plan effective immediately:

● The 56th Circuit Court, the 56–A District Court, and the Eaton County Probate Court.

The plan shall remain on file with the state court administrator.

Amendments to concurrent jurisdiction plans may be implemented by local administrative order pursuant to MCR 8.112. Plan amendments shall conform to the requirements of Administrative Order No. 2003–1 and MCL 600.401 *et seq.*

[Adopted effective May 1, 2013, 493 Mich.]

Order 2013–5 Adoption of Concurrent Jurisdiction Plan for the 54th Circuit Court, the 71–B District Court, and the Tuscola County Probate Court

Administrative Order No. 2003–1 and MCL 600.401 *et seq.* authorize Michigan trial courts to adopt concurrent jurisdiction plans within a county or judicial circuit, subject to approval of the Court.

The Court hereby approves adoption of the following concurrent jurisdiction plan effective immediately:

● The 54th Circuit Court, the 71–B District Court, and the Tuscola County Probate Court.

The plan shall remain on file with the state court administrator.

Amendments to concurrent jurisdiction plans may be implemented by local administrative order pursuant to MCR 8.112. Plan amendments shall conform to the requirements of Administrative Order No. 2003–1 and MCL 600.401 *et seq.*

[Adopted effective May 1, 2013, 493 Mich.]

Order 2013–6   Implementation of Business Court Standards

Business courts, as defined by MCL 600.8031, are specialized dockets within a circuit court. Business courts are intended to provide a case management structure that facilitates timely, effective, and predictable resolution of complex business cases. Specialized dockets improve the efficiency of the courts, which benefits all litigants. This order provides specific direction to circuit courts in the establishment of their business courts.

1. Each business court shall develop a local administrative order for operation of its business court docket. That local administrative order must be approved by the State Court Administrative Office in accordance with MCR 8.112(B).

2. Judges appointed to the business court must attend training provided by the Michigan Judicial Institute. Business court judges are encouraged also to participate in training provided by other organizations as local funding permits.

3. A business court judge should preside over the assigned business court cases from filing through disposition of the matter. If the business court judge is unable to preside over a business court matter, the chief judge may temporarily assign another judge to preside over the business court matter pursuant to MCR 8.111(C).

4. Courts shall establish specific case management practices for business court matters. These practices should reflect the specialized pretrial requirements for business court cases, and will typically include provisions relating to scheduling conferences, alternative dispute resolution (with an emphasis on mediation scheduled early in the proceeding), discovery cutoff dates, case evaluation, and final settlement conferences.

5. Case management and scheduling conferences shall be conducted by the assigned business court judge. Courts should facilitate the processing of business court cases by utilizing electronic filing (if authorized by the Supreme Court), telephonic and video conferencing.

6. Business court opinions shall be transmitted to the SCAO within 7 days after the trial court enters the opinion. Court opinions generated as part of the business court docket must meet the requirements established by the SCAO.

7. Business courts shall maintain data as prescribed by the SCAO, and shall provide data to the SCAO upon request.
[Adopted June 5, 2013, effective September 1, 2013, 494 Mich.]

Comments

Staff Comment to 2013 Adoption

The administrative order establishes procedures for courts that are required to or choose to implement a business court.

Order 2013–7   Adoption of Concurrent Jurisdiction Plan for the 38th Circuit Court, the 1st District Court, and the Monroe County Probate Court

Administrative Order No. 2003–1 and MCL 600.401 *et seq.* authorize Michigan trial courts to adopt concurrent jurisdiction plans within a county or judicial circuit, subject to approval of the Court.

The Court hereby approves adoption of the following concurrent jurisdiction plan effective immediately:

● The 38th Circuit Court, the 1st District Court, and the Monroe County Probate Court.

The plan shall remain on file with the state court administrator.

Amendments to concurrent jurisdiction plans may be implemented by local administrative order pursuant to MCR 8.112. Plan amendments shall conform to the requirements of Administrative Order No. 2003–1 and MCL 600.401 *et seq.*
[Adopted effective June 19, 2013, 494 Mich.]

Order 2013–8   Trial Court Requirements for Providing Meaningful Access to the Court for Limited English Proficient Persons

In order to ensure that those persons with limited English proficiency have meaningful access to Michigan courts, the Michigan Supreme Court adopts this order requiring courts to adopt a language access plan.

"Limited English proficient" person means a person who does not speak English as his or her primary language, and who has a limited ability to read, write, speak, or understand English, and by reason of his or her limitations, is not able to understand and meaningfully participate in the court process.

Within 90 days of the date of this order, each trial court shall adopt a language access plan. This plan must substantially conform to the model promulgated by the state court administrator. The plan must provide meaningful access to limited English proficient persons who have contacts with the court and its administrative staff. The plan shall be submitted to and approved by the State Court Administrative Office as a local administrative order under MCR 8.112.
[Adopted effective September 11, 2013, 495 Mich.]

Order 2013–9   Adoption of Concurrent Jurisdiction plan for the 40th Circuit Court, the 71–A District Court, and the Lapeer County Probate Court

Administrative Order No. 2003–1 and MCL 600.401 *et seq.* authorize Michigan trial courts to adopt concurrent jurisdiction plans within a county or judicial circuit, subject to approval of the Court.

The Court hereby approves adoption of the following concurrent jurisdiction plan effective immediately:

● The 40th Circuit Court, the 71–A District Court, and the Lapeer County Probate Court.

The plan shall remain on file with the state court administrator.

Amendments to concurrent jurisdiction plans may be implemented by local administrative order pursuant to MCR 8.112. Plan amendments shall conform to the requirements of Administrative Order No. 2003–1 and MCL 600.401 *et seq.*
[Adopted effective September 18, 2013, 495 Mich.]

Order 2013–10   Adoption of Concurrent Jurisdiction plan for the 44th Circuit Court, the 53rd District Court, and the Livingston County Probate Court

Administrative Order No. 2003–1 and MCL 600.401 *et seq.* authorize Michigan trial courts to adopt concurrent jurisdiction plans within a county or judicial circuit, subject to approval of the Court.

The Court hereby approves adoption of the following concurrent jurisdiction plan effective immediately:

• The 44th Circuit Court, the 53rd District Court, and the Livingston County Probate Court.

The plan shall remain on file with the state court administrator.

Amendments to concurrent jurisdiction plans may be implemented by local administrative order pursuant to MCR 8.112. Plan amendments shall conform to the requirements of Administrative Order No. 2003–1 and MCL 600.401 *et seq.*

[Adopted effective September 18, 2013, 495 Mich.]

Order 2013–11 Adoption of Concurrent Jurisdiction plan for the 1st Circuit Court, the 2–B District Court, and the Hillsdale County Probate Court

Administrative Order No. 2003–1 and MCL 600.401 *et seq.* authorize Michigan trial courts to adopt concurrent jurisdiction plans within a county or judicial circuit, subject to approval of the Court.

The Court hereby approves adoption of the following concurrent jurisdiction plan effective immediately:

• The 1st Circuit Court, the 2–B District Court, and the Hillsdale County Probate Court.

The plan shall remain on file with the state court administrator.

Amendments to concurrent jurisdiction plans may be implemented by local administrative order pursuant to MCR 8.112. Plan amendments shall conform to the requirements of Administrative Order No. 2003–1 and MCL 600.401 *et seq.*

[Adopted effective September 18, 2013, 495 Mich.]

Order 2013–12 Revised Caseflow Management Guidelines and Rescission of Administrative Order No. 2011–3

On order of the Court, notice of the proposed changes and an opportunity for comment in writing and at a public hearing having been provided, and consideration having been given to the comments received, Administrative Order No. 2013–12 is adopted, and Administrative Order No. 2011–3 is rescinded, effective January 1, 2014.

Administrative Order No. 2013–12

The management of the flow of cases in the trial court is the responsibility of the judiciary. In carrying out that responsibility, the judiciary must balance the rights and interests of individual litigants, the limited resources of the judicial branch and other participants in the justice system, and the interests of the citizens of this state in having an effective, fair, and efficient system of justice.

Accordingly, on order of the Court,

A. The State Court Administrator is Directed, within Available Resources, to:

1. assist trial courts in implementing caseflow management plans that incorporate case processing time guidelines established pursuant to this order;

2. gather information from trial courts on compliance with caseflow management guidelines; and

3. assess the effectiveness of caseflow management plans in achieving the guidelines established by this order.

B. Trial Courts are Directed to:

1. maintain current caseflow management plans consistent with case processing time guidelines established in this order, and in cooperation with the State Court Administrative Office;

2. report to the State Court Administrative Office caseflow management statistics and other caseflow management data required by that office; and

3. cooperate with the State Court Administrative Office in assessing caseflow management plans implemented pursuant to this order.

On further order of the Court, the following time guidelines for case processing are provided as goals for the administration of court caseloads. These are only guidelines and are not intended to supersede procedural requirements in court rules or statutes for specific cases, or to supersede reporting requirements in court rules or statutes. The trial courts shall not dismiss cases for the sole reason that the case is likely to exceed the guideline. In addition, these guidelines do not supplant judicial discretion if, for good cause, a specific case of any type requires a time line that extends beyond the maximum permitted under these guidelines.

Note: The phrase "adjudicated" refers to the date a case is reported in Part 2 of the caseload report forms and instructions. Aging of a case is suspended for the time a case is inactive as defined in Parts 2 and 4 of the caseload report forms and instructions. Refer to these specific definitions for details.

Matters Submitted to the Judge. Matters under submission to a judge or judicial officer should be promptly determined. Short deadlines should be set for presentation of briefs and affidavits and or production of transcripts. Decisions, when possible, should be made from the bench or within a few days of submission; otherwise a decision should be rendered no later than 35 days after submission.

Probate Court Guidelines

1. **Estate Proceedings.** 75% of all cases should be adjudicated within 35 days from the date of the initial filing, 90% within 182 days, and 98% within 364 days.

2. **Guardianship, Conservatorship, and Protective Order Proceedings.** 75% of all matters should be adjudicated within 90 days from the date of the initial filing and 95% within 364 days.

3. **Mental Illness Proceedings; Judicial Admission Proceedings.** 90% of all petitions should be adjudicated within 14 days from the date of filing and 98% within 28 days.

4. **Civil Proceedings and Trusts Proceedings.** 70% of all cases should be adjudicated within 364 days from the date of case filing and 95% within 728 days.

District Court Guidelines

1. **Civil Proceedings.**

a. *General Civil.* 90% of all general civil and miscellaneous civil cases should be adjudicated within 273 days from the date of case filing and 98% within 455 days.

b. *Summary Civil.* 95% of all small claims, landlord/tenant, and land contract actions should be adjudicated within 126 days from the date of case filing in those cases where there is no jury demand. 65% of all landlord/tenant and land contract actions where a jury is demanded should be adjudicated within 154 days from the date of case filing.

2. Felony, Misdemeanor, and Extradition Detainer Proceedings.

a. *Misdemeanor.* 85% of all statute and ordinance misdemeanor cases, including misdemeanor drunk driving and misdemeanor traffic, should be adjudicated within 63 days from the date of first appearance and 95% within 126 days.

b. *Felony and Extradition/Detainer.* 60% of all preliminary examinations in felony, felony drunk driving, felony traffic, and extradition/detainer cases should be concluded within 14 days of arraignment and 75% within 28 days.

3. Civil Infraction Proceedings. 90% of all civil infraction cases, including traffic, nontraffic, and parking cases, should be adjudicated within 35 days from the date of filing and 98% within 84 days.

Circuit Court Guidelines

1. Civil Proceedings. 70% of all cases should be adjudicated within 364 days from the date of case filing and 95% within 728 days.

2. Domestic Relations Proceedings.

a. *Divorce Without Children.* 85% of all divorce cases without children should be adjudicated within 182 days from the date of case filing and 98% within 364 days.

b. *Divorce With Children.* 85% of all divorce cases with children should be adjudicated within 301 days from the date of case filing and 95% within 364 days.

c. *Paternity.* 75% of all paternity cases should be adjudicated within 147 days from the date of case filing and 95% within 238 days.

d. *Responding Interstate Establishment.* 75% of all incoming interstate actions to establish support should be adjudicated within 147 days from the date of case filing and 95% within 238 days.

e. *Child Custody Issues, Other Support, and Other Domestic Relations Matters.* 75% of all child custody, other support, and other domestic relations issues not listed above should be adjudicated within 147 days from the date of case filing and 95% within 238 days.

3. Delinquency Proceedings. Where a minor is being detained or is held in court custody, 80% of all original petitions or complaints should have adjudication and disposition completed within 84 days from the authorization of the petition and 90% within 98 days. Where a minor is not being detained or held in court custody, 75% of all original petitions or complaints should have adjudication and disposition completed within 119 days from the authorization of the petition and 98% within 210 days.

4. Child Protective Proceedings. Where a child is in out-of-home placement (foster care), 75% of all original petitions should have adjudication and disposition completed within 84 days from the authorization of the petition and 85% within 98 days. Where a child is not in out-of-home placement (foster care), 75% of all original petitions should have adjudication and disposition within 119 days from the authorization of the petition and 95% within 210 days.

5. Designated Proceedings. 90% of all original petitions should be adjudicated within 154 days from the designation date and 98% within 301 days. Minors held in custody should be afforded priority for trial.

6. Juvenile Traffic and Ordinance Proceedings. 90% of all citations should have adjudication and disposition completed within 63 days from the date of first appearance and 98% within 126 days.

7. Adoption Proceedings.

a. *Petitions for Adoption.* 90% of all petitions for adoption should be finalized or otherwise concluded within 287 days from the date of filing and 98% within 364 days.

b. *Petitions to Rescind Adoption.* 98% of all petitions to rescind adoption should be adjudicated within 91 days from the date of filing.

8. Miscellaneous Family Proceedings.

a. *Name Change.* 98% of all petitions should be adjudicated within 126 days from the date of filing.

b. *Safe Delivery.* 98% of all petitions should be adjudicated within 273 days from the date of filing.

c. *Personal Protection.* 100% of all petitions requesting ex parte relief should be adjudicated within 24 hours of filing. 90% of all petitions not requesting ex parte relief or in which a hearing will be set should be adjudicated within 14 days from the date of filing and 100% within 21 days.

d. *Emancipation of Minors.* 98% of all petitions should be adjudicated within 91 days from the date of filing.

e. *Infectious Diseases.* 98% of all petitions should be adjudicated within 91 days from the date of filing.

f. *Parental Waiver.* 98% of all petitions should be adjudicated within 5 days from the date of filing.

9. Ancillary Proceedings.

a. *Guardianship, Conservatorship, and Protective Order Proceedings.* 75% of all matters should be adjudicated within 90 days from the date of the initial filing and 95% within 364 days.

b. *Mental Illness Proceedings; Judicial Admission.* 90% of all petitions should be adjudicated within 14 days from the date of filing and 98% within 28 days.

10. Criminal Proceedings. 70% of all felony cases should be adjudicated within 91 days from the date of entry of the order binding the defendant over to the circuit court; 85% within 154 days; and 98% within 301 days. Incarcerated persons should be afforded priority for trial.

With SCAO approval, circuit courts may establish by local administrative order an alternative guideline for criminal proceedings that would provide that 75% of all felony cases should be adjudicated within 154 days from the date of entry of the order binding the defendant over to the circuit court and 98% within 301 days. Incarcerated persons should be afforded priority for trial. Courts requesting the alternative guideline must give the sheriff the opportunity to comment on the proposed order.

11. Appellate, Administrative Review, and Extraordinary Writ Proceedings.

a. *Appeals from Courts of Limited Jurisdiction.* 98% of all appeals to circuit court from courts of limited jurisdiction should be adjudicated within 182 days from the filing of the claim of appeal.

b. *Appeals from Administrative Agencies.* 98% of all appeals to the circuit court from administrative agencies should be adjudicated within 182 days from the filing of the claim of appeal.

c. *Extraordinary Writs.* 90% of all extraordinary writ requests should be adjudicated within 35 days from the date of filing and 98% within 91 days.

[Adopted October 2, 2013, effective January 1, 2014, 495 Mich. Amended effective May 7, 2014, 495 Mich. Amended May 25, 2016, effective September 1, 2016, 499 Mich; June 15, 2016, effective September 1, 2016, 499 Mich.]

Comments

Staff Comment to January, 2014 Adoption

Administrative Order No. 2013–12 rescinds Administrative Order No. 2011–3 and updates the guidelines found in that order. The updates revise the guidelines to make them more reflective of disposition rates based on statewide court data and to accommodate the fact that there may be delay in any case type that would make 100 percent disposition nearly impossible. However, the 100 percent disposition expectation remains in place for personal protection petitions.

Staff Comment to May, 2014 Amendment

These amendments reflect changes that correct minor technical errors that have occurred in drafting or the changes respond to recent adopted rule revisions, which occasionally inadvertently create incorrect cross-references in other rules.

Staff Comment to First September, 2016 Amendment

The revisions of Administrative Order No. 2013–12 adjust the time guidelines in probate courts by applying disposition rates to cases filed in estate, trust, guardianship, and conservatorship proceedings instead of applying rates to only "contested matters" in those types of proceedings. The revisions also separate the guidelines for guardianship and conservatorship proceedings from other estate matters, and group them with protective order proceedings, and group trust proceedings with civil proceedings instead of the former grouping of trusts with proceedings for estates.

Staff Comment to Second September, 2016 Amendment

The revisions of the Circuit Court Guidelines reflect recent amendments in the Probate Court Guidelines.

Order 2013–13   Creation of Committee on Model Criminal Jury Instructions

For decades, criminal jury instructions in Michigan have been developed by the Standing Committee on Jury Instructions, Standard Criminal, of the State Bar of Michigan and then published by the Institute for Continuing Legal Education. The instructions were then made available for purchase. Now, however, recognizing their widespread use and the utility of the instructions for attorneys, litigants, and the courts, and in support of the notion that these materials should be readily available to all users, the Court desires to make use of the instructions mandatory and ensure that they are freely available to all, as are the model civil jury instructions.

In addition to the Court's adoption of proposed amendments of MCR 2.512 that will require the use of criminal jury instructions where appropriate, under this administrative order the Court creates a committee to propose new and to modify existing criminal jury instructions. The Court is appreciative of the long and distinguished service that members of the Standing Committee on Standard Criminal Jury Instructions have provided over the years. Their dedicated service has produced a set of criminal jury instructions that has become a valuable tool in criminal proceedings. The Court also acknowl-

edges the generous decision by the Institute of Continuing Legal Education to relinquish its copyright over the instructions, thus enabling this Court to make the instructions and much of their accompanying materials available to everyone for no charge on the Court's website.

The new Committee on Model Criminal Jury Instructions is established. The committee shall consist of 21 persons to be appointed by the Supreme Court. The Supreme Court will designate one member to serve as the chairperson of the committee. Generally members will be appointed for three-year terms and may be reappointed for two additional terms. However, to facilitate the transition and the staggering of terms, some initial appointments will be for abbreviated terms and those appointees who are members of the current State Bar of Michigan Standing Committee on Jury Instructions, Standard Criminal, will not be eligible for reappointment.

Effective January 1, 2014, the following persons are appointed to the new Committee on Model Criminal Jury Instructions:

For terms ending December 31, 2014:

The Honorable William J. Caprathe
The Honorable John T. Hammond
Ronald J. Bretz
Stephen M. Taratuta
Anica Letica
J. Mark Cooney
Torchio W. Feaster

For terms ending December 31, 2015:

The Honorable Brian R. Sullivan
William J. Vailliencourt, Jr.
Opolla Brown
The Honorable Annette M. Jurkiewicz–Berry
Louisa M. Papalas–Concessi
The Honorable Gene Schnelz
Lawrence B. Shulman

For terms ending December 31, 2016:

Rudolph A. Serra
Bonita S. Hoffman
The Honorable Paul J. Paruk
Christopher Smith
Stacia J. Buchanan
The Honorable Timothy G. Hicks
Timothy Baughman

Judge Caprathe is designated as chairperson for the duration of his term. Court staff will serve as reporter of the committee.

It shall be the duty of the committee to ensure that the Criminal Jury Instructions accurately state applicable law, and that the instructions are concise, understandable, conversational, unslanted, and not argumentative. The committee shall have the authority to amend or repeal existing instructions and, when necessary, to adopt new instructions. Before doing so, the committee shall provide a text of the proposal to the secretary of the State Bar of Michigan and the state court administrator, and shall post the proposal on the Court's website [http://courts.mi.gov/Courts/MichiganSupremeCourt/MCrimJI] for public comment. The notice and website posting shall state the time and method for commenting on the proposal. If the committee finds it necessary to take immediate action, the committee may adopt a new instruction or revision while the public comment period is pending.

By separate order, the Court is amending Rule 2.512 of the Michigan Court Rules to reflect the requirement to use the criminal jury instructions. The instructions, use notes, and history are expected to be posted on the Court's website by January 1, 2014. Additional supplemental commentary will be available shortly thereafter. Practitioners, litigants, and courts are encouraged to use the instructions as soon as practicable, but will be required to use them on the order's effective date of March 1, 2014.

[Adopted October 30, 2013, effective January 1, 2014, 495 Mich.]

Order 2013–14   Adoption of Concurrent Jurisdiction Plan for the 20th Circuit Court, the 58th District Court, and the Ottawa County Probate Court

Administrative Order No. 2003–1 and MCL 600.401 *et seq.* authorize Michigan trial courts to adopt concurrent jurisdiction plans within a county or judicial circuit, subject to approval of the Court.

The Court hereby approves adoption of the following concurrent jurisdiction plan effective immediately:

• The 20th Circuit Court, the 58th District Court, and the Ottawa County Probate Court.

The plan shall remain on file with the state court administrator.

Amendments to concurrent jurisdiction plans may be implemented by local administrative order pursuant to MCR 8.112. Plan amendments shall conform to the requirements of Administrative Order No. 2003–1 and MCL 600.401 *et seq.*

[Adopted effective November 6, 2013, 495 Mich.]

Order 2013–15   Adoption of Concurrent Jurisdiction Plan for the 31st Circuit Court, the 72nd District Court, and the St. Clair County Probate Court

Administrative Order No. 2003–1 and MCL 600.401 *et seq.* authorize Michigan trial courts to adopt concurrent jurisdiction plans within a county or judicial circuit, subject to approval of the Court.

The Court hereby approves adoption of the following concurrent jurisdiction plan effective immediately:

• The 31st Circuit Court, the 72nd District Court, and the St. Clair County Probate Court.

The plan shall remain on file with the state court administrator.

Amendments to concurrent jurisdiction plans may be implemented by local administrative order pursuant to MCR 8.112. Plan amendments shall conform to the requirements of Administrative Order No. 2003–1 and MCL 600.401 *et seq.*

[Adopted effective November 6, 2013, 495 Mich.]

Order 2013–16   Adoption of Concurrent Jurisdiction Plan for the 25th Circuit Court, the 96th District Court, and the Marquette County Probate Court

Administrative Order No. 2003–1 and MCL 600.401 *et seq.* authorize Michigan trial courts to adopt concurrent jurisdiction plans within a county or judicial circuit, subject to approval of the Court.

The Court hereby approves adoption of the following concurrent jurisdiction plan effective immediately:

• The 25th Circuit Court, the 96th District Court, and the Marquette County Probate Court.

The plan shall remain on file with the state court administrator.

Amendments to concurrent jurisdiction plans may be implemented by local administrative order pursuant to MCR 8.112. Plan amendments shall conform to the requirements of Administrative Order No. 2003–1 and MCL 600.401 *et seq.*

[Adopted effective November 27, 2013, 495 Mich.]

Order 2014–1   Adoption of Concurrent Jurisdiction Plan for the 15th Circuit Court, the 3–A District Court, and the Branch County Probate Court

Administrative Order No. 2003–1 and MCL 600.401 *et seq.* authorize Michigan trial courts to adopt concurrent jurisdiction plans within a county or judicial circuit, subject to approval of the Court.

The Court hereby approves adoption of the following concurrent jurisdiction plan effective immediately:

• The 15th Circuit Court, the 3–A District Court, and the Branch County Probate Court.

The plan shall remain on file with the state court administrator.

Amendments to concurrent jurisdiction plans may be implemented by local administrative order pursuant to MCR 8.112. Plan amendments shall conform to the requirements of Administrative Order No. 2003–1 and MCL 600.401 *et seq.*

[Adopted effective January 29, 2014, 495 Mich.]

Order 2014–2   Adoption of Concurrent Jurisdiction Plan for the 9th Circuit Court, the 8th District Court, and the Kalamazoo County Probate Court

Administrative Order No. 2003–1 and MCL 600.401 *et seq.* authorize Michigan trial courts to adopt concurrent jurisdiction plans within a county or judicial circuit, subject to approval of the Court.

The Court hereby approves adoption of the following concurrent jurisdiction plan effective immediately:

• The 9th Circuit Court, the 8th District Court, and the Kalamazoo County Probate Court.

The plan shall remain on file with the state court administrator.

Amendments to concurrent jurisdiction plans may be implemented by local administrative order pursuant to MCR 8.112. Plan amendments shall conform to the requirements of Administrative Order No. 2003–1 and MCL 600.401 *et seq.*

[Adopted effective January 29, 2014, 495 Mich.]

Order 2014–3   Adoption of Concurrent Jurisdiction Plan for the 29th Circuit Court, the 65A and 65B District Courts, and the Clinton County and Gratiot County Probate Courts

Administrative Order No. 2003–1 and MCL 600.401 *et seq.* authorize Michigan trial courts to adopt concurrent jurisdiction plans within a county or judicial circuit, subject to approval of the Court.

The Court hereby approves adoption of the following concurrent jurisdiction plan effective immediately:

● The 29th Circuit Court, the 65A and 65B District Courts, and the Clinton County and Gratiot County Probate Courts.

The plan shall remain on file with the state court administrator.

Amendments to concurrent jurisdiction plans may be implemented by local administrative order pursuant to MCR 8.112. Plan amendments shall conform to the requirements of Administrative Order No. 2003–1 and MCL 600.401 *et seq*.

[Adopted effective January 29, 2014, 495 Mich.]

Order 2014–4 Adoption of Concurrent Jurisdiction Plan for the 30th Circuit Court, the 54A, 54B, and 55th District Courts, and the Ingham County Probate Court

Administrative Order No. 2003–1 and MCL 600.401 *et seq*. authorize Michigan trial courts to adopt concurrent jurisdiction plans within a county or judicial circuit, subject to approval of the Court.

The Court hereby approves adoption of the following concurrent jurisdiction plan effective immediately:

● The 30th Circuit Court, the 54A, 54B, and 55th District Courts, and the Ingham County Probate Court.

The plan shall remain on file with the state court administrator.

Amendments to concurrent jurisdiction plans may be implemented by local administrative order pursuant to MCR 8.112. Plan amendments shall conform to the requirements of Administrative Order No. 2003–1 and MCL 600.401 *et seq*.

[Adopted effective January 29, 2014, 495 Mich.]

Order 2014–5 Order Creating the Task Force on the Role of the State Bar of Michigan

[T]he regulation of the practice of law, the maintenance of high standards in the legal profession, and the discharge of the profession's duty to protect and inform the public are, in the context of the present challenge, purposes in which the State of Michigan has a compelling interest ... [*Falk v State Bar of Michigan*, 411 Mich 63, 114; 305 NW2d 201 (1981) (opinion of RYAN, J.).]

[T]he compelled association and integrated bar are justified by the State's interest in regulating the legal profession and improving the quality of legal services. The State Bar may therefore constitutionally fund activities germane to those goals out of the mandatory dues of all members. It may not, however, in such manner fund activities of an ideological nature which fall outside of those areas of activity. [*Keller v State Bar of California*, 496 US 1, 13–14; 110 S Ct 2228; 110 L Ed 2d 1 (1990).]

The question having been raised about the appropriateness of the mandatory nature of the State Bar of Michigan, and the State Bar having requested that the Michigan Supreme Court facilitate this important discussion, pursuant to its exclusive constitutional authority to establish "practice and procedure," Const 1963, art 6, § 5, the Court establishes the Task Force on the Role of the State Bar of Michigan to address whether the State Bar's current programs and activities support its status as a mandatory bar.

The task force is charged with determining whether the State Bar's duties and functions "can[] be accomplished by means less intrusive upon the First Amendment rights of objecting individual attorneys" (*Falk*, 411 Mich at 112 [opinion of RYAN, J.]) under the First Amendment principles articulated in *Keller* and *Falk*. At the same time, the task force should keep in mind the importance of protecting the public through regulating the legal profession, and how this goal can be balanced with attorneys' First Amendment rights.

The task force shall examine existing State Bar programs and activities that are germane to the compelling state interests recognized in *Falk* and *Keller* to justify a mandatory bar. In addition, the task force shall examine what other programs the State Bar of Michigan ought to undertake to enhance its constitutionally-compelled mission. The task force is invited to examine how other mandatory bars satisfy their constitutionally-permitted mission and shall make its report and recommendations to the Court by June 2, 2014. The task force's report may also include proposed revisions of administrative orders and court rules governing the State Bar of Michigan in order to improve the governance and operation of the State Bar.

The members appointed to the task force are as follows:

Danielle Michelle Brown
Hon. Alfred M. Butzbaugh (Ret.)
Thomas W. Cranmer
Peter H. Ellsworth
John E. McSorley
Colleen A. Pero
John W. Reed
Hon. Michael J. Riordan
Thomas C. Rombach
Hon. John J. Walsh
Janet K. Welch
Vanessa Peterson Williams

Hon. Alfred M. Butzbaugh is appointed as chairperson of the task force.

Nelson Leavitt shall serve as the reporter of the task force. Justice McCormack shall serve as the Court's liaison to the task force.

[Adopted effective February 13, 2014, 495 Mich.]

Order 2014–6 Adoption of Concurrent Jurisdiction Plan for the 43rd Circuit Court, the 4th District Court, and the Cass County Probate Court

Administrative Order No. 2003–1 and MCL 600.401 *et seq*. authorize Michigan trial courts to adopt concurrent jurisdiction plans within a county or judicial circuit, subject to approval of the Court.

The Court hereby approves adoption of the following concurrent jurisdiction plan effective immediately:

● The 43rd Circuit Court, the 4th District Court, and the Cass County Probate Court.

The plan shall remain on file with the state court administrator.

Amendments to concurrent jurisdiction plans may be implemented by local administrative order pursuant to MCR 8.112.

Plan amendments shall conform to the requirements of Administrative Order No. 2003–1 and MCL 600.401 *et seq.*

[Adopted effective March 26, 2014, 495 Mich.]

Order 2014–7   Adoption of Concurrent Jurisdiction Plan for the 42nd Circuit Court, the 75th District Court, and the Midland County Probate Court

Administrative Order No. 2003–1 and MCL 600.401 *et seq.* authorize Michigan trial courts to adopt concurrent jurisdiction plans within a county or judicial circuit, subject to approval of the Court.

The Court hereby approves adoption of the following concurrent jurisdiction plan effective immediately:

• The 42nd Circuit Court, the 75th District Court, and the Midland County Probate Court.

The plan shall remain on file with the state court administrator.

Amendments to concurrent jurisdiction plans may be implemented by local administrative order pursuant to MCR 8.112. Plan amendments shall conform to the requirements of Administrative Order No. 2003–1 and MCL 600.401 *et seq.*

[Adopted effective March 26, 2014, 495 Mich.]

Order 2014–8   Adoption of Concurrent Jurisdiction Plan for the 27th Circuit Court, the 78th District Court, and the Newaygo County and Oceana County Probate Courts

Administrative Order No. 2003–1 and MCL 600.401 *et seq.* authorize Michigan trial courts to adopt concurrent jurisdiction plans within a county or judicial circuit, subject to approval of the Court.

The Court hereby approves adoption of the following concurrent jurisdiction plan effective immediately:

• The 27th Circuit Court, the 78th District Court, and the Newaygo County and Oceana County Probate Courts.

The plan shall remain on file with the state court administrator.

Amendments to concurrent jurisdiction plans may be implemented by local administrative order pursuant to MCR 8.112. Plan amendments shall conform to the requirements of Administrative Order No. 2003–1 and MCL 600.401 *et seq.*

[Adopted effective Entered March 26, 2014, 495 Mich.]

Order 2014–9   Adoption of Concurrent Jurisdiction Plan for the 24th Circuit Court, the 73A District Court, and the Sanilac County Probate Court

Administrative Order No. 2003–1 and MCL 600.401 *et seq.* authorize Michigan trial courts to adopt concurrent jurisdiction plans within a county or judicial circuit, subject to approval of the Court.

The Court hereby approves adoption of the following concurrent jurisdiction plan effective immediately:

• The 24th Circuit Court, the 73A District Court, and the Sanilac County Probate Court.

The plan shall remain on file with the state court administrator.

Amendments to concurrent jurisdiction plans may be implemented by local administrative order pursuant to MCR 8.112. Plan amendments shall conform to the requirements of Administrative Order No. 2003–1 and MCL 600.401 *et seq.*

[Adopted effective March 26, 2014, 495 Mich.]

Order 2014–10   Adoption of Concurrent Jurisdiction Plan for the 6th Circuit Court and the Oakland County Probate Court

Administrative Order No. 2003–1 and MCL 600.401 *et seq.* authorize Michigan trial courts to adopt concurrent jurisdiction plans within a county or judicial circuit, subject to approval of the Court.

The Court hereby approves adoption of the following concurrent jurisdiction plan effective immediately:

• The 6th Circuit Court and the Oakland County Probate Court.

The plan shall remain on file with the state court administrator.

Amendments to concurrent jurisdiction plans may be implemented by local administrative order pursuant to MCR 8.112. Plan amendments shall conform to the requirements of Administrative Order No. 2003–1 and MCL 600.401 *et seq.*

[Adopted effective April 2, 2014, 495 Mich.]

Order 2014–11   Adjustment of Discipline Portion of State Bar of Michigan Dues

In 2011, the Court directed that the discipline portion of the dues members pay to the State Bar of Michigan be reduced by $10 (to $110) in light of the $5 million surplus of the discipline system. Today, there is an even greater surplus. Therefore, the Court directs that the amount of discipline dues be adjusted to $90. This change will be reflected in the dues notice for the 2014–15 fiscal year that is distributed to all bar members under Rule 4 of the Rules Concerning the State Bar.

[Adopted effective June 20, 2014, 496 Mich.]

Order 2014–12   Order Creating the Michigan Tribal State Federal Judicial Forum

Michigan is privileged to be the home of 12 federally recognized Indian tribes and tribal court systems. Michigan has also enjoyed a long history of collaboration between state and tribal courts. The first Tribal State Court Forum, which was created in 1992, resulted in the creation of the "Enforcement of Tribal Judgments" court rule, MCR 2.615, and, most recently, the passage of the Michigan Indian Family Preservation Act of 2012 (MIFPA). Fostering continuing good relations between our state and tribal courts is of great interest to this Court.

For purposes of building on the past spirit of cooperation and of creating a dialogue among the state, tribal, and federal judiciaries, the Court recognizes the importance of establishing an ongoing forum that will address working relationships among the court systems and the interaction of state, tribal, and federal court jurisdiction in Michigan.

The Michigan Tribal State Federal Judicial Forum is established. The membership of the forum shall consist of: the chief tribal judge of each of Michigan's 12 federally recognized tribes, or their designated alternate judges, with membership to be expanded to accommodate any new federally recognized tribes; and 12 state court judges (or the same number as there are tribal judges), who will be appointed by the Michigan Supreme Court from among a pool of currently serving or retired Michigan judges or justices. In making appointments, the Court will consider geographic proximity to the tribes, Indian Child Welfare Act and MIFPA case load dockets, and current involvement with tribal court relations. The forum shall then pursue participation from federal judges and officials.

The specific charge of the forum is contained in its Naakoni-gewin (or Charter), but by majority vote, the members of the forum may designate any other duties that are in the best interests of state, tribal, and federal courts and the citizens who are served by these three systems.

Forum members will serve three-year terms, and member-ships are renewable at the discretion of the Chief Tribal Judges or Tribal Liaison Justice. To facilitate the staggering of terms, some initial appointments will be for abbreviated terms. The forum shall be led by co-chairs, who will be one tribal court judge and one state court judge and who shall be selected by the entire body of members for a three-year term. Work committees may be formed as needed, and decisions shall be made by consensus—defined as a majority of members present at each meeting. Meetings shall be held three times per year, including at least two in-person meetings.

Effective July 1, 2014, the following state court judges or justices are appointed to the new Michigan Tribal State Federal Judicial Forum:

For terms ending July 1, 2016:

1) Susan L. Dobrich, Chief Judge, Cass County Courts, 43rd Circuit Court Family Division

2) William A. Hupy, Chief Judge, Menominee County Pro-bate Court, 41st Circuit Court Family Division

3) Jeffrey C. Nellis, Judge, Mason County Probate Court, 51st Circuit Court Family Division

4) Larry J. Nelson, Chief Judge, Leelanau County Probate Court, 13th Circuit Court Family Division

5) George J. Quist, Judge, Kent County Probate Court, 17th Circuit Court Family Division

6) Frank S. Szymanski, Judge, Wayne County Probate Court, 3rd Circuit Court Family Division

7) Jeff J. Davis, Assistant U.S. Attorney, Western District of Michigan

For terms ending July 1, 2017:

1) Robert J. Butts, Judge, Cheboygan County Probate Court, 53rd Circuit Court Family Division

2) William T. Ervin, Judge, Isabella County Probate Court, 21st Circuit Court Family Division

3) Cheryl L. Hill, Judge, Marquette County Probate Court, 25th Circuit Court Family Division

4) James P. Lambros, Chief Judge, Chippewa County Courts, 50th Circuit Court Family Division

5) Timothy P. Connors, Judge, 22nd Circuit Court Family Division

6) Michael F. Cavanagh, Justice, Michigan Supreme Court

7) Timothy P. Greeley, U.S. Magistrate Judge

8) Hannah N. Bobee, Assistant U.S. Attorney (Western District of Michigan)

Effective July 1, 2014, tribal judges will be appointed by their respective Chief Tribal Court Judges to represent the following federally recognized Indian tribes:

1) Bay Mills Indian Community

2) The Grand Traverse Band of Ottawa and Chippewa Indians

3) Hannahville Indian Community

4) Nottawaseppi Huron Band of Potawatomi

5) Keweenaw Bay Indian Community

6) Lac Vieux Desert Band of Lake Superior Chippewa Indians

7) Little River Band of Ottawa Indians

8) Little Traverse Bay Bands of Odawa Indians

9) Pokagon Band of Potawatomi Indians

10) Saginaw Chippewa Indian Tribe

11) Sault Ste. Marie Tribe of Chippewa Indians

12) Match–E–Be–Nash–She–Wish Band of Pottawatomi Indians (Gun Lake Tribe)

Court staff shall serve as reporter of the forum.

Justice Bridget M. McCormack shall serve as the Supreme Court Tribal Liaison Justice to the forum.

[Adopted June 25, 2014, effective July 1, 2014, 496 Mich. Amended effective February 18, 2015, 497 Mich; September 16, 2015, 498 Mich.]

Order 2014–13   Automated Income Tax Garnishment Pilot Project in 36th District Court

On order of the Court, the 36th District Court (court) and the State Court Administrative Office (SCAO) developed this pilot project to automate the business process for issuing writs for income tax garnishment.

Effective immediately, the 36th District Court is authorized to operate a pilot program to process requests for writs of state income tax garnishment through a web-based system referred to as GarnIT. This administrative order governs the proce-dures associated with the transmission of requests and writs through GarnIT. This order also includes rules designed to address issues unique to the implementation of this program. Participation in this pilot program is voluntary for 2014.

The 36th District Court and SCAO will track the effective-ness of this pilot program and report the results to the Supreme Court after January 1, 2015.

1. Purpose and Construction. The purpose of the pilot is to determine whether it is feasible to automate the processing of income tax garnishments in the 36th District Court as a way to reduce overhead costs, streamline data storage require-ments, and improve user satisfaction. Except for matters related to transmission of requests and writs for state income tax garnishments through GarnIT during the pilot, the Michi-gan Court Rules govern all other postjudgment proceedings concerning the cases involved in the pilot.

2. Definitions.

(a) "ACH" means Automated Clearing House, an electronic network for financial transactions in the United States.

(b) "Batch" means an electronic submission that contains one or more case records.

(c) "CEPAS" means Centralized Electronic Payment Authorization System.

(d) "Clerk" means the clerk of the court for the 36th District Court.

(e) "Court" means the 36th District Court.

(f) "Department" means the Department of Treasury.

(g) "Electronic submission" means the submission of one or more requests which results in the recording of data into the 36th District Court's case management system.

(h) "File format" means the format for submitting income tax garnishment transactions to the Department of Treasury for processing.

(i) "GarnIT" means the web-based system for processing requests and writs for income tax garnishments.

(j) "MCR" means the Michigan Court Rules.

(k) "Pilot" means the court innovation initiative tested in the 36th District Court and the Michigan Department of Treasury in conjunction with IBM and under the supervision of the SCAO. This web-based application facilitates the electronic processing of income tax garnishments in the 36th District Court. The pilot program is expected to launch October 1, 2014 and will continue through November 30, 2014. If it is successful, the pilot will be discontinued and the program will be evaluated for statewide use.

(l) "Transaction" means the request and writ for income tax garnishment electronically processed pursuant to the pilot.

3. Participation in GarnIT. Use of GarnIT for filers who submit requests to the court for 2014 income tax garnishments begins on October 1, 2014, and shall be voluntary during the pilot.

4. Electronic Submission and Acceptance of Submission with the Court; Signature; Statutory Service and Process Fees.

(a) Plaintiffs who choose to use GarnIT will submit requests under the rules in this administrative order and agree to comply with GarnIT's technical requirements. GarnIT will reject requests that do not meet GarnIT's validation requirements and that do not conform to the technical requirements of GarnIT.

(b) Except when maintenance of the case management system or GarnIT is being performed, requests may be submitted to the court and will be processed 24–hours per day, seven days a week through GarnIT.

(c) A request submitted under these rules shall be deemed to have been signed by the plaintiff and filed with the clerk of the court. Electronic signatures shall use the following form: /s/ *John L. Smith.*

(d) By using GarnIT, the plaintiff acknowledges compliance with the rules of this administrative order and acceptance of the business process specified in this administrative order.

(e) The statutory service fee for issuing a writ (hereinafter referred to as filing fee) shall be paid electronically at the same time the writ is issued and in the same amount as required by statute.

(f) The court shall pay the fees associated with the use of credit cards or the court shall pay the cost of establishing Automated Clearing House (ACH) for payment of the filing fees for issuing the writs.

(g) Each plaintiff shall provide one email address with the functionality required by the GarnIT pilot.

5. Format and Form of Electronic Submission.

(a) A plaintiff may file only one request per case per defendant.

(b) A plaintiff may submit multiple transactions within a single batch, subject to subrule 5(a).

(c) All submissions shall comply with the technical requirements of GarnIT and MCR 1.109.

(d) The court will maintain a digital image of each order issued, in accordance with subrule (11).

6. Validation of Requests; Notice of Writs and Rejected Requests; Payment and Receipt.

(a) GarnIT will compare data from submitted requests against data in the Court's case management system and will validate:

(1) party information,

(2) case number,

(3) existence of an unsatisfied judgment on file,

(4) that the judgment has not expired,

(5) that the 21–day time frame before enforcing judgment has passed, and

(6) there is no bankruptcy case pending.

(b) If a request does not meet the validation criteria, GarnIT will display an error message to the filer indicating writ field validation failure. Instructions to the plaintiff for handling validation failure will be available through GarnIT. The instructions will include what steps, if any, the plaintiff can take to correct discrepancies in data between the court's case management system and the official court documents upon which the plaintiff is basing the request.

(c) Filing fees under MCL 600.2529(h) will be collected through CEPAS on each validated request.

(d) GarnIT will notify the plaintiff regarding the submitted requests including payment receipt numbers and a link for printing the writs for purposes of service on the department and the defendant in accordance with Rule 8.

7. Format and Generation of Writs; Payment Processing.

(a) For each validated request, GarnIT will produce an electronic equivalent of SCAO–approved form MC 52, Request and Writ for Garnishment (Income Tax Refund/Credit), which constitutes issuance of a signed writ.

(b) All writs issued will be recorded in data files in the format the department requires for use by the plaintiff.

(c) GarnIT will update the Court's case management system as to each writ issued.

(d) GarnIT will update the Court's case management system as to fees collected.

8. Service on the Department and the Defendant. The plaintiff shall print all issued writs and serve them on the department and the defendant in accordance with existing court rules and department requirements.

9. Correcting Data in the Court's Case Management System. If the plaintiff receives an error message as indicated in Rule 6b, the following procedure shall be followed by the plaintiff and the court:

(a) If the error is the result of incorrect data provided by the plaintiff, the plaintiff may correct the data and resubmit the request through GarnIT in accordance with the instructions and requirements of GarnIT.

(b) If the plaintiff believes the error is the result of incorrect data in the court's case management system, the plaintiff shall submit an email request to correct the data, along with supporting documentation, in accordance with the instructions and requirements of GarnIT. Within 24 hours after receipt of a request to correct data and supporting documentation, the court shall handle the request. If the court determines that the discrepancy is the result of clerical error by the court, the court will correct the data in the case management system and send an email response to the plaintiff indicating what action was taken and informing plaintiff that the request can be resubmitted in GarnIT. If the court determines that the discrepancy is not the result of clerical error by the court, the court will send an email response to the plaintiff indicating that fact.

(c) If the plaintiff wants to request a change in case data that is not the result of data entry error, plaintiff shall file a motion with the court under MCR 2.119.

10. Technical Malfunctions. The GarnIT website will provide instructions regarding what action to take if the plaintiff experiences a technical malfunction with use of GarnIT or has other technical difficulties using GarnIT that cannot be resolved by the plaintiff.

11. Official Court Record; Record Retention.

(a) For purposes of this pilot program, the electronic data and the electronic equivalent of SCAO–approved form MC 52, Request and Writ for Garnishment (Income Tax Refund/Credit), produced by and through the GarnIT transaction and subsequently maintained in the case management system, constitutes the official court record and meets the record retention and public access requirements of the court rules and General Records Retention and Disposal Schedule #16— Michigan Trial Courts.

(b) A request and writ processed by GarnIT can be generated or printed on demand by the clerk. The request and writ maintained by the court will not contain the social security numbers or federal identification numbers of the parties.

(c) If a request is made for a certified copy of a request and writ processed by GarnIT, the clerk shall print the document and certify it in compliance with the Michigan Trial Court Case File Management Standards.

12. Privacy Considerations. The plaintiff shall provide in each submission to GarnIT, the social security numbers and federal identification numbers of the parties for use in the data file and writs issued for service on the department. The social security number or federal identification number will not be retained by GarnIT or the Court after requests are validated

and writs are issued and printed in accordance with Rules 6 and 7.

13. Expiration. Unless otherwise directed by the Michigan Supreme Court, this pilot shall continue until November 30, 2014.

[Adopted effective June 25, 2014, 496 Mich.]

Order 2014–14   Adoption of Concurrent Jurisdiction Plan for the 47th Circuit Court, the 94th District Court, and the Delta County Probate Court

Administrative Order No. 2003–1 and MCL 600.401 *et seq.* authorize Michigan trial courts to adopt concurrent jurisdiction plans within a county or judicial circuit, subject to approval of the Court.

The Court hereby approves adoption of the following concurrent jurisdiction plan effective immediately:

● The 47th Circuit Court, the 94th District Court, and the Delta County Probate Court.

The plan shall remain on file with the state court administrator.

Amendments to concurrent jurisdiction plans may be implemented by local administrative order pursuant to MCR 8.112. Plan amendments shall conform to the requirements of Administrative Order No. 2003–1 and MCL 600.401 *et seq.*

[Adopted effective August 26, 2014, 497 Mich.]

Order 2014–15   Adoption of Concurrent Jurisdiction Plan for the 16th Circuit Court, the 42nd District Court, and the Macomb County Probate Court

Administrative Order No. 2003–1 and MCL 600.401 et seq. authorize Michigan trial courts to adopt concurrent jurisdiction plans within a county or judicial circuit, subject to approval of the Court.

The Court hereby approves adoption of the following concurrent jurisdiction plan effective immediately:

● The 16th Circuit Court, the 42nd District Court, and the Macomb County Probate Court.

The plan shall remain on file with the state court administrator.

Amendments to concurrent jurisdiction plans may be implemented by local administrative order pursuant to MCR 8.112. Plan amendments shall conform to the requirements of Administrative Order No. 2003–1 and MCL 600.401 et seq.

[Adopted effective August 26, 2014, 497 Mich.]

Order 2014–16   Adoption of Concurrent Jurisdiction Plan for the 32nd Circuit Court, the 98th District Court, and the Gogebic and Ontonagon County Probate Courts

Administrative Order No. 2003–1 and MCL 600.401 *et seq.* authorize Michigan trial courts to adopt concurrent jurisdiction plans within a county or judicial circuit, subject to approval of the Court.

The Court hereby revises Administrative Order No. 2005–1 and approves adoption of the following concurrent jurisdiction plan, effective immediately:

- The 32nd Circuit Court, the 98th District Court, and the Gogebic and Ontonagon County Probate Courts.

The plan shall remain on file with the state court administrator.

Amendments to concurrent jurisdiction plans may be implemented by local administrative order pursuant to MCR 8.112. Plan amendments shall conform to the requirements of Administrative Order No. 2003–1 and MCL 600.401 *et seq.*

[Adopted effective August 26, 2014, 497 Mich.]

Order 2014–17   Adoption of Concurrent Jurisdiction Plan for the 4th Circuit Court, the 12th District Court, and the Jackson County Probate Court

Administrative Order No. 2003–1 and MCL 600.401 *et seq.* authorize Michigan trial courts to adopt concurrent jurisdiction plans within a county or judicial circuit, subject to approval of the Court.

The Court hereby approves adoption of the following concurrent jurisdiction plan effective immediately:

- The 4th Circuit Court, the 12th District Court, and the Jackson County Probate Court.

The plan shall remain on file with the state court administrator.

Amendments to concurrent jurisdiction plans may be implemented by local administrative order pursuant to MCR 8.112. Plan amendments shall conform to the requirements of Administrative Order No. 2003–1 and MCL 600.401 *et seq.*

[Adopted effective August 26, 2014, 497 Mich.]

Order 2014–18   Merger of the State Appellate Defender Office (SADO) and Michigan Appellate Assigned Counsel System (MAACS)

1978 PA 620 authorized the Appellate Defender Commission to develop a system of indigent appellate defense services to include services provided by the State Appellate Defender Office and locally appointed private counsel. In Administrative Order No. 1981–7, the Court authorized the Appellate Defender Commission to establish an Appellate Assigned Counsel Administrator's Office to operate the roster of private attorneys providing appellate defense services. SADO and the Michigan Assigned Appellate Counsel System have operated separately until now. On order of the Court, at the request of the Appellate Defender Commission, effective immediately, to promote efficiency and improve the administration of assigned appellate counsel for indigent defendants, the Court orders that operations of the two offices be merged. The State Appellate Defender shall serve as administrator of the Michigan Assigned Appellate Counsel System. Further, the Court directs the Appellate Defender Commission to review operations of the MAACS and submit a proposed administrative order that reflects the consolidation of the two offices and incorporates proposed updates or revisions that the commission recommends. The commission shall submit the proposed administrative order to the Court no later than October 1, 2015.

[Adopted effective September 17, 2014, 497 Mich. Amended effective January 21, 2015, 497 Mich.]

Comments

Staff Comment to 2014 Adoption

MCL 780.711 *et seq.* charged the Appellate Defender Commission with development of a mixed system of appellate assigned defense representation, consisting of both a public defender office and roster of private attorneys qualified and willing to accept appellate assignments. The State Appellate Defender Office (SADO) was created in 1978 to function as the public defender office; in 1981, the Michigan Appellate Assigned Counsel System (MAACS) was authorized to function as administrator of the statewide roster of private attorneys. Administrative Order No. 1981–7 commentary recognized two administrative models for the system, one defender-administered and one with independent offices. Over time, the Appellate Defender Commission, overseer of both components, has recognized the benefits of the defender-administered model; as in the federal system, this model produces cost-effective and coordinated management of resources. To better serve the interests of appellate defendants, the Appellate Defender Commission has recommended the change.

Order 2014–19   Reporting Requirements of the 36th District Court [Terminated effective December 21, 2016.]

Order 2014–20   Adoption of Concurrent Jurisdiction Plan for the 35th Circuit Court, the 66th District Court, and the Shiawassee County Probate Court

Administrative Order No. 2003–1 and MCL 600.401 *et seq.* authorize Michigan trial courts to adopt concurrent jurisdiction plans within a county or judicial circuit, subject to approval of the Court.

The Court hereby approves adoption of the following concurrent jurisdiction plan effective immediately:

- The 35th Circuit Court, the 66th District Court, and the Shiawassee County Probate Court.

The plan shall remain on file with the state court administrator.

Amendments to concurrent jurisdiction plans may be implemented by local administrative order pursuant to MCR 8.112. Plan amendments shall conform to the requirements of Administrative Order No. 2003–1 and MCL 600.401 *et seq.*

[Adopted effective October 22, 2014, 497 Mich.]

Order 2014–21   Adoption of Concurrent Jurisdiction Plan for the 18th District Court and the 29th District Court

Administrative Order No. 2003–1 and MCL 600.401 *et seq.* authorize Michigan trial courts to adopt concurrent jurisdiction plans within a county or judicial circuit, subject to approval of the Court.

The Court hereby approves adoption of the following concurrent jurisdiction plan effective immediately:

- The 18th District Court and the 29th District Court.

The plan shall remain on file with the state court administrator.

Amendments to concurrent jurisdiction plans may be implemented by local administrative order pursuant to MCR 8.112. Plan amendments shall conform to the requirements of Administrative Order No. 2003–1 and MCL 600.401 *et seq.*

[Adopted effective October 22, 2014, 497 Mich.]

Order 2014–22   Rescission of Administrative Order No. 2006–3 (Michigan Uniform System of Citation)

On order of the Court, effective immediately, Administrative Order No. 2006–3, the order setting forth the Michigan

Uniform System of Citation, is rescinded. The Court currently uses, and encourages others to use, the Michigan Appellate Opinion Manual, which sets forth the Court's standards for citation of authority, quotation, and style in opinions of the Supreme Court and the Court of Appeals. The manual is now available in a searchable online format, and may be found at www.courts.mi.gov.

[Adopted effective November 5, 2014, 497 Mich.]

Order 2014–23 E–Filing System for the Michigan Supreme Court and the Michigan Court of Appeals

On order of the Court, effective February 1, 2020, all documents filed by or on behalf of attorneys who are licensed to practice law in the State of Michigan or who are admitted to temporarily appear and practice under MCR 8.126(A), must be filed electronically with the Michigan Supreme Court (MSC) and the Michigan Court of Appeals (COA) using the MiFILE system unless excused by court order upon a motion showing good cause. Self-represented litigants may, but are not required to, electronically file their documents with the Court.

Although this order sets out the manner in which e-filed documents are submitted to the courts or served on other parties to an action, it does not change the time periods required for taking action under the Michigan Court Rules, except as explicitly provided.

I. Definitions. For purposes of this order:

(A) "Authorized user" means a party, a party's attorney, or court staff who is registered in the MiFILE system (https://mifile.courts.michigan.gov/) and who has satisfied the requirements imposed by the courts relating to electronic filing and service procedures. A court may revoke user authorization for good cause as determined by the court, including but not limited to a security breach or failure to comply with system requirements. An authorized user must notify the court and ImageSoft, Inc., of any change in the authorized user's firm name, delivery address, telephone number, fax number, e-mail address, or other required registration information. This notice must occur as soon as practicable but no later than 7 days after the effective date of the change.

(B) "Electronic filing" or "e-filing" means the completed electronic transmission of documents or information to the court.

(C) "Electronic notice/notification" or "e–notice/notification" means the electronic transmission of documents or information from the court.

(D) "Electronic service" or "e-service" means the electronic transmission of documents or information to a party, a party's attorney, or a party's representative.

II. Scope.

(A) Consistent with the Michigan Court Rules and the provisions of this order, the MSC and the COA may:

(1) accept electronic filing and permit electronic service of documents from authorized users, except as provided in subsection (B) below;

(2) issue electronic filing guidelines consistent with this order. The guidelines must be posted prominently on the courts' electronic filing website; or

(3) electronically issue, file, and serve notices, orders, opinions, and other documents, subject to the provisions of this order.

Filers need not provide hard copies to the courts, as otherwise required by the court rules, of documents that are electronically filed.

(B) Registered users agree to accept e-service through the MiFILE system unless and until the user's registration is terminated. Service on nonregistered users must be accomplished in a manner allowed under the court rules, such as by first-class mail, hand delivery, or e-mail under MCR 2.107(C)(4).

III. Signatures.

(A) A document electronically filed or electronically served under this order shall be deemed to have been signed by the party, the party's attorney, or the declarant for all purposes provided in the Michigan Court Rules. A statutory or court rule requirement for an original signature in a document is satisfied by inserting a typed signature with "/s/ [Name]" or a graphic image of a handwritten signature, including an actual signature on a scanned document. A digital signature that authenticates digital information through computer cryptography may not be used.

(B) A document containing the signature of a third party (e.g., affidavits, stipulations) may also be filed electronically by indicating that the signed original is maintained by the filing party. Signed copies shall be provided to the parties or court upon request.

IV. Retention of Documents. Unless otherwise ordered by the court, copies of all documents electronically filed or served shall be maintained by the party filing those documents and shall be made available, upon reasonable notice, for inspection or copying. Parties shall retain such copies until final disposition of the case and the expiration of all appeal opportunities.

V. Official Case Record. The electronically filed documents maintained on the courts' servers are the official record of the court.

VI. Payment of Filing Fees and Costs.

(A) A filing fee is due and payable at the time of the transmission of the electronic document unless:

(1) the document type does not require a fee;

(2) the filing is accompanied by a motion to waive fees;

(3) the fee is waived by the court pursuant to statute or court rule; or

(4) payment is deferred pending an interagency transfer of funds.

Failure to timely pay a filing fee may result in the filing being rejected by the court.

(B) Fees and costs are paid electronically through the MiFILE system.

VII. Transmission Failures and System Outages.

(A) In the event of a transmission failure of an electronically filed document, a party may file a motion requesting that the court enter an order permitting a document to be deemed filed *nunc pro tunc* on the date of the unsuccessful transmission. The moving party must prove to the court's satisfaction that:

(1) the transmission was attempted on the date and at the time asserted by the party;

(2) the transmission failed because of the failure of the MiFILE system to process the electronic document or because of the court's computer system's failure to receive the document; and

(3) the transmission failure was not caused, in whole or in part, by the action or inaction of the party.

(B) Scheduled system outages, such as for system maintenance, shall be posted on the court and MiFILE websites and will be scheduled before 9:00 a.m. or after midnight on business days whenever feasible.

(C) Notice will be provided on the court and MiFILE websites if the MiFILE system becomes unavailable for an extended or uncertain period. The notice shall indicate whether filers are responsible for filing the documents conventionally in order to meet the deadlines imposed by statute or court rule.

VIII. Filing Completion.

(A) A document filed electronically shall be considered filed with the court when the transmission to the MiFILE system is complete and the system reflects a "Filed" status.

(B) If the court rejects an e-filed document pursuant to court rule, the court shall notify the filer of the rejection and the document shall not become part of the official court record.

(C) Upon completion of an e-filing transmission to the MiFILE system, the system shall issue to the filer and to the court a notification that includes the date and time of the transmission.

IX. Time for Filing. Filings may be transmitted to the MiFILE system twenty-four hours a day, seven days a week (with the exception of the system's downtime required for periodic maintenance). However, a document electronically filed or served after 11:59 p.m. Eastern Time, or on a Saturday, Sunday, or court holiday (see MCR 8.110[D][2]) shall be deemed to have been filed or served on the next business day. See MCR 1.108.

X. Format of Documents. The MiFILE system accepts the following file types for e-filed documents: Microsoft Word (DOC and DOCX), PDF, text files (TXT), images such as a TIFF, PNG or JPG. The courts strongly prefer that original pleadings be submitted as Word documents, text files, or searchable PDFs. Nonoriginal documents may be scanned into PDF as nonsearchable images.

[Adopted effective November 26, 2014, 497 Mich. Amended December 18, 2019, effective February 1, 2020, 503 Mich.]

Comments

Staff Comment to 2014 Adoption

Administrative Order No. 2014–23 authorizes implementation and sets out the basic requirements for voluntary e-filing in the Michigan Supreme Court and Michigan Court of Appeals.

Order 2014–24 Extension of Expiration Date for E–Filing Pilot Project in Oakland Circuit Court, Family Division

By revision of Administrative Order No. 2010–3, dated January 23, 2013, this Court extended the e-filing project of the Family Division of the Oakland Circuit Court through December 31, 2014. Since that time, the validity and scalability of e-

filing has been successfully demonstrated in Oakland Circuit Court's Family Division, and in six other courts participating in e-filing pilot projects. Recognizing that the "pilot" aspect of the projects would be ending before a statewide system is available, the State Court Administrator communicated to all pilot courts that their e-filing projects would end, at the latest, at the expiration of their administrative orders that authorized or extended their projects. Pilot projects would be replaced, as the State Court Administrator noted, with an accessible and affordable statewide system for all Michigan residents, litigants, and courts. To that end, the Court anticipates working with the Michigan Legislature and the Governor in 2015 for authorization and funding of a statewide system.

Given the looming expiration date of the Family Division's e-filing project, the Oakland Circuit Court has expressed its desire for a limited extension of that project. Consistent with this Court's long-term goals, the Oakland Circuit Court communicated an interest in "a uniform approach and consistent e-filing experience, no matter where, when, and in which court they file" and the court "firmly . . . support[s] . . . the statewide e-filing initiative." Considering Oakland Circuit Court's interest and willingness to partner with the State Court Administrative Office on this statewide effort, the State Court Administrator has recommended a limited extension of the pilot project "to ensure the continuity of e-filing services as [the Oakland Circuit Court, Family Division,] transition[s] from [its] local pilot to the statewide initiative."

On order of the Court, the e-filing pilot project operating in Oakland Circuit Court's Family Division, under Administrative Order No. 2010–3, is extended until June 30, 2015, which is the same expiration date for Oakland Circuit Court's e-filing pilot project authorized by Administrative Order No. 2007–3.

[Adopted effective November 26, 2014, 497 Mich.]

Order 2014–25 Establishment of Videoconferencing Standards

To ensure consistency in videoconferencing practices and procedures throughout the state of Michigan; to improve service to the public, other agencies, and the judiciary; and to improve the performance and efficiency of videoconferencing in the courts, it is ordered that the State Court Administrator establish Videoconferencing Standards and that appellate and trial courts conform to those standards. The State Court Administrative Office shall enforce the standards and assist courts in adopting practices to conform to those standards.

[Adopted November 26, 2014, effective January 1, 2015, 497 Mich.]

Comments

Staff Comment to 2015 Adoption

This administrative order requires the State Court Administrator to establish videoconferencing standards and requires that the appellate and trial courts conform to those standards. Please note that this administrative order is part of a group of orders issued today that relate to videoconferencing, including amendments adopted in MCR 3.210 and MCR 3.215, and adoption of new rule MCR 2.407, along with rescission of Administrative Order No. 2007–1.

Order 2015–1 Authorization of Pilot Project for Summary Jury Trials in the 16th Circuit Court and for Pilot Projects Testing Summary Jury Trials in Other Courts Approved by the Michigan Supreme Court

On order of the Court, the 16th Circuit Court and other courts approved by the Michigan Supreme Court are authorized to implement summary jury trial pilot projects. A summary jury trial is a voluntary, binding jury trial, typically conducted in a single day before a panel of six jurors and presided over by the assigned judge, a judge appointed by the court, or a special hearing officer selected jointly by the parties. The summary jury trial process is intended to afford parties an efficient and economical means of resolving their dispute. The pilot projects are established to study the effectiveness of the summary jury trial process in resolving civil cases without adjudication by the trial court. The pilot projects shall begin as soon as possible after the approval by the Court, and shall remain in effect for 24 months. The 16th Circuit Court and other pilot courts will track participation in and the effectiveness of their pilot programs and shall report to, and make such findings available to, the Michigan Supreme Court.

(A) Applicability. This administrative order governs summary jury trial practice in the pilot projects conducted in the 16th Circuit Court and other pilot courts. The pilot projects are intended to include cases that can be presented on a summary basis, including those tort, no-fault and business proceedings that do not involve complex facts or numerous witnesses, but each pilot site will establish its own standards for identifying eligible cases. Parties who agree to participate in the summary jury trial pilot projects must participate in the scheduled summary jury trial unless the parties reach a resolution before the summary jury trial.

(B) Procedure.

(1) *Stipulation.* At any time after the filing of a complaint, parties who agree to participate in a summary jury trial shall file with the court a Consent Order for Summary Jury Trial. The attorneys and/or parties may stipulate to any high/low parameters, which shall not be disclosed to the jury.

(2) *Presiding Officer.* The parties shall agree on who shall preside over the summary jury trial. The presiding officer may be the assigned trial court judge, a retired judge appointed to preside over the proceeding, or a special hearing officer. The trial court shall not appoint, recommend, direct or otherwise influence a party's or attorney's selection of a special hearing officer. If the parties agree that a retired judge should be assigned or a special hearing officer should preside, the court shall enter an order naming the presiding officer.

(3) *Appointment and Qualification of Special Hearing Officer.* The special hearing officer must be licensed to practice law in the State of Michigan. A special hearing officer is not authorized to enter judicial orders but must present them to the court's assigned judge for entry. The parties and the special hearing officer, by agreement, shall determine the compensation, if any, of the special hearing officer and how that cost will be allocated between the parties.

(4) *Mediation and Case Evaluation.* Upon entry of a Consent Order for Summary Jury Trial, the trial court shall not require that mediation under MCR 2.411 or case evaluation under MCR 2.403 take place prior to the summary jury trial. However, the parties may voluntarily engage in any ADR processes following the entry of the consent order and before the summary jury trial.

(5) *Scheduling.* The clerk of the court, in consultation with the parties, shall schedule the summary jury trial and provide notice of the scheduled summary jury trial to the parties and attorneys at least 56 days before the trial's date. The clerk of the court shall allocate such space or staff as may be available and suitable to conduct the summary jury trial. Once scheduled, the summary jury trial will be adjourned only upon written stipulation of the parties with approval of the presiding officer or upon good cause shown.

(6) *Pretrial Submissions.*

(a) Documentary Evidence. Any party intending to offer evidence at the summary jury trial shall serve copies of any proposed exhibits and a witness list upon all parties not less than 28 days before the scheduled date of the summary jury trial. Unless otherwise agreed by all parties, exhibits that are not served upon all parties as required under this provision are not admissible. Witnesses who have not been listed shall not be called at trial.

(b) Pretrial Conference. No later than 14 days before the scheduled date of the summary jury trial, the judge or special hearing officer assigned to the case shall conduct a pretrial conference, at which time the special hearing officer or judge shall address:

(i) objections to any evidence, including proposed redactions, motions in limine, and other evidentiary issues;

(ii) juror questionnaires and proposed voir dire questions;

(iii) whether the jury shall be permitted to take notes;

(iv) jury instructions and the jury verdict form; and,

(v) any other matters the judge, special hearing officer, or parties consider important in governing the summary jury trial process.

(7) *Record.* The summary jury trial shall not be recorded by the court's court reporter. However, any party may record or transcribe the proceedings at that party's expense.

(8) *Jury Composition.* The jury of a summary jury trial shall be comprised of six jurors, selected for examination in the regular term of court. Ten potential jurors shall be seated, and after questioning, plaintiff(s) shall strike one juror, defendant(s) shall strike one juror, plaintiff(s) shall strike a second juror and defendant(s) shall strike a second juror until six jurors remain and have been impaneled. Challenges for cause are not permitted.

(9) *Time Allocations.* It is expected that a summary jury trial shall last no longer than one day. Unless otherwise agreed to by the parties and the court under subrule (17) below, the summary jury trial shall be conducted within the following time allocations:

(a) Jury Selection. Jury selection shall take no longer than 30 minutes, which includes 10 minutes allocated to the special hearing officer or judge for an introduction and general questions to be given to all potential jurors agreed to by the parties, and 10 minutes for questions by each side.

(b) Opening Statements. Each side shall have 15 minutes for opening statements.

(c) Presentation of Proofs. Each side shall have up to 2 hours for presentation of proofs. This time allocation shall include the party's direct examination of witnesses, cross-examination of the other party's witnesses, admission of exhibits, and any time spent directing the jury's attention to specific aspects of documents that have been admitted.

(d) Closing Argument. Each side shall have up to 15 minutes for closing argument, and plaintiff shall have an additional 3 minutes for rebuttal.

(e) Jury Instruction. The parties shall make efforts to limit the number of instructions read to allow the instructions to be presented in 10 minutes or less.

(10) *Rules of Evidence.* The parties may offer evidence that is relevant and material to the dispute. The judge or hearing officer shall not require authentication of documentary evidence for purposes of admissibility. As part of the Consent Order for Summary Jury Trial, the parties may agree to modify the rules of evidence. The parties are encouraged to stipulate to modes and methods of presentation that will expedite the process, such as an agreement regarding the admissibility of video or written depositions, affidavits, written reports and ex parte depositions with any agreed upon redactions.

(11) *Jury Verdict.* The verdict of the jury shall be returned on a written verdict form and is binding, subject to any written high/low limitations agreed upon by the parties. A verdict will be received when five of the six jurors agree on a disposition.

(12) *Inconsistent Verdict.* In the case of an inconsistent verdict, the judge or special hearing officer shall recharge the jury as appropriate and require it to return to deliberation to resolve any inconsistency.

(13) *Posttrial Motions.* The only posttrial motion available to the parties shall be a motion for new trial, which must be filed with the trial court and served on the judge or special hearing officer as well as the other parties within seven days after entry of the jury's verdict. The judge or special hearing officer shall grant a new trial only under the following circumstances:

(a) an irregularity in the proceedings of the court, jury, or prevailing party, or an order of the court or abuse of discretion that denied the moving party a fair trial;

(b) misconduct of the jury or of the prevailing party during the trial;

(c) error of law occurring in the proceedings; or

(d) fraud (intrinsic or extrinsic) of an adverse party.

(14) *Order of Judgment.* The nonprevailing party shall pay the prevailing party the judgment amount within 28 days after the jury renders a verdict, subject to any high/low parameters established before the trial. After payment, the prevailing party shall submit an Order of Dismissal with Prejudice for entry by the court.

If payment is not made within 28 days after entry of the verdict, an Order of Judgment based upon the jury verdict, subject to any high/low agreement, shall be entered by the circuit court consistent with MCR 2.602.

(15) *Waiver of Costs and Sanctions.* Except in the case of fraud, the parties agree to waive taxation of costs and sanctions.

(16) *No Right to Appeal and Costs.* Except in the case of fraud, the parties agree to waive the right to appeal the jury's verdict. Any appeals shall be taken in accordance with the Appellate Rules found at MCR 7.201—7.219.

(17) *Modification of Procedures.* Any of the above described procedures may be modified by stipulation of the parties with approval of the judge or special hearing officer.
[Adopted effective March 25, 2015, 497 Mich. Amended effective June 21, 2017, 500 Mich.]

Order 2015–2   Adoption of Concurrent Jurisdiction Plan for the 52nd Circuit Court, the 73B District Court, and the Huron County Probate Court

Administrative Order No. 2003–1 and MCL 600.401 *et seq.* authorize Michigan trial courts to adopt concurrent jurisdiction plans within a county or judicial circuit, subject to approval of the Court.

The Court hereby approves adoption of the following concurrent jurisdiction plan effective immediately:

● The 52nd Circuit Court, the 73B District Court, and the Huron County Probate Court.

The plan shall remain on file with the state court administrator.

Amendments to concurrent jurisdiction plans may be implemented by local administrative order pursuant to MCR 8.112. Plan amendments shall conform to the requirements of Administrative Order No. 2003–1 and MCL 600.401 *et seq.*
[Adopted effective April 29, 2015, 497 Mich.]

Order 2015–3   Establishment of Michigan Trial Court Standards and Guidelines for Websites and Social Media

In order to guide trial courts that are considering the use of trial court websites and social media sites to improve their service to the public, other agencies, and the judiciary, and to meet the public's growing expectation that courts communicate directly with the public, while preserving fairness and judicial impartiality, it is ORDERED that the State Court Administrator establish Michigan Trial Court Standards and Guidelines for Websites and Social Media and that trial courts conform to the standards. The State Court Administrative Office shall enforce the standards and assist courts in adopting practices to conform to those standards.
[Adopted effective April 29, 2015, 497 Mich.]

Order 2015–4   Authorization for Use of GarnIT in the 36th, 46th, and 47th District Courts

Until further order of the Court, effective immediately, the 36th, 46th, and 47th District Courts are each authorized to operate the GarnIT system for processing requests for writs of state income tax garnishment. Participation by plaintiffs in this program is voluntary.

1. **Purpose and Construction.** The purpose of this order is to authorize continued use of GarnIT in the courts that piloted the system in 2015. The 2015 pilot was successful and it is beneficial to these three courts and the users to continue the GarnIT system while the Michigan Supreme Court determines its long-term strategy for e-filing and its plans for incorporating GarnIT into that strategy. Except for matters related to the transmission of requests and writs for state income tax garnishments through GarnIT, the Michigan Court Rules govern all other postjudgment proceedings concerning the cases involved in the GarnIT program.

2. Definitions.

(a) "ACH" means Automated Clearing House, an electronic network for financial transactions in the United States.

(b) "Batch" means an electronic submission that contains one or more case records.

(c) "CEPAS" means Centralized Electronic Payment Authorization System.

(d) "Clerk" means the clerk of the court for the 36th, 46th, or 47th District Courts.

(e) "Court" means the 36th, 46th, or 47th District Courts.

(f) "Department" means the Department of Treasury.

(g) "Electronic submission" means the submission of one or more requests that result in the recording of data into the courts' case management systems.

(h) "File format" means the format for submitting batch income tax garnishment transactions to the GarnIT for processing.

(i) "GarnIT" means the web-based system for processing requests and writs for state income tax garnishments.

(j) "MCR" means the Michigan Court Rules.

(k) "Transaction" means the request and writ for income tax garnishment electronically processed pursuant to the pilot.

3. Participation in GarnIT. Use of GarnIT for submitting requests for income tax garnishments in the 36th, 46th, and 47th District Courts shall be voluntary.

4. Electronic Submission and Acceptance of Submission with the Court; Signatures; Statutory Service and Process Fees.

(a) Plaintiffs who choose to use GarnIT will submit requests under the rules in this administrative order and agree to comply with GarnIT's technical requirements. GarnIT will reject requests that do not meet GarnIT's validation requirements and that do not conform to the technical requirements of GarnIT.

(b) Except when maintenance to the case management system or GarnIT is being performed, requests may be submitted to the court and will be processed 24 hours a day, seven days a week through GarnIT.

(c) A request submitted under these rules shall be deemed to have been signed by the plaintiff and filed with the clerk. Electronic signatures shall use the following form: /s/ *John L. Smith.*

(d) By using GarnIT, the plaintiff acknowledges compliance with the rules in this administrative order and acceptance of the business process as specified in this administrative order.

(e) The statutory service fee for issuing a writ (hereinafter referred to as the "filing fee") shall be paid electronically at the same time the writ is issued and in the same amount as required by statute.

(f) The court shall pay the fees associated with the use of credit cards or the cost of establishing Automated Clearing House (ACH) for payment of the filing fees.

(g) Each plaintiff shall provide one e-mail address with the functionality required for GarnIT.

5. Format and Form of Electronic Submission.

(a) A plaintiff may file only one request per case per defendant.

(b) A plaintiff may submit multiple transactions within a single batch, subject to subrule 5(a).

(c) All submissions must comply with the technical requirements of GarnIT and MCR 1.109.

(d) The court will maintain a digital image of each order issued, in accordance with subrule 11.

6. Validation of Requests; Notice of Writs and Rejected Requests; Payment and Receipt.

(a) GarnIT will compare data from submitted requests against data in the court's case management system and will validate:

(1) the party information,

(2) the name of the plaintiff's attorney, if one exists,

(3) the case number,

(4) the existence of an unsatisfied judgment on file,

(5) that the judgment has not expired,

(6) that the 21–day period required before enforcing the judgment has passed, and

(7) that there is no bankruptcy case pending.

(b) GarnIT will compare a plaintiff attorney name from a submitted request against data in the case management system, and if the name is validated, GarnIT will provide the address from the case management system. Judicial Information Systems will update the case management system with address information provided by the State Bar of Michigan on a quarterly basis.

(c) If a plaintiff's attorney is designated to receive money from a garnished income tax refund on behalf of the plaintiff, GarnIT will omit the plaintiff's address from the validation requirements. The plaintiff's name will be validated and included in the request, but the plaintiff's address on file with the court, if any, will not be included in the request.

(d) If a request does not meet the validation criteria, GarnIT will display an error message to the filer indicating a validation failure in the writ field. Instructions to the plaintiff for handling validation failure will be available through GarnIT. The instructions will include what steps, if any, the plaintiff can take to correct discrepancies in data between the court's case management system and the official court documents on which the plaintiff is basing the request.

(e) GarnIT will apply a formula to the amount of costs supplied by the plaintiff, and if they exceed the programmed threshold, GarnIT will display a message to the filer indicating that the amounts appear to be inaccurate. Instructions for how to proceed will be available through GarnIT. The filer can correct the amounts and proceed with the submission or, if the filer believes that the amounts are accurate, may file the request with the court manually.

(f) Filing fees under MCL 600.2529(1)(h) will be collected through CEPAS on each validated request.

(g) GarnIT will notify the plaintiff regarding the submitted requests including payment receipt numbers and a link for printing the writs for purposes of service on the department and the defendant in accordance with Rule 8.

7. Format and Generation of Writs; Payment Processing.

(a) For each validated request, GarnIT will produce a secure electronic equivalent of SCAO–approved form MC 52, Request and Writ for Garnishment (Income Tax Refund/Credit), which constitutes issuance of a signed writ.

(b) GarnIT will update the court's case management system with respect to each writ issued.

(c) GarnIT will update the court's case management system with respect to fees collected.

8. Service on the Department and the Defendant.

(a) The plaintiff shall print all issued writs and serve them on the department and the defendant in accordance with existing court rules.

(b) After service is completed, the plaintiff shall record proof of service in GarnIT by completing an attestation for each recipient that service was completed, including the date of service and the amount of any fee charged.

(c) The plaintiff shall maintain the proof of service so that it can be produced upon request if necessary in further proceedings in the case.

9. Correcting Data in the Court's Case Management System. If the plaintiff receives an error message as indicated in Rule 6b, the following procedure shall be followed by the plaintiff and the court:

(a) If the error is the result of incorrect data provided by the plaintiff, the plaintiff may correct the data and resubmit the request through GarnIT in accordance with the instructions and requirements of GarnIT.

(b) If the plaintiff believes the error is the result of incorrect data in the court's case management system, the plaintiff shall submit an e-mail request to correct the data, along with supporting documentation, in accordance with the instructions and requirements of GarnIT. Within 24 hours after receipt of a request to correct data and supporting documentation, the court shall handle the request. If the court determines that the discrepancy is the result of clerical error by the court, the court will correct the data in the case management system and send an e-mail response to the plaintiff indicating what action was taken and informing the plaintiff that the request can be resubmitted in GarnIT. If the court determines that the discrepancy is not the result of clerical error by the court, the court will send an e-mail response to the plaintiff indicating that fact.

(c) If the plaintiff wants to request that data in a case be changed for a reason other than a data entry error, the plaintiff must file a notice of the change with the court.

10. Technical Malfunctions. The GarnIT website will provide instructions regarding what action to take if the plaintiff experiences a technical malfunction using GarnIT or has other technical difficulties using GarnIT that cannot be resolved by the plaintiff.

11. Official Court Record; Record Retention.

(a) The electronic data and the electronic equivalent of SCAO–approved form MC 52, Request and Writ for Garnishment (Income Tax Refund/Credit), produced by and through the GarnIT transaction and subsequently maintained in the case management system constitutes the official court record and meets the record retention and public access requirements of the court rules and General Records Retention and Disposal Schedule #16—Michigan Trial Courts.

(b) A request and writ processed by GarnIT can be generated or printed on demand by the clerk. The request and writ maintained by the court will not contain the social security numbers or federal identification numbers of the parties.

(c) If a request is made for a certified copy of a request and writ processed by GarnIT, the clerk shall print the document and certify it in compliance with the Michigan Trial Court Case File Management Standards.

12. Privacy Considerations. In each submission to GarnIT, the plaintiff shall provide the social security numbers and federal identification numbers of the parties for use in the data file and writs issued for service on the department. The social security numbers or federal identification numbers will not be retained by GarnIT or the court after requests are validated and writs are issued and printed in accordance with rules 6 and 7 of this order.

13. Expiration. This pilot project will continue until further order of the Court.

[Adopted effective May 27, 2015, 498 Mich. Amended effective May 25, 2016, 499 Mich.]

Order 2015–5   Adoption of Administrative Order Requiring Trial Courts to Comply with Certain ADA–Related Practices

Trial Court Requirements for Providing Equal and Full Access to Courts for Persons With Disabilities

On order of the Court, to ensure that persons with disabilities have equal and full access to Michigan courts and that all trial courts and court-operated programs and services have implemented procedures in compliance with the Americans with Disabilities Act of 1990, the ADA Amendments Act of 2008, Michigan's Deaf Persons' Interpreters Act (1982 PA 204), and the Persons with Disabilities Civil Rights Act (1976 PA 220), the Michigan Supreme Court orders that each trial court shall:

Adopt a local administrative order that describes the procedure to be followed for a person to request accommodations in that court. The local administrative order shall include the provisions incorporated in Model LAO 35, but may include additional provisions. The local administrative order shall be submitted to and approved by the State Court Administrative Office as a local administrative order under MCR 8.112.

Designate a court employee to be the court's ADA coordinator.

Ensure that the chief judge and ADA coordinator participate in training regarding the duties and obligations of a court in compliance with the ADA, the ADA Amendments Act of 2008, the Deaf Persons' Interpreters Act, and the Persons with Disabilities Civil Rights Act.

Further, courts shall comply with any additional requirements established by the SCAO regarding compliance with these acts.

The requirements established in this order shall become effective 90 days after the date this order enters.

[Adopted September 16, 2015, effective December 15, 2015, 498 Mich.]

Order 2015–6   Adoption of Concurrent Jurisdiction Plan for the 23rd Circuit Court, the 81st District Court, and the Alcona, Arenac, Iosco, and Oscoda County Probate Courts

On order of the Court, adoption of this concurrent jurisdiction plan replaces the plan for the 23rd Circuit Court, the 81st District Court, and the Alcona, Arenac, Iosco, and Oscoda County Probate Courts originally adopted in Administrative Order No. 2004–4, which has been revised to eliminate references to these courts.

Administrative Order No. 2003–1 and MCL 600.401 *et seq.* authorize Michigan trial courts to adopt concurrent jurisdiction plans within a county or judicial circuit, subject to approval of the Court.

The Court hereby approves adoption of the following concurrent jurisdiction plan effective immediately:

• The 23rd Circuit Court, the 81st District Court, and the Alcona, Arenac, Iosco, and Oscoda County Probate Courts.

The plan shall remain on file with the state court administrator.

Amendments to concurrent jurisdiction plans may be implemented by local administrative order pursuant to MCR 8.112. Plan amendments shall conform to the requirements of Administrative Order No. 2003–1 and MCL 600.401 *et seq.*

[Adopted effective September 16, 2015, 498 Mich.]

Order 2015–7   Adoption of Concurrent Jurisdiction Plan for the 26th Circuit Court, the 88th District Court, and the Montmorency County Probate Court

Administrative Order No. 2003–1 and MCL 600.401 *et seq.* authorize Michigan trial courts to adopt concurrent jurisdiction plans within a county or judicial circuit, subject to approval of the Court.

The Court hereby approves adoption of the following concurrent jurisdiction plan effective immediately:

• the 26th Circuit Court, the 88th District Court, and the Montmorency County Probate Court.

The plan shall remain on file with the state court administrator.

Amendments to concurrent jurisdiction plans may be implemented by local administrative order pursuant to MCR 8.112. Plan amendments shall conform to the requirements of Administrative Order No. 2003–1 and MCL 600.401 *et seq.*

[Adopted effective September 16, 2015, 498 Mich.]

Order 2015–8   Authorization of Pilot Project to Study Feasibility and Effectiveness of Mediation in the Court of Appeals

On order of the Court, the Court of Appeals is authorized to implement a mediation pilot project. As provided below, selection for mediation before an outside mediator would be by order of the Court of Appeals and parties could request to have their appeal included in the program or removed from the program. The program is intended to afford parties an efficient and economical means of resolving their appeal. This pilot project is established to study the feasibility and effective-

ness of appellate mediation. The program shall begin October 1, 2015, and shall remain in effect for 12 months. The Court of Appeals will track participation in, and effectiveness of, the program and shall report to, and make such findings available to, the Michigan Supreme Court.

(A) Selection for Mediation.

(1) At any time during the pendency of an appeal before the Court of Appeals, the chief judge or another designated judge may order an appeal submitted to mediation. When a case is selected for mediation, participation is mandatory, however, the chief judge or another designated judge may remove the case on finding that mediation would be inappropriate.

(2) To identify cases for mediation, the Court of Appeals will review civil appeals to determine if mediation would be of assistance to the court or the parties. At any time, a party to a pending civil appeal may file a written request that the appeal be submitted to mediation. Such a request may be made without formal motion and shall be confidential.

(3) A party to a case that has been selected for mediation may file a request to have the case removed from mediation. Such a request may be made without formal motion and shall be confidential. If the request to remove is premised on a desire to avoid the cost of mediation, it is not necessary to demonstrate an inability to pay such costs.

(4) The submission of an appeal to mediation will not toll any filing deadlines in the appeal unless the court orders otherwise.

(B) Mediation Procedure.

(1) Mediation shall be conducted by a mediator selected by stipulation of the parties or designated by the court. A mediator designated by the court shall be an attorney, licensed in Michigan, who has met the qualifications of mediators provided in MCR 2.411(F).

(2) Mediation shall consider the possibility of settlement, the simplification of the issues, and any other matters which the mediator determines may aid in the handling or disposition of the appeal.

(3) The order referring the case to mediation shall specify the time within which the mediation is to be completed. Within the time stated in the order, the mediator shall file a notice with the clerk stating only the date of completion of mediation, who participated in the mediation, whether settlement was reached, and whether any further mediation is warranted.

(4) If mediation results in full or partial settlement of the case, within 21 days after the filing of the notice by the mediator, the parties shall file a stipulation to dismiss pursuant to MCR 7.218(B).

(5) The mediator may charge a reasonable fee, which shall be divided and borne equally by the parties unless agreed otherwise and paid by the parties directly to the mediator. If a party does not agree upon the fee requested by the mediator, upon motion of the party, the chief judge or another designated judge shall set a reasonable fee. In all other respects, mediator fees shall be governed by MCR 2.411(D).

(6) The statements and comments made during mediation are confidential as provided in MCR 2.412 and may not be disclosed in the notice filed by the mediator under (B)(3) of this order or by the participants in briefs or in argument.

(7) Upon failure by a party or attorney to comply with a provision of this order or the order submitting the case to mediation, the chief judge or another designated judge may assess reasonable expenses, including attorney's fees, caused by the failure, may assess all or a portion of appellate costs, or may dismiss the appeal.

(C) Selection of Mediator.

(1) Except as otherwise provided in this order, the selection of a mediator shall be governed by MCR 2.411(B).

(2) Within the time provided in the order referring a case to mediation, the parties may stipulate to the selection of a mediator. Such stipulation shall be filed with the clerk of the court. If the parties do not file a stipulation agreeing to a mediator within the time provided, the court shall appoint a mediator from the roster of approved mediators maintained by the circuit court in which the case originated.

[Adopted September 16, 2015, effective October 1, 2015, 498 Mich.]

Order 2015–9 Authorization of a One–Year Pilot Project Related to the SADO/MAACS Merger

In Administrative Order No. 2014–18, the Court ordered the merger of the State Appellate Defender Office (SADO) and the Michigan Appellate Assigned Counsel System (MAACS), and further ordered the Appellate Defender Commission "to review operations of the MAACS and submit a proposed administrative order that reflects the consolidation of the two offices and incorporates proposed updates or revisions that the commission recommends."

On order of the Court, and upon the request of the Appellate Defender Commission, MAACS is authorized to implement a one-year pilot project to assess the feasibility, costs, and benefits associated with structural reforms currently under consideration for permanent statewide implementation. These reforms would consolidate the individual "local lists" of roster attorneys, which currently exist in all 57 circuit courts, into a smaller number of regional lists to be maintained and administered by MAACS. The pilot will assess the extent to which this consolidation results in greater speed and efficiency in the assignment process, by reducing the number of lists to maintain and allowing MAACS to assume the responsibility of prescreening counsel, preparing appointment orders, and sending notification of appointments to defendants and their attorneys.

The reforms under consideration will depend upon the standardization of appellate assigned counsel policies among the circuit courts, most notably including the voluntary adoption of a standard attorney fee and expense policy. The pilot will assess the extent to which uniformity in attorney fee policies allows more meaningful data analysis related to attorney performance and efficiency, as well as the potential financial impact of these reforms on the circuit courts and their funding units. The pilot will also assess the extent to which standardization of attorney fees affects MAACS's attorney recruitment and retention efforts.

The pilot shall begin as soon as possible as authorized by this order and when there is participation by a sufficient number of circuit courts to constitute two geographic regions, as identified and approved by MAACS. The pilot shall remain in effect for 12 months, unless extended with the approval of this Court and participating circuit courts. [1] MAACS shall track the effectiveness of the reforms by quantitative and qualitative analysis, and

shall make its findings available to the Michigan Supreme Court.

For the duration of the pilot project, all participating circuit courts shall comply with the following regulations, which supplement Section 3 of the MAACS regulations as adopted by this Court in Administrative Order No. 1989–3:

(1) Upon the consent of all affected circuit courts and MAACS, local lists of MAACS roster attorneys may be consolidated by geographic region in whatever manner MAACS deems appropriate, with MAACS assuming certain administrative responsibilities that have traditionally been handled by individual circuit courts.

(2) In order to facilitate the consolidation of local lists, any affected circuit court shall adopt the following administrative procedures:

(a) Within one business day after receiving a request for appellate counsel, the trial court shall provide a copy to MAACS, along with the judgment of sentence, the register of actions, and the identities of all court reporters not named on the register of actions.

(b) Within seven days after the filing of a timely request for counsel, MAACS shall provide to the trial court a proposed order of appointment naming a qualified attorney who has been selected by list rotation or approved specific selection, and directing the court reporter(s) to prepare and file all transcripts as required by MCR 6.425(G) within the time limits specified in MCR 7.210.

(c) Within seven days after receiving a proposed appointment order naming appellate counsel, and within the deadline provided by MCR 6.425(G)(1)(a), the trial court shall issue an order appointing counsel or denying the request for counsel. If the court denies the request for counsel, it shall accompany its ruling with a statement of reasons. The court shall provide copies of its order to MAACS, the prosecutor, and the court reporter(s). MAACS shall provide copies of the trial court's order to the defendant and appointed counsel, thereby satisfying the trial court's responsibilities under MCR 6.425(G)(2).

(d) Within 28 days after receiving a timely request for payment detailing the time and expenses related to the representation in a manner approved by MAACS, the trial court shall order reimbursement pursuant to a standard attorney fee and expense policy that has been approved by the appellate defender commission and the trial court.

[Adopted effective September 16, 2015, 498 Mich. Pilot project extended until December 31, 2017 by order dated September 21, 2016, 500 Mich.]

[1] **Publisher's Note:** By order 2014–36, dated September 21, 2016, the Michigan Supreme Court extended the MAACS Regional Pilot Project until December 31, 2017.

Order 2015–10 Adoption of Concurrent Jurisdiction Plan for the 51st Circuit Court, the 79th District Court, and the Mason County Probate Court

Administrative Order No. 2003–1 and MCL 600.401 *et seq.* authorize Michigan trial courts to adopt concurrent jurisdiction plans within a county or judicial circuit, subject to approval of the Court.

The Court hereby approves adoption of the following concurrent jurisdiction plan effective immediately:

- the 51st Circuit Court, the 79th District Court, and the Mason County Probate Court.

The plan shall remain on file with the state court administrator.

Amendments to concurrent jurisdiction plans may be implemented by local administrative order pursuant to MCR 8.112. Plan amendments shall conform to the requirements of Administrative Order No. 2003–1 and MCL 600.401 *et seq.*

[Adopted effective October 14, 2015, 498 Mich.]

Order 2016–1   Authorizes the 7th Circuit Court to Require Parties and Attorneys to Submit Pleadings in Electronic Format in Personal Injury or Other Civil Cases Arising from Allegations of Lead or Other Contaminants in Flint Water

On order of the Court, at the request of the 7th Circuit Court, and pursuant to MCR 1.109(C)(1), the 7th Circuit Court is authorized to require parties and attorneys in personal injury or other civil cases arising from allegations of lead or other contaminants in Flint water to submit pleadings in electronic format. The 7th Circuit Court shall submit a local administrative order to the State Court Administrative Office describing the manner in which such pleadings are to be submitted. This order is effective immediately, and shall remain in effect until further order of the Court.

[Adopted effective May 25, 2016, 499 Mich.]

Order 2016–2   Regulations Governing a System for Appointment of Counsel for Indigent Defendants in Criminal Cases and Minimum Standards for Indigent Criminal Defense Services

Pursuant to the Michigan Indigent Defense Commission Act, 2013 PA 93, the Michigan Indigent Defense Commission submitted to this Court proposed standards that would regulate the manner in which counsel would be appointed to represent indigent defendants in criminal cases, and would further impose specific training, experience and continuing legal education requirements on attorneys who seek appointment as counsel in these types of cases. The Court published the proposed standards for comment, and after due consideration, conditionally approves the standards as set forth below.[1]

This approval is subject to and contingent on legislative revision of the MIDC Act to address provisions that the Court deems to be of uncertain constitutionality. These provisions include:

1. MCL 780.985 creates the MIDC as an "autonomous entity" and places it within "the judicial branch." Employees of the judicial branch are subject to this Court's exclusive constitutional authority to exercise general supervisory control. See Const 1963, art 6, §§ 1, 4, and 7; *Judicial Attorneys Ass'n v Michigan*, 459 Mich 291, 298; 586 NW2d 635 (1998). We are concerned that placing the MIDC within the judicial branch, while denying the Court the ability to supervise and direct the commission's activities and employment, may contravene the general principle of separation of powers under the Michigan Constitution, Const 1963, art 3, § 2, and impinge upon the specific constitutional function of this Court to supervise the judicial branch.

2. MCL 780.983(f) defines "indigent criminal defense system," an entity subject to the authority of the MIDC, in a manner that includes trial courts, and combines trial courts with nonjudicial local governments. In addition, MCL 780.989(1)(a) allows the MIDC to "[d]evelop[] and oversee[] the implementation, enforcement, and modification of minimum standards, rules, and procedures to ensure that indigent criminal defense services providing effective assistance of counsel are consistently delivered to all indigent adults in this state;" and MCL 780.989(1)(b) allows the MIDC "to assure compliance with the commission's minimum standards, rules, and procedures." We are concerned that these provisions might contain enforcement mechanisms that present an unconstitutional usurpation of this Court's authority under Const 1963, art 6, § 4, which provides that the Supreme Court "shall have general superintending control over all courts." They also raise general separation of powers concerns under Const 1963, art 3, § 2.

3. MCL 780.989(1)(f) and (2) and MCL 780.991(2) arguably allow the MIDC to regulate the legal profession. The Constitution exclusively assigns regulation of the legal profession to the judiciary. See Const 1963, art 6, § 5; *Grievance Administrator v Lopatin*, 462 Mich 235; 612 NW2d 120 (2000); *Attorney General v Michigan Public Serv Comm*, 243 Mich App 487, 517; 625 NW2d 16 (2000).

To promote the goal of providing effective assistance of counsel for indigent defendants in criminal cases without disruption, the Court urges legislative revision of the MIDC Act to address the constitutional concerns raised herein by this Court. If this Court determines before December 31, 2016, that legislative revisions of the MIDC Act have sufficiently addressed our concerns, the standards approved conditionally by this Court today will then take full effect. Otherwise, this Court's conditional approval of these standards will be automatically withdrawn on December 31, 2016. The Court will then determine what, if any, further action it may take to preserve its constitutional authority.

The conditionally approved standards and requirements, together with the commentary of the MIDC and the MIDC's description of the principles governing the creation of the standards, are as follows:

Minimum Standards for Appointed Counsel under the MIDC Act

Standard 1.   Education and Training of Defense Counsel. The MIDC Act requires adherence to the principle that "[d]efense counsel is required to attend continuing legal education relevant to counsel's indigent defense clients." MCL 780.991(2)(e). The United States Supreme Court has held that the constitutional right to counsel guaranteed by the Sixth Amendment includes the right to the effective assistance of counsel. The mere presence of a lawyer at a trial "is not enough to satisfy the constitutional command." *Strickland v Washington*, 466 US 668, 685; 104 S Ct 2052, 2063; 80 L Ed 2d 674 (1984). Further, the Ninth Principle of The American Bar Association's *Ten Principles of a Public Defense Delivery System* provides that a public defense system, in order to provide effective assistance of counsel, must ensure that "Defense counsel is provided with and required to attend continuing legal education."

The MIDC proposed a minimum standard for the education and training of defense counsel. The version conditionally approved by the Court is as follows:

A. *Knowledge of the Law.* Counsel shall have reasonable knowledge of substantive Michigan and federal law, constitutional law, criminal law, criminal procedure, rules of evidence, ethical rules and local practices. Counsel has a continuing obligation to have reasonable knowledge of the changes and developments in the law. "Reasonable knowledge" as used in this standard means knowledge of which a lawyer competent under MRPC 1.1 would be aware.

B. *Knowledge of Scientific Evidence and Applicable Defenses.* Counsel shall have reasonable knowledge of the forensic and scientific issues that can arise in a criminal case, the legal issues concerning defenses to a crime, and be reasonably able to effectively litigate those issues.

C. *Knowledge of Technology.* Counsel shall be reasonably able to use office technology commonly used in the legal community, and technology used within the applicable court system. Counsel shall be reasonably able to thoroughly review materials that are provided in an electronic format.

D. *Continuing Education.* Counsel shall annually complete continuing legal education courses relevant to the representation of the criminally accused. Counsel shall participate in skills training and educational programs in order to maintain and enhance overall preparation, oral and written advocacy, and litigation and negotiation skills. Lawyers can discharge this obligation for annual continuing legal education by attending local trainings or statewide conferences. Attorneys with fewer than two years of experience practicing criminal defense in Michigan shall participate in one basic skills acquisition class. All attorneys shall annually complete at least twelve hours of continuing legal education. Training shall be funded through compliance plans submitted by the local delivery system or other mechanism that does not place a financial burden on assigned counsel. The MIDC shall collect or direct the collection of data regarding the number of hours of continuing legal education offered to and attended by assigned counsel, shall analyze the quality of the training, and shall ensure that the effectiveness of the training be measurable and validated. A report regarding these data shall be submitted to the Court annually by April 1 for the previous calendar year.

> *Comment: The minimum of twelve hours of training represents typical national and some local county requirements, and is accessible in existing programs offered statewide.*

Standard 2. Initial Interview. The MIDC Act requires adherence to the principle that "[d]efense counsel is provided sufficient time and a space where attorney-client confidentiality is safeguarded for meetings with defense counsel's client." MCL 780.991(2)(a). United States Supreme Court precedent and American Bar Association Principles recognize that the "lack of time for adequate preparation and the lack of privacy for attorney-client consultation" can preclude "any lawyer from providing effective advice." *See United States v Morris,* 470 F3d 596, 602 (CA 6, 2006) (citing *United States v Cronic,* 466 US 648; 104 S Ct 2039; 80 L Ed 2d 657 (1984)). Further, the Fourth Principle of The American Bar Association's *Ten Principles of a Public Defense Delivery System* provides that a public defense system, in order to provide effective assistance

of counsel, must ensure that "Defense counsel is provided sufficient time and a confidential space within which to meet with the client."

The MIDC proposed a minimum standard for the initial client interview. The version conditionally approved by the Court is as follows:

A. *Timing and Purpose of the Interview.* Counsel shall conduct a client interview as soon as practicable after appointment to represent the defendant in order to obtain information necessary to provide quality representation at the early stages of the case and to provide the client with information concerning counsel's representation and the case proceedings. The purpose of the initial interview is to: (1) establish the best possible relationship with the indigent client; (2) review charges; (3) determine whether a motion for pretrial release is appropriate; (4) determine the need to start-up any immediate investigations; (5) determine any immediate mental or physical health needs or need for foreign language interpreter assistance; and (6) advise that clients should not discuss the circumstances of the arrest or allegations with cellmates, law enforcement, family or anybody else without counsel present. Counsel shall conduct subsequent client interviews as needed. Following appointment, counsel shall conduct the initial interview with the client sufficiently before any subsequent court proceeding so as to be prepared for that proceeding. When a client is in local custody, counsel shall conduct an initial client intake interview within three business days after appointment. When a client is not in custody, counsel shall promptly deliver an introductory communication so that the client may follow-up and schedule a meeting. If confidential videoconference facilities are made available for trial attorneys, visits should at least be scheduled within three business days. If an indigent defendant is in the custody of the Michigan Department of Corrections (MDOC) or detained in a different county from where the defendant is charged, counsel should arrange for a confidential client visit in advance of the first pretrial hearing.

B. *Setting of the Interview.* All client interviews shall be conducted in a private and confidential setting to the extent reasonably possible. The indigent criminal defense system shall ensure the necessary accommodations for private discussions between counsel and clients in courthouses, lock-ups, jails, prisons, detention centers, and other places where clients must confer with counsel.

C. *Preparation.* Counsel shall obtain copies of any relevant documents which are available, including copies of any charging documents, recommendations and reports concerning pretrial release, and discoverable material.

D. *Client Status.*

1. Counsel shall evaluate whether the client is capable of participation in his/her representation, understands the charges, and has some basic comprehension of criminal procedure. Counsel has a continuing responsibility to evaluate, and, where appropriate, raise as an issue for the court the client's capacity to stand trial or to enter a plea pursuant to MCR 6.125 and MCL 330.2020. Counsel shall take appropriate action where there are any questions about a client's competency.

2. Where counsel is unable to communicate with the client because of language or communication differences, counsel shall take whatever steps are necessary to fully

explain the proceedings in a language or form of communication the client can understand. Steps include seeking the appointment of an interpreter to assist with pretrial preparation, interviews, investigation, and in-court proceedings, or other accommodations pursuant to MCR. 1.111.

Comments:

1. The MIDC recognizes that counsel cannot ensure communication prior to court with an out of custody indigent client. For out of custody clients the standard instead requires the attorney to notify clients of the need for a prompt interview.

2. The requirement of a meeting within three business days is typical of national requirements (Florida Performance Guidelines suggest 72 hours; in Massachusetts, the Committee for Public Counsel Services Assigned Counsel Manual requires a visit within three business days for custody clients; the Supreme Court of Nevada issued a performance standard requiring an initial interview within 72 hours of appointment).

3. Certain indigent criminal defense systems only pay counsel for limited client visits in custody. In these jurisdictions, compliance plans with this standard will need to guarantee funding for multiple visits.

4. In certain systems, counsel is not immediately notified of appointments to represent indigent clients. In these jurisdictions, compliance plans must resolve any issues with the failure to provide timely notification.

5. Some jurisdictions do not have discovery prepared for trial counsel within three business days. The MIDC expects that this minimum standard can be used to push for local reforms to immediately provide electronic discovery upon appointment.

6. The three-business-day requirement is specific to clients in "local" custody because some indigent defendants are in the custody of the Michigan Department of Corrections (MDOC) while other defendants might be in jail in a different county from the charging offense.

7. In jurisdictions with a large client population in MDOC custody or rural jurisdictions requiring distant client visits compliance plans might provide for visits through confidential videoconferencing.

8. Systems without adequate settings for confidential visits for either in-custody or out-of-custody clients will need compliance plans to create this space.

9. This standard only involves the initial client interview. Other confidential client interviews are expected, as necessary.

Standard 3. Investigation and Experts. The United States Supreme Court has held: (1) "counsel has a duty to make reasonable investigations or to make a reasonable decision that makes particular investigations unnecessary." *Strickland v Washington*, 466 US 668, 691; 104 S Ct 2052, 2066; 80 L Ed 2d 674 (1984); and (2) "[c]riminal cases will arise where the only reasonable and available defense strategy requires consul-

tation with experts or introduction of expert evidence, whether pretrial, at trial, or both." *Harrington v Richter*, 562 US 86, 106; 131 S Ct 770, 788; 178 L Ed 2d 624 (2011). The MIDC Act authorizes "minimum standards for the local delivery of indigent criminal defense services providing effective assistance of counsel..." MCL 780.985(3).

The MIDC proposed a minimum standard for investigations and experts. The version conditionally approved by the Court is as follows:

A. Counsel shall conduct an independent investigation of the charges and offense as promptly as practicable.

B. When appropriate, counsel shall request funds to retain an investigator to assist with the client's defense. Reasonable requests must be funded.

C. Counsel shall request the assistance of experts where it is reasonably necessary to prepare the defense and rebut the prosecution's case. Reasonable requests must be funded as required by law.

D. Counsel has a continuing duty to evaluate a case for appropriate defense investigations or expert assistance. Decisions to limit investigation must take into consideration the client's wishes and the client's version of the facts.

Comments:

1. The MIDC recognizes that counsel can make "a reasonable decision that makes particular investigations unnecessary" after a review of discovery and an interview with the client. Decisions to limit investigation should not be made merely on the basis of discovery or representations made by the government.

2. The MIDC emphasizes that a client's professed desire to plead guilty does not automatically alleviate the need to investigate.

3. Counsel should inform clients of the progress of investigations pertaining to their case.

4. Expected increased costs from an increase in investigations and expert use will be tackled in compliance plans.

Standard 4. Counsel at First Appearance and other Critical Stages. The MIDC Act provides that standards shall be established to effectuate the following: (1) "All adults, except those appearing with retained counsel or those who have made an informed waiver of counsel, shall be screened for eligibility under this act, and counsel shall be assigned as soon as an indigent adult is determined to be eligible for indigent criminal defense services." MCL 780.991(1)(c); (2) "A preliminary inquiry regarding, and the determination of, the indigency of any defendant shall be made by the court not later than at the defendant's first appearance in court. MCL 780.991(3)(a); (3) ...counsel continuously represents and personally appears at *every court appearance* throughout the pendency of the case." MCL 780.991(2)(d)(emphasis added).

The MIDC proposed a minimum standard on counsel at first appearance and other critical stages. The version conditionally approved by the Court is as follows:

A. Counsel shall be assigned as soon as the defendant is determined to be eligible for indigent criminal defense services. The indigency determination shall be made and counsel appointed to provide assistance to the defendant as soon as the defendant's liberty is subject to restriction by a magistrate or judge. Representation includes but is not limited to the arraignment on the complaint and warrant. Where there are case-specific interim bonds set, counsel at arraignment shall be prepared to make a de novo argument regarding an appropriate bond regardless of and, indeed, in the face of, an interim bond set prior to arraignment which has no precedential effect on bond-setting at arraignment. Nothing in this paragraph shall prevent the defendant from making an informed waiver of counsel.

B. All persons determined to be eligible for indigent criminal defense services shall also have appointed counsel at pre-trial proceedings, during plea negotiations and at other critical stages, whether in court or out of court.

Comments:

1. The proposed standard addresses an indigent defendant's right to counsel at every court appearance and is not addressing vertical representation (same defense counsel continuously represents) which will be the subject of a future minimum standard as described in MCL 780.991(2)(d).

2. One of several potential compliance plans for this standard may use an on-duty arraignment attorney to represent defendants. This appointment may be a limited appearance for arraignment only with subsequent appointment of different counsel for future proceedings. In this manner, actual indigency determinations may still be made during the arraignment.

3. Among other duties, lawyering at first appearance should consist of an explanation of the criminal justice process, advice on what topics to discuss with the judge, a focus on the potential for pre-trial release, or achieving dispositions outside of the criminal justice system via civil infraction or dismissal. In rare cases, if an attorney has reviewed discovery and has an opportunity for a confidential discussion with her client, there may be a criminal disposition at arraignment.

4. The MIDC anticipates creative and cost-effective compliance plans like representation and advocacy through videoconferencing or consolidated arraignment schedules between multiple district courts.

5. This standard does not preclude the setting of interim bonds to allow for the release of in-custody defendants. The intent is not to lengthen any jail stays. The MIDC believes that case-specific interim bond determinations should be discouraged. Formal arraignment and the formal setting of bond should be done as quickly as possible.

6. Any waiver of the right to counsel must be both unequivocal and knowing, intelligent, and voluntary. People v Anderson, 398 Mich 361; 247 NW2d 857 (1976). The uncounseled defendant must have sufficient information to make an intelligent choice dependent on a range of case-specific factors, including his education or sophistication, the complexity or easily grasped nature of the charge, and the stage of the proceeding.

[Adopted effective June 1, 2016, 499 Mich.]

[1] The conditional approval reflects the Court's ongoing authority to establish, implement, and impose professional standards. See Administrative Order No. 1981–7 (approving regulations and standards for the appellate indigent defense system); Administrative Order No. 2004–6 (altering the standards of AO No. 1981–7).

Order 2016–3   Prisoner Electronic Filing Program with the Michigan Supreme Court and the Michigan Department of Corrections

On order of the Court, effective immediately, the Michigan Supreme Court ("Court") is authorized to implement a Prisoner Electronic Filing Program with the Michigan Department of Corrections.

Participants in the Prisoner Electronic Filing Program consist of the Clerk's Office of the Michigan Supreme Court, the correctional facilities operated by the Michigan Department of Corrections ("MDOC") identified in Exhibit A to this order, and the prisoner litigants housed in the identified correctional facilities who are or who seek to be parties to litigation filed in the Michigan Supreme Court. Additional facilities may be made part of this program at the discretion of the Clerk's Office and the MDOC.

For the initial phase of the Prisoner Electronic Filing Program, the Court will provide to the MDOC, and retain ownership of, digital equipment for use in the identified correctional facilities with the sole purpose of transmitting authorized documents between the Court and the identified correctional facilities. The digital equipment will be programmed with an email address used by the Clerk's Office for receiving electronic filings from the MDOC. The MDOC will provide the Clerk's Office with email addresses for receiving electronic notices from the Court on behalf of the prisoner litigants at the identified correctional facilities.

Filings by prisoner litigants during the initial phase of the program will be limited to applications for leave to appeal and related documents in criminal cases. Prisoner litigants must utilize the form created by the Clerk's Office for self-represented litigants and made available to the MDOC.

All filings by prisoner litigants must be submitted electronically to the Clerk's Office unless the system is not operational when the documents are presented to the MDOC for e-filing. If the system is not operational at the time of presentment, the filing shall be submitted by mail, unless the system is expected to resume operation before the filing deadline. A prisoner litigant transferred from a correctional facility with e-filing capability to a correctional facility without e-filing capability must submit all future filings by mail via the U.S. Postal Service. A prisoner litigant who is transferred into a correctional facility with e-filing capability must electronically transmit all subsequent filings to the Court. The prisoner litigant must notify the Clerk's Office immediately of any change of address.

MDOC staff will scan the prisoner litigant's filings at the correctional facility and transmit them, with a time stamp applied by the digital equipment, to the Clerk's Office email address. An automated email reply will be immediately sent to the MDOC email address acknowledging receipt of the filing. The original documents will be returned to the prisoner litigant, who must retain them in their original form and produce them at a later time if ordered by the Court.

The Clerk's Office will review filings as soon as practicable (usually by 5:00 p.m. if received in the morning on a business day or by 12:00 p.m. the following business day if received in the afternoon) for jurisdiction and compliance with the court rules. If the Court does not have jurisdiction or if the filing does not substantially comply with the court rules, the Clerk's Office will transmit a Notice of Rejection to the MDOC that specifies the reason(s) for the rejection.

If the filing is accepted, it will be docketed in the Court's case management system and electronically served on those persons or entities that the prisoner litigant has identified as parties to the litigation if they are registered users of TrueFiling or have provided an official email address to the Court. The Clerk's Office will mail copies of the prisoner litigant's filing via the U.S. Postal Service to identified parties who cannot be e-served. For accepted filings, the Clerk's Office will transmit a Notice of Electronic Filing to the MDOC that identifies, among other things, the names and service information of parties who were served with the filing. The Notice of Electronic Filing also will be electronically transmitted or mailed to the Michigan Court of Appeals and the trial court/tribunal as notice of the appeal under MCR 7.305(A)(3).

The MDOC will provide a copy of the Notice of Rejection or Notice of Electronic Filing to the prisoner litigant as soon as practicable.

Exhibit A

Correctional Facilities Participating in the Prisoner Electronic Filing Program:

Carson City Correctional Facility, 10274 Boyer Road, Carson City, MI 48811

St. Louis Correctional Facility, 8585 N. Croswell Road, St. Louis, MI 48880

[Adopted effective November 2, 2016, 500 Mich.]

Order 2016–4   Adoption of Administrative Order to Expedite Disposition of Pending Probate Appeals in Circuit Court

Expedited Consideration of Probate Appeals in Circuit Court

2016 PA 186 provides that all final orders issued by the probate court are appealable to the Court of Appeals beginning September 27, 2016. To facilitate disposition of the appeals of orders pending in the circuit court on September 27, 2016, each circuit judge is directed to:

(1) Insofar as possible, expedite the consideration of pending appeals from orders of the probate court; and

(2) On March 1, 2017, and every 6 months thereafter, file a report with the State Court Administrator listing each such appeal that remains pending, including a statement of the reasons the appeal has not been concluded.

[Adopted effective November 23, 2016, 500 Mich.]

Comment

Staff Comment to 2016 Adoption

This administrative order directs circuit courts to expedite disposition of pending appeals, and report unresolved appeals beginning March 1, 2017.

Order 2016–5   Adoption of New Antinepotism Policy and Rescission of AO No. 1996–11

Antinepotism Order

1. Policy. All courts in Michigan are committed to make all business decisions—including decisions regarding employment, contracting with vendors, and selecting interns—on the basis of qualifications and merit, and to avoid circumstances in which the appearance of impropriety or possibility of favoritism exist. On the basis of this policy, the following situations are prohibited:

(a) A superior-subordinate relationship existing at or developing after the time of employment between any related employees;

(b) A related chief judge and a court administrator working in the same court, regardless of whether there is a superior-subordinate relationship;

(c) Except as waived under this order, a related judge and court employee working in the same court.

All other relatives of court personnel who meet established requirements for job vacancies, court contract, or internship opportunities based on their qualifications and performance are eligible for judiciary employment, contracts, or internships in the same court. But advocacy of one relative on behalf of the other is prohibited in all circumstances.

2. Definitions. For purposes of this order, the following definitions apply:

(a) "Relative" includes spouse, child, parent, brother, sister, grandparent, grandchild, first cousin, uncle, aunt, niece, nephew, brother-in-law, sister-in-law, daughter-in-law, son-in-law, mother-in-law, and father-in-law, whether natural, adopted, step or foster. The term also includes same-sex or different-sex individuals who have a relationship of a romantic, intimate, committed, or dating nature, which relationship arises after the effective date of this policy. The definition of relative does not include two related judges who are elected to or appointed to serve in the same court.

(b) "Court Administrator" includes the highest level of administrator, clerk, or director of the court who functions under the general direction of the chief justice or chief judge, including but not limited to state court administrator, circuit court administrator, friend of the court, probate court administrator, juvenile court administrator, probate register and district court administrator/clerk.

(c) A "superior-subordinate relationship" is one in which one employee is the direct supervisor of the other employee.

(d) An intern is a student or trainee who works for the court, with or without pay, to gain work experience.

(e) A vendor is an individual or someone appearing on behalf of a corporation or other entity that offers to provide or provides goods or services to the court.

3. Application. This policy applies to all applicants for employment, as well as all full-time and part-time employees, temporary employees, and contractual employees, including independent contractors, interns, vendors, and personal service contracts.

4. Affected Employees. No person shall be transferred, promoted, or rehired following separation in a position that would create a nepotic relationship in violation of this policy.

5. Collective Bargaining Agreements. After the date this order enters, chief judges and court administrators are prohibited from entering into collective bargaining agreements inconsistent with this policy.

6. Conflicts; Waiver. The chief judge of a court shall resolve any employment situations that conflict with or would conflict with this policy, unless the conflict involves a relative of the chief judge. In such a situation, the State Court Administrator shall resolve the issue.

In making a hiring decision, a chief judge (or the State Court Administrator, if the chief judge of a court is a relative of the prospective employee) may waive the prohibition in Paragraph 1(c) if the following requirements are met:

(a) The position for which the waiver is sought must have been announced or advertised to the public in the same manner and for the same duration as other vacancies within the court.

(b) The prospective employee's judge relative cannot have participated in any way in the selection process.

(c) Other qualified applicants must have been considered.

(d) Selection of a candidate who is related to a judge must have been based on merit and qualifications, including evidence that the candidate meets the minimum requirements for the position.

(e) The chief judge (or the State Court Administrator, if applicable) completes and files with the State Court Administrative Office a form approved by the State Court Administrative Office in which the chief judge affirms that the court has followed this procedure.

If an employee is employed by a court and a relative of the employee subsequently becomes a judge in that court, the prohibition does not apply as long as the judge is not in a superior-subordinate position with the employee and as long as the employee retains the current employment status. If the employee seeks a different position, a court may seek a waiver only if it complies with the waiver procedure outlined above.

In making a decision about a waiver, the chief judge or State Court Administrator must determine whether the requirements listed above have been met, and whether such employment would create an appearance of impropriety or possibility of favoritism.

A decision rendered by a chief judge or the State Court Administrator under this order is not appealable or otherwise subject to review.

7. Chief Judge Appointments. Nothing in this policy prohibits the Supreme Court from selecting any judge as a chief judge of a court. If such selection occurs, and such selection creates a nepotic relationship, the putative chief judge shall provide to the Court, and the Court shall approve, an alternative means by which the relative of the chief judge shall be supervised.

8. No New Rights Created. Adoption of this policy creates no new rights for employees or prospective employees.

9. Grandfather Clause. This policy shall not apply to any person who is an employee of a court on the date this order enters. However, from the date this order enters, no person may be transferred, promoted, or enter into a nepotic relationship in violation of this policy, except as provided herein.

[Adopted December 7, 2016, effective January 1, 2017, 500 Mich.]

Order 2017–1   Adjustment of Discipline Portion of State Bar of Michigan Dues

In light of an attorney discipline system reserve of about $5 million, the Court lowered the discipline portion of the State Bar of Michigan annual dues from $120 to $110 (in 2011) and then to $90 (in 2014), intending that those reserve funds be used to offset annual operating expenses until the fund was reduced to a more reasonable level. With the reserve now projected to be approximately $1.86 million by the end of fiscal year 2016–2017, the Court has determined that bar dues should be restored, albeit in a phased-in fashion.

Therefore, on order of the Court, the amount of discipline dues is increased to $105 in the 2017–18 fiscal year, and further increased to $120 in the 2018–19 fiscal year, unless otherwise ordered by the Court. These changes will be reflected in the dues notices that are communicated to all bar members under Rule 4 of the Rules Concerning the State Bar.

[Adopted effective July 12, 2017, 500 Mich.]

Order 2017–2   Adoption of Concurrent Jurisdiction (Plan for the 19th Circuit Court, the 85th District Court, and the Benzie and Manistee County Probate Courts)

Administrative Order No. 2003–1 and MCL 600.401 *et seq.* authorize Michigan trial courts to adopt concurrent jurisdiction plans within a county or judicial circuit, subject to approval of the Court.

The Court hereby approves adoption of the following concurrent jurisdiction plan effective immediately:

● The 19th Circuit Court, the 85th District Court, and the Benzie and Manistee County Probate Courts.

The plan shall remain on file with the state court administrator.

Amendments to concurrent jurisdiction plans may be implemented by local administrative order pursuant to MCR 8.112. Plan amendments shall conform to the requirements of Administrative Order No. 2003–1 and MCL 600.401 *et seq.*

[Adopted effective September 20, 2017, 501 Mich.]

Order 2017–3   Merger of the State Appellate Defender Office (SADO) and Michigan Appellate Assigned Counsel System (MAACS)

Michigan's Appellate Defender Act, 1978 PA 620, established an Appellate Defender Commission to oversee a system of criminal appellate defense services for indigents. The Act provides in part that "[t]he appointment of criminal appellate defense services for indigents shall be made by the trial court from the roster provided by the commission or shall be referred to the office of the state appellate defender." MCL 780.712(6).

In Administrative Order No. 1981–7, this Court directed the Commission to "establish an Appellate Assigned Counsel Administrator's Office which shall be coordinated with but separate from the State Appellate Defender Office." The office was "to compile and maintain a statewide roster of attorneys eligible and willing to accept criminal appellate defense assignments," and the Court approved regulations to govern both the appointment process and the assigned counsel roster. In 1985, however, the Court determined that under the Appellate Defender Act, "the regulations governing a system for appointment of appellate counsel for indigents in criminal cases" should fall to "the Appellate Defender Commission and not to this Court." See Administrative Order No. 1985-3. See also Administrative Order No. 1989-3. The same year, the Michigan Appellate Assigned Counsel System (MAACS) began operating as an independent state agency under regulations adopted by the Commission.

In 2014, at the request of the Appellate Defender Commission, the Court ordered an operational merger of MAACS with the State Appellate Defender Office (SADO) under the management of the State Appellate Defender "to promote efficiency and improve the administration of assigned appellate counsel for indigent defendants." Administrative Order No. 2014-18. The Court directed the Commission "to review operations of the MAACS and submit a proposed administrative order that reflects the consolidation of the two offices and incorporates proposed updates or revisions that the commission recommends."

The Commission has overseen the merger of SADO and MAACS and conducted an exhaustive review of operations to improve indigent criminal appellants' access to competent counsel with shared resources and expertise. As part of that review, the Commission has monitored a pilot project approved by the Court to "assess the feasibility, costs, and benefits associated with structural reforms" including the regional consolidation of trial court assignment lists, the voluntary implementation of a uniform attorney fee policy, the trial courts' delegation of certain administrative responsibilities to MAACS, the pre-screening of counsel, and the electronic transfer of documents related to the appointment process. See Administrative Order No. 2015-9. The Commission reports that these reforms have improved the speed and efficiency of the assignment process as well as the quality of assigned appellate representation, and have been well-received by courts and counsel alike.

Therefore, at the request of the Appellate Defender Commission, the Court orders that the Commission shall remain responsible for enacting regulations to govern the MAACS roster and the selection of felony appellate assigned counsel, including SADO's appropriate share of appellate appointments under MCL 780.716(c). The Commission may approve policies to facilitate the regional consolidation of appellate assignment lists for private assigned counsel, including a voluntary attorney fee and expense policy for participating trial courts.

Trial courts shall address all requests for the appointment of felony appellate counsel under the regulations and procedures approved by the Commission and in conformity with applicable court rules. The Court has reviewed the regulations adopted by the Commission on September 20, 2017, and directs the Commission to notify the Court of any updates or changes to these regulations.

This Order supersedes Administrative Orders 1981-7, 1985-3, and 1989-3.

[Adopted effective November 15, 2017.]

Order 2018-1 Adoption of Concurrent Jurisdiction Plan for the 34th Circuit Court, the 82nd District Court, the Ogemaw and Roscommon County Probate Courts

Administrative Order No. 2003-1 and MCL 600.401, *et seq.* authorize Michigan trial courts to adopt concurrent jurisdiction plans within a county or judicial circuit, subject to approval of the Court.

The Court hereby approves adoption of the following concurrent jurisdiction plan, effective immediately:

● The 34th Circuit Court, the 82nd District Court, and the Ogemaw County and Roscommon County Probate Courts.

The plan shall remain on file with the state court administrator.

Amendments to concurrent jurisdiction plans may be implemented by local administrative order pursuant to MCR 8.112. Plan amendments shall conform to the requirements of Administrative Order No. 2003-1 and MCL 600.401, *et seq.*

[Adopted effective March 14, 2018, 501 Mich.]

Order 2018-2 Adoption of Concurrent Jurisdiction Plan for the 8th Circuit Court, the 64th District Court, the Ionia and Montcalm County Probate Courts

Administrative Order No. 2003-1 and MCL 600.401, *et seq.* authorize Michigan trial courts to adopt concurrent jurisdiction plans within a county or judicial circuit, subject to approval of the Court.

The Court hereby approves adoption of the following concurrent jurisdiction plan, effective immediately:

● The 8th Circuit Court, the 64th District Court, and the Ionia County and Montcalm County Probate Courts.

The plan shall remain on file with the state court administrator.

Amendments to concurrent jurisdiction plans may be implemented by local administrative order pursuant to MCR 8.112. Plan amendments shall conform to the requirements of Administrative Order No. 2003-1 and MCL 600.401, *et seq.*

[Adopted effective May 16, 2018, 501 Mich.]

Order 2019-1. Establishment of Court Security Committees

The issue of courthouse security is of vital importance to ensure the safety of the public, litigants, and the judicial employees of this state. Therefore, it is ordered that each chief judge or, in any facility with multiple chief judges, one chief judge as designated by consensus of the chief judges, establish a standing courthouse security committee to be chaired by the chief judge or his/her designee. The members of the committee shall include representatives of the court's funding unit, local law enforcement, the Clerk of Court, and other facility stakeholders. The courthouse security committee is responsible for creating and promoting policies and procedures to improve the safety and security of the courthouse.

Each court shall submit to the State Court Administrative Office (SCAO) a local administrative order that establishes the courthouse security committee in accordance with the model local administrative order developed by the SCAO. Courts with multiple chief judges in one location and courts that have multiple locations must follow the instructions provided by the SCAO for establishing the standing courthouse security committee. In developing the security committee, courts are directed to work with local funding units and to collaborate with other entities in shared facilities, where appropriate.

Proposed local administrative orders must be submitted to the SCAO no later than September 1, 2019.

[Adopted effective March 13, 2019, 502 Mich.]

Order 2019-2   Trial Court Requirements for Providing Meaningful Access to the Court for Mandated Electronic Filers

To ensure that those individuals required to electronically file court documents have meaningful access to Michigan courts, the Michigan Supreme Court adopts this order requiring courts that seek permission to mandate that all litigants e-File to first submit an e-Filing Access Plan for approval by the State Court Administrative Office.

Each plan must conform to the model promulgated by the State Court Administrator and ensure access to at least one computer workstation per county. The plan shall be submitted to and approved by the State Court Administrative Office as a local administrative order under MCR 8.112. The State Court Administrative Office may revoke approval of an e-Filing Access Plan due to litigant grievances.

[Adopted June 5, 2019, effective September 1, 2019, 503 Mich.]

Order 2019-3.   Concurrent Jurisdiction Plan for the 41st Circuit Court

Administrative Order No. 2003–1 and MCL 600.401 *et seq.* authorize Michigan trial courts to adopt concurrent jurisdiction plans within a county or judicial circuit, subject to approval of the Court.

The Court hereby rescinds Administrative Order No. 2005–1 and approves adoption of the following concurrent jurisdiction plan, effective immediately:

• The 41st Circuit Court, the 95A District Court, the 95B District Court, and the Dickinson, Iron, and Menominee County Probate Courts.

The plan shall remain on file with the State Court Administrator.

Amendments to concurrent jurisdiction plans may be implemented by local administrative order pursuant to MCR 8.112. Plan amendments shall conform to the requirements of Administrative Order No. 2003–1 and MCL 600.401 *et seq.*

[Adopted effective August 14, 2019, 503 Mich.]

Order 2019-4.   Electronic Filing in the 3rd, 6th, 13th, 16th, and 20th Circuit Courts

On order of the Court, the 3rd, 6th, 13th, 16th, and 20th Circuit Courts are authorized to continue their e-Filing programs in accordance with this order while the State Court Administrative Office develops and implements a statewide e-Filing system (known as MiFILE). This order rescinds and replaces Michigan Supreme Court Administrative Orders 2007-3 (Oakland County), 2010-4 (the 13th Judicial Circuit), 2010-6 (the 16th Judicial Circuit), 2011-1 (the 3rd Circuit Court), and 2011-4 (Ottawa County).

1. **Construction.** Until each court is fully implemented on MiFILE, each court shall operate its current e-Filing system in accordance with this order and Michigan Court Rules 1.109(G) and 8.119. This includes that each court may continue to exercise its discretion to grant necessary relief to avoid the consequences of error so as not to affect the substantial rights of the parties until the court is fully implemented on MiFILE. The Michigan Rules of Court govern all other aspects of the cases that are required to be filed electronically.

2. **Participation in E-Filing.**

a. *Mandatory Participation.* Participation in the e-Filing system is mandatory for the case types in place and for parties currently required to e-File in each court, as of the date of this order. Each court shall post on its website and in the clerk's office a list of the case types, mandated filers, and types of filings as specified in State Court Administrative Office Memo 2019–4. The State Court Administrative Office shall also maintain this information on its One Court of Justice website.

On or before the date a pilot court is transitioned to MiFILE, the court must have in place an approved e-Filing access plan as required by Administrative Order 2019–2. Approval of the e-Filing plan means that the court has demonstrated full access for self-represented litigants. Nothing in this order precludes a court from implementing an e-Filing access plan before full implementation of MiFILE.

b. *Exemption from E-Filing Participation.* Circumstances may arise that will prevent a party from e-Filing where e-Filing is mandated by these courts. A filer may file a request for exemption from e-Filing under MCR 1.109(G)(3). The court shall consider those requests with factors described in MCR 1.109(G)(3)(g)-(h) and shall comply with all other requirements in the rule. The clerk of the court must promptly mail or hand-deliver the order of exemption to the individual.

3. **E-Filing Rules, Standards, and Local Requirements**

a. *Court Responsibility.* With the exception of the e-Filing requirements in the Michigan Court Rules and any e-Filing standards prescribed by the State Court Administrative Office, each court will comply with the requirements of this order and, to the extent possible, continue to accept and process e-Filed documents for the case types, case initiation procedures, subsequent filing procedures, and filer requirements in place in each court as of the date of this order. Each court shall make this information readily available to filers from the court's website and at the clerk's office.

b. *Filer Responsibility.* With the exception of the e-Filing requirements in the Michigan Court Rules and any e-Filing standards prescribed by the State Court Administrative Office, filers will comply with the requirements of this order and the e-Filing procedures and requirements in place in each court as of the date of this order.

4. **Personal Identifying Information**

a. With respect to any document submitted through the e-Filing system, the following requirements for personal identifying information apply:

i. Social Security Numbers: Pursuant to Administrative Order No. 2006–2, full social security numbers shall not be included in public documents. If an individual's social security number must be referenced in a public document, only the last four digits of that number may be used, with the number specified in the following format: XXX–XX–1234.

ii. Names of Minor Children: Unless named as a party or otherwise required by statute, court rule, or administrative order, the identity of minor children shall not be included in a public document. If a non-party minor child must be mentioned, only the initials of that child's name may be used.

iii. Dates of Birth: Except as required by statute, court rule, or administrative order, an individual's full birth date shall not be included in a public document. If an individual's date of birth must be referenced in a public document, only the year may be used, with the date specified in the following format: XX/XX/1998.

iv. Financial Account Numbers: Full financial account numbers shall not be included in public documents unless required by statute, court rule, or other authority. If a financial account number must be referenced in a public document, only the last four digits of these numbers may be used, with the number specified in the following format: XXXXX1234.

v. Driver's License Numbers and State–Issued Personal Identification Card Numbers: A person's full driver's license number and state issued personal identification number shall not be included in a public document. If an individual's driver's license number or state-issued personal identification card number must be referenced in a public document, only the last four digits of that number may be used, with the number specified in the following format: X–XXX–XXX–XX1–234.

vi. Home Addresses: With the exception of a self-represented party, full home addresses shall not be included in e-Filings. If an individual's home address must be referenced in an e-Filing, only the city and state should be used. For a party whose address has been made confidential by court order pursuant to MCR 3.203(F), the alternate address shall be treated as specified above.

b. Parties wanting to file a pleading containing a complete personal data identifier as listed above may:

i. Pursuant to and in accordance with the MCR and the LAO, file a motion to file a traditional paper version of the document under seal. The court, in granting the motion to file the document under seal, may still require that an e-Filing that does not reveal the complete personal data identifier be filed for the public files; or,

ii. Pursuant to and in accordance with the applicable MCR and LAO, obtain a court order to file a traditional paper reference list under seal. The reference list shall contain the complete personal data identifiers and the redacted identifiers used in the e-Filing. All references in the case to the redacted identifiers included in the reference list shall be construed to refer to the corresponding complete personal data identifiers. The reference list must be filed under seal, and may be amended as of right.

c. Parties should exercise caution when filing papers that contain private or confidential information, including, but not limited to, the information covered above and listed below:

i. Medical records, treatment, and diagnosis;

ii. Employment history;

iii. Individual financial information;

iv. Insurance information;

v. Proprietary or trade secret information;

vi. Information regarding an individual's cooperation with the government; and

vii. Personal information regarding the victim of any criminal activity.

d. These rules are designed to protect the private personal identifiers and information of individuals involved or referenced in actions before the court. Nothing in these rules should be interpreted as authority for counsel or a self-represented litigant to deny discovery to the opposing party.

e. These rules regarding personal information will remain in effect until they are superseded by amendments of MCR 1.109, MCR 8.119, and Administrative Order 1999–4. Those amendments, adopted by the Court on May 22, 2019, are effective on January 1, 2021.

[Adopted effective October 23, 2019, 503 Mich.]

Order 2019-5. Concurrent Jurisdiction Plan for the 17th Circuit Court and the Kent County Probate Court

Administrative Order No. 2003–1 and MCL 600.401, *et seq.* authorize Michigan trial courts to adopt concurrent jurisdiction plans within a county or judicial circuit, subject to approval of the Court.

The Court hereby approves adoption of the following concurrent jurisdiction plan, effective immediately:

● The 17th Circuit Court and the Kent County Probate Court.

The plan shall remain on file with the State Court Administrator.

Amendments to concurrent jurisdiction plans may be implemented by local administrative order pursuant to MCR 8.112. Plan amendments shall conform to the requirements of Administrative Order No. 2003–1 and MCL 600.401, *et seq.*

[Adopted effective October 23, 2019, 503 Mich.]

Order 2019–6. Briefs Formatted for Optimized Reading on Electronic Displays

On order of the Court, effective immediately, the Michigan Supreme Court and Court of Appeals are authorized to implement a pilot program in which lawyers and self-represented parties may file briefs that are formatted, within the parameters set forth below, to be more readable on electronic displays, such as computer monitors, laptops, and tablets, instead of complying with the current formatting rules. This pilot program will run for two years from the effective date above, after which the Courts will make recommendations for future practice. The Courts have the discretion to terminate the pilot program early.

(A) Application.

(1) This pilot program shall apply to the length and formatting of briefs, applications for leave to appeal, responses, replies, and other pleadings (collectively "briefs") that are required to be filed in conformity with MCR 7.212 or 7.312.

(2) Filing briefs under the pilot program is optional. Briefs filed under the pilot program must include the words, in bold, "Filed under AO 2019–6" on the caption of the brief and must

comply with the following requirements in place of MCR 7.212(B) or 7.312(A). Any requirements not addressed by subsection (B) of this administrative order shall be governed by MCR 7.212 or 7.312.

(B) Length and Format of Briefs.

(1) *Length.* Unless otherwise lengthened or shortened by the Court of Appeals on motion, the principal briefs of the appellant(s) and appellee(s) and the briefs of amici curiae shall be no longer than 16,000 words, and the reply briefs of the appellant shall be no longer than 3,200 words. Briefs shall contain pagination as specified by MCR 7.212(B). The title page, table of contents, index of authorities, statement of the basis of jurisdiction, statement of the questions involved, signature block and listing of counsel at the end of the brief, certificate of compliance, proof of service, exhibits, and appendices do not count toward the word limit. Footnotes within the non-excluded sections also count toward the word total, as do any words contained in embedded graphics.

Each brief shall contain a certificate of compliance after the signature block, signed by the attorney or self-represented party, stating the number of countable words in the document and the typeface and size used. The person preparing the certificate may rely on the word count of the word-processing system used to prepare the document.

(2) *Font.* The body text of briefs shall be set in a proportional font no smaller than 12 point. Narrow-tyle or compressed fonts and condensed spacing are prohibited. Other fonts may be used in captions and headings.

(3) *Line Spacing.* The line spacing of all text must be set between 133% and 150% of the point size of the text. For example, text set in a 12–point font must be set with line spacing between 16 and 18 points. There shall be a minimum of 6 points of additional spacing between paragraphs and around headings.

(4) *Line Length and Margins.* The left and right side margins may not be less than 1.5 inches each. This does not apply to captions or headings, which may be formatted with 1–inch side margins.

(5) *Electronic Format.* Briefs must be filed in a text-searchable PDF format that is created electronically by a word processor or similar program. An unsearchable image file of a scanned document is not acceptable.

The electronic brief must be bookmarked to include, at a minimum, all major divisions and headings, and should track the table of contents.

Page numbers in the electronic brief must correspond to the PDF page numbers.

[Adopted effective October 23, 2019, 503 Mich.]

LOCAL COURT RULES

JUDICIAL CIRCUIT COURTS

THIRD JUDICIAL CIRCUIT [WAYNE COUNTY]

Rule 2.100   Praecipes—Forms and Procedure

(A) At Issue Praecipes—Forms.   The following forms shall be used for "At Issue Praecipes":

(1) *Yellow Form.*   Domestic relations default judgments.

(2) *Blue Form.*   Contested domestic relations actions.

(3) *White Form.*   All other civil actions.

(B) At Issue Praecipes—Filing.   An "At Issue Praecipe" shall be filed with Docket Management and a copy served on the attorneys of record or parties in propria persona, with the answer to the complaint.

(C) Added Parties or Appearance After Praecipe is Filed (Notice to Docket Management).   If any party is added to an action or an attorney appears in an action after the "At Issue Praecipe" is filed, the party or attorney shall immediately notify Docket Management.

(D) Domestic Relations Actions.   In uncontested domestic relations actions the action shall be considered "at issue" when the default has been taken, and an "At Issue Praecipe" shall be filed with the affidavit of default.

[Amended effective May 15, 2001, 464 Mich.]

Comments

Staff Comment to 2001 Amendment

The May 15, 2001 amendments of Local Court Rules 2.100 and 8.108 of the Third Judicial Circuit were made at the request of that court, effective immediately.

Rule 2.107   Service and Filing of Pleadings and Other Papers

(A) Service of Pleadings.   Except for cases subject to e-filing, at the time of service of the summons and complaint, the plaintiff shall serve upon the opposing parties the preprinted caption labels provided pursuant to LCR 2.113(C).

[Adopted effective April 1, 1987, 428 Mich.   Amended effective March 25, 1988, 430 Mich; August 24, 2012, 492 Mich.]

Comments

Staff Comment to 2012 Amendment

The changes in LCR 2.107 and LCR 2.113 are intended to clarify that the requirement to distribute and use preprinted caption labels does not apply to cases that are e-filed.

Rule 2.113   Form of Pleadings and Other Papers

(C) Pleadings—Requirement of Preprinted Labels.   Except for cases subject to e-filing, all pleadings hereinafter filed shall bear on the face thereof preprinted caption labels to be furnished by the Office of the County Clerk.

[Adopted effective April 1, 1987, 428 Mich.   Amended effective March 25, 1988, 430 Mich; August 24, 2012, 492 Mich.]

Comments

Staff Comment to 2012 Amendment

The changes in LCR 2.107 and LCR 2.113 are intended to clarify that the requirement to distribute and use preprinted caption labels does not apply to cases that are e-filed.

Rule 2.119   Motion Practice

(A) Motion Praecipe Forms.   A white form is to be used for a general motion praecipe and a yellow form for a domestic relations motion praecipe.

(B) Additional Motion Requirements.

(1) *Certification by Attorney.*   The following certificate signed by the attorney of record or the party in propria persona must be placed on the face sheet of each motion filed in the county clerk's office:

I hereby certify that I have complied with all provisions of LCR 2.119(B) on motion practice.

_____

Attorney of Record

(2) *Ascertaining Opposition; Contents.*   The moving party must ascertain whether a contemplated motion will be opposed. The motion must affirmatively state that the concurrence of counsel in the relief sought has been requested on a specified date, and that concurrence has been denied or has not been acquiesced in, and hence, that it is necessary to present the motion.

(C) Motions and Orders to Show Cause in Domestic Relations Cases; Objections to Friend of the Court Recommendations; Referee Hearings [Rescinded effective April 2, 2003].

(D) Motions and Orders to Show Cause in Civil Cases Other Than Domestic Relations Cases.   The original motion must be filed with the county clerk, who shall indicate payment of the motion fee on the praecipe.   The praecipe, with a copy of the motion or order to show cause and the brief, if any, attached, must be delivered to the judge who is to hear the motion or order to show cause.   Any party filing any pleading, brief, or other document relating to a pending motion or order to show cause shall indicate the hearing date and time for oral argument of the motion or order to show cause in the upper right corner of the front page of each document, file the original with the county clerk, and deliver a copy to the judge who is to hear the motion or order to show cause.

[Amended February 3, 1992, effective April 1, 1992, 439 Mich.   Amended effective April 30, 1993, 442 Mich; April 2, 2003, 468 Mich.]

Comments

Staff Comment to 1992 Amendment

The 1992 amendment of Local Rule 2.119(D) added the final sentence of subrule (D).

Rule 2.503   Adjournments [Repealed]

[Repealed effective May 15, 2001.]

Rule 3.204   Proceedings Affecting Children

(A) In any action involving a child custody dispute that falls under the "DC" case type code, the plaintiff/petitioner shall file a completed Third Circuit Court child custody action cover sheet.

(B) In any action seeking registration, enforcement, or modification of another state's or a foreign country's child custody determination, the parties shall use the most recent local Court Uniform Child Custody Jurisdiction and Enforcement Act forms or the most recent equivalent State Court Administrative Office forms.

[Adopted September 19, 2012, effective January 1, 2013, 493 Mich.]

Comments

Staff Comment to 2012 Adoption

These local court rule provisions of the 3rd Circuit Court have been adopted in an effort to better process cases filed with a case-type suffix of "DC." Subrule (A) requires the use of uniform Child Custody Cover Sheets when an action is filed in a child custody dispute. Subrule (B) requires the use of the most recent local Court Uniform Child Custody Jurisdiction and Enforcement Act forms or the equivalent most recent State Court Administrative Office forms in an action seeking registration, enforcement, or modification of another state's or a foreign country's child custody determination.

Rule 3.206   Certificate on Behalf of Plaintiff Regarding Ex Parte Interim Support Order

A completed "Certificate on Behalf of Plaintiff Regarding Ex Parte Interim Support Order" must be filed in all actions for divorce, separate maintenance or annulment of marriage, where the complaint alleges that minor children were born to the parties or during the marriage. The original must be filed with the county clerk. Copies must be served on the Friend of the Court and the defendant. A proof of service must be provided to the Friend of the Court.

[Formerly Rule 3.204, adopted effective October 1, 1987, 428 Mich. Amended effective October 1, 1987, 429 Mich; April 30, 1993, 442 Mich. Renumbered Rule 3.206, effective February 23, 2006, 474 Mich.]

Rule 3.207   Ex Parte Interim Orders for Support, Custody of Children and Attorney Fees; Notice of Dispute

(A) Before an ex parte interim order for the support of minor children or for attorney fees in a domestic relations action is presented to the judge, the party seeking the order must complete a "Certificate on Behalf of Plaintiff Regarding Ex Parte Interim Support Order," and a "Certificate of Conformity." The originals must be filed with the county clerk, and copies provided to the Friend of the Court. The party also must submit a Verified Statement as required by MCR 3.204(B).

(B) After the ex parte interim order for support is entered, the party who obtained the order must serve on the opposite party completed copies of the "Certificate on Behalf of Plaintiff Regarding Ex Parte Interim Support Order," the "Certificate of Conformity," the complaint (or counterclaim or petition), the custody affidavit required by MCL 600.659, and the ex parte interim order for support. A proof of service of these documents must be filed with the county clerk and the Friend of the Court.

(C) In all cases in which there is a dispute as to child custody, visitation, child support, or alimony, a party who requests the temporary or final order shall file with the Friend of the Court a written Notice of Dispute which shall include the information required by MCR 3.204 and the nature of the dispute. (Forms to be supplied by the Friend of the Court's Office.)

[Formerly Rule 3.206, adopted effective October 1, 1987, 428 Mich. Amended effective October 1, 1987, 429 Mich; April 30, 1993, 442 Mich. Renumbered Rule 3.207, effective February 23, 2006, 474 Mich.]

Rule 3.211(B).   Judgments and Orders [Rescinded effective October 23, 2019]

Rule 3.920(B)(4)   Simultaneous Attempts at Service in Juvenile Proceedings

(b) Service of a summons on the persons listed in MCR 3.920(B)(2) shall be attempted simultaneously by:

(i) personal service in accord with MCR 3.920(B)(4)(a);

(ii) registered mail directed to the person's last known address; and

(iii) publication in accord with MCR 3.920(B)(4)(b).

Personal service, service by registered mail, and service by publication shall be made in accord with the time standards in MCR 3.920(B)(5). If the court finds on the record that reasonable attempts have been made to personally serve persons required to be served and that personal service is impracticable or has not been achieved, the court may then rely on the service by registered mail or publication.

[Adopted June 27, 2006, effective September 1, 2006, 475 Mich.]

Comments

Staff comment to 2006 Adoption

LCR 3.920(B)(4)(b) allows simultaneous service of process by personal service, registered mail, and publication. If a court finds personal service is impracticable or cannot be achieved, service by one of the other methods may be relied on.

Rule 6.100   Rules Applicable in the Third Judicial Circuit

(A) **Criminal Division, Assignment of Judges, Case Processing.** The Criminal Division of the Third Judicial Circuit shall consist of a presiding judge and such other judges as may be assigned by the chief judge. The number and term of said judges shall be determined by the chief judge.

(B) **Appearance in Lower Court Constitutes Appearance in Circuit Court.** Appearance by an attorney in a municipal or district court in any criminal action where the defendant is bound over to the Third Judicial Circuit shall constitute an appearance in the Third Judicial Circuit in said criminal action. An attorney may by motion for cause shown be permitted to withdraw from further representation of said defendant.

(C) **Method of Assignment, Reassignment; Adjournments.** Cases shall be assigned by lot to a trial judge. If the trial judge is unavailable on the date set for trial, the case shall be reassigned to an available judge within the Criminal Division or, if no such judge is available, then to a judge available in the Civil Division.

No trial of a criminal case shall be adjourned except by the presiding judge for good cause shown upon motion of the party seeking the adjournment or by the presiding judge for good cause.

(D) **Implementation of Court-Administered Final Plea Conference in Criminal Felony Matters.** A final plea conference shall be held prior to trial of all criminal felony cases bound over to the Third Judicial Circuit. The final plea conference shall be scheduled by the court after the conclusion of the arraignment on the information and no later than 3 weeks prior to the scheduled trial date. The final plea conference shall be administered by the presiding judge of the criminal division. The defendants, defense attorneys, and the Wayne County Prosecuting Attorney's office shall be notified in writing of the court-scheduled final conference and shall appear at the time and location specified in the notice. The failure of the defendant to appear for the final conference may result in the issuance of a warrant for his or her arrest and the revocation of bond. All requests for adjournment of the final conference are to be taken in open court before the presiding judge of the Criminal Division.

Rule 6.410 Selection of Juries for Trials of Former Recorder's Court Cases

(A) Application. This rule only applies to defendants who are

(1) charged with committing a felony in the City of Detroit, and

(2) arraigned on the warrant or complaint before October 1, 1997.

(B) Selection of Jurors. For trials of defendants described in subrule (A), the court will draw potential jurors from all of Wayne County, unless the defendant elects in writing, on or before the final pretrial conference, to be tried by a jury composed of persons drawn only from the City of Detroit.

[Adopted September 25, 1997, effective October 1, 1997, 456 Mich.]

Comments

Staff Comment to 1997 Adoption

Local Rule 6.410 was adopted at the request of the Wayne Circuit Court.

Rule 8.108 Transcript for Appeal

A request or order for a transcript of proceedings in the Third Judicial Circuit for use on appeal must be made to Court Reporting Services or a designee of that office by completing and filing the required form with Court Reporting Services.

All transcripts will be filed with and can be obtained through Court Reporting Services by the ordering party, upon completion.

[Amended effective May 15, 2001, 464 Mich.]

Comments

Staff Comment to 2001 Amendment

The May 15, 2001 amendments of Local Court Rules 2.100 and 8.108 of the Third Judicial Circuit were made at the request of that court, effective immediately.

Rule 8.115 Courthouse Decorum

(A) This court rule applies to the conduct and dress of those who attend court or engage in business in the court offices, including attorneys, litigants, witnesses, jurors, and interested persons.

(B) Court proceedings shall be conducted in a manner that protects the dignity and seriousness of the proceedings. Conduct by any person that may interfere with the decorum of the court is prohibited and may result in removal of that person from the court and/or a finding of contempt of court.

(C) Attorneys shall wear proper business attire while attending court, unless excused from doing so by the court.

(D) Jurors, parties, witnesses, and interested persons should wear appropriate attire while attending court, unless excused from doing so by the court.

(E) The jury clerk shall assist the court in ensuring compliance with this rule and may require a juror whose clothing does not comply with subsection (D) to obtain appropriate attire or to report for service on a later date. A juror who fails to return to court as directed may be found in contempt of court and is subject to the penalties permitted by statute and court rule.

(F) Persons attending court are required to abide by the following guidelines, which are representative rather than all inclusive.

(1) Smoking or the use of electronic smoking devices, eating, drinking beverages other than water, and gum chewing are not allowed in any courtroom at any time, whether during sessions of the court or during a recess.

(2) Taking photographs or making other audio or video recordings is not allowed in the courtroom without the express permission of the court.

(3) All conversations and reading of non-case related materials like books, newspapers, and periodicals, except as necessary for the matter before the court, are prohibited in the courtroom during sessions of the court.

(4) Cellular telephones, beepers, and electronic communication devices that have the capacity to disrupt court proceedings must be turned off or set for silent notification during sessions of the court. Individuals shall not answer or send messages from telephones, beepers, or other electronic communication devices while the court is in session. Failure to comply with this section may result in the seizure of the device, a fine, incarceration, or both for contempt of court.

(G) Each business office of the court may set a policy regarding the use of cellular telephones, beepers, and other electronic communication devices in that office.

(H) It is within the discretion of the judge to have an individual removed from the courtroom if the individual's conduct or dress does not comport with this rule.

[Adopted effective July 1, 2017.]

Comments

Staff Comment to 2017 Amendment

These local court rule provisions of the Third Judicial Circuit Court have been adopted to reinforce the solemnity and importance of court proceedings, clearly enunciate to all court users the conduct expected or prohibited in court facilities, and establish a single standard.

FOURTH JUDICIAL CIRCUIT [JACKSON COUNTY]

Rule 2.402   Fascimile Transmission of Documents [Rescinded]

[Rescinded effective January 1, 2004.]

Rule 2.403   Mediation

(A) Obtaining Briefs or Summary. The mediation clerk shall, immediately after the deadline for filing a document, brief, or summary, make those received available to the assigned mediators. The assigned mediators shall thereafter obtain the same as soon as possible from the administrative office of the court.

(B) Disposition and Adjournment.

(1) Adjournment of mediation hearings is to be avoided whenever possible. Adjournments are to be approved by the judge assigned to the case or, in the absence of the assigned judge, the chief judge or, in the absence of the chief judge, the chief judge pro tempore.

Whenever possible, the attorney in principal charge of the case shall delegate responsibility for attendance at the hearing to another attorney when necessary so as to avoid adjournment.

(2) When a case is set for mediation as provided in MCR 2.403, and is thereafter settled or otherwise disposed of before the mediation, it shall be the responsibility of both counsel immediately to notify the mediation clerk of the disposition, and to provide the mediation clerk with a signed, true copy of the judge's order of disposition as soon as possible.

(3) When a true copy of a final order of disposition is submitted to the mediation clerk before the documents, briefs, or summaries have been turned over to the assigned mediators, the fees paid for that hearing shall be returned to the parties paying such fee, except for those fees subject to penalty under the terms of this rule.

SIXTH JUDICIAL CIRCUIT [OAKLAND COUNTY]

Rule 2.119   Motion Practice

(A) Miscellaneous Calendar. Motions and petitions shall be heard on Wednesday mornings unless otherwise ordered by the court. An attorney desiring to have a hearing on any pro confesso, default, motion, or miscellaneous matter shall file a praecipe with the assignment clerk on or before the Wednesday preceding the Wednesday of the desired hearing. Each Thursday the assignment clerk shall, under the direction of the chief judge, prepare a list of all matters to be heard the following Wednesday. The list shall show the name of the judge before whom the matter will be heard. A copy of the list shall be published in a newspaper as defined in MCR 2.106(F) before the Wednesday on which the matters will be heard.

(B) Motion Praecipe; Motion Certification by Attorney.

(1) A motion praecipe must be filed at least 7 days before the hearing.

(2) Motion certification by attorney.

(a) The following certificate signed by the attorney of record or by the party in propria persona shall be attached to or incorporated in the praecipe filed with the assignment clerk:

> I HEREBY CERTIFY that I have made personal contact with _____ on _____, 20__, requesting concurrence in the relief sought with this motion and that concurrence has been denied or that I have made reasonable and diligent attempts to contact counsel requesting concurrence in the relief sought with this motion.

(C) Appearance at the Hearing. If counsel for the moving party on a motion praeciped for hearing does not check in with the court clerk by 9:30 a.m., the court may dismiss the motion praecipe on its own motion or upon request of counsel for the opposing party.

If counsel for the opposing party in a motion praeciped for hearing does not check in with the clerk by 9:30 a.m., upon request of the moving party the clerk shall call the motion for hearing. If appropriate, the court shall grant the requested relief.

Rule 2.202   Substitution of Parties; Substitution of Counsel

(A) Substitution of Parties. Any attorney granted leave to add or delete a party to or from a pending case shall promptly notify the assignment office.

(B) Substitution of Counsel. Any attorney granted leave to substitute into a pending case shall promptly notify the assignment office.

Rule 2.315   Video Tape Depositions

(A) Filing of Petition. A producer of a video-taped deposition or a party may file a petition in a closed case, identifying the tape produced for use in the case, stating facts showing the case is closed, and requesting return of the video tape.

(B) Filing of Affidavit and Stipulation. Along with the petition, the following shall be filed:

(1) An affidavit by the petitioner affirming there is a written transcript in the court file for each requested video-taped deposition, and stating that the petitioner is the owner of the requested video tape or that the owner has waived any rights to the requested video tape;

(2) A stipulation from each party litigant or all counsel of record agreeing there is no objection to releasing the requested video tape and stating there is no appeal pending or contemplated.

(C) Discretion of Court. Upon review of the petition and supporting documents, the court may enter an order permitting release of the requested video tape, may refuse to return the video tape, or may order release of the video tape upon any conditions it deems appropriate.

Rule 2.612   Social Security Number Redaction Local Court Rule

I. Scope. This local rule is issued in accordance with Michigan Court Rules 2.119 and 2.612(A) and Supreme Court Administrative Order No. 2006–2. The local rule establishes the procedure by which the court will process motions to redact identified social security numbers and other personal information from specified documents filed on or after March 1, 2006.

II. Procedure.

A. A party [1] may file a motion to redact one's social security number [2] (SSN) or other personal information from any document in which it is not required by statute, court rule, court order, or as required for identification purposes.

   1. A party requesting redaction of an SSN or other personal information shall identify the document containing the SSN or other personal information, the date the document was filed with the Court, and the page and line number where the SSN or other personal information is located.

   2. Multiple documents and locations may be identified in a single motion.

   3. Pursuant to Michigan Court Rules (MCR) 2.119 and Administrative Order (AO) No. 2006–2, a separate motion is required for each case that contains one's SSN or other personal information.

B. A party shall serve a copy of the motion to redact an SSN or other personal information on opposing parties as required by MCR 2.119(C). In addition, when the person files the motion for redaction, the person shall provide an extra copy for the court administrator marked "court administrator copy." The court clerk must transmit the copy to the court administrator's office.

   1. Opposing parties may object to the motion within seven days after service of the motion. An objecting party shall also notice the objections for hearing and file a praecipe before the assigned judge.

   2. Unless otherwise ordered by the Court, all motions to redact an SSN or other personal information shall be decided without oral argument as provided at MCL 2.119(E)(2).

C. After the period to respond to the motion has elapsed, the motion to redact the SSN or other personal information and any response shall be reviewed by the Court. The standards shall include that the motion complies with the requirements of MCR 2.119, MCR 2.612(A), AO 2006–2, and this order and shall be limited to motions to redact an SSN and other personal information. If the court grants the motion, the court shall enter an order allowing the information to be redacted. The order shall be made part of the court record.

[Adopted effective October 13, 2009, 485 Mich.]

[1] As used in this local administrative order, "party" includes the named party, counsel representing the named party, the next friend, a guardian ad litem, a personal representative, a guardian, and a conservator. This definition also includes individuals who discover their social security number (SSN) or other personal information included in a case file.

[2] Social security number means a complete, unredacted nine-digit social security number.

Rule 3.205   Prior and Subsequent Orders and Judgments Affecting Minors

(A) Venue. This rule applies whenever the prior and subsequent courts are Oakland County courts.

(B) Notice to Prior Court, Friend of the Court, Juvenile/Probate Register or Prosecuting Attorney.

(1) As used in this rule, "appropriate official" means the friend of the court, juvenile/probate register, or Prosecuting Attorney, depending on the nature of the prior or subsequent action and the court involved.

(2) If a minor is known to be subject to the prior continuing jurisdiction of an Oakland County court, the plaintiff or other initiating party must file written notice of proceedings in the subsequent court with

   (a) the clerk or register of the prior court, and

   (b) the appropriate official of the prior court.

(3) The notice must be filed at least 21 days before the date set for hearing. If the fact of continuing jurisdiction is not then known, notice must be given immediately when it becomes known.

(4) The notice requirement of this subrule is not jurisdictional and does not preclude the subsequent court from entering interim orders before the expiration of the 21–day period, if required by the best interests of the minor.

(C) Prior Orders.

(1) Each provision of a prior order remains in effect until the provision is superseded, changed, or terminated by a subsequent order.

(2) A subsequent court must give due consideration to prior continuing orders of other courts, and may not enter orders contrary to or inconsistent with such orders, except as provided by law.

(D) Duties of Officials of Prior and Subsequent Courts.

(1) Upon receipt of the notice required by subrule (B), the appropriate official of the prior court

   (a) must provide the assigned judge of the subsequent court with the docket sheet;

   (b) may appear in person at proceedings in the subsequent court, as the welfare of the minor and the interests of justice require.

(2) The appropriate official of the prior court shall furnish documents upon request of the subsequent court.

(3) Upon request of the prior court, the appropriate official of the subsequent court

   (a) must notify the appropriate official of the prior court of all proceedings in the subsequent court, and

   (b) must send copies of all orders entered in the subsequent court to the attention of the clerk or register and the appropriate official of the prior court.

(4) If a circuit court awards custody of a minor pursuant to MCL 722.26b, the clerk of the circuit court must send a copy of the judgment or order of disposition to the probate court that has prior or continuing jurisdiction of the minor as a result of the guardianship proceedings, regardless of whether there is a request.

(5) Upon receipt of an order from the subsequent court, the appropriate official of the prior court must take the steps necessary to implement the order in the prior court.

[Adopted effective November 1, 1995, 450 Mich.]

Comments

Staff Comment to 1995 Adoption

Local Court Rule 3.205 of the Sixth Judicial Circuit and the Oakland County Probate Court was adopted at the joint request of those courts.

Rule 3.208 Powers and Duties of Friend of the Court

(B) Friend of the Court Pre–Arraignment Review.

(1) All bench warrants issued for failure to appear pursuant to an order to show cause in friend of the court matters must contain a provision for bail and be returnable to a friend of the court referee.

(2) A person arrested pursuant to such a bench warrant will be brought before a referee for review at the Oakland County Jail. The referee is empowered to:

(a) enter into a consent agreement for payment of support;

(b) lower the bond if appropriate; and

(c) continue the bond until the next court date for friend of the court matters.

(3) Either party may request an immediate arraignment before the court.

[Adopted effective April 30, 1993, 442 Mich.]

Rule 6.101 Termination of Circuit Court Appointment of Attorneys and Submission of Fee Vouchers

(A) Termination of Circuit Court Appointment of Attorneys. The appointment of counsel in indigent cases shall terminate at the time of dismissal or sentencing, whether the dismissal or sentencing has occurred at circuit or district court.

(B) Date Certain for Attorney Fee Vouchers. Appointed attorneys shall submit their vouchers to the court administrator no later than one month after dismissal of the case or sentencing of their client.

(C) For purposes of this rule, sentencing shall include granting of YTA status and delayed sentence.

Rule 6.107 Grand Juries

Petitions for a grand jury shall be presented to the chief judge and submitted by him or her to the bench for decision. No such petition shall be granted except by affirmative majority action of the bench. If a one-man grand jury is called, the judges of the circuit, by majority action, shall designate the judge who shall act as the grand juror.

Rule 8.115 Courtroom Decorum

(A) This court rule applies to the conduct and dress of those who attend court or engage in business in the courthouse, including attorneys, litigants, witnesses, jurors, and interested persons.

(B) Court proceedings shall be conducted in a manner that protects the dignity and seriousness of the proceedings. Conduct by any person that may interfere with the decorum of the court is prohibited and may result in removal of that person from the court.

(C) Persons attending court are required to abide by the following guidelines, which are representative rather than all-inclusive.

(1) Smoking, eating, drinking (including bottled water), and gum chewing are not allowed in any courtroom at any time, whether during sessions of the court or at recess.

(2) Taking photographs is not allowed in the courtroom without the express permission of the court.

(3) All conversations and reading of books, newspapers, and periodicals, except as necessary for the trial of an issue, are prohibited in the courtroom during sessions of the court.

(4) Demonstrations, placards, badges, T-shirts, and clothing that espouse a position on an issue before the court shall not be allowed without the express permission of the judge.

(5) Individuals other than attorneys, court personnel, and jurors shall refrain from using the corridors between the courtrooms and chambers unless expressly authorized to do so by the court.

(6) Cellular telephones, beepers, and electronic or communication devices that have the capacity to disrupt court proceedings must be turned off or set for silent notification during sessions of the court. Individuals shall not answer telephones, beepers, or other electronic communication devices while the court is in session. Failure to comply with this section may result in a fine, incarceration, or both for contempt of court.

(D) Dress

(1) Attorneys shall wear proper business attire while attending court, unless excused from doing so by the court.

(2) Jurors, parties, and witnesses should wear proper attire while attending court, unless excused from doing so by the court.

(3) Clothing such as short shorts, halter tops, sweat suits, camouflage garments, swimwear, exercise garb, and revealing garments such as tank tops shall not be permitted in the courtroom.

(4) Men are required to remove hats, caps, and hoods in the courtroom.

(5) The jury clerk shall assist the court in ensuring compliance with this subrule, and may require a juror whose clothing does not comport with (D)(2) and (3) to obtain appropriate attire or to report for service on a later date. A juror who fails to return to court as directed may be found in contempt of court and is subject to the penalties permitted by statute and court rule.

(E) It is within the judge's discretion to have an individual removed from the courtroom if the individual's conduct or dress does not comport with this rule.

(F) Individuals other than those giving testimony shall stand at all times when addressing the court or jury, or when examining witnesses, unless excused from doing so by the court.

(G) Each business office of the court may set a policy regarding the use of cellular telephones, beepers, and other electronic or communication devices in that office.

[Adopted November 25, 2003, effective January 1, 2004, 469 Mich.]

Comments

Staff Comment to 2004 Adoption

Rule 8.115 of the Local Court Rules of the Sixth Judicial Circuit Court was adopted November 25, 2003, at the request of that circuit, to be effective January 1, 2004.

SEVENTH JUDICIAL CIRCUIT [GENESEE COUNTY]

Rule 2.119   Motion Practice

(A) Motion Certification by Attorney. The following certificate signed by the attorney of record or by the party *in propria persona* shall be attached to or incorporated in the motion and notice of hearing filed with the clerk:

I hereby certify that I have made personal contact with _____ [name] on _____ [date], requesting concurrence in the relief sought with this motion and that concurrence has been denied, or that I have made reasonable and diligent attempts to contact counsel requesting concurrence in the relief sought with this motion.

(B) Proposed Orders. A proposed order must be attached to and served with the motion.

(C) Application. This rule applies to all motions filed in the circuit court and to motions filed in civil actions in the probate court.

[Adopted February 2, 1999, effective March 1, 1999, 459 Mich.]

Comments

Staff Comment to 1998 Adoption

Local Court Rule 2.119 of the Seventh Judicial Circuit and the Genesee Probate Court was adopted February 2, 1999, effective March 1, 1999, at the request of those courts.

NINTH JUDICIAL CIRCUIT [KALAMAZOO COUNTY]

Rule 2.119   Motion Practice [Rescinded]
[Rescinded effective January 1, 2004.]

Rule 2.401   Pretrial Procedures—Civil [Rescinded]
[Rescinded effective May 2, 1995.]

Rule 2.403   Mediation [Rescinded]
[Rescinded effective May 2, 1995.]

Rule 2.501   Court Calendar: Civil and Domestic Hearings [Rescinded]
[Rescinded effective January 1, 2004.]

Rule 3.200   Domestic Cases: Judgments; Support and Custody Orders [Rescinded]
[Rescinded effective May 1, 1993.]

Rule 6.000   Court Calendar: Evidentiary Hearings—Criminal Cases [Rescinded]
[Rescinded effective January 1, 2004.]

Rule 6.001   Criminal Procedures— Pretrials [Rescinded]
[Rescinded effective January 1, 2004.]

THIRTEENTH JUDICIAL CIRCUIT [GRAND TRAVERSE COUNTY]

Rule 3.800   Notice for Court Appointed Special Advocates

In the interest of justice, the Court Appointed Special Advocate appointed to work for a child in any abuse and neglect case shall be afforded notice of any adoption hearing that may occur on behalf of the child.

[Adopted June 20, 2012, effective July 1, 2012, 491 Mich.]

Comments

Staff Comment to 2012 Adoption

This local court rule allows a Court Appointed Special Advocate who works with a child as part of an abuse/neglect proceeding to receive notice of an adoption hearing that also involves the child.

SIXTEENTH JUDICIAL CIRCUIT [MACOMB COUNTY]

Rule 2.119   Motion Practice

(A) Motion Day. Monday of each week shall be motion day, except when on a legal holiday, in which case it will be the day following. Uncontested matters will be given preference over contested matters at the morning session.

(B) Filing. Counsel shall notice motions for hearing by filing a praecipe with the County Clerk at least 7 days prior to the scheduled hearing date. The praecipe shall contain the following information:

1. Names of the parties and the number of the case.
2. Nature of the motion.
3. Names of the attorneys.
4. Scheduled hearing date.
5. Name of the judge to whom the case is assigned.

If an order to show cause has been issued and a hearing scheduled for a Monday, 7 days or more from the date of issuance, a praecipe shall be filed to notify the clerk of that fact.

The original motion must be filed with the County Clerk, who shall indicate payment of the motion fee on the praecipe. If not consented to by the opposing party, a copy of the motion and brief, if any, must be filed with the judge who is to hear the motion. The same procedure shall apply for any responses made to the motion by the opposing party.

All motions shall be scheduled for 9:00 a.m. unless otherwise scheduled by or with the approval of the court, and opposing counsel has been so notified.

(C) Opening of Court. Motions will be called by the court clerk in the order as attorneys appear. All counsel entering the courtroom should notify the court clerk of their readiness for hearing.

(D) Dismissal for Non-appearance. Motions not responded to when called by the court clerk may be dismissed without prejudice one hour after being called. The court clerk will grant consent adjournments if notified by telephone or written stipulation.

(E) Assignment. By 8:45 a.m. each motion day, the assignment clerk and respective court clerks will have posted on the main floor bulletin board of the court building and on each court bulletin board the list of matters scheduled for that day and before which judge the case is assigned.

(F) Hearing on Other Than Motion Day. All motions should be specifically noticed before the judge assigned to the case. Short matters may be heard on days other than motion days promptly at 9:00 a.m. but only when confirmed and scheduled in advance by the judge and when properly noticed for hearing.

(G) Duty to Examine File. Counsel are charged with the responsibility of examining the court file to see that all papers necessary to the hearing are in the file, including proof of service or notice of hearing.

(H) Motion Certification. The attorney of record or the party in propria persona shall certify on the notice of hearing that the attorney or party either has made personal contact with the other party or the party's attorney and requested concurrence in the relief sought, but concurrence has been denied, or that the attorney or party has made reasonable and diligent attempts to contact the other party or the party's

attorney, but was unable to do so. The certification must specify the date or dates that contact was made or attempted. [Adopted January 30, 1986, effective February 6, 1986, 424 Mich. Amended September 19, 1991, effective November 1, 1991, 438 Mich; November 2, 1999, effective December 1, 1999, 461 Mich.]

Comments

Staff Comment to 1999 Amendment

Subrule (H) was added to Local Court Rule 2.119, effective December 1, 1999, at the request of the Sixteenth Circuit Court (Macomb County).

Rule 2.402   Facsimile Transmission of Documents [Rescinded]

[Rescinded effective January 1, 2004.]

Rule 2.602   Orders and Judgments

(A) Presentation for Signature. Judgments and orders to which all parties have consented in writing as to form or form and substance shall be presented for the signature or attention of the judge through the court clerk, the court officer, or the judge's secretary. Such documents shall be presented before court convenes, during recess, at the close of court in the forenoon or afternoon, or left at the judge's chambers for presentation to the judge. If the document is presented for signature while the judge is on the bench and it would be a hardship upon the attorney to return later to pick up the signed document, it may be given to the court clerk who will present it to the judge as soon as possible.

(B) Distracting Conduct. Papers should not be presented to the clerk in the court during trial arguments to the court or jury.

NINETEENTH JUDICIAL CIRCUIT [BENZIE AND MANISTEE COUNTIES]

Rule 2.402   Facsimile Transmission of Documents [Rescinded]

[Rescinded effective January 1, 2004.]

Rule 6.445   Probation Violations; Authority of Probation Agent to Apprehend, Detain and Confine

(A) Authorization to Apprehend. Probation officers assigned to the Manistee/Benzie Circuit Court are, pursuant to MCL 771.4, authorized without further order of the court to apprehend, detain, and confine any probationer of the Manis-

tee/Benzie Circuit Court accused of violating a term of probation.

(B) Prompt Arraignment. A probationer apprehended, detained or confined under this rule must be brought promptly before the court for arraignment.

(C) Written Charges and Hearing. A probationer apprehended, detained, or confined under this rule is entitled to a written copy of the charge, setting forth the alleged violation of probation, and is entitled to a hearing conducted in accordance with law and the court rules.

[Adopted effective June 24, 1997, 455 Mich.]

TWENTY-FIRST JUDICIAL CIRCUIT [ISABELLA]

Rule 2.402   Facsimile Transmission of Documents [Rescinded]

[Rescinded effective January 1, 2004.]

TWENTY–THIRD JUDICIAL CIRCUIT [ALCONA, ARENAC, IOSCO, AND OSCODA COUNTIES]

Rule 2.119   Motion Practice [Rescinded]

[Rescinded effective January 1, 2004.]

Rule 2.402   Facsimile Transmission of Documents [Rescinded]

[Rescinded effective January 1, 2004.]

Rule 3.208   Taking of Cash Bonds and Modification of Cash Bonds in Friend of the Court Bench Warrant Cases

(A) In addition to the sheriff or his deputy, court officers authorized by the chief judge may accept the payment of money in fulfillment of a cash bond from a person arrested pursuant to a bench warrant issued under MCL 552.631 or MCR 3.208(B)(4) and (6), immediately upon arrest or at any point thereafter prior to court appearance, subject to the conditions set forth at MCL 552.632.

(B) If the respondent is not brought before the court within 24 hours of arrest and is unable, thereafter, to post the required cash bond, or if the respondent cannot be lodged at the county jail because of a declared jail overcrowding emergency and a circuit judge is not readily available to arraign the respondent, the friend of the court or deputy friend of the court may conduct a prearraignment bond review and authorize a lower cash bond, pending the respondent's arraignment on the bench warrant before the court.

(C) In determining whether to lower a cash bond, the friend of the court or deputy friend of the court must take into account factors such as the respondent's available resources and the likelihood that he or she will appear before the court as further

directed by the friend of the court or deputy friend of the court. The friend of the court or deputy friend of the court may authorize release upon personal recognizance pending arraignment before the court.

[Adopted effective April 26, 2000, 461 Mich.]

Comments

Staff Comment to 2000 Adoption

Local Court Rules 3.208, 6.113, and 6.445 were approved by the Supreme Court, effective April 26, 2000, at the request of the 23rd Circuit Court.

Rule 6.113   Pretrial Conferences [Rescinded]

[Rescinded effective January 1, 2004.]

Rule 6.445   Probation Violations; Authority of Probation Agent to Apprehend, Detain and Confine [Rescinded]

[Rescinded effective January 1, 2004.]

TWENTY–FOURTH JUDICIAL CIRCUIT [SANILAC COUNTY]

Rule 2.401   Pretrial Conferences; Trial Date Assignments

The assignment clerk shall, based upon the term calendar, determine which cases are ready for pretrial conference and notify counsel of record as to the date, time, and place thereof; however, all pretrial conferences shall, as far as practicable, be held a reasonable time prior to trial. Failure of counsel to appear at pretrial conferences without notice may result in such action as is provided by the Michigan Court Rules. The pretrial conference may be waived in writing by both counsel through stipulation, except where a pretrial conference is expressly ordered by the court. All counsel for the respective parties shall attend the pretrial hearing, unless excused by the court, and they may, at their discretion, and the discretion of the court, be accompanied by their respective clients. As far as possible, trial dates will be assigned to counsel at the pretrial

conference, and no further notice of trial shall be given. Post pretrial discovery shall be allowed; however, failure to complete discovery prior to trial shall not be a basis for adjournment of the trial date set at the pretrial hearing, except for good cause shown.

Rule 2.602   Signing of Proposed Judgments and Orders

All proposed judgments or orders shall be delivered to the assignment clerk or the county clerk, who shall attach them to the appropriate court file. However, if an attorney is desirous of obtaining a signed order or judgment without delay, the appropriate file may be checked out of the county clerk's office with the proposed order or judgment attached and presented to the judge for signature.

TWENTY–EIGHTH JUDICIAL CIRCUIT [MISSAUKEE AND WEXFORD COUNTIES]

Rule 2.401   Pretrial Conferences

(A) Pretrial Conferences in Criminal Cases.

(1) On the date scheduled for arraignment pursuant to Local Administrative Order No. 1985–2, a pretrial conference shall be held unless the defendant enters a plea of guilty or nolo contendere when arraigned.

(a) The pretrial conference may be adjourned or continued by order of the court.

(b) The defendant shall be present at the pretrial conference unless excused by order of the court.

(2) *Scope of Conference.* At the pretrial conference, the court shall:

(a) Determine the need for pretrial motions, establish a cutoff date for the filing of said motions, and schedule said motions for hearing;

(b) Determine whether or not there are additional witnesses sought to be endorsed by the prosecution or defendant;

(c) Determine whether the defendant is raising any defense which requires notice (alibi, insanity, or incompetency) and require the filing of such notice as required by law;

(d) Estimate the time required for trial;

(e) Determine whether plea negotiations are completed;

(f) Determine whether the defense will waive any endorsed witness;

(g) Determine whether there will be any unusual legal issues or requested special jury instructions;

(h) Consider all other matters that may aid in the disposition of the action; and

(i) Fix a date certain for trial.

THIRTIETH JUDICIAL CIRCUIT [INGHAM COUNTY]

Rule 2.119   Motion Practice

(A) An attorney of record may secure a date for hearing from the trial judge's secretary for matters such as uncontested divorce cases, brief motion arguments, and hearings.

(B) Motion day shall be Wednesday. If a legal holiday coincides in some manner, the assignment clerk shall set a new motion day and provide appropriate notice.

(C) Any hearing time secured by telephone shall be cancelled if a written notice of hearing is not filed within seven days with a copy to the assignment clerk or judge's secretary, as appropriate.

(D) Any matter requiring testimony or hearings of more than 15 minutes shall be scheduled by the assignment clerk other than on motion day.

[Amended September 19, 1985, effective September 4, 1985, 422 Mich.]

Rule 2.510   Impaneling the Jury

Jurors: Term of Service.

(1) All persons summoned to appear as circuit court petit jurors shall serve a term of one calendar week, or for the duration of the trial, if selected to serve on a trial jury.

(2) During the term of the jury service jurors shall report for actual jury service only when so directed by the court.

Rule 6.107   Grand Jury

(A) Grand Juries; Presentation of Petition; Granting of Petition.

(1) Petitions for a grand jury shall be presented to the chief judge, and submitted to the bench for decision.

(2) No such petition shall be granted except by affirmative majority action of the entire bench.

(B) Grand Juries; One-Person Grand Jury. If a one-person grand jury is called, the judge who shall act as the grand juror shall be selected by blind draw.

(C) Grand Juries; Citizens' Grand Jury; Selection. If a citizens' grand jury is called, the chief judge shall direct the jury board to draw the names of a specified number of persons to appear for selection to serve as grand jurors. A judge shall be selected by blind draw and shall preside over the selection of a sufficient number of the persons to serve as grand jurors and subsequent grand jury proceedings.

THIRTY–SEVENTH JUDICIAL CIRCUIT [CALHOUN COUNTY]

Rule 2.119   Motion Practice [Rescinded]

[Rescinded effective September 28, 2011, 490 Mich.]

Rule 2.401   Pretrial Conferences [Rescinded]

[Rescinded effective September 20, 1993.]

Rule 2.402   Facsimile Transmission of Documents [Rescinded]

[Rescinded effective January 1, 2004.]

Rule 2.403   Mediation [Rescinded]

[Rescinded effective September 28, 2011, 490 Mich.]

Rule 3.208(B)   Taking of Cash Bonds and Modification of Cash Bonds in Friend of the Court Bench Warrant Cases

(1) In addition to the sheriff or his deputy, court officers authorized by the chief judge may accept the payment of money in fulfillment of a cash bond from a person arrested pursuant to a bench warrant issued under MCL 552.631 or MCR 3.207(D)(5) [MCR 3.208(B)(6)], immediately upon arrest or at any point thereafter prior to court appearance, subject to the conditions set forth at MCL 552.632.

(2) If the respondent is not brought before the court within 24 hours of arrest and is unable, thereafter, to post the required cash bond, or if the respondent cannot be lodged at the county jail because of a declared jail overcrowding emergency and a circuit judge is not readily available to arraign the respondent, a friend of the court referee may conduct a pre-arraignment bond review and authorize a lower cash bond pending the respondent's arraignment on the bench warrant before the court.

(3) In determining whether to lower a cash bond, the referee must take into account factors such as the respondent's available resources and the likelihood that he or she will appear before the court as further directed by the referee. The referee is without authority to authorize release upon personal recognizance pending arraignment before the court.

[Formerly Rule 3.207(D), adopted effective April 12, 1993. Renumbered Rule 3.208(B), effective May 1, 1993, 442 Mich.]

Rule 6.445   Probation Violations; Authority of Probation Agent to Apprehend, Detain and Confine

(A) Authorization to Apprehend. Probation officers assigned to the Calhoun Circuit Court are, pursuant to MCL 771.4, authorized without further order of the court to apprehend, detain, and confine any probationer of the Calhoun Circuit Court accused of violating a term of probation. The director and the assistant director of the Calhoun Community Alternatives Program Residential Probation Center may apprehend, detain, and confine a probationer of this court who is assigned to that program and who is accused of violating a term of probation.

(B) Prompt Arraignment. A probationer apprehended, detained or confined under this rule must be brought promptly before the court for arraignment.

(C) Written Charges and Hearing. A probationer apprehended, detained, or confined under this rule is entitled to a written copy of the charge, setting forth the alleged violation of probation, and is entitled to a hearing conducted in accordance with law and the court rules.

[Adopted effective September 20, 1993, 443 Mich.]

THIRTY–EIGHTH JUDICIAL CIRCUIT [MONROE COUNTY]

Rule 2.119   Motion Practice

(C) Time for Service of Motion Praecipe. Except in an emergency, a motion praecipe must be filed at least 7 days before the scheduled hearing date.

THIRTY–NINTH JUDICIAL CIRCUIT [LENAWEE COUNTY]

Rule 8.110   Chief Judge Rule

(A) Terms and Sessions. There shall be four terms of court each year beginning the first Monday of January, April, July, and October, unless falling on a legal holiday, in which case the next weekday of the month shall be the first day of the term. Each term of the court shall be deemed to continue from the first day of the term until the first day of the succeeding term.

(B) Arraignments. When the district court binds any respondent over to the circuit court for trial, said respondent shall be ordered to appear before the Thirty-Ninth Circuit Court on the Tuesday or Friday morning next following four days after the district court orders said respondent bound over. The appearance shall be at 8:15 a.m. on said Tuesday or Friday.

(C) Nonsupport Orders. Nonsupport orders to show cause will be noticed at 8:30 a.m., Monday.

(D) Motions. Motions, petitions, defaults, pro confesso, ex parte, and miscellaneous matters, and other short causes not requiring more than 20 minutes, shall be heard on Monday of each week beginning at 9:00 a.m., unless a legal holiday, in which case they shall be heard the following day at 9:00 a.m.

(E) Monday Matters. Monday matters will be heard by the court. If other attorneys are waiting, a matter being heard will be recessed after 20 minutes until all other matters are heard.

FORTIETH JUDICIAL CIRCUIT [LAPEER COUNTY]

Rule 1.101   Scope of Rules

(A) These rules govern the practice of the Fortieth Judicial Circuit in civil and criminal cases.

(B) These rules are supplemental to the Michigan Court Rules of 1985, which shall be controlling in the event of any conflict in the rules.

(C) These rules shall supersede all earlier local court rules of this circuit and shall rescind all related administrative orders of this circuit.

Rule 1.102   Number of Rules

(A) These rules are numbered in conformity with the Michigan Court Rules of 1985 as closely as is feasible.

(B) These rules may be cited as "LCR," i.e., this rule may be referred to as LCR 1.102(B).

Rule 2.119   Motion Day Practice

(A) Motion days shall be held on the first four Mondays of each month. If a Monday is a legal holiday, then the following day shall be motion day, unless otherwise designated.

(B) The chief judge shall determine on which motion days criminal matters will be heard.

(C) All motion day matters shall be noticed for hearing on a regularly scheduled motion day of the judge to whom the action is assigned.

(D) Matters may be scheduled for hearing on motion days by filing a motion praecipe no later than noon of the previous Thursday.

(E) Unless otherwise provided by notice published in the term calendar, criminal matters (including appeals), paternity, arraignments, family support matters, and driver's license petitions shall be noticed for hearing on assigned motion days at 1:30 p.m.; all other matters shall be heard at 9:00 a.m.

(F) At each session of motion day, attorneys shall notify the court clerk when their matters are ready for hearing and those matters shall be called in the order in which notice is received.

Rule 2.401   Civil Pretrial Conference Procedures

(A) Preparing for Pretrial Conference. Attorneys or parties in propria persona shall be prepared to participate in a pretrial conference pursuant to MCR 2.401 and these rules.

(B) Submitting Pretrial Statements. Each party shall submit to the court and to the opposing counsel, at the beginning of every scheduled pretrial conference, a pretrial statement that sets forth:

(1) a brief statement of the party's claims and defenses;

(2) a statement of factual issues;

(3) a statement of legal issues;

(4) citations of law in support of the party's positions including, in negligence actions, all statutes the other party is claimed to have violated;

(5) a statement of required amendments to pleadings and the reasons of the delayed request to amend pleadings;

(6) a statement of required discovery;

(7) an estimate of the time required for trials; and

(8) any other information that will enable the court and parties to conduct a meaningful pretrial conference.

(C) Using Forms in Lieu of Statement. Blank forms for pretrial statements for different types of actions shall be available in the clerk's office and may be completed and submitted in lieu of the pretrial statement described in subrule (B).

Rule 2.602   Presenting Orders and Judgments for Signature of Judge

Proposed judgments and orders shall be deposited with the clerk, who will check them against the clerk's minutes before they are presented to the judge for signature; this procedure need not be followed with respect to the following judgments and orders:

(1) those approved by opposing counsel,

(2) those presented for signature at the same session of court, and

(3) interim support orders.

Rule 6.100   Criminal Procedure

(A) Criminal Pretrial Conferences.

(1) Pretrial conferences shall be held in all criminal cases to be tried in circuit court. The purposes of a pretrial conference shall be:

   (a) to determine whether the parties intend to proceed to trial or to enter a plea to the original charge, a lesser charge, or an added charge;

   (b) to determine whether pretrial motions have been completed;

   (c) to stipulate which witnesses will be called at trial and which witnesses will be waived, if any;

   (d) to determine the number of trial days required;

   (e) to determine when the case will be ready for trial and disclose any scheduling problems.

(2) The defendant and his or her attorney, as well as the prosecuting attorney or a representative, shall attend the pretrial conference. The defendant shall not participate in the conference, but shall be immediately available for consultation. Incarcerated defendants need not be present, unless required by the judge.

(3) Copies of the pretrial conference summary shall be available from the clerk on request.

(B) Arraignments and Motions.

(1) Arraignments shall be noticed for a regularly scheduled motion day of the judge to whom the case is assigned. The district court judge who binds the case over to circuit court for arraignment will ordinarily assign a date for arraignment. If no date is assigned, the case will automatically be noticed by the clerk for the next regularly scheduled criminal motion day of the assigned judge.

(2) A defendant represented by a lawyer may enter a plea of not guilty or stand mute without arraignment in accordance with the provisions of MCR 6.101(D)(2). In such a case, the defendant shall state, in addition, what pretrial motions will be filed, how much time will be required to hear them, and the earliest date the defendant will be ready to proceed with them. A copy of the statement shall be served on the prosecuting attorney no later than the date set for arraignment.

(3) At the arraignment or on receipt of the statement required in subsection (2), the court shall set a date for hearing pretrial motions. Except in the discretion of the trial court for good cause and not as the result of failure to exercise due diligence on the part of counsel or the parties and in those matters concerning jurisdiction, no pretrial motions shall be accepted by the court for hearing after the pretrial conference is completed.

FORTY–FIRST JUDICIAL CIRCUIT [DICKINSON, IRON, AND MENOMINEE COUNTIES]

Rule 2.402   Facsimile Transmission of Documents [Rescinded]

[Rescinded effective January 1, 2004.]

FORTY–SECOND JUDICIAL CIRCUIT [MIDLAND COUNTY]

Rule 2.402   Facsimile Transmission of Documents [Rescinded]

[Rescinded effective January 1, 2004.]

FORTY–FIFTH JUDICIAL CIRCUIT [ST. JOSEPH COUNTY]

Rule 2.403   Mediation

(A) All mediation procedures shall be in accordance with MCR 2.403.

(B) After a mediation order is entered, the parties must serve upon the mediation clerk a copy of any motion, stipulation, order, or pleading concerning scheduling.

(C) The parties may object to the form of mediation or to the composition of a mediation panel by following the procedures and time periods specified in MCR 2.403(C).

(G) Mediation shall be conducted in the courthouse on the last Friday of each month or, by stipulation, at any other time and place convenient to the mediators.

(H) If a matter is settled or otherwise concluded, and a notice of disposition is given to the mediation clerk at least 14 days prior to the hearing date, any fees paid pursuant to MCR 2.403(H) shall be returned. Failure to notify the mediation clerk within the specified time shall preclude the return of fees.

[Adopted effective January 21, 1987, 428 Mich.]

Rule 2.502   Dismissal for Lack of Progress

(A) Notice of Proposed Dismissal. If an attorney or party is directed to appear in court pursuant to MCR 2.502(A) in order to prevent an action from being dismissed for lack of progress, such appearance may be made either by letter or in person.

FORTY–SIXTH JUDICIAL CIRCUIT [KALKASKA, CRAWFORD AND OTSEGO COUNTIES]

Rule 2.403   Mediation

(A) All mediation procedures shall be in accordance with MCR 2.403.

(B) After a mediation order is entered, the parties must serve upon the mediation clerk a copy of any motion, stipulation, order, or pleading concerning scheduling.

(C) Adjournment of mediation hearings is to be avoided whenever possible. Adjournments are to be approved by the judge assigned to the case or, in the absence of the assigned judge, the chief judge. Whenever possible, the attorney in principal charge of the case shall delegate responsibility for attendance to another attorney so as to avoid adjournment.

(D) If a matter is adjourned, settled or otherwise disposed of before mediation, it shall be the responsibility of both counsel to immediately notify the mediation clerk of the disposition. If a notice of disposition or adjournment is given to the mediation clerk at least 7 days prior to the hearing date, any fees paid pursuant to MCR 2.403(H) shall be returned. Failure to notify the mediation clerk within the specified time shall preclude the return of fees; any subsequent rescheduled hearing shall require the parties to pay an additional $75 fee per party.

FORTY–EIGHTH JUDICIAL CIRCUIT [ALLEGAN COUNTY]

Rule 2.402   Facsimile Transmission of Documents [Rescinded]

[Rescinded effective January 1, 2004.]

Rule 2.503   Adjournments [Rescinded]

[Rescinded effective January 1, 2004.]

Rule 3.206   Pleading

All new cases filed in the family division of the 48th Circuit Court must be accompanied by a completed case file information form, in addition to any other document or information required by statute or court rule. Forms may be obtained from the Office of the County Clerk.

[Adopted October 7, 1998, effective January 1, 1999, 459 Mich.]

Comments

Staff Comment to 1998 Adoption

Local Court Rule 3.206 was adopted October 7, 1998, at the request of the circuit court, to be effective January 1, 1999.

FIFTIETH JUDICIAL CIRCUIT [CHIPPEWA COUNTY]

Rule 2.402   Facsimile Transmission of Documents [Rescinded]

[Rescinded effective January 1, 2004.]

FIFTY–SIXTH JUDICIAL CIRCUIT [EATON COUNTY]

Rule 2.402   Facsimile Filing and Transmission of Court Documents [Rescinded]

[Rescinded effective January 1, 2004.]

RECORDER'S COURTS
LOCAL RULES OF THE RECORDER'S COURT [CITY OF DETROIT]

Rule 2.302   Discovery of Documents and Exhibits

(A) On a motion in open court at the arraignment on the information or by a subsequent proper motion, the trial court may order that the prosecution make copies of the following available to defense counsel:

(1) All statements known to the police and prosecutor by all endorsed witnesses;

(2) All statements by the defendant which have been recorded or written;

(3) The investigator's report and all preliminary complaint reports (PCR's) concerning the case;

(4) The defendant's arrest and conviction record;

(5) All scientific and laboratory reports;

(6) All corporeal and photographic lineup sheets.

(B) The trial court may also order that the prosecution permit defense counsel to view the following:

(1) All photographs, diagrams, or other visual evidence pertaining to the case that are in police custody;

(2) All physical or tangible evidence pertaining to the case that are in police custody.

(C) Additionally, the court may order that the prosecution permit defense counsel to view or receive copies of any and all other documents pertaining to the case that are in the possession or control of the police or prosecution. This shall be in effect whenever such documents or items may be material to the defense, regardless of whether they are intended for evidence at trial.

Rule 2.401   Pretrial Conferences

(A) The pretrial stage begins after the arraignment on the information. The purpose of the pretrial conference is to review the legal issues, to advise the court of any motions, and to fix time limitations on such motions and filings. Guilty plea possibilities are to be discussed as well as other matters the court may determine to be necessary to expedite the orderly progression of the case. The pretrial stage consists of three phases:

(1) The calendar conference for setting the calendar of events;

(2) Motion and evidentiary hearings; and

(3) Final conference for terminating plea negotiations, certifying readiness for trial, and setting a firm trial date.

(B) Attendance is required. The presence of the defendant, defense counsel, and the prosecutor is required at each conference.

Rule 2.503   Continuances and Adjournments

Adjournments, postponements, or continuances of any trial or other proceeding shall occur only on a written order of the chief judge or a designee.

Rule 2.506   Witnesses and Subpoenas

(A) Filing of Witness Lists. The court clerk may assume responsibility for the service of subpoenas on witnesses for either party provided that either party, the prosecution, or defense, files in the clerk's office, no later than 28 days prior to the scheduled trial date, a complete list of the respective witnesses for whom subpoenas are sought, together with their addresses.

(B) Subpoenas, Preparation, and Service. When witness lists are filed in accordance with subrule (A), the court clerk shall direct the timely and proper preparation of subpoenas for each of the witnesses listed and shall be responsible for seeing that the proper officers of the Detroit Police Department receive the subpoenas timely with directions that they be promptly served and that a return of service for each subpoena is filed with the court before the trial date or the date of such other proceeding for which the attendance of the witness is required.

(C) Whenever the procedure for service of subpoenas which is outlined in this rule is not followed, and due diligence is not shown with respect to the service of subpoenas on any witness, no adjournment, postponement, or continuance will be granted because of the failure of the witness to appear.

Rule 2.511   Jurors;   Jury Service

(A) Supervision of Jurors. The chief judge shall supervise persons summoned for jury duty in Recorder's Court and shall exercise the other responsibilities required by law or court rules pertaining to jury service. The trial judge, however, shall supervise jurors summoned before him or her for voir dire and the entire jury selection process, and shall supervise those jurors selected to sit on a case until they are discharged by the trial judge.

(B) Term of Juror Services. Persons summoned for jury duty shall serve one day, or the duration of any trial for which they are jurors.

(C) Communication Between Jurors, Attorneys, and Court Personnel. Deputy clerks, prosecuting or defense attorneys, police officers, or other officials or employees on duty in the Recorder's Court building who must perform any duty, directly or indirectly, with or for any jurors or panel of jurors, shall not converse with them at any time or place during their period of service. Only necessary social civility or the transaction of necessary court business are excepted from this rule.

Rule 6.101   Pretrial Proceedings;   Arraignment on the Information

(A) Immediately after a defendant is bound over for trial, the defendant, the defense counsel, and the prosecuting attorney shall be notified of the date and time of arraignment on the information.

(B) When a defendant is confined in jail, he or she shall be arraigned on the information before the chief judge or a designee on the seventh calendar day after the magistrate signs the return; when a defendant is free on bail or recognizance, he or she shall be arraigned on the fourteenth calendar day after the magistrate signs the return. Court holidays shall not be counted in computing time.

(C) At the arraignment on the information, the chief judge, or a designee, may accept a plea of guilty and may consider an application for youthful trainee or diversionary status.

JUDICIAL DISTRICT COURTS
FIRST JUDICIAL DISTRICT COURT [MONROE COUNTY]

Rule 4.201   Summary Proceedings to Recover Possession of Premises

(C) Summons. The summons must comply with MCR 2.102, and shall command the defendant to appear in accord with MCL 600.5735(4), as follows:

(a) within 10 days after service of the summons upon the defendant, in proceedings under MCL 600.5726;

(b) within 5 days after service of the summons upon the defendant in all other proceedings.

[Adopted effective March 30, 2004, 469 Mich.]

Comments

Staff Comment to 2004 Adoption

Local Court Rule 4.201(C) of the First Judicial District Court was adopted March 30, 2004, at the request of that court, to be effective immediately.

2–A JUDICIAL DISTRICT [LENAWEE COUNTY]

Rule 4.201   Summary Proceedings to Recover Possession of Premises

(C) Summons.

(1) The summons must comply with MCR 2.102, and shall command the defendant to appear in accord with MCL 600.5735(4), as follows:

(a) within 10 days after service of the summons upon the defendant, in proceedings under MCL 600.5726;

(b) within 5 days after service of the summons upon the defendant in all other proceedings.

[Adopted effective November 2, 1999, 461 Mich.]

Comments

Staff Comment to 1999 Adoption

Local Rule 4.201(C) of the 2A District Court was adopted November 2, 1999, at the request of that court, to be effective immediately.

3–B JUDICIAL DISTRICT [ST. JOSEPH COUNTY]

Rule 2.402   Facsimile Transmission of Documents [Rescinded]

[Rescinded effective January 1, 2004.]

TWELFTH JUDICIAL DISTRICT [JACKSON COUNTY]

Rule 2.402   Facsimile Transmission of Documents [Rescinded]

[Rescinded effective January 1, 2004.]

Rule 4.201   Summary Proceedings to Recover Possession of Premises

(C) Summons. The summons must comply with MCR 2.102, and shall command the defendant to appear in accord with MCL 600.5735(4), as follows:

(a) within 10 days after service of the summons upon the defendant, in proceedings under MCL 600.5726;

(b) within 5 days after service of the summons upon the defendant in all other proceedings.

[Adopted January 15, 2002, effective May 1, 2002, 465 Mich.]

Comments

Staff Comment to 2002 Adoption

Local Rule 4.201(C) of the 12th District Court was adopted January 15, 2002, at the request of that court, to be effective May 1, 2002.

EIGHTEENTH JUDICIAL DISTRICT [CITY OF WESTLAND]

Rule 2.402   Facsimile Transmission of Documents [Rescinded effective January 1, 2004]

Rule 4.201   Summary Proceedings to Recover Possession of Premises

(C) Summons.

(1) The summons must comply with MCR 2.102, and shall command the defendant to appear in accord with MCL 600.5735(4), as follows:

(a) within 10 days after service of the summons upon the defendant, in proceedings under MCL 600.5726;

(b) within 5 days after service of the summons upon the defendant in all other proceedings.

[Adopted effective December 2, 1992, 441 Mich.]

Comments

Staff Comment to 1992 Adoption

Local Rule 4.201(C)(1) of the 18th District Court was adopted in 1992 at the request of that court.

TWENTY–SEVENTH JUDICIAL DISTRICT [CITY OF RIVERVIEW]

Rule 4.201   Summary Proceedings to Recover Possession of Premises [Rescinded]

[Rescinded effective January 1, 2004.]

THIRTY–SIXTH JUDICIAL DISTRICT [CITY OF DETROIT]

Rule 2.113   Form of Pleading and Other Papers [Rescinded]

[Rescinded effective March 25, 1991.]

Rule 2.119   Motion Practice for Motions in General Civil Cases

(A) Application. The provisions of this rule apply to motions filed in general civil cases in the 36th District Court. This rule does not apply to motions filed in small claims, real estate, traffic, or criminal cases. The judge's copy of motions and responses shall be filed with the clerk at the same time as the originals.

(B) Motion Praecipe Forms. A motion praecipe form provided by the clerk of the court must be attached to the judge's copy of all motions.

(C) No Oral Argument; Decision/Review Date; Notice. There is no oral argument on motions unless a request is made and is granted by the assigned judge. The moving party shall choose a decision/review date that shall be a Tuesday and shall constitute "the time set for hearing" under MCR 2.119(C) and MCR 2.116(B)(2) for purposes of providing adequate notice to the opposing party. The moving party must provide notice of the decision/review date to the opposing party or that party's attorney. The notice must advise that there will be no oral argument unless the assigned judge grants a request.

(D) Certification of Attempt to Obtain Concurrence. The attorney for the moving party or the moving party must certify on the praecipe form that the opposing party or that party's attorney has been contacted and asked to concur in the relief sought, and that concurrence has been denied or otherwise not obtained.

(E) Responses; Notation of Decision/Review Date. A response to a motion must be filed no later than 3 days before the decision/review date. That date must appear on the upper right corner of the first page of any pleading, brief, or other document relating to a pending motion.

[Adopted September 11, 2002, effective January 1, 2003, 467 Mich.]

Comments

Staff Comment to 2003 Adoption

Local Rule 2.119 of the 36th District Court was adopted September 11, 2002, at the request of that court, to be effective January 1, 2003.

Rule 2.603   Default and Default Judgments [Rescinded]

[Rescinded effective January 1, 2004.]

Rule 3.101   Garnishment after Judgment

(F) Service of Writ. The writ of garnishment and the disclosure form, and a copy of the writ for each principal defendant, must be served on the garnishee defendant in the manner provided for the service of a summons and complaint in MCR 2.105 within 14 days after the writ was issued.

Rule 4.201   Summary Proceedings to Recover Possession of Premises [Rescinded]

[Rescinded effective January 1, 2004.]

Rule 4.202   Summary Proceedings; Land Contract Forfeiture [Rescinded]

[Rescinded effective January 1, 2004.]

FORTY–EIGHTH JUDICIAL DISTRICT [OAKLAND, BLOOMFIELD, AND HILLS COUNTIES]

Rule 2.402   Facsimile Transmission of Documents [Rescinded]

[Rescinded effective January 1, 2004.]

54–A JUDICIAL DISTRICT [CITY OF LANSING]

Rule 2.402   Use of Facsimile Communication Equipment [Rescinded]

[Rescinded effective January 1, 2004.]

54–B JUDICIAL DISTRICT [CITY OF EAST LANSING]

Rule 2.402   Facsimile Transmission of Documents [Rescinded]

[Rescinded effective January 1, 2004.]

FIFTY–FIFTH JUDICIAL DISTRICT [INGHAM COUNTY]

Rule 4.201   Summary Proceedings to Recover Possession of Premises [Rescinded]

[Rescinded effective January 1, 2004.]

56–1 JUDICIAL DISTRICT, FIRST DIVISION [EATON COUNTY]

Rule 2.402   Facsimile Transmission of Documents [Rescinded]

[Rescinded effective January 1, 2004.]

SIXTY–FIRST JUDICIAL DISTRICT [CITY OF GRAND RAPIDS]

Rule 2.402   Use of Facsimile and Communication Equipment for the Filing and Transmission of Court Documents [Rescinded]

[Rescinded effective January 1, 2004.]

62–A JUDICIAL DISTRICT [CITY OF WYOMING]

Rule 2.402   Facsimile Transmission of Documents [Rescinded]

[Rescinded effective January 1, 2004.]

65–1 JUDICIAL DISTRICT, FIRST DIVISION [CLINTON AND ST. JOHNS COUNTIES]

Rule 2.402   Facsimile Transmission of Documents [Rescinded]

[Rescinded effective January 1, 2004.]

SIXTY–EIGHT JUDICIAL DISTRICT [CITY OF FLINT]

Rule 2.503   Adjournment Policy

Requests must be made by motion or stipulation in writing or orally in open court based on good cause, except as specifically exempted below:

(1) Felony pretrial can be adjourned by the prosecutor who shall note the adjournment and new date on the Register of Actions.

(2) The clerk's office can grant adjournment of misdemeanor arraignments for a period not exceeding 1 week from the originally scheduled date. At the option of the defendant, the new date can be set for any day within the period at 8:30 a.m. or 3:00 p.m.

(3) Alias dates (i.e., no service by date originally scheduled) can be given by the clerk's office, however, this cannot be done on the phone. All copies of the summons must be returned to the clerk's office so the new date and time can be noted on the stipulation. The person making the change must put his or her initials on the stipulation, and, at the bottom, put the date the change was made and the initials again.

(4) The scheduling office may adjourn initial misdemeanor pretrials as necessary, except that it must occur prior to the final pretrial. Final misdemeanor pretrials may not be adjourned except pursuant to MCR 2.503.

(5) The scheduling office may adjourn civil pretrials no more than two times upon receipt of written stipulation and order.

(6) The scheduling office may adjourn nonjury trials no more than one time upon receipt of written stipulation and order.

(7) Jury trials may not be adjourned except pursuant to MCR 2.503.

SEVENTY–FOURTH JUDICIAL DISTRICT [BAY COUNTY]

Rule 2.402   Facsimile Transmission of Documents [Rescinded]

[Rescinded effective January 1, 2004.]

EIGHTY–FIRST JUDICIAL DISTRICT [ALCONA, ARENAC, IOSCO, AND OSCODA COUNTIES]

Rule 4.201   Summary Proceedings to Recover Possession of Premises

(C) Summons.

(1) The summons must comply with MCR 2.102, and shall command the defendant to appear in accord with MCL 600.5735(4), as follows:

(a) within 10 days after service of the summons upon the defendant, in proceedings under MCL 600.5726;

(b) within 5 days after service of the summons upon the defendant in all other proceedings.

Comments

Staff Comment to 1993 Adoption

Local Rule 4.201(C)(1) of the 81st District Court was adopted in 1993 at the request of that court.

EIGHTY–SECOND JUDICIAL DISTRICT [OGEMAW COUNTY]

Rule 2.402   Facsimile Transmission of Documents [Rescinded]

[Rescinded effective January 1, 2004.]

Rule 4.201   Summary Proceedings to Recover Possession of Premises

(C) Summons.

(1) The summons must comply with MCR 2.102, and shall command the defendant to appear in accord with MCL 600.5735(4), as follows:

(a) within 10 days after service of the summons upon the defendant, in proceedings under MCL 600.5726;

(b) within 5 days after service of the summons upon the defendant in all other proceedings.

EIGHTY–NINTH JUDICIAL DISTRICT [CHEBOYGAN AND PRESQUE ISLE COUNTIES]

Rule 2.402   Facsimile Transmission of Documents [Rescinded]

[Rescinded effective January 1, 2004.]

95–B JUDICIAL DISTRICT [DICKINSON AND IRON COUNTIES]

Rule 4.201   Summary Proceedings to Recover Possession of Premises

(C) Summons.

(1) The summons must comply with MCR 2.102, and shall command the defendant to appear in accord with MCL 600.5735(4), as follows:

(a) within 10 days after service of the summons upon the defendant, in proceedings under MCL 600.5726;

(b) within 5 days after service of the summons upon the defendant in all other proceedings.

Comments

Staff Comment to 1992 Adoption

Local Rule 4.201(C)(1) of the 95–B Judicial District Court was adopted in 1992 at the request of that court.

PROBATE COURTS
ALLEGAN PROBATE COURT
Effective July 6, 1995

Rule 2.402   Facsimile Transmission of Documents [Rescinded]
[Rescinded effective January 1, 2004.]

BARRY PROBATE COURT
Effective July 6, 1995

Rule 2.402   Facsimile Transmission of Documents [Rescinded]
[Rescinded effective January 1, 2004.]

EATON PROBATE COURT
Effective September 21, 1994

Rule 2.402   Use of Communication Equipment [Rescinded]
[Rescinded effective January 1, 2004.]

GENESEE PROBATE COURT
Effective March 1, 1999

Rule 2.119   Motion Practice

(A) Motion Certification by Attorney. The following certificate signed by the attorney of record or by the party *in propria persona* shall be attached to or incorporated in the motion and notice of hearing filed with the clerk:

I hereby certify that I have made personal contact with _____ [name] on _____ [date], requesting concurrence in the relief sought with this motion and that concurrence has been denied, or that I have made reasonable and diligent attempts to contact counsel requesting concurrence in the relief sought with this motion.

(B) Proposed Orders. A proposed order must be attached to and served with the motion.

(C) Application. This rule applies to all motions filed in the circuit court and to motions filed in civil actions in the probate court.

[Adopted February 2, 1999, effective March 1, 1999.]

Comments
Staff Comment to 1999 Adoption

Local Court Rule 2.119 of the Seventh Judicial Circuit and the Genesee Probate Court was adopted February 2, 1999, effective March 1, 1999, at the request of those courts.

GRAND TRAVERSE PROBATE COURT
Effective July 1, 2012

Rule 3.800   Notice for Court Appointed Special Advocates

In the interest of justice, the Court Appointed Special Advocate appointed to work for a child in any abuse and neglect case shall be afforded notice of any adoption hearing that may occur on behalf of the child.

[Adopted June 20, 2012, effective July 1, 2012, 491 Mich.]

Comments
Staff Comment to 2012 Adoption

This local court rule allows a Court Appointed Special Advocate who works with a child as part of an abuse/neglect proceeding to receive notice of an adoption hearing that also involves the child.

INGHAM PROBATE COURT
Effective March 3, 1995

Rule 2.402   Facsimile Transmission of Documents [Rescinded]

[Rescinded effective January 1, 2004.]

KALAMAZOO PROBATE COURT
Effective March 3, 1995

Rule 2.402   Facsimile Transmission of Documents [Rescinded]

[Rescinded effective January 1, 2004.]

MENOMINEE PROBATE COURT
Effective March 3, 1995

Rule 2.402   Facsimile Transmission of Documents [Rescinded]

[Rescinded effective January 1, 2004.]

OAKLAND PROBATE COURT
Effective May 1, 1992

Rule 2.402   Use of Communication Equipment [Rescinded]

[Rescinded effective January 1, 2004.]

Rule 3.205   Prior and Subsequent Orders and Judgments Affecting Minors

(A) Venue. This rule applies whenever the prior and subsequent courts are Oakland County courts.

(B) Notice to Prior Court, Friend of the Court, Juvenile/Probate Register or Prosecuting Attorney.

(1) As used in this rule, "appropriate official" means the Friend of the Court, juvenile/probate register or Prosecuting Attorney, depending on the nature of the prior or subsequent action and the court involved.

(2) If a minor is known to be subject to the prior continuing jurisdiction of an Oakland County court, the plaintiff or other initiating party must file written notice of proceedings in the subsequent court with

(a) the clerk or register of the prior court, and

(b) the appropriate official of the prior court.

(3) The notice must be filed at least 21 days before the date set for hearing. If the fact of continuing jurisdiction is not then known, notice must be given immediately when it becomes known.

(4) The notice requirement of this subrule is not jurisdictional and does not preclude the subsequent court from entering interim orders before the expiration of the 21–day period, if required by the best interests of the minor.

(C) Prior Orders.

(1) Each provision of a prior order remains in effect until the provision is superseded, changed, or terminated by a subsequent order.

(2) A subsequent court must give due consideration to prior continuing orders of other courts, and may not enter orders contrary to or inconsistent with such orders, except as provided by law.

(D) Duties of Officials of Prior and Subsequent Courts.

(1) Upon receipt of the notice required by subrule (B), the appropriate official of the prior court

(a) must provide the assigned judge of the subsequent court with the docket sheet;

(b) may appear in person at proceedings in the subsequent court, as the welfare of the minor and the interests of justice require.

(2) The appropriate official of the prior court shall furnish documents upon request of the subsequent court.

(3) Upon request of the prior court, the appropriate official of the subsequent court

(a) must notify the appropriate official of the prior court of all proceedings in the subsequent court, and

(b) must send copies of all orders entered in the subsequent court to the attention of the clerk or register and the appropriate official of the prior court.

(4) If a circuit court awards custody of a minor pursuant to MCL 722.26b, the clerk of the circuit court must send a copy of the judgment or order of disposition to the probate court that has prior or continuing jurisdiction of the minor as a result of the guardianship proceedings, regardless of whether there is a request.

(5) Upon receipt of an order from the subsequent court, the appropriate official of the prior court must take the steps necessary to implement the order in the prior court.

[Adopted effective November 1, 1995, 450 Mich.]

Comments

Staff Comment to 1995 Adoption

Local Court Rule 3.205 of the Sixth Judicial Circuit and the Oakland County Probate Court was adopted at the joint request of those courts.

Rule 5.503   Adjournments in the Estates Division [Rescinded]

[Rescinded effective January 1, 2004.]

OSCODA PROBATE COURT
Effective September 21, 1994

Rule 2.402   Facsimile Transmission of Documents [Rescinded]

[Rescinded effective January 1, 2004.]

ST. JOSEPH PROBATE COURT
Effective September 21, 1994

Rule 2.402   Use of Facsimile Communication Equipment for Purposes of Filing Court Documents [Rescinded]

[Rescinded effective January 1, 2004.]

COURT OF CLAIMS

Rule 2.119. Motion Practice

(A) Form of Motions.

(1) An application to the court for an order in a pending action must be by motion. Unless made during a hearing or trial, a motion must

(a) be in writing,

(b) state with particularity the grounds and authority on which it is based,

(c) state the relief or order sought, and

(d) be signed by the party or attorney as provided in MCR 2.114.

(2) The moving party must affirmatively state that he or she requested opposing counsel's concurrence in the relief sought on a specified date, and that opposing counsel has denied or not acquiesced in the relief sought, and therefore, that it is necessary to present the motion.

(3) A motion or response to a motion that presents an issue of law must be accompanied by a brief citing the authority on which it is based. Except as permitted by the court, the combined length of any motion and brief, or of a response and brief, may not exceed 20 pages double spaced, exclusive of attachments and exhibits. Exhibits and attachments are to be abridged to include only the portions that are relevant to the motion or response. But, each exhibit and attachment shall fully provide identification of parties, witnesses, attorneys participating, date, and location. A set of unabridged exhibits and attachments shall be filed contemporaneously and separately with the Clerk of the Court at the time of filing a motion or response. Quotations and footnotes may be single-spaced. At least one-inch margins must be used, and printing shall not be smaller than 12–point type. A copy of a motion or response (including brief) filed under this rule must be provided by counsel to the office of the judge hearing the motion. The judge's copy must be clearly marked judge's copy on the cover sheet; that notation may be handwritten.

(4) If a contested motion is filed after rejection of a proposed order under subrule (D), a copy of the rejected order and an affidavit establishing the rejection must be filed with the motion.

(5) All motions and responses shall include as part of the title the date of filing of the motion. (For example, DATE [mm/dd/yyyy] followed by MOTION FOR ... or RESPONSE TO THE [mm/dd/yyyy] MOTION FOR ...).

(6) There is no oral argument on motions unless a request is made in the motion or response, and the request is granted by the assigned judge. A notice of hearing, if any, will be provided by the court.

(7) The motion will be deemed submitted for decision 21 days after the date of filing as appears in the title of the motion unless otherwise specified by the court or noticed for hearing by the court.

(B) Form of Affidavits.

(1) If an affidavit is filed in support of or in opposition to a motion, it must:

(a) be made on personal knowledge;

(b) state with particularity facts admissible as evidence establishing or denying the grounds stated in the motion; and

(c) show affirmatively that the affiant, if sworn as a witness, can testify competently to the facts stated in the affidavit.

(2) Sworn or certified copies of all papers or parts of papers referred to in an affidavit must be attached to the affidavit unless the papers or copies:

(a) have already been filed in the action;

(b) are matters of public record in the county in which the action is pending;

(c) are in the possession of the adverse party, and this fact is stated in the affidavit or the motion; or

(d) are of such nature that attaching them would be unreasonable or impracticable, and this fact and the reasons are stated in the affidavit or the motion.

(C) Time for Service and Filing of Motions, Responses, and Reply Briefs.

(1) Unless a different period is set by these rules or by the court for good cause, a written motion (other than one that may be heard ex parte) and any supporting brief or affidavits must be served within 5 days after the date of filing as appears in the title of the motion, and in accordance with MCR 2.107.

(2) Unless a different period is set by these rules or by the court for good cause, any response to a motion (including a brief or affidavits) required or permitted by these rules must be filed with the court and served within 14 days after the date of filing as appears in the title of the motion and in accordance with MCR 2.107.

(3) The failure to file a response to a motion will result in the treatment of the motion as uncontested.

(4) Unless a different period is set by the court for good cause, any reply brief filed pursuant to MCR 2.116(G)(1)(a)(iii) must be filed and served within 4 days after the response is filed.

(5) If the court sets a different time for serving a motion or response its authorization must be endorsed in writing on the face of the motion or response, or made by separate order.

(6) Unless the court sets a different time, any discovery motion must be filed at least 21 days before the discovery cut-off date.

(D) Uncontested Orders.

(1) Before filing a motion, a party may serve on the opposite party a copy of a proposed order and a request to stipulate to the court's entry of the proposed order.

(2) On receipt of a request to stipulate, a party may

(a) stipulate to the entry of the order by signing the following statement at the end of the proposed order: "I stipulate to the entry of the above order"; or

(b) waive notice and hearing on the entry of an order by signing the following statement at the end of the proposed order: "Notice and hearing on entry of the above order is waived."

A proposed order is deemed rejected unless it is stipulated to or notice and hearing are waived within 7 days after it is served.

(3) If the parties have stipulated to the entry of a proposed order or waived notice and hearing, the court may enter the order. If the court declines to enter the order, it shall notify the parties by written order or notice a hearing on the motion. If a hearing is noticed by the court, the matter then proceeds as a contested motion under subrule (E).

(4) Notwithstanding the provisions of subrule (D)(3), stipulations and orders for adjournment are governed by MCR 2.503.

(E) Contested Motions.

(1) Contested motions will be deemed submitted for decision 21 days after the date of filing as appears in the title of the motion unless otherwise specified by the court or noticed for hearing by the court.

(2) When a motion is based on facts not appearing of record, the court may hear the motion on affidavits presented by the parties, or may direct that the motion be heard wholly or partly on oral testimony or deposition.

(3) In its discretion, the court may grant, dispense with, or limit oral arguments on motions; and may require the parties to file supplemental briefs in support of and in opposition to a motion.

(4) Appearance at a hearing noticed by the court is governed by the following:

(a) A party who, pursuant to subrule (D)(2), has previously rejected the proposed order before the court, and the court thereafter notices a hearing, must

(i) appear at the hearing held on the motion, and

(ii) before the hearing, if no response to the motion has been filed, file a response containing a concise statement of reasons and supporting authorities in opposition to the motion.

A party who fails to comply with this subrule is subject to assessment of costs under subrule (E)(4)(c).

(b) Unless excused by the court, the moving party must appear at a hearing on the motion. A moving party who fails to appear is subject to assessment of costs under subrule (E)(4)(c); in addition, the court may assess a penalty not to exceed $100, payable to the clerk of the court.

(c) If a party violates the provisions of subrule (E)(4)(a) or (b), the court shall assess costs against the offending party, that party's attorney, or both, equal to the expenses reasonably incurred by the opposing party in appearing at the hearing, including reasonable attorney fees, unless the circumstances make an award of expenses unjust.

(F) Motions for Rehearing or Reconsideration.

(1) Unless another rule provides a different procedure for reconsideration of a decision (see, e.g., MCR 2.604[A], 2.612), a motion for rehearing or reconsideration of the decision on a motion must be served and filed not later than 21 days after entry of an order deciding the motion.

(2) No response to the motion may be filed, and there is no oral argument, unless the court otherwise directs.

(3) Generally, and without restricting the discretion of the court, a motion for rehearing or reconsideration which merely presents the same issues ruled on by the court, either expressly or by reasonable implication, will not be granted. The moving party must demonstrate a palpable error by which the court and the parties have been misled and show that a different disposition of the motion must result from correction of the error.

(G) Motion Fees. The following provisions apply to actions in which a motion fee is required:

(1) A motion fee must be paid on the filing of any request for an order in a pending action, whether the request is entitled "motion," "petition," "application," or otherwise.

(2) The clerk shall charge a single motion fee for all motions filed at the same time in an action regardless of the number of separately captioned documents filed or the number of distinct or alternative requests for relief included in the motions.

(3) A motion fee may not be charged:

(a) in criminal cases;

(b) for a notice of settlement of a proposed judgment or order under MCR 2.602(B);

(c) for a request for an order waiving fees under MCR 2.002 or MCL 600.2529(4) or MCL 600.8371(6);

(d) if the motion is filed at the same time as another document in the same action as to which a fee is required; or

(e) for entry of an uncontested order under subrule (D).

[Adopted effective May 21, 2014, 495 Mich. Amended effective March 21, 2018, 501 Mich; November 20, 2019, effective January 1, 2020, 503 Mich.]

Comments

Staff Comment to 2014 Adoption

Local Court Rule 2.119 for the Court of Claims is adopted May 21, 2014, at the request of that court, effective immediately.

Staff Comment to 2018 Amendment

These amendments update cross-references and make other nonsubstantive revisions to clarify the rules. The amendment of MCR 6.110(B)(1) addresses an inadvertent omission from the last amendment of this rule that was intended to be shown in overstrike. Accordingly, the current rule does not match the published version. Striking the clause "for good cause shown" will provide consistency with other published versions of the rule and with the statute, MCL 766.7, which allows a magistrate to adjourn a preliminary examination with the consent of the parties without the need for good cause to be shown.

Staff Comment to 2020 Amendment

The amendment of LCR 2.119 for the Court of Claims requires a moving party to affirmatively state that he or she has sought concurrence in the relief sought on a specific date, and opposing counsel denied concurrence in the relief sought.

CHAPTER 600

REVISED JUDICATURE ACT OF 1961

For the remainder of the section analysis containing Chapter 600, relating to the Revised Judicature Act of 1961, see any of the section analyses in the M.C.L.A. volumes containing §§ 600.2101 to 600.9947.

P.A.1961, No. 236, effective January 1, 1963, repealed the Judicature Act of 1915 (P.A.1915, No. 314 (§§ 600.1, 600.2, and 601.1 to 681.3)) and various other acts on the subject of courts and the judicial procedure, and enacted the Revised Judicature Act of 1961.

The General Court Rules of 1963, effective January 1, 1963, supplemented the Revised Judicature Act of 1961. The General Court Rules of 1963 have been superceded by the Michigan Court Rules of 1985 (MCR), effective March 1, 1985.

CHAPTER 64. COURT OF CLAIMS

600.6401. Short title

Sec. 6401. This chapter shall be known and may be cited as "the court of claims act".

600.6404. Judges; jurisdiction; transfer of pending matters; transfer notice; assignment; disability, disqualification, or death of judge; term; chief judge

Sec. 6404. (1) The court of claims consists of 4 court of appeals judges from at least 2 court of appeals districts assigned by the supreme court. A court of appeals judge while sitting as a judge of the court of claims may exercise the jurisdiction of the court of claims as provided by law.

(2) All matters pending in the court of claims as of the effective date of the amendatory act that added this subsection [1] shall be transferred to the clerk of the court of appeals, acting as the clerk of the court of claims, for assignment to a court of appeals judge sitting as a court of claims judge pursuant to section 6410.[2] The transfer shall be effective on the effective date of the amendatory act that added this subsection.

(3) Beginning on the effective date of the amendatory act that added this subsection,[1] any matter within the jurisdiction of the court of claims described in section 6419(1)[3] pending or later filed in any court must, upon notice of the state or a department or officer of the state, be transferred to the court of claims described in subsection (1). The transfer shall be effective upon the filing of the transfer notice. The state or a department or officer of this state shall file a copy of the transfer notice with the clerk of the court of appeals, who shall act as the clerk of the court of claims, for assignment to a court of appeals judge sitting as a court of claims judge pursuant to section 6410.

778

(4) If a judge assigned to serve on the court of claims is disabled, disqualified, or otherwise unable to attend to a matter, another judge assigned to sit as a judge of the court of claims may continue, hear, determine, and sign orders and other documents in the matter.

(5) In case a court of appeals judge designated to sit as the judge of the court of claims dies before signing a judgment and after filing a finding of fact or rendering an opinion upon proof submitted and argument of counsel disposing of all or part of the issues in the case involved, a successor as judge of the court of claims may proceed with that action in a manner consistent with the finding or opinion and the judge is given the same powers as if the finding of fact had been made or the opinion had been rendered by the successor judge.

(6) A judge assigned as a judge of the court of claims shall be assigned for a term of 2 years and may be reassigned at the expiration of that term.

(7) The term of a judge of the court of claims expires on May 1 of each odd-numbered year.

(8) When a judge who is sitting as a judge of the court of claims leaves office or is otherwise unable to serve as a judge of the court of claims, the supreme court may assign a court of appeals judge to serve for the remainder of the judge's term on the court of claims.

(9) The supreme court shall select a chief judge of the court of claims from among the court of appeals judges assigned to the court of claims.

Amended by P.A.2013, No. 164, Imd. Eff. Nov. 12, 2013.

1 P.A.2013, No. 164, Imd. Eff. Nov. 12, 2013.
2 M.C.L.A. § 600.6410.
3 M.C.L.A. § 600.6419.

600.6407. Sessions; location; space and equipment

Sec. 6407. The court shall hold at least 4 sessions in each year. Sessions of the court of claims may be held in the various court of appeals districts in the state as the supreme court administrator may determine. The department of technology, management, and budget shall furnish the court with suitable space and equipment.

Amended by P.A.2013, No. 164, Imd. Eff. Nov. 12, 2013.

600.6410. Clerk; filing cause of action; assignment to judge; copies of records, proceedings, and testimony; fees; service of process

Sec. 6410. (1) The clerk of the court of appeals shall serve as the clerk of the court of claims.

(2) A plaintiff may file a cause of action in the court of claims in any court of appeals district.

(3) The clerk of the court of claims shall, by blind draw, assign a cause of action filed in the court of claims to a court of appeals judge sitting as a court of claims judge.

(4) For making copies of records, proceedings, and testimony and furnishing the same at the request of the claimant, or any other person, the clerk of the court of claims or any reporter or recorder serving in the court of claims shall be entitled, in addition to salary, to the same fees as are by law provided for court reporters or recorders in the circuit court. No charge shall be made against the state for services rendered for

furnishing copies of records, proceedings, or testimony or other papers to the attorney general.

(5) Process issued by the court may be served by any member of the Michigan state police as well as any other officer or person authorized to serve process issued out of the circuit court.

Amended by P.A.1986, No. 308, § 1, Eff. Jan. 1, 1987; P.A.2013, No. 164, Imd. Eff. Nov. 12, 2013.

600.6413. Location of court of claims

Sec. 6413. The court of claims shall sit in the court of appeals district where a court of appeals judge serving as a judge of the court of claims sits, unless otherwise determined by the chief judge of the court of claims.

Amended by P.A.2013, No. 164, Imd. Eff. Nov. 12, 2013.

600.6416. Representation of state by attorney general or assistants

Sec. 6416. The attorney general, or his assistants, shall appear for and represent the interests of the state in all matters before the court.

600.6419. Exclusive jurisdiction; claims against state or its department or officers; powers and jurisdictions; judgments; claim for compensation; jurisdiction of circuit court over certain actions and proceedings

Sec. 6419. (1) Except as provided in sections 6421 and 6440,[1] the jurisdiction of the court of claims, as conferred upon it by this chapter, is exclusive. All actions initiated in the court of claims shall be filed in the court of appeals. The state administrative board is vested with discretionary authority upon the advice of the attorney general to hear, consider, determine, and allow any claim against the state in an amount less than $1,000.00. Any claim so allowed by the state administrative board shall be paid in the same manner as judgments are paid under section 6458[2] upon certification of the allowed claim by the secretary of the state administrative board to the clerk of the court of claims. Except as otherwise provided in this section, the court has the following power and jurisdiction:

(a) To hear and determine any claim or demand, statutory or constitutional, liquidated or unliquidated, ex contractu or ex delicto, or any demand for monetary, equitable, or declaratory relief or any demand for an extraordinary writ against the state or any of its departments or officers notwithstanding another law that confers jurisdiction of the case in the circuit court.

(b) To hear and determine any claim or demand, statutory or constitutional, liquidated or unliquidated, ex contractu or ex delicto, or any demand for monetary, equitable, or declaratory relief or any demand for an extraordinary writ that may be pleaded by way of counterclaim on the part of the state or any of its departments or officers against any claimant who may bring an action in the court of claims. Any claim of the state or any of its departments or officers may be pleaded by way of counterclaim in any action brought against the state or any of its departments or officers.

(c) To appoint and utilize a special master as the court considers necessary.

(d) To hear and determine any action challenging the validity of a notice of transfer described in section 6404(2) or (3).[3]

(2) The judgment entered by the court of claims upon any claim described in subsection (1), either against or in favor of the state or any of its departments or officers, upon becoming final is res judicata of that claim. Upon the trial of any cause in which any demand is made by the state or any of its departments or officers against the claimant either by way of setoff, recoupment, or cross declaration, the court shall hear and determine each claim or demand, and if the court finds a balance due from the claimant to the state, the court shall render judgment in favor of the state for the balance. Writs of execution or garnishment may issue upon the judgment the same as from the circuit court of this state. The judgment entered by the court of claims upon any claim, either for or against the claimant, is final unless appealed from as provided in this chapter.

(3) The court of claims does not have jurisdiction of any claim for compensation under either of the following:

(a) The worker's disability compensation act of 1969, 1969 PA 317, MCL 418.101 to 418.941.

(b) 1937 PA 329, MCL 419.101 to 419.104.

(4) This chapter does not deprive the circuit court of this state of jurisdiction over actions brought by the taxpayer under the general sales tax act, 1933 PA 167, MCL 205.51 to 205.78, upon the circuit court, or proceedings to review findings as provided in the Michigan employment security act, 1936 (Ex Sess) PA 1, MCL 421.1 to 421.75, or any other similar tax or employment security proceedings expressly authorized by the statutes of this state.

(5) This chapter does not deprive the circuit court of exclusive jurisdiction over appeals from the district court and administrative agencies as authorized by law.

(6) This chapter does not deprive the circuit court of exclusive jurisdiction to issue, hear, and determine prerogative and remedial writs consistent with section 13 of article VI of the state constitution of 1963.

(7) As used in this section, "the state or any of its departments or officers" means this state or any state governing, legislative, or judicial body, department, commission, board, institution, arm, or agency of the state, or an officer, employee, or volunteer of this state or any governing, legislative, or judicial body, department, commission, board, institution, arm, or agency of this state, acting, or who reasonably believes that he or she is acting, within the scope of his or her authority while engaged in or discharging a government function in the course of his or her duties.

Amended by P.A.1984, No. 212, § 1, Imd. Eff. July 9; P.A.2013, No. 164, Imd. Eff. Nov. 12, 2013.

1 M.C.L.A. §§ 600.6421 and 600.6440.
2 M.C.L.A. § 600.6458.
3 M.C.L.A. § 600.6404.

600.6419a. Repealed by P.A.2013, No. 164, § 1, Imd. Eff. Nov. 12, 2013

600.6420. Claims of $500 or less, delegation of state administrative board's authority to determine and allow claims; payment

Sec. 6420. The state administrative board may delegate the authority vested in it by section 6419(1)[1] for any claim of $500.00 or less for damage or loss of personal property by a claimant who is an employee of the state, to the head of the department in which the claimant was employed. Payment of the claim shall be made upon the written certificate of the department head that the loss or damage occurred in the course of the claimant's employment, without fault on the part of the claimant and that the claimant has not otherwise been reimbursed for the loss.

Amended by P.A.1984, No. 212, § 1, Imd. Eff. July 9.

1 M.C.L.A. § 600.6419.

600.6421. Trial by jury; declaratory or equitable relief or demand for extraordinary writ; joinder; jurisdiction

Sec. 6421. (1) Nothing in this chapter eliminates or creates any right a party may have to a trial by jury, including any right that existed before November 12, 2013. Nothing in this chapter deprives the circuit, district, or probate court of jurisdiction to hear and determine a claim for which there is a right to a trial by jury as otherwise provided by law, including a claim against an individual employee of this state for which there is a right to a trial by jury as otherwise provided by law. Except as otherwise provided in this section, if a party has the right to a trial by jury and asserts that right as required by law, the claim may be heard and determined by a circuit, district, or probate court in the appropriate venue.

(2) For declaratory or equitable relief or a demand for extraordinary writ sought by a party within the jurisdiction of the court of claims described in section 6419(1)[1] and arising out of the same transaction or series of transactions with a matter asserted for which a party has the right to a trial by jury under subsection (1), unless joined as provided in subsection (3), the court of claims shall retain exclusive jurisdiction over the matter of declaratory or equitable relief or a demand for extraordinary writ until a final judgment has been entered, and the matter asserted for which a party has the right to a trial by jury under subsection (1) shall be stayed until final judgment on the matter of declaratory or equitable relief or a demand for extraordinary writ.

(3) With the approval of all parties, any matter within the jurisdiction of the court of claims described in section 6419(1) may be joined for trial with cases arising out of the same transaction or series of transactions that are pending in any of the various trial courts of the state. A case in the court of claims that has been joined with the approval of all parties shall be tried and determined by the judge even though the trial court action with which it may be joined is tried to a jury under the supervision of the same trial judge.

(4) Except as provided in subsection (5), the court of claims' jurisdiction in a matter within its jurisdiction as described in section 6419(1) and pending in any circuit, district, or probate court on November 12, 2013 is as follows:

(a) If the matter is not transferred under section 6404(3),[2] the jurisdiction of the court of claims is not exclusive and the circuit, district, or probate court may continue to exercise jurisdiction over that matter.

(b) If the matter is transferred to the court of claims under section 6404(3), the court of claims has exclusive jurisdiction over the matter, subject to subsection (1).

(5) Subsection (4) does not apply to matters transferred to the court of claims under section 6404(2).

Amended by P.A.1984, No. 212, § 1, Imd. Eff. July 9; P.A.2013, No. 164, Imd. Eff. Nov. 12, 2013; P.A.2013, No. 205, Imd. Eff. Dec. 18, 2013.

1 M.C.L.A. § 600.6419.
2 M.C.L.A. § 600.6404.

600.6422. Practice and procedure; adoption of special rules; fees

Sec. 6422. (1) Practice and procedure in the court of claims shall be in accordance with the statutes and court rules prescribing the practice in the circuit courts of this state, except as otherwise provided in this section.

(2) The supreme court may adopt special rules for the court of claims.

(3) All fees in the court of claims shall be at the rate established by statute or court rule for actions in the circuit courts of this state and shall be paid to the clerk of the court of claims.

Amended by P.A.2013, No. 164, Imd. Eff. Nov. 12, 2013.

600.6425. Depositions

Sec. 6425. The statutes and rules governing the taking of depositions in suits in the circuit courts of this state shall govern in the court of claims, except that it is not sufficient that the witness resides more than 50 miles from the place of holding court to enable the deposition to be used for any purpose.

600.6428. Witnesses, power to compel attendance

Sec. 6428. The court of claims is hereby given the same power to subpoena witnesses and require the production of books, papers, records, documents and any other evidence and to punish for contempt as the circuit courts of this state now have or may hereafter have. The judge and clerk of said court may administer oaths and affirmations, and take acknowledgments of instruments in writing.

600.6431. Notice of intention to file claim, contents, time, verification, copies

Sec. 6431. (1) No claim may be maintained against the state unless the claimant, within 1 year after such claim has accrued, files in the office of the clerk of the court of claims either a written claim or a written notice of intention to file a claim against the state or any of its departments, commissions, boards, institutions, arms or agencies, stating the time when and the place where such claim arose and in detail the nature of the same and of the items of damage alleged or claimed to have been sustained, which claim or notice shall be signed and verified by the claimant before an officer authorized to administer oaths.

(2) Such claim or notice shall designate any department, commission, board, institution, arm or agency of the state involved in connection with such claim, and a copy of such claim or notice shall be furnished to the clerk at the time of the filing of the original for transmittal to the attorney general and to each of the departments, commissions, boards, institutions, arms or agencies designated.

(3) In all actions for property damage or personal injuries, claimant shall file with the clerk of the court of claims a notice of intention to file a claim or the claim itself within 6 months following the happening of the event giving rise to the cause of action.

600.6434. Pleadings, service, copies

Sec. 6434. (1) Except as provided in this section, the pleadings shall conform to the rules for pleadings in the circuit courts.

(2) The complaint shall be verified. The pleadings of the state need not be verified.

(3) The complaint shall be served upon any department, commission, board, institution, arm, or agency of the state involved in the litigation, in the same manner as a complaint filed in the circuit court.

(4) With each paper, including the original complaint filed by the claimant, 1 copy of each shall be furnished to the clerk who shall immediately transmit the copy to the attorney general.

Amended by P.A.1984, No. 212, § 1, Imd. Eff. July 9.

600.6437. Judgment on stipulated facts

Sec. 6437. The court may order entry of judgment against the state or any of its departments, commissions, boards, institutions, arms or agencies based upon facts as stipulated by counsel after taking such proofs in support thereof as may be necessary to satisfy the court as to the accuracy of such facts and upon being satisfied that such judgment is in accordance with applicable law.

600.6440. Remedy in federal court as bar to jurisdiction

Sec. 6440. No claimant may be permitted to file claim in said court against the state nor any department, commission, board, institution, arm or agency thereof who has an adequate remedy upon his claim in the federal courts, but it is not necessary in the complaint filed to allege that claimant has no such adequate remedy, but that fact may be put in issue by the answer or motion filed by the state or the department, commission, board, institution, arm or agency thereof.

600.6443. Trial by court without jury; new trial

Sec. 6443. The case shall be heard by the judge without a jury. The court may grant a new trial upon the same terms and under the same conditions and for the same reasons as prevail in the case of the circuit courts of this state, in a case at law without a jury.

600.6446. Appeal to court of appeals; procedure

Sec. 6446. (1) Appeals shall lie from the court of claims to the court of appeals in all respects as if the court of claims was a circuit court.

(2) The procedure for the taking of appeals to the court of appeals from the court of claims shall be governed by the statutes and court rules governing the taking of appeals from a circuit court to the court of appeals in a case at law, without a jury.

(3) The clerk of the court of claims shall immediately furnish the parties to every action with a notice of entry of any final order or judgment, and the time within which an appeal as of

right may be taken shall be governed by the Michigan court rules.

Amended by P.A.1984, No. 212, § 1, Imd. Eff. July 9.

600.6449. Costs, security for costs on appeal

Sec. 6449. (1) If the state shall put in issue the right of claimant to recover, the court may allow costs to the prevailing party from the time of the joining of the issue. The costs, however, shall include only witness fees and officers' fees for service of subpoenas actually paid, and attorney fees in the same amount as is provided for trial of cases in circuit court.

(2) Costs upon an appeal to the court of appeals shall be allowed in like amounts and for the same items as in a case appealed to the court of appeals from the circuit court.

(3) In the case of costs allowed against a claimant, judgment shall be entered thereon and writs of execution or garnishment may issue as from the circuit court.

(4) In the event of an appeal to the court of appeals by a claimant the judge may, upon motion by the attorney general, require security for costs from the claimant in connection with such an appeal.

Amended by P.A.1984, No. 212, § 1, Imd. Eff. July 9.

600.6452. Limitation of actions; rights of attorney general, petitions for administration of estate or appointment of guardian

Sec. 6452. (1) **Filing of claim.** Every claim against the state, cognizable by the court of claims, shall be forever barred unless the claim is filed with the clerk of the court or suit instituted thereon in federal court as authorized in section 6440,[1] within 3 years after the claim first accrues.

(2) **Limitation of actions.** Except as modified by this section, the provisions of RJA chapter 58,[2] relative to the limitation of actions, shall also be applicable to the limitation prescribed in this section.

(3) **Attorney general; petition for administration of estate of a deceased person.** The attorney general shall have the same right as a creditor under the provisions of the statutes of the state of Michigan in such case made and provided, to petition for the granting of letters of administration of the estate of any deceased person.

(4) **Petition for appointment of guardian of minor or person under disability.** The attorney general shall have the same right as a superintendent of the poor under the provisions of the statutes of the state of Michigan in such case made and provided, to petition for the appointment of a guardian of the estate of a minor or any other person under disability.

[1] M.C.L.A. § 600.6440.
[2] M.C.L.A. § 600.5801 et seq.

600.6455. Court of claims; judgment, interest

Sec. 6455. (1) Interest shall not be allowed upon any claim up to the date of the rendition of judgment by the court, unless upon a contract expressly stipulating for the payment of interest. All judgments from the date of the rendition of the judgment shall carry interest at the rate of 12% per annum compounded annually, except that judgment upon a contract expressly providing for interest shall carry interest at the rate provided by the contract in which case provision to that effect

shall be incorporated in the judgment entered. This subsection shall apply to any civil action based on tort filed on or after July 9, 1984 but before January 1, 1987 and any action pending before the court of claims on July 9, 1984. This subsection shall apply to any action, other than a civil action based on tort, filed on or after July 1, 1984 and any action pending before the court of claims on July 9, 1984.

(2) Except as otherwise provided in this subsection, for complaints filed on or after January 1, 1987, interest on a money judgment recovered in a civil action shall be calculated from the date of filing the complaint at a rate of interest which is equal to 1% plus the average interest rate paid at auctions of 5–year United States treasury notes during the 6 months immediately preceding July 1 and January 1, as certified by the state treasurer, and compounded annually, pursuant to this section.

(3) For complaints filed on or after October 1, 1986, interest shall not be allowed on future damages from the date of filing the complaint to the date of entry of the judgment.

(4) If a bona fide, reasonable written offer of settlement in a civil action based on tort is made by the party against whom the judgment is subsequently rendered, the court shall order that interest shall not be allowed beyond the date the written offer of settlement which is made and rejected by the plaintiff, and is filed with the court.

(5) Except as otherwise provided in subsection (3), if a bona fide, reasonable written offer of settlement in a civil action based on tort is not made by the party against whom the judgment is subsequently rendered, or is made and that offer is not filed with the court, the court shall order that interest be calculated from the date of filing the complaint to the date of satisfaction of the judgment.

(6) Except as otherwise provided in subsection (3), if a bona fide, reasonable written offer of settlement in a civil action based on tort is made by a plaintiff for whom the judgment is subsequently rendered and that offer is rejected and the offer is filed with the court, the court shall order that interest be calculated from the date of the rejection of the offer to the date of satisfaction of the judgment at a rate of interest equal to 2% plus the rate of interest computed under subsection (2).

(7) An offer made pursuant to this section which is not accepted within 21 days after the offer is made shall be considered rejected. A rejection, under this subsection or otherwise, does not preclude a later offer by either party.

(8) As used in this section:

(a) "Bona fide, reasonable written offer of settlement" means:

(*i*) With respect to an offer of settlement made by a defendant against whom judgment is subsequently rendered, an offer of settlement that is not less than 90% of the amount actually received by the plaintiff in the action through judgment.

(*ii*) With respect to an offer of settlement made by a plaintiff, an offer of settlement that is not more than 110% of the amount actually received by the plaintiff in the action through judgment.

(b) "Defendant" means a defendant, a counter-defendant, or a cross-defendant.

(c) "Party" means a plaintiff or a defendant.

(d) "Plaintiff" means a plaintiff, a counter-plaintiff, or a cross-plaintiff.

Amended by P.A.1984, No. 212, § 1, Imd. Eff. July 9; P.A.1986, No. 178, § 1, Eff. Oct. 1.

600.6458. Judgment against state, payment

Sec. 6458. (1) In rendering any judgment against the state, or any department, commission, board, institution, arm, or agency, the court shall determine and specify in that judgment the department, commission, board, institution, arm, or agency from whose appropriation that judgment shall be paid.

(2) Upon any judgment against the state or any department, commission, board, institution, arm, or agency becoming final, or upon allowance of any claim by the state administrative board and upon certification by the secretary of the state administrative board to the clerk of the court of claims, the clerk of the court shall certify to the state treasurer the fact that that judgment was entered or that the claim was allowed and the claim shall thereupon be paid from the unencumbered appropriation of the department, commission, board, institution, arm, or agency if the state treasurer determines the unencumbered appropriation is sufficient for the payment. In the event that funds are not available to pay the judgment or allowed claim, the state treasurer shall instruct the clerk of the court of claims to issue a voucher against an appropriation made by the legislature for the payment of judgment claims and allowed claims. In the event that funds are not available to pay the judgment or allowed claim, that fact, together with the name of the claimant, date of judgment, date of allowance of claim by the state administrative board and amount shall be reported to the legislature at its next session, and the judgment or allowed claim shall be paid as soon as money is available for that purpose. The clerk shall not certify any judgment to the state treasurer until the period for appeal from that judgment shall have expired, unless written stipulation between the attorney general and the claimant or his or her attorney, waiving any right of appeal or new trial, is filed with the clerk of the court.

(3) The clerk shall approve vouchers under the direction of the court for the payment of the several judgments rendered by the court. All warrants issued in satisfaction of those judgments shall be transmitted to the clerk for distribution; and all warrants issued in satisfaction of claims allowed by the state administrative board shall be transmitted to the secretary of the state administrative board for distribution.

Amended by P.A.2002, No. 429, Imd. Eff. June 5, 2002.

600.6461. Clerk's report to legislature, state treasurer, and budget director

Sec. 6461. (1) At the commencement of each session of the legislature and at such other times during the session as he or she may consider proper, the clerk of the court shall report to the legislature the claims upon which the court has finally acted, with a statement of the judgment rendered in each case.

(2) The clerk shall submit a detailed statement of the amount of each claim allowed by the court to the state treasurer and the budget director.

Amended by P.A.2002, No. 429, Imd. Eff. June 5, 2002.

600.6464. Judgment, discharge

Sec. 6464. The payment of any amount due as found by the judgment of the court of claims, including interest and costs, shall operate as a discharge of such judgment.

600.6467. State agencies to furnish information upon request

Sec. 6467. The court shall have power to call upon any officer, department, institution, board, arm or agency of the state government for any examination, information or papers pertinent to the issues involved in any case then pending before the court. No state employee shall receive any additional fees or compensation for rendering such services or appearing as a witness before the court upon behalf of the state.

600.6470. Fraud in connection with claim; forfeiture

Sec. 6470. Any person who corruptly practices, or attempts to practice, any fraud against the state of Michigan, in the proof, statement, establishment, or allowance of any claim or of any part of a claim, against the state, shall thereby forfeit the same to the state and it shall be the duty of the court of claims in such case to find specifically that such fraud was practiced, or attempted to be practiced, and thereupon to give judgment that such claim is forfeited to the state and that the claimant be forever barred from prosecuting the same.

600.6475. Actions involving negligent operation of motor vehicles or aircraft; defense of governmental function

Sec. 6475. In all actions brought in the court of claims against the state to recover damages resulting from the negligent operation by an officer, agent or employee of the state of a motor vehicle or an aircraft, other than a military aircraft, of which the state is owner, the fact that the state, in the ownership or operation of such motor vehicle or aircraft, was engaged in a governmental function shall not be a defense to such action. This act shall not be construed to impose upon the state a liability other or greater than the liability imposed by law upon other owners of motor vehicles or aircraft.

RULES OF PROFESSIONAL CONDUCT

Adopted Effective October 1, 1988

Rule 1.0. Scope and Applicability of Rules and Commentary

(a) These are the Michigan Rules of Professional Conduct. The form of citation for this rule is MRPC 1.0.

(b) Failure to comply with an obligation or prohibition imposed by a rule is a basis for invoking the disciplinary process. The rules do not, however, give rise to a cause of action for enforcement of a rule or for damages caused by failure to comply with an obligation or prohibition imposed by a rule. In a civil or criminal action, the admissibility of the Rules of Professional Conduct is governed by the Michigan Rules of Evidence and other provisions of law.

(c) The text of each rule is authoritative. The comment that accompanies each rule does not expand or limit the scope of the obligations, prohibitions, and counsel found in the text of the rule.

Preamble: A Lawyer's Responsibilities

This preamble is part of the comment to Rule 1.0, and provides a general introduction to the Rules of Professional Conduct.

A lawyer is a representative of clients, an officer of the legal system and a public citizen having special responsibility for the quality of justice.

As a representative of clients, a lawyer performs various functions. As advisor, a lawyer provides a client with an informed understanding of the client's legal rights and obligations and explains their practical implications. As advocate, a lawyer zealously asserts the client's position under the rules of the adversary system. As negotiator, a lawyer seeks a result advantageous to the client but consistent with requirements of honest dealing with others. As intermediary between clients, a lawyer seeks to reconcile their divergent interests as an advisor and, to a limited extent, as a spokesperson for each client. A lawyer acts as evaluator by examining a client's legal affairs and reporting about them to the client or to others.

In all professional functions a lawyer should be competent, prompt and diligent. A lawyer should maintain communication with a client concerning the representation. A lawyer should keep in confidence information relating to representation of a client except so far as disclosure is required or permitted by the Rules of Professional Conduct or other law.

A lawyer's conduct should conform to the requirements of the law, both in professional service to clients and in the lawyer's business and personal affairs. A lawyer should use the law's procedures only for legitimate purposes and not to harass or intimidate others. A lawyer should demonstrate respect for the legal system and for those who serve it, including judges, other lawyers and public officials. While it is a lawyer's duty, when necessary, to challenge the rectitude of official action, it is also a lawyer's duty to uphold legal process.

As a public citizen, a lawyer should seek improvement of the law, the administration of justice and the quality of service rendered by the legal profession. As a member of a learned profession, a lawyer should cultivate knowledge of the law beyond its use for clients, employ that knowledge in reform of the law and work to strengthen legal education. A lawyer should be mindful of deficiencies in the administration of justice and of the fact that the poor, and sometimes persons who are not poor, cannot afford adequate legal assistance, and should therefore devote professional time and civic influence in their behalf. A lawyer should aid the legal profession in pursuing these objectives and should help the bar regulate itself in the public interest.

Many of a lawyer's professional responsibilities are prescribed in the Rules of Professional Conduct, as well as substantive and procedural law. However, a lawyer is also guided by personal conscience and the approbation of professional peers. A lawyer should strive to attain the highest level of skill, to improve the law and the legal profession and to exemplify the legal profession's ideals of public service.

A lawyer's responsibilities as a representative of clients, an officer of the legal system, and a public citizen are usually harmonious. Thus, when an opposing party is well represented, a lawyer can be a zealous advocate on behalf of a client and at the same time assume that justice is being done. So also, a lawyer can be sure that preserving client confidences ordinarily serves the public interest because people are more likely to seek legal advice, and thereby heed their legal obligations, when they know their communications will be private.

In the nature of law practice, however, conflicting responsibilities are encountered. Virtually all difficult ethical problems arise from conflict between a lawyer's responsibilities to clients, to the legal system, and to the lawyer's own interest in remaining an upright person while earning a satisfactory living. The Rules of Professional Conduct prescribe terms for resolving such conflicts. Within the framework of these rules many difficult issues of professional discretion can arise. Such issues must be resolved through the exercise of sensitive professional

and moral judgment guided by the basic principles underlying the rules.

The legal profession is largely self-governing. Although other professions also have been granted powers of self-government, the legal profession is unique in this respect because of the close relationship between the profession and the processes of government and law enforcement. This connection is manifested in the fact that ultimate authority over the legal profession is vested largely in the courts.

To the extent that lawyers meet the obligations of their professional calling, the occasion for government regulation is obviated. Self-regulation also helps maintain the legal profession's independence from government domination. An independent legal profession is an important force in preserving government under law, for abuse of legal authority is more readily challenged by a profession whose members are not dependent on government for the right to practice.

The legal profession's relative autonomy carries with it special responsibilities of self-government. The profession has a responsibility to assure that its regulations are conceived in the public interest and not in furtherance of parochial or self-interested concerns of the bar. Every lawyer is responsible for observance of the Rules of Professional Conduct. A lawyer should also aid in securing their observance by other lawyers. Neglect of these responsibilities compromises the independence of the profession and the public interest which it serves.

Lawyers play a vital role in the preservation of society. The fulfillment of this role requires an understanding by lawyers of their relationship to our legal system. The Rules of Professional Conduct, when properly applied, serve to define that relationship.

Scope

The Rules of Professional Conduct are rules of reason. They should be interpreted with reference to the purposes of legal representation and of the law itself. Some of the rules are imperatives, cast in the terms "shall" or "shall not." These define proper conduct for purposes of professional discipline. Others, generally cast in the term "may," are permissive and define areas under the rules in which the lawyer has professional discretion. No disciplinary action should be taken when the lawyer acts or chooses not to act within the bounds of such discretion. Other rules define the nature of relationships between the lawyer and others. The rules are thus partly obligatory and disciplinary and partly constitutive and descriptive in that they define a lawyer's professional role. Many of the comments use the term "should." Comments do not add obligations to the rules, but provide guidance for practicing in compliance with the rules.

The rules presuppose a larger legal context shaping the lawyer's role. That context includes court rules and statutes relating to matters of licensure, laws defining specific obligations of lawyers, and substantive and procedural law in general. Compliance with the rules, as with all law in an open society, depends primarily upon understanding and voluntary compliance, secondarily upon reinforcement by peer and public opinion, and finally, when necessary, upon enforcement through disciplinary proceedings. The rules do not, however, exhaust the moral and ethical considerations that should inform a lawyer, for no worthwhile human activity can be completely defined by legal rules. The rules simply provide a framework for the ethical practice of law.

Furthermore, for purposes of determining the lawyer's authority and responsibility, principles of substantive law external to these rules determine whether a client-lawyer relationship exists. Most of the duties flowing from the client-lawyer relationship attach only after the client has requested the lawyer to render legal services and the lawyer has agreed to do so. But there are some duties, such as that of confidentiality under Rule 1.6, that may attach when the lawyer agrees to consider whether a client-lawyer relationship shall be established. Whether a client-lawyer relationship exists for any specific purpose can depend on the circumstances and may be a question of fact.

Under various legal provisions, including constitutional, statutory and common-law, the responsibilities of government lawyers may include authority concerning legal matters that ordinarily reposes in the client in private client-lawyer relationships. For example, a lawyer for a government agency may have authority on behalf of the government to decide upon settlement or whether to appeal from an adverse judgment. Such authority in various respects is generally vested in the attorney general and the prosecuting attorney in state government, and their federal counterparts, and the same may be true of other government law officers. Also, lawyers under the supervision of these officers may be authorized to represent several government agencies in intragovernmental legal controversies in circumstances where a private lawyer could not represent multiple private clients. They also may have authority to represent the "public interest" in circumstances where a private lawyer would not be authorized to do so. These rules do not abrogate any such authority.

As indicated earlier in this comment, a failure to comply with an obligation or prohibition imposed by a rule is a basis for invoking the disciplinary process. The rules presuppose that disciplinary assessment of a lawyer's conduct will be made on the basis of the facts and circumstances as they existed at the time of the conduct in question and in recognition of the fact that a lawyer often has to act upon uncertain or incomplete evidence of the situation. Moreover, the rules presuppose that whether or not discipline should be imposed for a violation, and the severity of a sanction, depend on all the circumstances, such as the wilfulness and seriousness of the violation, extenuating factors and whether there have been previous violations.

As also indicated earlier in this comment, a violation of a rule does not give rise to a cause of action, nor does it create any presumption that a legal duty has been breached. The rules are designed to provide guidance to lawyers and to provide a structure for regulating conduct through disciplinary agencies. They are not designed to be a basis for civil liability. Furthermore, the purposes of the rules can be subverted when they are invoked by opposing parties as procedural weapons. The fact that a rule is a just basis for a lawyer's self-assessment, or for sanctioning a lawyer under the administration of a disciplinary authority, does not imply that an antagonist in a collateral proceeding or transaction has standing to seek enforcement of the rule. Accordingly, nothing in the rules should be deemed to augment any substantive legal duty of lawyers or the extradisciplinary consequences of violating such a duty.

Moreover, these rules are not intended to govern or affect judicial application of either the client-lawyer or work-product privilege. Those privileges were developed to promote compliance with law and fairness in litigation. In reliance on the client-lawyer privilege, clients are entitled to expect that communications within the scope of the privilege will be protected against compelled disclosure. The client-lawyer privilege is that of the client and not of the lawyer. The fact that in exceptional situations the lawyer under the rules has a limited discretion to disclose a client confidence does not vitiate the proposition that, as a general matter, the client has a reasonable expectation that information relating to the client will not be voluntarily disclosed and that disclosure of such information may be judicially compelled only in accordance with recognized exceptions to the client-lawyer and work-product privileges.

The lawyer's exercise of discretion not to disclose information under Rule 1.6 should not be subject to reexamination. Permitting such reexamination would be incompatible with the general policy of promoting compliance with law through assurances that communications will be protected against disclosure.

The comment accompanying each rule explains and illustrates the meaning and purpose of the rule. The Preamble and this note on scope provide general orientation. The comments are intended as guides to interpretation, but the text of each rule is authoritative.

Terminology

"Belief" or "believes" denotes that the person involved actually supposed the fact in question to be true. A person's belief may be inferred from circumstances.

"Confirmed in writing," when used in reference to the informed consent of a person, denotes informed consent that is given in writing confirming an oral informed consent. If it is not feasible to obtain or transmit the writing at the time the person gives informed consent, then the lawyer must obtain or transmit it within a reasonable time thereafter.

"Consult" or "consultation" denotes communication of information reasonably sufficient to permit the client to appreciate the significance of the matter in question.

"Firm" or "law firm" denotes a lawyer or lawyers in a private firm, lawyers employed in the legal department of a corporation or other organization, and lawyers employed in a legal services organization. See comment, Rule 1.10.

"Fraud" or "fraudulent" denotes conduct having a purpose to deceive and not merely negligent misrepresentation or failure to apprise another of relevant information.

"Informed consent" denotes the agreement by a person to a proposed course of conduct after the lawyer has communicated adequate information and explanation about the material risks of and reasonably available alternatives to the proposed course of conduct.

"Knowingly," "known," or "knows" denotes actual knowledge of the fact in question. A person's knowledge may be inferred from circumstances.

"Partner" denotes a member of a partnership and a shareholder in a law firm organized as a professional corporation.

"Reasonable" or "reasonably," when used in relation to conduct by a lawyer, denotes the conduct of a reasonably prudent and competent lawyer.

"Reasonable belief" or "reasonably believes," when used in reference to a lawyer, denotes that the lawyer believes the matter in question and that the circumstances are such that the belief is reasonable.

"Reasonably should know," when used in reference to a lawyer, denotes that a lawyer of reasonable prudence and competence would ascertain the matter in question.

"Substantial," when used in reference to degree or extent, denotes a material matter of clear and weighty importance.
[Amended September 20, 2017, effective January 1, 2018, 501 Mich.]

Official Comment

The rules and comments were largely drawn from the American Bar Association's Model Rules of Professional Conduct. Prior to submission of those Model Rules to the Michigan Supreme Court, the State Bar of Michigan made minor changes in the rules and the comments to conform them to Michigan law and preferred practice. The Supreme Court then adopted the rules, with such substantive changes as appeared proper to the Court. Additional changes in the comments were then made by staff to conform the comments to the rules as adopted by the Supreme Court. The Supreme Court has authorized publication of the comments as an aid to the reader, but the rules alone comprise the Supreme Court's authoritative statement of a lawyer's ethical obligations.

Comments

Staff Comment to 2017 Amendment

The amendments of Rules 1.0, 1.2, 4.2, and 4.3 of the Michigan Rules of Professional Conduct and Rules 2.107, 2.117, and 6.001 of the Michigan Court Rules were submitted to the Court by the State Bar of Michigan Representative Assembly. The rules are intended to provide guidance for attorneys and clients who would prefer to engage in a limited scope representation. The rules allow for such an agreement "preferably in writing," and enable an attorney to file a notice of LSR with the court when the representation is undertaken as well as a termination notice when the representation has ended. The rules also explicitly allow attorneys to provide document preparation services for a self-represented litigant without having to file an appearance with the court.

CLIENT–LAWYER RELATIONSHIP

Rule 1.1 Competence

A lawyer shall provide competent representation to a client. A lawyer shall not:

(a) handle a legal matter which the lawyer knows or should know that the lawyer is not competent to handle, without associating with a lawyer who is competent to handle it;

(b) handle a legal matter without preparation adequate in the circumstances; or

(c) neglect a legal matter entrusted to the lawyer.
Comment amended September 18, 2019, effective January 1, 2020, 503 Mich.

Official Comment

Legal Knowledge and Skill. In determining whether a lawyer is able to provide competent representation in a particular matter, relevant factors include the relative complexity and specialized nature of the matter, the lawyer's general experience, the lawyer's training and experience in the field in question, the preparation and study the lawyer is able to give the matter, and whether it is feasible to refer the matter to, or associate or consult with, a lawyer of established competence in the field in question. In many instances, the required proficiency is that of a general practitioner. Expertise in a particular field of law may be required in some circumstances.

A lawyer need not necessarily have special training or prior experience to handle legal problems of a type with which the lawyer is unfamiliar. A newly admitted lawyer can be as competent as a practitioner with long experience. Some important legal skills, such as the analysis of precedent, the evaluation of evidence and legal drafting, are required in all legal problems. Perhaps the most fundamental legal skill consists of determining what kind of legal problems a situation may involve, a skill that necessarily transcends any particular specialized knowledge. A lawyer can provide adequate representation in a wholly novel field through necessary study. Competent representation can also be provided through the association of a lawyer of established competence in the field in question.

In an emergency, a lawyer may give advice or assistance in a matter in which the lawyer does not have the skill ordinarily required where referral to or consultation or association with another lawyer would be impractical. Even in an emergency, however, assistance should be limited to that reasonably necessary in the circumstances, for ill-considered action under emergency conditions can jeopardize the client's interest.

A lawyer may offer representation where the requisite level of competence can be achieved by reasonable preparation. This applies as well to a lawyer who is appointed as counsel for an unrepresented person. See also Rule 6.2.

Thoroughness and Preparation. Competent handling of a particular matter includes inquiry into and analysis of the factual and legal elements of the problem, and use of methods and procedures meeting the standards of competent practitioners. It also includes adequate preparation. The required attention and preparation are determined in part by what is at stake; major litigation and complex transactions ordinarily require more elaborate treatment than matters of lesser consequence.

Maintaining Competence. To maintain the requisite knowledge and skill, a lawyer should engage in continuing study and education, including the knowledge and skills regarding existing and developing technology that are reasonably necessary to provide competent representation for the client in a particular matter. If a system of peer review has been established, the lawyer should consider making use of it in appropriate circumstances.

Comments

Staff Comment to 2020 Amendment

The amendments of the comments of MRPC 1.1 and MRPC 1.6 address a lawyer's obligation to maintain reasonable competence in relevant technology and ensure reasonable efforts to maintain confidentiality of documents.

Rule 1.2.   Scope of Representation

(a) A lawyer shall seek the lawful objectives of a client through reasonably available means permitted by law and these rules. A lawyer does not violate this rule by acceding to reasonable requests of opposing counsel that do not prejudice the rights of the client, by being punctual in fulfilling all professional commitments, or by avoiding offensive tactics. A lawyer shall abide by a client's decision whether to accept an offer of settlement or mediation evaluation of a matter. In a criminal case, the lawyer shall abide by the client's decision, after consultation with the lawyer, with respect to a plea to be entered, whether to waive jury trial, and whether the client will testify. In representing a client, a lawyer may, where permissible, exercise professional judgment to waive or fail to assert a right or position of the client.

(b) A lawyer licensed to practice in the State of Michigan may limit the scope of a representation, file a limited appearance in a civil action, and act as counsel of record for the limited purpose identified in that appearance, if the limitation is reasonable under the circumstances and the client gives informed consent, preferably confirmed in writing.

(1) A lawyer licensed to practice in the State of Michigan may draft or partially draft pleadings, briefs, and other papers to be filed with the court. Such assistance does not require the signature or identification of the lawyer, but does require the following statement on the document: "This document was drafted or partially drafted with the assistance of a lawyer licensed to practice in the State of Michigan, pursuant to Michigan Rule of Professional Conduct 1.2(b)."

(2) The filing of such documents is not and shall not be deemed an appearance by the lawyer in the case. Any filing prepared pursuant to this rule shall be signed by the party designated as "self-represented" and shall not be signed by the lawyer who provided drafting preparation assistance. Further, the lawyer providing document preparation assistance without entering a general appearance may rely on the client's representation of the facts, unless the lawyer has reason to believe that such representation is false, seeks objectives that are inconsistent with the lawyer's obligation under the Rules of Professional Conduct, or asserts claims or defenses pursuant to pleadings or papers that would, if signed by the lawyer, violate MCR 1.109, or which are materially insufficient.

(c) A lawyer shall not counsel a client to engage, or assist a client, in conduct that the lawyer knows is illegal or fraudulent, but a lawyer may discuss the legal consequences of any proposed course of conduct with a client and may counsel or assist a client to make a good-faith effort to determine the validity, scope, meaning, or application of the law.

(d) When a lawyer knows that a client expects assistance not permitted by the Rules of Professional Conduct or other law, the lawyer shall consult with the client regarding the relevant limitations on the lawyer's conduct.

[Amended July 16, 1993, effective October 1, 1993, 443 Mich; September 20, 2017 effective January 1, 2018, 501 Mich; August 30, 2018, effective September 1, 2018, 502 Mich.]

Official Comment

Scope of Representation. Both the lawyer and the client have authority and responsibility in the objectives and means of representation. The client has ultimate authority to determine the purposes to be served by legal representation, within the limits imposed by law and the lawyer's professional obligations. Within those limits, a client also has a right to consult with the lawyer about the means to be used in pursuing those objectives. At the same time, a lawyer is not required to pursue objectives or employ means simply because a client may wish that the lawyer do so. A clear distinction between objectives and means sometimes cannot be drawn, and in many cases the client-lawyer relationship partakes of a joint undertaking. In questions of means, the lawyer should assume responsibility for technical and legal tactical issues, but should defer to the client regarding such questions as the expense to be incurred and concern for third persons who might be adversely affected.

In a case in which the client appears to be suffering mental disability, the lawyer's duty to abide by the client's decisions is to be guided by reference to Rule 1.14.

Independence from Client's Views or Activities. Legal representation should not be denied to people who are unable to afford legal services or whose cause is controversial or the subject of popular disapproval. By the same token, representation of a client, including representation by appointment, does not constitute an endorsement of the client's political, economic, social, or moral views or activities.

Services Limited in Objectives or Means. The objectives or scope of services provided by a lawyer may be limited by agreement with the client or by the terms under which the lawyer's services are made available to the client. For example, a retainer may be for a specifically defined purpose. Representation provided through a legal-aid agency may be subject to limitations on the types of cases the agency handles. When a lawyer has been retained by an insurer to represent an insured, the representation may be limited to matters related to the insurance coverage. The terms upon which representation is undertaken may exclude specific objectives or means. Such limitations may exclude objectives or means that the lawyer regards as repugnant or imprudent.

An agreement concerning the scope of representation must accord with the Rules of Professional Conduct and other law. Thus, the client may not be asked to agree to representation so limited in scope as to violate Rule 1.1, or to surrender the right to terminate the lawyer's services or the right to settle litigation that the lawyer might wish to continue.

Reasonable under the Circumstances. Factors to weigh in deciding whether the limitation is reasonable under the circumstances according to the facts communicated to the attorney include the apparent capacity of the person to proceed effectively with the limited scope assistance given the complexity and type of matter and other self-help resources available. For example, some self-represented persons may seek objectives that are inconsistent with an attorney's obligation under the Rules of Professional Conduct, or assert claims or defenses pursuant to pleadings or motions that would, if signed by an attorney, violate MCR 1.109. Attorneys must be reasonably diligent to ensure a limited scope representation does not advance improper objectives, and the commentary should help inform lawyers of these considerations.

Illegal, Fraudulent and Prohibited Transactions. A lawyer is required to give an honest opinion about the actual consequences that appear likely to result from a client's conduct. The fact that a client uses advice in a course of action that is illegal or fraudulent does not, of itself, make a lawyer a party to the course of action. However, a lawyer may not knowingly assist a client in illegal or fraudulent conduct. There is a critical distinction between presenting an analysis of legal aspects of questionable conduct and recommending the means by which an illegal act or fraud might be committed with impunity.

When the client's course of action has already begun and is continuing, the lawyer's responsibility is especially delicate. The lawyer is not permitted to reveal the client's wrongdoing, except where permitted by Rule 1.6. However, the lawyer is required to avoid furthering the purpose, for example, by suggesting how it might be concealed. A lawyer may not continue assisting a client in conduct that the lawyer originally supposes is legally proper but then discovers is illegal or fraudulent. Withdrawal from the representation, therefore, may be required.

Where the client is a fiduciary, the lawyer may be charged with special obligations in dealings with a beneficiary.

Paragraph (c) applies whether or not the defrauded party is a party to the transaction. Hence, a lawyer should not participate in a sham transaction; for example, a transaction to effectuate criminal or fraudulent escape of tax liability. Paragraph (c) does not preclude undertaking a criminal defense incident to a general retainer for legal services to a lawful enterprise. The last clause of paragraph (c) recognizes that determining the validity or interpretation of a statute or regulation may require a course of action involving disobedience of the statute or regulation or of the interpretation placed upon it by governmental authorities.

Comments

Staff Comment to January, 2018 Amendment

The amendments of Rules 1.0, 1.2, 4.2, and 4.3 of the Michigan Rules of Professional Conduct and Rules 2.107, 2.117, and 6.001 of the Michigan Court Rules were submitted to the Court by the State Bar of Michigan Representative Assembly. The rules are intended to provide guidance for attorneys and clients who would prefer to engage in a limited scope representation. The rules allow for such an agreement "preferably in writing," and enable an attorney to file a notice of LSR with the court when the representation is undertaken as well as a termination notice when the representation has ended. The rules also explicitly allow attorneys to provide document preparation services for a self-represented litigant without having to file an appearance with the court.

Staff Comment to September, 2018 Amendment

These amendments update cross-references in the rules, and are intended to reflect changes that are necessary as a result of the Court's recent e-Filing rules amendments.

Rule 1.3. Diligence

A lawyer shall act with reasonable diligence and promptness in representing a client.

Official Comment

A lawyer should pursue a matter on behalf of a client despite opposition, obstruction or personal inconvenience to the lawyer, and may take whatever lawful and ethical measures are required to vindicate a client's cause or endeavor. A lawyer should act with commitment and dedication to the interests of the client and with zeal in advocacy upon the client's behalf. However, a lawyer is not bound to press for every advantage that might be realized for a client. A lawyer has professional discretion in determining the means by which a matter should be pursued. See Rule 1.2. A lawyer's workload should be controlled so that each matter can be handled adequately.

Perhaps no professional shortcoming is more widely resented than procrastination. A client's interests often can be adversely affected by the passage of time or the change of conditions; in extreme instances, as when a lawyer overlooks a statute of limitations, the client's legal position may be destroyed. Even when the client's interests are not affected in substance, however, unreasonable delay can cause a client needless anxiety and undermine confidence in the lawyer's trustworthiness.

Unless the relationship is terminated as provided in Rule 1.16, a lawyer should carry through to conclusion all matters undertaken for a client. If a lawyer's employment is limited to a specific matter, the relationship terminates when the matter has been resolved. If a lawyer has served a client over a substantial period in a variety of matters, the client sometimes may assume that the lawyer will continue to serve on a continuing basis unless the lawyer gives notice of withdrawal. Doubt about whether a client-lawyer relationship still exists should be clarified by the lawyer, preferably in writing, so that the client will not mistakenly suppose the lawyer is looking after the client's affairs when the lawyer has ceased to do so. For example, if a lawyer has handled a judicial or administrative proceeding that produced a result adverse to the client but has not been specifically instructed concerning pursuit of an appeal, the lawyer should advise the client of the possibility of appeal before relinquishing responsibility for the matter.

Rule 1.4.   Communication

(a) A lawyer shall keep a client reasonably informed about the status of a matter and comply promptly with reasonable requests for information. A lawyer shall notify the client promptly of all settlement offers, mediation evaluations, and proposed plea bargains.

(b) A lawyer shall explain a matter to the extent reasonably necessary to permit the client to make informed decisions regarding the representation.

Official Comment

The client should have sufficient information to participate intelligently in decisions concerning the objectives of the representation and the means by which they are to be pursued to the extent the client is willing and able to do so. For example, a lawyer negotiating on behalf of a client should provide the client with facts relevant to the matter, inform the client of communications from another party, and take other reasonable steps that permit the client to make a decision regarding an offer from another party. A lawyer who receives an offer of settlement or a mediation evaluation in a civil controversy, or a proffered plea bargain in a criminal case, must promptly inform the client of its substance. See Rule 1.2(a). Even when a client delegates authority to the lawyer, the client should be kept advised of the status of the matter.

Adequacy of communication depends in part on the kind of advice or assistance involved. For example, in negotiations where there is time to explain a proposal, the lawyer should review all important provisions with the client before proceeding to an agreement. In litigation, a lawyer should explain the general strategy and prospects of success and ordinarily should consult the client on tactics that might injure or coerce others. On the other hand, a lawyer ordinarily cannot be expected to describe trial or negotiation strategy in detail. The guiding principle is that the lawyer should fulfill reasonable client expectations for information consistent with the duty to act in the client's best interests and consistent with the client's overall requirements as to the character of representation.

Ordinarily, the information to be provided is that appropriate for a client who is a comprehending and responsible adult. However, fully informing the client according to this standard may be impracticable, for example, where the client is a child or suffers from mental disability. See Rule 1.14. When the client is an organization or group, it is often impossible or inappropriate to inform every one of its members about its legal affairs; ordinarily, the lawyer should address communications to the appropriate officials of the organization. See Rule 1.13. Where many routine matters are involved, a system of limited or occasional reporting may be arranged with the client. Practical exigency may also require a lawyer to act for a client without prior consultation.

Withholding Information. In some circumstances, a lawyer may be justified in delaying transmission of information when the client would be likely to react imprudently to an immediate communication. Thus, a lawyer might withhold a psychiatric diagnosis of a client when the examining psychiatrist indicates that disclosure would harm the client. A lawyer may not withhold information to serve the lawyer's own interest or convenience. Rules or court orders governing litigation may provide that information supplied to a lawyer may not be disclosed to the client. Rule 3.4(c) directs compliance with such rules or orders.

Rule 1.5.   Fees

(a) A lawyer shall not enter into an agreement for, charge, or collect an illegal or clearly excessive fee. A fee is clearly excessive when, after a review of the facts, a lawyer of ordinary prudence would be left with a definite and firm conviction that the fee is in excess of a reasonable fee. The factors to be considered in determining the reasonableness of a fee include the following:

(1) the time and labor required, the novelty and difficulty of the questions involved, and the skill requisite to perform the legal service properly;

(2) the likelihood, if apparent to the client, that the acceptance of the particular employment will preclude other employment by the lawyer;

(3) the fee customarily charged in the locality for similar legal services;

(4) the amount involved and the results obtained;

(5) the time limitations imposed by the client or by the circumstances;

(6) the nature and length of the professional relationship with the client;

(7) the experience, reputation, and ability of the lawyer or lawyers performing the services; and

(8) whether the fee is fixed or contingent.

(b) When the lawyer has not regularly represented the client, the basis or rate of the fee shall be communicated to the client, preferably in writing, before or within a reasonable time after commencing the representation.

(c) A fee may be contingent on the outcome of the matter for which the service is rendered, except in a matter in which a contingent fee is prohibited by paragraph (d) or by other law. A contingent-fee agreement shall be in writing and shall state the method by which the fee is to be determined. Upon conclusion of a contingent-fee matter, the lawyer shall provide the client with a written statement of the outcome of the matter and, if there is a recovery, show the remittance to the client and the method of its determination. See also MCR 8.121 for additional requirements applicable to some contingent-fee agreements.

(d) A lawyer shall not enter into an arrangement for, charge, or collect:

(1) any fee in a domestic relations matter, the payment or amount of which is contingent upon the securing of a divorce or upon the amount of alimony or support, or property settlement in lieu thereof, the lawyer's success, results obtained, value added, or any factor to be applied that leaves the client unable to discern the basis or rate of the fee or the method by which the fee is to be determined, or

(2) a contingent fee for representing a defendant in a criminal case.

(e) A division of a fee between lawyers who are not in the same firm may be made only if:

(1) the client is advised of and does not object to the participation of all the lawyers involved; and

(2) the total fee is reasonable.

[Amended February 5, 1998, effective April 1, 1998, 456 Mich; April 5, 2017 effective May 1, 2017, 500 Mich.]

Official Comment

Basis or Rate of Fee. When the lawyer has regularly represented a client, they ordinarily will have evolved an understanding concerning the basis or rate of the fee. In a new client-lawyer relationship, however, an understanding as to the fee should be promptly established. It is not necessary to recite all the factors that underlie the basis of the fee, but only those that are directly involved in its computation. It is sufficient, for example, to state that the basic rate is an hourly charge or a fixed amount or an estimated amount, or to identify the factors that may be taken into account in finally fixing the fee. When developments occur during the representation that render an earlier estimate substantially inaccurate, a revised estimate should be provided to the client. A written statement concerning the fee reduces the possibility of misunderstanding. Furnishing the client with a simple memorandum or a copy of the lawyer's customary fee schedule is sufficient if the basis or rate of the fee is set forth.

Prohibited Contingent Fees. Paragraph (d) prohibits a lawyer from charging a fee in a domestic relations matter when payment is contingent upon the securing of a divorce, or upon the amount of alimony or support or property settlement to be obtained. The amount of alimony, support or property awarded to a client shall not be used by a lawyer as a basis for enhancing the fee. This provision does not preclude a contract for a contingent fee for legal representation in connection with the recovery of postjudgment balances due under support, alimony or other financial orders because such contracts do not implicate the same policy concerns.

Terms of Payment. A lawyer may require advance payment of a fee, but is obliged to return any unearned portion. See Rule 1.16(d). A lawyer may accept property in payment for services, such as an ownership interest in an enterprise, providing this does not involve acquisition of a proprietary interest in the cause of action or subject matter of the litigation contrary to Rule 1.8(j). However, a fee paid in property instead of money may be subject to special scrutiny because it involves questions concerning both the value of the services and the lawyer's special knowledge of the value of the property.

An agreement may not be made whose terms might induce the lawyer improperly to curtail services for the client or perform them in a way contrary to the client's interest. For example, a lawyer should not enter into an agreement whereby services are to be provided only up to a stated amount when it is foreseeable that more extensive services probably will be required, unless the situation is adequately explained to the client. Otherwise, the client might have to bargain for further assistance in the midst of a proceeding or transaction. However, it is proper to define the extent of services in light of the client's ability to pay. A lawyer should not exploit a fee arrangement based primarily on hourly charges by using wasteful procedures. When there is doubt whether a contingent fee is consistent with the client's best interest, the lawyer should offer the client alternative bases for the fee and explain their implications. Applicable law may impose limitations on contingent fees, such as a ceiling on the percentage. See MCR 8.121.

Division of Fee. A division of fee is a single billing to a client covering the fee of two or more lawyers who are not in the same firm. A division of fee facilitates association of more than one lawyer in a matter in which neither alone could serve the client as well, and most often is used when the fee is contingent and the division is between a referring lawyer and a trial specialist. Paragraph (e) permits the lawyers to divide a fee on agreement between the participating lawyers if the client is advised and does not object. It does not require disclosure to the client of the share that each lawyer is to receive.

Disputes Over Fees. If a procedure has been established for resolution of fee disputes, such as an arbitration or mediation procedure established by the bar, the lawyer should conscientiously consider submitting to it. Law may prescribe a procedure for determining a lawyer's fee, for example, in representation of an executor or administrator, of a class, or of a person entitled to a reasonable fee as part of the measure of damages. The lawyer entitled to such a fee and a lawyer representing another party concerned with the fee should comply with the prescribed procedure.

Comments

Staff Comment to 1998 Amendment

The amendment of paragraph c, adopted February 5, 1998, and effective April 1, 1998, clarified that this rule's provisions apply to all contingent fee agreements, not just to those covered by MCR 8.121.

Staff Comment to 2017 Amendment

At the invitation of the Supreme Court, the Attorney Grievance Commission, the Family Law Council of the State Bar of Michigan, and the Bar's Committee on Professional Ethics submitted individual proposals to revise MRPC 1.5(d) related to the ability of an attorney to charge "results obtained" or "value-added fees" in a domestic relations case. Proposals by the AGC and Committee on Professional Ethics were combined for purposes of publication, and that proposal was published along with the Family Law Council's proposal for comment. The Court adopted the AGC–proposed language that clarifies that a lawyer is prohibited from charging a contingent fee in a domestic relations action based on the "results obtained" or "value added."

Rule 1.6.   Confidentiality of Information

(a) "Confidence" refers to information protected by the client-lawyer privilege under applicable law, and "secret" refers to other information gained in the professional relationship that the client has requested be held inviolate or the disclosure of which would be embarrassing or would be likely to be detrimental to the client.

(b) Except when permitted under paragraph (c), a lawyer shall not knowingly:

(1) reveal a confidence or secret of a client;

(2) use a confidence or secret of a client to the disadvantage of the client; or

(3) use a confidence or secret of a client for the advantage of the lawyer or of a third person, unless the client consents after full disclosure.

(c) A lawyer may reveal:

(1) confidences or secrets with the consent of the client or clients affected, but only after full disclosure to them;

(2) confidences or secrets when permitted or required by these rules, or when required by law or by court order;

(3) confidences and secrets to the extent reasonably necessary to rectify the consequences of a client's illegal or fraudulent act in the furtherance of which the lawyer's services have been used;

(4) the intention of a client to commit a crime and the information necessary to prevent the crime; and

(5) confidences or secrets necessary to establish or collect a fee, or to defend the lawyer or the lawyer's employees or associates against an accusation of wrongful conduct.

(d) A lawyer shall exercise reasonable care to prevent employees, associates, and others whose services are utilized by the lawyer from disclosing or using confidences or secrets of a client, except that a lawyer may reveal the information allowed by paragraph (c) through an employee.

Comment amended September 18, 2019, effective January 1, 2020, 503 Mich.

Official Comment

The lawyer is part of a judicial system charged with upholding the law. One of the lawyer's functions is to advise clients so that they avoid any violation of the law in the proper exercise of their rights.

The observance of the ethical obligation of a lawyer to hold inviolate confidential information of the client not only facilitates the full development of facts essential to proper representation of the client, but also encourages people to seek early legal assistance.

Almost without exception, clients come to lawyers in order to determine what their rights are and what is, in the maze of laws and regulations, deemed to be legal and correct. The common law recognizes that the client's confidences must be protected from disclosure. Upon the basis of experience, lawyers know that almost all clients follow the advice given and that the law is upheld.

A fundamental principle in the client-lawyer relationship is that the lawyer maintain confidentiality of information relating to the representation. The client is thereby encouraged to communicate fully and frankly with the lawyer even as to embarrassing or legally damaging subject matter.

The principle of confidentiality is given effect in two related bodies of law, the client-lawyer privilege (which includes the work-product doctrine) in the law of evidence and the rule of confidentiality established in professional ethics. The client-lawyer privilege applies in judicial and other proceedings in which a lawyer may be called as a witness or otherwise required to produce evidence concerning a client. The rule of client-lawyer confidentiality applies in situations other than those where evidence is sought from the lawyer through compulsion of law. The confidentiality rule applies to confidences and secrets as defined in the rule. A lawyer may not disclose such information except as authorized or required by the Rules of Professional Conduct or other law. See also Scope, ante.

The requirement of maintaining confidentiality of information relating to representation applies to government lawyers who may disagree with the policy goals that their representation is designed to advance.

Authorized Disclosure. A lawyer is impliedly authorized to make disclosures about a client when appropriate in carrying out the representation, except to the extent that the client's instructions or special circumstances limit that authority. In litigation, for example, a lawyer may disclose information by admitting a fact that cannot properly be disputed, or, in negotiation, by making a disclosure that facilitates a satisfactory conclusion.

Lawyers in a firm may, in the course of the firm's practice, disclose to each other information relating to a client of the firm, unless the client has instructed that particular information be confined to specified lawyers, or unless the disclosure would breach a screen erected within the firm in accordance with Rules 1.10(b), 1.11(a), or 1.12(c).

Disclosure Adverse to Client. The confidentiality rule is subject to limited exceptions. In becoming privy to information about a client, a lawyer may foresee that the client intends to commit a crime. To the extent a lawyer is prohibited from making disclosure, the interests of the potential victim are sacrificed in favor of preserving the client's confidences even though the client's purpose is wrongful. To the extent a lawyer is required or permitted to disclose a client's purposes, the client may be inhibited from revealing facts which would enable the lawyer to counsel against a wrongful course of action. A rule governing disclosure of threatened harm thus involves balancing the interests of one group of potential victims against those of another. On the assumption that lawyers generally fulfill their duty to advise against the commission of deliberately wrongful acts, the public is better protected if full and open communication by the client is encouraged than if it is inhibited.

Generally speaking, information relating to the representation must be kept confidential as stated in paragraph (b). However, when the client is or will be engaged in criminal conduct or the integrity of the lawyer's own conduct is involved, the principle of confidentiality may appropriately yield, depending on the lawyer's knowledge about and relationship to the conduct in question, and the seriousness of that conduct. Several situations must be distinguished.

First, the lawyer may not counsel or assist a client in conduct that is illegal or fraudulent. See Rule 1.2(c). Similarly, a lawyer has a duty under Rule 3.3(a)(4) not to use false evidence. This duty is essentially a special instance of the duty prescribed in Rule 1.2(c) to avoid assisting a client in illegal or fraudulent conduct. The same is true of compliance with Rule 4.1 concerning truthfulness of a lawyer's own representations.

Second, the lawyer may have been innocently involved in past conduct by the client that was criminal or fraudulent. In such a situation the lawyer has not violated Rule 1.2(c), because to "counsel or assist" criminal or fraudulent conduct requires knowing that the conduct is of that character. Even if the involvement was innocent, however, the fact remains that the lawyer's professional services were made the instrument of the client's crime or fraud. The lawyer, therefore, has a legitimate interest in being able to rectify the consequences of such conduct, and has the professional right, although not a professional duty, to rectify the situation. Exercising that right may require revealing information relating to the representation. Paragraph (c)(3) gives the lawyer professional discretion to reveal such information to the extent necessary to accomplish rectification. However, the constitutional rights of defendants in criminal cases may limit the extent to which counsel for a defendant may correct a misrepresentation that is based on information provided by the client. See comment to Rule 3.3.

Third, the lawyer may learn that a client intends prospective conduct that is criminal. Inaction by the lawyer is not a violation of Rule 1.2(c), except in the limited circumstances where failure to act constitutes assisting the client. See comment to Rule 1.2(c). However, the lawyer's knowledge of the client's purpose may enable the lawyer to prevent commission of the prospective crime. If the prospective crime is likely to result in substantial injury, the lawyer may feel a moral obligation to take preventive action. When the threatened injury is grave, such as homicide or serious bodily injury, a lawyer may have an obligation under tort or criminal law to take reasonable preventive measures. Whether the lawyer's concern is based on moral or legal considerations, the interest in preventing the harm may be more compelling than the interest in preserving confidentiality of information relating to the client. As stated in paragraph (c)(4), the lawyer has professional discretion to reveal information in order to prevent a client's criminal act.

It is arguable that the lawyer should have a professional obligation to make a disclosure in order to prevent homicide or serious bodily injury which the lawyer knows is intended by the client. However, it is very difficult for a lawyer to "know" when such a heinous purpose will actually be carried out, for the client may have a change of mind. To require disclosure when the client intends such an act, at the risk of professional discipline if the assessment of the client's purpose turns out to be wrong, would be to impose a penal risk that might interfere with the lawyer's resolution of an inherently difficult moral dilemma.

The lawyer's exercise of discretion requires consideration of such factors as magnitude, proximity, and likelihood of the contemplated wrong; the nature of the lawyer's relationship with the client and with those who might be injured by the client; the lawyer's own involvement in the transaction; and factors that may extenuate the conduct in question. Where practical, the lawyer should seek to persuade the client to take suitable action. In any case, a disclosure adverse to the client's interest should be no greater than the lawyer reasonably believes necessary to the purpose. A lawyer's decision not to make a disclosure permitted by paragraph (c) does not violate this rule.

Where the client is an organization, the lawyer may be in doubt whether contemplated conduct will actually be carried out by the organization. Where necessary to guide conduct in connection with this rule, the lawyer should make an inquiry within the organization as indicated in Rule 1.13(b).

Paragraph (c)(3) does not apply where a lawyer is employed after a crime or fraud has been committed to represent the client in matters ensuing therefrom.

Withdrawal. If the lawyer's services will be used by the client in materially furthering a course of criminal or fraudulent conduct, the lawyer must withdraw, as stated in Rule 1.16(a)(1).

After withdrawal the lawyer is required to refrain from making disclosure of the client's confidences, except as otherwise provided in Rule 1.6. Neither this rule nor Rule 1.8(b) nor Rule 1.16(d) prevents the lawyer from giving notice of the fact of withdrawal, and the lawyer may also withdraw or disaffirm any opinion, document, affirmation, or the like.

Dispute Concerning Lawyer's Conduct. Where a legal claim or disciplinary charge alleges complicity of the lawyer in a client's conduct or other misconduct of the lawyer involving representation of the client, the lawyer may respond to the extent the lawyer reasonably believes necessary to establish a defense. The same is true with respect to a claim involving the conduct or representation of a former client. The lawyer's right to respond arises when an assertion of complicity or other misconduct has been made. Paragraph (c)(5) does not require the lawyer to await the commencement of an action or proceeding that charges complicity or other misconduct, so that the defense may be established by responding directly to a third party who has made such an assertion. The right to defend, of course, applies where a proceeding has been commenced. Where practicable and not prejudicial to the lawyer's ability to establish the defense, the lawyer should advise the client of the third party's assertion and request that the client respond appropriately. In any event, disclosure should be no greater than the lawyer reasonably believes is necessary to vindicate innocence, the disclosure should be made in a manner which limits access to the information to the tribunal or other persons having a need to know it, and appropriate protective orders or other arrangements should be sought by the lawyer to the fullest extent practicable.

If the lawyer is charged with wrongdoing in which the client's conduct is implicated, the rule of confidentiality should not prevent the lawyer from defending against the charge. Such a charge can arise in a civil, criminal, or professional disciplinary proceeding, and can be based on a wrong allegedly committed by the lawyer against the client, or on a wrong alleged by a third person, for example, a person claiming to have been defrauded by the lawyer and client acting together.

A lawyer entitled to a fee is permitted by paragraph (c)(5) to prove the services rendered in an action to collect it. This aspect of the rule expresses the principle that the beneficiary of a fiduciary relationship may not exploit it to the detriment of the fiduciary. As stated above, the lawyer must make every effort practicable to avoid unnecessary disclosure of information relating to a representation, to limit disclosure to those having the need to know it, and to obtain protective orders or make other arrangements minimizing the risk of disclosure.

Disclosures Otherwise Required or Authorized. The scope of the client-lawyer privilege is a question of law. If a lawyer is called as a witness to give testimony concerning a client, absent waiver by the client, paragraph (b)(1) requires the lawyer to invoke the privilege when it is applicable. The lawyer must comply with the final orders of a court or other tribunal of competent jurisdiction requiring the lawyer to give information about the client.

The Rules of Professional Conduct in various circumstances permit or require a lawyer to disclose information relating to the representation. See Rules 2.2, 2.3, 3.3 and 4.1. In addition to these provisions, a lawyer may be obligated or permitted by other provisions of law to give information about a client. Whether another provision of law supersedes Rule 1.6 is a matter of interpretation beyond the scope of these rules, but a presumption should exist against such a supersession.

Former Client. The duty of confidentiality continues after the client-lawyer relationship has terminated. See Rule 1.9.

Confidentiality of Information. When transmitting a communication that contains confidential and/or privileged information relating to the representation of a client, the lawyer should take reasonable measures and act competently so that the confidential and/or privileged client information will not be revealed to unintended third parties.

Comments

Staff Comment to 2020 Amendment

The amendments of the comments of MRPC 1.1 and MRPC 1.6 address a lawyer's obligation to maintain reasonable competence in relevant technology and ensure reasonable efforts to maintain confidentiality of documents.

Rule 1.7. Conflict of Interest: General Rule

(a) A lawyer shall not represent a client if the representation of that client will be directly adverse to another client, unless:

(1) the lawyer reasonably believes the representation will not adversely affect the relationship with the other client; and

(2) each client consents after consultation.

(b) A lawyer shall not represent a client if the representation of that client may be materially limited by the lawyer's responsibilities to another client or to a third person, or by the lawyer's own interests, unless:

(1) the lawyer reasonably believes the representation will not be adversely affected; and

(2) the client consents after consultation. When representation of multiple clients in a single matter is undertaken, the consultation shall include explanation of the implications of the common representation and the advantages and risks involved.
[Amended effective June 7, 1989, 432 Mich.]

Official Comment

Loyalty to a Client. Loyalty is an essential element in the lawyer's relationship to a client. An impermissible conflict of interest may exist before representation is undertaken, in which event the representation should be declined. The lawyer should adopt reasonable procedures, appropriate for the size and type of firm and practice, to determine in both litigation and nonlitigation matters the parties and issues involved and to determine whether there are actual or potential conflicts of interest.

If such a conflict arises after representation has been undertaken, the lawyer should withdraw from the representation. See Rule 1.16. Where more than one client is involved and the lawyer withdraws because a conflict arises after representation, whether the lawyer may continue to represent any of the clients is determined by Rule 1.9. See also Rule 2.2(c). As to whether a client-lawyer relationship exists or, having once been established, is continuing, see comment to Rule 1.3 and Scope, ante.

As a general proposition, loyalty to a client prohibits undertaking representation directly adverse to that client without that client's consent. Paragraph (a) expresses that general rule. Thus, a lawyer ordinarily may not act as advocate against a person the lawyer represents in some other matter, even if it is wholly unrelated. On the other hand, simultaneous representation in unrelated matters of clients whose interests are only generally adverse, such as competing economic enterprises, does not require consent of the respective clients. Paragraph (a) applies only when the representation of one client would be directly adverse to the other.

Loyalty to a client is also impaired when a lawyer cannot consider, recommend, or carry out an appropriate course of action for the client because of the lawyer's other responsibilities or interests. The conflict in effect forecloses alternatives that would otherwise be available to the client. Paragraph (b) addresses such situations. A possible conflict does not itself preclude the representation. The critical questions are the likelihood that a conflict will eventuate and, if it does, whether it will materially interfere with the lawyer's independent professional judgment in considering alternatives or foreclose courses of action that reasonably should be pursued on behalf of the client. Consideration should be given to whether the client wishes to accommodate the other interest involved.

Consultation and Consent. A client may consent to representation notwithstanding a conflict. However, as indicated in paragraph (a)(1) with respect to representation directly adverse to a client, and paragraph (b)(1) with respect to

material limitations on representation of a client, when a disinterested lawyer would conclude that the client should not agree to the representation under the circumstances, the lawyer involved cannot properly ask for such agreement or provide representation on the basis of the client's consent. When more than one client is involved, the question of conflict must be resolved as to each client. Moreover, there may be circumstances where it is impossible to make the disclosure necessary to obtain consent. For example, when the lawyer represents different clients in related matters and one of the clients refuses to consent to the disclosure necessary to permit the other client to make an informed decision, the lawyer cannot properly ask the latter to consent.

Lawyer's Interests. The lawyer's own interests should not be permitted to have adverse effect on representation of a client. For example, a lawyer's need for income should not lead the lawyer to undertake matters that cannot be handled competently and at a reasonable fee. See Rules 1.1 and 1.5. If the probity of a lawyer's own conduct in a transaction is in serious question, it may be difficult or impossible for the lawyer to give a client detached advice. A lawyer may not allow related business interests to affect representation, for example, by referring clients to an enterprise in which the lawyer has an undisclosed interest.

Conflicts in Litigation. Paragraph (a) prohibits representation of opposing parties in litigation. Simultaneous representation of parties whose interests in litigation may conflict, such as coplaintiffs or codefendants, is governed by paragraph (b). An impermissible conflict may exist by reason of substantial discrepancy in the parties' testimony, incompatibility in positions in relation to an opposing party, or the fact that there are substantially different possibilities of settlement of the claims or liabilities in question. Such conflicts can arise in criminal cases as well as civil. The potential for conflict of interest in representing multiple defendants in a criminal case is so grave that ordinarily a lawyer should decline to represent more than one codefendant. On the other hand, common representation of persons having similar interests is proper if the risk of adverse effect is minimal and the requirements of paragraph (b) are met. Compare Rule 2.2 involving intermediation between clients.

Ordinarily, a lawyer may not act as advocate against a client the lawyer represents in some other matter, even if the other matter is wholly unrelated. However, there are circumstances in which a lawyer may act as advocate against a client. For example, a lawyer representing an enterprise with diverse operations may accept employment as an advocate against the enterprise in an unrelated matter if doing so will not adversely affect the lawyer's relationship with the enterprise or conduct of the suit and if both clients consent upon consultation. By the same token, government lawyers in some circumstances may represent government employees in proceedings in which a government agency is the opposing party. The propriety of concurrent representation can depend on the nature of the litigation. For example, a suit charging fraud entails conflict to a degree not involved in a suit for a declaratory judgment concerning statutory interpretation.

Interest of Person Paying for a Lawyer's Service. A lawyer may be paid from a source other than the client if the client is informed of that fact and consents and the arrangement does not compromise the lawyer's duty of loyalty to the client. See Rule 1.8(f). For example, when an insurer and its insured have conflicting interests in a matter arising from a liability insurance agreement, and the insurer is required to provide special counsel for the insured, the arrangement should assure the special counsel's professional independence. So also, when a corporation and its directors or employees are involved in a controversy in which they have conflicting interests, the corporation may provide funds for separate legal representation of the directors or employees if the clients consent after consultation and the arrangement ensures the lawyer's professional independence.

Other Conflict Situations. Conflicts of interest in contexts other than litigation sometimes may be difficult to assess. Relevant factors in determining whether there is potential for adverse effect include the duration and intimacy of the lawyer's relationship with the client or clients involved, the functions being performed by the lawyer, the likelihood that actual conflict will arise, and the likely prejudice to the client from the conflict if it does arise. The question is often one of proximity and degree.

For example, a lawyer may not represent multiple parties in a negotiation whose interests are fundamentally antagonistic to each other, but common representation is permissible where the clients are generally aligned in interest even though there is some difference of interest among them.

Conflict questions may also arise in estate planning and estate administration. A lawyer may be called upon to prepare wills for several family members, such as husband and wife, and, depending upon the circumstances, a conflict of interest may arise. In estate administration the identity of the client may be a question of law. The lawyer should make clear the relationship to the parties involved.

A lawyer for a corporation or other organization who is also a member of its board of directors should determine whether the responsibilities of the two roles may conflict. The lawyer may be called on to advise the corporation in matters involving actions of the directors. Consideration should be given to the frequency with which such situations may arise, the potential intensity of the conflict, the effect of the lawyer's resignation from the board, and the possibility of the corporation's obtaining legal advice from another lawyer in such situations. If there is material risk that the dual role will compromise the lawyer's independence of professional judgment, the lawyer should not serve as a director.

Conflict Charged by an Opposing Party. Resolving questions of conflict of interest is primarily the responsibility of the lawyer undertaking the representation. In litigation, a court may raise the question when there is reason to infer that the lawyer has neglected the responsibility. In a criminal case, inquiry by the court is generally required when a lawyer represents multiple defendants. See MCR 6.101(C)(4). Where the conflict is such as clearly to call in question the fair or efficient administration of justice, opposing counsel may properly raise the question. Such an objection should be viewed with caution, however, for it can be misused as a technique of harassment. See Scope, *ante.*

Comments

Staff Comment to 1989 Amendment

The 1989 amendment inserts a phrase ("the relationship with") that was part of Rule 1.7(a)(1) of the American Bar Association's Model Rules, but which was omitted when Rule 1.7 was originally promulgated by the Michigan Supreme Court.

Rule 1.8.   Conflict of Interest: Prohibited Transactions

(a) A lawyer shall not enter into a business transaction with a client or knowingly acquire an ownership, possessory, security, or other pecuniary interest adverse to a client unless:

(1) the transaction and terms on which the lawyer acquires the interest are fair and reasonable to the client and are fully disclosed and transmitted in writing to the client in a manner that can be reasonably understood by the client;

(2) the client is given a reasonable opportunity to seek the advice of independent counsel in the transaction; and

(3) the client consents in writing thereto.

(b) A lawyer shall not use information relating to representation of a client to the disadvantage of the client unless the client consents after consultation, except as permitted or required by Rule 1.6 or Rule 3.3.

(c) A lawyer shall not prepare an instrument giving the lawyer or a person related to the lawyer as parent, child, sibling, or spouse any substantial gift from a client, including a testamentary gift, except where the client is related to the donee.

(d) Prior to the conclusion of representation of a client, a lawyer shall not make or negotiate an agreement giving the lawyer literary or media rights to a portrayal or account based in substantial part on information relating to the representation.

(e) A lawyer shall not provide financial assistance to a client in connection with pending or contemplated litigation, except that

(1) a lawyer may advance court costs and expenses of litigation, the repayment of which shall ultimately be the responsibility of the client; and

(2) a lawyer representing an indigent client may pay court costs and expenses of litigation on behalf of the client.

(f) A lawyer shall not accept compensation for representing a client from one other than the client unless:

(1) the client consents after consultation;

(2) there is no interference with the lawyer's independence of professional judgment or with the client-lawyer relationship; and

(3) information relating to representation of a client is protected as required by Rule 1.6.

(g) A lawyer who represents two or more clients shall not participate in making an aggregate settlement of the claims of or against the clients, or, in a criminal case, an aggregated agreement as to guilty or nolo contendere pleas, unless each client consents after consultation, including disclosure of the existence and nature of all the claims or pleas involved and of the participation of each person in the settlement.

(h) A lawyer shall not:

(1) make an agreement prospectively limiting the lawyer's liability to a client for malpractice unless permitted by law and the client is independently represented in making the agreement; or

(2) settle a claim for such liability with an unrepresented client or former client without first advising that person in writing that independent representation is appropriate in connection therewith.

(i) A lawyer related to another lawyer as parent, child, sibling, or spouse shall not represent a client in a representation directly adverse to a person whom the lawyer knows is represented by the other lawyer except upon consent by the client after consultation regarding the relationship.

(j) A lawyer shall not acquire a proprietary interest in the cause of action or subject matter of litigation the lawyer is conducting for a client, except that the lawyer may:

(1) acquire a lien granted by law to secure the lawyer's fee or expenses; and

(2) contract with a client for a reasonable contingent fee in a civil case, as permitted by Rule 1.5 and MCR 8.121.

[Comment amended effective October 15, 1998.]

Official Comment

Transactions Between Client and Lawyer. As a general principle, all transactions between client and lawyer should be fair and reasonable to the client. In such transactions a review by independent counsel on behalf of the client is often advisable. Furthermore, a lawyer may not exploit information relating to the representation to the client's disadvantage. For example, a lawyer who has learned that the client is investing in specific real estate may not, without the client's consent, seek to acquire nearby property where doing so would adversely affect the client's plan for investment. Paragraph (a) does not, however, apply to standard commercial transactions between the lawyer and the client for products or services that the client generally markets to others, for example, banking or brokerage services, medical services, products manufactured or distributed by the client, and utilities' services. In such transactions, the lawyer has no advantage in dealing with the client, and the restrictions in paragraph (a) are unnecessary and impracticable.

A lawyer may accept a gift from a client if the transaction meets general standards of fairness. For example, a simple gift such as a present given at a holiday or as a token of appreciation is permitted. If effectuation of a substantial gift requires preparing a legal instrument such as a will or conveyance, however, the client should have the detached advice that another lawyer can provide. Paragraph (c) recognizes an exception where the client is a relative of the donee or the gift is not substantial.

Literary Rights. An agreement by which a lawyer acquires literary or media rights concerning the conduct of the representation creates a conflict between the interests of the client and the personal interests of the lawyer. Measures suitable in the representation of the client may detract from the publication value of an account of the representation. Paragraph (d) does not prohibit a lawyer representing a client in a transaction concerning literary property from agreeing that the lawyer's fee shall consist of a share in ownership in the property, if the arrangement conforms to Rule 1.5 and paragraph (j).

Person Paying for Lawyer's Services. Paragraph (f) requires disclosure of the fact that the lawyer's services are being paid for by a third party. Such an arrangement must also conform to the requirements of Rule 1.6 concerning confidentiality and Rule 1.7 concerning conflict of interest. Where the client is a class, consent may be obtained on behalf of the class by court-supervised procedure.

Limiting Liability. Paragraph (h) is not intended to apply to customary qualifications and limitations in legal opinions and memoranda.

Family Relationships Between Lawyers. Paragraph (i) applies to related lawyers who are in different firms. Related lawyers in the same firm are governed by Rules 1.7, 1.9, and 1.10. The disqualification stated in paragraph (i) is personal and is not imputed to members of firms with whom the lawyers are associated.

Acquisition of Interest in Litigation. Paragraph (j) states the traditional general rule that lawyers are prohibited from acquiring a proprietary interest in litigation. This general rule, which has its basis in common-law champerty and maintenance, is subject to specific exceptions developed in decisional law and continued in these rules, such as the exception for reasonable contingent fees set forth in Rule 1.5 and the exception for certain advances of the costs of litigation set forth in paragraph (e).

Sexual Relations with Clients. After careful study, the Supreme Court declined in 1998 to adopt a proposal to amend Rule 1.8 to limit sexual relationships between lawyers and clients. The Michigan Rules of Professional Conduct adequately prohibit representation that lacks competence or diligence, or that is shadowed by a conflict of interest. With regard to sexual behavior, the Michigan Court Rules provide that a lawyer may be disciplined for "conduct that is contrary to justice, ethics, honesty, or good morals." MCR 9.104(3). Further, the Legislature has enacted criminal penalties for certain types of sexual misconduct. In this regard, it should be emphasized that a lawyer bears a fiduciary responsibility toward the client. A lawyer who has a conflict of interest, whose actions interfere with effective representation, who takes advantage of a client's vulnerability, or whose behavior is immoral risks severe sanctions under the existing Michigan Court Rules and Michigan Rules of Professional Conduct.

Rule 1.9. Conflict of Interest: Former Client

(a) A lawyer who has formerly represented a client in a matter shall not thereafter represent another person in the same or a substantially related matter in which that person's interests are materially adverse to the interests of the former client unless the former client consents after consultation.

(b) Unless the former client consents after consultation, a lawyer shall not knowingly represent a person in the same or a substantially related matter in which a firm with which the lawyer formerly was associated has previously represented a client

(1) whose interests are materially adverse to that person, and

(2) about whom the lawyer had acquired information protected by Rules 1.6 and 1.9(c) that is material to the matter.

(c) A lawyer who has formerly represented a client in a matter or whose present or former firm has formerly represented a client in a matter shall not thereafter:

(1) use information relating to the representation to the disadvantage of the former client except as Rule 1.6 or Rule 3.3 would permit or require with respect to a client, or when the information has become generally known; or

(2) reveal information relating to the representation except as Rule 1.6 or Rule 3.3 would permit or require with respect to a client.

[Amended May 22, 1990, effective August 1, 1990, 434 Mich.]

Official Comment

After termination of a client-lawyer relationship, a lawyer may not represent another client except in conformity with this rule. The principles in Rule 1.7 determine whether the interests of the present and former client are adverse.

Thus, a lawyer could not properly seek to rescind on behalf of a new client a contract drafted on behalf of the former client. So also a lawyer who has prosecuted an accused person could not properly represent the accused in a subsequent civil action against the government concerning the same transaction.

The scope of a "matter" for purposes of this rule may depend on the facts of a particular situation or transaction. The lawyer's involvement in a matter can also be a question of degree. When a lawyer has been directly involved in a specific transaction, subsequent representation of other clients with materially adverse interests clearly is prohibited. On the other hand, a lawyer who recurrently handled a type of problem for a former client is not precluded from later representing another client in a wholly distinct problem of that type even though the subsequent representation involves a position adverse to the prior client. Similar considerations can apply to the reassignment of military lawyers between defense and prosecution functions within the same military jurisdiction. The underlying question is whether the lawyer was so involved in the matter that the subsequent representation can be justly regarded as a changing of sides in the matter in question.

Lawyers Moving Between Firms. When lawyers have been associated in a firm but then end their association, the problem is more complicated. First, the client previously represented must be reasonably assured that the principle of loyalty to the client is not compromised. Second, the rule of disqualification should not be so broadly cast as to preclude other persons from having reasonable choice of legal counsel. Third, the rule of disqualification should not unreasonably hamper lawyers from forming new associations and taking on new clients after having left a previous association. In this connection, it should be recognized that today many lawyers practice in firms, that many, to some degree, limit their practice to one field or another, and that many move from one association to another several times in their careers. If the concept of imputed disqualification were applied with unqualified rigor, the result would be radical curtailment of the opportunity of lawyers to move from one practice setting to another and of the opportunity of clients to change counsel.

Reconciliation of these competing principles in the past has been attempted under two rubrics. One approach has been to seek rules of disqualification per se. For example, it has been held that a partner in a law firm is conclusively presumed to have access to all confidences concerning all clients of the firm. Under this analysis, if a lawyer has been a partner in one law firm and then becomes a partner in another law firm, there is a presumption that all confidences known by a partner in the first firm are known to all partners in the second firm. This presumption might properly be applied in some circumstances, especially where the client has been extensively represented, but may be unrealistic where the client was represented only for limited purposes. Furthermore, such a rigid rule exaggerates the difference between a partner and an associate in modern law firms.

The other rubric formerly used for dealing with vicarious disqualification is the appearance of impropriety proscribed in Canon 9 of the former Michigan Code of Professional Responsibility. Two problems can arise under this rubric. First, the appearance of impropriety might be understood to include any new client-lawyer relationship that might make a former client feel anxious. If that meaning were adopted, disqualification would become little more than a question of subjective judgment by the former client. Second, since "impropriety" is undefined, the term "appearance of impropriety" begs the question. Thus, the problem of imputed disqualification cannot readily be resolved either by simple analogy to a lawyer practicing alone or by the very general concept of appearance of impropriety.

A rule based on a functional analysis is more appropriate for determining the question of vicarious disqualification. Two functions are involved: preserving confidentiality and avoiding positions adverse to a client.

Under Rule 1.10(b), screening may be employed to preserve the confidences of a client when a lawyer has moved from one firm to another. Rule 1.10(b) applies not just to cases in which a lawyer's present and former firms are involved on the date the lawyer moves. The paragraph also applies where the lawyer's present firm later wishes to enter a case from which the lawyer is barred because of information acquired while associated with the prior firm.

Confidentiality. Preserving confidentiality is a question of access to information. Access to information, in turn, is essentially a question of fact in particular circumstances. The determination of that question of fact can be aided by inferences, deductions, or assumptions that reasonably may be made about the way in which lawyers work together. A lawyer may have general access to files of all clients of a law firm and may regularly participate in discussions of their affairs; it should be inferred that such a lawyer in fact is privy to all information about all the firm's clients. In contrast, another lawyer may have access to the files of only a limited number of clients and participate in discussion of the affairs of no other clients; in the absence of information to the contrary, it should be inferred that such a lawyer in fact is privy to information about the clients actually served but not those of other clients.

Application of paragraph (b) depends on a situation's particular facts. In any such inquiry, the burden of proof should rest upon the lawyer whose disqualification is sought.

Rule 1.10(b), incorporating paragraph (b) of this rule, operates to disqualify the firm only when the lawyer involved has actual knowledge of information protected by Rules 1.6 and 1.9(c). Thus, if a lawyer while with one firm acquired no knowledge of information relating to a particular client of the firm, and that lawyer later joined another firm, neither the lawyer individually nor the second firm is disqualified from representing another client in the same or a related matter even though the interests of the two clients conflict. See Rule 1.10(c) for the restrictions on a firm once a lawyer has terminated association with the firm.

Independent of the question of disqualification of a firm, a lawyer changing professional association has a continuing duty to preserve confidentiality of information about a client formerly represented. See Rule 1.6.

Adverse Positions. The second aspect of loyalty to a client is the lawyer's obligation to decline subsequent representations involving positions adverse to a former client arising in substantially related matters. This obligation requires abstention from adverse representation by the individual lawyer involved, but does not properly entail abstention of other lawyers through imputed disqualification. Thus, if a lawyer left one firm for another, the new affiliation would not preclude the firms involved from continuing to represent clients with adverse interests in the same or related matters, so long as the conditions of Rule 1.10(b) and (c) have been met.

Information acquired by the lawyer in the course of representing a client may not subsequently be used or revealed by the lawyer to the disadvantage of the client. However, the fact that a lawyer has once served a client does not preclude the lawyer from using generally known information about that client when later representing another client.

Disqualification from subsequent representation is for the protection of clients and can be waived by them. A waiver is effective only if there is disclosure of the circumstances, including the lawyer's intended role in behalf of the new client.

With regard to an opposing party raising a question of conflict of interest, see comment to Rule 1.7. With regard to disqualification of a firm with which a lawyer is or was formerly associated, see Rule 1.10.

Rule 1.10. Imputed Disqualification: General Rule

(a) While lawyers are associated in a firm, none of them shall knowingly represent a client when any one of them practicing alone would be prohibited from doing so by Rules 1.7, 1.8(c), 1.9(a), or 2.2. If a lawyer leaves a firm and becomes associated with another firm, MRPC 1.10(b) governs whether the new firm is imputedly disqualified because of the newly hired lawyer's prior services in or association with the lawyer's former law firm.

(b) When a lawyer becomes associated with a firm, the firm may not knowingly represent a person in the same or a substantially related matter in which that lawyer, or a firm with which the lawyer was associated, is disqualified under Rule 1.9(b), unless:

(1) the disqualified lawyer is screened from any participation in the matter and is apportioned no part of the fee therefrom; and

(2) written notice is promptly given to the appropriate tribunal to enable it to ascertain compliance with the provisions of this rule.

(c) When a lawyer has terminated an association with a firm, the firm is not prohibited from thereafter representing a person with interests materially adverse to those of a client represented by the formerly associated lawyer, and not currently represented by the firm, unless:

(1) the matter is the same or substantially related to that in which the formerly associated lawyer represented the client; and

(2) any lawyer remaining in the firm has information protected by Rules 1.6 and 1.9(c) that is material to the matter.

(d) A disqualification prescribed by this rule may be waived by the affected client under the conditions stated in Rule 1.7.

[Amended May 22, 1990, effective August 1, 1990, 434 Mich. Amended effective November 14, 2006, 477 Mich; May 22, 2007, 478 Mich.]

Official Comment

Definition of "Firm". For purposes of these rules, the term "firm" includes lawyers in a private firm and lawyers employed in the legal department of a corporation or other organization or in a legal services organization. Whether two or more lawyers constitute a firm within this definition can depend on the specific facts. For example, two practitioners who share office space and occasionally consult or assist each other ordinarily would not be regarded as constituting a firm. However, if they present themselves to the public in a way suggesting that they are a firm or conduct themselves as a firm, they should be regarded as a firm for purposes of the rules. The terms of any formal agreement between associated lawyers are relevant in determining whether they are a firm, as is the fact that they have mutual access to confidential information concerning the clients they serve. Furthermore, it is relevant in doubtful cases to consider the underlying purpose of the rule that is involved. A group of lawyers could be regarded as a firm for purposes of the rule that the same lawyer should not represent opposing parties in litigation, while it might not be so regarded for purposes of the rule that information acquired by one lawyer is attributed to another.

With respect to the law department of an organization, there is ordinarily no question that the members of the department constitute a firm within the meaning of the Rules of Professional Conduct. However, there can be uncertainty as to the identity of the client. For example, it may not be clear whether the law department of a corporation represents a subsidiary or an affiliated corporation, as well as the corporation by which the members of the department are directly employed. A similar question can arise concerning an unincorporated association and its local affiliates.

Similar questions can also arise with respect to lawyers in legal aid. Lawyers employed in the same unit of a legal service organization constitute a firm, but not necessarily those employed in separate units. As in the case of independent practitioners, whether the lawyers should be treated as being associated with each other can depend on the particular rule that is involved and on the specific facts of the situation.

Where a lawyer has joined a private firm after having represented the government, the situation is governed by Rule 1.11(a) and (b); where a lawyer represents the government after having served private clients, the situation is governed by Rule 1.11(c)(1). The individual lawyer involved is bound by the rules generally, including Rules 1.6, 1.7, and 1.9.

Principles of Imputed Disqualification. The rule of imputed disqualification stated in paragraph (a) gives effect to the principle of loyalty to the client as it applies to lawyers who practice in a law firm. Such situations can be considered from the premise that a firm of lawyers is essentially one lawyer for purposes of the rules governing loyalty to the client, or from the premise that each lawyer is vicariously bound by the obligation of loyalty owed by each lawyer with whom the lawyer is associated. Paragraph (a) operates only among the lawyers currently associated in a firm. When a lawyer moves or has recently moved from one firm to another, the situation is governed by Rules 1.9(b) and 1.10(b).

Rule 1.10(c) operates to permit a law firm, under certain circumstances, to represent a person with interests directly adverse to those of a client represented by a lawyer who formerly was associated with the firm. The rule applies regardless of when the formerly associated lawyer represented the client. However, the law firm may not represent a person with interests adverse to those of a present client of the firm, which would violate Rule 1.7. Moreover, the firm may not represent the person where the matter is the same or substantially related to that in which the formerly associated lawyer represented the client and any other lawyer currently in the firm has material information protected by Rules 1.6 and 1.9(c), unless the provisions of this rule are followed. [Amended May 22, 2007.]

Comments

Staff Comment to 2006 Amendment

This amendment clarifies that when an attorney associates with a new firm, the attorney's disqualification does not necessarily disqualify the attorney's new firm by imputed disqualification, if the new firm imposes timely and appropriate screening under MRPC 1.10(b). The amendment clarifies that MRPC 1.10(b) governs the issue of imputed disqualification following the transfer of an attorney to a new firm, which was the intent of the rule and has been the practice since the rule was adopted in 1988 and further amendments were adopted in 1990. This proposal was prompted by the decision issued in *Nat'l Union Fire Ins Co v Alticor, Inc*, ___ F3d ___; 2006 WL 2956522 (CA 6, 2006).

MRPC 1.10(a) requires that if a lawyer practicing alone is prohibited from representing a person in particular situations (including under MRPC 1.9, which prohibits representation if such representation would create a conflict of interest with a former client), then no lawyers associated with that attorney may represent such a client. The amendment of MRPC 1.10(a) removes a reference to a provision (MRPC 1.9[c]) that is unrelated to the question whether a lawyer is prohibited from representing a client. MRPC 1.9(c) prohibits a lawyer from using or revealing information gained during representation of a former client, and does not prohibit representation based on a conflict of interest. Thus, it is misplaced to use it as a basis for imputed disqualification in MRPC 1.10(a).

In addition, this order makes a correction to the reference to Rule 1.10 in the final paragraph of the current staff comment. That paragraph relates to application of the rule after a lawyer leaves a firm, which is covered by MRPC 1.10(c), and not to circumstances surrounding when a lawyer becomes associated with a firm, which is covered by MRPC 1.10(b).

Rule 1.11. Successive Government and Private Employment

(a) Except as law may otherwise expressly permit, a lawyer shall not represent a private client in connection with a matter in which the lawyer participated personally and substantially as a public officer or employee, unless the appropriate government agency consents after consultation. No lawyer in a firm with which that lawyer is associated may knowingly undertake or continue representation in such a matter, unless:

(1) the disqualified lawyer is screened from any participation in the matter and is apportioned no part of the fee therefrom; and

(2) written notice is promptly given to the appropriate government agency to enable it to ascertain compliance with the provisions of this rule.

(b) Except as law may otherwise expressly permit, a lawyer having information that the lawyer knows is confidential government information about a person, acquired when the lawyer was a public officer or employee, may not represent a private client whose interests are adverse to that person in a matter in which the information could be used to the material disadvantage of that person. A firm with which that lawyer is associated may undertake or continue representation in the matter only if the disqualified lawyer is screened from any participation in the matter and is apportioned no part of the fee therefrom.

(c) Except as law may otherwise expressly permit, a lawyer serving as a public officer or employee shall not:

(1) participate in a matter in which the lawyer participated personally and substantially while in private practice or non-governmental employment, unless under applicable law no one is, or by lawful delegation may be, authorized to act in the lawyer's stead in the matter; or

(2) negotiate for private employment with any person who is involved as a party or as an attorney for a party in a matter in which the lawyer is participating personally and substantially, except that a lawyer serving as a law clerk to a judge, other adjudicative officer, or arbitrator may negotiate for private employment in accordance with Rule 1.12(b).

(d) As used in this rule, the term "matter" includes:

(1) any judicial or other proceeding, application, request for a ruling or other determination, contract, claim, controversy, investigation, charge, accusation, arrest, or other particular matter involving a specific party or parties; and

(2) any other matter covered by the conflict of interest rules of the appropriate government agency.

(e) As used in this rule, the term "confidential government information" means information that has been obtained under governmental authority and that, at the time this rule is applied, the government is prohibited by law from disclosing to the public or has a legal privilege not to disclose, and that is not otherwise available to the public.

Official Comment

This rule prevents a lawyer from exploiting public office for the advantage of a private client. It is a counterpart of Rule 1.10(b), which applies to lawyers moving from one firm to another.

A lawyer representing a government agency, whether employed or specially retained by the government, is subject to the Rules of Professional Conduct, including the prohibition against representing adverse interests stated in Rule 1.7 and the protections afforded former clients in Rule 1.9. In addition, such a lawyer is subject to Rule 1.11 and to statutes and government regulations regarding conflict of interest. Such statutes and regulations may circumscribe the extent to which the government agency may give consent under this rule.

Where the successive clients are a public agency and a private client, the risk exists that power or discretion vested in public authority might be used for the special benefit of a private client. A lawyer should not be in a position where benefit to a private client might affect performance of the lawyer's professional functions on behalf of public authority. Also, unfair advantage could accrue to the private client by reason of access to confidential government information about the client's adversary obtainable only through the lawyer's government service. However, the rules governing lawyers presently or formerly employed by a government agency should not be so restrictive as to inhibit transfer of employment to and from the government. The government has a legitimate need to attract qualified lawyers as well as to maintain high ethical standards. The provisions for screening and waiver are necessary to prevent the disqualification rule from imposing too severe a deterrent against entering public service.

When the client is an agency of one government, that agency should be treated as a private client for purposes of this rule if the lawyer thereafter represents an agency of another government, as when a lawyer represents a city and subsequently is employed by a federal agency.

Paragraphs (a)(1) and (b) do not prohibit a lawyer from receiving a salary or partnership share established by prior independent agreement. They prohibit directly relating the attorney's compensation to the fee in the matter in which the lawyer is disqualified.

Paragraph (a)(2) does not require that a lawyer give notice to the government agency at a time when premature disclosure would injure the client; a requirement for premature disclosure might preclude engagement of the lawyer. Such notice is, however, required to be given as soon as practicable in order that the government agency will have a reasonable opportunity to ascertain that the lawyer is complying with Rule 1.11 and to take appropriate action if it believes the lawyer is not complying.

Paragraph (b) operates only when the lawyer in question has knowledge of the information, which means actual knowledge; it does not operate with respect to information that merely could be imputed to the lawyer.

Paragraphs (a) and (c) do not prohibit a lawyer from jointly representing a private party and a government agency when doing so is permitted by Rule 1.7 and is not otherwise prohibited by law.

Paragraph (c) does not disqualify other lawyers in the agency with which the lawyer in question has become associated.

Rule 1.12. Former Judge or Arbitrator

(a) Except as stated in paragraph (d), a lawyer shall not represent anyone in connection with a matter in which the lawyer participated personally and substantially as a judge or other adjudicative officer, arbitrator, or law clerk to such a person, unless all parties to the proceeding consent after consultation.

(b) A lawyer shall not negotiate for employment with any person who is involved as a party, or as an attorney for a party, in a matter in which the lawyer is participating personally and substantially as a judge or other adjudicative officer or arbitrator. A lawyer serving as a law clerk to a judge, other adjudicative officer, or arbitrator may negotiate for employment with a party or attorney involved in a matter in which the clerk is participating personally and substantially, but only after the lawyer has notified the judge, other adjudicative officer, or arbitrator.

(c) If a lawyer is disqualified by paragraph (a), no lawyer in a firm with which that lawyer is associated may knowingly undertake or continue representation in the matter, unless:

(1) the disqualified lawyer is screened from any participation in the matter and is apportioned no part of the fee therefrom; and

(2) written notice is promptly given to the appropriate tribunal to enable it to ascertain compliance with the provisions of this rule.

(d) An arbitrator selected as a partisan of a party in a multimember arbitration panel is not prohibited from subsequently representing that party.

Official Comment

This rule generally parallels Rule 1.11. The term "personally and substantially" signifies that a judge who was a member of a multimember court, and thereafter left judicial office to practice law, is not prohibited from representing a client in a matter pending in the court, but in which the former judge did not participate. So also the fact that a former judge exercised administrative responsibility in a court does not prevent the former judge from acting as a lawyer in a matter where the judge had previously exercised remote or incidental administrative responsibility that did not affect the merits. Compare the comment to Rule 1.11. The term "adjudicative officer" includes such officials as judges pro tempore, referees, special masters, hearing officers and other parajudicial officers, and also lawyers who serve as part-time judges.

Rule 1.13.   Organization as Client

(a) A lawyer employed or retained to represent an organization represents the organization as distinct from its directors, officers, employees, members, shareholders, or other constituents.

(b) If a lawyer for an organization knows that an officer, employee, or other person associated with the organization is engaged in action, intends to act, or refuses to act in a matter related to the representation that is a violation of a legal obligation to the organization, or a violation of law which reasonably might be imputed to the organization, and that is likely to result in substantial injury to the organization, the lawyer shall proceed as is reasonably necessary in the best interest of the organization. In determining how to proceed, the lawyer shall give due consideration to the seriousness of the violation and its consequences, the scope and nature of the lawyer's representation, the responsibility in the organization, and the apparent motivation of the person involved, the policies of the organization concerning such matters, and any other relevant considerations. Any measures taken shall be designed to minimize disruption of the organization and the risk of revealing information relating to the representation to persons outside the organization. Such measures may include among others:

(1) asking reconsideration of the matter;

(2) advising that a separate legal opinion on the matter be sought for presentation to appropriate authority in the organization; and

(3) referring the matter to higher authority in the organization, including, if warranted by the seriousness of the matter,

referral to the highest authority that can act in behalf of the organization as determined by applicable law.

(c) When the organization's highest authority insists upon action, or refuses to take action, that is clearly a violation of a legal obligation to the organization or a violation of law which reasonably might be imputed to the organization, and that is likely to result in substantial injury to the organization, the lawyer may take further remedial action that the lawyer reasonably believes to be in the best interest of the organization. Such action may include revealing information otherwise protected by Rule 1.6 only if the lawyer reasonably believes that

(1) the highest authority in the organization has acted to further the personal or financial interests of members of that authority which are in conflict with the interests of the organization; and

(2) revealing the information is necessary in the best interest of the organization.

(d) In dealing with an organization's directors, officers, employees, members, shareholders, or other constituents, a lawyer shall explain the identity of the client when the lawyer believes that such explanation is necessary to avoid misunderstandings on their part.

(e) A lawyer representing an organization may also represent any of its directors, officers, employees, members, shareholders, or other constituents, subject to the provisions of Rule 1.7. If the organization's consent to the dual representation is required by Rule 1.7, the consent shall be given by an appropriate official of the organization other than the individual who is to be represented, or by the shareholders.

Official Comment

The Entity as the Client. In transactions with their lawyers, clients who are individuals can speak and decide for themselves, finally and authoritatively. In transactions between an organization and its lawyer, however, the organization can speak and decide only through agents, such as its officers or employees. In effect, the client-lawyer relationship is maintained through an intermediary between the client and the lawyer. This fact requires the lawyer under certain conditions to be concerned whether the intermediary legitimately represents the client.

When officers or employees of the organization make decisions for it, the decisions ordinarily must be accepted by the lawyer even if their utility or prudence is doubtful. Decisions concerning policy and operations, including ones entailing serious risk, are not as such in the lawyer's province. However, different considerations arise when the lawyer knows that the organization may be substantially injured by action of an officer or employee that is in violation of law. In such a circumstance, it may be reasonably necessary for the lawyer to ask the officer, employee, or other agent to reconsider the matter. If that fails, or if the matter is of sufficient seriousness and importance to the organization, it may be reasonably necessary for the lawyer to take steps to have the matter reviewed by a higher authority in the organization. Clear justification should exist for seeking review over the head of the officer or employee normally responsible for it. The stated policy of the organization may define circumstances and prescribe channels for such review, and a lawyer should encourage formulation of such a policy. Even in the absence of organization policy, however, the lawyer may have an obligation to refer a matter to higher authority, depending on the seriousness of the matter and whether the officer in question has apparent motives to act at variance with the organization's interest. Review by the chief executive officer or by the board of directors may be required when the matter is of importance commensurate with their authority. At some point it may be useful or essential to obtain an independent legal opinion.

In an extreme case, it may be reasonably necessary for the lawyer to refer the matter to the organization's highest authority. Ordinarily, that is the board of directors or similar governing body. However, applicable law may prescribe that under certain conditions highest authority reposes elsewhere, for example, in the independent directors of a corporation. The ultimately difficult question is whether the lawyer should be permitted to circumvent the organization's highest authority when it persists in a course of action that is clearly violative of law or a legal obligation to the organization and that is likely to result in substantial injury to the organization.

In such a situation, if the lawyer can take remedial action without a disclosure of information that might adversely affect the organization, the lawyer as a matter of professional discretion may take such actions as the lawyer reasonably believes to be in the best interest of the organization. For example, a lawyer for a close corporation may find it reasonably necessary to disclose misconduct by the board to the shareholders. However, taking such action could entail disclosure of information relating to the representation with consequent risk of injury to the client. When such is the case, the organization is threatened by alternative injuries: the injury that may result from the governing board's action or refusal to act, and the injury that may result if the lawyer's remedial efforts entail disclosure of confidential information. The lawyer may pursue remedial efforts even at the risk of disclosure in the circumstances stated in subparagraphs (c)(1) and (c)(2).

Relation to Other Rules. The authority and responsibility provided in Rules 1.13(b) and (c) are concurrent with the authority and responsibility provided in other rules. In particular, this rule does not limit the lawyer's authority under Rule 1.6, the responsibilities to the client under Rules 1.8 and 1.16 and the responsibilities of the lawyer under Rule 3.3 or 4.1. If the lawyer's services are being used by an organization to further an illegal act or fraud by the organization, Rule 1.2(c) can be applicable. In connection with complying with Rule 1.2(c), 3.3 or 4.1, or exercising the discretion conferred by Rule 1.6(c), a lawyer for an organization may be in doubt whether the conduct will actually be carried out by the organization. To guide conduct in such circumstances, the lawyer ordinarily should make inquiry within the organization as indicated in Rule 1.13(b).

When the lawyer involved is a member of a firm, the firm's procedures may require referral of difficult questions to a superior in the firm. In that event, Rule 5.2 may be applicable.

Unincorporated Associations. The duty defined in this rule applies to unincorporated associations.

Governmental Agency. The duty defined in this rule applies to governmental organizations. However, when the client is a governmental organization, a different balance may be appropriate between maintaining confidentiality and assuring that the wrongful official act is prevented or rectified because public business is involved. In addition, duties of lawyers employed by the government or lawyers in military service may be defined by statutes and regulations. Therefore, defining precisely the identity of the client and prescribing the resulting obligations of such lawyers may be more difficult in the government context. In some circumstances, it may be a specific agency, but in others it may be the government as a whole. For example, if the action or failure to act involves the head of a bureau, the department of which the bureau is a part may be the client for purpose of this rule. With these qualifications, the lawyer's substantive duty to the client and reasonable courses of action are essentially the same as when the client is a private organization.

Clarifying the Lawyer's Role. The fact that the organization is the client may be quite unclear to the organization's officials and employees. An organization official accustomed to working with the organization's lawyer may forget that the lawyer represents the organization and not the official. The result of such a misunderstanding can be embarrassing or prejudicial to the individual if, for example, the situation is such that the client-lawyer privilege will not protect the individual's communications to the lawyer. The lawyer should take reasonable care to prevent such consequences. The measures required depend on the circumstances. In routine legal matters, a lawyer for a large corporation does not have to explain to a corporate official that the corporation is the client. On the other hand, if the lawyer is conducting an inquiry involving possible illegal activity, a warning might be essential to prevent unfairness to a corporate employee. See also Rule 4.3.

Dual Representation. Paragraph (e) recognizes that a lawyer for an organization may also represent a principal officer or major shareholder. Such common representation, although often undertaken in practice, can entail serious potential conflicts of interest.

Derivative Actions. Under generally prevailing law, the shareholders or members of a corporation may bring suit to compel the directors to perform their legal obligations in the supervision of the organization. Members of unincorporated associations have essentially the same right. Such an action may be brought nominally by the organization, but usually is, in fact, a legal controversy over management of the organization.

The question can arise whether counsel for the organization may defend such an action. The proposition that the organization is the lawyer's client does not alone resolve the issue. Most derivative actions are a normal incident of an organization's affairs, to be defended by the organization's lawyer like any other suit. However, if the claim involves serious charges of wrongdoing by those in control of the organization, a conflict may arise between the lawyer's duty to the

organization and the lawyer's relationship with the board. In those circumstances, Rule 1.7 governs whether independent counsel should represent the directors.

Rule 1.14.   Client Under a Disability

(a) When a client's ability to make adequately considered decisions in connection with the representation is impaired, whether because of minority or mental disability or for some other reason, the lawyer shall, as far as reasonably possible, maintain a normal client-lawyer relationship with the client.

(b) A lawyer may seek the appointment of a guardian or take other protective action with respect to a client only when the lawyer reasonably believes that the client cannot adequately act in the client's own interest.

Official Comment

The normal client-lawyer relationship is based on the assumption that the client, when properly advised and assisted, is capable of making decisions about important matters. When the client is a minor or suffers from a mental disorder or disability, however, maintaining the ordinary client-lawyer relationship may not be possible in all respects. In particular, an incapacitated person may have no power to make legally binding decisions. Nevertheless, a client lacking legal competence often has the ability to understand, deliberate upon, and reach conclusions about matters affecting the client's own well-being. Furthermore, to an increasing extent the law recognizes intermediate degrees of competence. For example, children as young as five or six years of age, and certainly those of ten or twelve, are regarded as having opinions that are entitled to weight in legal proceedings concerning their custody. So also, it is recognized that some persons of advanced age can be quite capable of handling routine financial matters while needing special legal protection concerning major transactions.

The fact that a client suffers a disability does not diminish the lawyer's obligation to treat the client with attention and respect. If the person has no guardian or legal representative, the lawyer often must act de facto as guardian. Even if the person does have a legal representative, the lawyer should as far as possible accord the represented person the status of client, particularly in maintaining communication.

If a legal representative has already been appointed for the client, the lawyer should ordinarily look to the representative for decisions on behalf of the client. If a legal representative has not been appointed, the lawyer should see to such an appointment where it would serve the client's best interests. Thus, if a disabled client has substantial property that should be sold for the client's benefit, effective completion of the transaction ordinarily requires appointment of a legal representative. In many circumstances, however, appointment of a legal representative may be expensive or traumatic for the client. Evaluation of these considerations is a matter of professional judgment on the lawyer's part.

If the lawyer represents the guardian as distinct from the ward, and is aware that the guardian is acting adversely to the ward's interest, the lawyer may have an obligation to prevent or rectify the guardian's misconduct. See Rule 1.2(c).

If the lawyer seeks the appointment of a legal representative for the client, the filing of the request itself, together with the facts upon which it is predicated, may constitute the disclosure of confidential information which could be used against the client. If the court to whom the matter is submitted thereafter determines that a legal representative is not necessary, the harm befalling the client as the result of the disclosure may be irreparable. Consequently, consideration should be given to initially filing the petition seeking the appointment of a legal representative ex parte so that the court can decide how best to proceed to minimize the potential adverse consequences to the client by, for example, issuing a protective order limiting the disclosure of the confidential information upon which the request is predicated.

Disclosure of the Client's Condition. Rules of procedure in litigation generally provide that minors or persons suffering mental disability shall be represented by a guardian or next friend if they do not have a general guardian. However, disclosure of the client's disability can adversely affect the client's interests. For example, raising the question of disability could, in some circumstances, lead to proceedings for involuntary commitment. The lawyer's position in such cases is an unavoidably difficult one. The lawyer may seek guidance from an appropriate diagnostician.

Rule 1.15.   Safekeeping Property

(a) Definitions.

(1) "Allowable reasonable fees" for IOLTA accounts are per check charges, per deposit charges, a fee in lieu of a minimum balance, federal deposit insurance fees, sweep fees, and a reasonable IOLTA account administrative or maintenance fee. All other fees are the responsibility of, and may be charged to, the lawyer maintaining the IOLTA account. Fees or charges in excess of the interest or dividends earned on the account for any month or quarter shall not be taken from interest or dividends earned on other IOLTA accounts or from the principal of the account.

(2) An "eligible institution" for IOLTA accounts is a bank, credit union, or savings and loan association authorized by federal or state law to do business in Michigan, the deposits of which are insured by an agency of the federal government, or is an open-end investment company registered with the Securities and Exchange Commission authorized by federal or state law to do business in Michigan. The eligible institution must pay no less on an IOLTA account than the highest interest rate or dividend generally available from the institution to its non–IOLTA customers when the IOLTA account meets the same minimum balance or other eligibility qualifications. Interest or dividends and fees shall be calculated in accordance with the eligible institution's standard practice, but institutions may elect to pay a higher interest or dividend rate and may elect to waive any fees on IOLTA accounts.

(3) "IOLTA account" refers to an interest- or dividend-bearing account, as defined by the Michigan State Bar Foundation, at an eligible institution from which funds may be withdrawn upon request as soon as permitted by law. An IOLTA account shall include only client or third person funds that cannot earn income for the client or third person in excess of the costs incurred to secure such income while the funds are held.

(4) "Non-IOLTA account" refers to an interest- or dividend-bearing account from which funds may be withdrawn upon request as soon as permitted by law in banks, savings and loan associations, and credit unions authorized by federal or state law to do business in Michigan, the deposits of which are insured by an agency of the federal government. Such an account shall be established as:

(A) a separate client trust account for the particular client or matter on which the net interest or dividend will be paid to the client or third person, or

(B) a pooled client trust account with subaccounting by the bank or savings and loan association or by the lawyer, which will provide for computation of net interest or dividend earned by each client or third person's funds and the payment thereof to the client or third person.

(5) "Lawyer" includes a law firm or other organization with which a lawyer is professionally associated.

(b) A lawyer shall:

(1) promptly notify the client or third person when funds or property in which a client or third person has an interest is received;

(2) preserve complete records of such account funds and other property for a period of five years after termination of the representation; and

(3) promptly pay or deliver any funds or other property that the client or third person is entitled to receive, except as stated in this rule or otherwise permitted by law or by agreement with the client or third person, and, upon request by the client or third person, promptly render a full accounting regarding such property.

(c) When two or more persons (one of whom may be the lawyer) claim interest in the property, it shall be kept separate by the lawyer until the dispute is resolved. The lawyer shall promptly distribute all portions of the property as to which the interests are not in dispute.

(d) A lawyer shall hold property of clients or third persons in connection with a representation separate from the lawyer's own property. All client or third person funds shall be deposited in an IOLTA or non-IOLTA account. Other property shall be identified as such and appropriately safeguarded.

(e) In determining whether client or third person funds should be deposited in an IOLTA account or a non-IOLTA account, a lawyer shall consider the following factors:

(1) the amount of interest or dividends the funds would earn during the period that they are expected to be deposited in light of (a) the amount of the funds to be deposited; (b) the expected duration of the deposit, including the likelihood of delay in the matter for which the funds are held; and (c) the rates of interest or yield at financial institutions where the funds are to be deposited;

(2) the cost of establishing and administering non-IOLTA accounts for the client or third person's benefit, including service charges or fees, the lawyer's services, preparation of tax reports, or other associated costs;

(3) the capability of financial institutions or lawyers to calculate and pay income to individual clients or third persons; and

(4) any other circumstances that affect the ability of the funds to earn a net return for the client or third person.

(f) A lawyer may deposit the lawyer's own funds in a client trust account only in an amount reasonably necessary to pay financial institution service charges or fees or to obtain a waiver of service charges or fees.

(g) Legal fees and expenses that have been paid in advance shall be deposited in a client trust account and may be withdrawn only as fees are earned or expenses incurred.

(h) No interest or dividends from the client trust account shall be available to the lawyer.

(i) The lawyer shall direct the eligible institution to:

(1) remit the interest and dividends from an IOLTA account, less allowable reasonable fees, if any, to the Michigan State Bar Foundation at least quarterly;

(2) transmit with each remittance a report that shall identify each lawyer for whom the remittance is sent, the amount of remittance attributable to each IOLTA account, the rate and type of interest or dividends applied, the amount of interest or dividends earned, the amount and type of fees deducted, if any, and the average account balance for the period in which the report is made; and

(3) transmit to the depositing lawyer a report in accordance with normal procedures for reporting to its depositors.

(j) A lawyer's good-faith decision regarding the deposit or holding of such funds in an IOLTA account is not reviewable by a disciplinary body. A lawyer shall review the IOLTA account at reasonable intervals to determine whether changed circumstances require the funds to be deposited prospectively in a non-IOLTA account.

[Amended February 21, 1990, effective October 1, 1990, 434 Mich. Amended effective June 15, 2005, 472 Mich; October 18, 2005, 474 Mich; February 4, 2015, 497 Mich; September 23, 2015, 498 Mich.]

Official Comment

A lawyer should hold property of others with the care required of a professional fiduciary. Securities should be kept in a safe deposit box, except when some other form of safekeeping is warranted by special circumstances. All property which is the property of a client or a third person should be kept separate from the lawyer's business and personal property and, if funds, should be kept in one or more trust accounts. Separate trust accounts may be warranted when administering estate funds or acting in similar fiduciary capacities.

Lawyers often receive from third persons funds from which the lawyer's fee will be paid. If there is risk that the client may divert the funds without paying the fee, the lawyer is not required to remit the portion from which the fee is to be paid. However, a lawyer may not hold funds to coerce a client into accepting the lawyer's contention. The disputed portion of the funds should be kept in trust and the lawyer should suggest means for prompt resolution of the dispute, such as arbitration. The undisputed portion of the funds shall be promptly distributed.

A third person, such as a client's creditors, may have a just claim against funds or other property in a lawyer's custody. A lawyer may have a duty under applicable law to protect such a third-party claim against wrongful interference by the client, and accordingly may refuse to surrender the property to the client. However, a lawyer should not unilaterally assume to arbitrate a dispute between the client and the third person.

The obligations of a lawyer under this rule are independent of those arising from activity other than rendering legal services. For example, a lawyer who serves as an escrow agent is governed by the applicable law relating to fiduciaries even though the lawyer does not render legal services in the transaction.

Comments

Staff Comment to June, 2005 Amendment

The amendments to MRPC 1.15, effective immediately, are intended to provide interest rate parity with investments in non-IOLTA accounts in order to maximize the return on the investments for the benefit of the Michigan Bar Foundation.

Staff Comment to October, 2005 Amendment

The amendment of MRPC 1.15 conforms with the decision in Brown v Legal Foundation of Washington, 538 US 216; 123 S Ct 1406; 155 L Ed 2d 376 (2003), to create interest rate parity with non-IOLTA investments consistent with changes in financial products presently available in the market, and to make other revenue enhancing modifications to the IOLTA program.

Staff Comment to 2015 Amendment

The amendment of MRPC 1.15 adds "credit union" to the definition of "eligible institution" for deposit of IOLTA funds. This change reflects a recent federal statutory amendment that extends federal insurance protection to IOLTA deposits held in credit unions. PL 113–252.

Rule 1.15A.   Trust Account Overdraft Notification

(a) Scope. Lawyers who practice law in this jurisdiction shall deposit all funds held in trust in accordance with Rule 1.15. Funds held in trust include funds held in any fiduciary capacity in connection with a representation, whether as trustee, agent, guardian, executor or otherwise.

(1) "Lawyer" includes a law firm or other organization with which a lawyer is professionally associated.

(2) For any trust account which is an IOLTA account pursuant to Rule 1.15, the "Notice to Eligible Financial Institution" shall constitute notice to the depository institution that such account is subject to this rule. Lawyers shall clearly identify any other accounts in which funds are held in trust as "trust" or "escrow" accounts, and lawyers must inform the depository institution in writing that such other accounts are trust accounts for the purposes of this rule.

(b) Overdraft Notification Agreement Required. In addition to meeting the requirements of Rule 1.15, each bank, credit union, savings and loan association, savings bank, or open-end investment company registered with the Securities and Exchange Commission (hereinafter "financial institution") referred to in Rule 1.15 must be approved by the State Bar of Michigan in order to serve as a depository for lawyer trust accounts. To apply for approval, financial institutions must file with the State Bar of Michigan a signed agreement, in a form provided by the State Bar of Michigan, that it will submit the reports required in paragraph (d) of this rule to the Grievance Administrator and the trust account holder when any properly payable instrument is presented against a lawyer trust account containing insufficient funds or when any other debit to such account would create a negative balance in the account, whether or not the instrument or other debit is honored and irrespective of any overdraft protection or other similar privileges that may attach to such account. The agreement shall apply to the financial institution for all of its locations in Michigan and cannot be canceled except on 120 days notice in writing to the State Bar of Michigan. Upon notice of cancellation or termination of the agreement, the financial institution must notify all holders of trust accounts subject to the provisions of this rule at least 90 days before termination of approved status that the financial institution will no longer be approved to hold such trust accounts.

(c) The State Bar of Michigan shall establish guidelines regarding the process of approving and terminating "approved status" for financial institutions, and for other operational procedures to effectuate this rule in consultation with the Grievance Administrator. The State Bar of Michigan shall periodically publish a list of approved financial institutions. No trust account shall be maintained in any financial institution that has not been so approved. Approved status under this rule does not substitute for "eligible financial institution" status under Rule 1.15.

(d) Overdraft Reports. The overdraft notification agreement must provide that all reports made by the financial institution contain the following information in a form acceptable to the State Bar of Michigan:

(1) The identity of the financial institution

(2) The identity of the account holder

(3) The account number

(4) Information identifying the transaction item

(5) The amount and date of the overdraft and either the amount of the returned instrument or other dishonored debit to the account and the date returned or dishonored, or the date of presentation for payment and the date paid.

The financial institution must provide the information required by the notification agreement within five banking days after the date the item was paid or returned unpaid.

(e) Costs. The overdraft notification agreement must provide that a financial institution is not prohibited from charging the lawyer for the reasonable cost of providing the reports and records required by this rule, but those costs may not be charged against principal, nor against interest or dividends earned on trust accounts, including earnings on IOLTA accounts payable to the Michigan State Bar Foundation under Rule 1.15. Such costs, if charged, shall not be borne by clients.

(f) Notification by Lawyers. Every lawyer who receives notification that any instrument presented against the trust account was presented against insufficient funds or that any other debit to such account would create a negative balance in the account, whether or not the instrument or other debit was honored, shall, upon receipt of a request for investigation from the Grievance Administrator, provide the Grievance Administrator, in writing, within 21 days after issuance of such request, a full and fair explanation of the cause of the overdraft and how it was corrected.

(g) Every lawyer practicing or admitted to practice in this jurisdiction shall, as a condition thereof, be conclusively deemed to have consented to the requirements mandated by this rule and shall be deemed to have consented under applicable privacy laws, including but not limited to those of the Gramm–Leach–Bliley Act, 15 USC 6801, to the reporting of information required by this rule.

[Adopted December 15, 2009, effective September 15, 2010, 485 Mich.]

Comments

Staff Comment to 2010 Adoption

This new rule, submitted by the State Bar of Michigan and supported by the Attorney Grievance Commission, requires attorneys to maintain client trust accounts in approved financial institutions. The State Bar of Michigan will establish guidelines for approving and terminating "approved status" for financial institutions, and will periodically publish a list of approved financial institutions. The financial institutions become approved by, among other requirements, agreeing to notify the Grievance Administrator and the lawyer if a lawyer's trust account is overdrawn. If the Grievance Administrator sends the lawyer a request for investigation based on the overdraft, the lawyer is required to submit an explanation of the overdraft to the Grievance Administrator within 21 days.

Rule 1.16. Declining or Terminating Representation

(a) Except as stated in paragraph (c), a lawyer shall not represent a client or, where representation has commenced, shall withdraw from the representation of a client if:

(1) the representation will result in violation of the Rules of Professional Conduct or other law;

(2) the lawyer's physical or mental condition materially impairs the lawyer's ability to represent the client; or

(3) the lawyer is discharged.

(b) Except as stated in paragraph (c), after informing the client that the lawyer cannot do so without permission from the tribunal for the pending case, a lawyer may withdraw from representing a client if withdrawal can be accomplished without material adverse effect on the interests of the client, or if:

(1) the client persists in a course of action involving the lawyer's services that the lawyer reasonably believes is criminal or fraudulent;

(2) the client has used the lawyer's services to perpetrate a crime or fraud;

(3) the client insists upon pursuing an objective that the lawyer considers repugnant or imprudent;

(4) the client fails substantially to fulfill an obligation to the lawyer regarding the lawyer's services and has been given reasonable warning that the lawyer will withdraw unless the obligation is fulfilled;

(5) the representation will result in an unreasonable financial burden on the lawyer or has been rendered unreasonably difficult by the client; or

(6) other good cause for withdrawal exists.

(c) When ordered to do so by a tribunal, a lawyer shall continue representation notwithstanding good cause for terminating the representation.

(d) Upon termination of representation, a lawyer shall take reasonable steps to protect a client's interests, such as giving reasonable notice to the client, allowing time for employment of other counsel, surrendering papers and property to which the client is entitled, and refunding any advance payment of fee that has not been earned. The lawyer may retain papers relating to the client to the extent permitted by law.

[Amended May 23, 2018, effective September 1, 2018, 501 Mich.]

Official Comment

A lawyer should not accept representation in a matter unless it can be performed competently, promptly, without improper conflict of interest and to completion.

Mandatory Withdrawal. A lawyer ordinarily must decline or withdraw from representation if the client demands that the lawyer engage in conduct that is illegal or violates the Rules of Professional Conduct or other law. The lawyer is not obliged to decline or withdraw simply because the client suggests such a course of conduct; a client may make such a suggestion in the hope that a lawyer will not be constrained by a professional obligation.

When a lawyer has been appointed to represent a client, withdrawal ordinarily requires approval of the appointing authority. See also Rule 6.2. Difficulty may be encountered if withdrawal is based on the client's demand that the lawyer engage in unprofessional conduct. The court may wish an explanation for the withdrawal, while the lawyer may be bound to keep confidential the facts that would constitute such an explanation. The lawyer's statement that professional considerations require termination of the representation ordinarily should be accepted as sufficient.

Discharge. A client has a right to discharge a lawyer at any time, with or without cause, subject to liability for payment for the lawyer's services. Where future dispute about the withdrawal may be anticipated, it may be advisable to prepare a written statement reciting the circumstances.

Whether a client can discharge appointed counsel may depend on applicable law. A client seeking to do so should be given a full explanation of the consequences. These consequences may include a decision by the appointing authority that appointment of successor counsel is unjustified, thus requiring the client to represent himself.

If the client is mentally incompetent, the client may lack the legal capacity to discharge the lawyer, and in any event the discharge may be seriously adverse to the client's interests. The lawyer should make special effort to help the client consider the consequences and, in an extreme case, may initiate proceedings for a conservatorship or similar protection of the client. See Rule 1.14.

Optional Withdrawal. A lawyer may withdraw from representation in some circumstances. The lawyer has the option to withdraw if it can be accomplished without material adverse effect on the client's interests. Withdrawal is also justified if the client persists in a course of action that the lawyer reasonably believes is illegal or fraudulent, for a lawyer is not required to be associated with such conduct even if the lawyer does not further it. Withdrawal is also permitted if the lawyer's services were misused in the past even if that would materially prejudice the client. The lawyer also may withdraw where the client insists on a repugnant or imprudent objective.

A lawyer may withdraw if the client refuses to abide by the terms of an agreement relating to the representation, such as an agreement concerning fees or court costs, or an agreement limiting the objectives of the representation.

Assisting the Client Upon Withdrawal. Even if the lawyer has been unfairly discharged by the client, a lawyer must take all reasonable steps to mitigate the consequences to the client. The lawyer may retain papers as security for a fee only to the extent permitted by law.

Whether a lawyer for an organization may under certain unusual circumstances have a legal obligation to the organization after withdrawing or being discharged by the organization's highest authority is beyond the scope of these rules.

Comments

Staff Comment to 2018 Amendment

The amendment of MRPC 1.16 addresses the concern raised during the Court's consideration of *People v Townsend*, docket 153153, to ensure that criminal defendants are made aware of the fact that an attorney cannot withdraw without the court's permission.

Rule 1.17.   Sale of a Law Practice

(a) A lawyer or a law firm may sell or purchase a private law practice, including good will, pursuant to this rule.

(b) The fees charged clients shall not be increased by reason of the sale, and a purchaser shall not pass on the cost of good will to a client. The purchaser may, however, refuse to undertake the representation unless the client consents to pay fees regularly charged by the purchaser for rendering substantially similar services to other clients prior to the initiation of the purchase negotiations.

(c) Actual written notice of a pending sale shall be given at least 91 days prior to the date of the sale to each of the seller's clients, and the notice shall include:

(1) notice of the fact of the proposed sale;

(2) the identity of the purchaser;

(3) the terms of any proposed change in the fee agreement permitted under paragraph (b);

(4) notice of the client's right to retain other counsel or to take possession of the file; and

(5) notice that the client's consent to the transfer of the client's file to the purchaser will be presumed if the client does not retain other counsel or otherwise object within 90 days of receipt of the notice.

If the purchaser has identified a conflict of interest that the client cannot waive and that prohibits the purchaser from undertaking the client's matter, the notice shall advise that the client should retain substitute counsel to assume the representation and arrange to have the substitute counsel contact the seller.

(d) If a client cannot be given actual notice as required in paragraph (c), the representation of that client may be transferred to the purchaser only upon entry of an order so authorizing by a judge of the judicial circuit in which the seller maintains the practice. The seller or the purchaser may disclose to the judge in camera information relating to the representation only to the extent necessary to obtain an order authorizing the transfer of a file.

(e) The sale of the good will of a law practice may be conditioned upon the seller ceasing to engage in the private practice of law for a reasonable period of time within the geographical area in which the practice had been conducted.

[Adopted May 31, 1991, effective October 1, 1991, 437 Mich.]

Official Comment

This rule permits a selling lawyer or law firm to obtain compensation for the reasonable value of a private law practice in the same manner as withdrawing partners of law firms. See MRPC 5.4 and 5.6. This rule does not apply to the transfer of responsibility for legal representation from one lawyer or firm to another when such transfers are unrelated to the sale of a practice; for transfer of individual files in other circumstances, see MRPC 1.5(e) and 1.16. Admission to or retirement from a law partnership or professional association, retirement plans and similar arrangements, and a sale of tangible assets of a law practice, do not constitute a sale or purchase governed by this rule.

A lawyer participating in the sale of a law practice is subject to the ethical standards that apply when involving another lawyer in the representation of a client. These include, for example, the seller's obligation to act competently in identifying a purchaser qualified to assume the representation of the client and

the purchaser's obligation to undertake the representation competently, MRPC 1.1, the obligation to avoid disqualifying conflicts and to secure client consent after consultation for those conflicts that can be waived, MRPC 1.7, and the obligation to protect information relating to the representation, MRPC 1.6 and 1.9.

If approval of the substitution of the purchasing attorney for the selling attorney is required by the rules of any tribunal in which a matter is pending, such approval must be obtained before the matter can be included in the sale, MRPC 1.16. See also MCR 2.117(C).

All the elements of client autonomy, including the client's absolute right to discharge a lawyer and transfer the representation to another, survive the sale of the practice.

Selling Entire Practice. When a lawyer is closing a private practice, the lawyer may negotiate with a purchaser for the reasonable value of the practice that has been developed by the seller. A seller may agree to transfer matters in one legal field to one purchaser, while transferring matters in another legal field to a separate purchaser. However, a lawyer may not sell individual files piecemeal. A seller closing a practice to accept employment with another firm may take certain matters to the new employer while selling the remainder of the practice.

Although the rule contemplates the sale of substantially all of the law practice, a seller retiring from private practice generally may continue to represent a small number of clients while transferring the balance of the practice.

The seller remains responsible for handling all client matters until the files are transferred under this rule.

Termination of Practice by the Seller. The rule allows the parties to agree that the seller cease practice in the geographical area for a reasonable time as a condition of the sale. In certain situations, a blanket prohibition on the seller's practice would not be appropriate or warranted, such as a judicial appointee who might subsequently be defeated for reelection, or a seller elected full-time prosecutor. The parties should be allowed to negotiate, for instance, whether any geographical or duration restrictions apply to the seller's employment as a lawyer on the staff of a public agency or of a legal services entity that provides legal services to the poor, or as inside counsel to a business.

Conflicts. The practice may be sold to one or more lawyers or firms, provided that the seller assures that all clients are afforded competent representation. Since the number of client matters and their nature directly bear on the valuation of good will and therefore directly relate to selling the law practice, conflicts that cannot be waived by the client and that prevent the prospective purchaser from undertaking the client's matter should be determined promptly. If the purchaser identifies a conflict that the client cannot waive, information should be provided to the client to assist in locating substitute counsel. If the conflict can be waived by the client, the purchaser should explain the implications and determine whether the client consents to the purchaser undertaking the representation. Initial screening with regard to conflicts, for the purpose of determining the good will of the practice, need be no more intrusive than conflict screening of a walk-in prospective client at the purchaser's firm.

Client Confidences, Consent, and Notice. Negotiations between the seller and prospective purchaser prior to disclosure of information relating to a specific representation of an identifiable client can be conducted in a manner that does not violate the confidentiality provisions of MRPC 1.6, just as preliminary discussions are permissible concerning the possible association of another lawyer or mergers between firms, with respect to which client consent is not required. Providing the purchaser access to client-specific information relating to the representation and to the file, however, requires client consent. The rule provides that before such information can be disclosed by the seller to the purchaser the client must be given actual written notice of the fact of the contemplated sale, including the identity of the purchaser, and must be told that the decision to consent or make other arrangements must be made within 90 days. If nothing is heard from the client within that time, consent to the transfer of the client's file to the identified purchaser is presumed.

A lawyer or law firm ceasing to practice cannot be required to remain in practice because some clients cannot be given actual notice of the proposed purchase. Since these clients are not available to consent to the purchase or direct any other disposition of their files, the rule requires an order from a judge of the judicial circuit in which the seller maintains the practice, authorizing their transfer or other disposition. The court can be expected to determine whether reasonable efforts to locate the client have been exhausted, and whether the absent client's legitimate interests will be served by authorizing the transfer of the file so that the purchaser may continue the representation. Preservation of client confidences requires that the petition for a court order be considered in camera.

The client should be told the identity of the purchaser before being asked to consent to disclosure of confidences and secrets or to consent to transfer of the file.

MCR 9.119(G) provides a mechanism for handling client matters when a lawyer dies and there is no one else at the firm to take responsibility for the file.

Fee Arrangements Between Client and Purchaser. Paragraph (b) is intended to prohibit a purchaser from charging the former clients of the seller a higher fee than the purchaser is charging the purchaser's existing clients. The sale may not be financed by increases in fees charged the clients of the practice that is purchased. Existing agreements between the seller and the client as to fees and the scope of the work must be honored by the purchaser, unless the client consents after consultation.

Adjustments for differences in the fee schedules of the seller and the purchaser should be made between the seller and purchaser in valuing good will, and not between the client and the purchaser. The purchaser may, however, advise the client that the purchaser will not undertake the representation unless the client consents to pay the higher fees the purchaser usually charges. To prevent client financing of the sale, the higher fee the purchaser may charge must not exceed the fees charged by the purchaser for substantially similar service rendered prior to the initiation of the purchase negotiations.

Deceased Lawyer. Even though a nonlawyer seller representing the estate of a deceased lawyer is not subject to the Michigan Rules of Professional Conduct, a lawyer who participates in a sale of a law practice must conform to this rule. Therefore, the purchasing lawyer can be expected to see that its requirements are met.

Rule 1.18.   Duties to Prospective Client

(a) A person who consults with a lawyer about the possibility of forming a client-lawyer relationship with respect to a matter is a prospective client.

(b) Even when no client-lawyer relationship ensues, a lawyer who has learned information from a prospective client shall not use or reveal that information, except as Rule 1.9 would permit with respect to information of a former client.

(c) A lawyer subject to paragraph (b) shall not represent a client with interests materially adverse to those of a prospective client in the same or a substantially related matter if the lawyer received information from the prospective client that could be significantly harmful to that person in the matter, except as provided in paragraph (d). If a lawyer is disqualified from representation under this paragraph, no lawyer in a firm with which that lawyer is associated may knowingly undertake or continue representation in such a matter, except as provided in paragraph (d).

(d) When the lawyer has received disqualifying information as defined in paragraph (c), representation is permissible if:

(1) both the affected client and the prospective client have given informed consent, confirmed in writing, or:

(2) the lawyer who received the information took reasonable measures to avoid exposure to more disqualifying information than was reasonably necessary to determine whether to represent the prospective client; and

> **(i)** the disqualified lawyer is timely screened from any participation in the matter and is apportioned no part of the fee therefrom; and

> **(ii)** written notice is promptly given to the prospective client.

[Adopted May 23, 2018, effective September 1, 2018, 501 Mich.]

Official Comment

Prospective clients, like clients, may disclose information to a lawyer, place documents or other property in the lawyer's custody, or rely on the lawyer's advice. A lawyer's consultations with a prospective client usually are limited in time and depth and leave both the prospective client and the lawyer free (and sometimes required) to proceed no further. Hence, prospective clients should receive some but not all of the protection afforded clients.

A person becomes a prospective client by consulting with a lawyer about the possibility of forming a client-lawyer relationship with respect to a matter. Whether communications, including written, oral, or electronic communications, constitute a consultation depends on the circumstances. For example, a consultation is likely to have occurred if a lawyer, either in person or through the lawyer's advertising in any medium, specifically requests or invites the submission of information about a potential representation without clear and reasonably understandable warnings and cautionary statements that limit the lawyer's obligations, and a person provides information in response. In contrast, a consultation does not occur if a person provides information to a lawyer in response to advertising that merely describes the lawyer's education, experience, areas of practice, and contact information, or provides legal information of general interest. Such a person communicates information unilaterally to a lawyer, without any reasonable expectation that the lawyer is willing to discuss the possibility of forming a client-lawyer relationship, and is thus not a "prospective client." Moreover, a person who communicates with a lawyer for the purpose of disqualifying the lawyer is not a "prospective client."

It is often necessary for a prospective client to reveal information to the lawyer during an initial consultation prior to the decision about formation of a client-lawyer relationship. The lawyer often must learn such information to determine whether there is a conflict of interest with an existing client and whether the matter is one that the lawyer is willing to undertake. Paragraph (b) prohibits the lawyer from using or revealing that information, except as permitted by Rule 1.9, even if the client or lawyer decides not to proceed with the representation. The duty exists regardless of how brief the initial conference may be.

In order to avoid acquiring disqualifying information from a prospective client, a lawyer considering whether or not to undertake a new matter should limit the initial consultation to only such information as reasonably appears necessary for that purpose. Where the information indicates that a conflict of interest or other reason for non-representation exists, the lawyer should so inform the prospective client or decline the representation. If the prospective client wishes to retain the lawyer, and if consent is possible under Rule 1.7, then consent from all affected present or former clients must be obtained before accepting the representation.

A lawyer may condition a consultation with a prospective client on the person's informed consent that no information disclosed during the consultation will prohibit the lawyer from representing a different client in the matter. If the agreement expressly so provides, the prospective client may also consent to the lawyer's subsequent use of information received from the prospective client.

Even in the absence of an agreement, under paragraph (c), the lawyer is not prohibited from representing a client with interests adverse to those of the prospective client in the same or a substantially related matter unless the lawyer has received from the prospective client information that could be significantly harmful if used in the matter.

Under paragraph (c), the prohibition in this Rule is imputed to other lawyers as provided in Rule 1.10, but, under paragraph (d)(l), imputation may be avoided if the lawyer obtains the informed consent, confirmed in writing, of both the prospective and affected clients. In the alternative, imputation may be avoided if the conditions of paragraph (d)(2) are met and all disqualified lawyers are timely screened and written notice is promptly given to the prospective client. Paragraph (d)(2)(i) does not prohibit the screened lawyer from receiving a salary or partnership share established by prior independent agreement, but that lawyer may not receive compensation directly related to the matter in which the lawyer is disqualified.

Notice, including a general description of the subject matter about which the lawyer was consulted, and of the screening procedures employed, generally should be given as soon as practicable after the need for screening becomes apparent.

Comments

Staff Comment to 2018 Adoption

The addition of new rule MRPC 1.18 and amendment of MRPC 7.3 clarifies the ethical duties that lawyers owe to prospective clients and creates consistency in the use of the term "prospective client." This proposal was submitted to the Court by the Representative Assembly of the State Bar of Michigan.

COUNSELOR

Rule 2.1. Advisor

In representing a client, a lawyer shall exercise independent professional judgment and shall render candid advice. In rendering advice, a lawyer may refer not only to law but to other considerations such as moral, economic, social, and political factors that may be relevant to the client's situation.

Comments

Scope of Advice. A client is entitled to straightforward advice expressing the lawyer's honest assessment. Legal advice often involves unpleasant facts and alternatives that a client may be disinclined to confront. In presenting advice, a lawyer endeavors to sustain the client's morale and may put advice in as acceptable a form as honesty permits. However, a lawyer should not be deterred from giving candid advice by the prospect that the advice will be unpalatable to the client.

Advice couched in narrowly legal terms may be of little value to a client, especially where practical considerations, such as cost or effects on other people, are predominant. Purely technical legal advice, therefore, can sometimes be inadequate. It is proper for a lawyer to refer to relevant moral and ethical considerations in giving advice. Although a lawyer is not a moral advisor as such, moral and ethical considerations impinge upon most legal questions and may decisively influence how the law will be applied.

A client may expressly or impliedly ask the lawyer for purely technical advice. When such a request is made by a client experienced in legal matters, the lawyer may accept it at face value. When such a request is made by a client inexperienced in legal matters, however, the lawyer's responsibility as advisor may include indicating that more is involved than strictly legal considerations.

Matters that go beyond strictly legal questions may also be in the domain of another profession. Family matters can involve problems within the professional competence of psychiatry, clinical psychology, or social work; business matters can involve problems within the competence of the accounting profession or of financial specialists. Where consultation with a professional in another field is itself something a competent lawyer would recommend, the lawyer should make such a recommendation. At the same time, a lawyer's advice at its best often consists of recommending a course of action in the face of conflicting recommendations of experts.

Offering Advice. In general, a lawyer is not expected to give advice until asked by the client. However, when a lawyer knows that a client proposes a course of action that is likely to result in substantial adverse legal consequences to the client, the duty to the client under Rule 1.4 may require that the lawyer act if the client's course of action is related to the representation. A lawyer ordinarily has no duty to initiate investigation of a client's affairs or to give advice that the client has indicated is unwanted, but a lawyer may initiate advice to a client when doing so appears to be in the client's interest.

Rule 2.2. Intermediary

(a) A lawyer may act as intermediary between clients if:

(1) the lawyer consults with each client concerning the implications of the common representation, including the advantages and risks involved and the effect on the client-lawyer privileges, and obtains each client's consent to the common representation;

(2) the lawyer reasonably believes that the matter can be resolved on terms compatible with the clients' best interests, that each client will be able to make adequately informed decisions in the matter, and that there is little risk of material prejudice to the interests of any of the clients if the contemplated resolution is unsuccessful; and

(3) the lawyer reasonably believes that the common representation can be undertaken impartially and without improper effect on other responsibilities the lawyer has to any of the clients.

(b) While acting as intermediary, the lawyer shall consult with each client concerning the decisions to be made and the considerations relevant in making them, so that each client can make adequately informed decisions.

(c) A lawyer shall withdraw as intermediary if any of the clients so requests, or if any of the conditions stated in paragraph (a) is no longer satisfied. Upon withdrawal, the lawyer shall not continue to represent any of the clients in the matter that was the subject of the intermediation.

Official Comment

A lawyer acts as intermediary under this rule when the lawyer represents two or more parties with potentially conflicting interests. A key factor in defining the relationship is whether the parties share responsibility for the lawyer's fee, but the common representation may be inferred from other circumstances. Because confusion can arise as to the lawyer's role where each party is not separately represented, it is important that the lawyer make clear the relationship.

The rule does not apply to a lawyer acting as arbitrator or mediator between or among parties who are not clients of the lawyer, even where the lawyer has been appointed with the concurrence of the parties. In performing such a role the lawyer may be subject to applicable codes of ethics, such as the Code of Ethics for Arbitration in Commercial Disputes prepared by a joint committee of the American Bar Association and the American Arbitration Association.

A lawyer acts as intermediary in seeking to establish or adjust a relationship between clients on an amicable and mutually advantageous basis, for example, in helping to organize a business in which two or more clients are entrepreneurs, working out the financial reorganization of an enterprise in which two or more clients have an interest, arranging a property distribution in settlement of an estate, or mediating a dispute between clients. The lawyer seeks to resolve potentially conflicting interests by developing the parties' mutual interests. The alternative can be that each party may have to obtain separate representation, with the possibility in some situations of incurring additional cost, complication, or even litigation. Given these and other relevant factors, all the clients may prefer that the lawyer act as intermediary.

In considering whether to act as intermediary between clients, a lawyer should be mindful that if the intermediation fails the result can be additional cost, embarrassment, and recrimination. In some situations the risk of failure is so great that intermediation is plainly impossible. For example, a lawyer cannot undertake common representation of clients between whom contentious litigation is imminent or who contemplate contentious negotiations. More generally, if the relationship between the parties has already assumed definite antagonism, the possibility that the clients' interests can be adjusted by intermediation ordinarily is not very good.

The appropriateness of intermediation can depend on its form. Forms of intermediation include informal arbitration (where each client's case is presented by the respective client and the lawyer decides the outcome), mediation, and common representation where the clients' interests are substantially, though not entirely, compatible. One form may be appropriate in circumstances where another would not. Other relevant factors are whether the lawyer subsequently will represent both parties on a continuing basis and whether the situation involves creating a relationship between the parties or terminating one.

Confidentiality and Privilege. A particularly important factor in determining the appropriateness of intermediation is the effect on client-lawyer confidentiality and the client-lawyer privilege. In a common representation, the lawyer is still required both to keep each client adequately informed and to maintain confidentiality of information relating to the representation. See Rules 1.4 and 1.6. Complying with both requirements while acting as intermediary requires a delicate balance. If the balance cannot be maintained, the common representation is improper. With regard to the client-lawyer privilege, the prevailing rule is that as between commonly represented clients the privilege does not attach. Hence, it must be assumed that if litigation eventuates between the clients, the privilege will not protect any such communications, and the clients should be so advised.

Since the lawyer is required to be impartial between commonly represented clients, intermediation is improper when that impartiality cannot be maintained. For example, a lawyer who has represented one of the clients for a long period and in a variety of matters might have difficulty being impartial between that client and one to whom the lawyer has only recently been introduced.

Consultation. In acting as intermediary between clients, the lawyer is required to consult with the clients on the implications of doing so, and proceed only upon consent based on such a consultation. The consultation should make clear that the lawyer's role is not that of partisanship normally expected in other circumstances.

Paragraph (b) is an application of the principle expressed in Rule 1.4. Where the lawyer is intermediary, the clients ordinarily must assume greater responsibility for decisions than when each client is independently represented.

Withdrawal. Common representation does not diminish the rights of each client in the client-lawyer relationship. Each has the right to loyal and diligent representation, the right to discharge the lawyer stated in Rule 1.16, and the protection of Rule 1.9 concerning obligations to a former client.

Rule 2.3. Evaluation for Use by Third Persons

(a) A lawyer may, for the use of someone other than the client, undertake an evaluation of a matter affecting a client if:

(1) the lawyer reasonably believes that making the evaluation is compatible with other aspects of the lawyer's relationship with the client; and

(2) the client consents after consultation.

(b) Except as disclosure is required in connection with a report of an evaluation, information relating to the evaluation is protected by Rule 1.6.

Official Comment

Definition. An evaluation may be performed at the client's direction, but for the primary purpose of establishing information for the benefit of third parties; for example, an opinion concerning the title of property rendered at the behest of a vendor for the information of a prospective purchaser, or at the behest of a borrower for the information of a prospective lender. In some situations, the evaluation may be required by a government agency, for example, an opinion concerning the legality of the securities registered for sale under the securities laws. In other instances, the evaluation may be required by a third person, such as a purchaser of a business.

Lawyers for the government may be called upon to give a formal opinion on the legality of contemplated government agency action. In making such an evaluation, the government lawyer acts at the behest of the government as the client, but for the purpose of establishing the limits of the agency's authorized activity. Such an opinion is to be distinguished from confidential legal advice given agency officials. The critical question is whether the opinion is to be made public.

A legal evaluation should be distinguished from an investigation of a person with whom the lawyer does not have a client-lawyer relationship. For example, a lawyer retained by a purchaser to analyze a vendor's title to property does not have a client-lawyer relationship with the vendor. So also, an investigation into a person's affairs by a government lawyer, or by special counsel employed by the government, is not an evaluation as that term is used in this rule. The question is whether the lawyer is retained by the person whose affairs are being examined. When the lawyer is retained by that person, the general rules concerning loyalty to client and preservation of confidences apply, which is not the case if the lawyer is retained by someone else. For this reason, it is essential to identify the person by whom the lawyer is retained. This should be made clear not only to the person under examination, but also to others to whom the results are to be made available.

Duty to Third Person. When the evaluation is intended for the information or use of a third person, a legal duty to that person may or may not arise. That legal question is beyond the scope of this rule. However, since such an evaluation involves a departure from the normal client-lawyer relationship, careful analysis of the situation is required. The lawyer must be satisfied as a matter of professional judgment that making the evaluation is compatible with other functions undertaken in behalf of the client. For example, if the lawyer is acting as advocate in defending the client against charges of fraud, it would normally be incompatible with that responsibility for the lawyer to perform an evaluation for others concerning the same or a related transaction. Assuming no such impediment is apparent, however, the lawyer should advise the client of the implications of the evaluation, particularly the lawyer's responsibilities to third persons and the duty to disseminate the findings.

Access to and Disclosure of Information. The quality of an evaluation depends on the freedom and extent of the investigation upon which it is based. Ordinarily a lawyer should have whatever latitude of investigation seems necessary as a matter of professional judgment. Under some circumstances, however, the terms of the evaluation may be limited. For example, certain issues or sources may be categorically excluded, or the scope of search may be limited by time constraints or the noncooperation of persons having relevant information. Any such limitations which are material to the evaluation should be described in the report. If after a lawyer has commenced an evaluation the client refuses to comply with the terms upon which it was understood the evaluation was to have been made, the lawyer's obligations are determined by law, having reference to the terms of the client's agreement and the surrounding circumstances.

Financial Auditors' Requests for Information. When a question concerning the legal situation of a client arises at the instance of the client's financial auditor and the question is referred to the lawyer, the lawyer's response may be made in accordance with procedures recognized in the legal profession. Such a procedure is set forth in the American Bar Association Statement of Policy Regarding Lawyers' Responses to Auditors' Requests for Information, adopted in 1975.

Rule 2.4. Lawyer Serving as Third–Party Neutral

(a) A lawyer serves as a third-party neutral when the lawyer assists two or more persons who are not clients of the lawyer to reach a resolution of a dispute or other matter that has arisen between them. Service as a third-party neutral may include service as an arbitrator, a mediator, or in such other capacity as will enable the lawyer to assist the parties to resolve the matter.

(b) A lawyer serving as a third-party neutral must inform unrepresented parties that the lawyer is not representing them. When the lawyer knows or reasonably should know that a party does not understand the lawyer's role in the matter, the lawyer must explain the difference between the lawyer's role as a third-party neutral and a lawyer's role as one who represents a client.

[Adopted October 26, 2010, effective January 1, 2011, 487 Mich.]

Official Comment

Alternative dispute resolution has become a substantial part of the civil justice system. Aside from representing clients in dispute-resolution processes, lawyers often serve as third-party neutrals. A third-party neutral is a person, such as a mediator, an arbitrator, a conciliator, or an evaluator, who assists the parties, represented or unrepresented, in the resolution of a dispute or in the arrangement of a transaction. Whether a third-party neutral serves primarily as a facilitator, an evaluator, or a decision maker depends on the particular process that is selected by the parties or mandated by a court.

The role of a third-party neutral is not unique to lawyers, although, in some court-connected contexts, only lawyers are allowed to serve in this role or to handle certain types of cases. In performing this role, the lawyer may be subject to court rules or other law that apply either to third-party neutrals generally or to lawyers serving as third-party neutrals. Lawyer-neutrals also may be subject to various codes of ethics, such as the Code of Ethics for Arbitration in Commercial Disputes prepared by a joint committee of the American Bar Association and the American Arbitration Association, or the Model Standards of Conduct for Mediators jointly prepared by the American Bar Association, the American Arbitration Association, and the Society of Professionals in Dispute Resolution.

Unlike nonlawyers who serve as third-party neutrals, lawyers serving in this role may experience unique problems as a result of differences between the role of a third-party neutral and a lawyer's service as a client representative. The potential for confusion is significant when the parties are unrepresented in the process. Thus, paragraph (b) requires a lawyer-neutral to inform unrepresented parties that the lawyer is not representing them. For some parties, particularly parties who frequently use dispute-resolution processes, this information will be sufficient. For others, particularly those who are using the process for the first time, more information will be required. Where appropriate, the lawyer should inform unrepresented parties of the important differences between the lawyer's role as third-party neutral and a lawyer's role as a client representative, including the inapplicability of the attorney-client evidentiary privilege. The extent of disclosure required under this paragraph will depend on the particular parties involved and the subject matter of the proceeding, as well as the particular features of the dispute-resolution process selected.

A lawyer who serves as a third-party neutral subsequently may be asked to serve as a lawyer representing a client in the same matter. The conflicts of interest that arise for both the individual lawyer and the lawyer's law firm are addressed in Rule 1.12.

Lawyers who represent clients in alternative dispute resolution are governed by the Michigan Rules of Professional Conduct. When the dispute-resolution process takes place before a tribunal, as in binding arbitration, the lawyer's duty of candor is governed by Rule 3.3. Otherwise, the lawyer's duty of candor toward both the third-party neutral and other parties is governed by Rule 4.1.

Comments
Staff Comment to 2011 Amendment
There is no equivalent to MRPC 2.4 in the current Michigan Rules of Professional Conduct. The rule is designed to help parties involved in alternative dispute resolution to better understand the role of a lawyer serving as a third-party neutral.

ADVOCATE

Rule 3.1.   Meritorious Claims and Contentions

A lawyer shall not bring or defend a proceeding, or assert or controvert an issue therein, unless there is a basis for doing so that is not frivolous. A lawyer may offer a good-faith argument for an extension, modification, or reversal of existing law. A lawyer for the defendant in a criminal proceeding, or the respondent in a proceeding that could result in incarceration, may so defend the proceeding as to require that every element of the case be established.

[Comment amended October 26, 2010, effective January 1, 2011, 487 Mich.]

Official Comment

The advocate has a duty to use legal procedure for the fullest benefit of the client's cause, but also has a duty not to abuse legal procedure. The law, both procedural and substantive, establishes the limits within which an advocate may proceed. However, the law is not always clear and never is static. Accordingly, in determining the proper scope of advocacy, account must be taken of the law's ambiguities and potential for change.

The filing of an action or defense or similar action taken for a client is not frivolous merely because the facts have not first been fully substantiated or because the lawyer expects to develop vital evidence only by discovery. What is required of lawyers is that they inform themselves about the facts of their clients' cases and the applicable law and determine that they can make good-faith arguments in support of their clients' positions. Such action is not frivolous even though the lawyer believes that the client's position ultimately will not prevail. The action is frivolous, however, if the lawyer is unable either to make a good-faith argument on the merits of the action taken or to support the action taken by a good-faith argument for an extension, modification, or reversal of existing law.

Comments
Staff Comment to 2010 Amendment
The amendments of MRPC 3.1 make no changes in the current rule, but modify the accompanying commentary to clarify that a lawyer is not responsible for a client's subjective motivation.

Rule 3.2.   Expediting Litigation

A lawyer shall make reasonable efforts to expedite litigation consistent with the interests of the client.

Official Comment

Although a judge bears the responsibility of assuring the progress of a court's docket, dilatory practices by a lawyer can bring the administration of justice into disrepute. Delay should not be indulged merely for the convenience of the advocates, or for the purpose of frustrating an opposing party's attempt to obtain rightful redress or repose. It is not a justification that similar conduct is often tolerated by the bench and bar. Even though it causes delay, a course of action is proper if a competent lawyer acting in good faith would regard the course of action as having some substantial purpose other than delay. Realizing financial or other benefit from otherwise improper delay in litigation is not a legitimate interest of the client.

Rule 3.3.   Candor Toward the Tribunal

(a) A lawyer shall not knowingly:

(1) make a false statement of material fact or law to a tribunal or fail to correct a false statement of material fact or law previously made to the tribunal by the lawyer;

(2) fail to disclose to a tribunal controlling legal authority in the jurisdiction known to the lawyer to be directly adverse to the position of the client and not disclosed by opposing counsel; or

(3) offer evidence that the lawyer knows to be false. If a lawyer has offered material evidence and comes to know of its falsity, the lawyer shall take reasonable remedial measures, including, if necessary, disclosure to the tribunal.

(b) If a lawyer knows that the lawyer's client or other person intends to engage, is engaging, or has engaged in criminal or fraudulent conduct related to an adjudicative proceeding involving the client, the lawyer shall take reasonable remedial measures, including, if necessary, disclosure to the tribunal.

(c) The duties stated in paragraphs (a) and (b) continue to the conclusion of the proceeding, and apply even if compliance requires disclosure of information otherwise protected by Rule 1.6.

(d) In an ex parte proceeding, a lawyer shall inform the tribunal of all material facts that are known to the lawyer and that will enable the tribunal to make an informed decision, whether or not the facts are adverse.

(e) When false evidence is offered, a conflict may arise between the lawyer's duty to keep the client's revelations confidential and the duty of candor to the court. Upon ascertaining that material evidence is false, the lawyer should seek to persuade the client that the evidence should not be offered or, if it has been offered, that its false character should immediately be disclosed. If the persuasion is ineffective, the lawyer must take reasonable remedial measures. The advocate should seek to withdraw if that will remedy the situation. If withdrawal from the representation is not permitted or will not remedy the effect of the false evidence, the lawyer must make such disclosure to the tribunal as is reasonably necessary to remedy the situation, even if doing so requires the lawyer to reveal information that otherwise would be protected by Rule 1.6.

[Amended October 26, 2010, effective January 1, 2011, 487 Mich.]

Official Comment

This rule governs the conduct of a lawyer who is representing a client in a tribunal. It also applies when the lawyer is representing a client in an ancillary proceeding conducted pursuant to the tribunal's adjudicative authority, such as a deposition. Thus, subrule (a) requires a lawyer to take reasonable remedial measures if the lawyer comes to know that a client who is testifying in a deposition has offered evidence that is false.

As officers of the court, lawyers have special duties to avoid conduct that undermines the integrity of the adjudicative process. A lawyer acting as an advocate in an adjudicative proceeding has an obligation to present the client's case with persuasive force. Performance of that duty while maintaining confidences of the client is qualified, however, by the advocate's duty of candor to the tribunal. Consequently, although a lawyer in an adversary proceeding is not required to present an impartial exposition of the law or to vouch for the evidence submitted in a cause, the lawyer must not allow the tribunal to be misled by false statements of law or fact or evidence that the lawyer knows to be false.

Representations by a Lawyer. An advocate is responsible for pleadings and other documents prepared for litigation, but is usually not required to have personal knowledge of matters asserted therein, because litigation documents ordinarily present assertions by the client or by someone on the client's behalf and not assertions by the lawyer. Compare Rule 3.1. However, an assertion purporting to be on the lawyer's own knowledge, as in an affidavit by the lawyer or in a statement in open court, may properly be made only when the lawyer knows the assertion is true or believes it to be true on the basis of a reasonably diligent inquiry. There are circumstances where failure to make a disclosure is the equivalent of an affirmative misrepresentation. The obligation prescribed in Rule 1.2(c) not to counsel a client to commit or assist the client in committing a fraud applies in litigation. Regarding compliance with Rule 1.2(c), see the comment to that rule. See also the comment to Rule 8.4(b).

Legal Argument. Legal argument based on a knowingly false representation of law constitutes dishonesty toward the tribunal. A lawyer is not required to make a disinterested exposition of the law, but must recognize the existence of pertinent legal authorities. Furthermore, as stated in paragraph (a)(2), an advocate has a duty to disclose directly controlling adverse authority that has not been disclosed by the opposing party. The underlying concept is that legal argument is a discussion seeking to determine the legal premises properly applicable to the case.

Offering Evidence. Paragraph (a)(3) requires that a lawyer refuse to offer evidence that the lawyer knows to be false, regardless of the client's wishes. This duty is premised on the lawyer's obligation as an officer of the court to prevent the trier of fact from being misled by false evidence. A lawyer does not violate this rule if the lawyer offers the evidence for the purpose of establishing its falsity.

If a lawyer knows that the client intends to testify falsely or wants the lawyer to introduce false evidence, the lawyer should seek to persuade the client that the evidence should not be offered. If the persuasion is ineffective and the lawyer continues to represent the client, the lawyer must refuse to offer the false evidence. If only a portion of a witness' testimony will be false, the lawyer may call the witness to testify but may not elicit or otherwise permit the witness to present the testimony that the lawyer knows is false. A lawyer's knowledge that evidence is false can be inferred from the circumstances. Thus, although a lawyer should resolve doubts about the veracity of testimony or other evidence in favor of the client, the lawyer cannot ignore an obvious falsehood.

Remedial Measures. Having offered material evidence in the belief that it was true, a lawyer may subsequently come to know that the evidence is false. Or a lawyer may be surprised when the lawyer's client, or another witness called by the lawyer, offers testimony the lawyer knows to be false, either during the lawyer's direct examination or in response to cross-examination by the opposing lawyer. In such situations, or if the lawyer knows of the falsity of testimony elicited from the client during a deposition, the lawyer must take reasonable remedial measures. If that fails, the lawyer must take further remedial action. It is for the tribunal then to determine what should be done—making a statement about the matter to the trier of fact, ordering a mistrial, or perhaps nothing.

The disclosure of a client's false testimony can result in grave consequences to the client, including a sense of betrayal, the loss of the case, or perhaps a prosecution for perjury. However, the alternative is that the lawyer aids in the deception of the court, thereby subverting the truth-finding process that the adversarial system is designed to implement. See Rule 1.2(c). Furthermore, unless it is clearly understood that the lawyer must remediate the disclosure of false evidence, the client could simply reject the lawyer's counsel to reveal the false evidence and require that the lawyer remain silent. Thus, the client could insist that the lawyer assist in perpetrating a fraud on the court.

Preserving Integrity of Adjudicative Process. Lawyers have a special obligation to protect a tribunal against criminal or fraudulent conduct that undermines the integrity of the adjudicative process, such as bribing, intimidating, or otherwise unlawfully communicating with a witness, juror, court official, or other participant in the proceeding, unlawfully destroying or concealing documents or other evidence, or failing to disclose information to the tribunal when required by law to do so. Thus, paragraph (b) requires a lawyer to take reasonable remedial measures, including disclosure, if necessary, whenever the lawyer knows that a person, including the lawyer's client, intends to engage, is engaging, or has engaged in criminal or fraudulent conduct related to the proceeding. See Rule 3.4.

Duration of Obligation. A practical time limit on the obligation to rectify the presentation of false evidence or false statements of law and fact must be established. The conclusion of the proceeding is a reasonably definite point for the termination of the obligation.

Ex Parte Proceedings. Ordinarily, an advocate has the limited responsibility of presenting one side of the matters that a tribunal should consider in reaching a decision; the conflicting position is expected to be presented by the opposing party. However, in an ex parte proceeding, such as an application for a temporary restraining order, there is no balance of presentation by opposing advocates. The object of an ex parte proceeding is nevertheless to yield a substantially just result. The judge has an affirmative responsibility to accord the absent party just consideration. The lawyer for the represented party has the correlative duty to make disclosures of material facts that are known to the

lawyer and that the lawyer reasonably believes are necessary to an informed decision.

Withdrawal. Normally, a lawyer's compliance with the duty of candor imposed by this rule does not require that the lawyer withdraw from the representation of a client whose interests will be or have been adversely affected by the lawyer's disclosure. The lawyer may, however, be required by Rule 1.16(a) to seek permission of the tribunal to withdraw if the lawyer's compliance with this rule's duty of candor results in such an extreme deterioration of the client-lawyer relationship that the lawyer can no longer competently represent the client. Also see Rule 1.16(b) for the circumstances in which a lawyer will be permitted to seek a tribunal's permission to withdraw. In connection with a request for permission to withdraw that is premised on a client's misconduct, a lawyer may reveal information relating to the representation only to the extent reasonably necessary to comply with this rule or as otherwise permitted by Rule 1.6.

Comments
Staff Comment to 2010 Amendment

The changes in MRPC 3.3 specify in paragraph (a)(1) that a lawyer shall not knowingly "fail to correct a false statement of material fact or law," and substitute paragraph (b) for current paragraph (a)(2), which deals with a disclosure that is "necessary to avoid assisting a criminal or fraudulent act by the client." In addition, several paragraphs from the comment relating to remedial actions a lawyer must take upon learning that false testimony has been offered have been combined and inserted into the body of the rule as new subsection (e).

Rule 3.4. Fairness to Opposing Party and Counsel

A lawyer shall not:

(a) unlawfully obstruct another party's access to evidence; unlawfully alter, destroy, or conceal a document or other material having potential evidentiary value; or counsel or assist another person to do any such act;

(b) falsify evidence, counsel or assist a witness to testify falsely, or offer an inducement to a witness that is prohibited by law;

(c) knowingly disobey an obligation under the rules of a tribunal except for an open refusal based on an assertion that no valid obligation exists;

(d) in pretrial procedure, make a frivolous discovery request or fail to make reasonably diligent efforts to comply with a legally proper discovery request by an opposing party;

(e) during trial, allude to any matter that the lawyer does not reasonably believe is relevant or that will not be supported by admissible evidence, assert personal knowledge of facts in issue except when testifying as a witness, or state a personal opinion as to the justness of a cause, the credibility of a witness, the culpability of a civil litigant, or the guilt or innocence of an accused; or

(f) request a person other than a client to refrain from voluntarily giving relevant information to another party, unless:

(1) the person is an employee or other agent of a client for purposes of MRE 801(d)(2)(D); and

(2) the lawyer reasonably believes that the person's interests will not be adversely affected by refraining from giving such information.

[Amended October 26, 2010, effective January 1, 2011, 487 Mich.]

Official Comment

The procedure of the adversary system contemplates that the evidence in a case is to be marshaled competitively by the contending parties. Fair competition in the adversary system is secured by prohibitions against destruction or concealment of evidence, improper influence of witnesses, obstructive tactics in discovery procedure, and the like.

Documents and other items of evidence are often essential to establish a claim or defense. Subject to evidentiary privileges, the right of an opposing party, including the government, to obtain evidence through discovery or subpoena is an important procedural right. The exercise of that right can be frustrated if relevant material is altered, concealed or destroyed. Other law makes it an offense to destroy material for purpose of impairing its availability in a pending proceeding or one whose commencement can be foreseen. Falsifying evidence is also generally a criminal offense. Paragraph (a) applies to evidentiary material generally, including computerized information.

With regard to paragraph (b), it is not improper to pay a witness' expenses or to compensate an expert witness on terms permitted by law. It is, however, improper to pay an occurrence witness any fee for testifying beyond that authorized by law, and it is improper to pay an expert witness a contingent fee.

Comments

Staff Comment to 2010 Amendment

The amendments of MRPC 3.4 clarify in paragraph (f)(1) that a lawyer may not ask someone other than a client to refrain from voluntarily giving relevant information to another party unless the person is "an employee or other agent of a client for the purposes of MRE 801(d)(2)(D)."

Rule 3.5. Impartiality and Decorum of the Tribunal

A lawyer shall not:

(a) seek to influence a judge, juror, prospective juror, or other official by means prohibited by law;

(b) communicate ex parte with such a person concerning a pending matter, unless authorized to do so by law or court order;

(c) communicate with a juror or prospective juror after discharge of the jury if:

(1) the communication is prohibited by law or court order;

(2) the juror has made known to the lawyer a desire not to communicate; or

(3) the communication constitutes misrepresentation, coercion, duress or harassment; or

(d) engage in undignified or discourteous conduct toward the tribunal.

[Amended October 26, 2010, effective January 1, 2011, 487 Mich.]

Official Comment

Many forms of improper influence upon a tribunal are proscribed by criminal law. Others are specified in the Michigan Code of Judicial Conduct, with which an advocate should be familiar. A lawyer is required to avoid contributing to a violation of such provisions.

During a proceeding a lawyer may not communicate ex parte with persons serving in an official capacity in the proceeding, such as judges, masters, or jurors, unless authorized to do so by law or court order.

A lawyer may on occasion want to communicate with a juror or prospective juror after the jury has been discharged. The lawyer may do so, unless the communication is prohibited by law or a court order, but must respect the desire of the juror not to talk with the lawyer. The lawyer may not engage in improper conduct during the communication.

The advocate's function is to present evidence and argument so that the cause may be decided according to law. Refraining from undignified or discourteous conduct is a corollary of the advocate's right to speak on behalf of litigants. A lawyer may stand firm against abuse by a judge, but should avoid reciprocation; the judge's default is no justification for similar dereliction by an advocate. An advocate can present the cause, protect the record for subsequent review, and preserve professional integrity by patient firmness no less effectively than by belligerence or theatrics.

Comments

Staff Comment to 2010 Amendment

The amendments of MRPC 3.5 add paragraph (c), which clarifies the rule regarding lawyers' contact of jurors and prospective jurors after the jury is discharged.

Rule 3.6. Trial Publicity

(a) A lawyer who is participating or has participated in the investigation or litigation of a matter shall not make an extrajudicial statement that the lawyer knows or reasonably should know will be disseminated by means of public communication and will have a substantial likelihood of materially prejudicing an adjudicative proceeding in the matter. A statement is likely to have a substantial likelihood of materially prejudicing an adjudicative proceeding when it refers to a civil matter triable to a jury, a criminal matter, or any other proceeding that could result in incarceration, and the statement relates to:

(1) the character, credibility, reputation, or criminal record of a party, of a suspect in a criminal investigation or of a witness, or the identity of a witness, or the expected testimony of a party or witness;

(2) in a criminal case or proceeding that could result in incarceration, the possibility of a plea of guilty to the offense or the existence or contents of any confession, admission, or statement given by a defendant or suspect, or that person's refusal or failure to make a statement;

(3) the performance or results of any examination or test, or the refusal or failure of a person to submit to an examination or test, or the identity or nature of physical evidence expected to be presented;

(4) any opinion as to the guilt or innocence of a defendant or suspect in a criminal case or proceeding that could result in incarceration;

(5) information that the lawyer knows or reasonably should know is likely to be inadmissible as evidence in a trial and that would, if disclosed, create a substantial risk of prejudicing an impartial trial; or

(6) the fact that a defendant has been charged with a crime, unless there is included therein a statement explaining that the charge is merely an accusation and that the defendant is presumed innocent until and unless proven guilty.

(b) Notwithstanding paragraph (a), a lawyer who is participating or has participated in the investigation or litigation of a matter may state without elaboration:

(1) the nature of the claim, offense, or defense involved;

(2) information contained in a public record;

(3) that an investigation of a matter is in progress;

(4) the scheduling or result of any step in litigation;

(5) a request for assistance in obtaining evidence and information necessary thereto;

(6) a warning of danger concerning the behavior of a person involved, when there is reason to believe that there exists the likelihood of substantial harm to an individual or to the public interest; and

(7) in a criminal case, also:

(i) the identity, residence, occupation, and family status of the accused;

(ii) if the accused has not been apprehended, information necessary to aid in apprehension of that person;

(iii) the fact, time and place of arrest; and

(iv) the identity of investigating and arresting officers or agencies and the length of the investigation.

(c) No lawyer associated in a firm or government agency with a lawyer subject to paragraph (a) shall make a statement prohibited by paragraph (a).

[Amended October 26, 2010, effective January 1, 2011, 487 Mich.]

Official Comment

It is difficult to strike a balance between protecting the right to a fair trial and safeguarding the right of free expression. Preserving the right to a fair trial necessarily entails some curtailment of the information that may be disseminated about a party before trial, particularly where trial by jury is involved. If there were no such limits, the result would be the practical nullification of the protective effect of the rules of forensic decorum and the exclusionary rules of evidence. On the other hand, there are vital social interests served by the free dissemination of information about events having legal consequences and about legal proceedings themselves. The public has a right to know about threats to its safety and measures aimed at assuring its security. It also has a legitimate interest in the conduct of judicial proceedings, particularly in matters of general public concern. Furthermore, the subject matter of legal proceedings is often of direct significance in debate and deliberation over questions of public policy.

Special rules of confidentiality may validly govern juvenile, domestic relations, and mental disability proceedings, in addition to other types of litigation. Rule 3.4(c) requires compliance with such rules.

Rule 3.6 sets forth a basic general prohibition against a lawyer's making statements that the lawyer knows or should know will have a substantial likelihood of materially prejudicing an adjudicative proceeding. Recognizing that the public value of informed commentary is great and the likelihood of prejudice to a proceeding by the commentary of a lawyer who is not involved in the proceeding is small, the rule applies only to lawyers who are, or who have been, involved in the investigation or litigation of a case, and their associates.

See Rule 3.8(e) for additional duties of prosecutors in connection with extrajudicial statements about criminal proceedings.

Comments

Staff Comment to 2010 Amendment

The amendments in this rule expand the current rule considerably by moving substantial portions of the current commentary into the rule itself. See, for example, paragraph (b), and the latter portion of paragraph (a). The initial part of paragraph (a) is substantially the same as the current rule, except that the "reasonable lawyer" standard is substituted for the "reasonable person" standard.

Rule 3.7.   Lawyer as Witness

(a) A lawyer shall not act as advocate at a trial in which the lawyer is likely to be a necessary witness except where:

(1) the testimony relates to an uncontested issue;

(2) the testimony relates to the nature and value of legal services rendered in the case; or

(3) disqualification of the lawyer would work substantial hardship on the client.

(b) A lawyer may act as advocate in a trial in which another lawyer in the lawyer's firm is likely to be called as a witness unless precluded from doing so by Rule 1.7 or Rule 1.9.

Official Comment

Combining the roles of advocate and witness can prejudice the opposing party and can involve a conflict of interest between the lawyer and client.

The opposing party may properly object where the combination of roles may prejudice that party's rights in the litigation. A witness is required to testify on the basis of personal knowledge, while an advocate is expected to explain and comment on evidence given by others. It may not be clear whether a statement by an advocate-witness should be taken as proof or as an analysis of the proof.

Paragraph (a)(1) recognizes that if the testimony will be uncontested, the ambiguities in the dual role are purely theoretical. Paragraph (a)(2) recognizes that where the testimony concerns the extent and value of legal services rendered in the action in which the testimony is offered, permitting the lawyers to testify avoids the need for a second trial with new counsel to resolve that issue. Moreover, in such a situation the judge has firsthand knowledge of the matter in

issue; hence, there is less dependence on the adversary process to test the credibility of the testimony.

Apart from these two exceptions, paragraph (a)(3) recognizes that a balancing is required between the interests of the client and those of the opposing party. Whether the opposing party is likely to suffer prejudice depends on the nature of the case, the importance and probable tenor of the lawyer's testimony, and the probability that the lawyer's testimony will conflict with that of other witnesses. Even if there is risk of such prejudice, in determining whether the lawyer should be disqualified due regard must be given to the effect of disqualification on the lawyer's client. It is relevant that one or both parties could reasonably foresee that the lawyer would probably be a witness. The principle of imputed disqualification stated in Rule 1.10 has no application to this aspect of the problem.

Whether the combination of roles involves an improper conflict of interest with respect to the client is determined by Rule 1.7 or 1.9. For example, if there is likely to be substantial conflict between the testimony of the client and that of the lawyer or a member of the lawyer's firm, the representation is improper. The problem can arise whether the lawyer is called as a witness on behalf of the client or is called by the opposing party. Determining whether or not such a conflict exists is primarily the responsibility of the lawyer involved. See comment to Rule 1.7. If a lawyer who is a member of a firm may not act as both advocate and witness by reason of conflict of interest, Rule 1.10 disqualifies the firm also.

Rule 3.8.   Special Responsibilities of a Prosecutor

The prosecutor in a criminal case shall:

(a) refrain from prosecuting a charge that the prosecutor knows is not supported by probable cause;

(b) make reasonable efforts to assure that the accused has been advised of the right to, and the procedure for obtaining, counsel and has been given reasonable opportunity to obtain counsel;

(c) not seek to obtain from an unrepresented accused a waiver of important pretrial rights, such as the right to a preliminary hearing;

(d) make timely disclosure to the defense of all evidence or information known to the prosecutor that tends to negate the guilt of the accused or mitigates the degree of the offense, and, in connection with sentencing, disclose to the defense and to the tribunal all unprivileged mitigating information known to the prosecutor, except when the prosecutor is relieved of this responsibility by a protective order of the tribunal; and

(e) exercise reasonable care to prevent investigators, law enforcement personnel, employees, or other persons assisting or associated with the prosecutor in a criminal case from making an extrajudicial statement that the prosecutor would be prohibited from making under Rule 3.6.

(f) When a prosecutor knows of new, credible, and material evidence creating a reasonable likelihood that a convicted defendant is innocent of the crime for which the defendant was convicted, the prosecutor shall:

(1) promptly disclose that evidence to an appropriate court or authority, and

(2) if the conviction was obtained in the prosecutor's jurisdiction,

(i) promptly disclose that evidence to the defendant unless a court authorizes delay, and

(ii) undertake further investigation, or make reasonable efforts to cause an investigation, to determine whether the defendant is innocent of the crime.

(g) When a prosecutor knows of clear and convincing evidence establishing that a defendant in the prosecutor's jurisdiction is innocent of the crime for which defendant was prosecuted, the prosecutor shall seek to remedy the conviction.

(h) A prosecutor's independent judgment, made in good faith, that the new evidence is not of such nature as to trigger the obligations of section (f) and (g), though subsequently determined to have been erroneous, does not constitute a violation of this Rule.

[Amended September 24, 2018, effective January 1, 2019, 502 Mich.]

Official Comment

A prosecutor has the responsibility of a minister of justice and not simply that of an advocate. This responsibility carries with it specific obligations to see that the defendant is accorded procedural justice and that guilt is decided upon the basis of sufficient evidence. Precisely how far the prosecutor is required to go in this direction is a matter of debate. Cf. Rule 3.3(d), governing ex parte proceedings, among which grand jury proceedings are included. Applicable law may require other measures by the prosecutor, and knowing disregard of those obligations or a systematic abuse of prosecutorial discretion could constitute a violation of Rule 8.4.

Paragraph (c) does not apply to an accused appearing pro se with the approval of the tribunal. Nor does it forbid the lawful questioning of a suspect who has knowingly waived the rights to counsel and silence.

The exception in paragraph (d) recognizes that a prosecutor may seek an appropriate protective order from the tribunal if disclosure of information to the defense could result in substantial harm to an individual or to the public interest.

In paragraphs (b) and (e), this rule imposes on a prosecutor an obligation to make reasonable efforts and to take reasonable care to assure that a defendant's rights are protected. Of course, not all of the individuals who might encroach upon those rights are under the control of the prosecutor. The prosecutor cannot be held responsible for the actions of persons over whom the prosecutor does not exercise authority. The prosecutor's obligation is discharged if the prosecutor has taken reasonable and appropriate steps to assure that the defendant's rights are protected.

Comments

Staff Comment to 2019 Amendment

The amendments make several substantive changes in MCR 6.502 regarding postjudgment relief from judgment motions. First, the new language in MCR 6.502(G)(2) inserts a discretionary "actual innocence" waiver provision similar to that in MCR 6.508(D)(3). Further, MCR 6.502(G)(3) is added to clarify that shifts in science are included in the definition of "new evidence" for purposes of the exemption from the successive motion limitation. Finally, new language is added to MRPC 3.8 to require certain actions by a prosecutor who knows of new, credible, and material evidence creating a reasonable likelihood that defendant is innocent of the crime for which defendant was convicted, or who knows of clear and convincing evidence that shows defendant is innocent of the crime. The additional language of MRPC 3.8 is taken largely from the ABA Model Rules of Professional Conduct 3.8, and includes the "safe harbor" provision as a separate provision of the rule (as opposed to being part of the comments as in the model rule).

Rule 3.9. Advocate in Nonadjudicative Proceedings

A lawyer representing a client before a legislative or administrative tribunal in a nonadjudicative proceeding shall disclose that the appearance is in a representative capacity and shall conform to the provisions of Rules 3.3(a) through (c), 3.4(a) through (c), and 3.5.

Official Comment

In representation before bodies such as legislatures, municipal councils, and executive and administrative agencies acting in a rule-making or policy-making capacity, lawyers present facts, formulate issues, and advance argument in the matters under consideration. The decision-making body, like a court, should be able to rely on the integrity of the submissions made to it. A lawyer appearing before such a body should deal with the tribunal honestly and in conformity with applicable rules of procedure.

Lawyers have no exclusive right to appear before nonadjudicative bodies, as they do before a court. The requirements of this rule therefore may subject lawyers to regulations inapplicable to advocates who are not lawyers. However, legislatures and administrative agencies have a right to expect lawyers to deal with them as they deal with courts.

This rule does not apply to representation of a client in a negotiation or other bilateral transaction with a governmental agency; representation in such a transaction is governed by Rules 4.1 through 4.4.

TRANSACTIONS WITH PERSONS OTHER THAN CLIENTS

Rule 4.1. Truthfulness in Statements to Others

In the course of representing a client, a lawyer shall not knowingly make a false statement of material fact or law to a third person.

Official Comment

Misrepresentation. A lawyer is required to be truthful when dealing with others on a client's behalf, but generally has no affirmative duty to inform an opposing party of relevant facts. A misrepresentation can occur if the lawyer incorporates or affirms a statement of another person that the lawyer knows is false.

Statements of Fact. This rule refers to statements of fact. Whether a particular statement should be regarded as one of fact can depend on the circumstances. Under generally accepted conventions in negotiation, certain types of statements ordinarily are not taken as statements of material fact. Estimates of price or value placed on the subject of a transaction and a party's intentions as to an acceptable settlement of a claim are in this category, and so is the existence of an undisclosed principal except where nondisclosure of the principal would constitute fraud.

Fraud by Client. Making a false statement may include the failure to make a statement in circumstances in which silence is equivalent to making such a statement. Thus, where the lawyer has made a statement that the lawyer believed to be true when made but later discovers that the statement was not true, in some circumstances failure to correct the statement may be equivalent to making a statement that is false. When the falsity of the original statement by the lawyer resulted from reliance upon what was told to the lawyer by the client and if the original statement if left uncorrected may further a criminal or fraudulent act by the client, the provisions of Rule 1.6(c)(3) give the lawyer discretion to make the disclosure necessary to rectify the consequences.

Rule 4.2. Communication with a Person Represented by Counsel

(a) In representing a client, a lawyer shall not communicate about the subject of the representation with a person whom the lawyer knows to be represented in the matter by another lawyer, unless the lawyer has the consent of the other lawyer or is authorized by law to do so.

(b) An otherwise self-represented person receiving limited representation in accordance with Rule 1.2(b) is considered to be self-represented for purposes of this rule unless the opposing lawyer knows of, or has been provided with, a written notice of limited appearance comporting with MCR 2.117(B)(2)(c) or other written communication advising of the limited scope representation. Oral communication shall be made first to the limited scope representation lawyer, who may, after consultation with the client, authorize oral communications directly with the client as agreed.

(c) Until a notice of termination of limited scope representation comporting with MCR 2.117(B)(2)(c) is filed, or other written communication terminating the limited scope representation is provided, all written communication, both court filings and otherwise, shall be served upon both the client and the limited scope representation attorney.

[Amended September 20, 2017, effective January 1, 2018, 501 Mich.]

Official Comment

This rule does not prohibit communication with a party, or an employee or agent of a party, concerning matters outside the representation. For example, the existence of a controversy between a government agency and a private party, or between two organizations, does not prohibit a lawyer for either from communicating with nonlawyer representatives of the other regarding a separate matter. Also, parties to a matter may communicate directly with each other and a lawyer having independent justification for communicating with the other party is permitted to do so. Communications authorized by law include, for example, the right of a party to a controversy with a government agency to speak with government officials about the matter.

In the case of an organization, this rule prohibits communications by a lawyer for one party concerning the matter in representation with persons having a managerial responsibility on behalf of the organization, and with any other person whose act or omission in connection with that matter may be imputed to the organization for purposes of civil or criminal liability or whose statement may constitute an admission on the part of the organization. If an agent or employee of the organization is represented in the matter by separate counsel, the consent by that counsel to a communication will be sufficient for purposes of this rule. Compare Rule 3.4(f).

This rule also covers any person, whether or not a party to a formal proceeding, who is represented by counsel concerning the matter in question.

Comments

Staff Comment to 2017 Amendment

The amendments of Rules 1.0, 1.2, 4.2, and 4.3 of the Michigan Rules of Professional Conduct and Rules 2.107, 2.117, and 6.001 of the Michigan Court Rules were submitted to the Court by the State Bar of Michigan Representative Assembly. The rules are intended to provide guidance for attorneys and clients who would prefer to engage in a limited scope representation. The rules allow for such an agreement "preferably in writing," and enable an attorney to file a notice of LSR with the court when the representation is undertaken as well as a termination notice when the representation has ended. The rules also explicitly allow attorneys to provide document preparation services for a self-represented litigant without having to file an appearance with the court.

Rule 4.3. Dealing with a Self–Represented Person

(a) In dealing on behalf of a client with a person who is not represented by counsel, a lawyer shall not state or imply that the lawyer is disinterested. When the lawyer knows or reasonably should know that the self-represented person misunderstands the lawyer's role in the matter, the lawyer shall make reasonable efforts to correct the misunderstanding.

(b) Clients receiving representation under a notice of limited appearance comporting with MCR 2.117(B)(2)(c) or other written communication advising of the limited scope representation are not self-represented persons for matters within the scope of the limited appearance, until a notice of termination of limited appearance representation comporting with MCR 2.117(B)(2)(c) is filed or other written communication terminating the limited scope representation is in effect. See Rule 4.2.
[Amended September 20, 2017, effective January 1, 2018, 501 Mich.]

Official Comment

An unrepresented person, particularly one not experienced in dealing with legal matters, might assume that a lawyer is disinterested in loyalties or is a disinterested authority on the law even when the lawyer represents a client. During the course of a lawyer's representation of a client, the lawyer should not give advice to an unrepresented person other than the advice to obtain counsel.

Comments

Staff Comment to 2017 Amendment

The amendments of Rules 1.0, 1.2, 4.2, and 4.3 of the Michigan Rules of Professional Conduct and Rules 2.107, 2.117, and 6.001 of the Michigan Court Rules were submitted to the Court by the State Bar of Michigan Representative Assembly. The rules are intended to provide guidance for attorneys and clients who would prefer to engage in a limited scope representation. The rules allow for such an agreement "preferably in writing," and enable an attorney to file a notice of LSR with the court when the representation is undertaken as well as a termination notice when the representation has ended. The rules also explicitly allow attorneys to provide document preparation services for a self-represented litigant without having to file an appearance with the court.

Rule 4.4. Respect for Rights of Third Persons

In representing a client, a lawyer shall not use means that have no substantial purpose other than to embarrass, delay, or burden a third person, or use methods of obtaining evidence that violate the legal rights of such a person.

Official Comment

Responsibility to a client requires a lawyer to subordinate the interests of others to those of the client, but that responsibility does not imply that a lawyer may disregard the rights of third persons. It is impractical to catalogue all such rights, but they include legal restrictions on methods of obtaining evidence from third persons.

LAW FIRMS AND ASSOCIATIONS

Rule 5.1. Responsibilities of a Partner or Supervisory Lawyer

(a) A partner in a law firm shall make reasonable efforts to ensure that the firm has in effect measures giving reasonable assurance that all lawyers in the firm conform to the Rules of Professional Conduct.

(b) A lawyer having direct supervisory authority over another lawyer shall make reasonable efforts to ensure that the other lawyer conforms to the Rules of Professional Conduct.

(c) A lawyer shall be responsible for another lawyer's violation of the rules of professional conduct if:

(1) the lawyer orders or, with knowledge of the relevant facts and the specific conduct, ratifies the conduct involved; or

(2) the lawyer is a partner in the law firm in which the other lawyer practices or has direct supervisory authority over the other lawyer, and knows of the conduct at a time when its consequences can be avoided or mitigated but fails to take reasonable remedial action.

Official Comment

Paragraphs (a) and (b) refer to lawyers who have supervisory authority over the professional work of a firm or a legal department of a government agency. This includes members of a partnership and the shareholders in a law firm organized as a professional corporation. This also includes lawyers having supervisory authority in the law department of an enterprise or government agency and lawyers who have intermediate managerial responsibilities in a firm.

The measures required to fulfill the responsibility prescribed in paragraphs (a) and (b) can depend on the firm's structure and the nature of its practice. In a small firm, informal supervision and occasional admonition ordinarily might be sufficient. In a large firm, or in practice situations in which intensely difficult ethical problems frequently arise, more elaborate procedures may be necessary. Some firms, for example, have a procedure whereby junior lawyers can make confidential referral of ethical problems directly to a designated senior partner or special committee. See Rule 5.2. Firms, whether large or small, may also rely on continuing legal education in professional ethics. In any event, the ethical atmosphere of a firm can influence the conduct of all its members and a lawyer having authority over the work of another may not assume that the subordinate lawyer will inevitably conform to the rules.

Paragraph (c)(1) expresses a general principle concerning responsibility for acts of another. See also Rule 8.4(a).

Paragraph (c)(2) defines the duty of a lawyer having direct supervisory authority over performance of specific legal work by another lawyer. Whether a lawyer has such supervisory authority in particular circumstances is a question of fact. Partners of a private firm have at least indirect responsibility for all work being done by the firm, while a partner in charge of a particular matter ordinarily has direct authority over other firm lawyers engaged in the matter. Appropriate remedial action by a partner would depend on the immediacy of the partner's involvement and the seriousness of the misconduct. The supervisor is required to intervene to prevent avoidable consequences of misconduct if the supervisor knows that the misconduct occurred. Thus, if a supervising lawyer knows that a subordinate misrepresented a matter to an opposing party in negotiation, the supervisor as well as the subordinate has a duty to correct the resulting misapprehension.

Professional misconduct by a lawyer under supervision could reveal a violation of paragraph (b) on the part of the supervisory lawyer even though it does not entail a violation of paragraph (c) because there was no direction, ratification, or knowledge of the violation.

Apart from this rule and Rule 8.4(a), a lawyer does not have disciplinary liability for the conduct of a partner, associate, or subordinate. Whether a lawyer may be liable civilly or criminally for another lawyer's conduct is a question of law beyond the scope of these rules.

Rule 5.2. Responsibilities of a Subordinate Lawyer

(a) A lawyer is bound by the rules of professional conduct notwithstanding that the lawyer acted at the direction of another person.

(b) A subordinate lawyer does not violate the rules of professional conduct if that lawyer acts in accordance with a supervisory lawyer's reasonable resolution of an arguable question of professional duty.

Official Comment

Although a lawyer is not relieved of responsibility for a violation by the fact that the lawyer acted at the direction of a supervisor, that fact may be relevant in determining whether a lawyer had the knowledge required to render conduct a violation of the rules. For example, if a subordinate filed a frivolous pleading at the direction of a supervisor, the subordinate would not be guilty of a professional violation unless the subordinate knew of the document's frivolous character.

When lawyers in a supervisor-subordinate relationship encounter a matter involving professional judgment as to ethical duty, the supervisor may assume responsibility for making the judgment. Otherwise a consistent course of action or position could not be taken. If the question can reasonably be answered only one way, the duty of both lawyers is clear and they are equally responsible for fulfilling it. However, if the question is reasonably arguable, someone has to decide upon the course of action. That authority ordinarily reposes in the supervisor, and a subordinate may be guided accordingly. For example, if a question arises whether the interests of two clients conflict under Rule 1.7, the supervisor's reasonable resolution of the question should protect the subordinate professionally if the resolution is subsequently challenged.

Rule 5.3. Responsibilities Regarding Nonlawyer Assistants

With respect to a nonlawyer employed by, retained by, or associated with a lawyer:

(a) a partner in a law firm shall make reasonable efforts to ensure that the firm has in effect measures giving reasonable assurance that the person's conduct is compatible with the professional obligations of the lawyer;

(b) a lawyer having direct supervisory authority over the nonlawyer shall make reasonable efforts to ensure that the person's conduct is compatible with the professional obligations of the lawyer; and

(c) a lawyer shall be responsible for conduct of such a person that would be a violation of the rules of professional conduct if engaged in by a lawyer if:

(1) the lawyer orders or, with knowledge of the relevant facts and the specific conduct, ratifies the conduct involved; or

(2) the lawyer is a partner in the law firm in which the person is employed or has direct supervisory authority over the

person and knows of the conduct at a time when its consequences can be avoided or mitigated but fails to take reasonable remedial action.

Official Comment

Lawyers generally employ assistants in their practice, including secretaries, investigators, law student interns, and paraprofessionals. Such assistants, whether employees or independent contractors, act for the lawyer in rendition of the lawyer's professional services. A lawyer should give such assistants appropriate instruction and supervision concerning the ethical aspects of their employment, particularly regarding the obligation not to disclose information relating to representation of the client, and should be responsible for their work product. The measures employed in supervising nonlawyers should take account of the fact that they do not have legal training and are not subject to professional discipline.

As does Rule 3.8, this rule may in certain situations impose on a prosecutor an obligation to make reasonable efforts to assure that a defendant's rights are protected. Of course, not all of the individuals who might encroach upon those rights are under the control of the prosecutor, but where this rule applies, the prosecutor must take reasonable and appropriate steps to assure that the defendant's rights are protected.

Rule 5.4. Professional Independence of Lawyer

(a) A lawyer or law firm shall not share legal fees with a nonlawyer, except that:

(1) an agreement by a lawyer with the lawyer's firm, partner, or associate may provide for the payment of money, over a reasonable period of time after the lawyer's death, to the lawyer's estate, or to one or more specified persons;

(2) a lawyer who purchases the practice of a deceased, disabled, or disappeared lawyer may, pursuant to the provisions of Rule 1.17, pay to the estate or other representative of that lawyer the agreed-upon purchase price;

(3) a lawyer or law firm may include nonlawyer employees in a compensation or retirement plan, even though the plan is based in whole or in part on a profit-sharing arrangement; and

(4) a lawyer may share court-awarded legal fees with a nonprofit organization that employed, retained, or recommended employment of the lawyer in the matter.

(b) A lawyer shall not form a partnership with a nonlawyer if any of the activities of the partnership consist of the practice of law.

(c) A lawyer shall not permit a person who recommends, employs, or pays the lawyer to render legal services for another to direct or regulate the lawyer's professional judgment in rendering such legal services.

(d) A lawyer shall not practice with or in the form of a professional corporation or association authorized to practice law for a profit, if:

(1) a nonlawyer owns any interest therein, except that a fiduciary representative of the estate of a lawyer may hold the stock or interest of the lawyer for a reasonable time during administration;

(2) a nonlawyer is a corporate director or officer thereof, or one who occupies a position of similar responsibility in any form of association other than a corporation; or

(3) a nonlawyer has the right to direct or control the professional judgment of a lawyer.

[Amended effective October 1, 1991. Amended June 8, 2010, effective September 1, 2010, 486 Mich.]

The provisions of this rule express traditional limitations on sharing fees. These limitations are to protect the lawyer's professional independence of judgment. Where someone other than the client pays the lawyer's fee or salary, or recommends employment of the lawyer, that arrangement does not modify the lawyer's obligation to the client. As stated in paragraph (c), such arrangements should not interfere with the lawyer's professional judgment.

This rule also expresses traditional limitations on permitting a third party to direct or regulate the lawyer's professional judgment in rendering legal services to another. See also Rule 1.8(f) (lawyer may accept compensation from a third party as long as there is no interference with the lawyer's independent professional judgment and the client gives consent).

Comments

Staff Comment to 2010 Amendment

The primary amendment of MRPC 5.4 adds proposed paragraph (a)(4), which specifically allows a lawyer to "share court-awarded legal fees with a nonprofit organization that employed, retained, or recommended employment of the lawyer in the matter."

Rule 5.5. Unauthorized Practice of Law; Multijurisdictional Practice of Law

(a) A lawyer shall not practice law in a jurisdiction in violation of the regulation of the legal profession in that jurisdiction, or assist another in doing so.

(b) A lawyer who is not admitted to practice in this jurisdiction shall not:

(1) except as authorized by law or these rules, establish an office or other systematic and continuous presence in this jurisdiction for the practice of law; or

(2) hold out to the public or otherwise represent that the lawyer is admitted to practice law in this jurisdiction.

(c) A lawyer admitted in another jurisdiction of the United States and not disbarred or suspended from practice in any jurisdiction may provide temporary legal services in this jurisdiction that:

(1) are undertaken in association with a lawyer who is admitted to practice in this jurisdiction and who actively participates in the matter;

(2) are in or reasonably related to a pending or potential proceeding before a tribunal in this or another jurisdiction, if the lawyer or a person the lawyer is assisting is authorized by law to appear in such proceeding or reasonably expects to be so authorized;

(3) are in or reasonably related to a pending or potential arbitration, mediation, or other alternative dispute resolution proceeding in this or another jurisdiction, if the services arise out of or are reasonably related to the lawyer's practice in a jurisdiction in which the lawyer is admitted to practice and are not services for which the forum requires pro hac vice admission; or

(4) are not covered by paragraphs (c)(2) or (c)(3) and arise out of or are reasonably related to the lawyer's practice in a jurisdiction in which the lawyer is admitted to practice.

(d) A lawyer admitted in another jurisdiction of the United States and not disbarred or suspended from practice in any jurisdiction may provide legal services in this jurisdiction that:

(1) are provided to the lawyer's employer or its organizational affiliates and are not services for which the forum requires pro hac vice admission; or

(2) are services that the lawyer is authorized by law to provide in this jurisdiction.
[Amended October 26, 2010, effective January 1, 2011, 487 Mich.]

A lawyer may practice law only in a jurisdiction in which the lawyer is authorized to practice. A lawyer may be admitted to practice law in a jurisdiction on a regular basis or may be authorized by law, order, or court rule to practice for a limited purpose or on a restricted basis. See, for example, MCR 8.126, which permits, under certain circumstances, the temporary admission to the bar of a person who is licensed to practice law in another jurisdiction, and Rule 5(E) of the Rules for the Board of Law Examiners, which permits a lawyer who is admitted to practice in a foreign country to practice in Michigan as a special legal consultant, without examination, provided certain conditions are met.

Paragraph (a) applies to the unauthorized practice of law by a lawyer, whether through the lawyer's direct action or by the lawyer assisting another person. The definition of the practice of law is established by law and varies from one jurisdiction to another. Whatever the definition, limiting the practice of law to members of the bar protects the public against rendition of legal services by unqualified persons. This rule does not prohibit a lawyer from employing the services of paraprofessionals and delegating functions to them, so long as the lawyer supervises the delegated work and retains responsibility for it. See Rule 5.3.

A lawyer may provide professional advice and instruction to nonlawyers whose employment requires knowledge of the law, for example, claims adjusters, employees of financial or commercial institutions, social workers, accountants and persons employed in government agencies. Lawyers also may assist independent nonlawyers, such as paraprofessionals, who are authorized by the law of a jurisdiction to provide particular law-related services. In addition, a lawyer may counsel nonlawyers who wish to proceed pro se.

Other than as authorized by law or this rule, a lawyer who is not admitted to practice generally in this jurisdiction violates paragraph (b) if the lawyer establishes an office or other systematic and continuous presence in this jurisdiction for the practice of law. Presence may be systematic and continuous even if the lawyer is not physically present here. Such a lawyer must not hold out to the public or otherwise represent that the lawyer is admitted to practice law in this jurisdiction. See also Rules 7.1(a) and 7.5(b).

There are occasions on which a lawyer admitted to practice in another jurisdiction of the United States and not disbarred or suspended from practice in any jurisdiction may provide legal services on a temporary basis in this jurisdiction under circumstances that do not create an unreasonable risk to the interests of clients, the public, or the courts. Paragraph (c) identifies four such circumstances. The fact that conduct is not so identified does not indicate whether the conduct is authorized. With the exception of paragraphs (d)(1) and (d)(2), this rule does not authorize a lawyer to establish an office or other systematic and continuous presence in this jurisdiction without being admitted here to practice generally.

There is no single test to determine whether a lawyer's services are provided on a "temporary basis" in this jurisdiction and, therefore, may be permissible under paragraph (c). Services may be "temporary" even though the lawyer provides services in this jurisdiction on a recurring basis or for an extended period of time, as when the lawyer is representing a client in a single lengthy negotiation or litigation.

Paragraphs (c) and (d) apply to lawyers who are admitted to practice law in any jurisdiction of the United States, including the District of Columbia and any state, territory, or commonwealth. The word "admitted" in paragraph (c) contemplates that the lawyer is authorized to practice and is in good standing to practice in the jurisdiction in which the lawyer is admitted and excludes a lawyer who, while technically admitted, is not authorized to practice because, for example, the lawyer is on inactive status or is suspended for nonpayment of dues.

Paragraph (c)(1) recognizes that the interests of clients and the public are protected if a lawyer admitted only in another jurisdiction associates with a lawyer licensed to practice in this jurisdiction. For this paragraph to apply, however, the lawyer admitted to practice in this jurisdiction must actively participate in and share responsibility for the representation of the client.

Lawyers not admitted to practice generally in a jurisdiction may be authorized by law or order of a tribunal or an administrative agency to appear before the tribunal or agency. This authority may be granted pursuant to formal rules governing admission pro hac vice, such as MCR 8.126, or pursuant to informal practice of the tribunal or agency. Under paragraph (c)(2), a lawyer does not violate this rule when the lawyer appears before a tribunal or agency pursuant to such authority. To the extent that a law or court rule of this jurisdiction requires that a lawyer who is not admitted to practice in this jurisdiction obtain admission pro hac vice before appearing before a tribunal or administrative agency, this rule requires the lawyer to obtain that authority.

Paragraph (c)(2) also provides that a lawyer rendering services in this jurisdiction on a temporary basis does not violate this rule when the lawyer engages in conduct in anticipation of a proceeding or hearing in a jurisdiction in which the lawyer is authorized to practice law or in which the lawyer reasonably expects to be admitted pro hac vice under MCR 8.126. Examples of such conduct include meetings with a client, interviews of potential witnesses, and the review of documents. Similarly, a lawyer admitted only in another jurisdiction may engage temporarily in this jurisdiction in conduct related to pending litigation in another jurisdiction in which the lawyer is or reasonably expects to be authorized to appear, including taking depositions in this jurisdiction.

When a lawyer has been or reasonably expects to be admitted to appear before a court or administrative agency, paragraph (c)(2) also permits conduct by lawyers who are associated with that lawyer in the matter but who do not expect to appear before the court or administrative agency. For example, subordinate lawyers may conduct research, review documents, and attend meetings with witnesses in support of the lawyer responsible for the litigation.

Paragraph (c)(3) permits a lawyer admitted to practice law in another jurisdiction to perform services on a temporary basis in this jurisdiction, provided that those services are in or are reasonably related to a pending or potential arbitration, mediation, or other alternative dispute resolution proceeding in this or another jurisdiction and the services arise out of or are reasonably related to the lawyer's practice in a jurisdiction in which the lawyer is admitted to practice. The lawyer, however, must obtain admission pro hac vice under MCR 8.126 in the case of a court-annexed arbitration or mediation, or otherwise if required by court rule or law.

Paragraph (c)(4) permits a lawyer admitted in another jurisdiction to provide certain legal services on a temporary basis in this jurisdiction if they arise out of or are reasonably related to the lawyer's practice in a jurisdiction in which the lawyer is admitted but are not covered by paragraphs (c)(2) or (c)(3). These services include both legal services and services performed by nonlawyers that would be considered the practice of law if performed by lawyers.

Paragraphs (c)(3) and (c)(4) require that the services arise out of or be reasonably related to the lawyer's practice in a jurisdiction in which the lawyer is admitted. A variety of factors indicate such a relationship. The lawyer's client previously may have been represented by the lawyer or may reside in or have substantial contacts with the jurisdiction in which the lawyer is admitted. The matter, although involving other jurisdictions, may have a significant connection with that jurisdiction. In other cases, significant aspects of the lawyer's work may be conducted in that jurisdiction or a significant aspect of the matter may involve the law of that jurisdiction. The necessary relationship may arise when the client's activities or the legal issues involve multiple jurisdictions, such as when the officers of a multinational corporation survey potential business sites and seek the services of the corporation's lawyer in assessing the relative merits of each. In addition, the services may draw on the lawyer's recognized expertise, as developed through the regular practice of law on behalf of clients in matters involving a particular body of federal, nationally uniform, foreign, or international law.

Paragraph (d) identifies two circumstances in which a lawyer who is admitted to practice in another jurisdiction of the United States and is not disbarred or suspended from practice in any jurisdiction may establish an office or other systematic and continuous presence in this jurisdiction for the practice of law as well as to provide legal services on a temporary basis. Except as provided in paragraphs (d)(1) and (d)(2), a lawyer who is admitted to practice law in another jurisdiction and who establishes an office or other systematic or continuous presence in this jurisdiction must become admitted to practice law generally in this jurisdiction.

Paragraph (d)(1) applies to a lawyer who is employed by a client to provide legal services to the client or its organizational affiliates, i.e., entities that control, are controlled by, or are under common control with the employer. This paragraph does not authorize the provision of personal legal services to the employer's officers or employees. This paragraph applies to in-house corporate lawyers, government lawyers, and others who are employed to render legal services to the employer. The lawyer's ability to represent the employer outside the jurisdiction in which the lawyer is licensed generally serves the interests of the employer and does not create an unreasonable risk to the client and others because the employer is well situated to assess the lawyer's qualifications and the quality of the lawyer's work.

If an employed lawyer establishes an office or other systematic presence in this jurisdiction for the purpose of rendering legal services to the employer, the lawyer may be subject to registration or other requirements, including assessments for client protection funds and mandatory continuing legal education.

Paragraph (d)(2) recognizes that a lawyer may provide legal services in a jurisdiction in which the lawyer is not licensed when authorized to do so by statute, court rule, executive regulation, or judicial precedent.

A lawyer who practices law in this jurisdiction is subject to the disciplinary authority of this jurisdiction. See Rule 8.5(a).

In some circumstances, a lawyer who practices law in this jurisdiction pursuant to paragraphs (c) or (d) may be required to inform the client that the lawyer is not licensed to practice law in this jurisdiction. For example, such disclosure may be required when the representation occurs primarily in this jurisdiction and requires knowledge of the law of this jurisdiction. See Rule 1.4(b).

Paragraphs (c) and (d) do not authorize lawyers who are admitted to practice in other jurisdictions to advertise legal services to prospective clients in this jurisdiction. Whether and how lawyers may communicate the availability of their services to prospective clients in this jurisdiction is governed by Rules 7.1 to 7.5.

Comments

Staff Comment to 2010 Amendment

The amended rule sets specific guidelines for out-of-state lawyers who are appearing temporarily in Michigan, and is intended to work in conjunction with MRPC 8.5. See, also, MCR 8.126 and MCR 9.108(E)(8).

Rule 5.6. Restrictions on Right to Practice

A lawyer shall not participate in offering or making:

(a) a partnership or employment agreement that restricts the right of a lawyer to practice after termination of the relationship, except an agreement concerning benefits upon retirement or as permitted in Rule 1.17; or

(b) an agreement in which a restriction on the lawyer's right to practice is part of the settlement of a controversy between private parties.

[Amended May 31, 1991, effective October 1, 1991, 437 Mich.]

Official Comment

An agreement restricting the right of a lawyer to practice after leaving a firm not only limits the lawyer's professional autonomy but also limits the freedom of clients to choose a lawyer. Paragraph (a) prohibits such agreements except for restrictions incident to provisions concerning retirement benefits for service with the firm or restrictions included in the terms of a sale pursuant to MRPC 1.17.

Paragraph (b) prohibits a lawyer from agreeing not to represent other persons in connection with settling a claim on behalf of a client.

Rule 5.7. Responsibilities Regarding Law–Related Services

(a) A lawyer shall be subject to the Michigan Rules of Professional Conduct with respect to the provision of law-related services, as defined in paragraph (b), if the law-related services are provided:

(1) by the lawyer in circumstances that are not distinct from the lawyer's provision of legal services to clients; or

(2) in other circumstances by an entity controlled by the lawyer individually or with others if the lawyer fails to take reasonable measures to assure that a person obtaining the law-related services knows that the services are not legal services and that the protections of the client-lawyer relationship do not exist.

(b) The term "law-related services" denotes services that might reasonably be performed in conjunction with and in substance are related to the provision of legal services, and that are not prohibited as unauthorized practice of law when provided by a nonlawyer.

[Adopted October 26, 2010, effective January 1, 2011, 487 Mich.]

Official Comment

When a lawyer performs law-related services or controls an organization that does so, there exists the potential for ethical problems. Principal among these is the possibility that the person for whom the law-related services are performed fails to understand that the services may not carry with them the protections normally afforded as part of the client-lawyer relationship. The recipient of the law-related services may expect, for example, that the protection of client confidences, prohibitions against representation of persons with conflicting interests, and obligations of a lawyer to maintain professional independence apply to the provision of law-related services when that may not be the case.

Rule 5.7 applies to the provision of law-related services by a lawyer even when the lawyer does not provide any legal services to the person for whom the law-related services are performed, and regardless of whether the law-related services are performed through a law firm or a separate entity. This rule identifies the circumstances in which all the Michigan Rules of Professional Conduct apply to the provision of law-related services. Even when those circumstances do not exist, however, the conduct of a lawyer involved in the provision of law-related services is subject to those rules that apply generally to lawyer conduct, regardless whether the conduct involves the provision of legal services. See, e.g., Rule 8.4.

When law-related services are provided by a lawyer under circumstances that are not distinct from the lawyer's provision of legal services to clients, the lawyer providing the law-related services must adhere to the requirements of the Michigan Rules of Professional Conduct as provided in paragraph (a)(1). Even when the law-related and legal services are provided in circumstances that are distinct from each other, for example through separate entities or different support staff within the law firm, the Michigan Rules of Professional Conduct apply to the lawyer as provided in paragraph (a)(2) unless the lawyer takes reasonable measures to assure that the recipient of the law-related services knows that the services are not legal services and that the protections of the client-lawyer relationship do not apply.

Law-related services also may be provided through an entity that is distinct from that through which the lawyer provides legal services. If the lawyer individually or with others has control of such an entity's operations, this rule requires the lawyer to take reasonable measures to assure that each person using the services of the entity knows that the services provided by the entity are not legal services and that the Michigan Rules of Professional Conduct that relate to the client-lawyer relationship do not apply. A lawyer's control of an entity extends to the ability to direct its operation. Whether a lawyer has such control will depend upon the circumstances of the particular case.

When a client-lawyer relationship exists with a person who is referred by a lawyer to a separate law-related service entity controlled by the lawyer, individually or with others, the lawyer must comply with Rule 1.8(a).

In taking the reasonable measures referred to in paragraph (a)(2) to assure that a person using law-related services understands the practical effect or significance of the inapplicability of the Michigan Rules of Professional Conduct, the lawyer should communicate to the person receiving the law-related services, in a manner sufficient to assure that the person understands the significance of the fact, that the relationship of the person to the business entity will not be a client-lawyer relationship. The communication should be made, preferably in writing, before law-related services are provided or before an agreement is reached for provision of such services.

The burden is upon the lawyer to show that the lawyer has taken reasonable measures under the circumstances to communicate the desired understanding. For instance, a sophisticated user of law-related services, such as a publicly held corporation, may require a lesser explanation than someone unaccustomed to

making distinctions between legal services and law-related services, such as an individual seeking tax advice from a lawyer-accountant or investigative services in connection with a lawsuit.

Regardless of the sophistication of potential recipients of law-related services, a lawyer should take special care to keep separate the provision of law-related and legal services in order to minimize the risk that the recipient will assume that the law-related services are legal services. The risk of such confusion is especially acute when the lawyer renders both types of services with respect to the same matter. Under some circumstances, the legal and law-related services may be so closely entwined that they cannot be distinguished from each other, and the requirement of disclosure and consultation imposed by paragraph (a)(2) of the rule cannot be met. In such a case, a lawyer will be responsible for assuring that both the lawyer's conduct and, to the extent required by Rule 5.3, that of nonlawyer employees in the distinct entity that the lawyer controls, comply in all respects with the Michigan Rules of Professional Conduct.

A broad range of economic and other interests of clients may be served by lawyers' engaging in the delivery of law-related services. Examples of law-related services include providing title insurance, financial planning, accounting, trust services, real estate counseling, legislative lobbying, economic analysis, social work, psychological counseling, tax preparation, and patent, medical, or environmental consulting.

When a lawyer is obliged to accord the recipients of such services the protections of those rules that apply to the client-lawyer relationship, the lawyer must take special care to heed the proscriptions of the rules addressing conflicts of interest, and to scrupulously adhere to the requirements of Rule 1.6 relating to disclosure of confidential information. The promotion of the law-related services must also in all respects comply with Rules 7.1 through 7.3, dealing with advertising and solicitation. In that regard, lawyers should take special care to identify the obligations that may be imposed as a result of a jurisdiction's decisional law.

When the full protections of all the Michigan Rules of Professional Conduct do not apply to the provision of law-related services, principles of law external to the rules, for example, the law of principal and agent, govern the legal duties owed to those receiving the services. Those other legal principles may establish a different degree of protection for the recipient with respect to confidentiality of information, conflicts of interest, and permissible business relationships with clients. See also Rule 8.4 (Misconduct).

Comments

Staff Comment to 2011 Amendment

This is a new rule. The underlying presumption of the rule is that the Michigan Rules of Professional Conduct apply whenever a lawyer performs law-related services or controls an entity that performs law-related services. The accompanying commentary explains that the presumption may be rebutted only if the lawyer carefully informs the consumer and identifies the services that are law related and clarifies that no client-lawyer relationship exists with respect to ancillary services.

PUBLIC SERVICE

Rule 6.1.   Pro Bono Publico Service

A lawyer should render public interest legal service. A lawyer may discharge this responsibility by providing professional services at no fee or a reduced fee to persons of limited means, or to public service or charitable groups or organizations. A lawyer may also discharge this responsibility by service in activities for improving the law, the legal system, or the legal profession, and by financial support for organizations that provide legal services to persons of limited means.

Official Comment

The ABA House of Delegates has formally acknowledged "the basic responsibility of each lawyer engaged in the practice of law to provide public interest legal services" without fee, or at a substantially reduced fee, in one or more of the following areas: poverty law, civil rights law, public rights law, charitable organization representation and the administration of justice. This rule expresses that policy, but is not intended to be enforced through disciplinary process.

The rights and responsibilities of individuals and organizations in the United States are increasingly defined in legal terms. As a consequence, legal assistance

in coping with the web of statutes, rules and regulations is imperative for persons of modest and limited means, as well as for the relatively well-to-do.

The basic responsibility for providing legal services for those unable to pay ultimately rests upon the individual lawyer, and personal involvement in the problems of the disadvantaged can be one of the most rewarding experiences in the life of a lawyer. Every lawyer, regardless of professional prominence or professional workload, should find time to participate in or otherwise support the provision of legal services to the disadvantaged. The provision of free legal services to those unable to pay reasonable fees continues to be an obligation of each lawyer as well as the profession generally, but the efforts of individual lawyers are often not enough to meet the need. Thus, it has been necessary for the profession and government to institute additional programs to provide legal services. Accordingly, legal aid offices, lawyer referral services and other related programs have been developed, and others will be developed by the profession and government. Every lawyer should support all proper efforts to meet this need for legal services.

Rule 6.2.   Accepting Appointments

A lawyer shall not seek to avoid appointment by a tribunal to represent a person except for good cause, such as:

(a) representing the client is likely to result in violation of the Rules of Professional Conduct or other law;

(b) representing the client is likely to result in an unreasonable financial burden on the lawyer; or

(c) the client or the cause is so repugnant to the lawyer as to be likely to impair the client-lawyer relationship or the lawyer's ability to represent the client.

Official Comment

A lawyer ordinarily is not obliged to accept a client whose character or cause the lawyer regards as repugnant. The lawyer's freedom to select clients is, however, qualified. All lawyers have a responsibility to assist in providing pro bono publico service. See Rule 6.1. An individual lawyer fulfills this responsibility by accepting a fair share of unpopular matters or indigent or unpopular clients. A lawyer may also be subject to appointment by a court to serve unpopular clients or persons unable to afford legal services.

Appointed Counsel. For good cause, a lawyer may seek to decline an appointment to represent a person who cannot afford to retain counsel or whose cause is unpopular. Good cause exists if the lawyer could not handle the matter competently (see Rule 1.1) or if undertaking the representation would result in an improper conflict of interest. Good cause also exists if the client or the cause is so repugnant to the lawyer as to be likely to impair the client-lawyer relationship or the lawyer's ability to represent the client. A lawyer may also seek to decline an appointment if acceptance would be unreasonably burdensome, for example, when it would impose a financial sacrifice so great as to be unjust.

An appointed lawyer has the same obligations to the client as retained counsel, including the obligations of loyalty and confidentiality, and is subject to the same limitations on the client-lawyer relationship, such as the obligation to refrain from assisting the client in violation of the rules.

Rule 6.3. Legal Services Organizations and Lawyer Referral Services

(a) A lawyer may serve as a director, officer, or member of a legal services organization, apart from the law firm in which the lawyer practices, notwithstanding that the organization serves persons having interests adverse to a client of the lawyer. The lawyer shall not knowingly participate in a decision or action of the organization:

(1) if participating in the decision or action would be incompatible with the lawyer's obligations to a client under Rule 1.7; or

(2) where the decision or action could have a material adverse effect on the representation of a client of the organization whose interests are adverse to a client of the lawyer.

(b) A lawyer may participate in and pay the usual charges of a not-for-profit lawyer referral service that recommends legal services to the public if that service:

(1) maintains registration as a qualified service with the State Bar, under such rules as may be adopted by the State Bar, consistent with these rules;

(2) is operated in the public interest for the purpose of referring prospective clients to lawyers; pro bono and public service legal programs; and government, consumer or other agencies that can best provide the assistance needed by clients, in light of their financial circumstances, spoken language, any disability, geographical convenience, and the nature and complexity of their problems;

(3) is open to all lawyers licensed and eligible to practice in this state who maintain an office within the geographical area served, and who:

(i) meet reasonable and objective requirements of experience, as established by the service;

(ii) pay reasonable registration and membership fees not to exceed an amount established by the State Bar to encourage widespread lawyer participation; and

(iii) maintain a policy of errors and omissions insurance, or provide proof of financial responsibility, in an amount at least equal to the minimum established by the State Bar;

(4) ensures that the combined fees and expenses charged a prospective client by a qualified service and a lawyer to whom the client is referred not exceed the total charges the client would have incurred had no referral service been involved; and

(5) makes no fee-generating referral to any lawyer who has an ownership interest in, or who operates or is employed by, the qualified service, or who is associated with a law firm that has an ownership interest in, or operates or is employed by, a qualified service.

(c) The requirements of subrule (b) do not apply to

(1) a plan of prepaid legal services insurance authorized to operate in the state, or a group or prepaid legal plan, whether operated by a union, trust, mutual benefit or aid association, corporation or other entity or person, which provides unlimited or a specified amount of telephone advice or personal communications at no charge to the members or beneficiaries, other than a periodic membership or beneficiary fee, and furnishes to or pays for legal services for its members or beneficiaries;

(2) individual lawyer-to-lawyer referrals;

(3) lawyers jointly advertising their services in a manner that discloses that such advertising is solely to solicit clients for themselves; or

(4) any pro bono legal assistance program that does not accept fees from lawyers or clients for referrals.

(d) The State Bar or any aggrieved person may seek an injunction in the circuit court to enjoin violations of subrule (b). In the event the injunction is granted, the petitioner shall be entitled to reasonable costs and attorney fees.

(e) A lawyer may participate in and pay the usual charges of a plan or organization defined in subrule (c)(1), if that plan or organization:

(1) has filed with the State Bar of Michigan a written plan disclosing the name under which it operates; the name, address, and telephone number of its chief operating officer; and the plan terms, conditions of eligibility, schedule of benefits, subscription charges and agreements with counsel;

(2) updates its filings within 30 days of any material change;

(3) in January of each year following its inception files a statement representing that it continues to do business under the terms and conditions reflected in its filings as amended to date.

These filing requirements shall not apply to not-for-profit legal aid associations.

[Amended October 23, 1989, effective January 1, 1990, 433 Mich; January 30, 1990, effective March 1, 1990, 434 Mich; January 21, 1998, effective April 1, 1998, 456 Mich.]

Official Comment

Lawyers should be encouraged to support and participate in legal service organizations. A lawyer who is an officer or a member of such an organization does not thereby have a client-lawyer relationship with persons served by the organization. However, there is potential conflict between the interests of such persons and the interests of the lawyer's clients. If the possibility of such conflict disqualified a lawyer from serving on the board of a legal services organization, the profession's involvement in such organizations would be severely curtailed.

It may be necessary in appropriate cases to reassure a client of the organization that the representation will not be affected by conflicting loyalties of a member of the board. Established, written policies in this respect can enhance the credibility of such assurances.

The restriction on lawyer participation with legal services and lawyer referral service organizations to those that file their plans with the State Bar of Michigan is intended to facilitate the establishment of a single, central repository of all such organizations in Michigan and of the terms and conditions under which they operate. The existence of that repository would make it possible for the State Bar of Michigan annually to prepare and make publicly available a directory of legal services and lawyer referral service organizations in Michigan. Absent such a central repository, reliable information concerning the status of all such organizations might not be available.

Comments

Staff Comment to 1990 Amendment

The 1990 amendment to MRPC 6.3(b) was made at the request of the State Bar of Michigan.

Staff Comment to 1998 Amendment

The April 1998 amendment of MRPC 6.3 was recommended by the State Bar of Michigan. The amended rule provides that a lawyer referral service may not make fee-generating referrals to lawyers who have an ownership or employment interest in the service. The rule also distinguishes services established and operated in the public interest from for-profit ventures and those of private law firms; establishes minimum uniform standards for making referrals and operating the referral business in the public interest; and helps clarify the public understanding of the types of services advertised and offered by different delivery systems.

Rule 6.4. Law Reform Activities Affecting Client Interests

A lawyer may serve as a director, officer, or member of an organization involved in reform of the law or administration of the law notwithstanding that the reform may affect the interests of a client of the lawyer. When the lawyer knows that the interests of a client may be materially benefited by a decision in which the lawyer participates, the lawyer shall disclose that fact but need not identify the client.

Official Comment

Lawyers involved in organizations seeking law reform generally do not have a client-lawyer relationship with the organization. Otherwise, it might follow that a lawyer could not be involved in a bar association law reform program that might indirectly affect a client. See also the comment to Rule 1.2. For example, a lawyer specializing in antitrust litigation might be regarded as disqualified from participating in drafting revisions of rules governing that subject. In determining the nature and scope of participation in such activities, a lawyer should be mindful of obligations to clients under other rules, particularly Rule 1.7. A lawyer is professionally obligated to protect the integrity of the program by making an appropriate disclosure within the organization when the lawyer knows a private client might be materially benefitted.

Rule 6.5. Professional Conduct

(a) A lawyer shall treat with courtesy and respect all persons involved in the legal process. A lawyer shall take particular care to avoid treating such a person discourteously or disrespectfully because of the person's race, gender, or other protected personal characteristic. To the extent possible, a lawyer shall require subordinate lawyers and nonlawyer assistants to provide such courteous and respectful treatment.

(b) A lawyer serving as an adjudicative officer shall, without regard to a person's race, gender, or other protected personal characteristic, treat every person fairly, with courtesy and

respect. To the extent possible, the lawyer shall require staff and others who are subject to the adjudicative officer's direction and control to provide such fair, courteous, and respectful treatment to persons who have contact with the adjudicative tribunal.

[Adopted July 16, 1993, effective October 1, 1993, 443 Mich.]

Official Comment

Duties of the Lawyer. A lawyer is an officer of the court who has sworn to uphold the federal and state constitutions, to proceed only by means that are truthful and honorable, and to avoid offensive personality. It follows that such a professional must treat clients and third persons with courtesy and respect. For many citizens, contact with a lawyer is the first or only contact with the legal system. Respect for law and for legal institutions is diminished whenever a lawyer neglects the obligation to treat persons properly. It is increased when the obligation is met.

A lawyer must pursue a client's interests with diligence. This often requires the lawyer to frame questions and statements in bold and direct terms. The obligation to treat persons with courtesy and respect is not inconsistent with the lawyer's right, where appropriate, to speak and write bluntly. Obviously, it is not possible to formulate a rule that will clearly divide what is properly challenging from what is impermissibly rude. A lawyer's professional judgment must be employed here with care and discretion.

A lawyer must take particular care to avoid words or actions that appear to be improperly based upon a person's race, gender, or other protected personal characteristic. Legal institutions, and those who serve them, should take leadership roles in assuring equal treatment for all.

A judge must act "[a]t all times" in a manner that promotes public confidence in the impartiality of the judiciary. Canon 2(B) of the Code of Judicial Conduct. See also Canon 5. By contrast, a lawyer's private conduct is largely beyond the scope of these rules. See Rule 8.4. However, a lawyer's private conduct should not cast doubt on the lawyer's commitment to equal justice under law.

A supervisory lawyer should make every reasonable effort to ensure that subordinate lawyers and nonlawyer assistants, as well as other agents, avoid discourteous or disrespectful behavior toward persons involved in the legal process. Further, a supervisory lawyer should make reasonable efforts to ensure that the firm has in effect policies and procedures that do not discriminate against members or employees of the firm on the basis of race, gender, or other protected personal characteristic. See Rules 5.1 and 5.3.

Duties of Adjudicative Officers. The duties of an adjudicative officer are included in these rules, since many legislatively created adjudicative positions, such as administrative hearing officer, are not covered by the Code of Judicial Conduct. For parallel provisions for judges, see the Code of Judicial Conduct.

Rule 6.6. Nonprofit and Court–Annexed Limited Legal Services Programs

(a) A lawyer who, under the auspices of a program sponsored by a nonprofit organization or court, provides short-term limited legal services to a client without expectation by either the lawyer or the client that the lawyer will provide continuing representation in the matter:

(1) is subject to Rules 1.7 and 1.9(a) only if the lawyer knows that the representation of the client involves a conflict of interest; and

(2) is subject to Rule 1.10 only if the lawyer knows that another lawyer associated with the lawyer in a law firm is disqualified by Rule 1.7 or 1.9(a) with respect to the matter.

(b) Except as provided in paragraph (a)(2), Rule 1.10 is inapplicable to a representation governed by this rule.

[Adopted October 26, 2010, effective January 1, 2011, 487 Mich.]

Official Comment

Legal services organizations, courts, and various nonprofit organizations have established programs through which lawyers provide short-term limited legal services, such as advice or the completion of legal forms, that will help persons address their legal problems without further representation by a lawyer. In these programs, such as legal-advice hotlines, advice-only clinics, or pro se counseling programs, a client-lawyer relationship may or may not be established as a matter of law, but regardless there is no expectation that the lawyer's representation of the client will continue beyond the limited consultation. Such programs are normally operated under circumstances in which it is not feasible for a lawyer to systematically screen for conflicts of interest as is generally required before undertaking a representation. See, e.g., Rules 1.7, 1.9, and 1.10.

A lawyer who provides short-term limited legal services pursuant to this rule must secure the client's consent to the scope of the representation. See Rule 1.2. If a short-term limited representation would not be reasonable under the circumstances, the lawyer may offer advice to the client but must also advise the client of the need for further assistance of counsel. Except as provided in this rule, the Michigan Rules of Professional Conduct, including Rules 1.6 and 1.9(c), are applicable to the limited representation.

Because a lawyer who is representing a client in the circumstances addressed by this rule ordinarily is not able to check systematically for conflicts of interest, paragraph (a) requires compliance with Rules 1.7 or 1. 9(a) only if the lawyer knows that the representation presents a conflict of interest for the lawyer, and with Rule 1.10 only if the lawyer knows that another lawyer in the lawyer's firm is disqualified by Rules 1.7 or 1.9(a) in the matter.

Because the limited nature of the services significantly reduces the risk of conflicts of interest with other matters being handled by the lawyer's firm,

paragraph (b) provides that Rule 1.10 is inapplicable to a representation governed by this rule except as provided by paragraph (a)(2). Paragraph (a)(2) requires the participating lawyer to comply with Rule 1.10 when the lawyer knows that the lawyer's firm is disqualified by Rules 1.7 or 1.9(a). By virtue of paragraph (b), however, a lawyer's participation in a short-term limited legal services program will not preclude the lawyer's firm from undertaking or continuing the representation of a client with interests adverse to a client being represented under the program's auspices. Nor will the personal disqualification of a lawyer participating in the program be imputed to other lawyers participating in the program.

If, after commencing a short-term limited representation in accordance with this rule, a lawyer undertakes to represent the client in the matter on an ongoing basis, Rules 1.7, 1.9(a), and 1.10 become applicable.

Comments

Staff Comment to 2011 Adoption

MRPC 6.6 is a new rule. The rule addresses concerns that a strict application of conflict-of-interest rules may deter lawyers from volunteering to provide short-term legal services through nonprofit organizations, court-related programs, and similar other endeavors such as legal-advice hotlines.

INFORMATION ABOUT LEGAL SERVICES

Rule 7.1. Communications Concerning a Lawyer's Services

A lawyer may, on the lawyer's own behalf, on behalf of a partner or associate, or on behalf of any other lawyer affiliated with the lawyer or the lawyer's law firm, use or participate in the use of any form of public communication that is not false, fraudulent, misleading, or deceptive. A communication shall not:

(a) contain a material misrepresentation of fact or law, or omit a fact necessary to make the statement considered as a whole not materially misleading;

(b) be likely to create an unjustified expectation about results the lawyer can achieve, or state or imply that the lawyer can achieve results by means that violate the Rules of Professional Conduct or other law; or

(c) compare the lawyer's services with other lawyers' services, unless the comparison can be factually substantiated.

Except as otherwise provided in this rule, a lawyer who is a retired or former justice, judge, referee, or magistrate may use the title ("justice," "judge," "referee," or "magistrate") only when the title is preceded by the word "retired" or "former." A justice, judge, referee, or magistrate who is removed from office or terminated on grounds of misconduct is prohibited from using the title.

[Amended September 20, 2018, effective January 1, 2019, 502 Mich.]

Official Comment

This rule governs all communications about a lawyer's services, including advertising permitted by Rule 7.2. Whatever means are used to make known a lawyer's services, statements about them should be truthful. The prohibition in paragraph (b) of statements that may create "an unjustified expectation" would ordinarily preclude advertisements about results obtained on behalf of a client, such as the amount of a damage award or the lawyer's record in obtaining favorable verdicts, and would ordinarily preclude advertisements containing client endorsements. Such information may create the unjustified expectation that similar results can be obtained for others without reference to the specific factual and legal circumstances.

Comments

Staff Comment to 2019 Amendment

The amendment of MRPC 7.1 restricts and regulates the use of the terms "retired" or "former" for a justice, judge, referee, or magistrate who returns to

the practice of law. It applies only where a lawyer is communicating information about the lawyer's services, and thus, would not apply to a former judge who does not return to I, Larry S. Royster, Clerk of the Michigan Supreme Court, certify that the foregoing is a true and complete copy of the order entered at the direction of the Court. the practice of law. This amendment is a narrower version than one submitted by the State Bar of Michigan Representative Assembly.

Rule 7.2. Advertising

(a) Subject to the provisions of these rules, a lawyer may advertise.

(b) A copy or recording of an advertisement or communication shall be kept for two years after its last dissemination along with a record of when and where it was used.

(c) A lawyer shall not give anything of value to a person for recommending the lawyer's services, except that a lawyer may:

(i) pay the reasonable cost of advertising or communication permitted by this rule;

(ii) participate in, and pay the usual charges of, a not-for-profit lawyer referral service or other legal service organization that satisfies the requirements of Rule 6.3(b); and

(iii) pay for a law practice in accordance with Rule 1.17.

(d) For purposes of media advertising, services of a lawyer or law firm that are advertised under the heading of a phone number, web address, icon, or trade name shall identify the name and contact information of at least one lawyer responsible for the content of the advertisement. The identification shall appear on or in the advertisement itself; or, if that is not practical due to space limitations, the identification shall be prominently displayed on the home page of the law firm's website and any other website used by the law firm for advertising purposes.

[Amended October 23, 1989, effective January 1, 1990, 433 Mich; May 31, 1991, effective October 1, 1991, 437 Mich; May 30, 2018, effective September 1, 2018, 501 Mich; March 27, 2019, effective May 1, 2019, 502 Mich.]

Official Comment

To assist the public in obtaining legal services, lawyers should be allowed to make known their services not only through reputation but also through organized information campaigns in the form of advertising. Advertising involves an active quest for clients, contrary to the tradition that a lawyer should not seek clientele. However, the public's need to know about legal services can be fulfilled in part through advertising. This need is particularly acute in the case of persons of moderate means who have not made extensive use of legal services. The interest in expanding public information about legal services ought to prevail over considerations of tradition. Nevertheless, advertising by lawyers entails the risk of practices that are misleading or overreaching.

Neither this rule nor Rule 7.3 prohibits communications authorized by law, such as notice to members of a class in a class action.

Record of Advertising. Paragraph (b) requires that a record of the content and use of advertising be kept in order to facilitate enforcement of these rules.

Paying Others to Recommend a Lawyer. A lawyer is allowed to pay for advertising permitted by these rules and for the purchase of a law practice in accordance with the provisions of MRPC 1.17, but otherwise is not permitted to pay another person for channeling professional work. But see MRPC 1.5(e). This restriction does not prevent an organization or person other than the lawyer from advertising or recommending the lawyer's services. Thus, a legal aid agency or prepaid legal services plan may pay to advertise legal services provided under its auspices. Likewise, a lawyer may participate in not-for-profit lawyer referral programs and pay the usual fees charged by such programs. Paragraph (c) does not prohibit paying regular compensation to an assistant, such as a secretary, to prepare communications permitted by these rules.

Comments

Staff Comment to 2018 Amendment

The amendment of MRPC Rule 7.2 requires certain lawyer advertisements to identify the lawyer or law firm responsible for the advertisement's content. This new language is a revised version of a proposal submitted by the State Bar of Michigan Representative Assembly, and is intended to identify at least one lawyer responsible for the advertisement's content as a way to provide potential clients with important information when the services are advertised under the heading of a phone number, web address, or trade name.

Staff Comment to 2019 Amendment

The amendment of MRPC 7.2 requires lawyer media advertisements under the heading of a phone number, web address, icon, or trade name to identify the name and contact information of at least one lawyer responsible for the content of the advertisement. The identification shall appear in the advertisement or, if not practical because of size restrictions, on the homepage of the law firm's website.

Rule 7.3. Solicitation

(a) A lawyer shall not solicit professional employment from a person with whom the lawyer has no family or prior professional relationship when a significant motive for the lawyer's doing so is the lawyer's pecuniary gain. The term "solicit" includes contact in person, by telephone or telegraph, by letter or other writing, or by other communication directed to a specific recipient, but does not include letters addressed or advertising circulars distributed generally to persons not known to need legal services of the kind provided by the lawyer in a particular matter, but who are so situated that they might in general find such services useful, nor does the term "solicit" include "sending truthful and nondeceptive letters to potential clients known to face particular legal problems" as elucidated in *Shapero v Kentucky Bar Ass'n*, 486 US 466, 468; 108 S Ct 1916; 100 L Ed 2d 475 (1988).

(b) A lawyer shall not solicit professional employment from a person by written or recorded communication or by in-person or telephone contact even when not otherwise prohibited by paragraph (a), if:

(1) the person has made known to the lawyer a desire not to be solicited by the lawyer; or

(2) the solicitation involves coercion, duress or harassment.

[Amended October 23, 1989, effective January 1, 1990, 433 Mich. Comment amended May 23, 2018, effective September 1, 2018, 501 Mich.]

Official Comment

There is a potential for abuse inherent in direct contact by a lawyer with a person known to need legal services. These forms of contact subject a person to the private importuning of the trained advocate in a direct interpersonal

encounter. A person, who may already feel overwhelmed by the circumstances giving rise to the need for legal services, may find it difficult to evaluate fully all available alternatives with reasoned judgment and appropriate self-interest in the face of a lawyer's presence and insistence upon being retained immediately. The situation is fraught with the possibility of undue influence, intimidation, and overreaching.

However, the United States Supreme Court has modified the traditional ban on written solicitation. *Shapero v Kentucky Bar Ass'n*, 486 US 466; 108 S Ct 1916; 100 L Ed 2d 475 (1988). Paragraph (a) of this rule is therefore modified to the extent required by the Shapero decision.

The potential for abuse inherent in direct solicitation justifies its partial prohibition, particularly since lawyer advertising and the communication permitted under these rules are alternative means of communicating necessary information to those who may be in need of legal services.

Advertising and permissible communication make it possible for a person to be informed about the need for legal services, and about the qualifications of available lawyers and law firms, without subjecting a person to impermissible persuasion that may overwhelm a person's judgment.

The use of general advertising and communications permitted under *Shapero*, rather than impermissible direct contact, will help to assure that the information flows cleanly as well as freely. Advertising is out in public view, thus subject to scrutiny by those who know the lawyer. The contents of advertisements and communications permitted under Rule 7.2 are permanently recorded so that they cannot be disputed and may be shared with others who know the lawyer. This potential for informal review is itself likely to help guard against statements and claims that might constitute false or misleading communications, in violation of Rule 7.1. The contents of some impermissible direct conversations can be disputed and are not subject to third-party scrutiny. Consequently they are much more likely to approach (and occasionally cross) the dividing line between accurate representations and those that are false and misleading.

There is far less likelihood that a lawyer would engage in abusive practices against an individual with whom the lawyer has a prior family or professional relationship or where the lawyer is motivated by considerations other than the lawyer's pecuniary gain. Consequently, the general prohibition in Rule 7.3(a) is not applicable in those situations.

This rule is not intended to prohibit a lawyer from contacting representatives of organizations or groups that may be interested in establishing a group or prepaid legal plan for its members, insureds, beneficiaries, or other third parties for the purpose of informing such entities of the availability of, and detail concerning, the plan or arrangement that the lawyer or the lawyer's firm is willing to offer. This form of communication is not directed to a specific person known to need legal services related to a particular matter. Rather, it is usually addressed to an individual acting in a fiduciary capacity seeking a supplier of legal services for others who may, if they choose, become clients of the lawyer. Under these circumstances, the activity which the lawyer undertakes in communicating with such representatives and the type of information transmitted to the individual are functionally similar to and serve the same purpose as advertising permitted under these rules.

Comments

Staff Comment to 1990 Amendment

The 1989 amendment to MRPC 6.3 [effective January 1, 1990] and the corresponding amendment to 7.2(c) [effective January 1, 1990] were made in response to a proposal by the State Bar of Michigan. As indicated in the revised commentary for MRPC 6.3, the changes are intended to facilitate the establishment of a single, central repository of information concerning programs of the sort described in the rule, and of the terms and conditions under which they operate. With such a repository, it will be possible for the State Bar of Michigan annually to prepare and make publicly available a directory of such organizations in Michigan.

The 1989 amendment to MRPC 7.3 [effective January 1, 1990], a corresponding change in MRPC 7.2, and the accompanying changes in the commentary are in response to the U.S. Supreme Court's decision in *Shapero v Kentucky Bar Ass'n*, 486 US 466; 108 S Ct 1916; 100 LEd2d 475 (1988).

Staff Comment to 2018 Amendment

The addition of new rule MRPC 1.18 and amendment of MRPC 7.3 clarifies the ethical duties that lawyers owe to prospective clients and creates consistency in the use of the term "prospective client." This proposal was submitted to the Court by the Representative Assembly of the State Bar of Michigan.

Rule 7.4. Communication of Fields of Practice

A lawyer may communicate the fact that the lawyer does or does not practice in particular fields of law.

Official Comment

This rule permits a lawyer to indicate areas of practice in communications about the lawyer's services, for example, in a telephone directory or other advertising. If a lawyer practices only in certain fields, or will not accept matters except in such fields, the lawyer is permitted to indicate that fact.

Rule 7.5.   Firm Names and Letterheads

(a) A lawyer shall not use a firm name, letterhead or other professional designation that violates Rule 7.1. A trade name may be used by a lawyer in private practice if it does not imply a connection with a government agency or with a public or charitable legal services organization and it is not otherwise in violation of Rule 7.1.

(b) A law firm with offices in more than one jurisdiction may use the same name in each jurisdiction, but identification of the lawyers in an office of the firm shall indicate the jurisdictional limitations on those not licensed to practice in the jurisdiction where the office is located.

(c) The name of a lawyer holding a public office shall not be used in the name of a law firm, or in communications on its behalf, during any substantial period in which the lawyer is not actively and regularly practicing with the firm.

(d) Lawyers may state or imply that they practice in a partnership or other organization only when that is the fact.

Official Comment

A firm may be designated by the names of all or some of its members, by the names of deceased members where there has been a continuing succession in the firm's identity or by a trade name such as the "ABC Legal Clinic." Although the United States Supreme Court has held that legislation may prohibit the use of trade names in professional practice, use of such names in law practice is acceptable so long as it is not misleading. If a private firm uses a trade name that includes a geographical name such as "Springfield Legal Clinic," an express disclaimer that it is a public legal aid agency may be required to avoid a misleading implication. It may be observed that any firm name including the name of a deceased partner is, strictly speaking, a trade name. The use of such names to designate law firms has proven a useful means of identification. However, it is misleading to use the name of a lawyer not associated with the firm or with a predecessor of the firm.

With regard to paragraph (d), lawyers sharing office facilities, but who are not in fact partners, may not denominate themselves as, for example, "Smith and Jones," for that title suggests partnership in the practice of law.

MAINTAINING THE INTEGRITY OF THE PROFESSION

Rule 8.1.   Bar Admission and Disciplinary Matters

(a) An applicant for admission to the bar, or a lawyer in connection with a bar admission application or in connection with a disciplinary matter, shall not

(1) knowingly make a false statement of material fact, or

(2) fail to disclose a fact necessary to correct a misapprehension known by the person to have arisen in the matter, or knowingly fail to respond to a lawful demand for information from an admissions or disciplinary authority, except that this rule does not require disclosure of information protected by Rule 1.6.

(b) An applicant for admission to the bar

(1) shall not engage in the unauthorized practice of law (this does not apply to activities permitted under MCR 8.120), and

(2) has a continuing obligation, until the date of admission, to inform the standing committee on character and fitness, in writing, if any answers in the applicant's affidavit of personal history change or cease to be true.

[Amended effective July 30, 2001, 465 Mich.]

Official Comment

The duty imposed by this rule extends to persons seeking admission to the bar as well as to lawyers. Hence, if a person makes a material false statement in connection with an application for admission, it may be the basis for subsequent disciplinary action if the person is admitted, and in any event may be relevant in a subsequent admission application. The duty imposed by this rule applies to a lawyer's own admission or discipline as well as that of others. Thus, it is a separate professional offense for a lawyer to knowingly make a misrepresentation or omission in connection with a disciplinary investigation of the lawyer's own conduct. This rule also requires affirmative clarification of any misunderstanding on the part of the admissions or disciplinary authority of which the person involved becomes aware.

This rule is subject to the provisions of the Fifth Amendment of the United States Constitution and to article 1, section 17 of the Michigan Constitution. A person relying on such a provision in response to a question, however, should do so openly and not use the right of nondisclosure as a justification for failure to comply with this rule.

A lawyer representing an applicant for admission to the bar, or representing a lawyer who is the subject of a disciplinary inquiry or proceeding, is governed by the rules applicable to the client-lawyer relationship.

Comments

Staff Comment to 2001 Amendment

The July 30, 2001 amendment of MRPC 8.1 expressly precluded bar applicants from engaging in the unauthorized practice of law, and stated an applicant's continuing obligation to update the affidavit of personal history. The structure of MCR 9.104 was changed for greater clarity.

Rule 8.2 .   Judicial and Legal Officials

(a) A lawyer shall not make a statement that the lawyer knows to be false or with reckless disregard as to its truth or falsity concerning the qualifications or integrity of a judge, adjudicative officer, or public legal officer, or of a candidate for election or appointment to judicial or legal office.

(b) A lawyer who is a candidate for judicial office shall comply with the applicable provisions of the Code of Judicial Conduct as provided under Canon 5.

[Amended May 1, 2013, effective August 1, 2013, 493 Mich.]

Official Comment

Assessments by lawyers are relied on in evaluating the professional or personal fitness of persons being considered for election or appointment to judicial office and to public legal offices, such as attorney general, prosecuting attorney and public defender. Expressing honest and candid opinions on such matters contributes to improving the administration of justice. Conversely, false statements by a lawyer can unfairly undermine public confidence in the administration of justice.

To maintain the fair and independent administration of justice, lawyers are encouraged to continue traditional efforts to defend judges and courts unjustly criticized.

Comments

Staff Comment to 2013 Amendment

These amendments reflect an effort to make the judicial canons consistent regarding law-related and nonlaw-related extrajudicial activities in which judges may participate, and to clarify the activities that are allowed or prohibited. The proposal retains the explicit prohibition on a judge individually soliciting funds, and likewise prohibits the use of the prestige of the office for that purpose. The newly-constituted Canon 4, which consolidates previous Canon 4 and Canon 5 into one canon, permits a judge to engage in various specific activities, including serving as a member of an honorary committee or joining a general appeal, speaking at or receiving an award at an organization's event, and allowing the judge's name to be used in support of a fundraising event. The proposal also includes several suggested revisions that were recommended during the public comment period.

In addition to combining Canons 4 and 5 into one canon, the amendments eliminate the language of Canon 7C that prohibited a judge from accepting a testimonial, and move the reformulated language from Canon 7C(2) prohibiting a judge from accepting a contribution of money to Canon 2G. Also, the proposal clarifies Canon 2 so that activities allowed under Canon 4 are not considered a violation of the principle of use of the prestige of office. Further, the amendments clarify that certain canons of the Code of Judicial Conduct (specifically Canons 1, 2, 4[A]–[D] and 7) apply to all candidates for judicial office as part of the new language inserted as Canon 5. Finally, MRPC 8.2 (which applies to lawyers) is amended to reflect that the judicial canons applicable to judicial candidates are set out in new Canon 5.

Nearly all of the current language in Canon 2, 4, 5, and 7 is retained in this proposal. The new language adds explicit provisions to describe the types of activities that are allowed or prohibited for judges which until now had been undefined and therefore the source of confusion.

Rule 8.3. Reporting Professional Misconduct

(a) A lawyer having knowledge that another lawyer has committed a significant violation of the Rules of Professional Conduct that raises a substantial question as to that lawyer's honesty, trustworthiness, or fitness as a lawyer shall inform the Attorney Grievance Commission.

(b) A lawyer having knowledge that a judge has committed a significant violation of the Code of Judicial Conduct that raises a substantial question as to the judge's honesty, trustworthiness, or fitness for office shall inform the Judicial Tenure Commission.

(c) This rule does not require disclosure of:

(1) information otherwise protected by Rule 1.6; or

(2) information gained by a lawyer while serving as an employee or volunteer of the substance abuse counseling program of the State Bar of Michigan, to the extent the information would be protected under Rule 1.6 from disclosure if it were a communication between lawyer and client.
[Amended effective January 6, 1993, 441 Mich.]

Official Comment

Self-regulation of the legal profession requires that members of the profession initiate disciplinary investigation when they know of a violation of the Rules of Professional Conduct. Lawyers have a similar obligation with respect to judicial misconduct. An apparently isolated violation may indicate a pattern of misconduct that only a disciplinary investigation can uncover. Reporting a violation is especially important where the victim is unlikely to discover the offense.

A report about misconduct is not required where it would involve violation of Rule 1.6. However, a lawyer should encourage a client to consent to disclosure where prosecution would not substantially prejudice the client's interests. Because confidentiality is essential to encourage lawyers and judges to seek treatment, information received in the course of providing counseling services in the State Bar's lawyers and judges assistance program is exempt from the reporting requirement to the extent it would be protected under Rule 1.6 if it were a communication between lawyer and client.

If a lawyer were obliged to report every violation of the rules, the failure to report any violation would itself be a professional offense. Such a requirement existed in many jurisdictions but proved to be unenforceable. This rule limits the reporting obligation to those offenses that a self-regulating profession must vigorously endeavor to prevent. A measure of judgment is, therefore, required in complying with the provisions of this rule. The term "substantial" refers to the seriousness of the possible offense and not the quantum of evidence of which the lawyer is aware.

The duty to report professional misconduct does not apply to a lawyer retained to represent a lawyer whose professional conduct is in question. Such a situation is governed by the rules applicable to the client-lawyer relationship.

Rule 8.4. Misconduct

It is professional misconduct for a lawyer to:

(a) violate or attempt to violate the Rules of Professional Conduct, knowingly assist or induce another to do so, or do so through the acts of another;

(b) engage in conduct involving dishonesty, fraud, deceit, misrepresentation, or violation of the criminal law, where such conduct reflects adversely on the lawyer's honesty, trustworthiness, or fitness as a lawyer;

(c) engage in conduct that is prejudicial to the administration of justice;

(d) state or imply an ability to influence improperly a government agency or official; or

(e) knowingly assist a judge or judicial officer in conduct that is a violation of the Code of Judicial Conduct or other law.

Official Comment

Many kinds of illegal conduct reflect adversely on fitness to practice law, such as offenses involving fraud and the offense of wilful failure to file an income tax return. However, some kinds of offenses carry no such implication. Traditionally, the distinction was drawn in terms of offenses involving "moral turpitude." That concept can be construed to include offenses concerning some matters of personal morality, such as adultery and comparable offenses, that have no specific connection to fitness for the practice of law. Although a lawyer is personally answerable to the entire criminal law, a lawyer should be professionally answerable only for offenses that indicate lack of those characteristics relevant to law practice. Offenses involving violence, dishonesty, breach of trust, or serious interference with the administration of justice are in that category. A pattern of repeated offenses, even ones of minor significance when considered separately, can indicate indifference to legal obligation.

A lawyer may refuse to comply with an obligation imposed by law upon a good-faith belief that no valid obligation exists. The provisions of Rule 1.2(c) concerning a good-faith challenge to the validity, scope, meaning, or application of the law apply to challenges of legal regulation of the practice of law. See also Rule 3.4(c).

Lawyers holding public office assume legal responsibilities going beyond those of other citizens. A lawyer's abuse of public office can suggest an inability to fulfill the professional role of attorney. The same is true of abuse of positions of private trust such as trustee, executor, administrator, guardian, agent, and such as officer, director, or manager of a corporation or other organization.

Rule 8.5. Disciplinary Authority; Choice of Law

(a) Disciplinary Authority. A lawyer admitted to practice in this jurisdiction is subject to the disciplinary authority of this jurisdiction, regardless where the lawyer's conduct occurs. A lawyer not admitted in this jurisdiction is also subject to the disciplinary authority of this jurisdiction if the lawyer provides or offers to provide any legal services in this jurisdiction. A lawyer may be subject to the disciplinary authority of both this jurisdiction and another jurisdiction for the same conduct.

(b) Choice of Law. In any exercise of the disciplinary authority of this jurisdiction, the rules of professional conduct to be applied shall be as follows:

(1) for conduct in connection with a matter pending before a tribunal, the rules of the jurisdiction in which the tribunal sits, unless the rules of the tribunal provide otherwise; and

(2) for any other conduct, the rules of the jurisdiction in which the conduct occurred, or, if the predominant effect of the conduct is in a different jurisdiction, the rules of that jurisdiction shall be applied to the conduct; a lawyer shall not be subject to discipline if the lawyer's conduct conforms to the

rules of a jurisdiction in which the lawyer reasonably believes the predominant effect of the lawyer's conduct will occur.

[Amended effective October 6, 1995, 450 Mich. Amended October 26, 2010, effective January 1, 2011, 487 Mich.]

Official Comment

Disciplinary Authority. It is longstanding law that the conduct of a lawyer admitted to practice in this jurisdiction is subject to the disciplinary authority of this jurisdiction. Extension of the disciplinary authority of this jurisdiction to other lawyers who provide or offer to provide legal services in this jurisdiction is for the protection of the citizens of this jurisdiction. Reciprocal enforcement of a jurisdiction's disciplinary findings and sanctions will further advance the purposes of this rule. The fact that a lawyer is subject to the disciplinary authority of this jurisdiction may be a factor in determining whether personal jurisdiction may be asserted over the lawyer in civil matters.

Choice of Law. A lawyer potentially may be subject to more than one set of rules of professional conduct that impose different obligations. The lawyer may be licensed to practice in more than one jurisdiction with differing rules, or may be admitted to practice before a particular court with rules that differ from those of the jurisdiction or jurisdictions in which the lawyer is licensed to practice. Additionally, the lawyer's conduct may involve significant contacts with more than one jurisdiction.

Paragraph (b) seeks to resolve such potential conflicts. Its premise is that minimizing conflicts between rules, as well as uncertainty about which rules are applicable, is in the best interests of clients, the profession, and those who are authorized to regulate the profession. Accordingly, paragraph (b) provides that any particular conduct of a lawyer shall be subject to only one set of rules of professional conduct; makes the determination of which set of rules applies to particular conduct as straightforward as possible, consistent with recognition of appropriate regulatory interests of relevant jurisdictions; and protects from discipline those lawyers who act reasonably in the face of uncertainty.

Paragraph (b)(1) provides, as to a lawyer's conduct relating to a proceeding pending before a tribunal, that the lawyer shall be subject only to the rules of the jurisdiction in which the tribunal sits unless the rules of the tribunal, including its choice of law rule, provide otherwise. As to all other conduct, including conduct in anticipation of a proceeding not yet pending before a tribunal, paragraph (b)(2) provides that a lawyer shall be subject to the rules of the jurisdiction in which the lawyer's conduct occurred or, if the predominant effect of the conduct is in another jurisdiction, the lawyer shall be subject to the rules of that jurisdiction. In the case of conduct in anticipation of a proceeding that is likely to be before a tribunal, the predominant effect of such conduct could be either where the conduct occurred, where the tribunal sits, or in another jurisdiction.

When a lawyer's conduct involves significant contacts with more than one jurisdiction, it may not be clear initially whether the predominant effect of the lawyer's conduct will occur in a jurisdiction other than the one in which the conduct actually did occur. So long as the lawyer's conduct conforms to the rules of a jurisdiction in which the lawyer reasonably believes the predominant effect will occur, the lawyer shall not be subject to discipline under this rule.

If two admitting jurisdictions were to proceed against a lawyer for the same conduct, they should, applying this rule, identify the same governing ethics rules. They should take all appropriate steps to see that they do apply the same rule to the same conduct and should avoid proceeding against a lawyer on the basis of inconsistent rules.

The choice of law provision applies to lawyers engaged in transnational practice, unless international law, treaties, or other agreements between regulatory authorities in the affected jurisdictions provide otherwise.

Comments

Staff Comment to 1995 Amendment

The 1995 amendment of Rule 8.5 was based on a proposal from the State Bar of Michigan. The word "licensed" was substituted for the word "admitted" in the first sentence and the beginning part of the second sentence; the words "regardless of whether the lawyer is" were substituted for the word "although" in the first sentence; and the words "admitted to practice" were substituted for the word "practicing" in the second part of the second sentence.

Staff Comment to 2010 Amendment

The amendments of MRPC 8.5 add a separate section on choice of law. The rule specifically gives discipline authorities jurisdiction to investigate and prosecute the ethics violations of attorneys temporarily admitted to practice in Michigan. The rule is intended to work in conjunction with MRPC 5.5. See, also, MCR 8.126 and MCR 9.108(E)(8).

RULES CONCERNING THE STATE BAR

Effective January 12, 1972

Rule 1.   State Bar of Michigan

The State Bar of Michigan is the association of the members of the bar of this State, organized and existing as a public body corporate pursuant to powers of the Supreme Court over the bar of the State.   The State Bar of Michigan shall, under these rules, aid in promoting improvements in the administration of justice and advancements in jurisprudence, in improving relations between the legal profession and the public, and in promoting the interests of the legal profession in this State.

Comments

For the reasons stated above, IT IS ORDERED that the State Bar of Michigan shall not include a solicitation for funds for any PAC on any mailing to its membership.

This order does not prevent individual attorneys from exercising their rights to contribute to any PAC, including LAWPAC.

IT IS FURTHER ORDERED that this order shall be effective immediately.

IT IS FURTHER ORDERED that Administrative Order No. 1993–5 shall remain in effect.

Rule 2.   Membership

Those persons who are licensed to practice law in this state shall constitute the membership of the State Bar of Michigan, subject to the provisions of these rules.   Law students may become section members of the State Bar Law Student Section. None other than a member's correct name shall be entered upon the official register of attorneys of this state.   Each member, upon admission to the State Bar and in the annual dues notice, must provide the State Bar with the member's correct name, physical address, and email address, that can be used, among other things, for the annual dues notice and to effectuate electronic service as authorized by court rule, and such additional information as may be required.   If the physical address provided is a mailing address only, the member also must provide a street or building address for the member's business or residence.   No member shall practice law in this state until the information required in this Rule has been provided.   Members shall promptly update the State Bar with any change of name, physical address, or email address.   The State Bar shall be entitled to due notice of, and to intervene and be heard in, any proceeding by a member to alter or change the member's name.   The name and address on file with the State Bar at the time shall control in any matter arising under these rules involving the sufficiency of notice to a member or the propriety of the name used by the member in the practice of law or in a judicial election or in an election for any other public office.   Every active member shall annually provide a certification as to whether the member or the member's law firm has a policy to maintain interest-bearing trust accounts for deposit of client and third-party funds.   The certification shall be included on the annual dues notice and shall require the member's signature or electronic signature.

[Amended effective December 11, 1975, 395 Mich.   Amended June 11, 1991, effective August 1, 1991, 437 Mich.   Amended effective August 19, 1993, 443 Mich; September 26, 2001, 465 Mich; May 10, 2005, 472 Mich.   Amended November 20, 2019, effective January 1, 2020, 503 Mich.]

Comments

Staff Comment to 2001 Amendment

The September 26, 2001 amendment of Rule 2 was made at the request of the State Bar of Michigan.   The amendment eliminated the requirement that members of the Bar provide their home addresses to the Bar.   Under the amendment, a business address will be sufficient unless it is a mailing address only.   Although Rule 2 had included a "residence address" requirement since its inception, the Bar had not requested such information for many years.   The other changes were made for clarity and style.

Staff Comment to 2005 Amendment

By order dated May 10, 2005, this Court adopted the amendments of Rules 2, 5, and 6 of the Rules Concerning the State Bar of Michigan with immediate effect. 472 Mich cxii-cxv (2005).   Notice and an opportunity for comment at the September 29, 2005, public hearing having been provided, and consideration having been given, the amendments of Rules 2, 5, and 6 of the Rules Concerning the State Bar of Michigan are retained.

Staff Comment to 2020 Amendment

The amendment of Rule 2 of the Rules Concerning the State Bar of Michigan updates and expands the rule slightly to include reference to a member's email address.

Rule 3.   Membership Classes

(A) Active.   A person engaged in the practice of law in Michigan must be an active member of the State Bar.   In addition to its traditional meaning, the term "person engaged in the practice of law" in this rule includes a person licensed to practice law in Michigan or another jurisdiction and employed in Michigan in the administration of justice or in a position which requires that the person be a law school graduate, but does not include (1) a judicial law clerk who is a member or is seeking to become a member of the bar of another jurisdiction and who does not intend to practice in Michigan after the clerkship ends, or (2) an instructor in law. Only an active member may vote in a State Bar election or hold a State Bar office. A person not an active member who engages in the practice of law is subject to discipline or prosecution for unauthorized practice.

(B) Inactive. An active member may request an inactive classification.

(1) If the period of inactivity is less than 3 years, the member may be reclassified as active by

(a) applying to the State Bar secretary;

(b) paying the full amount of the annual dues for the current fiscal year; and

(c) demonstrating that no disciplinary action has been taken or is currently pending in another jurisdiction.

(2) If the period of inactivity is 3 years or more, the member must, in addition to fulfilling the requirements of subrule (B)(1)(a)–(c), obtain a certificate from the Board of Law Examiners that the member possesses sufficient ability and learning in the law to enable the member to properly practice as an attorney and counselor in Michigan.

If the inactive member has been or is currently subject to disciplinary action in another jurisdiction, the application must be referred to the Attorney Discipline Board and action on the application delayed until the board makes a decision.

(C) Law Student. A student in good standing at a law school approved by the Board of Law Examiners or the American Bar Association may be a member of the law student section.

(D) Affiliate. A legal assistant as defined in the State Bar bylaws may become an affiliate member of the State Bar of Michigan and shall thereupon be a member of the legal assistants section. A legal administrator as defined in the State Bar bylaws may become an affiliate member of the State Bar of Michigan and shall thereupon be a member of the legal administrators section.

(E) Resignation. An active or inactive member who is not subject to pending disciplinary action in this state or any other jurisdiction may resign from membership by notifying the secretary of the State Bar in writing. The secretary shall notify the member when the request is accepted, whereupon the member no longer will be qualified to practice law in Michigan and no longer will be eligible to receive any other member benefits. The secretary of the State Bar also shall notify the clerk of the Supreme Court of the resignation. To be readmitted as a member of the State Bar, a person who has voluntarily resigned and who is not otherwise eligible for admission without examination under Rule 5 of the Rules for the Board of Law Examiners must reapply for admission, satisfy the Board of Law Examiners that the person possesses the requisite character and fitness to practice law, obtain a passing score on the Michigan Bar Examination, and pay applicable fees and dues. Resignation does not deprive the Attorney Grievance Commission or the Attorney Discipline Board of jurisdiction over the resignee with respect to misconduct that occurred before the effective date of resignation.

(F) Emeritus Membership. Effective October 1, 2004, an active or inactive member who is 70 years of age or older or has been a member of the State Bar for at least 30 years, and who is not subject to pending disciplinary action in this state or any other jurisdiction, may elect emeritus status by notifying the secretary of the State Bar in writing. The secretary shall notify the member when the request is accepted, whereupon the member no longer will be qualified to practice law in Michigan, but will be eligible to receive other member benefits as directed by the Board of Commissioners of the State Bar. The secretary of the State Bar also shall notify the clerk of the Supreme Court when a member is given emeritus status. Members who were age 70 or older as of October 1, 2003, who resigned or were suspended from membership after October 1, 2003, but before September 30, 2004, for nonpayment of dues are to be automatically reinstated as emeritus members, effective October 1, 2004, unless they notify the secretary of the State Bar that they do not wish to be reinstated.

(1) *Grievances and Discipline.* Emeritus status does not deprive the Attorney Grievance Commission or the Attorney Discipline Board of jurisdiction over the emeritus member.

(2) *Readmission.* To be readmitted as an active member of the State Bar, a member who has voluntarily elected emeritus status and who is not otherwise eligible for admission without examination under Rule 5 of the Rules for the Board of Law Examiners must reapply for admission, satisfy the Board of Law Examiners that the person possesses the requisite character and fitness to practice law, obtain a passing score on the Michigan Bar Examination, and pay applicable fees and dues.

[Amended effective May 12, 1972, 387 Mich; December 12, 1975, 395 Mich; October 1, 1978, 402 Mich; May 3, 1979, 406 Mich; Amended October 23, 1989, effective April 1, 1990, 433 Mich; June 11, 1991, effective August 1, 1991, 437 Mich; July 22, 2003, effective September 1, 2003, 469 Mich. Amended effective June 1, 2004, 470 Mich. Amended May 17, 2011, effective September 1, 2011, 489 Mich.]

Comments

Staff Comment to 2003 Amendment

The July 22, 2003, amendments of Rule 3 of the Rules Concerning the State Bar of Michigan, effective September 1, 2003, imposed a dues requirement on inactive members for the first time and also added a provision allowing members of the State Bar to resign their membership. Rule 4 was amended to add a separate dues component for the client security fund administered by the State Bar–money for the client security fund previously came from the general fund. In addition, a dues exemption for persons who are members of the Bar for at least 50 years was substituted for an exemption for members 70 years of age and older. The dues set by the Court for most members were: (1) $120 for the Attorney Grievance Commission and the Attorney Discipline Board; (2) $15 for the client security fund; and (3) $180 for other State Bar expenses.

Staff Comment to 2004 Amendment

The June 1, 2004, amendments of the Rules Concerning the State Bar of Michigan add new subrule 3(F), which creates an emeritus membership status for State Bar members who are 70 years old or older or have been State Bar members for at least 30 years. Beginning October 1, 2004, such members may elect that status as long as there are no pending disciplinary actions against the member in any state. Rule 4(D) is amended to exempt emeritus members from paying State Bar dues. Emeritus members will not be qualified to practice law in Michigan, but will be eligible to receive certain other member benefits.

Staff Comment to 2011 Amendment

The amendment of SBR 3(E), submitted by the State Bar of Michigan, would clarify that an out-of-state attorney who voluntarily resigned from the Michigan bar would not be required to retake the Michigan Bar Examination if the person meets the criteria for admission without examination under Rule 5 of the Rules for the Board of Law Examiners. A similar change also is made in SBR 3(F) regarding emeritus members. Finally, Rule 8 of the Rules for the Board of Law

Examiners is amended to reflect that resigned or emeritus members who seek readmission are covered under Rule 8, which allows for recertification.

Rule 4. Membership Dues

(A) An active member's dues for each fiscal year (October 1 through September 30) are payable at the State Bar's principal office by October 1 of each year. The dues consist of three separate amounts to be set by the Supreme Court to fund: (1) the Attorney Grievance Commission and the Attorney Discipline Board, (2) the client security fund administered by the State Bar, and (3) other State Bar expenses. Each amount shall be listed separately in the dues notice. An inactive member shall be assessed one-half the amounts assessed an active member for the client security fund and general expenses, but the full amount designated for the discipline agencies.

(B) A member who is admitted to the State Bar between April 1 and September 30 shall be assessed one-half the full amount of dues for that fiscal year.

(C) Dues notices must be sent to all members before September 20. A $50 late charge will be added to a dues payment postmarked after November 30. The State Bar must send a written notice of delinquency to the last recorded address provided as required by Rule 2 to a member who fails to pay dues by November 30. Active members must be notified by registered or certified mail. Inactive members must be notified by first class mail. If the dues and the late charge are not paid within 30 days after the notice is sent, the individual is suspended from membership in the State Bar. If an individual is not subject to a disciplinary order and the suspension is for less than 3 years, the member will be reinstated on the payment of dues, a $100 reinstatement fee, and late charges owing from the date of the suspension to the date of the reinstatement. If the suspension is for 3 years or more, the individual must also apply for recertification under Rule 8 for the Board of Law Examiners.

(D) A person who has been a member of the State Bar for at least 50 years shall not be assessed general expenses, but shall pay the full amount assessed other members for the client security fund and the discipline agencies. A member who elects emeritus status pursuant to Rule 3(F) is exempt from paying dues.

(E) An active or inactive member in good standing serving in the United States Armed Forces in full-time active-duty status, as defined by the United States Department of Defense, is eligible for a waiver of payment of dues, including the attorney discipline system fee and the client security fund assessment. An application for a waiver of dues that includes a copy of military orders showing federal active-duty status must be made for each year for which a dues waiver is requested, and a waiver will be granted up to a total of four times. A member for whom a waiver of dues is granted continues to be subject to the disciplinary system.

(F) Annual dues for affiliate members and law student section members are established annually by the Board of Commissioners in an amount not to exceed one-third of the portion of dues for active members which fund State Bar activities other than the attorney discipline system and are payable at the State Bar's principal office by October 1 of each year.

(G) All dues are paid into the State Bar treasury and maintained in segregated accounts to pay State Bar expenses authorized by the Board of Commissioners and the expenses of the attorney discipline system within the budget approved by the Supreme Court, respectively.

[Amended effective March 15, 1973, 389 Mich; December 12, 1975, 395 Mich; December 28, 1976, 399 Mich; December 28, 1976, 399 Mich; October 1, 1978, 402 Mich. Amended June 23, 1989, effective October 1, 1989, 423 Mich; October 23, 1989, effective April 1, 1990, 433 Mich; June 11, 1991, effective August 1, 1991, 437 Mich; July 30, 1993, effective October 1, 1993, 443 Mich; July 22, 2003, effective September 1, 2003, 469 Mich. Amended effective January 26, 2004, 469 Mich; June 1, 2004, 470 Mich. Amended July 3, 2008, effective October 1, 2008, 481 Mich.]

Comments

Staff Comment to 1993 Amendment

The July 30, 1993, amendment of State Bar Rule 4 bifurcates State Bar dues into two components, one for State Bar activities other than the attorney discipline system and the other to fund the Attorney Grievance Commission and the Attorney Discipline Board. This change had been recommended by the State Bar Representative Assembly. In addition, the amendment sets the nondiscipline component at $160.

Staff Comment to 2003 Amendment

The July 22, 2003, amendments of Rule 3 of the Rules Concerning the State Bar of Michigan, effective September 1, 2003, imposed a dues requirement on inactive members for the first time and also added a provision allowing members of the State Bar to resign their membership. Rule 4 was amended to add a separate dues component for the client security fund administered by the State Bar–money for the client security fund previously came from the general fund. In addition, a dues exemption for persons who are members of the Bar for at least 50 years was substituted for an exemption for members 70 years of age and older. The dues set by the Court for most members were: (1) $120 for the Attorney Grievance Commission and the Attorney Discipline Board; (2) $15 for the client security fund; and (3) $180 for other State Bar expenses.

Staff Comment to January, 2004 Amendment

The January 26, 2004, amendment of Rule 4(C), of the Rules Concerning the State Bar of Michigan, which was given immediate effect, was based on a recommendation from the Executive Director of the State Bar of Michigan. The amendment permits the Bar to send notice of nonpayment of dues to inactive members by first class mail. The Bar is still required to send notice of nonpayment of dues to active members by registered or certified mail to the last recorded address.

Staff Comment to June, 2004 Amendment

The June 1, 2004, amendments of the Rules Concerning the State Bar of Michigan add new subrule 3(F), which creates an emeritus membership status for State Bar members who are 70 years old or older or have been State Bar members for at least 30 years. Beginning October 1, 2004, such members may elect that status as long as there are no pending disciplinary actions against the member in any state. Rule 4(D) is amended to exempt emeritus members from paying State Bar dues. Emeritus members will not be qualified to practice law in Michigan, but will be eligible to receive certain other member benefits.

Staff Comment to 2008 Amendment

This proposal, submitted by the State Bar of Michigan, would allow for a waiver of bar dues for up to four year for members who are in full-time active-duty status in the United States Armed Forces.

Rule 5. Board of Commissioners

Section 1. Powers, Functions, and Duties.

(a) The Board of Commissioners shall

(1) implement policy adopted by the assembly;

(2) establish policy for the State Bar between assembly meetings not inconsistent with prior action of the assembly;

(3) manage the State Bar, adopt a budget for it, and supervise receipt and disbursements of State Bar funds;

(4) prescribe the function and duties of committees;

(5) provide for the organization of sections (including a law student section) of the State Bar, membership in which is

voluntary, and determine the amount and regulate the collection and disbursement of section dues;

(6) receive and review committee and section reports and recommendations proposing action by the board and take interim or final action that the board finds feasible, in the public interest, and germane to the functions and purposes of the State Bar; and

(7) arrange for the publication of a journal to be issued at least 4 times a year and sent to the active members without charge.

(b) The Board of Commissioners may

(1) adopt bylaws;

(2) appoint standing and special committees, including

(A) character and fitness,

(B) civil procedure,

(C) court administration,

(D) criminal jurisprudence,

(E) fiscal,

(F) grievance,

(G) judicial qualifications,

(H) legal education,

(I) legislation,

(J) professional and judicial ethics,

(K) scope and correlation, and

(L) unauthorized practice of law;

(3) at the request of the governor, the legislature, or the supreme court, or on its own initiative, conduct an investigation of any matter relating to the state's courts or tribunals, to the practice and procedure in them, or to the administration of justice, and report to the officer or body making the request;

(4) acquire and hold real and personal estate by lease, purchase, gift, devise, or bequest, and sell, convey, mortgage, pledge, or release property;

(5) borrow money and pledge for repayment in annual installments, in anticipation of future revenues from annual membership dues, and issue notes, but the total indebtedness outstanding may not at any time exceed 40 percent and the principal installment due in one year may not exceed 8 percent of the revenues from required annual membership dues for the 5 preceding fiscal years;

(6) accept and hold real and personal estate in trust for any use or purpose germane to the general functions and purposes of the State Bar;

(7) bring an action or proceeding at law or in equity in a state or federal court or tribunal and intervene and be heard on an issue involving the membership or affairs of the State Bar in an action or proceeding pending in a state or federal court or tribunal.

(c) The board may assign these powers, functions, and duties to another State Bar agency but the board may reverse or modify the exercise of a power, function, or duty by a delegated agency.

Section 2. Membership; Terms. The board consists of:

(1) 20 elected members, each serving a 3-year term commencing upon the adjournment of the meeting of the outgoing

Board of Commissioners held at the annual meeting following the member's election.

(2) 5 members appointed by the Supreme Court, each serving a 3-year term commencing upon the adjournment of the meeting of the outgoing Board of Commissioners held at the annual meeting following the member's appointment. In the event that a commissioner appointed by the Supreme Court is not appointed before the adjournment of the annual meeting at which time he or she would ordinarily take office, that member shall begin to serve immediately upon appointment. Except where appointment is made under Section 5, such appointed commissioner shall be considered to have been in office at the beginning of the term for which the appointment is made.

(3) The chairperson-elect, the chairperson and the immediate past chairperson of the State Bar young lawyers section, each serving for the years during which they hold those positions.

(4) The chairperson, vice-chairperson, and clerk of the assembly, each serving for the years during which they hold those positions.

Section 3. Election Districts; Apportionment. The board shall establish commissioner election districts consisting of contiguous judicial circuits and containing, as nearly as practicable, an equal lawyer population. The largest geographic area may have the highest deviation from population equality.

The board shall review and revise election districts every 6 years. If, as the result of a revision in election districts, no elected commissioner maintains his or her principal office in a district or a district has fewer elected commissioners than it is entitled to, the board may designate an elected commissioner or commissioner at large for the district until the next annual election when the vacancy will be filled.

To provide for an orderly transition and to preserve the requirement that approximately one-third of the elected board members are elected each year, the board may extend the term of an elected commissioner for a period not exceeding one year and the authorized membership of the board will be enlarged for the period affected.

An elected commissioner whose district is merged with another district as the result of a revision of commissioner election districts may nevertheless serve the full term for which the commissioner was elected and the authorized membership of the board will be temporarily enlarged for that purpose.

Section 4. Nomination and Election of Commissioners. A commissioner is elected by the active members having their principal offices in the election district. To be nominated, a member must have his or her principal office in the election district and file a petition signed by at least 5 persons entitled to vote for the nominee with the secretary at the principal office of the State Bar between April 1 and April 30. Voting eligibility is determined annually on May 1. Before June 2, the secretary shall mail or electronically deliver a ballot to everyone entitled to vote. A ballot will not be counted unless marked and returned to the secretary at the principal office of the State Bar in a sealed envelope bearing a postmark date not later than June 15, or returned electronically or telephonically in conformity with State Bar election procedure not later than June 15. A board of 3 tellers appointed by the president shall canvass the ballots, and the secretary shall certify the count to the supreme court clerk. A member of or a candidate for the board may not be a teller. The candidate receiving the highest number of votes will be declared elected. In the case of a tie vote, the tellers shall determine the successful candidate by lot. In an election in which terms of differing length are to be filled, the successful candidate with the lowest vote shall serve the shortest term to be filled.

Section 5. Vacancy. The board shall fill a vacancy among the elected commissioners and the Supreme Court shall fill a vacancy among the appointed commissioners, to serve the remainder of an unexpired term. If an elected commissioner moves his or her principal office out of his or her election district, the board shall declare that a vacancy exists. If an elected or appointed commissioner does not attend two consecutive meetings of the board without being excused by the president because of a personal or professional emergency, the president shall declare that a vacancy exists.

Section 6. Meetings. The board shall meet during the annual meeting of the State Bar and before the convening of the assembly and shall hold not less than 4 meetings each year. The interval between board meetings may not be greater than 3 months. A special meeting may be held at the president's call and must be held at the secretary's call at the request of three or more board members. At a meeting, a majority of the board constitutes a quorum.

Section 7. Voting. Each member of the board may cast only one vote. Voting by proxy is not permitted.

[Amended effective October 24, 1972, 388 Mich; March 15, 1973, 389 Mich; April 22, 1975, 394 Mich; May 28, 1975, 394 Mich; December 12, 1975, 395 Mich; November 28, 1977, 402 Mich; June 29, 1979, 406 Mich; February 11, 1986, 424 Mich; January 10, 1989, 423 Mich. Amended June 11, 1991, effective August 1, 1991, 437 Mich. Amended effective May 16, 1995, 448 Mich; May 10, 1996, 451 Mich; May 10, 2005, 472 Mich.]

Comments

Staff Comment to 1996 Amendment

The May 10, 1996, amendment rescinds the prohibition on service by judges on the State Bar Board of Commissioners or in the Representative Assembly. However, judges may not be elected or appointed officers of either body.

Staff Comment to 2005 Amendment

By order dated May 10, 2005, this Court adopted the amendments of Rules 2, 5, and 6 of the Rules Concerning the State Bar of Michigan with immediate effect. 472 Mich cxii-cxv (2005). Notice and an opportunity for comment at the September 29, 2005, public hearing having been provided, and consideration having been given, the amendments of Rules 2, 5, and 6 of the Rules Concerning the State Bar of Michigan are retained.

Rule 6. Representative Assembly

Section 1. Powers, Functions and Duties. The Representative Assembly is the final policy-making body of the State Bar. No petition may be made for an increase in State Bar dues except as authorized by the Representative Assembly.

Section 2. Membership. The assembly consists of:

(1) 142 elected representatives.

(2) 8 commissioner representatives who are the members of the executive committee of the Board of Commissioners. No other member of the board may serve in the assembly.

Notwithstanding the provisions of this section, all representatives previously appointed by the Supreme Court shall serve until the end of their terms. The provisions of Section 6 with regard to the declaration of a vacancy shall also apply, where applicable, to the remaining appointed representatives. Vacan-

cies in appointed positions shall not be filled. In order to achieve the increase in the number of elected representatives from 130 to 142, the assembly shall allocate additional seats each year as necessary to replace former appointed representatives whose terms expire or whose seats have become vacant.

Section 3. Election Districts; Apportionment. The assembly shall apportion the representatives every 6 years. The judicial circuits are the election districts. Each judicial circuit is entitled to one representative. The remaining seats are to be apportioned among the circuits on the basis of lawyer population, determined on February 1 of the reapportionment year. If as a result of the reapportionment any circuit becomes entitled to fewer representatives than are currently elected therefrom, the assembly representatives from that circuit may nevertheless serve the full terms for which they were elected and the authorized membership of the assembly will be temporarily enlarged for that purpose.

Section 4. Nomination and Election of Representatives. A representative is elected by the active members having their principal offices in a judicial circuit. To be nominated, a member must have his or her principal office in the judicial circuit and file a petition signed by at least 5 persons entitled to vote for the nominee with the secretary at the principal office of the State Bar between April 1 and April 30. Voting eligibility is determined annually on May 1. Before June 2, the secretary shall mail or electronically deliver a ballot to everyone entitled to vote. When an assembly member seeks reelection, the election notification must disclose his or her incumbency and the number of meetings of the assembly that the incumbent has attended in the following form: "has attended _____ of _____ meetings during the period of [*his or her*] incumbency." A ballot may not be counted unless marked and returned to the secretary at the principal office of the State Bar in a sealed envelope bearing a postmark date not later than June 15, or returned electronically or telephonically in conformity with State Bar election procedure not later than June 15. A board of tellers appointed by the president shall canvass the ballots and the secretary shall certify the count to the supreme court clerk. A member of or candidate for the assembly may not be a teller. The candidate receiving the highest number of votes will be declared elected. In the case of a tie vote, the tellers shall determine the successful candidate by lot. An election will occur in each judicial circuit every 3 years, except that in a judicial circuit entitled to 3 or more representatives, one-third will be elected each year. If a short-term representative is to be elected at the same election as a full-term one, the member with the higher vote total is elected to the longer term.

Section 5. Terms. An elected representative shall serve a three-year term beginning with the adjournment of the annual meeting following the representative's election and until his or her successor is elected. A representative may not continue to serve after completing two successive three-year terms unless service is extended under the provisions of Rule 7, Section 2.2.

Section 6. Vacancy. If an elected representative ceases to be a member of the State Bar of Michigan, dies during his or her term of office, moves his or her principal office out of the judicial circuit he or she represents, or submits a written resignation acceptable to the chairperson, the chairperson shall declare that a vacancy exists. If an elected representative does not attend two consecutive meetings of the assembly without being excused by the chairperson because of a personal or professional emergency, or does not attend three consecutive meetings of the assembly for any reason or reasons, the chairperson shall declare that a vacancy exists.

When a vacancy exists, the remaining representatives from the affected judicial circuit or, if there are none, the State Bar-recognized local bar associations in the affected judicial circuit, shall nominate a successor prior to the next meeting of the assembly. The assembly may appoint such nominee or, in the event of failure to receive such nomination, any lawyer from the affected judicial circuit, to fill the vacancy, effective immediately upon such appointment and continuing until the position is filled by the election process.

In the event that at the time a vacancy arises under this rule more than eighteen months remain in the term of an elected representative, there will be an election for the unexpired term at the next annual election of representatives. If there are less than eighteen months remaining in the term of an elected representative when a vacancy arises, no interim election will be held. The interim appointment ends when the secretary certifies the election count, and the person elected shall take his or her seat immediately.

Section 7. Meetings. The assembly shall meet:

(1) during the annual meeting of the State Bar;

(2) annually in March or April; and

(3) at any other time and place it determines.

A special meeting may be called by the Board of Commissioners, or by the chairperson and clerk, who shall determine the time and place of such meeting. A special meeting must be called by the chairperson on the written request of a quorum of the Representative Assembly. Fifty members constitute a quorum. The chairperson of the assembly presides at all of its meetings. The assembly may adopt rules and procedures for the transaction of its business not inconsistent with these rules or the bylaws of the State Bar. A section chairperson is entitled to floor privileges without a vote when the assembly considers a matter falling within the section's jurisdiction.

Section 8. Voting. Each member of the assembly may cast only one vote. Voting by proxy is not permitted.

[Amended effective September 10, 1974, 392 Mich; April 22, 1975, 394 Mich; April 29, 1976, 396 Mich; June 29, 1979, 406 Mich; February 2, 1981, 410 Mich; February 11, 1986, 424 Mich; January 10, 1989, 423 Mich; May 16, 1995, 448 Mich; May 10, 1996, 451 Mich; May 10, 2005, 472 Mich.]

Comments

Staff Comment to 1996 Amendment

The May 10, 1996, amendment rescinds the prohibition on service by judges on the State Bar Board of Commissioners or in the Representative Assembly. However, judges may not be elected or appointed officers of either body.

Staff Comment to 2005 Amendment

By order dated May 10, 2005, this Court adopted the amendments of Rules 2, 5, and 6 of the Rules Concerning the State Bar of Michigan with immediate effect. 472 Mich cxii-cxv (2005). Notice and an opportunity for comment at the September 29, 2005, public hearing having been provided, and consideration having been given, the amendments of Rules 2, 5, and 6 of the Rules Concerning the State Bar of Michigan are retained.

Rule 7.   Officers

Section 1. President, President-elect, Vice-president, Secretary, and Treasurer. The officers of the Board of Commissioners of the State Bar of Michigan are the president,

the president-elect, the vice-president, the secretary, and the treasurer. The officers serve for the year beginning with the adjournment of the annual meeting following their election and ending with the adjournment of the next annual meeting. A person may serve as president only once.

After the election of board members but before the annual meeting each year, the Board of Commissioners shall elect from among its members, by majority vote of those present and voting, if a quorum is present:

(1) a vice-president who, after serving a one-year term, automatically succeeds to the office of president-elect for a one-year term, and then to the office of president, for a one-year term;

(2) a secretary; and

(3) a treasurer.

If a vice-president is not able to assume the duties of president-elect, the Board of Commissioners also shall elect from among its members, by majority vote of those present and voting, if a quorum is present, a president-elect who becomes president on the adjournment of the next succeeding annual meeting.

A commissioner whose term expires at the next annual meeting is not eligible for election as an officer unless the commissioner has been reelected or reappointed for another term as a commissioner. If the remaining term of a commissioner elected vice-president or president-elect will expire before the commissioner completes a term as president, the term shall be extended to allow the commissioner to complete the term as president. If the term of an elected commissioner is so extended, the authorized membership of the board is increased by one for that period; a vacancy in the district the vice-president or president-elect represents exists when the term as a commissioner would normally expire, and an election to choose a successor is to be held in the usual manner.

No person holding judicial office may be elected or appointed an officer of the Board of Commissioners. A judge presently serving as an officer may complete that term but may not thereafter, while holding judicial office, be elected or appointed an officer. A person serving as an officer who, after the effective date of this amendment, is elected or appointed to a judicial office, must resign as an officer of the board on or before the date that person assumes judicial office.

Section 2. Chairperson, Vice-Chairperson, and Clerk of the Assembly. A clerk of the Representative Assembly chosen from the elected or appointed membership of the assembly must be elected by the assembly at each annual meeting by majority vote of those present and voting, if there is a quorum present. The clerk serves a one-year term beginning with the adjournment of the annual meeting at which he or she is elected and ending with the adjournment of the next annual meeting at which he or she becomes vice-chairperson for a one-year term concluding with the next annual meeting, at which time he or she becomes chairperson for a one-year term concluding with the next annual meeting. If a representative is elected clerk of the assembly with only one or two years of his or her term remaining, the term of the representative is extended for an additional year or years to permit him or her to serve consecutive terms as vice-chairperson, and chairperson. If the term of an elected representative is so extended, the authorized membership of the assembly is increased by one for the appropriate period; a vacancy in the judicial circuit the chairperson-elect or chairperson represents exists when his or her term would normally expire and an election conducted to choose a successor having the vote to which the representative for that judicial circuit is entitled is to be held in the usual manner. Assembly officers may not concurrently hold another State Bar office and may not be reelected as assembly officers.

No person holding judicial office may be elected or appointed an officer of the Representative Assembly. A judge presently serving as an officer may complete that term but may not thereafter, while holding judicial office, be elected or appointed an officer. A person serving as an officer who, after the effective date of this amendment, is elected or appointed to a judicial office, must resign as an officer of the assembly on or before the date that person assumes judicial office.

Section 3. Duties. The president shall preside at all State Bar meetings and at all meetings of the Board of Commissioners and perform other duties that are usually incident to that office.

The president-elect shall perform the duties assigned by the president. If the president is unable to perform his or her duties or is absent from a meeting of the board or the State Bar, the president-elect shall perform the duties of the president while the disability or absence continues.

The vice-president shall perform the duties assigned by the president and if the president and president-elect are unable to perform their duties or are absent from a meeting of the board or the State Bar, the vice-president shall perform the duties of the president while the disability or absence continues.

The secretary shall act as secretary of the Board of Commissioners, prepare an annual report, and perform the duties usually incident to that office.

The treasurer shall prepare an annual report and perform the duties usually incident to that office. The treasurer will furnish bond that the Board of Commissioners directs.

The Board of Commissioners may assign other duties to the president, president-elect, vice-president, secretary, and treasurer.

The chairperson of the Representative Assembly shall preside at all of its meetings and perform the other duties usually incident to that office, together with additional duties the assembly may assign. The vice-chairperson shall perform duties assigned by the chairperson or as the assembly may assign. The clerk of the assembly shall act as secretary of the assembly and perform the other duties the assembly assigns. If the chairperson is unable to perform his or her duties or is absent from a meeting of the assembly, the vice-chairperson shall perform the chairperson's duties while the disability or absence continues.

Section 4. Vacancies. If any office other than that of president or chairperson or vice-chairperson or clerk of the Representative Assembly becomes vacant, the Board of Commissioners shall fill the office for the unexpired term. If the office of president becomes vacant, the president-elect becomes president for the unexpired term, and may continue as president at the adjournment of the next annual meeting. If the office of president becomes vacant when the office of president-elect is also vacant, the Board of Commissioners shall fill both

vacancies for the unexpired term. If the office of chairperson of the Representative Assembly becomes vacant, the vice-chairperson becomes chairperson for the unexpired term, and may continue as chairperson at the adjournment of the next annual meeting. If the office of chairperson becomes vacant when the office of vice-chairperson or clerk is also vacant, the assembly shall fill all vacancies for the unexpired term at its next meeting; the secretary shall convene and preside at the meeting until successors are elected.

[Amended effective May 24, 1978, 402 Mich; June 29, 1979, 406 Mich. Amended June 11, 1991, effective August 1, 1991, 437 Mich. Amended effective May 10, 1996, 451 Mich. Amended April 3, 2001, effective July 1, 2001, 463 Mich.]

Comments

Staff Comment to 1996 Amendment

The May 10, 1996, amendment rescinds the prohibition on service by judges on the State Bar Board of Commissioners or in the Representative Assembly. However, judges may not be elected or appointed officers of either body.

Staff Comment to 2001 Amendment

The April 3, 2001 amendment of § 1, effective July 1, 2001, provides that persons elected vice president of the Board of Commissioners succeed to the office of president-elect and then to the office of president.

Rule 8.   Executive Director

The Board of Commissioners may appoint an Executive Director, and such assistants, who shall serve on a full-time or part-time basis during such period and for such compensation as the Board of Commissioners may determine, but shall at all times be subject to removal by the board with or without cause. The Executive Director shall perform such duties as the Board of Commissioners may from time to time prescribe. The Executive Director shall have the privilege of the floor at all meetings of the Board of Commissioners, Representative Assembly, sections, section councils, committees, or subcommittees, without vote.

[Amended June 11, 1991, effective August 1, 1991, 437 Mich.]

Comments

Staff Comment to 1991 Amendment

The 1991 amendments effected several changes. They added a vice-chairperson for the Representative Assembly, and gave this new officer a seat on the Board of Commissioners. They also altered the membership of the Board of Commissioners by assigning a seat to the chairperson-elect of the Young Lawyers Section, in addition to the immediate past chairperson and the chairperson of the section. They increased the number of Supreme Court appointees on the Board of Commissioners from three to five. Finally, the 1991 amendments rendered these rules in gender-neutral language.

Rule 9.   Disbursements

The Board of Commissioners shall make the necessary appropriations for disbursements from the funds of the treasury to pay the necessary expenses of the State Bar of Michigan, its officers, and committees. It shall be the duty of the board to cause proper books of account to be kept and to have them audited annually by a certified public accountant. On or before December 31 each year the board shall cause to be presented an audited financial statement of the receipts and expenditures of the State Bar of Michigan for the fiscal year ending the preceding September 30. Such a statement shall also be filed with the Clerk of the Supreme Court and shall be published in the January issue of the official publication of the State Bar of Michigan.

No officer, member of the Board of Commissioners, member of the Representative Assembly, or member of a committee or

section of the State Bar of Michigan shall receive compensation for services rendered in connection with the performance of his or her duties. They may, however, be reimbursed for the necessary expenses incurred in connection with the performance of their duties.
[Amended effective February 11, 1986, 424 Mich.]

Rule 10. Annual Meeting

The State Bar shall hold an annual meeting, which shall include a meeting of the Board of Commissioners and the Representative Assembly and, if requested, the annual congress, as well as meetings of sections and committees that the Board of Commissioners may set. The Board of Commissioners shall designate the time (no later than November 1) and place of the annual meeting.
[Amended effective June 29, 1979, 406 Mich.]

Rule 11. Committees

Section 1. Appointment. Committees of the State Bar of Michigan may be established for the promotion of the objects of the State Bar of Michigan, and shall consist of limited numbers of members appointed by the President with their number, jurisdiction, method of selection and tenure determined in accordance with the bylaws and the resolution establishing the committee. In the event of the resignation, death or disqualification of any member of a committee, the President shall appoint a successor to serve for the unexpired term.

Section 2. Classes. The classes of committees of the State Bar of Michigan shall be:

(a) Standing committees, for the investigation and study of matters relating to the accomplishment of the general purposes, business and objects of the State Bar of Michigan of a continuous and recurring character, within the limitation of the powers conferred.

(b) Special committees, created by resolution of the Board of Commissioners defining the powers and duties of such committees, to investigate and study matters relating to the specific purposes, business and objects of the State Bar of Michigan of an immediate or non-recurring character. The life of any special committee shall expire at the end of the next annual meeting following its creation unless continued by action of the Board.

Section 3. Powers. The Committee on Arbitration of Disputes Among Lawyers, which has the authority to arbitrate disputes voluntarily submitted by lawyers, has the power to issue subpoenas (including subpoenas duces tecum), to take testimony under oath, and to rule on the admissibility of evidence according to the rules of evidence applicable to civil cases.
[Amended effective May 4, 1977, 400 Mich.]

Rule 12. Sections

Section 1. Establishment and Discontinuance. New sections may be established and existing sections may be combined or discontinued or their names changed by the Board of Commissioners in a manner provided by the bylaws.

Section 2. Bylaws. Each section shall have bylaws not inconsistent with these Rules or the bylaws of the State Bar of Michigan. Section bylaws or amendments thereof shall become effective when approved by the Board of Commissioners.

Section 3. Existing Sections. Sections in existence at the time of the adoption of these Rules shall continue unless changed by action of the Board of Commissioners.

Rule 13. Initiative

Three percent or more of the active members of the State Bar may by written petition require consideration by the Representative Assembly of any question of public policy germane to the function and purposes of the State Bar; the assembly may take action on it that it finds proper. The petition must be filed with the clerk at least 90 days before any meeting of the Representative Assembly at which the subject matter is to be considered.
[Amended effective June 29, 1979, 406 Mich.]

Rule 14. Congress

Section 1. Membership and Meeting. Twenty-five or more active members of the State Bar may file a written petition with the secretary at the principal office of the State Bar no later than 90 days before the annual meeting of the State Bar, to require the convening of a congress of the active members of the State Bar in conjunction with the annual meeting to consider the subject matter raised in the petition. One hundred active members constitute a quorum. The president is the presiding officer of the congress and the secretary is the secretary of the congress.

Section 2. Agenda. The congress shall consider all matters proposed for inclusion on its agenda in the petition requesting its convening. The congress may take action on the matters arising on its agenda that it deems warranted. The action is advisory only and must be communicated to the Board of Commissioners and to the Representative Assembly, but the congress may by a two-thirds vote place an issue on the agenda of the board or assembly. If an issue so initiated is first considered by the board, the board shall notify the assembly of its action, and the assembly shall concur with, modify, or reverse the board's action.
[Amended effective April 22, 1975, 394 Mich; June 29, 1979, 406 Mich.]

Rule 15. Admission to the Bar

Section 1. Character and Fitness Committees.

(1) A standing committee on character and fitness consisting of 18 active members of the bar shall be appointed annually by the president of the State Bar of Michigan, who shall designate its chairperson. District character and fitness committees consisting of active members of the bar in each commissioner election district shall be appointed, and their chairpersons designated, by the State Bar commissioners within the respective districts, subject to approval by the State Bar Board of Commissioners.

(2) The standing committee and the district committees under its supervision shall investigate and make recommendations with respect to the character and fitness of every applicant for admission to the bar by bar examination and, upon request of the Board of Law Examiners, the character and fitness of any other applicant for admission.

(3) The State Bar of Michigan shall assign staff to assist the standing and district committees in the discharge of their duties.

(4) The standing committee and each district committee shall meet at the times and places designated by their respective chairpersons. Five members of the standing committee or 3 members of a district committee shall constitute a quorum. The action of a majority of those present constitutes the action of a committee.

(5) State Bar recommendations concerning the character and fitness of an applicant for admission to the bar shall be transmitted to the Board of Law Examiners in accordance with the following procedure:

(a) An applicant shall be recommended favorably by State Bar staff without referral to committee when investigation of all past conduct discloses no significant adverse factual information.

(b) In all other instances, applicants shall be referred to the appropriate district committee for personal interview unless the chairperson or other member of the standing committee designated by the chairperson determines that any adverse information reflected in the file would under no circumstance justify a committee determination that the applicant does not possess the character and fitness requisite for admission, in which event the application shall be transmitted to the Board of Law Examiners with a favorable recommendation.

(c) District committees shall, under the supervision and direction of the standing committee, investigate the character and fitness (other than scholastic) of every applicant referred to them. They shall do so by informal interview and any additional investigation which to them seems appropriate. District committees shall make a written report and recommendation to the standing committee concerning each applicant referred to them.

(d) Upon receiving a district committee report and recommendation, the standing committee shall endorse the recommendation, take the recommendation under advisement pending the receipt of additional information that it deems necessary, remand the recommendation to the district committee with instructions for further proceedings, or reject the recommendation and conduct a hearing de novo.

(e) If the standing committee endorses a report and recommendation of a district committee that an applicant has the requisite character and fitness for admission to the bar, it shall transmit that recommendation to the Board of Law Examiners.

(f) If the standing committee endorses a report and recommendation of a district committee that an applicant does not have the requisite character and fitness for admission to the bar, it shall furnish the applicant with a copy of the report and recommendation and advise the applicant of the right to a formal hearing before the standing committee provided request therefor is made in writing within 20 days. If the applicant requests a formal hearing within the time permitted, a hearing shall be scheduled before the standing committee. If the applicant does not request a formal hearing before the standing committee within the time permitted, the standing committee shall thereupon transmit the report and recommendation of the district committee to the Board of Law Examiners.

(g) At the conclusion of any hearing conducted by the standing committee it shall transmit its report and recommendation to the Board of Law Examiners.

(6) Each applicant is entitled to be represented by counsel at the applicant's own expense at any stage of character and fitness processing.

(7) Information obtained in the course of processing an application for admission to the bar may not be used for any other purpose or otherwise disclosed without the consent of the applicant or by order of the Supreme Court.

(8) Notwithstanding any prohibition against disclosure in this rule or elsewhere, the committee on character and fitness shall disclose information concerning a bar application to the Attorney Grievance Commission during the course of the commission's investigation of a disciplined lawyer's request for reinstatement to the practice of law. Upon receiving a request for character and fitness information and proof that a disciplined lawyer is seeking reinstatement to the practice of law, the committee shall notify the lawyer that the commission has requested the lawyer's confidential file. The committee then shall disclose to the commission all information relating to the lawyer's bar application. The commission and the grievance administrator shall protect such information, as provided in MCR 9.126(D). The administrator shall submit to a hearing panel, under seal, any information obtained under this rule that the administrator intends to use in a reinstatement proceeding. The hearing panel shall determine whether the information is relevant to the proceeding, and only upon such a determination may the administrator use the information in a public pleading or proceeding.

(9) Any information pertaining to an application for admission to the bar submitted to a district committee, the standing committee, the Board of Law Examiners or the Supreme Court must also be disclosed to the applicant.

(10) A person is absolutely immune from suit for statements and communications transmitted solely to the State Bar staff, the district committee, the standing committee or the Board of Law Examiners, or given in the course of an investigation or proceeding concerning the character and fitness of an applicant for admission to the bar. The State Bar staff, the members of the district and standing committees and the members and staff of the Board of Law Examiners are absolutely immune from suit for conduct arising out of the performance of their duties.

(11) The standing committee has the power to issue subpoenas (including subpoenas duces tecum), to take testimony under oath, and to rule on the admissibility of evidence guided, but not strictly bound, by the rules of evidence applicable to civil cases. An applicant is entitled to use the committee's subpoena power to obtain relevant evidence by request submitted to the chairperson of the standing committee.

(12) Formal hearings conducted by the standing committee shall be suitably recorded for the later production of transcripts, if necessary.

(13) An applicant is entitled to a copy of the entire record of proceedings before the standing committee at the applicant's expense.

(14) An applicant is entitled to at least 10 days notice of scheduled district committee interviews and standing commit-

tee hearings. The notice shall contain the following information:

(a) The time and place of the interview or hearing;

(b) A statement of the conduct which is to be the subject of the interview or hearing;

(c) The applicant's right to be represented by counsel; and

(d) A description of the procedures to be followed at the interview or hearing, together with copies of any applicable rules.

(15) An applicant has the burden of proving by clear and convincing evidence that he or she has the current good moral character and general fitness to warrant admission to the bar.

(16) Upon request made no later than 5 days prior to a scheduled interview or hearing, the applicant and State Bar staff may demand of the other that they be furnished with the identity of any witnesses to be produced at the interview or hearing as well as an opportunity for inspecting or copying any documentary evidence to be offered or introduced.

(17) If an application is withdrawn following an adverse recommendation by a district committee or the standing committee, or, if following such an adverse recommendation the applicant fails to appear for further proceedings or takes no further action, the standing committee shall notify the applicant that the application for admission to the bar may not be renewed until the expiration of two years from the date of the adverse recommendation by the district committee or by the standing committee, or such greater period as the committee specifies, up to a maximum period of five years. The notification shall specify the reasons for the imposition of a waiting period that is longer than two years.

(18) An applicant who has been denied character and fitness certification for admission to the bar by the Board of Law Examiners may not reapply for character and fitness certification for a period of two years following the denial or such greater period specified in the decision denying certification, up to a maximum period of five years. The decision shall specify the reasons for the imposition of a waiting period that is longer than two years.

(19) The standing committee may adopt rules of procedure governing the processing and investigation of applications for admission to the bar and proceedings before district committees and the standing committee not inconsistent with these rules.

(20) An applicant is entitled to review by the Board of Law Examiners of any report and recommendation filed with the Board concluding that the applicant does not have the character and fitness requisite for admission.

(21) Every applicant for admission by examination and any other applicant whose application is submitted to the standing committee on character and fitness for evaluation and recommendation shall pay to the State Bar of Michigan a fee of $375 for the character and fitness investigation authorized by this rule. An additional fee of $175 shall be required for character and fitness evaluations related to applications for the February examination that are submitted after November 1, and applications for the July examination that are submitted after March 1.

Section 2. Foreign Attorney; Temporary Permission. Any person who is duly licensed to practice law in another state or territory, or in the District of Columbia, of the United States of America, or in any foreign country, may be temporarily admitted under MCR 8.126.

Section 3. Procedure for Admission; Oath of Office.

(1) Each applicant to whom a certificate of qualification has been issued by the Board of Law Examiners is required to appear personally and present such certificate to the Supreme Court or one of the circuit courts of this State. Upon motion made in open court by an active member of the State Bar of Michigan, the court may enter an order admitting such applicant to the bar of this State. The clerk of such court is required to forthwith administer to such applicant in open court the following oath of office:

I do solemnly swear (or affirm):

I will support the Constitution of the United States and the Constitution of the State of Michigan;

I will maintain the respect due to courts of justice and judicial officers;

I will not counsel or maintain any suit or proceeding which shall appear to me to be unjust, nor any defense except such as I believe to be honestly debatable under the law of the land;

I will employ for the purpose of maintaining the causes confided to me such means only as are consistent with truth and honor, and will never seek to mislead the judge or jury by any artifice or false statement of fact or law;

I will maintain the confidence and preserve inviolate the secrets of my client, and will accept no compensation in connection with my client's business except with my client's knowledge and approval;

I will abstain from all offensive personality, and advance no fact prejudicial to the honor or reputation of a party or witness, unless required by the justice of the cause with which I am charged;

I will never reject, from any consideration personal to myself, the cause of the defenseless or oppressed, or delay any cause for lucre or malice;

I will in all other respects conduct myself personally and professionally in conformity with the high standards of conduct imposed on members of the bar as conditions for the privilege to practice law in this State.

(2) The applicant is required to subscribe to such oath of office by signing a copy and to register membership in the State Bar of Michigan in the manner prescribed in Rule 2 of these rules and to pay the required dues before practicing law in this State. The clerk shall record such admission, in the journal of such court, and shall preserve such oath of office in the records of the court. A roll of all persons admitted to the bar shall be kept in the office of the clerk of the Supreme Court.

(3) Admission to the bar of this State is an authorization to practice as an attorney and counselor in every court in this State.

[Amended effective June 29, 1979, 406 Mich; October 4, 1985, 422 Mich; February 10, 1987, 428 Mich; September 25, 1987, 429 Mich; July 30, 1992, 440 Mich. Amended June 4, 1976, effective November 1, 1996, 451 Mich; September 22, 1998, effective December 1, 1998, 459 Mich. Amended effective July 18, 2001, 464 Mich; September 12, 2001, 464 Mich; November 1, 2002, 467 Mich; October 8, 2003, 469 Mich. Amended June 27, 2008, effective September 1, 2008, 481 Mich; February 3, 2016, effective May 1, 2016, 499 Mich; December 12, 2018, effective January 1, 2019, 502 Mich.]

Comments

Staff Comment to 1996 Amendment

The November 1, 1996 amendment of Rule 15, section 1, paragraph (20), was requested by the State Bar of Michigan. The amendment will permit the State Bar to charge an additional fee for character and fitness evaluations related to late applications.

Staff Comment to 1998 Amendment

The December 1, 1998 amendment of MCR 9.126 and 9.222 made mandatory the disclosure of information, upon request, between the Attorney Grievance Commission and the Judicial Tenure Commission. The amendment of State Bar Rule 15, § 1 authorized the State Bar's Committee on Character and Fitness to disclose to the Attorney Grievance Commission information concerning the bar application of a disciplined lawyer who is requesting reinstatement to the practice of law. Under the amendment, the lawyer must be notified of the request, and the hearing panel must determine the relevancy of the information before permitting it to be used in a public document or proceeding.

Staff Comment to 2001 Amendment

The July 18, 2001, amendment of Rule 15, § 1, ¶ 21 was proposed by the State Bar of Michigan to more accurately reflect the actual cost of character and fitness investigations. It was approved by the Supreme Court as to new applications for the February 2002 bar examination and any other applications submitted to the character and fitness committee of the State Bar during that time period. The request to make the fee increase permanent remained under consideration by the Court. [The amendment was made permanent by order of the Court effective September 12, 2001.]

Staff Comment to 2002 Amendment

The November 1, 2002, amendment of Rule 15 of the Rules Concerning the State Bar of Michigan increased the number of members on the Standing Committee on Character and Fitness from 12 to 18.

Staff Comment to 2003 Amendment

The October 8, 2003, amendment of Rule 15, § 1, of the Rules Concerning the State Bar of Michigan, which was given immediate effect, was based on a recommendation from the Board of Commissioners of the State Bar of Michigan. The amendment made uniform the length of time that an unsuccessful bar candidate must wait before reapplying for admission. The period for reapplication after an adverse determination by a district character and fitness committee or the Standing Committee on Character and Fitness was changed to two years from three years, unless the committee specifies a longer period of up to five years. Similarly, the period for reapplication after an adverse determination by the Board of Law Examiners was changed to two years from five years, unless the Board of Law Examiners specifies a longer period of up to five years. If a waiting period longer than two years is imposed, the notification or Board decision must specify the reasons for the longer waiting period.

Staff Comment to 2008 Amendment

The adoption of MCR 8.126 and the amendments of MCR 9. 108 and Rule 15 of the Rules Concerning the State Bar of Michigan apply to out-of-state attorneys who seek temporary admission to the bar on or after September 1, 2008. They allow an out-of-state attorney to be authorized to appear temporarily (also known as pro hac vice appearance) in no more than five cases within a 365-day period. Because misconduct will subject the out-of-state attorney to disciplinary action in Michigan, a fee equal to the discipline and client-protection fund portions of a bar member's annual dues is imposed. The fee is required to be paid only once in each fiscal year of the State Bar of Michigan for which the attorney seeks admission. The Attorney Grievance Commission is required to keep a record of all such temporary appearances ordered by Michigan courts and administrative tribunals and agencies, and the attorney discipline system is entitled to receipt of the discipline portion of the fee paid in applying for the temporary admission. The Client Protection Fund is entitled to receipt of the portion of the fee representing the client protection fund fee. The State Bar of Michigan will apprise the Attorney Grievance Commission of any fees paid for temporary admissions.

The Court plans to review these rules again within two years of their effective dates in light of the information gathered by the Attorney Grievance Commission.

Staff Comment to 2016 Amendment

These rule revisions combine and transfer the ministerial functions of processing the payment and monitoring the number of cases for which an out-of-state attorney is temporarily admitted in Michigan to the State Bar of Michigan. In addition, the Michigan attorney associated with the out-of-state attorney is required to submit a copy of the order granting permission to the out-of-state attorney to the state bar for purposes of monitoring.

Staff Comment to 2018 Amendment

The amendment of Rule 15 of the Rules Concerning the State Bar of Michigan (submitted by the SBM Representative Assembly) increases the fee for Character & Fitness investigations to more accurately reflect the costs of performing the investigations and updates the language to reflect the online application process. According to the Bar, this is the first increase in these fees in more than 15 years.

Rule 16. Unauthorized Practice of the Law

The State Bar of Michigan is hereby authorized and empowered to investigate matters pertaining to the unauthorized practice of law and, with the authority of its Board of Commissioners, to file and prosecute actions and proceedings with regard to such matters.

[Amended effective June 29, 1979, 406 Mich.]

Rule 17. Mandatory Legal Education Program for New Admittees to the Michigan Bar [Rescinded effective April 1, 1994]

[Rescinded March 22, 1994, effective April 1, 1994, 444 Mich.]

Rule 19. Confidentiality of State Bar Records

Section 1. Except as provided below, in Rule 15, or as otherwise provided by law, records maintained by the state bar are open to the public pursuant to the State Bar of Michigan Access to Information Policy.

Section 2. Records and information of the Client Protection Fund, Ethics Program, Lawyers and Judges Assistance Program, Practice Management Resource Center Program, and Unauthorized Practice of Law Program that contain identifying information about a person who uses, is a participant in, is subject to, or who inquires about participation in, any of these programs, are confidential and are not subject to disclosure, discovery, or production, except as provided in section (3) and (4).

Section 3. Records and information made confidential under section (1) or (2) shall be disclosed:

(a) pursuant to a court order;

(b) to a law enforcement agency in response to a lawfully issued subpoena or search warrant, or;

(c) to the attorney grievance commission or attorney discipline board in connection with an investigation or hearing conducted by the commission or board, or sanction imposed by the board.

Section 4. Records and information made confidential under section (1) or (2) may be disclosed:

(a) upon request of the state bar and approval by the Michigan Supreme Court where the public interest in disclosure outweighs the public interest in nondisclosure in the particular instance, or

(b) at the discretion of the state bar, upon written permission of all persons who would be identified by the requested information.

[Adopted December 19, 2007, effective January 1, 2008, 480 Mich.]

Comments

Staff Comment to 2008 Adoption

This new rule was submitted for consideration to the Supreme Court by the State Bar of Michigan to clarify and set out the rules regarding confidentiality of documents and records of the bar. This rule requires that internal information that contains identifying information, including information that relates to the Client Protection Fund, the Ethics Program, the Lawyers and Judges Assistance Program, the Practice Management Resource Center Program, and the Unauthorized Practice of Law Program, be confidential. However, records and documents must be disclosed pursuant to a court order, to a law enforcement agency that submits a warrant or subpoena, or to the Attorney Grievance Commission and Attorney Discipline Board. Confidential information may be disclosed if the public interest in disclosure outweighs the public interest in nondisclosure, or at the discretion of the SBM, with the approval of all persons who would be identified by the requested information.

RULES FOR THE BOARD OF
LAW EXAMINERS

Revised August 26, 1976

Rule 1.   General Requirements

An applicant for admission to the practice of law must

(A) be 18 years old or older;

(B) possess good moral character; and

(C) have completed, before entering law school, at least 60 semester hours or 90 quarter hours toward an undergraduate degree from an accredited school or while attending an accredited junior or community college.

Rule 2.   Admission by Examination

(A) An application must be filed by November 1 for the February examination, or March 1 for the July examination. Late applications will be accepted until December 15 for the February examination, or May 15 for the July examination. An application must be accompanied by payment of the fee. All materials filed are confidential.

(B) Before taking the examination, an applicant must obtain a JD degree from a reputable and qualified law school that

(1) is incorporated in the United States, its territories, or the District of Columbia; and

(2) requires for graduation 3 school years of study for full-time students, and 4 school years of study for part-time or night students. A school year must be at least 30 weeks.

A law school approved by the American Bar Association is reputable and qualified. Other schools may ask the Board to approve the school as reputable and qualified. In the event the law school has ceased operations since an applicant's graduation, the request for approval may be made by the applicant. The Board may in its discretion permit applicants who do not possess a JD degree from an ABA-approved law school to take the examination based upon factors including, but not limited to, relevant legal education, such as an LLM degree from a reputable and qualified law school, and experience that otherwise qualifies the applicant to take the examination.

(C) The State Bar character and fitness committee will investigate each applicant. The applicant must disclose any criminal conviction which carries a possible penalty of incarceration in jail or prison that has not been reversed or vacated and comply with the committee's requirements and requests. The committee will report the results of its investigation to the Board. If the committee report shows that an applicant lacks the necessary character and fitness, the Board will review the application, record, and report. If the Board accepts the report, the applicant is entitled to a hearing before the Board and may use the Board's subpoena power. The Board may permit an applicant to take the examination before the character and fitness committee reports. The Board will release the applicant's grade if character and fitness committee approval is obtained.

(D) Every applicant for admission must achieve a passing score, as determined by the Board, on the Multistate Professional Responsibility Examination.

(E) The Board may permit an applicant entering the armed forces before the examination immediately following graduation to take an earlier examination. The applicant must have completed, before the examination, 2½ years full-time or 3½ years part-time study. The Board will release the applicant's grade when the school certifies the applicant's graduation.

(F) The applicant is responsible for meeting all requirements before the examination. The Board may act on information about an applicant's character whenever the information is received.

[Amended effective July 11, 1979, 406 Mich; January 15, 1981, 410 Mich. Amended August 19, 1988, effective January 1, 1990, 431 Mich; May 1, 1995, effective June 1, 1995, 448 Mich; August 26, 1994, effective February 1, 1996, 446 Mich. Amended effective June 30, 2004, 470 Mich.]

Comments

Staff Comment to 1990 Amendment

The [January 1, 1990] amendment conforms the Rules for the Board of Law Examiners concerning admission to the practice of law by examination to the requirements of MCL 600.940, which requires, inter alia, that every applicant for the bar examination be a graduate of a reputable and qualified law school. The amendment rescinds the summer school exception which allowed students attending summer law school to sit for the bar exam if the student would be graduated at the end of the summer term.

Staff Comment to 1996 Amendment

This rule change in section 2(D), effective February 1, 1996, replaces present Rule 2(D) in its entirety as of that date and requires all applicants for admission to the State Bar of Michigan to receive a passing score on the Multistate Professional Responsibility Examination.

Staff Comment to 2004 Amendment

The June 30, 2004, amendments, which were given immediate effect, eliminate the so-called "LLM exception" to the requirement that an applicant possess a JD degree from an ABA-approved law school to sit for the Michigan bar examination. The language added to Rule 2(B)(2) gives the Board of Law Examiners discretion to permit an applicant who does not possess a JD degree from an approved law school to take the bar examination based upon relevant experience and legal education, such as an LLM degree from an approved law school. The new language also permits an applicant whose law school is no longer in operation to request approval of the law school as reputable and qualified.

Rule 3.   Examination Subjects and Grading

(A) The examination consists of two sections:

(1) The Multistate Bar Examination prepared by the National Conference of Bar Examiners and administered on dates and under regulations set by the Conference.

(2) An essay examination prepared by or under the supervision of the Board or by law professors selected by the Board, on these subjects:

  (a) Real and Personal Property
  (b) Wills and Trusts
  (c) Contracts
  (d) Constitutional Law
  (e) Criminal Law and Procedure
  (f) Corporations, Partnerships, and Agency
  (g) Evidence
  (h) Creditor's Rights, including mortgages, garnishments and attachments
  (i) Practice and Procedure, trial and appellate, state and federal
  (j) Equity
  (k) Torts (including no-fault)
  (*l*) The sales, negotiable instruments, and secured transactions articles of the Uniform Commercial Code
  (m) Michigan Rules of Professional Conduct
  (n) Domestic Relations
  (*o*) Conflicts of Laws
  (p) Worker's Compensation.

(B) The National Conference of Bar Examiners will grade the Multistate section. The Board or its agents will grade the essay section, with the Board having final responsibility. The Board will determine a method for combining the grades and select a passing score.

[Amended effective August 10, 1995, 449 Mich; April 21, 1998, 457 Mich. Amended October 30, 1998, effective January 1, 2000, 459 Mich.]

Comments

Staff Comment to April, 1998 Amendment

The rule change gives Board Members the authority to author their own questions and model answers for the essay portion of the bar exam.

Staff Comment to October, 1998 Amendment

The October 1998 amendment of Rule 3(A)(2) of the Rules for the Board of Law Examiners, effective January 1, 2000, adds to the list of subjects for essay questions. The category of "no fault" is added to the subject of "Torts." See (k). In addition, the categories of "Domestic Relations", "Conflicts of Laws" and "Worker's Compensation" have been added.

Rule 4.   Post–Examination Procedures

(A) The Executive Director will release examination results at the Board's direction. Blue books will be kept for 3 months after results are released.

(B) Within 30 days after the day the results are released, the applicant may ask the Board to reconsider the applicant's essay grades. The applicant shall file with the Executive Director two (2) copies of

(1) the request;

(2) the answer given in the applicant's blue books; and

(3) an explanation why the applicant deserves a higher grade.

(C) An applicant for re-examination may obtain an application from the Executive Director. The application must be filed at least sixty (60) days before the examination. If the applicant's clearance is more than three (3) years old, the applicant must be approved by the State Bar Committee on Character and Fitness.

[Amended May 1, 1995, effective June 1, 1995, 448 Mich. Amended effective July 7, 1995, 449 Mich; August 10, 1995, 449 Mich; September 5, 2013, 495 Mich.]

Comments

Staff Comment to 2013 Amendment

These amendments reflect changes that correct minor technical errors that have occurred in drafting or the changes respond to recent adopted rule revisions, which occasionally inadvertently create incorrect cross-references in other rules.

Rule 5.   Admission without Examination

(A) An applicant for admission without examination must

(1) qualify under Rules 1 and 2(B);

(2) be licensed to practice law in the United States, its territories, or the District of Columbia;

(3) be a member in good standing of the Bar where admitted;

(4) intend to practice law in Michigan, or to be a full-time instructor in a reputable and qualified Michigan law school; and

(5) have, after being licensed and for 3 of the 5 years preceding the application,

  (a) actively practiced law as a principal business or occupation in a jurisdiction where admitted (the practice of law under a special certificate pursuant to Rule 5[D] or as a special legal consultant pursuant to Rule 5[E] does not qualify as the practice of law required by this rule);

  (b) been employed as a full-time instructor in a reputable and qualified law school in the United States, its districts, or its territories; or

  (c) been on active duty (other than for training or reserve duty) in the United States armed forces as a judge advocate, legal specialist, or legal officer. The judge advocate general (or a comparable officer) or delegate must certify the assignment and the inclusive dates.

The Supreme Court may, for good cause, increase the 5–year period. Active duty in the United States armed forces not satisfying Rule 5(A)(5)(c) may be excluded when computing the 5–year period.

(B) An applicant must submit the National Conference of Bar Examiners' Request for Preparation of a Character Report along with other material required by the Board and payment of the fees.

(C) An applicant not satisfying Rule 5(A) will be notified and given an opportunity to appear before the Board. The applicant may use the Board's subpoena power.

(D) An attorney

(1) ineligible for admission without examination because of the inability to satisfy Rule 5(A)(5); and

(2) practicing law in an institutional setting, e.g., counsel to a corporation or instructor in a law school, may apply to the

Board for a special certificate of qualification to practice law. The applicant must satisfy Rule 5(A)(1)–(3), and comply with Rule 5(B). The Board may then issue the special certificate, which will entitle the attorney to continue current employment if the attorney becomes an active member of the State Bar. If the attorney leaves the current employment, the special certificate automatically expires; if the attorney's new employment is also institutional, the attorney may reapply for another special certificate.

(E) Special Legal Consultants.

(a) To qualify for admission without examination to practice as a special legal consultant one must:

(1) be admitted to practice in a foreign country and have actually practiced, and be in good standing, as an attorney or counselor at law or the equivalent in such foreign country for at least 3 of the 5 years immediately preceding the application; and

(2) possess the good moral character and general fitness requisite for a member of the bar of this state; and

(3) fulfill the requirements of MCL 600.934 and 600.937; and

(4) be a resident of this or another state of the United States, its territories or the District of Columbia and maintain an office in this state for the practice of law; and

(5) be over 18 years of age.

(b) In considering whether to license an applicant to practice pursuant to Rule 5(E), the Board may in its discretion take into account whether a member of the bar of this state would have a reasonable and practical opportunity to establish an office for the giving of legal advice to clients in the applicant's country of admission (as referred to in Rule 5[E][a][1]), if there is pending with the Board a request to take this factor into account from a member of the bar of this state actively seeking to establish such an office in that country which raises a serious question as to the adequacy of the opportunity for such a member to establish such an office.

(c) An applicant for a license as a special legal consultant shall submit to the Board:

(1) a certificate from the authority in such foreign country having final jurisdiction over professional discipline, certifying as to the applicant's admission to practice and the date thereof and as to the good standing of such attorney or counselor at law or the equivalent, together with a duly authenticated English translation of such certificate if it is not in English; and

(2) a letter of recommendation from one of the judges of the highest law court or intermediate appellate court of such foreign country, together with a duly authenticated English translation of such letter if it is not in English; and

(3) the National Conference of Bar Examiners questionnaire and affidavit along with the payment of the requisite fee and such other evidence of the applicant's educational and professional qualifications, good moral character and general fitness, and compliance with the requirements of Rule 5(E)(a)(1)–(5) as the Board may require; and

(4) shall execute and file with the Executive Director of the State Board of Law Examiners, in such form and manner as the Board may prescribe,

(i) a duly acknowledged instrument in writing setting forth the special legal consultant's address in the state of Michigan and designating the Executive Director of the State Board of Law Examiners an agent upon whom process may be served, with like effect as if served personally upon the special legal consultant, in any action or proceeding thereafter brought against the special legal consultant and arising out of or based upon any legal services rendered or offered to be rendered by the special legal consultant within or to residents of the state of Michigan whenever after due diligence service cannot be made upon the special legal consultant at such address or at such new address in the state of Michigan as the special legal consultant shall have filed in the office of the Executive Director of the State Board of Law Examiners by means of a duly acknowledged supplemental instrument in writing; and

(ii) the special legal consultant's commitment to notify the Executive Director of the State Board of Law Examiners of any resignation or revocation of the special legal consultant's admission to practice in the foreign country of admission, or of any censure, suspension or expulsion in respect of such admission.

Service of process on the Executive Director of the State Board of Law Examiners shall be made by personally delivering to and leaving with the Executive Director, or with a deputy or assistant authorized by the Executive Director to receive such service, at the Executive Director's office, duplicate copies of such process together with a fee of $10.00. Service of process shall be complete when the Executive Director has been so served. The Executive Director shall promptly send one of such copies to the special legal consultant to whom the process is directed, by certified mail, return receipt requested, addressed to such special legal consultant at the address specified by the special legal consultant as aforesaid.

(d) A person licensed to practice as a special legal consultant must maintain active membership in the State Bar of Michigan and must discharge the responsibilities of State Bar membership and is authorized to render professional legal advice:

(1) on the law of the foreign country where the legal consultant is admitted to practice;

(2) may use the title "special legal consultant" either singly or in connection with the authorized title or firm name in the foreign country of the legal consultant's admission to practice, provided that in each case the name of such foreign country be identified.

[Amended effective October 1, 1978, 402 Mich; March 26, 1982, 413 Mich; August 23, 1983, 417 Mich; November 27, 1985, 423 Mich; September 9, 1988, 431 Mich. Amended May 1, 1995, effective June 1, 1995, 448 Mich. Amended effective August 10, 1995, 449 Mich. Amended July 16, 1996, effective September 1, 1996, 452 Mich; June 13, 2012, effective January 1, 2013, 491 Mich. Amended effective September 5, 2013, 495 Mich.]

Comments

Staff Comment to 1988 Amendment

The amendment conforms the Rules for the Board of Law Examiners concerning admission to the practice of law without examination to the requirements of MCL 600.946, which requires, inter alia, that for admission to the practice of law without examination, an applicant must intend in good faith either to maintain an office in the state for the practice of law and to practice actively in this state, or to engage in the teaching of law as a full-time instructor in a reputable and qualified law school duly incorporated under the laws of this state.

The residency requirement formerly a part of Rule 5(A)(4) of the Rules for the Board of Law Examiners is rescinded so that the Rules conform with MCL 600.946, and the United States Supreme Court decision of *Supreme Court of Virginia v Friedman*, 487 US 59; 108 SCt 2260; 101 LEd2d 56 (1988).

Staff Comment to 1996 Amendment

The July 16, 1996 amendment of subrule 5(A)(5), proposed by the State Bar of Michigan, eliminated the requirement that applicants for admission without examination intend to practice law in Michigan "as a principal occupation."

Staff Comment to 2012 Amendment

The amendment of BLE Rule 5 eliminates the requirement that an applicant for admission by motion be required to express an intention to maintain an office in the state.

Staff Comment to 2013 Amendment

These amendments reflect changes that correct minor technical errors that have occurred in drafting or the changes respond to recent adopted rule revisions, which occasionally inadvertently create incorrect cross-references in other rules.

Rule 6.   Fees

The fees are: an application for examination, $400 and an additional fee for the late filing of an application or transfer of an application for examination, $100; an application for re-examination, $300; an application for recertification, $300; an application for admission without examination, $800 plus the requisite fee for the National Conference of Bar Examiners' character report. Certified checks or money orders must be payable to the State of Michigan. Online bar examination payments for first time takers must be paid by credit card.

[Adopted effective January 15, 1981, 410 Mich. Amended effective July 5, 1989, 432 Mich; September 30, 2008, 482 Mich. Amended May 25, 2016, effective August 1, 2016, 499 Mich.]

Comments

Staff Comment to 1989 Amendment

The [July 5, 1989] amendments reflect increases in filing fees required by 1989 PA 100, signed by the Governor on June 21, 1989, and given immediate effect.

Staff Comment to 2008 Amendment

The amendment of Rule 6 of the Rules for the Board of Law Examiners increases the fees for application for the bar examination from $300 to $340, and for reexamination from $200 to $240.

Staff Comment to 2016 Amendment

The amendment of BLE Rule 6 increases the fees for application for the bar examination from $340 to $400, reexamination from $240 to $300, application for recertification from $200 to $300, and application for admission without examination from $600 to $800.

Rule 7.   Exceptions

An applicant may ask the Board to waive any requirement except the payment of fees. The applicant must demonstrate why the request should be granted.

[Amended May 1, 1995, effective June 1, 1995, 448 Mich.]

Rule 8.   Recertification

An applicant for recertification shall file an application and other material required by the Board. After a hearing the Board shall either recertify the applicant or require that the applicant pass the examination described in Rule 3. An applicant may use the Board's subpoena power for the hearing. An applicant who is an inactive State Bar member or who had previously voluntarily resigned from the State Bar or who previously elected emeritus status, and who has been employed in another jurisdiction in one of the ways listed in Rule 5(A)(5) is entitled to recertification by the Board.

[Amended effective October 1, 1978, 402 Mich. Amended May 1, 1995, effective June 1, 1995, 448 Mich; May 17, 2011, effective September 1, 2011, 489 Mich. Amended effective September 5, 2013, 495 Mich.]

Comments

Staff Comment to 2011 Amendment

The amendment of SBR 3(E), submitted by the State Bar of Michigan, would clarify that an out-of-state attorney who voluntarily resigned from the Michigan bar would not be required to retake the Michigan Bar Examination if the person meets the criteria for admission without examination under Rule 5 of the Rules for the Board of Law Examiners. A similar change also is made in SBR 3(F) regarding emeritus members. Finally, Rule 8 of the Rules for the Board of Law Examiners is amended to reflect that resigned or emeritus members who seek readmission are covered under Rule 8, which allows for recertification.

Staff Comment to 2013 Amendment

These amendments reflect changes that correct minor technical errors that have occurred in drafting or the changes respond to recent adopted rule revisions, which occasionally inadvertently create incorrect cross-references in other rules.

CODE OF JUDICIAL CONDUCT

Adopted October 1, 1974

---

1. A Judge Should Uphold the Integrity and Independence of the Judiciary.
2. A Judge Should Avoid Impropriety and the Appearance of Impropriety in All Activities.
3. A Judge Should Perform the Duties of Office Impartially and Diligently.
4. A Judge May Engage in Extrajudicial Activities.
5. Applicability of the Code of Judicial Conduct to Judicial Candidates.
6. A Judge Should Regularly File Reports of Compensation Received for Quasi-Judicial and Extra-Judicial Activities and of Monetary Contributions.
7. A Judge or a Candidate for Judicial Office Should Refrain from Political Activity Inappropriate to Judicial Office.
8. Collective Activity by Judges.
   Judicial Conference Rules.
   Michigan Uniform System of Citation [Rescinded].

CANON 1. A Judge Should Uphold the Integrity and Independence of the Judiciary

An independent and honorable judiciary is indispensable to justice in our society. A judge should participate in establishing, maintaining, and enforcing, and should personally observe, high standards of conduct so that the integrity and independence of the judiciary may be preserved. A judge should always be aware that the judicial system is for the benefit of the litigant and the public, not the judiciary. The provisions of this code should be construed and applied to further those objectives.

[Amended July 16, 1993, effective October 1, 1993, 443 Mich.]

CANON 2. A Judge Should Avoid Impropriety and the Appearance of Impropriety in All Activities

A. Public confidence in the judiciary is eroded by irresponsible or improper conduct by judges. A judge must avoid all impropriety and appearance of impropriety. A judge must expect to be the subject of constant public scrutiny. A judge must therefore accept restrictions on conduct that might be viewed as burdensome by the ordinary citizen and should do so freely and willingly.

B. A judge should respect and observe the law. At all times, the conduct and manner of a judge should promote public confidence in the integrity and impartiality of the judiciary. Without regard to a person's race, gender, or other protected personal characteristic, a judge should treat every person fairly, with courtesy and respect.

C. A judge should not allow family, social, or other relationships to influence judicial conduct or judgment. A judge should not use the prestige of office to advance personal business interests or those of others, but participation in activities allowed in Canon 4 is not a violation of this principle.

D. A judge should not appear as a witness in a court proceeding unless subpoenaed.

E. A judge may respond to requests for personal references.

F. A judge should not allow activity as a member of an organization to cast doubt on the judge's ability to perform the function of the office in a manner consistent with the Michigan Code of Judicial Conduct, the laws of this state, and the Michigan and United States Constitutions. A judge should be particularly cautious with regard to membership activities that discriminate, or appear to discriminate, on the basis of race, gender, or other protected personal characteristic. Nothing in this paragraph should be interpreted to diminish a judge's right to the free exercise of religion.

G. No judge may accept any contribution of money, directly or indirectly, for a campaign deficit or for expenses associated with judicial office. Requests for payment of membership dues or fees in a judicial association do not constitute solicitation of funds for purposes of this provision.

[Amended July 16, 1993, effective October 1, 1993, 443 Mich; May 1, 2013, effective August 1, 2013, 493 Mich.]

Comments

Staff Comment to 2013 Amendment

These amendments reflect an effort to make the judicial canons consistent regarding law-related and nonlaw-related extrajudicial activities in which judges may participate, and to clarify the activities that are allowed or prohibited. The proposal retains the explicit prohibition on a judge individually soliciting funds, and likewise prohibits the use of the prestige of the office for that purpose. The newly-constituted Canon 4, which consolidates previous Canon 4 and Canon 5 into one canon, permits a judge to engage in various specific activities, including serving as a member of an honorary committee or joining a general appeal, speaking at or receiving an award at an organization's event, and allowing the judge's name to be used in support of a fundraising event. The proposal also includes several suggested revisions that were recommended during the public comment period.

In addition to combining Canons 4 and 5 into one canon, the amendments eliminate the language of Canon 7C that prohibited a judge from accepting a testimonial, and move the reformulated language from Canon 7C(2) prohibiting a judge from accepting a contribution of money to Canon 2G. Also, the proposal clarifies Canon 2 so that activities allowed under Canon 4 are not considered a violation of the principle of use of the prestige of office. Further, the amendments clarify that certain canons of the Code of Judicial Conduct (specifically Canons 1, 2, 4[A]–[D] and 7) apply to all candidates for judicial office as part of the new language inserted as Canon 5. Finally, MRPC 8.2 (which applies to lawyers) is amended to reflect that the judicial canons applicable to judicial candidates are set out in new Canon 5.

Nearly all of the current language in Canon 2, 4, 5, and 7 is retained in this proposal. The new language adds explicit provisions to describe the types of activities that are allowed or prohibited for judges which until now had been undefined and therefore the source of confusion.

CANON 3. A Judge Should Perform the Duties of Office Impartially and Diligently

The judicial duties of a judge take precedence over all other activities. Judicial duties include all the duties of office prescribed by law. In the performance of these duties, the following standards apply:

A. Adjudicative Responsibilities.

(1) A judge should be faithful to the law and maintain professional competence in it. A judge should be unswayed by partisan interests, public clamor, or fear of criticism.

(2) A judge may require lawyers, court personnel, and litigants to be appropriately attired for court and should enforce reasonable rules of conduct in the courtroom.

(3) A judge should be patient, dignified, and courteous to litigants, jurors, witnesses, lawyers, and others with whom the judge deals in an official capacity, and should require similar conduct of lawyers, and of staff, court officials, and others subject to the judge's direction and control.

(4) A judge shall not initiate, permit, or consider ex parte communications, or consider other communications made to the judge outside the presence of the parties concerning a pending or impending proceeding, except as follows:

(a) A judge may allow ex parte communications for scheduling, administrative purposes, or emergencies that do not deal with substantive matters or issues on the merits, provided:

(i) the judge reasonably believes that no party or counsel for a party will gain a procedural or tactical advantage as a result of the ex parte communication, and

(ii) the judge makes provision promptly to notify all other parties and counsel for parties of the substance of the ex parte communication and allows an opportunity to respond.

(b) A judge may obtain the advice of a disinterested expert on the law applicable to a proceeding before the judge if the judge gives notice to the parties of the person consulted and the substance of the advice, and affords the parties reasonable opportunity to respond.

(c) A judge may consult with court personnel whose function is to aid the judge in carrying out the judge's adjudicative responsibilities or with other judges.

(d) A judge may, with the consent of the parties, confer separately with the parties and their lawyers in an effort to mediate or settle matters pending before the judge.

(e) A judge may initiate or consider any ex parte communications when expressly authorized by law to do so.

(5) A judge should dispose promptly of the business of the court.

(6) A judge shall not make any public statement that might reasonably be expected to affect the outcome or impair the fairness of a matter pending or impending in any court.

(7) A judge shall not, in connection with cases, controversies, or issues that are likely to come before the court, make pledges, promises, or commitments that are inconsistent with the impartial performance of the adjudicative duties of judicial office.

(8) A judge shall require court staff, court officials, and others subject to the judge's direction and control to refrain from making statements that the judge would be prohibited from making by paragraphs (6) and (7).

(9) Notwithstanding the restrictions in paragraph (6), a judge may make public statements in the course of official duties, may explain court procedures, and may comment on any proceeding in which the judge is a litigant in a personal capacity.

(10) Subject to the requirements of paragraph (6), a judge may respond directly or through a third party to allegations in the media or other forms of communication concerning the judge's conduct in a matter.

(11) A judge should prohibit broadcasting, televising, recording, or taking of photographs in or out of the courtroom during sessions of court or recesses between sessions except as authorized by the Supreme Court. [1]

(12) A judge may properly intervene in a trial of a case to promote expedition, and prevent unnecessary waste of time, or to clear up some obscurity, but the judge should bear in mind that undue interference, impatience, or participation in the examination of witnesses, or a severe attitude on the judge's part toward witnesses, especially those who are excited or terrified by the unusual circumstances of a trial, may tend to prevent the proper presentation of the cause, or the ascertainment of truth in respect thereto.

Conversation between the judge and counsel in court is often necessary, but the judge should be studious to avoid controversies that are apt to obscure the merits of the dispute between litigants and lead to its unjust disposition. In addressing counsel, litigants, or witnesses, the judge should avoid a controversial manner or tone.

A judge should avoid interruptions of counsel in their arguments except to clarify their positions, and should not be tempted to the unnecessary display of learning or a premature judgment.

(13) A judge should adopt the usual and accepted methods of doing justice; avoid the imposition of humiliating acts or discipline, not authorized by law in sentencing and endeavor to conform to a reasonable standard of punishment and not seek popularity or publicity either by exceptional severity or undue leniency.

(14) Without regard to a person's race, gender, or other protected personal characteristic, a judge should treat every person fairly, with courtesy and respect. To the extent possible, a judge should require staff, court officials, and others who are subject to the judge's direction and control to provide such fair, courteous, and respectful treatment to persons who have contact with the court.

B. Administrative Responsibilities.

(1) A judge should diligently discharge administrative responsibilities, maintain professional competence in judicial administration, and facilitate the performance of the administrative responsibilities of other judges and court officials.

(2) A judge should direct staff and court officials subject to the judge's control to observe high standards of fidelity, diligence, and courtesy to litigants, jurors, witnesses, lawyers, and others with whom they deal in their official capacity.

(3) A judge should take or initiate appropriate disciplinary measures against a judge or lawyer for unprofessional conduct of which the judge may become aware.

(4) A judge should not cause unnecessary expense by making unnecessary appointments. All appointments shall be based upon merit.

(5) A judge should not approve compensation beyond the fair value of services rendered.

C. Disqualification. A judge should raise the issue of disqualification whenever the judge has cause to believe that grounds for disqualification may exist under MCR 2.003(C).

D. Waiver of Disqualification. A disqualification of a judge may be waived as provided by MCR 2.003(E).

[Amended July 16, 1993, effective October 1, 1993, 443 Mich. Amended effective January 18, 1994. Amended July 10, 1995, effective September 1, 1995, 449 Mich. Amended effective March 9, 2016, 499 Mich; October 25, 2018, 502 Mich.]

1 Administrative Order 1990–7, Videotape Record of Court Proceedings, supra, which authorized an exception to this paragraph was rescinded December 12, 2006.

Comments

Staff Comment to 1994 Amendment

The 1994 amendment of Canon 3.B(3) was proposed by the State Bar of Michigan. It was designed to parallel the language of MRPC 8.3(c)(2), and to help assure confidentiality for those seeking assistance in the Bar's substance-abuse counseling program.

Staff Comment to 1995 Amendment

The July 7, 1995, amendments of MCR 2.003, and Rules 3A, 3D, 6C, and 7B of the Michigan Code of Judicial Conduct, and new MCR 9.227 and Rule 7D of the Michigan Code of Judicial Conduct, are based on the proposed revision of the Michigan Code of Judicial Conduct submitted by the State Bar Representative Assembly. See 442 Mich 1216 (1993). They are effective September 1, 1995.

Staff Comment to 2016 Amendment

These amendments update cross-references that changed after the rule was adopted and make other nonsubstantive revisions.

Staff Comment to 2018 Amendment

The amendments of Canon 3 and Canon 7 of the Code of Judicial Conduct incorporate most of the ABA Model Code of Judicial Conduct 2.10 language and clarify its application to public comments made by judges.

CANON 4. A Judge May Engage in Extrajudicial Activities

As a judicial officer and person specially learned in the law, a judge is in a unique position to contribute to the improvement of the law, the legal system, and the administration of justice, including revision of substantive and procedural law and improvement of criminal and juvenile justice. To the extent that time permits, the judge is encouraged to do so, either independently or through a bar association, judicial conference, or other organization dedicated to the improvement of the law. A judge should regulate extrajudicial activities to minimize the risk of conflict with judicial duties.

A judge may engage in the following activities:

A. Law–Related Activities.

(1) A judge may speak, write, lecture, teach, and participate in other activities concerning the law, the legal system, and the administration of justice.

(2) A judge may appear at a public hearing before an executive or legislative body or official on matters concerning the law, the legal system, and the administration of justice, and may otherwise consult with such executive or legislative body or official on such matters.

(3) A judge may serve as a member, officer, or director of an organization or governmental agency devoted to the improve-ment of the law, the legal system, or the administration of justice. A judge may participate in the management and investment of such an organization's funds.

(4) A judge may make recommendations to public and private fund-granting agencies on projects and programs concerning the law, the legal system, and the administration of justice.

B. Avocational Activities. A judge may write, lecture, teach, speak, and consult on nonlegal subjects, appear before public nonlegal bodies, and engage in the arts, sports, and other social and recreational activities, if such avocational activities do not detract from the dignity of the office or interfere with the performance of judicial duties.

C. Civic and Charitable Activities. A judge may participate in civic and charitable activities that do not reflect adversely upon the judge's impartiality or interfere with the performance of judicial duties. A judge may serve and be listed as an officer, director, trustee, or nonlegal advisor of a bona fide educational, religious, charitable, fraternal, or civic organization. A judge should not serve if it is likely that the organization will be engaged in proceedings that would ordinarily come before the judge or will be regularly engaged in adversary proceedings in any court.

D. Fundraising Activities. A judge should not individually solicit funds for any educational, religious, charitable, fraternal, or civic organization or any organization or governmental agency devoted to the improvement of the law, the legal system, or the administration of justice or use or permit the use of the prestige of the office for that purpose. A judge may, however, serve as a member of an honorary committee or may join a general appeal on behalf of such an organization. A judge may speak or receive an award or other recognition in connection with an event of such an organization. A judge may allow his or her name or title to be used in advertising the judge's involvement in an event so long as the judge does not individually solicit funds.

E. Financial Activities.

(1) A judge should refrain from financial and business dealings that tend to reflect adversely on the judge's impartiality or judicial office, interfere with the proper performance of judicial duties, exploit the judicial position, or involve the judge in frequent transactions with lawyers or persons likely to come before the court on which the judge serves.

(2) Subject to the requirements of E(1), a judge may hold and manage investments, including real estate, and engage in other remunerative activity, but should not serve as director, officer, manager, advisor, or employee of any business. Provided, however, with respect to a judge holding office and serving as an officer, director, manager, advisor, or employee of any business not prohibited heretofore by law or judicial canon, the effective date of the prohibition contained herein shall be the date of expiration of the judge's current judicial term of office.

(3) A judge should manage investments and other financial interests to minimize the number of cases in which the judge is disqualified. As soon as it can be done without serious financial detriment, the judge should dispose of investments and other financial interests that require frequent disqualification.

(4) Neither a judge nor a family member residing in the judge's household should accept a gift, bequest, favor, or loan from anyone except as follows:

(a) A judge may accept a gift or gifts not to exceed a total value of $375, incident to a public testimonial; books supplied by publishers on a complimentary basis for official use; or an invitation to the judge and spouse to attend a bar-related function or activity devoted to the improvement of the law, the legal system, or the administration of justice.

(b) A judge or a family member residing in the judge's household may accept ordinary social hospitality; a gift, bequest, favor, or loan from a relative; a wedding or engagement gift; a loan from a lending institution in its regular course of business on the same terms generally available to persons who are not judges; or a scholarship or fellowship awarded on the same terms applied to other applicants.

(c) A judge or a family member residing in the judge's household may accept any other gift, bequest, favor, or loan only if the donor is not a party or other person whose interests have come or are likely to come before the judge, and if the aggregate value of gifts received by a judge or family member residing in the judge's household from any source exceeds $375, the judge reports it in the same manner as compensation is reported in Canon 6C. For purposes of reporting gifts under this subsection, any gift with a fair market value of $150 or less need not be aggregated to determine if the $375 reporting threshold has been met.

(5) For the purposes of this section, "family member residing in the judge's household" means any relative of a judge by blood or marriage, or a person treated by a judge as a family member, who resides in the judge's household.

(6) A judge is not required by this code to disclose income, debts, or investments, except as provided in this canon and Canons 3 and 6.

(7) Information acquired by a judge in a judicial capacity should not be used or disclosed by the judge in financial dealings or for any other purpose not related to judicial duties.

F. Fiduciary Activities. A judge should not serve as an executor, administrator, testamentary trustee, or guardian, except for the estate, testamentary trust, or person of a member of the judge's immediate family, and then only if such service will not interfere with the proper performance of judicial duties. As a family fiduciary, a judge is subject to the following restrictions:

(1) A judge should not serve if it is likely that as such fiduciary the judge will be engaged in proceedings that would ordinarily come before the judge or if the estate, trust, or ward becomes involved in adversary proceedings in the court on which the judge serves or one under its appellate jurisdiction.

(2) While acting as such fiduciary, a judge is subject to the same restrictions on financial activities that apply in the judge's personal capacity.

G. Arbitration. A judge should not act as an arbitrator or mediator, except in the performance of judicial duties.

H. Practice of Law. A judge should not practice law for compensation except as otherwise provided by law.

I. Extra–judicial Appointments. A judge should not accept appointment to a governmental committee, commission, or other position that is concerned with issues of fact or policy on matters other than the improvement of the law, the legal system, or the administration of justice. A judge, however, may represent the country, state, or locality on ceremonial occasions or in connection with historical, educational, and cultural activities.

[Adopted May 1, 2013, effective August 1, 2013, 493 Mich. Amended effective February 28, 2018, 501 Mich.]

Comments

Staff Comment to 2013 Adoption

These amendments reflect an effort to make the judicial canons consistent regarding law-related and non-law-related extrajudicial activities in which judges may participate, and to clarify the activities that are allowed or prohibited. The proposal retains the explicit prohibition on a judge individually soliciting funds, and likewise prohibits the use of the prestige of the office for that purpose. The newly-constituted Canon 4, which consolidates previous Canon 4 and Canon 5 into one canon, permits a judge to engage in various specific activities, including serving as a member of an honorary committee or joining a general appeal, speaking at or receiving an award at an organization's event, and allowing the judge's name to be used in support of a fundraising event. The proposal also includes several suggested revisions that were recommended during the public comment period.

In addition to combining Canons 4 and 5 into one canon, the amendments eliminate the language of Canon 7C that prohibited a judge from accepting a testimonial, and move the reformulated language from Canon 7C(2) prohibiting a judge from accepting a contribution of money to Canon 2G. Also, the proposal clarifies Canon 2 so that activities allowed under Canon 4 are not considered a violation of the principle of use of the prestige of office. Further, the amendments clarify that certain canons of the Code of Judicial Conduct (specifically Canons 1, 2, 4[A]–[D] and 7) apply to all candidates for judicial office as part of the new language inserted as Canon 5. Finally, MRPC 8.2 (which applies to lawyers) is amended to reflect that the judicial canons applicable to judicial candidates are set out in new Canon 5.

Nearly all of the current language in Canon 2, 4, 5, and 7 is retained in this proposal. The new language adds explicit provisions to describe the types of activities that are allowed or prohibited for judges which until now had been undefined and therefore the source of confusion.

Staff Comment to 2018 Amendment

This amendment increases the acceptable value for a gift given incident to a public testimonial, and likewise increases the threshold amount for disclosure of a gift. This increase is the first revision since the $100 value threshold was adopted in 1974.

The threshold amount for reporting gifts is widely variable among the states and federal government. The disclosure threshold for reporting gifts in other states, established by statute or court rule, ranges from $50 to $500. Many states do not have a threshold amount at all; instead, such states may prohibit the acceptance of gifts from certain classes of donors, or alternatively allow judges to accept a certain class of gifts without regard to value for specific events, such as a wedding, or 25th or 50th wedding anniversary. The Court also considered the increase in the value of money since the $100 threshold was adopted. According to the American Institute for Economic Research, the value of $100 in today's economy is $495.92.

The Court used the federal disclosure rule and threshold as its model. For federal judges, the gift disclosure amount is $375, as established by the Judicial Conference. The instructions for submitting the annual disclosure report require a federal judge to:

Report information on gifts aggregating more than $375 in value received by the filer, spouse and dependent child from any source other than a relative during the reporting period. Any gift with a fair market value of $150 or less need not be aggregated to determine if the $375 reporting threshold has been met.

Thus, similar to the federal rule, the amendment increases the disclosure threshold to $375, but requires gifts to the judge and his family members from a single source to be aggregated for purposes of reporting. Gifts with value less than $150 would not need to be included in this aggregate amount. Further, the amendment does not change the restriction that a gift may be accepted under this subsection only if the donor is not a party or other person whose interests have come or are likely to come before the judge.

CANON 5. Applicability of the Code of Judicial Conduct to Judicial Candidates

All judicial candidates are subject to Canon 1, Canon 2, Canon 4A–4D and Canon 7 of the Code of Judicial Conduct as applicable during a judicial campaign. A successful candidate, whether or not an incumbent, and an unsuccessful candidate who is a judge, are subject to judicial discipline for campaign misconduct. An unsuccessful candidate who is a lawyer is subject to lawyer discipline for judicial campaign misconduct.

[Adopted May 1, 2013, effective August 1, 2013, 493 Mich.]

Comments

Staff Comment to 2013 Adoption

These amendments reflect an effort to make the judicial canons consistent regarding law-related and nonlaw-related extrajudicial activities in which judges may participate, and to clarify the activities that are allowed or prohibited. The proposal retains the explicit prohibition on a judge individually soliciting funds, and likewise prohibits the use of the prestige of the office for that purpose. The newly-constituted Canon 4, which consolidates previous Canon 4 and Canon 5 into one canon, permits a judge to engage in various specific activities, including serving as a member of an honorary committee or joining a general appeal, speaking at or receiving an award at an organization's event, and allowing the judge's name to be used in support of a fundraising event. The proposal also includes several suggested revisions that were recommended during the public comment period.

In addition to combining Canons 4 and 5 into one canon, the amendments eliminate the language of Canon 7C that prohibited a judge from accepting a testimonial, and move the reformulated language from Canon 7C(2) prohibiting a judge from accepting a contribution of money to Canon 2G. Also, the proposal clarifies Canon 2 so that activities allowed under Canon 4 are not considered a violation of the principle of use of the prestige of office. Further, the amendments clarify that certain canons of the Code of Judicial Conduct (specifically Canons 1, 2, 4[A]–[D] and 7) apply to all candidates for judicial office as part of the new language inserted as Canon 5. Finally, MRPC 8.2 (which applies to lawyers) is amended to reflect that the judicial canons applicable to judicial candidates are set out in new Canon 5.

Nearly all of the current language in Canon 2, 4, 5, and 7 is retained in this proposal. The new language adds explicit provisions to describe the types of activities that are allowed or prohibited for judges which until now had been undefined and therefore the source of confusion.

CANON 6. A Judge Should Regularly File Reports of Compensation Received for Quasi-Judicial and Extra-Judicial Activities and of Monetary Contributions

A judge may receive compensation and reimbursement of expenses for the quasi-judicial and extra-judicial activities permitted by this code, if the source of such payments does not give the appearance of influencing the judge in judicial duties or otherwise give the appearance of impropriety, subject to the following restrictions:

A. Compensation. Compensation should not exceed a reasonable amount nor should it exceed what a person who is not a judge would receive for the same activity.

B. Expense Reimbursement. Expense reimbursement should be limited to the actual cost of travel, food, and lodging reasonably incurred by the judge and, where appropriate to the occasion, by the judge's spouse. Any payment in excess of such an amount is compensation.

C. Public Reports. A judge shall report the date, place, and nature of any activity for which the judge received compensation, and the name of the payor and the amount of compensation so received. The judge's report shall be made at least annually and shall be filed as a public document in the office of the State Court Administrator or other office designated by law.

[Amended effective April 18, 1980, 408 Mich. Amended July 16, 1993, effective October 1, 1993, 443 Mich; July 10, 1995, effective September 1, 1995, 449 Mich.]

Comments

Staff Comment to 1995 Amendment

The July 7, 1995, amendments of MCR 2.003, and Rules 3A, 3D, 6C, and 7B of the Michigan Code of Judicial Conduct, and new MCR 9.227 and Rule 7D of the Michigan Code of Judicial Conduct, are based on the proposed revision of the Michigan Code of Judicial Conduct submitted by the State Bar Representative Assembly. See 442 Mich 1216 (1993). They are effective September 1, 1995.

CANON 7. A Judge or a Candidate for Judicial Office Should Refrain From Political Activity Inappropriate to Judicial Office

A. Political Conduct in General.

(1) A judge or candidate for judicial office should not:

(a) hold any office in a political party;

(b) make speeches on behalf of a political party or nonjudicial candidate or publicly endorse a candidate for nonjudicial office.

(2) A judge or candidate for judicial office may:

(a) attend political gatherings;

(b) speak to such gatherings on the judge's own behalf or on behalf of other judicial candidates;

(c) contribute to a political party.

(3) A judge should resign the judicial office before becoming a candidate either in a party primary or in a general election for nonjudicial office.

B. Campaign Conduct.

(1) A candidate, including an incumbent judge, for a judicial office:

(a) should maintain the dignity appropriate to judicial office, and should encourage family members to adhere to the same standards of political conduct that apply to the judge;

(b) should prohibit public employees subject to the judge's direction or control from doing for the judge what the judge is prohibited from doing under this canon;

(c) shall not, in connection with cases, controversies, or issues that are likely to come before the court, make pledges, promises, or commitments about conduct in office that are inconsistent with the impartial performance of the adjudicative duties of judicial office.

(d) should not knowingly, or with reckless disregard, use or participate in the use of any form of public communication that is false.

(2) These provisions govern a candidate, including an incumbent judge, for a judicial office:

(a) A candidate should not personally solicit or accept campaign funds, or solicit publicly stated support by improper use of the judicial office in violation of B(1)(c). A candidate may send a thank-you note to a contributor.

(b) A candidate may establish committees of responsible persons to secure and manage the expenditure of funds for the campaign and to obtain public statements of support (including support from lawyers) for the candidacy.

(c) Such committees may solicit and accept campaign contributions from the public, including lawyers, as permitted by law.

(d) A candidate's committee may not directly or indirectly accept funds from any committee that was established in connection with the candidate's attempt to secure any other judicial or nonjudicial office. The committee may solicit funds for the campaign no earlier than February 15 of the year of the election, and may not solicit or accept funds after the date of the general election.

(e) A candidate should not use or permit the use of campaign contributions for the private benefit of the candidate or the candidate's family.

(f) If a candidate is not opposed for such judicial office, the candidate or the candidate's committee shall return to the contributors funds raised in excess of the actual costs incurred or contribute such funds to the client security fund of the State Bar of Michigan, not later than January 1 following the election. Likewise, any candidate or committee having funds remaining after payment of all campaign expenses shall either return such funds to the contributors thereof or donate the funds to the client security fund of the State Bar of Michigan, not later than January 1 following the election.

(g) A candidate for judicial office may not pay an endorsing organization for its ranking or endorsement. However, a candidate for judicial office may contribute campaign funds to pay some of the costs associated with the publication of the endorsement or ranking of the candidate, provided the candidate secures from the endorsing organization an assurance, before the endorsement or ranking is made, that the endorsing organization will not:

    (i) demand payment from the candidate or the candidate's agent as a condition of the endorsement or favorable ranking,

    (ii) seek any assurance from the candidate before the endorsement or ranking is made that it will be paid if it endorses or ranks the candidate favorably,

    (iii) add an endorsement or favorable ranking of a different candidate in the event that the initially supported candidate decides not to pay the endorsing organization for publicizing its endorsement and favorable ranking,

    (iv) prevent the candidate from publicizing the endorsement or favorable ranking independent of the endorsing organization, regardless of whether the endorsing organization itself publicizes its endorsement or favorable ranking.

(3) No judge should personally sell or permit any court or public employee working for or assigned to any court to sell fund-raising tickets or accept contributions of any kind on the judge's behalf or on behalf of any other judicial candidate.

C. Wind up of Law Practice.

(1) A successful elected candidate who was not an incumbent has until midnight December 31 following the election to wind up the candidate's law practice, and has until June 30 following the election to resign from organizations and activities, and divest interests that do not qualify under Canon 4.

(2) Upon notice of appointment to judicial office, a candidate shall wind up the candidate's law practice prior to taking office,

and has six months from the date of taking office to resign from organizations and activities and divest interests that do not qualify under Canon 4.

[Amended July 16, 1993, effective October 1, 1993, 443 Mich; July 10, 1995, effective September 1, 1995, 449 Mich; December 28, 1999, effective January 1, 2000, 461 Mich. Amended effective March 30, 2000, 461 Mich. Amended September 30, 2003, effective January 1, 2004, 469 Mich; June 9, 2004, effective January 1, 2005, 470 Mich; May 1, 2013, effective August 1, 2013, 493 Mich. Amended effective October 25, 2018, 502 Mich. Amended March 13, 2019, effective May 1, 2019, 502 Mich.]

Comments

Staff Comment to 1995 Amendment

The July 7, 1995, amendments of MCR 2.003, and Rules 3A, 3D, 6C, and 7B of the Michigan Code of Judicial Conduct, and new MCR 9.227 and Rule 7D of the Michigan Code of Judicial Conduct, are based on the proposed revision of the Michigan Code of Judicial Conduct submitted by the State Bar Representative Assembly. See 442 Mich 1216 (1993). They are effective September 1, 1995.

Staff Comment to 1999 Amendment

With regard to the December 28, 1999 amendment of Canon 7B(2)(a), effective January 1, 2000, both the Michigan Judges Association and the State Bar of Michigan Standing Committee on Professional and Judicial Ethics supported this clarification concerning thank-you notes. Further, several witnesses at the Supreme Court's public hearings questioned how a simple expression of common courtesy could be unethical. As attorney John Felton stated during the hearing on November 4, 1999, in Gaylord:

"One other comment, if I might, with respect to thank you notes. Having donated to campaigns, and I know I have talked to other lawyers that donate to campaigns, I just can't conceive of how the good manners our mother taught us would lead to bad ethics. So I think it's perfectly appropriate, and I don't think as a lawyer I would draw any inference from a judge thanking a lawyer for a contribution."

The Court considered concerns expressed by some members of the State Bar Representative Assembly that a thank-you note might circumvent the intent of the code to prohibit a candidate's personal involvement in fund-raising, but was persuaded that the requirement of the Michigan Campaign Finance Act, 1976 PA 388, that judicial candidates verify the truth of campaign finance statements that list contributors, MCL 169.237, effectively negates that concern. The reference in the proposed rule that would have allowed "other acknowledgments" was not adopted.

With regard to Canon 7B(2)(c), the $100 limitation concerning solicitation of lawyers had been the rule since 1974. If adjusted for inflation, the amount would have been in excess of $300. Nevertheless, the Court declined to raise the amount judicial candidate committees may solicit from lawyers from $100 to $300 for the year 2000 judicial elections. The Court explained, however, that its duty to keep its rules in compliance with the United States Supreme Court's understanding of First Amendment law concerning free speech and rights of association might require it to revisit this question after the United States Supreme Court decides *Shrink Missouri Government PAC v Nixon*, 161 F3d 519 (CA 8, 1998) cert granted 119 S Ct 901; 142 L Ed 2d 901 (1999), because that case involves a constitutional challenge to limits on contributions that have not been raised for many years to account for the effects of inflation.

The Court adopted language in Canon 7B(2)(c) allowing for a disclaimer in solicitation letters in excess of $100 that may inadvertently be sent to lawyers because it is virtually impossible for a candidate to assure that a solicitation sent to any group believed to consist primarily of nonlawyers will not include at least one lawyer.

With regard to Canon 7B(2)(d)-(f), the Court established a fixed date that made clear to the public and to candidate committees, when fund-raising may begin, eliminating the need to count backwards 180 days from the date of the primary election or the varying dates of the parties' nominating conventions in order to arrive at the applicable date. As the Court had no desire to increase the length of time for fund-raising, it chose February 15 as the starting date, a change that has the effect of decreasing the amount of time available for fund-raising, given the historic practice of using the primary election date as the applicable date from which to count back.

The Court rejected the proposal to allow solicitation or acceptance of funds up to 45 days after the general election because of comments suggesting that such a rule could lead to abuses and the appearance of impropriety.

Parts of Canon 7B(2)(d)-(f) also were restructured.

The December 28, 1999 amendment of Canon 7C, effective January 1, 2000, eliminated obsolete language pertaining to campaign year 1974.

Staff Comment to 2000 Amendment

The March 30, 2000 amendment of Canon 7 is explained in *In re Chmura*, 461 Mich [517]; [608] NW2d [31] (2000).

Staff Comment to 2004 Amendment

The September 30, 2003 amendment of Canon 7B(2)(a) and (b), effective January 1, 2004, clarified that Canon 7B applies to all candidates for judicial office, not just incumbent judges. (ADM File No. 2003-09.

The amendment of Canon 7B(2)(d) precludes a judicial campaign committee from accepting funds from another committee that was set up for that candidate in connection with an attempt to secure any other judicial or nonjudicial office. Although Canon 7B(2) prohibits judicial campaign committees from raising funds before February 15 of an election year and from soliciting more than $100 per individual lawyer, these provisions potentially could have been evaded under the previous version of 7B(2)(d). For example, the rule did not expressly preclude the transfer to a judicial campaign committed of funds solicited before February 15 of an election year for a nonjudicial campaign. Nor did it expressly prohibit the transfer of a contribution solicited from an individual lawyer for a nonjudicial campaign to a subsequently established judicial committee for that same candidate. In that situation, the lawyer might have contributed $500 to the nonjudicial campaign, more than the judicial campaign committee could solicit, and the judicial campaign committee then could solicit a new, direct $100 contribution from the lawyer. The amendment eliminated these flaws, as well as potential violations of the contribution limits set by the Michigan Campaign Finance Act, MCL 169.201 *et seq.* (ADM File No. 2002-50.)

Staff Comment to 2005 Amendment

The amendment of Canon 7(B)(4) concerns endorsements of judicial candidates. It prohibits judicial candidates from paying for endorsements or favorable ratings from a person or entity. It also regulates the manner in which a candidate may pay the cost associated with publication of an endorsement or ranking. The amendment is effective January 1, 2005, so as not to take effect in the middle of the current election cycle.

Staff Comment to 2013 Amendment

These amendments reflect an effort to make the judicial canons consistent regarding law-related and nonlaw-related extrajudicial activities in which judges may participate, and to clarify the activities that are allowed or prohibited. The proposal retains the explicit prohibition on a judge individually soliciting funds, and likewise prohibits the use of the prestige of the office for that purpose. The newly-constituted Canon 4, which consolidates previous Canon 4 and Canon 5 into one canon, permits a judge to engage in various specific activities, including serving as a member of an honorary committee or joining a general appeal, speaking at or receiving an award at an organization's event, and allowing the judge's name to be used in support of a fundraising event. The proposal also

includes several suggested revisions that were recommended during the public comment period.

In addition to combining Canons 4 and 5 into one canon, the amendments eliminate the language of Canon 7C that prohibited a judge from accepting a testimonial, and move the reformulated language from Canon 7C(2) prohibiting a judge from accepting a contribution of money to Canon 2G. Also, the proposal clarifies Canon 2 so that activities allowed under Canon 4 are not considered a violation of the principle of use of the prestige of office. Further, the amendments clarify that certain canons of the Code of Judicial Conduct (specifically Canons 1, 2, 4[A]–[D] and 7) apply to all candidates for judicial office as part of the new language inserted as Canon 5. Finally, MRPC 8.2 (which applies to lawyers) is amended to reflect that the judicial canons applicable to judicial candidates are set out in new Canon 5.

Nearly all of the current language in Canon 2, 4, 5, and 7 is retained in this proposal. The new language adds explicit provisions to describe the types of activities that are allowed or prohibited for judges which until now had been undefined and therefore the source of confusion.

Staff Comment to 2018 Amendment

The amendments of Canon 3 and Canon 7 of the Code of Judicial Conduct incorporate most of the ABA Model Code of Judicial Conduct 2.10 language and clarify its application to public comments made by judges.

Staff Comment to 2019 Amendment

The amendment of Canon 7 of the Code of Judicial Conduct explicitly allows judicial campaign solicitation as permitted by law, eliminates the $100 per lawyer limitation, and removes the disclaimer requirement. This change brings Michigan's canons into conformity with the majority of states that have moved away from solicitation restrictions and instead opted to refer to statutory campaign provisions.

CANON 8. Collective Activity By Judges

The canons of this Code concerning the conduct of individual judges and judicial candidates also apply to judges' associations or any other organization consisting exclusively of judges.
[Adopted December 28, 1999, effective January 1, 2000, 461 Mich.]

Comments

Staff Comment to 2000 Adoption

The addition of Canon 8 on December 28, 1999, effective January 1, 2000, clarified that judges remain accountable for their actions under the Code of Judicial Conduct when acting collectively in concert with other judges.

RULES CONCERNING THE JUDICIAL CONFERENCE

Effective November 1, 1955

JUDICIAL CONFERENCE RULES

1. There is hereby constituted the judicial conference of Michigan, hereinafter called the conference, of which the justices of the Supreme Court and the judges of the circuit courts, recorder's court of the city of Detroit, and superior court of Grand Rapids shall be members. The chief justice, with the approval of the Supreme Court, may invite lawyers and laymen to attend sessions of the conference or to participate in its programs.

2. The directors of the conference shall consist of the chief justice, as chairman, the court administrator, as secretary, the president of the Michigan Judges' Association, the president of the State Bar, the president of the State Bar Foundation, the attorney general of Michigan, the chairman of the senate judiciary committee, the chairman of the house judiciary committee, 3 other members of the conference designated, with the approval of the Supreme Court, by the chief justice, and such others as the chief justice, with the approval of the Supreme Court, may from time to time determine.

3. The directors shall meet at the call of the chief justice. They shall assign subjects to the conference study committees for study, report and recommendations. The directors shall receive and consider the reports of such committees and refer them, together with their own recommendations thereon, to the Supreme Court. The directors may, either on the basis of such committee reports or otherwise, make recommendations to the Supreme Court for amendments, changes or additions to the Michigan Court Rules, and, with the approval of the Supreme Court, make recommendations to the judges who are members of this conference with respect to local practice, and to the governor, the legislature and the people for statutory or constitutional amendments, enactments or changes. The directors shall also, subject to the direction, approval and control of the Supreme Court, inaugurate and maintain, in behalf of the conference and its members, a program of relations with the Michigan State Bar, the State Bar Foundation, the Federal courts, the governor, the legislature and the public.

4. The study committees of the conference shall consist of the following and such others as the chief justice, with the approval of the Supreme Court, shall from time to time determine, namely, study committees on:

(a) Civil procedure.

(b) Criminal jurisprudence.

(c) Substantive law.

(d) Local court organization and administration.

(e) Professional and judicial ethics.

(f) Domestic relations.

(g) Miscellaneous and special questions.

Each study committee shall be composed of a chairman and members designated, with the approval of the Supreme Court, by the chief justice, including the following: A justice of the Supreme Court, at least 2 trial judges who are members of the conference, at least 2 members of the bar, and at least 2 laymen, and shall meet at the call of its chairman.

5. The study committees shall study subjects assigned to them by the chief justice or the directors and make reports and recommendations thereon to the directors, for consideration by the latter and reference to the Supreme Court. Such recommendations may include proposed amendments, changes and additions to the statutory and constitutional law and Court Rules of Michigan.

6. Each member of the conference shall from time to time, as he encounters problems in the administration of justice and operation of the courts, forward a statement thereof to the court administrator for consideration by the directors and assignment to the appropriate study committee.

7. At the annual meeting of the conference, the directors shall make a report of their work and that of the several study committees during the preceding year.

8. The Supreme Court shall from time to time make such other and further provisions with respect to the conference as it shall deem necessary and proper.

9. The foregoing rules are promulgated pursuant to the general superintending control of the Court over all inferior courts, its powers over the bar of the State and the members thereof, and P.A. 1954, No. 195. They shall take effect on November 1, 1955, and remain in effect until altered or abrogated.

UNIFORM SYSTEM OF CITATION [RESCINDED]

MICHIGAN UNIFORM SYSTEM OF CITATION [RESCINDED]

Comments
Publisher's Note

Rescinded effective November 5, 2014 by order entered November 5, 2014, 497 Mich. See now Administrative Order 2014–22, which reads:

"On order of the Court, effective immediately, Administrative Order No. 2006–3, the order setting forth the Michigan Uniform System of Citation, is rescinded. The Court currently uses, and encourages others to use, the Michigan Appellate Opinion Manual, which sets forth the Court's standards for citation of authority, quotation, and style in opinions of the Supreme Court and the Court of Appeals. The manual is now available in a searchable online format, and may be found at www.courts.mi.gov."